WOMEN'S WO

An Anthology of American Literature

Man may work from sun to sun,
But woman's work is never done.

Traditional saying

WOMEN'S WORK

An Anthology of American Literature

Barbara Perkins
University of Toledo

Robyn Warhol
University of Vermont

George Perkins
Eastern Michigan University

McGraw-Hill, Inc.

New York   St. Louis   San Francisco   Auckland   Bogotá   Caracas
Lisbon   London   Madrid   Mexico City   Milan   Montreal   New Delhi
San Juan   Singapore   Sydney   Tokyo   Toronto

This book was developed by STEVEN PENSINGER, Inc.

WOMEN'S WORK: An Anthology of American Literature

This book was set in Janson by ComCom, Inc.
The editors were Steve Pensinger and David Dunham;
the design was done by A Good Thing, Inc.;
the production supervisor was Richard A. Ausburn.
R. R. Donnelley & Sons Company was printer and binder.

Library of Congress Cataloging-in-Publication Data

Women's work: an anthology of American literature / Barbara Perkins,
   Robyn Warhol, George Perkins.
       p.   cm.
   Includes bibliographical references and index.
   ISBN 0-07-049364-2 (acid-free paper)
   1. American literature—Women authors.   2. Women—United States—
Literary collections.   I. Perkins, Barbara, (date).   II. Warhol,
Robyn R.   III. Perkins, George B., (date).
PS508.W7W65   1994
810.8'09287—dc20   93-26558

About the Editors

Barbara Perkins is Adjunct Professor of English at the University of Toledo and Associate Editor of *Narrative*. Since its founding she has served as Secretary-Treasurer of the Society for the Study of Narrative Literature. She received her Ph.D. from the University of Pennsylvania and has taught at Baldwin-Wallace College, The University of Pennsylvania, Fairleigh Dickinson University, Eastern Michigan University, and the University of Newcastle, Australia. She has contributed essays to several reference works including *Contemporary Novelists, Great Writers of the English Language*, and *The World Book Encyclopedia*. Her books include *Contemporary American Literature* (with George Perkins), *Benet's Reader's Encyclopedia of American Literature* (with George Perkins and Phillip Leininger), *Kaleidoscope: Stories of the American Experience* (with George Perkins), and *The American Tradition in Literature*, 8th edition (with George Perkins).

Robyn Warhol is Associate Professor and Director of Graduate Studies at the University of Vermont. She holds the Ph.D. from Stanford University and is a Phi Beta Kappa graduate of Pomona College. Author of *Gendered Interventions: Narrative Discourse in the Victorian Novel* (Rutgers UP, 1989), she is also coeditor (with Diane Price Herndl) of *Feminisms: An Anthology of Feminist Theory and Criticism* (Rutgers, 1992) and has published essays on women writers in *PMLA, Novel, Essays in Literature*, and the *Psychohistory Review*. She is currently President of the Society for the Study of Narrative Literature, an Allied Organization of the Modern Language Association.

George Perkins is Professor of English at Eastern Michigan University and an Associate Editor of *Narrative*. He holds degrees from Tufts and Duke universities and received his Ph.D. from Cornell. He has been a Fulbright Lecturer at the University of Newcastle in Australia and has held a Fellowship at the Institute for Advanced Studies in the Humanities at the University of Edinburgh. In addition to Newcastle and Edinburgh, he has taught at Washington University, Baldwin-Wallace College and Fairleigh Dickinson University. His books include *The Theory of the American Novel, Realistic American Short Fiction, American Poetic Theory, The Harper Handbook to Literature* (with Northrop Frye and Sheridan Baker), *The Practical Imagination* (compact edition with Frye, Baker, and Barbara Perkins), *Benet's Reader's Encyclopedia of American Literature* (with Barbara Perkins and Phillip Leininger), *Contemporary American Literature* (with Barbara Perkins), *Kaleidoscope: Stories of the American Experience* (with Barbara Perkins), and *The American Tradition in Literature*, 8th edition (with Barbara Perkins).

We dedicate this book, with warm affection, to Laura, Suzanne, and Alison Perkins, and to Patricia Warhol.

Contents

Preface / xvii

American Women in the Eighteenth and Nineteenth Centuries / 1

Anne Bradstreet (1612–1672) / 8

The Prologue / 9

In Honour of That High and Mighty Princess Queen Elizabeth of Happy Memory / 10

Contemplations / 14

The Flesh and the Spirit / 20

The Author to Her Book / 23

Before the Birth of One of Her Children / 23

To My Dear and Loving Husband / 24

A Letter to Her Husband, Absent upon Public Employment / 24

Another / 25

In Reference to Her Children, 23 June, 1659 / 26

In Memory of My Dear Grandchild Elizabeth Bradstreet, Who Deceased August, 1665, Being a Year and Half Old / 28

In Memory of My Dear Grandchild Anne Bradstreet Who Deceased June 20, 1669, Being Three Years and Seven Months Old / 29

On My Dear Grandchild Simon Bradstreet, Who Died on 16

November, 1669, Being but a Month, and One Day Old / 29

Upon My Son Samuel His Going for England, Nov. 6, 1657 / 30

Here Follows Some Verses upon the Burning of Our House July 10th, 1666. Copied Out of a Loose Paper / 30

As Weary Pilgrim / 32

Mary Rowlandson (1636?–1711?) / 33

The Narrative of the Captivity and Restoration of Mrs. Mary Rowlandson / 34

Sarah Kemble Knight (1666–1727) / 60

The Journal of Madam Knight / 61

Mercy Otis Warren (1728–1814) / 76

The Group / 77

Abigail Adams (1744–1818) / 97

Letters / 98

Phillis Wheatley (c. 1753?–1784) / 109

To the University of Cambridge, in New-England / 110

On Being Brought from Africa to America / 111

On the Death of the Reverend Mr.
George Whitefield / 111

An Hymn to the Morning / 112

An Hymn to the Evening / 113

To the Right Honourable William,
Earl of Dartmouth, His Majesty's
Principal Secretary of State for North
America, & c. / 113

On the Death of Dr. Samuel
Marshall / 114

To S. M. a Young African Painter,
on Seeing His Works / 115

To His Excellency General
Washington / 116

On the Death of General
Wooster / 117

**Susanna Haswell Rowson
(1762–1824) / 118**

[from] *Charlotte Temple: A Tale
of Truth* / 120

**Catherine Maria Sedgwick
(1789–1867) / 177**

[from] *Hope Leslie* / 178

**Sojourner Truth (c.
1797–1883) / 191**

Reminiscences by Frances D.
Gage / 192

What Time of Night It Is / 194

**Caroline Stansbury Kirkland
(1801–1864) / 195**

[from] *A New Home* / 196

**Margaret Fuller
(1810–1850) / 205**

[from] *Woman in the Nineteenth
Century* / 206

[from] *Memoirs* of *Margaret Fuller
Ossoli* / 217

**Fanny Fern (Sarah Payson
Willis) (1811–1872) / 224**

[from] *Ruth Hall* / 226

Male Criticism on Ladies' Books / 243

The "Coming" Woman / 244

The Working-Girls of New
York / 245

**Harriet Beecher Stowe
(1811–1896) / 246**

[from] *Uncle Tom's Cabin, or Life among
the Lowly* / 248

**Harriet Jacobs
(1813–1897) / 313**

[from] *Incidents in the Life of a Slave
Girl* / 315

**Susan Warner
(1819–1885) / 350**

[from] *The Wide, Wide World* / 352

Alice Cary (1820–1871) / 378

The Wildermings / 378

**Rose Terry Cooke
(1827–1897) / 383**

How Celia Changed Her Mind / 383

**Emily Dickinson
(1830–1886) / 394**

49 [I never lost as much but
twice] / 396

67 [Success is counted sweetest] / 396

130 [These are the days when Birds
come back—] / 396

185 ["Faith" is a fine invention] / 397

211 [Come slowly—Eden!] / 397

214 [I taste a liquor never
brewed—] / 397

216 [Safe in their Alabaster Chambers—] / 397

241 [I like a look of Agony] / 398

249 [Wild Nights—Wild Nights!] / 398

254 ["Hope" is the thing with feathers—] / 398

258 [There's a certain Slant of Light] / 398

280 [I felt a Funeral, in my Brain] / 398

285 [The Robin's my Criterion for Tune—] / 399

288 [I'm Nobody! Who are you?] / 399

303 [The Soul selects her own Society—] / 399

315 [He fumbles at your Soul] / 399

322 [There came a Day at Summer's full] / 399

324 [Some keep the Sabbath going to Church—] / 400

328 [A Bird came down the Walk—] / 400

338 [I know that He exists] / 400

341 [After great pain, a formal feeling comes—] / 401

376 [Of Course—I prayed—] / 401

401 [What Soft—Cherubic Creatures—] / 401

435 [Much Madness is divinest Sense—] / 401

441 [This is my letter to the World] / 401

448 [This was a Poet—It is That] / 401

449 [I died for Beauty—but was scarce] / 402

465 [I heard a Fly buzz—when I died—] / 402

501 [This World is not Conclusion] / 402

508 [I'm ceded—I've stopped being Theirs—] / 402

510 [It was not Death, for I stood up] / 403

511 [If you were coming in the Fall] / 403

520 [I started Early—Took my Dog—] / 403

528 [Mine—by the Right of the White Election!] / 404

536 [The Heart asks Pleasure—first—] / 404

547 [I've seen a Dying Eye] / 404

569 [I reckon—when I count at all—] / 404

579 [I had been hungry, all the Years—] / 404

585 [I like to see it lap the Miles—] / 405

632 [The Brain—is wider than the Sky—] / 405

640 [I cannot live with You—] / 405

650 [Pain—has an Element of Blank—] / 405

657 [I dwell in Possibility—] / 406

664 [Of all the Souls that stand create—] / 406

670 [One need not be a Chamber—to be Haunted—] / 406

709 [Publication—is the Auction] / 407

712 [Because I could not stop for Death—] / 407

732 [She rose to His Requirement—dropt] / 407

754 [My Life had stood—a Loaded Gun—] / 408

986 [A narrow Fellow in the Grass] / 408

1052 [I never saw a Moor—] / 408

1078 [The Bustle in a House] / 408

1100 [The last Night that She lived] / 409

1129 [Tell all the Truth but tell it slant—] / 409

1207 [He preached upon "Breadth" til it argued him narrow—] / 409

1463 [A Route of Evanescence] / 409

1540 [As imperceptibly as Grief] / 409

1545 [The Bible is an antique Volume—] / 410

1624 [Apparently with no surprise] / 410

1651 [A Word made Flesh is seldom] / 410

1670 [In Winter in my Room] / 410

1732 [My life closed twice before its close—] / 411

1737 [Rearrange a "Wife's" affection!] / 411

1755 [To make a prairie it takes a clover and one bee] / 411

1760 [Elysium is as far as to] / 411

Letters / 412

To recipient unknown, about 1858

To recipient unknown, about 1861

To recipient unknown, early 1862?

To T. W. Higginson, 15 April 1862

To T. W. Higginson, 25 April 1862

To T. W. Higginson, 7 June 1862

To T. W. Higginson, July 1862

To T. W. Higginson, August 1862

Rebecca Harding Davis (1831–1910) / 418

Life in the Iron-Mills / 419

Louisa May Alcott (1832–1888) / 440

[from] Little Women / 442

Constance Fenimore Woolson (1840–1894) / 543

Miss Grief / 545

Sarah Morgan (1842–1909) / 557

[from] The Civil War Diary of Sarah Morgan / 558

Sarah Winnemucca Hopkins (1844–1891) / 576

[from] Life among the Piutes / 577

Sarah Orne Jewett (1849–1909) / 582

The Town Poor / 583

Kate Chopin (1850–1904) / 590

A Pair of Silk Stockings / 591

The Storm: A Sequel to "The 'Cadian Ball" / 594

Mary Noailles Murfree (1850–1922) / 597

Over on T'other Mounting / 598

Grace Elizabeth King (1851–1932) / 609

A Crippled Hope / 610

Mary E. Wilkins Freeman (1852–1930) / 615

The Revolt of "Mother" / 616

A New England Nun / 625

Sarah Pratt McLean Greene (1856–1935) / 632

[from] Cape Cod Folks / 633

Charlotte Perkins Gilman (1860–1935) / 639

The Yellow Wallpaper / 640

Twentieth-Century Women Writers / 651

Edith Wharton (1862–1937) / 655

The Muse's Tragedy / 657
The Other Two / 665

Mary Austin (1868–1934) / 676

The Fakir / 677

Willa Cather (1873–1947) / 683

Paul's Case / 685

Ellen Glasgow (1873–1945) / 696

Jordan's End / 697

Amy Lowell (1874–1925) / 706

A Lady / 707
Patterns / 708
Opal / 710
A Decade / 710
Meeting-House Hill / 710
Lilacs / 711

Gertrude Stein (1874–1946) / 713

The Gentle Lena / 715

Susan Glaspell (1876?–1948) / 731

A Jury of Her Peers / 733

Mary Antin (1881–1949) / 745

[from] *The Promised Land* / 746

Anzia Yezierska (c. 1881–1970) / 751

The Free Vacation House / 752

Elinor Wylie (1885–1928) / 757

The Eagle and the Mole / 758
Wild Peaches / 758
Sanctuary / 760
Prophecy / 760
Let No Charitable Hope / 761
O Virtuous Light / 761
Pastiche / 762

H. D. (Hilda Doolittle) (1886–1961) / 762

Sea Rose / 763
Mid-day / 764
Garden / 765
Orchard / 765
Pear Tree / 766
Oread / 767
Helen / 767
[from] *The Walls Do Not Fall* / 767
[from] *Tribute to the Angels* / 772

Marianne Moore (1887–1972) / 775

Poetry / 776
In the Days of Prismatic Color / 778
Peter / 778
A Grave / 779
An Egyptian Pulled Glass Bottle in the Shape of a Fish / 780
The Past Is the Present / 781
Silence / 781
No Swan So Fine / 781
The Frigate Pelican / 782
The Pangolin / 783
Nevertheless / 786
The Mind Is an Enchanting Thing / 786
In Distrust of Merits / 787
A Jelly-Fish / 789

Katherine Anne Porter
(1890–1980) / 790

Pale Horse, Pale Rider / 791

Zora Neale Hurston
(1891–1960) / 818

[from] *Their Eyes Were Watching God* / 819
[The Yellow Mule]

Edna St. Vincent Millay
(1892–1950) / 824

First Fig / 825
Second Fig / 825
Recuerdo / 825
The Spring and the Fall / 826
[Oh, Oh, you will be sorry for that word!] / 826
[What lips my lips have kissed, and where, and why,] / 827
[from] Sonnets from an Ungrafted Tree / 827
  VII [One way there was of muting in the mind]
  XIV [She had a horror he would die at night]
Justice Denied in Massachusetts / 828
[from] *Fatal Interview* / 829
  II [This beast that rends me in the sight of all]
  XIV [Since of no creature living the last breath]
  XXX [Love is not all: it is not meat nor drink]
  XLVI [Even in the moment of our earliest kiss]
[Those hours when happy hours were my estate,—] / 831
[I will put Chaos into fourteen lines] / 831

Caroline Gordon
(1895–1981) / 831

The Ice House / 832

Mari Sandoz (1896–1966) / 836

[from] *Crazy Horse* / 837
The Song of a Good Name

Louise Bogan (1897–1970) / 847

The Alchemist / 848
Men Loved Wholly Beyond Wisdom / 848
The Crows / 848
Women / 849
Dark Summer / 849
Roman Fountain / 850
Evening in the Sanitarium / 850
The Dragonfly / 851
Night / 851

Meridel Le Sueur
(1900–   ) / 852

[from] *The Girl* / 853
[The Bank Robbery]

Lillian Hellman
(1905–1984) / 868

Watch on the Rhine / 869

Eudora Welty
(1909–   ) / 910

Livvie / 911

Mary McCarthy
(1912–1989) / 919

Artists in Uniform / 920

Tillie Olsen (1913?–   ) / 928

[from] *Yonnondio* / 929
  The Iron Throat

Gwendolyn Brooks
(1917–) / 936

A Song in the Front Yard / 937
The Vacant Lot / 938
Queen of the Blues / 938
The Bean Eaters / 940
We Real Cool / 941
Jessie Mitchell's Mother / 941
The Lovers of the Poor / 942
The Crazy Woman / 944

Amy Clampitt
(1920–) / 944

The Kingfisher / 945
What the Light Was Like / 946
Urn-Burial and the Butterfly
Migration / 949
Margaret Fuller, 1847 / 951
The Field Pansy / 953
A Winter Burial / 954
Amherst / 955

Hisaye Yamamoto
(1921–) / 956

Seventeen Syllables / 957

Denise Levertov
(1923–) / 964

The Third Dimension / 965
To the Snake / 966
Illustrious Ancestors / 967
About Marriage / 967
In Mind / 968
A Note to Olga / 969
Intrusion / 970
The 90th Year / 970
The Well / 971

Flannery O'Connor
(1925–1964) / 972

The Life You Save May Be Your
Own / 973

Maya Angelou
(1928–) / 979

[from] *I Know Why the Caged Bird
Sings* / 980

Anne Sexton (1928–1974) / 987

Her Kind / 988
For John, Who Begs Me Not to
Enquire Further / 989
The Double Image / 990
The Truth the Dead Know / 995
All My Pretty Ones / 996
With Mercy for the Greedy / 997
Self in 1958 / 998

Adrienne Rich
(1929–) / 999

Aunt Jennifer's Tigers / 1000
Living in Sin / 1000
Snapshots of a
Daughter-in-Law / 1001
"I Am in Danger—Sir—" / 1004
Face to Face / 1005
Diving into the Wreck / 1005
From a Survivor / 1007
For the Dead / 1008
[from] Twenty-One Love
Poems / 1009
    XVIII [Rain on the West Side
    Highway]
Upper Broadway / 1009

Lorraine Hansberry
(1930–1965) / 1010

A Raisin in the Sun / 1011

Toni Morrison
(1931–   ) / 1068

[from] *Beloved* / 1069
[Denver's Secrets]

Sylvia Plath
(1932–1963) / 1078

Black Rook in Rainy Weather / 1080
Morning Song / 1081
Blackberrying / 1081
The Arrival of the Bee Box / 1082
Wintering / 1083
Daddy / 1084
Lady Lazarus / 1086
Child / 1088
Mystic / 1088
Words / 1089

Joyce Carol Oates
(1938–   ) / 1090

Nairobi / 1091

Maxine Hong Kingston
(1940–   ) / 1095

[from] *The Woman Warrior* / 1096
No Name Woman

Bobbie Ann Mason
(1940–   ) / 1103

Hunktown / 1103

Bharati Mukherjee
(1940–   ) / 1114

The Management of Grief / 1115

Louise Glück
(1943–   ) / 1124

The School Children / 1124
Dedication to Hunger / 1125
The Drowned Children / 1127
Lamentations / 1127
Brooding Likeness / 1129
Terminal Resemblance / 1129

Alice Walker
(1944–   ) / 1130

Everyday Use for Your
Grandma / 1131

Anne Beattie
(1947–   ) / 1136

Skeletons / 1137

Leslie Marmon Silko
(1948–   ) / 1139

Lullaby / 1140

Rita Dove (1952–   ) / 1145

ö / 1146
Dusting / 1146
Roast Possum / 1147
Daystar / 1148
Crab-Boil / 1149

Amy Tan (1952–   ) / 1150

[from] *The Joy Luck Club* / 1150
Rules of the Game

Louise Erdrich
(1954–   ) / 1157

Fleur / 1157

Bibliography / 1167

Index / 1171

Preface

Changing attitudes toward women's history, together with increasing attention to the evolving roles of women in contemporary society, have long mandated serious study of women's thoughts and imaginings as recorded, chiefly, in their words. For Americans, the record of American literary history is of paramount importance, and, within limits, the accomplishments of American women may be studied in the larger context provided by books that have helped to lay the foundations for this one, including *The American Tradition in Literature* (8th edition, 1994), *Contemporary American Literature* (1988), and *Kaleidoscope: Stories of the American Experience* (1993). For extended study of the accomplishments of women, however, such books and the courses constructed around them are not enough.

We have designed *Women's Work* to meet the need for a comprehensive survey of the writings of American women from colonial days to the present. Chief among our guiding principles has been a desire to represent women's writing at its highest level of accomplishment. In making our selections, however, we have tried to give due consideration to different kinds of accomplishment and to varying criteria for literary and historical excellence, weighing our personal judgments against the best wisdom, as we understand it, of the community of scholars in American literature and women's studies.

In order to represent the varied nature of women's writing, we have added to the usual anthology genres—fiction, poetry, drama, and essays—some representation of diaries, letters, autobiographies, oratory, and journalism. We have preferred works that stand complete in our presentation, but we have also enriched the offerings with portions of major writings too long for full inclusion; in these instances, the intent is to provide a substantial flavor of the whole.

The order of presentation is chronological. A brief overview, "American Women in the Eighteenth and Nineteenth Centuries," introduces the selections from colonial times to the end of the nineteenth century. Another, "Twentieth-Century Women Writers," introduces the writings of the twentieth century. For each writer, we have supplied a brief biographic, critical, and bibliographic introduction. At the end of the volume, a longer bibliography provides sources of information generally on American literature and more specifically on the literature of American women.

For each selection, we have tried to provide a faithful copy of the text that in our judgment supplies the best reading. Unless it is obvious, the source of each text is indicated in the author introductions or footnotes. Our omissions from the copy text are indicated by spaced asterisks. Footnotes are our own, except for those found in the originals, where the name of the author is given in square brackets. Some early texts have been newly edited for this book, as indicated in headnotes or footnotes, and we have occasionally normalized spelling or punctuation, but the diction remains as found, with archaic usages explained in footnotes. Titles are those of the original except where printed between square brackets. Important dates are given at the end of each selection: At the right margin appears the date of first publication in a book by the author; a date preceding that, separated by a comma, is the date of first periodical publication; a date at the left margin is the date of composition.

Woman's Work owes much to those scholars of women's literature whose names appear in the bibliographies throughout its pages. It owes more to the women represented within it and others for whom we could find no space. The generous support of McGraw-Hill has placed no limitations on the inclusion of writers and works that suited our plans within the physical scope of the book; we regret only the omission of Elizabeth Bishop, whose estate refused permission to reproduce her poems. We owe special thanks to the vision of Steve Pensinger, who was quick to see the value of the project. Thanks also are due for the diligent editorial assistance of David Dunham and the research assistance of Kathleen Gormly and Elizabeth Halley.

Barbara Perkins
Robyn Warhol
George Perkins

WOMEN'S WORK

An Anthology of American Literature

American Women in the Eighteenth and Nineteenth Centuries

Women's Place in American Literary History

Until recently, anthologies of women writers were rare, and were seldom adopted in the college classroom. In the traditional history of American literature, a small number of exceptional women sparkled in the firmament of literary stars: Emily Dickinson, Edith Wharton, Willa Cather, and Adrienne Rich, for example, are "canonical" authors, whose names have appeared on the unofficial lists of writers whose literary works are widely considered valuable enough to be studied in courses. Often, though, these women's literary reputations have suffered from prejudices about their personalities (Dickinson is supposed to have been an eccentric recluse, whose peculiar behavior has always colored critics' reception of her work.) or from comparisons with male writers whose work resembles theirs but is traditionally considered "greater." (Wharton at times worked closely with Henry James, and though their fiction takes similar forms, James has always held a higher position in critics' estimation.) Even canonized women writers have traditionally held a tenuous position in the history of "great works": their writings have long been in the margins, not at the center, of literary studies.

Women writers who are not part of the canon—the great majority of the authors represented in this volume—have been dismissed or overlooked for many reasons, even when their writings maintained a large popular audience. Such novelists as Harriet Beecher Stowe (author of *Uncle Tom's Cabin*) and Louisa May Alcott (who wrote *Little Women*) have been as widely read as any author in American history, but before the late 1970s, their works were virtually absent from college curricula: Stowe's novel was pushed aside as "propaganda," which could not be great art; Alcott's dismissed as a "girls' book," which focused too much on intimate domestic details to be of "universal" importance or interest. Poets such as Anne Bradstreet or Phillis Wheatley were considered too "conventional" to be interesting; fiction writers such as Sarah Orne Jewett, Kate Chopin, and Mary Wilkins Freeman were considered too "regional" to compete with important works that were supposed to hold broader appeal; writers representing diverse ethnicities such as Sarah Winnemucca Hopkins and Zora Neale Hurston were often simply overlooked. Though women writers have always been present in American literary history, they have been resolutely assigned to its margins.

Beginning in the late 1970s, feminist criticism began to ask questions about why "women's work" was assigned so little value; through the 1980s, feminism developed theories to explain women's place in the history of literature. To understand the role of feminism in the history of women's writing, one must begin with a working definition of "feminism." A "feminist" is *not* someone who is antimen, nor is it necessarily someone who believes women to be superior to men (though some people who consider themselves feminists do hold this position). Many different feminisms exist, and many have existed throughout American history: the priorities of a nineteenth-century feminist are not those of a 1990s feminist, nor are the values held by a working-class, African-American lesbian feminist necessarily identical to those of her middle-class, white, heterosexual counterpart. At the bottom line, though, most feminists in the present day agree that women are, and have historically been, oppressed within culture and society, and all feminists agree that such oppression is unacceptable. Feminists hold that men and women should be treated equally under the law, at the same time that they insist women are not identical to men. Most feminists in the 1990s try to recognize the diversity inherent in the word "woman" and try not to universalize from their own experience of race, class, or sexual preference. As the constitution of the National Women's Studies Association puts it, feminist goals include working to eliminate "sexism, racism, anti-Semitism, heterosexism, and oppression based on age, class, religion, ethnicity, disability, and national origin, as well as other barriers to liberation in our social structure."

If these are the sociohistorical implications of "feminist," the word holds philosophical resonances that are important to literary history as well. Feminist theorists have called into question the binary oppositions that structure much of literary criticism and, for that matter, much of Western thought. If such oppositions as "good/evil," "body/spirit," "illusion/reality," and "self/other" can be shown to be more slippery and less fixed than traditional empirical philosophy has assumed, so can the oppositions between "high art/popular culture," "universal/local," "central/marginal," and "masculine/feminine" that have operated to keep women's writing out of the mainstream of literary studies.

Joanna Russ, in *How to Suppress Women's Writing* (1983), wittily summarizes the process by which women's work has traditionally been devalued. The long subtitle to her book parodies the reasoning of critics who dismiss women writers from the ranks of the greats: First they claim . . .

. . . she didn't write it. But if it's clear she did the deed. . . . She wrote it, but she shouldn't have. (It's political, sexual, masculine, feminist.) She wrote it, but look what she wrote about. (The bedroom, the kitchen, her family. Other women!) She wrote it, but she wrote only one of it. (*Jane Eyre.* Poor dear, that's all she ever . . . .") She wrote it, but she isn't really an artist, and it isn't really art. (It's a thriller, a romance, a children's book. It's sci fi!) She wrote it, but she had help. (Robert Browning. Branwell Brontë. Her own "masculine side.") She wrote it, but she's an anomaly. (Woolf. With Leonard's help . . . .) She wrote it BUT . . . .

Russ, a popular writer of science fiction as well as an astute literary scholar, illustrates each of these positions with ample quotations from other critics. To demonstrate such patterns of oppression is one goal of American feminist literary criticism. Another is to uncover the tradition of women writers that has been suppressed (whether consciously or unconsciously) and to appreciate women writers on their own terms, rather than comparing and contrasting them always to men. Although this may sound like "special treatment" or an unfair way to evaluate literature, the history of women in the United States (as opposed to the history of men) justifies this approach. During the eighteenth and nineteenth centuries, women's experience in U.S. society was distinctly different from men's; it stands to reason that women's literary productions would be different, too.

The Public and Private Spheres

Since colonial times (the period in the late seventeenth century when America was first settled by English-speaking colonists), American society has been arranged around the principles of patriarchy and capitalism. "Patriarchy" means that men hold property and official political power and (usually) pass it on to their sons, and that women are economically and socially dependent on male relations for the definition of their social identities. (One lingering sign of patriarchy in American culture, for instance, is that women are born with their fathers' surnames and usually take their husbands' surnames in marriage, even though women now can earn money and hold independent property). "Capitalism" is the free-market system that has historically structured the American economy, where individuals accrue economic profit through "work," production, and investment.

The confluence of these two principles meant, in eighteenth- and nineteenth-century America, that people's social functions were strictly divided along gender lines. In early America, women were involved in home-based production of goods, but women's main economic function was reproduction, or having babies. Men participated in the marketplace, in politics, and in higher education, thus dominating the public sphere; women stayed home, reigning over the private sphere. From a late twentieth-century perspective, this arrangement seems obviously to assign the greater degree of power to men, but that is not how nineteenth-century Americans viewed it. Middle-class "domestic ideology" (as feminist historians have called it) held that the woman who stayed home was in many ways morally superior to her husband, because she was protected from the competition and scrambling for profit of the world of commerce and the professions. She could devote herself to Christian principles of spirituality and would not have to compromise her moral values as her husband necessarily might. She could wield a positive ethical influence over her husband, and especially over her children, who would carry the marks of her training with them into the public world, if they were boys, or into their own child-rearing, if they were girls. This was women's power: the power of influence, as opposed to men's public power of action. The private sphere was a world supposedly dominated by women's concerns and women's activities: from Anne Bradstreet's

time to the end of the nineteenth century, women formed strong relationships and networks of mutual support within their private communities.

Middle-class domestic ideology also emphasized the differences between the sexes and worked to uphold certain ideas about female nature: women were supposed to be more spiritual, more virtuous, less intellectual, and less sexual than men; they were supposed to hold strong maternal instincts and no professional ambitions; and they were supposed to be physically frail and delicate. (These assumptions were deeply enough rooted in the culture to lead to a nineteenth-century medical belief that the female brain and the womb were intricately connected, and that the overdevelopment of the thinking organ would result in the shriveling of the reproductive one.) Sexual difference was strongly emphasized in middle-class fashions of the eighteenth and nineteenth centuries: women's dresses of the late eighteenth century uniformly emphasized the bustline (a clear sign of biological sexual difference and of the mother's nurturing function) and obscured the lower part of the body under billowing skirts; nineteenth-century fashions tended to cover up more of the upper body as well as the legs, while maintaining an emphasis on the hourglass shape. The contrast within the female figure between ample bust and wide hips on the one hand and comparatively smaller waist on the other is one biological sign of the difference between men and women; nineteenth-century fashions emphasized that difference as much as possible with elaborate women's corsets that often resulted in faintness and shortness of breath or even permanent damage to ribs and internal organs. Men's clothing, by contrast, has remained quite standard in its outlines during the past two centuries: nineteenth-century men's wear looked very similar to today's shirts and trousers, suits, and "evening clothes" or tuxedos. Today, an American woman is as free as a man to wear pants whenever she pleases, though she may expose herself to comment in certain circumstances by doing so. But throughout the eighteenth and nineteenth centuries, women in pants were unthinkable: using clothes to uphold a visible difference between men and women was crucial to maintaining the separate-spheres status quo.

Of course, such definitions of women excluded more female Americans than they included. While middle-class and privileged women were supposed to be so delicate that they must be "confined" for weeks or months during pregnancy, for instance, women who worked as servants or in the fields or factories were somehow considered to be immune from this inherent delicacy and were generally expected to work regardless of their actual physical condition, whether they were pregnant, sick, or well. The intensely Anglo-American focus of separate-spheres assumptions about women's moral superiority had no reference point in the Native American, Spanish American, or African-American cultures that were developing simultaneously with what we have traditionally called "American literature." As Sojourner Truth pointed out at a women's rights convention in her famous speech "Ain't I A Woman?" the slave woman was defined out of "womanhood" altogether by such middle-class assumptions about femininity.

By the middle of the nineteenth century, there were approximately 2 million African-American women living as slaves, and another 200,000 black women who were free. The slave woman's experience contradicted received notions of femininity on almost every count. Under the system of slavery, African Americans could not enter into legal marriages, and while many slave women did form emotional bonds with the men they were paired with, many others were hindered from becoming the wives of the men of their choice. Slave women had no legal claim to their children, either; the laws of slavery held that a child of a slave "followed the condition of the mother," which meant that her child would be the property of her master, even when (as happened too frequently) the child was the master's own offspring, the product of sexual harassment or rape. Some had domestic assignments in masters' homes, while others worked alongside men in the fields. African-American women who had gained their freedom, either by individual acts of emancipation or by escape, faced racial oppression as well as gender discrimination as they struggled to support themselves in the free states and to bring their families to freedom.

Historical Periods and Literary Movements

Just as traditional definitions of "woman" exclude more female persons in American history than they include, "American literature," too, has been very narrowly defined. Only recently have courses in English departments begun to acknowledge that the first American "authors" were not colonialists, but the Native Americans who preceded them, creating and passing on a rich oral culture of narrative, myth, and music. Slave narratives—the autobiographies of escaped or emancipated African-American slaves—are another recent entry in the American literary canon, as are the "domestic novels" written by white, middle-class women about their experience of the private sphere. Seen from the margin, American history takes on a different form, as does American literature.

Official accounts of American literary history begin with the colonial period, when British settlers began populating the American South (Jamestown, Virginia, was established in 1607) and New England (the first Massachusetts colonies were founded in 1620 and 1630). Male writers of the period were generally civic leaders, Puritan ministers, or politicians, who addressed a public audience in their works. Women of Puritan New England—such as Anne Bradstreet, a poet; or Mary Rowlandson, who wrote an account of her being taken captive by Native Americans—wrote more often about private experience. It was rare for women in the colonial period to write for publication or public dissemination: that was men's work.

The Revolutionary War (1776), in which the United States declared political independence from Great Britain, inaugurated a period in which some women announced their own independence by writing to an audience beyond their private circle. Mercy Otis Warren wrote plays—and politically motivated ones, at that—as did Susanna Rowson, who was to become primarily famous for writing didactic, sentimental novels aimed at the moral improvement of young people. Other women novelists followed suit, among them Hannah Webster Foster and Catherine Maria Sedgwick, who wrote a frontier novel that has been compared to the works of James Fenimore Cooper. Phillis Wheatley, a slave, later freed, wrote "occasional poems" about public events, as well as working within the more personal and devotional modes that women typically practiced; she wrote for publication, speaking both for herself and for the many American slaves whose voices had no access to the literary public's ear.

The early part of the nineteenth century—usually called the "Romantic" period in literary history—brought with it a divergence between men's and women's forms of writing. The canonical male writers of the pre–Civil War period (from 1800 to the 1860s)—Washington Irving, James Fenimore Cooper, Nathaniel Hawthorne, Edgar Allan Poe, Ralph Waldo Emerson, Henry David Thoreau, Herman Melville, and Walt Whitman, for example—share many thematic concerns with the British Romantics, including a strong affinity for nature, a spirit of rebellion, a focus on individual development and achievement, a faith in the power of imagination, and an idealization of the "common man." The United States during this period was economically prosperous and expanding: "manifest destiny" suggested that America's ever-broadening frontiers could reach no boundaries until they extended to the west coast. Of course, westward movement meant the suppression and near-extermination of many native cultures and societies, and while the Romantic vision of the "noble savage" expressed an idealized nostalgia for the cultures that were being rapidly wiped out, American literature did little to subvert what seemed like the inevitable march of history.

Parallel to American Romanticism as it expressed itself in the writings of male authors, American domesticity found a voice in women's works. Some writers, such as Caroline Stansbury Kirkland, wrote of the westward expansion from the perspective of women intent upon making homes on the frontier; others—including Susan Warner and Harriet Beecher Stowe—chronicled the home-centered experience of middle-class women whose families did not move west. Part novel of manners, part *Bildungsroman*, part didactic sentimental fiction, the domestic novel was widely popular in its day—more popular among readers, in fact, than the literature of that period which is now considered canonical—though it has fallen away from critical approval in the twentieth century.

Domestic fiction intersected in the pre–Civil War period with protest fiction in antislavery novels like Harriet Beecher Stowe's *Uncle Tom's Cabin* and in the feminist writing of the first professional female journalist in America, "Fanny Fern"; her novel *Ruth Hall* begins as a sentimental portrait of a middle-class heroine who marries and starts a family, but turns into a tale of economic difficulty that reveals the struggles a woman without a husband or a sympathetic father had to undergo to support herself and her children. The element of protest, as well as domesticity, is present in such antislavery autobiographical narratives as Harriet Jacobs's *Incidents in the Life of a Slave Girl*, and it carries over later in the century into middle-class women's writing on behalf of oppressed factory workers, as in Rebecca Harding Davis's *Life in the Iron Mills*. Given that women were barred from speaking in public forums—unless, like Sojourner Truth, they were willing to compromise their "respectability" to do so—they used fiction as the most effective available means of communicating with the body politic on such urgent matters as abolition and social reform. Not every woman writer intended her work for public consumption, however; Emily Dickinson, now considered among the most important American poets of any period, sewed her hundreds of poems into private volumes and submitted only a handful for critical appraisal or publication during her lifetime.

Women's involvement with the abolition and temperance movements before and during the Civil War coincided, in the northern states, with the early movement for women's rights. Many middle-class white women spoke out publicly against the institution of slavery through the 1830s and thereafter; many of those same women began organizing for their own emancipation concurrently, and in 1848 a group of feminists held the first Woman's Rights Convention in Seneca Falls, New York. Their goal was to gain women the right to vote, a right that was not achieved in the majority of the United States until 1920. Margaret Fuller was among the female intellectuals of the period who argued eloquently in her essays for women's rights.

Although women did not win the right to vote until well into the twentieth century, the nineteenth century saw significant advances in professional and educational opportunities for women of the privileged classes. In the eighteenth century, middle-class women were educated at home or in primary schools, and their curriculum focused on "accomplishments": drawing, music, embroidery, "conversational" foreign languages, and a smattering of history, geography, and arithmetic. Colleges in the United States were closed to women until 1833, when Oberlin College admitted women to the first coeducational student body. The first women's college to be established was Mount Holyoke in Massachusetts, which opened in 1837; a number of other rigorously academic colleges for women were established throughout the nineteenth century, including Vassar, Wellesley, Smith, Radcliffe, and Bryn Mawr. During the period, middle-class women were expected either to marry or to undertake the only "respectable" profession, teaching. The women's colleges, however, began to assist educated women in making inroads into the other professions and helped develop the field of "domestic science" (more recently known as home economics) as a means of giving academic credibility to such "women's work" as nutrition and home design. They also provided predominantly female communities where some women could remain as instructors or administrators, making it possible for them to choose an alternative to the mainstream heterosexual destiny of marriage and family.

Higher education did have an impact on many women's decisions to flout convention and reject marriage. Between 1880 and 1900, half of all college-educated women remained single, while only 10 percent of all American women did so. Not all these women entered what the twentieth century would call lesbian relationships instead of marriage, although many did. Intimate, physically affectionate, exclusive relationships between pairs of women occurred throughout the nineteenth century, without necessarily carrying sexual overtones. The ideology of femininity posited women as asexual creatures in any case, so close relationships between women—even those who exchanged effusive endearments, and openly lived or slept together—were not considered shocking or scandalous during the period. The institution of the "Boston marriage"—two middle-class or upper-class educated women living alone together in a lifelong, committed relationship—was at least marginally respectable, as was "romantic friendship" among young women. Not until the turn of the century, when sexologists and psychoanalysts began theorizing lesbianism as a pathology, did same-sex companionship between women become unacceptable in mainstream American society.

The Civil War meant great loss and familial destruction for women in both the northern and southern states, many of whom directly involved themselves in relief efforts. American literary history mainly remembers the northern white and African-American women writers who wrote in support of the antislavery movement, but southern women wrote, too, to support the antebellum world they were a part of. The Civil War diaries of Sarah Morgan address the conflict from a woman's perspective, but most women writers experienced and wrote about the conflict from a position far beyond the sidelines. For example, Louisa May Alcott, mainly known for her domestic novels, had a brief experience in a war hospital which led to her *Hospital Sketches;* her treatment of the war in *Little Women*—as an off-stage episode that functions to keep the father absent from the first volume of the March family's story—is more typical of female authors' perspective.

The period after the Civil War known as Reconstruction was another period of economic growth and territorial expansion for the United States, whose population was made increasingly diverse by the influx of immigrants from Europe and Asia. Many working-class women became active in labor reform movements, while middle-class women worked through churches and civic organizations for social welfare issues, including public health and birth control. New technologies began to make housekeeping less labor-intensive, and opened opportunities for women to spend time in other pursuits. Shifts in the economy and in social expectations about women's role made it increasingly possible for a woman to support herself by writing.

Some women authors of the period participated in the literary movement known as realism, the attempt to represent everyday life as accurately as possible in fiction. Realist fiction presents psychologically detailed portraits of characters in ordinary, plausible situations which are communicated to the reader as if they were true. Realism can carry a pessimistic tone, as it does in Constance Fenimore Woolson's stories, or it can convey a moderated message of hope, as in Rebecca Harding Davis. Edith Wharton is considered by many critics to be a master of the realist genre, in terms of both the technique and the thematic material of her fiction.

By the end of the century, realism had developed for some authors into naturalism, a literary movement based on the scientific theory of evolution. The naturalists held that human character was nothing more nor less than the combined product of inherited traits ("race"), social circumstances ("milieu"), and historical period, and that each individual's fate is in a sense predetermined by the confluence of these factors. Some critics see signs of naturalism in the writing of Kate Chopin; Charlotte Perkins Gilman's "The Yellow Wallpaper" could also be read as an example of naturalist fiction. Gilman joined many others in writing utopian fiction as well (*Herland*, for instance, is a story of a society populated and ruled exclusively by women), pulling against the grain of the realist and naturalist movements that dominated the period in mainstream literature.

Regionalism, another outgrowth of realism, has had special significance for female American writers. Regional writing is realistic fiction that self-consciously locates itself in a particular section of the country, drawing heavily on dialect, setting, local mythology, and sometimes an external narrative perspective (for instance, an "outsider" narrator or focal character) to establish the distinctness of the world it describes. Sarah Winnemucca Hopkins (writing about the American West); Sarah Orne Jewett, Sarah Pratt McLean Greene, and Mary Wilkins Freeman (writing about New England); Kate Chopin and Mary Noailles Murfree (writing about different regions of the American South); and many other women writers have been identified as regionalists. The label functions both to praise and to damn the writer who receives it. Regionalism is valued for its "authenticity" to local experience, but it is particularly praised when its themes transcend region and address what critics call "universal" concerns. (This is how William Faulkner, for instance, whose fiction is intensely regional in its characterizations and settings, has escaped being labeled exclusively a regionalist.) In other words, regionalism is supposed to be of the highest literary value when it is least regional. Feminist critics have asked why so many nineteenth-century female realists have been labeled regionalists, a term which seems to call the broader applicability and value of women's work into question.

"Regional," "domestic," "conventional": whatever terms are used to designate the work of women writers in the centuries before our own, by 1900 women had created a vast body of literature that merits our attention. As the nineteenth century turned into the twentieth, American women writers had laid firm foundations for the work to follow.

Anne Bradstreet

(1612–1672)

Born in England into the home of a wealthy mother and an educated father, Anne Dudley had the childhood advantage of a good home library and parental encouragement. At 16 she married Simon Bradstreet, a graduate of Cambridge whom she had known since she was very young. Two years later the Dudley and Bradstreet families sailed for Massachusetts on the ship *Arbella;* Anne and Simon lived first in Cambridge (called Newtown in 1630) and later settled in Andover.

Anne's family achieved political eminence in the colonies: her father, Thomas Dudley, served as the second governor of the Massachusetts Bay Colony, and after Anne's death, her husband, Simon Bradstreet, was also elected to the post. Anne gave birth to eight children; despite the widespread disease and infant mortality of the period, all but one of her offspring outlived their mother.

Prejudice against intellectual women was particularly strong among the Puritans. Anne Hutchinson's antinomian challenges to Puritan orthodoxy had scandalized the colony before her expulsion in 1637, and in 1645 Governor John Winthrop recounted the sad fate of a Mrs. Hopkins, who was driven mad by "giving herself wholly to reading and writing." In this climate, Bradstreet had reason to be wary of "each carping tongue who says my hand a needle better fits," but she was writing poetry within a year of her arrival in the New World and continued to write verse and prose throughout her life.

In 1650, the Reverend John Woodbridge, husband of Anne's sister Mercy, took manuscript copies of Bradstreet's work with him on a return trip to England and had them published under the title *The Tenth Muse, Lately Sprung Up in America.* In the preface, Woodbridge noted that though the reader might doubt the poems could really have been written by a member of "the inferior Sex," he could be reassured that the author is "a Woman, honoured, and esteemed where she lives, for her gracious demeanour, her eminent parts, her pious conversation, her courteous disposition, her exact diligence in her place, and discreet mannaging of her family occasions, and more than so, these poems are the fruit but of some few houres, curtailed from her sleep, and other refreshments."

In "The Author to Her Book," a poem added to the second edition, Bradstreet expresses herself as embarrassed to have her uncorrected work, "my rambling brat," exposed to the world, but vows to clean it up and, dressed in "homespun cloth," send it "out of door." She did undertake corrections with subsequent publication evidently in mind.

The poems in this first collection give evidence of wide reading and express the writer's Puritan religious sentiments. They were intended particularly for her father's eyes. Indeed, her quaternions—four poems each on the four elements, four humors, four ages, and four seasons—echo the structure of a Thomas Dudley poem, now lost, "On the Four Parts of the World."

Her shorter lyrics, contained in a family manuscript, display her emotional experience as they deal with everyday life, health, and family. In addition to her verse, Bradstreet left a prose journal intended to provide moral and spiritual guidance to her children. From these writings come most of our information about Bradstreet's biography, for though her male relatives were mentioned in histories of the period, she was not. No portrait of her survives, and the site of her grave is unknown.

The posthumous first American edition, *Several Poems Compiled with Great Variety of Wit and Learning* (1678), included the verses of *The Tenth Muse* with the author's corrections and additional poems; the editor is unknown. In 1867, John Harvard Ellis collated the two editions and added the previously unpublished poetry and prose from the family manuscript for his edition of *The Works of Anne Bradstreet*. Jeannine Hensley edited *The Works of Anne Bradstreet*

(1967), the source of the following texts. Anne Stanford's *Anne Bradstreet: The Worldly Puritan* (1974) is a critical study. Bradstreet was one of the three poets studied by Wendy Martin in *An American Triptych* (1984).

The Prologue[1]

1

To sing of wars, of captains, and of kings,
Of cities founded, commonwealths begun,
For my mean pen are too superior things:
Or how they all, or each their dates have run
Let poets and historians set these forth,   5
My obscure lines shall not so dim their worth.

2

But when my wond'ring eyes and envious heart
Great Bartas'[2] sugared lines do but read o'er,
Fool I do grudge the Muses did not part
'Twixt him and me that overfluent store;   10
A Bartas can do what a Bartas will
But simple I according to my skill.

3

From schoolboy's tongue no rhet'ric we expect,
Nor yet a sweet consort from broken strings,
Nor perfect beauty where's a main defect: 15
My foolish, broken, blemished Muse so sings,
And this to mend, alas, no art is able,
'Cause nature made it so irreparable.

4

Nor can I, like that fluent sweet tongued Greek,
Who lisped at first, in future times speak plain.   20
By art he gladly found what he did seek,
A full requital of his striving pain.
Art can do much, but this maxim's most sure:
A weak or wounded brain admits no cure.

1. Apparently intended as a prologue to the quaternions, this was the second poem in the 1650 edition; it came after a poem of dedication to the author's father, Thomas Dudley.
2. Guillaume de Salluste du Bartas (1544–1590),

French Huguenot poet best known for *La Septmaine; ou Creation du Monde* (1578); a translation of this book was owned by Thomas Dudley. Bradstreet was greatly influenced by it.

5

I am obnoxious to each carping tongue   25
Who says my hand a needle better fits,
A poet's pen all scorn I should thus wrong,
For such despite they cast on female wits:
If what I do prove well, it won't advance,
They'll say it's stol'n, or else it was by chance.   30

6

But sure the antique Greeks were far more mild
Else of our sex, why feigned they those nine[3]
And poesy made Calliope's own child;
So 'mongst the rest they placed the arts divine:
But this weak knot they will full soon untie,   35
The Greeks did nought, but play the fools and lie.

7

Let Greeks be Greeks, and women what they are
Men have precedency and still excel,
It is but vain unjustly to wage war;
Men can do best, and women know it well.   40
Preeminence in all and each is yours;
Yet grant some small acknowledgement of ours.

8

And oh ye high flown quills[4] that soar the skies,
And ever with your prey still catch your praise,
If e'er you deign these lowly lines your eyes,   45
Give thyme or parsley wreath, I ask no bays;
This mean and unrefined ore of mine
Will make your glist'ring gold but more to shine.

1650

In Honour of That High and Mighty Princess Queen Elizabeth of Happy Memory[5]

The Proem

Although, great Queen, thou now in silence lie
Yet thy loud herald Fame doth to the sky

---

3. The muses of Greek mythology were all female. Calliope, referred to in line 33, was the muse of heroic epic verse.
4. Quill pens.
5. Elizabeth I (1533–1603). One of the queen's first actions when she assumed the throne in 1558 was to reestablish Protestantism; though Puritans distrusted the Church of England, they feared Catholicism more.

Thy wondrous worth proclaim in every clime,
And so hath vowed while there is world or time.
So great's thy glory and thine excellence,   5
The sound thereof rapts[6] every human sense,
That men account it no impiety,
To say thou wert a fleshly deity.
Thousands bring offerings (though out of date)
Thy world of honours to accumulate;   10
'Mongst hundred hecatombs of roaring verse,
Mine bleating stands before thy royal herse.
Thou never didst nor canst thou now disdain
T' accept the tribute of a loyal brain.
Thy clemency did erst esteem as much   15
The acclamations of the poor as rich,
Which makes me deem my rudeness is no wrong,
Though I resound thy praises 'mongst the throng.

The Poem

No Phoenix pen, nor Spenser's poetry,
No Speed's nor Camden's learned history,   20
Eliza's works wars, praise, can e'er compact;
The world's the theatre where she did act.
No memories nor volumes can contain
The 'leven Olympiads[7] of her happy reign.
Who was so good, so just, so learn'd, so wise,   25
From all the kings on earth she won the prize.
Nor say I more than duly is her due,
Millions will testify that this is true.
She hath wiped off th' aspersion of her sex,
That women wisdom lack to play the rex.   30
Spain's monarch, says not so, nor yet his host;[8]
She taught them better manners, to their cost.
The Salic[9] law, in force now had not been,
If France had ever hoped for such a queen.
But can you, doctors, now this point dispute,   35
She's argument enough to make you mute.
Since first the Sun did run his ne'er run race,
And earth had, once a year, a new old face,
Since time was time, and man unmanly man,
Come show me such a Phoenix if you can.   40
Was ever people better ruled than hers?
Was ever land more happy freed from stirs?[1]
Did ever wealth in England more abound?
Her victories in foreign coasts resound;
Ships more invincible than Spain's, her foe,   45
She wracked, she sacked, she sunk his Armado;

6. Enraptures.
7. Four-year spans, as between Olympic games.
8. The Spanish Armada, sent by Phillip II of Spain, was defeated by English forces and storms off the Irish coast in 1588.

9. A rule of succession forbidding women or heirs of the female line from assuming titles. It was strongly enforced by the House of Valois and later the House of Bourbon in France.
1. Dissension.

Her stately troops advanced to Lisbon's wall,
Don Anthony in's right there to install.
She frankly helped Frank's brave distressed king;
The states united now her fame do sing.[2]   50
She their protectrix was; they well do know
Unto our dread virago, what they owe.
Her nobles sacrificed their noble blood,
Nor men nor coin she spared to do them good.
The rude untamed Irish, she did quell,   55
Before her picture the proud Tyrone[3] fell.
Had ever prince such counsellors as she?
Herself Minerva caused them so to be.
Such captains and such soldiers never seen,
As were the subjects of our Pallas queen.   60
Her seamen through all straits the world did round;
Terra incognita might know the sound.
Her Drake[4] came laden home with Spanish gold;
Her Essex took Cadiz, their Herculean hold.[5]
But time would fail me, so my tongue would too,   65
To tell of half she did, or she could do.
Semiramis to her is but obscure,
More infamy than fame she did procure.
She built her glory but on Babel's walls,
World's wonder for a while, but yet it falls.   70
Fierce Tomris (Cyrus' headsman) Scythians' queen,
Had put her harness off, had she but seen
Our Amazon in th' Camp of Tilbury,
Judging all valour and all majesty
Within that princess to have residence,   75
And prostrate yielded to her excellence.
Dido, first foundress of proud Carthage walls
(Who living consummates her funerals),
A great Eliza, but compared with ours,
How vanisheth her glory, wealth, and powers.   80
Profuse, proud Cleopatra, whose wrong name,
Instead of glory, proved her country's shame,
Of her what worth in stories to be seen,
But that she was a rich Egyptian queen.
Zenobya, potent empress of the East,   85
And of all these without compare the best,

2. Elizabeth supported Protestant claimants or
   rulers, including Don Antonio, claimant to the
   throne of Portugal; Henry IV of France,
   attacked by Catholic rebels; and the Dutch,
   who won their freedom from Spain and united
   their provinces in 1581.
3. Hugh O'Neill Tyrone (1540?–1616), leader of
   an Irish rebellion allied with Spain. Tyrone
   accepted peace with England in 1603.
4. Sir Francis Drake (1540?–1596). He explored
   the West Indies, Central and South America,
   and the west coast of the United States,

returning to England by the Pacific route. In
South America he plundered the Spanish
colonies and ships. Elizabeth knighted him
aboard his ship *The Golden Hind*. He was vice
admiral of the fleet that defeated the Spanish
Armada.
5. Robert Devereux, second earl of Essex
   (1567–1601), was co-commander of the
   expedition against Cadiz (1596), but failed to
   quell the Irish rebellion. Implicated in a plot
   against the queen, he was found guilty and
   executed.

Whom none but great Aurelius could quell;
Yet for our Queen is no fit parallel.[6]
She was a Phoenix queen, so shall she be,
Her ashes not revived, more Phoenix she.   90
Her personal perfections, who would tell
Must dip his pen in th' Heleconian[7] well,
Which I may not, my pride doth but aspire
To read what others write and so admire.
Now say, have women worth? or have they none?   95
Or had they some, but with our Queen is't gone?
Nay masculines, you have thus taxed us long,
But she, though dead, will vindicate our wrong.
Let such as say our sex is void of reason,
Know 'tis a slander now but once was treason.   100
But happy England which had such a queen;
Yea happy, happy, had those days still been.
But happiness lies in a higher sphere,
Then wonder not Eliza moves not here.
Full fraught with honour, riches and with days   105
She set, she set, like Titan in his rays.
No more shall rise or set so glorious sun
Until the heaven's great revolution;[8]
If then new things their old forms shall retain,
Eliza shall rule Albion once again.   110

Her Epitaph

Here sleeps the queen, this is the royal bed
Of th' damask rose, sprung from the white and red,[9]
Whose sweet perfume fills the all-filling air.
This rose is withered, once so lovely fair.
On neither tree did grow such rose before,   115
The greater was our gain, our loss the more.

Another

Here lies the pride of queens, pattern of kings,
So blaze it, Fame, here's feathers for thy wings.
Here lies the envied, yet unparalleled prince,
Whose living virtues speak (though dead long since).   120
If many worlds, as that fantastic framed,
In every one be her great glory famed.

1650

6. The queens of antiquity are Semiramis of Assyria, said to be the founder of Babylon; Tomyris, Queen of the Massaqetes, who defeated Cyrus of Persia; Dido of Carthage, also called Elissa; Cleopatra of Egypt; Zenobia of Palmyra (Syria), conquered by Emperor Aurelian.

7. On the slopes of Mount Helicon, where the Temple of the Muses was located.

8. The Last Judgment.

9. The Tudor monarchs, of which Elizabeth was the last, came to power at the end of the War of the Roses, fought between the House of Lancaster (the red rose) and the House of York (the white rose).

Contemplations

1

Some time now past in the autumnal tide,
When Phoebus[1] wanted but one hour to bed,
The trees all richly clad, yet void of pride,
Where gilded o'er by his rich golden head.
Their leaves and fruits seemed painted, but was true,   5
Of green, of red, of yellow, mixed hue;
Rapt were my senses at this delectable view.

2

I wist not what to wish, yet sure thought I,
If so much excellence abide below,
How excellent is He that dwells on high,   10
Whose power and beauty by his works we know?
Sure he is goodness, wisdom, glory, light,
That hath this under world so richly dight;
More heaven than earth was here, no winter and no night.

3

Then on a stately oak I cast mine eye,   15
Whose ruffling top the clouds seemed to aspire;
How long since thou wast in thine infancy?
Thy strength, and stature, more thy years admire,
Hath hundred winters past since thou wast born?
Or thousand since thou brakest thy shell of horn?   20
If so, all these as nought, eternity doth scorn.

4

Then higher on the glistering Sun I gazed,
Whose beams was shaded by the leavie tree;
The more I looked, the more I grew amazed,
And softly said, "What glory's like to thee?"   25
Soul of this world, this universe's eye,
No wonder some made thee a deity;
Had I not better known, alas, the same had I.

5

Thou as a bridegroom from thy chamber rushes,[2]
And as a strong man, joys to run a race;   30
The morn doth usher thee with smiles and blushes;

1. An epithet for the Greek god of the Sun, Apollo.
2. Psalm 19 begins, "The heavens declare the glory of God . . ." Verse 5 has the image of the sun as a bridegroom.

The Earth reflects her glances in thy face.
Birds, insects, animals with vegative,
Thy heat from death and dullness doth revive,
And in the darksome womb of fruitful nature dive.   35

6

Thy swift annual and diurnal course,
Thy daily straight and yearly oblique path,
Thy pleasing fervor and thy scorching force,
All mortals here the feeling knowledge hath.
Thy presence makes it day, thy absence night,   40
Quaternal seasons caused by thy might:
Hail creature, full of sweetness, beauty, and delight.

7

Art thou so full of glory that no eye
Hath strength thy shining rays once to behold?
And is thy splendid throne erect so high,   45
As to approach it, can no earthly mould?
How full of glory then must thy Creator be,
Who gave this bright light luster unto thee?
Admired, adored for ever, be that Majesty.

8

Silent alone, where none or saw, or heard,   50
In pathless paths I lead my wand'ring feet,
My humble eyes to lofty skies I reared
To sing some song, my mazed Muse thought meet.
My great Creator I would magnify,
That nature had thus decked liberally;   55
But Ah, and Ah, again, my imbecility![3]

9

I heard the merry grasshopper then sing.
The black-clad cricket bear a second part;
They kept one tune and played on the same string,
Seeming to glory in their little art.   60
Shall creatures abject thus their voices raise
And in their kind resound their Maker's praise,
Whilst I, as mute, can warble forth no higher lays?

10

When present times look back to ages past,
And men in being fancy those are dead,   65
It makes things gone perpetually to last,

---

3. Inadequacy.

And calls back months and years that long since fled.
It makes a man more aged in conceit
Than was Methuselah, or's grandsire great,[4]
While of their persons and their acts his mind doth treat.   70

11

Sometimes in Eden fair he seems to be,
Sees glorious Adam there made lord of all,
Fancies the apple, dangle on the tree,
That turned his sovereign to a naked thrall.
Who like a miscreant's driven from that place,   75
To get his bread with pain and sweat of face,
A penalty imposed on his backsliding race.

12

Here sits our grandame in retired place,
And in her lap her bloody Cain new-born;
The weeping imp oft looks her in the face,   80
Bewails his unknown hap and fate forlorn;
His mother sighs to think of Paradise,
And how she lost her bliss to be more wise,
Believing him that was, and is, father of lies.[5]

13

Here Cain and Abel come to sacrifice,   85
Fruits of the earth and fatlings each do bring,
On Abel's gift the fire descends from skies,
But no such sign on false Cain's offering;
With sullen hateful looks he goes his ways,
Hath thousand thoughts to end his brother's days,   90
Upon whose blood his future good he hopes to raise.

14

There Abel keeps his sheep, no ill he thinks;
His brother comes, then acts his fratricide;
The virgin Earth of blood her first draught drinks,[6]
But since that time she often hath been cloyed.   95
The wretch with ghastly face and dreadful mind
Thinks each he sees will serve him in his kind,
Though none on earth but kindred near then could he find.

15

Who fancies not his looks now at the bar,
His face like death, his heart with horror fraught,   100

4. According to the Old Testament, Jared lived
962 years and his grandson Methuselah lived
969 years (Genesis 5:20–27).
5. Satan is the father of lies; Cain is bloody
because he killed his brother Abel (Genesis
4:8).
6. Genesis 4:1–16.

Nor malefactor ever felt like war,
When deep despair with wish of life hath fought,
Branded with guilt and crushed with treble woes,
A vagabond to Land of Nod he goes.
A city builds, that walls might him secure from foes.   105

16

Who thinks not oft upon the father's ages,
Their long descent, how nephews' sons they saw,
The starry observations of those sages,
And how their precepts to their sons were law,
How Adam sighed to see his progeny,   110
Clothed all in his black sinful livery,
Who neither guilt nor yet the punishment could fly.

17

Our life compare we with their length of days
Who to the tenth of theirs doth now arrive?
And though thus short, we shorten many ways,   115
Living so little while we are alive;
In eating, drinking, sleeping, vain delight
So unawares comes on perpetual night,
And puts all pleasures vain unto eternal flight.

18

When I behold the heavens as in their prime,   120
And then the earth (though old) still clad in green,
The stones and trees, insensible of time,
Nor age nor wrinkle on their front are seen;
If winter come and greenness then do fade,
A spring returns, and they more youthful made;   125
But man grows old, lies down, remains where once he's laid.

19

By birth more noble than those creatures all,
Yet seems by nature and by custom cursed,
No sooner born, but grief and care makes fall
That state obliterate he had at first;   130
Nor youth, nor strength, nor wisdom spring again,
Nor habitations long their names retain,
But in oblivion to the final day remain.

20

Shall I then praise the heavens, the trees, the earth
Because their beauty and their strength last longer?   135
Shall I wish there, or never to had birth,
Because they're bigger, and their bodies stronger?
Nay, they shall darken, perish, fade and die,

And when unmade, so ever shall they lie,
But man was made for endless immortality.   140

21

Under the cooling shadow of a stately elm
Close sat I by a goodly river's side,
Where gliding streams the rocks did overwhelm,
A lonely place, with pleasures dignified.
I once that loved the shady woods so well,   145
Now thought the rivers did the trees excel,
And if the sun would ever shine, there would I dwell.

22

While on the stealing stream I fixt mine eye,
Which to the longed-for ocean held its course,
I marked, nor crooks, nor rubs that there did lie   150
Could hinder ought, but still augment its force.
"O happy flood," quoth I, "that holds thy race
Till thou arrive at thy beloved place,
Nor is it rocks or shoals that can obstruct thy pace,

23

Nor is't enough, that thou alone mayst slide,   155
But hundred brooks in thy clear waves do meet,
So hand in hand along with thee they glide
To Thetis'[7] house, where all embrace and greet.
Thou emblem true of what I count the best,
O could I lead my rivulets to rest,   160
So may we press to that vast mansion, ever blest."

24

Ye fish, which in this liquid region 'bide,
That for each season have your habitation,
Now salt, now fresh where you think best to glide
To unknown coasts to give a visitation,   165
In lakes and ponds you leave your numerous fry;
So nature taught, and yet you know not why,
You wat'ry folk that know not your felicity.

25

Look how the wantons frisk to taste the air,
Then to the colder bottom straight they dive;   170
Eftsoon to Neptune's glassy hall repair
To see what trade they great ones there do drive,
Who forage o'er the spacious sea-green field,

7. A water nymph, mother of Achilles.

And take the trembling prey before it yield,
Whose armour is their scales, their spreading fins their shield.   175

26

While musing thus with contemplation fed,
And thousand fancies buzzing in my brain.
The sweet-tongued Philomel[8] perched o'er my head
And chanted forth a most melodious strain
Which rapt me so with wonder and delight,   180
I judged my hearing better than my sight,
And wished me wings with her a while to take my flight.

27

"O merry Bird," said I, "that fears no snares,
That neither toils nor hoards up in thy barn,
Feels no sad thoughts nor cruciating cares   185
To gain more good or shun what might thee harm.
Thy clothes ne'er wear, thy meat is everywhere,
Thy bed a bough, thy drink the water clear,
Reminds not what is past, nor what's to come dost fear."

28

"The dawning morn with songs thou dost prevent,[9]   190
Sets hundred notes unto thy feathered crew,
So each one tunes his pretty instrument,
And warbling out the old, begin anew,
And thus they pass their youth in summer season,
Then follow thee into a better region,   195
Where winter's never felt by that sweet airy legion."

29

Man at the best a creature frail and vain,
In knowledge ignorant, in strength but weak,
Subject to sorrows, losses, sickness, pain,
Each storm his state, his mind, his body break,   200
From some of these he never finds cessation,
But day or night, within, without, vexation,
Troubles from foes, from friends, from dearest, near'st relation.

30

And yet this sinful creature, frail and vain,
This lump of wretchedness, of sin and sorrow,   205
This weatherbeaten vessel wracked with pain,

---

8. According to myth, Philomel, a princess of
Athens, was turned into a nightingale. A staple
of English pastoral verse, the nightingale is not
native to New England.
9. Anticipate or come before.

Joys not in hope of an eternal morrow;
Nor all his losses, crosses, and vexation,
In weight, in frequency and long duration
Can make him deeply groan for that divine translation.   210

31

The mariner that on smooth waves doth glide
Sings merrily and steers his bark with ease,
As if he had command of wind and tide,
And now become great master of the seas:
But suddenly a storm spoils all the sport,   225
And makes him long for a more quiet port,
Which 'gainst all adverse winds may serve for fort.

32

So he that saileth in this world of pleasure,
Feeding on sweets, that never bit of th' sour,
That's full of friends, of honour, and of treasure,   220
Fond fool, he takes this earth ev'n for heav'n's bower.
But sad affliction comes and makes him see
Here's neither honour, wealth, nor safety;
Only above is found all with security.

33

O Time the fatal wrack of mortal things,   225
That draws oblivion's curtains over kings;
Their sumptuous monuments, men know them not,
Their names without a record are forgot,
Their parts, their ports, their pomp's all laid in th' dust
Nor wit nor gold, nor buildings scape times rust;   230
But he whose name is graved in the white stone[1]
Shall last and shine when all of these are gone.

                1678

The Flesh and the Spirit[2]

In secret place where once I stood
Close by the banks of Lacrim[3] flood,
I heard two sisters reason on
Things that are past and things to come;

1. A reference to Rev. 2:17 in which Jesus promises "to him that overcometh" a white stone with a name engraved on it that only the receiver will know.
2. The debate between the body and the soul was an established poetic convention in the Middle Ages. See also the discussion in Saint Paul's Epistle to the Romans, Chapter 8.
3. Tears, cf. Latin *Lacrima*.

One flesh was called, who had her eye   5
On worldly wealth and vanity;
The other Spirit, who did rear
Her thoughts unto a higher sphere:
Sister, quoth Flesh, what liv'st thou on,
Nothing but meditation?   10
Doth contemplation feed thee so
Regardlessly to let earth go?
Can speculation satisfy
Notion without reality?
Dost dream of things beyond the moon,   15
And dost thou hope to dwell there soon?
Hast treasures there laid up in store
That all in th' world thou count'st but poor?
Art fancy sick, or turned a sot
To catch at shadows which are not?   20
Come, come, I'll show unto thy sense,
Industry hath its recompense.
What canst desire, but thou may'st see
True substance in variety?
Dost honour like? Acquire the same,   25
As some to their immortal fame,
And trophies to thy name erect
Which wearing time shall ne'er deject.
For riches doth thou long full sore?
Behold enough of precious store.   30
Earth hath more silver, pearls, and gold,
Than eyes can see or hands can hold.
Affect's thou pleasure? Take thy fill,
Earth hath enough of what you will.
Then let not go, what thou may'st find   35
For things unknown, only in mind.
Spir: *Spirit.* Be still thou unregenerate part,
Disturb no more my settled heart,
For I have vowed (and so will do)
Thee as a foe still to pursue.   40
And combat with thee will and must,
Until I see thee laid in th' dust.
Sisters we are, yea, twins we be,
Yet deadly feud 'twixt thee and me;
For from one father are we not,   45
Thou by old Adam wast begot,
But my arise is from above,
Whence my dear Father I do love.
Thou speak'st me fair, but hat'st me sore,
Thy flatt'ring shows I'll trust no more.   50
How oft thy slave, hast thou me made,
When I believed what thou hast said,
And never had more cause of woe
Than when I did what thou bad'st do.
I'll stop mine ears at these thy charms,   55
And count them for my deadly harms.

Thy sinful pleasures I do hate,
Thy riches are to me no bait,
Thine honours do, nor will I love;
For my ambition lies above.   60
My greatest honour it shall be
When I am victor over thee,
And triumph shall with laurel head,
When thou my captive shalt be led,
How I do live, thou need'st not scoff,   65
For I have meat thou know'st not of;
The hidden manna[4] I do eat,
The word of life it is my meat.
My thoughts do yield me more content
Than can thy hours in pleasure spent.   70
Nor are they shadows which I catch,
Nor fancies vain at which I snatch,
But reach at things that are so high,
Beyond thy dull capacity;
Eternal substance I do see,   75
With which enriched I would be.
Mine eye doth pierce the heavens and see
What is invisible to thee.
My garments are not silk nor gold,
Nor such like trash which earth doth hold,   80
But royal robes I shall have on,
More glorious than the glist'ring sun;
My crown not diamonds, pearls, and gold,
But such as angels' heads enfold.
The city[5] where I hope to dwell,   85
There's none on earth can parallel;
The stately walls both high and strong,
Are made of precious jasper stone;
The gates of pearl, both rich and clear,
And angels are for porters there;   90
The streets thereof transparent gold,
Such as no eye did e'er behold;
A crystal river there doth run,
Which doth proceed from the Lamb's throne.
Of life, there are the waters sure,   95
Which shall remain forever pure,
Nor sun, nor moon, they have no need,
For glory doth from God proceed.
No candle there, nor yet torchlight,
For there shall be no darksome night.   100
From sickness and infirmity
For evermore they shall be free;
Nor withering age shall e'er come there,
But beauty shall be bright and clear;
This city pure is not for thee,   105

4. Food sent by God.
5. The City of God (described in Revelations

21–22) was described by Saint Augustine
(354–430), in the book of that title.

For things unclean there shall not be.
If I of heaven may have my fill,
Take thou the world and all that will.

1678

The Author to Her Book

Thou ill-formed offspring of my feeble brain,
Who after birth didst by my side remain,
Till snatched from thence by friends, less wise than true,
Who thee abroad, exposed to public view,
Made thee in rags, halting to th' press to trudge,   5
Where errors were not lessened (all may judge).
At thy return my blushing was not small,
My rambling brat (in print) should mother call,
I cast thee by as one unfit for light,
Thy visage was so irksome in my sight;   10
Yet being mine own, at length affection would
Thy blemishes amend, if so I could:
I washed thy face, but more defects I saw,
And rubbing off a spot still made a flaw.
I stretched thy joints to make thee even feet,   15
Yet still thou run'st more hobbling than is meet;
In better dress to trim thee was my mind,
But nought save homespun cloth i' th' house I find.
In this array 'mongst vulgars may'st thou roam.
In critic's hands beware thou dost not come,   20
And take thy way where yet thou art not known;
If for thy father asked, say thou hadst none;
And for thy mother, she alas is poor,
Which caused her thus to send thee out of door.

1678

Before the Birth of One[6] of Her Children

All things within this fading world hath end,
Adversity doth still our joys attend;
No ties so strong, no friends so dear and sweet,
But with death's parting blow is sure to meet.
The sentence past is most irrevocable,   5
A common thing, yet oh, inevitable.
How soon, my Dear, death may my steps attend,

---

6. In the 1678 American edition, the unknown editor included this poem and others found among Bradstreet's papers after her death.

How soon't may be thy lot to lose thy friend,
We both are ignorant, yet love bids me
These farewell lines to recommend to thee,   10
That when that knot's untied that made us one,
I may seem thine, who in effect am none.
And if I see not half my days that's due,
What nature would, God grant to yours and you;
The many faults that well you know I have   15
Let be interred in my oblivious grave;
If any worth or virtue were in me,
Let that live freshly in thy memory
And when thou feel'st no grief, as I no harms,
Yet love thy dead, who long lay in thine arms.   20
And when thy loss shall be repaid with gains
Look to my little babes, my dear remains.
And if thou love thyself, or loved'st me,
These O protect from step-dame's injury.
And if chance to thine eyes shall bring this verse,   25
With some sad sighs honour my absent hearse;
And kiss this paper for thy love's dear sake,
Who with salt tears this last farewell did take.

                                                1678

To My Dear and Loving Husband

If ever two were one, then surely we.
If ever man were loved by wife, then thee;
If ever wife was happy in a man,
Compare with me, ye women, if you can.
I prize thy love more than whole mines of gold   5
Or all the riches that the East doth hold.
My love is such that rivers cannot quench,
Nor ought but love from thee, give recompense.
Thy love is such I can no way repay,
The heavens reward thee manifold, I pray.   10
Then while we live, in love let's so persevere
That when we live no more, we may live ever.

                                                1678

A Letter to Her Husband, Absent upon Public Employment

My head, my heart, mine eyes, my life, nay, more,
My joy, my magazine of earthly store,

On whom I placed no small delight;
Coupled with mate loving and true,
Hath also bid her dam adieu;
And where Aurora first appears,   25
She now hath perched to spend her years.
One to the academy flew[4]
To chat among that learned crew;
Ambition moves still in his breast
That he might chant above the rest,   30
Striving for more than to do well,
That nightingales he might excel,
My fifth, whose down is yet scarce gone,
Is 'mongst the shrubs and bushes flown,
And as his wings increase in strength,   35
On higher boughs he'll perch at length.
My other three still with me nest,
Until they're grown, then as the rest,
Or here or there they'll take their flight,
As is ordained, so shall they light.   40
If birds could weep, then would my tears
Let others know what are my fears
Lest this my brood some harm should catch,
And be surprised for want of watch,
Whilst pecking corn and void of care,   45
They fall un'wares in fowler's snare,
Or whilst on trees they sit and sing,
Some untoward boy at them do fling,
Or whilst allured with bell and glass,
The net be spread, and caught, alas.   50
Or lest by lime-twigs they be foiled,
Or by some greedy hawks be spoiled.
O would my young, ye saw my breast,
And knew what thoughts there sadly rest,
Great was my pain when I you bred,   55
Great was my care when I you fed,
Long did I keep you soft and warm,
And with my wings kept off all harm,
My cares are more and fears than ever,
My throbs such now as 'fore were never.   60
Alas, my birds, you wisdom want,
Of perils you are ignorant;
Oft times in grass, on trees, in flight,
Sore accidents on you may light.
O to your safety have an eye,   65
So happy may you live and die.
Meanwhile my days in tunes I'll spend,
Till my weak lays with me shall end.
In shady woods I'll sit and sing,
And things that past to mind I'll bring.   70
Once young and pleasant, as are you,

4. Simon entered Harvard on June 25, 1656.

But former toys (no joys) adieu.
My age I will not once lament,
But sing, my time so near is spent.
And from the top bough take my flight   75
Into a country beyond sight,
Where old ones instantly grow young,
And there with seraphims set song;
No seasons cold, nor storms they see;
But spring lasts to eternity.   80
When each of you shall in your nest
Among your young ones take your rest,
In chirping language, oft them tell,
You had a dam that loved you well,
That did what could be done for young,   85
And nursed you up till you were strong,
And 'fore she once would let you fly,
She showed you joy and misery;
Taught what was good, and what was ill,
What would save life, and what would kill.   90
Thus gone, amongst you I may live,
And dead, yet speak, and counsel give:
Farewell, my birds, farewell adieu,
I happy am, if well with you.

1678

In Memory of My Dear Grandchild Elizabeth Bradstreet, Who Deceased August, 1665, Being a Year and Half Old

1

Farewell dear babe, my heart's too much content,
Farewell sweet babe, the pleasure of mine eye,
Farewell fair flower that for a space was lent,
Then t'en away unto eternity.
Blest babe, why should I once bewail thy fate,   5
Or sigh thy days so soon were terminate,
Sith⁵ thou art settled in an everlasting state.

2

By nature trees do rot when they are grown,
And plums and apples thoroughly ripe do fall,
And corn and grass are in their season mown,   10
And time brings down what is both strong and tall.

---

5. Since.

But plants new set to be eradicate,
And buds new blown to have so short a date,
Is by His hand alone that guides nature and fate.

1678

In Memory of My Dear Grandchild Anne Bradstreet Who Deceased June 20, 1669, Being Three Years and Seven Months Old

With troubled heart and trembling hand I write,
The heavens have changed to sorrow my delight.
How oft with disappointment have I met,
When I on fading things my hopes have set.
Experience might 'fore this have made me wise,   5
To value things according to their price.
Was ever stable joy yet found below?
Or perfect bliss without mixture of woe?
I knew she was but as a withering flower,
That's here today, perhaps gone in an hour;   10
Like as a bubble, or the brittle glass,
Or like a shadow turning as it was.
More fool then I to look on that was lent
As if mine own, when thus impermanent.
Farewell dear child, thou ne'er shall come to me,   15
But yet a while, and I shall go to thee;
Mean time my throbbing heart's cheered up with this:
Thou with thy Saviour art in endless bliss.

1678

On My Dear Grandchild Simon Bradstreet, Who Died On 16 November, 1669, Being but a Month, and One Day Old

No sooner came, but gone, and fall'n asleep,
Acquaintance short, yet parting caused us weep;
Three flowers, two scarcely blown, the last i' th' bud,
Cropt by th' Almighty's hand; yet is He good.
With dreadful awe before Him let's be mute,   5
Such was His will, but why, let's not dispute,
With humble hearts and mouths put in the dust,
Let's say He's merciful as well as just.
He will return and make up all our losses,

And smile again after our bitter crosses 10
Go pretty babe, go rest with sisters twain;
Among the blest in endless joys remain.

1678

Upon My Son Samuel His Going for England, Nov. 6, 1657

Thou mighty God of sea and land,
I here resign into Thy hand
The son of prayers, of vows, of tears,
The child I stayed for many years.
Thou heard'st me then and gav'st him me; 5
Hear me again, I give him Thee.
He's mine, but more, O Lord, Thine own,
For sure Thy grace on him is shown.
No friend I have like Thee to trust,
For mortal helps are brittle dust. 10
Preserve, O Lord, from storms and wrack,
Protect him there, and bring him back,
And if Thou shalt spare me a space
That I again may see his face,
Then shall I celebrate Thy praise 15
And bless Thee for't even all my days.
If otherwise I go to rest,
Thy will be done, for that is best.
Persuade my heart I shall him see
Forever happified with Thee. 20

1867

Here Follows Some Verses upon the Burning of Our House July 10th, 1666. Copied out of a Loose Paper[6]

In silent night when rest I took
For sorrow near I did not look
I wakened was with thund'ring noise
And piteous shrieks of dreadful voice.
That fearful sound of "Fire!" and "Fire!" 5
Let no man know is my desire.

6. Most of Bradstreet's papers, including a version
of the unfinished "Four Monarchies," were
destroyed. The extant manuscript of this poem
is in the handwriting of her son Simon,
presumably copied from a manuscript written
by Mrs. Bradstreet.

I, starting up, the light did spy,
And to my God my heart did cry
To strengthen me in my distress
And not to leave me succorless.   10
Then, coming out, beheld a space
The flame consume my dwelling place.
And when I could no longer look,
I blest His name that gave and took,[7]
That laid my goods now in the dust.   15
Yea, so it was, and so 'twas just.
It was His own, it was not mine,
Far be it that I should repine;
He might of all justly bereft
But yet sufficient for us left.   20
When by the ruins oft I past
My sorrowing eyes aside did cast,
And here and there the places spy
Where oft I sat and long did lie:
Here stood that trunk, and there that chest, 25
There lay that store I counted best.
My pleasant things in ashes lie,
And them behold no more shall I.
Under thy roof no guest shall sit,
Nor at thy table eat a bit.   30
No pleasant tale shall e'er be told,
Nor things recounted done of old.
No candle e'er shall shine in thee,
Nor bridegroom's voice e'er heard shall be.
In silence ever shall thou lie,   35
Adieu, Adieu, all's vanity.
Then straight I 'gin my heart to chide,
And did thy wealth on earth abide?
Didst fix thy hope on mold'ring dust?[8]
The arm of flesh didst make thy trust?   40
Raise up thy thoughts above the sky
That dunghill mists away may fly.
Thou hast an house on high erect,
Framed by that mighty Architect,
With glory richly furnished,   45
Stands permanent though this be fled.
It's purchased and paid for too
By Him who hath enough to do.
A price so vast as is unknown
Yet by His gift is made thine own;   50
There's wealth enough, I need no more,
Farewell, my pelf,[9] farewell my store.

---

7. Compare to Job 1:21 "The Lord gave, and the Lord hath taken away; blessed be the name of the Lord."
8. Compare to the Sermon on the Mount (Matthew 6 and 7 or Luke 12): "lay up for yourselves treasures in heaven, where neither moth nor rust doth corrupt. . . . For where your treasure is, there will your heart be also" (Matthew 6:20–21).
9. Pejorative term for wealth.

The world no longer let me love,
My hope and treasure lies above.

1867

As Weary Pilgrim

As weary pilgrim, now at rest,
   Hugs with delight his silent nest,
His wasted limbs now lie full soft
   That mirey steps have trodden oft,
Blesses himself to think upon   5
   His dangers past, and travails done.
The burning sun no more shall heat,
   Nor stormy rains on him shall beat.
The briars and thorns no more shall scratch,
   Nor hungry wolves at him shall catch.   10
He erring paths no more shall tread,
   Nor wild fruits eat instead of bread.
For waters cold he doth not long
   For thirst no more shall parch his tongue.
No rugged stones his feet shall gall,   15
   Nor stumps nor rocks cause him to fall.
All cares and fears he bids farewell
   And means in safety now to dwell.
A pilgrim I, on earth perplexed
   With sins, with cares and sorrows vext,   20
By age and pains brought to decay,
   And my clay house mold'ring away.[1]
Oh, how I long to be at rest
   And soar on high among the blest.
This body shall in silence sleep,   25
   Mine eyes no more shall ever weep,
No fainting fits shall me assail,
   Nor grinding pains my body frail,
With cares and fears ne'er cumb'red be
   Nor losses know, nor sorrows see.   30
What though my flesh shall there consume,
   It is the bed Christ did perfume,
And when a few years shall be gone,
   This mortal shall be clothed upon.
A corrupt carcass down it lays,   35
   A glorious body it shall rise.

---

1. Mrs. Bradstreet suffered ill health throughout most of her life from smallpox (a life-threatening disease in the seventeenth century) at 16 through repeated attacks of fainting and weakness, consumptionlike symptoms, and lameness.

In weakness and dishonour sown,
  In power 'tis raised by Christ alone.
Then soul and body shall unite
  And of their Maker have the sight.   40
Such lasting joys shall there behold
  As ear ne'er heard nor tongue e'er told.
Lord make me ready for that day,
  Then come, dear Bridegroom, come away.

Aug. 31, 1669.   1867   45

Mary Rowlandson
(1636?–1711?)

When Mary White Rowlandson wrote the story of her four-month captivity among the Wampanoag Indians during King Philip's War, she became the first female author of an American best-seller. Aside from the written record she left, little is known of Rowlandson's life. She was born in England to prosperous parents, John and Joane (West) White, who migrated first to Salem around 1638, and later to Lancaster, Massachusetts, in 1653. One of seven siblings, Mary married a minister, Joseph Rowlandson, in 1656. Although we know nothing of her education or the details of her later life—even the date of her death is uncertain—her narrative gives voice to a strong, Calvinistic faith; a witty, feisty personality; and a deeply embedded cultural and racial revulsion against the Native Americans, whom she believed— as her text asserts—to be instruments of Satan.

Rowlandson's was the first in a tradition of "captivity narratives" recounting English colonists' experiences among Native Americans who seized them during raids on New England towns. In form it is similar to the slave narratives later written or dictated by African Americans who had achieved their individual freedom, in that it strives to find a meaning in the experience of bondage and forced labor. Rowlandson's focus resembles that of slave mothers who wrote of their concern for their children, devoting equal attention to their family affections and to the facts of their own fear, starvation, and bodily injury. Beginning, like a proper epic, *in medias res* with the massacre and capture of Rowlandson's friends and family, the narrative does not flinch from representing violence. It found a wide readership in the Northeast, and was reprinted twenty-six times between 1682 and 1888.

Like many African-American slaves who told their stories, Rowlandson seeks to understand her captivity in terms of her religious faith. She intersperses her accounts of daily incidents among the Wampanoags with quotations from scripture, drawing parallels between her own trials and those recounted in the Old and New Testaments of the Bible. In so doing, she exemplifies the Puritanism which leads her to read her life typologically, in terms of biblical prophecies. Rowlandson conceives of each incident—from being taken captive and having her wounded 6-year-old daughter die on the ensuing march through northern Massachusetts, New Hampshire, and Vermont to being spared from getting her feet wet when crossing a river in cold weather—as a test or a blessing from God. When her captors treat her brutally, she assumes it is God's will; when they treat her well, she remarks on God's goodness in inspiring them to do so.

The point of view of Rowlandson's text

is strictly limited to what she herself observed or was told by others. Throughout her account of her horrific experience, Rowlandson constructs her captors as "other" from the English; indeed, from her perspective, they are hardly human. Full of biblical allusion and quotation, her *Narrative* can be seen as a spiritual autobiography; simultaneously, it is a record of profound racial polarization in early America.

A useful recent text is the National Bicentennial Edition produced in 1975 by Robert Diebold and the town of Lancaster, Massachusetts. Diebold's edition contains detailed historical annotations helpful to understanding. Only one full-length study of Rowlandson exists: Mitchell Breitweiser's *American Puritanism and the Defense of Mourning: Religion, Grief, and Ethnology in Mary White Rowlandson's Captivity Narrative* (1990). See also *The Indian Captivity Narrative: An American Genre* (1983) by Richard VanDerBeets and *Puritans among the Indians* (1981) by Alden T. Vaughan and Edward W. Clark.

The Narrative of the Captivity and Restoration of Mrs. Mary Rowlandson[1]

On the tenth of February, 1675,[2] came the Indians with great numbers upon Lancaster. Their first coming was about sun-rising. Hearing the noise of some guns, we looked out: several houses were burning and the smoke ascending to Heaven. There were five persons taken in one house. The father and the mother and a sucking child they knocked on the head; the other two they took and carried away alive. There were two others who, being out of their garrison[3] upon some occasion, were set upon: one was knocked on the head; the other escaped. Another there was who running along was shot and wounded and fell down. He begged of them his life, promising them money (as they told me), but they would not hearken to him, but knocked him in head, stripped him naked, and split open his bowels. Another, seeing many of the Indians about his barn, ventured and went out, but was quickly shot down. There were three others belonging to the same garrison who were killed. The Indians, getting up upon the roof of the barn, had advantage to shoot down upon them over their fortification. Thus these murtherous wretches went on, burning and destroying before them.

At length they came and beset our own house, and quickly it was the dolefullest day that ever mine eyes saw. The house stood upon the edge of a hill. Some of the Indians got behind the hill, others into the barn, and others behind anything that would shelter them, from all which places they shot against the house, so that the bullets seemed to fly like hail. And quickly they wounded one man among us, then another, and then a third. About two hours (according to my observation in that amazing time) they had been about the house before they prevailed to fire it (which they did with flax and hemp which they brought out of the barn—and there being no defence about the house, only two flankers at two opposite corners, and one of them not finished). They fired it once, and one ventured out and quenched it; but they quickly fired it again, and that took.

Now is that dreadful Hour come that I have often heard of (in the time of the war, as it was the case of others), but now mine eyes see it. Some in our house were fighting for their lives, others wallowing in their blood, the house on fire over our heads, and the bloody

---

1. The full title is *The Sovereignty and Goodness of God and the Faithfulness of His Promises Displayed, Being the Narrative of the Captivity and Restoration of Mrs. Mary Rowlandson.*

2. February 20, 1676, according to modern calendars.

3. Fortress.

heathen ready to knock us on the head if we stirred out. Now might we hear mothers and children crying out for themselves and one another, *Lord, what shall we do?*

Then I took my children[4] (and one of my sisters, hers) to go forth and leave the house. But as soon as we came to the door and appeared, the Indians shot so thick that the bullets rattled against the house as if one had taken a handful of stones and threw them, so that we were fain to give back. We had six stout dogs belonging to our garrison, but none of them would stir, though another time if an Indian had come to the door, they were ready to fly upon him and tear him down. The Lord hereby would make us the more to acknowledge his hand and to see that our help is always in him. But out we must go, the fire increasing and coming along behind us roaring and the Indians gaping before us with their guns, spears, and hatchets to devour us. No sooner were we out of the house, but my brother-in-law (being before wounded, in defending the house, in or near the throat) fell down dead, whereat the Indians scornfully shouted and hallowed and were presently upon him, stripping off his clothes. The bullets flying thick, one went through my side, and the same (as would seem) through the bowels and hand of my dear child in my arms.[5] One of my elder sister's children (named William) had then his leg broken—which the Indians perceiving, they knocked him on head.

Thus were we butchered by those merciless heathen, standing amazed, with the blood running down to our heels. My elder sister being yet in the house and seeing those woeful sights—the infidels haling mothers one way and children another, and some wallowing in their blood, and her elder son telling her that (her son) William was dead, and myself was wounded—she said, And *Lord, let me die with them.* Which was no sooner said, but she was struck with a bullet and fell down dead over the threshold. I hope she is reaping the fruit of her good labors, being faithful to the service of God in her place. In her younger years she lay under much trouble upon spiritual accounts, till it pleased God to make that precious scripture take hold of her heart, *2 Cor. 12, 9, And he said unto me, My grace is sufficient for thee.* More than twenty years after, I have heard her tell how sweet and comfortable that place was to her. But to return: the Indians laid hold of us, pulling me one way and the children another, and said, *Come, go along with us.* I told them they would kill me. They answered, *If I were willing to go along with them, they would not hurt me.*

O the doleful sight that now was to behold at this house! *Come, behold the works of the Lord, what desolations he has made in the earth.*[6] Of thirty-seven persons who were in this one house, none escaped either present death or a bitter captivity, save only one, who might say as he (*Job* 1, 15): *And I only am escaped alone to tell the news.* There were twelve killed—some shot, some stabbed with their spears, some knocked down with their hatchets. When we are in prosperity, Oh the little that we think of such dreadful sights and to see our dear friends and relations lie bleeding out their heart-blood upon the ground! There was one who was chopped into the head with a hatchet and stripped naked, and yet was crawling up and down. It is a solemn sight to see so many Christians lying in their blood, some here and some there, like a company of sheep torn by wolves, all of them stripped naked by a company of hell hounds, roaring, singing, ranting and insulting, as if they would have torn our very hearts out. Yet the Lord by his almighty power preserved a number of us from death, for there were twenty four of us taken alive and carried captive.

I had often before this said that if the Indians should come, I should choose rather to be killed by them than taken alive; but when it came to the trial, my mind changed. Their glittering weapons so daunted my spirit that I chose rather to go along with those (as I may say) ravenous bears than that moment to end my days. And that I may the better declare what happened to me during that grievous captivity, I shall particularly speak of the several removes we had up and down the wilderness.

---

4. Joseph, Jr., born 1661; Mary, born 1665; Sarah, born 1669.

5. Sarah.

6. Psalm 46:8.

The First Remove[7]

Now away we must go with those barbarous creatures, with our bodies wounded and bleeding, and our hearts no less than our bodies. About a mile we went that night, up upon a hill within sight of the town, where they intended to lodge. There was hard by a vacant house (deserted by the English before, for fear of the Indians). I asked them whether I might not lodge in the house that night. To which they answered, What, will you love Englishmen still?

This was the dolefullest night that ever my eyes saw. Oh the roaring, and singing, and dancing, and yelling of those black creatures in the night, which made the place a lively resemblance of hell. And as miserable was the waste that was there made of horses, cattle, sheep, swine, calves, lambs, roasting pigs, and fowls (which they had plundered in the town), some roasting, some lying and burning, and some boiling, to feed our merciless enemies, who were joyful enough though we were disconsolate. To add to the dolefulness of the former day and the dismalness of the present night, my thoughts ran upon my losses and sad, bereaved condition. All was gone: my husband gone (at least separated from me, he being in the Bay—and to add to my grief, the Indians told me they would kill him as he came homeward), my children gone, my relations and friends gone, our house and home and all our comforts within door and without—all was gone except my life, and I knew not but the next moment that might go too.

There remained nothing to me but one poor, wounded babe, and it seemed at present worse than death that it was in such a pitiful condition, bespeaking compassion, and I had no refreshing for it, nor suitable things to revive it. Little do many think what is the savageness and brutishness of this barbarous enemy, even those that seem to profess more than others among them,[8] when the English have fallen into their hands.

Those seven that were killed at Lancaster the summer before upon a Sabbath day and the one that was afterward killed upon a weekday were slain and mangled in a barbarous manner by One-eyed John and Marlborough's Praying Indians,[9] which Capt. Mosely[1] brought to Boston, as the Indians told me.

The Second Remove

But now (the next morning) I must turn my back upon the town and travel with them into the vast and desolate wilderness—I know not whither. It is not my tongue or pen can express the sorrows of my heart and bitterness of my spirit that I had at this departure. But God was with me, in a wonderful manner, carrying me along and bearing up my spirit, that it did not quite fail. One of the Indians carried my poor wounded babe upon a horse. It went moaning all along, I shall die, I shall die. I went on foot after it, with sorrow that cannot be expressed. At length I took it off the horse and carried it in my arms till my strength failed, and I fell down with it. Then they set me upon a horse with my wounded child in my lap, and there being no furniture upon the horse's back. As we were going down a steep hill, we both fell over the horse's head—at which they like inhuman creatures laughed and rejoiced to see it, though I thought we should there have ended our days, as overcome with so many difficulties. But the Lord renewed my strength still and

7. Archaic term for changing one's place of residence. The twenty "removes" took Rowlandson from Lancaster, Massachusetts, to southern Vermont and back. The captivity lasted from February 1676 until Rowlandson was ransomed in May of that year.
8. To affirm belief in Christianity; a reference to

"Praying Indians."
9. Historians dispute the responsibility of Christian Indians for the massacre at Lancaster in 1675. See Diebold, p. 66.
1. A popular, brutal officer in the colonial army, known for terrorizing Native Americans.

carried me along that I might see more of his power, yea, so much that I could never have thought of, had I not experienced it.

After this, it quickly began to snow, and when night came on they stopped. And now I must sit in the snow (by a little fire, and a few boughs behind me) with my sick child in my lap, and calling much for water, being now (through the wound) fallen into a violent fever (my own wound also growing so stiff that I could scarce sit down or rise up). Yet so it must be that I must sit all this cold winter night upon the cold snowy ground with my sick child in my arms, looking that every hour would be the last of its life, and having no Christian friend near me, either to comfort or help me. Oh, I may see the wonderful power of God, that my spirit did not utterly sink under my afflictions. Still the Lord upheld me with his gracious and merciful spirit, and we were both alive to see the light of the next morning.

The Third Remove

The morning being come, they prepared to go on their way. One of the Indians got up upon a horse, and they set me up behind him with my poor sick babe in my lap. A very wearisome and tedious day I had of it, what with my own wound and my child's being so exceeding sick and in a lamentable condition with her wound. It may easily be judged what a poor, feeble condition we were in, there being not the least crumb of refreshing that came within either of our mouths from Wednesday to Saturday night, except only a little cold water.[2]

This day in the afternoon, about an hour by sun, we came to the place where they intended, *viz.*, an Indian town called Wenimesset, northward of Quabaug.[3] When we were come, Oh the number of pagans (now merciless enemies) that there came about me, that I may say, as David, Psal. 27, 13, *I had fainted, unless I had believed etc.* The next day was the Sabbath. I then remembered how careless I had been of God's holy time: how many Sabbaths I had lost and misspent, and how evilly I had walked in God's sight—which lay so close upon my spirit that it was easy for me to see how righteous it was with God to cut off the thread of my life and cast me out of his presence forever. Yet the Lord still showed mercy to me and upheld me, and as he wounded me with one hand, so he healed me with the other.

This day there came to me one Robert Pepper (a man belonging to Roxbury), who was taken in Capt. Beers's fight[4] and had been now a considerable time with the Indians and up with them almost as far as Albany to see King Philip, as he told me, and was now very lately come with them into these parts. Hearing, I say, that I was in the Indian town, he obtained leave to come and see me. He told me he himself was wounded in the leg at Capt. Beers's fight and was not able sometime to go but as they carried him, and that he took oaken leaves and laid to his wound and through the blessing of God he was able to travel again. Then I took oaken leaves and laid to my side, and with the blessing of God it cured me also. Yet before the cure was wrought, I may say as it is in Psal. 38. 5,6, *My wounds stink and are corrupt; I am troubled; I am bowed down greatly; I go mourning all the day long.* I sat much alone with a poor wounded child in my lap, which moaned night and day, having nothing to revive the body or cheer the spirits of her; but instead of that sometimes one Indian would come and tell her, One hour and your master will knock your child in the head; and then a second, and then a third, your master will quickly knock your child in the head.

This was the comfort I had from them. Miserable comforters are ye all, as he said.[5] Thus nine days I sat upon my knees with my babe in my lap, till my flesh was raw again. My child being even ready to depart this sorrowful world, they bade me carry it out to another wigwam

2. Later, the text mentions that Sarah was given some cake.
3. Brookfield.
4. An attempt in September 1675 to evacuate Northfield ended in an ambush; Beers and half

his thirty-six men were killed, and others—including Pepper—were taken captive by the Indians.

5. Job 16:2.

(I suppose because they would not be troubled with such spectacles). Whither I went with a very heavy heart, and down I sat with the picture of death in my lap. About two hours in the night, my sweet babe like a lamb departed this life, on Feb. 18, 1675, it being about six years and five months old. It was nine days (from the first wounding) in this miserable condition, without any refreshing of one nature or other, except a little cold water. I cannot but take notice how at another time I could not bear to be in the room where any dead person was, but now the case is changed. I must and could lie down by my dead babe, side by side, all the night after. I have thought since of the wonderful goodness of God to me, in preserving me so in the use of my reason and senses in that distressed time that I did not use wicked and violent means to end my own miserable life.

In the morning, when they understood that my child was dead, they sent for me home to my master's wigwam (by my master in this writing must be understood Quannopin, who was a sagamore and married King Philip's wife's sister—not that he first took me, but I was sold to him by another Narraganset Indian, who took me when first I came out of the garrison). I went to take up my dead child in my arms to carry it with me, but they bade me let it alone. There was no resisting, but go I must and leave it. When I had been a while at my master's wigwam, I took the first opportunity I could get to go look after my dead child. When I came, I asked them what they had done with it. They told me it was upon the hill. Then they went and showed me where it was, where I saw the ground was newly digged, and there they told me they had buried it. There I left that child in the wilderness, and must commit it, and myself also in this wilderness condition, to him who is above all.

God having taken away this dear child, I went to see my daughter Mary, who was at this same Indian town, at a wigwam not very far off, though we had little liberty or opportunity to see one another. She was about ten years old, and taken from the door at first by a Praying Indian, and afterward sold for a gun. When I came in sight, she would fall a-weeping; at which they were provoked and would not let me come near her, but bade me be gone: which was a heart-cutting word to me. I had one child dead, another in the wilderness I knew not where, the third they would not let me come near to. *Me* (as he said) *have ye bereaved of my children: Joseph is not, and Simeon is not, and ye will take Benjamin also; all these things are against me.*[6] I could not sit still in this condition, but kept walking from one place to another. And as I was going along, my heart was even overwhelmed with the thoughts of my condition, and that I should have children and a nation which I knew not ruled over them. Whereupon I earnestly entreated the Lord that he would consider my low estate and show me a token for good and, if it were his blessed will, some sign and hope of some relief.

And indeed quickly the Lord answered in some measure my poor prayer. For as I was going up and down mourning and lamenting my condition, my son came to me and asked me how I did. I had not seen him before, since the destruction of the town, and I knew not where he was, till I was informed by himself that he was amongst a smaller parcel of Indians, whose place was about six miles off. With tears in his eyes, he asked me whether his sister Sarah was dead and told me he had seen his sister Mary, and prayed me that I would not be troubled in reference to himself. The occasion of his coming to see me at this time was this: there was, as I said, about six miles from us a small plantation of Indians, where it seems he had been during his captivity. And at this time, there were some forces of the Indians gathered out of our company and some also from them (amongst whom was my son's master) to go to assault and burn Medfield. In this time of the absence of his master, his dame brought him to see me. I took this to be some gracious answer to my earnest and unfeigned desire.

The next day, *viz.* to this, the Indians returned from Medfield (all the company, for those that belonged to the other smaller company came through the town that now we were at). But before they came to us, Oh the outrageous roaring and hooping that there was! They began their din about a mile before they came to us. By their noise and hooping they signified

6. Genesis 42:36.

how many they had destroyed (which was at that time twenty three). Those that were with us at home were gathered together as soon as they heard the hooping, and every time that the other went over their number, those at home gave a shout, that the very earth rang again. And thus they continued till those that had been upon the expedition were come up to the sagamore's wigwam; and then Oh the hideous insulting and triumphing that there was over some Englishmen's scalps that they had taken (as their manner is) and brought with them!

I cannot but take notice of the wonderful mercy of God to me in those afflictions, in sending me a Bible. One of the Indians that came from Medfield fight and had brought some plunder came to me and asked me if I would have a Bible; he had got one in his basket. I was glad of it and asked him whether he thought the Indians would let me read. He answered yes; so I took the Bible, and in that melancholy time it came into my mind to read first the 28 chapter of Deuteronomy, which I did, and when I had read it, my dark heart wrought on this manner: that there was no mercy for me, that the blessings were gone, and the curses came in their room, and that I had lost my opportunity. But the Lord helped me still to go on reading till I came to Chap. 30, the seven first verses, where I found there was mercy promised again, if we would return to him by repentance; and though we were scattered from one end of the earth to the other, yet the Lord would gather us together and turn all those curses upon our enemies. I do not desire to live to forget this Scripture and what comfort it was to me.

Now the Indians began to talk of removing from this place, some one way and some another. There were now besides myself nine English captives in this place (all of them children, except one woman). I got an opportunity to go and take leave of them, they being to go one way and I another. I asked them whether they were earnest with God for deliverance; they all told me they did as they were able; and it was some comfort to me that the Lord stirred up children to look to him. The woman, viz., Goodwife Joslin,[7] told me she should never see me again, and that she could find in her heart to run away. I wished her not to run away by any means, for we were near thirty miles from any English town and she very big with child and had but one week to reckon, and another child in her arms, two years old, and bad rivers there were to go over, and we were feeble with our poor and coarse entertainment. I had my Bible with me; I pulled it out and asked her whether she would read. We opened the Bible and lighted on Psal. 27, in which Psalm we especially took notice of that *ver. ult.: Wait on the Lord; be of good courage, and he shall strengthen thine heart; wait I say on the Lord.*[8]

The Fourth Remove

And now must I part with that little company that I had. Here I parted from my daughter Mary (whom I never saw again till I saw her in Dorchester, returned from captivity) and from four little cousins and neighbors, some of which I never saw afterward—the Lord only knows the end of them. Amongst them also was that poor woman before mentioned,[9] who came to a sad end, as some of the company told me in my travel. She having much grief upon her spirit about her miserable condition, being so near her time, she would be often asking the Indians to let her go home. They, not being willing to that and yet vexed with her importunity, gathered a great company together about her and stripped her naked, and set her in the midst of them. And when they had sung and danced about her (in their hellish manner) as long as they pleased, they knocked her on the head, and the child in her arms with her. When they had done that, they made a fire and put them both into it, and told the other children that were with them that if they attempted to go home, they would serve them in

7. Mrs. Joslin, the female head of a household.　　9. Goodwife Joslin.
8. Psalm 27:14.

like manner. The children said she did not shed one tear, but prayed all the while. But to return to my own journey: we travelled about half a day or a little more and came to a desolate place in the wilderness, where there were no wigwams or inhabitants before. We came about the middle of the afternoon to this place, cold and wet and snowy and hungry and weary, and no refreshing (for man) but the cold ground to sit on, and our poor Indian cheer.

Heart-aching thoughts here I had about my poor children, who were scattered up and down among the wild beasts of the forest. My head was light and dizzy (either through hunger or hard lodging or trouble, or all together), my knees feeble, my body raw by sitting double night and day, that I cannot express to man the affliction that lay upon my spirit; but the Lord helped me at that time to express it to himself. I opened my Bible to read, and the Lord brought that precious Scripture to me, Jer. 31:16: *Thus saith the Lord: refrain thy voice from weeping and thine eyes from tears, for thy work shall be rewarded, and they shall come again from the land of the enemy.* This was a sweet cordial to me when I was ready to faint; many and many a time have I sate down and wept sweetly over this Scripture. At this place we continued about four days.

The Fifth Remove

The occasion (as I thought) of their moving at this time was the English army, its being near and following them. For they went as if they had gone for their lives for some considerable way, and then they made a stop and chose out some of their stoutest men, and sent them back to hold the English army in play whilst the rest escaped. And then like Jehu they marched on furiously,[1] with their old and with their young. Some carried their old decrepit mothers; some carried one, and some another. Four of them carried a great Indian upon a bier, but, going through a thick wood with him, they were hindered and could make no haste; whereupon they took him upon their backs and carried him, one at a time, till we came to Bacquaug River. Upon a Friday a little after noon we came to this river. When all the company was come up and were gathered together, I thought to count the number of them, but they were so many, and being somewhat in motion it was beyond my skill. In this travel because of my wound, I was somewhat favored in my load: I carried only my knitting-work and two quarts of parched meal. Being very faint, I asked my mistress to give me one spoonful of the meal, but she would not give me a taste. They quickly fell to cutting dry trees to make rafts to carry them over the river, and soon my turn came to go over. By the advantage of some brush which they had laid upon the raft to sit, I did not wet my foot (when many of themselves at the other end were mid-leg-deep)—which cannot but be acknowledged as a favor of God to my weakened body, it being a very cold time. I was not before acquainted with such kind of doings or dangers. *When thou passest through the waters, I will be with thee, and through the rivers, they shall not overflow thee.* Isai. 43:2. A certain number of us got over the river that night, but it was the night after the Sabbath before all the company was got over. On the Saturday, they boiled an old horse's leg (which they had got), and so we drank of the broth as soon as they thought it was ready, and when it was almost all gone, they filled it up again.

The first week of my being among them I hardly ate anything. The second week I found my stomach grow very faint for want of something, and yet 'twas very hard to get down their filthy trash. But the third week (though I could think how formerly my stomach would turn against this or that, and I could starve and die before I could eat such things, yet) they were pleasant and savory to my taste. I was at this time knitting a pair of white cotton stockings for my mistress,[2] and I had not yet wrought upon the Sabbath day. When the Sabbath day came, they bade me go to work; I told them it was Sabbath day and desired them to let me

---

1. An allusion to 2 Kings 10:20.   2. Weetamoo.

rest, and told them I would do as much more tomorrow. To which they answered me, they would break my face.

And here I cannot but take notice of the strange providence of God in preserving the heathen. They were many hundreds, old and young, some sick and some lame; many had papooses at their backs. The greatest number (at this time with us) were squaws, and they travelled with all they had, bag and baggage. And yet they got over this river aforesaid; and on Monday they set their wigwams on fire, and away they went. On that very day came the English army after them to this river and saw the smoke of their wigwams, and yet this river put a stop to them. God did not give them courage or activity to go over after us. We were not ready for so great a mercy as victory and deliverance; if we had been, God would have found out a way for the English to have passed this river as well as for the Indians with their squaws and children and all their luggage. *Oh that my people had hearkened to me, and Israel had walked in my ways: I should soon have subdued their enemies and turned my hand against their adversaries.* Psal. 81:13,14.

The Sixth Remove

On Monday (as I said) they set their wigwams on fire and went away. It was a cold morning, and before us there was a great brook with ice on it. Some waded through it, up to the knees and higher; but others went till they came to a beaver dam, and I amongst them, where through the good providence of God, I did not wet my foot. I went along that day, mourning and lamenting, leaving farther my own country and travelling into the vast and howling wilderness; and I understood something of Lot's wife's temptation, when she looked back.[3] We came that day to a great swamp, by the side of which we took up our lodging that night. When I came to the brow of the hill that looked toward the swamp, I thought we had come to a great Indian town (though there were none but our own company): the Indians were as thick as the trees. It seemed as if there had been a thousand hatchets going at once; if one looked before one, there was nothing but Indians, and behind one, nothing but Indians, and so on either hand, I myself in the midst, and no Christian soul near me. And yet how hath the Lord preserved me in safety! Oh the experience that I have had of the goodness of God to me and mine!

The Seventh Remove

After a restless and hungry night there, we had a wearisome time of it the next day. The swamp by which we lay was, as it were, a deep dungeon, and an exceeding high and steep hill before it. Before I got to the top of the hill, I thought my heart and legs and all would have broken and failed me. What through faintness and soreness of body, it was a grievous day of travel to me. As we went along, I saw a place where English cattle had been; that was comfort to me, such as it was. Quickly after that we came to an English path, which so took with me that I thought I could there have freely lain down and died.

That day, a little after noon, we came to Squaukheag,[4] where the Indians quickly spread themselves over the deserted English fields, gleaning what they could find. Some picked up ears of wheat that were crickled down; some found ears of Indian corn; some found ground-nuts[5] and others sheaves of wheat that were frozen together in the shock, and went to threshing of them out. Myself got two ears of Indian corn, and whilst I did but turn my back, one of them was stolen from me, which much troubled me. There came an Indian to them

3. Genesis 19:26. Forbidden to turn back to look while leaving the city, Lot's wife looks and is turned into a pillar of salt.
4. Northfield.
5. Small, edible tubers growing underground.

at that time with a basket of horse liver. I asked him to give me a piece. What (says he), can you eat horse liver? I told him I would try if he would give a piece, which he did, and I laid it on the coals to roast; but before it was half ready, they got half of it away from me, so that I was fain to take the rest and eat it as it was, with the blood around my mouth. And yet a savory bit it was to me, for to the hungry soul every bitter thing is sweet.[6] A solemn sight methought it was, to see whole fields of wheat and Indian corn forsaken and spoiled, and the remainders of them to be food for our merciless enemies. That night we had a mess of wheat for our supper.

The Eighth Remove

On the morrow morning we must go over the river, i.e., Connecticut, to meet with King Philip. Two canoes full they had carried over; the next turn I myself was to go. But as my foot was upon the canoe to step in, there was a sudden outcry among them, and I must step back; and instead of going over the river, I must go four or five miles up the river farther northward. Some of the Indians ran one way and some another. The cause of this rout was, as I thought, their espying some English scouts who were thereabout.

In this travel up the river, about noon the company made a stop and sat down, some to eat and others to rest them. As I sat amongst them, musing of things past, my son, Joseph, unexpectedly came to me. We asked of each other's welfare, bemoaning our doleful condition and the change that had come upon us. We had husband and father, and children and sisters, and friends and relations, and house and home, and many comforts of this life; but now we might say as Job: *Naked came I out of my mother's womb, and naked shall I return; the Lord gave, and the Lord hath taken away: blessed be the name of the Lord.*[7] I asked him whether he would read; he told me he earnestly desired it. I gave him my Bible, and he lighted upon that comfortable Scripture, Psal. 118:17,18: *I shall not die, but live, and declare the works of the Lord; the Lord hath chastened me sore, yet he hath not given me over to death.* Look here, Mother (says he), did you read this? And here I may take occasion to mention one principal ground of my setting forth these few lines: even as the Psalmist says, to declare the works of the Lord and his wonderful power in carrying us along, preserving us in the wilderness while under the enemies' hand and returning of us in safety again. And his goodness in bringing to my hand so many comfortable and suitable Scriptures in my distress.

But to return: we travelled on till night, and in the morning we must go over the river to Philip's crew. When I was in the canoe, I could not but be amazed at the numerous crew of pagans that were on the bank on the other side. When I came ashore, they gathered all about me, I sitting alone in the midst; I observed they asked one another questions and laughed, and rejoiced over their gains and victories. Then my heart began to fail, and I fell a-weeping—which was the first time to my remembrance that I wept before them. Although I had met with so much affliction, and my heart was many times ready to break, yet could I not shed one tear in their sight, but rather had been all the while in a maze and like one astonished. But now I may say, as Psal. 137:1: *By the rivers of Babylon, there we sat down; yea, we wept when we remembered Zion.* There one of them asked me why I wept. I could hardly tell what to say, yet I answered, they would kill me. No, said he, none will hurt you. Then came one of them and gave me two spoonfuls of meal (to comfort me), and another gave me half a pint of peas, which was more worth than many bushels at another time.

Then I went to see King Philip; he bade me come in and sit down, and asked me whether I would smoke it (a usual compliment nowadays amongst saints and sinners). But this no way suited me. For though I had formerly used tobacco, yet I had left it ever since I was first taken. *It seems to be a bait the devil lays to make men lose their precious time.* I remember with shame how

6. Proverbs 27:7.　　　　　　　7. Job 1:21.

formerly, when I had taken two or three pipes, I was presently ready for another, such a bewildering thing it is. But I thank God he has now given me power over it. Surely, there are many who may be better employed than to lie sucking a stinking tobacco pipe.

Now the Indians gather their forces to go against Northampton; over night, one went about yelling and hooting to give notice of the design. Whereupon they fell to boiling of ground-nuts and parching of corn (as many as had it) for their provision. And in the morning away they went. During my abode in this place, Philip spoke to me to make a shirt for his boy—which I did, for which he gave me a shilling. I offered the money to my master, but he bade me keep it, and with it I bought a piece of horse flesh. Afterwards he asked me to make a cap for his boy, for which he invited me to dinner. I went, and he gave me a pancake about as big as two fingers; it was made of parched wheat, beaten and fried in bear's grease, but I thought I never tasted pleasanter meat in my life. There was a squaw who spoke to me to make a shirt for her sannup,[8] for which she gave me a piece of bear. Another asked me to knit a pair of stockings, for which she gave me a quart of peas. I boiled my peas and bear together and invited my master and mistress to dinner; but the proud gossip,[9] because I served them both in one dish, would eat nothing, except one bit that he gave her upon the point of his knife.

Hearing that my son was come to this place, I went to see him and found him lying flat upon the ground. I asked him how he could sleep so. He answered me that he was not asleep, but at prayer, and lay so, that they might not observe what he was doing. I pray, God he may remember these things now he is returned in safety. At this place (the sun now getting higher), what with the beams and heat of the sun and the smoke of the wigwams, I thought I should have been blind: I could scarce discern one wigwam from another. There was here one Mary Thurston of Medfield, who, seeing how it was with me, lent me a hat to wear; but as soon as I was gone, the squaw (who owned that Mary Thurston) came running after me and got it away again. Here there was a squaw who gave me one spoonful of meal. I put it in my pocket to keep it safe; yet notwithstanding somebody stole it, but put five Indian corns in the room of it—which corns were the greatest provision I had in my travel for one day.

The Indians returning from Northampton brought with them some horses and sheep and other things which they had taken. I desired them that they would carry me to Albany upon one of those horses and sell me for powder, for so they had sometimes discoursed. I was utterly hopeless of getting home on foot the way that I came. I could hardly bear to think of the many weary steps I had taken to come to this place.

The Ninth Remove

But instead of going either to Albany or homeward, we must go five miles up the river and then go over it. Here we abode a while. Here lived a sorry Indian who spoke to me to make him a shirt; when I had done it, he would pay me nothing. But he living by the river side, where I often went to fetch water, I would often be putting of him in mind and calling for my pay. At last he told me if I would make another shirt, for a papoose not yet born, he would give me a knife, which he did when I had done it. I carried the knife in, and my master asked me to give it him, and I was not a little glad that I had anything that they would accept of and be pleased with. When we were at this place, my master's maid came home; she had been gone three weeks into the Narraganset country to fetch corn where they had stored up some in the ground. She brought home about a peck, and half of corn. This was about the time that their great captain (Naananto) was killed in the Narragansett country.[1]

---

8. A married Native American man, especially in New England.
9. Archaic term for "companion."

1. Naananto, or Canonchet, was a war chief of the Narragansetts, known for having died heroically.

My son being now about a mile from me, I asked liberty to go and see him; they bade me go, and away I went, but quickly lost myself travelling over hills and through swamps, and could not find the way to him. And I cannot but admire at the wonderful power and goodness of God to me in that, though I was gone from home and met with all sorts of Indians, and those I had no knowledge of, and there being no Christian soul near me, yet not one of them offered the least imaginable miscarriage to me. I turned homeward again and met with my master; he showed me the way to my son. When I came to him I found him not well; and withal he had a boil on his side which much troubled him. We bemoaned one another a while, as the Lord helped us, and then I returned again. When I was returned, I found myself as unsatisfied as I was before. I went up and down moaning and lamenting, and my spirit was ready to sink with the thoughts of my poor children: my son was ill, and I could not but think of his mournful looks, and no Christian friend was near him to do any office of love for him, either for soul or body. And my poor girl—I knew not where she was, nor whether she was sick or well, or alive or dead. I repaired under these thoughts to my Bible (my great comforter in that time), and that Scripture came to my hand, *Cast thy burden upon the Lord and he shall sustain thee*, Psal. 55:22.

But I was fain to go and look after something to satisfy my hunger, and going among the wigwams I went into one and there found a squaw who showed herself very kind to me and gave me a piece of bear. I put it into my pocket and came home, but could not find an opportunity to broil it, for fear they would get it from me, and there it lay all that day and night in my stinking pocket. In the morning I went again to the same squaw, who had a kettle of ground-nuts boiling. I asked her to let me boil my piece of bear in her kettle, which she did and gave me some ground-nuts to eat with it; and I cannot but think how pleasant it was to me. I have sometime seen bear baked very handsomely amongst the English, and some like it, but the thoughts that it was bear made me tremble; but now that was savory to me that one would think was enough to turn the stomach of a brute creature.

One bitter cold day I could find no room to sit down before the fire. I went out and could not tell what to do, but I went into another wigwam, where they were also sitting round the fire. But the squaw laid a skin for me and bade me sit down, and gave me some ground-nuts and bade me come again, and told me they would buy me if they were able; and yet these were strangers to me that I never knew before.

The Tenth Remove

That day a small part of the company removed about three quarters of a mile, intending farther the next day. When they came to the place where they intended to lodge and had pitched their wigwams, being hungry I went again back to the place we were before at, to get something to eat, being encouraged by the squaw's kindness, who bade me come again. When I was there, there came an Indian to look after me, who, when he had found me, kicked me all along. I went home and found venison roasting that night, but they would not give me one bit of it. Sometimes I met with favor and sometimes with nothing but frowns.

The Eleventh Remove

The next day in the morning they took their travel, intending a day's journey up the river. I took my load at my back, and quickly we came to wade over a river and passed over tiresome and wearisome hills. One hill was so steep that I was fain to creep up upon my knees and to hold by the twigs and bushes to keep myself from falling backward. My head also was so light that I usually reeled as I went, but I hope all those wearisome steps that I have taken are but a forwarding of me to the Heavenly rest. *I know, O Lord, that thy judgments are right and that thou in faithfulness hast afflicted me*, Psal. 119:75.

The Twelfth Remove

It was upon a Sabbath day morning that they prepared for their travel. This morning I asked my master whether he would sell me to my husband. He answered, *Nux*,[2] which did much rejoice my spirit. My mistress, before we went, was gone to the burial of a papoose, and returning she found me sitting and reading in my Bible; she snatched it hastily out of my hand and threw it out of doors. I ran out and catched it up, and put it into my pocket and never let her see it afterward. Then they packed up their things to be gone and gave me my load; I complained it was too heavy, whereupon she gave me a slap in the face and bade me go. I lifted up my heart to God, hoping that redemption was not far off, and the rather because their insolency grew worse and worse.

But the thoughts of my going homeward (for so we bent our course) much cheered my spirit and made my burden seem light, and almost nothing at all. But (to my amazement and great perplexity) the scale was soon turned: for when we had gone a little way, on a sudden my mistress gives out she would go no further, but turn back again, and said I must go back again with her. And she called her sannup[3] and would have had him gone back also, but he would not, but said he would go on and come to us again in three days. My spirit was upon this (I confess) very impatient and almost outrageous.[4] I thought I could as well have died as went back. I cannot declare the trouble that I was in about it; but yet back again I must go. As soon as I had an opportunity, I took my Bible to read, and that quieting Scripture came to my hand, Psal. 46:10: *Be still, and know that I am God*—which stilled my spirit for the present. But a sore time of trial I concluded I had to go through: my master being gone, who seemed to me the best friend that I had of an Indian, both in cold and hunger, and quickly so it proved.

Down I sat, with my heart as full as it could hold and yet so hungry that I could not sit neither, but going out to see what I could find, and walking among the trees, I found six acorns and two chestnuts, which were some refreshment to me. Towards night I gathered me some sticks for my own comfort, that I might not lie a-cold; but when we came to lie down, they bade me go out and lie somewhere else, for they had company (they said) come in more than their own. I told them I could not tell where to go; they bade me go look. I told them if I went to another wigwam, they would be angry and send me home again. Then one of the company drew his sword and told me he would run me through if I did not go presently. Then was I fain to stoop to this rude fellow and to go out in the night I knew not whither. Mine eyes have seen that fellow afterwards walking up and down in Boston under the appearance of a friend-Indian, and several others of the like cut.

I went to one wigwam, and they told me they had no room. Then I went to another, and they said the same. At last an old Indian bade me come to him, and his squaw gave me some ground-nuts; she gave me also something to lay under my head, and a good fire we had. And through the good providence of God, I had a comfortable lodging that night. In the morning another Indian bade me come at night, and he would give me six ground-nuts—which I did. We were at this place and time about two miles from Connecticut River. We went in the morning (to gather ground-nuts) to the river and went back again at night. I went with a great load at my back (for they, when they went, though but a little way, would carry all their trumpery with them). I told them the skin was off my back, but I had no other comforting answer from them that this: that it would be no matter if my head were off too.

The Thirteenth Remove

Instead of going toward the Bay (which was that I desired), I must go with them five or six miles down the river into a mighty thicket of brush, where we abode almost a fortnight. Here

---

2. Yes.
3. Quanopen.

4. Violent, unrestrained; immoderate, extreme.

one asked me to make a shirt for her papoose, for which she gave me a mess of broth which was thickened with meal made of the bark of a tree; and to make it the better she had put into it about a handful of peas and a few roasted ground-nuts. I had not seen my son a pretty while, and here was an Indian of whom I made inquiry after him and asked him when he saw him. He answered me that such a time his master roasted him and that himself did eat a piece of him as big as his two fingers, and that he was very good meat; but the Lord upheld my spirit under this discouragement, and I considered their horrible addictedness to lying, and that there is not one of them that makes the least conscience of speaking the truth.

In this place on a cold night, as I lay by the fire, I removed a stick which kept the heat from me; a squaw moved it down again, at which I looked up, and she threw an handful of ashes in my eyes. I thought I should have been quite blinded and have never seen more; but, lying down, the water run out of my eyes and carried the dirt with it, that by the morning I recovered my sight again. Yet upon this and the like occasions, I hope it is not too much to say with Job: *Have pity upon me; have pity upon me, Oh ye my friends, for the hand of the Lord has touched me.*[5] And here I cannot but remember how many times sitting in their wigwams and musing on things past, I should suddenly leap up and run out as if I had been at home, forgetting where I was and what my condition was. But when I was without and saw nothing but wilderness and woods, and a company of barbarous heathen, my mind quickly returned to me, which made me think of that spoken concerning Samson, who said: *I will go out and shake myself as at other times, but he wist not that the Lord was departed from him.*[6]

About this time I began to think that all my hopes of restoration would come to nothing. I thought of the English army and hoped for their coming and being retaken by them, but that failed. I hoped to be carried to Albany as the Indians had discoursed, but that failed also. I thought of being sold to my husband, as my master spoke; but instead of that my master himself was gone and I left behind, so that my spirit was now quite ready to sink. I asked them to let me go out and pick up some sticks, that I might get alone and pour out my heart unto the Lord. Then also I took my Bible to read, but I found no comfort here neither—which many times I was wont to find. So easie a thing it is with God to dry up the streams of Scripture-comfort from us. Yet I can say that in all my sorrows and afflictions, God did not leave me to have my impatience work towards himself, as if his ways were unrighteous; but I knew that he laid upon me less than I deserved. Afterward, before this doleful time ended with me, I was turning the leaves of my Bible, and the Lord brought to me some Scriptures which did a little revive me, as that, Isai. 55:8: *For my thoughts are not your thoughts; neither are your ways my ways, saith the Lord.* And also that, Ps. 37:5: *Commit thy way unto the Lord; trust also in him, and he shall bring it to pass.*

About this time they came yelping from Hadley, having there killed three Englishmen and brought one captive with them, *viz.* Thomas Read.[7] They all gathered about the poor man, asking him many questions. I desired also to go and see him, and when I came he was crying bitterly, supposing they would quickly kill him. Whereupon I asked one of them whether they intended to kill him. He answered me they would not. He being a little cheered with that, I asked him about the welfare of my husband; he told me he saw him such a time in the Bay, and he was well, but very melancholy. By which I certainly understood (though I suspected it before) that whatsoever the Indians told me respecting him was vanity and lies. Some of them told me he was dead, and they had killed him; some said he was married again and that the Governor wished him to marry and told him he should have his choice, and that all persuaded him I was dead. So like were these barbarous creatures to him who was a liar from the beginning.

As I was sitting once in the wigwam here, Philip's maid came in with the child in her arms and asked me to give her a piece of my apron to make a flap for it; I told her I would not.

5. Job 19:21.
6. Judges 16:20.

7. A soldier assigned to guard the settlers; he later escaped.

Then my mistress bade me give it, but still I said no. The maid told me if I would not give her a piece, she would tear a piece off it; I told her I would tear her coat then. With that, my mistress rises up and takes up a stick big enough to have killed me and struck at me with it, but I stepped out, and she struck the stick into the mat of the wigwam. But while she was pulling of it out, I ran to the maid and gave her all my apron, and so that storm went over.

Hearing that my son was come to this place, I went to see him and told him his father was well, but very melancholy; he told me he was as much grieved for his father as for himself. I wondered at his speech, for I thought I had enough upon my spirit in reference to myself to make me mindless of my husband and everyone else, they being safe among their friends. He told me also that, a while before, his master (together with other Indians) were going to the French for powder; but by the way the Mohawks[8] met with them and killed four of their company, which made the rest turn back again—for which I desire that myself and he may bless the Lord. For it might have been worse with him had he been sold to the French than it proved to be in his remaining with the Indians.

I went to see an English youth in this place, one John Gilberd of Springfield.[9] I found him lying without doors upon the ground; I asked him how he did. He told me he was very sick of a flux with eating so much blood. They had turned him out of the wigwam and with him an Indian papoose, almost dead (whose parents had been killed), in a bitter cold day, without fire or clothes; the young man himself had nothing on but his shirt and waistcoat. This sight was enough to melt a heart of flint. There they lay, quivering in the cold, the youth round like a dog, the papoose stretched out, with his eyes and nose and mouth full of dirt, and yet alive and groaning. I advised John to go and get to some fire; he told me he could not stand, but I persuaded him still, lest he should lie there and die. And with much ado I got him to a fire and went myself home. As soon as I was got home, his master's daughter came after me to know what I had done with the Englishman. I told her I had got him to a fire in such a place. Now had I need to pray Paul's prayer, 2 Thess. 3:2: *That we may be delivered from unreasonable and wicked men.* For her satisfaction I went along with her and brought her to him; but before I got home again it was noised about that I was running away and getting the English youth along with me, that as soon as I came in, they began to rant and domineer, asking me where I had been and what I had been doing, and saying they would knock me on the head. I told them I had been seeing the English youth and that I would not run away; they told me I lied, and, taking up a hatchet, they came to me and said they would knock me down if I stirred out again, and so confined me to the wigwam. Now may I say with David, 2 Sam. 24:14: *I am in a great strait.* If I keep in, I must die with hunger, and if I go out, I must be knocked in the head.

This distressed condition held that day and half the next, and then the Lord remembered me, whose mercies are great. Then came an Indian to me with a pair of stockings which were too big for him, and he would have me ravel them out and knit them fit for him. I showed myself willing and bade him ask my mistress if I might go along with him a little way. She said, Yes, I might, but I was not a little refreshed with that news, that I had my liberty again. Then I went along with him, and he gave me some roasted ground-nuts, which did again revive my feeble stomach.

Being got out of her sight, I had time and liberty again to look into my Bible—which was my guide by day and my pillow by night. Now that comfortable Scripture presented itself to me, Isai. 54:7: *For a small moment have I forsaken thee, but with great mercies will I gather thee.* Thus the Lord carried me along from one time to another and made good to me this precious promise and many others. Then my son came to see me, and I asked his master to let him stay a while with me, that I might comb his head and look over him, for he was almost overcome with lice. He told me, when I had done, that he was very hungry, but I had nothing

---

8. Evidently the Mohawks were fighting on the English side.

9. A 17-year-old, captured early in March, who later escaped.

to relieve him, but bid him go into the wigwams as he went along and see if he could get anything among them. Which he did, and (it seems) tarried a little too long, for his master was angry with him and beat him, and then sold him. Then he came running to tell me he had a new master and that he had given him some groundnuts already. Then I went along with him to his new master, who told me he loved him, and he should not want. So his master carried him away, and I never saw him afterward till I saw him at Piscataqua in Portsmouth.

That night they bade me go out of the wigwam again; my mistress's papoose was sick, and it died that night. And there was one benefit in it, that there was more room. I went to a wigwam, and they bade me come in and gave me a skin to lie upon and a mess of venison and ground-nuts, which was a choice dish among them. On the morrow, they buried the papoose, and afterward, both morning and evening, there came a company to mourn and howl with her, though I confess I could not much condole with them. Many sorrowful days I had in this place, often getting alone: *like a crane or a swallow, so did I chatter; I did mourn as a dove; mine eyes fail with looking upward. Oh Lord, I am oppressed; undertake for me*, Isai. 38:14. I could tell the Lord, as Hezechiah, ver. 3: *Remember now, O Lord, I beseech thee, how I have walked before thee in truth.*[1] Now had I time to examine all my ways; my conscience did not accuse me of unrighteousness toward one or another, yet I saw how in my walk with God I had been a careless creature. As David said: *Against thee, thee only, have I sinned,*[2] and I might say with the poor publican: *God be merciful unto me, a sinner.*[3]

On the Sabbath days, I could look upon the sun and think how people were going to the house of God to have their souls refreshed, and then home, and their bodies also; but I was destitute of both and might say as the poor Prodigal: *he would fain have filled his belly with the husks that the swine did eat, and no man gave unto him*, Luke 15:16. For I must say with him: *Father, I have sinned against Heaven and in thy sight*, ver. 21.[4] I remembered how on the night before and after the Sabbath, when my family was about me, and relations and neighbours with us, we could pray and sing, and then refresh our bodies with the good creatures of God, and then have a comfortable bed to lie down on; but instead of all this I had only a little swill for the body, and then like a swine must lie down on the ground. I cannot express to man the sorrow that lay upon my spirit—the Lord knows it. Yet that comfortable Scripture would often come to my mind: *For a small moment have I forsaken thee, but with great mercies will I gather thee.*[5]

The Fourteenth Remove

Now must we pack up and be gone from this thicket, bending our course toward the Bay towns—I having nothing to eat by the way this day but a few crumbs of cake that an Indian gave my girl the same day we were taken. She gave it me, and I put it into my pocket; there it lay till it was so mouldy (for want of good baking) that one could not tell what it was made of. It fell all to crumbs and grew so dry and hard that it was like little flints; and this refreshed me many times when I was ready to faint. It was in my thoughts when I put it into my mouth that, if ever I returned, I would tell the world what a blessing the Lord gave to such mean food. As we went along, they killed a deer with a young one in her; they gave me a piece of the fawn, and it was so young and tender that one might eat the bones as well as the flesh, and yet I thought it very good. When night came on, we sat down; it rained, but they quickly got up a bark wigwam, where I lay dry that night. I looked out in the morning, and many of them had lain in the rain all night, I saw by their reeking. Thus the Lord dealt mercifully with me many times, and I fared better than many of them. In the morning, they took the

---

1. Isaiah 38:2,3.
2. Psalm 51:4.
3. Luke 18:13.
4. Luke 15:21.
5. Isaiah 54:7.

blood of the deer and put it into the paunch and so boiled it; I could eat nothing of that, though they ate it sweetly. And yet they were so nice in other things that, when I had fetched water and had put the dish I dipped the water with into the kettle of water which I brought, they would say they would knock me down; for they said it was a sluttish trick.

The Fifteenth Remove

We went on our travel. I having got one handful of ground-nuts for my support that day, they gave me my load, and I went on cheerfully (with the thoughts of going homeward), having my burden more on my back than my spirit; we came to Baquaug river again that day, near which we abode a few days. Sometimes one of them would give me a pipe, another a little tobacco, another a little salt, which I would change for a little victuals. I cannot but think what a wolvish appetite persons have in a starving condition, for many times when they gave me that which was hot I was so greedy that I should burn my mouth, that it would trouble me hours after; and yet I should quickly do the same again. And after I was thoroughly hungry, I was never again satisfied. For though sometimes it fell out that I got enough and did eat till I could eat no more, yet I was as unsatisfied as I was when I began. And now could I see that Scripture verified (there being many Scriptures which we do not take notice of or understand till we are afflicted), *Mic. 6:14: Thou shalt eat and not be satisfied.* Now might I see more than ever before the miseries that sin hath brought upon us.

Many times I should be ready to run out against the heathen, but that Scripture would quiet me again, Amos 3:6: *Shall there be evil in the city, and the Lord hath not done it?* The Lord help me to make a right improvement of his word and that I might learn that great lesson, Mic. 6:8,9: *He hath showed thee, O Man, what is good, and what doth the Lord require of thee but to do justly and love mercy, and walk humbly with thy God? Hear ye the rod and who hath appointed it.*

The Sixteenth Remove

We began this remove with wading over Baquaug river. The water was up to the knees, and the stream very swift and so cold that I thought it would have cut me in sunder. I was so weak and feeble that I reeled as I went along and thought there I must end my days at last, after my bearing and getting through so many difficulties. The Indians stood laughing to see me staggering along, but in my distress the Lord gave me experience of the truth and goodness of that promise, Isai. 43:2: *When thou passest through the waters, I will be with thee, and through the rivers, they shall not overflow thee.* Then I sat down to put on my stockings and shoes, with the tears running down my eyes and many sorrowful thoughts in my heart; but I got up to go along with them.

Quickly there came up to us an Indian who informed them that I must go to Wachuset to my master, for there was a letter come from the Council to the sagamores about redeeming the captives, and that there would be another in fourteen days and that I must be there ready. My heart was so heavy before that I could scarce speak or go in the path, and yet now so light that I could run. My strength seemed to come again and to recruit my feeble knees and aching heart; yet it pleased them to go but one mile that night, and there we stayed two days.

In that time came a company of Indians to us, near thirty, all on horseback. My heart skipped within me, thinking they had been Englishmen at the first sight of them; for they were dressed in English apparel, with hats, white neckcloths, and sashes about their waists, and ribbons upon their shoulders. But when they came near, there was a vast difference between the lovely faces of Christians and the foul looks of those heathens, which much damped my spirit again.

The Seventeenth Remove

A comfortable remove it was to me, because of my hopes. They gave me my pack, and along we went cheerfully; but quickly my will proved more than my strength. Having little or no refreshing, my strength failed, and my spirits were almost quite gone. Now may I say as David, Psal. 109: 22, 23, 24: *I am poor and needy, and my heart is wounded within me. I am gone like the shadow when it declineth; I am tossed up and down like the locust. My knees are weak through fasting, and my flesh faileth of fatness.*

At night we came to an Indian town, and the Indians sat down by a wigwam discoursing, but I was almost spent and could scarce speak. I laid down my load and went into the wigwam, and there sat an Indian boiling of horse's feet (they being wont to eat the flesh first, and when the feet were old and dried and they had nothing else they would cut off the feet and use them). I asked him to give me a little of his broth or water they were boiling in; he took a dish and gave me one spoonful of samp,[6] and bid me take as much of the broth as I would. Then I put some of the hot water to the samp and drank it up, and my spirit came again. He gave me also a piece of the ruffe or ridding[7] of the small guts, and I broiled it on the coals; and now may I say with Jonathan: *See, I pray you, how mine eyes have been enlightened because I tasted a little of this honey,* I Sam. 14:29. Now is my spirit revived again; though means be never so inconsiderable, yet if the Lord bestow his blessing upon them they shall refresh both soul and body.

The Eighteenth Remove

We took up our packs, and along we went. But a wearisome day I had of it. As we went along, I saw an Englishman stripped naked and lying dead upon the ground, but knew not who it was. Then we came to another Indian town, where I stayed all night. In this town, there were four English children, captives, and one of them my own sister's. I went to see how she did, and she was well, considering her captive-condition. I would have tarried that night with her, but they that owned her would not suffer it. Then I went to another wigwam, where they were boiling corn and beans, which was a lovely sight to see; but I could not get a taste thereof. Then I went into another wigwam, where there were two of the English children; the squaw was boiling horse's feet. Then she cut me off a little piece and gave one of the English children a piece also. Being very hungry, I had quickly eat up mine, but the child could not bite it—it was so tough and sinewy—but lay sucking, gnawing, chewing, and slobbering of it in the mouth and hand; then I took it of the child and eat it myself, and savory it was to my taste.

That I may say as Job, Chap. 6:7: *The things that my soul refused to touch are as my sorrowful meat.* Thus the Lord made that pleasant and refreshing which another time would have been an abomination. Then I went home to my mistress's wigwam, and they told me I disgraced my master with begging and, if I did so any more, they would knock me in head; I told them they had as good knock me in head as starve me to death.

The Nineteenth Remove

They said, when we went out, that we must travel to Wachuset this day. But a bitter weary day I had of it, travelling now three days together, without resting any day between. At last, after many weary steps. I saw Wachuset hills, but many miles off. Then we came to a great swamp, through which we travelled up to the knees in mud and water—which was heavy going to one tired before. Being almost spent, I thought I should have sunk down at last and

---

6. Porridge made from coarse hominy.   7. The unwanted parts; the refuse.

never get out; but I may say, as in Psal. 94:18: *When my foot slipped, thy mercy O Lord held me up.* Going along, having indeed my life, but little spirit, Philip (who was in the company) came up and took me by the hand, and said, *two weeks more and you shall be mistress again.* I asked him if he spoke true. He answered, *Yes, and quickly you shall come to your master again*—who had been gone from us three weeks.

After many weary steps, we came to Wachuset, where he was; and glad I was to see him. He asked me when I washed me. I told him not this month; then he fetched me some water himself and bid me wash, and gave me the glass to see how I looked and bade his squaw[8] give me something to eat. So she gave me a mess of beans and meat, and a little ground-nut cake. I was wonderfully revived with this favor showed me, Psal. 106:46: *He made them also to be pitied of all those that carried them captives.*

My master had three squaws, living sometimes with one and sometimes with another— one, this old squaw at whose wigwam I was, and with whom my master had been those three weeks. Another was Wettimore,[9] with whom I had lived and served all this while. A severe and proud dame she was, bestowing every day in dressing herself near as much time as any of the gentry of the land—powdering her hair and painting her face, going with her necklaces, with jewels in her ears and bracelets upon her hands. When she had dressed herself, her work was to make girdles of wampum and beads. The third squaw was a younger one, by whom he had two papooses.

By that time I was refreshed by the old squaw with whom my master was, Wettimore's maid came to call me home, at which I fell a-weeping; then the old squaw told me, to encourage me, that if I wanted victuals, I should come to her, and that I should lie there in her wigwam. Then I went with the maid and quickly came again and lodged there. The squaw laid a mat under me and a good rug over me, the first time I had any such kindness showed me. I understood that Wettimore thought that, if she should let me go and serve with the old squaw, she would be in danger to lose not only my service, but the redemption pay also. And I was not a little glad to hear this—being by it raised in my hopes that in God's due time there would be an end of this sorrowful hour. Then came an Indian and asked me to knit him three pair of stockings, for which I had a hat and a silk handkerchief. Then another asked me to make her a shirt, for which she gave me an apron.

Then came Tom and Peter[1] with the second letter from the Council about the captives. Though they were Indians, I got them by the hand and burst out into tears; my heart was so full that I could not speak to them. But, recovering myself, I asked them how my husband did, and all my friends and acquaintances. They said they were well, but very melancholy. They brought me two biscuits and a pound of tobacco. The tobacco I quickly gave away; when it was all gone, one asked me to give him a pipe of tobacco. I told him it was all gone; then began he to rant and threaten. I told him when my husband came I would give him some. *Hang him, Rogue* (says he), *I will knock out his brains if he comes here.* And then again in the same breath they would say that if there should came an hundred without guns, they would do them no hurt. So unstable and like madmen they were. So that, fearing the worst, I durst not send to my husband, though there were some thoughts of his coming to redeem and fetch me, not knowing what might follow; for there was little more trust to them than to the Master they served.

When the letter was come, the sagamores met to consult about the captives and called me to them to inquire how much my husband would give to redeem me. When I came, I sat down among them as I was wont to do, as their manner is. Then they bade me stand up and said they were the *General Court.* They bid me speak what I thought he would give. Now knowing

---

8. Evidently the "old squaw," mentioned later.
9. Also called Weetamoo. A leader (squaw sachem) of the Pocasset Wampanoags, formerly married to King Philip's brother, Wamsutta.

1. Tom Dublet (Nepanet) and Peter Conway (Tataquinea), Christian Indians of the Nashoba village.

that all we had was destroyed by the Indians, I was in a great strait. I thought if I should speak of but a little, it would be slighted and hinder the matter; if of a great sum, I knew not where it would be procured. Yet at a venture I said, *Twenty pounds,* yet desired them to take less; but they would not hear of that, but sent that message to Boston that for twenty pounds I should be redeemed. It was a Praying Indian that wrote their letter for them.

There was another Praying Indian, who told me that he had a brother that would not eat horse—his conscience was so tender and scrupulous (though as large as hell for the destruction of poor Christians). Then he said he read that Scripture to him, 2 King 6:25: *There was a famine in Samaria, and behold they besieged it until an ass's head was sold for fourscore pieces of silver and the fourth part of a kab of dove's dung for five pieces of silver.* He expounded this place to his brother and showed him that it was lawful to eat that in a famine which is not at another time. And now, says he, he will eat horse with any Indian of them all. There was another Praying Indian who, when he had done all the mischief that he could, betrayed his own father into the English's hands, thereby to purchase his own life. Another Praying Indian was at Sudbury fight,[2] though, as he deserved, he was afterward hanged for it. There was another Praying Indian so wicked and cruel as to wear a string about his neck strung with Christian fingers.

Another Praying Indian, when they went to Sudbury fight, went with them, and his squaw also with him with her papoose at her back; before they went to that fight, they got a company together to powwow.[3] The manner was as followeth. There was one that kneeled upon a deer-skin, with the company round him in a ring, who kneeled, striking upon the ground with their hands and with sticks, and muttering or humming with their mouths. Besides him who kneeled in the ring, there also stood one with a gun in his hand. Then he on the deerskin made a speech, and all manifested assent to it; and so they did many times together. Then they bade him with the gun go out of the ring, which he did; but when he was out they called him in again. But he seemed to make a stand; then they called the more earnestly, till he returned again. Then they all sang. Then they gave him two guns, in either hand one. And so he on the deer-skin began again, and at the end of every sentence in his speaking they all assented, humming or muttering with their mouths and striking upon the ground with their hands. Then they bade him with the two guns go out of the ring again—which he did a little way. Then they called him in again, but he made a stand, so they called him with greater earnestness; but he stood reeling and wavering, as if he knew not whether he should stand or fall or which way to go. Then they called him with exceeding great vehemency, all of them, one and another; after a little while, he turned in, staggering as he went, with his arms stretched out, in either hand a gun. As soon as he came in, they all sang and rejoiced exceedingly a while. And then he upon the deer-skin made another speech, unto which they all assented in a rejoicing manner; and so they ended their business and forthwith went to Sudbury fight.

To my thinking, they went without any scruple but that they should prosper and gain the victory. And they went out not so rejoicing, but they came home with as great a victory. For they said they had killed two captains and almost an hundred men. One Englishman they brought alive with them, and he said it was too true, for they had made sad work at Sudbury, as indeed it proved. Yet they came home without that rejoicing and triumphing over their victory which they were wont to show at other times, but rather like dogs (as they say) which have lost their ears. Yet I could not perceive that it was for their own loss of men; they said they had not lost above five or six, and I missed none, except in one wigwam. When they went, they acted as if the Devil had told them that they should gain the victory; and now they acted as if the Devil had told them that they should have a fall. Whether it were so or no

2. A significant victory for the Indians, whose casualties were few in comparison with the English.

3. Native American ceremony in which incantations and dancing are used to invoke divine aid in battle, in hunting, or against disease.

I cannot tell, but so it proved; for quickly they began to fall and so held on that summer till they came to utter ruin. They came home on a Sabbath day, and the Powwow[4] that kneeled upon the deer-skin came home (I may say, without any abuse) as black as the Devil.

When my master came home, he came to me and bid me make a shirt for his papoose of a Hollandlaced pillowbeer.[5] About that time there came an Indian to me and bid me come to his wigwam at night, and he would give me some pork and ground-nuts. Which I did, and as I was eating another Indian said to me, *he seems to be your good friend, but he killed two Englishmen at Sudbury, and there lie their clothes behind you.* I looked behind me, and there I saw bloody clothes, with bullet holes in them; yet the Lord suffered not this wretch to do me any hurt. Yea, instead of that, he many times refreshed me; five or six times did he and his squaw refresh my feeble carcass. If I went to their wigwam at any time, they would always give me something, and yet they were strangers that I never saw before. Another squaw gave me a piece of fresh pork and a little salt with it, and lent me her frying pan to fry it in; and I cannot but remember what a sweet, pleasant, and delightful relish that bit had to me, to this day. So little do we prize common mercies when we have them to the full.

The Twentieth Remove

It was their usual manner to remove when they had done any mischief, lest they should be found out, and so they did at this time. We went about three or four miles, and there they built a great wigwam, big enough to hold an hundred Indians, which they did in preparation to a great day of dancing. They would say amongst themselves that the Governor would be so angry for his loss at Sudbury that he would send no more about the captives—which made me grieve and tremble. My sister, being not far from the place where we now were and hearing that I was here, desired her master to let her come and see me, and he was willing to it and would go with her; but she, being ready before him, told him she would be before and was come within a mile or two of the place. Then he overtook her and began to rant as if he had been mad, and made her go back again in the rain, so that I never saw her till I saw her in Charlestown. But the Lord requited many of their ill-doings, for this Indian, her master, was hanged afterward at Boston.

The Indians now began to come from all quarters against their merry dancing day. Amongst some of them came one Goodwife Kettle. I told her my heart was so heavy that it was ready to break. *So is mine too,* said she, but yet said, *I hope we shall hear some good news shortly.* I could hear how earnestly my sister desired to see me, and I as earnestly desired to see her; and yet neither of us could get an opportunity. My daughter was also now but about a mile off, and I had not seen her in nine or ten weeks, as I had not seen my sister since our first taking. I earnestly desired them to let me go and see them; yea, I entreated, begged, and persuaded them but to let me see my daughter. And yet so hardhearted were they that they would not suffer it. They made use of their tyrannical power whilst they had it, but through the Lord's wonderful mercy their time was short.

On a Sabbath day, the sun being about an hour high in the afternoon, came Mr. John Hoar (the Council permitting him and his own forward spirit inclining him), together with the two forementioned Indians, Tom and Peter, with the third letter from the Council. When they came near, I was abroad; though I saw them not, they presently called me in and bade me sit down, and not stir. Then they catched up their guns, and away they ran, as if an enemy had been at hand, and the guns went off apace. I manifested some great trouble, and they asked me what was the matter. I told them I thought they had killed the Englishman (for they had in the meantime informed me that an Englishman was come); they said, *No.* They shot over his horse and under, and before his horse; and they pushed

4. Medicine man.   5. Linen pillowcase.

him this way and that way at their pleasure, showing what they could do. Then they let them come to their wigwams.

I begged of them to let me see the Englishman, but they would not. But there was I fain to sit their pleasure. When they had talked their fill with him, they suffered me to go to him. We asked each other of our welfare and how my husband did, and all my friends. He told me they were all well and would be glad to see me. Amongst other things which my husband sent me there came a pound of tobacco, which I sold for nine shillings in money; for many of the Indians, for want of tobacco, smoked hemlock and ground-ivy. It was a great mistake in any who thought I sent for tobacco; for through the favor of God that desire was overcome. I now asked them whether I should go home with Mr. Hoar. They answered, *No*, one and another of them; and it being night, we lay down with that answer. In the morning Mr. Hoar invited the sagamores to dinner, but when we went to get it ready, we found that they had stolen the greatest part of the provision Mr. Hoar had brought out of his bags in the night. And we may see the wonderful power of God in that one passage, in that, when there was such a great number of the Indians together and so greedy of a little good food, and no English there but Mr. Hoar and myself, that there they did not knock us in the head and take what we had—there being not only some provision, but also trading cloth, a part of the twenty pounds agreed upon. But instead of doing us any mischief, they seemed to be ashamed of the fact and said it were some *matchit*[6] Indians that did it. O that we could believe that there is nothing too hard for God! God showed his power over the heathen in this as he did over the hungry lions when Daniel was cast into the den.[7]

Mr. Hoar called them betime to dinner, but they ate very little, they being so busy in dressing themselves and getting ready for their dance, which was carried on by eight of them, four men and four squaws, my master and mistress being two. He was dressed in his Holland shirt, with great laces sewed at the tail of it; he had his silver buttons, his white stockings. His garters were hung round with shillings, and he had girdles of wampum upon his head and shoulders. She had a kersey coat[8] covered with girdles of wampum from the loins upward. Her arms from her elbows to her hands were covered with bracelets; there were handfuls of necklaces about her neck and several sorts of jewels in her ears. She had fine red stockings and white shoes, her hair powdered and her face painted red, that was always before black. And all the dancers were after the same manner. There were two others singing and knocking on a kettle for their music. They kept hopping up and down one after another, with a kettle of water in the midst standing warm upon some embers, to drink of when they were dry. They held on till it was almost night, throwing out wampum to the standers by.

At night I asked them again if I should go home. They all as one said no, except my husband would come for me. When we were lain down, my master went out of the wigwam and by and by sent in an Indian called James the Printer,[9] who told Mr. Hoar that my master would let me go home tomorrow if he would let him have one pint of liquors. Then Mr. Hoar called his own Indians, Tom and Peter, and bid them all go and see whether he would promise it before them three; and, if he would, he should have it—which he did, and had it. Then Philip, smelling the business, called me to him and asked me what I would give him to tell me some good news and to speak a good word for me, that I might go home tomorrow. I told him I could not tell what to give him—I would anything I had—and asked him what he would have. He said two coats and twenty shillings in money, and half a bushel of seed-corn and some tobacco. I thanked him for his love, but I knew the good news as well as that crafty fox.

My master, after he had had his drink, quickly came ranting into the wigwam again and

6. Wicked.
7. See Daniel 6.
8. Made of twilled woolen fabric, perhaps with a cotton warp, often used for coats.
9. A Christian Indian who was to work as a compositor on the 1682 Cambridge edition of Rowlandson's text.

called for Mr. Hoar, drinking to him and saying he was a good man; and then again he would say, *Hang him, Rogue.* Being almost drunk, he would drink to him and yet presently say he should be hanged. Then he called for me; I trembled to hear him, yet I was fain to go to him. And he drank to me, showing no incivility. He was the first Indian I saw drunk all the while that I was amongst them. At last his squaw ran out and he after her, round the wigwam, with his money jingling at his knees; but she escaped him. But, having an old squaw, he ran to her, and so through the Lord's mercy we were no more troubled with him that night.

Yet I had not a comfortable night's rest; for I think I can say I did not sleep for three nights together. The night before the letter came from the Council I could not rest—I was so full of fears and troubles (God many times leaving us most in the dark when deliverance is nearest); yea, at this time I could not rest night nor day. The next night I was over-joyed, Mr. Hoar being come, and that with such good tidings. The third night I was even swallowed up with the thoughts of things, *viz.,* that ever I should go home again and that I must go leaving my children behind me in the wilderness, so that sleep was now almost departed from mine eyes.

On Tuesday morning they called their General Court (as they styled it) to consult and determine whether I should go home or no; and they all as one man did seemingly consent to it, that I should go home, except Philip, who would not come among them.

But before I go any further, I would take leave to mention a few remarkable passages of Providence which I took special notice of in my afflicted time.

1. Of the fair opportunity lost in the long march, a little after the fort-fight, when our English army was so numerous and in pursuit of the enemy, and so near as to overtake several and destroy them; and the enemy in such distress for food that our men might track them by their rooting in the earth for ground-nuts, whilst they were flying for their lives—I say that then our army should want provision and be forced to leave their pursuit, and return homeward. And the very next week the enemy came upon our town like bears bereft of their whelps or so many ravenous wolves, rending us and our lambs to death. But what shall I say? God seemed to leave his people to themselves and ordered all things for his own holy ends. *Shall there be evil in the city, and the Lord hath not done it? They are not grieved for the affliction of Joseph; therefore they shall go captive with the first that go captive. It is the Lord's doing, and it should be marvellous in our eyes.*[1]

2. I cannot but remember how the Indians derided the slowness and dullness of the English army in its setting out. For after the desolations at Lancaster and Medfield, as I went along with them, they asked me when I thought the English army would come after them. I told them I could not tell; *it may be they will come in May,* said they. Thus did they scoff at us, as if the English army would be a quarter of a year getting ready.

3. Which also I have hinted before: when the English army with new supplies were sent forth to pursue after the enemy and they understanding it fled before them till they came to Baquaug River, where they forthwith went over safely, that that river should be impassable to the English; I can but admire to see the wonderful providence of God in preserving the heathen for farther affliction to our poor country. They could go in great numbers over, but the English must stop. God had an overruling hand in all those things.

4. It was thought if their corn were cut down, they would starve and die with hunger, and all their corn that could be found was destroyed and they driven from that little they had in store, into the woods in the midst of winter; and yet how to admiration did the Lord preserve them for his holy ends and the destruction of many still amongst the English! Strangely did the Lord provide for them, that I did not see (all the time I was among them) one man or woman or child die with hunger.

Though many times they would that that a hog or a dog would hardly touch, yet by that God strengthened them to be a scourge to his people.

1. See Amos 3:6, Amos 6:6, 7, and Psalm 118:23.

Their chief and commonest food was ground-nuts; they ate also nuts and acorns, artichokes, lily-roots, ground-beans, and several other weeds and roots that I know not.

They would pick up old bones and cut them in pieces at the joints, and, if they were full of worms and maggots, they would scald them over the fire to make the vermin come out, and then boil them and drink up the liquor, and then beat the great ends of them in a mortar and so eat them. They would eat horse's guts and ears and all sorts of wild birds, which they could catch—also bear, venison, beavers, tortoise, frogs, squirrels, dogs, skunks, rattlesnakes, yea, the very barks of trees, besides all sorts of creatures and provision which they plundered from the English. I can but stand in admiration to see the wonderful power of God in providing for such a vast number of our enemies in the wilderness, where there was nothing to be seen but from hand to mouth. Many times in a morning, the generality of them would eat up all they had and yet have some further supply against they wanted. It is said, Psal. 81: 13, 14: *O that my people had hearkened to me and Israel had walked in my ways: I should soon have subdued their enemies and turned my hand against their adversaries*. But now our perverse and evil carriages in the sight of the Lord have so offended him that, instead of turning his hand against them, the Lord feeds and nourishes them up to be a scourge to the whole land.

5. Another thing that I would observe is the strange providence in God in turning things about when the Indians were at the highest and the English at the lowest.[2] I was with the enemy eleven weeks and five days, and not one week passed without the fury of the enemy and some desolation by fire and sword upon one place or other. They mourned (with their black faces) for their own losses, yet triumphed and rejoiced in their inhumane (and many times devilish) cruelty to the English. They would boast much of their victories, saying that in two hours time they had destroyed such a captain and his company in such a place, and such a captain and his company in such a place, and boast how many towns they had destroyed, and then scoff and say they had done them a good turn to send them to Heaven so soon. Again they would say this summer they would knock all the rogues in the head or drive them into the sea, or make them fly the country, thinking surely, Agag-like, *The bitterness of death is past*.[3] Now the heathen begin to think all is their own, and the poor Christians' hopes to fail (as to man), and now their eyes are more to God, and their hearts sigh heavenward, and to say in good earnest: *Help, Lord, or we perish*.[4] When the Lord had brought his people to this, that they saw no help in anything but himself, then he takes the quarrel into his own hand; and though they had made a pit (in their imaginations) as deep as hell for the Christians that summer, yet the Lord hurled themselves into it. And the Lord had not so many ways before to preserve them, but now he hath as many to destroy them.

But to return again to my going home, where we may see a remarkable change of Providence: at first they were all against it except my husband would come for me, but afterwards they assented to it and seemed much to rejoice in it, some asking me to send them some bread, others some tobacco, others shaking me by the hand, offering me a hood and scarf to ride in, not one moving hand or tongue against it. Thus hath the Lord answered my poor desires and the many earnest requests of others put up unto God for me. In my travels, an Indian came to me and told me if I were willing, he and his squaw would run away and go home along with me. I told him, *No;* I was not willing to run away, but desired to wait God's time, that I might go home quietly and without fear. And now God hath granted my desire.

O the wonderful power of God that I have seen, and the experiences that I have had! I have been in the midst of those roaring lions and savage bears that feared neither God nor man nor the devil, by night and day, alone and in company, sleeping all sorts together, and yet not one of them ever offered the least abuse of unchastity to me in word or action. Though some are ready to say I speak it for my own credit, but I speak it in the presence of God and to his glory. God's power is as great now and as sufficient to save as when he preserved Daniel

2. Shortly after their Sudbury victory, the Indians   3. 1 Samuel 16:32.
   began to suffer defeats by the English.   4. Matthew 8:25; Luke 8:24.

in the lion's den or the three children in the fiery furnace. I may well say, as he, Psal. 107: 1, 2: *Oh give thanks unto the Lord, for he is good; for his mercy endureth forever. Let the redeemed of the Lord say so, whom he hath redeemed from the hand of the enemy*—especially that I should come away in the midst of so many hundreds of enemies quietly and peacably, and not a dog moving his tongue. So I took my leave of them, and in coming along my heart melted into tears, more than all the while I was with them, and I was almost swallowed up with the thoughts that ever I should go home again.

About the sun's going down, Mr. Hoar and myself, and the two Indians, came to Lancaster, and a solemn sight it was to me. There had I lived many comfortable years amongst my relations and neighbors, and now not one Christian to be seen nor one house left standing. We went on to a farm-house that was yet standing, where we lay all night; and a comfortable lodging we had, though nothing but straw to lie on. The Lord preserved us in safety that night and raised us up again in the morning, and carried us along, that before noon we came to Concord. Now was I full of joy and yet not without sorrow to see such a lovely sight, so many Christians together and some of them my neighbors. There I met with my brother and my brother-in-law, who asked me if I knew where his wife was. Poor heart! He had helped to bury her and knew it not; she, being shot down by the house, was partly burnt, so that those who were at Boston at the desolation of the town, and came back afterward and buried the dead, did not know her. Yet I was not without sorrow to think how many were looking and longing, and my own children amongst the rest, to enjoy that deliverance that I had now received; and I did not know whether I should ever see them again.

Being recruited with food and raiment, we went to Boston that day, where I met with my dear husband; but the thoughts of our dear children, one being dead and the other we could not tell where, abated our comfort in each other. I was not before so much hemmed in with the merciless and cruel heathen, but now as much with pitiful, tender-hearted, and compassionate Christians. In that poor and distressed and beggarly condition I was received in, I was kindly entertained in several houses; so much love I received from several (some of whom I knew and others I knew not) that I am not capable to declare it. But the Lord knows them all by name; the Lord reward them sevenfold into their bosoms of his spirituals for their temporals. The twenty pounds, the price of my redemption, was raised by some Boston gentlewomen and Mr. Usher,[5] whose bounty and religious charity I would not forget to make mention of. Then Mr. Thomas Shepard of Charlestown received us into his house, where we continued eleven weeks—and a father and mother they were unto us. And many more tender-hearted friends we met with in that place. We were now in the midst of love, yet not without much and frequent heaviness of heart for our poor children and other relations who were still in affliction.

The week following, after my coming in, the Governor[6] and Council sent forth to the Indians again—and that not without success, for they brought in my sister and Goodwife Kettle. Their not knowing where our children were was a sore trial to us still, and yet we were not without secret hopes that we should see them again. That which was dead lay heavier upon my spirit than those which were alive amongst the heathen—thinking how it suffered with its wounds and I was no way able to relieve it, and how it was buried by the heathen in the wilderness, from among all Christians. We were hurried up and down in our thoughts: sometime we should hear a report that they were gone this way and sometimes that, and that they were come in in this place or that. We kept inquiring and listening to hear concerning them, but no certain news as yet.

About this time the Council had ordered a day of public Thanksgiving, though I thought I had still cause of mourning; and, being unsettled in our minds, we thought we would ride toward the eastward to see if we could hear anything concerning our children. And as we

---

5. A bookseller in Boston, instrumental in printing the Indian Bible.

6. John Leverett.

were riding along (God is the wise disposer of all things) between Ipswich and Rowley, we met with Mr. William Hubbard,[7] who told us our son, Joseph, was come in to Major Waldron's,[8] and another with him, which was my sister's son. I asked him how he knew it. He said the Major himself told him so. So along we went till we came to Newbury; and, their minister being absent, they desired my husband to preach the Thanksgiving for them. But he was not willing to stay there that night, but would go over to Salisbury to hear farther and come again in the morning—which he did and preached there that day. At night, when he had done, one came and told him that his daughter was come in at Providence: here was mercy on both hands. Now hath God fulfilled that precious Scripture, which was such a comfort to me in my distressed condition. When my heart was ready to sink into the earth (my children being gone I could not tell whither), and my knees trembled under me, and I was walking through the valley of the shadow of death, then the Lord brought, and now has fulfilled, that reviving word unto me: *Thus saith the Lord: Refrain thy voice from weeping and thy eyes from tears, for thy work shall be rewarded, saith the Lord, and they shall come again from the land of the enemy.*[9]

Now we were between them: the one on the east and the other on the west. Our son being nearest, we went to him first, to Portsmouth, where we met with him and with the Major also, who told us he had done what he could, but could not redeem him under seven pounds, which the good people thereabouts were pleased to pay. The Lord reward the Major and all the rest, though unknown to me, for their labor of love. My sister's son was redeemed for four pounds, which the Council gave order for the payment of. Having now received one of our children, we hastened toward the other; going back through Newbury, my husband preached there on the Sabbath day, for which they rewarded him manifold.

On Monday we came to Charlestown, where we heard that the Governor of Rhode Island[1] had sent over for our daughter, to take care of her, being now within his jurisdiction—which should not pass without our acknowledgments. But she being nearer Rehoboth than Rhode Island, Mr. Newman went over and took care of her, and brought her to his own house. And the goodness of God was admirable to us in our low estate in that he raised up compassionate friends on every side to us when we had nothing to recompence any for their love. The Indians were now gone that way, that it was apprehended dangerous to go to her; but the carts which carried provision to the English army, being guarded, brought her with them to Dorchester, where we received her safe. Blessed be the Lord for it, for great is his power, and he can do whatsoever seemeth him good.

Her coming in was after this manner: she was travelling one day with the Indians, with her basket at her back. The company of Indians were got before her and gone out of sight, all except one squaw; she followed the squaw till night, and then both of them lay down, having nothing over them but the heavens, nor under them but the earth. Thus she travelled three days together, not knowing whither she was going, having nothing to eat or drink, but water and green hirtleberries.[2] At last they came into Providence, where she was kindly entertained by several of that town. The Indians often said that I should never have her under twenty pounds, but now the Lord hath brought her in upon free cost and given her to me the second time. The Lord make us a blessing indeed, each to others. Now have I seen that Scripture also fulfilled, Deut. 30: 4, 7: *If any of thine be driven out to the utmost parts of Heaven, from thence will the Lord thy God gather thee, and from thence will he fetch thee. And the Lord thy God will put all these curses upon thine enemies and on them which hate thee, which persecuted thee.* Thus hath the Lord brought me and mine out of that horrible pit and hath set us in the midst of tender-hearted

---

7. Author of the contemporary account of King Philip's War, *A Narrative of the Troubles with the Indians.*
8. Richard Waldron operated a trading post in Dover, New Hampshire.
9. Jeremiah 31:16.
1. William Coddington.
2. Bilberries or whortleberries, which are black when ripe.

and compassionate Christians. 'Tis the desire of my soul that we may walk worthy of the mercies received and which we are receiving.

Our family being now gathered together (those of us that were living), the South Church in Boston hired an house for us; then we removed from Mr. Shepard's (those cordial friends) and went to Boston, where we continued about three quarters of a year. Still the Lord went along with us and provided graciously for us. I thought it somewhat strange to set up housekeeping with bare walls, but, as Solomon says, *Money answers all things,*[3] and that we had through the benevolence of Christian friends, some in this town and some in that and others, and some from England, that in a little time we might look and see the house furnished with love. The Lord hath been exceeding good to us in our low estate, in that when we had neither house nor home, nor other necessaries, the Lord so moved the hearts of these and those towards us that we wanted neither food nor raiment for ourselves or ours, Prov. 18: 24. *There is a friend which sticketh closer than a brother.* And how many such friends have we found, and now living amongst! And truly such a friend have we found him to be unto us, in whose house we lived, *viz.,* Mr. James Whitcomb,[4] a friend unto us near hand and afar off.

I can remember the time when I used to sleep quietly, without workings in my thoughts, whole nights together; but now it is otherwise with me. When all are fast about me and no eye open but his who ever waketh, my thoughts are upon things past, upon the awful dispensations of the Lord towards us, upon his wonderful power and might in carrying of us through so many difficulties, in returning us in safety and suffering none to hurt us. I remember in the night season how the other day I was in the midst of thousands of enemies and nothing but death before me; it was then hard work to persuade myself that ever I should be satisfied with bread again. But now we are fed with the finest of the wheat and (as I may say) with honey out of the rock;[5] instead of the husk, we have the fatted calf.[6] The thoughts of these things in the particulars of them, and of the love and goodness of God towards us, make it true of me, what David said of himself, Psal. 6:6: *I water my couch with my tears.* Oh the wonderful power of God that mine eyes have seen, affording matter enough for my thoughts to run in: that when others are sleeping, mine eyes are weeping.

I have seen the extreme vanity of this world: one hour I have been in health and wealth, wanting nothing, but the next hour in sickness and wounds and death, having nothing but sorrow and affliction.

Before I knew what affliction meant, I was ready sometimes to wish for it. When I lived in prosperity, having the comforts of this world about me, my relations by me, and my heart cheerful and taking little care for anything, and yet seeing many (whom I preferred before myself) under many trials and afflictions, in sickness, weakness, poverty, losses, crosses, and cares of the world, I should be sometimes jealous lest I should have my portion in this life; and that Scripture would come to my mind, Heb. 12:6: *For whom the Lord loveth he chasteneth, and scourgeth every son whom he receiveth.* But now I see the Lord had his time to scourge and chasten me. The portion of some is to have their affliction by drops, now one drop and then another; but the dregs of the cup, the wine of astonishment,[7] like a sweeping rain that leaveth no food, did the Lord prepare to be my portion. Affliction I wanted, and affliction I had, full measure (I thought) pressed down and running over;[8] yet I see when God calls a person to anything and through never so many difficulties, yet he is fully able to carry them through and make them see and say they have been gainers thereby. And I hope I can say in some measure, as David did: *It is good for me that I have been afflicted.*[9] The Lord hath showed me the vanity of these outward things, that they are the *Vanity of vanities,* and *vexation of spirit;*[1] that

---

3. Ecclesiastes 10:19.
4. A wealthy Bostonian who was, by the way, a trafficker in Indian slaves.
5. An allusion to Psalm 81:16.
6. Allusions to Luke 15.

7. Images drawn from Psalm 60:3 and Isaiah 51:22.
8. Allusion to Luke 6:38.
9. Psalm 119:71
1. Phrases drawn from Ecclesiastes.

they are but a shadow, a blast, a bubble, and things of no continuance; that we must rely on God himself, and our whole dependence must be upon him. If trouble from smaller matters begin to arise in me, I have something at hand to check myself with and say, *Why am I troubled?* It was but the other day that, if I had had the world, I would have given it for my freedom or to have been a servant to a Christian. I have learned to look beyond present and smaller troubles and to be quieted under them, as Moses said, Exod. 14:13: *Stand still, and see the salvation of the Lord.*[2]

Finis

1682

Sarah Kemble Knight
(1666–1727)

Among the literary remains of American life in the seventeenth century are the diaries kept to record the daily affairs of the colonists. Most are quotidian accounts of weather, commerce, religion, and governmental affairs as they touch the lives of the writers, who are men. Some formed the basis for political and social histories of the time by major participants, such as William Bradford's *History of Plymouth Plantation* (written 1630–1650; first published in 1856) and John Winthrop's *The History of New England from 1630 to 1649* (written 1630–1649; first published in 1825–1826). One, *The Diary of Samuel Sewell* (written 1673–1729; first published in 1878–1882), is especially noteworthy for its portrayal of incidents of everyday life, including courtship. The eighteenth century had hardly begun, however, when a Boston woman added to the record a brief account of her journey to Connecticut and New York. Witty and irreverent, it was actually in print before the more famous writings of Bradford, Winthrop, and Sewell.

Born in Boston, Sarah Kemble was the daughter of an English merchant who had settled in Boston and his American-born wife. Little is known of her early life. By 1689 she had married Richard Knight, a shipmaster who was probably considerably older than she and who died in London in 1706. The mother of only one child, she seems to have helped her husband in his business and kept a shop in Boston's North End. The trip recorded in her *Journal* was undertaken primarily to settle the estate of a cousin. On her return, she conducted a school, where, according to tradition, her pupils included Benjamin Franklin and Samuel Mather. In 1712 she moved to Connecticut, where she apparently kept a shop and an inn. Prosperous at her death, she left a substantial estate.

Although King Philip's War (1675–1676), fought in Sarah Kemble's childhood, had effectively put an end to the power of Native Americans in New England and rendered the forest much less threatening by the time she made her journey than it had been to early Puritans, much of the terrain was still wilderness. Nevertheless, she traveled alone, except for hired guides or chance companions, over a route that took her five days from Boston to New Haven, another two days from New Haven to New York, and similar time for return. Tired as she was at the end of each day, sometimes ill, sometimes unable to eat or keep down

---

2. The verse continues, "which he will shew to you to day: for the Egyptians whom ye have seen to day, ye shall see them no more for ever." Rowlandson's text thus compares her own bondage to that of the Israelites under Egypt.

the food, she found time to keep the notes that became *The Journal of Madam Knight*.

The *Journal* was first published in 1825, with an introduction by Theodore Dwight. The source of the present text is the George Parker Winthrop edition (1920, 1935), but spelling and punctuation have been modernized. Biographical information may be found in Winthrop's introduction and in Sidney Gunn's essay in the *Dictionary of American Biography* (1933).

The Journal of Madam Knight

Monday, October the second, 1704.

About three o'clock afternoon, I begun my journey from Boston to New Haven; being about two hundred mile. My kinsman, Capt. Robert Luist, waited on me as far as Dedham, where I was to meet the Western post.

I visited the Reverend Mr. Belcher, the Minister of the town, and tarried there till evening, in hopes the post would come along. But he not coming, I resolved to go to Billingses where he used to lodge, being 12 miles further. But being ignorant of the way, Madam Belcher,[1] seeing no persuasions of her good spouses or hers could prevail with me to lodge there that night, very kindly went with me to the tavern, where I hoped to get my guide, and desired the hostess to inquire of her guests whether any of them would go with me. But they, being tied by the lips to a pewter engine, scarcely allowed themselves time to say what clownish ***.[2]

Pieces of eight, I told her no, I would not be accessory to such extortion.

Then John shan't go, says she. No, indeed, shan't he; and held forth at that rate a long time, that I began to fear I was got among the Quaking tribe, believing not a limber-tongued sister among them could outdo Madam Hostess.

Upon this, to my no small surprise, son John arose, and gravely demanded what I would give him to go with me? Give you, says I, are you John? Yes, says he, for want of a better; and behold! this John looked as old as my host, and perhaps had been a man in the last century. Well, Mr. John, says I, make your demands. Why, half a piece of eight and a dram, says John. I agreed, and gave him a Dram (now) in hand to bind the bargain.

My hostess catechised John for going so cheap, saying his poor wife would break her heart ***.[3]

His shade on his horse resembled a globe on a gate post. His habit, horse and furniture, its looks and goings, incomparably answered the rest.

Thus jogging on with an easy pace, my guide telling me it was dangerous to ride hard in the night, (which his horse had the sense to avoid,) he entertained me with the adventures he had passed by late riding, and eminent dangers he had escaped, so that, remembering the heroes in Parismus and the Knight of the Oracle,[4] I didn't know but I had met with a prince disguised.

When we had rid about an hour, we come into a thick swamp, which by reason of a great fog very much startled me, it being now very dark. But nothing dismayed John: he had encountered a thousand and a thousand such swamps, having a universal knowledge in the woods; and readily answered all my inquiries, which were not a few.

In about an hour, or something more, after we left the swamp, we come to Billinges, where I was to lodge. My guide dismounted and very complacently helped me down and showed

1. The text has "Billings."
2. A half-page of the manuscript is missing here.
3. Another half-page of manuscript is missing

here.
4. Sixteenth- and seventeenth-century romances.

the door, signing to me with his hand to go in; which I gladly did—but had not gone many steps into the room, ere I was interrogated by a young lady I understood afterwards was the eldest daughter of the family, with these, or words to this purpose, *(viz.)* Law for me—what in the world brings you here at this time a night?—I never see a woman on the road so dreadful late, in all the days of my versal[5] life. Who are you? Where are you going? I'm scared out of my wits—with much now of the same kind. I stood aghast, preparing to reply, when in comes my guide—to him madam turned roaring out: lawful heart, John, is it you?—how de do! Where in the world are you going with this woman? Who is she? John made no answer but sat down in the corner, fumbled out his black junk,[6] and saluted that instead of Debb; she then turned again to me and fell anew into her silly questions, without asking me to sit down.

I told her she treated me very rudely, and I did not think it my duty to answer her unmannerly questions. But to get rid of them, I told her I come there to have the post's company with me tomorrow on my journey, &c. Miss stared awhile, drew a chair, bid me sit, And then run upstairs and puts on two or three rings (or else I had not seen them before) and returning, set herself just before me, showing the way to reding,[7] that I might see her ornaments, perhaps to gain the more respect. But her Granam's new rung[8] sow, had it appeared, would affected me as much. I paid honest John with money and dram according to contract, and dismissed him, and prayed Miss to show me where I must lodge. She conducted me to a parlor in a little back lean-to, which was almost filled with the bedstead, which was so high that I was forced to climb on a chair to git up to the wretched bed that lay on it; on which having stretched my tired limbs, and layed my head on a sad-colored pillow, I began to think on the transactions of the past day.

Tuesday, October the third,

about 8 in the morning, I with the post proceeded forward without observing anything remarkable; and about two, afternoon, arrived at the post's second stage, where the western post met him and exchanged letters. Here, having called for something to eat, the woman brought in a twisted thing like a cable, but something whiter; and laying it on the board, tugged for life to bring it into a capacity to spread; which having with great pains accomplished, she served in a dish of pork and cabbage, I suppose the remains of dinner. The sauce was of a deep purple, which I thought was boiled in her dye kettle; the bread was Indian, and every thing on the table service agreeable to these. I, being hungry, got a little down; but my stomach was soon cloyed, and what cabbage I swallowed served me for a cud the whole day after.

Having here discharged the ordinary[9] for self and guide, (as I understood was the custom,) about three, afternoon, went on with my third guide, who rode very hard; and having crossed Providence ferry, we come to a river which they generally ride through. But I dare not venture; so the post got a lad and canoe to carry me to tother side, and he rid through and led my horse. The canoe was very small and shallow, so that when we were in she seemed ready to take in water, which greatly terrified me, and caused me to be very circumspect, sitting with my hands fast on each side, my eyes steady, not daring so much as to lodge my tongue a hair's breadth more on one side of my mouth than tother, nor so much as think on Lot's wife,[1] for a wry thought would have overset our wherry: but was soon put out of this pain, by feeling the canoe on shore, which I as soon almost saluted with my feet; and rewarding my sculler, again mounted and made the best of our way forwards. The road here was very even and the day pleasant, it being now near sunset. But the post told me we had

---

5. Universal, entire.
6. Here, a twist of tobacco.
7. Slang: making a display.
8. Having a ring in its nose.

9. A tavern with set meals and prices.
1. Fleeing the wicked city of Sodom, Lot's wife looked back, contrary to instructions, and "became a pillar of salt" (Genesis 19:26).

near 14 miles to ride to the next stage, (where we were to lodge.) I asked him of the rest of the road, foreseeing wee must travail in the night. He told me there was a bad river we were to ride through, which was so very fierce a horse could sometimes hardly stem it: but it was but narrow, and we should soon be over. I cannot express the concern of mind this relation set me in: no thoughts but those of the dangerous river could entertain my imagination, and they were as formidable as various still tormenting me with blackest ideas of my approaching fate—sometimes seeing my self drowning, otherwhiles drowned, and at the best like a holy Sister just come out of a spiritual bath in dripping garments.

Now was the glorious luminary, with his swift coursers arrived at his stage, leaving poor me with the rest of this part of the lower world in darkness, with which we were soon surrounded. The only glimmering we now had was from the spangled skies, whose imperfect reflections rendered every object formidable. Each lifeless trunk, with its shattered limbs, appeared an armed enemy; and every little stump like a ravenous devourer. Nor could I so much as discern my guide, when at any distance, which added to the terror.

Thus, absolutely lost in thought, and dying with the very thoughts of drowning, I come up with the post, who I did not see till even with his horse: he told me he stopped for me; and we rode on very deliberatly a few paces, when we entred a thicket of trees and shrubs, and I perceived by the horse's going, we were on the descent of a hill, which, as we come nearer the bottom, 'twas totally dark with the trees that surrounded it. But I knew by the going of the horse we had entered the water, which my guide told me was the hazardous river he had told me of; and he, riding up close to my side, bid me not fear—we should be over immediately. I now rallied all the courage I was mistress of, knowing that I must either venture my fate of drowning, or be left like the children in the wood. So, as the post bid me, I gave reins to my nag; and sitting as steady as just before in the canoe, in a few minutes got safe to the other side, which he told me was the Narragansett country.

Here we found great difficulty in travailing, the way being very narrow, and on each side the trees and bushes gave us very unpleasent welcomes with their branches and boughs, which we could not avoid, it being so exceeding dark. My guide, as before so now, put on harder than I, with my weary bones, could follow; so left me and the way behind him. Now returned my distressed apprehensions of the place where I was: the dolesome woods, my company next to none, going I knew not whither, and encompassed with terrifying darkness; the least of which was enough to startle a more masculine courage. Added to which the reflections, as in the afternoon of the day, that my call was very questionable, which till then I had not so prudently as I ought considered. Now, coming to the foot of a hill, I found great difficulty in ascending; but being got to the top, was there amply recompensed with the friendly appearance of the kind conductress of the night, just then advancing above the horizontal line. The raptures which the sight of that fair planet produced in me, caused me, for the moment, to forget my present weariness and past toils; and inspired me for most of the remaining way with very divirting thoughts, some of which, with the other occurances of the day, I reserved to note down when I should come to my stage. My thoughts on the sight of the moon were to this purpose:

> Fair Cynthia, all the homage that I may
> Unto a creature, unto thee I pay;
> In lonesome woods to meet so kind a guide,
> To me's more worth than all the world beside.
> Some joy I felt just now, when safe got o'er
> Yon surly river to this rugged shore,
> Deeming rough welcomes from these clownish trees
> Better than lodgings with Nereides.[2]

2.   Sea nymphs of classical mythology.

Yet swelling fears surprise; all dark appears—
Nothing but light can dissipate those fears.
My fainting vitals can't lend strength to say,
But softly whisper, O I wish 'twere day.
The murmer hardly warm'd the ambient air,
E're thy bright aspect rescues from dispair:
Makes the old hag her sable mantle loose,
And a bright joy does through my soul diffuse.
The boisterous trees now lend a passage free,
And pleasent prospects thou giv'st light to see.

From hence we kept on, with more ease than before: the way being smooth and even, the night warm and serene, and the tall and thick trees at a distance, especially when the moon glared light through the branches, filled my imagination with the pleasant delusion of a sumptuous city, filled with famous buildings and churches, with their spiring steeples, balconies, galleries and I know not what: granduers which I had heard of, and which the stories of foreign countries had given me the idea of.

Here stood a lofty church—there is a steeple,
And there the grand parade—O see the people!
That famous castle there, were I but nigh,
To see the moat and bridge and walls so high—
They're very fine! says my deluded eye.

Being thus agreeably entertained without a thought of any thing but thoughts themselves, I on a sudden was roused from these pleasing imaginations, by the post's sounding his horn, which assured me he was arrived at the stage, where we were to lodge: and that music was then most musical and agreeable to me.

Being come to Mr. Havens', I was very civilly received, and courteously entertained, in a clean comfortable house; and the good woman was very active in helping off my riding clothes, and then asked what I would eat. I told her I had some chocolate, if she would prepare it; which with the help of some milk, and a little clean brass kettle, she soon effected to my satisfaction. I then betook me to my apartment, which was a little room parted from the kitchen by a single board partition; where, after I had noted the occurrences of the past day, I went to bed, which, though pretty hard, yet neat and handsome. But I could get no sleep, because of the clamor of some of the town topers in next room, who were entered into a strong debate concerning the signification of the name of their country, *(viz.) Narraganset.* One said it was named so by the Indians, because there grew a brier there, of a prodigious height and bigness, the like hardly ever known, called by the Indians Narragansett; and quotes an Indian of so barbarous a name for his author, that I could not write it. His antagonist replied no—It was from a spring it had its name, which he well knew where it was, which was extream cold in summer, and as hot as could be imagined in the winter, which was much resorted too by the natives, and by them called Narragansett, (hot and cold,) and that was the original of their place's name—with a thousand impertinances not worth notice, which He uttered with such a roaring voice and thundering blows with the fist of wickedness on the table, that it pierced my very head. I heartily fretted, and wished 'um tongue tied; but with as little success as a friend of mine once, who was (as she said) kept a whole night awake, on a journey, by a country left.[3] and a sergeant, insigne[4] and a deacon, contriving how to bring a triangle into a square. They kept calling for tother gill, which while they were swallowing, was some intermission; but presently, like oil to fire, increased the flame. I set my candle on

---

3. For leftenant, or lieutenant.   4. Ensign.

a chest by the bed side, and setting up, fell to my old way of composing my resentments, in the following manner:

> I ask thy aid, O potent Rum!
> To charm these wrangling topers Dum.
> Thou hast their giddy brains possest—
> The man confounded with the Beast—
> And I, poor I, can get no rest.
> Intoxicate them with thy fumes:
> O still their tongues till morning comes!

And I know not but my wishes took effect; for the dispute soon ended with 'tother dram; and so good night!

Wednesday, October 4th.

About four in the morning, we set out for Kingston (for so was the town called) with a French doctor in our company. He and the post put on very furiously, so that I could not keep up with them, only as now and then they'd stop till they see me. This road was poorly furnished with accommodations for travellers, so that we were forced to ride 22 miles by the post's account, but nearer thirty by mine, before we could bait[5] so much as our horses, which I exceedingly complained of. But the post encouraged me, by saying we should be well accommodated anon at Mr. Devil's, a few miles further. But I questioned whether we ought to go to the Devil to be helped out of affliction. However, like the rest of deluded souls that post to the infernal den, we made all possible speed to this Devil's habitation; where alighting, in full assurance of good accommodation, we were going in. But meeting his two daughters, as I supposed twins, they so nearly resembled each other, both in features and habit, and looked as old as the Devil himself, and quite as ugly, We desired entertainment, but could hardly get a word out of 'um, till with our importunity, telling them our necessity, &c. they called the old sophister, who was as sparing of his words as his daughters had been, and no, or none, was the replies he made us to our demands. He differed only in this from the old fellow in t'other country: he let us depart. However, I thought it proper to warn poor travailers to endeavor to avoid falling into circumstances like ours, which at our next stage I sat down and did as followeth:

> May all that dread the cruel fiend of night
> Keep on, and not at this curs't mansion light.
> 'Tis Hell; 'tis Hell! and Devils here do dwell:
> Here dwells the Devil—surely this's Hell.
> Nothing but Wants: a drop to cool your tongue
> Can't be procured these cruel fiends among.
> Plenty of horrid grins and looks severe,
> Hunger and thirst, but pity's bannished here—
> The right hand keep, if Hell on earth you fear!

Thus leaving this habitation of cruelty, we went forward; and arriving at an ordinary about two mile further, found tolerable accommodation. But our hostess, being a pretty full mouthed old creature, entertained our fellow travailer, the French doctor, with unnumerable complaints of her bodily infirmities; and whispered to him so loud, that all the house had as full a hearing as he: which was very divirting to the company, (of which there was a great

---

5. Feed and water.

many,) as one might see by their sneering. But poor weary I slipped out to enter my mind in my journal, and left my great landlady with her talkative guests to themselves.

From hence we proceeded (about ten forenoon) through the Narragansett country, pretty leisurely; and about one afternoon come to Paukataug River, which was about two hundred paces over, and now very high, and no way over to t'other side but this. I dared not venture to ride through, my courage at best in such cases but small, and now at the lowest ebb, by reason of my weary, very weary, hungry and uneasy circumstances. So taking leave of my company, though with no little reluctance, that I could not proceed with them on my journey, stopped at a little cottage just by the river, to wait the water's falling, which the old man that lived there said would be in a little time, and he would conduct me safe over. This little hut was one of the wretchedest I ever saw a habitation for human creatures. It was supported with shores enclosed with clapboards, laid on lengthways, and so much asunder, that the light come through everywhere; the door tyied on with a cord in the place of hinges; the floor the bare earth; no windows but such as the thin covering afforded, nor any furniture but a bed with a glass bottle hanging at the head on't; an earthen cup, a small pewter Basin, a board with sticks to stand on, instead of a table, and a block or two in the corner instead of chairs. The family were the old man, his wife and two children; all and every part being the picture of poverty. Notwithstanding both the hut and its inhabitance were very clean and tidy: to the crossing the old proverb, that bare walls make giddy housewives.

I blessed myself that I was not one of this miserable crew; and the impressions their wretchedness formed in me caused me on the very spot to say:

> Tho' ill at ease, a stranger and alone,
> All my fatigues shall not extort a groan.
> These indigents have hunger with their ease;
> Their best is worse by half than my disease.
> Their miserable hut which heat and cold
> Alternately without repulse do hold;
> Their lodgings thin and hard, their Indian fare,
> The mean apparel which the wretches wear,
> And their ten thousand ills which can't be told,
> Makes nature er'e 'tis midle age'd look old.
> When I reflect, my late fatigues do seem
> Only a notion or forgotten dream.

I had scarce done thinking, when an Indian-like animal come to the door, on a creature very much like himself, in mien and feature, as well as ragged clothing; and having 'lit, makes an awkward scratch with his Indian shoe, and a nod, sits on the block, fumbles out his black junk, dips it in the ashes, and presents it piping hot to his muscheeto's, and fell to sucking like a calf, without speaking, for near a quarter of an hour. At length the old man said how does Sarah do? who I understood was the wretch's wife, and daughter to the old man: he replied— as well as can be expected, &c. So I remembred the old say, and supposed I knew Sarah's case. But he being, as I understood, going over the river, as ugly as he was, I was glad to ask him to show me the way to Saxton's, at Stonington; which he promising, I ventur'd over with the old man's assistance; who having rewarded to content, with my tattertailed guide, I rid on very slowly through Stonington, where the road was very stony and uneven. I asked the fellow, as we went, divers questions of the place and way, &c. I being arrived at my country Saxton's, at Stonington, was very well accommodated both as to victuals and lodging, the only good of both I had found since my setting out. Here I heard there was an old man and his daughter to come that way, bound to N. London; and being now destitute of a guide, gladly waited for them, being in so good a harbor, and accordingly,

Thursday, October the 5th,

about 3 in the afternoon, I sat forward with neighbor Polly and Jemima, a girl about 18 years old, who he said he had been to fetch out of the Narragansetts, and said they had rode thirty miles that day, on a sorry lean jade, with only a bag under her for a pillion, which the poor girl often complain'd was very uneasy.

We made good speed along, which made poor Jemima make many a sour face, the mare being a very hard trotter; and after many a hearty and bitter Oh, she at length lowed out: Lawful heart father! this bare mare hurts me dingely,[6] I'm direful sore I vow; with many words to that purpose: poor child says Gaffer—she used to serve your mother so. I don't care how mother used to do, quoth Jemima, in a passionate tone. At which the old man laughed, and kicked his jade o' the side, which made her jolt ten times harder.

About seven that evening, we come to New London ferry: here, by reason of a very high wind, we met with great difficulty in getting over—the boat tossed exceedingly, and our horses capered at a very surprising rate, and set us all in a fright; especially poor Jemima, who desired her father to say "so Jack" to the jade, to make her stand. But the careless parent, taking no notice of her repeated desires, she roared out in a passionate manner: Pray sooth father, are you deaf? Say "so Jack" to the jade, I tell you. The dutiful parent obey's; saying "so Jack, so Jack," as gravely as if he'd been to saying catechism after young Miss, who with her fright looked of all colors in the rainbow.

Being safely arrived at the house of Mrs. Prentice's in N. London, I treated neighbor Polly and daughter for their diverting company, and bid them farewell; and between nine and ten at night waited on the Reverend Mr. Gurdon Saltonstall, minister of the town, who kindly invited me to stay that night at his house, where I was very handsomely and plentifully treated and lodged; and made good the great character I had before heard concerning him: viz. that he was the most affable, courteous, generous and best of men.

Friday, October 6th.

I got up very early, in order to hire somebody to go with me to New Haven, being in great perplexity at the thoughts of proceeding alone; which my most hospitable entertainer observing, himself went, and soon returned with a young gentleman of the town, who he could confide in to go with me; and about eight this morning, with Mr. Joshua Wheeler my new guide, taking leave of this worthy gentleman, we advanced on towards Seabrook. The roads all along this way are very bad, encumbered with rocks and mountainous passages, which were very disagreeable to my tired carcass; but we went on with a moderate pace which made the journey more pleasant. But after about eight miles riding, in going over a bridge under which the river run very swift, my horse stumbled, and very narrowly escaped falling over into the water; which extremely frightened me. But through God's goodness I met with no harm, and mounting again, in about half a mile's riding, come to an ordinary, were well entertained by a woman of about seventy and vantage, but of as sound intellectuals as one of seventeen. She entertained Mr. Wheeler with some passages of a wedding awhile ago at a place hard by, the brides-groom being about her age or something above, saying his children was dreadfully against their father's marrying, which she condemned them extremely for.

From hence we went pretty briskly forward, and arrived at Saybrook ferry about two of the clock afternoon; and crossing it, we called at an inn to bait, (foreseeing we should not have such another opportunity till we come to Killingsworth.) Landlady come in, with her hair about her ears, and hands at full pay scratching. She told us she had some mutton which she would broil, which I was glad to hear; But I suppose forgot to wash her scratchers; in a little

---

6. With repeated thumps.

time she brought it in; but it being pickled, and my guide said it smelt strong of head sauce, we left it, and paid sixpence apiece for our dinners, which was only smell.

So we put forward with all speed, and about seven at night come to Killingsworth, and were tolerably well with travellers fare, and lodged there that night.

Saturday, October 7th,

we set out early in the morning, and being something unaquainted with the way, having asked it of some we met, they told us we must ride a mile or two and turn down a lane on the right hand; and by their direction we rode on but not yet coming to the turning, we met a young fellow and asked him how far it was to the lane which turned down towards Guilford. He said we must ride a little further, and turn down by the corner of uncle Sam's lot. My guide vented his spleen at the lubber; and we soon after came into the road, and keeping still on, without any thing further remarkable, about two a clock afternoon we arrived at New Haven, where I was received with all possible respects and civility. Here I discharged Mr. Wheeler with a reward to his satisfaction, and took some time to rest after so long and toilsome a journey; and informed myself of the manners and customs of the place, and at the same time employed myself in the affair I went there upon.

They are governed by the same laws as we in Boston, (or little differing,) throughout this whole colony of Connecticut, and much the same way of church government, and many of them good, sociable people, and I hope religious too: but a little too much independant in their principles, and, as I have been told, were formerly in their zeal very rigid in their administrations towards such as their laws made offenders, even to a harmless kiss or innocent merriment among young people. Whipping being a frequent and counted an easy punishment, about which as other crimes, the judges were absolute in their sentences. They told me a pleasant story about a pair of justices in those parts, which I may not omit the relation of.

A Negro slave belonging to a man in the town, stole a hogshead from his master, and gave or sold it to an Indian, native of the place. The Indian sold it in the neighborhood, and so the theft was found out. Thereupon the heathen was seized, and carried to the justice's house to be examined. But his worship (it seems) was gone into the field, with a brother in office, to gather in his pompions.[7] Whither the malefactor is hurried, and complaint made, and satisfaction in the name of justice demanded. Their worships can't proceed in form without a bench: whereupon they order one to be immediately erected, which, for want of fitter materials, they made with pompions—which being finished, down sets their worships, and the malefactor called, and by the senior justice interrogated after the following manner. You Indian why did you steal from this man? You shouldn't do so—it's a grandy wicked thing to steal. Hol't hol't cries justice junior brother, You speak Negro to him. I'll ask him. You sirrah, why did you steal this man's hogshead? Hogshead? (replies the Indian,) me no stomany. No? says his worship; and pulling off his hat, patted his own head with his hand, says, Tatapa—You, Tatapa—you; all one this. Hogshead all one this. Hah! says Netop, now me stomany that. Whereupon the company fell into a great fit of laughter, even to roaring. Silence is commanded, but to no effect: for they continued perfectly shouting. Nay, says his worship, in an angry tone, if it be so, *take me off the bench.*

Their diversions in this part of the country are on lecture days and training days[8] mostly: on the former there is riding from town to town.

And on training days the youth divert themselves by shooting at the target, as they call it (but it very much resembles a pillory) where he that hits nearest the white has some yards of red ribbon presented him which being tied to his hatband, the two ends streaming down his back, he is led away in triumph, with great applause, as the winners of the Olympic

7. Pumpkins.
8. Days for religious lectures and military training.

Games. They generally marry very young: the males oftener as I am told under twenty than above; they generally make public wedings, and have a way something singular (as they say) in some of them, *viz.* just before joining hands the bridegroom quits the place, who is soon followed by the bridesmen, and as it were, dragged back to duty—being the reverse to the former practice among us, to steal Ms. Pride.

There are great plenty of oysters all along by the seaside, as far as I rode in the colony, and those very good. And they generally lived very well and comfortably in their families. But too indulgent (especially the farmers) to their slaves: suffering too great familiarity from them, permitting them to sit at table and eat with them, (as they say to save time,) and into the dish goes the black hoof as freely as the white hand. They told me that there was a farmer lived near the town where I lodged who had some difference with his slave, concerning something the master had promised him and did not punctualy perform; which caused some hard words between them; but at length they put the matter to arbitration and bound themselves to stand to the award of such as they named—which done, the arbitrators having heard the allegations of both parties, order the master to pay 40s to black face, and acknowledge his fault. And so the matter ended: the poor master very honestly standing to the award.

There are everywhere in the towns as I passed, a number of Indians the natives of the country, and are the most savage of all the savages of that kind that I had ever seen: little or no care taken (as I heard upon enquiry) to make them otherwise. They have in some places lands of their own, and governed by laws of their own making;—they marry many wives and at pleasure put them away, and on the least dislike or fickle humor, on either side, saying *stand away* to one another is a sufficient divorce. And indeed those uncomely *stand aways* are too much in vogue among the English in this (indulgent colony) as their records plentifully prove, and that on very trivial matters, of which some have been told me, but are not proper to be related by a female pen, though some of that foolish sex have had too large a share in the story.

If the natives commit any crime on their own precincts among themselves, the English takes no cognizance of. But if on the English ground, they are punishable by our laws. They mourn for their dead by blacking their faces, and cutting their hair, after an awkward and frightful manner; but can't bear you should mention the names of their dead relations to them: they trade most for rum, for which they'd hazard their very lives; and the English fit them generally as well, by seasoning it plentifully with water.

They give the title of merchant to every trader; who rate their goods according to the time and specie they pay in: *viz.* pay, money, pay as money, and trusting. *Pay* is grain, pork, beef, &c. at the prices set by the General Court that year; *money* is pieces of eight, reals, or Boston or Bay shillings (as they call them,) or good hard money, as sometimes silver coin is termed by them; also wampum, *viz.* Indian beads which serves for change. *Pay as money* is provisions, as aforesaid one third cheaper than as the Assembly or General Court sets it; and *Trust* as they and the merchant agree for time.

Now, when the buyer comes to ask for a commodity, sometimes before the merchant answers that he has it, he says, *is your pay ready?* Perhaps the chap replies yes: what do you pay in? says the merchant. The buyer having answered, then the price is set; as suppose he wants a sixpenny knife, in pay it is 12d—in pay as money eight pence, and hard money its own price, *viz.* 6d. It seems a very intricate way of trade and what *Lex Mercatoria*[9] had not thought of.

Being at a merchants house, in comes a tall country fellow, with his alforjas[1] full of tobacco; for they seldom loose their cud, but keep chewing and spitting as long as their eyes are open,—he advanced to the midle of the room, makes an awkward nod, and spitting a large deal of aromatic tincture, he gave a scrape with his shovel-like shoe, leaving a small shovel full of dirt on the floor, made a full stop, hugging his own pretty body with his hands under

9. The law of merchants.   1. Saddlebags, but here, humorously, cheeks.

his arms, stood staring round him, like a cat let out of a basket. At last, like the creature Balaam rode on, he opened his mouth and said: have you any ribbons for hatbands to sell I pray? The questions and answers about the pay being past, the ribbon is brought and opened. Bumpkin simpers, cries it's confounded gay I vow; and beckoning to the door, in comes Joan Tawdry, dropping about 50 curtsies, and stands by him: he shows her the ribbon. *Law you,* says she, *it's right gent,* do you, take it, 'tis dreadful pretty. Then she enquires, *have you any hood silk I pray?* which being brought and bought, have you any *thread silk to sew it with* says she, which being accommodated with they departed. They generally stand after they come in a great while speechless, and sometimes don't say a word till they are asked what they want, which I impute to the awe they stand in of the merchants, who they are constantly almost indebted to; and must take what they bring without liberty to choose for themselves; but they serve them as well, making the merchants stay long enough for their pay.

We may observe here the great necessity and benefit both of education and conversation; for these people have as large a portion of mother wit, and sometimes a larger, than those who have been brought up in cities; but for want of improvements, render themselves almost ridiculous, as above. I should be glad if they would leave such follies, and am sure all that love clean houses (at least) would be glad on't too.

They are generally very plain in their dress, throuout all the colony, as I saw, and follow one another in their modes; that you may know where they belong, especially the women, meet them where you will.

Their chief red letter day is St. Election, which is annually observed according to charter, to choose their governor: a blessing they can never be thankful enough for, as they will find, if ever it be their hard fortune to lose it. The present governor in Connecticut is the Honorable John Winthrop, Esq., a gentleman of an ancient and honorable family, whose father was governor here sometime before, and his grandfather had been governor of the Massachusetts. This gentleman is a very courteous and affable person, much given to hospitality, and has by his good services gained the affection of the people as much as any who had been before him in that post.

December 6th.

Being by this time well recruited and rested after my journey, my business lying unfinished by some concerns at New York depending thereupon, my kinsman, Mr. Thomas Trowbridge of New Haven, must needs take a journey there before it could be accomplished. I resolved to go there in company with him, and a man of the town which I engaged to wait on me there. Accordingly, Dec. 6th we set out from New Haven, and about 11 same morning came to Stratford ferry; which crossing, about two miles on the other side baited our horses and would have eat a morsel ourselves, but the pumpkin and Indian mixed bread had such an aspect, and the bare-legged punch so awkward or rather awful a sound, that we left both, and proceeded forward, and about seven at night come to Fairfield, where we met with good entertainment and lodged; and early next morning set forward to Norwalk, from its half Indian name *North-walk,* when about 12 at noon we arrived, and had a dinner of fried venison, very savory. Landlady wanting some pepper in the seasoning, bid the girl hand her the spice in the little *gay* cup on the shelfe. From hence we hasted towards Rye, walking and leading our horses near a mile together, up a prodigious high hill; and so riding till about nine at night, and there arrived and took up our lodgings at an ordinary, which a French family kept. Here being very hungry, I desired a fricassee, which the Frenchman undertaking, managed so contrary to my notion of cookery, that I hastened to bed supperless; and being showed the way up a pair of stairs which had such a narrow passage that I had almost stopped by the bulk of my body; but arriving at my apartment found it to be a little lean-to chamber furnished amongst other rubbish with a high bed and a low one, a long table, a bench and a bottomless chair,—Little Miss went to scratch up my kennel, which rustled as if she'd been in the barn amongst the husks, and suppose such was the contents of the ticking—nevertheless being exceeding weary, down I laid my poor carcass (never more tired) and found my covering as scanty as my bed was hard. Anon I heard another rustling noise in the room—called to know the matter—Little Miss said she was making a bed for the men; who, when they were in bed, complained their legs lay out of it by reason of its shortness—my poor bones complained bitterly not being used to such lodgings, and so did the man who was with us; and poor I made but one groan, which was from the time I went to bed to the time I rose, which was about three in the morning, setting up by the fire till light, and having discharged our ordinary, which was as dear as if we had had far better fare—we took our leave of Monsieur and about seven in the morn come to New Rochelle a French town, where we had a good breakfast. And in the strength of that about an hour before sunset got to York. Here I applied myself to Mr. Burroughs, a merchant to whom I was recommended by my kinsman Capt. Prout, and received great civilities from him and his spouse, who were now both deaf but very agreeable in their conversation, diverting me with pleasant stories of their knowledge in Britain, from whence they both come, one of which was above the rest very pleasant to me viz. my Lord Darcy had a very extravagant brother who had mortgaged what estate he could not sell, and in good time died leaving only one son. Him his Lordship (having none of his own) took and made him heir of his whole estate, which he was to receive at the death of his aunt. He and his aunt in her widowhood held a right understanding and lived as become such relations, she being a discreet gentlewoman and he an ingenious young man. One day he fell into some company though far his inferiors, very freely told him of the ill circumstances his father's estate lay under, and the many debts he left unpaid to the wrong of poor people with whom he had dealt. The young gentleman was put out of countenance—no way he could think of to redress himself—his whole dependance being on the Lady his aunt, and how to speak to her he knew not—He went home, sat down to dinner and as usual sometimes with her when the chaplain was absent, she desired him to say grace, which he did after this manner:

> Pray God in Mercy take my Lady Darcy
>   Unto his Heavenly Throne,
>   That Little John may live like a man,
>   And pay every man his own.

The prudent Lady took no present notice, But finishd dinner, after which having sat and talked awhile (as customary) he rose, took his hat and going out she desired him to give her leave to speak to him in her closet, where being come she desired to know why he prayed for her death in the manner aforesaid, and what part of her deportment towards him merited such desires. He replied, none at all, but he was under such disadvantages that nothing but that could do him service, and told her how he had been affronted as above, and what impressions it had made upon him. The Lady made him a gentle reprimand that he had not informed her after another manner, bid him see what his father owed and he should have money to pay it to a penny, and always to let her know his wants and he should have a ready supply. The young gentleman charmed with his aunt's discreet management, begged her pardon and accepted her kind offer and retrieved his father's estate, &c. and said he hoped his aunt would never die, for she had done better by him than he could have done for himself.—Mr. Burroughs went with me to vendue[2] where I bought about 100 ream of paper which was retaken in a flyboat from Holland and sold very reasonably here—some ten, some eight shillings per ream by the lot, which was ten ream in a lot. And at the vendue I made a great many acquaintances amongst the good women of the town, who courteously invited me to their houses and generously entertained me.

The City of New York is a pleasant, well compacted place, situated on a commodious river

2. A public auction or sale.

which is a fine harbor for shipping. The buildings brick generally, very stately and high, though not altogether like ours in Boston. The bricks in some of the houses are of divers colors and laid in checkers, being glazed look very agreeable. The inside of them are neat to admiration, the wooden work, for only the walls are plastered, and the summers and gist[3] are planed and kept very white scoured as so is all the partitions if made of boards. The fireplaces have no jambs (as ours have) but the backs run flush with the walls, and the hearth is of tiles and is as far out into the room at the ends as before the fire, which is generally five foot in the lower rooms, and the peice over where the mantel tree should be is made as ours with joiner's work, and as I suppose is fastened to iron rods inside. The house where the vendue was had chimney corners like ours, and they and the hearths were laid with the finest tile that I ever see, and the staircases laid all with white tile which is ever clean, and so are the walls of the kitchen which had a brick floor. They were making great preparations to receive their governor, Lord Cornbury from the Jerseys, and for that end raised the militia to guard him on shore to the fort.

They are generally of the Church of England and have a New England gentleman for their minister, and a very fine church set out with all customary requisites. There are also a Dutch and divers conventicles as they call them, *viz.* Baptist, Quakers, &c. They are not strict in keeping the sabbath as in Boston and other places where I had been, but seem to deal with great exactness as far as I see or deal with. They are sociable to one another and curteous and civil to strangers and fare well in their houses. The English go very fashionable in their dress. But the Dutch, especially the middling sort, differ from our women, in their habit go loose, French muches[4] which are like a cap and a head band in one, leaving their ears bare, which are set out with jewels of a large size and many in number. And their fingers hooped with rings, some with large stones in them of many colors as were their pendants in their ears, which you should see very old women wear as well as young.

They have vendues very frequently and make their earnings very well by them, for they treat with good liquor liberally, and the customers drink as liberally and generally pay for't as well, by paying for that which they bid up briskly for, after the sack[5] has gone plentifully about, though sometimes good penny worths are got there. Their diversions in the winter is riding sleighs about three or four miles out of town, where they have houses of entertainment at a place called the Bowery, and some go to friend's houses who handsomely treat them. Mr. Burroughs carried his spouse and daughter and myself out to one Madame Dowes, a gentlewoman that lived at a farm house, who gave us a handsome entertainment of five or six dishes and choice beer and metheglin,[6] cider, &c. all which she said was the produce of her farm. I believe we met 50 or 60 sleighs that day—they fly with great swiftness and some are so furious that they'll turn out of the path for none except a loaden cart. Nor do they spare for any diversion the place affords, and sociable to a degree, their tables being as free to their neighbors as to themselves.

Having here transacted the affair I went upon and some other that fell in the way, after about a fortnight's stay there I left New York with no little regret,

Thursday, December 21,

set out for New Haven with my kinsman Trowbridge, and the man that waited on me about one afternoon, and about three come to half-way house about ten miles out of town, where we baited and went forward, and about 5 come to Spiting Devil,[7] Else Kings bridge, where

3. Beams and joists.	7. Spuyten Duyvil Creek, at the north end of
4. Mouchoirs, kerchiefs.	Manhattan, connecting the Hudson and
5. Any of several light-colored wines.	Harlem rivers.
6. Mead, a fermented honey drink.	

they pay three pence for passing over with a horse, which the man that keeps the gate set up at the end of the bridge receives.

We hoped to reach the French town and lodge there that night, but unhappily lost our way about four miles short, and being overtaken by a great storm of wind and snow which set full in our faces about dark, we were very uneasy. But meeting one Gardner who lived in a cottage thereabout, offered us his fire to set by, having but one poor bed, and his wife not well, &c. or he would go to a house with us, where he thought we might be better accommodated—thither we went, But a surly old she creature, not worthy the name of woman, who would hardly let us go into her door, though the weather was so stormy none but she would have turnd out a dog. But her son, whose name was Gallop, who lived just by invited us to his house and showed me two pair of stairs, *viz.* one up the loft and t'other up the bed, which was as hard as it was high, and warmed it with a hot stone at the feet. I lay very uncomfortably, insomuch that I was so very cold and sick I was forced to call them up to give me something to warm me. They had nothing but milk in the house, which they boiled, and to make it better sweetened with molasses, which I not knowing or thinking of till it was down and coming up again, which it did in so plentiful a manner that my host was soon paid double for his portion, and that in specie.[8] But I believe it did me service in clearing my stomach. So after this sick and weary night at East Chester, (a very miserable poor place,) the weather being now fair,

Friday the 22^d December

we set out for New Rochelle, where being come we had good entertainment and recruited ourselves very well. This is a very pretty place well compact, and good handsome houses, clean, good and passable roads, and situated on a navigable river, abundance of land well fined and cleared all along as we passed, which caused in me a love to the place, which I could have been content to live in it. Here we rid over a bridge made of one entire stone of such a breadth that a cart might pass with safety, and to spare—it lay over a passage cut through a rock to convey water to a mill not far off. Here are three fine taverns within call of each other, very good provision for Travailers.

Thence we travailed through Merrinak, a neat, though little place, with a navigable river before it, one of the pleasantest I ever see—here were good buildings, especially one, a very fine seat, which they told me was Col. Hethcoat's, who I had heard was a very fine gentleman. From hence we come to Horse Neck, where wee baited, and they told me that one Church of England parson officiated in all these three towns once every Sunday in turns throughout the year; and that they all could but poorly maintain him which they grudged to do, being a poor and quarrelsome crew as I understand by our host; their quarrelling about their choice of minister, they chose to have none—but caused the government to send this gentleman to them. Here we took leave of York government, and descending the mountainous passage that almost broke my heart in ascending before, we come to Stamford, a well compact town, but miserable meeting house, which we passed, and through many and great difficulties, as bridges which were exceeding high and very tottering and of vast length, steep and rocky hills and precipices, (bugbears to a fearful female travailer.) About nine at night we come to Norwalk, having crept over a timber of a broken bridge about thirty foot long, and perhaps fifty to the water. I was exceeding tired and cold when we come to our inn, and could get nothing there but poor entertainment, and the impertinant babble of one of the worst of men, among many others of which our host made one, who, had he been one degree impudenter, would have outdone his grandfather. And this I think is the most perplexed night I have yet had. From hence,

8. In the same kind.

Saturday, December 23,

a very cold and windy day, after an intolerable night's lodging, we hasted forward only observing in our way the town to be situated on a navigable river with indiferent buildings and people more refined than in some of the country towns we had passed, though vicious enough, the church and tavern being next neighbors. Having rid through a difficult river we come to Fairfield where we baited and were much refreshed as well with the good things which gratified our appetites as the time took to rest our wearied limbs, which latter I employed in enquiring concerning the town and manners of the people, &c. This is a considerable town, and filled as they say with wealthy people—have a spacious meeting house and good buildings. But the inhabitants are litigious, nor do they well agree with their minister, who (they say) is a very worthy gentleman.

They have abundance of sheep, whose very dung brings them great gain, with part of which they pay their parson's salary. And they grudge that, prefering their dung before their minister. They let out their sheep at so much as they agree upon for a night; the highest bidder always carries them, And they will sufficiently dung a large quantity of land before morning. But were once bit by a sharper who had them a night and sheared them all before morning—From hence we went to Stratford, the next town, in which I observed but few houses, and those not very good ones. But the people that I conversed with were civil and good natured. Here we stayed till late at night, being to cross a dangerous river ferry, the river at that time full of ice; but after about four hours waiting with great difficulty we got over. My fears and fatigues prevented my here taking any particular observation. Being got to Milford, it being late in the night, I could go no further; my fellow travailer going forward, I was invited to lodge at Mrs. ———, a very kind and civil gentlewoman, by whom I was handsomely and kindly entertained till the next night. The people here go very plain in their apparel (more plain than I had observed in the towns I had passed) and seem to be very grave and serious. They told me there was a singing Quaker lived there, or at least had a strong inclination to be so, his spouse not at all affected that way. Some of the singing crew come there one day to visit him, who being then abroad, they sat down (to the woman's no small vexation) humming and singing and groaning after their conjuring way—Says the woman are you singing Quakers? Yea says they—Then take my squalling brat of a child here and sing to it, says she, for I have almost split my throat with singing to him and cant get the rogue to sleep. They took this as a great indignity, and immediately departed. Shaking the dust from their heels left the good woman and her child among the number of the wicked.

This is a seaport place and accommodated with a good harbor, But I had not opportunity to make particular observations because it was sabbath day—This evening,

December 24,

I set out with the gentlewoman's son who she very civilly offered to go with me when she see no persuasions would cause me to stay, which she pressingly desired, and crossing a ferry having but nine miles to New Haven in a short time arrived there and was kindly received and well accommodated amongst my friends and relations.

The government of Connecticut colony begins westward towards York at Stanford (as I am told) and so runs eastward towards Boston (I mean in my range, because I don't intent to extend my description beyond my own travails) and ends that way at Stonington—and has a great many large towns lying more northerly. It is a plentiful country for provisions of all sorts and it's generally healthy. No one that can and will be diligent in this place need fear poverty nor the want of food and raiment.

January 6th.

Being now well recruited and fit for business I discoursed the persons I was concerned with, that we might finish in order to my return to Boston. They delayed as they had hitherto done, hoping to tire my patience. But I was resolute to stay and see an end of the matter, let it be never so much to my disadvantage—So January 9th they come again and promise the Wednesday following to go through with the distribution of the estate which they delayed till Thursday and then come with new amusements. But at length by the mediation of that holy good gentleman, the Rev. Mr. James Pierpont, the minister of New Haven, and with the advice and assistance of other our good friends we come to an accommodation and distribution, which having finished, though not till February, the man that waited on me to York taking the charge of me I set out for Boston. We went from New Haven upon the ice (the ferry being not passable thereby) and the Rev. Mr. Pierpont with Madam Prout Cuzin Trowbridge and divers others were taking leave we went onward without any thing remarkable till we come to New London and lodged again at Mr. Saltonstall's—and here I dismissed my guide, and my generous entertainer provided me Mr. Samuel Rogers of that place to go home with me—I stayed a day here longer than I intended by the commands of the Honorable Governor Winthrop to stay and take a supper with him whose wonderful civility I may not omit. The next morning I crossed the ferry to Groton, having had the honor of the company, of Madam Livingston (who is the Governor's daughter) and Mary Christophers and divers others to the boat—and that night lodged at Stonington and had roast beef and pumpkin sauce for supper. The next night at Haven's and had roast fowl, and the next day we come to a river which by reason of the freshets coming down was swelled so high we feared it impassable and the rapid stream was very terrifying—however, we must over and that in a small canoe. Mr. Rogers assuring me of his good conduct, I after a stay of near an hour on the shore for consultation went into the canoe, and Mr. Rogers paddled about 100 yards up the creek by the shore side, turned into the swift stream and dexterously steering her in a moment we come to the other side as swiftly passing as an arrow shot out of the bow by a strong arm. I stayed on the shore till he returned to fetch our horses, which he caused to swim over, himself bringing the furniture in the canoe. But it is past my skill to express the exceeding fright all their transactions formed in me. We were now in the colony of the Massachusetts and taking lodgings at the first inn we come to had a pretty difficult passage the next day, which was the second of March, by reason of the sloughy ways then thawed by the sun. Here I met Capt. John Richards of Boston, who was going home, so being very glad of his company we rode something harder than hitherto, and missing my way in going up a very steep hill, my horse dropped down under me as dead; this new surprise no little hurt me, meeting it just at the entrance into Dedham from whence we intended to reach home that night. But was now obliged to get another horse there and leave my own, resolving for Boston that night if possible. But in going over the causeway at Dedham, the bridge being overflowed by the high waters comming down, I very narrowly escaped falling over into the river horse and all, which 'twas almost a miracle I did not—now it grew late in the afternoon and the people having very much discouraged us about the sloughy way which they said we should find very difficult and hazardous, it so wrought on me being tired and dispirited and disappointed of my desires of going home that I agreed to lodge there that night, which we did at the house of one Draper, and the next day being March 3d we got safe home to Boston, where I found my aged and tender mother and my dear and only child in good health with open arms ready to receive me, and my kind relations and friends flocking in to welcome me and hear the story of my transactions and travails, I having this day been five months from home, and now I cannot fully express my joy and satisfaction. But de-

sire sincerely to adore my Great Benefactor for thus graciously carrying forth and returning in safety his unworthy handmaid.

1704–1705   1825

Mercy Otis Warren
(1728–1814)

Born in Barnstable on Cape Cod, Mercy
Otis had the good fortune to be educated,
along with her two older brothers, by a
clergyman uncle. From her childhood she
was associated with men who were at the
center of colonial political activity: her father was a judge and a colonel in the militia, her brother James was active in the
movement toward independence, and her
husband James Warren was the organizer
of the Committees of Correspondence.
She and her family were friends of the
John Adams family, Joseph Warren, John
Hancock, and George and Martha Washington. In the pre-Revolutionary period,
Mercy Warren's home in Plymouth was
the meeting place for leading activists.

James Otis introduced his sister to the
liberal ideas of John Locke, a major philosophical influence on the framers of the
Declaration of Independence, the Constitution, and the Bill of Rights. As a prominent attorney and leader of the colonial
assembly, Otis was an outspoken defender
of the rights of the colonists against the
British crown until, in 1769, he was beaten
over the head during a quarrel with loyal-
ist Tories. He never fully recovered from
his wounds.

After her brother's injury, Mercy Warren began writing political satire for newspapers and pamphlets. Her play The Adulateur, strongly attacking Governor Thomas
Hutchinson, was published in 1773. In
1772 Benjamin Franklin had revealed covert letters from Hutchinson (called
Rapatio in Warren's plays) to friends in
England urging that King George III and
his prime minister, Lord North, dispatch
troops to subdue the colonists with martial
law. This treachery was particularly galling because Hutchinson, a native-born

American and descendant of the religious
dissenter Anne Hutchinson, had taken the
public stance that the crown had no right
to tax the colonies. In 1773, after his refusal to allow the offending ships to leave
the harbor brought on the Boston Tea
Party, he fled to England.

In March 1774, the British Parliament
passed the Boston Port Bill, initiating a
siege of the city, and abrogated the Massachusetts Bay charter; the colony's elected
assembly was disbanded and a crown-ap-
pointed assembly was put in place. The
following month, General Thomas Gage,
in command of four regiments of troops,
was sent to Boston. In September the First
Continental Congress met in Philadelphia,
and the process of colonial unification was
underway.

The Group was probably written in the
first quarter of 1775; it seems to predict the
April 19 battles at Lexington and Concord,
but makes no specific references to them.
It mentions the series of letters printed in
the Massachusetts Gazette and Post Boy under
the pen name Massachusettensis, written
by the Tory Daniel Leonard, which were
answered by John Adams, calling himself
Novanglus, in the Boston Gazette from December 1774 to April 1775. In May, Adams
wrote to James Warren that an abbreviated
form of The Group was being published in
Philadelphia, and if Warren could send a
copy of the complete Boston edition, "it
will be greedily reprinted here."

The group of the title is the assembly
appointed by royal mandamus after the
highly prized colonial charter was nulli-
fied. The public resentment against anyone who accepted appointment was so
great that the author had no need to identify individuals by name, but later readers

need help with identification. The following table devised by Arthur Hobson Quinn is based on a comparison of the notes in four of the extant copies of the first edition of the play. The most complete list is in the handwriting of John Adams.

Lord Chief Justice Hazlerod	Peter Oliver
Judge Meagre	Foster Hutchinson
Brigadier Hateall	Timothy Ruggles
Hum Humbug, Esq.	John Erving, Jr.
Sir Sparrow Spendall	William Pepperell
Hector Mushroom	Colonel John Murray
Beau Trumps	Daniel Leonard
Dick, the publican	Richard Lechmere
Simple Sapling, Esq.	Nathaniel Ray Thomas
Monsieur de Francois	James Boutineau
Crusty Crowbar, Esq.	Josiah Edson
Dupe, secretary of state	Thomas Flucker
Scriblerius Fribble	Harrison Gray
Commodore Batteau	Josiah Loring

Foster Hutchinson, the brother of the departed governor, was a judge of the Supreme Court until he fled to Nova Scotia with other loyalists in 1776. Boutineau and Lechmere had at first spoken out against British encroachments, but later they recanted. Boutineau acted as attorney for his son-in-law, John Robinson, who was convicted for the attack on James Otis. Timothy Ruggles, as a delegate to the first American Congress in 1765, had refused to sign a resolution of unity. Peter Oliver had been made chief justice of Massachusetts despite the fact that he was not a lawyer. Leonard, the writer of the Massachuset-

tensis letters, appears as Beau Trumps. General Gage, called Sylla in the play, is treated in a relatively sympathetic light. The patriots referred to as Brutus and Cassius are James Warren and John Adams.

In addition to satiric drama, Warren wrote a three-volume *History of the Rise, Progress, and Termination of the American Revolution* (1805) and a collection of patriotic verse, *Poems Dramatic and Miscellaneous* (1790). For a biography, see Katherine Anthony's *First Lady of the Revolution: Mercy Otis Warren* (1958).

The following text has been edited, with some regularization of spelling and punctuation, from a first edition of the play printed by Edes and Gill, Queen Street, Boston in 1775.

As the great business of the polite world is the eager pursuit of amusement, and as the Public diversions of the season have been interrupted by the hostile parade in the capital[1]; the exhibition of a new farce may not be unentertaining.

The Group

As lately acted, and to be re-acted to the wonder of all superior intelligences, nigh head-quarters at Amboyne.

The author has thought proper to borrow the following spirited lines from a late celebrated poet, and offer to the public by way of PROLOGUE, which cannot fail of pleasing at this crisis.

1. Boston was the capital of the Massachusetts Bay Colony.

What! arm'd for virtue and not point the pen,
Brand the bold front of shameless guilty men,
Dash the proud Gamester from his gilded car,
Bare the mean heart which lurks beneath a Star.

. . . .

Shall I not strip the gilding off a knave,
Unplac'd, unpension'd, no man's heir or slave?
I will or perish in the gen'rous cause;
Hear this and tremble, ye who 'scape the laws;
Yes, while I live, no rich or noble knave,
Shall walk the world in credit to his grave;
To virtue only, and her friends, a friend,
The world beside may murmur, or commend.

Dramatis Personae

Lord Chief Justice Hazlerod	Simple Sapling, Esquire
Judge Meagre	Monsieur de Francois
Brigadier Hateall	Crusty Crowbar, Esquire
Hum Humbug, Esquire	Dupe, Secretary of State
Sir Sparrow Spendall	Scriblerius Fribble
Hector Mushroom, Colonel	Collateralis, a new made Judge
Beau Trumps	Commodore Batteau
Dick, the Publican	[Sylla]

Attended by a swarm of court sycophants, hungry harpies, and unprincipled danglers, collected from the neighboring villages, hovering over the stage in the shape of locusts, led by Massachusettensis in the form of a basilisk;[2] the rear brought up by Proteus,[3] bearing a torch in one hand, and a powder-flask in the other. The whole supported by a mighty army and navy, from Blunderland, for the laudible purpose of enslaving its best friends.

Act I, Scene 1

Scene, a little dark parlour, guards standing at the door.
Hazlerod, Crusty Crowbar, Simple Sapling, Hateall, and Hector Mushroom.

SIMPLE

I know not what to think of these sad times,
The people arm'd—and all resolv'd to die
E're they'll submit.—

CRUSTY CROWBAR

I too am almost sick of the parade
Of honours purchas'd at the price of peace.

SIMPLE

Fond as I am of greatness and her charms,
Elate with prospects of my rising name,

---

2. A mythical creature, variously described as a serpent or dragon, said to kill by its breath or look.

3. A sea god noted for his ability to prophesy and change shape.

Pushed into place,—a place I ne'er expected,
My bounding heart leapt in my feeble breast
And extasies entranc'd my slender brain.—
But yet, e're this I hop'd more solid gains,
As my low purse demands a quick supply—
Poor Sylvia weeps,—and urges my return
To rural peace and humble happiness,
As my ambition beggars all her babes.

CRUSTY

When first I listed in the desp'rate cause,
And blindly swore obedience to his will,
So wise, so just, so good I thought Rapatio,[4]
That if salvation rested on his word
I'd pin my faith and risk my hopes thereon.

HAZLEROD

And why not now?—What staggers thy belief?

CRUSTY

Himself—his perfidy appears—
It is too plain he has betray'd his country.
And we're the wretched tools by him mark'd out
To seal its ruins—tear up the ancient forms,
And every vestige treacherously destroy,
Nor leave a trait of freedom in the land.
Nor did I think hard fate wou'd call me up
From drudging o'er my acres,—
Treading the glade, and sweating at the plough,
To dangle at the tables of the great;
At bowls and cards, to spend my frozen years;
To sell my friends, my country, and my conscience;
Prophane the sacred sabbaths of my God;
Scorn'd by the very men who want my aid
To spread distress o'er this devoted people

HAZLEROD

Pho—What misgivings—why these idle qualms
This shrinking backwards at the bugbear conscience?
In early life I heard the phantom nam'd,
And the grave sages prate of moral sense
Presiding in the bosom of the just;
Or panting thongs about the guilty heart.
Bound by these shackles, long my lab'ring mind
Obscurely trod the lower walks of life,
In hopes by honesty my bread to gain;
But neither commerce, or my conjuring rods,
Nor yet mechanics, or new fangled drills,

---

4. The departed governor of the colony, Thomas Hutchinson, also referred to in Crusty's next speech as "Himself."

Or all the Iron-monger's curious arts,
Gave me a competence of shining ore,
Or gratify'd my itching palm for more,
Till I dismiss'd the bold intruding guest,
And banish'd conscience from my wounded breast.

CRUSTY

Happy expedient!—Could I gain the art,
Then balmy sleep might soothe my waking lids,
And rest once more refresh my weary soul.—

HAZLEROD

Resolv'd more rapidly to gain my point,
I mounted high in justice's sacred seat,
With flowing robes, and head equip'd without,
A heart unfeelling and a stubborn soul,
As qualify'd as e'er a Jefferies[5] was;
Save in the knotty rudiments of law,
The smallest requisite for modern times,
When wisdom, law, and justice, are supply'd
By swords, dragoons, and ministerial nods,
Sanctions most sacred in the pander's creed,
I sold my country for a splendid bribe.
Now let her sink—and all the dire alarms
Of war, confusion, pestilence and blood,
And tenfold mis'ry be her future doom—
Let civil discord lift her sword on high,
Nay sheathe its hilt e'en in my brother's blood;
It ne'er shall move the purpose of my soul;
Tho' once I trembled at a thought so bold;
By Philalethes's[6] arguments, convinc'd
We may live Demons, as we die like brutes,
I give my tears, and conscience to the winds.

HATEALL

Curse on their coward fears, and dastard souls,
Their soft compunctions and relenting qualms,
Compassion ne'er shall seize my steadfast breast
Though blood and carnage spread thro' all the land
Till streaming purple tinge the verdant turf,
Till ev'ry street shall float with human gore,
I Nero like, the capital in flames,
Could laugh to see her glotted sons expire,
Tho' much too rough my soul to touch the lyre.

5. George Jeffreys (1645?–1689) was a judge under the Stuart kings Charles II and James II. Jeffreys was notorious for cruelty, once condemning over 200 people to be hanged. Made Lord Chancellor by James II, he was imprisoned when the king fled (1688) and died in the Tower of London.

6. A pseudonym that could be translated "lover of oblivion," unidentified.

SIMPLE

I fear the brave, the injur'd multitude;
Repeated wrongs, arouse then to resent,
And every patriot like old Brutus[7] stands,
The shining steel half drawn—its glitt'ring point
Scarce hid beneath the scabbard's friendly cell
Resolv'd to die, or see their country free.

HATEALL

Then let them die—*The dogs we will keep down*—
While N_ _ _ _'s my friend, and G_ _ _ _ _[8] approves the deed.
Tho' hell and all its hell-hounds should unite,
I'll not recede to save from swift perdition
My wife, my country, family or friends.
G_ _ _ _ _'s mandamus I more highly prize
Than all the mandates of th'etherial king.

HECTOR MUSHROOM

Will our abettors in the distant towns
Support us long against the common cause,
When they shall see from Hampshire's[9] northern bounds
Thro' the wide western plains to southern shores
The whole united continent in arms?—

HATEALL

They shall—as sure as oaths or bonds can bind;
I've boldly sent my new-born brat abroad,
Th' association of my morbid brain,
To which each minion must affix his name.
As all our hope depends on brutal force
On quick destruction, misery and death,
Soon may we see dark ruin stalk around,
With murder, rapine, and inflicted pains,
Estates confiscate, slav'ry and despair,
Wrecks, halters, axes, gibbeting and chains,
All the dread ills that wait on civil war;—
How I could glut my vengeful eyes to see
The weeping maid thrown helpless on the world,
Her sire cut off.—Her orphan brothers stand
While the big tear rolls down the manly cheek.
Robb'd of maternal care by grief's keen shaft,
The sorrowing mother mourns her starving babes,
Her murder'd lord torn guiltless from her side,
And flees for shelter to the pitying grave
To screen at once from slavery and pain.

---

7. James Warren, the author's husband, is called
by this name in her earlier play *The Adulateur.*
8. The initial letter and blanks refer to Lord
Frederick North (1732–1792), prime minister,
and King George III (1738–1820).
9. A county in western Massachusetts along the
Connecticut River.

HAZLEROD

But more compleat I view this scene of woe,
By the incursions of a savage foe,
Of which I warn'd them, if they dare refuse
The badge of slaves, and bold resistance use.
Now let them suffer—I'll no pity feel.

HATEALL

Nor I—But had I power, as I have the Will
I'd send them murm'ring to the shades of hell.

Act II

The scene changes to a large dining room. The table furnished with bowls, bottles, glasses, and cards. The group appear sitting round in a restless attitude. In one corner of the room is discovered a small cabinet of books, for the use of the studious and contemplative: containing Hobbes's Leviathan, Sipthrop's Sermons, Hutchinson's History, Fable of the Bees, Philalethes on Philanthrop, with an appendix by Massachusettensis, Hoyle on Whist, Lives of the Stewarts, Statutes of Henry the Eighth and William the Conqueror, Wedderburn's Speeches, and Acts of Parliament for 1774.[1]

Scene 1

Hateall, Hazlerod, Monsieur, Beau Trumps, Simple, Humbug, Sir Sparrow, etc.

SCRIBLERIUS

—Thy toast Monsieur,
Pray why that solemn phiz?—
Art thou, too, balancing 'twixt right and wrong?
Hast thou a thought so mean as to give up
Thy present good, for promise in reversion?
'Tis true hereafter has some feeble terrors,
But e'er our grizley heads are wrapt in clay
We may compound, and make our peace with Heav'n.

MONSIEUR

Could I give up the dread of retribution,
The awful reck'ning of some future day,
Like surly Hateall I might curse mankind,
And dare the threat'ned vengeance of the skies,
Or like yon apostate—[*pointing to Hazlerod, retired to a corner to read Massachusettensis*[2]] feel
but slight remorse

1. This library, satirically described as for "the studious and contemplative," advocates frivolous activities, glorifies ruthless monarchs, or presents humankind as a degraded species. *The Leviation* (1651) by Thomas Hobbes (1588–1679) depicts man as a selfish being who must be controlled by external power; *Fable of the Bees* (1744) by Bernard de Mandeville (1670–1733) argues that humans

are naturally acquisitive and love luxury; Hutchinson, the absent governor, wrote a three-volume history of the Massachusetts Bay Colony; the Parliament of 1774 had passed several acts detrimental to the colony.

2. Pen name of the Tory pamphleteer Daniel Leonard, who also appears in the play as Beau Trumps; he constantly refers to card playing.

To sell my country for a grasp of Gold,
But the impressions of my early youth,
Infix'd by precepts of my pious sire,
Are stings and scorpions in my goaded breast;
Oft have I hung upon my parent's knee
And heard him tell of his escape from France;
He left the land of slaves, and wooden shoes;
From place to place he sought a safe retreat,
Till fair Bostonia stretched her friendly arm
And gave the refugee both bread and peace,
(Shall I ungrateful 'rase the sacred bonds,
And help to clank the tyrant's iron chains
O'er these blest shores—once the sure asylum
From all the ills of arbitrary sway?)
With his expiring breath he bade his sons
If e'er oppression reach'd the western world
Resist its force, and break the servile yoke.

SCRIBLERIUS

Well quit thy post;—Go make thy flatt'ring court
To Freedom's Son's and tell thy baby fears;
Shew the soft traces in thy puny heart,
Made by the trembling tongue and quiv'ring lip
Of an old grandsire's superstitious whims.

MONSIEUR

No,—I never can—
So great the itch I feel for titl'd place
Some honorary post, some small distinction,
To save my name from dark oblivion's jaws,
I'll Hazard all, but ne'er give up my place,
For that I'll see Rome's antient rites restor'd,
And flame and faggot blaze in ev'ry street.

BEAU TRUMPS

—That's right, Monsieur,
There's nought on earth that has such tempting charms
As rank and show, and pomp, and glitt'ring dress,
Save the dear counters at belov'd quadrill,[3]
Viner unsoil'd and Littleton may sleep,
And Coke[4] lie mould'ring on the dusty shelf,
If I by shuffling draw some lucky card
That wins the livers, or lucrative place.

HUM-HUMBUG

When sly Rapatio shew'd his friends the scroll,
I wonder'd much to see thy patriot name

3. A card game played by four people.
4. Viner, Littleton, and Coke were English legal writers. Coke's edition of Littleton's *Tenures* was a standard text on property law.

Among the list of rebels to the state,
I thought thee one of Rusticus's[5] sworn friends.

BEAU TRUMPS

When first I enter'd on the public stage
My country groan'd beneath base Brundo's[6] hand,
Virtue look'd fair and beckon'd to her lure,
Thro' truth's bright mirror I beheld her charms
And wish'd to tread the patriotic path,
And wear the Laurels that adorn his fame;
I walk'd a while and tasted solid peace
With Cassius,[7] Rusticus and good Hortensius,
And many more, whose names will be rever'd
When you and I, and all the venal herd
Weigh'd in Nemesis's[8] just, impartial scale,
Are mark'd with infamy till time blot out
And in oblivion sink our hated names.
But 'twas a poor unprofitable path,
Nought to be gain'd, save solid peace of mind,
No pensions, place or title there I found;
I saw Rapatio's arts had struck so deep
And giv'n his country such a fatal wound
None but its foes promotion could expect;
I trim'd, and pimp'd, and veer'd, and wav'ring stood
But half resolv'd to show myself a knave,
Till the Arch Traitor prowling round for aid
Saw my suspense and bid me doubt no more;—
He gently bow'd, and smiling took my hand,
And whispering softly in my listening ear,
Shew'd me my name among his chosen band,
And laugh'd at virtue dignify'd by fools,
Clear'd all my doubts, and bid me persevere
In spite of the restraints, or hourly checks
Of wounded friendship, and a goaded mind,
Or all the sacred ties of truth and honour.

COLLATERALIS

Come 'mongst ourselves we'll e'en speak out the truth.
Can you suppose there yet is such a dupe
As still believes that wretch an honest man?
    The latter strokes of his serpentine brain
Outvie the arts of Machiavel[9] himself;

---

5. The name suggests a patriot known as a farmer. Several of the Virginia planters, such as Washington and Jefferson, were so known. The specific reference is unknown.

6. Sir Francis Bernard (1712–1779), royal governor before Hutchinson. His enforcement of the Stamp Act made him unpopular; he was recalled in 1769.

7. John Adams was called Cassius in Warren's earlier play. The other two names are not clearly identified with specific persons.

8. Greek goddess of divine retribution.

9. Niccolo Machiavelli (1469–1527), Italian statesman, author of *The Prince* (1513), in which he advocated political expediency over moral considerations.

His Borgian[1] model here is realiz'd,
And the stale tricks of politicians play'd
Beneath a vizard fair—
————Drawn from the Heav'nly form
Of blest religion weeping o'er the land
For virtue fall'n, and for freedom lost.

BEAU TRUMPS

I think with you————
————Unparalleled his effront'ry,
When by chican'ry and specious art,
Mid'st the distress in which he'd brought the city,
He found a few (by artifice and cunning,
By much industry of his wily friend
The false Philanthrop—sly undermining tool,
Who with the Syren's voice—
Deals daily round the poison of his tongue)
To speak him fair—and overlook his guilt.
They by reiterated promise made
To stand their friend at Britain's mighty court,
And vindicate his native injur'd land,
Lent him their names to sanctify his deeds.
But mark the traitor—his high crime gloss'd o'er
Conceals the tender feelings of the man,
The social ties that bind the human heart;
He strikes a bargain with his country's foes,
And joins to wrap America in flames.
Yet with feign'd pity, and Satanic grin,
As if more deep to fix the keen insult,
Or make his life a farce still more compleat,
He sends a groan across the broad Atlantic,
And with a phiz of Crocodilian[2] stamp,
Can weep, and wreathe, still hoping to deceive,
He cries the gath'ring clouds hang thick about her,
But laughs within—then sobs
————Alas! my country!

HUM-HUMBUG

Why so severe, or why exclaim at all,
Against the man who made thee what thou art?

BEAU TRUMPS

I know his guilt,—I ever knew the man,
Thy father knew him e're we trod the stage;
I only speak to such as know him well;
Abroad I tell the World he is a saint.
But as for interest, I betray'd my own

---

1. The Borgia family included several powerful
   political figures of Renaissance Italy, especially
   Cardinal Cesare Borgia (1476?–1507).

2. According to myth, crocodiles can weep;
   crocodile tears are signs of hypocrisy.

With the same views, I rank'd among his friends;
But my ambition sighs for something more.
What merits has Sir Sparrow[3] of his own,
And yet a feather graces the Fool's cap;
Which did he wear for what himself atchiev'd,
'Twould stamp some honour on his latest heir—
But I'll suspen'd my murm'ring rays awhile;
Come t'other glass—and try our luck at loo,[4]
And if before the dawn your gold I win,
Or e'er bright Phoebus[5] does his course begin,
The eastern breeze from Britain's hostile shore
Should waft her lofty floating towers o'er,
Whose waving pendants sweep the wat'ry main,
Dip their proud beaks and dance towards the plain,
The destin'd plains of slaughter and distress,
Laden with troops from Hanover and Hess,[6]
I would invigorate my sinking soul,
For then the continent we might controul;
Not all the millions that she vainly boasts
Can cope with Veteran Barbarian hosts;—
But the brave sons of Albion's warlike race,
Their arms, and honours, never can disgrace,
Or draw their swords in such a hated cause
In blood to seal a N_ _ _ _'s oppressive laws.
They'll spurn the service:—Britons must recoil,
And show themselves the natives of an isle
Who sought for freedom, in the worst of times
Produc'd her Hampdens, Fairfaxes and Pyms.[7]
But if by carnage we should win the game,
Perhaps by my abilities and fame,
I might attain a splendid glitt'ring car,
And mount aloft, and sail in liquid air;
Like Phaeton,[8] I'd then out-strip the wind,
And leave my low competitors behind.

Act II, Scene 2

Collateralis, Dick the Publican

PUBLICAN

This dull inaction will no longer do;
Month after Month the idle troops have lain,

3. Sir William Pepperell had adopted the surname of his wealthy, famous maternal grandfather. His real name was Sparhawk, on which Warren bases her sarcastic name for the character.
4. A card game in which forfeits are paid into a pool.
5. Phoebus Apollo, the Greek god who rides the chariot of the sun across the sky.
6. Mercenary soldiers from the German provinces were employed by the British.

7. Puritan heroes: John Hampden (1594–1643), parliamentary leader killed during the English Civil War; General Thomas Fairfax (1612–1617), led the army against Charles I; John Pym (1583?–1643), parliamentary opponent of Charles I.
8. In Greek myth, Phaeton drove the sun chariot for one day, but when he drove too close to earth, Zeus struck him down with a thunderbolt.

Nor struck one stroke that leads us to our wish.
    The trifling bickerings at the city gates,
Or bold outrages of their midnight routs,
Bring us no nearer to the point in view.
Though much the daily suff'rings of the people,
Commerce destroy'd, and government unhing'd,
No talk of tame submission yet I hear.

COLLATERALIS

No————not the least————
————they're more resolv'd than ever,
They're firm, united, bold, undaunted, brave,
And every villa boasts their marshall'd ranks.
The warlike Clarion sounds through ev'ry street;
Both vig'rous youth, and the grey headed sir
Bear the Fusee, in regimental garbs,
Repairing to defend invaded right,
And if push'd hard, by manly force repel;
And tho' Britannia sends her legions o'er,
To plant her daggers in her children's breast,
It will rebound————New whetted, the keen point,
Will find a sheath in ev'ry tyrant's heart.

PUBLICAN

————What then is to be done?
My finances too low to stand it long.
You well remember————
When station'd there to gripe the honest trade,
How much I plunder'd from your native town.
Under the sanctions of the laws of trade,
I the hard earnings of industry
Filch'd from their hands, and built my nest on high.
And on the spoils I rioted a while,
But soon the unrighteous pelf slip'd through my hand.
Nor longer idly could I waste my time,
A num'rous flock was rising round my Board,
Who urg'd to something that might give them bread.
My only game was hither to repair,
And court the proud oppressors of my Country,
By the parade of pompous luxury,
To win their favour, and obtain a place;
That (with my limbeck[9]) might have kept me on,
But for the cursed, persevering spirit
Of Freedom's sons—who triumph o'er distress,
Nor will comply with requisitions, made
By haughty mandates from corrupted courts,
To pay the workmen for the chains, they'd Forg'd.

COLLATERALIS

No—tho' proud Britain wafts her wooden walls
O'er the broad waves—and plants them round these Coasts,

9. An alembic is a closed vessel; it could be employed in distilling liquor.

Shuts up their Ports, and robs them of their bread,
They're not dismay'd—nor servilely comply
To pay the hunters of the Nabob[1] shores
Their high demand for India's pois'nous weed,
Long since a sacrifice to *Thetis*[2] made,
A rich regale—Now all the wat'ry dames
May snuff Souchong, and sip in flowing bowls,
The higher flavour'd choice Hysonian[3] stream,
And leave their Nectar to old Homer's Gods.

PUBLICAN

The Group this morn were summon'd to the camp;
The council early meets at Sylla's[4] tent,
But for what purpose yet I cannot learn.

COLLATERALIS

Then Then let us haste, 'tis novel to be call'd
By Sylla's order, summon'd to attend,
So close he keeps his counsels in his breast,
Nor trusts us with the manoeuvers of state,
I fear he half despises us himself.
And if he does, we cannot wonder much,
We're made the jest of ev'ry idle boy:
Most of us hunted from our rural seats,
Drove from our homes, a prey to guilty fears,
When————When dare we return!
    And now shut up in this devoted City,
Amidst the pestilence[5] on either hand,
Pursued by every dreadful Execration
That the bold Tongue of innocence oppress'd,
Pours forth in anguish for a ruin'd state.

Scene 3

The fragments of the broken Council appear with trembling servile gestures, shewing several applications to the General from the Under-Tools in the distant Counties, begging each a guard of myrmidons[6] to protect them from the armed multitudes (which the guilty horrors of their wounded consciences hourly presented to their frighted imaginations) approaching to take speedy vengeance on the Court Parasites, who had fled for refuge to the Camp, by immediate destruction to their Pimps, Panders and Sycophants left behind. Sylla, walking in great Perplexity.

SYLLA

Pray, how will it comport with my pretence
For building walls, and shutting up the Town,
Erecting fortresses, and strong redoubts,

---

1. Another name for India. The lines in this speech refer to the Boston Tea Party.
2. A sea nymph, mother of Achilles.
3. Both Souchong and Hyson are varieties of Chinese tea.
4. General Thomas Gage (1721–1787), the commander of British forces.
5. There were serious outbreaks of disease, especially dysentery, in Boston.
6. The warlike followers of Achilles in the Trojan War.

To keep my troops from any bold inroads
A brave insulted people might attempt,
If I send out my little scatter'd parties,
And the long suff'ring, gen'rous patriot's Care
Prevents a Skirmish?
   Though they're the sport of wanton cruel power,
And Hydra[7] headed ills start up around,
Till the last hope of a redress cut off
Their humane feeling, Urge them to forbear,
And wait some milder means to bring relief.

HATEALL

'Tis now the time to try their daring tempers.
Send out a few—and if they are cut off,
What are a thousand souls, sent swiftly down
To Pluto's gloomy shades,—to tell in anguish
Half their compeers shall sit pandimonic,
E're we will suffer Liberty to reign,
Or see her sons triumphant win the day.
   I feign would push them to the last extreme,
To draw their swords against their legal King;
Then short's the process to compleat destruction.

SECRETARY DUPE

Be not so sanguine—the day is not our own,
And much I fear it never will be won.
Their discipline is equal to our own,
Their valour has been try'd, and in a field
They're not less brave than are a Fred'rick's[8] troops,
Those members formidable pour along,
While virtue's banners shroud each warrior's head
Stern Justice binds the helmet on his brow,
And Liberty sits perch'd on ev'ry shield.
But who's apply'd, and ask'd the General's aid,
Or wish'd his peaceful Villa such a curse,
As posting Troops beside the peasant's cot?

JUDGE MEAGRE

None but the very dregs of all mankind,
The Stains of nature,—The blots of human race,
Yet that's no matter, still they are our friends,
"Twill help our projects if we give them aid.

SIMPLE SAPLING

Though my paternal Acres are eat up,
My patrimony spent, I've yet an house
My lenient creditors let me improve.

---

7. The Hydra was a mythical water serpent; each
time one of its nine heads was cut off, two new
ones would grow. Hercules killed it by
cauterizing each bloody stump before new
heads could grow.

8. Frederick II or Frederick the Great
(1712–1786), king of Prussia, was considered
the foremost military power of Europe.

Send up the Troops, 'twill serve them well for Barracks.
I somehow think 'twould bear a noble sound,
To have my mansion guarded by the King.

SYLLA

Hast thou no sons or blooming daughters there,
To call up all the feelings of a Father,
Least their young minds contaminate by vice,
Caught from such inmates, dangerous and vile,
Devoid of virtue, rectitude, or honour
Save what accords with military fame?
 Hast thou no wife who asks thy tender care,
To guard her from Belona's[9] hardy sons?
Who when not toiling in the hostile field,
Are faithful vot'ries to the Cyprian Queen.
Or is her soul of such materials made,
Indelicate, and thoughtless of her fame:
So void of either sentiment or sense,
As makes her a companion fit for thee!

SIMPLE SAPLING

Sylvia's good natur'd, and no doubt will yield,
And take the brawny vet'rans to her board,
When she's assur'd 'twill help her husband's fame.
 If she complains or murmurs at the plan,
Let her solicit charity abroad;
Let her go out and seek some pitying friend
To give her shelter from the wint'ry blast,
Disperse her children round the neighb'ring cots,
And then————.

PUBLICAN

————Then weep thy folly, and her own hard fate!
I pity Sylvia, I knew the beauteous maid
E'er she descended to become thy wife:
She silent mourns the weakness of her lord,
For she's too virtuous to approve thy deeds.

HATEALL

Pho—what's a woman's tears,
Or all the whinings of that trifling sex?
I never felt one tender thought towards them.
 When young, indeed, I wedded nut brown Kate,
(Blyth buxom Dowager, the jockey's prey)
But all I wish'd was to secure her dower.
I broke her spirits when I'd won her purse;
For which I'll give a recipe most sure
To ev'ry hen peck'd husband round the board;

---

9. Bellona, the Roman goddess of war.

If crabbed words or surly looks won't tame
The haughty shrew, nor bend the stubborn mind,
Then the green Hick'ry, or the willow twig,
Will prove a curse for each rebellious dame
Who dare oppose her lord's superior will.

SYLLA

Enough of this, ten thousand harrowing cares
Tear up my peace, and swell my anxious breast.
  I see some mighty victim must appease
An injured nation, tott'ring on the verge
Of wide destruction, made the wanton sport
Of hungry Harpies,[1] gaping for their prey;
Which if by misadventures they should miss,
The disappointed vultures' angry Fang,
Will seize the lesser gudgeons[2] of the state,
And sacrifice to mad Alecto's[3] rage;
Lest the tide turning, with a rapid course
The booming torrent rushes o'er their heads,
And sweeps the "cawing cormorants from earth."

HATEALL

Then strike some sudden blow, and if hereafter
Dangers should rise—then set up for thyself,
And make thy name as famous in Columbia,
As ever Caesar's[4] was in ancient Gaul.
Who would such distant Provinces subdue,
And then resign them to a foreign lord!
With such an armament at thy command
Why all this cautious prudence?

SYLLA

I only wish to serve my Sov'reign well,
And bring new glory to my master's crown,
Which can't be done by spreading ruin round
This loyal country———
———Wro't up to madness by oppression's hand.
How much deceiv'd my royal master is
By those he trusts!—but more of this anon.
  Were it consistent with my former plan,
I'd gladly send my sickly troops abroad
Out from the stench of this infected town,
To breathe some air more free from putrefaction;
To brace their nerves against approaching spring,
If my ill stars should destine a campaign,

1. A mythical monster with a woman's head and
   a bird's body.
2. A small fish of the minnow family; therefore, a
   person easily duped or cheated.
3. In mythology, one of the Furies who punished

crimes at the instigation of the victims.
4. Caesar made his reputation by conquering
   Gaul (France) and other distant provinces of
   the Roman Empire.

And call me forth to fight in such a cause.
  To quench the gen'rous spark, the innate love
Of glorious freedom, planted in the breast
Of ev'ry man who boasts a Briton's name,
Until some base born lust of foreign growth
Contaminate his soul, till false ambition,
Or the sordid hope of swelling coffers,
Poison the mind, and brutalize the man.

COLLATERALIS

I almost wish I never had engag'd
To rob my country of her native rights,
Nor strove to mount on justice's solemn bench,
By mean submission cringing for a place.
  How great the pain, and yet how small the purchase!
Had I been dumb, or my right hand cut off,
E'er I so servilely held it up,
Or giv'n my voice abjectly to rescind
The wisest step that mortal man could take
To curb the talons of tyrannic power,
Outstretch'd, rapacious, ready to devour
The fair possessions, by our Maker giv'n
Confirmed by compacts—ratify'd by Heav'n.

SYLLA

Look o'er the annals of our virtuous sires,
And search the story of Britannia's deeds,
From Caesar's ravages to Hambden's fall;
From the good Hambden down to glorious Wolfe,[5]
Whose soul took wing on Abraham's fatal plain,
Where the young Hero fought Britannia's foes,
And vanquish'd Bourbon's dark ferocious hosts,
Till the slaves trembled at a George's name.
  'Twas love of freedom drew a Marlborough's[6] sword;
This glorious passion mov'd a Sydney's pen;
And crown'd with Bayes a Harrington and Locke;[7]
'Tis freedom wreathes the Garlands o'er their tombs.
  For her how oft have bleeding Heroes fall'n!
With the warm fluid, gushing from their wounds,
Convey'd the purchase to their distant heirs!
  And shall I rashly draw my guilty sword,
And dip its hungry hilt in the rich blood
Of the best subjects that a Brunswick[8] boasts,
And for no cause, but that they nobly scorn

5. General James Wolfe (1727–1759), killed at
    the siege of Quebec while fighting the French
    (Bourbons) commanded by Montcalm on the
    plains of Abraham.
6. John Churchill, first Duke of Marlborough,
    military hero and supporter of the Protestant
    King William of Orange against the Catholic
    James II.
7. Sir Philip Sidney (1554–1586), soldier and
    poet; James Harrington (1611–1677), English
    utopian writer; John Locke (1632–1704),
    philosopher of freedom and human rights.
8. Brunswick, a Saxon state; George III was of
    German ancestry.

To wear the fetters of his venal slaves!
   But swift time rolls, and on his rapid wheel
Bears the winged hours, and the circling years.
The cloud cap'd morn, the dark, short, wintry day,
And the keen blasts of roughened Borea's[9] breath,
Will soon evanish, and approaching spring
Opes with the fate of empires on her wing.

Exit Sylla
Hazlerod rises in great agitation.

HAZLEROD

This ballancing of passion ne'er will do,
And by the scale which virtue hold to reason,
Weighing the business e'er he executes,
Doubting, deliberating, half resolv'd
To be the saviour of a virtuous state,
Instead of guarding refugees and knaves,
The buzzing reptiles that crawl round his court,
And lick his hand for some delicious crumb,
Or painted plume to grace the guilty brow,
Stain'd with ten thousand falsities, trumped up
To injure every good and virtuous name
Who won't strike hands and be his country's foe:
I'll hasten after, and stir up his soul,
To dire revenge and bloody resolutions,
Or the whole fabrick falls, on which we hang,
And down the pit of infamy we plunge,
Without the spoils we long have hop'd to reap.

He crosses the stage hastily and goes out after Sylla.
Meagre and Secretary Dupe at the further part of the stage.

MEAGRE

As Sylla pass'd I mark'd his anxious brow;
I fear his soul is with compassion mov'd
For suff'ring virtue, wounded and betray'd;
For freedom hunted down in this fair field,
The only soil, in these degenerate days,
In which the heavenly goddess can exist.

SECRETARY

Humanity recoils—his heart relucts
To execute the black, the accurst design.
Such I must call it, though thy guilty friends,
Thy subtle brother, laid the artful plan,
"And like the toad squat at the ear of Eve"[1]

9. Boreas, the Greek personification of the north
   wind.
1. From Milton's *Paradise Lost*, 4. 800, describing
Satan's tempting of the Sleeping Eve, slightly
misquoted here.

Infusing poisons by his snaky tongue,
Push'd Brundo on to tread the thorny path,
And plunge his country in ten thousand woes;
Then slyly justling him behind the scenes,
Step'd in his place for which he long had sigh'd.

MEAGRE

Yes, all allow he play'd a master game,
And dealt his cards with such peculiar skill,
That every dangler about the court,
As you and I and all might well suppose,
Thought the chains fix'd which Brundo only clank'd.
    But yet unless some speedy method's found
To break the union, and dissolve the bonds
That bind this mighty continent so firm,
Their Congresses, their Covenants, and leagues,
With their Committees,[2] working in each town
With unremitting vigilance and care,
To baffle ev'ry evil machination
Of all state rooks, who peck about the land,
If not broke up, will ruin all at last.
    Amidst the many scriblers of the age,
Can none be found to set their schemes afloat,
To sow dissention—and distrust abroad,
Sap that cement that bears down all before it,
And makes America a match for all
The hostile powers that proud Europa[3] boasts?

SECRETARY

Not all the swarms of prostituted pens,
Nor hireling smatterers scribbling for gain,
From the first pension'd on the northern list
To bigot Priests—who write from southern shores,
With all their phantoms, bugbears, threats or smiles,
Will e'er persuade them to renounce their claim
To freedom, purchas'd with their fathers' blood.
    How various are the arts already try'd,
What pains unwearied to write men to sleep,
Or rock them in the cradle of despair,
To doze supinely, 'til they should believe
They'd neither eyes, nor tongues, or strength to move
But at the nod of some despotic lord!
    What shifts, evasions, what delusive tales,
What poor prevarication for rash oaths,
What nightly watchings, and what daily cares
To dress up falshood in some fair disguise,

2. The Committees of Correspondence, organized
   to facilitate communications between the
   colonies. In her three-volume history of the
   American Revolution, Mercy Warren credits

her husband with the idea for them.
3. A mythical figure courted by Zeus in the form
   of a bull; the continent is named for her.

Or wrap the bantling of their midnight dreams
In the soft vest of friendship, to betray,
Then send it forth in every fairy form,
To stalk at noon tide, giddy with fond hope
That some new gambols might deceive again
Men broad awake, who see through all the cheat.

MEAGRE

There still is hope—why need we yet despair?
The doughty champion of our sinking cause,
The deep "arcana"[4] of whose winding brain
Is fraught with dark expedients to betray,
By the long labours of his vet'ran quill,
By scattering scraps from ev'ry musty code
Of canon, civil, or draconian laws,
Quoting old statutes or defining new,
Treasons, misprisions, riots, routs, cabals,
And insurrections of these stubborn times,
He'll sure prevail and terrify at last,
By bringing precedents from those blest days
When royal Stewarts,[5] Britain's sceptre sway'd,
And taught her sons the right divine of Kings.
When pains and forfeitures an hundred fold
Were dealt to traitors, puny when compared
To the bold rebels of this continent,
From Merrimack[6] to Messisipi's—Banks
Who dare resist a ministerial frown,
    In spite of all the truths *Novanglus*[7] tells,
And his cool reas'ning argumentive stile,
Or master strokes of his unrival'd pen,
They will divide, and wav'ring will submit
And take the word of *Massachusettensis*
That men were born all ready bitted, curb'd,
And on their backs the saddles prominent,
For every upstart sycophant to mount.

SECRETARY

Not *Massachusettensis* oily tongue,
Or retail'd nonsense of a *Philarene*
Nor *Senec's* rant, nor yet dull *Grotius's*[8] pen,
Or the whole Group of selfish venal men,
If gather'd from cold Zembla's frozen shore,
To the warm zone where rapid rivers roar,

4. A term from alchemy meaning mysteries.
5. The House of Stuart ruled England from 1603 to 1649 and from 1660 to 1714. From 1649 to 1660, after the beheading of Charles I, the Puritans, led by Oliver Cromwell, were in power.
6. The Merrimack River runs through New Hampshire and Massachusetts.
7. A pen name of John Adams.
8. Seneca (c. 60 BC–AD 37), Roman writer whose tragedies were known for highly emotional speeches; Hugo Grotius (1583–1648), Dutch jurist, author of *De Jure Bellia ac Pacis* (1625), considered to be the first text on international law.

Can either coax them, or the least control
The val'rous purpose of their roman souls.

MEAGRE

Let not thy soft timidity of heart
Urge thee to terms, till the last stake is thrown.
T'is not my temper ever to forgive,
When once resentment's kindled in my breast.
    I hated Brutus for his noble stand
Against the oppressors of his injur'd country.
    I hate the leaders of these restless factions,
For all their gen'rous efforts to be free.
    I curse the senate which defeats our bribes,
Who Hazlerod impeach'd for the same crime.
    I hate the people, who, no longer gull'd,
See through the schemes of our aspiring clan.
And from the rancour of my venom'd mind,
I look askance on all the human race,
And if they're not to be appall'd by fear,
I wish the earth might drink that vital stream
That warms the heart, and feeds the manly glow,
The love inherent, planted in the breast,
To equal liberty, confer'd on man,
By him who form'd the peasant and the King!
    Could we erase these notions from their minds,
Then (paramount to these ideal whimeal whims,
Utopian dreams, of patriot virtue,
Which long has danc'd in their distemper'd brains)
We'd smoothly glide on midst a race of slaves,
Nor heave one sigh tho' all the human race
Were plung'd in darkness, slavery and vice.
If we could keep our foot-hold in the stirrup,
And, like the noble Claudia of old,
Ride o'er the people, if they don't give way:
Or wish their fates were all involv'd in one;
For Iv'e a Brother, as the roman dame,
Who would strike off the rebel neck at once.

SECRETARY

No, all is o'er unless the sword decides,
Which cuts down Kings, and kingdoms oft divides.
By that appeal I think we can't prevail,
Their valour's great, and justice holds the scale.
They fight for freedom, while we stab the breast
Of every man, who is her friend profest.
They fight in virtue's ever sacred cause,
While we tread on divine and human laws.
Glory and victory, and lasting fame,
Will crown their arms and bless each Hero's name!

MEAGRE

Away with all thy foolish, trifling cares;
And to the winds give all thy empty fears;
Let us repair and urge brave Sylla on,
I long to see the sweet revenge begun.
As fortune is a fickle, sportive dame,
She may for us the victory proclaim,
And with success our busy ploddings crown,
Though injured justice stern and solemn frown.
    Then they shall smart for ev'ry bold offence,
Estates confiscated will pay th'expense;
On their lost fortunes we a while will plume
And strive to think there is no after doom.

Ex. Om—
*As they pass off the stage the curtain draws up, and discovers to the audience a Lady
nearly connected with one of the principals actors in the group, reclined in an adjoining
alcove, who in mournful accents accosts them—thus—*

What painful scenes are hov'ring o'er the morn,
When spring again invigorates the lawn!
    Instead of the gay landscape's beautious dies,
Must the stain'd field salute our weeping eyes,
Must the green turf, and all the mournful glades,
Drench'd in the stream, absorb their dewy heads,
Whilst the tall oak, and quiv'ring willow bends
To make a covert for their country's friends,
Deny'd a grave!—amid the hurrying scene
Of routed armies scouring o'er the plain.
    Till British troops shall to Columbia yield,
And freedom's sons are Masters of the field;
Then o'er the purpl'd plain the victors tread
Among the slain to seek each patriot dead,
(While freedom weeps that merit could not save
But conq'ring Heroes must enrich the Grave)
    An adamantine monument they rear
With this inscription—*Virtue's sons lie here!*

Finis

1775   1775

Abigail Adams

(1744–1818)

Abigail Smith was one of three daughters
of Reverend William Smith and his wife,
Elizabeth Quincy. The Smiths' Weymouth home was on the road linking Boston, center of the Massachusetts Bay Colony, with the Plymouth settlements.

Denied formal schooling by the customs of the time, Mary, Abigail, and Elizabeth Smith were taught at home and profited from the attention of their maternal grandparents and family friends.

Exposed to animated debates on current events in their home, all three developed a lively civic concern. As Mary expressed it in 1800, "so totally secluded as we were in childhood from the world, we came to be so interested in the politics of it at so early a period of life." Abigail particularly credited Richard Cranch, who would become Mary's husband, with helping her become "a lover of literature" by introducing her to the works of Shakespeare, Milton, Pope, Richardson, and the philosophy of John Locke. Cranch was also the person who introduced a serious young Braintree attorney named John Adams into the parsonage social circle.

By the spring of 1764, when John Adams was confined to Boston for two months by the ordeal of being inoculated against smallpox, his letters to Abigail claimed she had "softened and warmed my heart." They were married in October of that year by the bride's father and took a house near the groom's widowed mother in Braintree.

In the first two decades of the marriage, John Adams was absent much of the time, serving as a circuit-riding attorney, delegate to the Continental Congress, and diplomat. The correspondence of this period documents Abigail's management skills, civic concern, shrewd political instincts, and strong love of family.

As a private citizen, vice president's wife, and First Lady, Mrs. Adams carried on extensive correspondence with her sisters, daughters, daughters-in-law, and friends such as Mercy Otis Warren. With these correspondents, she shared her interest in the status of women, equality and companionship between the sexes, and the education of the young.

Louisa Johnson Adams (Mrs. John Quincy Adams), the second Adams woman to preside over the White House, predicted that the ideas expressed in her mother-in-law's published correspondence would "gladden the hearts of many a timid female whose rays too feebly shine, not for want of merit but for want of confidence in the powers and encouragement in the exercise of those capacities with which the Almighty has gifted them."

In 1840, Charles Francis Adams prepared a selection of his grandmother's letters for publication. The complete Adams family papers, including letters and journal entries by Abigail, are housed in the Massachusetts Historical Society archives in Boston and are available on microfilm.

The following selections are taken from *The Book of Abigail and John: Selected Letters of the Adams Family, 1762–1784,* edited by L. H. Butterfield, Marc Friedlaender, and Mary-Jo Kline (Harvard University Press, 1975). L. Withey's *Dearest Friend: A Life of Abigail Adams* appeared in 1981.

Letters

Abigail Adams to John Adams

24 May B[raintre]e 1775

Suppose you have had a formidable account of the alarm we had last Sunday morning. When I rose about six oclock I was told that the Drums had been some time beating and that 3 allarm Guns were fired, that Weymouth Bell had been ringing, and Mr. Welds was then ringing.[1] I immediately sent of an express to know the occasion, and found the whole Town in confusion. 3 Sloops and one cutter had come out, and droped anchor just below Great Hill.

1. Reverend Ezra Weld was pastor of a church on the border of Braintree near Weymouth.

It was difficult to tell their design, some supposed they were comeing to Germantown others to Weymouth. People women children from the Iron Works flocking down this Way—every woman and child above or from below my Fathers. My Fathers family flying, the Drs.[2] in great distress, as you may well immagine for my Aunt had her Bed thrown into a cart, into which she got herself, and orderd the boy to drive her of to Bridgwater which he did. The report was to them, that 300 hundred had landed, and were upon their march into Town. The allarm flew [like] lightning, and men from all parts came flocking down till 2000 were collected—but it seems their expidition was to Grape Island for *Levet's* hay. There it was impossible to reach them for want of Boats, but the sight of so many persons, and the fireing at them prevented their getting more than 3 ton of Hay, tho they had carted much more down to the water. At last they musterd a Lighter, and a Sloop from Hingham which had six port holes. Our men eagerly jumpt on board, and put of for the Island. As soon as they perceived it, they decamped. Our people landed upon [the] Island, and in an instant set fire to the Hay which with the Barn was soon consumed, about 80 ton tis said. We expect soon to be in continual alarms, till something decisive takes place. We wait with longing Expectation in hopes to hear the best accounts from you with regard to union and harmony &c. We rejoice greatly on the Arival of Doctor Franklin, as he must certainly be able to inform you very perticuliarly of the situation of affairs in England. I wish you would [write] if you can get time; be as perticuliar as you *may*, when you write—every one here abouts come[s] to me to hear what accounts I have. I was so unlucky as not to get the Letter you wrote at New York. Capn. Beals forgot it, and left it behind. We have a flying report here with regard to New York, but cannot give any credit to, as yet, that they had been engaged with the Ships which Gage sent there and taken them with great looss upon both sides.

Yesterday we have an account of 3 Ships comeing in to Boston. I believe it is true, as there was a Salute from the other Ships, tho I have not been able to learn from whence they come. Suppose you have had an account of the fire which did much damage to the Warehouses, and added greatly to the distresses of the inhabitants whilst it continued. The bad conduct of General Gage was the means of its doing so much damage.

Tis a fine growing Season having lately had a charming rain, which was much wanted as we had none before for a fortnight. Your meadow is almost fit to mow. Isaac talks of leaving you, and going into the Army. I believe he will. Mr. Rice has a prospect of an *adjutant* place in the Army. I believe he will not be a very hardy Soldier. He has been sick of a fever above this week, and has not been out of his chamber. He is upon the recovery now.

Our House has been upon this alarm in the same Scene of confusion that it was upon the first—Soldiers comeing in for lodging, for Breakfast, for Supper, for Drink &c. &c. Sometimes refugees from Boston tierd and fatigued, seek an assilum for a Day or Night, a week—you can hardly imagine how we live.

> "Yet to the Houseless child of want
> Our doors are open still.
> And tho our portions are but scant
> We give them with good will."

I want to know how you do? How are your Eyes? Is not the weather very hot where you are? The children are well and send Duty to Pappa. This day Month you set of. I have never once inquired when you think it possible to return; as I think you could not give me any satisfactory answer. I have according to your direction wrote to Mr. Dilly, and given it to the care of Capn. Beals who will deliver it with his own hand; I got Mr. Thaxter to take a coppy for me, as I had not time amidst our confusions; I send it to you for your approbation. You will be careful of it as I have no other coppy. My best wishes attend you both for your Health

2. Dr. Cotton Tufts was the husband of Abigail's maternal aunt, Lucy Quincy.

and happiness, and that you may be directed into the wisest and best measures for our Safety, and the Security of our posterity. I wish you was nearer to us. We know not what a day will bring forth, nor what distress one hour may throw us into. Heitherto I have been able to mantain a calmness and presence of Mind, and hope I shall, let the Exigency of the time be what they will.

Mrs. W[arre]n[3] desires to be rememberd to you with her sincere regards. Mr. C[ranc]h[4] and family send their Love. He poor man has a fit of his old disorder. I have not heard one Syllable from Providence since I wrote you last. I wait to hear from you, then shall act accordingly. I dare not discharge any debts with what I have except to Isaac, least you should be dissapointed of the remainder. Adieu Breakfast calls your affectionate

Portia[5]

Sister Betsy is with me, and desires her kindest Wishes, and most affectionate Regards may be presented to you.

Abigail Adams to John Adams

Dearest Friend   Braintree July 16 1775

I have this afternoon had the pleasure of receiving your Letter by your Friends Mr. Collins and Kaighn[6] and an English Gentle man his Name I do not remember. It was next to seeing my dearest Friend. Mr. Collins could tell me more perticuliarly about you and your Health than I have been able to hear since you left me. I rejoice in his account of your better Health, and of your spirits, tho he says I must not expect to see you till next spring. I hope he does not speak the truth. I know (I think I do, for am not I your Bosome Friend?) your feelings, your anxieties, your exertions, &c. more than those before whom you are obliged to wear the face of chearfulness.[7]

I have seen your Letters to Col. Palmer and Warren.[8] I pity your Embaresments. How difficult the task to quench out the fire and the pride of private ambition, and to sacrifice ourselfs and all our hopes and expectations to the publick weal. How few have souls capable of so noble an undertaking—how often are the lawrels worn by those who have had no share in earning them, but there is a future recompence of reward to which the upright man looks, and which he will most assuredly obtain provided he perseveres unto the end.—The appointment of the Generals Washington and Lee,[9] gives universal satisfaction. The people have the highest opinion of Lees abilities, but you know the continuation of the popular Breath, depends much upon favorable events.

I had the pleasure of seeing both the Generals and their Aid de camps soon after their arrival and of being personally made known to them. They very politely express their regard for you. Major Miflin[1] said he had orders from you to visit me at Braintree. I told him I should be very happy to see him there, and accordingly sent Mr. Thaxter[2] to Cambridge with a card to him and Mr. Read [Reed] to dine with me. Mrs. Warren and her Son were to be with me. They very politely received the Message and lamented that they were not able to upon account of Expresses which they were that day to get in readiness to send of.

3. Mercy Otis Warren.
4. Richard Cranch, husband of Abigail's sister Mary.
5. Mrs. Adams addressed her letters to her husband most often "Dearest Friend" and signed them "Portia." Some letters written to him before their marriage were signed "Diana."
6. Stephen Collins and John Cain were Quakers from Philadelphia.
7. Parentheses added for clarity in the Butterfield edition.
8. Joseph Palmer and James Warren, husband of Mercy O. Warren.
9. George Washington was named commander-in-chief on June 15, 1775; Charles Lee, his adjutant, was a major general.
1. Major General Thomas Mifflin.
2. John Thaxter, one of the law students who studied with John and stayed in the Adams's household. He was Abigail's cousin.

I was struck with General Washington. You had prepaired me to entertain a favorable opinion of him, but I thought the one half was not told me. Dignity with ease, and complacency, the Gentleman and Soldier look agreably blended in him. Modesty marks every line and feture of his face. Those lines of Dryden instantly occurd to me

> "Mark his Majestick fabrick! he's a temple
> Sacred by birth, and built by hands divine
> His Souls the Deity that lodges there.
> Nor is the pile unworthy of the God."

General Lee looks like a careless hardy Veteran and from his appeerence brought to my mind his namesake Charls the 12, king of Sweeden. The Elegance of his pen far exceeds that of his person. I was much pleased with your Friend Collins. I persuaded them to stay coffe with me, and he was as unreserved and social as if we had been old acquaintances, and said he was very loth to leave the house. I would have detaind them till morning, but they were very desirous of reaching Cambridge.

You have made often and frequent complaints that your Friends do not write to you. I have stired up some of them. Dr. Tufts, Col. Quincy, Mr. Tudor, Mr. Thaxter all have wrote you now, and a Lady whom I am willing you should value preferable to all others save one.[3] May not I in my turn make complaints? All the Letters I receive from you seem to be wrote in so much haste, that they scarcely leave room for a social feeling. They let me know that you exist, but some of them contain scarcely six lines. I want some sentimental Effusions of the Heart. I am sure you are not destitute of them or are they all absorbed in the great publick. Much is due to that I know, but being part of the whole I lay claim to a Larger Share than I have had. You used to be more communicative a Sundays. I always loved a Sabeth days letter, for then you had a greater command of your time— but hush to all complaints.

I am much surprized that you have not been more accurately informd of what passes in the camps. As to intelegance from Boston, tis but very seldom we are able to collect any thing that may be relied upon, and to report the vague flying rumours would be endless. I heard yesterday by one Mr. Rolestone [Roulstone] a Goldsmith who got out in a fishing Schooner, that there distress encreased upon them fast, their Beaf is all spent, their Malt and Sider all gone, all the fresh provisions they can procure they are obliged to give to the sick and wounded. 19 of our Men who were in Jail and were wounded at the Battle of Charlstown were Dead. No Man dared now to be seen talking to his Friend in the Street, they were obliged to be within every evening at ten o clock according to Martial Law, nor could any inhabitant walk any Street in Town after that time without a pass from Gage. He has orderd all the melasses to be stilld up into rum for the Soldiers, taken away all Licences, and given out others obligeing to a forfeiture of ten pounds L M if any rum is sold without written orders from the General. He give much the same account of the kill'd and wounded we have had from others. The Spirit he says which prevails among the Soldiers is a Spirit of Malice and revenge, there is no true courage and bravery to be observed among them, their Duty is hard allways mounting guard with their packs at their back ready for an alarm which they live in continual hazard of. Doctor Eliot is not on bord a man of war, as has been reported, but perhaps was left in Town as the comfort and support of those who cannot escape, he was constantly with our prisoners. Mr. Lovel and Leach with others are certainly in Jail. A poor Milch cow was last week kill'd in Town and sold for a shilling stearling per pound. The transports arrived last week from York, but every additional Man adds to their distress.—

3. Mercy Otis Warren was a close friend of both Abigail and John Adams; comments about John Adams's politics in Warren's *History of the* *Revolution* (1805) put a strain on the friendship in later years.

There has been a little Expidition this week to Long Island.[4] There has been before several attempts to go on but 3 men of war lay near, and cutters all round the Island that they could not succeed. A number of whale boats lay at Germantown; 300 volenters commanded by one Capt. Tupper came on monday evening and took the boats, went on and brought of 70 odd Sheep, 15 head of cattle, and 16 prisoners 13 of whom were sent by Simple Sapling[5] to mow the Hay which they had very badly executed. They were all a sleep in the house and barn when they were taken. There were 3 women with them. Our Heroes came of in triumph not being observed by their Enimies. This spiritted up other[s]. They could not endure the thought that the House and barn should afford them any shelter. They did not distroy them the night before for fear of being discoverd. Capt. Wild of this Town with about 25 of his company, Capt. Gold [Gould] of Weymouth with as many of his, and some other volenters to the amount of an 100, obtain leave to go on and distroy the Hay together with the House and barn and in open day in full view of the men of war they set of from the Moon so call'd coverd by a number of men who were placed there, went on, set fire to the Buildings and Hay. A number of armed cutters immediately Surrounded the Island, fired upon our Men. They came of with a hot and continued fire upon them, the Bullets flying in every direction and the Men of Wars boats plying them with small arms. Many in this Town who were spectators expected every moment our Men would all be sacrificed, for sometimes they were so near as to be calld to and damnd by their Enimies and orderd to surrender yet they all returnd in safty, not one Man even wounded. Upon the Moon we lost one Man from the cannon on board the Man of War. On the Evening of the same day a Man of War came and anchord near Great Hill, and two cutters came to Pig Rocks.[6] It occasiond an alarm in this Town and we were up all Night. They remain there yet, but have not ventured to land any men.

This Town have chosen their Representative. Col. Palmer is the Man. There was a considerable musture upon Thayers side, and Vintons company marched up in order to assist, but got sadly dissapointed. Newcomb insisted upon it that no man should vote who was in the army—he had no notion of being under the Military power—said we might be so situated as to have the greater part of the people engaged in the Military, and then all power would be wrested out of the hands of the civil Majestrate. He insisted upon its being put to vote, and carried his point immediately. It brought Thayer to his Speach who said all he could against it.[7]—As to the Situation of the camps, our Men are in general Healthy, much more so at Roxbury than Cambridge, and the Camp in vastly better order. General Thomas has the character of an Excelent officer. His Merit has certainly been overlook'd, as modest merrit generally is. I hear General Washington is much pleased with his conduct.

Every article here in the West india way is very scarce and dear. In six week[s] we shall not be able to purchase any article of the kind. I wish you would let Bass get me one pound of peper, and 2 yd. of black caliminco for Shooes. I cannot wear leather if I go bare foot the reason I need not mention. Bass may make a fine profit if he layes in a stock for himself. You can hardly immagine how much we want many common small articles which are not manufactured amongst ourselves, but we will have them in time. Not one pin is to be purchased for love nor money. I wish you could convey me a thousand by any Friend travelling this way. Tis very provoking to have such a plenty so near us, but tantulus like not able to touch. I should have been glad to have laid in a small stock of the West India articles, but I cannot get one copper. No person thinks of paying any thing, and I do not chuse to run

4. Long Island and "the Moon" mentioned below are islands in Boston Harbor.
5. The Tory Nathaniel Ray Thomas was given the name Simple Sapling in Mercy Warren's satire *The Group*. Thomas's home in Marshfield had been used by British troops in the winter of 1774–1775.
6. Great Hill is in Quincy; Pig Island is located about half a mile off shore.
7. Two elections were held for a seat in the House of Representatives. When Joseph Palmer, who won the July 10 vote, was elevated to the Council, a new election was held on August 14. Ebenezer Thayer was elected to the House.

in debt. I endeavour to live in the most frugal manner posible, but I am many times distressed.—Mr. Trot I have accommodated by removeing the office into my own chamber, and after being very angry and sometimes persuaideding I obtaind the mighty concession of the Bed room, but I am now so crouded as not to have a Lodging for a Friend that calls to see me. I must beg you would give them[8] warning to seek a place before Winter. Had that house been empty I could have had an 100 a year for it. Many person[s] had applied before Mr. Trot, but I wanted some part of it my self, and the other part it seems I have no command of.—We have since I wrote you had many fine showers, and altho the crops of grass have been cut short, we have a fine prospect of Indian corn and English grain. Be not afraid, ye beasts of the field, for the pastures of the Wilderness do spring, the Tree beareth her fruit, the vine and the olive yeald their increase.

We have not yet been much distressed for grain. Every thing at present looks blooming. O that peace would once more extend her olive Branch.

> "This Day be Bread and peace my lot
> All Else beneath the Sun
> Thou knowst if best bestowed or not
> And let thy will be done."
>
> But is the Almighty ever bound to please
> Ruild by my wish or studious of my ease.
> Shall I determine where his frowns shall fall
> And fence my Grotto from the Lot of all?
> Prostrate his Sovereign Wisdom I adore
> Intreat his Mercy, but I dare no more.

Our little ones send Duty to pappa. You would smile to see them all gather round mamma upon the reception of a letter to hear from pappa, and Charls with open mouth, What does par say—did not he write no more. And little Tom says I wish I could see par. Upon Mr. Rice's going into the army he asked Charls if he should get him a place, he catchd at it with great eagerness and insisted upon going. We could not put him of, he cryed and beged, no obstical we could raise was suffcent to satisfy him, till I told him he must first obtain your consent. Then he insisted that I must write about it, and has been every day these 3 weeks insisting upon my asking your consent. At last I have promised to write to you, and am obliged to be as good as my word.—I have now wrote you all I can collect from every quarter. Tis fit for no eye but yours, because you can make all necessary allowances. I cannot coppy.

There are yet in Town 4 of the Selectmen and some thousands of inhabitants tis said.—I hope to hear from you soon. Do let me know if there is any prospect of seeing you? Next Wedensday is 13 weeks since you went away.

I must bid you adieu. You have many Friends tho they have not noticed you by writing. I am sorry they have been so neglegent. I hope no share of that blame lays upon your most affectionate

Portia

Mr. Cranch has in his possession a Barrel of Mrs. Wilkings Beer which belonged to the late Dr. Warren.[9] He does not know what to do with it. Suppose you should take it and give credit for it, as there will be neither wine, lemmons or any thing else to be had but what we make ourselves. Write me your pleasure about it.

8. The Hayden family had come to live in the Adams house.
9. General Joseph Warren (1741–1775) was a Boston physician active in the Revolutionary cause. He had sent Paul Revere and William Dawes on their ride to warn the outlying towns of British troop movement. He was killed in the Battle of Bunker Hill.

Abigail Adams to John Adams

Braintree March 31, 1776

I wish you would ever write me a Letter half as long as I write you; and tell me if you may where your Fleet are gone? What sort of Defence Virginia can make against our common Enemy? Whether it is so situated as to make an able Defence? Are not the Gentery Lords and the common people vassals, are they not like the uncivilized Natives Brittain represents us to be? I hope their Riffel Men who have shewen themselves very savage and even Blood thirsty; are not a specimen of the Generality of the people.

I am willing to allow the Colony great merrit for having produced a Washington but they have been shamefully duped by a Dunmore.[1]

I have sometimes been ready to think that the passion for Liberty cannot be Eaquelly Strong in the Breasts of those who have been accustomed to deprive their fellow Creatures of theirs. Of this I am certain that it[2] is not founded upon that generous and christian principal of doing to others as we would that others should do unto us.

Do not you want to see Boston; I am fearfull of the small pox, or I should have been in before this time. I got Mr. Crane to go to our House and see what state it was in. I find it has been occupied by one of the Doctors of a Regiment, very dirty, but no other damage has been done to it. The few things which were left in it are all gone. Cranch[3] has the key which he never deliverd up. I have wrote to him for it and am determined to get it cleand as soon as possible and shut it up. I look upon it a new acquisition of property, a property which one month ago I did not value at a single Shilling, and could with pleasure have seen it in flames.

The Town in General is left in a better state than we expected, more oweing to a percipitate flight than any Regard to the inhabitants, tho some individuals discoverd a sense of honour and justice and have left the rent of the Houses in which they were, for the owners and the furniture unhurt, or if damaged sufficient to make it good.

Others have committed abominable Ravages. The Mansion House of your President[4] is safe and the furniture unhurt whilst both the House and Furniture of the Solisiter General[5] have fallen a prey to their own merciless party. Surely the very Fiends feel a Reverential awe for Virtue and patriotism, whilst they Detest the paricide and traitor.

I feel very differently at the approach of spring to what I did a month ago. We knew not then whether we could plant or sow with safety, whether when we had toild we could reap the fruits of our own industery, whether we could rest in our own Cottages, or whether we should not be driven from the sea coasts to seek shelter in the wilderness, but now we feel as if we might sit under our own vine and eat the good of the land.

I feel a gaieti de Coar[6] to which before I was a stranger. I think the Sun looks brighter, the Birds sing more melodiously, and Nature puts on a more chearfull countance. We feel a temporary peace, and the poor fugitives are returning to their deserted habitations.

Tho we felicitate ourselves, we sympathize with those who are trembling least the Lot of Boston should be theirs. But they cannot be in similar circumstances unless pusilanimity and cowardise should take possession of them. They have time and warning given them to see the Evil and shun it.—I long to hear that you have declared an independancy—and by the way in the new Code of Laws which I suppose it will be necessary for you to make I desire

1. John Murray, fourth earl of Dunmore, was Virginia's royal governor. When news of the battles at Lexington and Concord reached him, he confiscated the Virginia Colony's gunpowder supply, declared martial law, sent troops against resisters, and attacked Norfolk from the sea. In July 1776 he was forced to flee to Britain.

2. Slavery.

3. Probably a slip of the pen for Crane. Elsewhere AA always refers to her brother-in-law as Mr. Cranch, and he would be an unlikely custodian for her Boston house.

4. John Hancock.

5. Samuel Quincy.

6. *gaieté du coeur*, liveliness of heart.

you would Remember the Ladies, and be more generous and favourable to them than your ancestors. Do not put such unlimited power into the hands of the Husbands. Remember all Men would be tyrants if they could. If perticuliar care and attention is not paid to the Laidies we are determined to foment a Rebelion, and will not hold ourselves bound by any Laws in which we have no voice, or Representation.

That your Sex are Naturally Tyrannical is a Truth so thoroughly established as to admit of no dispute, but such of you as wish to be happy willingly give up the harsh title of Master for the more tender and endearing one of Friend. Why then, not put it out of the power of the vicious and the Lawless to use us with cruelty and indignity with impunity. Men of Sense in all Ages abhor those customs which treat us only as the vassals of your Sex. Regard us then as Beings placed by providence under your protection and in immitation of the Supreem Being make use of that power only for our happiness.

April 5

Not having an opportunity of sending this I shall add a few lines more; tho not with a heart so gay. I have been attending the sick chamber of our Neighbour Trot whose affliction I most sensibly feel but cannot discribe, striped of two lovely children in one week. Gorge the Eldest died on weduesday and Billy the youngest on fryday, with the Canker fever, a terible disorder so much like the thr[o]at distemper, that it differs but little from it. Betsy Cranch has been very bad, but upon the recovery. Becky Peck they do not expect will live out the day. Many grown person[s] are now sick with it, in this [street?] 5. It rages much in other Towns. The Mumps too are very frequent. Isaac is now confined with it. Our own little flock are yet well. My Heart trembles with anxiety for them. God preserve them.

I want to hear much oftener from you than I do. March 8 was the last date of any that I have yet had.—You inquire of whether I am making Salt peter.[7] I have not yet attempted it, but after Soap making believe I shall make the experiment. I find as much as I can do to manufacture cloathing for my family which would else be Naked. I know of but one person in this part of the Town who has made any, that is Mr. Tertias Bass as he is calld who has got very near an hundred weight which has been found to be very good. I have heard of some others in the other parishes. Mr. Reed of Weymouth has been applied to, to go to Andover to the mills which are now at work, and has gone. I have lately seen a small Manuscrip de[s]cribing the proportions for the various sorts of powder, fit for cannon, small arms and pistols. If it would be of any Service your way I will get it transcribed and send it to you.—Every one of your Friend[s] send their Regards, and all the little ones. Your Brothers youngest child lies bad with convulsion fitts.[8] Adieu. I need not say how much I am Your ever faithfull Friend.

Abigail Adams to Mercy Otis Warren

Braintree April 27 1776

I set myself down to comply with my Friends request, who I think seem's rather low spiritted.

I did write last week, but not meeting with an early conveyance I thought the Letter of But little importance and tos'd it away. I acknowledg my Thanks due to my Friend for the entertainment she so kindly afforded me in the Characters drawn in her Last Letter, and if coveting my Neighbours Goods was not prohibited by the Sacred Law, I should be most certainly tempted to envy her the happy talant she possesses above the rest of her Sex, by adorning with her pen even trivial occurances, as well as dignifying the most important.

---

7. Potassium nitrate, used in the manufacture of gunpowder.

8. Susanna, daughter of Peter B. Adams, born in July 1775. She died in April 1776.

Cannot you communicate some of those Graces to your Friend and suffer her to pass them upon the World for her own that she may feel a little more upon an Eaquality with you?—Tis true I often receive large packages from P[hiladelphi]a. They contain as I said before more News papers than Letters, tho they are not forgotton. It would be hard indeed if absence had not some alleviations.

I dare say he writes to no one unless to Portia oftner than to your Friend,[9] because I know there is no one besides in whom he has an eaquel confidence. His Letters to me have been generally short, but he pleads in Excuse the critical state of affairs and the Multiplicity of avocations and says further that he has been very Busy, and writ near ten Sheets of paper, about some affairs which he does not chuse to Mention for fear of accident.

He is very sausy to me in return for a List of Female Grievances which I transmitted to him. I think I will get you to join me in a petition to Congress. I thought it was very probable our wise Statesmen would erect a New Government and form a new code of Laws. I ventured to speak a word in behalf of our Sex, who are rather hardly dealt with by the Laws of England which gives such unlimitted power to the Husband to use his wife Ill.

I requested that our Legislators would consider our case and as all Men of Delicacy and Sentiment are averse to Exercising the power they possess, yet as there is a natural propensity in Humane Nature to domination, I thought the most generous plan was to put it out of the power of the Arbitary and tyranick to injure us with impunity by Establishing some Laws in our favour upon just and Liberal principals.

I believe I even threatned fomenting a Rebellion in case we were not considerd, and assured him we would not hold ourselves bound by any Laws in which we had neither a voice, nor representation.

In return he tells me he cannot but Laugh at My Extrodonary Code of Laws. That he had heard their Struggle had loosned the bands of Government, that children and apprentices were dissabedient, that Schools and Colledges were grown turbulant, that Indians slighted their Guardians, and Negroes grew insolent to their Masters. But my Letter was the first intimation that another Tribe more numerous and powerfull than all the rest were grown discontented. This is rather too coarse a complement, he adds, but that I am so sausy he wont blot it out.

So I have help'd the Sex abundantly, but I will tell him I have only been making trial of the Disintresstedness of his Virtue, and when weigh'd in the balance have found it wanting.

It would be bad policy to grant us greater power say they since under all the disadvantages we Labour we have the assendancy over their Hearts

> And charm by accepting, by submitting sway.

I wonder Apollo and the Muses could not have indulged me with a poetical Genious. I have always been a votary to her charms but never could assend Parnassus myself.

I am very sorry to hear of the indisposition of your Friend. I am affraid it will hasten his return, and I do not think he can be spaired.

> "Though certain pains attend the cares of State
> A Good Man owes his Country to be great
> Should act abroad the high distinguishd part
> or shew at least the purpose of his heart."

Good Night my Friend. You will be so good as to remember me to our worthy Friend Mrs. W———e[1] when you see her and write soon to your

Portia

---

9. Mercy Warren's husband James.   1. Mrs. John Winthrop.

Abigail Adams to John Adams

August 14 1776

I wrote you to day by Mr. Smith but as I suppose this will reach you sooner, I omitted mentioning any thing of my family in it.

Nabby has enough of the small Pox for all the family beside. She is pretty well coverd, not a spot but what is so soar that she can neither walk sit stand or lay with any comfort. She is as patient as one can expect, but they are a very soar sort. If it was a disorder to which we could be subject more than once I would go as far as it was possible to avoid it. She is sweld a good deal. You will receive a perticuliar account before this reaches you of the uncommon manner in which the small Pox acts, it bafels the skill of the most Experience'd here. Billy Cranch is now out with about 40, and so well as not to be detaind at Home an hour for it. Charlly remains in the same state he did.

Your Letter of August 3 came by this days Post. I find it very conveniant to be so handy. I can receive a Letter at Night, sit down and reply to it, and send it of in the morning.

You remark upon the deficiency of Education in your Countrymen. It never I believe was in a worse state, at least for many years. The Colledge is not in the state one could wish, the Schollars complain that their professer in Philosophy is taken of by publick Business to their great detriment.[2] In this Town I never saw so great a neglect of Education. The poorer sort of children are wholly neglected, and left to range the Streets without Schools, without Buisness, given up to all Evil. The Town is not as formerly divided into Wards. There is either too much Buisness left upon the hands of a few, or too little care to do it. We daily see the Necessity of a regular Government.—You speak of our Worthy Brother.[3] I often lament it that a Man so peculiarly formed for the Education of youth, and so well qualified as he is in many Branches of Litrature, excelling in Philosiphy and the Mathematicks, should not be imployd in some publick Station. I know not the person who would make half so good a Successor to Dr. Winthrope. He has a peculiar easy manner of communicating his Ideas to Youth, and the Goodness of his Heart, and the purity of his morrals without an affected austerity must have a happy Effect upon the minds of Pupils.

If you complain of neglect of Education in sons, What shall I say with regard to daughters, who every day experience the want of it. With regard to the Education of my own children, I find myself soon out of my debth, and destitute and deficient in every part of Education.

I most sincerely wish that some more liberal plan might be laid and executed for the Benefit of the rising Generation, and that our new constitution may be distinguished for Learning and Virtue. If we mean to have Heroes, Statesmen and Philosophers, we should have learned women. The world perhaps would laugh at me, and accuse me of vanity, But you I know have a mind too enlarged and liberal to disregard the Sentiment. If much depends as is allowed upon the early Education of youth and the first principals which are instilld take the deepest root, great benifit must arise from litirary accomplishments in women.

Excuse me my pen has run away with me. I have no thoughts of comeing to P[hiladelphi]a. The length of time I have [and] shall be detaind here would have prevented me, even if you had no thoughts of returning till December, but I live in daily Expectation of seeing you here. Your Health I think requires your immediate return. I expected Mr. Gerry would have set off before now, but he finds it perhaps very hard to leave his Mistress—I wont say harder than some do to leave their wives. Mr. Gerry stood very high in my Esteem—what is meat for one is not for an other—no accounting for fancy. She is a queer dame and leads people wild dances.

But hush—Post, dont betray your trust and loose my Letter.

Nabby is poorly this morning. The pock are near the turn, 6 or 7 hundred boils are no

---

2. John Winthrop, a Harvard professor of mathematics and natural philosophy, was also a member of the Massachusetts Council.

3. Richard Cranch, husband of Abigail's sister Mary.

agreable feeling. You and I know not what a feeling it is. Miss Katy can tell. I had but 3 they were very clever and fill'd nicely. The Town instead of being clear of this distemper are now in the height of it, hundreds having it in the natural way through the deceitfulness of innoculation.

Adieu ever yours. Breakfast waits.

Portia

Abigail Adams to John Adams

Dearest of Friends   *June 30 [1778]*[4]

Shall I tell my dearest that tears of joy filld my Eyes this morning at the sight of his well known hand, the first line which has bless[ed] my Sight since his four months absence during which time I have never been able to learn a word from him, or my dear son till about ten days ago an english paper taken in a prize and brought into Salem containd an account under the Paris News of your arrival at the abode of Dr. Franklin, and last week a Carteel from Halifax brought Capt. Welch of the Boston who informd that he left you well the Eleventh of March, that he had Letters for me but distroyed them, when he was taken,[5] and this is all the information I have ever been able to obtain. Our Enemies have told us the vessel was taken and named the frigate which took her and that she was carried into Plimouth. I have lived a life of fear and anxiety ever since you left me, not more than a week after your absence the Horrid Story of Doctor Franklins assassination was received from France and sent by Mr. Purveyance of Baltimore to Congress and to Boston. Near two months before that was contradicted, then we could not hear a word from the Boston, and most people gave her up as taken or lost, thus has my mind been agitated like a troubled sea. You will easily Conceive how gratefull to me your favour of April 25 and those of our Son were to me and mine, tho I regret your short warning and the little time you had to write, by which means I know not how you fared upon your Voiage, what reception you have met with, (not even from the Ladies, tho you profess yourself an admirer of them,) and a thousand circumstances which I wish to know, and which are always perticuliarly interesting to [a] near connexion. I must request you always to be minute and to write me by every conveyance. Some perhaps which may appear unlikely to reach [me] will be the first to arrive. I own I was mortified at so Short a Letter, but I quiet my Heart with thinking there are many more upon their passage to me. I have wrote Seven before this and some of them very long. Now I know you are Safe I wish myself with you. Whenever you entertain such a wish recollect that I would have willingly hazarded all dangers to have been your companion, but as that was not permitted you must console me in your absence by a Recital of all your adventures, tho methinks I would not have them in all respects too similar to those related of your venerable Colleigue,[6] Whose Mentor like appearence, age and philosiphy must certainly lead the polite scientifick Ladies of France to suppose they are embraceing the God of Wisdom, in a Humane Form, but I who own that I never yet wish'd an Angle whom I loved a Man, shall be full as content if those divine Honours are omitted. The whole Heart of my Friend is in the Bosom of his partner, more than half a score of years has so riveted [it] there that the fabrick which contains it must crumble into Dust e'er the particles can be separated. I can hear of the Brilliant accomplishment[s] of any of my Sex with pleasure and rejoice in that Liberality of Sentiment which

4. John Adams had been appointed commissioner to France in 1777; he and John Quincy Adams had sailed there on the ship *Boston*.

5. The *Boston* captured the ship *Martha*; Hezekiah Welch was put in charge of the captured ship's voyage to America. John Adams gave him

   personal and official correspondence to bring back. The British recaptured the ship.

6. Benjamin Franklin was admired by the aristocratic ladies of France, where learned females enjoyed greater toleration.

acknowledges them. At the same time I regret the trifling narrow contracted Education of the Females of my own country. I have entertaind a superiour opinion of the accomplishments of the French Ladies ever since I read the Letters of Dr. Sherbear,[7] who professes that he had rather take the opinion of an accomplished Lady in matters of polite writing than the first wits of Italy and should think himself safer with her approbation than of a long List of Literati, and he give[s] this reason for it that Women have in general more delicate Sensations than Men, what touches them is for the most part true in Nature, whereas men warpt by Education, judge amiss from previous prejudice and refering all things to the model of the ancients, condemn that by comparison where no true Similitud ought to be expected.

But in this country you need not be told how much female Education is neglected, nor how fashonable it has been to ridicule Female learning, tho I acknowled[ge] it my happiness to be connected with a person of a more generous mind and liberal Sentiments. I cannot forbear transcribing a few Generous Sentiments which I lately met with upon this Subject. If women says the writer are to be esteemed our Enemies, methinks it is an Ignoble Cowardice thus to disarm them and not allow them the same weapons we use ourselves, but if they deserve the title of our Friends tis an inhumane Tyranny to debar them of priviliges of ingenious Education which would also render their Friendship so much the more delightfull to themselves and us. Nature is seldom observed to be niggardly of her choisest Gifts to the Sex, their Senses are generally as quick as ours, their Reason as nervious,[8] their judgment as mature and solid. Add but to these natural perfections the advantages of acquired learning what polite and charming creatures would they prove whilst their external Beauty does the office of a Crystal to the Lamp not shrowding but discloseing their Brighter intellects. Nor need we fear to loose our Empire over them by thus improveing their native abilities since where there is most Learning, Sence and knowledge there is always observed to be the most modesty and Rectitude of manners.[9]

Phillis Wheatley

(1753?–1784)

Born in West Africa, probably in what is now Gambia or Senegal, Phillis Wheatley was brought as a slave to Boston at age 7 or 8 and sold to the family of John Wheatley, a prosperous merchant. Raised in the Wheatley house on King Street (now State Street), she was nominally a personal maid to Wheatley's wife, Susanna, but she was treated, she wrote, "more like her child than her servant." With the assistance of the Wheatley daughter, Mary, she soon learned English and some Latin and was encouraged in wide reading in the Bible, Milton, Pope, Horace, Ovid, and other classics of her day. In 1767, only six years after her arrival in Boston, she published

her first poem. Others followed, including "On the Death of the Rev. George Whitefield" in 1770, when she was 17; this earned her some fame both in America and England, and two years later she had material for a book, but found no publisher in Boston.

Poems on Various Subjects, Religious and Moral (1773) was published in London and advertised on its title page as *By Phillis Wheatley, Negro Servant to Mr. John Wheatley, of Boston, in New England.* Mrs. Wheatley fostered the book by sending the poems to a friend, the Countess of Huntingdon, then arranging for Phillis to sail to England for her health. Treated in London as a celeb-

---

7. John Shebbeare, *Letters on the English Nation,* 2 vols., London, 1775. The Adamses owned a copy of this book.
8. Full of vigor or nerve.

9. The source of these ideas is unidentified. This is a draft copy of a letter which is not acknowledged in any John Adams reply. It may never have been sent.

rity, she would probably have been presented at the court of George III, but news of the illness of Susanna Wheatley brought her back to Boston. In the autumn of 1773, Phillis was granted her freedom, and a few months later Susanna Wheatley died.

Phillis Wheatley had been close to New England's movement toward freedom from Great Britain almost from the dawning of her intellectual awareness. The Wheatley home was so close to the site that it is possible she witnessed the Boston Massacre in 1770. She wrote on that occasion a poem now lost, wrote other poems dedicated to the glory of Columbia, and addressed one of her poems to George Washington. Her personal freedom, however, proved a mixed blessing. Mr. Wheatley died in 1778 and in the same year Phillis married John Peters, a free black who ran a grocery business that soon

failed. She lived only a few more years, mostly forgotten, mostly in poverty. Most of her poetry had been written before she was 20. Her book, however, continued in print. At least five English and American editions appeared before 1800, and printings continued throughout the nineteenth century and into the twentieth. From the 1960s onward Wheatley's verse has attracted attention, especially of students of African-American and women's literature.

Recent editions and studies include *The Collected Works of Phillis Wheatley*, ed. John C. Shields, 1988; *Phillis Wheatley and Her Writings*, ed. William H. Robinson, 1984; and *The Poems of Phillis Wheatley*, ed. John D. Mason, Jr., 1966. Earlier collections and studies include *Phillis Wheatley (Phillis Peters): Poems and Letters*, ed. Charles F. Heartman, 1915; G. Herbert Renfro, *The Life and Works of Phillis Wheatley* (1916); and *The Poems of Phillis Wheatley*, ed. Charlotte Ruth Wright (1930).

To the University of Cambridge, in New-England[1]

While an intrinsic ardor prompts to write,
The muses promise to assist my pen;
'Twas not long since I left my native shore
The land of errors, and *Egyptian* gloom:
Father of mercy, 'twas thy gracious hand   5
Brought me in safety from those dark abodes.

Students, to you 'tis giv'n to scan the heights
Above, to traverse the ethereal space,
And mark the systems of revolving worlds.
Still more, ye sons of science ye receive   10
The blissful news by messengers from heav'n,
How *Jesus'* blood for your redemption flows.
See him with hands out-stretcht upon the cross;
Immense compassion in his bosom glows;
He hears revilers, nor resents their scorn: 15
What matchless mercy in the Son of God!
When the whole human race by sin had fall'n,
He deign'd to die that they might rise again,
And share with him in the sublimest skies,
Life without death, and glory without end.   20

Improve your privileges while they stay,
Ye pupils, and each hour redeem, that bears
Or good or bad report of you to heav'n.

1. Texts of this and all the following poems but one are taken from *Poems on Various Subjects* (1773).

Let sin, that baneful evil to the soul,
By you be shunn'd, nor once remit your guard;   25
Suppress the deadly serpent in its egg.
Ye blooming plants of human race devine,
An *Ethiop* tells you 'tis your greatest foe;
Its transient sweetness turns to endless pain,
And in immense perdition sinks the soul.   30

1767   1773

On Being Brought from Africa to America

'Twas mercy brought me from my *Pagan* land,
Taught my benighted soul to understand
That there's a God, that there's a *Saviour* too:
Once I redemption neither sought nor knew.
Some view our sable race with scornful eye,   5
"Their colour is a diabolic die."[2]
Remember, *Christians, Negroes*, black as *Cain*,
May be refin'd, and join th' angelic train.

1768   1773

On the Death of the Reverend Mr. George Whitefield[3]

Hail, happy saint, on thine immortal throne,
Possest of glory, life, and bliss unknown;
We hear no more the music of thy tongue,
Thy wonted[4] auditories cease to throng.
Thy sermons in unequall'd accents flow'd,   5
And ev'ry bosom with devotion glow'd;
Thou didst in strains of eloquence refin'd
Inflame the heart, and captivate the mind.
Unhappy we the setting sun deplore,
So glorious once, but ah! it shines no more.   10

Behold the prophet in his tow'ring flight!
He leaves the earth for heav'n's unmeasur'd height,
And worlds unknown receive him from our sight.
There *Whitefield* wings with rapid course his way,
And sails to *Zion* through vast seas of day.   15
Thy pray'rs, great saint, and thine incessant cries
Have pierc'd the bosom of thy native skies.
Thou moon hast seen, and all the stars of light,
How he has wrestled with his God by night.

2. Dye.
3. English Methodist evangelist (1714–1770),
   prominent during America's "Great
   Awakening." He was chaplain to the Countess
of Huntingdon, who became Phillis Wheatley's
English sponsor. The poem was widely
reprinted in America and England.
4. Accustomed.

He pray'd that grace in ev'ry heart might dwell,   20
He long'd to see *America* excel;
He charg'd its youth that ev'ry grace divine
Should with full lustre in their conduct shine;
That Saviour, which his soul did first receive,
The greatest gift that ev'n a God can give,   25
He freely offer'd to the num'rous throng,
That on his lips with list'ning pleasure hung.

    "Take him, ye wretched, for your only good,
"Take him ye starving sinners, for your food;
"Ye thirsty, come to this life-giving stream,   30
"Ye preachers, take him for your joyful theme;
"Take him my dear *Americans,* he said,
"Be your complaints on his kind bosom laid:
"Take him, ye *Africans,* he longs for you,
"Impartial Saviour is his title due: 35
"Wash'd in the fountain of redeeming blood,
"You shall be sons, and kings, and priests to God."

    Great *Countess,* we *Americans* revere
Thy name, and mingle in thy grief sincere;
New England deeply feels, the *Orphans* mourn,   40
Their more than father will no more return.

    But, though arrested by the hand of death,
Whitefield no more exerts his lab'ring breath,
Yet let us view him in th' eternal skies,
Let ev'ry heart to this bright vision rise;   45
While the tomb safe retains its sacred trust,
Till life divine re-animates his dust.

1770   1770, 1773

An Hymn to the Morning.

ATTEND my lays, ye ever honour'd nine,[5]
Assist my labours, and my strains refine;
In smoothest numbers pour the notes along,
For bright *Aurora* now demands my song.

    Aurora hail, and all the thousands dies,   5
Which deck thy progress through the vaulted skies:
The morn awakes, and wide extends her rays,
On ev'ry leaf the gentle zephyr plays;
Harmonious lays the feather'd race resume.
Dart the bright eye, and shake the painted plume.   10

    Ye shady groves, your verdant gloom display
To shield your poet from the burning day:

5.   The nine muses of classical mythology presided over the arts. Calliope, line 13, was muse of epic poetry.

Calliope awake the sacred lyre,
While thy fair sisters fan the pleasing fire:
The bow'rs, the gales, the variegated skies   15
In all their pleasures in my bosom rise.

   See in the east th' illustrious king of day!
His rising radiance drives the shades away—
But Oh! I feel his fervid beams too strong,
And scarce begun, concludes th' abortive song.   20

1773

An Hymn to the Evening

Soon as the sun forsook the eastern main
The pealing thunder shook the heav'nly plain;
Majestic grandeur! From the zephyr's wing,
Exhales the incense of the blooming spring.
Soft purl the streams, the birds renew their notes,   5
And through the air their mingled music floats.

   Through all the heav'ns what beauteous dies are spread!
But the west glories in the deepest red:
So may our breasts with ev'ry virtue glow,
The living temples of our God below!   10

   Fill'd with the praise of him who gives the light,
And draws the sable curtains of the night,
Let placid slumbers sooth each weary mind,
At morn to wake more heav'nly, more refin'd;
So shall the labours of the day begin   15
More pure, more guarded from the snares of sin.

   Night's leaden sceptre seals my drowsy eyes,
Then cease, my song, till fair *Aurora* rise.

1773

To the Right Honourable WILLIAM, Earl of DARTMOUTH,[6] His Majesty's Principal Secretary of State for North America, &c.

HAIL, happy day, when, smiling like the morn,
Fair *Freedom* rose *New-England* to adorn:
The northern clime beneath her genial ray,
Dartmouth, congratulates thy blissful sway:
Elate with hope her race no longer mourns,   5

---

6. William Legge (1731–1801), second earl of Dartmouth. His appointment in 1772 as secretary of state for North America was thought a good omen for American causes.

Each soul expands, each grateful bosom burns,
While in thine hand with pleasure we behold
The silken reins, and *Freedom's* charms unfold.
Long lost to realms beneath the northern skies
She shines supreme, while hated *faction* dies: 10
Soon as appear'd the *Goddess* long desir'd,
Sick at the view, she languish'd and expir'd;
Thus from the splendors of the morning light
The owl in sadness seeks the caves of night.

No more, *America,* in mournful strain 15
Of wrongs, and grievance unredress'd complain,
No longer shall thou dread the iron chain,
Which wanton *Tyranny* with lawless hand
Had made, and with it meant t' enslave the land.

Should you, my lord, while you peruse my song, 20
Wonder from whence my love of *Freedom* sprung,
Whence flow these wishes for the common good,
By feeling hearts alone best understood,
I, young in life, by seeming cruel fate
Was snatch d from *Afric's* fancy'd happy seat: 25
What pangs excruciating must molest,
What sorrows labour in my parent's breast?
Steel'd was that soul and by no misery mov'd
That from a father seiz'd his babe belov'd:
Such, such my case. And can I then but pray 30
Others may never feel tyrannic sway?

For favours past, great Sir, our thanks are due,
and thee we ask thy favours to renew,
Since in thy pow'r, as in thy will before,
To sooth the griefs, which thou did'st once deplore. 35
May heav'nly grace the sacred sanction give
To all thy works, and thou for ever live
Not only on the wings of fleeting *Fame,*
Though praise immortal crowns the patriot's name,
But to conduct to heav'ns refulgent fane, 40
May fiery coursers sweep th' ethereal plain,
And bear thee upwards to that blest abode,
Where, like the prophet, thou shalt find thy God.

1772   1773

On the Death of Dr. Samuel Marshall.[7]

1771.

THROUGH thickest glooms look back, immortal shade,
On that confusion which thy death has made;
Or from *Olympus'* height look down, and see

---

7. A relative of Susanna Wheatley, Dr. Marshall (1735–1771) had perhaps served as a physician to Phillis. The Lucy Tyler mentioned in the poem was his wife.

A *Town* involv'd in grief bereft of thee.
Thy *Lucy* sees thee mingle with the dead,   5
And rends the graceful tresses from her head,
Wild in her woe, with grief unknown opprest
Sigh follows sigh deep heaving from her breast.

Too quickly fled, ah! whither art thou gone?
Ah! lost for ever to thy wife and son!   10
The hapless child, thine only hope and heir,
Clings round his mother's neck, and weeps his sorrows there.
The loss of thee on *Tyler's* soul returns,
And *Boston* for her dear physician mourns.

When sickness call'd for *Marshall's* healing hand,   15
With what compassion did his soul expand?
In him we found the father and the friend:
In life how lov'd! how honour'd in his end!

And must not then our *Æsculapius*[8] stay
To bring his ling'ring infant into day?   20
The babe unborn in the dark womb is tost,
And seems in anguish for its father lost.

Gone is *Apollo*[9] from his house of earth,
But leaves the sweet memorials of his worth:
The common parent, whom we all deplore,   25
From yonder world unseen must come no more,
Yet 'midst our woes immortal hopes attend
The spouse, the sire, the universal friend.

1771   1771, 1773

To S. M.[1] a Young African Painter, on Seeing His Works

To show the lab'ring bosom's deep intent,
And thought in living characters to paint,
When first thy pencil did those beauties give,
And breathing figures learnt from thee to live,
How did those prospects give my soul delight,   5
A new creation rushing on my sight?
Still, wond'rous youth! each noble path pursue,
On deathless glories fix thine ardent view:
Still may the painter's and the poet's fire
To aid thy pencil, and thy verse conspire!   10
And may the charms of each seraphic theme
Conduct thy footsteps to immortal fame!
High to the blissful wonders of the skies
Elate thy soul, and raise thy wishful eyes.
Thrice happy, when exalted to survey   15

8. Roman god of healing.
9. Greek and Roman god of light, also associated
    with healing.

1. Probably Scipio Moorhead, servant to the
    Reverend John Moorhead of Boston.

That splendid city, crown'd with endless day,
Whose twice six gates on radiant hinges ring:
Celestial *Salem*[2] blooms in endless spring.

Calm and serene thy moments glide along,
And may the muse inspire each future song!   20
Still, with the sweets of contemplation bless'd,
May peace with balmy wings your soul invest!
But when these shades of time are chas'd away,
And darkness ends in everlasting day,
On what seraphic pinions shall we move,   25
And view the landscapes in the realms above?
There shall thy tongue in heav'nly murmurs flow,
And there my muse with heav'nly transport glow:
No more to tell of *Damon's*[3] tender sighs,
Or rising radiance of *Aurora's* eyes,   30
For nobler themes demand a nobler strain,
And purer language on th' ethereal plain.
Cease, gentle muse! the solemn gloom of night
Now seals the fair creation from my sight.

1773

To His Excellency General Washington[4]

Celestial choir! enthron'd in realms of light,
  Columbia's scenes of glorious toils I write.
While freedom's cause her anxious breast alarms,
She flashes dreadful in refulgent arms.
See mother earth her offspring's fate bemoan,   5
And nations gaze at scenes before unknown!
See the bright beams of heaven's revolving light
Involved in sorrows and the veil of night!
  The goddess comes, she moves divinely fair,
Olive and laurel binds her golden hair: 10
Wherever shines this native of the skies,
Unnumber'd charms and recent graces rise.
  Muse! bow propitious while my pen relates
How pour her armies through a thousand gates,
As when Eolus[5] heaven's fair face deforms,   15
Enwrapp'd in tempest and a night of storms;
Astonish'd ocean feels the wild uproar,
The refluent surges beat the sounding shore;
Or thick as leaves in Autumn's golden reign,

2. Jerusalem.
3. Damon and Pythias were famous friends in an
   oft-told classical story.
4. Wheatley sent the poem with a letter to
   Washington in October 1775. He replied,
   praising her "genius" and inviting her to meet
   him in Cambridge, where she was received in
   1776. The poem was printed in the *Virginia
   Gazette*, March 20, 1776, and, by Thomas
   Paine, in *The Pennsylvania Magazine* for April
   1776.
5. In classical mythology, the ruler of the winds.

Such, and so many, moves the warrior's train.   20
In bright array they seek the work of war,
Where high unfurl'd the ensign waves in air.
Shall I to Washington their praise recite?
Enough thou know'st them in the fields of fight.
Thee, first in peace and honours,—we demand   25
The grace and glory of thy martial band.
Fam'd for thy valour, for thy virtues more,
Hear every tongue thy guardian aid implore!
   One century scarce perform'd its destined round,
When Gallic powers Columbia's fury found;[6]   30
And so may you, whoever dares disgrace
The land of freedom's heaven-defended race!
Fix'd are the eyes of nations on the scales,
For in their hopes Columbia's arm prevails.
Anon Britannia droops the pensive head,   35
While round increase the rising hills of dead.
Ah! cruel blindness to Columbia's state!
Lament thy thirst of boundless power too late.
   Proceed, great chief, with virtue on thy side,
Thy ev'ry action let the goddess guide.   40
A crown, a mansion, and a throne that shine,
With gold unfading, WASHINGTON! be thine.

1775   1776, 1834

On the Death of General Wooster[7]

From this the Muse rich consolation draws
He nobly perish'd in his Country's cause
His Country's Cause that ever fir'd his mind
Where martial flames, and Christian virtues join'd.
How shall my pen his warlike deeds proclaim   5
Or paint them fairer on the list of Fame—
Enough, great Chief—now wrapt in Shades around,
Thy grateful Country shall thy praise resound—
Tho not with mortals' empty praise elate
That vainest vapour to th' immortal State   10
Inly serene the expiring hero lies
And thus (while heav'nward roll his swimming eyes):

   "Permit, great power, while yet my fleeting breath
And Spirits wander to the verge of Death—
Permit me yet to point fair freedom's charms
For her the Continent shines bright in arms,   15
By thy high will, celestial prize she came—

---

6. During the French and Indian War.
7. David Wooster (1711–1777). Wheatley
enclosed the poem in a letter to Mary

Wooster, the poet's widow. The present text is
from *The Collected Works* (1988), ed. John C.
Shields.

For her we combat on the field of fame
Without her presence vice maintains full sway
And social love and virtue wing their way   20
O still propitious be thy guardian care
And lead Columbia thro' the toils of war.
With thine own hand conduct them and defend
And bring the dreadful contest to an end—
For ever grateful let them live to thee   25
And keep them ever Virtuous, brave, and free—
But how, presumptuous shall we hope to find
Divine acceptance with th' Almighty mind—
While yet (O deed Ungenerous!) they disgrace
And hold in bondage Afric's blameless race?   30
Let Virtue reign—And thou accord our prayers
Be victory our's, and generous freedom theirs."
The hero pray'd—the wond'ring spirits fled
And sought the unknown regions of the dead—
Tis thine, fair partner of his life, to find   35
His virtuous path and follow close behind—
A little moment steals him from thy sight
He waits thy coming to the realms of light
Freed from his labours in the ethereal Skies
Where in succession endless pleasures rise!   40

1778   1980, 1988

Susanna Haswell Rowson

(1762–1824)

Remembered primarily as the author of *Charlotte Temple* (1794), the first best-selling novel written by an American woman, Susanna Rowson could not have been more different from the hapless, tragic heroine of her masterpiece of eighteenth-century sentimentalism. As a playwright, actress, manager, novelist, songwriter, and educator, Rowson defied stereotypes of female helplessness in her life as well as in literary works other than her most famous one.

Born in Portsmouth, England, Susanna Haswell—whose mother, also named Susanna, died in bearing her—came to the colonies as a young child with her father, William Haswell, and her American stepmother. They lived in Nantasket until the Revolutionary War, when her father's lieutenancy in the British navy motivated their return to England in 1778. The first of Susanna's many jobs was to serve as governess to the Duchess of Devonshire, who encouraged her in 1786 to publish her first novel, *Victoria*. The novel's subtitle— *taken from real Life, and Calculated to Improve the Morals of the Female Sex, By impressing them with a just Sense of the Merits of Filial Piety*—describes much of Rowson's early work, with its fictive emphasis on "truth" and its didactic targeting of young women readers.

In 1786 Susanna married William Rowson, a member of the Horse Guard and a hardware merchant. Contrary to eighteenth-century middle-class expectations, William Rowson proved unable to support his wife and family. His business failed and was never recovered. Eventually, as scholar Cathy N. Davidson puts it, Susanna "was the breadwinner for herself, her husband, his sister, his sister's children, his illegitimate son, and two adopted children of her own."

One way Rowson made money was to write. During her early adult life in England, she produced a volume of poetry, *Poems on Various Subjects* (1788); a long critical poem, *A Trip to Parnassus; or, The Judgement of Apollo on Dramatic Authors and Performers* (1788); two sets of short fictions, *The Inquisitor* (1788, 1793) and *Mentoria; or The Young Lady's Friend* (1791, 1794); and three novels, *The Test of Honour* (1789); *Charlotte. A Tale of Truth* (1794), more commonly known as *Charlotte Temple;* and *The Fille de Chambre* (1794). Another source of income was the theater. Both Susanna and her husband joined a company of actors; first they toured Britain, and then they came to the United States to the stage of the New Theater in Philadelphia. They remained in the United States for the rest of their careers. In addition to acting, to modest reviews, Susanna wrote a musical play, *Slaves in Algiers; or, A Struggle for Freedom* (1794), and over forty popular songs, including "America, Commerce, and Freedom," a hit in 1794. In 1796 she transferred to an acting company in Boston.

In 1797 Rowson made the unlikely transition from stage actress (not a highly respectable profession in the eighteenth century) to school mistress, when she opened the Young Ladies' Academy in Boston. The academy was a success, and Rowson remained at its helm until her retirement in 1822. In her role as teacher she wrote numerous textbooks for young women's education, and she continued writing fiction. Her last novel, published posthumously in 1828, was *Charlotte's Daughter; or, the Three Orphans,* a sequel to *Charlotte Temple.*

Rowson's best-seller remained popular throughout the nineteenth century, finding American audiences at all social and economic levels. In the tradition of Samuel Richardson's *Clarissa* (though notably shorter), *Charlotte Temple* recounts the trials of an innocent young woman seduced away from her loving parents' protection by a charming, though not irredeemable man. Unlike the heroine of Hannah Webster Foster's American novel *The Coquette* (1797), Charlotte is no conscious rebel against the constraints of conventional marriage. She is only "weak," but her story exposes the powerful sexual double standard of her day. Addressed to young women, the novel makes a case for chastity and filial duty, regardless of personal desires; it argues that young women will pay a far higher price than their male counterparts if they lose their virginity outside of marriage. Some critics see the story as an allegory of early American ambivalence about independence from Britain: perhaps the complicity of the French teacher, Mlle La Rue, in Charlotte's "treasonous" abandonment of her parents suggests the historical parallel. To most of Rowson's devoted audience, however, *Charlotte Temple* was a "true" account of a young woman's sufferings. Admirers of the novel used to visit a grave at New York City's Trinity churchyard that bore the inscription "Charlotte Temple" to weep over their favorite character's fate.

The novel is "sentimental" in its plot structure—the pattern of innocence ruined, repentant, and expiated—and in its writing style. In scenes of high emotion Rowson often employs poetic diction, including alliteration, personification, and allusions to classical mythology. The narrator frequently addresses her target audiences, especially "my dear young readers," to enforce their identification with her heroine. The tale itself contains many "sentiments," of two distinct kinds: there are the high passions the characters fall into, and there are also the phrases (or "sentiments") that characters like Mr. Temple utter to sum up circumstances in philosophical terms (as when Charlotte's father remarks that "the truly brave soul is tremblingly alive to the feelings of humanity," or that "light and shade are not more happily blended than are the pleasures and pains of life; and the horrors of the one serve only to increase the splendor of the other"). Although the modern reader might be moved to chuckle at all the shrieking and fainting, all the "falling prostrate to the floor" (indeed, such action is reminiscent of *Love and Freindship*, the parody of sentimental fiction Jane Austen wrote as a teenager), Rowson's readers generally took Charlotte's experiences with high gravity.

In addition to those named above, Rowson's novels include *Trials of the Human Heart* (1795); *Reuben and Rachel; or, Tales of Old Times* (1798, 1799); and *Sarah, or The Exemplary Wife* (1813). She published *Miscellaneous Poems* in 1804. She wrote at least six plays that were produced on stage, but not published. Her textbooks include *An Abridgment of Universal Geography, Together With Sketches of History* (1806); *A Spelling Dictionary, Divided into Short Lessons, for the Easier Committing to Memory by Children and Young Persons; and Calculated to Assist Youth in Comprehending What They Read* (1807); *A Present for Young Ladies; Containing Poems,*

Dialogues, Addresses . . . (1811); *Youth's First Steps in Geography, Being a Series of Exercises Making the Tour of the Habitable Globe* (1818); *Biblical Dialogues between a Father and his Family: Comprising Sacred History, From the Creation to the Death of our Saviour Christ. The Lives of the Apostles, and the Promulgation of the Gospel; With a Sketch of the History of the Church Down to the Reformation. The Whole Carried on in Conjunction with Profane History,* 2 volumes (1822); and *Exercises in History, Chronology, and Biography, in Question and Answer. For the Use of Schools. Comprising, Ancient History, Greece, Rome, &c. Modern History, England, France, Spain, Portugal, &c. The Discovery of America, Rise, Progress and Final Independence of the United States* (1822).

For biographies of Rowson, see Ellen B. Brandt, *Susanna Haswell Rowson, America's First Best-Selling Novelist* (1975), and Dorothy Weil, *In Defense of Women: Susanna Rowson (1762–1824)* (1976). Patricia Parker published a full-length critical study, *Susanna Rowson* (1986). The very interesting results of Cathy N. Davidson's research on *Charlotte Temple* are to be found in her introduction to the 1986 Oxford University Press edition of the novel, in *Revolution and the Word* (1986), and in "The Life and Times of *Charlotte Temple*: The Biography of a Book" in Davidson's edited collection, *Reading in America* (1989).

FROM CHARLOTTE TEMPLE:
A TALE OF TRUTH

To
Ladies and Gentlemen,
Patrons of Entertaining Literature.

The great encouragement and support our Plan of a LITERARY MUSEUM, *or* NOVEL REPOSITORY, *has received from a generous public, demands the utmost tribute of gratitude; and it is with pleasure announced, that since its commencement Manuscripts have been introduced receiving general approbation. The manner in which we have printed Works committed to our care will better speak our attention and praise than any eulogium of language.*

Ladies and Gentlemen, from this specimen of our conduct, will be sure to have the efforts of their genius and productions of their pen introduced to the world in a style of superiority: the printing will be executed with expedition, correctness, accuracy and elegance, and the paper equally correspondent; and we presume to assert that no pains, care, assiduity, or expence, shall be spared to merit the continuance of the approbation we have obtained; and we also affirm, that we have never introduced any subjects but such as are founded on the basis of Virtue, and have tended to improve the understanding and to amend the heart.—Our study shall be to please; as this will equally add to our interest as reflect to our honor.

In addition to this proposal, Authors who wish to derive emolument from their studies, are informed, that five hundred pounds is placed at an eminent bankers, for the sole purpose of purchasing literary productions; and notwithstanding we are now unrivalled in the public estimation, for Novels, Tales, Romances, Adventures, etc. yet, in this undertaking, works of a general nature, whether Originals, Translations, or Compilations, which can entertain or improve the mind, elucidate the sciences, or be of any utility, will find an asylum.

From the great encrease and general encouragement

CIRCULATING LIBRARIES

have received, and which are now established in all parts of England, Scotland, and Ireland, (an employ both respectable and lucrative), such as are desirous of embarking in that line of business are informed that books suitable for that purpose are kept ready bound, in History, Voyages, Novels, Plays, etc. containing from One Hundred to Five Thousand Volumes, which may be had at a few days notice, with a catalogue for their subscribers, and instructions and directions how to plan, systemize, and conduct the same.

Such are the general outlines of this spirited undertaking: a plan founded on propriety, and sanctioned by the liberal approbation of the public; and we shall be happy farther to improve the same, so as to render it the Museum of Entertainment, and a Repository of Sciences, Arts, and Polite Literature.

Minerva Printing Office,
Leadenhall-Street.

Preface

For the perusal of the young and thoughtless of the fair sex, this Tale of Truth is designed; and I could wish my fair readers to consider it as not merely the effusion of Fancy, but as a reality.[1] The circumstances on which I have founded this novel were related to me some little time since by an old lady who had personally known Charlotte, though she concealed the real names of the characters, and likewise the place where the unfortunate scenes were acted: yet, as it was impossible to offer a relation to the public in such an imperfect state, I have thrown over the whole a slight veil of fiction, and substituted names and places according to my own fancy. The principal characters in this little tale are now consigned to the silent tomb: it can therefore hurt the feelings of no one; and may, I flatter myself, be of service to some who are so unfortunate as to have neither friends to advise, or understanding to direct them, through the various and unexpected evils that attend a young and unprotected woman in her first entrance into life.

While the tear of compassion still trembled in my eye for the fate of the unhappy Charlotte, I may have Children of my own, said I, to whom this recital may be of use, and if to your own children, said Benevolence, why not to the many daughters of Misfortune who, deprived of natural friends, or spoilt by a mistaken education, are thrown on an unfeeling world without the least power to defend themselves from the snares, not only of the other sex, but from the more dangerous arts of the profligate of their own:

Sensible as I am that a novel writer, at a time when such a variety of works are ushered into the world under that name, stands but a poor chance for fame in the annals of litera-ture, I shall therefore shelter myself from the shafts of criticism under the friendly shade of obscurity: and conscious that I wrote with a mind anxious for the happiness of that sex whose morals and conduct have so powerful an influence on mankind in general; and convinced that I have not wrote a line that conveys a wrong idea to the head or a corrupt

1. The story is supposed to have been based on a scandalous affair between Charlotte Stanley (whose grandfather was an English earl) and a wealthy cousin of Rowson's, John Montresor.

wish to the heart, I shall rest satisfied in the purity of my own intentions, and if I merit not applause, I feel that I dread not censure.

If the following tale should save one hapless fair one from the errors which ruined poor Charlotte, or rescue from impending misery the heart of one anxious parent, I shall feel a much higher gratification in reflecting on this trifling performance, than could possibly result from the applause which might attend the most elegant, finished piece of literature whose tendency might deprave the heart or mislead the understanding.

Chapter I.
A Boarding School.

"Are you for a walk," said Montraville to his companion, as they arose from table; "are you for a walk? or shall we order the chaise[2] and proceed to Portsmouth?" Belcour preferred the former; and they sauntered out to view the town, and to make remarks on the inhabitants as they returned from church.

Montraville was a Lieutenant in the army: Belcour was his brother officer: they had been to take leave of their friends previous to their departure for America, and were now returning to Portsmouth, where the troops waited orders for embarkation. They had stopped at Chichester to dine; and knowing they had sufficient time to reach the place of destination before dark, and yet allow them a walk, had resolved, it being Sunday afternoon, to take a survey of the Chichester ladies as they returned from their devotions.

They had gratified their curiosity, and were preparing to return to the inn without honoring any of the belles with particular notice, when Madame Du Pont, at the head of her school, descended from the church. Such an assemblage of youth and innocence naturally attracted the young soldiers: they stopped; and as the little cavalcade passed almost involuntarily pulled off their hats. A tall, elegant girl looked at Montraville and blushed: he instantly recollected the features of Charlotte Temple, whom he had once seen and danced with at a ball at Portsmouth. At that time he thought on her only as a very lovely child, she being then only thirteen; but the improvement two years had made in her person, and the blush of recollection which suffused her cheeks as she passed, awakened in his bosom new and pleasing ideas. Vanity led him to think that pleasure at again beholding him might have occasioned the emotion he had witnessed, and the same vanity led him to wish to see her again.

"She is the sweetest girl in the world," said he, as he entered the inn. Belcour stared. "Did you not notice her?" continued Montraville: "she had on a blue bonnet, and with a pair of lovely eyes of the same colour, has contrived to make me feel devilish odd about the heart."

"Pho," said Belcour, "a musket-ball from our friends the Americans may, in less than two months make you feel worse."

"I never think of the future," replied Montraville; "but am determined to make the most of the present, and would willingly compound with any kind Familiar who would inform me who the girl is and how I might be likely to obtain an interview."

But no kind Familiar[3] at that time appearing, and the chaise which they had ordered driving up to the door, Montraville and his companion were obliged to take leave of Chichester and its fair inhabitant and proceed on their journey.

But Charlotte had made too great an impression on his mind to be easily eradicated: having therefore spent three whole days in thinking on her, and in endeavouring to form some plan

---

2. Two-wheeled carriage drawn by one horse.
3. Close friend; attendant spirit, often taking animal form.

for seeing her, he determined to set off for Chichester, and trust to chance either to favour or frustrate his designs. Arriving at the verge of the town, he dismounted, and sending the servant forward with the horses, proceeded toward the place, where in the midst of an extensive pleasure ground, stood the mansion which contained the lovely Charlotte Temple. Montraville leaned on a broken gate, and looked earnestly at the house. The wall which surrounded it was high, and perhaps the Arguses who guarded the Hesperian fruit within were more watchful than those famed of old.[4]

" 'Tis a romantic attempt," said he; "and should I even succeed in seeing and conversing with her, it can be productive of no good: I must of necessity leave England in a few days, and probably may never return; why then should I endeavour to engage the affections of this lovely girl only to leave her a prey to a thousand inquietudes of which at present she has no idea? I will return to Portsmouth, and think no more about her."

The evening now was closed; a serene stillness reigned, and the chaste Queen of Night with her silver crescent faintly illuminated the hemisphere. The mind of Montraville was hushed into composure by the serenity of the surrounding objects. "I will think on her no more," said he, and turned with an intention to leave the place; but as he turned he saw the gate which led to the pleasure grounds open and two women come out, who walked arm in arm across the field.

"I will at least see who these are," said he. He overtook them, and giving them the compliments of the evening, begged leave to see them into the more frequented parts of the town: but how was he delighted, when, waiting for an answer, he discovered, under the concealment of a large bonnet, the face of Charlotte Temple.

He soon found means to ingratiate himself with her companion, who was a French teacher at the school, and at parting slipped a letter he had purposely written into Charlotte's hand, and five guineas[5] into that of Mademoiselle, who promised she would endeavour to bring her young charge into the field again the next evening.

Chapter II.
Domestic Concerns.

Mr. Temple was the youngest son of a nobleman, whose fortune was by no means adequate to the antiquity, grandeur, and, I may add, pride of the family. He saw his elder brother made completely wretched by marrying a disagreeable woman, whose fortune helped to prop the sinking dignity of the house, and he beheld his sisters legally prostituted to old, decrepit men, whose titles gave them consequence in the eyes of the world, and whose affluence rendered them splendidly miserable. "I will not sacrifice internal happiness for outward show," said he; "I will seek Content; and if I find her in a cottage will embrace her with as much cordiality as I should if seated on a throne."

Mr. Temple possessed a small estate of about five hundred pounds a year, and with that he resolved to preserve independence, to marry where the feelings of his heart should direct him, and to confine his expenses within the limits of his income. He had a heart open to every generous feeling of humanity, and a hand ready to dispense to those who wanted part of the blessings he enjoyed himself.

As he was universally known to be the friend of the unfortunate, his advice and bounty

---

4. In Greek mythology, Argus was a hundred-eyed giant who guarded Io; the guards of the garden of the golden apples in the Isles of the Blest were nymphs known as the Hesperides.

5. A guinea is a gold British coin worth 1 pound plus 1 shilling; it was generally used for high-prestige purchases.

was frequently solicited, nor was it seldom that he sought out indigent merit and raised it from obscurity, confining his own expenses within a very narrow compass.

"You are a benevolent fellow," said a young officer to him one day, "and I have a great mind to give you a fine subject to exercise the goodness of your heart upon."

"You cannot oblige me more," said Temple, "than to point out any way by which I can be serviceable to my fellow creatures."

"Come along, then," said the young man, "we will go and visit a man who is not in so good a lodging as he deserves, and were it not that he has an angel with him, who comforts and supports him, he must long since have sunk under his misfortunes." The young man's heart was too full to proceed, and Temple, unwilling to irritate his feelings by making further inquiries, followed him in silence, till they arrived at the Fleet Prison.[6]

The officer enquired for Captain Eldridge: a person led them up several pair of dirty stairs, and pointing to a door which led to a miserable, small apartment, said that was the Captain's room, and retired.

The officer, whose name was Blackney, tapped at the door, and was bid to enter by a voice melodiously soft. He opened the door, and discovered to Temple a scene which rivetted him to the spot with astonishment.

The apartment, though small, and bearing strong marks of poverty, was neat in the extreme. In an armchair, his head reclined upon his hand, his eyes fixed on a book which lay open before him, sat an aged man in a Lieutenant's uniform, which, though threadbare, would sooner call a blush of shame into the face of those who could neglect real merit, than cause the hectic of confusion to glow on the cheeks of him who wore it.

Beside him sat a lovely creature, busied in painting a fan mount. She was fair as the lily, but sorrow had nipped the rose in her cheek before it was half blown. Her eyes were blue; and her hair, which was light brown, was slightly confined under a plain muslin cap, tied round with a black ribbon;[7] a white linen gown and plain lawn handkerchief composed the remainder of her dress; and in this simple attire she was more irresistibly charming to such a heart as Temple's than she would have been if adorned with all the splendour of a birth-night belle.

When they entered, the old man arose from his seat, and, shaking Blackney by the hand with great cordiality, offered Temple his chair, and there being but three in the room, seated himself on the side of his little bed with evident composure.

"This is a strange place," said he to Temple, "to receive visitors of distinction in; but we must fit our feelings to our station. While I am not ashamed to own the cause which brought me here, why should I blush at my situation. Our misfortunes are not our faults; and were it not for that poor girl—"

Here the philosopher was lost in the father. He rose hastily from his seat, and, walking toward the window, brushed off a tear which he was afraid would tarnish the cheek of a sailor.

Temple cast his eye on Miss Eldridge; a pellucid drop had stolen from her eyes and fallen upon a rose she was painting. It blotted and discoloured the flower. " 'Tis emblematic," said he mentally: "the rose of youth and health soon fades when watered by the tear of affliction."

"My friend Blackney," said he, addressing the old man, "told me I could be of service to you: be so kind, then, dear Sir, as to point out some way in which I can relieve the anxiety of your heart and increase the pleasures of my own."

"My good young man," said Eldridge, "you know not what you offer. While deprived of my liberty I cannot be free from anxiety on my own account; but that is a trifling concern; my anxious thoughts extend to one more dear a thousand times than life: I am a poor weak

6. One of London's three debtor prisons. Until 1869, anyone unable to pay a debt could be imprisoned at the suit of the person to whom the money was owed. The point was not

punishment for the debtor, but security for the creditor.

7. A sign of mourning.

old man, and must expect in a few years to sink into silence and oblivion; but when I am gone, who will protect that fair bud of innocence from the blasts of adversity, or from the cruel hand of insult and dishonour?"

"Oh, my father!" cried Miss Eldridge, tenderly taking his hand, "be not anxious on that account; for daily are my prayers offered to heaven that our lives may terminate at the same instant, and one grave receive us both; for why should I live when deprived of my only friend."

Temple was moved even to tears. "You will both live many years," said he, "and, I hope, see much happiness. Chearly, my friend, chearly; these passing clouds of adversity will serve only to make the sunshine of prosperity more pleasing. But we are losing time: you might ere this have told me who were your creditors, what were their demands, and other particulars necessary to your liberation."

"My story is short," said Mr. Eldridge, "but there are some particulars which will wring my heart barely to remember; yet to one whose offers of friendship appear so open and disinterested, I will relate every circumstance that led to my present painful situation. But my child," continued he, addressing his daughter, "let me prevail on you to take this opportunity, while my friends are with me, to enjoy the benefit of air and exercise. Go, my love; leave me now; tomorrow at your usual hour I will expect you."

Miss Eldridge impressed on his cheek the kiss of filial affection, and obeyed.

Chapter III.
Unexpected Misfortunes.

"My life," said Mr. Eldridge, "till within these few years was marked by no particular circumstance deserving notice. I early embraced the life of a sailor, and have served my king with unremitted ardour for many years. At the age of twenty five I married an amiable woman; one son, and the girl who just now left us, were the fruits of our union. My boy had genius and spirit. I straitened my little income to give him a liberal education, but the rapid progress he made in his studies amply compensated for the inconvenience. At the academy where he received his education, he commenced an acquaintance with a Mr. Lewis, a young man of affluent fortune: as they grew up their intimacy ripened into friendship, and they became almost inseparable companions.

"George chose the profession of a soldier. I had neither friends or money to procure him a commission,[8] and had wished him to embrace a nautical life: but this was repugnant to his wishes, and I ceased to urge him on the subject.

"The friendship subsisting between Lewis and my son was of such a nature as gave him free access to our family; and so specious[9] was his manner that we hesitated not to state to him all our little difficulties in regard to George's future views. He listened to us with attention, and offered to advance any sum necessary for his first setting out.

"I embraced the offer, and gave him my note for the payment of it, but he would not suffer me to mention any stipulated time, as he said I might do it whenever most convenient to myself. About this time my dear Lucy returned from school, and I soon began to imagine Lewis looked at her with eyes of affection. I gave my child a caution to beware of him, and to look on her mother as her friend. She was unaffectedly artless; and when, as I suspected, Lewis made professions of love, she confided in her parents, and assured us her heart was perfectly unbiased in his favour, and she would cheerfully submit to our direction.

---

8. Commissions to officer status were purchased, not won by education or merit.

9. Seemingly true, but actually deceptive.

"I took an early opportunity of questioning him concerning his intentions towards my child: he gave an equivocal answer, and I forbade him the house.

"The next day he sent and demanded payment of his money. It was not in my power to comply with the demand. I requested three days to endeavour to raise it, determining in that time to mortgage my half pay,[1] and live on a small annuity which my wife possessed, rather than be under an obligation to so worthless a man: but this short time was not allowed me; for that evening, as I was sitting down to supper, unsuspicious of danger, an officer entered and tore me from the embraces of my family.

"My wife had been for some time in a declining state of health: ruin at once so unexpected and inevitable was a stroke she was not prepared to bear, and I saw her faint into the arms of our servant as I left my own habitation for the comfortless walls of a prison. My poor Lucy, distracted with her fears for us both, sunk on the floor and endeavoured to detain me by her feeble efforts: but in vain; they forced open her arms; she shrieked and fell prostrate. But pardon me. The horrors of that night unman me. I can not proceed."

He rose from his seat and walked several times across the room: at length, attaining more composure, he cried—"What a mere infant I am. Why, Sir, I never felt thus in the day of battle."

"No," said Temple; "but the truly brave soul is tremblingly alive to the feelings of humanity."

"True," replied the old man (something like satisfaction darting across his features) "and painful as these feelings are, I would not exchange them for that torpor which the stoic mistakes for philosophy. How many exquisite delights I should have passed by unnoticed but for these keen sensations, this quick sense of happiness or misery. Then let us, my friend, take the cup of life as it is presented to us, tempered by the hand of a wise Providence, be thankful for the good, patient under the evil, and presume not to enquire why the latter predominates."

"This is true philosophy," said Temple.

" 'Tis the only way to reconcile ourselves to the cross events of life," replied he. "But I forget myself. I will not longer intrude on your patience, but proceed in my melancholy tale.

"The very evening that I was taken to prison my son arrived from Ireland, where he had been some time with his regiment. From the distracted expressions of his mother and sister he learnt by whom I had been arrested; and late as it was, flew on the wings of wounded affection to the house of his false friend, and earnestly enquired the cause of this cruel conduct. With all the calmness of a cool, deliberate villain, he avowed his passion for Lucy, declared her situation in life would not permit him to marry her, but offered to release me immediately, and make any settlement on her, if George would persuade her to live, as he impiously termed it, a life of honour.

"Fired at the insult offered to a man and a soldier, my boy struck the villain, and a challenge ensued.[2] He then went to a coffee house in the neighbourhood and wrote a long, affectionate letter to me, blaming himself severely for ever introducing Lewis into the family, or permitting him to confer an obligation which had brought inevitable ruin on us all. He begged me, whatever might be the event of the ensuing morning, not to suffer regret or unavailing sorrow for his fate to encrease the anguish of my heart, which he greatly feared was already insupportable.

"This letter was delivered to me early in the morning. It would be vain to attempt describing my feelings on the perusal of it; suffice it to say, that a merciful Providence interposed, and I was for three weeks insensible to miseries almost beyond the strength of human nature to support.

"A fever and strong delirium seized me, and my life was despaired of. At length nature,

---

1.   Military pension.   2.   That is, a challenge to a duel.

overpowered with fatigue, gave way to the salutary power of rest, and a quiet slumber of some hours restored me to reason, though the extreme weakness of my frame prevented my feeling my distress so acutely as I otherwise should.

"The first object that struck me on awaking was Lucy sitting by my bedside; her pale countenance and sable dress prevented my enquiries for poor George: for the letter I had received from him was the first thing that occurred to my memory. By degrees the rest returned: I recollected being arrested, but could no ways account for being in this apartment, whither they had conveyed me during my illness.

"I was so weak as to be almost unable to speak. I pressed Lucy's hand, and looked earnestly round the apartment in search of another dear object.

" 'Where is your mother?' said I, faintly.

"The poor girl could not answer: she shook her head in expressive silence; and throwing herself on the bed, folded her arms about me and burst into tears.

" 'What! both gone?' said I.

" 'Both,' she replied, endeavouring to restrain her emotions: 'but they are happy, no doubt.' "

Here Mr. Eldridge paused: the recollection of the scene was too painful to permit him to proceed.

Chapter IV.
Change of Fortune.

"It was some days," continued Mr. Eldridge, recovering himself, "before I could venture to enquire the particulars of what had happened during my illness: at length I assumed courage to ask my dear girl how long her mother and brother had been dead: she told me that the morning after my arrest, George came home early to enquire after his mother's health, staid with them but a few minutes, seemed greatly agitated at parting, but gave them strict charge to keep up their spirits, and hope everything would turn out for the best. In about two hours after, as they were sitting at breakfast and endeavouring to strike out some plan to attain my liberty, they heard a loud rap at the door, which Lucy running to open, she met the bleeding body of her brother, borne in by two men who had lifted him from a litter[3] on which they had brought him from the place where he fought. Her poor mother, weakened by illness and the struggles of the preceding night, was not able to support this shock: gasping for breath, her looks wild and haggard, she reached the apartment where they had carried her dying son. She knelt by the bed side; and taking his cold hand, 'My poor boy,' said she, 'I will not be parted from thee: husband! son! both at once lost. Father of mercies spare me!' She fell into a strong convulsion, and expired in about two hours. In the mean time a surgeon had dressed George's wounds, but they were in such situations as to bar the smallest hopes of recovery. He never was sensible from the time he was brought home, and died that evening in the arms of his sister.

"Late as it was when this event took place, my affectionate Lucy insisted on coming to me. 'What must he feel,' said she, 'at our apparent neglect, and how shall I inform him of the afflictions with which it has pleased heaven to visit us.'

"She left the care of the dear departed ones to some neighbours, who had kindly come in to comfort and assist her; and coming to the house where I was confined, found me in the situation I have mentioned.

"How she supported herself in these trying moments I know not: heaven no doubt was

3. A stretcher.

with her; and her anxiety to preserve the life of one parent in some measure abated her affliction for the loss of the other.

"My circumstances were greatly embarrassed, my acquaintance few, and those few utterly unable to assist me. When my wife and son were committed to their kindred earth, my creditors seized my house and furniture, which not being sufficient to discharge all their demands, detainers were lodged against me. No friend stepped forward to my relief, and from the grave of her mother, my beloved Lucy followed an almost dying father to this melancholy place.

"Here we have been nearly a year and a half. My half pay I have given up to satisfy my creditors, and my child supports me by her industry: sometimes by fine needlework, sometimes painting. She leaves me every night, and goes to a lodging near the bridge, but returns in the morning to chear me with her smiles, and bless me by her duteous affection. A lady once offered her an asylum in her family; but she would not leave me. 'We are all the world to each other,' said she. 'I thank God I have health and spirits to improve the talents with which nature has endowed me; and I trust if I employ them in the support of a beloved parent, I shall not be thought an unprofitable servant. While he lives, I pray for strength to pursue my employment; and when it pleases heaven to take one of us, may it give the survivor resignation to bear the separation as we ought: till then I will never leave him.' "

"But where is this inhuman persecutor?" said Temple.

"He has been abroad ever since," replied the old man; "though he has left orders with his lawyer never to give up the note until the utmost farthing is paid."

"And how much is the amount of your debts in all?" said Temple.

"Five hundred pounds," he replied.

Temple started; it was more than he expected. "But something must be done," said he: "that sweet maid must not wear out her life in a prison. I will see you again to-morrow, my friend," said he, shaking Eldridge's hand: "keep up your spirits: light and shade are not more happily blended than are the pleasures and pains of life; and the horrors of the one serve only to encrease the splendour of the other."

"You never lost a wife and son," said Eldridge.

"No," replied he, "but I can feel for those that have." Eldridge pressed his hand, as they went toward the door, and they parted in silence.

When they got without the walls of the prison, Temple thanked his friend Blackney for introducing him to so worthy a character; and telling him he had a particular engagement in the city, wished him a good evening.

"And what is to be done for this distressed man?" said Temple, as he walked up Ludgate Hill. "Would to heaven I had a fortune that would enable me instantly to discharge his debt: what exquisite transport to see the expressive eyes of Lucy beaming at once with pleasure for her father's deliverance and gratitude for her deliverer: but is not my fortune affluence," continued he, "nay superfluous wealth, when compared to the extreme indigence of Eldridge; and what have I done to deserve ease and plenty, while a brave worthy officer starves in a prison? Three hundred a year is surely sufficient for all my wants and wishes: at any rate Eldridge must be relieved."

When the heart has will the hands can soon find means to execute a good action.

Temple was a young man, his feelings warm and impetuous; unacquainted with the world, his heart had not been rendered callous by being convinced of its fraud and hypocrisy. He pitied their sufferings, overlooked their faults, thought every bosom as generous as his own, and would cheerfully have divided his last guinea with an unfortunate fellow creature.

No wonder then that such a man (without waiting a moment for the interference of Madame Prudence) should resolve to raise money sufficient for the relief of Eldridge by mortgaging part of his fortune.

We will not enquire too minutely into the cause which might actuate him in this instance: suffice it to say, he immediately put the plan in execution; and in three days from the time he first saw the unfortunate Lieutenant, he had the superlative felicity of seeing him at liberty, and receiving an ample reward in the tearful eye and half articulated thanks of the grateful Lucy.

"And pray, young man," said his father to him one morning, "what are your designs in visiting thus constantly that old man and his daughter?"

Temple was at a loss for a reply: he had never asked himself the question: he hesitated, and his father continued—

"It was not till within these few days that I heard in what manner your acquaintance first commenced, and cannot suppose any thing but attachment to the daughter could carry you such imprudent lengths for the father: it certainly must be her art[4] that drew you in to mortgage part of your fortune."

"Art, Sir." cried Temple, eagerly. "Lucy Eldridge is as free from art as she is from every other error: she is—"

"Every thing that is amiable and lovely," said his father, interrupting him ironically: "no doubt in your opinion she is a pattern of excellence for all her sex to follow; but come, Sir, pray tell me what are your designs toward this paragon? I hope you do not intend to complete your folly by marrying her."

"Were my fortune such as would support her according to her merit, I don't know a woman more formed to insure happiness in the marriage state."

"Then prithee, my dear lad," said his father, "since your rank and fortune are so much beneath what your *Princess* might expect, be so kind as to turn your eyes on Miss Weatherby; who, having only an estate of three thousand a year, is more upon a level with you, and whose father yesterday solicited the mighty honour of your alliance. I shall leave you to consider on this offer; and pray remember that your union with Miss Weatherby will put it in your power to be more liberally the friend of Lucy Eldridge."

The old gentleman walked in a stately manner out of the room, and Temple stood almost petrified with astonishment, contempt, and rage.

Chapter V.
Such Things Are.

Miss Weatherby was the only child of a wealthy man, almost idolized by her parents, flattered by her dependents, and never contradicted even by those who called themselves her friends: I cannot give a better description than by the following lines from a late ingenious female pen:

> The gay but gaudy morning flowers,
> That bloom and die within few hours,
> That dying leave no trace behind,
> Bring to the deep reflecting mind
> The lovely maid whose form and face
> Nature has deck'd with every grace,
> But in whose breast no virtues glow,
> Whose heart ne'er felt another's woe,
> Whose hand ne'er smooth'd the bed of pain,
> Or eas'd the captive's galling chain;
> But like the tulip caught the eye,
> Born just to be admir'd and die;

4. Manipulative flirtatiousness.

When gone, no one regrets its loss,
Or scarce remembers that it was.

Such was Miss Weatherby: her form lovely as nature could make it, but her mind uncultivated, her heart unfeeling, her passions impetuous, and her brain almost turned with flattery, dissipation, and pleasure; and such was the girl whom a partial grandfather left independent mistress of the fortune before mentioned.

She had seen Temple frequently; and fancying she could never be happy without him, nor once imagining he could refuse a girl of her beauty and fortune, she prevailed on her fond father to offer the alliance to the old Earl of D———, Mr. Temple's father.

The Earl had received the offer courteously: he thought it a great match for Henry, and was too fashionable a man to suppose a wife could be any impediment to the friendship he professed for Eldridge and his daughter.

Unfortunately for Temple he thought quite otherwise: the conversation he had just had with his father discovered to him the situation of his heart; and he found that the most affluent fortune would bring no encrease of happiness unless Lucy Eldridge shared it with him; and the knowledge of the purity of her sentiments, and the integrity of his own heart, made him shudder at the idea his father had started of marrying a woman for no other reason than because the affluence of her fortune would enable him to injure her by maintaining in splendour the woman to whom his heart was devoted: he therefore resolved to refuse Miss Weatherby, and let what would be the consequence offer his heart and hand to Lucy Eldridge.

Full of this determination, he sought his father, declared his resolution, and was commanded never more to appear in his presence. Temple bowed; his heart was too full to permit him to speak; he left the house precipitately, and hastened to relate the cause of his sorrows to his good old friend and his amiable daughter.

In the mean time, the Earl, vexed to the soul that such a fortune should be lost, determined to offer himself a candidate for Miss Weatherby's favour.

What wonderful changes are wrought by that reigning power, ambition: the lovesick girl, when first she heard of Temple's refusal, wept, raved, tore her hair, and vowed to found a protestant nunnery with her fortune; and by commencing abbess, shut herself up from the sight of cruel, ungrateful man forever.

Her father was a man of the world: he suffered this first transport[5] to subside, and then very deliberately unfolded to her the offers of the old Earl, expatiated on the many benefits arising from an elevated title, painted in glowing colours the surprise and vexation of Temple when he should see her figuring as a Countess and his mother in law, and begged her to consider well before she made any rash vows.

The *distressed* fair one dried her tears, listened patiently, and at length declared she believed the surest method to revenge the slight put on her by the son, would be to accept the father: so said so done, and in a few days she became the Countess D———.

Temple heard the news with emotion: he had lost his father's favour by avowing his passion for Lucy, and he saw now there was no hope of regaining it: "but it shall not make me miserable," said he. "Lucy and I have not any ambitious notions: we can live on three hundred a year for some little time, till the mortgage is paid off, and then we shall have sufficient not only for the comforts but many of the little elegancies of life. We will purchase a little cottage, my Lucy," said he, "and thither with your reverend father we will retire; we will forget there are such things as splendour, profusion, and dissipation: we will have some cows, and you shall be queen of the dairy; in a morning while I look after my garden you shall take a basket on your arm and sally forth to feed your poultry; and as they flutter round you in token of humble gratitude, your father shall smoke his pipe in a woodbine alcove, and viewing the serenity of your countenance, feel such real pleasure dilate his own heart, as shall make him forget he had ever been unhappy."

5.   State of being carried away by strong emotion.

Lucy smiled, and Temple saw it was the smile of approbation. He sought and found a cottage suited to his taste: thither, attended by Love and Hymen,[6] the happy trio retired; where, during many years of uninterrupted felicity, they cast not a wish beyond the little boundaries of their own tenement. Plenty and her hand-maid Prudence presided at their board; Hospitality stood at their gate; Peace smiled on each face, Content reigned in each heart, and Love and Health strewed roses on their pillows.

Such were the parents of Charlotte Temple, who was the only pledge of their mutual love, and who, at the earnest entreaty of a particular friend, was permitted to finish the education her mother had begun, at Madame Du Pont's school, where we first introduced her to the acquaintance of the reader.

Chapter VI.
French Teachers not Always the Best Women in the World.

Madame Du Pont was a woman every way calculated to take the care of young ladies, had that care devolved entirely on herself; but it was impossible to attend the education of a numerous school without proper assistants, and those assistants were not always the kind of people whose conversation and morals were exactly such as parents of delicacy and refinement could wish a daughter to copy. Among the teachers at Madame Du Pont's school was Mademoiselle La Rue, who added to a pleasing person and insinuating address, a liberal education and the manners of a gentlewoman. She was recommended to the school by a lady whose humanity overstepped the bounds of discretion; for though she knew Miss La Rue had eloped from a convent with a young officer, and on coming to England had lived with several different men in open defiance of all moral and religious duties, yet finding her reduced to the most abject want, and believing the penitence which she professed to be sincere, she took her into her own family, and from thence recommended her to Madame Du Pont, as thinking the situation more suitable for a woman of her abilities. But Mademoiselle possessed too much of the spirit of intrigue to remain long without adventures. At church, where she constantly appeared, her person attracted the attention of a young man who was upon a visit at a gentleman's seat[7] in the neighbourhood: she had met him several times clandestinely; and being invited to come out that evening, and eat some fruit and pastry in a summerhouse belonging to the gentleman he was visiting, and requested to bring some of the ladies with her, Charlotte being her favourite, was fixed on to accompany her.

The mind of youth eagerly catches at promised pleasure: pure and innocent by nature, it thinks not of the dangers lurking beneath those pleasures till too late to avoid them: when Mademoiselle asked Charlotte to go with her, she mentioned the gentleman as a relation, and spoke in such high terms of the elegance of his gardens, the sprightliness of his conversation, and the liberality with which he ever entertained his guests, that Charlotte thought only of the pleasure she should enjoy in the visit,—not on the imprudence of going without her governess's knowledge, or of the danger to which she exposed herself in visting the house of a gay young man of fashion.

Madame Du Pont was gone out for the evening, and the rest of the ladies retired to rest, when Charlotte and the teacher stole out of the back gate, and in crossing the field, were accosted by Montraville, as mentioned in the first chapter.

Charlotte was disappointed in the pleasure she had promised herself from this visit. The levity of the gentlemen and the freedom of their conversation disgusted her. She was

---

6.   Love is Cupid; Hymen, in Greek mythology, is
the god of marriage.

7.   A large residence, usually part of an estate.

astonished at the liberties Mademoiselle permitted them to take; grew thoughtful and uneasy, and heartily wished herself at home again in her own chamber.

Perhaps one cause of that wish might be an earnest desire to see the contents of the letter which had been put into her hand by Montraville.

Any reader who has the least knowledge of the world will easily imagine the letter was made up of encomiums on her beauty, and vows of everlasting love and constancy; nor will he be surprised that a heart open to every gentle, generous sentiment, should feel itself warmed by gratitude for a man who professed to feel so much for her, nor is it improbable but her mind might revert to the agreeable person and martial appearance of Montraville.

In affairs of love a young heart is never in more danger than when attempted by a handsome young soldier. A man naturally ordinary, when arrayed in a military habit, will make a tolerable apperance; but when beauty of person, elegance of manner, and an easy method of paying compliments, are united to the scarlet coat, smart cockade, and military sash, ah! well a day for the poor girl who gazes on him: she is in imminent danger; but if she listens to him with pleasure, 'tis all over with her, and from that moment she has neither eyes nor ears for any other object.

Now, my dear sober matron, (if a sober matron should deign to turn over these pages before she trusts them to the eye of a darling daughter,) let me entreat you not to put on a grave face and throw down the book in a passion and declare 'tis enough to turn the heads of half the girls in England; I do solemnly protest, my dear madam, I mean no more by what I have here advanced than to ridicule those romantic girls who foolishly imagine a red coat and silver epaulet constitute the fine gentleman; and should that fine gentleman make half a dozen fine speeches to them, they will imagine themselves so much in love as to fancy it a meritorious action to jump out of a two pair of stairs window, abandon their friends, and trust entirely to the honour of a man who perhaps hardly knows the meaning of the word, and if he does will be too much the modern man of refinement to practise it in their favour.

Gracious heaven! when I think on the miseries that must rend the heart of a doating parent when he sees the darling of his age at first seduced from his protection, and afterwards abandoned by the very wretch whose promises of love decoyed her from the paternal roof; when he sees her poor and wretched, her bosom torn between remorse for her crime and love for her vile betrayer; when fancy paints to me the good old man stooping to raise the weeping penitent, while every tear from her eye is numbered by drops from his bleeding heart, my bosom glows with honest indignation, and I wish for power to extirpate those monsters of seduction from the earth.

Oh my dear girls, for to such only am I writing, listen not to the voice of love unless sanctioned by paternal approbation: be assured it is now past the days of romance: no woman can be run away with contrary to her own inclination: then kneel down each morning and request kind heaven to keep you free from temptation, or should it please to suffer you to be tried, pray for fortitude to resist the impulse of inclination when it runs counter to the precepts of religion and virtue.

Chapter VII.
Natural Sense of Propriety Inherent in the Female Bosom.

"I cannot think we have done exactly right in going out this evening, Mademoiselle," said Charlotte, seating herself when she entered her apartment: "nay I am sure it was not right; for I expected to be very happy, but was sadly disappointed."

"It was your own fault then," replied Mademoiselle: "for I am sure my cousin omitted nothing that could serve to render the evening agreeable."

"True," said Charlotte: "but I thought the gentlemen were very free in their manner: I wonder you would suffer them to behave as they did."

"Prithee don't be such a foolish little prude," said the artful French woman, affecting anger: "I invited you to go in hopes it would divert you, and be an agreeable change of scene; however if your delicacy was hurt by the behavior of the gentlemen, you need not go again; so there let it rest."

"I do not intend to go again," said Charlotte, gravely taking off her bonnet, and beginning to prepare for bed: "I am sure if Madame Du Pont knew we had been out tonight she would be very angry; and it is ten to one but she hears of it by some means or other."

"Nay, Miss," said La Rue, "perhaps your mighty sense of propriety may lead you to tell her yourself; and in order to avoid the censure you would incur, should she hear of it by accident, throw the blame on me: but I confess I deserve it: it will be a very kind return for that partiality which led me to prefer you before any of the rest of the ladies; but perhaps it will give you pleasure," continued she, letting fall some hypocritical tears, "to see me deprived of bread, and for an action which by the most rigid could only be esteemed an inadvertency, lose my place and character, and be drove again into the world, where I have already suffered all the evils attendant on poverty."

This was touching Charlotte in the most vulnerable part: she rose from her seat, and taking Mademoiselle's hand—"You know, my dear La Rue," said she, "I love you too well to do anything that would injure you in my governess's opinion: I am only sorry we went out this evening."

"I don't believe it, Charlotte," said she, assuming a little vivacity; "for if you had not gone out you would not have seen the gentleman who met us crossing the field, and I rather think you were pleased with his conversation."

"I had seen him once before," replied Charlotte, "and thought him an agreeable man; and you know one is always pleased to see a person with whom one has passed several chearful hours. But," said she pausing and drawing the letter from her pocket, while a general suffusion of vermillion tinged her neck and face, "he gave me this letter; what shall I do with it?"

"Read it to be sure," returned Mademoiselle.

"I am afraid I ought not," said Charlotte: "my mother has often told me I should never read a letter given me by a young man without first giving it to her."

"Lord bless you, my dear girl!" cried the teacher smiling, "have you a mind to be in leading strings all your life time. Prithee open the letter, read it, and judge for yourself; if you shew it your mother the consequence will be you will be taken from school, and a strict guard kept over you, so you will stand no chance of ever seeing the smart young officer again."

"I should not like to leave school yet," replied Charlotte, "till I have attained a greater proficiency in my Italian and music. But you can if you please, Mademoiselle, take the letter back to Montraville, and tell him I wish him well but cannot with any propriety enter into a clandestine correspondence with him." She laid the letter on the table, and began to undress herself.

"Well," said La Rue, "I vow you are an unaccountable girl: have you no curiosity to see the inside now? for my part I could no more let a letter addressed to me lie unopened so long, than I could work miracles: he writes a good hand," continued she, turning the letter to look at the superscription.

" 'Tis well enough," said Charlotte, drawing it towards her.

"He is a genteel young fellow," said La Rue carelessly, folding up her apron at the same time; "but I think he is marked with the small pox."

"Oh you are greatly mistaken," said Charlotte eagerly; "he has a remarkable clear skin and fine complexion."

"His eyes, if I could judge by what I saw," said La Rue, "are grey, and want expression."

"By no means," replied Charlotte; "they are the most expressive eyes I ever saw."

"Well, child, whether they are grey or black is of no consequence: you have determined not to read his letter, so it is likely you will never either see or hear from him again."

Charlotte took up the letter, and Mademoiselle continued—

"He is most probably going to America; and if ever you should hear any account of him it may possibly be that he is killed; and though he loved you ever so fervently, though his last breath should be spent in a prayer for your happiness, it can be nothing to you: you can feel nothing for the fate of the man whose letters you will not open, and whose sufferings you will not alleviate by permitting him to think you would remember him when absent, and pray for his safety."

Charlotte still held the letter in her hand: her heart swelled at the conclusion of Mademoiselle's speech, and a tear dropped upon the wafer that closed it.

"The wafer is not dry yet," said she, "and sure there can be no great harm—" She hesitated. La Rue was silent. "I may read it, Mademoiselle, and return it afterward."

"Certainly," replied Mademoiselle.

"At any rate I am determined not to answer it," continued Charlotte, as she cut the paper round the wafer.

Here let me stop to make one remark, and trust me my very heart aches while I write it; but certain I am that when once a woman has stifled the sense of shame in her own bosom, when once she has lost sight of the basis on which reputation, honour, everything that should be dear to the female heart, rests, she grows hardened in guilt, and will spare no pains to bring down innocence and beauty to the shocking level with herself: and this proceeds from that diabolical spirit of envy, which repines at seeing another in the full possession of that respect and esteem which she can no longer hope to enjoy.

Mademoiselle eyed the unsuspecting Charlotte, as she perused the letter, with a malignant pleasure. She saw that the contents had awakened new emotions in her youthful bosom: she encouraged her hopes, calmed her fears, and before they parted for the night it was determined that she should meet Montraville the ensuing evening.

Chapter VIII.
Domestic Pleasures Planned.

"I think, my dear," said Mrs. Temple, laying her hand on her husband's arm as they were walking together in the garden, "I think next Wednesday is Charlotte's birth day: now I have formed a little scheme in my own mind to give her an agreeable surprise, and if you have no objection we will send for her home on that day." Temple pressed his wife's hand in token of approbation, and she proceeded—"You know the little alcove at the bottom of the garden, of which Charlotte is so fond? I have an inclination to deck this out in a fanciful manner, and invite all her little friends to partake of a collation of fruit, sweetmeats, and other things suitable to the general taste of young guests, and by way of making it more pleasing to Charlotte, she shall be mistress of the feast, and entertain her visitors in this alcove. I know she will be delighted; and to complete all, they shall have some music and finish with a dance."

"A very fine plan indeed," said Temple, smiling; "and you really suppose I will wink at[8] your indulging the girl in this manner? You will quite spoil her, Lucy; indeed you will."

"She is the only child we have," said Mrs. Temple, the whole tenderness of a mother adding animation to her fine countenance, but it was withal tempered so sweetly with the

---

8.   That is, pretend not to see.

meek affection and submissive duty of the wife, that as she paused expecting her husband's answer, he gazed at her tenderly, and found he was unable to refuse her request.

"She is a good girl," said Temple.

"She is indeed," replied the fond mother exultingly, "a grateful, affectionate girl, and I am sure will never lose sight of the duty she owes her parents."

"If she does," said he, "she must forget the example set her by the best of mothers."

Mrs. Temple could not reply, but the delightful sensation that delighted her heart sparkled in her intelligent eyes and heightened the vermillion on her cheeks.

Of all the pleasures of which the human mind is sensible, there is none equal to that which warms and expands the bosom when listening to commendations bestowed on us by a beloved object, and are conscious of having deserved them.

Ye giddy flutterers in the fantastic round of dissipation, who eagerly seek pleasure in the lofty dome, rich treat, and midnight revel—tell me, ye thoughtless daughters of folly, have ye ever found the phantom you have so long sought with such unremitted assiduity? Has she not always eluded your grasp, and when you have reached your hand to take the cup she extends to her deluded votaries, have you not found the long expected draught strongly tinctured with the bitter dregs of disappointment? I know you have: I see it in the wan cheek, sunk eye, and air of chagrin, which ever mark the children of dissipation. Pleasure is a vain illusion; she draws you on to a thousand follies, errors, and I may say vices, and then leaves you to deplore your thoughtless credulity.

Look, my dear friends, at yonder lovely Virgin, arrayed in a white robe, devoid of ornament; behold the meekness of her countenance, the modesty of her gait; her handmaids are *Humility, Filial Piety, Conjugal Affection, Industry,* and *Benevolence;* her name is *Content;* she holds in her hand the cup of true felicity, and when once you have formed an intimate acquaintance with these her attendants, nay you must admit them as your bosom friends and chief counsellors, then, whatever may be your situation in life, the meek eyed Virgin will immediately take up her abode with you.

Is poverty your portion?—she will lighten your labours, preside at your frugal board, and watch your quiet slumbers.

Is your state mediocrity?—she will heighten every blessing you enjoy, by informing you how grateful you should be to that bountiful Providence who might have placed you in the most abject situation, and by teaching you to weigh your blessings against your deserts, shew you how much more you receive than you have a right to expect.

Are you possessed of affluence?—what an inexhaustible fund of happiness she will lay before you. To relieve the distressed, redress the injured, in short, to perform all the good works of peace and mercy.

Content, my dear friends, will blunt even the arrows of adversity so that they can not materially harm you. She will dwell in the humblest cottage; she will attend you even to a prison. Her parent is Religion; her sisters, Patience and Hope. She will pass with you through life, smoothing the rough paths and tread to earth those thorns which every one must meet with as they journey onward to the appointed goal. She will soften the pains of sickness, continue with you even in the cold, gloomy hour of death, and chearing you with the smiles of her heaven born sister Hope, lead you triumphant to a blissful eternity.

I confess I have rambled strangely from my story: but what of that? if I have been so lucky as to find the road to happiness, why should I be such a niggard as to omit so good an opportunity of pointing out the way to others. The very basis of true peace of mind is a benevolent wish to see all the world as happy as itself; and from my soul do I pity the selfish churl, who remembering the little bickerings of anger, envy, and fifty other disagreeables to which frail mortality is subject, would wish to revenge the affront which pride whispers him he has received. For my own part, I can safely declare, there is not a human being in the universe whose prosperity I should not rejoice in, and to whose happiness I would not contribute to the utmost limit of my power: and may my offenses be no more remembered in the day of general retribution than as from my soul I forgive every offense or injury received from a fellow creature.

Merciful heaven! who would exchange the rapture of such a reflection for all the gaudy tinsel which the world calls pleasure!

But to return.—Content dwelt in Mrs. Temple's bosom, and spread a charming animation over her countenance, as her husband led her in, to lay the plan she had formed (for the celebration of Charlotte's birth day,) before Mr. Eldridge.

Chapter IX.
We Know Not What a Day May Bring Forth.

Various were the sensations which agitated the mind of Charlotte during the day preceding the evening in which she was to meet Montraville. Several times did she almost resolve to go to her governess, shew her the letter, and be guided by her advice: but Charlotte had taken one step in the ways of imprudence, and when that is once done there are always innumerable obstacles to prevent the erring person returning to the path of rectitude: yet these objections, however forcible they may appear in general, exist chiefly in the imagination.

Charlotte feared the anger of her governess: she loved her mother, and the very idea of incurring her displeasure gave her the greatest uneasiness: but there was a more forcible reason still remaining: should she shew the letter to Madame Du Pont, she must confess the means by which it came into her possession, and what would be the consequence? Mademoiselle would be turned out of doors.

"I must not be ungrateful," said she. "La Rue is very kind to me; besides I can, when I see Montraville, inform him of the impropriety of our continuing to see or correspond with each other, and request him to come no more to Chichester."

However prudent Charlotte might be in these resolutions, she certainly did not take a proper method to confirm herself in them. Several times in the course of the day she indulged herself in reading over the letter, and each time she read it the contents sunk deeper in her heart. As evening drew near, she caught herself frequently consulting her watch. "I wish this foolish meeting was over," said she, by way of apology to her own heart, "I wish it was over; for when I have seen him, and convinced him my resolution is not to be shaken, I shall feel my mind much easier."

The appointed hour arrived. Charlotte and Mademoiselle eluded the eye of vigilance; and Montraville, who had waited their coming with impatience, received them with rapturous and unbounded acknowledgments for their condescension: he had wisely brought Belcour with him to entertain Mademoiselle while he enjoyed an uninterrupted conversation with Charlotte.

Belcour was a man whose character might be comprised in a few words; and as he will make some figure in the ensuing pages, I shall here describe him. He possessed a genteel fortune, and had a liberal education; dissipated, thoughtless, and capricious, he paid little regard to the moral duties, and less to religious ones: eager in the pursuit of pleasure, he minded not the miseries he inflicted on others, so that his own wishes, however extravagant, were gratified. Self, darling self, was the idol he worshiped, and to that he would have sacrificed the interest and happiness of all mankind. Such was the friend of Montraville: will not the reader be ready to imagine that the man who could regard such a character must be actuated by the same feelings, follow the same pursuits, and be equally unworthy with the person to whom he thus gave his confidence?

But Montraville was a different character: generous in his disposition, liberal in his opinions, and good natured almost to a fault; yet eager and impetuous in the pursuit of a favourite object, he staid not to reflect on the consequence which might follow the attainment of his wishes; with a mind ever open to conviction, had he been so fortunate as to possess a friend who would have pointed out the cruelty of endeavouring to gain the heart of an innocent artless girl, when he knew it was utterly impossible for him to marry her, and when the gratification of his passion would be unavoidable infamy and misery to her, and a cause of never ceasing remorse to himself: had these dreadful consequences been placed before him in a proper light, the humanity of his nature would have urged him to give up the pursuit: but Belcour was not this friend; he rather encouraged the growing passion of Montraville; and being pleased with the vivacity of Mademoiselle, resolved to leave no argument untried which he thought might prevail on her to be the companion of their intended voyage, and he made no doubt but her example, added to the rhetoric of Montraville, would persuade Charlotte to go with them.

Charlotte had, when she went out to meet Montraville, flattered herself that her resolution was not to be shaken, and that conscious of the impropriety of her conduct in having a clandestine intercourse with a stranger, she would never repeat the indiscretion.

But alas! poor Charlotte, she knew not the deceitfulness of her own heart, or she would have avoided the trial of her stability.

Montraville was tender, eloquent, ardent, and yet respectful. "Shall I not see you once more," said he, "before I leave England? Will you not bless me by an assurance that when we are divided by a vast expanse of sea I shall not be forgotten?"

Charlotte sighed.

"Why that sigh, my dear Charlotte? Could I flatter myself that a fear for my safety, or a wish for my welfare occasioned it, how happy would it make me."

"I shall ever wish you well, Montraville," said she, "but we must meet no more."

"Oh, say not so, my lovely girl: reflect that when I leave my native land, perhaps a few short weeks may terminate my existence; the perils of the ocean—the dangers of war——"

"I can hear no more," said Charlotte, in a tremulous voice. "I must leave you."

"Say you will see me once again."

"I dare not," said she.

"Only for one half hour to-morrow evening: 'tis my last request. I shall never trouble you again, Charlotte."

"I know not what to say," cried Charlotte, struggling to draw her hands from him: "let me leave you now."

"And will you come to-morrow?" said Montraville.

"Perhaps I may," said she.

"Adieu then. I will live upon that hope till we meet again."

He kissed her hand. She sighed an adieu, and catching hold of Mademoiselle's arm, hastily entered the garden gate.

Chapter X.
When We Have Excited Curiosity, It Is but an Act of Good Nature to Gratify It.

Montraville was the youngest son of a gentleman of fortune: but his family being numerous, he was obliged to bring up his sons to genteel professions, by the exercise of which they might hope to raise themselves into notice.

"My daughters," said he, "have been educated like gentlewomen; and should I die before they are settled, they must have some provision made to place them above the snares and temptations which vice ever holds out to the elegant, accomplished female, when oppressed by the frowns of poverty and the sting of dependence: my boys, with only moderate incomes, when placed in the church, at the bar, or in the field, may exert their talents, make themselves friends, and raise their fortunes on the basis of merit."

When Montraville chose the profession of arms, his father presented him with a commission, and made him a handsome provision for his private purse. "Now, my boy," said he; "go! seek glory in the field of battle. You have received from me all I shall ever have it in my power to bestow: it is certain I have interest[9] to gain you promotion; but be assured that interest shall never be exerted unless by your future conduct you deserve it. Remember therefore your success in life depends entirely on yourself. There is one thing I think it my duty to caution you against; the precipitancy with which young men frequently rush into matrimonial engagements, and by their thoughtlessness draw many a deserving woman into scenes of poverty and distress. A soldier has no business to think of a wife till his rank is such as to place him above the fear of bringing into the world a train of helpless innocents, heirs only to penury and affliction. If indeed, a woman, whose fortune is sufficient to preserve you in that state of independence I would teach you to prize, should generously bestow herself on a young soldier, whose chief hope of future prosperity depended on his success in the field; if such a woman should offer, every barrier is removed, and I should rejoice in an union which would promise so much felicity. But mark me, boy, if on the contrary you rush into a precipitate union with a girl of little or no fortune, take the poor creature from a comfortable home and kind friends, and plunge her into all the evils a narrow income and encreasing family can inflict, I will leave you to enjoy the blessed fruits of your rashness; for by all that is sacred, neither my interest or fortune shall ever be exerted in your favour. I am serious," continued he, "therefore imprint this conversation on your memory, and let it influence your future conduct. Your happiness will always be dear to me, and I wish to warn you of a rock on which the peace of many an honest fellow has been wrecked; for believe me the difficulties and dangers of the longest winter campaign are much easier to be borne than the pangs that would seize your heart when you beheld the woman of your choice, the children of your affection, involved in penury and distress, and reflected that it was your own folly and precipitancy had been the prime cause of their sufferings."

As this conversation passed but a few hours before Montraville took leave of his father, it was deeply impressed on his mind: when therefore Belcour came with him to the place of assignation with Charlotte, he directed him to enquire of the French woman what were Miss Temple's expectations in regard to fortune.

Mademoiselle informed him, that though Charlotte's father possessed a genteel independence, it was by no means probable that he could give his daughter more than a thousand pounds; and in case she did not marry to his liking, it was possible he might not give her a single *sous*;[1] nor did it appear the least likely that Mr. Temple would agree to her union with a young man on the point of embarking for the seat of war.

Montraville therefore concluded it was impossible he should ever marry Charlotte Temple; and what end he proposed to himself by continuing the acquaintance he had commenced with her he did not at that moment give himself time to enquire.

Chapter XI.
Conflict of Love and Duty.

Almost a week was now gone, and Charlotte continued every evening to meet Montraville, and in her heart every meeting was resolved to be the last; but alas! when Montraville at

---

9. Influence.   1. French coin of little value.

parting would earnestly entreat one more interview, that treacherous heart betrayed her; and forgetful of its resolution, pleaded the cause of the enemy so powerfully, that Charlotte was unable to resist. Another and another meeting succeeded; and so well did Montraville improve each opportunity, that the heedless girl at length confessed no idea could be so painful to her as that of never seeing him again.

"Then we will never be parted," said he.

"Ah, Montraville," replied Charlotte, forcing a smile, "how can it be avoided? My parents would never consent to our union; and even could they be brought to approve of it, how should I bear to be separated from my kind, my beloved mother?"

"Then you love your parents more than you do me, Charlotte?"

"I hope I do," said she, blushing and looking down, "I hope my affection for them will ever keep me from infringing the laws of filial duty."

"Well, Charlotte," said Montraville, gravely, and letting go her hand, "since that is the case, I find I have deceived myself with fallacious hopes. I had flattered my fond heart that I was dearer to Charlotte than any thing in the world besides. I thought that you would for my sake have braved the danger of the ocean, that you would, by your affection and smiles, have softened the hardships of war, and had it been my fate to fall, your tenderness would cheer the hour of death, and smooth my passage to another world. But farewell, Charlotte! I see you never loved me. I shall now welcome the friendly ball that deprives me of the sense of my misery."

"Oh stay, unkind Montraville," cried she, catching hold of his arm, as he pretended to leave her, "stay, and to calm your fears I will here protest that was it not for the fear of giving pain to the best of parents, and returning their kindness with ingratitude, I would follow you through every danger, and in studying to promote your happiness, insure my own. But I can not break my mother's heart, Montraville; I must not bring the grey hairs of my doating grandfather with sorrow to the grave, or make my beloved father perhaps curse the hour that gave me birth." She covered her face with her hands, and burst into tears.

"All these distressing scenes, my dear Charlotte," cried Montraville, "are merely the chimeras of a disturbed fancy. Your parents might perhaps grieve at first, but when they heard from your own hand that you was with a man of honour, and that it was to insure your felicity by a union with him, to which you feared they would never have given their assent, that you left their protection, they will, be assured, forgive an error which love alone occasioned, and when we return from America, receive you with open arms and tears of joy."

Belcour and Mademoiselle heard this last speech, and conceiving it a proper time to throw in their advice and persuasions, approached Charlotte, and so well seconded the entreaties of Montraville, that finding Mademoiselle intended going with Belcour, and feeling her own treacherous heart too much inclined to accompany them, the hapless Charlotte, in an evil hour, consented that the next evening they should bring a chaise to the end of the town, and that she would leave her friends, and throw herself entirely on the protection of Montraville. "But should you," said she, looking earnestly at him, her eyes full of tears, "should you, forgetful of your promises, and repenting the engagements you here voluntarily enter into, forsake and leave me on a foreign shore—"

"Judge not so meanly of me," said he. "The moment we reach our place of destination, Hymen shall sanctify our love; and when I shall forget your goodness, may heaven forget me!"

"Ah," said Charlotte, leaning on Mademoiselle's arm, as they walked up the garden together, "I have forgot all that I ought to have remembered, in consenting to this intended elopement."

"You are a strange girl," said Mademoiselle: "you never know your own mind two minutes at a time. Just now you declared Montraville's happiness was what you prized most in the world; and now I suppose you repent having insured that happiness by agreeing to accompany him abroad."

"Indeed I do repent," replied Charlotte, "from my soul; but while discretion points out the impropriety of my conduct, inclination urges me on to ruin."

"Ruin! fiddlesticks!" said Mademoiselle; "am not I going with you? and do I feel any of these qualms?"

"You do not renounce a tender father and mother," said Charlotte.

"But I hazard my dear reputation," replied Mademoiselle, bridling.

"True," replied Charlotte, "but you do not feel what I do." She then bade her good night: but sleep was a stranger to her eyes, and the tear of anguish watered her pillow.

Chapter XII.

Nature's last, best gift:
Creature in whom excell'd, whatever could
To sight or thought be nam'd!
Holy, divine! good, amiable, and sweet!
How thou art fall'n!——[2]

When Charlotte left her restless bed, her languid eye and pale cheek discovered to Madame Du Pont the little repose she had tasted.

"My dear child," said the affectionate governess, "what is the cause of the langour so apparent in your frame? Are you not well?"

"Yes, my dear Madame, very well," replied Charlotte, attempting to smile, "but I know not how it was I could not sleep last night, and my spirits are depressed this morning."

"Come cheer up, my love," said the governess; "I believe I have brought a cordial to revive them. I have just received a letter from your good mama, and here is one for yourself."

Charlotte hastily took the letter: it contained these words—

> "As to-morrow is the anniversary of the happy day that gave my beloved girl
> to the anxious wishes of a maternal heart, I have requested your governess to let
> you come home and spend it with us; and as I know you to be a good affectionate
> child, and make it your study to improve in those branches of education which
> you know will give most pleasure to your delighted parents, as a reward for your
> diligence and attention I have prepared an agreeable surprise for your reception.
> Your grandfather, eager to embrace the darling of his aged heart, will come in the
> chaise for you; so hold yourself in readiness to attend him by nine o'clock. Your
> dear father joins in every tender wish for your health and future felicity which
> warms the heart of my dear Charlotte's affectionate mother.   "L. Temple."

"Gracious heaven!" cried Charlotte, forgetting where she was, and raising her streaming eyes as in earnest supplication.

Madame Du Pont was surprised. "Why these tears, my love?" said she. "Why this seeming agitation? I thought the letter would have rejoiced instead of distressing you."

"It does rejoice me," replied Charlotte, endeavouring at composure, "but I was praying for merit to deserve the unremitted attentions of the best of parents."

"You do right," said Madame Du Pont, "to ask the assistance of heaven that you may continue to deserve their love. Continue, my dear Charlotte, in the course you have ever pursued, and you will insure at once their happiness and your own."

"Oh!" cried Charlotte, as her governess left her, "I have forfeited both forever! Yet let me reflect:—the irrevocable step is not yet taken: it is not too late to recede from the brink of a precipice, from which I can only behold the dark abyss of ruin, shame, and remorse!"

2. Loosely quoted from John Milton, *Paradise Lost*, 9. 896–900.

She arose from her seat and flew to the apartment of La Rue. "Oh Mademoiselle!" said she, "I am snatched by a miracle from destruction! This letter has saved me: it has opened my eyes to the folly I was so near committing. I will not go, Mademoiselle; I will not wound the hearts of those dear parents who make my happiness the whole study of their lives."

"Well," said Mademoiselle, "do as you please, Miss; but pray understand that my resolution is taken, and it is not in your power to alter it. I shall meet the gentlemen at the appointed hour, and shall not be surprised at any outrage which Montraville may commit when he finds himself disappointed. Indeed I should not be astonished was he to come immediately here and reproach you for your instability in the hearing of the whole school: and what will be the consequence? you will bear the odium of having formed the resolution of eloping, and every girl of spirit will laugh at your want of fortitude to put it in execution, while prudes and fools will load you with reproach and contempt. You will have lost the confidence of your parents, incurred their anger, and the scoffs of the world; and what fruit do you expect to reap from this piece of heroism (for such no doubt you think it is) you will have the pleasure to reflect that you have deceived the man who adores you, and whom in your heart you prefer to all other men, and that you are separated from him for ever."

This eloquent harangue was given with such volubility, that Charlotte could not find an opportunity to interrupt her, or to offer a single word till the whole was finished, and then found her ideas so confused that she knew not what to say.

At length she determined that she would go with Mademoiselle to the place of assignation, convince Montraville of the necessity of her adhering to her resolution of remaining behind; assure him of her affection, and bid him adieu.

Charlotte formed this plan in her mind and exulted in the certainty of its success. "How shall I rejoice," said she, "in this triumph of reason over inclination, and when in the arms of my affectionate parents, lift up my soul in gratitude to heaven as I look back on the dangers I have escaped!"

The hour of assignation arrived: Mademoiselle put what money and valuables she possessed in her pocket, and advised Charlotte to do the same; but she refused; "my resolution is fixed;" said she; "I will sacrifice love to duty."

Mademoiselle smiled internally, and they proceeded softly down the back stairs and out of the garden gate. Montraville and Belcour were ready to receive them.

"Now," said Montraville, taking Charlotte in his arms, "you are mine forever."

"No," said she, withdrawing from his embrace; "I am come to take an everlasting farewell."

It would be useless to repeat the conversation that here ensued; suffice it to say, that Montraville used every argument that had formerly been successful, Charlotte's resolution began to waver, and he drew her almost imperceptibly toward the chaise.

"I can not go," said she: "cease, dear Montraville, to persuade. I must not: religion, duty, forbid."

"Cruel Charlotte!" said he, "if you disappoint my ardent hopes, by all that is sacred this hand shall put a period to my existence. I can not—will not live without you."

"Alas! my torn heart!" said Charlotte, "how shall I act?"

"Let me direct you," said Montraville, lifting her into the chaise.

"Oh! my dear, forsaken parents!" cried Charlotte.

The chaise drove off. She shrieked, and fainted into the arms of her betrayer.

Chapter XIII.
Cruel Disappointment.

"What pleasure!" cried Mr. Eldridge, as he stepped into the chaise to go for his granddaughter, "what pleasure expands the heart of an old man, when he beholds the progeny of a beloved child growing up in every virtue that adorned the minds of her parents. I foolishly thought, some few years since, that every sense of joy was buried in the graves of my dear partner and my son, but my Lucy by her filial affection soothed my soul to peace, and this dear Charlotte has twined herself around my heart, and opened such new scenes of delight to my view, that I almost forget I have ever been unhappy."

When the chaise stopped he alighted with the alacrity of youth; so much do the emotions of the soul influence the body.

It was half past eight o'clock: the ladies were assembled in the school room, and Madame Du Pont was preparing to offer the morning sacrifice of prayer and praise, when it was discovered that Mademoiselle and Charlotte were missing.

"She is busy no doubt," said the governess, "in preparing Charlotte for her little excursion; but pleasure should never make us forget our duty to our Creator. Go one of you and bid them both attend prayers."

The lady who went to summon them soon returned, and informed the governess that the room was locked, and that she had knocked repeatedly but obtained no answer.

"Good heaven!" cried Madame Du Pont, "this is very strange:" and turning pale with terror, she went hastily to the door and ordered it to be forced open. The apartment instantly discovered the fact that no person had been in it the preceding night, the beds appearing as though just made. The house was instantly a scene of confusion: the garden, the pleasure grounds, were searched to no purpose, every apartment rang with the names of Miss Temple and Mademoiselle; but they were too distant to hear, and every face wore the marks of disappointment.

Mr. Eldridge was sitting in the parlour, eagerly expecting his granddaughter to descend, ready equipped for her journey: he heard the confusion that reigned in the house; he heard the name of Charlotte frequently repeated. "What can be the matter?" said he, rising and opening the door. "I fear some accident has befallen my dear girl."

The governess entered. The visible agitation of her countenance discovered that something extraordinary had happened.

"Where is Charlotte?" said he. "Why does not my child come to welcome her doating parent?"

"Be composed, my dear Sir," said Madame Du Pont, "do not frighten yourself unnecessarily. She is not in the house at present; but as Mademoiselle is undoubtedly with her, she will speedily return in safety, and I hope they will both be able to account for this unseasonable absence in such a manner as shall remove our present uneasiness."

"Madam," cried the old man, with an angry look, "has my child been accustomed to go out without leave, with no other company or protector than that French woman? Pardon me, Madam, I mean no reflection on your country, but I never did like Mademoiselle La Rue; I think she was a very improper person to be entrusted with the care of such a girl as Charlotte Temple, or to be suffered to take her from under your immediate protection."

"You wrong me, Mr. Eldridge," replied she, "if you suppose I have ever permitted your granddaughter to go out unless with the other ladies. I would to heaven I could form any probable conjecture concerning her absence this morning, but it is a mystery which her return can alone unravel."

Servants were now dispatched to every place where there was the least hope of hearing any tidings of the fugitives, but in vain. Dreadful were the hours of horrid suspense which Mr. Eldridge passed till twelve o'clock, when that suspense was reduced to a shocking certainty, and every spark of hope which till then they had indulged, was in a moment extinguished.

Mr. Eldridge was preparing, with a heavy heart, to return to his anxiously expecting children, when Madame Du Pont received the following note without either name or date:

"Miss Temple is well, and wishes to relieve the anxiety of her parents by letting them know she has voluntarily put herself under the protection of a man whose future study shall be to make her happy. Pursuit is needless; the measures taken to avoid discovery are too effectual to be eluded. When she thinks her friends are reconciled to this precipitate step, they may perhaps be informed of her place of residence. Mademoiselle is with her."

As Madame Du Pont read these cruel lines, she turned pale as ashes, her limbs trembled, and she was forced to call for a glass of water. She loved Charlotte truly; and when she reflected on the innocence and gentleness of her disposition, she concluded that it must have been the advice and machinations of La Rue which led her to this imprudent action; she recollected her agitation at the receipt of her mother's letter, and saw in it the conflict of her mind.

"Does that letter relate to Charlotte?" said Mr. Eldridge, having waited some time in expectation of Madame Du Pont's speaking.

"It does," said she. "Charlotte is well, but cannot return to-day."

"Not return, Madam? where is she? who will detain her from her fond expecting parents?"

"You distract me with these questions, Mr. Eldridge. Indeed I know not where she is, or who has seduced her from her duty."

The whole truth now rushed at once upon Mr. Eldridge's mind. "She has eloped then," said he. "My child is betrayed, the darling, the comfort of my aged heart, is lost. Oh would to heaven I had died but yesterday."

A violent gush of grief in some measure relieved him, and after several vain attempts, he at length assumed sufficient composure to read the note.

"And how shall I return to my children?" said he: "how approach that mansion so late the habitation of peace? Alas! my dear Lucy, how will you support these heart-rending tidings? or how shall I be enabled to console you, who need so much consolation myself?"

The old man returned to the chaise, but the light step and chearful countenance were no more; sorrow filled his heart and guided his motions; he seated himself in the chaise, his venerable head reclined upon his bosom, his hands were folded, his eye fixed on vacancy, and the large drops of sorrow rolled silently down his cheeks. There was a mixture of anguish and resignation depicted in his countenance, as he would say, henceforth who shall dare to boast his happiness, or even in idea contemplate his treasure, least in the very moment his heart is exulting in its own felicity the object which constitutes that felicity should be torn from him.

Chapter XIV.
Maternal Sorrow.

Slow and heavy passed the time while the carriage was conveying Mr. Eldridge home; and yet when he came in sight of the house, he wished a longer reprieve from the dreadful task of informing Mr. and Mrs. Temple of their daughter's elopement.

It is easy to judge the anxiety of these affectionate parents, when they found the return of their father delayed so much beyond the expected time. They were now met in the dining parlour, and several of the young people who had been invited were already arrived. Each different part of the company were employed in the same manner, looking out at the windows which faced the road. At length the long expected chaise appeared. Mrs. Temple ran out to receive and welcome her darling: her young companions flocked around the door, each one eager to give her joy on the return of her birth day. The door of the chaise was opened: Charlotte was not there. "Where is my child?" cried Mrs. Temple, in breathless agitation.

Mr. Eldridge could not answer: he took hold of his daughter's hand, led her into the house; and sinking on the first chair he came to, burst into tears and sobbed aloud.

"She is dead," cried Mrs. Temple. "Oh my dear Charlotte!" and clasping her hands in an agony of distress, fell into strong hysterics.

Mr. Temple, who had stood speechless with surprise and fear, now ventured to enquire if indeed his Charlotte was no more. Mr. Eldridge led him into another apartment; and putting the fatal note into his hand, cried—"Bear it like a Christian," and turned from him, endeavouring to suppress his own too visible emotions.

It would be vain to attempt describing what Mr. Temple felt whilst he hastily ran over the dreadful lines: when he had finished, the paper dropped from his unnerved hand. "Gracious heaven!" said he. "could Charlotte act thus?" Neither tear or sigh escaped him; and he sat the image of mute sorrow, till roused from his stupor by the repeated shrieks of Mrs. Temple. He rose hastily, and rushing into the apartment where she was, folded his arms about her, and saying—"Let us be patient, my dear Lucy," nature relieved his almost bursting heart by a friendly gush of tears.

Should any one, presuming on his own philosophic temper, look with an eye of contempt on the man who could indulge a woman's weakness, let him remember that man was a father, and he will then pity the misery which wrung those drops from a noble, generous heart.

Mrs. Temple beginning to be a little more composed, but still imagining her child was dead, her husband, gently taking her hand, cried—"You are mistaken, my love. Charlotte is not dead."

"Then she is very ill; else why did she not come? But I will go to her; the chaise is still at the door: let me go instantly to the dear girl. If I was ill she would fly to attend me, to alleviate my sufferings, and chear me with her love."

"Be calm, my dearest Lucy, and I will tell you all," said Mr. Temple. "You must not go, indeed you must not; it will be of no use."

"Temple," said she, assuming a look of firmness and composure, "tell me the truth I beseech you. I can not bear this dreadful suspense. What misfortune has befallen my child? Let me know the worst, and I will endeavour to bear it as I ought."

"Lucy," replied Mr. Temple, "imagine your daughter alive, and in no danger of death: what misfortune would you then dread?"

"There is one misfortune which is worse than death. But I know my child too well to suspect——"

"Be not too confident, Lucy."

"Oh heavens!" said she, "what horrid images do you start: is it possible she should forget—"

"She has forgot us all, my love; she has preferred the love of a stranger to the affectionate protection of her friends."

"Not eloped!" cried she, eagerly.

Mr. Temple was silent.

"You cannot contradict it," said she. "I see my fate in those tearful eyes. Oh Charlotte! Charlotte! how ill have you requited our tenderness. But Father of Mercies," continued she, sinking on her knees, and raising her streaming eyes and clasped hands to heaven, "this once vouchsafe to hear a fond, a distracted mother's prayer. Oh let thy bounteous Providence watch over and protect the dear thoughtless girl, save her from the miseries which I fear will be her portion, and, oh! of thine infinite mercy make her not a mother, least she should one day feel what I now suffer."

The last words faltered on her tongue, and she fell fainting into the arms of her husband, who had involuntarily dropped on his knees beside her.

A mother's anguish, when disappointed in her tenderest hopes, none but a mother can conceive. Yet, my dear young readers, I would have you read this scene with attention, and reflect that you may yourselves one day be mothers. Oh my friends, as you value your eternal happiness, wound not, by thoughtless ingratitude, the peace of the mother who bore you: remember the tenderness, the care, the unremitting anxiety with which she has attended to all your wants and wishes from earliest infancy to the present day; behold the mild ray of affectionate applause that beams from her eye on the performance of your duty; listen to her reproofs with silent attention; they proceed from a heart anxious for your future felicity: you must love her; nature, all powerful nature, has planted the seeds of filial affection in your bosoms.

Then once more read over the sorrows of poor Mrs. Temple, and remember, the mother whom you so dearly love and venerate will feel the same, when you, forgetful of the respect due to your maker and yourself, forsake the paths of virtue, for those of vice and folly.

Chapter XV.
Embarkation.

It was with the utmost difficulty that the united efforts of Mademoiselle and Montraville could support Charlotte's spirits during their short ride from Chichester to Portsmouth, where a boat waited to take them immediately on board the ship in which they were to embark for America.

As soon as she became tolerably composed, she entreated pen and ink to write to her parents. This she did in the most affecting, artless manner, entreating their pardon and blessing, and describing the dreadful situation of her mind, the conflict she suffered in endeavouring to conquer this unfortunate attachment, and concluded with saying her only hope of future comfort consisted in the (perhaps delusive) idea she indulged of being once more folded in their protecting arms, and hearing the words of peace and pardon from their lips.

The tears streamed incessantly while she was writing, and she was frequently obliged to lay down her pen: but when the task was completed, and she had committed the letter to the care of Montraville to be sent to the post office, she became more calm, and indulging the delightful hope of soon receiving an answer that would seal her pardon, she in some measure assumed her usual chearfulness.

But Montraville knew too well the consequences that must unavoidably ensue should this letter reach Mr. Temple: he therefore wisely resolved to walk on the deck, tear it in pieces, and commit the fragments to the care of Neptune,[3] who might or might not, as it suited his convenience, convey them on shore.

All Charlotte's hopes and wishes were now concentered in one, namely that the fleet might be detained at Spithead till she could receive a letter from her friends: but in this she was disappointed, for the second morning after she went on board the signal was made, the fleet weighed anchor, and in a few hours (the wind being favourable) they bid adieu to the white cliffs of Albion.[4]

In the mean time every enquiry that could be thought of was made by Mr. and Mrs. Temple; for many days did they indulge the fond hope that she was merely gone off to be married, and that when the indissoluble knot was once tied, she would return with the partner she had chosen, and entreat their blessing and forgiveness.

"And shall we not forgive her?" said Mr. Temple.

"Forgive her!" exclaimed the mother. "Oh yes, whatever be her errors, is she not our child? and though bowed to the earth even with shame and remorse, is it not our duty to raise the

---

3. Roman god of the Sea.   4. A poetic name for Britain.

poor penitent, and whisper peace and comfort to her desponding soul? would she but return, with rapture would I fold her to my heart, and bury every remembrance of her faults in the dear embrace."

But still day after day passed on, and Charlotte did not appear, nor were any tidings to be heard of her: yet each rising morning was welcomed by some new hope—the evening brought with it disappointment. At length hope was no more; despair usurped her place; and the mansion which was once the mansion of peace, became the habitation of pale dejected melancholy.

The chearful smile that was wont to adorn the face of Mrs. Temple was fled, and had it not been for the support of unaffected piety, and a consciousness of having ever set before her child the fairest example, she must have sunk under this heavy affliction.

"Since," said she, "the severest scrutiny cannot charge me with any breach of duty to have deserved this severe chastisement, I will bow before the power who inflicts it with humble resignation to his will; nor shall the duty of a wife be totally absorbed in the feelings of the mother; I will endeavour to appear more chearful, and by appearing in some measure to have conquered my own sorrow, alleviate the sufferings of my husband, and rouse him from that torpor into which this misfortune has plunged him. My father too demands my care and attention: I must not, by a selfish indulgence of my own grief, forget the interest those two dear objects take in my happiness or misery: I will wear a smile on my face, though the thorn rankles in my heart; and if by so doing I in the smallest degree contribute to restore their peace of mind, I shall be amply rewarded for the pain the concealment of my own feelings may occasion."

Thus argued this excellent woman: and in the execution of so laudable a resolution we shall leave her, to follow the fortunes of the hapless victim of imprudence and evil counsellors.

Chapter XVI.
Necessary Digression.

On board of the ship on which Charlotte and Mademoiselle were embarked, was an officer of large unencumbered fortune and elevated rank, and whom I shall call Crayton.

He was one of those men, who, having travelled in their youth, pretend to have contracted a peculiar fondness for every thing foreign, and to hold in contempt the productions of their own country; and this affected partiality extended even to the women.

With him therefore the blushing modesty and unaffected simplicity of Charlotte passed unnoticed; but the forward pertness of La Rue, the freedom of her conversation, the elegance of her person, mixed with a certain engaging *je ne sais quoi*,[6] perfectly enchanted him.

The reader no doubt has already developed the character of La Rue: designing, artful and selfish, she had accepted the devoirs[7] of Belcour because she was heartily weary of the retired life she led at the school, wished to be released from what she deemed a slavery, and to return to that vortex of folly and dissipation which had once plunged her into the deepest misery; but her plan she flattered herself was now better formed: she resolved to put herself under the protection of no man till she had first secured a settlement; but the clandestine manner in which she left Madame Du Pont's prevented her putting this plan into execution, though Belcour solemnly protested he would make her a handsome settlement the moment they arrived at Portsmouth. This he afterward contrived to evade by a pretended hurry of business; La Rue readily conceiving he never meant to fulfill his promise, determined to

---

6. "I know not what," in French.   7. Courteous attentions; compliments.

change her battery and attack the heart of Colonel Crayton. She soon discovered the partiality he entertained for her nation; and having imposed on him a feigned tale of distress, representing Belcour as a villain who had seduced her from her friends under promise of marriage, and afterward betrayed her, pretending great remorse for the errors she had committed, and declaring whatever her affection might have been, it was now entirely extinguished, and she wished for nothing more than an opportunity to leave a course of life which her soul abhorred; but she had no friends to apply to, they had all renounced her, and guilt and misery would undoubtedly be her future portion through life.

Crayton was possessed of many amiable qualities, though the peculiar trait in his character, which we have already mentioned, in a great measure threw a shade over them. He was beloved for his humanity and benevolence by all who knew him, but he was easy and unsuspicious himself, and easily became a dupe to the artifice of others.

He was, when very young, united to an amiable Parisian lady, and perhaps it was his affection for her that laid the foundation for the partiality he ever retained for the whole nation. He had by her one daughter, who entered into the world but a few hours before her mother left it. This lady was universally beloved and admired, being endowed with all the virtues of her mother without the weakness of the father: she was married to Major Beauchamp, and was at this time in the same fleet with her father, attending her husband to New York.

Crayton was melted by the affected contrition and distress of La Rue: he would converse with her for hours, read to her, play cards with her, listen to all her complaints, and promise to protect her to the utmost of his power. La Rue easily saw his character; her sole aim was to awaken a passion in his bosom that might turn out to her advantage, and in this aim she was but too successful, for before the voyage was finished, the infatuated Colonel gave her from under his hand a promise of marriage on their arrival at New York, under forfeiture of five thousand pounds.

And how did our poor Charlotte pass her time during a tedious and tempestuous passage? Naturally delicate, the fatigue and sickness which she endured rendered her so weak as to be almost entirely confined to her bed: yet the kindness and attention of Montraville in some measure contributed to alleviate her sufferings, and the hope of hearing from her friends soon after her arrival, kept up her spirits, and cheared many a gloomy hour.

But during the voyage a great revolution took place, not only in the fortune of La Rue but in the bosom of Belcour: whilst in the pursuit of his amour with Mademoiselle, he had attended little to the interesting inobtrusive charms of Charlotte, but when, cloyed by possession, and disgusted with the art and dissimulation of one, he beheld the simplicity and gentleness of the other, the contrast became too striking not to fill him at once with surprise and admiration. He frequently conversed with Charlotte; he found her sensible, well informed, but diffident and unassuming. The langour which the fatigue of her body and perturbation of her mind spread over her delicate features, served only in his opinion to render her more lovely: he knew that Montraville did not design to marry her, and he formed a resolution to endeavour to gain her himself whenever Montraville should leave her.

Let not the reader imagine Belcour's designs were honourable. Alas! when once a woman has forgot the respect due to herself, by yielding to the solicitations of illicit love, they lose all the consequence, even in the eyes of the man whose art has betrayed them, and for whose sake they have sacrificed every valuable consideration.

The heedless Fair, who stoops to guilty joys,
A man may pity—but he must despise.

Nay, every libertine will think he has a right to insult her with his licentious passions; and should the unhappy creature shrink from the insolent overture, he will sneeringly taunt her with pretence of modesty.

Chapter XVII.
A Wedding.

On the day before their arrival at New York, after dinner, Crayton arose from his seat, and placing himself by Mademoiselle, thus addressed the company—

"As we are now nearly arrived at our destined port, I think it but my duty to inform you, my friends, that this lady," (taking her hand), "has placed herself under my protection. I have seen and severely felt the anguish of her heart, and through every shade which cruelty or malice may throw over her, can discover the most amiable qualities. I thought it but necessary to mention my esteem for her before our disembarkation, as it is my fixed resolution, the morning after we land, to give her an undoubted title to my favour and protection by honourably uniting my fate to hers. I would wish every gentleman here, therefore to remember that her honour henceforth is mine, and," continued he, looking at Belcour, "should any man presume to speak in the least disrespectfully of her, I shall not hesitate to pronounce him a scoundrel."

Belcour cast at him a smile of contempt, and bowing profoundly low, wished Mademoiselle much joy in the proposed union; and assuring the Colonel that he need not be in the least apprehensive of any one throwing the least odium on the character of his lady, shook him by the hand with ridiculous gravity, and left the cabin.

The truth was, he was glad to be rid of La Rue, and so he was but freed from her he cared not who fell a victim to her infamous arts.

The inexperienced Charlotte was astonished at what she heard. She thought La Rue had, like herself, only been urged by the force of her attachment to Belcour, to quit her friends, and follow him to the seat of war: how wonderful then, that she should resolve to marry another man. It was certainly extremely wrong. It was indelicate. She mentioned her thoughts to Montraville. He laughed at her simplicity, called her a little idiot, and patting her on the cheek, said she knew nothing of the world. "If the world sanctifies such things, 'tis a very bad world, I think," said Charlotte. "Why I always understood they were to have been married when they arrived at New York. I am sure Mademoiselle told me Belcour promised to marry her."

"Well, and suppose he did?"

"Why he should be obliged to keep his word I think."

"Well, but I suppose he has changed his mind," said Montraville, "and then, you know, the case is altered."

Charlotte looked at him attentively for a moment. A full sense of her own situation rushed upon her mind. She burst into tears, and remained silent. Montraville too well understood the cause of her tears. He kissed her cheek, and bidding her not make herself uneasy, unable to bear the silent but keen remonstrance, hastily left her.

The next morning by sun rise they found themselves at anchor before the city of New York. A boat was ordered to convey the ladies on shore. Crayton accompanied them; and they were shewn to a house of public entertainment.[8] Scarcely were they seated, when the door opened, and the Colonel found himself in the arms of his daughter, who had landed a few minutes before him. The first transport of meeting subsided, Crayton introduced his daughter to Mademoiselle La Rue, as an old friend of her mother's, (for the artful French woman had really made it appear to the credulous Colonel that she was in the same convent with his first wife, and tho' much younger, received many tokens of her esteem and regard).

"If, Mademoiselle," said Mrs. Beauchamp, "you were the friend of my mother, you must be worthy the esteem of all good hearts."

8. A tavern or inn.

"Mademoiselle will soon honour our family," said Crayton, "by supplying the place that valuable woman filled; and as you are married, my dear, I think you will not blame—"

"Hush, my dear Sir," replied Mrs. Beauchamp: "I know my duty too well to scrutinize your conduct. Be assured, my dear father, your happiness is mine. I shall rejoice in it, and sincerely love the person who contributes to it. But tell me," continued she, turning to Charlotte, "who is this lovely girl? Is she your sister, Mademoiselle?"

A blush deep as the glow of the carnation suffused the cheeks of Charlotte.

"It is a young lady," replied the Colonel, "who came in the same vessel with us from England." He then drew his daughter aside, and told her in a whisper that Charlotte was the mistress of Montraville.

"What a pity!" said Mrs. Beauchamp, softly, (casting a most compassionate glance at her). "But surely her mind is not depraved. The goodness of her heart is depicted in her ingenuous countenance."

Charlotte caught the word pity. "And am I already fallen so low?" said she. A sigh escaped her, and a tear was ready to start, but Montraville appeared, and she checked the rising emotion. Mademoiselle went with the Colonel and his daughter to another apartment. Charlotte remained with Montraville and Belcour. The next morning the Colonel performed his promise, and La Rue became in due form Mrs. Crayton, exulted in her good fortune, and dared to look with an eye of contempt on the unfortunate but far less guilty Charlotte.

Chapter XVIII.
Reflections.

"And am I indeed fallen so low," said Charlotte, "as to be only pitied? Will the voice of approbation no more meet my ear? and shall I never again possess a friend whose face will wear a smile of joy whenever I approach? Alas! how thoughtless, how dreadfully imprudent have I been! I know not which is most painful to endure, the sneer of contempt, or the glance of compassion, which is depicted in the various countenances of my own sex: they are both equally humiliating. Ah! my dear parents, could you now see the child of your affections, the daughter whom you so dearly loved, a poor solitary being, without society, here wearing out her heavy hours in deep regret and anguish of heart, no kind friend of her own sex to whom she can unbosom her griefs, no beloved mother, no woman of character will appear in my company, and low as your Charlotte is fallen, she can not associate with infamy."

These were the painful reflections which occupied the mind of Charlotte. Montraville had placed her in a small house a few miles from New York: he gave her one female attendant, and supplied her with what money she wanted; but business and pleasure so entirely occupied his time, that he had little to devote to the woman whom he had brought from all her connections and robbed of innocence. Sometimes indeed he would steal out at the close of the evening and pass a few hours with her; and then so much was she attached to him, that all her sorrows were forgotten while blessed with his society: she would enjoy a walk by moonlight, or sit by him in a little arbour at the bottom of the garden, and play on the harp, accompanying it with her plaintive, harmonious voice. But often, very often, did he promise to renew his visits, and forgetful of his promise leave her to mourn her disappointment. What painful hours of expectation would she pass; she would sit at a window which looked toward a field he used to cross, counting the minutes and straining her eyes to catch the first glimpse of his person, till blinded with tears of disappointment, she would lean her head on her hands, and give free vent to her sorrows: then catching at some new hope, she would again renew her watchful position, till the shades of evening enveloped every object in a dusky cloud: she would then renew her complaints, and with a heart bursting with disappointed love and wounded sensibility, retire to a bed which remorse had strewed with thorns, and court in vain that comforter of weary nature (who seldom visits the unhappy) to come and steep her senses in oblivion.

Who can form an adequate idea of the sorrow that preyed upon the mind of Charlotte? The wife whose breast glows with affection to her husband, and who in return meets only indifference, can but faintly conceive her anguish. Dreadfully painful is the situation of such a woman, but she has many comforts of which our poor Charlotte was deprived. The duteous, faithful wife, though treated with indifference, has one solid pleasure within her own bosom, she can reflect that she has not deserved neglect—that she has ever fulfilled the duties of her station with the strictest exactness; she may hope, by constant assiduity and unremitted attention, to recall her wanderer, and be doubly happy in his returning affection; she knows he can not leave her to unite himself to another: he can not cast her out to poverty and contempt; she looks around her and sees the smile of friendly welcome, or the tear of affectionate consolation on the face of every person whom she favours with her esteem, and from all these circumstances she gathers comfort: but the poor girl by thoughtless passion led astray, who in parting with her honour has forfeited the esteem of the very man to whom she has sacrificed every thing dear and valuable in life, feels his indifference in the fruit of her own folly, and laments her want of power to recall his lost affection; she knows there is no tie but honour, and that in a man who has been guilty of seduction is but very feeble: he may leave her in a moment to shame and want; he may marry and forsake her for ever; and should he, she has no redress, no friendly soothing companion to pour into her wounded mind the balm of consolation, no benevolent hand to lead her back to the path of rectitude; she has disgraced her friends, forfeited the good opinion of the world, and undone herself: she feels herself a poor solitary being in the midst of surrounding multitudes; shame bows her to the earth, remorse tears her distracted mind, and guilt, poverty, and disease, close the dreadful scene: she sinks unnoticed to oblivion. The finger of contempt may point out to some passing daughter of youthful mirth the humble bed where lies this frail sister of mortality; and will she, in the unbounded gaiety of her heart, exult in her own unblemished fame, and triumph over the silent ashes of the dead? Oh no! has she a heart of sensibility she will stop and thus address the unhappy victim of folly—

"Thou had'st thy faults, but sure thy sufferings have expatiated them: thy errors brought thee to an early grave; but thou wert a fellow creature—thou hast been unhappy—then be those errors forgotten."

Then as she stoops to pluck the noxious weed from off the sod, a tear will fall and consecrate the spot to Charity.

For ever honoured be the sacred drop of humanity; the angel of mercy shall record its source, and the soul from whence it sprang shall be immortal.

My dear Madam, contract not your brow into a frown of disapprobation. I mean not to extenuate the faults of those unhappy women who fall victims to guilt and folly; but surely when we reflect how many errors we are ourselves subject to, how many secret faults lie hid in the recesses of our hearts, which we should blush to have brought into open day, (and yet those faults require the lenity and pity of a benevolent judge, or awful would be our prospect of futurity) I say, my dear Madam, when we consider this, we surely may pity the faults of others.

Believe me many an unfortunate female, who has once strayed into the thorny paths of vice, would gladly return to virtue was any generous friend to endeavour to raise and reassure her; but alas! it cannot be you say; the world would deride and scoff. Then let me tell you, Madam, 'tis a very unfeeling world, and does not deserve half the blessings which a bountiful Providence showers upon it.

Oh thou benevolent giver of all good! how shall we erring mortals dare to look up to thy mercy in the great day of retribution if we now uncharitably refuse to overlook the errors, or alleviate the miseries of our fellow creatures.

Chapter XIX.
A Mistake Discovered.

Julia Franklin was the only child of a man of large property, who at the age of eighteen left her independent mistress of an unencumbered income of seven hundred a year; she was a girl of a lively disposition, and humane susceptible heart: she resided in New York with an uncle, who loved her too well, and had too high an opinion of her prudence to scrutinize her actions so much as would have been necessary with many young ladies who were not blest with her discretion: she was at the time Montraville arrived at New York the life of society and the universal toast. Montraville was introduced to her by the following accident.

One night when he was upon guard, a dreadful fire broke out near Mr. Franklin's house, which in a few hours reduced that and several others to ashes; fortunately no lives were lost, and by the assiduity of the soldiers much valuable property was saved from the flames. In the midst of the confusion an old gentleman came up to Montraville, and putting a small box into his hands, cried—"Keep it, my good Sir, till I come to you again;" and then rushing again into the thickest of the croud, Montraville saw him no more. He waited till the fire was quite extinguished and the mob dispersed; but in vain: the old gentleman did not appear to claim his property; and Montraville fearing to make any enquiry least he should meet with impostors who might lay claim, without any legal right, to the box, carried it to his lodgings and locked it up: he naturally imagined that the person who committed it to his care knew him, and would in a day or two reclaim it; but several weeks passed on, and no enquiry being made, he began to be uneasy, and resolved to examine the contents of the box, and if they were, as he supposed, valuable, to spare no pains to discover, and restore them to the owner. Upon opening it, he found it contained jewels to a large amount, about two hundred pounds in money, and a miniature picture set for a bracelet. On examining the picture he thought he had somewhere seen features very like it, but could not recollect where. A few days after, being at a public assembly, he saw Miss Franklin, and the likeness was too evident to be mistaken: he enquired among his brother officers if any of them knew her, and found one who was upon terms of intimacy in the family: "then introduce me to her immediately," said he, "for I am certain I can inform her of something which will give her peculiar pleasure."

He was immediately introduced, found she was the owner of the jewels, and was invited to breakfast the next morning in order to [make] their restoration. This whole evening Montraville was honour'd with Julia's hand; the lively sallies of her wit, the elegance of her manner, powerfully charmed him: he forgot Charlotte, and indulged himself in saying every thing that was polite and tender to Julia. But on retiring, recollection returned. "What am I about?" said he: "though I can not marry Charlotte, I can not be villain enough to forsake her, nor must I dare to trifle with the heart of Julia Franklin. I will return this box," said he, "which has been the source of so much uneasiness already, and in the evening pay a visit to my poor melancholy Charlotte, and endeavour to forget this fascinating Julia."

He arose, dressed himself, and taking the picture out, "I will reserve this from the rest," said he, "and by presenting it to her when she thinks it is lost, enhance the value of the obligation." He repaired to Mr. Franklin's and found Julia in the breakfast parlour alone.

"How happy am I, Madam," said he, "that being the fortunate instrument of saving these jewels has been the means of procuring me the acquaintance of so amiable a lady. There are the jewels and money all safe."

"But where is the picture, Sir?" said Julia.

"Here, Madam. I would not willingly part with it."

"It is the portrait of my mother," said she, taking it from him; " 'tis all that remains." She pressed it to her lips, and a tear trembled in her eyes. Montraville glanced his eye on her grey night-gown and black ribbon, and his own feelings prevented a reply.

Julia Franklin was the very reverse of Charlotte Temple: she was tall, elegantly shaped, and possessed much of the air and manner of a woman of fashion; her complexion was a clear brown, enlivened with the glow of health, her eyes, full, black, and sparkling, darted their intelligent glances through long silken lashes; her hair was shining brown, and her features regular and striking; there was an air of innocent gaiety [that] played about her countenance, where good humour sat triumphant.

"I have been mistaken," said Montraville. "I imagined I loved Charlotte: but, alas! I am now too late convinced my attachment to her was merely the impulse of the moment. I fear I have not only entailed[9] lasting misery on that poor girl, but also thrown a barrier in the way of my own happiness, which it will be impossible to surmount. I feel I love Julia Franklin with ardour and sincerity; yet when in her presence I am sensible of my own inability to offer a heart worthy her acceptance and remain silent."

Full of these painful thoughts, Montraville walked out to see Charlotte: she saw him approach, and ran out to meet him: she banished from her countenance the air of discontent which ever appeared when he was absent, and met him with a smile of joy.

"I thought you had forgotten me, Montraville," said she, "and was very unhappy."

"I shall never forget you, Charlotte," he replied, pressing her hand.

The uncommon gravity of his countenance, and the brevity of his reply, alarmed her.

"You are not well," said she; "your hand is hot, your eyes are heavy; you are very ill."

"I am a villain," said he mentally, as he turned from her to hide his emotions.

"But come," continued she tenderly, "you shall go to bed, and I will sit by and watch you; you will be better when you have slept."

Montraville was glad to retire, and by pretending to sleep, hide the agitation of his mind from her penetrating eye. Charlotte watched[1] by him till a late hour, and then, laying softly down by his side, sunk into a profound sleep, from whence she awoke not till late the next morning.

Chapter XX.

Virtue never appears so amiable as when reaching forth her hand to raise a fallen sister.
Chapter of Accidents.

When Charlotte awoke, she missed Montraville; but thinking he might have arisen early to enjoy the beauties of the morning, she was preparing to follow him, when casting her eye on the table, she saw a note, and opening it hastily, found these words—

> "My dear Charlotte must not be surprised if she does not see me again for some time: unavoidable business will prevent me that pleasure: be assured I am quite well this morning; and what your fond imagination magnified into illness was nothing more than fatigue, which a few hours rest has entirely removed. Make yourself happy, and be certain of the unalterable friendship of
>
> "Montraville."

"Friendship!" said Charlotte emphatically as she finished the note, "is it come to this at last. Alas! poor forsaken Charlotte, thy doom is now but too apparent. Montraville is no longer interested in thy happiness, and shame, remorse, and disappointed love will henceforth be thy only attendants."

Though these were the ideas that involuntarily rushed upon the mind of Charlotte as she

---

9. To impose upon.   1. Stayed awake.

perused the fatal note, yet after a few hours had elapsed, the syren[2] Hope again took possession of her bosom, and she flattered herself she could, on a second perusal, discover an air of tenderness in the few lines he had left which at first had escaped her notice. "He certainly can not be so base as to leave me," said she; "and in styling himself[3] my friend, does he not promise to protect me. I will not torment myself with these causeless fears; I will place a confidence in his honour; and sure he will not be so unjust as to abuse it."

Just as she had by this manner of reasoning brought her mind to some tolerable degree of composure, she was surprised by a visit from Belcour. The dejection visible in Charlotte's countenance, her swollen eyes and neglected attire, at once told him she was unhappy: he made no doubt but Montraville had by his coldness alarmed her suspicions, and was resolved if possible to rouse her to jealousy, urge her to reproach him, and by that means occasion a breach between them. "If I can once convince her that she has a rival," said he, "she will listen to my passion if it is only to revenge his slights." Belcour knew but little of the female heart; and what he did know was only of those of loose and dissolute lives. He had no idea that a woman might fall a victim to imprudence, and yet retain so strong a sense of honour as to reject with horror and contempt every solicitation to a second fault. He never imagined that a gentle, generous female heart, once tenderly attached, when treated with unkindness might break, but would never harbour a thought of revenge.

His visit was not long, but before he went he fixed a scorpion in the heart of Charlotte, whose venom embittered every future hour of her life.

We will now return for a moment to Colonel Crayton. He had been three months married, and in that little time had discovered that the conduct of his lady was not so prudent as it ought to have been: but remonstrance was vain: her temper was violent; and to the Colonel's great misfortune he had conceived a sincere affection for her: she saw her own power, and with the art of a Circe,[4] made every action appear to him in what light she pleased: his acquaintances laughed at his blindness, his friends pitied his infatuation, his amiable daughter, Mrs. Beauchamp, in secret deplored the loss of her father's affection, and grieved that he should be so entirely swayed by an artful and, she much feared, infamous woman.

Mrs. Beauchamp was mild and engaging; she loved not the hurry and bustle of a city, and had prevailed on her husband to take a house a few miles from New York. Chance led her into the same neighbourhood with Charlotte; their houses stood within a short space of each other, and their gardens joined: she had not been long in her new habitation before the figure of Charlotte struck her; she recollected her interesting features; she saw the melancholy so conspicuous in her countenance, and her heart bled at the reflection, that perhaps deprived of honour, friends, all that was valuable in life, she was doomed to linger out a wretched existence in a strange land, and sink broken hearted into an untimely grave. "Would to heaven I could snatch her from so hard a fate," said she; "but the merciless world have barred the doors of compassion against a poor weak girl who perhaps had she one kind friend to raise and re-assure her, would gladly return to peace and virtue; nay even the woman who dares to pity and endeavour to recall a wandering sister, incurs the sneer of contempt and ridicule, for an action in which even angels are said to rejoice."

The longer Mrs. Beauchamp was a witness to the solitary life Charlotte led, the more she wished to speak to her, and often as she saw her cheeks wet with the tears of anguish, she would say—"Dear sufferer, how gladly would I pour into your heart the balm of consolation, were it not for the fear of derision."

But an accident soon happened which made her resolve to brave even the scoffs of the world rather than not enjoy the heavenly satisfaction of comforting a desponding fellow creature.

2. In Greek mythology, the sirens are sea nymphs who sing sweetly, luring mariners to destruction on the rocks of their island.

3. To "style oneself" is to profess to be.

4. In Homer's *Odyssey*, Circe is an enchantress who detains Odysseus for a year and turns his men into pigs.

Mrs. Beauchamp was an early riser. She was one morning walking in the garden, leaning on her husband's arm, when the sound of a harp attracted their notice: they listened attentively, and heard a soft melodious voice distinctly sing the following stanzas:

> *Thou glorious orb supremely bright,*
> *Just rising from the sea,*
> *To chear all nature with thy light*
> *What are thy beams to me?*
>
> *In vain thy glories bid me rise,*
> *To hail the new born day,*
> *Alas! my morning sacrifice*
> *Is still to weep and pray.*
>
> *For what are nature's charms combin'd,*
> *To one whose weary breast*
> *Can neither peace nor comfort find,*
> *Nor friend whereon to rest?*
>
> *Oh! never! never! whilst I live*
> *Can my heart's anguish cease;*
> *Come, friendly death, thy mandate give,*
> *And let me be at peace.*

" 'Tis poor Charlotte!" said Mrs. Beauchamp, the pellucid drop of humanity stealing down her cheek.

Captain Beauchamp was alarmed at her emotion. "What, Charlotte?" said he; "do you know her?"

In the accent of a pitying angel did she disclose to her husband Charlotte's unhappy situation, and the frequent wish she had formed of being serviceable to her. "I fear," continued she, "the poor girl has been basely betrayed; and if I thought you would not blame me, I would pay her a visit, offer her my friendship, and endeavour to restore to her heart that peace she seems to have lost, and so pathetically laments. Who knows, my dear," laying her hand affectionately on his arm, "who knows but she has left some kind affectionate parents to lament her errors, and would she return, they might with rapture receive the poor penitent, and wash away her faults in tears of joy. Oh! what a glorious reflection would it be for me could I be the happy instrument of restoring her. Her heart may not be depraved, Beauchamp."

"Exalted woman!" cried Beauchamp, embracing her, "how dost thou rise every moment in my esteem. Follow the impulse of thy generous heart, my Emily. Let prudes and fools censure, if they dare, and blame a sensibility they never felt, I will exultingly tell them that the heart that is truly virtuous is ever inclined to pity and forgive the errors of its fellow creatures."

A beam of exulting joy played round the animated countenance of Mrs. Beauchamp at these encomiums bestowed on her by a beloved husband; the most delightful sensations pervaded her heart; and having breakfasted, she prepared to visit Charlotte.

Chapter XXI.

> *Teach me to feel another's woe,*
> *To hide the fault I see,*
> *That mercy I to others show*
> *That mercy shew to me.*
>
> —Pope.

When Mrs. Beauchamp was dressed she began to feel embarrassed at the thought of beginning an acquaintance with Charlotte, and was distressed how to make the first visit. "I cannot go without some introduction," said she. "It will look so like impertinent curiosity." At length recollecting herself, she stepped into the garden, and gathering a few fine cucumbers, took them in her hand by way of apology for her visit.

A glow of conscious shame vermilioned Charlotte's face as Mrs. Beauchamp entered.

"You will pardon me, Madam," said she, "for not having before paid my respects to so amiable a neighbour; but we English people always keep up that reserve which is the characteristic of our nation wherever we go. I have taken the liberty to bring you a few cucumbers, for I had observed you had none in your garden."

Charlotte, though naturally polite and well bred, was so confused she could hardly speak. Her kind visitor endeavoured to relieve her by not noticing her embarrassment. "I am come, Madam," continued she, "to request you will spend the day with me. I shall be alone; and as we are both strangers in this country we may hereafter be extremely happy in each other's friendship."

"Your friendship, Madam," said Charlotte blushing, "is an honour to all who are favoured with it. Little as I have seen of this part of the world I am no stranger to Mrs. Beauchamp's goodness of heart and known humanity; but my friendship——" She paused, glanced her eye upon her own visible situation,[5] and in spite of her endeavours to suppress them burst into tears.

Mrs. Beauchamp guessed the source from whence those tears flowed. "You seem unhappy, Madam," said she: "shall I be thought worthy your confidence? will you entrust me with the cause of your sorrow and rest on my assurances to exert my utmost power to serve you." Charlotte returned a look of gratitude, but could not speak, and Mrs. Beauchamp continued—"My heart was interested in your behalf the first moment I saw you, and I only lament I had not made earlier overtures towards an acquaintance, but I flatter myself you will henceforth consider me as your friend."

"Oh Madam!" cried Charlotte, "I have forfeited the good opinion of all my friends; I have forsaken them and undone myself."

"Come, come, my dear," said Mrs. Beauchamp, "you must not indulge these gloomy thoughts: you are not I hope so miserable as you imagine yourself: endeavour to be composed, and let me be favoured with your company at dinner, when if you can bring yourself to think me your friend and repose a confidence in me, I am ready to convince you it shall not be abused." She then arose and bade her good morning.

At the dining hour Charlotte repaired to Mrs. Beauchamp's, and during dinner assumed as composed an aspect as possible; but when the cloth was removed, she summoned all her resolution and determined to make Mrs. Beauchamp acquainted with every circumstance preceding her unfortunate elopement, and the earnest desire she had to quit a way of life so repugnant to her feelings.

With the benignant aspect of an angel of mercy did Mrs. Beauchamp listen to the artless tale: she was shocked to the soul to find how large a share La Rue had in the seduction of this amiable girl, and a tear fell when she reflected so vile a woman was now the wife of her father. When Charlotte had finished, she gave her a little time to collect her scattered spirits, and then asked her if she had never written to her friends.

"Oh yes, Madam," said she, "frequently: but I have broke their hearts: they are all either dead or have cast me off for ever, for I have never received a single line from them."

"I rather suspect," said Mrs. Beauchamp, "they have never had your letters: but suppose you were to hear from them, and they were willing to receive you, would you then leave this cruel Montraville and return to them?"

"Would I?" said Charlotte, clasping her hands; "would not the poor sailor tossed on a tempestuous ocean, threatened every moment with death, gladly return to the shore he had

5. Her pregnancy.

left to trust to its deceitful calmness? Oh, my dear Madam, I would return, though to do it I were obliged to walk barefoot over a burning desert, and beg a scanty pittance of each traveller to support my existence. I would endure it all chearfully could I but once more see my dear blessed mother, hear her pronounce my pardon, and bless me before I died; but alas! I shall never see her more; she has blotted the ungrateful Charlotte from her remembrance, and I shall sink to the grave loaded with her's and my father's curse."

Mrs. Beauchamp endeavoured to soothe her. "You shall write to them again," said she, "and I will see that the letter is sent by the first pacquet that sails for England; in the mean time keep up your spirits, and hope every thing, by daring to deserve it."

She then turned the conversation, and Charlotte having taken a cup of tea wished her benevolent friend a good-evening.

Chapter XXII.
Sorrows of the Heart.

When Charlotte got home she endeavoured to collect her thoughts, and took up a pen in order to address those dear parents whom, spite of her errors, she still loved with the utmost tenderness, but vain was every effort to write with the least coherence; her tears fell so fast they almost blinded her; and as she proceeded to describe her unhappy situation she became so agitated she was obliged to give over the attempt and retire to bed, where, overcome with the fatigue her mind had undergone, she fell into a slumber which greatly refreshed her, and she arose in the morning with spirits more adequate to the painful task she had to perform, and after several attempts at length concluded the following letter to her mother:

To Mrs. Temple.   New York.

"Will my once kind, my ever beloved mother, deign to receive a letter from her guilty, but repentant child? or has she justly incensed at my ingratitude, driven the unhappy Charlotte from her remembrance? Alas! thou much injured mother! shouldst thou even disown me, I dare not complain, because I know I have deserved it: but yet, believe me, guilty as I am, and cruelly as I have disappointed the hopes of the fondest parents that ever girl had, even in the moment when, forgetful of my duty, I fled from you and happiness, even then I loved you most, and my heart bled at the thought of what you would suffer. Oh! never, never! whilst I have existence, will the agony of that moment be erased from my memory. It seemed like the separation of soul and body. What can I plead in excuse for my conduct? alas! nothing! That I loved my seducer is but too true; yet powerful as that passion is when operating in a young heart glowing with sensibility, it never would have conquered my affection to you, my beloved parents, had I not been encouraged, nay urged to take the fatally imprudent step, by one of my own sex who under the mask of friendship drew me on to ruin. Yet think not your Charlotte was so lost as to voluntarily rush into a life of infamy, no, my dear mother, deceived by the specious appearance of my betrayer, and every suspicion lulled asleep by the most solemn promises of marriage, I thought not those promises would so easily be forgotten. I never once reflected that the man who could stoop to seduction would not hesitate to forsake the wretched object of his passion, whenever his capricious heart grew weary of her tenderness. When we arrived at this place, I vainly expected him to fulfil his engagements, but was at last fatally convinced he had never intended to make me his wife, or if he had once thought of it, his mind was now altered. I scorned to claim from his humanity what I could not obtain from his love: I was conscious of having forfeited the only gem that could render me respectable in the eye of the world.[6] I locked my sorrows in my own bosom, and bore my injuries in silence. But how shall I proceed? This man, this cruel Montraville, for whom I sacrificed honour, happiness, and the love of my friends, no longer looks on me with affection, but scorns the credulous girl whom his art has made miserable. Could you see me, my dear parents, without society, without friends, stung with remorse, and (I feel the burning blush of shame dye my cheeks while I write it) tortured with the pangs of disappointed love; cut to the soul by the indifference of him, who, having deprived me of every other comfort, no longer thinks it worth his while to soothe the heart where he has planted the thorn of never ceasing regret. My daily employment is to think of you and weep, to pray for your happiness, and deplore my own folly: my nights are scarce more happy, for if by chance I close my weary eyes and hope some small forgetfulness of sorrow, some little time to pass in sweet oblivion, fancy, still waking, wafts me home to you: I see your beloved forms, I kneel and hear the blessed words of peace and pardon. Extatic joy pervades my soul; I reach my arms to catch your dear embraces; the motion chases the illusive dream; I wake to real misery. At other times I see my father angry and frowning, point to horrid caves, where, on the cold damp ground, in the agonies of death, I see my dear mother and my revered grandfather. I strive to raise you; you push me from you, and shrieking cry—"Charlotte thou hast murdered me!" Horror and despair tear every tortured nerve; I start and leave my restless bed weary and unrefreshed.

"Shocking as these reflections are, I have yet one more dreadful than the rest. Mother, my dear mother! do not let me quite break your heart when I tell you, in a few months I shall bring into the world an innocent witness of my guilt. Oh my bleeding heart, I shall bring a poor little helpless creature, heir to infamy and shame.

"This alone has urged me once more to address you, to interest you in behalf of this poor unborn, and beg you to extend your protection to the child of your lost Charlotte; for my own part I have wrote so often, so frequently have pleaded for forgiveness, and entreated to be received once more beneath the paternal roof, that having received no answer, not even one line, I much fear you have cast me from you for ever.

"But sure you cannot refuse to protect my innocent infant: it partakes not of its mother's guilt. Oh my father, oh beloved mother, now do I feel the anguish I inflicted on your hearts recoiling with double force upon my own.

"If my child should be a girl (which heaven forbid) tell her the unhappy fate of her mother, and teach her to avoid my errors; if a boy, teach him to lament my miseries, but tell him not who inflicted them, least in wishing to revenge his mother's injuries he should wound the peace of his father.

"And now, dear friends of my soul, kind guardians of my infancy, farewell. I feel I never more must hope to see you; the anguish of my heart strikes at the strings of life, and in a short time I shall be at rest. Oh could I but receive your blessing and forgiveness before I died, it would smooth my passage to the peaceful grave, and be a blessed foretaste of a happy eternity. I beseech you curse me not, my adored parents, but let a tear of pity and pardon fall to the memory of your lost

Charlotte.

6. Her virginity.

Chapter XXIII.
A Man May Smile and Smile and Be a Villain.[7]

While Charlotte was enjoying some small degree of comfort in the consoling friendship of Mrs. Beauchamp, Montraville was advancing rapidly in his affection toward Miss Franklin. Julia was an amiable girl; she saw only the fair side of his character; she possessed an independent fortune, and resolved to be happy with the man of her heart though his rank and fortune were by no means so exalted as she had a right to expect; she saw the passion which Montraville struggled to conceal; she wondered at his timidity, but imagined the distance fortune had placed between them occasioned his backwardness,[8] and made every advance which strict prudence and a becoming modesty would permit. Montraville saw with pleasure he was not indifferent to her; but a spark of honour which animated his bosom would not suffer him to take advantage of her partiality. He was well acquainted with Charlotte's situation, and he thought there would be a double cruelty in forsaking her at such a time; and to marry Miss Franklin, while honour, humanity, every sacred law, obliged him still to protect and support Charlotte, was a baseness which his soul shuddered at.

He communicated his uneasiness to Belcour: it was the very thing this pretended friend had wished. "And do you really," said he, laughing, "hesitate at marrying the lovely Julia and becoming master of her fortune, because a little, foolish, fond girl chose to leave her friends and run away with you to America. Dear Montraville, act more like a man of sense: this whining, pining Charlotte, who occasions you so much uneasiness, would have eloped with somebody else, if she had not with you."

"Would to heaven," said Montraville, "I had never seen her; my regard for her was but the momentary passion of desire; but I feel I shall love and revere Julia Franklin as long as I live; yet to leave poor Charlotte in her present situation would be cruel beyond description."

"Oh my good sentimental friend," said Belcour, "do you imagine nobody has a right to provide for the brat but yourself."

Montraville started. "Sure," said he, "you cannot mean to insinuate that Charlotte is false!"

"I don't insinuate it," said Belcour, "I know it."

Montraville turned pale as ashes. "Then there is no faith in woman," said he.

"While I thought you were attached to her," said Belcour with an air of indifference, "I never wished to make you uneasy by mentioning her perfidy, but as I know you love and are beloved by Miss Franklin, I was determined not to let these foolish scruples of honour step between you and happiness, or your tenderness for the peace of a perfidious girl prevent your uniting yourself to a woman of honour."

"Good heavens!" said Montraville, "what poignant reflections does a man endure who sees a lovely woman plunged in infamy, and is conscious he was her first seducer; but are you certain of what you say, Belcour?"

"So far," replied he, "that I myself have received advances from her which I would not take advantage of out of regard to you: but hang it, think no more about her. I dined at Franklin's to-day, and Julia bid me seek and bring you to tea: so come along, my lad, make good use of opportunity, and seize the gifts of fortune while they are within your reach."

Montraville was too much agitated to pass a happy evening even in the company of Julia Franklin: he determined to visit Charlotte early the next morning, tax her with her falsehood and take an everlasting leave of her; but when the morning came, he was commanded on duty, and for six weeks was prevented from putting his design in execution. At length he found an hour to spare, and walked out to spend it with Charlotte: it was near four o'clock in the afternoon when he arrived at her cottage; she was not in the parlour, and without calling the

---

7. *Hamlet*, 1.5.   8. Shyness, reluctance.

servant he walked up stairs, thinking to find her in her bed room. He opened the door, and the first object that met his eyes was Charlotte asleep on the bed and Belcour by her side.

"Death and distraction," said he, stamping, "this is too much. Rise, villain, and defend yourself." Belcour sprang from the bed. The noise awoke Charlotte; terrified at the furious appearance of Montraville and seeing Belcour with him in the chamber, she caught hold of his arm as he stood by the bed side, and eagerly asked what was the matter.

"Treacherous, infamous girl," said he, "can you ask? How came he here?" pointing to Belcour.

"As heaven is my witness," replied she weeping, "I do not know. I have not seen him for these three weeks."

"Then you confess he sometimes visits you?"

"He came sometimes by your desire."

" 'Tis false; I never desired him to come, and you know I did not; but mark me, Charlotte, from this instant our connection is at an end. Let Belcour or any other of your favoured lovers take you and provide for you, I have done with you forever."

He was then going to leave her; but starting wildly from the bed, she threw herself on her knees before him, protesting her innocence, and entreating him not to leave her. "Oh Montraville" said she, "kill me, for pity's sake kill me, but do not doubt my fidelity. Do not leave me in this horrid situation; for the sake of your unborn child, oh! spurn not the wretched mother from you."

"Charlotte," said he, with a firm voice, "I shall take care that neither you nor your child want any thing in the approaching painful hour; but we meet no more." He then endeavoured to raise her from the ground; but in vain; she clung about his knees, entreating him to believe her innocent, and conjuring Belcour to clear up the dreadful mystery.

Belcour cast on Montraville a smile of contempt: it irritated him almost to madness; he broke from the feeble arms of the distressed girl; she shrieked and fell prostrate on the floor.

Montraville instantly left the house and returned hastily to the city.

Chapter XXIV.
Mystery Developed.

Unfortunately for Charlotte, about three weeks before this unhappy rencontre,[9] Captain Beauchamp, being ordered to Rhode Island, his lady had accompanied him, so that Charlotte was deprived of her friendly advice and consoling society. The afternoon on which Montraville had visited her she had found herself languid and fatigued, and after making a very slight dinner, had lain down to endeavour to recruit her exhausted spirits, and contrary to her expectations had fallen asleep. She had not long been laid down, when Belcour arrived, for he took every opportunity of visiting her, and striving to awaken her resentment against Montraville. He enquired of the servant where her mistress was, and being told she was asleep, took up a book to amuse himself: having sat a few minutes, he by chance cast his eyes towards the road, and saw Montraville approaching; he instantly conceived the diabolical scheme of ruining the unhappy Charlotte in his opinion for ever; he therefore stole softly up stairs, and laying himself by her side with the greatest precaution for fear she should awake, was in that situation discovered by his credulous friend.

When Montraville spurned the weeping Charlotte from him, and left her almost distracted with terror and despair, Belcour raised her from the floor, and leading her down stairs, assumed the part of a tender, consoling friend; she listened to the arguments he advanced

9. Unplanned meeting.

with apparent composure; but this was only the calm of a moment: the remembrance of Montraville's recent cruelty again rushed upon her mind: she pushed him from her with some violence, and crying—"Leave me, Sir, I beseech you leave me, for much I fear you have been the cause of my fidelity being suspected; go, leave me to the accumulated miseries my own imprudence has brought upon me."

She then left him with precipitation, and retiring to her own apartments, threw herself on the bed, and gave vent to an agony of grief which it is impossible to describe.

It now occurred to Belcour that she might possibly write to Montraville and endeavour to convince him of her innocence: he was well aware of her pathetic remonstrances, and sensible of the tenderness of Montraville's heart, resolved to prevent any letters ever reaching him: he therefore called the servant, and by the powerful persuasion of a bribe prevailed with her to promise whatever letters her mistress might write should be sent to him. He then left a polite, tender note for Charlotte, and returned to New York. His first business was to seek Montraville, and endeavour to convince him that what had happened would ultimately tend to his happiness: he found him in his apartment, solitary, pensive, and wrapped in disagreeable reflections.

"Why how now, whining, pining lover?" said he, clapping him on the shoulder. Montraville started; a momentary flush of resentment crossed his cheek, but instantly gave place to a deathlike paleness, occasioned by painful remembrance—remembrance awakened by that monitor, whom, though we may in vain endeavour, we can never entirely silence.

"Belcour," said he, "you have injured me in a tender point."

"Prithee, Jack," replied Belcour, "do not make a serious matter of it: how could I refuse the girl's advances? and thank heaven she is not your wife."

"True," said Montraville; "but she was innocent when I first knew her. It was I seduced her, Belcour. Had it not been for me she had still been virtuous and happy in the affection and protection of her family."

"Pshaw," replied Belcour, laughing, "if you had not taken advantage of her easy nature, some other would, and where is the difference, pray?"

"I wish I had never seen her," cried he passionately, and starting from his seat. "Oh that cursed French woman," added he with vehemence, "had it not been for her, I might have been happy—" He paused.

"With Julia Franklin," said Belcour. The name, like a sudden spark of electric fire, seemed for a moment to suspend his faculties—for a moment he was transfixed; but recovering, he caught Belcour's hand and cried—"Stop! stop! I beseech you name not the lovely Julia and the wretched Montraville in the same breath. I am a seducer, a mean, ungenerous seducer of unsuspecting innocence. I dare not hope that purity like hers would stoop to unite itself with black premeditated guilt: yet by heavens I swear, Belcour, I thought I loved the lost, abandoned Charlotte till I saw Julia—I thought I never could forsake her; but the heart is deceitful, and I now can plainly discriminate between the impulse of a youthful passion, and the pure flame of disinterested affection."

At that instant Julia Franklin passed the window, leaning on her uncle's arm. She courtesied as she passed, and with the bewitching smile of modest chearfulness cried—"Do you bury yourselves in the house this fine evening, gents?" There was something in the voice! the manner! the look! that was altogether irresistible. "Perhaps she wishes my company," said Montraville mentally, as he snatched up his hat: "if I thought she loved me, I would confess my errors, and trust to her generosity to pity and pardon me." He soon overtook her, and offering her his arm they sauntered to pleasant, but unfrequented walks. Belcour drew Mr. Franklin on one side and entered into a political discourse: they walked faster than the young people, and Belcour by some means, contrived entirely to lose sight of them. It was a fine evening in the beginning of autumn; the last remains of day light faintly streaked the western sky, while the moon with pale and virgin luster in the room of gorgeous gold and purple, ornamented the canopy of heaven with silver fleecy clouds which now and then half hid her lovely face, and by partly concealing heightened every beauty; the zephyrs[1] whispered softly through the trees, which now began to shed their leafy honours; a solemn silence reigned: and to a happy mind an evening such as this would give serenity and calm unruffled pleasure: but to Montraville, while it soothed the turbulence of his passions it brought increase of melancholy reflections. Julia was leaning on his arm: he took her hand in his, and pressing it tenderly, sighed deeply, but continued silent. Julia was embarrassed; she wished to break a silence so unaccountable, but was unable; she loved Montraville, she saw he was unhappy, and wished to know the cause of his uneasiness, but that innate modesty which nature has implanted in the female breast prevented her enquiring. "I am bad company, Miss Franklin," said he, at last recollecting himself; "but I have met with something to-day that has greatly distressed me, and I can not shake off the disagreeable impression it has made on my mind."

"I am sorry," she replied, "that you have any cause of inquietude. I am sure if you were as happy as you deserve, and as all your friends wish you——" She hesitated. "And might I," replied he, with some animation, "presume to rank the amiable Julia in that number?"

"Certainly," said she, "the service you have rendered me, the knowledge of your worth, all combine to make me esteem you."

"Esteem! my lovely Julia," said he passionately, "is but a poor cold word. I would if I dared, if I thought I merited your attention—but no I must not—honour forbids. I am beneath your notice, Julia, I am miserable, and can not hope to be otherwise."

"Alas!" said Julia, "I pity you."

"Oh thou condescending[2] charmer," said he, "how that sweet word chears my sad heart. Indeed if you knew all, you would pity; but at the same time I fear you would despise me."

Just then they were again joined by Mr. Franklin and Belcour. It had interrupted an interesting discourse. They found it impossible to converse on indifferent subjects, and proceeded home in silence. At Mr. Franklin's door Montraville again pressed Julia's hand, and faintly articulating "good-night," retired to his lodgings, dispirited and wretched, from a consciousness that he deserved not the affection with which he plainly saw he was honoured.

Chapter XXV.
Reception of a Letter.

"And where now is our poor Charlotte?" said Mr. Temple one evening as the cold blasts of autumn whistled rudely over the heath, and the yellow appearance of the distant wood spoke the near approach of winter. In vain the chearful fire blazed on the hearth, in vain was he surrounded by all the comforts of life; the parent was still alive in his heart, and when he thought that perhaps his once darling child was ere this exposed to all the miseries of want in a distant land, without a friend to sooth and comfort her, without the benignant look of compassion to chear, or the angelic voice of pity to pour the balm of consolation on her wounded heart; when he thought of this, his whole soul dissolved in tenderness; and while he wiped the tear of anguish from the eye of his patient uncomplaining Lucy, he struggled to suppress the sympathizing drop that started in his own. "Oh my poor girl," said Mrs. Temple, "how must she be altered, else surely she would have relieved our agonizing minds by one line to say she lived—to say she had not quite forgot the parents who almost idolized her."

"Gracious heaven," said Mr. Temple, starting from his seat, "who would wish to be a father, to experience the agonizing pangs inflicted on a parent's heart by the ingratitude of

---

1. Gentle breezes.
2. The word did not have the negative connotations it holds in modern usage.

a child?" Mrs. Temple wept: her father took her hand: he would have said, "be comforted, my child," but the words died on his tongue. The sad silence that ensued was interrupted by a loud rap at the door. In a moment a servant entered with a letter in his hand.

Mrs. Temple took it from him: she cast her eyes upon the superscription; she knew the writing. " 'Tis Charlotte," said she, eagerly breaking the seal, "she has not quite forgot us." But before she had half gone through the contents, a sudden sickness seized her; she grew cold and giddy, and putting it into her husband's hands, she cried—"Read it: I cannot." Mr. Temple attempted to read it aloud, but frequently paused to give vent to his tears. "My poor deluded child," said he, when he had finished.

"Oh shall we not forgive the dear penitent?" said Mrs. Temple. "We must, we will, my love; she is willing to return, and 'tis our duty to receive her."

"Father of mercy," said Mr. Eldridge, raising his clasped hands, "let me but live once more to see the dear wanderer restored to her afflicted parents, and take me from this world of sorrow whenever it seemeth best to thy wisdom."

"Yes, we will receive her," said Mr. Temple; "we will endeavour to heal her wounded spirit, and speak peace and comfort to her agitated soul. I will write to her to return immediately."

"Oh!" said Mrs. Temple, "I would, if possible, fly to her, support and chear the dear sufferer in the approaching hour of distress, and tell her how nearly penitence is allied to virtue. Cannot we go and conduct her home, my love?" continued she, laying her hand on his arm. "My father will surely forgive our absence if we go to bring home his darling."

"You cannot go, my Lucy," said Mr. Temple: "the delicacy of your frame would but poorly sustain the fatigue of a long voyage; but I will go and bring the gentle penitent to your arms: we may still see many years of happiness."

The struggle in the bosom of Mrs. Temple between maternal and conjugal tenderness was long and painful. At length the former triumphed, and she consented that her husband should set forward to New York by the first opportunity: she wrote to her Charlotte in the tenderest, most consoling manner, and looked forward to the happy hour when she would again embrace her with the most animated hope.

Chapter XXVI.
What Might Be Expected.

In the mean time the passion Montraville had conceived for Julia Franklin daily encreased, and he saw evidently how much he was beloved by that amiable girl: he was likewise strongly prepossessed with an idea of Charlotte's perfidy. What wonder then if he gave himself up to the delightful sensation which pervaded his bosom; and finding no obstacle arise to oppose his happiness, he solicited and obtained the hand of Julia. A few days before his marriage, he thus addressed Belcour:

"Though Charlotte, by her abandoned conduct, has thrown herself from my protection, I still hold myself bound to support her till relieved from her present condition, and also to provide for the child. I do not intend to see her again, but I will place a sum of money in your hands, which will amply supply her with every convenience; but should she require more let her have it, and I will see it repaid. I wish I could prevail on the poor deluded girl to return to her friends: she was an only child, and I make no doubt but they would joyfully receive her; it would shock me greatly to see her henceforth leading a life of infamy, as I should always accuse myself as being the primary cause of all her errors. If she should choose to remain under your protection, be kind to her, Belcour, I conjure you. Let not satiety prompt you to treat her in such a manner as may drive her to actions which necessity might urge her to, while her better reason disapprove them: she shall never want a friend while I live, but I never more desire to behold her; her presence would be always painful to me, and a glance from her eye would call the blush of conscious guilt into my cheek.

"I will write a letter to her, which you may deliver when I am gone, as I shall go to St. Eustatia the day after my union with Julia, who will accompany me."

Belcour promised to fulfil the request of his friend, though nothing was further from his intentions than the least design of delivering the letter, or making Charlotte acquainted with the provision Montraville had made for her; he was bent on the complete ruin of the unhappy girl, and supposed, by reducing her to an entire dependence on him, to bring her by degrees to consent to gratify his ungenerous passion.

The evening before the day appointed for the nuptials of Montraville and Julia, the former retired early to his apartment, and ruminating on the past scenes of his life, suffered the keenest remorse in the remembrance of Charlotte's seduction. "Poor girl," said he, "I will at least write and bid her adieu; I will too endeavour to awaken that love of virtue in her bosom which her unfortunate attachment to me has extinguished." He took up the pen and began to write, but words were denied him. How could he address the woman whom he had seduced, and whom, though he thought unworthy his tenderness, he was about to bid adieu for ever? How should he tell her that he was going to abjure her, to enter into the most indissoluble ties with another, and that he could not even own the infant which she bore as his child? Several letters were begun and destroyed: at length he completed the following:

To Charlotte.

"Though I have taken up my pen to address you, my poor injured girl, I feel I am inadequate to the task: yet however painful the endeavour, I could not resolve upon leaving you forever without one kind line to bid you adieu, to tell you how my heart bleeds at the remembrance of what you was before you saw the hated Montraville. Even now imagination paints the scene, when, torn by contending passions, when, struggling between love and duty, you fainted in my arms, and I lifted you into the chaise: I see the agony of your mind, when, recovering, you found yourself on the road to Portsmouth: but how, my gentle girl, how could you, when so justly impressed with the value of virtue, how could you, when loving as I thought you loved me, yield to the solicitation of Belcour?

"Oh Charlotte, conscience tells me it was I, villain that I am; who first taught you the allurements of guilty pleasure, it was I dragged you from the calm repose which innocence and virtue ever enjoy; and can I, dare I tell you, it was not love prompted to the horrid deed? No, thou dear fallen angel, believe your repentant Montraville when he tells you that the man who truly loves will never betray the object of his affection. Adieu, Charlotte: could you still find charms in a life of unoffending innocence, return to your parents; you shall never want[3] the means of support both for yourself and child. Oh! gracious heaven! may that child be entirely free from the vices of its father and the weakness of its mother.

"To-morrow—but no, I can not tell you what to-morrow will produce; Belcour will inform you: he also has cash for you, which I beg you will ask for whenever you may want it. Once more adieu: believe me could I hear you was returned to your friends, and enjoying that tranquility of which I have robbed you, I should be as completely happy as even you, in your fondest hours, could wish me, but till then a gloom will obscure the brightest prospects of

                                                 "Montraville."

3. Lack.

After he had sealed this letter he threw himself on the bed and enjoyed a few hours repose. Early in the morning Belcour tapped at his door: he arose hastily, and prepared to meet his Julia at the altar.

"This is the letter to Charlotte," said he, giving it to Belcour: "take it to her when we are gone to Eustatia; and I conjure you, my dear friend, not to use any sophistical[4] arguments to prevent her return to virtue; but should she incline that way, encourage her in the thought, and assist her to put her design in execution."

Chapter XXVII.

Pensive she mourn'd and hung her languid head,
Like a fair lilly overcharg'd with dew.

Charlotte had now been left almost three months a prey to her own melancholy reflections— sad companions indeed; nor did any one break in upon her solitude but Belcour, who once or twice called to enquire after her health, and tell her he had in vain endeavoured to bring Montraville to hear reason; and once, but only once, was her mind cheared by the receipt of an affectionate letter from Mrs. Beauchamp. Often had she wrote to her perfidious seducer, and with the most persuasive eloquence endeavoured to convince him of her innocence; but these letters were never suffered to reach the hands of Montraville, or they must, though on the very eve of marriage, have prevented his deserting the wretched girl. Real anguish of heart had in a great measure faded her charms; her cheeks were pale from want of rest, and her eyes, by frequent, indeed almost continued weeping, were sunk and heavy. Sometimes a gleam of hope would play about her heart when she thought of her parents—"They cannot surely," she would say, "refuse to forgive me; or should they deny their pardon to me, they will not hate my innocent infant on account of its mother's errors." How often did the poor mourner wish for the consoling presence of the benevolent Mrs. Beauchamp. "If she were here," she would cry, "she would certainly comfort me, and sooth the distraction of my soul."

She was sitting one afternoon wrapped in these melancholy reflections, when she was interrupted by the entrance of Belcour. Great as the alteration was which incessant sorrow had made on her person, she was still interesting, still charming, and the unhallowed flame which had urged Belcour to plant dissension between her and Montraville still raged in his bosom: he was determined, if possible, to make her his mistress; nay he had even conceived the diabolical scheme of taking her to New York, and making her appear in every public place where it was likely she should meet Montraville, that he might be a witness to his unmanly triumph.

When he entered the room where Charlotte was sitting, he assumed the look of tender consolatory friendship. "And how does my lovely Charlotte?" said he, taking her hand: "I fear you are not so well as I could wish."

"I am not well, Mr. Belcour," said she, "very far from it; but the pains and infirmities of the body I could easily bear, nay submit to them with patience, were they not aggravated by the almost insupportable anguish of my mind."

"You are not happy, Charlotte," said he, with a look of well dissembled sorrow.

"Alas!" replied she, mournfully shaking her head, "how can I be happy, deserted and forsaken as I am, without a friend of my own sex to whom I can unburthen my full heart, nay my fidelity suspected by the very man for whom I have sacrificed every thing valuable in life, for whom I have made myself a poor despised creature, an outcast from society, an object only of contempt and pity."

---

4. Specious, fallacious.

"You think too meanly of yourself, Miss Temple: there is no one who would dare to treat you with contempt: all who have the pleasure of knowing you must admire and esteem. You are lonely here, my dear girl; give me leave to conduct you to New York, where the agreeable society of some ladies, to whom I will introduce you, will dispel these sad thoughts, and I shall again see returning chearfulness animate those lovely features."

"Oh never! never!" cried Charlotte, emphatically: "the virtuous part of my sex will scorn me, and I will never associate with infamy. No, Belcour, here let me hide my shame and sorrow; here let me spend my few remaining days in obscurity, unknown and unpitied: here let me die unlamented, and my name sink to oblivion." Here her tears stopped her utterance. Belcour was awed to silence: he dared not interrupt her; and after a moment's pause she proceeded—"I once had conceived the thought of going to New York to seek out the still dear though cruel, ungenerous Montraville, to throw myself at his feet and entreat his compassion; heaven knows, not for myself; if I am no longer beloved, I will not be indebted to his pity to redress my injuries, but I would have knelt and entreated him not to forsake my poor unborn——" She could say no more; a crimson glow rushed over her cheeks, and covering her face with her hands she sobbed aloud.

Something like humanity was awakened in Belcour's breast by this pathetic[5] speech: he arose and walked toward the window; but the selfish passion which had taken possession of his heart soon stifled these finer emotions; and he thought if Charlotte was once convinced she had no longer any dependence on Montraville, she would more readily throw herself on his protection. Determined, therefore, to inform her of all that had happened, he again resumed his seat; and finding she began to be more composed, enquired if she had ever heard from Montraville since the unfortunate rencontre[6] in her bed chamber.

"Ah no!" said she, "I fear I shall never hear from him again."

"I am greatly of your opinion," said Belcour, "for he has been for some time past greatly attached——"

At the word "attached," a deathlike paleness overspread the countenance of Charlotte, but she applied to some hartshorn which stood beside her, and Belcour proceeded.

"He has been for some time past greatly attached to one Miss Franklin, a pleasing, lively girl, with a large fortune."

"She may be richer, may be handsomer," cried Charlotte, "but cannot love him so well. Oh may she beware of his art and not trust him too far as I have done."

"He addresses her publicly," said he, "and it was rumoured they were to be married before he sailed for Eustatia, whither his company is ordered."

"Belcour," said Charlotte, seizing his hand and gazing at him earnestly, while her pale lips trembled with convulsive agony, "tell me, and tell me truly, I beseech you, do you think he can be such a villain as to marry another woman, and leave me to die with want and misery in a strange land: tell me what you think; I can bear it very well; I will not shrink from this heaviest stroke of fate; I have deserved my afflictions, and I will endeavour to bear them as I ought."

"I fear," said Belcour, "he can be that villain."

"Perhaps," cried she, eagerly interrupting him, "perhaps he is married already: come let me know the worst," continued she with an affected look of composure: "you need not be afraid, I shall not send the fortunate lady a bowl of poison."

"Well then, my dear girl," said he, deceived by her appearance, "they were married on Thursday, and yesterday morning they sailed for Eustatia."

"Married—gone—say you?" cried she, in a distracted accent; "what without a last farewell, without one thought on my unhappy situation. Oh Montraville, may God forgive your perfidy." She shrieked, and Belcour sprang forward just in time to prevent her falling to the

---

5. In the context of sentimental fiction, "pathetic"   6. Sudden meeting.
    holds positive connotations.

floor. Alarming faintings now succeeded each other and she was conveyed to her bed, from whence she earnestly prayed she might never more arise. Belcour stayed with her that night, and in the morning found her in a high fever. The fits she had been seized with had greatly terrified him; and confined as she now was to a bed of sickness, she was no longer an object of desire: it is true for several days he went constantly to see her, but her pale, emaciated appearance disgusted him: his visits became less frequent; he forgot the solemn charge given him by Montraville; he even forgot the money entrusted to his care; and, the burning blush of indignation and shame tinges my cheek while I write it, this disgrace to humanity and manhood at length forgot even the injured Charlotte; and attracted by the blooming health of a farmer's daughter, whom he had seen in his frequent excursions to the country, he left the unhappy girl to sink unnoticed to the grave, a prey to sickness, grief, and penury; while he, having triumphed over the virtue of the artless cottager, rioted in all the intemperance of luxury and lawless pleasure.

Chapter XXVIII.
A Trifling Retrospect.

"Bless my heart," cries my young, volatile reader, "I shall never have patience to get through these volumes, there are so many ahs! and ohs! so much fainting, tears and distress, I am sick to death of the subject." My dear, chearful, innocent girl, for innocent I will suppose you to be, or you would acutely feel the woes of Charlotte, did conscience say thus might it have been with me, had not Providence interposed to snatch me from destruction: therefore my lively, innocent girl, I must request your patience: I am writing a tale of truth: I mean to write it to the heart: but if perchance the heart is rendered impenetrable by unbounded prosperity, or a continuance in vice, I expect not my tale to please, nay I even expect it will be thrown by with disgust. But softly, gentle fair one; I pray you throw it not aside till you have perused the whole; mayhap you may find something therein to repay you for the trouble. Methinks I see a sarcastic smile sit on your countenance—"And what," cry you, "does the conceited author suppose we can glean from these pages, if Charlotte is held up as an object of terror, to prevent us from falling into guilty errors? does not La Rue triumph in her shame, and, by adding art to guilt, obtain the affection of a worthy man and rise to a station where she is beheld with respect, and chearfully received into all companies. What then is the moral you would inculcate? Would you wish us to think that a deviation from virtue, if covered by art and hypocrisy, is not an object of detestation, but on the contrary shall raise us to fame and honour? while the hapless girl who falls a victim to her too great sensibility, shall be loaded with ignominy and shame?" No, my fair querist, I mean no such thing. Remember the endeavours of the wicked are often suffered to prosper, that in the end their fall may be attended with more bitterness of heart; while the cup of affliction is poured out for wise and salutary ends, and they who are compelled to drain it even to the bitter dregs, often find comfort at the bottom; the tear of penitence blots their offences from the book of fate, and they rise from the heavy, painful trial, purified and fit for a mansion in the kingdom of eternity.

Yes, my young friends, the tear of compassion shall fall for the fate of Charlotte, while the name of La Rue shall be detested and despised. For Charlotte, the soul melts with sympathy; for La Rue, it feels nothing but horror and contempt. But perhaps your gay hearts would rather follow the fortunate Mrs. Crayton through the scenes of pleasure and dissipation in which she was engaged, than listen to the complaints and miseries of Charlotte. I will for once oblige you; I will for once follow her to midnight revels, balls, and scenes of gaiety, for in such was she constantly engaged.

I have said her person was lovely; let us add that she was surrounded by splendor and affluence, and he must know but little of the world who can wonder, (however faulty such a woman's conduct), at her being followed by the men and her company courted by the women: in short Mrs. Crayton was the universal favorite: she set the fashions, she was toasted by all the gentlemen, and copied by all the ladies.

Colonel Crayton was a domestic man. Could he be happy with such a woman? impossible! Remonstrance was vain: he might as well have preached to the winds as endeavour to persuade her from any action, however ridiculous, on which she had set her mind: in short, after a little ineffectual struggle, he gave up the attempt, and left her to follow the bent of her own inclinations: what those were, I think the reader must have seen enough of her character to form a just idea. Among the number who paid their devotions at her shrine, she singled one, a young Ensign, of mean birth, indifferent education, and weak intellects. How such a man came into the army, we hardly know to account for, and how he afterward rose to posts of honour is likewise strange and wonderful.[7] But fortune is blind, and so are those too frequently who have the power of dispensing her favours: else why do we see fools and knaves at the very top of the wheel, while patient merit sinks to the extreme of the opposite abyss. But we may form a thousand conjectures on this subject, and yet never hit on the right. Let us therefore endeavour to deserve her smiles, and whether we succeed or not we shall feel more innate satisfaction than thousands of those who bask in the sunshine of her favour unworthily. But to return to Mrs. Crayton: this young man, whom I shall distinguish by the name of Corydon, was the reigning favourite of her heart. He escorted her to the play, danced with her at every ball, and when indisposition prevented her going out, it was he alone who was permitted to chear the gloomy solitude to which she was obliged to confine herself. Did she ever think of poor Charlotte?—if she did, my dear Miss, it was only to laugh at the poor girl's want of spirit in consenting to be moped up in the country, while Montraville was enjoying all the pleasures of a gay, dissipated city. When she heard of his marriage, she smiling said, "So there's an end of Madame Charlotte's hopes. I wonder who will take her now, or what will become of the little affected prude?"

But as you have lead to the subject, I think we may as well return to the distressed Charlotte, and not like the unfeeling Mrs. Crayton shut our hearts to the call of humanity.

Chapter XXIX.
We Go Forward Again.

The strength of Charlotte's constitution combated against her disorder, and she began slowly to recover, though she still laboured under a violent depression of spirits: how must that depression be encreased, when, upon examining her little store, she found herself reduced to one solitary guinea, and that during her illness the attendance of an apothecary and nurse, together with many other unavoidable expenses, had involved her in debt, from which she saw no method of extricating herself. As to the faint hope which she had entertained of hearing from and being relieved by her parents; it now entirely forsook her, for it was above four months since her letter was dispatched, and she had received no answer: she therefore imagined that her conduct had either entirely alienated their affection from her, or broken their hearts, and she must never more hope to receive their blessing.

Never did any human being wish for death with greater fervency or with juster cause; yet she had too just a sense of the duties of the christian religion to attempt to put a period to her own existence. "I have but to be patient a little longer," she would cry, "and nature,

---

7. To be wondered at.

fatigued and fainting, will throw off this heavy load of mortality, and I shall be relieved from all my sufferings."

It was one cold stormy day in the latter end of December, as Charlotte sat by a handful of fire, the low state of her finances not allowing her to replenish her stock of fuel, and prudence teaching her to be careful of what she had, when she was surprised by the entrance of a farmer's wife, who, without much ceremony, seated herself, and began this curious harangue.

"I'm come to see if as how you can pay your rent, because as how we hear Captain Montable is gone away, and it's fifty to one if he b'ant killed afore he comes back again; and then, Miss or Ma'am, or whatever you may be, as I was saying to my husband, where are we to look for our money."

This was a stroke altogether unexpected by Charlotte: she knew so little of the ways of the world that she had never bestowed a thought on the payment for the rent of the house; she knew indeed that she owed a good deal, but this was never reckoned among the others: she was thunderstruck; she hardly knew what answer to make, yet it was absolutely necessary that she should say something; and judging of the gentleness of every female disposition by her own, she thought the best way to interest the woman in her favour would be to tell her candidly to what a situation she was reduced, and how little probability there was of her ever paying any body.

Alas poor Charlotte, how confined was her knowledge of human nature, or she would have been convinced that the only way to insure the friendship and assistance of your surrounding acquaintance is to convince them that you do not require it, for when once the petrifying aspect of distress and penury appear, whose qualities, like Medusa's head, can change to stone all that look upon it;[8] when once this Gorgon claims acquaintance with us, the phantom of friendship, that before courted our notice, will vanish into unsubstantial air, and the whole world before us appears a barren waste. Pardon me, ye dear spirits of benevolence, whose benign smiles and chearful giving hand have strewed sweet flowers on many a thorny path through which my wayward fate forced me to pass; think not, that, in condemning the unfeeling texture of the human heart, I forget the spring from whence flow all the comforts I enjoy: oh, no; I look up to you as to bright constellations, gathering new splendours from the surrounding darkness; but, ah! whilst I adore the benignant rays that cheared and illumined my heart, I mourn that their influence cannot extend to all the sons and daughters of affliction.

"Indeed, Madam," said poor Charlotte in a tremulous accent, "I am at a loss what to do. Montraville placed me here, and promised to defray all my expenses: but he has forgot his promise, he has forsaken me, and I have no friend who has either power or will to relieve me. Let me hope, as you see my unhappy situation, your charity——"

"Charity," cried the woman impatiently interrupting her, "charity indeed: why, Mistress, charity begins at home, and I have seven children at home, *honest, lawful* children, and it is my duty to keep them; and do you think I will give away my property to a nasty impudent hussy to maintain her and her bastard; an I was saying to my husband the other day what will this world come to; honest women are nothing now adays, while the harlotings are set up for fine ladies, and look upon us no more nor the dirt they walk upon: but let me tell you, my fine spoken Ma'am, I must have my money; so seeing as how you can't pay it, why you must troop, and leave all your fine gimcracks and fal der ralls behind you. I don't ask for no more nor my right, and nobody shall dare for to go for to hinder me of it."

"Oh heavens," cried Charlotte, clasping her hands, "what will become of me?"

"Come on ye!" retorted the unfeeling wretch: "why go to the barracks and work for a morsel of bread; wash and mend the soldiers cloaths, an cook their victuals, and not expect

---

8. In Greek mythology, a female gorgon with snakes for hair; a glimpse of her eyes turned the beholder into stone.

to live in idleness on honest people's means. Oh I wish I could see the day when all such cattle were obliged to work hard and eat little; it's only what they deserve."

"Father of mercy," cried Charlotte, "I acknowledge thy correction just; but prepare me, I beseech thee, for the portion of misery thou may'st please to lay upon me."

"Well," said the woman, "I shall go an tell my husband as how you can't pay; and so d'ye see, Ma'am, get ready to be packing away this very night, for you should not stay another night in this house, though I were sure you would lay in the street."

Charlotte bowed her head in silence; but the anguish of her heart was too great to permit her to articulate a single word.

Chapter XXX.

And what is friendship but a name,
A charm that lulls to sleep,
A shade that follows wealth and fame,
But leaves the wretch to weep.

When Charlotte was left to herself, she began to think what course she must take, or to whom she should apply, to prevent her perishing for want, or perhaps that very night falling a victim to the inclemency of the season. After many perplexed thoughts, she at last determined to set out for New York, and enquire out Mrs. Crayton, from whom she had no doubt but she should obtain immediate relief as soon as her distress was made known; she had no sooner formed this resolution than she resolved immediately to put it in execution: she therefore wrote the following little billet to Mrs. Crayton, thinking if she should have company with her, it would be better to send it in than to request to see her.

To Mrs. Crayton.

"Madam,

"When we left our native land, that dear, happy land which now contains all that is dear to the wretched Charlotte, our prospects were the same; we both, pardon me, Madam, if I say we both too easily followed the impulse of our treacherous hearts, and trusted our happiness on a tempestuous ocean, where mine has been wrecked and lost forever; you have been more fortunate—you are united to a man of honour and humanity, united by the most sacred ties, re-spected, esteemed, and admired, and surrounded by innumerable blessings of which I am bereaved, enjoying those pleasures which have fled my bosom never to return; alas! sorrow and deep regret have taken their place. Behold me, Madam, a poor forsaken wanderer, who has not where to lay her weary head, wherewith to supply the wants of nature, or to shield her from the inclemency of the weather. To you I sue, to you I look for pity and relief. I ask not to be received as an intimate or an equal; only for charity's sweet sake receive me into your hospitable mansion, allot me the meanest apartment in it, and let me breathe out my soul in prayers for your happiness; I cannot, I feel I cannot long bear up under the accumulated woes that pour in upon me; but oh! my dear Madam, for the love of heaven suffer me not to expire in the street; and when I am at peace, as soon I shall be, extend your compassion to my helpless offspring, should it please Heaven that it should survive its unhappy mother. A gleam of joy breaks in on my benighted soul while I reflect that you cannot, will not refuse your protection to the heart broken

"Charlotte."

When Charlotte had finished this letter, late as it was in the afternoon, and though the snow began to fall very fast, she tied up a few necessaries, which she had prepared against her expected confinement, and terrified least she should be again exposed to the insults of her barbarous landlady, more dreadful to her wounded spirit than either storm or darkness, she set forward for New York.

It may be asked by those who, in a work of this kind, love to cavil at every trifling omission, whether Charlotte did not possess any valuable of which she could have disposed, and by that means have supported herself till Mrs. Beauchamp's return, when she would have been certain of receiving every tender attention which compassion and friendship could dictate: but let me entreat these wise, penetrating gentlemen to reflect that when Charlotte left England it was in such haste that there was no time to purchase any thing more than what was wanted for immediate use on the voyage, and after her arrival at New York, Montraville's affection soon began to decline, so that her whole wardrobe consisted of only necessaries; and as to the baubles, with which fond lovers often load their mistresses, she possessed not one, except a plain gold locket of small value which contained a lock of her mother's hair, and which the greatest extremity of want could not have forced her to part with.

I hope, Sir, your prejudices are now removed in regard to the probability of my story? Oh they are. Well then, with your leave, I will proceed.

The distance from the house which our suffering heroine occupied, to New York, was not very great; yet the snow fell so fast, and the cold so intense, that being unable from her situation to walk quick, she found herself almost sinking with cold and fatigue before she reached the town; her garments, which were merely suitable to the summer season, being an undress robe[9] of plain white muslin, were wet through, and a thin black cloak and bonnet, very improper habiliments for such a climate, but poorly defended her from the cold. In this situation she reached the city, and enquired of a footsoldier whom she met, the way to Colonel Crayton's.

"Bless you, my sweet lady," said the soldier with a voice and look of compassion, "I will shew you the way with all my heart; but if you are going to make a petition to Madame Crayton it is all to no purpose I assure you: if you please I will conduct you to Mr. Franklin's: though Miss Julia is married and gone now, yet the old gentleman is very good."

"Julia Franklin," said Charlotte; "is she not married to Montraville?"

"Yes," replied the soldier, "and may God bless them, for a better officer never lived, he is so good to us all; and as to Miss Julia, all the poor folks almost worshiped her."

"Gracious heaven," cried Charlotte, "is Montraville unjust then to none but me."

The soldier now shewed her Colonel Crayton's door, and with a beating heart she knocked for admission.

Chapter XXXI.
Subject Continued.

When the door was opened, Charlotte, in a voice rendered scarcely articulate through cold and the extreme agitation of her mind, demanded whether Mrs. Crayton was at home. The servant hesitated: he knew that his lady was engaged at a game of picquet[1] with her dear Corydon, nor could he think she would like to be disturbed by a person whose appearance spoke her of so little consequence as Charlotte; yet there was something in her countenance

9. An informal gown.   1. A card game for two people.

that rather interested him in her favour, and he said his lady was engaged, but if she had any particular message he would deliver it.

"Take up this letter," said Charlotte: "tell her the unhappy writer of it waits in her hall for an answer."

The tremulous accent, the tearful eye, must have moved any heart not composed of adamant. The man took the letter from the poor suppliant, and hastily ascended the stair case.

"A letter, Madam," said he, presenting it to his lady: "an immediate answer is required."

Mrs. Crayton glanced her eye carelessly over the contents. "What stuff is this," cried she haughtily; "have not I told you a thousand times that I will not be plagued with beggars, and petitions from people one knows nothing about? Go tell the woman I can't do any thing in it. I'm sorry, but one can't relieve every body."

The servant bowed, and heavily returned with this chilling message to Charlotte.

"Surely," said she, "Mrs. Crayton has not read my letter. Go, my good friend, pray go back to her; tell her it is Charlotte Temple who requests beneath her hospitable roof to find shelter from the inclemency of the season."

"Prithee, don't plague me, man," cried Mrs. Crayton impatiently, as the servant advanced something in behalf of the unhappy girl. "I tell you I don't know her."

"Not know me," cried Charlotte, rushing into the room, (for she had followed the man up stairs) "not know me, not remember the ruined Charlotte Temple, who but for you perhaps might still have been innocent, still have been happy. Oh! La Rue, this is beyond every thing I could have believed possible."

"Upon my honour, Miss," replied the unfeeling woman with the utmost effrontery, "this is a most unaccountable address: it is beyond my comprehension. John," continued she, turning to the servant, "the young woman is certainly out of her senses; do pray take her away, she terrifies me to death."

"Oh God," cried Charlotte, clasping her hands in an agony, "this is too much; what will become of me? but I will not leave you; they shall not tear me from you; here on my knees I conjure you to save me from perishing in the streets; if you really have forgot me, oh for charity's sweet sake this night let me be sheltered from the winter's piercing cold."

The kneeling figure of Charlotte in her affecting situation might have moved the heart of a stoic to compassion; but Mrs. Crayton remained inflexible. In vain did Charlotte recount the time they had known each other at Chichester, in vain mention their being in the same ship; in vain were the names of Montraville and Belcour mentioned. Mrs. Crayton could only say she was sorry for her imprudence, but could not think of having her own reputation endangered by encouraging a woman of that kind in her own house, besides she did not know what trouble and expense she might bring upon her husband by giving shelter to a woman in her situation.

"I can at least die here," said Charlotte. "I feel I can not long survive this dreadful conflict. Father of mercy, here let me finish my existence." Her agonizing sensations overpowered her, and she fell senseless on the floor.

"Take her away," said Mrs. Crayton, "she will really frighten me into hysterics; take her away I say this instant."

"And where must I take the poor creature?" said the servant, with a voice and look of compassion.

"Any where," cried she hastily, "only don't let me ever see her again. I declare she has flurried me so I shan't be myself again this fortnight."

John, assisted by his fellow servant, raised and carried her down stairs. "Poor soul," said he, "you shall not lay in the street this night. I have a bed and a poor little hovel, where my wife and her little ones rest them, but they shall watch tonight, and you shall be sheltered from danger." They placed her in a chair; and the benevolent man, assisted by one of his comrades, carried her to the place where his wife and children lived. A surgeon was sent for: he bled her,[2] she gave signs of returning life, and before the dawn gave birth to a female infant. After this event she lay for some hours in a kind of stupor; and if at any time she spoke it was with a quickness and incoherence that plainly evinced the total deprivation of her reason.

Chapter XXXII.
Reasons Why and Wherefore.

The reader of sensibility may perhaps be astonished to find Mrs. Crayton could so positively deny any knowledge of Charlotte; it is therefore but just that her conduct should in some measure be accounted for. She had ever been fully sensible of the superiority of Charlotte's sense and virtue; she was conscious that she had never swerved from rectitude had it not been for her bad precepts and worse example. These were things as yet unknown to her husband, and she wished not to have that part of her conduct exposed to him, as she had great reason to fear she had already lost considerable part of that power she once maintained over him. She trembled whilst Charlotte was in the house, least the Colonel should return; she perfectly well remembered how much he seemed interested in her favour whilst on their passage from England, and made no doubt but should he see her in her present distress he would offer her an asylum, and protect her to the utmost of his power. In that case she feared the unguarded nature of Charlotte might discover to the Colonel the part she had taken in the unhappy girl's elopement, and she well knew the contrast between her own and Charlotte's conduct would make the former appear in no very respectable light. Had she reflected properly, she would have afforded the poor girl protection; and by enjoining her silence, ensured it by acts of repeated kindness; but vice in general blinds its votaries, and they discover their real characters to the world when they are most studious to preserve appearances.

Just so it happened with Mrs. Crayton: her servants made no scruple of mentioning the cruel conduct of their lady to a poor distressed lunatic who claimed her protection; every one joined in reprobating her inhumanity; nay even Corydon thought she might at least have ordered her to be taken care of, but he dare not even hint it to her, for he lived but in her smiles, and drew from her lavish fondness large sums to support an extravagance to which the state of his own finances was very inadequate: it cannot therefore be supposed that he wished Mrs. Crayton to be very liberal in her bounty to the afflicted suppliant; yet vice had not so entirely seared over his heart but the sorrows of Charlotte could find a vulnerable part.

Charlotte had now been three days with her humane preservers, but she was totally insensible of everything; she raved incessantly for Montraville and her father: she was not conscious of being a mother, nor took the least notice of her child except to ask whose it was, and why it was not carried to its parents.

"Oh," said she one day, starting up on hearing the infant cry, "why, why will you keep that child here; I am sure you would not if you knew how hard it was for a mother to be parted from her infant: it is like tearing the cords of life asunder. Oh could you see the horrid sight which I now behold—there—there stands my dear mother, her poor bosom bleeding at every vein; her gentle, affectionate heart torn in a thousand pieces, and all for the loss of a ruined, ungrateful child. Save me—save me—from her frown. I dare not—indeed I dare not speak to her."

Such were the dreadful images that haunted her distracted mind, and nature was sinking fast under the dreadful malady which medicine had no power to remove. The surgeon who

2. Certain disorders were thought to be brought on by an excess of blood. A surgeon would drain the blood from the patient, often with leeches.

attended her was a humane man; he exerted his utmost abilities to save her, but he saw she was in want of many necessaries and comforts which the poverty of her hospitable host rendered him unable to provide: he therefore determined to make her situation known to some of the officers ladies, and endeavour to make a collection for her relief.

When he returned home after making this resolution, he found a message from Mrs. Beauchamp, who had just arrived from Rhode Island, requesting he would call and see one of her children, who was very unwell. "I do not know," said he, as he was hastening to obey the summons, "I do not know a woman to whom I could apply with more hope of success than Mrs. Beauchamp. I will endeavour to interest her in this poor girl's behalf; she wants the soothing balm of friendly consolation: we may perhaps save her; we will try at least."

"And where is she," cried Mrs. Beauchamp when he had prescribed something for the child, and told his little pathetic tale, "where is she, Sir? we will go to her immediately. Heaven forbid that I should be deaf to the calls of humanity. Come we will go this instant." Then seizing the doctor's arm, they sought the habitation that contained the dying Charlotte.

Chapter XXXIII.
Which People Void of Feeling Need Not Read.

When Mrs. Beauchamp entered the apartment of the poor sufferer, she started back with horror. On a wretched bed, without hangings and but poorly supplied with covering, lay the emaciated figure of what still retained the semblance of a lovely woman, though sickness had so altered her features that Mrs. Beauchamp had not the least recollection of her person. In one corner of the room stood a woman washing, and, shivering over a small fire, two healthy but half naked children; the infant was asleep beside its mother, and on a chair by the bedside stood a porrenger[3] and wooden spoon containing a little gruel, and a tea cup with about two spoonfuls of wine in it. Mrs. Beauchamp had never before beheld such a scene of poverty; she shuddered involuntarily, and exclaiming—"heaven preserve us!" leaned on the back of a chair ready to sink to the earth. The doctor repented having so precipitately brought her into this affecting scene; but there was no time for apologies: Charlotte caught the sound of her voice, and starting almost out of bed exclaimed—"Angel of peace and mercy, art thou come to deliver me? Oh I know you are, for whenever you was near me I felt eased of half my sorrows; but you don't know me, nor can I, with all the recollection I am mistress of, remember your name just now; but I know that benevolent countenance, and the softness of that voice which has so often comforted the wretched Charlotte."

Mrs. Beauchamp had, during the time Charlotte was speaking, seated herself on the bed and taken one of her hands; she looked at her attentively, and at the name of Charlotte she perfectly conceived the whole shocking affair. A faint sickness came over her. "Gracious heaven," said she, "is this possible?" and bursting into tears, she reclined the burning head of Charlotte on her own bosom; and folding her arms about her, wept over her in silence. "Oh," said Charlotte, "you are very good to weep thus for me: it is a long time since I shed a tear for myself: my head and heart are both on fire, but these tears of yours seem to cool and refresh it. Oh now I remember you said you would send a letter to my poor father: do you think he ever received it? or perhaps you have brought me an answer: why don't you speak, Madam? Does he say I may go home? Well he is very good; I shall soon be ready."

She then made an effort to get out of bed; but being prevented, her frenzy again returned, and she raved with the greatest wildness and incoherence. Mrs. Beauchamp, finding it was impossible for her to be removed, contented herself with ordering the apartment to be made

3. A shallow cup or bowl with a handle.

more comfortable, and procuring a proper nurse for both mother and child; and having learned the particulars of Charlotte's fruitless application to Mrs. Crayton from honest John, she amply rewarded him for his benevolence, and returned home with a heart oppressed with many painful sensations, but yet rendered easy by the reflection that she had performed her duty towards a distressed fellow creature.

Early the next morning she again visited Charlotte, and found her tolerably composed; she called her by name, thanked her for her goodness, and when her child was brought to her, pressed it in her arms, wept over it, and called it the offspring of disobedience. Mrs. Beauchamp was delighted to see her so much amended, and began to hope she might recover, and spite of her former errors become an useful and respectable member of society; but the arrival of the doctor put an end to these delusive hopes: he said nature was making her last effort, and a few hours would most probably consign the unhappy girl to her kindred dust.

Being asked how she found herself, she replied—"Why better, much better, doctor. I hope now I have but little more to suffer. I had last night a few hours sleep, and when I awoke recovered the full power of recollection. I am quite sensible of my weakness; I feel I have but little longer to combat with the shafts of affliction. I have an humble confidence in the mercy of him who died to save the world, and trust that my sufferings in this state of mortality, joined to my unfeigned repentance, through his mercy, have blotted my offences from the sight of my offended maker. I have but one care—my poor infant! Father of mercy," continued she, raising her eyes, "of thy infinite goodness grant that the sins of the parent be not visited on the unoffending child. May those who taught me to despise thy laws be forgiven; lay not my offences to their charge I beseech thee; and oh! shower the choicest of thy blessings on those whose pity has soothed the afflicted heart, and made easy even the bed of pain and sickness."

She was exhausted by this fervent address to the throne of mercy, and though her lips still moved her voice became inarticulate: she lay for some time as it were in a doze, and then recovering faintly pressed Mrs. Beauchamp's hand, and requested that a clergyman might be sent for.

On his arrival she joined fervently in the pious office, frequently mentioning her ingratitude to her parents as what lay most heavy at her heart. When she had performed the last solemn duty, and was preparing to lie down, a little bustle on the outside door occasioned Mrs. Beauchamp to open it, and enquire the cause. A man, in appearance about forty, presented himself, and asked for Mrs. Beauchamp.

"That is my name, Sir," said she.

"Oh then, my dear Madam," cried he, "tell me where I may find my poor, ruined, but repentant child."

Mrs. Beauchamp was surprised and affected; she knew not what to say; she foresaw the agony this interview would occasion Mr. Temple, who had just arrived in search of his Charlotte, and yet was sensible that the pardon and blessing of her father would soften even the agonies of death to the daughter.

She hesitated. "Tell me, Madam," cried he wildly, "tell me, I beseech thee, does she live? shall I see my darling once again? Perhaps she is in this house. Lead, lead me to her, that I may bless her, and then lie down and die."

The ardent manner in which he uttered these words occasioned him to raise his voice. It caught the ear of Charlotte: she knew the beloved sound: and uttering a loud shriek, she sprang forward as Mr. Temple entered the room. "My adored father." "My long lost child." Nature could support no more, and they both sunk lifeless into the arms of the attendants.

Charlotte was again put into bed, and a few moments restored Mr. Temple: but to describe the agony of his sufferings is past the power of any one, who though they may readily conceive, cannot delineate the dreadful scene. Every eye gave testimony of what each heart felt—but all were silent.

When Charlotte recovered, she found herself supported in her father's arms. She cast on him a most expressive look, but was unable to speak. A reviving cordial was administered. She then asked in a low voice for her child: it was brought to her: she put it in her father's arms. "Protect her," said she, "and bless your dying——"

Unable to finish the sentence, she sunk back on her pillow: her countenance was serenely composed; she regarded her father as he pressed the infant to his breast with a steadfast look; a sudden beam of joy passed across her languid features, she raised her eyes to heaven—and then closed them for ever.

Chapter XXXIV.
Retribution.

In the mean time Montraville having received orders to return to New York, arrived, and having still some remains of compassionate tenderness for the woman whom he regarded as brought to shame by himself, he went out in search of Belcour, to enquire whether she was safe, and whether the child lived. He found him immersed in dissipation, and could gain no other intelligence than that Charlotte had left him, and that he knew not what was become of her.

"I can not believe it possible," said Montraville, "that a mind once so pure as Charlotte Temple's should so suddenly become the mansion of vice. Beware, Belcour," continued he, "beware if you have dared to behave either unjustly or dishonourably to that poor girl, your life shall pay the forfeit.—I will revenge her cause."

He immediately went into the country, to the house where he had left Charlotte. It was desolate. After much enquiry he at length found the servant girl who had lived with her. From her he learnt the misery Charlotte had endured from the complicated evils of illness, poverty, and a broken heart, and that she had set out on foot for New York on a cold winter's evening; but she could inform him no further.

Tortured almost to madness by this shocking account, he returned to the city, but before he reached it the evening was drawing to a close. In entering the town he was obliged to pass several little huts, the residences of poor women, who supported themselves by washing the cloaths of the officers and soldiers. It was nearly dark: he heard from a neighbouring steeple a solemn toll that seemed to say some poor mortal was going to their last mansion: the sound struck on the heart of Montraville, and he involuntarily stopped, when, from one of the houses, he saw the appearance of a funeral. Almost unknowing what he did, he followed at a small distance; and as they let the coffin into the grave, he enquired of a soldier who stood by, and had just brushed off a tear that did honour to his heart, who it was that was just buried. "An please your honour," said the man, " 'tis a poor girl that was brought from her friends by a cruel man, who left her when she was big with child and married another." Montraville stood motionless, and the man proceeded—"I met her myself not a fortnight since one night all wet and cold in the streets; she went to Madam Crayton's, but she would not take her in, and so the poor thing went raving mad." Montraville could bear no more; he struck his hands against his forehead with violence; and exclaiming "poor murdered Charlotte!" ran with precipitation towards the place where they were heaping the earth on her remains. "Hold, hold, one moment," said he, "Close not the grave of the injured Charlotte Temple, till I have taken vengeance on her murderer."

"Rash young man," said Mr. Temple, "who art thou that thus disturbest the last mournful rites of the dead, and rudely breaks in upon the grief of an afflicted father."

"If thou art the father of Charlotte Temple," said he, gazing at him with mingled horror and amazement—"if thou art her father—I am Montraville." Then falling on his knees, he continued—"Here is my bosom. I bare it to receive the stroke I merit. Strike—strike now, and save me from the misery of reflection."

"Alas!" said Mr. Temple, "if thou wert the seducer of my child, thy own reflections be thy punishment. I wrest not the power from the hand of omnipotence. Look on that little heap of earth, there hast thou buried the only joy of a fond father. Look at it often; and may thy heart feel such true sorrow as shall merit the mercy of heaven." He turned from him; and Montraville starting up from the ground, where he had thrown himself, and at that instant remembering the perfidy of Belcour, flew like lightning to his lodgings. Belcour was intoxicated; Montraville impetuous: they fought, and the sword of the latter entered the heart of his adversary. He fell, and expired almost instantly. Montraville had received a slight wound: and overcome with the agitation of his mind and loss of blood, was carried in a state of insensibility to his distracted wife. A dangerous illness and obstinate delirium ensued, during which he raved incessantly for Charlotte: but a strong constitution and the tender assiduities of Julia, in time overcome the disorder. He recovered; but to the end of his life was subject to severe fits of melancholy, and while he remained at New York frequently retired to the church yard, where he would weep over the grave, and regret the untimely fate of the lovely Charlotte Temple.

Chapter XXXV.
Conclusion.

Shortly after the interment of his daughter, Mr. Temple, with his dear little charge and her nurse, set forward for England. It would be impossible to do justice to the meeting scene between him, his Lucy, and her aged father. Every heart of sensibility can easily conceive their feelings. After the first tumult of grief was subsided, Mrs. Temple gave up the chief of her time to her grandchild, and as she grew up and improved, began to almost fancy she again possessed her Charlotte.

It was about ten years after these painful events, that Mr. and Mrs. Temple, having buried their father, were obliged to come to London on particular business, and brought the little Lucy with them. They had been walking one evening, when on their return they found a poor wretch sitting on the steps of the door. She attempted to rise as they approached, but from extreme weakness was unable, and after several fruitless efforts fell back in a fit. Mr. Temple was not one of those men who stand to consider whether by assisting an object in distress they shall not inconvenience themselves, but instigated by the impulse of a noble feeling heart, immediately ordered her to be carried into the house, and proper restoratives applied.

She soon recovered; and fixing her eyes on Mrs. Temple, cried—"You know not, Madam, what you do; you know not whom you are relieving, or you would curse me in the bitterness of your heart. Come not near me, Madam, I shall contaminate you. I am the viper that stung your peace. I am the woman who turned the poor Charlotte out to perish in the street. Heaven have mercy! I see her now," continued she looking at Lucy; "such, such was the fair bud of innocence that my vile arts blasted ere it was half blown."

It was in vain that Mr. and Mrs. Temple entreated her to be composed and to take some refreshment. She only drank half a glass of wine; and then told them that she had been separated from her husband seven years, the chief of which she had passed in riot, dissipation, and vice, till overtaken by poverty and sickness, she had been reduced to part with every valuable, and thought only of ending her life in a prison; when a benevolent friend paid her debts and released her; but that her illness increasing, she had no possible means of supporting herself, and her friends were weary of relieving her. "I have fasted," said she, "two days, and last night laid my aching head on the cold pavement: indeed it was but just that I should experience those miseries myself which I had unfeelingly inflicted on others."

Greatly as Mr. Temple had reason to detest Mrs. Crayton, he could not behold her in this distress without some emotions of pity. He gave her shelter that night beneath his hospitable roof, and the next day got her admission into an hospital: where having lingered a few weeks, she died, a striking example that vice, however prosperous in the beginning, in the end leads only to misery and shame.

Finis.

1794

Catherine Maria Sedgwick
(1789–1867)

Born in Stockbridge, Massachusetts, Catherine Sedgwick was the daughter of Theodore and Pamela Dwight Sedgwick. Her mother was descended from distinguished western Massachusetts families, and her father, a lawyer, was a leading Federalist, serving as Speaker of the House of Representatives during the administration of George Washington. Because of her mother's chronic illness and the early marriages of her two older sisters she spent much of her childhood in the company of her father and four brothers; as she later wrote, "their daily habits and pursuits and pleasures were intellectual—and I naturally imbibed from them a kindred taste." She was educated in Stockbridge and at private schools for young ladies in New York City, Albany, and Boston, but her "school life," she wrote, "was a waste—my home life my only education." From the time she was very young she was listening to her father's readings from Cervantes and Shakespeare; later he encouraged her to "devote your mornings to reading—there are few who can make such improvements by it and it would be lamented if this precious time should be lost." Her family's support continued throughout her life, as, unmarried, she was welcomed into the homes of her brothers and encouraged by them to write and publish.

From the beginning, her aim was to create for Americans a native strain of fiction imbued with the morality of her adopted Unitarianism. With the encouragement of her brothers, she turned a religious tract into *A New England Tale* (1822), a novel that focuses in part on religious hypocrisy. In her next novel, *Redwood* (1824), she set some of her most interesting scenes in the Shaker community at Hancock, not far from her home, as she again examined questions of faith. Her third novel is her masterpiece. *Hope Leslie: or Early Times in the Massachusetts* (1827) is a historical romance, modeled on Scott and Cooper, set in the Connecticut River valley and Boston; most of the action takes place in the mid-1640s, the period that Hawthorne later focused on in *The Scarlet Letter* (1850) and others of his works. In *Hope Leslie* an elaborately coincidental plot brings together love entanglements, kidnappings, imprisonments, escapes, disguises, and mistaken identities to advance ideas of the proper roles for women, the rule of law versus individual and natural morality, and relations between Native Americans and English colonists. Especially remarkable is the portrait of the Indian heroine, Magawisca. Another novel, *The Linwoods: or, "Sixty Years Since" in America* (1835), set during the American Revolution, displays in its title its debt to the idea of Scott's

Waverley, or 'Tis Sixty Years Since, a time of turmoil examined from a perspective that places it not quite outside the bounds of living memory.

Widely read in the nineteenth century, Sedgwick wrote her first novels when American literature was just emerging from its infancy; she stood for a while with Bryant, Irving, and Cooper at the head of the few American authors read with respect in Europe. Later, she occupied the center of the literary community in the Berkshires in the 1840s and 1850s, a gathering that perhaps owed its attraction to the area, at least in part, to the fine descriptions of local scenery that form much of the appeal of her best works. She was a friend and neighbor of Melville and earned the respect of Hawthorne, who

called her "our most truthful novelist." An early feminist, she wrote an 1839 article on "The Rights of Women," but generally confined her opinions to her novels, where she wrote often of strong-willed women whose choices are in the end not entirely limited by their circumstances.

Other novels include *Clarence: or, A Tale of Our Own Times* (1830) and *Married or Single?* (1857). Short fiction is collected in *Tales and Sketches* (1835) and *Tales and Sketches, Second Series* (1844). Other titles are *Home: Scenes and Characters Illustrating Christian Truth* (1835), *The Poor Rich Man and Rich Poor Man* (1836), *Live and Let Live* (1837), *Means and Ends, or Self-Training* (1839), and *Letters from Abroad to Kindred at Home* (1841). Mary E. Dewey edited *Life and Letters of Catherine Maria Sedgwick* (1872). A study is Edward Halsey Foster, *Catherine Maria Sedgwick* (1974).

FROM HOPE LESLIE[1]
Volume One: Chapter IV

***Digby had not a very strong conviction of the actual presence of an enemy, as was evident from his giving no alarm to his auxiliaries in the house; and he believed that if there were hostile Indians prowling about them, they were few in number, and fearful;[2] still he deemed it prudent to persevere in their precautionary measures. "I will remain here," he said, "Mr. Everell, and do you follow Magawisca; sift what you can from her. Depend on't, there's something wrong. Why should she have turned away on seeing us? and did you not observe her hide something beneath her mantle?"

Everell acceded to Digby's proposition; not with the expectation of confirming his suspicions, but in the hope that Magawisca would shew they were groundless. He followed her to the front of the house, to which she seemed involuntarily to have bent her steps on perceiving him.

"You have taken the most difficult part of our duty on yourself, Magawisca," he said, on coming up to her. "You have acted as vidette,[3] while I have been quiet at my post."

Perhaps Magawisca did not understand him, at any rate she made no reply.

"Have you met an enemy in your reconnoitering? Digby and I fancied that we both heard and saw the foe."

"When and where?" exclaimed Magawisca, in a hurried, alarmed tone.

"Not many minutes since, and just at the very edge of the wood."

"What! when Digby raised his gun? I thought that had been in sport to startle me."

1. The text is that of the 1827 edition, with some normalization of spelling and punctuation.
2. The scene is Springfield, Massachusetts, not long after the defeat of the Pequots (in 1637, though Sedgwick gives the date as 1636).

Magawisca, the 15-year-old daughter of the Pequot chief Mononotto, has become a servant of the Fletcher family. Everell is their 14-year-old son, and Digby is a servant.

3. Sentry.

"No—Magawisca. Sporting does not suit our present case. My mother and her little ones are in peril, and Digby is a faithful servant."

"Faithful!" echoed Magawisca, as if there were more in Everell's expression than met the ear; "he surely may walk straight who hath nothing to draw him aside. Digby hath but one path, and that is plain before him—but one voice from his heart, and why should he not obey it?" The girl's voice faltered as she spoke, and as she concluded she burst into tears. Everell had never before witnessed this expression of feeling from her. She had an habitual self-command that hid the motions of her heart from common observers, and veiled them even from those who most narrowly watched her. Everell's confidence in Magawisca had not been in the least degree weakened by all the appearances against her. He did not mean to imply suspicion by his commendation of Digby, but merely to throw out a leading observation which she might follow if she would.

He felt reproached and touched by her distress, but struck by the clew, which, as he thought, her language afforded to the mystery of her conduct, and confident that she would in no way aid or abet any mischief that her own people might be contriving against them, he followed the natural bent of his generous temper, and assured her again, and again, of his entire trust in her. This seemed rather to aggravate than abate her distress. She threw herself on the ground, drew her mantle over her face, and wept convulsively. He found he could not allay the storm he had raised, and he seated himself beside her. After a little while, either exhausted by the violence of her emotion, or comforted by Everell's silent sympathy, she became composed; and raised her face from her mantle, and as she did so, something fell from beneath its folds. She hastily recovered and replaced it, but not till Everell had perceived it was an eagle's feather. He knew this was the badge of her tribe, and he had heard her say, that "a tuft from the wing of the monarch-bird was her father's crest." A suspicion flashed through his mind, and was conveyed to Magawisca's, by one bright glance of inquiry. She said nothing, but her responding look was rather sorrowful than confused, and Everell, anxious to believe what he wished to be true, came, after a little consideration, to the conclusion, that the feather had been dropped in her path by a passing bird. He did not scrutinise her motive in concealing it; he could not think her capable of evil, and anxious to efface from her mind the distrust his countenance might have expressed—"This beautiful moon and her train of stars," he said, "look as if they were keeping their watch over our dwelling. There are those, Magawisca, who believe the stars have a mysterious influence on human destiny. I know nothing of the grounds of their faith, and my imagination is none of the brightest, but I can almost fancy they are stationed there as guardian angels, and I feel quite sure that nothing evil could walk abroad in their light."

"They do look peaceful," she replied mournfully; "but ah! Everell, man is ever breaking the peace of nature. It was such a night as this—so bright and still, when your English came upon our quiet homes."

"You have never spoken to me of that night Magawisca."

"No—Everell, for our hands have taken hold of the chain of friendship, and I feared to break it by speaking of the wrongs your people laid on mine."

"You need not fear it; I can honour noble deeds though done by our enemies, and see that cruelty is cruelty, though inflicted by our friends."

"Then listen to me; and when the hour of vengeance comes, if it should come, remember it was provoked."

She paused for a few moments, sighed deeply, and then began the recital of the last acts in the tragedy of her people; the principal circumstances of which are detailed in the chronicles of the times, by the witnesses of the bloody scenes. "You know," she said, "our fortress-homes were on the level summit of a hill. Thence we could see as far as the eye could stretch, our hunting-grounds, and our gardens, which lay beneath us on the borders of a stream that glided around our hill, and so near to it, that in the still nights we could hear its gentle voice. Our fort and wigwams were encompassed with a palisade, formed of young trees, and branches interwoven and sharply pointed. No enemy's foot had ever approached this nest, which the eagles of the tribe had built for their mates and their young. Sassacus[4] and my father were both away on that dreadful night. They had called a council of our chiefs, and old men; our young men had been out in their canoes, and when they returned they had danced and feasted, and were now in deep sleep. My mother was in her hut with her children, not sleeping, for my brother Samoset had lingered behind his companions, and had not yet returned from the water-sport. The warning spirit, that ever keeps its station at a mother's pillow, whispered that some evil was near; and my mother, bidding me lie still with the little ones, went forth in quest of my brother. All the servants of the Great Spirit spoke to my mother's ear and eye of danger and death. The moon, as she sunk behind the hills, appeared a ball of fire; strange lights darted through the air; to my mother's eye they seemed fiery arrows; to her ear the air was filled with death-sighs.

"She had passed the palisade, and was descending the hill, when she met old Cushmakin. "Do you know aught of my boy?" she asked.

"Your boy is safe, and sleeps with his companions; he returned by the Sassafras knoll; that way can only be trodden by the strong-limbed, and light-footed." "My boy is safe," said my mother; "then tell me, for thou art wise, and canst see quite through the dark future, tell me, what evil is coming to our tribe?" She then described the omens she had seen. "I know not," said Cushmakin, "of late darkness hath spread over my soul, and all is black there, as before these eyes, that the arrows of death have pierced; but tell me, Monoco, what see you now in the fields of heaven?"

"Oh, now," said my mother, "I see nothing but the blue depths, and the watching stars. The spirits of the air have ceased their moaning, and steal over my cheek like an infant's breath. The water-spirits are rising, and will soon spread their soft wings around the nest of our tribe."

"The boy sleeps safely," muttered the old man, "and I have listened to the idle fear of a doating mother."

"I come not of a fearful race," said my mother.

"Nay, that I did not mean," replied Cushmakin, "but the panther watching her young is fearful as a doe." The night was far spent, and my mother bade him go home with her, for our powwows have always a mat in the wigwam of their chief. "Nay," he said, "the day is near, and I am always abroad at the rising of the sun." It seemed that the first warm touch of the sun opened the eye of the old man's soul, and he saw again the flushed hills, and the shaded valleys, the sparkling waters, the green maize, and the gray old rocks of our home. They were just passing the little gate of the palisade, when the old man's dog sprang from him with a fearful bark. A rushing sound was heard. "Owanox! Owanox! (the English! the English!)" cried Cushmakin. My mother joined her voice to his, and in an instant the cry of alarm spread through the wigwams. The enemy were indeed upon us. They had surrounded the palisade, and opened their fire.

"Was it so sudden? Did they so rush on sleeping women and children?" asked Everell, who was unconsciously lending all his interest to the party of the narrator.

"Even so; they were guided to us by the traitor Wequash; he from whose bloody hand my mother had shielded the captive English maidens—he who had eaten from my father's dish, and slept on his mat. They were flanked by the cowardly Narragansetts, who shrunk from the sight of our tribe—who were pale as white men at the thought of Sassacus, and so feared him, that when his name was spoken, they were like an unstrung bow, and they said, 'He is all one God—no man can kill him.' These cowardly allies waited for the prey they dared not attack."

"Then," said Everell, "as I have heard, our people had all the honour of the fight."

"Honour! was it, Everell—ye shall hear. Our warriors rushed forth to meet the foe; they

---

4. Sassacus, another chief, and Mononotto were both historical figures.

surrounded the huts of their mothers, wives, sisters, children; they fought as if each man had a hundred lives, and would give each, and all, to redeem their homes. Oh! the dreadful fray, even now, rings in my ears! Those fearful guns that we had never heard before—the shouts of your people—our own battle yell—the piteous cries of the little children—the groans of our mothers, and, oh! worse—worse than all—the silence of those that could not speak— The English fell back; they were driven to the palisade; some beyond it, when their leader gave the cry to fire our huts, and led the way to my mother's. Samoset, the noble boy, defended the entrance with a prince-like courage, till they struck him down; prostrate and bleeding he again bent his bow, and had taken deadly aim at the English leader, when a sabre-blow severed his bowstring. Then was taken from our hearth-stone, where the English had been so often warmed and cherished, the brand to consume our dwellings. They were covered with mats, and burnt like dried straw. The enemy retreated without the palisade. In vain did our warriors fight for a path by which we might escape from the consuming fire; they were beaten back; the fierce element gained on us; the Naragansetts pressed on the English, howling like wolves for their prey. Some of our people threw themselves into the midst of the crackling flames, and their courageous souls parted with one shout of triumph; others mounted the palisade, but they were shot and dropped like a flock of birds smitten by the hunter's arrows. Thus did the strangers destroy, in our own homes, hundreds of our tribe."

"And how did you escape in that dreadful hour, Magawisca—you were not then taken prisoner?"

"No; there was a rock at one extremity of our hut, and beneath it a cavity into which my mother crept, with Oneco, myself, and the two little ones that afterwards perished. Our simple habitations were soon consumed; we heard the foe retiring, and when the last sound had died away, we came forth to a sight that made us lament to be among the living. The sun was scarce an hour from his rising, and yet in this brief space our homes had vanished. The bodies of our people were strewn about the smouldering ruin; and all around the palisade lay the strong and valiant warriors—cold—silent—powerless as the unformed clay."

Magawisca paused; she was overcome with the recollection of this scene of desolation. She looked upward with an intent gaze, as if she held communion with an invisible being. "Spirit of my mother!" burst from her lips. "Oh! that I could follow thee to that blessed land where I should no more dread the war-cry, nor the death-knife." Everell dashed the gathering tears from his eyes, and Magawisca proceeded in her narrative.

"While we all stood silent and motionless, we heard footsteps and cheerful voices. They came from my father and Sassacus, and their band, returning from the friendly council. They approached on the side of the hill that was covered with a thicket of oaks, and their ruined homes at once burst upon their view. Oh! what horrid sounds then pealed on the air! shouts of wailing, and cries for vengeance. Every eye was turned with suspicion and hatred on my father. *He* had been the friend of the English; *he* had counselled peace and alliance with them; *he* had protected their traders; delivered the captives taken from them, and restored them to their people; now *his* wife and children alone were living, and they called him traitor. I heard an angry murmur, and many hands were lifted to strike the death-blow. He moved not— 'Nay, nay,' cried Sassacus, beating them off. 'Touch him not; his soul is bright as the sun; sooner shall you darken that, than find treason in his breast. If he hath shown the dove's heart to the English when he believed them friends, he will show himself the fierce eagle now he knows them enemies. Touch him not, warriors; remember my blood runneth in his veins.'

"From that moment my father was a changed man. He neither spoke nor looked at his wife, or children; but placing himself at the head of one band of the young men he shouted his war-cry, and then silently pursued the enemy. Sassacus went forth to assemble the tribe, and we followed my mother to one of our villages."

"You did not tell me, Magawisca," said Everell, "how Samoset perished; was he consumed in the flames, or shot from the palisade?"

"Neither—neither. He was reserved to whet my father's revenge to a still keener edge. He had forced a passage through the English, and hastily collecting a few warriors, they pursued the enemy, sprung upon them from a covert, and did so annoy them that the English turned and gave them battle. All fled save my brother, and him they took prisoner. They told him they would spare his life if he would guide them to our strong holds; he refused. He had, Everell, lived but sixteen summers; he loved the light of the sun even as we love it; his manly spirit was tamed by wounds and weariness; his limbs were like a bending reed, and his heart beat like a woman's; but the fire of his soul burnt clear. Again they pressed him with offers of life and reward; he faithfully refused, and with one sabre-stroke they severed his head from his body."

Magawisca paused—she looked at Everell and said with a bitter smile—"You English tell us, Everell, that the book of your law is better than that written on our hearts, for ye say it teaches mercy, compassion, forgiveness—if ye had such a law and believed it, would ye thus have treated a captive boy?"

Magawisca's reflecting mind suggested the most serious obstacle to the progress of the Christian religion, in all ages and under all circumstances; the contrariety between its divine principles and the conduct of its professors; which, instead of always being a medium for the light that emanates from our holy law, is too often the darkest cloud that obstructs the passage of its rays to the hearts of heathen men. Everell had been carefully instructed in the principles of his religion, and he felt Magawisca's relation to be an awkward comment on them, and her inquiry natural; but though he knew not what answer to make, he was sure there must be a good one, and mentally resolving to refer the case to his mother, he begged Magawisca to proceed with her narrative.

"The fragments of our broken tribe," she said, "were collected, and some other small dependent tribes persuaded to join us. We were obliged to flee from the open grounds, and shelter ourselves in a dismal swamp. The English surrounded us; they sent in to us a messenger and offered life and pardon to all who had not shed the blood of Englishmen. Our allies listened, and fled from us, as frightened birds fly from a falling tree. My father looked upon his warriors; they answered that look with their battle shout. 'Tell your people,' said my father to the messenger, 'that we have shed and drank English blood, and that we will take nothing from them but death.'

"The messenger departed and again returned with offers of pardon, if we would come forth and lay our arrows and our tomahawks at the feet of the English. 'What say you, warriors,' cried my father—'shall we take *pardon* from those who have burned your wives and children, and given your homes to the beasts of prey—who have robbed you of your hunting grounds, and driven your canoes from their waters?' A hundred arrows were pointed to the messenger. 'Enough—you have your answer,' said my father, and the messenger returned to announce the fate we had chosen."

"Where was Sassacus?—had he abandoned his people?" asked Everell.

"Abandoned them! No—his life was in theirs; but accustomed to attack and victory, he could not bear to be thus driven, like a fox to his hole. His soul was sick within him, and he was silent and left all to my father. All day we heard the strokes of the English axes felling the trees that defended us, and when night came, they had approached so near that we could see the glimmering of their watch-lights through the branches of the trees. All night they were pouring in their bullets, alike on warriors, women, and children. Old Cushmakin was lying at my mother's feet, when he received a death-wound. Gasping for breath he called on Sassacus and my father—'Stay not here,' he said; 'look not on your wives and children, but burst your prison bound; sound through the nations the cry of revenge! Linked together, ye shall drive the English into the sea. I speak the word of the Great Spirit—obey it!' While he was yet speaking he stiffened in death. 'Obey him, warriors,' cried my mother; 'see,' she said, pointing to the mist that was now wrapping itself around the wood like a thick curtain—'see, our friends have come from the spirit-land to shelter you. Nay, look not on us—our hearts have been tender in the wigwam, but we can die before our enemies without a groan. Go forth and avenge us.'

" 'Have we come to the counsel of old men and old women!' said Sassacus, in the bitterness of his spirit.

" 'When women put down their womanish thoughts and counsel like men, they should be obeyed,' said my father. 'Follow me, warriors.'

"They burst through the enclosure. We saw nothing more, but we heard the shout from the foe, as they issued from the wood—the momentary fierce encounter—and the cry, 'they have escaped!' Then it was that my mother, who had listened with breathless silence, threw herself down on the mossy stones, and laying her hot cheek to mine—'Oh, my children—my children!' she said, 'would that I could die for you! But fear not death—the blood of a hundred chieftains, that never knew fear, runneth in your veins. Hark, the enemy comes nearer and nearer. Now lift up your heads, my children, and show them that even the weak ones of our tribe are strong in soul.'

"We rose from the ground—all about sat women and children in family clusters, awaiting unmoved their fate. The English had penetrated the forest-screen, and were already on the little rising-ground where we had been entrenched. Death was dealt freely. None resisted— not a movement was made—not a voice lifted—not a sound escaped, save the wailings of the dying children.

"One of your soldiers knew my mother, and a command was given that her life and that of her children should be spared. A guard was stationed round us.

"You know that, after our tribe was thus cut off, we were taken, with a few other captives, to Boston. Some were sent to the Islands of the Sun,[5] to bend their free limbs to bondage like your beasts of burden. There are among your people those who have not put out the light of the Great Spirit; they can remember a kindness, albeit done by an Indian; and when it was known to your Sachems that the wife of Mononotto, once the protector and friend of your people, was a prisoner, they treated her with honour and gentleness. But her people were extinguished—her husband driven to distant forests—forced on earth to the misery of wicked souls—to wander without a home; her children were captives—and her heart was broken. You know the rest."

THIS WAR, SO FATAL to the Pequods, had transpired the preceding year. It was an important event to the infant colonies, and its magnitude probably somewhat heightened to the imaginations of the English, by the terror this resolute tribe had inspired. All the circumstances attending it were still fresh in men's minds, and Everell had heard them detailed with the interest and particularity that belongs to recent adventures; but he had heard them in the language of the enemies and conquerors of the Pequods; and from Magawisca's lips they took a new form and hue; she seemed, to him, to embody nature's best gifts, and her feelings to be the inspiration of heaven. This new version of an old story reminded him of the man and the lion in the fable. But here it was not merely changing sculptors to give the advantage to one or the other of the artist's subjects; but it was putting the chisel into the hands of truth, and giving it to whom it belonged.

He had heard this destruction of the original possessors of the soil described, as we find it in the history of the times, where, we are told, "the number destroyed was about four hundred;" and "it was a fearful sight to see them thus frying in the fire, and the streams of blood quenching the same, and the horrible scent thereof; but the victory seemed a sweet sacrifice, and they gave the priase thereof to God."

In the relations of their enemies, the courage of the Pequods was distorted into ferocity, and their fortitude, in their last extremity, thus set forth: "many were killed in the swamp, like sullen dogs, that would rather, in their self-willedness and madness, sit still to be shot

5. Some of the defeated Indians were sold into slavery in the West Indies.

or cut in pieces, than receive their lives for asking, at the hands of those into whose power they had now fallen."

Everell's imagination, touched by the wand of feeling, presented a very different picture of those defenceless families of savages, pent in the recesses of their native forests, and there exterminated, not by superior natural force, but by the adventitious circumstances of arms, skill, and knowledge; from that offered by those who "then living and worthy of credit did affirm, that in the morning entering into the swamp, they saw several heaps of them [the Pequods] sitting close together, upon whom they discharged their pieces, laden with ten or twelve pistol bullets at a time, putting the muzzles of their pieces under the boughs, within a few yards of them."[6]

Everell did not fail to express to Magawisca, with all the eloquence of a heated imagination, his sympathy and admiration of her heroic and suffering people. She listened with a mournful pleasure, as one listens to the praise of a departed friend. Both seemed to have forgotten the purpose of their vigil, which they had marvellously kept without apprehension, or heaviness, when they were roused from their romantic abstraction by Digby's voice: "Now to your beds, children," he said; "the family is stirring, and the day is at hand. See the morning star hanging just over those trees, like a single watch-light in all the wide canopy. As you have not to look in a prayer-book for it, master Everell, don't forget to thank the Lord for keeping us safe, as your mother, God bless her, would say, through the night-watches. Stop one moment," added Digby, lowering his voice to Everell as he rose to follow Magawisca, "did she tell you?"

"Tell me! what?"

"What! Heaven's mercy! what ails the boy! Why, did she tell you what brought her out tonight? Did she explain all the mysterious actions we have seen? Are you crazy? Did not you ask her?"

Everell hesitated—fortunately for him the light was too dim to expose to Digby's eyes the blushes that betrayed his consciousness that he had forgotten his duty. "Magawisca did not tell me," he said, "but I am sure Digby that"——

"That she can do no wrong—hey, Master Everell, well, that may be very satisfactory to you—but it does not content me. I like not her secret ways—'it's bad ware that needs a dark store.'"

Everell had tried the force of his own convictions on Digby, and knew it to be unavailing, therefore having no reply to make, he very discreetly retreated without attempting any.

Magawisca crept to her bed, but not to repose—neither watching nor weariness procured sleep for her. Her mind was racked with apprehensions, and conflicting duties, the cruellest rack to an honourable mind.***

Chapter VII

***As the fugitives[7] emerged from the narrow defile, a new scene opened upon them; a scene of valley and hill, river and meadow, surrounded by mountains, whose encircling embrace, expressed protection and love to the gentle spirits of the valley. A light summer shower had just fallen, and the clouds, "in thousand liveries dight," had risen from the western horizon, and hung their rich draperies about the clear sun. The horizontal rays passed over the valley,

6. Although Sedgwick does not often cite sources, this and the quotations immediately above were probably taken from William Hubbard's *A Narrative of the Indian Wars in New England* (1814) or his *General History of New England* (1815).

7. Everell has been taken captive by a band of Indians led by Mononotto, who has also rescued his daughter, Magawisca.

and flushed the upper branches of the trees, the summits of the hills, and the mountains, with a flood of light, whilst the low grounds reposing in deep shadow, presented one of those striking and accidental contrasts in nature, that a painter would have selected to give effect to his art.

The gentle Housatonick wound through the depths of the valley, in some parts contracted to a narrow channel, and murmuring over the rocks that rippled its surface; and in others, spreading wide its clear mirror, and lingering like a lover amidst the vines, trees, and flowers, that fringed its banks. Thus it flows now—but not as then in the sylvan freedom of nature, when no clattering mills and bustling factories, threw their prosaic shadows over the silver waters—when not even a bridge spanned their bosom—when not a trace of man's art was seen save the little bark canoe that glided over them or lay idly moored along the shore. The savage was rather the vassal, than the master of nature; obeying her laws, but never usurping her dominion. He only used the land she prepared, and cast in his corn but where she seemed to invite him by mellowing and upheaving the rich mould. He did not presume to hew down her trees, the proud crest of her uplands, and convert them into "russet lawns and fallows grey." The axman's stroke, that music to the *settler's* ear, never then violated the peace of nature, or made discord in her music.

Imagination may be indulged in lingering for a moment in those dusky regions of the past; but it is not permitted to reasonable instructed man, to admire or regret tribes of human beings, who lived and died, leaving scarcely a more enduring memorial, than the forsaken nest that vanishes before one winter's storms.

But to return to our wanderers. They had entered the expanded vale, by following the windings of the Housatonick around a hill, conical and easy of ascent, excepting on that side which overlooked the river, where, half-way from the base to the summit, rose a perpendicular rock, bearing on its beetling front the age of centuries. On every other side, the hill was garlanded with laurels, now in full and profuse bloom; here and there surmounted by an intervening pine, spruce, or hemlock, whose seared winter foliage was fringed with the bright tender sprouts of spring. We believe there is a chord, even in the heart of savage man, that responds to the voice of nature. Certain it is, the party paused, as it appeared from a common instinct, at a little grassy nook, formed by the curve of the hill, to gaze on this singularly beautiful spot. Everell looked on the smoke that curled from the huts of the village, embosomed in pine trees, on the adjacent plain. The scene, to him, breathed peace and happiness, and gushing thoughts of home filled his eyes with tears. Oneco plucked clusters of laurels, and decked his little favourite, and the old chief fixed his melancholy eye on a solitary pine, scathed and blasted by tempests, that rooted in the ground where he stood, lifted its topmost branches to the bare rock, where they seemed, in their wild desolation, to brave the elemental fury that had stripped them of beauty and life.

The leafless tree was truly, as it appeared to the eye of Mononotto, a fit emblem of the chieftain of a ruined tribe. "See you, child," he said, addressing Magawisca, "those unearthed roots? the tree must fall—hear you the death-song that wails through those blasted branches?"

"Nay, father, listen not to the sad strain; it is but the spirit of the tree mourning over its decay; rather turn thine ear to the glad song of this bright stream, image of the good. She nourishes the aged trees, and cherishes the tender flowrets, and her song is ever of happiness, till she reaches the great sea—image of our eternity."

"Speak not to me of happiness, Magawisca; it has vanished with the smoke of our homes. I tell ye, the spirits of our race are gathered about this blasted tree. Samoset points to that rock—that sacrifice-rock." His keen glance turned from the rock to Everell.

Magawisca understood its portentous meaning, and she clasped her hands in mute and agonizing supplication. He answered to the silent entreaty. "It is in vain—my purpose is fixed, and here it shall be accomplished. Why hast thou linked thy heart, foolish girl, to this English boy? I have sworn, kneeling on the ashes of our hut, that I would never spare a son of our enemy's race. The lights of heaven witnessed my vow, and think you, that now this boy is given into my hands to avenge thy brother, I will spare him for thy prayer? No— though thou lookest on me with thy mother's eye, and speakest with her voice, I will not break my vow."

Mononotto had indeed taken a final and fatal resolution; and prompted, as he fancied, by supernatural intimations, and, perhaps, dreading the relentings of his own heart, he determined on its immediate execution. He announced his decision to the Mohawks. A brief and animated consultation followed, during which they brandished their tomahawks, and cast wild and threatening glances at Everell, who at once comprehended the meaning of these menacing looks and gestures. He turned an appealing glance to Magawisca. She did not speak. "Am I to die now?" he asked; she turned shuddering from him.

Everell had expected death from his savage captors, but while it was comparatively distant, he thought he was indifferent to it, or rather, he believed he should welcome it as a release from the horrible recollection of the massacre at Bethel,[8] which haunted him day and night. But now that his fate seemed inevitable, nature was appalled, and shrunk from it; and the impassive spirit, for a moment, endured a pang that there cannot be in any "corp'ral sufferance." The avenues of sense were closed, and past and future were present to the mind, as if it were already invested with the attributes of its eternity. From this agonizing excitement, Everell was roused by a command from the savages to move onward. "It is then deferred," thought Magawisca, and heaving a deep sigh, as if for a moment relieved from a pressure on her over-burthened heart, she looked to her father for an explanation; he said nothing, but proceeded in silence towards the village.

The lower valley of the Housatonick, at the period to which our history refers, was inhabited by a peaceful, and, as far as that epithet could ever be applied to our savages, an agricultural tribe, whose territory, situate midway between the Hudson and the Connecticut, was bounded and defended on each side by mountains, then deemed impracticable to a foe. These inland people had heard from the hunters of distant tribes, who occasionally visited them, of the aggressions and hostility of the English strangers, but regarding it as no concern of theirs, they listened, much as we listen to news of the Burmese war—Captain Symmes' theory—or lectures on phrenology. One of their hunters, it is true, had penetrated to Springfield, and another had passed over the hills to the Dutch fort at Albany, and returned with the report that the strangers' skin was the colour of cowardice—that they served their women, and spoke an unintelligible language. There was little in this account to interest those who were so ignorant as to be scarcely susceptible of curiosity, and they hardly thought of the dangerous strangers at all, or only thought of them as a people from whom they had nothing to hope or fear, when the appearance of the ruined Pequod chief, with his English captives, roused them from their apathy.

The village was on a level, sandy plain, extending for about half a mile, and raised by a natural and almost perpendicular bank fifty feet above the level of the meadows. At one extremity of the plain, was the hill we have described; the other was terminated by a broad green, appropriated to sports and councils.

The huts of the savages were irregularly scattered over the plain—some on cleared ground, and others just peeping out of copses of pine trees—some on the very verge of the plain, overlooking the meadows—and others under the shelter of a high hill that formed the northern boundary of the valley, and seemed stationed there to defend the inhabitants from their natural enemies—cold, and wind.

The huts were the simplest structures of human art; but, as in no natural condition of society a perfect equality obtains, some were more spacious and commodious than others. All were made with flexible poles, firmly set in the ground, and drawn and attached together at the top. Those of the more indolent, or least skilful, were filled in with branches of trees and

8. His home in Springfield.

hung over with coarse mats; while those of the better order were neatly covered with bark, prepared with art, and considerable labour for the purpose. Little garden patches adjoined a few of the dwellings, and were planted with beans, pumpkins, and squashes; the seeds of these vegetables, according to an Indian tradition (in which we may perceive the usual admixture of fable and truth), having been sent to them, in the bill of a bird, from the south-west, by the Great Spirit.

The Pequod chief and his retinue passed, just at twilight, over the plain, by one of the many foot-paths that indented it. Many of the women were still at work with their stone-pointed hoes, in their gardens. Some of the men and children were at their sports on the green. Here a straggler was coming from the river with a string of fine trout; another fortunate sportsman appeared from the hill-side with wild turkeys and partridges; while two emerged from the forest with still more noble game, a fat antlered buck.

This village, as we have described it, and perhaps from the affection its natural beauty inspired, remained the residence of the savages long after they had vanished from the surrounding country. Within the memory of the present generation the remnant of the tribe migrated to the west; and even now some of their families make a summer pilgrimage to this, their Jerusalem, and are regarded with a melancholy interest by the present occupants of the soil.

Mononotto directed his steps to the wigwam of the Housatonick chief, which stood on one side of the green. The chief advanced from his hut to receive him, and by the most animated gestures expressed to Mononotto his pleasure in the success of his incursion, from which it seemed that Mononotto had communicated with him on his way to the Connecticut.

A brief and secret consultation succeeded, which appeared to consist of propositions from the Pequod, and assent on the part of the Housatonick chief, and was immediately followed by a motion to separate the travellers. Mononotto and Everell were to remain with the chief, and the rest of the party to be conducted to the hut of his sister.

Magawisca's prophetic spirit too truly interpreted this arrangement; and thinking or hoping there might be some saving power in her presence, since her father tacitly acknowledged it by the pains he took to remove her, she refused to leave him. He insisted vehemently; but finding her unyielding, he commanded the Mohawks to force her away.

Resistance was vain, but resistance she would still have made, but for the interposition of Everell. "Go with them, Magawisca," he said, "and leave me to my fate.—We shall meet again."

"Never!" she shrieked; "your fate is death."

"And after death we shall meet again," replied Everell, with a calmness that evinced his mind was already in a great degree resigned to the event that now appeared inevitable. "Do not fear for me, Magawisca. Better thoughts have put down my fears. When it is over, think of me."

"And what am I to do with this scorching fire till then?" she asked, pressing both her hands on her head. "Oh, my father, has your heart become stone?"

Her father turned from her appeal, and motioned to Everell to enter the hut. Everell obeyed; and when the mat dropped over the entrance and separated him from the generous creature, whose heart had kept true time with his through all his griefs, who he knew would have redeemed his life with her own, he yielded to a burst of natural and not unmanly tears.

If this could be deemed a weakness, it was his last. Alone with his God, he realized the sufficiency of His presence and favour. He appealed to that mercy which is never refused, nor given in stinted measure to the humble suppliant. Every expression of pious confidence and resignation, which he had heard with the heedless ear of childhood, now flashed like an illumination upon his mind.

His mother's counsels and instructions, to which he had often lent a wearied attention— the passages from the sacred book he had been compelled to commit to memory, when his truant thoughts were ranging forest and field, now returned upon him as if a celestial spirit breathed them into his soul. Stillness and peace stole over him. He was amazed at his own tranquility. 'It may be,' he thought, 'that my mother and sisters are permitted to minister to me.'

He might have been agitated by the admission of the least ray of hope; but hope was utterly excluded, and it was only when he thought of his bereft father, that his courage failed him.

But we must leave him to his solitude and silence, only interrupted by the distant hootings of the owl, and the heavy tread of the Pequod chief, who spent the night in slowly pacing before the door of the hut.

Magawisca and her companions were conducted to a wigwam standing on that part of the plain on which they had first entered. It was completely enclosed on three sides by dwarf oaks. In front there was a little plantation of the edible luxuries of the savages. On entering the hut, they perceived it had but one occupant, a sick emaciated old woman, who was stretched on her mat covered with skins. She raised her head, as the strangers entered, and at the sight of Faith Leslie,[9] uttered a faint exclamation, deeming the fair creature a messenger from the spirit-land—but being informed who they were and whence they came, she made every sign and expression of courtesy to them, that her feeble strength permitted.

Her hut contained all that was essential to savage hospitality. A few brands were burning on a hearth-stone in the middle of the apartment. The smoke that found egress, passed out by a hole in the centre of the roof, over which a mat was skilfully adjusted, and turned to the windward-side by a cord that hung within. The old woman, in her long pilgrimage, had accumulated stores of Indian riches: piles of sleeping-mats laid in one corner; nicely dressed skins garnished the walls; baskets, of all shapes and sizes, gaily decorated with rude images of birds and flowers, contained dried fruits, medicinal herbs, Indian corn, nuts, and game. A covered pail, made of folds of birch-bark, was filled with a kind of beer—a decoction of various roots and aromatic shrubs. Neatly turned wooden spoons and bowls, and culinary utensils of clay supplied all the demands of the inartificial housewifery of savage life.

The travellers, directed by their old hostess, prepared their evening repast, a short and simple process to an Indian; and having satisfied the cravings of hunger, they were all, with the exception of Magawisca and one of the Mohawks, in a very short time, stretched on their mats and fast asleep.

Magawisca seated herself at the feet of the old woman, and had neither spoken nor moved since she entered the hut. She watched anxiously and impatiently the movements of the Indian, whose appointed duty it appeared to be, to guard her. He placed a wooden bench against the mat which served for a door, and stuffing his pipe with tobacco from the pouch slung over his shoulder, and then filling a gourd with the liquor in the pail and placing it beside him, he quietly sat himself down to his night-watch.

The old woman became restless, and her loud and repeated groans, at last, withdrew Magawisca from her own miserable thoughts. She inquired if she could do aught to allay her pain; the sufferer pointed to a jar that stood on the embers in which a medicinal preparation was simmering. She motioned to Magawisca to give her a spoonful of the liquor; she did so, and as she took it, "it is made," she said, "of all the plants on which the spirit of sleep has breathed," and so it seemed to be; for she had scarcely swallowed it, when she fell asleep.

Once or twice she waked and murmured something, and once Magawisca heard her say, "Hark to the wekolis![1]—he is perched on the old oak, by the sacrifice-rock, and his cry is neither musical, nor merry—a bad sign in a bird."

But all signs and portents were alike to Magawisca—every sound rung a death-peal to her ear, and the hissing silence had in it the mystery and fearfulness of death. The night wore slowly and painfully away, as if, as in the fairy tale, the moments were counted by drops of

9. An English child captured in the attack on Bethel; later in the novel, as a counterpoint to the doomed relationship of Everell and

Magawisca, Faith Leslie is happily married to Magawisca's brother, Oneco.

1. Whip-poor-will [Sedgwick's note].

heart's-blood. But the most wearisome nights will end; the morning approached; the familiar notes of the birds of earliest dawn were heard, and the twilight peeped through the crevices of the hut, when a new sound fell on Magawisca's startled ear. It was the slow measured tread of many feet. The poor girl now broke silence, and vehemently entreated the Mohawk to let her pass the door, or at least to raise the mat.

He shook his head with a look of unconcern, as if it were the petulant demand of a child, when the old woman, awakened by the noise, cried out that she was dying—that she must have light and air, and the Mohawk started up, impulsively, to raise the mat. It was held between two poles that formed the door-posts, and while he was disengaging it, Magawisca, as if inspired, and quick as thought, poured the liquor from the jar on the fire into the hollow of her hand, and dashed it into the gourd which the Mohawk had just replenished. The narcotic was boiling hot, but she did not cringe; she did not even feel it; and she could scarcely repress a cry of joy, when the savage turned round and swallowed, at one draught, the contents of the cup.

Magawisca looked eagerly through the aperture, but though the sound of the footsteps had approached nearer, she saw no one. She saw nothing but a gentle declivity that sloped to the plain, a few yards from the hut, and was covered with a grove of trees; beyond and peering above them, was the hill, and the sacrifice-rock: the morning star, its rays not yet dimmed in the light of day, shed a soft trembling beam on its summit. This beautiful star, alone in the heavens, when all other lights were quenched, spoke to the superstitious, or, rather, the imaginative spirit of Magawisca. 'Star of promise,' she thought, 'thou dost still linger with us when day is vanished, and now thou art there, alone, to proclaim the coming sun; thou dost send in upon my soul a ray of hope; and though it be but as the spider's slender pathway, it shall sustain my courage.' She had scarcely formed this resolution, when she needed all its efficacy, for the train, whose footsteps she had heard, appeared in full view.

First came her father, with the Housatonick chief; next, alone, and walking with a firm undaunted step, was Everell; his arms folded over his breast, and his head a little inclined upward, so that Magawisca fancied she saw his full eye turned heavenward; after him walked all the men of the tribe, ranged according to their age, and the rank assigned to each by his own exploits.

They were neither painted nor ornamented according to the common usage at festivals and sacrifices, but every thing had the air of hasty preparation. Magawisca gazed in speechless despair. The procession entered the wood, and for a few moments, disappeared from her sight—again they were visible, mounting the acclivity of the hill, by a winding narrow foot-path, shaded on either side by laurels. They now walked singly and slowly, but to Magawisca, their progress seemed rapid as a falling avalanche. She felt that, if she were to remain pent in that prison-house, her heart would burst, and she sprang towards the door-way in the hope of clearing her passage, but the Mohawk caught her arm in his iron grasp, and putting her back, calmly retained his station. She threw herself on her knees to him—she entreated—she wept—but in vain: he looked on her with unmoved apathy. Already she saw the foremost of the party had reached the rock, and were forming a semicircle around it—again she appealed to her determined keeper, and again he denied her petition, but with a faltering tongue, and a drooping eye.

Magawisca, in the urgency of a necessity that could brook no delay, had forgotten, or regarded as useless, the sleeping potion she had infused into the Mohawk's draught; she now saw the powerful agent was at work for her, and with that quickness of apprehension that made the operations of her mind as rapid as the impulses of instinct, she perceived that every emotion she excited but hindered the effect of the potion, suddenly seeming to relinquish all purpose and hope of escape, she threw herself on a mat, and hid her face, burning with agonizing impatience, in her mantle. There we must leave her, and join that fearful company who were gathered together to witness what they believed to be the execution of exact and necessary justice.

Seated around their sacrifice-rock—their holy of holies—they listened to the sad story of the Pequod chief, with dejected countenances and downcast eyes, save when an involuntary glance turned on Everell, who stood awaiting his fate, cruelly aggravated by every moment's delay, with a quiet dignity and calm resignation, that would have become a hero, or a saint. Surrounded by this dark cloud of savages, his fair countenance kindled by holy inspiration, he looked scarcely like a creature of earth.

There might have been among the spectators, some who felt the silent appeal of the helpless courageous boy; some whose hearts moved them to interpose to save the selected victim; but they were restrained by their interpretation of natural justice, as controlling to them as our artificial codes of laws to us.

Others of a more cruel, or more irritable disposition, when the Pequod described his wrongs, and depicted his sufferings, brandished their tomahawks, and would have hurled them at the boy, but the chief said—"Nay, brothers—the work is mine—he dies by my hand—for my firstborn—life for life—he dies by a single stroke, for thus was my boy cut off. The blood of sachems is in his veins. He has the skin, but not the soul of that mixed race, whose gratitude is like that vanishing mist," and he pointed to the vapour that was melting from the mountain tops into the transparent ether; "and their promises are like this," and he snapped a dead branch from the pine beside which he stood, and broke it in fragments. "Boy, as he is, he fought for his mother, as the eagle fights for its young. I watched him in the mountain-path, when the blood gushed from his torn feet; not a word from his smooth lip, betrayed his pain."

Mononotto embellished his victim with praises, as the ancients wreathed theirs with flowers. He brandished his hatchet over Everell's head, and cried, exultingly, "See, he flinches not. Thus stood my boy, when they flashed their sabres before his eyes, and bade him betray his father. Brothers—My people have told me I bore a woman's heart towards the enemy. Ye shall see. I will pour out this English boy's blood to the last drop, and give his flesh and bones to the dogs and wolves."

He then motioned to Everell to prostrate himself on the rock, his face downward. In this position the boy would not see the descending stroke. Even at this moment of dire vengeance, the instincts of a merciful nature asserted their rights.

Everell sunk calmly on his knees, not to supplicate life, but to commend his soul to God. He clasped his hands together. He did not—he could not speak: his soul was

> "Rapt in still communion that transcends
> The imperfect offices of prayer."

At this moment a sun-beam penetrated the trees that enclosed the area, and fell athwart his brow and hair, kindling it with an almost supernatural brightness. To the savages, this was a token that the victim was accepted, and they sent forth a shout that rent the air. Everell bent forward, and pressed his forehead to the rock. The chief raised the deadly weapon, when Magawisca, springing from the precipitous side of the rock, screamed—"Forbear!" and interposed her arm. It was too late. The blow was levelled—force and direction given—the stroke aimed at Everell's neck, severed his defender's arm, and left him unharmed. The lopped quivering member dropped over the precipice. Mononotto staggered and fell senseless, and all the savages, uttering horrible yells, rushed toward the fatal spot.

"Stand back!" cried Magawisca. "I have bought his life with my own. Fly, Everell—nay, speak not, but fly—thither—to the east!" she cried, more vehemently.

Everell's faculties were paralyzed by a rapid succession of violent emotions. He was conscious only of a feeling of mingled gratitude and admiration for his preserver. He stood motionless, gazing on her. "I die in vain then," she cried, in an accent of such despair, that he was roused. He threw his arms around her, and pressed her to his heart, as he would a sister that had redeemed his life with her own, and then tearing himself from her, he disappeared. No one offered to follow him. The voice of nature rose from every heart, and responding to the justice of Magawisca's claim, bade him "God speed!" To all it seemed that his deliverance had been achieved by miraculous aid. All—the dullest and coldest, paid involuntary homage to the heroic girl, as if she were a superior being, guided and upheld by supernatural power.

Every thing short of miracle she had achieved. The moment the opiate dulled the senses of her keeper, she escaped from the hut; and aware that, if she attempted to penetrate to her father through the semicircular line of spectators that enclosed him, she would be repulsed, and probably borne off the ground, she had taken the desperate resolution of mounting the rock, where only her approach would be unperceived. She did not stop to ask herself if it were possible, but impelled by a determined spirit, or rather, we would believe, by that inspiration that teaches the bird its unknown path, and leads the goat, with its young, safely over the mountain crags, she ascended the rock. There were crevices in it, but they seemed scarcely sufficient to support the eagle with his grappling talon, and twigs issuing from the fissures, but so slender, that they waved like a blade of grass under the weight of the young birds that made a rest on them, and yet, such is the power of love, stronger than death, that with these inadequate helps, Magawisca scaled the rock, and achieved her generous purpose.

1827

Sojourner Truth
(c. 1797–1883)

To call Sojourner Truth an American "writer" is to take some liberties with the literal meaning of the word, for—raised a slave whose first language was not English but Dutch, and who received no education in reading or writing—she was illiterate. By all reports, however, she was a distinguished orator, brilliant in her ability to move even hostile crowds to agreement.

Sojourner Truth was born Isabella, a slave on Colonel Johannes Hardenbergh's farm in Ulster County, New York, sometime in the late 1790s. She had a number of owners in New York state, one of whom promised to free her. When he broke that promise, she fled in 1827 with two infant daughters to the farm of the Van Wagenen family, who sheltered and later purchased her. She sued her former master for having illegally sold her 5-year-old son to an Alabama planter; in 1827 she won the precedent-setting case, and her son was freed. She herself achieved her freedom in that same year under the terms of the New York Emancipation Act and took the name Isabella Van Wagenen.

From 1829 to 1843, she lived in New York City, becoming involved in churches and making a living as a house servant. Changing her name to Sojourner Truth in 1843, she followed a "call" to leave the city and to travel, preaching and speaking against slavery and for women's suffrage. Her sojourns took her before audiences in Connecticut, Massachusetts, Ohio, Indiana, Illinois, and Kansas. Sometimes she spoke alongside such prominent abolitionists as Frederick Douglass, sometimes alone; she spoke, too, at rallies for women's rights, where middle-class white women wrote down what she said. The surviving texts of "Ain't I a Woman" and "What Time of Night It Is" are the results of such transcriptions. Although we have no unmediated versions of her speeches, we can find the traces of an oral preaching tradition in what survives. Rhetorical questions, repetition and variation, biblical allusion, and witty remarks about the audience characterize her style.

"Ain't I a Woman" was recorded by Frances Gage, a suffragist, after Sojourner

Truth spoke at a women's rights convention in Akron, Ohio, in 1851. We have reproduced the full text of Gage's "reminiscence" to provide the context for this representation of Truth's appearance and manner of speaking. The heavy dialect of the speech is Gage's rendition of how Truth sounded to her; the commentary on Truth's gestures and the audience's response reflect Gage's own impressions. The speech known as "What Time of Night It Is," probably written down by Elizabeth Cady Stanton, was delivered at a similar convention in New York City in 1853. This text displays another mode of transcription: Stanton has partially standardized Truth's usage and diction, avoiding the near-caricature of Gage's account. Both texts can be found in *History of Woman Suffrage* (1889), edited by Stanton, Susan B. Anthony, and Matilda Joslyn Gage.

Stanton describes Truth on the speaker's platform: "Sojourner combined in herself, as an individual, the two most hated elements of humanity. She was black, and she was a woman, and all the insults that could be cast upon color and sex were together hurled at her; but there she stood, calm and dignified; a grand, wise woman, who could neither read nor write, and yet with deep insight could penetrate the very soul of the universe about her." Readers who never saw her came to know Truth through an influential essay by Harriet Beecher Stowe, "Sojourner Truth, the Libyan Sibyl" (1863), and through *The Narrative of Sojourner Truth* (1875), a biography written by Olive Gilbert.

Eventually Truth met Abraham Lincoln, who appointed her counselor to the freedmen in Washington, D.C. She continued speaking and working on behalf of free African Americans until she died in 1883 in Michigan, where she spent the last years of her life.

For more information about Sojourner Truth, see *Sojourner Truth: God's Faithful Pilgrim* (1938) by Arthur Huff Fauset and *Women and Sisters: The Antislavery Feminists in American Culture* (1989) by Jean Fagan Yellin.

Reminiscences by Frances D. Gage

Sojourner Truth.

The leaders of the movement[1] trembled on seeing a tall, gaunt black woman in a gray dress and white turban, surmounted with an uncouth sun-bonnet, march deliberately into the church, walk with the air of a queen up the aisle, and take her seat upon the pulpit steps. A buzz of disapprobation was heard all over the house, and there fell on the listening ear, "An abolition affair!" "Woman's rights and niggers!" "I told you so!" "Go it, darkey!"

I chanced on that occasion to wear my first laurels in public life as president of the meeting. At my request order was restored, and the business of the Convention went on. Morning, afternoon, and evening exercises came and went. Through all these sessions old Sojourner, quiet and reticent as the "Lybian Statue,"[2] sat crouched against the wall on the corner of the pulpit stairs, her sun-bonnet shading her eyes, her elbows on her knees, her chin resting upon her broad, hard palms. At intermission she was busy selling the "Life of Sojourner Truth,"[3] a narrative of her own strange and adventurous life. Again and again, timorous and trembling ones came to me and said, with earnestness, "Don't let her speak, Mrs. Gage, it will ruin us.

1. The movement for gaining women the right to vote.
2. Probably a reference to "The Libyan Sibyl," by sculptor William Wetmore Story, at the Smithsonian. The semi-nude African-featured female figure sits thoughtfully, with chin in hand and elbow on knee. Story said Stowe's description of Sojourner Truth inspired the piece.
3. By Olive Gilbert.

Every newspaper in the land will have our cause mixed up with abolition and niggers, and we shall be utterly denounced." My only answer was, "We shall see when the time comes."

The second day the work waxed warm. Methodist, Baptist, Episcopal, Presbyterian, and Universalist ministers came in to hear and discuss the resolutions presented. One claimed superior rights and privileges for man, on the ground of "superior intellect"; another, because of the "manhood of Christ; if God had desired the equality of woman, He would have given some token of His will through the birth, life, and death of the Saviour." Another gave us a theological view of the "sin of our first mother."

There were very few women in those days who dared to "speak in meeting"[4]; and the august teachers of the people were seemingly getting the better of us, while the boys in the galleries, and the sneerers among the pews, were hugely enjoying the discomfiture, as they supposed, of the "strong-minded." Some of the tender-skinned friends were on the point of losing dignity, and the atmosphere betokened a storm. When, slowly from her seat in the corner rose Sojourner Truth, who, till now, had scarcely lifted her head. "Don't let her speak!" gasped half a dozen in my ear. She moved slowly and solemnly to the front, laid her old bonnet at her feet, and turned her great speaking eyes to me. There was a hissing sound of disapprobation above and below. I rose and announced "Sojourner Truth," and begged the audience to keep silence for a few moments.

The tumult subsided at once, and every eye was fixed on this almost Amazon[5] form, which stood nearly six feet high, head erect, and eyes piercing the upper air like one in a dream. At her first word there was a profound hush. She spoke in deep tones, which, though not loud, reached every ear in the house, and away through the throng at the doors and windows.

"Wall, chilern, whar dar is so much racket dar must be somethin' out o' kilter. I tink dat 'twixt de niggers of de Souf and de womin at de Norf, all talkin' 'bout rights, de white men will be in a fix pretty soon. But what's all dis here talkin' 'bout?

"Dat man ober dar say dat womin needs to be helped into carriages, and lifted ober ditches, and to hab de best place everywhar. Nobody eber helps me into carriages, or ober mud-puddles, or gibs me any best place!" And raising herself to her full height, and her voice to a pitch like rolling thunder, she asked. "And a'n't I a woman? Look at me! Look at my arm! (and she bared her right arm to the shoulder, showing her tremendous muscular power). I have ploughed, and planted, and gathered into barns, and no man could head me! And a'n't I a woman? I could work as much and eat as much as a man—when I could get it—and bear de lash as well! And a'n't I a woman? I have borne thirteen chilern, and seen 'em mos' all sold off to slavery, and when I cried out with my mother's grief, none but Jesus heard me! And a'n't I a woman?

"Den dey talks 'bout dis ting in de head; what dis dey call it?" ("Intellect," whispered some one near.) "Dat's it, honey. What's dat got to do wid womin's rights or nigger's rights? If my cup won't hold but a pint, and yourn holds a quart, wouldn't ye be mean not to let me have my little half-measure full?" And she pointed her significant finger, and sent a keen glance at the minister who had made the argument. The cheering was long and loud.

"Den dat little man in black dar, he say women can't have as much rights as men, 'cause Christ wan't a woman! Whar did your Christ come from?" Rolling thunder couldn't have stilled that crowd, as did those deep, wonderful tones, as she stood there with outstretched arms and eyes of fire. Raising her voice still louder, she repeated, "Whar did your Christ come from? From God and a woman! Man had nothin' to do wid Him." Oh, what a rebuke that was to that little man.

Turning again to another objector, she took up the defense of Mother Eve. I can not follow her through it all. It was pointed, and witty, and solemn; eliciting at almost every sentence deafening applause; and she ended by asserting: "If de fust woman God ever made was strong

4. To speak out in church.
5. In Greek mythology, a member of a nation of female warriors.

enough to turn de world upside down all alone, dese women togedder (and she glanced her eye over the platform) ought to be able to turn it back, and get it right side up again! And now dey is asking to do it, de men better let 'em." Long-continued cheering greeted this. " 'Bleeged[6] to ye for hearin' on me, and now ole Sojourner han't got nothin' more to say."

Amid roars of applause, she returned to her corner, leaving more than one of us with streaming eyes, and hearts beating with gratitude. She had taken us up in her strong arms and carried us safely over the slough of difficulty turning the whole tide in our favor. I have never in my life seen anything like the magical influence that subdued the mobbish spirit of the day, and turned the sneers and jeers of an excited crowd into notes of respect and admiration. Hundreds rushed up to shake hands with her, and congratulate the glorious old mother, and bid her God-speed on her mission of "testifyin' agin concerning the wickedness of this 'ere people."

1859

"What Time of Night It Is"

Is it not good for me to come and draw forth a spirit, to see what kind of spirit people are of? I see that some of you have got the spirit of a goose, and some have got the spirit of a snake.[7] I feel at home here. I come to you, citizens of New York, as I suppose you ought to be. I am a citizen of the State of New York; I was born in it, and I was a slave in the State of New York; and now I am a good citizen of this State. I was born here, and I can tell you I feel at home here. I've been lookin' round and watchin' things, and I know a little mite 'bout Woman's Rights, too. I come forth to speak 'bout Woman's Rights, and want to throw in my little mite, to keep the scales a-movin'. I know that it feels a kind o' hissin' and ticklin' like to see a colored woman get up and tell you about things, and Woman's Rights. We have all been thrown down so low that nobody thought we'd ever get up again; but we have been long enough trodden now; we will come up again, and now I am here.

I was a-thinkin', when I see women contendin' for their rights, I was a-thinkin' what a difference there is now, and what there was in old times. I have only a few minutes to speak; but in the old times the kings of the earth would hear a woman. There was a king in the Scriptures; and then it was the kings of the earth would kill a woman if she come into their presence; but Queen Esther come forth, for she was oppressed, and felt there was a great wrong, and she said I will die or I will bring my complaint before the king.[8] Should the king of the United States be greater, or more crueler, or more harder? But the king, he raised up his sceptre and said: "Thy request shall be granted unto thee—to the half of my kingdom will I grant it to thee!" Then he said he would hang Haman on the gallows he had made up high. But that is not what women come forward to contend. The women want their rights as Esther. She only wanted to explain her rights. And he was so liberal that he said, "the half of my kingdom shall be granted to thee," and he did not wait for her to ask, he was so liberal with her.

Now, women do not ask half of a kingdom, but their rights, and they don't get 'em. When she comes to demand 'em, don't you hear how sons hiss their mothers like snakes, because they ask for their rights; and can they ask for anything less? The king ordered Haman to be hung on the gallows which he prepared to hang others; but I do not want any man to be killed, but I am sorry to see them so short-minded. But we'll have our rights; see if we don't; and

6. Obliged.
7. Probably an allusion to audience members' hissing.
8. In the Old Testament book of Esther, the queen intercedes with her husband, the king, on behalf of her oppressed people; at her request, the king hangs Haman, the oppressor.

you can't stop us from them; see if you can. You may hiss as much as you like, but it is comin'. Women don't get half as much rights as they ought to; we want more, and we will have it. Jesus says: "What I say to one, I say to all—watch!"[9] I'm a-watchin'. God says: "Honor your father and your mother."[1] Sons and daughters ought to behave themselves before their mothers, but they do not. I can see them a-laughin', and pointin' at their mothers up here on the stage. They hiss when an aged woman comes forth. If they'd been brought up proper they'd have known better than hissing like snakes and geese. I'm 'round watchin' these things, and I wanted to come up and say these few things to you, and I'm glad of the hearin' you give me. I wanted to tell you a mite about Woman's Rights, and so I came out and said so. I am sittin' among you to watch; and every once and awhile I will come out and tell you what time of night it is.[2]

1853   1859

Caroline Stansbury Kirkland

(1801–1864)

Born in New York City to a socially prominent family, Caroline Stansbury was thoroughly educated by her aunt, a school headmistress. She planned a career in teaching and began by assisting her aunt. The family moved to Clinton, New York, after the death of Mr. Stansbury in 1822. In 1828 she married William Kirkland, a professor of classics at Hamilton College; the couple soon moved to Geneva, New York, and founded a girls' school. Mrs. Kirkland gave birth to four children there.

In 1835 Mr. Kirkland was offered the job of principal in the new Detroit Female Seminary, and they moved to Michigan. Two more children were born in Detroit and one died there. In early 1836 the Kirklands began acquiring land in Livingston County, about 60 miles northwest of the city, and started to plan the community to be known as Montacute in Mrs. Kirkland's books, near the present village of Pinckney. They moved to the frontier settlement in 1837 and stayed until 1843, when they returned to New York. *A New Home— Who'll Follow?* was published under the pen name Mrs. Mary Clavers in 1839, followed by *Forest Life* (1842) and *Western Clearings* (1845).

Back east, Mrs. Kirkland opened a school and Mr. Kirkland went into newspaper work. After she was widowed in 1846, Mrs. Kirkland became a professional writer and editor. She edited *The Union Magazine*, a literary journal, and compiled books for a wide female audience. Not only prominent in New York circles, she was received by Charles Dickens and Robert and Elizabeth Browning when she traveled to Britain and carried on a correspondence with social activist Harriet Martineau. Her son, the novelist Joseph Kirkland, served in the Union Army, and she was active in Civil War relief work.

With *A New Home*, Kirkland had opened up a fresh subject for American literature, and her work was very favorably received. Edgar Allan Poe, in *Literati of New York*, written for *Godey's Lady's Book*, called her "one of our best writers." At the time of her death, her literary reputation was still strong. She counted the poet William Cullen Bryant among her friends; he served as one of her pallbearers and wrote her obituary. By the turn of the century, however, her name was nearly forgotten.

Kirkland intended to depict frontier life as she had experienced and observed it,

9. Mark 13:37.
1. Exodus 20:12.

2. To "watch" is to stay awake as well as to observe.

without romance or sentiment. As she wrote to a friend in 1848, "I love the West, and shall be glad to do it good by telling the truth." Because she came from a background of genteel living and was a very educated woman for her day—able to read Latin, French, Italian, and German—Kirkland was not the typical frontier wife and mother. Her reporter's eye took in both humor and tragedy in backwoods life. Alongside the beauty of oak clearings, she could see the mudholes and marshes. In neighboring cabins, she observed nobility and dignity, selfishness and crudity.

The following text is taken from an 1872 reprint of *A New Home*, retitled *Our New Home in the West; or Glimpses of Life among the Early Settlers.*

FROM A NEW HOME.

Chapter I

Here are seen
No traces of man's pomp and pride; no silks
Rustle, nor jewels shine, nor envious eyes
Encounter. . . .
 Oh, there is not lost
One of earth's charms; upon her bosom yet
After the flight of untold centuries
The freshness of her far beginning lies.
 Bryant.

Our friends in the 'settlements' have expressed so much interest in such of our letters to them as happened to convey any account of the peculiar features of western life, and have asked so many questions, touching particulars which we had not thought worthy of mention, that I have been for some time past contemplating the possibility of something like a detailed account of our experiences. And I have determined to give them to the world, in a form not very different from that in which they were originally recorded for our private delectation; nothing doubting, that a veracious history of actual occurrences, an unvarnished transcript of real characters, and an impartial record of every-day forms of speech (taken down in many cases from the lips of the speaker) will be pronounced 'graphic' by at least a fair proportion of the journalists of the day.

It is true there are but meagre materials for anything that might be called a story. I have never seen a cougar—nor been bitten by a rattlesnake. The reader who has patience to go with me to the close of my desultory sketches, must expect nothing beyond a meandering recital of common-place occurrences—mere gossip about everyday people, little enhanced in value by any fancy or ingenuity of the writer; in short, a very ordinary pen-drawing; which, deriving no interest from coloring, can be valuable only for its truth.

A home on the outskirts of civilization—habits of society which allow the maid and her mistress to do the honors in complete equality, and to make the social tea visit in loving conjunction—such a distribution of the duties of life as compels all, without distinction, to rise with the sun or before him—to breakfast with the chickens—then,

"Count the slow clock, and dine exact at noon"—

to be ready for tea at four, and for bed at eight—may certainly be expected to furnish some curious particulars for the consideration of those whose daily course almost reverses this primitive arrangement—who 'call night day and day night,' and who are apt occasionally to forget, when speaking of a particular class, that 'those creatures' are partakers with themselves of a common nature.

I can only wish, like other modest chroniclers, my respected prototypes, that so fertile a theme had fallen into worthier hands. If Miss Mitford,[1] who has given us such charming glimpses of Aberleigh, Hilton Cross, and the Loddon, had, by some happy chance, been translated to Michigan, what would she not have made of such materials as Tinkerville, Montacute, and the Turnip?

When my husband purchased two hundred acres of wild land on the banks of this to-be-celebrated stream, and drew with a piece of chalk on the bar-room table at Danforth's the plan of a village, I little thought I was destined to make myself famous by handing down to posterity a faithful record of the advancing fortunes of that favored spot.

'The madness of the people' in those days of golden dreams took more commonly the form of city-building; but there were a few who contented themselves with planning villages, on the banks of streams which certainly never could be expected to bear navies, but which might yet be turned to account in the more homely way of grinding or sawing—operations which must necessarily be performed somewhere, for the well-being of those very cities. It is of one of these humble attempts that it is my lot to speak, and I make my confession at the outset, warning any fashionable reader, who may have taken up my book, that I intend to be 'decidedly low.'

Whether the purchaser of *our* village would have been as moderate under all possible circumstances, I am not prepared to say, since, never having enjoyed a situation under government, his resources have not been unlimited; and for this reason any remark which may be hazarded in the course of these my lucubrations touching the more magnificent plans of wealthier aspirants, must be received with some grains of allowance. 'Il est plus aisé d'être sage pour les autres, que de l'être pour soi-même.'[2]

When I made my first visit to these remote and lonely regions, the scattered woods through which we rode for many miles were gay in their first gosling-green suit of half-opened leaves, and the forest odors which exhaled with the dews of morning and evening, were beyond measure delicious to one 'long in populous cities pent.' I desired much to be a little sentimental at the time, and feel tempted to indulge to some small extent even here—but I forbear; and shall adhere closely to matters more in keeping with my subject.

I think, to be precise, the time was the last, the very last of April, and I recollect well that even at that early season, by availing myself with sedulous application, of those times when I was fain to quit the vehicle through fear of the perilous mud-holes, or still more perilous half-bridged marshes, I picked upwards of twenty varieties of wild-flowers—some of them of rare and delicate beauty;—and sure I am, that if I had succeeded in inspiring my companion with one spark of my own floral enthusiasm, our hundred miles of travel would have occupied a week's time.

The wild-flowers of Michigan deserve a poet of their own. Shelley who sang so quaintly of 'the pied wind-flowers and the tulip tall,' would have found many a fanciful comparison and deep-drawn meaning for the thousand gems of the road-side. Charles Lamb could have written charming volumes about the humblest among them. Bulwer would find means to associate the common three-leaved white lily so closely with the Past, the Present, and the Future—the Wind, the Stars, and the Tripod of Delphos, that all future botanists, and eke all future philosophers, might fail to unravel the 'linked sweetness.'[3] We must have a poet of our own.

Since I have casually alluded to a Michigan mud-hole, I may as well enter into a detailed memoir on the subject, for the benefit of future travellers, who, flying over the soil on

---

1. Mary Russell Mitford (1787–1855), English writer whose work included country and village sketches.
2. It's easier to be wise for others than for yourself.

3. Percy Bysshe Shelley (1792–1822), Charles Lamb (1775–1834), and Edward Bulwer-Lytton (1803–1873) are English writers widely read in the United States.

railroads, may look slightingly back upon the achievements of their predecessors. In the 'settlements,' a mud-hole is considered as apt to occasion an unpleasant jolt—a breaking of the thread of one's reverie—or in extreme cases, a temporary stand-still, or even an overturn of the rash and unwary. Here, on approaching one of these characteristic features of the 'West'—(how much does that expression mean to include? I have never been able to discover its limits)—the driver stops—alights—walks up to the dark gulf—and around it, if he can get around it. He then seeks a long pole and sounds it, measures it across to ascertain how its width compares with the length of his wagon—tries whether its sides are perpendicular, as is usually the case if the road is much used. If he find it not more than three feet deep, he remounts cheerily, encourages his team, and in they go, with a plunge and a shock, rather apt to damp the courage of the inexperienced. If the hole be narrow, the hinder wheels will be quite lifted off the ground by the depression of their precedents, and so remain until by unwearied chiruping and some judicious touches of 'the string' the horses are induced to struggle as for their lives; and if the Fates are propitious they generally emerge on the opposite side, dragging the vehicle, or, at least, the forewheels, after them. When I first 'penetrated the interior,' (to use an indigenous phrase,) all I knew of the wilds was from Hoffman's Tour, or Captain Hall's[4] 'graphic' delineations. I had some floating idea of 'driving a barouche-and-four any where through the oak-openings'—and seeing 'the murdered Banquos of the forest' haunting the scenes of their departed strength and beauty. But I confess these pictures, touched by the glowing pencil of fancy, gave me but incorrect notions of a real journey through Michigan.

Our vehicle was not perhaps very judiciously chosen—at least we have since thought so. It was a light, high-hung carriage—of the description commonly known as a buggy or shandrydan—names, of which I would be glad to learn the etymology. I seriously advise any of my friends, who are about flitting to Wisconsin or Oregon, to prefer a heavy lumber wagon, even for the use of the ladies of the family; very little aid or consolation being derived from making a 'genteel' appearance in such cases.

At the first encounter of such a mud-hole as I have attempted to describe, we stopped in utter despair. My companion indeed would fain have persuaded me that the many wheel tracks which passed through the formidable gulf were proof positive that it might be forded. I insisted with all a woman's obstinacy that I could not and would not make the attempt, and alighted accordingly, and tried to find a path on one side or the other. But in vain, even putting out of the question my paper-soled shoes—sensible things for the woods. The ditch on each side was filled with water and quite too wide to jump over; and we were actually contemplating a return, when a man in an immense bear-skin cap and a suit of deer's hide, sprang from behind a stump just within the edge of the forest. He 'poled' himself over the ditch in a moment, and stood beside us, rifle in hand, as wild and rough a specimen of humanity as one would wish to encounter in a strange and lonely road, just at the shadowy dusk of the evening. I did *not* scream, though I own I was prodigiously frightened. But our stranger said immediately, in a gentle tone and with a French accent, 'Me watch deer—you want to cross?' On receiving an answer in the affirmative, he ran in search of a rail, which he threw over the terrific mud-hole—aided me to walk across by the help of his pole— showed my husband where to plunge—waited till he had gone safely through, and 'slow circles dimpled o'er the quaking mud'—then took himself off by the way he came, declining any compensation with a most polite 'rien! rien!'[5] This instance of true and genuine and generous politeness I record for the benefit of all bearskin caps, leathern jerkins, and cowhide boots, which ladies from the eastward world may hereafter encounter in Michigan.

---

4. Charles Fenno Hoffman (1806–1884) wrote descriptions of crossing the Alleghenies and prairies in *A Winter in the West* (1835); James Hall (1793–1868) edited *Western Monthly* *Magazine* (1832–1836) and presented Western stories in such books as *Legends from the West* (1828).

5. "Nothing! nothing!"

Our journey was marked by no incident more alarming than the one I have related, though one night passed in a wretched inn, deep in the 'timbered land'—as all woods are called in Michigan—was not without its terrors, owing to the horrible drunkenness of the master of the house, whose wife and children were in constant fear of their lives from his insane fury. I can never forget the countenance of that desolate woman, sitting trembling, and with white compressed lips, in the midst of her children. The father raving all night, and coming through our sleeping apartment with the earliest ray of morning in search of more of the poison already boiling in his veins. The poor wife could not forbear telling me her story—her change of lot—from a well-stored and comfortable home in Connecticut to this wretched den in the wilderness—herself and children worn almost to shadows with the ague,[6] and her husband such as I have described him. I may mention here, that not very long after, I heard of this man in prison in Detroit, for stabbing a neighbor in a drunken brawl, and ere the year was out, he died of delirium tremens, leaving his family destitute. So much for turning our fields of golden grain into 'fire water'—a branch of business in which Michigan is fast improving.

Our ride being a deliberate one, I felt, after the third day, a little wearied, and began to complain of the sameness of the oak openings, and to wish we were fairly at our journey's end. We were crossing a broad expanse of what seemed, at a little distance, a smooth shaven lawn of the most brilliant green, but which proved on trial little better than a quaking bog—embracing within its ridgy circumference all possible varieties of

'Muirs and mosses, slaps and styles'—

I had just indulged in something like a yawn, and wished that I could see our hotel. At the word, my companion's face assumed rather a comical expression, and I was preparing to inquire somewhat testily what there was so laughable—I was getting tired and cross, reader—when down came our good horse to the very chin in a bog-hole, green as Erin on the top, but giving way on the touch, and seeming deep enough to have engulfed us entirely, if its width had been proportionate. Down came the horse—and this was not all—down came the driver; and I could not do less than follow, though at a little distance—our good steed kicking and floundering—covering us with hieroglyphics, which would be readily deciphered by any Wolverine[7] we should meet, though perchance strange to the eyes of our friends at home. This mishap was soon amended. Tufts of long marsh grass served to assoilzie our habiliments a little, and a clear stream which rippled through the marsh aided in removing the eclipse from our faces. We journeyed on cheerily, watching the splendid changes in the west, but keeping a bright look out for bog-holes.

Chapter II.

Think us no churls, nor measure our good minds
By this rude place we live in.

Cymbeline.

The sun had just set when we stopped at the tavern, and I then read the cause of my companion's quizzical look. My hotel was a log-house, of diminutive size, with corresponding appurtenances; and from the moment we entered its door I was in a fidget to know where we could possibly sleep. I was then new in Michigan. Our good hostess rose at once with a nod of welcome.

6. A malarial fever.
7. Nickname for natives or inhabitants of Michigan.

'Well! is this Miss Clavers!' (my husband had been there before)—'well! I want to know! why do tell if you have been upsot in the mash? why I want to know!—and did n't ye hurt ye none? Come, gals, fly round, and let's git some supper.'

'But you'll not be able to lodge us, Mrs. Danforth,' said I, glancing at three young men and some boys, who appeared to have come in from their work, and who were lounging on one side of the immense open chimney.

'Why, bless your heart! yes I shall; don't you fret yourself; I'll give you as good a bed as anybody need want.'

I cast an exploring look, and now discovered a door opposite the fire.

'Jist step in here,' said Mrs. Danforth, opening this door, 'jist come in and take off your things, and lop down, if you're a mind to, while we're a getting supper.'

I followed her into the room, if room it might be called, a strip partitioned off, just six feet wide, so that a bed was accurately fitted in at each end, and a square space remained vacant between the two.

'We've been getting this room made lately, and I tell you it's real nice, so private like!' said our hostess, with a complacent air. 'Here,' she continued, 'in this bed the gals sleeps, and that's my bed and the old man's; and then here's a trundle-bed for Sally and Jane,' and suiting the action to the word, she drew out the trundle-bed as far as our standing-place would allow, to show me how convenient it was.

Here was my grand problem still unsolved! If 'me and the old man,' and the girls, and Sally and Jane, slept in this strip, there certainly could be no room for more, and I thought with dismay of the low-browed roof, which had seemed to me to rest on the tops of the window-frames. And, to make a long story short, though manifold were the runnings up and down, and close the whisperings, before all was ready, I was at length ushered up a steep and narrow stick ladder into the sleeping apartment. Here, surrounded by beds of all sizes spread on the floor, was a bedstead, placed under the peak of the roof in order to gain space for its height; and round this state-bed, for such it evidently was, although not supplied with pillows at each end, all the men and boys I had seen below stairs were to repose. Sundry old quilts were fastened by forks to the rafters in such a way as to serve as a partial screen, and with this I was obliged to be content. Excessive fatigue is not fastidious. I called to mind some canal-boat experiences, and resigned myself to the 'honey-heavy dew of slumber.'

I awoke with a sense of suffocation—started up—all was dark as the Hall of Eblis.[8] I called; no answer came; I shrieked! and up ran one of the 'gals.'

'What on airth's the matter?'

'Where am I? What ails me?' said I, beginning to feel a little awkward when I heard the damsel's voice.

'Why, I guess you was scairt, wa'n't ye?'

'Why am I in the dark? Is it morning?'

'Morning? why, the boys has been gone away this hour, and, you see, there a'n't no winder up here, but I'll take down this here quilt, and then I guess you'll be able to see some.'

She did so, and I began to discern

'A faint shadow of uncertain light,'

which, after my eyes had become somewhat accustomed to it, served very well to dress by.

Upon descending the ladder, I found our breakfast prepared on a very neat-looking table, and Mrs. Danforth with her clean apron on, ready to do the honors.

Seeing me looking round with inquiring eye, she said, 'O, you'm looking for a wash-dish, a'n't ye?' and forthwith put some water into a little iron skillet, and carried it out to a bench

8. In Islamic myth, Eblis or Iblis is the chief of the wicked jinns.

which stood under the eaves, where I performed my very limited ablutions *al fresco,*[9] not at all pleased with this part of country habits.

I bethought me of a story I had heard before we crossed the line, of a gentleman travelling in Michigan, who, instead of a 'wash-dish,' was directed to the spring, and when he requested a towel received for answer—'why, I should think you had a hankercher.'

After breakfast I expressed a wish to accompany Mr. Clavers to the village tract; but he thought a very bad marsh would make the ride unpleasant.

'Lord bless ye!' said Mr. Danforth, 'that mash has got a real handsome bridge over it since you was here last.'

So we set out in the buggy and rode several miles through an alternation of open glades with fine walnut trees scattered over them, and 'bosky dells' fragrant as 'Araby the blest' at that delicious hour, when the dews filled the air with the scent of the bursting leaves.

By-and-by we came to the 'beautiful bridge,' a newly-laid causeway of large round logs, with a 'slough of despond'[1] to be crossed, in order to reach it. I would not consent to turn back, however, and in we went, the buggy standing it most commendably. When we reached the first log our poor Rozinante[2] stopped in utter despair, and some persuasion was necessary to induce him to rear high enough to place his fore-feet upon the bridge; and when he accomplished this feat, and after a rest essayed to make the buggy rear too, it was neck or nothing. Yet up we went, and then came the severe part of the achievement, a 'beautiful bridge' half a mile long!

Half a rod was enough for me; I cried for quarter, and was permitted to pick my way over its slippery eminences, to the utter annihilation of a pair of Lane's shoes.

Chapter V.

Such soon-speeding geer
As will dispense itself through all the veins.
Shakespeare.

By her help I also now
Make this churlish place allow
Some things that may sweeten gladness
In the very heart of sadness.
Withers.

The next day I was to spend in the society of my hostess; and I felt in no haste to quit my eyrie, although it was terribly close, but waited a call from one of the little maidens before I attempted my twilight toilet. When I descended the ladder, nobody was visible but the womankind.

After breakfast Mrs. Danforth mentioned that she was going about a mile into the woods to visit a neighbor whose son had been bitten by a massisaugas,[3] (I spell the word by ear), and was not expected to live.

I inquired of course—'Why, law! it's a rattlesnake; the Indians call them massisaugas, and so *folks* calls 'em so too.'

'Are they often seen here?'

---

9. "In the fresh air."
1. A reference to John Bunyon's *Pilgrim's Progress,* where Christian must get through a "slough of despond."

2. Don Quixote's horse's name.
3. The Massasauga rattlesnake, a small variety native to Michigan, ranges from the Great Lakes to the Mexican border.

'Why, no not very; as far from the *mash* as this. I hadn't seen but two this spring, and them was here in the garden, and I killed 'em both.'

'*You* killed them!'

'Why, law, yes!—Betsey come in one night after tea[4] and told me on 'em, and we went out, and she held the candle while I killed them. But I tell you we had a real chase after them!'

My desire for a long walk through the woods was somewhat cooled by this conversation; nevertheless, upon the good dame's reiterated assurance that there was no danger, and that she would 'as lief meet forty on 'em as not,' I consented to accompany her, and our path through the dim forest was as enchanting as one of poor Shelley's gemmed and leafy dreams. The distance seemed nothing, and I scarcely remembered the rattlesnakes.

We found the poor boy in not quite so sad a case as had been expected. A physician had arrived from————, about fourteen miles off, and had brought with him a quantity of spirits of hartshorn,[5] with which the poisoned limb had now been constantly bathed for some hours, while frequent small doses of the same specific had been administered. This course had produced a change, and the pale and weary mother had begun to hope.

This boy had been fishing in the stream which was to make the fortune of Montacute, and in kneeling to search for bait had roused the snake which bit him just above the knee. The entire limb was frightfully swollen and covered with large livid spots 'exactly like the snake,' as the woman stated with an air of mysterious meaning.

When I saw the body of the snake, which the father had found without difficulty, and killed very near the scene of the accident—so slow are these creatures generally—I found it difficult to trace the resemblance between its brilliant colors and the purplish brown blotches on the poor boy's leg. But the superstition once received, imagination supplies all deficiencies. A firm belief in some inscrutable connexion between the spots on the snake and the spots on the wounded person is universal in this region, as I have since frequently heard.

During our walk homeward, sauntering as we did to prolong the enjoyment, my hostess gave me a little sketch of her own early history, and she had interested me so strongly by her unaffected kindliness, and withal a certain dash of espiéglerie,[6] that I listened to the homely recital with a good deal of pleasure.

'I was always pretty lucky,' she began—and as I looked at her benevolent countenance with its broad expansive brow and gentle eyes, I thought such people are apt to be 'lucky' even in this world of disappointments.

'My mother didn't live to bring me up,' she continued, 'but a man by the name of Spangler, that had no children, took me and did for me as if I had been his own; sent me to school and all. His wife was a real mother to me. She was a weakly woman, hardly ever able to sit up all day. I don't believe she ever spun a hank of yarn in her life; but she was a proper nice woman, and Spangler loved her just as well as if she had been ever so smart.'[7]

Mrs. Danforth seemed to dwell on this point in her friend's character with peculiar respect,—that he should love a wife who could not do her own work. I could not help telling her she reminded me of a man weeping for the loss of his partner—his neighbors trying to comfort him, by urging the usual topics; he cut them short, looking up at the same time with an inconsolable air—'Ah! but she was such a dreadful good creature to work!'

Mrs. Danforth said gravely, 'Well, I suppose the poor feller had a family of children to do for;' and after a reflective pause continued—'Well, *Miss* Spangler had a little one after all, when I was quite a big girl, and you never see folks so pleased as they! Mr. Spangler seemed as if he could not find folks enough to be good to, that winter. He had the prayers of the poor, I tell ye. There wasn't a baby born anywheres in our neighborhood, that whole blessed winter, but what he found out whether the mother had what would make her comfortable, and sent whatever was wanted.

---

4. The evening meal.
5. Ground deer antler used as a source of ammonia; ammonium carbonate.
6. Mischievousness.
7. Capable.

'He little thought that baby that he thought so much on was going to cost him so dear. His wife was never well again! She only lived through the summer and died when the frost came, just like the flowers; and he never held up his head afterwards. He had been a professor[8] for a good many years, but he did n't seem then to have neither faith nor hope. He would n't hear reason from nobody. I always thought that was the reason the baby died. It only lived about a year. Well, I had the baby to bring up by hand, and so I was living there yet when Mr. Spangler took sick. He seemed always like a broken-hearted man, but still he took comfort with the baby, and by and by the little dear took the croup and died all in a minute like. It began to be bad after tea and it was dead before sunrise. Then I saw plain enough nothing could be done for the father. He wasted away just like an April snow. I took as good care on him as I could, and when it came towards the last, he would n't have any body else give him even so much as a cup of tea. He settled up his business and gave receipts to many poor folks that owed him small debts, besides giving away a great many things, and paying all those that had helped take care of him. I think he knew what kind of a feller his nephew was, that was to have all when he was gone.

'Well, all this is neither here nor there. George Danforth and I had been keeping company then a good while, and Mr. Spangler knew we'd been only waiting till I could be spared, so he sent for George one day and told him that he had long intended to give me a small house and lot jist back of where he lived, but seein' things stood jist as they did, he advised George to buy a farm of his that was for sale on the edge of the village, and he would credit him for as much as the house and lot would have been worth, and he could pay the rest by his labor in the course of two or three years. Sure enough, he gave him a deed and took a mortgage, and it was so worded, that he could not be hurried to pay, and every body said it was the greatest bargain that ever was. And Mr. Spangler gave me a nice settin out besides.—But if there is n't the boys coming in to dinner,[9] and I bet there's nothin ready for 'em!' So saying, the good woman quickened her pace, and for the next hour her whole attention was absorbed by the 'savory cates,' fried pork and parsnips.

Chapter VI.

A trickling stream from high rock tumbling down,
And ever drizzling rain upon the loft,
Mixt with a murmuring wind much like the sound
Of swarming bees.

Spenser—House of Sleep

While pensive memory traces back the round
Which fills the varied interval between;
Much pleasure, more of sorrow, marks the scene.

Warton

When we were quietly seated after dinner, I requested some further insight into Mrs. Danforth's early history, the prosy flow of which was just in keeping with the long dreamy course of the afternoon, unbroken as it was by any sound more awakening than the ceaseless click of knitting-needles, or an occasional yawn from the town lady, who found the *farniente*[1] rather burdensome.

She smiled complacently, and took up the broken thread at the right place, evidently quite pleased to find she had excited so much interest.

---

8. A professor of religion or a believer.   1. Idleness.
9. Midday meal.

'When Mr. Spangler's nephew came after he was dead and gone, he was very close in asking all about the business, and seein' after the mortgages and such like. Now, George had never got his deed recorded. He felt as if it was n't worth while to lose a day's work, as he could send it any time by one of his neighbors. But when we found what sort of a man Mr. Wilkins was, we tho't it was high time to set about it. He had talked a good deal about the place, and said the old man must have been crazy to let us have it so cheap, and once went so far as to offer my husband a hundred dollars for his bargain. So John Green, a good neighbor of ours, sent us word one morning that he was going, and would call and get the deed, as he knew we wanted to send it up; and I got it out and laid it ready on the stand, and put the big Bible on it to keep it safe. But he did not come; something happened that he could not go that day: and I had jist took up the deed to put it back in the chest, when in came Wilkins. He had an eye like a hawk; and I was afraid he would see that it was a deed, and ask to look at it, and then I could n't refuse to hand it to him, you know; so I jist slipped it back under the Bible before I turned to ask him what was his will.

"Did n't John Saunderson leave my bridle here?' says he. So I stepped into the other room and got it, and he took it and walked off without speaking a word; and when I went to put away the deed, it was gone!

'My husband came in while I sat crying fit to break my heart; but all I could do I could not make him believe that Wilkins had got it. He said I had put it somewhere else without thinking, that people often felt just as sure as I did, and found themselves mistaken after all. But I knew better, and though I hunted high and low to please him, I knew well enough where it was. When he found he must give it up he never gave me a word of blame, but charged me not to say anything about the loss, for, wherever the deed was, Wilkins was just the man to take advantage if he knew we had lost it.

'Well, things went on this way for a while, and I had many a good cryin' spell, I tell ye! and one evening when George was away, in comes Wilkins, I was sittin' alone at my knittin', heavy hearted enough, and the schoolmaster was in the little room; for that was his week to board with us.

"Is your man at home?' says he; I said—No; but I expect him soon, so he sat down and began the old story about the place, and at last he says,

"I'd like to look at that deed if you've no objection, Mrs. Danforth.' I was so mad, I forgot what George had told me, and spoke right out.

'I should think, says I, you'd had it long enough to know it all by heart.'

"What does the woman mean?' says he.

'You know well enough what I mean, says I, you know you took it off this table, and from under this blessed book, the very last time you was in this house.

'If I had not known it before, I should have been certain then, for his face was as white as the wall, and he trembled when he spoke in spite of his impudence. But I could have bit off my own tongue when I tho't how imprudent I had been, and what my husband would say. He talked very angry as you may think.

"Only say that where anybody else can hear you,' says he, 'and I'll will make it cost your husband all he is worth in the world.'

'He spoke so loud that Mr. Peeler, the master, came out of the room to see what was the matter, and Wilkins bullied away and told Peeler what I had said, and dared me to say it over again. The master looked as if he knew something about it but did not speak. Just then the door opened, and in came George Danforth, led between two men, as pale as death, and dripping wet from head to foot. You may think how I felt! Well, they would n't give no answer about what was the matter till they got George into bed—only one of 'em said he had been in the canal. Wilkins pretended to be too angry to notice my husband, but kept talking away to himself—and was jist a beginning at me again, when one of the men said, 'Squire, I guess Henry'll want some looking after; for Mr. Danforth has just got him out of the water.'

'If I live to be a hundred years old, I shall never forget how Wilkins looked. There was everything in his face at once. He seemed as if he would pitch head-foremost out of the door, when he started to go home—for Henry was his only child.

'When he was gone, and my husband had got warm and recovered himself a little, he told us that he had seen Henry fall into the lock, and soused right in after him, and they had come very near drowning together, and so stayed in so long that they were about senseless when they got into the air again. Then I told him all that had happened—and then Peeler, he up, and told that he saw Wilkins take a paper off the stand the time I opened the bed-room door to get the bridle, for he was at our house then.

'I was very glad to hear it, to be sure; but the very next morning came a new deed and the mortgage, with a few lines from Mr. Wilkins, saying how thankful he was, and that he hoped George would oblige him by accepting some compensation. George sent back the mortgage, saying he would rather not take it, but thanked him kindly for the deed. So then I was glad Peeler had n't spoke, 'cause it would have set Wilkins against him. After that we thought it was best to sell out and come away, for such feelings, you know, a'in't pleasant among neighbors, and we had talked some of coming to Michigan afore.

'We had most awful hard times at first. Many's the day I've worked from sunrise till dark in the fields, gathering brush-heaps and burning stumps. But that's all over now; and we've got four times as much land as we ever should have owned in York state.'

I have since had occasion to observe that this forms a prominent and frequent theme of self-gratulation among the settlers in Michigan. The possession of a large number of acres is esteemed a great good, though it makes but little difference in the owner's mode of living. Comforts do not seem to abound in proportion to landed increase, but often, on the contrary, are really diminished for the sake of it; and the habit of selling out so frequently, makes that *home*-feeling, which is so large an ingredient in happiness elsewhere, almost a nonentity in Michigan. The man who holds himself ready to accept the first advantageous offer, will not be very solicitous to provide those minor accommodations, which, though essential to domestic comfort, will not add to the moneyed value of his farm, which he considers merely an article of trade, and which he knows his successor will look upon in the same light. I have sometimes thought that our neighbors forget that 'the days of man's life are three score years and ten,' since they spend all their lives in getting ready to begin.

1839

Margaret Fuller
(1810–1850)

Born in Cambridgeport, Massachusetts, the eldest of nine children, Margaret Fuller began her education at home under the tutelage of her father, whose expectations of her were much what they might have been for a son. Treated as a child prodigy, she was introduced to Latin at age 6 and was soon reading in Horace, Virgil, and Ovid. The pressures placed upon her, however, led to sleeplessness, nightmares, and headaches. "I look back on these glooms and terrors, wherein I was enveloped," she wrote later, "and perceive that I had no natural childhood." Despite the stress, she learned to love the Roman authors, as she also did Shakespeare when she came upon *Romeo and Juliet* at the age of 8. Her education was continued when she was 13 at a boarding school for young ladies in Groton, and later at a school in Cambridgeport, where her schoolfellows included Oliver Wendell Holmes and Richard Henry Dana. Living not far from Harvard, she was a part of a social and intellectual circle of students and faculty; among them was her cousin James Freeman Clarke, who introduced her to the writings of Goethe. Before long, she was planning a translation of his *Tasso*. This period of her life ended in 1833, when her family moved to Groton and she took over the education of four of her younger siblings. Two years later, upon the death of her father, she became largely responsible for the support of her family.

In the years that followed her father's death, Fuller wrote for newspapers and journals, taught at schools in Boston and Providence, and gravitated toward the transcendentalism of Ralph Waldo Emerson, whom she first visited in 1836, the year his *Nature* was published. Acclaimed by almost all who knew her as an unparalleled conversationalist, from 1839 to 1844 she conducted "conversations" for pay in Boston—a learning experience for women akin to the vogue for public lectures that helped support Emerson. Meanwhile, with Emerson and others she founded, and for its first two years edited, the transcendental journal *The Dial* (1840–1844). She took little part in the Brook Farm experiment, but she formed at least part of the model for Zenobia in *The Marble Faun* (1860), Hawthorne's fictional account of the experience. In 1844 she moved to New York City, where she wrote for Horace Greeley's *Tribune*, and two years later she sailed for Europe as a foreign correspondent for the same journal. She met Wordsworth and Carlyle and the Italian patriot Giuseppi Mazzini in England, as well as George Sand and the Polish patriot Adam Mickiewicz in France. In Italy she fell in love with and had a child by a younger man, Giovanni

Angelo, Marchese Ossoli. Subsequently married, they were on the way to the United States when their ship was wrecked off Fire Island and she, her husband, and her child were all drowned.

Summer on the Lakes (1844) first gained her notice outside the circle of her transcendental friends. An account of her travels in the Midwest in 1843, with comments on the plight of the Native Americans, it led to her job with Horace Greeley. *Woman in the Nineteenth Century* (1845), her next book, was an expansion of her essay "The Great Lawsuit: Man *versus* Men, Woman *versus* Women," published in *The Dial* in 1843. In it she argued for an equality of the sexes based upon a recognition of the essential oneness of humanity. In *Papers on Literature and Art* (1846) she collected essays and reviews. Remembered in the nineteenth century primarily for her association with the New England transcendentalists, she has been hailed in the twentieth century for her pioneering attempts to question the prescribed roles of women.

Memoirs of Margaret Fuller Ossoli (2 vols., 1852) contains edited versions of her memoirs, letters, and journals, as well as observations by J. F. Clarke, Emerson, and W. H. Channing. *At Home and Abroad* was edited by Arthur B. Fuller (1856). A multivolume *Letters of Margaret Fuller* is being edited by Robert N. Hudspeth (1983–). *"These Sad But Glorious Days": Dispatches from Europe, 1846–1850* was edited by Larry J. Reynolds and Susan Belasco Smith (1991). Studies include Madeleine B. Stern, *The Life of Margaret Fuller* (1942); Bell Gale Chevigny, *The Woman and the Myth: Margaret Fuller's Life and Writings* (1976); Paula Blanchard, *Margaret Fuller: From Transcendentalism to Revolution* (1978); and Margaret V. Allen *The Achievement of Margaret Fuller* (1979).

FROM WOMAN IN THE NINETEENTH CENTURY[1]

***It should be remarked that, as the principle of liberty is better understood, and more nobly interpreted, a broader protest is made in behalf of Woman. As men become aware that few men have had a fair chance, they are inclined to say that no women have had a fair chance.

1. The text is that of the 1845 edition, with some normalization of spelling and punctuation.

The French Revolution, that strangely disguised angel, bore witness in favor of woman, but interpreted her claims no less ignorantly than those of man. Its idea of happiness did not rise beyond outward enjoyment, unobstructed by the tyranny of others. The title it gave was citoyen, citoyenne, and it is not unimportant to woman that even this species of equality was awarded her. Before, she could be condemned to perish on the scaffold for treason, not as a citizen, but as a subject. The right with which this title then invested a human being, was that of bloodshed and license. The Goddess of Liberty was impure. As we read the poem addressed to her not long since, by Beranger,[2] we can scarcely refrain from tears as painful as the tears of blood that flowed when "such crimes were committed in her name."[3] Yes! Man, born to purify and animate the unintelligent and the cold, can, in his madness, degrade and pollute no less the fair and the chaste. Yet truth was prophesied in the ravings of that hideous fever, caused by long ignorance and abuse. Europe is conning a valued lesson from the blood-stained page. The same tendencies, farther unfolded, will bear good fruit in this country.

Yet, by men in this country, as by the Jews, when Moses was leading them to the promised land, every thing has been done that inherited depravity could do, to hinder the promise of Heaven from its fulfilment. The cross, here as elsewhere, has been planted only to be blasphemed by cruelty and fraud. The name of the Prince of Peace has been profaned by all kinds of injustice toward the Gentile whom he said he came to save. But I need not speak of what has been done towards the red man, the black man. Those deeds are the scoff of the world; and they have been accompanied by such pious words that the gentlest would not dare to intercede with "Father, forgive them, for they know not what they do."[4]

Here, as elsewhere, the gain of creation consists always in the growth of individual minds, which live and aspire, as flowers bloom and birds sing, in the midst of morasses; and in the continual development of that thought, the thought of human destiny, which is given to eternity adequately to express, and which ages of failure only seemingly impede. Only seemingly, and whatever seems to the contrary, this country is as surely destined to elucidate a great moral law, as Europe was to promote the mental culture of man.***

"Is it not enough," cries the irritated trader, "that you have done all you could to break up the national union, and thus destroy the prosperity of our country, but now you must be trying to break up family union, to take my wife away from the cradle and the kitchen hearth to vote at polls, and preach from a pulpit? Of course, if she does such things, she cannot attend to those of her own sphere. She is happy enough as she is. She has more leisure than I have, every means of improvement, every indulgence."

"Have you asked her whether she was satisfied with these *indulgences?*"

"No, but I know she is. She is too amiable to wish what would make me unhappy, and too judicious to wish to step beyond the sphere of her sex. I will never consent to have our peace disturbed by any such discussions."

" 'Consent—you?' it is not consent from you that is in question, it is assent from your wife."

"Am not I the head of my house?"

"You are not the head of your wife. God has given her a mind of her own."

"I am the head and she the heart."

"God grant you play true to one another then. I suppose I am to be grateful that you did not say she was only the hand. If the head represses no natural pulse of the heart, there can be no question as to your giving your consent. Both will be of one accord, and there needs but to present any question to get a full and true answer. There is no need of precaution, of indulgence, or consent. But our doubt is whether the heart *does* consent with the head, or only obeys its decrees with a passiveness that precludes the exercise of its natural powers, or a

---

2. Pierre-Jean de Béranger (1780–1857), French poet, author of "La Liberté."

3. Attributed to Madame Roland (1754–1793),

French revolutionary.

4. Christ's words on the cross, according to Luke 24:34.

repugnance that turns sweet qualities to bitter, or a doubt that lays waste the fair occasions of life. It is to ascertain the truth, that we propose some liberating measures."

Thus vaguely are these questions proposed and discussed at present. But their being proposed at all implies much thought and suggests more. Many women are considering within themselves, what they need that they have not, and what they can have, if they find they need it. Many men are considering whether women are capable of being and having more than they are and have, *and*, whether, if so, it will be best to consent to improvement in their condition.

This morning, I open the Boston "Daily Mail," and find in its "poet's corner," a translation of Schiller's[5] "Dignity of Woman." In the advertisement of a book on America, I see in the table of contents this sequence, "Republican Institutions. American Slavery. American Ladies."

I open the *"Deutsche Schnellpost,"* published in New-York, and find at the head of a column, *Judenund Frauen-emancipation in Ungarn.* Emancipation of Jews and Women in Hungary.

The past year has seen action in the Rhode-Island legislature, to secure married women rights over their own property, where men showed that a very little examination of the subject could teach them much; an article in the Democratic Review[6] on the same subject more largely considered, written by a woman, impelled, it is said, by glaring wrong to a distinguished friend having shown the defects in the existing laws, and the state of opinion from which they spring; and an answer from the revered old man, J.Q. Adams,[7] in some respects the Phocion[8] of his time, to an address made him by some ladies. To this last I shall again advert in another place.

These symptoms of the times have come under my view quite accidentally: one who seeks, may, each month or week, collect more.

The numerous party, whose opinions are already labelled and adjusted too much to their mind to admit of any new light, strive, by lectures on some model-woman of bride-like beauty and gentleness, by writing and lending little treatises, intended to mark out with precision the limits of woman's sphere, and woman's mission, to prevent other than the rightful shepherd from climbing the wall, or the flock from using any chance to go astray.

Without enrolling ourselves at once on either side, let us look upon the subject from the best point of view which to-day offers. No better, it is to be feared, than a high house-top. A high hill-top, or at least a cathedral spire, would be desirable.

It may well be an Anti-Slavery party that pleads for woman, if we consider merely that she does not hold property on equal terms with men; so that, if a husband dies without making a will, the wife, instead of taking at once his place as head of the family, inherits only a part of his fortune, often brought him by herself, as if she were a child, or ward only, not an equal partner.

We will not speak of the innumerable instances in which profligate and idle men live upon the earnings of industrious wives; or if the wives leave them, and take with them the children, to perform the double duty of mother and father, follow from place to place, and threaten to rob them of the children, if deprived of the rights of a husband, as they call them, planting themselves in their poor lodgings, frightening them into paying tribute by taking from them the children, running into debt at the expense of these otherwise so overtasked helots.[9] Such instances count up by scores within my own memory. I have seen the husband who had stained himself by a long course of low vice, till his wife was wearied from her heroic forgiveness, by finding that his treachery made it useless, and that if she would provide bread

---

5. Johann Christoph Friedrich von Schiller (1759–1805), German poet.
6. "The Legal Wrongs of Women," *United States Magazine and Democratic Review*, May 1844.
7. John Quincy Adams (1767–1868), sixth

president of the United States.
8. (402?–317 B.C.), Athenian general and statesman, remembered in part for his scorn for the fickle public and popular leaders.
9. Serfs or slaves.

for herself and her children, she must be separate from his ill fame—I have known this man come to install himself in the chamber of a woman who loathed him and say she should never take food without his company. I have known these men steal their children whom they knew they had no means to maintain, take them into dissolute company, expose them to bodily danger, to frighten the poor woman, to whom, it seems, the fact that she alone had borne the pangs of their birth, and nourished their infancy, does not give an equal right to them. I do believe that this mode of kidnapping, and it is frequent enough in all classes of society, will be by the next age viewed as it is by Heaven now, and that the man who avails himself of the shelter of men's laws to steal from a mother her own children, or arrogate any superior right in them, save that of superior virtue, will bear the stigma he deserves, in common with him who steals grown men from their mother land, their hopes, and their homes.

I said, we will not speak of this now, yet I have spoken, for the subject makes me feel too much. I could give instances that would startle the most vulgar and callous, but I will not, for the public opinion of their own sex is already against such men, and where cases of extreme tyranny are made known, there is private action in the wife's favor. But she ought not to need this, nor, I think, can she long. Men must soon see that, on their own ground, that woman is the weaker party, she ought to have legal protection, which would make such oppression impossible. But I would not deal with "atrocious instances" except in the way of illustration, neither demand from men a partial redress in some one matter, but go to the root of the whole. If principles could be established, particulars would adjust themselves aright. Ascertain the true destiny of woman, give her legitimate hopes, and a standard within herself; marriage and all other relations would by degrees be harmonized with these.

But to return to the historical progress of this matter. Knowing that there exists in the minds of men a tone of feeling towards women as towards slaves, such as is expressed in the common phrase, "Tell that to women and children," that the infinite soul can only work through them in already ascertained limits; that the gift of reason, man's highest prerogative, is allotted to them in much lower degree; that they must be kept from mischief and melancholy by being constantly engaged in active labor, which is to be furnished and directed by those better able to think, &c. &c; we need not multiply instances, for who can review the experience of last week without recalling words which imply, whether in jest or earnest, these views or views like these; knowing this, can we wonder that many reformers think that measures are not likely to be taken in behalf of women, unless their wishes could be publicly represented by women?

That can never be necessary, cry the other side. All men are privately influenced by women; each has his wife, sister, or female friends, and is too much biased by these relations to fail of representing their interests, and, if this is not enough, let them propose and enforce their wishes with the pen. The beauty of home would be destroyed, the delicacy of the sex be violated, the dignity of halls of legislation degraded by an attempt to introduce them there. Such duties are inconsistent with those of a mother; and then we have ludicrous pictures of ladies in hysterics at the polls, and senate chambers filled with cradles.

But if, in reply, we admit as truth that woman seems destined by nature rather for the inner circle, we must add that the arrangements of civilized life have not been, as yet, such as to secure it to her. Her circle, if the duller, is not the quieter. If kept from "excitement," she is not from drudgery. Not only the Indian squaw carries the burdens of the camp, but the favorites of Louis the Fourteenth[1] accompany him in his journeys, and the washerwoman stands at her tub and carries home her work at all seasons, and in all states of health. Those who think the physical circumstances of woman would make a part in the affairs of national government unsuitable, are by no means those who think it impossible for the negresses to endure field work, even during pregnancy, or the sempstresses to go through their killing labors.

---

1. (1638–1715), "the Sun King" of France from 1643 to 1715.

As to the use of the pen, there was quite as much opposition to woman's possessing herself of that help to free agency, as there is now to her seizing on the rostrum or the desk; and she is likely to draw, from a permission to plead her cause that way, opposite inferences to what might be wished by those who now grant it.

As to the possibility of her filling with grace and dignity, any such position, we should think those who had seen the great actresses, and heard the Quaker preachers of modern times, would not doubt, that woman can express publicly the fulness of thought and creation, without losing any of the peculiar beauty of her sex. What can pollute and tarnish is to act thus from any motive except that something needs to be said or done. Woman could take part in the processions, the songs, the dances of old religion; no one fancied their delicacy was impaired by appearing in public for such a cause.

As to her home, she is not likely to leave it more than she now does for balls, theatres, meetings for promoting missions, revival meetings, and others to which she flies, in hope of an animation for her existence, commensurate with what she sees enjoyed by men. Governors of ladies' fairs are no less engrossed by such a change, than the Governor of the state by his; presidents of Washingtonian societies[2] no less away from home than presidents of conventions. If men look straitly to it, they will find that, unless their lives are domestic, those of the women will not be. A house is no home unless it contain food and fire for the mind as well as for the body. The female Greek, of our day, is as much in the street as the male to cry, What news? We doubt not it was the same in Athens of old. The women, shut out from the market-place, made up for it at the religious festivals. For human beings are not so constituted that they can live without expansion. If they do not get it one way, they must another, or perish.

As to men's representing women fairly at present, while we hear from men who owe to their wives not only all that is comfortable or graceful, but all that is wise in the arrangement of their lives, the frequent remark, "You cannot reason with a woman," when from those of delicacy, nobleness, and poetic culture, the contemptuous phrase "women and children," and that in no light sally of the hour, but in works intended to give a permanent statement of the best experiences, when not one man, in the million, shall I say? no, not in the hundred million, can rise above the belief that woman was made *for man*, when such traits as these are daily forced upon the attention, can we feel that man will always do justice to the interests of woman? Can we think that he takes a sufficiently discerning and religious view of her office and destiny, *ever* to do her justice, except when prompted by sentiment, accidentally or transiently, that is, for the sentiment will vary according to the relations in which he is placed. The lover, the poet, the artist, are likely to view her nobly. The father and the philosopher have some chance of liberality; the man of the world, the legislator for expediency, none.

Under these circumstances, without attaching importance, in themselves, to the changes demanded by the champions of woman, we hail them as signs of the times. We would have every arbitrary barrier thrown down. We would have every path laid open to woman as freely as to man. Were this done and a slight temporary fermentation allowed to subside, we should see crystallizations more pure and of more various beauty. We believe the divine energy would pervade nature to a degree unknown in the history of former ages, and that no discordant collision, but a ravishing harmony of the spheres would ensue.

Yet, then and only then, will mankind be ripe for this, when inward and outward freedom for woman as much as for man shall be acknowledged as a right, not yielded as a concession. As the friend of the negro assumes that one man cannot by right, hold another in bondage, so should the friend of woman assume that man cannot, by right, lay even well-meant restrictions on woman. If the negro be a soul, if the woman be a soul, appareled in flesh, to one Master only are they accountable. There is but one law for souls, and if there is to be an interpreter of it, he must come not as man, or son of man, but as son of God.

2. Temperance societies of the time.

Were thought and feeling once so far elevated that man should esteem himself the brother and friend, but nowise the lord and tutor of woman, were he really bound with her in equal worship, arrangements as to function and employment would be of no consequence. What woman needs is not as a woman to act or rule, but as a nature to grow, as an intellect to discern, as a soul to live freely and unimpeded, to unfold such powers as were given her when we left our common home. If fewer talents were given her, yet if allowed the free and full employment of these, so that she may render back to the giver his own with usury, she will not complain; nay, I dare to say she will bless and rejoice in her earthly birth-place, her earthly lot. Let us consider what obstructions impede this good era, and what signs give reason to hope that it draws near.

I was talking on this subject with Miranda, a woman, who, if any in the world could, might speak without heat and bitterness of the position of her sex. Her father was a man who cherished no sentimental reverence for woman, but a firm belief in the equality of the sexes. She was his eldest child, and came to him at an age when he needed a companion. From the time she could speak and go alone, he addressed her not as a plaything, but as a living mind. Among the few verses he ever wrote was a copy addressed to this child, when the first locks were cut from her head, and the reverence expressed on this occasion for that cherished head, he never belied. It was to him the temple of immortal intellect. He respected his child, however, too much to be an indulgent parent. He called on her for clear judgment, for courage, for honor and fidelity; in short, for such virtues as he knew. In so far as he possessed the keys to the wonders of this universe, he allowed free use of them to her, and by the incentive of a high expectation, he forbade, as far as possible, that she should let the privilege lie idle.

Thus this child was early led to feel herself a child of the spirit. She took her place easily, not only in the world of organized being, but in the world of mind. A dignified sense of self-dependence was given as all her portion, and she found it a sure anchor. Herself securely anchored, her relations with others were established with equal security. She was fortunate in a total absence of those charms which might have drawn to her bewildering flatteries, and in a strong electric nature, which repelled those who did not belong to her, and attracted those who did. With men and women her relations were noble, affectionate without passion, intellectual without coldness. The world was free to her, and she lived freely in it. Outward adversity came, and inward conflict, but that faith and self-respect had early been awakened which must always lead at last, to an outward serenity and an inward peace.

Of Miranda I had always thought as an example, that the restraints upon the sex were insuperable only to those who think them so, or who noisily strive to break them. She had taken a course of her own, and no man stood in her way. Many of her acts had been unusual, but excited no uproar. Few helped, but none checked her, and the many men, who knew her mind and her life, showed to her confidence, as to a brother, gentleness as to a sister. And not only refined, but very coarse men approved and aided one in whom they saw resolution and clearness of design. Her mind was often the leading one, always effective.

When I talked with her upon these matters, and had said very much what I have written, she smilingly replied: "And yet we must admit that I have been fortunate, and this should not be. My good father's early trust gave the first bias, and the rest followed of course. It is true that I have had less outward aid, in after years, than most women; but that is of little consequence. Religion was early awakened in my soul, a sense that what the soul is capable to ask it must attain, and that, though I might be aided and instructed by others, I must depend on myself as the only constant friend. This self dependence, which was honored in me, is deprecated as a fault in most women. They are taught to learn their rule from without, not to unfold it from within.

"This is the fault of man, who is still vain, and wishes to be more important to woman than, by right, he should be."

"Men have not shown this disposition toward you," I said.

"No! because the position I early was enabled to take was one of self-reliance.[3] And were all women as sure of their wants as I was, the result would be the same. But they are so overloaded with precepts by guardians, who think that nothing is so much to be dreaded for a woman as originality of thought or character, that their minds are impeded by doubts till they lose their chance of fair, free proportions. The difficulty is to get them to the point from which they shall naturally develope self-respect, and learn self-help.

"Once I thought that men would help to forward this state of things more than I do now. I saw so many of them wretched in the connections they had formed in weakness and vanity. They seemed so glad to esteem women whenever they could.

" 'The soft arms of affection' said one of the most discerning spirits, 'will not suffice for me, unless on them I see the steel bracelets of strength.'

"But early I perceived that men never, in any extreme of despair, wished to be women. On the contrary they were ever ready to taunt one another, at any sign of weakness, with,

" 'Art thou not like the women, who'—

The passage ends various ways, according to the occasion and rhetoric of the speaker. When they admired any woman they were inclined to speak of her as 'above her sex.' Silently I observed this, and feared it argued a rooted scepticism, which for ages had been fastening on the heart, and which only an age of miracles could eradicate. Ever I have been treated with great sincerity; and I look upon it as a signal instance of this, that an intimate friend of the other sex said, in a fervent moment, that I 'deserved in some star to be a man.' He was much surprised when I disclosed my view of my position and hopes, when I declared my faith that the feminine side, the side of love, of beauty, of holiness, was now to have its full chance, and that, if either were better, it was better now to be a woman, for even the slightest achievement of good was furthering an especial work of our time. He smiled incredulous. 'She makes the best she can of it,' thought he. 'Let Jews believe the pride of Jewry, but I am of the better sort, and know better.'

"Another used as highest praise, in speaking of a character in literature, the words 'a manly woman.'

"So in the noble passage of Ben Jonson:[4]

> *I meant the day-star should not brighter ride,*
> *Nor shed like influence from its lucent seat;*
> *I meant she should be courteous, facile, sweet,*
> *Free from that solemn vice of greatness, pride;*
> *I meant each softest virtue there should meet,*
> *Fit in that softer bosom to abide,*
> *Only a learned and a* manly *soul*
> *I purposed her, that should with even powers,*
> *The rock, the spindle, and the shears control*
> *Of destiny, and spin her own free hours.'* "

"Methinks," said I, "you are too fastidious in objecting to this. Jonson, in using the word 'manly,' only meant to heighten the picture of this, the true, the intelligent fate, with one of the deeper colors."

"And yet," said she, "so invariable is the use of this word where a heroic quality is to be described, and I feel so sure that persistence and courage are the most womanly no less than

---

3. Compare Emerson's essay, "Self-Reliance," a discussion of a concept central to New England transcendental thought.

4. English poet (c. 1573–1637). The lines are from Epigram 76, "On Lucy, Countess of Bedford," with Fuller's emphasis on "manly."

the most manly qualities, that I would exchange these words for others of a larger sense at the risk of marring the fine tissue of the verse. Read, 'A heavenward and instructed soul,' and I should be satisfied. Let it not be said, wherever there is energy or creative genius, 'She has a masculine mind.' "****

There are two aspects of woman's nature, represented by the ancients as Muse and Minerva.[5] It is the former to which the writer in the Pathfinder looks.[6] It is the latter which Wordsworth has in mind, when he says,

> *"With a placid brow,*
> *Which woman ne'er should forfeit, keep thy vow."*[7]

The especial genius of woman I believe to be electrical in movement, intuitive in function, spiritual in tendency. She excels not so easily in classification, or recreation, as in an instinctive seizure of causes, and a simple breathing out of what she receives that has the singleness of life, rather than the selecting and energizing of art.

More native is it to her to be the living model of the artist than to set apart from herself any one form in objective reality; more native to inspire and receive the poem, than to create it. In so far as soul is in her completely developed, all soul is the same; but in so far as it is modified in her as woman, it flows, it breathes, it sings, rather than deposits soil, or finishes work, and that which is especially feminine flushes, in blossom, the face of earth, and pervades, like air and water, all this seeming solid globe, daily renewing and purifying its life. Such may be the especially feminine element spoken of as Femality. But it is no more the order of nature that it should be incarnated pure in any form, than that the masculine energy should exist unmingled with it in any form.

Male and female represent the two sides of the great radical dualism. But, in fact, they are perpetually passing into one another. Fluid hardens to solid, solid rushes to fluid. There is no wholly masculine man, no purely feminine woman.

History jeers at the attempts of physiologists to bind great original laws by the forms which flow from them. They make a rule; they say from observation what can and cannot be. In vain! Nature provides exceptions to every rule. She sends women to battle, and sets Hercules[8] spinning; she enables women to bear immense burdens, cold, and frost; she enables the man, who feels maternal love, to nourish his infant like a mother. Of late she plays still gayer pranks. Not only she deprives organizations, but organs, of a necessary end. She enables people to read with the top of the head, and see with the pit of the stomach. Presently she will make a female Newton,[9] and a male Syren.[1]

Man partakes of the feminine in the Apollo,[2] Woman of the masculine as Minerva.***

A little while since, I was at one of the most fashionable places of public resort. I saw there many women, dressed without regard to the season or the demands of the place, in apery, or, as it looked, in mockery, of European fashions. I saw their eyes restlessly courting attention. I saw the way in which it was paid, the style of devotion, almost an open sneer, which it pleased those ladies to receive from men whose expression marked their own low position in the moral and intellectual world. Those women went to their pillows with their heads full of folly, their hearts of jealousy, or gratified vanity; those men, with the low opinion

5. The muses of Greek mythology presided over the arts. Minerva was a Roman goddess associated with wisdom, handicrafts, and war.
6. Two articles on "Femality" appeared in the *New York Pathfinder*, March 1843.
7. From "Liberty: Sequel to the Preceding" (1835) by William Wordsworth (1770–1850), English poet.
8. In classical mythology, celebrated for his strength.
9. Sir Isaac Newton (1642–1727), English scientist.
1. In classical mythology, a sea nymph capable of luring men to destruction.
2. Greek god of light, healing, music, and poetry.

they already entertained of woman confirmed. These were American *ladies,* i.e., they were of that class who have wealth and leisure to make full use of the day, and confer benefits on others. They were of that class whom the possession of external advantages makes of pernicious example to many, if these advantages be misused.

Soon after, I met a circle of women, stamped by society as among the most degraded of their sex. "How," it was asked of them, "did you come here?" for, by the society that I saw in the former place, they were shut up in a prison. The causes were not difficult to trace: love of dress, love of flattery, love of excitement. They had not dresses like the other ladies, so they stole them; they could not pay for flattery by distinctions, and the dower of a worldly marriage, so they paid by the profanation of their persons. In excitement, more and more madly sought from day to day, they drowned the voice of conscience.

Now I ask you, my sisters, if the women at the fashionable house be not answerable for those women being in the prison?

As to position in the world of souls, we may suppose the women of the prison stood fairest, both because they had misused less light, and because loneliness and sorrow had brought some of them to feel the need of better life, nearer truth and good. This was no merit in them, being an effect of circumstance, but it was hopeful. But you, my friends, (and some of you I have already met), consecrate yourselves without waiting for reproof, in free love and unbroken energy, to win and to diffuse a better life. Offer beauty, talents, riches, on the altar; thus shall ye keep spotless your own hearts, and be visibly or invisibly the angels to others.

I would urge upon those women who have not yet considered this subject, to do so. Do not forget the unfortunates who dare not cross your guarded way. If it do not suit you to act with those who have organized measures of reform, then hold not yourself excused from acting in private. Seek out these degraded women, give them tender sympathy, counsel, employment. Take the place of mothers, such as might have saved them originally.

If you can do little for those already under the ban of the world, and the best considered efforts have often failed, from a want of strength in those unhappy ones to bear up against the sting of shame and the prejudices of the world, which makes them seek oblivion again in their old excitements, you will at least leave a sense of love and justice in their hearts, that will prevent their becoming utterly embittered and corrupt. And you may learn the means of prevention for those yet uninjured. There will be found in a diffusion of mental culture, simple tastes, best taught by your example, a genuine self-respect, and above all, what the influence of man tends to hide from woman, the love and fear of a divine, in preference to a human tribunal.

But suppose you save many who would have lost their bodily innocence (for as to mental, the loss of that is incalculably more general) through mere vanity and folly; there still remain many, the prey and spoil of the brute passions of man. For the stories frequent in our newspapers outshame antiquity, and vie with the horrors of war.

As to this, it must be considered that, as the vanity and proneness to seduction of the imprisoned women represented a general degradation in their sex; so do these acts a still more general and worse in the male. Where so many are weak it is natural there should be many lost, where legislators admit that ten thousand prostitutes are a fair proportion to one city, and husbands tell their wives that it is folly to expect chastity from men, it is inevitable that there should be many monsters of vice.***

And now I have designated in outline, if not in fulness, the stream which is ever flowing from the heights of my thought.

In the earlier tract,[3] I was told, I did not make my meaning sufficiently clear. In this I have consequently tried to illustrate it in various ways, and may have been guilty of much

---

3. "The Great Lawsuit: Man *versus* Men, Woman *versus* Women," *The Dial,* April 1843.

repetition. Yet, as I am anxious to leave no room for doubt, I shall venture to retrace, once more, the scope of my design in points, as was done in old-fashioned sermons.

Man is a being of two-fold relations, to nature beneath, and intelligences above him. The earth is his school, if not his birth-place; God his object; life and thought his means of interpreting nature, and aspiring to God.

Only a fraction of this purpose is accomplished in the life of any one man. Its entire accomplishment is to be hoped only from the sum of the lives of men, or man considered as a whole.

As this whole has one soul and one body, any injury or obstruction to a part, or to the meanest member, affects the whole. Man can never be perfectly happy or virtuous, till all men are so.

To address man wisely, you must not forget that his life is partly animal, subject to the same laws with nature.

But you cannot address him wisely unless you consider him still more as soul and appreciate the conditions and destiny of soul.

The growth of man is two-fold, masculine and feminine.

As far as these two methods can be distinguished they are so as

Energy and Harmony;

Power and Beauty;

Intellect and Love;

or by some such rude classification, for we have not language primitive and pure enough to express such ideas with precision.

These two sides are supposed to be expressed in man and woman, that is, as the more and less, for the faculties have not been given pure to either, but only in preponderance. There are also exceptions in great number, such as men of far more beauty than power, and the reverse. But as a general rule, it seems to have been the intention to give a preponderance on the one side, that is called masculine, and on the other, one that is called feminine.

There cannot be a doubt that, if these two developments were in perfect harmony, they would correspond to and fulfil one another, like hemispheres, or the tenor and bass in music.

But there is no perfect harmony in human nature; and the two parts answer one another only now and then, or, if there be a persistent consonance, it can only be traced, at long intervals, instead of discoursing an obvious melody.

What is the cause of this?

Man, in the order of time, was developed first; as energy comes before harmony; power before beauty.

Woman was therefore under his care as an elder. He might have been her guardian and teacher.

But as human nature goes not straight forward, but by excessive action and then reaction in an undulated course, he misunderstood and abused his advantages, and became her temporal master instead of her spiritual sire.

On himself came the punishment. He educated woman more as a servant than a daughter, and found himself a king without a queen.

The children of this unequal union showed unequal natures, and, more and more, men seemed sons of the hand-maid, rather than princess.

At last there were so many Ishmaelites that the rest grew frightened and indignant. They laid the blame on Hagar, and drove her forth into the wilderness.[4]

But there were none the fewer Ishmaelites for that.

At last men became a little wiser, and saw that the infant Moses was, in every case, saved by the pure instincts of woman's breast.[5] For, as too much adversity is better for the moral

---

4. The story is told in Genesis 16, 17, and 21.
5. The rescue of the infant Moses is told in Exodus 2:1–10.

nature than too much prosperity, woman, in this respect, dwindled less than man, though in other respects, still a child in leading strings.

So man did her more and more justice, and grew more and more kind.

But yet, his habits and his will corrupted by the past, he did not clearly see that woman was half himself, that her interests were identical with his, and that, by the law of their common being, he could never reach his true proportions while she remained in any wise shorn of hers.

And so it has gone on to our day; both ideas developing, but more slowly than they would under a clearer recognition of truth and justice, which would have permitted the sexes their due influence on one another, and mutual improvement from more dignified relations.***

I believe that, at present, women are the best helpers of one another.

Let them think; let them act; till they know what they need.

We only ask of men to remove arbitrary barriers. Some would like to do more. But I believe it needs for woman to show herself in her native dignity, to teach them how to aid her; their minds are so encumbered by tradition.

When Lord Edward Fitzgerald[6] travelled with the Indians, his manly heart obliged him at once to take the packs from the squaws and carry them. But we do not read that the red men followed his example, though they are ready enough to carry the pack of the white woman, because she seems to them a superior being.

Let woman appear in the mild majesty of Ceres,[7] and rudest churls will be willing to learn from her.

You ask, what use will she make of liberty, when she has so long been sustained and restrained?

I answer; in the first place, this will not be suddenly given. I read yesterday a debate of this year on the subject of enlarging women's rights over property. It was a leaf from the class-book that is preparing for the needed instruction. The men learned visibly as they spoke. The champions of woman saw the fallacy of arguments on the opposite side, and were startled by their own convictions. With their wives at home, and the readers of the paper, it was the same. And so the stream flows on; thought urging action, and action leading to the evolution of still better thought.

But, were this freedom to come suddenly, I have no fear of the consequences. Individuals might commit excesses, but there is not only in the sex a reverence for decorums and limits inherited and enhanced from generation to generation, which many years of other life could not efface, but a native love, in woman as woman, of proportion, of "the simple art of not too much," a Greek moderation, which would create immediately a restraining party, the natural legislators and instructors of the rest, and would gradually establish such rules as are needed to guard, without impeding, life.

The Graces[8] would lead the choral dance, and teach the rest to regulate their steps to the measure of beauty.

But if you ask me what offices they may fill, I reply—any. I do not care what case you put; let them be sea-captains, if you will. I do not doubt there are women well fitted for such an office, and, if so, I should be glad to see them in it, as to welcome the maid of Saragossa, or the maid of Missolonghi, or the Suliote heroine, or Emily Plater.[9]

I think women need, especially at this juncture, a much greater range of occupation than they have, to rouse their latent powers. A party of travellers lately visited a lonely hut on a

6. (1763–1798); Irish traveler in the American West.
7. Roman goddess of agriculture.
8. In classical mythology, three goddesses of beauty and charm.
9. Women heroines in wars: in Saragossa, Spain, during a French seige (1808–1809); in Greece, under Turkish seige at various times (1821–1833); in Greece, under seige by the Albanians (1803); Emily Plater led a Polish regiment against the Russians (1831).

mountain. There they found an old woman that told them she and her husband had lived there forty years. "Why," they said, "did you choose so barren a spot?" She "did not know; *it was the man's notion.*"

And, during forty years, she had been content to act, without knowing why, upon "the man's notion." I would not have it so.***

1845

FROM MEMOIRS OF MARGARET FULLER OSSOLI[1]

Death in the House.

My earliest recollection is of a death,—the death of a sister, two years younger than myself. Probably there is a sense of childish endearments, such as belong to this tie, mingled with that of loss, of wonder, and mystery; but these last are prominent in memory. I remember coming home and meeting our nursery-maid, her face streaming with tears. That strange sight of tears made an indelible impression. I realize how little I was of stature, in that I looked up to this weeping face;—and it has often seemed since, that—full-grown for the life of this earth, I have looked up just so, at times of threatening, of doubt, and distress, and that just so has some being of the next higher order of existences looked down, aware of a law unknown to me, and tenderly commiserating the pain I must endure in emerging from my ignorance.

She took me by the hand and led me into a still and dark chamber,—then drew aside the curtain and showed me my sister. I see yet that beauty of death! The highest achievements of sculpture are only the reminder of its severe sweetness. Then I remember the house all still and dark,—the people in their black clothes and dreary faces,—the scent of the newly-made coffin,—my being set up in a chair and detained by a gentle hand to hear the clergyman,—the carriages slowly going, the procession slowly doling out their steps to the grave. But I have no remembrance of what I have since been told I did,—insisting, with loud cries, that they should not put the body in the ground. I suppose that my emotion was spent at the time, and so there was nothing to fix that moment in my memory.

I did not then, nor do I now, find any beauty in these ceremonies. What had they to do with the sweet playful child? Her life and death were alike beautiful, but all this sad parade was not. Thus my first experience of life was one of death. She who would have been the companion of my life was severed from me, and I was left alone. This has made a vast difference in my lot. Her character, if that fair face promised right, would have been soft, graceful and lively; it would have tempered mine to a gentler and more gradual course.

Overwork.

My father,—all whose feelings were now concentred on me,—instructed me himself. The effect of this was so far good that, not passing through the hands of many ignorant and weak persons as so many do at preparatory schools, I was put at once under discipline of considerable severity, and, at the same time, had a more than ordinarily high standard presented to me. My father was a man of business, even in literature; he had been a high scholar at college, and was warmly attached to all he had learned there, both from the pleasure he had derived in the exercise of his faculties and the associated memories of success and good repute. He

---

1. The text is that of the 1852 edition.

was, beside, well read in French literature, and in English, a Queen Anne's man.[2] He hoped to make me the heir of all he knew, and of as much more as the income of his profession enabled him to give me means of acquiring. At the very beginning, he made one great mistake, more common, it is to be hoped, in the last generation, than the warnings of physiologists will permit it to be with the next. He thought to gain time, by bringing forward the intellect as early as possible. Thus I had tasks given me, as many and various as the hours would allow, and on subjects beyond my age; with the additional disadvantage of reciting to him in the evening, after he returned from his office. As he was subject to many interruptions, I was often kept up till very late; and as he was a severe teacher, both from his habits of mind and his ambition for me, my feelings were kept on the stretch till the recitations were over. Thus frequently, I was sent to bed several hours too late, with nerves unnaturally stimulated. The consequence was a premature development of the brain, that made me a "youthful prodigy" by day, and by night a victim of spectral illusions, nightmare, and somnambulism, which at the time prevented the harmonious development of my bodily powers and checked my growth, while, later, they induced continual headache, weakness and nervous affections, of all kinds. As these again re-acted on the brain, giving undue force to every thought and every feeling, there was finally produced a state of being both too active and too intense, which wasted my constitution, and will bring me,—even although I have learned to understand and regulate my now morbid temperament,—to a premature grave.

No one understood this subject of health then. No one knew why this child, already kept up so late, was still unwilling to retire. My aunts cried out upon the "spoiled child, the most unreasonable child that ever was,—if brother could but open his eyes to see it,—who was never willing to go to bed." They did not know that, so soon as the light was taken away, she seemed to see colossal faces advancing slowly towards her, the eyes dilating, and each feature swelling loathsomely as they came, till at last, when they were about to close upon her, she started up with a shriek which drove them away, but only to return when she lay down again. They did not know that, when at last she went to sleep, it was to dream of horses trampling over her, and to awake once more in fright; or, as she had just read in her Virgil,[3] of being among trees that dripped with blood, where she walked and walked and could not get out, while the blood became a pool and plashed over her feet, and rose higher and higher, till soon she dreamed it would reach her lips. No wonder the child arose and walked in her sleep, moaning all over the house, till once, when they heard her, and came and waked her, and she told what she had dreamed, her father sharply bid her "leave off thinking of such nonsense, or she would be crazy,"—never knowing that he was himself the cause of all these horrors of the night. Often she dreamed of following to the grave the body of her mother, as she had done that of her sister, and woke to find the pillow drenched in tears. These dreams softened her heart too much, and cast a deep shadow over her young days; for then, and later, the life of dreams,—probably because there was in it less to distract the mind from its own earnestness,—has often seemed to her more real, and been remembered with more interest, than that of waking hours.

Poor child! Far remote in time, in thought, from that period, I look back on these glooms and terrors, wherein I was enveloped; and perceive that I had no natural childhood.

Books

Thus passed my first years. My mother was in delicate health, and much absorbed in the care of her younger children. In the house was neither dog nor bird, nor any graceful

---

2. That is, he favored the writers of the reign of Queen Anne (1702–1714), including Swift, Pope, Addison, Steele, and Defoe.

3. (70–19 B.C.); Roman poet, author of the *Aeneid.*

animated form of existence. I saw no persons who took my fancy, and real life offered no attraction. Thus my already over-excited mind found no relief from without, and was driven for refuge from itself to the world of books. I was taught Latin and English grammar at the same time, and began to read Latin at six years old, after which, for some years, I read it daily. In this branch of study, first by my father, and afterwards by a tutor, I was trained to quite a high degree of precision. I was expected to understand the mechanism of the language thoroughly, and in translating to give the thoughts in as few well-arranged words as possible, and without breaks or hesitation,—for with these my father had absolutely no patience.

Indeed, he demanded accuracy and clearness in everything: you must not speak, unless you can make your meaning perfectly intelligible to the person addressed; must not express a thought, unless you can give a reason for it, if required; must not make a statement, unless sure of all particulars—such were his rules. "But," "if," "unless," "I am mistaken," and "it may be so," were words and phrases excluded from the province where he held sway. Trained to great dexterity in artificial methods, accurate, ready, with entire command of his resources, he had no belief in minds that listen, wait, and receive. He had no conception of the subtle and indirect motions of imagination and feeling. His influence on me was great, and opposed to the natural unfolding of my character, which was fervent, of strong grasp, and disposed to infatuation, and self-forgetfulness. He made the common prose world so present to me, that my natural bias was controlled. I did not go mad, as many would do, at being continually roused from my dreams. I had too much strength to be crushed,—and since I must put on the fetters, could not submit to let them impede my motions. My own world sank deep within, away from the surface of my life; in what I did and said I learned to have reference to other minds. But my true life was only the dearer that it was secluded and veiled over by a thick curtain of available intellect, and that coarse, but wearable stuff woven by the ages,—Common Sense.

In accordance with this discipline in heroic common sense, was the influence of those great Romans, whose thoughts and lives were my daily food during those plastic years. The genius of Rome displayed itself in Character, and scarcely needed an occasional wave of the torch of thought to show its lineaments, so marble strong they gleamed in every light. Who, that has lived with those men, but admires the plain force of fact, of thought passed into action? They take up things with their naked hands. There is just the man, and the block he casts before you,—no divinity, no demon, no unfulfilled aim, but just the man and Rome, and what he did for Rome. Everything turns your attention to what a man can become, not by yielding himself freely to impressions, not by letting nature play freely through him, but by a single thought, an earnest purpose, an indomitable will, by hardihood, self-command, and force of expression. Architecture was the art in which Rome excelled, and this corresponds with the feeling these men of Rome excite. They did not grow,—they built themselves up, or were built up by the fate of Rome, as a temple for Jupiter Stator.[4] The ruined Roman sits among the ruins; he flies to no green garden; he does not look to heaven; if his intent is defeated, if he is less than he meant to be, he lives no more. The names which end in "us," seem to speak with lyric cadence. That measured cadence,—that tramp and march,—which are not stilted, because they indicate real force, yet which seem so when compared with any other language,—make Latin a study in itself of mighty influence. The language alone, without the literature, would give one the *thought* of Rome. Man present in nature, commanding nature too sternly to be inspired by it, standing like the rock amid the sea, or moving like the fire over the land, either impassive, or irresistible; knowing not the soft mediums or fine flights of life, but by the force which he expresses, piercing to the centre.***

I steadily loved this ideal in my childhood, and this is the cause, probably, why I have always felt that man must know how to stand firm on the ground, before he can fly. In vain

4. Roman supreme god.

for me are men more, if they are less, than Romans. Dante[5] was far greater than any Roman, yet I feel he was right to take the Mantuan[6] as his guide through hell, and to heaven.

Horace[7] was a great deal to me then, and is so still. Though his words do not abide in memory, his presence does: serene, courtly, of darting hazel eye, a self-sufficient grace, and an appreciation of the world of stern realities, sometimes pathetic, never tragic. He is the natural man of the world; he is what he ought to be, and his darts never fail of their aim. There is a perfume and raciness, too, which makes life a banquet, where the wit sparkles no less that the viands were bought with blood.

Ovid[8] gave me not Rome, nor himself, but a view into the enchanted gardens of the Greek mythology. This path I followed, have been following ever since; and now, life half over, it seems to me, as in my childhood, that every thought of which man is susceptible, is intimated there. In those young years, indeed, I did not see what I now see, but loved to creep from amid the Roman pikes to lie beneath this great vine, and see the smiling and serene shapes go by, woven from the finest fibres of all the elements. I knew not why, at that time,—but I loved to get away from the hum of the forum, and the mailed clang of Roman speech, to these shifting shows of nature, these Gods and Nymphs born of the sunbeam, the wave, the shadows on the hill.

As with Rome I antedated the world of deeds, so I lived in those Greek forms the true faith of a refined and intense childhood. So great was the force of reality with which these forms impressed me, that I prayed earnestly for a sign,—that it would lighten in some particular region of the heavens, or that I might find a bunch of grapes in the path, when I went forth in the morning. But no sign was given, and I was left a waif stranded upon the shores of modern life!

Of the Greek language, I knew only enough to feel that the sounds told the same story as the mythology;—that the law of life in that land was beauty, as in Rome it was a stern composure. I wish I had learned as much of Greece as of Rome,—so freely does the mind play in her sunny waters, where there is no chill, and the restraint is from within out; for these Greeks, in an atmosphere of ample grace, could not be impetuous, or stern, but loved moderation as equable life always must, for it is the law of beauty.

With these books I passed my days. The great amount of study exacted of me soon ceased to be a burden, and reading became a habit and a passion. The force of feeling, which, under other circumstances, might have ripened thought, was turned to learn the thoughts of others. This was not a tame state, for the energies brought out by rapid acquisition gave glow enough. I thought with rapture of the all-accomplished man, him of the many talents, wide resources, clear sight, and omnipotent will. A Caesar seemed great enough. I did not then know that such men impoverish the treasury to build the palace. I kept their statues as belonging to the hall of my ancestors, and loved to conquer obstacles, and fed my youth and strength for their sake.

[Garden]

Still, though this bias was so great that in earliest years I learned, in these ways, how the world takes hold of a powerful nature, I had yet other experiences. None of these were deeper than what I found in the happiest haunt of my childish years,—our little garden. Our house, though comfortable, was very ugly, and in a neighborhood which I detested,—every dwelling and its appurtenances having a *mesquin*[9] and huddled look. I liked nothing about us except the tall graceful elms before the house, and the dear little garden behind. Our back door

5. Dante Alighieri (1265–1321), Italian poet.
6. Virgil (70–19 B.C.), Roman poet who appears in Dante's *Divine Comedy* as Dante's guide.
7. (65–8 B.C.); Roman poet and satirist.
8. (43 B.C.–A.D. 17?); Roman poet.
9. Shabby (French).

opened on a high flight of steps, by which I went down to a green plot, much injured in my ambitious eyes by the presence of the pump and tool-house. This opened into a little garden, full of choice flowers and fruit-trees, which was my mother's delight, and was carefully kept. Here I felt at home. A gate opened thence into the fields,—a wooden gate made of boards, in a high, unpainted board wall, and embowered in the clematis creeper. This gate I used to open to see the sunset heaven; beyond this black frame I did not step, for I liked to look at the deep gold behind it. How exquisitely happy I was in its beauty, and how I loved the silvery wreaths of my protecting vine! I never would pluck one of its flowers at that time, I was so jealous of its beauty, but often since I carry off wreaths of it from the wild-wood, and it stands in nature to my mind as the emblem of domestic love.

Of late I have thankfully felt what I owe to that garden, where the best hours of my lonely childhood were spent. Within the house everything was socially utilitarian; my books told of a proud world, but in another temper were the teachings of the little garden. There my thoughts could lie callow in the nest, and only be fed and kept warm, not called to fly or sing before the time. I loved to gaze on the roses, the violets, the lilies, the pinks; my mother's hand had planted them, and they bloomed for me. I culled the most beautiful. I looked at them on every side. I kissed them, I pressed them to my bosom with passionate emotions, such as I have never dared express to any human being. An ambition swelled my heart to be as beautiful, as perfect as they. I have not kept my vow. Yet, forgive, ye wild asters, which gleam so sadly amid the fading grass; forgive me, ye golden autumn flowers, which so strive to reflect the glories of the departing distant sun; and ye silvery flowers, whose moonlight eyes I knew so well, forgive! Living and blooming in your unchecked law, ye know nothing of the blights, the distortions, which beset the human being; and which at such hours it would seem that no glories of free agency could ever repay!

[Library, Reading]

There was, in the house, no apartment appropriated to the purpose of a library, but there was in my father's room a large closet filled with books, and to these I had free access when the task-work of the day was done. Its window overlooked wide fields, gentle slopes, a rich and smiling country, whose aspect pleased without much occupying the eye, while a range of blue hills, rising at about twelve miles distance, allured to reverie. "Distant mountains," says Tieck,[1] "excite the fancy, for beyond them we place the scene of our Paradise." Thus, in the poems of fairy adventure, we climb the rocky barrier, pass fearless its dragon caves, and dark pine forests, and find the scene of enchantment in the vale behind. My hopes were never so definite, but my eye was constantly allured to that distant blue range, and I would sit, lost in fancies, till tears fell on my cheek. I loved this sadness; but only in later years, when the realities of life had taught me moderation, did the passionate emotions excited by seeing them again teach how glorious were the hopes that swelled my heart while gazing on them in those early days.

Melancholy attends on the best joys of a merely ideal life, else I should call most happy the hours in the garden, the hours in the book closet. Here were the best French writers of the last century; for my father had been more than half a Jacobin, in the time when the French Republic cast its glare of promise over the world. Here, too, were the Queen Anne authors, his models, and the English novelists; but among them I found none that charmed me. Smollett, Fielding,[2] and the like, deal too broadly with the coarse actualities of life. The best

1. Ludwig Tieck (1773–1853), German writer.
2. Tobias George Smollett (1721–1771) and Henry Fielding (1707–1754), English authors.

of their men and women—so merely natural, with the nature found every day—do not meet our hopes. Sometimes the simple picture, warm with life and the light of the common sun, cannot fail to charm,—as in the wedded love of Fielding's Amelia,—but it is at a later day, when the mind is trained to comparison, that we learn to prize excellence like this as it deserves. Early youth is prince-like: it will bend only to "the king, my father." Various kinds of excellence please, and leave their impression, but the most commanding, alone, is duly acknowledged at that all-exacting age.

Three great authors it was my fortune to meet at this important period,—all, though of unequal, yet congenial powers,—all of rich and wide, rather than aspiring genius,—all free to the extent of the horizon their eye took in,—all fresh with impulse, racy with experience; never to be lost sight of, or superseded, but always to be apprehended more and more.

Ever memorable is the day on which I first took a volume of SHAKSPEARE in my hand to read. It was on a Sunday.

—This day was punctiliously set apart in our house. We had family prayers, for which there was no time on other days. Our dinners were different, and our clothes. We went to church. My father put some limitations on my reading, but—bless him for the gentleness which has left me a pleasant feeling for the day!—he did not prescribe what was, but only what was *not*, to be done. And the liberty this left was a large one. "You must not read a novel, or a play;" but all other books, the worst, or the best, were open to me. The distinction was merely technical. The day was pleasing to me, as relieving me from the routine of tasks and recitations; it gave me freer play than usual, and there were fewer things occurred in its course, which reminded me of the divisions of time; still the church-going, where I heard nothing that had any connection with my inward life, and these rules, gave me associations with the day of empty formalities, and arbitrary restrictions; but though the forbidden book or walk always seemed more charming then, I was seldom tempted to disobey.—

This Sunday—I was only eight years old—I took from the book-shelf a volume lettered SHAKESPEARE. It was not the first time I had looked at it, but before I had been deterred from attempting to read, by the broken appearance along the page, and preferred smooth narrative. But this time I held in my hand "Romeo and Juliet" long enough to get my eye fastened to the page. It was a cold winter afternoon. I took the book to the parlor fire, and had there been seated an hour or two, when my father looked up and asked what I was reading so intently. "Shakspeare," replied the child, merely raising her eye from the page. "Shakspeare,—that won't do; that's no book for Sunday; go put it away and take another." I went as I was bid, but took no other. Returning to my seat, the unfinished story, the personages to whom I was but just introduced, thronged and burnt my brain. I could not bear it long; such a lure it was impossible to resist. I went and brought the book again. There were several guests present, and I had got half through the play before I again attracted attention. "What is that child about that she don't hear a word that's said to her?" quoth my aunt. "What are you reading?" said my father. "Shakspeare" was again the reply, in a clear, though somewhat impatient, tone. "How?" said my father angrily,—then restraining himself before his guests,—"Give me the book and go directly to bed."

Into my little room no care of his anger followed me. Alone, in the dark, I thought only of the scene placed by the poet before my eye, where the free flow of life, sudden and graceful dialogue, and forms, whether grotesque or fair, seen in the broad lustre of his imagination, gave just what I wanted, and brought home the life I seemed born to live. My fancies swarmed like bees, as I contrived the rest of the story;—what all would do, what say, where go. My confinement tortured me. I could not go forth from this prison to ask after these friends; I could not make my pillow of the dreams about them which yet I could not forbear to frame. Thus was I absorbed when my father entered. He felt it right, before going to rest, to reason with me about my disobedience, shown in a way, as he considered, so insolent. I listened, but could not feel interested in what he said, nor turn my mind from what engaged it. He went away really grieved at my impenitence, and quite at a loss to understand conduct in me so unusual.

—Often since I have seen the same misunderstanding between parent and child,—the parent thrusting the morale, the discipline, of life upon the child, when just engrossed by some game of real importance and great leadings to it. That is only a wooden horse to the father,—the child was careering to distant scenes of conquest and crusade, through a country of elsewhere unimagined beauty. None but poets remember their youth; but the father who does not retain poetical apprehension of the world, free and splendid as it stretches out before the child, who cannot read his natural history, and follow out its intimations with reverence, must be a tyrant in his home, and the purest intentions will not prevent his doing much to cramp him. Each new child is a new Thought, and has bearings and discernings, which the Thoughts older in date know not yet, but must learn.—

My attention thus fixed on Shakspeare, I returned to him at every hour I could command. Here was a counterpoise to my Romans, still more forcible than the little garden. My author could read the Roman nature too,—read it in the sternness of Coriolanus, and in the varied wealth of Caesar. But he viewed these men of will as only one kind of men; he kept them in their place, and I found that he, who could understand the Roman, yet expressed in Hamlet a deeper thought.

In CERVANTES,[3] I found far less productive talent,—indeed, a far less powerful genius,— but the same wide wisdom, a discernment piercing the shows and symbols of existence, yet rejoicing in them all, both for their own life, and as signs of the unseen reality. Not that Cervantes philosophized,—his genius was too deeply philosophical for that; he took things as they came before him, and saw their actual relations and bearings. Thus the work he produced was of deep meaning, though he might never have expressed that meaning to himself. It was left implied in the whole. A Coleridge[4] comes and calls Don Quixote the pure Reason, and Sancho the Understanding. Cervantes made no such distinctions in his own mind; but he had seen and suffered enough to bring out all his faculties, and to make him comprehend the higher as well as the lower part of our nature. Sancho is too amusing and sagacious to be contemptible; the Don too noble and clear-sighted towards absolute truth, to be ridiculous. And we are pleased to see manifested in this way, how the lower must follow and serve the higher, despite its jeering mistrust and the stubborn realities which break up the plans of this pure-minded champion.

The effect produced on the mind is nowise that described by Byron[5]:—

"Cervantes smiled Spain's chivalry away," &c.

On the contrary, who is not conscious of a sincere reverence for the Don, prancing forth on his gaunt steed? Who would not rather be he than any of the persons who laugh at him?—Yet the one we would wish to be is thyself, Cervantes, unconquerable spirit! gaining flavor and color like wine from every change, while being carried round the world; in whose eye the serene sagacious laughter could not be dimmed by poverty, slavery, or unsuccessful authorship. Thou art to us still more the Man, though less the Genius, than Shakspeare; thou dost not evade our sight, but, holding the lamp to thine own magic shows, dost enjoy them with us.

My third friend was MOLIÉRE,[6] one very much lower, both in range and depth, than the others, but, as far as he goes, of the same character. Nothing secluded or partial is there about his genius,—a man of the world, and a man by himself, as he is. It was, indeed, only the poor social world of Paris that he saw, but he viewed it from the firm foundations of his manhood, and every lightest laugh rings from a clear perception, and teaches life anew.

These men were all alike in this,—they loved the *natural history* of man. Not what he

3. Miguel de Cervantes (1547–1616), Spanish novelist.
4. Samuel Taylor Coleridge (1772–1834), English poet and critic.
5. George Gordon, Lord Byron (1788–1824) English poet.
6. Pseudonym of Jean Baptiste Poquelin (1622–1673), French actor and playwright.

should be, but what he is, was the favorite subject of their thought. Whenever a noble leading opened to the eye new paths of light, they rejoiced; but it was never fancy, but always fact, that inspired them. They loved a thorough penetration of the murkiest dens, and most tangled paths of nature; they did not spin from the desires of their own special natures, but reconstructed the world from materials which they collected on every side. Thus their influence upon me was not to prompt me to follow out thought in myself so much as to detect it everywhere, for each of these men is not only a nature, but a happy interpreter of many natures. They taught me to distrust all invention which is not based on a wide experience. Perhaps, too, they taught me to overvalue an outward experience at the expense of inward growth; but all this I did not appreciate till later.

It will be seen that my youth was not unfriended, since those great minds came to me in kindness. A moment of action in one's self, however, is worth an age of apprehension through others; not that our deeds are better, but that they produce a renewal of our being. I have had more productive moments and of deeper joy, but never hours of more tranquil pleasure than those in which these demi-gods visited me,—and with a smile so familiar, that I imagined the world to be full of such. They did me good, for by them a standard was early given of sight and thought, from which I could never go back, and beneath which I cannot suffer patiently my own life or that of any friend to fall. They did me harm, too, for the child fed with meat instead of milk becomes too soon mature. Expectations and desires were thus early raised, after which I must long toil before they can be realized. How poor the scene around, how tame one's own existence, how meagre and faint every power, with these beings in my mind! Often I must cast them quite aside in order to grow in my small way, and not sink into despair. Certainly I do not wish that instead of these masters I had read baby books, written down to children, and with such ignorant dulness that they blunt the senses and corrupt the tastes of the still plastic human being. But I do wish that I had read no books at all till later,—that I had lived with toys, and played in the open air. Children should not cull the fruits of reflection and observation early, but expand in the sun, and let thoughts come to them. They should not through books antedate their actual experiences, but should take them gradually, as sympathy and interpretation are needed. With me, much of life was devoured in the bud.***

1852

Fanny Fern (Sara Payson Willis)
(1811–1872)

Although Nathaniel Hawthorne referred to the popular women novelists of his day as that "damned mob of scribbling women," he made an exception for Fanny Fern. He wrote to his publisher that he had been reading her novel, *Ruth Hall*, "and I must say I enjoyed it a good deal. The woman writes as if the Devil was in her; and that is the only condition under which a woman ever writes anything worth reading.*** When they throw off the restraints of decency and come before the public stark naked, as it were—then their books are sure to possess character and value." Not all of Fern's contemporaries appreciated her lack of reserve as much as Hawthorne did, but she was very popular: she was the first American woman employed as a regular newspaper columnist and became one of the most highly paid journalists of her time. *Ruth Hall*, based on her life story, was as controversial as it was successful.

Fern was born Sara Payson Willis, closely related to two prominent newspapermen who played no part in furthering her career. Her father was Nathaniel Willis, who founded and edited two newspapers in Boston, where the family moved from Portland, Maine, when Fern was 6 months old; her brother was N. P. Willis, an essayist, poet, and journalist based in New York. Fern was a middle child, the fifth of nine siblings; she attended several schools, including one of the most renowned schools for young women, Catharine Beecher's Hartford Female Seminary, which she left in 1829.

Fern lived with her parents until 1837, when she married Charles Eldredge, a cashier at the Merchant's Bank in Boston. She bore three children, and her life seemed to have reached a heroine's happily-ever-after end. But when Fern was 33, her situation changed radically: over the course of two years, her youngest sister, her mother, her eldest daughter (7 years old at the time), and her husband all died. As if the emotional disaster were not enough, Fern faced financial ruin as well, as her husband's estate went entirely to creditors.

With no financial resources to support herself and her two surviving children, Fern received small pensions from her father and father-in-law. Under pressure from her relatives, Fern agreed in 1849 to make a second marriage—evidently for economic reasons—to Samuel P. Farrington, whose wife had died, leaving him with two small daughters. The marriage quickly crumbled under the pressure of Farrington's jealousies and their mutual incompatibility: in 1851 Fern walked out on her husband. The breach ended in divorce, still unusual at that time. Her family, scandalized, refused to support her after that.

Like Ruth Hall, her fictional heroine, Fern tried to make a living by taking in sewing and teaching school. And, like Ruth, she found much more success when she began to write. The episode of Ruth's submitting some sample essays to her journalist brother for advice is based on an experience of Fern's: her brother rebuffed her, criticized her work for "vulgarity" and "indecency," and refused to help her place

it. But Fern persisted and, in a manner that was highly atypical for a Victorian-era woman, followed the American individualist ideal of the self-made man: on her own, she found editors willing to publish her articles and began to build a wide readership.

Fern collected her columns in book form: *Fern Leaves from Fanny's Portfolio* (1853) was a best-seller, followed by a second series a year later. In all, she published eight volumes of essays and two novels, *Ruth Hall* (1855) and *Rose Clark* (1856). Her first novel, fiercely critical of the family members and acquaintances who fail to aid Ruth in her time of need, raised a scandal among readers who recognized Fern's father and brother—as well as other prominent editors—among the caricatures. One offended editor's vituperative attack on her personal history and writings—sarcastically called *The Life and Beauties of Fanny Fern* (1855)—did little to erode her popularity; in fact, it increased her novel's appeal as a *roman à clef.* Fern was severely criticized for her irreverent attitude toward hypocritical, prosperous people, particularly men; she was taken to task for the self-flattery some critics saw in her portrayal of Ruth; and she was attacked for the frankness of her treatment of such topics as prostitution and birth control. Twentieth-century readers have also objected to the overtly emotional quality—or "sentimentality"—of her writing. But all these factors contributed to her popularity among her reading public.

Ruth Hall is an unusual heroine for a nineteenth-century novel: whereas most novels about a woman ended either in her marriage or her death, Ruth's story follows neither convention. In the end she is resourceful, independent, and financially self-sufficient. Ultimately, Fern's path diverged from Ruth's: in 1856 she married again, this time quite happily. Her third husband, the biographer James Parton, was eleven years her junior. They lived together while Fern continued writing weekly columns until she died in 1872, of cancer.

Fern's collections include *Little Ferns for Fanny's Little Friends* (1853); *The Play-Day Book* (1857); *Fresh Leaves* (1857); *A New Story Book for Children* (1864); *Folly As It Flies* (1868); *Ginger-Snaps* (1870); and *Caper-Sauce* (1872). The best available edition of her work is *Ruth Hall & Other Writings* (1986), edited by Joyce W. Warren.

In addition to Warren's biography, *Fanny Fern: An Independent Woman* (1992), the major works on Fanny Fern include *Fanny Fern, or a Pair of Flaming Shoes* (1966) by Florence Adams; sections of *A Portrait of the Artist as a Young Woman: The Writer as Heroine in American Literature* (1983) by Linda Huf; and *Private Woman, Public Stage: Literary Domesticity in Nineteenth-Century America* (1984) by Mary Kelley.

FROM RUTH HALL

Chapter I

The old church clock rang solemnly out on the midnight air. Ruth started. For hours she had sat there, leaning her cheek upon her hand, and gazing through the open space between the rows of brick walls, upon the sparkling waters of the bay, glancing and quivering 'neath the moonbeams. The city's busy hum had long since died away; myriad restless eyes had closed in peaceful slumber; Ruth could not sleep. This was the last time she would sit at that little window. The morrow would find her in a home of her own. On the morrow Ruth would be a bride.

Ruth was not sighing because she was about to leave her father's roof, (for her childhood had been anything but happy,) but she was vainly trying to look into a future, which God has mercifully veiled from curious eyes. Had that craving heart of her's at length found its ark of refuge? Would clouds or sunshine, joy or sorrow, tears or smiles, predominate in her future? Who could tell? The silent stars returned her no answer. Would a harsh word ever fall from lips which now breathed only love? Would the step whose lightest footfall now made her heart leap, ever sound in her ear like a death-knell? As time, with its ceaseless changes, rolled on, would love flee affrighted from the bent form, and silver locks, and faltering footstep? Was there no talisman to keep him?

"Strange questions," were they, "for a young girl!" Ah, but Ruth could remember when she was no taller than a rosebush, how cravingly her little heart cried out for love! How a careless word, powerless to wound one less sensitive, would send her, weeping, to that little room for hours; and, young as she was, life's pains seemed already more to her than life's pleasures. Would it *always* be so? Would she find more thorns than roses in her *future* pathway?

Then, Ruth remembered how she used to wish she were beautiful,—not that she might be admired, but that she might be loved. But Ruth was "very plain,"—so her brother Hyacinth told her, and "awkward," too; she had heard that ever since she could remember; and the recollection of it dyed her cheek with blushes, whenever a stranger made his appearance in the home circle.

So, Ruth was fonder of being alone by herself; and then, they called her "odd," and "queer," and wondered if she would "ever make anything;" and Ruth used to wonder, too; and sometimes she asked herself why a sweet strain of music, or a fine passage in a poem, made her heart thrill, and her whole frame quiver with emotion?

The world smiled on her brother Hyacinth. He was handsome, and gifted. He could win fame, and what was better, love. Ruth wished he would love her a little. She often used to steal into his room and "right" his papers, when the stupid housemaid had displaced them; and often she would prepare him a tempting little lunch, and carry it to his room, on his return from his morning walk; but Hyacinth would only say, "Oh, it is you, Ruth, is it? I thought it was Bridget;" and go on reading his newspaper.

Ruth's mother was dead. Ruth did not remember a great deal about her—only that she always looked uneasy about the time her father was expected home; and when his step was heard in the hall, she would say in a whisper, to Hyacinth and herself, "Hush! hush! your father is coming;" and then Hyacinth would immediately stop whistling, or humming, and Ruth would run up into her little room, for fear she should, in some unexpected way, get into disgrace.

Ruth, also, remembered when her father came home and found company to tea, how he frowned and complained of headache, although he always ate as heartily as any of the company; and how after tea he would stretch himself out upon the sofa and say, "I think I'll take a nap;" and then, he would close his eyes, and if the company commenced talking, he would start up and say to Ruth, who was sitting very still in the corner, *"Ruth*, don't make such a noise;" and when Ruth's mother would whisper gently in his ear, "Wouldn't it be better, dear, if you laid down up stairs? It is quite comfortable and quiet there," her father would say, aloud, "Oh yes, oh yes, you want to get rid of me, do you?" And then her mother would say, turning to the company, "How very fond Mr. Ellet is of a joke!" But Ruth remembered that her mother often blushed when she said so, and that her laugh did not sound natural.

After her mother's death, Ruth was sent to boarding-school, where she shared a room with four strange girls, who laid awake all night, telling the most extraordinary stories, and ridiculing Ruth for being such an old maid that she could not see "where the laugh came in." Equally astonishing to the unsophisticated Ruth, was the demureness with which they would bend over their books when the pale, meek-eyed widow, employed as duenna,[1] went the rounds after tea, to see if each inmate was preparing the next day's lessons, and the coolness with which they would jump up, on her departure, put on their bonnets and shawls, and slip out at the sidestreet door to meet expectant lovers; and when the pale widow went the rounds again at nine o'clock, she would find them demurely seated, just where she left them, apparently busily conning[2] their lessons! Ruth wondered if *all* girls were as mischievous, and if fathers and mothers ever stopped to think what companions their daughters would have for roommates and bed-fellows, when they sent them away from home. As to the Principal, Madame Moreau, she contented herself with sweeping her flounces, once a day, through the recitation rooms; so it was not a difficult matter, in so large an establishment, to pass muster with the sub-teachers at recitations.

Composition day was the general bugbear. Ruth's madcap roommates were struck with the most unqualified amazement and admiration at the facility with which "the old maid" executed this frightful task. They soon learned to put her services in requisition; first, to help them out of this slough of despond;[3] next, to save them the necessity of wading in at all, by writing their compositions for them.

In the all-absorbing love affairs which were constantly going on between the young ladies of Madame Moreau's school and their respective admirers, Ruth took no interest; and on the occasion of the unexpected reception of a bouquet, from a smitten swain, accompanied by a copy of amatory verses, Ruth crimsoned to her temples and burst into tears, that any one could be found so heartless as to burlesque the "awkward" Ruth. Simple child! She was unconscious that, in the freedom of that atmosphere where a "prophet out of his own country is honored," her lithe form had rounded into symmetry and grace, her slow step had become light and elastic, her eye bright, her smile winning, and her voice soft and melodious. Other bouquets, other notes, and glances of involuntary admiration from passers-by, at length opened her eyes to the fact, that she was "plain, awkward Ruth" no longer. Eureka! She had arrived at the first epoch in a young girl's life,—she had found out her power! Her manners became assured and self-possessed. *She*, Ruth, could inspire love! Life became dear to her.

1. Chaperone.
2. Memorizing.

3. Image drawn from John Bunyan's *Pilgrim's Progress* (1678).

There was something worth living for—something to look forward to. She had a motive—an aim; she should *some* day make somebody's heart glad,—somebody's hearth-stone bright; somebody should be proud of her; and oh, how she *could* love that somebody! History, astronomy, mathematics, the languages, were all pastime now. Life wore a new aspect; the skies were bluer, the earth greener, the flowers more fragrant;—her twin-soul existed somewhere.

When Ruth had been a year at school, her elegant brother Hyacinth came to see her. Ruth dashed down her books, and bounded down three stairs at a time, to meet him; for she loved him, poor child, just as well as if he were worth loving. Hyacinth drew languidly back a dozen paces, and holding up his hands, drawled out imploringly, "kiss me if you insist on it, Ruth, but for heaven's sake, don't tumble my dickey." He also remarked, that her shoes were too large for her feet, and that her little French apron was "slightly askew;" and told her, whatever else she omitted, to be sure to learn "to waltz." He was then introduced to Madame Moreau, who remarked to Madame Chicchi, her Italian teacher, what a very *distingué* looking person he was; after which he yawned several times, then touched his hat gracefully, praised "the very superior air of the establishment," brushed an imperceptible atom of dust from his beaver, kissed the tips of his fingers to his demonstrative sister, and tip-toed Terpsichoreally[4] over the academic threshold.

In addition to this, Ruth's father wrote occasionally when a term-bill became due, or when his tradesmen's bills came in, on the first of January; on which occasion an annual fit of poverty seized him, an almshouse loomed up in perspective, he reduced the wages of his cook two shillings, and advised Ruth either to get married or teach school.

Three years had passed under Madame Moreau's roof; Ruth's schoolmates wondering the while why she took so much pains to bother her head with those stupid books, when she was every day growing prettier, and all the world knew that it was quite unnecessary for a pretty woman to be clever. When Ruth once more crossed the paternal threshold, Hyacinth levelled his eye-glass at her, and exclaimed, " 'Pon honor, Ruth, you've positively had a narrow escape from being handsome." Whether old Mr. Ellet was satisfied with her physical and mental progress, Ruth had no means of knowing.

AND NOW, as we have said before, it is the night before Ruth's bridal; and there she sits, though the old church bell has long since chimed the midnight hour, gazing at the moon, as she cuts a shining path through the waters; and trembling, while she questions the dim, uncertain future. Tears, Ruth? Have phantom shapes of terror glided before those gentle prophet eyes? Has death's dark wing even now fanned those girlish temples?

Chapter II

"*It was so odd* in Ruth to have no one but the family at the wedding. It was just one of her queer freaks! Where was the use of her white satin dress and orange wreath? what the use of her looking handsomer than she ever did before, when there was nobody there to see her?"

"Nobody to see her?" Mark that manly form at her side; see his dark eye glisten, and his chiselled lip quiver, as he bends an earnest gaze on her who realizes all his boyhood dreams. Mistaken ones! it is not admiration which that young beating heart craves; it is love.

"A very fine-looking, presentable fellow," said Hyacinth, as the carriage rolled away with his new brother-in-law. "Really, love is a great beautifier. Ruth looked quite handsome

---

4. Terpsichore, in Greek myth, is the muse of dancing and singing.

to-night. Lord bless me! how immensely tiresome it must be to sit opposite the same face three times a day, three hundred and sixty-five days in a year! I should weary of Venus[5] herself. I'm glad my handsome brother-in-law is in such good circumstances. Duns[6] *are* a bore. I must keep on the right side of him. Tom, was that tailor here again yesterday? Did you tell him I was out of town? Right, Tom."

Chapter III

"Well, I *hope* Harry will be happy," said Ruth's mother-in-law, old Mrs. Hall, as she untied her cap-strings, and seated herself in the newly-furnished parlor, to await the coming of the bride and bridegroom. "I can't say, though, that I see the need of his being married. I always mended his socks. He has sixteen bran new shirts, eight linen and eight cotton. I made them myself out of the Hamilton long-cloth. Hamilton long-cloth is good cotton, too; strong, firm, and wears well. Eight cotton and eight linen shirts! Can anybody tell what he got married for? *I* don't know. If he tired of his boarding-house, of course he could always come home. As to Ruth, I don't know anything about her. Of course she is perfect in *his* eyes. I remember the time when he used to think *me* perfect. I suppose I shall be laid on the shelf now. Well, what beauty he can find in that pale, golden hair, and those blue-gray eyes, I don't know. I can't say I fancy the family either. Proud as Lucifer, all of 'em. Nothing to be proud of, either. The father next to nothing when he began life. The son, a conceited jackanapes, who divides his time between writing rhymes and inventing new ties for his cravat. Well, well, we shall see; but I doubt if this bride is anything but a well-dressed doll. I've been peeping into her bureau drawers to-day. What is the use of all those ruffles on her under-clothes, I'd like to know? Who's going to wash and iron them? *Presents* to her! Well, why don't people make *sensible* presents,—a dozen of dish towels, some crash rollers, a ball of wick-yarn, or the like of that?"[7]

"O-o-oh d-e-a-r! there's the carriage! Now, for one month to come, to say the least, I shall be made perfectly sick with their billing and cooing. I shouldn't be surprised if Harry didn't speak to me oftener than once a day. Had he married a practical woman I wouldn't have cared—somebody who looked as if God made her for something; but that little yellow-haired simpleton—umph!"

Poor Ruth, in happy ignorance of the state of her new mother-in-law's feelings, moved about her apartments in a sort of blissful dream. How odd it seemed, this new freedom, this being one's own mistress. How odd to see that shaving-brush and those razors lying on *her* toilet table! then that saucy looking smoking-cap, those slippers and that dressing-gown, those fancy neckties, too, and vests and coats, in unrebuked proximity to her muslins, laces, silks and de laines![8]

Ruth liked it.

Chapter IV

"Good morning, Ruth; Mrs. Hall I suppose *I should* call you, only that I can't get used to being shoved one side quite so suddenly," said the old lady, with a faint attempt at a laugh.

---

5. The Roman name for Aphrodite, Greek goddess of love.
6. Bill collectors.

7. Crash is a coarse fabric used for towels and curtains; wick yarn is used in candlemaking.
8. Woollens (the allusion is to undergarments).

"Oh, pray don't say Mrs. Hall to *me*," said Ruth, handing her a chair; "call me any name that best pleases you; I shall be quite satisfied."

"I suppose you feel quite lonesome when Harry is away, attending to business, and as if you hardly knew what to do with yourself; don't you?"

"Oh, no," said Ruth, with a glad smile, "not at all. I was just thinking whether I was not glad to have him gone a little while, so that I could sit down and think how much I love him."

The old lady moved uneasily in her chair. "I suppose you understand all about housekeeping, Ruth?"

Ruth blushed. "No," said she, "I have but just returned from boarding school. I asked Harry to wait till I had learned house-keeping matters, but he was not willing."

The old lady untied her cap-strings, and patted the floor restlessly with her foot.

"It is a great pity you were not brought up properly," said she. "I learned all that a girl should learn, before I married. Harry has his fortune yet to make, you know. Young people, now-a-days, seem to think that money comes in showers, whenever it is wanted; that's a mistake; a penny at a time—that's the way we got ours; that's the way Harry and you will have to get yours. Harry has been brought up sensibly. He has been taught economy; he is like me, naturally of a very generous turn; he will occasionally offer you pin-money. In those cases, it will be best for you to pass it over to me to keep; of course you can always have it again, by telling me how you wish to spend it. I would advise you, too, to lay by all your handsome clothes. As to the silk stockings you were married in, of course you will never be so extravagant as to wear them again. I never had a pair of silk stockings in my life; they have a very silly, frivolous look. Do you know how to iron, Ruth?"

"Yes," said Ruth; "I have sometimes clear-starched my own muslins and laces."

"Glad to hear it; did you ever seat a pair of pantaloons?"

"No," said Ruth, repressing a laugh, and yet half inclined to cry; "you forget that I am just home from boarding-school."

"Can you make bread? When I say *bread* I *mean* bread—old fashioned, yeast riz bread; none of your sal-soda, salaeratus, sal-volatile poisonous mixtures, that must be eaten as quick as baked, lest it should dry up; *yeast* bread—do you know how to make it?"

"No," said Ruth, with a growing sense of her utter good-for-nothingness; "people in the city always buy baker's bread; my father did."

"Your father! land's sake, child, you mustn't quote your father now you're married; you haven't any father."

I never had, thought Ruth.

"To be sure; what does the Bible say? 'Forsaking father and mother, cleave to your wife,' (or husband, which amounts to the same thing, I take it;) and speaking of that, I hope you won't be always running home, or running anywhere in fact. Wives should be keepers at home. Ruth," continued the old lady after a short pause, "do you know I should like your looks better, if you didn't curl your hair?"

"I don't curl it," said Ruth, "it curls naturally."

"That's a pity," said the old lady, "you should avoid everything that looks frivolous; you must try and pomatum it down.[9] And Ruth, if you should feel the need of exercise, don't gad in the streets. Remember there is nothing like a broom and a dust-pan to make the blood circulate."

"You keep a rag bag, I suppose," said the old lady; "many's the glass dish I've peddled away my scissors-clippings for. 'Waste not, want not.' I've got that framed somewhere. I'll hunt it up, and put it on your wall. It won't do you any harm to read it now and then."

"I hope," continued the old lady, "that you don't read novels and such trash. I have a very select little library, when you feel inclined to read, consisting of a treatise on 'The Complaints of Women,' an excellent sermon on Predestination, by our old minister, Dr. Diggs, and Seven

9. Use a heavy hair oil.

Reasons why John Rogers, the martyr, must have had *ten* children instead of *nine* (as is *generally* supposed); any time that you stand in need of *rational* reading come to me;" and the old lady, smoothing a wrinkle in her black silk apron, took a dignified leave.

Chapter V

Poor Ruth! her sky so soon overcast! As the door closed on the prim, retreating figure of her mother-in-law, she burst into tears. But she was too sensible a girl to weep long. She wiped her eyes, and began to consider what was to be done. It would never do to complain to Harry—dear Harry. He would have to take sides; oh no, that would never do; she could never complain to him of his *own* mother. But why did he bring them together? knowing, as he must have known, how little likely they were to assimilate. This thought she smothered quickly, but not before it had given birth to a sigh, close upon the heels of which love framed this apology: It was so long since Harry had lived under the same roof with his mother he had probably forgotten her eccentricities; and then she was so dotingly fond of him, that probably no points of collision ever came up between the two.

In the course of an hour, what with cold bathing and philosophy, Ruth's eyes and equanimity were placed beyond the suspicion even of a newly-made husband, and when she held up her lips to him so temptingly, on his return, he little dreamed of the self-conquest she had so tearfully achieved for his sake.

Chapter LVI

It was a sultry morning in July.[1] Ruth had risen early, for her cough seemed more troublesome in a reclining posture. "I wonder what that noise can be?" said she to herself; whir—whir—whir, it went, all day long in the attic overhead. She knew that Mrs. Waters had one other lodger beside herself, an elderly gentleman by the name of Bond, who cooked his own food, and whom she often met on the stairs, coming up with a pitcher of water, or a few eggs in a paper bag, or a pie that he had bought of Mr. Flake, at the little black grocery-shop at the corner. On these occasions he always stepped aside, and with a deferential bow waited for Ruth to pass. He was a thin, spare man, slightly bent; his hair and whiskers curiously striped like a zebra, one lock being jet black, while the neighboring one was as distinct a white. His dress was plain, but very neat and tidy. He never seemed to have any business out-doors, as he stayed in his room all day, never leaving it at all till dark, when he paced up and down, with his hands behind him, before the house. "Whir—whir—whir." It was early sunrise; but Ruth had heard that odd noise for two hours at least. What *could* it mean? Just then a carrier passed on the other side of the street with the morning papers, and slipped one under the crack of the house door opposite.

A thought! why could not Ruth write for the papers? How very odd it had never occurred to her before? Yes, write for the papers—why not? She remembered that while at boarding-school, an editor of a paper in the same town used often to come in and take down her compositions in short-hand as she read them aloud, and transfer them to the columns of his

---

1. In the intervening chapters, Ruth has three children; her eldest daughter and her husband have died. To support her remaining daughters, Ruth tries needlework and teaching but fails to find work. Receiving no support from her relations, Ruth lives in a boardinghouse.

paper. She certainly *ought* to write better now than she did when an inexperienced girl. She would begin that very night; but where to make a beginning? who would publish her articles? how much would they pay her? to whom should she apply first? There was her brother Hyacinth, now the prosperous editor of the Irving Magazine; oh, if he would only employ her? Ruth was quite sure she could write as well as some of his correspondents, whom he had praised with no niggardly pen. She would prepare samples to send immediately, announcing her intention, and offering them for his acceptance. This means of support would be so congenial, so absorbing. At the needle one's mind could still be brooding over sorrowful thoughts.

Ruth counted the days and hours impatiently, as she waited for an answer. Hyacinth surely would not refuse *her* when in almost every number of his magazine he was announcing some new contributor; or, if *he* could not employ her *himself,* he surely would be brotherly enough to point out to her some one of the many avenues so accessible to a man of extensive newspaperial and literary acquaintance. She would so gladly support herself, so cheerfully toil day and night, if need be, could she only win an independence; and Ruth recalled with a sigh Katy's last visit to her father,[2] and then she rose and walked the floor in her impatience; and then, her restless spirit urging her on to her fate, she went again to the post office to see if there were no letter. How long the clerk made her wait! Yes, there was a letter for her, and in her brother's hand-writing too. Oh, how long since she had seen it!

Ruth heeded neither the jostling of office-boys, porters, or draymen, as she held out her eager hand for the letter. Thrusting it hastily in her pocket, she hurried in breathless haste back to her lodgings. The contents were as follows:

> "I have looked over the pieces you sent me, Ruth. It is very evident that writing never can be *your* forte; you have no talent that way. You may possibly be employed by some inferior newspapers, but be assured your articles never will be heard of out of your own little provincial city. For myself I have plenty of contributors, nor do I know of any of my literary acquaintances who would employ you. I would advise you, therefore, to seek some *unobtrusive* employment. Your brother,

> "Hyacinth Ellet."

A bitter smile struggled with the hot tear that fell upon Ruth's cheek. "I have tried the unobtrusive employment," said Ruth; "the wages are six cents a day, Hyacinth;" and again the bitter smile disfigured her gentle lip.

"No talent!"

"At another tribunal than his will I appeal."

"Never be heard of out of my own little provincial city!" The cold, contemptuous tone stung her.

"But they shall be heard of," and Ruth leaped to her feet. "Sooner than he dreams of, too. I *can* do it, I *feel* it, I *will* do it," and she closed her lips firmly; "but there will be a desperate struggle first," and she clasped her hands over her heart as if it had already commenced; "there will be scant meals, and sleepless nights, and weary days, and a throbbing brow, and an aching heart; there will be the chilling tone, the rude repulse; there will be ten backward steps to one forward. *Pride* must sleep! but—" and Ruth glanced at her children—"it shall be *done.* They shall be proud of their mother. *Hyacinth shall yet be proud to claim his sister."*

"What is it, mamma?" asked Katy, looking wonderingly at the strange expression of her mother's face.

"What is it, my darling?" and Ruth caught up the child with convulsive energy; "what is

---

2. The elder of Ruth's surviving daughters had appealed unsuccessfully to Ruth's father for financial help.

it? only that when you are a woman you shall remember this day, my little pet;" and as she kissed Katy's upturned brow a bright spot burned on her cheek, and her eye glowed like a star.

Chapter LVII

"Doctor?" said Mrs. Hall, "put down that book, will you? I want to talk to you a bit; there you've sat these three hours, without stirring, except to brush the flies off your nose, and my tongue actually aches keeping still."

"Sh-sh-sh," said the doctor, running his forefinger along to guide his purblind eyes safely to the end of the paragraph. "Sh-sh. 'It—is es-ti-ma-ted by Captain Smith—that— there — are — up'ards — of — ten — hundred — human — critters — in — the — Nor-West — sett-le-ment.' Well—Mis. Hall—well—" said the doctor, laying a faded ribbon mark between the leaves of the book, and pushing his spectacles back on his forehead, "what's to pay now? what do you want of me?"

"I've a great mind as ever I had to eat," said the old lady, pettishly, "to knit twice round the heel of this stocking, before I answer you; what do you think I care about Captain Smith? Travelers always lie; it is a part of their trade, and if they don't it's neither here nor there to me. I wish that book was in the Red Sea."

"I thought you didn't want it *read,*" retorted the irritating old doctor.

"Now I suppose you call that funny," said the old lady. "I call it simply ridiculous for a man of your years to play on words in such a frivolous manner. What I was going to say was this, *i.e.* if I can get a chance to say it, if *you* have given up all idea of getting Harry's children, *I* haven't, and now is the time to apply for Katy again; for, according to all accounts, Ruth is getting along poorly enough."

"How did you hear?" asked the doctor.

"Why, my milliner, Miss Tiffkins, has a nephew who tends in a little grocery-shop near where Ruth boards, and he says that she buys a smaller loaf every time she comes to the store, and that the milkman told him that she only took a pint of milk a day of him now; then Katy has not been well, and what she did for doctors and medicines is best known to herself; she's so independent that she never would complain if she had to eat paving stones. The best way to get the child will be to ask her here on a visit, and say we want to cure her up a little with country air. You understand? that will throw dust in Ruth's eyes, and then we will take our own time about letting her go back you know. Miss Tiffkins says her nephew says that people who come into the grocery-shop are very curious to know who Ruth is; and old Mr. Flake, who keeps it, says that it wouldn't hurt her any, if she is a lady, to stop and talk a little, like the rest of his customers; he says, too, that her children are as close-mouthed as their mother, for when he just asked Katy what business her father used to do, and what supported them now he was dead, and if they lived all the time on bread and milk, and a few such little questions, Katy answered, 'Mamma does not allow me to talk to strangers,' and went out of the shop, with her loaf of bread, as dignified as a little duchess."

"Like mother, like child," said the doctor; "proud and poor, proud and poor; that tells the whole story. Well, shall I write to Ruth, Mis. Hall, about Katy?"

"No," said the old lady, "let me manage that; you will upset the whole business if you do. I've a plan in my head, and to-morrow, after breakfast, I'll take the old chaise, and go in after Katy."

In pursuance of this plan, the old lady, on the following day, climbed up into an old-fashioned chaise, and turned the steady old horse's nose in the direction of the city; jerking at the reins, and clucking and gee-ing him up, after the usual awkward fashion of sexegenarian female drivers. Using Miss Tiffkins's land-mark, the little black grocery-shop, for a guide-board, she soon discovered Ruth's abode; and so well did she play her part in commiserating Ruth's misfortunes, and Katy's sickly appearance, that the widow's kind heart was immediately tortured with the most unnecessary self-reproaches, which prepared the way for an acceptance of her invitation for Katy "for a week or two;" great promises, meanwhile, being held out to the child of "a little pony to ride," and various other tempting lures of the same kind. Still little Katy hesitated, clinging tightly to her mother's dress, and looking, with her clear, searching eyes, into her grandmother's face, in a way that would have embarrassed a less artful manœuverer. The old lady understood the glance, and put it on file, to be attended to at her leisure; it being no part of her present errand to play the unamiable. Little Katy, finally won over, consented to make the visit, and the old chaise was again set in motion for home.

Chapter LVIII

"How d'ye do, Ruth? asked Mr. Ellet, the next morning, as he ran against Ruth in the street; "glad you have taken my advice, and done a sensible thing at last."

"I don't know what you mean," answered Ruth.

"Why, the doctor told me yesterday that you had given Katy up to them, to bring up; you would have done better if you had sent off Nettie too."

"I have not 'given Katy up,' " said Ruth, starting and blushing deeply; "and they could not have understood it so; she has only gone on a visit of a fortnight, to recruit a little."

"Pooh—pooh!" replied Mr. Ellet. "The thing is quietly over with; now don't make a fuss. The old folks expect to keep her. They wrote to me about it, and I approved of it. It's the best thing all round; and, as I just said, it would have been better still if Nettie had gone, too. Now don't make a fool of yourself; you can go once in awhile, I suppose, to see the child."

"How can I go?" asked Ruth, looking her father calmly in the face; "it costs fifty cents every trip, by railroad, and you know I have not the money."

"That's for you to decide," answered the father coldly; "I can't be bothered about such trifles. It is the way you always do, Ruth, whenever I see you; but it is time I was at my office. Don't make a fool of yourself, now; mind what I tell you, and let well alone."

"Father," said Ruth; "father—"

"Can't stop—can't stop," said Mr. Ellet, moving rapidly down street, to get out of his daughter's way.

"Can it be possible," thought Ruth, looking after him, "that he could connive at such duplicity? Was the old lady's sympathy a mere stratagem to work upon my feelings? How unnecessarily I reproached myself with my supposed injustice to her? Can *good* people do such things? Is religion only a fable? No, no; 'let God be true, and every man a liar.' "

Chapter LIX

"Is this 'The Daily Type' office?" asked Ruth of a printer's boy, who was rushing down five steps at a time, with an empty pail in his hand.

"All you have to do is to ask, mem. You've got a tongue in your head, haven't ye? women folks generally has," said the little ruffian.

Ruth, obeying this civil invitation, knocked gently at the office door. A whir of machinery, and a bad odor of damp paper and cigar smoke, issued through the half-open crack.

"I shall have to walk in," said Ruth, "they never will hear my feeble knock amid all this racket and bustle;" and pushing the door ajar, she found herself in the midst of a group of smokers, who, in slippered feet, and with heels higher than their heads, were whiffing and laughing, amid the pauses of conversation, most uproariously. Ruth's face crimsoned as heels and cigars remained, in *status quo,* and her glance was met by a rude stare.

"I called to see if you would like a new contributor to your paper," said Ruth; "if so, I will leave a few samples of my articles for your inspection."

"What do you say, Bill?" said the person addressed; "drawer full as usual, I suppose, isn't it? more chaff than wheat, too, I'll swear; don't want any, ma'am; come now, Jo, let's hear the rest of that story; shut the door, ma'am, if you please."

"Are you the editor of the 'Parental Guide'?" said Ruth, to a thin, cadaverous-looking gentleman, in a white neck-cloth, and green spectacles, whose editorial sanctum was not far from the office she had just left.

"I am."

"Do you employ contributors for your paper?"

"Sometimes."

"Shall I leave you this MS. for your inspection, sir?"

"Just as you please."

"Have you a copy of your paper here, sir, from which I could judge what style of articles you prefer?"

At this, the gentleman addressed raised his eyes for the first time, wheeled his editorial arm-chair round, facing Ruth, and peering over his green spectacles, remarked:

"Our paper, madam, is most em-phat-i-cal-ly a paper devoted to the interests of religion; no frivolous jests, no love-sick ditties, no fashionable sentimentalism, finds a place in its columns. This is a serious world, madam, and it ill becomes those who are born to die, to go dancing through it. Josephus remarks that the Saviour of the world was never known to smile. *I* seldom smile. Are you a religious woman, madam?"

"I endeavor to become so," answered Ruth.

"V-e-r-y good; what sect?"

"Presbyterian."

At this the white neck-clothed gentleman moved back his chair: "Wrong, madam, all wrong; I was educated by the best of fathers, but he was *not* a Presbyterian; his son is not a Presbyterian; his son's paper sets its face like a flint against that heresy; no, madam, we shall have no occasion for your contributions; a hope built on a Presbyterian foundation, is built on the sand. Good morning, madam."

Did Ruth despair? No! but the weary little feet which for so many hours had kept pace with hers, needed a reprieve. Little Nettie must go home, and Ruth must read the office signs as she went along, to prepare for new attempts on the morrow.

To-morrow? Would a brighter morrow *ever* come? Ruth thought of her children, and said again with a strong heart—*it will;* and taking little Nettie upon her lap she divided with her their frugal supper—a scanty bowl of bread and milk.

Ruth could not but acknowledge to herself that she had thus far met with but poor encouragement, but she knew that to climb, she must begin at the lowest round of the ladder. It were useless to apply to a long-established leading paper for employment, unless endorsed by some influential name. Her brother had coolly, almost contemptuously, set her aside; and yet in the very last number of his Magazine, which accident threw in her way, he pleaded for public favor for a young actress, whom he said had been driven by fortune from the sheltered privacy of home, to earn her subsistence upon the stage, and whose earnest, strong-souled nature, he thought, should meet with a better welcome than mere curiosity.

"Oh, why not one word for me?" thought Ruth; "and how can I ask of strangers a favor which a brother's heart has so coldly refused?"

It was very disagreeable applying to the small papers, many of the editors of which, accustomed to dealing with hoydenish contributors, were incapable of comprehending that their manner towards Ruth had been marked by any want of that respectful courtesy due to a dignified woman. From all such contact Ruth shrank sensitively; their free-and-easy tone fell upon her ear so painfully, as often to bring the tears to her eyes. Oh, if Harry—but she must not think of him.

The next day Ruth wandered about the business streets, looking into office-entries, reading signs, and trying to gather from their "know-nothing" hieroglyphics, some light to illumine her darkened pathway. Day after day chronicled only repeated failures, and now, notwithstanding she had reduced their already meagre fare, her purse was nearly empty.

Chapter LX

It was a warm, sultry Sabbath morning; not a breath of air played over the heated roofs of the great, swarming city. Ruth sat in her little, close attic, leaning her head upon her hand, weary, languid and dejected. Life seemed to her scarce worth the pains to keep its little flame flickering. A dull pain was in her temples, a heavy weight upon her heart. Other Sabbaths, *happy* Sabbaths, came up to her remembrance; earth looked so dark to her now, heaven so distant, God's ways so inscrutable.

Hark to the Sabbath-bell!

Ruth took little Nettie by the hand, and led her slowly to church. Other families, *unbroken* families, passed her on their way; families whose sunny thresholds the destroying angel had never crossed. Oh why the joy to them, the pain to her? Sadly she entered the church, and took her accustomed seat amid the worshippers. The man of God opened the holy book. Sweet and clear fell upon Ruth's troubled ear these blessed words: "There remaineth, therefore, a rest for the people of God."[3]

The bliss, the joy of heaven was pictured; life,—mysterious, crooked, unfathomable life, made clear to the eye of faith; sorrow, pain, suffering, ignominy even, made sweet for His sake, who suffered all for us.

Ruth weeps! weeps that her faith was for an instant o'erclouded; weeps that she shrank from breasting the foaming waves at the bidding of Him who said, "It is I, be not afraid." And she, who came there fluttering with a broken wing, went away singing, soaring.

Oh man of God! pressed down with many cares, anxious and troubled, sowing but not reaping, fearing to bring in no sheaves for the harvest, be of good courage. The arrow shot at a venture may to thine eye fall aimless; but in the Book of Life shalt thou read many an answer to the wrestling prayer, heard in thy closet by God alone.

Chapter LXII

Ruth had found employment. Ruth's MSS. had been accepted at the office of "The Standard." Yes, an article of hers was to be published in the very next issue. The remuneration was not what Ruth had hoped, but it was at least a *beginning,* a stepping-stone. What a pity that Mr.

3. Hebrews 4:9.

Lescom's (the editor's) rule was, not to pay a contributor, even after a piece was accepted, until it was printed—and Ruth so short of funds. Could she hold out to work so hard, and fare so rigidly? for often there was only a crust left at night; but, God be thanked, she should now *earn* that crust! It was a pity that oil was so dear, too, because most of her writing must be done at night, when Nettie's little prattling voice was hushed, and her innumerable little wants forgotten in sleep. Yes, it *was* a pity that good oil was so dear, for the cheaper kind crusted so soon on the wick, and Ruth's eyes, from excessive weeping, had become quite tender, and often very painful. Then it would be so mortifying should a mistake occur in one of her articles. She must write very legibly, for type-setters were sometimes sad bunglers, making people accountable for words that would set Worcester's or Webster's hair on end; but, poor things, *they* worked hard too—they had *their* sorrows, thinking, long into the still night, as they scattered the types, more of their dependent wives and children, than of the orthography of a word, or the rhetoric of a sentence.

Scratch—scratch—scratch, went Ruth's pen; the dim lamp flickering in the night breeze, while the deep breathing of the little sleepers was the watchword, *On!* to her throbbing brow and weary fingers. One o'clock—two o'clock—three o'clock—the lamp burns low in the socket. Ruth lays down her pen, and pushing back the hair from her forehead, leans faint and exhausted against the window-sill, that the cool night-air may fan her heated temples. How impressive the stillness! Ruth can almost hear her own heart beat. She looks upward, and the watchful stars seem to her like the eyes of gentle friends. No, God would *not* forsake her! A sweet peace steals into her troubled heart, and the overtasked lids droop heavily over the weary eyes.

Ruth sleeps.

Daylight! Morning *so* soon? All night Ruth has leaned with her head on the window-sill, and now she wakes unrefreshed from the constrained posture; but she has no time to heed *that,* for little Nettie lies moaning in her bed with pain; she lifts the little creature in her lap, rocks her gently, and kisses her cheek; but still little Nettie moans. Ruth goes to the drawer and looks in her small purse (Harry's gift); it is empty! then she clasps her hands and looks again at little Nettie. Must Nettie die for want of care? Oh, if Mr. Lescom would *only* advance her the money for the contributions he had accepted, but he said so decidedly that "it was a rule he *never* departed from;" and there were yet five long days before the next paper would be out. Five days! what might not happen to Nettie in five days? There was her cousin, Mrs. Millet, but she had muffled her furniture in linen wrappers, and gone to the springs with her family, for the summer months; there was her father, but had he not said "Remember, if you *will* burden yourself with your children, you must not look to me for help." Kissing little Nettie's cheek she lays her gently on the bed, whispering in a husky voice, "only a few moments, Nettie; mamma will be back soon." She closes the door upon the sick child, and stands with her hand upon her bewildered brow, thinking.

"I beg your pardon, madam; the entry is so very dark I did not see you," said Mr. Bond;[4] "you are as early a riser as myself."

"My child is sick," answered Ruth, tremulously; "I was just going out for medicine."

"If you approve of Homœopathy,[5] said Mr. Bond, "and will trust me to prescribe, there will be no necessity for your putting yourself to that trouble; I always treat myself homœ-opathically in sickness, and happen to have a small supply of those medicines by me."

Ruth's natural independence revolted at the idea of receiving a favor from a stranger.

"Perhaps you disapprove of Homœopathy," said Mr. Bond, mistaking the cause of her

---

4. Ruth's boardinghouse neighbor.
5. System of treatment based on using tiny quantities of remedies that in massive doses produce effects similar to those of the illness being treated.

momentary hesitation; "it works like a charm with children; but if you prefer not to try it, allow me to go out and procure you whatever you desire in the way of medicine; you will not then be obliged to leave your child."

Here was another dilemma—what *should* Ruth do? Why, clearly accept his first offer; there was an air of goodness and sincerity about him, which, added to his years, seemed to invite her confidence.

Mr. Bond stepped in, looked at Nettie, and felt her pulse. "Ah, little one, we will soon have you better," said he, as he left the room to obtain his little package of medicines.

"Thank you," said Ruth, with a grateful smile, as he administered to Nettie some infinitesimal pills.

"Not in the least," said Mr. Bond. "I learned two years since to doctor myself in this way, and I have often had the pleasure of relieving others in emergencies like this, from my little Homœopathic stores. You will find that your little girl will soon fall into a sweet sleep, and awake much relieved; if you are careful with her, she will, I think, need nothing more in the way of medicine, or if she should, my advice is quite at your service;" and, taking his pitcher of water in his hand, he bowed respectfully, and wished Ruth good morning.

Who was he? what was he? Whir—whir—there was the noise again! That he was a man of refined and courteous manners, was very certain. Ruth felt glad he was so much her senior; he seemed so like what Ruth had sometimes dreamed a kind father might be, that it lessened the weight of the obligation. Already little Nettie had ceased moaning; her little lids began to droop, and her skin, which had been hot and feverish, became moist and cool. "May God reward him, whoever he may be," said Ruth. "Surely it *is* blessed to *trust!*"

Chapter LXIII

It was four o'clock of a hot August afternoon. The sun had crept round to the front piazza of the doctor's cottage. No friendly trees warded off his burning rays, for the doctor "liked a prospect;" *i.e.* he liked to sit at the window and count the different trains which whizzed past in the course of the day; the number of wagons, and gigs, and carriages, that rolled lazily up the hill; to see the village engine, the "Cataract," drawn out on the green for its weekly ablutions, and to count the bundles of shingles that it took to roof over Squire Ruggles' new barn. No drooping vines, therefore, or creepers, intruded between him and this pleasant "prospect." The doctor was an utilitarian; he could see "no use" in such things, save to rot timber and harbor vermin. So a wondrous glare of white paint, (carefully renewed every spring,) blinded the traveler whose misfortune it was to pass the road by the doctor's house. As I said, it was now four o'clock. The twelve o'clock dinner was long since over. The Irish girl had rinsed out her dish-towels, hung them out the back door to dry, and gone down to the village store to buy some new ribbons advertised as selling at an "immense sacrifice" by the disinterested village shopkeeper.

Let us peep into the doctor's sitting room; the air of this room is close and stifled, for the windows must be tightly closed, lest some audacious fly should make his mark on the old lady's immaculate walls. A centre table stands in the middle of the floor, with a copy of "The Religious Pilot," last year's Almanac, A Directory, and "The remarkable Escape of Eliza Cook, who was partially scalped by the Indians." On one side of the room hangs a piece of framed needle-work, by the virgin fingers of the old lady, representing an unhappy female, weeping over a very high and very perpendicular tombstone, which is hieroglyphiced over with untranslateable characters in red worsted, while a few herbs, not mentioned by botanists, are struggling for existence at its base. A friendly willow-tree, of a most extraordinary shade of blue green, droops in sympathy over the afflicted female, while a nondescript looking bird, resembling a dropsical bull-frog, suspends his song and one leg, in the foreground.[6] It was principally to preserve this chef-d'oeuvre of art, that the windows were hermetically sealed to the entrance of vagrant flies.

The old doctor, with his spectacles awry and his hands drooping listlessly at his side, snored from the depths of his arm-chair, while opposite him the old lady, peering out from behind a very stiffly-starched cap border, was "scaming," "widening," and "narrowing," with a precision and perseverance most painful to witness. Outside, the bee hummed, the robin twittered, the shining leaves of the village trees danced and whispered to the shifting clouds; the free, glad breeze swept the tall meadowgrass, and the village children, as free and fetterless, danced and shouted at their sports; but there sat little Katy, with her hands crossed in her lap, as she *had* sat for many an hour, listening to the never-ceasing click of her grandmother's needles, and the sonorous breathings of the doctor's rubicund nose. Sometimes she moved uneasily in her chair, but the old lady's uplifted finger would immediately remind her that "little girls must be seen and not heard." It was a great thing for Katy when a mouse scratched on the wainscot, or her grandmother's ball rolled out of her lap, giving her a chance to stretch her little cramped limbs. And now the village bell began to toll, with a low, booming, funereal sound, sending a cold shudder through the child's nervous and excited frame. What if *her* mother should die way off in the city? What if she should *always* live in this terrible way at her grandmother's? with nobody to love her, or kiss her, or pat her little head kindly, and say, "Katy, dear;" and again the bell boomed out its mournful sound, and little Katy, unable longer to bear the torturing thoughts it called up, sobbed aloud.

It was all in vain, that the frowning old lady held up her warning finger; the flood-gates were opened, and Katy could not have stopped her tears had her life depended on it.

Hark! a knock at the door! a strange footstep!

"Mother!" shrieked the child hysterically, "mother!" and flew into Ruth's sheltering arms.

"What shall we do, doctor?" asked the old lady, the day after Ruth's visit. "I trusted to her not being able to get the money to come out here, and her father, I knew, wouldn't give it to her, and now here she has walked the whole distance, with Nettie in her arms, except a lift a wagoner or two gave her on the road; and I verily believe she would have done it, had it been twice the distance it is. I never shall be able to bring up that child according to my notions, while *she* is round. I'd forbid her the house, (she deserves it,) only that it won't sound well if she tells of it. And to think of that ungrateful little thing's flying into her mother's arms as if she was in the last extremity, after all we have done for her. I don't suppose Ruth would have left her with us, as it is, if she had the bread to put in her mouth. She might as well give her up, though, first as last, for she never will be able to support her."

"She's fit for nothing but a parlor ornament," said the doctor, "never was. No more business talent in Ruth Ellet, than there is in that chany image[7] of yours on the mantle-tree, Mis. Hall. That tells the whole story."

Chapter LXIV

"I have good news for you," said Mr. Lescom to Ruth, at her next weekly visit; "your very first articles are copied, I see, into many of my exchanges, even into the ———, which seldom contains anything but politics. A good sign for you Mrs. Hall; a good test of your popularity."

6. Such funerary images were popular in middle-class Victorian decor.

7. China ornament.

Ruth's eyes sparkled, and her whole face glowed.

"Ladies *like* to be praised," said Mr. Lescom, good-humoredly, with a mischievous smile.

"Oh, it is not that—not that, sir," said Ruth, with a sudden moistening of the eye, "it is because it will be bread for my children."

Mr. Lescom checked his mirthful mood, and said, "Well, here is something good for me, too; a letter from Missouri, in which the writer says, that if "Floy" (a pretty *nom-de-plume* that of yours, Mrs. Hall) is to be a contributor for the coming year, I may put him down as a subscriber, as well as S. Jones, E. May, and J. Noyes, all of the same place. That's good news for *me*, you see," said Mr. Lescom, with one of his pleasant, beaming smiles.

"Yes," replied Ruth, abstractedly. She was wondering if her articles were to be the means of swelling Mr. Lescom's subscription list, whether *she* ought not to profit by it as well as himself, and whether she should not ask him to increase her pay. She pulled her gloves off and on, and finally mustered courage to clothe her thought in words.

"Now that's just *like* a woman," replied Mr. Lescom, turning it off with a joke; "give them the least foot-hold, and they will want the whole territory. Had I not shown you that letter, you would have been quite contented with your present pay. Ah! I see it won't do to talk so unprofessionally to you; and you needn't expect," said he, smiling, "that I shall ever speak of letters containing new subscribers on your account. I could easily get you the offer of a handsome salary by publishing such things. No—no, I have been foolish enough to lose two or three valuable contributors in that way; I have learned better than that, 'Floy';" and taking out his purse, he paid Ruth the usual sum for her articles.

Ruth bowed courteously, and put the money in her purse; but she sighed as she went down the office stairs. Mr. Lescom's view of the case was a business one, undoubtedly; and the same view that almost any other business man would have taken, viz.: to retain her at her present low rate of compensation, till he was necessitated to raise it by a higher bid from a rival quarter. And so she must plod wearily on till that time came, and poor Katy must still be an exile; for she had not enough to feed her, her landlady having raised the rent of her room two shillings, and Ruth being unable to find cheaper accommodations. It *was* hard, but what could be done? Ruth believed she had exhausted all the offices she knew of. Oh! there was one, "The Pilgrim;" she had not tried there. She would call at the office on her way home.

The editor of "The Pilgrim" talked largely. He had, now, plenty of contributors; he didn't know about employing a new one. Had she ever written? and *what* had she written? Ruth showed him her article in the last number of "The Standard."

"Oh—hum—hum!" said Mr. Tibbetts, changing his tone; "so you are 'Floy,' are you?" (casting his eyes on her.) "What pay do they give you over there?"

Ruth was a novice in business-matters, but she had strong common sense, and that common sense said, he has no right to ask you that question; don't you tell him; so she replied with dignity, "My bargain, sir, with Mr. Lescom was a private one, I believe."

"Hum," said the foiled Mr. Tibbetts; adding in an under-tone to his partner, "sharp that!"

"Well, if I conclude to engage you," said Mr. Tibbetts, "I should prefer you would write for me over a different signature than the one by which your pieces are indicated at The Standard office, or you can write exclusively for my paper."

"With regard to your first proposal," said Ruth, "if I have gained any reputation by my first efforts, it appears to me that I should be foolish to throw it away by the adoption of another signature; and with regard to the last, I have no objection to writing exclusively for you, if you will make it worth my while."

"Sharp again," whispered Tibbetts to his partner.

The two editors then withdrawing into a further corner of the office, a whispered consultation followed, during which Ruth heard the words, "Can't afford it, Tom; hang it! we are head over ears in debt now to that paper man; good articles though—deuced good—must have her if we dispense with some of our other contributors. We had better begin low though, as to terms, for she'll go up now like a rocket, and when she finds out her value we shall have to increase her pay, you know."

(Thank you, gentlemen, thought Ruth, when the cards change hands, I'll take care to return the compliment.)

In pursuance of Mr. Tibbetts's shrewd resolution, he made known his "exclusive" terms to Ruth, which were no advance upon her present rate of pay at The Standard. This offer being declined, they made her another, in which, since she would not consent to do otherwise, they agreed she should write over her old signature, "Floy," furnishing them with two articles a week.

Ruth accepted the terms, poor as they were, because she could at present do no better, and because every pebble serves to swell the current.

Months passed away, while Ruth hoped and toiled, "Floy's" fame as a writer increasing much faster than her remuneration. There was rent-room to pay, little shoes and stockings to buy, oil, paper, pens, and ink to find; and now autumn had come, she could not write with stiffened fingers, and wood and coal were ruinously high, so that even with this new addition to her labor, Ruth seemed to retrograde pecuniarily, instead of advancing; and Katy still away! She must work harder—harder. Good, brave little Katy; she, too, was bearing and hoping on—mamma had promised, if she would stay there, patiently, she would certainly take her away just as soon as she had earned money enough; and mamma *never* broke her promise—*never;* and Katy prayed to God every night, with childish trust, to help her mother to earn money, that she might soon go home again.

And so, while Ruth scribbled away in her garret, the public were busying themselves in conjecturing who "Floy" might be. Letters poured in upon Mr. Lescom, with inquiries, even bribing him with the offer to procure a certain number of subscribers, if he would divulge her real name; to all of which the old man, true to his promise to Ruth, to keep her secret inviolate, turned a deaf ear. All sorts of rumors became rife about "Floy," some maintaining her to be a man, because she had the courage to call things by their right names, and the independence to express herself boldly on subjects which to the timid and clique-serving, were tabooed. Some said she was a disappointed old maid; some said she was a designing widow; some said she was a moon-struck girl; and all said she was a nondescript. Some tried to imitate her, and failing in this, abused and maligned her; the outwardly strait-laced and inwardly corrupt, puckered up their mouths and "blushed for her;" the hypocritical denounced the sacrilegious fingers which had dared to touch the Ark; the fashionist voted her a vulgar, plebeian thing; and the earnest and sorrowing, to whose burdened hearts she had given voice, cried God speed her. And still "Floy" scribbled on, thinking only of bread for her children, laughing and crying behind her mask,—laughing all the more when her heart was heaviest; but of this her readers knew little and would have cared less. Still her little bark breasted the billows, now rising high on the topmost wave, now merged in the shadows, but still steering with straining sides, and a heart of oak, for the nearing port of Independence.

Ruth's brother, Hyacinth, saw "Floy's" articles floating through his exchanges with marked dissatisfaction and uneasiness. That she should have succeeded in any degree without his assistance, was a puzzle, and the premonitory symptoms of her popularity, which his weekly exchanges furnished, in the shape of commendatory notices, were gall and wormwood to him. *Something* must be done, and that immediately. Seizing his pen, he despatched a letter to Mrs. Millet,[8] which he requested her to read to Ruth, alluding very contemptuously to Ruth's articles, and begging her to use her influence with Ruth to desist from scribbling, and seek some other employment. *What* employment, he did not condescend to state; in fact, it was a matter of entire indifference to him, provided she did not cross his track. Ruth listened to the contents of the letter, with the old bitter smile, and went on writing.

8. A pampered, fashionable friend of Hyacinth's, acquainted with Ruth.

Chapter LXV

A dull, drizzling rain spattered perseveringly against Ruth's windows, making her little dark room tenfold gloomier and darker than ever. Little Nettie had exhausted her slender stock of toys, and creeping up to her mother's side, laid her head wearily in her lap.

"Wait just a moment, Nettie, till mamma finishes this page," said Ruth, dipping her pen again in the old stone inkstand.

The child crept back again to the window, and watched the little pools of water in the streets, as the rain-drops dimpled them, and saw, for the hundredth time, the grocer's boy carrying home a brown-paper parcel for some customers, and eating something from it as he went along; and listened to the milkman, who thumped so loudly on the back gates, and seemed always in such a tearing hurry; and saw the baker open the lid of his boxes, and let the steam escape from the smoking hot cakes and pies. Nettie wished she could have some of them, but she had long since learned *only to wish;* and then she saw the two little sisters who went by to school every morning, and who were now cuddling, laughingly together, under a great big umbrella, which the naughty wind was trying to turn inside out, and to get away from them; and then Nettie thought of Katy, and wished she had Katy to play with her, when mamma wrote such a long, long time; and then little Nettie drew such a heavy sigh, that Ruth dashed down her pen, and taking her in her arms and kissing her, told her about,

> "Mistress McShuttle,
> Who lived in a coal-scuttle,
>   Along with her dog and her cat,
> What she did there, I can't tell,
> But I know very well,
>   That none of the party were fat."

And then she narrated the exciting adventures of "The Wise Men of Gotham," who went to sea in that rudderless bowl, and suffered shipwreck and "total *lass* of life," as the newsboys (God bless their rough-and-ready faces) call it; and then little Nettie's snowy lids drooped over her violet eyes, and she was far away in the land of dreams, where there are no little hungry girls, or tired, scribbling mammas.

Ruth laid the child gently on her little bed, and resumed her pen; but the spell was broken, and "careful and troubled about many things" she laid it down again, and her thoughts ran riot.

Pushing aside her papers, she discovered two unopened letters which Mr. Lescom had handed her, and which she had in the hurry of finishing her next article, quite forgotten. Breaking the seal of the first, she read as follows:

"To 'Floy.'

"I am a rough old man, Miss, and not used to writing or talking to ladies. I don't know who you are, and I don't ask; but I take 'The Standard,' and I like your pieces. I have a family of bouncing girls and boys; and when we've all done work, we get round the fire of an evening, while one of us reads your pieces aloud. It may not make much difference to you what an old man thinks, but I tell you those pieces have got the real stuff in 'em, and so I told my son John the other night; and *he* says, and *I* say, and neighbor Smith, who comes in to hear 'em, says, that you ought to make a book of them, so that your readers may keep them. You can put me down for three copies, to begin with; and if every subscriber to 'The Standard' feels as I do, you might make a plum by the operation. Suppose, now, you think of it?

"N.B.—John says, maybe you'll be offended at my writing to you, but I say you've got too much common sense.

Yours to command,

"John Stokes."

"Well, well," said Ruth, laughing, "that's a thought that never entered this busy head of mine, John Stokes. *I* publish a book? Why, John, are you aware that those articles were written for bread and butter, not fame; and tossed to the printer before the ink was dry, or I had time for a second reading? And yet, perhaps, there is more freshness about them than there would have been, had I leisure to have pruned and polished them—who knows? I'll put your suggestion on file, friend Stokes, to be turned over at my leisure. It strikes me, though, that it will keep awhile. Thank you, honest John. It is just such readers as you whom I like to secure. Well, what have we here?" and Ruth broke the seal of the second letter. It was in a delicate, beautiful, female hand; just such a one as you, dear Reader, might trace, whose sweet, soft eyes, and long, drooping tresses, are now bending over this page. It said:

"Dear 'Floy':
"For you *are* 'dear' to me, dear as a sister on whose loving breast I have leaned, though I never saw your face. I know not whether you are young and fair, or old and wrinkled, but I know that your heart is fresh, and guileless, and warm as childhood's; and that every week your printed words come to me, in my sick chamber, like the ministrations of some gentle friend, sometimes stirring to its very depths the fountain of tears, sometimes, by odd and quaint conceits, provoking the mirthful smile. But 'Floy,' I love you best in your serious moods; for as earth recedes, and eternity draws near, it is the real and tangible, my soul yearns after. And sure I am, 'Floy,' that I am not mistaken in thinking that we both lean on the same Rock of Ages; both discern, through the mists and clouds of time, the Sun of Righteousness. I shall never see you, 'Floy,' on earth;—mysterious voices, audible only to the dying ear, are calling me away; and yet, before I go, I would send you this token of my love, for all the sweet and soul-strengthening words you have unconsciously sent to my sick chamber, to wing the weary, waiting hours. We shall *meet*, 'Floy'; but it will be where 'tears are wiped away.'
"God bless you, my unknown sister.

"Mary R. ———."

Ruth's head bowed low upon the table, and her lips moved; but He to whom the secrets of all hearts are known, alone heard that grateful prayer.

1855

Male Criticism on Ladies' Books[9]

"Courtship and marriage, servants and children, these are the great objects of a woman's thoughts, and they necessarily form the staple topics of their writings and their conversation. We have no right to expect anything else in a woman's book."

—N.Y. Times

9. This and the following two essays represent the periodical columns that made Fern's reputation. The first two appeared in the *New York Ledger*, the third in Fern's collection, *Folly As It Flies*.

Is it in feminine novels *only* that courtship, marriage, servants and children are the staple? Is not this true of all novels?—of Dickens, of Thackery, of Bulwer and a host of others?[1] Is it peculiar to feminine pens, most astute and liberal of critics? Would a novel be a novel if it did not treat of courtship and marriage? and if it could be so recognized, would it find readers? When I see such a narrow, snarling criticism as the above, I always say to myself, the writer is some unhappy man, who has come up without the refining influence of mother, or sister, or reputable female friends; who has divided his migratory life between boarding-houses, restaurants, and the outskirts of editorial sanctums; and who knows as much about reviewing a woman's book, as I do about navigating a ship, or engineering an omnibus from the South Ferry, through Broadway, to Union Park. I think I see him writing that paragraph in a fit of spleen—of *male* spleen—in his small boarding-house upper chamber, by the cheerful light of a solitary candle, flickering alternately on cobwebbed walls, dusty wash-stand, begrimed bowl and pitcher, refuse cigar stumps, boot-jacks, old hats, buttonless coats, muddy trousers, and all the wretched accompaniments of solitary, selfish male existence, not to speak of his own puckered, unkissable face; perhaps, in addition, his boots hurt, his cravat-bow persists in slipping under his ear for want of a pin, and a wife to pin it (poor wretch!) or he has been refused by some pretty girl, as he deserved to be (narrow-minded old vinegar-cruet!) or snubbed by some lady authoress; or, more trying than all to the male constitution, has had a weak cup of coffee for that morning's breakfast.

But seriously—we have had quite enough of this shallow criticism (?) on lady-books. Whether the book which called forth the remark above quoted, was a good book or a bad one, I know not: I should be inclined to think the *former* from the dispraise of such a pen. Whether ladies can write novels or not, is a question I do not intend to discuss; but that some of them have no difficulty in finding either publishers or readers is a matter of history; and that gentlemen often write over feminine signatures would seem also to argue that feminine literature is, after all, in good odor with the reading public. Granted that lady-novels are not all that they should be—is such shallow, unfair, wholesale, sneering criticism (?) the way to reform them? Would it not be better and more manly to point out a better way kindly, justly, *and above all, respectfully?* or—what would be a much harder task for such critics—write a better book!

1857

The "Coming" Woman

Men often say, "When *I* marry, my wife must be this, that and the other," enumerating all physical, mental, and moral perfections. One cannot but smile to look at the men who say these things; smile to think of the equivalent they will bring for all the amiability, beauty, health, intellectuality, domesticity, and faithfulness they so modestly require; smile to think of the perforated hearts, damaged morals, broken-down constitutions, and irritable tempers, which the bright, pure, innocent girl is to receive with her wedding ring. If one half the girls knew the previous life of the men they marry, the list of old maids would be wonderfully increased.

Doubted? Well, if there is room for a doubt now, thank God the "coming" woman's Alpha and Omega will not be matrimony. *She* will not of necessity sour into a pink-nosed old maid, or throw herself at any rickety old shell of humanity, whose clothes are as much out of repair

---

1. Charles Dickens, William Makepeace Thackeray, and Edward Bulwer-Lytton were popular British novelists of the period.

as his morals. No, the future man will have to "step lively;" *this* wife is not to be had for the whistling. He will have a long canter round the pasture for her, and then she will leap the fence and leave him limping on the ground. Thick-soled boots and skating are coming in, and "nerves," novels and sentiment (by consequence) are going out. The coming woman, as I see her, is not to throw aside her needle; neither is she to sit embroidering worsted dogs and cats, or singing doubtful love ditties, and rolling up her eyes to "the chaste moon."

Heaven forbid she should stamp round with a cigar in her mouth, elbowing her fellows, and puffing smoke in their faces; or stand on the free-love platform, *public or private—call it by what specious name you will*—wooing men who, low as they may have sunk in their own self-respect, would die before they would introduce her to the unsullied sister who shared their cradle.

Heaven forbid the coming woman should not have warm blood in her veins, quick to rush to her cheek, or tingle at her fingers' ends when her heart is astir. No, the coming woman shall be no cold, angular, flat-chested, narrow-shouldered, skimpy sharp-visaged Betsey, but she shall be a bright-eyed, full-chested, broad-shouldered, large-souled, intellectual being; able to walk, able to eat, able to fulfill her maternal destiny, and able—if it so please God—to go to her grave happy, self-poised and serene, though unwedded.

1859

The Working-Girls of New York

Nowhere more than in New York does the contest between squalor and splendor so sharply present itself. This is the first reflection of the observing stranger who walks its streets. Particularly is this noticeable with regard to its women. Jostling on the same pavement with the dainty fashionist is the care-worn working-girl. Looking at both these women, the question arises, which lives the more miserable life—she whom the world styles "fortunate," whose husband belongs to three clubs, and whose only meal with his family is an occasional breakfast, from year's end to year's end; who is as much a stranger to his own children as to the reader; whose young son of seventeen has already a detective on his track employed by his father to ascertain where and how he spends his nights and his father's money; swift retribution for that father who finds food, raiment, shelter, equipages for his household; but love, sympathy, companionship—never? Or she—this other woman—with a heart quite as hungry and unappeased, who also faces day by day the same appalling question: *Is this all life has for me?*

A great book is yet unwritten about women. Michelet has aired his wax-doll theories regarding them.[2] The defender of "woman's rights" has given us her views. Authors and authoresses of little, and big repute, have expressed themselves on this subject, and none of them as yet have begun to grasp it: men—because they lack spirituality, rightly and justly to interpret women; women—because they dare not, or will not tell us that which most interests us to know. Who shall write this bold, frank, truthful book remains to be seen. Meanwhile woman's millennium is yet a great way off; and while it slowly progresses, conservatism and indifference gaze through their spectacles at the seething elements of to-day, and wonder "what ails all our women?"

Let me tell you what ails the working-girls. While yet your breakfast is progressing, and

2. Jules Michelet (1798–1874) wrote, among other historical works, *L'amour* (1858) and *La Femme*. His views on women correspond to the "cult of true womanhood," holding that women should be restricted to the domestic sphere and subordinate to their husbands.

your toilet unmade,[3] comes forth through Chatham Street and the Bowery, a long procession of them by twos and threes to their daily labor. Their breakfast, so called, has been hastily swallowed in a tenement house, where two of them share, in a small room, the same miserable bed. Of its quality you may better judge, when you know that each of these girls pays but three dollars a week for board, to the working man and his wife where they lodge.

The room they occupy is close and unventilated, with no accommodations for personal cleanliness, and so near to the little Flinegans that their Celtic night-cries are distinctly heard. They have risen unrefreshed, as a matter of course, and their ill-cooked breakfast does not mend the matter. They emerge from the doorway where their passage is obstructed by "nanny goats" and ragged children rooting together in the dirt, and pass out into the street. They shiver as the sharp wind of early morning strikes their temples. There is no look of youth on their faces; hard lines appear there. Their brows are knit; their eyes are sunken; their dress is flimsy, and foolish, and tawdry; always a hat, and feather or soiled artificial flower upon it; the hair dressed with an abortive attempt at style; a soiled petticoat; a greasy dress, a well-worn sacque[4] or shawl, and a gilt breast-pin and earrings.

Now follow them to the large, black-looking building, where several hundred of them are manufacturing hoop-skirts. If you are a woman you have worn plenty; but you little thought what passed in the heads of these girls as their busy fingers glazed the wire, or prepared the spools for covering them, or secured the tapes which held them in their places. *You* could not stay five minutes in that room, where the noise of the machinery used is so deafening, that only by the motion of the lips could you comprehend a person speaking.

Five minutes! Why, these young creatures bear it, from seven in the morning till six in the evening; week after week, month after month, with only half an hour at midday to eat their dinner of a slice of bread and butter or an apple, which they usually eat in the building, some of them having come a long distance. As I said, the roar of machinery in that room is like the roar of Niagara. Observe them as you enter. Not one lifts her head. They might as well be machines, for any interest or curiosity they show, save always to know *what o'clock it is.* Pitiful! pitiful, you almost sob to yourself, as you look at these young girls. *Young?* Alas! it is only in years that they are young.

1868

Harriet Beecher Stowe
(1811–1896)

The most sensational and widely circulated novel of the nineteenth century is still controversial. No one denies that Harriet Beecher Stowe's *Uncle Tom's Cabin* (1851–1852) argues powerfully against the institution of slavery, on the grounds that it should not be tolerated in a nation that considered itself Christian. But is it a racist book, perpetuating stereotypes of African-American characters? Or is it complex and realistic in its portrayals? Is it objectionable for its sentimentality? Or do its emotional renditions of the effects of slavery on the family make an effective point? Does it uphold feminist ideals? Or does it relegate heroic women to passive domestic roles and helpless, early death?

No stranger to controversy, Stowe was born into the Beecher family in Litchfield, Connecticut, in 1811. Her mother, Roxana Foote, died when Harriet was 4; her father, Lyman Beecher—a noted Calvinist preacher—raised Harriet and her seven siblings (who included Henry Ward

---

3. "Before you are dressed."

4. A sack; a short, loose-fitting coat.

Beecher, later to become a famous minister; Catharine Beecher, an educator of women and proponent of domestic science; and Isabella Beecher Hooker, an abolitionist and suffragist) according to strict religious principles. When Harriet was 7, her father remarked: "Hattie is a genius. I would give a hundred dollars if she was a boy." In her early teens, Harriet was already teaching such traditionally masculine subjects as Latin and composition at the school her sister ran, the Hartford Female Seminary.

The Beecher family moved from Connecticut to Boston in 1826, and from there to Cincinnati in 1832. Harriet's father became president of Lane Theological Seminary, and her sister Catharine opened another school, the Western Female Institute, where Harriet continued teaching and began writing textbooks and brief essays. One of her father's colleagues at Lane was Calvin Stowe, a professor of biblical literature; he and his wife became close friends of the Beecher family, and when his wife died in 1836, he rapidly wooed and married Harriet that same year. Bearing five children during the first seven years of her marriage, Harriet assumed the heavy child-rearing and housekeeping duties of a middle-class woman of the period.

She did not, however, let family demands interfere with her writing. As she put it, she continued to write "for the pay. I have determined not to be a mere domestic slave." The money Stowe brought in with essays and sketches about life in New England made it possible for her to pay for some household help, but—in spite of what she said—she also wrote because she had political views she wanted to communicate. In 1850, shortly after moving to Maine, where her husband had been appointed to the faculty of Bowdoin College, Stowe wanted to speak out against slavery. The Fugitive Slave Law, requiring Northerners to return escaped slaves to their Southern "owners," had just been passed. Stowe had been reading the autobiography of Josiah Henson, an escaped slave whom many regard as the original for Uncle

Tom; and she had a vision in church of a black man being whipped to death by a white man. As a Victorian-era woman concerned about her respectability, she could neither get involved in electoral politics, nor give public lectures against slavery, nor get into a pulpit to preach. She did the only thing she could do to register a public protest: she wrote a novel.

Uncle Tom's Cabin was first serialized in 1851–1852; its structure suggests the "cliff-hanger" effect of being published in parts. It was immediately published as a two-volume book and was lauded in the North and reviled in the South. Many Southern readers questioned the accuracy of the novel's representation of slaves' lives; to support her fiction's contentions, Stowe published *A Key to Uncle Tom's Cabin* (a compendium of documentation for her claims) in 1853. By 1852 its characters and stories were already being adapted for the popular stage, and the broad caricatures of the stage versions are partly responsible for the novel's reputation for racism. Traveling versions of the play continued being produced until the early twentieth century.

Since *Uncle Tom's Cabin* is primarily responsible for Stowe's reputation, we have excerpted it here rather than choosing to reprint a complete, short, but less influential work. The selection includes the first ten chapters of the forty-five chapter novel, introducing Tom and Eliza, slaves on a plantation in Kentucky, whose departures from that plantation mark two very different paths to "freedom." The novel raises the question of whether freedom in the material world is possible for every enslaved person and holds out the hope of a triumph over oppression in a Christian version of life after death. These opening chapters set out the characteristic patterns of the novel: they drive home the anguish of the slave family divided by masters' whims; they set up alternate responses to the slave experience, in George Harris's decision to flee and in Tom's resolution to "do his duty"; and they establish both positive and negative models for white Americans' behavior in the face of the slaves' plight. Alternating rapidly between humor and pathos, realism and melodrama, and pausing occasionally to address the reading audience directly, Stowe pulls out all the emotional stops to get her abolitionist point across. The final selection is the last chapter of the book, "Concluding Remarks," in which the novelist makes her agenda perfectly clear.

Stowe wrote only one other book on slavery. Her *Dred; A Tale of the Great Dismal Swamp* (1856) won praise from George Eliot in an anonymous review titled "Silly Novels by Lady Novelists." According to Eliot, the realism, moral seriousness, and technical skill of Stowe's work were exceptional. Most of Stowe's later novels are categorized as "local color" works, domestic fictions focusing on small-town life in New England. As such, they form an early and important part of the realistic movement in American literature. These novels include *The Minister's Wooing* (1859), *The Pearl of Orr's Island* (1862), *Oldtown Folks* (1869), and *Poganuc People* (1878). She also wrote travel books, including an account of her trip to Europe after the publication of *Uncle Tom—Sunny Memories of Foreign Lands* (1854)—and a description of life in

Florida, where she and her husband spent the winter months in their later years, called *Palmetto-Leaves* (1873). Her nonfiction writing also included domestic manuals, written sometimes in collaboration with her sister Catharine, sometimes under the pseudonym Christopher Crowfield. Surviving her husband by a decade, Stowe died in Hartford, Connecticut; their home—next door to Mark Twain's mansion—is open for public tours today.

Stowe's other publications include *Agnes of Sorrento* (1862); *House and Home Papers* (1865); *Little Foxes*, as Christopher Crowfield (1866); *Religious Poems* (1867); *The Chimney-Corner*, as Christopher Crowfield (1868); *The American Woman's Home* by Stowe and Catharine Beecher (1869); *Lady Byron Vindicated* (1870); *My Wife and I* (1871); *Pink and White Tyranny* (1871); *Woman in Sacred History* (1874); *We and Our Neighbors* (1875); and *Footsteps of the Master* (1877).

A full biography of Stowe is *Crusader in Crinoline* (1941) by Forrest Wilson; Milton Rugoff's more recent *The Beechers: An American Family in the Nineteenth Century* (1981) is less condescending. Major studies of Stowe's work include sections of Ann Douglas's *The Feminization of American Culture* (1977); Leslie Fiedler's *What Was Literature?* (1982); Jane Tompkins's *Sensational Designs* (1985); and Gillian Brown's *Domestic Individualism* (1990). See also *Uncle Tom's Cabin and American Culture* (1985) by Thomas Gossett and *New Essays on Uncle Tom's Cabin* (1986), edited by Eric J. Sundquist.

FROM UNCLE TOM'S CABIN, OR

LIFE AMONG THE LOWLY

Chapter 1
In Which the Reader Is Introduced to a Man of Humanity

Late in the afternoon of a chilly day in February, two gentlemen were sitting alone over their wine, in a well-furnished dining parlor, in the town of P——, in Kentucky. There were no servants present, and the gentlemen, with chairs closely approaching, seemed to be discussing some subject with great earnestness.

For convenience' sake, we have said, hitherto, two *gentlemen*. One of the parties, however, when critically examined, did not seem, strictly speaking, to come under the species. He was a short thick-set man, with coarse commonplace features, and that swaggering air of pretension which marks a low man who is trying to elbow his way upward in the world. He was much overdressed, in a gaudy vest of many colors, a blue neckerchief, bedropped gayly with yellow spots, and arranged with a flaunting tie, quite in keeping with the general air of the man. His hands, large and coarse, were plentifully bedecked with rings; and he wore a heavy gold watch-chain, with a bundle of seals[1] of portentous size, and a great variety of colors, attached to it,—which, in the ardor of conversation, he was in the habit of flourishing and jingling with evident satisfaction. His conversation was in free and easy defiance of Murray's Grammar, and was garnished at convenient intervals with various profane expressions, which not even the desire to be graphic in our account shall induce us to transcribe.

His companion, Mr. Shelby, had the appearance of a gentleman; and the arrangements of the house, and the general air of the housekeeping, indicated easy, and even opulent circumstances. As we before stated, the two were in the midst of an earnest conversation.

"That is the way I should arrange the matter," said Mr. Shelby.

"I can't make trade that way,—I positively can't, Mr. Shelby," said the other, holding up a glass of wine between his eye and the light.

"Why, the fact is, Haley, Tom is an uncommon fellow; he is certainly worth that sum anywhere,—steady, honest, capable, manages my whole farm like a clock."

"You mean honest, as niggers go," said Haley, helping himself to a glass of brandy.

"No; I mean, really, Tom is a good, steady, sensible, pious fellow. He got religion at a camp-meeting, four years ago; and I believe he really *did* get it. I've trusted him, since then, with everything I have,—money, house, horses,—and let him come and go round the country; and I always found him true and square in everything."

"Some folks don't believe there is pious niggers, Shelby," said Haley, with a candid flourish of his hand, "but *I do.* I had a fellow, now, in this yer last lot I took to Orleans,—'twas as good as a meetin', now, really, to hear that critter pray; and he was quite gentle and quiet like. He fetched me a good sum, too, for I bought him cheap of a man that was 'bliged to sell out; so I realized six hundred on him. Yes, I consider religion a valeyable thing in a nigger, when it's the genuine article, and no mistake."

Well, Tom's got the real article, if ever a fellow had," rejoined the other. "Why, last fall, I let him go to Cincinnati alone, to do business for me, and bring home five hundred dollars. 'Tom,' says I to him, 'I trust you, because I think you're a Christian,—I know you wouldn't cheat.' Tom comes back, sure enough; I knew he would. Some low fellows, they say, said to him, 'Tom, why don't you make tracks for Canada?' 'Ah, master trusted me, and I couldn't,'—they told me about it. I am sorry to part with Tom, I must say. You ought to let him cover the whole balance of the debt; and you would, Haley, if you had any conscience."

"Well, I've got just as much conscience as any man in business can afford to keep,—just a little, you know, to swear by, as 'twere," said the trader, jocularly; "and, then, I'm ready to do anything in reason to 'blige friends; but this yer, you see, is a leetle too hard on a fellow,—a leetle too hard." The trader sighed contemplatively, and poured out some more brandy.

"Well then, Haley, how will you trade?" said Mr. Shelby, after an uneasy interval of silence.

"Well, haven't you a boy or gal that you could throw in with Tom?"

"Hum!—none that I could well spare; to tell you the truth, it's only hard necessity makes me willing to sell at all. I don't like parting with any of my hands, that's a fact."

Here the door opened, and a small quadroon[2] boy, between four and five years of age, entered the room. There was something in his appearance remarkably beautiful and engaging. His black hair, fine as floss silk, hung in glossy curls about his round dimpled face, while

1. Signets used for stamping sealing wax.
2. A person having one-quarter African-American ancestry; legally black.

a pair of large dark eyes, full of fire and softness, looked out from beneath the rich, long lashes, as he peered curiously into the apartment. A gay robe of scarlet and yellow plaid, carefully made and neatly fitted, set off to advantage the dark and rich style of his beauty; and a certain comic air of assurance, blended with bashfulness, showed that he had been not unused to being petted and noticed by his master.

"Hulloa, Jim Crow!"[3] said Mr. Shelby, whistling, and snapping a bunch of raisins towards him, "pick that up, now!"

The child scampered, with all his little strength, after the prize, while his master laughed.

"Come here, Jim Crow," said he. The child came up, and the master patted the curly head, and chucked him under the chin.

"Now, Jim, show this gentleman how you can dance and sing." The boy commenced one of those wild, grotesque songs common among the negroes, in a rich, clear voice, accompanying his singing with many comic evolutions of the hands, feet, and whole body, all in perfect time to the music.

"Bravo!" said Haley, throwing him a quarter of an orange.

"Now, Jim, walk like old Uncle Cudjoe when he has the rheumatism," said his master.

Instantly the flexible limbs of the child assumed the appearance of deformity and distortion, as, with his back humped up, and his master's stick in his hand, he hobbled about the room, his childish face drawn into a doleful pucker, and spitting from right to left, in imitation of an old man.

Both gentlemen laughed uproariously.

"Now, Jim," said his master, "show us how old Elder Robbins leads the psalm." The boy drew his chubby face down to a formidable length, and commenced toning a psalm tune through his nose with imperturbable gravity.

"Hurrah! bravo! what a young 'un!" said Haley; "that chap's a case, I'll promise. Tell you what," said he, suddenly clapping his hand on Mr. Shelby's shoulder, "fling in that chap and I'll settle the business,—I will. Come, now, if that an't doing the thing up about the rightest!"

At this moment, the door was pushed gently open, and a young quadroon woman, apparently about twenty-five, entered the room.

There needed only a glance from the child to her, to identify her as its mother. There was the same rich, full, dark eye, with its long lashes; the same ripples of silky black hair. The brown of her complexion gave way on the cheek to a perceptible flush, which deepened as she saw the gaze of the strange man fixed upon her in bold and undisguised admiration. Her dress was of the neatest possible fit, and set off to advantage her finely moulded shape; a delicately formed hand and a trim foot and ankle were items of appearance that did not escape the quick eye of the trader, well used to run up at a glance the points of a fine female article.

"Well, Eliza?" said her master, as she stopped and looked hesitatingly at him.

"I was looking for Harry, please, sir"; and the boy bounded toward her, showing his spoils, which he had gathered in the skirt of his robe.

"Well, take him away, then," said Mr. Shelby; and hastily she withdrew, carrying the child on her arm.

"By Jupiter," said the trader, turning to him in admiration, "there's an article, now! You might make your fortune on that ar gal in Orleans, any day. I've seen over a thousand, in my day, paid down for gals not a bit handsomer."

"I don't want to make my fortune on her," said Mr. Shelby, dryly; and, seeking to turn the conversation, he uncorked a bottle of fresh wine, and asked his companion's opinion of it.

"Capital, sir—first chop!" said the trader; then turning, and slapping his hand familiarly on Shelby's shoulder, he added,—

3. A character in an act by an entertainer, Thomas D. Rice, who based it on an anonymous nineteenth-century song.

"Come, how will you trade about the gal?—what shall I say for her,—what'll you take?"

"Mr. Haley, she is not to be sold," said Shelby. "My wife would not part with her for her weight in gold."

"Ay, ay! women always say such things, cause they han't no sort of calculation. Just show 'em how many watches, feathers, and trinkets one's weight in gold would buy, and that alters the case, *I* reckon."

"I tell you, Haley, this must not be spoken of; I say no, and I mean no," said Shelby, decidedly.

"Well, you'll let me have the boy, though," said the trader; "you must own I've come down pretty handsomely for him."

"What on earth can you want with the child?" said Shelby.

"Why, I've got a friend that's going into this yer branch of the business,—wants to buy up handsome boys to raise for the market. Fancy articles entirely,—sell for waiters, and so on, to rich 'uns, that can pay for handsome 'uns. It sets off one of yer great places,—a real handsome boy to open door, wait and tend. They fetch a good sum; and this little devil is such a comical, musical concern, he's just the article."

"I would rather not sell him," said Mr. Shelby, thoughtfully; "the fact is, sir, I'm a humane man, and I hate to take the boy from his mother, sir."

"O, you do?—La! yes,—something of that ar natur. I understand, perfectly. It is mighty onpleasant getting on with women, sometimes. I al'ays hates these yer screechin', screamin' times. They are *mighty* onpleasant; but, as I manages business, I generally avoids 'em, sir. Now, what if you get the girl off for a day, or a week, or so; then the thing's done quietly,—all over before she comes home. Your wife might get her some ear-rings, or a new gown, or some such truck, to make up with her."

"I'm afraid not."

"Lor bless ye, yes! These critters an't like white folks, you know; they gets over things, only manage right. Now, they say," said Haley, assuming a candid and confidential air, "that this kind o' trade is hardening to the feelings; but I never found it so. Fact is, I never could do things up the way some fellers manage the business. I've seen 'em as would pull a woman's child out of her arms, and set him up to sell, and she screechin' like mad all the time; very bad policy,—damages the article,—makes 'em quite unfit for service sometimes. I knew a real handsome gal once, in Orleans, as was entirely ruined by this sort o' handling. The fellow that was trading for her didn't want her baby; and she was one of your real high sort, when her blood was up. I tell you, she squeezed up her child in her arms, and talked, and went on real awful. It kinder makes my blood run cold to think on 't; and when they carried off the child, and locked her up, she jest went ravin' mad, and died in a week. Clear waste, sir, of a thousand dollars, just for want of management,—there's where 'tis. It's always best to do the humane thing, sir; that's been *my* experience." And the trader leaned back in his chair, and folded his arm, with an air of virtuous decision, apparently considering himself a second Wilberforce.[4]

The subject appeared to interest the gentleman deeply; for while Mr. Shelby was thoughtfully peeling an orange, Haley broke out afresh, with becoming diffidence, but as if actually driven by the force of truth to say a few words more.

"It don't look well, now, for a feller to be praisin' himself; but I say it jest because it's the truth. I believe I'm reckoned to bring in about the finest droves of niggers that is brought in,—at least, I've been told so; if I have once, I reckon I have a hundred times,—all in good case,—fat and likely, and I lose as few as any man in the business. And I lays it all to my management, sir; and humanity, sir, I may say, is the great pillar of *my* management."

Mr Shelby did not know what to say, and so he said, "Indeed!"

4.   British philanthropist and abolitionist (1759–1833).

"Now, I've been laughed at for my notions, sir, and I've been talked to. They an't pop'lar, and they an't common; but I stuck to 'em, sir; I've stuck to 'em, and realized well on 'em; yes, sir, they have paid their passage, I may say," and the trader laughed at his joke.

There was something so piquant and original in these elucidations of humanity, that Mr. Shelby could not help laughing in company. Perhaps you laugh too, dear reader; but you know humanity comes out in a variety of strange forms nowadays, and there is no end to the odd things that humane people will say and do.

Mr. Shelby's laugh encouraged the trader to proceed.

"It's strange now, but I never could beat this into people's heads. Now, there was Tom Loker, my old partner, down in Natchez; he was a clever fellow, Tom was, only the very devil with niggers,—on principle 'twas, you see, for a better-hearted feller never broke bread; 'twas his *system*, sir. I used to talk to Tom. 'Why, Tom,' I used to say, 'when your gals takes on and cry, what's the use o' crackin' on 'em over the head, and knockin' on 'em round? It's ridiculous,' says I, 'and don't do no sort o' good. Why, I don't see no harm in their cryin',' says I; 'it's natur,' says I, 'and if natur can't blow off one way, it will another. Besides, Tom,' says I, 'it jest spiles your gals; they get sickly, and down in the mouth; and sometimes they gets ugly,—particularly yellow⁵ gals do,—and it's the devil and all gettin' on 'em broke in. Now,' says I, 'why can't you kinder coax 'em up, and speak 'em fair? Depend on it, Tom, a little humanity, thrown in along, goes a heap further than all your jawin' and crackin'; and it pays better,' says I, 'depend on't.' But Tom couldn't get the hang on't; and he spiled so many for me, that I had to break off with him, though he was a good-hearted fellow, and as fair a business hand as is goin'."

"And do you find your ways o' managing do the business better than Tom's?" said Mr. Shelby.

"Why, yes, sir, I may say so. You see, when I any ways can, I takes a leetle care about the onpleasant parts, like selling young uns and that,—get the gals out of the way,—out of sight, out of mind, you know,—and when it's clean done, and can't be helped, they naturally gets used to it. 'Tan't, you know, as if it was white folks, that's brought up in the way of 'spectin' to keep their children and wives, and all that. Niggers, you know, that's fetched up properly han't no kind of 'spectations of no kind; so all these things comes easier."

"I'm afraid mine are not properly brought up, then," said Mr. Shelby.

"S'pose not; you Kentucky folks spile your niggers. You mean well by 'em, but 'tan't no real kindness, arter all. Now, a nigger, you see, what's got to be hacked and tumbled round the world, and sold to Tom, and Dick, and the Lord knows who, 'tan't no kindness to be givin' on him notions and expectations, and bringin' on him up too well, for the rough and tumble comes all the harder on him arter. Now, I venture to say, your niggers would be quite chop-fallen in a place where some of your plantation niggers would be singing and whooping like all possessed. Every man, you know, Mr. Shelby, naturally thinks well of his own ways; and I think I treat niggers just about as well as it's ever worth while to treat 'em."

"It's a happy thing to be satisfied," said Mr. Shelby, with a slight shrug, and some perceptible feelings of a disagreeable nature.

"Well," said Haley, after they had both silently picked their nuts for a season, "what do you say?"

"I'll think the matter over, and talk with my wife," said Mr. Shelby. "Meantime, Haley, if you want the matter carried on in the quiet way you speak of, you'd best not let your business in this neighborhood be known. It will get out among my boys, and it will not be a particularly quiet business getting away any of my fellows, if they know it, I'll promise you."

"O, certainly, by all means, mum! of course. But I'll tell you, I'm in a devil of a hurry, and shall want to know, as soon as possible, what I may depend on," said he, rising and putting on his overcoat.

---

5. Yellow, those with some Caucasian ancestry.

"Well, call up this evening, between six and seven, and you shall have my answer," said Mr. Shelby, and the trader bowed himself out of the apartment.

"I'd like to have been able to kick the fellow down the steps," said he to himself, as he saw the door fairly closed, "with his impudent assurance; but he knows how much he has me at advantage. If anybody had ever said to me that I should sell Tom down south to one of those rascally traders, I should have said, 'Is thy servant a dog, that he should do this thing?'[6] And now it must come, for aught I see. And Eliza's child, too! I know that I shall have some fuss with wife about that; and, for that matter, about Tom, too. So much for being in debt,—heigh-ho. The fellow sees his advantage, and means to push it."

Perhaps the mildest form of the system of slavery is to be seen in the State of Kentucky. The general prevalence of agricultural pursuits of a quiet and gradual nature, not requiring those periodic seasons of hurry and pressure that are called for in the business of more southern districts, makes the task of the negro a more healthful and reasonable one; while the master, content with a more gradual style of acquisition, has not those temptations to hard-heartedness which always overcome frail human nature when the prospect of sudden and rapid gain is weighed in the balance, with no heavier counterpoise than the interests of the helpless and unprotected.

Whoever visits some estates there, and witnesses the good-humored indulgence of some masters and mistresses and the affectionate loyalty of some slaves, might be tempted to dream the oft-fabled poetic legend of a patriarchal institution, and all that; but over and above the scene there broods a portentous shadow,—the shadow of *law*. So long as the law considers all these human beings, with beating hearts and living affections, only as so many *things* belonging to a master,—so long as the failure, or misfortune, or imprudence, or death of the kindest owner may cause them any day to exchange a life of kind protection and indulgence for one of hopeless misery and toil,—so long it is impossible to make anything beautiful or desirable in the best-regulated administration of slavery.

Mr. Shelby was a fair average kind of man, good-natured and kindly, and disposed to easy indulgence of those around him, and there had never been a lack of anything which might contribute to the physical comfort of the negroes on his estate. He had, however, speculated largely and quite loosely; had involved himself deeply, and his notes to a large amount had come into the hands of Haley; and this small piece of information is the key to the preceding conversation.

Now, it had so happened that, in approaching the door, Eliza had caught enough of the conversation to know that a trader was making offers to her master for somebody.

She would gladly have stopped at the door to listen, as she came out; but her mistress just then calling, she was obliged to hasten away.

Still she thought she heard the trader make an offer for her boy;—could she be mistaken? Her heart swelled and throbbed, and she involuntarily strained him so tight that the little fellow looked up into her face in astonishment.

"Eliza, girl, what ails you to-day?" said her mistress, when Eliza had upset the wash-pitcher, knocked down the workstand, and finally was abstractedly offering her mistress a long nightgown in place of the silk dress she had ordered her to bring from the wardrobe.

Eliza started. "O, missis!" she said, raising her eyes; then, bursting into tears, she sat down in a chair, and began sobbing.

"Why, Eliza, child! what ails you?" said her mistress.

"O, missis, missis," said Eliza, "there's been a trader talking with master in the parlor! I heard him."

"Well, silly child, suppose there has."

"O, missis, *do* you suppose mas'r would sell my Harry?" And the poor creature threw herself into a chair, and sobbed convulsively.

6. 2 Kings 8:13.

"Sell him! No, you foolish girl! You know your master never deals with those southern traders, and never means to sell any of his servants, as long as they behave well. Why, you silly child, who do you think would want to buy your Harry? Do you think all the world are set on him as you are, you goosie? Come, cheer up, and hook my dress. There now, put my back hair up in that pretty braid you learnt the other day, and don't go listening at doors any more."

"Well, but, missis, *you* never would give your consent—to—to—"

"Nonsense, child! to be sure I shouldn't. What do you talk so for? I would as soon have one of my own children sold. But really, Eliza, you are getting altogether too proud of that little fellow. A man can't put his nose into the door, but you think he must be coming to buy him."

Reassured by her mistress's confident tone, Eliza proceeded nimbly and adroitly with her toilet, laughing at her own fears, as she proceeded.

Mrs. Shelby was a woman of a high class, both intellectually and morally. To that natural magnanimity and generosity of mind which one often marks as characteristic of the women of Kentucky, she added high moral and religious sensibility and principle, carried out with great energy and ability into practical results. Her husband, who made no professions to any particular religious character, nevertheless reverenced and respected the consistency of hers, and stood, perhaps, a little in awe of her opinion. Certain it was that he gave her unlimited scope in all her benevolent efforts for the comfort, instruction, and improvement of her servants, though he never took any decided part in them himself. In fact, if not exactly a believer in the doctrine of the efficiency of the extra good works of saints, he really seemed somehow or other to fancy that his wife had piety and benevolence enough for two,—to indulge a shadowy expectation of getting into heaven through her superabundance of qualities to which he made no particular pretension.

The heaviest load on his mind, after his conversation with the trader, lay in the foreseen necessity of breaking to his wife the arrangement contemplated,—meeting the importunities and opposition which he knew he should have reason to encounter.

Mrs. Shelby, being entirely ignorant of her husband's embarrassments, and knowing only the general kindliness of his temper, had been quite sincere in the entire incredulity with which she had met Eliza's suspicions. In fact, she dismissed the matter from her mind, without a second thought; and being occupied in preparations for an evening visit, it passed out of her thoughts entirely.

Chapter 2
The Mother

Eliza had been brought up by her mistress, from girlhood, as a petted and indulged favorite.

The traveller in the south must often have remarked that peculiar air of refinement, that softness of voice and manner, which seems in many cases to be a particular gift to the quadroon and mulatto women. These natural graces in the quadroon are often united with beauty of the most dazzling kind, and in almost every case with a personal appearance prepossessing and agreeable. Eliza, such as we have described her, is not a fancy sketch, but taken from remembrance, as we saw her, years ago, in Kentucky. Safe under the protecting care of her mistress, Eliza had reached maturity without those temptations which make beauty so fatal an inheritance to a slave. She had been married to a bright and talented young mulatto man, who was a slave on a neighboring estate, and bore the name of George Harris.

This young man had been hired out by his master to work in a bagging factory, where his adroitness and ingenuity caused him to be considered the first hand in the place. He had invented a machine for the cleaning of the hemp, which, considering the education and circumstances of the inventor, displayed quite as much mechanical genius as Whitney's cotton-gin.[7]

He was possessed of a handsome person and pleasing manners, and was a general favorite in the factory. Nevertheless, as this young man was in the eye of the law not a man, but a thing, all these superior qualifications were subject to the control of a vulgar, narrow-minded, tyrannical master. This same gentleman, having heard of the fame of George's invention, took a ride over to the factory, to see what this intelligent chattel had been about. He was received with great enthusiasm by the employer, who congratulated him on possessing so valuable a slave.

He was waited upon over the factory, shown the machinery by George, who, in high spirits, talked so fluently, held himself so erect, looked so handsome and manly, that his master began to feel an uneasy consciousness of inferiority. What business had his slave to be marching round the country, inventing machines, and holding up his head among gentlemen? He'd soon put a stop to it. He'd take him back, and put him to hoeing and digging, and "see if he'd step about so smart." Accordingly, the manufacturer and all hands concerned were astounded when he suddenly demanded George's wages, and announced his intention of taking him home.

"But, Mr. Harris," remonstrated the manufacturer, "isn't this rather sudden?"

"What if it is?—isn't the man *mine?*"

"We would be willing, sir, to increase the rate of compensation."

"No object at all, sir. I don't need to hire any of my hands out, unless I've a mind to."

"But, sir, he seems peculiarly adapted to this business."

"Dare say he may be; never was much adapted to anything that I set him about, I'll be bound."

"But only think of his inventing this machine," interposed one of the workmen, rather unluckily.

"O yes!—a machine for saving work, is it? He'd invent that, I'll be bound; let a nigger alone for that, any time. They are all labor-saving machines themselves, every one of 'em. No, he shall tramp!"

George had stood like one transfixed, at hearing his doom thus suddenly pronounced by a power that he knew was irresistible. He folded his arms, tightly pressed in his lips, but a whole volcano of bitter feelings burned in his bosom, and sent streams of fire through his veins. He breathed short, and his large dark eyes flashed like live coals; and he might have broken out into some dangerous ebullition, had not the kindly manufacturer touched him on the arm, and said, in a low tone,—

"Give way, George; go with him for the present. We'll try to help you, yet."

The tyrant observed the whisper, and conjectured its import, though he could not hear what was said; and he inwardly strengthened himself in his determination to keep the power he possessed over his victim.

George was taken home, and put to the meanest drudgery of the farm. He had been able to repress every disrespectful word; but the flashing eye, the gloomy and troubled brow, were part of a natural language that could not be repressed,—indubitable signs, which showed too plainly that the man could not become a thing.

It was during the happy period of his employment in the factory that George had seen and married his wife. During that period,—being much trusted and favored by his employer,— he had free liberty to come and go at discretion. The marriage was highly approved of by Mrs. Shelby, who, with a little womanly complacency in match-making, felt pleased to unite her handsome favorite with one of her own class who seemed in every way suited to her; and

7. A machine of this description was really the invention of a young colored man in Kentucky. [author's note]

so they were married in her mistress's great parlor, and her mistress herself adorned the bride's beautiful hair with orange-blossoms, and threw over it the bridal veil, which certainly could scarce have rested on a fairer head; and there was no lack of white gloves, and cake and wine,—of admiring guests to praise the bride's beauty, and her mistress's indulgence and liberality. For a year or two Eliza saw her husband frequently, and there was nothing to interrupt their happiness, except the loss of two infant children, to whom she was passionately attached, and whom she mourned with a grief so intense as to call for gentle remonstrance from her mistress, who sought, with maternal anxiety, to direct her naturally passionate feelings within the bounds of reason and religion.

After the birth of little Harry, however, she had gradually become tranquillized and settled; and every bleeding tie and throbbing nerve, once more entwined with that little life, seemed to become sound and healthful, and Eliza was a happy woman up to the time that her husband was rudely torn from his kind employer, and brought under the iron sway of his legal owner.

The manufacturer, true to his word, visited Mr. Harris a week or two after George had been taken away, when, as he hoped, the heat of the occasion had passed away, and tried every possible inducement to lead him to restore him to his former employment.

"You needn't trouble to talk any longer," said he doggedly; "I know my own business, sir."

"I did not presume to interfere with it, sir. I only thought that you might think it for your interest to let your man to us on the terms proposed."

"O, I understand the matter well enough. I saw your winking and whispering, the day I took him out of the factory; but you don't come it over me that way. It's a free country, sir; the man's *mine*, and I do what I please with him,—that's it!"

And so fell George's last hope;—nothing before him but a life of toil and drudgery, rendered more bitter by every little smarting vexation and indignity which tyrannical ingenuity could devise.

A very humane jurist once said, The worst use you can put a man to is to hang him. No; there is another use that a man can be put to that is worse!

Chapter 3
The Husband and Father

Mrs. Shelby had gone on her visit, and Eliza stood in the veranda, rather dejectedly looking after the retreating carriage, when a hand was laid on her shoulder. She turned, and a bright smile lighted up her fine eyes.

"George, is it you? How you frightened me! Well; I am so glad you's come! Missis is gone to spend the afternoon; so come into my little room, and we'll have the time all to ourselves."

Saying this, she drew him into a neat little apartment opening on the veranda, where she generally sat at her sewing, within call of her mistress.

"How glad I am!—why don't you smile?—and look at Harry,—how he grows." The boy stood shyly regarding his father through his curls, holding close to the skirts of his mother's dress. "Isn't he beautiful?" said Eliza, lifting his long curls and kissing him.

"I wish he'd never been born!" said George, bitterly. "I wish I'd never been born myself!"

Surprised and frightened, Eliza sat down, leaned her head on her husband's shoulder, and burst into tears.

"There now, Eliza, it's too bad for me to make you feel so, poor girl!" said he, fondly; "it's too bad. O, how I wish you never had seen me,—you might have been happy!"

"George! George! how can you talk so? What dreadful thing has happened, or is going to happen? I'm sure we've been very happy, till lately."

"So we have, dear," said George. Then drawing his child on his knee, he gazed intently on his glorious dark eyes, and passed his hands through his long curls.

"Just like you, Eliza; and you are the handsomest woman I ever saw, and the best one I ever wish to see; but, O, I wish I'd never seen you, nor you me!"

"O, George, how can you!"

"Yes, Eliza, it's all misery, misery, misery! My life is bitter as wormwood; the very life is burning out of me. I'm a poor, miserable, forlorn drudge; I shall only drag you down with me, that's all. What's the use of our trying to do anything, trying to know anything, trying to be anything? What's the use of living? I wish I was dead!"

"O, now, dear George, that is really wicked! I know how you feel about losing your place in the factory, and you have a hard master; but pray be patient, and perhaps something—"

"Patient!" said he, interrupting her; "haven't I been patient? Did I say a word when he came and took me away, for no earthly reason, from the place where everybody was kind to me? I'd paid him truly every cent of my earnings,—and they all say I worked well."

"Well, it *is* dreadful," said Eliza; "but, after all, he is your master, you know."

"My master! and who made him my master? That's what I think of,—what right has he to me? I'm a man as much as he is. I'm a better man than he is. I know more about business than he does; I am a better manager than he is; I can read better than he can; I can write a better hand,—and I've learned it all myself, and no thanks to him,—I've learned it in spite of him; and now what right has he to make a dray-horse of me?—to take me from things I can do, and do better than he can, and put me to work that any horse can do? He tries to do it; he says he'll bring me down and humble me, and he puts me to just the hardest, meanest, and dirtiest work, on purpose!"

"O, George! George! you frighten me! Why, I never heard you talk so; I'm afraid you'll do something dreadful. I don't wonder at your feelings, at all; but O, do be careful—do, do—for my sake,—for Harry's!"

"I have been careful, and I have been patient, but it's growing worse and worse; flesh and blood can't bear it any longer;—every chance he can get to insult and torment me, he takes. I thought I could do my work well, and keep on quiet, and have some time to read and learn out of work hours; but the more he sees I can do, the more he loads on. He says that though I don't say anything, he sees I've got the devil in me, and he means to bring it out; and one of these days it will come out in a way that he won't like, or I'm mistaken!"

"O dear! what shall we do?" said Eliza, mournfully.

"It was only yesterday," said George, "as I was busy loading stones into a cart, that young Mas'r Tom stood there, slashing his whip so near the horse that the creature was frightened. I asked him to stop, as pleasant as I could,—he just kept right on. I begged him again, and then he turned on me, and began striking me. I held his hand, and then he screamed and kicked and ran to his father, and told him that I was fighting him. He came in a rage, and said he'd teach me who was my master; and he tied me to a tree, and cut switches for young master, and told him that he might whip me till he was tired;—and he did do it! If I don't make him remember it, some time!" and the brow of the young man grew dark, and his eyes burned with an expression that made his young wife tremble. "Who made this man my master? That's what I want to know!" he said.

"Well," said Eliza, mournfully, "I always thought that I must obey my master and mistress, or I couldn't be a Christian."

"There is some sense in it, in your case; they have brought you up like a child, fed you, clothed you, indulged you, and taught you, so that you have a good education; that is some reason why they should claim you. But I have been kicked and cuffed and sworn at, and at the best only let alone; and what do I owe? I've paid for all my keeping a hundred times over. I *won't* bear it. No, I *won't!*" he said, clenching his hand with a fierce frown.

Eliza trembled, and was silent. She had never seen her husband in this mood before; and her gentle system of ethics seemed to bend like a reed in the surges of such passions.

"You know poor little Carlo, that you gave me," added George; "the creature has been about all the comfort that I've had. He has slept with me nights, and followed me around days, and kind o' looked at me as if he understood how I felt. Well, the other day I was just feeding him with a few old scraps I picked up by the kitchen door, and Mas'r came along, and said I was feeding him up at his expense, and that he couldn't afford to have every nigger keeping his dog, and ordered me to tie a stone to his neck and throw him in the pond."

"O, George, you didn't do it!"

"Do it? not I!—but he did. Mas'r and Tom pelted the poor drowning creature with stones. Poor thing! he looked at me so mournful, as if he wondered why I didn't save him. I had to take a flogging because I wouldn't do it myself. I don't care. Mas'r will find out that I'm one that whipping won't tame. My day will come yet, if he don't look out."

"What are you going to do? O, George, don't do anything wicked; if you only trust in God, and try to do right, he'll deliver you."

"I an't a Christian like you, Eliza; my heart's full of bitterness; I can't trust in God. Why does he let things be so?"

"O, George, we must have faith. Mistress says that when all things go wrong to us, we must believe that God is doing the very best."

"That's easy to say for people that are sitting on their sofas and riding in their carriages; but let 'em be where I am, I guess it would come some harder. I wish I could be good; but my heart burns, and can't be reconciled, anyhow. You couldn't, in my place,—you can't now, if I tell you all I've got to say. You don't know the whole yet."

"What can be coming now?"

"Well, lately Mas'r has been saying that he was a fool to let me marry off the place; that he hates Mr. Shelby and all his tribe, because they are proud, and hold their heads up above him, and that I've got proud notions from you; and he says he won't let me come here any more, and that I shall take a wife and settle down on his place. At first he only scolded and grumbled these things; but yesterday he told me that I should take Mina for a wife, and settle down in a cabin with her, or he would sell me down river."

"Why—but you were married to *me*, by the minister, as much as if you'd been a white man!" said Eliza, simply.

"Don't you know a slave can't be married? There is no law in this country for that; I can't hold you for my wife if he chooses to part us. That's why I wish I'd never seen you,—why I wish I'd never been born; it would have been better for us both,—it would have been better for this poor child if he had never been born. All this may happen to him yet!"

"O, but master is so kind!"

"Yes, but who knows?—he may die,—and then he may be sold to nobody knows who. What pleasure is it that he is handsome, and smart, and bright? I tell you, Eliza, that a sword will pierce through your soul for every good and pleasant thing your child is or has; it will make him worth too much for you to keep!"

The words smote heavily on Eliza's heart; the vision of the trader came before her eyes, and, as if some one had struck her a deadly blow, she turned pale and gasped for breath. She looked nervously out on the veranda, where the boy, tired of the grave conversation, had retired, and where he was riding triumphantly up and down on Mr. Shelby's walking-stick. She would have spoken to tell her husband her fears, but checked herself.

"No, no,—he has enough to bear, poor fellow!" she thought. "No, I won't tell him; besides, it an't true. Missis never deceives us."

"So, Eliza, my girl," said the husband, mournfully, "bear up, now; and good by, for I'm going."

"Going, George! Going where?"

"To Canada," said he, straightening himself up; "and when I'm there, I'll buy you; that's all the hope that's left us. You have a kind master, that won't refuse to sell you. I'll buy you and the boy;—God helping me, I will!"

"O, dreadful! if you should be taken?"

"I won't be taken, Eliza; I'll *die* first! I'll be free, or I'll die!"

"You won't kill yourself!"

"No need of that. They will kill me, fast enough; they never will get me down the river alive!"

"O, George, for my sake, do be careful! Don't do anything wicked; don't lay hands on yourself, or anybody else. You are tempted too much—too much; but don't—go you must—but go carefully, prudently; pray God to help you."

"Well, then, Eliza, hear my plan. Mas'r took it into his head to send me right by here, with a note to Mr. Symmes, that lives a mile past. I believe he expected I should come here to tell you what I have. It would please him if he thought it would aggravate 'Shelby's folks,' as he calls 'em. I'm going home quite resigned, you understand, as if all was over. I've got some preparations made,—and there are those that will help me; and, in the course of a week or so, I shall be among the missing, some day. Pray for me, Eliza; perhaps the good Lord will hear *you.*"

"O, pray yourself, George, and go trusting in him; then you won't do anything wicked."

"Well, now, *good by,*" said George, holding Eliza's hands, and gazing into her eyes, without moving. They stood silent; then there were last words, and sobs, and bitter weeping,—such parting as those may make whose hope to meet again is as the spider's web,—and the husband and wife were parted.

Chapter 4
An Evening in Uncle Tom's Cabin

The cabin of Uncle Tom was a small log building, close adjoining to "the house," as the negro *par excellence* designates his master's dwelling. In front it had a neat garden-patch, where, every summer, strawberries, raspberries, and a variety of fruits and vegetables flourished under careful tending. The whole front of it was covered by a large scarlet bignonia and a native multiflora rose, which, entwisting and interlacing, left scarce a vestige of the rough logs to be seen. Here, also, in summer, various brilliant annuals, such as marigolds, petunias, four-o'clocks, found an indulgent corner in which to unfold their splendors, and were the delight and pride of Aunt Chloe's heart.

Let us enter the dwelling. The evening meal at the house is over, and Aunt Chloe, who presided over its preparation as head cook, has left to inferior officers in the kitchen the business of clearing away and washing dishes, and come out into her own snug territories, to "get her ole man's supper"; therefore, doubt not that it is she you see by the fire, presiding with anxious interest over certain frizzling items in a stewpan, and anon with grave consideration lifting the cover of a bake-kettle, from whence steam forth indubitable intimations of "something good." A round, black, shining face is hers, so glossy as to suggest the idea that she might have been washed over with white of eggs, like one of her own tea rusks. Her whole plump countenance beams with satisfaction and contentment from under her well-starched checked turban, bearing on it, however, if we must confess it, a little of that tinge of self-consciousness which becomes the first cook of the neighborhood, as Aunt Chloe was universally held and acknowledged to be.

A cook she certainly was, in the very bone and centre of her soul. Not a chicken or turkey or duck in the barnyard but looked grave when they saw her approaching, and seemed evidently to be reflecting on their latter end; and certain it was that she was always meditating on trussing, stuffing, and roasting, to a degree that was calculated to inspire terror in any reflecting fowl living. Her corn-cake, in all its varieties of hoe-cake, dodgers, muffins, and other species too numerous to mention, was a sublime mystery to all less practised compounders; and she would shake her fat sides with honest pride and merriment, as she would narrate the fruitless efforts that one and another of her compeers had made to attain to her elevation.

The arrival of company at the house, the arranging of dinners and suppers "in style," awoke all the energies of her soul; and no sight was more welcome to her than a pile of travelling trunks launched on the veranda, for then she foresaw fresh efforts and fresh triumphs.

Just at present, however, Aunt Chloe is looking into the bake-pan; in which congenial operation we shall leave her till we finish our picture of the cottage.

In one corner of it stood a bed, covered neatly with a snowy spread; and by the side of it was a piece of carpeting, of some considerable size. On this piece of carpeting Aunt Chloe took her stand, as being decidedly in the upper walks of life; and it and the bed by which it lay, and the whole corner, in fact, were treated with distinguished consideration, and made, so far as possible, sacred from the marauding inroads and desecrations of little folks. In fact, that corner was the *drawing-room* of the establishment. In the other corner was a bed of much humbler pretensions, and evidently designed for *use*. The wall over the fireplace was adorned with some very brilliant scriptural prints, and a portrait of General Washington, drawn and colored in a manner which would certainly have astonished that hero, if ever he had happened to meet with its like.

On a rough bench in the corner, a couple of woolly-headed boys, with glistening black eyes and fat shining cheeks, were busy in superintending the first walking operations of the baby, which, as is usually the case, consisted in getting up on its feet, balancing a moment, and then tumbling down,—each successive failure being violently cheered, as something decidedly clever.

A table, somewhat rheumatic in its limbs, was drawn out in front of the fire, and covered with a cloth, displaying cups and saucers of a decidedly brilliant pattern, with other symptoms of an approaching meal. At this table was seated Uncle Tom, Mr. Shelby's best hand, who, as he is to be the hero of our story, we must daguerreotype[8] for our readers. He was a large, broad-chested, powerfully made man, of a full glossy black, and a face whose truly African features were characterized by an expression of grave and steady good sense, united with much kindliness and benevolence. There was something about his whole air self-respecting and dignified, yet united with a confiding and humble simplicity.

He was very busily intent at this moment on a slate lying before him, on which he was carefully and slowly endeavoring to accomplish a copy of some letters, in which operation he was overlooked by young Mas'r George, a smart, bright boy of thirteen, who appeared fully to realize the dignity of his position as instructor.

"Not that way, Uncle Tom,—not that way," said he, briskly, as Uncle Tom laboriously brought up the tail of his *g* the wrong side out; "that makes a *q*, you see."

"La sakes, now, does it?" said Uncle Tom, looking with a respectful, admiring air, as his young teacher flourishingly scrawled *q*'s and *g*'s innumerable for his edification; and then, taking the pencil in his big, heavy fingers, he patiently recommenced.

"How easy white folks al'us does things!" said Aunt Chloe, pausing while she was greasing a griddle with a scrap of bacon on her fork, and regarding young Master George with pride. "The way he can write, now! and read, too! and then to come out here evenings and read his lessons to us,—it's mighty interestin'!"

"But, Aunt Chloe, I'm getting mighty hungry," said George. "Isn't that cake in the skillet almost done?"

"Mose done, Mas'r George," said Aunt Chloe, lifting the lid and peeping in,—"browning beautiful,—a real lovely brown. Ah! let me alone for dat. Missis let Sally try to make some

8. An early form of photography.

cake, t'other day, jes to *larn* her, she said. 'O, go way, Missis,' says I; 'it really hurts my feelin's, now, to see good vittle spiled dat ar way! Cake ris all to one side,—no shape at all; no more than my shoe;—go way!' "

And with this final expression of contempt for Sally's greenness, Aunt Chloe whipped the cover off the bake-kettle, and disclosed to view a neatly baked pound-cake, of which no city confectioner need to have been ashamed. This being evidently the central point of the entertainment, Aunt Chloe began now to bustle about earnestly in the supper department.

"Here you, Mose and Pete! get out de way, you niggers! Get away, Polly, honey,— mammy'll give her baby somefin, by and by. Now, Mas'r George, you jest take off dem books, and set down now with my old man, and I'll take up de sausages, and have de first griddle full of cakes on your plates in less dan no time."

"They wanted me to come to supper in the house," said George; "but I knew what was what too well for that, Aunt Chloe."

"So you did,—so you did, honey," said Aunt Chloe, heaping the smoking batter-cakes on his plate; "you know'd your old aunty'd keep the best for you. O, let you alone for dat! Go way!" and, with that, aunty gave George a nudge with her finger, designed to be immensely facetious, and turned again to her griddle with great briskness.

"Now for the cake," said Mas'r George, when the activity of the griddle department had somewhat subsided; and, with that, the youngster flourished a large knife over the article in question.

"La bless you, Mas'r George!" said Aunt Chloe, with earnestness, catching his arm, "you wouldn't be for cuttin' it wid dat ar great heavy knife! Smash all down,—spile all de pretty rise of it. Here, I've got a thin old knife, I keeps sharp a purpose. Dar now, see! comes apart light as a feather! Now eat away,—you won't get anything to beat dat ar."

"Tom Lincon says," said George, speaking with his mouth full, "that their Jinny is a better cook than you."

"Dem Lincons an't much 'count, no way!" said Aunt Chloe, contemptuously; "I mean, set alongside *our* folks. They's 'spectable folks enough in a kinder plain way; but, as to gettin' up anything in style, they don't begin to have a notion on't. Set Mas'r Lincon, now, alongside Mas'r Shelby! Good Lor! and Missis Lincon,—can she kinder sweep it into a room like my missis,—so kinder splendid, yer know! O, go way! don't tell me nothin' of dem Lincons!"— and Aunt Chloe tossed her head as one who hoped she did know something of the world.

"Well, though, I've heard you say," said George, "that Jinny was a pretty fair cook."

"So I did," said Aunt Chloe,—"I may say dat. Good, plain, common cookin' Jinny'll do;—make a good pone o' bread,—bile her taters *far*,—her corn cakes isn't extra, not extra now, Jinny's corncakes isn't, but then they's far,—but, Lor, come to de higher branches, and what *can* she do? Why, she makes pies,—sartin she does; but what kinder crust? Can she make your real flecky paste, as melts in your mouth, and lies all up like a puff? Now, I went over thar when Miss Mary was gwine to be married, and Jinny she jest showed me de weddin' pies. Jinny and I is good friends, ye know. I never said nothin'; but go long, Mas'r George! Why, I shouldn't sleep a wink for a week, if I had a batch of pies like dem ar. Why, dey warn't no 'count 'tall."

"I suppose Jinny thought they were ever so nice," said George.

"Thought so!—didn't she? Thar she was, showing 'em as innocent,—ye see, it's jest here, Jinny *don't know*. Lor, the family an't nothing! She can't be spected to know! 'Tan't no fault o' hern. Ah, Mas'r George, you doesn't know half your privileges in yer family and bringin' up!" Here Aunt Chloe sighed, and rolled up her eyes with emotion.

"I'm sure, Aunt Chloe, I understand all my pie and pudding privileges," said George. "Ask Tom Lincon if I don't crow over him, every time I meet him."

Aunt Chloe sat back in her chair, and indulged in a hearty guffaw of laughter, at this witticism of young Mas'r's, laughing till the tears rolled down her black, shining cheeks, and varying the exercise with playfully slapping and poking Mas'r Georgey, and telling him to go way, and that he was a case,—that he was fit to kill her, and that he sartin would kill her, one of these days; and, between each of these sanguinary predictions, going off into a laugh, each longer and stronger than the other, till George really began to think that he was a very dangerously witty fellow, and that it became him to be careful how he talked "as funny as he could."

"And so ye telled Tom, did ye? O, Lor! what young uns will be up ter! Ye crowed over Tom? O, Lor! Mas'r George, if ye wouldn't make a hornbug laugh!"

"Yes," said George, "I says to him, 'Tom, you ought to see some of Aunt Chloe's pies; they're the right sort,' says I."

"Pity, now, Tom couldn't," said Aunt Chloe, on whose benevolent heart the idea of Tom's benighted condition seemed to make a strong impression. "Ye oughter just ask him here to dinner, some o' these times, Mas'r George," she added; "it would look quite pretty of ye. Ye know, Mas'r George, ye oughtenter feel 'bove nobody, on 'count yer privileges, 'cause all our privileges is gi'n to us; we ought al'ays to 'member that," said Aunt Chloe, looking quite serious.

"Well, I mean to ask Tom here, some day next week," said George; "and you do your prettiest, Aunt Chloe, and we'll make him stare. Won't we make him eat so he won't get over it for a fortnight?"

"Yes, yes,—sartin," said Aunt Chloe, delighted; "you'll see. Lor! to think of some of our dinners! Yer mind dat ar great chicken-pie I made when we guv de dinner to General Knox? I and Missis, we come pretty near quarrelling about dat ar crust. What does get into ladies sometimes, I don't know; but, sometimes, when a body has de heaviest kind o' 'sponsibility on 'em, as ye may say, and is all kinder *'seris'* and taken up, dey takes dat ar time to be hangin' round and kinder interferin'! Now, Missis, she wanted me to do dis way, and she wanted me to do dat way; and, finally, I got kinder sarcy, and, says I, 'Now, Missis, do jist look at dem beautiful white hands o' yourn with long fingers, and all a sparkling with rings, like my white lilies when de dew's on 'em; and look at my great black stumpin' hands. Now, don't ye think dat de Lord must have meant *me* to make de piecrust, and you to stay in de parlor?' Dar! I was jist so sarcy,[9] Mas'r George."

"And what did mother say?" said George.

"Say?—why, she kinder larfed in her eyes,—dem great handsome eyes o' hern; and, says she, 'Well, Aunt Chloe, I think you are about in the right on't,' says she; and she went off in de parlor. She oughter cracked me over de head for bein' so sarcy; but dar's whar 'tis,—I can't do nothin' with ladies in de kitchen!"

"Well, you made out well with that dinner,—I remember everybody said so," said George.

"Didn't I? And wan't I behind de dinin'-room door dat bery day? and didn't I see de General pass his plate three times for some more dat bery pie?—and, says he, 'You must have an uncommon cook, Mrs. Shelby.' Lor! I was fit to split myself.

"And de Gineral, he knows what cookin' is," said Aunt Chloe, drawing herself up with an air. "Bery nice man, de Gineral! He comes of one of de bery *fustest* families in Old Virginny! He knows what's what, now, as well as I do,—de Gineral. Ye see, there's *pints*[1] in all pies, Mas'r George; but 'tan't everybody knows what they is, or orter be. But the Gineral, he knows; I knew by his 'marks he made. Yes, he knows what de pints is!"

By this time, Master George had arrived at that pass to which even a boy can come (under uncommon circumstances), when he really could not eat another morsel, and, therefore, he was at leisure to notice the pile of woolly heads and glistening eyes which were regarding their operations hungrily from the opposite corner.

"Here, you Mose, Pete," he said, breaking off liberal bits, and throwing it at them; "you want some, don't you? Come, Aunt Chloe bake them some cakes."

And George and Tom moved to a comfortable seat in the chimney-corner, while Aunt

9. Saucy; impudent, disrespectful. 1. Points.

Chloe, after baking a goodly pile of cakes, took her baby on her lap, and began alternately filling its mouth and her own, and distributing to Mose and Pete, who seemed rather to prefer eating theirs as they rolled about on the floor under the table, tickling each other, and occasionally pulling the baby's toes.

"O, go long, will ye?" said the mother, giving now and then a kick, in a kind of general way, under the table, when the movement became too obstreperous. "Can't ye be decent when white folks comes to see ye? Stop dat ar, now, will ye? Better mind yerselves, or I'll take ye down a button-hole lower, when Mas'r George is gone!"

What meaning was couched under this terrible threat, it is difficult to say; but certain it is that its awful indistinctness seemed to produce very little impression on the young sinners addressed.

"La, now!" said Uncle Tom, "they are so full of tickle all the while, they can't behave theirselves."

Here the boys emerged from under the table, and, with hands and faces well plastered with molasses, began a vigorous kissing of the baby.

"Get along wid ye!" said the mother, pushing away their woolly heads. "Ye'll all stick together, and never get clar, if ye do dat fashion. Go long to de spring and wash yerselves!" she said, seconding her exhortations by a slap, which resounded very formidably, but which seemed only to knock out so much more laugh from the young ones, as they tumbled precipitately over each other out of doors, where they fairly screamed with merriment.

"Did ye ever see such aggravating young uns?" said Aunt Chloe, rather complacently, as, producing an old towel, kept for such emergencies, she poured a little water out of the cracked teapot on it, and began rubbing off the molasses from the baby's face and hands; and, having polished her till she shone, she set her down in Tom's lap, while she busied herself in clearing away supper. The baby employed the intervals in pulling Tom's nose, scratching his face, and burying her fat hands in his woolly hair, which last operation seemed to afford her special content.

"An't she a peart young un?" said Tom, holding her from him to take a full-length view; then, getting up, he set her on his broad shoulder and began capering and dancing with her, while Mas'r George snapped at her with his pocket-handkerchief, and Mose and Pete, now returned again, roared after her like bears, till Aunt Chloe declared that they "fairly took her head off" with their noise. As, according to her own statement, this surgical operation was a matter of daily occurrence in the cabin, the declaration no whit abated the merriment, till every one had roared and tumbled and danced themselves down to a state of composure.

"Well, now, I hopes you're done," said Aunt Chloe, who had been busy in pulling out a rude box of a trundle-bed; "and now, you Mose and you Pete, get into thar; for we's goin' to have the meetin'."

"O mother, we don't wanter. We wants to sit up to meetin',—meetin's is so curis. We likes 'em,"

"La, Aunt Chloe, shove it under, and let 'em sit up," said Mas'r George, decisively, giving a push to the rude machine.

Aunt Chloe, having thus saved appearances, seemed highly delighted to push the thing under, saying, as she did so, "Well, mebbe 'twill do 'em some good."

The house now resolved itself into a committee of the whole, to consider the accommodations and arrangements for the meeting.

"What we's to do for cheers, now, *I* declar I don't know," said Aunt Chloe. As the meeting had been held at Uncle Tom's, weekly, for an indefinite length of time, without any more "cheers," there seemed some encouragement to hope that a way would be discovered at present.

"Old Uncle Peter sung both de legs out of dat oldest cheer, last week," suggested Mose.

"You go long; I'll boun' you pulled 'em out; some o' your shines," said Aunt Chloe.

"Well, it'll stand, if it only keeps jam up agin de wall!" said Mose.

"Den Uncle Peter musn't sit in it, cause he al'ays hitches when he gets a singing. He hitched pretty nigh across de room, t'other night," said Pete.

"Good Lor! get him in it, then," said Mose, "and den he'd begin, 'Come saints and sinners, hear me tell,' and den down he'd go,"—and Mose imitated precisely the nasal tones of the old man, tumbling on the floor, to illustrate the supposed catastrophe.

"Come now, be decent, can't ye?" said Aunt Chloe; "an't yer shamed?"

Mas'r George, however, joined the offender in the laugh, and declared decidedly that Mose was a "buster." So the maternal admonition seemed rather to fail of effect.

"Well, ole man," said Aunt Chloe, "you'll have to tote in them ar bar'ls."

'Mother's bar'ls is like dat ar widder's, Mas'r George was reading 'bout, in de good book,—dey never fails," said Mose, aside to Pete.

"I'm sure one on 'em caved in last week," said Pete, "and let 'em all down in de middle of de singin'; dat ar was failin', warn't it?"

During this aside between Mose and Pete two empty casks had been rolled into the cabin, and being secured from rolling, by stones on each side, boards were laid across them, which arrangement, together with the turning down of certain tubs and pails, and the disposing of the rickety chairs, at last completed the preparation.

"Mas'r George is such a beautiful reader, now, I know he'll stay to read for us," said Aunt Chloe; " 'pears like 'twill be so much more interestin'."

George very readily consented, for your boy is always ready for anything that makes him of importance.

The room was soon filled with a motley assemblage, from the old gray-headed patriarch of eighty, to the young girl and lad of fifteen. A little harmless gossip ensued on various themes, such as where old Aunt Sally got her new red headkerchief, and how "Missis was a going to give Lizzy that spotted muslin gown, when she'd got her new berage up"; and how Mas'r Shelby was thinking of buying a new sorrel colt, that was going to prove an addition to the glories of the place. A few of the worshippers belonged to families hard by,[2] who had got permission to attend, and who brought in various choice scraps of information, about the sayings and doings at the house and on the place, which circulated as freely as the same sort of small change does in higher circles.

After a while the singing commenced, to the evident delight of all present. Not even all the disadvantages of nasal intonation could prevent the effect of the naturally fine voices, in airs at once wild and spirited. The words were sometimes the well-known and common hymns sung in the churches about, and sometimes of a wilder, more indefinite character, picked up at camp-meetings.

The chorus of one of them, which ran as follows, was sung with great energy and unction:—

> "Die on the field of battle,
> Die on the field of battle,
> Glory in my soul."

Another special favorite had oft repeated the words,—

> "O, I'm going to glory,—won't you come along with me?
> Don't you see the angels beck'ning, and a calling me away?
> Don't you see the golden city and the everlasting day?"

There were others, which made incessant mention of "Jordan's banks," and "Canaan's fields," and the "New Jerusalem"; for the negro mind, impassioned and imaginative, always

2. Nearby.

attaches itself to hymns and expressions of a vivid and pictorial nature; and, as they sung, some laughed, and some cried, and some clapped hands, or shook hands rejoicingly with each other, as if they had fairly gained the other side of the river.

Various exhortations, or relations of experience, followed, and intermingled with the singing. One old gray-headed woman, long past work, but much revered as a sort of chronicle of the past, rose, and leaning on her staff, said,—

"Well, chil'en! Well, I'm mighty glad to hear ye all and see ye all once more, 'cause I don't know when I'll be gone to glory; but I've done got ready, chil'en; 'pears like I'd got my little bundle all tied up, and my bonnet on, jest a waitin' for the stage to come along and take me home; sometimes, in the night, I think I hear the wheels a rattlin', and I'm lookin' out all the time; now, you jest be ready too, for I tell ye all, chil'en," she said, striking her staff hard on the floor, "dat ar *glory* is a mighty thing; It's a mighty thing, chil'en,—you don'no nothing about it,—it's *wonderful*." And the old creature sat down, with streaming tears, as wholly overcome, while the whole circle struck up,—

> *"O, Canaan, bright Canaan,*
> *I'm bound for the land of Canaan."*

Mas'r George, by request, read the last chapters of Revelation, often interrupted by such exclamations as "The *sakes* now!" "Only hear that!" "Jest think on't" "Is all that a comin' sure enough?"

George, who was a bright boy, and well trained in religious things by his mother, finding himself an object of general admiration, threw in expositions of his own, from time to time, with a commendable seriousness and gravity, for which he was admired by the young and blessed by the old; and it was agreed, on all hands, that "a minister couldn't lay it off better than he did"; that "'twas reely 'mazin'!"

Uncle Tom was a sort of patriarch in religious matters, in the neighborhood. Having, naturally, an organization in which the *morale* was strongly predominant, together with a greater breadth and cultivation of mind than obtained among his companions, he was looked up to with great respect, as a sort of minister among them; and the simple, hearty, sincere style of his exhortations might have edified even better educated persons. But it was in prayer that he especially excelled. Nothing could exceed the touching simplicity, the childlike earnestness of his prayer, enriched with the language of Scripture, which seemed so entirely to have wrought itself into his being, as to have become a part of himself, and to drop from his lips unconsciously; in the language of a pious old negro, he "prayed right up." And so much did his prayer always work on the devotional feelings of his audiences, that there seemed often a danger that it would be lost altogether in the abundance of the responses which broke out everywhere around him.

While this scene was passing in the cabin of the man, one quite otherwise passed in the halls of the master.

The trader and Mr. Shelby were seated together in the dining-room aforenamed, at a table covered with papers and writing utensils.

Mr. Shelby was busy in counting some bundles of bills, which, as they were counted, he pushed over to the trader, who counted them likewise.

"All fair," said the trader; "and now for signing these yer."

Mr. Shelby hastily drew the bills of sale towards him, and signed them, like a man that hurries over some disagreeable business, and then pushed them over with the money. Haley produced, from a well-worn valise, a parchment, which, after looking over it a moment, he handed to Mr. Shelby, who took it with a gesture of suppressed eagerness.

"Wal, now, the thing's *done!*" said the trader, getting up.

"It's *done!*" said Mr. Shelby, in a musing tone; and, fetching a long breath, he repeated, *"It's done!"*

"Yer don't seem to feel much pleased with it, 'pears to me," said the trader.

"Haley," said Mr. Shelby, "I hope you'll remember that you promised, on your honor, you wouldn't sell Tom, without knowing what sort of hands he's going into."

"Why, you've just done it, sir," said the trader.

"Circumstances, you well know, *obliged* me," said Shelby, haughtily.

"Wal, you know, they may 'blige *me,* too," said the trader. "Howsomever, I'll do the very best I can in gettin' Tom a good berth; as to my treatin' on him bad, you needn't be a grain afeard. If there's anything that I thank the Lord for, it is that I'm never noways cruel."

After the expositions which the trader had previously given of his humane principle, Mr. Shelby did not feel particularly reassured by these declarations; but, as they were the best comfort the case admitted of, he allowed the trader to depart in silence, and betook himself to a solitary cigar.

Chapter 5
Showing the Feelings of Living Property on Changing Owners

Mr. and Mrs. Shelby had retired to their apartment for the night. He was lounging in a large easy chair, looking over some letters that had come in the afternoon mail, and she was standing before her mirror, brushing out the complicated braids and curls in which Eliza had arranged her hair; for, noticing her pale cheeks and haggard eyes, she had excused her attendance that night, and ordered her to bed. The employment, naturally enough, suggested her conversation with the girl in the morning; and, turning to her husband, she said, carelessly,—

"By the by, Arthur, who was that low-bred fellow that you lugged in to our dinner-table to-day?"

"Haley is his name," said Shelby, turning himself rather uneasily in his chair, and continuing with his eyes fixed on a letter.

"Haley! Who is he, and what may be his business here, pray?"

"Well, he's a man that I transacted some business with, last time I was at Natchez," said Shelby.

"And he presumed on it to make himself quite at home, and call and dine here, ay?"

"Why, I invited him; I had some accounts with him," said Shelby.

"Is he a negro-trader?" said Mrs. Shelby, noticing a certain embarrassment in her husband's manner.

"Why, my dear, what put that into your head?" said Shelby, looking up.

"Nothing,—only Eliza came in here, after dinner, in a great worry, crying and taking on, and said you were talking with a trader, and that she heard him make an offer for her boy,—the ridiculous little goose!"

"She did, hey?" said Mr. Shelby, returning to his paper, which he seemed for a few moments quite intent upon, not perceiving that he was holding it bottom upwards.

"It will have to come out," said he, mentally; "as well now as ever."

"I told Eliza," said Mrs. Shelby, as she continued brushing her hair, "that she was a little fool for her pains, and that you never had anything to do with that sort of person. Of course, I knew you never meant to sell any of our people,—least of all, to such a fellow."

"Well, Emily," said her husband, "so I have always felt and said; but the fact is that my business lies so that I cannot get on without. I shall have to sell some of my hands."

"To that creature? Impossible! Mr. Shelby, you cannot be serious."

"I'm sorry to say that I am," said Mr. Shelby. "I've agreed to sell Tom."

"What! our Tom?—that good, faithful creature!—been your faithful servant from a boy! O, Mr. Shelby!—and you have promised him his freedom, too,—you and I have spoken to him a hundred times of it. Well, I can believe anything now,—I can believe *now* that you could sell little Harry, poor Eliza's only child!" said Mrs. Shelby, in a tone between grief and indignation.

"Well, since you must know all, it is so. I have agreed to sell Tom and Harry both; and I don't know why I am to be rated, as if I were a monster, for doing what every one does every day."

"But why, of all others, choose these?" said Mrs. Shelby. "Why sell them, of all on the place, if you must sell at all?"

"Because they will bring the highest sum of any,—that's why. I could choose another, if you say so. The fellow made me a high bid on Eliza, if that would suit you any better," said Mr. Shelby.

"The wretch!" said Mrs. Shelby, vehemently.

"Well, I didn't listen to it, a moment,—out of regard to your feelings, I wouldn't—so give me some credit."

"My dear," said Mrs. Shelby, recollecting herself, "forgive me. I have been hasty. I was surprised, and entirely unprepared for this;—but surely you will allow me to intercede for these poor creatures. Tom is a noble-hearted, faithful fellow, if he is black. I do believe, Mr. Shelby, that if he were put to it, he would lay down his life for you."

"I know it,—I dare say;—but what's the use of all this?—I can't help myself."

"Why not make a pecuniary sacrifice? I'm willing to bear my part of the inconvenience. O, Mr. Shelby, I have tried—tried most faithfully, as a Christian woman should—to do my duty to these poor, simple, dependent creatures. I have cared for them, instructed them, watched over them, and known all their little cares and joys, for years; and how can I ever hold up my head again among them, if, for the sake of a little paltry gain, we sell such a faithful, excellent, confiding creature as poor Tom, and tear from him in a moment all we have taught him to love and value? I have taught them the duties of the family, of parent and child, and husband and wife; and how can I bear to have this open acknowledgment that we care for no tie, no duty, no relation, however sacred, compared with money? I have talked with Eliza about her boy,—her duty to him as a Christian mother, to watch over him, pray for him, and bring him up in a Christian way; and now what can I say, if you tear him away, and sell him, soul and body, to a profane, unprincipled man, just to save a little money? I have told her that one soul is worth more than all the money in the world; and how will she believe me when she sees us turn round and sell her child?—sell him, perhaps, to certain ruin of body and soul!"

"I'm sorry you feel so about it, Emily,—indeed I am," said Mr. Shelby; "and I respect your feelings, too, though I don't pretend to share them to their full extent; but I tell you now, solemnly, it's of no use,—I can't help myself. I didn't mean to tell you this, Emily; but, in plain words, there is no choice between selling these two and selling everything. Either they must go, or *all* must. Haley has come into possession of a mortgage, which, if I don't clear off with him directly, will take everything before it. I've raked, and scraped, and borrowed, and all but begged,—and the price of these two was needed to make up the balance, and I had to give them up. Haley fancied the child; he agreed to settle the matter that way, and no other. I was in his power, and *had* to do it. If you feel so to have them sold, would it be any better to have *all* sold?"

Mrs. Shelby stood like one stricken. Finally, turning to her toilet,[3] she rested her face in her hands, and gave a sort of groan.

"This is God's curse on slavery!—a bitter, bitter, most accursed thing!—a curse to the master and a curse to the slave! I was a fool to think I could make anything good out of such a deadly evil. It is a sin to hold a slave under laws like ours,—I always felt it was,—I always thought so when I was a girl,—I thought so still more after I joined the church; but I thought I could gild it over,—I thought, by kindness, and care, and instruction, I could make the condition of mine better than freedom,—fool that I was!"

"Why, wife, you are getting to be an abolitionist, quite."

"Abolitionist; if they knew all I know about slavery they *might* talk! We don't need them to tell us; you know I never thought that slavery was right,—never felt willing to own slaves."

"Well, therein you differ from many wise and pious men," said Mr. Shelby. "You remember Mr. B.'s sermon, the other Sunday?"

"I don't want to hear such sermons; I never wish to hear Mr. B. in our church again. Ministers can't help the evil, perhaps,—can't cure it, any more than we can,—but defend it!—it always went against my common sense. And I think you didn't think much of that sermon, either."

"Well," said Shelby, "I must say these ministers sometimes carry matters further than we poor sinners would exactly dare to do. We men of the world must wink pretty hard at various things, and get used to a deal that isn't the exact thing. But we don't quite fancy, when women and ministers come out broad and square, and go beyond us in matters of either modesty or morals, that's a fact. But now, my dear, I trust you see the necessity of the thing, and you see that I have done the very best that circumstances would allow."

"O yes, yes!" said Mrs. Shelby, hurriedly and abstractedly fingering her gold watch,—"I haven't any jewelry of any amount," she added, thoughtfully; "but would not this watch do something?—it was an expensive one when it was bought. If I could only at least save Eliza's child, I would sacrifice anything I have."

"I'm sorry, very sorry, Emily," said Mr. Shelby. "I'm sorry this takes hold of you so; but it will do no good. The fact is, Emily, the thing's done; the bills of sale are already signed, and in Haley's hands; and you must be thankful it is no worse. That man has had it in his power to ruin us all,—and now he is fairly off. If you knew the man as I do, you'd think that we had had a narrow escape."

"Is he so hard, then?"

"Why, not a cruel man, exactly, but a man of leather,—a man alive to nothing but trade and profit,—cool, and unhesitating, and unrelenting, as death and the grave. He'd sell his own mother at a good percentage,—not wishing the old woman any harm, either."

"And this wretch owns that good, faithful Tom, and Eliza's child!"

"Well, my dear, the fact is that this goes rather hard with me; it's a thing I hate to think of. Haley wants to drive matters, and take possession to-morrow. I'm going to get out my horse bright and early, and be off. I can't see Tom, that's a fact; and you had better arrange a drive somewhere, and carry Eliza off. Let the thing be done when she is out of sight."

"No, no," said Mrs. Shelby; "I'll be in no sense accomplice or help in this cruel business. I'll go and see poor old Tom, God help him, in his distress! They shall see, at any rate, that their mistress can feel for and with them. As to Eliza, I dare not think about it. The Lord forgive us! What have we done, that this cruel necessity should come on us?"

There was one listener to this conversation whom Mr. and Mrs. Shelby little suspected.

Communicating with their apartment was a large closet, opening by a door into the outer passage. When Mrs. Shelby had dismissed Eliza for the night, her feverish and excited mind had suggested the idea of this closet; and she had hidden herself there, and, with her ear pressed close against the crack of the door, had lost not a word of the conversation.

3.   Dressing table.

When the voices died into silence, she rose and crept stealthily away. Pale, shivering, with rigid features and compressed lips, she looked an entirely altered being from the soft and timid creature she had been hitherto. She moved cautiously along the entry, paused one moment at her mistress's door, and raised her hands in mute appeal to Heaven, and then turned and glided into her own room. It was a quiet, neat apartment, on the same floor with her mistress. There was the pleasant sunny window, where she had often sat singing at her sewing; there a little case of books, and various little fancy articles, ranged by them, the gifts of Christmas holidays; there was her simple wardrobe in the closet and in the drawers:—here was, in short, her home; and, on the whole, a happy one it had been to her. But there, on the bed, lay her slumbering boy, his long curls falling negligently around his unconscious face, his rosy mouth half open, his little fat hands thrown out over the bedclothes, and a smile spread like a sunbeam over his whole face.

"Poor boy! poor fellow!" said Eliza; "they have sold you! but your mother will save you yet!"

No tear dropped over that pillow; in such straits as these the heart has no tears to give,—it drops only blood, bleeding itself away in silence. She took a piece of paper and a pencil, and wrote hastily,—

"O, Missis dear Missis! don't think me ungrateful,—don't think hard of me, any way,—I heard all you and master said to-night. I am going to try to save my boy,—you will not blame me! God bless and reward you for all your kindness!"

Hastily folding and directing this, she went to a drawer and made up a little package of clothing for her boy, which she tied with a handkerchief firmly round her waist; and, so fond is a mother's remembrance, that, even in the terrors of that hour, she did not forget to put in the little package one or two of his favorite toys, reserving a gayly painted parrot to amuse him, when she should be called on to awaken him. It was some trouble to arouse the little sleeper; but, after some effort, he sat up, and was playing with his bird, while his mother was putting on her bonnet and shawl.

"Where are you going, mother?" said he, as she drew near the bed, with his little coat and cap.

His mother drew near, and looked so earnestly into his eyes, that he at once divined that something unusual was the matter.

"Hush, Harry," she said; "mustn't speak loud, or they will hear us. A wicked man was coming to take little Harry away from his mother, and carry him 'way off in the dark; but mother won't let him,—she's going to put on her little boy's cap and coat, and run off with him, so the ugly man can't catch him."

Saying these words, she had tied and buttoned on the child's simple outfit, and, taking him in her arms, she whispered to him to be very still; and, opening a door in her room which led into the outer veranda, she glided noiselessly out.

It was a sparkling, frosty, starlight night, and the mother wrapped the shawl close round her child, as, perfectly quiet with vague terror, he clung round her neck.

Old Bruno, a great Newfoundland, who slept at the end of the porch, rose, with a low growl, as she came near. She gently spoke his name, and the animal, an old pet and playmate of hers, instantly, wagging his tail, prepared to follow her, though apparently revolving much, in his simple dog's head, what such an indiscreet midnight promenade might mean. Some dim idea of imprudence or impropriety in the measure seemed to embarrass him considerably; for he often stopped, as Eliza glided forward, and looked wistfully, first at her and then at the house, and then, as if reassured by reflection, he pattered along after her again. A few minutes brought them to the window of Uncle Tom's cottage, and Eliza, stopping, tapped lightly on the window-pane.

The prayer-meeting at Uncle Tom's had, in the order of hymn-singing, been protracted to a very late hour; and, as Uncle Tom had indulged himself in a few lengthy solos afterwards, the consequence was, that, although it was now between twelve and one o'clock, he and his worthy helpmeet were not yet asleep.

"Good Lord! what's that?" said Aunt Chloe, starting up and hastily drawing the curtain. "My sakes alive, if it an't Lizy! Get on your clothes, old man, quick!—there's old Bruno, too, a pawin' round; what on airth! I'm gwine to open the door."

And, suiting the action to the word, the door flew open, and the light of the tallow candle, which Tom had hastily lighted, fell on the haggard face and dark, wild eyes of the fugitive.

"Lord bless you!—I'm skeered to look at ye, Lizy! Are ye tuck sick, or what's come over ye?"

"I'm running away,—Uncle Tom and Aunt Chloe,—carrying off my child,—Master sold him!"

"Sold him?" echoed both, lifting up their hands in dismay.

"Yes, sold him!" said Eliza, firmly; "I crept into the closet by Mistress's door to-night, and I heard Master tell Missis that he had sold my Harry, and you, Uncle Tom, both, to a trader; and that he was going off this morning on his horse, and that the man was to take possession to-day."

Tom had stood, during this speech, with his hands raised, and his eyes dilated, like a man in a dream. Slowly and gradually, as its meaning came over him, he collapsed, rather than seated himself, on his old chair, and sunk his head down upon his knees.

"The good Lord have pity on us!" said Aunt Chloe. "O, it don't seem as if it was true! What has he done, that Mas'r should sell *him?*"

"He hasn't done anything,—it isn't for that. Master don't want to sell; and Missis,—she's always good. I heard her plead and beg for us; but he told her 'twas no use; that he was in this man's debt, and that this man had got the power over him; and that if he didn't pay him off clear, it would end in his having to sell the place and all the people, and move off. Yes, I heard him say there was no choice between selling these two and selling all, the man was driving him so hard. Master said he was sorry; but O, Missis,—you ought to have heard her talk! If she an't a Christian and an angel, there never was one. I'm a wicked girl to leave her so; but, then, I can't help it. She said, herself, one soul was worth more than the world; and this boy has a soul, and if I let him be carried off, who knows what'll become of it? It must be right; but, if it an't right, the Lord forgive me, for I can't help doing it!"

"Well, old man!" said Aunt Chloe, "why don't you go, too? Will you wait to be toted down river, where they kill niggers with hard work and starving? I'd a heap rather die than go there, any day! There's time for ye,—be off with Lizy,—you've got a pass to come and go any time. Come, bustle up, and I'll get your things together."

Tom slowly raised his head, and looked sorrowfully but quietly around, and said,—

"No, no,—I an't going. Let Eliza go,—it's her right! I wouldn't be the one to say no,—'tan't in *natur* for her to stay; but you heard what she said! If I must be sold, or all the people on the place, and everything go to rack, why, let me be sold. I s'pose I can b'ar it as well as any on 'em," he added, while something like a sob and a sigh shook his broad, rough chest convulsively. "Mas'r always found me on the spot,—he always will. I never have broke trust, nor used my pass no ways contrary to my word, and I never will. It's better for me alone to go, than to break up the place and sell all. Mas'r an't to blame, Chloe, and he'll take care of you and the poor—"

Here he turned to the rough trundle-bed full of little woolly heads, and broke fairly down. He leaned over the back of the chair, and covered his face with his large hands. Sobs, heavy, hoarse, and loud, shook the chair, and great tears fell through his fingers on the floor; just such tears, sir, as you dropped into the coffin where lay your first-born son; such tears, woman, as you shed when you heard the cries of your dying babe. For, sir, he was a man,—and you are but another man. And, woman, though dressed in silk and jewels, you are but a woman, and, in life's great straits and mighty griefs, ye feel but one sorrow!

"And now," said Eliza, as she stood in the door, "I saw my husband only this afternoon, and I little knew then what was to come. They have pushed him to the very last standing-place, and he told me, to-day, that he was going to run away. Do try, if you can, to get word to him. Tell him how I went, and why I went; and tell him I'm going to try and find Canada. You must give my love to him, and tell him, if I never see him again,"—she turned away, and stood with her back to them for a moment, and then added, in a husky voice, "tell him to be as good as he can, and try and meet me in the kingdom of heaven."

"Call Bruno in there," she added. "Shut the door on him, poor beast! He mustn't go with me!"

A few last words and tears, a few simple adieus and blessings, and, clasping her wondering and afrighted child in her arms, she glided noiselessly away.

Chapter 6
Discovery

Mr. and Mrs. Shelby, after their protracted discussion of the night before, did not readily sink to repose, and, in consequence, slept somewhat later than usual, the ensuing morning.

"I wonder what keeps Eliza," said Mrs. Shelby, after giving her bell repeated pulls, to no purpose.

Mr. Shelby was standing before his dressing-glass, sharpening his razor; and just then the door opened, and a colored boy entered, with his shaving-water.

"Andy," said his mistress, "step to Eliza's door, and tell her I have rung for her three times. Poor thing!" she added to herself, with a sigh.

Andy soon returned, with eyes very wide in astonishment.

"Lor, Missis! Lizy's drawers is all open, and her things all lying every which way; and I believe she's just done clared out!"

The truth flashed upon Mr. Shelby and his wife at the same moment. He exclaimed,—

"Then she suspected it, and she's off!"

"The Lord be thanked!" said Mrs. Shelby. "I trust she is."

"Wife, you talk like a fool! Really, it will be something pretty awkward for me, if she is. Haley saw that I hesitated about selling this child, and he'll think I connived at it, to get him out of the way. It touches my honor!" And Mr. Shelby left the room hastily.

There was great running and ejaculating, and opening and shutting of doors, and appearance of faces in all shades of color in different places, for about a quarter of an hour. One person only, who might have shed some light on the matter, was entirely silent, and that was the head cook, Aunt Chloe. Silently, and with a heavy cloud settled down over her once joyous face, she proceeded making out her breakfast biscuits, as if she heard and saw nothing of the excitement around her.

Very soon, about a dozen young imps were roosting, like so many crows, on the veranda railings, each one determined to be the first one to apprize the strange Mas'r of his ill luck.

"He'll be rael mad, I'll be bound," said Andy.

"*Won't* he swar!" said little black Jake.

"Yes, for he *does* swar," said woolly-headed Mandy. "I hearn him yesterday, at dinner. I hearn all about it then, 'cause I got into the closet where Missis keeps the great jugs, and I hearn every word." And Mandy, who had never in her life thought of the meaning of a word she had heard, more than a black cat, now took airs of superior wisdom, and strutted about, forgetting to state that, though actually coiled up among the jugs at the time specified, she had been fast asleep all the time.

When, at last, Haley appeared, booted and spurred, he was saluted with the bad tidings on every hand. The young imps on the veranda were not disappointed in their hope of hearing him "swar," which he did with a fluency and fervency which delighted them all amazingly, as they ducked and dodged hither and thither, to be out of the reach of his riding-whip; and, all whooping off together, they tumbled, in a pile of immeasurable giggle, on the withered turf under the veranda, where they kicked up their heels and shouted to their full satisfaction.

"If I had the little devils!" muttered Haley, between his teeth.

"But you han't got 'em, though!" said Andy, with a triumphant flourish, and making a string of indescribable mouths at the unfortunate trader's back, when he was fairly beyond hearing.

"I say now, Shelby, this yer's a most extro'rnary business!" said Haley, as he abruptly entered the parlor. "It seems that gal's off, with her young un."

"Mr. Haley, Mrs. Shelby is present," said Mr. Shelby.

"I beg pardon, ma'am," said Haley, bowing slightly, with a still lowering brow; "but still I say, as I said before, this yer's a sing'lar report. Is it true, sir?"

"Sir," said Mr. Shelby, "if you wish to communicate with me, you must observe something of the decorum of a gentleman. Andy, take Mr. Haley's hat and riding-whip. Take a seat, sir. Yes, sir; I regret to say that the young woman, excited by overhearing, or having reported to her, something of this business, has taken her child in the night, and made off."

"I did expect fair dealing in this matter, I confess," said Haley.

"Well, sir," said Mr. Shelby, turning sharply round upon him, "what am I to understand by that remark? If any man calls my honor in question, I have but one answer for him."

The trader cowered at this, and in a somewhat lower tone said that "it was plaguy hard on a fellow, that had made a fair bargain, to be gulled that way."

"Mr. Haley," said Mr. Shelby, "if I did not think you had some cause for disappointment, I should not have borne from you the rude and unceremonious style of your entrance into my parlor this morning. I say thus much, however, since appearances call for it, that I shall allow of no insinuations cast upon me, as if I were at all partner to any unfairness in this matter. Moreover, I shall feel bound to give you every assistance, in the use of horses, servants, etc., in the recovery of your property. So, in short, Haley," said he suddenly dropping from the tone of dignified coolness to his ordinary one of easy frankness, "the best way for you is to keep good-natured and eat some breakfast, and we will then see what is to be done."

Mrs. Shelby now rose, and said her engagements would prevent her being at the breakfast-table that morning; and, deputing a very respectable mulatto woman to attend to the gentlemen's coffee at the sideboard, she left the room.

"Old lady don't like your humble servant, over and above," said Haley, with an uneasy effort to be very familiar.

"I am not accustomed to hear my wife spoken of with such freedom," said Mr. Shelby, dryly.

"Beg pardon; of course, only a joke, you know," said Haley, forcing a laugh.

"Some jokes are less agreeable than others," rejoined Shelby.

"Devilish free, now I've signed those papers, cuss him!" muttered Haley to himself; "quite grand, since yesterday!"

Never did fall of any prime minister at court occasion wider surges of sensation than the report of Tom's fate among his compeers on the place. It was the topic in every mouth, everywhere; and nothing was done in the house or in the field, but to discuss its probable results. Eliza's flight—an unprecedented event on the place—was also a great accessory in stimulating the general excitement.

Black Sam, as he was commonly called, from his being about three shades blacker than any other son of ebony on the place, was revolving the matter profoundly in all its phases and bearings, with a comprehensiveness of vision and a strict lookout to his own personal well-being, that would have done credit to any white patriot in Washington.

"It's an ill wind dat blows nowhar,—dat ar a fact," said Sam, sententiously, giving an additional hoist to his pantaloons, and adroitly substituting a long nail in place of a missing suspender-button, with which effort of mechanical genius he seemed highly delighted.

"Yes, it's an ill wind blows nowhar," he repeated. "Now, dar, Tom's down,—wal, course der's room for some nigger to be up,—and why not dis nigger?—dat's de idee. Tom, a ridin' round de country,—boots blacked,—pass in his pocket,—all grand as Cuffee,—who but he? Now, why shouldn't Sam?—dat's what I want to know."

"Halloo, Sam,—O Sam! Mas'r wants you to cotch Bill and Jerry," said Andy, cutting short Sam's soliloquy.

"High! what's afoot now, young un?"

"Why, you don't know, I s'pose, that Lizy's cut stick, and clared out, with her young un?"

"You teach your granny!" said Sam, with infinite contempt; "knowed it a heap sight sooner than you did; this nigger an't so green, now!"

"Well, anyhow, Mas'r wants Bill and Jerry geared right up; and you and I's to go with Mas'r Haley, to look arter her."

"Good, now! dat's de time o' day!" said Sam. "It's Sam dat's called for in dese yer times. He's de nigger. See if I don't cotch her, now; Mas'r'll see what Sam can do!"

"Ah! but, Sam," said Andy, "you'd better think twice; for Missis don't want her cotched, and she'll be in yer wool."

"High!" said Sam, opening his eyes. "How you know dat?"

"Heard her say so, my own self, dis blessed mornin', when I bring in Mas'rs shaving-water. She sent me to see why Lizy didn't come to dress her; and when I told her she was off, she jest ris up, and ses she, 'The Lord be praised'; and Mas'r, he seemed rael mad, and ses he, 'Wife, you talk like a fool.' But Lor! she'll bring him to! I knows well enough how that'll be—it's allers best to stand Missis' side the fence, now I tell yer."

Black Sam, upon this, scratched his woolly pate, which, if it did not contain very profound wisdom, still contained a great deal of a particular species much in demand among politicians of all complexions and countries, and vulgarly denominated "knowing which side the bread is buttered"; so, stopping with grave consideration, he again gave a hitch to his pantaloons, which was his regularly organized method of assisting his mental perplexities.

"Der an't no sayin'—never—'bout no kind o' thing in *dis* yer world," he said, at last.

Sam spoke like a philosopher, emphasizing *this*,—as if he had had a large experience in different sorts of worlds, and therefore had come to his conclusions advisedly.

"Now, sartin I'd a said that Missis would a scoured the varsal world after Lizy," added Sam, thoughtfully.

"So she would," said Andy; "but can't you see through a ladder, ye black nigger? Missis don't want dis yer Mas'r Haley to get Lizy's boy; dat's de go!"

"High!" said Sam, with an indescribable intonation, known only to those who have heard it among the negroes.

"And I'll tell yer more 'n all," said Andy; "I spect you'd better be making tracks for dem hosses,—mighty sudden, too,—for I hearn Missis 'quirin' arter yer,—so you've stood foolin' long enough."

Sam, upon this, began to bestir himself in real earnest, and after a while appeared, bearing down gloriously towards the house, with Bill and Jerry in a full canter, and adroitly throwing himself off before they had any idea of stopping, he brought them up alongside of the horse-post like a tornado. Haley's horse, which was a skittish young colt, winced, and bounced, and pulled hard at his halter.

"Ho, ho!" said Sam, "skeery, ar ye?" and his black visage lighted up with a curious, mischievous gleam. "I'll fix ye now!" said he.

There was a large beech-tree overshadowing the place, and the small, sharp, triangular beechnuts lay scattered thickly on the ground. With one of these in his fingers, Sam approached the colt, stroked and patted, and seemed apparently busy in soothing his agitation. On pretence of adjusting the saddle, he adroitly slipped under it the sharp little nut, in such a manner that the least weight brought upon the saddle would annoy the nervous sensibilities of the animal, without leaving any perceptible graze or wound.

"Dar!" he said, rolling his eyes with an approving grin; "me fix 'em!"

At this moment Mrs. Shelby appeared on the balcony, beckoning to him. Sam approached with as good a determination to pay court as did ever suitor after a vacant place at St. James's or Washington.

"Why have you been loitering so, Sam? I sent Andy to tell you to hurry."

"Lord bless you, Missis!" said Sam, "horses won't be cotched all in a minnit; they'd done clared out way down to the south pasture, and the Lord knows whar!"

"Sam, how often must I tell you not to say 'Lord bless you, and the Lord knows,' and such things? It's wicked."

"O, Lord bless my soul! I done forgot, Missis! I won't say nothing of de sort no more."

"Why, Sam, you just *have* said it again."

"Did I? O, Lord! I mean,—I didn't go fur to say it."

"You must be *careful*, Sam."

"Just let me get my breath, Missis, and I'll start fair. I'll be berry careful."

"Well, Sam, you are to go with Mr. Haley, to show him the road, and help him. Be careful of the horses, Sam; you know Jerry was a little lame last week; *don't ride them too fast.*"

Mrs. Shelby spoke the last words with a low voice, and strong emphasis.

"Let dis child alone for dat!" said Sam, rolling up his eyes with a volume of meaning. "Lord knows! High! Didn't say dat!" said he, suddenly catching his breath, with a ludicrous flourish of apprehension, which made his mistress laugh, spite of herself. "Yes, Missis, I'll look out for de hosses!"

"Now, Andy," said Sam, returning to his stand under the beech-trees, "you see I wouldn't be 'tall surprised if dat ar gen'lman's crittur should gib a fling, by and by, when he comes to be a gettin' up. You know, Andy, critturs *will* do such things"; and therewith Sam poked Andy in the side, in a highly suggestive manner.

"High!" said Andy, with an air of instant appreciation.

"Yes, you see, Andy, Missis wants to make time,—dat ar's clar to der most or'nary 'bserver. I jis make a little for her. Now, you see, get all dese yer hosses loose, caperin' permiscus round dis yer lot and down to de wood dar, and I spec Mas'r won't be off in a hurry."

Andy grinned.

"Yer see," said Sam, "yer see, Andy, if any such thing should happen as that Mas'r Haley's horse *should* begin to act contrary, and cut up, you and I jist let's go of our'n to help him, and *we'll help him,*—O yes!" And Sam and Andy laid their heads back on their shoulders, and broke into a low, immoderate laugh, snapping their fingers and flourishing their heels with exquisite delight.

At this instant, Haley appeared on the veranda. Somewhat mollified by certain cups of very good coffee, he came out smiling and talking, in tolerably restored humor. Sam and Andy, clawing for certain fragmentary palm-leaves, which they were in the habit of considering as hats, flew to the horse-posts, to be ready to "help Mas'r."

Sam's palm-leaf had been ingeniously disentangled from all pretensions to braid, as respects its brim; and the slivers starting apart, and standing upright, gave it a blazing air of freedom and defiance, quite equal to that of any Fejee[4] chief; while the whole brim of Andy's being departed bodily, he rapped the crown on his head with a dexterous thump, and looked about well pleased, as if to say, "Who says I haven't got a hat?"

"Well, boys," said Haley, "look alive now; we must lose no time."

"Not a bit of him, Mas'r!" said Sam, putting Haley's rein in his hand, and holding his stirrup, while Andy was untying the other two horses.

The instant Haley touched the saddle, the mettlesome creature bounded from the earth with a sudden spring, that threw his master sprawling, some feet off, on the soft, dry turf. Sam, with frantic ejaculations, made a dive at the reins, but only succeeded in brushing the blazing

4. A native of the Fiji Islands in the southwestern Pacific.

palm-leaf aforenamed into the horse's eyes, which by no means tended to allay the confusion of his nerves. So, with great vehemence, he overturned Sam, and, giving two or three contemptuous snorts, flourished his heels vigorously in the air, and was soon prancing away towards the lower end of the lawn, followed by Bill and Jerry, whom Andy had not failed to let loose, according to contract, speeding them off with various direful ejaculations. And now ensued a miscellaneous scene of confusion. Sam and Andy ran and shouted,—dogs barked here and there,—and Mike, Mose, Mandy, Fanny, and all the smaller specimens on the place, both male and female, raced, clapped hands, whooped, and shouted, with outrageous officiousness and untiring zeal.

Haley's horse, which was a white one, and very fleet and spirited, appeared to enter into the spirit of the scene with great gusto; and having for his coursing ground a lawn of nearly half a mile in extent, gently sloping down on every side into indefinite woodland, he appeared to take infinite delight in seeing how near he could allow his pursuers to approach him, and then, when within a hand's breadth, whisk off with a start and a snort, like a mischievous beast as he was, and career far down into some alley of the wood-lot. Nothing was further from Sam's mind than to have any one of the troop taken until such season as should seem to him most befitting,—and the exertions that he made were certainly most heroic. Like the sword of Cœur de Lion,[5] which always blazed in the front and thickest of the battle, Sam's palm-leaf was to be seen everywhere when there was the least danger that a horse could be caught;—there he would bear down full tilt, shouting, "Now for it! cotch him!" in a way that would set everything to indiscriminate rout in a moment.

Haley ran up and down, and cursed and swore and stamped miscellaneously. Mr. Shelby in vain tried to shout directions from the balcony, and Mrs. Shelby from her chamber window alternately laughed and wondered,—not without some inkling of what lay at the bottom of all this confusion.

At last, about twelve o'clock, Sam appeared triumphant, mounted on Jerry, with Haley's horse by his side, reeking with sweat, but with flashing eyes and dilated nostrils, showing that the spirit of freedom had not yet entirely subsided.

"He's cotched!" he exclaimed triumphantly. "If 't hadn't been for me, they might a bust theirselves, all on 'em; but I cotched him!"

"You!" growled Haley, in no amiable mood. "If it hadn't been for you, this never would have happened."

"Lord bless us, Mas'r," said Sam, in a tone of the deepest concern, "and me that has been racin' and chasin' till the sweat jest pours off me!"

"Well, well!" said Haley, "you've lost me near three hours, with your cursed nonsense. Now let's be off, and have no more fooling."

"Why, Mas'r," said Sam, in a deprecating tone, "I believe you mean to kill us all clar, horses and all. Here we are all just ready to drop down, and the critturs all in a reek of sweat. Why, Mas'r won't think of startin' on now till arter dinner. Mas'r's hoss wants rubben' down; see how he splashed hisself; and Jerry limps too; don't think Missis would be willin' to have us start dis yer way, no how. Lord bless you, Mas'r, we can ketch up, if we do stop. Lizy never was no great of a walker."

Mrs. Shelby, who, greatly to her amusement, had overheard this conversation from the veranda, now resolved to do her part. She came forward, and, courteously expressing her concern for Haley's accident, pressed him to stay to dinner, saying that the cook should bring it on the table immediately.

Thus, all things considered, Haley, with rather an equivocal grace, proceeded to the parlor, while Sam, rolling his eyes after him with unutterable meaning, proceeded gravely with the horses to the stable-yard.

"Did yer see him, Andy? *did* yer see him?" said Sam, when he had got fairly beyond the

5.   Richard the Lionhearted, king of England 1189–1199.

shelter of the barn, and fastened the horse to a post. "O, Lor, if it warn't as good as a meetin', now, to see him a dancin' and kickin' and swarin' at us. Didn't I hear him? Swar away, ole fellow (says I to myself); will yer have yer hoss now, or wait till you cotch him? (says I). Lor, Andy, I think I can see him now." And Sam and Andy leaned up against the barn, and laughed to their hearts' content.

"Yer oughter seen how mad he looked, when I brought the hoss up. Lord, he'd a killed me, if he durs' to; and there I was a standin' as innercent and as humble."

"Lor, I seed you," said Andy; "an't you an old hoss, Sam?"

"Rather specks I am," said Sam; "did yer see Missis up stars at the winder? I seed her laughin'."

"I'm sure, I was racin' so, I didn't see nothing," said Andy.

"Well, yer see," said Sam, proceeding gravely to wash down Haley's pony. "I'se 'quired what yer may call a habit o' *bobservation*, Andy. It's a very 'portant habit, Andy, and I 'commend yer to be cultivatin' it, now yer young. Hist up that hind foot, Andy. Yer see, Andy, it's *bobservation* makes all de difference in niggers. Didn't I see which way the wind blew dis yer mornin'? Didn't I see what Missis wanted, though she never let on? Dat ar's bobservation, Andy. I spects it's what you may call a faculty. Faculties is different in different peoples, but cultivation of 'em goes a great way."

"I guess if I hadn't helped your bobservation dis mornin', yer wouldn't have seen your way so smart," said Andy.

"Andy," said Sam, "you's a promisin' child, der an't no manner o' doubt. I think lots of yer, Andy; and I don't feel no ways ashamed to take idees from you. We oughtenter overlook nobody, Andy, cause the smartest on us gets tripped up sometimes. And so, Andy, let's go up to the house now. I'll be boun' Missis'll give us an uncommon good bite, dis yer time."

Chapter 7
The Mother's Struggle

It is impossible to conceive of a human creature more wholly desolate and forlorn than Eliza, when she turned her footsteps from Uncle Tom's cabin.

Her husband's suffering and dangers, and the danger of her child, all blended in her mind, with a confused and stunning sense of the risk she was running, in leaving the only home she had ever known, and cutting loose from the protection of a friend whom she loved and revered. Then there was the parting from every familiar object,—the place where she had grown up, the trees under which she had played, the groves where she had walked many an evening in happier days, by the side of her young husband,—everything, as it lay in the clear, frosty starlight, seemed to speak reproachfully to her, and ask her whither could she go from a home like that?

But stronger than all was maternal love, wrought into a paroxysm of frenzy by the near approach of a fearful danger. Her boy was old enough to have walked by her side, and, in an indifferent case, she would only have led him by the hand; but now the bare thought of putting him out of her arms made her shudder, and she strained him to her bosom with a convulsive grasp, as she went rapidly forward.

The frosty ground creaked beneath her feet, and she trembled at the sound; every quaking leaf and fluttering shadow sent the blood backward to her heart, and quickened her footsteps. She wondered within herself at the strength that seemed to be come upon her; for she felt the weight of her boy as if it had been a feather, and every flutter of fear seemed to increase the supernatural power that bore her on, while from her pale lips burst forth, in frequent ejaculations, the prayer to a Friend above,—"Lord, help! Lord, save me!"

If it were *your* Harry, mother, or your Willie, that were going to be torn from you by a brutal trader, to-morrow morning,—if you had seen the man, and heard that the papers were signed and delivered, and you had only from twelve o'clock till morning to make good your escape,—how fast could *you* walk? How many miles could you make in those few brief hours, with the darling at your bosom,—the little sleepy head on your shoulder,—the small, soft arms trustingly holding on to your neck?

For the child slept. At first, the novelty and alarm kept him waking; but his mother so hurriedly repressed every breath or sound, and so assured him that if he were only still she would certainly save him, that he clung quietly round her neck, only asking, as he found himself sinking to sleep,—

"Mother, I don't need to keep awake, do I?"

"No, my darling; sleep, if you want to."

"But, mother, if I do get asleep, you won't let him get me?"

"No! so may God help me!" said his mother, with a paler cheek, and a brighter light in her large dark eyes.

"You're *sure*, an't you, mother?"

"Yes, *sure!*" said the mother, in a voice that startled herself; for it seemed to her to come from a spirit within, that was no part of her; and the boy dropped his little weary head on her shoulder, and was soon asleep. How the touch of those warm arms, the gentle breathings that came in her neck, seemed to add fire and spirit to her movements! It seemed to her as if strength poured into her in electric streams, from every gentle touch and movement of the sleeping, confiding child. Sublime is the dominion of the mind over the body, that, for a time, can make flesh and nerve impregnable, and string the sinews like steel, so that the weak become so mighty.

The boundaries of the farm, the grove, the wood-lot, passed by her dizzily, as she walked on; and still she went, leaving one familiar object after another, slacking not, pausing not, till reddening daylight found her many a long mile from all traces of any familiar objects upon the open highway.

She had often been, with her mistress, to visit some connections, in the little village of T———, not far from the Ohio river, and knew the road well. To go thither, to escape across the Ohio river, were the first hurried outlines of her plan of escape; beyond that, she could only hope in God.

When horses and vehicles began to move along the highway, with that alert perception peculiar to a state of excitement, and which seems to be a sort of inspiration, she became aware that her headlong pace and distracted air might bring on her remark and suspicion. She therefore put the boy on the ground, and, adjusting her dress and bonnet, she walked on at as rapid a pace as she thought consistent with the preservation of appearances. In her little bundle she had provided a store of cakes and apples, which she used as expedients for quickening the speed of the child, rolling the apple some yards before them, when the boy would run with all his might after it; and this ruse, often repeated, carried them over many a half-mile.

After a while, they came to a thick patch of woodland, through which murmured a clear brook. As the child complained of hunger and thirst, she climbed over the fence with him; and, sitting down behind a large rock which concealed them from the road, she gave him a breakfast out of her little package. The boy wondered and grieved that she could not eat; and when, putting his arms round her neck, he tried to wedge some of his cake into her mouth, it seemed to her that the rising in her throat would choke her.

"No, no, Harry darling! mother can't eat till you are safe! We must go on,—on,—till we come to the river!" And she hurried again into the road, and again constrained herself to walk regularly and composedly forward.

She was many miles past any neighborhood where she was personally known. If she should chance to meet any who knew her, she reflected that the well-known kindness of the family would be of itself a blind to suspicion, as making it an unlikely supposition that she could be a fugitive. As she was also so white as not to be known as of colored lineage, without a critical survey, and her child was white also, it was much easier for her to pass on unsuspected.

On this presumption, she stopped at noon at a neat farmhouse, to rest herself, and buy some dinner for her child and self; for, as the danger decreased with the distance, the supernatural tension of the nervous system lessened, and she found herself both weary and hungry.

The good woman, kindly and gossiping, seemed rather pleased than otherwise with having somebody come in to talk with; and accepted, without examination, Eliza's statement, that she "was going on a little piece, to spend a week with her friends,"—all which she hoped in her heart might prove strictly true.

An hour before sunset, she entered the village of T——, by the Ohio river, weary and footsore, but still strong in heart. Her first glance was at the river, which lay, like Jordan, between her and the Canaan of liberty on the other side.[6]

It was now early spring, and the river was swollen and turbulent; great cakes of floating ice were swinging heavily to and fro in the turbid waters. Owing to the peculiar form of the shore on the Kentucky side, the land bending far out into the water, the ice had been lodged and detained in great quantities, and the narrow channel which swept round the bend was full of ice, piled one cake over another, thus forming a temporary barrier to the descending ice, which lodged, and formed a great, undulating raft, filling up the whole river, and extending almost to the Kentucky shore.

Eliza stood, for a moment, contemplating this unfavorable aspect of things, which she saw at once must prevent the usual ferry-boat from running, and then turned into a small public house on the bank, to make a few inquiries.

The hostess, who was busy in various fizzing and stewing operations over the fire, preparatory to the evening meal, stopped, with a fork in her hand, as Eliza's sweet and plaintive voice arrested her.

"What is it?" she said.

"Isn't there any ferry or boat, that takes people over to B——, now?" she said.

"No, indeed!" said the woman; "the boats has stopped running."

Eliza's look of dismay and disappointment struck the woman, and she said, inquiringly,—

"May be you're wanting to get over?—anybody sick? Ye seem mighty anxious?"

"I've got a child that's very dangerous," said Eliza. "I never heard of it till last night, and I've walked quite a piece to-day, in hopes to get to the ferry."

"Well, now, that's onlucky," said the woman, whose motherly sympathies were much aroused; "I'm re'lly consarned for ye. Solomon!" she called, from the window, towards a small back building. A man, in leather apron and very dirty hands, appeared at the door.

"I say, Sol," said the woman, "is that ar man going to tote them bar'ls over to-night?"

"He said he should try, if 'twas any way prudent," said the man.

"There's a man a piece down here, that's going over with some truck this evening, if he durs' to; he'll be in here to supper to-night, so you'd better set down and wait. That's a sweet little fellow," added the woman, offering him a cake.

But the child, wholly exhausted, cried with weariness.

"Poor fellow! he isn't used to walking, and I've hurried him on so," said Eliza.

"Well, take him into this room," said the woman, opening into a small bedroom, where stood a comfortable bed. Eliza laid the weary boy upon it, and held his hands in hers till he was fast asleep. For her there was no rest. As a fire in her bones, the thought of the pursuer urged her on; and she gazed with longing eyes on the sullen, surging waters that lay between her and liberty.

Here we must take our leave of her for the present, to follow the course of her pursuers.

6. In biblical times, Canaan was the part of Palestine between the Jordan River and the Mediterranean Sea: the "Promised Land."

Though Mrs. Shelby had promised that the dinner should be hurried on table, yet it was soon seen, as the thing has often been seen before, that it required more than one to make a bargain. So, although the order was fairly given out in Haley's hearing, and carried to Aunt Chloe by at least half a dozen juvenile messengers, that dignitary only gave certain very gruff snorts, and tosses of her head, and went on with every operation in an unusually leisurely and circumstantial manner.

For some singular reason, an impression seemed to reign among the servants generally that Missis would not be particularly disobliged by delay; and it was wonderful what a number of counter accidents occurred constantly, to retard the course of things. One luckless wight[7] contrived to upset the gravy; and then gravy had to be got up *de novo*, with due care and formality, Aunt Chloe watching and stirring with dogged precision, answering shortly, to all suggestions of haste, that she "warn't a going to have raw gravy on the table, to help nobody's catchings." One tumbled down with the water, and had to go to the spring for more; and another precipitated the butter into the path of events; and there was from time to time giggling news brought into the kitchen that "Mas'r Haley was mighty oneasy, and that he couldn't sit in his cheer no ways, but was a walkin' and stalkin' to the winders and through the porch."

"Sarves him right!" said Aunt Chloe, indignantly. "He'll get wus nor oneasy, one of these days, if he don't mend his ways. *His* master'll be sending for him, and then see how he'll look!"

"He'll go to torment, and no mistake," said little Jake.

"He desarves it!" said Aunt Chloe, grimly; "he's broke a many, many, many hearts,—I tell ye all!" she said, stopping, with a fork uplifted in her hands; "it's like what Mas'r George reads in Ravelations,—souls a callin' under the altar! and a callin' on the Lord for vengeance on sich!(8)—and by and by the Lord he'll hear 'em,—so he will!"

Aunt Chloe, who was much revered in the kitchen, was listened to with open mouth; and, the dinner being now fairly sent in, the whole kitchen was at leisure to gossip with her, and to listen to her remarks.

"Sich'll be burnt up forever, and no mistake; won't ther?" said Andy.

"I'd be glad to see it, I'll be boun'," said little Jake.

"Chil'en!" said a voice, that made them all start. It was Uncle Tom, who had come in, and stood listening to the conversation at the door.

"Chil'en!" he said, "I'm afeard you don't know what ye're sayin'. Forever is a *dre'ful* word, chil'en; it's awful to think on't. You oughtenter wish that ar to any human crittur."

"We wouldn't to anybody but the soul-drivers," said Andy; "nobody can help wishing it to them, they's so awful wicked."

"Don't natur herself kinder cry out on 'em?" said Aunt Chloe. "Don't dey tear der suckin' baby right off his mother's breast, and sell him, and der little children as is crying and holding on by her clothes,—don't dey pull 'em off and sells 'em? Don't dey tear wife and husband apart?" said Aunt Chloe, beginning to cry, "when it's jest takin' the very life on 'em?—and all the while does they feel one bit,—don't dey drink and smoke, and take it oncommon easy? Lor', if the devil don't get them, what's he good for?" And Aunt Chloe covered her face with her checked apron, and began to sob in good earnest.

"Pray for them that 'spitefully use you, the good book says," says Tom.

"Pray for 'em!" said Aunt Chloe; "Lor, it's too tough! I can't pray for 'em."

"It's natur, Chloe, and natur's strong," said Tom, "but the Lord's grace is stronger; besides, you oughter think what an awful state a poor crittur's soul's in that'll do them ar things,—you oughter thank God that you an't *like* him, Chloe. I'm sure I'd rather be sold, ten thousand times over, than to have all that ar poor crittur's got to answer for."

"So'd I, a heap," said Jake. "Lor, *shouldn't* we cotch it, Andy?"

Andy shrugged his shoulders, and gave an acquiescent whistle.

"I'm glad Mas'r didn't go off this morning, as he looked to," said Tom; "that ar hurt me

---

7. Archaic term for human being.   8. See Revelations 6:9–10.

more than sellin', it did. Mebbe it might have been natural for him, but 't would have come desp't hard on me, as has known him from a baby; but I've seen Mas'r, and I begin ter feel sort o' reconciled to the Lord's will now. Mas'r couldn't help hisself; he did right, but I'm feared things will be kinder goin' to rack, when I'm gone. Mas'r can't be spected to be a pryin' round everywhar, as I've done, a keepin' up all the ends. The boys all means well, but they's powerful car'less. That ar troubles me."

The bell here rang, and Tom was summoned to the parlor.

"Tom," said his master, kindly, "I want you to notice that I give this gentleman bonds to forfeit a thousand dollars if you are not on the spot when he wants you; he's going to-day to look after his other business, and you can have the day to yourself. Go anywhere you like, boy."

"Thank you, Mas'r," said Tom.

"And mind yourself," said the trader, "and don't come it over your master with any o' yer nigger tricks; for I'll take every cent out of him, if you an't thar. If he'd hear to me, he wouldn't trust any on ye,—slippery as eels!"

"Mas'r," said Tom,—and he stood very straight,—"I was jist eight years old when ole Missis put you into my arms, and you wasn't a year old. 'Thar,' says she, 'Tom, that's to be *your* young Mas'r; take good care on him,' says she. And now I jist ask you, Mas'r, have I ever broke word to you, or gone contrary to you, 'specially since I was a Christian?"

Mr. Shelby was fairly overcome, and the tears rose to his eyes.

"My good boy," said he, "the Lord knows you say but the truth; and if I was able to help it, all the world shouldn't buy you."

"And sure as I am a Christian woman," said Mrs. Shelby, "you shall be redeemed as soon as I can any way bring together means. Sir," she said to Haley, "take good account of whom you sell him to, and let me know."

"Lor, yes, for that matter," said the trader, "I may bring him up in a year, not much the wuss for wear, and trade him back."

"I'll trade with you then, and make it for your advantage," said Mrs. Shelby.

"Of course," said the trader, "all's equal with me; li'ves trade 'em up as down, so I does a good business. All I want is a livin', you know, ma'am; that's all any on us wants, I s'pose."

Mr. and Mrs. Shelby both felt annoyed and degraded by the familiar impudence of the trader, and yet both saw the absolute necessity of putting a constraint on their feelings. The more hopelessly sordid and insensible he appeared, the greater became Mrs. Shelby's dread of his succeeding in recapturing Eliza and her child, and of course the greater her motive for detaining him by every female artifice. She therefore graciously smiled, assented, chatted familiarly, and did all she could to make time pass imperceptibly.

At two o'clock Sam and Andy brought the horses up to the posts, apparently greatly refreshed and invigorated by the scamper of the morning.

Sam was there new oiled from dinner, with an abundance of zealous and ready officious-ness. As Haley approached, he was boasting, in flourishing style, to Andy, of the evident and eminent success of the operation, now that he had "farly come to it."

"Your master, I s'pose, don't keep no dogs," said Haley, thoughtfully, as he prepared to mount.

"Heaps on 'em," said Sam, triumphantly; "thar's Bruno,—he's a roarer! and, besides that, 'bout every nigger of us keeps a pup of some natur or uther."

"Poh!" said Haley,—and he said something else, too, with regard to the said dogs, at which Sam muttered,—

"I don't see no use cussin' on 'em, no way."

"But your master don't keep no dogs (I pretty much know he don't) for trackin' out niggers."

Sam knew exactly what he meant, but he kept on a look of earnest and desperate simplicity.

"Our dogs all smells round consid'able sharp. I spect they's the kind, though they han't never had no practice. They's *far* dogs, though, at most anything, if you'd get 'em started. Here, Bruno," he called, whistling to the lumbering Newfoundland, who came pitching tumultuously toward them.

"You go hang!" said Haley, getting up. "Come, tumble up now."

Sam tumbled up accordingly, dexterously contriving to tickle Andy as he did so, which occasioned Andy to split out into a laugh, greatly to Haley's indignation, who made a cut at him with his riding-whip.

"I's 'stonished at yer, Andy," said Sam, with awful gravity. "This yer's a seris bisness, Andy. Yer mustn't be makin' game. This yer an't no way to help Mas'r."

"I shall take the straight road to the river," said Haley, decidedly, after they had come to the boundaries of the estate. "I know the way of all of 'em,—they makes tracks for the underground."

"Sartin," said Sam, "dat's de idee. Mas'r Haley hits de thing right in de middle. Now, der's two roads to de river,—de dirt road and der pike,⁹—which Mas'r mean to take?"

Andy looked up innocently at Sam, surprised at hearing this new geographical fact, but instantly confirmed what he said by a vehement reiteration.

" 'Cause," said Sam, "I'd rather be 'clined to 'magine that Lizy'd take de dirt road, bein' it's the least travelled."

Haley, notwithstanding that he was a very old bird, and naturally inclined to be suspicious of chaff, was rather brought up by this view of the case.

"If yer warn't both on yer such cussed liars, now!" he said, contemplatively, as he pondered a moment.

The pensive, reflective tone in which this was spoken appeared to amuse Andy prodigiously, and he drew a little behind, and shook so as apparently to run a great risk of falling off his horse, while Sam's face was immovably composed into the most doleful gravity.

"Course," said Sam, "Mas'r can do as he'd ruther; go de straight road, if Mas'r thinks best,—it's all one to us. Now, when I study 'pon it, I think de straight road de best, *deridedly.*"

"She would naturally go a lonesome way," said Haley, thinking aloud, and not minding Sam's remark.

"Dar an't no sayin'," said Sam; "gals is pecular; they never does nothin' ye thinks they will; mose gen'lly the contrar. Gals is nat'lly made contrary; and so, if you thinks they've gone one road, it is sartin you'd better go t'other, and then you'll be sure to find 'em. Now, my private 'pinion is, Lizy took der dirt road; so I think we'd better take de straight one."

This profound generic view of the female sex did not seem to dispose Haley particularly to the straight road; and he announced decidedly that he should go the other, and asked Sam when they should come to it.

"A little piece ahead," said Sam, giving a wink to Andy with the eye which was on Andy's side of the head; and he added, gravely, "but I've studded on de matter, and I'm quite clar we ought not to go dat ar way. I nebber been over it no way. It's despit lonesome, and we might lose our way,—whar we'd come to, de Lord only knows."

"Nevertheless," said Haley, "I shall go that way."

"Now I think on't, I think I hearn 'em tell that dat ar road was all fenced up and down by der creek, and thar, an't it, Andy?"

Andy wasn't certain; he'd only "hearn tell" about that road, but never been over it. In short, he was strictly noncommittal.

Haley, accustomed to strike the balance of probabilities between lies of greater or lesser magnitude, thought that it lay in favor of the dirt road aforesaid. The mention of the thing he thought he perceived was involuntary on Sam's part at first, and his confused attempts to dissuade him he set down to a desperate lying on second thoughts, as being unwilling to implicate Eliza.

9. Turnpike; toll road.

When, therefore, Sam indicated the road, Haley plunged briskly into it, followed by Sam and Andy.

Now, the road, in fact, was an old one, that had formerly been a thoroughfare to the river, but abandoned for many years after the laying of the new pike. It was open for about an hour's ride, and after that it was cut across by various farms and fences. Sam knew this fact perfectly well,—indeed, the road had been so long closed up, that Andy had never heard of it. He therefore rode along with an air of dutiful submission, only groaning and vociferating occasionally that 'twas "desp't rough, and bad for Jerry's foot."

"Now, I jest give yer warning," said Haley, "I know yer; yer won't get me to turn off this yer road, with all yer fussin',—so you shet up!"

"Mas'r will go his own way!" said Sam, with rueful submission, at the same time winking most portentously to Andy, whose delight was now very near the explosive point.

Sam was in wonderful spirits,—professed to keep a very brisk lookout,—at one time exclaiming that he saw "a gal's bonnet" on the top of some distant eminence, or calling to Andy "if that thar wasn't 'Lizy' down in the hollow"; always making these exclamations in some rough or craggy part of the road, where the sudden quickening of speed was a special inconvenience to all parties concerned, and thus keeping Haley in a state of constant commotion.

After riding about an hour in this way, the whole party made a precipitate and tumultuous descent into a barnyard belonging to a large farming establishment. Not a soul was in sight, all the hands being employed in the fields; but, as the barn stood conspicuously and plainly square across the road, it was evident that their journey in that direction had reached a decided finale.

"Warn't dat ar what I told Mas'r?" said Sam, with an air of injured innocence. "How does strange gentleman spect to know more about a country dan de natives born and raised?"

"You rascal!" said Haley, "you knew all about this."

"Didn't I tell yer I *know'd*, and yer wouldn't believe me? I told Mas'r was all shet up, and fenced up, and I didn't spect we could get through,—Andy heard me."

It was all too true to be disputed, and the unlucky man had to pocket his wrath with the best grace he was able, and all three faced to the right about, and took up their line of march for the highway.

In consequence of all the various delays, it was about three quarters of an hour after Eliza had laid her child to sleep in the village tavern that the party came riding into the same place. Eliza was standing by the window, looking out in another direction, when Sam's quick eye caught a glimpse of her. Haley and Andy were two yards behind. At this crisis, Sam contrived to have his hat blown off, and uttered a loud and characteristic ejaculation, which startled her at once; she drew suddenly back; the whole train swept by the window, round to the front door.

A thousand lives seemed to be concentrated in that one moment to Eliza. Her room opened by a side door to the river. She caught her child, and sprang down the steps towards it. The trader caught a full glimpse of her, just as she was disappearing down the bank; and throwing himself from his horse, and calling loudly on Sam and Andy, he was after her like a hound after a deer. In that dizzy moment her feet to her scarce seemed to touch the ground, and a moment brought her to the water's edge. Right on behind they came; and, nerved with strength such as God gives only to the desperate, with one wild cry and flying leap, she vaulted sheer over the turbid current by the shore, on to the raft of ice beyond. It was a desperate leap,—impossible to anything but madness and despair; and Haley, Sam, and Andy instinctively cried out, and lifted up their hands, as she did it.

The huge green fragment of ice on which she alighted pitched and creaked as her weight came on it, but she stayed there not a moment. With wild cries and desperate energy she leaped to another and still another cake;—stumbling,—leaping,—slipping,—springing upwards again! Her shoes are gone,—her stockings cut from her feet,—while blood marked every step; but she saw nothing, felt nothing, till dimly, as in a dream, she saw the Ohio side, and a man helping her up the bank.

"Yer a brave gal, now, whoever ye ar!" said the man, with an oath.

Eliza recognized the voice and face of a man who owned a farm not far from her old home.

"O, Mr. Symmes!—save me,—do save me,—do hide me!" said Eliza.

"Why, what's this?" said the man. "Why, if 'tan't Shelby's gal!"

"My child!—this boy!—he'd sold him! There is his Mas'r," said she, pointing to the Kentucky shore. "O, Mr. Symmes, you've got a little boy!"

"So I have," said the man, as he roughly, but kindly, drew her up the steep bank. "Besides, you're a right brave gal. I like grit, wherever I see it."

When they had gained the top of the bank, the man paused. "I'd be glad to do something for ye," said he; "but then there's nowhar I could take ye. The best I can do is to tell ye to go *thar*," said he, pointing to a large white house which stood by itself, off the main street of the village. "Go thar; they're kind folks. Thar's no kind o' danger but they'll help you,—they're up to all that sort o' thing."

"The Lord bless you!" said Eliza, earnestly.

"No 'casion, no 'casion in the world," said the man. "What I've done's of no 'count."

"And, O, surely, sir, you won't tell any one!"

"Go to thunder, gal! What do you take a feller for? In course not," said the man. "Come, now, go along like a likely, sensible gal, as you are. You've arnt your liberty, and you shall have it, for all me."

The woman folded her child to her bosom, and walked firmly and swiftly away. The man stood and looked after her.

"Shelby, now, mebbe won't think this yer the most neighborly thing in the world; but what's a feller to do? If he catches one of my gals in the same fix, he's welcome to pay back. Somehow I never could see no kind o' crittur a strivin' and pantin', and trying to clar theirselves, with the dogs arter 'em, and go agin 'em. Besides, I don't see no kind of 'casion for me to be hunter and catcher for other folks, neither."

So spoke this poor, heathenish Kentuckian, who had not been instructed in his constitutional relations, and consequently was betrayed into acting in a sort of Christianized manner, which, if he had been better situated and more enlightened, he would not have been left to do.

Haley had stood a perfectly amazed spectator of the scene, till Eliza had disappeared up the bank, when he turned a blank, inquiring look on Sam and Andy.

"That ar was a tolable fair stroke of business," said Sam.

"The gal's got seven devils in her, I believe!" said Haley. "How like a wildcat she jumped!"

"Wal, now," said Sam, scratching his head, "I hope Mas'r'll scuse us tryin' dat ar road. Don't think I feel spry enough for dat ar, no way!" and Sam gave a hoarse chuckle.

"*You* laugh!" said the trader, with a growl.

"Lord bless you, Mas'r, I couldn't help it, now," said Sam, giving way to the long pent-up delight of his soul. "She looked so curi's, a leapin' and springin'—ice a crackin'—and only to hear her,—plump! ker chunk! ker splash! Spring! Lord! how she goes it!" and Sam and Andy laughed till the tears rolled down their cheeks.

"I'll make yer laugh t'other side yer mouths!" said the trader, laying about their heads with his riding-whip.

Both ducked, and ran shouting up the bank, and were on their horses before he was up.

"Good evening, Mas'r;" said Sam, with much gravity. "I berry much spect Missis be anxious 'bout Jerry. Mas'r Haley won't want us no longer. Missis wouldn't hear of our ridin' the critturs over Lizy's bridge to-night"; and, with a facetious poke into Andy's ribs, he started off, followed by the latter, at full speed,—their shouts of laughter coming faintly on the wind.

Chapter 8
Eliza's Escape

Eliza made her desperate retreat across the river just in the dusk of twilight. The gray mist of evening, rising slowly from the river, enveloped her as she disappeared up the bank, and the swollen current and floundering masses of ice presented a hopeless barrier between her and her pursuer. Haley therefore slowly and discontentedly returned to the little tavern, to ponder further what was to be done. The woman opened to him the door of a little parlor, covered with a rag carpet, where stood a table with a very shining black oil-cloth, sundry lank, high-backed wood chairs, with some plaster images in resplendent colors on the mantel-shelf, above a very dimly smoking grate; a long hard-wood settle extended its uneasy length by the chimney, and here Haley sat him down to meditate on the instability of human hopes and happiness in general.

"What did I want with the little cuss, now," he said to himself, "that I should have got myself treed like a coon, as I am, this yer way?" and Haley relieved himself by repeating over a not very select litany of imprecations on himself, which, though there was the best possible reason to consider them as true, we shall, as a matter of taste, omit.

He was startled by the loud and dissonant voice of a man who was apparently dismounting at the door. He hurried to the window.

"By the land! if this yer an't the nearest, now, to what I've heard folks call Providence," said Haley. "I do b'lieve that ar's Tom Loker."

Haley hastened out. Standing by the bar, in the corner of the room, was a brawny, muscular man, full six feet in height and broad in proportion. He was dressed in a coat of buffalo-skin, made with the hair outward, which gave him a shaggy and fierce appearance, perfectly in keeping with the whole air of his physiognomy.[1] In the head and face every organ and lineament expressive of brutal and unhesitating violence was in a state of the highest possible development. Indeed, could our readers fancy a bull-dog come unto man's estate, and walking about in a hat and coat, they would have no unapt idea of the general style and effect of his physique. He was accompanied by a travelling companion, in many respects an exact contrast to himself. He was short and slender, lithe and catlike in his motions, and had a peering, mousing expression about his keen black eyes, with which every feature of his face seemed sharpened into sympathy; his thin, long nose ran out as if it was eager to bore into the nature of things in general; his sleek, thin, black hair was stuck eagerly forward, and all his motions and evolutions expressed a dry, cautious acuteness. The great big man poured out a big tumbler half full of raw spirits, and gulped it down without a word. The little man stood tiptoe, and putting his head first to one side and then to the other, and snuffing considerably in the directions of the various bottles, ordered at last a mint julep, in a thin and quivering voice, and with an air of great circumspection. When poured out, he took it and looked at it with a sharp, complacent air, like a man who thinks he has done about the right thing, and hit the nail on the head, and proceeded to dispose of it in short and well-advised sips.

"Wal, now, who'd a thought this yer luck 'ad come to me? Why, Loker, how are ye?" said Haley, coming forward, and extending his hand to the big man.

"The devil!" was the civil reply. "What brought you here, Haley?"

The mousing man, who bore the name of Marks, instantly stopped his sipping, and, poking his head forward, looked shrewdly on the new acquaintance, as a cat sometimes looks at a moving dry leaf, or some other possible object of pursuit.

"I say, Tom, this yer's the luckiest thing in the world. I'm in a devil of a hobble, and you must help me out."

---

1. Facial features, regarded in the nineteenth century as revealing personality.

"Ugh? aw! like enough!" grunted his complacent acquaintance "A body may be pretty sure of that, when *you*'re glad to see 'em; something to be made off of 'em. What's the blow now?"

"You've got a friend here?" said Haley, looking doubtfully at Marks; "partner, perhaps?"

"Yes, I have. Here, Marks! here's that ar feller that I was in with in Natchez."

"Shall be pleased with his acquaintance," said Marks, thrusting out a long, thin hand, like a raven's claw. "Mr. Haley, I believe?"

"The same, sir," said Haley. "And now, gentlemen, seein' as we've met so happily, I think I'll stand up to a small matter of a treat in this here parlor. So now, old coon," said he to the man at the bar, "get us hot water, and sugar, and cigars, and plenty of the *real stuff*, and we'll have a blowout."

Behold, then, the candles lighted, the fire stimulated to the burning point in the grate, and our three worthies seated round a table, well spread with all the accessories to good-fellowship enumerated before.

Haley began a pathetic recital of his peculiar troubles. Loker shut up his mouth, and listened to him with gruff and surly attention. Marks, who was anxiously and with much fidgeting compounding a tumbler of punch to his own peculiar taste, occasionally looked up from his employment, and, poking his sharp nose and chin almost into Haley's face, gave the most earnest heed to the whole narrative. The conclusion of it appeared to amuse him extremely, for he shook his shoulders and sides in silence, and perked up his thin lips with an air of great internal enjoyment.

"So, then, ye'r fairly sewed up, ain't ye?" he said; "he! he! he! It's neatly done, too."

"This yer young-un business makes lots of trouble in the trade," said Haley, dolefully.

"If we could get a breed of gals that didn't care, now, for their young uns," said Marks; "tell ye I think 'twould be 'bout the greatest mod'rn improvement I knows on,"—and Marks patronized his joke by a quiet introductory sniggle.

"Jes so," said Haley; "I never couldn't see into it; young uns is heaps of trouble to 'em; one would think, now, they'd be glad to get clar on 'em; but they arn't. And the more trouble a young un is, and the more good for nothing, as a gen'l thing, the tighter they sticks to 'em."

"Wal, Mr. Haley," said Marks, "jest pass the hot water. Yes, sir; you say jest what I feel and allers have. Now, I bought a gal once, when I was in the trade,—a tight, likely wench she was, too, and quite considerable smart,—and she had a young un that was mis'able sickly; it had a crooked back, or something or other; and I jest gin't away to a man that thought he'd take his chance raising on't, being it didn't cost nothin';—never thought, yer know, of the gal's takin' on about it,—but, Lord, yer oughter seen how she went on. Why, re'lly she did seem to me to valley the child more 'cause 'twas sickly and cross, and plagued her; and she warn't making b'lieve, neither,—cried about it, she did, and lopped round, as if she'd lost every friend she had. It re'lly was droll to think on't. Lord, there an't no end to women's notions."

"Wal, jest so with me," said Haley. "Last summer, down on Red river, I got a gal traded off on me, with a likely lookin' child enough, and his eyes looked as bright as yourn; but, come to look, I found him stone blind. Fact,—he was stone blind. Wal, ye see, I thought there warn't no harm in my jest passing him along, and not sayin' nothin'; and I'd got him nicely swapped off for a keg o' whiskey; but come to get him away from the gal, she was jest like a tiger. So 'twas before we started, and I hadn't got my gang chained up; so what should she do but ups on a cotton-bale, like a cat, ketches a knife from one of the deck hands, and, I tell ye, she made all fly for a minnit, till she saw 'twarn't no use; and she jest turns round, and pitches head first, young un and all, into the river,—went down plump, and never ris."

"Bah!" said Tom Loker, who had listened to these stories with ill-repressed disgust,—"shif'less,[2] both on ye! *my* gals don't cut up no such shines, I tell ye!"

"Indeed! how do you help it?" said Marks, briskly.

"Help it? why, I buys a gal, and if she's got a young un to be sold, I jest walks up and puts

---

2. Shiftless; lacking capacities or abilities.

my fist to her face, and says 'Look here, now, if you give me one word out of your head, I'll smash yer face in. I won't hear one word,—not the beginning of a word.' I says to 'em, 'This yer, young un's mine, and not yourn, and you've no kind o' business with it. I'm going to sell it, first chance; mind, you don't cut up none o' yer shines about it, or I'll make ye wish ye'd never been born.' I tell ye, they sees it an't no play, when I gets hold. I makes 'em as whist as fishes; and if one of 'em begins and gives a yelp, why—" and Mr. Loker brought down his fist with a thump that fully explained the hiatus.

"That ar's what ye may call *emphasis,*" said Marks, poking Haley in the side, and going into another small giggle. "An't Tom peculiar? he! he! he! I say, Tom, I spect you make 'em *understand,* for all niggers' heads is woolly. They don't never have no doubt o' your meaning, Tom. If you an't the devil, Tom, you's his twin brother, I'll say that for ye!"

Tom received the compliment with becoming modesty, and began to look as affable as was consistent, as John Bunyan[3] says, "with his doggish nature."

Haley, who had been imbibing very freely of the staple of the evening, began to feel a sensible elevation and enlargement of his moral faculties,—a phenomenon not unusual with gentlemen of a serious and reflective turn, under similar circumstances.

"Wal, now, Tom," he said, "ye re'lly is too bad, as I al'ays have told ye; ye know, Tom, you and I used to talk over these yer matters down in Natchez, and I used to prove to ye that we made full as much, and was as well off for this yer world, by treatin' on 'em well, besides keepin' a better chance for comin' in the kingdom at last, when wust come to wust, and thar an't nothing else left to get, ye know."

"Boh!" said Tom, *"don't* I know?—don't make me too sick with any yer stuff,—my stomach is a leetle riled now"; and Tom drank half a glass of raw brandy.

"I say," said Haley, and leaning back in his chair and gesturing impressively, "I'll say this now, I al'ays meant to drive my trade so as to make money on't, *fust and foremost,* as much as any man; but, then, trade an't everything, and money an't everything, 'cause we's all got souls. I don't care, now, who hears me say it,—and I think a cussed sight on it,—so I may as well come out with it. I b'lieve in religion, and one of these days, when I've got matters tight and snug, I calculates to tend to my soul and them ar matters; and so what's the use of doin' any more wickedness than's re'lly necessary?—it don't seem to me it's 'tall prudent."

"Tend to yer soul!" repeated Tom, contemptuously; "take a bright lookout to find a soul in you,—save yourself any care on that score. If the devil sifts you through a hair sieve, he won't find one."

"Why, Tom, you're cross," said Haley; "why can't ye take it pleasant, now, when a feller's talking for your good?"

"Stop that ar jaw o' yourn, there," said Tom, gruffly. "I can stand most any talk o' yourn but your pious talk,—that kills me right up. After all, what's the odds between me and you? 'Tan't that you care one bit more, or have a bit more feelin', it's clean, sheer, dog meanness, wanting to cheat the devil and save your own skin; don't I see through it? And you 'gettin' religion,' as you call it, arter all, is too p'isin mean for any crittur;—run up a bill with the devil all your life, and then sneak out when pay-time comes! Boh!"

"Come, come, gentlemen, I say; this isn't business," said Marks. "There's different ways, you know, of looking at all subjects. Mr. Haley is a very nice[4] man, no doubt, and has his own conscience; and Tom, you have your ways, and very good ones, too, Tom; but quarrelling, you know, won't answer no kind of purpose. Let's go to business. Now, Mr. Haley, what is it?—you want us to undertake to catch this yer gal?"

"The gal's no matter of mine,—she's Shelby's; it's only the boy. I was a fool for buying the monkey!"

"You're generally a fool!" said Tom, gruffly.

---

3. Author of *Pilgrim's Progress* (1678–1684), an allegory popular among Protestant readers of Stowe's era.

4. Fastidious.

"Come, now, Loker, none of your huffs," said Marks, licking his lips; "you see, Mr. Haley's a puttin' us in a way of a good job, I reckon; just hold still,—these yer arrangements is my forte. This yer gal, Mr. Haley, who is she? what is she?"

"Wal! white and handsome,—well brought up. I'd a gin Shelby eight hundred or a thousand, and then made well on her."

"White and handsome,—well brought up!" said Marks, his sharp eyes, nose and mouth, all alive with enterprise. "Look here, now, Loker, a beautiful opening. We'll do a business here on our own account;—we does the catchin'; the boy, of course, goes to Mr. Haley,—we takes the gal to Orleans to speculate on. An't it beautiful?"

Tom, whose great heavy mouth had stood ajar during this communication, now suddenly snapped it together, as a big dog closes on a piece of meat, and seemed to be digesting the idea at his leisure.

"Ye see," said Marks to Haley, stirring his punch as he did so, "ye see, we has justices convenient at all p'ints alongshore, that does up any little jobs in our line quite reasonable. Tom, he does the knockin' down and that ar; and I come in all dressed up,—shining boots,—everything first chop, when the swearin' 's to be done. You oughter see, now," said Marks, in a glow of professional pride, "how I can tone it off. One day, I'm Mr. Twickem, from New Orleans; 'nother day, I'm just come from my plantation on Pearl river, where I works seven hundred niggers; then, again, I come out a distant relation of Henry Clay,[5] or some old cock in Kentuck. Talents is different, you know. Now, Tom's a roarer when there's any thumping or fighting to be done; but at lying he an't good, Tom an't,—ye see it don't come natural to him; but, Lord, if thar's a feller in the country that can swear to anything and everything, and put in all the circumstances and flourishes with a longer face, and carry't through better'n I can, why, I'd like to see him, that's all! I b'lieve my heart, I could get along and snake through, even if justices were more particular than they is. Sometimes I rather wish they was more particular; 'twould be a heap more relishin' if they was,—more fun, yer know."

Tom Loker, who, as we have made it appear, was a man of slow thoughts and movements, here interrupted Marks by bringing his heavy fist down on the table, so as to make all ring again. *"It'll do!"* he said.

"Lord bless ye, Tom, ye needn't break all the glasses!" said Marks; "save your fist for time o' need."

"But, gentlemen, an't I to come in for a share of the profits?" said Haley.

"An't it enough we catch the boy for ye?" said Loker. "What do ye want?"

"Wal," said Haley, "if I gives you the job, it's worth something,—say ten per cent on the profits, expenses paid."

"Now," said Loker, with a tremendous oath, and striking the table with his heavy fist, "don't I know *you*, Dan Haley? Don't you think to come it over me! Suppose Marks and I have taken up the catchin' trade, jest to 'commodate gentlemen like you, and get nothin' for ourselves?—Not by a long chalk! we'll have the gal out and out, and you keep quiet, or, ye see, we'll have both,—what's to hinder? Han't you show'd us the game? It's as free to us as you, I hope. If you or Shelby wants to chase us, look where the partridges was last year; if you find them or us, you're quite welcome."

"O, wal, certainly, jest let it go at that," said Haley, alarmed; "you catch the boy for the job;—you allers did trade *far* with me, Tom, and was up to yer word."

"Ye know that," said Tom; "I don't pretend none of your snivelling ways, but I won't lie in my 'counts with the devil himself. What I ses I'll do, I will do,—you know *that*, Dan Haley."

"Jes so, jes so,—I said so, Tom," said Haley; "and if you'd only promise to have the boy for me in a week, at any point you'll name, that's all I want."

"But it an't all I want, by a long jump," said Tom. "Ye don't think I did business with you,

5.   U.S. Secretary of State, 1825–1829; died in 1852.

down in Natchez, for nothing, Haley; I've learned to hold an eel, when I catch him. You've got to fork over fifty dollars, flat down, or this child don't start a peg. I know yer."

"Why, when you have a job in hand that may bring a clean profit of somewhere about a thousand or sixteen hundred, why, Tom, you're onreasonable," said Haley.

"Yes, and hasn't we business booked for five weeks to come—all we can do? And suppose we leaves all, and goes to bushwacking round arter yer young un, and finally doesn't catch the gal,—and gals allers is the devil *to* catch,—what's then? would you pay us a cent,—would you? I think I see you a doin' it,—ugh! No, no; flap down your fifty. If we get the job, and it pays, I'll hand it back; if we don't, it's for our trouble,—that's *far*, an't it, Marks?"

"Certainly, certainly," said Marks, with a conciliatory tone; "it's only a retaining fee, you see,—he! he! he!—we lawyers, you know. Wall, we must all keep good-natured,—keep easy, yer know. Tom'll have the boy for yer, anywhere ye'll name; won't ye, Tom?"

"If I find the young un, I'll bring him on to Cincinnati, and leave him at Granny Belcher's, on the landing," said Loker.

Marks had got from his pocket a greasy pocket-book, and taking a long paper from thence, he sat down, and fixing his keen black eyes on it, began mumbling over its contents: "Barnes,—Shelby County,—boy Jim, three hundred dollars for him, dead or alive.

"Edwards,—Dick and Lucy,—man and wife, six hundred dollars; wench Polly and two children,—six hundred for her or her head.

"I'm jest a runnin' over our business, to see if we can take up this yer handily. Loker," he said, after a pause, "we must set Adams and Springer on the track of these yer; they've been booked some time."

"They'll charge too much," said Tom.

"I'll manage that ar; they's young in the business, and must spect to work cheap," said Marks, as he continued to read. "There's three on 'em easy cases, 'cause all you've got to do is to shoot 'em, or swear they is shot; they couldn't, of course, charge much for that. Them other cases," he said, folding the paper, "will bear puttin' off a spell. So now let's come to the particulars. Now, Mr. Haley, you saw this yer gal when she landed?"

"To be sure,—plain as I see you."

"And a man helpin' on her up the bank?" said Loker.

"To be sure, I did."

"Most likely," said Marks, "she's took in somewhere; but where, 's a question. Tom, what do you say?"

"We must cross the river to-night, no mistake," said Tom.

"But there's no boat about," said Marks. "The ice is running awfully, Tom; an't it dangerous?"

"Don'no nothing 'bout that,—only it's got to be done," said Tom, decidedly.

"Dear me," said Marks, fidgeting, "it'll be—I say," he said, walking to the window, "it's dark as a wolf's mouth and, Tom—"

"The long and short is, you're scared, Marks; but I can't help that,—you've got to go. Suppose you want to lie by a day or two, till the gal's been carried on the underground line up to Sandusky or so, before you start."

"Oh, no; I an't a grain afraid," said Marks, "only—"

"Only what?" said Tom.

"Well, about the boat. Yer see there an't any boat."

"I heard the woman say there was one coming along this evening, and that a man was going to cross over in it. Neck or nothing, we must go with him," said Tom.

"I s'pose you've got good dogs," said Haley.

"First rate," said Marks. "But what's the use? you han't got nothin' o' hers to smell on."

"Yes, I have," said Haley, triumphantly. "Here's her shawl she left on the bed in her hurry; she left her bonnet, too."

"That ar's lucky," said Loker; "fork over."

"Though the dogs might damage the gal, if they come on her unawars," said Haley.

"That ar's a consideration," said Marks. "Our dogs tore a feller half to pieces, once, down in Mobile, 'fore we could get 'em off."

"Well, ye see, for this sort that's to be sold for their looks, that are won't answer, ye see," said Haley.

"I do see," said Marks. "Besides, if she's got took in, 'tan't no go, neither. Dogs is no 'count in these yer up states where these critturs gets carried; of course, ye can't get on their track. They only does down in plantations, where niggers, when they runs, has to do their own running, and don't get no help."

"Well," said Loker, who had just stepped out to the bar to make some inquiries, "they say the man's come with the boat; so, Marks—"

That worthy cast a rueful look at the comfortable quarters he was leaving, but slowly rose to obey. After exchanging a few words of further arrangement, Haley, with visible reluctance, handed over the fifty dollars to Tom, and the worthy trio separated for the night.

If any of our refined and Christian readers object to the society into which this scene introduces them, let us beg them to begin and conquer their prejudices in time. The catching business, we beg to remind them, is rising to the dignity of a lawful and patriotic profession. If all the broad land between the Mississippi and the Pacific becomes one great market for bodies and souls, and human property retains the locomotive tendencies of this nineteenth century, the trader and catcher may yet be among our aristocracy.

While this scene was going on at the tavern, Sam and Andy, in a state of high felicitation, pursued their way home.

Sam was in the highest possible feather, and expressed his exultation by all sorts of supernatural howls and ejaculations, by divers odd motions and contortions of his whole system. Sometimes he would sit backward, with his face to the horse's tail and sides, and then, with a whoop and a somerset, come right side up in his place again, and, drawing on a grave face, begin to lecture Andy in high-sounding tones for laughing and playing the fool. Anon,[6] slapping his sides with his arms, he would burst forth in peals of laughter, that made the old woods ring as they passed. With all these evolutions, he contrived to keep the horses up to the top of their speed, until, between ten and eleven, their heels resounded on the gravel at the end of the balcony. Mrs. Shelby flew to the railings.

"Is that you, Sam? Where are they?"

"Mas'r Haley's a-restin' at the tavern; he's dreful fatigued, Missis."

"And Eliza, Sam?"

"Wal, she's clar 'cross Jordan. As a body may say, in the land o' Canaan."

"Why, Sam, what *do* you mean?" said Mrs. Shelby, breathless, and almost faint, as the possible meaning of these words came over her.

"Wal, Missis, de Lord he presarves his own. Lizy's done gone over the river into 'Hio, as 'markably as if de Lord took her over in a charrit of fire and two hosses."

Sam's vein of piety was always uncommonly fervent in his mistress's presence; and he made great capital of scriptural figures and images.[7]

"Come up here, Sam," said Mr. Shelby, who had followed on to the veranda, "and tell your mistress what she wants. Come, come, Emily," said he, passing his arm around her, "you are cold and all in a shiver; you allow yourself to feel too much."

"Feel too much! Am not I a woman,—a mother? Are we not both responsible to God for this poor girl? My God! lay not this sin to our charge."

"What sin, Emily? You see yourself that we have only done what we were obliged to."

"There's an awful feeling of guilt about it, though," said Mrs. Shelby. "I can't reason it away."

6. Archaic for "immediately."   7. See Psalms 46:9.

"Here, Andy, you nigger, be alive!" called Sam, under the veranda; "take these yer hosses to der barn; don't ye hear Mas'r a callin'?" and Sam soon appeared, palm-leaf in hand, at the parlor door.

"Now, Sam, tell us distinctly how the matter was," said Mr. Shelby. "Where is Eliza, if you know?"

"Wal, Mas'r, I saw her, with my own eyes a crossin' on the floatin' ice. She crossed most 'markably; it wasn't no less nor a miracle; and I saw a man help her up the 'Hio side, and then she was lost in the dusk."

"Sam, I think this rather apocryphal,—this miracle. Crossing on floating ice isn't so easily done," said Mr. Shelby.

"Easy! couldn't nobody a done it, widout de Lord. Why, now," said Sam, " 'twas jist dis yer way. Mas'r Haley, and me, and Andy, we comes up to de little tavern by the river, and I rides a leetle ahead,—(I's so zealous to be a cotchin' Lizy, that I couldn't hold in, no way),—and when I comes by the tavern winder, sure enough there she was, right in plain sight, and dey diggin' on behind. Wal, I loses off my hat, and sings out nuff to raise the dead. Course Lizy she hars, and she dodges back, when Mas'r Haley he goes past the door; and then, I tell ye, she clared out de side door; she went down de river bank;—Mas'r Haley he seed her, and yelled out, and him, and me, and Andy, we took arter. Down she come to the river, and thar was the current running ten feet wide by the shore, and over t' other side ice a sawin' and a jigging up and down, kinder as 'twere a great island. We come right behind her, and I thought my soul he'd got her sure enough,—when she gin sich a screech as I never hearn, and thar she was, clar over t'other side the current, on the ice, and then on she went, a screeching and a jumpin'—the ice went crack! c'wallop! cracking! chung! and she a boundin' like a buck! Lord, the spring that ar gal's got in her an't common, I'm o' 'pinion."

Mrs. Shelby sat perfectly silent, pale with excitement, while Sam told his story.

"God be praised, she isn't dead!" she said; "but where is the poor child now?"

"De Lord will pervide," said Sam, rolling up his eyes piously. "As I've been a sayin', dis yer's a providence and no mistake, as Missis has allers been a instructin' on us. Thar's allers instruments ris up to do de Lord's will. Now, if 't hadn't been for me to-day, she'd a been took a dozen times. Warn't it I started off de hosses, dis yer mornin', and kept 'em chasin' till nigh dinner-time? And didn't I car Mas'r Haley nigh five miles out of de road, dis evening, or else he'd a come up with Lizy as easy as a dog arter a coon? These yer's all providences."

"They are a kind of providences that you'll have to be pretty sparing of, Master Sam. I allow no such practices with gentlemen on my place," said Mr. Shelby, with as much sternness as he could command, under the circumstances.

Now, there is no more use in making believe be angry with a negro than with a child; both instinctively see the true state of the case, through all attempts to affect the contrary; and Sam was in no wise disheartened by this rebuke, though he assumed an air of doleful gravity, and stood with the corners of his mouth lowered in most penitential style.

"Mas'r's quite right,—quite, it was ugly on me,—there's no disputin' that ar; and of course Mas'r and Misses wouldn't encourage no such works. I'm sensible of dat ar; but a poor nigger like me's 'mazin' tempted to act ugly sometimes, when fellers will cut up such shines as dat ar Mas'r Haley; he an't no gen'l'man no way; anybody's been raised as I've been can't help a seein' dat ar."

"Well, Sam," said Mrs. Shelby, "as you appear to have a proper sense of your errors, you may go now and tell Aunt Chloe she may get you some of that cold ham that was left of dinner to-day. You and Andy must be hungry."

"Missis is a heap too good for us," said Sam, making his bow with alacrity, and departing.

It will be perceived, as has been before intimated, that Master Sam had a native talent that might, undoubtedly, have raised him to eminence in political life—a talent of making capital out of everything that turned up, to be invested for his own especial praise and glory; and having done up his piety and humility, as he trusted, to the satisfaction of the parlor, he clapped his palm-leaf on his head, with a sort of rakish, free-and-easy air, and proceeded to the dominions of Aunt Chloe, with the intention of flourishing largely in the kitchen.

"I'll speechify these yer niggers," said Sam to himself, "now I've got a chance. Lord, I'll reel it off to make 'em stare!"

It must be observed that one of Sam's especial delights had been to ride in attendance on his master to all kinds of political gatherings, where, roosted on some rail fence, or perched aloft in some tree, he would sit watching the orators, with the greatest apparent gusto, and then, descending among the various brethren of his own color, assembled on the same errand, he would edify and delight them with the most ludicrous burlesques and imitations, all delivered with the most imperturbable earnestness and solemnity; and though the auditors immediately about him were generally of his own color, it not unfrequently happened that they were fringed pretty deeply with those of a fairer complexion, who listened, laughing and winking, to Sam's great self-congratulation. In fact, Sam considered oratory as his vocation, and never let slip an opportunity of magnifying his office.

Now, between Sam and Aunt Chloe there had existed, from ancient times, a sort of chronic feud, or rather a decided coolness; but, as Sam was meditating something in the provision department, as the necessary and obvious foundation of his operations, he determined, on the present occasion, to be eminently conciliatory; for he well knew that although "Missis' orders" would undoubtedly be followed to the letter, yet he should gain a considerable deal by enlisting the spirit also. He therefore appeared before Aunt Chloe with a touchingly subdued, resigned expression, like one who has suffered immeasurable hardships in behalf of a persecuted fellow-creature,—enlarged upon the fact that Missis had directed him to come to Aunt Chloe for whatever might be wanting to make up the balance in his solids and fluids,—and thus unequivocally acknowledged her right and supremacy in the cooking department, and all thereto pertaining.

The thing took accordingly. No poor, simple, virtuous body was ever cajoled by the attentions of an electioneering politician with more ease than Aunt Chloe was won over by Master Sam's suavities; and if he had been the prodigal son himself, he could not have been overwhelmed with more maternal bountifulness; and he soon found himself seated, happy and glorious, over a large tin pan, containing a sort of *olla podrida* of all that had appeared on the table for two or three days past. Savory morsels of ham, golden blocks of corn-cake, fragments of pie of every conceivable mathematical figure, chicken wings, gizzards, and drumsticks, all appeared in picturesque confusion; and Sam, as monarch of all he surveyed, sat with his palm-leaf cocked rejoicingly to one side, and patronizing Andy at his right hand.

The kitchen was full of all his compeers, who had hurried and crowded in, from the various cabins, to hear the termination of the day's exploits. Now was Sam's hour of glory. The story of the day was rehearsed with all kinds of ornament and varnishing which might be necessary to heighten its effect; for Sam, like some of our fashionable dilettanti, never allowed a story to lose any of its gilding by passing through his hands. Roars of laughter attended the narration, and were taken up and prolonged by all the smaller fry, who were lying, in any quantity, about on the floor, or perched in every corner. In the height of the uproar and laughter, Sam, however, preserved an immovable gravity, only from time to time rolling his eyes up, and giving his auditors divers inexpressibly droll glances, without departing from the sententious elevation of his oratory.

"Yer see, fellow-countrymen," said Sam, elevating a turkey's leg, with energy, "yer see, now, what dis yer chile's up ter for 'fendin' yer all,—yes, all on yer. For him as tries to get one o' our people, is as good as tryin' to get all; yer see the principle's de same,—dat ar's clar. And any one o' these yer drivers that comes smelling round arter any our people, why, he's got *me* in his way; *I'm* the feller he's got to set in with,—I'm the feller for yer all to come to, bredren,—I'll stand up for yer rights,—I'll 'fend 'em to the last breath!"

"Why, but, Sam, yer told me, only this mornin', that you'd help this yer Mas'r to cotch Lizy; seems to me yer talk don't hang together," said Andy.

"I tell you now, Andy," said Sam, with awful superiority, "don't yer be a talkin' 'bout what yer don't know nothin' on; boys like you, Andy, means well, but they can't be spected to collusitate the great principles of action."

Andy looked rebuked, particularly by the hard word collusitate, which most of the youngerly members of the company seemed to consider as a settler in the case, while Sam proceeded.

"Dat ar was *conscience*, Andy; when I thought of gwine arter Lizy, I railly spected Mas'r was sot dat way. When I found Missis was sot de contrar, dat ar was conscience *more yet*,—'cause fellers allers gets more by stickin' to Missis' side,—so yer see I's persistent either way, and sticks up to conscience, and holds on to principles. Yes, *principles*," said Sam, giving an enthusiastic toss to a chicken's neck,—"what's principles good for, if we isn't persistent, I wanter know? Thar, Andy, you may have dat ar bone,—'tan't picked quite clean."

Sam's audience hanging on his words with open mouth, he could not but proceed.

"Dis yer matter 'bout persistence, feller-niggers," said Sam, with the air of one entering into an abstruse subject, "dis yer 'sistency's a thing what an't seed into very clar, by most anybody. Now, yer see, when a feller stands up for a thing one day and night, de contrar de next, folks ses (and nat'rally enough dey ses), why he an't persistent—hand me dat ar bit o' corn-cake, Andy. But let's look inter it. I hope the gen'lmen and der fair sex will scuse my usin' an or'nary sort o' 'parison. Here! I'm a tryin' to get top o' der hay. Wal, I puts up my larder dis yer side; 'tan't no go;—den, 'cause I don't try dere no more, but puts my larder right de contrar side, an't I persistent? I'm persistent in wantin' to get up which ary side my larder is; don't you see, all on yer?"

"It's the only thing ye ever was persistent in, Lord knows!" muttered Aunt Chloe, who was getting rather restive; the merriment of the evening being to her somewhat after the Scripture comparison,—like "vinegar upon nitre."[8]

"Yes, indeed!" said Sam, rising, full of supper and glory, for a closing effort. "Yes, my feller-citizens and ladies of de other sex in general, I has principles,—I'm proud to 'oon 'em,—they's perquisite to dese yer times, and ter *all* times. I has principles, and I sticks to 'em like forty,—jest anything that I thinks is principle, I goes in to't;—I wouldn't mind if dey burnt me 'live,—I'd walk right up to de stake, I would, and say, here I comes to shed my last blood fur my principles, fur my country, fur der gen'l interests of s'ciety."

"Well," said Aunt Chloe, "one o' yer principles will have to be to get to bed some time to-night, and not be a keepin' everybody up till mornin'; now, every one of you young uns that don't want to be cracked, had better be scase,[9] mighty sudden."

"Niggers! all on ye," said Sam, waving his palm-leaf with benignity, "I give yer my blessin'; go to bed now, and be good boys."

And, with this pathetic benediction, the assembly dispersed.

Chapter 9
In which it Appears that a Senator is but a Man

The light of the cheerful fire shone on the rug and carpet of a cosey parlor, and glittered on the sides of the teacups and well-brightened teapot, as Senator Bird was drawing off his boots, preparatory to inserting his feet in a pair of new handsome slippers, which his wife had been working for him while away on his senatorial tour. Mrs. Bird, looking the very picture of delight, was superintending the arrangements of the table, ever and anon mingling admoni-

8. Nitre is saltpeter, used in making gunpowder.　　9. Scarce.

tory remarks to a number of frolicsome juveniles, who were effervescing in all those modes of untold gambol and mischief that have astonished mothers ever since the flood.

"Tom, let the door-knob alone,—there's a man! Mary! Mary! don't pull the cat's tail,—poor pussy! Jim, you mustn't climb on that table,—no, no!—You don't know, my dear, what a surprise it is to us all, to see you here to-night!" said she, at last, when she found a space to say something to her husband.

"Yes, yes, I thought I'd just make a run down, spend the night, and have a little comfort at home. I'm tired to death, and my head aches!"

Mrs. Bird cast a glance at a camphor-bottle, which stood in the half-open closet, and appeared to meditate an approach to it, but her husband interposed.

"No, no, Mary, no doctoring! a cup of your good hot tea, and some of our good home living, is what I want. It's a tiresome business, this legislating!"

And the senator smiled, as if he rather liked the idea of considering himself a sacrifice to his country.

"Well," said his wife, after the business of the tea-table was getting rather slack, "and what have they been doing in the Senate?"

Now, it was a very unusual thing for gentle little Mrs. Bird ever to trouble her head with what was going on in the house of the state, very wisely considering that she had enough to do to mind her own. Mr. Bird, therefore, opened his eyes in surprise, and said,—

"Not very much of importance."

"Well; but is it true that they have been passing a law forbidding people to give meat and drink to those poor colored folks that come along? I heard they were talking of some such law, but I didn't think any Christian legislature would pass it!"

"Why, Mary, you are getting to be a politician, all at once."

"No, nonsense! I wouldn't give a fig for all your politics, generally, but I think this is something downright cruel and unchristian. I hope, my dear, no such law has been passed."

"There has been a law passed forbidding people to help off the slaves that come over from Kentucky, my dear; so much of that thing has been done by these reckless Abolitionists, that our brethren in Kentucky are very strongly excited, and it seems necessary, and no more than Christian and kind, that something should be done by our state to quiet the excitement."

"And what is the law? It don't forbid us to shelter these poor creatures a night, does it, and to give 'em something comfortable to eat, and a few old clothes, and send them quietly about their business?"

"Why, yes, my dear; that would be aiding and abetting, you know."

Mrs. Bird was a timid, blushing little woman, of about four feet in height, and with mild blue eyes, and a peach-blow complexion, and the gentlest, sweetest voice in the world;—as for courage, a moderate-sized cock-turkey had been known to put her to rout at the very first gobble, and a stout house-dog, of moderate capacity, would bring her into subjection merely by a show of his teeth. Her husband and children were her entire world, and in these she ruled more by entreaty and persuasion than by command or argument. There was only one thing that was capable of arousing her, and that provocation came in on the side of her usually gentle and sympathetic nature;—anything in the shape of cruelty would throw her into a passion, which was the more alarming and inexplicable in proportion to the general softness of her nature. Generally the most indulgent and easy to be entreated of all mothers, still her boys had a very reverent remembrance of a most vehement chastisement she once bestowed on them, because she found them leagued with several graceless boys of the neighborhood, stoning a defenceless kitten.

"I'll tell you what," Master Bill used to say, "I was scared that time. Mother came at me so that I thought she was crazy, and I was whipped and tumbled off to bed, without any supper, before I could get over wondering what had come about; and after that, I heard mother crying outside the door, which made me feel worse than all the rest. I'll tell you what," he'd say, "we boys never stoned another kitten!"

On the present occasion, Mrs. Bird rose quickly, with very red cheeks, which quite improved her general appearance, and walked up to her husband, with quite a resolute air, and said, in a determined tone,—

"Now, John, I want to know if you think such a law as that is right and Christian?"

"You won't shoot me, now, Mary, if I say I do!"

"I never could have thought it of you, John; you didn't vote for it?"

"Even so, my fair politician."

"You ought to be ashamed, John! Poor, homeless, houseless creatures! It's a shameful, wicked, abominable law, and I'll break it, for one, the first time I get a chance; and I hope I *shall* have a chance, I do! Things have got to a pretty pass, if a woman can't give a warm supper and a bed to poor, starving creatures, just because they are slaves, and have been abused and oppressed all their lives, poor things!"

"But, Mary, just listen to me. Your feelings are all quite right, dear, and interesting, and I love you for them; but, then, dear we mustn't suffer our feelings to run away with our judgment; you must consider it's not a matter of private feeling,—there are great public interests involved,—there is such a state of public agitation rising, that we must put aside our private feelings."

"Now, John, I don't know anything about politics, but I can read my Bible; and there I see that I must feed the hungry, clothe the naked, and comfort the desolate; and that Bible I mean to follow."

"But in cases where your doing so would involve a great public evil—"

"Obeying God never brings on public evils. I know it can't. It's always safest, all round, to *do as he* bids us."

"Now, listen to me, Mary, and I can state to you a very clear argument, to show—"

"O, nonsense, John! you can talk all night, but you wouldn't do it. I put it to you, John,—would *you*, now, turn away a poor, shivering, hungry creature from your door, because he was a runaway? *Would* you now?"

Now, if the truth must be told, our senator had the misfortune to be a man who had a particularly humane and accessible nature, and turning away anybody that was in trouble never had been his forte; and what was worse for him in this particular pinch of the argument was, that his wife knew it, and, of course, was making an assault on rather an indefensible point. So he had recourse to the usual means of gaining time for such cases made and provided; he said "ahem," and coughed several times, took out his pocket-handkerchief, and began to wipe his glasses. Mrs. Bird, seeing the defenceless condition of the enemy's territory, had no more conscience than to push her advantage.

"I should like to see you doing that, John,—I really should! Turning a woman out of doors in a snow-storm, for instance; or, may be you'd take her up and put her in jail, wouldn't you? You would make a great hand at that!"

"Of course, it would be a very painful duty," began Mr. Bird, in a moderate tone.

"Duty, John! don't use that word! You know it isn't a duty,—it can't be a duty! If folks want to keep their slaves from running away, let 'em treat 'em well,—that's my doctrine. If I had slaves (as I hope I never shall have), I'd risk their wanting to run away from me, or you either, John. I tell you folks don't run away when they are happy; and when they do run, poor creatures! they suffer enough with cold and hunger and fear, without everybody's turning against them; and, law or no law, I never will, so help me God!"

"Mary! Mary! My dear, let me reason with you."

"I hate reasoning, John,—especially reasoning on such subjects. There's a way you political folks have of coming round and round a plain right thing; and you don't believe in it yourselves, when it comes to practice. I know *you* well enough, John. You don't believe it's right any more than I do; and you wouldn't do it any sooner than I."

At this critical juncture, old Cudjoe, the black man-of-all-work, put his head in at the door, and wished "Missis would come into the kitchen"; and our senator, tolerably relieved, looked after his little wife with a whimsical mixture of amusement and vexation, and, seating himself in the armchair, began to read the papers.

After a moment, his wife's voice was heard at the door, in a quick, earnest tone,—"John! John! I do wish you'd come here, a moment."

He laid down his paper, and went into the kitchen, and startled, quite amazed at the sight that presented itself:—A young and slender woman, with garments torn and frozen, with one shoe gone, and the stocking torn away from the cut and bleeding foot, was laid back in a deadly swoon upon two chairs. There was the impress of the despised race on her face, yet none could help feeling its mournful and pathetic beauty, while its stony sharpness, its cold, fixed, deathly aspect, struck a solemn chill over him. He drew his breath short, and stood in silence. His wife, and their only colored domestic, old Aunt Dinah, were busily engaged in restorative measures; while old Cudjoe had got the boy on his knee, and was busy pulling off his shoes and stockings, and chafing his little cold feet.

"Sure, now, if she an't a sight to behold!" said old Dinah, compassionately; " 'pears like 'twas the heat that made her faint. She was tol'able peart when she cum in, and asked if she couldn't warm herself here a spell; and I was just a askin' her where she cum from, and she fainted right down. Never done much hard work, guess, by the looks of her hands."

"Poor creature!" said Mrs. Bird, compassionately, as the woman slowly unclosed her large, dark eyes, and looked vacantly at her. Suddenly an expression of agony crossed her face, and she sprang up, saying, "O, my Harry! Have they got him?"

The boy, at this, jumped from Cudjoe's knee, and, running to her side, put up his arms. "O, he's here; he's here!" she exclaimed.

"O ma'am!" said she, wildly, to Mrs. Bird, "do protect us! don't let them get him!"

"Nobody shall hurt you here, poor woman," said Mrs. Bird, encouragingly. "You are safe; don't be afraid."

"God bless you" said the woman, covering her face and sobbing; while the little boy, seeing her crying, tried to get into her lap.

With many gentle and womanly offices, which none knew better how to render than Mrs. Bird, the poor woman was, in time, rendered more calm. A temporary bed was provided for her on the settle, near the fire; and, after a short time, she fell into a heavy slumber, with the child, who seemed no less weary, soundly sleeping on her arm; for the mother resisted, with nervous anxiety, the kindest attempts to take him from her; and, even in sleep, her arm encircled him with an unrelaxing clasp, as if she could not even then be beguiled of her vigilant hold.

Mr. and Mrs. Bird had gone back to the parlor, where strange as it may appear, no reference was made, on either side, to the preceding conversation; but Mrs. Bird busied herself with her knitting-work, and Mr. Bird pretended to be reading the paper.

"I wonder who and what she is!" said Mr. Bird, at last, as he laid it down.

"When she wakes up and feels a little rested, we will see," said Mrs. Bird.

"I say, wife!" said Mr. Bird, after musing in silence over his newspaper.

"Well, dear!"

"She couldn't wear one of your gowns, could she, by any letting down, or such matter? She seems to be rather larger than you are."

A quite perceptible smile glimmered on Mrs. Bird's face, as she answered, "We'll see."

Another pause, and Mr. Bird again broke out,—

"I say, wife!"

"Well! what now?"

"Why, there's that old bombazine cloak, that you keep on purpose to put over me when I take my afternoon's nap; you might as well give her that,—she needs clothes."

At this instant, Dinah looked in to say that the woman was awake, and wanted to see Missis.

Mr. and Mrs. Bird went into the kitchen, followed by the two eldest boys, the smaller fry having, by this time, been safely disposed of in bed.

The woman was now sitting up on the settle, by the fire. She was looking steadily into the blaze, with a calm, heartbroken expression, very different from her former agitated wildness.

"Did you want me?" said Mrs. Bird, in gentle tones. "I hope you feel better now, poor woman!"

A long-drawn, shivering sigh was the only answer; but she lifted her dark eyes, and fixed them on her with such a forlorn and imploring expression, that the tears came into the little woman's eyes.

"You needn't be afraid of anything; we are friends here, poor woman! Tell me where you came from, and what you want," said she.

"I came from Kentucky," said the woman.

"When?" said Mr. Bird, taking up the interrogatory.

"To-night."

"How did you come?"

"I crossed on the ice."

"Crossed on the ice!" said every one present.

"Yes," said the woman, slowly, "I did. God helping me, I crossed on the ice; for they were behind me,—right behind,—and there was no other way!"

"Law, Missis," said Cudjoe, "the ice is all in broken-up blocks, a swinging and a teetering up and down in the water."

"I know it was,—I know it!" said she, wildly; "but I did it! I wouldn't have thought I could,—I didn't think I should get over, but I didn't care! I could but die, if I didn't. The Lord helped me; nobody knows how much the Lord can help 'em, till they try," said the woman, with a flashing eye.

"Were you a slave?" said Mr. Bird.

"Yes, sir; I belonged to a man in Kentucky."

"Was he unkind to you?"

"No, sir; he was a good master."

"And was your mistress unkind to you?"

"No, sir,—no! my mistress was always good to me."

"What could induce you to leave a good home, then, and run away, and go through such dangers?"

The woman looked up at Mrs. Bird with a keen, scrutinizing glance, and it did not escape her that she was dressed in deep mourning.

"Ma'am," she said, suddenly, "have you ever lost a child?"

The question was unexpected, and it was a thrust on a new wound; for it was only a month since a darling child of the family had been laid in the grave.

Mr. Bird turned around and walked to the window, and Mrs. Bird burst into tears; but, recovering her voice, she said,—

"Why do you ask that? I have lost a little one."

"Then you will feel for me. I have lost two, one after another,—left 'em buried there when I came away; and I had only this one left. I never slept a night without him; he was all I had. He was my comfort and pride, day and night; and, ma'am, they were going to take him away from me,—to *sell* him,—sell him down south, ma'am, to go all alone,—a baby that had never been away from his mother in his life! I couldn't stand it, ma'am. I knew I never should be good for anything, if they did; and when I knew the papers were signed, and he was sold, I took him and came off in the night; and they chased me,—the man that bought him, and some of Mas'r's folk,—and they were coming down right behind me, and I heard 'em. I jumped right on to the ice; and how I got across, I don't know,—but, first I knew, a man was helping me up the bank."

The woman did not sob nor weep. She had gone to a place where tears are dry; but every one around her was, in some way characteristic of themselves, showing signs of hearty sympathy.

The two little boys, after a desperate rummaging in their pockets, in search of those pocket-handkerchiefs which mothers know are never to be found there, had thrown themselves disconsolately into the skirts of their mother's gown, where they were sobbing, and wiping their eyes and noses, to their hearts' content;—Mrs. Bird had her face fairly hidden in her pocket-handkerchief; and old Dinah, with tears streaming down her black, honest face, was ejaculating, "Lord have mercy on us!" with all the fervor of a camp-meeting;—while old Cudjoe, rubbing his eyes very hard with his cuffs, and making a most uncommon variety of wry faces, occasionally responded in the same key, with great fervor. Our senator was a statesman, and of course could not be expected to cry, like other mortals; and so he turned his back to the company, and looked out of the window, and seemed particularly busy in clearing his throat and wiping his spectacle-glasses, occasionally blowing his nose in a manner that was calculated to excite suspicion, had any one been in a state to observe critically.

"How came you to tell me you had a kind master?" he suddenly exclaimed, gulping down very resolutely some kind of rising in his throat, and turning suddenly round upon the woman.

"Because he *was* a kind master; I'll say that of him, any way;—and my mistress was kind; but they couldn't help themselves. They were owing money; and there was some way, I can't tell how, that a man had a hold on them, and they were obliged to give him his will. I listened, and heard him telling mistress that, and she begging and pleading for me,—and he told her he couldn't help himself, and that the papers were all drawn;—and then it was I took him and left my home, and came away. I knew 'twas no use of my trying to live, if they did it; for 't 'pears like this child is all I have."

"Have you no husband?"

"Yes, but he belongs to another man. His master is real hard to him, and won't let him come to see me, hardly ever; and he's grown harder and harder upon us, and he threatens to sell him down south;—it's like I'll never see *him* again!"

The quiet tone in which the woman pronounced these words might have led a superficial observer to think that she was entirely apathetic; but there was a calm, settled depth of anguish in her large, dark eye, that spoke of something far otherwise.

"And where do you mean to go, my poor woman?" said Mrs. Bird.

"To Canada, if I only knew where that was. Is it very far off, is Canada?" said she, looking up, with a simple, confiding air, to Mrs. Bird's face.

"Poor thing!" said Mrs. Bird, involuntarily.

"Is't a very great way off, think?" said the woman, earnestly.

"Much further than you think, poor child!" said Mrs. Bird; "but we will try to think what can be done for you. Here, Dinah, make her up a bed in your own room, close by the kitchen, and I'll think what to do for her in the morning. Meanwhile, never fear, poor woman; put your trust in God; he will protect you."

Mrs. Bird and her husband re-entered the parlor. She sat down in her little rocking-chair before the fire, swaying thoughtfully to and fro. Mr. Bird strode up and down the room, grumbling to himself. "Pish! pshaw! confounded awkward business!" At length, striding up to his wife, he said,—

"I say, wife, she'll have to get away from here, this very night. That fellow will be down on the scent bright and early to-morrow morning; if 'twas only the woman, she could lie quiet till it was over; but that little chap can't be kept still by a troop of horse and foot, I'll warrant me; he'll bring it all out, popping his head out of some window or door. A pretty kettle of fish it would be for me, too, to be caught with them both here, just now! No; they'll have to be got off to-night."

"To-night! How is it possible?—where to?"

"Well, I know pretty well where to," said the senator, beginning to put on his boots, with a reflective air; and, stopping when his leg was half in, he embraced his knee with both hands, and seemed to go off in deep meditation.

"It's a confounded awkward, ugly business," said he, at last, beginning to tug at his boot-straps again, "and that's a fact!" After one boot was fairly on, the senator sat with the other in his hand, profoundly studying the figure of the carpet. "It will have to be done, though, for aught I see,—hang it all!" and he drew the other boot anxiously on, and looked out of the window.

Now, little Mrs. Bird was a discreet woman,—a woman who never in her life said, "I told you so!" and, on the present occasion, though pretty well aware of the shape her husband's meditations were taking, she very prudently forbode to meddle with them, only sat very quietly in her chair, and looked quite ready to hear her liege lord's intentions, when he should think proper to utter them.

"You see," he said, "there's my old client, Van Trompe, has come over from Kentucky, and set all his slaves free; and he has bought a place seven miles up the creek, here, back in the woods, where nobody goes, unless they go on purpose; and it's a place that isn't found in a hurry. There she'd be safe enough; but the plague of the thing is, nobody could drive a carriage there to-night, but *me.*"

"Why not? Cudjoe is an excellent driver."

"Ay, ay, but here it is. The creek has to be crossed twice; and the second crossing is quite dangerous, unless one knows it as I do. I have crossed it a hundred times on horseback, and know exactly the turns to take. And so, you see, there's no help for it. Cudjoe must put in the horses, as quietly as may be, about twelve o'clock, and I'll take her over; and then, to give color to the matter, he must carry me on to the next tavern, to take the stage for Columbus, that comes by about three or four, and so it will look as if I had had the carriage only for that. I shall get into business bright and early in the morning. But I'm thinking I shall feel rather cheap there, after all that's been said and done; but, hang it, I can't help it!"

"Your heart is better than your head, in this case, John," said the wife, laying her little white hand on his. "Could I ever have loved you, had I not known you better than you know yourself?" And the little woman looked so handsome, with the tears sparkling in her eyes, that the senator thought he must be a decidedly clever fellow, to get such a pretty creature into such a passionate admiration of him; and so, what could he do but walk off soberly, to see about the carriage. At the door, however, he stopped a moment, and then coming back, he said, with some hesitation,—

"Mary, I don't know how you'd feel about it, but there's that drawer full of things—of—of—poor little Henry's." So saying, he turned quickly on his heel, and shut the door after him.

His wife opened the little bedroom door adjoining her room, and, taking the candle, set it down on the top of a bureau there; then from a small recess she took a key, and put it thoughtfully in the lock of a drawer, and made a sudden pause, while two boys, who, boy-like, had followed close on her heels, stood looking, with silent, significant glances, at their mother. And O, mother that reads this, has there never been in your house a drawer, or a closet, the opening of which has been to you like the opening again of a little grave? Ah! happy mother that you are, if it has not been so.

Mrs. Bird slowly opened the drawer. There were little coats of many a form and pattern, piles of aprons, and rows of small stockings; and even a pair of little shoes, worn and rubbed at the toes, were peeping from the folds of a paper. There was a toy horse and wagon, a top, a ball,—memorials gathered with many a tear and many a heart-break! She sat down by the drawer, and, leaning her head on her hands over it, wept till the tears fell through her fingers into the drawer; then suddenly raising her head, she began, with nervous haste, selecting the plainest and most substantial articles, and gathering them into a bundle.

"Mamma," said one of the boys, gently touching her arm, "are you going to give away *those* things?"

"My dear boys," she said, softly and earnestly, "if our dear, loving little Henry looks down from heaven, he would be glad to have us do this. I could not find it in my heart to give them away to any common person,—to anybody that was happy; but I give them to a mother more heart-broken and sorrowful than I am; and I hope God will send his blessings with them!"

There are in this world blessed souls, whose sorrows all spring up into joys for others; whose earthly hopes, laid in the grave with many tears, are the seed from which spring healing flowers and balm for the desolate and the distressed. Among such was the delicate woman who sits there by the lamp, dropping slow tears, while she prepares the memorials of her own lost one for the outcast wanderer.

After a while, Mrs. Bird opened a wardrobe, and, taking from thence a plain, serviceable dress or two, she sat down busily to her work-table, and, with needle, scissors, and thimble, at hand, quietly commenced the "letting down" process[1] which her husband had recommended, and continued busily at it till the old clock in the corner struck twelve, and she heard the low rattling of wheels at the door.

"Mary," said her husband, coming in, with his overcoat in his hand, "you must wake her up now; we must be off."

Mrs. Bird hastily deposited the various articles she had collected in a small plain trunk, and locking it, desired her husband to see it in the carriage, and then proceeded to call the woman. Soon, arrayed in a cloak, bonnet, and shawl, that had belonged to her benefactress, she appeared at the door with her child in her arms. Mr. Bird hurried her into the carriage, and Mrs. Bird pressed on after her to the carriage steps. Eliza leaned out of the carriage, and put out her hand,—a hand as soft and beautiful as was given in return. She fixed her large, dark eyes, full of earnest meaning, on Mrs. Bird's face, and seemed going to speak. Her lips moved,—she tried once or twice, but there was no sound,—and pointing upward, with a look never to be forgotten, she fell back in the seat, and covered her face. The door was shut, and the carriage drove on.

What a situation, now, for a patriotic senator, that had been all the week before spurring up the legislature of his native state to pass more stringent resolutions against escaping fugitives, their harborers and abettors!

Our good senator in his native state had not been exceeded by any of his brethren at Washington, in the sort of eloquence which has won for them immortal renown! How sublimely he had sat with his hands in his pockets, and scouted all sentimental weakness of those who would put the welfare of a few miserable fugitives before great state interests!

He was as bold as a lion about it, and "mightily convinced" not only himself, but everybody that heard him;—but then his idea of a fugitive was only an idea of the letters that spell the word,—or, at the most, the image of a little newspaper picture of a man with a stick and bundle, with "Ran away from the subscriber" under it. The magic of the real presence of distress,—the imploring human eye, the frail, trembling human hand, the despairing appeal of helpless agony,—these he had never tried. He had never thought that a fugitive might be a hapless mother, a defenceless child,—like that one which was now wearing his lost boy's little well-known cap; and so, as our poor senator was not stone or steel,—as he was a man, and a downright noble-hearted one, too,—he was, as everybody must see, in a sad case for his patriotism. And you need not exult over him, good brother of the Southern States; for we have some inklings that many of you, under similar circumstances, would not do much better. We have reason to know, in Kentucky, as in Mississippi, are noble and generous hearts, to whom never was tale of suffering told in vain. Ah, good brother! is it fair for you to expect of us services which your own brave, honorable heart would not allow you to render, were you in our place?

Be that as it may, if our good senator was a political sinner, he was in a fair way to expiate it by his night's penance. There had been a long continuous period of rainy weather, and the soft, rich earth of Ohio, as every one knows, is admirably suited to the manufacture of mud,—and the road was an Ohio railroad of the good old times.

1. Taking out a hem to lengthen a garment.

"And pray, what sort of a road may that be?" says some eastern traveller, who has been accustomed to connect no ideas with a railroad but those of smoothness or speed.

Know, then, innocent eastern friend, that in benighted regions of the west, where the mud is of unfathomable and sublime depth, roads are made of round rough logs, arranged transversely side by side, and coated over in their pristine freshness with earth, turf, and whatsoever may come to hand, and then the rejoicing native calleth it a road, and straightway essayeth to ride thereupon. In process of time, the rains wash off all the turf and grass aforesaid, move the logs hither and thither, in picturesque positions, up, and down, and crosswise, with divers chasms and ruts of black mud intervening.

Over such a road as this our senator went stumbling along, making moral reflections as continuously as under the circumstances could be expected,—the carriage proceeding along much as follows,—bump! bump! bump! slush! down in the mud!—the senator, woman, and child reversing their positions so suddenly as to come, without any very accurate adjustment, against the windows of the down-hill side. Carriage sticks fast, while Cudjoe on the outside is heard making a great muster among the horses. After various ineffectual pullings and twitchings, just as the senator is losing all patience, the carriage suddenly rights itself with a bounce,—two front wheels go down into another abyss, and senator, woman, and child all tumble promiscuously on to the front seat,—senator's hat is jammed over his eyes and nose quite unceremoniously, and he considers himself fairly extinguished;—child cries, and Cudjoe on the outside delivers animated addresses to the horses, who are kicking, and floundering, and straining, under repeated cracks of the whip. Carriage springs up, with another bounce,—down go the hind wheels,—senator, woman, and child fly over on to the back seat, his elbows encountering her bonnet, and both her feet being jammed into his hat, which flies off in the concussion. After a few moments the "slough" is passed, and the horses stop, panting;—the senator finds his hat, the woman straightens her bonnet and hushes her child, and they brace themselves firmly for what is yet to come.

For a while only the continuous bump! bump! intermingled, just by way of variety, with divers side plunges and compound shakes; and they begin to flatter themselves that they are not so badly off, after all. At last, with a square plunge, which puts all on to their feet and then down into their seats with incredible quickness, the carriage stops,—and, after much outside commotion, Cudjoe appears at the door.

"Please, sir, it's powerful bad spot, this yer. I don't know how we's to get clar out. I'm a thinkin' we'll have to be a gettin' rails."

The senator despairingly steps out, picking gingerly for some firm foothold; down goes one foot an immeasurable depth,—he tries to pull it up, loses his balance, and tumbles over into the mud, and is fished out, in a very despairing condition, by Cudjoe.

But we forbear, out of sympathy to our readers' bones. Western travellers, who have beguiled the midnight hour in the interesting process of pulling down rail fences, to pry their carriages out of mud-holes, will have a respectful and mournful sympathy with our unfortunate hero. We beg them to drop a silent tear, and pass on.

It was full late in the night when the carriage emerged, dripping and bespattered, out of the creek, and stood at the door of a large farm-house.

It took no inconsiderable perseverance to arouse the inmates; but at last the respectable proprietor appeared, and undid the door. He was a great, tall, bristling Orson of a fellow, full six feet and some inches in his stockings, and arrayed in a red flannel hunting-shirt. A very heavy *mat* of sandy hair, in a decidedly tousled condition, and a beard of some days' growth, gave the worthy man an appearance, to say the least, not particularly prepossessing. He stood for a few minutes holding the candle aloft, and blinking on our travellers with a dismal and mystified expression that was truly ludicrous. It cost some effort of our senator to induce him to comprehend the case fully; and while he is doing his best at that, we shall give him a little introduction to our readers.

Honest old John Van Trompe was once quite a considerable land-holder and slave-owner in the State of Kentucky. Having "nothing of the bear about him but the skin," and being gifted by nature with a great, honest, just heart, quite equal to his gigantic frame, he had been for some years witnessing with repressed uneasiness the workings of a system equally bad for oppressor and oppressed. At last, one day, John's great heart had swelled altogether too big to wear his bonds any longer; so he just took his pocket-book out of his desk, and went over into Ohio, and bought a quarter of a township of good, rich land, made out free papers for all his people,—men, women, and children,—packed them up in wagons, and sent them off to settle down; and then honest John turned his face up the creek, and sat quietly down on a snug, retired farm, to enjoy his conscience and his reflections.

"Are you the man that will shelter a poor woman and child from slave-catchers?" said the senator, explicitly.

"I rather think I am," said honest John, with some considerable emphasis.

"I thought so," said the senator.

"If there's anybody comes," said the good man, stretching his tall, muscular form upward, "why here I'm ready for him; and I've got seven sons, each six foot high, and they'll be ready for 'em. Give our respects to 'em," said John; "tell 'em it's no matter how soon they call,—make no kinder difference to us," said John, running his fingers through the shock of hair that thatched his head, and bursting out into a great laugh.

Weary, jaded, and spiritless, Eliza dragged herself up to the door, with her child lying in a heavy sleep on her arm. The rough man held the candle to her face, and uttering a kind of compassionate grunt, opened the door of a small bedroom adjoining to the large kitchen where they were standing, and motioned her to go in. He took down a candle, and lighting it, set it upon the table, and then addressed himself to Eliza.

"Now, I say, gal, you needn't be a bit afeard, let who will come here. I'm up to all that sort o' thing," said he, pointing to two or three goodly rifles over the mantel-piece; "and most people that know me know that 'twouldn't be healthy to try to get anybody out o' my house when I'm agin it. So *now* you jist go to sleep now, as quiet as if yer mother was a rockin' ye," said he, as he shut the door.

"Why, this is an uncommon handsome un," he said to the senator. "Ah, well; handsome uns has the greatest cause to run, sometimes, if they has any kind o' feelin', such as decent women should. I know all about that."

The senator, in a few words, briefly explained Eliza's history.

"Oh! ou! aw! now, I want to know?" said the good man, pitifully; "sho! now sho! That's natur now, poor crittur! hunted down now like a deer,—hunted down, jest for havin' natural feelin's, and doin' what no kind o' mother could help a doin'! I tell ye what, these yer things make me come the nighest to swearin', now, o' most anything," said honest John, as he wiped his eyes with the back of a great, freckled, yellow hand. "I tell yer what, stranger, it was years and years before I'd jine the church, 'cause the ministers round in our parts used to preach that the Bible went in for these ere cuttings up,—and I couldn't be up to 'em with their Greek and Hebrew, and so I took up agin 'em, Bible and all. I never jined the church till I found a minister that was up to 'em all in Greek and all that, and he said right the contrary; and then I took right hold, and jined the church,—I did now, fact," said John, who had been all this time uncorking some very frisky bottled cider, which at this juncture he presented.

"Ye'd better jest put up here, now, till daylight," said he, heartily, "and I'll call up the old woman, and have a bed got ready for you in no time."

"Thank you, my good friend," said the senator. "I must be along, to take the night stage for Columbus."

"Ah! well, then, if you must, I'll go a piece with you, and show you a cross road that will take you there better than the road you came on. That road's mighty bad."

John equipped himself, and, with a lantern in hand, was soon seen guiding the senator's carriage towards a road that ran down in a hollow, back of his dwelling. When they parted, the senator put into his hand a ten-dollar bill.

"It's for her," he said, briefly.

"Ay, ay," said John, with equal conciseness.

They shook hands, and parted.

Chapter 10
The Property is Carried off

The February morning looked gray and drizzling through the window of Uncle Tom's cabin. It looked on downcast faces, the images of mournful hearts. The little table stood out before the fire, covered with an ironing-cloth; a coarse but clean shirt or two, fresh from the iron, hung on the back of a chair by the fire, and Aunt Chloe had another spread out before her on the table. Carefully she rubbed and ironed every fold and every hem, with the most scrupulous exactness, every now and then raising her hand to her face to wipe off the tears that were coursing down her cheeks.

Tom sat by, with his Testament open on his knee, and his head leaning upon his hand;—but neither spoke. It was yet early, and the children lay all asleep together in their little rude trundle-bed.

Tom, who had, to the full, the gentle, domestic heart, which, woe for them! has been a peculiar characteristic of his unhappy race, got up and walked silently to look at his children.

"It's the last time," he said.

Aunt Chloe did not answer, only rubbed away over and over on the coarse shirt, already as smooth as hands could make it; and finally setting her iron suddenly down with a despairing plunge, she sat down to the table, and "lifted up her voice and wept."[2]

"S'pose we must be resigned; but, O Lord! how ken I? If I know'd anything whar you's goin', or how they'd sarve you! Missis says she'll try and 'deem ye, in a year or two; but Lor! nobody never comes up that goes down thar! They kills 'em! I've hearn 'em tell how dey works 'em up on dem ar plantations."

"There'll be the same God there, Chloe, that there is here."

"Well," said Aunt Chloe, "s'pose dere will; but de Lord lets dreful things happen, sometimes. I don't seem to get no comfort dat way."

"I'm in the Lord's hands," said Tom; "nothin' can go no furder than he lets it;—and thar's *one* thing I can thank him for. It's *me* that's sold and going down, and not you nur the chil'en. Here you're safe;—what comes will come only on me; and the Lord, he'll help me,—I know he will."

Ah, brave, manly heart,—smothering thine own sorrow, to comfort thy beloved ones! Tom spoke with a thick utterance, and with a bitter choking in his throat,—but he spoke brave and strong.

"Let's think on our marcies!" he added, tremulously, as if he was quite sure he needed to think on them very hard indeed.

"Marcies!" said Aunt Chloe; "don't see no marcy in't! 'tan't right! 'tan't right it should be so! Mas'r never ought ter left it so that ye *could* be took for his debts. Ye've arnt him all he gets for ye, twice over. He owed ye yer freedom, and ought ter gin 't to yer years ago. Mebbe he can't help himself now, but I feel it's wrong. Nothing can't beat that ar out o' me. Sich a faithful crittur as ye've been,—and allers sot his business 'fore yer own every way,—and reckoned on him more than yer own wife and chil'en! Them as sells heart's love and heart's blood, to get out thar scrapes, de Lord'll be up to 'em!"

"Chloe! now, if ye love me, ye won't talk so, when perhaps jest the last time we'll ever have together! And I'll tell ye, Chloe, it goes agin me to hear one word agin Mas'r. Warn't he put

---

2. Compare Isaiah 42.2.

in my arms a baby?—it's natur I should think a heap of him. And he couldn't be spected to think so much of poor Tom. Mas'rs is used to havin' all these yer things done for 'em, and nat'lly they don't think so much on't. They can't be spected to, no way. Set him 'longside of other Mas'rs,—who's had the treatment and the livin' I've had? And he never would have let this yer come on me, if he could have seed it aforehand. I know he wouldn't."

"Wal, any way, thar's wrong about it *somewhar,*" said Aunt Chloe, in whom a stubborn sense of justice was a predominant trait; "I can't jest make out whar 'tis, but thar's wrong somewhar, I'm *clar* o' that."

"Yer ought ter look up to the Lord above,—he's above all,—thar don't a sparrow fall without him."[3]

"It don't seem to comfort me, but I spect it orter," said Aunt Chloe. "But dar's no use talkin'; I'll jes wet up de corncake, and get ye one good breakfast, 'cause nobody knows when you'll get another."

In order to appreciate the sufferings of the negroes sold south, it must be remembered that all the instinctive affections of that race are peculiarly strong. Their local attachments are very abiding. They are not naturally daring and enterprising, but home-loving and affection-ate. Add to this all the terrors with which ignorance invests the unknown, and add to this, again, that selling to the south is set before the negro from childhood as the last severity of punishment. The threat that terrifies more than whipping or torture of any kind is the threat of being sent down river. We have ourselves heard this feeling expressed by them, and seen the unaffected horror with which they will sit in their gossiping hours, and tell frightful stories of that "down river," which to them is

> "That undiscovered country, from whose bourn
> No traveller returns."[4]

A missionary among the fugitives in Canada told us that many of the fugitives confessed themselves to have escaped from comparatively kind masters, and that they were induced to brave the perils of escape, in almost every case, by the desperate horror with which they regarded being sold south,—a doom which was hanging either over themselves or their husbands, their wives or children. This nerves the African, naturally patient, timid, and unenterprising, with heroic courage, and leads him to suffer hunger, cold, pain, the perils of the wilderness, and the more dread penalties of recapture.

The simple morning meal now smoked on the table, for Mrs. Shelby had excused Aunt Chloe's attendance at the great house that morning. The poor soul had expended all her little energies on this farewell feast,—had killed and dressed her choicest chicken, and prepared her corn-cake with scrupulous exactness, just to her husband's taste, and brought out certain mysterious jars on the mantel-piece, some preserves that were never produced except on extreme occasions.

"Lor, Pete," said Mose, triumphantly, "han't we got a buster of a breakfast!" at the same time catching at a fragment of the chicken.

Aunt Chloe gave him a sudden box on the ear. "Thar now! crowing over the last breakfast yer poor daddy's gwine to have to home!"

"O, Chloe!" said Tom, gently.

"Wal, I can't help it," said Aunt Chloe, hiding her face in her apron; "I's so tossed about, it makes me act ugly."

The boys stood quite still, looking first at their father and then at their mother, while the baby, climbing up her clothes, began an imperious, commanding cry.

"Thar!" said Aunt Chloe, wiping her eyes and taking up the baby; "now I's done, I hope,—now do eat something. This yer's my nicest chicken. Thar, boys, ye shall have some, poor critturs! Yer mammy's been cross to yer."

---

3. See Matthew 10:29–31.   4. *Hamlet,* 3.1, lines 369–370.

The boys needed no second invitation, and went in with great zeal for the eatables; and it was well they did so, as otherwise there would have been very little performed to any purpose by the party.

"Now," said Aunt Chloe, bustling about after breakfast, "I must put up yer clothes. Jest like as not, he'll take 'em all away. I know thar ways,—mean as dirt, they is! Wal, now, yer flannels for rhumatis is in this corner; so be car'ful, 'cause there won't nobody make ye no more. Then here's yer old shirts, and these yer is new ones. I toed off these yer stockings last night, and put de ball in 'em to mend with. But Lor! who'll ever mend for ye?" and Aunt Chloe, again overcome, laid her head on the box side, and sobbed. "To think on't! no crittur to do for ye, sick or well! I don't railly think I ought ter be good now!"

The boys, having eaten everything there was on the breakfast-table, began now to take some thought of the case; and, seeing their mother crying, and their father looking very sad, began to whimper and put their hands to their eyes. Uncle Tom had the baby on his knee, and was letting her enjoy herself to the utmost extent, scratching his face and pulling his hair, and occasionally breaking out into clamorous explosions of delight, evidently arising out of her own internal reflections.

"Ay, crow away, poor crittur!" said Aunt Chloe; "ye'll have to come to it, too! ye'll live to see yer husband sold, or mebbe be sold yerself; and these yer boys, they's to be sold, I s'pose, too, jest like as not, when dey gets good for somethin'; an't no use in niggers havin' nothin'!"

Here one of the boys called out, "Thar's Missis a-comin' in!"

"She can't do no good; what's she coming for?" said Aunt Chloe.

Mrs. Shelby entered. Aunt Chloe set a chair for her in a manner decidedly gruff and crusty. She did not seem to notice either the action or the manner. She looked pale and anxious.

"Tom," she said, "I come to—" and stopping suddenly, and regarding the silent group, she sat down in the chair, and, covering her face with her handkerchief, began to sob.

"Lor, now, Missis, don't—don't!" said Aunt Chloe, bursting out in her turn; and for a few moments they all wept in company. And in those tears they all shed together, the high and the lowly, melted away all the heart-burnings and anger of the oppressed. O, ye who visit the distressed, do ye know that everything your money can buy, given with a cold, averted face, is not worth one honest tear shed in real sympathy?

"My good fellow," said Mrs. Shelby, "I can't give you anything to do you any good. If I give you money, it will only be taken from you. But I tell you solemnly, and before God, that I will keep trace of you, and bring you back as soon as I can command the money;—and, till then, trust in God!"

Here the boys called out that Mas'r Haley was coming, and then an unceremonious kick pushed open the door. Haley stood there in very ill humor, having ridden hard the night before, and being not at all pacified by his ill success in recapturing his prey.

"Come," said he, "ye nigger, ye 'r ready? Servant, ma'am!" said he, taking off his hat, as he saw Mrs. Shelby.

Aunt Chloe shut and corded the box, and, getting up, looked gruffly on the trader, her tears seeming suddenly turned to sparks of fire.

Tom rose up meekly, to follow his new master, and raised up his heavy box on his shoulder. His wife took the baby in her arms to go with him to the wagon, and the children, still crying, trailed on behind.

Mrs. Shelby, walking up to the trader, detained him for a few moments, talking with him in an earnest manner; and while she was thus talking, the whole family party proceeded to a wagon, that stood ready harnessed at the door. A crowd of all the old and young hands on the place stood gathered around it, to bid farewell to their old associate. Tom had been looked up to, both as a head servant and a Christian teacher, by all the place, and there was much honest sympathy and grief about him, particularly among the women.

"Why, Chloe, you bar it better'n we do!" said one of the women, who had been weeping freely, noticing the gloomy calmness with which Aunt Chloe stood by the wagon.

"I's done *my* tears!" she said, looking grimly at the trader, who was coming up. "I does not feel to cry 'fore dat ar old limb,⁵ no how!"

"Get in!" said Haley to Tom, as he strode through the crowd of servants, who looked at him with lowering brows.

Tom got in, and Haley, drawing out from under the wagon-seat a heavy pair of shackles, made them fast around each ankle.

A smothered groan of indignation ran through the whole circle, and Mrs. Shelby spoke from the veranda,—

"Mr. Haley, I assure you that precaution is entirely unnecessary."

"Don' know, ma'am; I've lost one five hundred dollars from this yer place, and I can't afford to run no more risks."

"What else could she spect on him?" said Aunt Chloe, indignantly, while the two boys, who now seemed to comprehend at once their father's destiny, clung to her gown, sobbing and groaning vehemently.

"I'm sorry," said Tom, "that Mas'r George happened to be away."

George had gone to spend two or three days with a companion on a neighboring estate, and having departed early in the morning, before Tom's misfortune had been made public; had left without hearing of it.

"Give my love to Mas'r George," he said, earnestly.

Haley whipped up the horse, and, with a steady, mournful look, fixed to the last on the old place, Tom was whirled away.

Mr. Shelby at this time was not at home. He had sold Tom under the spur of a driving necessity, to get out of the power of a man whom he dreaded,—and his first feeling, after the consummation of the bargain, had been that of relief. But his wife's expostulations awoke his half-slumbering regrets; and Tom's manly disinterestedness increased the unpleasantness of his feelings. It was in vain that he said to himself that he had a *right* to do it,—that everybody did it,—and that some did it without even the excuse of necessity;—he could not satisfy his own feelings; and that he might not witness the unpleasant scenes of the consummation, he had gone on a short business tour up the country, hoping that all would be over before he returned.

Tom and Haley rattled on along the dusty road, whirling past every old familiar spot, until the bounds of the estate were fairly passed, and they found themselves out on the open pike. After they had ridden about a mile, Haley suddenly drew up at the door of a blacksmith's shop, when, taking out with him a pair of handcuffs, he stepped into the shop, to have a little alteration in them.

"These yer 's a little too small for his build," said Haley, showing the fetters, and pointing out to Tom.

"Lor! now, if thar an't Shelby's Tom. He han't sold him, now?" said the smith.

"Yes, he has," said Haley.

"Now, ye don't! well, reely," said the smith, "who'd a thought it! Why, ye needn't go to fetterin' him up this yer way. He's the faithfullest, best crittur—"

"Yes, yes," said Haley; "but your good fellers are just the critturs to want ter run off. Them stupid ones, as doesn't care whar they go, and shifless, drunken ones, as don't care for nothin', they'll stick by, and like as not be rather pleased to be toted round; but these yer prime fellers, they hates it like sin. No way but to fetter 'em; got legs—they'll use 'em,—no mistake."

"Well," said the smith, feeling among his tools, "them plantations down thar, stranger, an't jest the place a Kentuck nigger wants to go to; they dies thar tol'able fast, don't they?"

"Wal, yes, tol'able fast, ther dying is; what with the 'climating and one thing and another, they dies so as to keep the market up pretty brisk," said Haley.

---

5. "Limb of Satan"; worthless person.

"Wal, now, a feller can't help thinkin' it's a mighty pity to have a nice, quiet, likely feller, as good un as Tom is, go down to be fairly ground up on one of them ar sugar plantations."

"Wal, he's got a fa'r chance. I promised to do well by him. I'll get him in house-servant in some good old family, and then, if he stands the fever and 'climating, he'll have a berth good as any nigger ought ter ask for."

"He leaves his wife and chil'en up here, s'pose?"

"Yes; but he'll get another thar. Lord, thar's women enough everywhar," said Haley.

Tom was sitting very mournfully on the outside of the shop while this conversation was going on. Suddenly he heard the quick, short click of a horse's hoof behind him; and, before he could fairly awake from his surprise, young Master George sprang into the wagon, threw his arms tumultuously round his neck, and was sobbing and scolding with energy.

"I declare, it's real mean! I don't care what they say, any of 'em! It's a nasty, mean shame! If I was a man, they shouldn't do it,—they should not, *so!*" said George, with a kind of subdued howl.

"O, Mas'r George! this does me good!" said Tom. "I couldn't bar to go off without seein' ye! It does me real good, ye can't tell!" Here Tom made some movement of his feet, and George's eye fell on the fetters.

"What a shame!" he exclaimed, lifting his hands. "I'll knock that old fellow down,—I will!"

"No, you won't, Mas'r George; and you must not talk so loud. It won't help me any, to anger him."

"Well, I won't, then, for your sake; but only to think of it,—isn't it a shame? They never sent for me, nor sent me any word, and, if it hadn't been for Tom Lincon, I shouldn't have heard it. I tell you, I blew 'em up well, all of 'em, at home!"

"That ar wasn't right, I'm 'feared, Mas'r George."

"Can't help it! I say it's a shame! Look here, Uncle Tom," said he, turning his back to the shop, and speaking in a mysterious tone, *"I've brought you my dollar!"*

"O, I couldn't think o' takin' on 't, Mas'r George, no ways in the world!" said Tom, quite moved.

"But you *shall* take it!" said George; "look here,—I told Aunt Chloe I'd do it, and she advised me just to make a hole in it, and put a string through, so you could hang it round your neck, and keep it out of sight; else this mean scamp would take it away. I tell ye, Tom, I want to blow him up! it would do me good!"

"No, don't, Mas'r George, for it won't do *me* any good."

"Well, I won't, for your sake," said George, busily tying his dollar round Tom's neck; "but there, now, button your coat tight over it, and keep it, and remember, every time you see it, that I'll come down after you, and bring you back. Aunt Chloe and I have been talking about it. I told her not to fear; I'll see to it, and I'll tease father's life out, if he don't do it."

"O, Mas'r George, ye mustn't talk so 'bout yer father!"

"Lor, Uncle Tom, I don't mean anything bad."

"And now, Mas'r George," said Tom, "ye must be a good boy; 'member how many hearts is sot on ye. Al'ays keep close to yer mother. Don't be gettin' into any of them foolish ways boys has of gettin' too big to mind their mothers. Tell ye what, Mas'r George, the Lord gives good many things twice over; but he don't give ye a mother but once. Ye'll never see sich another woman, Mas'r George, if ye live to be a hundred years old. So, now, you hold on to her, and grow up, and be a comfort to her, thar's my own good boy,—you will now, won't ye?"

"Yes, I will, Uncle Tom," said George, seriously.

"And be careful of yer speaking, Mas'r George. Young boys, when they comes to your age, is wilful, sometimes,—it's natur they should be. But real gentlemen, such as I hopes you'll be, never lets fall no words that isn't 'spectful to thar parents. Ye an't 'fended, Mas'r George?"

"No, indeed, Uncle Tom; you always did give me good advice."

"I's older, ye know," said Tom, stroking the boy's fine, curly head with his large, strong hand, but speaking in a voice as tender as a woman's, "and I sees all that's bound up in you. O, Mas'r George, you has everything,—l'arnin', privileges, readin', writin',—and you'll grow up to be a great, learned, good man, and all the people on the place and your mother and father'll be so proud on ye! Be a good Mas'r, like yer father; and be a Christian, like yer mother. 'Member yer Creator in the days o' yer youth, Mas'r George."

"I'll be *real* good, Uncle Tom, I tell you," said George. "I'm going to be a *first-rater;* and don't you be discouraged. I'll have you back to the place yet. As I told Aunt Chloe this morning, I'll build your house all over, and you shall have a room for a parlor with a carpet on it, when I'm a man. O, you'll have good times yet!"

Haley now came to the door, with the handcuffs in his hands.

"Look here, now, Mister," said George, with an air of great superiority, as he got out, "I shall let father and mother know how you treat Uncle Tom!"

"You're welcome," said the trader.

"I should think you'd be ashamed to spend all your life buying men and women, and chaining them, like cattle! I should think you'd feel mean!" said George.

"So long as your grand folks wants to buy men and women, I'm as good as they is," said Haley; " 'tan't any meaner sellin' on 'em, than 'tis buyin'!"

"I'll never do either, when I'm a man," said George; "I'm ashamed, this day, that I'm a Kentuckian. I always was proud of it before"; and George sat very straight on his horse, and looked round with an air, as if he expected the state would be impressed with his opinion.

"Well, good by, Uncle Tom; keep a stiff upper lip," said George.

"Good by, Mas'r George," said Tom, looking fondly and admiringly at him. "God Almighty bless you! Ah! Kentucky han't got many like you!" he said, in the fulness of his heart, as the frank, boyish face was lost to his view. Away he went, and Tom looked, till the clatter of his horse's heels died away, the last sound or sight of his home. But over his heart there seemed to be a warm spot, where those young hands had placed that precious dollar. Tom put up his hand, and held it close to his heart.

"Now, I tell ye what, Tom," said Haley, as he came up to the wagon, and threw in the handcuffs, "I mean to start fa'r with ye, as I gen'ally do with my niggers; and I'll tell ye now, to begin with, you treat me fa'r, and I'll treat you fa'r; I an't never hard on my niggers. Calculates to do the best for 'em I can. Now, ye see, you'd better jest settle down comfortable, and not be tryin' no tricks; because niggers' tricks of all sorts I'm up to, and it's no use. If niggers is quiet, and don't try to get off, they has good times with me; and if they don't, why, it's thar fault, and not mine."

Tom assured Haley that he had no present intentions of running off. In fact, the exhortation seemed rather a superfluous one to a man with a great pair of iron fetters on his feet. But Mr. Haley had got in the habit of commencing his relations with his stock with little exhortations of this nature, calculated, as he deemed, to inspire cheerfulness and confidence, and prevent the necessity of any unpleasant scenes.

And here, for the present, we take our leave of Tom, to pursue the fortunes of other characters in our story.

Chapter 45
Concluding Remarks[6]

The writer has often been inquired of, by correspondents from different parts of the country, whether this narrative is a true one; and to these inquiries she will give one general answer.

---

6. This follows thirty-four more chapters of narrative, which alternate irregularly between George and Eliza's movements toward Canada and Uncle Tom's placement first in the St. Clair mansion in New Orleans (home of his child-mistress Eva and the irrepressible slave Topsy) and later on the plantation of Simon Legree. Chapter 45 is the author's postscript, coming after the story's denouement.

The separate incidents that compose the narrative are, to a very great extent, authentic, occurring, many of them, either under her own observation or that of her personal friends. She or her friends have observed characters the counterpart of almost all that are here introduced; and many of the sayings are word for word as heard herself, or reported to her.

The personal appearance of Eliza, the character ascribed to her, are sketches drawn from life. The incorruptible fidelity, piety, and honesty of Uncle Tom had more than one development, to her personal knowledge. Some of the most deeply tragic and romantic, some of the most terrible incidents, have also their parallel in reality. The incident of the mother's crossing the Ohio river on the ice is a well-known fact. The story of "old Prue" (Chapter 19.)[7] was an incident that fell under the personal observation of a brother of the writer, then collecting-clerk to a large mercantile house in New Orleans. From the same source was derived the character of the planter Legree. Of him her brother thus wrote, speaking of visiting his plantation, on a collecting tour: "He actually made me feel of his fist, which was like a blacksmith's hammer, or a nodule of iron, telling me that it was 'calloused with knocking down niggers.' When I left the plantation, I drew a long breath, and felt as if I had escaped from an ogre's den."

That the tragical fate of Tom, also, has too many times had its parallel, there are living witnesses, all over our land, to testify. Let it be remembered that in all southern states, it is a principle of jurisprudence that no person of colored lineage can testify in a suit against a white, and it will be easy to see that such a case may occur, wherever there is a man whose passions outweigh his interests, and a slave who has manhood or principle enough to resist his will. There is, actually, nothing to protect the slave's life, but the *character* of the master. Facts too shocking to be contemplated occasionally force their way to the public ear, and the comment that one often hears made on them is more shocking than the thing itself. It is said, "Very likely such cases may now and then occur, but they are no sample of general practice." If the laws of New England were so arranged that a master could *now and then* torture an apprentice to death, without a possibility of being brought to justice, would it be received with equal composure? Would it be said, "These cases are rare, and no samples of general practice"? This injustice is an *inherent* one in the slave system,—it cannot exist without it.

The public and shameless sale of beautiful mulatto and quadroon girls has acquired a notoriety, from the incidents following the capture of the Pearl. We extract the following from the speech of Hon. Horace Mann, one of the legal counsel for the defendants in that case. He says: "In that company of seventy-six persons, who attempted, in 1848, to escape from the District of Columbia, in the schooner Pearl, and whose officers I assisted in defending, there were several young and healthy girls, who had those peculiar attractions of form and feature which connoisseurs prize so highly. Elizabeth Russel was one of them. She immediately fell into the slave-trader's fangs, and was doomed for the New Orleans market. The hearts of those that saw her were touched with pity for her fate. They offered eighteen hundred dollars to redeem her; and some there were who offered to give, that would not have much left after the gift; but the fiend of a slave-trader was inexorable. She was despatched to New Orleans; but when about half-way there, God had mercy on her, and smote her with death. There were two girls named Edmundson in the same company. When about to be sent to the same market, an older sister went to the shambles,[8] to plead with the wretch who owned them, for the love of God, to spare his victims. He bantered her, telling what fine dresses and fine furniture they would have. 'Yes,' she said, 'that may do very well in this life, but what will become of them in the next?' They too were sent to New Orleans; but were afterwards redeemed, at an enormous ransom, and brought back." Is it not plain, from this, that the histories of Emmeline and Cassy may have many counterparts?[9]

7. An abused slave Tom meets in New Orleans.
8. Slaughterhouse; here, the slave market.

9. Emmeline and Cassy are mulatto women Legree buys to use as concubines.

Justice, too, obliges the author to state that the fairness of mind and generosity attributed to St. Clare[1] are not without a parallel, as the following anecdote will show. A few years since, a young Southern gentleman was in Cincinnati, with a favorite servant, who had been his personal attendant from a boy. The young man took advantage of this opportunity to secure his own freedom, and fled to the protection of a Quaker, who was quite noted in affairs of this kind. The owner was exceedingly indignant. He had always treated the slave with such indulgence, and his confidence in his affection was such, that he believed he must have been practised upon to induce him to revolt from him. He visited the Quaker, in high anger, but, being possessed of uncommon candor and fairness, was soon quieted by his arguments and representations. It was a side of the subject which he never had heard,—never had thought on; and he immediately told the Quaker that, if his slave would, to his own face, say that it was his desire to be free, he would liberate him. An interview was forthwith procured, and Nathan was asked by his young master whether he had ever had any reason to complain of his treatment, in any respect.

"No, Mas'r," said Nathan; "you've always been good to me."

"Well, then why do you want to leave me?"

"Mas'r may die, and then who get me?—I'd rather be a free man."

After some deliberation, the young master replied, "Nathan, in your place, I think I should feel very much so, myself. You are free."

He immediately made him out free papers; deposited a sum of money in the hands of the Quaker, to be judiciously used in assisting him to start in life, and left a very sensible and kind letter of advice to the young man. That letter was for some time in the writer's hands.

The author hopes she has done justice to that nobility, generosity, and humanity, which in many cases characterize individuals at the South. Such instances save us from utter despair of our kind. But, she asks any person, who knows the world, are such characters *common,* anywhere?

For many years of her life, the author avoided all reading upon or allusion to the subject of slavery, considering it as too painful to be inquired into, and one which advancing light and civilization would certainly live down. But, since the legislative act of 1850, when she heard, with perfect surprise and consternation, Christian and humane people actually recommending the remanding escaped fugitives into slavery, as a duty binding on good citizens,—when she heard, on all hands, from kind, compassionate, and estimable people, in the free states of the North, deliberations and discussions as to what Christian duty could be on this head,—she could only think, These men and Christians cannot know what slavery is; if they did, such a question could never be open for discussion. And from this arose a desire to exhibit it in a *living dramatic reality.* She has endeavored to show it fairly, in its best and its worst phases. In its *best* aspect, she has, perhaps, been successful; but, oh! who shall say what yet remains untold in that valley and shadow of death, that lies the other side?

To you, generous, noble-minded men and women, of the South,—you, whose virtue, and magnanimity, and purity of character, are the greater for the severer trial it has encountered,—to you is her appeal. Have you not, in your own secret souls, in your own private conversings, felt that there are woes and evils, in this accursed system, far beyond what are here shadowed, or can be shadowed? Can it be otherwise? Is *man* ever a creature to be trusted with wholly irresponsible power? And does not the slave system, by denying the slave all legal right of testimony, make every individual owner an irresponsible despot? Can anybody fail to make the inference what the practical result will be? If there is, as we admit, a public sentiment among you, men of honor, justice, and humanity, is there not also another kind of public sentiment among the ruffian, the brutal, and debased? And cannot the ruffian, the brutal, the debased, by slave law, own just as many slaves as the best and purest? Are the honorable, the just, the high-minded and compassionate, the majority anywhere in this world?

---

1.   Tom's forward-thinking (but ineffectual) New Orleans owner.

The slave-trade[2] is now, by American law, considered as piracy. But a slave-trade, as systematic as ever was carried on on the coast of Africa, is an inevitable attendant and result of American slavery. And its heart-break and its horrors, *can* they be told?

The writer has given only a faint shadow, a dim picture, of the anguish and despair that are, at this very moment, riving thousands of hearts, shattering thousands of families, and driving a helpless and sensitive race to frenzy and despair. There are those living who know the mothers whom this accursed traffic has driven to the murder of their children; and themselves seeking in death a shelter from woes more dreaded than death. Nothing of tragedy can be written, can be spoken, can be conceived, that equals the frightful reality of scenes daily and hourly acting on our shores, beneath the shadow of American law, and the shadow of the cross of Christ.

And now, men and women of America, is this a thing to be trifled with, apologized for, and passed over in silence? Farmers of Massachusetts, of New Hampshire, of Vermont, of Connecticut, who read this book by the blaze of your winter-evening fire,—strong-hearted, generous sailors and ship-owners of Maine,—is this a thing for you to countenance and encourage? Brave and generous men of New York, farmers of rich and joyous Ohio, and ye of the wide prairie states,—answer, is this a thing for you to protect and countenance? And you, mothers of America,—you, who have learned, by the cradles of your own children, to love and feel for all mankind,—by the sacred love you bear your child; by your joy in his beautiful, spotless infancy; by the motherly pity and tenderness with which you guide his growing years; by the anxieties of his education; by the prayers you breathe for his soul's eternal good;—I beseech you, pity the mother who has all your affections, and not one legal right to protect, guide, or educate the child of her bosom! By the sick hour of your child; by those dying eyes, which you can never forget; by those last cries, that wrung your heart when you could neither help not save; by the desolation of that empty cradle, that silent nursery,—I beseech you, pity those mothers that are constantly made childless by the American slave-trade! And say, mothers of America, is this a thing to be defended, sympathized with, passed over in silence?

Do you say that the people of the free states have nothing to do with it, and can do nothing? Would to God this were true! But it is not true. The people of the free states have defended, encouraged, and participated; and are more guilty for it, before God, than the South, in that they have *not* the apology of education or custom.

If the mothers of the free states had all felt as they should, in times past, the sons of the free states would not have been the holders, and, proverbially, the hardest masters of slaves; the sons of the free states would not have connived at the extension of slavery, in our national body; the sons of the free states would not, as they do, trade the souls and bodies of men as an equivalent to money, in their mercantile dealings. There are multitudes of slaves temporarily owned, and sold again, by merchants in Northern cities; and shall the whole guilt or obloquy of slavery fall only on the South?

Northern men, Northern mothers, Northern Christians, have something more to do than denounce their brethren at the South; they have to look to the evil among themselves.

But, what can any individual do? Of that, every individual can judge. There is one thing that every individual can do,—they can see to it that *they feel right.* An atmosphere of sympathetic influence encircles every human being; and the man or woman who *feels* strongly, healthily, and justly on the great interests of humanity, is a constant benefactor to the human race. See, then, to your sympathies in this matter! Are they in harmony with the sympathies of Christ? or are they swayed and perverted by the sophistries of worldly policy?

Christian men and women of the North! still further,—you have another power; you can *pray!* Do you believe in prayer? or has it become an indistinct apostolic tradition? You pray

2. Kidnapping people in Africa to be sold into slavery.

for the heathen abroad; pray also for the heathen at home. And pray for those distressed Christians whose whole chance of religious improvement is an accident of trade and sale; from whom any adherence to the morals of Christianity is, in many cases, an impossibility, unless they have given them, from above, the courage and grace of martyrdom.

But, still more. On the shores of our free states are emerging the poor, shattered, broken remnants of families,—men and women, escaped, by miraculous providences, from the surges of slavery,—feeble in knowledge, and, in many cases, infirm in moral constitution, from a system which confounds and confuses every principle of Christianity and morality. They come to seek a refuge among you; they come to seek education, knowledge, Christianity.

What do you owe to these poor unfortunates, O Christians? Does not every American Christian owe to the African race some effort at reparation for the wrongs that the American nation has brought upon them? Shall the doors of churches and school-houses be shut upon them? Shall states arise and shake them out? Shall the Church of Christ hear in silence the taunt that is thrown at them, and shrink away from the helpless hand that they stretch out; and, by her silence, encourage the cruelty that would chase them from our borders? If it must be so, it will be a mournful spectacle. If it must be so, the country will have reason to tremble, when it remembers that the fate of nations is in the hands of One who is very pitiful, and of tender compassion.

Do you say, "We don't want them here; let them go to Africa"?

That the providence of God has provided a refuge in Africa, is, indeed, a great and noticeable fact;[3] but that is no reason why the Church of Christ should throw off that responsibility to this outcast race which her profession demands of her.

To fill up Liberia with an ignorant, inexperienced, half-barbarized race, just escaped from the chains of slavery, would be only to prolong, for ages, the period of struggle and conflict which attends the inception of new enterprises. Let the Church of the North receive these poor sufferers in the spirit of Christ; receive them to the educating advantages of Christian republican society and schools, until they have attained to somewhat of a moral and intellectual maturity, and then assist them in their passage to those shores, where they may put into practice the lessons they have learned in America.

There is a body of men at the North, comparatively small, who have been doing this; and, as the result, this country has already seen examples of men, formerly slaves, who have rapidly acquired property, reputation, and education. Talent has been developed, which, considering the circumstances, is certainly remarkable; and, for moral traits of honesty, kindness, tenderness of feeling,—for heroic efforts and self-denials, endured for the ransom of brethren and friends yet in slavery,—they have been remarkable to a degree that, considering the influence under which they were born, is surprising.

The writer has lived, for many years, on the frontier-line of slave states, and has had great opportunities of observation among those who formerly were slaves. They have been in her family as servants; and, in default of any other school to receive them, she has, in many cases, had them instructed in a family school, with her own children. She has also the testimony of missionaries, among the fugitives in Canada, in coincidence with her own experience; and her deductions, with regard to the capabilities of the race, are encouraging in the highest degree.

The first desire of the emancipated slave, generally, is for *education*. There is nothing that they are not willing to give or do to have their children instructed; and, so far as the writer has observed herself, or taken the testimony of teachers among them, they are remarkably intelligent and quick to learn. The results of schools, founded for them by benevolent individuals in Cincinnati, fully establish this.

3. A reference to Liberia, founded in 1847 by American slaves who had gained their freedom.

The author gives the following statement of facts, on the authority of Professor C. E. Stowe,[4] then of Lane Seminary, Ohio, with regard to emancipated slaves, now resident in Cincinnati; given to show the capability of the race, even without any very particular assistance or encouragement.

The initial letters alone are given. They are all residents of Cincinnati.

"B———. Furniture-maker; twenty years in the city; worth ten thousand dollars, all his own earnings; a Baptist.

"C———. Full black; stolen from Africa; sold in New Orleans; been free fifteen years; paid for himself six hundred dollars; a farmer; owns several farms in Indiana; Presbyterian; probably worth fifteen or twenty thousand dollars, all earned by himself.

"K———. Full black; dealer in real estate; worth thirty thousand dollars; about forty years old; free six years; paid eighteen hundred dollars for his family; member of the Baptist church; received a legacy from his master, which he has taken good care of, and increased.

"G———. Full black; coal-dealer; about thirty years old; worth eighteen thousand dollars; paid for himself twice, being once defrauded to the amount of sixteen hundred dollars; made all his money by his own efforts,—much of it while a slave, hiring his time of his master, and doing business for himself; a fine, gentlemanly fellow.

"W———. Three fourths black; barber and waiter; from Kentucky; nineteen years free; paid for self and family over three thousand dollars; worth twenty thousand dollars, all his own earnings; deacon in the Baptist church.

"G. D———. Three fourths black; whitewasher; from Kentucky; nine years free; paid fifteen hundred dollars for self and family; recently died, aged sixty; worth six thousand dollars."

Professor Stowe says, "With all these, except G———, I have been, for some years personally acquainted, and make my statements from my own knowledge."

The writer well remembers an aged colored woman, who was employed as a washer-woman in her father's family. The daughter of this woman married a slave. She was a remarkably active and capable young woman, and, by her industry and thrift, and the most persevering self-denial, raised nine hundred dollars for her husband's freedom, which she paid, as she raised it, into the hands of his master. She yet wanted a hundred dollars of the price, when he died. She never recovered any of the money.

These are but few facts, among multitudes which might be adduced, to show the self-denial, energy, patience, and honesty, which the slave has exhibited in a state of freedom.

And let it be remembered that these individuals have thus bravely succeeded in conquering for themselves comparative wealth and social position, in the face of every disadvantage and discouragement. The colored man, by the law of Ohio, cannot be a voter, and, till within a few years, was even denied the right of testimony in legal suits with the white. Nor are these instances confined to the State of Ohio. In all states of the Union we see men, but yesterday burst from the shackles of slavery, who, by a self-educating force, which cannot be too much admired, have risen to highly respectable stations in society. Pennington, among clergymen, Douglas and Ward, among editors, are well-known instances.

If this persecuted race, with every discouragement and disadvantage, have done thus much, how much more they might do, if the Christian Church would act towards them in the spirit of her Lord!

This is an age of the world when nations are trembling and convulsed.[5] A mighty influence is abroad, surging and heaving the world, as with an earthquake. And is America safe? Every nation that carries in its bosom great and unredressed injustice has in it the elements of this last convulsion.

4.　The novelist's husband, Calvin Stowe.
5.　A reference to the European revolutions of 1848 and thereafter.

For what is this mighty influence thus rousing in all nations and languages those groanings that cannot be uttered, for man's freedom and equality?

O, Church of Christ, read the signs of the times! Is not this power the spirit of HIM whose kingdom is yet to come, and whose will to be done on earth as it is in heaven?

But who may abide the day of his appearing? "For that day shall burn as an oven: and he shall appear as a swift witness against those that oppress the hireling in his wages, the widow and the fatherless, and that *turn aside the stranger in his right:* and he shall break in pieces the oppressor."[6]

Are not these dread words for a nation bearing in her bosom so mighty an injustice? Christians! every time that you pray that the kingdom of Christ may come, can you forget that prophecy associates, in dread fellowship, the *day of vengeance* with the year of his redeemed?

A day of grace is yet held out to us. Both North and South have been guilty before God; and the *Christian Church* has a heavy account to answer. Not by combining together, to protect injustice and cruelty, and making a common capital of sin, is this Union to be saved,—but by repentance, justice, and mercy; for, not surer is the eternal law by which the millstone sinks in the ocean, than that stronger law, by which injustice and cruelty shall bring on nations the wrath of Almighty God!

The End

1852

Harriet Jacobs

(1813–1897)

Born a slave in Edenton, North Carolina, Harriet Jacobs grew up to live—and to write—a dramatic story of captivity and escape into freedom. Her *Incidents in the Life of a Slave Girl* has only recently been confirmed as a genuine autobiography; generations of scholars believed it to have been written by Lydia Maria Child, a novelist who edited Jacobs's text. In its emphasis on family relationships and the theme of "home," *Incidents* seems to resemble the sentimental domestic novels such authors as Child produced, more than the slave narratives in the tradition of Frederick Douglass's. But it is Jacobs's own story, "written"—as her subtitle declares—"by herself."

Jacobs learned to read and write from the woman who owned her in childhood. As her autobiography explains, after her mother died when she was 6, Jacobs was much influenced by her grandmother, a slave who eventually obtained her freedom, owned a home, and supported herself as a baker. Though Jacobs hoped her mistress would free her when her mistress died, she was bequeathed to a very young girl. The girl's father, Dr. James Norcom ("Dr. Flint" in the autobiography), relentlessly harassed Jacobs for sexual favors from the time she was 14 years old. Having no positive recourse, since no law protected slaves from owners' sexual assaults, and desperate to put Dr. Norcom off, Jacobs became pregnant by another white man, Samuel Treadwell Sawyer ("Mr. Sands"), eventually bearing him two children, one when she was 19 and one at 20.

Despite Jacobs's motherhood, Dr. Norcom continued his pursuit; in 1835 he sent her to a plantation, from which she escaped. As revenge, he put those of her

6.   An adaptation of verses from Malachi 3:2–5 and Malachi 4:1.

family members whom he owned in jail, including her two small children. Sawyer bought Jacobs's children and brother, who went to live with Jacobs's grandmother, but Norcom would not consent to sell Jacobs. Unwilling either to leave the vicinity of her children or to subject herself to Norcom's harassment, Jacobs hid in an attic crawl space in her grandmother's home for a grueling seven years.

In 1842 Jacobs escaped to the North, where she worked as a nursemaid in the home of Nathaniel P. Willis (the brother of Fanny Fern and original of "Hyacinth Ellis" in *Ruth Hall*) and lived alternately in New York and in Boston. In the employ of the Willis family she traveled to England in 1845. In 1849 she left Boston for Rochester, working for her brother John S. Jacobs (an antislavery activist and lecturer) and making connections with many white feminists who were active in the abolition movement. Returning to New York in 1850, Jacobs worked once again as a nursemaid for the Willis family. From the time of her escape, Jacobs had repeatedly been troubled by attempts on the part of the Norcoms to return her to slavery. In 1852, ten years after arriving in the North, Jacobs was purchased and freed by her friend and employer, Mrs. Willis.

One of Jacobs's abolitionist friends, Amy Post, having suggested to her that she write the story of her life, arranged for Jacobs to talk to Harriet Beecher Stowe in 1853, shortly after the publication of *Uncle Tom's Cabin*. Offended at Stowe's suggestion that her story should be subsumed in the *Key to Uncle Tom's Cabin* that Stowe was then writing, she decided to try to write it herself, without help in getting it published from Stowe or from Willis (who, by the way, was no more useful in furthering Jacobs's writing career than he was in Fanny Fern's). A publisher's request that she get a preface from Lydia Maria Child started a helpful literary relationship. Child is supposed to have rearranged the manuscript of *Incidents* a little, "so as to bring the story into continuous *order* and

the remarks into *appropriate* places," as she wrote to Jacobs. But she said she "had very little occasion to alter the language, which is wonderfully good, for one whose opportunities for education have been so limited." The autobiography was published in 1861.

Just before the Emancipation Proclamation was passed in 1863, Jacobs moved to Washington, D.C., where she did relief work. She did similar work under the sponsorship of Philadelphia's and New York's Quakers in Alexandria, Virginia, and Savannah, Georgia, and traveled to London in 1868 on a charitable fund-raising tour. From 1870 to 1885, Jacobs ran a boardinghouse in Cambridge, Massachusetts. Although she moved back to Washington in 1885, she was buried in Mount Auburn Cemetery at Cambridge.

Incidents in the Life of a Slave Girl follows Jacobs's experiences up to 1860, drawing explicit contrasts between the life of the protagonist, "Linda Brent," and the story of the typical heroine: "Reader, my story ends with freedom; not in the usual way, with marriage," she asserts in the conclusion. Self-consciously addressing the narrative to white women reading in the North, the autobiography resembles *Uncle Tom's Cabin* in that it draws many parallels between the feelings of the slave woman and those of her presumed readers. But here it is the voice of the African-American woman herself, rather than that of a white intercessor, which speaks to the reader. Conforming to some Victorian proprieties, the autobiography leaves significant gaps in Linda Brent's experience, notably omitting any details about the conception of her two children. But the master's persecution of the young female slave and the long, crippling imprisonment in her attic "loophole of retreat" are graphically depicted, almost Gothic in their representation. Jacobs's style reveals the breadth of her own reading; her voice participates vividly in the tradition of American women's writing in her period.

Jacobs published no other text. The most comprehensive study of her work is Jean Fagan Yellin's edition of *Incidents in the Life of a Slave Girl* (1987), which
is extensively annotated.

FROM INCIDENTS IN THE LIFE OF A SLAVE GIRL

I.
Childhood

I was born a slave; but I never knew it till six years of happy childhood had passed away. My father was a carpenter, and considered so intelligent and skilful in his trade, that, when buildings out of the common line were to be erected, he was sent for from long distances, to be head workman. On condition of paying his mistress two hundred dollars a year, and supporting himself, he was allowed to work at his trade, and manage his own affairs. His strongest wish was to purchase his children; but, though he several times offered his hard earnings for that purpose, he never succeeded. In complexion my parents were a light shade of brownish yellow, and were termed mulattoes. They lived together in a comfortable home; and, though we were all slaves, I was so fondly shielded that I never dreamed I was a piece of merchandise, trusted to them for safe keeping, and liable to be demanded of them at any moment. I had one brother, William, who was two years younger than myself—a bright, affectionate child. I had also a great treasure in my maternal grandmother, who was a remarkable woman in many respects. She was the daughter of a planter in South Carolina, who, at his death, left her mother and his three children free, with money to go to St. Augustine, where they had relatives. It was during the Revolutionary War; and they were captured on their passage, carried back, and sold to different purchasers. Such was the story my grandmother used to tell me; but I do not remember all the particulars. She was a little girl when she was captured and sold to the keeper of a large hotel. I have often heard her tell how hard she fared during childhood. But as she grew older she evinced so much intelligence, and was so faithful, that her master and mistress could not help seeing it was for their interest to take care of such a valuable piece of property. She became an indispensable personage in the household, officiating in all capacities, from cook and wet nurse to seamstress. She was much praised for her cooking; and her nice crackers became so famous in the neighborhood that many people were desirous of obtaining them. In consequence of numerous requests of this kind, she asked permission of her mistress to bake crackers at night, after all the household work was done; and she obtained leave to do it, provided she would clothe herself and her children from the profits. Upon these terms, after working hard all day for her mistress, she began her midnight bakings, assisted by her two oldest children. The business proved profitable; and each year she laid by a little, which was saved for a fund to purchase her children. Her master died, and the property was divided among his heirs. The widow had her dower in the hotel, which she continued to keep open. My grandmother remained in her service as a slave; but her children were divided among her master's children. As she had five, Benjamin, the youngest one, was sold, in order that each heir might have an equal portion of dollars and cents. There was so little difference in our ages that he seemed more like my brother than my uncle. He was a bright, handsome lad, nearly white; for he inherited the complexion my grandmother had derived from Anglo-Saxon ancestors. Though only ten years old, seven hundred and twenty dollars were paid for him. His sale was a terrible blow to my grandmother; but she was naturally hopeful, and she went to work with renewed energy, trusting in time to be able to purchase some of her children. She had laid up three hundred dollars, which her mistress one day begged as a loan, promising to pay her soon. The reader probably knows that no promise or writing given to a slave is legally binding; for, according to Southern laws, a slave, *being* property, can *hold* no property. When my grandmother lent her hard earnings to her mistress, she trusted solely to her honor. The honor of a slaveholder to a slave!

To this good grandmother I was indebted for many comforts. My brother Willie and I often received portions of the crackers, cakes, and preserves, she made to sell; and after we ceased to be children we were indebted to her for many more important services.

Such were the unusually fortunate circumstances of my early childhood. When I was six years old, my mother died; and then, for the first time, I learned, by the talk around me, that I was a slave. My mother's mistress was the daughter of my grandmother's mistress. She was the foster sister of my mother; they were both nourished at my grandmother's breast. In fact, my mother had been weaned at three months old, that the babe of the mistress might obtain sufficient food. They played together as children; and, when they became women, my mother was a most faithful servant to her whiter foster sister. On her death-bed her mistress promised that her children should never suffer for any thing; and during her lifetime she kept her word. They all spoke kindly of my dead mother, who had been a slave merely in name, but in nature was noble and womanly. I grieved for her, and my young mind was troubled with the thought who would now take care of me and my little brother. I was told that my home was now to be with her mistress; and I found it a happy one. No toilsome or disagreeable duties were imposed upon me. My mistress was so kind to me that I was always glad to do her bidding, and proud to labor for her as much as my young years would permit. I would sit by her side for hours, sewing diligently, with a heart as free from care as that of any free-born white child. When she thought I was tired, she would send me out to run and jump; and away I bounded, to gather berries or flowers to decorate her room. Those were happy days—too happy to last. The slave child had no thought for the morrow; but there came that blight, which too surely waits on every human being born to be a chattel.

When I was nearly twelve years old, my kind mistress sickened and died. As I saw the cheek grow paler, and the eye more glassy, how earnestly I prayed in my heart that she might live! I loved her; for she had been almost like a mother to me. My prayers were not answered. She died, and they buried her in the little churchyard, where, day after day, my tears fell upon her grave.

I was sent to spend a week with my grandmother. I was now old enough to begin to think of the future; and again and again I asked myself what they would do with me. I felt sure I should never find another mistress so kind as the one who was gone. She had promised my dying mother that her children should never suffer for any thing; and when I remembered that, and recalled her many proofs of attachment to me, I could not help having some hopes that she had left me free. My friends were almost certain it would be so. They thought she would be sure to do it, on account of my mother's love and faithful service. But, alas! we all know that the memory of a faithful slave does not avail much to save her children from the auction block.

After a brief period of suspense, the will of my mistress was read, and we learned that she had bequeathed me to her sister's daughter, a child of five years old. So vanished our hopes. My mistress had taught me the precepts of God's Word: "Thou shalt love thy neighbor as thyself."[1] "Whatsoever ye would that men should do unto you, do ye even so unto them."[2] But I was her slave, and I suppose she did not recognize me as her neighbor. I would give much to blot out from my memory that one great wrong. As a child, I loved my mistress; and, looking back on the happy days I spent with her, I try to think with less bitterness of this act of injustice. While I was with her, she taught me to read and spell; and for this privilege, which so rarely falls to the lot of a slave, I bless her memory.

1. Mark 12:31.   2. Matthew 7:12.

She possessed but few slaves; and at her death those were all distributed among her relatives. Five of them were my grandmother's children, and had shared the same milk that nourished her mother's children. Notwithstanding my grandmother's long and faithful service to her owners, not one of her children escaped the auction block. These God-breathing machines are no more, in the sight of their masters, than the cotton they plant, or the horses they tend.

II.
The New Master and Mistress

Mr. Flint, a physician in the neighborhood, had married the sister of my mistress, and I was now the property of their little daughter. It was not without murmuring that I prepared for my new home; and what added to my unhappiness, was the fact that my brother William was purchased by the same family. My father, by his nature, as well as by the habit of transacting business as a skilful mechanic, had more of the feelings of a freeman than is common among slaves. My brother was a spirited boy; and being brought up under such influences, he early detested the name of master and mistress. One day, when his father and his mistress both happened to call him at the same time, he hesitated between the two; being perplexed to know which had the strongest claim upon his obedience. He finally concluded to go to his mistress. When my father reproved him for it, he said, "You both called me, and I didn't know which I ought to go to first."

"You are *my* child," replied our father, "and when I call you, you should come immediately, if you have to pass through fire and water."

Poor Willie! He was now to learn his first lesson of obedience to a master. Grandmother tried to cheer us with hopeful words, and they found an echo in the credulous hearts of youth.

When we entered our new home we encountered cold looks, cold words, and cold treatment. We were glad when the night came. On my narrow bed I moaned and wept, I felt so desolate and alone.

I had been there nearly a year, when a dear little friend of mine was buried. I heard her mother sob, as the clods fell on the coffin of her only child, and I turned away from the grave, feeling thankful that I still had something left to love. I met my grandmother, who said, "Come with me, Linda;" and from her tone I knew that something sad had happened. She led me apart from the people, and then said, "My child, your father is dead." Dead! How could I believe it? He had died so suddenly I had not even heard that he was sick. I went home with my grandmother. My heart rebelled against God, who had taken from me mother, father, mistress, and friend. The good grandmother tried to comfort me. "Who knows the ways of God?" said she. "Perhaps they have been kindly taken from the evil days to come." Years afterwards I often thought of this. She promised to be a mother to her grandchildren, so far as she might be permitted to do so; and strengthened by her love, I returned to my master's. I thought I should be allowed to go to my father's house the next morning; but I was ordered to go for flowers, that my mistress's house might be decorated for an evening party. I spent the day gathering flowers and weaving them into festoons, while the dead body of my father was lying within a mile of me. What cared my owners for that? he was merely a piece of property. Moreover, they thought he had spoiled his children, by teaching them to feel that they were human beings. This was blasphemous doctrine for a slave to teach; presumptuous in him, and dangerous to the masters.

The next day I followed his remains to a humble grave beside that of my dear mother. There were those who knew my father's worth, and respected his memory.

My home now seemed more dreary than ever. The laugh of the little slave-children sounded harsh and cruel. It was selfish to feel so about the joy of others. My brother moved about with a very grave face. I tried to comfort him, by saying, "Take courage, Willie; brighter days will come by and by."

"You don't know any thing about it, Linda," he replied. "We shall have to stay here all our days; we shall never be free."

I argued that we were growing older and stronger, and that perhaps we might, before long, be allowed to hire our own time, and then we could earn money to buy our freedom. William declared this was much easier to say than to do; moreover, he did not intend to *buy* his freedom. We held daily controversies upon this subject.

Little attention was paid to the slaves' meals in Dr. Flint's house. If they could catch a bit of food while it was going, well and good. I gave myself no trouble on that score, for on my various errands I passed my grandmother's house, where there was always something to spare for me. I was frequently threatened with punishment if I stopped there; and my grandmother, to avoid detaining me, often stood at the gate with something for my breakfast or dinner. I was indebted to *her* for all my comforts, spiritual or temporal. It was *her* labor that supplied my scanty wardrobe. I have a vivid recollection of the linsey-woolsey[3] dress given me every winter by Mrs. Flint. How I hated it! It was one of the badges of slavery.

While my grandmother was thus helping to support me from her hard earnings, the three hundred dollars she had lent her mistress were never repaid. When her mistress died, her son-in-law, Dr. Flint, was appointed executor. When grandmother applied to him for payment, he said the estate was insolvent, and the law prohibited payment. It did not, however, prohibit him from retaining the silver candelabra, which had been purchased with that money. I presume they will be handed down in the family, from generation to generation.

My grandmother's mistress had always promised her that, at her death, she should be free; and it was said that in her will she made good the promise. But when the estate was settled, Dr. Flint told the faithful old servant that, under existing circumstances, it was necessary she should be sold.

On the appointed day, the customary advertisement was posted up, proclaiming that there would be a "public sale of negroes, horses, &c." Dr. Flint called to tell my grandmother that he was unwilling to wound her feelings by putting her up at auction, and that he would prefer to dispose of her at private sale. My grandmother saw through his hypocrisy; she understood very well that he was ashamed of the job. She was a very spirited woman, and if he was base enough to sell her, when her mistress intended she should be free, she was determined the public should know it. She had for a long time supplied many families with crackers and preserves; consequently, "Aunt Marthy," as she was called, was generally known, and every body who knew her respected her intelligence and good character. Her long and faithful service in the family was also well known, and the intention of her mistress to leave her free. When the day of sale came, she took her place among the chattels, and at the first call she sprang upon the auction-block. Many voices called out, "Shame! Shame! Who is going to sell *you*, aunt Marthy? Don't stand there! That is no place for *you*." Without saying a word, she quietly awaited her fate. No one bid for her. At last, a feeble voice said, "Fifty dollars." It came from a maiden lady, seventy years old, the sister of my grandmother's deceased mistress. She had lived forty years under the same roof with my grandmother; she knew how faithfully she had served her owners, and how cruelly she had been defrauded of her rights; and she resolved to protect her. The auctioneer waited for a higher bid; but her wishes were respected; no one bid above her. She could neither read nor write; and when the bill of sale was made out, she signed it with a cross. But what consequence was that, when she had a big heart overflowing with human kindness? She gave the old servant her freedom.

At that time, my grandmother was just fifty years old. Laborious years had passed since then; and now my brother and I were slaves to the man who had defrauded her of her money,

---

3. Coarse fabric woven of cotton or linen and wool.

and tried to defraud her of her freedom. One of my mother's sisters, called Aunt Nancy, was also a slave in his family. She was a kind, good aunt to me; and supplied the place of both housekeeper and waiting maid to her mistress. She was, in fact, at the beginning and end of every thing.

Mrs. Flint, like many southern women, was totally deficient in energy. She had not strength to superintend her household affairs; but her nerves were so strong, that she could sit in her easy chair and see a woman whipped, till the blood trickled from every stroke of the lash. She was a member of the church; but partaking of the Lord's supper did not seem to put her in a Christian frame of mind. If dinner was not served at the exact time on that particular Sunday, she would station herself in the kitchen, and wait till it was dished, and then spit in all the kettles and pans that had been used for cooking. She did this to prevent the cook and her children from eking out their meagre fare with the remains of the gravy and other scrapings. The slaves could get nothing to eat except what she chose to give them. Provisions were weighed out by the pound and ounce, three times a day. I can assure you she gave them no chance to eat wheat bread from her flour barrel. She knew how many biscuits a quart of flour would make, and exactly what size they ought to be.

Dr. Flint was an epicure. The cook never sent a dinner to his table without fear and trembling; for if there happened to be a dish not to his liking, he would either order her to be whipped, or compel her to eat every mouthful of it in his presence. The poor, hungry creature might not have objected to eating it; but she did object to having her master cram it down her throat till she choked.

They had a pet dog, that was a nuisance in the house. The cook was ordered to make some Indian mush for him. He refused to eat, and when his head was held over it, the froth flowed from his mouth into the basin. He died a few minutes after. When Dr. Flint came in, he said the mush had not been well cooked, and that was the reason the animal would not eat it. He sent for the cook, and compelled her to eat it. He thought that the woman's stomach was stronger than the dog's; but her sufferings afterwards proved that he was mistaken. This poor woman endured many cruelties from her master and mistress; sometimes she was locked up, away from her nursing baby, for a whole day and night.

When I had been in the family a few weeks, one of the plantation slaves was brought to town, by order of his master. It was near night when he arrived, and Dr. Flint ordered him to be taken to the work house, and tied up to the joist, so that his feet would just escape the ground. In that situation he was to wait till the doctor had taken his tea. I shall never forget that night. Never before, in my life, had I heard hundreds of blows fall, in succession, on a human being. His piteous groans, and his "O, pray don't, massa," rang in my ear for months afterwards. There were many conjectures as to the cause of this terrible punishment. Some said master accused him of stealing corn; others said the slave had quarrelled with his wife, in presence of the overseer, and had accused his master of being the father of her child. They were both black, and the child was very fair.

I went into the work house next morning, and saw the cowhide still wet with blood, and the boards all covered with gore. The poor man lived, and continued to quarrel with his wife. A few months afterwards Dr. Flint handed them both over to a slave-trader. The guilty man put their value into his pocket, and had the satisfaction of knowing that they were out of sight and hearing. When the mother was delivered into the trader's hands, she said, "You *promised* to treat me well." To which he replied, "You have let your tongue run too far; damn you!" She had forgotten that it was a crime for a slave to tell who was the father of her child.

From others than the master persecution also comes in such cases. I once saw a young slave girl dying soon after the birth of a child nearly white. In her agony she cried out, "O Lord, come and take me!" Her mistress stood by, and mocked at her like an incarnate fiend. "You suffer, do you?" she exclaimed. "I am glad of it. You deserve it all, and more too."

The girl's mother said, "The baby is dead, thank God; and I hope my poor child will soon be in heaven, too."

"Heaven!" retorted the mistress. "There is no such place for the like of her and her bastard."

The poor mother turned away, sobbing. Her dying daughter called her, feebly, and as she bent over her, I heard her say, "Don't grieve so, mother; God knows all about it; and HE will have mercy upon me."

Her sufferings, afterwards, became so intense, that her mistress felt unable to stay; but when she left the room, the scornful smile was still on her lips. Seven children called her mother. The poor black woman had but the one child, whose eyes she saw closing in death, while she thanked God for taking her away from the greater bitterness of life.

III.
The Slaves' New Year's Day

Dr. Flint owned a fine residence in town, several farms, and about fifty slaves, besides hiring a number by the year.

Hiring-day at the south takes place on the 1st of January. On the 2d, the slaves are expected to go to their new masters. On a farm, they work until the corn and cotton are laid. They then have two holidays. Some masters give them a good dinner under the trees. This over, they work until Christmas eve. If no heavy charges are meantime brought against them, they are given four or five holidays, whichever the master or overseer may think proper. Then comes New Year's eve; and they gather together their little alls, or more properly speaking, their little nothings, and wait anxiously for the dawning of day. At the appointed hour the grounds are thronged with men, women, and children, waiting, like criminals, to hear their doom pronounced. The slave is sure to know who is the most humane, or cruel master, within forty miles of him.

It is easy to find out, on that day, who clothes and feeds his slaves well; for he is surrounded by a crowd, begging, "Please, massa, hire me this year. I will work *very* hard, massa."

If a slave is unwilling to go with his new master, he is whipped, or locked up in jail, until he consents to go, and promises not to run away during the year. Should he chance to change his mind, thinking it justifiable to violate an extorted promise, woe unto him if he is caught! The whip is used till the blood flows at his feet; and his stiffened limbs are put in chains, to be dragged in the field for days and days!

If he lives until the next year, perhaps the same man will hire him again, without even giving him an opportunity of going to the hiring-ground. After those for hire are disposed of, those for sale are called up.

O, you happy free women, contrast *your* New Year's day with that of the poor bond-woman! With you it is a pleasant season, and the light of the day is blessed. Friendly wishes meet you every where, and gifts are showered upon you. Even hearts that have been estranged from you soften at this season, and lips that have been silent echo back, "I wish you a happy New Year." Children bring their little offerings, and raise their rosy lips for a caress. They are your own, and no hand but that of death can take them from you.

But to the slave mother New Year's day comes laden with peculiar sorrows. She sits on her cold cabin floor, watching the children who may all be torn from her the next morning; and often does she wish that she and they might die before the day dawns. She may be an ignorant creature, degraded by the system that has brutalized her from childhood; but she has a mother's instincts, and is capable of feeling a mother's agonies.

On one of these sale days, I saw a mother lead seven children to the auction-block. She knew that *some* of them would be taken from her; but they took *all*. The children were sold to a slave-trader, and their mother was bought by a man in her own town. Before night her children were all far away. She begged the trader to tell her where he intended to take them; this he refused to do. How *could* he, when he knew he would sell them, one by one, wherever he could command the highest price? I met that mother in the street, and her wild, haggard face lives to-day in my mind. She wrung her hands in anguish, and exclaimed, "Gone! All gone! Why *don't* God kill me?" I had no words wherewith to comfort her. Instances of this kind are of daily, yea, of hourly occurrence.

Slaveholders have a method, peculiar to their institution, of getting rid of *old* slaves, whose lives have been worn out in their service. I knew an old woman, who for seventy years faithfully served her master. She had become almost helpless, from hard labor and disease. Her owners moved to Alabama, and the old black woman was left to be sold to any body who would give twenty dollars for her.

IV.
The Slave Who Dared to Feel Like a Man

Two years had passed since I entered Dr. Flint's family, and those years had brought much of the knowledge that comes from experience, though they had afforded little opportunity for any other kinds of knowledge.

My grandmother had, as much as possible, been a mother to her orphan grandchildren. By perseverance and unwearied industry, she was now mistress of a snug little home, surrounded with the necessaries of life. She would have been happy could her children have shared them with her. There remained but three children and two grandchildren, all slaves. Most earnestly did she strive to make us feel that it was the will of God: that He had seen fit to place us under such circumstances; and though it seemed hard, we ought to pray for contentment.

It was a beautiful faith, coming from a mother who could not call her children her own. But I, and Benjamin, her youngest boy, condemned it. We reasoned that it was much more the will of God that we should be situated as she was. We longed for a home like hers. There we always found sweet balsam for our troubles. She was so loving, so sympathizing! She always met us with a smile, and listened with patience to all our sorrows. She spoke so hopefully, that unconsciously the clouds gave place to sunshine. There was a grand big oven there, too, that baked bread and nice things for the town, and we knew there was always a choice bit in store for us.

But, alas! even the charms of the old oven failed to reconcile us to our hard lot. Benjamin was now a tall, handsome lad, strongly and gracefully made, and with a spirit too bold and daring for a slave. My brother William, now twelve years old, had the same aversion to the word master that he had when he was an urchin of seven years. I was his confidant. He came to me with all his troubles. I remember one instance in particular. It was on a lovely spring morning, and when I marked the sunlight dancing here and there, its beauty seemed to mock my sadness. For my master, whose restless, craving, vicious nature roved about day and night, seeking whom to devour, had just left me, with stinging, scorching words; words that scathed ear and brain like fire. O, how I despised him! I thought how glad I should be, if some day when he walked the earth, it would open and swallow him up, and disencumber the world of a plague.

When he told me that I was made for his use, made to obey his command in *every* thing; that I was nothing but a slave, whose will must and should surrender to his, never before had my puny arm felt half so strong.

So deeply was I absorbed in painful reflections afterwards, that I neither saw nor heard the entrance of any one, till the voice of William sounded close beside me. "Linda," said he, "what makes you look so sad? I love you. O, Linda, isn't this a bad world? Every body seems so cross and unhappy. I wish I had died when poor father did."

I told him that every body was *not* cross, or unhappy; that those who had pleasant homes, and kind friends, and who were not afraid to love them, were happy. But we, who were slave-children, without father or mother, could not expect to be happy. We must be good; perhaps that would bring us contentment.

"Yes," he said, "I try to be good; but what's the use? They are all the time troubling me." Then he proceeded to relate his afternoon's difficulty with young master Nicholas. It seemed that the brother of master Nicholas had pleased himself with making up stories about William. Master Nicholas said he should be flogged, and he would do it. Whereupon he went to work; but William fought bravely, and the young master, finding he was getting the better of him, undertook to tie his hands behind him. He failed in that likewise. By dint of kicking and fisting, William came out of the skirmish none the worse for a few scratches.

He continued to discourse on his young master's *meanness;* how he whipped the *little* boys, but was a perfect coward when a tussle ensued between him and white boys of his own size. On such occasions he always took to his legs. William had other charges to make against him. One was his rubbing up pennies with quicksilver, and passing them off for quarters of a dollar on an old man who kept a fruit stall. William was often sent to buy fruit, and he earnestly inquired of me what he ought to do under such circumstances. I told him it was certainly wrong to deceive the old man, and that it was his duty to tell him of the impositions practised by his young master. I assured him the old man would not be slow to comprehend the whole, and there the matter would end. William thought it might with the old man, but not with *him.* He said he did not mind the smart of the whip, but he did not like the *idea* of being whipped.

While I advised him to be good and forgiving I was not unconscious of the beam in my own eye.[4] It was the very knowledge of my own shortcomings that urged me to retain, if possible, some sparks of my brother's God-given nature. I had not lived fourteen years in slavery for nothing. I had felt, seen, and heard enough, to read the characters, and question the motives, of those around me. The war of my life had begun; and though one of God's most powerless creatures, I resolved never to be conquered. Alas, for me!

If there was one pure, sunny spot for me, I believed it to be in Benjamin's heart, and in another's, whom I loved with all the ardor of a girl's first love. My owner knew of it, and sought in every way to render me miserable. He did not resort to corporal punishment, but to all the petty, tyrannical ways that human ingenuity could devise.

I remember the first time I was punished. It was in the month of February. My grandmother had taken my old shoes, and replaced them with a new pair. I needed them; for several inches of snow had fallen, and it still continued to fall. When I walked through Mrs. Flint's room, their creaking grated harshly on her refined nerves. She called me to her, and asked what I had about me that made such a horrid noise. I told her it was my new shoes. "Take them off," said she; "and if you put them on again, I'll throw them into the fire."

I took them off, and my stockings also. She then sent me a long distance, on an errand. As I went through the snow, my bare feet tingled. That night I was very hoarse; and I went to bed thinking the next day would find me sick, perhaps dead. What was my grief on waking to find myself quite well!

I had imagined if I died, or was laid up for some time, that my mistress would feel a twinge of remorse that she had so hated "the little imp," as she styled me. It was my ignorance of that mistress that gave rise to such extravagant imaginings.

Dr. Flint occasionally had high prices offered for me; but he always said, "She don't belong to me. She is my daughter's property, and I have no right to sell her." Good, honest man! My

---

4. Compare Luke 6:42: "Cast first the beam out of thine own eye, and then shalt thou see clearly to pull out the mote that is in thy brother's eye."

young mistress was still a child, and I could look for no protection from her. I loved her, and she returned my affection. I once heard her father allude to her attachment to me; and his wife promptly replied that it proceeded from fear. This put unpleasant doubts into my mind. Did the child feign what she did not feel? or was her mother jealous of the mite of love she bestowed on me? I concluded it must be the latter. I said to myself, "Surely, little children are true."

One afternoon I sat at my sewing, feeling unusual depression of spirits. My mistress had been accusing me of an offence, of which I assured her I was perfectly innocent; but I saw, by the contemptuous curl of her lip, that she believed I was telling a lie.

I wondered for what wise purpose God was leading me through such thorny paths, and whether still darker days were in store for me. As I sat musing thus, the door opened softly, and William came in. "Well, brother," said I, "what is the matter this time?"

"O Linda, Ben and his master have had a dreadful time!" said he.

My first thought was that Benjamin was killed. "Don't be frightened, Linda," said William; "I will tell you all about it."

It appeared that Benjamin's master had sent for him, and he did not immediately obey the summons. When he did, his master was angry, and began to whip him. He resisted. Master and slave fought, and finally the master was thrown. Benjamin had cause to tremble; for he had thrown to the ground his master—one of the richest men in town. I anxiously awaited the result.

That night I stole to my grandmother's house, and Benjamin also stole thither from his master's. My grandmother had gone to spend a day or two with an old friend living in the country.

"I have come," said Benjamin, "to tell you good by. I am going away."

I inquired where.

"To the north," he replied.

I looked at him to see whether he was in earnest. I saw it all in his firm, set mouth. I implored him not to go, but he paid no heed to my words. He said he was no longer a boy, and every day made his yoke more galling. He had raised his hand against his master, and was to be publicly whipped for the offence. I reminded him of the poverty and hardships he must encounter among strangers. I told him he might be caught and brought back; and that was terrible to think of.

He grew vexed, and asked if poverty and hardships with freedom, were not preferable to our treatment in slavery. "Linda," he continued, "we are dogs here; foot-balls, cattle, every thing that's mean. No, I will not stay. Let them bring me back. We don't die but once."

He was right; but it was hard to give him up. "Go," said I, "and break your mother's heart."

I repented of my words ere they were out.

"Linda," said he, speaking as I had not heard him speak that evening, "how *could* you say that? Poor mother! be kind to her, Linda; and you, too, cousin Fanny."

Cousin Fanny was a friend who had lived some years with us.

Farewells were exchanged, and the bright, kind boy, endeared to us by so many acts of love, vanished from our sight.

It is not necessary to state how he made his escape. Suffice it to say, he was on his way to New York when a violent storm overtook the vessel. The captain said he must put into the nearest port. This alarmed Benjamin, who was aware that he would be advertised in every port near his own town. His embarrassment was noticed by the captain. To port they went. There the advertisement met the captain's eye. Benjamin so exactly answered its description, that the captain laid hold on him, and bound him in chains. The storm passed, and they proceeded to New York. Before reaching that port Benjamin managed to get off his chains and throw them overboard. He escaped from the vessel, but was pursued, captured, and carried back to his master.

When my grandmother returned home and found her youngest child had fled, great was her sorrow; but, with characteristic piety, she said, "God's will be done." Each morning, she inquired if any news had been heard from her boy. Yes, news *was* heard. The master was rejoicing over a letter, announcing the capture of his human chattel.

That day seems but as yesterday, so well do I remember it. I saw him led through the streets in chains, to jail. His face was ghastly pale, yet full of determination. He had begged one of the sailors to go to his mother's house and ask her not to meet him. He said the sight of her distress would take from him all self-control. She yearned to see him, and she went; but she screened herself in the crowd, that it might be as her child had said.

We were not allowed to visit him; but we had known the jailer for years, and he was a kind-hearted man. At midnight he opened the jail door for my grandmother and myself to enter, in disguise. When we entered the cell not a sound broke the stillness. "Benjamin, Benjamin!" whispered my grandmother. No answer. "Benjamin!" she again faltered. There was a jingle of chains. The moon had just risen, and cast an uncertain light through the bars of the window. We knelt down and took Benjamin's cold hands in ours. We did not speak. Sobs were heard, and Benjamin's lips were unsealed; for his mother was weeping on his neck. How vividly does memory bring back that sad night! Mother and son talked together. He asked her pardon for the suffering he had caused her. She said she had nothing to forgive; she could not blame his desire for freedom. He told her that when he was captured, he broke away, and was about casting himself into the river, when thoughts of *her* came over him, and he desisted. She asked if he did not also think of God. I fancied I saw his face grow fierce in the moonlight. He answered, "No, I did not think of him. When a man is hunted like a wild beast he forgets there is a God, a heaven. He forgets every thing in his struggle to get beyond the reach of the bloodhounds."

"Don't talk so, Benjamin," said she. "Put your trust in God. Be humble, my child, and your master will forgive you."

"Forgive me for *what*, mother? For not letting him treat me like a dog? No! I will never humble myself to him. I have worked for him for nothing all my life, and I am repaid with stripes and imprisonment. Here I will stay till I die, or till he sells me."

The poor mother shuddered at his words. I think he felt it; for when he next spoke, his voice was calmer. "Don't fret about me, mother. I ain't worth it," said he. "I wish I had some of your goodness. You bear every thing patiently, just as though you thought it was all right. I wish I could."

She told him she had not always been so; once, she was like him; but when sore troubles came upon her, and she had no arm to lean upon, she learned to call on God, and he lightened her burdens. She besought him to do likewise.

We overstaid our time, and were obliged to hurry from the jail.

Benjamin had been imprisoned three weeks, when my grandmother went to intercede for him with his master. He was immovable. He said Benjamin should serve as an example to the rest of his slaves; he should be kept in jail till he was subdued, or be sold if he got but one dollar for him. However, he afterwards relented in some degree. The chains were taken off, and we were allowed to visit him.

As his food was of the coarsest kind, we carried him as often as possible a warm supper, accompanied with some little luxury for the jailer.

Three months elapsed, and there was no prospect of release or of a purchaser. One day he was heard to sing and laugh. This piece of indecorum was told to his master, and the overseer was ordered to re-chain him. He was now confined in an apartment with other prisoners, who were covered with filthy rags. Benjamin was chained near them, and was soon covered with vermin. He worked at his chains till he succeeded in getting out of them. He passed them through the bars of the window, with a request that they should be taken to his master, and he should be informed that he was covered with vermin.

This audacity was punished with heavier chains, and prohibition of our visits.

My grandmother continued to send him fresh changes of clothes. The old ones were burned up. The last night we saw him in jail his mother still begged him to send for his master, and beg his pardon. Neither persuasion nor argument could turn him from his purpose. He calmly answered, "I am waiting his time."

Those chains were mournful to hear.

Another three months passed, and Benjamin left his prison walls. We that loved him waited to bid him a long and last farewell. A slave trader had bought him. You remember, I told you what price he brought when ten years of age. Now he was more than twenty years old, and sold for three hundred dollars. The master had been blind to his own interest. Long confinement had made his face too pale, his form too thin; moreover, the trader had heard something of his character, and it did not strike him as suitable for a slave. He said he would give any price if the handsome lad was a girl. We thanked God that he was not.

Could you have seen that mother clinging to her child, when they fastened the irons upon his wrists; could you have heard her heart-rending groans, and seen her bloodshot eyes wander wildly from face to face, vainly pleading for mercy; could you have witnessed that scene as I saw it, you would exclaim, *Slavery is damnable!*

Benjamin, her youngest, her pet, was forever gone! She could not realize it. She had had an interview with the trader for the purpose of ascertaining if Benjamin could be purchased. She was told it was impossible, as he had given bonds not to sell him till he was out of the state. He promised that he would not sell him till he reached New Orleans.

With a strong arm and unvaried trust, my grandmother began her work of love. Benjamin must be free. If she succeeded, she knew they would still be separated; but the sacrifice was not too great. Day and night she labored. The trader's price would treble that he gave; but she was not discouraged.

She employed a lawyer to write to a gentleman, whom she knew, in New Orleans. She begged him to interest himself for Benjamin, and he willingly favored her request. When he saw Benjamin, and stated his business, he thanked him; but said he preferred to wait a while before making the trader an offer. He knew he had tried to obtain a high price for him, and had invariably failed. This encouraged him to make another effort for freedom. So one morning, long before day, Benjamin was missing. He was riding over the blue billows, bound for Baltimore.

For once his white face did him a kindly service. They had no suspicion that it belonged to a slave; otherwise, the law would have been followed out to the letter, and the *thing* rendered back to slavery. The brightest skies are often overshadowed by the darkest clouds. Benjamin was taken sick, and compelled to remain in Baltimore three weeks. His strength was slow in returning; and his desire to continue his journey seemed to retard his recovery. How could he get strength without air and exercise? He resolved to venture on a short walk. A by-street was selected, where he thought himself secure of not being met by any one that knew him; but a voice called out, "Halloo, Ben, my boy! what are you doing *here?*"

His first impulse was to run; but his legs trembled so that he could not stir. He turned to confront his antagonist, and behold, there stood his old master's next door neighbor! He thought it was all over with him now; but it proved otherwise. That man was a miracle. He possessed a goodly number of slaves, and yet was not quite deaf to that mystic clock, whose ticking is rarely heard in the slaveholder's breast.

"Ben, you are sick," said he. "Why, you look like a ghost. I guess I gave you something of a start. Never mind, Ben, I am not going to touch you. You had a pretty tough time of it, and you may go on your way rejoicing for all me. But I would advise you to get out of this place plaguy quick, for there are several gentlemen here from our town." He described the nearest and safest route to New York, and added, "I shall be glad to tell your mother I have seen you. Good by, Ben."

Benjamin turned away, filled with gratitude, and surprised that the town he hated contained such a gem—a gem worthy of a purer setting.

This gentleman was a Northerner by birth, and had married a southern lady. On his return, he told my grandmother that he had seen her son, and of the service he had rendered him.

Benjamin reached New York safely, and concluded to stop there until he had gained strength enough to proceed further. It happened that my grandmother's only remaining son had sailed for the same city on business for his mistress. Through God's providence, the brothers met. You may be sure it was a happy meeting. "O Phil," exclaimed Benjamin, "I am here at last." Then he told him how near he came to dying, almost in sight of free land, and how he prayed that he might live to get one breath of free air. He said life was worth something now, and it would be hard to die. In the old jail he had not valued it; once, he was tempted to destroy it; but something, he did not know what, had prevented him; perhaps it was fear. He had heard those who profess to be religious declare there was no heaven for self-murderers; and as his life had been pretty hot here, he did not desire a continuation of the same in another world. "If I die now," he exclaimed, "thank God, I shall die a freeman!"

He begged my uncle Phillip not to return south; but stay and work with him, till they earned enough to buy those at home. His brother told him it would kill their mother if he deserted her in her trouble. She had pledged her house, and with difficulty had raised money to buy him. Would he be bought?

"No, never!" he replied. "Do you suppose, Phil, when I have got so far out of their clutches, I will give them one red cent? No! And do you suppose I would turn mother out of her home in her old age? That I would let her pay all those hard-earned dollars for me, and never to see me? For you know she will stay south as long as her other children are slaves. What a good mother! Tell her to buy *you*, Phil. You have been a comfort to her, and I have been a trouble. And Linda, poor Linda; what'll become of her? Phil, you don't know what a life they lead her. She has told me something about it, and I wish old Flint was dead, or a better man. When I was in jail, he asked her if she didn't want *him* to ask my master to forgive me, and take me home again. She told him, No; that I didn't want to go back. He got mad, and said we were all alike. I never despised my own master half as much as I do that man. There is many a worse slaveholder than my master; but for all that I would not be his slave."

While Benjamin was sick, he had parted with nearly all his clothes to pay necessary expenses. But he did not part with a little pin I fastened in his bosom when we parted. It was the most valuable thing I owned, and I still thought none more worthy to wear it. He had it still.

His brother furnished him with clothes, and gave him what money he had.

They parted with moistened eyes; and as Benjamin turned away, he said, "Phil, I part with all my kindred." And so it proved. We never heard from him again.

Uncle Phillip came home; and the first words he uttered when he entered the house were, "Mother, Ben is free! I have seen him in New York." She stood looking at him with a bewildered air. "Mother, don't you believe it?" he said, laying his hand softly upon her shoulder. She raised her hands, and exclaimed, "God be praised! Let us thank him." She dropped on her knees, and poured forth her heart in prayer. Then Phillip must sit down and repeat to her every word Benjamin had said. He told her all; only he forbore to mention how sick and pale her darling looked. Why should he distress her when she could do him no good?

The brave old woman still toiled on, hoping to rescue some of her other children. After a while she succeeded in buying Phillip. She paid eight hundred dollars, and came home with the precious document that secured his freedom. The happy mother and son sat together by the old hearthstone that night, telling how proud they were of each other, and how they would prove to the world that they could take care of themselves, as they had long taken care of others. We all concluded by saying, "He that is *willing* to be a slave, let him be a slave."

V.
The Trials of Girlhood

During the first years of my service in Dr. Flint's family, I was accustomed to share some indulgences with the children of my mistress. Though this seemed to me no more than right, I was grateful for it, and tried to merit the kindness by the faithful discharge of my duties. But I now entered on my fifteenth year—a sad epoch in the life of a slave girl. My master began to whisper foul words in my ear. Young as I was, I could not remain ignorant of their import. I tried to treat them with indifference or contempt. The master's age, my extreme youth, and the fear that his conduct would be reported to my grandmother, made him bear this treatment for many months. He was a crafty man, and resorted to many means to accomplish his purposes. Sometimes he had stormy, terrific ways, that made his victims tremble; sometimes he assumed a gentleness that he thought must surely subdue. Of the two, I preferred his stormy moods, although they left me trembling. He tried his utmost to corrupt the pure principles my grandmother had instilled. He peopled my young mind with unclean images, such as only a vile monster could think of. I turned from him with disgust and hatred. But he was my master. I was compelled to live under the same roof with him—where I saw a man forty years my senior daily violating the most sacred commandments of nature. He told me I was his property; that I must be subject to his will in all things. My soul revolted against the mean tyranny. But where could I turn for protection? No matter whether the slave girl be as black as ebony or as fair as her mistress. In either case, there is no shadow of law to protect her from insult, from violence, or even from death; all these are inflicted by fiends who bear the shape of men. The mistress, who ought to protect the helpless victim, has no other feelings towards her but those of jealousy and rage. The degradation, the wrongs, the vices, that grow out of slavery, are more than I can describe. They are greater than you would willingly believe. Surely, if you credited one half the truths that are told you concerning the helpless millions suffering in this cruel bondage, you at the north would not help to tighten the yoke. You surely would refuse to do for the master, on your own soil, the mean and cruel work which trained bloodhounds and the lowest class of whites do for him at the south.[5]

Every where the years bring to all enough of sin and sorrow; but in slavery the very dawn of life is darkened by these shadows. Even the little child, who is accustomed to wait on her mistress and her children, will learn, before she is twelve years old, why it is that her mistress hates such and such a one among the slaves. Perhaps the child's own mother is among those hated ones. She listens to violent outbreaks of jealous passion, and cannot help understanding what is the cause. She will become prematurely knowing in evil things. Soon she will learn to tremble when she hears her master's footfall. She will be compelled to realize that she is no longer a child. If God has bestowed beauty upon her, it will prove her greatest curse. That which commands admiration in the white woman only hastens the degradation of the female slave. I know that some are too much brutalized by slavery to feel the humiliation of their position; but many slaves feel it most acutely, and shrink from the memory of it. I cannot tell how much I suffered in the presence of these wrongs, nor how I am still pained by the retrospect. My master met me at every turn, reminding me that I belonged to him, and swearing by heaven and earth that he would compel me to submit to him. If I went out for a breath of fresh air, after a day of unwearied toil, his footsteps dogged me. If I knelt by my mother's grave, his dark shadow fell on me even there. The light heart which nature had given me became heavy with sad forebodings. The other slaves in my master's house noticed the change. Many of them pitied me; but none dared to ask the cause. They had no need to

5.   A reference to the Fugitive Slave Law, passed in 1850, which required Northerners to return escaped slaves to captivity.

inquire. They knew too well the guilty practices under that roof; and they were aware that to speak of them was an offence that never went unpunished.

I longed for some one to confide in. I would have given the world to have laid my head on my grandmother's faithful bosom, and told her all my troubles. But Dr. Flint swore he would kill me, if I was not as silent as the grave. Then, although my grandmother was all in all to me, I feared her as well as loved her. I had been accustomed to look up to her with a respect bordering upon awe. I was very young, and felt shamefaced about telling her such impure things, especially as I knew her to be very strict on such subjects. Moreover, she was a woman of a high spirit. She was usually very quiet in her demeanor; but if her indignation was once roused, it was not very easily quelled. I had been told that she once chased a white gentleman with a loaded pistol, because he insulted one of her daughters. I dreaded the consequences of a violent outbreak; and both pride and fear kept me silent. But though I did not confide in my grandmother, and even evaded her vigilant watchfulness and inquiry, her presence in the neighborhood was some protection to me. Though she had been a slave, Dr. Flint was afraid of her. He dreaded her scorching rebukes. Moreover, she was known and patronized by many people; and he did not wish to have his villany made public. It was lucky for me that I did not live on a distant plantation, but in a town not so large that the inhabitants were ignorant of each other's affairs. Bad as are the laws and customs in a slaveholding community, the doctor, as a professional man, deemed it prudent to keep up some outward show of decency.

O, what days and nights of fear and sorrow that man caused me! Reader, it is not to awaken sympathy for myself that I am telling you truthfully what I suffered in slavery. I do it to kindle a flame of compassion in your hearts for my sisters who are still in bondage, suffering as I once suffered.

I once saw two beautiful children playing together. One was a fair white child; the other was her slave, and also her sister. When I saw them embracing each other, and heard their joyous laughter, I turned sadly away from the lovely sight. I foresaw the inevitable blight that would fall on the little slave's heart. I knew how soon her laughter would be changed to sighs. The fair child grew up to be a still fairer woman. From childhood to womanhood her pathway was blooming with flowers, and overarched by a sunny sky. Scarcely one day of her life had been clouded when the sun rose on her happy bridal morning.

How had those years dealt with her slave sister, the little playmate of her childhood? She, also, was very beautiful; but the flowers and sunshine of love were not for her. She drank the cup of sin, and shame, and misery, whereof her persecuted race are compelled to drink.

In view of these things, why are ye silent, ye free men and women of the north? Why do your tongues falter in maintenance of the right? Would that I had more ability! But my heart is so full, and my pen is so weak! There are noble men and women who plead for us, striving to help those who cannot help themselves. God bless them! God give them strength and courage to go on! God bless those, every where, who are laboring to advance the cause of humanity!

VI.
The Jealous Mistress

I would ten thousand times rather that my children should be the half-starved paupers of Ireland than to be the most pampered among the slaves of America. I would rather drudge out my life on a cotton plantation, till the grave opened to give me rest, than to live with an unprincipled master and a jealous mistress. The felon's home in a penitentiary is preferable. He may repent, and turn from the error of his ways, and so find peace; but it is not so with a favorite slave. She is not allowed to have any pride of character. It is deemed a crime in her to wish to be virtuous.

Mrs. Flint possessed the key to her husband's character before I was born. She might have used this knowledge to counsel and to screen the young and the innocent among her slaves; but for them she had no sympathy. They were the objects of her constant suspicion and malevolence. She watched her husband with unceasing vigilance; but he was well practised in means to evade it. What he could not find opportunity to say in words he manifested in signs. He invented more than were ever thought of in a deaf and dumb asylum. I let them pass, as if I did not understand what he meant; and many were the curses and threats bestowed on me for my stupidity. One day he caught me teaching myself to write. He frowned, as if he was not well pleased; but I suppose he came to the conclusion that such an accomplishment might help to advance his favorite scheme. Before long, notes were often slipped into my hand. I would return them, saying, "I can't read them, sir." "Can't you?" he replied; "then I must read them to you." He always finished the reading by asking, "Do you understand?" Sometimes he would complain of the heat of the tea room, and order his supper to be placed on a small table in the piazza. He would seat himself there with a well-satisfied smile, and tell me to stand by and brush away the flies. He would eat very slowly, pausing between the mouthfuls. These intervals were employed in describing the happiness I was so foolishly throwing away, and in threatening me with the penalty that finally awaited my stubborn disobedience. He boasted much of the forbearance he had exercised towards me, and reminded me that there was a limit to his patience. When I succeeded in avoiding opportunities for him to talk to me at home, I was ordered to come to his office, to do some errand. When there, I was obliged to stand and listen to such language as he saw fit to address to me. Sometimes I so openly expressed my contempt for him that he would become violently enraged, and I wondered why he did not strike me. Circumstanced as he was, he probably thought it was better policy to be forbearing. But the state of things grew worse and worse daily. In desperation I told him that I must and would apply to my grandmother for protection. He threatened me with death, and worse than death, if I made any complaint to her. Strange to say, I did not despair. I was naturally of a buoyant disposition, and always I had a hope of somehow getting out of his clutches. Like many a poor, simple slave before me, I trusted that some threads of joy would yet be woven into my dark destiny.

I had entered my sixteenth year, and every day it became more apparent that my presence was intolerable to Mrs. Flint. Angry words frequently passed between her and her husband. He had never punished me himself, and he would not allow any body else to punish me. In that respect, she was never satisfied; but, in her angry moods, no terms were too vile for her to bestow upon me. Yet I, whom she detested so bitterly, had far more pity for her than he had, whose duty it was to make her life happy. I never wronged her, or wished to wrong her; and one word of kindness from her would have brought me to her feet.

After repeated quarrels between the doctor and his wife, he announced his intention to take his youngest daughter, then four years old, to sleep in his apartment. It was necessary that a servant should sleep in the same room, to be on hand if the child stirred. I was selected for that office, and informed for what purpose that arrangement had been made. By managing to keep within sight of people, as much as possible, during the day time, I had hitherto succeeded in eluding my master, though a razor was often held to my throat to force me to change this line of policy. At night I slept by the side of my great aunt, where I felt safe. He was too prudent to come into her room. She was an old woman, and had been in the family many years. Moreover, as a married man, and a professional man, he deemed it necessary to save appearances in some degree. But he resolved to remove the obstacle in the way of his scheme; and he thought he had planned it so that he should evade suspicion. He was well aware how much I prized my refuge by the side of my old aunt, and he determined to dispossess me of it. The first night the doctor had the little child in his room alone. The next morning, I was ordered to take my station as nurse the following night. A kind Providence interposed in my favor. During the day Mrs. Flint heard of this new arrangement, and a storm followed. I rejoiced to hear it rage.

After a while my mistress sent for me to come to her room. Her first question was, "Did you know you were to sleep in the doctor's room?"

"Yes, ma'am."

"Who told you?"

"My master."

"Will you answer truly all the questions I ask?"

"Yes, ma'am."

"Tell me, then, as you hope to be forgiven, are you innocent of what I have accused you?"

"I am."

She handed me a Bible, and said, "Lay your hand on your heart, kiss this holy book, and swear before God that you tell me the truth."

I took the oath she required, and I did it with a clear conscience.

"You have taken God's holy word to testify your innocence," said she. "If you have deceived me, beware! Now take this stool, sit down, look me directly in the face, and tell me all that has passed between your master and you."

I did as she ordered. As I went on with my account her color changed frequently, she wept, and sometimes groaned. She spoke in tones so sad, that I was touched by her grief. The tears came to my eyes; but I was soon convinced that her emotions arose from anger and wounded pride. She felt that her marriage vows were desecrated, her dignity insulted; but she had no compassion for the poor victim of her husband's perfidy. She pitied herself as a martyr; but she was incapable of feeling for the condition of shame and misery in which her unfortunate, helpless slave was placed.

Yet perhaps she had some touch of feeling for me; for when the conference was ended, she spoke kindly, and promised to protect me. I should have been much comforted by this assurance if I could have had confidence in it; but my experiences in slavery had filled me with distrust. She was not a very refined woman, and had not much control over her passions. I was an object of her jealousy, and, consequently, of her hatred; and I knew I could not expect kindness or confidence from her under the circumstances in which I was placed. I could not blame her. Slaveholders' wives feel as other women would under similar circumstances. The fire of her temper kindled from small sparks, and now the flame became so intense that the doctor was obliged to give up his intended arrangement.

I knew I had ignited the torch, and I expected to suffer for it afterwards; but I felt too thankful to my mistress for the timely aid she rendered me to care much about that. She now took me to sleep in a room adjoining her own. There I was an object of her especial care, though not of her especial comfort, for she spent many a sleepless night to watch over me. Sometimes I woke up, and found her bending over me. At other times she whispered in my ear, as though it was her husband who was speaking to me, and listened to hear what I would answer. If she startled me, on such occasions, she would glide stealthily away; and the next morning she would tell me I had been talking in my sleep, and ask who I was talking to. At last, I began to be fearful for my life. It had been often threatened; and you can imagine, better than I can describe, what an unpleasant sensation it must produce to wake up in the dead of night and find a jealous woman bending over you. Terrible as this experience was, I had fears that it would give place to one more terrible.

My mistress grew weary of her vigils; they did not prove satisfactory. She changed her tactics. She now tried the trick of accusing my master of crime, in my presence, and gave my name as the author of the accusation. To my utter astonishment, he replied, "I don't believe it; but if she did acknowledge it, you tortured her into exposing me." Tortured into exposing him! Truly, Satan had no difficulty in distinguishing the color of his soul! I understood his object in making this false representation. It was to show me that I gained nothing by seeking the protection of my mistress; that the power was still all in his own hands. I pitied Mrs. Flint.

She was a second wife, many years the junior of her husband; and the hoary-headed miscreant was enough to try the patience of a wiser and better woman. She was completely foiled, and knew not how to proceed. She would gladly have had me flogged for my supposed false oath; but, as I have already stated, the doctor never allowed any one to whip me. The old sinner was politic. The application of the lash might have led to remarks that would have exposed him in the eyes of his children and grandchildren. How often did I rejoice that I lived in a town where all the inhabitants knew each other! If I had been on a remote plantation, or lost among the multitude of a crowded city, I should not be a living woman at this day.

The secrets of slavery are concealed like those of the Inquisition.[6] My master was, to my knowledge, the father of eleven slaves. But did the mothers dare to tell who was the father of their children? Did the other slaves dare to allude to it, except in whispers among themselves? No, indeed! They knew too well the terrible consequences.

My grandmother could not avoid seeing things which excited her suspicions. She was uneasy about me, and tried various ways to buy me; but the never-changing answer was always repeated: "Linda does not belong to *me*. She is my daughter's property, and I have no legal right to sell her." The conscientious man! He was too scrupulous to *sell* me; but he had no scruples whatever about committing a much greater wrong against the helpless young girl placed under his guardianship, as his daughter's property. Sometimes my persecutor would ask me whether I would like to be sold. I told him I would rather be sold to any body than to lead such a life as I did. On such occasions he would assume the air of a very injured individual, and reproach me for my ingratitude. "Did I not take you into the house, and make you the companion of my own children?" he would say. "Have I ever treated you like a negro? I have never allowed you to be punished, not even to please your mistress. And this is the recompense I get, you ungrateful girl!" I answered that he had reasons of his own for screening me from punishment, and that the course he pursued made my mistress hate me and persecute me. If I wept, he would say, "Poor child! Don't cry! don't cry! I will make peace for you with your mistress. Only let me arrange matters in my own way. Poor, foolish girl! you don't know what is for your own good. I would cherish you. I would make a lady of you. Now go, and think of all I have promised you."

I did think of it.

Reader, I draw no imaginary pictures of southern homes. I am telling you the plain truth. Yet when victims make their escape from this wild beast of Slavery, northerners consent to act the part of bloodhounds, and hunt the poor fugitive back into his den, "full of dead men's bones, and all uncleanness." Nay, more, they are not only willing, but proud, to give their daughters in marriage to slaveholders. The poor girls have romantic notions of a sunny clime, and of the flowering vines that all the year round shade a happy home. To what disappointments are they destined! The young wife soon learns that the husband in whose hands she has placed her happiness pays no regard to his marriage vows. Children of every shade of complexion play with her own fair babies, and too well she knows that they are born unto him of his own household. Jealousy and hatred enter the flowery home, and it is ravaged of its loveliness.

Southern women often marry a man knowing that he is the father of many little slaves. They do not trouble themselves about it. They regard such children as property, as marketable as the pigs on the plantation; and it is seldom that they do not make them aware of this by passing them into the slave-trader's hands as soon as possible, and thus getting them out of their sight. I am glad to say there are some honorable exceptions.

I have myself known two southern wives who exhorted their husbands to free those slaves towards whom they stood in a "parental relation;" and their request was granted. These husbands blushed before the superior nobleness of their wives' natures. Though they had only counselled them to do that which it was their duty to do, it commanded their respect, and

6. Notorious tribunal of the Roman Catholic Church, designed to suppress heresy.

rendered their conduct more exemplary. Concealment was at an end, and confidence took the place of distrust.

Though this bad institution deadens the moral sense, even in white women, to a fearful extent, it is not altogether extinct. I have heard southern ladies say of Mr. Such a one, "He not only thinks it no disgrace to be the father of those little niggers, but he is not ashamed to call himself their master. I declare, such things ought not to be tolerated in any decent society!"

VII.
The Lover

Why does the slave ever love? Why allow the tendrils of the heart to twine around objects which may at any moment be wrenched away by the hand of violence? When separations come by the hand of death, the pious soul can bow in resignation, and say, "Not my will, but thine be done, O Lord!"[7] But when the ruthless hand of man strikes the blow, regardless of the misery he causes, it is hard to be submissive. I did not reason thus when I was a young girl. Youth will be youth. I loved, and I indulged the hope that the dark clouds around me would turn out a bright lining. I forgot that in the land of my birth the shadows are too dense for light to penetrate. A land

> *"Where laughter is not mirth; nor thought the mind;*
> *Nor words a language; nor e'en men mankind.*
> *Where cries reply to curses, shrieks to blows,*
> *And each is tortured in his separate hell."*[8]

There was in the neighborhood a young colored carpenter; a free born man. We had been well acquainted in childhood, and frequently met together afterwards. We became mutually attached, and he proposed to marry me. I loved him with all the ardor of a young girl's first love. But when I reflected that I was a slave, and that the laws gave no sanction to the marriage of such, my heart sank within me. My lover wanted to buy me; but I knew that Dr. Flint was too wilful and arbitrary a man to consent to that arrangement. From him, I was sure of experiencing all sorts of opposition, and I had nothing to hope from my mistress. She would have been delighted to have got rid of me, but not in that way. It would have relieved her mind of a burden if she could have seen me sold to some distant state, but if I was married near home I should be just as much in her husband's power as I had previously been,—for the husband of a slave has no power to protect her. Moreover, my mistress, like many others, seemed to think that slaves had no right to any family ties of their own; that they were created merely to wait upon the family of the mistress. I once heard her abuse a young slave girl, who told her that a colored man wanted to make her his wife. "I will have you peeled and pickled,[9] my lady," said she, "if I ever hear you mention that subject again. Do you suppose that I will have you tending *my* children with the children of that nigger?" The girl to whom she said this had a mulatto child, of course not acknowledged by its father. The poor black man who loved her would have been proud to acknowledge his helpless offspring.

Many and anxious were the thoughts I revolved in my mind. I was at a loss what to do. Above all things, I was desirous to spare my lover the insults that had cut so deeply into my own soul. I talked with my grandmother about it, and partly told her my fears. I

7. Luke 22:42.   Tasso," 4. 7–10.
8. George Gordon, Lord Byron, "The Lament of   9. Whipped and washed with brine.

did not dare to tell her the worst. She had long suspected all was not right, and if I confirmed her suspicions I knew a storm would rise that would prove the overthrow of all my hopes.

This love-dream had been my support through many trials; and I could not bear to run the risk of having it suddenly dissipated. There was a lady in the neighborhood, a particular friend of Dr. Flint's, who often visited the house. I had a great respect for her, and she had always manifested a friendly interest in me. Grandmother thought she would have great influence with the doctor. I went to this lady, and told her my story. I told her I was aware that my lover's being a free-born man would prove a great objection; but he wanted to buy me; and if Dr. Flint would consent to that arrangement, I felt sure he would be willing to pay any reasonable price. She knew that Mrs. Flint disliked me; therefore, I ventured to suggest that perhaps my mistress would approve of my being sold, as that would rid her of me. The lady listened with kindly sympathy, and promised to do her utmost to promote my wishes. She had an interview with the doctor, and I believe she pleaded my cause earnestly; but it was all to no purpose.

How I dreaded my master now! Every minute I expected to be summoned to his presence; but the day passed, and I heard nothing from him. The next morning, a message was brought to me: "Master wants you in his study." I found the door ajar, and I stood a moment gazing at the hateful man who claimed a right to rule me, body and soul. I entered, and tried to appear calm. I did not want him to know how my heart was bleeding. He looked fixedly at me, with an expression which seemed to say, "I have half a mind to kill you on the spot." At last he broke the silence, and that was a relief to both of us.

"So you want to be married, do you?" said he, "and to a free nigger."

"Yes, sir."

"Well, I'll soon convince you whether I am your master, or the nigger fellow you honor so highly. If you *must* have a husband, you may take up with one of my slaves."

What a situation I should be in, as the wife of one of *his* slaves, even if my heart had been interested!

I replied, "Don't you suppose, sir, that a slave can have some preference about marrying? Do you suppose that all men are alike to her?"

"Do you love this nigger?" said he, abruptly.

"Yes, sir."

"How dare you tell me so!" he exclaimed, in great wrath. After a slight pause, he added, "I supposed you thought more of yourself; that you felt above the insults of such puppies."[1]

"I replied, "If he is a puppy I am a puppy, for we are both of the negro race. It is right and honorable for us to love each other. The man you call a puppy never insulted me, sir; and he would not love me if he did not believe me to be a virtuous woman."

He sprang upon me like a tiger, and gave me a stunning blow. It was the first time he had ever struck me; and fear did not enable me to control my anger. When I had recovered a little from the effects, I exclaimed, "You have struck me for answering you honestly. How I despise you!"

There was silence for some minutes. Perhaps he was deciding what should be my punishment; or, perhaps, he wanted to give me time to reflect on what I had said, and to whom I had said it. Finally, he asked, "Do you know what you have said?"

"Yes, sir; but your treatment drove me to it."

"Do you know that I have a right to do as I like with you,—that I can kill you, if I please?"

"You have tried to kill me, and I wish you had; but you have no right to do as you like with me."

"Silence!" he exclaimed, in a thundering voice. "By heavens, girl, you forget yourself too far! Are you mad? If you are, I will soon bring you to your senses. Do you think any other

1. "Puppy" is slang for an arrogant, insolent young man.

master would bear what I have borne from you this morning? Many masters would have killed you on the spot. How would you like to be sent to jail for your insolence?"

"I know I have been disrespectful, sir," I replied; "but you drove me to it; I couldn't help it. As for the jail, there would be more peace for me there than there is here."

"You deserve to go there," said he, "and to be under such treatment, that you would forget the meaning of the word *peace*. It would do you good. It would take some of your high notions out of you. But I am not ready to send you there yet, notwithstanding your ingratitude for all my kindness and forbearance. You have been the plague of my life. I have wanted to make you happy, and I have been repaid with the basest ingratitude; but though you have proved yourself incapable of appreciating my kindness, I will be lenient towards you, Linda. I will give you one more chance to redeem your character. If you behave yourself and do as I require, I will forgive you and treat you as I always have done; but if you disobey me, I will punish you as I would the meanest slave on my plantation. Never let me hear that fellow's name mentioned again. If I ever know of your speaking to him, I will cowhide you both; and if I catch him lurking about my premises, I will shoot him as soon as I would a dog. Do you hear what I say? I'll teach you a lesson about marriage and free niggers! Now go, and let this be the last time I have occasion to speak to you on this subject."

Reader, did you ever hate? I hope not. I never did but once; and I trust I never shall again. Somebody has called it "the atmosphere of hell;" and I believe it is so.

For a fortnight the doctor did not speak to me. He thought to mortify me; to make me feel that I had disgraced myself by receiving the honorable addresses of a respectable colored man, in preference to the base proposals of a white man. But though his lips disdained to address me, his eyes were very loquacious. No animal ever watched its prey more narrowly than he watched me. He knew that I could write, though he had failed to make me read his letters; and he was now troubled lest I should exchange letters with another man. After a while he became weary of silence; and I was sorry for it. One morning, as he passed through the hall, to leave the house, he contrived to thrust a note into my hand. I thought I had better read it, and spare myself the vexation of having him read it to me. It expressed regret for the blow he had given me, and reminded me that I myself was wholly to blame for it. He hoped I had become convinced of the injury I was doing myself by incurring his displeasure. He wrote that he had made up his mind to go to Louisiana; that he should take several slaves with him, and intended I should be one of the number. My mistress would remain where she was; therefore I should have nothing to fear from that quarter. If I merited kindness from him, he assured me that it would be lavishly bestowed. He begged me to think over the matter, and answer the following day.

The next morning I was called to carry a pair of scissors to his room. I laid them on the table, with the letter beside them. He thought it was my answer, and did not call me back. I went as usual to attend my young mistress to and from school. He met me in the street, and ordered me to stop at his office on my way back. When I entered, he showed me his letter, and asked me why I had not answered it. I replied, "I am your daughter's property, and it is in your power to send me, or take me, wherever you please." He said he was very glad to find me so willing to go, and that we should start early in the autumn. He had a large practice in the town, and I rather thought he had made up the story merely to frighten me. However that might be, I was determined that I would never go to Louisiana with him.

Summer passed away, and early in the autumn Dr. Flint's eldest son was sent to Louisiana to examine the country, with a view to emigrating. That news did not disturb me. I knew very well that I should not be sent with *him*. That I had not been taken to the plantation before this time, was owing to the fact that his son was there. He was jealous of his son; and jealousy of the overseer had kept him from punishing me by sending me into the fields to work. Is it strange that I was not proud of these protectors? As for the overseer, he was a man for whom I had less respect than I had for a bloodhound.

Young Mr. Flint did not bring back a favorable report of Louisiana, and I heard no more of that scheme. Soon after this, my lover met me at the corner of the street, and I stopped to speak to him. Looking up, I saw my master watching us from his window. I hurried home, trembling with fear. I was sent for, immediately, to go to his room. He met me with a blow. "When is mistress to be married?" said he, in a sneering tone. A shower of oaths and imprecations followed. How thankful I was that my lover was a free man! that my tyrant had no power to flog him for speaking to me in the street!

Again and again I revolved in my mind how all this would end. There was no hope that the doctor would consent to sell me on any terms. He had an iron will, and was determined to keep me, and to conquer me. My lover was an intelligent and religious man. Even if he could have obtained permission to marry me while I was a slave, the marriage would give him no power to protect me from my master. It would have made him miserable to witness the insults I should have been subjected to. And then, if we had children, I knew they must "follow the condition of the mother."[2] What a terrible blight that would be on the heart of a free, intelligent father! For *his* sake, I felt that I ought not to link his fate with my own unhappy destiny. He was going to Savannah to see about a little property left him by an uncle; and hard as it was to bring my feelings to it, I earnestly entreated him not to come back. I advised him to go to the Free States, where his tongue would not be tied, and where his intelligence would be of more avail to him. He left me, still hoping the day would come when I could be bought. With me the lamp of hope had gone out. The dream of my girlhood was over. I felt lonely and desolate.

Still I was not stripped of all. I still had my good grandmother, and my affectionate brother. When he put his arms round my neck, and looked into my eyes, as if to read there the troubles I dared not tell, I felt that I still had something to love. But even that pleasant emotion was chilled by the reflection that he might be torn from me at any moment, by some sudden freak of my master. If he had known how we loved each other, I think he would have exulted in separating us. We often planned together how we could get to the north. But, as William remarked, such things are easier said than done. My movements were very closely watched, and we had no means of getting any money to defray our expenses. As for grandmother, she was strongly opposed to her children's undertaking any such project. She had not forgotten poor Benjamin's sufferings, and she was afraid that if another child tried to escape, he would have a similar or a worse fate. To me, nothing seemed more dreadful than my present life. I said to myself, "William *must* be free. He shall go to the north, and I will follow him." Many a slave sister has formed the same plans.

VIII.
What Slaves Are Taught to Think of the North

Slaveholders pride themselves upon being honorable men; but if you were to hear the enormous lies they tell their slaves, you would have small respect for their veracity. I have spoken plain English. Pardon me. I cannot use a milder term. When they visit the north, and return home, they tell their slaves of the runaways they have seen, and describe them to be in the most deplorable condition. A slaveholder once told me that he had seen a runaway friend of mine in New York, and that she besought him to take her back to her master, for she was literally dying of starvation; that many days she had only one cold potato to eat, and at other times could get nothing at all. He said he refused to take her, because he knew her master would not thank him for bringing such a miserable wretch to his house. He ended by

---

2.   A slave mother's children were legally slaves, a free mother's children were free.

saying to me, "This is the punishment she brought on herself for running away from a kind master."

This whole story was false. I afterwards staid with that friend in New York, and found her in comfortable circumstances. She had never thought of such a thing as wishing to go back to slavery. Many of the slaves believe such stories, and think it is not worth while to exchange slavery for such a hard kind of freedom. It is difficult to persuade such that freedom could make them useful men, and enable them to protect their wives and children. If those heathen in our Christian land had as much teaching as some Hindoos, they would think otherwise. They would know that liberty is more valuable than life. They would begin to understand their own capabilities, and exert themselves to become men and women.

But while the Free States sustain a law which hurls fugitives back into slavery, how can the slaves resolve to become men? There are some who strive to protect wives and daughters from the insults of their masters; but those who have such sentiments have had advantages above the general mass of slaves. They have been partially civilized and Christianized by favorable circumstances. Some are bold enough to *utter* such sentiments to their masters. O, that there were more of them!

Some poor creatures have been so brutalized by the lash that they will sneak out of the way to give their masters free access to their wives and daughters. Do you think this proves the black man to belong to an inferior order of beings? What would *you* be, if you had been born and brought up a slave, with generations of slaves for ancestors? I admit that the black man *is* inferior. But what is it that makes him so? It is the ignorance in which white men compel him to live; it is the torturing whip that lashes manhood out of him; it is the fierce bloodhounds of the South, and the scarcely less cruel human bloodhounds of the north, who enforce the Fugitive Slave Law. *They* do the work.

Southern gentlemen indulge in the most contemptuous expressions about the Yankees, while they, on their part, consent to do the vilest work for them, such as the ferocious bloodhounds and the despised negro-hunters are employed to do at home. When southerners go to the north, they are proud to do them honor; but the northern man is not welcome south of Mason and Dixon's line, unless he suppresses every thought and feeling at variance with their "peculiar institution." Nor is it enough to be silent. The masters are not pleased, unless they obtain a greater degree of subservience than that; and they are generally accommodated. Do they respect the northerner for this? I trow not. Even the slaves despise "a northern man with southern principles;" and that is the class they generally see. When northerners go to the south to reside, they prove very apt scholars. They soon imbibe the sentiments and disposition of their neighbors, and generally go beyond their teachers. Of the two, they are proverbially the hardest masters.

They seem to satisfy their consciences with the doctrine that God created the Africans to be slaves. What a libel upon the heavenly Father, who "made of one blood all nations of men!"[3] And then who *are* Africans? Who can measure the amount of Anglo-Saxon blood coursing in the veins of American slaves?

I have spoken of the pains slaveholders take to give their slaves a bad opinion of the north; but, notwithstanding this, intelligent slaves are aware that they have many friends in the Free States. Even the most ignorant have some confused notions about it. They knew that I could read; and I was often asked if I had seen any thing in the newspapers about white folks over in the big north, who were trying to get their freedom for them. Some believe that the abolitionists have already made them free, and that it is established by law, but that their masters prevent the law from going into effect. One woman begged me to get a newspaper and read it over. She said her husband told her that the black people had sent word to the queen of 'Merica that they were all slaves; that she didn't believe it, and went to Washington

3. Acts 17:26.

city to see the president about it. They quarrelled; she drew her sword upon him, and swore that he should help her to make them all free.

That poor, ignorant woman thought that America was governed by a Queen, to whom the President was subordinate. I wish the President was subordinate to Queen Justice.[4]

X.
A Perilous Passage in the Slave Girl's Life

After my lover went away, Dr. Flint contrived a new plan. He seemed to have an idea that my fear of my mistress was his greatest obstacle. In the blandest tones, he told me that he was going to build a small house for me, in a secluded place, four miles away from the town. I shuddered; but I was constrained to listen, while he talked of his intention to give me a home of my own, and to make a lady of me. Hitherto, I had escaped my dreaded fate, by being in the midst of people. My grandmother had already had high words with my master about me. She had told him pretty plainly what she thought of his character, and there was considerable gossip in the neighborhood about our affairs, to which the open-mouthed jealousy of Mrs. Flint contributed not a little. When my master said he was going to build a house for me, and that he could do it with little trouble and expense, I was in hopes something would happen to frustrate his scheme; but I soon heard that the house was actually begun. I vowed before my Maker that I would never enter it. I had rather toil on the plantation from dawn till dark; I had rather live and die in jail, than drag on, from day to day, through such a living death. I was determined that the master, whom I so hated and loathed, who had blighted the prospects of my youth, and made my life a desert, should not, after my long struggle with him, succeed at last in trampling his victim under his feet. I would do any thing, every thing, for the sake of defeating him. What *could* I do? I thought and thought, till I became desperate, and made a plunge into the abyss.

And now, reader, I come to a period in my unhappy life, which I would gladly forget if I could. The remembrance fills me with sorrow and shame. It pains me to tell you of it; but I have promised to tell you the truth, and I will do it honestly, let it cost me what it may. I will not try to screen myself behind the plea of compulsion from a master; for it was not so. Neither can I plead ignorance or thoughtlessness. For years, my master had done his utmost to pollute my mind with foul images, and to destroy the pure principles inculcated by my grandmother, and the good mistress of my childhood. The influences of slavery had had the same effect on me that they had on other young girls; they had made me prematurely knowing, concerning the evil ways of the world. I knew what I did, and I did it with deliberate calculation.

But, O, ye happy women, whose purity has been sheltered from childhood, who have been free to choose the objects of your affection, whose homes are protected by law, do not judge the poor desolate slave girl too severely! If slavery had been abolished, I, also, could have married the man of my choice; I could have had a home shielded by the laws; and I should have been spared the painful task of confessing what I am now about to relate; but all my prospects had been blighted by slavery. I wanted to keep myself pure; and, under the most adverse circumstances, I tried hard to preserve my self-respect; but I was struggling alone in the powerful grasp of the demon Slavery; and the monster proved too strong for me. I felt as if I was forsaken by God and man; as if all my efforts must be frustrated; and I became reckless in my despair.

---

4. The following chapter, omitted here, details atrocities against slaves in Jacobs's neighborhood, emphasizing that "nothing was said" against the perpetrators.

I have told you that Dr. Flint's persecutions and his wife's jealousy had given rise to some gossip in the neighborhood. Among others, it chanced that a white unmarried gentleman had obtained some knowledge of the circumstances in which I was placed. He knew my grandmother, and often spoke to me in the street. He became interested for me, and asked questions about my master, which I answered in part. He expressed a great deal of sympathy, and a wish to aid me. He constantly sought opportunities to see me, and wrote to me frequently. I was a poor slave girl, only fifteen years old.

So much attention from a superior person was, of course, flattering; for human nature is the same in all. I also felt grateful for his sympathy, and encouraged by his kind words. It seemed to me a great thing to have such a friend. By degrees, a more tender feeling crept into my heart. He was an educated and eloquent gentleman; too eloquent, alas, for the poor slave girl who trusted in him. Of course I saw whither all this was tending. I knew the impassable gulf between us; but to be an object of interest to a man who is not married, and who is not her master, is agreeable to the pride and feelings of a slave, if her miserable situation has left her any pride or sentiment. It seems less degrading to give one's self, than to submit to compulsion. There is something akin to freedom in having a lover who has no control over you, except that which he gains by kindness and attachment. A master may treat you as rudely as he pleases, and you dare not speak; moreover, the wrong does not seem so great with an unmarried man, as with one who has a wife to be made unhappy. There may be sophistry in all this; but the condition of a slave confuses all principles of morality, and, in fact, renders the practice of them impossible.

When I found that my master had actually begun to build the lonely cottage, other feelings mixed with those I have described. Revenge, and calculations of interest, were added to flattered vanity and sincere gratitude for kindness. I knew nothing would enrage Dr. Flint so much as to know that I favored another; and it was something to triumph over my tyrant even in that small way. I thought he would revenge himself by selling me, and I was sure my friend, Mr. Sands, would buy me. He was a man of more generosity and feeling than my master, and I thought my freedom could be easily obtained from him. The crisis of my fate now came so near that I was desperate. I shuddered to think of being the mother of children that should be owned by my old tyrant. I knew that as soon as a new fancy took him, his victims were sold far off to get rid of them; especially if they had children. I had seen several women sold, with his babies at the breast. He never allowed his offspring by slaves to remain long in sight of himself and his wife. Of a man who was not my master I could ask to have my children well supported; and in this case, I felt confident I should obtain the boon. I also felt quite sure that they would be made free. With all these thoughts revolving in my mind, and seeing no other way of escaping the doom I so much dreaded, I made a headlong plunge. Pity me, and pardon me, O virtuous reader! You never knew what it is to be a slave; to be entirely unprotected by law or custom; to have the laws reduce you to the condition of a chattel, entirely subject to the will of another. You never exhausted your ingenuity in avoiding the snares, and eluding the power of a hated tyrant; you never shuddered at the sound of his footsteps, and trembled within hearing of his voice. I know I did wrong. No one can feel it more sensibly than I do. The painful and humiliating memory will haunt me to my dying day. Still, in looking back, calmly, on the events of my life, I feel that the slave woman ought not to be judged by the same standard as others.

The months passed on. I had many unhappy hours. I secretly mourned over the sorrow I was bringing on my grandmother, who had so tried to shield me from harm. I knew that I was the greatest comfort of her old age, and that it was a source of pride to her that I had not degraded myself, like most of the slaves. I wanted to confess to her that I was no longer worthy of her love; but I could not utter the dreaded words.

As for Dr. Flint, I had a feeling of satisfaction and triumph in the thought of telling *him*.

From time to time he told me of his intended arrangements, and I was silent. At last, he came and told me the cottage was completed, and ordered me to go to it. I told him I would never enter it. He said, "I have heard enough of such talk as that. You shall go, if you are carried by force; and you shall remain there."

I replied, "I will never go there. In a few months I shall be a mother."

He stood and looked at me in dumb amazement, and left the house without a word. I thought I should be happy in my triumph over him. But now that the truth was out, and my relatives would hear of it, I felt wretched. Humble as were their circumstances, they had pride in my good character. Now, how could I look them in the face? My self-respect was gone! I had resolved that I would be virtuous, though I was a slave. I had said, "Let the storm beat! I will brave it till I die." And now, how humiliated I felt!

I went to my grandmother. My lips moved to make confession, but the words stuck in my throat. I sat down in the shade of a tree at her door and began to sew. I think she saw something unusual was the matter with me. The mother of slaves is very watchful. She knows there is no security for her children. After they have entered their teens she lives in daily expectation of trouble. This leads to many questions. If the girl is of a sensitive nature, timidity keeps her from answering truthfully, and this well-meant course has a tendency to drive her from maternal counsels. Presently, in came my mistress, like a mad woman, and accused me concerning her husband. My grandmother, whose suspicions had been previously awakened, believed what she said. She exclaimed, "O Linda! has it come to this? I had rather see you dead than to see you as you now are. You are a disgrace to your dead mother." She tore from my fingers my mother's wedding ring and her silver thimble. "Go away!" she exclaimed, "and never come to my house, again." Her reproaches fell so hot and heavy, that they left me no chance to answer. Bitter tears, such as the eyes never shed but once, were my only answer. I rose from my seat, but fell back again, sobbing. She did not speak to me; but the tears were running down her furrowed cheeks, and they scorched me like fire. She had always been so kind to me! *So* kind! How I longed to throw myself at her feet, and tell her all the truth! But she had ordered me to go, and never to come there again. After a few minutes, I mustered strength, and started to obey her. With what feelings did I now close that little gate, which I used to open with such an eager hand in my childhood! It closed upon me with a sound I never heard before.

Where could I go? I was afraid to return to my master's. I walked on recklessly, not caring where I went, or what would become of me. When I had gone four or five miles, fatigue compelled me to stop. I sat down on the stump of an old tree. The stars were shining through the boughs above me. How they mocked me, with their bright, calm light! The hours passed by, and as I sat there alone a chilliness and deadly sickness came over me. I sank on the ground. My mind was full of horrid thoughts. I prayed to die; but the prayer was not answered. At last, with great effort I roused myself, and walked some distance further, to the house of a woman who had been a friend of my mother. When I told her why I was there, she spoke soothingly to me; but I could not be comforted. I thought I could bear my shame if I could only be reconciled to my grandmother. I longed to open my heart to her. I thought if she could know the real state of the case, and all I had been bearing for years, she would perhaps judge me less harshly. My friend advised me to send for her. I did so; but days of agonizing suspense passed before she came. Had she utterly forsaken me? No. She came at last. I knelt before her, and told her the things that had poisoned my life; how long I had been persecuted; that I saw no way of escape; and in an hour of extremity I had become desperate. She listened in silence. I told her I would bear any thing and do any thing, if in time I had hopes of obtaining her forgiveness. I begged of her to pity me, for my dead mother's sake. And she did pity me. She did not say, "I forgive you;" but she looked at me lovingly, with her eyes full of tears. She laid her old hand gently on my head, and murmured, "Poor child! Poor child!"

XI.
The New Tie to Life

I returned to my good grandmother's house. She had an interview with Mr. Sands. When she asked him why he could not have left her one ewe lamb,—whether there were not plenty of slaves who did not care about character,—he made no answer; but he spoke kind and encouraging words. He promised to care for my child, and to buy me, be the conditions what they might.

I had not seen Dr. Flint for five days. I had never seen him since I made the avowal to him. He talked of the disgrace I had brought on myself; how I had sinned against my master, and mortified my old grandmother. He intimated that if I had accepted his proposals, he, as a physician, could have saved me from exposure. He even condescended to pity me. Could he have offered wormwood more bitter? He, whose persecutions had been the cause of my sin!

"Linda," said he, "though you have been criminal towards me, I feel for you, and I can pardon you if you obey my wishes. Tell me whether the fellow you wanted to marry is the father of your child. If you deceive me, you shall feel the fires of hell."

I did not feel as proud as I had done. My strongest weapon with him was gone. I was lowered in my own estimation, and had resolved to bear his abuse in silence. But when he spoke contemptuously of the lover who had always treated me honorably; when I remembered that but for *him* I might have been a virtuous, free, and happy wife, I lost my patience. "I have sinned against God and myself," I replied; "but not against you."

He clinched his teeth, and muttered, "Curse you!" He came towards me, with ill-suppressed rage, and exclaimed, "You obstinate girl! I could grind your bones to powder! You have thrown yourself away on some worthless rascal. You are weak-minded, and have been easily persuaded by those who don't care a straw for you. The future will settle accounts between us. You are blinded now; but hereafter you will be convinced that your master was your best friend. My lenity towards you is a proof of it. I might have punished you in many ways. I might have had you whipped till you fell dead under the lash. But I wanted you to live; I would have bettered your condition. Others cannot do it. You are my slave. Your mistress, disgusted by your conduct, forbids you to return to the house; therefore I leave you here for the present; but I shall see you often. I will call tomorrow."

He came with frowning brows, that showed a dissatisfied state of mind. After asking about my health, he inquired whether my board was paid, and who visited me. He then went on to say that he had neglected his duty; that as a physician there were certain things that he ought to have explained to me. Then followed talk such as would have made the most shameless blush. He ordered me to stand up before him. I obeyed. "I command you," said he, "to tell me whether the father of your child is white or black." I hesitated. "Answer me this instant!" he exclaimed. I did answer. He sprang upon me like a wolf, and grabbed my arm as if he would have broken it. "Do you love him?" said he, in a hissing tone.

"I am thankful that I do not despise him," I replied.

He raised his hand to strike me; but it fell again. I don't know what arrested the blow. He sat down, with lips tightly compressed. At last he spoke. "I came here," said he, "to make you a friendly proposition; but your ingratitude chafes me beyond endurance. You turn aside all my good intentions towards you. I don't know what it is that keeps me from killing you." Again he rose, as if he had a mind to strike me.

But he resumed. "On one condition I will forgive your insolence and crime. You must henceforth have no communication of any kind with the father of your child. You must not ask any thing from him, or receive any thing from him. I will take care of you and your child. You had better promise this at once, and not wait till you are deserted by him. This is the last act of mercy I shall show towards you."

I said something about being unwilling to have my child supported by a man who had cursed it and me also. He rejoined, that a woman who had sunk to my level had no right to expect any thing else. He asked, for the last time, would I accept his kindness? I answered that I would not.

"Very well," said he; "then take the consequences of your wayward course. Never look to me for help. You are my slave, and shall always be my slave. I will never sell you, that you may depend upon."

Hope died away in my heart as he closed the door after him. I had calculated that in his rage he would sell me to a slave-trader; and I knew the father of my child was on the watch to buy me.

About this time my uncle Phillip was expected to return from a voyage. The day before his departure I had officiated as bridesmaid to a young friend. My heart was then ill at ease, but my smiling countenance did not betray it. Only a year had passed; but what fearful changes it had wrought! My heart had grown gray in misery. Lives that flash in sunshine, and lives that are born in tears, receive their hue from circumstances. None of us know what a year may bring forth.

I felt no joy when they told me my uncle had come. He wanted to see me, though he knew what had happened. I shrank from him at first; but at last consented that he should come to my room. He received me as he always had done. O, how my heart smote me when I felt his tears on my burning cheeks! The words of my grandmother came to my mind,—"Perhaps your mother and father are taken from the evil days to come." My disappointed heart could now praise God that it was so. But why, thought I, did my relatives ever cherish hopes for me? What was there to save me from the usual fate of slave girls? Many more beautiful and more intelligent than I had experienced a similar fate, or a far worse one. How could they hope that I should escape?

My uncle's stay was short, and I was not sorry for it. I was too ill in mind and body to enjoy my friends as I had done. For some weeks I was unable to leave my bed. I could not have any doctor but my master, and I would not have him sent for. At last, alarmed by my increasing illness, they sent for him. I was very weak and nervous; and as soon as he entered the room, I began to scream. They told him my state was very critical. He had no wish to hasten me out of the world, and he withdrew.

When my babe was born, they said it was premature. It weighed only four pounds; but God let it live. I heard the doctor say I could not survive till morning. I had often prayed for death; but now I did not want to die, unless my child could die too. Many weeks passed before I was able to leave my bed. I was a mere wreck of my former self. For a year there was scarcely a day when I was free from chills and fever. My babe also was sickly. His little limbs were often racked with pain. Dr. Flint continued his visits, to look after my health; and he did not fail to remind me that my child was an addition to his stock of slaves.

I felt too feeble to dispute with him, and listened to his remarks in silence. His visits were less frequent; but his busy spirit could not remain quiet. He employed my brother in his office, and he was made the medium of frequent notes and messages to me. William was a bright lad, and of much use to the doctor. He had learned to put up medicines, to leech, cup, and bleed. He had taught himself to read and spell. I was proud of my brother; and the old doctor suspected as much. One day, when I had not seen him for several weeks, I heard his steps approaching the door. I dreaded the encounter, and hid myself. He inquired for me, of course; but I was nowhere to be found. He went to his office, and despatched William with a note. The color mounted to my brother's face when he gave it to me; and he said, "Don't you hate me, Linda, for bringing you these things?" I told him I could not blame him; he was a slave, and obliged to obey his master's will. The note ordered me to come to his office. I went. He demanded to know where I was when he called. I told him I was at home. He flew into a passion, and said he knew better. Then he launched out upon his usual themes,—my crimes against him, and my ingratitude for his forbearance. The laws were laid down to me anew, and I was dismissed. I felt humiliated that my brother should stand by, and listen to such language as would be addressed only to a slave. Poor boy! He was powerless to defend me; but I saw the tears, which he vainly strove to keep back. This manifestation of feeling irritated the doctor. William could do nothing to please him. One morning he did not arrive at the office so early as usual; and that circumstance afforded his master an opportunity to vent his spleen. He was put in jail. The next day my brother sent a trader to the doctor, with a request to be sold. His master was greatly incensed at what he called his insolence. He said he had put him there to reflect upon his bad conduct, and he certainly was not giving any evidence of repentance. For two days he harassed himself to find somebody to do his office work; but every thing went wrong without William. He was released, and ordered to take his old stand, with many threats, if he was not careful about his future behavior.

As the months passed on, my boy improved in health. When he was a year old, they called him beautiful. The little vine was taking deep root in my existence, though its clinging fondness excited a mixture of love and pain. When I was most sorely oppressed I found a solace in his smiles. I loved to watch his infant slumbers; but always there was a dark cloud over my enjoyment. I could never forget that he was a slave. Sometimes I wished that he might die in infancy. God tried me. My darling became very ill. The bright eyes grew dull, and the little feet and hands were so icy cold that I thought death had already touched them. I had prayed for his death, but never so earnestly as I now prayed for his life; and my prayer was heard. Alas, what mockery it is for a slave mother to try to pray back her dying child to life! Death is better than slavery. It was a sad thought that I had no name to give my child. His father caressed him and treated him kindly, whenever he had a chance to see him. He was not unwilling that he should bear his name; but he had no legal claim to it; and if I had bestowed it upon him, my master would have regarded it as a new crime, a new piece of insolence, and would, perhaps, revenge it on the boy. O, the serpent of Slavery has many and poisonous fangs![5]

XXI.
The Loophole of Retreat

A small shed had been added to my grandmother's house years ago. Some boards were laid across the joists at the top, and between these boards and the roof was a very small garret, never occupied by any thing but rats and mice. It was a pent roof, covered with nothing but shingles, according to the southern custom for such buildings. The garret was only nine feet long and seven wide. The highest part was three feet high, and sloped down abruptly to the loose board floor. There was no admission for either light or air. My uncle Philip, who was a carpenter, had very skillfully made a concealed trap-door, which communicated with the storeroom. He had been doing this while I was waiting in the swamp. The storeroom opened upon a piazza. To this hole I was conveyed as soon as I entered the house. The air was stifling; the darkness total. A bed had been spread on the floor. I could sleep quite comfortably on one side; but the slope was so sudden that I could not turn on the other without hitting the roof. The rats and mice ran over my bed; but I was weary, and I slept such sleep as the wretched may, when a tempest has passed over them. Morning came. I knew it only by the

---

5. In subsequent chapters, Linda comments on the repercussions of Nat Turner's insurrection in 1831, on the attitude of the church toward slavery, and her own affairs. She bears a second child, remains subject to Dr. Flint's persecution, gets sent to his plantation, and escapes. When a plan for her to travel North falls through, Linda resolves to stay near her children, whom Mr. Sands has bought from Dr. Flint.

noises I heard; for in my small den day and night were all the same. I suffered for air even more than for light. But I was not comfortless. I heard the voices of my children. There was joy and there was sadness in the sound. It made my tears flow. How I longed to speak to them! I was eager to look on their faces; but there was no hole, no crack, through which I could peep. This continued darkness was oppressive. It seemed horrible to sit or lie in a cramped position day after day, without one gleam of light. Yet I would have chosen this, rather than my lot as a slave though white people considered it an easy one; and it was so compared with the fate of others. I was never cruelly over-worked; I was never lacerated with the whip from head to foot; I was never so beaten and bruised that I could not turn from one side to the other; I never had my heel-strings cut to prevent my running away; I was never chained to a log and forced to drag it about, while I toiled in the fields from morning till night; I was never branded with hot iron, or torn by bloodhounds. On the contrary, I had always been kindly treated, and tenderly cared for, until I came into the hands of Dr. Flint. I had never wished for freedom till then. But though my life in slavery was comparatively devoid of hardships, God pity the woman who is compelled to lead such a life!

My food was passed up to me through the trap-door my uncle had contrived; and my grandmother, my uncle Phillip, and aunt Nancy would seize such opportunities as they could, to mount up there and chat with me at the opening. But of course this was not safe in the daytime. It must all be done in darkness. It was impossible for me to move in an erect position, but I crawled about my den for exercise. One day I hit my head against something, and found it was a gimlet.[6] My uncle had left it sticking there when he made the trap-door. I was as rejoiced as Robinson Crusoe[7] could have been at finding such a treasure. It put a lucky thought into my head. I said to myself, "Now I will have some light. Now I will see my children." I did not dare to begin my work during the daytime, for fear of attracting attention. But I groped round; and having found the side next the street, where I could frequently see my children, I stuck the gimlet in and waited for evening. I bored three rows of holes, one above another; then I bored out the interstices between. I thus succeeded in making one hole about an inch long and an inch broad. I sat by it till late into the night, to enjoy the little whiff of air that floated in. In the morning I watched for my children. The first person I saw in the street was Dr. Flint. I had a shuddering, superstitious feeling that it was a bad omen. Several familiar faces passed by. At last I heard the merry laugh of children, and presently two sweet little faces were looking up at me, as though they knew I was there, and were conscious of the joy they imparted. How I longed to *tell* them I was there!

My condition was now a little improved. But for weeks I was tormented by hundreds of little red insects, fine as a needle's point, that pierced through my skin, and produced an intolerable burning. The good grandmother gave me herb teas and cooling medicines, and finally I got rid of them. The heat of my den was intense, for nothing but thin shingles protected me from the scorching summer's sun. But I had my consolations. Through my peeping-hole I could watch the children, and when they were near enough, I could hear their talk. Aunt Nancy brought me all the news she could hear at Dr. Flint's. From her I learned that the doctor had written to New York to a colored woman, who had been born and raised in our neighborhood, and had breathed his contaminating atmosphere. He offered her a reward if she could find out any thing about me. I know not what was the nature of her reply; but he soon after started for New York in haste, saying to his family that he had business of importance to transact. I peeped at him as he passed on his way to the steamboat. It was a satisfaction to have miles of land and water between us, even for a little while; and it was a still greater satisfaction to know that he believed me to be in the Free States. My little den seemed less dreary than it had done. He returned, as he did from his former journey to New

6. Small handtool for boring holes.
7. The hero of Daniel Defoe's 1719 novel, a castaway who builds a home on a desert island out of materials salvaged from his wrecked ship.

York, without obtaining any satisfactory information. When he passed our house next morning, Benny was standing at the gate. He had heard them say that he had gone to find me, and he called out, "Dr. Flint, did you bring my mother home? I want to see her." The doctor stamped his foot at him in a rage, and exclaimed, "Get out of the way, you little damned rascal! If you don't, I'll cut off your head."

Benny ran terrified into the house, saying, "You can't put me in jail again. I don't belong to you now." It was well that the wind carried the words away from the doctor's ear. I told my grandmother of it, when we had our next conference at the trap-door; and begged of her not to allow the children to be impertinent to the irascible old man.

Autumn came, with a pleasant abatement of heat. My eyes had become accustomed to the dim light, and by holding my book or work in a certain position near the aperture I contrived to read and sew. That was a great relief to the tedious monotony of my life. But when winter came, the cold penetrated through the thin shingle roof, and I was dreadfully chilled. The winters there are not so long, or so severe, as in northern latitudes; but the houses are not built to shelter from cold, and my little den was peculiarly comfortless. The kind grandmother brought me bed-clothes and warm drinks. Often I was obliged to lie in bed all day to keep comfortable; but with all my precautions, my shoulders and feet were frostbitten. O, those long, gloomy days, with no object for my eye to rest upon, and no thoughts to occupy my mind, except the dreary past and the uncertain future! I was thankful when there came a day sufficiently mild for me to wrap myself up and sit at the loophole to watch the passers by. Southerners have the habit of stopping and talking in the streets, and I heard many conversations not intended to meet my ears. I heard slave-hunters planning how to catch some poor fugitive. Several times I heard allusions to Dr. Flint, myself, and the history of my children, who, perhaps, were playing near the gate. One would say, "I wouldn't move my little finger to catch her, as old Flint's property." Another would say, "I'll catch *any* nigger for the reward. A man ought to have what belongs to him, if he *is* a damned brute." The opinion was often expressed that I was in the Free States. Very rarely did any one suggest that I might be in the vicinity. Had the least suspicion rested on my grandmother's house, it would have been burned to the ground. But it was the last place they thought of. Yet there was no place, where slavery existed, that could have afforded me so good a place of concealment.

Dr. Flint and his family repeatedly tried to coax and bribe my children to tell something they had heard said about me. One day the doctor took them into a shop, and offered them some bright little silver pieces and gay handkerchiefs if they would tell where their mother was. Ellen shrank away from him, and would not speak; but Benny spoke up, and said, "Dr. Flint, I don't know where my mother is. I guess she's in New York; and when you go there again, I wish you'd ask her to come home, for I want to see her; but if you put her in jail, or tell her you'll cut her head off, I'll tell her to go right back."[8]

XXIII.
Still in Prison

When spring returned, and I took in the little patch of green the aperture commanded, I asked myself how many more summers and winters I must be condemned to spend thus. I longed to draw in a plentiful draught of fresh air, to stretch my cramped limbs, to have room to stand erect, to feel the earth under my feet again. My relatives were constantly on the lookout for a chance of escape; but none offered that seemed practicable, and even tolerably safe. The hot summer came again, and made the turpentine drop from the thin roof over my head.

8. Chapter 22 details Linda's first Christmas in her hiding place.

During the long nights I was restless for want of air, and I had no room to toss and turn. There was but one compensation; the atmosphere was so stifled that even mosquitos would not condescend to buzz in it. With all my detestation of Dr. Flint, I could hardly wish him a worse punishment, either in this world or that which is to come, than to suffer what I suffered in one single summer. Yet the laws allowed *him* to be out in the free air, while I, guiltless of crime, was pent up here, as the only means of avoiding the cruelties the laws allowed him to inflict upon me! I don't know what kept life within me. Again and again, I thought I should die before long; but I saw the leaves of another autumn whirl through the air, and felt the touch of another winter. In summer the most terrible thunder storms were acceptable, for the rain came through the roof, and I rolled up my bed that it might cool the hot boards under it. Later in the season, storms sometimes wet my clothes through and through, and that was not comfortable when the air grew chilly. Moderate storms I could keep out by filling the chinks with oakum.[9]

But uncomfortable as my situation was, I had glimpses of things out of doors, which made me thankful for my wretched hiding-place. One day I saw a slave pass our gate, muttering, "It's his own, and he can kill it if he will." My grandmother told me that woman's history. Her mistress had that day seen her baby for the first time, and in the lineaments of its fair face she saw a likeness to her husband. She turned the bondwoman and her child out of doors, and forbade her ever to return. The slave went to her master, and told him what had happened. He promised to talk with her mistress, and make it all right. The next day she and her baby were sold to a Georgia trader.

Another time I saw a woman rush wildly by, pursued by two men. She was a slave, the wet nurse of her mistress's children. For some trifling offence her mistress ordered her to be stripped and whipped. To escape the degradation and the torture, she rushed to the river, jumped in, and ended her wrongs in death.

Senator Brown, of Mississippi, could not be ignorant of many such facts as these, for they are of frequent occurrence in every Southern State. Yet he stood up in the Congress of the United States, and declared that slavery was "a great moral, social, and political blessing; a blessing to the master, and a blessing to the slave!"

I suffered much more during the second winter than I did during the first. My limbs were benumbed by inaction, and the cold filled them with cramp. I had a very painful sensation of coldness in my head; even my face and tongue stiffened, and I lost the power of speech. Of course it was impossible, under the circumstances, to summon any physician. My brother William came and did all he could for me. Uncle Phillip also watched tenderly over me; and poor grandmother crept up and down to inquire whether there were any signs of returning life. I was restored to consciousness by the dashing of cold water in my face, and found myself leaning against my brother's arm, while he bent over me with streaming eyes. He afterwards told me he thought I was dying, for I had been in an unconscious state sixteen hours. I next became delirious, and was in great danger of betraying myself and my friends. To prevent this, they stupefied me with drugs. I remained in bed six weeks, weary in body and sick at heart. How to get medical advice was the question. William finally went to a Thompsonian doctor, and described himself as having all my pains and aches.[1] He returned with herbs, roots, and ointment. He was especially charged to rub on the ointment by a fire; but how could a fire be made in my little den? Charcoal in a furnace was tried, but there was no outlet for the gas, and it nearly cost me my life. Afterwards coals, already kindled, were brought up in an iron pan, and placed on bricks. I was so weak, and it was so long since I had enjoyed the warmth of a fire, that those few coals actually made me weep. I think the medicines did me some good; but my recovery was very slow. Dark thoughts passed through my mind as I lay there day after day. I tried to be thankful for my little cell, dismal as it was, and even

---

9. Loose hemp, used for caulking.
1. Samuel Thompson (1763–1843) advocated raising the body temperature to treat illness.

to love it, as part of the price I had paid for the redemption of my children. Sometimes I thought God was a compassionate Father, who would forgive my sins for the sake of my sufferings. At other times, it seemed to me there was no justice or mercy in the divine government. I asked why the curse of slavery was permitted to exist, and why I had been so persecuted and wronged from youth upward. These things took the shape of mystery, which is to this day not so clear to my soul as I trust it will be hereafter.

In the midst of my illness, grandmother broke down under the weight of anxiety and toil. The idea of losing her, who had always been my best friend and a mother to my children, was the sorest trial I had yet had. O, how earnestly I prayed that she might recover! How hard it seemed, that I could not tend upon her, who had so long and so tenderly watched over me!

One day the screams of a child nerved me with strength to crawl to my peeping-hole, and I saw my son covered with blood. A fierce dog, usually kept chained, had seized and bitten him. A doctor was sent for, and I heard the groans and screams of my child while the wounds were being sewed up. O, what torture to a mother's heart, to listen to this and be unable to go to him!

But childhood is like a day in spring, alternately shower and sunshine. Before night Benny was bright and lively, threatening the destruction of the dog; and great was his delight when the doctor told him the next day that the dog had bitten another boy and been shot. Benny recovered from his wounds; but it was long before he could walk.

When my grandmother's illness became known, many ladies, who were her customers, called to bring her some little comforts, and to inquire whether she had every thing she wanted. Aunt Nancy one night asked permission to watch with her sick mother, and Mrs. Flint replied, "I don't see any need of your going. I can't spare you." But when she found other ladies in the neighborhood were so attentive, not wishing to be outdone in Christian charity, she also sallied forth, in magnificent condescension, and stood by the bedside of her who had loved her in her infancy, and who had been repaid by such grievous wrongs. She seemed surprised to find her so ill, and scolded uncle Phillip for not sending for Dr. Flint. She herself sent for him immediately, and he came. Secure as I was in my retreat, I should have been terrified if I had known he was so near me. He pronounced my grandmother in a very critical situation, and said if her attending physician wished it, he would visit her. Nobody wished to have him coming to the house at all hours, and we were not disposed to give him a chance to make out a long bill.

As Mrs. Flint went out, Sally told her the reason Benny was lame was, that a dog had bitten him. "I'm glad of it," replied she. "I wish he had killed him. It would be good news to send to his mother. *Her* day will come. The dogs will grab *her* yet." With these Christian words she and her husband departed, and, to my great satisfaction, returned no more.

I heard from uncle Phillip, with feelings of unspeakable joy and gratitude, that the crisis was passed and grandmother would live. I could now say from my heart, "God is merciful. He has spared me the anguish of feeling that I caused her death."[2]

XXXIV.
The Old Enemy Again

My young mistress, Miss Emily Flint,[3] did not return any answer to my letter requesting her to consent to my being sold. But after a while, I received a reply, which purported to be

---

2. Linda finally escapes to the North after seven years' hiding; she and her daughter live with the Bruce family, where Linda serves as

nursemaid.
3. Dr. Flint's daughter, to whom Linda had been bequeathed in childhood.

written by her younger brother. In order rightly to enjoy the contents of this letter, the reader must bear in mind that the Flint family supposed I had been at the north many years. They had no idea that I knew of the doctor's three excursions to New York in search of me; that I had heard his voice, when he came to borrow five hundred dollars for that purpose; and that I had seen him pass on his way to the steamboat. Neither were they aware that all the particulars of aunt Nancy's death and burial were conveyed to me at the time they occurred.[4] I have kept the letter, of which I herewith subjoin a copy:—

"Your letter to sister was received a few days ago. I gather from it that you are desirous of returning to your native place, among your friends and relatives. We were all gratified with the contents of your letter; and let me assure you that if any members of the family have had any feeling of resentment towards you, they feel it no longer. We all sympathize with you in your unfortunate condition, and are ready to do all in our power to make you contented and happy. It is difficult for you to return home as a free person. If you were purchased by your grandmother, it is doubtful whether you would be permitted to remain, although it would be lawful for you to do so. If a servant should be allowed to purchase herself, after absenting herself so long from her owners, and return free, it would have an injurious effect. From your letter, I think your situation must be hard and uncomfortable. Come home. You have it in your power to be reinstated in our affections. We would receive you with open arms and tears of joy. You need not apprehend any unkind treatment, as we have not put ourselves to any trouble or expense to get you. Had we done so, perhaps we should feel otherwise. You know my sister was always attached to you, and that you were never treated as a slave. You were never put to hard work, nor exposed to field labor. On the contrary, you were taken into the house, and treated as one of us, and almost as free; and we, at least, felt that you were above disgracing yourself by running away. Believing you may be induced to come home voluntarily has induced me to write for my sister. The family will be rejoiced to see you; and your poor old grandmother expressed a great desire to have you come, when she heard your letter read. In her old age she needs the consolation of having her children round her. Doubtless you have heard of the death of your aunt. She was a faithful servant, and a faithful member of the Episcopal church. In her Christian life she taught us how to live—and, O, too high the price of knowledge, she taught us how to die! Could you have seen us round her death bed, with her mother, all mingling our tears in one common stream, you would have thought the same heartfelt tie existed between a master and his servant, as between a mother and her child. But this subject is too painful to dwell upon. I must bring my letter to a close. If you are contented to stay away from your old grandmother, your child, and the friends who love you, stay where you are. We shall never trouble ourselves to apprehend you. But should you prefer to come home, we will do all that we can to make you happy. If you do not wish to remain in the family, I know that father, by our persuasion, will be induced to let you be purchased by any person you may choose in our community. You will please answer this as soon as possible, and let us know your decision. Sister sends much love to you. In the mean time believe me your sincere friend and well wisher."

This letter was signed by Emily's brother, who was as yet a mere lad. I knew, by the style, that it was not written by a person of his age, and though the writing was disguised, I had been made too unhappy by it, in former years, not to recognize at once the hand of Dr. Flint. O, the hypocrisy of slaveholders! Did the old fox suppose I was goose enough to go into such a trap? Verily, he relied too much on "the stupidity of the African race." I did not return the family of Flints any thanks for their cordial invitation—a remissness for which I was, no doubt, charged with base ingratitude.

Not long afterwards I received a letter from one of my friends at the south, informing me that Dr. Flint was about to visit the north. The letter had been delayed, and I supposed he might be already on the way. Mrs. Bruce did not know I was a fugitive. I told her that

4. Aunt Nancy is Linda's aunt, a slave in the Flint household.

important business called me to Boston, where my brother then was, and asked permission to bring a friend to supply my place as nurse, for a fortnight. I started on my journey immediately; and as soon as I arrived, I wrote to my grandmother that if Benny came, he must be sent to Boston. I knew she was only waiting for a good chance to send him north, and, fortunately, she had the legal power to do so, without asking leave of any body. She was a free woman; and when my children were purchased, Mr. Sands preferred to have the bill of sale drawn up in her name. It was conjectured that he advanced the money, but it was not known. At the south, a gentleman may have a shoal of colored children without any disgrace; but if he is known to purchase them, with the view of setting them free, the example is thought to be dangerous to their "peculiar institution,"[5] and he becomes unpopular.

There was a good opportunity to send Benny in a vessel coming directly to New York. He was put on board with a letter to a friend, who was requested to see him off to Boston. Early one morning, there was a loud rap at my door, and in rushed Benjamin, all out of breath. "O mother!" he exclaimed, "here I am! I run all the way; and I come all alone. How d'you do?"

O reader, can you imagine my joy? No, you cannot, unless you have been a slave mother. Benjamin rattled away as fast as his tongue could go. "Mother, why don't you bring Ellen here? I went over to Brooklyn to see her, and she felt very bad when I bid her good by. She said, 'O Ben, I wish I was going too.' I thought she'd know ever so much; but she don't know so much as I do; for I can read, and she can't. And, mother, I lost all my clothes coming. What can I do to get some more? I 'spose free boys can get along here at the north as well as white boys."

I did not like to tell the sanguine, happy little fellow how much he was mistaken. I took him to a tailor, and procured a change of clothes. The rest of the day was spent in mutual asking and answering of questions, with the wish constantly repeated that the good old grandmother was with us, and frequent injunctions from Benny to write to her immediately, and be sure to tell her every thing about his voyage, and his journey to Boston.

Dr. Flint made his visit to New York, and made every exertion to call upon me, and invite me to return with him; but not being able to ascertain where I was, his hospitable intentions were frustrated, and the affectionate family, who were waiting for me with "open arms," were doomed to disappointment.

As soon as I knew he was safely at home, I placed Benjamin in the care of my brother William, and returned to Mrs. Bruce. There I remained through the winter and spring, endeavoring to perform my duties faithfully, and finding a good degree of happiness in the attractions of baby Mary, the considerate kindness of her excellent mother, and occasional interviews with my darling daughter.

But when summer came, the old feeling of insecurity haunted me. It was necessary for me to take little Mary out daily, for exercise and fresh air, and the city was swarming with Southerners, some of whom might recognize me. Hot weather brings out snakes and slave-holders, and I like one class of the venomous creatures as little as I do the other. What a comfort it is, to be free to *say* so!

XXXV.
Prejudice Against Color

It was a relief to my mind to see preparations for leaving the city.[6] We went to Albany in the steamboat Knickerbocker. When the gong sounded for tea, Mrs. Bruce said, "Linda, it

---

5. A common euphemism for slavery.   6. For a Bruce family vacation.

is late, and you and baby had better come to the table with me." I replied, "I know it is time baby had her supper, but I had rather not go with you, if you please. I am afraid of being insulted." "O no, not if you are with *me,*" she said. I saw several white nurses go with their ladies, and I ventured to do the same. We were at the extreme end of the table. I was no sooner seated, than a gruff voice said, "Get up! You know you are not allowed to sit here." I looked up, and, to my astonishment and indignation, saw that the speaker was a colored man. If his office required him to enforce the by-laws of the boat, he might, at least, have done it politely. I replied, "I shall not get up, unless the captain comes and takes me up." No cup of tea was offered me, but Mrs. Bruce handed me hers and called for another. I looked to see whether the other nurses were treated in a similar manner. They were all properly waited on.

Next morning, when we stopped at Troy for breakfast, every body was making a rush for the table. Mrs. Bruce said, "Take my arm, Linda, and we'll go in together." The landlord heard her, and said, "Madam, will you allow your nurse and baby to take breakfast with my family?" I knew this was to be attributed to my complexion; but he spoke courteously, and therefore I did not mind it.

At Saratoga we found the United States Hotel crowded, and Mr. Bruce took one of the cottages belonging to the hotel. I had thought, with gladness, of going to the quiet of the country, where I should meet few people, but here I found myself in the midst of a swarm of Southerners. I looked round me with fear and trembling, dreading to see some one who would recognize me. I was rejoiced to find that we were to stay but a short time.

We soon returned to New York, to make arrangements for spending the remainder of the summer at Rockaway. While the laundress was putting the clothes in order, I took an opportunity to go over to Brooklyn to see Ellen. I met her going to a grocery store, and the first words she said, were, "O, mother, don't go to Mrs. Hobbs's. Her brother, Mr. Thorne, has come from the south, and may be he'll tell where you are."[7] I accepted the warning. I told her I was going away with Mrs. Bruce the next day, and would try to see her when I came back.

Being in servitude to the Anglo-Saxon race, I was not put into a "Jim Crow car,"[8] on our way to Rockaway, neither was I invited to ride through the streets on the top of trunks in a truck; but every where I found the same manifestations of that cruel prejudice, which so discourages the feelings, and represses the energies of the colored people. We reached Rockaway before dark, and put up at the Pavilion—a large hotel, beautifully situated by the sea-side—a great resort of the fashionable world. Thirty or forty nurses were there, of a great variety of nations. Some of the ladies had colored waiting-maids and coachmen, but I was the only nurse tinged with the blood of Africa. When the tea bell rang, I took little Mary and followed the other nurses. Supper was served in a long hall. A young man, who had the ordering of things, took the circuit of the table two or three times, and finally pointed me to a seat at the lower end of it. As there was but one chair, I sat down and took the child in my lap. Whereupon the young man came to me and said, in the blandest manner possible, "Will you please to seat the little girl in the chair, and stand behind it and feed her? After they have done, you will be shown to the kitchen, where you will have a good supper."

This was the climax! I found it hard to preserve my self-control, when I looked round, and saw women who were nurses, as I was, and only one shade lighter in complexion, eyeing me with a defiant look, as if my presence were a contamination. However, I said nothing. I quietly took the child in my arms, went to our room, and refused to go to the table again. Mr. Bruce ordered meals to be sent to the room for little Mary and I. This answered for a few days; but the waiters of the establishment were white, and they soon began to complain, saying they were not hired to wait on negroes. The landlord requested Mr. Bruce to send me down to

7. Mrs. Hobbs is a cousin of Mr. Sands, who "gave" his daughter Ellen to Mrs. Hobbs's daughter, to serve as a maid.

8. A railway car for blacks only.

my meals, because his servants rebelled against bringing them up, and the colored servants of other boarders were dissatisfied because all were not treated alike.

My answer was that the colored servants ought to be dissatisfied with *themselves*, for not having too much self-respect to submit to such treatment; that there was no difference in the price of board for colored and white servants, and there was no justification for difference of treatment. I staid a month after this, and finding I was resolved to stand up for my rights, they concluded to treat me well. Let every colored man and woman do this, and eventually we shall cease to be trampled under foot by our oppressors.***

1861

Susan Warner
(1819–1885)

Like Ellen Montgomery, the heroine of her first and most popular novel, Susan Warner was born into a prominent and wealthy New York City family, and like Ellen, Susan saw her family's fortunes fall before she herself reached adulthood. Her father, Henry Whiting Warner, was a successful lawyer who enjoyed profitable investments in real estate; her mother, Anna Marsh Bartlett, was the stepdaughter of a family more well-to-do than the Warners. Susan was raised at home with her younger sister Anna, under the tutelage of her father, who instructed his daughters in classical and modern languages, English literature, history, and geography. Evidently she was closer to her father than her mother, who died when Susan was 10 years old.

Just as her education resembled one that would be considered appropriate for a boy of her generation, so did Susan's temperament. Her sister Anna wrote that Susan in her youth possessed "a strong temper, an imperious will, a masterful love of power that very ill brooked curbing, and a relish for the right of way that might have served a boy." In an era that demanded self-sacrifice and submissiveness from virtuous women, learning to curb such traits was part of a young woman's education. The Warner sisters fully expected to marry well and to take their places among the upper-middle-class social ranks of New York City wives.

In the financial crash of 1837, however, Susan's father lost the better part of his fortune, and his daughters' expectations fell accordingly. The family—including the girls' Aunt Fanny, who had come to live with them when their mother died—moved to a farmhouse on Constitution Island on the Hudson River, across from West Point. Susan and Anna learned to help support the household by sewing, cooking, and cleaning. Neither daughter married. Absorbed in Presbyterian church activities, they became increasingly cut off from the fashionable social circles they had once known. When the family's poverty became so extreme that creditors came after their furniture, the sisters decided to follow a suggestion of their aunt's: they tried their hand at novel writing to earn some money for the household.

Susan Warner published her first novel, *The Wide, Wide World,* in 1850 under the pen name Elizabeth Wetherell. Although it was phenomenally successful (its sales were surpassed in its day only by those of *Uncle Tom's Cabin*), the novel did not make the Warners rich. Susan sold the manuscript outright, rather than waiting for royalties. This was to become the pattern for her and for Anna, as they wrote and sold books both separately and together.

Almost forgotten until recently, *The Wide, Wide World* has become a classic case in the feminist reconstruction of the literary canon. It falls into the genre of domestic fiction, which has not been considered equal in literary interest to the more "serious" novels of Warner's contemporaries, Hawthorne and Melville. At first glance, the story—centering around the experiences of a preadolescent girl whose parents have lost their fortune, gone to Europe, and left her with an indifferent and exploitative aunt—looks like a children's book, although Warner did not intend her work primarily for a juvenile audience. Over 600 pages long, the novel details the routines of nineteenth-century middle-class female life in New York City, in small-town New England, and in Scotland as it traces the heroine's spiritual development and emotional maturing. Ellen Montgomery is a child with strong passions who learns to submit with relative meekness to the correction—both just and unjust—she receives from her "elders and betters." At the same time, she learns to do housework, and to think of her experience in terms of a strongly felt and rigidly practiced protestant Christianity.

Because of its earnest Christian message and intense emotionality, modernist critics dismissed The Wide, Wide World as an insignificant piece of sentimentality. Even today, culturally conservative critics contend that the novel is "almost devoid of literary value." But feminist critics interested in rehabilitating the history and literature of American women have celebrated the novel as a repository of feminine experience and values of its period. Some feminists go so far as to see the novel as "subversive," finding in it an implicit critique of domineering male characters who seek to control Ellen, including the hero, John Humphreys, who is depicted as being morally perfect, but who shows excessive force in "breaking" his horse. Readers who admire the novel

emphasize its value as a reflection of a culture different in many ways from our own, a culture that has indelibly influenced current ideas about femininity and moral values.

The Wide, Wide World was Warner's most popular novel, followed by Queechy (1852), a similar tale of a young girl's spiritual development. Her other novels are mainly didactic, some of them falling into the category of protest fiction. One series of novels embraces the abolitionist cause: Melbourne House (1864), Daisy (1868), and Daisy in the Field (1869). Another, written with Anna, proposed a plan for the relief of factory workers: Wych Hazel (1876) and The Gold of Chickaree (1876). In addition to collaborating with her sister on numerous books, Anna Warner wrote her biography, Susan Warner, in 1909.

Susan Warner's other publications include: American Female Patriotism: A Prize Essay (1852); The Law and the Testimony (1853); Carl Krinken: His Christmas Stocking, with Anna Warner (1853); The Hills of Shatemuc (1856); Say and Seal, with Anna Warner (1860); The Old Helmet (1863); Walks from Eden (1865); The House of Israel (1866); The Broken Walls of Jerusalem and the Rebuilding of Them (1870); "What She Could" (1870); The House in Town (1870); Opportunities (1871); Lessons on the Standard Bearers of the Old Testament (1872); Trading (1872); The Little Camp on Eagle Hill (1873); Sceptres and Crowns (1874); Willow Brook (1874); Bread and Oranges (1875); The Flag of Truce (1875); The Rapids of Niagara (1876); Pine Needles (1877); Diana (1877); The Kingdom of Judah (1878); My Desire (1879); The End of a Coil (1880); The Letter of Credit (1881); Nobody (1882); Stephen, M.D. (1883); A Red Wallflower (1884); and Daisy Plains (1885).

Critical studies include Nina Baym, Woman's Fiction: A Guide to Novels by and about Women in America, 1820–1870 (1978); Mary Kelley, Private Woman, Public Stage: Literary Domesticity in Nineteenth-Century America (1984); and Jane Tompkins, Sensational Designs: The Cultural Work of American Fiction 1790–1860 (1985). See also Mabel Baker, The Warner Family and the Warner Books (1971) and Edward Halsey Foster, Susan and Anna Warner (1978).

FROM THE WIDE, WIDE WORLD

Chapter I

Enjoy the spring of love and youth,
To some good angel leave the rest,
For time will teach thee soon the truth,
"There are no birds in last year's nest."
Longfellow.[1]

"Mamma, what was that I heard papa saying to you this morning about his lawsuit?"

"I cannot tell you just now. Ellen, pick up that shawl, and spread it over me."

"Mamma!—are you cold in this warm room?"

"A little,—there, that will do. Now, my daughter, let me be quiet awhile—don't disturb me."

There was no one else in the room. Driven thus to her own resources, Ellen betook herself to the window and sought amusement there. The prospect without gave little promise of it. Rain was falling, and made the street and everything in it look dull and gloomy. The foot-passengers plashed through the water, and the horses and carriages plashed through the mud; gayety had forsaken the sidewalks, and equipages were few, and the people that were out were plainly there only because they could not help it. But yet Ellen, having seriously set herself to study everything that passed, presently became engaged in her occupation; and her thoughts travelling dreamily from one thing to another, she sat for a long time with her little face pressed against the windowframe, perfectly regardless of all but the moving world without.

Daylight gradually faded away, and the street wore a more and more gloomy aspect. The rain poured, and now only an occasional carriage or footstep disturbed the sound of its steady pattering. Yet still Ellen sat with her face glued to the window as if spellbound, gazing out at every dusky form that passed, as though it had some strange interest for her. At length, in the distance, light after light began to appear; presently Ellen could see the dim figure of the lamplighter crossing the street, from side to side, with his ladder; then he drew near enough for her to watch him as he hooked his ladder on the lamp-irons, ran up and lit the lamp, then shouldered the ladder and marched off quick, the light glancing on his wet oil-skin[2] hat, rough great coat and lantern, and on the pavement and iron railings. The veriest moth could not have followed the light with more perseverance than did Ellen's eyes, till the lamplighter gradually disappeared from view, and the last lamp she could see was lit; and not till then did it occur to her that there was such a place as in-doors. She took her face from the window. The room was dark and cheerless; and Ellen felt stiff and chilly. However, she made her way to the fire, and having found the poker, she applied it gently to the Liverpool coal with such good effect that a bright ruddy blaze sprang up, and lighted the whole room. Ellen smiled at the result of her experiment. "That is something like," said she to herself; "who says I can't poke the fire? Now, let us see if I can't do something else. Do but see how those chairs are standing—one would think we had had a sewing-circle here—there, go back to your places,—that looks a little better; now these curtains must come down, and I may as well shut the shutters too; and now this table-cloth must be content to hang straight, and mamma's box and the books must lie in their places, and not all helter-skelter. Now, I wish mamma would wake up; I should think she might. I don't believe she is asleep either, she don't look as if she was."

---

1. Henry Wadsworth Longfellow, "It Is Not Always May."

2. Waterproof oilcloth.

Ellen was right in this; her mother's face did not wear the look of sleep, nor indeed of repose at all: the lips were compressed, and the brow not calm. To try, however, whether she was asleep or not, and with the half-acknowledged intent to rouse her at all events, Ellen knelt down by her side and laid her face close to her mother's on the pillow. But this failed to draw either word or sign. After a minute or two Ellen tried stroking her mother's cheek very gently; and this succeeded, for Mrs. Montgomery arrested the little hand as it passed her lips, and kissed it fondly two or three times.

"I haven't disturbed you, mamma, have I?" said Ellen.

Without replying, Mrs. Montgomery raised herself to a sitting posture, and lifting both hands to her face, pushed back the hair from her forehead and temples, with a gesture which Ellen knew meant that she was making up her mind to some disagreeable or painful effort. Then taking both Ellen's hands, as she still knelt before her, she gazed in her face with a look even more fond than usual, Ellen thought, but much sadder too; though Mrs. Montgomery's cheerfulness had always been of a serious kind.

"What question was that you were asking me awhile ago, my daughter?"

"I thought, mamma, I heard papa telling you this morning, or yesterday, that he had lost that lawsuit."

"You heard right, Ellen,—he has lost it," said Mrs. Montgomery, sadly.

"Are you sorry, mamma?—does it trouble you?"

"You know, my dear, that I am not apt to concern myself overmuch about the gain or the loss of money. I believe my Heavenly Father will give me what is good for me."

"Then, mamma, why are you troubled?"

"Because, my child, I cannot carry out this principle in other matters, and leave quietly my *all* in His hands."

"What is the matter, dear mother? What makes you look so?"

"This lawsuit, Ellen, has brought upon us more trouble than I ever thought a lawsuit could,—the loss of it, I mean."

"How, mamma?"

"It has caused an entire change of all our plans. Your father says he is too poor now to stay here any longer; and he has agreed to go soon on some government or military business to Europe."

"Well, mamma, that is bad; but he has been away a great deal before, and I am sure we were always very happy."

"But, Ellen, he thinks now, and the doctor thinks too, that it is very important for my health that I should go with him."

"Does he, mamma?—and do you mean to go?"

"I am afraid I must, my dear child."

"Not, and leave *me*, mother?"

The imploring look of mingled astonishment, terror, and sorrow with which Ellen uttered these words, took from her mother all power of replying. It was not necessary; her little daughter understood only too well the silent answer of her eye. With a wild cry she flung her arms round her mother, and hiding her face in her lap, gave way to a violent burst of grief that seemed for a few moments as if it would rend soul and body in twain. For her passions were by nature very strong, and by education very imperfectly controlled; and time, "that rider that breaks youth," had not as yet tried his hand upon her. And Mrs. Montgomery, in spite of the fortitude and calmness to which she had steeled herself, bent down over her, and folding her arms about her, yielded to sorrow deeper still, and for a little while scarcely less violent in its expression than Ellen's own.

Alas! she had too good reason. She knew that the chance of her ever returning to shield the little creature who was nearest her heart from the future evils and snares of life was very, very small. She had at first absolutely refused to leave Ellen, when her husband proposed it: declaring that she would rather stay with her and die than take the chance of recovery at such a cost. But her physician assured her she could not live long without a change of climate; Captain Montgomery urged that it was better to submit to a temporary separation, than to cling obstinately to her child for a few months and then leave her for ever; said he must himself go speedily to France, and that now was her best opportunity; assuring her, however, that his circumstances would not permit him to take Ellen along, but that she would be secure of a happy home with his sister during her mother's absence; and to the pressure of argument Captain Montgomery added the weight of authority, insisting on her compliance. Conscience also asked Mrs. Montgomery whether she had a *right* to neglect any chance of life that was offered her; and at last she yielded to the combined influence of motives no one of which would have had power sufficient to move her, and, though with a secret consciousness it would be in vain, she consented to do as her friends wished. And it was for Ellen's sake she did it, after all.

Nothing but necessity had given her the courage to open the matter to her little daughter. She had foreseen and endeavored to prepare herself for Ellen's anguish; but nature was too strong for her, and they clasped each other in a convulsive embrace, while tears fell like rain.

It was some minutes before Mrs. Montgomery recollected herself, and then, though she struggled hard, she could not immediately regain her composure. But Ellen's deep sobs at length fairly alarmed her; she saw the necessity, for both their sakes, of putting a stop to this state of violent excitement; self-command was restored at once.

"Ellen! Ellen! listen to me," she said; "my child, this is not right. Remember, my darling, who it is that brings this sorrow upon us; though we *must* sorrow, we must not rebel."

Ellen sobbed more gently; but that and the mute pressure of her arms was her only answer.

"You will hurt both yourself and me, my daughter, if you cannot command yourself. Remember, dear Ellen, God sends no trouble upon his children but in love; and though we cannot see how, he will no doubt make all this work for our good."

"I know it, dear mother," sobbed Ellen, "but it's just as hard!"

Mrs. Montgomery's own heart answered so readily to the truth of Ellen's words that for the moment she could not speak.

"Try, my daughter," she said, after a pause,—"try to compose yourself. I am afraid you will make me worse, Ellen, if you cannot,—I am, indeed."

Ellen had plenty of faults, but amidst them all love to her mother was the strongest feeling her heart knew. It had power enough now to move her as nothing else could have done; and exerting all her self-command, of which she had sometimes a good deal, she *did* calm herself; ceased sobbing; wiped her eyes; arose from her crouching posture, and seating herself on the sofa by her mother, and laying her head on her bosom, she listened quietly to all the soothing words and cheering considerations with which Mrs. Montgomery endeavoured to lead her to take a more hopeful view of the subject. All she could urge, however, had but very partial success, though the conversation was prolonged far into the evening. Ellen said little, and did not weep any more; but in secret her heart refused consolation.

Long before this the servant had brought in the tea-things. Nobody regarded it at the time, but the little kettle hissing away on the fire now by chance attracted Ellen's attention, and she suddenly recollected her mother had had no tea. To make her mother's tea was Ellen's regular business. She treated it as a very grave affair, and loved it as one of the pleasantest in the course of the day. She used in the first place to make sure that the kettle really boiled; then she carefully poured some water into the tea-pot and rinsed it, both to make it clean and to make it hot; then she knew exactly how much tea to put into the tiny little tea-pot, which was just big enough to hold two cups of tea, and having poured a very little boiling water to it, she used to set it by the side of the fire while she made half a slice of toast. How careful Ellen was about that toast! The bread must not be cut too thick, nor too thin; the fire must, if possible, burn clear and bright, and she herself held the bread on a fork, just at the right distance from the coals to get nicely browned without burning. When this was done to her satisfaction (and if the first piece failed she would take another), she filled up the little tea-pot from the boiling kettle, and proceeded to make a cup of tea. She knew, and was very careful to put in, just the quantity of milk and sugar that her mother liked; and then she used to carry the tea and toast on a little tray to her mother's side, and very often held it there for her while she eat.[3] All this Ellen did with the zeal that love gives, and though the same thing was to be gone over every night of the year, she was never wearied. It was a real pleasure; she had the greatest satisfaction in seeing that the little her mother could eat was prepared for her in the nicest possible manner; she knew her hands made it taste better; her mother often said so.

But this evening other thoughts had driven this important business quite out of poor Ellen's mind. Now, however, when her eyes fell upon the little kettle, she recollected her mother had not had her tea, and must want it very much; and silently slipping off the sofa, she set about getting it as usual. There was no doubt this time whether the kettle boiled or no; it had been hissing for an hour and more, calling as loud as it could to somebody to come and make the tea. So Ellen made it, and then began the toast. But she began to think, too, as she watched it, how few more times she would be able to do so,—how soon her pleasant tea-makings would be over,—and the desolate feeling of separation began to come upon her before the time. These thoughts were too much for poor Ellen; the thick tears gathered so fast she could not see what she was doing; and she had no more than just turned the slice of bread on the fork when the sickness of heart quite overcame her; she could not go on. Toast and fork and all dropped from her hand into the ashes; and rushing to her mother's side, who was now lying down again, and throwing herself upon her, she burst into another fit of sorrow; not so violent as the former, but with a touch of hopelessness in it which went yet more to her mother's heart. Passion in the first said, "I cannot;" despair now seemed to say, "I must."

But Mrs. Montgomery was too exhausted to either share or soothe Ellen's agitation. She lay in suffering silence; till after some time she said, faintly, "Ellen, my love, I cannot bear this much longer."

Ellen was immediately brought to herself by these words. She arose, sorry and ashamed that she should have given occasion for them; and tenderly kissing her mother, assured her most sincerely and resolutely that she would not do so again. In a few minutes she was calm enough to finish making the tea, and having toasted another piece of bread, she brought it to her mother. Mrs. Montgomery swallowed a cup of tea, but no toast could be eaten that night.

Both remained silent and quiet awhile after this, till the clock struck ten. "You had better go to bed, my daughter," said Mrs. Montgomery.

"I will, mamma."

"Do you think you can read me a little before you go?"

"Yes, indeed, mamma;" and Ellen brought the book. "Where shall I read?"

"The twenty-third psalm."[4]

Ellen began it, and went through it steadily and slowly, though her voice quavered a little.

" 'The Lord is my Shepherd; I shall not want.

" 'He maketh me to lie down in green pastures: He leadeth me beside the still waters.

" 'He restoreth my soul: He leadeth me in the paths of righteousness for his name's sake.

" 'Yea, though I walk through the valley of the shadow of death, I will fear no evil: for Thou art with me; thy rod and thy staff they comfort me.

" 'Thou preparest a table before me in the presence of mine enemies: Thou anointest my head with oil; my cup runneth over.

" 'Surely goodness and mercy shall follow me all the days of my life: and I will dwell in the house of the Lord forever.' "

Long before she had finished, Ellen's eyes were full, and her heart too. "If I only could feel these words as mamma does!" she said to herself. She did not dare look up till the traces of

---

3.   Common nineteenth-century spelling for "ate."   4.   Psalms 23:1–6.

tears had passed away; then she saw that her mother was asleep. Those first sweet words had fallen like balm upon the sore heart; and mind and body had instantly found rest together.

Ellen breathed the lightest possible kiss upon her forehead, and stole quietly out of the room to her own little bed. . . .[5]

Chapter III

Sweetheart, we shall be rich ere we depart,
If fairings come thus plentifully in.
                    —Shakespeare.[6]

Ellen had to wait some time for the desired fine day. The equinoctial storms would have their way as usual, and Ellen thought they were longer than ever this year. But after many stormy days had tried her patience, there was at length a sudden change, both without and within doors. The clouds had done their work for that time, and fled away before a strong northerly wind, leaving the sky bright and fair. And Mrs. Montgomery's deceitful disease took a turn, and for a little space raised the hopes of her friends. All were rejoicing but two persons; Mrs. Montgomery was not deceived, neither was the doctor. The shopping project was kept a profound secret from him and from everybody except Ellen.

Ellen watched now for a favourable day. Every morning as soon as she rose she went to the window to see what was the look of the weather; and about a week after the change above noticed, she was greatly pleased one morning, on opening her window as usual, to find the air and sky promising all that could be desired. It was one of those beautiful days in the end of September, that sometimes herald October before it arrives,—cloudless, brilliant, and breathing balm. "This will do," said Ellen to herself, in great satisfaction. "I think this will do; I hope mamma will think so."

Hastily dressing herself, and a good deal excited already, she ran down-stairs; and after the morning salutations, examined her mother's looks with as much anxiety as she had just done those of the weather. All was satisfactory there also, and Ellen ate her breakfast with an excellent appetite; but she said not a word of the intended expedition till her father should be gone. She contented herself with strengthening her hopes by making constant fresh inspections of the weather and her mother's countenance alternately; and her eyes, returning from the window on one of these excursions and meeting her mother's face, saw a smile there which said all she wanted. Breakfast went on more vigorously than ever. But after breakfast it seemed to Ellen that her father never would go away. He took the newspaper, an uncommon thing for him, and pored over it most perseveringly, while Ellen was in a perfect fidget of impatience. Her mother, seeing the state she was in, and taking pity on her, sent her up-stairs to do some little matters of business in her own room. These Ellen despatched with all possible zeal and speed; and coming down again found her father gone and her mother alone. She flew to kiss her in the first place, and then make the inquiry, "Don't you think to-day will do, mamma?"

"As fine as possible, daughter; we could not have a better; but I must wait till the doctor has been here."

"Mamma," said Ellen, after a pause, making a great effort of self-denial, "I am afraid you oughtn't to go out to get these things for me. Pray don't, mamma, if you think it will do you harm. I would rather go without them; indeed I would."

5. In Chapter 2, Ellen learns she is to stay with her father's sister in a rural town. She and her mother try to resign themselves to their separation and plan to go shopping for a Bible and other necessities for Ellen's trip.

6. *Love's Labours Lost,* 1.1, line 386.

"Never mind that, daughter," said Mrs. Montgomery, kissing her. "I am bent upon it; it would be quite as much of a disappointment to me as to you not to go. We have a lovely day for it, and we will take our time and walk slowly, and we haven't far to go, either. But I must let Dr. Green make his visit first."

To fill up the time till he came, Mrs. Montgomery employed Ellen in reading to her as usual. And this morning's reading Ellen long after remembered. Her mother directed her to several passages in different parts of the Bible that speak of heaven and its enjoyments; and though, when she began, her own little heart was full of excitement, in view of the day's plans, and beating with hope and pleasure, the sublime beauty of the words and thoughts, as she went on, awed her into quiet, and her mother's manner at length turned her attention entirely from herself. Mrs. Montgomery was lying on the sofa, and for the most part listened in silence, with her eyes closed, but sometimes saying a word or two that made Ellen feel how deep was the interest her mother had in the things she read of, and how pure and strong the pleasure she was even now taking in them; and sometimes there was a smile on her face that Ellen scarce liked to see; it gave her an indistinct feeling that her mother would not be long away from that heaven to which she seemed already to belong. Ellen had a sad consciousness, too, that she had no part with her mother in this matter. She could hardly go on. She came to that beautiful passage in the seventh of Revelation:

"And one of the elders answered, saying unto me, What are these which are arrayed in white robes? and whence came they? And I said unto him, Sir, thou knowest. And he said unto me, These are they which came out of great tribulation, and have washed their robes, and made them white in the blood of the Lamb. Therefore are they before the throne of God, and serve him day and night in his temple: and he that sitteth on the throne shall dwell among them. They shall hunger no more, neither thirst any more; neither shall the sun light on them, nor any heat. For the Lamb which is in the midst of the throne shall feed them, and shall lead them unto living fountains of waters: and God shall wipe away all tears from their eyes."[7]

With difficulty, and a husky voice, Ellen got through it. Lifting then her eyes to her mother's face, she saw again the same singular sweet smile. Ellen felt that she could not read another word; to her great relief the door opened, and Dr. Green came in. His appearance changed the whole course of her thoughts. All that was grave or painful fled quickly away; Ellen's head was immediately full again of what had filled it before she began to read.

As soon as the doctor had retired and was fairly out of hearing, "Now, mamma, shall we go?" said Ellen. "You needn't stir, mamma; I'll bring all your things to you, and put them on; may I, mamma? then you won't be a bit tired before you set out."

Her mother assented; and with a great deal of tenderness and a great deal of eagerness, Ellen put on her stockings and shoes, arranged her hair, and did all that she could toward changing her dress and putting on her bonnet and shawl; and greatly delighted she was when the business was accomplished.

"Now, mamma, you look like yourself; I haven't seen you look so well this great while. I'm so glad you're going out again," said Ellen, putting her arms round her; "I do believe it will do you good. Now, mamma, I'll go and get ready; I'll be very quick about it; you shan't have to wait long for me."

In a few minutes the two set forth from the house. The day was as fine as could be; there was no wind, there was no dust; the sun was not oppressive; and Mrs. Montgomery did feel refreshed and strengthened during the few steps they had to take to their first stopping-place.

It was a jeweller's store. Ellen had never been in one before in her life, and her first feeling on entering was of dazzled wonderment at the glittering splendours around; this was presently forgotten in curiosity to know what her mother could possibly want there. She soon discovered that she had come to sell and not to buy. Mrs. Montgomery drew a ring from her finger, and after a little chaffering parted with it to the owner of the store for eighty dollars,

7. Revelation 7:13–17.

being about three-quarters of its real value. The money was counted out, and she left the store.

"Mamma," said Ellen, in a low voice, "wasn't that grandmamma's ring, which I thought you loved so much?"

"Yes, I did love it, Ellen, but I love you better."

"Oh, mamma, I am very sorry!" said Ellen.

"You need not be sorry, daughter. Jewels in themselves are the merest nothings to me; and as for the rest, it doesn't matter; I can remember my mother without any help from a trinket."

There were tears, however, in Mrs. Montgomery's eyes, that showed the sacrifice had cost her something; and there were tears in Ellen's that told it was not thrown away upon her.

"I am sorry you should know of this," continued Mrs. Montgomery; "you should not if I could have helped it. But set your heart quite at rest, Ellen; I assure you this use of my ring gives me more pleasure on the whole than any other I could have made of it."

A grateful squeeze of her hand and glance into her face was Ellen's answer.

Mrs. Montgomery had applied to her husband for the funds necessary to fit Ellen comfortably for the time they should be absent; and in answer he had given her a sum barely sufficient for her mere clothing. Mrs. Montgomery knew him better than to ask for a further supply, but she resolved to have recourse to other means to do what she had determined upon. Now that she was about to leave her little daughter, and it might be forever, she had set her heart upon providing her with certain things which she thought important to her comfort and improvement, and which Ellen would go very long without if *she* did not give them to her, and *now*. Ellen had had very few presents in her life, and those always of the simplest and cheapest kind; her mother resolved that in the midst of the bitterness of this time she would give her one pleasure, if she could; it might be the last.

They stopped next at a bookstore. "Oh, what a delicious smell of new books!" said Ellen, as they entered. "Mamma, if it wasn't for one thing, I should say I never was so happy in my life."

Children's books, lying in tempting confusion near the door, immediately fastened Ellen's eyes and attention. She opened one, and was already deep in the interest of it, when the word *"Bibles"* struck her ear. Mrs. Montgomery was desiring the shopman to show her various kinds and sizes that she might choose from among them. Down went Ellen's book, and she flew to the place, where a dozen different Bibles were presently displayed. Ellen's wits were ready to forsake her. Such beautiful Bibles she had never seen; she pored in ecstasy over their varieties of type and binding, and was very evidently in love with them all.

"Now, Ellen," said Mrs. Montgomery, "look and choose; take your time, and see which you like best."

It was not likely that Ellen's "time" would be a short one. Her mother, seeing this, took a chair at a little distance to await patiently her decision; and while Ellen's eyes were riveted on the Bibles, her own very naturally were fixed upon her. In the excitement and eagerness of the moment, Ellen had thrown off her light bonnet, and with flushed cheek and sparkling eye, and a brow grave with unusual care, as though a nation's fate were deciding, she was weighing the comparative advantages of large, small, and middle-sized; black, blue, purple, and red; gilt and not gilt; clasp and no clasp. Everything but the Bibles before her Ellen had forgotten utterly; she was deep in what was to her the most important of business; she did not see the bystanders smile; she did not know there were any. To her mother's eye it was a most fair sight. Mrs. Montgomery gazed with rising emotions of pleasure and pain that struggled for the mastery, but pain at last got the better and rose very high. "How can I give thee up!" was the one thought of her heart. Unable to command herself, she rose and went to a distant part of the counter, where she seemed to be examining books; but tears, some of the bitterest she had ever shed, were falling thick upon the dusty floor, and she felt her heart like to break. Her little daughter at one end of the counter had forgotten there ever was such a thing as sorrow in the world; and she at the other was bowed beneath a weight of it that was nigh to crush her. But in her extremity she betook herself to that refuge she had never known to fail; it did not fail her now. She remembered the words Ellen had been reading to her but that very morning, and they came like the breath of heaven upon the fever of her soul. "Not my will, but thine be done."[8] She strove and prayed to say it, and not in vain; and after a little while she was able to return to her seat. She felt that she had been shaken by a tempest, but she was calmer now than before.

Ellen was just as she had left her, and apparently just as far from coming to any conclusion. Mrs. Montgomery was resolved to let her take her way. Presently Ellen came over from the counter with a large royal octavo Bible, heavy enough to be a good lift for her. "Mamma," said she, laying it on her mother's lap and opening it, "what do you think of that? isn't that splendid?"

"A most beautiful page, indeed; is this your choice, Ellen?"

"Well, mamma, I don't know; what do you think?"

"I think it is rather inconveniently large and heavy for everyday use. It is quite a weight upon my lap. I shouldn't like to carry it in my hands long. You would want a little table on purpose to hold it."

"Well, that wouldn't do at all," said Ellen, laughing; "I believe you are right, mamma; I wonder I didn't think of it. I might have known that myself."

She took it back; and there followed another careful examination of the whole stock; and then Ellen came to her mother with a beautiful miniature edition in two volumes, gilt and clasped, and very perfect in all respects, but of exceeding small print.

"I think I'll have this, mamma," said she; "isn't it a beauty? I could put it in my pocket, you know, and carry it anywhere with the greatest ease."

"It would have one great objection to me," said Mrs. Montgomery, "inasmuch as I cannot possibly see to read it."

"Cannot you, mamma! But I can read it perfectly."

"Well, my dear, take it; that is, if you will make up your mind to put on spectacles before your time."

"Spectacles, mamma! I hope I shall never wear spectacles."

"What do you propose to do when your sight fails, if you shall live so long?"

"Well, mamma,—if it comes to that,—but you don't advise me, then, to take this little beauty?"

"Judge for yourself; I think you are old enough."

"I know what you think, though, mamma, and I dare say you are right, too; I won't take it, though it's a pity. Well, I must look again."

Mrs. Montgomery came to her help, for it was plain Ellen had lost the power of judging amidst so many tempting objects. But she presently simplified the matter by putting aside all that were decidedly too large, or too small, or of too fine print. There remained three, of moderate size and sufficiently large type, but different binding. "Either of these I think will answer your purpose nicely," said Mrs. Montgomery.

"Then, mamma, if you please, I will have the red one. I like that best, because it will put me in mind of yours."

Mrs. Montgomery could find no fault with this reason. She paid for the red Bible, and directed it to be sent home. "Shan't I carry it, mamma?" said Ellen.

"No, you would find it in the way; we have several things to do yet."

"Have we, mamma? I thought we only came to get a Bible."

"That is enough for one day, I confess; I am a little afraid your head will be turned; but I must run the risk of it. I dare not lose the opportunity of this fine weather; I may not have such another. I wish to have the comfort of thinking, when I am away, that I have left you with everything necessary to the keeping up of good habits,—everything that will make them

8. Luke 22:42.

pleasant and easy. I wish you to be always neat, and tidy, and industrious; depending upon others as little as possible; and careful to improve yourself by every means, and especially by writing to me. I will leave you no excuse, Ellen, for failing in any of these duties. I trust you will not disappoint me in a single particular."

Ellen's heart was too full to speak; she again looked up tearfully and pressed her mother's hand.

"I do not expect to be disappointed, love," returned Mrs. Montgomery.

They now entered a large fancy store. "What are we to get here, mamma?" said Ellen.

"A box to put your pens and paper in," said her mother, smiling.

"Oh, to be sure," said Ellen; "I had almost forgotten that." She quite forgot it a minute after. It was the first time she had ever seen the inside of such a store; and the articles displayed on every side completely bewitched her. From one thing to another she went, admiring and wondering; in her wildest dreams she had never imagined such beautiful things. The store was fairy-land.

Mrs. Montgomery meanwhile attended to business. Having chosen a neat little japanned[9] dressing-box, perfectly plain, but well supplied with everything a child could want in that line, she called Ellen from the delightful journey of discovery she was making round the store, and asked her what she thought of it. "I think it's a little beauty," said Ellen; "but I never saw such a place for beautiful things."

"You think it will do, then?" said her mother.

"For me, mamma! You don't mean to give it to me? Oh, mother, how good you are! But I know what is the best way to thank you, and I'll do it. What a perfect little beauty! Mamma, I'm too happy."

"I hope not," said her mother, "for you know I haven't got you the box for your pens and paper yet."

"Well, mamma, I'll try and bear it," said Ellen, laughing. "But do get me the plainest little thing in the world, for you're giving me too much."

Mrs. Montgomery asked to look at writing-desks, and was shown to another part of the store for the purpose. "Mamma," said Ellen, in a low tone, as they went, "you're not going to get me a writing-desk?"

"Why, that is the best kind of box for holding writing materials," said her mother, smiling; "don't you think so?"

"I don't know what to say!" exclaimed Ellen. "I can't thank you, mamma; I haven't any words to do it. I think I shall go crazy."

She was truly overcome with the weight of happiness. Words failed her, and tears came instead.

From among a great many desks of all descriptions, Mrs. Montgomery with some difficulty succeeded in choosing one to her mind. It was of mahogany, not very large, but thoroughly well made and finished, and very convenient and perfect in its internal arrangements. Ellen was speechless; occasional looks at her mother, and deep sighs, were all she had now to offer. The desk was quite empty. "Ellen," said her mother, "do you remember the furniture of Miss Allen's desk, that you were so pleased with a while ago."

"Perfectly, mamma; I know all that was in it."

"Well, then, you must prompt me if I forget anything. Your desk will be furnished with every thing really useful. Merely showy matters we can dispense with. Now, let us see.— Here is a great empty place that I think wants some paper to fill it. Show me some of different sizes, if you please."

The shopman obeyed, and Mrs. Montgomery stocked the desk well with letter paper, large and small. Ellen looked on in great satisfaction. "That will do nicely," she said;—"that large paper will be beautiful whenever I am writing to you, mamma, you know, and the other will

9. Lacquered.

do for other times when I haven't so much to say; though I am sure I don't know who there is in the world I should ever send letters to except you."

"If there is nobody now, perhaps there will be at some future time," replied her mother. "I hope I shall not always be your only correspondent. Now what next?"

"Envelopes, mamma?"

"To be sure; I had forgotten them. Envelopes of both sizes to match."

"Because, mamma, you know I might, and I certainly shall, want to write upon the fourth page of my letter, and I couldn't do it unless I had envelopes."

A sufficient stock of envelopes was laid in.

"Mamma," said Ellen, "what do you think of a little notepaper?"

"Who are the notes to be written to, Ellen?" said Mrs. Montgomery, smiling.

"You needn't smile, mamma; you know, as you said, if I don't now know, perhaps I shall by and by. Miss Allen's desk had notepaper; that made me think of it."

"So shall yours, daughter; while we are about it we will do the thing well. And your note-paper will keep quite safely in this nice little place provided for it, even if you should not want to use a sheet of it in half a dozen years."

"How nice that is!" said Ellen, admiringly.

"I suppose the note-paper must have envelopes too," said Mrs. Montgomery.

"To be sure, mamma; I suppose so," said Ellen, smiling; "Miss Allen's had."

"Well now we have got all the paper we want, I think," said Mrs. Montgomery; "the next thing is ink,—or an inkstand rather."

Different kinds were presented for her choice.

"Oh, mamma, that one won't do," said Ellen, anxiously; "you know the desk will be knocking about in a trunk, and the ink would run out, and spoil every thing. It should be one of those that shut tight. I don't see the right kind here."

The shopman brought one.

"There, mamma, do you see?" said Ellen; "it shuts with a spring, and nothing can possibly come out; do you see, mamma? You can turn it topsy turvy."

"I see you are quite right, daughter; it seems I should get on very ill without you to advise me. Fill the inkstand, if you please."

"Mamma, what shall I do when my ink is gone? that inkstand will hold but a little, you know."

"Your aunt will supply you, of course, my dear, when you are out."

"I'd rather take some of my own by half," said Ellen.

"You could not carry a bottle of ink in your desk without great danger to every thing else in it. It would not do to venture."

"We have excellent ink-powder," said the shopman, "in small packages, which can be very conveniently carried about. You see, ma'am, there is a compartment in the desk for such things; and the ink is very easily made at any time."

"Oh, that will do nicely," said Ellen, "that is just the thing."

"Now what is to go in this other square place opposite the inkstand?" said Mrs. Montgomery.

"That is the place for the box of lights, mamma."

"What sort of lights?"

"For sealing letters, mamma, you know. They are not like your wax taper at all; they are little wax matches, that burn just long enough to seal one or two letters; Miss Allen showed me how she used them. Hers were in a nice little box just like the inkstand on the outside; and there was a place to light the matches, and a place to set them in while they are burning. There, mamma, that's it," said Ellen, as the shopman brought forth the article which she was describing, "that's it, exactly; and that will just fit. Now, mamma, for the wax."

"You want to seal your letter before you have written it," said Mrs. Montgomery,—"we have not got the pens yet."

"That's true, mamma; let us have the pens. And some quills too, mamma?"

"Do you know how to make a pen, Ellen?"

"No, mamma, not yet; but I want to learn very much. Miss Pichegru says that every lady ought to know how to make her own pens."

"Miss Pichegru is very right; but I think you are rather too young to learn. However, we will try. Now here are steel points enough to last you a great while,—and as many quills as it is needful you should cut up for one year at least;—we haven't a penhandle yet."

"Here, mamma," said Ellen, holding out a plain ivory one,—"don't you like this? I think that it is prettier than these that are all cut and fussed, or those other gay ones either."

"I think so too, Ellen; the plainer the prettier. Now what comes next?"

"The knife, mamma, to make the pens," said Ellen, smiling.

"True, the knife. Let us see some of your best pen-knives. Now, Ellen, choose. That one won't do, my dear; it should have two blades,—a large as well as a small one. You know you want to mend a pencil sometimes."

"So I do, mamma, to be sure, you're very right; here's a nice one. Now, mamma, the wax."

"There is a box full; choose your own colours." Seeing it was likely to be a work of time, Mrs. Montgomery walked away to another part of the store. When she returned Ellen had made up an assortment of the oddest colours she could find.

"I won't have any red, mamma, it is so common," she said.

"I think it is the prettiest of all," said Mrs. Montgomery.

"Do you, mamma? then I will have a stick of red on purpose to seal to you with."

"And who do you intend shall have the benefit of the other colours?" inquired her mother.

"I declare, mamma," said Ellen, laughing; "I never thought of that; I am afraid they will have to go to you. You must not mind, mamma, if you get green and blue and yellow seals once in a while."

"I dare say I shall submit myself to it with a good grace," said Mrs. Montgomery. "But come, my dear, have we got all that we want? This desk has been very long in furnishing."

"You haven't given me a seal yet, mamma."

"Seals! There are a variety before you; see if you can find one that you like. By the way, you cannot seal a letter, can you?"

"Not yet, mamma," said Ellen, smiling again; "that is another of the things I have got to learn."

"Then I think you had better have some wafers in the mean time."

While Ellen was picking out her seal, which took not a little time, Mrs. Montgomery laid in a good supply of wafers of all sorts; and then went on further to furnish the desk with an ivory leaf-cutter, a paper-folder, a pounce-box,[1] a ruler, and a neat little silver pencil; also, some drawing-pencils, India-rubber, and sheets of drawing-paper. She took a sad pleasure in adding every thing she could think of that might be for Ellen's future use or advantage; but as with her own hands she placed in the desk one thing after another, the thought crossed her mind how Ellen would make drawings with those very pencils, on those very sheets of paper, which her eyes would never see! She turned away with a sigh, and receiving Ellen's seal from her hand, put that also in its place. Ellen had chosen one with her own name.

"Will you send these things *at once?*" said Mrs. Montgomery. "I particularly wish them at home as early in the day as possible."

The man promised. Mrs. Montgomery paid the bill, and she and Ellen left the store.

They walked a little way in silence.

"I cannot thank you, mamma," said Ellen.

"It is not necessary, my dear child," said Mrs. Montgomery, returning the pressure of her hand; "I know all that you would say."

---

1. Small box with a perforated top, used for sprinkling sand on writing paper to dry the ink.

There was as much sorrow as joy at that moment in the heart of the joyfullest of the two.

"Where are we going now, mamma?" said Ellen again, after a while.

"I wished and intended to have gone to St. Clair and Fleury's, to get you some merino[2] and other things; but we have been detained so long already that I think I had better go home. I feel somewhat tired."

"I am very sorry, dear mamma," said Ellen; "I am afraid I kept you too long about that desk."

"You did not keep me, daughter, any longer than I chose to be kept. But I think I will go home now, and take the chance of another fine day for the merino."[3]

Chapter XXXVII

Thou must run to him; for thou hast stayed so long that going will scarce serve the turn.
—Shakespeare.

Captain Montgomery did *not* come the next week, nor the week after; and what is more, the Duck Dorleens, as his sister called the ship in which he had taken passage, was never heard of from that time.[4] She sailed duly on the fifth of April, as they learned from the papers; but whatever became of her she never reached port. It remained a doubt whether Captain Montgomery had actually gone in her; and Ellen had many weeks of anxious watching, first for himself, and then for news of him in case he were still in France. None ever came. Anxiety gradually faded into uncertainty; and by midsummer no doubt of the truth remained in any mind. If Captain Montgomery had been alive, he would certainly have written, if not before, on learning the fate of the vessel in which he had told his friends to expect him home.

Ellen rather felt that she was an orphan than that she had lost her father. She had never learned to love him, he had never given her much cause. Comparatively a small portion of her life had been passed in his society, and she looked back to it as the least agreeable of all; and it had not been possible for her to expect with pleasure his return to America and visit to Thirlwall; she dreaded it. Life had nothing now worse for her than a separation from Alice and John Humphreys; she feared her father might take her away and put her in some dreadful boarding-school, or carry her about the world wherever he went, a wretched wanderer from every thing good and pleasant. The knowledge of his death had less pain for her than the removal of this fear brought relief.

Ellen felt sometimes, soberly and sadly, that she was thrown upon the wide world now. To all intents and purposes so she had been a year and three-quarters before; but it was something to have a father and mother living even on the other side of the world. Now Miss Fortune was her sole guardian and owner. However, she could hardly realize that, with Alice and John so near at hand. Without reasoning much about it, she felt tolerably secure that they would take care of her interests, and make good their claim to interfere if ever need were.

Ellen and her little horse grew more and more fond of each other.[5] This friendship, no doubt, was a comfort to the Brownie; but to his mistress it made a large part of the pleasure of her every-day life. To visit him was her delight, at all hours, early and late; and it is to the Brownie's credit that he always seemed as glad to see her as she was to see him. At any time Ellen's voice would bring him from the far end of the meadow where he was allowed

---

2. A soft, lightweight fabric of fine wool.
3. In subsequent chapters, Ellen moves to her Aunt Fortune's rural home. Her aunt is hypercritical and uncooperative and withholds Ellen's mother's letters. Ellen learns housekeeping and befriends her aunt's handyman, Mr. Van Brunt, as well as the

grown children of a neighboring clergyman, Alice and John Humphreys.
4. Ellen has had little news of either of her parents, except for word that her mother has died in Europe.
5. She received the horse as a gift from the Humphreys' friend, Mr. Marshman.

to run. He would come trotting up at her call, and stand to have her scratch his forehead or pat him and talk to him; and though the Brownie could not answer her speeches he certainly seemed to hear them with pleasure. Then throwing up his head he would bound off, take a turn in the field, and come back again to stand as still as a lamb as long as she stayed there herself. Now and then, when she had a little more time, she would cross the fence and take a walk with him; and there, with his nose just at her elbow, wherever she went the Brownie went after her. After a while there was no need that she should call him; if he saw or heard her at a distance it was enough; he would come running up directly. Ellen loved him dearly.

She gave him more proof of it than words and caresses. Many were the apples and scraps of bread hoarded up for him; and if these failed, Ellen sometimes took him a little salt to show that he was not forgotten. There were not certainly many scraps left at Miss Fortune's table; nor apples to be had at home for such a purpose, except what she gathered up from the poor ones that were left under the trees for the hogs; but Ellen had other sources of supply. Once she had begged from Jenny Hitchcock a waste bit that she was going to throw away; Jenny found what she wanted to do with it, and after that many a basket of apples and many a piece of cold shortcake was set by for her. Margery, too, remembered the Brownie when disposing of her odds and ends; likewise did Mrs. Van Brunt; so that among them all Ellen seldom wanted something to give him.[6] Mr. Marshman did not know what happiness he was bestowing when he sent her that little horse. Many, many, were the hours of enjoyment she had upon his back. Ellen went nowhere but upon the Brownie. Alice made her a riding-dress of dark gingham; and it was the admiration of the country to see her trotting or cantering by, all alone, and always looking happy. Ellen soon found that if the Brownie was to do her much good she must learn to saddle and bridle him herself. This was very awkward at first, but there was no help for it. Mr. Van Brunt showed her how to manage, and after a while it became quite easy. She used to call the Brownie to the bar-place, put the bridle on, and let him out; and then he would stand motionless before her while she fastened the saddle on; looking round sometimes as if to make sure that it was she herself, and giving a little kind of satisfied neigh when he saw that it was. Ellen's heart began to dance as soon as she felt him moving under her; and once off and away on the docile and spirited little animal, over the roads, through the lanes, up and down the hills, her horse her only companion, but having the most perfect understanding with him, both Ellen and the Brownie cast care to the winds. "I do believe," said Mr. Van Brunt, "that critter would a *leetle* rather have Ellen on his back than not." He was the Brownie's next best friend. Miss Fortune never said any thing to him or of him.

Ellen however reaped a reward for her faithful steadiness to duty while her aunt was ill. Things were never after that as they had been before. She was looked on with a different eye. To be sure Miss Fortune tasked her as much as ever, spoke as sharply, was as ready to scold if any thing went wrong;—all that was just as it used to be; but beneath all that Ellen felt with great satisfaction that she was trusted and believed. She was no longer an interloper, in every body's way; she was not watched and suspected; her aunt treated her as one of the family and a person to be depended on. It was a very great comfort to little Ellen's life. Miss Fortune even owned that "she believed she was an honest child and meant to do right,"—a great deal from her; Miss Fortune was never over forward to give any one the praise of *honesty*. Ellen now went out and came in without feeling she was an alien. And though her aunt was always bent on keeping herself and every body else at work, she did not now show any particular desire for breaking off Ellen from her studies; and was generally willing when the work was pretty well done up that she should saddle the Brownie and be off to Alice or Mrs. Vawse.[7]

Though Ellen was happy, it was a sober kind of happiness;—the sun shining behind a

6. Jenny and Mrs. Van Brunt are neighbors of Fortune's; Margery is the Humphreys' housekeeper.

7. Another neighbor.

cloud. And if others thought her so, it was not because she laughed loudly or wore a merry face.

"I can't help but think," said Mrs. Van Brunt, "that that child has something more to make her happy than what she gets in this world."

There was a quilting party gathered that afternoon at Mrs. Van Brunt's house.

"There is no doubt of that, neighbour," said Mrs. Vawse; "nobody ever found enough here to make him happy yet."

"Well I don't want to see a prettier girl than that," said Mrs. Lowndes;—"you'll never catch her, working at home or riding along on that handsome little critter of hers, that she ha'n't a pleasant look and a smile for you, and as pretty behaved as can be. I never see her look sorrowful but once."

"Ain't that a pretty horse?" said Mimy Lawson.

"*I've* seen her look sorrowful though," said Sarah Lowndes; "I've been up at the house when Miss Fortune was hustling every body round, and as sharp as vinegar, and you'd think it would take Job's patience to stand it;—and for all there wouldn't be a bit of crossness in that child's face,—she'd go round, and not say a word that wasn't just so;—you'd ha' thought her bread was all spread with honey; and every body knows it ain't. I don't see how she could do it, for my part. I know *I* couldn't."

"Ah, neighbour," said Mrs. Vawse, "Ellen looks higher than to please her aunt; she tries to please her God; and one can bear people's words or looks when one is pleasing him.—She is a dear child!"

"And there's 'Brahm," said Mrs. Van Brunt,[8]—"he thinks the hull world of her. I never see him take so to any one. There ain't an airthly thing he wouldn't do to please her. If she was his own child I've no idea he could set her up more than he does."

"Very well!" said Nancy coming up,—"good reason! Ellen don't set *him* up any, does she? I wish you'd just seen her once, the time when Miss Fortune was abed,—the way she'd look out for him! Mr. Van Brunt's as good as at home in that house sure enough; whoever's down stairs."

"Bless her dear little heart!" said his mother.

"A good name is better than precious ointment."

August had come, and John was daily expected home. One morning Miss Fortune was in the lower kitchen, up to the elbows in making a rich fall cheese; Ellen was busy up stairs, when her aunt shouted to her to "come and see what was all that splashing and crashing in the garden." Ellen ran out.

"Oh, aunt Fortune," said she,—"Timothy has broken down the fence and got in."

"Timothy!" said Miss Fortune,—"what Timothy?"

"Why Timothy, the near ox," said Ellen laughing;—"he has knocked down the fence over there where it was low, you know."

"The near ox!" said Miss Fortune,—"I wish he warn't quite so near this time. Mercy! he'll be at the corn and over every thing. Run and drive him into the barnyard, can't you?"

But Ellen stood still and shook her head. "He wouldn't stir for me," she said;—"and besides I am as afraid of that ox as can be. If it was Clover I wouldn't mind."

"But he'll have every bit of the corn eaten up in five minutes! Where's Mr. Van Brunt?"

"I heard him say he was going home till noon," said Ellen.

"And Sam Larkens is gone to mill—and Johnny Low is laid up with the shakes. Very careless of Mr. Van Brunt!" said Miss Fortune, drawing her arms out of the cheese-tub wringing off the whey,—"I wish he'd mind his own oxen. There was no business to be a low place in the fence! Well come along! you ain't afraid with me, I suppose."

Ellen followed, at a respectful distance. Miss Fortune however feared the face of neither man nor beast; she pulled up a bean pole, and made such a show of fight that Timothy after

8. Mr. Van Brunt, her son.

looking at her a little, fairly turned tail, and marched out at the breach he had made. Miss Fortune went after, and rested not till she had driven him quite into the meadow;—get him into the barnyard she could not.

"You ain't worth a straw, Ellen!" said she when she came back;—"couldn't you ha' headed him and driv' him into the barnyard? Now that plaguy beast will just be back again by the time I get well to work. He ha'n't done much mischief yet—there's Mr. Van Brunt's salary[9] he's made a pretty mess of; I'm glad on't! He should ha' put potatoes, as I told him. I don't know what's to be done—I can't be leaving my cheese to run and mind the garden every minute, if it was full of Timothys; and *you'd* be scared if a mosquito flew at you;—you had better go right off for Mr. Van Brunt and fetch him straight home—serve him right! he has no business to leave things so. Run along,—and don't let the grass grow under your feet!"

Ellen wisely thought her pony's feet would do the business quicker. She ran and put on her gingham dress and saddled and bridled the Brownie in three minutes; but before setting off she had to scream to her aunt that Timothy was just coming round the corner of the barn again; and Miss Fortune rushed out to the garden as Ellen and the Brownie walked down to the gate.

The weather was fine, and Ellen thought with herself it was an ill wind that blew no good. She was getting a nice ride in the early morning, that she would not have had but for Timothy's lawless behaviour. To ride at that time was particularly pleasant and rare; and forgetting how she had left poor Miss Fortune between the ox and the cheese-tub, Ellen and the Brownie cantered on in excellent spirits.

She looked in vain as she passed his grounds to see Mr. Van Brunt in the garden or about the barn. She went on to the little gate of the courtyard, dismounted, and led the Brownie in. Here she was met by Nancy[1] who came running from the way of the barnyard.

"How d'ye do, Nancy?" said Ellen;—"where's Mr. Van Brunt?"

"Goodness! Ellen!—what do you want?"

"I want Mr. Van Brunt,—where is he?"

"Mr. Van Brunt!—he's out in the barn,—but he's used himself up."

"Used himself up! what do you mean?"

"Why he's fixed himself in fine style; he's fell through the trap-door and broke his leg."

"Oh, Nancy!" screamed Ellen,—"he hasn't! how could he?"

"Why easy enough if he didn't look where he was going,—there's so much hay on the floor. But it's a pretty bad place to fall."

"How do you know his leg is broken?"

" 'Cause he says so, and any body with eyes can see it must be. I'm going over to Hitchcock's to get somebody to come and help in with him; for you know me and Mrs. Van Brunt ain't Samsons."

"Where is Mrs. Van Brunt?"

"She's out there—in a terrible to do."

Nancy sped on to the Hitchcock's; and greatly frightened and distressed Ellen ran over to the barn, trembling like an aspen. Mr. Van Brunt was lying in the lower floor, just where he had fallen; one leg doubled under him in such a way as left no doubt it must be broken. He had lain there some time before any one found him; and on trying to change his position when he saw his mother's distress, he had fainted from pain. She sat by weeping most bitterly. Ellen could bear but one look at Mr. Van Brunt; that one sickened her. She went up to his poor mother and getting down on her knees by her side put both arms round her neck.

"Don't cry so, dear Mrs. Van Brunt," (Ellen was crying so she could hardly speak herself,)— "pray don't do so!—he'll be better—Oh, what shall we do?"

"Oh, ain't it dreadful!" said poor Mrs. Van Brunt;—"oh, 'Brahm! 'Brahm! my son!—the best son that ever was to me—oh, to see him there—ain't it dreadful? he's dying!"

---

9. Celery.   1. Mrs. Vawse's mischievous granddaughter.

"Oh, no he isn't," said Ellen,—"oh, no he isn't!—what shall we do, Mrs. Van Brunt?—what shall we do?"

"The doctor!" said Mrs. Van Brunt,—"he said 'send for the doctor;'—but I can't go, and there's nobody to send. Oh, he'll die!—oh, my dear 'Brahm! I wish it was me!"

"What doctor?" said Ellen;—"I'll find somebody to go; what doctor?"

"Dr. Gibson, he said; but he's away off to Thirlwall; and he's been lying here all the morning a'ready!—nobody found him—he couldn't make us hear. Oh, isn't it dreadful!"

"Oh, don't cry so, dear Mrs. Van Brunt," said Ellen, pressing her cheek to the poor old lady's; "he'll be better—he will! I've got the Brownie here and I'll ride over to Mrs. Hitchcock's and get somebody to go right away for the doctor. I won't be long,—we'll have him here in a little while! *don't* feel so bad!"

"You're a dear blessed darling!" said the old lady, hugging and kissing her,—"if ever there was one. Make haste dear, if you love him!—he loves you."

Ellen stayed but to give her another kiss. Trembling so that she could hardly stand she made her way back to the house, led out the Brownie again, and set off full speed for Mrs. Hitchcock's. It was well her pony was sure-footed, for letting the reins hang, Ellen bent over his neck crying bitterly, only urging him now and then to greater speed; till at length the feeling that she had something to do came to her help. She straightened herself, gathered up her reins, and by the time she reached Mrs. Hitchcock's was looking calm again, though very sad and very earnest. She did not alight, but stopped before the door and called Jenny. Jenny came out, expressing her pleasure.

"Dear Jenny," said Ellen,—"isn't there somebody here that will go right off to Thirlwall for Dr. Gibson? Mr. Van Brunt has broken his leg, I am afraid, and wants the doctor directly."

"Why dear Ellen," said Jenny, "the men have just gone off this minute to Mrs. Van Brunt. Nancy was here for them to come and help move him in a great hurry. How did it happen? I couldn't get any thing out of Nancy."

"He fell down through the trap-door. But dear Jenny, isn't there *any body* about? Oh," said Ellen clasping her hands,—"I want somebody to go for the doctor *so* much!"

"There ain't a living soul!" said Jenny; "two of the men and all the teams are 'way on the other side of the hill ploughing, and pa and June and Black Bill have gone over, as I told you; but I don't believe they'll be enough. Where's his leg broke?"

"I didn't meet them," said Ellen;—"I came away only a little while after Nancy."

"They went 'cross lots I guess,—that's how it was, and that's the way Nancy got the start of you."

"What shall I do?" said Ellen. She could not bear to wait till they returned; if she rode back she might miss them again, besides the delay; and then a man on foot would make a long journey of it. Jenny told her of a house or two where she might try for a messenger; but they were strangers to her; she could not make up her mind to ask such a favour of them. Her friends were too far out of the way.

"I'll go myself!" she said suddenly. "Tell 'em, dear Jenny, will you, that I have gone for Dr. Gibson and that I'll bring him back as quick as ever I can. I know the road to Thirlwall."

"But Ellen! you mustn't," said Jenny;—"I am afraid to have you go all that way alone. Wait till the men come back,—they won't be long."

"No I can't, Jenny," said Ellen,—"I can't wait; I must go. You needn't be afraid. Tell 'em I'll be as quick as I can."

"But see, Ellen!" cried Jenny as she was moving off,—"I don't like to have you!"

"I must, Jenny. Never mind."

"But see, Ellen!" cried Jenny again,—"if you *will* go—if you don't find Dr. Gibson just get Dr. Marshchalk,—he's every bit as good and some folks think he's better;—he'll do just as well. Good-by!"

Ellen nodded and rode off. There was a little fluttering of the heart at taking so much upon herself; she had never been to Thirlwall but once since the first time she saw it. But she thought of Mr. Van Brunt, suffering for help which could not be obtained, and it was impossible for her to hesitate. "I am sure I am doing right," she thought,—"and what is there to be afraid of? If I ride two miles alone, why shouldn't I four?—And I am doing right—God will take care of me." Ellen earnestly asked him to do so; and after that she felt pretty easy. "Now dear Brownie," said she, patting his neck,—"you and I have work to do to-day; behave like a good little horse as you are." The Brownie answered with a little cheerful kind of neigh, as much as to say, Never fear me!—They trotted on nicely.

But nothing could help that's being a disagreeable ride. Do what she would, Ellen felt a little afraid when she found herself on a long piece of road where she had never been alone before. There were not many houses on the way; the few there were looked strange; Ellen did not know exactly where she was, or how near the end of her journey; it seemed a long one. She felt rather lonely;—a little shy of meeting people, and yet a little unwilling to have the intervals between them so very long. She repeated to herself, "I am doing right—God will take care of me,"—still there was a nervous trembling at heart. Sometimes she would pat her pony's neck and say, "Trot on, dear Brownie! we'll soon be there!"—by way of cheering herself; for certainly the Brownie needed no cheering, and was trotting on bravely. Then the thought of Mr. Van Brunt as she had seen him lying on the barn-floor, made her feel sick and miserable; many tears fell during her ride when she remembered him. "Heaven will be a good place," thought little Ellen as she went;—"there will be no sickness, no pain, no sorrow; but Mr. Van Brunt!—I wonder if he is fit to go to heaven?"—This was a new matter of thought and uneasiness, not now for the first time in Ellen's mind; and so the time passed till she crossed the bridge over the little river and saw the houses of Thirlwall stretching away in the distance. Then she felt comfortable.

Long before, she had bethought her that she did not know where to find Dr. Gibson, and had forgotten to ask Jenny. For one instant Ellen drew bridle, but it was too far to go back, and she recollected any body could tell her where the doctor lived. When she got to Thirlwall however Ellen found that she did not like to ask *any body*; she remembered her old friend Mrs. Forbes of the Star inn,[2] and resolved she would go there in the first place. She rode slowly up the street, and looking carefully till she came to the house. There was no mistaking it; there was the very same big star over the front door that had caught her eye from the coach-window, and there was the very same boy or man, Sam, lounging on the sidewalk. Ellen reigned up and asked him to ask Mrs. Forbes if she would be so good as to come out to her for one minute. Sam gave her a long Yankee look and disappeared, coming back again directly with the landlady.

"How d'ye do, Mrs. Forbes?" said Ellen, holding out her hand;—"don't you know me? I am Ellen Montgomery—that you were so kind to, and gave me bread and milk,—when I first came here,—Miss Fortune's——"

"Oh, bless your dear little heart," cried the landlady; "don't I know you! and ain't I glad to see you! I must have a kiss. Bless you! I couldn't mistake you in Jerusalem, but the sun was in my eyes in that way I was a'most blind. But ain't you grown though! Forget you? I guess I ha'n't! there's one o' your friends wouldn't let me do that in a hurry; if I ha'n't seen you I've heered on you. But what are you sitting there in the sun for? come in—come in—and I'll give you something better than bread and milk this time. Come! jump down."

"Oh, I can't, Mrs. Forbes," said Ellen,—"I am in a great hurry;—Mr. Van Brunt has broken his leg, and I want to find the doctor."

"Mr. Van Brunt!" cried the landlady. "Broken his leg! The land's sakes! how did he do that? *he* too!"

"He fell down through the trap-door in the barn; and I want to get Dr. Gibson as soon as I can to come to him. Where does he live, Mrs. Forbes?"

---

2.   The innkeeper had treated Ellen kindly when she arrived alone in Thirlwall.

"Dr. Gibson? you won't catch him to hum,[3] dear; he's flying round somewheres. But how come the trap-door to be open? and how happened Mr. Van Brunt not to see it afore he put his foot in it? Dear! I declare I'm real sorry to hear you tell. How happened it, darlin'? I'm cur'ous to hear."

"I don't know, Mrs. Forbes," said Ellen,—"but oh, where shall I find Dr. Gibson? Do tell me!—he ought to be there now;—oh, help me! where shall I go for him?"

"Well, I declare," said the landlady stepping back a pace,—"I don't know as I can tell—there ain't no sort o' likelihood that he's to hum at this time o' day—Sam! you lazy feller, you ha'n't got nothing to do but to gape at folks, ha' you seen the doctor go by this forenoon?"

"I seen him go down to Mis' Perriman's," said Sam,—"Mis' Perriman was a dyin'—Jim Barstow said."

"How long since?" said his mistress.

But Sam shuffled and shuffled, looked every way but at Ellen or Mrs. Forbes, and "didn't know."

"Well then," said Mrs. Forbes turning to Ellen,—"I don' know but you might about as well go down to the post-office—but if *I* was you, I'd just get Dr. Marshchalk instead! he's a smarter man than Dr. Gibson any day in the year; and he ain't quite so awful high neither, and that's something. *I'd* get Dr. Marshchalk; they say there ain't the like o' him in the country for settin' bones; it's quite a gift;—he takes to it natural like."

But Ellen said Mr. Van Brunt wanted Dr. Gibson, and if she could she must find him.

"Well," said Mrs. Forbes, "every one has their fancies;—*I* wouldn't let Dr. Gibson come near me with a pair of tongs;—but any how if you must have him, your best way is to go right straight down to the post-office and ask for him there,—maybe you'll catch him."

"Thank you, ma'am," said Ellen;—"where is the post-office?"

"It's that white-faced house down street," said the landlady, pointing with her finger where Ellen saw no lack of white-faced houses,—"you see that big red store with the man standing out in front?—the next white house below that is Mis' Perriman's; just run right in and ask for Dr. Gibson. Good-by, dear, I'm real sorry you can't come in;—that first white house."

Glad to get free, Ellen rode smartly down to the post-office. Nobody before the door; there was nothing for it but to get off here and go in; she did not know the people either. "Never mind! wait for me a minute, dear Brownie, like a good little horse as you are!"

No fear of the Brownie. He stood as if he did not mean to budge again in a century. At first going in Ellen saw nobody in the post-office; presently, at an opening in a kind of boxed-up place in one corner a face looked out and asked what was wanted.

"Is Dr. Gibson here?"

"No," said the owner of the face, with a disagreeable kind of smile.

"Isn't this Miss Perriman's house?"

"You are in the right box, my dear, and no mistake," said the young man,—"but then it ain't Dr. Gibson's house, you know."

"Can you tell me, sir, where I can find him?"

"Can't indeed—the doctor never tells me where he is going, and I never ask him. I am sorry I didn't this morning, for your sake."

The way, and the look, made the words extremely disagreeable, and furthermore Ellen had an uncomfortable feeling that neither was new to her. Where *had* she seen the man before? she puzzled herself to think. Where but in a dream had she seen that bold ill-favoured face, that horrible smile, that sandy hair,—she knew! It was Mr. Saunders, the man who had sold her the merino at St. Clair and Fleury's.[4] She knew him; and she was very sorry to see that he knew her. All she desired now was to get out of the house and away; but on turning she

---

3. At home.
4. He had upset Ellen by treating her scornfully while she was on an errand for her mother in the city.

saw another man, older and respectable-looking, whose face encouraged her to ask again if Dr. Gibson was there. He was not, the man said; he had been there and gone.

"Do you know where I should be likely to find him, sir?"

"No, I don't," said he;—"who wants him?"

"I want to see him, sir."

"For yourself?"

"No, sir; Mr. Van Brunt has broken his leg and wants Dr. Gibson to come directly and set it."

"Mr. Van Brunt!" said he,—"Farmer Van Brunt that lives down toward the Cat's back? I'm very sorry! How did it happen?"

Ellen told as shortly as possible, and again begged to know where she might look for Dr. Gibson.

"Well," said he, "the best plan I can think of will be for you—How did you come here?"

"I came on horseback, sir."

"Ah—well—the best plan will be for you to ride up to his house; maybe he'll have left word there, and any how *you* can leave word for him to come down as soon as he gets home. Do you know where the doctor lives?"

"No, sir."

"Come here," said he, pulling her to the door,—"you can't see it from here; but you must ride up street till you have passed two churches, one on the right hand first, and then a good piece beyond you'll come to another red brick one on the left hand;—and Dr. Gibson lives in the next block but one after that, on the other side;—any body will tell you the house. Is that your horse?"

"Yes, sir. I'm very much obliged to you."

"Well I will say!—if you ha'n't the prettiest fit out in Thirlwall—shall I help you? will you have a cheer?"

"No, I thank you, sir; I'll bring him up to this step; it will do just as well. I am *very* much obliged to you, sir."

He did not seem to hear her thanks; he was all eyes; and with his clerk stood looking after her till she was out of sight.

Poor Ellen found it a long way up to the doctor's. The post-office was near the lower end of the town and the doctor's house was near the upper; she passed one church, and then the other, but there was a long distance between, or what she thought so. Happily the Brownie did not seem tired at all; his little mistress *was* tired and disheartened too. And there, all this time, was poor Mr. Van Brunt lying without a doctor! She could not bear to think of it.

She jumped down when she came to the block she had been told of, and easily found the house where Dr. Gibson lived. She knocked at the door. A grey-haired woman with a very dead-and-alive face presented herself. Ellen asked for the doctor.

"He ain't to hum."

"When will he be at home?"

"Couldn't say."

"Before dinner?"

The woman shook her head—"Guess not till late in the day."

"Where is he gone?"

"He is gone to Babcock—gone to 'attend a consummation,' I guess, he told me—Babcock is a considerable long way."

Ellen thought a minute.

"Can you tell me where Dr. Marshchalk lives?"

"I guess you'd better wait till Dr. Gibson comes back, ha'n't you?" said the woman coaxingly;—"he'll be along by and by. If you'll leave me your name I'll give it to him."

"I cannot wait," said Ellen,—"I am in a dreadful hurry. Will you be so good as to tell me where Dr. Marshchalk lives?"

"Well—if so be you're in such a takin' you can't wait—you know where Miss Forbes lives?"

"At the inn?—the Star—yes."

"He lives a few doors this side o' her'n; you'll know it the first minute you set your eyes on it—it's painted a bright yaller."

Ellen thanked her, once more mounted, and rode down the street.

Chapter XXXVIII

And he had ridden o'er dale and down
By eight o'clock in the day,
When he was ware of a bold Tanner,
Came riding along the way.
         Old Ballad..

The yellow door, as the old woman had said, was not to be mistaken. Again Ellen dismounted and knocked; then she heard a slow step coming along the entry, and the pleasant kind face of Miss Janet appeared at the open door. It was a real refreshment, and Ellen wanted one.

"Why it's dear little—ain't it?—her that lives down to Miss Fortune Emerson's?—yes, it is:—come in, dear; I'm very glad to see you. How's all at your house?"

"Is the doctor at home, ma'am?"

"No dear, he ain't to home just this minute, but he'll be in directly; Come in;—is that your horse?—just hitch him to the post there so he won't run away, and come right in. Who did you come along with?"

"Nobody, ma'am; I came alone," said Ellen while she obeyed Miss Janet's directions.

"Alone!—on that 'ere little skittish creeter?—he's as handsome as a picture too—why do tell if you warn't afraid? it a'most scares me to think of it."

"I was a little afraid," said Ellen, as she followed Miss Janet along the entry,—"but I couldn't help that. You think the doctor will soon be in, ma'am?"

"Yes, dear, sure of it," said Miss Janet, kissing Ellen and taking off her bonnet;—"he won't be five minutes, for it's a'most dinner time. What's the matter dear? is Miss Fortune sick again?"

"No, ma'am," said Ellen sadly,—"Mr. Van Brunt has fallen through the trap-door in the barn and broken his leg."

"Oh!" cried the old lady with a face of real horror,—"you don't tell me! Fell through the trap-door! and he ain't a light weight neither;—oh, that is a lamentable event! And how is the poor old mother, dear?"

"She is very much troubled, ma'am," said Ellen, crying at the remembrance;—"and he has been lying ever since early this morning without anybody to set it; I have been going round and round for a doctor this ever so long."

"Why, warn't there nobody to come but you, you poor lamb?" said Miss Janet.

"No, ma'am; nobody quick enough; and I had the Brownie there, and so I came."

"Well, cheer up, dear! the doctor will be here now and we'll send him right off; he won't be long about his dinner, I'll engage. Come and set in this big cheer—do!—it'll rest you; I see you're a'most tired out, and it ain't a wonder. There—don't that feel better? now I'll give you a little sup of dinner, for you won't want to swallow it at the rate Leander will his'n. Dear! dear!—to think of poor Mr. Van Brunt. He's a likely man too;[5]—I'm very sorry for him and his poor mother. A kind body she is as ever the sun shined upon."

---

5. A promising fellow, capable of doing well.

"And so is he," said Ellen.

"Well, so I dare say," said Miss Janet,—"but I don't know so much about him; however he's got every body's good word as far as I know;—he's a likely man."

The little room in which Miss Janet had brought Ellen was very plainly furnished indeed, but as neat as hands could make it. The carpet was as crumbless and lintless as if meals were never taken there nor work seen; and yet a little table ready set for dinner forbade the one conclusion, and a huge basket of naperies[6] in one corner showed that Miss Janet's industry did not spend itself in housework alone. Before the fire stood a pretty good-sized kettle, and a very appetizing smell came from it to Ellen's nose. In spite of sorrow and anxiety her ride had made her hungry. It was not without pleasure that she saw her kind hostess arm herself with a deep plate and tin dipper, and carefully taking off the pot-cover so that no drops might fall on the hearth, proceed to ladle out a goodly supply of what Ellen knew was that excellent country dish called pot-pie. Excellent it is when well made, and that was Miss Janet's. The pieces of crust were white and light like new bread; the very tit-bits of the meat she culled out for Ellen; and the soup gravy poured over all would have met even Miss Fortune's wishes, from its just degree of richness and exact seasoning. Smoking hot it was placed before Ellen on a little stand by her easy chair, with some nice bread and butter; and presently Miss Janet poured her out a cup of tea; "for," she said, "Leander never could take his dinner without it." Ellen's appetite needed no silver fork. Tea and pot-pie were never better liked; yet Miss Janet's enjoyment was perhaps greater still. She sat talking and looking at her little visitor with secret but immense satisfaction.

"Have you heard what fine doings we're a going to have here by and by?" said she. "The doctor's tired of me; he's going to get a new housekeeper;—he's going to get married some of these days."

"Is he!" said Ellen. "Not to Jenny!"

"Yes indeed he is—to Jenny—Jenny Hitchcock; and a nice little wife she'll make him. You're a great friend of Jenny, I know."

"How soon?" said Ellen.

"Oh, not just yet—by and by—after we get a little smarted up, I guess;—before a great while. Don't you think he'll be a happy man?"

Ellen could not help wondering, as the doctor just then came in and she looked up at his unfortunate three-cornered face, whether Jenny would be a happy woman? But as people often do, she only judged from the outside; Jenny had not made such a bad choice after all.

The doctor said he would go directly to Mr. Van Brunt after he had been over to Mrs. Sibnorth's; it wouldn't be a minute. Ellen meant to ride back in his company; and having finished her dinner waited now only for him. But the one minute passed—two minutes—ten—twenty—she waited impatiently, but he came not.

"I'll tell you how it must be," said his sister,—"he's gone off without his dinner calculating to get it at Miss Hitchcock's,—he'd be glad of the chance. That's how it is, dear; and you'll have to ride home alone; I'm real sorry. S'pose you stop till evening, and I'll make the doctor go along with you. But oh, dear! maybe he wouldn't be able to neither; he's got to go up to that tiresome Mrs. Robin's; it's too bad. Well, take good care of yourself, darling;—couldn't you stop till it's cooler?—well, come and see me as soon as you can again, but don't come without some one else along! Good-by! I wish I could keep you."

She went to the door to see her mount, and smiled and nodded her off.

Ellen was greatly refreshed with her rest and her dinner; it grieved her that the Brownie had not fared as well. All the refreshment that kind words and patting could give him, she gave; promised him the freshest of water and the sweetest of hay when he should reach home; and begged him to keep up his spirits and hold on for a little longer. It may be doubted whether the Brownie understood the full sense of her words, but he probably knew what the

6. Household linens, especially for the table.

kind tones and gentle hand meant. He answered cheerfully; threw up his head and gave a little neigh, as much as to say, *he* wasn't going to mind a few hours of sunshine; and trotted on as if he knew his face was toward home,—which no doubt he did. Luckily it was not a very hot day; for August, it was remarkably cool and beautiful; indeed, there was little very hot weather ever known in Thirlwall. Ellen's heart felt easier, now that her business was done! and when she had left the town behind her and was again in the fields, she was less timid than she had been before; she was going toward home; that makes a great difference; and every step was bringing her nearer. "I am glad I came after all," she thought;—"but I hope I shall never have to do such a thing again. But I am glad I came."

She had no more than crossed the little bridge, however, when she saw what brought her heart into her mouth. It was Mr. Saunders, lolling under a tree. What could he have come there for at that time of day? A vague feeling crossed her mind that if she could only get past him she should pass a danger; she thought to ride by without seeming to see him, and quietly gave the Brownie a pat to make him go faster. But as she drew near Mr. Saunders rose up, came to the middle of the road, and taking hold of her bridle, checked her pony's pace so that he could walk alongside; to Ellen's unspeakable dismay.

"What's kept you so long?" said he;—"I've been looking out for you this great while. Had hard work to find the doctor?"

"Won't you please to let go of my horse," said Ellen, her heart beating very fast;—"I am in a great hurry to get home;—please don't keep me."

"Oh, I want to see you a little," said Mr. Saunders;—"you ain't in such a hurry to get away from me as that comes to, are you?"

Ellen was silent.

"It's quite a long time since I saw you last," said he;—"how have the merinoes worn?"

Ellen could not bear to look at his face and did not see the expression which went with these words, yet she *felt* it.

"They have worn very well," said she, "but I want to get home very much—*please* let me go."

"Not yet—not yet," said he,—"oh, no, not yet. I want to talk to you; why, what are you in such a devil of a hurry for? I came out on purpose; do you think I am going to have all my long waiting for nothing?"

Ellen did not know what to say; her heart sprang with a nameless pang to the thought, if she ever got free from this! Meanwhile she was not free.

"Whose horse is that you're on?"

"Mine," said Ellen.

"Your'n! that's a likely story. I guess he ain't your'n, and so you won't mind if I touch him up a little;—I want to see how well you can sit on a horse."

Passing his arm through the bridle as he said these words, Mr. Saunders led the pony down to the side of the road where grew a clump of high bushes; and with some trouble cut off a long stout sapling. Ellen looked in every direction while he was doing this, despairing, as she looked, of aid from any quarter of the broad quiet open country. Oh, for wings! But she could not leave the Brownie if she had them.

Returning to the middle of the road, Mr. Saunders amused himself as they walked along with stripping off all the leaves and little twigs from his sapling, leaving it when done a very good imitation of an ox-whip in size and length, with a fine lash-like point. Ellen watched him in an ecstasy of apprehension, afraid alike to speak or to be silent.

"There! what do you think of that?" said he, giving it two or three switches in the air to try its suppleness and toughness;—"don't that look like a whip? Now we'll see how he'll go!"

"Please don't do any thing with it," said Ellen earnestly;—"I never touch him with a whip,—he doesn't need it,—he isn't used to it; pray, pray do not!"

"Oh, we'll just tickle him a little with it," said Mr. Saunders coolly,—"I want to see how well you'll sit him;—just make him caper a little bit."

He accordingly applied the switch lightly to the Brownie's heels, enough to annoy without hurting him. The Brownie showed signs of uneasiness, quitted his quiet pace, and took to little starts and springs and whisking motions, most unpleasing to his rider.

"Oh, do not!" cried Ellen, almost beside herself,—"he's very spirited, and I don't know what he will do if you trouble him."

"You let me take care of that," said Mr. Saunders;—"if he troubles *me* I'll give it to him! If he rears up, only you catch hold of his mane and hold on tight, and you won't fall off;—I want to see him rear."

"But you'll give him bad tricks!" said Ellen. "Oh, pray don't do so! It's very bad for him to be teased. I am afraid he will kick if you do so, and he'd be ruined if he got a habit of kicking. Oh, *please* let us go!" said she with the most acute accent of entreaty,—"I want to be home."

"You keep quiet," said Mr. Saunders coolly;—"if he kicks I'll give him such a lathering as he never had yet; he won't do it but once. I ain't a going to hurt him, but I am a going to make him rear;—no, I won't,—I'll make him leap over a rail, the first bar-place we come to; that'll be prettier."

"Oh, you mustn't do that," said Ellen;—"I have not learned to leap yet; I couldn't keep on; you mustn't do that if you please."

"You just hold fast and hold your tongue. Catch hold of his ears, and you'll stick on fast enough; if you can't you may get down, for I am going to make him take the leap whether you will or no."

Ellen feared still more to get off and leave the Brownie to her tormentor's mercy than to stay where she was and take her chance. She tried in vain, as well as she could, to soothe her horse; the touches of the whip coming now in one place and now in another, and some of them pretty sharp, he began to grow very frisky indeed; and she began to be very much frightened for fear she should suddenly be jerked off. With a good deal of presence of mind, though wrought up to a terrible pitch of excitement and fear, Ellen gave her best attention to keeping her seat as the Brownie sprang and started and jumped to one side and the other; Mr. Saunders holding the bridle as loose as possible so as give him plenty of room. For some little time he amused himself with this game, the horse growing more and more irritated. At length a smart stroke of the whip upon his haunches made the Brownie spring in a way that brought Ellen's heart into her mouth, and almost threw her off.

"Oh, don't!" cried Ellen, bursting into tears for the first time,—she had with great effort commanded them back until now;—"poor Brownie!—How can you! Oh, please let us go!—please let us go!"

For one minute she dropped her face in her hands.

"Be quiet!" said Mr. Saunders. "Here's a bar-place—now for the leap!"

Ellen wiped away her tears, forced back those that were coming, and began the most earnest remonstrance and pleading with Mr. Saunders that she knew how to make. He paid her no sort of attention. He led the Brownie to the side of the road, let down all the bars but the lower two, let go the bridle, and stood a little off prepared with his whip to force the horse to take the spring.

"I tell you I shall fall," said Ellen, reining him back. "How can you be so cruel!—I want to go home!"

"Well, you ain't a going home yet. Get off, if you are afraid."

But though trembling in every nerve from head to foot, Ellen fancied the Brownie was safer so long as he had her on his back; she would not leave him. She pleaded her best, which Mr. Saunders heard as if it was amusing, and without making any answer kept the horse capering in front of the bars, pretending every minute he was going to whip him up to take the leap. His object however was merely to gratify the smallest of minds by teasing a child he had a spite against;[7] he had no intention to risk breaking her bones by a fall from her horse; so in

---

7. He had been reprimanded by a superior at the store for mistreating Ellen, after a mysterious but kindly old man intervened on her behalf.

time he had enough of the bar-place; took the bridle again and walked on. Ellen drew breath a little more freely.

"Did you hear how I handled your old gentleman after that time?" said Mr. Saunders. Ellen made no answer.

"No one ever affronts me that don't hear news of it afterwards, and so he found to his cost. *I* paid him off, to my heart's content. I gave the old fellow a lesson to behave in future. I forgive him now entirely. By the way I've a little account to settle with you—didn't you ask Mr. Perriman this morning if Dr. Gibson was in the house?"

"I don't know who it was," said Ellen.

"Well, hadn't I told you just before he warn't there?"
Ellen was silent.

"What did you do that for, eh? Didn't you believe me?"
Still she did not speak.

"I say!" said Mr. Saunders, touching the Brownie as he spoke,—"did you think I told you a lie about it?—eh?"

"I didn't know but he might be there," Ellen forced herself to say.

"Then you didn't believe me?" said he, always with that same smile upon his face; Ellen knew that.

"Now that warn't handsome of you—and I'm a going to punish you for it, somehow or 'nother; but it ain't pretty to quarrel with ladies, so Brownie and me'll settle it together. You won't mind that I dare say."

"What are you going to do?" said Ellen, as he once more drew her down to the side of the fence.

"Get off and you'll see," said he, laughing;—"get off and you'll see."

"What do you want to do?" repeated Ellen, though scarce able to speak the words.

"I'm just going to tickle Brownie a little, to teach you to believe honest folks when they speak the truth; get off."

"No I won't," said Ellen, throwing both arms round the neck of her pony;—"poor Brownie!—you shan't do it. He hasn't done any harm, nor I either; you are a bad man!"

"Get off!" repeated Mr. Saunders.

"I will not!" said Ellen, still clinging fast.

"Very well," said he coolly,—"then I will take you off; it don't make much difference. We'll go along a little further till I find a nice stone for you to sit down upon. If you had got off then I wouldn't ha' done much to him, but I'll give it to him now! If he hasn't been used to a whip he'll know pretty well what it means by the time I have done with him; and then you may go home as fast as you can."

It is very likely Mr. Saunders would have been as good or as bad, as his word. His behavior to Ellen in the store at New York, and the measures taken by the old gentleman who had befriended her, had been the cause of his dismissal from the employ of Messrs. St. Clair and Fleury. Two or three other attempts to get into business had come to nothing, and he had been obliged to return to his native town. Ever since, Ellen and the old gentleman had lived in his memory as objects of the deepest spite;—the one for interfering, the other for having been the innocent cause; and he no sooner saw her in the post-office than he promised himself revenge, such revenge as only the meanest and most cowardly spirit could have taken pleasure in. His best way of distressing Ellen, he found, was through her horse; he had almost satisfied himself; but very naturally his feeling of spite had grown stronger and blunter with indulgence, and he meant to wind up with such a treatment of her pony, real or seeming, as he knew would give great pain to the pony's mistress. He was prevented.

As they went slowly along, Ellen still clasping the Brownie's neck and resolved to cling to him to the last, Mr. Saunders making him caper in a way very uncomfortable to her, one was too busy and the other too deafened by fear to notice the sound of fast-approaching hoofs behind them. It happened that John Humphreys had passed the night at Ventnor; and having an errand to do for a friend at Thirlwall had taken that road, which led him but a few miles out of his way, and was now at full speed on his way home. He had never made the Brownie's acquaintance, and did not recognise Ellen as he came up; but in passing them some strange notion crossing his mind he wheeled his horse round directly in front of the astonished pair. Ellen quitted her pony's neck, and stretching out both arms toward him exclaimed, almost shrieked, "Oh, John! John! send him away! make him let me go!"

"What are you about, sir?" said the new-comer sternly.

"It's none of your business!" answered Mr. Saunders, in whom rage for the time overcame cowardice.

"Take your hand off the bridle!"—with a slight touch of the riding-whip upon the hand in question.

"Not for you, brother," said Mr. Saunders sneeringly;—"I'll walk with any lady I've a mind to. Look out for yourself!"

"We will dispense with your further attendance," said John coolly. "Do you hear me?—do as I order you!"

The speaker did not put himself in a passion, and Mr. Saunders, accustomed for his own part to make bluster serve instead of prowess, despised a command so calmly given.— Ellen, who knew the voice, and still better could read the eye, drew conclusions very different. She was almost breathless with terror. Saunders was enraged and mortified at an interference that promised to baffle him; he was a stout young man, and judged himself the stronger of the two, and took notice besides that the stranger had nothing in his hand but a slight riding-whip. He answered very insolently and with an oath; and John saw that he was taking the bridle in his left hand and shifting his sapling whip so as to bring the club end of it uppermost. The next instant he aimed a furious blow at his adversary's horse. The quick eye and hand of the rider disappointed that with a sudden swerve. In another moment, and Ellen hardly saw how, it was so quick,—John had dismounted, taken Mr. Saunders by the collar, and hurled him quite over into the gully at the side of the road, where he lay at full length without stirring.

"Ride on, Ellen!" said her deliverer.

She obeyed. He stayed a moment to say to his fallen adversary a few words of pointed warning as to ever repeating his offence; then remounted and spurred forward to join Ellen. All her power of keeping up was gone, now that the necessity was over. Her head was once more bowed on her pony's neck, her whole frame shaking with convulsive sobs; she could scarce with great effort keep from crying out aloud.

"Ellie!"—said her adopted brother,[8] in a voice that could hardly be known for the one that had last spoken. She had no words, but as he gently took one of her hands, the convulsive squeeze it gave him showed the state of nervous excitement she was in. It was very long before his utmost efforts could soothe her, or she could command herself enough to tell him her story. When at last told, it was with many tears.

"Oh, how could he! how could he!" said poor Ellen;—"how could he do so!—it was very hard!"——

An involuntary touch of the spurs made John's horse start.

"But what took you to Thirlwall alone?" said he;—"you have not told me that yet."

Ellen went back to Timothy's invasion of the cabbages, and gave him the whole history of the morning.

"I thought when I was going for the doctor, at first," said she,—"and then afterwards when I had found him, what a good thing it was that Timothy broke down the garden fence and got in this morning; for if it had not been for that I should not have gone to Mr. Van Brunt's;—and then again after that I thought, if he only hadn't!"

"Little things often draw after them long trains of circumstances," said John,—"and that shows the folly of those people who think that God does not stoop to concern himself about

8. The Humphreys have "adopted" Ellen in affection, but not in law.

trifles;—life, and much more than life, may hang upon the turn of a hand. But Ellen, you must ride no more alone.—Promise me that you will not."

"I will not to Thirlwall, certainly," said Ellen,—"but mayn't I to Alice?—how can I help it?"

"Well—to Alice's—that is a safe part of the country;—but I should like to know a little more of your horse before trusting you even there."

"Of the Brownie?" said Ellen;—"Oh, he is as good as he can be; you need not be afraid of him; he has no trick at all; there never was such a good little horse."

John smiled. "How do you like mine?" said he.

"Is that your new one? Oh, what a beauty!—Oh, me, what a beauty! I didn't look at him before. Oh, I like him very much! he's handsomer than the Brownie;—do you like him?"

"Very well!—this is the first trial I have made of him. I was at Mr. Marshman's last night, and they detained me this morning, or I should have been here much earlier. I am very well satisfied with him, so far."

"And if you had *not* been detained!"—said Ellen.

"Yes, Ellie—I should not have fretted at my late breakfast and having to try Mr. Marshman's favourite mare, if I had known what good purpose the delay was to serve. I wish I could have been here half an hour sooner, though."

"Is his name the Black Prince?" said Ellen, returning to the horse.

"Yes, I believe so; but you shall change it, Ellie, if you can find one you like better."

"Oh, I cannot!—I like that very much. How beautiful he is! Is he good?"

"I hope so," said John, smiling;—"if he is not I shall be at the pains to make him so. We are hardly acquainted yet."

Ellen looked doubtfully at the black horse and his rider, and patting the Brownie's neck, observed with great satisfaction that *he* was very good.

John had been riding very slowly on Ellen's account; they now mended their pace. He saw however that she still looked miserably, and exerted himself to turn her thoughts from every thing disagreeable. Much to her amusement he rode round her two or three times, to view her horse and show her his own; commended the Brownie; praised her bridle hand; corrected several things about her riding; and by degrees engaged her in a very animated conversation. Ellen roused up; the colour came back to her cheeks; and when they reached home and rode round to the glass door she looked almost like herself.

She sprang off as usual without waiting for any help. John scarce saw that she had done so, when Alice's cry of joy brought him to the door, and from that together they went in to their father's study. Ellen was left alone on the lawn. Something was the matter; for she stood with swimming eyes and a trembling lip, rubbing her stirrup, which really needed no polishing, and forgetting the tired horses, which would have had her sympathy at any other time. What *was* the matter? Only—that Mr. John had forgotten the kiss he always gave her on going or coming. Ellen was jealous of it as a pledge of sistership, and could not want it;[9] and though she tried as hard as she could to get her face in order, so that she might go in and meet them, somehow it seemed to take a great while. She was still busy with her stirrup, when she suddenly felt two hands on her shoulders, and looking up received the very kiss the want of which she had been lamenting. But John saw the tears in her eyes, and asked her, she thought with somewhat of a comical look, what the matter was? Ellen was ashamed to tell, but he had her there by the shoulders, and besides, whatever that eye demanded she never knew how to keep back, so with some difficulty she told him.

"You are a foolish child, Ellie," said he gently, and kissing her again. "Run in out of the sun while I see to the horses."

Ellen ran in, and told her long story to Alice; and then feeling very weary and weak she sat on the sofa and lay resting in her arms in a state of the most entire and unruffled happiness.

9. Go without it.

Alice however after a while transferred her to bed, thinking with good reason that a long sleep would be the best thing for her.

1850

Alice Cary
(1820–1871)

Born on a farm near Cincinnati, Alice Cary received a scant education at a local school. At 18 she had a poem published in a Cincinnati newspaper, and in the next few years she and her younger sister Phoebe (1824–1871) gained enough of a reputation for newspaper verse to win them an invitation from Rufus Griswold to contribute to his anthology *The Female Poets of America* (1848). Reviewing the volume, Edgar Allan Poe gave particular praise to Alice's "Pictures of Memory," which he called the "noblest" poem in the book. *Poems of Alice and Phoebe Cary* (1849) followed, and soon the sisters were living in New York, supporting themselves as writers. Alice, particularly, won popular success in national magazines and with succeeding volumes of poetry; she also wrote short stories, novels, and nonfiction. Together, the sisters hosted a weekly literary and intellectual salon that brought to their home on New York's East 20th Street many of the famous people of their day.

Alice Cary is primarily remembered now, however, not for her poetry but for the prose of two volumes: *Clovernook, or Recollections of Our Neighborhood in the West* (1852) and *Clovernook, Second Series* (1853). Southwestern Ohio was still nearly a wilderness in her childhood. Cincinnati, 8 miles from her father's farm, had been founded only in 1788 and had attained the status of a city only the year before her birth. Her sketches tell simply and effectively of country isolation and hardship at an early period of that region's history.

Additional sketches are collected in *Sketches of Country Life* (1859). Novels include *Hagar, a Story of To-Day* (1852); *Married, Not Mated* (1856); and *The Bishop's Son* (1867). Her own volumes of poems are *Lyra and Other Poems* (1852); *Collected Poems* (1855); *Ballads, Lyrics and Hymns* (1866); and *A Lover's Diary* (1868). Her sister's books include *Poems and Parodies* (1854) and *Poems of Faith, Hope, and Love* (1868). A selection, with a useful introduction, is Judith Fetterley, ed., *Clovernook Sketches and Other Stories* (1987).

The Wildermings[1]

There came to reside in the neighborhood a family consisting of three persons—an old lady, a young man, and a child some fourteen years of age. The place they took was divided by a little strip of woods from Clovernook, and I well remember how rejoiced I was on first seeing the blue smoke curling up from the high red chimneys; for the cottage had been a long time vacant, and the prospect of having people so near us, gave me delight. Perhaps, too, I was not the less pleased that they were to be new acquaintances. We are likely to underestimate persons and things we have continually about us; but let separation come, and we learn what they were to us. *Apropos* of this—in the little grove I have spoken of I remember there was an oak tree, taller by a great deal than its fellows; and a thousand times I have felt as though its mates must be oppressed with a painful sense of inferiority, and really wished the

---

1. "The Wildermings," first published as "A Reminiscence" by "Patty Lee" in the *National Era*, June 5, 1851, was collected in *Clovernook* (1852), the source of the present text.

axe laid at its root. At last, one day, I heard the ringing strokes of that destroyer—and, on inquiry, was told that the woodman had orders no longer to spare the great oak. Eagerly I listened at first—every stroke was like the song of victory; then the gladness subsided, and I began to marvel how the woods would look with the monarch fallen; then I thought, their glory will have departed, and began to reflect on myself as having sealed the warrant of its death, so that when the crash, telling that it was fallen, woke the sleeping echoes from the hills, I cannot tell how sad a feeling it induced in my heart. If I could see it standing once more, just once more! but I could not, and till this day I feel a regretful pang when I think of that grand old tree.

But the new neighbors. Some curiosity mingled with my pleasure, and so, as soon as I thought they were settled, and feeling at home, I made my toilet with unusual care for a first call.

The cottage was a little way from the main road, and access to it was by a narrow grass-grown lane, bordered on one side by a green belt of meadow land, and on the other by the grove, sloping upward and backward to a clayey hill, where, with children and children's children about them,

"The rude forefathers of the hamlet slept."[2]

A little farther on, but in full view of its stunted cypresses and white headstones, was the cottage. Of burial grounds generally I have no dread, but from this particular one I was accustomed, from childhood, to turn away with something of superstitious horror. I could never forget how Laura Hastings saw a light burning there all one winter night, after the death of John Hine, a wild, roving fellow, who never did any real harm in his life to any one but himself, hastening his own death by foolish excesses. Nevertheless, his ghost had been seen more than once, sitting on the cold mound beneath which the soul's expression was fading and crumbling: so, at least, said some of the oldest and most pious inhabitants of our neighborhood. There, too, Mary Wildermings, a fair young girl who died, more sinned against than sinning, had been heard to sing sad lullabies under the waning moon sometimes, and at other times had been seen sitting by her sunken grave, and braiding roses in her hair, as for a bridal. *I* never saw any of these wonderful things; but a spot more likely to be haunted by the unresting spirits of the bad could not readily be imagined. The woods, thick and full of birds, along the roadside, thinned away toward the desolate ridge, where briers grew over the mounds, and about and through the fallen fences, as they would, with here and there a little clearing among weeds and thistles and high matted grass, for the making of a new grave.

It was the twilight of a beautiful summer day, as I walked down the grassy lane and past the lonesome cemetery, to make this first call at the cottage, feeling, I scarcely knew why, strangely sad. By an old broken bridge in the hollow, between the cottage and the field of death I remember that I sat down, and for a long time listened to the trickling of the water over the pebbles, and watched golden spots of sunlight till they quite faded out, and "came still evening on, and twilight gray, that in her sober livery all things clad."[3]

So quietly I sat, that the mole, beginning its blind work at sunset, loosened and stirred the ground beneath my feet, and the white, thickwinged moths, coming from beneath the dusty weeds, fluttered about me, and lightened in my lap, and the dull beating of the bat came almost in my face.

The first complaint of the owl sounded along the hollow and died over the next hill, warning me to proceed, when I heard,—as it were the echo of my own thought, repeated in

2. Thomas Gray (1716–1771), English poet, "Elegy Written in a Country Churchyard." This and the following quotation, from Milton, are slightly changed by Cary to accommodate her syntactical context.

3. John Milton (1608–1674), English poet, *Paradise Lost*, 4.

a low, melancholy voice—the conclusion of that beautiful stanza of the elegy in reference to that moping bird. I distinctly caught the lines—

"Of such as wandering near her sacred bower,
Molest her ancient, solitary reign."[4]

Looking up, I saw approaching slowly, with arms folded and eyes on the ground, a young and seemingly handsome man. He passed without noticing me at all, and I think without seeing me. But I had the better opportunity of observing him, though I would have foregone that privilege to win one glance. He interested me, and I felt humiliated that he should pass me with his unkind indifference. His face was pale and very sad, and his forehead shaded with a heavy mass of black hair, pushed away from one temple, and falling neglectedly over the other.

"Well!" said I, as I watched him ascending the opposite hill, feeling very much as though he had wantonly disregarded some claim I had on him, though I could not possibly have had the slightest; and, turning ill-humoredly away, I walked with a quick step toward the cottage.

A golden-haired young girl sat in the window reading, and on my approach arose and received me with easy gracefulness and well-bred courtesy, but during my stay her manner did not once border on cordiality. She was very beautiful, but her beauty was like that of statuary. The mother I did not see. She was, I was told, indisposed, and, on begging that she might not be disturbed, the daughter readily acquiesced. Every thing about the place indicated refinement and elegant habits, but whence the family came, how long they proposed to remain, and what relation the young man sustained to the rest, I would gladly have known.

Seeing a flute on the table, I spoke of music, for I suspected it to belong to the absent gentleman. I received no information, however; and as the twilight was already falling deeply, I felt a necessity to take leave, without obtaining even a glimpse of the person whom I had pictured in my fancy as so young and fair, and, of course so agreeable.

The sun had been set some time, but the moon had risen full and bright, so that I had no fear even in passing the graveyard, but walked more slowly than I had done before, till, reaching the gate, I paused to think of the awful mysteries of life and death.

This is not a very desolate spot after all, I thought, as, leaning over the gate, something of the quiet of the place infused itself into my spirits. Here, I felt, the wicked cease from troubling, and the weary are at rest; the long train of evils that attach to the best phases of humanity, is quite forgotten; the thorn-crown is loosened from the brow of sorrow by the white hand of peace, and the hearts that were all their lifetime under the shadows of great and haply unpitied afflictions never ache any more. And here, best of all! the frailties of the unresisting tempted, are folded away beneath the shroud, from the humiliating glances of pity, and the cold eyes of pride. We have need to be thankful that when man brought on the primal glory of his nature the mildew of sin, God did not cast us utterly from him, but in the unsearchable riches of his mercy struck open the refuge of the grave. If there were no fountain where our sins of scarlet might be washed white as wool, if the black night of death were not bordered by the golden shadows of the morning of immortality, if deep in the darkness were not sunken the foundations of the white bastions of peace, it were yet an inestimable privilege to lay aside the burden of life, for life becomes, sooner or later, a burden, and an echo among ruins.

In the corner of the burial ground, where the trees are thickest, a little apart from the rest, was the grave of Mary Wildermings, and year after year, the blue thistles bloomed and faded in its sunken sod.

The train of my reflections naturally suggested her, and, turning my eyes in the direction of her resting place, I saw, or thought I saw, the outline of a human figure. I remembered the

4. Gray's "Elegy."

story of her unresting ghost, and at first little doubted that I beheld it, and felt a tumult of strange emotions on finding myself thus alone near so questionable a shape.

Then, I said, this is some delusion of the senses; and I passed my hand over my eyes, for an uncertain glimmer had followed the intensity of my gaze. I looked towards the cottage to reassure myself by the light of a human habitation, but all there was dark; a cloud had passed over the moon, and, without venturing to look towards the haunted grave, I withdrew from the gate, very lightly, though it creaked as I did so. Any sound save the beating of my own heart gave me courage; and when I had walked a little way, I turned and looked again, but the dense shadow would have prevented my seeing any thing, if any thing had been there. Certain it is, I saw nothing.

On reaching home, I asked the housekeeper, a garrulous person usually, if she remembered Mary Wildermings, and what she could tell me of her burial, in the graveyard across the wood.

"Yes, I remember her, and she is buried in the corner of the ground, on the hill. They came to my house, I know, to get a cup, or something of the sort, with which to dip the water from her grave, for it rained terribly all the day of her funeral. She added, "But what do you want to talk of the dead and gone for, when there are living folks enough to talk about?"

Truth is, she wanted me to say something of our new neighbors, and was vexed that I did not, though I probably should have done so had they not been quite driven from my mind by the more absorbing event of the evening; so, as much vexed and disappointed as herself, I retired. The night was haunted with some troublous dreams, but a day of sunshine succeeded, and my thoughts flowed back to a more pleasing channel.

Days and weeks went by, and we neither saw nor heard anything of our new neighbors, for my call was not returned, nor did I make any further overtures towards an acquaintance. But often, as I sat under the apple tree by the door, in the twilight, I heard the mellow music of the distant flute.

"Is that at the cottage?" said the housekeeper to me, one night: "it sounds to me as though it were in the corner of the graveyard."

I smiled as she turned her head a little to one side, and encircling the right ear with her hand, listened some minutes eagerly, and then proceeded to express her conviction that the music was the result of no mortal agency.

"Did you ever hear of a ghost playing the flute?" I said.

"A flute!" she answered, indignantly, "it's a flute, just as much as you are a flute; and for the sake of enlightening your blind understanding, I'll go to the graveyard, night as it is, if you will go with me."

"Very well," I said; "let us go."

So, under the faint light of the crescent moon, we took our way together. Gradually the notes became lower and sadder, and at length quite died away. I urged my trembling companion to walk faster, lest the ghost should vanish too; and she acceded to my wish with a silent alacrity, that convinced me at once of the sincerity of her expressed belief. Just as we began to ascend the hill, she stopped suddenly, saying, "There! did you hear that?"

I answered, that I heard a noise, but that it was no unusual thing to hear such sounds in an inhabited neighborhood, at so early an hour. "It was the latching of the gate at the graveyard," she answered solemnly. "As you value your immortal soul, go no further."

In vain I argued, that a ghost would have no need to unlatch the gate. She positively refused to go farther, and with a courage not very habitual to me, I walked on alone.

"Do you think I don't know that sound?" she called after me. "I would know if I had forgotten everything else. Oh, stop, till I tell you! The night Mary Wildermings died," I heard her say; but I knew the sound of the gate as well as she, and would not wait even for a ghost story. I have since wished I had, for I could never afterwards persuade her to proceed with it.

Gaining the summit of the hill, I saw, a little way before me, a dark figure, receding slowly; but so intent was I on the superhuman, that I paid little heed to the human; though afterward, in recalling the circumstance, the individual previously seen while I sat on the bridge became in some way associated with this one.

How hushed and solemn the graveyard seemed! I was half afraid, as I looked in—quite startled, in fact, when, latching and unlatching the gate, to determine whether the sound I had heard were that or not, a rabbit, roused from its light sleep, under the fallen grass, sped fleetly across the still mounds to the safer shelter of the woods. I saw nothing else, save that the grass was trampled to a narrow path all the way leading toward Mary's grave.

During the summer, I sometimes saw the young girl in the woods, and I noticed that she neither gathered flowers nor sang with the birds; but would sit for hours in some deep shadow, without moving her position in the least, not even to push away the light curls which the wind blew over her cheeks and forehead, as they would. She seemed neither to love nor seek human companionship. Once only I noticed, and it was the last time she ever walked in the woods, that he whom I supposed to be her brother was with her. She did not sit in the shade, as usual, but walked languidly, and leaning heavily on the arm of her attendant, who several times swept off the curls from her forehead, and bent down, as if kissing her.

A few days afterwards, being slightly indisposed, I called in the village doctor. Our conversation, naturally, was of who was sick and who was dead.

"Among my patients," he said, "there is none that interests me so deeply as a little girl at the cottage—indeed, I have scarcely thought of anything else, since I knew that she must die. A strange child," he continued; "she seems to feel neither love of life nor fear of death, nor does she either weep or smile; and though I have been with her much of late, I have never seen her sleep. She suffers no pain—her face wears the same calm expression, but her melancholy eyes are wide open all the time."

The second evening after this, though not quite recovered myself, I called at the cottage, in the hope of being of some service to the sick girl. The snowy curtain was dropped over the window of her chamber, the sash partly raised, and all within still—very still. The door was a little way open, and, pausing, I heard from within a low, stifled moan, which I could not misunderstand, and pushing the door aside, I entered, without rapping.

In the white sheet, drawn straight over the head and the feet, I recognised at once the fearful truth—the little girl was dead. By the head of the bed, and still as one stricken into stone, sat the person I so often wished to see. The room was nearly dark, and his face was buried in his hands—nevertheless, I knew him—it was he who had passed me on the bridge.

Presently the housekeeper, or one that I took to be her, entered, and whispering to him, he arose and went out, so that I saw him but imperfectly. When he was gone, the woman folded the covering away from the face, and to my horror I saw that the eyes were still unclosed. Seeing my surprise, she said, as she folded a napkin, and pinned it close over the lids—

"It is strange, but the child would never in life close her eyes—her mother, they say, died in watching for one who never came, and the baby was watchful and sleepless from the first."

The next day, and the next, it was dull and rainy—excitement and premature exposure had induced a return of my first indisposition, so that I was not at the funeral. I saw, however, from my window, preparations for the burial—to my surprise, in the lonesome little grave-yard by the woods.

In the course of a fortnight, I prepared for a visit of condolence to the cottage, but on reaching it, found the inhabitants gone—the place still and empty.

Returning, I stopped at the haunted ground: close by the grave of Mary Wildermings was that of the stranger child. The briers and thistles had been carefully cut away, there was no slab and no name over either, but the blue and white violets were planted thickly about both. That they slept well, was all I knew.

1851, 1852

Rose Terry Cooke
(1827–1892)

Rose Terry was born in Connecticut and educated at the Hartford Female Seminary, which had been founded three years before her birth by Catharine E. Beecher, an elder sister of Harriet Beecher Stowe. Thrown largely on her own resources while still a teenager, she taught school, served as a governess, and wrote poetry and fiction. She published her first story at 18 and by her late twenties was a regular contributor to *Putnam's Monthly Magazine*; when that journal ceased publication in 1857 she found a ready market in the new *Atlantic Monthly*, edited by James Russell Lowell and soon to be acclaimed as the premier literary magazine in the United States. In 1873 she married a bank clerk, Rollin H. Cooke. After her marriage she continued to produce stories in great numbers and with apparent ease, publishing her most famous collection, *Huckleberries Gathered from New England Hills* (1891), in

the year before her death, over four decades after she had begun to write.

With Harriet Beecher Stowe she helped establish the tradition of realistic stories of New England life that was further developed in the work of a number of other women, including Sarah Orne Jewett and Mary E. Wilkins Freeman. Like these others, her texts derive much of their strength from close observation of regional characteristics, including speech patterns, and from detailed representations of the lives of women and of the interchanges between the sexes in rural New England in the latter half of the nineteenth century.

Cooke's other collections include *Somebody's Neighbors* (1881), *Root-Bound and Other Sketches* (1885), and *The Sphinx's Children and Other People's* (1886). A brief study appears in *The Dictionary of Literary Biography*, vol. 12: *American Realists and Naturalists*, eds. Donald Pizer and Earl N. Harbert (1982).

How Celia Changed Her Mind.[1]

"If there's anything on the face of the earth I *do* hate, it's an old maid!"

Mrs. Stearns looked up from her sewing in astonishment.

"Why, Miss Celia!"

"Oh, yes! I know it. I'm one myself, but all the same, I hate 'em worse than p'ison. They ain't nothing nor nobody; they're cumberers of the ground." And Celia Barnes laid down her scissors with a bang, as if she might be Atropos[2] herself, ready to cut the thread of life for all the despised class of which she was a notable member.

The minister's wife was genuinely surprised at this outburst; she herself had been well along in life before she married, and though she had been fairly happy in the uncertain relationship to which she had attained, she was, on the whole, inclined to agree with St. Paul, that the woman who did not marry "doeth better."[3] "I don't agree with you, Miss Celia," she said gently. "Many, indeed, most of my best friends are maiden ladies, and I respect and love them just as much as if they were married women."

"Well, I don't. A woman that's married is somebody; she's got a place in the world; she ain't everybody's tag; folks don't say, 'Oh, it's nobody but that old maid Celye Barnes;' it's 'Mis'

1. First collected in *Huckleberries Gathered from New England Hills* (1891), the source of the present text.
2. In Greek mythology, the Fate who ends life.

3. 1 Corinthians, 7:38: "So then he that giveth her in marriage doeth well; but he that giveth her not in marriage doeth better."

Price,' and 'Mis' Simms,' or 'Thomas Smith's wife,' as though you was somebody. I don't know how 't is elsewheres, but here in Bassett you might as well be a dog as an old maid. I allow it might be better if they all had means or eddication: money's 'a dreadful good thing to have in the house,' as I see in a book once, and learning is sort of comp'ny to you if you're lonesome; but then lonesome you be, and you've got to be, if you're an old maid, and it can't be helped noway."

Mrs. Stearns smiled a little sadly, thinking that even married life had its own loneliness when your husband was shut up in his study, or gone off on a long drive to see some sick parishioner or conduct a neighborhood prayer-meeting, or even when he was the other side of the fireplace absorbed in a religious paper or a New York daily, or meditating on his next sermon, while the silent wife sat unnoticed at her mending or knitting. "But married women have more troubles and responsibilities than the unmarried, Miss Celia," she said. "You have no children to bring up and be anxious about, no daily dread of not doing your duty by the family whom you preside over, and no fear of the supplies giving out that are really needed. Nobody but your own self to look out for."

"That's jest it," snapped Celia, laying down the boy's coat she was sewing with a vicious jerk of her thread. "There 't is! Nobody to home to care if you live or die; nobody to peek out of the winder to see if you're comin', or to make a mess of gruel or a cup of tea for you, or to throw ye a feelin' word if you're sick nigh unto death. And old maids is just as li'ble to up and die as them that's married. And as to responsibility, I ain't afraid to tackle that. Never! I don't hold with them that cringe and crawl and are skeert at a shadder, and won't do a living thing that they had ought to do because they're 'afraid to take the responsibility.' Why, there's Mrs. Deacon Trimble, she durst n't so much as set up a prayer-meetin' for missions or the temp'rance cause, because 't was 'sech a reesponsibility to take the lead in them matters.' I suppose it's somethin' of a responsible chore to preach the gospel to the heathen, or grab a drinkin' feller by the scruff of his neck and haul him out of the horrible pit anyway, but if it's dooty it's got to be done, whether or no; and I ain't afraid of pitchin' into anything the Lord sets me to do!"

"Except being an old maid," said Mrs. Stearns.

Celia darted a sharp glance at her over her silver-rimmed spectacles, and pulled her needle through and through the seams of Willy's jacket with fresh vigor, while a thoughtful shadow came across her fine old face. Celia was a candid woman, for all her prejudices, a combination peculiarly characteristic of New England, for she was a typical Yankee. Presently she said abruptly, "I had n't thought on 't in that light." But then the minister opened the door, and the conversation stopped.

Parson Stearns was tired and hungry and cross, and his wife knew all that as soon as she saw his face. She had learned long ago that ministers, however good they may be, are still men; so to-day she had kept her husband's dinner warm in the under-oven, and had the kettle boiling to make him a cup of tea on the spot to assuage his irritation in the shortest and surest way; but though the odor of a savory stew and the cheerful warmth of the cooking-stove greeted him as he preceded her through the door into the kitchen, he snapped out, sharply enough for Celia to hear him through the half-closed door, "What do you have that old maid here for so often?"

"There!" said Celia to herself,—"there 't is! He don't look upon 't as a dispensation, if she doos. Men-folks run the world, and they know it. There ain't one of the hull caboodle but what despises an onmarried woman! Well, 't ain't altogether my fault. I would n't marry them that I could; I could n't—not and be honest; and them that I would hev had did n't ask me. I don't know as I'm to blame, after all, when you look into 't."

And she went on sewing Willy's jacket, contrived with pains and skill out of an old coat of his father's, while Mrs. Stearns poured out her husband's tea in the kitchen, replenished his plate with stew, and cut for him more than one segment of the crisp, fresh apple-pie, and urged upon him the squares of new cheese that legitimately accompany this deleterious viand of the race and country, the sempiternal, insistent, flagrant, and alas! also fragrant pie.

Celia Barnes was the tailoress of the little scattered country town of Bassett. Early left an orphan, without near relatives or money, she had received the scantiest measure of education that our town authorities deal to the pauper children of such organizations. She was ten years old when her mother, a widow for almost all those ten years, left her to the tender mercies of the selectmen of Bassett. The selectmen of our country towns are almost irresponsible governors of their petty spheres, and gratify the instinct of oligarchy peculiar to, and conservative of, the human race. Men must be governed and tyrannized over,—it is an inborn necessity of their nature; and while a republic is a beautiful theory, eminently fitted for a race who are "non Angli, sed Angeli,"[4] it has in practice the effect of producing more than Russian tyranny, but on smaller scales and in far and scattered localities. Nowhere are there more despots than among village selectmen in New England. Those who have wrestled with their absolute monarchism in behalf of some charity that might abstract a few of the almighty dollars made out of poverty and distress from their official pockets know how positive and dogmatic is their use of power—*experto crede.*[5] The Bassett "first selectman" promptly bound out little Celia Barnes to a hard, imperious woman, who made a white slave of the child, and only dealt out to her the smallest measure of schooling demanded by law, because the good old minister, Father Perkins, interfered in the child's behalf.

As she was strong and hardy and resolute, Celia lived through her bondage, and at the "free" age of eighteen apprenticed herself to old Miss Polly Mariner, the Bassett tailoress, and being deft with her fingers and quick of brain, soon outran her teacher, and when Polly died, succeeded to her business.

She was a bright girl, not particularly noticeable among others, for she had none of that delicate flower-like New England beauty which is so peculiar, so charming, and so evanescent; her features were tolerably regular, her forehead broad and calm, her gray eyes keen and perceptive, and she had abundant hair of an uncertain brown; but forty other girls in Bassett might have been described in the same way; Celia's face was one to improve with age; its strong sense, capacity for humor, fine outlines of a rugged sort, were always more the style of fifty than fifteen, and what she said of herself was true.

She had been asked to marry an old farmer with five uproarious boys, a man notorious in East Bassett for his stinginess and bad temper, and she had promptly declined the offer. Once more fate had given her a chance. A young fellow of no character, poor, "shiftless," and given to cider as a beverage, had considered it a good idea to marry some one who would make a home for him and earn his living. Looking about him for a proper person to fill this pleasant situation, he pounced on Celia—and she returned the attention!

"Marry *you?* I wonder you've got the sass to ask any decent girl to marry ye, Alfred Hatch! What be you good for, anyway? I don't know what under the canopy the Lord spares you for,—only He doos let the tares grow amongst the wheat, Scripter says,[6] and I'm free to suppose He knows why, but I don't. No, *sir!* Ef you was the last man in the livin' universe I would n't tech ye with the tongs. If you'd got a speck of grit into you, you'd be ashamed to ask a woman to take ye in and support ye, for that's what it comes to. You go 'long! I can make my hands save my head so long as I hev the use of 'em, and I have n't no call to set up a private poor-house!"

So Alfred Hatch sneaked off, much like a cur that has sought to share the kennel of a mastiff, and been shortly and sharply convinced of his presumption.

---

4. Latin for "Not Angles, but Angels," attributed to Pope Gregory I (590–604) when he first saw the "Angles," English slaves brought to Rome.

5. Latin for "Believe the voice of experience" (Virgil, *Aeneid,* 11.283).

6. See Matthew 13:30: "In the time of harvest I will say to the reapers, Gather ye together first the tares, and bind them in bundles to burn them: but gather the wheat into my barn." Tares are weeds.

Here ended Celia's "chances," as she phrased it. Young men were few in Bassett; the West had drawn them away with its subtle attraction of unknown possibilities, just as it does to-day, and Celia grew old in the service of those established matrons who always want clothes cut over for their children, carpet rags sewed, quilts quilted, and comfortables tacked. She was industrious and frugal, and in time laid up some money in the Dartford Savings' Bank; but she did not, like many spinsters, invest her hard-earned dollars in a small house. Often she was urged to do so, but her reasons were good for refusing.

"I should be so independent? Well, I'm as independent now as the law allows. I've got two good rooms to myself, south winders, stairs of my own and outside door, and some privileges. If I had a house there'd be taxes, and insurance, and cleanin' off snow come winter-time, and hoein' paths; and likely enough I should be so fur left to myself that I should set up a garden, and make my succotash cost a dollar a pint a-hirin' of a man to dig it up and hoe it down. Like enough, too, I should be gettin' flower seeds and things; I'm kinder fond of blows[7] in the time of 'em. My old fish-geran'um is a sight of comfort to me as 't is, and there would be a bill of expense again. Then you can't noway build a house with only two rooms in 't, it would be all outside; and you might as well try to heat the universe with a cookin'-stove as such a house. Besides, how lonesome I should be! It's forlorn enough to be an old maid anyway, but to have it sort of ground into you, as you may say, by livin' all alone in a hull house, that ain't necessary nor agreeable. Now, if I'm sick or sorry, I can just step downstairs and have aunt Nabby to help or hearten me. Deacon Everts he did set to work one time to persuade me to buy a house; he said 't was a good thing to be able to give somebody shelter 't was poorer 'n I was. Says I, 'Deacon, I've worked for my livin' ever sence I remember, and I know there 's no use in anybody bein' poorer than I be. I have n't no call to take any sech in and do for 'em. I give what I can to missions,—home ones,—and I'm willin', cheerfully willin', to do a day's work now and again for somebody that is strivin' with too heavy burdens; but as for keepin' free lodgin' and board, I sha'n't do it.' 'Well, well, well,' says he, kinder as if I was a fractious young one, and a-sawin' his fat hand up and down in the air till I wanted to slap him, 'just as you'd ruther, Celye,—just as you'd ruther. I don't mean to drive ye a mite, only, as Scripter says, "Provoke one another to love and good works." '[8]

"That did rile me! Says I: 'Well, you've provoked me full enough, though I don't know as you've done it in the Scripter sense; and mabbe I should n't have got so fur provoked if I had n't have known that little red house your grandsir' lived and died in was throwed back on your hands just now, and advertised for sellin'. I see the "Mounting County Herald," Deacon Everts.' He shut up, I tell ye. But I sha'n't never buy no house so long as aunt Nabby lets me have her two south chambers, and use the back stairway and the north door continual."

So Miss Celia had kept on in her way till now she was fifty, and to-day making over old clothes at the minister's. The minister's wife had, as we have seen, little romance or wild happiness in her life; it is not often the portion of country ministers' wives; and, moreover, she had two step-daughters who were girls of sixteen and twelve when she married their father. Katy was married herself now, this ten years, and doing her hard duty by an annual baby and a struggling parish in Dakota; but Rosabel, whose fine name had been the only legacy her dying mother left the day-old child she had scarce had time to kiss and christen before she went to take her own "new name" above, was now a girl of twenty-two, pretty, headstrong, and rebellious. Nature had endowed her with keen dark eyes, crisp dark curls, a long chin, and a very obstinate mouth, which only her red lips and white even teeth redeemed from ugliness; her bright color and her sense of fun made her attractive to young men wherever she encountered one of that rare species. Just now she was engaged in a serious flirtation with the station-master at Bassett Centre,—an impecunious youth of no special interest to other people and quite unable to maintain a wife. But out of the "strong necessity of loving," as it is called, and the want of young society or settled occupation, Rosa Stearns

---

7. Blossoms.   8. Hebrews 10:24.

chose to fall in love with Amos Barker, and her father considered it a "fall" indeed. So, with the natural clumsiness of a man and a father, Parson Stearns set himself to prevent the matter, and began by forbidding Rosabel to see or speak or write to the youth in question, and thereby inspired in her mind a burning desire to do all three. Up to this time she had rather languidly amused herself by mild and gentle flirtations with him, such as looking at him sidewise in church on Sunday, meeting him accidentally on his way to and from the station, for she spent at least half her time at her aunt's in Bassett Centre, and had even taught the small school there during the last six months. She had also sent him her tintype, and his own was secreted in her bureau drawer. He had invited her to go with him to two sleigh-rides and one sugaring-off, and always came home with her from prayer-meeting and singing-school; but like a wise youth he had never yet proposed to marry her in due form, not so much because he was wise as because he was thoughtless and lazy; and while he enjoyed the society of a bright girl, and liked to dangle after the prettiest one in Bassett, and the minister's daughter too, he did not love work well enough to shoulder the responsibility of providing for another those material but necessary supplies that imply labor of an incessant sort.

Rosabel, in her first inconsiderate anger at her father's command, sat down and wrote a note to Amos, eminently calculated to call out his sympathy with her own wrath, and promptly mailed it as soon as it was written. It ran as follows:—

> Dear Friend,—Pa has forbidden me to speak to you any more, or to correspond with you. I suppose I must submit so far; but he did not say I must return your picture [the parson had not an idea that she possessed that precious thing], so I shall keep it to remind me of the pleasant hours we have passed together.
>
> *"Fare thee well, and if forever,*
> *Still forever fare thee well!"* [9]
>
>   Your true friend,   Rosabel Stearns.
> P.S.—I think pa is *horrid!*

So did Amos as he read this heart-rending missive, in which the postscript, according to the established sneer at woman's postscripts, carried the whole force of the epistle.

Now Amos had made a friend of Miss Celia by once telegraphing for her trunk, which she had lost on her way home from the only journey of her life, a trip to Boston, whither she had gone, on the strength of the one share of B. & A. R. R. stock she held, to spend the allotted three days granted to stockholders on their annual excursions, presumably to attend the annual meeting. Amos had put himself to the immense trouble of sending two messages for Miss Celia, and asked her nothing for the civility, so that ever after, in the fashion of solitary women, she held herself deeply in his debt. He knew that she was at work for Mrs. Stearns when he received Rosa's epistle, for he had just been over to Bassett on the train—there was but a mile to traverse—to get her to repair his Sunday coat, and not found her at home, but had no time to look her up at the parson's, as he must walk back to his station. Now he resolved to take his answer to Rosa to Miss Celia in the evening, and so be sure that his abused sweetheart received it, for he had read too many dime novels to doubt that her tyrannic father would intercept their letters, and drive them both to madness and despair. That well-meaning but rather dull divine never would have thought of such a thing; he was a puffy, absent-minded, fat little man, with a weak, squeaky voice, and a sudden temper that blazed up like a bunch of dry weeds at a passing spark, and went out at once in flattest ashes. It had been Mrs. Stearns's step-motherly interference that drove him into his harshness to Rosa. She meant well and he meant well, but we all know what good intentions with no

9. "Fare Thee Well," by Lord Byron (1788–1824), English poet.

further sequel of act are good for, and nobody did more of that "paving" than these two excellent but futile people.

Miss Celia was ready to do anything for Amos Barker, and she considered it little less than a mortal sin to stand in the way of any marriage that was really desired by two parties. That Amos was poor did not daunt her at all; she had the curious faith that possesses some women, that any man can be prosperous if he has the will so to be; and she had a high opinion of this youth, based on his civility to her. It may be said of men, as of elephants, that it is lucky they do not know their own power; for how many more women would become their worshipers and slaves than are so to-day if they knew the abject gratitude the average woman feels for the least attention, the smallest kindness, the faintest expression of affection or good will. We are all, like the Syrophenician woman,[1] glad and ready to eat of the crumbs which fall from the children's table, so great is our faith—in men.

Miss Celia took the note in her big basket over to the minister's the very next day after that on which we introduced her to our readers. She was perhaps more rejoiced to contravene that reverend gentleman's orders than if she had not heard his querulous and contemptuous remark about her through the crack of the door on the previous afternoon; and it was with a sense of joy that, after all, an old maid could do something, that she slipped the envelope into Rosa's hands, and told her to put it quickly into her pocket, the very first moment she found herself alone with that young woman.

Many a hasty word had Parson Stearns spoken in the suddenness of his petulant temper, but never one that bore direr fruit than that when he called Celia Barnes "that old maid."

For of course Amos and Rosabel found in her an ardent friend. They had the instinct of distressed lovers to cajole her with all their confidences, caresses, and eager gratitude, and for once she felt herself dear and of importance. Amos consulted her on his plans for the future, which of course pointed westward, where he had a brother editing and owning a newspaper. This brother had before offered him a place in his office, but Amos had liked better the easy work of a station-master in a tiny village. Now his ambition was aroused, for the time at least. He wanted to make a home for Rosabel, but, alack! he had not one cent to pay their united expenses to Peoria, and a lion stood in the way. Here again Celia stepped in: she had some money laid up; she would lend it to them.

I do not say that at this stage she had no misgivings, but even these were set at rest by a conversation she had with Mrs. Stearns some six weeks after the day on which Celia had so fully expressed her scorn of spinsters. She was there again to tack a comfortable for Rosabel's bed, and bethought herself that it was a good time to feel her way a little concerning Mrs. Stearns's opinion of things.

"They do say," she remarked, stopping to snip off her thread and twist the end of it through her needle's eye, "that your Rosy don't go with Amos Barker no more. Is that so?"

"Yes," said Mrs. Stearns, with a half sigh. "Husband was rather prompt about it; he don't think Amos Barker ever'll amount to much, and he thinks his people are not just what they should be. You know his father never was very much of a man, and his grandfather is a real old reprobate. Husband says he never knew anything but crows come out of a crow's nest, and so he told Rosa to break acquaintance with him."

"Who does he like to hev come to see her?" asked Celia, with a grim set of her lips, stabbing her needle fiercely through the unoffending calico.

Mrs. Stearns laughed rather feebly. "I don't think he has anybody on his mind, Miss Celia. I don't think there are any young men in Bassett. I dare say Rosa will never marry. I wish she would, for she is n't happy here, and I can't do much to help it, with all my cares."

"And you can't feel for her as though she was your own, if you try ever so," confidently asserted Celia.

"No, I suppose not. I try to do my duty by her, and I am sorry for her; but I know all the

1. See Mark 7:24–30.

time an own mother would understand her better and make it easier for her. Mr. Stearns is peculiar, and men don't know just how to manage girls."

It was a cautious admission, but Miss Celia had sharp eyes, and knew very well that Rosabel neither loved nor respected her father, and that they were now on terms of real if unavowed hostility.

"Well," said she, "I don' know but you will have to have one of them onpleasant creturs, an old maid, in your fam'ly. I declare for 't, I'd hold a Thanksgiving Day all to myself ef I'd escaped that marcy."

"You may not always think so, Celia."

"I don't know what'll change me. 'T will be something I don't look forrard to now," answered Celia obstinately.

Mrs. Stearns sighed. "I hope Rosa will do nothing worse than to live unmarried," she said; but she could not help wishing silently that some worthy man would carry the perverse and annoying girl out of the parsonage for good.

After this Celia felt a certain freedom to help Rosabel; she encouraged the lovers to meet at her house, helped plan their elopement, sewed for the girl, and at last went with them as far as Brimfield when they stole away one evening, saw them safely married at the Methodist parsonage there, and bidding them good-speed, returned to Bassett Centre on the midnight train, and walked over to her own dwelling in the full moonshine of the October night, quite fearless and entirely exultant.

But she was not to come off unscathed. There was a scene of wild commotion at the parsonage next day, when Rosa's letter, modeled on that of the last novel heroine she had become acquainted with, was found on her bureau, as per novel aforesaid.

With her natural thoughtlessness she assured her parents that she "fled not uncompanioned," that her "kind and all but maternal friend, Miss Celia Barnes, would accompany her to the altar, and give her support and her countenance to the solemn ceremony that should make Rosabel Stearns the blessed wife of Amos Barker!"

It was all the minister could do not to swear as he read this astounding letter. His flabby face grew purple; his fat, sallow hands shook with rage; he dared not speak, he only sputtered, for he knew that profane and unbecoming words would surely leap from his tongue if he set it free; but he must—he really must—do or say something! So he clapped on his old hat, and with coat tails flying in the breeze, and rage in every step, set out to find Celia Barnes; and find her he did.

It would be unpleasant, and it is needless, to depict this encounter; language both unjust and unsavory smote the air and reverberated along the highway, for he met the spinster on her road to an engagement at Deacon Stiles's. Suffice it to say that both freed their minds with great enlargement of opinion, and the parson wound up with,—

"And I never want to see you again inside of my house, you confounded old maid!"

"There! that's it!" retorted Celia. "Ef I was n't an old maid, you would n't no more have darst to 'a' talked to me this way than nothin'. Ef I'd had a man to stand up to ye you'd have been dumber 'n Balaam's ass[2] a great sight,—afore it seen the angel, I mean. I swow to man, I b'lieve I'd marry a hitchin'-post if 't was big enough to trounce ye. You great lummox, if I could knock ye over you would n't peep nor mutter agin, if I be a woman!"

And with a burst of furious tears that asserted her womanhood Miss Celia went her way. Her hands were clinched under her blanket-shawl, her eyes red with angry rain, and as she walked on she soliloquized aloud:—

"I declare for 't, I b'lieve I'd marry the Old Boy himself if he'd ask me. I'm sicker 'n ever of bein' an old maid!"

"Be ye?" queried a voice at her elbow. "P'r'aps, then, you might hear to me if I was to speak my mind, Celye."

2. See Numbers 22:21–34.

Celia jumped. As she said afterward, "I vum I thought 't was the Enemy, for certain; and to think 't was only Deacon Everts!"

"Mercy me!" she said now; "is 't you, deacon?"

"Yes, it's me; and I think 't is a real providence I come up behind ye just in the nick of time. I've sold my farm only last week, and I've come to live on the street in that old red house of grandsir's, that you mistrusted once I wanted you to buy. I'm real lonesome sence I lost my partner" (he meant his wife), "and I've been a-hangin' on by the edges the past two year; hired help is worse than nothing onto a farm, and hard to get at that; so I sold out, and I'm a-movin' yet, but the old house looks forlorn enough, and I was intendin' to look about for a second; so if you'll have me, Celye, here I be."

Celia looked at him sharply; he was an apple-faced little man, with shrewd, twinkling eyes, a hard, dull red still lingering on his round cheeks in spite of the deep wrinkles about his pursed-up lips and around his eyelids; his mouth gave him a consequential and self-important air, to which the short stubbly hair, brushed up "like a blaze" above his forehead, added; and his old blue coat with brass buttons, his homespun trousers, the old-fashioned aspect of his unbleached cotton shirt, all attested his frugality. Indeed, everybody knew that Deacon Everts was "near," and also that he had plenty of money, that is to say, far more than he could spend. He had no children, no near relations; his first wife had died two years since, after long invalidism, and all her relations had moved far west. All this Celia knew and now recalled; her wrath against Parson Stearns was yet fresh and vivid; she remembered that Simeon Everts was senior deacon of the church, and had it in his power to make the minister extremely uncomfortable if he chose. I have never said Celia was a very good woman; her religion was of the dormant type not uncommon nowadays; she kept up its observances properly, and said her prayers every day, bestowed a part of her savings on each church collection, and was rated as a church-member "in good and regular standing;" but the vital transforming power of that Christianity which means to "love the Lord thy God with all thy heart, and mind, and soul, and strength, and thy neighbor as thyself,"[3] had no more entered into her soul than it had into Deacon Everts's; and while she would have honestly admitted that revenge was a very wrong sentiment, and entirely improper for any other person to cherish, she felt that she did well to be angry with Parson Stearns, and had a perfect right to "pay him off" in any way she could.

Now here was her opportunity. If she said "Yes" to Deacon Everts, he would no doubt take her part. Her objections to housekeeping were set aside by the fact that the house-owner himself would have to do those heavy labors about the house which she must otherwise have hired a man to do; and the cooking and the indoor work for two people could not be so hard as to sew from house to house for her daily bread. In short, her mind was slowly turning favorably toward this sudden project, but she did not want this wooer to be too sure; so she said: "W-e-ll, 't is a life sentence, as you may say, deacon, and I want to think on 't a spell. Let's see,—to-day's Tuesday; I'll let ye know Thursday night, after prayer-meetin'."

"Well," answered the deacon.

Blessed Yankee monosyllable that means so much and so little; that has such shades of phrase and intention in its myriad inflections; that is "yes," or "no," or "perhaps," just as you accent it; that is at once preface and peroration, evasion and definition! What would all New England speech be without "well"? Even as salt without any savor, or pepper with no pungency.

Now it meant to Miss Celia assent to her proposition; and in accordance the deacon escorted her home from meeting Thursday night, and received for reward a consenting answer. This was no love affair, but a matter of mere business. Deacon Everts needed a housekeeper, and did not want to pay out wages for one; and Miss Celia's position she expressed herself as she put out her tallow candle on that memorable night, and breathed

3. A paraphrase of Matthew 12:37–39.

out on the darkness the audible aspiration, "Thank goodness, I sha'n't hev to die an old maid!"

There was no touch of sanctifying love or consoling affection, or even friendly comradeship, in this arrangement; it was as truly a *marriage de convenance* as was ever contracted in Paris itself, and when the wedding day came, a short month afterward, the sourest aspect of November skies threatening a drenching pour, the dead and sodden leaves that strewed the earth, the wailing northeast wind, even the draggled and bony old horse behind which they jogged over to Bassett Centre, seemed fit accompaniments to the degraded ceremony performed by a justice of the peace, who concluded this merely legal compact, for Miss Celia stoutly refused to be married by Parson Stearns; she would not be accessory to putting one dollar in his pocket, even as her own wedding fee. So she went home to the little red house on Bassett Street, and begun her married life by scrubbing the dust and dirt of years from the kitchen table, making biscuit for tea, washing up the dishes, and at last falling asleep during the deacon's long nasal prayer, wherein he wandered to the ends of the earth, and prayed fervently for the heathen, piteously unconscious that he was little better than a heathen himself.

It did not take many weeks to discover to Celia what is meant by "the curse of a granted prayer." She could not at first accept the situation at all; she was accustomed to enough food, if it was plain and simple, when she herself provided it; but now it was hard to get such viands as would satisfy a healthy appetite.

"You've used a sight of pork, Celye," the deacon would remonstrate. "My first never cooked half what you do. We shall come to want certain, if you're so free-handed."

"Well, Mr. Everts, there was n't a mite left to set by. We eat it all, and I did n't have no more'n I wanted, if you did."

"We must mortify the flesh, Celye. It's hullsome to get up from your victuals hungry. Ye know what Scripter says, 'Jeshurun waxed fat an' kicked.' "[4]

"Well, I ain't Jeshurun, but I expect I shall be more likely to kick if I don't have enough to eat, when it's only pork 'n' potatoes."

"My first used to say them was the best, for steady victuals, of anything, and she never used but two codfish and two quarts of m'lasses the year round; and as for butter, she was real sparin'; she'd fry our bread along with the salt pork, and 't was just as good."

"Look here!" snapped Celia. "I don't want to hear no more about your 'first.' I'm ready to say I wish 't she'd ha' been your last too."

"Well, well, well! this is onseemly contention, Celye," sputtered the alarmed deacon. "Le' 's dwell together in unity so fur as we can, Mis' Everts. I have n't no intention to starve ye, none whatever. I only want to be keerful, so as we sha'n't have to fetch up in the poor-us."

"No need to have a poor-house to home," muttered Celia.

But this is only a mild specimen of poor Celia's life as a married woman. She did not find the honor and glory of "Mrs." before her name a compensation for the thousand evils that she "knew not of" when she fled to them as a desirable change from her single blessedness. Deacon Everts entirely refused to enter into any of her devices against Parson Stearns; he did not care a penny about Celia's wrongs, and he knew very well that no other man than dreamy, unpractical Mr. Stearns, who eked out his minute pittance by writing schoolbooks of a primary sort, would put up with four hundred dollars a year from his parish; yet that was all Bassett people would pay. If they must have the gospel, they must have it at the lowest living rates, and everybody would not assent to that.

So Celia found her revenge no more feasible after her marriage than before, and, gradually absorbed in her own wrongs and sufferings, her desire to reward Mr. Stearns in kind for his treatment of her vanished; she thought less of his futile wrath and more of her present distresses every day.

4. Deuteronomy, 32:15.

For Celia, like everybody who profanes the sacrament of marriage, was beginning to suffer the consequences of her misstep. As her husband's mean, querulous, loveless character unveiled itself in the terrible intimacy of constant and inevitable companionship, she began to look woefully back to the freedom and peace of her maiden days. She learned that a husband is by no means his wife's defender always, not even against reviling tongues. It did not suit Deacon Everts to quarrel with any one, whatever they said to him, or of him and his; he "did n't want no enemies," and Celia bitterly felt that she must fight her own battles; she had not even an ally in her husband. She became not only defiant, but also depressed; the consciousness of a vital and life-long mistake is not productive of cheer or content; and now, admitted into the free-masonry of married women, she discovered how few among them were more than household drudges, the servants of their families, worked to the verge of exhaustion, and neither thanked nor rewarded for their pains. She saw here a woman whose children were careless of, and ungrateful to her, and her husband coldly indifferent; there was one on whom the man she had married wreaked all his fiendish temper in daily small injuries, little vexatious acts, petty tyrannies, a "street-angel, house-devil" of a man, of all sorts the most hateful. There were many whose lives had no other outlook than hard work until the end should come, who rose up to labor and lay down in sleepless exhaustion, and some whose days were a constant terror to them from the intemperate brutes to whom they had intrusted their happiness, and indeed their whole existence.

It was no worse with Celia than with most of her sex in Bassett; here and there, there were of course exceptions, but so rare as to be shining examples and objects of envy. Then, too, after two years, there came forlorn accounts of poor Rosabel's situation at the west. Amos Barker had done his best at first to make his wife comfortable, but change of place or new motives do not at once, if ever, transform an indolent man into an active and efficient one. He found work in his brother's office, but it was the hard work of collecting bills all about the country; the roads were bad, the weather as fluctuating as weather always is, the climate did not agree with him, and he got woefully tired of driving about from dawn till after dark, to dun unwilling debtors. Rosa had chills and fever and babies with persistent alacrity; she had indeed enough to eat, with no appetite, and a house, with no strength to keep it. She grew untidy, listless, hysterical; and her father, getting worried by her despondent and infrequent letters, actually so far roused himself as to sell his horse, and with this sacrificial money betook himself to Mound Village, where he found Rosabel with two babies in her arms, dust an inch deep on all her possessions, nothing but pork, potatoes, and corn bread in the pantry, and a slatternly negress washing some clothes in a kitchen that made the parson shudder.

The little man's heart was bigger than his soul. He put his arms about Rosa and the dingy babies, and forgave her all; but he had to say, even while he held them closely and fondly to his breast, "Oh, Rosy, I told you what would happen if you married that fellow."

Of course Rosa resented the speech, for, after all, she had loved Amos; perhaps could love him still if the poverty and malaria and babies could have all been eliminated from her daily life.

Fortunately the parson's horse had sold well, for it was strong and young, and the rack of venerable bones with which he replaced it was bought very cheap at a farmer's auction, so he had money enough to carry Rosa and the two children home to Bassett, where two months after she added another feeble, howling cipher to the miserable sum of humanity.

Miss—no, Mrs.—Celia's conscience stung her to the quick when she encountered this ghastly wreck of pretty Rosabel Stearns, now called Mrs. Barker. She remembered with deep regret how she had given aid and comfort to the girl who had defied and disobeyed parental counsel and authority, and so brought on herself all this misery. She fancied that Parson Stearns glared at her with eyes of bitter accusation and reproach, and not improbably he did, for beside his pity and affection for his daughter, it was no slight burden to take into his house a feeble woman with two children helpless as babies, and to look forward to the expense and anxiety of another soon to come. And Mrs. Stearns had never loved Rosa well enough to be complacent at this addition to her family cares. She gave the parson no sympathy. It would have been her way to let Rosabel lie on the bed she had made, and die there if need be. But the poor worn-out creature died at home, after all, and the third baby lay on its mother's breast in her coffin: they had gone together.

Celia felt almost like a murderess when she heard that Rosabel Barker was dead. She did not reflect that in all human probability the girl would have married Amos if she, Celia, had refused to help or encourage her. It began to be an importunate question in our friend's mind whether she herself had not made a mistake too; whether the phrase "single blessedness" was not an expression of a vital truth rather than a scoff. Celia was changing her mind no doubt, surely if slowly.

Meantime Deacon Everts did not find all the satisfaction with his "second" that he had anticipated. Celia had a will of her own, quite undisciplined, and it was too often asserted to suit her lord and master. Secretly he planned devices to circumvent her purposes, and sometimes succeeded. In prayer-meeting and in Sunday-school the idea haunted him; his malice lay down and rose up with him. Even when he propounded to his Bible class the important question, "How fur be the heathen *ree*-sponsible for what they dun know?" and asked them "to ponder on 't through the comin' week," he chuckled inwardly at the thought that Celia could not evade *her* responsibility; she knew enough, and would be judged accordingly: the deacon was not a merciful man.

At last he hit upon that great legal engine whereby men do inflict the last deadly kick upon their wives: he would remodel his will. Yes, he would leave those gathered thousands to foreign missions; he would leave behind him the indisputable testimony and taunt that he considered the wife of his bosom less than the savages and heathen afar off. He forgot conveniently that the man "who provideth not for his own household hath denied the faith, and is worse than an infidel."[5] And in his delight of revenge he also forgot that the law of the land provides for a man's wife and children in spite of his wicked will. Nor did he remember that his life-insurance policy for five thousand dollars was made out in his wife's name, simply as his wife, her own name not being specified. He had paid the premium always from his "first's" small annual income, and agreed that it should be written for her benefit, but he supposed that at her death it had reverted to him. He forgot that he still had a wife when he mentioned that policy in his assets recorded in the will, and to save money he drew that evil document up himself, and had it signed down at "the store" by three witnesses.

Celia had borne her self-imposed yoke for four years, when it was suddenly broken. A late crop of grass was to be mowed in mid-July on the meadow which appertained to the old house, and the deacon, now some seventy years old, to save hiring help, determined to do it by himself. The grass was heavy and over-ripe, the day extremely hot and breathless, and the grim Mower of Man trod side by side with Simeon Everts, and laid him too, all along by the rough heads of timothy and the purpled feather-tops of the blue-grass. He did not come home at noon or at night, and when Celia went down to the lot to call him she heard no summons of hers; he had answered a call far more imperative and final.

After the funeral Celia found his will pushed back in the deep drawer of an old secretary, where he kept his one quill pen, a bottle of dried ink, a lump of chalk, some rat-poison, and various other odds and ends.

She was indignant enough at its tenor; but it was easily broken, and she not only had her "thirds,"[6] but the life policy reverted to her also, as it was made out to Simeon Everts's wife, and surely she had occupied that position for four wretched years. Then, also, she had a right to her support for one year out of the estate, and the use of the house for that time.

Oh, how sweet was her freedom! With her characteristic honesty she refused to put on mourning, and even went to the funeral in her usual gray Sunday gown and bonnet. "I won't

---

5. A paraphrase of 1 Timothy, 5:8.
6. The one-third of the man's estate allotted by law to his widow.

lie, anyhow!" she answered to Mrs. Stiles's remonstrance. "I ain't a mite sorry nor mournful. I could ha' wished he'd had time to repent of his sins, but sence the Lord saw fit to cut him short, I don't feel to rebel ag'inst it. I wish 't I'd never married him, that's all!"

"But, Celye, you got a good livin'."

"I earned it."

"And he's left ye with means too."

"He done his best not to. I don't owe him nothing for that; and I earned that too,—the hull on 't. It's poor pay for what I've lived through; and I'm a'most a mind to call it the wages of sin, for I done wrong, ondeniably wrong, in marryin' of him; but the Lord knows I've repented, and said my lesson, if I did get it by the hardest."

Yet all Bassett opened eyes and mouth both when on the next Thanksgiving Day Celia invited every old maid in town—seven all told—to take dinner with her. Never before had she celebrated this old New England day of solemn revel. A woman living in two small rooms could not "keep the feast," and rarely had she been asked to any family conclave. We Yankees are conservative at Thanksgiving if nowhere else, and like to gather our own people only about the family hearth; so Celia had but once or twice shared the turkeys of her more fortunate neighbors.

Now she called in Nabby Hyde and Sarah Gillett, Ann Smith, Celestia Potter, Delia Hills, Sophronia Ann Jenkins and her sister Adelia Ann, ancient twins, who lived together on next to nothing, and were happy.

Celia bloomed at the head of the board, not with beauty, but with gratification. "Well," she said, as soon as they were seated, "I sent for ye all to come because I wanted to have a good time, for one thing, and because it seems as though I'd ought to take back all the sassy and disagreeable things I used to be forever flingin' at old maids. 'I spoke in my haste,'[7] as Scripter says, and also in my ignorance. I'm free to confess. I feel as though I could keep Thanksgivin' to-day with my hull soul. I'm so thankful to be an old maid ag'in!"

"I thought you was a widder," snapped Sally Gillett.

Celia flung a glance of wrath at her, but scorned to reply.

"And I'm thankful too that I'm spared to help ondo somethin' done in that ignorance. I've got means, and, as I've said before, I earned 'em. I don't feel noway obleeged to him for 'em; he did n't mean it. But now I can I'm goin' to adopt Rosy Barker's two children, and fetch 'em up to be dyed-in-the-wool old maids; and every year, so long as I live, I'm goin' to keep an old maids' Thanksgivin' for a kind of a burnt-offering, sech as the Bible tells about,[8] for I've changed my mind clear down to the bottom, and I go the hull figure with the 'postle Paul when he speaks about the onmarried. 'It is better if she so abide.'[9] Now let's go to work at the victuals."

1891

Emily Dickinson

(1830–1886)

America's most admired and influential woman poet and one of its major writers in any genre and of either sex was unrecognized while alive. Indeed, fewer than a dozen of her poems appeared in print during her lifetime; and even if she had published considerably more, it is doubtful that she would have found a place in the

7.   Psalms 31:22.
8.   Leviticus 1:1–17.
9.   1 Corinthians 7:40.

hearts and minds of Americans attuned to the voices of those New England poets whose faces for many years graced the walls of classrooms across the country: William Cullen Bryant, Henry Wadsworth Longfellow, John Greenleaf Whittier, Ralph Waldo Emerson, Oliver Wendell Holmes, and James Russell Lowell. Hers was a genius—voice, matter, and sensibility—that had to await discovery in a later time, by a different set of readers.

She was born and lived out her years in Amherst, Massachusetts, leaving only occasionally and briefly. Her grandfather had been one of the founders of Amherst College, and her father, Edward Dickinson, was for nearly forty years the college's treasurer. The family lived on the town's main street, a few blocks from the college, in a house that still stands and is, on occasion, open for visitors. Edward Dickinson, a lawyer, prospered in business and served for many years in the Massachusetts legislature and for two years in Washington as a representative from Massachusetts. Emily Norcross Dickinson, the poet's mother, was for years a semi-invalid. Emily was the middle child of three. Austin, her older brother, received a man's education with the expectation that he would play a man's role in the public sphere. Although Emily and her younger sister, Lavinia, were also well educated, the family expectations for them were much more limiting. Emily graduated from Amherst Academy and attended Mount Holyoke Female Seminary for a year. Returning home after an intellectual and spiritual crisis, she assumed the duties of running her father's household. Thereafter, she left home for only a few brief visits to Washington, Philadelphia, and Boston while she was still relatively young. Her life seems to have turned inward. At times she seems to have chosen to avoid the distractions of social life as she composed, largely unknown to her family and friends, the huge numbers of poems that were eventually to bring her fame.

There may have been disappointed sexual passion in her life, as some of the poems hint, but no love object has been positively identified. Guesses include a minister, Charles Wadsworth of Philadelphia, and a newspaper editor, Samuel Bowles of the Springfield *Daily Republican*. From 1862 onward she maintained a close friendship with Thomas Wentworth Higginson, an author who served as a literary adviser, and she was especially close to her sister-in-law, Austin's wife, who lived next door. Nobody around her seems to have thought of her as more than an occasional poet, a woman with a minor talent.

Upon her death, her sister Lavinia found that Emily had preserved in a box about 900 poems, neatly tied with twine into 60 packets. A selection of these, edited by Mabel Loomis Todd and Thomas Wentworth Higginson, became *Poems by Emily Dickinson* in 1890. Two more volumes in the 1890s established her, posthumously, as one of the significant American poets of that decade and brought the number of her poems in print to over 500. Nobody knew then, however, the full extent of her work, or understood how many of her irregular meters and rhymes had been smoothed over by the editors. In Thomas H. Johnson's variorum edition, *The Poems of Emily Dickinson* (3 vols., 1955), the total of poems and fragments is 1775 and the variations presented make clear how difficult it is to establish, for many of the poems, what precisely is the preferred text.

It is clear, however, that the regular meters and rhymes preferred by the nineteenth century and by the editors of the pre-Johnson texts are frequently not the meters and rhymes employed by Dickinson in her most interesting and characteristic work. Her meters are less akin to the relatively regular iambics of the major English and American tradition than they are to the irregular iambics carried by the music of hymns and folk songs. Her off-rhymes seem out of place for a period when full rhyme was the rule. From the perspective granted by twentieth-century experimentation, however, her poetic practice seems not peculiar but sparkling with originality.

In her content, too, she seems in some ways more a woman of the twentieth century than the nineteenth. Her "I" is central, her voice witty, her approach oblique, her vision clear and not much cluttered by the poetic or social conventions of her day. In other ways she belongs to her own time as she looks at what is near in nature or human feeling with an eye that sees "New Englandly"—that is, in her case, with a provincialism not far removed from the Emersonian transcendentalism that finds large things mirrored in small, the all in the one. Like Thoreau, who had traveled much in Concord, she discovered at home in Amherst most of what she needed to stir the imaginations of readers around the world.

Thomas H. Johnson, ed., *The Complete Poems of Emily Dickinson* (1960), with reading texts of all the poems in the variorum edition noted above, is the source of the selections below. Facsimiles of the poems as Dickinson wrote them may be found in R. W. Franklin's edition of *The Manuscript Books of Emily Dickinson* (2 vols., 1981). Thomas H. Johnson edited *Letters of Emily Dickinson* (3 vols., 1958); and *Emily Dickinson: Selected Letters* (1971). Biographies include Cynthia Griffin Wolff, *Emily Dickinson* (1986); and Richard B. Sewall, *Emily Dickinson* (1974). Among studies are Albert Gelpi, *Emily Dickinson: The Mind of the Poet* (1965); David T. Porter, *The Art of Emily Dickinson's Early Poetry* (1966); Ruth Miller, *The Poetry of Emily Dickinson* (1968); John Cody, *The Inner Life of Emily Dickinson* (1971); John Evangelist Walsh, *The Hidden Life of Emily Dickinson* (1971); Robert Weisbuch, *Emily Dickinson's Poetry* (1975); Joanne F. Diehl, *Dickinson and the Romantic Imagination* (1981); David Porter, *Dickinson: The Modern Idiom* (1981); Suzanne Juhasz, *The Undiscovered Continent: Emily Dickinson and the Space of the Mind* (1983); Jerome Loving, *Emily Dickinson: The Poet on the Second Story* (1986); and Christanne Miller, *Emily Dickinson: A Poet's Grammar* (1987).

49

I never lost as much but twice,
And that was in the sod.
Twice have I stood a beggar
Before the door of God!

Angels—twice descending   5
Reimbursed my store—
Burglar! Banker—Father!
I am poor once more!

c. 1858   1890

67

Success is counted sweetest
By those who ne'er succeed.
To comprehend a nectar
Requires sorest need.

Not one of all the purple Host   5
Who took the Flag today

Can tell the definition
So clear of Victory

As he defeated—dying—
On whose forbidden ear   10
The distant strains of triumph
Burst agonized and clear!

c. 1859   1878, 1890

130

These are the days when Birds come back—
A very few—a Bird or two—
To take a backward look.

These are the days when skies resume
The old—old sophistries of June—   5
A blue and gold mistake.

Oh fraud that cannot cheat the Bee—
Almost thy plausibility
Induces my belief.

Till ranks of seeds their witness bear— 10
And softly thro' the altered air
Hurries a timid leaf.

Oh Sacrament of summer days,
Oh Last Communion in the Haze—
Permit a child to join. 15

Thy sacred emblems to partake—
Thy consecrated bread to take
And thine immortal wine!

c. 1859   1890

185

"Faith" is a fine invention
When Gentlemen can *see*—
But *Microscopes* are prudent
In an Emergency.

c. 1860   1891

211

Come slowly—Eden!
Lips unused to Thee—
Bashful—sip thy Jessamines—
As the fainting Bee—

Reaching late his flower, 5
Round her chamber hums—
Counts his nectars—
Enters—and is lost in Balms.

c. 1860   1890

214

I taste a liquor never brewed—
From Tankards scooped in Pearl—

Not all the Vats upon the Rhine
Yield such an Alcohol!

Inebriate of Air—am I— 5
And Debauchee of Dew—

Reeling—thro endless summer days—
From inns of Molten Blue—

When "Landlords" turn the drunken Bee
Out of the Foxglove's door— 10
When Butterflies—renounce their
    "drams"—
I shall but drink the more!

Till Seraphs swing their snowy Hats—
And Saints—to windows run—
To see the little Tippler 15
Leaning against the—Sun—

c. 1860   1861, 1890

216

Safe in their Alabaster Chambers—
Untouched by Morning
And untouched by Noon—
Sleep the meek members of the
    Resurrection—
Rafter of satin, 5
And Roof of stone.

Light laughs the breeze
In her Castle above them—
Babbles the Bee in a stolid Ear,
Pipe the Sweet Birds in ignorant
    cadence— 10
Ah, what sagacity perished here!

version of 1859   1862

Safe in their Alabaster Chambers—
Untouched by Morning—
And untouched by Noon—
Lie the meek members of the
    Resurrection—
Rafter of Satin—and Roof of Stone! 5

Grand go the Years—in the
    Crescent—above them—
Worlds scoop their Arcs—
And Firmaments—row—
Diadems—drop—and
    Doges—surrender— 10
Soundless as dots—on a Disc of Snow—

version of 1861   1890

241

I like a look of Agony,
Because I know it's true—
Men do not sham Convulsion,
Nor simulate, a Throe—

The Eyes glaze once—and that is
  Death—   5
Impossible to feign
The Beads upon the Forehead
By homely Anguish strung

c. 1861   1890

249

Wild Nights—Wild Nights!
Were I with thee
Wild Nights should be
Our luxury!

Futile—the Winds—   5
To a Heart in port—
Done with the Compass—
Done with the Chart!

Rowing in Eden—
Ah, the Sea!   10
Might I but moor—Tonight—
In Thee!

c. 1861   1891

254

"Hope" is the thing with feathers—
That perches in the soul—
And sings the tune without the words—
And never stops—at all—

And sweetest—in the Gale—is
  heard—   5
And sore must be the storm—
That could abash the little Bird
That kept so many warm—

I've heard it in the chillest land—
And on the strangest Sea—   10

Yet, never, in Extremity,
It asked a crumb—of Me.

c. 1861   1891

258

There's a certain Slant of light,
Winter Afternoons—
That oppresses, like the Heft
Of Cathedral Tunes—

Heavenly Hurt, it gives us—   5
We can find no scar,
But internal difference,
Where the Meanings, are—

None may teach it—Any—
'Tis the Seal Despair—   10
An imperial affliction
Sent us of the Air—

When it comes, the Landscape listens—
Shadows—hold their breath—
When it goes, 'tis like the Distance   15
On the look of Death—

c. 1861   1890

280

I felt a Funeral, in my Brain,
And Mourners to and fro
Kept treading—treading—till it seemed
That Sense was breaking through—

And when they all were seated,   5
A Service, like a Drum—
Kept beating—beating—till I thought
My Mind was going numb—

And then I heard them lift a Box
And creak across my Soul   10
With those same Boots of Lead, again,
Then Space—began to toll,

As all the Heavens were a Bell,
And Being, but an Ear,
And I, and Silence, some strange Race   15
Wrecked, solitary, here—

And then a Plank in Reason, broke,
And I dropped down, and down—
And hit a World, at every plunge,
And Finished knowing—then—   20

c. 1861   1896

285

The Robin's my Criterion for
    Tune—
Because I grow—where Robins do—
But, were I Cuckoo born—
I'd swear by him—

The ode familiar—rules the Noon—   5
The Buttercup's, my Whim for
    Bloom—
Because, we're Orchard sprung—
But, were I Britain born,
I'd Daisies spurn—
None but the Nut—October fit—   10
Because, through dropping it,
The Seasons flit—I'm taught—
Without the Snow's Tableau
Winter, were lie—to me—
Because I see—New Englandly—   15
The Queen, discerns like me—
Provincially—

c. 1861   1929

288

I'm Nobody! Who are you?
Are you—Nobody—Too?
Then there's a pair of us?
Don't tell! they'd advertise—you know!

How dreary—to be—Somebody!   5
How public—like a Frog—
To tell one's name—the livelong
    June—
To an admiring Bog!

c. 1861   1891

303

The Soul selects her own Society—
Then—shuts the Door—
To her divine Majority—
Present no more—

Unmoved—she notes the
    Chariots—pausing   5
At her low Gate—
Unmoved—an Emperor be kneeling
Upon her Mat—

I've known her—from an ample nation—
Choose One—   10
Then—close the Valves of her attention—
Like Stone—

c. 1862   1890

315

He fumbles at your Soul
As Players at the Keys
Before they drop full Music on—
He stuns you by degrees—
Prepares your brittle Nature   5
For the Ethereal Blow
By fainter Hammers—further heard—
Then nearer—Then so slow
Your Breath has time to straighten—
Your Brain—to bubble Cool—   10
Deals—One—imperial—Thunderbolt—
That scalps your naked Soul—

When Winds take Forests in their Paws—
The Universe—is still—

c. 1862   1896

322

There came a Day at Summer's full,
Entirely for me—
I thought that such were for the Saints,
Where Resurrections—be—

The Sun, as common, went abroad,   5
The flowers, accustomed, blew,
As if no soul the solstice passed
That maketh all things new—

The time was scarce profaned, by
  speech—
The symbol of a word—   10
Was needless, as at Sacrament,
The Wardrobe—of our Lord—

Each was to each The Sealed Church,
Permitted to commune this—time—
Lest we too awkward show   15
At Supper of the Lamb.

The Hours slid fast—as Hours will,
Clutched tight, by greedy hands—
So faces on two Decks, look back,
Bound to opposing lands—   20

And so when all the time had leaked,
Without external sound
Each bound the Other's Crucifix—
We gave no other Bond—

Sufficient troth, that we shall rise—   25
Deposed—at length, the Grave—
To that new Marriage,
Justified—through Calvaries of Love—

c. 1861   1890

324

Some keep the Sabbath going to
  Church—
I keep it, staying at Home—
With a Bobolink for a Chorister—
And an Orchard, for a Dome—

Some keep the Sabbath in Surplice—   5
I just wear my Wings—
And instead of tolling the Bell, for Church,
Our little Sexton—sings.

God preaches, a noted Clergyman—
And the sermon is never long,   10
So instead of getting to Heaven, at last—
I'm going, all along.

c. 1860   1864

328

A Bird came down the Walk—
He did not know I saw—
He bit an Angleworm in halves
And ate the fellow, raw,

And then he drank a Dew   5
From a convenient Grass—
And then hopped sidewise to the Wall
To let a Beetle pass—

He glanced with rapid eyes
That hurried all around—   10
They looked like frightened Beads, I
  thought—
He stirred his Velvet Head

Like one in danger, Cautious,
I offered him a Crumb
And he unrolled his feathers   15
And rowed him softer home—

Than Oars divide the Ocean,
Too silver for a seam—
Or Butterflies, off Banks of Noon
Leap, plashless as they swim.   20

c. 1862   1891

338

I know that He exists.
Somewhere—in Silence—
He has hid his rare life
From our gross eyes.

'Tis an instant's play.   5
'Tis a fond Ambush—
Just to make Bliss
Earn her own surprise!

But—should the play
Prove piercing earnest—   10
Should the glee—glaze—
In Death's—stiff—stare—

Would not the fun
Look too expensive!
Would not the jest—   15
Have crawled too far!

c. 1862   1891

341

After great pain, a formal feeling comes—
The Nerves sit ceremonious, like
    Tombs—
The stiff Heart questions was it He, that
    bore,
And Yesterday, or Centuries before?

The Feet, mechanical, go round—   5
Of Ground, or Air, or Ought—
A Wooden way
Regardless grown,
A Quartz contentment, like a stone—

This is the Hour of Lead—   10
Remembered, if outlived,
As Freezing persons, recollect the Snow—
First—Chill—then Stupor—then the
    letting go—

c. 1862   1929

376

Of Course—I prayed—
And did God Care?
He cared as much as on the Air
A Bird—had stamped her foot—
And cried "Give Me"—   5
My Reason—Life—
I had not had—but for Yourself—
'Twere better Charity
To leave me in the Atom's Tomb—
Merry, and Nought, and gay, and
    numb—   10
Than this smart Misery.

c. 1862   1929

401

What Soft—Cherubic Creatures—
These Gentlewomen are—
One would as soon assault a Plush—
Or violate a Star—

Such Dimity Convictions—   5
A Horror so refined
Of freckled Human Nature—
Of Deity—ashamed—

It's such a common—Glory—
A Fisherman's—Degree—   10
Redemption—Brittle Lady—
Be so—ashamed of Thee—

c. 1862   1896

435

Much Madness is divinest Sense—
To a discerning Eye—
Much Sense—the starkest Madness—
'Tis the Majority
In this, as All, prevail—   5
Assent—and you are sane—
Demur—you're straightway dangerous—
And handled with a Chain—

c. 1862   1890

441

This is my letter to the World
That never wrote to Me—
The simple News that Nature told—
With tender Majesty

Her Message is committed   5
To Hands I cannot see—
For love of Her—Sweet—countrymen—
Judge tenderly—of Me

c. 1862   1890

448

This was a Poet—It is That
Distills amazing sense
From ordinary Meanings—
And Attar so immense

From the familiar species   5
That perished by the Door—
We wonder it was not Ourselves
Arrested it—before—

Of Pictures, the Discloser—
The Poet—it is He—   10
Entitles Us—by Contrast—
To ceaseless Poverty—

Of Portion—so unconscious—
The Robbing—could not harm—
Himself—to Him—a Fortune—   15
Exterior—to Time—

c. 1862   1929

449

I died for Beauty—but was scarce
Adjusted in the Tomb
When One who died for Truth, was lain
In an adjoining Room—

He questioned softly "Why I failed"?   5
"For Beauty", I replied—
"And I—for Truth—Themself Are One—
We Brethren, are", He said—

And so, as Kinsmen, met a Night—
We talked between the Rooms—   10
Until the Moss had reached our lips—
And covered up—our names—

c. 1862   1890

465

I heard a Fly buzz—when I died—
The Stillness in the Room
Was like the Stillness in the Air—
Between the Heaves of Storm—

The Eyes around—had wrung them
     dry—   5
And Breaths were gathering firm
For that last Onset—when the King
Be witnessed—in the Room—

I willed my Keepsakes—Signed away
What portion of me be   10
Assignable—and then it was
There interposed a Fly—

With Blue—uncertain stumbling Buzz—
Between the light—and me—
And then the Windows failed—and
     then   15
I could not see to see—

c. 1862   1890

501

This World is not Conclusion.
A Species stands beyond—
Invisible, as Music—
But positive, as Sound—
It beckons, and it baffles—   5
Philosophy—don't know—
And through a Riddle, at the last—
Sagacity, must go—
To guess it, puzzles scholars—
To gain it, Men have borne   10
Contempt of Generations
And Crucifixion, shown—
Faith slips—and laughs, and rallies—
Blushes, if any see—
Plucks at a twig of Evidence—   15
And asks a Vane, the way—
Much Gesture, from the Pulpit—
Strong Hallelujahs roll—
Narcotics cannot still the Tooth
That nibbles at the soul—   20

c. 1862   1896

508

I'm ceded—I've stopped being Theirs—
The name They dropped upon my face
With water, in the country church
Is finished using, now,
And They can put it with my Dolls,   5
My childhood, and the string of spools,
I've finished threading—too—

Baptized, before, without the choice,
But this time, consciously, of Grace—
Unto supremest name— 10
Called to my Full—The Crescent
dropped—
Existence's whole Arc, filled up,
With one small Diadem.

My second Rank—too small the first—
Crowned—Crowing—on my Father's
breast— 15
A half unconscious Queen—
But this time—Adequate—Erect,
With Will to choose, or to reject,
And I choose, just a Crown—

c. 1862   1890

510

It was not Death, for I stood up,
And all the Dead, lie down—
It was not Night, for all the Bells
Put out their Tongues, for Noon.

It was not Frost, for on my Flesh 5
I felt Siroccos—crawl—
Nor Fire—for just my Marble feet
Could keep a Chancel, cool—

And yet, it tasted, like them all,
The Figures I have seen 10
Set orderly, for Burial,
Reminded me, of mine—

As if my life were shaven,
And fitted to a frame,
And could not breathe without a key, 15
And 'twas like Midnight, some—

When everything that ticked—has
stopped—
And Space stares all around—
Or Grisly frosts—first Autumn morns,
Repeal the Beating Ground— 20

But, most, like Chaos—Stopless—cool—
Without a Chance, or Spar—
Or even a Report of Land—
To justify—Despair.

c. 1862   1891

511

If you were coming in the Fall,
I'd brush the Summer by
With half a smile, and half a spurn,
As Housewives do, a Fly.

If I could see you in a year, 5
I'd wind the months in balls—
And put them each in separate Drawers,
For fear the numbers fuse—

If only Centuries delayed,
I'd count them on my Hand, 10
Subtracting, till my fingers dropped
Into Van Dieman's Land.[1]

If certain, when this life was out—
That yours and mine, should be
I'd toss it yonder, like a Rind, 15
And take Eternity—

But, now, uncertain of the length
Of this, that is between,
It goads me, like the Goblin Bee—
That will not state—its sting. 20

c. 1862   1890

520

I started Early—Took my Dog—
And visited the Sea—
The Mermaids in the Basement
Came out to look at me—

And Frigates—in the Upper Floor 5
Extended Hempen Hands—
Presuming Me to be a Mouse—
Aground—upon the Sands—

But no Man moved Me—till the Tide
Went past my simple Shoe— 10
And past my Apron—and my Belt
And past my Bodice—too—

And made as He would eat me up—
As wholly as a Dew

1. Tasmania, an island off the southern coast of
Australia.

Upon a Dandelion's Sleeve—   15
And then—I started—too—

And He—He followed—close
     behind—
I felt His Silver Heel
Upon my Ankle—Then my Shoes
Would overflow with Pearl—   20

Until We met the Solid Town—
No One He seemed to know—
And bowing—with a Mighty look—
At me—The Sea withdrew—

c. 1862   1891

528

Mine—by the Right of the White
     Election!
Mine—by the Royal Seal!
Mine—by the Sign in the Scarlet
     prison—
Bars—cannot conceal!

Mine—here—in Vision—and in Veto!   5
Mine—by the Grave's Repeal—
Titled—Confirmed—
Delirious Charter!
Mine—long as Ages steal!

c. 1862   1890

536

The Heart asks Pleasure—first—
And then—Excuse from Pain—
And then—those little Anodynes
That deaden suffering—

And then—to go to sleep—   5
And then—if it should be
The will of its Inquisitor
The privilege to die—

c. 1862   1890

547

I've seen a Dying Eye
Run round and round a Room—
In search of Something—as it seemed—
Then Cloudier become—
And then—obscure with Fog—   5
And then—be soldered down
Without disclosing what it be
'Twere blessed to have seen—

c. 1862   1890

569

I reckon—when I count at all—
First—Poets—Then the Sun—
Then Summer—Then the Heaven of
     God—
And then—the List is done—

But, looking back—the First so seems   5
To Comprehend the Whole—
The Others look a needless Show—
So I write—Poets—All—

Their Summer—lasts a Solid Year—
They can afford a Sun   10
The East—would deem extravagant—
And if the Further Heaven—

Be Beautiful as they prepare
For Those who worship Them—
It is too difficult a Grace—
To justify the Dream—   15

c. 1862   1929

579

I had been hungry, all the Years—
My Noon had Come—to dine—
I trembling drew the Table near—
And touched the Curious Wine—

'Twas this on Tables I had seen—   5
When turning, hungry, Home

I looked in Windows, for the Wealth
I could not hope—for Mine—

I did not know the ample Bread—
'Twas so unlike the Crumb   10
The Birds and I, had often shared
In Nature's—Dining Room—

The Plenty hurt me—'twas so new—
Myself felt ill—and odd—
As Berry—of a Mountain Bush—   15
Transplanted—to the Road—

Nor was I hungry—so I found
That Hunger—was a way
Of Persons outside Windows—
The Entering—takes away—   20

c. 1862   1891

585

I like to see it lap the Miles—
And lick the Valleys up—
And stop to feed itself at Tanks—
And then—prodigious step

Around a Pile of Mountains—   5
And supercilious peer
In Shanties—by the sides of
    Roads—
And then a Quarry pare

To fit its Ribs
And crawl between   10
Complaining all the while
In horrid—hooting stanza—
Then chase itself down Hill—

And neigh like Boanerges²
Then—punctual as a Star   15
Stop—docile and omnipotent
At its own stable door—

c. 1862   1891

2. A surname meaning "sons of thunder," given by
   Jesus to James and John (Mark 3:17) and sometimes used to designate a vociferous preacher or
   orator.

632

The Brain—is wider than the Sky—
For—put them side by side—
The one the other will contain
With ease—and You—beside—

The Brain is deeper than the sea—   5
For—hold them—Blue to Blue—
The one the other will absorb—
As Sponges—Buckets—do—

The Brain is just the weight of God—
For—Heft them—Pound for Pound—   10
And they will differ—if they do—
As Syllable from Sound—

c. 1862   1896

640

I cannot live with You—
It would be Life—
And Life is over there—
Behind the Shelf

The Sexton keeps the Key to—   5
Putting up
Our Life—His Porcelain—
Like a Cup—

Discarded of the Housewife—
Quaint—or Broke—   10
A newer Sevres³ pleases—
Old Ones crack—

I could not die—with You—
For One must wait
To shut the Other's Gaze down—   15
You—could not—

And I—Could I stand by
And see You—freeze—
Without my Right of Frost—
Death's privilege?   20

Nor could I rise—with You—
Because Your Face

3. Fine porcelain from Sèvres, France.

Would put out Jesus'—
That New Grace

Glow plain—and foreign   25
On my homesick Eye—
Except that You than He
Shone closer by—

They'd judge Us—How—
For You—served Heaven—You
    know,   30
Or sought to—
I could not—

Because You saturated Sight—
And I had no more Eyes
For sordid excellence   35
As Paradise

And were You lost, I would be—
Though My Name
Rang loudest
On the Heavenly fame—   40

And were You—saved—
And I—condemned to be
Where You were not—
That self—were Hell to Me—

So We must meet apart—   45
You there—I—here—
With just the Door ajar
That Oceans are—and Prayer—

And that White Sustenance—
Despair—   50

c. 1862   1890

650

Pain—has an Element of Blank—
It cannot recollect
When it begun—or if there were
A time when it was not—

It has no Future—but itself—   5
Its Infinite contain
Its Past—enlightened to perceive
New Periods—of Pain.

c. 1862   1890

657

I dwell in Possibility—
A fairer House than Prose—
More numerous of Windows—
Superior—for Doors—

Of Chambers as the Cedars—   5
Impregnable of Eye—
And for an Everlasting Roof
The Gambrels of the Sky—

Of Visitors—the fairest—
For Occupation—This—   10
The spreading wide my narrow Hands
To gather Paradise—

c. 1862   1929

664

Of all the Souls that stand create—
I have elected—One—
When Sense from Spirit—files away—
And Subterfuge—is done—
When that which is—and that which
    was—   5
Apart—intrinsic—stand—
And this brief Drama in the flesh—
Is shifted—like a Sand—
When Figures show their royal Front—
And Mists—are carved away,   10
Behold the Atom—I preferred—
To all the lists of Clay!

c. 1862   1891

670

One need not be a Chamber—to be
    Haunted—
One need not be a House—
The Brain has Corridors—surpassing
Material Place—

Far safer, of a Midnight Meeting   5
External Ghost
Than its interior Confronting—
That Cooler Host.

Far safer, through an Abbey gallop,
The Stones a'chase—   10
Than Unarmed, one's a'self encounter—
In lonesome Place—

Ourself behind ourself, concealed—
Should startle most—
Assassin hid in our Apartment   15
Be Horror's least.

The Body—borrows a Revolver—
He bolts the Door—
O'erlooking a superior spectre—
Or More—   20

c. 1863   1891

709

Publication—is the Auction
Of the Mind of Man—
Poverty—be justifying
For so foul a thing

Possibly—but We—would rather   5
From Our Garret go
White—Unto the White Creator—
Than invest—Our Snow—

Thought belong to Him who gave it—
Then—to Him Who bear   10
Its Corporeal illustration—Sell
The Royal Air—

In the Parcel—Be the Merchant
Of the Heavenly Grace—
But reduce no Human Spirit   15
To Disgrace of Price—

c. 1863   1929

712

Because I could not stop for Death—
He kindly stopped for me—

The Carriage held but just Ourselves—
And Immortality.

We slowly drove—He knew no haste   5
And I had put away
My labor and my leisure too,
For His Civility—

We passed the School, where Children strove
At Recess—in the Ring—   10
We passed the Fields of Gazing Grain—
We passed the Setting Sun—

Or rather—He passed Us—
The Dews drew quivering and chill—
For only Gossamer, my Gown—   15
My Tippet—only Tulle—

We paused before a House that seemed
A Swelling of the Ground—
The Roof was scarcely visible—
The Cornice—in the Ground—   20

Since then—'tis Centuries—and yet
Feels shorter than the Day
I first surmised the Horses' Heads
Were toward Eternity—

c. 1863   1890

732

She rose to His Requirement—dropt
The Playthings of Her Life
To take the honorable Work
Of Woman, and of Wife—

If ought She missed in Her new Day,   5
Of Amplitude, or Awe—
Or first Prospective—Or the Gold
In using, wear away,

It lay unmentioned—as the Sea
Develop Pearl, and Weed,   10
But only to Himself—be known
The Fathoms they abide—

c. 1863   1890

754

My Life had stood—a Loaded Gun—
In Corners—till a Day
The Owner passed—identified—
And carried Me away—

And now We roam in Sovereign
   Woods—   5
And now We hunt the Doe—
And every time I speak for Him—
The Mountains straight reply—

And do I smile, such cordial light
Upon the Valley glow—   10
It is as a Vesuvian face
Had let its pleasure through—

And when at Night—Our good Day
   done—
I guard My Master's Head—
'Tis better than the Eider-Duck's   15
Deep Pillow—to have shared—

To foe of His—I'm deadly foe—
None stir the second time—
On whom I lay a Yellow Eye—
Or an emphatic Thumb—   20

Though I than He—may longer live
He longer must—than I—
For I have but the power to kill,
Without—the power to die—

c. 1863   1929

986

A narrow Fellow in the Grass
Occasionally rides—
You may have met Him—did you not
His notice sudden is—

The Grass divides as with a Comb—   5
A spotted shaft is seen—
And then it closes at your feet
And opens further on—

He likes a Boggy Acre
A Floor too cool for Corn—   10
Yet when a Boy, and Barefoot—
I more than once at Noon

Have passed, I thought, a Whip lash
Unbraiding in the Sun
When stooping to secure it   15
It wrinkled, and was gone—

Several of Nature's People
I know, and they know me—
I feel for them a transport
Of cordiality—   20

But never met this Fellow
Attended, or alone
Without a tighter breathing
And Zero at the Bone—

c. 1865   1866, 1891

1052

I never saw a Moor—
I never saw the Sea—
Yet know I how the Heather looks
And what a Billow be

I never spoke with God   5
Nor visited in Heaven—
Yet certain am I of the spot
As if the Checks were given—

c. 1865   1890

1078

The Bustle in a House
The Morning after Death
Is solemnest of industries
Enacted upon Earth—

The Sweeping up the Heart   5
And putting Love away
We shall not want to use again
Until Eternity.

c. 1866   1890

1100

The last Night that She lived[4]
It was a Common Night
Except the Dying—this to Us
Made Nature different

We noticed smallest things—   5
Things overlooked before
By this great light upon our Minds
Italicized—as 'twere.

As We went out and in
Between Her final Room   10
And Rooms where Those to be alive
Tomorrow were, a Blame

That Others could exist
While She must finish quite
A Jealousy for Her arose   15
So nearly infinite—

We waited while She passed—
It was a narrow time—
Too jostled were Our Souls to speak
At length the notice came.   20

She mentioned, and forgot—
Then lightly as a Reed
Bent to the Water, struggled
  scarce—
Consented, and was dead—

And We—We placed the Hair—   25
And drew the Head erect—
And then an awful leisure was
Belief to regulate—

c. 1866   1890

1129

Tell all the Truth but tell it
  slant—
Success in Circuit lies

Too bright for our infirm Delight
The Truth's superb surprise

As Lightning to the Children eased   5
With explanation kind
The Truth must dazzle gradually
Or every man be blind—

c. 1868   1945

1207

He preached upon "Breadth" till it argued
  him narrow—
The Broad are too broad to define
And of "Truth" until it proclaimed him a
  Liar—
The Truth never flaunted a Sign—

Simplicity fled from his counterfeit
  presence   5
As Gold the Pyrites would shun—
What confusion would cover the innocent
  Jesus
To meet so enabled a Man!

1872   1891

1463

A Route of Evanescence
With a revolving Wheel—
A Resonance of Emerald—
A Rush of Cochineal[5]—
And every Blossom on the Bush   5
Adjusts its tumbled Head—
The mail from Tunis, probably,
An easy Morning's Ride—

c. 1879   1891

1540

As imperceptibly as Grief
The Summer lapsed away—

---

4. "On Thursday, 3 May 1866, Laura Dickey (Mrs.
    Frank W.) of Michigan, youngest daughter of Mr.
    and Mrs. L. M. Hills, died at her parents' home in
    Amherst. The Hills land lay next to the Dickin-
    sons on the East" [Johnson's note].

5. A red dye.

Too imperceptible at last
To seem like Perfidy—
A Quietness distilled   5
As Twilight long begun,
Or Nature spending with herself
Sequestered Afternoon—
The Dusk drew earlier in—
The Morning foreign shone—   10
A courteous, yet harrowing Grace,
As Guest, that would be gone—
And thus, without a Wing
Or service of a Keel
Our Summer made her light escape   15
Into the Beautiful.

c. 1865   1891

1545

The Bible is an antique Volume—
Written by faded Men
At the suggestion of Holy Spectres—
Subjects—Bethlehem—
Eden—the ancient Homestead—   5
Satan—the Brigadier—
Judas—the Great Defaulter—
David—the Troubadour—
Sin—a distinguished Precipice
Others must resist—   10
Boys that "believe" are very lonesome—
Other Boys are "lost"—
Had but the Tale a warbling Teller—
All the Boys would come—
Orpheus' Sermon captivated—   15
It did not condemn—

c. 1882   1924

1624

Apparently with no surprise
To any happy Flower
The Frost beheads it at its play—
In accidental power—
The blonde Assassin passes on—   5

The Sun proceeds unmoved
To measure off another Day
For an Approving God.

c. 1884   1890

1651

A Word made Flesh is seldom
And tremblingly partook
Nor then perhaps reported
But have I not mistook
Each one of us has tasted   5
With ecstasies of stealth
The very food debated
To our specific strength—

A Word that breathes distinctly
Has not the power to die   10
Cohesive as the Spirit
It may expire if He—
"Made Flesh and dwelt among us"
Could condescension be
Like this consent of Language   15
This loved Philology.

?   1955

1670

In Winter in my Room
I came upon a Worm—
Pink, lank and warm—
But as he was a worm
And worms presume   5
Not quite with him at home—
Secured him by a string
To something neighboring
And went along.

A Trifle afterward   10
A thing occurred
I'd not believe it if I heard
But state with creeping blood—
A snake with mottles rare
Surveyed my chamber floor.   15

In feature as the worm before
But ringed with power—
The very string with which
I tied him—too
When he was mean and new   20
That string was there—

I shrank—"How fair you are"!
Propitiation's claw—
"Afraid," he hissed
"Of me"?   25
"No cordiality"—
He fathomed me—
Then to a Rhythm *Slim*
Secreted in his Form
As Patterns swim   30
Projected him.

That time I flew
Both eyes his way
Lest he pursue
Nor ever ceased to run   35
Till in a distant Town
Towns on from mine
I set me down
This was a dream.

?   1914

1732

My life closed twice before its close—
It yet remains to see
If Immortality unveil
A third event to me
So huge, so hopeless to conceive   5
As these that twice befell.
Parting is all we know of heaven,
And all we need of hell.

?   1896

1737

Rearrange a "Wife's" affection!
When they dislocate my Brain!
Amputate my freckled Bosom!
Make me bearded like a man!

Blush, my spirit, in thy Fastness—   5
Blush, my unacknowledged clay—
Seven years of troth have taught thee
More than Wifehood ever may!

Love that never leaped its socket—
Trust entrenched in narrow pain—   10
Constancy thro' fire—awarded—
Anguish—bare of anodyne!

Burden—borne so far triumphant—
None suspect me of the crown,
For I wear the "Thorns" till *Sunset*—   15
Then—my Diadem put on.

Big my Secret but it's *bandaged*—
It will never get away
Till the Day its Weary Keeper
Leads it through the Grave to thee.   20

?   1945

1755

To make a prairie it takes a clover and
    one bee,
One clover, and a bee,
And revery.
The revery alone will do,
If bees are few.   5

?   1896

1760

Elysium[6] is as far as to
The very nearest Room
If in that Room a Friend await
Felicity or Doom—

What fortitude the Soul contains,   5
That it can so endure
The accent of a coming Foot—
The opening of a Door—

c. 1882   1890

6. Paradise.

Letters

To recipient unknown / about 1858

Dear Master[7]

I am ill, but grieving more that you are ill, I make my stronger hand work long eno' to tell you. I thought perhaps you were in Heaven, and when you spoke again, it seemed quite sweet, and wonderful, and surprised me so—I wish that you were well.

I would that all I love, should be weak no more. The Violets are by my side, the Robin very near, and "Spring"—they say, Who is she—going by the door—

Indeed it is God's house—and these are gates of Heaven, and to and fro, the angels go, with their sweet postillions—I wish that I were great, like Mr. Michael Angelo, and could paint for you. You ask me what my flowers said—then they were disobedient—I gave them messages. They said what the lips in the West, say, when the sun goes down, and so says the Dawn.

Listen again, Master. I did not tell you that today had been the Sabbath Day.

Each Sabbath on the Sea, makes me count the Sabbaths, till we meet on shore—and (will the) whether the hills will look as blue as the sailors say. I cannot talk any more (stay any longer) tonight (now), for this pain denies me.

How strong when weak to recollect, and easy, quite, to love. Will you tell me, please to tell me, soon as you are well.

To recipient unknown / about 1861

Master.

If you saw a bullet hit a Bird—and he told you he was'nt shot—you might weep at his courtesy, but you would certainly doubt his word.

One drop more from the gash that stains your Daisy's bosom—then would you *believe?* Thomas' faith in Anatomy, was stronger than his faith in faith. God made me—[Sir] Master—I did'nt be—myself. I dont know how it was done. He built the heart in me—Bye and bye it outgrew me—and like the little mother—with the big child—I got tired holding him. I heard of a thing called "Redemption"—which rested men and women. You remember I asked you for it—you gave me something else. I forgot the Redemption [in the Redeemed—I did'nt tell you for a long time, but I knew you had altered me—I] and was tired—no more—[so dear did this stranger become that were it, or my breath—the Alternative—I had tossed the fellow away with a smile.] I am older—tonight, Master—but the love is the same—so are the moon and the crescent. If it had been God's will that I might breathe where you breathed—and find the place—myself—at night—if I (can) never forget that I am not with you—and that sorrow and frost are nearer than I—if I wish with a might I cannot repress—that mine were the Queen's place—the love of the Plantagenet is my only apology—To come nearer than presbyteries—and nearer than the new Coat—that the Tailor made—the prank of the Heart at play on the Heart—in holy Holiday—is forbidden me—You make me say it over—I fear you laugh—when I do not see—[but] "Chillon" is not funny. Have you the Heart in your breast—Sir—is it set like mine—a little to the

---

7. This draft was left among ED's own papers, and no one knows whether a fair copy was made or sent to the person addressed. That it was meant as a reply to one from him is shown by the allusion to his question. She may have had the Reverend Charles Wadsworth in mind as "Master" [Johnson's note]. The texts for this and the following letters are as given in Johnson's *The Letters of Emily Dickinson*. Johnson gives alternative readings in parentheses, words crossed out in brackets.

left—has it the misgiving—if it wake in the night—perchance—itself to it—a timbrel is it—itself to it a tune?

These things are [reverent] holy, Sir, I touch them [reverently] hallowed, but persons who pray—dare remark [our] "Father"! You say I do not tell you all—Daisy confessed—and denied not.

Vesuvius dont talk—Etna—dont—[Thy] one of them—said a syllable—a thousand years ago, and Pompeii heard it, and hid forever—She could'nt look the world in the face, afterward—I suppose—Bashfull Pompeii! "Tell you of the want"—you know what a leech is, dont you—and [remember that] Daisy's arm is small—and you have felt the horizon hav'nt you—and did the sea—never come so close as to make you dance?

I dont know what you can do for it—thank you—Master—but if I had the Beard on my cheek—like you—and you—had Daisy's petals—and you cared so for me—what would become of you? Could you forget me in fight, or flight—or the foreign land? Could'nt Carlo,[8] and you and I walk in the meadows an hour—and nobody care but the Bobolink—and *his*—a *silver* scruple? I used to think when I died—I could see you—so I died as fast as I could—but the "Corporation" are going Heaven too so [Eternity] wont be sequestered— now [at all]—Say I may wait for you—say I need go with no stranger to the to me—untried [country] fold—I waited a long time—Master—but I can wait more—wait till my hazel hair is dappled—and you carry the cane—then I can look at my watch—and if the Day is too far declined—we can take the chances [of] for Heaven—What would you do with me if I came "in white?" Have you the little chest to put the Alive—in?

I want to see you more—Sir—than all I wish for in this world—and the wish—altered a little—will be my only one—for the skies.

Could you come to New England—[this summer—could] would you come to Amherst— Would you like to come—Master?

[Would it do harm—yet we both fear God—] Would Daisy disappoint you—no—she would'nt—Sir—it were comfort forever—just to look in your face, while you looked in mine—then I could play in the woods till Dark—till you take me where Sundown cannot find us—and the true keep coming—till the town is full. [Will you tell me if you will?]

I did'nt think to tell you, you did'nt come to me "in white," nor ever told me why,

> No Rose, yet felt myself a'bloom,
> No Bird—yet rode in Ether.

To recipient unknown / early 1862?

Oh, did I offend it—[Did'nt it want me to tell it the truth] Daisy—Daisy—offend it—who bends her smaller life to his (it's) meeker (lower) every day—who only asks—a task—[who] something to do for love of it—some little way she cannot guess to make that master glad—

A love so big it scares her, rushing among her small heart—pushing aside the blood and leaving her faint (all) and white in the gust's arm—

Daisy—who never flinched thro' that awful parting, but held her life so tight he should not see the wound—who would have sheltered him in her childish bosom (Heart)—only it was'nt big eno' for a Guest so large—*this* Daisy—grieve her Lord—and yet it (she) often blundered—Perhaps she grieved (grazed) his taste—perhaps her odd—Backwoodsman [life] ways [troubled] teased his finer nature (sense). Daisy [fea] knows all that—but must she go unpardoned—teach her, preceptor grace—teach her majesty—Slow (Dull) at patrician things—Even the wren upon her nest learns (knows) more than Daisy dares—

Low at the knee that bore her once unto [royal] wordless rest [now] Daisy [stoops a] kneels

8. Her dog.

a culprit—tell her her [offence] fault—Master—if it is [not so] small eno' to cancel with her life, [Daisy] she is satisfied—but punish [do not] dont banish her—shut her in prison, Sir—only pledge that you will forgive—sometime—before the grave, and Daisy will not mind—She will awake in [his] your likeness.

Wonder stings me more than the Bee—who did never sting me—but made gay music with his might wherever I [may] [should] did go—Wonder wastes my pound, you said I had no size to spare—

You send the water over the Dam in my brown eyes—

I've got a cough as big as a thimble—but I dont care for that—I've got a Tomahawk in my side but that dont hurt me much. [If you] Her master stabs her more—

Wont he come to her—or will he let her seek him, never minding [whatever] so long wandering [out] if to him at last.

Oh how the sailor strains, when his boat is filling—Oh how the dying tug, till the angel comes. Master—open your life wide, and take me in forever, I will never be tired—I will never be noisy when you want to be still. I will be [glad] [as the] your best little girl—nobody else will see me, but you—but that is enough—I shall not want any more—and all that Heaven only will disappoint me—will be because it's not so dear

To T. W. Higginson[9] / 15 April 1862

Mr Higginson,

Are you too deeply occupied to say if my Verse is alive?

The Mind is so near itself—it cannot see, distinctly—and I have none to ask—

Should you think it breathed—and had you the leisure to tell me, I should feel quick gratitude—

If I make the mistake—that you dared to tell me—would give me sincere honor—toward you—

I enclose my name—asking you, if you please—Sir—to tell me what is true?

That you will not betray me—it is needless to ask—since Honor is it's own pawn—

To T. W. Higginson / 25 April 1862

Mr Higginson,

Your kindness claimed earlier gratitude—but I was ill—and write today, from my pillow.

Thank you for the surgery—it was not so painful as I supposed. I bring you others—as you ask—though they might not differ—

While my thought is undressed—I can make the distinction, but when I put them in the Gown—they look alike, and numb.

You asked how old I was? I made no verse—but one or two—until this winter—Sir—

I had a terror—since September—I could tell to none—and so I sing, as the Boy does by the Burying Ground—because I am afraid—You inquire my Books—For Poets—I have Keats—and Mr and Mrs Browning. For Prose—Mr Ruskin—Sir Thomas Browne—and the

9. In place of a signature, ED enclosed a card (in its own envelope) on which she wrote her name. This first letter to Higginson, which begins a correspondence that lasted until the month of her death, she wrote because she had just read his "Letter to a Young Contributor," the lead article in the *Atlantic Monthly* for April, offering practical advice to beginning writers. She also enclosed four poems: "Safe in their Alabaster Chambers," "The nearest Dream recedes unrealized," "We play at Paste," and "I'll tell you how the Sun rose" [Johnson's note]. Thomas Wentworth Higginson (1823–1911) was a prolific writer who became Dickinson's close friend and adviser.

Revelations.[1] I went to school—but in your manner of the phrase—had no education. When a little Girl, I had a friend,[2] who taught me Immortality—but venturing too near, himself—he never returned—Soon after, my Tutor, died—and for several years, my Lexicon—was my only companion—Then I found one more—but he was not contented I be his scholar—so he left the Land.

You ask of my Companions Hills—Sir—and the Sundown—and a Dog—large as myself, that my Father bought me—They are better than Beings—because they know—but do not tell—and the noise in the Pool, at Noon—excels my Piano. I have a Brother and Sister—My Mother does not care for thought—and Father, too busy with his Briefs—to notice what we do—He buys me many Books—but begs me not to read them—because he fears they joggle the Mind. They are religious—except me—and address an Eclipse, every morning—whom they call their "Father." But I fear my story fatigues you—I would like to learn—Could you tell me how to grow—or is it unconveyed—like Melody—or Witchcraft?

You speak of Mr Whitman—I never read his Book[3]—but was told that he was disgraceful—

I read Miss Prescott's "Circumstance,"[4] but it followed me, in the Dark—so I avoided her—

Two Editors[5] of Journals came to my Father's House, this winter—and asked me for my Mind—and when I asked them "Why," they said I was penurious—and they, would use it for the World—

I could not weigh myself—Myself—

My size felt small—to me—I read your Chapters in the Atlantic—and experienced honor for you—I was sure you would not reject a confiding question—

Is this—Sir—what you asked me to tell you?

Your friend,
E—Dickinson.

To T. W. Higginson / 7 June 1862

Dear friend.

Your letter gave no Drunkenness, because I tasted Rum before—Domingo[6] comes but once—yet I have had few pleasures so deep as your opinion, and if I tried to thank you, my tears would block my tongue—

My dying Tutor told me that he would like to live till I had been a poet, but Death was much of Mob as I could master—then—And when far afterward—a sudden light on Orchards, or a new fashion in the wind troubled my attention—I felt a palsy, here—the Verses just relieve—

Your second letter surprised me, and for a moment, swung—I had not supposed it. Your first—gave no dishonor, because the True—are not ashamed—I thanked you for your justice—but could not drop the Bells whose jingling cooled my Tramp—Perhaps the Balm, seemed better, because you bled me, first.

1. John Keats (1795–1821), Robert Browning (1812–1889), Elizabeth Barrett Browning (1806–1861), John Ruskin (1819–1900), and Sir Thomas Browne (1605–1682), English writers. Revelations is the concluding book of the New Testament.
2. Probably Benjamin Franklin Newton (1821–1853), one-time student of law in her father's office, who died of consumption.
3. *Leaves of Grass.*

4. "Circumstance," by Harriet Prescott Spofford, was a story published in the *Atlantic Monthly* in May 1860.
5. Perhaps Samuel Bowles (1826–1878) and Josiah Gilbert Holland (1819–1881) of the Springfield *Daily Republican.* The paper had already published some of Dickinson's poetry, anonymously.
6. Rum from Santo Domingo, the Dominican Republic.

I smile when you suggest that I delay "to publish"—that being foreign to my thought, as Firmament to Fin—

If fame belonged to me, I could not escape her—if she did not, the longest day would pass me on the chase—and the approbation of my Dog, would forsake me—then—My Barefoot-Rank is better—

You think my gait "spasmodic"—I am in danger—Sir—

You think me "uncontrolled"—I have no Tribunal.

Would you have time to be the "friend" you should think I need? I have a little shape—it would not crowd your Desk—nor make much Racket as the Mouse, that dents your Galleries—

If I might bring you what I do—not so frequent to trouble you—and ask you if I told it clear—'twould be control, to me—

The Sailor cannot see the North—but knows the Needle can—

The "hand you stretch me in the Dark," I put mine in, and turn away—I have no Saxon, now[7]—

> As if I asked a common Alms,
> And in my wondering hand
> A Stranger pressed a Kingdom,
> And I, bewildered, stand—
> As if I asked the Orient
> Had it for me a Morn—
> And it should lift it's purple Dikes,
> And shatter me with Dawn!

But, will you be my Preceptor, Mr Higginson?

Your friend
E Dickinson—

To T. W. Higginson / July 1862

Could you believe me—without? I had no portrait, now, but am small, like the Wren, and my Hair is bold, like the Chestnut Bur—and my eyes, like the Sherry in the Glass, that the Guest leaves—Would this do just as well?

It often alarms Father—He says Death might occur, and he has Molds of all the rest—but has no Mold of me, but I noticed the Quick wore off those things, in a few days, and forestall the dishonor—You will think no caprice of me—

You said "Dark." I know the Butterfly—and the Lizard—and the Orchis[8]—

Are not those *your* Countrymen?

I am happy to be your scholar, and will deserve the kindness, I cannot repay.

If you truly consent, I recite, now—

Will you tell me my fault, frankly as to yourself, for I had rather wince, than die. Men do not call the surgeon, to commend—the Bone, but to set it, Sir, and fracture within, is more critical. And for this, Preceptor, I shall bring you—Obedience—the Blossom from my Garden, and every gratitude I know. Perhaps you smile at me. I could not stop for that—My Business is Circumference—An ignorance, not of Customs, but if caught with the Dawn—or

---

7. The phrase "I have no Saxon" means "Language fails me": see *Poems* (1955) 197, where in poem no. 276 she offers "English language" as her alternative for "Saxon" [Johnson's note].

8. A small purple flower.

the Sunset see me—Myself the only Kangaroo among the Beauty, Sir, if you please, it afflicts me, and I thought that instruction would take it away.

Because you have much business, beside the growth of me—you will appoint, yourself, how often I shall come—without your inconvenience. And if at any time—you regret you received me, or I prove a different fabric to that you supposed—you must banish me—

When I state myself, as the Representative of the Verse—it does not mean—me—but a supposed person. You are true, about the "perfection."

Today, makes Yesterday mean.

You spoke of Pippa Passes[9]—I never heard anybody speak of Pippa Passes—before.

You see my posture is benighted.

To thank you, baffles me. Are you perfectly powerful? Had I a pleasure you had not, I could delight to bring it.

Your Scholar

To T. W. Higginson   /   August 1862

Dear friend—

Are these[1] more orderly? I thank you for the Truth—

I had no Monarch in my life, and cannot rule myself, and when I try to organize—my little Force explodes—and leaves me bare and charred—

I think you called me "Wayward." Will you help me improve?

I suppose the pride that stops the Breath, in the Core of Woods, is not of Ourself—

You say I confess the little mistake, and omit the large—Because I can see Orthography—but the Ignorance out of sight—is my Preceptor's charge—

Of "shunning Men and Women"—they talk of Hallowed things, aloud—and embarrass my Dog—He and I dont object to them, if they'll exist their side. I think Carl[o] would please you—He is dumb, and brave—I think you would like the Chestnut Tree, I met in my walk. It hit my notice suddenly—and I thought the Skies were in Blossom—

Then there's a noiseless noise in the Orchard—that I let persons hear—You told me in one letter, you could not come to see me, "now," and I made no answer, not because I had none, but did not think myself the price that you should come so far—

I do not ask so large a pleasure, lest you might deny me—

You say "Beyond your knowledge." You would not jest with me, because I believe you—but Preceptor—you cannot mean it? All men say "What" to me, but I thought it a fashion—

When much in the Woods as a little Girl, I was told that the Snake would bite me, that I might pick a poisonous flower, or Goblins kidnap me, but I went along and met no one but Angels, who were far shyer of me, than I could be of them, so I hav'nt that confidence in fraud which many exercise.

I shall observe your precept—though I dont understand it, always.

I marked a line in One Verse—because I met it after I made it—and never consciously touch a paint, mixed by another person—

I do not let go it, because it is mine.

Have you the portrait of Mrs Browning? Persons sent me three—If you had none, will you have mine?

Your Scholar—

9. A poem by Robert Browning.
1. Poems enclosed with this letter were "Before I got my Eye put out" and "I cannot dance upon my Toes."

Rebecca Harding Davis
(1831–1910)

Remembered as one of the first American realists, Rebecca Harding Davis achieved her literary reputation with the first story she published, "Life in the Iron Mills." When she wrote the story at age 30, she was an unmarried woman living with her prosperous parents in Wheeling, Virginia (now part of West Virginia), where she had lived since early childhood. She had been sent to school in her birthplace, Washington, Pennsylvania, and had graduated as the valedictorian of her class at the Washington Female Seminary in 1848. She returned from school with an enthusiasm for writing, and—in addition to taking on the duties of a grown daughter in a busy household—she worked at her craft through her young adulthood.

"Life in the Iron Mills" was published in the *Atlantic Monthly*, where it received national acclaim. Drawing on the British tradition of the novels of social protest (or the "social problem novels") written by Elizabeth Gaskell, Charles Kingsley, Benjamin Disraeli, and Charles Dickens, Davis wrote the story of a doomed young factory worker whose untrained genius for sculpture draws brief but temporary attention from a representative group of middle-class men. Like Gaskell and Harriet Beecher Stowe, Davis uses a narrator that speaks from a distinctly middle-class perspective to an audience of her social peers, beseeching them to confront the reality of workers' impoverished lives. Unlike Gaskell and Stowe, however, Davis's narrator neither aims to work up readers' emotions nor endorses a Christian faith that might transcend the misery of this world. Instead, she proposes activist intervention in the problems of individual workers. Her minimally emotional tone and her depiction of "environmental determinism" in her characters' personalities and fates point toward the method and themes of such American naturalists of the next generation as Theo-

dore Dreiser, Stephen Crane, and Frank Norris.

On the strength of the public reception of her first story, Davis published a first novel, *Margaret Howth: A Story of To-Day* (1862). She traveled for the first time to Boston and met Louisa May and Bronson Alcott, Ralph Waldo Emerson, and Nathaniel Hawthorne. Among her enthusiastic readers was L. Clarke Davis, a lawyer's apprentice who wrote her a fan letter about "Life in the Iron Mills." They married shortly after they met in 1863. Later that year Davis took a "rest cure" for a mysterious illness (see the introduction to Charlotte Perkins Gilman for details about S. Weir Mitchell's now-infamous treatment of neurasthenic women). Davis's husband became the editor of the *Philadelphia Public Ledger* and an activist for abolition, but she herself did not become involved in activism against slavery or for women's rights, though themes of race- and gender-based oppression frequently come up in her writing. Happily married until her husband's death in 1904, Davis bore three children and continued her career as a professional author up to the time of her own death in 1910. Ironically, she wrote stories advocating that women turn their backs on their artistic potential to devote themselves to domestic duty. Her 1864 "The Wife's Story" concludes that "a woman has no better work in life than *** to make herself a visible Providence to her husband and child." Unlike the heroine of that story, she did not abandon authorship herself.

Davis wrote articles and columns for journals and newspapers, as well as novels. In 1867 she wrote *Waiting for the Verdict*, a study of the Civil War. Her other books include *David Gaunt* (1862); *Dallas Galbraith* (1868); *Pro Aris et Focis: A Plea for Our Altars and Hearths* (1870); *John Andross* (1874); *Kitty's Choice: A Story of Berrytown* (1874); *A Law Unto Herself* (1878); *Natasqua* (1887); *Silhouettes of American Life* (1892); *Kent*

Hampden (1892); *Doctor Warwick's Daughters* (1896); *Frances Waldeaux* (1897); and a memoir called *Bits of Gossip* (1904).

The standard biography of Davis combines her life story with that of her son, the journalist Richard Harding Davis; see Gerald Langford, *The Richard Harding Davis Years: A Biography of a Mother and Son* (1961). For a comprehensive treatment of Davis's literary output, see Sharon Harris, *Rebecca Harding Davis and American Realism* (1991).

Life in the Iron-Mills

"Is this the end?
O Life, as futile, then, as frail!
What hope of answer or redress?"[1]

A cloudy day: do you know what that is in a town of iron-works? The sky sank down before dawn, muddy, flat, immovable. The air is thick, clammy with the breath of crowded human beings. It stifles me. I open the window, and, looking out, can scarcely see through the rain the grocer's shop opposite, where a crowd of drunken Irishmen are puffing Lynchburg tobacco[2] in their pipes. I can detect the scent through all the foul smells ranging loose in the air.

The idiosyncrasy of this town is smoke. It rolls sullenly in slow folds from the great chimneys of the iron-foundries, and settles down in black, slimy pools on the muddy streets. Smoke on the wharves, smoke on the dingy boats, on the yellow river,—clinging in a coating of greasy soot to the house-front, the two faded poplars, the faces of the passers-by. The long train of mules, dragging masses of pig-iron[3] through the narrow street, have a foul vapor hanging to their reeking sides. Here, inside, is a little broken figure of an angel pointing upward from the mantel-shelf; but even its wings are covered with smoke, clotted and black. Smoke everywhere! A dirty canary chirps desolately in a cage beside me. Its dream of green fields and sunshine is a very old dream,—almost worn out, I think.

From the back-window I can see a narrow brick-yard sloping down to the river-side, strewed with rain-butts[4] and tubs. The river, dull and tawny-colored, (*la belle rivière!*)[5] drags itself sluggishly along, tired of the heavy weight of boats and coal-barges. What wonder? When I was a child, I used to fancy a look of weary, dumb appeal upon the face of the negro-like river slavishly bearing its burden day after day. Something of the same idle notion comes to me to-day, when from the street-window I look on the slow stream of human life creeping past, night and morning, to the great mills. Masses of men, with dull, besotted faces bent to the ground, sharpened here and there by pain or cunning; skin and muscle and flesh begrimed with smoke and ashes; stooping all night over boiling caldrons of metal, laired by day in dens of drunkenness and infamy; breathing from infancy to death an air saturated with fog and grease and soot, vileness for soul and body. What do you make of a case like that, amateur psychologist? You call it an altogether serious thing to be alive: to these men it is a drunken jest, a joke,—horrible to angels perhaps, to them commonplace enough. My fancy about the river was an idle one: it is no type of such a life. What if it be stagnant and slimy here? It knows that beyond there waits for it odorous sunlight,—quaint old gardens, dusky

---

1. Davis has added her own first line to a couplet from Alfred, Lord Tennyson's poem, *In Memoriam* 56:25–27.
2. Cheap tobacco.
3. Crude iron cast in blocks or "pigs."
4. Barrels that catch rainwater.
5. French for "the beautiful river."

with soft, green foliage of apple-trees, and flushing crimson with roses,—air, and fields, and mountains. The future of the Welsh puddler[6] passing just now is not so pleasant. To be stowed away, after his grimy work is done, in a hole in the muddy graveyard, and after that,—*not* air, nor green fields, nor curious roses.

Can you see how foggy the day is? As I stand here, idly tapping the window-pane, and looking out through the rain at the dirty back-yard and the coal-boats below, fragments of an old story float up before me,—a story of this old house into which I happened to come to-day. You may think it a tiresome story enough, as foggy as the day, sharpened by no sudden flashes of pain or pleasure.—I know: only the outline of a dull life, that long since, with thousands of dull lives like its own, was vainly lived and lost: thousands of them,— massed, vile, slimy lives, like those of the torpid lizards in yonder stagnant water-butt.—Lost? There is a curious point for you to settle, my friend, who study psychology in a lazy, *dilettante* way. Stop a moment. I am going to be honest. This is what I want you to do. I want you to hide your disgust, take no heed to your clean clothes, and come right down with me,—here, into the thickest of the fog and mud and foul effluvia. I want you to hear this story. There is a secret down here, in this nightmare fog, that has lain dumb for centuries: I want to make it a real thing to you. You, Egoist, or Pantheist, or Arminian,[7] busy in making straight paths for your feet on the hills, do not see it clearly,—this terrible question which men here have gone mad and died trying to answer. I dare not put this secret into words. I told you it was dumb. These men, going by with drunken faces and brains full of unawakened power, do not ask it of Society or of God. Their lives ask it; their deaths ask it. There is no reply. I will tell you plainly that I have a great hope; and I bring it to you to be tested. It is this: that this terrible dumb question is its own reply; that it is not the sentence of death we think it, but, from the very extremity of its darkness, the most solemn prophecy which the world has known of the Hope to come. I dare make my meaning no clearer, but will only tell my story. It will, perhaps, seem to you as foul and dark as this thick vapor about us, and as pregnant with death; but if your eyes are free as mine are to look deeper, no perfume-tinted dawn will be so fair with promise of the day that shall surely come.

My story is very simple,—only what I remember of the life of one of these men,—a furnace-tender in one of Kirby & John's rolling-mills,[8]—Hugh Wolfe. You know the mills? They took the great order for the Lower Virginia railroads there last winter; run usually with about a thousand men. I cannot tell why I choose the half-forgotten story of this Wolfe more than that of myriads of these furnace-hands. Perhaps because there is a secret underlying sympathy between that story and this day with its impure fog and thwarted sunshine,—or perhaps simply for the reason that this house is the one where the Wolfes lived. There were the father and son,—both hands, as I said, in one of Kirby & John's mills for making railroad-iron,—and Deborah, their cousin, a picker[9] in some of the cotton-mills. The house was rented then to half a dozen families. The Wolfes had two of the cellar-rooms. The old man, like many of the puddlers and feeders[1] of the mills, was Welsh,—had spent half of his life in the Cornish tin-mines.[2] You may pick the Welsh emigrants, Cornish miners, out of the throng passing the windows, any day. They are a trifle more filthy; their muscles are not so brawny; they stoop more. When they are drunk, they neither yell, nor shout, nor stagger, but

6. To "puddle" is to purify pig iron by agitation of a molten bath of the metal in an oxidizing atmosphere.
7. An egoist believes in the preeminence of the self; a pantheist sees God in the forces and workings of nature; an Arminian believes in individual free will as opposed to predestination.
8. Mills for processing metal.
9. A "picker" in a cotton mill separated and cleaned the unprocessed fibers of cotton; however, Deborah is later represented as "standing twelve hours at the spools," suggesting another meaning of "to pick" in textile mills, namely, "throwing the shuttle across the loom."
1. Workers who keep molten metal flowing into casts.
2. Mines in Cornwall, located in western England.

skulk along like beaten hounds. A pure, unmixed blood, I fancy: shows itself in the slight angular bodies and sharply-cut facial lines. It is nearly thirty years since the Wolfes lived here. Their lives were like those of their class: incessant labor, sleeping in kennel-like rooms, eating rank pork and molasses, drinking—God and the distillers only know what; with an occasional night in jail, to atone for some drunken excess. Is that all of their lives?—of the portion given to them and these their duplicates swarming the streets to-day?—nothing beneath?—all? So many a political reformer will tell you,—and many a private reformer, too, who has gone among them with a heart tender with Christ's charity, and come out outraged, hardened.

One rainy night, about eleven o'clock, a crowd of half-clothed women stopped outside of the cellar-door. They were going home from the cotton-mill.

"Good-night, Deb," said one, a mulatto,[3] steadying herself against the gas-post. She needed the post to steady her. So did more than one of them.

"Dah's a ball to Miss Potts' to-night. Ye'd best come."

"Inteet, Deb, if hur'll[4] come, hur'll hef fun," said a shrill Welsh voice in the crowd.

Two or three dirty hands were thrust out to catch the gown of the woman, who was groping for the latch of the door.

"No."

"No? Where's Kit Small, then?"

"Begorra! on the spools.[5] Alleys behint, though we helped her, we dud. An wid ye! Let Deb alone! It's ondacent frettin' a quite body. Be the powers, an' we'll have a night of it! there'll be lashin's[6] o' drink,—the Vargent[7] be blessed and praised for 't!"

They went on, the mulatto inclining for a moment to show fight, and drag the woman Wolfe off with them; but, being pacified, she staggered away.

Deborah groped her way into the cellar, and, after considerable stumbling, kindled a match, and lighted a tallow dip, that sent a yellow glimmer over the room. It was low, damp,—the earthen floor covered with a green, slimy moss,—a fetid air smothering the breath. Old Wolfe lay asleep on a heap of straw, wrapped in a torn horse-blanket. He was a pale, meek little man, with a white face and red rabbit-eyes. The woman Deborah was like him; only her face was even more ghastly, her lips bluer, her eyes more watery. She wore a faded cotton gown and a slouching bonnet. When she walked, one could see that she was deformed, almost a hunchback. She trod softly, so as not to waken him, and went through into the room beyond. There she found by the half-extinguished fire an iron saucepan filled with cold boiled potatoes, which she put upon a broken chair with a pint-cup of ale. Placing the old candlestick beside this dainty repast, she untied her bonnet, which hung limp and wet over her face, and prepared to eat her supper. It was the first food that had touched her lips since morning. There was enough of it, however: there is not always. She was hungry,—one could see that easily enough,—and not drunk, as most of her companions would have been found at this hour. She did not drink, this woman,—her face told that, too,—nothing stronger than ale. Perhaps the weak, flaccid wretch had some stimulant in her pale life to keep her up,—some love or hope, it might be, or urgent need. When that stimulant was gone, she would take to whiskey. Man cannot live by work alone. While she was skinning the potatoes, and munching them, a noise behind her made her stop.

"Janey!" she called, lifting the candle and peering into the darkness. "Janey, are you there?"

A heap of ragged coats was heaved up, and the face of a young girl emerged, staring sleepily at the woman.

"Deborah," she said, at last, "I'm here the night."

"Yes, child. Hur's welcome," she said, quietly eating on.

---

3. A person of partly Caucasian, partly African ancestry.
4. The dialect substitutes "hur" for "you."
5. Working in the cotton mill.
6. Lavish quantities.
7. The Virgin Mary.

The girl's face was haggard and sickly; her eyes were heavy with sleep and hunger: real Milesian[8] eyes they were, dark, delicate blue, glooming out from black shadows with a pitiful fright.

"I was alone," she said, timidly.

"Where's the father?" asked Deborah, holding out a potato, which the girl greedily seized.

"He's beyant,—wid Haley,—in the stone house." (Did you ever hear the word *jail* from an Irish mouth?) "I came here. Hugh told me never to stay me-lone."

"Hugh?"

"Yes."

A vexed frown crossed her face. The girl saw it, and added quickly,—

"I have not seen Hugh the day, Deb. The old man says his watch[9] lasts till the mornin'."

The woman sprang up, and hastily began to arrange some bread and flitch[1] in a tin pail, and to pour her own measure of ale into a bottle. Tying on her bonnet, she blew out the candle.

"Lay ye down, Janey dear," she said, gently, covering her with the old rags. "Hur can eat the potatoes, if hur's hungry."

"Where are ye goin', Deb? The rain's sharp."

"To the mill, with Hugh's supper."

"Let him bide till th' morn. Sit ye down."

"No, no,"—sharply pushing her off. "The boy'll starve."

She hurried from the cellar, while the child wearily coiled herself up for sleep. The rain was falling heavily, as the woman, pail in hand, emerged from the mouth of the alley, and turned down the narrow street, that stretched out, long and black, miles before her. Here and there a flicker of gas lighted an uncertain space of muddy footwalk and gutter; the long rows of houses, except an occasional lager-bier[2] shop, were closed; now and then she met a band of mill-hands skulking to or from their work.

Not many even of the inhabitants of a manufacturing town know the vast machinery of system by which the bodies of workmen are governed, that goes on unceasingly from year to year. The hands of each mill are divided into watches that relieve each other as regularly as the sentinels of an army. By night and day the work goes on, the unsleeping engines groan and shriek, the fiery pools of metal boil and surge. Only for a day in the week, in half-courtesy to public censure, the fires are partially veiled; but as soon as the clock strikes midnight, the great furnaces break forth with renewed fury, the clamor begins with fresh, breathless vigor, the engines sob and shriek like "gods in pain."

As Deborah hurried down through the heavy rain, the noise of these thousand engines sounded through the sleep and shadow of the city like far-off thunder. The mill to which she was going lay on the river, a mile below the city-limits. It was far, and she was weak, aching from standing twelve hours at the spools. Yet it was her almost nightly walk to take this man his supper, though at every square she sat down to rest, and she knew she should receive small word of thanks.

Perhaps, if she had possessed an artist's eye, the picturesque oddity of the scene might have made her step stagger less, and the path seem shorter; but to her the mills were only "summat deilish[3] to look at by night."

The road leading to the mills had been quarried from the solid rock, which rose abrupt and bare on one side of the cinder-covered road, while the river, sluggish and black, crept past on the other. The mills for rolling iron are simply immense tent-like roofs, covering acres of ground, open on every side. Beneath these roofs Deborah looked in on a city of fires, that burned hot and fiercely in the night. Fire in every horrible form: pits of flame waving in the

8. Native to Ireland.
9. Shift at the factory.
1. Salted and cured side of bacon.

2. German ale.
3. "Something devilish."

wind; liquid metal-flames writhing in tortuous streams through the sand; wide caldrons filled with boiling fire, over which bent ghastly wretches stirring the strange brewing; and through all, crowds of half-clad men, looking like revengeful ghosts in the red light, hurried, throwing masses of glittering fire. It was like a street in Hell. Even Deborah muttered, as she crept through, " 'T looks like t' Devil's place!" It did,—in more ways than one.

She found the man she was looking for, at last, heaping coal on a furnace. He had not time to eat his supper; so she went behind the furnace, and waited. Only a few men were with him, and they noticed her only by a "Hyur comes t' hunchback, Wolfe."

Deborah was stupid with sleep; her back pained her sharply; and her teeth chattered with cold, with the rain that soaked her clothes and dripped from her at every step. She stood, however, patiently holding the pail, and waiting.

"Hout, woman! ye look like a drowned cat. Come near to the fire,"—said one of the men, approaching to scrape away the ashes.

She shook her head. Wolfe had forgotten her. He turned, hearing the man, and came closer.

"I did no' think; gi' me my supper, woman."

She watched him eat with a painful eagerness. With a woman's quick instinct, she saw that he was not hungry,—was eating to please her. Her pale, watery eyes began to gather a strange light.

"Is't good, Hugh? T'ale was a bit sour, I feared."

"No, good enough." He hesitated a moment. "Ye're tired, poor lass! Bide here till I go. Lay down there on that heap of ash, and go to sleep."

He threw her an old coat for a pillow, and turned to his work. The heap was the refuse of the burnt iron, and was not a hard bed; the half-smothered warmth, too, penetrated her limbs, dulling their pain and cold shiver.

Miserable enough she looked, lying there on the ashes like a limp, dirty rag,—yet not an unfitting figure to crown the scene of hopeless discomfort and veiled crime: more fitting, if one looked deeper into the heart of things,—at her thwarted woman's form, her colorless life, her waking stupor that smothered pain and hunger,—even more fit to be a type of her class. Deeper yet if one could look, was there nothing worth reading in this wet, faded thing, half-covered with ashes? no story of a soul filled with groping passionate love, heroic unselfishness, fierce jealousy? of years of weary trying to please the one human being whom she loved, to gain one look of real heart-kindness from him? If anything like this were hidden beneath the pale, bleared eyes, and dull, washed-out-looking face, no one had ever taken the trouble to read its faint signs: not the half-clothed furnace-tender, Wolfe, certainly. Yet he was kind to her: it was his nature to be kind, even to the very rats that swarmed in the cellar; kind to her in just the same way. She knew that. And it might be that very knowledge had given to her face its apathy and vacancy more than her low, torpid life. One sees that dead, vacant look steal sometimes over the rarest, finest of women's faces,—in the very midst, it may be, of their warmest summer's day; and then one can guess at the secret of intolerable solitude that lies hid beneath the delicate laces and brilliant smile. There was no warmth, no brilliancy, no summer for this woman; so the stupor and vacancy had time to gnaw into her face perpetually. She was young, too, though no one guessed it; so the gnawing was the fiercer.

She lay quiet in the dark corner, listening, through the monotonous din and uncertain glare of the works, to the dull plash of the rain in the far distance,—shrinking back whenever the man Wolfe happened to look towards her. She knew, in spite of all his kindness, that there was that in her face and form which made him loathe the sight of her. She felt by instinct, although she could not comprehend it, the finer nature of the man, which made him among his fellow-workmen something unique, set apart. She knew, that, down under all the vileness and coarseness of his life, there was a groping passion for whatever was beautiful and pure,—that his soul sickened with disgust at her deformity, even when his words were kindest. Through this dull consciousness, which never left her, came, like a sting, the recollection of the dark blue eyes and lithe figure of the little Irish girl she had left in the cellar. The recollection struck through even her stupid intellect with a vivid glow of beauty and of grace. Little Janey, timid, helpless, clinging to Hugh as her only friend: that was the sharp thought, the bitter thought, that drove into the glazed eyes a fierce light of pain. You laugh at it? Are pain and jealousy less savage realities down here in this place I am taking you to than in your own house or your own heart,—your heart, which they clutch at sometimes? The note is the same, I fancy, be the octave high or low.

If you could go into this mill where Deborah lay, and drag out from the hearts of these men the terrible tragedy of their lives, taking it as a symptom of the disease of their class, no ghost Horror would terrify you more. A reality of soul-starvation, of living death, that meets you every day under the besotted faces on the street,—I can paint nothing of this, only give you the outside outlines of a night, a crisis in the life of one man: whatever muddy depth of soul-history lies beneath you can read according to the eyes God has given you.

Wolfe, while Deborah watched him as a spaniel its master, bent over the furnace with his iron pole, unconscious of her scrutiny, only stopping to receive orders. Physically, Nature had promised the man but little. He had already lost the strength and instinct vigor of a man, his muscles were thin, his nerves weak, his face (a meek, woman's face) haggard, yellow with consumption.[4] In the mill he was known as one of the girl-men: "Molly Wolfe" was his *sobriquet.*[5] He was never seen in the cockpit,[6] did not own a terrier, drank but seldom; when he did, desperately. He fought sometimes, but was always thrashed, pommelled to a jelly. The man was game enough, when his blood was up: but he was no favorite in the mill; he had the taint of school-learning on him,—not to a dangerous extent, only a quarter or so in the free-school in fact, but enough to ruin him as a good hand in a fight.

For other reasons, too, he was not popular. Not one of themselves, they felt that, though outwardly as filthy and ash-covered; silent, with foreign thoughts and longings breaking out through his quietness in innumerable curious ways: this one, for instance. In the neighboring furnace-buildings lay great heaps of the refuse from the ore after the pig-metal is run. *Korl* we call it here: a light, porous substance, of a delicate, waxen, flesh-colored tinge. Out of the blocks of this korl, Wolfe, in his off-hours from the furnace, had a habit of chipping and moulding figures,—hideous, fantastic enough, but sometimes strangely beautiful: even the mill-men saw that, while they jeered at him. It was a curious fancy in the man, almost a passion. The few hours for rest he spent hewing and hacking with his blunt knife, never speaking, until his watch came again,—working at one figure for months, and, when it was finished, breaking it to pieces perhaps, in a fit of disappointment. A morbid, gloomy man, untaught, unled, left to feed his soul in grossness and crime, and hard, grinding labor.

I want you to come down and look at this Wolfe, standing there among the lowest of his kind, and see him just as he is, that you may judge him justly when you hear the story of this night. I want you to look back, as he does every day, at his birth in vice, his starved infancy; to remember the heavy years he has groped through as boy and man,—the slow, heavy years of constant, hot work. So long ago he began, that he thinks sometimes he has worked there for ages. There is no hope that it will ever end. Think that God put into this man's soul a fierce thirst for beauty,—to know it, to create it; to *be*—something, he knows not what,—other than he is. There are moments when a passing cloud, the sun glinting on the purple thistles, a kindly smile, a child's face, will rouse him to a passion of pain,—when his nature starts up with a mad cry of rage against God, man, whoever it is that has forced this vile, slimy life upon him. With all this groping, this mad desire, a great blind intellect stumbling through wrong, a loving poet's heart, the man was by habit only a coarse, vulgar laborer, familiar with sights and words you would blush to name. Be just: when I tell you about this night, see him

4. Nineteenth-century term for tuberculosis.
5. Nickname.

6. Pit for holding cockfights, a popular form of gambling in which roosters battled to the death.

as he is. Be just,—not like man's law, which seizes on one isolated fact, but like God's judging angel, whose clear, sad eye saw all the countless cankering days of this man's life, all the countless nights, when, sick with starving, his soul fainted in him, before it judged him for this night, the saddest of all.

I called this night the crisis of his life. If it was, it stole on him unawares. These great turning-days of life cast no shadow before, slip by unconsciously. Only a trifle, a little turn of the rudder, and the ship goes to heaven or hell.

Wolfe, while Deborah watched him, dug into the furnace of melting iron with his pole, dully thinking only how many rails the lump would yield. It was late,—nearly Sunday morning; another hour, and the heavy work would be done,—only the furnaces to replenish and cover for the next day. The workmen were growing more noisy, shouting, as they had to do, to be heard over the deep clamor of the mills. Suddenly they grew less boisterous,—at the far end, entirely silent. Something unusual had happened. After a moment, the silence came nearer; the men stopped their jeers and drunken choruses. Deborah, stupidly lifting up her head, saw the cause of the quiet. A group of five or six men were slowly approaching, stopping to examine each furnace as they came. Visitors often came to see the mills after night: except by growing less noisy, the men took no notice of them. The furnace where Wolfe worked was near the bounds of the works; they halted there hot and tired: a walk over one of these great foundries is no trifling task. The woman, drawing out of sight, turned over to sleep. Wolfe, seeing them stop, suddenly roused from his indifferent stupor, and watched them keenly. He knew some of them: the overseer, Clarke,—a son of Kirby, one of the mill-owners,—and a Doctor May, one of the town-physicians. The other two were strangers. Wolfe came closer. He seized eagerly every chance that brought him into contact with this mysterious class that shone down on him perpetually with the glamour of another order of being. What made the difference between them? That was the mystery of his life. He had a vague notion that perhaps to-night he could find it out. One of the strangers sat down on a pile of bricks, and beckoned young Kirby to his side.

"This *is* hot, with a vengeance. A match, please?"—lighting his cigar. "But the walk is worth the trouble. If it were not that you must have heard it so often, Kirby, I would tell you that your works look like Dante's Inferno."[7]

Kirby laughed.

"Yes. Yonder is Farinata himself in the burning tomb,"[8]—pointing to some figure in the shimmering shadows.

"Judging from some of the faces of your men," said the other, "they bid fair to try the reality of Dante's vision, some day."

Young Kirby looked curiously around, as if seeing the faces of his hands for the first time.

"They're bad enough, that's true. A desperate set, I fancy. Eh, Clarke?"

The overseer did not hear him. He was talking of net profits just then,—giving, in fact, a schedule of the annual business of the firm to a sharp peering little Yankee, who jotted down notes on a paper laid on the crown of his hat: a reporter for one of the city-papers, getting up a series of reviews of the leading manufactories. The other gentlemen had accompanied them merely for amusement. They were silent until the notes were finished, drying their feet at the furnaces, and sheltering their faces from the intolerable heat. At last the overseer concluded with—

"I believe that is a pretty fair estimate, Captain."

"Here, some of you men!" said Kirby, "bring up those boards. We may as well sit down, gentlemen, until the rain is over. It cannot last much longer at this rate."

"Pig-metal,"—mumbled the reporter,—"um!—coal facilities,—um!—hands employed,

7. That is, like the depiction of hell in the *Divine Comedy* by Dante Alighieri (1265–1321).

8. In canto 10 of Dante's *Inferno*, Farinata is a heretic who burns in hell.

twelve hundred,—bitumen,[9]—um!—all right, I believe, Mr. Clarke;—sinking-fund,—what did you say was your sinking-fund?"[1]

"Twelve hundred hands?" said the stranger, the young man who had first spoken. "Do you control their votes, Kirby?"

"Control? No." The young man smiled complacently. "But my father brought seven hundred votes to the polls for his candidate last November. No force-work, you understand,—only a speech or two, a hint to form themselves into a society, and a bit of red and blue bunting to make them a flag. The Invincible Roughs,—I believe that is their name. I forget the motto: 'Our country's hope,' I think."

There was a laugh. The young man talking to Kirby sat with an amused light in his cool gray eye, surveying critically the half-clothed figures of the puddlers, and the slow swing of their brawny muscles. He was a stranger in the city,—spending a couple of months in the borders of a Slave State, to study the institutions of the South,[2]—a brother-in-law of Kirby's—Mitchell. He was an amateur gymnast,—hence his anatomical eye; a patron, in a *blasé* way, of the prize-ring; a man who sucked the essence out of a science or philosophy in an indifferent, gentlemanly way; who took Kant, Novalis, Humboldt,[3] for what they were worth in his own scales; accepting all, despising nothing, in heaven, earth, or hell, but one-idead men; with a temper yielding and brilliant as summer water, until his Self was touched, when it was ice, though brilliant still. Such men are not rare in the States.

As he knocked the ashes from his cigar, Wolfe caught with a quick pleasure the contour of the white hand, the blood-glow of a red ring he wore. His voice, too, and that of Kirby's, touched him like music,—low, even, with chording cadences. About this man Mitchell hung the impalpable atmosphere belonging to the thoroughbred gentleman. Wolfe, scraping away the ashes beside him, was conscious of it, did obeisance to it with his artist sense, unconscious that he did so.

The rain did not cease. Clarke and the reporter left the mills; the others, comfortably seated near the furnace, lingered, smoking and talking in a desultory way. Greek would not have been more unintelligible to the furnace-tenders, whose presence they soon forgot entirely. Kirby drew out a newspaper from his pocket and read aloud some article, which they discussed eagerly. At every sentence, Wolfe listened more and more like a dumb, hopeless animal, with a duller, more stolid look creeping over his face, glancing now and then at Mitchell, marking acutely every smallest sign of refinement, then back to himself, seeing as in a mirror his filthy body, his more stained soul.

Never! He had no words for such a thought, but he knew now, in all the sharpness of the bitter certainty, that between them there was a great gulf never to be passed.[4] Never!

The bells of the mills rang for midnight. Sunday morning had dawned. Whatever hidden message lay in the tolling bells floated past these men unknown. Yet it was there. Veiled in the solemn music ushering the risen saviour was a key-note to solve the darkest secrets of a world gone wrong,—even this social riddle which the brain of the grimy puddler grappled with madly to-night.

The men began to withdraw the metal from the caldrons. The mills were deserted on Sundays, except by the hands who fed the fires, and those who had no lodgings and slept usually on the ash-heaps. The three strangers sat still during the next hour, watching the men cover the furnaces, laughing now and then at some jest of Kirby's.

"Do you know," said Mitchell, "I like this view of the works better than when the glare

<hr>

9. A substance used in making asphalt and tar.
1. Fund accumulated to pay off a public or corporate debt.
2. Namely, slavery.
3. Influential German writers of the eighteenth

and nineteenth centuries; the first two are philosophers, the third a naturalist, explorer, and statesman.

4. Compare Luke 16:26.

was fiercest? These heavy shadows and the amphitheatre of smothered fires are ghostly, unreal. One could fancy these red smouldering lights to be the half-shut eyes of wild beasts, and the spectral figures their victims in the den."

Kirby laughed. "You are fanciful. Come, let us get out of the den. The spectral figures, as you call them, are a little too real for me to fancy a close proximity in the darkness,— unarmed, too."

The others rose, buttoning their over-coats, and lighting cigars.

"Raining, still," said Doctor May, "and hard. Where did we leave the coach, Mitchell?"

"At the other side of the works.—Kirby, what's that?"

Mitchell started back, half-frightened, as, suddenly turning a corner, the white figure of a woman faced him in the darkness,—a woman, white, of giant proportions, crouching on the ground, her arms flung out in some wild gesture of warning.

"Stop! Make that fire burn there!" cried Kirby, stopping short.

The flame burst out, flashing the gaunt figure into bold relief.

Mitchell drew a long breath.

"I thought it was alive," he said, going up curiously.

The others followed.

"Not marble, eh?" asked Kirby, touching it.

One of the lower overseers stopped.

"Korl, Sir."

"Who did it?"

"Can't say. Some of the hands; chipped it out in off-hours."

"Chipped to some purpose, I should say. What a flesh-tint the stuff has! Do you see, Mitchell?"

"I see."

He had stepped aside where the light fell boldest on the figure, looking at it in silence. There was not one line of beauty or grace in it: a nude woman's form, muscular, grown coarse with labor, the powerful limbs instinct with some one poignant longing. One idea: there it was in the tense, rigid muscles, the clutching hands, the wild, eager face, like that of a starving wolf's. Kirby and Doctor May walked around it, critical, curious. Mitchell stood aloof, silent. The figure touched him strangely.

"Not badly done," said Doctor May. "Where did the fellow learn that sweep of the muscles in the arm and hand? Look at them! They are groping,—do you see?—clutching: the peculiar action of a man dying of thirst."

"They have ample facilities for studying anatomy," sneered Kirby, glancing at the half-naked figures.

"Look," continued the Doctor, "at this bony wrist, and the strained sinews of the instep! A working-woman,—the very type of her class."

"God forbid!" muttered Mitchell.

"Why?" demanded May. "What does the fellow intend by the figure? I cannot catch the meaning."

"Ask him," said the other, dryly. "There he stands,"—pointing to Wolfe, who stood with a group of men, leaning on his ash-rake.

The Doctor beckoned him with the affable smile which kind-hearted men put on, when talking with these people.

"Mr. Mitchell has picked you out as the man who did this,—I'm sure I don't know why. But what did you mean by it?"

"She be hungry."

Wolfe's eyes answered Mitchell, not the Doctor.

"Oh-h! But what a mistake you have made, my fine fellow! You have given no sign of starvation to the body. It is strong,—terribly strong. It has the mad, half-despairing gesture of drowning."

Wolfe stammered, glanced appealingly at Mitchell, who saw the soul of the thing, he knew. But the cool, probing eyes were turned on himself now,—mocking, cruel, relentless.

"Not hungry for meat," the furnace-tender said at last.

"What then? Whiskey?" jeered Kirby, with a coarse laugh.

Wolfe was silent a moment, thinking.

"I dunno," he said, with a bewildered look. "It mebbe. Summat to make her live, I think,—like you. Whiskey ull do it, in a way."

The young man laughed again. Mitchell flashed a look of disgust somewhere,—not at Wolfe.

"May," he broke out impatiently, "are you blind? Look at that woman's face! It asks questions of God, and says, 'I have a right to know.' Good God, how hungry it is!"

They looked a moment; then May turned to the mill-owner:—

"Have you many such hands as this? What are you going to do with them? Keep them at puddling iron?"

Kirby shrugged his shoulders. Mitchell's look had irritated him.

"Ce n'est pas mon affaire.[5] I have no fancy for nursing infant geniuses. I suppose there are some stray gleams of mind and soul among these wretches. The Lord will take care of his own; or else they can work out their own salvation. I have heard you call our American system a ladder which any man can scale. Do you doubt it? Or perhaps you want to banish all social ladders, and put us all on a flat table-land,—eh, May?"

The Doctor looked vexed, puzzled. Some terrible problem lay hid in this woman's face, and troubled these men. Kirby waited for an answer, and, receiving none, went on, warming with his subject.

"I tell you, there's something wrong that no talk of *'Liberté'* or *'Égalité'* will do away.[6] If I had the making of men, these men who do the lowest part of the world's work should be machines,—nothing more,—hands. It would be kindness. God help them! What are taste, reason, to creatures who must live such lives as that?" He pointed to Deborah, sleeping on the ash-heap. "So many nerves to sting them to pain. What if God had put your brain, with all its agony of touch, into your fingers, and bid you work and strike with that?"

"You think you could govern the world better?" laughed the Doctor.

"I do not think at all."

"That is true philosophy. Drift with the stream, because you cannot dive deep enough to find bottom, eh?"

"Exactly," rejoined Kirby. "I do not think. I wash my hands of all social problems,—slavery, caste, white or black. My duty to my operatives[7] has a narrow limit,—the pay-hour on Saturday night. Outside of that, if they cut korl, or cut each other's throats, (the more popular amusement of the two,) I am not responsible."

The Doctor sighed,—a good honest sigh, from the depths of his stomach.

"God help us! Who is responsible?"

"Not I, I tell you," said Kirby, testily. "What has the man who pays them money to do with their souls' concerns, more than the grocer or butcher who takes it?"

"And yet," said Mitchell's cynical voice, "look at her! How hungry she is!"

Kirby tapped his boot with his cane. No one spoke. Only the dumb face of the rough image looking into their faces with the awful question, "What shall we do to be saved?"[8] Only Wolfe's face, with its heavy weight of brain, its weak, uncertain mouth, its desperate eyes, out of which looked the soul of his class,—only Wolfe's face turned towards Kirby's. Mitchell laughed,—a cool, musical laugh.

---

5. "It's not my business."

6. "Liberty, Equality, Brotherhood" was a motto of the French Revolution.

7. Workers.

8. In Acts 16:30, a prisonkeeper asks this question after God opens his prison with an earthquake, releasing the Apostles.

"Money has spoken!" he said, seating himself lightly on a stone with the air of an amused spectator at a play. "Are you answered?"—turning to Wolfe his clear, magnetic face.

Bright and deep and cold as Arctic air, the soul of the man lay tranquil beneath. He looked at the furnace-tender as he had looked at a rare mosaic in the morning; only the man was the more amusing study of the two.

"Are you answered? Why, May, look at him! *De profundis clamavi.*⁹ Or, to quote in English, 'Hungry and thirsty, his soul faints in him.' And so Money sends back its answer into the depths through you, Kirby! Very clear the answer, too!—I think I remember reading the same words somewhere:—washing your hands in Eau de Cologne, and saying, 'I am innocent of the blood of this man. See ye to it!' "¹

Kirby flushed angrily.

"You quote Scripture freely."

"Do I not quote correctly? I think I remember another line, which may amend my meaning: 'Inasmuch as ye did it unto one of the least of these, ye did it unto me.'² Deist?³ Bless you, man, I was raised on the milk of the Word. Now, Doctor, the pocket of the world having uttered its voice, what has the heart to say? You are a philanthropist, in a small way,—*n'est-ce pas?*⁴ Here, boy, this gentleman can show you how to cut korl better,—or your destiny. Go on, May!"

"I think a mocking devil possesses you to-night," rejoined the Doctor, seriously.

He went to Wolfe and put his hand kindly on his arm. Something of a vague idea possessed the Doctor's brain that much good was to be done here by a friendly word or two: a latent genius to be warmed into life by a waited-for sun-beam. Here it was: he had brought it. So he went on complacently:—

"Do you know, boy, you have it in you to be a great sculptor, a great man?—do you understand?" (talking down to the capacity of his hearer: it is a way people have with children, and men like Wolfe,)—"to live a better, stronger life than I, or Mr. Kirby here? A man may make himself anything he chooses. God has given you stronger powers than many men,—me, for instance."

May stopped, heated, glowing with his own magnanimity. And it was magnanimous. The puddler had drunk in every word, looking through the Doctor's flurry, and generous heat, and self-approval, into his will, with those slow, absorbing eyes of his.

"Make yourself what you will. It is your right."

"I know," quietly. "Will you help me?"

Mitchell laughed again. The Doctor turned now, in a passion,—

"You know, Mitchell, I have not the means. You know, if I had, it is in my heart to take this boy and educate him for"—

"The glory of God, and the glory of John May."

May did not speak for a moment; then, controlled, he said,—

"Why should one be raised, when myriads are left?—I have not the money, boy," to Wolfe, shortly.

"Money?" He said it over slowly, as one repeats the guessed answer to a riddle, doubtfully. "That is it? Money?"

"Yes, money,—that is it," said Mitchell, rising, and drawing his furred coat about him. "You've found the cure for all the world's diseases.—Come, May, find your good-humor, and come home. This damp wind chills my very bones. Come and preach your Saint-

---

9. Latin for "Out of the depths have I cried unto thee"; Psalms 130:1.

1. Pontius Pilate speaks these words to disown responsibility for the crucifixion of Jesus, which he does not prevent, in Matthew 27:24.

2. Matthew 25:40, quoting Jesus.

3. A "deist" cites the evidence of reason in believing God created the universe, then abandoned it, assumed no control over nature, and gave no supernatural revelation.

4. "Isn't that so?"

Simonian[5] doctrines to-morrow to Kirby's hands. Let them have a clear idea of the rights of the soul, and I'll venture next week they'll strike for higher wages. That will be the end of it."

"Will you send the coach-driver to this side of the mills?" asked Kirby, turning to Wolfe.

He spoke kindly: it was his habit to do so. Deborah, seeing the puddler go, crept after him. The three men waited outside. Doctor May walked up and down, chafed. Suddenly he stopped.

"Go back, Mitchell! You say the pocket and the heart of the world speak without meaning to these people. What has its head to say? Taste, culture, refinement? Go!"

Mitchell was leaning against a brick wall. He turned his head indolently, and looked into the mills. There hung about the place a thick, unclean odor. The slightest motion of his hand marked that he perceived it, and his insufferable disgust. That was all. May said nothing, only quickened his angry tramp.

"Besides," added Mitchell, giving a corollary to his answer, "it would be of no use. I am not one of them."

"You do not mean"—said May, facing him.

"Yes, I mean just that. Reform is born of need, not pity. No vital movement of the people's has worked down, for good or evil; fermented, instead, carried up the heaving, cloggy mass. Think back through history, and you will know it. What will this lowest deep—thieves, Magdalens,[6] negroes—do with the light filtered through ponderous Church creeds, Baconian theories, Goethe schemes?[7] Some day, out of their bitter need will be thrown up their own light-bringer,—their Jean Paul, their Cromwell, their Messiah."[8]

"Bah!" was the Doctor's inward criticism. However, in practice, he adopted the theory; for, when, night and morning, afterwards, he prayed that power might be given these degraded souls to rise, he glowed at heart, recognizing an accomplished duty.

Wolfe and the woman had stood in the shadow of the works as the coach drove off. The Doctor had held out his hand in a frank, generous way, telling him to "take care of himself, and to remember it was his right to rise." Mitchell had simply touched his hat, as to an equal, with a quiet look of thorough recognition. Kirby had thrown Deborah some money, which she found, and clutched eagerly enough. They were gone now, all of them. The man sat down on the cinder-road, looking up into the murky sky.

" 'T be late, Hugh. Wunnot hur come?"

He shook his head doggedly, and the woman crouched out of his sight against the wall. Do you remember rare moments when a sudden light flashed over yourself, your world, God? when you stood on a mountain-peak, seeing your life as it might have been, as it is? one quick instant, when custom lost its force and every-day usage? when your friend, wife, brother, stood in a new light? your soul was bared, and the grave,—a foretaste of the nakedness of the Judgment-Day? So it came before him, his life, that night. The slow tides of pain he had borne gathered themselves up and surged against his soul. His squalid daily life, the brutal coarseness eating into his brain, as the ashes into his skin: before, these things had been a dull aching into his consciousness; to-night, they were reality. He gripped the filthy red shirt that clung, stiff with soot, about him, and tore it savagely from his arm. The flesh beneath was muddy with grease and ashes,—and the heart beneath that! And the soul? God knows.

Then flashed before his vivid poetic sense the man who had left him,—the pure face, the delicate, sinewy limbs, in harmony with all he knew of beauty or truth. In his cloudy fancy he had pictured a Something like this. He had found it in this Mitchell, even when he idly scoffed at his pain: a Man all-knowing, all-seeing, crowned by Nature, reigning,—the keen

---

5. Saint-Simon was an eighteenth-century French socialist.
6. Prostitutes.
7. Francis Bacon was a sixteenth-century English philosopher; Johann Wolfgang von Goethe was

a German Romantic poet.
8. Jean-Paul Richter (1763–1825) was a German novelist; Oliver Cromwell (1599–1658) was the "commoner" who led a successful revolution against the monarchy of England.

glance of his eye falling like a sceptre on other men. And yet his instinct taught him that he too—He! He looked at himself with sudden loathing, sick, wrung his hands with a cry, and then was silent. With all the phantoms of his heated, ignorant fancy, Wolfe had not been vague in his ambitions. They were practical, slowly built up before him out of his knowledge of what he could do. Through years he had day by day made this hope a real thing to himself,—a clear, projected figure of himself, as he might become.

Able to speak, to know what was best, to raise these men and women working at his side up with him: sometimes he forgot this defined hope in the frantic anguish to escape,—only to escape,—out of the wet, the pain, the ashes, somewhere, anywhere,—only for one moment of free air on a hill-side, to lie down and let his sick soul throb itself out in the sunshine. But to-night he panted for life. The savage strength of his nature was roused; his cry was fierce to God for justice.

"Look at me!" he said to Deborah, with a low, bitter laugh, striking his puny chest savagely. "What am I worth, Deb? Is it my fault that I am no better? My fault? My fault?"

He stopped, stung with a sudden remorse, seeing her hunchback shape writhing with sobs. For Deborah was crying thankless tears, according to the fashion of women.

"God forgi' me, woman! Things go harder wi' you nor me. It's a worse share."

He got up and helped her to rise; and they went doggedly down the muddy street, side by side.

"It's all wrong," he muttered, slowly,—"all wrong! I dunnot understan'. But it'll end some day."

"Come home, Hugh!" she said, coaxingly; for he had stopped, looking around bewildered.

"Home,—and back to the mill!" He went on saying this over to himself, as if he would mutter down every pain in this dull despair.

She followed him through the fog, her blue lips chattering with cold. They reached the cellar at last. Old Wolfe had been drinking since she went out, and had crept nearer the door. The girl Janey slept heavily in the corner. He went up to her, touching softly the worn white arm with his fingers. Some bitterer thought stung him, as he stood there. He wiped the drops from his forehead, and went into the room beyond, livid, trembling. A hope, trifling, perhaps, but very dear, had died just then out of the poor puddler's life, as he looked at the sleeping, innocent girl,—some plan for the future, in which she had borne a part. He gave it up that moment, then and forever. Only a trifle, perhaps, to us: his face grew a shade paler,—that was all. But, somehow, the man's soul, as God and the angels looked down on it, never was the same afterwards.

Deborah followed him into the inner room. She carried a candle, which she placed on the floor, closing the door after her. She had seen the look on his face, as he turned away: her own grew deadly. Yet, as she came up to him her eyes glowed. He was seated on an old chest, quiet, holding his face in his hands.

"Hugh!" she said, softly.

He did not speak.

"Hugh, did hur hear what the man said,—him with the clear voice? Did hur hear? Money, money,—that it wud do all?"

He pushed her away,—gently, but he was worn out; her rasping tone fretted him.

"Hugh!"

The candle flared a pale yellow light over the cobwebbed brick walls, and the woman standing there. He looked at her. She was young, in deadly earnest; her faded eyes, and wet, ragged figure caught from their frantic eagerness a power akin to beauty.

"Hugh, it is true! Money ull do it! Oh, Hugh, boy, listen till me! He said it true! It is money!"

"I know. Go back! I do not want you here."

"Hugh, it is t' last time. I'll never worrit hur again."[9]

9. "I'll never bother you again."

There were tears in her voice now, but she choked them back.

"Hear till me only to-night! If one of t'witch people wud come, them we heard of t' home, and gif hur all hur wants, what then? Say, Hugh!"

"What do you mean?"

"I mean money."

Her whisper shrilled through his brain.

"If one of t' witch dwarfs wud come from t' lane moors to-night, and gif hur money, to go out,—*out*, I say,—out, lad, where t' sun shines, and t' heath grows, and t' ladies walk in silken gownds, and God stays all t' time,—where t' man lives that talked to us to-night,—Hugh knows,—Hugh could walk there like a king!"

He thought the woman mad, tried to check her, but she went on, fierce in her eager haste.

"If *I* were t' witch dwarf, if I had t' money, wud hur thank me? Wud hur take me out o' this place wid hur and Janey? I wud not come into the gran' house hur wud build, to vex hur wid t' hunch,—only at night, when t' shadows were dark, stand far off to see hur."

Mad? Yes! Are many of us mad in this way?

"Poor Deb! poor Deb!" he said, soothingly.

"It is here," she said, suddenly jerking into his hand a small roll. "I took it! I did it! Me, me!—not hur! I shall be hanged, I shall be burnt in hell, if anybody knows I took it! Out of his pocket, as he leaned against t' bricks. Hur knows?"

She thrust it into his hand, and then, her errand done, began to gather chips together to make a fire, choking down hysteric sobs.

"Has it come to this?"

That was all he said. The Welsh Wolfe blood was honest. The roll was a small green pocket-book containing one or two gold pieces, and a check for an incredible amount, as it seemed to the poor puddler. He laid it down, hiding his face again in his hands.

"Hugh, don't be angry wud me! It's only poor Deb,—hur knows?"

He took the long skinny fingers kindly in his.

"Angry? God help me, no! Let me sleep. I am tired."

He threw himself heavily down on the wooden bench, stunned with pain and weariness. She brought some old rags to cover him.

It was late on Sunday evening before he awoke. I tell God's truth, when I say he had then no thought of keeping this money. Deborah had hid it in his pocket. He found it there. She watched him eagerly, as he took it out.

"I must gif it to him," he said, reading her face.

"Hur knows," she said with a bitter sigh of disappointment. "But it is hur right to keep it."

His right! The word struck him. Doctor May had used the same. He washed himself, and went out to find this man Mitchell. His right! Why did this chance word cling to him so obstinately? Do you hear the fierce devils whisper in his ear, as he went slowly down the darkening street?

The evening came on, slow and calm. He seated himself at the end of an alley leading into one of the larger streets. His brain was clear to-night, keen, intent, mastering. It would not start back, cowardly, from any hellish temptation, but meet it face to face. Therefore the great temptation of his life came to him veiled by no sophistry, but bold, defiant, owning its own vile name, trusting to one bold blow for victory.

He did not deceive himself. Theft! That was it. At first the word sickened him; then he grappled with it. Sitting there on a broken cartwheel, the fading day, the noisy groups, the church-bells' tolling passed before him like a panorama, while the sharp struggle went on within. This money! He took it out, and looked at it. If he gave it back, what then? He was going to be cool about it.

People going by to church saw only a sickly mill-boy watching them quietly at the alley's mouth. They did not know that he was mad, or they would not have gone by so quietly: mad with hunger; stretching out his hands to the world, that had given so much to them, for leave to live the life God meant him to live. His soul within him was smothering to death; he wanted so much, thought so much, and *knew*—nothing. There was nothing of which he was certain, except the mill and things there. Of God and heaven he had heard so little, that they were to him what fairy-land is to a child: something real, but not here; very far off. His brain, greedy, dwarfed, full of thwarted energy and unused powers, questioned these men and women going by, coldly, bitterly, that night. Was it not his right to live as they,—a pure life, a good, true-hearted life, full of beauty and kind words? He only wanted to know how to use the strength within him. His heart warmed, as he thought of it. He suffered[1] himself to think of it longer. If he took the money?

Then he saw himself as he might be, strong, helpful, kindly. The night crept on, as this one image slowly evolved itself from the crowd of other thoughts and stood triumphant. He looked at it. As he might be! What wonder, if it blinded him to delirium,—the madness that underlies all revolution, all progress, and all fall?

You laugh at the shallow temptation? You see the error underlying its argument so clearly,—that to him a true life was one of full development rather than self-restraint? that he was deaf to the higher tone in a cry of voluntary suffering for truth's sake than in the fullest flow of spontaneous harmony? I do not plead his cause. I only want to show you the mote in my brother's eye: then you can see clearly to take it out.[2]

The money,—there it lay on his knee, a little blotted slip of paper, nothing in itself; used to raise him out of the pit; something straight from God's hand. A thief! Well, what was it to be a thief? He met the question at last, face to face, wiping the clammy drops of sweat from his forehead. God made this money—the fresh air, too—for his children's use. He never made the difference between poor and rich. The Something who looked down on him that moment through the cool gray sky had a kindly face, he knew,—loved his children alike. Oh, he knew that!

There were times when the soft floods of color in the crimson and purple flames, or the clear depth of amber in the water below the bridge, had somehow given him a glimpse of another world than this,—of an infinite depth of beauty and of quiet somewhere,—somewhere,—a depth of quiet and rest and love. Looking up now, it became strangely real. The sun had sunk quite below the hills, but his last rays struck upward, touching the zenith. The fog had risen, and the town and river were steeped in its thick, gray damp; but overhead, the sun-touched smoke-clouds opened like a cleft ocean,—shifting, rolling seas of crimson mist, waves of billowy silver veined with blood-scarlet, inner depths unfathomable of glancing light. Wolfe's artist-eye grew drunk with color. The gates of that other world! Fading, flashing before him now! What, in that world of Beauty, Content, and Right, were the petty laws, the mine and thine, of mill-owners and mill-hands?

A consciousness of power stirred within him. He stood up. A man,—he thought, stretching out his hands,—free to work, to live, to love! Free! His right! He folded the scrap of paper in his hand. As his nervous fingers took it in, limp and blotted, so his soul took in the mean temptation, lapped it in fancied rights, in dreams of improved existences, drifting and endless as the cloud-seas of color. Clutching it, as if the tightness of his hold would strengthen his sense of possession, he went aimlessly down the street. It was his watch at the mill. He need not go, need never go again, thank God!—shaking off the thought with unspeakable loathing.

Shall I go over the history of the hours of that night? how the man wandered from one to another of his old haunts, with a half-consciousness of bidding them farewell,—lanes and alleys and back-yards where the mill-hands lodged,—noting, with a new eagerness, the filth and drunkenness, the pig-pens, the ash-heaps covered with potato-skins, the bloated, pimpled women at the doors,—with a new disgust, a new sense of sudden triumph, and, under all, a new, vague dread, unknown before, smothered down, kept under, but still there? It left him

1. Permitted.   2. See Matthew 7:3–4.

but once during the night, when, for the second time in his life, he entered a church. It was a sombre Gothic pile,[3] where the stained light lost itself in far-retreating arches; built to meet the requirements and sympathies of a far other class than Wolfe's. Yet it touched, moved him uncontrollably. The distances, the shadows, the still, marble figures, the mass of silent kneeling worshippers, the mysterious music, thrilled, lifted his soul with a wonderful pain. Wolfe forgot himself, forgot the new life he was going to live, the mean terror gnawing underneath. The voice of the speaker strengthened the charm; it was clear, feeling, full, strong. An old man, who had lived much, suffered much; whose brain was keenly alive, dominant; whose heart was summer-warm with charity. He taught it to-night. He held up Humanity in its grand total; showed the great world-cancer to his people. Who could show it better? He was a Christian reformer; he had studied the age thoroughly; his outlook at man had been free, world-wide, over all time. His faith stood sublime upon the Rock of Ages;[4] his fiery zeal guided vast schemes by which the gospel was to be preached to all nations. How did he preach it to-night? In burning, light-laden words he painted the incarnate Life, Love, the universal Man: words that became reality in the lives of these people,—that lived again in beautiful words and actions, trifling, but heroic. Sin, as he defined it, was a real foe to them; their trials, temptations, were his. His words passed far over the furnace-tender's grasp, toned to suit another class of culture; they sounded in his ears a very pleasant song in an unknown tongue. He meant to cure this world-cancer with a steady eye that had never glared with hunger, and a hand that neither poverty nor strychnine-whiskey had taught to shake. In this morbid, distorted heart of the Welsh puddler he had failed.

Wolfe rose at last, and turned from the church down the street. He looked up; the night had come on foggy, damp; the golden mists had vanished, and the sky lay dull and ash-colored. He wandered again aimlessly down the street, idly wondering what had become of the cloud-sea of crimson and scarlet. The trial-day of this man's life was over, and he had lost the victory. What followed was mere drifting circumstance,—a quicker walking over the path,—that was all. Do you want to hear the end of it? You wish me to make a tragic story out of it? Why, in the police-reports of the morning paper you can find a dozen such tragedies: hints of shipwrecks unlike any that ever befell on the high seas; hints that here a power was lost to heaven,—that there a soul went down where no tide can ebb or flow. Commonplace enough the hints are,—jocose sometimes, done up in rhyme.

Doctor May, a month after the night I have told you of, was reading to his wife at breakfast from this fourth column of the morning-paper: an unusual thing,—these police-reports not being, in general, choice reading for ladies; but it was only one item he read.

"Oh, my dear! You remember that man I told you of, that we saw at Kirby's mill?—that was arrested for robbing Mitchell? Here he is; just listen:—'Circuit Court. Judge Day. Hugh Wolfe, operative in Kirby & John's Loudon Mills. Charge, grand larceny. Sentence, nineteen years hard labor in penitentiary.'—Scoundrel! Serves him right! After all our kindness that night! Picking Mitchell's pocket at the very time!"

His wife said something about the ingratitude of that kind of people, and then they began to talk of something else.

Nineteen years! How easy that was to read! What a simple word for Judge Day to utter! Nineteen years! Half a lifetime!

Hugh Wolfe sat on the window-ledge of his cell, looking out. His ankles were ironed. Not usual in such cases; but he had made two desperate efforts to escape. "Well," as Haley, the jailer, said, "small blame to him! Nineteen years' imprisonment was not a pleasant thing to look forward to." Haley was very good-natured about it, though Wolfe had fought him savagely.

"When he was first caught," the jailer said afterwards, in telling the story, "before the trial,

---

3. A large building, in the style of a medieval cathedral.

4. An allusion to a hymn extolling Christian faith.

the fellow was cut down at once,—laid there on that pallet like a dead man, with his hands over his eyes. Never saw a man so cut down in my life. Time of the trial, too, came the queerest dodge of any customer I ever had. Would choose no lawyer. Judge gave him one, of course. Gibson it was. He tried to prove the fellow crazy; but it wouldn't go. Thing was plain as day-light: money found on him. 'Twas a hard sentence,—all the law allows; but it was for 'xample's sake. These mill-hands are gettin' onbearable. When the sentence was read, he just looked up, and said the money was his by rights, and that all the world had gone wrong. That night, after the trial, a gentleman came to see him here, name of Mitchell,—him as he stole from. Talked to him for an hour. Thought he came for curiosity, like. After he was gone, thought Wolfe was remarkable quiet, and went into his cell. Found him very low; bed all bloody. Doctor said he had been bleeding at the lungs. He was as weak as a cat; yet, if ye'll b'lieve me, he tried to get a-past me and get out. I just carried him like a baby, and threw him on the pallet. Three days after, he tried it again: that time reached the wall. Lord help you! he fought like a tiger,—giv' some terrible blows. Fightin' for life, you see; for he can't live long, shut up in the stone crib[5] down yonder. Got a death-cough now. 'T took two of us to bring him down that day; so I just put the irons on his feet. There he sits, in there. Goin' to-morrow, with a batch more of 'em. That woman, hunchback, tried with him,—you remember?—she's only got three years. 'Complice. But *she's* a woman, you know. He's been quiet ever since I put on irons: giv' up, I suppose. Looks white, sick-lookin'. It acts different on 'em, bein' sentenced. Most of 'em gets reckless, devilish-like. Some prays awful, and sings them vile songs of the mills, all in a breath. That woman, now, she's desper't'. Been beggin' to see Hugh, as she calls him, for three days. I'm a-going' to let her in. She don't go with him. Here she is in this next cell. I'm a-goin' now to let her in."

He let her in. Wolfe did not see her. She crept into a corner of the cell, and stood watching him. He was scratching the iron bars of the window with a piece of tin which he had picked up, with an idle, uncertain, vacant stare, just as a child or idiot would do.

"Tryin' to get out, old boy?" laughed Haley. "Them irons will need a crow-bar beside your tin, before you can open 'em."

Wolfe laughed, too, in a senseless way.

"I think I'll get out," he said.

"I believe his brain's touched," said Haley, when he came out.

The puddler scraped away with the tin for half an hour. Still Deborah did not speak. At last she ventured nearer, and touched his arm.

"Blood?" she said, looking at some spots on his coat with a shudder.

He looked up at her. "Why, Deb!" he said, smiling,—such a bright, boyish smile, that it went to poor Deborah's heart directly, and she sobbed and cried out loud.

"Oh, Hugh, lad! Hugh! dunnot look at me, when it wur my fault! To think I brought hur to it! And I loved hur so! Oh, lad, I dud!"

The confession, even in this wretch, came with the woman's blush through the sharp cry.

He did not seem to hear her,—scraping away diligently at the bars with the bit of tin.

Was he going mad? She peered closely into his face. Something she saw there made her draw suddenly back,—something which Haley had not seen, that lay beneath the pinched, vacant look it had caught since the trial, or the curious gray shadow that rested on it. That gray shadow,—yes, she knew what that meant. She had often seen it creeping over women's faces for months, who died at last of slow hunger or consumption. That meant death, distant, lingering: but this—Whatever it was the woman saw, or thought she saw, used as she was to crime and misery, seemed to make her sick with a new horror. Forgetting her fear of him, she caught his shoulders, and looked keenly, steadily, into his eyes.

"Hugh!" she cried, in a desperate whisper,—"oh, boy, not that! for God's sake, not *that!*"

The vacant laugh went off his face, and he answered her in a muttered word or two that

5. Small, crude cottage or room.

drove her away. Yet the words were kindly enough. Sitting there on his pallet, she cried silently a hopeless sort of tears, but did not speak again. The man looked up furtively at her now and then. Whatever his own trouble was, her distress vexed him with a momentary sting.

It was market-day. The narrow window of the jail looked down directly on the carts and wagons drawn up in a long line, where they had unloaded. He could see, too, and hear distinctly the clink of money as it changed hands, the busy crowd of whites and blacks shoving, pushing one another, and the chaffering[6] and swearing at the stalls. Somehow, the sound, more than anything else had done, wakened him up,—made the whole real to him. He was done with the world and the business of it. He let the tin fall, and looked out, pressing his face close to the rusty bars. How they crowded and pushed! And he,—he should never walk that pavement again! There came Neff Sanders, one of the feeders at the mill, with a basket on his arm. Sure enough, Neff was married the other week. He whistled, hoping he would look up; but he did not. He wondered if Neff remembered he was there,—if any of the boys thought of him up there, and thought that he never was to go down that old cinder-road again. Never again! He had not quite understood it before; but now he did. Not for days or years, but never!—that was it.

How clear the light fell on that stall in front of the market! and how like a picture it was, the dark-green heaps of corn, and the crimson beets, and golden melons! There was another with game: how the light flickered on that pheasant's breast, with the purplish blood dripping over the brown feathers! He could see the red shining of the drops, it was so near. In one minute he could be down there. It was just a step. So easy, as it seemed, so natural to go! Yet it could never be—not in all the thousands of years to come—that he should put his foot on that street again! He thought of himself with a sorrowful pity, as of some one else. There was a dog down in the market, walking after his master with such a stately, grave look!—only a dog, yet he could go backwards and forwards just as he pleased: he had good luck! Why, the very vilest cur, yelping there in the gutter, had not lived his life, had been free to act out whatever thought God had put into his brain; while he—No, he would not think of that! He tried to put the thought away, and to listen to a dispute between a countryman and a woman about some meat; but it would come back. He, what had he done to bear this?

Then came the sudden picture of what might have been, and now. He knew what it was to be in the penitentiary,—how it went with men there. He knew how in these long years he should slowly die, but not until soul and body had become corrupt and rotten,—how, when he came out, if he lived to come, even the lowest of the mill-hands would jeer him,—how his hands would be weak, and his brain senseless and stupid. He believed he was almost that now. He put his hand to his head, with a puzzled, weary look. It ached, his head, with thinking. He tried to quiet himself. It was only right, perhaps; he had done wrong. But was there right or wrong for such as he? What was right? And who had ever taught him? He thrust the whole matter away. A dark, cold quiet crept through his brain. It was all wrong; but let it be! It was nothing to him more than the others. Let it be!

The door grated, as Haley opened it.

"Come, my woman! Must lock up for t' night. Come, stir yerself!"

She went up and took Hugh's hand.

"Good-night, Deb," he said, carelessly.

She had not hoped he would say more; but the tired pain on her mouth just then was bitterer than death. She took his passive hand and kissed it.

"Hur'll never see Deb again!" she ventured, her lips growing colder and more bloodless.

What did she say that for? Did he not know it? Yet he would not be impatient with poor old Deb. She had trouble of her own, as well as he.

"No, never again," he said, trying to be cheerful.

She stood just a moment, looking at him. Do you laugh at her, standing there, with her

6. Bargaining, haggling.

hunchback, her rags, her bleared, withered face, and the great despised love tugging at her heart?

"Come, you!" called Haley, impatiently.

She did not move.

"Hugh!" she whispered.

It was to be her last word. What was it?

"Hugh, boy, not *THAT!*"

He did not answer. She wrung her hands, trying to be silent, looking in his face in an agony of entreaty. He smiled again, kindly.

"It is best, Deb. I cannot bear to be hurted any more."

"Hur knows," she said, humbly.

"Tell my father good-bye; and—and kiss little Janey."

She nodded, saying nothing, looked in his face again, and went out of the door. As she went, she staggered.

"Drinkin' to-day?" broke out Haley, pushing her before him. "Where the Devil did you get it? Here, in with ye!" and he shoved her into her cell, next to Wolfe's, and shut the door.

Along the wall of her cell there was a crack low down by the floor, through which she could see the light from Wolfe's. She had discovered it days before. She hurried in now, and, kneeling down by it, listened, hoping to hear some sound. Nothing but the rasping of the tin on the bars. He was at his old amusement again. Something in the noise jarred on her ear, for she shivered as she heard it. Hugh rasped away at the bars. A dull old bit of tin, not fit to cut korl with.

He looked out of the window again. People were leaving the market now. A tall mulatto girl, following her mistress, her basket on her head, crossed the street just below, and looked up. She was laughing; but, when she caught sight of the haggard face peering out through the bars, suddenly grew grave, and hurried by. A free, firm, step, a clear-cut olive face, with a scarlet turban tied on one side, dark, shining eyes, and on the head the basket poised, filled with fruit and flowers, under which the scarlet turban and bright eyes looked out half-shadowed. The picture caught his eye. It was good to see a face like that. He would try to-morrow, and cut one like it. *To-morrow!* He threw down the tin, trembling, and covered his face with his hands. When he looked up again, the daylight was gone.

Deborah, crouching near by on the other side of the wall, heard no noise. He sat on the side of the low pallet, thinking. Whatever was the mystery which the woman had seen on his face, it came out now slowly, in the dark there, and became fixed,—a something never seen on his face before. The evening was darkening fast. The market had been over for an hour; the rumbling of the carts over the pavement grew more infrequent: he listened to each, as it passed, because he thought it was to be for the last time. For the same reason, it was, I suppose, that he strained his eyes to catch a glimpse of each passer-by, wondering who they were, what kind of homes they were going to, if they had children,—listening eagerly to every chance word in the street, as if—(God be merciful to the man! what strange fancy was this?)—as if he never should hear human voices again.

It was quite dark at last. The street was a lonely one. The last passenger, he thought, was gone. No,—there was a quick step: Joe Hill, lighting the lamps. Joe was a good old chap; never passed a fellow without some joke or other. He remembered once seeing the place where he lived with his wife. "Granny Hill" the boys called her. Bedridden she was; but so kind as Joe was to her! kept the room so clean!—and the old woman, when he was there, was laughing at "some of t' lad's foolishness." The step was far down the street; but he could see him place the ladder, run up, and light the gas. A longing seized him to be spoken to once more.

"Joe!" he called, out of the grating. "Good-bye, Joe!"

The old man stopped a moment, listening uncertainly; then hurried on. The prisoner thrust his hand out of the window, and called again, louder; but Joe was too far down the street. It was a little thing; but it hurt him,—this disappointment.

"Good-bye, Joe!" he called, sorrowfully enough.

"Be quiet!" said one of the jailers, passing the door, striking on it with his club.

Oh, that was the last, was it?

There was an inexpressible bitterness on his face, as he lay down on the bed, taking the bit of tin, which he had rasped to a tolerable degree of sharpness, in his hand,—to play with, it may be. He bared his arms, looking intently at their corded veins and sinews. Deborah, listening in the next cell, heard a slight clicking sound, often repeated. She shut her lips tightly, that she might not scream, the cold drops of sweat broke over her, in her dumb agony.

"Hur knows best," she muttered at last, fiercely clutching the boards where she lay.

If she could have seen Wolfe, there was nothing about him to frighten her. He lay quite still, his arms outstretched, looking at the pearly stream of moonlight coming into the window. I think in that one hour that came then he lived back over all the years that had gone before. I think that all the low, vile life, all his wrongs, all his starved hopes, came then, and stung him with a farewell poison that made him sick unto death. He made neither moan nor cry, only turned his worn face now and then to the pure light, that seemed so far off, as one that said, "How long, O Lord? how long?"

The hour was over at last. The moon, passing over her nightly path, slowly came nearer, and threw the light across his bed on his feet. He watched it steadily, as it crept up, inch by inch, slowly. It seemed to him to carry with it a great silence. He had been so hot and tired there always in the mills! The years had been so fierce and cruel! There was coming now quiet and coolness and sleep. His tense limbs relaxed, and settled in a calm languor. The blood ran fainter and slow from his heart. He did not think now with a savage anger of what might be and was not; he was conscious only of deep stillness creeping over him. At first he saw a sea of faces: the mill-men,—women he had known, drunken and bloated,—Janeys timid and pitiful,—poor old Debs: then they floated together like a mist, and faded away, leaving only the clear, pearly moonlight.

Whether, as the pure light crept up the stretched-out figure, it brought with it calm and peace, who shall say? His dumb soul was alone with God in judgment. A Voice may have spoken for it from far-off Calvary, "Father, forgive them, for they know not what they do!"[7] Who dare say? Fainter and fainter the heart rose and fell, slower and slower the moon floated from behind a cloud, until, when at last its full tide of white splendor swept over the cell, it seemed to wrap and fold into a deeper stillness the dead figure that never should move again. Silence deeper than the Night! Nothing that moved, save the black nauseous stream of blood dripping slowly from the pallet to the floor!

There was outcry and crowd enough in the cell the next day. The coroner and his jury, the local editors, Kirby himself, and boys with their hands thrust knowingly into their pockets and heads on one side, jammed into the corners. Coming and going all day. Only one woman. She came late, and outstayed them all. A Quaker, or Friend, as they call themselves.[8] I think this woman was known by that name in heaven. A homely body, coarsely dressed in gray and white. Deborah (for Haley had let her in) took notice of her. She watched them all—sitting on the end of the pallet, holding his head in her arms—with the ferocity of a watch-dog, if any of them touched the body. There was no meekness, or sorrow, in her face; the stuff out of which murderers are made, instead. All the time Haley and the woman were laying straight the limbs and cleaning the cell, Deborah sat still, keenly watching the Quaker's face. Of all the crowd there that day, this woman alone had not spoken to her,—only once or twice had put some cordial to her lips. After they all were gone, the woman, in the same still, gentle way, brought a vase of wood-leaves and berries, and placed it by the pallet, then opened the narrow window. The fresh air blew in, and swept the woody fragrance over the dead face. Deborah looked up with a quick wonder.

7. Words spoken by Jesus from the cross, in Luke
    23:34.

8. Quakers are known among themselves as the
    Society of Friends.

"Did hur know my boy wud like it? Did hur know Hugh?"

"I know Hugh now."

The white fingers passed in a slow, pitiful way over the dead, worn face. There was a heavy shadow in the quiet eyes.

"Did hur know where they'll bury Hugh?" said Deborah in a shrill tone, catching her arm. This had been the question hanging on her lips all day.

"In t' town-yard? Under t' mud and ash? T' lad'll smother, woman! He wur born on t' lane moor, where t' air is frick[9] and strong. Take hur out, for God's sake, take hur out where t' air blows!"

The Quaker hesitated, but only for a moment. She put her strong arm around Deborah and led her to the window.

"Thee sees the hills, friend, over the river?[1] Thee sees how the light lies warm there, and the winds of God blow all the day? I live there,—where the blue smoke is, by the trees. Look at me." She turned Deborah's face to her own, clear and earnest. "Thee will believe me? I will take Hugh and bury him there to-morrow."

Deborah did not doubt her. As the evening wore on, she leaned against the iron bars, looking at the hills that rose far off, through the thick sodden clouds, like a bright, unattainable calm. As she looked, a shadow of their solemn repose fell on her face: its fierce discontent faded into a pitiful, humble quiet. Slow, solemn tears gathered in her eyes: the poor weak eyes turned so hopelessly to the place where Hugh was to rest, the grave heights looking higher and brighter and more solemn than ever before. The Quaker watched her keenly. She came to her at last, and touched her arm.

"When thee comes back," she said, in a low, sorrowful tone, like one who speaks from a strong heart deeply moved with remorse or pity, "thee shall begin thy life again,—there on the hills. I came too late; but not for thee,—by God's help, it may be."

Not too late. Three years after, the Quaker began her work. I end my story here. At evening-time it was light. There is no need to tire you with the long years of sunshine, and fresh air, and slow, patient Christ-love, needed to make healthy and hopeful this impure body and soul. There is a homely pine house, on one of these hills, whose windows overlook broad, wooded slopes and clover-crimsoned meadows,—niched into the very place where the light is warmest, the air freest. It is the Friends' meeting-house. Once a week they sit there, in their grave, earnest way, waiting for the Spirit of Love to speak, opening their simple hearts to receive His words. There is a woman, old, deformed, who takes a humble place among them: waiting like them: in her gray dress, her worn face, pure and meek, turned now and then to the sky. A woman much loved by these silent, restful people; more silent than they, more humble, more loving. Waiting: with her eyes turned to hills higher and purer than these on which she lives,—dim and far off now, but to be reached some day. There may be in her heart some latent hope to meet there the love denied her here,—that she shall find him whom she lost, and that then she will not be all-unworthy. Who blames her? Something is lost in the passage of every soul from one eternity to the other,—something pure and beautiful, which might have been and was not: a hope, a talent, a love, over which the soul mourns, like Esau[2] deprived of his birthright. What blame to the meek Quaker, if she took her lost hope to make the hills of heaven more fair?

Nothing remains to tell that the poor Welsh puddler once lived, but this figure of the mill-woman cut in korl. I have it here in a corner of my library. I keep it hid behind a curtain,—it is such a rough, ungainly thing. Yet there are about it touches, grand sweeps of outline, that show a master's hand. Sometimes,—to-night, for instance,—the curtain is accidentally drawn back, and I see a bare arm stretched out imploringly in the darkness, and

---

9. Fresh.
1. Traditionally, Quakers use the familiar "thee" rather than the formal "you," as a sign of the

equality of all persons.
2. In Genesis 25:25, Esau sold his birthright to his brother.

an eager, wolfish face watching mine: a wan, woful face, through which the spirit of the dead korl-cutter looks out, with its thwarted life, its mighty hunger, its unfinished work. Its pale, vague lips seem to tremble with a terrible question. "Is this the End?" they say,—"nothing beyond?—no more?" Why, you tell me you have seen that look in the eyes of dumb brutes,—horses dying under the lash. I know.

The deep of the night is passing while I write. The gas-light wakens from the shadows here and there the objects which lie scattered through the room: only faintly, though; for they belong to the open sunlight. As I glance at them, they each recall some task or pleasure of the coming day. A half-moulded child's head; Aphrodite;[3] a bough of forest-leaves; music; work; homely fragments, in which lie the secrets of all eternal truth and beauty. Prophetic all! Only this dumb, woful face seems to belong to and end with the night. I turn to look at it. Has the power of its desperate need commanded the darkness away? While the room is yet steeped in heavy shadow, a cool, gray light suddenly touches its head like a blessing hand, and its groping arm points through the broken cloud to the far East, where, in the flickering, nebulous crimson, God has set the promise of the Dawn.

1861

Louisa May Alcott
(1832–1888)

Feminist and abolitionist, supporter of women's suffrage and dress reform, self-supporting woman and professional author, Louisa May Alcott lived a life very different from the domestic idyll portrayed in her most famous novel, *Little Women*. Although many remember her as an author of didactic children's novels, recent critics have rediscovered the "alternative Alcott," a writer of sensational shockers, gothic thrillers, and grittily realistic accounts of the lives of working women. *Little Women* is autobiographical in its portrayal of four sisters' adolescent struggles toward Victorian womanhood, but the career of Jo March differs strikingly from that of her model and creator.

Like her famous creations, Alcott was the daughter of a well-connected Boston lady, Abigail May, and her idealistic, impractical, transcendentalist husband, Amos Bronson Alcott. Louisa and her older sister Anna were born in Germantown, Pennsylvania, where her father opened an experimental school for boys. They returned with their parents to the Boston area in 1834 when the school failed and the family

fell deeply into debt. With help from friends, including Ralph Waldo Emerson, Bronson opened another school in Boston, but it, too, failed. In 1840 the Alcotts settled in Concord, Massachusetts, where they supported themselves by farming and taking in sewing.

Bronson undertook the girls' education and introduced them to such family friends as Emerson, Henry David Thoreau, Margaret Fuller, William Lloyd Garrison, and Lydia Maria Child. In 1843, when Louisa was 11, the family moved with a group of friends to Fruitlands, a house in Harvard, Massachusetts, that Bronson hoped would be a model utopian community. Life there was very spartan, lived according to strict principles of health and morality. For example, the diet was vegetarian, and no animal products were allowed to be consumed; sugar, caffeine, chocolate, and salt were also forbidden. Making a living off the New England land was prohibitively difficult; the commune broke up in 1844 and the Alcott family bought a house in Concord in 1845. Louisa later wrote a satirical essay about

3. The Greek goddess of love.

the experience, called "Transcendental Wild Oats."

Throughout her teenage years, Louisa wrote. She worked on poems, plays, essays, and stories and thought of a future as an author. At 17 she said, "I'm not looking to be married . . . not having seen very many truly happy ones." She began teaching as a means of bringing income into the financially strapped family, but she also began to publish. Her first story, "The Rival Painters," appeared in a magazine in 1852, and her first book, *Flower Fables* (1855), a collection of fairy stories, launched her career as a children's writer, though it received little or no notice from readers or reviewers. By 1856 she had earned enough from the sales of romantic tales and poems to leave home and establish herself in a boardinghouse room in Boston. Tutoring, taking in sewing, and writing, she managed to support herself. By the early 1860s she was finding particular success with the sensational stories she called "blood and thunder" tales, full of intrigue, murder, and violence.

The Alcott family had always been active in the abolition movement, and in 1862 Louisa May Alcott resolved to contribute to the Northern cause in the Civil War. She contracted typhoid fever in Washington, D.C., while working as an army nurse. The disease and its treatment (with mercury) poisoned her health and left her with debilitating headaches for the rest of her life. From the experience came *Hospital Sketches* (1863), Alcott's first book to meet with significant critical praise and sales. Her next book, a psychological novel called *Moods* (1865), was less well received, but Alcott recovered from the disappointment on a trip to Europe with her youngest sister, May, and a mutual friend.

In 1868 Alcott returned home to Concord for a visit and began work on a project her publisher had suggested, a book expressly for girls. In just 6 weeks she wrote the first volume of *Little Women*, basing the characters on her own family but moving their experience up in history by two decades. Neither she nor her editor had much enthusiasm for the result, but the editor asked a 20-year-old woman to read and judge the manuscript: she (and several of her friends) cried copiously over it, and declared it the best girls' book they had ever read. The public agreed, and both sales and reviews were very strong.

Under pressure from the public to reveal the marital fates of her four heroines, Alcott brought out the second volume the next year. She followed autobiography in rendering the death of the third sister, Beth, and the marriage of the eldest sister, Meg, but she adapted her family's history to the exigencies of the marriage plot by marrying Jo to an unglamorous German professor and Amy to the eligible bachelor of the tale, Laurie. Eventually the novel became part of a trilogy, following the story of Jo's life as headmistress of a progressive boys' school in *Little Men: Life at Plumfield with Jo's Boys* (1871) and *Jo's Boys, and How They Turned Out* (1886). She consolidated her reputation as an author of novels for young people with other successes, including *An Old-Fashioned Girl* (1870); *Eight Cousins; or The Aunt-Hill* (1875) and its sequel, *Rose in Bloom* (1876); and a series known as *Aunt Jo's Scrap-Bag* (1872–1882). Though all these novels extol the feminine Victorian virtues of practicing good housekeeping and self-denial, they do so in a context that promotes progressive education, physical activity, and open-ended career possibilities for women.

Having returned to Boston, Alcott published a more explicitly feminist novel for adults, *Work: A Story of Experience* (1873). She drew on her experience in the Civil War to write of Christie, a woman who becomes an army nurse immediately after marriage, and who survives her young husband's death to become a public speaker at rallies for women's rights. Alcott privately said she did not have time to become directly involved in such rallies herself: she was too busy proving "women's right to labor" to try to prove "women's right to vote."

Though Alcott never married or had children, she raised a niece as her own daughter. Her youngest sister May

("Amy") had been married in Europe at age 38 to a Swiss man fifteen years her junior, and had died in 1879 a few weeks after giving birth to their first child. Louisa adopted "Lulu," and—after her own mother had died—headed a household including her widowed sister Anna and her children. Her health, never recovered after the war, broke down when she was 55; she died just five days after her father, in 1888.

Little Women has remained a best-selling children's classic since its first appearance, and many critics have praised the "universal" appeal of Alcott's depictions of youthful joys and tribulations. The character of the androgynous Jo, with her "gentlemanly" and "boyish" manners, her passionate temper, and her powerfully nonconformist desires, has been a particular success with readers and with critics of both sexes. Although some scholars dismiss the novel as overly sentimental, preferring Alcott's less domestic "adult" writing, others admire its ability to move readers as well as its portrayal of an empowering community of women. The novel's broadly Christian structure (loosely based on John Bunyan's *Pilgrim's Progress*), its details of home life in Victorian New England, its insistence on suppressing personal pride and promoting self-sacrifice, and its inevitable march toward death or marriage for each of the four heroines offer vivid insight into the ideologies that shaped middle-class women's lives as Alcott knew them.

Alcott's other publications include *The Rose Family. A Fairy Tale* (1864); *On Picket Duty, and Other Tales* (1864); *Nelly's Hospital* (1865); *The Mysterious Key, and What It Opened* (1867); *Morning-Glories, and Other Stories* (1868); *Louisa M. Alcott's Proverb Stories* (1868); *Hospital Sketches and Camp and Fireside Stories* (1869); *Will's Wonder Book* (1870); *V. V.: or, Plots and Counterplots* (circa 1870); *Something to Do* (1873); *Silver Pitchers: And Independence, A Centennial Love Story* (1876); *A Modern Mephistopheles* (1877); *Jack and Jill: A Village Story* (1880); *Spinning-Wheel Stories* (1884); *Lulu's Library. Vol. I. A Christmas Dream* (1886); *Lulu's Library. Vol. II. The Frost King* (1887); *A Garland for Girls* (1887); *A Modern Mephistopheles and A Whisper in the Dark* (1889); *Lulu's Library. Vol. III. Recollections* (1889); and *Comic Tragedies Written by "Jo" and "Meg" and Acted by the Little Women* (1893). Modern reprints of her periodical fiction include *Behind a Mask; The Unknown Thrillers of Louisa May Alcott,* edited by Madeleine B. Stern (1975); *Louisa's Wonder Book: An Unknown Alcott Juvenile,* edited by Stern (1975); and *Plots and Counterplots; More Unknown Thrillers of Louisa May Alcott,* edited by Stern (1976).

Authoritative biographies are *Louisa May: A Modern Biography of Louisa May Alcott* (1977) by Martha Saxton and *The Alcotts* by Madelon Bedell (1981). Gloria T. Delamar's *Louisa May Alcott and "Little Women"* (1990) collects materials on the reception of the novel. Useful critical sources include *Communities of Women* (1978) by Nina Auerbach; *A Hunger for Home: Louisa May Alcott and Little Women* (1984) by Sarah Elbert; *Critical Essays on Louisa May Alcott* (1984), edited by Madeleine B. Stern; and *Alternative Alcott* (1988), edited and with an introduction by Elaine Showalter.

FROM LITTLE WOMEN

Part I

1

Playing Pilgrims

"Christmas won't be Christmas without any presents," grumbled Jo, lying on the rug.
"It's so dreadful to be poor!" sighed Meg, looking down at her old dress.

"I don't think it's fair for some girls to have lots of pretty things, and other girls nothing at all," added little Amy, with an injured sniff.

"We've got father and mother, and each other, anyhow," said Beth, contentedly, from her corner.

The four young faces on which the firelight shone brightened at the cheerful words, but darkened again as Jo said sadly,—

"We haven't got father, and shall not have him for a long time." She didn't say "perhaps never," but each silently added it, thinking of father far away, where the fighting was.[1]

Nobody spoke for a minute; then Meg said in an altered tone,—

"You know the reason mother proposed not having any presents this Christmas, was because it's going to be a hard winter for every one; and she thinks we ought not to spend money for pleasure, when our men are suffering so in the army. We can't do much, but we can make our little sacrifices, and ought to do it gladly. But I am afraid I don't;" and Meg shook her head, as she thought regretfully of all the pretty things she wanted.

"But I don't think the little we should spend would do any good. We've each got a dollar, and the army wouldn't be much helped by our giving that. I agree not to expect anything from mother or you, but I do want to buy Undine and Sintram[2] for myself; I've wanted it so long," said Jo, who was a bookworm.

"I planned to spend mine in new music," said Beth, with a little sigh, which no one heard but the hearth-brush and kettle-holder.

"I shall get a nice box of Faber's drawing pencils; I really need them," said Amy, decidedly.

"Mother didn't say anything about our money, and she won't wish us to give up everything. Let's each buy what we want, and have a little fun; I'm sure we grub hard enough to earn it," cried Jo, examining the heels of her boots in a gentlemanly manner.

"I know I do,—teaching those dreadful children nearly all day, when I'm longing to enjoy myself at home," began Meg, in the complaining tone again.

"You don't have half such a hard time as I do," said Jo. "How would you like to be shut up for hours with a nervous, fussy old lady, who keeps you trotting, is never satisfied, and worries you till you're ready to fly out of the window or box her ears?"[3]

"It's naughty to fret,—but I do think washing dishes and keeping things tidy is the worst work in the world. It makes me cross; and my hands get so stiff, I can't practise good a bit." And Beth looked at her rough hands with a sigh that any one could hear that time.

"I don't believe any of you suffer as I do," cried Amy; "for you don't have to go to school with impertinent girls, who plague you if you don't know your lessons, and laugh at your dresses, and label your father if he isn't rich, and insult you when your nose isn't nice."

"If you mean *libel* I'd say so, and not talk about *labels*, as if pa was a pickle-bottle," advised Jo, laughing.

"I know what I mean, and you needn't be 'statirical' about it. It's proper to use good words, and improve your *vocabilary*," returned Amy, with dignity.

"Don't peck at one another, children. Don't you wish we had the money papa lost when we were little, Jo? Dear me, how happy and good we'd be, if we had no worries," said Meg, who could remember better times.

"You said the other day you thought we were a deal happier than the King children, for they were fighting and fretting all the time, in spite of their money."

"So I did, Beth. Well, I guess we are; for though we do have to work, we make fun for ourselves, and are a pretty jolly set, as Jo would say."

"Jo does use such slang words," observed Amy, with a reproving look at the long figure stretched on the rug. Jo immediately sat up, put her hands in her apron pockets, and began to whistle.

---

1. Allusion to the Civil War. The opening scene is set in 1861.
2. *Undine* (1811) and *Sintram* (1815) are romantic

tales by German author Friedrich de la Motte Fouqué.

3. That is, to slap her face.

"Don't, Jo; it's so boyish."

"That's why I do it."

"I detest rude, unlady-like girls."

"I hate affected, niminy piminy chits."

"Birds in their little nests agree," sang Beth, the peace-maker, with such a funny face that both sharp voices softened to a laugh, and the "pecking" ended for that time.

"Really, girls, you are both to be blamed," said Meg, beginning to lecture in her elder sisterly fashion. "You are old enough to leave off boyish tricks, and behave better, Josephine. It didn't matter so much when you were a little girl; but now you are so tall, and turn up your hair, you should remember that you are a young lady."

"I ain't! and if turning up my hair makes me one, I'll wear it in two tails till I'm twenty," cried Jo, pulling off her net, and shaking down a chestnut mane. "I hate to think I've got to grow up and be Miss March, and wear long gowns, and look as prim as a China-aster.[4] It's bad enough to be a girl, any-way, when I like boy's games, and work, and manners. I can't get over my disappointment in not being a boy, and it's worse than ever now, for I'm dying to go and fight with papa, and I can only stay at home and knit like a poky old woman;" and Jo shook the blue army-sock till the needles rattled like castanets, and her ball bounded across the room.

"Poor Jo; it's too bad! But it can't be helped, so you must try to be contented with making your name boyish, and playing brother to us girls," said Beth, stroking the rough head at her knee with a hand that all the dishwashing and dusting in the world could not make ungentle in its touch.

"As for you, Amy," continued Meg, "you are altogether too particular and prim. Your airs are funny now, but you'll grow up an affected little goose if you don't take care. I like your nice manners, and refined ways of speaking, when you don't try to be elegant; but your absurd words are as bad as Jo's slang."

"If Jo is a tom-boy, and Amy a goose, what am I, please?" asked Beth, ready to share the lecture.

"You're a dear, and nothing else," answered Meg, warmly; and no one contradicted her, for the "Mouse" was the pet of the family.

As young readers like to know "how people look," we will take this moment to give them a little sketch of the four sisters, who sat knitting away in the twilight, while the December snow fell quietly without, and the fire crackled cheerfully within. It was a comfortable old room, though the carpet was faded and the furniture very plain, for a good picture or two hung on the walls, books filled the recesses, chrysanthemums and Christmas roses bloomed in the windows, and a pleasant atmosphere of home-peace pervaded it.

Margaret, the eldest of the four, was sixteen, and very pretty, being plump and fair, with large eyes, plenty of soft brown hair, a sweet mouth, and white hands, of which she was rather vain. Fifteen-year-old Jo was very tall, thin and brown, and reminded one of a colt; for she never seemed to know what to do with her long limbs, which were very much in her way. She had a decided mouth, a comical nose, and sharp gray eyes, which appeared to see everything, and were by turns fierce, funny, or thoughtful. Her long, thick hair was her one beauty; but it was usually bundled into a net, to be out of her way. Round shoulders had Jo, big hands and feet, a fly-away look to her clothes, and the uncomfortable appearance of a girl who was rapidly shooting up into a woman, and didn't like it. Elizabeth,—or Beth, as every one called her,—was a rosy, smooth-haired, bright-eyed girl of thirteen, with a shy manner, a timid voice, and a peaceful expression, which was seldom disturbed. Her father called her "Little Tranquillity," and the name suited her excellently; for she seemed to live in a happy world of her own, only venturing out to meet the few whom she trusted and loved. Amy, though the youngest, was a most important person, in her own opinion at least. A regular

---

4. A plant cultivated for its showy, colorful flowers.

snow maiden, with blue eyes, and yellow hair curling on her shoulders; pale and slender, and always carrying herself like a young lady mindful of her manners. What the characters of the four sisters were, we will leave to be found out.

The clock struck six; and, having swept up the hearth, Beth put a pair of slippers down to warm. Somehow the sight of the old shoes had a good effect upon the girls, for mother was coming, and every one brightened to welcome her. Meg stopped lecturing, and lit the lamp, Amy got out of the easy-chair without being asked, and Jo forgot how tired she was as she sat up to hold the slippers nearer to the blaze.

"They are quite worn out; Marmee must have a new pair."

"I thought I'd get her some with my dollar," said Beth.

"No, I shall!" cried Amy.

"I'm the oldest," began Meg, but Jo cut in with a decided—

"I'm the man of the family now papa is away, and *I* shall provide the slippers, for he told me to take special care of mother while he was gone."

"I'll tell you what we'll do," said Beth; "let's each get her something for Christmas, and not get anything for ourselves."

"That's like you, dear! What will we get?" exclaimed Jo.

Every one thought soberly for a minute; then Meg announced, as if the idea was suggested by the sight of her own pretty hands, "I shall give her a nice pair of gloves."

"Army shoes, best to be had," cried Jo.

"Some handkerchiefs, all hemmed," said Beth.

"I'll get a little bottle of Cologne; she likes it, and it won't cost much, so I'll have some left to buy something for me," added Amy.

"How will we give the things?" asked Meg.

"Put 'em on the table, and bring her in and see her open the bundles. Don't you remember how we used to do on our birthdays?" answered Jo.

"I used to be so frightened when it was my turn to sit in the big chair with a crown on, and see you all come marching round to give the presents, with a kiss. I liked the things and the kisses, but it was dreadful to have you sit looking at me while I opened the bundles," said Beth, who was toasting her face and the bread for tea, at the same time.

"Let Marmee think we are getting things for ourselves, and then surprise her. We must go shopping to-morrow afternoon, Meg; there is lots to do about the play for Christmas night," said Jo, marching up and down with her hands behind her back, and her nose in the air.

"I don't mean to act any more after this time; I'm getting too old for such things," observed Meg, who was as much a child as ever about "dressing up" frolics.

"You won't stop, I know, as long as you can trail round in a white gown with your hair down, and wear gold-paper jewelry. You are the best actress we've got, and there'll be an end of everything if you quit the boards," said Jo. "We ought to rehearse to-night; come here, Amy, and do the fainting scene, for you are as stiff as a poker in that."

"I can't help it; I never saw any one faint, and I don't choose to make myself all black and blue, tumbling flat as you do. If I can go down easily, I'll drop; if I can't, I shall fall into a chair and be graceful; I don't care if Hugo does come at me with a pistol," returned Amy, who was not gifted with dramatic power, but was chosen because she was small enough to be borne out shrieking by the hero of the piece.

"Do it this way; clasp your hands so, and stagger across the room, crying frantically, 'Roderigo! save me! save me!'" and away went Jo, with a melodramatic scream which was truly thrilling.

Amy followed, but she poked her hands out stiffly before her, and jerked herself along as if she went by machinery; and her "Ow!" was more suggestive of pins being run into her than of fear and anguish. Jo gave a despairing groan, and Meg laughed outright, while Beth let her bread burn as she watched the fun, with interest.

"It's no use! do the best you can when the time comes, and if the audience shout, don't blame me. Come on, Meg."

Then things went smoothly, for Don Pedro defied the world in a speech of two pages without a single break; Hagar, the witch, chanted an awful incantation over her kettleful of simmering toads, with weird effect; Roderigo rent his chains asunder manfully, and Hugo died in agonies of remorse and arsenic, with a wild "Ha! ha!"

"It's the best we've had yet," said Meg, as the dead villain sat up and rubbed his elbows.

"I don't see how you can write and act such splendid things, Jo. You're a regular Shakespeare!" exclaimed Beth, who firmly believed that her sisters were gifted with wonderful genius in all things.

"Not quite," replied Jo, modestly. "I do think 'The Witch's Curse, an Operatic Tragedy,' is rather a nice thing; but I'd like to try Macbeth, if we only had a trapdoor for Banquo. I always wanted to do the killing part. 'Is that a dagger that I see before me?' " muttered Jo, rolling her eyes and clutching at the air, as she had seen a famous tragedian do.

"No, it's the toasting fork, with ma's shoe on it instead of the bread. Beth's stage struck!" cried Meg, and the rehearsal ended in a general burst of laughter.

"Glad to find you so merry, my girls," said a cheery voice at the door, and actors and audience turned to welcome a stout, motherly lady, with a "can-I-help-you" look about her which was truly delightful. She wasn't a particularly handsome person, but mothers are always lovely to their children, and the girls thought the gray cloak and unfashionable bonnet covered the most splendid woman in the world.

"Well, dearies, how have you got on to-day? There was so much to do, getting the boxes ready to go to-morrow, that I didn't come home to dinner. Has any one called, Beth? How is your cold, Meg? Jo, you look tired to death. Come and kiss me, baby."

While making these maternal inquiries Mrs. March got her wet things off, her hot slippers on, and sitting down in the easy-chair, drew Amy to her lap, preparing to enjoy the happiest hour of her busy day. The girls flew about, trying to make things comfortable, each in her own way. Meg arranged the tea-table; Jo brought wood and set chairs, dropping, overturning, and clattering everything she touched; Beth trotted to and fro between parlor and kitchen, quiet and busy; while Amy gave directions to every one, as she sat with her hands folded.

As they gathered about the table, Mrs. March said, with a particularly happy face, "I've got a treat for you after supper."

A quick, bright smile went round like a streak of sunshine. Beth clapped her hands, regardless of the hot biscuit she held, and Jo tossed up her napkin, crying, "A letter! a letter! Three cheers for father!"

"Yes, a nice long letter. He is well, and thinks he shall get through the cold season better than we feared. He sends all sorts of loving wishes for Christmas, and an especial message to you girls," said Mrs. March, patting her pocket as if she had got a treasure there.

"Hurry up, and get done. Don't stop to quirk your little finger, and prink over your plate, Amy," cried Jo, choking in her tea, and dropping her bread, butter side down, on the carpet, in her haste to get at the treat.

Beth ate no more, but crept away, to sit in her shadowy corner and brood over the delight to come, till the others were ready.

"I think it was so splendid in father to go as a chaplain when he was too old to be draughted, and not strong enough for a soldier," said Meg, warmly.

"Don't I wish I could go as a drummer, a *vivan*—what's its name?[5] or a nurse, so I could be near him and help him," exclaimed Jo, with a groan.

"It must be very disagreeable to sleep in a tent, and eat all sorts of bad-tasting things, and drink out of a tin mug," sighed Amy.

"When will he come home, Marmee?" asked Beth, with a little quiver in her voice.

5. Probably a *vivandière*, a woman who accompanied troops to sell them provisions.

"Not for many months, dear, unless he is sick. He will stay and do his work faithfully as long as he can, and we won't ask for him back a minute sooner than he can be spared. Now come and hear the letter."

They all drew to the fire, mother in the big chair with Beth at her feet, Meg and Amy perched on either arm of the chair, and Jo leaning on the back, where no one would see any sign of emotion if the letter should happen to be touching.

Very few letters were written in those hard times that were not touching, especially those which fathers sent home. In this one little was said of the hardships endured, the dangers faced, or the homesickness conquered; it was a cheerful, hopeful letter, full of lively descriptions of camp life, marches, and military news; and only at the end did the writer's heart overflow with fatherly love and longing for the little girls at home.

"Give them all my dear love and a kiss. Tell them I think of them by day, pray for them by night, and find my best comfort in their affection at all times. A year seems very long to wait before I see them, but remind them that while we wait we may all work, so that these hard days need not be wasted. I know they will remember all I said to them, that they will be loving children to you, will do their duty faithfully, fight their bosom enemies bravely, and conquer themselves so beautifully, that when I come back to them I may be fonder and prouder than ever of my little women."

Everybody sniffed when they came to that part; Jo wasn't ashamed of the great tear that dropped off the end of her nose, and Amy never minded the rumpling of her curls as she hid her face on her mother's shoulder and sobbed out, "I *am* a selfish pig! but I'll truly try to be better, so he mayn't be disappointed in me by and by."

"We all will!" cried Meg. "I think too much of my looks, and hate to work, but won't any more, if I can help it."

"I'll try and be what he loves to call me, 'a little woman,' and not be rough and wild; but do my duty here instead of wanting to be somewhere else," said Jo, thinking that keeping her temper at home was a much harder task than facing a rebel or two down South.

Beth said nothing, but wiped away her tears with the blue army-sock, and began to knit with all her might, losing no time in doing the duty that lay nearest her, while she resolved in her quiet little soul to be all that father hoped to find her when the year brought round the happy coming home.

Mrs. March broke the silence that followed Jo's words, by saying in her cheery voice, "Do you remember how you used to play Pilgrim's Progress when you were little things? Nothing delighted you more than to have me tie my piece-bags on your backs for burdens, give you hats and sticks, and rolls of paper, and let you travel through the house from the cellar, which was the City of Destruction, up, up, to the house-top, where you had all the lovely things you could collect to make a Celestial City."[6]

"What fun it was, especially going by the lions, fighting Apollyon, and passing through the Valley where the hobgoblins were," said Jo.

"I liked the place where the bundles fell off and tumbled down stairs," said Meg.

"My favorite part was when we came out on the flat roof where our flowers and arbors, and pretty things were, and all stood and sung for joy up there in the sunshine," said Beth, smiling, as if that pleasant moment had come back to her.

"I don't remember much about it, except that I was afraid of the cellar and the dark entry, and always liked the cake and milk we had up at the top. If I wasn't too old for such things, I'd rather like to play it over again," said Amy, who began to talk of renouncing childish things at the mature age of twelve.

"We never are too old for this, my dear, because it is a play we are playing all the time in one way or another. Our burdens are here, our road is before us, and the longing for goodness and happiness is the guide that leads us through many troubles and mistakes to the

6. Their game is based on John Bunyan's Christian allegory, published in two parts, in 1678 and 1684.

peace which is a true Celestial City. Now, my little pilgrims, suppose you begin again, not in play, but in earnest, and see how far on you can get before father comes home."

"Really, mother? where are our bundles?" asked Amy, who was a very literal young lady.

"Each of you told what your burden was just now, except Beth; I rather think she hasn't got any," said her mother.

"Yes, I have; mine is dishes and dusters, and envying girls with nice pianos, and being afraid of people."

Beth's bundle was such a funny one that everybody wanted to laugh; but nobody did, for it would have hurt her feelings very much.

"Let us do it," said Meg, thoughtfully. "It is only another name for trying to be good, and the story may help us; for though we do want to be good, it's hard work, and we forget, and don't do our best."

"We were in the Slough of Despond to-night, and mother came and pulled us out as Help did in the book. We ought to have our roll of directions, like Christian. What shall we do about that?" asked Jo, delighted with the fancy which lent a little romance to the very dull task of doing her duty.

"Look under your pillows, Christmas morning, and you will find your guide-book," replied Mrs. March.

They talked over the new plan while old Hannah cleared the table; then out came the four little workbaskets, and the needles flew as the girls made sheets for Aunt March. It was uninteresting sewing, but to-night no one grumbled. They adopted Jo's plan of dividing the long seams into four parts, and calling the quarters Europe, Asia, Africa and America, and in that way got on capitally, especially when they talked about the different countries as they stitched their way through them.

At nine they stopped work, and sung, as usual, before they went to bed. No one but Beth could get much music out of the old piano; but she had a way of softly touching the yellow keys, and making a pleasant accompaniment to the simple songs they sung. Meg had a voice like a flute, and she and her mother led the little choir. Amy chirped like a cricket, and Jo wandered through the airs at her own sweet will, always coming out at the wrong place with a crook or a quaver that spoilt the most pensive tune. They had always done this from the time they could lisp

"Crinkle, crinkle, 'ittle 'tar,"

and it had become a household custom, for the mother was a born singer. The first sound in the morning was her voice, as she went about the house singing like a lark; and the last sound at night was the same cheery sound, for the girls never grew too old for that familiar lullaby.

2
A Merry Christmas

Jo was the first to wake in the gray dawn of Christmas morning. No stockings hung at the fireplace, and for a moment she felt as much disappointed as she did long ago, when her little sock fell down because it was so crammed with goodies. Then she remembered her mother's promise, and slipping her hand under her pillow, drew out a little crimson-covered book. She knew it very well, for it was that beautiful old story of the best life ever lived,[7] and Jo felt

---

7. Probably a New Testament, chronicling the life of Jesus.

that it was a true guide-book for any pilgrim going the long journey. She woke Meg with a "Merry Christmas," and bade her see what was under her pillow. A green-covered book appeared, with the same picture inside, and a few words written by their mother, which made their one present very precious in their eyes. Presently Beth and Amy woke, to rummage and find their little books also,—one dove-colored, the other blue; and all sat looking at and talking about them, while the East grew rosy with the coming day.

In spite of her small vanities, Margaret had a sweet and pious nature, which unconsciously influenced her sisters, especially Jo, who loved her very tenderly, and obeyed her because her advice was so gently given.

"Girls," said Meg, seriously, looking from the tumbled head beside her to the two little night-capped ones in the room beyond, "mother wants us to read and love and mind these books, and we must begin at once. We used to be faithful about it; but since father went away, and all this war trouble unsettled us, we have neglected many things. You can do as you please; but *I* shall keep my book on the table here, and read a little every morning as soon as I wake, for I know it will do me good, and help me through the day."

Then she opened her new book and began to read. Jo put her arm round her, and, leaning cheek to cheek, read also, with the quiet expression so seldom seen on her restless face.

"How good Meg is! Come, Amy, let's do as they do. I'll help you with the hard words, and they'll explain things if we don't understand," whispered Beth, very much impressed by the pretty books and her sisters' example.

"I'm glad mine is blue," said Amy; and then the rooms were very still while the pages were softly turned, and the winter sunshine crept in to touch the bright heads and serious faces with a Christmas greeting.

"Where is mother?" asked Meg, as she and Jo ran down to thank her for their gifts, half an hour later.

"Goodness only knows. Some poor creeter come a-beggin', and your ma went straight off to see what was needed. There never *was* such a woman for givin' away vittles and drink, clothes and firin'," replied Hannah, who had lived with the family since Meg was born, and was considered by them all more as a friend than a servant.

"She will be back soon, I guess; so do your cakes, and have everything ready," said Meg, looking over the presents which were collected in a basket and kept under the sofa, ready to be produced at the proper time. "Why, where is Amy's bottle of Cologne?" she added, as the little flask did not appear.

"She took it out a minute ago, and went off with it to put a ribbon on it, or some such notion," replied Jo, dancing about the room to take the first stiffness off the new army-slippers.

"How nice my handkerchiefs look, don't they? Hannah washed and ironed them for me, and I marked them all myself," said Beth, looking proudly at the somewhat uneven letters which had cost her such labor.

"Bless the child, she's gone and put 'Mother' on them instead of 'M. March;' how funny!" cried Jo, taking up one.

"Isn't it right? I thought it was better to do it so, because Meg's initials are 'M. M.,' and I don't want any one to use these but Marmee," said Beth, looking troubled.

"It's all right, dear, and a very pretty idea; quite sensible, too, for no one can ever mistake now. It will please her very much, I know," said Meg, with a frown for Jo, and a smile for Beth.

"There's mother; hide the basket, quick!" cried Jo, as a door slammed, and steps sounded in the hall.

Amy came in hastily, and looked rather abashed when she saw her sisters all waiting for her.

"Where have you been, and what are you hiding behind you?" asked Meg, surprised to see, by her hood and cloak, that lazy Amy had been out so early.

"Don't laugh at me, Jo, I didn't mean any one should know till the time came. I only meant to change the little bottle for a big one, and I gave *all* my money to get it, and I'm truly trying not to be selfish any more."

As she spoke, Amy showed the handsome flask which replaced the cheap one; and looked so earnest and humble in her little effort to forget herself, that Meg hugged her on the spot, and Jo pronounced her "a trump," while Beth ran to the window, and picked her finest rose to ornament the stately bottle.

"You see I felt ashamed of my present, after reading and talking about being good this morning, so I ran round the corner and changed it the minute I was up; and I'm *so* glad, for mine is the handsomest now."

Another bang of the street-door sent the basket under the sofa, and the girls to the table eager for breakfast.

"Merry Christmas, Marmee! Lots of them! Thank you for our books; we read some, and mean to every day," they cried, in chorus.

"Merry Christmas, little daughters! I'm glad you began at once, and hope you will keep on. But I want to say one word before we sit down. Not far away from here lies a poor woman with a little newborn baby. Six children are huddled into one bed to keep from freezing, for they have no fire. There is nothing to eat over there; and the oldest boy came to tell me they were suffering hunger and cold. My girls, will you give them your breakfast as a Christmas present?"

They were all unusually hungry, having waited nearly an hour, and for a minute no one spoke; only a minute, for Jo exclaimed impetuously,—

"I'm so glad you came before we began!"

"May I go and help carry the things to the poor little children?" asked Beth, eagerly.

"*I* shall take the cream and the muffins," added Amy, heroically giving up the articles she most liked.

Meg was already covering the buckwheats, and piling the bread into one big plate.

"I thought you'd do it," said Mrs. March, smiling as if satisfied. "You shall all go and help me, and when we come back we will have bread and milk for breakfast, and make it up at dinner-time."

They were soon ready, and the procession set out. Fortunately it was early, and they went through back streets, so few people saw them, and no one laughed at the funny party.

A poor, bare, miserable room it was, with broken windows, no fire, ragged bed-clothes, a sick mother, wailing baby, and a group of pale, hungry children cuddled under one old quilt, trying to keep warm. How the big eyes stared, and the blue lips smiled, as the girls went in!

"Ach, mein Gott! it is good angels come to us!" cried the poor woman, crying for joy.

"Funny angels in hoods and mittens," said Jo, and set them laughing.

In a few minutes it really did seem as if kind spirits had been at work there. Hannah, who had carried wood, made a fire, and stopped up the broken panes with old hats, and her own shawl. Mrs. March gave the mother tea and gruel, and comforted her with promises of help, while she dressed the little baby as tenderly as if it had been her own. The girls, meantime, spread the table, set the children round the fire, and fed them like so many hungry birds; laughing, talking, and trying to understand the funny broken English.

"Das ist gute!" "Der angel-kinder!" cried the poor things, as they ate, and warmed their purple hands at the comfortable blaze. The girls had never been called angel children before, and thought it very agreeable, especially Jo, who had been considered "a Sancho"[8] ever since she was born. That was a very happy breakfast, though they didn't get any of it; and when they went away, leaving comfort behind, I think there were not in all the city four merrier

---

8.   Perhaps an allusion to Sancho Panza, the clownish companion of Don Quixote in Cervantes's satirical romance, published 1605–1615.

people than the hungry little girls who gave away their breakfasts, and contented themselves with bread and milk on Christmas morning.

"That's loving our neighbor better than ourselves, and I like it," said Meg, as they set out their presents, while their mother was upstairs collecting clothes for the poor Hummels.

Not a very splendid show, but there was a great deal of love done up in the few little bundles; and the tall vase of red roses, white chrysanthemums, and trailing vines, which stood in the middle, gave quite an elegant air to the table.

"She's coming! strike up, Beth, open the door, Amy. Three cheers for Marmee!" cried Jo, prancing about, while Meg went to conduct mother to the seat of honor.

Beth played her gayest march, Amy threw open the door, and Meg enacted escort with great dignity. Mrs. March was both surprised and touched; and smiled with her eyes full as she examined her presents, and read the little notes which accompanied them. The slippers went on at once, a new handkerchief was slipped into her pocket, well scented with Amy's Cologne, the rose was fastened in her bosom, and the nice gloves were pronounced "a perfect fit."

There was a good deal of laughing, and kissing, and explaining, in the simple, loving fashion which makes these home-festivals so pleasant at the time, so sweet to remember long afterward, and then all fell to work.

The morning charities and ceremonies took so much time, that the rest of the day was devoted to preparations for the evening festivities. Being still too young to go often to the theatre, and not rich enough to afford any great outlay for private performances, the girls put their wits to work, and, necessity being the mother of invention, made whatever they needed. Very clever were some of their productions; paste-board guitars, antique lamps made of old-fashioned butter-boats, covered with silver paper, gorgeous robes of old cotton, glittering with tin spangles from a pickle factory, and armor covered with the same useful diamond-shaped bits, left in sheets when the lids of tin preserve-pots were cut out. The furniture was used to being turned topsy-turvy, and the big chamber was the scene of many innocent revels.

No gentlemen were admitted; so Jo played male parts to her heart's content, and took immense satisfaction in a pair of russet-leather boots given her by a friend, who knew a lady who knew an actor. These boots, an old foil, and a slashed doublet once used by an artist for some picture, were Jo's chief treasures, and appeared on all occasions. The smallness of the company made it necessary for the two principal actors to take several parts apiece; and they certainly deserved some credit for the hard work they did in learning three or four different parts, whisking in and out of various costumes, and managing the stage besides. It was excellent drill for their memories, a harmless amusement, and employed many hours which otherwise would have been idle, lonely, or spent in less profitable society.

On Christmas night, a dozen girls piled on to the bed, which was the dress circle, and sat before the blue and yellow chintz curtains, in a most flattering state of expectancy. There was a good deal of rustling and whispering behind the curtain, a trifle of lampsmoke, and an occasional giggle from Amy, who was apt to get hysterical in the excitement of the moment. Presently a bell sounded, the curtains flew apart, and the Operatic Tragedy began.

"A gloomy wood," according to the one play-bill, was represented by a few shrubs in pots, a green baize[9] on the floor, and a cave in the distance. This cave was made with a clothes-horse for a roof, bureaus for walls; and in it was a small furnace in full blast, with a black pot on it, and an old witch bending over it. The stage was dark, and the glow of the furnace had a fine effect, especially as real steam issued from the kettle when the witch took off the cover. A moment was allowed for the first thrill to subside; then Hugo, the villain, stalked in with a clanking sword at his side, a slouched hat, black beard, mysterious cloak, and the boots. After pacing to and fro in much agitation, he struck his forehead, and burst out in a wild strain, singing of his hatred for Roderigo, his love for Zara, and his pleasing resolution to kill the

---

9. A bright green, feltlike table cover.

one and win the other. The gruff tones of Hugo's voice, with an occasional shout when his feelings overcame him, were very impressive, and the audience applauded the moment he paused for breath. Bowing with the air of one accustomed to public praise, he stole to the cavern and ordered Hagar to come forth with a commanding "What ho! minion! I need thee!"

Out came Meg, with gray horse-hair hanging about her face, a red and black robe, a staff, and cabalistic[1] signs upon her cloak. Hugo demanded a potion to make Zara adore him, and one to destroy Roderigo. Hagar, in a fine dramatic melody, promised both, and proceeded to call up the spirit who would bring the love philter:—

> "Hither, hither, from they home,
> Airy sprite, I bid thee come!
> Born of roses, fed on dew,
> Charms and potions canst thou brew?
> Bring me here, with elfin speed,
> The fragrant philter which I need;
> Make it sweet, and swift and strong;
> Spirit, answer now my song!"

A soft strain of music sounded, and then at the back of the cave appeared a little figure in cloudy white, with glittering wings, golden hair, and a garland of roses on its head. Waving a wand, it sung:—

> "Hither I come,
> From my airy home,
> Afar in the silver moon;
> Take the magic spell,
> Oh, use it well!
> Or its power will vanish soon!"

and dropping a small gilded bottle at the witch's feet, the spirit vanished. Another chant from Hagar produced another apparition,—not a lovely one, for, with a bang, an ugly, black imp appeared, and having croaked a reply, tossed a dark bottle at Hugo, and disappeared with a mocking laugh. Having warbled his thanks, and put the potions in his boots, Hugo departed; and Hagar informed the audience that, as he had killed a few of her friends in times past, she has cursed him, and intends to thwart his plans, and be revenged on him. Then the curtain fell, and the audience reposed and ate candy while discussing the merits of the play.

A good deal of hammering went on before the curtain rose again; but when it became evident what a masterpiece of stage carpentering had been got up, no one murmured at the delay. It was truly superb! A tower rose to the ceiling; half-way up appeared a window with a lamp burning at it, and behind the white curtain appeared Zara in a lovely blue and silver dress, waiting for Roderigo. He came, in gorgeous array, with plumed cap, red cloak, chestnut lovelocks,[2] a guitar, and the boots, of course. Kneeling at the foot of the tower, he sung a serenade in melting tones. Zara replied, and after a musical dialogue, consented to fly. Then came the grand effect of the play. Roderigo produced a rope-ladder with five steps to it, threw up one end, and invited Zara to descend. Timidly she crept from her lattice, put her hand on Roderigo's shoulder, and was about to leap gracefully down, when, "alas, alas for Zara!" she forgot her train,—it caught in the window; the tower tottered, leaned forward, fell with a crash, and buried the unhappy lovers in the ruins!

1. Occult, mysterious.
2. A curled lock of hair tied with a ribbon, worn by fashionable men in the seventeenth and eighteenth centuries.

A universal shriek arose as the russet boots waved wildly from the wreck, and a golden head emerged, exclaiming "I told you so! I told you so!" With wonderful presence of mind Don Pedro, the cruel sire, rushed in, dragged out his daughter with a hasty aside,—

"Don't laugh, act as if it was all right!" and ordering Roderigo up, banished him from the kingdom with wrath and scorn. Though decidedly shaken by the fall of the tower upon him, Roderigo defied the old gentleman, and refused to stir. This dauntless example fired Zara; she also defied her sire, and he ordered them both to the deepest dungeons of the castle. A stout little retainer came in with chains, and led them away, looking very much frightened, and evidently forgetting the speech he ought to have made.

Act third was the castle hall; and here Hagar appeared, having come to free the lovers and finish Hugo. She hears him coming, and hides; sees him put the potions into two cups of wine, and bid the timid little servant "Bear them to the captives in their cells, and tell them I shall come anon." The servant takes Hugo aside to tell him something, and Hagar changes the cups for two others which are harmless. Ferdinando, the "minion," carries them away, and Hagar puts back the cup which holds the poison meant for Roderigo. Hugo, getting thirsty after a long warble, drinks it, loses his wits, and after a good deal of clutching and stamping, falls flat and dies; while Hagar informs him what she has done in a song of exquisite power and melody.

This was a truly thrilling scene; though some persons might have thought that the sudden tumbling down of a quantity of long hair rather marred the effect of the villain's death. He was called before the curtain, and with great propriety appeared leading Hagar, whose singing was considered more wonderful than all the rest of the performance put together.

Act fourth displayed the despairing Roderigo on the point of stabbing himself, because he has been told that Zara has deserted him. Just as the dagger is at his heart, a lovely song is sung under his window, informing him that Zara is true, but in danger, and he can save her if he will. A key is thrown in, which unlocks the door, and in a spasm of rapture he tears off his chains, and rushes away to find and rescue his lady-love.

Act fifth opened with a stormy scene between Zara and Don Pedro. He wishes her to go into a convent, but she won't hear of it; and, after a touching appeal, is about to faint, when Roderigo dashes in and demands her hand. Don Pedro refuses, because he is not rich. They shout and gesticulate tremendously, but cannot agree, and Roderigo is about to bear away the exhausted Zara, when the timid servant enters with a letter and a bag from Hagar, who has mysteriously disappeared. The latter informs the party that she bequeaths untold wealth to the young pair, and an awful doom to Don Pedro if he doesn't make them happy. The bag is opened, and several quarts of tin money shower down upon the stage, till it is quite glorified with the glitter. This entirely softens the "stern sire;" he consents without a murmur, all join in a joyful chorus, and the curtain falls upon the lovers kneeling to receive Don Pedro's blessing, in attitudes of the most romantic grace.

Tumultuous applause followed, but received an unexpected check; for the cot-bed on which the "dress circle" was built, suddenly shut up, and extinguished the enthusiastic audience. Roderigo and Don Pedro flew to the rescue, and all were taken out unhurt, though many were speechless with laughter. The excitement had hardly subsided when Hannah appeared, with "Mrs. March's compliments, and would the ladies walk down to supper."

This was a surprise, even to the actors; and when they saw the table they looked at one another in rapturous amazement. It was like "Marmee" to get up a little treat for them, but anything so fine as this was unheard of since the departed days of plenty. There was ice cream, actually two dishes of it,—pink and white,—and cake, and fruit, and distracting French bonbons, and in the middle of the table four great bouquets of hot-house flowers!

It quite took their breath away; and they stared first at the table and then at their mother, who looked as if she enjoyed it immensely.

"Is it fairies?" asked Amy.

"It's Santa Claus," said Beth.

"Mother did it;" and Meg smiled her sweetest, in spite of her gray beard and white eyebrows.

"Aunt March had a good fit, and sent the supper," cried Jo, with a sudden inspiration.

"All wrong; old Mr. Laurence sent it," replied Mrs. March.

"The Laurence boy's grandfather! What in the world put such a thing into his head? We don't know him," exclaimed Meg.

"Hannah told one of his servants about your breakfast party; he is an odd old gentleman, but that pleased him. He knew my father, years ago, and he sent me a polite note this afternoon, saying he hoped I would allow him to express his friendly feeling toward my children by sending them a few trifles in honor of the day. I could not refuse, and so you have a little feast at night to make up for the bread and milk breakfast."

"That boy put it into his head, I know he did! He's a capital fellow, and I wish we could get acquainted. He looks as if he'd like to know us; but he's bashful, and Meg is so prim she won't let me speak to him when we pass," said Jo, as the plates went round, and the ice began to melt out of sight, with ohs! and ahs! of satisfaction.

"You mean the people who live in the big house next door, don't you?" asked one of the girls. "My mother knows old Mr. Laurence, but says he's very proud, and don't like to mix with his neighbors. He keeps his grandson shut up when he isn't riding or walking with his tutor, and makes him study dreadful hard. We invited him to our party, but he didn't come. Mother says he's very nice, though he never speaks to us girls."

"Our cat ran away once, and he brought her back, and we talked over the fence, and were getting on capitally, all about cricket, and so on, when he saw Meg coming, and walked off. I mean to know him some day, for he needs fun, I'm sure he does," said Jo, decidedly.

"I like his manners, and he looks like a little gentleman, so I've no objection to your knowing him if a proper opportunity comes. He brought the flowers himself, and I should have asked him in if I had been sure what was going on upstairs. He looked so wistful as he went away, hearing the frolic, and evidently having none of his own."

"It's a mercy you didn't mother," laughed Jo, looking at her boots. "But we'll have another play some time, that he *can* see. Maybe he'll help act; wouldn't that be jolly?"

"I never had a bouquet before; how pretty it is," and Meg examined her flowers with great interest.

"They *are* lovely, but Beth's roses are sweeter to me," said Mrs. March, sniffing at the half dead posy in her belt.

Beth nestled up to her, and whispered, softly, "I wish I could send my bunch to father. I'm afraid he isn't having such a merry Christmas as we are."

3
The Laurence Boy

"Jo! Jo! where are you?" cried Meg, at the foot of the garret stairs.

"Here," answered a husky voice from above; and running up, Meg found her sister eating apples and crying over the "Heir of Redcliffe,"[3] wrapped up in a comforter on an old three-legged sofa by the sunny window. This was Jo's favorite refuge; and here she loved to retire with half a dozen russets and a nice book, to enjoy the quiet and the society of a pet rat who lived near by, and didn't mind her a particle. As Meg appeared, Scrabble whisked into his hole. Jo shook the tears off her cheeks, and waited to hear the news.

3. *The Heir of Redclyffe* (1853), a British novel by Charlotte Yonge, who specialized in domestic fiction.

"Such fun! only see! a regular note of invitation from Mrs. Gardiner for to-morrow night!" cried Meg, waving the precious paper, and then proceeding to read it, with girlish delight.

" 'Mrs. Gardiner would be happy to see Miss March and Miss Josephine at a little dance on New-Year's-Eve.' Marmee is willing we should go; now what *shall* we wear?"

"What's the use of asking that, when you know we shall wear our poplins, because we haven't got anything else," answered Jo, with her mouth full.

"If I only had a silk!" sighed Meg; "mother says I may when I'm eighteen, perhaps; but two years is an everlasting time to wait."

"I'm sure our pops look like silk, and they are nice enough for us. Yours is as good as new, but I forgot the burn and the tear in mine; whatever shall I do? the burn shows horridly, and I can't take any out."

"You must sit still all you can, and keep your back out of sight; the front is all right. I shall have a new ribbon for my hair, and Marmee will lend me her little pearl pin, and my new slippers are lovely, and my gloves will do, though they aren't as nice as I'd like."

"Mine are spoilt with lemonade, and I can't get any new ones, so I shall have to go without," said Jo, who never troubled herself much about dress.

"You *must* have gloves, or I won't go," cried Meg, decidedly. "Gloves are more important than anything else; you can't dance without them, and if you don't I should be *so* mortified."

"Then I'll stay still; I don't care much for company dancing; it's no fun to go sailing round, I like to fly about and cut capers."

"You can't ask mother for new ones, they are so expensive, and you are so careless. She said, when you spoilt the others, that she shouldn't get you any more this winter. Can't you fix them any way?" asked Meg, anxiously.

"I can hold them crunched up in my hand, so no one will know how stained they are; that's all I can do. No! I'll tell you how we can manage—each wear one good one and carry a bad one; don't you see?"

"Your hands are bigger than mine, and you will stretch my glove dreadfully," began Meg, whose gloves were a tender point with her.

"Then I'll go without. I don't care what people say," cried Jo, taking up her book.

"You may have it, you may! only don't stain it, and do behave nicely; don't put your hands behind you, or stare, or say 'Christopher Columbus!' will you?"

"Don't worry about me; I'll be as prim as a dish, and not get into any scrapes, if I can help it. Now go and answer your note, and let me finish this splendid story."

So Meg went away to "accept with thanks," look over her dress, and sing blithely as she did up her one real lace frill; while Jo finished her story, her four apples, and had a game of romps with Scrabble.

On New-Year's-Eve the parlor was deserted, for the two younger girls played dressing maids, and the two elder were absorbed in the all-important business of "getting ready for the party." Simple as the toilets were, there was a great deal of running up and down, laughing and talking, and at one time a strong smell of burnt hair pervaded the house. Meg wanted a few curls about her face, and Jo undertook to pinch the papered locks with a pair of hot tongs.

"Ought they to smoke like that?" asked Beth, from her perch on the bed.

"It's the dampness drying," replied Jo.

"What a queer smell! it's like burnt feathers," observed Amy, smoothing her own pretty curls with a superior air.

"There, now I'll take off the papers and you'll see a cloud of little ringlets," said Jo, putting down the tongs.

She did take off the papers, but no cloud of ringlets appeared, for the hair came with the papers, and the horrified hair-dresser laid a row of little scorched bundles on the bureau before her victim.

"Oh, oh, oh! what *have* you done? I'm spoilt! I can't go! my hair, oh my hair!" wailed Meg, looking with despair at the uneven frizzle on her forehead.

"Just my luck! you shouldn't have asked me to do it; I always spoil everything. I'm no end sorry, but the tongs were too hot, and so I've made a mess," groaned poor Jo, regarding the black pancakes with tears of regret.

"It isn't spoilt; just frizzle it, and tie your ribbon so the ends come on your forehead a bit, and it will look like the last fashion. I've seen lots of girls do it so," said Amy, consolingly.

"Serves me right for trying to be fine. I wish I'd let my hair alone," cried Meg, petulantly.

"So do I, it was so smooth and pretty. But it will soon grow out again," said Beth, coming to kiss and comfort the shorn sheep.

After various lesser mishaps, Meg was finished at last, and by the united exertions of the family Jo's hair was got up, and her dress on. They looked very well in their simple suits, Meg in silvery drab, with a blue velvet snood, lace frills, and the pearl pin;[4] Jo in maroon, with a stiff, gentlemanly linen collar, and a white chrysanthemum or two for her only ornament. Each put on one nice light glove, and carried one soiled one, and all pronounced the effect "quite easy and nice." Meg's high-heeled slippers were dreadfully tight, and hurt her, though she would not own it, and Jo's nineteen hair-pins all seemed stuck straight into her head, which was not exactly comfortable; but, dear me, let us be elegant or die.

"Have a good time, dearies," said Mrs. March, as the sisters went daintily down the walk. "Don't eat much supper, and come away at eleven, when I send Hannah for you." As the gate clashed behind them, a voice cried from a window,—

"Girls, girls! *have* you both got nice pocket-handkerchiefs?"

"Yes, yes, spandy nice, and Meg has Cologne on hers," cried Jo, adding, with a laugh, as they went on, "I do believe Marmee would ask that if we were all running away from an earthquake."

"It is one of her aristocratic tastes, and quite proper, for a real lady is always known by neat boots, gloves, and handkerchief," replied Meg, who had a good many little "aristocratic tastes" of her own.

"Now don't forget to keep the bad breadth out of sight, Jo. Is my sash right; and does my hair look *very* bad?" said Meg, as she turned from the glass in Mrs. Gardiner's dressing-room, after a prolonged prink.[5]

"I know I shall forget. If you see me doing anything wrong, you just remind me by a wink, will you?" returned Jo, giving her collar a twitch and her head a hasty brush.

"No, winking isn't lady-like; I'll lift my eyebrows if anything is wrong, and nod if you are all right. Now hold your shoulders straight, and take short steps, and don't shake hands if you are introduced to any one, it isn't the thing."

"How *do* you learn all the proper quirks? I never can. Isn't that music gay?"

Down they went, feeling a trifle timid, for they seldom went to parties, and, informal as this little gathering was, it was an event to them. Mrs. Gardiner, a stately old lady, greeted them kindly, and handed them over to the eldest of her six daughters. Meg knew Sallie, and was at her ease very soon; but Jo, who didn't care much for girls or girlish gossip, stood about with her back carefully against the wall, and felt as much out of place as a colt in a flower-garden. Half a dozen jovial lads were talking about skates in another part of the room, and she longed to go and join them, for skating was one of the joys of her life. She telegraphed her wish to Meg, but the eyebrows went up so alarmingly that she dared not stir. No one came to talk to her, and one by one the group near her dwindled away, till she was left alone. She could not roam about and amuse herself, for the burnt breadth would show, so she stared at people rather forlornly till the dancing began. Meg was asked at once, and the tight slippers tripped about so briskly that none would have guessed the pain their wearer suffered

---

4. "Drab" is unbleached, natural-color wool or   5. Primping.
    cotton fabric; a "snood" is a hairnet.

smilingly. Jo saw a big red-headed youth approaching her corner, and fearing he meant to engage her, she slipped into a curtained recess, intending to peep and enjoy herself in peace. Unfortunately, another bashful person had chosen the same refuge; for, as the curtain fell behind her, she found herself face to face with the "Laurence boy."

"Dear me, I didn't know any one was here!" stammered Jo, preparing to back out as speedily as she had bounced in.

But the boy laughed, and said, pleasantly, though he looked a little startled,—

"Don't mind me; stay, if you like."

"Shan't I disturb you?"

"Not a bit; I only came here because I don't know many people, and felt rather strange at first, you know."

"So did I. Don't go away, please, unless you'd rather."

The boy sat down again and looked at his boots, till Jo said, trying to be polite and easy,—

"I think I've had the pleasure of seeing you before; you live near us, don't you?"

"Next door;" and he looked up and laughed outright, for Jo's prim manner was rather funny when he remembered how they had chatted about cricket when he brought the cat home.

That put Jo at her ease; and she laughed too, as she said, in her heartiest way,—

"We did have such a good time over your nice Christmas present."

"Grandpa sent it."

"But you put it into his head, didn't you, now?"

"How is your cat, Miss March?" asked the boy, trying to look sober, while his black eyes shone with fun.

"Nicely, thank you, Mr. Laurence; but I ain't Miss March, I'm only Jo," returned the young lady.

"I'm not Mr. Laurence, I'm only Laurie."

"Laurie Laurence; what an odd name."

"My first name is Theodore, but I don't like it, for the fellows called me Dora, so I made them say Laurie instead."

"I hate my name, too—so sentimental! I wish every one would say Jo, instead of Josephine. How did you make the boys stop calling you Dora?"

"I thrashed 'em."

"I can't thrash Aunt March, so I suppose I shall have to bear it;" and Jo resigned herself with a sigh.

"Don't you like to dance, Miss Jo?" asked Laurie, looking as if he thought the name suited her.

"I like it well enough if there is plenty of room, and every one is lively. In a place like this I'm sure to upset something, tread on people's toes, or do something dreadful, so I keep out of mischief, and let Meg do the pretty. Don't you dance?"

"Sometimes; you see I've been abroad a good many years, and haven't been about enough yet to know how you do things here."

"Abroad!" cried Jo, "oh, tell me about it! I love dearly to hear people describe their travels."

Laurie didn't seem to know where to begin; but Jo's eager questions soon set him going, and he told her how he had been at school in Vevey, where the boys never wore hats, and had a fleet of boats on the lake, and for holiday fun went on walking trips about Switzerland with their teachers.

"Don't I wish I'd been there!" cried Jo. "Did you go to Paris?"

"We spent last winter there."

"Can you talk French?"

"We were not allowed to speak anything else at Vevey."

"Do say some. I can read it, but can't pronounce."

"Quel nom a cette jeune demoiselle en les pantoufles jolis?" said Laurie, good-naturedly.

"How nicely you do it! Let me see—you said, 'Who is the young lady in the pretty slippers,' didn't you?"

"Oui, mademoiselle."

"It's my sister Margaret, and you knew it was! Do you think she is pretty?"

"Yes; she makes me think of the German girls, she looks so fresh and quiet, and dances like a lady."

Jo quite glowed with pleasure at this boyish praise of her sister, and stored it up to repeat to Meg. Both peeped, and criticised, and chatted, till they felt like old acquaintances. Laurie's bashfulness soon wore off, for Jo's gentlemanly demeanor amused and set him at his ease, and Jo was her merry self again, because her dress was forgotten, and nobody lifted their eyebrows at her. She liked the "Laurence boy" better than ever, and took several good looks at him, so that she might describe him to the girls; for they had no brothers, very few male cousins, and boys were almost unknown creatures to them.

Curly black hair, brown skin, big black eyes, long nose, nice teeth, little hands and feet, tall as I am; very polite for a boy, and altogether jolly. Wonder how old he is?

It was on the tip of Jo's tongue to ask; but she checked herself in time, and, with unusual tact, tried to find out in a roundabout way.

"I suppose you are going to college soon? I see you pegging away at your books—no, I mean studying hard;" and Jo blushed at the dreadful "pegging" which had escaped her.

Laurie smiled, but didn't seem shocked, and answered, with a shrug,—

"Not for two or three years yet; I won't go before seventeen, any-way."

"Aren't you but fifteen?" asked Jo, looking at the tall lad, whom she had imagined seventeen already.

"Sixteen, next month."

"How I wish I was going to college; you don't look as if you liked it."

"I hate it! nothing but grinding or sky-larking; and I don't like the way fellows do either, in this country."

"What do you like?"

"To live in Italy, and to enjoy myself in my own way."

Jo wanted very much to ask what his own way was; but his black brows looked rather threatening as he knit them, so she changed the subject by saying, as her foot kept time, "That's a splendid polka; why don't you go and try it?"

"If you will come too," he answered, with a queer little French bow.

"I can't; for I told Meg I wouldn't because—" there Jo stopped, and looked undecided whether to tell or to laugh.

"Because what?" asked Laurie, curiously.

"You won't tell?"

"Never!"

"Well, I have a bad trick of standing before the fire, and so I burn my frocks, and I scorched this one; and, though it's nicely mended, it shows, and Meg told me to keep still, so no one would see it. You may laugh if you want to; it is funny, I know."

But Laurie didn't laugh; he only looked down a minute, and the expression of his face puzzled Jo, when he said very gently,—

"Never mind that; I'll tell you how we can manage: there's a long hall out there, and we can dance grandly, and no one will see us. Please come."

Jo thanked him, and gladly went, wishing she had two neat gloves, when she saw the nice pearl-colored ones her partner put on. The hall was empty, and they had a grand polk, for Laurie danced well, and taught her the German step, which delighted Jo, being full of swing and spring. When the music stopped they sat down on the stairs to get their breath, and Laurie was in the midst of an account of a students' festival at Heidelberg, when Meg appeared in search of her sister. She beckoned, and Jo reluctantly followed her into a side-room, where she found her on a sofa holding her foot, and looking pale.

"I've sprained my ankle. That stupid high heel turned, and gave me a horrid wrench. It aches so, I can hardly stand, and I don't know how I'm ever going to get home," she said, rocking to and fro in pain.

"I knew you'd hurt your foot with those silly things. I'm sorry; but I don't see what you can do, except get a carriage, or stay here all night," answered Jo, softly rubbing the poor ankle, as she spoke.

"I can't have a carriage without its costing ever so much; I dare say I can't get one at all, for most people come in their own, and it's a long way to the stable, and no one to send."

"I'll go."

"No, indeed; it's past ten, and dark as Egypt. I can't stop here, for the house is full; Sallie has some girls staying with her. I'll rest till Hannah comes, and then do the best I can."

"I'll ask Laurie; he will go," said Jo, looking relieved as the idea occurred to her.

"Mercy, no! don't ask or tell any one. Get me my rubbers,[6] and put these slippers with our things. I can't dance any more; but as soon as supper is over, watch for Hannah, and tell me the minute she comes."

"They are going out to supper now. I'll stay with you; I'd rather."

"No, dear; run along, and bring me some coffee. I'm so tired, I can't stir."

So Meg reclined, with the rubbers well hidden, and Jo went blundering away to the dining-room, which she found after going into a china-closet and opening the door of a room where old Mr. Gardiner was taking a little private refreshment. Making a dive at the table, she secured the coffee, which she immediately spilt, thereby making the front of her dress as bad as the back.

"Oh dear! what a blunderbuss I am!" exclaimed Jo, finishing Meg's glove by scrubbing her gown with it.

"Can I help you?" said a friendly voice; and there was Laurie, with a full cup in one hand and a plate of ice in the other.

"I was trying to get something for Meg, who is very tired, and some one shook me, and here I am, in a nice state," answered Jo, glancing, dismally, from the stained skirt to the coffee-colored glove.

"Too bad! I was looking for some one to give this to; may I take it to your sister?"

"Oh, thank you; I'll show you where she is. I don't offer to take it myself, for I should only get into another scrape if I did."

Jo led the way; and, as if used to waiting on ladies, Laurie drew up a little table, brought a second instalment of coffee and ice for Jo, and was so obliging that even particular Meg pronounced him a "nice boy." They had a merry time over the bonbons and mottos, and were in the midst of a quiet game of "buzz" with two or three other young people who had strayed in, when Hannah appeared. Meg forgot her foot, and rose so quickly that she was forced to catch hold of Jo, with an exclamation of pain.

"Hush! don't say anything," she whispered; adding aloud, "It's nothing; I turned my foot a little,—that's all," and limped up stairs to put her things on.

Hannah scolded, Meg cried, and Jo was at her wits' end, till she decided to take things into her own hands. Slipping out, she ran down, and finding a servant, asked if he could get her a carriage. It happened to be a hired waiter, who knew nothing about the neighborhood; and Jo was looking round for help, when Laurie, who had heard what she did, came up and offered his grandfather's carriage, which had just come for him, he said.

"It's so early,—you can't mean to go yet," began Jo, looking relieved, but hesitating to accept the offer.

"I always go early,—I do, truly. Please let me take you home; it's all on my way, you know, and it rains, they say."

That settled it; and telling him of Meg's mishap, Jo gratefully accepted, and rushed up to bring down the rest of the party. Hannah hated rain as much as a cat does; so she made no trouble, and they rolled away in the luxurious close carriage, feeling very festive and elegant.

6.   Overshoes.

Laurie went on the box, so Meg could keep her foot up, and the girls talked over their party in freedom.

"I had a capital time; did you?" asked Jo, rumpling up her hair, and making herself comfortable.

"Yes, till I hurt myself. Sallie's friend, Annie Moffat, took a fancy to me, and asked me to come and spend a week with her when Sallie does. She is going in the spring, when the opera comes, and it will be perfectly splendid if mother only lets me go," answered Meg, cheering up at the thought.

"I saw you dancing with the red-headed man I ran away from; was he nice?"

"Oh, very! his hair is auburn, not red; and he was very polite, and I had a delicious *redowa*[7] with him!"

"He looked like a grasshopper in a fit, when he did the new step. Laurie and I couldn't help laughing; did you hear us?"

"No, but it was very rude. What *were* you about all that time, hidden away there?"

Jo told her adventures, and by the time she had finished they were at home. With many thanks, they said "Good-night," and crept in, hoping to disturb no one; but the instant their door creaked, two little night-caps bobbed up, and two sleepy but eager voices cried out,—

"Tell about the party! tell about the party!"

With what Meg called "a great want of manners," Jo had saved some bonbons for the little girls, and they soon subsided, after hearing the most thrilling events of the evening.

"I declare, it really seems like being a fine young lady, to come home from my party in my carriage, and sit in my dressing-gown with a maid to wait on me," said Meg, as Jo bound up her foot with arnica,[8] and brushed her hair.

"I don't believe fine young ladies enjoy themselves a bit more than we do, in spite of our burnt hair, old gowns, one glove apiece, and tight slippers, that sprain our ankles when we are silly enough to wear them." And I think Jo was quite right.

4
Burdens

"Oh dear, how hard it does seem to take up our packs and go on," sighed Meg, the morning after the party; for now the holidays were over, the week of merry-making did not fit her for going on easily with the task she never liked.

"I wish it was Christmas or New-Year all the time; wouldn't it be fun?" answered Jo, yawning dismally.

"We shouldn't enjoy ourselves half so much as we do now. But it does seem so nice to have little suppers and bouquets, and go to parties, and drive home in a carriage, and read and rest, and not grub. It's like other people, you know, and I always envy girls who do such things; I'm so fond of luxury," said Meg, trying to decide which of two shabby gowns was the least shabby.

"Well, we can't have it, so don't let's grumble, but shoulder our bundles and trudge along as cheerfully as Marmee does. I'm sure Aunt March is a regular Old Man of the Sea to me, but I suppose when I've learned to carry her without complaining, she will tumble off, or get so light that I shan't mind her."[9]

7. A fast, East European-style dance.
8. An herbal tincture used to treat sprains and bruises.
9. In "Sinbad the Sailor," from *A Thousand and* *One Nights,* Sinbad has trouble getting rid of an old man he has agreed to carry on his shoulders.

This idea tickled Jo's fancy, and put her in good spirits; but Meg didn't brighten, for her burden, consisting of four spoilt children, seemed heavier than ever. She hadn't heart enough to make herself pretty, as usual, by putting on a blue neck-ribbon, and dressing her hair in the most becoming way.

"Where's the use of looking nice, when no one sees me but those cross midgets, and no one cares whether I'm pretty or not," she muttered, shutting her drawer with a jerk. "I shall have to toil and moil all my days, with only little bits of fun now and then, and get old and ugly and sour, because I'm poor, and can't enjoy my life as other girls do. It's a shame!"

So Meg went down, wearing an injured look, and wasn't at all agreeable at breakfast-time. Every one seemed rather out of sorts, and inclined to croak. Beth had a headache, and lay on the sofa trying to comfort herself with the cat and three kittens; Amy was fretting because her lessons were not learned, and she couldn't find her rubbers; Jo *would* whistle, and make a great racket getting ready; Mrs. March was very busy trying to finish a letter, which must go at once; and Hannah had the grumps, for being up late didn't suit her.

"There never *was* such a cross family!" cried Jo, losing her temper when she had upset an inkstand, broken both boot-lacings, and sat down upon her hat.

"You're the crossest person in it!" returned Amy, washing out the sum, that was all wrong, with the tears that had fallen on her slate.

"Beth, if you don't keep these horrid cats down cellar I'll have them drowned," exclaimed Meg, angrily, as she tried to get rid of the kitten, who had swarmed up her back, and stuck like a burr just out of reach.

Jo laughed, Meg scolded, Beth implored, and Amy wailed, because she couldn't remember how much nine times twelve was.

"Girls! girls! do be quiet one minute. I *must* get this off by the early mail, and you drive me distracted with your worry," cried Mrs. March, crossing out the third spoilt sentence in her letter.

There was a momentary lull, broken by Hannah, who bounced in, laid two hot turn-overs on the table, and bounced out again. These turn-overs were an institution; and the girls called them "muffs," for they had no others, and found the hot pies very comforting to their hands on cold mornings. Hannah never forgot to make them, no matter how busy or grumpy she might be, for the walk was long and bleak; the poor things got no other lunch, and were seldom home before three.

"Cuddle your cats, and get over your headache, Bethy. Good-by, Marmee; we are a set of rascals this morning, but we'll come home regular angels. Now then, Meg," and Jo tramped away, feeling that the pilgrims were not setting out as they ought to do.

They always looked back before turning the corner, for their mother was always at the window, to nod, and smile, and wave her hand to them. Somehow it seemed as if they couldn't have got through the day without that, for whatever their mood might be, the last glimpse of that motherly face was sure to affect them like sunshine.

"If Marmee shook her fist instead of kissing her hand to us, it would serve us right, for more ungrateful minxes than we are were never seen," cried Jo, taking a remorseful satisfaction in the slushy road and bitter wind.

"Don't use such dreadful expressions," said Meg, from the depths of the veil in which she had shrouded herself like a nun sick of the world.

"I like good, strong words, that mean something," replied Jo, catching her hat as it took a leap off her head, preparatory to flying away altogether.

"Call yourself any names you like; but *I* am neither a rascal nor a minx, and I don't choose to be called so."

"You're a blighted being, and decidedly cross today, because you can't sit in the lap of luxury all the time. Poor dear! just wait till I make my fortune, and you shall revel in carriages, and ice-cream, and high-heeled slippers, and posies, and red-headed boys to dance with."

"How ridiculous you are, Jo!" but Meg laughed at the nonsense, and felt better in spite of herself.

"Lucky for you I am; for if I put on crushed airs, and tried to be dismal, as you do, we should be in a nice state. Thank goodness, I can always find something funny to keep me up. Don't croak any more, but come home jolly, there's a dear."

Jo gave her sister an encouraging pat on the shoulder as they parted for the day, each going a different way, each hugging her little warm turn-over, and each trying to be cheerful in spite of wintry weather, hard work, and the unsatisfied desires of pleasure-loving youth.

When Mr. March lost his property in trying to help an unfortunate friend, the two oldest girls begged to be allowed to do something toward their own support, at least. Believing that they could not begin too early to cultivate energy, industry, and independence, their parents consented, and both fell to work with the hearty good-will which, in spite of all obstacles, is sure to succeed at last. Margaret found a place as nursery governess, and felt rich with her small salary. As she said, she *was* "fond of luxury," and her chief trouble was poverty. She found it harder to bear than the others, because she could remember a time when home was beautiful, life full of ease and pleasure, and want of any kind unknown. She tried not to be envious or discontented, but it was very natural that the young girl should long for pretty things, gay friends, accomplishments, and a happy life. At the Kings she daily saw all she wanted, for the children's older sisters were just out,[1] and Meg caught frequent glimpses of dainty ball-dresses and bouquets, heard lively gossip about theatres, concerts, sleighing parties and merry-makings of all kinds, and saw money lavished on trifles which would have been so precious to her. Poor Meg seldom complained, but a sense of injustice made her feel bitter toward every one sometimes, for she had not yet learned to know how rich she was in the blessings which alone can make life happy.

Jo happened to suit Aunt March, who was lame, and needed an active person to wait upon her. The childless old lady had offered to adopt one of the girls when the troubles came, and was much offended because her offer was declined. Other friends told the Marches that they had lost all chance of being remembered in the rich old lady's will; but the unworldly Marches only said,—

"We can't give up our girls for a dozen fortunes. Rich or poor, we will keep together and be happy in one another."

The old lady wouldn't speak to them for a time, but, happening to meet Jo at a friend's, something in her comical face and blunt manners struck the old lady's fancy, and she proposed to take her for a companion. This did not suit Jo at all; but she accepted the place, since nothing better appeared, and, to every one's surprise, got on remarkably well with her irascible relative. There was an occasional tempest, and once Jo had marched home, declaring she couldn't bear it any longer; but Aunt March always cleared up quickly, and sent for her back again with such urgency that she could not refuse, for in her heart she rather liked the peppery old lady.

I suspect that the real attraction was a large library of fine books, which was left to dust and spiders since Uncle March died. Jo remembered the kind old gentleman who used to let her build railroads and bridges with his big dictionaries, tell her stories about the queer pictures in his Latin books, and buy her cards of gingerbread whenever he met her in the street. The dim, dusty room, with the busts staring down from the tall book-cases, the cosy chairs, the globes, and, best of all, the wilderness of books, in which she could wander where she liked, made the library a region of bliss to her. The moment Aunt March took her nap, or was busy with company, Jo hurried to this quiet place, and, curling herself up in the big chair, devoured poetry, romance, history, travels, and pictures, like a regular book-worm. But, like all happiness, it did not last long; for as sure as she had just reached the heart of the story, the sweetest verse of the song, or the most perilous adventure of her traveller, a shrill voice

---

1. They had made their social debut, and were now officially eligible for marriage.

called, "Josy-phine! Josy-phine!" and she had to leave her paradise to wind yarn, wash the poodle, or read Belsham's Essays, by the hour together.[2]

Jo's ambition was to do something very splendid; what it was she had no idea, but left it for time to tell her; and, meanwhile, found her greatest affliction in the fact that she couldn't read, run, and ride as much as she liked. A quick temper, sharp tongue, and restless spirit were always getting her into scrapes, and her life was a series of ups and downs, which were both comic and pathetic. But the training she received at Aunt March's was just what she needed; and the thought that she was doing something to support herself made her happy, in spite of the perpetual "Josy-phine!"

Beth was too bashful to go to school; it had been tried, but she suffered so much that it was given up, and she did her lessons at home, with her father. Even when he went away, and her mother was called to devote her skill and energy to Soldiers' Aid Societies, Beth went faithfully on by herself, and did the best she could. She was a housewifely little creature, and helped Hannah keep home neat and comfortable for the workers, never thinking of any reward but to be loved. Long, quiet days she spent, not lonely nor idle, for her little world was peopled with imaginary friends, and she was by nature a busy bee. There were six dolls to be taken up and dressed every morning, for Beth was a child still, and loved her pets as well as ever; not one whole or handsome one among them; all were outcasts till Beth took them in; for, when her sisters outgrew these idols, they passed to her, because Amy would have nothing old or ugly. Beth cherished them all the more tenderly for that very reason, and set up a hospital for infirm dolls. No pins were ever stuck into their cotton vitals; no harsh words or blows were ever given them; no neglect ever saddened the heart of the most repulsive, but all were fed and clothed, nursed and caressed, with an affection which never failed. One forlorn fragment of *dollanity* had belonged to Jo; and, having led a tempestuous life, was left a wreck in the rag-bag, from which dreary poorhouse it was rescued by Beth, and taken to her refuge. Having no top to its head, she tied on a neat little cap, and, as both arms and legs were gone, she hid these deficiencies by folding it in a blanket, and devoting her best bed to this chronic invalid. If any one had known the care lavished on that dolly, I think it would have touched their hearts, even while they laughed. She brought it bits of bouquets; she read to it, took it out to breathe the air, hidden under her coat; she sung it lullabys, and never went to bed without kissing its dirty face, and whispering tenderly, "I hope you'll have a good night, my poor dear."

Beth had her troubles as well as the others; and not being an angel, but a very human little girl, she often "wept a little weep," as Jo said, because she couldn't take music lessons and have a fine piano. She loved music so dearly, tried so hard to learn, and practised away so patiently at the jingling old instrument, that it did seem as if some one (not to hint Aunt March) ought to help her. Nobody did, however, and nobody saw Beth wipe the tears off the yellow keys, that wouldn't keep in tune when she was all alone. She sung like a little lark about her work, never was too tired to play for Marmee and the girls, and day after day said hopefully to herself, "I know I'll get my music some time, if I'm good."

There are many Beths in the world, shy and quiet, sitting in corners till needed, and living for others so cheerfully, that no one sees the sacrifices till the little cricket on the hearth stops chirping, and the sweet, sunshiny presence vanishes, leaving silence and shadow behind.

If anybody had asked Amy what the greatest trial of her life was, she would have answered at once, "My nose." When she was a baby, Jo had accidentally dropped her into the coal-hod, and Amy insisted that the fall had ruined her nose forever. It was not big, nor red, like poor "Petrea's;"[3] it was only rather flat, and all the pinching in the world could not give it an aristocratic point. No one minded it but herself, and it was doing its best to grow, but Amy

2. *Essays, Philosophical, Historical, and Literary* by William Belsham, published in two volumes in 1789 and 1791.

3. "Petrea" is a stock name for Arabs; here, the allusion is obscure.

felt deeply the want of a Grecian nose, and drew whole sheets of handsome ones to console herself.

"Little Raphael," as her sisters called her, had a decided talent for drawing, and was never so happy as when copying flowers, designing fairies, or illustrating stories with queer specimens of art. Her teachers complained that instead of doing her sums, she covered her slate with animals; the blank pages of her atlas were used to copy maps on, and caricatures of the most ludicrous description came fluttering out of all her books at unlucky moments. She got through her lessons as well as she could, and managed to escape reprimands by being a model of deportment. She was a great favorite with her mates, being good-tempered, and possessing the happy art of pleasing without effort. Her little airs and graces were much admired, so were her accomplishments; for beside her drawing, she could play twelve tunes, crochet, and read French without mispronouncing more than two-thirds of the words. She had a plaintive way of saying, "When papa was rich we did so-and-so," which was very touching; and her long words were considered "perfectly elegant" by the girls.

Amy was in a fair way to be spoilt; for every one petted her, and her small vanities and selfishnesses were growing nicely. One thing, however, rather quenched the vanities; she had to wear her cousin's clothes. Now Florence's mamma hadn't a particle of taste, and Amy suffered deeply at having to wear a red instead of a blue bonnet, unbecoming gowns, and fussy aprons that did not fit. Everything was good, well made, and little worn; but Amy's artistic eyes were much afflicted, especially this winter, when her school dress was a dull purple, with yellow dots, and no trimming.

"My only comfort," she said to Meg, with tears in her eyes, "is, that mother don't take tucks in my dresses whenever I'm naughty, as Maria Parks' mother does. My dear, it's really dreadful; for sometimes she is so bad, her frock is up to her knees, and she can't come to school. When I think of this *deggerredation*, I feel that I can bear even my flat nose and purple gown, with yellow sky-rockets[4] on it."

Meg was Amy's confidant and monitor, and, by some strange attraction of opposites, Jo was gentle Beth's. To Jo alone did the shy child tell her thoughts; and over her big, harum-scarum sister, Beth unconsciously exercised more influence than any one in the family. The two older girls were a great deal to each other, but both took one of the younger into their keeping, and watched over them in their own way; "playing mother" they called it, and put their sisters in the places of discarded dolls, with the maternal instinct of little women.

"Has anybody got anything to tell? It's been such a dismal day I'm really dying for some amusement," said Meg, as they sat sewing together that evening.

"I had a queer time with aunt to-day, and, as I got the best of it, I'll tell you about it," began Jo, who dearly loved to tell stories. "I was reading that everlasting Belsham, and droning away as I always do, for aunt soon drops off, and then I take out some nice book, and read like fury, till she wakes up. I actually made myself sleepy; and, before she began to nod, I gave such a gape that she asked me what I meant by opening my mouth wide enough to take the whole book in at once.

" 'I wish I could, and be done with it,' " said I, trying not to be saucy.

"Then she gave me a long lecture on my sins, and told me to sit and think them over while she just 'lost' herself for a moment. She never finds herself very soon; so the minute her cap began to bob, like a top-heavy dahlia, I whipped the 'Vicar of Wakefield' out of my pocket, and read away, with one eye on him, and one on aunt.[5] I'd just got to where they all tumbled into the water, when I forgot, and laughed out loud. Aunt woke up; and, being more good-natured after her nap, told me to read a bit, and show what frivolous work I preferred to the worthy and instructive Belsham. I did my very best, and she liked it, though she only said,—

4. Fireworks.
5. A British novel by Oliver Goldsmith, published in 1766, about a family who, like the Marches, lose their fortune.

" 'I don't understand what it's all about; go back and begin it, child.'

"Back I went, and made the Primroses as interesting as ever I could. Once I was wicked enough to stop in a thrilling place, and say meekly, 'I'm afraid it tires you, ma'am; shan't I stop now?'

"She caught up her knitting which had dropped out of her hands, gave me a sharp look through her specs, and said, in her short way,—

" 'Finish the chapter, and don't be impertinent, miss.' "

"Did she own she liked it?" asked Meg.

"Oh, bless you, no! but she let old Belsham rest; and, when I ran back after my gloves this afternoon, there she was, so hard at the Vicar, that she didn't hear me laugh as I danced a jig in the hall, because of the good time coming. What a pleasant life she might have, if she only chose. I don't envy her much, in spite of her money, for after all rich people have about as many worries as poor ones, I guess," added Jo.

"That reminds me," said Meg, "that I've got something to tell. It isn't funny, like Jo's story, but I thought about it a good deal as I came home. At the Kings to-day I found everybody in a flurry, and one of the children said that her oldest brother had done something dreadful, and papa had sent him away. I heard Mrs. King crying, and Mr. King talking very loud, and Grace and Ellen turned away their faces when they passed me, so I shouldn't see how red their eyes were. I didn't ask any questions, of course; but I felt so sorry for them, and was rather glad I hadn't any wild brothers to do wicked things, and disgrace the family."

"I think being disgraced in school is a great deal try*inger* than anything bad boys can do," said Amy, shaking her head, as if her experience of life had been a deep one. "Susie Perkins came to school to-day with a lovely red carnelian ring; I wanted it dreadfully, and wished I was her with all my might. Well, she drew a picture of Mr. Davis, with a monstrous nose and a hump, and the words, 'Young ladies, my eye is upon you!' coming out of his mouth in a balloon thing. We were laughing over it, when all of a sudden his eye *was* on us, and he ordered Susie to bring up her slate. She was *parry*lized with fright, but she went, and oh, what *do* you think he did? He took her by the ear, the ear! just fancy how horrid! and led her to the recitation platform, and made her stand there half an hour, holding that slate so every one could see."

"Didn't the girls shout at the picture?" asked Jo, who relished the scrape.

"Laugh! not a one; they sat as still as mice, and Susie cried quarts, I know she did. I didn't envy her then, for I felt that millions of carnelian rings wouldn't have made me happy after that. I never, never should have got over such an agonizing mortification;" and Amy went on with her work, in the proud consciousness of virtue, and the successful utterance of two long words in a breath.

"I saw something that I liked this morning, and I meant to tell it at dinner, but I forgot," said Beth, putting Jo's topsy-turvy basket in order as she talked. "When I went to get some oysters for Hannah, Mr. Laurence was in the fish shop, but he didn't see me, for I kept behind a barrel, and he was busy with Mr. Cutter, the fish-man. A poor woman came in with a pail and a mop, and asked Mr. Cutter if he would let her do some scrubbing for a bit of fish, because she hadn't any dinner for her children, and had been disappointed of a day's work. Mr. Cutter was in a hurry, and said 'No,' rather crossly; so she was going away, looking hungry and sorry, when Mr. Laurence hooked up a big fish with the crooked end of his cane, and held it out to her. She was so glad and surprised she took it right in her arms, and thanked him over and over. He told her to 'go along and cook it,' and she hurried off, so happy! wasn't it nice of him? Oh, she did look so funny, hugging the big, slippery fish, and hoping Mr. Laurence's bed in heaven would be 'aisy.' "

When they had laughed at Beth's story, they asked their mother for one; and, after a moment's thought, she said soberly,—

"As I sat cutting out blue flannel jackets to-day, at the rooms, I felt very anxious about father, and thought how lonely and helpless we should be if anything happened to him. It was not a wise thing to do, but I kept on worrying, till an old man came in with an order for some things. He sat down near me, and I began to talk to him, for he looked poor, and tired, and anxious.

"'Have you sons in the army?' I asked, for the note he brought was not to me.

"'Yes, ma'am; I had four, but two were killed; one is a prisoner, and I'm going to the other, who is very sick in a Washington hospital,' he answered, quietly.

"'You have done a great deal for your country, sir,' I said, feeling respect now, instead of pity.

"'Not a mite more than I ought, ma'am. I'd go myself, if I was any use; as I ain't, I give my boys, and give 'em free.'

"He spoke so cheerfully, looked so sincere, and seemed so glad to give his all, that I was ashamed of myself. I'd given one man, and thought it too much, while he gave four, without grudging them; I had all my girls to comfort me at home, and his last son was waiting, miles away, to say 'good-by' to him, perhaps. I felt so rich, so happy, thinking of my blessings, that I made him a nice bundle, gave him some money, and thanked him heartily for the lesson he had taught me."

"Tell another story, mother; one with a moral to it, like this. I like to think about them afterwards, if they are real, and not too preachy," said Jo, after a minute's silence.

Mrs. March smiled, and began at once; for she had told stories to this little audience for many years, and knew how to please them.

"Once upon a time there were four girls, who had enough to eat, and drink, and wear; a good many comforts and pleasures, kind friends and parents, who loved them dearly, and yet they were not contented." (Here the listeners stole sly looks at one another, and began to sew diligently.) "These girls were anxious to be good, and made many excellent resolutions, but somehow they did not keep them very well, and were constantly saying, 'If we only had this,' or 'if we could only do that,' quite forgetting how much they already had, and how many pleasant things they actually could do; so they asked an old woman what spell they could use to make them happy, and she said, 'When you feel discontented, think over your blessings, and be grateful.'" (Here Jo looked up quickly, as if about to speak, but changed her mind, seeing that the story was not done yet.)

"Being sensible girls, they decided to try her advice, and soon were surprised to see how well off they were. One discovered that money couldn't keep shame and sorrow out of rich people's houses; another that though she was poor, she was a great deal happier with her youth, health, and good spirits, than a certain fretful, feeble old lady, who couldn't enjoy her comforts; a third, that, disagreeable as it was to help get dinner, it was harder still to have to go begging for it; and the fourth, that even carnelian rings were not so valuable as good behavior. So they agreed to stop complaining, to enjoy the blessings already possessed, and try to deserve them, lest they should be taken away entirely, instead of increased; and I believe they were never disappointed, or sorry that they took the old woman's advice."

"Now, Marmee, that is very cunning of you to turn our own stories against us, and give us a sermon instead of a 'spin,'" cried Meg.

"I like that kind of sermon; it's the sort father used to tell us," said Beth, thoughtfully, putting the needles straight on Jo's cushion.

"I don't complain near as much as the others do, and I shall be more careful than ever now, for I've had warning from Susie's downfall," said Amy, morally.

"We needed that lesson, and we won't forget it. If we do, you just say to us as Old Chloe[6] did in Uncle Tom,—'Tink ob yer marcies, chillen, tink ob yer marcies.'" added Jo, who could not for the life of her help getting a morsel of fun out of the little sermon, though she took it to heart as much as any of them.

6. One of the heroines of Harriet Beecher Stowe's *Uncle Tom's Cabin* (1851–1852), the wife of Tom.

5
Being Neighborly

"What in the world are you going to do now, Jo?" asked Meg, one snowy afternoon, as her sister came clumping through the hall, in rubber boots, old sack and hood, with a broom in one hand and a shovel in the other.

"Going out for exercise," answered Jo, with a mischievous twinkle in her eyes.

"I should think two long walks, this morning, would have been enough. It's cold and dull out, and I advise you to stay, warm and dry, by the fire, as I do," said Meg, with a shiver.

"Never take advice; can't keep still all day, and not being a pussy-cat, I don't like to doze by the fire. I like adventures, and I'm going to find some."

Meg went back to toast her feet, and read "Ivanhoe,"[7] and Jo began to dig paths with great energy. The snow was light; and with her broom she soon swept a path all round the garden, for Beth to walk in when the sun came out; and the invalid dolls needed air. Now the garden separated the Marches' house from that of Mr. Laurence; both stood in a suburb of the city, which was still country-like, with groves and lawns, large gardens, and quiet streets. A low hedge parted the two estates. On one side was an old brown house, looking rather bare and shabby, robbed of the vines that in summer covered its walls, and the flowers which then surrounded it. On the other side was a stately stone mansion, plainly betokening every sort of comfort and luxury, from the big coach-house and well-kept grounds to the conservatory, and the glimpses of lovely things one caught between the rich curtains. Yet it seemed a lonely, lifeless sort of house; for no children frolicked on the lawn, no motherly face ever smiled at the windows, and few people went in and out, except the old gentleman and his grandson.

To Jo's lively fancy this fine house seemed a kind of enchanted palace, full of splendors and delights, which no one enjoyed. She had long wanted to behold these hidden glories, and to know the "Laurence boy," who looked as if he would like to be known, if he only knew how to begin. Since the party she had been more eager than ever, and had planned many ways of making friends with him; but he had not been lately seen, and Jo began to think he had gone away, when she one day spied a brown face at an upper window, looking wistfully down into their garden, where Beth and Amy were snow-balling one another.

"That boy is suffering for society and fun," she said to herself. "His grandpa don't know what's good for him, and keeps him shut up all alone. He needs a lot of jolly boys to play with, or somebody young and lively. I've a great mind to go over and tell the old gentleman so."

The idea amused Jo, who liked to do daring things, and was always scandalizing Meg by her queer performances. The plan of "going over" was not forgotten; and, when the snowy afternoon came, Jo resolved to try what could be done. She saw Mr. Laurence drive off, and then sallied out to dig her way down to the hedge, where she paused, and took a survey. All quiet; curtains down at the lower windows; servants out of sight, and nothing human visible but a curly black head leaning on a thin hand, at the upper window.

"There he is," thought Jo; "poor boy! all alone, and sick, this dismal day! It's a shame! I'll toss up a snow-ball, and make him look out, and then say a kind word to him."

Up went a handful of soft snow, and the head turned at once, showing a face which lost its listless look in a minute, as the big eyes brightened, and the mouth began to smile. Jo nodded, and laughed, and flourished her broom as she called out,—

"How do you do? Are you sick?"

Laurie opened the window and croaked out as hoarsely as a raven,—

"Better, thank you. I've had a horrid cold, and been shut up a week."

"I'm sorry. What do you amuse yourself with?"

---

7. Sir Walter Scott's 1819 historical romance.

"Nothing; it's as dull as tombs up here."

"Don't you read?"

"Not much; they won't let me."

"Can't somebody read to you?"

"Grandpa does, sometimes; but my books don't interest him, and I hate to ask Brooke all the time."

"Have some one come and see you, then."

"There isn't any one I'd like to see. Boys make such a row, and my head is weak."

"Isn't there some nice girl who'd read and amuse you? Girls are quiet, and like to play nurse."

"Don't know any."

"You know me," began Jo, then laughed, and stopped.

"So I do! Will you come, please?" cried Laurie.

"I'm not quiet and nice; but I'll come, if mother will let me. I'll go ask her. Shut that window, like a good boy, and wait till I come."

With that, Jo shouldered her broom and marched into the house, wondering what they would all say to her. Laurie was in a little flutter of excitement at the idea of having company, and flew about to get ready; for, as Mrs. March said, he was "a little gentleman," and did honor to the coming guest by brushing his curly pate, putting on a fresh collar, and trying to tidy up the room, which, in spite of half a dozen servants, was anything but neat. Presently, there came a loud ring, then a decided voice, asking for "Mr. Laurie," and a surprised-looking servant came running up to announce a young lady.

"All right, show her up, it's Miss Jo," said Laurie, going to the door of his little parlor to meet Jo, who appeared, looking rosy and kind, and quite at her ease, with a covered dish in one hand, and Beth's three kittens in the other.

"Here I am, bag and baggage," she said, briskly. "Mother sent her love, and was glad if I could do anything for you. Meg wanted me to bring some of her blanc-mange;[8] she makes it very nice, and Beth thought her cats would be comforting. I knew you'd shout at them, but I couldn't refuse, she was so anxious to do something."

It so happened that Beth's funny loan was just the thing; for, in laughing over the kits, Laurie forgot his bashfulness, and grew sociable at once.

"That looks too pretty to eat," he said, smiling with pleasure, as Jo uncovered the dish, and showed the blanc-mange, surrounded by a garland of green leaves, and the scarlet flowers of Amy's pet geranium.

"It isn't anything, only they all felt kindly, and wanted to show it. Tell the girl to put it away for your tea; it's so simple, you can eat it; and, being soft, it will slip down without hurting your sore throat. What a cosy room this is."

"It might be, if it was kept nice; but the maids are lazy, and I don't know how to make them mind. It worries me, though."

"I'll right it up in two minutes; for it only needs to have the hearth brushed, so,—and the things stood straight on the mantelpiece, so,—and the books put here, and the bottles there, and your sofa turned from the light, and the pillows plumped up a bit. Now, then, you're fixed."

And so he was; for, as she laughed and talked, Jo had whisked things into place, and given quite a different air to the room. Laurie watched her in respectful silence; and, when she beckoned him to his sofa, he sat down with a sigh of satisfaction, saying, gratefully,—

"How kind you are! Yes, that's what it wanted. Now please take the big chair, and let me do something to amuse my company."

"No; I came to amuse you. Shall I read aloud?" and Jo looked affectionately toward some inviting books near by.

8. A bland, white gelatin dessert.

"Thank you; I've read all those, and if you don't mind, I'd rather talk," answered Laurie.

"Not a bit; I'll talk all day if you'll only set me going. Beth says I never know when to stop."

"Is Beth the rosy one, who stays at home a good deal, and sometimes goes out with a little basket?" asked Laurie, with interest.

"Yes, that's Beth; she's my girl, and a regular good one she is, too."

"The pretty one is Meg, and the curly-haired one is Amy, I believe?"

"How did you find that out?"

Laurie colored up, but answered frankly, "Why, you see, I often hear you calling to one another, and when I'm alone up here, I can't help looking over at your house, you always seem to be having such good times. I beg your pardon for being so rude, but sometimes you forget to put down the curtain at the window where the flowers are; and, when the lamps are lighted, it's like looking at a picture to see the fire, and you all round the table with your mother; her face is right opposite, and it looks so sweet behind the flowers, I can't help watching it. I haven't got any mother, you know;" and Laurie poked the fire to hide a little twitching of the lips that he could not control.

The solitary, hungry look in his eyes went straight to Jo's warm heart. She had been so simply taught that there was no nonsense in her head, and at fifteen she was as innocent and frank as any child. Laurie was sick and lonely; and, feeling how rich she was in home-love and happiness, she gladly tried to share it with him. Her brown face was very friendly, and her sharp voice unusually gentle, as she said,—

"We'll never draw that curtain any more, and I give you leave to look as much as you like. I just wish, though, instead of peeping, you'd come over and see us. Mother is so splendid, she'd do you heaps of good, and Beth would sing to you if *I* begged her to, and Amy would dance; Meg and I would make you laugh over our funny stage properties, and we'd have jolly times. Wouldn't your grandpa let you?"

"I think he would, if your mother asked him. He's very kind, though he don't look it; and he lets me do what I like, pretty much, only he's afraid I might be a bother to strangers," began Laurie, brightening more and more.

"We ain't strangers, we are neighbors, and you needn't think you'd be a bother. We *want* to know you, and I've been trying to do it this ever so long. We haven't been here a great while, you know, but we have got acquainted with all our neighbors but you."

"You see grandpa lives among his books, and don't mind much what happens outside. Mr. Brooke, my tutor, don't stay here, you know, and I have no one to go round with me, so I just stop at home and get on as I can."

"That's bad; you ought to make a dive, and go visiting everywhere you are asked; then you'll have lots of friends, and pleasant places to go to. Never mind being bashful, it won't last long if you keep going."

Laurie turned red again, but wasn't offended at being accused of bashfulness; for there was so much good-will in Jo, it was impossible not to take her blunt speeches as kindly as they were meant.

"Do you like your school?" asked the boy, changing the subject, after a little pause, during which he stared at the fire, and Jo looked about her well pleased.

"Don't go to school; I'm a business man—girl, I mean. I go to wait on my aunt, and a dear, cross old soul she is, too," answered Jo.

Laurie opened his mouth to ask another question; but remembering just in time that it wasn't manners to make too many inquiries into people's affairs, he shut it again, and looked uncomfortable. Jo liked his good breeding, and didn't mind having a laugh at Aunt March, so she gave him a lively description of the fidgety old lady, her fat poodle, the parrot that talked Spanish, and the library where she revelled. Laurie enjoyed that immensely; and when she told about the prim old gentleman who came once to woo Aunt March, and, in the middle of a fine speech, how Poll had tweaked his wig off to his great dismay, the boy lay back and laughed till the tears ran down his cheeks, and a maid popped her head in to see what was the matter.

"Oh! that does me lots of good; tell on, please," he said, taking his face out of the sofa-cushion, red and shining with merriment.

Much elated with her success, Jo did "tell on," all about their plays and plans, their hopes and fears for father, and the most interesting events of the little world in which the sisters lived. Then they got to talking about books; and to Jo's delight she found that Laurie loved them as well as she did, and had read even more than herself.

"If you like them so much, come down and see ours. Grandpa is out, so you needn't be afraid," said Laurie, getting up.

"I'm not afraid of anything," returned Jo, with a toss of the head.

"I don't believe you are!" exclaimed the boy, looking at her with much admiration, though he privately thought she would have good reason to be a trifle afraid of the old gentleman, if she met him in some of his moods.

The atmosphere of the whole house being summer-like, Laurie led the way from room to room, letting Jo stop to examine whatever struck her fancy; and so at last they came to the library, where she clapped her hands, and pranced, as she always did when especially delighted. It was lined with books, and there were pictures and statues, and distracting little cabinets full of coins and curiosities, and Sleepy-Hollow chairs,[9] and queer tables, and bronzes; and, best of all, a great, open fireplace, with quaint tiles all around it.

"What richness!" sighed Jo, sinking into the depths of a velvet chair, and gazing about her with an air of intense satisfaction. "Theodore Laurence, you ought to be the happiest boy in the world," she added, impressively.

"A fellow can't live on books," said Laurie, shaking his head, as he perched on a table opposite.

Before he could say more, a bell rung, and Jo flew up, exclaiming with alarm, "Mercy me! it's your grandpa!"

"Well, what if it is? You are not afraid of anything, you know," returned the boy, looking wicked.

"I think I am a little bit afraid of him, but I don't know why I should be. Marmee said I might come, and I don't think you're any the worse for it," said Jo, composing herself, though she kept her eyes on the door.

"I'm a great deal better for it, and ever so much obliged. I'm only afraid you are very tired of talking to me; it was *so* pleasant, I couldn't bear to stop," said Laurie, gratefully.

"The doctor to see you, sir," and the maid beckoned as she spoke.

"Would you mind if I left you for a minute? I suppose I must see him," said Laurie.

"Don't mind me. I'm as happy as a cricket here," answered Jo.

Laurie went away, and his guest amused herself in her own way. She was standing before a fine portrait of the old gentleman, when the door opened again, and, without turning, she said decidedly, "I'm sure now that I shouldn't be afraid of him, for he's got kind eyes, though his mouth is grim, and he looks as if he had a tremendous will of his own. He isn't as handsome as *my* grandfather, but I like him."

"Thank you, ma'am," said a gruff voice behind her; and there, to her great dismay, stood old Mr. Laurence.

Poor Jo blushed till she couldn't blush any redder, and her heart began to beat uncomfortably fast as she thought what she had said. For a minute a wild desire to run away possessed her; but that was cowardly, and the girls would laugh at her; so she resolved to stay, and get out of the scrape as she could. A second look showed her that the living eyes, under the bushy gray eyebrows, were kinder even than the painted ones; and there was a sly twinkle in them, which lessened her fear a good deal. The gruff voice was gruffer than

9. A type of comfortable, deeply upholstered armchair.

ever, as the old gentleman said abruptly, after that dreadful pause, "So, you're not afraid of me, hey?"

"Not much, sir."

"And you don't think me as handsome as your grandfather?"

"Not quite, sir."

"And I've got a tremendous will, have I?"

"I only said I thought so."

"But you like me, in spite of it?"

"Yes, I do, sir."

That answer pleased the old gentleman; he gave a short laugh, shook hands with her, and putting his finger under her chin, turned up her face, examined it gravely, and let it go, saying, with a nod, "You've got your grandfather's spirit, if you haven't his face. He *was* a fine man, my dear; but, what is better, he was a brave and an honest one, and I was proud to be his friend."

"Thank you, sir;" and Jo was quite comfortable after that, for it suited her exactly.

"What have you been doing to this boy of mine, hey?" was the next question, sharply put.

"Only trying to be neighborly, sir;" and Jo told how her visit came about.

"You think he needs cheering up a bit, do you?"

"Yes, sir; he seems a little lonely, and young folks would do him good, perhaps. We are only girls, but we should be glad to help if we could, for we don't forget the splendid Christmas present you sent us," said Jo, eagerly.

"Tut, tut, tut; that was the boy's affair. How is the poor woman?"

"Doing nicely, sir;" and off went Jo, talking very fast, as she told all about the Hummels, in whom her mother had interested richer friends than they were.

"Just her father's way of doing good. I shall come and see your mother some fine day. Tell her so. There's the tea-bell; we have it early, on the boy's account. Come down, and go on being neighborly."

"If you'd like to have me, sir."

"Shouldn't ask you, if I didn't;" and Mr. Laurence offered her his arm with old-fashioned courtesy.

"What *would* Meg say to this?" thought Jo, as she was marched away, while her eyes danced with fun as she imagined herself telling the story at home.

"Hey! why what the dickens has come to the fellow?" said the old gentleman, as Laurie came running down stairs, and brought up with a start of surprise at the astonishing sight of Jo arm in arm with his redoubtable grandfather.

"I didn't know you'd come, sir," he began, as Jo gave him a triumphant little glance.

"That's evident, by the way you racket down stairs. Come to your tea, sir, and behave like a gentleman;" and having pulled the boy's hair by way of a caress, Mr. Laurence walked on, while Laurie went through a series of comic evolutions behind their backs, which nearly produced an explosion of laughter from Jo.

The old gentleman did not say much as he drank his four cups of tea, but he watched the young people, who soon chatted away like old friends, and the change in his grandson did not escape him. There was color, light and life in the boy's face now, vivacity in his manner, and genuine merriment in his laugh.

"She's right; the lad *is* lonely. I'll see what these little girls can do for him," thought Mr. Laurence, as he looked and listened. He liked Jo, for her odd, blunt ways suited him; and she seemed to understand the boy almost as well as if she had been one herself.

If the Laurences had been what Jo called "prim and poky," she would not have got on at all, for such people always made her shy and awkward; but finding them free and easy, she was so herself, and made a good impression. When they rose she proposed to go, but Laurie said he had something more to show her, and took her away to the conservatory, which had been lighted for her benefit. It seemed quite fairy-like to Jo, as she went up and down the walks, enjoying the blooming walls on either side,—the soft light, the damp, sweet air, and the wonderful vines and trees that hung above her,—while her new friend cut the finest flowers till his hands were full; then he tied them up, saying, with the happy look Jo liked to see, "Please give these to your mother, and tell her I like the medicine she sent me very much."

They found Mr. Laurence standing before the fire in the great drawing-room, but Jo's attention was entirely absorbed by a grand piano which stood open.

"Do you play?" she asked, turning to Laurie with a respectful expression.

"Sometimes," he answered, modestly.

"Please do now; I want to hear it, so I can tell Beth."

"Won't you first?"

"Don't know how; too stupid to learn, but I love music dearly."

So Laurie played, and Jo listened, with her nose luxuriously buried in heliotrope and tea roses. Her respect and regard for the "Laurence boy" increased very much, for he played remarkably well, and didn't put on any airs. She wished Beth could hear him, but she did not say so; only praised him till he was quite abashed, and his grandfather came to the rescue. "That will do, that will do, young lady; too many sugar-plums are not good for him. His music isn't bad, but I hope he will do as well in more important things. Going? Well, I'm much obliged to you, and I hope you'll come again. My respects to your mother; good-night, Doctor Jo."

He shook hands kindly, but looked as if something did not please him. When they got into the hall, Jo asked Laurie if she had said anything amiss; he shook his head.

"No, it was me; he don't like to hear me play."

"Why not?"

"I'll tell you some day. John is going home with you, as I can't."

"No need of that; I ain't a young lady, and it's only a step. Take care of yourself, won't you?"

"Yes, but you will come again, I hope?"

"If you promise to come and see us after you are well."

"I will."

"Good-night, Laurie."

"Good-night, Jo, good-night."

When all the afternoon's adventures had been told, the family felt inclined to go visiting in a body, for each found something very attractive in the big house on the other side of the hedge. Mrs. March wanted to talk of her father with the old man who had not forgotten him; Meg longed to walk in the conservatory; Beth sighed for the grand piano, and Amy was eager to see the fine pictures and statues.

"Mother, why didn't Mr. Laurence like to have Laurie play?" asked Jo, who was of an inquiring disposition.

"I am not sure, but I think it was because his son, Laurie's father, married an Italian lady, a musician, which displeased the old man, who is very proud. The lady was good and lovely and accomplished, but he did not like her, and never saw his son after he married. They both died when Laurie was a little child, and then his grandfather took him home. I fancy the boy, who was born in Italy, is not very strong, and the old man is afraid of losing him, which makes him so careful. Laurie comes naturally by his love of music, for he is like his mother, and I dare say his grandfather fears that he may want to be a musician; at any rate, his skill reminds him of the woman he did not like, and so he 'glowered,' as Jo said."

"Dear me, how romantic!" exclaimed Meg.

"How silly," said Jo; "let him be a musician, if he wants to, and not plague his life out sending him to college, when he hates to go."

"That's why he has such handsome black eyes and pretty manners, I suppose; Italians are always nice," said Meg, who was a little sentimental.

"What do you know about his eyes and his manners? you never spoke to him, hardly;" cried Jo, who was *not* sentimental.

"I saw him at the party, and what you tell shows that he knows how to behave. That was a nice little speech about the medicine mother sent him."

"He meant the blanc-mange, I suppose."

"How stupid you are, child; he meant you, of course."

"Did he?" and Jo opened her eyes as if it had never occurred to her before.

"I never saw such a girl! You don't know a compliment when you get it," said Meg, with the air of a young lady who knew all about the matter.

"I think they are great nonsense, and I'll thank you not to be silly, and spoil my fun. Laurie's a nice boy, and I like him, and I won't have any sentimental stuff about compliments and such rubbish. We'll all be good to him, because he hasn't got any mother, and he *may* come over and see us, mayn't he, Marmee?"

"Yes, Jo, your little friend is very welcome, and I hope Meg will remember that children should be children as long as they can."

"I don't call myself a child, and I'm not in my teens yet," observed Amy. "What do you say, Beth?"

"I was thinking about our 'Pilgrim's Progress,'" answered Beth, who had not heard a word. "How we got out of the Slough and through the Wicket Gate by resolving to be good, and up the steep hill, by trying; and that maybe the house over there, full of splendid things, is going to be our Palace Beautiful."

"We have got to get by the lions, first," said Jo, as if she rather liked the prospect.

6
Beth Finds the Palace Beautiful

The big house did prove a Palace Beautiful, though it took some time for all to get in, and Beth found it very hard to pass the lions. Old Mr. Laurence was the biggest one; but, after he had called, said something funny or kind to each one of the girls, and talked over old times with their mother, nobody felt much afraid of him, except timid Beth. The other lion was the fact that they were poor and Laurie rich; for this made them shy of accepting favors which they could not return. But after a while they found that he considered them the benefactors, and could not do enough to show how grateful he was for Mrs. March's motherly welcome, their cheerful society, and the comfort he took in that humble home of theirs; so they soon forgot their pride, and interchanged kindnesses without stopping to think which was the greater.

All sorts of pleasant things happened about that time, for the new friendship flourished like grass in spring. Every one liked Laurie, and he privately informed his tutor that "the Marches were regularly splendid girls." With the delightful enthusiasm of youth, they took the solitary boy into their midst, and made much of him, and he found something very charming in the innocent companionship of these simple-hearted girls. Never having known mother or sisters, he was quick to feel the influences they brought about him; and their busy, lively ways made him ashamed of the indolent life he led. He was tired of books, and found people so interesting now, that Mr. Brooke was obliged to make very unsatisfactory reports; for Laurie was always playing truant, and running over to the Marches.

"Never mind, let him take a holiday, and make it up afterward," said the old gentleman. "The good lady next door says he is studying too hard, and needs young society, amusement, and exercise. I suspect she is right, and that I've been coddling the fellow as if I'd been his grandmother. Let him do what he likes, as long as he is happy; he can't get into mischief in that little nunnery over there, and Mrs. March is doing more for him than we can."

What good times they had, to be sure! Such plays and tableaux;[1] such sleigh-rides and skating frolics; such pleasant evenings in the old parlor, and now and then such gay little parties at the great house. Meg could walk in the conservatory whenever she liked, and revel in bouquets; Jo browsed over the new library voraciously, and convulsed the old gentleman with her criticisms; Amy copied pictures and enjoyed beauty to her heart's content, and Laurie played lord of the manor in the most delightful style.

But Beth, though yearning for the grand piano, could not pluck up courage to go to the "mansion of bliss," as Meg called it. She went once with Jo, but the old gentleman, not being aware of her infirmity, stared at her so hard from under his heavy eyebrows, and said "hey!" so loud, that he frightened her so much her "feet chattered on the floor," she told her mother; and she ran away, declaring she would never go there any more, not even for the dear piano. No persuasions or enticements could overcome her fear, till the fact coming to Mr. Laurence's ear in some mysterious way, he set about mending matters. During one of the brief calls he made, he artfully led the conversation to music, and talked away about great singers whom he had seen, fine organs he had heard, and told such charming anecdotes, that Beth found it impossible to stay in her distant corner, but crept nearer and nearer, as if fascinated. At the back of his chair she stopped, and stood listening with her great eyes wide open, and her cheeks red with the excitement of this unusual performance. Taking no more notice of her than if she had been a fly, Mr. Laurence talked on about Laurie's lessons and teachers; and presently, as if the idea had just occurred to him, he said to Mrs. March,—

"The boy neglects his music now, and I'm glad of it, for he was getting too fond of it. But the piano suffers for want of use; wouldn't some of your girls like to run over, and practice on it now and then, just to keep it in tune, you know, ma'am?"

Beth took a step forward, and pressed her hands tightly together, to keep from clapping them, for this was an irresistible temptation; and the thought of practising on that splendid instrument quite took her breath away. Before Mrs. March could reply, Mr. Laurence went on with an odd little nod and smile,—

"They needn't see or speak to any one, but run in at any time, for I'm shut up in my study at the other end of the house. Laurie is out a great deal, and the servants are never near the drawing-room after nine o'clock." Here he rose, as if going, and Beth made up her mind to speak, for that last arrangement left nothing to be desired. "Please tell the young ladies what I say, and if they don't care to come, why, never mind;" here a little hand slipped into his, and Beth looked up at him with a face full of gratitude, as she said, in her earnest, yet timid way,—

"Oh, sir! they do care, very, very much!"

"Are you the musical girl?" he asked, without any startling "hey!" as he looked down at her very kindly.

"I'm Beth; I love it dearly, and I'll come if you are quite sure nobody will hear me—and be disturbed," she added, fearing to be rude, and trembling at her own boldness as she spoke.

"Not a soul, my dear; the house is empty half the day, so come and drum away as much as you like, and I shall be obliged to you."

"How kind you are, sir."

Beth blushed like a rose under the friendly look he wore, but she was not frightened now, and gave the big hand a grateful squeeze, because she had no words to thank him for the precious gift he had given her. The old gentleman softly stroked the hair off her forehead, and, stooping down, he kissed her, saying, in a tone few people ever heard,—

"I had a little girl once with eyes like these; God bless you, my dear; good-day, madam," and away he went, in a great hurry.

Beth had a rapture with her mother, and then rushed up to impart the glorious news to her family of invalids, as the girls were not at home. How blithely she sung that evening, and

---

1. A "tableau vivant" is a silent scene presented on a stage by actors in costume: a "living picture."

how they all laughed at her, because she woke Amy in the night, by playing the piano on her face in her sleep. Next day, having seen both the old and young gentleman out of the house, Beth, after two or three retreats, fairly got in at the side-door, and made her way as noiselessly as any mouse to the drawing-room, where her idol stood. Quite by accident, of course, some pretty, easy music lay on the piano; and, with trembling fingers, and frequent stops to listen and look about, Beth at last touched the great instrument, and straightway forgot her fear, herself, and everything else but the unspeakable delight which the music gave her, for it was like the voice of a beloved friend.

She stayed till Hannah came to take her home to dinner; but she had no appetite, and could only sit and smile upon every one in a general state of beatitude.

After that, the little brown hood slipped through the hedge nearly every day, and the great drawing-room was haunted by a tuneful spirit that came and went unseen. She never knew that Mr. Laurence often opened his study door to hear the old-fashioned airs he liked; she never saw Laurie mount guard in the hall, to warn the servants away; she never suspected that the exercise-books and new songs which she found in the rack were put there for her especial benefit; and when he talked to her about music at home, she only thought how kind he was to tell things that helped her so much. So she enjoyed herself heartily, and found, what isn't always the case, that her granted wish was all she had hoped. Perhaps it was because she was so grateful for this blessing that a greater was given her; at any rate, she deserved both.

"Mother, I'm going to work Mr. Laurence a pair of slippers. He is so kind to me I must thank him, and I don't know any other way. Can I do it?" asked Beth, a few weeks after that eventful call of his.

"Yes, dear; it will please him very much, and be a nice way of thanking him. The girls will help you about them, and I will pay for the making up," replied Mrs. March, who took peculiar pleasure in granting Beth's requests, because she so seldom asked anything for herself.

After many serious discussions with Meg and Jo, the pattern was chosen, the materials bought, and the slippers begun. A cluster of grave yet cheerful pansies, on a deeper purple ground, was pronounced very appropriate and pretty, and Beth worked away early and late, with occasional lifts over hard parts. She was a nimble little needle-woman, and they were finished before any one got tired of them. Then she wrote a very short, simple note, and, with Laurie's help, got them smuggled on to the study-table one morning before the old gentleman was up.

When this excitement was over, Beth waited to see what would happen. All that day passed, and a part of the next, before any acknowledgment arrived, and she was beginning to fear she had offended her crotchety friend. On the afternoon of the second day she went out to do an errand, and give poor Joanna, the invalid doll, her daily exercise. As she came up the street on her return she saw three—yes, four heads popping in and out of the parlor windows; and the moment they saw her several hands were waved, and several joyful voices screamed,—

"Here's a letter from the old gentleman; come quick, and read it!"

"Oh, Beth! he's sent you—" began Amy, gesticulating with unseemly energy; but she got no further, for Jo quenched her by slamming down the window.

Beth hurried on in a twitter of suspense; at the door her sisters seized and bore her to the parlor in a triumphal procession, all pointing, and all saying at once, "Look there! look there!" Beth did look, and turned pale with delight and surprise; for there stood a little cabinet piano, with a letter lying on the glossy lid, directed like a sign-board, to "Miss Elizabeth March."

"For me?" gasped Beth, holding on to Jo, and feeling as if she should tumble down, it was such an overwhelming thing altogether.

"Yes; all for you, my precious! Isn't it splendid of him? Don't you think he's the dearest old man in the world? Here's the key in the letter; we didn't open it, but we are dying to know what he says," cried Jo, hugging her sister, and offering the note.

"You read it; I can't, I feel so queer. Oh, it is too lovely!" and Beth hid her face in Jo's apron, quite upset by her present.

Jo opened the paper, and began to laugh, for the first words she saw were:—

"Miss March:

"Dear Madam—"

"How nice it sounds! I wish some one would write to me so!" said Amy, who thought the old-fashioned address very elegant.

" 'I have had many pairs of slippers in my life, but I never had any that suited me so well as yours,' "

continued Jo.

" 'Heart's-ease is my favorite flower, and these will always remind me of the gentle giver. I like to pay my debts, so I know you will allow "the old gentleman" to send you something which once belonged to the little granddaughter he lost. With hearty thanks, and best wishes, I remain,

" 'Your grateful friend and humble servant,

" 'James Laurence.' "

"There, Beth, that's an honor to be proud of, I'm sure! Laurie told me how fond Mr. Laurence used to be of the child who died, and how he kept all her little things carefully. Just think; he's given you her piano! That comes of having big blue eyes and loving music," said Jo, trying to soothe Beth, who trembled, and looked more excited than she had ever been before.

"See the cunning brackets to hold candles, and the nice green silk, puckered up with a gold rose in the middle, and the pretty rack and stool, all complete," added Meg, opening the instrument, and displaying its beauties.

" 'Your humble servant, James Laurence;' only think of his writing that to you. I'll tell the girls; they'll think it's killing," said Amy, much impressed by the note.

"Try it, honey; let's hear the sound of the baby pianny," said Hannah, who always took a share in the family joys and sorrows.

So Beth tried it, and every one pronounced it the most remarkable piano ever heard. It had evidently been newly tuned, and put in apple-pie order; but, perfect as it was, I think the real charm of it lay in the happiest all happy faces which leaned over it, as Beth lovingly touched the beautiful black and white keys, and pressed the shiny pedals.

"You'll have to go and thank him," said Jo, by way of a joke; for the idea of the child's really going, never entered her head.

"Yes, I mean to; I guess I'll go now, before I get frightened thinking about it;" and, to the utter amazement of the assembled family, Beth walked deliberately down the garden, through the hedge, and in at the Laurences' door.

"Well, I wish I may die, if it ain't the queerest thing I ever see! The pianny has turned her head; she'd never have gone, in her right mind," cried Hannah, staring after her, while the girls were rendered quite speechless by the miracle.

They would have been still more amazed, if they had seen what Beth did afterward. If you will believe me, she went and knocked at the study door, before she gave herself time to think; and when a gruff voice called out, "Come in!" she did go in, right up to Mr. Laurence, who looked quite taken aback, and held out her hand, saying, with only a small quaver in her voice,

"I came to thank you, sir, for—" but she didn't finish, for he looked so friendly that she forgot her speech; and, only remembering that he had lost the little girl he loved, she put both arms round his neck, and kissed him.

If the roof of the house had suddenly flown off, the old gentleman wouldn't have been more astonished; but he liked it—oh dear, yes! he liked it amazingly; and was so touched and pleased by that confiding little kiss, that all his crustiness vanished; and he just set her on his knee, and laid his wrinkled cheek against her rosy one, feeling as if he had got his own little granddaughter back again. Beth ceased to fear him from that moment, and sat there talking to him as cosily as if she had known him all her life; for love casts out fear, and gratitude can conquer pride.[2] When she went home, he walked with her to her own gate, shook hands cordially, and touched his hat as he marched back again, looking very stately and erect, like a handsome, soldierly old gentleman, as he was.

When the girls saw that performance, Jo began to dance a jig, by way of expressing her satisfaction; Amy nearly fell out of the window in her surprise, and Meg exclaimed, with uplifted hands, "Well, I do believe the world is coming to an end!"

7
Amy's Valley of Humiliation[3]

"That boy is a perfect Cyclops,[4] isn't he?" said Amy, one day, as Laurie clattered by on horseback, with a flourish of his whip as he passed.

"How dare you say so, when he's got both his eyes? and very handsome ones they are, too;" cried Jo, who resented any slighting remarks about her friend.

"I didn't say anything about his eyes, and I don't see why you need fire up when I admire his riding."

"Oh, my goodness! that little goose means a centaur,[5] and she called him a Cyclops," exclaimed Jo, with a burst of laughter.

"You needn't be so rude, it's only a 'lapse of lingy,' as Mr. Davis says," retorted Amy, finishing Jo with her Latin. "I just wish I had a little of the money Laurie spends on that horse," she added, as if to herself, yet hoping her sisters would hear.

"Why?" asked Meg, kindly, for Jo had gone off in another laugh at Amy's second blunder.

"I need it so much; I'm dreadfully in debt, and it won't be my turn to have the rag-money for a month."

"In debt, Amy; what do you mean?" and Meg looked sober.

"Why, I owe at least a dozen pickled limes, and I can't pay them, you know, till I have money, for Marmee forbid my having anything charged at the shop."

"Tell me all about it. Are limes the fashion now? It used to be pricking bits of rubber to make balls;" and Meg tried to keep her countenance, Amy looked so grave and important.

"Why, you see, the girls are always buying them, and unless you want to be thought mean,[6] you must do it, too. It's nothing but limes now, for every one is sucking them in their desks in school-time, and trading them off for pencils, bead-rings, paper dolls, or something else, at recess. If one girl likes another, she gives her a lime; if she's mad with her, she eats one before her face, and don't offer even a suck. They treat by turns; and I've had ever so many, but haven't returned them, and I ought, for they are debts of honor, you know."

---

2. See 1 John 4:18.
3. In *Pilgrim's Progress,* one of the difficult territories Christian crosses.
4. In Greek mythology, a one-eyed giant.

5. Mythological creature who is human above the waist and horse below.
6. Stingy.

"How much will pay them off, and restore your credit?" asked Meg, taking out her purse.

"A quarter would more than do it, and leave a few cents over for a treat for you. Don't you like limes?"

"Not much; you may have my share. Here's the money,—make it last as long as you can, for it isn't very plenty, you know."

"Oh, thank you! it must be so nice to have pocket-money. I'll have a grand feast, for I haven't tasted a lime this week. I felt delicate about taking any, as I couldn't return them, and I'm actually suffering for one."

Next day Amy was rather late at school; but could not resist the temptation of displaying, with pardonable pride, a moist brown paper parcel, before she consigned it to the inmost recesses of her desk. During the next few minutes the rumor that Amy March had got twenty-four delicious limes (she ate one on the way), and was going to treat, circulated through her "set," and the attentions of her friends became quite overwhelming. Katy Brown invited her to her next party on the spot; Mary Kingsley insisted on lending her her watch till recess, and Jenny Snow, a satirical young lady who had basely twitted Amy upon her limeless state, promptly buried the hatchet, and offered to furnish answers to certain appalling sums. But Amy had not forgotten Miss Snow's cutting remarks about "some persons whose noses were not too flat to smell other people's limes, and stuck-up people, who were not too proud to ask for them;" and she instantly crushed "that Snow girl's" hopes by the withering telegram, "You needn't be so polite all of a sudden, for you won't get any."

A distinguished personage happened to visit the school that morning, and Amy's beautifully drawn maps received praise, which honor to her foe rankled in the soul of Miss Snow, and caused Miss March to assume the airs of a studious young peacock. But, alas, alas! pride goes before a fall,[7] and the revengeful Snow turned the tables with disastrous success. No sooner had the guest paid the usual stale compliments, and bowed himself out, than Jenny, under pretence of asking an important question, informed Mr. Davis, the teacher, that Amy March had pickled limes in her desk.

Now Mr. Davis had declared limes a contraband article, and solemnly vowed to publicly ferule[8] the first person who was found breaking the law. This much-enduring man had succeeded in banishing gum after a long and stormy war, had made a bonfire of the confiscated novels and newspapers, had suppressed a private post-office, had forbidden distortions of the face, nicknames, and caricatures, and done all that one man could do to keep half a hundred rebellious girls in order. Boys are trying enough to human patience, goodness knows! but girls are infinitely more so, especially to nervous gentlemen with tyrannical tempers and no more talent for teaching than "Dr. Blimber."[9] Mr. Davis knew any quantity of Greek, Latin, Algebra, and ologies of all sorts, so he was called a fine teacher; and manners, morals, feelings, and examples were not considered of any particular importance. It was a most unfortunate moment for denouncing Amy, and Jenny knew it. Mr. Davis had evidently taken his coffee too strong that morning; there was an east wind, which always affected his neuralgia, and his pupils had not done him the credit which he felt he deserved; therefore, to use the expressive, if not elegant, language of a school-girl, "he was as nervous as a witch and as cross as a bear." The word "limes" was like fire to powder; his yellow face flushed, and he rapped on his desk with an energy which made Jenny skip to her seat with unusual rapidity.

"Young ladies, attention, if you please!"

At the stern order the buzz ceased, and fifty pairs of blue, black, gray, and brown eyes were obediently fixed upon his awful countenance.

---

7. See Proverbs 16:18.
8. To flog with a stick or cane that has a metal cap at the end.

9. In Charles Dickens's *Dombey and Son* (1846–1848), Dr. Blimber is the conceited schoolmaster.

"Miss March, come to the desk."

Amy rose to comply, with outward composure, but a secret fear oppressed her, for the limes weighed upon her conscience.

"Bring with you the limes you have in your desk," was the unexpected command which arrested her before she got out of her seat.

"Don't take all," whispered her neighbor, a young lady of great presence of mind.

Amy hastily shook out half a dozen, and laid the rest down before Mr. Davis, feeling that any man possessing a human heart would relent when that delicious perfume met his nose. Unfortunately, Mr. Davis particularly detested the odor of the fashionable pickle, and disgust added to his wrath.

"Is that all?"

"Not quite," stammered Amy.

"Bring the rest, immediately."

With a despairing glance at her set she obeyed.

"You are sure there are no more?"

"I never lie, sir."

"So I see. Now take these disgusting things, two by two, and throw them out of the window."

There was a simultaneous sigh, which created quite a little gust as the last hope fled, and the treat was ravished from their longing lips. Scarlet with shame and anger, Amy went to and fro twelve mortal times; and as each doomed couple, looking, oh, so plump and juicy! fell from her reluctant hands, a shout from the street completed the anguish of the girls, for it told them that their feast was being exulted over by the little Irish children, who were their sworn foes. This—this was too much; all flashed indignant or appealing glances at the inexorable Davis, and one passionate lime-lover burst into tears.

As Amy returned from her last trip, Mr. Davis gave a portentous "hem," and said, in his most impressive manner,—

"Young ladies, you remember what I said to you a week ago. I am sorry this has happened; but I never allow my rules to be infringed, and I *never* break my word. Miss March, hold out your hand."

Amy started, and put both hands behind her, turning on him an imploring look, which pleaded for her better than the words she could not utter. She was rather a favorite with "old Davis," as, of course, he was called, and it's my private belief that he *would* have broken his word if the indignation of one irrepressible young lady had not found vent in a hiss. That hiss, faint as it was, irritated the irascible gentleman, and sealed the culprit's fate.

"Your hand, Miss March!" was the only answer her mute appeal received; and, too proud to cry or beseech, Amy set her teeth, threw back her head defiantly, and bore without flinching several tingling blows on her little palm. They were neither many nor heavy, but that made no difference to her. For the first time in her life she had been struck; and the disgrace, in her eyes, was as deep as if he had knocked her down.

"You will now stand on the platform till recess," said Mr. Davis, resolved to do the thing thoroughly, since he had begun.

That was dreadful; it would have been bad enough to go to her seat and see the pitying faces of her friends, or the satisfied ones of her few enemies; but to face the whole school, with that shame fresh upon her, seemed impossible, and for a second she felt as if she could only drop down where she stood, and break her heart with crying. A bitter sense of wrong, and the thought of Jenny Snow, helped her to bear it; and, taking the ignominious place, she fixed her eyes on the stove-funnel above what now seemed a sea of faces, and stood there so motionless and white, that the girls found it very hard to study, with the pathetic little figure before them.

During the fifteen minutes that followed, the proud and sensitive little girl suffered a shame and pain which she never forgot. To others it might seem a ludicrous or trivial affair, but to her it was a hard experience; for during the twelve years of her life she had been governed by love alone, and a blow of that sort had never touched her before. The smart of her hand, and the ache of her heart, were forgotten in the sting of the thought,—

"I shall have to tell at home, and they will be so disappointed in me!"

The fifteen minutes seemed an hour; but they came to an end at last, and the word "recess!" had never seemed so welcome to her before.

"You can go, Miss March," said Mr. Davis, looking, as he felt, uncomfortable.

He did not soon forget the reproachful look Amy gave him, as she went, without a word to any one, straight into the anteroom, snatched her things, and left the place "forever," as she passionately declared to herself. She was in a sad state when she got home; and when the older girls arrived, some time later, an indignation meeting was held at once. Mrs. March did not say much, but looked disturbed, and comforted her afflicted little daughter in her tenderest manner. Meg bathed the insulted hand with glycerine and tears; Beth felt that even her beloved kittens would fail as a balm for griefs like this, and Jo wrathfully proposed that Mr. Davis be arrested without delay, while Hannah shook her fist at the "villain," and pounded potatoes for dinner as if she had him under her pestle.

No notice was taken of Amy's flight, except by her mates; but the sharp-eyed demoiselles discovered that Mr. Davis was quite benignant in the afternoon, also unusually nervous. Just before school closed, Jo appeared, wearing a grim expression, as she stalked up to the desk, and delivered a letter from her mother; then collected Amy's property, and departed, carefully scraping the mud from her boots on the door-mat, as if she shook the dust of the place off her feet.

"Yes, you can have a vacation from school, but I want you to study a little every day, with Beth," said Mrs. March, that evening. "I don't approve of corporal punishment, especially for girls. I dislike Mr. Davis' manner of teaching, and don't think the girls you associate with are doing you any good, so I shall ask your father's advice before I send you anywhere else."

"That's good! I wish all the girls would leave, and spoil his old school. It's perfectly maddening to think of those lovely limes," sighed Amy, with the air of a martyr.

"I am not sorry you lost them, for you broke the rules, and deserved some punishment for disobedience," was the severe reply, which rather disappointed the young lady, who expected nothing but sympathy.

"Do you mean you are glad I was disgraced before the whole school?" cried Amy.

"I should not have chosen that way of mending a fault," replied her mother; "but I'm not sure that it won't do you more good than a milder method. You are getting to be altogether too conceited and important, my dear, and it is quite time you set about correcting it. You have a good many little gifts and virtues, but there is no need of parading them, for conceit spoils the finest genius. There is not much danger that real talent or goodness will be overlooked long; even if it is, the consciousness of possessing and using it well should satisfy one, and the great charm of all power is modesty."

"So it is," cried Laurie, who was playing chess in a corner with Jo. "I knew a girl, once, who had a really remarkable talent for music, and she didn't know it; never guessed what sweet little things she composed when she was alone, and wouldn't have believed it if any one had told her."

"I wish I'd known that nice girl, maybe she would have helped me, I'm so stupid," said Beth, who stood beside him, listening eagerly.

"You do know her, and she helps you better than any one else could," answered Laurie, looking at her with such mischievous meaning in his merry black eyes, that Beth suddenly turned very red, and hid her face in the sofa-cushion, quite overcome by such an unexpected discovery.

Jo let Laurie win the game, to pay for that praise of her Beth, who could not be prevailed upon to play for them after her compliment. So Laurie did his best, and sung delightfully, being in a particularly lively humor, for to the Marches he seldom showed the moody side of his character. When he was gone, Amy, who had been pensive all the evening, said, suddenly, as if busy over some new idea,—

"Is Laurie an accomplished boy?"

"Yes; he has had an excellent education, and has much talent; he will make a fine man, if not spoilt by petting," replied her mother.

"And he isn't conceited, is he?" asked Amy.

"Not in the least; that is why he is so charming, and we all like him so much."

"I see; it's nice to have accomplishments, and be elegant; but not to show off, or get perked up,[1]" said Amy, thoughtfully.

"These things are always seen and felt in a person's manner and conversation, if modestly used; but it is not necessary to display them," said Mrs. March.

"Any more than it's proper to wear all your bonnets, and gowns, and ribbons, at once, that folks may know you've got 'em," added Jo; and the lecture ended in a laugh.

8
Jo Meets Apollyon[2]

"Girls, where are you going?" asked Amy, coming into their room one Saturday afternoon, and finding them getting ready to go out, with an air of secrecy which excited her curiosity.

"Never mind; little girls shouldn't ask questions," returned Jo, sharply.

Now if there is anything mortifying to our feelings, when we are young, it is to be told that; and to be bidden to "run away, dear," is still more trying to us. Amy bridled up at this insult, and determined to find out the secret, if she teased for an hour. Turning to Meg, who never refused her anything very long, she said, coaxingly, "Do tell me! I should think you might let me go, too; for Beth is fussing over her dolls, and I haven't got anything to do, and am *so* lonely."

"I can't, dear, because you aren't invited," began Meg; but Jo broke in impatiently, "Now, Meg, be quiet, or you will spoil it all. You can't go, Amy; so don't be a baby, and whine about it."

"You are going somewhere with Laurie, I know you are; you were whispering and laughing together, on the sofa, last night, and you stopped when I came in. Aren't you going with him?"

"Yes, we are; now do be still, and stop bothering."

Amy held her tongue, but used her eyes, and saw Meg slip a fan into her pocket.

"I know! I know! you're going to the theatre to see the 'Seven Castles!'" she cried; adding, resolutely, "and I *shall* go, for mother said I might see it; and I've got my rag-money, and it was mean not to tell me in time."

"Just listen to me a minute, and be a good child," said Meg, soothingly. "Mother doesn't wish you to go this week, because your eyes are not well enough yet to bear the light of this fairy piece. Next week you can go with Beth and Hannah, and have a nice time."

"I don't like that half as well as going with you and Laurie. Please let me; I've been sick with this cold so long, and shut up, I'm dying for some fun. Do, Meg! I'll be ever so good," pleaded Amy, looking as pathetic as she could.

"Suppose we take her. I don't believe mother would mind, if we bundle her up well," began Meg.

"If *she* goes *I* shan't; and if I don't, Laurie won't like it; and it will be very rude, after he invited only us, to go and drag in Amy. I should think she'd hate to poke herself where she

---

1. Carry oneself in a lively or jaunty manner.
2. In *Pilgrim's Progress,* an especially strong devil

Christian must defeat in hand-to-hand combat.

isn't wanted," said Jo, crossly, for she disliked the trouble of overseeing a fidgety child, when she wanted to enjoy herself.

Her tone and manner angered Amy, who began to put her boots on, saying, in her most aggravating way, "I *shall* go; Meg says I may; and if I pay for myself, Laurie hasn't anything to do with it."

"You can't sit with us, for our seats are reserved, and you mustn't sit alone; so Laurie will give you his place, and that will spoil our pleasure; or he'll get another seat for you, and that isn't proper, when you weren't asked. You shan't stir a step; so you may just stay where you are," scolded Jo, crosser than ever, having just pricked her finger in her hurry.

Sitting on the floor, with one boot on, Amy began to cry, and Meg to reason with her, when Laurie called from below, and the two girls hurried down, leaving their sister wailing; for now and then she forgot her grown-up ways, and acted like a spoilt child. Just as the party was setting out, Amy called over the banisters, in a threatening tone, "You'll be sorry for this, Jo March! see if you ain't."

"Fiddlesticks!" returned Jo, slamming the door.

They had a charming time, for "The Seven Castles of the Diamond Lake" were as brilliant and wonderful as a heart could wish. But, in spite of the comical red imps, sparkling elves, and gorgeous princes and princesses, Jo's pleasure had a drop of bitterness in it; the fairy queen's yellow curls reminded her of Amy; and between the acts she amused herself with wondering what her sister would do to make her "sorry for it." She and Amy had had many lively skirmishes in the course of their lives, for both had quick tempers, and were apt to be violent when fairly roused. Amy teased Jo, and Jo irritated Amy, and semi-occasional explosions occurred, of which both were much ashamed afterward. Although the oldest,[3] Jo had the least self-control, and had hard times trying to curb the fiery spirit which was continually getting her into trouble; her anger never lasted long, and, having humbly confessed her fault, she sincerely repented, and tried to do better. Her sisters used to say, that they rather liked to get Jo into a fury, because she was such an angel afterward. Poor Jo tried desperately to be good, but her bosom enemy was always ready to flame up and defeat her; and it took years of patient effort to subdue it.

When they got home, they found Amy reading in the parlor. She assumed an injured air as they came in; never lifted her eyes from her book, or asked a single question. Perhaps curiosity might have conquered resentment, if Beth had not been there to inquire, and receive a glowing description of the play. On going up to put away her best hat, Jo's first look was toward the bureau; for, in their last quarrel, Amy had soothed her feelings by turning Jo's top drawer upside down, on the floor. Everything was in its place, however; and after a hasty glance into her various closets, bags and boxes, Jo decided that Amy had forgiven and forgotten her wrongs.

There Jo was mistaken; for next day she made a discovery which produced a tempest. Meg, Beth and Amy were sitting together, late in the afternoon, when Jo burst into the room, looking excited, and demanding, breathlessly, "Has any one taken my story?"

Meg and Beth said "No," at once, and looked surprised; Amy poked the fire, and said nothing. Jo saw her color rise, and was down upon her in a minute.

"Amy, you've got it!"

"No, I haven't."

"You know where it is, then!"

"No, I don't."

"That's a fib!" cried Jo, taking her by the shoulders, and looking fierce enough to frighten a much braver child than Amy.

"It isn't. I haven't got it, don't know where it is now, and don't care."

"You know something about it, and you'd better tell at once, or I'll make you," and Jo gave her a slight shake.

3. The older of the two. (Meg is the eldest daughter.)

"Scold as much as you like, you'll never get your silly old story again," cried Amy, getting excited in her turn.

"Why not?"

"I burnt it up."

"What! my little book I was so fond of, and worked over, and meant to finish before father got home? Have you really burnt it?" said Jo, turning very pale, while her eyes kindled and her hands clutched Amy nervously.

"Yes, I did! I told you I'd make you pay for being so cross yesterday, and I have, so—"

Amy got no farther, for Jo's hot temper mastered her, and she shook Amy till her teeth chattered in her head; crying, in a passion of grief and anger,—

"You wicked, wicked girl! I never can write it again, and I'll never forgive you as long as I live."

Meg flew to rescue Amy, and Beth to pacify Jo, but Jo was quite beside herself; and, with a parting box on her sister's ear, she rushed out of the room up to the old sofa in the garret, and finished her fight alone.

The storm cleared up below, for Mrs. March came home, and, having heard the story, soon brought Amy to a sense of the wrong she had done her sister. Jo's book was the pride of her heart, and was regarded by her family as a literary sprout of great promise. It was only half a dozen little fairy tales, but Jo had worked over them patiently, putting her whole heart into her work, hoping to make something good enough to print. She had just copied them with great care, and had destroyed the old manuscript, so that Amy's bonfire had consumed the loving work of several years. It seemed a small loss to others, but to Jo it was a dreadful calamity, and she felt that it never could be made up to her. Beth mourned as for a departed kitten, and Meg refused to defend her pet; Mrs. March looked grave and grieved, and Amy felt that no one would love her till she had asked pardon for the act which she now regretted more than any of them.

When the tea-bell rung, Jo appeared, looking so grim and unapproachable, that it took all Amy's courage to say, meekly,—

"Please forgive me, Jo; I'm very, very sorry."

"I never shall forgive you," was Jo's stern answer; and, from that moment, she ignored Amy entirely.

No one spoke of the great trouble,—not even Mrs. March,—for all had learned by experience that when Jo was in that mood words were wasted; and the wisest course was to wait till some little accident, or her own generous nature, softened Jo's resentment, and healed the breach. It was not a happy evening; for, though they sewed as usual, while their mother read aloud from Bremer, Scott, or Edgeworth,[4] something was wanting, and the sweet home-peace was disturbed. They felt this most when singing-time came; for Beth could only play, Jo stood dumb as a stone, and Amy broke down, so Meg and mother sang alone. But, in spite of their efforts to be as cheery as larks, the flute-like voices did not seem to chord as well as usual, and all felt out of tune.

As Jo received her good-night kiss, Mrs. March whispered, gently,—

"My dear, don't let the sun go down upon your anger; forgive each other, help each other, and begin again to-morrow."

Jo wanted to lay her head down on that motherly bosom, and cry her grief and anger all away; but tears were an unmanly weakness, and she felt so deeply injured that she really *couldn't* quite forgive yet. So she winked hard, shook her head, and said, gruffly, because Amy was listening,—

"It was an abominable thing, and she don't deserve to be forgiven."

---

4. Frederika Bremer (1801–1865), a domestic novelist from Sweden; Sir Walter Scott (1771–1832), the enormously popular writer of historical romances, ballads, and plays from Scotland; and Maria Edgeworth (1767–1849), a writer of novels and didactic children's books from Ireland.

With that she marched off to bed, and there was no merry or confidential gossip that night.

Amy was much offended that her overtures of peace had been repulsed, and began to wish she had not humbled herself, to feel more injured than ever, and to plume herself on her superior virtue in a way which was particularly exasperating. Jo still looked like a thunder-cloud, and nothing went well all day. It was bitter cold in the morning; she dropped her precious turn-over in the gutter, Aunt March had an attack of fidgets, Meg was pensive, Beth *would* look grieved and wistful when she got home, and Amy kept making remarks about people who were always talking about being good, and yet wouldn't try, when other people set them a virtuous example.

"Everybody is so hateful, I'll ask Laurie to go skating. He is always kind and jolly, and will put me to rights, I know," said Jo to herself, and off she went.

Amy heard the clash of skates, and looked out with an impatient exclamation,—

"There! she promised I should go next time, for this is the last ice we shall have. But it's no use to ask such a cross patch to take me."

"Don't say that; you *were* very naughty, and it is hard to forgive the loss of her precious little book; but I think she might do it now, and I guess she will, if you try her at the right minute," said Meg. "Go after them; don't say anything till Jo has got good-natured with Laurie, then take a quiet minute, and just kiss her, or do some kind thing, and I'm sure she'll be friends again, with all her heart."

"I'll try," said Amy, for the advice suited her; and, after a flurry to get ready, she ran after the friends, who were just disappearing over the hill.

It was not far to the river, but both were ready before Amy reached them. Jo saw her coming, and turned her back; Laurie did not see, for he was carefully skating along the shore, sounding the ice, for a warm spell had preceded the cold snap.

"I'll go on to the first bend, and see if it's all right, before we begin to race," Amy heard him say, as he shot away, looking like a young Russian, in his fur-trimmed coat and cap.

Jo heard Amy panting after her run, stamping her feet, and blowing her fingers, as she tried to put her skates on; but Jo never turned, and went slowly zigzagging down the river, taking a bitter, unhappy sort of satisfaction in her sister's troubles. She had cherished her anger till it grew strong, and took possession of her, as evil thoughts and feelings always do, unless cast out at once. As Laurie turned the bend, he shouted back,—

"Keep near the shore; it isn't safe in the middle."

Jo heard, but Amy was just struggling to her feet, and did not catch a word. Jo glanced over her shoulder, and the little demon she was harboring said in her ear,—

"No matter whether she heard or not, let her take care of herself."

Laurie had vanished round the bend; Jo was just at the turn, and Amy, far behind, striking out toward the smoother ice in the middle of the river. For a minute Jo stood still, with a strange feeling at her heart; then she resolved to go on, but something held and turned her round, just in time to see Amy throw up her hands and go down, with the sudden crash of rotten ice, the splash of water, and a cry that made Jo's heart stand still with fear. She tried to call Laurie, but her voice was gone; she tried to rush forward, but her feet seemed to have no strength in them; and, for a second, she could only stand motionless, staring, with a terror-stricken face, at the little blue hood above the black water. Something rushed swiftly by her, and Laurie's voice cried out,—

"Bring a rail; quick, quick!"

How she did it, she never knew; but for the next few minutes she worked as if possessed, blindly obeying Laurie, who was quite self-possessed; and, lying flat, held Amy up by his arm and hockey, till Jo dragged a rail from the fence, and together they got the child out, more frightened than hurt.

"Now then, we must walk her home as fast as we can; pile our things on her, while I get off these confounded skates," cried Laurie, wrapping his coat round Amy, and tugging away at the straps, which never seemed so intricate before.

Shivering, dripping, and crying, they got Amy home; and, after an exciting time of it, she fell asleep, rolled in blankets, before a hot fire. During the bustle Jo had scarcely spoken; but flown about, looking pale and wild, with her things half off, her dress torn, and her hands cut and bruised by ice and rails, and refractory buckles. When Amy was comfortably asleep, the house quiet, and Mrs. March sitting by the bed, she called Jo to her, and began to bind up the hurt hands.

"Are you sure she is safe?" whispered Jo, looking remorsefully at the golden head, which might have been swept away from her sight forever, under the treacherous ice.

"Quite safe, dear; she is not hurt, and won't even take cold, I think, you were so sensible in covering and getting her home quickly," replied her mother, cheerfully.

"Laurie did it all; I only let her go. Mother, if she *should* die, it would be my fault;" and Jo dropped down beside the bed, in a passion of penitent tears, telling all that had happened, bitterly condemning her hardness of heart, and sobbing out her gratitude for being spared the heavy punishment which might have come upon her.

"It's my dreadful temper! I try to cure it; I think I have, and then it breaks out worse than ever. Oh, mother! what shall I do! what shall I do?" cried poor Jo, in despair.

"Watch and pray, dear; never get tired of trying; and never think it is impossible to conquer your fault," said Mrs. March, drawing the blowzy head to her shoulder, and kissing the wet cheek so tenderly, that Jo cried harder than ever.

"You don't know; you can't guess how bad it is! It seems as if I could do anything when I'm in a passion; I get so savage, I could hurt any one, and enjoy it. I'm afraid I *shall* do something dreadful some day, and spoil my life, and make everybody hate me. Oh, mother! help me, do help me!"

"I will, my child; I will. Don't cry so bitterly, but remember this day, and resolve, with all your soul, that you will never know another like it. Jo, dear, we all have our temptations, some far greater than yours, and it often takes us all our lives to conquer them. You think your temper is the worst in the world; but mine used to be just like it."

"Yours, mother? Why, you are never angry!" and, for the moment, Jo forgot remorse in surprise.

"I've been trying to cure it for forty years, and have only succeeded in controlling it. I am angry nearly every day of my life, Jo; but I have learned not to show it; and I still hope to learn not to feel it, though it may take me another forty years to do so."

The patience and the humility of the face she loved so well, was a better lesson to Jo than the wisest lecture, the sharpest reproof. She felt comforted at once by the sympathy and confidence given her; the knowledge that her mother had a fault like hers, and tried to mend it, made her own easier to bear, and strengthened her resolution to cure it; though forty years seemed rather a long time to watch and pray, to a girl of fifteen.

"Mother, are you angry when you fold your lips tight together, and go out of the room sometimes, when Aunt March scolds, or people worry you?" asked Jo, feeling nearer and dearer to her mother than ever before.

"Yes, I've learned to check the hasty words that rise to my lips; and when I feel that they mean to break out against my will, I just go away a minute, and give myself a little shake, for being so weak and wicked," answered Mrs. March, with a sigh and a smile, as she smoothed and fastened up Jo's dishevelled hair.

"How did you learn to keep still? That is what troubles me—for the sharp words fly out before I know what I'm about; and the more I say the worse I get, till it's a pleasure to hurt people's feelings, and say dreadful things. Tell me how you do it, Marmee dear."

"My good mother used to help me—"

"As you do us—" interrupted Jo, with a grateful kiss.

"But I lost her when I was a little older than you are, and for years had to struggle on alone, for I was too proud to confess my weakness to any one else. I had a hard time, Jo, and shed a good many bitter tears over my failures; for, in spite of my efforts, I never seemed to get on. Then your father came, and I was so happy that I found it easy to be good. But by and by, when I had four little daughters round me, and we were poor, then the old trouble began again; for I am not patient by nature, and it tried me very much to see my children wanting anything."

"Poor mother! what helped you then?"

"Your father, Jo. He never loses patience,—never doubts or complains,—but always hopes, and works and waits so cheerfully, that one is ashamed to do otherwise before him. He helped and comforted me, and showed me that I must try to practise all the virtues I would have my little girls possess, for I was their example. It was easier to try for your sakes than for my own; a startled or surprised look from one of you, when I spoke sharply, rebuked me more than any words could have done; and the love, respect, and confidence of my children was the sweetest reward I could receive for my efforts to be the woman I would have them copy."

"Oh, mother! if I'm ever half as good as you, I shall be satisfied," cried Jo, much touched.

"I hope you will be a great deal better, dear; but you must keep watch over your 'bosom enemy,' as father calls it, or it may sadden, if not spoil your life. You have had a warning; remember it, and try with heart and soul to master this quick temper, before it brings you greater sorrow and regret than you have known today."

"I will try, mother; I truly will. But you must help me, remind me, and keep me from flying out. I used to see father sometimes put his finger on his lips, and look at you with a very kind, but sober face; and you always folded your lips tight, or went away; was he reminding you then?" asked Jo, softly.

"Yes; I asked him to help me so, and he never forgot it, but saved me from many a sharp word by that little gesture and kind look."

Jo saw that her mother's eyes filled, and her lips trembled, as she spoke; and, fearing that she had said too much, she whispered anxiously, "Was it wrong to watch you, and to speak of it? I didn't mean to be rude, but it's so comfortable to say all I think to you, and feel so safe and happy here."

"My Jo, you may say anything to your mother, for it is my greatest happiness and pride to feel that my girls confide in me, and know how much I love them."

"I thought I'd grieved you."

"No, dear; but speaking of father reminded me how much I miss him, how much I owe him, and how faithfully I should watch and work to keep his little daughters safe and good for him."

"Yet you told him to go, mother, and didn't cry when he went, and never complain now, or seem as if you needed any help," said Jo, wondering.

"I gave my best to the country I love, and kept my tears till he was gone. Why should I complain, when we both have merely done our duty, and will surely be the happier for it in the end? If I don't seem to need help, it is because I have a better friend, even than father, to comfort and sustain me. My child, the troubles and temptations of your life are beginning, and may be many; but you can overcome and outlive them all, if you learn to feel the strength and tenderness of your Heavenly Father as you do that of your earthly one. The more you love and trust Him, the nearer you will feel to Him, and the less you will depend on human power and wisdom. His love and care never tire or change, can never be taken from you, but may become the source of lifelong peace, happiness, and strength. Believe this heartily, and go to God with all your little cares, and hopes, and sins, and sorrows, as freely and confidingly as you come to your mother."

Jo's only answer was to hold her mother close, and, in the silence which followed, the sincerest prayer she had ever prayed left her heart, without words; for in that sad, yet happy hour, she had learned not only the bitterness of remorse and despair, but the sweetness of self-denial and self-control; and, led by her mother's hand, she had drawn nearer to the Friend who welcomes every child with a love stronger than that of any father, tenderer than that of any mother.

Amy stirred, and sighed in her sleep; and, as if eager to begin at once to mend her fault, Jo looked up with an expression on her face which it had never worn before.

"I let the sun go down on my anger; I wouldn't forgive her, and today, if it hadn't been for Laurie, it might have been too late! How could I be so wicked?" said Jo, half aloud, as she leaned over her sister, softly stroking the wet hair scattered on the pillow.

As if she heard, Amy opened her eyes, and held out her arms, with a smile that went straight to Jo's heart. Neither said a word, but they hugged one another close, in spite of the blankets, and everything was forgiven and forgotten in one hearty kiss.

9
Meg Goes to Vanity Fair[5]

"I do think it was the most fortunate thing in the world, that those children should have the measles just now," said Meg, one April day, as she stood packing the "go abroady" trunk in her room, surrounded by her sisters.

"And so nice of Annie Moffat, not to forget her promise. A whole fortnight of fun will be regularly splendid," replied Jo, looking like a windmill, as she folded skirts with her long arms.

"And such lovely weather; I'm so glad of that," added Beth, tidily sorting neck and hair ribbons in her best box, lent for the great occasion.

"I wish I was going to have a fine time, and wear all these nice things," said Amy, with her mouth full of pins, as she artistically replenished her sister's cushion.

"I wish you were all going; but, as you can't, I shall keep my adventures to tell you when I come back. I'm sure it's the least I can do, when you have been so kind, lending me things, and helping me get ready," said Meg, glancing round the room at the very simple outfit, which seemed nearly perfect in their eyes.

"What did mother give you out of the treasure-box?" asked Amy, who had not been present at the opening of a certain cedar chest, in which Mrs. March kept a few relics of past splendor, as gifts for her girls when the proper time came.

"A pair of silk stockings, that pretty carved fan, and a lovely blue sash. I wanted the violet silk; but there isn't time to make it over, so I must be contented with my old tarleton."[6]

"It will look nicely over my new muslin skirt, and the sash will set it off beautifully. I wish I hadn't smashed my coral bracelet, for you might have had it," said Jo, who loved to give and lend, but whose possessions were usually too dilapidated to be of much use.

"There is a lovely old-fashioned pearl set in the treasure-box; but mother said real flowers were the prettiest ornament for a young girl, and Laurie promised to send me all I want," replied Meg. "Now, let me see; there's my new gray walking-suit,—just curl up the feather in my hat, Beth,—then my poplin, for Sunday, and the small party,—it looks heavy for spring, don't it? the violet silk would be so nice; oh, dear!"

"Never mind; you've got the tarleton for the big party, and you always look like an angel in white," said Amy, brooding over the little store of finery in which her soul delighted.

"It isn't low-necked, and it doesn't sweep enough, but it will have to do. My blue house-dress looks so well, turned and freshly trimmed, that I feel as if I'd got a new one. My silk sacque[7] isn't a bit the fashion, and my bonnet don't look like Sallie's; I didn't like to say anything, but I was dreadfully disappointed in my umbrella. I told mother black, with a white handle, but she forgot, and bought a green one, with an ugly yellowish handle. It's strong and neat, so

5. In *Pilgrim's Progress*, an urban marketplace Christian must traverse on his way to paradise.
6. "Tarletan" is thin, stiffly starched, open-weave muslin; in this case, a dress.
7. Short, loose-fitting coat.

I ought not to complain, but I know I shall feel ashamed of it beside Annie's silk one, with a gold top," sighed Meg, surveying the little umbrella with great disfavor.

"Change it," advised Jo.

"I won't be so silly, or hurt Marmee's feelings, when she took so much pains to get my things. It's a nonsensical notion of mine, and I'm not going to give up to it. My silk stockings and two pairs of spandy gloves are my comfort. You are a dear, to lend me yours, Jo; I feel so rich, and sort of elegant, with two new pairs, and the old ones cleaned up for common;" and Meg took a refreshing peep at her glove-box.

"Annie Moffat has blue and pink bows on her night-caps; would you put some on mine?" she asked, as Beth brought up a pile of snowy muslins, fresh from Hannah's hands.

"No, I wouldn't; for the smart caps won't match the plain gowns, without any trimming on them. Poor folks shouldn't rig," said Jo, decidedly.

"I wonder if I shall *ever* be happy enough to have real lace on my clothes, and bows on my caps?" said Meg, impatiently.

"You said the other day that you'd be perfectly happy if you could only go to Annie Moffat's," observed Beth, in her quiet way.

"So I did! Well, I *am* happy, and I *won't* fret; but it does seem as if the more one gets the more one wants, don't it? There, now, the trays are ready, and everything in but my ball-dress, which I shall leave for mother," said Meg, cheering up, as she glanced from the half-filled trunk to the many-times pressed and mended white tarleton, which she called her "ball-dress," with an important air.

The next day was fine, and Meg departed, in style, for a fortnight of novelty and pleasure. Mrs. March had consented to the visit rather reluctantly, fearing that Margaret would come back more discontented than she went. But she had begged so hard, and Sallie had promised to take good care of her, and a little pleasure seemed so delightful after a winter of hard work, that the mother yielded, and the daughter went to take her first taste of fashionable life.

The Moffats *were* very fashionable, and simple Meg was rather daunted, at first, by the splendor of the house, and the elegance of its occupants. But they were kindly people, in spite of the frivolous life they led, and soon put their guest at her ease. Perhaps Meg felt, without understanding why, that they were not particularly cultivated or intelligent people, and that all their gilding could not quite conceal the ordinary material of which they were made. It certainly was agreeable to fare sumptuously, drive in a fine carriage, wear her best frock every day, and do nothing but enjoy herself. It suited her exactly; and soon she began to imitate the manners and conversation of those about her; to put on little airs and graces, use French phrases, crimp her hair, take in her dresses, and talk about the fashions, as well as she could. The more she saw of Annie Moffat's pretty things, the more she envied her, and sighed to be rich. Home now looked bare and dismal as she thought of it, work grew harder than ever, and she felt that she was a very destitute and much injured girl, in spite of the new gloves and silk stockings.

She had not much time for repining, however, for the three young girls were busily employed in "having a good time." They shopped, walked, rode, and called all day; went to theatres and operas, or frolicked at home in the evening; for Annie had many friends, and knew how to entertain them. Her older sisters were very fine young ladies, and one was engaged, which was extremely interesting and romantic, Meg thought. Mr. Moffat was a fat, jolly old gentleman, who knew her father; and Mrs. Moffat, a fat, jolly old lady, who took as great a fancy to Meg as her daughter had done. Every one petted her; and "Daisy," as they called her, was in a fair way to have her head turned.[8]

When the evening for the "small party" came, she found that the poplin wouldn't do at all, for the other girls were putting on thin dresses, and making themselves very fine indeed; so out came the tarleton, looking older, limper, and shabbier than ever, beside Sallie's crisp

8. To become conceited.

new one. Meg saw the girls glance at it, and then at one another, and her cheeks began to burn; for, with all her gentleness, she was very proud. No one said a word about it, but Sallie offered to do her hair, and Annie to tie her sash, and Belle, the engaged sister, praised her white arms; but, in their kindness, Meg saw only pity for her poverty, and her heart felt very heavy as she stood by herself, while the others laughed and chattered, prinked, and flew about like gauzy butterflies. The hard, bitter feeling was getting pretty bad, when the maid brought in a box of flowers. Before she could speak, Annie had the cover off, and all were exclaiming at the lovely roses, heath, and ferns within.

"It's for Belle, of course; George always sends her some, but these are altogether ravishing," cried Annie, with a great sniff.

"They are for Miss March," the man said. "And here's a note," put in the maid, holding it to Meg.

"What fun! Who are they from? Didn't know you had a lover," cried the girls, fluttering about Meg in a high state of curiosity and surprise.

"The note is from mother, and the flowers from Laurie," said Meg, simply, yet much gratified that he had not forgotten her.

"Oh, indeed!" said Annie, with a funny look, as Meg slipped the note into her pocket, as a sort of talisman against envy, vanity, and false pride; for the few loving words had done her good, and the flowers cheered her up by their beauty.

Feeling almost happy again, she laid by a few ferns and roses for herself, and quickly made up the rest in dainty bouquets for the breasts, hair, or skirts of her friends, offering them so prettily, that Clara, the elder sister, told her she was "the sweetest little thing she ever saw;" and they looked quite charmed with her small attention. Somehow the kind act finished her despondency; and, when all the rest went to show themselves to Mrs. Moffat, she saw a happy, bright-eyed face in the mirror, as she laid her ferns against her rippling hair, and fastened the roses in the dress that didn't strike her as so *very* shabby now.

She enjoyed herself very much that evening, for she danced to her heart's content; every one was very kind, and she had three compliments. Annie made her sing, and some one said she had a remarkably fine voice; Major Lincoln asked who "the fresh little girl, with the beautiful eyes, was;" and Mr. Moffat insisted on dancing with her, because she "didn't dawdle, but had some spring in her," as he gracefully expressed it. So, altogether, she had a very nice time, till she overheard a bit of a conversation, which disturbed her extremely. She was sitting just inside the conservatory, waiting for her partner to bring her an ice, when she heard a voice ask, on the other side of the flowery wall,—

"How old is he?"

"Sixteen or seventeen, I should say," replied another voice.

"It would be a grand thing for one of those girls, wouldn't it? Sallie says they are very intimate now, and the old man quite dotes on them."

"Mrs. M. has laid her plans, I dare say, and will play her cards well, early as it is. The girl evidently doesn't think of it yet," said Mrs. Moffat.

"She told that fib about her mamma, as if she did know, and colored up when the flowers came, quite prettily. Poor thing! she'd be so nice if she was only got up in style. Do you think she'd be offended if we offered to lend her a dress for Thursday?" asked another voice.

"She's proud, but I don't believe she'd mind, for that dowdy tarleton is all she has got. She may tear it to-night, and that will be a good excuse for offering a decent one."

"We'll see; I shall ask that Laurence, as a compliment to her, and we'll have fun about it afterward."

Here Meg's partner appeared, to find her looking much flushed, and rather agitated. She was proud, and her pride was useful just then, for it helped her hide her mortification, anger, and disgust, at what she had just heard; for, innocent and unsuspicious as she was, she could not help understanding the gossip of her friends. She tried to forget it, but could not, and kept repeating to herself, "Mrs. M. has her plans," "that fib about her mamma," and "dowdy tarleton," till she was ready to cry, and rush home to tell her troubles, and ask for advice. As that was impossible, she did her best to seem gay; and, being rather excited, she succeeded so well, that no one dreamed what an effort she was making. She was very glad when it was all over, and she was quiet in her bed, where she could think and wonder and fume till her head ached, and her hot cheeks were cooled by a few natural tears. Those foolish, yet well-meant words, had opened a new world to Meg, and much disturbed the peace of the old one, in which, till now, she had lived as happily as a child. Her innocent friendship with Laurie was spoilt by the silly speeches she had overheard; her faith in her mother was a little shaken by the worldly plans attributed to her by Mrs. Moffat, who judged others by herself; and the sensible resolution to be contented with the simple wardrobe which suited a poor man's daughter, was weakened by the unnecessary pity of girls, who thought a shabby dress one of the greatest calamities under heaven.

Poor Meg had a restless night, and got up heavy-eyed, unhappy, half resentful toward her friends, and half ashamed of herself for not speaking out frankly, and setting everything right. Everybody dawdled that morning, and it was noon before the girls found energy enough even to take up their worsted work. Something in the manner of her friends struck Meg at once; they treated her with more respect, she thought; took quite a tender interest in what she said, and looked at her with eyes that plainly betrayed curiosity. All this surprised and flattered her, though she did not understand it till Miss Belle looked up from her writing, and said, with a sentimental air,—

"Daisy, dear, I've sent an invitation to your friend, Mr. Laurence, for Thursday. We should like to know him, and it's only a proper compliment to you."

Meg colored, but a mischievous fancy to tease the girls made her reply, demurely,—

"You are very kind, but I'm afraid he won't come."

"Why not, chérie?" asked Miss Belle.

"He's too old."

"My child, what do you mean? What is his age, I beg to know!" cried Miss Clara.

"Nearly seventy, I believe," answered Meg, counting stitches, to hide the merriment in her eyes.

"You sly creature! of course, we meant the young man," exclaimed Miss Belle, laughing.

"There isn't any; Laurie is only a little boy," and Meg laughed also at the queer look which the sisters exchanged, as she thus described her supposed lover.

"About your age," Nan said.

"Nearer my sister Jo's; *I* am seventeen in August," returned Meg, tossing her head.

"It's very nice of him to send you flowers, isn't it?" said Annie, looking wise about nothing.

"Yes, he often does, to all of us; for their house is full, and we are so fond of them. My mother and old Mr. Laurence are friends, you know, so it is quite natural that we children should play together;" and Meg hoped they would say no more.

"It's evident Daisy isn't out yet," said Miss Clara to Belle, with a nod.

"Quite a pastoral state of innocence all round," returned Miss Belle, with a shrug.

"I'm going out to get some little matters for my girls; can I do anything for you, young ladies?" asked Mrs. Moffat, lumbering in, like an elephant, in silk and lace.

"No, thank you, ma'am," replied Sallie; "I've got my new pink silk for Thursday, and I don't want a thing."

"Nor I—" began Meg, but stopped, because it occurred to her that she *did* want several things, and could not have them.

"What shall you wear?" asked Sallie.

"My old white one again, if I can mend it fit to be seen; it got sadly torn last night," said Meg, trying to speak quite easily, but feeling very uncomfortable.

"Why don't you send home for another?" said Sallie, who was not an observing young lady.

"I haven't got any other." It cost Meg an effort to say that, but Sallie did not see it, and exclaimed, in amiable surprise,—

"Only that? how funny—." She did not finish her speech, for Belle shook her head at her, and broke in, saying, kindly,—

"Not at all; where is the use of having a lot of dresses when she isn't out? There's no need of sending home, Daisy, even if you had a dozen, for I've got a sweet blue silk laid away, which I've outgrown, and you shall wear it, to please me; won't you, dear?"

"You are very kind, but I don't mind my old dress, if you don't; it does well enough for a little girl like me," said Meg.

"Now do let me please myself by dressing you up in style. I admire to do it, and you'd be a regular little beauty, with a touch here and there. I shan't let any one see you till you are done, and then we'll burst upon them like Cinderella and her godmother, going to the ball," said Belle, in her persuasive tone.

Meg couldn't refuse the offer so kindly made, for a desire to see if she would be "a little beauty" after touching up caused her to accept, and forget all her former uncomfortable feelings towards the Moffats.

On the Thursday evening, Belle shut herself up with her maid; and, between them, they turned Meg into a fine lady. They crimped and curled her hair, they polished her neck and arms with some fragrant powder, touched her lips with coralline salve, to make them redder, and Hortense would have added "a *soupçon* of rouge," if Meg had not rebelled. They laced her into a sky-blue dress, which was so tight she could hardly breathe, and so low in the neck that modest Meg blushed at herself in the mirror. A set of silver filagree was added, bracelets, necklace, brooch, and even ear-rings, for Hortense tied them on, with a bit of pink silk, which did not show. A cluster of tea rose-buds at the bosom, and a *ruche,*[9] reconciled Meg to the display of her pretty white shoulders, and a pair of high-heeled blue silk boots satisfied the last wish of her heart. A laced handkerchief, a plumy fan, and a bouquet in a silver holder, finished her off; and Miss Belle surveyed her with the satisfaction of a little girl with a newly dressed doll.

"Mademoiselle is charmante, très jolie,[1] is she not?" cried Hortense, clasping her hands in an affected rapture.

"Come and show yourself," said Miss Belle, leading the way to the room where the others were waiting.

As Meg went rustling after, with her long skirts trailing, her ear-rings tinkling, her curls waving, and her heart beating, she felt as if her "fun" had really begun at last, for the mirror had plainly told her that she *was* "a little beauty." Her friends repeated the pleasing phrase enthusiastically; and, for several minutes, she stood, like the jackdaw in the fable, enjoying her borrowed plumes, while the rest chattered like a party of magpies.

"While I dress, do you drill her, Nan, in the management of her skirt, and those French heels, or she will trip herself up. Put your silver butterfly in the middle of that white barbe, and catch up that long curl on the left side of her head, Clara, and don't any of you disturb the charming work of my hands," said Belle, as she hurried away, looking well pleased with her success.

"I'm afraid to go down, I feel so queer and stiff, and half-dressed," said Meg to Sallie, as the bell rang, and Mrs. Moffat sent to ask the young ladies to appear at once.

"You don't look a bit like yourself, but you are very nice. I'm nowhere beside you, for Belle has heaps of taste, and you're quite French, I assure you. Let your flowers hang; don't be so careful of them, and be sure you don't trip," returned Sallie, trying not to care that Meg was prettier than herself.

Keeping that warning carefully in mind, Margaret got safely down stairs, and sailed into the drawing-rooms, where the Moffats and a few early guests were assembled. She very soon discovered that there is a charm about fine clothes which attracts a certain class of people, and secures their respect. Several young ladies, who had taken no notice of her before, were

9. A cluster of lace, often worn tucked into the neckline of a low-cut garment.　　1. Charming, very pretty.

very affectionate all of a sudden; several young gentlemen, who had only stared at her at the other party, now not only stared, but asked to be introduced, and said all manner of foolish, but agreeable things to her; and several old ladies, who sat on sofas, and criticised the rest of the party, inquired who she was, with an air of interest. She heard Mrs. Moffat reply to one of them,—

"Daisy March—father a colonel in the army—one of our first families, but reverses of fortune, you know; intimate friends of the Laurences; sweet creature, I assure you; my Ned is quite wild about her."

"Dear me!" said the old lady, putting up her glass for another observation of Meg, who tried to look as if she had not heard, and been rather shocked at Mrs. Moffat's fibs.

The "queer feeling" did not pass away, but she imagined herself acting the new part of fine lady, and so got on pretty well, though the tight dress gave her a side-ache,[2] the train kept getting under her feet, and she was in constant fear lest her ear-rings should fly off, and get lost or broken. She was flirting her fan, and laughing at the feeble jokes of a young gentleman who tried to be witty, when she suddenly stopped laughing, and looked confused; for, just opposite, she saw Laurie. He was staring at her with undisguised surprise, and disapproval also, she thought; for, though he bowed and smiled, yet something in his honest eyes made her blush, and wish she had her old dress on. To complete her confusion, she saw Belle nudge Annie, and both glance from her to Laurie, who, she was happy to see, looked unusually boyish and shy.

"Silly creatures, to put such thoughts into my head! I won't care for it, or let it change me a bit," thought Meg, and rustled across the room to shake hands with her friend.

"I'm glad you came, for I was afraid you wouldn't," she said, with her most grown-up air.

"Jo wanted me to come, and tell her how you looked, so I did;" answered Laurie, without turning his eyes upon her, though he half smiled at her maternal tone.

"What shall you tell her?" asked Meg, full of curiosity to know his opinion of her, yet feeling ill at ease with him, for the first time.

"I shall say I didn't know you; for you look so grown-up, and unlike yourself, I'm quite afraid of you," he said, fumbling at his glove-button.

"How absurd of you! the girls dressed me up for fun, and I rather like it. Wouldn't Jo stare if she saw me?" said Meg, bent on making him say whether he thought her improved or not.

"Yes, I think she would," returned Laurie, gravely.

"Don't you like me so?" asked Meg.

"No, I don't," was the blunt reply.

"Why not?" in an anxious tone.

He glanced at her frizzled head, bare shoulders, and fantastically trimmed dress, with an expression that abashed her more than his answer, which had not a particle of his usual politeness about it.

"I don't like fuss and feathers."

That was altogether too much from a lad younger than herself; and Meg walked away, saying, petulantly,—

"You are the rudest boy I ever saw."

Feeling very much ruffled, she went and stood at a quiet window, to cool her cheeks, for the tight dress gave her an uncomfortably brilliant color. As she stood there, Major Lincoln passed by; and, a minute after, she heard him saying to his mother,—

"They are making a fool of that little girl; I wanted you to see her, but they have spoilt her entirely; she's nothing but a doll, to-night."

"Oh, dear!" sighed Meg; "I wish I'd been sensible, and worn my own things; then I should not have disgusted other people, or felt so uncomfortable and ashamed of myself."

She leaned her forehead on the cool pane, and stood half hidden by the curtains, never

2. Victorian-era corsets, if worn habitually, could fracture ribs and even displace internal organs.

minding that her favorite waltz had begun, till some one touched her; and, turning, she saw Laurie looking penitent, as he said, with his very best bow, and his hand out,—

"Please forgive my rudeness, and come and dance with me."

"I'm afraid it will be too disagreeable to you," said Meg, trying to look offended, and failing entirely.

"Not a bit of it; I'm dying to do it. Come, I'll be good; I don't like your gown, but I do think you are—just splendid;" and he waved his hands, as if words failed to express his admiration.

Meg smiled, and relented, and whispered, as they stood waiting to catch the time.

"Take care my skirt don't trip you up; it's the plague of my life, and I was a goose to wear it."

"Pin it round your neck, and then it will be useful," said Laurie, looking down at the little blue boots, which he evidently approved of.

Away they went, fleetly and gracefully; for, having practised at home, they were well matched, and the blithe young couple were a pleasant sight to see, as they twirled merrily round and round, feeling more friendly than ever after their small tiff.

"Laurie, I want you to do me a favor; will you?" said Meg, as he stood fanning her, when her breath gave out, which it did, very soon, though she would not own why.

"Won't I!" said Laurie, with alacrity.

"Please don't tell them at home about my dress to-night. They won't understand the joke, and it will worry mother."

"Then why did you do it?" said Laurie's eyes, so plainly, that Meg hastily added,—

"I shall tell them, myself, all about it, and 'fess' to mother how silly I've been. But I'd rather do it myself; so you'll not tell, will you?"

"I give you my word I won't; only what shall I say when they ask me?"

"Just say I looked nice, and was having a good time."

"I'll say the first, with all my heart; but how about the other? You don't look as if you were having a good time; are you?" and Laurie looked at her with an expression which made her answer, in a whisper,—

"No; not just now. Don't think I'm horrid; I only wanted a little fun, but this sort don't pay, I find, and I'm getting tired of it."

"Here comes Ned Moffat; what does he want?" said Laurie, knitting his black brows, as if he did not regard his young host in the light of a pleasant addition to the party.

"He put his name down for three dances, and I suppose he's coming for them; what a bore!" said Meg, assuming a languid air, which amused Laurie immensely.

He did not speak to her again till supper-time, when he saw her drinking champagne with Ned, and his friend Fisher, who were behaving "like a pair of fools," as Laurie said to himself, for he felt a brotherly sort of right to watch over the Marches, and fight their battles, whenever a defender was needed.

"You'll have a splitting headache to-morrow, if you drink much of that. I wouldn't, Meg; your mother don't like it, you know," he whispered, leaning over her chair, as Ned turned to refill her glass, and Fisher stooped to pick up her fan.

"I'm not Meg, to-night; I'm 'a doll,' who does all sorts of crazy things. To-morrow I shall put away my 'fuss and feathers,' and be desperately good again," she answered, with an affected little laugh.

"Wish to-morrow was here, then," muttered Laurie, walking off, ill-pleased at the change he saw in her.

Meg danced and flirted, chattered and giggled, as the other girls did; after supper she undertook the German,[3] and blundered through it, nearly upsetting her partner with her long skirt, and romping in a way that scandalized Laurie, who looked on and meditated a lecture. But he got no chance to deliver it, for Meg kept away from him till he came to say good-night.

3. A lively cotillion or quadrille, involving elaborate steps and the frequent exchange of dancing partners.

"Remember!" she said, trying to smile, for the splitting headache had already begun.

"Silence à la mort," replied Laurie, with a melodramatic flourish, as he went away.

This little bit of by-play excited Annie's curiosity; but Meg was too tired for gossip, and went to bed, feeling as if she had been to a masquerade, and hadn't enjoyed herself as much as she expected. She was sick all the next day, and on Saturday went home, quite used up with her fortnight's fun, and feeling that she had sat in the lap of luxury long enough.

"It does seem pleasant to be quiet, and not have company manners on all the time. Home *is* a nice place, though it isn't splendid," said Meg, looking about her with a restful expression, as she sat with her mother and Jo on the Sunday evening.

"I'm glad to hear you say so, dear, for I was afraid home would seem dull and poor to you, after your fine quarters," replied her mother, who had given her many anxious looks that day; for motherly eyes are quick to see any change in children's faces.

Meg had told her adventures gaily, and said over and over what a charming time she had had; but something still seemed to weigh upon her spirits, and, when the younger girls were gone to bed, she sat thoughtfully staring at the fire, saying little, and looking worried. As the clock struck nine, and Jo proposed bed, Meg suddenly left her chair, and, taking Beth's stool, leaned her elbows on her mother's knee, saying, bravely,—

"Marmee, I want to ' 'fess.' "

"I thought so; what is it, dear?"

"Shall I go away?" asked Jo, discreetly.

"Of course not; don't I always tell you everything? I was ashamed to speak of it before the children, but I want you to know all the dreadful things I did at the Moffats."

"We are prepared," said Mrs. March, smiling, but looking a little anxious.

"I told you they rigged me up, but I didn't tell you that they powdered, and squeezed, and frizzled, and made me look like a fashion-plate. Laurie thought I wasn't proper; I know he did, though he didn't say so, and one man called me 'a doll.' I knew it was silly, but they flattered me, and said I was a beauty, and quantities of nonsense, so I let them make a fool of me."

"Is that all?" asked Jo, as Mrs. March looked silently at the downcast face of her pretty daughter, and could not find it in her heart to blame her little follies.

"No; I drank champagne, and romped, and tried to flirt, and was, altogether, abominable," said Meg, self-reproachfully.

"There is something more, I think;" and Mrs. March smoothed the soft cheek, which suddenly grew rosy, as Meg answered, slowly,—

"Yes; it's very silly, but I want to tell it, because I hate to have people say and think such things about us and Laurie."

Then she told the various bits of gossip she had heard at the Moffats; and, as she spoke, Jo saw her mother fold her lips tightly, as if ill pleased that such ideas should be put into Meg's innocent mind.

"Well, if that isn't the greatest rubbish I ever heard," cried Jo, indignantly. "Why didn't you pop out and tell them so, on the spot?"

"I couldn't, it was so embarrassing for me. I couldn't help hearing, at first, and then I was so angry and ashamed, I didn't remember that I ought to go away."

"Just wait till *I* see Annie Moffat, and I'll show you how to settle such ridiculous stuff. The idea of having 'plans,' and being kind to Laurie, because he's rich, and may marry us by and by! Won't he shout, when I tell him what those silly things say about us poor children?" and Jo laughed, as if, on second thoughts, the thing struck her as a good joke.

"If you tell Laurie, I'll never forgive you! She mustn't, must she, mother?" said Meg, looking distressed.

"No; never repeat that foolish gossip, and forget it as soon as you can," said Mrs. March, gravely. "I was very unwise to let you go among people of whom I know so little; kind, I dare say, but worldly, ill-bred, and full of these vulgar ideas about young people. I am more sorry than I can express, for the mischief this visit may have done you, Meg."

"Don't be sorry, I won't let it hurt me; I'll forget all the bad, and remember only the good; for I did enjoy a great deal, and thank you very much for letting me go. I'll not be sentimental or dissatisfied, mother; I know I'm a silly little girl, and I'll stay with you till I'm fit to take care of myself. But it *is* nice to be praised and admired, and I can't help saying I like it," said Meg, looking half ashamed of the confession.

"That is perfectly natural, and quite harmless, if the liking does not become a passion, and lead one to do foolish or unmaidenly things. Learn to know and value the praise which is worth having, and to excite the admiration of excellent people, by being modest as well as pretty, Meg."

Margaret sat thinking a moment, while Jo stood with her hands behind her, looking both interested and a little perplexed; for it was a new thing to see Meg blushing and talking about admiration, lovers, and things of that sort, and Jo felt as if during that fortnight her sister had grown up amazingly, and was drifting away from her into a world where she could not follow.

"Mother, do you have 'plans,' as Mrs. Moffat said?" asked Meg, bashfully.

"Yes, my dear, I have a great many; all mothers do, but mine differ somewhat from Mrs. Moffat's, I suspect. I will tell you some of them, for the time has come when a word may set this romantic little head and heart of yours right, on a very serious subject. You are young, Meg; but not too young to understand me, and mothers' lips are the fittest to speak of such things to girls like you. Jo, your turn will come in time, perhaps, so listen to my 'plans,' and help me carry them out, if they are good."

Jo went and sat on one arm of the chair, looking as if she thought they were about to join in some very solemn affair. Holding a hand of each, and watching the two young faces wistfully, Mrs. March said, in her serious yet cheery way,—

"I want my daughters to be beautiful, accomplished, and good; to be admired, loved, and respected, to have a happy youth, to be well and wisely married, and to lead useful, pleasant lives, with as little care and sorrow to try them as God sees fit to send. To be loved and chosen by a good man is the best and sweetest thing which can happen to a woman; and I sincerely hope my girls may know this beautiful experience. It is natural to think of it, Meg; right to hope and wait for it, and wise to prepare for it; so that, when the happy time comes, you may feel ready for the duties, and worthy of the joy. My dear girls, I *am* ambitious for you, but not to have you make a dash in the world,—marry rich men merely because they are rich, or have splendid houses, which are not homes, because love is wanting. Money is a needful and precious thing,—and, when well used, a noble thing,—but I never want you to think it is the first or only prize to strive for. I'd rather see you poor men's wives, if you were happy, beloved, contented, than queens on thrones, without self-respect and peace."

"Poor girls don't stand any chance, Belle says, unless they put themselves forward," sighed Meg.

"Then we'll be old maids," said Jo, stoutly.

"Right, Jo; better be happy old maids than unhappy wives, or unmaidenly girls, running about to find husbands," said Mrs. March, decidedly. "Don't be troubled, Meg; poverty seldom daunts a sincere lover. Some of the best and most honored women I know were poor girls, but so love-worthy that they were not allowed to be old maids. Leave these things to time; make this home happy, so that you may be fit for homes of your own, if they are offered you, and contented here if they are not. One thing remember, my girls, mother is always ready to be your confidant, father to be your friend; and both of us trust and hope that our daughters, whether married or single, will be the pride and comfort of our lives."

"We will, Marmee, we will!" cried both, with all their hearts, as she bade them good-night.[4]

---

4. The chapters omitted here contain a replica of an Alcott family newspaper, an account of cooking experiments, a picnic, and a scene in which the girls tell Laurie about their "Pilgrim's Progress" game. We also omit a reference to Jo's crying over Susan Warner's *The Wide, Wide World.*

14
Secrets

Jo was very busy up in the garret, for the October days began to grow chilly, and the afternoons were short. For two or three hours the sun lay warmly in at the high window, showing Jo seated on the old sofa writing busily, with her papers spread out upon a trunk before her, while Scrabble, the pet rat, promenaded the beams overhead, accompanied by his oldest son, a fine young fellow, who was evidently very proud of his whiskers. Quite absorbed in her work, Jo scribbled away till the last page was filled, when she signed her name with a flourish, and threw down her pen, exclaiming,—

"There, I've done my best! If this don't suit I shall have to wait till I can do better."

Lying back on the sofa, she read the manuscript carefully through, making dashes here and there, and putting in many exclamation points, which looked like little balloons; then she tied it up with a smart red ribbon, and sat a minute looking at it with a sober, wistful expression, which plainly showed how earnest her work had been. Jo's desk up here was an old tin kitchen, which hung against the wall. In it she kept her papers, and a few books, safely shut away from Scrabble, who, being likewise of a literary turn, was fond of making a circulating library of such books as were left in his way, by eating the leaves. From this tin receptacle Jo produced another manuscript; and, putting both in her pocket, crept quietly down stairs, leaving her friends to nibble her pens and taste her ink.

She put on her hat and jacket as noiselessly as possible, and, going to the back entry window, got out upon the roof of a low porch, swung herself down to the grassy bank, and took a round-about way to the road. Once there she composed herself, hailed a passing omnibus, and rolled away to town, looking very merry and mysterious.

If any one had been watching her, he would have thought her movements decidedly peculiar; for, on alighting, she went off at a great pace till she reached a certain number in a certain busy street; having found the place with some difficulty, she went into the door-way, looked up the dirty stairs, and, after standing stock still a minute, suddenly dived into the street, and walked away as rapidly as she came. This manœuvre she repeated several times, to the great amusement of a black-eyed young gentleman lounging in the window of a building opposite. On returning for the third time, Jo gave herself a shake, pulled her hat over her eyes, and walked up the stairs, looking as if she was going to have all her teeth out.

There was a dentist's sign, among others, which adorned the entrance, and, after staring a moment at the pair of artificial jaws which slowly opened and shut to draw attention to a fine set of teeth, the young gentleman put on his coat, took his hat, and went down to post himself in the opposite door-way, saying, with a smile and a shiver,—

"It's like her to come alone, but if she has a bad time she'll need some one to help her home."

In ten minutes Jo came running down stairs with a very red face, and the general appearance of a person who had just passed through a trying ordeal of some sort. When she saw the young gentleman she looked anything but pleased, and passed him with a nod; but he followed, asking with an air of sympathy,—

"Did you have a bad time?"

"Not very."

"You got through quick."

"Yes, thank goodness!"

"Why did you go alone?"

"Didn't want any one to know."

"You're the oddest fellow I ever saw. How many did you have out?"

Jo looked at her friend as if she did not understand him; then began to laugh, as if mightily amused at something.

"There are two which I want to have come out, but I must wait a week."

"What are you laughing at? You are up to some mischief, Jo," said Laurie, looking mystified.

"So are you. What were you doing, sir, up in that billiard saloon?"

"Begging your pardon, ma'am, it wasn't a billiard saloon, but a gymnasium, and I was taking a lesson in fencing."

"I'm glad of that!"

"Why?"

"You can teach me; and then, when we play Hamlet, you can be Laertes, and we'll make a fine thing of the fencing scene."

Laurie burst out with a hearty boy's laugh, which made several passers-by smile in spite of themselves.

"I'll teach you, whether we play Hamlet or not; it's grand fun, and will straighten you up capitally. But I don't believe that was your only reason for saying 'I'm glad,' in that decided way; was it, now?"

"No, I was glad you were not in the saloon, because I hope you never go to such places. Do you?"

"Not often."

"I wish you wouldn't."

"It's no harm, Jo, I have billiards at home, but it's no fun unless you have good players; so, as I'm fond of it, I come sometimes and have a game with Ned Moffat or some of the other fellows."

"Oh dear, I'm so sorry, for you'll get to liking it better and better, and will waste time and money, and grow like those dreadful boys. I did hope you'd stay respectable, and be a satisfaction to your friends," said Jo, shaking her head.

"Can't a fellow take a little innocent amusement now and then without losing his respectability?" asked Laurie, looking nettled.

"That depends upon how and where he takes it. I don't like Ned and his set, and wish you'd keep out of it. Mother won't let us have him at our house, though he wants to come, and if you grow like him she won't be willing to have us frolic together as we do now."

"Won't she?" asked Laurie, anxiously.

"No, she can't bear fashionable young men, and she'd shut us all up in bandboxes rather than have us associate with them."

"Well, she needn't get out her bandboxes yet; I'm not a fashionable party, and don't mean to be; but I do like harmless larks now and then, don't you?"

"Yes, nobody minds them, so lark away, but don't get wild, will you? or there will be an end of all our good times."

"I'll be a double distilled saint."

"I can't bear saints; just be a simple, honest, respectable boy, and we'll never desert you. I don't know what I *should* do if you acted like Mr. King's son; he had plenty of money, but didn't know how to spend it, and got tipsey, and gambled, and ran away, and forged his father's name, I believe, and was altogether horrid."

"You think I'm likely to do the same? Much obliged."

"No I don't—oh, *dear*, no!—but I hear people talking about money being such a temptation, and I sometimes wish you were poor; I shouldn't worry then."

"Do you worry about me, Jo?"

"A little, when you look moody or discontented, as you sometimes do, for you've got such a strong will if you once get started wrong, I'm afraid it would be hard to stop you."

Laurie walked in silence a few minutes, and Jo watched him, wishing she had held her tongue, for his eyes looked angry, though his lips still smiled as if at her warnings.

"Are you going to deliver lectures all the way home?" he asked, presently.

"Of course not; why?"

"Because if you are, I'll take a 'bus; if you are not, I'd like to walk with you, and tell you something very interesting."

"I won't preach any more, and I'd like to hear the news immensely."

"Very well, then; come on. It's a secret, and if I tell you, you must tell me yours."

"I haven't got any," began Jo, but stopped suddenly, remembering that she had.

"You know you have; you can't hide anything, so up and 'fess, or I won't tell," cried Laurie. "Is your secret a nice one?"

"Oh, isn't it! all about people you know, and such fun! You ought to hear it, and I've been aching to tell this long time. Come! you begin."

"You'll not say anything about it at home, will you?"

"Not a word."

"And you won't tease me in private?"

"I never tease."

"Yes, you do; you get everything you want out of people. I don't know how you do it, but you are a born wheedler."

"Thank you; fire away!"

"Well, I've left two stories with a newspaper man, and he's to give his answer next week," whispered Jo, in her confidant's ear.

"Hurrah for Miss March, the celebrated American authoress!" cried Laurie, throwing up his hat and catching it again, to the great delight of two ducks, four cats, five hens, and half a dozen Irish children; for they were out of the city now.

"Hush! it won't come to anything, I dare say; but I couldn't rest till I had tried, and I said nothing about it, because I don't want any one else to be disappointed."

"It won't fail! Why, Jo, your stories are works of Shakespeare compared to half the rubbish that's published every day. Won't it be fun to see them in print; and shan't we feel proud of our authoress?"

Jo's eyes sparkled, for it's always pleasant to be believed in; and a friend's praise is always sweeter than a dozen newspaper puffs.

"Where's *your* secret? Play fair, Teddy, or I'll never believe you again," she said, trying to extinguish the brilliant hopes that blazed up at a word of encouragement.

"I may get into a scrape for telling; but I didn't promise not to, so I will, for I never feel easy in my mind till I've told you any plummy bit of news I get. I know where Meg's glove is."

"Is that all?" said Jo, looking disappointed, as Laurie nodded and twinkled, with a face full of mysterious intelligence.

"It's quite enough for the present, as you'll agree when I tell you where it is."

"Tell, then."

Laurie bent and whispered three words in Jo's ear, which produced a comical change. She stood and stared at him for a minute, looking both surprised and displeased, then walked on, saying sharply, "How do you know?"

"Saw it."

"Where?"

"Pocket."

"All this time?"

"Yes; isn't that romantic?"

"No, it's horrid."

"Don't you like it?"

"Of course I don't; it's ridiculous; it won't be allowed. My patience! what would Meg say?"

"You are not to tell any one; mind that."

"I didn't promise."

"That was understood, and I trusted you."

"Well, I won't for the present, anyway; but I'm disgusted, and wish you hadn't told me."

"I thought you'd be pleased."

"At the idea of anybody coming to take Meg away? No, thank you."

"You'll feel better about it when somebody comes to take you away."

"I'd like to see any one try it," cried Jo, fiercely.

"So should I!" and Laurie chuckled at the idea.

"I don't think secrets agree with me; I feel rumpled up in my mind since you told me that," said Jo, rather ungratefully.

"Race down this hill with me, and you'll be all right," suggested Laurie.

No one was in sight; the smooth road sloped invitingly before her, and, finding the temptation irresistible, Jo darted away, soon leaving hat and comb behind her, and scattering hair-pins as she ran. Laurie reached the goal first, and was quite satisfied with the success of his treatment; for his Atlanta[5] came panting up with flying hair, bright eyes, ruddy cheeks, and no signs of dissatisfaction in her face.

"I wish I was a horse; then I could run for miles in this splendid air, and not lose my breath. It was capital; but see what a guy[6] it's made me. Go, pick up my things, like a cherub as you are," said Jo, dropping down under a maple tree, which was carpeting the bank with crimson leaves.

Laurie leisurely departed to recover the lost property, and Jo bundled up her braids, hoping no one would pass by till she was tidy again. But some one did pass, and who should it be but Meg, looking particularly lady-like in her state and festival suit, for she had been making calls.

"What in the world are you doing here?" she asked, regarding her dishevelled sister with well-bred surprise.

"Getting leaves," meekly answered Jo, sorting the rosy handful she had just swept up.

"And hair-pins," added Laurie, throwing half a dozen into Jo's lap. "They grow on this road, Meg; so do combs and brown straw hats."

"You have been running, Jo; how could you? When *will* you stop such romping ways?" said Meg, reprovingly, as she settled her cuffs and smoothed her hair, with which the wind had taken liberties.

"Never till I'm stiff and old, and have to use a crutch. Don't try to make me grow up before my time, Meg; it's hard enough to have you change all of a sudden; let me be a little girl as long as I can."

As she spoke, Jo bent over her work to hide the trembling of her lips; for lately she had felt that Margaret was fast getting to be a woman, and Laurie's secret made her dread the separation which must surely come some time, and now seemed very near. He saw the trouble in her face, and drew Meg's attention from it by asking, quickly, "Where have you been calling, all so fine?"

"At the Gardiners; and Sallie has been telling me all about Belle Moffat's wedding. It was very splendid, and they have gone to spend the winter in Paris; just think how delightful that must be!"

"Do you envy her, Meg?" said Laurie.

"I'm afraid I do."

"I'm glad of it!" muttered Jo, tying on her hat with a jerk.

"Why?" asked Meg, looking surprised.

"Because, if you care much about riches, you will never go and marry a poor man," said Jo, frowning at Laurie, who was mutely warning her to mind what she said.

"I shall never 'go and marry' any one," observed Meg, walking on with great dignity, while the others followed, laughing, whispering, skipping stones, and "behaving like children," as

5. In Greek mythology, Atalanta promised to marry any man who could outrun her; her successful suitor wins by throwing golden apples in her path to distract her.

6. A person who is odd or grotesque in appearance.

Meg said to herself, though she might have been tempted to join them if she had not had her best dress on.

For a week or two Jo behaved so queerly, that her sisters got quite bewildered. She rushed to the door when the postman rang; was rude to Mr. Brooke whenever they met; would sit looking at Meg with a woe-begone face, occasionally jumping up to shake, and then to kiss her, in a very mysterious manner; Laurie and she were always making signs to one another, and talking about "Spread Eagles," till the girls declared they had both lost their wits. On the second Saturday after Jo got out of the window, Meg, as she sat sewing at her window, was scandalized by the sight of Laurie chasing Jo all over the garden, and finally capturing her in Amy's bower. What went on there, Meg could not see, but shrieks of laughter were heard, followed by the murmur of voices, and a great flapping of newspapers.

"What shall we do with that girl? She never *will* behave like a young lady," sighed Meg, as she watched the race with a disapproving face.

"I hope she won't; she is so funny and dear as she is," said Beth, who had never betrayed that she was a little hurt at Jo's having secrets with any one but her.

"It's very trying, but we never can make her *comme la fo,*" added Amy, who sat making some new frills for herself, with her curls tied up in a very becoming way,—two agreeable things, which made her feel unusually elegant and lady-like.

In a few minutes Jo bounced in, laid herself on the sofa, and affected to read.

"Have you anything interesting there?" asked Meg, with condescension.

"Nothing but a story; don't amount to much, I guess," returned Jo, carefully keeping the name of the paper out of sight.

"You'd better read it loud; that will amuse us, and keep you out of mischief," said Amy, in her most grown-up tone.

"What's the name?" asked Beth, wondering why Jo kept her face behind the sheet.

"The Rival Painters."[8]

"That sounds well; read it," said Meg.

With a loud "hem!" and a long breath, Jo began to read very fast. The girls listened with interest, for the tale was romantic, and somewhat pathetic, as most of the characters died in the end.

"I like that about the splendid picture," was Amy's approving remark, as Jo paused.

"I prefer the lovering part. Viola and Angelo are two of our favorite names; isn't that queer?" said Meg, wiping her eyes, for the "lovering part" was tragical.

"Who wrote it?" asked Beth, who had caught a glimpse of Jo's face.

The reader suddenly sat up, cast away the paper, displayed a flushed countenance, and, with a funny mixture of solemnity and excitement, replied in a loud voice, "Your sister!"

"You?" cried Meg, dropping her work.

"It's very good," said Amy, critically.

"I knew it! I knew it! oh, my Jo, I *am* so proud!" and Beth ran to hug her sister and exult over this splendid success.

Dear me, how delighted they all were, to be sure; how Meg wouldn't believe it till she saw the words, "Miss Josephine March," actually printed in the paper; how graciously Amy criticised the artistic parts of the story, and offered hints for a sequel, which unfortunately couldn't be carried out, as the hero and heroine were dead; how Beth got excited, and skipped and sung with joy; how Hannah came in to exclaim, "Sakes alive, well I never!" in great astonishment at "that Jo's doin's;" how proud Mrs. March was when she knew it; how Jo laughed, with tears in her eyes, as she declared she might as well be a peacock and done with it; and how the "Spread Eagle" might be said to flap his wings triumphantly over the house of March, as the paper passed from hand to hand.

---

7. *Comme il faut,* or fashionable.

8. Jo's story has the same title as Alcott's first published story, which appeared in 1852.

"Tell us about it." "When did it come?" "How much did you get for it?" "What *will* father say?" "Won't Laurie laugh?" cried the family, all in one breath, as they clustered about Jo; for these foolish, affectionate people made a jubilee of every little household joy.

"Stop jabbering, girls, and I'll tell you everything," said Jo, wondering if Miss Burney felt any grander over her "Evelina" than she did over her "Rival Painters."[9] Having told how she disposed of her tales, Jo added,—"And when I went to get my answer the man said he liked them both, but didn't pay beginners, only let them print in his paper, and noticed the stories. It was good practice, he said; and, when the beginners improved, any one would pay. So I let him have the two stories, and today this was sent to me, and Laurie caught me with it, and insisted on seeing it, so I let him; and he said it was good, and I shall write more, and he's going to get the next paid for, and oh—I *am* so happy, for in time I may be able to support myself and help the girls."

Jo's breath gave out here; and, wrapping her head in the paper, she bedewed her little story with a few natural tears; for to be independent, and earn the praise of those she loved, were the dearest wishes of her heart, and this seemed to be the first step toward that happy end.

15
A Telegram

"November is the most disagreeable month in the whole year," said Margaret, standing at the window one dull afternoon, looking out at the frost-bitten garden.

"That's the reason I was born in it," observed Jo, pensively, quite unconscious of the blot on her nose.

"If something very pleasant should happen now, we should think it a delightful month," said Beth, who took a hopeful view of everything, even November.

"I dare say; but nothing pleasant ever *does* happen in this family," said Meg, who was out of sorts. "We go grubbing along day after day, without a bit of change, and very little fun. We might as well be in a tread-mill."

"My patience, how blue we are!" cried Jo. "I don't much wonder, poor dear, for you see other girls having splendid times, while you grind, grind, year in and year out. Oh, don't I wish I could fix things for you as I do for my heroines! you're pretty enough and good enough already, so I'd have some rich relation leave you a fortune unexpectedly; then you'd dash out as an heiress, scorn every one who has slighted you, go abroad, and come home my Lady Something, in a blaze of splendor and elegance."

"People don't have fortunes left them in that style now-a-days; men have to work, and women to marry for money. It's a dreadfully unjust world," said Meg, bitterly.

"Jo and I are going to make fortunes for you all; just wait ten years, and see if we don't," said Amy, who sat in a corner making "mud pies," as Hannah called her little clay models of birds, fruit and faces.

"Can't wait, and I'm afraid I haven't much faith in ink and dirt, though I'm grateful for your good intentions."

Meg sighed, and turned to the frost-bitten garden again; Jo groaned, and leaned both elbows on the table in a despondent attitude, but Amy spatted away energetically; and Beth, who sat at the other window, said, smiling, "Two pleasant things are going to happen right away; Marmee is coming down the street, and Laurie is tramping through the garden as if he had something nice to tell."

9. Frances ("Fanny") Burney published *Evelina* (1778), her first novel, anonymously, waiting to hear her father praise it before confessing her authorship to him.

In they both came, Mrs. March with her usual question, "Any letter from father, girls?" and Laurie to say, in his persuasive way, "Won't some of you come for a drive? I've been pegging away at mathematics till my head is in a muddle, and I'm going to freshen my wits by a brisk turn. It's a dull day, but the air isn't bad, and I'm going to take Brooke home, so it will be gay inside, if it isn't out. Come, Jo, you and Beth will go, won't you?"

"Of course we will."

"Much obliged, but I'm busy;" and Meg whisked out her workbasket, for she had agreed with her mother that it was best, for her at least, not to drive often with the young gentleman.

"Can I do anything for you, Madam Mother?" asked Laurie, leaning over Mrs. March's chair, with the affectionate look and tone he always gave her.

"No, thank you, except call at the office, if you'll be so kind, dear. It's our day for a letter, and the penny postman hasn't been. Father is as regular as the sun, but there's some delay on the way, perhaps."

A sharp ring interrupted her, and a minute after Hannah came in with a letter.

"It's one of them horrid telegraph things, mum," she said, handling it as if she was afraid it would explode, and do some damage.

At the word "telegraph," Mrs. March snatched it, read the two lines it contained, and dropped back into her chair as white as if the little paper had sent a bullet to her heart. Laurie dashed down stairs for water, while Meg and Hannah supported her, and Jo read aloud, in a frightened voice,—

> "Mrs. March:
> "Your husband is very ill. Come at once.
> "S. Hale,
> "Blank Hospital, Washington"

How still the room was as they listened breathlessly! how strangely the day darkened outside! and how suddenly the whole world seemed to change, as the girls gathered about their mother, feeling as if all the happiness and support of their lives was about to be taken from them. Mrs. March was herself again directly; read the message over, and stretched out her arms to her daughters, saying, in a tone they never forgot, "I shall go at once, but it may be too late; oh, children, children! help me to bear it!"

For several minutes there was nothing but the sound of sobbing in the room, mingled with broken words of comfort, tender assurances of help, and hopeful whispers, that died away in tears. Poor Hannah was the first to recover, and with unconscious wisdom she set all the rest a good example; for, with her, work was the panacea for most afflictions.

"The Lord keep the dear man! I won't waste no time a cryin', but git your things ready right away, mum," she said, heartily, as she wiped her face on her apron, gave her mistress a warm shake of the hand with her own hard one, and went away to work, like three women in one.

"She's right; there's no time for tears now. Be calm, girls, and let me think."

They tried to be calm, poor things, as their mother sat up, looking pale, but steady, and put away her grief to think and plan for them.

"Where's Laurie?" she asked presently, when she had collected her thoughts, and decided on the first duties to be done.

"Here, ma'am; oh, let me do something!" cried the boy, hurrying from the next room, whither he had withdrawn, feeling that their first sorrow was too sacred for even his friendly eyes to see.

"Send a telegram saying I will come at once. The next train goes early in the morning; I'll take that."

"What else? The horses are ready; I can go anywhere,—do anything," he said, looking ready to fly to the ends of the earth.

"Leave a note at Aunt March's. Jo, give me that pen and paper."

Tearing off the blank side of one of her newly-copied pages, Jo drew the table before her mother, well knowing that money for the long, sad journey, must be borrowed, and feeling as if she could do anything to add a little to the sum for her father.

"Now go, dear; but don't kill yourself driving at a desperate pace; there is no need of that."

Mrs. March's warning was evidently thrown away; for five minutes later Laurie tore by the window, on his own fleet horse, riding as if for his life.

"Jo, run to the rooms, and tell Mrs. King that I can't come. On the way get these things. I'll put them down; they'll be needed, and I must go prepared for nursing. Hospital stores are not always good. Beth, go and ask Mr. Laurence for a couple of bottles of old wine; I'm not too proud to beg for father; he shall have the best of everything. Amy, tell Hannah to get down the black trunk; and Meg, come and help me find my things, for I'm half bewildered."

Writing, thinking, and directing all at once, might well bewilder the poor lady, and Meg begged her to sit quietly in her room for a little while, and let them work. Every one scattered, like leaves before a gust of wind; and the quiet, happy household was broken up as suddenly as if the paper had been an evil spell.

Mr. Laurence came hurrying back with Beth, bringing every comfort the kind old gentleman could think of for the invalid, and friendliest promises of protection for the girls, during the mother's absence, which comforted her very much. There was nothing he didn't offer, from his own dressing-gown to himself as escort. But that last was impossible. Mrs. March would not hear of the old gentleman's undertaking the long journey; yet an expression of relief was visible when he spoke of it, for anxiety ill fits one for travelling. He saw the look, knit his heavy eyebrows, rubbed his hands, and marched abruptly away, saying he'd be back directly. No one had time to think of him again till, as Meg ran through the entry, with a pair of rubbers in one hand and a cup of tea in the other, she came suddenly upon Mr. Brooke.

"I'm very sorry to hear of this, Miss March," he said, in the kind, quiet tone which sounded very pleasantly to her perturbed spirit. "I came to offer myself as escort to your mother. Mr. Laurence has commissions for me in Washington, and it will give me real satisfaction to be of service to her there."

Down dropped the rubbers, and the tea was very near following, as Meg put out her hand, with a face so full of gratitude, that Mr. Brooke would have felt repaid for a much greater sacrifice than the trifling one of time and comfort, which he was about to make.

"How kind you all are! Mother will accept, I'm sure; and it will be such a relief to know that she has some one to take care of her. Thank you very, very much!"

Meg spoke earnestly, and forgot herself entirely till something in the brown eyes looking down at her made her remember the cooling tea, and lead the way into the parlor, saying she would call her mother.

Everything was arranged by the time Laurie returned with a note from Aunt March, enclosing the desired sum, and a few lines repeating what she had often said before, that she had always told them it was absurd for March to go into the army, always predicted that no good would come of it, and she hoped they would take her advice next time. Mrs. March put the note in the fire, the money in her purse, and went on with her preparations, with her lips folded tightly, in a way which Jo would have understood if she had been there.

The short afternoon wore away; all the other errands were done, and Meg and her mother busy at some necessary needle-work, while Beth and Amy got tea, and Hannah finished her ironing with what she called a "slap and a bang," but still Jo did not come. They began to get anxious; and Laurie went off to find her, for no one ever knew what freak Jo might take into her head. He missed her, however, and she came walking in with a very queer expression of countenance, for there was a mixture of fun and fear, satisfaction and regret in it, which puzzled the family as much as did the roll of bills she laid before her mother, saying, with a little choke in her voice, "That's my contribution towards making father comfortable, and bringing him home!"

"My dear, where did you get it! Twenty-five dollars! Jo, I hope you haven't done anything rash?"

"No, it's mine honestly; I didn't beg, borrow, nor steal it. I earned it; and I don't think you'll blame me, for I only sold what was my own."

As she spoke, Jo took off her bonnet, and a general outcry arose, for all her abundant hair was cut short.

"Your hair! Your beautiful hair!" "Oh, Jo, how could you? Your one beauty," "My dear girl, there was no need of this." "She don't look like my Jo any more, but I love here dearly for it!"

As every one exclaimed, and Beth hugged the cropped head tenderly, Jo assumed an indifferent air, which did not deceive any one a particle, and said, rumpling up the brown bush, and trying to look as if she liked it, "It doesn't affect the fate of the nation, so don't wail, Beth. It will be good for my vanity; I was getting too proud of my wig. It will do my brains good to have that mop taken off; my head feels deliciously light and cool, and the barber said I could soon have a curly crop, which will be boyish, becoming, and easy to keep in order. I'm satisfied; so please take the money, and let's have supper."

"Tell me all about it, Jo; *I* am not quite satisfied, but I can't blame you, for I know how willingly you sacrificed your vanity, as you call it, to your love. But, my dear, it was not necessary, and I'm afraid you will regret it, one of these days," said Mrs. March.

"No I won't!" returned Jo, stoutly, feeling much relieved that her prank was not entirely condemned.

"What made you do it?" asked Amy, who would as soon have thought of cutting off her head as her pretty hair.

"Well, I was wild to do something for father," replied Jo, as they gathered about the table, for healthy young people can eat even in the midst of trouble. "I hate to borrow as much as mother does, and I knew Aunt March would croak; she always does, if you ask for a ninepence. Meg gave all her quarterly salary toward the rent, and I only got some clothes with mine, so I felt wicked, and was bound to have some money, if I sold the nose off my face to get it."

"You needn't feel wicked, my child, you had no winter things, and got the simplest, with your own hard earnings," said Mrs. March, with a look that warmed Jo's heart.

"I hadn't the least idea of selling my hair at first, but as I went along I kept thinking *what* I could do, and feeling as if I'd like to dive into some of the rich stores and help myself. In a barber's window I saw tails of hair with the prices marked; and one black tail, longer, but not so thick as mine, was forty dollars. It came over me all of a sudden that I had one thing to make money out of, and, without stopping to think, I walked in, asked if they bought hair, and what they would give for mine."

"I don't see how you dared to do it," said Beth, in a tone of awe.

"Oh, he was a little man who looked as if he merely lived to oil his hair. He rather stared, at first, as if he wasn't used to having girls bounce into his shop and ask him to buy their hair. He said he didn't care about mine, it wasn't the fashionable color, and he never paid much for it in the first place; the work put into it made it dear, and so on. It was getting late, and I was afraid, if it wasn't done right away, that I shouldn't have it done at all, and you know, when I start to do a thing, I hate to give it up; so I begged him to take it, and told him why I was in such a hurry. It was silly, I dare say, but it changed his mind, for I got rather excited, and told the story in my topsy-turvy way, and his wife heard, and said so kindly,"—

" 'Take it, Thomas, and oblige the young lady; I'd do as much for our Jimmy any day if I had a spire of hair worth selling.' "

"Who was Jimmy?" asked Amy, who liked to have things explained as they went along.

"Her son, she said, who is in the army. How friendly such things make strangers feel, don't they? She talked away all the time the man clipped, and diverted my mind nicely."

"Didn't you feel dreadfully when the first cut came?" asked Meg, with a shiver.

"I took a last look at my hair while the man got his things, and that was the end of it. I never snivel over trifles like that; I will confess, though, I felt queer when I saw the dear old hair laid out on the table, and felt only the short, rough ends on my head. It almost seemed as if I'd an arm or a leg off. The woman saw me look at it, and picked out a long lock for me to keep. I'll give it to you, Marmee, just to remember past glories by; for a crop is so comfortable I don't think I shall ever have a mane again."

Mrs. March folded the wavy, chestnut lock, and laid it away with a short gray one in her desk. She only said "Thank you, deary," but something in her face made the girls change the subject, and talk as cheerfully as they could about Mr. Brooke's kindness, the prospect of a fine day to-morrow, and the happy times they would have when father came home to be nursed.

No one wanted to go to bed, when, at ten o'clock, Mrs. March put by the last finished job, and said, "Come, girls." Beth went to the piano and played the father's favorite hymn; all began bravely, but broke down one by one till Beth was left alone, singing with all her heart, for to her music was always a sweet consoler.

"Go to bed, and don't talk, for we must be up early, and shall need all the sleep we can get. Good-night, my darlings," said Mrs. March, as the hymn ended, for no one cared to try another.

They kissed her quietly, and went to bed as silently as if the dear invalid lay in the next room. Beth and Amy soon fell asleep in spite of the great trouble, but Meg lay awake thinking the most serious thoughts she had ever known in her short life. Jo lay motionless, and her sister fancied that she was asleep, till a stifled sob made her exclaim, as she touched a wet cheek,—

"Jo, dear, what is it? Are you crying about father?"

"No, not now."

"What then?"

"My—my hair," burst our poor Jo, trying vainly to smother her emotion in the pillow.

It did not sound at all comical to Meg, who kissed and caressed the afflicted heroine in the tenderest manner.

"I'm not sorry," protested Jo, with a choke. "I'd do it again to-morrow, if I could. It's only the vain, selfish part of me that goes and cries in this silly way. Don't tell any one, it's all over now. I thought you were asleep, so I just made a little private moan for my one beauty. How came you to be awake?"

"I can't sleep, I'm so anxious," said Meg.

"Think about something pleasant and you'll soon drop off."

"I tried it, but felt wider awake than ever."

"What did you think of?"

"Handsome faces; eyes particularly," answered Meg smilingly, to herself, in the dark.

"What color do you like best?"

"Brown—that is sometimes—blue are lovely."

Jo laughed, and Meg sharply ordered her not to talk, then amiably promised to make her hair curl, and fell asleep to dream of living in her castle in the air.

The clocks were striking midnight, and the rooms were very still, as a figure glided quietly from bed to bed, smoothing a coverlid here, setting a pillow there, and pausing to look long and tenderly at each unconscious face, to kiss each with lips that mutely blessed, and to pray the fervent prayers which only mothers utter. As she lifted the curtain to look out into the dreary night, the moon broke suddenly from behind the clouds, and shone upon her like a bright benignant face, which seemed to whisper in the silence, "Be comforted, dear heart! there is always light behind the clouds."

16
Letters

In the cold gray dawn the sisters lit their lamp, and read their chapter with an earnestness never felt before, for now the shadow of a real trouble had come, showing them how rich in sunshine their lives had been. The little books were full of help and comfort; and, as they dressed, they agreed to say good-by cheerfully, hopefully, and send their mother on her anxious journey unsaddened by tears or complaints from them. Everything seemed very strange when they went down; so dim and still outside, so full of light and bustle within. Breakfast at that early hour seemed odd, and even Hannah's familiar face looked unnatural as she flew about her kitchen with her night cap on. The big trunk stood ready in the hall, mother's cloak and bonnet lay on the sofa, and mother herself sat trying to eat, but looking so pale and worn with sleeplessness and anxiety, that the girls found it very hard to keep their resolution. Meg's eyes kept filling in spite of herself; Jo was obliged to hide her face in the kitchen roller more than once, and the little girls' young faces wore a grave, troubled expression, as if sorrow was a new experience to them.

Nobody talked much, but, as the time drew very near, and they sat waiting for the carriage, Mrs. March said to the girls, who were all busied about her, one folding her shawl, another smoothing out the strings of her bonnet, a third putting on her over-shoes, and a fourth fastening up her travelling bag,—

"Children, I leave you to Hannah's care, and Mr. Laurence's protection; Hannah is faithfulness itself, and our good neighbor will guard you as if you were his own. I have no fears for you, yet I am anxious that you should take this trouble rightly. Don't grieve and fret when I am gone, or think that you can comfort yourselves by being idle, and trying to forget. So on with your work as usual, for work is a blessed solace. Hope, and keep busy; and, whatever happens, remember that you never can be fatherless."

"Yes, mother."

"Meg dear, be prudent, watch over your sisters, consult Hannah, and, in any perplexity, go to Mr. Laurence. Be patient, Jo, don't get despondent, or do rash things; write to me often, and be my brave girl, ready to help and cheer us all. Beth, comfort yourself with your music, and be faithful to the little home duties; and you, Amy, help all you can, be obedient, and keep happy safe at home."

"We will, mother! we will!"

The rattle of an approaching carriage made them all start and listen. That was the hard minute, but the girls stood it well; no one cried, no one ran away, or uttered a lamentation, though their hearts were very heavy as they sent loving messages to father, remembering, as they spoke, that it might be too late to deliver them. They kissed their mother quietly, clung about her tenderly, and tried to wave their hands cheerfully, when she drove away.

Laurie and his grandfather came over to see her off, and Mr. Brooke looked so strong, and sensible, and kind, that the girls christened him "Mr. Greatheart," on the spot.[1]

"Good-by, my darlings! God bless and keep us all," whispered Mrs. March, as she kissed one dear little face after the other, and hurried into the carriage.

As she rolled away, the sun came out, and, looking back, she saw it shining on the group at the gate, like a good omen. They saw it also, and smiled and waved their hands; and the last thing she beheld, as she turned the corner, was the four bright faces, and behind them, like a body-guard, old Mr. Laurence, faithful Hannah, and devoted Laurie.

"How kind every one is to us," she said, turning to find fresh proof of it in the respectful sympathy of the young man's face.

"I don't see how they can help it," returned Mr. Brooke, laughing so infectiously that Mrs.

1. A hero in *Pilgrim's Progress* who helps Christiana and her children on their trip to Celestial City.

March could not help smiling; and so the long journey began with the good omens of sunshine, smiles, and cheerful words.

"I feel as if there had been an earthquake," said Jo, as their neighbors went home to breakfast, leaving them to rest and refresh themselves.

"It seems as if half the house was gone," added Meg, forlornly.

Beth opened her lips to say something, but could only point to the pile of nicely-mended hose which lay on mother's table, showing that even in her last hurried moments she had thought and worked for them. It was a little thing, but it went straight to their hearts; and, in spite of their brave resolutions, they all broke down, and cried bitterly.

Hannah wisely allowed them to relieve their feelings; and, when the shower showed signs of clearing up, she came to the rescue, armed with a coffee-pot.

"Now, my dear young ladies, remember what your ma said, and don't fret; come and have a cup of coffee all round, and then let's fall to work, and be a credit to the family."

Coffee was a treat, and Hannah showed great tact in making it that morning. No one could resist her persuasive nods, or the fragrant invitation issuing from the nose of the coffee-pot. They drew up to the table, exchanged their handkerchiefs for napkins, and, in ten minutes, were all right again.

" 'Hope and keep busy;' that's the motto for us, so let's see who will remember it best. I shall go to Aunt March, as usual; oh, won't she lecture, though!" said Jo, as she sipped, with returning spirit.

"I shall go to my Kings, though I'd much rather stay at home and attend to things here," said Meg, wishing she hadn't made her eyes so red.

"No need of that; Beth and I can keep house perfectly well," put in Amy, with an important air.

"Hannah will tell us what to do; and we'll have everything nice when you come home," added Beth, getting out her mop and dishtub without delay.

"I think anxiety is very interesting," observed Amy, eating sugar, pensively.

The girls couldn't help laughing, and felt better for it, though Meg shook her head at the young lady who could find consolation in a sugar-bowl.

The sight of the turn-overs made Jo sober again; and, when the two went out to their daily tasks; they looked sorrowfully back at the window where they were accustomed to see their mother's face. It was gone; but Beth had remembered the little household ceremony, and there she was, nodding away at them like a rosy-faced mandarin.

"That's so like my Beth!" said Jo, waving her hat, with a grateful face. "Good-by, Meggy; I hope the Kings won't train to-day. Don't fret about father, dear," she added, as they parted.

"And I hope Aunt March won't croak. Your hair *is* becoming, and it looks very boyish and nice," returned Meg, trying not to smile at the curly head, which looked comically small on her tall sister's shoulders.

"That's my only comfort;" and, touching her hat à la Laurie, away went Jo, feeling like a shorn sheep on a wintry day.

News from their father comforted the girls very much; for, though dangerously ill, the presence of the best and tenderest of nurses had already done him good. Mr. Brooke sent a bulletin every day, and, as the head of the family, Meg insisted on reading the despatches, which grew more and more cheering as the week passed. At first, every one was eager to write, and plump envelopes were carefully poked into the letter-box, by one or other of the sisters, who felt rather important with their Washington correspondence. As one of these packets contained characteristic notes from the party, we will rob an imaginary mail, and read them:—

"My Dearest Mother,—

"It is impossible to tell you how happy your last letter made us, for the news was so good we couldn't help laughing and crying over it. How very kind Mr.

Brooke is, and how fortunate that Mr. Laurence's business detains him near you so long, since he is so useful to you and father. The girls are all as good as gold. Jo helps me with the sewing, and insists on doing all sorts of hard jobs. I should be afraid she might overdo, if I didn't know that her 'moral fit' wouldn't last long. Beth is as regular about her tasks as a clock, and never forgets what you told her. She grieves about father, and looks sober, except when she is at her little piano. Amy minds me nicely, and I take great care of her. She does her own hair, and I am teaching her to make button-holes, and mend her stockings. She tries very hard, and I know you will be pleased with her improvement when you come. Mr. Laurence watches over us like a motherly old hen, as Jo says; and Laurie is very kind and neighborly. He and Jo keep us merry, for we get pretty blue sometimes, and feel like orphans, with you so far away. Hannah is a perfect saint; she does not scold at all, and always calls me 'Miss Margaret,' which is quite proper, you know, and treats me with respect. We are all well and busy; but we long, day and night, to have you back. Give my dearest love to father, and believe me, ever your own

Meg."

    This note, prettily written on scented paper, was a great contrast to the next, which was scribbled on a big sheet of thin, foreign paper, ornamented with blots, and all manner of flourishes and curly-tailed letters:—

"My Precious Marmee,—

    "Three cheers for dear old father! Brooke was a trump to telegraph right off, and let us know the minute he was better. I rushed up garret when the letter came, and tried to thank God for being so good to us; but I could only cry, and say, 'I'm glad! I'm glad!' Didn't that do as well as a regular prayer? for I felt a great many in my heart. We have such funny times; and now I can enjoy 'em, for every one is so desperately good, it's like living in a nest of turtle-doves. You'd laugh to see Meg head the table, and try to be motherish. She gets prettier every day, and I'm in love with her sometimes. The children are regular archangels, and I—well, I'm Jo, and never shall be anything else. Oh, I must tell you that I came near having a quarrel with Laurie. I freed my mind about a silly little thing, and he was offended. I was right, but didn't speak as I ought, and he marched home, saying he wouldn't come again till I begged pardon. I declared I wouldn't, and got mad. It lasted all day; I felt bad, and wanted you very much. Laurie and I are both so proud, it's hard to beg pardon; but I thought he'd come to it, for I *was* in the right. He didn't come; and just at night I remembered what you said when Amy fell into the river. I read my little book, felt better, resolved not to let the sun set on *my* anger, and ran over to tell Laurie I was sorry. I met him at the gate, coming for the same thing. We both laughed, begged each other's pardon, and felt all good and comfortable again.

    "I made a 'pome' yesterday, when I was helping Hannah wash; and, as father likes my silly little things, I put it in to amuse him. Give him the lovingest hug that ever was, and kiss yourself a dozen times, for your

"Topsy-Turvy Jo.

"A Song from the Suds.

"Queen of my tub, I merrily sing,
    While the white foam rises high;
And sturdily wash, and rinse, and wring,
    And fasten the clothes to dry;
Then out in the free fresh air they swing,
    Under the sunny sky.

"I wish we could wash from our hearts and souls
The stains of the week away,
And let water and air by their magic make
Ourselves as pure as they;
Then on the earth there would be indeed
A glorious washing-day!

"Along the path of a useful life,
Will heart's-ease ever bloom;
The busy mind has no time to think
Of sorrow, or care, or gloom;
And anxious thoughts may be swept away,
As we busily wield a broom.

"I am glad a task to me is given,
To labor at day by day;
For it brings me health, and strength, and hope,
And I cheerfully learn to say,—
'Head you may think, Heart you may feel,
But Hand you shall work alway!'"

"Dear Mother:

"There is only room for me to send my love, and some pressed pansies from the root I have been keeping safe in the house, for father to see. I read every morning, try to be good all day, and sing myself to sleep with father's tune. I can't sing 'Land of the Leal' now; it makes me cry. Every one is very kind, and we are as happy as we can be without you. Amy wants the rest of the page, so I must stop. I didn't forget to cover the holders, and I wind the clock and air the rooms every day.

"Kiss dear father on the cheek he calls mine. Oh, do come soon to your loving

"Little Beth."

"Ma Chere Mamma:

"We are all well I do my lessons always and never corroberate the girls—Meg says I mean contradick so I put in both words and you can take the properest. Meg is a great comfort to me and lets me have jelly every night at tea its so good for me Jo says because it keeps me sweet tempered. Laurie is not as respeckful as he ought to be now I am almost in my teens, he calls me Chick and hurts my feelings by talking French to me very fast when I say Merci or Bon jour as Hattie King does. The sleeves of my blue dress were all worn out and Meg put in new ones but the full front came wrong and they are more blue than the dress. I felt bad but did not fret I bear my troubles well but I do wish Hannah would put more starch in my aprons and have buck wheats every day. Can't she? Didn't I make that interrigation point nice. Meg says my punchtuation and spelling are disgraceful and I am mortyfied but dear me I have so many things to do I can't stop. Adieu, I send heaps of love to Papa.

"Your affectionate daughter,

"Amy Curtis March."

"Dear Mis March:

"I jes drop a line to say we git on fust rate. The girls is clever and fly round right smart. Miss Meg is goin to make a proper good housekeeper; she hes the liking for it, and gits the hang of things surprisin quick. Jo doos beat all for goin ahead, but she don't stop to cal'k'late fust, and you never know where she's like to bring up. She done out a tub of clothes on Monday, but she starched em afore they was wrenched, and blued a pink calico dress till I thought I should a died a laughin. Beth is the best of little creeters, and a sight of help to me, being so forehanded and dependable. She tries to learn everything, and really goes to market beyond her years; likewise keeps accounts, with my help, quite wonderful. We have got on very economical so fur; I don't let the girls hev coffee only once a week, according to your wish, and keep em on plain wholesome vittles. Amy does well about frettin, wearin her best clothes and eatin sweet stuff. Mr. Laurie is as full of didoes[2] as usual, and turns the house upside down frequent; but he heartens up the girls, and so I let em hev full swing. The old man sends heaps of things, and is rather wearin, but means wal, and it aint my place to say nothing. My bread is riz, so no more at this time. I send my duty to Mr. March, and hope he's seen the last of his Pewmonia.

    "Yours respectful,

"Hannah Mullet"

"Head Nurse of Ward II:

    "All serene on the Rappahannock,[3] troops in fine condition, commissary department well conducted, the Home Guard under Colonel Teddy always on duty, Commander-in-chief General Laurence reviews the army daily, Quartermaster Mullett keeps order in camp, and Major Lion does picket duty at night. A salute of twenty-four guns was fired on receipt of good news from Washington, and a dress parade took place at headquarters. Commander-in-chief sends best wishes, in which he is heartily joined by

Colonel Teddy."

"Dear Madam:

    "The little girls are all well; Beth and my boy report daily; Hannah is a model servant, guards pretty Meg like a dragon. Glad the fine weather holds; pray make Brooke useful, and draw on me for funds if expenses exceed your estimate. Don't let your husband want anything. Thank God he is mending.

    "Your sincere friend and servant,

"James Laurence."

17
Little Faithful

For a week the amount of virtue in the old house would have supplied the neighborhood. It was really amazing, for every one seemed in a heavenly frame of mind, and self-denial was all the fashion. Relieved of their first anxiety about their father, the girls insensibly relaxed their praiseworthy efforts a little, and began to fall back into the old ways. They did not forget their motto, but hoping and keeping busy seemed to grow easier; and, after such tremendous exertions, they felt that Endeavor deserved a holiday, and gave it a good many.

    Jo caught a bad cold through neglecting to cover the shorn head enough, and was ordered to stay at home till she was better, for Aunt March didn't like to hear people read with colds in their heads. Jo liked this, and after an energetic rummage from garret to cellar, subsided on to the sofa to nurse her cold with arsenicum[4] and books. Amy found that house-work and

---

2. Mischievous pranks, antics.
3. A river in Virginia, flowing from the Blue Ridge Mountains to Chesapeake Bay; location of several battles in the Civil War.
4. "Aresenical" was a drug containing arsenic, a poisonous metallic element.

art did not go well together, and returned to her mud pies. Meg went daily to her kingdom, and sewed, or thought she did, at home, but much time was spent in writing long letters to her mother, or reading the Washington despatches over and over. Beth kept on with only slight relapses into idleness or grieving. All the little duties were faithfully done each day, and many of her sisters' also, for they were forgetful, and the house seemed like a clock, whose pendulum was gone a-visiting. When her heart got heavy with longings for mother, or fears for father, she went away into a certain closet, hid her face in the folds of a certain dear old gown, and made her little moan, and prayed her little prayer quietly by herself. Nobody knew what cheered her up after a sober fit, but every one felt how sweet and helpful Beth was, and fell into a way of going to her for comfort or advice in their small affairs.

All were unconscious that this experience was a test of character; and, when the first excitement was over, felt that they had done well, and deserved praise. So they did; but their mistake was in ceasing to do well, and they learned this lesson through much anxiety and regret.

"Meg, I wish you'd go and see the Hummels; you know mother told us not to forget them," said Beth, ten days after Mrs. March's departure.

"I'm too tired to go this afternoon," replied Meg, rocking comfortably, as she sewed.

"Can't you, Jo?" asked Beth.

"Too stormy for me, with my cold."

"I thought it was most well."

"It's well enough for me to go out with Laurie, but not well enough to go to the Hummels," said Jo, laughing, but looking a little ashamed of her inconsistency.

"Why don't you go yourself?" asked Meg.

"I *have* been every day, but the baby is sick, and I don't know what to do for it. Mrs. Hummel goes away to work, and Lottchen takes care of it; but it gets sicker and sicker, and I think you or Hannah ought to go."

Beth spoke earnestly, and Meg promised she would go tomorrow.

"Ask Hannah for some nice little mess, and take it round, Beth, the air will do you good;" said Jo, adding apologetically, "I'd go, but I want to finish my story."

"My head aches, and I'm tired, so I thought maybe some of you would go," said Beth.

"Amy will be in presently, and she will run down for us," suggested Meg.

"Well, I'll rest a little, and wait for her."

So Beth lay down on the sofa, the others returned to their work, and the Hummels were forgotten. An hour passed, Amy did not come; Meg went to her room to try on a new dress; Jo was absorbed in her story, and Hannah was sound asleep before the kitchen fire, when Beth quietly put on her hood, filled her basket with odds and ends for the poor children, and went out into the chilly air with a heavy head, and a grieved look in her patient eyes. It was late when she came back, and no one saw her creep upstairs and shut herself into her mother's room. Half an hour after, Jo went to "mother's closet" for something, and there found Beth sitting on the medicine chest, looking very grave, with red eyes, and a camphor bottle in her hand.

"Christopher Columbus! what's the matter?" cried Jo, as Beth put out her hand as if to warn her off, and asked quickly,—

"You've had scarlet fever, haven't you?"

"Years ago, when Meg did. Why?"

"Then I'll tell you—oh, Jo, the baby's dead!"

"What baby?"

"Mrs. Hummel's; it died in my lap before she got home," cried Beth, with a sob.

"My poor dear, how dreadful for you! I ought to have gone," said Jo, taking her sister in her lap as she sat down in her mother's big chair, with a remorseful face.

"It wasn't dreadful, Jo, only so sad! I saw in a minute that it was sicker, but Lottchen said her mother had gone for a doctor, so I took baby and let Lotty rest. It seemed asleep, but all of a sudden it gave a little cry, and trembled, and then lay very still. I tried to warm its feet, and Lotty gave it some milk, but it didn't stir, and I knew it was dead."

"Don't cry, dear! what did you do?"

"I just sat and held it softly till Mrs. Hummel came with the doctor. He said it was dead, and looked at Heinrich and Minna, who have got sore throats. 'Scarlet fever, ma'am; ought to have called me before,' he said, crossly. Mrs. Hummel told him she was poor, and had tried to cure baby herself, but now it was too late, and she could only ask him to help the others, and trust to charity for his pay. He smiled then, and was kinder, but it was very sad, and I cried with them till he turned round all of a sudden, and told me to go home and take belladonna[5] right away, or I'd have the fever."

"No you won't!" cried Jo, hugging her close, with a frightened look. "Oh, Beth, if you should be sick I never could forgive myself! What *shall* we do?"

"Don't be frightened, I guess I shan't have it badly; I looked in mother's book, and saw that it begins with headache, sore throat, and queer feelings like mine, so I did take some belladonna, and I feel better," said Beth, laying her cold hands on her hot forehead, and trying to look well.

"If mother was only at home!" exclaimed Jo, seizing the book, and feeling that Washington was an immense way off. She read a page, looked at Beth, felt her head, peeped into her throat, and then said, gravely, "You've been over the baby every day for more than a week, and among the others who are going to have it, so I'm afraid you're going to have it, Beth. I'll call Hannah; she knows all about sickness."

"Don't let Amy come; she never had it, and I should hate to give it to her. Can't you and Meg have it over again?" asked Beth, anxiously.

"I guess not; don't care if I do; serve me right, selfish pig, to let you go, and stay writing rubbish myself!" muttered Jo, as she went to consult Hannah.

The good soul was wide awake in a minute, and took the lead at once, assuring Jo that there was no need to worry; every one had scarlet fever, and, if rightly treated, nobody died; all of which Jo believed, and felt much relieved as they went up to call Meg.

"Now I'll tell you what we'll do," said Hannah, when she had examined and questioned Beth; "we will have Dr. Bangs, just to take a look at you, dear, and see that we start right; then we'll send Amy off to Aunt March's, for a spell, to keep her out of harm's way, and one of you girls can stay at home and amuse Beth for a day or two."

"I shall stay, of course, I'm oldest;" began Meg, looking anxious and self-reproachful.

"*I* shall, because it's my fault she is sick; I told mother I'd do the errands, and I haven't," said Jo, decidedly.

"Which will you have, Beth? there ain't no need of but one," said Hannah.

"Jo, please;" and Beth leaned her head against her sister, with a contented look, which effectually settled that point.

"I'll go and tell Amy," said Meg, feeling a little hurt, yet rather relieved, on the whole, for she did not like nursing, and Jo did.

Amy rebelled outright, and passionately declared that she had rather have the fever than go to Aunt March. Meg reasoned, pleaded, and commanded, all in vain. Amy protested that she would *not* go; and Meg left her in despair, to ask Hannah what should be done. Before she came back, Laurie walked into the parlor to find Amy sobbing, with her head in the sofa cushions. She told her story, expecting to be consoled; but Laurie only put his hands in his pockets and walked about the room, whistling softly, as he knit his brows in deep thought. Presently he sat down beside her, and said, in his most wheedlesome tone, "Now be a sensible little woman, and do as they say. No, don't cry, but hear what a jolly plan I've got. You go

---

5. A tincture prepared from the leaves and roots of Deadly Nightshade, a poisonous plant, used to treat
    asthma, colic, and hyperacidity.

to Aunt March's, and I'll come and take you out every day, driving or walking, and we'll have capital times. Won't that be better than moping here?"

"I don't wish to be sent off as if I was in the way," began Amy, in an injured voice.

"Bless your heart, child! it's to keep you well. You don't want to be sick, do you?"

"No, I'm sure I don't; but I dare say I shall be, for I've been with Beth all this time."

"That's the very reason you ought to go away at once, so that you may escape it. Change of air and care will keep you well, I dare say; or, if it don't entirely, you will have the fever more lightly. I advise you to be off as soon as you can, for scarlet fever is no joke, miss."

"But it's dull at Aunt March's, and she is so cross," said Amy, looking rather frightened.

"It won't be dull with me popping in every day to tell you how Beth is, and take you out gallivanting. The old lady likes me, and I'll be as clever as possible to her, so she won't peck at us, whatever we do."

"Will you take me out in the trotting wagon with Puck?"

"On my honor as a gentleman."

"And come every single day?"

"See if I don't."

"And bring me back the minute Beth is well?"

"The identical minute."

"And go to the theatre, truly?"

"A dozen theatres, if we may."

"Well—I guess—I will," said Amy, slowly.

"Good girl! Sing out for Meg, and tell her you'll give in," said Laurie, with an approving pat, which annoyed Amy more than the "giving in."

Meg and Jo came running down to behold the miracle which had been wrought; and Amy, feeling very precious and self-sacrificing, promised to go, if the doctor said Beth was going to be ill.

"How is the little dear?" asked Laurie; for Beth was his especial pet, and he felt more anxious about her than he liked to show.

"She is lying down on mother's bed, and feels better. The baby's death troubled her, but I dare say she has only got cold. Hannah *says* she thinks so; but she *looks* worried, and that makes me fidgety," answered Meg.

"What a trying world it is!" said Jo, rumpling up her hair in a fretful sort of way. "No sooner do we get out of one trouble than down comes another. There don't seem to be anything to hold on to when mother's gone; so I'm all at sea."

"Well, don't make a porcupine of yourself, it isn't becoming. Settle your wig, Jo, and tell me if I shall telegraph to your mother, or do anything?" asked Laurie, who never had been reconciled to the loss of his friend's one beauty.

"That is what troubles me," said Meg. "I think we ought to tell her if Beth is really ill, but Hannah says we mustn't, for mother can't leave father, and it will only make them anxious. Beth won't be sick long, and Hannah knows just what to do, and mother said we were to mind her, so I suppose we must, but it don't seem quite right to me."

"Hum, well, I can't say; suppose you ask grandfather, after the doctor has been."

"We will; Jo, go and get Dr. Bangs at once," commanded Meg; "we can't decide anything till he has been."

"Stay where you are, Jo; I'm errand boy to this establishment," said Laurie, taking up his cap.

"I'm afraid you are busy," began Meg.

"No, I've done my lessons for the day."

"Do you study in vacation time?" asked Jo.

"I follow the good example my neighbors set me," was Laurie's answer, as he swung himself out of the room.

"I have great hopes of my boy," observed Jo, watching him fly over the fence with an approving smile.

"He does very well—for a boy," was Meg's somewhat ungracious answer, for the subject did not interest her.

Dr. Bangs came, said Beth had symptoms of the fever, but thought she would have it lightly, though he looked sober over the Hummel story. Amy was ordered off at once, and provided with something to ward off danger; she departed in great state, with Jo and Laurie as escort.

Aunt March received them with her usual hospitality.

"What do you want now?" she asked, looking sharply over her spectacles, while the parrot, sitting on the back of her chair, called out,—

"Go away; no boys allowed here."

Laurie retired to the window, and Jo told her story.

"No more than I expected, if you are allowed to go poking about among poor folks. Amy can stay and make herself useful if she isn't sick, which I've no doubt she will be,—looks like it now. Don't cry, child, it worries me to hear people sniff."

Amy *was* on the point of crying, but Laurie slyly pulled the parrot's tail, which caused Polly to utter an astonished croak, and call out,—

"Bless my boots!" in such a funny way, that she laughed instead.

"What do you hear from your mother?" asked the old lady, gruffly.

"Father is much better," replied Jo, trying to keep sober.

"Oh, is he? Well, that won't last long, I fancy; March never had any stamina," was the cheerful reply.

"Ha, ha! never say die, take a pinch of snuff, good-by, good-by!" squalled Polly, dancing on her perch, and clawing at the old lady's cap as Laurie tweaked him in the rear.

"Hold your tongue, you disrespectful old bird! and, Jo, you'd better go at once; it isn't proper to be gadding about so late with a rattle-pated boy like—"

"Hold your tongue, you disrespectful old bird!" cried Polly, tumbling off the chair with a bounce, and running to peck the "rattle-pated" boy, who was shaking with laughter at the last speech.

"I don't think I *can* bear it, but I'll try," thought Amy, as she was left alone with Aunt March.

"Get along, you're a fright!" screamed Polly, and at that rude speech Amy could not restrain a sniff.

18
Dark Days

Beth did have the fever, and was much sicker than any one but Hannah and the doctor suspected. The girls knew nothing about illness, and Mr. Laurence was not allowed to see her, so Hannah had everything all her own way, and busy Dr. Bangs did his best, but left a good deal to the excellent nurse. Meg stayed at home, lest she should infect the Kings, and kept house, feeling very anxious, and a little guilty, when she wrote letters in which no mention was made of Beth's illness. She could not think it right to deceive her mother, but she had been bidden to mind Hannah, and Hannah wouldn't hear of "Mrs. March bein' told, and worried just for sech a trifle." Jo devoted herself to Beth day and night; not a hard task, for Beth was very patient, and bore her pain uncomplainingly as long as she could control herself. But there came a time when during the fever fits she began to talk in a hoarse, broken voice, to play on the coverlet, as if on her beloved little piano, and try to sing with a throat so swollen, that there was no music left; a time when she did not know the familiar faces round her, but addressed them by wrong names, and called imploringly for her mother. Then Jo grew frightened, Meg begged to be allowed to write the truth, and even Hannah said she "would think of it, though there was no danger *yet.*" A letter from Washington added to their trouble, for Mr. March had had a relapse, and could not think of coming home for a long while.

How dark the days seemed now, how sad and lonely the house, and how heavy were the hearts of the sisters as they worked and waited, while the shadow of death hovered over the once happy home! Then it was that Margaret, sitting alone with tears dropping often on her work, felt how rich she had been in things more precious than any luxuries money could buy; in love, protection, peace and health, the real blessings of life. Then it was that Jo, living in the darkened room with that suffering little sister always before her eyes, and that pathetic voice sounding in her ears, learned to see the beauty and the sweetness of Beth's nature, to feel how deep and tender a place she filled in all hearts, and to acknowledge the worth of Beth's unselfish ambition, to live for others, and make home happy by the exercise of those simple virtues which all may possess, and which all should love and value more than talent, wealth or beauty. And Amy, in her exile, longed eagerly to be at home, that she might work for Beth, feeling now that no service would be hard or irksome, and remembering, with regretful grief, how many neglected tasks those willing hands had done for her. Laurie haunted the house like a restless ghost, and Mr. Laurence locked the grand piano, because he could not bear to be reminded of the young neighbor who used to make the twilight pleasant for him. Every one missed Beth. The milk-man, baker, grocer and butcher inquired how she did; poor Mrs. Hummel came to beg pardon for her thoughtlessness, and to get a shroud for Minna; the neighbors sent all sorts of comforts and good wishes, and even those who knew her best, were surprised to find how many friends shy little Beth had made.

Meanwhile she lay on her bed with old Joanna at her side, for even in her wanderings she did not forget her forlorn *protége*. She longed for her cats, but would not have them brought, lest they should get sick; and, in her quiet hours, she was full of anxiety about Jo. She sent loving messages to Amy, bade them tell her mother that she would write soon; and often begged for pencil and paper to try to say a word, that father might not think she had neglected him. But soon even these intervals of consciousness ended, and she lay hour after hour tossing to and fro with incoherent words on her lips, or sank into a heavy sleep which brought her no refreshment. Dr. Bangs came twice a day, Hannah sat up at night, Meg kept a telegram in her desk all ready to send off at any minute, and Jo never stirred from Beth's side.

The first of December was a wintry day indeed to them, for a bitter wind blew, snow fell fast, and the year seemed getting ready for its death. When Dr. Bangs came that morning, he looked long at Beth, held the hot hand in both his own a minute, and laid it gently down, saying, in a low tone, to Hannah,—

"If Mrs. March *can* leave her husband, she'd better be sent for."

Hannah nodded without speaking, for her lips twitched nervously; Meg dropped down into a chair as the strength seemed to go out of her limbs at the sound of those words, and Jo, after standing with a pale face for a minute, ran to the parlor, snatched up the telegram, and, throwing on her things, rushed out into the storm. She was soon back, and, while noiselessly taking off her cloak, Laurie came in with a letter, saying that Mr. March was mending again. Jo read it thankfully, but the heavy weight did not seem lifted off her heart, and her face was so full of misery that Laurie asked, quickly,—

"What is it? is Beth worse?"

"I've sent for mother," said Jo, tugging at her rubber boots with a tragical expression.

"Good for you, Jo! Did you do it on your own responsibility?" asked Laurie, as he seated her in the hall chair and took off the rebellious boots, seeing how her hands shook.

"No, the doctor told us to."

"Oh, Jo, it's not so bad as that?" cried Laurie, with a startled face.

"Yes, it is; she don't know us, she don't even talk about the flocks of green doves, as she calls the vine leaves on the wall; she don't look like my Beth, and there's nobody to help us bear it; mother and father both gone, and God seems so far away I can't find Him."

As the tears streamed fast down poor Jo's cheeks, she stretched out her hand in a helpless sort of way, as if groping in the dark, and Laurie took it in his, whispering, as well as he could, with a lump in his throat,—

"I'm here, hold on to me, Jo, dear!"

She could not speak, but she did "hold on," and the warm grasp of the friendly human hand comforted her sore heart, and seemed to lead her nearer to the Divine arm which alone could uphold her in her trouble. Laurie longed to say something tender and comfortable, but no fitting words came to him, so he stood silent, gently stroking her bent head as her mother used to do. It was the best thing he could have done; far more soothing than the most eloquent words, for Jo felt the unspoken sympathy, and, in the silence, learned the sweet solace which affection administers to sorrow. Soon she dried the tears which had relieved her, and looked up with a grateful face.

"Thank you, Teddy, I'm better now; I don't feel so forlorn, and will try to bear it if it comes."

"Keep hoping for the best; that will help you lots, Jo. Soon your mother will be here, and then everything will be right."

"I'm so glad father is better; now she won't feel so bad about leaving him. Oh, me! it does seem as if all the troubles came in a heap, and I got the heaviest part on my shoulders," sighed Jo, spreading her wet handkerchief over her knees, to dry.

"Don't Meg pull fair?" asked Laurie, looking indignant.

"Oh, yes; she tries to, but she don't love Bethy as I do; and she won't miss her as I shall. Beth is my conscience, and I *can't* give her up; I can't! I can't!"

Down went Jo's face into the wet handkerchief, and she cried despairingly; for she had kept up bravely till now, and never shed a tear. Laurie drew his hand across his eyes, but could not speak till he had subdued the choky feeling in his throat, and steadied his lips. It might be unmanly, but he couldn't help it, and I am glad of it. Presently, as Jo's sobs quieted, he said, hopefully, "I don't think she will die; she's so good, and we all love her so much, I don't believe God will take her away yet."

"The good and dear people always do die," groaned Jo, but she stopped crying, for her friend's words cheered her up, in spite of her own doubts and fears.

"Poor girl! you're worn out. It isn't like you to be forlorn. Stop a bit; I'll hearten you up in a jiffy."

Laurie went off two stairs at a time, and Jo laid her wearied head down on Beth's little brown hood, which no one had thought of moving from the table where she left it. It must have possessed some magic, for the submissive spirit of its gentle owner seemed to enter into Jo; and, when Laurie came running down with a glass of wine, she took it with a smile, and said, bravely, "I drink—Health to my Beth! You are a good doctor, Teddy, and *such* a comfortable friend; how can I ever pay you?" she added, as the wine refreshed her body, as the kind words had done her troubled mind.

"I'll send in my bill, by and by; and to-night I'll give you something that will warm the cockles of your heart better than quarts of wine," said Laurie, beaming at her with a face of suppressed satisfaction at something.

"What is it?" cried Jo, forgetting her woes for a minute, in her wonder.

"I telegraphed to your mother yesterday, and Brooke answered she'd come at once, and she'll be here to-night, and everything will be all right. Aren't you glad I did it?"

Laurie spoke very fast, and turned red and excited all in a minute, for he had kept his plot a secret, for fear of disappointing the girls or harming Beth. Jo grew quite white, flew out of her chair, and the moment he stopped speaking she electrified him by throwing her arms round his neck, and crying out, with a joyful cry, "Oh, Laurie! oh, mother! I *am* so glad!" She did not weep again, but laughed hysterically, and trembled and clung to her friend as if she was a little bewildered by the sudden news. Laurie, though decidedly amazed, behaved with great presence of mind; he patted her back soothingly, and, finding that she was recovering, followed it up by a bashful kiss or two, which brought Jo round at once. Holding on to the banisters, she put him gently away, saying, breathless, "Oh, don't! I didn't mean to; it was dreadful of me; but you were such a dear to go and do it in spite of Hannah, that I couldn't help flying at you. Tell me all about it, and don't give me wine again; it makes me act so."

"I don't mind!" laughed Laurie, as he settled his tie. "Why, you see I got fidgety, and so did grandpa. We thought Hannah was overdoing the authority business, and your mother ought to know. She'd never forgive us if Beth,—well, if anything happened, you know. So I got grandpa to say it was high time we did something, and off I pelted to the office yesterday, for the doctor looked sober, and Hannah most took my head off when I proposed a telegram. I never *can* bear to be 'marmed over;' so that settled my mind, and I did it. Your mother will come, I know, and the late train is in at two, A.M. I shall go for her; and you've only got to bottle up your rapture, and keep Beth quiet, till that blessed lady gets here."

"Laurie, you're an angel! How shall I ever thank you?"

"Fly at me again; I rather like it," said Laurie, looking mischievous,—a thing he had not done for a fortnight.

"No, thank you. I'll do it by proxy, when your grandpa comes. Don't tease, but go home and rest, for you'll be up half the night. Bless you, Teddy; bless you!"

Jo had backed into a corner; and, as she finished her speech, she vanished precipitately into the kitchen, where she sat down upon a dresser, and told the assembled cats that she was "happy, oh, *so* happy!" while Laurie departed, feeling that he had made rather a neat thing of it.

"That's the interferingest chap I ever see; but I forgive him, and do hope Mrs. March is coming on right away," said Hannah, with an air of relief, when Jo told the good news.

Meg had a quiet rapture, and then brooded over the letter, while Jo set the sick room in order, and Hannah "knocked up a couple of pies in case of company unexpected." A breath of fresh air seemed to blow through the house, and something better than sunshine brightened the quiet rooms; everything appeared to feel the hopeful change; Beth's bird began to chirp again, and a half-blown rose was discovered on Amy's bush in the window; the fires seemed to burn with unusual cheeriness, and every time the girls met their pale faces broke into smiles as they hugged one another, whispering, encouragingly, "Mother's coming, dear! mother's coming!" Every one rejoiced but Beth; she lay in that heavy stupor, alike unconscious of hope and joy, doubt and danger. It was a piteous sight,—the once rosy face so changed and vacant,—the once busy hands so weak and wasted,—the once smiling lips quite dumb,—and the once pretty, well-kept hair scattered rough and tangled on the pillow. All day she lay so, only rousing now and then to mutter, "Water!" with lips so parched they could hardly shape the word; all day Jo and Meg hovered over her, watching, waiting, hoping, and trusting in God and mother; and all day the snow fell, the bitter wind raged, and the hours dragged slowly by. But night came at last; and every time the clock struck the sisters, still sitting on either side the bed, looked at each other with brightening eyes, for each hour brought help nearer. The doctor had been in to say that some change for better or worse would probably take place about midnight, at which time he would return.

Hannah, quite worn out, lay down on the sofa at the bed's foot, and fell fast asleep; Mr. Laurence marched to and fro in the parlor, feeling that he would rather face a rebel battery than Mrs. March's anxious countenance as she entered; Laurie lay on the rug, pretending to rest, but staring into the fire with the thoughtful look which made his black eyes beautifully soft and clear.

The girls never forgot that night, for no sleep came to them as they kept their watch, with that dreadful sense of powerlessness which comes to us in hours like those.

"If God spares Beth I never will complain again," whispered Meg, earnestly.

"If God spares Beth I'll try to love and serve Him all my life," answered Jo, with equal fervor.

"I wish I had no heart, it aches so," sighed Meg, after a pause.

"If life is often as hard as this, I don't see how we ever shall get through it," added her sister, despondently.

Here the clock struck twelve, and both forgot themselves in watching Beth, for they fancied a change passed over her wan face. The house was still as death, and nothing but the wailing of the wind broke the deep hush. Weary Hannah slept on, and no one but the sisters saw the pale shadow which seemed to fall upon the little bed. An hour went by, and nothing happened except Laurie's quiet departure for the station. Another hour,—still no one came; and anxious fears of delay in the storm, or accidents by the way, or, worst of all, a great grief at Washington, haunted the poor girls.

It was past two, when Jo, who stood at the window thinking how dreary the world looked in its winding-sheet of snow, heard a movement by the bed, and, turning quickly, saw Meg kneeling before their mother's easy-chair, with her face hidden. A dreadful fear passed coldly over Jo, as she thought, "Beth is dead, and Meg is afraid to tell me."

She was back at her post in an instant, and to her excited eyes a great change seemed to have taken place. The fever flush, and the look of pain, were gone, and the beloved little face looked so pale and peaceful in its utter repose, that Jo felt no desire to weep or lament. Leaning low over this dearest of her sisters, she kissed the damp forehead with her heart on her lips, and softly whispered, "Good-by, my Beth; good-by!"

As if waked by the stir, Hannah started out of her sleep, hurried to the bed, looked at Beth, felt her hands, listened at her lips, and then, throwing her apron over her head, sat down to rock to and fro, exclaiming, under her breath, "The fever's turned; she's sleepin' nat'ral; her skin's damp, and she breathes easy. Praise be given! Oh, my goodness me!"

Before the girls could believe the happy truth, the doctor came to confirm it. He was a homely man, but they thought his face quite heavenly when he smiled, and said, with a fatherly look at them, "Yes, my dears; I think the little girl will pull through this time. Keep the house quiet; let her sleep, and when she wakes, give her—"

What they were to give, neither heard; for both crept into the dark hall, and, sitting on the stairs, held each other close, rejoicing with hearts too full for words. When they went back to be kissed and cuddled by faithful Hannah, they found Beth lying, as she used to do, with her cheek pillowed on her hand, the dreadful pallor gone, and breathing quietly, as if just fallen asleep.

"If mother would only come now!" said Jo, as the winter night began to wane.

"See," said Meg, coming up with a white, half-opened rose, "I thought this would hardly be ready to lay in Beth's hand to-morrow if she—went away from us. But it has blossomed in the night, and now I mean to put it in my vase here, so that when the darling wakes, the first thing she sees will be the little rose, and mother's face."

Never had the sun risen so beautifully, and never had the world seemed so lovely, as it did to the heavy eyes of Meg and Jo, as they looked out in the early morning, when their long, sad vigil was done.

"It looks like a fairy world," said Meg, smiling to herself, as she stood behind the curtain watching the dazzling sight.

"Hark!" cried Jo, starting to her feet.

Yes, there was a sound of bells at the door below, a cry from Hannah, and then Laurie's voice, saying, in a joyful whisper, "Girls! she's come! she's come!"

19
Amy's Will

While these things were happening at home, Amy was having hard times at Aunt March's. She felt her exile deeply, and, for the first time in her life, realized how much she was beloved and petted at home. Aunt March never petted any one; she did not approve of it; but she meant to be kind, for the well-behaved little girl pleased her very much, and Aunt March had a soft place in her old heart for her nephew's children, though she didn't think proper to confess it. She really did her best to make Amy happy, but, dear me, what mistakes she made! Some old people keep young at heart in spite of wrinkles and gray hairs, can sympathize with children's little cares and joys, make them feel at home, and can hide wise lessons under pleasant plays, giving and receiving friendship in the sweetest way. But Aunt March had not this gift, and she worried Amy most to death with her rules and orders, her prim ways, and long, prosy talks. Finding the child more docile and amiable than her sister, the old lady felt it her duty to try and counteract, as far as possible, the bad effects of home freedom and indulgence. So she took Amy in hand, and taught her as she herself had been taught sixty years ago; a process which carried dismay to Amy's soul, and made her feel like a fly in the web of a very strict spider.

She had to wash the cups every morning, and polish up the old-fashioned spoons, the fat silver teapot, and the glasses, till they shone. Then she must dust the room, and what a trying job that was! Not a speck escaped Aunt March's eye, and all the furniture had claw legs, and much carving, which was never dusted to suit. Then Polly must be fed, the lap-dog combed, and a dozen trips upstairs and down, to get things or deliver orders, for the old lady was very lame, and seldom left her big chair. After these tiresome labors she must do her lessons, which was a daily trial of every virtue she possessed. Then she was allowed one hour for exercise or play, and didn't she enjoy it? Laurie came every day, and wheedled Aunt March till Amy was allowed to go out with him, when they walked and rode, and had capital times. After dinner she had to read aloud, and sit still while the old lady slept, which she usually did for an hour, as she dropped off over the first page. Then patchwork or towels appeared, and Amy sewed with outward meekness and inward rebellion till dusk, when she was allowed to amuse herself as she liked, till tea-time. The evenings were the worst of all, for Aunt March fell to telling long stories about her youth, which were so unutterably dull, that Amy was always ready to go to bed, intending to cry over her hard fate, but usually going to sleep before she had squeezed out more than a tear or two.

If it had not been for Laurie and old Esther, the maid, she felt that she never could have got through that dreadful time. The parrot alone was enough to drive her distracted, for he soon felt that she did not admire him, and revenged himself by being as mischievous as possible. He pulled her hair whenever she came near him, upset his bread and milk to plague her when she had newly cleaned his cage, made Mop bark by pecking at him while Madame dozed; called her names before company, and behaved in all respects like a reprehensible old bird. Then she could not endure the dog, a fat, cross beast, who snarled and yelped at her when she made his toilet,[6] and who laid on his back with all his legs in the air, and a most idiotic expression of countenance, when he wanted something to eat, which was about a dozen times a day. The cook was bad-tempered, the old coachman deaf, and Esther the only one who ever took any notice of the young lady.

Esther was a French woman, who had lived with "Madame," as she called her mistress, for many years, and who rather tyrannized over the old lady, who could not get along without her. Her real name was Estelle; but Aunt March ordered her to change it, and she obeyed,

---

6. When she groomed him.

on condition that she was never asked to change her religion. She took a fancy to Mademoi-selle, and amused her very much, with odd stories of her life in France, when Amy sat with her while she got up Madame's laces. She also allowed her to roam about the great house, and examine the curious and pretty things stored away in the big wardrobes and the ancient chests; for Aunt March hoarded like a magpie. Amy's chief delight was an Indian cabinet full of queer drawers, little pigeon-holes, and secret places in which were kept all sorts of ornaments, some precious, some merely curious, all more or less antique. To examine and arrange these things gave Amy great satisfaction, especially the jewel cases; in which, on velvet cushions, reposed the ornaments which had adorned a belle forty years ago. There was the garnet set which Aunt March wore when she came out, the pearls her father gave her on her wedding day, her lover's diamonds, the jet mourning rings and pins, the queer lockets, with portraits of dead friends, and weeping willows made of hair inside, the baby bracelets her one little daughter had worn; Uncle March's big watch, with the red seal so many childish hands had played with, and in a box, all by itself, lay Aunt March's wedding ring, too small now for her fat finger, but put carefully away, like the most precious jewel of them all.

"Which would Mademoiselle choose if she had her will?" asked Esther, who always sat near to watch over and lock up the valuables.

"I like the diamonds best, but there is no necklace among them, and I'm fond of necklaces, they are so becoming. I should choose this if I might," replied Amy, looking with great admiration at a string of gold and ebony beads, from which hung a heavy cross of the same.

"I, too, covet that, but not as a necklace; ah, no! to me it is a rosary, and as such I should use it like a good Catholic," said Esther, eyeing the handsome thing wistfully.

"Is it meant to use as you use the string of good-smelling wooden beads hanging over your glass?" asked Amy.

"Truly, yes, to pray with. It would be pleasing to the saints if one used so fine a rosary as this, instead of wearing it as a vain bijou."

"You seem to take a deal of comfort in your prayers, Esther, and always come down looking quiet and satisfied. I wish I could."

"If Mademoiselle was a Catholic, she would find true comfort; but, as that is not to be, it would be well if you went apart each day to meditate, and pray, as did the good mistress whom I served before Madame. She had a little chapel, and in it found solacement for much trouble."

"Would it be right for me to do so too?" asked Amy, who, in her loneliness, felt the need of help of some sort, and found that she was apt to forget her little book, now that Beth was not there to remind her of it.

"It would be excellent and charming; and I shall gladly arrange the little dressing-room for you, if you like it. Say nothing to Madame, but when she sleeps go you and sit alone a while to think good thoughts, and ask the dear God to preserve your sister."

Esther was truly pious, and quite sincere in her advice; for she had an affectionate heart, and felt much for the sisters in their anxiety. Amy liked the idea, and gave her leave to arrange the light closet next her room, hoping it would do her good.

"I wish I knew where all these pretty things would go when Aunt March dies," she said, as she slowly replaced the shining rosary, and shut the jewel cases one by one.

"To you and your sisters. I know it; Madame confides in me; I witnessed her will, and it is to be so," whispered Esther, smiling.

"How nice! but I wish she'd let us have them now. Pro-cras-ti-nation is not agreeable," observed Amy, taking a last look at the diamonds.

"It is too soon yet for the young ladies to wear these things. The first one who is affianced will have the pearls—Madame has said it; and I have a fancy that the little turquoise ring will be given to you when you go, for Madame approves your good behavior and charming manners."

"Do you think so? Oh, I'll be a lamb, if I can only have that lovely ring! It's ever so much prettier than Kitty Bryant's. I do like Aunt March, after all;" and Amy tried on the blue ring with a delighted face, and a firm resolve to earn it.

From that day she was a model of obedience, and the old lady complacently admired the success of her training. Esther fitted up the closet with a little table, placed a footstool before it, and over it a picture, taken from one of the shut-up rooms. She thought it was of no great value, but, being appropriate, she borrowed it, well knowing that Madame would never know it, nor care if she did. It was, however, a very valuable copy of one of the famous pictures of the world, and Amy's beauty-loving eyes were never tired of looking up at the sweet face of the divine mother, while tender thoughts of her own were busy at her heart. On the table she laid her little Testament and hymn-book, kept a vase always full of the best flowers Laurie brought her, and came every day to "sit alone, thinking good thoughts, and praying the dear God to preserve her sister." Esther had given her a rosary of black beads, with a silver cross, but Amy hung it up, and did not use it, feeling doubtful as to its fitness for Protestant prayers.

The little girl was very sincere in all this, for, being left alone outside the safe home-nest, she felt the need of some kind hand to hold by so sorely, that she instinctively turned to the strong and tender Friend, whose fatherly love most closely surrounds His little children. She missed her mother's help to understand and rule herself, but having been taught where to look, she did her best to find the way, and walk in it confidingly. But Amy was a young pilgrim, and just now her burden seemed very heavy. She tried to forget herself, to keep cheerful, and be satisfied with doing right, though no one saw or praised her for it. In her first effort at being very, very good, she decided to make her will, as Aunt March had done; so that if she *did* fall ill and die, her possessions might be justly and generously divided. It cost her a pang even to think of giving up the little treasures which in her eyes were as precious as the old lady's jewels.

During one of her play hours she wrote out the important document as well as she could, with some help from Esther as to certain legal terms; and, when the good-natured French woman had signed her name, Amy felt relieved, and laid it by to show Laurie, whom she wanted as a second witness. As it was a rainy day, she went upstairs to amuse herself in one of the large chambers, and took Polly with her for company. In this room there was a wardrobe full of old-fashioned costumes, with which Esther allowed her to play, and it was her favorite amusement to array herself in the faded brocades, and parade up and down before the long mirror, making stately courtesies, and sweeping her train about, with a rustle which delighted her ears. So busy was she on this day, that she did not hear Laurie's ring, nor see his face peeping in at her, as she gravely promenaded to and fro, flirting her fan and tossing her head, on which she wore a great pink turban, contrasting oddly with her blue brocade dress and yellow quilted petticoat. She was obliged to walk carefully, for she had on high-heeled shoes, and, as Laurie told Jo afterward, it was a comical sight to see her mince along in her gay suit, with Polly sidling and bridling just behind her, imitating her as well as he could, and occasionally stopping to laugh, or exclaim, "Ain't we fine? Get along you fright! Hold your tongue! Kiss me, dear; ha! ha!"

Having with difficulty restrained an explosion of merriment, lest it should offend her majesty, Laurie tapped, and was graciously received.

"Sit down and rest while I put these things away; then I want to consult you about a very serious matter," said Amy, when she had shown her splendor, and driven Polly into a corner. "That bird is the trial of my life," she continued, removing the pink mountain from her head, while Laurie seated himself astride of a chair. "Yesterday, when aunt was asleep, and I was trying to be as still as a mouse, Polly began to squall and flap about in his cage; so I went to let him out, and found a big spider there. I poked it out, and it ran under the book-case; Polly marched straight after it, stooped down and peeped under the book-case, saying, in his funny way, with a cock of his eye, 'Come out and take a walk, my dear.' I *couldn't* help laughing, which made Poll swear, and aunt woke up and scolded us both."

"Did the spider accept the old fellow's invitation?" asked Laurie, yawning.

"Yes; out it came, and away ran Polly, frightened to death, and scrambled up on aunt's chair, calling out, 'Catch her! catch her! catch her!' as I chased the spider."

"That's a lie! Oh lor!" cried the parrot, pecking at Laurie's toes.

"I'd wring your neck if you were mine, you old torment," cried Laurie, shaking his fist at the bird; who put his head on one side, and gravely croaked, "Allyluyer! bless your buttons, dear!"

"Now I'm ready," said Amy, shutting the wardrobe, and taking a paper out of her pocket. "I want you to read that, please, and tell me if it is legal and right. I felt that I ought to do it, for life is uncertain, and I don't want any ill-feeling over my tomb."

Laurie bit his lips, and turning a little from the pensive speaker, read the following document, with praiseworthy gravity, considering the spelling:—

"MY LAST WILL AND TESTIMENT.

"I, Amy Curtis March, being in my sane mind, do give and bequeethe all my earthly property—viz. to wit:—namely

"To my father, my best pictures, sketches, maps, and works of art, including frames. Also my $100, to do what he likes with.

"To my mother, all my clothes, except the blue apron with pockets,—also my likeness, and my medal, with much love.

"To my dear sister Margaret, I give my turkquoise ring (if I get it), also my green box with the doves on it, also my piece of real lace for her neck, and my sketch of her as a memorial of her 'little girl.'

"To Jo I leave my breast-pin, the one mended with sealing wax, also my bronze inkstand—she lost the cover,—and my most precious plaster rabbit, because I am sorry I burnt up her story.

"To Beth (if she lives after me) I give my dolls and the little bureau, my fan, my linen collars and my new slippers if she can wear them being thin when she gets well. And I herewith also leave her my regret that I ever made fun of old Joanna.

"To my friend and neighbor Theodore Laurence I bequeethe my paper marshay portfolio, my clay model of a horse though he did say it hadn't any neck. Also in return for his great kindness in the hour of affliction any one of my artistic works he likes, Noter Dame is the best.

"To our venerable benefactor Mr. Laurence I leave my purple box with a looking glass in the cover which will be nice for his pens and remind him of the departed girl who thanks him for his favors to her family, specially Beth.

"I wish my favorite playmate Kitty Bryant to have the blue silk apron and my gold-bead ring with a kiss.

"To Hannah I give the band-box she wanted and all the patch work I leave hoping she 'will remember me, when it you see.'

"And now having disposed of my most valuable property I hope all will be satisfied and not blame the dead. I forgive every one, and trust we may all meet when the trump shall sound. Amen.

"To this will and testiment I set my hand and seal on this 20th day of Nov. Anni Domino 1861.

"Amy Curtis March.

"*Witnesses:* Estelle Valnor, Theodore Laurence."

The last name was written in pencil, and Amy explained that he was to rewrite it in ink, and seal it up for her properly.

"What put it into your head? Did any one tell you about Beth's giving away her things?"

asked Laurie, soberly, as Amy laid a bit of red tape, with sealing-wax, a taper, and a standish before him.

She explained; and then asked, anxiously, "What about Beth?"

"I'm sorry I spoke; but as I did, I'll tell you. She felt so ill one day, that she told Jo she wanted to give her piano to Meg, her bird to you, and the poor old doll to Jo, who would love it for her sake. She was sorry she had so little to give, and left locks of hair to the rest of us, and her best love to grandpa. *She* never thought of a will."

Laurie was signing and sealing as he spoke, and did not look up till a great tear dropped on the paper. Amy's face was full of trouble; but she only said, "Don't people put sort of postscrips to their wills, sometimes."

"Yes; 'codicils,' they call them."

"Put one in mine then—that I wish *all* my curls cut off, and given round to my friends. I forgot it; but I want it done, though it will spoil my looks."

Laurie added it, smiling at Amy's last and greatest sacrifice. Then he amused her for an hour, and was much interested in all her trials. But when he came to go, Amy held him back to whisper, with trembling lips, "Is there really any danger about Beth?"

"I'm afraid there is; but we must hope for the best, so don't cry, dear;" and Laurie put his arm about her with a brotherly gesture, which was very comforting.

When he had gone, she went to her little chapel, and, sitting in the twilight, prayed for Beth with streaming tears and an aching heart, feeling that a million turquoise rings would not console her for the loss of her gentle little sister.

20
Confidential

I don't think I have any words in which to tell the meeting of the mother and daughters; such hours are beautiful to live, but very hard to describe, so I will leave it to the imagination of my readers; merely saying that the house was full of genuine happiness, and that Meg's tender hope was realized; for when Beth woke from that long, healing sleep, the first objects on which her eyes fell *were* the little rose and mother's face. Too weak to wonder at anything, she only smiled, and nestled close into the loving arms about her, feeling that the hungry longing was satisfied at last. Then she slept again, and the girls waited upon their mother, for she would not unclasp the thin hand which clung to hers, even in sleep. Hannah had "dished up" an astonishing breakfast for the traveller, finding it impossible to vent her excitement in any other way; and Meg and Jo fed their mother like dutiful young storks, while they listened to her whispered account of father's state, Mr. Brooke's promise to stay and nurse him, the delays which the storm occasioned on the homeward journey, and the unspeakable comfort Laurie's hopeful face had given her when she arrived, worn out with fatigue, anxiety and cold.

What a strange, yet pleasant day that was! so brilliant and gay without, for all the world seemed abroad to welcome the first snow; so quiet and reposeful within, for every one slept, spent with watching, and a Sabbath stillness reigned through the house, while nodding Hannah mounted guard at the door. With a blissful sense of burdens lifted off, Meg and Jo closed their weary eyes, and lay at rest like storm-beaten boats, safe at anchor in a quiet harbor. Mrs. March would not leave Beth's side, but rested in the big chair, waking often to look at, touch, and brood over her child, like a miser over some recovered treasure.

Laurie, meanwhile, posted off to comfort Amy, and told his story so well that Aunt March actually "sniffed" herself, and never once said, "I told you so." Amy came out so strong on this occasion, that I think the good thoughts in the little chapel really began to bear fruit. She dried her tears quickly, restrained her impatience to see her mother, and never even thought of the turquoise ring, when the old lady heartily agreed in Laurie's opinion, that she behaved "like a capital little woman." Even Polly seemed impressed, for he called her "good girl," blessed her buttons, and begged her to "come and take a walk, dear," in his most affable tone. She would very gladly have gone out to enjoy the bright wintry weather; but, discovering that Laurie was dropping with sleep in spite of manful efforts to conceal the fact, she persuaded him to rest on the sofa, while she wrote a note to her mother. She was a long time about it; and, when returned, he was stretched out with both arms under his head, sound asleep, while Aunt March had pulled down the curtains, and sat doing nothing in an unusual fit of benignity.

After a while, they began to think he was not going to wake till night, and I'm not sure that he would, had he not been effectually roused by Amy's cry of joy at sight of her mother. There probably were a good many happy little girls in and about the city that day, but it is my private opinion that Amy was the happiest of all, when she sat in her mother's lap and told her trials, receiving consolation and compensation in the shape of approving smiles and fond caresses. They were alone together in the chapel, to which her mother did not object when its purpose was explained to her.

"On the contrary, I like it very much, dear," she said, looking from the dusty rosary to the well-worn little book, and the lovely picture with its garland of evergreen. "It is an excellent plan to have some place where we can go to be quiet, when things vex or grieve us. There are a good many hard times in this life of ours, but we can always bear them if we ask help in the right way. I think my little girl is learning this?"

"Yes, mother; and when I go home I mean to have a corner in the big closet to put my books, and the copy of that picture which I've tried to make. The woman's face is not good, it's too beautiful for me to draw, but the baby is done better, and I love it very much. I like to think He was a little child once, for then I don't seem so far away, and that helps me."

As Amy pointed to the smiling Christ-child on his mother's knee, Mrs. March saw something on the lifted hand that made her smile. She said nothing, but Amy understood the look, and, after a minute's pause, she added, gravely,—

"I wanted to speak to you about this, but I forgot it. Aunt gave me the ring today; she called me to her and kissed me, and put it on my finger, and said I was a credit to her, and she'd like to keep me always. She gave that funny guard to keep the turquoise on, as it's too big. I'd like to wear them, mother; can I?"

"They are very pretty, but I think you're rather too young for such ornaments, Amy," said Mrs. March, looking at the plump little hand, with the band of sky-blue stones on the forefinger, and the quaint guard, formed of two tiny, golden hands clasped together.

"I'll try not to be vain," said Amy; "I don't think I like it, only because it's so pretty; but I want to wear it as the girl in the story wore her bracelet, to remind me of something."

"Do you mean Aunt March?" asked her mother, laughing.

"No, to remind me not to be selfish." Amy looked so earnest and sincere about it, that her mother stopped laughing, and listened respectfully to the little plan.

"I've thought a great deal lately about 'my bundle of naughties,' and being selfish is the largest one in it; so I'm going to try hard to cure it, if I can. Beth isn't selfish, and that's the reason every one loves her, and feels so bad at the thoughts of losing her. People wouldn't feel half so bad about me if I was sick, and I don't deserve to have them; but I'd like to be loved and missed by a great many friends, so I'm going to try and be like Beth all I can. I'm apt to forget my resolutions; but, if I had something always about me to remind me, I guess I should do better. May I try this way?"

"Yes; but I have more faith in the corner of the big closet. Wear your ring, dear, and do your best; I think you will prosper, for the sincere wish to be good is half the battle. Now, I must go back to Beth. Keep up your heart, little daughter, and we will soon have you home again."

That evening, while Meg was writing to her father, to report the traveller's safe arrival, Jo slipped upstairs into Beth's room, and, finding her mother in her usual place, stood a minute twisting her fingers in her hair, with a worried gesture and an undecided look.

"What is it, deary?" asked Mrs. March, holding out her hand with a face which invited confidence.

"I want to tell you something, mother."

"About Meg?"

"How quick you guessed! Yes, it's about her, and though it's a little thing, it fidgets me."

"Beth is asleep; speak low, and tell me all about it. That Moffat hasn't been here, I hope?" asked Mrs. March, rather sharply.

"No; I should have shut the door in his face if he had," said Jo, settling herself on the floor at her mother's feet. "Last summer Meg left a pair of gloves over at the Laurences, and only one was returned. We forgot all about it, till Teddy told me that Mr. Brooke had it. He kept it in his waistcoat pocket, and once it fell out, and Teddy joked him about it, and Mr. Brooke owned that he liked Meg, but didn't dare say so, she was so young and he so poor. Now isn't it a *dreadful* state of things?"

"Do you think Meg cares for him?" asked Mrs. March, with an anxious look.

"Mercy me! I don't know anything about love, and such nonsense!" cried Jo, with a funny mixture of interest and contempt. "In novels, the girls show it by starting and blushing, fainting away, growing thin, and acting like fools. Now Meg don't do anything of the sort; she eats and drinks, and sleeps, like a sensible creature; she looks straight in my face when I talk about that man, and only blushes a little bit when Teddy jokes about lovers. I forbid him to do it, but he don't mind me as he ought."

"Then you fancy that Meg is *not* interested in John?"

"Who?" cried Jo, staring.

"Mr. Brooke; I call him 'John' now; we fell into the way of doing so at the hospital, and he likes it."

"Oh, dear! I know you'll take his part; he's been good to father, and you won't send him away, but let Meg marry him, if she wants to. Mean thing! to go petting pa and truckling to you, just to wheedle you into liking him;" and Jo pulled her hair again with a wrathful tweak.

"My dear, don't get angry about it, and I will tell you how it happened. John went with me at Mr. Laurence's request, and was so devoted to poor father, that we couldn't help getting fond of him. He was perfectly open and honorable about Meg, for he told us he loved her; but would earn a comfortable home before he asked her to marry him. He only wanted our leave to love her and work for her, and the right to make her love him if he could. He is a truly excellent young man, and we could not refuse to listen to him; but I will not consent to Meg's engaging herself so young."

"Of course not; it would be idiotic! I knew there was mischief brewing; I felt it; and now it's worse than I imagined. I just wish I could marry Meg myself, and keep her safe in the family."

This odd arrangement made Mrs. March smile; but she said, gravely, "Jo, I confide in you, and don't wish you to say anything to Meg yet. When John comes back, and I see them together, I can judge better of her feelings toward him."

"She'll see his in those handsome eyes that she talks about, and then it will be all up with her. She's got such a soft heart, it will melt like butter in the sun if any one looks sentimentally at her. She read the short reports he sent more than she did your letters, and pinched me when I spoke of it, and likes brown eyes, and don't think John an ugly name, and she'll go and fall in love, and there's an end of peace and fun, and cosy times, together. I see it all! they'll go lovering round the house, and we shall have to dodge; Meg will be absorbed, and no good to me any more; Brooke will scratch up a fortune somehow,—carry her off and make a hole in the family; and I shall break my heart, and everything will be abominably uncomfortable. Oh, deary me! why weren't we all boys? then there wouldn't be any bother!"

Jo leaned her chin on her knees, in a disconsolate attitude, and shook her fist at the reprehensible John. Mrs. March sighed, and Jo looked up with an air of relief.

"You don't like it, mother? I'm glad of it; let's send him about his business, and not tell Meg a word of it, but all be jolly together as we always have been."

"I did wrong to sigh, Jo. It is natural and right you should all go to homes of your own, in time; but I do want to keep my girls as long as I can; and I am sorry that this happened so soon, for Meg is only seventeen, and it will be some years before John can make a home for her. Your father and I have agreed that she shall not bind herself in any way, nor be married, before twenty. If she and John love one another, they can wait, and test the love by doing so. She is conscientious, and I have no fear of her treating him unkindly. My pretty, tender-hearted girl! I hope things will go happily with her."

"Hadn't you rather have her marry a rich man?" asked Jo, as her mother's voice faltered a little over the last words.

"Money is a good and useful thing, Jo; and I hope my girls will never feel the need of it too bitterly, nor be tempted by too much. I should like to know that John was firmly established in some good business, which gave him an income large enough to keep free from debt, and make Meg comfortable. I'm not ambitious for a splendid fortune, a fashionable position, or a great name for my girls. If rank and money come with love and virtue, also, I should accept them gratefully, and enjoy your good fortune; but I know, by experience, how much genuine happiness can be had in a plain little house, where the daily bread is earned, and some privations give sweetness to the few pleasures; I am content to see Meg begin humbly, for, if I am not mistaken, she will be rich in the possession of a good man's heart, and that is better than a fortune."

"I understand, mother, and quite agree; but I'm disappointed about Meg, for I'd planned to have her marry Teddy by and by, and sit in the lap of luxury all her days. Wouldn't it be nice?" asked Jo, looking up with a brighter face.

"He is younger than she, you know," began Mrs. March; but Jo broke in,—

"Oh, that don't matter; he's old for his age, and tall; and can be quite grown-up in his manners, if he likes. Then he's rich, and generous, and good, and loves us all; and I say it's a pity my plan is spoilt."

"I'm afraid Laurie is hardly grown-up enough for Meg, and altogether too much of a weathercock, just now, for any one to depend on. Don't make plans, Jo; but let time and their own hearts mate your friends. We can't meddle safely in such matters, and had better not get 'romantic rubbish,' as you call it, into our heads, lest it spoil our friendship."

"Well, I won't; but I hate to see things going all criss-cross, and getting snarled up, when a pull here, and a snip there, would straighten it out. I wish wearing flat-irons on our heads would keep us from growing up. But buds will be roses, and kittens, cats,—more's the pity!"

"What's that about flat-irons and cats?" asked Meg, as she crept into the room, with the finished letter in her hand.

"Only one of my stupid speeches. I'm going to bed; come on, Peggy," said Jo, unfolding herself, like an animated puzzle.

"Quite right, and beautifully written. Please add that I send my love to John," said Mrs. March, as she glanced over the letter, and gave it back.

"Do you call him 'John'?" asked Meg, smiling, with her innocent eyes looking down into her mother's.

"Yes; he has been like a son to us, and we are very fond of him," replied Mrs. March, returning the look with a keen one.

"I'm glad of that; he is so lonely. Good-night, mother, dear. It is so inexpressibly comfortable to have you here," was Meg's quiet answer.

The kiss her mother gave her was a very tender one; and, as she went away, Mrs. March said, with a mixture of satisfaction and regret, "She does not love John yet, but will soon learn to."

21
Laurie Makes Mischief, and Jo Makes Peace

Jo's face was a study next day, for the secret rather weighed upon her, and she found it hard not to look mysterious and important. Meg observed it, but did not trouble herself to make inquiries, for she had learned that the best way to manage Jo was by the law of contraries, so she felt sure of being told everything if she did not ask. She was rather surprised, therefore, when the silence remained unbroken, and Jo assumed a patronizing air, which decidedly aggravated Meg, who in her turn assumed an air of dignified reserve, and devoted herself to her mother. This left Jo to her own devices; for Mrs. March had taken her place as nurse, and bid her rest, exercise, and amuse herself after her long confinement. Amy being gone, Laurie was her only refuge; and, much as she enjoyed his society, she rather dreaded him just then, for he was an incorrigible tease, and she feared he would coax her secret from her.

She was quite right; for the mischief-loving lad no sooner suspected a mystery, than he set himself to finding it out, and led Jo a trying life of it. He wheedled, bribed, ridiculed, threatened and scolded; affected indifference, that he might surprise the truth from her; declared he knew, then that he didn't care; and, at last, by dint of perseverance, he satisfied himself that it concerned Meg and Mr. Brooke. Feeling indignant that he was not taken into his tutor's confidence, he set his wits to work to devise some proper retaliation for the slight.

Meg meanwhile had apparently forgotten the matter, and was absorbed in preparations for her father's return; but all of a sudden a change seemed to come over her, and, for a day or two, she was quite unlike herself. She started when spoken to, blushed when looked at, was very quiet, and sat over her sewing with a timid, troubled look on her face. To her mother's inquiries she answered that she was quite well, and Jo's she silenced by begging to be let alone.

"She feels it in the air—love, I mean—and she's going very fast. She's got most of the symptoms, is twittery and cross, don't eat, lies awake, and mopes in corners. I caught her singing that song about 'the silver-voiced brook,' and once she said 'John,' as you do, and then turned as red as a poppy. Whatever shall we do?" said Jo, looking ready for any measures, however violent.

"Nothing but wait. Let her alone, be kind and patient, and father's coming will settle everything," replied her mother.

"Here's a note to you, Meg, all sealed up. How odd! Teddy never seals mine," said Jo, next day, as she distributed the contents of the little post-office.

Mrs. March and Jo were deep in their own affairs, when a sound from Meg made them look up to see her staring at her note, with a frightened face.

"My child, what is it?" cried her mother, running to her, while Jo tried to take the paper which had done the mischief.

"It's all a mistake—he didn't send it—oh, Jo, how could you do it?" and Meg hid her face in her hands, crying as if her heart was quite broken.

"Me! I've done nothing! What's she talking about?" cried Jo, bewildered.

Meg's mild eyes kindled with anger as she pulled a crumpled note from her pocket, and threw it at Jo, saying, reproachfully,—

"You wrote it, and that bad boy helped you. How could you be so rude, so mean, and cruel to us both?"

Jo hardly heard her, for she and her mother were reading the note, which was written in a peculiar hand.

> "My Dearest Margaret,—
>   "I can no longer restrain my passion, and must know my fate before I return.
> I dare not tell your parents yet, but I think they would consent if they knew that
> we adored one another. Mr. Laurence will help me to some good place, and then,

my sweet girl, you will make me happy. I implore you to say nothing to your family yet, but to send one word of hope through Laurie to

"Your devoted
"John."

"Oh, the little villain! that's the way he meant to pay me for keeping my word to mother. I'll give him a hearty scolding, and bring him over to beg pardon," cried Jo, burning to execute immediate justice. But her mother held her back, saying, with a look she seldom wore,—

"Stop, Jo, you must clear yourself first. You have played so many pranks, that I am afraid you had a hand in this."

"On my word, mother, I haven't! I never saw that note before, and don't know anything about it, as true as I live!" said Jo, so earnestly, that they believed her. "If I *had* taken a part in it I'd have done it better than this, and have written a sensible note. I should think you'd have known Mr. Brooke wouldn't write such stuff as that," she added, scornfully tossing down the paper.

"It's like his writing," faltered Meg, comparing it with the note in her hand.

"Oh, Meg, you didn't answer it?" cried Mrs. March, quickly.

"Yes, I did!" and Meg hid her face again, overcome with shame.

"Here's a scrape! *Do* let me bring that wicked boy over to explain, and be lectured. I can't rest till I get hold of him;" and Jo made for the door again.

"Hush! let me manage this, for it is worse than I thought. Margaret, tell me the whole story," commanded Mrs. March, sitting down by Meg, yet keeping hold of Jo, lest she should fly off.

"I received the first letter from Laurie, who didn't look as if he knew anything about it," began Meg, without looking up. "I was worried at first, and meant to tell you; then I remembered how you liked Mr. Brooke, so I thought you wouldn't mind if I kept my little secret for a few days. I'm so silly that I liked to think no one knew; and, while I was deciding what to say, I felt like the girls in books, who have such things to do. Forgive me, mother, I'm paid for my silliness now; I never can look him in the face again."

"What did you say to him?" asked Mrs. March.

"I only said I was too young to do anything about it yet; that I didn't wish to have secrets from you, and he must speak to father. I was very grateful for his kindness, and would be his friend, but nothing more, for a long while."

Mrs. March smiled, as if well pleased, and Jo clapped her hands, exclaiming, with a laugh,—

"You are almost equal to Caroline Percy, who was a pattern of prudence! Tell on, Meg. What did he say to that?"

"He writes in a different way entirely; telling me that he never sent any love-letter at all, and is very sorry that my roguish sister, Jo, should take such liberties with our names. It's very kind and respectful, but think how dreadful for me!"

Meg leaned against her mother, looking the image of despair, and Jo tramped about the room, calling Laurie names. All of a sudden she stopped, caught up the two notes, and, after looking at them closely, said, decidedly, "I don't believe Brooke ever saw either of these letters. Teddy wrote both, and keeps yours to crow over me with, because I wouldn't tell him my secret."

"Don't have any secrets, Jo; tell it to mother, and keep out of trouble, as I should have done," said Meg, warningly.

"Bless you, child! mother told me."

"That will do, Jo. I'll comfort Meg while you go and get Laurie. I shall sift the matter to the bottom, and put a stop to such pranks at once."

Away ran Jo, and Mrs. March gently told Meg Mr. Brooke's real feelings. "Now, dear, what are your own? Do you love him enough to wait till he can make a home for you, or will you keep yourself quite free for the present?"

"I've been so scared and worried, I don't want to have anything to do with lovers for a long while,—perhaps never," answered Meg, petulantly. "If John *doesn't* know anything about this nonsense, don't tell him, and make Jo and Laurie hold their tongues. I won't be deceived and plagued, and made a fool of,—it's a shame!"

Seeing that Meg's usually gentle temper was roused, and her pride hurt by this mischievous joke, Mrs. March soothed her by promises of entire silence, and great discretion for the future. The instant Laurie's step was heard in the hall, Meg fled into the study, and Mrs. March received the culprit alone. Jo had not told him why he was wanted, fearing he wouldn't come; but he knew the minute he saw Mrs. March's face, and stood twirling his hat with a guilty air, which convicted him at once. Jo was dismissed, but chose to march up and down the hall like a sentinel, having some fear that the prisoner might bolt. The sound of voices in the parlor rose and fell for half an hour; but what happened during that interview the girls never knew.

When they were called in, Laurie was standing by their mother with such a penitent face, that Jo forgave him on the spot, but did not think it wise to betray the fact. Meg received his humble apology, and was much comforted by the assurance that Brooke knew nothing of the joke.

"I'll never tell him to my dying day,—wild horses shan't drag it out of me; so you'll forgive me, Meg, and I'll do anything to show how out-and-out sorry I am," he added, looking very much ashamed of himself.

"I'll try; but it was a very ungentlemanly thing to do. I didn't think you could be so sly and malicious, Laurie," replied Meg, trying to hide her maidenly confusion under a gravely reproachful air.

"It was altogether abominable, and I don't deserve to be spoken to for a month; but you will, though, won't you?" and Laurie folded his hands together, with such an imploring gesture, and rolled up his eyes in such a meekly repentant way, as he spoke in his irresistibly persuasive tone, that it was impossible to frown upon him, in spite of his scandalous behavior. Meg pardoned him, and Mrs. March's grave face relaxed, in spite of her efforts to keep sober, when she heard him declare that he would atone for his sins by all sorts of penances, and abase himself like a worm before the injured damsel.

Jo stood aloof, meanwhile, trying to harden her heart against him, and succeeding only in primming up her face into an expression of entire disapprobation. Laurie looked at her once or twice, but, as she showed no sign of relenting, he felt injured, and turned his back on her till the others were done with him, when he made her a low bow, and walked off without a word.

As soon as he had gone, she wished she had been more forgiving; and, when Meg and her mother went upstairs, she felt lonely, and longed for Teddy. After resisting for some time, she yielded to the impulse, and, armed with a book to return, went over to the big house.

"Is Mr. Laurence in?" asked Jo, of a housemaid, who was coming down stairs.

"Yes, miss; but I don't believe he's seeable just yet."

"Why not; is he ill?"

"La, no, miss! but he's had a scene with Mr. Laurie, who is in one of his tantrums about something, which vexes the old gentleman, so I dursn't go nigh him."

"Where is Laurie?"

"Shut up in his room, and he won't answer, though I've been a-tapping. I don't know what's to become of the dinner, for it's ready, and there's no one to eat it."

"I'll go and see what the matter is. I'm not afraid of either of them."

Up went Jo, and knocked smartly on the door of Laurie's little study.

"Stop that, or I'll open the door and make you!" called out the young gentleman, in a threatening tone.

Jo immediately pounded again; the door flew open, and in she bounced, before Laurie could recover from his surprise. Seeing that he really *was* out of temper, Jo, who knew how to manage him, assumed a contrite expression, and, going artistically down upon her knees, said, meekly, "Please forgive me for being so cross. I came to make it up, and can't go away till I have."

"It's all right; get up, and don't be a goose, Jo," was the cavalier reply to her petition.

"Thank you; I will. Could I ask what's the matter? You don't look exactly easy in your mind."

"I've been shaken, and I won't bear it!" growled Laurie, indignantly.

"Who did it?" demanded Jo.

"Grandfather; if it had been any one else I'd have—" and the injured youth finished his sentence by an energetic gesture of the right arm.

"That's nothing; I often shake you, and you don't mind," said Jo, soothingly.

"Pooh! you're a girl, and it's fun; but I'll allow no man to shake *me.*"

"I don't think any one would care to try it, if you looked as much like a thunder-cloud as you do now. Why were you treated so?"

"Just because I wouldn't say what your mother wanted me for. I'd promised not to tell, and of course I wasn't going to break my word."

"Couldn't you satisfy your grandpa in any other way?"

"No; he *would* have the truth, the whole truth, and nothing but the truth. I'd have told my part of the scrape, if I could, without bringing Meg in. As I couldn't, I held my tongue, and bore the scolding till the old gentleman collared me. Then I got angry, and bolted, for fear I should forget myself."

"It wasn't nice, but he's sorry, I know; so go down and make up. I'll help you."

"Hanged if I do! I'm not going to be lectured and pummelled by every one, just for a bit of a frolic. I *was* sorry about Meg, and begged pardon like a man; but I won't do it again, when I wasn't in the wrong."

"He didn't know that."

"He ought to trust me, and not act as if I was a baby. It's no use, Jo; he's got to learn that I'm able to take care of myself, and don't need any one's apron-string to hold on by."

"What pepper-pots you are!" sighed Jo. "How do you mean to settle this affair?"

"Well, he ought to beg pardon, and believe me when I say I can't tell him what the row's about."

"Bless you! he won't do that."

"I won't go down till he does."

"Now, Teddy, be sensible; let it pass, and I'll explain what I can. You can't stay here, so what's the use of being melodramatic?"

"I don't intend to stay here long, any-way. I'll slip off and take a journey somewhere, and when grandpa misses me he'll come round fast enough."

"I dare say; but you ought not to go and worry him."

"Don't preach. I'll go to Washington and see Brooke; it's gay there, and I'll enjoy myself after the troubles."

"What fun you'd have! I wish I could run off too!" said Jo, forgetting her part of Mentor in lively visions of martial life at the capital.

"Come on, then! Why not? You go and surprise your father, and I'll stir up old Brooke. It would be a glorious joke; let's do it, Jo! We'll leave a letter saying we are all right, and trot off at once. I've got money enough; it will do you good, and be no harm, as you go to your father."

For a moment Jo looked as if she would agree; for, wild as the plan was, it just suited her. She was tired of care and confinement, longed for change, and thoughts of her father blended temptingly with the novel charms of camps and hospitals, liberty and fun. Her eyes kindled as they turned wistfully toward the window, but they fell on the old house opposite, and she shook her head with sorrowful decision.

"If I was a boy, we'd run away together, and have a capital time; but as I'm a miserable girl, I must be proper, and stop at home. Don't tempt me, Teddy, it's a crazy plan."

"That's the fun of it!" began Laurie, who had got a wilful fit on him, and was possessed to break out of bounds in some way.

"Hold your tongue!" cried Jo, covering her ears. 'Prunes and prisms'[7] are my doom, and I may as well make up my mind to it. I came here to moralize, not to hear about things that make me skip to think of."

"I knew Meg would wet-blanket such a proposal, but I thought you had more spirit," began Laurie, insinuatingly.

"Bad boy, be quiet. Sit down and think of your own sins, don't go making me add to mine. If I get your grandpa to apologize for the shaking, will you give up running away?" asked Jo, seriously.

"Yes, but you won't do it," answered Laurie, who wished to "make up," but felt that his outraged dignity must be appeased first.

"If I can manage the young one I can the old one," muttered Jo, as she walked away, leaving Laurie bent over a railroad map, with his head propped up on both hands.

"Come in!" and Mr. Laurence's gruff voice sounded gruffer than ever, as Jo tapped at his door.

"It's only me, sir, come to return a book," she said, blandly, as she entered.

"Want any more?" asked the old gentleman, looking grim and vexed, but trying not to show it.

"Yes, please, I like old Sam so well, I think I'll try the second volume," returned Jo, hoping to propitiate him by accepting a second dose of "Boswell's Johnson,"[8] as he had recommended that lively work.

The shaggy eyebrows unbent a little, as he rolled the steps toward the shelf where the Johnsonian literature was placed. Jo skipped up, and, sitting on the top step, affected to be searching for her book, but was really wondering how best to introduce the dangerous object of her visit. Mr. Laurence seemed to suspect that something was brewing in her mind; for, after taking several brisk turns about the room, he faced round on her, speaking so abruptly, that "Rasselas"[9] tumbled face downward on the floor.

"What has that boy been about? Don't try to shield him, now! I know he has been in mischief, by the way he acted when he came home. I can't get a word from him; and, when I threatened to shake the truth out of him, he bolted upstairs, and locked himself into his room."

"He did do wrong, but we forgave him, and all promised not to say a word to any one," began Jo, reluctantly.

"That won't do; he shall not shelter himself behind a promise from you soft-hearted girls. If he's done anything amiss, he shall confess, beg pardon, and be punished. Out with it, Jo! I won't be kept in the dark."

Mr. Laurence looked so alarming, and spoke so sharply, that Jo would have gladly run away, if she could, but she was perched aloft on the steps, and he stood at the foot, a lion in the path, so she had to stay and brave it out.

"Indeed, sir, I cannot tell, mother forbid it. Laurie has confessed, asked pardon, and been punished quite enough. We don't keep silence to shield him, but some one else, and it will

---

7. Young women were coached to say these words to hold their faces in a "proper" expression, with pursed lips.

8. James Boswell (1740–1795) wrote *The Life of*

Samuel Johnson in 1791, recording the opinions and experiences of the famous man of letters.

9. Johnson's 1759 novel, the philosophic tale of a Middle-Eastern prince's education.

make more trouble if you interfere. Please don't; it was partly my fault, but it's all right now, so let's forget it, and talk about the 'Rambler,'[1] or something pleasant."

"Hang the 'Rambler!' come down and give me your word that this harum-scarum boy of mine hasn't done anything ungrateful or impertinent. If he has, after all your kindness to him, I'll thrash him with my own hands."

The threat sounded awful, but did not alarm Jo, for she knew the irascible old man would never lift a finger against his grandson, whatever he might say to the contrary. She obediently descended, and made as light of the prank as she could without betraying Meg, or forgetting the truth.

"Hum! ha! well, if the boy held his tongue because he'd promised, and not from obstinacy, I'll forgive him. He's a stubborn fellow, and hard to manage," said Mr. Laurence, rubbing up his hair till it looked as if he'd been out in a gale, and smoothing the frown from his brow with an air of relief.

"So am I; but a kind word will govern me when all the king's horses and all the king's men couldn't," said Jo, trying to say a kind word for her friend, who seemed to get out of one scrape only to fall into another.

"You think I'm not kind to him, hey?" was the sharp answer.

"Oh, dear, no, sir; you are rather too kind sometimes, and then just a trifle hasty when he tries your patience. Don't you think you are?"

Jo was determined to have it out now, and tried to look quite placid, though she quaked a little after her bold speech. To her great relief and surprise, the old gentleman only threw his spectacles on to the table with a rattle, and exclaimed, frankly,—

"You're right, girl, I am! I love the boy, but he tries my patience past bearing, and I don't know how it will end, if we go on so."

"I'll tell you,—he'll run away." Jo was sorry for that speech the minute it was made; she meant to warn him that Laurie would not bear much restraint, and hoped he would be more forbearing with the lad.

Mr. Laurence's ruddy face changed suddenly, and he sat down with a troubled glance at the picture of a handsome man, which hung over his table. It was Laurie's father, who *had* run away in his youth, and married against the imperious old man's will. Jo fancied he remembered and regretted the past, and she wished she had held her tongue.

"He won't do it, unless he is very much worried, and only threatens it sometimes, when he gets tired of studying. I often think I should like to, especially since my hair was cut; so, if you ever miss us, you may advertise for two boys, and look among the ships bound for India."

She laughed as she spoke, and Mr. Laurence looked relieved, evidently taking the whole as a joke.

"You hussy, how dare you talk in that way? where's your respect for me, and your proper bringing up? Bless the boys and girls! what torments they are; yet we can't do without them," he said, pinching her cheeks good-humoredly.

"Go and bring that boy down to his dinner, tell him it's all right, and advise him not to put on tragedy airs with his grandfather; I won't bear it."

"He won't come, sir; he feels badly because you didn't believe him when he said he couldn't tell. I think the shaking hurt his feelings very much."

Jo tried to look pathetic, but must have failed, for Mr. Laurence began to laugh, and she knew the day was won.

"I'm sorry for that, and ought to thank him for not shaking *me*, I suppose. What the dickens does the fellow expect?" and the old gentleman looked a trifle ashamed of his own testiness.

"If I was you, I'd write him an apology, sir. He says he won't come down till he has one; and talks about Washington, and goes on in an absurd way. A formal apology will make him

---

1. A journal, consisting of essays written chiefly by Johnson, published from 1749 to 1751.

see how foolish he is, and bring him down quite amiable. Try it; he likes fun, and this way is better than talking. I'll carry it up, and teach him his duty."

Mr. Laurence gave her a sharp look, and put on his spectacles, saying, slowly, "You're a sly puss! but I don't mind being managed by you and Beth. Here, give me a bit of paper, and let us have done with this nonsense."

The note was written in the terms which one gentleman would use to another after offering some deep insult. Jo dropped a kiss on the top of Mr. Laurence's bald head, and ran up to slip the apology under Laurie's door, advising him, through the keyhole, to be submissive, decorous, and a few other agreeable impossibilities. Finding the door locked again, she left the note to do its work, and was going quietly away, when the young gentleman slid down the banisters, and waited for her at the bottom, saying, with his most virtuous expression of countenance, "What a good fellow you are, Jo! Did you get blown up?" he added, laughing.

"No; he was pretty clever, on the whole."

"Ah! I got it all around! even you cast me off over there, and I felt just ready to go to the deuce," he began, apologetically.

"Don't talk in that way; turn over a new leaf and begin again, Teddy, my son."

"I keep turning over new leaves, and spoiling them, as I used to spoil my copy-books; and I make so many beginnings there never will be an end," he said, dolefully.

"Go and eat your dinner; you'll feel better after it. Men always croak when they are hungry," and Jo whisked out at the front door after that.

"That's a 'label' on my 'sect,'" answered Laurie, quoting Amy, as he went to partake of humble-pie dutifully with his grandfather, who was quite saintly in temper, and overwhelmingly respectful in manner, all the rest of the day.

Every one thought the matter ended, and the little cloud blown over; but the mischief was done, for, though others forgot it, Meg remembered. She never alluded to a certain person, but she thought of him a good deal, dreamed dreams more than ever; and, once, Jo, rummaging her sister's desk for stamps, found a bit of paper scribbled over with the words, "Mrs. John Brooke;" whereat she groaned tragically, and cast it into the fire, feeling that Laurie's prank had hastened the evil day for her.

22
Pleasant Meadows

Like sunshine after storm were the peaceful weeks which followed. The invalids improved rapidly, and Mr. March began to talk of returning early in the new year. Beth was soon able to lie on the study sofa all day, amusing herself with the well-beloved cats, at first, and, in time, with doll's sewing, which had fallen sadly behindhand. Her once active limbs were so stiff and feeble that Jo took her a daily airing about the house, in her strong arms. Meg cheerfully blackened and burnt her white hands cooking delicate messes for "the dear;" while Amy, a loyal slave of the ring, celebrated her return by giving away as many of her treasures as she could prevail on her sisters to accept.

As Christmas approached, the usual mysteries began to haunt the house, and Jo frequently convulsed the family by proposing utterly impossible, or magnificently absurd ceremonies, in honor of this unusually merry Christmas. Laurie was equally impracticable, and would have had bonfires, sky-rockets, and triumphal arches, if he had had his own way. After many skirmishes and snubbings, the ambitious pair were considered effectually quenched, and went about with forlorn faces, which were rather belied by explosions of laughter when the two got together.

Several days of unusually mild weather fitly ushered in a splendid Christmas-day. Hannah "felt in her bones that it was going to be an uncommonly plummy day," and she proved herself a true prophetess, for everybody and everything seemed bound to produce a grand success. To begin with: Mr. March wrote that he should soon be with them; then Beth felt uncommonly well that morning, and, being dressed in her mother's gift,—a soft crimson merino wrapper,—was borne in triumph to the window, to behold the offering of Jo and Laurie. The Unquenchables had done their best to be worthy of the name, for, like elves, they had worked by night, and conjured up a comical surprise. Out in the garden stood a stately snow-maiden, crowned with holly, bearing a basket of fruit and flowers in one hand, a great roll of new music in the other, a perfect rainbow of an Afghan round her chilly shoulders, and a Christmas carol issuing from her lips, on a pink paper streamer:—

"The Jungfrau to Beth.

"God bless you, dear Queen Bess!
  May nothing you dismay;
But health, and peace, and happiness,
  Be yours, this Christmas-day.

"Here's fruit to feed our busy bee,
  And flowers for her nose;
Here's music for her pianee,—
  An Afghan for her toes.

"A portrait of Joanna, see,
  By Raphael No. 2,
Who labored with great industry,
  To make it fair and true.

"Accept a ribbon red I beg,
  For Madam Purrer's tail;
And ice cream made by lovely Peg,—
  A Mont Blanc in a pail.

"Their dearest love my makers laid
  Within my breast of snow,
Accept it, and the Alpine maid,
  From Laurie and from Jo."

How Beth laughed when she saw it! how Laurie ran up and down to bring in the gifts, and what ridiculous speeches Jo made as she presented them!

"I'm so full of happiness, that, if father was only here, I couldn't hold one drop more," said Beth, quite sighing with contentment as Jo carried her off to the study to rest after the excitement, and to refresh herself with some of the delicious grapes the "Jungfrau" had sent her.

"So am I," added Jo, slapping the pocket wherein reposed the long-desired Undine and Sintram.

"I'm sure I am," echoed Amy, poring over the engraved copy of the Madonna and Child, which her mother had given her, in a pretty frame.

"Of course I am," cried Meg, smoothing the silvery folds of her first silk dress; for Mr. Laurence had insisted on giving it.

"How can *I* be otherwise!" said Mrs. March, gratefully, as her eyes went from her husband's letter to Beth's smiling face, and her hand caressed the brooch made of gray and golden, chestnut and dark brown hair, which the girls had just fastened on her breast.

Now and then, in this work-a-day world, things do happen in the delightful story-book fashion, and what a comfort that is. Half an hour after every one had said they were so happy they could only hold one drop more, the drop came. Laurie opened the parlor door, and popped his head in very quietly. He might just as well have turned a somersault, and uttered an Indian war-whoop; for his face was so full of suppressed excitement, and his voice so treacherously joyful, that every one jumped up, though he only said, in a queer, breathless voice, "Here's another Christmas present for the March family."

Before the words were well out of his mouth, he was whisked away somehow, and in his place appeared a tall man, muffled up to the eyes, leaning on the arm of another tall man, who tried to say something and couldn't. Of course there was a general stampede; and for several minutes everybody seemed to lose their wits, for the strangest things were done, and no one said a word. Mr. March became invisible in the embrace of four pairs of loving arms; Jo disgraced herself by nearly fainting away, and had to be doctored by Laurie in the china closet; Mr. Brooke kissed Meg entirely by mistake, as he somewhat incoherently explained; and Amy, the dignified, tumbled over a stool, and, never stopping to get up, hugged and cried over her father's boots in the most touching manner. Mrs. March was the first to recover herself, and held up her hand with a warning, "Hush! remember Beth!"

But it was too late; the study door flew open,—the little red wrapper appeared on the threshold,—joy put strength into the feeble limbs,—and Beth ran straight into her father's arms. Never mind what happened just after that; for the full hearts overflowed, washing away the bitterness of the past, and leaving only the sweetness of the present.

It was not at all romantic, but a hearty laugh set everybody straight again,—for Hannah was discovered behind the door, sobbing over the fat turkey, which she had forgotten to put down when she rushed up from the kitchen. As the laugh subsided, Mrs. March began to thank Mr. Brooke for his faithful care of her husband, at which Mr. Brooke suddenly remembered that Mr. March needed rest, and, seizing Laurie, he precipitately retired. Then the two invalids were ordered to repose, which they did, by both sitting in one big chair, and talking hard.

Mr. March told how he had longed to surprise them, and how, when the fine weather came, he had been allowed by his doctor to take advantage of it; how devoted Brooke had been, and how he was altogether a most estimable and upright young man. Why Mr. March paused a minute just there, and, after a glance at Meg, who was violently poking the fire, looked at his wife with an inquiring lift of the eyebrows, I leave you to imagine; also why Mrs. March gently nodded her head, and asked, rather abruptly, if he wouldn't have something to eat. Jo saw and understood the look; and she stalked grimly away, to get wine and beef tea, muttering to herself, as she slammed the door, "I hate estimable young men with brown eyes!"

There never *was* such a Christmas dinner as they had that day. The fat turkey was a sight to behold, when Hannah sent him up, stuffed, browned and decorated. So was the plum-pudding, which quite melted in one's mouth; likewise the jellies, in which Amy revelled like a fly in a honey-pot. Everything turned out well; which was a mercy, Hannah said, "For my mind was that flustered, mum, that it's a merrycle I didn't roast the pudding and stuff the turkey with raisens, let alone bilin' of it in a cloth."

Mr. Laurence and his grandson dined with them; also Mr. Brooke,—at whom Jo glowered darkly, to Laurie's infinite amusement. Two easy-chairs stood side by side at the head of the table, in which sat Beth and her father, feasting, modestly, on chicken and a little fruit. They drank healths, told stories, sung songs, "reminisced," as the old folks say, and had a thoroughly good time. A sleigh-ride had been planned, but the girls would not leave their father; so the guests departed early, and, as twilight gathered, the happy family sat together round the fire.

"Just a year ago we were groaning over the dismal Christmas we expected to have. Do you remember?" asked Jo, breaking a short pause, which had followed a long conversation about many things.

"Rather a pleasant year on the whole!" said Meg, smiling at the fire, and congratulating herself on having treated Mr. Brooke with dignity.

"I think it's been a pretty hard one," observed Amy, watching the light shine on her ring, with thoughtful eyes.

"I'm glad it's over, because we've got you back," whispered Beth, who sat on her father's knee.

"Rather a rough road for you to travel, my little pilgrims, especially the latter part of it. But you have got on bravely; and I think the burdens are in a fair way to tumble off very soon," said Mr. March, looking, with fatherly satisfaction, at the four young faces gathered round him.

"How do you know? Did mother tell you?" asked Jo.

"Not much; straws show which way the wind blows; and I've made several discoveries today."

"Oh, tell us what they are!" cried Meg, who sat beside him.

"Here is one!" and, taking up the hand which lay on the arm of his chair, he pointed to the roughened forefinger, a burn on the back, and two or three little hard spots on the palm. "I remember a time when this hand was white and smooth, and your first care was to keep it so. It was very pretty then, but to me it is much prettier now,—for in these seeming blemishes I read a little history. A burnt offering has been made of vanity; this hardened palm has earned something better than blisters, and I'm sure the sewing done by these pricked fingers will last a long time, so much goodwill went into the stitches. Meg, my dear, I value the womanly skill which keeps home happy, more than white hands or fashionable accomplishments; I'm proud to shake this good, industrious little hand, and hope I shall not soon be asked to give it away."

If Meg had wanted a reward for hours of patient labor, she received it in the hearty pressure of her father's hand, and the approving smile he gave her.

"What about Jo? Please say something nice; for she has tried so hard, and been so very, very good to me," said Beth, in her father's ear.

He laughed, and looked across at the tall girl who sat opposite, with an unusually mild expression in her brown face.

"In spite of the curly crop, I don't see the 'son Jo' whom I left a year ago," said Mr. March. "I see a young lady who pins her collar straight, laces her boots neatly, and neither whistles, talks slang, nor lies on the rug, as she used to do. Her face is rather thin and pale, just now, with watching and anxiety; but I like to look at it, for it has grown gentler, and her voice is lower; she doesn't bounce, but moves quietly, and takes care of a certain little person in a motherly way, which delights me. I rather miss my wild girl; but if I get a strong, helpful, tender-hearted woman in her place, I shall feel quite satisfied. I don't know whether the shearing sobered our black sheep, but I do know that in all Washington I couldn't find anything beautiful enough to be bought with the five-and-twenty dollars which my good girl sent me."

Jo's keen eyes were rather dim for a minute, and her thin face grew rosy in the firelight, as she received her father's praise, feeling that she did deserve a portion of it.

"Now Beth," said Amy, longing for her turn, but ready to wait.

"There's so little of her I'm afraid to say much, for fear she will slip away altogether, though she is not so shy as she used to be," began their father, cheerfully; but, recollecting how nearly he *had* lost her, he held her close, saying, tenderly, with her cheek against his own, "I've got you safe, my Beth, and I'll keep you so, please God."

After a minute's silence, he looked down at Amy, who sat on the cricket at his feet, and said, with a caress of the shining hair,—

"I observed that Amy took drumsticks at dinner, ran errands for her mother all the afternoon, gave Meg her place to-night, and has waited on every one with patience and good-humor. I also observe that she does not fret much, nor prink at the glass, and has not even mentioned a very pretty ring which she wears; so I conclude that she has learned to think of other people more, and of herself less, and has decided to try and mould her character as carefully as she moulds her little clay figures. I am glad of this; for though I should be very proud of a graceful statue made by her, I shall be infinitely prouder of a lovable daughter, with a talent for making life beautiful to herself and others."

"What are you thinking of, Beth?" asked Jo, when Amy had thanked her father, and told about her ring.

"I read in 'Pilgrim's Progress' today, how, after many troubles, Christian and Hopeful came to a pleasant green meadow, where lilies bloomed all the year round, and there they rested happily, as we do now, before they went on to their journey's end," answered Beth; adding, as she slipped out of her father's arms, and went slowly to the instrument. "It's singing time now, and I want to be in my old place. I'll try to sing the song of the shepherd boy which the Pilgrims heard. I made the music for father, because he likes the verses."

So, sitting at the dear little piano, Beth softly touched the keys, and, in the sweet voice they had never thought to hear again, sung, to her own accompaniment, the quaint hymn, which was a singularly fitting song for her:—

> *"He that is down need fear no fall;*
> *He that is low no pride;*
> *He that is humble ever shall*
> *Have God to be his guide.*

> *"I am content with what I have,*
> *Little be it or much;*
> *And, Lord! contentment still I crave,*
> *Because Thou savest such.*

> *"Fulness to them a burden is,*
> *That go on Pilgrimage;*
> *Here little, and hereafter bliss,*
> *Is best from age to age!"*

23
Aunt March Settles the Question

Like bees swarming after their queen, mother and daughters hovered about Mr. March the next day, neglecting everything to look at, wait upon, and listen to, the new invalid, who was in a fair way to be killed by kindness. As he sat propped up in the big chair by Beth's sofa, with the other three close by, and Hannah popping in her head now and then, "to peek at the dear man," nothing seemed needed to complete their happiness. But something *was* needed, and the elder ones felt it, though none confessed the fact. Mr. and Mrs. March looked at one another with an anxious expression, as their eyes followed Meg. Jo had sudden fits of sobriety, and was seen to shake her fist at Mr. Brooke's umbrella, which had been left in the hall; Meg was absent-minded, shy and silent, started when the bell rang, and colored when John's name was mentioned; Amy said "Every one seemed waiting for something, and couldn't settle down, which was queer, since father was safe at home," and Beth innocently wondered why their neighbors didn't run over as usual.

Laurie went by in the afternoon, and, seeing Meg at the window, seemed suddenly possessed with a melodramatic fit, for he fell down upon one knee in the snow, beat his breast, tore his hair, and clasped his hands imploringly, as if begging some boon; and when Meg told him to behave himself, and go away, he wrung imaginary tears out of his handkerchief, and staggered round the corner as if in utter despair.

"What does the goose mean?" said Meg, laughing, and trying to look unconscious.

"He's showing you how your John will go on by and by. Touching, isn't it?" answered Jo, scornfully.

"Don't say *my John*, it isn't proper or true;" but Meg's voice lingered over the words as if they sounded pleasant to her. "Please don't plague me, Jo; I've told you I don't care *much* about him, and there isn't to be anything said, but we are all to be friendly, and go on as before."

"We can't, for something *has* been said, and Laurie's mischief has spoilt you for me. I see it, and so does mother; you are not like your old self a bit, and seem ever so far away from me. I don't mean to plague you, and will bear it like a man, but I do wish it was all settled. I hate to wait; so if you mean ever to do it, make haste, and have it over quick," said Jo, pettishly.

"*I* can't say or do anything till he speaks, and he won't, because father said I was too young," began Meg, bending over her work with a queer little smile, which suggested that she did not quite agree with her father on that point.

"If he did speak, you wouldn't know what to say, but would cry or blush, or let him have his own way, instead of giving a good, decided, No."

"I'm not so silly and weak as you think. I know just what I should say, for I've planned it all, so I needn't be taken unawares; there's no knowing what may happen, and I wished to be prepared."

Jo couldn't help smiling at the important air which Meg had unconsciously assumed, and which was as becoming as the pretty color varying in her cheeks.

"Would you mind telling me what you'd say?" asked Jo, more respectfully.

"Not at all; you are sixteen now, quite old enough to be my confidant, and my experience will be useful to you by and by, perhaps, in your own affairs of this sort."

"Don't mean to have any; it's fun to watch other people philander, but I should feel like a fool doing it myself," said Jo, looking alarmed at the thought.

"I guess not, if you liked any one very much, and he liked you," Meg spoke as if to herself, and glanced out at the lane where she had often seen lovers walking together in the summer twilight.

"I thought you were going to tell your speech to that man," said Jo, rudely shortening her sister's little reverie.

"Oh, I should merely say, quite calmly and decidedly, 'Thank you, Mr. Brooke, you are very kind, but I agree with father, that I am too young to enter into any engagement at present; so please say no more, but let us be friends as we were.' "

"Hum! that's stiff and cool enough. I don't believe you'll ever say it, and I know he won't be satisfied if you do. If he goes on like the rejected lovers in books, you'll give in, rather than hurt his feelings."

"No I won't! I shall tell him I've made up my mind, and shall walk out of the room with dignity."

Meg rose as she spoke, and was just going to rehearse the dignified exit, when a step in the hall made her fly into her seat, and begin to sew as if her life depended on finishing that particular seam in a given time. Jo smothered a laugh at the sudden change, and, when some one gave a modest tap, opened the door with a grim aspect, which was anything but hospitable.

"Good afternoon, I came to get my umbrella,—that is, to see how your father finds himself today," said Mr. Brooke, getting a trifle confused, as his eye went from one tell-tale face to the other.

"It's very well, he's in the rack, I'll get him, and tell it you are here," and having jumbled her father and the umbrella well together in her reply, Jo slipped out of the room to give Meg a chance to make her speech, and air her dignity. But the instant she vanished, Meg began to sidle toward the door, murmuring,—

"Mother will like to see you, pray sit down, I'll call her."

"Don't go; are you afraid of me, Margaret?" and Mr. Brooke looked so hurt, that Meg thought she must have done something very rude. She blushed up to the little curls on her forehead, for he had never called her Margaret before, and she was surprised to find how natural and sweet it seemed to hear him say it. Anxious to appear friendly and at her ease, she put out her hand with a confiding gesture, and said, gratefully,—

"How can I be afraid when you have been so kind to father? I only wish I could thank you for it."

"Shall I tell you how?" asked Mr. Brooke, holding the small hand fast in both his big ones, and looking down at Meg with so much love in the brown eyes, that her heart began to flutter, and she both longed to run away and to stop and listen.

"Oh no, please don't—I'd rather not," she said, trying to withdraw her hand, and looking frightened in spite of her denial.

"I won't trouble you, I only want to know if you care for me a little, Meg, I love you so much, dear," added Mr. Brooke, tenderly.

This was the moment for the calm, proper speech, but Meg didn't make it, she forgot every word of it, hung her head, and answered, "I don't know," so softly, that John had to stoop down to catch the foolish little reply.

He seemed to think it was worth the trouble, for he smiled to himself as if quite satisfied, pressed the plump hand gratefully, and said, in his most persuasive tone, "Will you try and find out? I want to know *so* much; for I can't go to work with any heart until I learn whether I am to have my reward in the end or not."

"I'm too young," faltered Meg, wondering why she was so fluttered, yet rather enjoying it.

"I'll wait; and, in the meantime, you could be learning to like me. Would it be a very hard lesson, dear?"

"Not if I chose to learn it, but—"

"Please choose to learn, Meg. I love to teach, and this is easier than German," broke in John, getting possession of the other hand, so that she had no way of hiding her face, as he bent to look at it.

His tone was properly beseeching; but, stealing a shy look at him, Meg saw that his eyes were merry as well as tender, and that he wore the satisfied smile of one who had no doubt of his success. This nettled her; Annie Moffat's foolish lessons in coquetry came into her mind, and the love of power, which sleeps in the bosoms of the best of little women, woke up all of a sudden, and took possession of her. She felt excited and strange, and, not knowing what else to do, followed a capricious impulse, and, withdrawing her hands, said, petulantly, "I *don't* choose; please go away, and let me be!"

Poor Mr. Brooke looked as if his lovely castle in the air was tumbling about his ears, for he had never seen Meg in such a mood before, and it rather bewildered him.

"Do you really mean that?" he asked, anxiously, following her as she walked away.

"Yes, I do; I don't want to be worried about such things. Father says I needn't; it's too soon, and I'd rather not."

"Mayn't I hope you'll change your mind by and by? I'll wait, and say nothing till you have had more time. Don't play with me, Meg. I didn't think that of you."

"Don't think of me at all. I'd rather you wouldn't," said Meg, taking a naughty satisfaction in trying her lover's patience and her own power.

He was grave and pale now, and looked decidedly more like the novel heroes whom she admired; but he neither slapped his forehead nor tramped about the room, as they did; he just stood looking at her so wistfully, so tenderly, that she found her heart relenting in spite of her. What would have happened next I cannot say, if Aunt March had not come hobbling in at this interesting minute.

The old lady couldn't resist her longing to see her nephew; for she had met Laurie as she took her airing, and, hearing of Mr. March's arrival, drove straight out to see him. The family were all busy in the back part of the house, and she had made her way quietly in, hoping to surprise them. She did surprise two of them so much, that Meg started as if she had seen a ghost, and Mr. Brooke vanished into the study.

"Bless me! what's all this?" cried the old lady, with a rap of her cane, as she glanced from the pale young gentleman to the scarlet young lady.

"It's father's friend. I'm *so* surprised to see you!" stammered Meg, feeling that she was in for a lecture now.

"That's evident," returned Aunt March, sitting down. "But what is father's friend saying, to make you look like a peony? There's mischief going on, and I insist upon knowing what it is!" with another rap.

"We were merely talking. Mr. Brooke came for his umbrella," began Meg, wishing that Mr. Brooke and the umbrella were safely out of the house.

"Brooke? That boy's tutor? Ah! I understand now. I know all about it. Jo blundered into a wrong message in one of your pa's letters, and I made her tell me. You haven't gone and accepted him, child?" cried Aunt March, looking scandalized.

"Hush! he'll hear! Shan't I call mother?" said Meg, much troubled.

"Not yet. I've something to say to you, and I must free my mind at once. Tell me, do you mean to marry this Cook? If you do, not one penny of my money ever goes to you. Remember that, and be a sensible girl," said the old lady, impressively.

Now Aunt March possessed, in perfection, the art of rousing the spirit of opposition in the gentlest people, and enjoyed doing it. The best of us have a spice of perversity in us, especially when we are young, and in love. If Aunt March had begged Meg to accept John Brooke, she would probably have declared she couldn't think of it; but, as she was peremptorily ordered *not* to like him, she immediately made up her mind that she would. Inclination as well as perversity made the decision easy, and, being already much excited, Meg opposed the old lady with unusual spirit.

"I shall marry whom I please, Aunt March, and you can leave your money to any one you like," she said, nodding her head with a resolute air.

"Highty tighty! Is that the way you take my advice, miss? You'll be sorry for it, by and by, when you've tried love in a cottage, and found it a failure."

"It can't be a worse one than some people find in big houses," retorted Meg.

Aunt March put on her glasses and took a look at the girl,—for she did not know her in this new mood. Meg hardly knew herself, she felt so brave and independent,—so glad to defend John, and assert her right to love him, if she liked. Aunt March saw that she had begun wrong, and, after a little pause, made a fresh start, saying, as mildly as she could, "Now, Meg, my dear, be reasonable, and take my advice. I mean it kindly, and don't want you to spoil your whole life by making a mistake at the beginning. You ought to marry well, and help your family; it's your duty to make a rich match, and it ought to be impressed upon you."

"Father and mother don't think so; they like John, though he *is* poor."

"Your pa and ma, my dear, have no more worldly wisdom than two babies."

"I'm glad of it," cried Meg, stoutly.

Aunt March took no notice, but went on with her lecture. "This Rook is poor, and hasn't got any rich relations, has he?"

"No; but he has many warm friends."

"You can't live on friends; try it, and see how cool they'll grow. He hasn't any business, has he?"

"Not yet; Mr. Laurence is going to help him."

"That won't last long. James Laurence is a crotchety old fellow, and not to be depended on. So you intend to marry a man without money, position, or business, and go on working harder than you do now, when you might be comfortable all your days by minding me, and doing better? I thought you had more sense, Meg."

"I couldn't do better if I waited half my life! John is good and wise; he's got heaps of talent; he's willing to work, and sure to get on, he's so energetic and brave. Every one likes and respects him, and I'm proud to think he cares for me, though I'm so poor, and young, and silly," said Meg, looking prettier than ever in her earnestness.

"He knows *you* have got rich relations, child; that's the secret of his liking, I suspect."

"Aunt March, how dare you say such a thing? John is above such meanness, and I won't listen to you a minute if you talk so," cried Meg, indignantly, forgetting everything but the injustice of the old lady's suspicions. "My John wouldn't marry for money, any more than I would. We are willing to work, and we mean to wait. I'm not afraid of being poor, for I've been happy so far, and I know I shall be with him, because he loves me, and I—"

Meg stopped there, remembering, all of a sudden, that she hadn't made up her mind; that she had told "her John" to go away, and that he might be overhearing her inconsistent remarks.

Aunt March was very angry, for she had set her heart on having her pretty niece make a fine match, and something in the girl's happy young face made the lonely old woman feel both sad and sour.

"Well, I wash my hands of the whole affair! You are a wilful child, and you've lost more than you know by this piece of folly. No, I won't stop; I'm disappointed in you, and haven't spirits to see your pa now. Don't expect anything from me when you are married; your Mr. Brooke's friends must take care of you. I'm done with you forever."

And, slamming the door in Meg's face, Aunt March drove off in high dudgeon. She seemed to take all the girl's courage with her; for, when left alone, Meg stood a moment undecided whether to laugh or cry. Before she could make up her mind, she was taken possession of by Mr. Brooke, who said, all in one breath, "I couldn't help hearing, Meg. Thank you for defending me, and Aunt March for proving that you *do* care for me a little bit."

"I didn't know how much, till she abused you," began Meg.

"And I needn't go away, but may stay and be happy—may I, dear?"

Here was another fine chance to make the crushing speech and the stately exit, but Meg never thought of doing either, and disgraced herself forever in Jo's eyes, by meekly whispering, "Yes, John," and hiding her face on Mr. Brooke's waistcoat.

Fifteen minutes after Aunt March's departure, Jo came softly down stairs, paused an instant at the parlor door, and, hearing no sound within, nodded and smiled, with a satisfied expression, saying to herself, "She has sent him away as we planned, and that affair is settled. I'll go and hear the fun, and have a good laugh over it."

But poor Jo never got her laugh, for she was transfixed upon the threshold by a spectacle which held her there, staring with her mouth nearly as wide open as her eyes. Going in to exult over a fallen enemy, and to praise a strong-minded sister for the banishment of an objectionable lover, it certainly *was* a shock to behold the aforesaid enemy serenely sitting on the sofa, with the strong-minded sister enthroned upon his knee, and wearing an expression of the most abject submission. Jo gave a sort of gasp, as if a cold shower-bath had suddenly fallen upon her,—for such an unexpected turning of the tables actually took her breath away. At the odd sound, the lovers turned and saw her. Meg jumped up, looking both proud and shy; but "that man," as Jo called him, actually laughed, and said, coolly, as he kissed the astonished new comer, "Sister Jo, congratulate us!"

That was adding insult to injury! it was altogether too much! and, making some wild demonstration with her hands, Jo vanished without a word. Rushing upstairs, she startled the invalids by exclaiming, tragically, as she burst into the room, "Oh, *do* somebody go down quick! John Brooke is acting dreadfully, and Meg likes it!"

Mr. and Mrs. March left the room with speed; and, casting herself upon the bed, Jo cried and scolded tempestuously as she told the awful news to Beth and Amy. The little girls, however, considered it a most agreeable and interesting event, and Jo got little comfort from them; so she went up to her refuge in the garret, and confided her troubles to the rats.

Nobody ever knew what went on in the parlor that afternoon; but a great deal of talking was done, and quiet Mr. Brooke astonished his friends by the eloquence and spirit with which he pleaded his suit, told his plans, and persuaded them to arrange everything just as he wanted it.

The tea-bell rang before he had finished describing the paradise which he meant to earn for Meg, and he proudly took her into supper, both looking so happy, that Jo hadn't the heart to be jealous or dismal. Amy was very much impressed by John's devotion and Meg's dignity. Beth beamed at them from a distance, while Mr. and Mrs. March surveyed the young couple with such tender satisfaction, that it was perfectly evident Aunt March was right in calling them as "unworldly as a pair of babies." No one ate much, but every one looked very happy, and the old room seemed to brighten up amazingly when the first romance of the family began there.

"You can't say 'nothing pleasant ever happens now,' can you, Meg?" said Amy, trying to decide how she would group the lovers in the sketch she was planning to make.

"No, I'm sure I can't. How much has happened since I said that! It seems a year ago," answered Meg, who was in a blissful dream, lifted far above such common things as bread and butter.

"The joys come close upon the sorrows this time, and I rather think the changes have begun," said Mrs. March. "In most families there comes, now and then, a year full of events; this has been such an one, but it ends well, after all."

"Hope the next will end better," muttered Jo, who found it very hard to see Meg absorbed in a stranger before her face; for Jo loved a few persons very dearly, and dreaded to have their affection lost or lessened in any way.

"I hope the third year from this *will* end better; I mean it shall, if I live to work out my plans," said Mr. Brooke, smiling at Meg, as if everything had become possible to him now.

"Doesn't it seem very long to wait?" asked Amy, who was in a hurry for the wedding.

"I've got so much to learn before I shall be ready, it seems a short time to me," answered Meg, with a sweet gravity in her face, never seen there before.

"You have only to wait. *I* am to do the work," said John, beginning his labors by picking up Meg's napkin, with an expression which caused Jo to shake her head, and then say to herself, with an air of relief, as the front door banged, "Here comes Laurie; now we shall have a little sensible conversation."

But Jo was mistaken; for Laurie came prancing in, overflowing with spirits, bearing a great bridal-looking bouquet for "Mrs. John Brooke," and evidently laboring under the delusion that the whole affair had been brought about by his excellent management.

"I knew Brooke would have it all his own way,—he always does; for when he makes up his mind to accomplish anything, it's done, though the sky falls," said Laurie, when he had presented his offering and his congratulations.

"Much obliged for that recommendation. I take it as a good omen for the future, and invite you to my wedding on the spot," answered Mr. Brooke, who felt at peace with all mankind, even his mischievous pupil.

"I'll come if I'm at the ends of the earth; for the sight of Jo's face alone, on that occasion, would be worth a long journey. You don't look festive, ma'am; what's the matter?" asked Laurie, following her into a corner of the parlor, whither all had adjourned to greet Mr. Laurence.

"I don't approve of the match, but I've made up my mind to bear it, and shall not say a word against it," said Jo, solemnly. "You can't know how hard it is for me to give up Meg," she continued, with a little quiver in her voice.

"You don't give her up. You only go halves," said Laurie, consolingly.

"It never can be the same again. I've lost my dearest friend," sighed Jo.

"You've got me, anyhow. I'm not good for much, I know; but I'll stand by you, Jo, all the days of my life; upon my word I will!" and Laurie meant what he said.

"I know you will, and I'm ever so much obliged; you are always a great comfort to me, Teddy," returned Jo, gratefully shaking hands.

"Well, now, don't be dismal, there's a good fellow. It's all right, you see. Meg is happy; Brooke will fly round and get settled immediately; grandpa will attend to him, and it will be very jolly to see Meg in her own little house. We'll have capital times after she is gone, for I shall be through college before long, and then we'll go abroad, or some nice trip or other. Wouldn't that console you?"

"I rather think it would; but there's no knowing what may happen in three years," said Jo, thoughtfully.

"That's true! Don't you wish you could take a look forward, and see where we shall all be then? I do," returned Laurie.

"I think not, for I might see something sad; and every one looks so happy now, I don't believe they could be much improved," and Jo's eyes went slowly round the room, brightening as they looked, for the prospect was a pleasant one.

Father and mother sat together quietly re-living the first chapter of the romance which for them began some twenty years ago. Amy was drawing the lovers, who sat apart in a beautiful world of their own, the light of which touched their faces with a grace the little artist could not copy. Beth lay on her sofa talking cheerily with her old friend, who held her little hand as if he felt that it possessed the power to lead him along the peaceful ways she walked. Jo lounged in her favorite low seat, with the grave, quiet look which best became her; and Laurie, leaning on the back of her chair, his chin on a level with her curly head, smiled with his friendliest aspect, and nodded at her in the long glass which reflected them both.

So grouped the curtain falls upon Meg, Jo, Beth and Amy. Whether it ever rises again, depends upon the reception given to the first act of the domestic drama, called "LITTLE WOMEN."[2]

1868

Constance Fenimore Woolson
(1840–1894)

Constance Fenimore Woolson was among the first generation of American women writers to regard themselves as artists, creating fiction for its cultural and aesthetic value rather than for moralistic or pecuniary reasons. Unlike such predecessors as Harriet Beecher Stowe, Susan Warner, Fanny Fern, and Louisa May Alcott, she did not need the money she earned by writing, nor did she see her short stories and novels as providing moral uplift for her readers. She was a close friend of Henry James's, and like him, she took her art seriously, for "art's sake" alone. In this respect she resembles the next generation of women writers, including Kate Chopin, Edith Wharton, and Gertrude Stein.

Born in 1840 in Claremont, New Hampshire, Woolson was a grandniece of James Fenimore Cooper. Woolson was the sixth child in her family, but after three of her older sisters died of scarlet fever, her parents moved the remaining children to Cleveland, Ohio, where Woolson grew up. Her father, Charles Woolson, manufactured stoves, making a good enough living to enable Woolson to attend Miss Hayden's School for Girls and the Cleveland Female Seminary. She was sent to Madame Chegaray's French "finishing school" in New York City in 1858 and graduated first in her class when she was 18 years old. Traveling with her family, she visited locations that were later to be featured in her fiction, including Mackinac

2. This first volume of *Little Women* was published in October 1868, the second in April 1869. The two volumes became one book in 1880; the second volume, omitted here, traces the March girls' progress toward marriage or death.

Island, between Lake Huron and Lake Michigan, and upstate New York.

During the Civil War, Woolson worked in a Union post office established for convalescent soldiers. After her father died in 1869, she became her mother's companion and traveled with her seasonally between New York and Florida. During her twenties, she wrote sketches, short fiction, and poems, but she did not pursue writing seriously until 1879, when her mother died and left her a small inheritance, enabling her to choose how and where she would live. Woolson went to Europe, where she spent the last fourteen years of her life, primarily in Italy. She began contributing sketches and short stories to American periodicals and was well received by editors and reviewers. Her first novel, *Anne* (1882), was a best-seller, selling 57,000 copies and making Woolson's name familiar among her contemporaries.

In Europe, Woolson met Henry James, whose novels she greatly admired, and the two became intimate friends, traveling together and exchanging ideas about writing projects. James borrowed the title of his story "The Figure in the Carpet" from Woolson's "Miss Grief," and he included her among such prominent novelists as George Eliot in his book of ruminative literary criticism, *Partial Portraits* (1888). Although James's biographer, Leon Edel, has portrayed Woolson as a lovesick spinster following the Master around Europe, recent biographical work on Woolson suggests a more balanced relation between the two authors. James is supposed to have suffered feelings of guilt over Woolson's death in 1894: she either jumped or fell from a second-story window in Venice, after weeks of feeling ill with influenza and a recurrent state of depression she battled every time she finished a major piece of writing.

Recent scholars tend to interpret Woolson's death as suicide, reading between the lines of her stories about doomed women artists and writers. Rejecting the traditional assumption that Woolson killed herself for thwarted love of Henry James, they point to themes in such stories as "Miss Grief" that reveal an acute awareness of the difficulties facing the nineteenth-century woman who wished to be taken seriously as a writer. In this story, the attitude of the narrator (a successful young male writer) and the publishers toward the woman writer's brilliant but "flawed" manuscripts reflect what Elaine Showalter has called the "critical double standard" of the literary establishment. The narrator's lack of interest in the faded, impoverished, unattractive woman he calls "Miss Grief" reflects the culture's evaluation of women: unless they are young and beautiful, they merit no attention. And when the narrator finally reads and admires the woman's inspired prose, he judges it by a masculine standard that ensures it will never find an audience. Woolson's own writing was less unconventional, more realistic than Miss Grief's visionary texts, and her own career far more successful than that of her fictional heroine. But the fact that her name has all but disappeared from literary history lends an element of allegorical truth to her heroine's fate.

Woolson's stories generally appeared first in periodicals, then in collections, including *The Old Stone House* (1872); *Castle Nowhere: Lake-Country Sketches* (1875); *Rodman the Keeper: Southern Sketches* (1880); *The Front Yard, and Other Italian Stories* (1896). In addition to *Anne*, her novels include *For the Major* (1883); *East Angels* (1886); *Jupiter Lights* (1889); and *Horace Chase* (1894).

An excellent literary biography is *Constance Fenimore Woolson: The Grief of Artistry* by Cheryl B. Torsney (1989); other studies include *Constance F. Woolson* by Rayburn Moore (1963) and *Constance Fenimore Woolson: Literary Pioneer* by John Dwight Kern (1934). Leon Edel's detailed account of her relationship with Henry James can be found in *Henry James: The Middle Years, 1882–1895* (1962).

"Miss Grief"

"A conceited fool" is a not uncommon expression. Now, I know that I am not a fool, but I also know that I am conceited. But, candidly, can it be helped if one happens to be young, well and strong, passably good looking, with some money that one has inherited and more that one has earned—in all, enough to make life comfortable—and if upon this foundation rests also the pleasant superstructure of a literary success? The success is deserved, I think: certainly it was not lightly gained. Yet even with this I fully appreciate its rarity. Thus, I find myself very well entertained in life: I have all I wish in the way of society, and a deep, though of course carefully concealed, satisfaction in my own little fame; which fame I foster by a gentle system of non-interference. I know that I am spoken of as "that quiet young fellow who writes those delightful little studies of society, you know"; and I live up to that definition.

A year ago I was in Rome, and enjoying life particularly. I had a large number of my acquaintances there, both American and English, and no day passed without its invitation. Of course I understood it: it is seldom that you find a literary man who is good tempered, well dressed, sufficiently provided with money, and amiably obedient to all the rules and require-ments of "society." "When found, make a note of it"; and the note was generally an invitation.

One evening, upon returning to my lodgings, my man Simpson informed me that a person had called in the afternoon, and upon learning that I was absent had left not a card, but her name—"Miss Grief." The title lingered—Miss Grief! "Grief has not so far visited me here," I said to myself, dismissing Simpson and seeking my little balcony for a final smoke, "and she shall not now. I shall take care to be 'not at home' to her if she continues to call." And then I fell to thinking of Isabel Abercrombie, in whose society I had spent that and many evenings: they were golden thoughts.

The next day there was an excursion; it was late when I reached my rooms, and again Simpson informed me that Miss Grief had called.

"Is she coming continuously?" I said, half to myself.

"Yes, sir: she mentioned that she should call again."

"How does she look?"

"Well, sir, a lady, but not so prosperous as she was, I should say," answered Simpson, discreetly.

"Young?"

"No, sir."

"Alone?"

"A maid with her, sir."

But once outside in my little high-up balcony with my cigar, I again forgot Miss Grief and whatever she might represent. Who would not forget in that moonlight, with Isabel Aber-crombie's face to remember?

The stranger came a third time, and I was absent; then she let two days pass, and began again. It grew to be a regular dialogue between Simpson and myself when I came in at night: "Grief today?"

"Yes, sir."

"What time?"

"Four, sir."

"Happy the man," I thought, "who can keep her confined to a particular hour!"

But I should not have treated my visitor so cavalierly if I had not felt sure that she was eccentric and unconventional—qualities extremely tiresome in a woman no longer young or attractive. If she were not eccentric, she would not have persisted in coming to my door day after day in this silent way, without stating her errand, leaving a note, or presenting her credentials in any shape. I made up my mind that she had something to sell—a bit of carving or some intaglio[1] supposed to be antique. It was known that I had a fancy for oddities. I said to myself, "She has read or heard of my 'Old Gold' story, or else 'The Buried God,' and she thinks me an idealizing ignoramus upon whom she can impose. Her sepulchral name is at least not Italian; probably she is a sharp countrywoman of mine, turning, by means of the present aesthetic craze, an honest penny when she can."

She had called seven times during a period of two weeks without seeing me, when one day I happened to be at home in the afternoon, owing to a pouring rain and a fit of doubt concerning Miss Abercrombie. For I had constructed a careful theory of that young lady's characteristics in my own mind, and she had lived up to it delightfully until the previous evening, when with one word she had blown it to atoms and taken flight, leaving me standing, as it were, on a desolate shore, with nothing but a handful of mistaken inductions wherewith to console myself. I do not know a more exasperating frame of mind, at least for a constructor of theories. I could not write, and so I took up a French novel (I model myself a little on Balzac).[2] I had been turning over its pages but a few moments when Simpson knocked, and, entering softly, said, with just a shadow of a smile on his well-trained face, "Miss Grief." I briefly consigned Miss Grief to all the Furies,[3] and then, as he still lingered—perhaps not knowing where they resided—I asked where the visitor was.

"Outside, sir—in the hall. I told her I would see if you were at home."

"She must be unpleasantly wet if she had no carriage."

"No carriage, sir; they always come on foot. I think she *is* a little damp, sir."

"Well, let her in; but I don't want the maid. I may as well see her now, I suppose, and end the affair."

"Yes, sir."

I did not put down my book. My visitor should have a hearing, but not much more: she had sacrificed her womanly claims by her persistent attacks upon my door. Presently Simpson ushered her in. "Miss Grief," he said, and then went out, closing the curtain behind him.

A woman—yes, a lady—but shabby, unattractive, and more than middle-aged.

I rose, bowed slightly, and then dropped into my chair again, still keeping the book in my hand. "Miss Grief?" I said interrogatively as I indicated a seat with my eyebrows.

"Not Grief," she answered—"Crief: my name is Crief."

She sat down, and I saw that she held a small flat box.

"Not carving, then," I thought—"Probably old lace, something that belonged to Tullia or Lucrezia Borgia."[4] But, as she did not speak, I found myself obliged to begin: "You have been here, I think, once or twice before?"

"Seven times; this is the eighth."

A silence.

"I am often out; indeed, I may say that I am never in," I remarked carelessly.

"Yes; you have many friends."

"—Who will perhaps buy old lace," I mentally added. But this time I too remained silent; why should I trouble myself to draw her out? She had sought me; let her advance her idea, whatever it was, now that entrance was gained.

But Miss Grief (I preferred to call her so) did not look as though she could advance anything: her black gown, damp with rain, seemed to retreat fearfully to her thin self, while her thin self retreated as far as possible from me, from the chair, from everything. Her eyes

1. A gemstone carved with a design cut beneath its surface.
2. Honoré de Balzac, a nineteenth-century French realist novelist, controversial in his day.
3. In Greek and Roman mythology, the Furies are the three serpent-haired goddesses who pursue and punish perpetrators of unavenged crimes.
4. The Borgias were a notorious family among the nobility of fifteenth- and sixteenth-century Italy, patrons of the arts.

were cast down; an old-fashioned lace veil with a heavy border shaded her face. She looked at the floor, and I looked at her.

I grew a little impatient, but I made up my mind that I would continue silent and see how long a time she would consider necessary to give due effect to her little pantomime. Comedy? Or was it tragedy? I suppose full five minutes passed thus in our double silence; and that is a long time when two persons are sitting opposite each other alone in a small still room.

At last my visitor, without raising her eyes, said slowly, "You are very happy, are you not, with youth, health, friends, riches, fame?"

It was a singular beginning. Her voice was clear, low, and very sweet as she thus enumerated my advantages one by one in a list. I was attracted by it, but repelled by her words, which seemed to me flattery both dull and bold.

"Thanks," I said, "for your kindness, but I fear it is undeserved. I seldom discuss myself even when with my friends."

"I am your friend," replied Miss Grief. Then, after a moment, she added slowly, "I have read every word you have written."

I curled the edges of my book indifferently; I am not a fop,[5] I hope, but—others have said the same.

"What is more, I know much of it by heart," continued my visitor. "Wait: I will show you"; and then, without pause, she began to repeat something of mine word for word, just as I had written it. On she went, and I—listened. I intended interrupting her after a moment, but I did not, because she was reciting so well, and also because I felt a desire gaining upon me to see what she would make of a certain conversation which I knew was coming—a conversation between two of my characters which was, to say the least, sphinx-like,[6] and somewhat incandescent as well. What won me a little, too, was the fact that the scene she was reciting (it was hardly more than that, though called a story) was secretly my favorite among all the sketches from my pen which a gracious public has received with favor. I never said so, but it was; and I had always felt a wondering annoyance that the aforesaid public, while kindly praising beyond their worth other attempts of mine, had never noticed the higher purpose of this little shaft, aimed not at the balconies and lighted windows of society, but straight up toward the distant stars. So she went on, and presently reached the conversation: my two people began to talk. She had raised her eyes now, and was looking at me soberly as she gave the words of the woman, quiet, gentle, cold, and the replies of the man, bitter, hot, and scathing. Her very voice changed, and took, though always sweetly, the different tones required, while no point of meaning, however small, no breath of delicate emphasis which I had meant, but which the dull types could not give, escaped an appreciative and full, almost overfull, recognition which startled me. For she had understood me—understood me almost better than I had understood myself. It seemed to me that while I had labored to interpret, partially, a psychological riddle, she, coming after, had comprehended its bearings better than I had, though confining herself strictly to my own words and emphasis. The scene ended (and it ended rather suddenly), she dropped her eyes, and moved her hand nervously to and fro over the box she held; her gloves were old and shabby, her hands small.

I was secretly much surprised by what I had heard, but my ill humor was deep-seated that day, and I still felt sure, besides, that the box contained something which I was expected to buy.

"You recite remarkably well," I said carelessly, "and I am much flattered also by your appreciation of my attempt. But it is not, I presume, to that alone that I owe the pleasure of this visit?"

5. A vain young man excessively preoccupied with his appearance.
6. Enigmatic. In Greek myth, the sphinx destroyed anyone who could not solve its riddle.

"Yes," she answered, still looking down, "it is, for if you had not written that scene I should not have sought you. Your other sketches are interiors—exquisitely painted and delicately finished, but of small scope. *This* is a sketch in a few bold, masterly lines—work of entirely different spirit and purpose."

I was nettled by her insight. "You have bestowed so much of your kind attention upon me that I feel your debtor," I said, conventionally. "It may be that there is something I can do for you—connected, possibly, with that little box?"

It was impertinent, but it was true; for she answered, "Yes."

I smiled, but her eyes were cast down and she did not see the smile.

"What I have to show you is a manuscript," she said after a pause which I did not break; "it is a drama. I thought that perhaps you would read it."

"An authoress! This is worse than old lace," I said to myself in dismay.—Then, aloud, "My opinion would be worth nothing, Miss Crief."

"Not in a business way, I know. But it might be—an assistance personally." Her voice had sunk to a whisper; outside, the rain was pouring steadily down. She was a very depressing object to me as she sat there with her box.

"I hardly think I have the time at present—" I began.

She had raised her eyes and was looking at me; then, when I paused, she rose and came suddenly toward my chair. "Yes, you will read it," she said with her hand on my arm—"you will read it. Look at this room; look at yourself; look at all you have. Then look at me, and have pity."

I had risen, for she held my arm, and her damp skirt was brushing my knees.

Her large dark eyes looked intently into mine as she went on: "I have no shame in asking. Why should I have? It is my last endeavor; but a calm and well-considered one. If you refuse I shall go away, knowing that Fate has willed it so. And I shall be content."

"She is mad," I thought. But she did not look so, and she had spoken quietly, even gently. "Sit down," I said, moving away from her. I felt as if I had been magnetized; but it was only the nearness of her eyes to mine, and their intensity. I drew forward a chair, but she remained standing.

"I cannot," she said in the same sweet, gentle tone, "unless you promise."

"Very well, I promise; only sit down."

As I took her arm to lead her to the chair, I perceived that she was trembling, but her face continued unmoved.

"You do not, of course, wish me to look at your manuscript now?" I said, temporizing; "it would be much better to leave it. Give me your address, and I will return it to you with my written opinion; though, I repeat, the latter will be of no use to you. It is the opinion of an editor or publisher that you want."

"It shall be as you please. And I will go in a moment," said Miss Grief, pressing her palms together, as if trying to control the tremor that had seized her slight frame.

She looked so pallid that I thought of offering her a glass of wine; then I remembered that if I did it might be a bait to bring her here again, and this I was desirous to prevent. She rose while the thought was passing through my mind. Her pasteboard box lay on the chair she had first occupied; she took it, wrote an address on the cover, laid it down, and then, bowing with a little air of formality, drew her black shawl round her shoulders and turned toward the door.

I followed, after touching the bell. "You will hear from me by letter," I said.

Simpson opened the door, and I caught a glimpse of the maid, who was waiting in the anteroom. She was an old woman, shorter than her mistress, equally thin, and dressed like her in rusty black. As the door opened she turned toward it a pair of small, dim, blue eyes with a look of furtive suspense. Simpson dropped the curtain, shutting me into the inner room; he had no intention of allowing me to accompany my visitor further. But I had the curiosity to go to a bay window in an angle from whence I could command the street door, and presently I saw them issue forth in the rain and walk away side by side, the mistress, being the taller, holding the umbrella: probably there was not much difference in rank between persons so poor and forlorn as these.

It grew dark. I was invited out for the evening, and I knew that if I should go I should meet Miss Abercrombie. I said to myself that I would not go. I got out my paper for writing, I made my preparations for a quiet evening at home with myself; but it was of no use. It all ended slavishly in my going. At the last allowable moment I presented myself, and—as a punishment for my vacillation, I suppose—I never passed a more disagreeable evening. I drove homeward in a murky temper; it was foggy without, and very foggy within. What Isabel really was, now that she had broken through my elaborately built theories, I was not able to decide. There was, to tell the truth, a certain young Englishman—But that is apart from this story.

I reached home, went up to my rooms, and had a supper. It was to console myself; I am obliged to console myself scientifically once in a while. I was walking up and down afterward, smoking and feeling somewhat better, when my eye fell upon the pasteboard box. I took it up; on the cover was written an address which showed that my visitor must have walked a long distance in order to see me: "A. Crief."—"A Grief," I thought; "and so she is. I positively believe she has brought all this trouble upon me: she has the evil eye." I took out the manuscript and looked at it. It was in the form of a little volume, and clearly written; on the cover was the word "Armor" in German text,[7] and, underneath, a pen-and-ink sketch of a helmet, breastplate, and shield.

"Grief certainly needs armor," I said to myself, sitting down by the table and turning over the pages. "I may as well look over the thing now; I could not be in a worse mood." And then I began to read.

Early the next morning Simpson took a note from me to the given address, returning with the following reply: "No; I prefer to come to you; at four; A. Crief." These words, with their three semicolons, were written in pencil upon a piece of coarse printing paper, but the handwriting was as clear and delicate as that of the manuscript in ink.

"What sort of a place was it, Simpson?"

"Very poor, sir, but I did not go all the way up. The elder person came down, sir, took the note, and requested me to wait where I was."

"You had no chance, then, to make inquiries?" I said, knowing full well that he had emptied the entire neighborhood of any information it might possess concerning these two lodgers.

"Well, sir, you know how these foreigners will talk, whether one wants to hear or not. But it seems that these two persons have been there but a few weeks; they live alone, and are uncommonly silent and reserved. The people round there call them something that signifies 'the Madames American, thin and dumb.'"

At four the "Madames American" arrived; it was raining again, and they came on foot under their old umbrella. The maid waited in the anteroom, and Miss Grief was ushered into my bachelor's parlor. I had thought that I should meet her with great deference; but she looked so forlorn that my deference changed to pity. It was the woman that impressed me then, more than the writer—the fragile, nerveless body more than the inspired mind. For it was inspired; I had sat up half the night over her drama, and had felt thrilled through and through more than once by its earnestness, passion, and power.

No one could have been more surprised than I was to find myself thus enthusiastic. I thought I had outgrown that sort of thing. And one would have supposed, too (I myself should have supposed so the day before), that the faults of the drama, which were many and prominent, would have chilled any liking I might have felt, I being a writer myself, and therefore critical; for writers are as apt to make much of the "how," rather than the "what," as painters, who, it is well known, prefer an exquisitely rendered representation of a commonplace theme to an imperfectly executed picture of even the most striking subject. But in this case, on the contrary, the scattered rays of splendor in Miss Grief's drama had made me

7. That is, in Fraktur, an elaborate, highly decorated typeface formerly used in German printing.

forget the dark spots, which were numerous and disfiguring; or, rather, the splendor had made me anxious to have the spots removed. And this also was a philanthropic state very unusual with me. Regarding unsuccessful writers, my motto had been "Væ victis!"[8]

My visitor took a seat and folded her hands; I could see, in spite of her quiet manner, that she was in breathless suspense. It seemed so pitiful that she should be trembling there before me—a woman so much older than I was, a woman who possessed the divine spark of genius, which I was by no means sure (in spite of my success) had been granted to me—that I felt as if I ought to go down on my knees before her, and entreat her to take her proper place of supremacy at once. But there! one does not go down on one's knees, combustively, as it were, before a woman over fifty, plain in feature, thin, dejected, and ill dressed. I contented myself with taking her hands (in their miserable old gloves) in mine, while I said cordially, "Miss Crief, your drama seems to me full of original power. It has roused my enthusiasm: I sat up half the night reading it."

The hands I held shook, but something (perhaps a shame for having evaded the knees business) made me tighten my hold and bestow upon her also a reassuring smile. She looked at me for a moment, and then, suddenly and noiselessly, tears rose and rolled down her cheeks. I dropped her hands and retreated. I had not thought her tearful: on the contrary, her voice and face had seemed rigidly controlled. But now here she was bending herself over the side of the chair with her head resting on her arms, not sobbing aloud, but her whole frame shaken by the strength of her emotion. I rushed for a glass of wine; I pressed her to take it. I did not quite know what to do, but, putting myself in her place, I decided to praise the drama; and praise it I did. I do not know when I have used so many adjectives. She raised her head and began to wipe her eyes.

"Do take the wine," I said, interrupting myself in my cataract[9] of language.

"I dare not," she answered; then added humbly, "that is, unless you have a biscuit here or a bit of bread."

I found some biscuit; she ate two, and then slowly drank the wine, while I resumed my verbal Niagara. Under its influence—and that of the wine too, perhaps—she began to show new life. It was not that she looked radiant—she could not—but simply that she looked warm. I now perceived what had been the principal discomfort of her appearance heretofore: it was that she had looked all the time as if suffering from a cold.

At last I could think of nothing more to say, and stopped. I really admired the drama, but I thought I had exerted myself sufficiently as an anti-hysteric, and that adjectives enough, for the present at least, had been administered. She had put down her empty wineglass, and was resting her hands on the broad cushioned arms of her chair with, for a thin person, a sort of expanded content.

"You must pardon my tears," she said, smiling; "it was the revulsion of feeling. My life was at a low ebb: if your sentence had been against me, it would have been my end."

"Your end?"

"Yes, the end of my life; I should have destroyed myself."

"Then you would have been a weak as well as wicked woman," I said in a tone of disgust. I do hate sensationalism.

"Oh no, you know nothing about it. I should have destroyed only this poor worn tenement of clay. But I can well understand how *you* would look upon it. Regarding the desirableness of life, the prince and the beggar may have different opinions. We will say no more of it, but talk of the drama instead." As she spoke the word "drama" a triumphant brightness came into her eyes.

8. Latin for "woe unto the vanquished" (Titus Livius, 5.8). The implication is that those who have been conquered are at the mercy of their conquerors.
9. A very large waterfall; a downpour.

I took the manuscript from a drawer and sat down beside her. "I suppose you know that there are faults," I said, expecting ready acquiescence.

"I was not aware that there were any," was her gentle reply.

Here was a beginning! After all my interest in her—and, I may say under the circumstances, my kindness—she received me in this way! However, my belief in her genius was too sincere to be altered by her whimsies; so I persevered. "Let us go over it together," I said. "Shall I read it to you, or will you read it to me?"

"I will not read it, but recite it."

"That will never do; you will recite it so well that we shall see only the good points, and what we have to concern ourselves with now is the bad ones."

"I will recite it," she repeated.

"Now, Miss Crief," I said bluntly, "for what purpose did you come to me? Certainly not merely to recite: I am no stage manager. In plain English, was it not your idea that I might help you in obtaining a publisher?"

"Yes, yes," she answered, looking at me apprehensively, all her old manner returning.

I followed up my advantage, opened the little paper volume and began. I first took the drama line by line, and spoke of the faults of expression and structure; then I turned back and touched upon two or three glaring impossibilities in the plot. "Your absorbed interest in the motive of the whole no doubt made you forget these blemishes," I said apologetically.

But, to my surprise, I found that she did not see the blemishes—that she appreciated nothing I had said, comprehended nothing. Such unaccountable obtuseness puzzled me. I began again, going over the whole with even greater minuteness and care. I worked hard: the perspiration stood in beads upon my forehead as I struggled with her—what shall I call it—obstinacy? But it was not exactly obstinacy. She simply could not see the faults of her own work, any more than a blind man can see the smoke that dims a patch of blue sky. When I had finished my task the second time, she still remained as gently impassive as before. I leaned back in my chair exhausted, and looked at her.

Even then she did not seem to comprehend (whether she agreed with it or not) what I must be thinking. "It is such a heaven to me that you like it!" she murmured dreamily, breaking the silence. Then, with more animation, "And *now* you will let me recite it?"

I was too weary to oppose her; she threw aside her shawl and bonnet, and standing in the center of the room, began.

And she carried me along with her: all the strong passages were doubly strong when spoken, and the faults, which seemed nothing to her, were made by her earnestness to seem nothing to me; at least for that moment. When it was ended, she stood looking at me with a triumphant smile.

"Yes," I said, "I like it, and you see that I do. But I like it because my taste is peculiar. To me originality and force are everything—perhaps because I have them not to any marked degree myself—but the world at large will not overlook as I do your absolutely barbarous shortcomings on account of them. Will you trust me to go over the drama and correct it at my pleasure?" This was a vast deal for me to offer; I was surprised at myself.

"No," she answered softly, still smiling. "There shall not be so much as a comma altered." Then she sat down and fell into a reverie as though she were alone.

"Have you written anything else?" I said after a while, when I had become tired of the silence.

"Yes."

"Can I see it? Or is it *them?*"

"It is *them*. Yes, you can see all."

"I will call upon you for the purpose."

"No, you must not," she said, coming back to the present nervously. "I prefer to come to you."

At this moment Simpson entered to light the room, and busied himself rather longer than was necessary over the task. When he finally went out, I saw that my visitor's manner had sunk into its former depression: the presence of the servant seemed to have chilled her.

"When did you say I might come?" I repeated, ignoring her refusal.

"I did not say it. It would be impossible."

"Well, then, when will you come here?" There was, I fear, a trace of fatigue in my tone.

"At your good pleasure, sir," she answered humbly.

My chivalry was touched by this: after all, she was a woman. "Come tomorrow," I said. "By the way, come and dine with me then; why not?" I was curious to see what she would reply.

"Why not, indeed? Yes, I will come. I am forty-three: I might have been your mother."

This was not quite true, as I am over thirty: but I look young, while she—Well, I had thought her over fifty. "I can hardly call you 'mother,' but we might compromise upon 'aunt,' " I said, laughing. "Aunt what?"

"My name is Aaronna," she gravely answered. "My father was much disappointed that I was not a boy, and gave me as nearly as possible the name he had prepared—Aaron."

"Then come and dine with me tomorrow, and bring with you the other manuscripts, Aaronna," I said, amused at the quaint sound of the name. On the whole, I did not like "aunt."

"I will come," she answered.

It was twilight and still raining, but she refused all offers of escort or carriage, departing with her maid, as she had come, under the brown umbrella. The next day we had the dinner. Simpson was astonished—and more than astonished, grieved—when I told him that he was to dine with the maid; but he could not complain in words, since my own guest, the mistress, was hardly more attractive. When our preparations were complete, I could not help laughing: the two prim little tables, one in the parlor and one in the anteroom, and Simpson disapprovingly going back and forth between them, were irresistible.

I greeted my guest hilariously[1] when she arrived, and, fortunately, her manner was not quite so depressed as usual: I could never have accorded myself with a tearful mood. I had thought that perhaps she would make, for the occasion, some change in her attire; I have never known a woman who had not some scrap of finery, however small, in reserve for that unexpected occasion of which she is ever dreaming. But no: Miss Grief wore the same black gown, unadorned and unaltered. I was glad that there was no rain that day, so that the skirt did not at least look so damp and rheumatic.

She ate quietly, almost furtively, yet with a good appetite, and she did not refuse the wine. Then, when the meal was over and Simpson had removed the dishes, I asked for the new manuscripts. She gave me an old green copybook filled with short poems, and a prose sketch by itself; I lit a cigar and sat down at my desk to look them over.

"Perhaps you will try a cigarette?" I suggested, more for amusement than anything else, for there was not a shade of Bohemianism[2] about her; her whole appearance was puritanical.

"I have not yet succeeded in learning to smoke."

"You have tried?" I said, turning round.

"Yes: Serena and I tried, but we did not succeed."

"Serena is your maid?"

"She lives with me."

I was seized with inward laughter, and began hastily to look over her manuscripts with my back toward her, so that she might not see it. A vision had risen before me of those two forlorn women, alone in their room with locked doors, patiently trying to acquire the smoker's art.

But my attention was soon absorbed by the papers before me. Such a fantastic collection of words, lines, and epithets I had never before seen, or even in dreams imagined. In truth,

---

1. With boisterous merriment.
2. A "Bohemian" is a person of artistic or literary

inclinations who disregards conventional behavior.

they were like the work of dreams: they were *Kubla Khan*,[3] only more so. Here and there was radiance like the flash of a diamond, but each poem, almost each verse and line, was marred by some fault or lack which seemed willful perversity, like the work of an evil sprite. It was like a case of jeweller's wares set before you, with each ring unfinished, each bracelet too large or too small for its purpose, each breastpin without its fastening, each necklace purposely broken. I turned the pages, marvelling. When about half an hour had passed, and I was leaning back for a moment to light another cigar, I glanced toward my visitor. She was behind me, in an easy chair before my small fire, and she was—fast asleep! In the relaxation of her unconsciousness I was struck anew by the poverty her appearance expressed; her feet were visible, and I saw the miserable worn old shoes which hitherto she had kept concealed.

After looking at her for a moment, I returned to my task and took up the prose story; in prose she must be more reasonable. She was less fantastic perhaps, but hardly more reasonable. The story was that of a profligate and commonplace man forced by two of his friends, in order not to break the heart of a dying girl who loves him, to live up to a high imaginary ideal of himself which her pure but mistaken mind has formed. He has a handsome face and sweet voice, and repeats what they tell them. Her long, slow decline and happy death, and his own inward ennui and profound weariness of the rôle he has to play, made the vivid points of the story. So far, well enough, but here was the trouble: through the whole narrative moved another character, a physician of tender heart and exquisite mercy, who practiced murder as a fine art, and was regarded (by the author) as a second Messiah! This was monstrous. I read it through twice, and threw it down; then, fatigued, I turned round and leaned back, waiting for her to wake. I could see her profile against the dark hue of the easy chair.

Presently she seemed to feel my gaze, for she stirred, then opened her eyes. "I have been asleep," she said, rising hurriedly.

"No harm in that, Aaronna."

But she was deeply embarrassed and troubled, much more so than the occasion required; so much so, indeed, that I turned the conversation back upon the manuscripts as a diversion. "I cannot stand that doctor of yours," I said, indicating the prose story; "no one would. You must cut him out."

Her self-possession returned as if by magic. "Certainly not," she answered haughtily.

"Oh, if you do not care—I had labored under the impression that you were anxious these things should find a purchaser."

"I am, I am," she said, her manner changing to deep humility with wonderful rapidity. With such alternations of feeling as this sweeping over her like great waves, no wonder she was old before her time.

"Then you must take out that doctor."

"I am willing, but do not know how," she answered, pressing her hands together helplessly. "In my mind he belongs to the story so closely that he cannot be separated from it."

Here Simpson entered, bringing a note for me: it was a line from Mrs. Abercrombie[4] inviting me for that evening—an unexpected gathering, and therefore likely to be all the more agreeable. My heart bounded in spite of me; I forgot Miss Grief and her manuscripts for the moment as completely as though they had never existed. But, bodily, being still in the same room with her, her speech brought me back to the present.

"You have had good news?" she said.

"Oh no, nothing especial—merely an invitation."

"But good news also," she repeated. "And now, as for me, I must go."

Not supposing that she would stay much later in any case, I had that morning ordered a

---

3. A fragment of a poem written by Samuel Taylor Coleridge in 1797. The poet recorded a series of vivid images that had come to him in a dream; but he lost the images when he was interrupted and could not finish the poem.

4. Isabel's mother.

carriage to come for her at about that hour. I told her this. She made no reply beyond putting on her bonnet and shawl.

"You will hear from me soon," I said; "I shall do all I can for you."

She had reached the door, but before opening it she stopped, turned and extended her hand. "You are good," she said: "I give you thanks. Do not think me ungrateful or envious. It is only that you are young, and I am so—so old." Then she opened the door and passed through the anteroom without pause, her maid accompanying her and Simpson with gladness lighting the way. They were gone. I dressed hastily and went out—to continue my studies in psychology.

Time passed; I was busy, amused and perhaps a little excited (sometimes psychology is exciting). But, though much occupied with my own affairs, I did not altogether neglect my self-imposed task of regarding Miss Grief. I began by sending her prose story to a friend, the editor of a monthly magazine, with a letter making a strong plea for its admittance. It should have a chance first on its own merits. Then I forwarded the drama to a publisher, also an acquaintance, a man with a taste for phantasms and a soul above mere common popularity, as his own coffers knew to their cost. This done, I waited with conscience clear.

Four weeks passed. During this waiting period I heard nothing from Miss Grief. At last one morning came a letter from my editor. "The story has force, but I cannot stand that doctor," he wrote. "Let her cut him out, and I might print it." Just what I myself had said. The package lay there on my table, travel worn and grimed; a returned manuscript is, I think, the most melancholy object on earth. I decided to wait, before writing to Aaronna, until the second letter was received. A week later it came. "Armor" was declined. The publisher had been "impressed" by the power displayed in certain passages, but the "impossibilities of the plot" rendered it "unavailable for publication"—in fact, would "bury it in ridicule" if brought before the public, a public "lamentably" fond of amusement, "seeking it, undaunted, even in the cannon's mouth." I doubt if he knew himself what he meant. But one thing, at any rate, was clear: "Armor" was declined.

Now, I am, as I have remarked before, a little obstinate. I was determined that Miss Grief's work should be received. I would alter and improve it myself, without letting her know: the end justified the means. Surely the sieve of my own good taste, whose mesh had been pronounced so fine and delicate, would serve for two. I began; and utterly failed.

I set to work first upon "Armor." I amended, altered, left out, put in, pieced, condensed, lengthened; I did my best, and all to no avail. I could not succeed in completing anything that satisfied me, or that approached, in truth, Miss Grief's own work just as it stood. I suppose I went over that manuscript twenty times: I covered sheets of paper with my copies. But the obstinate drama refused to be corrected; as it was it must stand or fall.

Wearied and annoyed, I threw it aside and took up the prose story: that would be easier. But, to my surprise, I found that the apparently gentle "doctor" would not out: he was so closely interwoven with every part of the tale that to take him out was like taking out one especial figure in a carpet: that is, impossible, unless you unravel the whole. At last I did unravel the whole, and then the story was no longer good, or Aaronna's: it was weak, and mine. All this took time, for of course I had much to do in connection with my own life and tasks. But, though slowly and at my leisure, I really did try my best as regarded Miss Grief, and without success. I was forced at last to make up my mind that either my own powers were not equal to the task, or else that her perversities were as essential a part of her work as her inspirations, and not to be separated from it. Once during this period I showed two of the short poems to Isabel, withholding of course the writer's name. "They were written by a woman," I explained.

"Her mind must have been disordered, poor thing!" Isabel said in her gentle way when she returned them—"at least, judging by these. They are hopelessly mixed and vague."

Now, they were not vague so much as vast. But I knew that I could not make Isabel comprehend it, and (so complex a creature is man) I do not know that I wanted her to comprehend it. These were the only ones in the whole collection that I would have shown her, and I was rather glad that she did not like even these. Not that poor Aaronna's poems were evil: they were simply unrestrained, large, vast, like the skies or the wind. Isabel was bounded on all sides, like a violet in a garden bed. And I liked her so.

One afternoon, about the time when I was beginning to see that I could not "improve" Miss Grief, I came upon the maid. I was driving, and she had stopped on the crossing to let the carriage pass. I recognized her at a glance (by her general forlornness), and called to the driver to stop. "How is Miss Grief?" I said. "I have been intending to write to her for some time."

"And your note, when it comes," answered the old woman on the crosswalk fiercely, "she shall not see."

"What?"

"I say she shall not see it. Your patronizing face shows that you have no good news, and you shall not rack and stab her any more on *this* earth, please God, while I have authority."

"Who has racked or stabbed her, Serena?"

"Serena, indeed! Rubbish! I'm no Serena: I'm her aunt. And as to who has racked and stabbed her, I say you, *you*—YOU literary men!" She had put her old head inside my carriage, and flung out these words at me in a shrill, menacing tone. "But she shall die in peace in spite of you," she continued. "Vampires! You take her ideas and fatten on them, and leave her to starve. You know you do—*you* who have had her poor manuscripts these months and months!"

"Is she ill?" I asked in real concern, gathering that much at least from the incoherent tirade.

"She is dying," answered the desolate old creature, her voice softening and her dim eyes filling with tears.

"Oh, I trust not. Perhaps something can be done. Can I help you in any way?"

"In all ways if you would," she said, breaking down and beginning to sob weakly, with her head resting on the sill of the carriage window. "Oh, what have we not been through together, we two! Piece by piece I have sold all."

I am goodhearted enough, but I do not like to have old women weeping across my carriage door. I suggested, therefore, that she should come inside and let me take her home. Her shabby old skirt was soon beside me, and, following her directions, the driver turned toward one of the most wretched quarters of the city, the abode of poverty, crowded and unclean. Here, in a large bare chamber up many flights of stairs, I found Miss Grief.

As I entered I was startled: I thought she was dead. There seemed no life present until she opened her eyes, and even then they rested upon us vaguely, as though she did not know who we were. But as I approached a light came into them: she recognized me, and this sudden revivification, this return of the soul to the almost deserted body, was the most wonderful thing I ever saw. "You have good news of the drama?" she whispered as I bent over her: "tell me. I *know* you have good news."

What was I to answer? Pray, what would you have answered, puritan?

"Yes, I have good news, Aaronna," I said. "The drama will appear." (And who knows? Perhaps it will in some other world.)

She smiled, and her now brilliant eyes did not leave my face.

"He knows I'm your aunt: I told him," said the old woman, coming to the bedside.

"Did you?" whispered Miss Grief, still gazing at me with a smile. "Then please, dear Aunt Martha, give me something to eat."

Aunt Martha hurried across the room, and I followed her. "It's the first time she's asked for food in weeks," she said in a husky tone.

She opened a cupboard door vaguely, but I could see nothing within. "What have you for her?" I asked with some impatience, though in a low voice.

"Please God, nothing!" answered the poor old woman, hiding her reply and her tears behind the broad cupboard door. "I was going out to get a little something when I met you."

"Good Heavens! is it money you need? Here, take this and send; or go yourself in the carriage waiting below."

She hurried out breathless, and I went back to the bedside, much disturbed by what I had seen and heard. But Miss Grief's eyes were full of life, and as I sat down beside her she whispered earnestly, "Tell me."

And I did tell her—a romance invented for the occasion. I venture to say that none of my published sketches could compare with it. As for the lie involved, it will stand among my few good deeds, I know, at the judgment bar.

And she was satisfied. "I have never known what it was," she whispered, "to be fully happy until now." She closed her eyes, and when the lids fell I again thought that she had passed away. But no, there was still pulsation in her small, thin wrist. As she perceived my touch she smiled. "Yes, I am happy," she said again, though without audible sound.

The old aunt returned; food was prepared, and she took some. I myself went out after wine that should be rich and pure. She rallied a little, but I did not leave her: her eyes dwelt upon me and compelled me to stay, or rather my conscience compelled me. It was a damp night, and I had a little fire made. The wine, fruit, flowers, and candles I had ordered made the bare place for the time being bright and fragrant. Aunt Martha dozed in her chair from sheer fatigue—she had watched many nights—but Miss Grief was awake, and I sat beside her.

"I make you my executor," she murmured, "as to the drama. But my other manuscripts place, when I am gone, under my head, and let them be buried with me. They are not many—those you have and these. See!"

I followed her gesture, and saw under her pillows the edges of two more copybooks like the one I had. "Do not look at them—my poor dead children!" she said tenderly. "Let them depart with me—unread, as I have been."

Later she whispered, "Did you wonder why I came to you? It was the contrast. You were young—strong—rich—praised—loved—successful: all that I was not. I wanted to look at you—and imagine how it would feel. You had success—but I had the greater power. Tell me, did I not have it?"

"Yes, Aaronna."

"It is all in the past now. But I am satisfied."

After another pause she said with a faint smile, "Do you remember when I fell asleep in your parlor? It was the good and rich food. It was so long since I had had food like that!"

I took her hand and held it, conscience stricken, but now she hardly seemed to perceive my touch. "And the smoking?" she whispered. "Do you remember how you laughed? I saw it. But I had heard that smoking soothed—that one was no longer tired and hungry—with a cigar."

In little whispers of this sort, separated by long rests and pauses, the night passed. Once she asked if her aunt was asleep, and when I answered in the affirmative she said, "Help her to return home—to America: the drama will pay for it. I ought never to have brought her away."

I promised, and she resumed her bright-eyed silence.

I think she did not speak again. Toward morning the change came, and soon after sunrise, with her old aunt kneeling by her side, she passed away.

All was arranged as she had wished. Her manuscripts, covered with violets, formed her pillow. No one followed her to the grave save her aunt and myself; I thought she would prefer it so. Her name was not "Crief," after all, but "Moncrief"; I saw it written out by Aunt Martha for the coffin plate, as follows: "Aaronna Moncrief, aged forty-three years, two months, and eight days."

I never knew more of her history than is written here. If there was more that I might have learned, it remained unlearned, for I did not ask.

And the drama? I keep it here in this locked case. I could have had it published at my own expense; but I think that now she knows its faults herself, perhaps, and would not like it.

I keep it; and, once in a while, I read it over—not as a *memento mori*[5] exactly, but rather as a memento of my own good fortune, for which I should continually give thanks. The want

5. A reminder of death.

of one grain made all her work void, and that one grain was given to me. She, with the greater power, failed—I, with the less, succeeded. But no praise is due to me for that. When I die "Armor" is to be destroyed unread: not even Isabel is to see it. For women will misunderstand each other; and, dear and precious to me as my sweet wife is, I could not bear that she or anyone should cast so much as a thought of scorn upon the memory of the writer, upon my poor dead, "unavailable," unaccepted "Miss Grief."

1880

Sarah Morgan
(1842–1909)

One of the most interesting Civil War diaries was begun in Baton Rouge, Louisiana, in January 1862 by Sarah Morgan, a woman not quite 20 years old. Not long before she began to write, her father had died, and not long before that she lost a favorite brother in a duel. Three other brothers were soon absent, fighting on the Confederate side; two did not survive the war. A brother-in-law was a Union army officer in California. A half-brother supported the Union cause in New Orleans. With her mother and a sister, she attempted to keep up the family home in Baton Rouge during the federal occupation, fled from it under threat of bombardment, returned to find it pillaged, and sought safety in other places in Louisiana, including, finally, New Orleans, where she lived under the protection of her pro-Union half-brother.

Born in New Orleans, Sarah Ida Fowler Morgan was the daughter of Thomas Gibbes Morgan, a lawyer, born in New Jersey and reared in Pennsylvania, who had come to Baton Rouge in the 1820s. Her mother, Thomas Morgan's second wife, was also a Northerner by birth, but the family owned slaves and considered themselves a part of the Southern aristocracy. Opposed to secession at first, they chose in the end to place their loyalties with the Confederacy.

After the war, Sarah Morgan never again lived in Baton Rouge. Living in South Carolina in the 1870s, she began a modest literary career, publishing essays on the role of women and a few pieces of fiction in newspapers and magazines. Her marriage to Frank Dawson, editor of the Charleston *News and Courier,* lasted fifteen years, ending when he was murdered in 1889. Ten years later, she went to live with her son Warrington Dawson in Paris, where she continued her literary activity and finally died.

Her diary invites comparison with Mary Chesnut's, also by a Southern woman. Chesnut was older and much closer to the affairs of the Confederacy and the progress of the war. Morgan's account of life far from the centers of power gives a good sense of the day-to-day life of an ordinary Southerner. It is also an account of an unrepentant rebel who is yet true to her feelings for relatives on the other side and honest enough to grant faults and report virtue and honor wherever she finds them. Not least interesting is her habit of continual introspection, questioning her own feelings and motivations in a work in which she once writes "I am so sick of me, me, everlasting Me! Can't I find a new subject?" In places her probing analysis is almost novelistic.

The diary first appeared, edited and with an introduction by her son Warrington Dawson, as Sarah

Morgan Dawson, *A Confederate Girl's Diary* (1915). More complete is *The Civil War Diary of Sarah Morgan* (1991), edited by Charles East. Selections below are from the East edition. A few of Sarah Morgan's irregularities of spelling have been here silently corrected.

FROM THE CIVIL WAR DIARY OF SARAH MORGAN

March 31st 1862. [Baton Rouge]

For a young woman who pretends to such a feeling of contempt for all egotism, and self conceit, it strikes me, on looking back a page or two, that I my self have displayed an inordinate amount of it. The question is where did it all come from? for really "public opinion" says I am not *very* egotistical, and of course no one would dispute the point, in consequence of that decree being infallible. Fact is, I am trying myself. I want to see how it feels to play "Ego sum" constantly, as well as occasionally. I would become a perfect bore if I talked of myself any more than I do, so I take refuge in writing all that is too preposterous to say aloud. Besides, one's diary is surely private property, and there is no more fitting place for talking about the only inexhaustible subject in the world, the only one of which we never tire, namely—yourself. I assume the right then, of talking about myself as much as I please, satisfied that no one will take the trouble of saying for me, what I do not first say for myself. I mean to record some few of my fancies now, that I may have the pleasure of contrasting them with those of a few years hence, to see whether I have become a better girl, or a worse.

April 26th 1862.

There is no word in the English language which can express the state in which we are all now, and have been for the last three days. Day before yesterday news came early in the morning of three of the enemy's boats passing the forts, and then the excitement commenced, and increased so rapidly on hearing of the sinking of eight of our gunboats in the engagement, the capture of the forts, and last night, of the burning of the wharves and cotton in the city,[1] while the Yankees were taking possession, that today the excitement has reached almost the crazy point. I believe that I am one of the most self possessed in my small circle of acquaintance, and yet, I feel such a craving for news from Miriam,[2] and mother and Jimmy,[3] who are in the city, such patriotic and enthusiastic sentiments, etc, that I believe I am as crazy as the rest, and it is all humbug when they tell me I am cool.

Nothing can be heard positively, for every report *except that our gunboats were sunk, and theirs coming up to the city,* has been contradicted, until we do not really know whether it is in their possession or not. We only know we had best be prepared for anything, so day before yesterday Lilly[4] and I secured what little jewelry we had, that may yet be of value to us if we *must* run. I vow I will not move one step, unless forced away! I remain here, come what will.

We went this morning to see the cotton burning, a sight which was never before presented to our view, and probably never will be again. Wagons and drays, and everything that could be driven, or rolled along were to be seen in every direction loaded with the bales, and taking

1. New Orleans. Once the Union fleet managed to pass Fort Jackson and Fort St. Philip, which guarded the river approach to New Orleans, the city's fate was decided. The Confederate river defense forces were no match for David G. Farragut's flotilla of sloops, gunboats, and mortar vessels. On April 29 the Federals occupied the city [East's note].
2. A sister.
3. A brother.
4. Another sister.

them a few squares back, to burn on the commons. Negroes were running around cutting them open, piling them up, and setting fire to them, all as busy as though they hoped to obtain their salvation by fooling the Yankees. Later, Charlie[5] sent for us to come to the river, and see him fire a flatboat loaded with the precious material for which the Yankees are risking their bodies and souls to obtain. Up and down the levee, as far as we could see, negroes were rolling it down to the brink of the river, where they would set them afire, and push them in, to float burning down the tide, each sending up its wreath of smoke and looking like so many little steamers puffing away—only I doubt that there are as many boats from the source, to the mouth of the river.

The flat boat was piled with as many bales as it could possibly hold without sinking, most of them cut open, while negroes staved in the heads of barrels of alcohol, whisky, etc. and dashed buckets of it over the cotton, while others built up little chimneys of wood every few feet, lined with pine knots and loose cotton, to set it afire. There, piled the length of the whole levee, or burning in the river, lay the work of thousands of negroes for more than a year gone by. It had come from all directions, but many men stood by who could claim an interest in the cotton that was burning, or was waiting to be burned, and either looked on, or helped with cheerfulness. Charlie only owned some sixteen bales—a matter of some fifteen hundred dollars, but he was head man of the whole affair, and burned other people's as well as his own. A single barrel of the whisky that was thrown on the cotton cost the man who gave it one hundred and twenty-five. It shows what a nation in earnest is capable of doing.

Only two men got on the flat boat with Charlie when it was ready, when it was towed into the middle of the river, set on fire in every direction, and then they jumped into a little skiff fastened in front, and rowed back to land, leaving the cotton floating down the Mississippi one sheet of living flame, even in the strong sunlight. It would have been a glorious sight at night; but we will have fun watching it this evening anyway, for they cannot get through to day, though no time is to be lost. Hundreds of bales remain still untouched, and they are all to go with the others. An incredible amount of property has been destroyed today, but nobody begrudges it. Every grog shop has been emptied, and gutters and pavements [are] floating with liquors of all kinds, so that if the Yankees are fond of strong drink, I fear they will fare ill.

Yesterday, Mr Hutchinson and a Dr Moffat stopped here to see me, but as I was not in, and they had but a moment to stay, they told their errand to Lilly. They wanted to tell me Jimmy was safe, that though sick in bed he had sprung up, and rushed to the wharf at the first tap of the alarm bell in the city; but as nothing was to be done, he would probably be home with Mother and Miriam today—I have seen or heard nothing of them since, though. The McRae,[6] he said went to the bottom, with the others; he did not know if any one had escaped. God be praised that Jimmy was not on her! The boat he was appointed to, is not yet finished, so he is saved. I was distressed about Capt Huger,[7] and could not help dropping just one tear; but then I remembered Miss Cammack might forget it was because I was grateful for his kindness to Jimmy, and might think it *too* tender, so I stopped. O I hope he escaped! I can tell him how frightened we were then, and have a laugh.

Mr Hutchinson was on his way above, on some ship, going to join the others where the final battle on the Mississippi is to be fought, and had not time to sit down even; and I felt doubly thankful to him for his kindness, remembering that this was the very man Jimmy thrashed not a month ago, on the McRae, and was sorry I could not see him to thank him in person. Lilly was so excited, that she gave him a letter I had written to George[8] just before going out, and begged of him to address it for me, and mail it at Vicksburg, or somewhere else, for no mail will ever leave *here* for Norfolk for some time to come. The fun of it is he

5. Her brother-in-law, John Charles LaNoue, husband of Lilly (Eliza Ann).
6. A Confederate ship that Jimmy Morgan had served on.
7. Commander of the *McRae*.
8. Another brother, serving in the Confederate army.

does not know George, though he gladly undertook the charge, and promised to remember the address which, Lilly told him, was *Richmond!*

Well! if the Yankees *do* get it, they will find only a crazy scrawl, for I was so intensely excited that though I wanted to calm his anxiety about us, I could write nothing but "dont mind us; we are safe; fight, George fight!" until the repetition was perfectly ludicrous. I hardly knew *what* I said, I was so anxious for him to remain where he is, and defend us. Ah Mr Yankee! if you had nothing in the world but your brothers, and their lives hanging on a thread, *you* would write crazy letters too! And if you want to know what an excited girl is capable of, call around, and I will show you the use of a small seven shooter, and large carving knife which vibrate between my belt, and pocket, always ready for use. ***

May 30th Greenwell.[9]

After all our trials and tribulations, here we are at last, and no limbs lost! How many weeks ago was it since I wrote here? It seems very long after all these events; let me try to recal[l] them. Wednesday the 28th—a day to be for ever remembered—as luck would have it, we rose very early, and had breakfast sooner than usual, it would seem for the express design of becoming famished before dinner. I picked up some of my letters and papers, and set them where I could find them whenever we were ready to go to Greenwell, burning a pile of trash, and leaving a quantity equally worthless, which were of no value even to myself, except from association. I was packing up my traveling desk with all Harry's little articles that were left me, and other things, and saying (to myself) that my affairs were in such confusion, that if obliged to run unexpectedly I would not know what to save, when I heard Lilly's voice down stairs crying as she ran in—she had been out shopping—"Mr Castle[1] has killed a Federal officer on a ship, and they are going to shell—" Bang! went a cannon at the word, and that was all our warning.

Mother had just come in, and was lying down, but sprang to her feet and added her screams to the general confusion. Miriam who had been searching the libraries ran up to quiet her. Lilly gathered her children crying hysterically all the time, and ran to the front door with them as they were; Lucy[2] saved the baby, naked as she took her from her bath, only throwing a quilt over her. I bethought me of my "running" bag which I had used on a former case, and in a moment my few precious articles were secured under my hoops, and with a sunbonnet on, [I] stood ready for any thing.

The firing still continued; they must have fired half a dozen times before we could coax mother off. What awful screams! I had hoped never to hear them again, after Harry[3] died. Charlie had gone to Greenwell before daybreak, to prepare the house, so we four women, with all these children and servants, were left to save ourselves. I did not forget my poor little Jimmy; (by the way, I always thought it a he-bird until she surprised me by laying ten eggs in rapid succession.) I caught up his cage, and ran down, just at this moment mother recovered enough to insist on saving father's papers—which was impossible, as she had not an idea of where the important ones were—I heard Miriam plead, argue, insist, command her to run, Lilly shriek, and cry she should go, the children screaming within, women running by without, crying and moaning, but I could not join in. I was going I knew not where; it was impossible to take my bird, for even if I could carry him, he would starve. So I took him out of his cage, kissed his little yellow head, and tossed him up. He gave one feeble little chirp as if uncertain where to go, and then for the first and last time I cried, laying my head against the gate post, and with my eyes too dim to see him. O how it hurt me to lose my little bird, one Jimmy had given me, too!

9. Greenwell Springs, 15 miles northeast of Baton Rouge.
1. A Confederate guerrilla.
2. One of the house slaves, or servants.
3. Her brother, killed in a duel in 1861.

But the next minute we were all off, in safety. A square from home, I discovered that boy shoes were not the most comfortable things to run in, so ran back, in spite of cannonading, entreaties, etc, to get another pair. I got home, found an old pair that were by no means respectable which I seized without hesitation, and being perfectly at ease, thought it would be so nice to save at least Miriam's, and my toothbrushes, so slipped them in my corsets. These in, of course we must have a comb—that was added—then how could we stand the sun without starch to cool our faces? This included the powder bag, then I must save that beautiful lace collar, and my hair was tumbling down, so in went the tucking comb and hair pins with the rest, until, if there had been any one to speculate, they would have wondered a long while at the singular appearance of a girl who is considered as very slight, usually. By this time, Miriam, alarmed for me, returned to find me, though urged by Dr Castleton not to risk her life by attempting it, and we started off together. We had hardly gone a square, when we decided to return a second time, and get at least a few articles for the children and ourselves, who had nothing except what we happened to have on when the shelling commenced. She picked up any little thing and threw them to me, while I filled a pillow-case jerked from the bed, and placed my powder and brushes in it with the rest. Before we could leave, mother, alarmed for both, came to find us, with Tiche.[4] All this time they had been shelling, but there was quite a lull when she got there, and she commenced picking up father's papers, vowing all the time she would not leave.

Every argument we could use, was of no avail, and we were desperate as to what course to pursue, when the shelling recommenced in a few minutes. Then mother recommenced her screams and was ready to fly any where, and holding her box of papers, with a faint idea of saving something, she picked up two dirty underskirts and an old cloak, and by dint of Miriam's vehement appeals, aided by a great deal of pulling, we got her down to the back door. We had given our pillow case to Tiche, who added another bundle, and all our silver to it, and had already departed.

As we stood in the door, four or five shells sailed over our heads at the same time, seeming to make a perfect corkscrew of the air—for it sounded as though it went in circles. Miriam cried never mind the door! Mother screamed anew, and I staid behind to lock the door, with this new music in my ears. We [had] reached the back gate, that was on the street, when another shell passed us, and Miriam jumped behind the fence for protection. We had only gone half a square when Dr Castleton begged of us to take another street, as they were firing up that one. We took his advice, but found our new street worse than the old, for the shells seemed to whistle their strange songs with redoubled vigor. The height of my ambition was now attained. I had heard Jimmy laugh about the singular sensation produced by the rifled balls spinning around one's head, and here I heard the same peculiar sound, ran the same risk, and was equal to the rest of the boys, for was I not in the midst of flying shells, in the middle of a bombardment? I think I was rather proud of it.

We were alone on the road; all had run away before, so I thought it was for our especial entertainment, this little affair. I cannot remember how long it lasted; I am positive that the clock struck ten before I left home, but I had been up so long, I know not what time it began, though I am told it was between eight and nine. We passed the graveyard; we did not even stop, and about a mile and a half from home, when mother was perfectly exhausted with fatigue and unable to proceed farther, we met a gentleman in a buggy who kindly took charge of her and our bundles. We could have walked miles beyond, then, for as soon as she was safe we felt as though a load had been removed from our shoulders; and after exhorting her not to be uneasy about us, and reminding her we had a pistol and a dagger—I had secured a "for true" one the day before, fortunately—she drove off, and we trudged on alone, the only people in sight, on foot, though occasionally carriages and buggies would pass, going towards town.

4. Catiche, a slave.

One party of gentlemen put their heads out and one said "There are Judge Morgan's daughters sitting by the road!" but I observed he did not offer them the slightest assistance. However others were very kind, and one I never heard of, volunteered to go for us, and bring us to mother, when she was uneasy about our staying so long, when we went home to get clothes. We heard him ring and knock, but thinking it must be next door, paid no attention so he went back, and mother came herself.

We were two miles away when we sat down by the road to rest, and have a laugh. Here were two women married, and able to take care of themselves, flying for their lives and leaving two lorn girls alone on the road, to protect each other! To be sure, neither could help us, and one was not able to walk, and the other had helpless children to save, but it was so funny when we talked about it, and thought how sorry both would be when they regained their reason! While we were yet resting, we saw a cart coming, and giving up all idea of our walking to Greenwell, called the people to stop. To our great delight, it proved to be a cart loaded with Mrs. Brunot's[5] affairs, driven by two of her negroes, who kindly took us up with them, on the top of their baggage, and we drove off in state, as much pleased at riding in that novel place, as though we were accustomed to ride in wheelbarrows. Miriam was in a hollow between a flour barrel and a mattress, and I at the end, astride, I am afraid, of a tremendous bundle; for my face was turned down the road, and each foot was resting very near the sides of the cart. I tried to make a better arrangement though, after a while. These servants were good enough to lend us their umbrella, with out which I am afraid we would have suffered severely, for the day was intensely warm.

Three miles from town we began to overtake the fugitives. Hundreds of women and children were walking along, some bare headed, and in all costumes. Little girls of twelve and fourteen were wandering on alone. I called to one I knew, and asked where her mother was; she didn't know; she would walk on until she found out. It seems her mother lost a nursing baby too, which was not found until ten that night. White and black were all mixed together, and were as confidential as though related. All called to us and asked where we were going, and many we knew, laughed at us for riding on a cart; but as they had walked only five miles, I imagined they would like even these poor accommodations, if they were in their reach.

The negroes deserve the greatest praise for their conduct. Hundreds were walking with babies, or bundles; ask them what they had saved, it was invariably "My mistress's clothes, or silver, or baby." Ask what they had for themselves, it was "Bless your heart honey, I was glad to get away with mistress things; I didn't think 'bout mine."

It was a heartrending scene. Women searching for their babies along the road, where they had been lost, others sitting in the dust crying and wringing their hands, for by this time, we had not an idea but what Baton Rouge was either in ashes, or being plundered, and we had saved nothing. I had one dress, Miriam two, but Tiche had them, and we had lost her, before we left home.

Presently we came on a Guerrilla camp. Men and horses were resting on each side of the road, some sick, some moving about carrying water to the women and children, and all looking like a monster Barbecue, for as far as the eye could see through the woods, was the same repetition of men and horses. They would ask us the news, and one, drunk with [words excised] excitement or whisky informed us that it was our own fault if we had saved nothing, the people must have been—fools not to know trouble would come before long, and that it was the fault of the men who were aware of it, that the women were thus forced to fly. In vain we pleaded that there was no warning, no means of forseeing this; he cried "*You* are ruined; so am I, and my brothers too! And by—there is nothing left but to die now, and I'll die!" "Good!" I said. "But die fighting for us!" He waved his hand black with powder and shouted "That I will!" after us, and that was the only swearing guerrilla we met; the others seemed to have too much respect for us to talk aloud.

5. Mrs. Sophia Brunot was a widow, a neighbor of the Morgans.

Lucy had met us before this; early in the action, Lilly had sent her back to get some baby clothes, but a shell exploding within a few feet of her, she took alarm, and ran up another road for three miles, when she cut across the plantations and regained the Greenwell route. It is fortunate that without consultation, the idea of running here should have seized us all. ***

August 25th. About 12 at night. [Linwood][6]

Sleep is impossible after all I have heard, so after vainly endeavoring to follow the example of the rest, and sleep like a stoic, I have lighted my candle and take to this to induce drowsiness. Just after supper, when Anna[7] and I were sitting with Mrs Carter in her room, I talking as usual of home, and saying I would be perfectly happy if mother would decide to remain in Baton Rouge and brave the occasional shellings, I heard a well known voice take up some sentence of mine from a dark part of the room, and with a cry of surprise, I was hugging Miriam until she was breathless. Such a forlorn creature! so dirty, tired, and fatigued, as to be hardly recognizable.

We thrust her in a chair, and made her speak. She had just come with Charlie, who went after them yesterday; and had left mother and the servants at a kind friend's, on the road. I never heard such a story as she told. I was heart sick; but I laughed until Mrs Badger grew furious with me and the Yankees, and abused me for not abusing them. She says when she entered the house, she burst into tears at the desolation. It was one scene of ruin. Libraries emptied, china smashed, sideboards split open with axes, three cedar chests cut open, plundered, and set up on end; all parlor ornaments carried off—even the alabaster Apollo and Diana that Hal valued so much. Her piano, dragged to the center of the parlor, had been abandoned as too heavy to carry off; her desk lay open with all letters and notes well thumbed and scattered around, while Will's last letter to her was open on the floor, with the Yankee stamp of dirty fingers.

Mother's portrait half cut from its frame stood on the floor. Margret[8] who was present at the sacking, told how she had saved father's. It seems that those who wrought the destruction in our house, were all officers. One jumped on the sofa to cut the picture down (Miriam saw the prints of his muddy feet) when Margret cried "For God's sake, gentlemen, let it be! I'll help you to anything here. He's dead, and the young ladies would rather see the house burn than lose it!" "I'll blow your damned brains out" was the "gentlemans" answer as he put a pistol to her head, which a brother officer dashed away, and the picture was abandoned for finer sport. All the others were cut up in shreds. Up stairs was the finest fun. Mother's beautiful mahogany armoir, whose single door was an extremely fine mirror, was entered by crashing through the glass, when it was emptied of every article, and the shelves half split, and half thrust back crooked. Letters labeled by the boys "Private," were strewn over the floor; they opened every armoir and drawer, collected every rag to be found and littered the whole house with them, until the wonder was, where so many rags had been found. Father's armoir was relieved of every thing; Gibbes'[9] handsome Damascus sword with the silver scabbard included. All his clothes, George's, Hal's, Jimmy's, were appropriated.

They entered my room, broke that fine mirror for sport, pulled down the rods from the bed, and with them, pulverized my toilet set, taking also all Lydia's[1] china ornaments I had packed in the washstand. The debris filled my basin, and ornamented my bed. My desk was broken open. Over it was spread all my letters, and private papers, a diary I kept when twelve years old, and sundry tokens of dried roses, etc., which must have been *very* funny, they all being labled with the donor's name, and the occasion! Fool! how I writhe when I think of all

---

6. The plantation of General Albert G. Carter, 20 miles north of Baton Rouge.
7. Anna Badger, a niece of General Carter.
8. A house slave.

9. Thomas Gibbes Morgan, Jr., another of Sarah's brothers.
1. Gibbes' wife.

they saw; the invitations to buggy rides, concerts, "Compliments of," etc.—! Lilly's sewing machine had disappeared; but as mother's was too heavy to move, they merely smashed the needles.

In the pillaging of the armoirs, they seized a pink flounced muslin of Miriam's, which one officer placed on the end of a bayonet, and paraded around with, followed by the others who slashed it with their swords crying "I have stuck the damned Secesh! that's the time I cut her!" and continued their sport until the rags could no longer be pierced. One seized my bonnet, with which he decked himself, and ran in the streets. Indeed, all who found such, rushed frantically around town by way of frolicking, with the things on their heads. They say no frenzy could surpass it. Another snatched one of my calico dresses, and a pair of vases that mother had when she was married, and was about to decamp, when a Mrs Jones jerked them away, and carried them to her boarding house, and restored them to mother the other day. Blessed be heaven! I have a calico dress! Our clothes were used for the vilest purposes, and spread in every corner—at least those few that were not stolen.

Aunt Barker's Charles[2] tried his best to defend the property. "Aint you 'shamed to destroy all dis here, that belongs to a poor widow lady who's got two daughters to support?" he asked of an officer who was foremost in the destruction. "Poor? Damn them! I dont know when I have seen a house furnished like this! look at that furniture! *they* poor!" was the retort, and thereupon the work went bravely on, of making us poor indeed.

It would have fared badly with us, had we been there. The servants say they broke in the house crying "Where are those damned Secesh women? We know they are hid in here, and we'll make them dance for hiding from Federal officers!" and they could not be convinced that we were not there, until they had searched the very garret. Wonder what they would have done? Charles caught a Captain Clark, in the streets, when the work was almost over, and begged him to put an end to it. The gentleman went readily, but though the devastation was quite evident, no one was to be seen, and he was about to leave, when insisting that there was someone there, Charles drew him in my room, dived under the bed, and drew from thence a Yankee Captain, by one leg, followed by a lieutenant, each with a bundle of the boys' clothes, which they instantly dropped, protesting they were only looking around the house. The gentleman Captain carried them off to their superior.

Ours was the most shockingly treated house in the whole town. We have the misfortune to be equally feared by both sides, because we will blackguard neither. So the Yankees selected the only house in town that sheltered three forlorn women, to wreak their vengeance on, just as our own people would have done, thanks for the reports of our kind relatives at Hope Estate, who Mr McHatton says, satisfied him that we were all Yankees. Bless their kind hearts!

From far and near, strangers and friends flocked in to see the ravages committed. Crowds rushed in before, crowds came in after, Miriam and mother arrived, all apologizing for the intrusion, but saying they had heard it was a sight never before seen. So they let them examine to their hearts content; and Miriam says the sympathy of all was extraordinary. A strange gentleman picked up a piece of mother's mirror, which was as thick as his finger, saying "Madame, I should like to keep this as a memento. I am about to travel through Mississippi, and having seen what a splendid piece of furniture this was, and the state your house is left in, should like to show this as a specimen of Yankee vandalism."

William Waller[3] flew to our home to try to save it; but was too late. They say he burst into tears as he looked around. While on his kind errand, another band of Yankees burst into his house, and left not one article of clothing to him, except the suit he had on. The whole talk is about our dreadful treatment at the Yankees hands. Dr Day, and Dr Ender's, in spite of the assertions of the former lost nothing.

Well! I am beggared! Strange to say, I dont feel it. Perhaps it is the satisfaction of knowing

2. A slave or former slave.   3. A cousin.

my fate, that makes me so cheerful that Mrs Carter envied my stoicism, while Mrs Badger felt like beating me because I did not agree that there was no such thing as a gentleman in the Yankee army. I know Major Drum[4] for one, and that Capt. Clark must be two, and Mr Biddle is three, and Gen Williams—God bless him where ever he is! for he certainly acted like a Christian. The Yankees boasted loudly that if it had not been for him, the work would have been done long ago.

And now, I am determined to see my home, before Yankee shells complete the work that Yankee axes spared. So by sunrise, I shall post over to Mr Elder's, and insist on Charlie taking me to town with him. I hardly think it is many hours off. I feel so settled, so calm! just as though I never meant to sleep again. If I only had a desk—a luxury I have not enjoyed since I left home,—I could write for hours still, without being sleepy; but this curved attitude is hard on my stiff back, so good night, while I lie down to gain strength for a sight they say will make me faint with distress. Nous verrons![5] if I say I Wont, I know I'll not cry.

The Brunots' lost nothing at all from their house, thank heaven for the mercy! Only they lost all their money in their flight. On the door, on their return, they found written "Ladies, I have done my best for you," signed by a Yankee soldier, which they suppose to be the one who has made it a habit of continually passing their house.

Forgot to say Miriam recovered my guitar from the Asylum,[6] our large trunk and father's papers (untouched) from Dr Ender's, and with her piano, the two portraits, a few mattresses (all that is left of housekeeping affairs) and father's law books, carried them out of town. For which I say in all humility, Blessed be God who has spared us so much. How ungrateful I would be, to complain when we have been so fortunate after all. Have I cause to complain? True, the house, furniture, clothing, etc., are lost but—trust in God!

Thursday Aug. 28.

I am satisfied. I have seen my home again. Tuesday I was up at sunrise, and my few preparations were soon completed, and before any one was awake, I walked over to Mr Elder's through mud and dew to meet Charlie. Fortunate was it for me that I started so early; for I found him hastily eating his breakfast and ready to leave. He was very much opposed to my going; and for some time I was afraid he would force me to remain; but at last he consented—perhaps because I did not insist—and with wet feet, and without a particle of breakfast, I at length found myself in the buggy on the road home. The ride afforded me a series of extraordinary surprises. Half the time I found myself half way out of the little low necked buggy when I thought I was safely in, and the other half, I was surprised to find myself really in, when I thought I was wholly out. And so on, for mile after mile, over muddy roads, until we came to a most terrific cross road, leading to the plank road, where we were obliged to pass, and which is best undescribed. Four miles from town we stopped at Mrs Brown's to see mother, and after a few moments' talk, went on our road.

I saw the first Yankee camp that Will Pinkney and Col. Bird had set fire to the day of the battle. Such a shocking sight of charred wood, burnt clothes, tents, and all imaginable articles strewn around, I had never before seen. I should have been very much excited, entering the town by the route our soldiers took; but I was not. It all seemed tame and familiar. I could hardly fancy I stood on the very spot where the severest struggle had taken place. The next turn of the road brought us to two graves, one on each side of the road, the resting place of two who fell that day. They were merely left in the ditch where they fell, and earth from the side was pulled over them. When Miriam passed, parts of their coats were sticking out of the grave; but some kind hand had scattered fresh earth over them when I saw them.

---

4. Major Richard C. Drum, married to Sarah's sister Lavinia.

5. "We shall see" (French).

6. The State Asylum for the Deaf and Blind, where Sarah had earlier taken refuge.

Beyond, the sight became more common. I was told that their hands and feet were visible from many. And one poor fellow lay unburied, just as he had fallen, with his horse across him, and both skeletons. That sight I was spared, as the road near which he was lying was blocked up by trees, so we were forced to go through the woods, to enter, instead of passing by the Catholic graveyard. In the woods, we passed another camp our men destroyed, while the torn branches above, testified to the number of shells our men had braved to do the work. Next to Mr Barbee's, were the remains of a third camp that was burned; and a few more steps made me suddenly hold my breath, for just before us lay a dead horse with the flesh still hanging, which was hardly endurable. Close by lay a skeleton, whether of man or horse, I did not wait to see.

Not a human being appeared until we reached the penitentiary, which was occupied by our men. After that, I saw crowds of wagons moving furniture out, but not a creature that I knew. Just back of our house was all that remained of a nice brick cottage—namely, four crumbling walls. The offense was that the husband was fighting for the Confederacy; so the wife was made to suffer, and is now homeless, like many thousands besides. It really seems as though God wanted to spare our homes. The frame dwelling adjoining was not touched, even. The town was hardly recognizable; and required some skill to avoid the corners blocked up by trees, so as to get in at all.

Our house could not be reached by the front, so we left the buggy in the back yard, and running through the lot without stopping to examine the store room and servants' rooms that opened wide, I went through the alley, and entered by the front door. Fortunate was it for this record that I undertook to describe the sacking only from Miriam's account. If I had waited until now, it would never have been mentioned; for as I looked around, to attempt such a thing seemed absurd. I stood in the parlor in silent amazement; and in answer to Charlie's "Well?" I could only laugh. It was so hard to realize. As I looked for each well known article, I could hardly believe that Abraham Lincoln's officers had really come so low down as to steal in such a wholesale manner. The papier maché workbox Miriam had given me, was gone. The baby sacque I was crocheting, with all knitting needles and wool, gone also. Of all the beautiful engravings of Annapolis that Will Pinkney had sent me, there remained a single one. Gentlemen, my name is written on each!

Not a book remained in the parlor, except Idylls of the King,[7] that contained my name also, and which, together with the door plate, was the only case in which the name of Morgan was spared. They must have thought we were related to John Morgan,[8] and wreaked their vengeance on us for that reason. Thanks for the honor, but there is not the slightest connection! Where they did not carry off articles bearing our name, they cut it off (as in the visiting cards) and left only the first name. Every book of any value or interest, except Hume and Gibbon, was "borrowed" permanently. I regretted Macaulay more than all the rest. Brother's splendid French histories went too; all except L'Histoir de la Bastille. However as they spared father's law libraries, (all except one volume they used to support a flour barrel with, while they emptied it near the parlor door) we ought to be thankful.

The dining room was *very* funny. I looked around for the cutglass celery and preserve dishes that were to be part of my "dot"[9] as mother always said, together with the champagne glasses that had figured on the table the day I was born; but there remained nothing. There was plenty of split up furniture though. I stood in mother's room before the shattered armoir, which I could hardly believe the same that I had smoothed my hair before, as I left home three weeks previously. Father's was split across, and the lock torn off, and in the place of the hundreds of articles it contained, I saw two bonnets at the sight of which I actually sat down to laugh. One was mother's velvet, which looked very much like a foot ball in its present condition. Mine was not to be found, as the officers forgot to return it. Wonder who has my

---

7. Arthurian romances by Alfred, Lord Tennyson (1809–1892), English poet.
8. John Hunt Morgan (1825–1864), already famous for his raids behind Union lines, later was made a general.
9. "Dowry" (French).

imperial? I know they never saw a handsomer one, with its black velvet, purple silk, and ostrich feathers.

I went to my room. Gone was my small paradise! Had this shocking place ever been habitable? The tall mirror squinted at me from a thousand broken angles. It looked so knowing! I tried to fancy the Yankee officers being dragged from under my bed by the leg, thanks to Charles; but it seemed too absurd; so I let them alone. My desk! What a sight! The central part I had kept as a little curiosity shop with all my little trinkets and keepsakes, of which a large proportion were from my gentlemen friends. I looked, and of all I had left, found only a piece of the McRae, which, as it was labled in full, I was surprised they had spared. Precious letters, I found under heaps of broken china and rags; all my notes were gone, with many letters. I looked for a letter of poor ——, in cipher, with the key attached, and name signed in plain hand. I knew it would hardly be agreeable to him to have it read, and it certainly would be unpleasant to me to have it published; but I could not find it. Miriam thinks she saw something answering the description, somewhere, though.

Bah! what is the use of describing such a scene? Many suffered along with us, though none so severely. Indeed, the Yankees cursed loudly at those who did not leave anything worth stealing. They cannot complain of us, on that score. All our handsome Brussels carpets, together with Lydia's four, were taken too. What did they not take? In the garret, in its darkest corner, a whole gilt edged china set of Lydia's had been over looked; so I set to work and packed it up, while Charlie packed her furniture in a wagon, to send to her father. It was now three o'clock; and with my light linen dress thrown off, I was standing over a barrel putting in cups and saucers as fast as I could wrap them in the rags that covered the floor, when Mr Larguier[1] sent me a nice little dinner. I had been so many hours with out eating—19, I think, during three of which I had slept, that I had lost all appetite; but nevertheless I eat it, to show my appreciation. If I should here-after think that the quantity of rags was exaggerated, let me here state that after I had packed the barrel and china with them, it made no perceptible diminution of the pile.

As soon as I had finished my task, Charlie was ready to leave again; so I left town without seeing, or hearing, any one, or any thing except what lay in my path. As we drove out of the gate, I begged Charlie to let me get my bird, as I heard Charles Barker had him. A man was dispatched, and in a few moments returned with my Jimmy. I have since heard that Tiche deserted him, the day of the battle, as I so much feared she would; and that Charles found him late in the evening and took charge of him. With my pet once more with me, we drove off again. I cast many a longing look at the graveyard; but knowing Charlie did not want to stop, I said nothing, though I had been there but once in three months, and that once, six weeks ago. I could see where the fence had been thrown down by our soldiers as they charged the Federals, but it was now replaced, though many a picket was gone.

Once more I stopped at Mrs Brown's, while Charlie went on to Clinton, leaving me to drive mother here in the morning. Early yesterday after seeing Miriam's piano and the mattresses packed up and on the road, we started off in the buggy, and after a tedious ride through a melting sun, arrived here about three o'clock, having again missed my dinner, which I kept a profound secret until supper time. I declare, by next Ash Wednesday, I will have learned how to fast without getting sick! Though very tired, I sat sewing until after sunset, dictating a page and a half to Anna, who was writing to Howell. ***[2]

Beech Grove. Sept 6th. Saturday.

I wanted to have a splendid dream last night, but failed. It was pleasant though to dream of welcoming George and Gibbes back. Jimmy I could not see; and George was in deep mourning. I dreamed of fainting when I saw him (a novel sensation, since I never experienced

1. A local merchant.
2. Howell Carter, who was fighting for the

Confederacy, was a cousin of Anna Badger.

it awake) but I speedily came to, and insisted on his "pulling Henry Walsh's red hair, for his insolence," which he promised to do instantly. How absurd! Dreams! dreams! That pathetic "Miss Sarah, do you ever dream?" comes vividly back to me sometimes.

Dream? Dont I! Not the dreams *he* meant; but royal, purple dreams, that De Quincy[3] could not purchase with his opium; dreams that I would not forgo for all the inducements that could be offered. I go to sleep, and pay a visit to heaven or fairy land. I have white wings, and, with another, float in rosy clouds, and look down on the moving world; or I have the power to raise myself in the air without wings, and silently float where ever I will, loving all things, and feeling that God loves me. I have heard Paul[4] preach to the people, while I stood on a fearful rock above. I have been to strange lands and great cities; I have talked with people I have never beheld. Charlotte Brontë has spent a week with me—in my dreams—and together we have talked of her sad life. Shakespeare and I have discussed his works, seated tête-à-tête over a small table. He pointed out the character of each of his heroines, explaining what I could not understand when awake; and closed the lecture with "*You* have the tenderest heart I have ever read, or sung of" which compliment, considering it as original with him, rather than myself, waked me up with surprise.

I see father and Harry in dreams. Once I walked with Hal through a garden of Paradise. Fountains, statues, flowers, surrounded us, as we wandered hand in hand. We stopped before a statue that held a finger to its lips, when he said "Did you ever see Fitch's celebrated picture of Eternity? No? Well let me show it to you. Nothing but that picture can give you an idea of the vastness of this eternity. Come!" I followed him through beautiful alleys until he stopped before an immense crystal wall. He held my hand without speaking, and we watched together. In the crystal, or the otherside, forms were moving, ever, always. What they were, I could not say; I only know that they were real, and forever moving! Over all, above, below, beyond, hovered a Something; a Something too great, awful, and mysterious for me to comprehend, though I struggled to understand. Striving still, I suddenly waked up, and the crystal painting disappeared. Dreams! who would give up the blessing? I would not care to sleep, if I could not dream. ***

Sunday Nov. 9th. [Linwood]

If Lincoln could spend the grinding season on a plantation, he would recall his proclamation.[5] As it is, he has only proved himself a fool, without injuring us. Why last evening I took old Wilson's place at the bagasse[6] chute, and kept the rollers free from cane until I had thrown down enough to fill several carts, and had my hands as black as his. What cruelty to slaves! And black Frank thinks me cruel too, when he meets me with a patronising grin, and shows me the nicest vats of candy, and peels cane for me! Oh! very cruel! And so does Jules, when he wipes the handle of his paddle on his apron, to give "Mamselle" a chance to skim the kettles and learn how to work! Yes! and so do all the rest who meet us with a courtesy[7] and "Howd'y young missus!"

Last night we girls sat on the wood just in front of the furnace—rather Miriam and Anna did while I sat in their laps—and with some twenty of all ages crowded around, we sang away to their great amusement. Poor oppressed devils! why did you not chunk us with the burning logs instead of looking happy, and laughing like fools? Really, some good old Abolitionist is needed here, to tell them how miserable they are. Cant mass Abe spare a few to enlighten his brethren? ***

3. Thomas De Quincey (1785–1859), author of *Confessions of an English Opium Eater* (1822).
4. (d. A.D. 64?), apostle to the gentiles and author of a number of the Epistles.
5. Although the Emancipation Proclamation was not issued until January 1, 1863, a preliminary draft had been made public.
6. Crushed sugarcane.
7. A curtsy.

Friday night. Jan. 23d [1863]

I am particularly happy today, for we have just heard from Brother[8] for the first time since last July. And he is well, and happy, and wants us to come to him in New Orleans, so he can take care of us, and no longer be so anxious for our safety. If we only could—!

To be sure the letter is from a gentleman who is just out of the city, who says he writes at Brother's earnest request; still it is something to hear, even indirectly. One hundred and fifty dollars he encloses, with the request that mother will draw for any amount she wishes. Dear Brother, money is the least thing we need; first of all, we are dying for want of a home. If we could see ours once more!

During the time we have heard incidentally of Brother; of his having taken the oath of allegiance—which I am confident he did not do until Butler's October decree[9]—of his being a prominent Union man, of his being a candidate for the Federal Congress, and of his withdrawal; and finally of his having gone to New York and Washington, from which places he only returned a few weeks since. That is all we ever heard. A very few people have been insolent enough to say to me "Your brother is as good a Yankee as any." My blood boils as [I] answer "Let him be President Lincoln if he will, and I would love him the same." And so I would. Politics cannot come between me and my father's son. What he thinks right, Is right, for him, though not for me. If he is for the Union, it is because he believes it to be in the right, and I honor him for acting from conviction, rather than from dread of public opinion.

If he were to take up the sword against us to-morrow, Miriam and I at least, would say "If he thinks it his duty, he is right; we will not forget he is our father's child." And we will not. From that sad day when the sun was setting for the first time on our father's grave, when the great, strong man sobbed in agony at the thought of what we had lost, and taking us both on his lap put his arms around us and said "Dear little sisters dont cry; I will be father and brother too, now," he has been both. And we love him as such, dont we Miriam? He respects our opinions, we shall respect his!

I confess my self a rebel, body and soul. *Confess?* I glory in it! Am proud of being one; would not forego the title for any other earthly one! Though none could regret the dismemberment of our old Union more than I did at the time, though I acknowledge that there never was a more unnecessary war than this in the beginning, yet once in earnest, from the secession of Louisiana I date my change of sentiment. I have never since then looked back; forward, forward! is the cry; and as the Federal States sink each day in more appalling folly and disgrace, I grow prouder still of my own country and rejoice that we can no longer be confounded with a nation which shows so little fortitude in calamity, so little magnanimity in its hour of triumph.

Yes! I am glad we are two distinct tribes! I am proud of my country; only wish I could fight in the ranks with our brave soldiers, to prove my enthusiasm; would think death, mutilation, glorious in such a cause; cry "war to all eternity before we submit!" But if I cant fight, being unfortunately a woman, which I now regret for the first time in my life, at least I can help in other ways. What fingers could do in knitting and sewing for them, I have done with the most intense delight; what words of encouragement and praise could accomplish, I have tried on more than one bold soldier boy, and not altogether in vain; I have lost my home and all its dear contents for our Southern Rights, have stood on its deserted hearth stone and looked at the ruin of all I loved without a murmur, almost glad of the sacrifice, if it would contribute its mite towards the salvation of the Confederacy.

8. Philip Hicky Morgan, son of Sarah's father by his first marriage.
9. General Benjamin Franklin Butler (1818–1893), military governor of New Orleans (May–December, 1862). Known as "Beast" Butler in the South, he imposed orders including ones requiring New Orleans citizens to swear allegiance to the United States or register as enemies subject to fine or imprisonment.

And so it did, indirectly; for the battle of Baton Rouge, which made the Yankees, drunk with rage, commit outrages in our homes that civilized Indians would blush to perpetrate, forced them to abandon the town as untenable, whereby we were enabled to fortify Port Hudson here, which now defies their strength. True they have reoccupied our town; that Yankees live in our house; but if our Generals said burn the whole concern, would I not put the torch to our home readily, though I love its bare skeleton still? Indeed I would, though I know what it is to be without one. Dont Lilly & mother live in a wretched cabin in vile Clinton while strangers rest under our father's roof? Yankees, I owe you one for that!

Well! I boast myself Rebel, sing Dixie, shout Southern Rights, pray for God's blessing on our cause, without ceasing, and would not live in this country if by any possible calamity we should be conquered; I am only a woman, and that is the way I feel. Brother may differ. What then? Shall I respect, love him less? No! God bless him! Union or Secession, he is always my dear, dear Brother, and tortures should not make me change my opinion. *****

Tuesday March 31st.

"To be, or not to be; that is the question," Whether 'tis nobler in the Confederacy to suffer the pangs of unappeasable hunger and never ending trouble, or to take passage to a Yankee port, and there remaining, end them. Which is best? I am so near daft that I cannot pretend to say; I only know that I shudder at the thought of going to New Orleans, and that my heart fails me when I think of the probable consequence to mother if I allow a mere outward sign of patriotism to over balance what should be my first consideration—her health. For Clinton is growing no better rapidly. To be hungry is there an every day occurrence. For ten days, mother writes, they have lived off just hominy enough to keep their bodies and souls from parting, without being able to procure another article—not even a potato.

Mother is not in a condition to stand such privation; day by day she grows weaker on her new régime; I am satisfied that two months more of danger, difficulties, perplexities, and starvation will lay her in her grave. The latter alone is enough to put a speedy end to her days. Lilly has been obliged to put her children to bed to make them forget they were supperless, and when she followed their example, could not sleep herself, for very hunger. The inhabitants of that abode of bliss would not put themselves out to sell them a mouthful to keep them from starving, such is their idea of Christianity. So with money enough to purchase a comfortable home among respectable people, they find it as serviceable as so many rags, and live on from day to day with empty stomachs and full pockets. Can any thing more aggravating be imagined?

We have tried in vain to find another home in the Confederacy. After three days spent in searching Augusta, Gibbes wrote that it was impossible to find a vacant room for us, as the city was already crowded with refugees. A kind Providence must have destined that disappointment in order to save my life, if there is any reason for Col. Steedman's fears.[1] We next wrote to Mobile, Brandon, and even that horrid little Liberty, besides making inquiries of every one we met, while Charlie too was endeavoring to find a place, and every where received the same answer—not a vacant room, and provisions hardly to be obtained at all.

The question has now resolved itself to whether we shall see mother die for want of food in Clinton, or, by sacrificing an outward show of patriotism, (the inward sentiment cannot be changed) go with her to New Orleans, as Brother begs in the few letters he contrives to smuggle through. It looks simple enough. Ought not mother's life to be our first considera-

---

1. Colonel I. G. W. Steedman had warned Sarah that a trip to Georgia might prove fatal to her. As a result of a carriage accident the previous November, she was a serious invalid, unable to walk without assistance.

tion? Undoubtedly! But suppose we could preserve her life and our free sentiments at the same time? If we could only find a resting place in the Confederacy! This, though is impossible. But to go to New Orleans; to live surrounded by Yankees; to cease singing Dixie; to be obliged to keep your sentiments to yourself—for I would not wound Brother by any Ultra Secession speech, and such could do me no good and only injure him. If he is as friendly with the Federals as they say he is—to listen to the scurrilous abuse heaped on those fighting for our homes and liberties, among them my three brothers—could I endure it? I fear not. Even if I did not go crazy, I would grow so restless, homesick and miserable, that I would pray for even Clinton again.

O I dont, dont want to go! If mother would only go alone, and leave us with Lilly! But she is as anxious to obtain Dr Stone's advice for me, as we are to secure her a comfortable home; and I wont go any where without Miriam, so we must all go together. Yet there is no disguising the fact that such a move will place us in a very doubtful position to both friends and enemies. However all our friends here warmly advocate the move, and Will Pinkney and Frank both promised to knock down anyone who shrugged their shoulders and said anything about it.

But what would the boys say? The fear of displeasing them is my chief distress. George writes in the greatest distress about my prolonged illness, and his alarm about my condition. "Of one thing I am sure" he writes, "and that is that she deserves to recover; for a better little sister never lived." God bless him! my eyes grew right moist over those few words. Loving words bring tears to them sooner than angry ones. Would he object to such a step when he knows that the very medicines necessary for my recovery are not to be procured in the whole country? Would he rather have mother dead, and me a cripple in the Confederacy, than both well out of it? I feel that if we go we are wrong; but I am satisfied that it is worse to stay. It is a distressing dilemma to be placed in, as we are certain to be blamed which ever course we pursue. But I don't want to go to New Orleans!

5th [February 1864, New Orleans]

Not dead! not dead! O my God! Gibbes is *not* dead! Where

O dear God! another? Only a few days ago came a letter so cheerful and hopeful—we have waited and prayed so patiently—at my feet lies one from Col. Steedman saying he is dead. Dead! suddenly and without a moment's warning summoned to God! No! it cannot be! I am mad! O God have mercy on us! my poor mother! And Lydia! Lydia! God comfort you! My brain seems fire. Am I mad? Not yet! God would not take him yet! He will come again! Hush! God is good! Not dead! not dead! O Gibbes come back to us!

11th [February]

O God O God have mercy on us! George is dead! Both in a week! George our sole hope—our sole dependence.

[p. 58] March

Dead! dead! Both dead! O my brothers! what have we lived for except you? We who would so gladly have laid down our lives for yours, are left desolate to mourn over all we loved and hoped for, weak and helpless; while you, so strong, noble, and brave, have gone before us without a murmur. God knows best. But it is hard—O so hard! to give them up without a murmur!

We cannot remember the day when our brothers were not all in all to us. What the boys would think; what the boys would say; what we would do when the boys came home, that has been our sole thought through life. A life time's hope wrecked in a moment—God help us! In our eyes, there is no one in the world quite so noble, quite so brave, quite so true as our brothers. And yet they are taken—and others useless to themselves and a curse to their families live on in safety, without fear of death. This is blasphemy. God knows best; I will not complain. But when I think of drunken, foolish, coarse Will Carter with horses and dogs his sole ambition, and drinking and gambling his idea of happiness, my heart swells within me. He lives, a torment to himself and a curse to others—he will live to a green old age as idle, as ignorant, as dissipated as he is now.

And Gibbes, Harry, and George, God's blessings he bestowed on us awhile—are dead. My brothers! my dear brothers! I would rather mourn over you in your graves, remembering what you were, than have you change places with that man. Death is nothing in comparison to dishonor.

If we had had any warning or preparation, this would not have been so unspeakably awful. But to shut ones eyes to all dangers and risks, and drown every rising fear with "God will send them back; I will not doubt his mercy," and then suddenly to learn that your faith has been presumption—and God wills that you shall undergo bitter affliction—it is a fearful awakening! What glory have we ever rendered to God that we should expect him to be so merciful to us? Are not all things His, and is He not infinitely more tender and compassionate than we deserve?

We have deceived ourselves willfully about both. After the first dismay on hearing of Gibbes' capture, we readily listened to the assertions of our friends that Johnson's Island[2] was the healthiest place in the world, that he would be better off, comfortably clothed and under shelter, than exposed to shot and shell, half fed, and lying on the bare ground during Ewell's[3] winter campaign. We were thankful for his safety, knowing Brother would leave nothing undone that could add to his comfort. And besides that, there was the sure hope of his having him paroled. On that hope we lived all winter—now confident that in a little while he would be with us, then again doubting for awhile, only to have the hope grow surer afterwards. And so we waited and prayed, never doubting he would come at last. He himself believed it, though striving not to be too hopeful lest he should disappoint us, as well as himself. Yet he wrote cheerfully and bravely to the last. Towards the middle of January, Brother was sure of succeeding, as all the prisoners had been placed under Butler's control. Ah me! How could we be so blind? We were sure he would be with us in a few weeks! I wrote to him that I had prepared his room.

On the 30th of January came his last letter, addressed to me, though meant for Sis. It was dated the 12th—the day George died. All his letters pleaded that I would write more frequently—he loved to hear from me; so I had been writing to him every ten days. On the third of February I sent my last. Friday the fifth, as I was running through Miriam's room, I saw Brother pass the door, and heard him ask Miriam for mother. The voice, the bowed head, the look of utter despair on his face, struck through me like a knife. "Gibbes! Gibbes!" was my sole thought; but Miriam and I stood motionless looking at each other without a word. "Gibbes is dead" said mother as he stood before her. He did not speak; and then we went in.

We did not ask how, or when. That he was dead was enough for us. But after a while he told us uncle James[4] had written that he had died at two o'clock on Thursday the twenty first. Still we did not know how he had died. Several letters that had been brought remained unopened on the floor. One, Brother opened, hoping to learn something more. It was from

---

2. Union prison near Sandusky, Ohio.
3. Richard Stoddert Ewell (1817–1872), Confederate general, and Gibbes Morgan's commanding officer. Ewell himself was still

commanding his men, though he had lost a leg at the second battle of Bull Run (August 1862).

4. James B. Morgan, Sarah's uncle, lived in Pittsburgh.

Col. Steedman to Miriam and me, written a few hours after his death, and contained the sad story of our dear brother's last hours. He had been in Col. Steedman's ward of the hospital for more than a week, with headache and sore throat; but it was thought nothing; he seemed to improve, and expected to be discharged in a few days. On the twenty first he complained that his throat pained him again. After prescribing for him, and talking cheerfully with him for some time, Col. Steedman left him surrounded by his friends, to attend to his other patients. He had hardly reached his room when someone ran to him saying Capt. Morgan was dying. He hurried to his bedside, and found him dead. Capt. Steedman,[5] sick in the next bed, and those around him said he had been talking pleasantly with them, when he sat up to reach his cup of water on the table. As soon as he drank it he seemed to suffocate; and after tossing his arms wildly in the air, and making several fearful efforts to breathe, he died.

O Gibbes! Gibbes! When you took me in your arms and cried so bitterly over that sad parting, it was indeed your last farewell! My brothers! my brothers! Dear Lord how can we live without our boys?

Sewed to the paper that contained the last words we should hear of our dear brother, was a lock of hair grown long during his imprisonment. I think it was a noble, tender heart that remembered that one little deed of kindness, and a gentle, pitying hand that cut it from his head as he lay cold and stark in death. Good heart that loved our brave brother, kind hand that soothed his pain, you will not be forgotten by us!

And keenly as we felt his loss, and deeply as we mourned over him who had fought with the bravest of the brave through more than thirty battles, to die a prisoner in a strange land—there was one for whom we felt a keener grief—the dear little wife who loved him so perfectly, whose life must henceforth be a blank before her, God help my poor little sister! "Hush, mother, hush," I said when I heard her cries. "We have Brother, and George and Jimmy left, and Lydia has lost all!" Heaven pity us! George had gone before—only He in mercy kept the knowledge of it from us for awhile longer.

On Thursday the eleventh, as we sat talking to mother, striving to make her forget the weary days we had cried through with that fearful sound of dead! dead! ringing ever in our ears, some one asked for Miriam. She went down, and presently I heard her thanking some body for a letter. "You could not have brought me anything more acceptable! It is from my sister, though she can hardly have heard from us yet!" I ran back, and sitting at mother's feet, told her Miriam was coming with a letter from Lydia. Mother cried at the mention of her name. O my little sister! you know how dear you are to us!

"Mother! Mother!" a horrible voice cried, and before I could think who it was, Miriam rushed in holding an open letter in her hand, and perfectly wild. "George is dead!" she shrieked and fell heavily to the ground. O my God! I could have prayed thee to take mother too, when I looked at her! I thought—I almost hoped she was dead, and that pang spared! But I was wild myself. I could have screamed!—laughed! "It is false! do you hear me mother? God would not take both! George is not dead!" I cried trying in vain to rouse her from her horrible state or bring one ray of reason to her eye. I spoke to a body alive only to pain; not a sound of my voice seemed to reach her; only fearful moans showed she was yet alive. Miriam lay raving on the ground. Poor Miriam! her heart's idol torn away. God help my darling! I did not understand that George *could* die until I looked at her. In vain I strove to raise her from the ground, or check her wild shrieks for death. "George! only George!" she would cry; until at last with the horror of seeing both die before me, I mastered strength enough to go for the servant and bid her run quickly for Brother.

How long I stood there alone, I never knew. I remember Ada coming in hurriedly and asking what it was. I told her George was dead. It was a relief to see her cry. I could not; but I felt the pain afresh, as though it were her brother she was crying over, not mine. And the

5. Seth D. Steedman, the colonel's brother.

sight of her tears brought mine too. We could only cry over mother and Miriam; we could not rouse them; we did not know what to do. Some one called me in the entry. I went, not understanding what I was doing. A lady came to me, told me her name, and said something about George; but I could not follow what she said. It was as though she were talking in a dream. I believe she repeated her words several times, for at last she shook me and said "Listen! Rouse yourself! the letter is about George!" Yes, I said; he is dead. She said I must read the letter; but I could not see, so she read it aloud.

It was from Dr Mitchell,[6] his friend who was with him when he died, telling of his sickness and death. He died on Tuesday the twelfth of January, after an illness of six days, conscious to the last and awaiting the end as only a Christian, and one who has led so beautiful a life, could, with the grace of God, look for it. He sent messages to his brothers and sisters, and bade them tell his mother his last thoughts were of her, and that he died trusting in the mercy of his Saviour. George! our pride! our beautiful, angel brother! *Could* he die? Surely God has sent all these afflictions within these three years to teach us that our hopes must be placed Above, and that it is blasphemy to have earthly idols!

The letter said that the physicians had mistaken his malady which was inflammation of the bowels, and he had died from being treated for something else. It seemed horrible cruelty to read me that part; I knew that if mother or Miriam ever heard of it, it would kill them. So I begged Mrs Mitchell never to let them hear of it. She seemed to think nothing of the pain it would inflict; how could she help telling if they asked? she said. I told her I must insist on her not mentioning it; it would only add suffering to what was already insupportable; if they asked for the letter, offer to read it aloud, but say positively that she would not allow any one to touch it except herself, and then she might pass it over in silence.

I roused Miriam then, and sent her to hear it read. She insisted on reading it herself; and half dead with grief held out her hands, begging piteously to be suffered to read it alone. I watched then until I was sure Mrs Mitchell would keep her promise. Horrible as I knew it to be from strange lips, I knew by what I experienced that I had saved her from a shock that might cost her her life; and then I went back to mother. No need to conceal what I felt there! She neither spoke nor saw. If I had shrieked that he died of ill treatment, she would not have understood. But I sat there silently with that horrible secret, wondering if God would help me bear it, or if despair would deprive me of self-control and force me presently to cry it aloud, though it should kill them both.

At last Brother came. I had to meet him downstairs and tell him. God spare me the sight of a strong man's grief! Then Sister[7] came in, knowing as little as he. Poor Sister! I could have blessed her for every tear she shed. It was a comfort to see some one who had life or feeling left. I felt as though the whole world was dead. Nothing was real, nothing existed except horrible speechless pain. Life was a fearful dream through which but one thought ran— "dead—dead."

Miriam had been taken to her room more dead than alive—mother lay speechless in hers. The shock of this second blow had obliterated, with them, all recollection of the first. It was a mercy I envied them; for I remembered both until loss of consciousness would have seemed a blessing. I shall never forget mother's shriek of horror when towards evening she recalled it. O those dreadful days of misery and wretchedness! It seems almost sacrilege to refer to them now. They are buried in our hearts with our boys—thought of with prayers and tears.

How will the world seem to us now? What will life be without the boys? When this terrible strife is over, and so many thousand return to their homes, what will peace bring us of all we hoped? Jimmy! dear Lord, spare us that one! but I have always felt Jimmy must

6. William S. Mitchell, surgeon to George's regiment.
7. Beatrice Ford Morgan, Brother's wife.

die young—and we have been so cast down that hope seems almost presumption in us. So we send our hearts over the waves after our last one, while our souls hardly dare pray "God spare him!" ***

April 19th. 1865. No. 211. Camp St.

Thursday the 13th, came the dreadful tidings of the surrender of Lee[8] and his army on the 9th. Every body cried, but I would not, satisfied that God will still save us, even though all should apparently be lost. Followed at intervals of two or three hours by the announcement of the capture of Richmond, Selma, Mobile, and Johnston's[9] army, even the staunchest Southerners were hopeless. Every one proclaimed Peace, and the only matter under consideration was whether Jeff. Davis,[1] all politicians, every man above the rank of Captain in the army, and above that of Lieutenant in the navy, should be hanged immediately, or *some* graciously pardoned. Henry Ward Beecher[2] humanely pleaded mercy for us, supported by a small minority. Davis and all leading men *must* be executed; the blood of the others, would serve to irrigate the country. Under this lively prospect, Peace! blessed Peace! was the cry. I whispered "Never! let a great earthquake swallow us up first! Let us leave our land and emigrate to any desert spot of the earth, rather than return to the Union, even as it Was!"

Six days this has lasted. Blessed with the silently obstinate disposition, I would not dispute, but felt my heart swell repeating "God is our refuge and our strength, a very present help in time of trouble," and could not for an instant believe this could end in our overthrow.

This morning when I went down to breakfast at seven, Brother read the announcement of the assassination of Lincoln and Secretary Seward.[3] "Vengence is mine; I will repay, saith the Lord." This is murder! God have mercy on those who did it! A while ago, Lincoln's chief occupation was thinking what death, thousands who ruled like lords when he was cutting logs, should die. A moment more, and the man who was progressing to murder countless human beings, is interrupted in his work by the shot of an assassin. Do I justify this murder? No! I shudder with horror, wonder, pity and fear, and then feeling that it is the salvation of all I love that has been purchased by this man's[4] crime, I long to thank God for those spared, and shudder to think that that is rejoicing against our enemy, being grateful for a fellow-creature's death. I am not! Seward was ill—dying—helpless. This was dastard murder. His throat was cut in bed. Horrible!

Charlotte Corday killed Marat[5] in his bath, and is held up in history as one of Liberty's martyrs, and one of the heroines of her country. To me, it is all Murder. Let historians extol blood shedding; it is woman's place to abhor it. And because I know that they would have apotheosized any man who had crucified Jeff Davis, I abhor this, and call it foul murder, unworthy of our cause—and God grant it was only the temporary insanity of a desperate man that committed this crime! Let not his blood be visited on our nation, Lord!

Across the way, a large building undoubtedly inhabited by officers is being draped in black. Immense streamers of black and white hang from the balcony. Down town, I understand all shops are closed, and all wrapped in mourning. And I hardly dare pray God to bless us, with the crape hanging over the way. It would have been banners, if our president had been killed,

8. Robert E. Lee (1807–1870), Confederate general.
9. Joseph Eggleston Johnston (1807–1891), Confederate general.
1. Jefferson Davis (1808–1889), president of the Confederate States of America (1861–1865).
2. Beecher (1813–1887) was a New England clergyman and prominent abolitionist.

3. William Henry Seward (1801–1872), wounded by stabbing in connection with Lincoln's assassination, survived the attack.
4. John Wilkes Booth (1838–1865), assassin of Lincoln.
5. Jean-Paul Marat (1743–1793), French revolutionary, stabbed to death by Charlotte Corday (1768–1793).

though! Now the struggle will be desperate, awful, short. Spare Jimmy, dear Lord! Have mercy on us as a people!

1915, 1991

Sarah Winnemucca Hopkins

(1844–1891)

The descendant and sister of Paiute chiefs, Sarah Winnemucca was born in Nevada and educated there. Her people, also known as "Digger Indians," spoke a dialect of the Shoshonean branch of the Uto-Aztecan linguistic family and lived in the Great Basin area. They subsisted in that arid country by gathering seeds, roots, and nuts and by snaring small animals. Using the fibers of desert plants, they wove clothing and mats; for winter they added rabbit pelts to their clothing. Their dwellings were made with frames of branches covered by grasses or earth. They were exceptionally skilled in basketry. Typically living in small family groups, they came together for tribal ceremonies and hunting.

Jedediah Smith, the mountain man, crossed the Great Basin about 1826, and in 1833 Joseph Reddeford Walker blazed a trail for later California gold seekers by following the Humboldt River through Paiute lands. Sarah Winnemucca recounts in her *Life among the Piutes* how elated her chieftain grandfather was at the news of sightings of white men. He believed them to be long alienated relatives of his tribal ancestors and hoped for reconciliation with his "white brothers," but others did not share his enthusiasm. Sarah, seeing European Americans for the first time as a child, was very frightened by their owl-like eyes and hairy faces. The tribe had heard rumors of the Donner party tragedy of 1846 and believed all white people to be cannibals, so the children were often hidden at the news of approaching settlers or soldiers. Nevertheless, young Sarah traveled with her grandfather to California, met many settlers, and became fluent in English. Throughout her life, she served as a translator and liaison between her tribe and settlers or military officers.

During her 1879 tour of the East, Hopkins gave over 300 lectures protesting federal government policy toward Native Americans. Among the many Eastern intellectuals who flocked to her support were Elizabeth Peabody Mann and Horace Mann, influential educators. Mrs. Mann edited the manuscript of *Life among the Piutes: Their Wrongs and Claims* and wrote a sympathetic introduction for the 1883 publication. Declaring the book to have "a single aim—*to tell the truth* as it lies in the heart and mind of a true patriot, and one whose knowledge of the two races gives her an opportunity of comparing them justly," Mann ventured the hope that its publication would serve to wake Americans to their "duty to the original possessors of our immense territory."

Unfortunately, Hopkins had little success in influencing federal policy or changing public apathy. She and her chieftain brother opened a school for Paiute children on the family farm, but because of financial failure and her ill health, they were forced to close it down in 1887. Sarah Winnemucca Hopkins died a disappointed woman; unable to bring about the reconciliation between Native Americans and whites her grandfather had dreamed of, she left her book to argue her case for justice.

The following description of the customs and education of her tribe is taken from the 1883 edition of *Life among the Piutes*. A study is Gae Whitney Canfield, *Sarah Winnemucca of the Northern Paiutes* (1983).

FROM LIFE AMONG THE PIUTES

Chapter II.
Domestic and Social Moralities.

Our children are very carefully taught to be good. Their parents tell them stories, traditions of old times, even of the first mother of the human race; and love stories, stories of giants, and fables; and when they ask if these last stories are true, they answer, "Oh, it is only coyote," which means that they are make-believe stories. Coyote is the name of a mean, crafty little animal, half wolf, half dog, and stands for everything low. It is the greatest term of reproach one Indian has for another. Indians do not swear,—they have no words for swearing till they learn them of white men. The worst they call each is bad or coyote; but they are very sincere with one another, and if they think each other in the wrong they say so.

We are taught to love everybody. We don't need to be taught to love our fathers and mothers. We love them without being told to. Our tenth cousin is as near to us as our first cousin; and we don't marry into our relations. Our young women are not allowed to talk to any young man that is not their cousin, except at the festive dances, when both are dressed in their best clothes, adorned with beads, feathers or shells, and stand alternately in the ring and take hold of hands. These are very pleasant occasions to all the young people.

Many years ago, when my people were happier than they are now, they used to celebrate the Festival of Flowers in the spring. I have been to three of them only in the course of my life.

Oh, with what eagerness we girls used to watch every spring for the time when we could meet with our hearts' delight, the young men, whom in civilized life you call beaux. We would all go in company to see if the flowers we were named for were yet in bloom, for almost all the girls are named for flowers. We talked about them in our wigwams, as if we were the flowers, saying, "Oh, I saw myself today in full bloom!" We would talk all the evening in this way in our families with such delight, and such beautiful thoughts of the happy day when we should meet with those who admired us and would help us to sing our flower-songs which we made up as we sang. But we were always sorry for those that were not named after some flower, because we knew they could not join in the flower-songs like ourselves, who were named for flowers of all kinds.[1]

At last one evening came a beautiful voice, which made every girl's heart throb with happiness. It was the chief, and every one hushed to hear what he said to-day.

"My dear daughters, we are told that you have seen yourselves in the hills and in the valleys, in full bloom. Five days from to-day your festival day will come. I know every young man's heart stops beating while I am talking. I know how it was with me many years ago. I used to wish the Flower Festival would come every day. Dear young men and young women, you are saying, 'Why put it off five days?' But you all know that is our rule. It gives you time to think, and to show your sweetheart your flower."

All the girls who have flower-names dance along together, and those who have not go together also. Our fathers and mothers and grandfathers and grandmothers make a place for us where we can dance. Each one gathers the flower she is named for, and then all weave them into wreaths and crowns and scarfs, and dress up in them.

Some girls are named for rocks and are called rock-girls, and they find some pretty rocks

---

1. Indian children are named from some passing circumstance; as, for instance, one of Mrs. Hopkins' brothers was named Black-eye, because when a very small child, sitting in a sister's lap, who had beautiful black eyes, he said, "What beautiful black eyes you have!" If they observed the flight of a bird, or an animal, in short, anything striking that became associated with them, that would be their appellation [E. P. Mann's note].

which they carry; each one such a rock as she is named for, or whatever she is named for. If she cannot, she can take a branch of sage-brush, or a bunch of rye-grass, which have no flower.

They all go marching along, each girl in turn singing of herself; but she is not a girl any more,—she is a flower singing. She sings of herself, and her sweetheart, dancing along by her side, helps her sing the song she makes.

I will repeat what we say of ourselves. "I, Sarah Winnemucca, am a shell-flower, such as I wear on my dress. My name is Thocmetony. I am so beautiful! Who will come and dance with me while I am so beautiful? Oh, come and be happy with me! I shall be beautiful while the earth lasts. Somebody will always admire me; and who will come and be happy with me in the Spirit-land? I shall be beautiful forever there. Yes, I shall be more beautiful than my shell-flower, my Thocmetony! Then, come, oh come, and dance and be happy with me!" The young men sing with us as they dance beside us.

Our parents are waiting for us somewhere to welcome us home. And then we praise the sage-brush and the rye-grass that have no flower, and the pretty rocks that some are named for; and then we present our beautiful flowers to these companions who could carry none. And so all are happy; and that closes the beautiful day.

My people have been so unhappy for a long time they wish now to *disincrease*, instead of multiply. The mothers are afraid to have more children, for fear they shall have daughters, who are not safe even in their mother's presence.

The grandmothers have the special care of the daughters just before and after they come to womanhood. The girls are not allowed to get married until they have come to womanhood; and that period is recognized as a very sacred thing, and is the subject of a festival, and has peculiar customs. The young woman is set apart under the care of two of her friends, somewhat older, and a little wigwam, called a teepee, just big enough for the three, is made for them, to which they retire. She goes through certain labors which are thought to be strengthening, and these last twenty-five days. Every day, three times a day, she must gather, and pile up as high as she can, five stacks of wood. This makes fifteen stacks a day. At the end of every five days the attendants take her to a river to bathe. She fasts from all flesh-meat during these twenty-five days, and continues to do this for five days in every month all her life. At the end of the twenty-five days she returns to the family lodge, and gives all her clothing to her attendants in payment for their care. Sometimes the wardrobe is quite extensive.

It is thus publicly known that there is another marriageable woman, and any young man interested in her, or wishing to form an alliance, comes forward. But the courting is very different from the courting of the white people. He never speaks to her, or visits the family, but endeavors to attract her attention by showing his horsemanship, etc. As he knows that she sleeps next to her grandmother in the lodge, he enters in full dress after the family has retired for the night, and seats himself at her feet. If she is not awake, her grandmother wakes her. He does not speak to either young woman or grandmother, but when the young woman wishes him to go away, she rises and goes and lies down by the side of her mother. He then leaves as silently as he came in. This goes on sometimes for a year or longer, if the young woman has not made up her mind. She is never forced by her parents to marry against her wishes. When she knows her own mind, she makes a confidant of her grandmother, and then the young man is summoned by the father of the girl, who asks him in her presence, if he really loves his daughter, and reminds him, if he says he does, of all the duties of a husband. He then asks his daughter the same question, and sets before her minutely all her duties. And these duties are not slight. She is to dress the game, prepare the food, clean the buckskins, make his moccasins, dress his hair, bring all the wood,—in short, do all the household work. She promises to "be himself," and she fulfils her promise. Then he is invited to a feast and all his relatives with him. But after the betrothal, a teepee is erected for the presents that pour in from both sides.

At the wedding feast, all the food is prepared in baskets. The young woman sits by the young man, and hands him the basket of food prepared for him with her own hands. He does not take it with his right hand; but seizes her wrist, and takes it with the left hand. This constitutes the marriage ceremony, and the father pronounces them man and wife. They go to a wigwam of their own, where they live till the first child is born. This event also is celebrated. Both father and mother fast from all flesh, and the father goes through the labor of piling the wood for twenty-five days, and assumes all his wife's household work during that time. If he does not do his part in the care of the child, he is considered an outcast. Every five days his child's basket is changed for a new one, and the five are all carefully put away at the end of the days, the last one containing the navel-string, carefully wrapped up, and all are put up into a tree, and the child put into a new and ornamented basket. All this respect shown to the mother and child makes the parents feel their responsibility, and makes the tie between parents and children very strong. The young mothers often get together and exchange their experiences about the attentions of their husbands; and inquire of each other if the fathers did their duty to their children, and were careful of their wives' health. When they are married they give away all the clothing they have ever worn, and dress themselves anew. The poor people have the same ceremonies, but do not make a feast of it, for want of means.

Our boys are introduced to manhood by their hunting of deer and mountain-sheep. Before they are fifteen or sixteen, they hunt only small game, like rabbits, hares, fowls, etc. They never eat what they kill themselves, but only what their father or elder brothers kill. When a boy becomes strong enough to use larger bows made of sinew, and arrows that are ornamented with eagle-feathers, for the first time, he kills game that is large, a deer or an antelope, or a mountain-sheep. Then he brings home the hide, and his father cuts it into a long coil which is wound into a loop, and the boy takes his quiver and throws it on his back as if he was going on a hunt, and takes his bow and arrows in his hand. Then his father throws the loop over him, and he jumps through it. This he does five times. Now for the first time he eats the flesh of the animal he has killed, and from that time he eats whatever he kills but he has always been faithful to his parents' command not to eat what he has killed before. He can now do whatever he likes, for now he is a man, and no longer considered a boy. If there is a war he can go to it; but the Piutes, and other tribes west of the Rocky Mountains, are not fond of going to war. I never saw a war-dance but once. It is always the whites that begin the wars, for their own selfish purposes. The government does not take care to send the good men; there are a plenty who would take pains to see and understand the chiefs and learn their characters, and their good will to the whites. But the whites have not waited to find out how good the Indians were, and what ideas they had of God, just like those of Jesus, who called him Father, just as my people do, and told men to do to others as they would be done by, just as my people teach their children to do. My people teach their children never to make fun of any one, no matter how they look. If you see your brother or sister doing something wrong, look away, or go away from them. If you make fun of bad persons, you make yourself beneath them. Be kind to all, both poor and rich, and feed all that come to your wigwam, and your name can be spoken of by every one far and near. In this way you will make many friends for yourself. Be kind both to bad and good, for you don't know your own heart. This is the way my people teach their children. It was handed down from father to son for many generations. I never in my life saw our children rude as I have seen white children and grown people in the streets.

The chief's tent is the largest tent, and it is the council-tent, where every one goes who wants advice. In the evenings the head men go there to discuss everything, for the chiefs do not rule like tyrants; they discuss everything with their people, as a father would in his family. Often they sit up all night. They discuss the doings of all, if they need to be advised. If a boy is not doing well they talk that over, and if the women are interested they can share in the talks. If there is not room enough inside, they all go out of doors, and make a great circle.

The men are in the inner circle, for there would be too much smoke for the women inside. The men never talk without smoking first. The women sit behind them in another circle, and if the children wish to hear, they can be there too. The women know as much as the men do, and their advice is often asked. We have a republic as well as you. The council-tent is our Congress, and anybody can speak who has anything to say, women and all. They are always interested in what their husbands are doing and thinking about. And they take some part even in the wars. They are always near at hand when fighting is going on, ready to snatch their husbands up and carry them off if wounded or killed. One splendid woman that my brother Lee married after his first wife died, went out into the battle-field after her uncle was killed, and went into the front ranks and cheered the men on. Her uncle's horse was dressed in a splendid robe made of eagles' feathers and she snatched it off and swung it in the face of the enemy, who always carry off everything they find, as much as to say, "You can't have that—I have it safe"; and she staid and took her uncle's place, as brave as any of the men. It means something when the women promise their fathers to make their husbands *themselves*. They faithfully keep with them in all the dangers they can share. They not only take care of their children together, but they do everything together; and when they grow blind, which I am sorry to say is very common, for the smoke they live in destroys their eyes at last, they take sweet care of one another. Marriage is a sweet thing when people love each other. If women could go into your Congress I think justice would soon be done to the Indians. I can't tell about all Indians; but I know my own people are kind to everybody that does not do them harm; but they will not be imposed upon, and when people are too bad they rise up and resist them. This seems to me all right. It is different from being revengeful. There is nothing cruel about our people. They never scalped a human being.

The chiefs do not live in idleness. They work with their people, and they are always poor for the following reason. It is the custom with my people to be very hospitable. When people visit them in their tents, they always set before them the best food they have, and if there is not enough for themselves they go without.

The chief's tent is the one always looked for when visitors come, and sometimes many come the same day. But they are all well received. I have often felt sorry for my brother, who is now the chief, when I saw him go without food for this reason. He would say, "We will wait and eat afterwards what is left." Perhaps little would be left, and when the agents did not give supplies and rations, he would have to go hungry.

At the council, one is always appointed to repeat at the time everything that is said on both sides, so that there may be no misunderstanding, and one person at least is present from every lodge, and after it is over, he goes and repeats what is decided upon at the door of the lodge, so all may be understood. For there is never any quarrelling in the tribe, only friendly counsels. The sub-chiefs are appointed by the great chief for special duties. There is no quarrelling about that, for neither sub-chief or great chief has any salary. It is this which makes the tribe so united and attached to each other, and makes it so dreadful to be parted. They would rather all die at once than be parted. They believe that in the Spirit-land those that die still watch over those that are living. When I was a child in California, I heard the Methodist minister say that everybody that did wrong was burned in hell forever. I was so frightened it made me very sick. He said the blessed ones in heaven looked down and saw their friends burning and could not help them. I wanted to be unborn, and cried so that my mother and the others told me it was not so, that it was only here that people did wrong and were in the hell that it made, and that those that were in the Spirit-land saw us here and were sorry for us. But we should go to them when we died, where there was never any wrongdoing, and so no hell. That is our religion.

My people capture antelopes by charming them, but only some of the people are charmers. My father was one of them, and once I went with him on an antelope hunt.

The antelopes move in herds in the winter, and as late in the spring as April. At this time there was said to be a large herd in a certain place, and my father told all his people to come together in ten days to go with him in his hunt. He told them to bring their wives with them, but no small children. When they came, at the end of ten days, he chose two men, who he said were to be his messengers to the antelopes. They were to have two large torches made of sage-brush bark, and after he had found a place for his camp, he marked out a circle around which the wigwams were to be placed, putting his own in the middle of the western side, and leaving an opening directly opposite in the middle of the eastern side, which was towards the antelopes.

The people who were with him in the camp then made another circle to the east of the one where their wigwams were, and made six mounds of sage-brush and stones on the sides of it, with a space of a hundred yards or more from one mound to the next one, but with no fence between the mounds. These mounds were made high, so that they could be seen from far off.

The women and boys and old men who were in the camp, and who were working on the mounds, were told to be very careful not to drop anything and not to stumble over a sage-brush root, or a stone, or anything, and not to have any accident, but to do everything perfectly and to keep thinking about the antelopes all the time, and not to let their thoughts go away to anything else. It took five days to charm the antelopes, and if anybody had an accident he must tell of it.

Every morning early, when the bright morning star could be seen, the people sat around the opening to the circle, with my father sitting in the middle of the opening, and my father lighted his pipe and passed it to his right, and the pipe went round the circle five times. And at night they did the same thing.

After they had smoked the pipe, my father took a kind of drum, which is used in this charming, and made music with it. This is the only kind of musical instrument which my people have, and it is only used for this antelope-charming. It is made of a hide of some large animal, stuffed with grass, so as to make it sound hollow, and then wound around tightly from one end to the other with a cord as large as my finger. One end of this instrument is large, and it tapers down to the other end, which is small, so that it makes a different sound on the different parts. My father took a stick and rubbed this stick from one end of the instrument to the other, making a penetrating, vibrating sound, that could be heard afar off, and he sang, and all his people sang with him.

After that the two men who were messengers went out to see the antelopes. They carried their torches in their right hands, and one of them carried a pipe in his left hand. They started from my father's wigwam and went straight across the camp to the opening; then they crossed, and one went around the second circle to the right and the other went to the left, till they met on the other side of the circle. Then they crossed again, and one went round the herd of antelopes one way and the other went round the other way, but they did not let the antelopes see them. When they met on the other side of the herd of antelopes, they stopped and smoked the pipe, and then they crossed, and each man came back on the track of the other to the camp, and told my father what they saw and what the antelopes were doing.

This was done every day for five days, and after the first day all the men and women and boys followed the messengers, and went around the circle they were to enter. On the fifth day the antelopes were charmed, and the whole herd followed the tracks of my people and entered the circle where the mounds were, coming in at the entrance, bowing and tossing their heads, and looking sleepy and under a powerful spell. They ran round and round inside the circle just as if there was a fence all around it and they could not get out, and they staid there until my people had killed every one. But if anybody had dropped anything, or had stumbled and had not told about it, then when the antelopes came to the place where he had done that, they threw off the spell and rushed wildly out of the circle at that place.

My brother can charm horses in the same way.

The Indian children amuse themselves a great deal by modelling in mud. They make herds of animals, which are modelled exceedingly well, and after setting them up, shoot at them with their little bows and arrows. They also string beads of different colors and show natural good taste.

1883

Sarah Orne Jewett
(1849–1909)

Berwick, Maine, had once been a thriving inland seaport, but at the time of Sarah Orne Jewett's birth, the region was in decline. The shipbuilding and fishing that had been its economic base were mostly gone, and the soil was not suitable for profitable farming. Accompanying her physician father on his rounds, Jewett saw the suffering of people whose livelihood had vanished. She was particularly struck by the plight of lone women, many the last remnants of once-prosperous families, living in isolation and poverty. She also observed how the increasing tide of summer tourists patronized the local people and looked down on them.

Her father was crucial to her intellectual development. Not only did she learn to observe people through his sympathetic eyes, his interest in botany and zoology helped focus her attention on her natural surroundings, and he made his extensive library of classic and contemporary writers available to her.

Because of chronic ill-health in childhood, Jewett had little formal education and had to abandon her dream of becoming a physician. Often, instead of attending classes at the local academy, she spent time with her beloved father, talked with people in the homes of his patients, read or explored the outdoors by herself. Her solitary observation, described in a letter as detail "that teases the mind over and over for years, and at last gets itself put down rightly on paper," proved to be her most effective preparation as a writer.

She read Harriet Beecher Stowe's novel *The Pearl of Orr's Island*, set on an island off the Maine coast, when she was a teenager.

For Jewett the book clarified the effectiveness of focusing on a specific geographical location, and she resolved that she would portray the denizens of her world with absolute realism and no romance. She hoped to illuminate "their grand, simple lives" and demonstrate "that country people were not the awkward, ignorant set" that summer tourists took them to be. Her first short stories, published before she was 20, appeared under the pseudonyms A. C. Eliot, Alice Eliot, and Sarah O. Sweet.

Frequently she traveled to Boston or New York, where prominent editors and authors were included among her circle of friends. Several of these men, especially James Russell Lowell, editor of *The Atlantic* from 1857 to 1861, and his successors, James T. Fields (1861–1871), William Dean Howells (1871–1881), and Thomas Bailey Aldrich (1881–1890), encouraged Jewett's career. Her story "Mr. Bruce" was published in the *Atlantic* in 1869, and with the encouragement of Howells she published *Deephaven*, her first volume of sketches, in 1877.

The death of Dr. Jewett (1878) was traumatic for his daughter, whose career as a writer was so newly begun. She dedicated *Country By-Ways* (1881) to him as "the best and wisest man I ever knew; who taught me many lessons and showed me many things as we went together along the country by-ways." The portrait of Dr. Leslie in *A Country Doctor* (1884) recreates his career; Jewett also wrote poetry expressing the desolation she felt at his loss.

With her father gone, her friendship with Annie Fields, the editor's wife, became her most important relationship.

After 1880, Jewett usually spent part of each winter in the Fields's Boston home and part of the summer at their summer cottage at Manchester-by-the-Sea. After James Fields died in 1881, the two women regularly traveled together in Florida, the Caribbean, and Europe. In successive European trips, they met some of the prominent British and American writers of the day, including Alfred, Lord Tennyson and Christina Rossetti (1882), Mrs. Humphry Ward and Mark Twain (1892), and Rudyard Kipling and Henry James (1898).

Jewett saw the villages of her region as microcosms of human experience, asserting that "the great plays of life, the comedies and tragedies, with their lovers and conspirators and clowns" were being constantly reenacted in farmhouses and streets. With gentle irony she reported the vanity, greed, and jealousy, as well as the selflessness and nobility of her characters. Jewett's collections of stories and sketches include *A White Heron and Other Stories* (1886); *The King of Folly Island and Other People* (1888); *Tales of New England* (1890); *Strangers and Wayfarers* (1890), the source of the story reprinted below; *A Native of Winby and Other Tales* (1893); *The Life of Nancy* (1895); and *The Queen's Twin and*

Other Stories (1899). Some stories were published in more than one collection. Her best known work, *The Country of the Pointed Firs*, appeared in 1896. Set in Dunnet Landing, a coastal village, it is narrated by a sympathetic summer visitor who encourages the inhabitants to recount their own experiences.

After a fall from a carriage in 1902, in which her head and spine were injured, Jewett's career as a writer was effectively ended, but she continued to carry on an active correspondence and travel to visit friends until her death following a stroke.

Jewett's fiction, in addition to titles named above, includes *Old Friends and New* (1879); *The Mate of the Daylight and Friends Ashore* (1883); *A Marsh Island* (1885); and *The Tory Lover* (1901), a historical romance. Collected editions include *Stories and Tales* (7 vols., 1910) and *The Best Short Stories of Sarah Orne Jewett*, ed. Willa Cather (2 vols., 1925). *The Uncollected Stories of Sarah Orne Jewett* was edited by Richard Cary (1971). *Letters* was edited by Richard Cary (1956, revised 1967).

Studies include F. O. Matthiessen, *Sarah Orne Jewett* (1929); Richard Cary, *Sarah Orne Jewett* (1962); Margaret Thorp, *Sarah Orne Jewett* (1966); Josephine Donovan, *Sarah Orne Jewett* (1980); and Sarah Way Sherman, *Sarah Orne Jewett, An American Persephone* (1989).

The Town Poor

Mrs. William Trimble and Miss Rebecca Wright were driving along Hampden east road, one afternoon in early spring. Their progress was slow. Mrs. Trimble's sorrel horse was old and stiff, and the wheels were clogged by clay mud. The frost was not yet out of the ground, although the snow was nearly gone, except in a few places on the north side of the woods, or where it had drifted all winter against a length of fence.

"There must be a good deal o' snow to the nor'ard of us yet," said weather-wise Mrs. Trimble. "I feel it in the air; 't is more than the ground-damp. We ain't goin' to have real nice weather till the upcountry snow's all gone."

"I heard say yesterday that there was good sleddin' yet, all up through Parsley," responded Miss Wright. "I shouldn't like to live in them northern places. My cousin Ellen's husband was a Parsley man, an' he was obliged, as you may have heard, to go up north to his father's second wife's funeral; got back day before yesterday. 'T was about twenty-one miles, an' they started on wheels; but when they'd gone nine or ten miles, they found 't was no sort o' use, an' left their wagon an' took a sleigh. The man that owned it charged 'em four an' six, too. I shouldn't have thought he would; they told him they was goin' to a funeral; an' they had their own buffaloes[1] an' everything."

"Well, I expect it's a good deal harder scratchin', up that way; they have to git money where they can; the farms is very poor as you go north," suggested Mrs. Trimble kindly. " 'T ain't none too rich a country where we be, but I've always been grateful I wa'n't born up to Parsley."

The old horse plodded along, and the sun, coming out from the heavy spring clouds, sent a sudden shine of light along the muddy road. Sister Wright drew her large veil forward over the high brim of her bonnet. She was not used to driving, or to being much in the open air; but Mrs. Trimble was an active business woman, and looked after her own affairs herself, in all weathers. The late Mr. Trimble had left her a good farm, but not much ready money, and it was often said that she was better off in the end than if he had lived. She regretted his loss deeply, however; it was impossible for her to speak of him, even to intimate friends, without emotion, and nobody had ever hinted that this emotion was insincere. She was most warm-hearted and generous, and in her limited way played the part of Lady Bountiful[2] in the town of Hampden.

"Why, there's where the Bray girls lives, ain't it?" she exclaimed, as, beyond a thicket of witch-hazel and scrub-oak, they came in sight of a weather-beaten, solitary farmhouse. The barn was too far away for thrift or comfort, and they could see long lines of light between the shrunken boards as they came nearer. The fields looked both stony and sodden. Somehow, even Parsley itself could be hardly more forlorn.

"Yes 'm," said Miss Wright, "that's where they live now, poor things. I know the place, though I ain't been up here for years. You don't suppose, Mis' Trimble—I ain't seen the girls out to meetin'[3] all winter. I've re'lly been covetin' "—

"Why, yes, Rebecca, of course we could stop," answered Mrs. Trimble heartily. "The exercises was over earlier 'n I expected, an' you're goin' to remain over night long o' me, you know. There won't be no tea till we git there, so we can't be late. I'm in the habit o' sendin' a basket to the Bray girls when any o' our folks is comin' this way, but I ain't been to see 'em since they moved up here. Why, it must be a good deal over a year ago. I know 't was in the late winter they had to make the move. 'T was cruel hard, I must say, an' if I hadn't been down with my pleurisy fever I'd have stirred round an' done somethin' about it. There was a good deal o' sickness at the time, an'—well, 't was kind o' rushed through, breakin' of 'em up, an' lots o' folks blamed the selec'men;[4] but when 't was done, 't was done, an' nobody took holt to undo it. Ann an' Mandy looked same 's ever when they come to meetin', 'long in the summer,—kind o' wishful, perhaps. They've always sent me word they was gittin' on pretty comfortable."

"That would be their way," said Rebecca Wright. "They never was any hand to complain, though Mandy's less cheerful than Ann. If Mandy'd been spared such poor eyesight, an' Ann hadn't got her lame wrist that wa'n't set right, they'd kep' off the town[5] fast enough. They both shed tears when they talked to me about havin' to break up, when I went to see 'em before I went over to brother Asa's. You see we was brought up neighbors, an' we went to school together, the Brays an' me. 'T was a special Providence brought us home this road, I've been so covetin' a chance to git to see 'em. My lameness hampers me."

---

1. Fur robes.
2. A wealthy character in Farquhar's play *The Beaux' Stratagem* (1707).
3. Church services.
4. A representative council of "selectmen" is the form of government in many New England villages. They are elected by the attendees at the "town meeting."
5. "Going on the town" describes a system of relief for the poor in which a fee is paid to a family who will provide a place to live; the person who accepts this town aid must give up his or her own home.

"I'm glad we come this way, myself," said Mrs. Trimble.

"I'd like to see just how they fare," Miss Rebecca Wright continued. "They give their consent to goin' on the town because they knew they'd got to be dependent, an' so they felt 't would come easier for all than for a few to help 'em. They acted real dignified an' right-minded, contrary to what most do in such cases, but they was dreadful anxious to see who would bid 'em off, town-meeting day; they did so hope 't would be somebody right in the village. I just sat down an' cried good when I found Abel Janes's folks had got hold of 'em. They always had the name of bein' slack an' poor-spirited, an' they did it just for what they got out o' the town. The selectmen this last year ain't what we have had. I hope they've been considerate about the Bray girls."

"I should have be'n more considerate about fetchin' of you over," apologized Mrs. Trimble. "I've got my horse, an' you're lame-footed; 't is too far for you to come. But time does slip away with busy folks, an' I forgit a good deal I ought to remember."

"There's nobody more considerate than you be," protested Miss Rebecca Wright.

Mrs. Trimble made no answer, but took out her whip and gently touched the sorrel horse, who walked considerably faster, but did not think it worth while to trot. It was a long, round-about way to the house, farther down the road and up a lane.

"I never had any opinion of the Bray girls' father, leavin' 'em as he did," said Mrs. Trimble.

"He was much praised in his time, though there was always some said his early life hadn't been up to the mark," explained her companion. "He was a great favorite of our then preacher, the Reverend Daniel Longbrother. They did a good deal for the parish, but they did it their own way. Deacon Bray was one that did his part in the repairs without urging. You know 't was in his time the first repairs was made, when they got out the old soundin'-board[6] an' them handsome square pews. It cost an awful sight o' money, too. They hadn't done payin' up that debt when they set to alter it again an' git the walls frescoed. My grandmother was one that always spoke her mind right out, an' she was dreadful opposed to breakin' up the square pews where she'd always set. They was countin' up what 't would cost in parish meetin', an' she riz right up an' said 't wouldn't cost nothin' to let 'em stay, an' there wa'n't a house carpenter left in the parish that could do such nice work, an' time would come when the great-grandchildren would give their eye-teeth to have the old meetin'-house look just as it did then. But haul the inside to pieces they would and did."

"There come to be a real fight over it, didn't there?" agreed Mrs. Trimble soothingly.

"Well, 't wa'n't good taste. I remember the old house well. I come here as a child to visit a cousin o' mother's, an' Mr. Trimble's folks was neighbors, an' we was drawed to each other then, young's we was. Mr. Trimble spoke of it many's the time,—that first time he ever see me, in a leghorn hat with a feather; 't was one that mother had, an' pressed over."

"When I think of them old sermons that used to be preached in that old meetin'-house of all, I'm glad it's altered over, so's not to remind folks," said Miss Rebecca Wright, after a suitable pause. "Them old brimstone discourses, you know, Mis' Trimble. Preachers is far more reasonable, nowadays. Why, I set an' thought, last Sabbath, as I listened, that if old Mr. Longbrother an' Deacon Bray could hear the difference they'd crack the ground over 'em like pole beans, an' come right up 'long side their headstones."

Mrs. Trimble laughed heartily, and shook the reins three or four times by way of emphasis. "There's no gitting round you," she said, much pleased. "I should think Deacon Bray would want to rise, any way, if 't was so he could, an' knew how his poor girls was farin'. A man ought to provide for his folks he's got to leave behind him, specially if they're women. To be sure, they had their little home; but we've seen how, with all their industrious ways, they hadn't means to keep it. I s'pose he thought he'd got time enough to lay by, when he give so generous in collections; but he didn't lay by, an' there they be. He might have took lessons from the squirrels: even them little wild creatur's makes them their winter hoards, an'

---

6. A structure over or around the pulpit intended to reflect the sound toward the congregation.

menfolks ought to know enough if squirrels does. 'Be just before you are generous:' that's what was always set for the B's in the copy-books, when I was to school, and it often runs through my mind."

" 'As for man, his days are as grass,'—that was for A; the two go well together," added Miss Rebecca Wright soberly. "My good gracious, ain't this a starved-lookin' place? It makes me ache to think them nice Bray girls has to brook it here."

The sorrel horse, though somewhat puzzled by an unexpected deviation from his homeward way, willingly came to a stand by the gnawed corner of the door-yard fence, which evidently served as hitching-place. Two or three ragged old hens were picking about the yard, and at last a face appeared at the kitchen window, tied up in a handkerchief, as if it were a case of toothache. By the time our friends reached the side door next this window, Mrs. Janes came disconsolately to open it for them, shutting it again as soon as possible, though the air felt more chilly inside the house.

"Take seats," said Mrs. Janes briefly. "You'll have to see me just as I be. I have been suffering these four days with the ague, and everything to do. Mr. Janes is to court, on the jury. 'T was inconvenient to spare him. I should be pleased to have you lay off your things."

Comfortable Mrs. Trimble looked about the cheerless kitchen, and could not think of anything to say; so she smiled blandly and shook her head in answer to the invitation. "We'll just set a few minutes with you, to pass the time o' day, an' then we must go in an' have a word with the Miss Brays, bein' old acquaintance. It ain't been so we could git to call on 'em before. I don't know's you're acquainted with Miss R'becca Wright. She's been out of town a good deal."

"I heard she was stopping over to Plainfields with her brother's folks," replied Mrs. Janes, rocking herself with irregular motion, as she sat close to the stove. "Got back some time in the fall, I believe?"

"Yes 'm," said Miss Rebecca, with an undue sense of guilt and conviction. "We've been to the installation[7] over to the East Parish, an' thought we'd stop in; we took this road home to see if 't was any better. How is the Miss Brays gettin' on?"

"They're well's common," answered Mrs. Janes grudgingly. "I was put out with Mr. Janes for fetchin' of 'em here, with all I've got to do, an' I own I was kind o' surly to 'em 'long to the first of it. He gits the money from the town, an' it helps him out; but he bid 'em off for five dollars a month, an' we can't do much for 'em at no such price as that. I went an' dealt with the selec'men, an' made 'em promise to find their firewood an' some other things extra. They was glad to get rid o' the matter the fourth time I went, an' would ha' promised 'most anything. But Mr. Janes don't keep me half the time in oven-wood, he's off so much, an' we was cramped o' room, any way. I have to store things up garrit a good deal, an' that keeps me trampin' right through their room. I do the best for 'em I can, Mis' Trimble, but 't ain't so easy for me as 't is for you, with all your means to do with."

The poor woman looked pinched and miserable herself, though it was evident that she had no gift at house or home keeping. Mrs. Trimble's heart was wrung with pain, as she thought of the unwelcome inmates of such a place; but she held her peace bravely, while Miss Rebecca again gave some brief information in regard to the installation.

"You go right up them back stairs," the hostess directed at last. "I'm glad some o' you church folks has seen fit to come an' visit 'em. There ain't been nobody here this long spell, an' they've aged a sight since they come. They always send down a taste out of your baskets, Mis' Trimble, an' I relish it, I tell you. I'll shut the door after you, if you don't object. I feel every draught o' cold air."

"I've always heard she was a great hand to make a poor mouth. Wa'n't she from somewheres up Parsley way?" whispered Miss Rebecca, as they stumbled in the half-light.

"Poor meechin' body, wherever she come from," replied Mrs. Trimble, as she knocked at the door.

---

7. Formal presentation of a new minister.

There was silence for a moment after this unusual sound; then one of the Bray sisters opened the door. The eager guests stared into a small, low room, brown with age, and gray, too, as if former dust and cobwebs could not be made wholly to disappear. The two elderly women who stood there looked like captives. Their withered faces wore a look of apprehension, and the room itself was more bare and plain than was fitting to their evident refinement of character and self-respect. There was an uncovered small table in the middle of the floor, with some crackers on a plate; and, for some reason or other, this added a great deal to the general desolation.

But Miss Ann Bray, the elder sister, who carried her right arm in a sling, with piteously drooping fingers, gazed at the visitors with radiant joy. She had not seen them arrive.

The one window gave only the view at the back of the house, across the fields, and their coming was indeed a surprise. The next minute she was laughing and crying together. "Oh, sister!" she said, "if here ain't our dear Mis' Trimble!—an' my heart o' goodness, 't is 'Becca Wright, too! What dear good creatur's you be! I've felt all day as if something good was goin' to happen, an' was just sayin' to myself 't was most sundown now, but I wouldn't let on to Mandany I'd give up hope quite yet. You see, the scissors stuck in the floor this very mornin' an' it's always a reliable sign. There, I've got to kiss ye both again!"

"I don't know where we can all set," lamented sister Mandana. "There ain't but the one chair an' the bed; t' other chair's too rickety; an' we've been promised another these ten days; but first they've forgot it, an' next Mis' Janes can't spare it,—one excuse an' another. I am goin' to git a stump o' wood an' nail a board on to it, when I can git outdoor again," said Mandana, in a plaintive voice. "There, I ain't goin' to complain o' nothin', now you've come," she added; and the guests sat down, Mrs. Trimble, as was proper, in the one chair.

"We've sat on the bed many's the time with you, 'Becca, an' talked over our girl nonsense, ain't we? You know where 't was—in the little back bedroom we had when we was girls, an' used to peek out at our beaux through the strings o' mornin'-glories," laughed Ann Bray delightedly, her thin face shining more and more with joy. "I brought some o' them mornin'-glory seeds along when we come away, we'd raised 'em so many years; an' we got 'em started all right, but the hens found 'em out. I declare I chased them poor hens, foolish as 't was; but the mornin'-glories I'd counted on a sight to remind me o' home. You see, our debts was so large, after my long sickness an' all, that we didn't feel 't was right to keep back anything we could help from the auction."

It was impossible for any one to speak for a moment or two; the sisters felt their own uprooted condition afresh, and their guests for the first time really comprehended the piteous contrast between that neat little village house, which now seemed a palace of comfort, and this cold, unpainted upper room in the remote Janes farmhouse. It was an unwelcome thought to Mrs. Trimble that the well-to-do town of Hampden could provide no better for its poor than this, and her round face flushed with resentment and the shame of personal responsibility. "The girls shall be well settled in the village before another winter, if I pay their board myself," she made an inward resolution, and took another almost tearful look at the broken stove, the miserable bed, and the sisters' one hair-covered trunk, on which Mandana was sitting. But the poor place was filled with a golden spirit of hospitality.

Rebecca was again discoursing eloquently of the installation; it was so much easier to speak of general subjects, and the sisters had evidently been longing to hear some news. Since the late summer they had not been to church, and presently Mrs. Trimble asked the reason.

"Now, don't you go to pouring out our woes, Mandy!" begged little old Ann, looking shy and almost girlish, and as if she insisted upon playing that life was still all before them and all pleasure. "Don't you go to spoilin' their visit with our complaints! They know well's we do that changes must come, an' we'd been so wonted[8] to our home things that this come hard at first; but then they felt for us, I know just as well's can be. 'T will soon be summer again,

8. Accustomed.

an' 't is real pleasant right out in the fields here, when there ain't too hot a spell. I've got to know a sight o' singin' birds since we come."

"Give me the folks I've always known," sighed the younger sister, who looked older than Miss Ann, and less even-tempered. "You may have your birds, if you want 'em. I do re'lly long to go to meetin' an' see folks go by up the aisle. Now, I will speak of it, Ann, whatever you say. We need, each of us, a pair o' good stout shoes an' rubbers,—ours are all wore out; an' we've asked an' asked, an' they never think to bring 'em, an' ' "—

Poor old Mandana, on the trunk, covered her face with her arms and sobbed aloud. The elder sister stood over her, and patted her on the thin shoulder like a child, and tried to comfort her. It crossed Mrs. Trimble's mind that it was not the first time one had wept and the other had comforted. The sad scene must have been repeated many times in that long, drear winter. She would see them forever after in her mind as fixed as a picture, and her own tears fell fast.

"You didn't see Mis' Janes's cunning little boy, the next one to the baby, did you?" asked Ann Bray, turning round quickly at last, and going cheerfully on with the conversation. "Now, hush, Mandy, dear; they'll think you're childish! He's a dear, friendly little creatur', an' likes to stay with us a good deal, though we feel's if it 't was too cold for him, now we are waitin' to get us more wood."

"When I think of the acres o' woodland in this town!" groaned Rebecca Wright. "I believe I'm goin' to preach next Sunday, 'stead o' the minister, an' I'll make the sparks fly. I've always heard the saying, 'What's everybody's business is nobody's business,' an' I've come to believe it."

"Now, don't you, 'Becca. You've happened on a kind of a poor time with us, but we've got more belongings than you see here, an' a good large cluset, where we can store those things there ain't room to have about. You an' Miss Trimble have happened on a kind of poor day, you know. Soon's I git me some stout shoes an' rubbers, as Mandy says, I can fetch home plenty o' little dry boughs o' pine; you remember I was always a great hand to roam in the woods? If we could only have a front room, so 't we could look out on the road an' see passin', an' was shod for meetin', I don' know's we should complain. Now we're just goin' to give you what we've got, an' make out with a good welcome. We make more tea 'n we want in the mornin', an' then let the fire go down, since 't has been so mild. We've got a *good* cluset" (disappearing as she spoke), "an' I know this to be good tea, 'cause it's some o' yourn, Mis' Trimble. An' here's our sprigged chiny cups that R'becca knows by sight, if Mis' Trimble don't. We kep' out four of 'em, an' put the even half dozen with the rest of the auction stuff. I've often wondered who'd got 'em, but I never asked, for fear 't would be somebody that would distress us. They was mother's, you know."

The four cups were poured, and the little table pushed to the bed, where Rebecca Wright still sat, and Mandana, wiping her eyes, came and joined her. Mrs. Trimble sat in her chair at the end, and Ann trotted about the room in pleased content for a while, and in and out of the closet, as if she still had much to do; then she came and stood opposite Mrs. Trimble. She was very short and small, and there was no painful sense of her being obliged to stand. The four cups were not quite full of cold tea, but there was a clean old tablecloth folded double, and a plate with three pairs of crackers neatly piled, and a small—it must be owned, a very small—piece of hard white cheese. Then, for a treat, in a glass dish, there was a little preserved peach, the last—Miss Rebecca knew it instinctively—of the household stores brought from their old home. It was very sugary, this bit of peach; and as she helped her guests and sister Mandy, Miss Ann Bray said, half unconsciously, as she often had said with less reason in the old days, "Our preserves ain't so good as usual this year; this is beginning to candy." Both the guests protested, while Rebecca added that the taste of it carried her back, and made her feel young again. The Brays had always managed to keep one or two peach-trees alive in their corner of a garden. "I've been keeping this preserve for a treat," said her friend. "I'm glad to have you eat some, 'Becca. Last summer I often wished you was home an' could come an' see us, 'stead o' being away off to Plainfields."

The crackers did not taste too dry. Miss Ann took the last of the peach on her own cracker; there could not have been quite a small spoonful, after the others were helped, but she asked them first if they would not have some more. Then there was a silence, and in the silence a wave of tender feeling rose high in the hearts of the four elderly women. At this moment the setting sun flooded the poor plain room with light; the unpainted wood was all of a golden-brown, and Ann Bray, with her gray hair and aged face, stood at the head of the table in a kind of aureole. Mrs. Trimble's face was all aquiver as she looked at her; she thought of the text about two or three being gathered together, and was half afraid.[9]

"I believe we ought to've asked Mis' Janes if she wouldn't come up," said Ann. "She's real good feelin', but she's had it very hard, an' gits discouraged. I can't find that she's ever had anything real pleasant to look back to, as we have. There, next time we'll make a good heartenin' time for her too."

The sorrel horse had taken a long nap by the gnawed fence-rail, and the cool air after sundown made him impatient to be gone. The two friends jolted homeward in the gathering darkness, through the stiffening mud, and neither Mrs. Trimble nor Rebecca Wright said a word until they were out of sight as well as out of sound of the Janes house. Time must elapse before they could reach a more familiar part of the road and resume conversation on its natural level.

"I consider myself to blame," insisted Mrs. Trimble at last. "I haven't no words of accusation for nobody else, an' I ain't one to take comfort in calling names to the board o' selec'*men*. I make no reproaches, an' I take it all on my own shoulders; but I'm goin' to stir about me, I tell you! I shall begin early to-morrow. They're goin' back to their own house,—it's been standin' empty all winter,—an' the town's goin' to give 'em the rent an' what firewood they need; it won't come to more than the board's payin' out now. An' you an' me'll take this same horse an' wagon, an' ride an' go afoot by turns, an' git means enough together to buy back their furniture an' whatever was sold at that plaguey auction; an' then we'll put it all back, an' tell 'em they've got to move to a new place, an' just carry 'em right back again where they come from. An' don't you never tell, R'becca, but here I be a widow woman, layin' up what I make from my farm for nobody knows who, an' I'm goin' to do for them Bray girls all I'm a mind to. I should be sca't to wake up in heaven, an' hear anybody there ask how the Bray girls was. Don't talk to me about the town o' Hampden, an' don't ever let me hear the name o' town poor! I'm ashamed to go home an' see what's set out for supper. I wish I'd brought 'em right along."

"I was goin' to ask if we couldn't git the new doctor to go up an' do somethin' for poor Ann's arm," said Miss Rebecca. "They say he's very smart. If she could get so's to braid straw or hook rugs again, she'd soon be earnin' a little somethin'. An' may be he could do somethin' for Mandy's eyes. They did use to live so neat an' ladylike. Somehow I couldn't speak to tell 'em there that 't was I bought them six best cups an' saucers, time of the auction; they went very low, as everything else did, an' I thought I could save it some other way. They shall have 'em back an' welcome. You're real whole-hearted, Mis' Trimble. I expect Ann'll be sayin' that her father's child'n wa'n't goin' to be left desolate, an' that all the bread he cast on the water's comin' back through you."

"I don't care what she says, dear creatur'!" exclaimed Mrs. Trimble. "I'm full o' regrets I took time for that installation, an' set there seepin' in a lot o' talk this whole day long, except for its kind of bringin' us to the Bray girls. I wish to my heart 't was to-morrow mornin' a'ready, an' I a-startin' for the selec'*men*."

1890

---

9. In Matthew 18:20 Jesus says, "For where two   in the midst of them."
    or three are gathered in my name, there am I

Kate Chopin
(1850–1904)

As the author of *The Awakening* (1899), a novel about a young wife's increasing dissatisfaction with the social and sexual conventionalities of late nineteenth-century upper middle-class life, Kate Chopin became a notorious woman. The scandal her novel aroused, the diminished attention to her works, and the recent heightened interest in her career form an important part of women's literary history.

Kate O'Flaherty was born into a privileged family in St. Louis at midcentury. Her mother was Eliza Faris O'Flaherty, whose upper-class Creole background prefigured Kate's own married life; her father, Thomas O'Flaherty, had immigrated from Ireland and found financial security as a merchant in St. Louis. Kate attended a Catholic school, the Academy of the Sacred Heart, and graduated in 1868, fluent in German and French.

Two years after graduation, Kate met and married a French-Creole gentleman, Oscar Chopin from Louisiana, who eventually made his fortune in the cotton business. After honeymooning in France, Switzerland, and Germany, the Chopins lived first in New Orleans, later in Cloutierville, Natchitoches Parish, Louisiana. Between 1871 and 1879, Chopin had six children. Although she had kept a diary in her youth, she found little time for writing as a young married woman.

A respectable wife and mother, Chopin was nevertheless unconventional. She was, for instance, a smoker, which was highly unusual for middle-class women of the period; she also thought nothing of traveling the city of New Orleans alone on the streetcars, exploring neighborhoods and coming into contact with people in all ranks of life. She ran her husband's plantation for over a year after he died of fever in 1882. Two years later she returned home with her children to St. Louis. She began studying contemporary philosophy, biology, and natural history, reading, for example, Charles Darwin's theories of evolution. She began writing stories of her own in 1888 and publishing them in periodicals.

The majority of Chopin's writings are set in Louisiana, detailing the settings, attitudes, and lifestyles of the Creoles (the socially prominent families of French extraction) and the Cajuns (the working-class descendants of French-speaking families who had emigrated from Acadia in Canada). Philosophically, she can be classed as a naturalist writer in the tradition of the French novelist Emile Zola. In common with Theodore Dreiser, Frank Norris, and Stephen Crane, she accepted naturalism's assumption that human character is the result of an individual's heredity and environment, its assertion that the individual will is helpless against those forces. For the naturalists, *"race"* (blood, or nature), *"milieu"* (setting and social status), and *"temps"* (era) constitute fate. Applying evolutionary theories to concepts of society and psychology, they held that the fittest would survive—and the fittest would not necessarily always be the most heroic. Hence they turned away from the moral uplift typical of American women's writing in the nineteenth century, where virtuous people receive their just rewards in the end.

Like other naturalists, Chopin takes an objective, almost scientific perspective in reporting characters' thoughts and actions. The narrator's comments stress the physical aspect of settings and record the characters' sensual responses to their surroundings. The narrator seldom, if ever, passes a judgment on the character's behavior: moral conclusions are conspicuously absent from the texts.

The reception of *The Awakening* demonstrates the risks of writing in this way. In her novel, Chopin traces the development of a new awareness of desire in her protagonist, Edna Pontellier, a married woman with two children who comes to realize how frustrated she is in her relation to her husband. She desires a creative outlet (in her case, painting), the freedom to determine how she will spend her own time, and sensual gratification. Gradually, Edna stops doing her "duty" as a wife, refusing to receive visitors, sleep with her husband on demand, or let her attention be consumed by her children. Edna leaves her husband, having conceived a passion for another, younger man, and begins pursuing life as an independent artist. Although in the end Edna drowns—perhaps in despair, perhaps in triumph over her fate— Chopin's contemporaries were outraged that the novel does not clearly condemn Edna's transgressions against conventional morality. When the book was published, the literary establishment condemned it and refused—in many cases—even to review it. It was banned from library shelves in Chopin's native St. Louis, and she was expelled from the St. Louis Fine Arts Club. Discouraged by the reaction to her novel, Chopin wrote only five more stories before her death of a cerebral hemorrhage in 1904.

The Awakening was neglected until the 1970s, when a newly awakened interest in women writers focused attention upon it. Until that time, Chopin had primarily been remembered as a "local-color" writer of short stories. Though Chopin collected many of her stories in volumes during her lifetime, the two reprinted below were not among them. "A Pair of Silk Stockings," published first in *Vogue* magazine in 1969, resembles *The Awakening* in its portrayal of a woman's succumbing to irresistible urges despite her family's claims upon her resources. It is typical, too, of Chopin in that the narrator remains completely neutral, allowing the reader to judge whether the protagonist's situation deserves sympathy or censure. *The Storm*, remarkable for its relative frankness about an adulterous sexual encounter between a Creole man and a Cajun woman, never appeared in print during Chopin's lifetime. It stands today as an unusual example of women's humor, drily ironic in its observation of the benefits that the lovers' families will derive from this illicit coupling. It is also an extremely early example of women's erotica, more surprising even than a smoking habit in a woman of Chopin's generation.

Chopin's first novel was *At Fault* (1890); her collections of stories include *Bayou Folk* (1894) and *A Night in Acadie* (1897). Her writings were collected in 1969 by Per Seyersted in the two-volume *Complete Works of Kate Chopin*; Seyersted and Emily Toth collaborated in collecting *A Kate Chopin Miscellany* (1979).

The most recent biography is *Kate Chopin* (1990) by Emily Toth; see also *Kate Chopin: A Critical Biography* (1969) by Per Seyersted; and *Kate Chopin and Her Creole Stories* (1932) by Daniel S. Rankin. For recent critical studies of Chopin, see *New Essays on The Awakening* (1988) edited by Wendy Martin; *Women on the Color Line* (1989) by Anna Shannon Elfenbein; *Gender, Race, and Region in the Writings of . . . Kate Chopin* (1989) by Helen Taylor; and *Verging on the Abyss* (1990) by Mary E. Papke.

A Pair of Silk Stockings

Little Mrs. Sommers one day found herself the unexpected possessor of fifteen dollars. It seemed to her a very large amount of money, and the way in which it stuffed and bulged her worn old *porte-monnaie*[1] gave her a feeling of importance such as she had not enjoyed for years.

The question of investment was one that occupied her greatly. For a day or two she walked about apparently in a dreamy state, but really absorbed in speculation and calculation. She

---

1. Coin purse.

did not wish to act hastily, to do anything she might afterward regret. But it was during the still hours of the night when she lay awake revolving plans in her mind that she seemed to see her way clearly toward a proper and judicious use of the money.

A dollar or two should be added to the price usually paid for Janie's shoes, which would insure their lasting an appreciable time longer than they usually did. She would buy so and so many yards of percale for new shirt waists for the boys and Janie and Mag.[2] She had intended to make the old ones do by skilful patching. Mag should have another gown. She had seen some beautiful patterns, veritable bargains in the shop windows. And still there would be left enough for new stockings—two pairs apiece—and what darning that would save for a while! She would get caps for the boys and sailor-hats for the girls. The vision of her little brood looking fresh and dainty and new for once in their lives excited her and made her restless and wakeful with anticipation.

The neighbors sometimes talked of certain "better days" that little Mrs. Sommers had known before she had ever thought of being Mrs. Sommers. She herself indulged in no such morbid retrospection. She had no time—no second of time to devote to the past. The needs of the present absorbed her every faculty. A vision of the future like some dim, gaunt monster sometimes appalled her, but luckily to-morrow never comes.

Mrs. Sommers was one who knew the value of bargains; who could stand for hours making her way inch by inch toward the desired object that was selling below cost. She could elbow her way if need be; she had learned to clutch a piece of goods and hold it and stick to it with persistence and determination till her turn came to be served, no matter when it came.

But that day she was a little faint and tired. She had swallowed a light luncheon—no! when she came to think of it, between getting the children fed and the place righted, and preparing herself for the shopping bout, she had actually forgotten to eat any luncheon at all!

She sat herself upon a revolving stool before a counter that was comparatively deserted, trying to gather strength and courage to charge through an eager multitude that was besieging breastworks of shirting and figured lawn.[3] An all-gone limp feeling had come over her and she rested her hand aimlessly upon the counter. She wore no gloves. By degrees she grew aware that her hand had encountered something very soothing, very pleasant to touch. She looked down to see that her hand lay upon a pile of silk stockings. A placard near by announced that they had been reduced in price from two dollars and fifty cents to one dollar and ninety-eight cents; and a young girl who stood behind the counter asked her if she wished to examine their line of silk hosiery. She smiled, just as if she had been asked to inspect a tiara of diamonds with the ultimate view of purchasing it. But she went on feeling the soft, sheeny luxurious things—with both hands now, holding them up to see them glisten, and to feel them glide serpent-like through her fingers.

Two hectic[4] blotches came suddenly into her pale cheeks. She looked up at the girl.

"Do you think there are any eights-and-a-half among these?"

There were any number of eights-and-a-half. In fact, there were more of that size than any other. Here was a light-blue pair; there were some lavender, some all black and various shades of tan and gray. Mrs. Sommers selected a black pair and looked at them very long and closely. She pretended to be examining their texture, which the clerk assured her was excellent.

"A dollar and ninety-eight cents," she mused aloud. "Well, I'll take this pair." She handed the girl a five-dollar bill and waited for her change and for her parcel. What a very small parcel it was! It seemed lost in the depths of her shabby old shopping-bag.

Mrs. Sommers after that did not move in the direction of the bargain counter. She took the elevator, which carried her to an upper floor into the region of the ladies' waiting-rooms. Here, in a retired corner, she exchanged her cotton stockings for the new silk ones which she

---

2. Percale is opaque cotton fabric; a shirtwaist is a tailored shirt, usually for women's wear.
3. Lawn is a fine, thin cotton or linen fabric;

"figured" cloth has a design or decorative pattern on it.
4. Feverish.

had just bought. She was not going through any acute mental process or reasoning with herself, nor was she striving to explain to her satisfaction the motive of her action. She was not thinking at all. She seemed for the time to be taking a rest from that laborious and fatiguing function and to have abandoned herself to some mechanical impulse that directed her actions and freed her of responsibility.

How good was the touch of the raw silk to her flesh! She felt like lying back in the cushioned chair and reveling for a while in the luxury of it. She did for a little while. Then she replaced her shoes, rolled the cotton stockings together and thrust them into her bag. After doing this she crossed straight over to the shoe department and took her seat to be fitted.

She was fastidious. The clerk could not make her out; he could not reconcile her shoes with her stockings, and she was not too easily pleased. She held back her skirts and turned her feet one way and her head another way as she glanced down at the polished, pointed-tipped boots. Her foot and ankle looked very pretty. She could not realize that they belonged to her and were a part of herself. She wanted an excellent and stylish fit, she told the young fellow who served her, and she did not mind the difference of a dollar or two more in the price so long as she got what she desired.

It was a long time since Mrs. Sommers had been fitted with gloves. On rare occasions when she had bought a pair they were always "bargains," so cheap that it would have been preposterous and unreasonable to have expected them to be fitted to the hand.

Now she rested her elbow on the cushion of the glove counter, and a pretty, pleasant young creature, delicate and deft of touch, drew a long-wristed "kid"[5] over Mrs. Sommers's hand. She smoothed it down over the wrist and buttoned it neatly, and both lost themselves for a second or two in admiring contemplation of the little symmetrical gloved hand. But there were other places where money might be spent.

There were books and magazines piled up in the window of a stall a few paces down the street. Mrs. Sommers bought two high-priced magazines such as she had been accustomed to read in the days when she had been accustomed to other pleasant things. She carried them without wrapping. As well as she could she lifted her skirts at the crossings. Her stockings and boots and well fitting gloves had worked marvels in her bearing—had given her a feeling of assurance, a sense of belonging to the well-dressed multitude.

She was very hungry. Another time she would have stilled the cravings for food until reaching her own home, where she would have brewed herself a cup of tea and taken a snack of anything that was available. But the impulse that was guiding her would not suffer her to entertain any such thought.

There was a restaurant at the corner. She had never entered its doors; from the outside she had sometimes caught glimpses of spotless damask and shining crystal, and soft-stepping waiters serving people of fashion.

When she entered her appearance created no surprise, no consternation, as she had half feared it might. She seated herself at a small table alone, and an attentive waiter at once approached to take her order. She did not want a profusion; she craved a nice and tasty bite—a half dozen blue-points, a plump chop with cress, a something sweet—a crème-frappée, for instance; a glass of Rhine wine, and after all a small cup of black coffee.

While waiting to be served she removed her gloves very leisurely and laid them beside her. Then she picked up a magazine and glanced through it, cutting the pages with a blunt edge of her knife.[6] It was all very agreeable. The damask was even more spotless than it had seemed through the window, and the crystal more sparkling. There were quiet ladies and gentlemen, who did not notice her, lunching at the small tables like her own. A soft, pleasing strain of music could be heard, and a gentle breeze was blowing through the window. She

---

5. Glove made from the hide of a young goat.
6. Books and magazines were printed on large sheets that were folded, then bound. The pages had to be cut with a paper knife before they could be read.

tasted a bite, and she read a word or two, and she sipped the amber wine and wiggled her toes in the silk stockings. The price of it made no difference. She counted the money out to the waiter and left an extra coin on his tray, whereupon he bowed before her as before a princess of royal blood.

There was still money in her purse, and her next temptation presented itself in the shape of a matinée poster.

It was a little later when she entered the theatre, the play had begun and the house seemed to her to be packed. But there were vacant seats here and there, and into one of them she was ushered, between brilliantly dressed women who had gone there to kill time and eat candy and display their gaudy attire. There were many others who were there solely for the play and acting. It is safe to say there was no one present who bore quite the attitude which Mrs. Sommers did to her surroundings. She gathered in the whole—stage and players and people in one wide impression, and absorbed it and enjoyed it. She laughed at the comedy and wept—she and the gaudy woman next to her wept over the tragedy. And they talked a little together over it. And the gaudy woman wiped her eyes and sniffled on a tiny square of filmy, perfumed lace and passed little Mrs. Sommers her box of candy.

The play was over, the music ceased, the crowd filed out. It was like a dream ended. People scattered in all directions. Mrs. Sommers went to the corner and waited for the cable car.

A man with keen eyes, who sat opposite to her, seemed to like the study of her small, pale face. It puzzled him to decipher what he saw there. In truth, he saw nothing—unless he were wizard enough to detect a poignant wish, a powerful longing that the cable car would never stop anywhere, but go on and on with her forever.

1897

The Storm: A Sequel to "The 'Cadian Ball"[1]

I

The leaves were so still that even Bibi thought it was going to rain. Bobinôt, who was accustomed to converse on terms of perfect equality with his little son, called the child's attention to certain sombre clouds that were rolling with sinister intention from the west, accompanied by a sullen, threatening roar. They were at Friedheimer's store and decided to remain there till the storm had passed. They sat within the door on two empty kegs. Bibi was four years old and looked very wise.

"Mama'll be 'fraid, yes," he suggested with blinking eyes.

"She'll shut the house. Maybe she got Sylvie helpin' her this evenin'," Bobinôt responded reassuringly.

"No; she ent got Sylvie. Sylvie was helpin' her yistiday," piped Bibi.

Bobinôt arose and going across to the counter purchased a can of shrimps, of which Calixta was very fond. Then he returned to his perch on the keg and sat stolidly holding the can of shrimps while the storm burst. It shook the wooden store and seemed to be ripping great furrows in the distant field. Bibi laid his little hand on his father's knee and was not afraid.

---

1. "At the 'Cadian Ball" (1892) takes place five or six years earlier, when Calixta and Alcée flirt at a ball until Clarisse interrupts them to take Alcée away. Acadians, or Cajuns, are residents of Louisiana descended from French Canadians in exile from the regions now called Nova Scotia and New Brunswick, formerly Acadia.

II

Calixta, at home, felt no uneasiness for their safety. She sat at a side window sewing furiously on a sewing machine. She was greatly occupied and did not notice the approaching storm. But she felt very warm and often stopped to mop her face on which the perspiration gathered in beads. She unfastened her white sacque at the throat. It began to grow dark, and suddenly realizing the situation she got up hurriedly and went about closing windows and doors.

Out on the small front gallery she had hung Bobinôt's Sunday clothes to air and she hastened out to gather them before the rain fell. As she stepped outside, Alcée Laballière rode in at the gate. She had not seen him very often since her marriage, and never alone. She stood there with Bobinôt's coat in her hands, and the big rain drops began to fall. Alcée rode his horse under the shelter of a side projection where the chickens had huddled and there were plows and a harrow piled up in the corner.

"May I come and wait on your gallery till the storm is over, Calixta?" he asked.

"Come 'long in, M'sieur Alcée."

His voice and her own startled her as if from a trance, and she seized Bobinôt's vest. Alcée, mounting to the porch, grabbed the trousers and snatched Bibi's braided jacket that was about to be carried away by a sudden gust of wind. He expressed an intention to remain outside, but it was soon apparent that he might as well have been out in the open: the water beat in upon the boards in driving sheets, and he went inside, closing the door after him. It was even necessary to put something beneath the door to keep the water out.

"My! what a rain! It's good two years since it rain' like that," exclaimed Calixta as she rolled up a piece of bagging and Alcée helped her to thrust it beneath the crack.

She was a little fuller of figure than five years before when she married; but she had lost nothing of her vivacity. Her blue eyes still retained their melting quality; and her yellow hair, dishevelled by the wind and rain, kinked more stubbornly than ever about her ears and temples.

The rain beat upon the low, shingled roof with a force and clatter that threatened to break an entrance and deluge them there. They were in the dining room—the sitting room—the general utility room. Adjoining was her bed room, with Bibi's couch along side her own. The door stood open, and the room with its white, monumental bed, its closed shutters, looked dim and mysterious.

Alcée flung himself into a rocker and Calixta nervously began to gather up from the floor the lengths of a cotton sheet which she had been sewing.

"If this keeps up, *Dieu sait*[2] if the levees goin' to stan' it!" she exclaimed.

"What have you got to do with the levees?"

"I got enough to do! An' there's Bobinôt with Bibi out in that storm—if he only didn' left Friedheimer's!"

"Let us hope, Calixta, that Bobinôt's got sense enough to come in out of a cyclone."

She went and stood at the window with a greatly disturbed look on her face. She wiped the frame that was clouded with moisture. It was stiflingly hot. Alcée got up and joined her at the window, looking over her shoulder. The rain was coming down in sheets obscuring the view of far-off cabins and enveloping the distant wood in a gray mist. The playing of the lightning was incessant. A bolt struck a tall chinaberry tree at the edge of the field. It filled all visible space with a blinding glare and the crash seemed to invade the very boards they stood upon.

Calixta put her hands to her eyes, and with a cry, staggered backward. Alcée's arm encircled her, and for an instant he drew her close and spasmodically to him.

"*Bonté!*"[3] she cried, releasing herself from his encircling arm and retreating from the

---

2. *"Dieu sait"* is French for "God knows"; a levee is an embankment raised to prevent a river from overflowing.

3. *"Bonté"* means "goodness," a mild curse.

window, "the house'll go next! If I only knew w'ere Bibi was!" She would not compose herself; she would not be seated. Alcée clasped her shoulders and looked into her face. The contact of her warm, palpitating body when he had unthinkingly drawn her into his arms, had aroused all the old-time infatuation and desire for her flesh.

"Calixta," he said, "don't be frightened. Nothing can happen. The house is too low to be struck, with so many tall trees standing about. There! aren't you going to be quiet? say, aren't you?" He pushed her hair back from her face that was warm and steaming. Her lips were as red and moist as pomegranate seed. Her white neck and a glimpse of her full, firm bosom disturbed him powerfully. As she glanced up at him the fear in her liquid blue eyes had given place to a drowsy gleam that unconsciously betrayed a sensuous desire. He looked down into her eyes and there was nothing for him to do but to gather her lips in a kiss. It reminded him of Assumption.

"Do you remember—in Assumption, Calixta?" he asked in a low voice broken by passion. Oh! she remembered; for in Assumption he had kissed her and kissed and kissed her; until his senses would well nigh fail, and to save her he would resort to a desperate flight. If she was not an immaculate dove in those days, she was still inviolate; a passionate creature whose very defenselessness had made her defense, against which his honor forbade him to prevail. Now—well, now—her lips seemed in a manner free to be tasted, as well as her round, white throat and her whiter breasts.

They did not heed the crashing torrents, and the roar of the elements made her laugh as she lay in his arms. She was a revelation in that dim, mysterious chamber; as white as the couch she lay upon. Her firm, elastic flesh that was knowing for the first time its birthright, was like a creamy lily that the sun invites to contribute its breath and perfume to the undying life of the world.

The generous abundance of her passion, without guile or trickery, was like a white flame which penetrated and found response in depths of his own sensuous nature that had never yet been reached.

When he touched her breasts they gave themselves up in quivering ecstasy, inviting his lips. Her mouth was a fountain of delight. And when he possessed her, they seemed to swoon together at the very borderland of life's mystery.

He stayed cushioned upon her, breathless, dazed, enervated, with his heart beating like a hammer upon her. With one hand she clasped his head, her lips lightly touching his forehead. The other hand stroked with a soothing rhythm his muscular shoulders.

The growl of the thunder was distant and passing away. The rain beat softly upon the shingles, inviting them to drowsiness and sleep. But they dared not yield.

The rain was over; and the sun was turning the glistening green world into a palace of gems. Calixta, on the gallery, watched Alcée ride away. He turned and smiled at her with a beaming face; and she lifted her pretty chin in the air and laughed aloud.

III

Bobinôt and Bibi, trudging home, stopped without at the cistern to make themselves presentable.

"My! Bibi, w'at will yo' mama say! You ought to be ashame'. You oughtn' put on those good pants. Look at 'em! An' that mud on yo' collar! How you got that mud on yo' collar, Bibi? I never saw such a boy!" Bibi was the picture of pathetic resignation. Bobinôt was the embodiment of serious solicitude as he strove to remove from his own person and his son's the signs of their tramp over heavy roads and through wet fields. He scraped the mud off Bibi's bare legs and feet with a stick and carefully removed all traces from his heavy brogans. Then, prepared for the worst—the meeting with an over-scrupulous housewife, they entered cautiously at the back door.

Calixta was preparing supper. She had set the table and was dripping coffee at the hearth. She sprang up as they came in.

"Oh, Bobinôt! You back! My! but I was uneasy. W'ere you been during the rain? An' Bibi? he ain't wet? he ain't hurt?" She had clasped Bibi and was kissing him effusively. Bobinôt's explanations and apologies which he had been composing all along the way, died on his lips as Calixta felt him to see if he were dry, and seemed to express nothing but satisfaction at their safe return.

"I brought you some shrimps, Calixta," offered Bobinôt, hauling the can from his ample side pocket and laying it on the table.

"Shrimps! Oh, Bobinôt! you too good fo' anything!" and she gave him a smacking kiss on the cheek that resounded. *"J'vous réponds,*[4] we'll have a feas' to-night! umph-umph!"

Bobinôt and Bibi began to relax and enjoy themselves, and when the three seated themselves at table they laughed much and so loud that anyone might have heard them as far away as Laballière's.

IV

Alcée Laballière wrote to his wife, Clarisse, that night. It was a loving letter, full of tender solicitude. He told her not to hurry back, but if she and the babies liked it at Biloxi, to stay a month longer. He was getting on nicely; and though he missed them, he was willing to bear the separation a while longer—realizing that their health and pleasure were the first things to be considered.

V

As for Clarisse, she was charmed upon receiving her husband's letter. She and the babies were doing well. The society was agreeable; many of her old friends and acquaintances were at the bay. And the first free breath since her marriage seemed to restore the pleasant liberty of her maiden days. Devoted as she was to her husband, their intimate conjugal life was something which she was more than willing to forego for a while.

So the storm passed and every one was happy.

1898   1969

Mary Noailles Murfree
(1850–1922)

Born on the family plantation of Grantland, near Murfreesboro, Tennessee, Mary Murfree was educated at the Nashville Female Academy and at a finishing school for young ladies, the Chegary Institute in Philadelphia. Lame from childhood, she became a voracious reader and observer. Summers were spent with her family at Beersheba Springs in the Cumberland Mountains, and at various times she visited the family's three Mississippi Delta plantations. During the Civil War the house at Grantland was destroyed. She observed Southern society in Nashville before, during, and after the war—and all became material for her books. Living at a newly built New Grantland after the war, she was encouraged to follow a literary

4. "I answer you."

career by her family. "Mary, stop sewing," her father is reported to have said. "Anyone that can write has no business sewing."

Murfree first gained attention with a story published under the male pseudonym Charles Egbert Craddock. Drawn from her summers at Beersheba Springs, "The Dancin' Party at Harrison's Cove" was printed in the *Atlantic Monthly* in 1878 and was collected with other stories in *In The Tennessee Mountains* (1884), a book that went through at least twenty editions. Not until 1885 was her identity as a woman known even to her publisher, and it was as "Craddock" that she continued to publish as one of the most celebrated writers of the American local-color movement. Most admired among her other works about mountain life is *The Prophet of the Great Smoky Mountains* (1885), a novel examining questions of justice and law, guilt and redemption. Additional mountain stories are collected in *The Mystery of Witch-Face Mountain* (1895) and *The Phantoms of the Foot-Bridge* (1895) and other books. A prolific author of some twenty-five books, she wrote also of the Civil War, the Tennessee frontier, and the postwar South in Mississippi, but it is as the author of *In the Tennessee Mountains* and *The Prophet of the Great Smoky Mountains* that she has been most remembered.

In addition to titles mentioned above, Murfree's novels include *Where the Battle Was Fought* (1884), about the Civil War battle that leveled her childhood home; *In the "Stranger People's" Country* (1891), about legendary little people of the mountains; and *The Story of Old Fort Loudon* (1899), set on the Tennessee frontier during the French and Indian War. Additional story collections include *The Bushwhackers* (1899), *The Frontiersmen* (1904), and *The Raid of the Guerilla* (1912). Studies include Edd Winfield Parks, *Charles Egbert Craddock (Mary Noailles Murfree)* (1941), and Richard Cary, *Mary N. Murfree* (1967).

Over on the T'other Mounting[1]

Stretching out laterally from a long oblique line of the Southern Alleghanies are two parallel ranges, following the same course through several leagues, and separated by a narrow strip of valley hardly half a mile in width. As they fare along arm in arm, so to speak, sundry differences between the close companions are distinctly apparent. One is much the higher, and leads the way; it strikes out all the bold curves and angles of the course, meekly attended by the lesser ridge; its shadowy coves and sharp ravines are repeated in miniature as its comrade falls into the line of march; it seems to have its companion in charge, and to conduct it away from the majestic procession of mountains that traverses the State.

But, despite its more imposing appearance, all the tangible advantages are possessed by its humble neighbor. When Old Rocky-Top, as the lower range is called, is fresh and green with the tender verdure of spring, the snow still lies on the summit of the T'other Mounting, and drifts deep into treacherous rifts and chasms, and muffles the voice of the singing pines; and all the crags are hung with gigantic glittering icicles, and the woods are gloomy and bleak. When the sun shines bright on Old Rocky-Top, clouds often hover about the loftier mountain, and storms brew in that higher atmosphere; the all-pervading winter winds surge wildly among the groaning forests, and wrench the limbs from the trees, and dash huge fragments of cliffs down deep gorges, and spend their fury before they reach the sheltered lower spur. When the kindly shades of evening slip softly down on drowsy Rocky-Top, and the work is laid by in the rough little houses, and the simple home-folks draw around the hearth, day

1. First collected in *In the Tennessee Mountains* (1884), the source of the present text.

still lingers in a weird, paralytic life among the tree-tops of the T'other Mounting; and the only remnant of the world visible is that stark black line of its summit, stiff and hard against the faint green and saffron tints of the sky. Before the birds are well awake on Old Rocky-Top, and while the shadows are still thick, the T'other Mounting has been called up to a new day. Lonely dawns these: the pale gleam strikes along the October woods, bringing first into uncertain twilight the dead yellow and red of the foliage, presently heightened into royal gold and crimson by the first ray of sunshine; it rouses the timid wild-fowl; it drives home the plundering fox; it meets, perhaps, some lumbering bear or skulking mountain wolf; it flecks with light and shade the deer, all gray and antlered; it falls upon no human habitation, for the few settlers of the region have a persistent predilection for Old Rocky-Top. Somehow, the T'other Mounting is vaguely in ill repute among its neighbors,—it has a bad name.

"It's the onluckiest place ennywhar nigh about," said Nathan White, as he sat one afternoon upon the porch of his log-cabin, on the summit of Old Rocky-Top, and gazed up at the heights of the T'other Mounting across the narrow valley. "I hev hearn tell all my days ez how, ef ye go up thar on the T'other Mounting, suthin' will happen ter ye afore ye kin git away. An' I knows myself ez how—'t war ten year ago an' better—I went up thar, one Jan'ry day, a-lookin' fur my cow, ez hed strayed off through not hevin' enny calf ter our house; an' I fund the cow, but jes' tuk an' slipped on a icy rock, an' bruk my ankle-bone. 'Twar sech a job a-gittin' off'n that thar T'other Mounting an' back over hyar, it hev l'arned me ter stay away from thar."

"Thar war a man," piped out a shrill, quavering voice from within the door,—the voice of Nathan White's father, the oldest inhabitant of Rocky-Top,—"thar war a man hyar, nigh on ter fifty year ago,—he war mightily gin ter thievin' horses; an' one time, while he war a-runnin' away with Pete Dilks's dapple-gray mare,—they called her Luce, five year old she war,—Pete, he war a-ridin' a-hint him on his old sorrel mare,—her name 't war Jane, an'—the Jeemes boys, they war a-ridin' arter the horse-thief too. Thar, now! I clar forgits what horses them Jeemes boys war a-ridin' of." He paused for an instant in anxious reflection. "Waal, sir! it do beat all that I can't remember them Jeemes boys' horses! Anyways, they got ter that thar tricky ford through Wild-Duck River, thar on the side o' the T'other Mounting, an' the horse-thief was ahead, an' he hed ter take it fust. An' that thar river,—it rises yander in them pines, nigh about," pointing with a shaking fore-finger,—"an' that thar river jes' spun him out 'n the saddle like a top, an' he war n't seen no more till he hed floated nigh ter Colbury, ez dead ez a door-nail, nor Pete's dapple-gray mare nuther; she bruk her knees agin them high stone banks. But he war a good swimmer, an' he war drowned. He war witched with the place, ez sure ez ye air born."

A long silence ensued. Then Nathan White raised his pondering eyes with a look of slow curiosity. "What did Tony Britt say he war a-doin' of, when ye kem on him suddint in the woods on the T'other Mounting?" he asked, addressing his son, a stalwart youth, who was sitting upon the step, his hat on the back of his head, and his hands in the pockets of his jeans trousers.

"He said he war a-huntin', but he hed n't hed no sort 'n luk. It 'pears ter me ez all the game thar is witched somehow, an' ye can't git no good shot at nuthin'. Tony tole me to-day that he got up three deer, an' hed toler'ble aim; an' he missed two, an' the t'other jes' trotted off with a rifle-ball in his flank, ez onconsarned ez ef he hed hit him with an acorn."

"I hev always hearn ez everything that belongs on that thar T'other Mounting air witched, an' ef ye brings away so much ez a leaf, or a stone, or a stick, ye fotches a curse with it," chimed in the old man, " 'kase thar heve been sech a many folks killed on the T'other Mounting."

"I tole Tony Britt that thar word," said the young fellow, "an' 'lowed ter him ez how he hed tuk a mighty bad spot ter go a-huntin'."

"What did he say?" demanded Nathan White.

"He say he never knowed ez thar war murders commit on T'other Mounting, an' ef thar war he 'spects 't war nuthin' but Injuns, long time ago. But he 'lowed the place war powerful onlucky, an' he believed the mounting war witched."

"Ef Tony Britt's arter enny harm," said the octogenarian, "he'll never come off'n that thar T'other Mounting. It's a mighty place fur bad folks ter make thar eend. Thar's that thar horse thief I war a-tellin' 'bout, an' that dapple-gray mare,—her name 't war Luce. An' folks ez is a-runnin' from the sheriff jes' takes ter the T'other Mounting ez nateral ez ef it war home; an' ef they don't git cotched, they is never hearn on no more." He paused impressively. "The rocks falls on 'em, an' kills 'em; an' I'll tell ye jes' how I knows," he resumed, oracularly. " 'T war sixty year ago, nigh about, an' me an' them Jeemes boys war a-burnin' of lime tergether over on the T'other Mounting. We hed a lime-kiln over thar, jes' under Piney Notch, an' never hed no luck, but jes' stuck ter it like fools, till Hiram Jeemes got one of his eyes put out. So we quit burnin' of lime on the T'other Mounting, 'count of the place bein' witched, an' kem over hyar ter Old Rocky-Top, an' got along toler'ble well, cornsiderin'. But one day, whilst we war a-workin' on the T'other Mounting, what d' ye think I fund in the rock? The print of a bare foot in the solid stone, ez plain an' ez nateral ez ef the track hed been lef' in the clay yestiddy. Waal, I knowed it war the track o' Jeremiah Stubbs, what shot his step-brother, an' gin the sheriff the slip, an' war las' seen on the T'other Mounting, 'kase his old shoe jes' fit the track, fur we tried it. An' a good while arterward I fund on that same T'other Mounting—in the solid stone, mind ye—a fish, what he had done br'iled fur supper, jes' turned ter a stone."

"So thar's the Bible made true," said an elderly woman, who had come to the door to hear this reminiscence, and stood mechanically stirring a hoe-cake batter in a shallow wooden bowl. "Ax fur a fish, an' ye'll git a stone."[2]

The secret history of the hills among which they lived was indeed as a sealed book to these simple mountaineers.

"The las' time I war ter Colbury," said Nathan White, "I hearn the sheriff a-talkin' 'bout how them evil-doers an' sech runs fur the T'other Mounting fust thing; though he 'lowed ez it war powerful foxy in 'em ter try ter hide thar, 'kase he said, ef they wunst reaches it, he mought ez well look fur a needle in a hay-stack. He 'lowed ef he hed a posse a thousand men strong he could n't git 'em out."

"He can't find 'em, 'kase the rocks falls on 'em, or swallers 'em in," said the old man. "Ef Tony Britt is up ter mischief he'll never come back no more. He'll git into worser trouble than ever he see afore."

"He hev done seen a powerful lot of trouble, fust one way an' another, 'thout foolin' round the T'other Mounting," said Nathan White. "They tells me ez he got hisself indicted, I believes they calls it, or suthin', down yander ter the court at Colbury,—that war year afore las',—an' he hed ter pay twenty dollars fine; 'kase when he war overseer of the road he jes' war constant in lettin' his friends, an' folks ginerally, off 'thout hevin' 'em fined, when they did n't come an' work on the road,—though that air the way ez the overseers hev always done, without nobody a-tellin' on 'em an' sech. But them ez warn't Tony Britt's friends seen a mighty differ. He war dead sure ter fine Caleb Hoxie seventy-five cents, 'cordin' ter the law, fur every day that he war summoned ter work an' never come; 'kase Tony an' Caleb hed some sort 'n grudge agin one another 'count of a spavined horse what Caleb sold ter Tony, makin' him out to be a sound critter,—though Caleb swears he never knowed the horse war spavined when he sold him ter Tony, no more 'n nuthin'. Caleb war mightily worked up 'bout this hyar finin' business, an' him an' Tony hed a tussle 'bout it every time they kem tergether. But Caleb war always sure ter git the worst of it, 'kase Tony, though he air toler'ble spindling sort o' build, he air somehow or other sorter stringy an' tough, an' makes a right smart show in a reg'lar knock-down an' drag-out fight. So Caleb he war beat every time, an' fined too.

2. Cf. Matthew 7:9–10.

An' he tried wunst ter shoot Tony Britt, but he missed his aim. An' when he war a-layin' off how ter fix Tony, fur treatin' him that way, he war a-stoppin', one day, at Jacob Green's blacksmith's shop, yander, a mile down the valley, an' he war a-talkin' 'bout it ter a passel o' folks thar. An' Lawyer Rood from Colbury war thar, an' Jacob war a-shoein' of his mare; an' he hearn the tale, an' axed Caleb why n't he report Tony ter the court, an' git him fined fur neglect of his duty, bein' overseer of the road. An' Caleb never knowed before that it war the law that everybody what war summonsed an' did n't come must be fined, or the overseer must be fined hisself; but he knowed that Tony hed been a-lettin' of his friends off, an' folks ginerally, an' he jes' 'greed fur Lawyer Rood ter stir up trouble fur Tony. An' he done it. An' the court fined Tony twenty dollars fur them ways o' his'n. An' it kept him so busy a-scufflin' ter raise the twenty dollars that he never hed a chance ter give Caleb Hoxie more'n one or two beatin's the whole time he war a-scrapin' up the money."

This story was by no means unknown to the little circle, nor did its narrator labor under the delusion that he was telling a new thing. It was merely a verbal act of recollection, and an attentive silence reigned as he related the familiar facts. To people who live in lonely regions this habit of retrospection (especially noticeable in them) and an enduring interest in the past may be something of a compensation for the scanty happenings of the present. When the recital was concluded, the hush for a time was unbroken, save by the rush of the winds, bringing upon their breath the fragrant woodland odors of balsams and pungent herbs, and a fresh and exhilarating suggestion of sweeping over a volume of falling water. They stirred the fringed shadow of a great pine that stood, like a sentinel, before Nathan White's door and threw its colorless simulacrum, a boastful lie twice its size, far down the sunset road. Now and then the faint clangor of a cow-bell came from out the tangled woods about the little hut, and the low of homeward-bound cattle sounded upon the air, mellowed and softened by the distance. The haze that rested above the long, narrow valley was hardly visible, save in the illusive beauty with which it invested the scene,—the tender azure of the far-away ranges; the exquisite tones of the gray and purple shadows that hovered about the darkening coves and along the deep lines marking the gorges; the burnished brilliance of the sunlight, which, despite its splendor, seemed lonely enough, lying motionless upon the lonely landscape and on the still figures clustered about the porch. Their eyes were turned toward the opposite steeps, gorgeous with scarlet oak and sumac, all in autumnal array, and their thoughts were busy with the hunter on the T'other Mounting and vague speculations concerning his evil intent.

"It 'pears ter me powerful strange ez Tony goes a-foolin' round that thar T'other Mount-ing, cornsiderin' what happened yander in its shadow," said the woman, coming again to the door, and leaning idly against the frame; the bread was baking over the coals. "That thar wife o' his'n, afore she died, war always frettin' 'kase way down thar on the backbone, whar her house war, the shadow o' the T'other Mounting laid on it fur an hour an' better every day of the worl'. She 'lowed ez it always put her in mind o' the shadow o' death. An' I thought 'bout that thar sayin' o' hern the day when I see her a-lyin' stiff an' cold on the bed, an' the shadow of the T'other Mounting drappin' in at the open door, an' a-creepin' an' a-creepin' over her face. An' I war plumb glad when they got that woman under ground, whar, ef the sunshine can't git ter her, neither kin the shadow. Ef ever thar war a murdered woman, she war one. After all that hed come an' gone with Caleb Hoxie, fur Tony Britt ter go arter him, 'kase he war a yerb-doctor,[3] ter git him ter physic his wife, who war nigh about dead with the lung fever, an' gin up by old Dr. Marsh!—it looks ter me like he war plumb crazy,— though him an' Caleb hed sorter made friends 'bout the spavined horse an' sech afore then. Jes' ez soon ez she drunk the stuff that Caleb fixed fur her she laid her head back an' shet her eyes, an' never opened 'em no more in this worl'. She war a murdered woman, an' Caleb Hoxie done it through the yerbs he fixed fur her."

3. An herb doctor, untrained, administered natural remedies.

A subtle amethystine mist had gradually overlaid the slopes of the T'other Mounting, mellowing the brilliant tints of the variegated foliage to a delicious hazy sheen of mosaics; but about the base the air seemed dun-colored, though transparent; seen through it, even the red of the crowded trees was but a sombre sort of magnificence, and the great masses of gray rocks, jutting out among them here and there, wore a darkly frowning aspect. Along the summit there was a blaze of scarlet and gold in the full glory of the sunshine; the topmost cliffs caught its rays, and gave them back in unexpected gleams of green or grayish-yellow, as of mosses, or vines, or huckleberry bushes, nourished in the heart of the deep fissures.

"Waal," said Nathan White, "I never did believe ez Caleb gin her ennythink ter hurt,— though I knows thar is them ez does. Caleb is the bes' yerb-doctor I ever see. The rheumatiz would nigh on ter hev killed me, ef it war n't fur him, that spell I hed las' winter. An' Dr. Marsh, what they hed up afore the gran' jury, swore that the yerbs what Caleb gin her war nuthin' ter hurt; *he* said, though, they couldn't holp nor hender. An' but fur Dr. Marsh they would hev jailed Caleb ter stand his trial, like Tony wanted 'em ter do. But Dr. Marsh said she died with the consumption, jes' the same, an' Caleb's yerbs war wholesome, though they war n't no 'count at all."

"I knows I ain't a-goin' never ter tech nuthin' he fixes fur me no more," said his wife, "an' I'll be bound nobody else in these hyar mountings will, nuther."

"Waal," drawled her son, "I knows fur true ez he air tendin' now on old Gideon Croft, what lives over yander in the valley on the t'other side of the T'other Mounting, an' is down with the fever. He went over thar yestiddy evening, late; I met him when he war goin', an' he tole me."

"He hed better look out how he comes across Tony Britt," said Nathan White; "fur I hearn, the las' time I war ter the Settlemint, how Tony hev swore ter kill him the nex' time he see him, fur a-givin' of pizenous yerbs ter his wife. Tony air mightily outdone 'kase the gran' jury let him off. Caleb hed better be sorter keerful how he goes a-foolin' round these hyar dark woods."

The sun had sunk, and the night, long held in abeyance, was coming fast. The glooms gathered in the valley; a soft gray shadow hung over the landscape, making familiar things strange. The T'other Mounting was all a dusky, sad purple under the faintly pulsating stars, save that high along the horizontal line of its summit gleamed the strange red radiance of the dead and gone sunset. The outline of the foliage was clearly drawn against the pure lapis lazuli tint of the sky behind it; here and there the uncanny light streamed through the bare limbs of an early leafless tree, which looked in the distance like some bony hand beckoning, or warning, or raised in horror.

"*Anythink* mought happen thar!" said the woman, as she stood on night-wrapped Rocky-Top and gazed up at the alien light, so red in the midst of the dark landscape. When she turned back to the door of the little hut, the meagre comforts within seemed almost luxury, in their cordial contrast to the desolate, dreary mountain yonder and the thought of the forlorn, wandering hunter. A genial glow from the hearth diffused itself over the puncheon floor; the savory odor of broiling venison filled the room as a tall, slim girl knelt before the fire and placed the meat upon the gridiron, her pale cheeks flushing with the heat; there was a happy suggestion of peace and unity when the four generations trooped in to their supper, grandfather on his grandson's arm, and a sedate two-year-old bringing up the rear. Nathan White's wife paused behind the others to bar the door, and once more, as she looked up at the T'other Mounting, the thought of the lonely wanderer smote her heart. The red sunset light had died out at last, but a golden aureola heralded the moon-rise, and a gleaming thread edged the masses of foliage; there was no faint suggestion now of mist in the valley, and myriads of stars filled a cloudless sky. "He hev done gone home by this time," she said to her daughter-in-law, as she closed the door, "an' ef he ain't, he'll hev a moon ter light him."

"Air ye a-studyin' 'bout Tony Britt yit?" asked Nathan White. "He hev done gone home a good hour by sun, I'll be bound. Jes' ketch Tony Britt a-huntin' till sundown, will ye! He air a mighty pore hand ter work. 'Stonishes me ter hear he air even a-huntin' on the T'other Mounting."

"I don't believe he's up ter enny harm," said the woman; "he hev jes' tuk ter the woods with grief."

" 'Pears ter me," said the daughter-in-law, rising from her kneeling posture before the fire, and glancing reproachfully at her husband,—" 'pears ter me ez ye mought hev brought him hyar ter eat his supper along of we-uns, stiddier a-leavin' him a-grievin' over his dead wife in them witched woods on the T'other Mounting."

The young fellow looked a trifle abashed at this suggestion. "I never wunst thought of it," he said. "Tony never stopped ter talk more 'n a minit, nohow."

The evening wore away; the octogenarian and the sedate two-year-old fell asleep in their chairs shortly after supper; Nathan White and his son smoked their cob-pipes, and talked fitfully of the few incidents of the day; the women sat in the firelight with their knitting, silent and absorbed, except that now and then the elder, breaking from her reverie, declared, "I can't git Tony Britt out'n my head nohow in the worl'."

The moon had come grandly up over the T'other Mounting, casting long silver lights and deep black shadows through all the tangled recesses and yawning chasms of the woods and rocks. In the vast wilderness the bright rays met only one human creature, the belated hunter making his way homeward through the dense forest with an experienced woodman's craft. For no evil intent had brought Tony Britt to the T'other Mounting; he had spent the day in hunting, urged by that strong necessity without which the mountaineer seldom makes any exertion. Dr. Marsh's unavailing skill had cost him dear; his only cow was sold to make up the twenty dollars fine which his revenge on Caleb Hoxie had entailed upon him; without even so much as a spavined horse tillage was impossible, and the bounteous harvest left him empty-handed, for he had no crops to gather. The hardships of extreme poverty had reinforced the sorrows that came upon him in battalions, and had driven him far through long aisles of the woods, where the night fell upon him unaware. The foliage was all embossed with exquisite silver designs that seemed to stand out some little distance from the dark masses of leaves; now and then there came to his eyes that emerald gleam never seen upon verdure in the day-time,—only shown by some artificial light, or the moon's sweet uncertainty. The wind was strong and fresh, but not cold; here and there was a glimmer of dew. Once, and once only, he thought of the wild traditions which peopled the T'other Mounting with evil spirits. He paused with a sudden chill; he glanced nervously over his shoulder down the illimitable avenues of the lonely woods. The grape-vines, hanging in festoons from tree to tree, were slowly swinging back and forth, stirred by the wind. There was a dizzy dance of shadows whirling on every open space where the light lay on the ground. The roar and fret of Wild-Duck River, hidden there somewhere in the pines, came on the breeze like a strange, weird, fitful voice, crying out amid the haunted solitudes of the T'other Mounting. He turned abruptly, with his gun on his shoulder, and pursued his way through the trackless desert in the direction of his home. He had been absorbed in his quest and his gloomy thoughts, and did not realize the distance he had traversed until it lay before him to be retraced; but his superstitious terror urged him to renewed exertions. "Ef ever I gits off'n this hyar witched mounting," he said to himself, as he tore away the vines and brambles that beset his course, "I'll never come back agin while I lives." He grew calmer when he paused on a huge projecting crag, and looked across the narrow valley at the great black mass opposite, which he knew was Old Rocky-Top; its very presence gave him a sense of companionship and blunted his fear, and he sat down to rest for a few minutes, gazing at the outline of the range he knew so well, so unfamiliar from a new stand-point. How low it seemed from the heights of the T'other Mounting! Could that faint gleam be the light in Nathan White's house? Tony Britt glanced further down the indistinct slope, where he knew his own desolate, deserted hut was crouched. "Jes' whar the shadow o' the T'other Mounting can reach it," he thought, with a new infusion of bitterness. He averted his eyes; he would look no longer; he threw himself at full length among the ragged clumps of grass and fragments of rock, and turned his face to the stars. It all came back to him then. Sometimes, in his sordid cares and struggles for his scanty existence, his past troubles were dwarfed by the present. But here on the lonely cliff, with the infinite spaces above him and the boundless forest below, he felt anew his isolation. No light on earth save the far gleam from another man's home, and in heaven only the drowning face of the moon, drifting slowly through the blue floods of the skies. He was only twenty-five; he had youth and health and strength, but he felt that he had lived his life; it seemed long, marked as it was by cares and privation and persistent failure. Little as he knew of life, he knew how hard his had been, even meted by those of the poverty-stricken wretches among whom his lot was cast. "An' sech luck!" he said, as his sad eyes followed the drifting dead face of the moon. "Along o' that thar step-mother o' mine till I war growed; an' then when I war married, an' we hed got the house put up, an' war beginnin' ter git along like other folks kin, an' Car'line's mother gin her that thar calf what growed ter a cow, an' through pinchin' an' savin' we made out ter buy that thar horse from Caleb Hoxie, jes' ez we war a-startin' ter work a crap he lays down an' dies; an' that cussed twenty dollars ez I hed ter pay ter the court; an' Car'line jes' a-gittin' sick, an' a-wastin' an' a-wastin' away, till I, like a fool, brung Caleb thar, an' he pizens her with his yerbs—God A'mighty! ef I could jes' lay my hands wunst on that scoundrel I would n't leave a mite of him, ef he war pertected by a hundred lyin', thievin' gran' juries! But he can't stay a-hidin' forevermo'. He's got ter 'count ter me, ef he ain't ter the law; an' he'll see a mighty differ atwixt us. I swear he'll never draw another breath!"

He rose with a set, stern face, and struck a huge bowlder beside him with his hard clenched hand as he spoke. He had not even an ignorant idea of an impressive dramatic pose; but if the great gaunt cliff had been the stage of a theatre his attitude and manner at that instant would have won him applause. He was all alone with his poverty and his anguished memories, as men with such burdens are apt to be.

The bowlder on which, in his rude fashion, he had registered his oath was harder than his hard hand, and the vehemence of the blow brought blood; but he had scarcely time to think of it. His absorbed reverie was broken by a rustling other than that of the eddying wind. He raised his head and looked about him, half expecting to see the antlers of a deer. Then there came to his ears the echo of the tread of man. His eyes mechanically followed the sound. Forty feet down the face of the crag a broad ledge jutted out, and upon it ran a narrow path, made by stray cattle, or the feet of their searching owners; it was visible from the summit for a distance of a hundred yards or so, and the white glamour of the moonbeams fell full upon it. Before a speculation had suggested itself, a man walked slowly into view along the path, and with starting eyes the hunter recognized his dearest foe. Britt's hand lay upon the bowlder; his oath was in his mind; his unconscious enemy had come within his power. Swifter than a flash the temptation was presented. He remembered the warnings of his lawyer at Colbury last week, when the grand jury had failed to find a true bill against Caleb Hoxie,— that he was an innocent man, and must go unscathed, that any revenge for fancied wrongs would be dearly rued; he remembered, too, the mountain traditions of the falling rocks burying evil-doers in the heart of the hills. Here was his opportunity. He would have a life for a life, and there would be one more legend of the very stones conspiring to punish malefactors escaped from men added to the terrible "sayin's" of the T'other Mounting. A strong belief in the supernatural influences of the place was rife within him; he knew nothing of Gideon Croft's fever and the errand that had brought the herb-doctor through the "witched mounting;" had he not been transported thither by some invisible agency, that the rocks might fall upon him and crush him?

The temptation and the resolve were simultaneous. With his hand upon the bowlder, his hot heart beating fast, his distended eyes burning upon the approaching figure, he waited for the moment to come. There lay the long, low, black mountain opposite, with only the moon beams upon it, for the lights in Nathan White's house were extinguished; there was the deep, dark gulf of the valley; there, forty feet below him, was the narrow, moon-flooded path on the ledge, and the man advancing carelessly. The bowlder fell with a frightful crash, the echoes rang with a scream of terror, and the two men—one fleeing from the dreadful danger he had barely escaped, the other from the hideous deed he thought he had done—ran wildly in opposite directions through the tangled autumnal woods.

Was every leaf of the forest endowed with a woful voice, that the echo of that shriek might never die from Tony Britt's ears? Did the storied, retributive rocks still vibrate with this new victim's frenzied cry? And what was this horror in his heart! Now,—so late,—was coming a terrible conviction of his enemy's innocence, and with it a fathomless remorse.

All through the interminable night he fled frantically along the mountain's summit, scarcely knowing whither, and caring for nothing except to multiply the miles between him and the frightful object that he believed lay under the bowlder which he had dashed down the precipice. The moon sank beneath the horizon; the fantastic shadows were merged in the darkest hour of the night; the winds died, and there was no voice in all the woods, save the wail of Wild-Duck River and the forever-resounding screams in the flying wretch's ears. Sometimes he answered them in a wild, hoarse, inarticulate cry; sometimes he flung his hands above his head and wrung them in his agony; never once did he pause in his flight. Panting, breathless, exhausted, he eagerly sped through the darkness; tearing his face upon the brambles; plunging now and then into gullies and unseen quagmires; sometimes falling heavily, but recovering himself in an instant, and once more struggling on; striving to elude the pursuing voices, and to distance forever his conscience and his memory.

And then came that terrible early daylight that was wont to dawn upon the T'other Mounting when all the world besides was lost in slumber; the wan, melancholy light showed dimly the solemn trees and dense undergrowth; the precarious pitfalls about his path; the long deep gorges; the great crags and chasms; the cascades, steely gray, and white; the huge mass, all hung about with shadows, which he knew was Old Rocky-Top, rising from the impenetrably dark valley below. It seemed wonderful to him, somehow, that a new day should break at all. If, in a revulsion of nature, that utter blackness had continued forever and ever it would not have been strange, after what had happened. He could have borne it better than the sight of the familiar world gradually growing into day, all unconscious of his secret. He had begun the descent of the T'other Mounting, and he seemed to carry that pale dawn with him; day was breaking when he reached the foot of Old Rocky-Top, and as he climbed up to his own deserted, empty little shanty, it too stood plainly defined in the morning light. He dragged himself to the door, and impelled by some morbid fascination he glanced over his shoulder at the T'other Mounting. There it was, unchanged, with the golden largess of a gracious season blazing upon every autumnal leaf. He shuddered, and went into the fireless, comfortless house. And then he made an appalling discovery. As he mechanically divested himself of his shotpouch and powder-horn he was stricken by a sudden consciousness that he did not have his gun! One doubtful moment, and he remembered that he had laid it upon the crag when he had thrown himself down to rest. Beyond question, it was there yet. His conscience was still now,—his remorse had fled. It was only a matter of time when his crime would be known. He recollected his meeting with young White while he was hunting, and then Britt cursed the gun which he had left on the cliff. The discovery of the weapon there would be strong evidence against him, taken in connection with all the other circumstances. True, he could even yet go back and recover it, but he was mastered by the fear of meeting some one on the unfrequented road, or even in the loneliness of the T'other Mounting, and strengthening the chain of evidence against him by the fact of being once more seen in the fateful neighborhood. He resolved that he would wait until night-fall, and then he would retrace his way, secure his gun, and all might yet be well with him. As to the bowlder,—were men never before buried under the falling rocks of the T'other Mounting?

Without food, without rest, without sleep, his limbs rigid with the strong tension of his nerves, his eyes bloodshot, haggard, and eager, his brain on fire, he sat through the long morning hours absently gazing across the narrow valley at the solemn, majestic mountain opposite, and that sinister jutting crag with the indistinctly defined ledges of its rugged surface.

After a time, the scene began to grow dim; the sun was still shining, but through a haze becoming momently more dense. The brilliantly tinted foliage upon the T'other Mounting was fading; the cliffs showed strangely distorted faces through the semi-transparent blue vapor, and presently they seemed to recede altogether; the valley disappeared, and all the country was filled with the smoke of distant burning woods. He was gasping when he first became sensible of the smoke-laden haze, for he had seen nothing of the changing aspect of the landscape. Before his vision was the changeless picture of a night of mingled moonlight and shadow, the ill-defined black mass where Old Rocky-Top rose into the air, the impenetrable gloom of the valley, the ledge of the crag, and the unconscious figure slowly coming within the power of his murderous hand. His eyes would look on no other scene, no other face, so long as he should live.

He had a momentary sensation of stifling, and then a great weight was lifted. For he had begun to doubt whether the unlucky locality would account satisfactorily for the fall of that bowlder and the horrible object beneath it; a more reasonable conclusion might be deduced from the fact that he had been seen in the neighborhood, and the circumstance of the deadly feud. But what wonder would there be if the dry leaves on the T'other Mounting should be ignited and the woods burned! What explanations might not such a catastrophe suggest!—a frantic flight from the flames toward the cliff and an accidental fall. And so he waited throughout the long day, that was hardly day at all, but an opaque twilight, through which could be discerned only the stony path leading down the slope from his door, only the blurred outlines of the bushes close at hand, only the great gaunt limbs of a lightning-scathed tree, seeming entirely severed from the unseen trunk, and swinging in the air sixty feet above the earth.

Toward night-fall the wind rose and the smoke-curtain lifted, once more revealing to the settlers upon Old Rocky-Top the sombre T'other Mounting, with the belated evening light still lurid upon the trees,—only a strange, faint resemblance of the sunset radiance, rather the ghost of a dead day. And presently this apparition was gone, and the deep purple line of the witched mountain's summit grew darker against the opaline skies, till it was merged in a dusky black, and the shades of the night fell thick on the landscape.

The scenic effects of the drama, that serve to widen the mental vision and cultivate the imagination of even the poor in cities, were denied these primitive, simple people; but that magnificent pageant of the four seasons, wherein was forever presented the imposing splendor of the T'other Mounting in an ever-changing grandeur of aspect, was a gracious recompense for the spectacular privileges of civilization. And this evening the humble family party on Nathan White's porch beheld a scene of unique impressiveness.

The moon had not yet risen; the winds were awhirl; the darkness draped the earth as with a pall. Out from the impenetrable gloom of the woods on the T'other Mounting there started, suddenly, a scarlet globe of fire; one long moment it was motionless, but near it the spectral outline of a hand appeared beckoning, or warning, or raised in horror,—only a leafless tree, catching in the distance a semblance of humanity. Then from the still ball of fire there streamed upward a long, slender plume of golden light, waving back and forth against the pale horizon. Across the dark slope of the mountain below, flashes of lightning were shooting in zigzag lines, and wherever they gleamed were seen those frantic skeleton hands raised and wrung in anguish. It was cruel sport for the cruel winds; they maddened over gorge and cliff and along the wooded steeps, carrying far upon their wings the sparks of desolation. From the summit, myriads of jets of flame reached up to the placid stars; about the base of the mountain lurked a lake of liquid fire, with wreaths of blue smoke hovering over it; ever and anon, athwart the slope, darted the sudden lightning, widening into sheets of flame as it conquered new ground.

The astonishment on the faces grouped about Nathan White's door was succeeded by a startled anxiety. After the first incoherent exclamations of surprise came the pertinent inquiry from his wife, "Ef Old Rocky-Top war ter ketch too, whar would we-uns run ter?"

Nathan White's countenance had in its expression more of astounded excitement than of bodily fear. "Why, bless my soul!" he said at length, "the woods away over yander, what hev been burnin' all day, ain't nigh enough ter the T'other Mounting ter ketch it,—nuthin' like it."

"The T'other Mounting would burn, though, ef fire war put ter it," said his son. The two men exchanged a glance of deep significance.

"Do ye mean ter say," exclaimed Mrs. White, her fire-lit face agitated by a sudden superstitious terror, "that that thar T'other Mounting is fired by witches an' sech?"

"Don't talk so loud, Matildy," said her husband. "Them knows best ez done it."

"Thar's one thing sure," quavered the old man: "that thar fire will never tech a leaf on Old Rocky-Top. Thar's a church on this hyar mounting,—bless the Lord fur it!—an' we lives in the fear o' God."

There was a pause, all watching with distended eyes the progress of the flames.

"It looks like it mought hev been kindled in torment," said the young daughter-in-law.

"It looks down thar," said her husband, pointing to the lake of fire, "like the pit itself."

The apathetic inhabitants of Old Rocky-Top were stirred into an activity very incongruous with their habits and the hour. During the conflagration they traversed long distances to reach each other's houses and confer concerning the danger and the questions of supernatural agency provoked by the mysterious firing of the woods. Nathan White had few neighbors, but above the crackling of the timber and the roar of the flames there rose the quick beat of running footsteps; the undergrowth of the forest near at hand was in strange commotion; and at last, the figure of a man burst forth, the light of the fire showing the startling pallor of his face as he staggered to the little porch and sank, exhausted, into a chair.

"Waal, Caleb Hoxie!" exclaimed Nathan White, in good-natured raillery; "ye 're skeered, fur true! What ails ye, ter think Old Rocky-Top air a-goin' ter ketch too? 'T ain't nigh dry enough, I'm a-thinkin'."

"Fire kindled that thar way can't tech a leaf on Old Rocky-Top," sleepily piped out the old man, nodding in his chair, the glare of the flames which rioted over the T'other Mounting gilding his long white hair and peaceful, slumberous face. "Thar's a church on Old Rocky-Top,—bless the"—The sentence drifted away with his dreams.

"Does ye believe—them—them"—Caleb Hoxie's trembling white lips could not frame the word—"them—done it?"

"Like ez not," said Nathan White. "But that ain't a-troublin' of ye an' me. I ain't never hearn o' them witches a-tormentin' of honest folks what ain't done nuthin' hurtful ter nobody," he added, in cordial reassurance.

His son was half hidden behind one of the rough cedar posts, that his mirth at the guest's display of cowardice might not be observed. But the women, always quick to suspect, glanced meaningly at each other with widening eyes, as they stood together in the door-way.

"I dunno,—I dunno," Caleb Hoxie declared huskily. "I ain't never done nuthin' ter nobody, an' what do ye s'pose them witches an' sech done ter me las' night, on that T'other Mounting? I war a-goin' over yander to Gideon Croft's fur ter physic him, ez he air mortal low with the fever; an' ez I war a-comin' alongside o' that thar high bluff"—it was very distinct, with the flames wreathing fantastically about its gray, rigid features—"they throwed a bowlder ez big ez this hyar porch down on ter me. It jes' grazed me, an' knocked me down, an' kivered me with dirt. An' I run home a-hollerin'; an' it seemed ter me ter-day ez I war a-goin' ter screech an' screech all my life, like some onsettled crazy critter. It 'peared like 't would take a bar'l o' hop tea ter git me quiet. An' now look yander!" and he pointed tremulously to the blazing mountain.

There was an expression of conviction on the women's faces. All their lives afterward it was there whenever Caleb Hoxie's name was mentioned; no more to be moved or changed than the stern, set faces of the crags among the fiery woods.

"Thar's a church on this hyar mounting," said the old man feebly, waking for a moment, and falling asleep the next.

Nathan White was perplexed and doubtful, and a superstitious awe had checked the laughing youngster behind the cedar post.

A great cloud of flame came rolling through the sky toward them, golden, pellucid, spangled through and through with fiery red stars; poising itself for one moment high above the valley, then breaking into myriads of sparks, and showering down upon the dark abysses below.

"Look-a-hyar!" said the elder woman in a frightened under-tone to her daughter-in-law; "this hyar wicked critter air too onlucky ter be a-sittin' 'longside of us; we'll all be burnt up afore he gits hisself away from hyar. An' who is that a-comin' yander?" For from the encompassing woods another dark figure had emerged, and was slowly approaching the porch. The wary eyes near Caleb Hoxie saw that he fell to trembling, and that he clutched at a post for support. But the hand pointing at him was shaken as with a palsy, and the voice hardly seemed Tony Britt's as it cried out, in an agony of terror, "What air ye a-doin' hyar, a-sittin' 'longside o' livin' folks? Yer bones air under a bowlder on the T'other Mounting, an' ye air a dead man!"

They said ever afterward that Tony Britt had lost his mind "through goin' a-huntin' jes' one time on the T'other Mounting. His spirit air all broke, an' he's a mighty tame critter nowadays." Through his persistent endeavor he and Caleb Hoxie became quite friendly, and he was even reported to " 'low that he war sati'fied that Caleb never gin his wife nuthin' ter hurt." "Though," said the gossips of Old Rocky-Top, "them women up ter White's will hev it no other way but that Caleb pizened her, an' they would n't take no yerbs from him no more 'n he war a rattlesnake. But Caleb always 'pears sorter skittish when he an' Tony air tergether, like he did n't know when Tony war a-goin' ter fotch him a lick. But law! Tony air that changed that ye can't make him mad 'thout ye mind him o' the time he called Caleb a ghost."

A dark, gloomy, deserted place was the charred T'other Mounting through all the long winter. And when spring came, and Old Rocky-Top was green with delicate fresh verdure, and melodious with singing birds and chorusing breezes, and bedecked as for some great festival with violets and azaleas and laurel-blooms, the T'other Mounting was stark and wintry and black with its desolate, leafless trees. But after a while the spring came for it, too: the buds swelled and burst; flowering vines festooned the grim gray crags; and the dainty freshness of the vernal season reigned upon its summit, while all the world below was growing into heat and dust. The circuit-rider[4] said it reminded him of a tardy change in a sinner's heart: though it come at the eleventh hour, the glorious summer is before it, and a full fruition; though it work but an hour in the Lord's vineyard, it receives the same reward as those who labored through all the day.[5]

"An' it always did 'pear ter me ez thar war mighty little jestice in that," was Mrs. White's comment.

But at the meeting when that sermon was preached Tony Britt told his "experience." It seemed a confession, for according to the gossips he " 'lowed that he hed flung that bowlder down on Caleb Hoxie,—what the witches flung, ye know,—'kase he believed then that Caleb hed killed his wife with pizenous yerbs; an' he went back the nex' night an' fired the woods, ter make folks think when they fund Caleb's bones that he war a-runnin' from the

---

4. A minister who makes a circuit, preaching from place to place.

5. For the parable of the laborers in the vineyard see Matthew 20:1–16.

blaze an' fell off'n the bluff." And everybody on Old Rocky-Top said incredulously, "Pore Tony Britt! He hev los' his mind through goin' a-huntin' jes' one time on the T'other Mounting."

1884

Grace Elizabeth King
(1851–1932)

Born into a prosperous and socially prominent New Orleans family, Grace King experienced the Union army's occupation of the city, the fall of the Confederacy, and the Reconstruction, events that precipitated a total collapse of her family's fortunes. When the city was captured in 1862, the 9-year-old girl fled with her mother and siblings to their L'Embarras Plantation near New Iberia. Returning four years later to find all their city property gone, they were forced to relocate in the working-class quarter near the Jackson Barracks, headquarters of the occupying troops. In the succeeding decades, while William Woodson King struggled to reestablish his law practice, the family lived in several temporary residences. It was not until 1904, after the death of both parents, that the brother and three unmarried sisters were able to afford a permanent home. In that shelter, Grace was able for the first time to have an attic study where she could write.

King was a product—both socially and intellectually—of the New Orleans Creole community. Though a Presbyterian, she was educated in French-speaking Catholic schools, where she received rigorous training in writing. Her family was intellectually active and regularly entertained scholars and writers in their home.

When the Cotton Centennial Exposition was held in New Orleans from 1884 to 1886, the King family played host to many Northern intellectuals, including Julia Ward Howe, Charles Dudley Warner, and the editor of the *Century Magazine,* Richard Watson Gilder. When she told him that Southerners resented the work of George Washington Cable as too slanted to a Northern audience, Gilder challenged Grace King to write her own version of life in New Orleans. She rose to the challenge: she had wanted to be a writer from the time she was a child, and after her father's death, the family was struggling financially. Though Gilder rejected her first manuscript, "Monsieur Motte," when it was sent to him anonymously, Charles Dudley Warner sponsored its publication in the *New Princeton Review* and served as her sponsor in placing later stories with *Harper's Magazine.* With the addition of three stories, King's first collection, *Monsieur Motte,* was published in 1888.

Mr. and Mrs. Warner invited her to visit them in Hartford, Connecticut, in 1887. There she met Mark Twain and his wife Olivia, Sarah Orne Jewett, and the aged Harriet Beecher Stowe. The contrast between the wealth of the North and the poverty of the South she had left behind made her feel very much the outsider; in contrast, she felt very much at home on her first trip to France (1891–1892).

Tales of a Time and Place (1892) and *Balcony Stories* (1893) are gatherings of most of King's local-color stories. Using realistic details, she treated themes of individuals suffering in genteel poverty, relations between the races, and the decline of Southern society. She was especially eager to depict instances of what she termed the "holy passion of the Negro women," demonstrated in "great instances of devotion . . . found among even the worst treated slaves." In "A Crippled Hope" from *Balcony Stories,* King describes such a woman, mistreated from childhood and ownerless at emancipation, who struggles to serve others.

The novel *The Pleasant Ways of St. Medard* (1916), detailing the experiences of a family very like the Kings, who must come back from losing their possessions and position in the war, is one of King's most successful works.

Equally accomplished as a historian, King wrote *Jean Baptiste le Moyne, sieur de Bienville* (1893), a bio-

graphy of the Canadian founder of Mobile and New Orleans; *A History of Louisiana* (1894); *New Orleans, The Place and the People* (1895); *De Soto and His Men in the Land of Florida* (1898); *Stories from Louisiana History* (1905); and *Creole Families of New Orleans* (1921). Her final work of fiction was the novel *La Dame de Sainte Hermine* (1924), a historical romance set in eighteenth-century New Orleans.

In her later years King was an honored citizen of the Louisiana establishment, and in her Greek revival home on Coliseum Place, she received many younger writers, including Sherwood Anderson and Edmund Wilson. *Memories of a Southern Woman of Letters* (1932), a gentle recapitulation of her experiences, was published a few months after her death.

A Crippled Hope

You must picture to yourself the quiet, dim-lighted room of a convalescent; outside, the dreary, bleak days of winter in a sparsely settled, distant country parish; inside, a slow, smoldering log-fire, a curtained bed, the infant sleeping well enough, the mother wakeful, restless, thought-driven, as a mother must be, unfortunately, nowadays, particularly in that parish, where cotton worms and overflows have acquired such a monopoly of one's future.

God is always pretty near a sick woman's couch; but nearer even than God seems the sick-nurse—at least in that part of the country, under those circumstances. It is so good to look through the dimness and uncertainty, moral and physical, and to meet those little black, steadfast, all-seeing eyes; to feel those smooth, soft, all-soothing hands; to hear, across one's sleep, that three-footed step—the flat-soled left foot, the tip-toe right, and the padded end of the broomstick; and when one is so wakeful and restless and thought-driven, to have another's story given one. God, depend upon it, grows stories and lives as he does herbs, each with a mission of balm to some woe.

She said she had, and in truth she had, no other name than "little Mammy"; and that was the name of her nature. Pure African, but bronze rather than pure black, and full-sized only in width, her growth having been hampered as to height by an injury to her hip, which had lamed her, pulling her figure awry, and burdening her with a protuberance of the joint. Her mother caused it by dropping her when a baby, and concealing it, for fear of punishment, until the dislocation became irremediable. All the animosity of which little Mammy was capable centered upon this unknown but never-to-be-forgotten mother of hers; out of this hatred had grown her love—that is, her destiny, a woman's love being her destiny. Little Mammy's love was for children.

The birth and infancy (the one as accidental as the other, one would infer) took place in—it sounds like the "Arabian Nights" now!—took place in the great room, caravansary, stable, behind a negro-trader's auction-mart, where human beings underwent literally the daily buying and selling of which the world now complains in a figure of speech—a great, square, dusty chamber where, sitting cross-legged, leaning against the wall, or lying on foul blanket pallets on the floor, the bargains of to-day made their brief sojourn, awaiting transformation into the profits of the morrow.

The place can be pointed out now, is often pointed out; but no emotion arises at sight of it. It is so plain, so matter-of-fact an edifice that emotion only comes afterward in thinking about it, and then in the reflection that such an edifice could be, then as now, plain and matter-of-fact.

For the slave-trader there was no capital so valuable as the physical soundness of his stock; the moral was easily enough forged or counterfeited. Little Mammy's good-for-nothing mother was sold as readily as a vote, in the parlance of to-day; but no one would pay for a crippled baby. The mother herself would not have taken her as a gift, had it been in the nature of a negro-trader to give away anything. Some doctoring was done,—so little Mammy heard traditionally,—some effort made to get her marketable. There were attempts to pair her off as a twin sister of various correspondencies in age, size, and color, and to palm her off, as a substitute, at migratory, bereaved, overfull breasts. Nothing equaled a negro-trader's will and power for fraud, except the hereditary distrust and watchfulness which it bred and maintained. And so, in the even balance between the two categories, the little cripple remained a fixture in the stream of life that passed through that back room, in the fluxes and refluxes of buying and selling; not valueless, however—rely upon a negro-trader for discovering values as substitutes, as panaceas. She earned her nourishment, and Providence did not let it kill the little animal before the emancipation of weaning arrived.

How much circumstances evoked, how much instinct responded, belongs to the secrets which nature seems to intend keeping. As a baby she had eyes, attention, solely for other babies. One cannot say while she was still crawling, for she could only crawl years after she should have been walking, but, before even precocious walking-time, tradition or the old gray-haired negro janitor relates, she would creep from baby to baby to play with it, put it to sleep, pat it, rub its stomach (a negro baby, you know, is all stomach, and generally aching stomach at that). And before she had a lap, she managed to force one for some ailing nursling. It was then that they began to call her "little Mammy." In the transitory population of the "pen" no one stayed long enough to give her another name; and no one ever stayed short enough to give her another one.

Her first recollection of herself was that she could not walk—she was past crawling; she cradled herself along, as she called sitting down flat, and working herself about with her hands and her one strong leg. Babbling babies walked all around her,—many walking before they babbled,—and still she did not walk, imitate them as she might and did. She would sit and "study" about it, make another trial, fall; sit and study some more, make another trial, fall again. Negroes, who believe that they must give a reason for everything even if they have to invent one, were convinced that it was all this studying upon her lameness that gave her such a large head.

And now she began secretly turning up the clothes of every negro child that came into that pen, and examining its legs, and still more secretly examining her own, stretched out before her on the ground. How long it took she does not remember; in fact, she could not have known, for she had no way of measuring time except by her thoughts and feelings. But in her own way and time the due process of deliberation was fulfilled, and the quotient made clear that, bowed or not, all children's legs were of equal length except her own, and all were alike, not one full, strong, hard, the other soft, flabby, wrinkled, growing out of a knot at the hip. A whole psychological period apparently lay between that conclusion and—a broom-handle walking-stick; but the broomstick came, as it was bound to come,—thank heaven!—from that premise, and what with stretching one limb to make it longer, and doubling up the other to make it shorter, she invented that form of locomotion which is still carrying her through life, and with no more exaggerated leg-crookedness than many careless negroes born with straight limbs display. This must have been when she was about eight or nine. Hobbling on a broomstick, with, no doubt, the same weird, wizened face as now, an innate sense of the fitness of things must have suggested the kerchief tied around her big head, and the burlap rag of an apron in front of her linsey-woolsey rag of a gown, and the bit of broken pipe-stem in the corner of her mouth, where the pipe should have been, and where it was in after years. That is the way she recollected herself, and that is the way one recalls her now, with a few modifications.

The others came and went, but she was always there. It wasn't long before she became "little Mammy" to the grown folks too; and the newest inmates soon learned to cry: "Where's little Mammy?" "Oh, little Mammy! little Mammy! Such a misery in my head [or my back, or my stomach]! Can't you help me, little Mammy?" It was curious what a quick eye she had for symptoms and ailments, and what a quick ear for suffering, and how apt she was at picking up, remembering, and inventing remedies. It never occurred to her not to crouch at the head or the foot of a sick pallet, day and night through. As for the nights, she said she dared not close her eyes of nights. The room they were in was so vast, and sometimes the negroes lay so thick on the floor, rolled in their blankets (you know, even in the summer they sleep under blankets), all snoring so loudly, she would never have heard a groan or a whimper any more than they did, if she had slept, too. And negro mothers are so careless and such heavy sleepers. All night she would creep at regular intervals to the different pallets, and draw the little babies from under, or away from, the heavy, inert impending mother forms. There is no telling how many she thus saved from being overlaid and smothered, or, what was worse, maimed and crippled.

Whenever a physician came in, as he was sometimes called, to look at a valuable investment or to furbish up some piece of damaged goods, she always managed to get near to hear the directions; and she generally was the one to apply them also, for negroes always would steal medicines most scurvily one from the other. And when death at times would slip into the pen, despite the trader's utmost alertness and precautions,—as death often "had to do," little Mammy said,—when the time of some of them came to die, and when the rest of the negroes, with African greed of eye for the horrible, would press around the lowly couch where the agonizing form of a slave lay writhing out of life, she would always to the last give medicines, and wipe the cold forehead, and soothe the clutching, fearsome hands, hoping to the end, and trying to inspire the hope that his or her "time" had not come yet; for, as she said, "Our time doesn't come just as often as it does come."

And in those sad last offices, which somehow have always been under reproach as a kind of shame, no matter how young she was, she was always too old to have the childish avoidance of them. On the contrary, to her a corpse was only a kind of baby, and she always strove, she said, to make one, like the other, easy and comfortable.

And in other emergencies she divined the mysteries of the flesh, as other precocities divine the mysteries of painting and music, and so become child wonders.

Others came and went. She alone remained there. Babies of her babyhood—the toddlers she, a toddler, had nursed—were having babies themselves now; the middle-aged had had time to grow old and die. Every week new families were coming into the great back chamber; every week they passed out; babies, boys, girls, buxom wenches, stalwart youths, and the middle-aged—the grave, serious ones whom misfortune had driven from their old masters, and the ill-reputed ones, the trickish, thievish, lazy, whom the cunning of the negro-trader alone could keep in circulation. All were marketable, all were bought and sold, all passed in one door and out the other—all except her, little Mammy. As with her lameness, it took time for her to recognize, to understand, the fact. She could study over her lameness, she could in the dull course of time think out the broomstick way of palliation. It would have been almost better, under the circumstances, for God to have kept the truth from her; only—God keeps so little of the truth from us women. It is his system.

Poor little thing! It was not now that her master *could* not sell her, but he *would* not! Out of her own intelligence she had forged her chains; the lameness was a hobble merely in comparison. She had become too valuable to the negro-trader by her services among his crew, and offers only solidified his determination not to sell her. Visiting physicians, after short acquaintance with her capacities, would offer what were called fancy prices for her. Planters who heard of her through their purchases would come to the city purposely to secure, at any cost, so inestimable an adjunct to their plantations. Even ladies—refined, delicate ladies—sometimes came to the pen personally to back money with influence. In vain. Little Mammy was worth more to the negro-trader, simply as a kind of insurance against accidents, than any sum, however glittering the figure, and he was no ignorant expert in human wares. She can tell it; no one else can for her. Remember that at times she had seen the streets outside. Remember that she could hear of the outside world daily from the passing chattels—of the plantations, farms, families; the green fields, Sunday woods, running streams; the camp-meetings, corn-shuckings, cotton-pickings, sugar-grindings; the baptisms, marriages, funerals, prayer-meetings; the holidays and holy days. Remember that, whether for liberty or whether for love, passion effloresces in the human being—no matter when, where, or how—with every spring's return. Remember that she was, even in middle age, young and vigorous. But no; do not remember anything. There is no need to heighten the coloring.

It would be tedious to relate, although it was not tedious to hear her relate it, the desperations and hopes of her life then. Hardly a day passed that she did not see, looking for purchases (rummaging among goods on a counter for bargains), some master whom she could have loved, some mistress whom she could have adored. Always her favorite mistresses were there—tall, delicate matrons, who came themselves, with great fatigue, to select kindly-faced women for nurses; languid-looking ladies with smooth hair standing out in wide *bandeaux* from their heads, and lace shawls dropping from their sloping shoulders, silk dresses carelessly held up in thumb and finger from embroidered petticoats that were spread out like tents over huge hoops which covered whole groups of swarming piccaninnies on the dirty floor; ladies, pale from illnesses that she might have nursed, and over-burdened with children whom she might have reared! And not a lady of that kind saw her face but wanted her, yearned for her, pleaded for her, coming back secretly to slip silver, and sometimes gold, pieces into her hand, patting her turbaned head, calling her "little Mammy" too, instantly, by inspiration, and making the negro-trader give them, with all sorts of assurances, the refusal of her. She had no need for the whispered "Buy me, master!" "Buy me, mistress!" "You'll see how I can work, master!" "You'll never be sorry, mistress!" of the others. The negro-trader—like hangmen, negro-traders are fitted by nature for their profession—it came into his head—he had no heart, not even a negro-trader's heart—that it would be more judicious to seclude her during these shopping visits, so to speak. She could not have had any hopes then at all; it must have been all desperations.

That auction-block, that executioner's block, about which so much has been written—Jacob's ladder,[1] in his dream, was nothing to what that block appeared nightly in her dreams to her; and the climbers up and down—well, perhaps Jacob's angels were his hopes, too.

At times she determined to depreciate her usefulness, mar her value, by renouncing her heart, denying her purpose. For days she would tie her kerchief over her ears and eyes, and crouch in a corner, strangling her impulses. She even malingered, refused food, became dumb. And she might have succeeded in making herself salable through incipient lunacy, if through no other way, had she been able to maintain her rôle long enough. But some woman or baby always was falling into some emergency of pain and illness.

How it might have ended one does not like to think. Fortunately, one does not need to think.

There came a night. She sat alone in the vast, dark caravansary—alone for the first time in her life. Empty rags and blankets lay strewn over the floor, no snoring, no tossing in them more. A sacrificial sale that day had cleared the counters. Alarm-bells rang in the streets, but she did not know them for alarm-bells; alarm brooded in the dim space around her, but she did not even recognize that. Her protracted tension of heart had made her fear-blind to all but one peradventure.

Once or twice she forgot herself, and limped over to some heap to relieve an imaginary struggling babe or moaning sleeper. Morning came. She had dozed. She looked to see the

---

1. See *Genesis* 28:12. In a dream, Jacob sees a ladder stretching from earth to heaven, with angels ascending and descending.

rag-heaps stir; they lay as still as corpses. The alarm-bells had ceased. She looked to see a new gang enter the far door. She listened for the gathering buzzing of voices in the next room, around the auction-block. She waited for the trader. She waited for the janitor. At nightfall a file of soldiers entered. They drove her forth, ordering her in the voice, in the tone, of the negro-trader. That was the only familiar thing in the chaos of incomprehensibility about her. She hobbled through the auction-room. Posters, advertisements, papers, lay on the floor, and in the torch-light glared from the wall. Her Jacob's ladder, her stepping-stone to her hopes, lay overturned in a corner.

You divine it. The negro-trader's trade was abolished, and he had vanished in the din and smoke of a war which he had not been entirely guiltless of producing, leaving little Mammy locked up behind him. Had he forgotten her? One cannot even hope so. She hobbled out into the street, leaning on her nine-year-old broomstick (she had grown only slightly beyond it; could still use it by bending over it), her head tied in a rag kerchief, a rag for a gown, a rag for an apron.

Free, she was free! But she had not hoped for freedom. The plantation, the household, the delicate ladies, the teeming children,—broomsticks they were in comparison to freedom, but,—that was what she had asked, what she had prayed for. God, she said, had let her drop, just as her mother had done. More than ever she grieved, as she crept down the street, that she had never mounted the auctioneer's block. An ownerless free negro! She knew no one whose duty it was to help her; no one knew her to help her. In the whole world (it was all she had asked) there was no white child to call her mammy, no white lady or gentleman (it was the extent of her dreams) beholden to her as to a nurse. And all her innumerable black beneficiaries! Even the janitor, whom she had tended as the others, had deserted her like his white prototype.

She tried to find a place for herself, but she had no indorsers, no recommenders. She dared not mention the name of the negro-trader; it banished her not only from the households of the whites, but from those of the genteel of her own color. And everywhere soldiers senti-neled the streets—soldiers whose tone and accent reminded her of the negro-trader.

Her sufferings, whether imaginary or real, were sufficiently acute to drive her into the only form of escape which once had been possible to friendless negroes. She became a runaway. With a bundle tied to the end of a stick over her shoulder, just as the old prints represent it, she fled from her homelessness and loneliness, from her ignoble past, and the heart-disappointing termination of it. Following a railroad track, journeying afoot, sleeping by the roadside, she lived on until she came to the one familiar landmark in life to her—a sick woman, but a white one. And so, progressing from patient to patient (it was a time when sick white women studded the country like mile-posts), she arrived at a little town, a kind of a refuge for soldiers' wives and widows. She never traveled further. She could not. Always, as in the pen, some emergency of pain and illness held her.

That is all. She is still there. The poor, poor women of that stricken region say that little Mammy was the only alleviation God left them after Sheridan[2] passed through; and the richer ones say very much the same thing—

But one should hear her tell it herself, as has been said, on a cold, gloomy winter day in the country, the fire glimmering on the hearth; the overworked husband in the fields; the baby quiet at last; the mother uneasy, restless, thought-driven; the soft black hand rubbing backward and forward, rubbing out aches and frets and nervousness.

The eyelids droop; the firelight plays fantasies on the bed-curtains; the ear drops words, sentences; one gets confused—one sleeps—one dreams.

1893

---

2. Philip Sheridan (1831–1888), Union general; his army pursued Lee's and cut off the Southern retreat at Appomattox, forcing Lee's surrender.

Mary E. Wilkins Freeman
(1852–1930)

In 1926 Mary Wilkins Freeman and Edith Wharton became the first women inducted into the National Institute of Arts and Letters. A professional author who supported herself by writing short stories for most of her adult life, Freeman is among the best known of the American regional realists, as her "local-color" stories provide insight into the details of New England domestic life. Recently she has also gained favor among feminist critics for her sympathetic portrayal of middle-class women who tread the fine line between their communities' expectations of them and their own desires. Her writings seldom conformed to the "marriage plot" that assumes every heroine's happy fate must end in matrimony. Her own life, too, diverged from that convention.

Freeman was born in Randolph, Massachusetts, a farming and shoe-manufacturing town, to parents from old New England families who were no longer prosperous. Her mother, Eleanor Lothrop Wilkins, and her father, Warren Wilkins, supported the family with the slim profits of her father's house-building and carpentry business. Raised as a strict Congregationalist, Mary was steeped in the religious tradition of her New England Puritan forebears. All three of her siblings died before adulthood, so Mary occupied the position of only child. She had a formal, classical education in Randolph, and, during her high school years in Brattleboro, Vermont, where her father had ventured into dry-goods retailing with a partner, Mary followed a college-preparatory curriculum of mathematics, rhetoric, Latin, and science.

After graduating from high school in 1870, Mary attended Mount Holyoke Female Seminary; like Emily Dickinson before her, she left that college after one uncomfortable year, to return home. She is supposed to have fallen in love with the son of family friends, but the romance ended when the young man traveled abroad and did not return, but married someone else. Her parents fell upon hard times, as her father's business failed. In 1877 the Freeman family moved in with the parents of Mary's former admirer, and her mother served as their housekeeper. Her mother died in 1880, and Mary took it upon herself to support her father with income from her writing. He died in 1883, leaving his daughter without family or financial means.

Freeman began her writing career as a children's author, making a small but steady income with the magazine stories that would be collected in *Goody Two-Shoes and Other Famous Nursery Tales* (with Clara Dote Bates, 1883); *The Crow with Golden Horns and Other Stories* (1886); and *The Adventures of Ann: Stories of Colonial Times* (1886). She won a $50 prize for adult fiction as early as 1882; by 1887 she had accumulated enough stories to publish *A Humble Romance and Other Stories*. She lived in Randolph with the family of her friend Mary Wales, who for twenty years took care of household details while Freeman wrote fiction, sometimes for ten hours a day. Her most highly respected stories appeared in *A New England Nun and Other Stories* (1891); her well-received novels include *Pembroke* (1894). She built a reputation and an income and traveled in the northeastern United States and Europe.

Wilkins did not marry until she was 49 years old, when she wed a physician without a practice, Dr. Charles Freeman. She had known him for ten years and had postponed the wedding more than once when it finally occurred in 1902. The marriage was troubled by the couple's respective addictions, hers to sedatives (prescribed for insomnia and night terrors) and his to alcohol. Dr. Freeman was institutionalized more than once for alcoholism and died in 1923 of its complications. Although his will left his entire estate to his chauffeur,

Mary Wilkins Freeman contested it, and eventually inherited a fortune large enough to live comfortably upon until her death in 1930. Her last book was published in 1918, twelve years before she died.

The two selections reprinted here are typical of Freeman's stories about New England women who negotiate between feminine submissiveness and duty on the one hand and independence and self-assertion on the other. Sarah Penn, in "The Revolt of 'Mother,' " has spent forty years dutifully keeping house in a decrepit building on her husband's farm, even though he promised her upon their marriage that he would build her a new house. When she learns he is building a new barn on the proposed homesite, she tries to argue him out of it; when words fail, she resorts to more drastic means to assert her needs. Louisa Ellis, of "A New England Nun," has lived alone for fifteen years, waiting for her fiancé to come back from a fortune-seeking trip abroad. His return disturbs her tranquil daily rituals, causing her to question her lifelong assumption that she ought to get married. Both stories are richly detailed accounts of middle-class women's activities, offering insight into the feminine realm of late Victorian housekeeping. They also suggest the power women could assert within that realm and celebrate women's potential for influencing their own fates.

Freeman's other publications include *The Pot of Gold and Other Stories* (1892); *Young Lucretia and Other Stories* (1892); *Jane Field* (1892); *Giles Corey, Yeoman: A Play* (1893); *Madelon* (1896); *Jerome, A Poor Man* (1897); *Silence and Other Stories* (1898); *The People of Our Neighborhood* (1898); *The Love of Parson Lord and Other Stories* (1900); *The Heart's Highway: A Romance of Virginia in the Seventeenth Century* (1900); *Understudies* (1901); *The Portion of Labor* (1901); *Six Trees* (1903); *The Wind in the Rose-bush and Other Stories of the Supernatural* (1903); *The Givers* (1904); *The Debtor* (1905); *"Doc." Gordon* (1906); *By the Light of the Soul* (1907); *The Fair Lavinia and Others* (1907); *The Shoulder of Atlas* (1908); *The Winning Lady and Others* (1909); *The Green Door* (1910); *The Butterfly House* (1912); *The Yates Pride* (1912); *The Copy-Cat & Other Stories* (1914); and *Edgewater People* (1918).

The standard biography of Freeman is Edward Foster's *Mary E. Wilkins Freeman* (1956). Studies of her work can be found in Ann Douglas, *The Feminization of American Culture* (1977); Josephine Donovan, *New England Local Color Literature: A Women's Tradition* (1983); Carol Ascher, et al., eds., *Between Women* (1984); Emily Toth, ed., *Regionalism and the Female Imagination* (1985).

The Revolt of "Mother"

"Father!"

"What is it?"

"What are them men diggin' over there in the field for?"

There was a sudden dropping and enlarging of the lower part of the old man's face, as if some heavy weight had settled therein; he shut his mouth tight, and went on harnessing the great bay mare. He hustled the collar on to her neck with a jerk.

"Father!"

The old man slapped the saddle upon the mare's back.

"Look here, father, I want to know what them men are diggin' over in the field for, an' I'm goin' to know."

"I wish you'd go into the house, mother, an' 'tend to your own affairs," the old man said then. He ran his words together, and his speech was almost as inarticulate as a growl.

But the woman understood; it was her most native tongue. "I ain't goin' into the house till you tell me what them men are doin' over there in the field," said she.

Then she stood waiting. She was a small woman, short and straight-waisted like a child in her brown cotton gown. Her forehead was mild and benevolent between the smooth curves of gray hair; there were meek downward lines about her nose and mouth; but her eyes, fixed upon the old man, looked as if the meekness had been the result of her own will, never of the will of another.

They were in the barn, standing before the wide open doors. The spring air, full of the smell of growing grass and unseen blossoms, came in their faces. The deep yard in front was littered with farm wagons and piles of wood; on the edges, close to the fence and the house, the grass was a vivid green, and there were some dandelions.

The old man glanced doggedly at his wife as he tightened the last buckles on the harness. She looked as immovable to him as one of the rocks in his pasture-land, bound to the earth with generations of blackberry vines. He slapped the reins over the horse, and started forth from the barn.

"Father!" said she.

The old man pulled up. "What is it?"

"I want to know what them men are diggin' over there in that field for."

"They're diggin' a cellar, I s'pose, if you've got to know."

"A cellar for what?"

"A barn."

"A barn? You ain't goin' to build a barn over there where we was goin' to have a house, father?"

The old man said not another word. He hurried the horse into the farm wagon, and clattered out of the yard, jouncing as sturdily on his seat as a boy.

The woman stood a moment looking after him, then she went out of the barn across a corner of the yard to the house. The house, standing at right angles with the great barn and a long reach of sheds and out-buildings, was infinitesimal compared with them. It was scarcely as commodious for people as the little boxes under the barn eaves were for doves.

A pretty girl's face, pink and delicate as a flower, was looking out of one of the house windows. She was watching three men who were digging over in the field which bounded the yard near the road line. She turned quietly when the woman entered.

"What are they digging for, mother?" said she. "Did he tell you?"

"They're diggin' for—a cellar for a new barn."

"Oh, mother, he ain't going to build another barn?"

"That's what he says."

A boy stood before the kitchen glass combing his hair. He combed slowly and painstakingly, arranging his brown hair in a smooth hillock over his forehead. He did not seem to pay any attention to the conversation.

"Sammy, did you know father was going to build a new barn?" asked the girl.

The boy combed assiduously.

"Sammy!"

He turned, and showed a face like his father's under his smooth crest of hair. "Yes, I s'pose I did," he said, reluctantly.

"How long have you known it?" asked his mother.

"'Bout three months, I guess."

"Why didn't you tell of it?"

"Didn't think 'twould do no good."

"I don't see what father wants another barn for," said the girl, in her sweet, slow voice. She turned again to the window, and stared out at the digging men in the field. Her tender, sweet face was full of a gentle distress. Her forehead was as bald and innocent as a baby's, with the light hair strained back from it in a row of curl-papers. She was quite large, but her soft curves did not look as if they covered muscles.

Her mother looked sternly at the boy. "Is he goin' to buy more cows?" said she.

The boy did not reply; he was tying his shoes.

"Sammy, I want you to tell me if he's goin' to buy more cows."

"I s'pose he is."

"How many?"

"Four, I guess."

His mother said nothing more. She went into the pantry, and there was a clatter of dishes. The boy got his cap from a nail behind the door, took an old arithmetic from the shelf, and started for school. He was lightly built, but clumsy. He went out of the yard with a curious spring in the hips, that made his loose homemade jacket tilt up in the rear.

The girl went to the sink, and began to wash the dishes that were piled up there. Her mother came promptly out of the pantry, and shoved her aside. "You wipe 'em," said she; "I'll wash. There's a good many this mornin'."

The mother plunged her hands vigorously into the water, the girl wiped the plates slowly and dreamily. "Mother," said she, "don't you think it's too bad father's going to build that new barn, much as we need a decent house to live in?"

Her mother scrubbed a dish fiercely. "You ain't found out yet we're women-folks, Nanny Penn," said she. "You ain't seen enough of men-folks yet to. One of these days you'll find it out, an' then you'll know that we know only what men-folks think we do, so far as any use of it goes, an' how we'd ought to reckon men-folks in with Providence, an' not complain of what they do any more than we do of the weather."

"I don't care; I don't believe George is anything like that, anyhow," said Nanny. Her delicate face flushed pink, her lips pouted softly, as if she were going to cry.

"You wait an' see. I guess George Eastman ain't no better than other men. You hadn't ought to judge father, though. He can't help it, 'cause he don't look at things jest the way we do. An' we've been pretty comfortable here, after all. The roof don't leak—ain't never but once—that's one thing. Father's kept it shingled right up."

"I do wish we had a parlor."

"I guess it won't hurt George Eastman any to come to see you in a nice clean kitchen. I guess a good many girls don't have as good a place as this. Nobody's ever heard me complain."

"I ain't complained either, mother."

"Well, I don't think you'd better, a good father an' a good home as you've got. S'pose your father made you go out an' work for your livin'? Lots of girls have to that ain't no stronger an' better able to than you be."

Sarah Penn washed the frying-pan with a conclusive air. She scrubbed the outside of it as faithfully as the inside. She was a masterly keeper of her box of a house. Her one living-room never seemed to have in it any of the dust which the friction of life with inanimate matter produces. She swept, and there seemed to be no dirt to go before the broom; she cleaned, and one could see no difference. She was like an artist so perfect that he has apparently no art. To-day she got out a mixing bowl and a board, and rolled some pies, and there was no more flour upon her than upon her daughter who was doing finer work. Nanny was to be married in the fall, and she was sewing on some white cambric[1] and embroidery. She sewed industriously while her mother cooked; her soft milk-white hands and wrists showed whiter than her delicate work.

"We must have the stove moved out in the shed before long," said Mrs. Penn. "Talk about not havin' things, it's been a real blessin' to be able to put a stove up in that shed in hot weather. Father did one good thing when he fixed that stove-pipe out there."

Sarah Penn's face as she rolled her pies had that expression of meek vigor which might have characterized one of the New Testament saints. She was making mince-pies. Her husband, Adoniram Penn, liked them better than any other kind. She baked twice a week. Adoniram often liked a piece of pie between meals. She hurried this morning. It had been

---

1. Finely woven white linen or cotton.

later than usual when she began, and she wanted to have a pie baked for dinner. However deep a resentment she might be forced to hold against her husband, she would never fail in sedulous attention to his wants.

Nobility of character manifests itself at loop-holes when it is not provided with large doors. Sarah Penn's showed itself to-day in flaky dishes of pastry. So she made the pies faithfully, while across the table she could see, when she glanced up from her work, the sight that rankled in her patient and steadfast soul—the digging of the cellar of the new barn in the place where Adoniram forty years ago had promised her their new house should stand.

The pies were done for dinner. Adoniram and Sammy were home a few minutes after twelve o'clock. The dinner was eaten with serious haste. There was never much conversation at the table in the Penn family. Adoniram asked a blessing, and they ate promptly, then rose up and went about their work.

Sammy went back to school, taking soft sly lopes out of the yard like a rabbit. He wanted a game of marbles before school, and feared his father would give him some chores to do. Adoniram hastened to the door and called after him, but he was out of sight.

"I don't see what you let him go for, mother," said he. "I wanted him to help me unload that wood."

Adoniram went to work out in the yard unloading wood from the wagon. Sarah put away the dinner dishes, while Nanny took down her curl-papers and changed her dress. She was going down to the store to buy some more embroidery and thread.

When Nanny was gone, Mrs. Penn went to the door. "Father!" she called.

"Well, what is it!"

"I want to see you jest a minute, father."

"I can't leave this wood nohow. I've got to git it unloaded an' go for a load of gravel afore two o'clock. Sammy had ought to helped me. You hadn't ought to let him go to school so early."

"I want to see you jest a minute."

"I tell ye I can't, nohow, mother."

"Father, you come here." Sarah Penn stood in the door like a queen; she held her head as if it bore a crown; there was the patience which makes authority royal in her voice. Adoniram went.

Mrs. Penn led the way into the kitchen, and pointed to a chair. "Sit down, father," said she; "I've got somethin' I want to say to you."

He sat down heavily; his face was quite stolid, but he looked at her with restive eyes. "Well, what is it, mother?"

"I want to know what you're buildin' that new barn for, father?"

"I ain't got nothin' to say about it."

"It can't be you think you need another barn?"

"I tell ye I ain't got nothin' to say about it, mother; an' I ain't goin' to say nothin'."

"Be you goin' to buy more cows?"

Adoniram did not reply; he shut his mouth tight.

"I know you be, as well as I want to. Now, father, look here"—Sarah Penn had not sat down; she stood before her husband in the humble fashion of a Scripture[2] woman—"I'm goin' to talk real plain to you; I never have sence I married you, but I'm goin' to now. I ain't never complained, an' I ain't goin' to complain now, but I'm goin' to talk plain. You see this room here, father; you look at it well. You see there ain't no carpet on the floor, an' you see the paper is all dirty, an' droppin' off the walls. We ain't had no new paper on it for ten year, an' then I put it on myself, an' it didn't cost but ninepence a roll. You see this room, father; it's all the one I've had to work in an' eat in an' sit in sence we was married. There ain't another woman in the whole town whose husband ain't got half the means you have but

2. A woman of the Old Testament.

what's got better. It's all the room Nanny's got to have her company in; an' there ain't one of her mates but what's got better, an' their fathers not so able as hers is. It's all the room she'll have to be married in. What would you have thought, father, if we had had our weddin' in a room no better than this? I was married in my mother's parlor, with a carpet on the floor, an' stuffed furniture, an' a mahogany card-table. An' this is all the room my daughter will have to be married in. Look here, father!"

Sarah Penn went across the room as though it were a tragic stage. She flung open a door and disclosed a tiny bedroom, only large enough for a bed and bureau, with a path between. "There, father," said she—"there's all the room I've had to sleep in forty year. All my children were born there—the two that died, an' the two that's livin'. I was sick with a fever there."

She stepped to another door and opened it. It led into the small, ill-lighted pantry. "Here," said she, "is all the buttery I've got—every place I've got for my dishes, to set away my victuals in, an' to keep my milk-pans in. Father, I've been takin' care of the milk of six cows in this place, an' now you're goin' to build a new barn, an' keep more cows, an' give me more to do in it."

She threw open another door. A narrow crooked flight of stairs wound upward from it. "There, father," said she, "I want you to look at the stairs that go up to them two unfinished chambers that are all the places our son an' daughter have had to sleep in all their lives. There ain't a prettier girl in town nor a more ladylike one than Nanny, an' that's the place she has to sleep in. It ain't so good as your horse's stall; it ain't so warm an' tight."

Sarah Penn went back and stood before her husband. "Now, father," said she, "I want to know if you think you're doin' right an' accordin' to what you profess. Here, when we was married, forty year ago, you promised me faithful that we should have a new house built in that lot over in the field before the year was out. You said you had money enough, an' you wouldn't ask me to live in no such place as this. It is forty year now, an' you've been makin' more money, an' I've been savin' of it for you ever since, an' you ain't built no house yet. You've built sheds an' cow-houses an' one new barn, an' now you're goin' to build another. Father, I want to know if you think it's right. You're lodgin' your dumb beasts better than you are your own flesh an' blood. I want to know if you think it's right."

"I ain't got nothin' to say."

"You can't say nothin' without ownin' it ain't right, father. An' there's another thing—I ain't complained; I've got along forty year, an' I s'pose I should forty more, if it wa'n't for that—if we don't have another house. Nanny she can't live with us after she's married. She'll have to go somewheres else to live away from us, an' it don't seem as if I could have it so, noways, father. She wa'n't ever strong. She's got considerable color, but there wa'n't ever any backbone to her. I've always took the heft of everything off her, an' she ain't fit to keep house an' do everything herself. She'll be all worn out inside of a year. Think of her doin' all the washin' an' ironin' an' bakin' with them soft white hands an' arms, an' sweepin'! I can't have it so, noways, father."

Mrs. Penn's face was burning; her mild eyes gleamed. She had pleaded her little cause like a Webster,[3] she had ranged from severity to pathos; but her opponent employed that obstinate silence which makes eloquence futile with mocking echoes. Adoniram arose clumsily.

"Father, ain't you got nothin' to say?" said Mrs. Penn.

"I've got to go off after that load of gravel. I can't stan' here talkin' all day."

"Father, won't you think it over, an' have a house built there instead of a barn?"

"I ain't got nothin' to say."

Adoniram shuffled out. Mrs. Penn went into her bedroom. When she came out, her eyes were red. She had a roll of unbleached cotton cloth. She spread it out on the kitchen table, and began cutting out some shirts for her husband. The men over in the field had a team to

---

3. Daniel Webster (1782–1852) was an American politician and diplomat, known for oratorical prowess.

help them this afternoon; she could hear their halloos. She had a scanty pattern for the shirts; she had to plan and piece the sleeves.

Nanny came home with her embroidery, and sat down with her needlework. She had taken down her curl-papers, and there was a soft roll of fair hair like an aureole[4] over her forehead; her face was as delicately fine and clear as porcelain. Suddenly she looked up, and the tender red flamed all over her face and neck. "Mother," said she.

"What say?"

"I've been thinking—I don't see how we're goin' to have any—wedding in this room. I'd be ashamed to have his folks come if we didn't have anybody else."

"Mebbe we can have some new paper before then; I can put it on. I guess you won't have no call to be ashamed of your belongin's."

"We might have the wedding in the new barn," said Nanny, with gentle pettishness. "Why, mother, what makes you look so?"

Mrs. Penn had started, and was staring at her with a curious expression. She turned again to her work, and spread out a pattern carefully on the cloth. "Nothin'," said she.

Presently Adoniram clattered out of the yard in his two-wheeled dump cart, standing as proudly upright as a Roman charioteer. Mrs. Penn opened the door and stood there a minute looking out; the halloos of the men sounded louder.

It seemed to her all through the spring months that she heard nothing but the halloos and the noises of saws and hammers. The new barn grew fast. It was a fine edifice for this little village. Men came on pleasant Sundays, in their meeting suits and clean shirt bosoms, and stood around it admiringly. Mrs. Penn did not speak of it, and Adoniram did not mention it to her, although sometimes, upon a return from inspecting it, he bore himself with injured dignity.

"It's a strange thing how your mother feels about the new barn," he said, confidentially, to Sammy one day.

Sammy only grunted after an odd fashion for a boy; he had learned it from his father.

The barn was all completed ready for use by the third week in July. Adoniram had planned to move his stock in on Wednesday; on Tuesday he received a letter which changed his plans. He came in with it early in the morning. "Sammy's been to the post-office," said he, "an' I've got a letter from Hiram." Hiram was Mrs. Penn's brother, who lived in Vermont.

"Well," said Mrs. Penn, "what does he say about the folks?"

"I guess they're all right. He says he thinks if I come up country right off there's a chance to buy jest the kind of horse I want." He stared reflectively out of the window at the new barn.

Mrs. Penn was making pies. She went on clapping the rolling-pin into the crust, although she was very pale, and her heart beat loudly.

"I dun' know but what I'd better go," said Adoniram. "I hate to go off jest now, right in the midst of hayin', but the ten-acre lot's cut, an' I guess Rufus an' the others can git along without me three or four days. I can't get a horse round here to suit me, nohow, an' I've got to have another for all that wood-haulin' in the fall. I told Hiram to watch out, an' if he got wind of a good horse to let me know. I guess I'd better go."

"I'll get out your clean shirt an' collar," said Mrs. Penn calmly.

She laid out Adoniram's Sunday suit and his clean clothes on the bed in the little bedroom. She got his shaving-water and razor ready. At last she buttoned on his collar and fastened his black cravat.

Adoniram never wore his collar and cravat except on extra occasions. He held his head high, with a rasped dignity. When he was all ready, with his coat and hat brushed, and a lunch of pie and cheese in a paper bag, he hesitated on the threshold of the door. He looked at his wife, and his manner was defiantly apologetic. "*If* them cows come to-day,

4. A halo.

Sammy can drive 'em into the new barn," said he; "an' when they bring the hay up, they can pitch it in there."

"Well," replied Mrs. Penn.

Adoniram set his shaven face ahead and started. When he had cleared the door-step, he turned and looked back with a kind of nervous solemnity. "I shall be back by Saturday if nothin' happens," said he.

"Do be careful, father," returned his wife.

She stood in the door with Nanny at her elbow and watched him out of sight. Her eyes had a strange, doubtful expression in them; her peaceful forehead was contracted. She went in, and about her baking again. Nanny sat sewing. Her wedding-day was drawing nearer, and she was getting pale and thin with her steady sewing. Her mother kept glancing at her.

"Have you got that pain in your side this mornin'?" she asked.

"A little."

Mrs. Penn's face, as she worked, changed, her perplexed forehead smoothed, her eyes were steady, her lips firmly set. She formed a maxim for herself, although incoherently with her unlettered thoughts. "Unsolicited opportunities are the guide-posts of the Lord to the new roads of life," she repeated in effect, and she made up her mind to her course of action.

"S'posin' I *had* wrote to Hiram," she muttered once, when she was in the pantry—"s'posin' I had wrote, an' asked him if he knew of any horse? But I didn't, an' father's goin' wa'n't none of my doin'. It looks like a providence." Her voice rang out quite loud at the last.

"What you talkin' about, mother?" called Nanny.

"Nothin'."

Mrs. Penn hurried her baking; at eleven o'clock it was all done. The load of hay from the west field came slowly down the cart track, and drew up at the new barn. Mrs. Penn ran out. "Stop!" she screamed—"stop!"

The men stopped and looked; Sammy upreared from the top of the load, and stared at his mother.

"Stop!" she cried out again. "Don't you put the hay in that barn; put it in the old one."

"Why, he said to put it in here," returned one of the hay-makers, wonderingly. He was a young man, a neighbor's son, whom Adoniram hired by the year to help on the farm.

"Don't you put the hay in the new barn; there's room enough in the old one, ain't there?" said Mrs. Penn.

"Room enough," returned the hired man, in his thick, rustic tones. "Didn't need the new barn, nohow, far as room's concerned. Well, I s'pose he changed his mind." He took hold of the horses' bridles.

Mrs. Penn went back to the house. Soon the kitchen windows were darkened, and a fragrance like warm honey came into the room.

Nanny laid down her work. "I thought father wanted them to put the hay into the new barn?" she said, wonderingly.

"It's all right," replied her mother.

Sammy slid down from the load of hay, and came in to see if dinner was ready.

"I ain't goin' to get a regular dinner to-day, as long as father's gone," said his mother. "I've let the fire go out. You can have some bread an' milk an' pie. I thought we could get along." She set out some bowls of milk, some bread and a pie on the kitchen table. "You'd better eat your dinner now," said she. "You might jest as well get through with it. I want you to help me afterward."

Nanny and Sammy stared at each other. There was something strange in their mother's manner. Mrs. Penn did not eat anything herself. She went into the pantry, and they heard her moving dishes while they ate. Presently she came out with a pile of plates. She got the clothes-basket out of the shed, and packed them in it. Nanny and Sammy watched. She brought out cups and saucers, and put them in with the plates.

"What you goin' to do, mother?" inquired Nanny, in a timid voice. A sense of something unusual made her tremble, as if it were a ghost. Sammy rolled his eyes over his pie.

"You'll see what I'm goin' to do," replied Mrs. Penn. "If you're through, Nanny, I want you to go up-stairs an' pack up your things; an' I want you, Sammy, to help me take down the bed in the bedroom."

"Oh, mother, what for?" gasped Nanny.

"You'll see."

During the next few hours a feat was performed by this simple, pious New England mother which was equal in its way to Wolfe's storming of the Heights of Abraham.[5] It took no more genius and audacity of bravery for Wolfe to cheer his wondering soldiers up those steep precipices, under the sleeping eyes of the enemy, than for Sarah Penn, at the head of her children, to move all their little household goods into the new barn while her husband was away.

Nanny and Sammy followed their mother's instructions without a murmur; indeed, they were overawed. There is a certain uncanny and superhuman quality about all such purely original undertakings as their mother's was to them. Nanny went back and forth with her light loads, and Sammy tugged with sober energy.

At five o'clock in the afternoon the little house in which the Penns had lived for forty years had emptied itself into the new barn.

Every builder builds somewhat for unknown purposes, and is in a measure a prophet. The architect of Adoniram Penn's barn, while he designed it for the comfort of four-footed animals, had planned better than he knew for the comfort of humans. Sarah Penn saw at a glance its possibilities. These great box-stalls, with quilts hung before them, would make better bedrooms than the one she had occupied for forty years, and there was a tight carriage-room. The harness-room, with its chimney and shelves, would make a kitchen of her dreams. The great middle space would make a parlor, by-and-by, fit for a palace. Up-stairs there was as much room as down. With partitions and windows, what a house would there be! Sarah looked at the row of stanchions before the allotted space for cows, and reflected that she would have her front entry there.

At six o'clock the stove was up in the harness-room, the kettle was boiling, and the table set for tea. It looked almost as home-like as the abandoned house across the yard had ever done. The young hired man milked, and Sarah directed him calmly to bring the milk to the new barn. He came gaping, dropping little blots of foam from the brimming pails on the grass. Before the next morning he had spread the story of Adoniram Penn's wife moving into the new barn all over the little village. Men assembled in the store and talked it over, women with shawls over their heads scuttled into each other's houses before their work was done. Any deviation from the ordinary course of life in this quiet town was enough to stop all progress in it. Everybody paused to look at the staid, independent figure on the side track. There was a difference of opinion with regard to her. Some held her to be insane; some, of a lawless and rebellious spirit.

Friday the minister went to see her. It was in the forenoon, and she was at the barn door shelling pease for dinner. She looked up and returned his salutation with dignity, then she went on with her work. She did not invite him in. The saintly expression of her face remained fixed, but there was an angry flush over it.

The minister stood awkwardly before her, and talked. She handled the pease as if they were bullets. At last she looked up, and her eyes showed the spirit that her meek front had covered for a lifetime.

"There ain't no use talkin', Mr. Hersey," said she. "I've thought it all over an' over, an' I

5. James Wolfe (1727–1759) was a British general mortally wounded in a victorious siege of Quebec during the Seven Years War.

believe I'm doin' what's right. I've made it the subject of prayer, an' it's betwixt me an' the Lord an' Adoniram. There ain't no call for nobody else to worry about it."

"Well, of course, if you have brought it to the Lord in prayer, and feel satisfied that you are doing right, Mrs. Penn," said the minister, helplessly. His thin gray-bearded face was pathetic. He was a sickly man; his youthful confidence had cooled; he had to scourge himself up to some of his pastoral duties as relentlessly as a Catholic ascetic, and then he was prostrated by the smart.

"I think it's right jest as much as I think it was right for our forefathers to come over from the old country 'cause they didn't have what belonged to 'em," said Mrs. Penn. She arose. The barn threshold might have been Plymouth Rock from her bearing. "I don't doubt you mean well, Mr. Hersey," said she, "but there are things people hadn't ought to interfere with. I've been a member of the church for over forty year. I've got my own mind an' my own feet, an' I'm goin' to think my own thoughts an' go my own ways, an' nobody but the Lord is goin' to dictate to me unless I've a mind to have him. Won't you come in an' set down? How is Mis' Hersey?"

"She is well, I thank you," replied the minister. He added some more perplexed apologetic remarks; then he retreated.

He could expound the intricacies of every character study in the Scriptures, he was competent to grasp the Pilgrim Fathers and all historical innovators, but Sarah Penn was beyond him. He could deal with primal cases, but parallel ones worsted him. But, after all, although it was aside from his province, he wondered more how Adoniram Penn would deal with his wife than how the Lord would. Everybody shared the wonder. When Adoniram's four new cows arrived, Sarah ordered three to be put in the old barn, the other in the house shed where the cooking-stove had stood. That added to the excitement. It was whispered that all four cows were domiciled in the house.

Towards sunset on Saturday, when Adoniram was expected home, there was a knot of men in the road near the new barn. The hired man had milked, but he still hung around the premises. Sarah Penn had supper all ready. There were brown-bread and baked beans and a custard pie; it was the supper Adoniram loved on a Saturday night. She had a clean calico, and she bore herself imperturbably. Nanny and Sammy kept close at her heels. Their eyes were large, and Nanny was full of nervous tremors. Still there was to them more pleasant excitement than anything else. An inborn confidence in their mother over their father asserted itself.

Sammy looked out of the harness-room window. "There he is," he announced, in an awed whisper. He and Nanny peeped around the casing. Mrs. Penn kept on about her work. The children watched Adoniram leave the new horse standing in the drive while he went to the house door. It was fastened. Then he went around to the shed. That door was seldom locked, even when the family was away. The thought how her father would be confronted by the cow flashed upon Nanny. There was a hysterical sob in her throat. Adoniram emerged from the shed and stood looking about in a dazed fashion. His lips moved; he was saying something, but they could not hear what it was. The hired man was peeping around a corner of the old barn, but nobody saw him.

Adoniram took the new horse by the bridle and led him across the yard to the new barn. Nanny and Sammy slunk close to their mother. The barn doors rolled back, and there stood Adoniram, with the long mild face of the great Canadian farm horse looking over his shoulder.

Nanny kept behind her mother, but Sammy stepped suddenly forward, and stood in front of her.

Adoniram stared at the group. "What on airth you all down here for?" said he. "What's the matter over to the house?"

"We've come here to live, father," said Sammy. His shrill voice quavered out bravely.

"What"—Adoniram sniffed—"what is it smells like cookin'?" said he. He stepped forward and looked in the open door of the harness-room. Then he turned to his wife. His old bristling face was pale and frightened. "What on airth does this mean, mother?" he gasped.

"You come in here, father," said Sarah. She led the way into the harness-room and shut the door. "Now, father," said she, "you needn't be scared. I ain't crazy. There ain't nothin' to be upset over. But we've come here to live, an' we're goin' to live here. We've got jest as good a right here as new horses an' cows. The house wa'n't fit for us to live in any longer, an' I made up my mind I wa'n't goin' to stay there. I've done my duty by you forty year, an' I'm goin' to do it now; but I'm goin' to live here. You've got to put in some windows and partitions; an' you'll have to buy some furniture."

"Why, mother!" the old man gasped.

"You'd better take your coat off an' get washed—there's the wash-basin—an' then we'll have supper."

"Why, mother!"

Sammy went past the window, leading the new horse to the old barn. The old man saw him, and shook his head speechlessly. He tried to take off his coat, but his arms seemed to lack the power. His wife helped him. She poured some water into the tin basin, and put in a piece of soap. She got the comb and brush, and smoothed his thin gray hair after he had washed. Then she put the beans, hot bread, and tea on the table. Sammy came in, and the family drew up. Adoniram sat looking dazedly at his plate, and they waited.

"Ain't you goin' to ask a blessin', father?" said Sarah.

And the old man bent his head and mumbled.

All through the meal he stopped eating at intervals, and stared furtively at his wife; but he ate well. The home food tasted good to him, and his old frame was too sturdily healthy to be affected by his mind. But after supper he went out, and sat down on the step of the smaller door at the right of the barn, through which he had meant his Jerseys to pass in stately file, but which Sarah designed for her front house door, and he leaned his head on his hands.

After the supper dishes were cleared away and the milk-pans washed, Sarah went out to him. The twilight was deepening. There was a clear green glow in the sky. Before them stretched the smooth level of field; in the distance was a cluster of hay-stacks like the huts of a village; the air was very cool and calm and sweet. The landscape might have been an ideal one of peace.

Sarah bent over and touched her husband on one of his thin, sinewy shoulders. "Father!"

The old man's shoulders heaved: he was weeping.

"Why, don't do so, father," said Sarah.

"I'll—put up the—partitions, an'—everything you—want, mother."

Sarah put her apron up to her face; she was overcome by her own triumph.

Adoniram was like a fortress whose walls had no active resistance, and went down the instant the right besieging tools were used. "Why, mother," he said, hoarsely, "I hadn't no idee you was so set on't as all this comes to."

1890

A New England Nun

It was late in the afternoon, and the light was waning. There was a difference in the look of the tree shadows out in the yard. Somewhere in the distance cows were lowing and a little bell was tinkling; now and then a farm-wagon tilted by, and the dust flew; some blue-shirted laborers with shovels over their shoulders plodded past; little swarms of flies were dancing up and down before the peoples' faces in the soft air. There seemed to be a gentle stir arising over everything for the mere sake of subsidence—a very premonition of rest and hush and night.

This soft diurnal commotion was over Louisa Ellis also. She had been peacefully sewing at her sitting-room window all the afternoon. Now she quilted her needle carefully into her work, which she folded precisely, and laid in a basket with her thimble and thread and scissors. Louisa Ellis could not remember that ever in her life she had mislaid one of these little feminine appurtenances, which had become, from long use and constant association, a very part of her personality.

Louisa tied a green apron round her waist, and got out a flat straw hat with a green ribbon. Then she went into the garden with a little blue crockery bowl, to pick some currants for her tea. After the currants were picked she sat on the back door-step and stemmed them, collecting the stems carefully in her apron, and afterwards throwing them into the hen-coop. She looked sharply at the grass beside the step to see if any had fallen there.

Louisa was slow and still in her movements; it took her a long time to prepare her tea; but when ready it was set forth with as much grace as if she had been a veritable guest to her own self. The little square table stood exactly in the centre of the kitchen, and was covered with a starched linen cloth whose border pattern of flowers glistened. Louisa had a damask napkin on her tea-tray, where were arranged a cut-glass tumbler full of teaspoons, a silver cream-pitcher, a china sugar-bowl, and one pink china cup and saucer. Louisa used china every day—something which none of her neighbors did. They whispered about it among themselves. Their daily tables were laid with common crockery, their sets of best china stayed in the parlor closet, and Louisa Ellis was no richer nor better bred than they. Still she would use the china. She had for her supper a glass dish full of sugared currants, a plate of little cakes, and one of light white biscuits. Also a leaf or two of lettuce, which she cut up daintily. Louisa was very fond of lettuce, which she raised to perfection in her little garden. She ate quite heartily, though in a delicate, pecking way; it seemed almost surprising that any considerable bulk of the food should vanish.

After tea she filled a plate with nicely baked thin corn-cakes, and carried them out into the back-yard.

"Caesar!" she called. "Caesar! Caesar!"

There was a little rush, and the clank of a chain, and a large yellow-and-white dog appeared at the door of his tiny hut, which was half hidden among the tall grasses and flowers. Louisa patted him and gave him the corn-cakes. Then she returned to the house and washed the tea-things, polishing the china carefully. The twilight had deepened; the chorus of the frogs floated in at the open window wonderfully loud and shrill, and once in a while a long sharp drone from a tree-toad pierced it. Louisa took off her green gingham apron, disclosing a shorter one of pink and white print. She lighted her lamp, and sat down again with her sewing.

In about half an hour Joe Dagget came. She heard his heavy step on the walk, and rose and took off her pink and white apron. Under that was still another—white linen with a little cambric edging on the bottom; that was Louisa's company apron. She never wore it without her calico sewing apron over it unless she had a guest. She had barely folded the pink and white one with methodical haste and laid it in a table-drawer when the door opened and Joe Dagget entered.

He seemed to fill up the whole room. A little yellow canary that had been asleep in his green cage at the south window woke up and fluttered wildly, beating his little yellow wings against the wires. He always did so when Joe Dagget came into the room.

"Good-evening," said Louisa. She extended her hand with a kind of solemn cordiality.

"Good-evening, Louisa," returned the man, in a loud voice.

She placed a chair for him, and they sat facing each other, with the table between them. He sat bolt-upright, toeing out his heavy feet squarely, glancing with a good-humored uneasiness around the room. She sat gently erect, folding her slender hands in her white-linen lap.

"Been a pleasant day," remarked Dagget.

"Real pleasant," Louisa assented, softly. "Have you been haying?" she asked, after a little while.

"Yes, I've been haying all day, down in the ten-acre lot. Pretty hot work."

"It must be."

"Yes, it's pretty hot work in the sun."

"Is your mother well to-day?"

"Yes, mother's pretty well."

"I suppose Lily Dyer's with her now?"

Dagget colored. "Yes, she's with her," he answered, slowly.

He was not very young, but there was a boyish look about his large face. Louisa was not quite as old as he, her face was fairer and smoother, but she gave people the impression of being older.

"I suppose she's a good deal of help to your mother," she said, further.

"I guess she is; I don't know how mother'd get along without her," said Dagget, with a sort of embarrassed warmth.

"She looks like a real capable girl. She's pretty-looking too," remarked Louisa.

"Yes, she is pretty fair-looking."

Presently Dagget began fingering the books on the table. There was a square red autograph album, and a Young Lady's Gift-Book[6] which had belonged to Louisa's mother. He took them up one after the other and opened them; then laid them down again, the album on the Gift-Book.

Louisa kept eying them with mild uneasiness. Finally she rose and changed the position of the books, putting the album underneath. That was the way they had been arranged in the first place.

Dagget gave an awkward little laugh. "Now what difference did it make which book was on top?" said he.

Louisa looked at him with a deprecating smile. "I always keep them that way," murmured she.

"You do beat everything," said Dagget, trying to laugh again. His large face was flushed.

He remained about an hour longer, then rose to take leave. Going out, he stumbled over a rug, and trying to recover himself, hit Louisa's work-basket on the table, and knocked it on the floor.

He looked at Louisa, then at the rolling spools; he ducked himself awkwardly toward them but she stopped him. "Never mind," said she; "I'll pick them up after you're gone."

She spoke with a mild stiffness. Either she was a little disturbed, or his nervousness affected her, and made her seem constrained in her effort to reassure him.

When Joe Dagget was outside he drew in the sweet evening air with a sigh, and felt much as an innocent and perfectly well-intentioned bear might after his exit from a china shop.

Louisa, on her part, felt much as the kind-hearted, long-suffering owner of the china shop might have done after the exit of the bear.

She tied on the pink, then the green apron, picked up all the scattered treasures and replaced them in her work-basket, and straightened the rug. Then she set the lamp on the floor, and began sharply examining the carpet. She even rubbed her fingers over it, and looked at them.

"He's tracked in a good deal of dust," she murmured. "I thought he must have." Louisa got a dust-pan and brush, and swept Joe Dagget's track carefully.

If he could have known it, it would have increased his perplexity and uneasiness, although it would not have disturbed his loyalty in the least. He came twice a week to see Louisa Ellis, and every time, sitting there in her delicately sweet room, he felt as if surrounded by a hedge

6. A keepsake book, full of quotations, poetry, and excerpts, published as appropriate gifts for women.

of lace. He was afraid to stir lest he should put a clumsy foot or hand through the fairy web, and he had always the consciousness that Louisa was watching fearfully lest he should.

Still the lace and Louisa commanded perforce his perfect respect and patience and loyalty. They were to be married in a month, after a singular courtship which had lasted for a matter of fifteen years. For fourteen out of the fifteen years the two had not once seen each other, and they had seldom exchanged letters. Joe had been all those years in Australia, where he had gone to make his fortune, and where he had stayed until he made it. He would have stayed fifty years if it had taken so long, and come home feeble and tottering, or never come home at all, to marry Louisa.

But the fortune had been made in the fourteen years, and he had come home now to marry the woman who had been patiently and unquestioningly waiting for him all that time.

Shortly after they were engaged he had announced to Louisa his determination to strike out into new fields, and secure a competency before they should be married. She had listened and assented with the sweet serenity which never failed her, not even when her lover set forth on that long and uncertain journey. Joe, buoyed up as he was by his sturdy determination, broke down a little at the last, but Louisa kissed him with a mild blush, and said good-by.

"It won't be for long," poor Joe had said, huskily; but it was for fourteen years.

In that length of time much had happened. Louisa's mother and brother had died, and she was all alone in the world. But the greatest happening of all—a subtle happening which both were too simple to understand—Louisa's feet had turned into a path, smooth maybe under a calm, serene sky, but so straight and unswerving that it could only meet a check at her grave, and so narrow that there was no room for any one at her side.

Louisa's first emotion when Joe Dagget came home (he had not apprised her of his coming) was consternation, although she would not admit it to herself, and he never dreamed of it. Fifteen years ago she had been in love with him—at least she considered herself to be. Just at that time, gently acquiescing with and falling into the natural drift of girlhood, she had seen marriage ahead as a reasonable feature and a probable desirability of life. She had listened with calm docility to her mother's views upon the subject. Her mother was remarkable for her cool sense and sweet, even temperament. She talked wisely to her daughter when Joe Dagget presented himself, and Louisa accepted him with no hesitation. He was the first lover she had ever had.

She had been faithful to him all these years. She had never dreamed of the possibility of marrying anyone else. Her life, especially for the last seven years, had been full of a pleasant peace, she had never felt discontented nor impatient over her lover's absence; still she had always looked forward to his return and their marriage as the inevitable conclusion of things. However, she had fallen into a way of placing it so far in the future that it was almost equal to placing it over the boundaries of another life.

When Joe came she had been expecting him, and expecting to be married for fourteen years, but she was as much surprised and taken aback as if she had never thought of it.

Joe's consternation came later. He eyed Louisa with an instant confirmation of his old admiration. She had changed but little. She still kept her pretty manner and soft grace, and was, he considered, every whit as attractive as ever. As for himself, his stent was done; he had turned his face away from fortune-seeking, and the old winds of romance whistled as loud and sweet as ever through his ears. All the song which he had been wont to hear in them was Louisa; he had for a long time a loyal belief that he heard it still, but finally it seemed to him that although the winds sang always that one song, it had another name. But for Louisa the wind had never more than murmured; now it had gone down, and everything was still. She listened for a little while with half-wistful attention; then she turned quietly away and went to work on her wedding-clothes.

Joe had made some extensive and quite magnificent alterations in his house. It was the old homestead; the newly-married couple would live there, for Joe could not desert his mother, who refused to leave her old home. So Louisa must leave hers. Every morning, rising and going about among her neat maidenly possessions, she felt as one looking her last upon the faces of dear friends. It was true that in a measure she could take them with her, but, robbed of their old environments, they would appear in such new guises that they would almost cease to be themselves. Then there were some peculiar features of her happy solitary life which she would probably be obliged to relinquish altogether. Sterner tasks than these graceful but half-needless ones would probably devolve upon her. There would be a large house to care for; there would be company to entertain; there would be Joe's rigorous and feeble old mother to wait upon; and it would be contrary to all thrifty village traditions for her to keep more than one servant. Louisa had a little still, and she used to occupy herself pleasantly in summer weather with distilling the sweet and aromatic essences from roses and peppermint and spearmint. By-and-by her still must be laid away. Her store of essences was already consider-able, and there would be no time for her to distil for the mere pleasure of it. Then Joe's mother would think it foolishness; she had already hinted her opinion in the matter. Louisa dearly loved to sew a linen seam, not always for use, but for the simple, mild pleasure which she took in it. She would have been loath to confess how more than once she had ripped a seam for the mere delight of sewing it together again. Sitting at her window during long sweet afternoons, drawing her needle gently through the dainty fabric, she was peace itself. But there was small chance of such foolish comfort in the future. Joe's mother, domineering, shrewd old matron that she was even in her old age, and very likely even Joe himself, with his honest masculine rudeness, would laugh and frown down all these pretty but senseless old maiden ways.

Louisa had almost the enthusiasm of an artist over the mere order and cleanliness of her solitary home. She had throbs of genuine triumph at the sight of the window-panes which she had polished until they shone like jewels. She gloated gently over her orderly bureau-drawers, with their exquisitely folded contents redolent with lavender and sweet clover and very purity. Could she be sure of the endurance of even this? She had visions, so startling that she half repudiated them as indelicate, of coarse masculine belongings strewn about in endless litter; of dust and disorder arising necessarily from a coarse masculine presence in the midst of all this delicate harmony.

Among her forebodings of disturbance, not the least was with regard to Caesar. Caesar was a veritable hermit of a dog. For the greater part of his life he had dwelt in his secluded hut, shut out from the society of his kind and all innocent canine joys. Never had Caesar since his early youth watched at a woodchuck's hole; never had he known the delights of a stray bone at a neighbor's kitchen door. And it was all on account of a sin committed when hardly out of his puppyhood. No one knew the possible depth of remorse of which this mild-visaged, altogether innocent-looking old dog might be capable; but whether or not he had encoun-tered remorse, he had encountered a full measure of righteous retribution. Old Caesar seldom lifted up his voice in a growl or a bark; he was fat and sleepy; there were yellow rings which looked like spectacles around his dim old eyes; but there was a neighbor who bore on his hand the imprint of several of Caesar's sharp white youthful teeth, and for that he had lived at the end of a chain, all alone in a little hut, for fourteen years. The neighbor, who was choleric and smarting with the pain of his wound, had demanded either Caesar's death or complete ostracism. So Louisa's brother, to whom the dog had belonged, had built him his little kennel and tied him up. It was now fourteen years since, in a flood of youthful spirits, he had inflicted that memorable bite, and with the exception of short excursions, always at the end of the chain, under the strict guardianship of his master or Louisa, the old dog had remained a close prisoner. It is doubtful if, with his limited ambition, he took much pride in the fact, but it is certain that he was possessed of considerable cheap fame. He was regarded by all the children in the village and by many adults as a very monster of ferocity. St. George's dragon[7] could hardly have surpassed in evil repute Louisa Ellis's old yellow dog. Mothers charged their

7. In legend, St. George vanquished a terrible dragon.

children with solemn emphasis not to go too near to him, and the children listened and believed greedily, with a fascinated appetite for terror, and ran by Louisa's house stealthily, with many sidelong and backward glances at the terrible dog. If perchance he sounded a hoarse bark, there was a panic. Wayfarers chancing into Louisa's yard eyed him with respect, and inquired if the chain were stout. Caesar at large might have seemed a very ordinary dog, and excited no comment whatever; chained, his reputation overshadowed him, so that he lost his own proper outlines and looked darkly vague and enormous. Joe Dagget, however, with his good-humored sense and shrewdness, saw him as he was. He strode valiantly up to him and patted him on the head, in spite of Louisa's soft clamor of warning, and even attempted to set him loose. Louisa grew so alarmed that he desisted, but kept announcing his opinion in the matter quite forcibly at intervals. "There ain't a better-natured dog in town," he would say, "and it's downright cruel to keep him tied up there. Some day I'm going to take him out."

Louisa had very little hope that he would not, one of these days, when their interests and possessions should be more completely fused in one. She pictured to herself Caesar on the rampage through the quiet and unguarded village. She saw innocent children bleeding in his path. She was herself very fond of the old dog, because he had belonged to her dead brother, and he was always very gentle with her; still she had great faith in his ferocity. She always warned people not to go too near him. She fed him on ascetic fare of corn-mush and cakes, and never fired his dangerous temper with a heating and sanguinary diet of flesh and bones. Louisa looked at the old dog munching his simple fare, and thought of her approaching marriage and trembled. Still, no anticipation of disorder and confusion in lieu of sweet peace and harmony, no forebodings of Caesar on the rampage, no wild fluttering of her little yellow canary, were sufficient to turn her a hair's-breadth. Joe Dagget had been fond of her and working for her all these years. It was not for her, whatever came to pass, to prove untrue and break his heart. She put the exquisite little stitches into her wedding-garments, and the time went on until it was only a week before her wedding-day. It was a Tuesday evening, and the wedding was to be a week from Wednesday.

There was a full moon that night. About nine o'clock Louisa strolled down the road a little way. There were harvest-fields on either hand, bordered by low stone walls. Luxuriant clumps of bushes grew beside the wall, and trees—wild cherry and old apple-trees—at intervals. Presently Louisa sat down on the wall and looked about her with mildly sorrowful reflectiveness. Tall shrubs of blueberry and meadow-sweet, all woven together and tangled with blackberry vines and horsebriers, shut her in on either side. She had a little clear space between them. Opposite her, on the other side of the road, was a spreading tree; the moon shone between its boughs, and the leaves twinkled like silver. The road was bespread with a beautiful shifting dapple of silver and shadow; the air was full of a mysterious sweetness. "I wonder if it's wild grapes?" murmured Louisa. She sat there some time. She was just thinking of rising, when she heard footsteps and low voices, and remained quiet. It was a lonely place, and she felt a little timid. She thought she would keep still in the shadow and let the persons, whoever they might be, pass her.

But just before they reached her the voices ceased, and the footsteps. She understood that their owners had also found seats upon the stone wall. She was wondering if she could not steal away unobserved, when the voice broke the stillness. It was Joe Dagget's. She sat still and listened.

The voice was announced by a loud sigh, which was as familiar as itself. "Well," said Dagget, "you've made up your mind, then, I suppose?"

"Yes," returned another voice; "I'm going day after to-morrow."

"That's Lily Dyer," thought Louisa to herself. The voice embodied itself in her mind. She saw a girl tall and full-figured, with a firm, fair face, looking fairer and firmer in the moonlight, her strong yellow hair braided in a close knot. A girl full of a calm rustic strength and bloom, with a masterful way which might have beseemed a princess. Lily Dyer was a favorite with the village folk; she had just the qualities to arouse the admiration. She was good and handsome and smart. Louisa had often heard her praises sounded.

"Well," said Joe Dagget, "I ain't got a word to say."

"I don't know what you could say," returned Lily Dyer.

"Not a word to say," repeated Joe, drawing out the words heavily. Then there was a silence. "I ain't sorry," he began at last, "that that happened yesterday—that we kind of let on how we felt to each other. I guess it's just as well we knew. Of course I can't do anything any different. I'm going right on an' get married next week. I ain't going back on a woman that's waited for me fourteen years, an' break her heart."

"If you should jilt her to-morrow, I wouldn't have you," spoke up the girl, with sudden vehemence.

"Well, I ain't going to give you the chance," said he; "but I don't believe you would, either."

"You'd see I wouldn't. Honor's honor, an' right's right. An' I'd never think anything of any man that went against 'em for me or any other girl; you'd find that out, Joe Dagget."

"Well, you'll find out fast enough that I ain't going against 'em for you or any other girl," returned he. Their voices sounded almost as if they were angry with each other. Louisa was listening eagerly.

"I'm sorry you feel as if you must go away," said Joe, "but I don't know but it's best."

"Of course it's best. I hope you and I have got common-sense."

"Well, I suppose you're right." Suddenly Joe's voice got an undertone of tenderness. "Say, Lily," said he, "I'll get along well enough myself, but I can't bear to think—You don't suppose you're going to fret much over it?"

"I guess you'll find out I sha'n't fret much over a married man."

"Well, I hope you won't—I hope you won't, Lily. God knows I do. And—I hope—one of these days—you'll—come across somebody else—"

"I don't see any reason why I shouldn't." Suddenly her tone changed. She spoke in a sweet, clear voice, so loud that she could have been heard across the street. "No, Joe Dagget," said she, "I'll never marry any other man as long as I live. I've got good sense, an' I ain't going to break my heart nor make a fool of myself; but I'm never going to be married, you can be sure of that. I ain't that sort of a girl to feel this way twice."

Louisa heard an exclamation and a soft commotion behind the bushes; then Lily spoke again—the voice sounded as if she had risen. "This must be put a stop to," said she. "We've stayed here long enough. I'm going home."

Louisa sat there in a daze, listening to their retreating steps. After a while she got up and slunk softly home herself. The next day she did her housework methodically; that was as much a matter of course as breathing; but she did not sew on her wedding-clothes. She sat at her window and meditated. In the evening Joe came. Louisa Ellis had never known that she had any diplomacy in her, but when she came to look for it that night she found it, although meek of its kind, among her little feminine weapons. Even now she could hardly believe that she had heard aright, and she would not do Joe a terrible injury should she break her troth-plight. She wanted to sound him without betraying too soon her own inclinations in the matter. She did it successfully, and they finally came to an understanding; but it was a difficult thing, for he was as afraid of betraying himself as she.

She never mentioned Lily Dyer. She simply said that while she had no cause of complaint against him, she had lived so long in one way that she shrank from making a change.

"Well, I never shrank, Louisa," said Dagget. "I'm going to be honest enough to say that I think maybe it's better this way; but if you'd wanted to keep on, I'd have stuck to you till my dying day. I hope you know that."

"Yes, I do," said she.

That night she and Joe parted more tenderly than they had done for a long time. Standing in the door, holding each other's hands, a last great wave of regretful memory swept over them.

"Well, this ain't the way we've thought it was all going to end, is it, Louisa?" said Joe. She shook her head. There was a little quiver on her placid face.

"You let me know if there's ever anything I can do for you," said he. "I ain't ever going to forget you, Louisa." Then he kissed her, and went down the path.

Louisa, all alone by herself that night, wept a little, she hardly knew why; but the next morning, on waking, she felt like a queen who, after fearing lest her domain be wrested away from her, sees it firmly insured in her possession.

Now the tall weeds and grasses might cluster around Caesar's little hermit hut, the snow might fall on its roof year in and year out, but he never would go on a rampage through the unguarded village. Now the little canary might turn itself into a peacefull yellow ball night after night, and have no need to wake and flutter with wild terror against its bars. Louisa could sew linen seams, and distil roses, and dust and polish and fold away in lavender, as long as she listed.[8] That afternoon she sat with her needle-work at the window, and felt fairly steeped in peace. Lily Dyer, tall and erect and blooming, went past; but she felt no qualm. If Louisa Ellis had sold her birthright she did not know it, the taste of the pottage[9] was so delicious, and had been her sole satisfaction for so long. Serenity and placid narrowness had become to her as the birthright itself. She gazed ahead through a long reach of future days strung together like pearls in a rosary,[1] every one like the others, and all smooth and flawless and innocent, and her heart went up in thankfulness. Outside was the fervid summer afternoon; the air was filled with the sounds of the busy harvest of men and birds and bees; there were halloos, metallic clatterings, sweet calls, and long hummings. Louisa sat, prayerfully numbering her days, like an uncloistered nun.

1891

Sarah Pratt McLean Greene

(1856–1935)

In 1874, at the age of 18, Sally McLean left her Connecticut home to teach for a term in a one-room school in Cedarville, Massachusetts. From that experience came *Cape Cod Folks* (1881), a novel that caused an immediate sensation and continued to be popular for over forty years. In its first year there were eight editions from three different publishers. Three years and a number of editions later, it was published in London. In 1904 an elaborate gift edition included fifty-seven illustrations, many of them engravings from photographs of Cape Cod scenes. In 1906 a dramatic version played in New York City. In 1924 the novel formed the basis for the Louis B. Mayer film *Women Who Give*, and in conjunction with the film there appeared yet another edition (at least the fourteenth), "Illustrated with scenes from the photoplay."

Born in Simsbury, Connecticut, Sarah Pratt McLean counted among her ancestors a Mayflower Pilgrim and other settlers with names prominent on Cape Cod from the early days. Her direct forebears, however, had moved to Connecticut in the eighteenth century, and her father was the minister of the Simsbury Congregational Church. After an early education supplemented at home by her mother, she entered Mount Holyoke Female Seminary, but she left after two years to take up a teaching position a friend was vacating on Cape Cod. Returning home after five months, she began the notes that became

8. As long as she desired or chose to.
9. A thick soup or stew.

1. A string of beads on which Catholics count their prayers.

Cape Cod Folks, her most enduring success. A second novel, *Towhead: The Story of a Girl* (1883), and a collection of short stories, *Some Other Folks* (1884), appeared before her marriage in 1887 to Franklin Greene.

In the next three years the couple lived near Chihuahua, Mexico, where Franklin Greene was engaged in silver mining, and in the territory of Washington and in California. Sarah Greene's novels *Lastchance Junction* (1898) and *Leon Pontifex* (1890) exploit this western experience, but after the death of her husband in 1890 she returned to New England and to the eastern materials that suited her best. *Vesty of the Basins* (1892), set on the Maine coast, was her second most popular work. Others followed, to mixed reviews. Among them, *Flood-Tide* (1901), another Maine novel, won praise from Mark Twain for its "delightful unworldly people."

Based in fact, *Cape Cod Folks* owed some of its early fame to lawsuits brought against the author by local people whose real names she used. It retained its popularity into the twentieth century for its place in the literature of local color, a realistic portrayal of qualities distinctive to a particular time and place. Today its interest comes at least in part from the rarity, for its time, of its story and manner of telling: a first-person woman narrator, gifted with a lightly ironic sense of humor, describes her situation alone in the working world.

Novels, in addition to those named above, include *Stuart and Bamboo* (1897), *The Moral Imbeciles* (1898), *Winslow Plain* (1902), *Deacon Lysander* (1904), *Power Lot* (1906), *The Long Green Road* (1911), and *Everbreeze* (1913).

FROM CAPE COD FOLKS[1]

Chapter IX.
Lovell "Pops the Question."

One morning, ere we had breakfasted at the Ark,[2] Lovell Barlow, like some new-fangled orb of day, was seen to surmount the ruddy verge of the horizon. He bore a gun upon his shoulders, and advanced with a singularly martial and self-confident tread. As he entered the Ark, he placed the gun against the wall, and sat down and folded his arms, and looked as though he could be brave without it.

"Well, Madeline," said he, with a determined gaze fixed straight before him on vacuity, and with a desperate affectation of spontaneity in his tone—"Well, Madeline, mother and father have gone to Aunt Marcia's, *I* suppose to spend a week, *I* suppose—ahem!—ahem!—*I* suppose so."

"You don't say so, Lovell!" exclaimed Madeline. "And what'll poor Robin do now, Lovell? Oh, what'll poor Robin do now?"

"Yes," said he gravely; "that's what *they* thought, ahem! *They* thought they should stay a week, *they* thought so, certainly."

"Wall, I declar' for't, Lovell," said Grandma; "now's the time you'd ought to have a wife. Jest to think how comf'table 'twould be fu ye, now, instead of stayin' there all alone, if ye only had a nice little wife to home, to cook for ye, and watch for ye, and keep ye company, and—"

"*I* think so," exclaimed Lovell, giving a quick glance backward in the direction of his gun. "Certainly, ahem! *I* think so. *I* do."

"Lookin' for game? Eh, Lovell?" inquired Grandpa.

---

1. The text is that of the 1904 edition.   2. The home where the narrator is a boarder.

"Pa," said Grandma, solemnly: "I wish you'd put another stick of wood in the stove."

Grandpa was awake now, and a youthful and satanic gleam shone from under his shaggy eyebrows; he glanced at me, too, as was his habit on such occasions, as though I had a sort of sympathy for and fellowship with him in his bold iniquities of speech.

But the guileless Lovell interpreted not the deeper meaning of Grandpa's words.

"I think some of it, Cap'n," he answered unsmilingly, and then continued: "It's been—ahem!—it's been a very mild winter on the—ahem!—I should say on the Cape. It's been a very mild winter on the Cape, Miss Hungerford."

Lovell's nervous glance falling again on his gun, took me in wildly on the way.

I had been directing some letters that I expected to have an opportunity to send that morning.

"I beg your pardon," I said, looking up. "Yes, you don't often have such mild winters on the Cape, Mr. Barlow!"

"No'm, we don't," said Lovell, "not very often, ahem!" He moved his chair a peg nearer the gun. "Quite a—ahem!—quite a little fall of snow we had last night, Miss Hungerford."

"Any deer tracks? Eh, Lovell?" inquired Grandpa.

"Pa," said Grandma; "I wish you'd fill Abigail—seems to me she smells sorter dry."

"She ain't, for sartin', ma," replied Grandpa, giving the tea-kettle a shake to verify his assertions; "and Rachel's chock full!"

Grandma then gave Grandpa a meaning look, and put her fingers on her lips.

"Well, Cap'n, I saw more rabbit tracks," replied Lovell, innocently amused at the ludicrousness of the old Captain's speech. "I did, rather—ahem!—yes, I saw more rabbit tracks—ahem!—ahem!" He gave his chair a desperate hitch gunward. "I don't suppose they ever do such a thing, where you live, Miss Hungerford, as to go—ahem!—to go sleigh-riding, now, do they, Miss Hungerford?"

"Why, yes," I said; "they always do in the winter. I haven't been home through the winter for a year or two past, but I remember what splendid times we used to have."

I was thinking particularly of a certain snow-fall, that came when I was seventeen years old, and John Cable had just returned from College, with a moustache and patriarchal airs.

Some grinning recollections of the past were also floating through Grandpa's mind. The look of reprehensible mirth was still in his eyes, and he showed his teeth, which gleamed oddly white and strong in contrast with his grizzled countenance.

"I remember"—he began.

"Pa," said Grandma, with an expressive wink of one eye, and only part of her face visible around the corner of the doorway, through which Madeline had already disappeared; "pa—I wish you'd come out here a minute, now—I want to see ye."

"Wall, wall, can't ye see me here, ma? What makes ye so dreadful anxious to see me all of a sudden?" inquired Grandpa. But his face did not lose its thoughtful illumination. "Wall, as I was a tellin' ye, teacher," he went on; "I was only a little shaver then—a little shaver—and my father had one of those 'ere pungs, as we used to call 'em, that he used to ride around in—and he was a dreadful man to swear, my father was, teacher—Lordy, how he would swear!—"

"Pa!" said the great calm voice at the door; "I'm a waitin' for you to come out, so't I can shet the door."

"Wall, wall, ma, shet the door if ye want to, I've no objections to havin' the door shet—and we had an old hoss, teacher. Lordy, how lean he was, lean as a skate, and—"

"Bijonah Keeler!"

"Yis, yis, I'm a comin', ma, I'm a comin'." And wonderful indeed, I thought must have been the tale, which, even under these exasperating circumstances, kept Grandpa's face a-grin as he ran and shuffled towards the door.

The door was quickly closed behind him by other hands than his own, and then I observed that Lovell's chair had been drawn into frightfully close proximity to his gun.

"I—I think it's pleasanter, that is—I—I sometimes think it's warmer for t-t-two in a sleigh, than —a—'tis—for one, don't you, Miss Hungerford?" said Lovell, and gasped for breath and continued; "Now, I think of it, you—you wouldn't think of such a thing as going to ride with me to-night, would you, Miss Hungerford? You—you wouldn't think of such a thing, would you now?"

"Why—if you are kind enough to invite me to go sleigh-riding with you, Mr. Barlow?"

"*I* think so;" said Lovell, grasping his gun, and becoming immediately pale, though composed. "Yes'm, *I* think so, certainly, *I* do."

"Thank you, I will go with pleasure," I said.

"Thank you, Miss Hungerford," said Lovell, rising hurriedly. "I wish you a pleasant day—*I* do, with pleasure, and I hope that nothing will happen to prevent!"

And Lovell marched back across the fields as valiantly as a man may, who, on occasions of doubt and peril, takes the precaution to go suitably armed.

During the day the Wallencampers indulged in a mode of recreation, suggestive of that unique sort of inspiration to which they not unfrequently fell victims.

They attached a horse to a boat, a demoralized old boat, which had hitherto occupied a modest place amid the *débris* surrounding the Ark, and thus equipped, they rode or sailed up and down the lane. It proved a stormy sea, and often, as the boat capsized, the air was rent with screams of mock terror and yells of unaffected delight.

Thus the youth of Wallencamp, yes, and those who heeded not the swift decline of years, by reason of the immortal freshness of their spirits, disported themselves. And I was not amazed, catching a glimpse through the school-house windows of this joyous boat on one of her return voyages up the lane, to see Grandma Keeler swaying wildly in the stern.

Meanwhile, I managed to keep my flock indoors. But when, at four o'clock, I took my ruler in hand to give the usual signal of dismissal, the Phenomenon's heels had already vanished through the window, and the repressed animal spirits of a whole barbaric epoch sounded in the whoop with which the Modoc shot through the door.

Finally, I myself, rode up the lane in the boat. The path was well worn by this time, and there was no danger of a catastrophe. It seemed to me a novel performance enough, but I had not yet been to ride in Lovell's sleigh.

Lovell came very early, and preferred to wait outside until I had finished eating my supper. Then, with that deep self-satisfaction which predominated in my soul, even over its appreciation of the novel and amusing, I donned my seal-brown cloak, and stepping out of the door, gathered up my skirts, and smiled at Mr. Lovell with a pair of seal-brown eyes, and was not surprised to hear him ejaculate, coughing slightly; "Ahem! *I* think so, certainly, yes'm, *I* think so; *I* do."

Lovell's was the only sleigh in Wallencamp, and, as he informed me, it was one that he had himself constructed. It had, indeed, already suggested to my mind the workings of no ordinary intellect. Perhaps its most impressive features were its lowness and its height—the general lowness and length of its body, into which one could step easily, the floor being covered with a carpet of straw, suggesting field-mice; and the unusual height to which it rose in the back, being surmounted by two glittering knobs, like those on the head-board of an old-fashioned bedstead. Half-way down the back of this imposing structure the arms or wings sprouted out, giving to the whole the appearance of an immense Pterodactyl, or some other fossil bird of fabulous proportions, and effectually shutting in the occupants of the sleigh from any contemplation of the possible charms of the scenery. The seat was made very low, and it was, perhaps, on this account that the horse seemed so abnormally high. It was a white horse, and from our lowly position, there seemed to be something awful and shadowy in the motions of its legs. The red of sunset had not gone out of the sky when we started, and a pale young moon was already getting up in the heavens, but we could see neither fading sky nor rising moon, nor rock, nor tree, nor snowy expanse, naught but the gigantic hoof-falls of our phantom steed.

Being thus hopelessly debarred from any communication with external nature, and fearing to give myself up to my own thoughts, which were of a somewhat dangerous character, I endeavored to engage my companion in lively and cheerful converse by the way; but he was in a position of actual physical suffering, for the reins were short—too short, that is, to form a happy connecting link between him and the horse, and poor Lovell was obliged to lean forward at an acute angle in order to grasp them at all. Whenever the ghostly quadruped made a plunge forward, as he not unfrequently did, Lovell was thrust violently down into the straw, and throughout all this he comported himself with such firm and hopeless dignity that, with the respect due to suffering, I was moved to witness the struggle, at length, with silent commiseration. Once, having kept his seat for a longer time than usual, Lovell said:—

"I'll give you a riddle, Miss Hungerford, *I* will. Ahem! 'Why—why does a hen go around the road,' Miss Hungerford?"

I posed my head in an attitude of deep thought.

"Because," Lovell hastened to say; "because she can't go across—no, that wasn't right—why—ahem! why does a hen go *across* the road, Miss Hungerford?" and the next instant he was wallowing in the straw at my feet.

My soul was filled with unutterable compassion for him.

"Because," I ventured, when Lovell reappeared again, affecting a tone of lively inspiration: "because she can't go around it?"

"You—you've heard of it before!" gravely protested Lovell.

"I confess," said I, "that I have. It used to be my favorite riddle."

"It—it used to be mine, too," said Lovell. "It *used* to be, Miss Hungerford—ahem! It *used* to be—You—you couldn't tell what I was thinking of when I—ahem—when I started from home to-night, now, could you, Miss Hungerford?" said Lovell, at length.

"I'm sure I couldn't, Mr. Barlow," said I: "but I hope it was something very agreeable."

"But it wasn't," said Lovell; "that is, not very, Miss Hungerford; ahem! not very. I was—I was—ahem! I was thinking of it, you know, of—of such a thing as getting married, you know."

"I hope," said I, cheerfully, after a pause; "that as you consider the subject longer, it will be a less painful one to you."

"I hope so, Miss Hungerford," said Lovell. "Ahem! I hope so, certainly;" but there was little of that sanguine quality expressed in his tones.

The great white horse made another plunge forward, and Lovell recovered himself with a desperate effort.

"What should you think now, Miss Hungerford," he continued, moistening his parched lips; "if I should do such a thing as to—ahem!—as to speak of such a thing as—ahem!—as something of that sort to you, now, Miss Hungerford? Now, what should you think of such a thing? now, really?"

"I should think you were very inconsiderate," I said, "and would probably regret your rashness afterwards."

"*I* think so," said Lovell; "ahem! *I* think so, Miss Hungerford; *I* do, certainly."

After this it seemed as though a weight had been lifted from Lovell's mind. He kept his seat better. His was not a buoyant spirit, but there was, on this occasion, an air of repressed cheerfulness about him such as I had never before seen him exhibit. I tried to think that it was a joyous mental rebound from the contemplation of those dark riddles which trouble humanity, "Why does the hen go across the road," etc.

After a brief pause, Lovell said; "You—you wouldn't mind if I should sing a little now, now would you, Miss Hungerford?"

I assured him that I should be very glad to have him do so, and he sang, I remember, all the rest of the way home. At the gate, I thanked him for the ride and its cheerful vocal accompaniment, and Lovell said; "Do you like to hear me sing, now? Do you—do you, really, now, Miss Hungerford?" and turned away with a smile on his face to seek his home by the sea.

But Lovell was not long lonely, for, in less than a week, his father and mother returned from their visit at Aunt Marcia's and brought to Lovell a wife.

Mrs. Barlow herself informed me that "it was an awful shock to him, at first, oh, dreadful! but he'd made up his mind to get married, and he'd never a' done it in the world, if we hadn't took it into our own hands. She was a good girl, and we knew it, and Lovell wasn't no more fit to pick out a wife, anyway, than a chicken, not a bit more fit than a chicken!"

This girl lived in the same town with Aunt Marcia, and was confidently recommended by her to Lovell's parents as one who would be likely to make him a wise and suitable helpmeet, and was, indeed, an uncommonly fair and wholesome looking individual. She had a mind, too, whose clear, practical common sense had never been obscured by the idle theories of romance. She was pure and hearty and substantial. She was neither diffident, nor slow of speech, nor vacillating. She came, at the invitation of Lovell's parents, to marry Lovell, and if he had refused, she would have boxed his ears as a wholesome means of correction, and married him on the spot.

So Lovell's destined wife was brought home to him in the morning, and in the afternoon of that same day the connubial knot was tied.

Half an hour after the arrival of the bride, it was known throughout the length and breadth of Wallencamp, to every one, I believe, save Lovell himself, who was gathering driftwood a mile or two down the beach, that Lovell was going to be married!

At three o'clock P. M., Brother Mark Barlow was despatched to West Wallen for a minister.

Small scouts had been sent out to watch, where the road from the beach winds into the main road, and when word was brought back that "Mark had gone by," the Wallencampers proceeded to make all due preparations; and soon might have been seen winding in a body towards the scene of interest.

The small paraphernalia of invitations and wedding cards were unknown in Wallencamp. The Wallencampers would have considered that there was little virtue in a ceremony of any sort, performed without the sanction and approval of their united presence.

In regard to the particular nature of this entertainment, there was some snickering in the corners of the room, but the general aspect was funereal.

The season during which, with Lovell at one end of the room, and the bride at the other, we sat waiting the arrival of the minister, was as solemn as anything I had ever known.

I made a congratulatory remark, in a low tone, to Mrs. Barlow, who sat at my side with her hands clasped, gazing first at Lovell and then at the bride; but I was forced to experience the uncomfortable sensation of one who has inadvertently spoken out loud in meeting. No one said anything.

The helpless snicker which started occasionally from Harvey Dole's corner, and was echoed faintly from other quarters of the room, only heightened, by contrast, the effect of the succeeding gloom.

The bride was perfectly composed, with a high, natural color in her cheeks, and an air of being duly impressed with the importance of the occasion.

She had assumed a large white bonnet, though I do not think that she and Lovell took so much as a stroll to the beach after the ceremony—and her plump and shapely hands were encased in a pair of green kid gloves. She gazed thoughtfully, at each occupant of the room in turn, not omitting Lovell, who never once stirred or lifted his eyes.

Mr. William Barlow was silently passing the water, when Brother Mark arrived with the minister.

That grave dignitary advanced with measured tread to a small stand, draped with a long white sheet, that had been prepared for him in the centre of the room.

He took off his gloves, and folded them; he took off his overcoat, and laid it on the back of a chair; and if he had then reached down into his pockets and taken out a rope, and proceeded to adjust a hanging-noose, his audience could not have shown a more ghastly and breathless interest in his performance.

"Will the parties"—his sonorous voice resounded through the awful stillness—"Will the parties—about—to be joined—in holy wedlock—now—come forward?"

As Lovell then arose and walked, with an automatic hitch in his legs, across the room to his bride, there was about him all the stiffness and pallor of the grave without its smile of peace.

"Lovell and Nancy"—arose the deep intonation—"will you—now—join hands?"

It was a warm strong hand in the green kid glove. Its grasp might have sent a thrill of life through Lovell's rigid frame, for when the minister inquired:

"And do you, Lovell, take this woman?" etc., etc.

Lovell bent his body, moved his lips, and replied in a strange, far-away tone, "Yes'm, *I* think so. *I* do, certainly."

But when the question was put to the bride, she, Nancy, promised to take Lovell to be her wedded husband, to love and cherish, yes, and to cleave to, with a round, full "I do," that left no possible room for doubt in the mind of any one present, and seemed to send back the flood of frozen terror to Lovell's veins.

Lovell and Nancy were pronounced man and wife, and Nancy then divested herself of her bonnet and gloves, and joined in the festivities which followed with a hearty good-will, that proved her to be quite at home among the Wallencampers, and won at once their affection and esteem. The manner, particularly, in which she carried beans from her plate to her mouth, gracefully balanced on the extreme verge of her knife, as an adroit and finished work of art, provoked the wonder and admiration of all those whose beans sometimes wandered and fell off by the way.

And all the while, Mrs. Barlow's adjectives flowed in a full and copious stream.

"Oh, Lovell had been so wild," she said to me. "Oh, dreadful! But didn't I think he looked like a husband now? So quick, too! Oh, yes, wasn't it beautiful! Abbie Ann said he looked as though he'd been a husband fifteen years!"

After the ceremony, Lovell had taken his pipe and retired a little from the active scenes which were being enacted around him.

I saw him, as I was going away, standing in the door and looking out upon the bay. I held out my hand to him, in passing. "I congratulate you, Mr. Barlow," I said. Lovell put his hand to his mouth and coughed slightly several times, as though he were striving to think of the polite thing to say. Then he replied: "I—I—ahem! I wish you the same, Miss Hungerford, *I* do, certainly."

Lovell was not so pale as he had been, but looked very serious and pensive with his eyes fixed on the mysterious depths of the ocean. Lovell had propounded riddles to me, but never before had I caught such a glimpse of the deeply philosophical workings of his mind.

"When you come to think of it, life—ahem—life is very uncertain, Miss Hungerford."

I replied that it was very uncertain.

"And short, too, when you come to think of it. It's very short, too, Miss Hungerford."

"Oh, yes," I answered, "very."

"Ahem! It was—it was dreadful sudden, somehow," said Lovell.

"I suppose so, Mr. Barlow," I replied gravely; "great and unexpected joys are sometimes said to be as benumbing in their first effects as griefs coming in the same way."

"*I* think so," said Lovell. "Ahem! *I* think so, Miss Hungerford, *I* do, certainly."

Madeline joined me at the door, and I bade Lovell good-night.

We clambered down the cliffs, walking a little while along on the beach on our way homeward.

It was growing dark, and the voice of the ocean was infinitely mournful and sublime. No wonder, I thought, that life had seemed very short and uncertain to Lovell as he stood in the door listening to the waves.

What a little thing it seemed indeed, comparatively—this life with its fears and hopes, its poor idle jests and fleeting shows.

"And there shall be no more sea"—but this poor human soul that looks out so blindly, and utters itself so feebly through the senses, shall live for ever and ever.

"Lovell's folks have picked out a good wife for him, anyhow," said Madeline, briskly. "She's got a sight more sense than anybody *he'd* ever a' picked out."

I crept back into my shell again. "I think so, certainly, Madeline," said I, smiling at having unconsciously repeated Lovell's favorite phrase.

"She'll make Lovell all over, and get some new ideas into him, I can tell you," said Madeline.

And though I did not stay in Wallencamp long enough to witness with my own eyes the fulfilment of this prophecy, I know that it was abundantly fulfilled—that Lovell soon recovered from the shock incident to his wedding; that under the influence of his wholesome, active wife, and with the weight of greater responsibilities, he grew more manly and admirable in character, as well as happier, with each succeeding year; and that Lovell's children—a joyful and robust group, adored of Mrs. Barlow, senior—play on the "broad window seat" that looks off towards the sea.

1881

Charlotte Perkins Gilman
(1860–1935)

"The one predominant duty is to find one's work and do it, and I have striven mightily at that." These words end the autobiography of Charlotte Perkins Gilman, who resisted her era's assignment of housekeeping to women as their sole appropriate work. Social theorist, economist, and fiction writer, Gilman strove to overturn what she saw as the oppression of middle-class American women.

Gilman was born in Hartford, Connecticut, and raised by a single mother, Mary Fritch Perkins; her father, Frederick Beecher Perkins, left home shortly after her birth. Charlotte had a sporadic education, culminating in a short stint at the Rhode Island School of Design. She began working early in life, writing poetry and serving as a commercial artist, governess, and teacher before she entered her twenties. At the age of 24 she married a fellow artist, Charles Walter Stetson, but the marriage was unhappy. Charlotte bore a daughter within her first year of marriage and experienced a serious postpartum depression.

By her own account, she "suffered from a severe and continuous nervous break-down tending to melancholia—and beyond." After three years of depression, she "went, in devout faith and some faint stir of hope, to a noted specialist in nervous diseases," S. Weir Mitchell, the inventor of the rest cure. Mitchell treated her in 1887, and "sent me home with solemn advice to 'live as domestic a life as far as possible,' to 'have but two hours' intellectual life a day,' and 'never to touch pen, brush, or pencil again' as long as I lived. . . . I went home and obeyed those directions for some three months, and came so near the borderline of utter mental ruin that I could see over." She decided to disregard the doctor's advice and "went to work again—work, the normal life of every human being; work, in which is joy and growth and service, without which one is a pauper and a parasite—ultimately recovering some measure of power."

As part of her recovery, Gilman moved to California in 1888. By 1894 she had ended her marriage in divorce. She began writing poetry—her first collection was *In This Our World* (1893)—and lecturing on social reform and women's rights. In 1898 she published *Women and Economics*, a critique of the "androcentric" (male-centered) emphasis of American social and economic arrangements. Gilman expanded her arguments for reform in *Concerning Children* (1900) and *The Home* (1904), where she argued for organized day care as a system that would enable women to work (either as paid care-givers or outside the home). Gilman maintained that children, as well as their mothers, would benefit from the arrangement.

The story Gilman based on her experience with the rest cure, "The Yellow Wallpaper," was written around 1890 and published in 1892 in the *New England Magazine*; it was published in a separate volume in 1899. Written in diary form, the story chronicles the mental and emotional changes a middle-class woman undergoes while shut up in an attic bedroom papered with an atrocious pattern. Some critics read the woman's state at the story's end as complete mental breakdown; others see the woman's rage—and her persistence in writing her diary after her husband has forbidden her to "work"—as a sign that she will enter a period of regeneration after this experience. In either case, it is important to remember that Gilman herself survived her experience and wrote the story to effect change in the treatment of depressive women.

Six years after her divorce from Stetson, Charlotte married George Gilman, a New York lawyer who supported her working during the thirty years of their union. In addition to editing a magazine, *The Forerunner*, for seven years, she continued writing novels (including *What Diantha Did* [1910] and *The Crux* [1911]), as well as social commentary. Her feminist-utopian novel, *Herland*, came out in the *Forerunner* in 1915. In *Human Work* (1904) she continued her argument that productive activity was essential to human happiness; in *The Man-Made World* (1911) and *His Religion and Hers* (1923) she pursued her theories about the differences between men's and women's values in Western culture and argued for women's full participation in political and social arenas. *The Living of Charlotte Perkins Gilman: An Autobiography* came out in 1935, the same year she committed suicide by chloroform, a choice she made because she had terminal cancer.

Book-length studies of Gilman include Mary A. Hill, *Charlotte Perkins Gilman: The Making of a Radical Feminist, 1860–1896* (1980); Polly W. Allen, *Building Domestic Liberty: Charlotte Perkins Gilman's Architectural Feminism* (1988); Sheryl L. Meyering, *Charlotte Perkins Gilman: The Woman and Her Work* (1989); and Ann J. Lane, *To Herland and Beyond* (1990).

The Yellow Wallpaper

It is very seldom that mere ordinary people like John and myself secure ancestral halls for the summer.

A colonial mansion, a hereditary estate, I would say a haunted house and reach the height of romantic felicity—but that would be asking too much of fate!

Still I will proudly declare that there is something queer about it.

Else, why should it be let so cheaply? And why have stood so long untenanted?

John laughs at me, of course, but one expects that.

John is practical in the extreme. He has no patience with faith, an intense horror of superstition, and he scoffs openly at any talk of things not to be felt and seen and put down in figures.

John is a physician, and *perhaps*—(I would not say it to a living soul, of course, but this is dead paper and a great relief to my mind)—*perhaps* that is one reason I do not get well faster.

You see, he does not believe I am sick! And what can one do?

If a physician of high standing, and one's own husband, assures friends and relatives that there is really nothing the matter with one but temporary nervous depression—a slight hysterical tendency[1]—what is one to do?

My brother is also a physician, and also of high standing, and he says the same thing.

So I take phosphates or phosphites—whichever it is—and tonics, and air and exercise, and journeys, and am absolutely forbidden to "work" until I am well again.

Personally, I disagree with their ideas.

Personally, I believe that congenial work, with excitement and change, would do me good. But what is one to do?

I did write for a while in spite of them; but it *does* exhaust me a good deal—having to be so sly about it, or else meet with heavy opposition.

I sometimes fancy that in my condition, if I had less opposition and more society and stimulus—but John says the very worst thing I can do is to think about my condition, and I confess it always makes me feel bad.

So I will let it alone and talk about the house.

The most beautiful place! It is quite alone, standing well back from the road, quite three miles from the village. It makes me think of English places that you read about, for there are hedges and walls and gates that lock, and lots of separate little houses for the gardeners and people.

There is a *delicious* garden! I never saw such a garden—large and shady, full of box-bordered paths, and lined with long grape-covered arbors with seats under them.

There were greenhouses, but they are all broken now.

There was some legal trouble, I believe, something about the heirs and co-heirs; anyhow, the place has been empty for years.

That spoils my ghostliness, I am afraid, but I don't care—there is something strange about the house—I can feel it.

I even said so to John one moonlight evening, but he said what I felt was a draught, and shut the window.

I get unreasonably angry with John sometimes. I'm sure I never used to be so sensitive. I think it is due to this nervous condition.

But John says if I feel so I shall neglect proper self-control; so I take pains to control myself—before him, at least, and that makes me very tired.

I don't like our room a bit. I wanted one downstairs that opened onto the piazza and had roses all over the window, and such pretty old fashioned chintz[2] hangings! But John would not hear of it.

He said there was only one window and not room for two beds, and no near room for him if he took another.

He is very careful and loving, and hardly lets me stir without special direction.

I have a schedule prescription for each hour in the day; he takes all care from me, and so I feel basely ungrateful not to value it more.

He said he came here solely on my account, that I was to have perfect rest and all the air I could get. "Your exercise depends on your strength, my dear," said he, "and your food somewhat on your appetite; but air you can absorb all the time." So we took the nursery at the top of the house.

It is a big, airy room, the whole floor nearly, with windows that look all ways, and air and sunshine galore. It was nursery first, and then playroom and gymnasium, I should judge, for the windows are barred for little children, and there are rings and things in the walls.

The paint and paper look as if a boys' school had used it. It is stripped off—the paper—in great patches all around the head of my bed, about as far as I can reach, and in a great place

1. Nervous disorders were supposed to be connected with the womb, the root of the word "hysteria."

2. Printed, brightly colored polished cotton.

on the other side of the room low down. I never saw a worse paper in my life. One of those sprawling, flamboyant patterns committing every artistic sin.

It is dull enough to confuse the eye in following, pronounced enough constantly to irritate and provoke study, and when you follow the lame uncertain curves for a little distance they suddenly commit suicide—plunge off at outrageous angles, destroy themselves in unheard-of contradictions.

The color is repellent, almost revolting: a smouldering unclean yellow, strangely faded by the slow-turning sunlight. It is a dull yet lurid orange in some places, a sickly sulphur tint in others.

No wonder the children hated it! I should hate it myself if I had to live in this room long.

There comes John, and I must put this away—he hates to have me write a word.

We have been here two weeks, and I haven't felt like writing before, since that first day.

I am sitting by the window now, up in this atrocious nursery, and there is nothing to hinder my writing as much as I please, save lack of strength.

John is away all day, and even some nights when his cases are serious.

I am glad my case is not serious!

But these nervous troubles are dreadfully depressing.

John does not know how much I really suffer. He knows there is no reason to suffer, and that satisfies him.

Of course it is only nervousness. It does weigh on me so not to do my duty in any way!

I meant to be such a help to John, such a real rest and comfort, and here I am a comparative burden already!

Nobody would believe what an effort it is to do what little I am able—to dress and entertain, and order things.

It is fortunate Mary is so good with the baby. Such a dear baby!

And yet I *cannot* be with him, it makes me so nervous.

I suppose John never was nervous in his life. He laughs at me so about this wallpaper!

At first he meant to repaper the room, but afterward he said that I was letting it get the better of me, and that nothing was worse for a nervous patient than to give way to such fancies.

He said that after the wallpaper was changed it would be the heavy bedstead, and then the barred windows, and then that gate at the head of the stairs, and so on.

"You know the place is doing you good," he said, "and really, dear. I don't care to renovate the house just for a three months' rental."

"Then do let us go downstairs," I said. "There are such pretty rooms there."

Then he took me in his arms and called me a blessed little goose, and said he would go down cellar, if I wished, and have it whitewashed into the bargain.

But he is right enough about the beds and windows and things.

It is as airy and comfortable a room as anyone need wish, and, of course, I would not be so silly as to make him uncomfortable just for a whim.

I'm really getting quite fond of the big room, all but that horrid paper.

Out of one window I can see the garden—those mysterious deep-shaded arbors, the riotous old-fashioned flowers, and bushes and gnarly trees.

Out of another I get a lovely view of the bay and a little private wharf belonging to the estate. There is a beautiful shaded lane that runs down there from the house. I always fancy I see people walking in these numerous paths and arbors, but John has cautioned me not to give way to fancy in the least. He says that with my imaginative power and habit of story-making, a nervous weakness like mine is sure to lead to all manner of excited fancies, and that I ought to use my will and good sense to check the tendency. So I try.

I think sometimes that if I were only well enough to write a little it would relieve the press of ideas and rest me.

But I find I get pretty tired when I try.

It is so discouraging not to have any advice and companionship about my work. When I get really well, John says we will ask Cousin Henry and Julia down for a long visit; but he says he would as soon put fireworks in my pillow-case as to let me have those stimulating people about now.

I wish I could get well faster.

But I must not think about that. This paper looks to me as if it *knew* what a vicious influence it had!

There is a recurrent spot where the pattern lolls like a broken neck and two bulbous eyes stare at you upside down.

I get positively angry with the impertinence of it and the everlastingness. Up and down and sideways they crawl, and those absurd unblinking eyes are everywhere. There is one place where two breadths didn't match, and the eyes go all up and down the line, one a little higher than the other.

I never saw so much expression in an inanimate thing before, and we all know how much expression they have! I used to lie awake as a child and get more entertainment and terror out of blank walls and plain furniture than most children could find in a toy-store.

I remember what a kindly wink the knobs of our big old bureau used to have, and there was one chair that always seemed like a strong friend.

I used to feel that if any of the other things looked too fierce I could always hop into that chair and be safe.

The furniture in this room is no worse than inharmonious, however, for we had to bring it all from downstairs. I suppose when this was used as a playroom they had to take the nursery things out, and no wonder! I never saw such ravages as the children have made here.

The wallpaper, as I said before, is torn off in spots, and it sticketh closer than a brother[3] —they must have had perseverance as well as hatred.

Then the floor is scratched and gouged and splintered, the plaster itself is dug out here and there, and this great heavy bed, which is all we found in the room, looks as if it had been through the wars.

But I don't mind it a bit—only the paper.

There comes John's sister. Such a dear girl as she is, and so careful of me! I must not let her find me writing.

She is a perfect and enthusiastic housekeeper, and hopes for no better profession. I verily believe she thinks it is the writing which made me sick!

But I can write when she is out, and see her a long way off from these windows.

There is one that commands the road, a lovely shaded winding road, and one that just looks off over the country. A lovely country, too, full of great elms and velvet meadows.

This wallpaper has a kind of sub-pattern in a different shade, a particularly irritating one, for you can only see it in certain lights, and not clearly then.

But in the places where it isn't faded and where the sun is just so—I can see a strange, provoking, formless sort of figure that seems to skulk about behind that silly and conspicuous front design.

There's sister on the stairs!

Well, the Fourth of July is over! The people are all gone, and I am tired out. John thought it might do me good to see a little company, so we just had Mother and Nellie and the children down for a week.

Of course I didn't do a thing. Jennie sees to everything now.

But it tired me all the same.

John says if I don't pick up faster he shall send me to Weir Mitchell[4] in the fall.

---

3. Allusion to Proverbs 18:24.
4. S. Weir Mitchell (1829–1914) was associated with the rest cure for nervous disorders. Gilman was among his patients.

But I don't want to go there at all. I had a friend who was in his hands once, and she says he is just like John and my brother, only more so!

Besides, it is such an undertaking to go so far.

I don't feel as if it was worthwhile to turn my hand over for anything, and I'm getting dreadfully fretful and querulous.

I cry at nothing, and cry most of the time.

Of course I don't when John is here, or anybody else, but when I am alone.

And I am alone a good deal just now. John is kept in town very often by serious cases, and Jennie is good and lets me alone when I want her to.

So I walk a little in the garden or down that lovely lane, sit on the porch under the roses, and lie down up here a good deal.

I'm getting really fond of the room in spite of the wallpaper. Perhaps *because* of the wallpaper.

It dwells in my mind so!

I lie here on this great immovable bed—it is nailed down, I believe—and follow that pattern about by the hour. It is as good as gymnastics, I assure you. I start, we'll say, at the bottom, down in the corner over there where it has not been touched, and I determine for the thousandth time that I *will* follow that pointless pattern to some sort of a conclusion.

I know a little of the principle of design, and I know this thing was not arranged on any laws of radiation, or alternation, or repetition, or symmetry, or anything else that I ever heard of.

It is repeated, of course, by the breadths, but not otherwise.

Looked at in one way, each breadth stands alone; the bloated curves and flourishes—a kind of "debased Romanesque" with delirium tremens[5]—go waddling up and down in isolated columns of fatuity.

But, on the other hand, they connect diagonally, and the sprawling outlines run off in great slanting waves of optic horror, like a lot of wallowing sea-weeds in full chase.

The whole thing goes horizontally, too, at least it seems so, and I exhaust myself trying to distinguish the order of its going in that direction.

They have used a horizontal breadth for a frieze,[6] and that adds wonderfully to the confusion.

There is one end of the room where it is almost intact, and there, when the crosslights fade and the low sun shines directly upon it, I can almost fancy radiation after all—the interminable grotesque seems to form around a common center and rush off in headlong plunges of equal distraction.

It makes me tired to follow it. I will take a nap, I guess.

I don't know why I should write this.

I don't want to.

I don't feel able.

And I know John would think it absurd. But I *must* say what I feel and think in some way—it is such a relief!

But the effort is getting to be greater than the relief.

Half the time now I am awfully lazy, and lie down ever so much. John says I mustn't lose my strength, and has me take cod liver oil and lots of tonics and things, to say nothing of ale and wine and rare meat.

Dear John! He loves me very dearly, and hates to have me sick. I tried to have a real earnest reasonable talk with him the other day, and tell him how I wish he would let me go and make a visit to Cousin Henry and Julia.

---

5. A state of anxiety, hallucinations, tremors, and   6. Horizontal band along the upper part of an
    delusions brought on by alcohol poisoning.   interior wall.

But he said I wasn't able to go, nor able to stand it after I got there; and I did not make out a very good case for myself, for I was crying before I had finished.

It is getting to be a great effort for me to think straight. Just this nervous weakness, I suppose.

And dear John gathered me up in his arms, and just carried me upstairs and laid me on the bed, and sat by me and read to me till it tired my head.

He said I was his darling and his comfort and all he had, and that I must take care of myself for his sake, and keep well.

He says no one but myself can help me out of it, that I must use my will and self-control and not let any silly fancies run away with me.

There's one comfort—the baby is well and happy, and does not have to occupy this nursery with the horrid wallpaper.

If we had not used it, that blessed child would have! What a fortunate escape! Why, I wouldn't have a child of mine, an impressionable little thing, live in such a room for worlds.

I never thought of it before, but it is lucky that John kept me here after all; I can stand it so much easier than a baby, you see.

Of course I never mention it to them any more—I am too wise—but I keep watch for it all the same.

There are things in that wallpaper that nobody knows about but me, or ever will.

Behind that outside pattern the dim shapes get clearer every day.

It is always the same shape, only very numerous.

And it is like a woman stooping down and creeping about behind that pattern. I don't like it a bit. I wonder—I begin to think—I wish John would take me away from here!

It is so hard to talk with John about my case, because he is so wise, and because he loves me so.

But I tried it last night.

It was moonlight. The moon shines in all around just as the sun does.

I hate to see it sometimes, it creeps so slowly, and always comes in by one window or another.

John was asleep and I hated to waken him, so I kept still and watched the moonlight on that undulating wallpaper till I felt creepy.

The faint figure behind seemed to shake the pattern, just as if she wanted to get out.

I got up softly and went to feel and see if the paper *did* move, and when I came back John was awake.

"What is it, little girl?" he said. "Don't go walking about like that—you'll get cold."

I thought it was a good time to talk, so I told him that I really was not gaining here, and that I wished he would take me away.

"Why, darling!" said he. "Our lease will be up in three weeks, and I can't see how to leave before.

"The repairs are not done at home, and I cannot possibly leave town just now. Of course, if you were in any danger, I could and would, but you really are better, dear, whether you can see it or not. I am a doctor, dear, and I know. You are gaining flesh and color, your appetite is better, I feel really much easier about you."

"I don't weigh a bit more," said I, "nor as much; and my appetite may be better in the evening when you are here but it is worse in the morning when you are away!"

"Bless her little heart!" said he with a big hug. "She shall be as sick as she pleases! But now let's improve the shining hours[7] by going to sleep, and talk about it in the morning!"

---

7. An allusion to an Isaac Watts (1674–1748) poem titled "Against Idleness and Mischief" that begins "How doth the little busy bee / Improve each shining hour"; parodied by Lewis Carroll (1832–1898) in "How doth the little crocodile."

"And you won't go away?" I asked gloomily.

"Why, how can I, dear? It is only three weeks more and then we will take a nice little trip of a few days while Jennie is getting the house ready. Really, dear, you are better!"

"Better in body perhaps—" I began, and stopped short, for he sat up straight and looked at me with such a stern, reproachful look that I could not say another word.

"My darling," said he, "I beg of you, for my sake and for our child's sake, as well as for your own, that you will never for one instant let that idea enter your mind! There is nothing so dangerous, so fascinating, to a temperament like yours. It is a false and foolish fancy. Can you not trust me as a physician when I tell you so?"

So of course I said no more on that score, and we went to sleep before long. He thought I was asleep first, but I wasn't and lay there for hours trying to decide whether that front pattern and the back pattern really did move together or separately.

On a pattern like this, by daylight, there is a lack of sequence, a defiance of law, that is a constant irritant to a normal mind.

The color is hideous enough, and unreliable enough, and infuriating enough, but the pattern is torturing.

You think you have mastered it, but just as you get well under way in following, it turns a back-somersault and there you are. It slaps you in the face, knocks you down, and tramples upon you. It is like a bad dream.

The outside pattern is a florid arabesque,[8] reminding one of a fungus. If you can imagine a toadstool in joints, an interminable string of toadstools, budding and sprouting in endless convolutions—why, that is something like it.

That is, sometimes!

There is one marked peculiarity about this paper, a thing nobody seems to notice but myself, and that is that it changes as the light changes.

When the sun shoots in through the east window—I always watch for that first long, straight ray—it changes so quickly that I never can quite believe it.

That is why I watch it always.

By moonlight—the moon shines in all night when there is a moon—I wouldn't know it was the same paper.

At night in any kind of light, in twilight, candlelight, lamplight, and worst of all by moonlight, it becomes bars! The outside pattern, I mean, and the woman behind it is as plain as can be.

I didn't realize for a long time what the thing was that showed behind, that dim sub-pattern, but now I am quite sure it is a woman.

By daylight she is subdued, quiet. I fancy it is the pattern that keeps her so still. It is so puzzling. It keeps me quiet by the hour.

I lie down ever so much now. John says it is good for me, and to sleep all I can.

Indeed he started the habit by making me lie down for an hour after each meal.

It is a very bad habit, I am convinced, for you see, I don't sleep.

And that cultivates deceit, for I don't tell them I'm awake—oh, no!

The fact is I am getting a little afraid of John.

He seems very queer sometimes, and even Jennie has an inexplicable look.

It strikes me occasionally, just as a scientific hypothesis, that perhaps it is the paper!

I have watched John when he did not know I was looking, and come into the room suddenly on the most innocent excuses, and I've caught him several times *looking at the paper!* And Jennie too. I caught Jennie with her hand on it once.

She didn't know I was in the room, and when I asked her in a quiet, a very quiet voice, with the most restrained manner possible, what she was doing with the paper, she turned

8. An intricate design combining flowers, leaves, and geometric figures.

around as if she had been caught stealing, and looked quite angry—asked me why I should frighten her so!

Then she said that the paper stained everything it touched, that she had found yellow smooches on all my clothes and John's and she wished we would be more careful!

Did not that sound innocent? But I know she was studying that pattern, and I am determined that nobody shall find it out but myself!

Life is very much more exciting now than it used to be. You see, I have something more to expect, to look forward to, to watch. I really do eat better, and am more quiet than I was.

John is so pleased to see me improve! He laughed a little the other day, and said I seemed to be flourishing in spite of my wallpaper.

I turned it off with a laugh. I had no intention of telling him it was *because* of the wallpaper—he would make fun of me. He might even want to take me away.

I don't want to leave now until I have found it out. There is a week more, and I think that will be enough.

I'm feeling so much better!

I don't sleep much at night, for it is so interesting to watch developments; but I sleep a good deal during the daytime.

In the daytime it is tiresome and perplexing.

There are always new shoots on the fungus, and new shades of yellow all over it. I cannot keep count of them, though I have tried conscientiously.

It is the strangest yellow, that wallpaper! It makes me think of all the yellow things I ever saw—not beautiful ones like buttercups, but old, foul, bad yellow things.

But there is something else about that paper—the smell! I noticed it the moment we came into the room, but with so much air and sun it was not bad. Now we have had a week of fog and rain, and whether the windows are open or not, the smell is here.

It creeps all over the house.

I find it hovering in the dining-room, skulking in the parlor, hiding in the hall, lying in wait for me on the stairs.

It gets into my hair.

Even when I go to ride, if I turn my head suddenly and surprise it—there is that smell!

Such a peculiar odor, too! I have spent hours in trying to analyze it, to find what it smelled like.

It is not bad—at first—and very gentle, but quite the subtlest, most enduring odor I ever met.

In this damp weather it is awful. I wake up in the night and find it hanging over me.

It used to disturb me at first. I thought seriously of burning the house—to reach the smell.

But now I am used to it. The only thing I can think of that it is like is the *color* of the paper! A yellow smell.

There is a very funny mark on this wall, low down, near the mopboard. A streak that runs round the room. It goes behind every piece of furniture, except the bed, a long, straight, even *smooch*, as if it had been rubbed over and over.

I wonder how it was done and who did it, and what they did it for. Round and round and round—round and round and round—it makes me dizzy!

I really have discovered something at last.

Through watching so much at night, when it changes so, I have finally found out.

The front pattern *does* move—and no wonder! The woman behind shakes it!

Sometimes I think there are a great many women behind, and sometimes only one, and she crawls around fast, and her crawling shakes it all over.

Then in the very bright spots she keeps still, and in the very shady spots she just takes hold of the bars and shakes them hard.

And she is all the time trying to climb through. But nobody could climb through that pattern—it strangles so; I think that is why it has so many heads.

They get through, and then the pattern strangles them off and turns them upside down, and makes their eyes white!

If those heads were covered or taken off it would not be half so bad.

I think that woman gets out in the daytime!

And I'll tell you why—privately—I've seen her!

I can see her out of every one of my windows!

It is the same woman, I know, for she is always creeping, and most women do not creep by daylight.

I see her in that long shaded lane, creeping up and down. I see her in those dark grape arbors, creeping all around the garden.

I see her on that long road under the trees, creeping along, and when a carriage comes she hides under the blackberry vines.

I don't blame her a bit. It must be very humiliating to be caught creeping by daylight!

I always lock the door when I creep by daylight. I can't do it at night, for I know John would suspect something at once.

And John is so queer now that I don't want to irritate him. I wish he would take another room! Besides, I don't want anybody to get that woman out at night but myself.

I often wonder if I could see her out of all the windows at once.

But, turn as fast as I can, I can only see out of one at one time.

And though I always see her, she *may* be able to creep faster than I can turn! I have watched her sometimes away off in the open country, creeping as fast as a cloud shadow in a wind.

If only that top pattern could be gotten off from the under one! I mean to try it, little by little.

I have found out another funny thing, but I shan't tell it this time! It does not do to trust people too much.

There are only two more days to get this paper off, and I believe John is beginning to notice. I don't like the look in his eyes.

And I heard him ask Jennie a lot of professional questions about me. She had a very good report to give.

She said I slept a good deal in the daytime.

John knows I don't sleep very well at night, for all I'm so quiet!

He asked me all sorts of questions, too, and pretended to be very loving and kind.

As if I couldn't see through him!

Still, I don't wonder he acts so, sleeping under this paper for three months.

It only interests me, but I feel sure John and Jennie are affected by it.

Hurrah! This is the last day, but it is enough. John is to stay in town over night, and won't be out until this evening.

Jennie wanted to sleep with me—the sly thing; but I told her I should undoubtedly rest better for a night all alone.

That was clever, for really I wasn't alone a bit! As soon as it was moonlight and that poor thing began to crawl and shake the pattern, I got up and ran to help her.

I pulled and she shook. I shook and she pulled, and before morning we had peeled off yards of that paper.

A strip about as high as my head and half around the room.

And then when the sun came and that awful pattern began to laugh at me, I declared I would finish it today!

We go away tomorrow, and they are moving all my furniture down again to leave things as they were before.

Jennie looked at the wall in amazement, but I told her merrily that I did it out of pure spite at the vicious thing.

She laughed and said she wouldn't mind doing it herself, but I must not get tired.

How she betrayed herself that time!

But I am here, and no person touches this paper but Me—not *alive!*

She tried to get me out of the room—it was too patent! But I said it was so quiet and empty and clean now that I believed I would lie down again and sleep all I could, and not to wake me even for dinner—I would call when I woke.

So now she is gone, and the servants are gone, and the things are gone, and there is nothing left but that great bedstead nailed down, with the canvas mattress we found on it.

We shall sleep downstairs tonight, and take the boat home tomorrow.

I quite enjoy the room, now it is bare again.

How those children did tear about here!

This bedstead is fairly gnawed!

But I must get to work.

I have locked the door and thrown the key down into the front path.

I don't want to go out, and I don't want to have anybody come in, till John comes.

I want to astonish him.

I've got a rope up here that even Jennie did not find. If that woman does get out, and tries to get away, I can tie her!

But I forgot I could not reach far without anything to stand on!

This bed will *not* move!

I tried to lift and push it until I was lame, and then I got so angry I bit off a little piece at one corner—but it hurt my teeth.

Then I peeled off all the paper I could reach standing on the floor. It sticks horribly and the pattern just enjoys it! All those strangled heads and bulbous eyes and waddling fungus growths just shriek with derision!

I am getting angry enough to do something desperate. To jump out of the window would be admirable exercise, but the bars are too strong even to try.

Besides I wouldn't do it. Of course not. I know well enough that a step like that is improper and might be misconstrued.

I don't like to *look* out of the windows even—there are so many of those creeping women, and they creep so fast.

I wonder if they all come out of that wallpaper as I did?

But I am securely fastened now by my well-hidden rope—you don't get *me* out in the road there!

I suppose I shall have to get back behind the pattern when it comes night, and that is hard!

It is so pleasant to be out in this great room and creep around as I please!

I don't want to go outside. I won't, even if Jennie asks me to.

For outside you have to creep on the ground, and everything is green instead of yellow.

But here I can creep smoothly on the floor, and my shoulder just fits in that long smooch around the wall, so I cannot lose my way.

Why, there's John at the door!

It is no use, young man, you can't open it!

How he does call and pound!

Now he's crying to Jennie for an axe.

It would be a shame to break down that beautiful door!

"John, dear!" said I in the gentlest voice. "The key is down by the front steps, under a plantain leaf!"

That silenced him for a few moments.

Then he said, very quietly indeed, "Open the door, my darling!"

"I can't," said I. "The key is down by the front door under a plantain leaf!" And then I said it again, several times, very gently and slowly, and said it so often that he had to go and see, and he got it of course, and came in. He stopped short by the door.

"What is the matter?" he cried. "For God's sake, what are you doing!"

I kept on creeping just the same, but I looked at him over my shoulder.

"I've got out at last," said I, "in spite of you and Jane.[9] And I've pulled off most of the paper, so you can't put me back!"

Now why should that man have fainted? But he did, and right across my path by the wall, so that I had to creep over him every time!

1890   1892

---

9. "Jennie" was a diminutive for "Jane." Some critics take "Jane" to be the narrator's name, however.

Twentieth-Century Women Writers

Women were defined almost wholly by family relationships in the nineteenth century. In middle-class families, any accomplishments not directly related to the roles of wife, mother, sister, or daughter were devalued in favor of the Victorian ideal of obedient and self-sacrificing True Womanhood. Though black and immigrant women worked outside the home in greater numbers than white middle-class women, their potential for individual achievement was curtailed by custom as well as financial restraints and bigotry. Because they had no effective control over their own reproductive systems, all females were subject to a social and economic dependency inimical to most personal ambitions. In the public sphere, women could not vote and were inadequately protected by the law in economic matters.

Though writing was the most visible professional activity practiced by women in the second half of the century, and Hawthorne, in 1855, complained he could not succeed against the competition of "a damned mob of scribbling women," published women authors were usually closely identified with home and family. At least 100 popular magazines dealt with domestic issues; widows and mothers of young children could write and still preside over their households; and middle-class matrons constituted the greatest market for the sentimental and didactic fiction that sold so well.

Change was slow to come, but a combination of access to higher education, better communication and easier travel, political and social reforms, and cultural reaction against Victorian strictures gradually opened a wider range of possibilities to women with professional ambitions, including those who aspired to be taken seriously as writers of literature.

As the new century dawned, a privileged group defined by Henry James as the "New Woman" emerged to claim a place in the professional world. Often products of newly available higher education, they were usually unmarried or childless and sometimes independently wealthy and had exerted their individualism to carve out careers in previously closed fields. Journalists such as Ida Tarbell, whose exposés led to the passage of health and safety laws, and social work professionals like Jane Addams, who tackled problems of urban poverty, flourished in the first decades of the twentieth century. The expansion of the work force was acknowledged when the first minimum wage laws applying to women and children were passed in 1912.

African-American women born after the Civil War also profited from greater access to education, later marriages, and strong professional orientation. The National Association for the Advancement of Colored People, founded in 1910, gave this new class of professional women a focus for action. Removed from the rigid social customs of Eastern urban areas, Mary Austin was free to chronicle the lives of Native Americans living close to nature in a series of books beginning with *Land of Little Rain* (1903). The hordes of immigrants who had been arriving from eastern and southern Europe began to find voice with books like Mary Antin's *The Promised Land* (1912), and the experience of women coping successfully with natural forces was described by such writers as Willa Cather, whose *O Pioneers!* appeared in 1913.

Edith Newbold Jones Wharton, like Henry James a product of New York wealth, loathed the fin de siècle socialization of upper-class women into ornamental, exploitive, and inarticulate creatures. In her 1920 Pulitzer Prize—winning novel *The Age of Innocence,* such women are defined by Newland Archer as "the subject creature, and versed in the arts of the enslaved." Educated by family governesses and well traveled, Wharton published her first poetry anonymously. Her socially prominent family studiously ignored her writing, and her first engagement was said to have been broken off because her fiancé objected to her "ambition." After success with a book on interior decoration cowritten with a man, a collection of stories, and three novels, Wharton struck out against social restrictions, leaving her mentally ill husband and her estate in Lenox, Massachusetts, to live in France (1907); there she continued to write fiction set, for the most part, in the United States and dealing with the struggles of women restricted by social custom.

Other writers of the period also reacted against their backgrounds of familial, financial, or social prominence. Ellen Glasgow, a product of Virginia aristocracy, treated the emergence of middle-class power in her native region in a series of novels written in the first four decades of the century. Amy Lowell and Gertrude Stein, born in the same year as Glasgow, were daughters of wealthy families—Lowell's was an inheritance long associated with Boston while Stein was born to a German-Jewish family in Pennsylvania. Lowell became a major advocate for the avant-garde imagist poets whose work came to prominence during World War I. Stein, after medical and scientific study at Radcliffe and Johns Hopkins, went to live in Paris (1902), where her home became an intellectual center for a gifted group of expatriate writers. Born a decade later, Elinor Wylie was also exiled from her socially prominent family because of her failed marriage, but living in Europe with her lover, she blossomed as a lyric poet. In the 1920s she published four substantial volumes of poetry.

World War I provided a strong impetus for changing sexual roles. In the emergency, young women filled jobs previously reserved for men. Most found experiences such as driving ambulances or producing munitions to be exhilarating. Even farm work had its compensations; middle-class women were taking on unprecedented responsibilities, exerting themselves physically, and facing danger. As battlefield nurses they were exposed to the male sexuality society had been so anxious to insulate them from in peacetime. In their new active roles women were able to experience the freedom of wearing less restrictive clothing, including pants. Artistic freedoms to treat previously forbidden subjects in experimental ways also flourished, and most were unwilling to relinquish these freedoms and return to the intellectual and social attitudes that had prevailed in the first decade of the century.

Some aspiring writers such as H. D. (Hilda Doolittle) spent the war years, like Wharton and Stein, in Europe. Others, including Edna St. Vincent Millay and Susan Glaspell, had settled in Greenwich Village, where, with the attraction of cheap rents in an area of immigrant populations, an American version of the Parisian Latin Quarter had grown up. "Little magazines" were founded, and community theaters such as the Provincetown Players produced the work of American playwrights. Such literary magazines as *Poetry,* founded in 1912 by Harriet Monroe, or *The Little Review,* edited by Margaret Anderson, offered publication to writers experimenting with new forms or clothing novel ideas in traditional styles. The Little Theater movement, transplanted from Europe, produced as many as fifty small, independent theaters hospitable to new playwrights of both sexes; the Provincetown Players, founded in New York and later headquartered on the fishing wharves of Provincetown, encouraged the work of Susan Glaspell as well as that of Eugene O'Neill. Women felt freer to express ideas about their own sexuality; Stein, Lowell, H. D., and others acknowledged their homosexual or bisexual orientation, while Glaspell and Millay expressed discontent with traditional monogamist relationships.

The battle for women's suffrage, begun in the middle of the nineteenth century, was finally won with the passage of the Nineteenth Amendment in 1920. The controversial and long-running trial of Nicola Sacco and Bartolomeo Vanzetti (1921–1927) attracted the sympathies of several prominent women authors, including Edna St. Vincent Millay and Katherine Anne Porter, both of whom wrote about the case. Marianne Moore and Elinor Wylie published their first collections in 1921, and *The Complete Poems of Emily Dickinson* (1924), even though it was by no means truly "complete," did much to elevate her reputation. The 1920s also brought the first transatlantic telephone cable and the promise of more convenient transportation in Lindbergh's solo flight from New York to Paris. Mass publishing ventures such as the Book of the Month Club and the Literary Guild presented more opportunities for writers.

The dominant voices of the modernist period, however, were male. Still under the influence of the past century's enthusiasm for science, the academy valorized objectivity as the correct intellectual approach, deriding the traditionally feminine modes of subjectivity and intuition. T. S. Eliot lauded the Western cultural heritage of elite education, still largely the domain of white males. Ernest Hemingway, in his spare masculine prose, made the case for character testing by exposure to the physical dangers experienced predominantly by men in the trenches, the bullring, or the hunting stand. Ezra Pound, whose boyhood ambition was to "know more about poetry than any man living," pressured Harriet Monroe and H. D., who was at one time his lover, to suppress their romantic or lyric impulses in order to attain intellectual dominance in the world of modern poetry. Sigmund Freud's phallocentric theories, while failing to explain "what women want," dominated public fascination with the workings of the human mind. Modernist women writers struggled to articulate ideas not being addressed by the loud and deep-toned voices around them, but their own voices were scarcely heard for half a century.

The stock market crash at the end of the decade was the prelude to an economic emergency that affected women writers as well as most other Americans. With the world in the grip of the Great Depression, Meridel Le Sueur began to record the stories of individual women's suffering that were transmuted years later into *The Girl*, while Tillie Olsen was retreating from writing to the manual labor she would need to support her family. Lillian Hellman's first New York production, *The Children's Hour* (1934), described the suffering of two schoolteachers whose attempt to be economically independent is doomed when they are falsely accused of lesbianism. While technical advances such as rural electrification promised to ease life for farm women, Mari Sandoz was turning the hardships of Nebraska frontier experience and the nearly forgotten history of the Plains Indians into a series of fictionalized accounts, beginning with *Old Jules* (1935). Zora Neale Hurston, trained in anthropology at Barnard College, used folk materials gathered in rural black communities as the basis for several works, including her best-known novel, *Their Eyes Were Watching God* (1937). Eudora Welty, supported by a job with the Works Progress Administration (WPA), published her first stories of Southern life in little magazines. In 1938, Pearl Buck won the Nobel Prize for her fictional rendering of the life of Chinese peasants. The Spanish Civil War (1936–1939) alerted many intellectuals, including Lillian Hellman, to the gathering threat of fascism, a theme she treated in *Watch on the Rhine* (1941).

The first peacetime conscription was passed in 1940, and European refugee children began to arrive in the United States. Under pressure to arm Europeans already at war against the Nazis, the United States became the "arsenal of democracy" and women once again began doing work previously reserved for men. Eleanor Roosevelt traveled the world on behalf of her disabled husband and wrote a newspaper column describing her daily activities. After the December 1941 bombing of Pearl Harbor, the United States entered World War II. The Women's Army Corps was founded the following year; by war's end nearly 100,000 women had served as medical technicians, cartographers, and cryptologists as well as drivers and clerical workers. A few were trained as pilots who transported planes between military bases. After the war, women volunteers continued to serve in all branches of the service.

The upheaval of a second global conflict brought decisive social changes on the home front. Mothers of young children and wives of servicemen took war industry jobs in large numbers for the first time. The lure of war work caused the rapid urbanization of the American population; Harriet Arnow described the experiences of Appalachian mountain women transplanted to the temporary towns built around the Willow Run bomber plant in Michigan in *The Dollmaker* (1954), and Gwendolyn Brooks described life in black urban neighborhoods in her first collection, *A Street in Bronzeville* (1945). Even women who stayed at home had to modify their traditionally passive roles by taking a greater share of responsibility to cope with rationing and shortages of food, air raid threats, and the drafting of their husbands and sons. Racial integration was fostered by urbanization, and the integration of the armed services was formalized in the aftermath of the war. The Supreme Court ruled, in 1954, that segregated public schools were unconstitutional. The pervasive threat of atomic warfare, heightened by the Korean war, disturbed the serenity of the traditional American family.

While popular culture of the 1950s emphasized the return of the traditional family, with Rosie the Riveter back in the kitchen, the mold had, in fact, been broken. Although they were not paid or promoted equally, women were in the work force to stay, and girl babies born in this "baby boom generation" would be socialized with a different set of assumptions about women's work. Adrienne Rich's career was launched in 1951 when her first collection, *A Change of World*, was published by the Yale Series of Younger Poets. Introduction of the birth control pill in 1955 gave women their first reliable family-planning tool. In the same year, Rosa Parks's refusal to give up her seat on a crowded bus started a chain of events that led to a nationwide campaign for equality in civil rights;

the signing of the Warsaw Pact signaled the beginning of the Cold War; and *A Good Man Is Hard to Find*, Flannery O'Connor's first story collection, appeared. By the end of the decade there were fifty stars on the flag, and Lorraine Hansberry had become the first African-American woman to have a play produced on Broadway.

The election of John Kennedy, with his glamorous and accomplished wife and small children, set the tone for the early 1960s. There were equal opportunities for both sexes in the Peace Corps, as well as the civil rights movement, although the first voyagers into outer space were all male. Anne Sexton's exploration of inner space in *To Bedlam and Part Way Back* (1960) joined books by Robert Lowell and W. D. Snodgrass to inaugurate the rage for "confessional poetry" that for many readers reached its culmination in the work of Sylvia Plath. Building on the accomplishments of O'Connor, Welty, and Carson McCullers, Tillie Olsen's publication of *Tell Me a Riddle* in 1961 promised continued success for women in the short story form. Joyce Carol Oates inaugurated a stunning career with a story collection, *By the North Gate* (1963). In the same year Mary McCarthy published *The Group*, her novel about female friends and their lives after college. Change was in the air; the assassinations of John and Robert Kennedy and Martin Luther King, reactions to the Vietnam war, and racial unrest characterized a decade in which many social and political assumptions—including the traditional roles of women—were dethroned.

Women writers have enjoyed unprecedented success in the last quarter of the twentieth century. Feminist critics rescued from oblivion such nineteenth-century texts as Harriet Jacobs's *Incidents in the Life of a Slave Girl* and Rebecca Harding Davis's *Life in the Iron Mills*. Other books, including *Uncle Tom's Cabin* and *The Awakening*, dismissed as sentimental or "unwomanly" by earlier critics, were studied anew with more sympathetic eyes. Women's writing began to receive more public recognition: in the last year of her life, for instance, Lorene Niedecker saw her first volume of poetry, *My Life by Water* (1970), into print. In her sixties, with the publication of her first collection, *The Kingfisher* (1983), Amy Clampitt joined the ranks of celebrated poets of the 1980s. In her seventies, Mona Van Duyn, author of five verse collections, was named Poet Laureate in 1992. Sales of Maya Angelou's books rose dramatically after she recited a poem at the inauguration of President William Clinton.

Short fiction has been a particularly fertile field for recent women writers. A scanning of the table of contents in *O. Henry Prize Stories* or *Best American Short Story* volumes of the 1980s or 1990s will reveal the dominance of women, including Joyce Carol Oates, Bobbie Anne Mason, Bharati Mukherjee, and Anne Beattie, in the short story genre

Increased visibility of women writers in the 1970s and 1980s has often been related to the increased visibility of writers of different ethnic and cultural backgrounds in the same period. Today, women with heritages based in diverse cultures are writing to illuminate the experience of growing up on the margin between traditions. Such African-American writers as Rita Dove, Toni Morrison, and Alice Walker enjoy wide acceptance. Asian Americans, including Gish Jen, Maxine Hong Kingston, Cathy Song, and Amy Tan, are exploring the relationship between immigrant parents and grandparents and their offspring educated in the United States. Native American writers of various tribal backgrounds, including Leslie Marmon Silko and Louise Erdrich, describe the conflict between the traditions of indigenous people and European customs.

The increased prominence of women's voices in the American chorus suggests that, in literary studies in the coming century, a better balance may finally be struck between the texts produced by women and men.

Edith Wharton
(1862–1937)

Among American women writers born in the nineteenth century, Edith Wharton stands with Emily Dickinson as an author whose work has long held an assured place in literary history. In the 1920s Wharton was one of the most acclaimed of American writers of fiction, having earned a Pulitzer Prize as well as having produced more than one best-seller. Her fiction's subject matter spans the two eras she lived in, both the late Victorian and the modern periods; her style is distinctly modern.

Edith Newbold Jones was born in 1862 into the most privileged class of old New York society, to George and Lucretia Rhinelander Jones, both of whom could trace their lineage back for three centuries. She inhabited the world of the very rich, spending winters in New York and summers in Newport, Rhode Island, and growing up with every expectation of taking her place as a prominent social figure in her turn. She had the typical upper-class young woman's private education, consisting of languages, liberal arts, and etiquette, and she had a formal social debut in 1879. Despite her conventional upbringing, however, she was a voracious reader and she experimented with writing poetry. She traveled in Europe often during her youth, thus preparing for her later sojourns there. In 1885 she married Edward Wharton, of an equally prestigious family, and she took up the duties of a high-society wife in their homes in New York; Newport; Lenox, Massachusetts; and France.

Edith and Edward ("Teddy") Wharton appear to have had little in common; he had no interest in her literary talents or aspirations. Nevertheless, Edith began writing short stories, which she placed in prominent periodicals; she also produced *The Decoration of Houses* (1897), written collaboratively with Ogden Codman, Jr., an architect from Boston. The book argues against Victorian principles of interior decoration and promotes openness, airiness, and light as the new standard of taste.

In 1894, despite her literary productivity, Edith had a breakdown and sought treatment from S. Weir Mitchell, the originator of the so-called rest cure.

After recovering from her depression, Wharton wrote steadily and tirelessly, completing an average of one book every year until her death. Her best-remembered novels are *The House of Mirth* (1905), *Ethan Frome* (1911), and *The Age of Innocence* (1920). The first tells the story of Lily Bart, a woman born and bred to be an upper-class wife whose circumstances make her marriage—and therefore her survival—impossible; the second presents a stark tragedy of love, frustration, and ironic sacrifice set in a New England village; the third chronicles the manners and mores of old New York society from an almost anthropological perspective, contrasting the range of available life choices in the period with those of the next generation of wealthy New Yorkers. An astute critic of conspicuous consumption, class snobbery, and prescribed gender roles, Wharton creates complex psychological portraits of the persons who inhabit her fictionalized social world.

Wharton is reported to have had a passionate affair with a fellow writer in 1910; her marriage ended in divorce in 1913. By that time she was living primarily in France, one of many American expatriate writers who were to settle there during the modern period. She had a close professional relationship with Henry James, who admired her writing, as well as with other writers and thinkers of the time. Like other modernists, she was self-conscious about the construction of stories and novels, which she discusses in *The Writing of Fiction* (1925). During World War I, she devoted her energies to charitable efforts, finding work, food, and shelter for refugees. When the war ended, she remained in France, where she died of a stroke at the age of 75, after completing her autobiography, *A Backward Glance* (1934).

Our two selections, "The Muse's Tragedy" (1899) and "The Other Two" (1904),

demonstrate one of Wharton's characteristic techniques in writing about women: she presents the central female character from the point of view of a man. "The Muse's Tragedy" introduces a woman who had been the inspiration for a fictional Victorian poet's masterpieces; she is portrayed first from the perspective of a young male admirer and then in a revelatory letter written by herself. In its unusual angle on women in literature, the story asks more questions than it answers. "The Other Two" leaves ambiguous the question of whether Alice Waythorn is culpable, as her husband ultimately finds her to be, for her evident ability to adapt herself to the various men she has married.

Wharton's other works include *Verses, Anonymous* (1878); *The Greater Inclination* (1899); *The Touchstone* (1900); *Crucial Instances* (1901); *The Valley of Decision* (1902); *Sanctuary* (1903); *Italian Villas and Their Gardens* (1904); *The Descent of Man and Other Stories* (1904); *Italian Backgrounds* (1905); *Madame de Treymes* (1907); *The Fruit of the Tree* (1907); *The Hermit and the Wild Woman and Other Stories* (1908); *A Motor-Flight through France* (1908); *Artemis to Actaeon and Other Verse* (1909); *Tales of Men and Ghosts* (1910); *The Reef* (1912); *The Custom of the Country* (1913); *Fighting France, from Dunkerque to Belfort* (1915); *Xingu and Other Stories* (1916); *Summer* (1917); *The Marne* (1918); *French Ways and Their Meaning* (1919); *In Morocco* (1920); *The Glimpses of the Moon* (1922); *A Son at the Front* (1923); *Old New York* (1924); *The Mother's Recompense* (1925); *Here and Beyond* (1926); *Twelve Poems* (1926); *Twilight Sleep* (1927); *The Children* (1928); *Hudson River Bracketed* (1929); *Certain People* (1930); *The Gods Arrive* (1932); *Human Nature* (1933); *The World Over* (1936); *Ghosts* (1937); and *The Buccaneers* (1938).

The main biographies of Wharton include Louis Auchincloss's *Edith Wharton: A Woman in Her Time* (1971), R. W. B. Lewis's *Edith Wharton: A Biography* (1975), and Cynthia Griffin Wolff's *A Feast of Words* (1977). Selected studies of her fiction include Blake Nevius, *Edith Wharton: A Study of Her Fiction* (1953); Gary Lindberg, *Edith Wharton and the Novel of Manners* (1975); Elizabeth Ammons, *Edith Wharton's Argument with America* (1980); Carol Wershoven, *The Female Intruder in the Novels of Edith Wharton* (1982); Judith Fryer, *Felicitous Space* (1986); Susan Goodman, *Edith Wharton's Women: Friends & Rivals* (1990); David Holbrook, *Edith Wharton and the Unsatisfactory Man* (1991); and Candace Waid, *Edith Wharton's Letters from the Underworld: Fictions of Women and Writing* (1991).

The Muse's Tragedy

Danyers afterwards liked to fancy that he had recognized Mrs. Anerton at once; but that, of course, was absurd, since he had seen no portrait of her—she affected a strict anonymity, refusing even her photograph to the most privileged—and from Mrs. Memorall, whom he revered and cultivated as her friend, he had extracted but the one impressionist phrase: "Oh, well, she's like one of those old prints where the lines have the value of color."

He was almost certain, at all events, that he had been thinking of Mrs. Anerton as he sat over his breakfast in the empty hotel restaurant, and that, looking up on the approach of the lady who seated herself at the table near the window, he had said to himself, *"That might be she."*

Ever since his Harvard days—he was still young enough to think of them as immensely remote—Danyers had dreamed of Mrs. Anerton, the Silvia of Vincent Rendle's immortal sonnet cycle, the Mrs. A. of the *Life and Letters*.[1] Her name was enshrined in some of the noblest English verse of the nineteenth century—and of all past or future centuries, as Danyers, from the standpoint of a maturer judgment, still believed. The first reading of certain poems—of the *Antinous,* the *Pia Tolomei,* the *Sonnets to Silvia*—had been epochs in Danyers' growth, and the verse seemed to gain in mellowness, in amplitude, in meaning as one brought to its interpretation more experience of life, a finer emotional sense. Where, in his boyhood, he had felt only the perfect, the almost austere beauty of form, the subtle interplay of vowel sounds, the rush and fullness of lyric emotion, he now thrilled to the close-packed significance of each line, the allusiveness of each word—his imagination lured hither and thither on fresh trails of thought, and perpetually spurred by the sense that, beyond what he had already discovered, more marvelous regions lay waiting to be explored. Danyers had written, at college, the prize essay on Rendle's poetry (it chanced to be the moment of the great man's death); he had fashioned the fugitive verse of his own Storm and Stress[2] period on the forms which Rendle had first given to English meter, and when two years later the *Life and Letters* appeared, and the Silvia of the sonnets took substance as Mrs. A., he had included in his worship of Rendle the woman who had inspired not only such divine verse but such playful, tender, incomparable prose.

Danyers never forgot the day when Mrs. Memorall happened to mention that she knew Mrs. Anerton. He had known Mrs. Memorall for a year or more, and had somewhat contemptuously classified her as the kind of woman who runs cheap excursions to celebrities; when one afternoon she remarked, as she put a second lump of sugar in his tea:

"Is it right this time? You're almost as particular as Mary Anerton."

"Mary Anerton?"

"Yes, I never *can* remember how she likes her tea. Either it's lemon *with* sugar, or lemon without sugar, or cream without either, and whichever it is must be put into the cup before the tea is poured in; and if one hasn't remembered, one must begin all over again. I suppose it was Vincent Rendle's way of taking his tea and has become a sacred rite."

"Do you *know* Mrs. Anerton?" cried Danyers, disturbed by this careless familiarity with the habits of his divinity.

" 'And did I once see Shelley plain?'[3] Mercy, yes! She and I were at school together—she's an American, you know. We were at a *pension*[4] near Tours[5] for nearly a year; then she went

---

1. Rendle is a fictional figure.
2. *"Sturm und Drang,"* an allusion to the eighteenth-century German romantic poets who glorified the struggles of the individual against conventional society.
3. The first lines of Robert Browning's poem

"Memorabilia" are "Ah, did you once see Shelley plain / And did he stop and speak to you . . . ?"
4. A boardinghouse.
5. City in western France.

back to New York, and I didn't see her again till after her marriage. She and Anerton spent a winter in Rome while my husband was attached to our Legation there, and she used to be with us a great deal." Mrs. Memorall smiled reminiscently. "It was *the* winter."

"The winter they first met?"

"Precisely—but unluckily I left Rome just before the meeting took place. Wasn't it too bad? I might have been in the *Life and Letters*. You know he mentions that stupid Madame Vodki, at whose house he first saw her."

"And did you see much of her after that?"

"Not during Rendle's life. You know she has lived in Europe almost entirely, and though I used to see her off and on when I went abroad, she was always so engrossed, so preoccupied, that one felt one wasn't wanted. The fact is, she cared only about his friends—she separated herself gradually from all her own people. Now, of course, it's different; she's desperately lonely; she's taken to writing to me now and then; and last year, when she heard I was going abroad, she asked me to meet her in Venice, and I spent a week with her there."

"And Rendle?"

Mrs. Memorall smiled and shook her head. "Oh, I never was allowed a peep at *him;* none of her old friends met him, except by accident. Ill-natured people say that was the reason she kept him so long. If one happened in while he was there, he was hustled into Anerton's study, and the husband mounted guard till the inopportune visitor had departed. Anerton, you know, was really much more ridiculous about it than his wife. Mary was too clever to lose her head, or at least to show she'd lost it—but Anerton couldn't conceal his pride in the conquest. I've seen Mary shiver when he spoke of Rendle as *our poet.* Rendle always had to have a certain seat at the dinner table, away from the draft and not too near the fire, and a box of cigars that no one else was allowed to touch, and a writing table of his own in Mary's sitting room—and Anerton was always telling one of the great man's idiosyncrasies: how he never would cut the ends of his cigars, though Anerton himself had given him a gold cutter set with a star sapphire, and how untidy his writing table was, and how the housemaid had orders always to bring the wastepaper basket to her mistress before emptying it, lest some immortal verse should be thrown into the dustbin."

"The Anertons never separated, did they?"

"Separated? Bless you, no. He never would have left Rendle! And besides, he was very fond of his wife."

"And she?"

"Oh, she saw he was the kind of man who was fated to make himself ridiculous, and she never interfered with his natural tendencies."

From Mrs. Memorall, Danyers further learned that Mrs. Anerton, whose husband had died some years before her poet, now divided her life between Rome, where she had a small apartment, and England, where she occasionally went to stay with those of her friends who had been Rendle's. She had been engaged, for some time after his death, in editing some juvenilia which he had bequeathed to her care; but that task being accomplished, she had been left without definite occupation, and Mrs. Memorall, on the occasion of their last meeting, had found her listless and out of spirits.

"She misses him too much—her life is too empty. I told her so—I told her she ought to marry."

"Oh!"

"Why not, pray? She's a young woman still—what many people would call young," Mrs. Memorall interjected, with a parenthetic glance at the mirror. "Why not accept the inevitable and begin over again? All the King's horses and all the King's men won't bring Rendle to life—and besides, she didn't marry *him* when she had the chance."

Danyers winced slightly at this rude fingering of his idol. Was it possible that Mrs. Memorall did not see what an anticlimax such a marriage would have been? Fancy Rendle "making an honest woman" of Silvia; for so society would have viewed it! How such a reparation would have vulgarized their past—it would have been like "restoring" a master-piece; and how exquisite must have been the perceptions of the woman who, in defiance of appearances, and perhaps of her own secret inclination, chose to go down to posterity as Silvia rather than as Mrs. Vincent Rendle!

Mrs. Memorall, from this day forth, acquired an interest in Danyers' eyes. She was like a volume of unindexed and discursive memoirs, through which he patiently plodded in the hope of finding embedded amid layers of dusty twaddle some precious allusion to the subject of his thought. When, some months later, he brought out his first slim volume, in which the remodeled college essay on Rendle figured among a dozen somewhat overstudied "apprecia-tions," he offered a copy to Mrs. Memorall; who surprised him, the next time they met, with the announcement that she had sent the book to Mrs. Anerton.

Mrs. Anerton in due time wrote to thank her friend. Danyers was privileged to read the few lines in which, in terms that suggested the habit of "acknowledging" similar tributes, she spoke of the author's "feeling and insight," and was "so glad of the opportunity," etc. He went away disappointed, without clearly knowing what else he had expected.

The following spring, when he went abroad, Mrs. Memorall offered him letters to every-body, from the Archbishop of Canterbury to Louise Michel.[6] She did not include Mrs. Anerton, however, and Danyers knew, from a previous conversation, that Silvia objected to people who "brought letters." He knew also that she traveled during the summer, and was unlikely to return to Rome before the term of his holiday should be reached, and the hope of meeting her was not included among his anticipations.

The lady whose entrance broke upon his solitary repast in the restaurant of the Hotel Villa d'Este[7] had seated herself in such a way that her profile was detached against the window; and thus viewed, her domed forehead, small arched nose, and fastidious lip suggested a silhouette of Marie Antoinette.[8] In the lady's dress and movements—in the very turn of her wrist as she poured out her coffee—Danyers thought he detected the same fastidiousness, the same air of tacitly excluding the obvious and unexceptional. Here was a woman who had been much bored and keenly interested. The waiter brought her a *Secolo*,[9] and as she bent above it Danyers noticed that the hair rolled back from her forehead was turning gray; but her figure was straight and slender, and she had the invaluable gift of a girlish back.

The rush of Anglo-Saxon travel had not set toward the lakes, and with the exception of an Italian family or two, and a hump-backed youth with an *abbé*,[1] Danyers and the lady had the marble halls of the Villa d'Este to themselves.

When he returned from his morning ramble among the hills he saw her sitting at one of the little tables at the edge of the lake. She was writing, and a heap of books and newspapers lay on the table at her side. That evening they met again in the garden. He had strolled out to smoke a last cigarette before dinner, and under the black vaulting of ilexes,[2] near the steps leading down to the boat landing, he found her leaning on the parapet above the lake. At the sound of his approach she turned and looked at him. She had thrown a black lace scarf over her head, and in this somber setting her face seemed thin and unhappy. He remembered afterwards that her eyes, as they met his, expressed not so much sorrow as profound discontent.

To his surprise she stepped toward him with a detaining gesture.

"Mr. Lewis Danyers, I believe?"

He bowed.

---

6. French writer of histories (1830–1905).
7. Elite hotel in Italy, on Lake Como.
8. Queen of France (1755–1793), beheaded during the French Revolution.
9. Aperitif.
1. French priest.
2. Holly trees.

"I am Mrs. Anerton. I saw your name on the visitors' list and wished to thank you for an essay on Mr. Rendle's poetry—or rather to tell you how much I appreciated it. The book was sent to me last winter by Mrs. Memorall."

She spoke in even melancholy tones, as though the habit of perfunctory utterance had robbed her voice of more spontaneous accents; but her smile was charming.

They sat down on a stone bench under the ilexes, and she told him how much pleasure his essay had given her. She thought it the best in the book—she was sure he had put more of himself into it than into any other; was she not right in conjecturing that he had been very deeply influenced by Mr. Rendle's poetry? *Pour comprendre il faut aimer,*[3] and it seemed to her that, in some ways, he had penetrated the poet's inner meaning more completely than any other critic. There were certain problems, of course, that he had left untouched; certain aspects of that many-sided mind that he had perhaps failed to seize—

"But then you are young," she concluded gently, "and one could not wish you, as yet, the experience that a fuller understanding would imply."

II

She stayed a month at Villa d'Este, and Danyers was with her daily. She showed an unaffected pleasure in his society; a pleasure so obviously founded on their common veneration of Rendle, that the young man could enjoy it without fear of fatuity. At first he was merely one more grain of frankincense on the altar of her insatiable divinity; but gradually a more personal note crept into their intercourse. If she still liked him only because he appreciated Rendle, she at least perceptibly distinguished him from the herd of Rendle's appreciators.

Her attitude toward the great man's memory struck Danyers as perfect. She neither proclaimed nor disavowed her identity. She was frankly Silvia to those who knew and cared; but there was no trace of the Egeria[4] in her pose. She spoke often of Rendle's books, but seldom of himself; there was no posthumous conjugality, no use of the possessive tense, in her abounding reminiscences. Of the master's intellectual life, of his habits of thought and work, she never wearied of talking. She knew the history of each poem; by what scene or episode each image had been evoked; how many times the words in a certain line had been transposed; how long a certain adjective had been sought, and what had at last suggested it; she could even explain that one impenetrable line, the torment of critics, the joy of detractors, the last line of *The Old Odysseus.*

Danyers felt that in talking of these things she was no mere echo of Rendle's thought. If her identity had appeared to be merged in his it was because they thought alike, not because he had thought for her. Posterity is apt to regard the women whom poets have sung as chance pegs on which they hung their garlands; but Mrs. Anerton's mind was like some fertile garden wherein, inevitably, Rendle's imagination had rooted itself and flowered. Danyers began to see how many threads of his complex mental tissue the poet had owed to the blending of her temperament with his; in a certain sense Silvia had herself created the *Sonnets to Silvia.*

To be the custodian of Rendle's inner self, the door, as it were, to the sanctuary, had at first seemed to Danyers so comprehensive a privilege that he had the sense, as his friendship with Mrs. Anerton advanced, of forcing his way into a life already crowded. What room was there, among such towering memories, for so small an actuality as his? Quite suddenly, after this, he discovered that Mrs. Memorall knew better: his fortunate friend was bored as well as lonely.

"You have had more than any other woman!" he had exclaimed to her one day: and her smile flashed a derisive light on his blunder. Fool that he was, not to have seen that she had

---

3. "To understand, it is necessary to love."   4. In Roman mythology, a female adviser.

not had enough! That she was young still—do years count?—tender, human, a woman; that the living have need of the living.

After that, when they climbed the alleys of the hanging park, resting in one of the little ruined temples, or watching, through a ripple of foliage, the remote blue flash of the lake, they did not always talk of Rendle or of literature. She encouraged Danyers to speak of himself; to confide his ambitions to her; she asked him the questions which are the wise woman's substitute for advice.

"You must write," she said, administering the most exquisite flattery that human lips could give.

Of course he meant to write—why not to do something great in his turn? His best, at least; with the resolve, at the outset, that his best should be *the* best. Nothing less seemed possible with that mandate in his ears. How she had divined him; lifted and disentangled his groping ambitions; laid the awakening touch on his spirit with her creative *Let there be light!*[5]

It was his last day with her, and he was feeling very hopeless and happy.

"You ought to write a book about *him*," she went on gently.

Danyers started; he was beginning to dislike Rendle's way of walking in unannounced.

"You ought to do it," she insisted. "A complete interpretation—a summing up of his style, his purpose, his theory of life and art. No one else could do it as well."

He sat looking at her perplexedly. Suddenly—dared he guess?

"I couldn't do it without you," he faltered.

"I could help you—I would help you, of course."

They sat silent, both looking at the lake.

It was agreed, when they parted, that he should rejoin her six weeks later in Venice. There they were to talk about the book.

III

Lago d'Iseo, August 14th.

When I said good-bye to you yesterday I promised to come back to Venice in a week: I was to give you your answer then. I was not honest in saying that; I didn't mean to go back to Venice or to see you again. I was running away from you—and I mean to keep on running! If *you* won't, *I* must. Somebody must save you from marrying a disappointed woman of—well, you say years don't count, and why should they, after all, since you are not to marry me?

That is what I dare not go back to say. *You are not to marry me.* We have had our month together in Venice (such a good month, was it not?) and now you are to go home and write a book—any book but the one we—didn't talk of!—and I am to stay here, attitudinizing among my memories like a sort of female Tithonus.[6] The dreariness of this enforced immortality!

But you shall know the truth. I care for you, or at least for your love, enough to owe you that.

You thought it was because Vincent Rendle had loved me that there was so little hope for you. I had had what I wanted to the full; wasn't that what you said? It is just when a man begins to think he understands a woman that he may be sure he doesn't! It is because Vincent Rendle *didn't love me* that there is no hope for you. I never had what I wanted, and never, never, never will I stoop to wanting anything else.

Do you begin to understand? It was all a sham then, you say? No, it was all real as far as it went. You are young—you haven't learned, as you will later, the thousand imper-

5. See Genesis 1:3.
6. In Greek mythology, a man who won
immortality from the gods, but neglected to
request eternal youthfulness.

ceptible signs by which one gropes one's way through the labyrinth of human nature; but didn't it strike you, sometimes, that I never told you any foolish little anecdotes about him? His trick, for instance, of twirling a paper knife round and round between his thumb and forefinger while he talked; his mania for saving the backs of notes; his greediness for wild strawberries, the little pungent Alpine ones; his childish delight in acrobats and jugglers; his way of always calling me *you*—*dear you,* every letter began—I never told you a word of all that, did I? Do you suppose I could have helped telling you, if he had loved me? These little things would have been mine, then, a part of my life—of our life—they would have slipped out in spite of me (it's only your unhappy woman who is always reticent and dignified). But there never was any "our life"; it was always "our lives" to the end. . . .

If you knew what a relief it is to tell someone at last, you would bear with me, you would let me hurt you! I shall never be quite so lonely again, now that someone knows.

Let me begin at the beginning. When I first met Vincent Rendle I was not twenty-five. That was twenty years ago. From that time until his death, five years ago, we were fast friends. He gave me fifteen years, perhaps the best fifteen years, of his life. The world, as you know, thinks that his greatest poems were written during those years; I am supposed to have "inspired" them, and in a sense I did. From the first, the intellectual sympathy between us was almost complete; my mind must have been to him (I fancy) like some perfectly tuned instrument on which he was never tired of playing. Someone told me of his once saying of me that I "always understood"; it is the only praise I ever heard of his giving me. I don't even know if he thought me pretty, though I hardly think my appearance could have been disagreeable to him, for he hated to be with ugly people. At all events he fell into the way of spending more and more of his time with me. He liked our house; our ways suited him. He was nervous, irritable; people bored him and yet he disliked solitude. He took sanctuary with us. When we traveled he went with us; in the winter he took rooms near us in Rome. In England or on the continent he was always with us for a good part of the year. In small ways I was able to help him in his work; he grew dependent on me. When we were apart he wrote to me continually—he liked to have me share in all he was doing or thinking; he was impatient for my criticism of every new book that interested him; I was a part of his intellectual life. The pity of it was that I wanted to be something more. I was a young woman and I was in love with him—not because he was Vincent Rendle, but just because he was himself!

People began to talk, of course—I was Vincent Rendle's Mrs. Anerton; when the *Sonnets to Silvia* appeared, it was whispered that I was Silvia. Wherever he went, I was invited; people made up to me in the hope of getting to know him; when I was in London my doorbell never stopped ringing. Elderly peeresses, aspiring hostesses, lovesick girls and struggling authors overwhelmed me with their assiduities. I hugged my success, for I knew what it meant—they thought that Rendle was in love with me! Do you know, at times, they almost made me think so too? Oh, there was no phase of folly I didn't go through. You can't imagine the excuses a woman will invent for a man's not telling her that he loves her—pitiable arguments that she would see through at a glance if any other woman used them! But all the while, deep down, I knew he had never cared. I should have known it if he had made love to me every day of his life. I could never guess whether he knew what people said about us—he listened so little to what people said; and cared still less, when he heard. He was always quite honest and straightforward with me; he treated me as one man treats another; and yet at times I felt he *must* see that with me it was different. If he did see, he made no sign. Perhaps he never noticed—I am sure he never meant to be cruel. He had never made love to me; it was no fault of his if I wanted more than he could give me. The *Sonnets to Silvia,* you say? But what are they? A cosmic philosophy, not a love poem; addressed to Woman, not to a woman!

But then, the letters? Ah, the letters! Well, I'll make a clean breast of it. You have noticed the breaks in the letters here and there, just as they seem to be on the point of growing a little—warmer? The critics, you may remember, praised the editor for his commendable delicacy and good taste (so rare in these days!) in omitting from the correspondence all personal allusions, all those *détails intimes*[7] which should be kept sacred from the public gaze. They referred, of course, to the asterisks in the letters to Mrs. A. Those letters I myself prepared for publication; that is to say, I copied them out for the editor, and every now and then I put in a line of asterisks to make it appear that something had been left out. You understand? The asterisks were a sham—*there was nothing to leave out.*

No one but a woman could understand what I went through during those years—the moments of revolt, when I felt I must break away from it all, fling the truth in his face and never see him again; the inevitable reaction, when not to see him seemed the one unendurable thing, and I trembled lest a look or word of mine should disturb the poise of our friendship; the silly days when I hugged the delusion that he *must* love me, since everybody thought he did; the long periods of numbness, when I didn't seem to care whether he loved me or not. Between these wretched days came others when our intellectual accord was so perfect that I forgot everything else in the joy of feeling myself lifted up on the wings of his thought. Sometimes, then, the heavens seemed to be opened.

All this time he was so dear a friend! He had the genius of friendship, and he spent it all on me. Yes, you were right when you said that I have had more than any other woman. *Il faut de l'adresse pour aimer,*[8] Pascal says; and I was so quiet, so cheerful, so frankly affectionate with him, that in all those years I am almost sure I never bored him. Could I have hoped as much if he had loved me?

You mustn't think of him, though, as having been tied to my skirts. He came and went as he pleased, and so did his fancies. There was a girl once (I am telling you everything), a lovely being who called his poetry "deep" and gave him *Lucile*[9] on his birthday. He followed her to Switzerland one summer, and all the time that he was dangling after her (a little too conspicuously, I always thought, for a Great Man), he was writing to *me* about his theory of vowel combinations—or was it his experiments in English hexameter? The letters were dated from the very places where I knew they went and sat by waterfalls together and he thought out adjectives for her hair. He talked to me about it quite frankly afterwards. She was perfectly beautiful and it had been a pure delight to watch her; but she *would* talk, and her mind, he said, was "all elbows." And yet, the next year, when her marriage was announced, he went away alone, quite suddenly . . . and it was just afterwards that he published *Love's Viaticum.* Men are queer!

After my husband died—I am putting things crudely, you see—I had a return of hope. It was because he loved me, I argued, that he had never spoken, because he had always hoped some day to make me his wife; because he wanted to spare me the "reproach." Rubbish! I knew well enough, in my heart of hearts, that my one chance lay in the force of habit. He had grown used to me; he was no longer young; he dreaded new people and new ways; *il avait pris son pli.*[1] Would it not be easier to marry me?

I don't believe he ever thought of it. He wrote me what people call "a beautiful letter"; he was kind, considerate, decently commiserating; then, after a few weeks, he slipped into his old ways of coming in every afternoon, and our interminable talks began again just where they had left off. I heard later that people thought I had shown "such good taste" in not marrying him.

7. "Intimate details."
8. "You must have skill to love."
9. Popular novel by Edward Bulwer-Lytton

(1831–1891), published under "Owen Meredith," a pseudonym.
1. "He was set in his ways."

So we jogged on for five years longer. Perhaps they were the best years, for I had given up hoping. Then he died.

After his death—this is curious—there came to me a kind of mirage of love. All the books and articles written about him, all the reviews of the *Life*, were full of discreet allusions to Silvia. I became again the Mrs. Anerton of the glorious days. Sentimental girls and dear lads like you turned pink when somebody whispered, "That was Silvia you were talking to." Idiots begged for my autograph—publishers urged me to write my reminiscences of him—critics consulted me about the reading of doubtful lines. And I knew that, to all these people, I was the woman Vincent Rendle had loved.

After a while that fire went out too and I was left alone with my past. Alone—quite alone; for he had never really been with me. The intellectual union counted for nothing now. It had been soul to soul, but never hand in hand, and there were no little things to remember him by.

Then there set in a kind of Arctic winter. I crawled into myself as into a snow hut. I hated my solitude and yet dreaded anyone who disturbed it. That phase, of course, passed like the others. I took up life again, and began to read the papers and consider the cut of my gowns. But here was one question that I could not be rid of, that haunted me night and day. Why had he never loved me? Why had I been so much to him, and no more? Was I so ugly, so essentially unlovable, that though a man might cherish me as his mind's comrade, he could not care for me as a woman? I can't tell you how that question tortured me. It became an obsession.

My poor friend, do you begin to see? I had to find out what some other man thought of me. Don't be too hard on me! Listen first—consider. When I first met Vincent Rendle I was a young woman, who had married early and led the quietest kind of life; I had had no "experiences." From the hour of our first meeting to the day of his death I never looked at any other man, and never noticed whether any other man looked at me. When he died, five years ago, I knew the extent of my powers no more than a baby. Was it too late to find out? Should I never know *why*?

Forgive me—forgive me. You are so young; it will be an episode, a mere "document," to you so soon! And, besides, it wasn't as deliberate, as cold-blooded as these disjointed lines have made it appear. I didn't plan it, like a woman in a book. Life is so much more complex than any rendering of it can be. I liked you from the first—I was drawn to you (you must have seen that)—I wanted you to like me; it was not a mere psychological experiment. And yet in a sense it was that, too—I must be honest. I had to have an answer to that question; it was a ghost that had to be laid.

At first I was afraid—oh, so much afraid—that you cared for me only because I was Silvia, that you loved me because you thought Rendle had loved me. I began to think there was no escaping my destiny.

How happy I was when I discovered that you were growing jealous of my past; that you actually hated Rendle! My heart beat like a girl's when you told me you meant to follow me to Venice.

After our parting at Villa d'Este my old doubts reasserted themselves. What did I know of your feeling for me, after all? Were you capable of analyzing it yourself? Was it not likely to be two-thirds vanity and curiosity, and one-third literary sentimentality? You might easily fancy that you cared for Mary Anerton when you were really in love with Silvia—the heart is such a hypocrite! Or you might be more calculating than I had supposed. Perhaps it was you who had been flattering *my* vanity in the hope (the pardonable hope!) of turning me, after a decent interval, into a pretty little essay with a margin.

When you arrived in Venice and we met again—do you remember the music on the lagoon, that evening, from my balcony?—I was so afraid you would begin to talk about the book—the book, you remember, was your ostensible reason for coming. You never spoke of it, and I soon saw your one fear was *I* might do so—might remind you of your object in being with me. Then I knew you cared for me! yes, at that moment really cared! We never mentioned the book once, did we, during that month in Venice?

I have read my letter over; and now I wish that I had said this to you instead of writing it. I could have felt my way then, watching your face and seeing if you understood. But, no, I could not go back to Venice; and I could not tell you (though I tried) while we were there together. I couldn't spoil that month—my one month. It was so good, for once in my life, to get away from literature.

You will be angry with me at first—but, alas! not for long. What I have done would have been cruel if I had been a younger woman; as it is, the experiment will hurt no one but myself. And it will hurt me horribly (as much as, in your first anger, you may perhaps wish), because it has shown me, for the first time, all that I have missed.

1899

The Other Two

Waythorn, on the drawing-room hearth, waited for his wife to come down to dinner.

It was their first night under his own roof, and he was surprised at his thrill of boyish agitation. He was not so old, to be sure—his glass gave him little more than the five-and-thirty years to which his wife confessed—but he had fancied himself already in the temperate zone; yet here he was listening for her step with a tender sense of all it symbolized, with some old trail of verse about the garlanded nuptial doorposts floating through his enjoyment of the pleasant room and the good dinner just beyond it.

They had been hastily recalled from their honeymoon by the illness of Lily Haskett, the child of Mrs. Waythorn's first marriage. The little girl, at Waythorn's desire, had been transferred to his house on the day of her mother's wedding, and the doctor, on their arrival, broke the news that she was ill with typhoid, but declared that all the symptoms were favorable. Lily could show twelve years of unblemished health, and the case promised to be a light one. The nurse spoke as reassuringly, and after a moment of alarm Mrs. Waythorn had adjusted herself to the situation. She was very fond of Lily—her affection for the child had perhaps been her decisive charm in Waythorn's eyes—but she had the perfectly balanced nerves which her little girl had inherited, and no woman ever wasted less tissue in unproductive worry. Waythorn was therefore quite prepared to see her come in presently, a little late because of a last look at Lily, but as serene and well-appointed as if her good-night kiss had been laid on the brow of health. Her composure was restful to him; it acted as ballast to his somewhat unstable sensibilities. As he pictured her bending over the child's bed he thought how soothing her presence must be in illness: her very step would prognosticate recovery.

His own life had been a gray one, from temperament rather than circumstance, and he had been drawn to her by the unperturbed gaiety which kept her fresh and elastic at an age when most women's activities are growing either slack or febrile. He knew what was said about her; for, popular as she was, there had always been a faint undercurrent of detraction. When she had appeared in New York, nine or ten years earlier, as the pretty Mrs. Haskett whom Gus Varick had unearthed somewhere—was it in Pittsburg or Utica?—society, while promptly accepting her, had reserved the right to cast a doubt on its own indiscrimination. Inquiry, however, established her undoubted connection with a socially reigning family, and explained her recent divorce as the natural result of a runaway match at seventeen; and as nothing was known of Mr. Haskett it was easy to believe the worst of him.

Alice Haskett's remarriage with Gus Varick was a passport to the set whose recognition she coveted, and for a few years the Varicks were the most popular couple in town. Unfortunately the alliance was brief and stormy, and this time the husband had his champions. Still, even Varick's stanchest supporters admitted that he was not meant for matrimony, and Mrs. Varick's grievances were of a nature to bear the inspection of the New York courts.[2] A New York divorce is in itself a diploma of virtue, and in the semiwidowhood of this second separation Mrs. Varick took on an air of sanctity, and was allowed to confide her wrongs to some of the most scrupulous ears in town. But when it was known that she was to marry Waythorn there was a momentary reaction. Her best friends would have preferred to see her remain in the role of the injured wife, which was as becoming to her as crepe to a rosy complexion. True, a decent time had elapsed, and it was not even suggested that Waythorn had supplanted his predecessor. People shook their heads over him, however, and one grudging friend, to whom he affirmed that he took the step with his eyes open, replied oracularly: "Yes—and with your ears shut."

Waythorn could afford to smile at these innuendoes. In the Wall Street phrase, he had "discounted" them. He knew that society has not yet adapted itself to the consequences of divorce, and that till the adaptation takes place every woman who uses the freedom the law accords her must be her own social justification. Waythorn had an amused confidence in his wife's ability to justify herself. His expectations were fulfilled, and before the wedding took place Alice Varick's group had rallied openly to her support. She took it all imperturbably: she had a way of surmounting obstacles without seeming to be aware of them, and Waythorn looked back with wonder at the trivialities over which he had worn his nerves thin. He had the sense of having found refuge in a richer, warmer nature than his own, and his satisfaction, at the moment, was humorously summed up in the thought that his wife, when she had done all she could for Lily, would not be ashamed to come down and enjoy a good dinner.

The anticipation of such enjoyment was not, however, the sentiment expressed by Mrs. Waythorn's charming face when she presently joined him. Though she had put on her most engaging tea gown she had neglected to assume the smile that went with it, and Waythorn thought he had never seen her look so nearly worried.

"What is it?" he asked. "Is anything wrong with Lily?"

"No; I've just been in and she's still sleeping." Mrs. Waythorn hesitated. "But something tiresome has happened."

He had taken her two hands, and now perceived that he was crushing a paper between them.

"This letter?"

"Yes—Mr. Haskett has written—I mean his lawyer has written."

Waythorn felt himself flush uncomfortably. He dropped his wife's hands.

"What about?"

"About seeing Lily. You know the courts—"

"Yes, yes," he interrupted nervously.

Nothing was known about Haskett in New York. He was vaguely supposed to have remained in the outer darkness from which his wife had been rescued, and Waythorn was one of the few who were aware that he had given up his business in Utica and followed her to New York in order to be near his little girl. In the days of his wooing, Waythorn had often met Lily on the doorstep, rosy and smiling, on her way "to see papa."

"I am so sorry," Mrs. Waythorn murmured.

He roused himself. "What does he want?"

"He wants to see her. You know she goes to him once a week."

"Well—he doesn't expect her to go to him now, does he?"

"No—he has heard of her illness; but he expects to come here."

2.   Adultery was the only legal grounds for divorce in New York state.

"Here?"

Mrs. Waythorn reddened under his gaze. They looked away from each other.

"I'm afraid he has the right. . . . You'll see. . . ." She made a proffer of the letter.

Waythorn moved away with a gesture of refusal. He stood staring about the softly-lighted room, which a moment before had seemed so full of bridal intimacy.

"I'm so sorry," she repeated. "If Lily could have been moved—"

"That's out of the question," he returned impatiently.

"I suppose so."

Her lip was beginning to tremble, and he felt himself a brute.

"He must come, of course," he said. "When is—his day?"

"I'm afraid—tomorrow."

"Very well. Send a note in the morning."

The butler entered to announce dinner.

Waythorn turned to his wife. "Come—you must be tired. It's beastly, but try to forget about it," he said, drawing her hand through his arm.

"You're so good, dear. I'll try," she whispered back.

Her face cleared at once, and as she looked at him across the flowers, between the rosy candleshades, he saw her lips waver back into a smile.

"How pretty everything is!" she sighed luxuriously.

He turned to the butler. "The champagne at once, please. Mrs. Waythorn is tired."

In a moment or two their eyes met above the sparkling glasses. Her own were quite clear and untroubled: he saw that she had obeyed his injunction and forgotten.

II

Waythorn, the next morning, went downtown earlier than usual. Haskett was not likely to come till the afternoon, but the instinct of flight drove him forth. He meant to stay away all day—he had thoughts of dining at his club. As his door closed behind him he reflected that before he opened it again it would have admitted another man who had as much right to enter it as himself, and the thought filled him with a physical repugnance.

He caught the elevated[3] at the employees' hour, and found himself crushed between two layers of pendulous humanity. At Eighth Street the man facing him wriggled out, and another took his place. Waythorn glanced up and saw that it was Gus Varick. The men were so close together that it was impossible to ignore the smile of recognition on Varick's handsome overblown face. And after all—why not? They had always been on good terms, and Varick had been divorced before Waythorn's attentions to his wife began. The two exchanged a word on the perennial grievance of the congested trains, and when a seat at their side was miraculously left empty the instinct of self-preservation made Waythorn slip into it after Varick.

The latter drew the stout man's breath of relief. "Lord—I was beginning to feel like a pressed flower." He leaned back, looking unconcernedly at Waythorn. "Sorry to hear that Sellers is knocked out again."

"Sellers?" echoed Waythorn, starting at his partner's name.

Varick looked surprised. "You didn't know he was laid up with the gout?"

"No. I've been away—I only got back last night." Waythorn felt himself reddening in anticipation of the other's smile.

"Ah—yes; to be sure. And Sellers' attack came on two days ago. I'm afraid he's pretty bad. Very awkward for me, as it happens, because he was just putting through a rather important thing for me."

"Ah?" Waythorn wondered vaguely since when Varick had been dealing in "important

3. The elevated train.

things." Hitherto he had dabbled only in the shallow pools of speculation, with which Waythorn's office did not usually concern itself.

It occurred to him that Varick might be talking at random, to relieve the strain of their propinquity. That strain was becoming momentarily more apparent to Waythorn, and when, at Cortlandt Street, he caught sight of an acquaintance and had a sudden vision of the picture he and Varick must present to an initiated eye, he jumped up with a muttered excuse.

"I hope you'll find Sellers better," said Varick civilly, and he stammered back: "If I can be of any use to you—" and let the departing crowd sweep him to the platform.

At his office he heard that Sellers was in fact ill with the gout, and would probably not be able to leave the house for some weeks.

"I'm sorry it should have happened so, Mr. Waythorn," the senior clerk said with affable significance. "Mr. Sellers was very much upset at the idea of giving you such a lot of extra work just now."

"Oh, that's no matter," said Waythorn hastily. He secretly welcomed the pressure of additional business, and was glad to think that, when the day's work was over, he would have to call at his partner's on the way home.

He was late for luncheon, and turned in at the nearest restaurant instead of going to his club. The place was full, and the waiter hurried him to the back of the room to capture the only vacant table. In the cloud of cigar smoke Waythorn did not at once distinguish his neighbors: but presently, looking about him, he saw Varick seated a few feet off. This time, luckily, they were too far apart for conversation, and Varick, who faced another way, had probably not even seen him; but there was an irony in their renewed nearness.

Varick was said to be fond of good living, and as Waythorn sat dispatching his hurried luncheon he looked across half enviously at the other's leisurely degustation of his meal. When Waythorn first saw him he had been helping himself with critical deliberation to a bit of Camembert at the ideal point of liquefaction, and now, the cheese removed, he was just pouring his *café double*[4] from its little two-storied earthen pot. He poured slowly, his ruddy profile bent over the task, and one beringed white hand steadying the lid of the coffeepot; then he stretched his other hand to the decanter of cognac at his elbow, filled a liqueur glass, took a tentative sip, and poured the brandy into his coffee cup.

Waythorn watched him in a kind of fascination. What was he thinking of—only of the flavor of the coffee and the liqueur? Had the morning's meeting left no more trace in his thoughts than on his face? Had his wife so completely passed out of his life that even this odd encounter with her present husband, within a week after her remarriage, was no more than an incident in his day? And as Waythorn mused, another idea struck him: had Haskett ever met Varick as Varick and he had just met? The recollection of Haskett perturbed him, and he rose and left the restaurant, taking a circuitous way out to escape the placid irony of Varick's nod.

It was after seven when Waythorn reached home. He thought the footman who opened the door looked at him oddly.

"How is Miss Lily?" he asked in haste.

"Doing very well, sir. A gentleman—"

"Tell Barlow to put off dinner for half an hour," Waythorn cut him off, hurrying upstairs.

He went straight to his room and dressed without seeing his wife. When he reached the drawing room she was there, fresh and radiant. Lily's day had been good; the doctor was not coming back that evening.

At dinner Waythorn told her of Sellers' illness and of the resulting complications. She listened sympathetically, adjuring him not to let himself be overworked, and asking vague feminine questions about the routine of the office. Then she gave him the chronicle of Lily's day; quoted the nurse and doctor, and told him who had called to inquire. He had never seen

4.   Strong, espresso-like coffee.

her more serene and unruffled. It struck him, with a curious pang, that she was very happy in being with him, so happy that she found a childish pleasure in rehearsing the trivial incidents of her day.

After dinner they went to the library, and the servant put the coffee and liqueurs on a low table before her and left the room. She looked singularly soft and girlish in her rosy-pale dress, against the dark leather of one of his bachelor armchairs. A day earlier the contrast would have charmed him.

He turned away now, choosing a cigar with affected deliberation.

"Did Haskett come?" he asked, with his back to her.

"Oh, yes—he came."

"You didn't see him, of course?"

She hesitated a moment. "I let the nurse see him."

That was all. There was nothing more to ask. He swung round toward her, applying a match to his cigar. Well, the thing was over for a week, at any rate. He would try not to think of it. She looked up at him, a trifle rosier than usual, with a smile in her eyes.

"Ready for your coffee, dear?"

He leaned against the mantelpiece, watching her as she lifted the coffeepot. The lamplight struck a gleam from her bracelets and tipped her soft hair with brightness. How light and slender she was, and how each gesture flowed into the next! She seemed a creature all compact of harmonies. As the thought of Haskett receded, Waythorn felt himself yielding again to the joy of possessorship. They were his, those white hands with their flitting motions, his the light haze of hair, the lips and eyes. . . .

She set down the coffeepot, and reaching for the decanter of cognac, measured off a liqueur glass and poured it into his cup.

Waythorn uttered a sudden exclamation.

"What is the matter?" she said, startled.

"Nothing; only—I don't take cognac in my coffee."

"Oh, how stupid of me," she cried.

Their eyes met, and she blushed a sudden agonized red.

III

Ten days later, Mr. Sellers, still housebound, asked Waythorn to call on his way downtown.

The senior partner, with his swaddled foot propped up by the fire, greeted his associate with an air of embarrassment.

"I'm sorry, my dear fellow; I've got to ask you to do an awkward thing for me."

Waythorn waited, and the other went on, after a pause apparently given to the arrangement of his phrases: "The fact is, when I was knocked out I had just gone into a rather complicated piece of business for—Gus Varick."

"Well?" said Waythorn, with an attempt to put him at his ease.

"Well—it's this way: Varick came to me the day before my attack. He had evidently had an inside tip from somebody, and had made about a hundred thousand. He came to me for advice, and I suggested his going in with Vanderlyn."

"Oh, the deuce!" Waythorn exclaimed. He saw in a flash what had happened. The investment was an alluring one, but required negotiation. He listened quietly while Sellers put the case before him, and, the statement ended, he said: "You think I ought to see Varick?"

"I'm afraid I can't as yet. The doctor is obdurate. And this thing can't wait. I hate to ask you, but no one else in the office knows the ins and outs of it."

Waythorn stood silent. He did not care a farthing for the success of Varick's venture, but the honor of the office was to be considered, and he could hardly refuse to oblige his partner.

"Very well," he said. "I'll do it."

That afternoon, apprised by telephone, Varick called at the office. Waythorn, waiting in his private room, wondered what the others thought of it. The newspapers, at the time of Mrs. Waythorn's marriage, had acquainted their readers with every detail of her previous matrimonial ventures, and Waythorn could fancy the clerks smiling behind Varick's back as he was ushered in.

Varick bore himself admirably. He was easy without being undignified, and Waythorn was conscious of cutting a much less impressive figure. Varick had no experience of business, and the talk prolonged itself for nearly an hour while Waythorn set forth with scrupulous precision the details of the proposed transaction.

"I'm awfully obliged to you," Varick said as he rose. "The fact is I'm not used to having much money to look after, and I don't want to make an ass of myself—" He smiled, and Waythorn could not help noticing that there was something pleasant about his smile. "It feels uncommonly queer to have enough cash to pay one's bills. I'd have sold my soul for it a few years ago!"

Waythorn winced at the allusion. He had heard it rumored that a lack of funds had been one of the determining causes of the Varick separation, but it did not occur to him that Varick's words were intentional. It seemed more likely that the desire to keep clear of embarrassing topics had fatally drawn him into one. Waythorn did not wish to be outdone in civility.

"We'll do the best we can for you," he said. "I think this is a good thing you're in."

"Oh, I'm sure it's immense. It's awfully good of you—" Varick broke off, embarrassed. "I suppose the thing's settled now—but if—"

"If anything happens before Sellers is about, I'll see you again," said Waythorn quietly. He was glad, in the end, to appear the more self-possessed of the two.

The course of Lily's illness ran smooth, and as the days passed Waythorn grew used to the idea of Haskett's weekly visit. The first time the day came round, he stayed out late, and questioned his wife as to the visit on his return. She replied at once that Haskett had merely seen the nurse downstairs, as the doctor did not wish anyone in the child's sickroom till after the crisis.

The following week Waythorn was again conscious of the recurrence of the day, but had forgotten it by the time he came home to dinner. The crisis of the disease came a few days later, with a rapid decline of fever, and the little girl was pronounced out of danger. In the rejoicing which ensued the thought of Haskett passed out of Waythorn's mind, and one afternoon, letting himself into the house with a latchkey, he went straight to his library without noticing a shabby hat and umbrella in the hall.

In the library he found a small effaced-looking man with a thinnish gray beard sitting on the edge of a chair. The stranger might have been a piano tuner, or one of those mysteriously efficient persons who are summoned in emergencies to adjust some detail of the domestic machinery. He blinked at Waythorn through a pair of gold-rimmed spectacles and said mildly: "Mr. Waythorn, I presume? I am Lily's father."

Waythorn flushed. "Oh—" he stammered uncomfortably. He broke off, disliking to appear rude. Inwardly he was trying to adjust the actual Haskett to the image of him projected by his wife's reminiscences. Waythorn had been allowed to infer that Alice's first husband was a brute.

"I am sorry to intrude," said Haskett, with his over-the-counter politeness.

"Don't mention it," returned Waythorn, collecting himself. "I suppose the nurse has been told?"

"I presume so. I can wait," said Haskett. He had a resigned way of speaking, as though life had worn down his natural powers of resistance.

Waythorn stood on the threshold, nervously pulling off his gloves.

"I'm sorry you've been detained. I will send for the nurse," he said; and as he opened the door he added with an effort: "I'm glad we can give you a good report of Lily." He winced as the *we* slipped out, but Haskett seemed not to notice it.

"Thank you, Mr. Waythorn, It's been an anxious time for me."

"Ah, well, that's past. Soon she'll be able to go to you." Waythorn nodded and passed out.

In his own room he flung himself down with a groan. He hated the womanish sensibility which made him suffer so acutely from the grotesque chances of life. He had known when he married that his wife's former husbands were both living, and that amid the multiplied contacts of modern existence there were a thousand chances to one that he would run against one or the other, yet he found himself as much disturbed by his brief encounter with Haskett as though the law had not obligingly removed all difficulties in the way of their meeting.

Waythorn sprang up and began to pace the room nervously. He had not suffered half as much from his two meetings with Varick. It was Haskett's presence in his own house that made the situation so intolerable. He stood still, hearing steps in the passage.

"This way, please," he heard the nurse say. Haskett was being taken upstairs, then: not a corner of the house but was open to him. Waythorn dropped into another chair, staring vaguely ahead of him. On his dressing table stood a photograph of Alice, taken when he had first known her. She was Alice Varick then—how fine and exquisite he had thought her! Those were Varick's pearls about her neck. At Waythorn's instance they had been returned before her marriage. Had Haskett ever given her any trinkets—and what had become of them, Waythorn wondered? He realized suddenly that he knew very little of Haskett's past or present situation; but from the man's appearance and manner of speech he could reconstruct with curious precision the surroundings of Alice's first marriage. And it startled him to think that she had, in the background of her life, a phase of existence so different from anything with which he had connected her. Varick, whatever his faults, was a gentleman, in the conventional, traditional sense of the term: the sense which at that moment seemed, oddly enough, to have most meaning to Waythorn. He and Varick had the same social habits, spoke the same language, understood the same allusions. But this other man . . . it was grotesquely uppermost in Waythorn's mind that Haskett had worn a made-up tie attached with an elastic. Why should that ridiculous detail symbolize the whole man? Waythorn was exasperated by his own paltriness, but the fact of the tie expanded, forced itself on him, became as it were the key to Alice's past. He could see her, as Mrs. Haskett, sitting in a "front parlor" furnished in plush, with a pianola, and copy of *Ben Hur*[5] on the center table. He could see her going to the theater with Haskett—or perhaps even to a "Church Sociable"—she in a "picture hat" and Haskett in a black frock coat, a little creased, with the made-up tie on an elastic. On the way home they would stop and look at the illuminated shop windows, lingering over the photographs of New York actresses. On Sunday afternoons Haskett would take her for a walk, pushing Lily ahead of them in a white enameled perambulator, and Waythorn had a vision of the people they would stop and talk to. He could fancy how pretty Alice must have looked, in a dress adroitly constructed from the hints of a New York fashion paper, and how she must have looked down on the other women, chafing at her life, and secretly feeling that she belonged in a bigger place.

For the moment his foremost thought was one of wonder at the way in which she had shed the phase of existence which her marriage with Haskett implied. It was as if her whole aspect, every gesture, every inflection, every allusion, were a studied negation of that period of her life. If she had denied being married to Haskett she could hardly have stood more convicted of duplicity than in this obliteration of the self which had been his wife.

Waythorn started up, checking himself in the analysis of her motives. What right had he to create a fantastic effigy of her and then pass judgment on it? She had spoken vaguely of her first marriage as unhappy, had hinted, with becoming reticence, that Haskett had wrought havoc among her young illusions. . . . It was a pity for Waythorn's peace of mind that Haskett's

5. Lew Wallace's popular novel (1892), set in Rome during the period of the Roman Empire.

very inoffensiveness shed a new light on the nature of those illusions. A man would rather think that his wife has been brutalized by her first husband than that the process has been reversed.

IV

"Mr. Waythorn, I don't like that French governess of Lily's."

Haskett, subdued and apologetic, stood before Waythorn in the library, revolving his shabby hat in his hand.

Waythorn, surprised in his armchair over the evening paper, stared back perplexedly at his visitor.

"You'll excuse my asking to see you," Haskett continued. "But this is my last visit, and I thought if I could have a word with you it would be a better way than writing to Mrs. Waythorn's lawyer."

Waythorn rose uneasily. He did not like the French governess either; but that was irrelevant.

"I am not so sure of that," he returned stiffly; "but since you wish it I will give your message to—my wife." He always hesitated over the possessive pronoun in addressing Haskett.

The latter sighed. "I don't know as that will help much. She didn't like it when I spoke to her."

Waythorn turned red. "When did you see her?" he asked.

"Not since the first day I came to see Lily—right after she was taken sick. I remarked to her then that I didn't like the governess."

Waythorn made no answer. He remembered distinctly that, after that first visit, he had asked his wife if she had seen Haskett. She had lied to him then, but she had respected his wishes since; and the incident cast a curious light on her character. He was sure she would not have seen Haskett that first day if she had divined that Waythorn would object, and the fact that she did not divine it was almost as disagreeable to the latter as the discovery that she had lied to him.

"I don't like the woman," Haskett was repeating with mild persistency. "She ain't straight, Mr. Waythorn—she'll teach the child to be underhand. I've noticed a change in Lily—she's too anxious to please—and she don't always tell the truth. She used to be the straightest child, Mr. Waythorn—" He broke off, his voice a little thick. "Not but what I want her to have a stylish education," he ended.

Waythorn was touched. "I'm sorry, Mr. Haskett; but frankly, I don't quite see what I can do."

Haskett hesitated. Then he laid his hat on the table, and advanced to the hearthrug, on which Waythorn was standing. There was nothing aggressive in his manner, but he had the solemnity of a timid man resolved on a decisive measure.

"There's just one thing you can do, Mr. Waythorn," he said. "You can remind Mrs. Waythorn that, by the decree of the courts, I am entitled to have a voice in Lily's bringing-up." He paused, and went on more deprecatingly: "I'm not the kind to talk about enforcing my rights, Mr. Waythorn. I don't know as I think a man is entitled to rights he hasn't known how to hold on to; but this business of the child is different. I've never let go there—and I never mean to."

The scene left Waythorn deeply shaken. Shamefacedly, in indirect ways, he had been finding out about Haskett; and all that he had learned was favorable. The little man, in order to be near his daughter, had sold out his share in a profitable business in Utica, and accepted a modest clerkship in a New York manufacturing house. He boarded in a shabby street and had few acquaintances. His passion for Lily filled his life. Waythorn felt that this exploration of Haskett was like groping about with a dark lantern in his wife's past; but he saw now that there were recesses his lantern had not explored. He had never inquired into the exact circumstances of his wife's first matrimonial rupture. On the surface all had been fair. It was she who had obtained the divorce, and the court had given her the child. But Waythorn knew how many ambiguities such a verdict might cover. The mere fact that Haskett retained a right over his daughter implied an unsuspected compromise. Waythorn was an idealist. He always refused to recognize unpleasant contingencies till he found himself confronted with them, and then he saw them followed by a spectral train of consequences. His next days were thus haunted, and he determined to try to lay the ghosts by conjuring them up in his wife's presence.

When he repeated Haskett's request a flame of anger passed over her face; but she subdued it instantly and spoke with a slight quiver of outraged motherhood.

"It is very ungentlemanly of him," she said.

The word grated on Waythorn. "That is neither here nor there. It's a bare question of rights."

She murmured: "It's not as if he could ever be a help to Lily—"

Waythorn flushed. This was even less to his taste. "The question is," he repeated, "what authority has he over her?"

She looked downward, twisting herself a little in her seat. "I am willing to see him—I thought you objected," she faltered.

In a flash he understood that she knew the extent of Haskett's claims. Perhaps it was not the first time she had resisted them.

"My objecting has nothing to do with it," he said coldly; "if Haskett has a right to be consulted you must consult him."

She burst into tears, and he saw that she expected him to regard her as a victim.

Haskett did not abuse his rights. Waythorn had felt miserably sure that he would not. But the governess was dismissed, and from time to time the little man demanded an interview with Alice. After the first outburst she accepted the situation with her usual adaptability. Haskett had once reminded Waythorn of the piano tuner, and Mrs. Waythorn, after a month or two, appeared to class him with that domestic familiar. Waythorn could not but respect the father's tenacity. At first he had tried to cultivate the suspicion that Haskett might be "up to" something, that he had an object in securing a foothold in the house. But in his heart Waythorn was sure of Haskett's single-mindedness; he even guessed in the latter a mild contempt for such advantages as his relation with the Waythorns might offer. Haskett's sincerity of purpose made him invulnerable, and his successor had to accept him as a lien on the property.

Mr. Sellers was sent to Europe to recover from his gout, and Varick's affairs hung on Waythorn's hands. The negotiations were prolonged and complicated; they necessitated frequent conferences between the two men, and the interests of the firm forbade Waythorn's suggesting that his client should transfer his business to another office.

Varick appeared well in the transaction. In moments of relaxation his coarse streak appeared, and Waythorn dreaded his geniality; but in the office he was concise and clear-headed, with a flattering deference to Waythorn's judgment. Their business relations being so affably established, it would have been absurd for the two men to ignore each other in society. The first time they met in a drawing room, Varick took up their intercourse in the same easy key, and his hostess' grateful glance obliged Waythorn to respond to it. After that they ran across each other frequently, and one evening at a ball Waythorn, wandering through the remoter rooms, came upon Varick seated beside his wife. She colored a little, and faltered in what she was saying; but Varick nodded to Waythorn without rising, and the latter strolled on.

In the carriage, on the way home, he broke out nervously: "I didn't know you spoke to Varick."

Her voice trembled a little. "It's the first time—he happened to be standing near me; I didn't know what to do. It's so awkward, meeting everywhere—and he said you had been very kind about some business."

"That's different," said Waythorn.

She paused a moment. "I'll do just as you wish," she returned pliantly. "I thought it would be less awkward to speak to him when we meet."

Her pliancy was beginning to sicken him. Had she really no will of her own—no theory about her relation to these men? She had accepted Haskett—did she mean to accept Varick? It was "less awkward," as she had said, and her instinct was to evade difficulties or to circumvent them. With sudden vividness Waythorn saw how the instinct had developed. She was "as easy as an old shoe"—a shoe that too many feet had worn. Her elasticity was the result of tension in too many different directions. Alice Haskett—Alice Varick—Alice Waythorn—she had been each in turn, and had left hanging to each name a little of her privacy, a little of her personality, a little of the inmost self where the unknown god abides.

"Yes—it's better to speak to Varick," said Waythorn wearily.

V

The winter wore on, and society took advantage of the Waythorns' acceptance of Varick. Harassed hostesses were grateful to them for bridging over a social difficulty, and Mrs. Waythorn was held up as a miracle of good taste. Some experimental spirits could not resist the diversion of throwing Varick and his former wife together, and there were those who thought he found a zest in the propinquity. But Mrs. Waythorn's conduct remained irreproachable. She neither avoided Varick nor sought him out. Even Waythorn could not but admit that she had discovered the solution of the newest social problem.

He had married her without giving much thought to that problem. He had fancied that a woman can shed her past like a man. But now he saw that Alice was bound to hers both by the circumstances which forced her into continued relation with it, and by the traces it had left on her nature. With grim irony Waythorn compared himself to a member of a syndicate. He held so many shares in his wife's personality and his predecessors were his partners in the business. If there had been any element of passion in the transaction he would have felt less deteriorated by it. The fact that Alice took her change of husbands like a change of weather reduced the situation to mediocrity. He could have forgiven her for blunders, for excesses; for resisting Haskett, for yielding to Varick; for anything but her acquiescence and her tact. She reminded him of a juggler tossing knives; but the knives were blunt and she knew they would never cut her.

And then, gradually, habit formed a protecting surface for his sensibilities. If he paid for each day's comfort with the small change of his illusions, he grew daily to value the comfort more and set less store upon the coin. He had drifted into a dulling propinquity with Haskett and Varick and he took refuge in the cheap revenge of satirizing the situation. He even began to reckon up the advantages which accrued from it, to ask himself if it were not better to own a third of a wife who knew how to make a man happy than a whole one who had lacked opportunity to acquire the art. For it *was* an art, and made up, like all others, of concessions, eliminations and embellishments; of lights judiciously thrown and shadows skillfully softened. His wife knew exactly how to manage the lights, and he knew exactly to what training she owed her skill. He even tried to trace the source of his obligations, to discriminate between the influences which had combined to produce his domestic happiness: he perceived that Haskett's commonness had made Alice worship good breeding, while Varick's liberal construction of the marriage bond had taught her to value the conjugal virtues; so that he was directly indebted to his predecessors for the devotion which made his life easy if not inspiring.

From this phase he passed into that of complete acceptance. He ceased to satirize himself because time dulled the irony of the situation and the joke lost its humor with its sting. Even the sight of Haskett's hat on the hall table had ceased to touch the springs of epigram. The hat was often seen there now, for it had been decided that it was better for Lily's father to visit her than for the little girl to go to his boardinghouse. Waythorn, having acquiesced in this arrangement, had been surprised to find how little difference it made. Haskett was never obtrusive, and the few visitors who met him on the stairs were unaware of his identity. Waythorn did not know how often he saw Alice, but with himself Haskett was seldom in contact.

One afternoon, however, he learned on entering that Lily's father was waiting to see him. In the library he found Haskett occupying a chair in his usual provisional way. Waythorn always felt grateful to him for not leaning back.

"I hope you'll excuse me, Mr. Waythorn," he said rising. "I wanted to see Mrs. Waythorn about Lily, and your man asked me to wait here till she came in."

"Of course," said Waythorn, remembering that a sudden leak had that morning given over the drawing room to the plumbers.

He opened his cigar case and held it out to his visitor, and Haskett's acceptance seemed to mark a fresh stage in their intercourse. The spring evening was chilly, and Waythorn invited his guest to draw up his chair to the fire. He meant to find an excuse to leave Haskett in a moment; but he was tired and cold, and after all the little man no longer jarred on him.

The two were enclosed in the intimacy of their blended cigar smoke when the door opened and Varick walked into the room. Waythorn rose abruptly. It was the first time that Varick had come to his house, and the surprise of seeing him, combined with the singular inopportuneness of his arrival, gave a new edge to Waythorn's blunted sensibilities. He stared at his visitor without speaking.

Varick seemed too preoccupied to notice his host's embarrassment.

"My dear fellow," he exclaimed in his most expansive tone, "I must apologize for tumbling in on you in this way, but I was too late to catch you downtown, and so I thought—"

He stopped short, catching sight of Haskett, and his sanguine color deepened to a flush which spread vividly under his scant blond hair. But in a moment he recovered himself and nodded slightly. Haskett returned the bow in silence, and Waythorn was still groping for speech when the footman came in carrying a tea table.

The intrusion offered a welcome vent to Waythorn's nerves. "What the deuce are you bringing this here for?" he said sharply.

"I beg your pardon, sir, but the plumbers are still in the drawing room, and Mrs. Waythorn said she would have tea in the library." The footman's perfectly respectful tone implied a reflection on Waythorn's reasonableness.

"Oh, very well," said the latter resignedly, and the footman proceeded to open the folding tea table and set out its complicated appointments. While this interminable process continued the three men stood motionless, watching it with a fascinated stare, till Waythorn, to break the silence, said to Varick, "Won't you have a cigar?"

He held out the case he had just tendered to Haskett, and Varick helped himself with a smile. Waythorn looked about for a match, and finding none, proffered a light from his own cigar. Haskett, in the background, held his ground mildly, examining his cigar tip now and then, and stepping forward at the right moment to knock its ashes into the fire.

The footman at last withdrew, and Varick immediately began: "If I could just say half a word to you about this business—"

"Certainly," stammered Waythorn; "in the dining room—"

But as he placed his hand on the door it opened from without, and his wife appeared on the threshold.

She came in fresh and smiling, in her street dress and hat, shedding a fragrance from the boa which she loosened in advancing.

"Shall we have tea in here, dear?" she began; and then she caught sight of Varick. Her smile deepened, veiling a slight tremor of surprise.

"Why, how do you do?" she said with a distinct note of pleasure.

As she shook hands with Varick she saw Haskett standing behind him. Her smile faded for a moment, but she recalled it quickly, with a scarcely perceptible side glance at Waythorn.

"How do you do, Mr. Haskett?" she said, and shook hands with him a shade less cordially.

The three men stood awkwardly before her, till Varick, always the most self-possessed, dashed into an explanatory phrase.

"We—I had to see Waythorn a moment on business," he stammered, brick-red from chin to nape.

Haskett stepped forward with his air of mild obstinacy. "I am sorry to intrude; but you appointed five o'clock—" he directed his resigned glance to the timepiece on the mantel.

She swept aside their embarrassment with a charming gesture of hospitality.

"I'm so sorry—I'm always late; but the afternoon was so lovely." She stood drawing off her gloves, propitiatory and graceful, diffusing about her a sense of ease and familiarity in which the situation lost its grotesqueness. "But before talking business," she added brightly, "I'm sure everyone wants a cup of tea."

She dropped into her low chair by the tea table, and the two visitors, as if drawn by her smile, advanced to receive the cups she held out.

She glanced about for Waythorn, and he took the third cup with a laugh.

1904

Mary Austin
(1868–1934)

Born in Carlinville, Illinois, the daughter of George and Susanna Hunter, Mary and her two brothers were raised by their widowed mother after their father died when Mary was 10. At 19 she graduated from Blackburn College in Carlinville, and almost immediately the Hunters moved to California to try homesteading in the Tejon area, south of Bakersfield. Here she first became attracted to the desert and to the history of the Native Americans and Spanish missions in California. She taught school, nursed her writing ambitions, and, in 1891, married Stafford W. Austin. In time they moved to the Owens River area, west of Death Valley, where they settled in Lone Pine. The birth of a retarded daughter in 1892 and her husband's general failure to provide adequate financial support forced her more and more to develop her own resources; eventually her daughter was placed in an institution, and after a long separation the parents divorced in 1914.

In 1892 she published her first story in the *Overland Monthly*. Others followed, and in *The Land of Little Rain* (1803), a collection of sketches of the Southwest, she had her first national success. Before long she had joined the artistic community at Carmel, California. In 1908 she left California to travel to Europe in search of spiritual healing, and when she returned she lived for twelve years in New York City before returning to the West. She spent her last ten years in Santa Fé, where her adobe home became a center of literary and cultural activity. A prolific writer, she published approximately thirty books and contributed over 200 pieces to the periodicals of her day.

Her most critically admired work, centered on the Southwest, has earned her a reputation as a skillful nature writer and a recorder of Western Americana, emphasizing the relationship between the land and its inhabitants. After *The Land of Little Rain* came *Isidro* (1905), a historical romance set in the days of Spanish rule of California, and *Lost Borders* (1909), stories set in the same general area. In *The Arrow Maker* (1911), a play, she portrayed a Paiute medicine woman at odds with her society. Stories drawing on Indian lore are collected in *The Basket Woman* (1910), *The Trail Book* (1918), and *One-Smoke Stories* (1934). Often her themes stress feminist views of the position of women, as in novels like *Santa Lucia: A Common Story* (1908), about three women and their problems in marriage, and *A Woman of Genius* (1912), about a woman's attempt to escape the restrictions of her Midwestern upbringing. Sometimes she turns to social reform, as in *The Ford* (1917), a novel about land usage and water rights in southern California. In her later years she capitalized on her fame in her role as social activist, working to advance women's and Native Americans' causes and representing New Mexico at the Boulder Dam Conference of 1927, where she argued for local control of the Colorado River water.

Austin's novels, in addition to those named above, include *Outland* (1910), a romance; *No. 26 Jayne Street* (1920), set in New York City; and *Starry Adventure* (1931), set in New Mexico. A mystical strain appears especially in *Christ in Italy* (1912); *The Man Jesus* (1915; reissued as *A Small Town Man*, 1925); and *Can Prayer Be Answered?* (1934). *Earth Horizon* (1932) is an autobiography. Useful collections of her work include *Western Trails*, ed. Melody Graulich (1987), and *Stories from the Country of Lost Borders*, ed. Marjorie Pryse (1987). A study is Esther Lanigan Stineman, *Mary Austin: Song of a Maverick* (1989).

The Fakir[1]

Whenever I come up to judgment, and am hard pushed to make good on my own account (as I expect to be), I shall mention the case of Netta Saybrick, for on the face of it, and by all the traditions in which I was bred, I behaved rather handsomely. I say on the face of it, for except in the matter of keeping my mouth shut afterward, I am not so sure I had anything to do with the affair. It was one of those incidents that from some crest of sheer inexplicableness seems about to direct the imagination over vast tracts of human experience, only to fall away into a pit of its own digging, all fouled with weed and sand. But, by keeping memory and attention fixed on its pellucid instant as it mounted against the sun, I can still see the Figure shining through it as I saw it that day at Posada, with the glimmering rails of the P. and S. running out behind it, thin lines of light toward the bar of Heaven.

Up till that time Netta Saybrick had never liked me, though I never laid it to any other account than Netta's being naturally a little fool; afterward she explained to me that it was because she thought I gave myself airs. The Saybricks lived in the third house from mine, around the corner, so that our back doors overlooked each other, and up till the coming of Doctor Challoner there had never been anything in Netta's conduct that the most censorious of the villagers could remark upon. Nor afterward, for that matter. The Saybricks had been married four years, and the baby was about two. He was not an interesting child to anybody but his mother, and even Netta was sometimes thought to be not quite absorbed in him.

Saybrick was a miner, one of the best drillers in our district, and consequently away from home much of the time. Their house was rather larger than their needs, and Netta, to avoid loneliness more than for profit, let out a room or two. That was the way she happened to fall into the hands of the Fakir.

Franklin Challoner had begun by being a brilliant and promising student of medicine. I had known him when his natural gifts prophesied the unusual, but I had known him rather better than most, and I was not surprised to have him turn up five years later at Maverick as a Fakir.

1. From *Lost Borders* (1909).

It had begun in his being poor, and having to work his way through the Medical College at the cost of endless pains and mortification to himself. Like most brilliant people, Challoner was sensitive and had an enormous egotism, and, what nearly always goes with it, the faculty of being horribly fascinating to women. It was thought very creditable of him to have put himself through college at his own charge, though in reality it proved a great social waste. I have a notion that the courage, endurance, and steadfastness which should have done Frank Challoner a lifetime was squeezed out of him by the stress of those overworked, starved, mortifying years. His egotism made it important to his happiness to keep the centre of any stage, and this he could do in school by sheer brilliance of scholarship and the distinction of his struggles. But afterward, when he had to establish himself without capital among strangers, he found himself impoverished of manliness. Always there was the compelling need of his temperament to stand well with people, and almost the only means of accomplishing it his poverty allowed was the dreadful facility with which he made himself master of women. I suppose this got his real ability discredited among his professional fellows. Between that and the sharp need of money, and the incredible appetite which people have for being fooled, somewhere in the Plateau of Fatigue between promise and accomplishment, Frank Challoner lost himself. Therefore, I was not surprised when he turned up finally at Maverick, lecturing on phrenology, and from the shape of their craniums advising country people of their proper careers at three dollars a sitting. He advertised to do various things in the way of medical practice that had a dubious sound.

It was court week when he came, and the only possible lodging to be found at Netta Saybrick's. Doctor Challoner took the two front rooms as being best suited to his clients and himself, and I believe he did very well. I was not particularly pleased to see him, on account of having known him before, not wishing to prosecute the acquaintance; and about that time Indian George brought me word that a variety of *redivivus* long sought was blooming that year on a certain clayey tract over toward Waban. It was not supposed to flower oftener than once in seven years, and I was five days finding it. That was why I never knew what went on at Mrs. Saybrick's. Nobody else did, apparently, for I never heard a breath of gossip, and *that* must have been Doctor Challoner's concern, for I am sure Netta would never have known how to avoid it.

Netta was pretty, and Saybrick had been gone five months. Challoner had a thin, romantic face, and eyes—even I had to admit the compelling attraction of his eyes; and his hands were fine and white. Saybrick's hands were cracked, broken-nailed, a driller's hands, and one of them was twisted from the time he was leaded, working on the Lucky Jim. If it came to that, though, Netta's husband might have been anything he pleased, and Challoner would still have had his way with her. He always did with women, as if to make up for not having it with the world. And the life at Maverick was deadly, appallingly dull. The stark houses, the rubbishy streets, the women who went about in them in calico wrappers, the draggling speech of the men, the wide, shadowless table-lands, the hard, bright skies, and the days all of one pattern, that went so stilly by that you only knew it was afternoon when you smelled the fried cabbage Mrs. Mulligan was cooking for supper.

At this distance I cannot say that I blamed Netta, am not sure of not being glad that she had her hour of the rose-red glow—*if* she had it. You are to bear in mind that all this time I was camping out in the creosote belt on the slope of Waban, and as to what had really happened neither Netta nor Challoner ever said a word. I keep saying things like this about Netta's being pretty and all, just as if I thought they had anything to do with it; truth is, the man had just a gift of taking souls, and I, even I, judicious and disapproving—but you shall hear.

At that time the stage from Maverick was a local affair going down to Posada, where passengers from the P. and S. booked for the Mojave line, returning after a wait of hours on the same day.

It happened that the morning I came back from Waban, Doctor Challoner left Maverick.

Being saddle weary, I had planned to send on the horses by Indian George, and take the stage where it crossed my trail an hour out from Posada, going home on it in the afternoon. I remember poking the botany-case under the front seat and turning round to be hit straight between the eyes, as it were, by Netta Saybrick and Doctor Challoner. The doctor was wearing his usual air of romantic mystery; wearing it a little awry—or perhaps it was only knowing the man that made me read the perturbation under it. But it was plain to see what Netta was about. Her hat was tilted by the jolting of the stage, while alkali dust lay heavy on the folds of her dress, and she never *would* wear hair-pins enough; but there was that in every turn and posture, in every note of her flat, childish voice, that acknowledged the man beside her. Her excitement was almost febrile. It was part of Netta's unsophistication that she seemed not to know that she gave herself away, and the witness of it was that she had brought the baby.

You would not have believed that any woman would plan to run away with a man like Frank Challoner and take that great, heavy-headed, drooling child. But that is what Netta had done. I am not sure it was maternal instinct, either; she probably did not know what else to do with him. He had pale, protruding eyes and reddish hair, and every time he clawed at the doctor's sleeve I could see the man withhold a shudder.

I suppose it was my being in a manner confounded by this extraordinary situation that made it possible for Doctor Challoner to renew his acquaintance with more warmth than the facts allowed. He fairly pitched himself into an intimacy of reminiscence, and it was partly to pay him for this, I suppose, and partly to gratify a natural curiosity, that made me so abrupt with him afterward. I remember looking around, when we got down, at the little station where I must wait two hours for the return stage, at the seven unpainted pine cabins, at the eating-house, and the store, and the two saloons, in the instant hope of refuge, and then out across the alkali flat fringed with sparse, unwholesome pickle-weed, and deciding that that would not do, and then turning round to take the situation by the throat, as it were. There was Netta, with that great child dragging on her arm and her hat still on one side, with a silly consciousness of Doctor Challoner's movements, and he still trying for the jovial note of old acquaintances met by chance. In a moment more I had him around the corner of the stationhouse and out with my question.

"Doctor Challoner, are you running away with Netta Saybrick?"

"Well, no," trying to carry it jauntily; "I think she is running away with me." Then, all his pretension suddenly sagging on him like an empty cayaque: "On my soul, I don't know what's got into the woman. I was as surprised as you were when she got on the stage with me"—on my continuing to look steadily at him—"she was a pretty little thing ... and the life is devilish dull there. . . . I suppose I flirted a little"—blowing himself out, as it were, with an assumption of honesty—"on my word, there was nothing more than that."

Flirted! He called it that; but women do not take their babies and run away from home for the sake of a little flirting. The life was devilish dull—did he need to tell me that! And she was pretty—well, whatever had happened he was bound to tell me that it was nothing, and I was bound to behave as if I believed him.

"She will go back," he began to say, looking bleak and drawn in the searching light. "She must go back! She must!"

"Well, maybe you can persuade her," said I; but I relented after that enough to take care of the baby while he and Netta went for a walk.

The whole mesa and the flat crawled with heat, and the steel rails ran on either side of them like thin fires, as if the slagged track were the appointed way that Netta had chosen to walk. They went out as far as the section-house and back toward the deserted station till I could almost read their faces clear, and turned again, back and forth through the heat-fogged atmosphere like the figures in a dream. I could see this much from their postures, that Challoner was trying to hold to some consistent attitude which he had adopted, and Netta wasn't understanding it. I could see her throw out her hands in a gesture of abandonment, and then I saw her stand as if the Pit yawned under her feet. The baby slept on a station bench, and I kept the flies from him with a branch of pickle-weed. I was out of it, smitten anew with the utter inutility of all the standards which were not bred of experience, but merely came down to me with the family teaspoons. Seen by the fierce desert light they looked like the spoons, thin and worn at the edges. I should have been ashamed to offer them to Netta Saybrick. It was this sense of detached helplessness toward the life at Maverick that Netta afterward explained she and the other women sensed but misread in me. They couldn't account for it on any grounds except that I felt myself above them. And all the time I was sick with the strained, meticulous inadequacy of my own soul. I understood well enough, then, that the sense of personal virtue comes to most women through an intervening medium of sedulous social guardianship. It is only when they love that it reaches directly to the centre of consciousness, as if it were ultimately nothing more than the instinctive movement of right love to preserve itself by a voluntary seclusion. It was not her faithlessness to Saybrick that tormented Netta out there between the burning rails; it was going back to him that was the intolerable offence. Passion had come upon her like a flame-burst, heaven-sent; she justified it on the grounds of its completeness, and lacked the sophistication for any other interpretation.

Challoner was a bad man, but he was not bad enough to reveal to Netta Saybrick the vulgar cheapness of his own relation to the incident. Besides, he hadn't time. In two hours the return stage for Maverick left the station, and he could never in that time get Netta Saybrick to realize the gulf between his situation and hers.

He came back to the station after a while on some pretext, and said, with his back to Netta, moving his lips with hardly any sound: "She must go back on the stage. She must!" Then with a sudden setting of his jaws, "You've got to help me." He sat down beside me, and began to devote himself to the baby and the flies.

Netta stood out for a while expecting him, and then came and sat provisionally on the edge of the station platform, ready at the slightest hint of an opportunity to carry him away into the glimmering heat out toward the station-house, and resume the supremacy of her poor charms.

She was resenting my presence as an interference, and I believe always cherished a thought that but for the accident of my being there the incident might have turned out differently. I could see that Challoner's attitude, whatever it was, was beginning to make itself felt. She was looking years older, and yet somehow pitifully puzzled and young, as if the self of her had had a wound which her intelligence had failed to grasp. I could see, too, that Challoner had made up his mind to be quit of her, quietly if he could, but at any risk of a scene, still to be quit. And it was forty minutes till stage-time.

Challoner sat on the bare station bench with his arm out above the baby protectingly—it was a manner always effective—and began to talk about "goodness," of all things in the world. Don't ask me what he said. It was the sort of talk many women would have called beautiful, and though it was mostly addressed to me, it was every word of it directed to Netta Saybrick's soul. Much of it went high and wide, but I could catch the pale reflection of it in her face like a miner guessing the sort of day it is from the glimmer of it on a puddle at the bottom of a shaft. In it Netta saw a pair of heroic figures renouncing a treasure they had found for the sake of the bitter goodness by which the world is saved. They had had the courage to take it while they could, but were much too exemplary to enjoy it at the cost of pain to any other heart. He started with the assumption that she meant to go back to Maverick, and recurred to it with a skilful and hypnotic insistence, painting upon her mind by large and general inference the picture of himself, helped greatly in his career by her noble renunciation of him. As a matter of fact, Saybrick, if his wife really had gone away with Doctor Challoner, would have followed him up and shot him, I suppose, and no end of vulgar and disagreeable things might have come from the affair; but Challoner managed to keep it on so high a plane that even I never thought of them until long afterward. And right here is where the uncertainty as to the part I really played begins. I can never make up my mind whether Challoner, from long practice in such affairs, had hit upon just the right note of extrication, or whether, cornered, he fell back desperately on the eternal rightness. And what was he, to know rightness at his need?

He was terribly in earnest, holding Netta's eyes with his own; his forehead sweated, hollows showed about his eyes, and the dreadful slackness of the corner of the mouth that comes of the whole mind being drawn away upon the object of attack to the neglect of its defences. He was so bent on getting Netta fixed in the idea that she must go back to Maverick that if she had not been a good deal of a fool she must have seen that he had given away the whole situation into my hands. I believed—I hope—I did the right thing, but I am not sure I could have helped taking the cue which was pressed upon me; he was as bad as they made them, but there I was lending my whole soul to the accomplishment of his purpose, which was, briefly, to get comfortably off from an occasion in which he had behaved very badly.

All this time Challoner kept a conscious attention on the stage stables far at the other end of the shadeless street. The moment he saw the driver come out of it with the horses, the man's soul fairly creaked with the release of tension. It released, too, an accession of that power of personal fascination for which he was remarkable.

Netta sat with her back to the street, and the beautiful solicitude with which he took up the baby at that moment, smoothed its dress and tied on its little cap, had no significance for her. It was not until she heard the rattle of the stage turning into the road that she stood up suddenly, alarmed. Challoner put the baby into my arms.

Did I tell you that all this time between me and this man there ran the inexplicable sense of being bonded together; the same suggestion of a superior and exclusive intimacy which ensnared poor Netta Saybrick no doubt, the absolute call of self and sex by which a man, past all reasonableness and belief, ranges a woman on his side. He was a Fakir, a common quack, a scoundrel if you will, but there was the call. I had answered it. I was under the impression, though not remembering what he said, when he had handed me that great lump of a child, that I had received a command to hold on to it, to get into the stage with it, and not to give it up on any consideration; and without saying anything, I had promised.

I do not know if it was the look that must have passed between us at that, or the squeal of the running-gear that shattered her dream, but I perceived on the instant that Netta had had a glimpse of where she stood. She saw herself for the moment a fallen woman, forsaken, despised. There was the Pit before her which Challoner's desertion and my knowledge of it had digged. She clutched once at her bosom and at her skirts as if already she heard the hiss of crawling shame. Then it was that Challoner turned toward her with the Look.

It rose in his face and streamed to her from his eyes as though it were the one thing in the world of a completeness equal to the anguish in her breast, as though, before it rested there, it had been through all the troubled intricacies of sin, and come upon the root of a superior fineness that every soul feels piteously to lie at the back of all its own affronting vagaries, brooding over it in a large, gentle way. It was the forgiveness—nay, the obliteration of offence—and the most Challoner could have known of forgiveness was his own great need of it. Out of that Look I could see the woman's soul rising rehabilitated, astonished, and on the instant, out there beyond the man and the woman, between the thin fiery lines of the rails, leading back to the horizon, the tall, robed Figure writing in the sand.

Oh, it was a hallucination, if you like, of the hour, the place, the perturbed mind, the dazzling glimmer of the alkali flat, of the incident of a sinful woman and a common fakir, faking an absolution that he might the more easily avoid an inconvenience, and I the tool made to see incredibly by some trick of suggestion how impossible it should be that any but the chief of sinners should understand forgiveness. But the Look continued to hold the moment in solution, while the woman climbed out of the Pit. I saw her put out her hand with the instinctive gesture of the sinking, and Challoner take it with the formality of farewell; and as the dust of the arriving stage billowed up between them, the Figure turned, fading, dissolving . . . but with the Look, consoling, obliterating. . . . He too . . . !

"It was very good of you, Mrs. Saybrick, to give me so much of a good-bye . . ." Challoner was saying as he put Netta into the stage; and then to me, "You must take good care of her . . . good-bye."

"Good-bye, Frank"—I had never called Doctor Challoner by his name before. I did not like him well enough to call him by it at any time, but there was the Look; it had reached out and enwrapped me in a kind of rarefied intimacy of extenuation and understanding. He stood on the station platform staring steadily after us, and as long as we had sight of him in the thick, bitter dust, the Look held.

If this were a story merely, or a story of Franklin Challoner, it would end there. He never thought of us again, you may depend, except to thank his stars for getting so lightly off, and to go on in the security of his success to other episodes from which he returned as scatheless.

But I found out in a very few days that whether it was to take rank as an incident or an event in Netta Saybrick's life depended on whether or not I said anything about it. Nobody had taken any notice of her day's ride to Posada. Saybrick came home in about ten days, and Netta seemed uncommonly glad to see him, as if in the preoccupation of his presence she found a solace for her fears.

But from the day of our return she had evinced an extraordinary liking for my company. She would be running in and out of the house at all hours, offering to help me with my sewing or to stir up a cake, kindly offices that had to be paid in kind; and if I slipped into the neighbors' on an errand, there a moment after would come Netta. Very soon it became clear to me that she was afraid of what I might tell. So long as she had me under her immediate eye she could be sure I was not taking away her character, but when I was not, she must have suffered horribly. I might have told, too, by the woman's code; she was really not respectable, and we made a great deal of that in Maverick. I might refuse to have anything to do with her and justified myself explaining why.

But Netta was not sure how much I knew, and could not risk betrayal by a plea. She had, too, the natural reticence of the villager, and though she must have been aching for news of Doctor Challoner, touch of him, the very sound of his name, she rarely ever mentioned it, but grew strained and thinner; watching, watching.

If that incident was known, Netta would have been ostracized and Saybrick might have divorced her. And I was going dumb with amazement to discover that nothing had come of it, nothing *could* come of it so long as I kept still. It was a deadly sin, as I had been taught, as I believed—of damnable potentiality; and as long as nobody told it was as if it had never been, as if that look of Challoner's had really the power as it had the seeming of absolving her from all soil and stain.

I cannot now remember if I was ever tempted to tell on Netta Saybrick, but I know with the obsession of that look upon my soul I never did. And in the mean time, from being so much in each other's company, Netta and I became very good friends. That was why, a little more than a year afterward, she chose to have me with her when her second child was born. In Maverick we did things for one another that in more sophisticated communities go to the service of paid attendants. That was the time when the suspicion that had lain at the bottom of Netta's shallow eyes whenever she looked at me went out of them forever.

It was along about midnight and the worst yet to come. I sat holding Netta's hands, and beyond in the room where the lamp was, the doctor lifted Saybrick through his stressful hour with cribbage and toddy. I could see the gleam of the light on Saybrick's red, hairy hands, a driller's hands, and whenever a sound came from the inner room, the uneasy lift of his shoulders and the twitching of his lip; then the doctor pushed the whiskey over toward him and jovially dealt the cards anew.

Netta, tossing on her pillow, came into range with Saybrick's blunt profile outlined against the cheaply papered wall, and I suppose her husband's distress was good to her to see. She looked at him a long time quietly.

"Henry's a good man," she said at last.

"Yes," I said; and then she turned to me narrowly with the expiring spark of anxious cunning in her eyes.

"And I've been a good wife to him," said she. It was half a challenge. And I, trapped by the hour, became a fakir in my turn, called instantly on all my soul and answered—with the Look—"Everybody knows that, Netta"—held on steadily until the spark went out. However I had done it I could not tell, but I saw the trouble go out of the woman's soul as the lids drooped, and with it out of my own heart the last of the virtuous resentment of the untempted. I had really forgiven her; how then was it possible for the sin to rise up and trouble her more? Mind you, I grew up in a church that makes a great deal of the forgiveness of sins and signifies it by a tremendous particularity about behavior, and the most I had learned of the efficient exercise of forgiveness was from the worst man I had ever known.

About an hour before dawn, when a wind began to stir, and out on the mesa the coyotes howled returning from the hunt, stooping to tuck the baby in her arms, I felt Netta's lips brush against my hand.

"You've been mighty good to me," she said. Well—if I were pushed for it, I should think it worth mentioning—but I am not so sure.

1909

Willa Cather
(1873–1947)

Acclaimed as a great American regional and historical novelist, a subtle modern stylist, a Romantic in an era of cynicism, and a prominent woman author whose ambiguous gender identification can be read in her texts, Willa Cather was a professional writer all her adult life. Journalist, novelist, and short story writer, Cather displayed a wide range in the subjects and forms of her writings.

Born on a farm in northern Virginia, Cather was the eldest child of Charles F. and Virginia B. Cather, who moved their family of seven children to Red Cloud, Nebraska, in 1883, when that region was still a frontier. Although the formal cultural resources of the small Western town were limited, Cather spent her adolescence immersed in the cultural diversity represented by her many immigrant neighbors, whose expertise in languages, music, history, and the arts left their mark

on her education. Cather graduated at age 16 from the new high school in Red Cloud and, after a year of prep school in Lincoln, Nebraska, went on to the University of Nebraska in 1891. She brought with her the persona of "William Cather, Jr.," a role she occasionally cross-dressed to play from her early adolescence. Although her original plan was to become a medical doctor, Cather received enough encouragement from instructors in writing classes to decide to pursue authorship as a career. She began working as a paid journalist in her junior year at college.

After graduating with her B.A. in 1895, Cather moved to Pittsburgh, Pennsylvania, to continue her work in journalism, but she took a break from paid writing to allow herself to pursue fiction. Cather maintained friendships with numerous women writers, including Dorothy Canfield Fisher (a college friend) and Sarah

Orne Jewett. She taught high school Latin and English in Pittsburgh for five years and published her first collection of short stories, *The Troll Garden* (1905). She moved to New York City the next year to work as an editor for *McClure's Magazine*. Although she was to travel to Europe, back to Nebraska, and to the American Southwest, New York City remained her lifelong home.

Cather's first great passion was for Isabelle McClung, a young woman of Pittsburgh who challenged her wealthy, respectable family's conventional attitudes by circulating among the city's "bohemian" (or artistic) circles, where she met Cather. The two shared a close companionship, living and traveling together intermittently until 1916, when Isabelle married. Cather had met Edith Lewis (of another conventionally middle-class family) in Lincoln, Nebraska, in 1903, and had helped her to a job on *McClure's* in 1906. In 1908 she and Edith began sharing an apartment in New York City's Greenwich Village, and the two were to live and travel together for the rest of Cather's life. Lewis wrote a memoir, *Willa Cather Living,* after Cather's death, which reveals very little of her own character or of the details of their relationship but demonstrates her devotion to her longtime companion.

Cather left the staff of *McClure's* in 1912 and committed herself exclusively to writing fiction. Over the years she produced five novels based on experiences and stories she remembered from her youth in Nebraska. *O Pioneers!* (1913), *The Song of the Lark* (1915), *My Ántonia* (1918), *One of Ours* (which won the Pulitzer Prize in 1922), and *A Lost Lady* (1923) received both critical and popular success. The novels stress the themes of family and community attachments, affection for the Midwest, respect for ethnicity and difference in the American population, and the redeeming possibilities of high culture and classic art. Cather's other major novels are set in the American Southwest. They include *The Professor's House* (1925) and *Death Comes for the Archbishop* (1927); the latter is an histor-

ical novel, a form with which Cather experimented further in *Shadows on the Rock* (1931), set in seventeenth-century Quebec, and in *Sapphira and the Slave Girl* (1940), which takes place in antebellum Virginia.

If the attitudes conveyed in her fiction are less cynically pessimistic than those of her male contemporaries, Cather's style is distinctly modern in its spareness. She practiced a form she called "the novel demeublé" ("the unfurnished novel"), limiting descriptive details to those which carry symbolic or allusive significance. The story reprinted here, "Paul's Case," was one of Cather's favorites; it was the only short story she allowed to be anthologized during her lifetime. Its rich fabric of artistic, musical, and literary allusion refers to Cather's early experience of the world of high culture in Pittsburgh and New York; its portrait of a young man who presents himself as an Oscar Wilde–style aesthete (complete with a red carnation in his jacket's buttonhole) and whose difference alienates him from his family and school surroundings has been read as a representation of ambivalent gayness. Cather revised the story later in her life, but the version found here comes from her first volume of short stories, *The Troll Garden*.

Cather's other publications include *April Twilights* (1903), *Alexander's Bridge* (1912), *Youth and the Bright Medusa* (1920), *My Mortal Enemy* (1926), *Obscure Destinies* (1932), *Lucy Gayheart* (1935), *Not Under Forty* (1936), *The Old Beauty and Others* (1948), and *Willa Cather on Writing* (1949).

Biographies of Cather (incorporating studies of her fiction) include James Woodress, *Willa Cather: Her Life and Art* (1970); Sharon O'Brien, *Willa Cather: The Emerging Voice* (1987); and Hermione Lee, *Willa Cather: Double Lives* (1989). Studies of her work include James Schroeder, ed., *Willa Cather and Her Critics* (1967); Linda Huf, *Portrait of the Artist as a Young Woman: The Writer as Heroine in American Literature* (1983); John J. Murphy, ed., *Critical Essays on Willa Cather* (1984); Judith Fryer, *Felicitous Space* (1986); Susan Danforth, *Understanding Willa Cather's 'A Lost Lady': Putting Your Finger on "The Thing Not Named"* (1987); John J. Adams et al., eds., *Willa Cather: Family, Community, and History* (1990); and Erik I. Thurin, *The Humanization of Willa Cather: Classicism in an American Classic* (1990).

Paul's Case

A Study in Temperament

It was Paul's afternoon to appear before the faculty of the Pittsburgh High School to account for his various misdemeanors. He had been suspended a week ago, and his father had called at the Principal's office and confessed his perplexity about his son. Paul entered the faculty room suave and smiling. His clothes were a trifle outgrown, and the tan velvet on the collar of his open overcoat was frayed and worn; but for all that there was something of the dandy about him, and he wore an opal pin in his neatly knotted black four-in-hand,[1] and a red carnation in his buttonhole. This latter adornment the faculty somehow felt was not properly significant of the contrite spirit befitting a boy under the ban of suspension.

Paul was tall for his age and very thin, with high, cramped shoulders and a narrow chest. His eyes were remarkable for a certain hysterical brilliancy, and he continually used them in a conscious, theatrical sort of way, peculiarly offensive in a boy. The pupils were abnormally large, as though he were addicted to belladonna,[2] but there was a glassy glitter about them which that drug does not produce.

When questioned by the Principal as to why he was there Paul stated, politely enough, that he wanted to come back to school. This was a lie, but Paul was quite accustomed to lying; found it, indeed, indispensable for overcoming friction. His teachers were asked to state their respective charges against him, which they did with such a rancor and aggrievedness as evinced that this was not a usual case. Disorder and impertinence were among the offenses named, yet each of his instructors felt that it was scarcely possible to put into words the real cause of the trouble, which lay in a sort of hysterically defiant manner of the boy's; in the contempt which they all knew he felt for them, and which he seemingly made not the least effort to conceal. Once, when he had been making a synopsis of a paragraph at the blackboard, his English teacher had stepped to his side and attempted to guide his hand. Paul had started back with a shudder and thrust his hands violently behind him. The astonished woman could scarcely have been more hurt and embarrassed had he struck at her. The insult was so involuntary and definitely personal as to be unforgettable. In one way and another he had made all his teachers, men and women alike, conscious of the same feeling of physical aversion. In one class he habitually sat with his hand shading his eyes; in another he always looked out of the window during the recitation; in another he made a running commentary on the lecture, with humorous intention.

His teachers felt this afternoon that his whole attitude was symbolized by his shrug and his flippantly red carnation flower, and they fell upon him without mercy, his English teacher leading the pack. He stood through it smiling, his pale lips parted over his white teeth. (His lips were continually twitching, and he had a habit of raising his eyebrows that was contemptuous and irritating to the last degree.) Older boys than Paul had broken down and shed tears under that baptism of fire, but his set smile did not once desert him, and his only sign of discomfort was the nervous trembling of the fingers that toyed with the buttons of his overcoat, and an occasional jerking of the other hand that held his hat. Paul was always smiling, always glancing about him, seeming to feel that people might be watching him and trying to detect something. This conscious expression, since it was as far as possible from boyish mirthfulness, was usually attributed to insolence or "smartness."[3]

As the inquisition proceeded one of his instructors repeated an impertinent remark of the boy's, and the Principal asked him whether he thought that a courteous speech to have made a woman. Paul shrugged his shoulders slightly and his eyebrows twitched.

1. A necktie.
2. A drug used to treat asthma, colic, and
       hyperacidity.
3. Impertinent cleverness.

"I don't know," he replied. "I didn't mean to be polite or impolite, either. I guess it's a sort of way I have of saying things regardless."

The Principal, who was a sympathetic man, asked him whether he didn't think that a way it would be well to get rid of. Paul grinned and said he guessed so. When he was told that he could go he bowed gracefully and went out. His bow was but a repetition of the scandalous red carnation.

His teachers were in despair, and his drawing master voiced the feeling of them all when he declared there was something about the boy which none of them understood. He added: "I don't really believe that smile of his comes altogether from insolence; there's something sort of haunted about it. The boy is not strong, for one thing. I happen to know that he was born in Colorado, only a few months before his mother died out there of a long illness. There is something wrong about the fellow."

The drawing master had come to realize that, in looking at Paul, one saw only his white teeth and the forced animation of his eyes. One warm afternoon the boy had gone to sleep at his drawing board, and his master had noted with amazement what a white, blue-veined face it was; drawn and wrinkled like an old man's about the eyes, the lips twitching even in his sleep, and stiff with a nervous tension that drew them back from his teeth.

His teachers left the building dissatisfied and unhappy; humiliated to have felt so vindictive toward a mere boy, to have uttered this feeling in cutting terms, and to have set each other on, as it were, in the gruesome game of intemperate reproach. Some of them remembered having seen a miserable street cat set at bay by a ring of tormentors.

As for Paul, he ran down the hill whistling the "Soldiers' Chorus" from *Faust*,[4] looking wildly behind him now and then to see whether some of his teachers were not there to writhe under his lightheartedness. As it was now late in the afternoon and Paul was on duty that evening as usher at Carnegie Hall, he decided that he would not go home to supper. When he reached the concert hall the doors were not yet open and, as it was chilly outside, he decided to go up into the picture gallery—always deserted at this hour—where there were some of Raffelli's gay studies of Paris streets and an airy blue Venetian scene or two that always exhilarated him. He was delighted to find no one in the gallery but the old guard, who sat in one corner, a newspaper on his knee, a black patch over one eye and the other closed. Paul possessed himself of the place and walked confidently up and down, whistling under his breath. After a while he sat down before a blue Rico and lost himself. When he bethought him to look at his watch, it was after seven o'clock, and he rose with a start and ran downstairs, making a face at Augustus, peering out from the cast room, and an evil gesture at the Venus de Milo as he passed her on the stairway.[5]

When Paul reached the ushers' dressing room half a dozen boys were there already, and he began excitedly to tumble into his uniform. It was one of the few that at all approached fitting, and Paul thought it very becoming—though he knew that the tight, straight coat accentuated his narrow chest, about which he was exceedingly sensitive. He was always considerably excited while he dressed, twanging all over to the tuning of the strings and the preliminary flourishes of the horns in the music room; but tonight he seemed quite beside himself, and he teased and plagued the boys until, telling him that he was crazy, they put him down on the floor and sat on him.

Somewhat calmed by his suppression, Paul dashed out to the front of the house to seat the early comers. He was a model usher; gracious and smiling he ran up and down the aisles; nothing was too much trouble for him; he carried messages and brought programs as though

4. Faust is the mythical alchemist and magician who sells his soul to the devil to gain knowledge and worldly experience; Charles Gounod composed an opera entitled *Faust* in 1859.

5. These are copies of a bust and a statue decorating the hall.

it were his greatest pleasure in life, and all the people in his section thought him a charming boy, feeling that he remembered and admired them. As the house filled, he grew more and more vivacious and animated, and the color came to his cheeks and lips. It was very much as though this were a great reception and Paul were the host. Just as the musicians came out to take their places, his English teacher arrived with checks for the seats which a prominent manufacturer had taken for the season. She betrayed some embarrassment when she handed Paul the tickets, and a hauteur which subsequently made her feel very foolish. Paul was startled for a moment, and had the feeling of wanting to put her out; what business had she here among all these fine people and gay colors? He looked her over and decided that she was not appropriately dressed and must be a fool to sit downstairs in such togs. The tickets had probably been sent her out of kindness, he reflected as he put down a seat for her, and she had about as much right to sit there as he had.

When the symphony began Paul sank into one of the rear seats with a long sigh of relief, and lost himself as he had done before the Rico. It was not that symphonies, as such, meant anything in particular to Paul, but the first sigh of the instruments seemed to free some hilarious and potent spirit within him; something that struggled there like the genie in the bottle found by the Arab fisherman. He felt a sudden zest of life; the lights danced before his eyes and the concert hall blazed into unimaginable splendor. When the soprano soloist came on Paul forgot even the nastiness of his teacher's being there and gave himself up to the peculiar stimulus such personages always had for him. The soloist chanced to be a German woman, by no means in her first youth, and the mother of many children; but she wore an elaborate gown and a tiara, and above all she had that indefinable air of achievement, that world-shine upon her, which, in Paul's eyes, made her a veritable queen of Romance.

After a concert was over Paul was always irritable and wretched until he got to sleep, and tonight he was even more than usually restless. He had the feeling of not being able to let down, of its being impossible to give up this delicious excitement which was the only thing that could be called living at all. During the last number he withdrew and, after hastily changing his clothes in the dressing room, slipped out to the side door where the soprano's carriage stood. Here he began pacing rapidly up and down the walk, waiting to see her come out.

Over yonder, the Schenley, in its vacant stretch, loomed big and square through the fine rain, the windows of its twelve stories glowing like those of a lighted cardboard house under a Christmas tree. All the actors and singers of the better class stayed there when they were in the city, and a number of the big manufacturers of the place lived there in the winter. Paul had often hung about the hotel, watching the people go in and out, longing to enter and leave schoolmasters and dull care behind him forever.

At last the singer came out, accompanied by the conductor, who helped her into her carriage and closed the door with a cordial *auf wiedersehen* which set Paul to wondering whether she were not an old sweetheart of his. Paul followed the carriage over to the hotel, walking so rapidly as not to be far from the entrance when the singer alighted, and disappeared behind the swinging glass doors that were opened by a Negro in a tall hat and a long coat. In the moment that the door was ajar it seemed to Paul that he, too, entered. He seemed to feel himself go after her up the steps, into the warm, lighted building, into an exotic, tropical world of shiny, glistening surfaces and basking ease. He reflected upon the mysterious dishes that were brought into the dining room, the green bottles in buckets of ice, as he had seen them in the supper party pictures of the *Sunday World* supplement. A quick gust of wind brought the rain down with sudden vehemence, and Paul was startled to find that he was still outside in the slush of the gravel driveway; that his boots were letting in the water and his scanty overcoat was clinging wet about him; that the lights in front of the concert hall were out and that the rain was driving in sheets between him and the orange glow of the windows above him. There it was, what he wanted—tangibly before him, like the fairy world of a Christmas pantomime—but mocking spirits stood guard at the doors, and, as the rain beat in his face, Paul wondered whether he were destined always to shiver in the black night outside, looking up at it.

He turned and walked reluctantly toward the car tracks. The end had to come sometime; his father in his nightclothes at the top of the stairs, explanations that did not explain, hastily improvised fictions that were forever tripping him up, his upstairs room and its horrible yellow wallpaper, the creaking bureau with the greasy plush collarbox, and over his painted wooden bed the pictures of George Washington and John Calvin, and the framed motto, "Feed my Lambs,"[6] which had been worked in red worsted by his mother.

Half an hour later Paul alighted from his car and went slowly down one of the side streets off the main thoroughfare. It was a highly respectable street, where all the houses were exactly alike, and where businessmen of moderate means begot and reared large families of children, all of whom went to Sabbath school and learned the shorter catechism, and were interested in arithmetic; all of whom were as exactly alike as their homes, and of a piece with the monotony in which they lived. Paul never went up Cordelia Street without a shudder of loathing. His home was next to the house of the Cumberland minister. He approached it tonight with the nerveless sense of defeat, the hopeless feeling of sinking back forever into ugliness and commonness that he had always had when he came home. The moment he turned into Cordelia Street he felt the waters close above his head. After each of these orgies of living he experienced all the physical depression which follows a debauch; the loathing of respectable beds, of common food, of a house penetrated by kitchen odors; a shuddering repulsion for the flavorless, colorless mass of everyday existence; a morbid desire for cool things and soft lights and fresh flowers.

The nearer he approached the house, the more absolutely unequal Paul felt to the sight of it all: his ugly sleeping chamber; the cold bathroom with the grimy zinc tub, the cracked mirror, the dripping spiggots; his father, at the top of the stairs, his hairy legs sticking out from his nightshirt, his feet thrust into carpet slippers. He was so much later than usual that there would certainly be inquiries and reproaches. Paul stopped short before the door. He felt that he could not be accosted by his father tonight; that he could not toss again on that miserable bed. He would not go in. He would tell his father that he had no carfare and it was raining so hard he had gone home with one of the boys and stayed all night.

Meanwhile, he was wet and cold. He went around to the back of the house and tried one of the basement windows, found it open, raised it cautiously, and scrambled down the cellar wall to the floor. There he stood, holding his breath, terrified by the noise he had made, but the floor above him was silent, and there was no creak on the stairs. He found a soapbox, and carried it over to the soft ring of light that streamed from the furnace door, and sat down. He was horribly afraid of rats, so he did not try to sleep, but sat looking distrustfully at the dark, still terrified lest he might have awakened his father. In such reactions, after one of the experiences which made days and nights out of the dreary blanks of the calendar, when his senses were deadened, Paul's head was always singularly clear. Suppose his father had heard him getting in at the window and had come down and shot him for a burglar? Then, again, suppose his father had come down, pistol in hand, and he had cried out in time to save himself, and his father had been horrified to think how nearly he had killed him? Then, again, suppose a day should come when his father would remember that night, and wish there had been no warning cry to stay his hand? With this last supposition Paul entertained himself until daybreak.

6. Calvin is the founder of a Protestant sect; the motto comes from John 21:15–17.

The following Sunday was fine; the sodden November chill was broken by the last flash of autumnal summer. In the morning Paul had to go to church and Sabbath school, as always. On seasonable Sunday afternoons the burghers of Cordelia Street always sat out on their front stoops and talked to their neighbors on the next stoop, or called to those across the street in neighborly fashion. The men usually sat on gay cushions placed upon the steps that led down to the sidewalk, while the women, in their Sunday "waists,"[7] sat in rockers on the cramped porches, pretending to be greatly at their ease. The children played in the streets; there were so many of them that the place resembled the recreation grounds of a kindergarten. The men on the steps—all in their shirt sleeves, their vests unbuttoned—sat with their legs well apart, their stomachs comfortably protruding, and talked of the prices of things, or told anecdotes of the sagacity of their various chiefs and overlords. They occasionally looked over the multitude of squabbling children, listened affectionately to their high-pitched, nasal voices, smiling to see their own proclivities reproduced in their offspring, and interspersed their legends of the iron kings with remarks about their sons' progress at school, their grades in arithmetic, and the amounts they had saved in their toy banks.

On this last Sunday of November Paul sat all the afternoon on the lowest step of his stoop, staring into the street, while his sisters, in their rockers, were talking to the minister's daughters next door about how many shirtwaists they had made in the last week, and how many waffles someone had eaten at the last church supper. When the weather was warm, and his father was in a particularly jovial frame of mind, the girls made lemonade, which was always brought out in a red-glass pitcher, ornamented with forget-me-nots in blue enamel. This the girls thought very fine, and the neighbors always joked about the suspicious colour of the pitcher.

Today Paul's father sat on the top step, talking to a young man who shifted a restless baby from knee to knee. He happened to be the young man who was daily held up to Paul as a model, and after whom it was his father's dearest hope that he would pattern. This young man was of a ruddy complexion, with a compressed, red mouth, and faded, nearsighted eyes, over which he wore thick spectacles, with gold bows that curved about his ears. He was clerk to one of the magnates of a great steel corporation, and was looked upon in Cordelia Street as a young man with a future. There was a story that, some five years ago—he was now barely twenty-six—he had been a trifle dissipated, but in order to curb his appetites and save the loss of time and strength that a sowing of wild oats might have entailed, he had taken his chief's advice, oft reiterated to his employees, and at twenty-one had married the first woman whom he could persuade to share his fortunes. She happened to be an angular schoolmistress, much older than he, who also wore thick glasses, and who had now borne him four children, all nearsighted, like herself.

The young man was relating how his chief, now cruising in the Mediterranean, kept in touch with all the details of the business, arranging his office hours on his yacht just as though he were at home, and "knocking off work enough to keep two stenographers busy." His father told, in turn, the plan his corporation was considering, of putting in an electric railway plant at Cairo. Paul snapped his teeth; he had an awful apprehension that they might spoil it all before he got there. Yet he rather liked to hear these legends of the iron kings that were told and retold on Sundays and holidays; these stories of palaces in Venice, yachts on the Mediterranean, and high play at Monte Carlo appealed to his fancy, and he was interested in the triumphs of these cash boys who had become famous, though he had no mind for the cash-boy stage.

After supper was over and he had helped to dry the dishes, Paul nervously asked his father whether he could go to George's to get some help in his geometry, and still more nervously

---

7. Shirtwaists, or blouses worn with skirts.

asked for carfare. This latter request he had to repeat, as his father, on principle, did not like to hear requests for money, whether much or little. He asked Paul whether he could not go to some boy who lived nearer, and told him that he ought not to leave his schoolwork until Sunday; but he gave him the dime. He was not a poor man, but he had a worthy ambition to come up in the world. His only reason for allowing Paul to usher was that he thought a boy ought to be earning a little.

Paul bounded upstairs, scrubbed the greasy odor of the dishwater from his hands with the ill-smelling soap he hated, and then shook over his fingers a few drops of violet water from the bottle he kept hidden in his drawer. He left the house with his geometry conspicuously under his arm, and the moment he got out of Cordelia Street and boarded a downtown car, he shook off the lethargy of two deadening days and began to live again.

The leading juvenile of the permanent stock company which played at one of the downtown theaters was an acquaintance of Paul's, and the boy had been invited to drop in at the Sunday-night rehearsals whenever he could. For more than a year Paul had spent every available moment loitering about Charley Edwards's dressing room. He had won a place among Edwards's following not only because the young actor, who could not afford to employ a dresser, often found him useful, but because he recognized in Paul something akin to what churchmen term "vocation."[8]

It was at the theater and at Carnegie Hall that Paul really lived; the rest was but a sleep and a forgetting.[9] This was Paul's fairy tale, and it had for him all the allurement of a secret love. The moment he inhaled the grassy, painty, dusty odor behind the scenes, he breathed like a prisoner set free, and felt within him the possibility of doing or saying splendid, brilliant, poetic things. The moment the cracked orchestra beat out the overture from *Martha*, or jerked at the serenade from *Rigoletto*,[1] all stupid and ugly things slid from him, and his senses were deliciously, yet delicately fired.

Perhaps it was because, in Paul's world, the natural nearly always wore the guise of ugliness that a certain element of artificiality seemed to him necessary in beauty. Perhaps it was because his experience of life elsewhere was so full of Sabbath-school picnics, petty economies, wholesome advice as to how to succeed in life, and the inescapable odors of cooking, that he found this existence so alluring, these smartly clad men and women so attractive, that he was so moved by these starry apple orchards that bloomed perennially under the limelight.

It would be difficult to put it strongly enough how convincingly the stage entrance of that theater was for Paul the actual portal of Romance. Certainly none of the company ever suspected it, least of all Charley Edwards. It was very like the old stories that used to float about London of fabulously rich Jews, who had subterranean halls there, with palms, and fountains, and soft lamps and richly appareled women who never saw the disenchanting light of London day. So, in the midst of that smoke-palled city, enamored of figures and grimy toil, Paul had his secret temple, his wishing carpet, his bit of blue-and-white Mediterranean shore bathed in perpetual sunshine.

Several of Paul's teachers had a theory that his imagination had been perverted by garish fiction, but the truth was that he scarcely ever read at all. The books at home were not such as would either tempt or corrupt a youthful mind, and as for reading the novels that some of his friends urged upon him—well, he got what he wanted much more quickly from music; any sort of music, from an orchestra to a barrel organ. He needed only the spark, the indescribable thrill that made his imagination master of his senses, and he could make plots and pictures enough of his own. It was equally true that he was not stagestruck—not, at any

8. A "calling" to a particular line of work.
9. A stanza in William Wordsworth's (1770–1850) "Ode: Intimations of Immortality" begins "Our birth is but a sleep and a forgetting" and ends

"Heaven lies about us in our infancy! / Shades of the prison-house begin to close / Upon the growing boy."
1. An opera by Giuseppi Verdi (1813–1901).

rate, in the usual acceptation of that expression. He had no desire to become an actor, any more than he had to become a musician. He felt no necessity to do any of these things; what he wanted was to see, to be in the atmosphere, float on the wave of it, to be carried out, blue league after blue league, away from everything.

After a night behind the scenes Paul found the schoolroom more than ever repulsive; the bare floors and naked walls; the prosy men who never wore frock coats, or violets in their buttonholes; the women with their dull gowns, shrill voices, and pitiful seriousness about prepositions that govern the dative. He could not bear to have the other pupils think, for a moment, that he took these people seriously; he must convey to them that he considered it all trivial, and was there only by way of a jest, anyway. He had autographed pictures of all the members of the stock company which he showed his classmates, telling them the most incredible stories of his familiarity with these people, of his acquaintance with the soloists who came to Carnegie Hall, his suppers with them and the flowers he sent them. When these stories lost their effect, and his audience grew listless, he became desperate and would bid all the boys good-by, announcing that he was going to travel for a while; going to Naples, to Venice, to Egypt. Then, next Monday, he would slip back, conscious and nervously smiling; his sister was ill, and he should have to defer his voyage until spring.

Matters went steadily worse with Paul at school. In the itch to let his instructors know how heartily he despised them and their homilies, and how thoroughly he was appreciated elsewhere, he mentioned once or twice that he had no time to fool with theorems; adding— with a twitch of the eyebrows and a touch of that nervous bravado which so perplexed them—that he was helping the people down at the stock company; they were old friends of his.

The upshot of the matter was that the Principal went to Paul's father, and Paul was taken out of school and put to work. The manager at Carnegie Hall was told to get another usher in his stead; the doorkeeper at the theater was warned not to admit him to the house; and Charley Edwards remorsefully promised the boy's father not to see him again.

The members of the stock company were vastly amused when some of Paul's stories reached them—especially the women. They were hardworking women, most of them supporting indigent husbands or brothers, and they laughed rather bitterly at having stirred the boy to such fervid and florid inventions. They agreed with the faculty and with his father that Paul's was a bad case.

The eastbound train was plowing through a January snowstorm; the dull dawn was beginning to show gray when the engine whistled a mile out of Newark. Paul started up from the seat where he had lain curled in uneasy slumber, rubbed the breath-misted window glass with his hand, and peered out. The snow was whirling in curling eddies above the white bottom lands, and the drifts lay already deep in the fields and along the fences, while here and there the long dead grass and dried weed stalks protruded black above it. Lights shone from the scattered houses, and a gang of laborers who stood beside the track waved their lanterns.

Paul had slept very little, and he felt grimy and uncomfortable. He had made the all-night journey in a day coach, partly because he was ashamed, dressed as he was, to go into a Pullman, and partly because he was afraid of being seen there by some Pittsburgh business-man, who might have noticed him in Denny & Carson's office. When the whistle awoke him, he clutched quickly at his breast pocket, glancing about him with an uncertain smile. But the little, clay-bespattered Italians were still sleeping, the slatternly women across the aisle were in open-mouthed oblivion, and even the crumby, crying babies were for the nonce stilled. Paul settled back to struggle with his impatience as best he could.

When he arrived at the Jersey City station he hurried through his breakfast, manifestly ill at ease and keeping a sharp eye about him. After he reached the Twenty-third Street station, he consulted a cabman and had himself driven to a men's-furnishings establishment that was just opening for the day. He spent upward of two hours there, buying with endless reconsidering and great care. His new street suit he put on in the fitting room; the frock coat and dress clothes he had bundled into the cab with his linen. Then he drove to a hatter's and a shoe house. His next errand was at Tiffany's, where he selected his silver and a new scarf pin. He would not wait to have his silver marked, he said. Lastly, he stopped at a trunk shop on Broadway and had his purchases packed into various traveling bags.

It was a little after one o'clock when he drove up to the Waldorf,[2] and after settling with the cabman, went into the office. He registered from Washington;[3] said his mother and father had been abroad, and that he had come down to await the arrival of their steamer. He told his story plausibly and had no trouble, since he volunteered to pay for them in advance, in engaging his rooms; a sleeping room, sitting room, and bath.

Not once, but a hundred times, Paul had planned this entry into New York. He had gone over every detail of it with Charley Edwards, and in his scrapbook at home there were pages of description about New York hotels, cut from the Sunday papers. When he was shown to his sitting room on the eighth floor he saw at a glance that everything was as it should be; there was but one detail in his mental picture that the place did not realize, so he rang for the bellboy and sent him down for flowers. He moved about nervously until the boy returned, putting away his new linen and fingering it delightedly as he did so. When the flowers came he put them hastily into water, and then tumbled into a hot bath. Presently he came out of his white bathroom, resplendent in his new silk underwear, and playing with the tassels of his red robe. The snow was whirling so fiercely outside his windows that he could scarcely see across the street, but within the air was deliciously soft and fragrant. He put the violets and jonquils on the taboret[4] beside the couch, and threw himself down, with a long sigh, covering himself with a Roman blanket. He was thoroughly tired; he had been in such haste, he had stood up to such a strain, covered so much ground in the last twenty-four hours, that he wanted to think how it had all come about. Lulled by the sound of the wind, the warm air, and the cool fragrance of the flowers, he sank into deep, drowsy retrospection.

It had been wonderfully simple; when they had shut him out of the theater and concert hall, when they had taken away his bone, the whole thing was virtually determined. The rest was a mere matter of opportunity. The only thing that at all surprised him was his own courage—for he realized well enough that he had always been tormented by fear, a sort of apprehensive dread that, of late years, as the meshes of the lies he had told closed about him, had been pulling the muscles of his body tighter and tighter. Until now he could not remember the time when he had not been dreading something. Even when he was a little boy it was always there—behind him, or before, or on either side. There had always been the shadowed corner, the dark place into which he dared not look, but from which something seemed always to be watching him—and Paul had done things that were not pretty to watch, he knew.

But now he had a curious sense of relief, as though he had at last thrown down the gauntlet to the thing in the corner.

Yet it was but a day since he had been sulking in the traces; but yesterday afternoon that he had been sent to the bank with Denny & Carson's deposit, as usual—but this time he was instructed to leave the book to be balanced. There was above two thousand dollars in checks, and nearly a thousand in the bank notes which he had taken from the book and quietly transferred to his pocket. At the bank he had made out a new deposit slip. His nerves had been steady enough to permit of his returning to the office, where he had finished his work and asked for a full day's holiday tomorrow, Saturday, giving a perfectly reasonable pretext. The bankbook, he knew, would not be returned before Monday or Tuesday, and his father would be out of town for the next week. From the time he slipped the bank notes into his

2. A luxurious New York hotel.
3. He gave his address as being in Washington,   D.C.
          4.   A low stand or cabinet.

pocket until he boarded the night train for New York, he had not known a moment's hesitation. It was not the first time Paul had steered through treacherous waters.

How astonishingly easy it had all been; here he was, the thing done; and this time there would be no awakening, no figure at the top of the stairs. He watched the snowflakes whirling by his window until he fell asleep.

When he awoke, it was three o'clock in the afternoon. He bounded up with a start; half of one of his precious days gone already! He spent more than an hour in dressing, watching every stage of his toilet carefully in the mirror. Everything was quite perfect; he was exactly the kind of boy he had always wanted to be.

When he went downstairs Paul took a carriage and drove up Fifth Avenue toward the Park. The snow had somewhat abated; carriages and tradesmen's wagons were hurrying sound-lessly to and fro in the winter twilight; boys in woolen mufflers were shoveling off the doorsteps; the avenue stages made fine spots of color against the white street. Here and there on the corners were stands, with whole flower gardens blooming under glass cases, against the sides of which the snowflakes stuck and melted; violets, roses, carnations, lilies of the valley—somehow vastly more lovely and alluring that they blossomed thus unnaturally in the snow. The Park itself was a wonderful stage winterpiece.

When he returned, the pause of the twilight had ceased and the tune of the streets had changed. The snow was falling faster, lights streamed from the hotels that reared their dozen stories fearlessly up into the storm, defying the raging Atlantic winds. A long, black stream of carriages poured down the avenue, intersected here and there by other streams, tending horizontally. There were a score of cabs about the entrance of his hotel, and his driver had to wait. Boys in livery were running in and out of the awning stretched across the sidewalk, up and down the red velvet carpet laid from the door to the street. Above, about, within it all was the rumble and roar, the hurry and toss of thousands of human beings as hot for pleasure as himself, and on every side of him towered the glaring affirmation of the omnipo-tence of wealth.

The boy set his teeth and drew his shoulders together in a spasm of realization; the plot of all dramas, the text of all romances, the nerve-stuff of all sensations was whirling about him like the snowflakes. He burnt like a faggot[5] in a tempest.

When Paul went down to dinner the music of the orchestra came floating up the elevator shaft to greet him. His head whirled as he stepped into the thronged corridor, and he sank back into one of the chairs against the wall to get his breath. The lights, the chatter, the perfumes, the bewildering medley of color—he had, for a moment, the feeling of not being able to stand it. But only for a moment; these were his own people, he told himself. He went slowly about the corridors, through the writing rooms, smoking rooms, reception rooms, as though he were exploring the chambers of an enchanted palace, built and peopled for him alone.

When he reached the dining room he sat down at a table near a window. The flowers, the white linen, the many-colored wineglasses, the gay toilettes of the women, the low popping of corks, the undulating repetitions of the *Blue Danube*[6] from the orchestra, all flooded Paul's dream with bewildering radiance. When the roseate tinge of his champagne was added—that cold, precious, bubbling stuff that creamed and foamed in his glass—Paul wondered that there were honest men in the world at all. This was what all the world was fighting for, he reflected; this was what all the struggle was about. He doubted the reality of his past. Had he ever known a place called Cordelia Street, a place where fagged-looking[7] businessmen got on the early car; mere rivets in a machine they seemed to Paul,—sickening men, with combings of children's hair always hanging to their coats, and the smell of cooking in their

---

5. A bundle of twigs ignited for use as a torch in a storm.
6. A waltz composed by the popular late

nineteenth-century Viennese composer, Johann Strauss (1825–1899).
7. Exhausted-looking.

clothes. Cordelia Street—Ah, that belonged to another time and country; had he not always been thus, had he not sat here night after night, from as far back as he could remember, looking pensively over just such shimmering textures and slowly twirling the stem of a glass like this one between his thumb and middle finger? He rather thought he had.

He was not in the least abashed or lonely. He had no especial desire to meet or to know any of these people; all he demanded was the right to look on and conjecture, to watch the pageant. The mere stage properties were all he contended for. Nor was he lonely later in the evening, in his lodge at the Metropolitan. He was now entirely rid of his nervous misgivings, of his forced aggressiveness, of the imperative desire to show himself different from his surroundings. He felt now that his surroundings explained him. Nobody questioned the purple; he had only to wear it passively. He had only to glance down at his attire to reassure himself that here it would be impossible for anyone to humiliate him.

He found it hard to leave his beautiful sitting room to go to bed that night, and sat long watching the raging storm from his turret window. When he went to sleep it was with the lights turned on in his bedroom; partly because of his old timidity, and partly so that, if he should wake in the night, there would be no wretched moment of doubt, no horrible suspicion of yellow wallpaper, or of Washington and Calvin above his bed.

Sunday morning the city was practically snowbound. Paul breakfasted late, and in the afternoon he fell in with a wild San Francisco boy, a freshman at Yale, who said he had run down for a "little flyer" over Sunday. The young man offered to show Paul the night side of the town, and the two boys went out together after dinner, not returning to the hotel until seven o'clock the next morning. They had started out in the confiding warmth of a champagne friendship, but their parting in the elevator was singularly cool. The freshman pulled himself together to make his train, and Paul went to bed. He awoke at two o'clock in the afternoon, very thirsty and dizzy, and rang for icewater, coffee, and the Pittsburgh papers.

On the part of the hotel management, Paul excited no suspicion. There was this to be said for him, that he wore his spoils with dignity and in no way made himself conspicuous. Even under the glow of his wine he was never boisterous, though he found the stuff like a magician's wand for wonder-building. His chief greediness lay in his ears and eyes, and his excesses were not offensive ones. His dearest pleasures were the gray winter twilights in his sitting room; his quiet enjoyment of his flowers, his clothes, his wide divan, his cigarette, and his sense of power. He could not remember a time when he had felt so at peace with himself. The mere release from the necessity of petty lying, lying every day and every day, restored his self-respect. He had never lied for pleasure, even at school; but to be noticed and admired, to assert his difference from other Cordelia Street boys; and he felt a good deal more manly, more honest, even, now that he had no need for boastful pretensions, now that he could, as his actor friends used to say, "dress the part." It was characteristic that remorse did not occur to him. His golden days went by without a shadow, and he made each as perfect as he could.

On the eighth day after his arrival in New York he found the whole affair exploited in the Pittsburgh papers, exploited with a wealth of detail which indicated that local news of a sensational nature was at a low ebb. The firm of Denny & Carson announced that the boy's father had refunded the full amount of the theft and that they had no intention of prosecuting. The Cumberland minister had been interviewed, and expressed his hope of yet reclaiming the motherless lad, and his Sabbath-school teacher declared that she would spare no effort to that end. The rumor had reached Pittsburgh that the boy had been seen in a New York hotel, and his father had gone East to find him and bring him home.

Paul had just come in to dress for dinner; he sank into a chair, weak to the knees, and clasped his head in his hands. It was to be worse than jail, even; the tepid waters of Cordelia Street were to close over him finally and forever. The gray monotony stretched before him in hopeless, unrelieved years; Sabbath school, Young People's Meeting, the yellow-papered room, the damp dishtowels; it all rushed back upon him with a sickening vividness. He had the old feeling that the orchestra had suddenly stopped, the sinking sensation that the play was over. The sweat broke out on his face, and he sprang to his feet, looked about him with his white, conscious smile, and winked at himself in the mirror. With something of the old childish belief in miracles with which he had so often gone to class, all his lessons unlearned, Paul dressed and dashed whistling down the corridor to the elevator.

He had no sooner entered the dining room and caught the measure of the music than his remembrance was lightened by his old elastic power of claiming the moment, mounting with it, and finding it all sufficient. The glare and glitter about him, the mere scenic accessories had again, and for the last time, their old potency. He would show himself that he was game, he would finish the thing splendidly. He doubted, more than ever, the existence of Cordelia Street, and for the first time he drank his wine recklessly. Was he not, after all, one of those fortunate beings born to the purple, was he not still himself and in his own place? He drummed a nervous accompaniment to the Pagliacci[8] music and looked about him, telling himself over and over that it had paid.

He reflected drowsily, to the swell of the music and the chill sweetness of his wine, that he might have done it more wisely. He might have caught an outbound steamer and been well out of their clutches before now. But the other side of the world had seemed too far away and too uncertain then; he could not have waited for it; his need had been too sharp. If he had to choose over again, he would do the same thing tomorrow. He looked affectionately about the dining room, now gilded with a soft mist. Ah, it had paid indeed!

Paul was awakened next morning by a painful throbbing in his head and feet. He had thrown himself across the bed without undressing, and had slept with his shoes on. His limbs and hands were lead heavy, and his tongue and throat were parched and burnt. There came upon him one of those fateful attacks of clearheadedness that never occurred except when he was physically exhausted and his nerves hung loose. He lay still, closed his eyes, and let the tide of things wash over him.

His father was in New York; "stopping at some joint or other," he told himself. The memory of successive summers on the front stoop fell upon him like a weight of black water. He had not a hundred dollars left; and he knew now, more than ever, that money was everything, the wall that stood between all he loathed and all he wanted. The thing was winding itself up; he had thought of that on his first glorious day in New York, and had even provided a way to snap the thread. It lay on his dressing table now; he had got it out last night when he came blindly up from dinner, but the shiny metal hurt his eyes, and he disliked the looks of it.

He rose and moved about with a painful effort, succumbing now and again to attacks of nausea. It was the old depression exaggerated; all the world had become Cordelia Street. Yet somehow he was not afraid of anything, was absolutely calm; perhaps because he had looked into the dark corner at last and knew. It was bad enough, what he saw there, but somehow not so bad as his long fear of it had been. He saw everything clearly now. He had a feeling that he had made the best of it, that he had lived the sort of life he was meant to live, and for half an hour he sat staring at the revolver. But he told himself that was not the way, so he went downstairs and took a cab to the ferry.

When Paul arrived at Newark he got off the train and took another cab, directing the driver to follow the Pennsylvania tracks out of the town. The snow lay heavy on the roadways and had drifted deep in the open fields. Only here and there the dead grass or dried weed stalks projected, singularly black, above it. Once well into the country, Paul dismissed the carriage and walked, floundering along the tracks, his mind a medley of irrelevant things. He seemed to hold in his brain an actual picture of everything he had seen that morning. He remembered every feature of both his drivers, of the toothless old woman from whom he had bought the red flowers in his coat, the agent from whom he had got his ticket, and all of his fellow passengers on the ferry. His mind, unable to cope with vital matters near at hand, worked feverishly and deftly at sorting and grouping these images. They made for him a part of the ugliness of the world, of the ache in his head, and the bitter burning on his tongue. He

8. *Pagliacci* ("The Clowns") is an 1892 opera by Ruggiero Leoncavallo (1858–1919).

stooped and put a handful of snow into his mouth as he walked, but that, too, seemed hot. When he reached a little hillside, where the tracks ran through a cut some twenty feet below him, he stopped and sat down.

The carnations in his coat were drooping with the cold, he noticed, their red glory all over. It occurred to him that all the flowers he had seen in the glass cases that first night must have gone the same way, long before this. It was only one splendid breath they had, in spite of their brave mockery at the winter outside the glass; and it was a losing game in the end, it seemed, this revolt against the homilies by which the world is run. Paul took one of the blossoms carefully from his coat and scooped a little hole in the snow, where he covered it up. Then he dozed a while, from his weak condition, seemingly insensible to the cold.

The sound of an approaching train awoke him, and he started to his feet, remembering only his resolution, and afraid lest he should be too late. He stood watching the approaching locomotive, his teeth chattering, his lips drawn away from them in a frightened smile; once or twice he glanced nervously sidewise, as though he were being watched. When the right moment came, he jumped. As he fell, the folly of his haste occurred to him with merciless clearness, the vastness of what he had left undone. There flashed through his brain, clearer than ever before, the blue of Adriatic water, the yellow of Algerian sands.

He felt something strike his chest, and that his body was being thrown swiftly through the air, on and on, immeasurably far and fast, while his limbs were gently relaxed. Then, because the picture-making mechanism was crushed, the disturbing visions flashed into black, and Paul dropped back into the immense design of things.

1905

Ellen Glasgow
(1873–1945)

Ellen Anderson Gholson Glasgow was born in Richmond, Virginia, the eighth of ten children in an upper-class family that, like others of its time and place, had to learn to adjust to the lessons of the Civil War and Reconstruction. Her father, the head of a Richmond ironworks, was descended from Scottish Covenanters who had escaped religious persecution in Scotland by settling in the western Virginia frontier in the 1760s. Her mother was descended from the English aristocracy of Tidewater Virginia; worn down for years by family cares and tensions, she died when Ellen was 20. Because of her frail health, Ellen was largely educated at home, where she read widely from youth. At 16 she began to lose her hearing. Her disability perhaps contributed to her introspectiveness, though she maintained many friendships throughout her life and was considered an engaging conversationalist, assisted in later years by a primitive hearing aid. She turned early to writing. By 18 she had completed a novel, which she destroyed after failing to find a publisher. Her next attempt became her first published novel, *The Descendant* (1897). This and the immediately subsequent book, *Phases of an Inferior Planet* (1898), were stories of New York society, which she knew from family visits. Her ultimate subject, however, had yet to emerge.

With *The Voice of the People*, published in 1900, she began an examination of Southern society that was to stretch through fifteen novels and constitute her major work for the next forty years. As the project evolved, she began to see it as

a well-rounded social record of Virginia from the decade before the Confederacy down to the period in which I was then living. *** My subject seemed to me to be fresh, and most certainly it remained untouched; for Southern novelists heretofore had been content to celebrate a dying culture. Yet the historic drama of a changing order, and the struggle of an emerging middle class were set against the many personal dramas of individual frustration. The world was full of fermenting processes, of mutability and of development, of decay and disintegration. The old agrarian civilization was passing; the new industrial system was but beginning to spring up from chaos.

Titles include *The Battle-Ground* (1902), about the Civil War; *The Deliverance* (1904), *The Miller of Old Church* (1911), and *Barren Ground* (1925), about the rise of the rural middle class at the expense of the old Tidewater aristocracy; *The Romance of a Plain Man* (1909), set in Richmond toward the end of the nineteenth century; *Virginia* (1913), a study of a Southern lady "capable of dying for an idea, but not of conceiving one"; *Life and Gabriella* (1916), about a stronger woman; *Barren Ground* (1925) and *Vein of Iron* (1935), two of her most well-received works, focused on the lives of forceful, independent women; the Queenborough trilogy, social comedies set in Richmond and consisting of *The Romantic Comedians* (1926), one of her best books, as well as *They Stooped to Folly* (1929) and *The Sheltered Life* (1932); and *In This Our Life* (1941), a study of a Southern community in the days preceding World War II, for which she won the Pulitzer Prize.

Writing of the South, she nevertheless aspired to be more than a regional writer, seeking universality in a basic human nature that transcends the merely local. Retaining throughout her life her base at the home in Richmond to which her family moved when she was 15, she also spent time in New York City and Europe and was acclaimed in her day for an achievement that remains unique. Hers is a valuable record—the most extensive before Faulkner—of the South in transition, a locale imbued with more than nostalgia and costume drama.

Her collected *Works*, both incomplete, include the Old Dominion Edition (8 vols., 1929–1933) and the Virginia Edition (12 vols., 1938). Prefaces to her novels, drawn from these editions, are collected in *A Certain Measure: An Interpretation of Prose Fiction* (1943). Novels, in addition to those named above, are *The Wheel of Life* (1906); *The Ancient Law* (1908); *The Builders* (1919); *One Man in His Time* (1922); and *Beyond Defeat* (1966), edited by Richard K. Meeker, a posthumous sequel to *In This Our Life*. The only collection of stories published while she was alive is *The Shadowy Third and Other Stories* (1923). *The Collected Stories* (1963) was edited by Richard K. Meeker. Verse is collected in *The Freeman and Other Poems* (1902). Her autobiography is *The Woman Within* (1954). *Letters of Ellen Glasgow* (1958) was edited by Blair Rouse.

Studies include F. W. McDowell, *Ellen Glasgow and the Ironic Art of Fiction* (1960); Blair Rouse, *Ellen Glasgow* (1962); Louis Auchincloss, *Ellen Glasgow* (1964); Julius R. Raper, *Without Shelter: The Early Career of Ellen Glasgow* (1971), and *From the Sunken Garden: The Fiction of Ellen Glasgow 1916–1945* (1980); E. Stanley Godbold, *Ellen Glasgow and the Woman Within* (1972); and Linda Wagner, *Ellen Glasgow: Beyond Convention* (1983).

Jordan's End[1]

At the fork of the road there was the dead tree where buzzards were roosting, and through its boughs I saw the last flare of the sunset. On either side the November woods were flung in broken masses against the sky. When I stopped they appeared to move closer and surround me with vague, glimmering shapes. It seemed to me that I had been driving for

1. First printed in *The Shadowy Third* (1923). The source of the present text is *The Collected Stories* (1963).

hours; yet the ancient negro who brought the message had told me to follow the Old Stage Road till I came to Buzzard's Tree at the fork. "F'om dar on hit's moughty nigh ter Marse Jur'dn's place," the old man had assured me, adding tremulously, "en young Miss she sez you mus' come jes' ez quick ez you kin." I was young then (that was more than thirty years ago), and I was just beginning the practice of medicine in one of the more remote counties of Virginia.

My mare stopped, and leaning out, I gazed down each winding road, where it branched off, under half bared boughs, into the autumnal haze of the distance. In a little while the red would fade from the sky, and the chill night would find me still hesitating between those dubious ways which seemed to stretch into an immense solitude. While I waited uncertainly there was a stir in the boughs overhead, and a buzzard's feather floated down and settled slowly on the robe over my knees. In the effort to drive off depression, I laughed aloud and addressed my mare in a jocular tone:

"We'll choose the most God-forsaken of the two, and see where it leads us."

To my surprise the words brought an answer from the trees at my back. "If you're goin' to Isham's store, keep on the Old Stage Road," piped a voice from the underbrush.

Turning quickly, I saw the dwarfed figure of a very old man, with a hunched back, who was dragging a load of pine knots out of the woods. Though he was so stooped that his head reached scarcely higher than my wheel, he appeared to possess unusual vigour for one of his age and infirmities. He was dressed in a rough overcoat of some wood brown shade, beneath which I could see his overalls of blue jeans. Under a thatch of grizzled hair his shrewd little eyes twinkled cunningly, and his bristly chin jutted so far forward that it barely escaped the descending curve of his nose. I remember thinking that he could not be far from a hundred; his skin was so wrinkled and weather-beaten that, at a distance, I had mistaken him for a negro.

I bowed politely. "Thank you, but I am going to Jordan's End," I replied.

He cackled softly. "Then you take the bad road. That's Jur'dn's turnout." He pointed to the sunken trail, deep in mud, on the right. "An' if you ain't objectin' to a little comp'ny, I'd be obleeged if you'd give me a lift. I'm bound thar on my own o' count, an' it's a long ways to tote these here lightwood knots."

While I drew back my robe and made room for him, I watched him heave the load of resinous pine into the buggy, and then scramble with agility to his place at my side.

"My name is Peterkin," he remarked by way of introduction. "They call me Father Peterkin along o' the gran'child'en." He was a garrulous soul, I suspected, and would not be averse to imparting the information I wanted.

"There's not much travel this way," I began, as we turned out of the cleared space into the deep tunnel of the trees. Immediately the twilight enveloped us, though now and then the dusky glow in the sky was still visible. The air was sharp with the tang of autumn; with the effluvium of rotting leaves, the drift of wood smoke, the ripe flavour of crushed apples.

"Thar's nary a stranger, thoughten he was a doctor, been to Jur'dn's End as fur back as I kin recollect. Ain't you the new doctor?"

"Yes, I am the doctor." I glanced down at the gnomelike shape in the wood brown overcoat. "Is it much farther?"

"Naw, suh, we're all but thar jest as soon as we come out of Whitten woods."

"If the road is so little travelled, how do you happen to be going there?"

Without turning his head, the old man wagged his crescent shaped profile. "Oh, I live on the place. My son Tony works a slice of the farm on shares, and I manage to lend a hand at the harvest or corn shuckin', and, now-and-agen, with the cider. The old gentleman used to run the place that away afore he went deranged, an' now that the young one is laid up, thar ain't nobody to look arter the farm but Miss Judith. Them old ladies don't count. Thar's three of 'em, but they're all addle-brained an' look as if the buzzards had picked 'em. I reckon that comes from bein' shut up with crazy folks in that thar old tumbledown house. The roof ain't been patched fur so long that the shingles have most rotted away, an' thar's times, Tony says, when you kin skearcely hear yo' years fur the rumpus the wrens an' rats are makin' overhead."

"What is the trouble with them—the Jordans, I mean?"

"Jest run to seed, such, I reckon."

"Is there no man of the family left?"

For a minute Father Peterkin made no reply. Then he shifted the bundle of pine knots, and responded warily. "Young Alan, he's still livin' on the old place, but I hear he's been took now, an' is goin' the way of all the rest of 'em. 'Tis a hard trial for Miss Judith, po' young thing, an' with a boy nine year old that's the very spit an' image of his pa. Wall, wall, I kin recollect away back yonder when old Mr. Timothy Jur'dn was the proudest man anywhar aroun' in these parts; but arter the War things sorter begun to go down hill with him, and he was obleeged to draw in his horns."

"Is he still living?"

The old man shook his head. "Mebbe he is, an' mebbe he ain't. Nobody knows but the Jur'dn's, an' they ain't tellin' fur the axin'."

"I suppose it was this Miss Judith who sent for me?"

" 'Twould most likely be she, suh. She was one of the Yardlys that lived over yonder at Yardly's Field; an' when young Mr. Alan begun to take notice of her, 'twas the first time sence way back that one of the Jur'dn's had gone courtin' outside the family. That's the reason the blood went bad like it did, I reckon. Thar's a sayin' down aroun' here that Jur'dn an' Jur'dn won't mix." The name was invariably called Jurdin by all classes; but I had already discovered that names are rarely pronounced as they are spelled in Virginia.

"Have they been married long?"

"Ten year or so, suh. I remember as well as if 'twas yestiddy the day young Alan brought her home as a bride, an' thar warn't a soul besides the three daft old ladies to welcome her. They drove over in my son Tony's old buggy, though 'twas spick an' span then. I was goin' to the house on an arrant, an' I was standin' right down thar at the ice pond when they come by. She hadn't been much in these parts, an' none of us had ever seed her afore. When she looked up at young Alan her face was pink all over and her eyes war shinin' bright as the moon. Then the front do' opened an' them old ladies, as black as crows, flocked out on the po'ch. Thar never was anybody as peart-lookin' as Miss Judith was when she come here; but soon arterwards she begun to peak an' pine, though she never lost her sperits an' went mopin' roun' like all the other women folks at Jur'dn's End. They married sudden, an' folks do say she didn't know nothin' about the family, an' young Alan didn't know much mo' than she did. The old ladies had kep' the secret away from him, sorter believin' that what you don't know cyarn' hurt you. Anyways they never let it leak out tell arter his chile was born. Thar ain't never been but that one, an' old Aunt Jerusly declars he was born with a caul over his face, so mebbe things will be all right fur him in the long run."

"But who are the old ladies? Are their husbands living?"

When Father Peterkin answered the question he had dropped his voice to a hoarse murmur. "Deranged. All gone deranged," he replied.

I shivered, for a chill depression seemed to emanate from the November woods. As we drove on, I remembered grim tales of enchanted forests filled with evil faces and whispering voices. The scents of wood earth and rotting leaves invaded my brain like a magic spell. On either side the forest was as still as death. Not a leaf quivered, not a bird moved, not a small wild creature stirred in the underbrush. Only the glossy leaves and the scarlet berries of the holly appeared alive amid the bare interlacing branches of the trees. I began to long for an autumn clearing and the red light of the afterglow.

"Are they living or dead?" I asked presently.

"I've hearn strange tattle," answered the old man nervously, "but nobody kin tell. Folks do say as young Alan's pa is shut up in a padded place, and that his gran'pa died thar arter thirty years. His uncles went crazy too, an' the daftness is beginnin' to crop out in the women.

Up tell now it has been mostly the men. One time I remember old Mr. Peter Jur'dn tryin' to burn down the place in the dead of the night. Thar's the end of the wood, suh. If you'll jest let me down here, I'll be gittin' along home across the old-field, an' thanky too."

At last the woods ended abruptly on the edge of an abandoned field which was thickly sown with scrub pine and broomsedge. The glow in the sky had faded now to a thin yellow-green, and a melancholy twilight pervaded the landscape. In this twilight I looked over the few sheep huddled together on the ragged lawn, and saw the old brick house crumbling beneath its rank growth of ivy. As I drew nearer I had the feeling that the surrounding desolation brooded there like some sinister influence.

Forlorn as it appeared at this first approach, I surmised that Jordan's End must have possessed once charm as well as distinction. The proportions of the Georgian front were impressive, and there was beauty of design in the quaint doorway, and in the steps of rounded stone which were brocaded now with a pattern of emerald moss. But the whole place was badly in need of repair. Looking up, as I stopped, I saw that the eaves were falling away, that crumbled shutters were sagging from loosened hinges, that odd scraps of hemp sacking or oil cloth were stuffed into windows where panes were missing. When I stepped on the floor of the porch, I felt the rotting boards give way under my feet.

After thundering vainly on the door, I descended the steps, and followed the beaten path that led round the west wing of the house. When I had passed an old boxwood tree at the corner, I saw a woman and a boy of nine years or so come out of a shed, which I took to be the smokehouse, and begin to gather chips from the woodpile. The woman carried a basket made of splits on her arm, and while she stooped to fill this, she talked to the child in a soft musical voice. Then, at a sound that I made, she put the basket aside, and rising to her feet, faced me in the pallid light from the sky. Her head was thrown back, and over her dress of some dark calico, a tattered gray shawl clung to her figure. That was thirty years ago; I am not young any longer; I have been in many countries since then, and looked on many women; but her face, with that wan light on it, is the last one I shall forget in my life. Beauty! Why, that woman will be beautiful when she is a skeleton, was the thought that flashed into my mind.

She was very tall, and so thin that her flesh seemed faintly luminous, as if an inward light pierced the transparent substance. It was the beauty, not of earth, but of triumphant spirit. Perfection, I suppose, is the rarest thing we achieve in this world of incessant compromise with inferior forms; yet the woman who stood there in that ruined place appeared to me to have stepped straight out of legend or allegory. The contour of her face was Italian in its pure oval; her hair swept in wings of dusk above her clear forehead; and, from the faintly shadowed hollows beneath her brows, the eyes that looked at me were purple-black, like dark pansies.

"I had given you up," she began in a low voice, as if she were afraid of being overheard. "You are the doctor?"

"Yes, I am the doctor. I took the wrong road and lost my way. Are you Mrs. Jordan?"

She bowed her head. "Mrs. Alan Jordan. There are three Mrs. Jordans besides myself. My husband's grandmother and the wives of his two uncles."

"And it is your husband who is ill?"

"My husband, yes. I wrote a few days ago to Doctor Carstairs." (Thirty years ago Carstairs, of Baltimore, was the leading alienist[2] in the country.) "He is coming to-morrow morning; but last night my husband was so restless that I sent for you to-day." Her rich voice, vibrating with suppressed feeling, made me think of stained glass windows and low organ music.

"Before we go in," I asked, "will you tell me as much as you can?"

Instead of replying to my request, she turned and laid her hand on the boy's shoulder. "Take the chips to Aunt Agatha, Benjamin," she said, "and tell her that the doctor has come."

While the child picked up the basket and ran up the sunken steps to the door, she watched

---

2. Before the advent of psychiatry, a physician who specialized in mental disorders.

him with breathless anxiety. Not until he had disappeared into the hall did she lift her eyes to my face again. Then, without answering my question, she murmured, with a sigh which was like the voice of that autumn evening, "We were once happy here." She was trying, I realized, to steel her heart against the despair that threatened it.

My gaze swept the obscure horizon, and returned to the mouldering woodpile where we were standing. The yellow-green had faded from the sky, and the only light came from the house where a few scattered lamps were burning. Through the open door I could see the hall, as bare as if the house were empty, and the spiral staircase which crawled to the upper story. A fine old place once, but repulsive now in its abject decay, like some young blood of former days who has grown senile.

"Have you managed to wring a living out of the land?" I asked, because I could think of no words that were less compassionate.

"At first a poor one," she answered slowly. "We worked hard, harder than any negro in the fields, to keep things together, but we were happy. Then three years ago this illness came, and after that everything went against us. In the beginning it was simply brooding, a kind of melancholy, and we tried to ward it off by pretending that it was not real, that we imagined it. Only of late, when it became so much worse, have we admitted the truth, have we faced the reality——"

This passionate murmur, which had almost the effect of a chant rising out of the loneliness, was addressed, not to me, but to some abstract and implacable power. While she uttered it her composure was like the tranquillity of the dead. She did not lift her hand to hold her shawl, which was slipping unnoticed from her shoulders, and her eyes, so like dark flowers in their softness, did not leave my face.

"If you will tell me all, perhaps I may be able to help you," I said.

"But you know our story," she responded. "You must have heard it."

"Then it is true? Heredity, intermarriage, insanity?"

She did not wince at the bluntness of my speech. "My husband's grandfather is in an asylum, still living after almost thirty years. His father—my husband's, I mean—died there a few years ago. Two of his uncles are there. When it began I don't know, or how far back it reaches. We have never talked of it. We have tried always to forget it— Even now I cannot put the thing into words— My husband's mother died of a broken heart, but the grandmother and the two others are still living. You will see them when you go into the house. They are old women now, and they feel nothing."

"And there have been other cases?"

"I do not know. Are not four enough?"

"Do you know if it has assumed always the same form?" I was trying to be as brief as I could.

She flinched, and I saw that her unnatural calm was shaken at last. "The same, I believe. In the beginning there is melancholy, moping, Grandmother calls it, and then——" She flung out her arms with a despairing gesture, and I was reminded again of some tragic figure of legend.

"I know, I know," I was young, and in spite of my pride, my voice trembled. "Has there been in any case partial recovery, recurring at intervals?"

"In his grandfather's case, yes. In the others none. With them it has been hopeless from the beginning."

"And Carstairs is coming?"

"In the morning. I should have waited, but last night——" Her voice broke, and she drew the tattered shawl about her with a shiver. "Last night something happened. Something happened," she repeated, and could not go on. Then, collecting her strength with an effort which made her tremble like a blade of grass in the wind, she continued more quietly, "To-day he has been better. For the first time he has slept, and I have been able to leave him. Two of the hands from the fields are in the room." Her tone changed suddenly, and a note of energy passed into it. Some obscure resolution brought a tinge of colour to her pale cheek. "I must know," she added, "if this is as hopeless as all the others."

I took a step toward the house. "Carstairs's opinion is worth as much as that of any man living," I answered.

"But will he tell me the truth?"

I shook my head. "He will tell you what he thinks. No man's judgment is infallible."

Turning away from me, she moved with an energetic step to the house. As I followed her into the hall the threshold creaked under my tread, and I was visited by an apprehension, or, if you prefer, by a superstitious dread of the floor above. Oh, I got over that kind of thing before I was many years older; though in the end I gave up medicine, you know, and turned to literature as a safer outlet for a suppressed imagination.

But the dread was there at that moment, and it was not lessened by the glimpse I caught, at the foot of the spiral staircase, of a scantily furnished room, where three lean black-robed figures, as impassive as the Fates,[3] were grouped in front of a wood fire. They were doing something with their hands. Knitting, crocheting, or plaiting straw?

At the head of the stairs the woman stopped and looked back at me. The light from the kerosene lamp on the wall fell over her, and I was struck afresh not only by the alien splendour of her beauty, but even more by the look of consecration, of impassioned fidelity that illumined her face.

"He is very strong," she said in a whisper. "Until this trouble came on him he had never had a day's illness in his life. We hoped that hard work, not having time to brood, might save us; but it has only brought the thing we feared sooner."

There was a question in her eyes, and I responded in the same subdued tone. "His health, you say, is good?" What else was there for me to ask when I understood everything?

A shudder ran through her frame. "We used to think that a blessing, but now——" She broke off and then added in a lifeless voice, "We keep two field hands in the room day and night, lest one should forget to watch the fire, or fall asleep."

A sound came from a room at the end of the hall, and, without finishing her sentence, she moved swiftly toward the closed door. The apprehension, the dread, or whatever you choose to call it, was so strong upon me, that I was seized by an impulse to turn and retreat down the spiral staircase. Yes, I know why some men turn cowards in battle.

"I have come back, Alan," she said in a voice that wrung my heartstrings.

The room was dimly lighted; and for a minute after I entered, I could see nothing clearly except the ruddy glow of the wood fire in front of which two negroes were seated on low wooden stools. They had kindly faces, these men; there was a primitive humanity in their features, which might have been modelled out of the dark earth of the fields.

Looking round the next minute, I saw that a young man was sitting away from the fire, huddled over in a cretonne-covered chair with a high back and deep wings. At our entrance the negroes glanced up with surprise; but the man in the winged chair neither lifted his head nor turned his eyes in our direction. He sat there, lost within the impenetrable wilderness of the insane, as remote from us and from the sound of our voices as if he were the inhabitant of an invisible world. His head was sunk forward; his eyes were staring fixedly at some image we could not see; his fingers, moving restlessly, were plaiting and unplaiting the fringe of a plaid shawl. Distraught as he was, he still possessed the dignity of mere physical perfection. At his full height he must have measured not under six feet three; his hair was the colour of ripe wheat, and his eyes, in spite of their fixed gaze, were as blue as the sky after rain. And this was only the beginning, I realized. With that constitution, that physical frame, he might live to be ninety.

"Alan!" breathed his wife again in her pleading murmur.

If he heard her voice, he gave no sign of it. Only when she crossed the room and bent over his chair, he put out his hand, with a gesture of irritation, and pushed her away, as if she were

---

3. In classical mythology, the three goddesses of human destiny.

a veil of smoke which came between him and the object at which he was looking. Then his hand fell back to its old place, and he resumed his mechanical plaiting of the fringe.

The woman lifted her eyes to mine. "His father did that for twenty years," she said in a whisper that was scarcely more than a sigh of anguish.

When I had made my brief examination, we left the room as we had come, and descended the stairs together. The three old women were still sitting in front of the wood fire. I do not think they had moved since we went upstairs; but, as we reached the hall below, one of them, the youngest, I imagine, rose from her chair, and came out to join us. She was crocheting something soft and small, an infant's sacque,[4] I perceived as she approached, of pink wool. The ball had rolled from her lap as she stood up, and it trailed after her now, like a woolen rose, on the bare floor. When the skein pulled at her, she turned back and stooped to pick up the ball, which she rewound with caressing fingers. Good God, an infant's sacque in that house!

"Is it the same thing?" she asked.

"Hush!" responded the younger woman kindly. Turning to me she added, "We cannot talk here," and opening the door, passed out on the porch. Not until we had reached the lawn, and walked in silence to where my buggy stood beneath an old locust tree, did she speak again.

Then she said only, "You know now?"

"Yes, I know," I replied, averting my eyes from her face while I gave my directions as briefly as I could. "I will leave an opiate," I said. "Tomorrow, if Carstairs should not come, send for me again. If he does come," I added, "I will talk to him and see you afterward."

"Thank you," she answered gently; and taking the bottle from my hand, she turned away and walked quickly back to the house.

I watched her as long as I could; and then getting into my buggy, I turned my mare's head toward the woods, and drove by moonlight, past Buzzard's Tree and over the Old Stage Road, to my home. "I will see Carstairs to-morrow," was my last thought that night before I slept.

But, after all, I saw Carstairs only for a minute as he was taking the train. Life at its beginning and its end had filled my morning; and when at last I reached the little station, Carstairs had paid his visit, and was waiting on the platform for the approaching express. At first he showed a disposition to question me about the shooting,[5] but as soon as I was able to make my errand clear, his jovial face clouded.

"So you've been there?" he said. "They didn't tell me. An interesting case, if it were not for that poor woman. Incurable, I'm afraid, when you consider the predisposing causes. The race is pretty well deteriorated, I suppose. God! what isolation! I've advised her to send him away. There are three others, they tell me, at Staunton."

The train came; he jumped on it, and was whisked away while I gazed after him. After all, I was none the wiser because of the great reputation of Carstairs.

All that day I heard nothing more from Jordan's End; and then, early next morning, the same decrepit negro brought me a message.

"Young Miss, she tole me ter ax you ter come along wid me jes' ez soon ez you kin git ready."

"I'll start at once, Uncle, and I'll take you with me."

My mare and buggy stood at the door. All I needed to do was to put on my overcoat, pick up my hat, and leave word, for a possible patient, that I should return before noon. I knew the road now, and I told myself, as I set out, that I would make as quick a trip as I could. For two nights I had been haunted by the memory of that man in the armchair, plaiting and unplaiting the fringe of the plaid shawl. And his father had done that, the woman had told me, for twenty years!

It was a brown autumn morning, raw, windless, with an overcast sky and a peculiar illusion of nearness about the distance. A high wind had blown all night, but at dawn it had dropped

---

4. A loose-fitting dress or cloak.   5. Hunting (in the area).

suddenly, and now there was not so much as a ripple in the broomsedge. Over the fields, when we came out of the woods, the thin trails of blue smoke were as motionless as cobwebs. The lawn surrounding the house looked smaller than it had appeared to me in the twilight, as if the barren fields had drawn closer since my last visit. Under the trees, where the few sheep were browsing, the piles of leaves lay in windrifts along the sunken walk and against the wings of the house.

When I knocked the door was opened immediately by one of the old women, who held a streamer of black cloth or rusty crape in her hands.

"You may go straight upstairs," she croaked; and, without waiting for an explanation, I entered the hall quickly, and ran up the stairs.

The door of the room was closed, and I opened it noiselessly, and stepped over the threshold. My first sensation, as I entered, was one of cold. Then I saw that the windows were wide open, and that the room seemed to be full of people, though, as I made out presently, there was no one there except Alan Jordan's wife, her little son, the two old aunts, and an aged crone of a negress. On the bed there was something under a yellowed sheet of fine linen (what the negroes call "a burial sheet," I suppose), which had been handed down from some more affluent generation.

When I went over, after a minute, and turned down one corner of the covering, I saw that my patient of the other evening was dead. Not a line of pain marred his features, not a thread of gray dimmed the wheaten gold of his hair. So he must have looked, I thought, when she first loved him. He had gone from life, not old, enfeebled and repulsive, but enveloped still in the romantic illusion of their passion.

As I entered, the two old women, who had been fussing about the bed, drew back to make way for me, but the witch of a negress did not pause in the weird chant, an incantation of some sort, which she was mumbling. From the rag carpet in front of the empty fireplace, the boy, with his father's hair and his mother's eyes, gazed at me silently, broodingly, as if I were trespassing; and by the open window, with her eyes on the ashen November day, the young wife stood as motionless as a statue. While I looked at her a redbird flew out of the boughs of a cedar, and she followed it with her eyes.

"You sent for me?" I said to her.

She did not turn. She was beyond the reach of my voice, of any voice, I imagine; but one of the palsied old women answered my question.

"He was like this when we found him this morning," she said. "He had a bad night, and Judith and the two hands were up with him until daybreak. Then he seemed to fall asleep, and Judith sent the hands, turn about, to get their breakfast."

While she spoke my eyes were on the bottle I had left there. Two nights ago it had been full, and now it stood empty, without a cork, on the mantelpiece. They had not even thrown it away. It was typical of the pervading inertia of the place that the bottle should still be standing there awaiting my visit.

For an instant the shock held me speechless; when at last I found my voice it was to ask mechanically.

"When did it happen?"

The old woman who had spoken took up the story. "Nobody knows. We have not touched him. No one but Judith has gone near him." Her words trailed off into unintelligible muttering. If she had ever had her wits about her, I dare-say fifty years at Jordan's End had unsettled them completely.

I turned to the woman at the window. Against the gray sky and the black intersecting branches of the cedar, her head, with its austere perfection, was surrounded by that visionary air of legend. So Antigone[6] might have looked on the day of her sacrifice, I reflected. I had

6. In Sophocles' *Antigone*, Antigone buries her dead brother in defiance of King Creon's order. Punished by being placed alive in a burial vault, she kills herself.

never seen a creature who appeared so withdrawn, so detached, from all human associations. It was as if some spiritual isolation divided her from her kind.

"I can do nothing," I said.

For the first time she looked at me, and her eyes were unfathomable. "No, you can do nothing," she answered. "He is safely dead."

The negress was still crooning on; the other old women were fussing helplessly. It was impossible in their presence, I felt, to put in words the thing I had to say.

"Will you come downstairs with me?" I asked. "Outside of this house?"

Turning quietly, she spoke to the boy. "Run out and play, dear. He would have wished it."

Then, without a glance toward the bed, or the old women gathered about it, she followed me over the threshold, down the stairs, and out on the deserted lawn. The ashen day could not touch her, I saw then. She was either so remote from it, or so completely a part of it, that she was impervious to its sadness. Her white face did not become more pallid as the light struck it; her tragic eyes did not grow deeper; her frail figure under the thin shawl did not shiver in the raw air. She felt nothing, I realized suddenly.

Wrapped in that silence as in a cloak, she walked across the windrifts of leaves to where my mare was waiting. Her step was so slow, so unhurried, that I remember thinking she moved like one who had all eternity before her. Oh, one has strange impressions, you know, at such moments!

In the middle of the lawn, where the trees had been stripped bare in the night, and the leaves were piled in long mounds like double graves, she stopped and looked in my face. The air was so still that the whole place might have been in a trance or asleep. Not a branch moved, not a leaf rustled on the ground, not a sparrow twittered in the ivy; and even the few sheep stood motionless, as if they were under a spell. Farther away, beyond the sea of broomsedge, where no wind stirred, I saw the flat desolation of the landscape. Nothing moved on the earth, but high above, under the leaden clouds, a buzzard was sailing.

I moistened my lips before I spoke. "God knows I want to help you!" At the back of my brain a hideous question was drumming. How had it happened? Could she have killed him? Had that delicate creature nerved her will to the unspeakable act? It was incredible. It was inconceivable. And yet. . . .

"The worst is over," she answered quietly, with that tearless agony which is so much more terrible than any outburst of grief. "Whatever happens, I can never go through the worst again. Once in the beginning he wanted to die. His great fear was that he might live too long, until it was too late to save himself. I made him wait then. I held him back by a promise."

So she had killed him, I thought. Then she went on steadily, after a minute, and I doubted again.

"Thank God, it was easier for him than he feared it would be," she murmured.

No, it was not conceivable. He must have bribed one of the negroes. But who had stood by and watched without intercepting? Who had been in the room? Well, either way! "I will do all I can to help you," I said.

Her gaze did not waver. "There is so little that any one can do now," she responded, as if she had not understood what I meant. Suddenly, without the warning of a sob, a cry of despair went out of her, as if it were torn from her breast. "He was my life," she cried, "and I must go on!"

So full of agony was the sound that it seemed to pass like a gust of wind over the broomsedge. I waited until the emptiness had opened and closed over it. Then I asked as quietly as I could:

"What will you do now?"

She collected herself with a shudder of pain. "As long as the old people live, I am tied here. I must bear it out to the end. When they die, I shall go away and find work. I am sending my boy to school. Doctor Carstairs will look after him, and he will help me when the time comes. While my boy needs me, there is no release."

While I listened to her, I knew that the question on my lips would never be uttered. I should always remain ignorant of the truth. The thing I feared most, standing there alone with her, was that some accident might solve the mystery before I could escape. My eyes left her face and wandered over the dead leaves at our feet. No, I had nothing to ask her.

"Shall I come again?" That was all.

She shook her head. "Not unless I send for you. If I need you, I will send for you," she answered; but in my heart I knew that she would never send for me.

I held out my hand, but she did not take it; and I felt that she meant me to understand, by her refusal, that she was beyond all consolation and all companionship. She was nearer to the bleak sky and the deserted fields than she was to her kind.

As she turned away, the shawl slipped from her shoulders to the dead leaves over which she was walking; but she did not stoop to recover it, nor did I make a movement to follow her. Long after she had entered the house I stood there, gazing down on the garment that she had dropped. Then climbing into my buggy, I drove slowly across the field and into the woods.

                                                                                            1923

Amy Lowell
(1874–1925)

In the years since her death, Amy Lowell's reputation has suffered from dismissive references to her figure and personal habits and from derisive comments by her contemporaries. She weighed over 200 pounds and she smoked cigars. Ezra Pound derided her as the leader not of "Imagism" but of "Amygism," and referred to her as a "hippopoetess." Yet she was highly influential in the decade from 1914 to the early 1920s, when American verse turned away from its heritage of nineteenth-century traditionalism. With her considerable help, poetic practice moved by way of imagism and free verse into the modernism that dominated the decade of her death, and she left behind some memorable poems.

Born into wealth and privilege in Brookline, Massachusetts, Amy Lowell was a member of one of the state's most prominent families. Her grandfathers were leaders of the textile industry that supplied much of the state's wealth from the 1830s onward. Her father served on the governing board of the Massachusetts Institute of Technology, and her brother Abbott Lawrence Lowell became president of Harvard. Another brother, Percival, was an

early Orientalist; he spent ten years in Japan and later founded the Lowell Observatory in Flagstaff, Arizona. Poets James Russell Lowell, earlier, and Robert Lowell, later, were relatives. Educated at home, in private schools, and through European travel, she early developed a preoccupation with what she perceived as her own inadequacies. Overweight and frequently suffering from ill health, she endured a prolonged depression in her twenties that lasted from about 1898 to 1905. In 1902, however, a performance by the Italian actress Eleanora Duse showed her the way to recovery through artistic expression. Enraptured by what she had seen, she returned home to write her first poetry: "It loosed a bolt in my brain and I found out where my true function lay."

In the same year as the publication of her first book, *A Dome of Many-Coloured Glass* (1912), a largely conventional collection of verse, Lowell met Ada Dwyer Russell, an older actress whose friendship and support became crucial to her development. In 1914 Russell moved into Sevenels, Lowell's home in Brookline, and remained with her until her death, encouraging her in the career that blossomed from that point onward. Meanwhile, the founding of *Poetry* magazine in Chicago had given an American presence to the new poetry then emerging, and Lowell and Russell traveled to London in 1913 and 1914 to meet such new poets as Ezra Pound, John Gould Fletcher, H. D., D. H. Lawrence, and Robert Frost. In her second book, *Sword Blades and Poppy Seed* (1914), she displayed her growth, including poems in free verse and the first examples of a new form she called "polyphonic prose," combining prose form and poetic sounds and rhythms. Committed now to experimentation, she became the major sponsor of the group Pound had earlier championed as *Les Imagistes,* producing three imagist anthologies between 1915 and 1917. Extraordinarily energetic in these years, she lectured, wrote, reviewed, and became a public personality, mocked by some, viewed as an inspirational leader by others. She published more polyphonic prose in *Can Grande's Castle* (1918), and short poems in *Pictures of a Floating World*

(1919). Her posthumous collection *What's O'Clock* (1925) was awarded a Pulitzer Prize. Meanwhile, she had published two works of pioneering criticism, *Six French Poets: Studies in Contemporary Criticism* (1915) and *Tendencies in Modern American Poetry* (1917). During her last years much of her effort went into the two volumes of her *John Keats* (1925).

The Complete Poetical Works was published in 1955. Individual titles, besides those named above, include *Men, Women and Ghosts* (1916), verse narratives, polyphonic prose, and dramatic monologues; *Fir Flower Tables* (1921), versions of Chinese poems drawn from English prose translations; and *A Critical Fable* (1922), discussions of contemporary poets in imitation of James Russell Lowell's *A Fable for Critics*. Ferris Greenslet edited *Poetry and Prose: Essays* (1930). Harley F. MacNair edited *Florence Ayscough and Amy Lowell: Correspondence and a Friendship* (1945). Studies include S. Foster Damon, *Amy Lowell: A Biography* (1935); Glenn Richard Ruihley, *The Thorn of a Rose: Amy Lowell Reconsidered* (1975); David Heymann, *American Aristocracy: The Lives and Times of James Russell, Amy, and Robert Lowell* (1980); and Richard Benvenuto, *Amy Lowell* (1985).

A Lady

You are beautiful and faded
Like an old opera tune
Played upon a harpsichord;
Or like the sun-flooded silks
Of an eighteenth-century boudoir.   5
In your eyes
Smolder the fallen roses of out-lived minutes,
And the perfume of your soul
Is vague and suffusing,
With the pungence of sealed spice-jars.   10
Your half-tones delight me,
And I grow mad with gazing
At your blent colors.

My vigor is a new-minted penny,
Which I cast at your feet.   15
Gather it up from the dust,
That its sparkle may amuse you.

1914

Patterns

I walk down the garden paths,
And all the daffodils
Are blowing, and the bright blue squills.
I walk down the patterned garden-paths
In my stiff, brocaded gown.   5
With my powdered hair and jewelled fan,
I too am a rare
Pattern. As I wander down
The garden paths.

My dress is richly figured;   10
And the train
Makes a pink and silver stain
On the gravel, and the thrift
Of the borders.
Just a plate of current fashion   15
Tripping by in high-heeled, ribboned shoes.
Not a softness anywhere about me,
Only whalebone and brocade.
And I sink on a seat in the shade
Of a lime tree. For my passion   20
Wars against the stiff brocade.
The daffodils and squills
Flutter in the breeze
As they please.
And I weep;   25
For the lime-tree is in blossom
And one small flower has dropped upon my bosom.

And the plashing of waterdrops
In the marble fountain
Comes down the garden-paths.   30
The dripping never stops.
Underneath my stiffened gown
Is the softness of a woman bathing in a marble basin,
A basin in the midst of hedges grown
So thick, she cannot see her lover hiding,   35
But she guesses he is near,
And the sliding of the water
Seems the stroking of a dear
Hand upon her.
What is Summer in a fine brocaded gown!   40
I should like to see it lying in a heap upon the ground.
All the pink and silver crumpled up on the ground.

I would be the pink and silver as I ran along the paths,
And he would stumble after,
Bewildered by my laughter.   45
I should see the sun flashing from his sword-hilt and buckles on his shoes.
I would choose
To lead him in a maze along the patterned paths,

A bright and laughing maze for my heavy-booted lover.
Till he caught me in the shade, 50
And the buttons of his waistcoat bruised my body as he clasped me,
Aching, melting, unafraid.
With the shadows of the leaves and the sundrops,
And the plopping of the waterdrops,
All about us in the open afternoon— 55
I am very like to swoon
With the weight of this brocade,
For the sun sifts through the shade.

Underneath the fallen blossom
In my bosom, 60
Is a letter I have hid.
It was brought to me this morning by a rider from the Duke.
"Madam, we regret to inform you that Lord Hartwell
Died in action Thursday se'nnight."
As I read it in the white, morning sunlight, 65
The letters squirmed like snakes.
"Any answer, Madam," said my footman.
"No," I told him.
"See that the messenger takes some refreshment.
No, no answer." 70
And I walked into the garden,
Up and down the patterned paths,
In my stiff, correct brocade.
The blue and yellow flowers stood up proudly in the sun,
Each one. 75
I stood upright too,
Held rigid to the pattern
By the stiffness of my gown.
Up and down I walked.
Up and down. 80

In a month he would have been my husband.
In a month, here, underneath this lime,
We would have broken the pattern;
He for me, and I for him,
He as Colonel, I as Lady, 85
On this shady seat.
He had a whim
That sunlight carried blessing.
And I answered, "It shall be as you have said."
Now he is dead. 90

In Summer and in Winter I shall walk
Up and down
The patterned garden-paths
In my stiff, brocaded gown.
The squills and daffodils 95
Will give place to pillared roses, and to asters, and to snow.
I shall go
Up and down,

In my gown.
Gorgeously arrayed,   100
Boned and stayed.
And the softness of my body will be guarded from embrace
By each button, hook, and lace.
For the man who should loose me is dead,
Fighting with the Duke in Flanders,   105
In a pattern called a war.
Christ! What are patterns for?

1916

Opal

You are ice and fire,
The touch of you burns my hands like snow.
You are cold and flame.
You are the crimson of amaryllis,
The silver of moon-touched magnolias.   5
When I am with you,
My heart is a frozen pond
Gleaming with agitated torches.

1919

A Decade

When you came, you were like red wine and honey,
And the taste of you burnt my mouth with its sweetness.
Now you are like morning bread,
Smooth and pleasant.
I hardly taste you at all for I know your savour,   5
But I am completely nourished.

1919

Meeting-House Hill

I must be mad, or very tired,
When the curve of a blue bay beyond a railroad track
Is shrill and sweet to me like the sudden springing of a tune,
And the sight of a white church above thin trees in a city square
Amazes my eyes as though it were the Parthenon.   5
Clear, reticent, superbly final,
With the pillars of its portico refined to a cautious elegance,

It dominates the weak trees,
And the shot of its spire
Is cool, and candid,   10
Rising into an unresisting sky.
Strange meeting-house
Pausing a moment upon a squalid hilltop.
I watch the spire sweeping the sky,
I am dizzy with the movement of the sky,   15
I might be watching a mast
With its royals set full
Straining before a two-reef breeze.
I might be sighting a tea-clipper,
Tacking into the blue bay,   20
Just back from Canton
With her hold full of green and blue porcelain,
And a Chinese coolie leaning over the rail
Gazing at the white spire
With dull, sea-spent eyes.   25

                                              1925

Lilacs

Lilacs,
False blue,
White,
Purple,
Colour of lilac,   5
Your great puffs of flowers
Are everywhere in this my New England.
Among your heart-shaped leaves
Orange orioles hop like music-box birds and sing
Their little weak soft songs;   10
In the crooks of your branches
The bright eyes of song sparrows sitting on spotted eggs
Peer restlessly through the light and shadow
Of all Springs.

Lilacs in dooryards   15
Holding quiet conversations with an early moon;
Lilacs watching a deserted house
Settling sideways into the grass of an old road;
Lilacs, wind-beaten, staggering under a lop-sided shock of bloom
Above a cellar dug into a hill.   20
You are everywhere.
You were everywhere.
You tapped the window when the preacher preached his sermon,
And ran along the road beside the boy going to school.
You stood by pasture-bars to give the cows good milking,   25
You persuaded the housewife that her dish pan was of silver

And her husband an image of pure gold.
You flaunted the fragrance of your blossoms
Through the wide doors of Custom Houses—
You, and sandal-wood, and tea,   30
Charging the noses of quill-driving clerks
When a ship was in from China.
You called to them: "Goose-quill men, goose-quill men,
May is a month for flitting."
Until they writhed on their high stools   35
And wrote poetry on their letter-sheets behind the propped-up ledgers.
Paradoxical New England clerks,
Writing inventories in ledgers, reading the "Song of Solomon" at night,
So many verses before bed-time,
Because it was the Bible.   40
The dead fed you
Amid the slant stones of graveyards.
Pale ghosts who planted you
Came in the night-time
And let their thin hair blow through your clustered stems.   45
You are of the green sea,
And of the stone hills which reach a long distance.
You are of elm-shaded streets with little shops where they sell kites and marbles,
You are of great parks where everyone walks and nobody is at home.
You cover the blind sides of greenhouses   50
And lean over the top to say a hurry-word through the glass
To your friends, the grapes, inside.

Lilacs,
False blue,
White,
Purple,   55
Colour of lilac,
You have forgotten your Eastern origin,
The veiled women with eyes like panthers,
The swollen, aggressive turbans of jewelled Pashas.   60
Now you are a very decent flower,
A reticent flower,
A curiously clear-cut, candid flower,
Standing beside clean doorways,
Friendly to a house-cat and a pair of spectacles,   65
Making poetry out of a bit of moonlight
And a hundred or two sharp blossoms.

Maine knows you,
Has for years and years;
New Hampshire knows you,   70
And Massachusetts
And Vermont.
Cape Cod starts you along the beaches to Rhode Island;
Connecticut takes you from a river to the sea.
You are brighter than apples,   75
Sweeter than tulips,
You are the great flood of our souls

Bursting above the leaf-shapes of our hearts,
You are the smell of all Summers,
The love of wives and children,   80
The recollection of the gardens of little children,
You are State Houses and Charters
And the familiar treading of the foot to and fro on a road it knows.
May is lilac here in New England,
May is a thrush singing "Sun up!" on a tip-top ash-tree,   85
May is white clouds behind pine-trees
Puffed out and marching upon a blue sky.
May is a green as no other,
May is much sun through small leaves,
May is soft earth,   90
And apple-blossoms,
And windows open to a South wind.
May is full light wind of lilac
From Canada to Narragansett Bay.

Lilacs,   95
False blue,
White,
Purple,
Colour of lilac.
Heart-leaves of lilac all over New England,   100
Roots of lilac under all the soil of New England,

Lilac in me because I am New England,
Because my roots are in it,
Because my leaves are of it,
Because my flowers are for it,   105
Because it is my country
And I speak to it of itself
And sing of it with my own voice
Since certainly it is mine.

1925

Gertrude Stein
(1874–1946)

Born in Allegheny, Pennsylvania, the seventh child of prosperous Jewish-American parents, Gertrude Stein lived most of her life in France. Occupying a central place in twentieth-century modernism, she inspired other writers and artists and served as a bridge between the ongoing lives of Americans and Europeans in a period when the world grew rapidly smaller. Asked why she chose Europe, she once replied, "the United States is a country the right age to be born in and the wrong age to live in." She was so famous when she returned to the United States briefly in 1934, three decades after she had left it for good, that Times Square was lit with the electric message, "GERTRUDE STEIN HAS ARRIVED IN NEW YORK." Although she had struggled all her life to be published, Random House now signed a contract with her for a book a year. Still, she said, "America is my country and Paris is my home town, and it is as it has come to be." Back in Europe, she lived out most of World War II in the French countryside; she returned to Paris as the war wound down, two years before her death.

In the year after her birth, the Stein family moved to Europe, where they spent the next four years, first in Vienna and then in Paris. In 1879, they moved briefly to Baltimore, but the next year they settled in Oakland, California ("There is no there there," she wrote later). Orphaned as a teenager—her mother died when she was 14, her father when she was 17—Stein became especially close to her older brother Leo, following him to school first at Harvard and then Johns Hopkins Medical School. At Harvard (the Harvard Annex when she entered, but soon Radcliffe College), she studied with the philosopher William James and graduated magna cum laude in 1897. After four years at Johns Hopkins she gave up her studies, and somewhat later, in 1903, she settled with Leo in an apartment at 27 rue de Fleurus, Paris, an address that became famous as a meeting place for avant-garde writers and artists. Alice B. Toklas, Stein's lifetime assistant and lover, joined the couple in 1909, and in 1913 Leo moved out. Sister and brother were never close thereafter.

For many years Stein's work found no large following. Leo, more interested in the art of modernists like Matisse, Braque, Cezanne, and Picasso that they both collected, belittled her writing. Much of her work remained unpublished and some appeared in private or limited editions. She held back her first substantial works, both completed by 1905: "Q.E.D.," a semi-autobiographical study of a lesbian triangle, appeared only after her death, as *Things As They Are* (1950), and "Fernhurst," based on a scandal at Bryn Mawr, appeared in revised form in *The Making of Americans* (1925). Her first book to see print, *Three*

Lives (1909), published at her own expense, has become one of her most admired works, an early example of experimental modernist prose that remains accessible to the average reader. *The Making of Americans*, in some ways her most ambitious work, was written next. From the three working-class American women of *Three Lives*, two immigrants and a black, she now moved to what she said was a history of every American "who ever can or is or was or will be living." Basing the account in the story of her own family, she completed it seventeen years before she was able to find a publisher in Robert McAlmon's Contact Press, and then it sold few copies. Meanwhile, *Tender Buttons* (1914), prose poems, showed how far she had advanced in creating verbal patterns that could stand as analogues in print for the graphic cubism she admired in Picasso. With two books in print, by World War I she had begun to attract the notice of critics, and she soon became an influence on younger writers like Sherwood Anderson and Ernest Hemingway.

Of the works that followed, *The Autobiography of Alice B. Toklas* (1933) remains most popular, the only one of her books that became a best-seller. Written as though from the pen of Toklas, it is largely about Stein herself and provides a lively, witty account of her Paris experiences. Other successes came quickly. Stein brought out a new, abridged edition of *The Making of Americans*, toured the United States in 1934–1935, saw *Three Lives* reprinted by Modern Library, and in rapid succession brought out Random House editions of *Four Saints in Three Acts* (1943), her libretto of a Virgil Thomson opera; *Portraits and Prayers* (1934); *Lectures in America* (1935); *The Geographical History of America* (1936); and *Everybody's Autobiography* (1937). After the war came *Wars I Have Seen* (1945), on the two world wars, and *Brewsie and Willie* (1946), inspired by the young American soldiers she met toward the end of the second.

The permanent value of Stein's enormous literary production is still being assessed. In recent years she has received concentrated attention from scholars interested in the interrelations of modernism as well as by those impelled by the concerns of feminism. Controversial in part because of the difficulty of much of her work, she seems nevertheless beyond controversy in the effects of some of her best writing, in demonstrations of the power of literary fragmentation, of reiteration, and of syntax bent to the will of a strong personality.

Major titles in addition to those named above include *Composition As Explanation* (1926), *Ida, a Novel* (1941), and *Four in America* (1947). Carl Van Vechten edited *Selected Writings*, 1946; and *The Yale Edition of the Unpublished Writings of Gertrude Stein*, eight vols., 1951–1958. Richard Kostalanetz edited *The Yale Ger-* *trude Stein: Selections*, 1980. A memoir is Alice B. Toklas, *What is Remembered*, 1963.

Biographical studies include Elizabeth Sprigge, *Gertrude Stein: Her Life and Work*, 1957; John Malcolm Brinnin, *The Third Rose: Gertrude Stein and Her World*, 1959; and Howard Greenfield, *Gertrude Stein: A Biography*, 1973. Critical studies include Donald Sutherland, *Gertrude Stein: A Biography of Her Work*, 1951, repr. 1972; J. Michael Hoffman, *The Development of Abstractionism in the Writings of Gertrude Stein*, 1965; Allegra Stewart, *Gertrude Stein and the Present*, 1967; Norman Weinstein, *Gertrude Stein and the Literature of Modern Consciousness*, 1970; Richard Bridgman, *Gertrude Stein in Pieces*, 1970; Robert B. Haas, *A Primer for the Gradual Understanding of Gertrude Stein*, 1971; James R. Mellow, *Charmed Circle: Gertrude Stein and Company*, 1974; Wendy Steiner, *Exact Resemblance to Exact Resemblance: The Literary Portraiture of Gertrude Stein*, 1978; Jayne L. Walker, *The Making of a Modernist: Gertrude Stein from Three Lives to Tender Buttons*, 1984; Harriett S. Chessman, *The Public Is Invited to the Dance: Representation, the Body, and Dialogue in Gertrude Stein*, 1989; and Lisa Ruddick, *Reading Gertrude Stein: Body, Text, Gnosis*, 1990.

The Gentle Lena[1]

Lena was patient, gentle, sweet and german. She had been a servant for four years and had liked it very well.

Lena had been brought from Germany to Bridgepoint by a cousin and had been in the same place there for four years.

This place Lena had found very good. There was a pleasant, unexacting mistress and her children, and they all liked Lena very well.

There was a cook there who scolded Lena a great deal but Lena's german patience held no suffering and the good incessant woman really only scolded so for Lena's good.

Lena's german voice when she knocked and called the family in the morning was as awakening, as soothing, and as appealing, as a delicate soft breeze in midday, summer. She stood in the hallway every morning a long time in her unexpectant and unsuffering german patience calling to the young ones to get up. She would call and wait a long time and then call again, always even, gentle, patient, while the young ones fell back often into that precious, tense, last bit of sleeping that gives a strength of joyous vigor in the young, over them that have come to the readiness of middle age, in their awakening.

Lena had good hard work all morning, and on the pleasant, sunny afternoons she was sent out into the park to sit and watch the little two year old girl baby of the family.

The other girls, all them that make the pleasant, lazy crowd, that watch the children in the sunny afternoons out in the park, all liked the simple, gentle, german Lena very well. They

1. The third of the three stories in *Three Lives*, "The Gentle Lena" was based in part on a servant girl Stein had known as a medical student at Johns Hopkins and influenced by Gustave Flaubert's "A Simple Heart."

all, too, liked very well to tease her, for it was so easy to make her mixed and troubled, and all helpless, for she could never learn to know just what the other quicker girls meant by the queer things they said.

The two or three of these girls, the ones that Lena always sat with, always worked together to confuse her. Still it was pleasant, all this life for Lena.

The little girl fell down sometimes and cried, and then Lena had to soothe her. When the little girl would drop her hat, Lena had to pick it up and hold it. When the little girl was bad and threw away her playthings, Lena told her she could not have them and took them from her to hold until the little girl should need them.

It was all a peaceful life for Lena, almost as peaceful as a pleasant leisure. The other girls, of course, did tease her, but then that only made a gentle stir within her.

Lena was a brown and pleasant creature, brown as blonde races often have them brown, brown, not with the yellow or the red or the chocolate brown of sun burned countries, but brown with the clear color laid flat on the light toned skin beneath, the plain, spare brown that makes it right to have been made with hazel eyes, and not too abundant straight, brown hair, hair that only later deepens itself into brown from the straw yellow of a german childhood.

Lena had the flat chest, straight back and forward falling shoulders of the patient and enduring working woman, though her body was now still in its milder girlhood and work had not yet made these lines too clear.

The rarer feeling that there was with Lena, showed in all the even quiet of her body movements, but in all it was the strongest in the patient, old-world ignorance, and earth made pureness of her brown, flat, soft featured face. Lena had eyebrows that were a wondrous thickness. They were black, and spread, and very cool, with their dark color and their beauty, and beneath them were her hazel eyes, simple and human, with the earth patience of the working, gentle, german woman.

Yes it was all a peaceful life for Lena. The other girls, of course, did tease her, but then that only made a gentle stir within her.

"What you got on your finger Lena," Mary, one of the girls she always sat with, one day asked her. Mary was good natured, quick, intelligent and Irish.

Lena had just picked up the fancy paper made accordion that the little girl had dropped beside her, and was making it squeak sadly as she pulled it with her brown strong, awkward finger.

"Why, what is it, Mary, paint?" said Lena, putting her finger to her mouth to taste the dirt spot.

"That's awful poison Lena, don't you know?" said Mary, "that green paint that you just tasted."

Lena had sucked a good deal of the green paint from her finger. She stopped and looked hard at the finger. She did not know just how much Mary meant by what she said.

"Ain't it poison, Nellie, that green paint, that Lena sucked just now," said Mary. "Sure it is Lena, it's real poison, I ain't foolin' this time anyhow."

Lena was a little troubled. She looked hard at her finger where the paint was, and she wondered if she had really sucked it.

It was still a little wet on the edges and she rubbed it off a long time on the inside of her dress, and in between she wondered and looked at the finger and thought, was it really poison that she had just tasted.

"Ain't it too bad, Nellie, Lena should have sucked that," Mary said.

Nellie smiled and did not answer. Nellie was dark and thin, and looked Italian. She had a big mass of black hair that she wore high up on her head, and that made her face look very fine.

Nellie always smiled and did not say much, and then she would look at Lena to perplex her.

And so they all three sat with their little charges in the pleasant sunshine a long time. And Lena would often look at her finger and wonder if it was really poison that she had just tasted and then she would rub her finger on her dress a little harder.

Mary laughed at her and teased her and Nellie smiled a little and looked queerly at her.

Then it came time, for it was growing cooler, for them to drag together the little ones, who had begun to wander, and to take each one back to its own mother. And Lena never knew for certain whether it was really poison, that green stuff that she had tasted.

During these four years of service, Lena always spent her Sundays out at the house of her aunt, who had brought her four years before to Bridgepoint.

This aunt, who had brought Lena, four years before, to Bridgepoint, was a hard, ambitious, well meaning, german woman. Her husband was a grocer in the town, and they were very well to do. Mrs. Haydon, Lena's aunt had two daughters who were just beginning as young ladies, and she had a little boy who was not honest and who was very hard to manage.

Mrs. Haydon was a short, stout, hard built, german woman. She always hit the ground very firmly and compactly as she walked. Mrs. Haydon was all a compact and well hardened mass, even to her face, reddish and darkened from its early blonde, with its hearty, shiny cheeks, and doubled chin well covered over with the up roll from her short, square neck.

The two daughters, who were fourteen and fifteen looked like unkneaded, unformed mounds of flesh beside her.

The elder girl, Mathilda, was blonde, and slow, and simple, and quite fat. The younger, Bertha, who was almost as tall as her sister, was dark, and quicker, and she was heavy, too, but not really fat.

These two girls the mother had brought up very firmly. They were well taught for their position. They were always both well dressed, in the same kinds of hats and dresses, as is becoming in two german sisters. The mother liked to have them dressed in red. Their best clothes were red dresses, made of good heavy cloth, and strongly trimmed with braid of a glistening black. They had stiff, red felt hats, trimmed with black velvet ribbon, and a bird. The mother dressed matronly, in a bonnet and in black, always sat between her two big daughters, firm, directing, and repressed.

The only weak spot in this good german woman's conduct was the way she spoiled her boy who was not honest and who was very hard to manage.

The father of this family was a decent, quiet, heavy, and uninterfering german man. He tried to cure the boy of his bad ways, and make him honest, but the mother could not make herself let the father manage, and so the boy was brought up very badly.

Mrs. Haydon's girls were now only just beginning as young ladies, and so to get her niece, Lena, married, was just then the most important thing that Mrs. Haydon had to do.

Mrs. Haydon had four years before gone to Germany to see her parents, and had taken the girls with her. This visit had been for Mrs. Haydon most successful, though her children had not liked it very well.

Mrs. Haydon was a good and generous woman, and she patronized her parents grandly, and all the cousins who came from all about to see her. Mrs. Haydon's people were of the middling class of farmers. They were not peasants, and they lived in a town of some pretension, but it all seemed very poor and smelly to Mrs. Haydon's american born daughters.

Mrs. Haydon liked it all. It was familiar, and then here she was so wealthy and important. She listened and decided, and advised all of her relations how to do things better. She arranged their present and their future for them, and showed them how in the past they had been wrong in all their methods.

Mrs. Haydon's only trouble was with her two daughters, whom she could not make behave well to her parents. The two girls were very nasty to all their numerous relations. Their mother could hardly make them kiss their grandparents, and every day the girls would get a scolding. But then Mrs. Haydon was so very busy that she did not have time to really manage her stubborn daughters.

These hard working, earth-rough german cousins were to these american born children, ugly and dirty and as far below them as were italian or negro workmen, and they could not see how their mother could ever bear to touch them, and then all the women dressed so funny, and were worked all rough and different.

The two girls stuck up their noses at them all, and always talked in English to each other about how they hated all these people and how they wished their mother would not do so. The girls could talk some German, but they never chose to use it.

It was her eldest brother's family that most interested Mrs. Haydon. Here there were eight children, and out of the eight, five of them were girls.

Mrs. Haydon thought it would be a fine thing to take one of these girls back with her to Bridgepoint and get her well started. Everybody liked that she should do so and they were all willing that it should be Lena.

Lena was the second girl in her large family. She was at this time just seventeen years old. Lena was not an important daughter in the family. She was always sort of dreamy and not there. She worked hard and went very regularly at it, but even good work never seemed to bring her near.

Lena's age just suited Mrs. Haydon's purpose. Lena could first go out to service, and learn how to do things, and then, when she was a little older, Mrs. Haydon could get her a good husband. And then Lena was so still and docile, she would never want to do things her own way. And then, too, Mrs. Haydon, with all her hardness had wisdom, and she could feel the rarer strain there was in Lena.

Lena was willing to go with Mrs. Haydon. Lena did not like her german life very well. It was not the hard work but the roughness that disturbed her. The people were not gentle, and the men when they were glad were very boisterous, and would lay hold of her and roughly tease her. They were good people enough around her, but it was all harsh and dreary for her.

Lena did not really know that she did not like it. She did not know that she was always dreamy and not there. She did not think whether it would be different for her away off there in Bridgepoint. Mrs. Haydon took her and got her different kinds of dresses, and then took her with them to the steamer. Lena did not really know what it was that had happened to her.

Mrs. Haydon, and her daughters, and Lena traveled second class on the steamer. Mrs. Haydon's daughters hated that their mother should take Lena. They hated to have a cousin, who was to them, little better than a nigger, and then everybody on the steamer there would see her. Mrs. Haydon's daughters said things like this to their mother, but she never stopped to hear them, and the girls did not dare to make their meaning very clear. And so they could only go on hating Lena hard, together. They could not stop her from going back with them to Bridgepoint.

Lena was very sick on the voyage. She thought, surely before it was over that she would die. She was so sick she could not even wish that she had not started. She could not eat, she could not moan, she was just blank and scared, and sure that every minute she would die. She could not hold herself in, nor help herself in her trouble. She just staid where she had been put, pale, and scared, and weak, and sick, and sure that she was going to die.

Mathilda and Bertha Haydon had no trouble from having Lena for a cousin on the voyage, until the last day that they were on the ship, and by that time they had made their friends and could explain.

Mrs. Haydon went down every day to Lena, gave her things to make her better, held her head when it was needful, and generally was good and did her duty by her.

Poor Lena had no power to be strong in such trouble. She did not know how to yield to her sickness nor endure. She lost all her little sense of being in her suffering. She was so scared, and then at her best, Lena, who was patient, sweet and quiet, had not self-control, nor any active courage.

Poor Lena was so scared and weak, and every minute she was sure that she would die.

After Lena was on land again a little while, she forgot all her bad suffering. Mrs. Haydon got her the good place, with the pleasant unexacting mistress, and her children and Lena began to learn some English and soon was very happy and content.

All her Sundays out Lena spent at Mrs. Haydon's house. Lena would have liked much better to spend her Sundays with the girls she always sat with, and who often asked her, and who teased her and made a gentle stir within her, but it never came to Lena's unexpectant and unsuffering german nature to do something different from what was expected of her, just because she would like it that way better. Mrs. Haydon had said that Lena was to come to her house every other Sunday, and so Lena always went there.

Mrs. Haydon was the only one of her family who took any interest in Lena. Mr. Haydon did not think much of her. She was his wife's cousin and he was good to her but she was for him stupid, and a little simple, and very dull, and sure some day to need help and to be in trouble. All young poor relations, who were brought from Germany to Bridgepoint were sure, before long, to need help and to be in trouble.

The little Haydon boy was always very nasty to her. He was a hard child for any one to manage, and his mother spoiled him very badly. Mrs. Haydon's daughters as they grew older did not learn to like Lena any better. Lena never knew that she did not like them either. She did not know that she was only happy with the other quicker girls, she always sat with in the park, and who laughed at her and always teased her.

Mathilda Haydon, the simple, fat, blonde, older daughter felt very badly that she had to say that this was her cousin Lena, this Lena who was little better for her than a nigger. Mathilda was an overgrown, slow, flabby, blonde, stupid, fat girl, just beginning as a woman; thick in her speech and dull and simple in her mind, and very jealous of all her family and of other girls, and proud that she could have good dresses and new hats and learn music, and hating very badly to have a cousin who was a common servant. And then Mathilda remembered very strongly that dirty nasty place that Lena came from and that Mathilda had so turned up her nose at, and where she had been made so angry because her mother scolded her and liked all those rough cow-smelly people.

Then, too, Mathilda would get very mad when her mother had Lena at their parties, and when she talked about how good Lena was, to certain german mothers in whose sons, perhaps, Mrs. Haydon might find Lena a good husband. All this would make the dull, blonde, fat Mathilda very angry. Sometimes she would get so angry that she would, in her thick, slow way, and with jealous anger blazing in her light blue eyes, tell her mother that she did not see how she could like that nasty Lena; and then her mother would scold Mathilda, and tell her that she knew her cousin Lena was poor and Mathilda must be good to poor people.

Mathilda Haydon did not like relations to be poor. She told all her girl friends what she thought of Lena, and so the girls would never talk to Lena at Mrs. Haydon's parties. But Lena in her unsuffering and unexpectant patience never really knew that she was slighted. When Mathilda was with her girls in the street or in the park and would see Lena, she always turned up her nose and barely nodded to her, and then she would tell her friends how funny her mother was to take care of people like that Lena, and how, back in Germany, all Lena's people lived just like pigs.

The younger daughter, the dark, large, but not fat, Bertha Haydon, who was very quick in her mind, and in her ways, and who was the favorite with her father, did not like Lena, either. She did not like her because for her Lena was a fool and so stupid, and she would let those Irish and Italian girls laugh at her and tease her, and everybody always made fun of Lena, and Lena never got mad, or even had sense enough to know that they were all making an awful fool of her.

Bertha Haydon hated people to be fools. Her father, too, thought Lena was a fool, and so neither the father nor the daughter ever paid any attention to Lena, although she came to their house every other Sunday.

Lena did not know how all the Haydons felt. She came to her aunt's house all her Sunday afternoons that she had out, because Mrs. Haydon had told her she must do so. In the same way Lena always saved all of her wages. She never thought of any way to spend it. The german cook, the good woman who always scolded Lena, helped her to put it in the bank each month, as soon as she got it. Sometimes before it got into the bank to be taken care of, somebody would ask Lena for it. The little Haydon boy sometimes asked and would get it, and sometimes some of the girls, the ones Lena always sat with, needed some more money; but the german cook, who always scolded Lena, saw to it that this did not happen very often. When it did happen she would scold Lena very sharply, and for the next few months she would not let Lena touch her wages, but put it in the bank for her on the same day that Lena got it.

So Lena always saved her wages, for she never thought to spend them, and she always went to her aunt's house for her Sundays because she did not know that she could do anything different.

Mrs. Haydon felt more and more every year that she had done right to bring Lena back with her, for it was all coming out just as she had expected. Lena was good and never wanted her own way, she was learning English, and saving all her wages, and soon Mrs. Haydon would get her a good husband.

All these four years Mrs. Haydon was busy looking around among all the german people that she knew for the right man to be Lena's husband, and now at last she was quite decided.

The man Mrs. Haydon wanted for Lena was a young german-american tailor, who worked with his father. He was good and all the family were very saving, and Mrs. Haydon was sure that this would be just right for Lena, and then too, this young tailor always did whatever his father and his mother wanted.

This old german tailor and his wife, the father and the mother of Herman Kreder, who was to marry Lena Mainz, were very thrifty, careful people. Herman was the only child they had left with them, and he always did everything they wanted. Herman was now twenty-eight years old, but he had never stopped being scolded and directed by his father and his mother. And now they wanted to see him married.

Herman Kreder did not care much to get married. He was a gentle soul and a little fearful. He had a sullen temper, too. He was obedient to his father and his mother. He always did his work well. He often went out on Saturday nights and on Sundays, with other men. He liked it with them but he never became really joyous. He liked to be with men and he hated to have women with them. He was obedient to his mother, but he did not care much to get married.

Mrs. Haydon and the elder Kreders had often talked the marriage over. They all three liked it very well. Lena would do anything that Mrs. Haydon wanted, and Herman was always obedient in everything to his father and his mother. Both Lena and Herman were saving and good workers and neither of them ever wanted their own way.

The elder Kreders, everybody knew, had saved up all their money, and they were hard, good german people, and Mrs. Haydon was sure that with these people Lena would never be in any trouble. Mr. Haydon would not say anything about it. He knew old Kreder had a lot of money and owned some good houses, and he did not care what his wife did with that simple, stupid Lena, so long as she would be sure never to need help or to be in trouble.

Lena did not care much to get married. She liked her life very well where she was working. She did not think much about Herman Kreder. She thought he was a good man and she always found him very quiet. Neither of them ever spoke much to the other. Lena did not care much just then about getting married.

Mrs. Haydon spoke to Lena about it very often. Lena never answered anything at all. Mrs. Haydon thought, perhaps Lena did not like Herman Kreder. Mrs. Haydon could not believe that any girl not even Lena, really had no feeling about getting married.

Mrs. Haydon spoke to Lena very often about Herman. Mrs. Haydon sometimes got very angry with Lena. She was afraid that Lena, for once, was going to be stubborn, now when it was all fixed right for her to be married.

"Why you stand there so stupid, why don't you answer, Lena," said Mrs. Haydon one Sunday, at the end of a long talking that she was giving Lena about Herman Kreder, and about Lena's getting married to him.

"Yes ma'am," said Lena, and then Mrs. Haydon was furious with this stupid Lena. "Why don't you answer with some sense, Lena, when I ask you if you don't like Herman Kreder. You stand there so stupid and don't answer just like you ain't heard a word what I been saying to you. I never see anybody like you, Lena. If you going to burst out at all, why don't you burst out sudden instead of standing there so silly and don't answer. And here I am so good to you, and find you a good husband so you can have a place to live in all your own. Answer me, Lena, don't you like Herman Kreder? He is a fine young fellow, almost too good for you, Lena, when you stand there so stupid and don't make no answer. There ain't many poor girls that get the chance you got now to get married."

"Why, I do anything you say, Aunt Mathilda. Yes. I like him. He don't say much to me, but I guess he is a good man, and I do anything you say for me to do."

"Well then Lena, why you stand there so silly all the time and not answer when I asked you."

"I didn't hear you say you wanted I should say anything to you. I didn't know you wanted me to say nothing. I do whatever you tell me it's right for me to do. I marry Herman Kreder, if you want me."

And so for Lena Mainz the match was made.

Old Mrs. Kreder did not discuss the matter with her Herman. She never thought that she needed to talk such things over with him. She just told him about getting married to Lena Mainz who was a good worker and very saving and never wanted her own way, and Herman made his usual little grunt in answer to her.

Mrs. Kreder and Mrs. Haydon fixed the day and made all the arrangements for the wedding and invited everybody who ought to be there to see them married.

In three months Lena Mainz and Herman Kreder were to be married.

Mrs. Haydon attended to Lena's getting all the things that she needed. Lena had to help a good deal with the sewing. Lena did not sew very well. Mrs. Haydon scolded because Lena did not do it better, but then she was very good to Lena, and she hired a girl to come and help her. Lena still stayed on with her pleasant mistress, but she spent all her evenings and her Sundays with her aunt and all the sewing.

Mrs. Haydon got Lena some nice dresses. Lena liked that very well. Lena liked having new hats even better, and Mrs. Haydon had some made for her by a real milliner who made them very pretty.

Lena was nervous these days, but she did not think much about getting married. She did not know really what it was, that, which was always coming nearer.

Lena liked the place where she was with the pleasant mistress and the good cook, who always scolded, and she liked the girls she always sat with. She did not ask if she would like being married any better. She always did whatever her aunt said and expected, but she was always nervous when she saw the Kreders with their Herman. She was excited and she liked her new hats, and everybody teased her and every day her marrying was coming nearer, and yet she did not really know what it was, this that was about to happen to her.

Herman Kreder knew more what it meant to be married and he did not like it very well. He did not like to see girls and he did not want to have to have one always near him. Herman always did everything that his father and his mother wanted and now they wanted that he should be married.

Herman had a sullen temper; he was gentle and he never said much. He liked to go out with other men, but he never wanted that there should be any women with them. The men all teased him about getting married. Herman did not mind the teasing but he did not like very well the getting married and having a girl always with him.

Three days before the wedding day, Herman went away to the country to be gone over

Sunday. He and Lena were to be married Tuesday afternoon. When the day came Herman had not been seen or heard from.

The old Kreder couple had not worried much about it. Herman always did everything they wanted and he would surely come back in time to get married. But when Monday night came, and there was no Herman, they went to Mrs. Haydon to tell her what had happened.

Mrs. Haydon got very much excited. It was hard enough to work so as to get everything all ready, and then to have that silly Herman go off that way, so no one could tell what was going to happen. Here was Lena and everything all ready, and now they would have to make the wedding later so that they would know that Herman would be sure to be there.

Mrs. Haydon was very much excited, and then she could not say much to the old Kreder couple. She did not want to make them angry, for she wanted very badly now that Lena should be married to their Herman.

At last it was decided that the wedding should be put off a week longer. Old Mr. Kreder would go to New York to find Herman, for it was very likely that Herman had gone there to his married sister.

Mrs. Haydon sent word around, about waiting until a week from that Tuesday, to everybody that had been invited, and then Tuesday morning she sent for Lena to come down to see her.

Mrs. Haydon was very angry with poor Lena when she saw her. She scolded her hard because she was so foolish, and now Herman had gone off and nobody could tell where he had gone to, and all because Lena always was so dumb and silly. And Mrs. Haydon was just like a mother to her, and Lena always stood there so stupid and did not answer what anybody asked her, and Herman was so silly too, and now his father had to go and find him. Mrs. Haydon did not think that any old people should be good to their children. Their children always were so thankless, and never paid any attention, and older people were always doing things for their good. Did Lena think it gave Mrs. Haydon any pleasure, to work so hard to make Lena happy, and get her a good husband, and then Lena was so thankless and never did anything that anybody wanted. It was a lesson to poor Mrs. Haydon not to do things any more for anybody. Let everybody take care of themselves and never come to her with any troubles; she knew better now than to meddle to make other people happy. It just made trouble for her and her husband did not like it. He always said she was too good, and nobody ever thanked her for it, and there Lena was always standing stupid and not answering anything anybody wanted. Lena could always talk enough to those silly girls she liked so much, and always sat with, but who never did anything for her except to take away her money, and here was her aunt who tried so hard and was so good to her and treated her just like one of her own children and Lena stood there, and never made any answer and never tried to please her aunt, or to do anything that her aunt wanted. "No, it ain't no use your standin' there and cryin', now, Lena. It's too late now to care about that Herman. You should have cared some before, and then you wouldn't have to stand and cry now, and be a disappointment to me, and then I get scolded by my husband for taking care of everybody, and nobody ever thankful. I am glad you got the sense to feel sorry now, Lena, anyway, and I try to do what I can to help you out in your trouble, only you don't deserve to have anybody take any trouble for you. But perhaps you know better next time. You go home now and take care you don't spoil your clothes and that new hat, you had no business to be wearin' that this morning, but you ain't got no sense at all, Lena. I never in my life see anybody be so stupid."

Mrs. Haydon stopped and poor Lena stood there in her hat, all trimmed with pretty flowers, and the tears coming out of her eyes, and Lena did not know what it was that she had done, only she was not going to be married and it was a disgrace for a girl to be left by a man on the very day she was to be married.

Lena went home all alone, and cried in the street car.

Poor Lena cried very hard all alone in the street car. She almost spoiled her new hat with her hitting it against the window in her crying. Then she remembered that she must not do so.

The conductor was a kind man and he was very sorry when he saw her crying. "Don't feel so bad, you get another feller, you are such a nice girl," he said to make her cheerful. "But Aunt Mathilda said now, I never get married," poor Lena sobbed out for her answer. "Why you really got trouble like that," said the conductor, "I just said that now to josh you. I didn't ever think you really was left by a feller. He must be a stupid feller. But don't you worry, he wasn't much good if he could go away and leave you, lookin' to be such a nice girl. You just tell all your trouble to me, and I help you." The car was empty and the conductor sat down beside her to put his arm around her, and to be a comfort to her. Lena suddenly remembered where she was, and if she did things like that her aunt would scold her. She moved away from the man into the corner. He laughed, "Don't be scared," he said, "I wasn't going to hurt you. But you just keep up your spirit. You are a real nice girl, and you'll be sure to get a real good husband. Don't you let nobody fool you. You're all right and I don't want to scare you."

The conductor went back to his platform to help a passenger get on the car. All the time Lena stayed in the street car, he would come in every little while and reassure her, about her not to feel so bad about a man who hadn't no more sense than to go away and leave her. She'd be sure yet to get a good man, she needn't be so worried, he frequently assured her.

He chatted with the other passenger who had just come in, a very well dressed old man, and then with another who came in later, a good sort of a working man, and then another who came in, a nice lady, and he told them all about Lena's having trouble, and it was too bad there were men who treated a poor girl so badly. And everybody in the car was sorry for poor Lena and the workman tried to cheer her, and the old man looked sharply at her, and said she looked like a good girl, but she ought to be more careful and not to be so careless, and things like that would not happen to her, and the nice lady went and sat beside her and Lena liked it, though she shrank away from being near her.

So Lena was feeling a little better when she got off the car, and the conductor helped her, and he called out to her, "You be sure you keep up a good heart now. He wasn't no good that feller and you were lucky for to lose him. You'll get a real man yet, one that will be better for you. Don't you be worried, you're a real nice girl as I ever see in such trouble," and the conductor shook his head and went back into his car to talk it over with the other passengers he had there.

The german cook, who always scolded Lena, was very angry when she heard the story. She never did think Mrs. Haydon would do so much for Lena, though she was always talking so grand about what she could do for everybody. The good german cook always had been a little distrustful of her. People who always thought they were so much never did really do things right for anybody. Not that Mrs. Haydon wasn't a good woman. Mrs. Haydon was a real, good, german woman, and she did really mean to do well by her niece Lena. The cook knew that very well, and she had always said so, and she always had liked and respected Mrs. Haydon, who always acted very proper to her, and Lena was so backward. When there was a man to talk to, Mrs. Haydon did have hard work when she tried to marry Lena. Mrs. Haydon was a good woman, only she did talk sometimes too grand. Perhaps this trouble would make her see it wasn't always so easy to do, to make everybody do everything just like she wanted. The cook was very sorry now for Mrs. Haydon. All this must be such a disappointment, and such a worry to her, and she really had always been very good to Lena. But Lena had better go and put on her other clothes and stop with all that crying. That wouldn't do nothing now to help her, and if Lena would be a good girl, and just be real patient, her aunt would make it all come out right yet for her. "I just tell Mrs. Aldrich, Lena, you stay here yet a little longer. You know she is always so good to you, Lena, and I know she let you, and I tell her all about that stupid Herman Kreder. I got no patience, Lena, with anybody who can be so stupid. You just stop now with your crying, Lena, and take off them good clothes and put them away so you don't spoil them when you need them, and you can help me with the dishes and everything will come off better for you. You see if I ain't right by what I tell you. You just stop crying now Lena quick, or else I scold you."

Lena still choked a little and was very miserable inside her but she did everything just as the cook told her.

The girls Lena always sat with were very sorry to see her look so sad with her trouble. Mary the Irish girl sometimes got very angry with her. Mary was always very hot when she talked of Lena's aunt Mathilda, who thought she was so grand, and had such stupid, stuck up daughters. Mary wouldn't be a fat fool like that ugly tempered Mathilda Haydon, not for anything anybody could ever give her. How Lena could keep on going there so much when they all always acted as if she was just dirt to them, Mary never could see. But Lena never had any sense of how she should make people stand round for her, and that was always all the trouble with her. And poor Lena, she was so stupid to be sorry for losing that gawky fool who didn't ever know what he wanted and just said "ja" to his mamma and his papa, like a baby, and was scared to look at a girl straight, and then sneaked away the last day like as if somebody was going to do something to him. Disgrace, Lena talking about disgrace! It was a disgrace for a girl to be seen with the likes of him, let alone to be married to him. But that poor Lena, she never did know how to show herself off for what she was really. Disgrace to have him go away and leave her. Mary would just like to get a chance to show him. If Lena wasn't worth fifteen like Herman Kreder, Mary would just eat her own head all up. It was a good riddance Lena had of that Herman Kreder and his stingy, dirty parents, and if Lena didn't stop crying about it,—Mary would just naturally despise her.

Poor Lena, she knew very well how Mary meant it all, this she was always saying to her. But Lena was very miserable inside her. She felt the disgrace it was for a decent german girl that a man should go away and leave her. Lena knew very well that her aunt was right when she said the way Herman had acted to her was a disgrace to everyone that knew her. Mary and Nellie and the other girls she always sat with were always very good to Lena but that did not make her trouble any better. It was a disgrace the way Lena had been left, to any decent family, and that could never be made any different to her.

And so the slow days wore on, and Lena never saw her Aunt Mathilda. At last on Sunday she got word by a boy to go and see her aunt Mathilda. Lena's heart beat quick for she was very nervous now with all this that had happened to her. She went just as quickly as she could to see her Aunt Mathilda.

Mrs. Haydon quick, as soon as she saw Lena, began to scold her for keeping her aunt waiting so long for her, and for not coming in all the week to see her, to see if her aunt should need her, and so her aunt had to send a boy to tell her. But it was easy, even for Lena, to see that her aunt was not really angry with her. It wasn't Lena's fault, went on Mrs. Haydon, that everything was going to happen all right for her. Mrs. Haydon was very tired taking all this trouble for her, and when Lena couldn't even take trouble to come and see her aunt, to see if she needed anything to tell her. But Mrs. Haydon really never minded things like that when she could do things for anybody. She was tired now, all the trouble she had been taking to make things right for Lena, but perhaps now Lena heard it she would learn a little to be thankful to her. "You get all ready to be married Tuesday Lena, you hear me," said Mrs. Haydon to her. "You come here Tuesday morning and I have everything all ready for you. You wear your new dress I got you, and your hat with all them flowers on it, and you be very careful coming you don't get your things all dirty, you so careless all the time, Lena, and not thinking, and you act sometimes you never got no head at all on you. You go home now, and you tell your Mrs. Aldrich that you leave her Tuesday. Don't you go forgetting now, Lena, anything I ever told you what you should do to be careful. You be a good girl now, Lena. You get married Tuesday to Herman Kreder." And that was all Lena ever knew of what had happened all this week to Herman Kreder. Lena forgot there was anything to know about it. She was really to be married Tuesday, and her Aunt Mathilda said she was a good girl, and now there was no disgrace left upon her.

Lena now fell back into the way she always had of being always dreamy and not there, the way she always had been, except for the few days she was so excited, because she had been left by a man the very day she was to have been married. Lena was a little nervous all these last days, but she did not think much about what it meant for her to be married.

Herman Kreder was not so content about it. He was quiet and was sullen and he knew he could not help it. He knew now he just had to let himself get married. It was not that Herman did not like Lena Mainz. She was as good as any other girl could be for him. She was a little better perhaps than other girls he saw, she was so very quiet, but Herman did not like to always have to have a girl around him. Herman had always done everything that his mother and his father wanted. His father had found him in New York, where Herman had gone to be with his married sister.

Herman's father when he had found him coaxed Herman a long time and went on whole days with his complaining to him, always troubled but gentle and quite patient with him, and always he was worrying to Herman about what was the right way his boy Herman should always do, always whatever it was his mother ever wanted from him, and always Herman never made him any answer.

Old Mr. Kreder kept on saying to him, he did not see how Herman could think now, it could be any different. When you make a bargain you just got to stick right to it, that was the only way old Mr. Kreder could ever see it, and saying you would get married to a girl and she got everything all ready, that was a bargain just like one you make in business and Herman he had made it, and now Herman he would just have to do it, old Mr. Kreder didn't see there was any other way a good boy like his Herman had, to do it. And then too that Lena Mainz was such a nice girl and Herman hadn't ought to really give his father so much trouble and make him pay out all that money, to come all the way to New York just to find him, and they both lose all that time from their working, when all Herman had to do was just to stand up, for an hour, and then he would be all right married, and it would be all over for him, and then everything at home would never be any different to him.

And his father went on; there was his poor mother saying always how her Herman always did everything before she ever wanted, and now just because he got notions in him, and wanted to show people how he could be stubborn, he was making all this trouble for her, and making them pay all that money just to run around and find him. "You got no idea Herman, how bad mama is feeling about the way you been acting Herman," said old Mr. Kreder to him. "She says she never can understand how you can be so thankless Herman. It hurts her very much you been so stubborn, and she finds you such a nice girl for you, like Lena Mainz who is always just so quiet and always saves up all her wages, and she never wanting her own way at all like some girls are always all the time to have it, and your mama trying so hard, just so you could be comfortable Herman to be married, and then you act so stubborn Herman. You like all young people Herman, you think only about yourself, and what you are just wanting, and your mama she is thinking only what is good for you to have, for you in the future. Do you think your mama wants to have a girl around to be a bother, for herself, Herman. It's just for you Herman she is always thinking, and she talks always about how happy she will be, when she sees her Herman married to a nice girl, and then when she fixed it all up so good for you, so it never would be any bother to you, just the way she wanted you should like it, and you say yes all right, I do it, and then you go away like this and act stubborn, and make all this trouble everybody to take for you, and we spend money, and I got to travel all round to find you. You come home now with me Herman and get married, and I tell your mama she better not say anything to you about how much it cost me to come all the way to look for you—Hey Herman," said his father coaxing, "Hey, you come home now and get married. All you got to do Herman is just to stand up for an hour Herman, and then you don't never to have any more bother to it—Hey Herman!—you come home with me to-morrow and get married. Hey Herman."

Herman's married sister liked her brother Herman, and she had always tried to help him, when there was anything she knew he wanted. She liked it that he was so good and always did everything that their father and their mother wanted, but still she wished it could be that he could have more his own way, if there was anything he ever wanted.

But now she thought Herman with his girl was very funny. She wanted that Herman should be married. She thought it would do him lots of good to get married. She laughed at Herman when she heard the story. Until his father came to find him, she did not know why it was Herman had come just then to New York to see her. When she heard the story she laughed a good deal at her brother Herman and teased him a good deal about his running away, because he didn't want to have a girl to be all the time around him.

Herman's married sister liked her brother Herman, and she did not want him not to like to be with women. He was good, her brother Herman, and it would surely do him good to get married. It would make him stand up for himself stronger. Herman's sister always laughed at him and always she would try to reassure him. "Such a nice man as my brother Herman acting like as if he was afraid of women. Why the girls all like a man like you Herman, if you didn't always run away when you saw them. It do you good really Herman to get married, and then you got somebody you can boss around when you want to. It do you good Herman to get married, you see if you don't like it, when you really done it. You go along home now with papa, Herman and get married to that Lena. You don't know how nice you like it Herman when you try once how you can do it. You just don't be afraid of nothing, Herman. You good enough for any girl to marry, Herman. Any girl be glad to have a man like you to be always with them Herman. You just go along home with papa and try it what I say, Herman. Oh you so funny Herman, when you sit there, and then run away and leave your girl behind you. I know she is crying like anything Herman for to lose you. Don't be bad to her Herman. You go along home with papa now and get married Herman. I'd be awful ashamed Herman, to really have a brother didn't have spirit enough to get married, when a girl is just dying for to have him. You always like me to be with you Herman. I don't see why you say you don't want a girl to be all the time around you. You always been good to me Herman, and I know you always be good to that Lena, and you soon feel just like as if she had always been there with you. Don't act like as if you wasn't a nice strong man, Herman. Really I laugh at you Herman, but you know I like awful well to see you real happy. You go home and get married to that Lena, Herman. She is a real pretty girl and real nice and good and quiet and she make my brother Herman very happy. You just stop your fussing now with Herman, papa. He go with you to-morrow papa, and you see he like it so much to be married, he make everybody laugh just to see him be so happy. Really truly, that's the way it will be with you Herman. You just listen to me what I tell you Herman." And so his sister laughed at him and reassured him, and his father kept on telling what the mother always said about her Herman, and he coaxed him and Herman never said anything in answer, and his sister packed his things up and was very cheerful with him, and she kissed him, and then she laughed and then she kissed him, and his father went and bought the tickets for the train, and at last late on Sunday he brought Herman back to Bridgepoint with him.

It was always very hard to keep Mrs. Kreder from saying what she thought, to her Herman, but her daughter had written her a letter, so as to warn her not to say anything about what he had been doing, to him, and her husband came in with Herman and said, "Here we are come home mama, Herman and me, and we are very tired it was so crowded coming," and then he whispered to her. "You be good to Herman, mama, he didn't mean to make us so much trouble," and so old Mrs. Kreder held in what she felt was so strong in her to say to her Herman. She just said very stiffly to him, "I'm glad to see you come home to-day, Herman." Then she went to arrange it all with Mrs. Haydon.

Herman was now again just like he always had been, sullen and very good, and very quiet, and always ready to do whatever his mother and his father wanted. Tuesday morning came, Herman got his new clothes on and went with his father and his mother to stand up for an hour and get married. Lena was there in her new dress, and her hat with all the pretty flowers, and she was very nervous for now she knew she was really very soon to be married. Mrs. Haydon had everything all ready. Everybody was there just as they should be and very soon Herman Kreder and Lena Mainz were married.

When everything was really over, they went back to the Kreder house together. They were all now to live together, Lena and Herman and the old father and the old mother, in the house where Mr. Kreder had worked so many years as a tailor, with his son Herman always there to help him.

Irish Mary had often said to Lena she never did see how Lena could ever want to have anything to do with Herman Kreder and his dirty stingy parents. The old Kreders were to an Irish nature, a stingy, dirty couple. They had not the free-hearted, thoughtless, fighting, mud bespattered, ragged, peat-smoked cabin dirt that irish Mary knew and could forgive and love. Theirs was the german dirt of saving, of being dowdy and loose and foul in your clothes so as to save them and yourself in washing, having your hair greasy to save it in the soap and drying, having your clothes dirty, not in freedom, but because so it was cheaper, keeping the house close and smelly because so it cost less to get it heated, living so poorly not only so as to save money but so they should never even know themselves that they had it, working all the time not only because from their nature they just had to and because it made them money but also that they never could be put in any way to make them spend their money.

This was the place Lena now had for her home and to her it was very different than it could be for an irish Mary. She too was german and was thrifty, though she was always so dreamy and not there. Lena was always careful with things and she always saved her money, for that was the only way she knew how to do it. She never had taken care of her own money and she never had thought how to use it.

Lena Mainz had been, before she was Mrs. Herman Kreder, always clean and decent in her clothes and in her person, but it was not because she ever thought about it or really needed so to have it, it was the way her people did in the german country where she came from, and her Aunt Mathilda and the good german cook who always scolded, had kept her on and made her, with their scoldings, always more careful to keep clean and to wash real often. But there was no deep need in all this for Lena and so, though Lena did not like the old Kreders, though she really did not know that, she did not think about their being stingy dirty people.

Herman Kreder was cleaner than the old people, just because it was his nature to keep cleaner, but he was used to his mother and his father, and he never thought that they should keep things cleaner. And Herman too always saved all his money, except for that little beer he drank when he went out with other men of an evening the way he always liked to do it, and he never thought of any other way to spend it. His father had always kept all the money for them and he always was doing business with it. And then too Herman really had no money, for he always had worked for his father, and his father had never thought to pay him.

And so they began all four to live in the Kreder house together, and Lena began soon with it to look careless and a little dirty, and to be more lifeless with it, and nobody ever noticed much what Lena wanted, and she never really knew herself what she needed.

The only real trouble that came to Lena with their living all four there together, was the way old Mrs. Kreder scolded. Lena had always been used to being scolded, but this scolding of old Mrs. Kreder was very different from the way she ever before had had to endure it.

Herman, now he was married to her, really liked Lena very well. He did not care very much about her but she never was a bother to him being there around him, only when his mother worried and was nasty to them because Lena was so careless, and did not know how to save things right for them with their eating, and all the other ways with money, that the old woman had to save it.

Herman Kreder had always done everything his mother and his father wanted but he did not really love his parents very deeply. With Herman it was always only that he hated to have any struggle. It was all always all right with him when he could just go along and do the same thing over every day with his working, and not to hear things, and not to have people make him listen to their anger. And now his marriage, and he just knew it would, was making trouble for him. It made him hear more what his mother was always saying, with her scolding. He had to really hear it now because Lena was there, and she was so scared and dull always when she heard it. Herman knew very well with his mother, it was all right if one ate very little and worked hard all day and did not hear her when she scolded, the way Herman always had done before they were so foolish about his getting married and having a girl there to be all the time around him, and now he had to help her so the girl could learn too, not to hear it when his mother scolded, and not to look so scared, and not to eat much, and always to be sure to save it.

Herman really did not know very well what he could do to help Lena to understand it. He could never answer his mother back to help Lena, that never would make things any better for her, and he never could feel in himself any way to comfort Lena, to make her strong not to hear his mother, in all the awful ways she always scolded. It just worried Herman to have it like that all the time around him. Herman did not know much about how a man could make a struggle with a mother, to do much to keep her quiet, and indeed Herman never knew much how to make a struggle against anyone who really wanted to have anything very badly. Herman all his life never wanted anything so badly, that he would really make a struggle against any one to get it. Herman all his life only wanted to live regular and quiet, and not talk much and to do the same way every day like every other with his working. And now his mother had made him get married to this Lena and now with his mother making all that scolding, he had all this trouble and this worry always on him.

Mrs. Haydon did not see Lena now very often. She had not lost her interest in her niece Lena, but Lena could not come much to her house to see her, it would not be right, now Lena was a married woman. And then too Mrs. Haydon had her hands full just then with her two daughters, for she was getting them ready to find them good husbands, and then too her own husband now worried her very often about her always spoiling that boy of hers, so he would be sure to turn out no good and be a disgrace to a german family, and all because his mother always spoiled him. All these things were very worrying now to Mrs. Haydon, but still she wanted to be good to Lena, though she could not see her very often. She only saw her when Mrs. Haydon went to call on Mrs. Kreder or when Mrs. Kreder came to see Mrs. Haydon, and that never could be very often. Then too these days Mrs. Haydon could not scold Lena, Mrs. Kreder was always there with her, and it would not be right to scold Lena when Mrs. Kreder was there, who had now the real right to do it. And so her aunt always said nice things now to Lena, and though Mrs. Haydon sometimes was a little worried when she saw Lena looking sad and not careful, she did not have time just then to really worry much about it.

Lena now never any more saw the girls she always used to sit with. She had no way now to see them and it was not in Lena's nature to search out ways to see them, nor did she now ever think much of the days when she had been used to see them. They never any of them had come to the Kreder house to see her. Not even Irish Mary had ever thought to come to see her. Lena had been soon forgotten by them. They had soon passed away from Lena and now Lena never thought any more that she had ever known them.

The only one of her old friends who tried to know what Lena liked and what she needed, and who always made Lena come to see her, was the good german cook who had always scolded. She now scolded Lena hard for letting herself go so, and going out when she was looking so untidy. "I know you going to have a baby Lena, but that's no way for you to be looking. I am ashamed most to see you come and sit here in my kitchen, looking so sloppy and like you never used to Lena. I never see anybody like you Lena. Herman is very good to you, you always say so, and he don't treat you bad even though you don't deserve to have anybody good to you, you so careless all the time, Lena, letting yourself go like you never had anybody tell you what was the right way you should know how to be looking. No, Lena, I don't see no reason you should let yourself go so and look so untidy Lena, so I am ashamed to see you sit there looking so ugly, Lena. No Lena that ain't no way ever I see a woman make things come out better, letting herself go so every way and crying all the time like as if you had real trouble. I never wanted to see you marry Herman Kreder, Lena, I knew what you got to stand with that old woman always, and that old man, he is so stingy too and he don't say things out but he ain't any better in his heart than his wife with her bad ways, I know that Lena, I know they don't hardly give you enough to eat, Lena, I am real sorry for you Lena, you know that Lena, but that ain't any way to be going round so untidy Lena, even if you have got all that trouble. You never see me do like that Lena, though sometimes I got a headache so I can't see to stand to be working hardly, and nothing comes right with all my cooking, but I always see Lena, I look decent. That's the only way a german girl can make things come out right Lena. You hear me what I am saying to you Lena. Now you eat something nice Lena, I got it all ready for you, and you wash up and be careful Lena and the baby will come all right to you, and then I make your Aunt Mathilda see that you live in a house soon all alone with Herman and your baby, and then everything go better for you. You hear me what I say to you Lena. Now don't let me ever see you come looking like this any more Lena, and you just stop with that always crying. You ain't got no reason to be sitting there now with all that crying, I never see anybody have trouble it did them any good to do the way you are doing, Lena. You hear me Lena. You go home now and you be good the way I tell you Lena, and I see what I can do. I make your Aunt Mathilda make old Mrs. Kreder let you be till you get your baby all right. Now don't you be scared and so silly Lena. I don't like to see you act so Lena when really you got a nice man and so many things really any girl should be grateful to be having. Now you go home Lena to-day and you do the way I say, to you, and I see what I can do to help you."

"Yes Mrs. Aldrich" said the good german woman to her mistress later. "Yes Mrs. Aldrich that's the way it is with them girls when they want so to get married. They dont know when they got it good Mrs. Aldrich. They never know what it is they're really wanting when they got it, Mrs. Aldrich. There's that poor Lena, she just been here crying and looking so careless so I scold her, but that was no good that marrying for that poor Lena, Mrs. Aldrich. She do look so pale and sad now Mrs. Aldrich, it just break my heart to see her. She was a good girl was Lena, Mrs. Aldrich, and I never had no trouble with her like I got with so many young girls nowadays, Mrs. Aldrich, and I never see any girl any better to work right than our Lena, and now she got to stand it all the time with that old woman Mrs. Kreder. My! Mrs. Aldrich, she is a bad old woman to her. I never see Mrs. Aldrich how old people can be so bad to young girls and not have no kind of patience with them. If Lena could only live with her Herman, he ain't so bad the way men are, Mrs. Aldrich, but he is just the way always his mother wants him, he ain't got no spirit in him, and so I don't really see no help for that poor Lena. I know her aunt, Mrs. Haydon, meant it all right for her Mrs. Aldrich, but poor Lena, it would be better for her if her Herman had stayed there in New York that time he went away to leave her. I don't like it the way Lena is looking now, Mrs. Aldrich. She looks like as if she don't have no life left in her hardly, Mrs. Aldrich, she just drags around and looks so dirty and after all the pains I always took to teach her and to keep her nice in her ways and looking. It don't do no good to them, for them girls to get married Mrs. Aldrich, they are much better when they only know it, to stay in a good place when they got it, and keep on regular with their working. I don't like it the way Lena looks now Mrs. Aldrich. I wish I knew some way to help that poor Lena, Mrs. Aldrich, but she is a bad old woman, that old Mrs. Kreder, Herman's mother. I speak to Mrs. Haydon real soon, Mrs. Aldrich. I see what we can do now to help that poor Lena."

These were really bad days for poor Lena. Herman always was real good to her and now he even sometimes tried to stop his mother from scolding Lena. "She ain't well now mama, you let her be now you hear me. You tell me what it is you want she should be doing, I tell her. I see she does it right just the way you want it mama. You let be, I say now mama, with that always scolding Lena. You let be, I say now, you wait till she is feeling better." Herman was getting really strong to struggle, for he could see that Lena with that baby working hard inside her, really could not stand it any longer with his mother and the awful ways she always scolded.

It was a new feeling Herman now had inside him that made him feel he was strong to make a struggle. It was new for Herman Kreder really to be wanting something, but Herman wanted strongly now to be a father, and he wanted badly that his baby should be a boy and healthy. Herman never had cared really very much about his father and his mother, though always, all his life, he had done everything just as they wanted, and he had never really cared much about his wife, Lena, though he always had been very good to her, and had always tried to keep his mother off her, with the awful way she always scolded, but to be really a father of a little baby, that feeling took hold of Herman very deeply. He was almost ready, so as to save his baby from all trouble, to really make a strong struggle with his mother and with his father, too, if he would not help him to control his mother.

Sometimes Herman even went to Mrs. Haydon to talk all this trouble over. They decided then together, it was better to wait there all four together for the baby, and Herman could make Mrs. Kreder stop a little with her scolding, and then when Lena was a little stronger, Herman should have his own house for her, next door to his father, so he could always be there to help him in his working, but so they could eat and sleep in a house where the old woman could not control them and they could not hear her awful scolding.

And so things went on, the same way, a little longer. Poor Lena was not feeling any joy to have a baby. She was scared the way she had been when she was so sick on the water. She was scared now every time when anything would hurt her. She was scared and still and lifeless, and sure that every minute she would die. Lena had no power to be strong in this kind of trouble, she could only sit still and be scared, and dull, and lifeless, and sure that every minute she would die.

Before very long, Lena had her baby. He was a good, healthy little boy, the baby. Herman cared very much to have the baby. When Lena was a little stronger he took a house next door to the old couple, so he and his own family could eat and sleep and do the way they wanted. This did not seem to make much change now for Lena. She was just the same as when she was waiting with her baby. She just dragged around and was careless with her clothes and all lifeless, and she acted always and lived on just as if she had no feeling. She always did everything regular with the work, the way she always had had to do it, but she never got back any spirit in her. Herman was always good and kind, and always helped her with her working. He did everything he knew to help her. He always did all the active new things in the house and for the baby. Lena did what she had to do the way she always had been taught it. She always just kept going now with her working, and she was always careless and dirty, and a little dazed, and lifeless. Lena never got any better in herself of this way of being that she had had ever since she had been married.

Mrs. Haydon never saw any more of her niece, Lena. Mrs. Haydon had now so much trouble with her own house, and her daughters getting married, and her boy, who was growing up, and who always was getting so much worse to manage. She knew she had done right by Lena. Herman Kreder was a good man, she would be glad to get one so good, sometimes, for her own daughters, and now they had a home to live in together, separate from the old people, who had made their trouble for them. Mrs. Haydon felt she had done very well by her niece Lena, and she never thought now she needed any more to go and see her. Lena would do very well now without her aunt to trouble herself any more about her.

The good german cook who had always scolded, still tried to do her duty like a mother to poor Lena. It was very hard now to do right by Lena. Lena never seemed to hear now what anyone was saying to her. Herman was always doing everything he could to help her. Herman always, when he was home, took good care of the baby. Herman loved to take care of his baby. Lena never thought to take him out or to do anything she didn't have to.

The good cook sometimes made Lena come to see her. Lena would come with her baby and sit there in the kitchen, and watch the good woman cooking, and listen to her sometimes a little, the way she used to, while the good german woman scolded her for going around looking so careless when now she had no trouble, and sitting there so dull, and always being just so thankless. Sometimes Lena would wake up a little and get back into her face her old, gentle, patient, and unsuffering sweetness, but mostly Lena did not seem to hear much when the good german woman scolded. Lena always liked it when Mrs. Aldrich her good mistress spoke to her kindly, and then Lena would seem to go back and feel herself to be like she was when she had been in service. But mostly Lena just lived along and was careless in her clothes, and dull, and lifeless.

By and by Lena had two more little babies. Lena was not so much scared now when she had the babies. She did not seem to notice very much when they hurt her, and she never seemed to feel very much now about anything that happened to her.

They were very nice babies, all these three that Lena had, and Herman took good care of them always. Herman never really cared much about his wife, Lena. The only things Herman ever really cared for were his babies. Herman always was very good to his children. He always had a gentle, tender way when he held them. He learned to be very handy with them. He spent all the time he was not working, with them. By and by he began to work all day in his own home so that he could have his children always in the same room with him.

Lena always was more and more lifeless and Herman now mostly never thought about her. He more and more took all the care of their three children. He saw to their eating right and their washing, and he dressed them every morning, and he taught them the right way to do things, and he put them to their sleeping, and he was now always every minute with them. Then there was to come to them, a fourth baby. Lena went to the hospital near by to have the baby. Lena seemed to be going to have much trouble with it. When the baby was come out at last, it was like its mother lifeless. While it was coming, Lena had grown very pale and sicker. When it was all over Lena had died, too, and nobody knew just how it had happened to her.

The good german cook who had always scolded Lena, and had always to the last day tried to help her, was the only one who ever missed her. She remembered how nice Lena had looked all the time she was in service with her, and how her voice had been so gentle and sweet-sounding, and how she always was a good girl, and how she never had to have any trouble with her, the way she always had with all the other girls who had been taken into the house to help her. The good cook sometimes spoke so of Lena when she had time to have a talk with Mrs. Aldrich, and this was all the remembering there now ever was of Lena.

Herman Kreder now always lived very happy, very gentle, very quiet, very well content alone with his three children. He never had a woman any more to be all the time around him. He always did all his own work in his house, when he was through every day with the work he was always doing for his father. Herman always was alone, and he always worked alone, until his little ones were big enough to help him. Herman Kreder was very well content now and he always lived very regular and peaceful, and with every day just like the next one, always alone now with his three good, gentle children.

1909

Susan Glaspell
(1876?–1948)

Although she never lived in the Midwest after leaving it in 1913, the region and especially her birthplace—Davenport, Iowa—strongly influenced Susan Glaspell's fiction. She was descended from one of Davenport's pioneer families and educated in its public schools. After graduating from Drake University and working two years as a reporter and columnist for the Des Moines *Daily News*, she returned to Davenport "to give all my time to my own writing."

Intending to support herself by writing fiction, Glaspell targeted an audience of popular magazine readers. Although her early fiction has not received much critical praise, she succeeded in crafting individualized characters and defining settings with realistic detail. Her stories, often constructed around opening flashbacks and surprise endings, proved popular enough that she was able to publish two or three every year between 1903 and 1922, when she stopped writing short fiction. Her early stories were collected in *Lifted Masks* (1912).

Glaspell's relationship with George Cram Cook was crucial to her life and her artistic development. A member of one of Davenport's first families, Cook was a free-thinking intellectual. His advocacy of political purposes for literature impressed her. The sentimental romance of her first novel, *The Glory of the Conquered* (1909), was replaced by explicit social purpose in her second, *The Visioning* (1911).

Cook was married when they met; after his divorce they married (1913) and moved to Provincetown, Massachusetts, at the tip of Cape Cod. In summers on the Cape and winters in Greenwich Village, they were at the center of a group of productive artists and intellectuals. After the publication of her third novel, *Fidelity* (1915), Glaspell turned her attention to writing for the theater, especially for the Provincetown Players, founded by Cook in 1915.

Producing original plays by American playwrights was the Players' stated purpose. In the summer of 1915, the group converted an old fish house at the end of a Provincetown wharf into a theater and presented Cook's and Glaspell's sophisticated satire on Freudian analysis, *Suppressed Desires*, and a play by Neith Boyce. The plays were so well received that by the next summer the founders had been joined by other New Yorkers, including the young playwright Eugene O'Neill.

For the Provincetown's second season,

Glaspell wrote her first solo play, a one-act drama called *Trifles*. Sitting on one of the wooden benches in the wharf theater, she remembered the bleak kitchen of an Iowa farmhouse where a killing had taken place; she had entered it years earlier as a reporter and the desolate image was engraved on her mind. The spare and concentrated drama, so appropriate for its intended theatrical setting, is her best-known play. Along with Eugene O'Neill's *Bound East for Cardiff*, it was the high point of the Players' second summer on Cape Cod. Back in New York, Glaspell adapted the material into a short story called "A Jury of Her Peers." It was published in *Every Week* (March 5, 1917) and selected by E. J. O'Brien for his *Best Short Stories of 1917*; the present text is taken from that volume.

Glaspell continued to write both one-act and full-length plays for the theater group, now established for its winter seasons in a building on MacDougal Street under the name The Playwright's Theater. She often took roles in its productions, and she was much admired for her acting. In addition she served as a business manager, set designer, and publicist. *The Outside*, a play set in a Cape Cod lifesaving station, was produced in 1917, and her first full-length play, *Bernice*, staged in 1919. A collection *Plays* was published in 1920. Among her most important writings for the theater are *The Inheritors* (1921), on the theme of preserving the values of the pioneer tradition, and *The Verge* (1921), treating a woman's rejection of social convention. *Chains of Dew* (1922) was the last Glaspell play produced by the Provincetown Players. This play, along with *The Comic Artist* (1928) and *Alison's House* (1930), inspired by Emily Dickinson and winner of a Pulitzer Prize, deals with the lives of artists.

In 1922 Cook, declaring that the Provincetown Players were too commercially successful to achieve their founding goals, quit the company and with Glaspell went to live in Greece, where he worked to establish a Greek national theater and regain the glories of its classic heritage. He died there in 1924. Glaspell's biography of him is entitled *The Road to the Temple* (1927). She was married from 1925 to 1931 to Norman Matson, with whom she wrote *The Comic Artist.*

Returning to Cape Cod after Cook's death, she also turned again to novels and the regionalist flavor of her earlier fiction. *Brook Evans* (1928) covers three generations of a Midwest family. *Fugitive's Return* (1929) treats the experience of living in Greece from a female vantage point. *Ambrose Holt and Family* (1931) is a dramatic novel based on the play *Chains of Dew.* The *Morning Is Near Us* (1939) is Glaspell's most successful evocation of the Midwest. *Cherished and Shared of Old* (1940) is a Christmas story. *Norma Ashe* (1942) and *Judd Rankin's Daughter* contain explicit criticism of Glaspell's native region.

Glaspell's most experimental writing was done for the theater, and it is this work that has primarily shaped her reputation.

Plays by Susan Glaspell (1987), edited by C. W. E. Bigsby, reprints four of her best-known works. Arthur E. Waterman's *Susan Glaspell* (1966) is a critical biography.

A Jury of Her Peers

When Martha Hale opened the storm-door and got a cut of the north wind, she ran back for her big woolen scarf. As she hurriedly wound that round her head her eye made a scandalized sweep of her kitchen. It was no ordinary thing that called her away—it was probably farther from ordinary than anything that had ever happened in Dickson County. But what her eye took in was that her kitchen was in no shape for leaving: her bread all ready for mixing, half the flour sifted and half unsifted.

She hated to see things half done; but she had been at that when the team from town stopped to get Mr. Hale, and then the sheriff came running in to say his wife wished Mrs. Hale would come too—adding, with a grin, that he guessed she was getting scarey and wanted another woman along. So she had dropped everything right where it was.

"Martha!" now came her husband's impatient voice. "Don't keep folks waiting out here in the cold."

She again opened the storm-door, and this time joined the three men and the one woman waiting for her in the big two-seated buggy.

After she had the robes tucked around her she took another look at the woman who sat beside her on the back seat. She had met Mrs. Peters the year before at the county fair, and the thing she remembered about her was that she didn't seem like a sheriff's wife. She was small and thin and didn't have a strong voice. Mrs. Gorman, sheriff's wife before Gorman went out and Peters came in, had a voice that somehow seemed to be backing up the law with every word. But if Mrs. Peters didn't look like a sheriff's wife, Peters made it up in looking like a sheriff. He was to a dot the kind of man who could get himself elected sheriff—a heavy man with a big voice, who was particularly genial with the law-abiding, as if to make it plain that he knew the difference between criminals and non-criminals. And right there it came into Mrs. Hale's mind, with a stab, that this man who was so pleasant and lively with all of them was going to the Wrights' now as a sheriff.

"The country's not very pleasant this time of year," Mrs. Peters at last ventured, as if she felt they ought to be talking as well as the men.

Mrs. Hale scarcely finished her reply, for they had gone up a little hill and could see the Wright place now, and seeing it did not make her feel like talking. It looked very lonesome this cold March morning. It had always been a lonesome-looking place. It was down in a hollow, and the poplar trees around it were lonesome-looking trees. The men were looking at it and talking about what had happened. The county attorney was bending to one side of the buggy, and kept looking steadily at the place as they drew up to it.

"I'm glad you came with me," Mrs. Peters said nervously, as the two women were about to follow the men in through the kitchen door.

Even after she had her foot on the door-step, her hand on the knob, Martha Hale had a moment of feeling she could not cross that threshold. And the reason it seemed she couldn't cross it now was simply because she hadn't crossed it before. Time and time again it had been in her mind, "I ought to go over and see Minnie Foster"—she still thought of her as Minnie Foster, though for twenty years she had been Mrs. Wright. And then there was always something to do and Minnie Foster would go from her mind. But *now* she could come.

The men went over to the stove. The women stood close together by the door. Young Henderson, the county attorney, turned around and said, "Come up to the fire, ladies."

Mrs. Peters took a step forward, then stopped. "I'm not—cold," she said.

And so the two women stood by the door, at first not even so much as looking around the kitchen.

The men talked for a minute about what a good thing it was the sheriff had sent his deputy out that morning to make a fire for them, and then Sheriff Peters stepped back from the stove, unbuttoned his outer coat, and leaned his hands on the kitchen table in a way that seemed to mark the beginning of official business. "Now, Mr. Hale," he said in a sort of semi-official voice, "before we move things about, you tell Mr. Henderson just what it was you saw when you came here yesterday morning."

The county attorney was looking around the kitchen.

"By the way," he said, "has anything been moved?" He turned to the sheriff. "Are things just as you left them yesterday?"

Peters looked from cupboard to sink; from that to a small worn rocker a little to one side of the kitchen table.

"It's just the same."

"Somebody should have been left here yesterday," said the county attorney.

"Oh—yesterday," returned the sheriff, with a little gesture as of yesterday having been more than he could bear to think of. "When I had to send Frank to Morris Center for that man who went crazy—let me tell you, I had my hands full *yesterday.* I knew you could get back from Omaha by to-day, George, and as long as I went over everything here myself—"

"Well, Mr. Hale," said the county attorney, in a way of letting what was past and gone go, "tell just what happened when you came here yesterday morning."

Mrs. Hale, still leaning against the door, had that sinking feeling of the mother whose child is about to speak a piece. Lewis often wandered along and got things mixed up in a story. She hoped he would tell this straight and plain, and not say unnecessary things that would just make things harder for Minnie Foster. He didn't begin at once, and she noticed that he looked queer—as if standing in that kitchen and having to tell what he had seen there yesterday morning made him almost sick.

"Yes, Mr. Hale?" the county attorney reminded.

"Harry and I had started to town with a load of potatoes," Mrs. Hale's husband began.

Harry was Mrs. Hale's oldest boy. He wasn't with them now, for the very good reason that those potatoes never got to town yesterday and he was taking them this morning, so he hadn't been home when the sheriff stopped to say he wanted Mr. Hale to come over to the Wright place and tell the county attorney his story there, where he could point it all out. With all Mrs. Hale's other emotions came the fear now that maybe Harry wasn't dressed warm enough—they hadn't any of them realized how that north wind did bite.

"We come along this road," Hale was going on, with a motion of his hand to the road over which they had just come, "and as we got in sight of the house I says to Harry, 'I'm goin' to see if I can't get John Wright to take a telephone.' You see," he explained to Henderson, "unless I can get somebody to go in with me they won't come out this branch road except for a price *I* can't pay. I'd spoke to Wright about it once before; but he put me off, saying folks talked too much anyway, and all he asked was peace and quiet—guess you know about how much he talked himself. But I thought maybe if I went to the house and talked about it before his wife, and said all the women-folks liked the telephones, and that in this lonesome stretch of road it would be a good thing—well, I said to Harry that that was what I was going to say—though I said at the same time that I didn't know as what his wife wanted made much difference to John—"

Now, there he was!—saying things he didn't need to say. Mrs. Hale tried to catch her husband's eye, but fortunately the county attorney interrupted with:

"Let's talk about that a little later, Mr. Hale. I do want to talk about that, but I'm anxious now to get along to just what happened when you got here."

When he began this time, it was very deliberately and carefully:

"I didn't see or hear anything. I knocked at the door. And still it was all quiet inside. I knew they must be up—it was past eight o'clock. So I knocked again, louder, and I thought I heard somebody say, 'Come in.' I wasn't sure—I'm not sure yet. But I opened the door—this door," jerking a hand toward the door by which the two women stood, "and there, in that rocker"—pointing to it—"sat Mrs. Wright."

Every one in the kitchen looked at the rocker. It came into Mrs. Hale's mind that that rocker didn't look in the least like Minnie Foster—the Minnie Foster of twenty years before. It was a dingy red, with wooden rungs up the back, and the middle rung was gone, and the chair sagged to one side.

"How did she—look?" the county attorney was inquiring.

"Well," said Hale, "she looked—queer."

"How do you mean—queer?"

As he asked it he took out a note-book and pencil. Mrs. Hale did not like the sight of that pencil. She kept her eye fixed on her husband, as if to keep him from saying unnecessary things that would go into that note-book and make trouble.

Hale did speak guardedly, as if the pencil had affected him too.

"Well, as if she didn't know what she was going to do next. And kind of—done up."

"How did she seem to feel about your coming?"

"Why, I don't think she minded—one way or other. She didn't pay much attention. I said, 'Ho' do, Mrs. Wright? It's cold, ain't it?' And she said, 'Is it?'—and went on pleatin' at her apron.

"Well, I was surprised. She didn't ask me to come up to the stove, or to sit down, but just set there, not even lookin' at me. And so I said: 'I want to see John.'

"And then she—laughed. I guess you would call it a laugh.

"I thought of Harry and the team outside, so I said, a little sharp, 'Can I see John?' 'No,' says she—kind of dull like. 'Ain't he home?' says I. Then she looked at me. 'Yes,' says she, 'he's home.' 'Then why can't I see him?' I asked her, out of patience with her now. ' 'Cause he's dead,' says she, just as quiet and dull—and fell to pleatin' her apron. 'Dead?' says I, like you do when you can't take in what you've heard.

"She just nodded her head, not getting a bit excited, but rockin' back and forth.

" 'Why—where is he?' says I, not knowing *what* to say.

"She just pointed upstairs—like this"—pointing to the room above.

"I got up, with the idea of going up there myself. By this time I—didn't know what to do. I walked from there to here; then I says: 'Why, what did he die of?'

" 'He died of a rope round his neck,' says she; and just went on pleatin' at her apron."

Hale stopped speaking, and stood staring at the rocker, as if he were still seeing the woman who had sat there the morning before. Nobody spoke; it was as if every one were seeing the woman who had sat there the morning before.

"And what did you do then?" the county attorney at last broke the silence.

"I went out and called Harry. I thought I might—need help. I got Harry in, and we went upstairs." His voice fell almost to a whisper. "There he was—lying over the—"

"I think I'd rather have you go into that upstairs," the county attorney interrupted, "where you can point it all out. Just go on now with the rest of the story."

"Well, my first thought was to get that rope off. It looked—"

He stopped, his face twitching.

"But Harry, he went up to him, and he said, 'No, he's dead all right, and we'd better not touch anything.' So we went downstairs.

"She was still sitting that same way. 'Has anybody been notified?' I asked. 'No,' says she, unconcerned.

" 'Who did this, Mrs. Wright?' said Harry. He said it businesslike, and she stopped pleatin' at her apron. 'I don't know,' she says. 'You don't *know?*' says Harry. 'Weren't you sleepin' in the bed with him?' 'Yes,' says she, 'but I was on the inside.' 'Somebody slipped a rope round his neck and strangled him, and you didn't wake up?' says Harry. 'I didn't wake up,' she said after him.

"We may have looked as if we didn't see how that could be, for after a minute she said, 'I sleep sound.'

"Harry was going to ask her more questions, but I said maybe that weren't our business; maybe we ought to let her tell her story first to the coroner or the sheriff. So Harry went fast as he could over to High Road—the Rivers' place, where there's a telephone."

"And what did she do when she knew you had gone for the coroner?" The attorney got his pencil in his hand all ready for writing.

"She moved from that chair to this one over here"—Hale pointed to a small chair in the corner—"and just sat there with her hands held together and looking down. I got a feeling that I ought to make some conversation, so I said I had come in to see if John wanted to put in a telephone, and at that she started to laugh, and then she stopped and looked at me—scared."

At sound of a moving pencil the man who was telling the story looked up.

"I dunno—maybe it wasn't scared," he hastened; "I wouldn't like to say it was. Soon Harry got back, and then Dr. Lloyd came, and you, Mr. Peters, and so I guess that's all I know that you don't."

He said that last with relief, and moved a little, as if relaxing. Every one moved a little. The county attorney walked toward the stair door.

"I guess we'll go upstairs first—then out to the barn and around there."

He paused and looked around the kitchen.

"You're convinced there was nothing important here?" he asked the sheriff. "Nothing that would—point to any motive?"

The sheriff too looked all around, as if to re-convince himself.

"Nothing here but kitchen things," he said, with a little laugh for the insignificance of kitchen things.

The county attorney was looking at the cupboard—a peculiar, ungainly structure, half closet and half cupboard, the upper part of it being built in the wall, and the lower part just the old-fashioned kitchen cupboard. As if its queerness attracted him, he got a chair and opened the upper part and looked in. After a moment he drew his hand away sticky.

"Here's a nice mess," he said resentfully.

The two women had drawn nearer, and now the sheriff's wife spoke.

"Oh—her fruit," she said, looking to Mrs. Hale for sympathetic understanding. She turned back to the county attorney and explained: "She worried about that when it turned so cold last night. She said the fire would go out and her jars might burst."

Mrs. Peters' husband broke into a laugh.

"Well, can you beat the women! Held for murder, and worrying about her preserves!"

The young attorney set his lips.

"I guess before we're through with her she may have something more serious than preserves to worry about."

"Oh, well," said Mrs. Hale's husband, with good-natured superiority, "women are used to worrying over trifles."

The two women moved a little closer together. Neither of them spoke. The county attorney seemed suddenly to remember his manners—and think of his future.

"And yet," said he, with the gallantry of a young politician, "for all their worries, what would we do without the ladies?"

The women did not speak, did not unbend. He went to the sink and began washing his hands. He turned to wipe them on the roller towel—whirled it for a cleaner place.

"Dirty towels! Not much of a housekeeper, would you say, ladies?"

He kicked his foot against some dirty pans under the sink.

"There's a great deal of work to be done on a farm," said Mrs. Hale stiffly.

"To be sure. And yet"—with a little bow to her—"I know there are some Dickson County farm-houses that do not have such roller towels." He gave it a pull to expose its full length again.

"Those towels get dirty awful quick. Men's hands aren't always as clean as they might be."

"Ah, loyal to your sex, I see," he laughed. He stopped and gave her a keen look. "But you and Mrs. Wright were neighbors. I suppose you were friends, too."

Martha Hale shook her head.

"I've seen little enough of her of late years. I've not been in this house—it's more than a year."

"And why was that? You didn't like her?"

"I liked her well enough," she replied with spirit. "Farmers' wives have their hands full, Mr. Henderson. And then—" She looked around the kitchen.

"Yes?" he encouraged.

"It never seemed a very cheerful place," said she, more to herself than to him.

"No," he agreed; "I don't think any one would call it cheerful. I shouldn't say she had the home-making instinct."

"Well, I don't know as Wright had, either," she muttered.

"You mean they didn't get on very well?" he was quick to ask.

"No; I don't mean anything," she answered, with decision. As she turned a little away from him, she added: "But I don't think a place would be any the cheerfuler for John Wright's bein' in it."

"I'd like to talk to you about that a little later, Mrs. Hale," he said. "I'm anxious to get the lay of things upstairs now."

He moved toward the stair door, followed by the two men.

"I suppose anything Mrs. Peters does'll be all right?" the sheriff inquired. "She was to take in some clothes for her, you know—and a few little things. We left in such a hurry yesterday."

The county attorney looked at the two women whom they were leaving alone there among the kitchen things.

"Yes—Mrs. Peters," he said, his glance resting on the woman who was not Mrs. Peters, the big farmer woman who stood behind the sheriff's wife. "Of course Mrs. Peters is one of us," he said, in a manner of entrusting responsibility. "And keep your eye out, Mrs. Peters, for anything that might be of use. No telling; you women might come upon a clue to the motive—and that's the thing we need."

Mr. Hale rubbed his face after the fashion of a show man getting ready for a pleasantry.

"But would the women know a clue if they did come upon it?" he said; and, having delivered himself of this, he followed the others through the stair door.

The women stood motionless and silent, listening to the footsteps, first upon the stairs, then in the room above them.

Then, as if releasing herself from something strange, Mrs. Hale began to arrange the dirty pans under the sink, which the county attorney's disdainful push of the foot had deranged.

"I'd hate to have men comin' into my kitchen," she said testily—"snoopin' round and criticizin'."

"Of course it's no more than their duty," said the sheriff's wife, in her manner of timid acquiescence.

"Duty's all right," replied Mrs. Hale bluffly; "but I guess that deputy sheriff that come out to make the fire might have got a little of this on." She gave the roller towel a pull. "Wish I'd thought of that sooner! Seems mean to talk about her for not having things slicked up, when she had to come away in such a hurry."

She looked around the kitchen. Certainly it was not "slicked up." Her eye was held by a bucket of sugar on a low shelf. The cover was off the wooden bucket, and beside it was a paper bag—half full.

Mrs. Hale moved toward it.

"She was putting this in there," she said to herself—slowly.

She thought of the flour in her kitchen at home—half sifted, half not sifted. She had been interrupted, and had left things half done. What had interrupted Minnie Foster? Why had that work been left half done? She made a move as if to finish it,—unfinished things always bothered her,—and then she glanced around and saw that Mrs. Peters was watching her— and she didn't want Mrs. Peters to get that feeling she had got of work begun and then—for some reason—not finished.

"It's a shame about her fruit," she said, and walked toward the cupboard that the county attorney had opened, and got on the chair, murmuring: "I wonder if it's all gone."

It was a sorry enough looking sight, but "Here's one that's all right," she said at last. She held it toward the light. "This is cherries, too." She looked again. "I declare I believe that's the only one."

With a sigh, she got down from the chair, went to the sink, and wiped off the bottle.

"She'll feel awful bad, after all her hard work in the hot weather. I remember the afternoon I put up my cherries last summer."

She set the bottle on the table, and, with another sigh, started to sit down in the rocker. But she did not sit down. Something kept her from sitting down in that chair. She straightened—stepped back, and, half turned away, stood looking at it, seeing the woman who had sat there "pleatin' at her apron."

The thin voice of the sheriff's wife broke in upon her: "I must be getting those things from the front room closet." She opened the door into the other room, started in, stepped back. "You coming with me, Mrs. Hale?" she asked nervously. "You—you could help me get them."

They were soon back—the stark coldness of that shut-up room was not a thing to linger in.

"My!" said Mrs. Peters, dropping the things on the table and hurrying to the stove.

Mrs. Hale stood examining the clothes the woman who was being detained in town had said she wanted.

"Wright was close![1]" she exclaimed, holding up a shabby black skirt that bore the marks of much making over. "I think maybe that's why she kept so much to herself. I s'pose she felt she couldn't do her part; and then, you don't enjoy things when you feel shabby. She used to wear pretty clothes and be lively—when she was Minnie Foster, one of the town girls, singing in the choir. But that—oh, that was twenty years ago."

With a carefulness in which there was something tender, she folded the shabby clothes and piled them at one corner of the table. She looked up at Mrs. Peters, and there was something in the other woman's look that irritated her.

"She don't care," she said to herself. "Much difference it makes to her whether Minnie Foster had pretty clothes when she was a girl."

_____

1. Stingy.

Then she looked again, and she wasn't so sure; in fact, she hadn't at any time been perfectly sure about Mrs. Peters. She had that shrinking manner, and yet her eyes looked as if they could see a long way into things.

"This all you was to take in?" asked Mrs. Hale.

"No," said the sheriff's wife; "she said she wanted an apron. Funny thing to want," she ventured in her nervous little way, "for there's not much to get you dirty in jail, goodness knows. But I suppose just to make her feel more natural. If you're used to wearing an apron—. She said they were in the bottom drawer of this cupboard. Yes—here they are. And then her little shawl that always hung on the stair door."

She took the small gray shawl from behind the door leading upstairs, and stood a minute looking at it.

Suddenly Mrs. Hale took a quick step toward the other woman.

"Mrs. Peters!"

"Yes, Mrs. Hale?"

"Do you think she—did it?"

A frightened look blurred the other thing in Mrs. Peters' eyes.

"Oh, I don't know," she said, in a voice that seemed to shrink away from the subject.

"Well, I don't think she did," affirmed Mrs. Hale stoutly. "Asking for an apron, and her little shawl. Worryin' about her fruit."

"Mr. Peters says—." Footsteps were heard in the room above; she stopped, looked up, then went on in a lowered voice: "Mr. Peters says—it looks bad for her. Mr. Henderson is awful sarcastic in a speech, and he's going to make fun of her saying she didn't—wake up."

For a moment Mrs. Hale had no answer. Then, "Well, I guess John Wright didn't wake up—when they was slippin' that rope under his neck," she muttered.

"No, it's *strange*," breathed Mrs. Peters. "They think it was such a—funny way to kill a man."

She began to laugh; at sound of the laugh, abruptly stopped.

"That's just what Mr. Hale said," said Mrs. Hale, in a resolutely natural voice. "There was a gun in the house. He says that's what he can't understand."

"Mr. Henderson said, coming out, that what was needed for the case was a motive. Something to show anger—or sudden feeling."

"Well, I don't see any signs of anger around here," said Mrs. Hale. "I don't—"

She stopped. It was as if her mind tripped on something. Her eye was caught by a dish-towel in the middle of the kitchen table. Slowly she moved toward the table. One half of it was wiped clean, the other half messy. Her eyes made a slow, almost unwilling turn to the bucket of sugar and the half empty bag beside it. Things begun—and not finished.

After a moment she stepped back, and said, in that manner of releasing herself:

"Wonder how they're finding things upstairs? I hope she had it a little more red up up there. You know,"—she paused, and feeling gathered,—"it seems kind of *sneaking*: locking her up in town and coming out here to get her own house to turn against her!"

"But, Mrs. Hale," said the sheriff's wife, "the law is the law."

"I s'pose 'tis," answered Mrs. Hale shortly.

She turned to the stove, saying something about that fire not being much to brag of. She worked with it a minute, and when she straightened up she said aggressively:

"The law is the law—and a bad stove is a bad stove. How'd you like to cook on this?"—pointing with the poker to the broken lining. She opened the oven door and started to express her opinion of the oven; but she was swept into her own thoughts, thinking of what it would mean, year after year, to have that stove to wrestle with. The thought of Minnie Foster trying to bake in that oven—and the thought of her never going over to see Minnie Foster—.

She was startled by hearing Mrs. Peters say: "A person gets discouraged—and loses heart."

The sheriff's wife had looked from the stove to the sink—to the pail of water which had been carried in from outside. The two women stood there silent, above them the footsteps of the men who were looking for evidence against the woman who had worked in that kitchen. That look of seeing into things, of seeing through a thing to something else, was in the eyes of the sheriff's wife now. When Mrs. Hale next spoke to her, it was gently:

"Better loosen up your things, Mrs. Peters. We'll not feel them when we go out."

Mrs. Peters went to the back of the room to hang up the fur tippet she was wearing. A moment later she exclaimed, "Why, she was piecing a quilt," and held up a large sewing basket piled high with quilt pieces.

Mrs. Hale spread some of the blocks out on the table.

"It's log-cabin pattern," she said, putting several of them together. "Pretty, isn't it?"

They were so engaged with the quilt that they did not hear the footsteps on the stairs. Just as the stair door opened Mrs. Hale was saying:

"Do you suppose she was going to quilt it or just knot it?"

The sheriff threw up his hands.

"They wonder whether she was going to quilt it or just knot it!"

There was a laugh for the ways of women, a warming of hands over the stove, and then the county attorney said briskly:

"Well, let's go right out to the barn and get that cleared up."

"I don't see as there's anything so strange," Mrs. Hale said resentfully, after the outside door had closed on the three men—"our taking up our time with little things while we're waiting for them to get the evidence. I don't see as it's anything to laugh about."

"Of course they've got awful important things on their minds," said the sheriff's wife apologetically.

They returned to an inspection of the block for the quilt. Mrs. Hale was looking at the fine, even sewing, and preoccupied with thoughts of the woman who had done that sewing, when she heard the sheriff's wife say, in a queer tone:

"Why, look at this one."

She turned to take the block held out to her.

"The sewing," said Mrs. Peters, in a troubled way. "All the rest of them have been so nice and even—but—this one. Why, it looks as if she didn't know what she was about!"

Their eyes met—something flashed to life, passed between them; then, as if with an effort, they seemed to pull away from each other. A moment Mrs. Hale sat there, her hands folded over that sewing which was so unlike all the rest of the sewing. Then she had pulled a knot and drawn the threads.

"Oh, what are you doing, Mrs. Hale?" asked the sheriff's wife, startled.

"Just pulling out a stitch or two that's not sewed very good," said Mrs. Hale mildly.

"I don't think we ought to touch things," Mrs. Peters said, a little helplessly.

"I'll just finish up this end," answered Mrs. Hale, still in that mild, matter-of-fact fashion.

She threaded a needle and started to replace bad sewing with good. For a little while she sewed in silence. Then, in that thin, timid voice, she heard:

"Mrs. Hale!"

"Yes, Mrs. Peters?"

"What do you suppose she was so—nervous about?"

"Oh, I don't know," said Mrs. Hale, as if dismissing a thing not important enough to spend much time on. "I don't know as she was—nervous. I sew awful queer sometimes when I'm just tired."

She cut a thread, and out of the corner of her eye looked up at Mrs. Peters. The small, lean face of the sheriff's wife seemed to have tightened up. Her eyes had that look of peering into something. But next moment she moved, and said in her thin, indecisive way:

"Well, I must get those clothes wrapped. They may be through sooner than we think. I wonder where I could find a piece of paper—and string."

"In that cupboard, maybe," suggested Mrs. Hale, after a glance around.

One piece of the crazy sewing remained unripped. Mrs. Peters' back turned, Martha Hale now scrutinized that piece, compared it with the dainty, accurate sewing of the other blocks. The difference was startling. Holding this block made her feel queer, as if the distracted thoughts of the woman who had perhaps turned to it to try and quiet herself were communicating themselves to her.

Mrs. Peters' voice roused her.

"Here's a bird-cage," she said. "Did she have a bird, Mrs. Hale?"

"Why, I don't know whether she did or not." She turned to look at the cage Mrs. Peters was holding up. "I've not been here in so long." She sighed. "There was a man round last year selling canaries cheap—but I don't know as she took one. Maybe she did. She used to sing real pretty herself."

Mrs. Peters looked around the kitchen.

"Seems kind of funny to think of a bird here." She half laughed—an attempt to put up a barrier. "But she must have had one—or why would she have a cage? I wonder what happened to it."

"I suppose maybe the cat got it," suggested Mrs. Hale, resuming her sewing.

"No; she didn't have a cat. She's got that feeling some people have about cats—being afraid of them. When they brought her to our house yesterday, my cat got in the room, and she was real upset and asked me to take it out."

"My sister Bessie was like that," laughed Mrs. Hale.

The sheriff's wife did not reply. The silence made Mrs. Hale turn round. Mrs. Peters was examining the bird-cage.

"Look at this door," she said slowly. "It's broke. One hinge has been pulled apart."

Mrs. Hale came nearer.

"Looks as if some one must have been—rough with it."

Again their eyes met—startled, questioning, apprehensive. For a moment neither spoke nor stirred. Then Mrs. Hale, turning away, said brusquely:

"If they're going to find any evidence, I wish they'd be about it. I don't like this place."

"But I'm awful glad you came with me, Mrs. Hale." Mrs. Peters put the bird-cage on the table and sat down. "It would be lonesome for me—sitting here alone."

"Yes, it would, wouldn't it?" agreed Mrs. Hale, a certain determined naturalness in her voice. She had picked up the sewing, but now it dropped in her lap, and she murmured in a different voice: "But I tell you what I *do* wish, Mrs. Peters. I wish I had come over sometimes when she was here. I wish—I had."

"But of course you were awful busy, Mrs. Hale. Your house—and your children."

"I could've come," retorted Mrs. Hale shortly. "I stayed away because it weren't cheerful—and that's why I ought to have come. I"—she looked around—"I've never liked this place. Maybe because it's down in a hollow and you don't see the road. I don't know what it is, but it's a lonesome place, and always was. I wish I had come over to see Minnie Foster sometimes. I can see now—." She did not put it into words.

"Well, you mustn't reproach yourself," counseled Mrs. Peters. "Somehow, we just don't see how it is with other folks till—something comes up."

"Not having children makes less work," mused Mrs. Hale, after a long silence, "but it makes a quiet house—and Wright out to work all day—and no company when he did come in. Did you know John Wright, Mrs. Peters?"

"Not to know him. I've seen him in town. They say he was a good man."

"Yes—good," conceded John Wright's neighbor grimly. "He didn't drink, and kept his word as well as most, I guess, and paid his debts. But he was a hard man, Mrs. Peters. Just to pass the time of day with him—." She stopped, shivered a little. "Like a raw wind that gets to the bone." Her eye fell upon the cage on the table before her, and she added, almost bitterly: "I should think she would've wanted a bird!"

Suddenly she leaned forward, looking intently at the cage. "But what do you s'pose went wrong with it?"

"I don't know," returned Mrs. Peters; "unless it got sick and died."

But after she said it she reached over and swung the broken door. Both women watched it as if somehow held by it.

"You didn't know—her?" Mrs. Hale asked, a gentler note in her voice.

"Not till they brought her yesterday," said the sheriff's wife.

"She—come to think of it, she was kind of like a bird herself. Real sweet and pretty, but kind of timid and—fluttery. How—she—did—change."

That held her for a long time. Finally, as if struck with a happy thought and relieved to get back to everyday things, she exclaimed:

"Tell you what, Mrs. Peters, why don't you take the quilt in with you? It might take up her mind."

"Why, I think that's a real nice idea, Mrs. Hale," agreed the sheriff's wife, as if she too were glad to come into the atmosphere of a simple kindness. "There couldn't possibly be any objection to that, could there? Now, just what will I take? I wonder if her patches are in here—and her things."

They turned to the sewing basket.

"Here's some red," said Mrs. Hale, bringing out a roll of cloth. Underneath that was a box. "Here, maybe her scissors are in here—and her things." She held it up. "What a pretty box! I'll warrant that was something she had a long time ago—when she was a girl."

She held it in her hand a moment; then, with a little sigh, opened it.

Instantly her hand went to her nose.

"Why—!"

Mrs. Peters drew nearer—then turned away.

"There's something wrapped up in this piece of silk," faltered Mrs. Hale.

"This isn't her scissors," said Mrs. Peters, in a shrinking voice.

Her hand not steady, Mrs. Hale raised the piece of silk. "Oh, Mrs. Peters!" she cried. "It's—"

Mrs. Peters bent closer.

"It's the bird," she whispered.

"But, Mrs. Peters!" cried Mrs. Hale. "*Look* at it! Its *neck*—look at its neck! It's all—other side *to.*"

She held the box away from her.

The sheriff's wife again bent closer.

"Somebody wrung its neck," said she, in a voice that was slow and deep.

And then again the eyes of the two women met—this time clung together in a look of dawning comprehension, of growing horror. Mrs. Peters looked from the dead bird to the broken door of the cage. Again their eyes met. And just then there was a sound at the outside door.

Mrs. Hale slipped the box under the quilt pieces in the basket, and sank into the chair before it. Mrs. Peters stood holding to the table. The county attorney and the sheriff came in from outside.

"Well, ladies," said the county attorney, as one turning from serious things to little pleasantries, "have you decided whether she was going to quilt it or knot it?"

"We think," began the sheriff's wife in a flurried voice, "that she was going to—knot it."

He was too preoccupied to notice the change that came in her voice on that last.

"Well, that's very interesting, I'm sure," he said tolerantly. He caught sight of the bird-cage. "Has the bird flown?"

"We think the cat got it," said Mrs. Hale in a voice curiously even.

He was walking up and down, as if thinking something out.

"Is there a cat?" he asked absently.

Mrs. Hale shot a look up at the sheriff's wife.

"Well, not *now*," said Mrs. Peters. "They're superstitious, you know; they leave." She sank into her chair.

The county attorney did not heed her. "No sign at all of any one having come in from the outside," he said to Peters, in the manner of continuing an interrupted conversation. "Their own rope. Now let's go upstairs again and go over it, piece by piece. It would have to have been some one who knew just the—"

The stair door closed behind them and their voices were lost.

The two women sat motionless, not looking at each other, but as if peering into something and at the same time holding back. When they spoke now it was as if they were afraid of what they were saying, but as if they could not help saying it.

"She liked the bird," said Martha Hale, low and slowly. "She was going to bury it in that pretty box."

"When I was a girl," said Mrs. Peters, under her breath, "my kitten—there was a boy took a hatchet, and before my eyes—before I could get there—" She covered her face an instant. "If they hadn't held me back I would have"—she caught herself, looked upstairs where footsteps were heard, and finished weakly—"hurt him."

Then they sat without speaking or moving.

"I wonder how it would seem," Mrs. Hale at last began, as if feeling her way over strange ground—"never to have had any children around?" Her eyes made a slow sweep of the kitchen, as if seeing what that kitchen had meant through all the years. "No, Wright wouldn't like the bird," she said after that—"a thing that sang. She used to sing. He killed that too." Her voice tightened.

Mrs. Peters moved uneasily.

"Of course we don't know who killed the bird."

"I knew John Wright," was Mrs. Hale's answer.

"It was an awful thing was done in this house that night, Mrs. Hale," said the sheriff's wife. "Killing a man while he slept—slipping a thing round his neck that choked the life out of him."

Mrs. Hale's hand went out to the bird-cage.

"His neck. Choked the life out of him."

"We don't *know* who killed him," whispered Mrs. Peters wildly. "We don't *know*."

Mrs. Hale had not moved. "If there had been years and years of—nothing, then a bird to sing to you, it would be awful—still—after the bird was still."

It was as if something within her not herself had spoken, and it found in Mrs. Peters something she did not know as herself.

"I know what stillness is," she said, in a queer, monotonous voice. "When we homesteaded in Dakota, and my first baby died—after he was two years old—and me with no other then—"

Mrs. Hale stirred.

"How soon do you suppose they'll be through looking for the evidence?"

"I know what stillness is," repeated Mrs. Peters, in just that same way. Then she too pulled back. "The law has got to punish crime, Mrs. Hale," she said in her tight little way.

"I wish you'd seen Minnie Foster," was the answer, "when she wore a white dress with blue ribbons, and stood up there in the choir and sang."

The picture of that girl, the fact that she had lived neighbor to that girl for twenty years, and had let her die for lack of life, was suddenly more than she could bear.

"Oh, I *wish* I'd come over here once in a while!" she cried. "That was a crime! That was a crime! Who's going to punish that?"

"We mustn't take on," said Mrs. Peters, with a frightened look toward the stairs.

"I might 'a' *known* she needed help! I tell you, it's *queer*, Mrs. Peters. We live close together, and we live far apart. We all go through the same things—it's all just a different kind of the same thing! If it weren't—why do you and I *understand?* Why do we *know*—what we know this minute?"

She dashed her hand across her eyes. Then, seeing the jar of fruit on the table, she reached for it and choked out:

"If I was you I wouldn't *tell* her her fruit was gone! Tell her it *ain't.* Tell her it's all right—all of it. Here—take this in to prove it to her! She—she may never know whether it was broke or not."

She turned away.

Mrs. Peters reached out for the bottle of fruit as if she were glad to take it—as if touching a familiar thing, having something to do, could keep her from something else. She got up, looked about for something to wrap the fruit in, took a petticoat from the pile of clothes she had brought from the front room, and nervously started winding that round the bottle.

"My!" she began, in a high, false voice, "it's a good thing the men couldn't hear us! Getting all stirred up over a little thing like a—dead canary." She hurried over that. "As if that could have anything to do with—with— My, wouldn't they *laugh?*"

Footsteps were heard on the stairs.

"Maybe they would," muttered Mrs. Hale—"maybe they wouldn't."

"No, Peters," said the county attorney incisively; "it's all perfectly clear, except the reason for doing it. But you know juries when it comes to women. If there was some definite thing—something to show. Something to make a story about. A thing that would connect up with this clumsy way of doing it."

In a covert way Mrs. Hale looked at Mrs. Peters. Mrs. Peters was looking at her. Quickly they looked away from each other. The outer door opened and Mr. Hale came in.

"I've got the team round now," he said. "Pretty cold out there."

"I'm going to stay here awhile by myself," the county attorney suddenly announced. "You can send Frank out for me, can't you?" he asked the sheriff. "I want to go over everything. I'm not satisfied we can't do better."

Again, for one brief moment, the two women's eyes found one another.

The sheriff came up to the table.

"Did you want to see what Mrs. Peters was going to take in?"

The county attorney picked up the apron. He laughed.

"Oh, I guess they're not very dangerous things the ladies have picked out."

Mrs. Hale's hand was on the sewing basket in which the box was concealed. She felt that she ought to take her hand off the basket. She did not seem able to. He picked up one of the quilt blocks which she had piled on to cover the box. Her eyes felt like fire. She had a feeling that if he took up the basket she would snatch it from him.

But he did not take it up. With another little laugh, he turned away, saying:

"No; Mrs. Peters doesn't need supervising. For that matter, a sheriff's wife is married to the law. Ever think of it that way, Mrs. Peters?"

Mrs. Peters was standing beside the table. Mrs. Hale shot a look up at her; but she could not see her face. Mrs. Peters had turned away. When she spoke, her voice was muffled.

"Not—just that way," she said.

"Married to the law!" chuckled Mrs. Peters' husband. He moved toward the door into the front room, and said to the county attorney:

"I just want you to come in here a minute, George. We ought to take a look at these windows."

"Oh—windows," said the county attorney scoffingly.

"We'll be right out, Mr. Hale," said the sheriff to the farmer, who was still waiting by the door.

Hale went to look after the horses. The sheriff followed the county attorney into the other room. Again—for one final moment—the two women were alone in that kitchen.

Martha Hale sprang up, her hands tight together, looking at that other woman, with whom it rested. At first she could not see her eyes, for the sheriff's wife had not turned back since she turned away at that suggestion of being married to the law. But now Mrs. Hale made her turn back. Her eyes made her turn back. Slowly, unwillingly, Mrs. Peters turned her head until her eyes met the eyes of the other woman. There was a moment when they held each other in a steady, burning look in which there was no evasion nor flinching. Then Martha Hale's eyes pointed the way to the basket in which was hidden the thing that would make certain the conviction of the other woman—that woman who was not there and yet who had been there with them all through that hour.

For a moment Mrs. Peters did not move. And then she did it. With a rush forward, she threw back the quilt pieces, got the box, tried to put it in her handbag. It was too big. Desperately she opened it, started to take the bird out. But there she broke—she could not touch the bird. She stood there helpless, foolish.

There was the sound of a knob turning in the inner door. Martha Hale snatched the box from the sheriff's wife, and got it in the pocket of her big coat just as the sheriff and the county attorney came back into the kitchen.

"Well, Henry," said the county attorney facetiously, "at least we found out that she was not going to quilt it. She was going to—what is it you call it, ladies?"

Mrs. Hale's hand was against the pocket of her coat.

"We call it—knot it, Mr. Henderson."

1917

Mary Antin
(1881–1949)

Born in Polotsk, in czarist Russia, inside the Jewish pale, Mary Antin came to the United States at age 14 with her mother, two sisters, and brother. Her father had gone a few years earlier to prepare the way. The Boston that they settled in was less crowded than the Lower East Side of New York in the 1890s as described by Abraham Cahan and Anzia Yezierska; possibly for this reason, possibly as a result of temperament or experience, Antin's is a largely affirmative response to the promise of America. For a while the family ran a concession at Revere Beach. When that failed, her father turned to storekeeping in Chelsea. Mary was immediately enrolled in school and soon treated as a prodigy (her older sister had to go to work). After Girls Latin School in Boston, she attended Columbia and Barnard College in New York and married a Columbia professor.

From Plotzk to Boston (1899), her first book, was published when she was not yet 20 and had not yet attended college. In it she translated into English letters she had written in Yiddish to an uncle in Russia. A dozen years later the material was enlarged as *The Promised Land* (1912), her major work. An autobiography (the first eight chapters described her family's life before their arrival in Boston and the rest recounted the early years of their new life), it was hugely popular for many years and received as a testimony to American opportunities and freedoms. Two years later, in *They Who Knock at Our Gates; A Complete Gospel of Immigration* (1914), she argued against restrictive immigration policies, preaching open doors as integral to "the loftiest interpretation of our duty as Americans." Although she continued to write for journals, she published no more books.

FROM THE PROMISED LAND

Chapter XVI
Dover Street

What happened next was Dover Street.

And what was Dover Street?

Ask rather, What was it not? Dover Street was my fairest garden of girlhood, a gate of paradise, a window facing on a broad avenue of life. Dover Street was a prison, a school of discipline, a battlefield of sordid strife. The air in Dover Street was heavy with evil odors of degradation, but a breath from the uppermost heavens rippled through, whispering of infinite things. In Dover Street the dragon poverty gripped me for a last fight, but I overthrew the hideous creature, and sat on his neck as on a throne. In Dover Street I was shackled with a hundred chains of disadvantage, but with one free hand I planted little seeds, right there in the mud of shame, that blossomed into the honeyed rose of widest freedom. In Dover Street there was often no loaf on the table, but the hand of some noble friend was ever in mine. The night in Dover Street was rent with the cries of wrong, but the thunders of truth crashed through the pitiful clamor and died out in prophetic silences.

Outwardly, Dover Street is a noisy thoroughfare cut through a South End slum, in every essential the same as Wheeler Street. Turn down any street in the slums, at random, and call it by whatever name you please, you will observe there the same fashions of life, death, and endurance. Every one of those streets is a rubbish heap of damaged humanity, and it will take a powerful broom and an ocean of soapsuds to clean it out.

Dover Street is intersected, near its eastern end, where we lived, by Harrison Avenue. That street is to the South End what Salem Street is to the North End. It is the heart of the South End ghetto, for the greater part of its length; although its northern end belongs to the realm of Chinatown. Its multifarious business bursts through the narrow shop doors, and overruns the basements, the sidewalk, the street itself, in pushcarts and open-air stands. Its multitudinous population bursts through the greasy tenement doors, and floods the corridors, the doorsteps, the gutters, the side streets, pushing in and out among the pushcarts, all day long and half the night besides.

Rarely as Harrison Avenue is caught asleep, even more rarely is it found clean. Nothing less than a fire or flood would cleanse this street. Even Passover cannot quite accomplish this feat. For although the tenements may be scrubbed to their remotest corners, on this one occasion, the cleansing stops at the curbstone. A great deal of the filthy rubbish accumulated in a year is pitched into the street, often through the windows; and what the ashman on his daily round does not remove is left to be trampled to powder, in which form it steals back into the houses from which it was so lately removed.

The City Fathers provide soap and water for the slums, in the form of excellent schools, kindergartens, and branch libraries. And there they stop: at the curbstone of the people's life. They cleanse and discipline the children's minds, but their bodies they pitch into the gutter. For there are no parks and almost no playgrounds in the Harrison Avenue district,—in my day there were none,—and such as there are have been wrenched from the city by public-spirited citizens who have no offices in City Hall. No wonder the ashman is not more thorough: he learns from his masters.

It is a pity to have it so, in a queen of enlightened cities like Boston. If we of the twentieth century do not believe in baseball as much as in philosophy, we have not learned the lesson of modern science, which teaches, among other things, that the body is the nursery of the soul; the instrument of our moral development; the secret chart of our devious progress from worm to man. The great achievement of recent science, of which we are so proud, has been the deciphering of the hieroglyphic of organic nature. To worship the facts and neglect the implications of the message of science is to applaud the drama without taking the moral to heart. And we certainly are not taking the moral to heart when we try to make a hero out of the boy by such foreign appliances as grammar and algebra, while utterly despising the fittest instrument for his uplifting—the boy's own body.

We had no particular reason for coming to Dover Street. It might just as well have been Applepie Alley. For my father had sold, with the goods, fixtures, and good-will of the Wheeler Street store, all his hopes of ever making a living in the grocery trade; and I doubt if he got a silver dollar the more for them. We had to live somewhere, even if we were not making a living, so we came to Dover Street, where tenements were cheap; by which I mean that rent was low. The ultimate cost of life in those tenements, in terms of human happiness, is high enough.

Our new home consisted of five small rooms up two flights of stairs, with the right of way through the dark corridors. In the "parlor" the dingy paper hung in rags and the plaster fell in chunks. One of the bedrooms was absolutely dark and air-tight. The kitchen windows looked out on a dirty court, at the back of which was the rear tenement of the estate. To us belonged, along with the five rooms and the right of way aforesaid, a block of upper space the length of a pulley line across this court, and the width of an arc described by a windy Monday's wash in its remotest wanderings.

The little front bedroom was assigned to me, with only one partner, my sister Dora. A mouse could not have led a cat much of a chase across this room; still we found space for a narrow bed, a crazy bureau, and a small table. From the window there was an unobstructed view of a lumberyard, beyond which frowned the blackened walls of a factory. The fence of the lumberyard was gay with theatre posters and illustrated advertisements of tobacco, whiskey, and patent baby foods. When the window was open, there was a constant clang and whirr of electric cars, varied by the screech of machinery, the clatter of empty wagons, or the rumble of heavy trucks.

There was nothing worse in all this than we had had before since our exile from Crescent Beach;[1] but I did not take the same delight in the propinquity of electric cars and arc lights that I had till now. I suppose the tenement began to pall on me.

It must not be supposed that I enjoyed any degree of privacy, because I had half a room to myself. We were six in the five rooms; we were bound to be always in each other's way. And as it was within our flat, so it was in the house as a whole. All doors, beginning with the street door, stood open most of the time; or if they were closed, the tenants did not wear out their knuckles knocking for admittance. I could stand at any time in the unswept entrance hall and tell, from an analysis of the medley of sounds and smells that issued from doors ajar, what was going on in the several flats from below up. That guttural, scolding voice, unremittent as the hissing of a steam pipe, is Mrs. Rasnosky. I make a guess that she is chastising the infant Isaac for taking a second lump of sugar in his tea. *Spam! Bam!* Yes, and she is rubbing in her objections with the flat of her hand. That blubbering and moaning, accompanying an elephantine tread, is fat Mrs. Casey, second floor, home drunk from an afternoon out, in fear of the vengeance of Mr. Casey; to propitiate whom she is burning a pan of bacon, as the choking fumes and outrageous sizzling testify. I hear a feeble whining, interrupted by long silences. It is that scabby baby on the third floor, fallen out of bed again, with nobody home to pick him up.

To escape from these various horrors I ascend to the roof, where bacon and babies and child-beating are not. But there I find two figures in calico wrappers, with bare red arms akimbo, a basket of wet clothes in front of each, and only one empty clothes-line between them. I do not want to be dragged in as a witness in a case of assault and battery, so I descend to the street again, grateful to note, as I pass, that the third-floor baby is still.

1. Now Revere Beach.

In front of the door I squeeze through a group of children. They are going to play tag, and are counting to see who should be "it":—

> "My-mother-and-your-mother-went-out-to-hang-clothes;
> My-mother-gave-your-mother-a-punch-in-the-nose."

If the children's couplet does not give a vivid picture of the life, manners, and customs of Dover Street, no description of mine can ever do so.

Frieda was married before we came to Dover Street, and went to live in East Boston. This left me the eldest of the children at home. Whether on this account, or because I was outgrowing my childish carelessness, or because I began to believe, on the cumulative evidence of the Crescent Beach, Chelsea, and Wheeler Street adventures, that America, after all, was not going to provide for my father's family,—whether for any or all of these reasons, I began at this time to take bread-and-butter matters more to heart, and to ponder ways and means of getting rich. My father sought employment wherever work was going on. His health was poor; he aged very fast. Nevertheless he offered himself for every kind of labor; he offered himself for a boy's wages. Here he was found too weak, here too old; here his imperfect English was in the way, here his Jewish appearance. He had a few short terms of work at this or that; I do not know the name of the form of drudgery that my father did not practise. But all told, he did not earn enough to pay the rent in full and buy a bone for the soup. The only steady source of income, for I do not know what years, was my brother's earnings from his newspapers.

Surely this was the time for me to take my sister's place in the workshop. I had had every fair chance until now: school, my time to myself, liberty to run and play and make friends. I had graduated from grammar school; I was of legal age to go to work. What was I doing, sitting at home and dreaming?

I was minding my business, of course; with all my might I was minding my business. As I understood it, my business was to go to school, to learn everything there was to know, to write poetry, become famous, and make the family rich. Surely it was not shirking to lay out such a programme for myself. I had boundless faith in my future. I was certainly going to be a great poet; I was certainly going to take care of the family.

Thus mused I, in my arrogance. And my family? They were as bad as I. My father had not lost a whit of his ambition for me. Since Graduation Day, and the school-committeeman's speech, and half a column about me in the paper, his ambition had soared even higher. He was going to keep me at school till I was prepared for college. By that time, he was sure, I would more than take care of myself. It never for a moment entered his head to doubt the wisdom or justice of this course. And my mother was just as loyal to my cause, and my brother, and my sister.

It is no wonder if I got along rapidly: I was helped, encouraged, and upheld by every one. Even the baby cheered me on. When I asked her whether she believed in higher education, she answered, without a moment's hesitation, "Ducka-ducka-da!" Against her I remember only that one day, when I read her a verse out of a most pathetic piece I was composing, she laughed right out, a most disrespectful laugh; for which I revenged myself by washing her face at the faucet, and rubbing it red on the roller towel.

It was just like me, when it was debated whether I would be best fitted for college at the High or the Latin School, to go in person to Mr. Tetlow, who was principal of both schools, and so get the most expert opinion on the subject. I never send a messenger, you may remember, where I can go myself. It was vacation time, and I had to find Mr. Tetlow at his home. Away out to the wilds of Roxbury I found my way—perhaps half an hour's ride on the electric car from Dover Street. I grew an inch taller and broader between the corner of Cedar Street and Mr. Tetlow's house, such was the charm of the clean, green suburb on a cramped waif from the slums. My faded calico dress, my rusty straw sailor hat, the color of my skin and all bespoke the waif. But never a bit daunted was I. I went up the steps to the porch, rang the bell, and asked for the great man with as much assurance as if I were a daily visitor on Cedar Street. I calmly awaited the appearance of Mr. Tetlow in the reception room, and stated my errand without trepidation.

And why not? I was a solemn little person for the moment, earnestly seeking advice on a matter of great importance. That is what Mr. Tetlow saw, to judge by the gravity with which he discussed my business with me, and the courtesy with which he showed me to the door. He saw, too, I fancy, that I was not the least bit conscious of my shabby dress; and I am sure he did not smile at my appearance, even when my back was turned.

A new life began for me when I entered the Latin School in September. Until then I had gone to school with my equals, and as a matter of course. Now it was distinctly a feat for me to keep in school, and my schoolmates were socially so far superior to me that my poverty became conspicuous. The pupils of the Latin School, from the nature of the institution, are an aristocratic set. They come from refined homes, dress well, and spend the recess hour talking about parties, beaux, and the matinée. As students they are either very quick or very hard-working; for the course of study, in the lingo of the school world, is considered "stiff." The girl with half her brain asleep, or with too many beaux, drops out by the end of the first year; or a one and only beau may be the fatal element. At the end of the course the weeding process has reduced the once numerous tribe of academic candidates to a cosy little family.

By all these tokens I should have had serious business on my hands as a pupil in the Latin School, but I did not find it hard. To make myself letter-perfect in my lessons required long hours of study, but that was my delight. To make myself at home in an alien world was also within my talents; I had been practising it day and night for the past four years. To remain unconscious of my shabby and ill-fitting clothes when the rustle of silk petticoats in the schoolroom protested against them was a matter still within my moral reach. Half a dress a year had been my allowance for many seasons; even less, for as I did not grow much I could wear my dresses as long as they lasted. And I had stood before editors, and exchanged polite calls with school-teachers, untroubled by the detestable colors and archaic design of my garments. To stand up and recite Latin declensions without trembling from hunger was something more of a feat, because I sometimes went to school with little or no breakfast; but even that required no special heroism,—at most it was a matter of self-control. I had the advantage of a poor appetite, too; I really did not need much breakfast. Or if I was hungry it would hardly show; I coughed so much that my unsteadiness was self-explained.

Everything helped, you see. My schoolmates helped. Aristocrats though they were, they did not hold themselves aloof from me. Some of the girls who came to school in carriages were especially cordial. They rated me by my scholarship, and not by my father's occupation. They teased and admired me by turns for learning the footnotes in the Latin grammar by heart; they never reproached me for my ignorance of the latest comic opera. And it was more than good breeding that made them seem unaware of the incongruity of my presence. It was a generous appreciation of what it meant for a girl from the slums to be in the Latin School, on the way to college. If our intimacy ended on the steps of the school-house, it was more my fault than theirs. Most of the girls were democratic enough to have invited me to their homes, although to some, of course, I was "impossible." But I had no time for visiting; school work and reading and family affairs occupied all the daytime, and much of the night time. I did not "go with" any of the girls, in the school-girl sense of the phrase. I admired some of them, either for good looks, or beautiful manners, or more subtle attributes; but always at a distance. I discovered something inimitable in the way the Back Bay girls carried themselves; and I should have been the first to perceive the incongruity of Commonwealth Avenue entwining arms with Dover Street. Some day, perhaps, when I should be famous and rich; but not just then. So my companions and I parted on the steps of the school-house, in mutual respect; they guiltless of snobbishness, I innocent of envy. It was a graciously American relation, and I am happy to this day to recall it.

The one exception to this rule of friendly distance was my chum, Florence Connolly. But I should hardly have said "chum." Florence and I occupied adjacent seats for three years, but we did not walk arm in arm, nor call each other nicknames, nor share our lunch, nor correspond in vacation time. Florence was quiet as a mouse, and I was reserved as an oyster; and perhaps we two had no more in common fundamentally than those two creatures in their natural state. Still, as we were both very studious, and never strayed far from our desks at recess, we practised a sort of intimacy of propinquity. Although Florence was of my social order, her father presiding over a cheap lunch room, I did not on that account feel especially drawn to her. I spent more time studying Florence than loving her, I suppose. And yet I ought to have loved her; she was such a good girl. Always perfect in her lessons, she was so modest that she recited in a noticeable tremor, and had to be told frequently to raise her voice. Florence wore her light brown hair brushed flatly back and braided in a single plait, at a time when pompadours were six inches high and braids hung in pairs. Florence had a pocket in her dress for her handkerchief, in a day when pockets were repugnant to fashion. All these things ought to have made me feel the kinship of humble circumstances, the comradeship of intellectual earnestness; but they did not.

The truth is that my relation to persons and things depended neither on social distinctions nor on intellectual or moral affinities. My attitude, at this time, was determined by my consciousness of the unique elements in my character and history. It seemed to me that I had been pursuing a single adventure since the beginning of the world. Through highways and byways, underground, overground, by land, by sea, ever the same star had guided me, I thought, ever the same purpose had divided my affairs from other men's. What that purpose was, where was the fixed horizon beyond which my star would not recede, was an absorbing mystery to me. But the current moment never puzzled me. What I chose instinctively to do I knew to be right and in accordance with my destiny. I never hesitated over great things, but answered promptly to the call of my genius. So what was it to me whether my neighbors spurned or embraced me, if my way was no man's way? Nor should any one ever reject me whom I chose to be my friend, because I would make sure of a kindred spirit by the coincidence of our guiding stars.

When, where in the harum-scarum life of Dover Street was there time or place for such self-communing? In the night, when everybody slept; on a solitary walk, as far from home as I dared to go.

I was not unhappy on Dover Street; quite the contrary. Everything of consequence was well with me. Poverty was a superficial, temporary matter; it vanished at the touch of money. Money in America was plentiful; it was only a matter of getting some of it, and I was on my way to the mint. If Dover Street was not a pleasant place to abide in, it was only a wayside house. And I was really happy, actively happy, in the exercise of my mind in Latin, mathematics, history, and the rest; the things that suffice a studious girl in the middle teens.

Still I had moments of depression, when my whole being protested against the life of the slum. I resented the familiarity of my vulgar neighbors. I felt myself defiled by the indecencies I was compelled to witness. Then it was I took to running away from home. I went out in the twilight and walked for hours, my blind feet leading me. I did not care where I went. If I lost my way, so much the better; I never wanted to see Dover Street again.

But behold, as I left the crowds behind, and the broader avenues were spanned by the open sky, my grievances melted away, and I fell to dreaming of things that neither hurt nor pleased. A fringe of trees against the sunset became suddenly the symbol of the whole world, and I stood and gazed and asked questions of it. The sunset faded; the trees withdrew. The wind went by, but dropped no hint in my ear. The evening star leaped out between the clouds, and sealed the secret with a seal of splendor.

A favorite resort of mine, after dark, was the South Boston Bridge, across South Bay and the Old Colony Railroad. This was so near home that I could go there at any time when the confusion in the house drove me out, or I felt the need of fresh air. I liked to stand leaning on the bridge railing, and look down on the dim tangle of railroad tracks below. I could barely see them branching out, elbowing, winding, and sliding out into the night in pairs. I was fascinated by the dotted lights, the significant red and green of signal lamps. These simple things stood for a complexity that it made me dizzy to think of. Then the blackness below me was split by the fiery eye of a monster engine, his breath enveloped me in blinding clouds, his long body shot by, rattling a hundred claws of steel; and he was gone, with an imperative shriek that shook me where I stood.

So would I be, swift on my rightful business, picking out my proper track from the million that cross it, pausing for no obstacles, sure of my goal.

After my watches on the bridge I often stayed up to write or study. It is late before Dover Street begins to go to bed. It is past midnight before I feel that I am alone. Seated in my stiff little chair before my narrow table, I gather in the night sounds through the open window, curious to assort and define them. As, little by little, the city settles down to sleep, the volume of sound diminishes, and the qualities of particular sounds stand out. The electric car lurches by with silent gong, taking the empty track by leaps, humming to itself in the invisible distance. A benighted team swings recklessly around the corner, sharp under my rattling window panes, the staccato pelting of hoofs on the cobblestones changed suddenly to an even pounding on the bridge. A few pedestrians hurry by, their heavy boots all out of step. The distant thoroughfares have long ago ceased their murmur, and I know that a million lamps shine idly in the idle streets.

My sister sleeps quietly in the little bed. The rhythmic dripping of a faucet is audible through the flat. It is so still that I can hear the paper crackling on the wall. Silence upon silence is added to the night; only the kitchen clock is the voice of my brooding thoughts,—ticking, ticking, ticking.

Suddenly the distant whistle of a locomotive breaks the stillness with a long-drawn wail. Like a threatened trouble, the sound comes nearer, piercingly near; then it dies out in a mangled silence, complaining to the last.

The sleepers stir in their beds. Somebody sighs, and the burden of all his trouble falls upon my heart. A homeless cat cries in the alley, in the voice of a human child. And the ticking of the kitchen clock is the voice of my troubled thoughts.

Many things are revealed to me as I sit and watch the world asleep. But the silence asks me many questions that I cannot answer; and I am glad when the tide of sound begins to return, by little and little, and I welcome the clatter of tin cans that announces the milkman. I cannot see him in the dusk, but I know his wholesome face has no problem in it.

It is one flight up to the roof; it is a leap of the soul to the sunrise. The morning mist rests lightly on chimneys and roofs and walls, wreathes the lampposts, and floats in gauzy streamers down the streets. Distant buildings are massed like palace walls, with turrets and spires lost in the rosy clouds. I love my beautiful city spreading all about me. I love the world. I love my place in the world.

1912

Anzia Yezierska
(c. 1881–1970)

Born in Russian Poland, Yezierska came with her family to the Lower East Side of New York when she was about 15. Her father, a Talmudic scholar, did little to advance the family fortunes, while his wife and children supported the family in the work available to them in sweatshops, laundries, and domestic service. Anzia's education, though minimal, was greater than that of many fellow immigrants. From night school she progressed to a training program for teaching "domestic science" (later called "home economics"), and by her late twenties she was working in an elementary school. Two brief marriages failed, and after the second she left her daughter to be raised by the child's father while she concentrated on her writing. Her first story, "The Free Vacation House," appeared in 1915. In the tension depicted between the needs of the poor and the condescension of the rich, she presented a sample of much that is best in her work. Drawing on experience and observation, she created an early voice for Jewish immigrants, particularly women, in New York.

In 1917 and 1918 her studies with John Dewey led to a brief romance, which prompted on his part a number of poems and provided for her both encouragement to write and the material for some of her later work. In 1919 her story "The Fat of the Land" was selected by Edward O'Brien as first among *The Best Short Stories of 1919;* in the following year it was collected with other stories of East Side life, including

her first, in the volume *Hungry Hearts,* one of her most highly acclaimed books. Success followed quickly. Both *Hungry Hearts* and *Salome of the Tenements* (1922), a novel, were sold to the movies, earning the author the then considerable sum of $25,000. Although she worked briefly in Hollywood, she found the life there unattractive and returned to Manhattan. Her most fertile period included two more books, *Children of Loneliness* (1923), short stories, and *Bread Givers* (1925), an autobiographical novel. Another novel is *Arrogant Beggar* (1927).

In later years she often had difficulty earning a living. In the 1930s she worked for the WPA Writers' Project and she wrote reviews into old age. Books were few, but included *All I Could Never Be* (1932), an autobiographical novel with a focus on a young woman's love for an older teacher, and *Red Ribbon on a White Horse* (1950), an autobiography.

Alice Kessler-Harris edited *The Open Cage: An Anzia Yezierska Collection* (1979). Studies include Carol B. Shoen, *Anzia Yezierska* (1982), and a book by her daughter, Louise Levitas Henrikson, *Anzia Yezierska: A Writer's Life* (1988).

The Free Vacation House

How came it that I went to the free vacation house was like this:

One day the visiting teacher from the school comes to find out for why don't I get the children ready for school in time; for why are they so often late.

I let out on her my whole bitter heart. I told her my head was on wheels from worrying. When I get up in the morning, I don't know on what to turn first: should I nurse the baby, or make Sam's breakfast, or attend on the older children. I only got two hands.

"My dear woman," she says, "you are about to have a nervous breakdown. You need to get away to the country for a rest and vacation."

"Gott im Himmel!"[1] says I. "Don't I know I need a rest? But how? On what money can I go to the country?"

"I know of a nice country place for mothers and children that will not cost you anything. It is free."

"Free! I never heard from it."

"Some kind people have made arrangements so no one need pay," she explains.

Later, in a few days, I just finished up with Masha and Mendel and Frieda and Sonya to

---

1. God in Heaven! (German).

send them to school, and I was getting Aby ready for kindergarten, when I hear a knock on the door, and a lady comes in. She had a white starched dress like a nurse and carried a black satchel in her hand.

"I am from the Social Betterment Society," she tells me. "You want to go to the country?"

Before I could say something, she goes over to the baby and pulls out the rubber nipple from her mouth, and to me, she says, "You must not get the child used to sucking this; it is very unsanitary."

"Gott im Himmel!" I beg the lady. "Please don't begin with that child, or she'll holler my head off. She must have the nipple. I'm too nervous to hear her scream like that."

When I put the nipple back again in the baby's mouth, the lady takes herself a seat, and then takes out a big black book from her satchel. Then she begins to question me. What is my first name? How old I am? From where come I? How long I'm already in this country? Do I keep any boarders? What is my husband's first name? How old he is? How long he is in this country? By what trade he works? How much wages he gets for a week? How much money do I spend out for rent? How old are the children, and everything about them.

"My goodness!" I cry out. "For why is it necessary all this to know? For why must I tell you all my business? What difference does it make already if I keep boarders, or I don't keep boarders? If Masha had the whooping-cough or Sonya had the measles? Or whether I spend out for my rent ten dollars or twenty? Or whether I come from Schnipishock or Kovner Gubernie?"

"We must make a record of all the applicants, and investigate each case," she tells me. "There are so many who apply to the charities, we can help only those who are most worthy."

"Charities!" I scream out. "Ain't the charities those who help the beggars out? I ain't no beggar. I'm not asking for no charity. My husband, he works."

"Miss Holcomb, the visiting teacher, said that you wanted to go to the country, and I had to make out this report before investigating your case."

"Oh! Oh!" I choke and bit my lips. "Is the free country from which Miss Holcomb told me, is it from the charities? She was telling me some kind people made arrangements for any mother what needs to go there."

"If your application is approved, you will be notified," she says to me, and out she goes.

When she is gone I think to myself, I'd better knock out from my head this idea about the country. For so long I lived, I did n't know nothing about the charities. For why should I come down among the beggars now?

Then I looked around me in the kitchen. On one side was the big wash-tub with clothes, waiting for me to wash. On the table was a pile of breakfast dishes yet. In the sink was the potatoes, waiting to be peeled. The baby was beginning to cry for the bottle. Aby was hollering and pulling me to take him to kindergarten. I felt if I did n't get away from here for a little while, I would land in a crazy house, or from the window jump down. Which was worser, to land in a crazy house, jump from the window down, or go to the country from the charities?

In about two weeks later around comes the same lady with the satchel again in my house.

"You can go to the country to-morrow," she tells me. "And you must come to the charity building to-morrow at nine o'clock sharp. Here is a card with the address. Don't lose it, because you must hand it to the lady in the office."

I look on the card, and there I see my name wrote; and by it, in big printed letters, that word "CHARITY."

"Must I go to the charity office?" I ask, feeling my heart to sink. "For why must I come there?"

"It is the rule that everybody comes to the office first, and from there they are taken to the country."

I shivered to think how I would feel, suppose somebody from my friends should see me walking into the charity office with my children. They would n't know that it is only for the country I go there. They might think I go to beg. Have I come down so low as to be seen by the charities? But what's the use? Should I knock my head on the walls? I had to go.

When I come to the office, I already found a crowd of women and children sitting on long benches and waiting. I took myself a seat with them, and we were sitting and sitting and looking on one another, sideways and crosswise, and with lowered eyes, like guilty criminals. Each one felt like hiding herself from all the rest. Each one felt black with shame in the face.

We may have been sitting and waiting for an hour or more. But every second was seeming years to me. The children began to get restless. Mendel wanted water. The baby on my arms was falling asleep. Aby was crying for something to eat.

"For why are we sittin' here like fat cats?" says the woman next to me. "Ain't we going to the country to-day yet?"

At last a lady comes to the desk and begins calling us our names, one by one. I nearly dropped to the floor when over she begins to ask: Do you keep boarders? How much do you spend out for rent? How much wages does your man get for a week?

Did n't the nurse tell them all about us already? It was bitter enough to have to tell the nurse everything, but in my own house nobody was hearing my troubles, only the nurse. But in the office there was so many strangers all around me. For why should everybody have to know my business? At every question I wanted to holler out: "Stop! Stop! I don't want no vacations! I'll better run home with my children." At every question I felt like she was stabbing a knife into my heart. And she kept on stabbing me more and more, but I could not help it, and they were all looking at me. I could n't move from her. I had to answer everything.

When she got through with me, my face was red like fire. I was burning with hurts and wounds. I felt like everything was bleeding in me.

When all the names was already called, a man doctor with a nurse comes in, and tells us to form a line, to be examined. I wish I could ease out my heart a little, and tell in words how that doctor looked on us, just because we were poor and had no money to pay. He only used the ends from his finger-tips to examine us with. From the way he was afraid to touch us or come near us, he made us feel like we had some catching sickness that he was trying not to get on him.

The doctor got finished with us in about five minutes, so quick he worked. Then we was told to walk after the nurse, who was leading the way for us through the street to the car. Everybody what passed us in the street turned around to look on us. I kept down my eyes and held down my head and I felt like sinking into the sidewalk. All the time I was trembling for fear somebody what knows me might yet pass and see me. For why did they make us walk through the street, after the nurse, like stupid cows? Were n't all of us smart enough to find our way without the nurse? Why should the whole world have to see that we are from the charities?

When we got into the train, I opened my eyes, and lifted up my head, and straightened out my chest, and again began to breathe. It was a beautiful, sunshiny day. I knocked open the window from the train, and the fresh-smelling country air rushed upon my face and made me feel so fine! I looked out from the window and instead of seeing the iron fire-escapes with garbage-cans and bedclothes, that I always seen when from my flat I looked—instead of seeing only walls and wash-lines between walls, I saw the blue sky, and green grass and trees and flowers.

Ah, how grand I felt, just on the sky to look! Ah, how grand I felt just to see the green grass—and the free space—and no houses!

"Get away from me, my troubles!" I said. "Leave me rest a minute. Leave me breathe and straighten out my bones. Forget the unpaid butcher's bill. Forget the rent. Forget the wash-tub and the cook-stove and the pots and pans. Forget the charities!"

"Tickets, please," calls the train conductor.

I felt knocked out from heaven all at once. I had to point to the nurse what held our tickets, and I was feeling the conductor looking on me as if to say, "Oh, you are only from the charities."

By the time we came to the vacation house I already forgot all about my knock-down. I was again filled with the beauty of the country. I never in all my life yet seen such a swell house like that vacation house. Like the grandest palace it looked. All round the front, flowers from all colors was smelling out the sweetest perfume. Here and there was shady trees with comfortable chairs under them to sit down on.

When I only came inside, my mouth opened wide and my breathing stopped still from wonder. I never yet seen such an order and such a cleanliness. From all the corners from the room, the cleanliness was shining like a looking-glass. The floor was so white scrubbed you could eat on it. You could n't find a speck of dust on nothing, if you was looking for it with eyeglasses on.

I was beginning to feel happy and glad that I come, when, Gott im Himmel! again a lady begins to ask us out the same questions what the nurse already asked me in my home and what was asked over again in the charity office. How much wages my husband makes out for a week? How much money I spend out for rent? Do I keep boarders?

We were hungry enough to faint. So worn out was I from excitement, and from the long ride, that my knees were bending under me ready to break from tiredness. The children were pulling me to pieces, nagging me for a drink, for something to eat and such like. But still we had to stand out the whole list of questionings. When she already got through asking us out everything, she gave to each of us a tag with our name written on it. She told us to tie the tag on our hand. Then like tagged horses at a horse sale in the street, they marched us into the dining-room.

There was rows of long tables, covered with pure-white oil-cloth. A vase with bought flowers was standing on the middle from each table. Each person got a clean napkin for himself. Laid out by the side from each person's plate was a silver knife and fork and spoon and teaspoon. When we only sat ourselves down, girls with white starched aprons was passing around the eatings.

I soon forgot again all my troubles. For the first time in ten years I sat down to a meal what I did not have to cook or worry about. For the first time in ten years I sat down to the table like a somebody. Ah, how grand it feels, to have handed you over the eatings and everything you need. Just as I was beginning to like it and let myself feel good, in comes a fat lady all in white, with a teacher's look on her face. I could tell already, right away by the way she looked on us, that she was the boss from this place.

"I want to read you the rules from this house, before you leave this room," says she to us.

Then she began like this: We dassen't stand on the front grass where the flowers are. We dassen't stay on the front porch. We dassen't sit on the chairs under the shady trees. We must stay always in the back and sit on those long wooden benches there. We dassen't come in the front sitting-room or walk on the front steps what have carpet on it—we must walk on the back iron steps. Everything on the front from the house must be kept perfect for the show for visitors. We dassen't lay down on the beds in the daytime, the beds must always be made up perfect for the show for visitors.

"Gott im Himmel!" thinks I to myself, "ain't there going to be no end to the things we dassen't do in this place?"

But still she went on. The children over two years dassen't stay around by the mothers. They must stay by the nurse in the play-room. By the meal-times, they can see their mothers. The children dassen't run around the house or tear up flowers or do anything. They dassen't holler or play rough in the play-room. They must always behave and obey the nurse.

We must always listen to the bells. Bell one was for getting up. Bell two, for getting babies' bottles. Bell three, for coming to breakfast. Bell four, for bathing the babies. If we come later, after the ring from the bell, then we'll not get what we need. If the bottle bell rings and we don't come right away for the bottle, then the baby don't get no bottle. If the breakfast bell rings, and we don't come right away down to the breakfast, then there won't be no breakfast for us.

When she got through with reading the rules, I was wondering which side of the house I was to walk on. At every step was some rule what said don't move here, and don't go there, don't stand there, and don't sit there. If I tried to remember the endless rules, it would only make me dizzy in the head. I was thinking for why, with so many rules, did n't they also have already another rule, about how much air in our lungs to breathe.

On every few days there came to the house swell ladies in automobiles. It was for them that the front from the house had to be always perfect. For them was all the beautiful smelling flowers. For them the front porch, the front sitting-room, and the easy stairs with the carpet on it.

Always when the rich ladies came the fat lady, what was the boss from the vacation house, showed off to them the front. Then she took them over to the back to look on us, where we was sitting together, on long wooden benches, like prisoners. I was always feeling cheap like dirt, and mad that I had to be there, when they smiled down on us.

"How nice for these poor creatures to have a restful place like this," I heard one lady say.

The next day I already felt like going back. The children what had to stay by the nurse in the play-room did n't like it neither.

"Mamma," says Mendel to me, "I wisht I was home and out in the street. They don't let us do nothing here. It's worser than school."

"Ain't it a play-room?" asks I. "Don't they let you play?"

"Gee wiss! play-room, they call it! The nurse hollers on us all the time. She don't let us do nothing."

The reason why I stayed out the whole two weeks is this: I think to myself, so much shame in the face I suffered to come here, let me at least make the best from it already. Let me at least save up for two weeks what I got to spend out for grocery and butcher for my back bills to pay out. And then also think I to myself, if I go back on Monday, I got to do the big washing; on Tuesday waits for me the ironing; on Wednesday, the scrubbing and cleaning, and so goes it on. How bad it is already in this place, it's a change from the very same sameness of what I'm having day in and day out at home. And so I stayed out this vacation to the bitter end.

But at last the day for going out from this prison came. On the way riding back, I kept thinking to myself: "This is such a beautiful vacation house. For why do they make it so hard for us? When a mother needs a vacation, why must they tear the insides out from her first, by making her come down to the charity office? Why drag us from the charity office through the streets? And when we live through the shame of the charities and when we come already to the vacation house, for why do they boss the life out of us with so many rules and bells? For why don't they let us lay down our heads on the bed when we are tired? For why must we always stick in the back, like dogs what have got to be chained in one spot? If they would let us walk around free, would we bite off something from the front part of the house?

"If the best part of the house what is comfortable is made up for a show for visitors, why ain't they keeping the whole business for a show for visitors? For why do they have to fool in worn-out mothers, to make them think they'll give them a rest? Do they need the worn-out mothers as part of the show? I guess that is it, already."

When I got back in my home, so happy and thankful I was I could cry from thankfulness. How good it was feeling for me to be able to move around my own house, like I pleased. I was always kicking that my rooms was small and narrow, but now my small rooms seemed to grow so big like the park. I looked out from my window on the fire-escapes, full with bedding and garbage-cans, and on the wash-lines full with the clothes. All these ugly things was grand in my eyes. Even the high brick walls all around made me feel like a bird what just jumped out from a cage. And I cried out, "Gott sei dank! Gott sei dank!"[2]

1915, 1920

2. Thank God! Thank God! (German).

Elinor Wylie

(1885–1928)

When Elinor Wylie burst upon the literary scene in 1921 with the verse of *Nets to Catch the Wind*, she inaugurated one of the most brilliant writing careers of the American 1920s. By the time of her death seven years later, she had completed three more books of verse and four novels. *Nets to Catch the Wind* won a prize from the Poetry Society of America. Her second novel, *The Orphan Angel* (1926), was a selection of the Book of the Month Club. Taken up by the literary establishment, she was friendly with writers and critics like Edmund Wilson, John Dos Passos, John Peale Bishop, and Edna St. Vincent Millay. From 1921 onward, she was a contributing editor of the *New Republic*, and from 1923 to 1925 she was poetry editor of *Vanity Fair*. In 1923 she married the poet and editor William Rose Benét, her third husband. From 1926 until her death she served as an editor of the fledgling Literary Guild. To admirers she seemed unmatched in an apparently effortless wit and creativity.

She did not arrive at her period of fame easily, and for many she was soon forgotten. Born Eleanor Morton Hoyt in Somerville, New Jersey, she was raised in Rosemont, Pennsylvania, and Washington, D.C., spending summers on Mount Desert Island, Maine. Daughter of a socially prominent family, she attended private schools, and in 1905 she married the son of an admiral, with whom she had a son in 1907. In 1910, however, she shocked the social world by eloping with a married man, Horace Wylie. For several years the two lived in England and the United States under assumed names. After her husband died and Wylie and his first wife were divorced, Elinor and Horace were married in 1916; but that marriage ended in divorce in 1923.

Popular as her verse was, it went against the grain of the modernism espoused by Pound and Eliot. Her poems are small, precise in language, brilliant in imagery, and carefully crafted within the restrictions of traditional forms. In an essay entitled "Jewelled Bindings," she described her own strengths and limitations as one of a class of poets satisfied to work elaborately in miniature forms: "I don't mean inferior or contemptible, or negligible. Nor do I mean great." Her novels, too, though richly inventive, have not found a wide readership since her day. Best known is *The Venetian Glass Nephew* (1925), in which a woman must be transformed into porcelain in order to become a suitable bride for her equally artificial husband. "The result, although miraculous," observes one of the characters, "is somewhat inhuman. I have known fathers who submitted their daughters to the ordeal, husbands who forced it upon their wives." The others are *Jennifer Lorn: A Sedate Extravaganza* (1923), set in eighteenth-century England and India; *The Orphan Angel* (1926), in which the poet Shelley escapes drowning and is carried to America on a Yankee ship; and *Mr. Hodge and Mr. Hazard* (1928), a satirical story of a long-lived romantic poet encountering the world of the Victorians.

Most of Wylie's verse may be found in *Collected Poems* (1932) and *Last Poems* (1943). Earlier titles, in addition to *Nets to Catch the Wind*, are *Incidental Numbers* (1912); *Black Armour* (1923); *Trivial Breath* (1928); and *Angels and Earthly Creatures* (1928). *Collected Prose* (1933) includes the four novels and stories and essays.

Her sister, Nancy Hoyt, wrote a memoir entitled *Elinor Wylie: The Portrait of an Unknown Lady* (1935). Studies include Thomas A. Gray, *Elinor Wylie* (1969); Stanley Olson, *Elinor Wylie: A Life Apart* (1979); and Judith Farr, *The Life and Art of Elinor Wylie* (1983).

The Eagle and the Mole

Avoid the reeking herd,
Shun the polluted flock,
Live like that stoic bird,
The eagle of the rock.

The huddled warmth of crowds   5
Begets and fosters hate;
He keeps, above the clouds,
His cliff inviolate.

When flocks are folded warm,
And herds to shelter run,   10
He sails above the storm,
He stares into the sun.

If in the eagle's track
Your sinews cannot leap,
Avoid the lathered pack,   15
Turn from the steaming sheep.

If you would keep your soul
From spotted sight or sound,
Live like the velvet mole;
Go burrow underground.   20

And there hold intercourse
With roots of trees and stones,
With rivers at their source,
And disembodied bones.

1921

Wild Peaches

1

When the world turns completely upside down
You say we'll emigrate to the Eastern Shore
Aboard a river-boat from Baltimore;
We'll live among wild peach trees, miles from town,
You'll wear a coonskin cap, and I a gown   5
Homespun, dyed butternut's dark gold colour.
Lost, like your lotus-eating ancestor,
We'll swim in milk and honey till we drown.

The winter will be short, the summer long,
The autumn amber-hued, sunny and hot,   10

Tasting of cider and of scuppernong;[1]
All seasons sweet, but autumn best of all.
The squirrels in their silver fur will fall
Like falling leaves, like fruit, before your shot.

2

The autumn frosts will lie upon the grass   15
Like bloom on grapes of purple-brown and gold.
The misted early mornings will be cold;
The little puddles will be roofed with glass.
The sun, which burns from copper into brass,
Melts these at noon, and makes the boys unfold   20
Their knitted mufflers; full as they can hold,
Fat pockets dribble chestnuts as they pass.

Peaches grow wild, and pigs can live in clover;
A barrel of salted herrings lasts a year;
The spring begins before the winter's over.   25
By February you may find the skins
Of garter snakes and water moccasins
Dwindled and harsh, dead-white and cloudy-clear.

3

When April pours the colours of a shell
Upon the hills, when every little creek   30
Is shot with silver from the Chesapeake
In shoals new-minted by the ocean swell,
When strawberries go begging, and the sleek
Blue plums lie open to the blackbird's beak,
We shall live well—we shall live very well.   35

The months between the cherries and the peaches
Are brimming cornucopias which spill
Fruits red and purple, sombre-bloomed and black;
Then, down rich fields and frosty river beaches
We'll trample bright persimmons, while you kill   40
Bronze partridge, speckled quail, and canvasback.

4

Down to the Puritan marrow of my bones
There's something in this richness that I hate.
I love the look, austere, immaculate,
Of landscapes drawn in pearly monotones.   45
There's something in my very blood that owns
Bare hills, cold silver on a sky of slate,

---

1. A wine, from the grape of the same name.

A thread of water, churned to milky spate
Streaming through slanted pastures fenced with stones.

I love those skies, thin blue or snowy gray,   50
Those fields sparse-planted, rendering meagre sheaves;
That spring, briefer than apple-blossom's breath,
Summer, so much too beautiful to stay,
Swift autumn, like a bonfire of leaves,
And sleepy winter, like the sleep of death.   55

                      1921

Sanctuary

This is the bricklayer; hear the thud
Of his heavy load dumped down on stone.
His lustrous bricks are brighter than blood,
His smoking mortar whiter than bone.

Set each sharp-edged, fire-bitten brick   5
Straight by the plumb-line's shivering length;
Make my marvellous wall so thick
Dead nor living may shake its strength.

Full as a crystal cup with drink
Is my cell with dreams, and quiet, and cool. . . .   10
Stop, old man! You must leave a chink;
How can I breathe? *You can't, you fool!*

                      1921

Prophecy

I shall lie hidden in a hut
In the middle of an alder wood,
With the back door blind and bolted shut,
And the front door locked for good.

I shall lie folded like a saint,   5
Lapped in a scented linen sheet,
On a bedstead striped with bright-blue paint,
Narrow and cold and neat.

The midnight will be glassy black
Behind the panes, with wind about   10
To set his mouth against a crack
And blow the candle out.

                    1923

Let No Charitable Hope

Now let no charitable hope
Confuse my mind with images
Of eagle and of antelope:
I am in nature none of these.

I was, being human, born alone;   5
I am, being woman, hard beset;
I live by squeezing from a stone
The little nourishment I get.

In masks outrageous and austere
The years go by in single file;   10
But none has merited my fear,
And none has quite escaped my smile.

1923

O Virtuous Light

A private madness has prevailed
Over the pure and valiant mind;
The instrument of reason failed
And the star-gazing eyes struck blind.

Sudden excess of light has wrought   5
Confusion in the secret place
Where the slow miracles of thought
Take shape through patience into grace.

Mysterious as steel and flint
The birth of this destructive spark   10
Whose inward growth has power to print
Strange suns upon the natural dark.

O break the walls of sense in half
And make the spirit fugitive!
This light begotten of itself   15
Is not a light by which to live!

The fire of farthing tallow dips
Dispels the menace of the skies
So it illuminate the lips
And enter the discerning eyes.   20

O virtuous light, if thou be man's
Or matter of the meteor stone,
Prevail against this radiance
Which is engendered of its own!

1929

Pastiche

Is not the woman moulded by your wish
A cockatrice[2] of a most intricate kind?
You have, my friend, the high fantastic mind
To clasp the cold enamel of a fish
As breastplate for a bosom tigerish;   5
To make a dove a dragon; or to bind
A panther skin upon the escaping hind:
You mix ambiguous spices in your dish.

Will there remain, when thus embellished I
Sprout wings, or am by cloven heels improved,   10
An atom of the lady that you loved?
Does Christ or Lucifer seal this alchemy?
Is there not lacking from your synthesis
Someone you may occasionally miss?

1932

H. D. (Hilda Doolittle)
(1886–1961)

When Ezra Pound provided the signature "H. D., *Imagiste*," for the poems he sponsored for publication in *Poetry* in 1913 he gave Hilda Doolittle both a name and an identity. For the rest of her life she published as H. D., and to the end of her life her fame as an Imagist overshadowed the reputation of her later work. Pound put her into his first Imagist anthology (1914). Amy Lowell included her in the three Imagist anthologies that she edited (1915, 1916, 1917) and praised her work in her *Tendencies in Modern American Poetry* (1917). When her *Collected Poems* (1925) appeared, coincidentally in the same year as the death of Lowell, it capped her career as a modernist poet skilled in a mode that later readers were to find brilliant but limited. Like Lowell, she began to be considered a minor poet in the modernist constellation headed by Pound and Eliot.

Only after the personal and public turmoil of the late 1920s, the Great Depression, and the beginning of World War II did she find her way to the longer poems that came to be widely admired in the decades after her death.

She was born in Bethlehem, Pennsylvania, the daughter of an astronomer who taught at Lehigh University and the University of Pennsylvania, and of a mother whose Moravian faith, with its emphasis on visionary experience, was to provide an important thread of influence for her poetry. Educated at private schools in Philadelphia and, from 1904 to 1906, Bryn Mawr, she met Pound when she was 15 and was briefly engaged to him. Through Pound, she met William Carlos Williams, who later wrote, "She fascinated me, not for her beauty which was unquestioned if bizarre to my sense, but for a provocative glance could kill.

2. A legendary monster, with a serpent's body and the head, tail, and wings of a cock. Its

indifference to rule and order which I liked." In 1911, she set out on a tour of Europe and soon joined the Pound circle in London (he had left the United States in 1906). Marriage to the English poet Richard Aldington followed in 1915, but proved unsuccessful, in part because of the separation forced by his war service. Meanwhile, she entered into friendships and emotional entanglements with Havelock Ellis and D. H. Lawrence, lost a brother in the war, came down with double pneumonia, gave birth to a daughter she named Perdita (fathered by a young Englishman), and was rescued from confusion and poverty by the loving friendship of Winifred Ellerman, illegitimate daughter of a wealthy Englishman. H. D. and Bryher, as Ellerman called herself, remained companions from 1919 to 1946, living in Switzerland much of the time between the wars. She wrote voluminously, underwent analysis with Freud in 1933–1934, returned with Bryher to London in 1939 for the war years, and eventually died in Zurich. She returned to the United States only a few times for visits during her life.

After the *Collected Poems* of 1925, H. D.'s poetic production was minimal until *The Walls Do Not Fall* (1944), *Tribute to the Angels* (1945), and *The Flowering of the Rod* (1946). Taken together as a trilogy, these works, deriving like Eliot's "Little Gidding" from the painful realities of wartime London, constitute H. D.'s major attempt to construct a sustaining myth in a time of cultural dissolution. Modernist in its fragmentation and wide-ranging allusiveness, discursive in its pursuit of an enlightenment experienced spiritually and intuitively, the trilogy is also feminist in its portrayal of the centrality of women's attributes, experience, and attitudes, especially as seen in the goddess figures of ancient worship. In a still later long poem, *Helen in Egypt* (1961), she attempted to give voice to Helen of Troy, for centuries depicted by men but now seen with the sympathetic eye of a woman who in some ways identified with her.

Collected Poems, 1912–1944, the source of the texts below, was edited by Louis L. Martz (1984). Books of verse not named above include *Sea Garden* (1916); *Heliodora and Other Poems* (1924); *Red Roses for Bronze* (1929); *By Avon River* (1949), a tribute to Shakespeare in prose and verse; and *Hermetic Definition* (1972). A verse drama is *Hippolytus Temporizes* (1927). Experimental prose fictions include *Palimpsest* (1926; rev. ed. 1968); *Hedylus* (1928); *Nights* (1935); and *Bid Me to Live: A Madrigal* (1960). *HERmione* (1981) is autobiographical. *Asphodel* (1992) and *Paint It Today* (1992) are autobiographical novels. Memoirs include *Tribute to Freud* (1956); *End to Torment: A Memoir of D. H. Lawrence*, ed. Norman Holmes Pearson and Michael King (1979); and *The Gift* (1982). H. D. also figures in Bryher's *The Heart of Artemis: A Writer's Memoirs* (1962).

A biography is Barbara Guest, *Herself Defined: The Poet H. D. and Her World* (1984). Biographical and critical studies include Thomas Burnett Swann, *The Classical World of H. D.* (1962); Vincent Quinn, *Hilda Doolittle (H. D.)* (1967); Susan Stanford Friedman, *Psyche Reborn: The Emergence of H. D.* (1981); Janice S. Robinson, *H. D.: The Life and Work of an American Poet* (1982); Rachel Blau DuPlessis, *H. D.: The Career of that Struggle* (1986); Angela DiPace Fritz, *Thought and Vision: A Critical Reading of H. D.'s Poetry* (1988); and Dianne Chisholm, *H. D.'s Freudian Poetics* (1992).

Sea Rose

Rose, harsh rose,
marred and with stint of petals,
meagre flower, thin,
sparse of leaf,

more precious   5
than a wet rose
single on a stem—
you are caught in the drift.

Stunted, with small leaf,
you are flung on the sand,   10
you are lifted
in the crisp sand
that drives in the wind.

Can the spice-rose
drip such acrid fragrance   15
hardened in a leaf?

1916

Mid-day

The light beats upon me.
I am startled—
a split leaf crackles on the paved floor—
I am anguished—defeated.

A slight wind shakes the seed-pods—   5
my thoughts are spent
as the black seeds.
My thoughts tear me,
I dread their fever.
I am scattered in its whirl.   10
I am scattered like
the hot shrivelled seeds.

The shrivelled seeds
are split on the path—
the grass bends with dust,   15
the grape slips
under its crackled leaf:
yet far beyond the spent seed-pods,
and the blackened stalks of mint,
the poplar is bright on the hill,   20
the poplar spreads out,
deep-rooted among trees.

O poplar, you are great
among the hill-stones,
while I perish on the path   25
among the crevices of the rocks.

1916

Garden

I

You are clear
O rose, cut in rock,
hard as the descent of hail.

I could scrape the colour
from the petals   5
like spilt dye from a rock.

If I could break you
I could break a tree.

If I could stir
I could break a tree—   10
I could break you.

II

O wind, rend open the heat,
cut apart the heat,
rend it to tatters.

Fruit cannot drop   15
through this thick air—
fruit cannot fall into heat
that presses up and blunts
the points of pears
and rounds the grapes.   20

Cut the heat—
plough through it,
turning it on either side
of your path.

                                    1916

Orchard

I saw the first pear
as it fell—
the honey-seeking, golden-banded,
the yellow swarm
was not more fleet than I,   5
(spare us from loveliness)
and I fell prostrate
crying:
you have flayed us

with your blossoms,   10
spare us the beauty
of fruit-trees.

The honey-seeking
paused not,
the air thundered their song,   15
and I alone was prostrate.

O rough-hewn
god of the orchard,
I bring you an offering—
do you, alone unbeautiful,   20
son of the god,
spare us from loveliness:

these fallen hazel-nuts,
stripped late of their green sheaths,
grapes, red-purple,   25
their berries
dripping with wine,
pomegranates already broken,
and shrunken figs
and quinces untouched,   30
I bring you as offering.

1913, 1916

Pear Tree

Silver dust
lifted from the earth,
higher than my arms reach,
you have mounted,
O silver,   5
higher than my arms reach
you front us with great mass;

no flower ever opened
so staunch a white leaf,
no flower ever parted silver   10
from such rare silver;

O white pear,
your flower-tufts
thick on the branch
bring summer and ripe fruits   15
in their purple hearts.

1916

Oread[1]

Whirl up, sea—
whirl your pointed pines,
splash your great pines
on our rocks,
hurl your green over us,   5
cover us with your pools of fir.

1914, 1924

Helen[2]

All Greece hates
the still eyes in the white face,
the lustre as of olives
where she stands,
and the white hands.   5

All Greece reviles
the wan face when she smiles,
hating it deeper still
when it grows wan and white,
remembering past enchantments   10
and past ills.

Greece sees unmoved,
God's daughter, born of love,
the beauty of cool feet
and slenderest knees,   15
could love indeed the maid,
only if she were laid,
white ash amid funereal cypresses.

1924

From The Walls Do Not Fall

To Bryher

for Karnak 1923
from London 1942

---

1. In classical mythology, a mountain nymph.
2. Daughter of Zeus and Leda, wife of King
   Menelaus, Helen was kidnapped by Paris and
   taken to Troy. Her abduction was the cause of
   the Trojan War.

[1]

An incident here and there,
and rails gone (for guns)
from your (and my) old town square:

mist and mist-grey, no colour,
still the Luxor³ bee, chick and hare   5
pursue unalterable purpose

in green, rose-red, lapis;
they continue to prophesy
from the stone papyrus:

there, as here, ruin opens   10
the tomb, the temple; enter,
there as here, there are no doors:

the shrine lies open to the sky,
the rain falls, here, there
sand drifts; eternity endures: 15

ruin everywhere, yet as the fallen roof
leaves the sealed room
open to the air,

so, through our desolation,
thoughts stir, inspiration stalks us   20
through gloom:

unaware, Spirit announces the Presence;
shivering overtakes us,
as of old, Samuel:

trembling at a known street-corner,   25
we know not nor are known;
the Pythian pronounces—we pass on

to another cellar, to another sliced wall
where poor utensils show
like rare objects in a museum;   30

Pompeii has nothing to teach us,
we know crack of volcanic fissure,
slow flow of terrible lava,

pressure on heart, lungs, the brain
about to burst its brittle case   35
(what the skull can endure!):

3. A town on the Nile in upper Egypt. Ruins of ancient Thebes are there and at Karnak. The poet contrasts present London, under German bombardment, with an ancient civilization, now in ruins. The poem invites comparison with T. S. Eliot's *Little Gidding* (1942). Later references within this first section link the thought to additional past civilizations, events, and prophecies: Samuel, a biblical prophet; Pythia, the priestess at Delphi who served as oracle; Pompeii, a town buried in lava when Mt. Vesuvius erupted in A.D. 79; the books of the Apocrypha, biblical texts usually omitted from Protestant versions of the Bible.

over us, Apocryphal fire,
under us, the earth sway, dip of a floor,
slope of a pavement

where men roll, drunk   40
with a new bewilderment,
sorcery, bedevilment:

the bone-frame was made for
no such shock knit within terror,
yet the skeleton stood up to it: 45

the flesh? it was melted away,
the heart burnt out, dead ember,
tendons, muscles shattered, outer husk dismembered,

yet the frame held:
we passed the flame: we wonder   50
what saved us? what for?

[2]

Evil was active in the land,
Good was improverished and sad;

Ill promised adventure,
Good was smug and fat;   55

Dev-ill was after us,
tricked up like Jehovah;

Good was the tasteless pod,
stripped from the manna-beans, pulse, lentils:

they were angry when we were so hungry   60
for the nourishment, God;

they snatched off our amulets,
charms are not, they said, grace;

but gods always face two-ways,
so let us search the old highways   65

for the true-rune, the right-spell,
recover old values;

nor listen if they shout out,
your beauty, Isis, Aset or Astarte,[4]

is a harlot; you are retrogressive,   70
zealot, hankering after old flesh-pots;

your heart, moreover,
is a dead canker,

they continue, and
your rhythm is the devil's hymn,   75

4. Goddesses of fertility: Isis in ancient Egypt, Astarte (or Aset) in ancient Phoenicia and Canaan.

your stylus is dipped in corrosive sublimate,
how can you scratch out

indelible ink of the palimpsest[5]
of past misadventure?

[3]

Let us, however, recover the Sceptre,   80
the rod of power:

it is crowned with the lily-head
or the lily-bud:

it is Caduceus;[6] among the dying
it bears healing: 85

or evoking the dead,
it brings life to the living.

[4]

There is a spell, for instance,
in every sea-shell:

continuous, the sea-thrust   90
is powerless against coral,

bone, stone, marble
hewn from within by that craftsman,

the shell-fish:
oyster, clam, mollusc   95

is master-mason planning
the stone marvel:

yet that flabby, amorphous hermit
within, like the planet

senses the finite,   100
it limits its orbit

of being, its house,
temple, fane, shrine:

it unlocks the portals
at stated intervals: 105

prompted by hunger,
it opens to the tide-flow:

but infinity? no,
of nothing-too-much:

5. A parchment or other writing surface with
earlier writing scratched away (but still
sometimes visible) and newer writing added.

6. The staff carried by Mercury, messenger of the
gods, frequently a symbol for the medical
profession.

I sense my own limit,   110
my shell-jaws snap shut

at invasion of the limitless,
ocean-weight; infinite water

can not crack me, egg in egg-shell;
closed in, complete, immortal   115

full-circle, I know the pull
of the tide, the lull

as well as the moon;
the octopus-darkness

is powerless against   120
her cold immortality;

so I in my own way know
that the whale

can not digest me:
be firm in your own small, static, limited   125

orbit and the shark-jaws
of outer circumstance

will spit you forth:
be indigestible, hard, ungiving.

so that, living within,   130
you beget, self-out-of-self,

selfless,
that pearl-of-great-price.[7]

[43]

Still the walls do not fall,
I do not know why;   135

there is zrr-hiss,
lightning in a not-known,

unregistered dimension;
we are powerless,

dust and powder fill our lungs   140
our bodies blunder

through doors twisted on hinges,
and the lintels slant

cross-wise;
we walk continually   145

7. See Matthew 13:45–46: "Again, the kingdom of heaven is like unto a merchant man, seeking goodly pearls: Who, when he found one pearl of great price, went and sold all that he had, and bought it."

on thin air
that thickens to a blind fog,

then step swiftly aside,
for even the air

is independable,   150
thick where it should be fine

and tenuous
where wings separate and open,

and the ether
is heavier than the floor,   155

and the floor sags
like a ship floundering;

we know no rule
of procedure,

we are voyagers, discoverers   160
of the not-known,

the unrecorded;
we have no map;

possibly we will reach haven,
heaven.   165

1944

From Tribute to the Angels

[6]

Never in Rome,
so many martyrs fell;

not in Jerusalem,
never in Thebes,

so many stood and watched   5
chariot-wheels turning,

saw with their very eyes,
the battle of the Titans,[8]

saw Zeus' thunderbolts in action
and how from giant hands,   10

the lightning shattered earth
and splintered sky, nor fled

to hide in caves,
but with unbroken will,

---

8. In Greek mythology, earlier gods defeated by Zeus.

with unbowed head, watched   15
and though unaware, worshipped

and knew not that they worshipped
and that they were

that which they worshipped,
had they known the fire   20

of strength, endurance, anger
in their hearts,

was part of that same fire
that in a candle on a candle-stick

or in a star,   25
is known as one of seven,

is named among the seven Angels,
Uriel.[9]

[7]

To Uriel, no shrine, no temple
where the red-death fell,   30

no image by the city-gate,
no torch to shine across the water,

no new fane in the market-place:
the lane is empty but the levelled wall

is purple as with purple spread   35
upon an altar,

this is the flowering of the rood,
this is the flowering of the reed,

where, Uriel, we pause to give
thanks that we rise again from death and live.   40

[8]

Now polish the crucible
and in the bowl distill

a word most bitter, *marah,*[1]
a word bitterer still, *mar,*

sea, brine, breaker, seducer,   45
giver of life, giver of tears;

---

9. Archangel mentioned in 2 Esdras (the second book of the Apocrypha) as well as in Milton's *Paradise Lost.*
1. "Marah" and "mar" are both forms of a Hebrew root meaning "bitter." After the Hebrews crossed the Red Sea, they wandered three days without water, and when they found it, they could not drink it. They called the place Marah (Exodus 15:22–33). H. D. invokes other associations below, including the French words for sea *(la mer)* and mother *(la mère)* and the name Mary.

now polish the crucible
and set the jet of flame

under, till *marah-mar*
are melted, fuse and join   50

and change and alter,
mer, mere, mère, mater, Maia, Mary,

Star of the Sea,
Mother.

[24]

Every hour, every moment   55
has its specific attendant Spirit;

the clock-hand, minute by minute,
ticks round its prescribed orbit;

but this curious mechanical perfection
should not separate but relate rather,   60

our life, this temporary eclipse
to that other . . .

[25]

. . . of the *no need*
of the moon to shine in it,

for it was ticking minute by minute   65
(the clock at my bed-head,

with its dim, luminous disc)
when the Lady knocked;

I was talking casually
with friends in the other room,   70

when we saw the outer hall
grow lighter—then we saw where the door was,

there was no door
(this was a dream, of course),

and she was standing there,   75
actually, at the turn of the stair.

[26]

One of us said, how odd,
she is actually standing there,

I wonder what brought her?
another of us said,   80

have we some power between us,
we three together,

that acts as a sort of magnet,
that attracts the super-natural?

(yet it was all natural enough,   85
we agreed);

I do not know what I said
or if I said anything,

for before I had time to speak,
I realized I had been dreaming,   90

that I lay awake now on my bed,
that the luminous light

was the phosphorescent face
of my little clock

and the faint knocking   95
was the clock ticking.

[27]

And yet in some very subtle way,
she was there more than ever,

as if she had miraculously
related herself to time here,   100

which is no easy trick, difficult
even for the experienced stranger,

of whom we must *be not forgetful*
for *some have entertained angels unawares.*

1945

Marianne Moore
(1887–1972)

Born in Kirkwood, Missouri, Marianne
Craig Moore lived as a child in the house
of a grandfather with her mother and
brother. In 1894, when the grandfather
died, her mother moved the small family
to Carlisle, Pennsylvania, and supported
them with a teaching position at Metzger
Institute. For the next two decades, Carlisle was the future poet's home. She was
educated at Metzger and Bryn Mawr,
where she met H. D., wrote for the campus
literary magazine, and graduated in 1909.

After studying briefly at Carlisle Commercial College, she toured Europe with
her mother, then returned to teach commercial studies at the United States Indian
School in Carlisle from 1911 to 1915. By
1915, she began to publish in *The Egoist*
(London) and *Poetry* (Chicago), and in
1918 she moved with her mother to New
York, where she lived with her most of the
rest of her life, first in Greenwich Village
and from 1929 on in Brooklyn.

In her early days she was associated

with the "Others" group, writers published in Alfred Kreymborg's short-lived journal *Others,* intended as an avant-garde alternative to *Poetry;* these included Ezra Pound and Amy Lowell, leaders of the new poetry, as well as Wallace Stevens and William Carlos Williams, poets whose fame, like Moore's, was to come much later. From 1921 to 1925 she worked in a public library in New York City, then from 1925 to 1929 edited *The Dial,* a leading literary journal.

Poems (1921), her first book, was published without her knowledge by H. D. and Bryher, who made the arrangements with the Egoist Press in London. "To issue my slight product—conspicuously tentative—seemed to me premature," she later wrote, but she soon had material for another volume, *Observations* (1924), which won the Dial Award. For a number of years, she published no further volumes of verse, but when her *Selected Poems* appeared in 1935, it contained an introduction in which T. S. Eliot proclaimed that "Miss Moore's poems form part of the small body of durable poetry written in our time." At this point, however, she had much more still to write. Important later collections include *What Are Years?* (1941), *Nevertheless* (1944), *Like a Bulwark* (1956), *O to Be a Dragon* (1959), and *Tell Me, Tell Me* (1966).

Especially in her early years, Moore's poetic practice puzzled many readers. Avoiding standard meters, she also for the most part avoided free verse, pioneering the syllabic verse that many saw as her trademark, though it was later adopted at times by Dylan Thomas and W. H. Auden,

among others. Setting up a pattern of syllable counts for each line of a stanza, without reference to stresses, she would repeat the pattern in subsequent stanzas of a given poem, though she would also vary the pattern, as traditional poets do with traditional metrics, and later her practice became much more loose. Fond of rhymes, she overturned tradition by finding them often on unstressed syllables or in the midst of words, rather than at the ends, so they are easily missed by a reader. Seeing little distinction between good prose and verse, she often quoted from books, newspapers, or overheard conversations, generally footnoting the sources. As her reputation grew, however, her peculiarities seemed less forbidding, and toward the end of her life she began to be accorded the status of a major poet.

Complete Poems (1981) contains about two-thirds of her published verse and includes five poems not contained in the 1967 edition. Individual titles, besides those named above, include *The Pangolin and Other Verse* (1936) and *The Arctic Ox* (1964). *The Fables of La Fontaine* (1954) is a translation. *The Complete Prose of Marianne Moore* (1986) was edited by Patricia C. Willis. *Predilictions* (1955) is an earlier collection of prose.

Studies include Donald Hall, *Marianne Moore: The Cage and the Animal* (1970); Pamela White Hadas, *Marianne Moore: Poet of Affection* (1977); Laurence Stapleton, *Marianne Moore: The Poet's Advance* (1978); Bonnie Costello, *Marianne Moore: Imaginary Possessions* (1982); John M. Slatin, *The Savage's Romance: The Poetry of Marianne Moore* (1986); Margaret Holley, *The Poetry of Marianne Moore: A Study in Voice and Value* (1987); Charles Molesworth, *Marianne Moore: A Literary Life* (1990); and Jeanne Heuving, *Omissions Are Not Accidents: Gender in the Art of Marianne Moore* (1992).

Poetry[1]

I, too, dislike it: there are things that are important beyond all
                                     this fiddle.
Reading it, however, with a perfect contempt for it, one
                                     discovers in

1. First published in *Poems* (1921) and condensed to two sentences in *Complete Poems,* the poem is given here in the text of the notes appended to that volume, which show the earlier form.

it after all, a place for the genuine.
    Hands that can grasp, eyes
      that can dilate, hair that can rise 5
        if it must, these things are important not because a

high-sounding interpretation can be put upon them but because
                              they are
useful. When they become so derivative as to become
                        unintelligible,
    the same thing may be said for all of us, that we 10
      do not admire what
      we cannot understand: the bat
        holding on upside down or in quest of something to

eat, elephants pushing, a wild horse taking a roll, a tireless wolf
                          under
    a tree, the immovable critic twitching his skin like a horse that
                feels a flea, the base-
ball fan, the statistician— 15
      nor is it valid
      to discriminate against "business documents and

school-books";[2] all these phenomena are important. One must
                make a distinction
    however: when dragged into prominence by half poets, the
                result is not poetry,
    nor till the poets among us can be 20
      "literalists of
      the imagination"[3]—above
        insolence and triviality and can present

for inspection, "imaginary gardens with real toads in them,"
                  shall we have
    it. In the meantime, if you demand on the one hand, 25
    the raw material of poetry in
      all its rawness and
      that which is on the other hand
        genuine, you are interested in poetry.

                        1921

2. *Diary of Tolstoy*, p. 84: "Where the boundary between prose and poetry lies, I shall never be able to understand. The question is raised in manuals of style, yet the answer to it lies beyond me. Poetry is verse: prose is not verse. Or else poetry is everything with the exception of business documents and school books" [Moore's note].
3. Yeats, *Ideas of Good and Evil* (A. H. Bullen, 1903), p. 182. "The limitation of his view was from the very intensity of his vision; he was a too literal realist of imagination, as others are of nature; and because he believed that the figures seen by the mind's eye, when exalted by inspiration, were 'eternal existences,' symbols of divine essences, he hated every grace of style that might obscure their lineaments." [Moore's note]. The reference is to the "vision" of William Blake.

In the Days of Prismatic Color

not in the days of Adam and Eve, but when Adam
  was alone; when there was no smoke and color was
fine, not with the refinement
  of early civilization art, but because
of its originality; with nothing to modify it but the   5

mist that went up, obliqueness was a variation
  of the perpendicular, plain to see and
to account for: it is no
  longer that; nor did the blue-red-yellow band
of incandescence that was color keep its stripe: it also is one of   10

those things into which much that is peculiar can be
  read; complexity is not a crime, but carry
it to the point of murkiness
  and nothing is plain. Complexity,
moreover, that has been committed to darkness, instead of   15

granting itself to be the pestilence that it is, moves all a-
  bout as if to bewilder us with the dismal
fallacy that insistence
  is the measure of achievement and that all
truth must be dark. Principally throat, sophistication is as it al-   20

ways has been—at the antipodes from the initial great truths. "Part of it was crawling, part of it
was about to crawl, the rest
  was torpid in its lair."[4] In the short-legged, fitful advance, the gurgling and all the minutiae—we have the   25
                                   classic

multitude of feet. To what purpose! Truth is no Apollo
  Belvedere,[5] no formal thing. The wave may go over it if it likes.
Know that it will be there when it says,
  "I shall be there when the wave has gone by."   30

                                             1924

Peter

    Strong and slippery,
      built for the midnight grass-party
    confronted by four cats, he sleeps his time away—
    the detached first claw on the foreleg corresponding
    to the thumb, retracted to its tip; the small tuft of fronds   5
    or katydid-legs above each eye numbering all units
    in each group; the shadbones regularly set about the mouth

4. Nestor. *Greek Anthology* (Loeb Classical
   Library), Vol. III, p. 129 [Moore's note].
5. The most famous statue from classical

antiquity, a Roman copy of a Greek original,
now in the Vatican.

to droop or rise in unison like porcupine-quills.
He lets himself be flattened out by gravity,
as seaweed is tamed and weakened by the sun,   10
compelled when extended, to lie stationary.
Sleep is the result of his delusion that one must
do as well as one can for oneself,
sleep—epitome of what is to him the end of life.
Demonstrate on him how the lady placed a forked stick   15
on the innocuous neck-sides of the dangerous southern snake.
One need not try to stir him up; his prune-shaped head
and alligator-eyes are not party to the joke.
Lifted and handled, he may be dangled like an eel
or set up on the forearm like a mouse;   20
his eyes bisected by pupils of a pin's width,
are flickeringly exhibited, then covered up.
May be? I should have said might have been;
when he has been got the better of in a dream—
as in a fight with nature or with cats, we all know it.   25
Profound sleep is not with him a fixed illusion.
Springing about with froglike accuracy, with jerky cries
when taken in hand, he is himself again;
to sit caged by the rungs of a domestic chair
would be unprofitable—human. What is the good of hypocrisy?   30
It is permissible to choose one's employment,
to abandon the nail, or roly-poly,
when it shows signs of being no longer a pleasure,
to score the nearby magazine with a double line of strokes.
He can talk but insolently says nothing. What of it?   35
When one is frank, one's very presence is a compliment.
It is clear that he can see the virtue of naturalness,
that he does not regard the published fact as a surrender.
As for the disposition invariably to affront,
an animal with claws should have an opportunity to use them.   40
The eel-like extension of trunk into tail is not an accident.
To leap, to lengthen out, divide the air, to purloin, to pursue.
To tell the hen: fly over the fence, go in the wrong way
in your perturbation—this is life;
to do less would be nothing but dishonesty.   45

                                  1924

A Grave

Man looking into the sea,
taking the view from those who have as much right to it as
                                you have to it yourself,
it is human nature to stand in the middle of a thing,
but you cannot stand in the middle of this;
the sea has nothing to give but a well excavated grave.   5

The firs stand in a procession, each with an emerald turkey-
                                        foot at the top,
reserved as their contours, saying nothing;
repression, however, is not the most obvious characteristic of
                                        the sea;
the sea is a collector, quick to return a rapacious look.
There are others besides you who have worn that look—   10
whose expression is no longer a protest; the fish no longer
                                        investigate them
for their bones have not lasted:
men lower nets, unconscious of the fact that they are
                                        desecrating a grave,
and row quickly away—the blades of the oars
moving together like the feet of water-spiders as if there were   15
                                        no such thing as death.
The wrinkles progress among themselves in a phalanx—
                                        beautiful under networks of foam,
and fade breathlessly while the sea rustles in and out of the
                                        seaweed;
the birds swim through the air at top speed, emitting cat-calls
                                        as heretofore—
the tortoise-shell scourges about the feet of the cliffs, in motion
                                        beneath them;
and the ocean, under the pulsation of lighthouses and noise of   20
                                        bell-buoys,

advances as usual, looking as if it were not that ocean in which
                                        dropped things are bound to sink—
in which if they turn and twist, it is neither with volition nor
                                        consciousness.

                                                        1924

An Egyptian Pulled Glass Bottle in the Shape of a Fish

Here we have thirst
and patience, from the first,
    and art, as in a wave held up for us to see
    in its essential perpendicularity;

not brittle but   5
intense—the spectrum, that
    spectacular and nimble animal the fish,
    whose scales turn aside the sun's sword by their polish.

                                                        1924

The Past Is the Present

If external action is effete
  and rhyme is outmoded,
    I shall revert to you,
Habakkuk,[6] as when in a Bible class
   · the teacher was speaking of unrhymed verse.   5
He said—and I think I repeat his exact words,
    "Hebrew poetry is prose
  with a sort of heightened consciousness."[7] Ecstasy affords
  the occasion and expediency determines the form.

1924

Silence

My father used to say,
"Superior people never make long visits,
have to be shown Longfellow's grave
or the glass flowers at Harvard.[8]
Self-reliant like the cat—   5
that takes its prey to privacy,
the mouse's limp tail hanging like a shoelace from its mouth—
they sometimes enjoy solitude,
and can be robbed of speech
by speech which has delighted them.   10
The deepest feeling always shows itself in silence;
not in silence, but restraint."
Nor was he insincere in saying, "Make my house your inn."[9]
Inns are not residences.

1924

No Swan So Fine[1]

"No water so still as the
    dead fountains of Versailles."[2] No swan,
  with swart blind look askance

---

6. A minor prophet from the seventh century B.C. whose name is given to one of the books of the Bible.
7. Dr. E. H. Kellogg in Bible class, Presbyterian Church, Carlisle, Pennsylvania [Moore's note].
8. "My father used to say, 'Superior people never make long visits. When I am visiting, I like to go about by myself. I never had to be shown Longfellow's grave or the glass flowers at Harvard.'" Miss A. M. Homans [Moore's note].
9. Edmund Burke, in *Burke's Life*, by Sir James

Prior (1872). " 'Throw yourself into a coach,' said he. 'Come down and make my house your inn' " [Moore's note].
1. An author's note suggests the poem was inspired by "A pair of Louis XV candelabra with Dresden figures of swans belonging to Lord Balfour."
2. *"There is no water so still as the dead fountains of Versailles."* Percy Phillip, *New York Times Magazine*, May 10, 1931 [Moore's note].

and gondoliering legs, so fine
  as the chintz china one with fawn-   5
brown eyes and toothed gold
collar on to show whose bird it was.

Lodged in the Louis Fifteenth
  candelabrum-tree of cockscomb-
tinted buttons, dahlias,   10
sea-urchins, and everlastings,
  it perches on the branching foam
of polished sculptured
flowers—at ease and tall. The king is dead.

1932, 1935

The Frigate Pelican

Rapidly cruising or lying on the air there is a bird
  that realizes Rasselas's friend's project
of wings uniting levity with strength.[3] This
  hell-diver, frigate-bird, hurricane-
bird; unless swift is the proper word   5
  for him, the storm omen when
he flies close to the waves, should be seen
  fishing, although oftener
  he appears to prefer

to take, on the wing, from industrious crude-winged species,   10
  the fish they have caught, and is seldom successless.
A marvel of grace, no matter how fast his
  victim may fly or how often may
turn. The others with similar ease,
  slowly rising once more,   15
  move out to the top
  of the circle and stop

and blow back, allowing the wind to reverse their direction—
  unlike the more stalwart swan that can ferry the
woodcutter's two children home. Make hay; keep   20
  the shop; I have one sheep; were a less
limber animal's mottoes. This one
  finds sticks for the swan's-down-dress
  of his child to rest upon and would
  not know Gretel from Hänsel.   25
  As impassioned Handel[4]—

meant for a lawyer and a masculine German domestic
  career—clandestinely studied the harpsichord

3. A friend of Rasselas, in Samuel Johnson's
  Rasselas (1759), devises wings for humans but
  will not share the secret for fear it will be put
to evil use.
4. George Frederick Handel (1685–1759),
  German composer.

and never was known to have fallen in love,
    the unconfiding frigate-bird hides 30

in the height and in the majestic
    display of his art. He glides
a hundred feet or quivers about
    as charred paper behaves—full
    of feints; and an eagle 35

of vigilance. . . . *Festina lente.* Be gay
    civilly? How so? "If I do well I am blessed
whether any bless me or not, and if I do
    ill I am cursed."[5] We watch the moon rise
on the Susquehanna.[6] In his way, 40
    this most romantic bird flies
to a more mundane place, the mangrove
    swamp to sleep. He wastes the moon.
    But he, and others, soon

rise from the bough and though flying, are able to foil the tired 45
    moment of danger that lays on heart and lungs the
    weight of the python that crushes to powder.

1934, 1935

The Pangolin

Another armored animal—scale
    lapping scale with spruce-cone regularity until they
form the uninterrupted central
    tail-row! This near artichoke with head and legs and
                grit-equipped gizzard,
    the night miniature artist engineer is, 5
        yes, Leonardo da Vinci's replica—
        impressive animal and toiler of whom we seldom hear.
    Armor seems extra. But for him,
        the closing ear-ridge[7]—
        or bare ear lacking even this small 10
        eminence and similarly safe

contracting nose and eye apertures
    impenetrably closable, are not;—a true ant-eater,
not cockroach-eater, who endures
    exhausting solitary trips through unfamiliar ground at night, 15
    returning before sunrise; stepping in the moonlight,
        on the moonlight peculiarly,[8] that the outside
        edges of his hands may bear the weight and save the
                claws

5. Hindu saying [Moore's note].
6. A river near Carlisle, Pennsylvania, the author's early home.
7. *"The closing ear-ridge,"* and certain other detail,

from "Pangolins" by Robert T. Hatt, *Natural History,* December 1935 [Moore's note].
8. *"Stepping . . . peculiarly."* See Lyddeker's *Royal Natural History* [Moore's note].

for digging. Serpentined about
   the tree, he draws
     away from danger unpugnaciously,
     with no sound but a harmless hiss; keeping   20

the fragile grace of the Thomas-
   of-Leighton Buzzard Westminster Abbey wrought-iron
                vine,[9] or

rolls himself into a ball that has   25
   power to defy all effort to unroll it; strongly intailed, neat
head for core, on neck not breaking off, with curled-in feet.
   Nevertheless he has sting-proof scales; and nest
     of rocks closed with earth from inside, which he can
                thus darken.
   Sun and moon and day and night and man and beast   30
     each with a splendor
     which man in all his vileness cannot
     set aside; each with an excellence!

"Fearful yet to be feared," the armored
   ant-eater met by the driver-ant does not turn back, but   35
engulfs what he can, the flattened sword-
   edged leafpoints on the tail and artichoke set leg- and
                body-plates
quivering violently when it retaliates
   and swarms on him. Compact like the furled fringed frill
     on the hat-brim of Gargallo's[1] hollow iron head of a   40
matador, he will drop and will
   then walk away
     unhurt, although if unintruded on,
     he cautiously works down the tree, helped

by his tail. The giant-pangolin-   45
   tail, graceful tool, as prop or hand or broom or ax, tipped like
an elephant's trunk with special skin,
     is not lost on this ant- and stone-swallowing uninjurable
     artichoke which simpletons thought a living fable
     whom the stones had nourished, whereas ants had done   50
      so. Pangolins are not aggressive animals; between
   dusk and day they have the not unchain-like machine-like
     form and frictionless creep of a thing
     made graceful by adversities, con-

versities. To explain grace requires   55
   a curious hand. If that which is at all were not forever,
why would those who graced the spires
   with animals and gathered there to rest, on cold luxurious
low stone seats—a monk and monk and monk—between the
               thus

---

9. Thomas of Leighton Buzzard's vine: a fragment
of iron-work in Westminster Abbey [Moore's
note].

1. Pablo Gargallo y Catalan (1881–1934), Spanish
sculptor.

ingenious roof-supports, have slaved to confuse   60
grace with a kindly manner, time in which to pay a
                debt;
the cure for sins, a graceful use
   of what are yet
      approved stone mullions[2] branching out across
      the perpendiculars? A sailboat   65

was the first machine.[3] Pangolins, made
   for moving quietly also, are models of exactness,
on four legs; on hind feet plantigrade,[4]
   with certain postures of a man. Beneath sun and moon,
                        man slaving
  to make his life more sweet, leaves half the flowers worth
                        having,   70
     needing to choose wisely how to use his strength;
      a paper-maker like the wasp; a tractor of foodstuffs,
   like the ant; spidering a length
     of web from bluffs
        above a stream; in fighting, mechanicked   75
        like the pangolin; capsizing in

disheartenment. Bedizened or stark
   naked, man, the self, the being we call human, writing-
master to this world, griffons a dark
   "Like does not like like that is obnoxious"; and writes error
                      with four   80
  r's. Among animals, *one* has a sense of humor.
     Humor saves a few steps, it saves years. Unignorant,
       modest and unemotional, and all emotion,
   he has everlasting vigor,
     power to grow,   85
        though there are few creatures who can make one
        breathe faster and make one erecter.

Not afraid of anything is he,
   and then goes cowering forth, tread paced to meet an obstacle
at every step. Consistent with the   90
   formula—warm blood, no gills, two pairs of hands and a few
                    hairs—that
  is a mammal; there he sits in his own habitat,
     serge-clad, strong-shod. The prey of fear, he, always
       curtailed, extinguished, thwarted by the dusk, work
                  partly done,
     says to the alternating blaze,   95
     "Again the sun!
       anew each day; and new and new and new,
       that comes into and steadies my soul."

                        1936

---

2. The bars dividing windows.
3. See F. L. Morse, *Power: Its Application from the 17th Dynasty to the 20th Century* [Moore's note].

4. Walking on the whole sole of the foot, like a man.

Nevertheless

you've seen a strawberry
　　that's had a struggle; yet
　　was, where the fragments met,

a hedgehog or a star-
　　fish for the multitude　　　　　　　5
　　of seeds. What better food

than apple-seeds—the fruit
　　within the fruit—locked in
　　like counter-curved twin

hazel-nuts? Frost that kills　　　　　10
　　the little rubber-plant-
　　leaves of *kok-saghyz*-stalks,⁵ can't

harm the roots; they still grow
　　in frozen ground. Once where
　　there was a prickly-pear-　　　　　15

leaf clinging to barbed wire,
　　a root shot down to grow
　　in earth two feet below;

as carrots form mandrakes⁶
　　or a ram's-horn root some-　　　　20
　　times. Victory won't come

to me unless I go
　　to it; a grape-tendril
　　ties a knot in knots till

knotted thirty times,—so　　　　　　25
　　the bound twig that's under-
　　gone and over-gone, can't stir.

The weak overcomes its
　　menace, the strong over-
　　comes itself. What is there　　　　30

like fortitude! What sap
　　went through that little thread
　　to make the cherry red!

　　　　　　　　　　　　　　　　1944

The Mind Is an Enchanting Thing

　　　　is an enchanted thing
　　　　　　like the glaze on a
　　　　　　katydid-wing

---

5. Russian dandelion.
6. European herbs with forked roots thought to resemble humans.

subdivided by sun
    till the nettings are legion.   5
Like Gieseking[7] playing Scarlatti[8];

like the apteryx-awl[9]
    as a beak, or the
kiwi's rain-shawl
      of haired feathers, the mind   10
    feeling its way as though blind,
walks along with its eyes on the ground.

It has memory's ear
    that can hear without
having to hear.   15
      Like the gyroscope's fall,
    truly unequivocal
because trued by regnant certainty,

it is a power of
    strong enchantment. It   20
is like the dove-
      neck animated by
    sun; it is memory's eye;
it's conscientious inconsistency.

It tears off the veil; tears   25
    the temptation, the
mist the heart wears,
      from its eyes—if the heart
    has a face; it takes apart
dejection. It's fire in the dove-neck's   30

iridescence; in the
    inconsistencies
of Scarlatti.
      Unconfusion submits
    its confusion to proof; it's   35
not a Herod's oath[1] that cannot change.

                 1944

In Distrust of Merits

Strengthened to live, strengthened to die for
    medals and positioned victories?
They're fighting, fighting, fighting the blind
    man who thinks he sees,—

---

7. Walter Gieseking (1895–1956), German
    pianist.
8. Domenico Scarletti (1685–1757), Italian
    composer.
9. "Apteryx" is the genus of birds containing the

kiwi, a bird from New Zealand, incapable of
flight, equipped with a long bill like an awl.
1. Herod ordered the beheading of John the
    Baptist because he would not change his oath
    (Mark 6:26).

who cannot see that the enslaver is   5
enslaved; the hater, harmed. O shining O
    firm star, O tumultuous
        ocean lashed till small things go
    as they will, the mountainous
        wave makes us who look, know   10

depth. Lost at sea before they fought! O
    star of David, star of Bethlehem,[2]
O black imperial lion
    of the Lord—emblem
of a risen world—be joined at last, be   15
joined. There is hate's crown beneath which all is
        death; there's love's without which none
            is king; the blessed deeds bless
        the halo. As contagion
            of sickness makes sickness,   20

contagion of trust can make trust. They're
    fighting in deserts and caves, one by
one, in battalions and squadrons;
    they're fighting that I
may yet recover from the disease, My   25
Self; some have it lightly; some will die. "Man's
        wolf to man" and we devour
            ourselves. The enemy could not
        have made a greater breach in our
            defenses. One pilot-   30

ing a blind man can escape him, but
    Job[3] disheartened by false comfort knew
that nothing can be so defeating
    as a blind man who
can see. O alive who are dead, who are   35
proud not to see, O small dust of the earth
        that walks so arrogantly,
            trust begets power and faith is
        an affectionate thing. We
            vow, we make this promise   40

to the fighting—it's a promise—"We'll
    never hate black, white, red, yellow, Jew,
Gentile, Untouchable." We are
    not competent to
make our vows. With set jaw they are fighting,   45
fighting, fighting,—some we love whom we know,
        some we love but know not—that
            hearts may feel and not be numb.
        It cures me; or am I what
            I can't believe in? Some   50

2. The two stars are invoked as symbols of   3.   The story is told in the Book of Job.
Judaism and Christianity.

in snow, some on crags, some in quicksands,
    little by little, much by much, they
are fighting fighting fighting that where
    there was death there may
be life. "When a man is prey to anger,   55
he is moved by outside things; when he holds
    his ground in patience patience
        patience, that is action or
    beauty," the soldier's defense
    and hardest armor for   60

the fight. The world's an orphans' home. Shall
    we never have peace without sorrow?
without pleas of the dying for
    help that won't come? O
quiet form upon the dust, I cannot   65
look and yet I must. If these great patient
    dyings—all these agonies
        and wound bearings and bloodshed—
    can teach us how to live, these
    dyings were not wasted.   70

Hate-hardened heart, O heart of iron,
    iron is iron till it is rust.
There never was a war that was
    not inward; I must
fight till I have conquered in myself what   75
causes war, but I would not believe it.
    I inwardly did nothing.
        O Iscariot-like crime![4]
    Beauty is everlasting
    and dust is for a time.   80

1944

A Jelly-Fish

    Visible, invisible,
      a fluctuating charm
    an amber-tinctured amethyst
      inhabits it, your arm
    approaches and it opens   5
      and it closes; you had meant
    to catch it and it quivers;
      you abandon your intent.

1959

---

4. Judas Iscariot was the apostle who betrayed Christ.

Katherine Anne Porter

(1890–1980)

Callie Russell Porter was born in a log cabin in Indian Creek, Texas, and grew up in poverty. When she was 2, her mother died and the family went to live with the paternal grandmother in Kyle, a small town between Austin and San Antonio. When she was 11, her grandmother died and the family moved several times before settling in San Antonio. Almost all her schooling was at home. Her grandmother, the first Katherine Anne Porter, was a storyteller, and young Callie took quickly to books. At 16, she left home for a marriage that did not last, but while married she converted to her husband's religion, Catholicism. During the World War I years, 1914 to 1918, the general convulsion in society was mirrored by several major events in her personal life. In 1915, she became Katherine Anne Porter, adopting the name of her grandmother. Seeking to support herself, she worked briefly for the film industry in Chicago. Ill with tuberculosis by 1916, she recovered with the aid of treatment in a Texas sanitorium. Beginning work as a journalist about that time, she went from Dallas, to Denver, to New York, and then to Mexico, but in Denver she nearly died from influenza in the epidemic that accompanied the end of the war.

Although she was married four times, hers was largely a life of self-sufficiency. From 1918 to 1924 she spent much of her time in Mexico, observing the attempts to bring about a just and stable society after the peak of revolutionary activity had passed, and gathering the impressions that prompted some of her best fiction. In the 1930s, she spent several years in Europe, living in Germany, France, and Switzerland. Fame came slowly but surely. Although she was 40 when her first book was published, she earned a substantial reputation with critics and other writers in the 1930s and 1940s, and taught and lectured at numerous colleges and universities from 1940 onward. Finally, *Ship of Fools* (1962), a best-seller and a major movie, provided her with the income to enjoy her last years in her home near Washington, D.C. It is her only novel, based on her 1931 steamer trip from Mexico to Germany; critics have generally not counted it among her most successful works.

Unlike some major American writers of her time—Hemingway, Faulkner, and Fitzgerald, for example—she wrote relatively little, but her finest stories rank with their best, and with the best of our century. In the success of her longer stories, developed well beyond the length most writers attempt in the genre, she is perhaps unparalleled. Most of the stories in her first collection, *Flowering Judas* (1930), fall within her shorter range; among masterworks included are the title story and "María Concepción," both set in Mexico, and "The Jilting of Granny Weatherall," set in Texas. The three much longer stories that make up *Pale Horse, Pale Rider* (1939) represent Porter's writing at the height of her powers. Two, the first and the last, form the major part of her exploration of the life of Miranda, a fictional character drawn in large part from the author's real experiences. In "Old Mortality," Miranda grows from a small child to a teenage rebel, married too young, but with, she thinks, "my own life yet to come." In "Pale Horse, Pale Rider," one of the greatest of World War I stories of life away from the front, she has become a writer in a Western city, is engaged in a foredoomed love affair, and almost dies from influenza. Between these Miranda stories—in some ways placed in counterpoint to them—lies "Noon Wine," a tale of oppressive isolation, ignorance, and sudden violence in Texas. In *The Leaning Tower and Other Stories* (1944), a sequence of seven stories gathered under the general title "The Old Order" explores Miranda's family background, with the child Miranda herself a character in several.

The Collected Stories (1965) adds four more stories to those of the earlier collections. *The Collected Essays and Occasional Writings* (1970) supersedes the earlier collection *The Days Before* (1952). Isabel Bayley edited *The Letters of Katherine Anne Porter* (1990).

A solid biography is Joan Givner, *Katherine Anne Porter: A Life* (1982). Other studies include Harry J. Mooney, *The Fiction and Criticism of Katherine Anne Porter* (1957; revised 1962); William L. Nance, *Katherine Anne Porter and the Art of Rejection* (1964); George Hendrick, *Katherine Anne Porter* (1965); M. M. Liberman, *Katherine Anne Porter's Fiction* (1971); Jane Krause DeMouey, *Katherine Anne Porter's Women: The Eye of Her Fiction* (1983); and Darlene Harbour Unrue, *Truth and Vision in Katherine Anne Porter's Fiction* (1985).

Pale Horse, Pale Rider[1]

In sleep she knew she was in her bed, but not the bed she had lain down in a few hours since, and the room was not the same but it was a room she had known somewhere. Her heart was a stone lying upon her breast outside of her; her pulses lagged and paused, and she knew that something strange was going to happen, even as the early morning winds were cool through the lattice, the streaks of light were dark blue and the whole house was snoring in its sleep.

Now I must get up and go while they are all quiet. Where are my things? Things have a will of their own in this place and hide where they like. Daylight will strike a sudden blow on the roof startling them all up to their feet; faces will beam asking, Where are you going, What are you doing, What are you thinking, How do you feel, Why do you say such things, What do you mean? No more sleep. Where are my boots and what horse shall I ride? Fiddler or Graylie or Miss Lucy with the long nose and the wicked eye? How I have loved this house in the morning before we are all awake and tangled together like badly cast fishing lines. Too many people have been born here, and have wept too much here, and have laughed too much, and have been too angry and outrageous with each other here. Too many have died in this bed already, there are far too many ancestral bones propped up on the mantelpieces, there have been too damned many antimacassars in this house, she said loudly, and oh, what accumulation of storied dust never allowed to settle in peace for one moment.

And the stranger? Where is that lank greenish stranger I remember hanging about the place, welcomed by my grandfather, my great-aunt, my five times removed cousin, my decrepit hound and my silver kitten? Why did they take to him, I wonder? And where are they now? Yet I saw him pass the window in the evening. What else besides them did I have in the world? Nothing. Nothing is mine, I have only nothing but it is enough, it is beautiful and it is all mine. Do I even walk about in my own skin or is it something I have borrowed to spare my modesty? Now what horse shall I borrow for this journey I do not mean to take, Graylie or Miss Lucy or Fiddler who can jump ditches in the dark and knows how to get the bit between his teeth? Early morning is best for me because trees are trees in one stroke, stones are stones set in shades known to be grass, there are no false shapes or surmises, the road is still asleep with the crust of dew unbroken. I'll take Graylie because he is not afraid of bridges.

Come now, Graylie, she said, taking his bridle, we must outrun Death and the Devil. You are no good for it, she told the other horses standing saddled before the stable gate, among them the horse of the stranger, gray also, with tarnished nose and ears. The stranger swung into his saddle beside her, leaned far towards her and regarded her without meaning, the blank still stare of mindless malice that makes no threats and can bide its time. She drew

1. The text is that of *The Collected Stories* (1965).

Graylie around sharply, urged him to run. He leaped the low rose hedge and the narrow ditch beyond, and the dust of the lane flew heavily under his beating hoofs. The stranger rode beside her, easily, lightly, his reins loose in his half-closed hand, straight and elegant in dark shabby garments that flapped upon his bones; his pale face smiled in an evil trance, he did not glance at her. Ah, I have seen this fellow before, I know this man if I could place him. He is no stranger to me.

She pulled Graylie up, rose in her stirrups and shouted, I'm not going with you this time—ride on! Without pausing or turning his head the stranger rode on. Graylie's ribs heaved under her, her own ribs rose and fell, Oh, why am I so tired, I must wake up. "But let me get a fine yawn first," she said, opening her eyes and stretching, "a slap of cold water in my face, for I've been talking in my sleep again, I heard myself but what was I saying?"

Slowly, unwillingly, Miranda drew herself up inch by inch out of the pit of sleep, waited in a daze for life to begin again. A single word struck in her mind, a gong of warning, reminding her for the day long what she forgot happily in sleep, and only in sleep. The war, said the gong, and she shook her head. Dangling her feet idly with their slippers hanging, she was reminded of the way all sorts of persons sat upon her desk at the newspaper office. Every day she found someone there, sitting upon her desk instead of the chair provided, dangling his legs, eyes roving, full of his important affairs, waiting to pounce about something or other. *"Why* won't they sit in the chair? Should I put a sign on it, saying, 'For God's sake, sit here'?"

Far from putting up a sign, she did not even frown at her visitors. Usually she did not notice them at all until their determination to be seen was greater than her determination not to see them. Saturday, she thought, lying comfortably in her tub of hot water, will be pay day, as always. Or I hope always. Her thoughts roved hazily in a continual effort to bring together and unite firmly the disturbing oppositions in her day-to-day existence, where survival, she could see clearly, had become a series of feats of sleight of hand. I owe—let me see, I wish I had pencil and paper—well, suppose I *did* pay five dollars now on a Liberty Bond, I couldn't possibly keep it up. Or maybe. Eighteen dollars a week. So much for rent, so much for food, and I mean to have a few things besides. About five dollars' worth. Will leave me twenty-seven cents. I suppose I can make it. I suppose I should be worried. I am worried. Very well, now I am worried and what next? Twenty-seven cents. That's not so bad. Pure profit, really. Imagine if they should suddenly raise me to twenty I should then have two dollars and twenty-seven cents left over. But they aren't going to raise me to twenty. They are in fact going to throw me out if I don't buy a Liberty Bond. I hardly believe that. I'll ask Bill. (Bill was the city editor.) I wonder if a threat like that isn't a kind of blackmail. I don't believe even a Lusk Committeeman can get away with that.

Yesterday there had been two pairs of legs dangling, on either side of her typewriter, both pairs stuffed thickly into funnels of dark expensive-looking material. She noticed at a distance that one of them was oldish and one was youngish, and they both of them had a stale air of borrowed importance which apparently they had got from the same source. They were both much too well nourished and the younger one wore a square little mustache. Being what they were, no matter what their business was it would be something unpleasant. Miranda had nodded at them, pulled out her chair and without removing her cap or gloves had reached into a pile of letters and sheets from the copy desk as if she had not a moment to spare. They did not move, or take off their hats. At last she had said "Good morning" to them, and asked if they were, perhaps, waiting for her?

The two men slid off the desk, leaving some of her papers rumpled, and the oldish man had inquired why she had not bought a Liberty Bond. Miranda had looked at him then, and got a poor impression. He was a pursy-faced man, gross-mouthed, with little lightless eyes, and Miranda wondered why nearly all of those selected to do the war work at home were of his sort. He might be anything at all, she thought; advance agent for a road show, promoter of a wildcat oil company, a former saloon keeper announcing the opening of a new cabaret, an automobile salesman—any follower of any one of the crafty, haphazard callings. But he was now all Patriot, working for the government. "Look here," he asked her, "do you know there's a war, or don't you?"

Did he expect an answer to that? Be quiet, Miranda told herself, this was bound to happen. Sooner or later it happens. Keep your head. The man wagged his finger at her, "Do you?" he persisted, as if he were prompting an obstinate child.

"Oh, the war," Miranda had echoed on a rising note and she almost smiled at him. It was habitual, automatic, to give that solemn, mystically uplifted grin when you spoke the words or heard them spoken. *"C'est la guerre,"* whether you could pronounce it or not, was even better, and always, always, you shrugged.

"Yeah," said the younger man in a nasty way, "the war." Miranda, startled by the tone, met his eye; his stare was really stony, really viciously cold, the kind of thing you might expect to meet behind a pistol on a deserted corner. This expression gave temporary meaning to a set of features otherwise nondescript, the face of those men who have no business of their own. "We're having a war, and some people are buying Liberty Bonds and others just don't seem to get around to it," he said. "That's what we mean."

Miranda frowned with nervousness, the sharp beginnings of fear. "Are you selling them?" she asked, taking the cover off her typewriter and putting it back again.

"No, we're not selling them," said the older man. "We're just asking you why you haven't bought one." The voice was persuasive and ominous.

Miranda began to explain that she had no money, and did not know where to find any, when the older man interrupted: "That's no excuse, no excuse at all, and you know it, with the Huns overrunning martyred Belgium."

"With our American boys fighting and dying in Belleau Wood[2]," said the younger man, "anybody can raise fifty dollars to help beat the Boche.[3]"

Miranda said hastily, "I have eighteen dollars a week and not another cent in the world. I simply cannot buy anything."

"You can pay for it five dollars a week," said the older man (they had stood there cawing back and forth over her head), "like a lot of other people in this office, and a lot of other offices besides are doing."

Miranda, desperately silent, had thought, "Suppose I were not a coward, but said what I really thought? Suppose I said to hell with this filthy war? Suppose I asked that little thug, What's the matter with you, why aren't you rotting in Belleau Wood? I wish you were . . ."

She began to arrange her letters and notes, her fingers refusing to pick up things properly. The older man went on making his little set speech. It was hard, of course. Everybody was suffering, naturally. Everybody had to do his share. But as to that, a Liberty Bond was the safest investment you could make. It was just like having the money in the bank. Of course. The government was back of it and where better could you invest?

"I agree with you about that," said Miranda, "but I haven't any money to invest."

And of course, the man had gone on, it wasn't so much her fifty dollars that was going to make any difference. It was just a pledge of good faith on her part. A pledge of good faith that she was a loyal American doing her duty. And the thing was safe as a church. Why, if he had a million dollars he'd be glad to put every last cent of it in these Bonds. . . . "You can't lose by it," he said, almost benevolently, "and you can lose a lot if you don't. Think it over. You're the only one in this whole newspaper office that hasn't come in. And every firm in this city has come in one hundred per cent. Over at the *Daily Clarion* nobody had to be asked twice."

2. In northern France, site of a victory over the Germans, largely fought by U.S. troops, June 6–25, 1918.

3. Disparaging term for German soldiers in World War I.

"They pay better over there," said Miranda. "But next week, if I can. Not now, next week."

"See that you do," said the younger man. "This ain't any laughing matter."

They lolled away, past the Society Editor's desk, past Bill the City Editor's desk, past the long copy desk where old man Gibbons sat all night shouting at intervals, "Jarge! Jarge!" and the copy boy would come flying. "Never say *people* when you mean *persons,*" old man Gibbons had instructed Miranda, "and never say *practically,* say *virtually,* and don't for God's sake ever so long as I am at this desk use the barbarism *inasmuch* under any circumstances whatsoever. Now you're educated, you may go." At the head of the stairs her inquisitors had stopped in their fussy pride and vainglory, lighting cigars and wedging their hats more firmly over their eyes.

Miranda turned over in the soothing water, and wished she might fall asleep there, to wake up only when it was time to sleep again. She had a burning slow headache, and noticed it now, remembering she had waked up with it and it had in fact begun the evening before. While she dressed she tried to trace the insidious career of her headache, and it seemed reasonable to suppose it had started with the war. "It's been a headache, all right, but not quite like this." After the Committeemen had left, yesterday, she had gone to the cloakroom and had found Mary Townsend, the Society Editor, quietly hysterical about something. She was perched on the edge of the shabby wicker couch with ridges down the center, knitting on something rose-colored. Now and then she would put down her knitting, seize her head with both hands and rock, saying, "My *God,*" in a surprised, inquiring voice. Her column was called Ye Towne Gossyp, so of course everybody called her Towney. Miranda and Towney had a great deal in common, and liked each other. They had both been real reporters once, and had been sent together to "cover" a scandalous elopement, in which no marriage had taken place, after all, and the recaptured girl, her face swollen, had sat with her mother, who was moaning steadily under a mound of blankets. They had both wept painfully and implored the young reporters to suppress the worst of the story. They had suppressed it, and the rival newspaper printed it all the next day. Miranda and Towney had then taken their punishment together, and had been degraded publicly to routine female jobs, one to the theaters, the other to society. They had this in common, that neither of them could see what else they could possibly have done, and they knew they were considered fools by the rest of the staff—nice girls, but fools. At sight of Miranda, Towney had broken out in a rage. "I can't do it, I'll never be able to raise the money, I told them, I can't, I can't, but they wouldn't listen."

Miranda said, "I knew I wasn't the only person in this office who couldn't raise five dollars. I told them I couldn't, too, and I can't."

"My *God,*" said Towney, in the same voice, "they told me I'd lose my job—"

"I'm going to ask Bill," Miranda said; "I don't believe Bill would do that."

"It's not up to Bill," said Towney. "He'd have to if they got after him. Do you suppose they could put us in jail?"

"I don't know," said Miranda. "If they do, we won't be lonesome." She sat down beside Towney and held her own head. "What kind of soldier are you knitting that for? It's a sprightly color, it ought to cheer him up."

"Like hell," said Towney, her needles going again. "I'm making this for myself. That's that."

"Well," said Miranda, "we won't be lonesome and we'll catch up on our sleep." She washed her face and put on fresh make-up. Taking clean gray gloves out of her pocket she went out to join a group of young women fresh from the country club dances, the morning bridge, the charity bazaar, the Red Cross workrooms, who were wallowing in good works. They gave tea dances and raised money, and with the money they bought quantities of sweets, fruit, cigarettes, and magazines for the men in the cantonment hospitals. With this loot they were now setting out, a gay procession of high-powered cars and brightly tinted faces to cheer the brave boys who already, you might very well say, had fallen in defense of their country. It must be frightfully hard on them, the dears, to be floored like this when they're all crazy to get overseas and into the trenches as quickly as possible. Yes, and some of them are the cutest things you ever saw, I didn't know there were so many good-looking men in this country, good heavens, I said, where do they come from? Well, my dear, you may ask yourself that question, who knows where they did come from? You're quite right, the way I feel about it is this, we must do everything we can to make them contented, but I draw the line at talking to them. I told the chaperons at those dances for enlisted men, I'll dance with them, every dumbbell who asks me, but I will NOT talk to them, I said, even if there is a war. So I danced hundreds of miles without opening my mouth except to say, Please keep your knees to yourself. I'm glad we gave those dances up. Yes, and the men stopped coming, anyway. But listen, I've heard that a great many of the enlisted men come from very good families; I'm not good at catching names, and those I did catch I'd never heard before, so I don't know . . . but it seems to me if they were from good families, you'd know it, wouldn't you? I mean, if a man is well bred he doesn't step on your feet, does he? At least not that. I used to have a pair of sandals ruined at every one of those dances. Well, I think any kind of social life is in very poor taste just now, I think we should all put on our Red Cross head dresses and wear them for the duration of the war—

Miranda, carrying her basket and her flowers, moved in among the young women, who scattered out and rushed upon the ward uttering girlish laughter meant to be refreshingly gay, but there was a grim determined clang in it calculated to freeze the blood. Miserably embarrassed at the idiocy of her errand, she walked rapidly between the long rows of high beds, set foot to foot with a narrow aisle between. The men, a selected presentable lot, sheets drawn up to their chins, not seriously ill, were bored and restless, most of them willing to be amused at anything. They were for the most part picturesquely bandaged as to arm or head, and those who were not visibly wounded invariably replied "Rheumatism" if some tactless girl, who had been solemnly warned never to ask this question, still forgot and asked a man what his illness was. The good-natured, eager ones, laughing and calling out from their hard narrow beds, were soon surrounded. Miranda, with her wilting bouquet and her basket of sweets and cigarettes, looking about, caught the unfriendly bitter eye of a young fellow lying on his back, his right leg in a cast and pulley. She stopped at the foot of his bed and continued to look at him, and he looked back with an unchanged, hostile face. Not having any, thank you and be damned to the whole business, his eyes said plainly to her, and will you be so good as to take your trash off my bed? For Miranda had set it down, leaning over to place it where he might be able to reach it if he would. Having set it down, she was incapable of taking it up again, but hurried away, her face burning, down the long aisle and out into the cool October sunshine, where the dreary raw barracks swarmed and worked with an aimless life of scurrying, dun-colored insects; and going around to a window near where he lay, she looked in, spying upon her soldier. He was lying with his eyes closed, his eyebrows in a sad bitter frown. She could not place him at all, she could not imagine where he came from nor what sort of being he might have been "in life," she said to herself. His face was young and the features sharp and plain, the hands were not laborer's hands but not well-cared-for hands either. They were good useful properly shaped hands, lying there on the coverlet. It occurred to her that it would be her luck to find him, instead of a jolly hungry puppy glad of a bite to eat and a little chatter. It is like turning a corner absorbed in your painful thoughts and meeting your state of mind embodied, face to face, she said. "My own feelings about this whole thing, made flesh. Never again will I come here, this is no sort of thing to be doing. This is disgusting," she told herself plainly. "Of course I would pick him out," she thought, getting into the back seat of the car she came in, "serves me right, I know better."

Another girl came out looking very tired and climbed in beside her. After a short silence, the girl said in a puzzled way, "I don't know what good it does, really. Some of them wouldn't take anything at all. I don't like this, do you?"

"I hate it," said Miranda.

"I suppose it's all right, though," said the girl, cautiously.

"Perhaps," said Miranda, turning cautious also.

That was for yesterday. At this point Miranda decided there was no good in thinking of yesterday, except for the hour after midnight she had spent dancing with Adam. He was in her mind so much, she hardly knew when she was thinking about him directly. His image was simply always present in more or less degree, he was sometimes nearer the surface of her thoughts, the pleasantest, the only really pleasant thought she had. She examined her face in the mirror between the windows and decided that her uneasiness was not all imagination. For three days at least she had felt odd and her expression was unfamiliar. She would have to raise that fifty dollars somehow, she supposed, or who knows what can happen? She was hardened to stories of personal disaster, of outrageous accusations and extraordinarily bitter penalties that had grown monstrously out of incidents very little more important than her failure—her refusal—to buy a Bond. No, she did not find herself a pleasing sight, flushed and shiny, and even her hair felt as if it had decided to grow in the other direction. I must do something about this, I can't let Adam see me like this, she told herself, knowing that even now at that moment he was listening for the turn of her door knob, and he would be in the hallway, or on the porch when she came out, as if by sheerest coincidence. The noon sunlight cast cold slanting shadows in the room where, she said, I suppose I live, and this day is beginning badly, but they all do now, for one reason or another. In a drowse, she sprayed perfume on her hair, put on her moleskin cap and jacket, now in their second winter, but still good, still nice to wear, again being glad she had paid a frightening price for them. She had enjoyed them all this time, and in no case would she have had the money now. Maybe she could manage for that Bond. She could not find the lock without leaning to search for it, then stood undecided a moment possessed by the notion that she had forgotten something she would miss seriously later on.

Adam was in the hallway, a step outside his own door; he swung about as if quite startled to see her, and said, "Hello. I don't have to go back to camp today after all—isn't that luck?"

Miranda smiled at him gaily because she was always delighted at the sight of him. He was wearing his new uniform, and he was all olive and tan and tawny, hay colored and sand colored from hair to boots. She half noticed again that he always began by smiling at her; that his smile faded gradually; that his eyes became fixed and thoughtful as if he were reading in a poor light.

They walked out together into the fine fall day, scuffling bright ragged leaves under their feet, turning their faces up to a generous sky really blue and spotless. At the first corner they waited for a funeral to pass, the mourners seated straight and firm as if proud in their sorrow.

"I imagine I'm late," said Miranda, "as usual. What time is it?"

"Nearly half past one," he said, slipping back his sleeve with an exaggerated thrust of his arm upward. The young soldiers were still self-conscious about their wrist watches. Such of them as Miranda knew were boys from southern and southwestern towns, far off the Atlantic seaboard, and they had always believed that only sissies wore wrist watches. "I'll slap you on the wrist watch," one vaudeville comedian would simper to another, and it was always a good joke, never stale.

"I think it's a most sensible way to carry a watch," said Miranda. "You needn't blush."

"I'm nearly used to it," said Adam, who was from Texas. "We've been told time and again how all the he-manly regular army men wear them. It's the horrors of war," he said; "are we downhearted? I'll say we are."

It was the kind of patter going the rounds. "You look it," said Miranda.

He was tall and heavily muscled in the shoulders, narrow in the waist and flanks, and he was infinitely buttoned, strapped, harnessed into a uniform as tough and unyielding in cut as a strait jacket, though the cloth was fine and supple. He had his uniforms made by the best tailor he could find, he confided to Miranda one day when she told him how squish he was looking in his new soldier suit. "Hard enough to make anything of the outfit, anyhow," he told her. "It's the least I can do for my beloved country, not to go around looking like a tramp." He was twenty-four years old and a Second Lieutenant in an Engineers Corps, on leave because his outfit expected to be sent over shortly. "Came in to make my will," he told Miranda, "and get a supply of toothbrushes and razor blades. By what gorgeous luck do you suppose," he asked her, "I happened to pick on your rooming house? How did I know you were there?"

Strolling, keeping step, his stout polished well-made boots setting themselves down firmly beside her thin-soled black suède, they put off as long as they could the end of their moment together, and kept up as well as they could their small talk that flew back and forth over little grooves worn in the thin upper surface of the brain, things you could say and hear clink reassuringly at once without disturbing the radiance which played and darted about the simple and lovely miracle of being two persons named Adam and Miranda, twenty-four years old each, alive and on the earth at the same moment: "Are you in the mood for dancing, Miranda?" and "I'm always in the mood for dancing, Adam!" but there were things in the way, the day that ended with dancing was a long way to go.

He really did look, Miranda thought, like a fine healthy apple this morning. One time or another in their talking, he had boasted that he had never had a pain in his life that he could remember. Instead of being horrified at this monster, she approved his monstrous uniqueness. As for herself, she had had too many pains to mention, so she did not mention them. After working for three years on a morning newspaper she had an illusion of maturity and experience; but it was fatigue merely, she decided, from keeping what she had been brought up to believe were unnatural hours, eating casually at dirty little restaurants, drinking bad coffee all night, and smoking too much. When she said something of her way of living to Adam, he studied her face a few seconds as if he had never seen it before, and said in a forthright way, "Why, it hasn't hurt you a bit, I think you're beautiful," and left her dangling there, wondering if he had thought she wished to be praised. She did wish to be praised, but not at that moment. Adam kept unwholesome hours too, or had in the ten days they had known each other, staying awake until one o'clock to take her out for supper; he smoked also continually, though if she did not stop him he was apt to explain to her exactly what smoking did to the lungs. "But," he said, "does it matter so much if you're going to war, anyway?"

"No," said Miranda, "and it matters even less if you're staying at home knitting socks. Give me a cigarette, will you?" They paused at another corner, under a half-foliaged maple, and hardly glanced at a funeral procession approaching. His eyes were pale tan with orange flecks in them, and his hair was the color of a haystack when you turn the weathered top back to the clear straw beneath. He fished out his cigarette case and snapped his silver lighter at her, snapped it several times in his own face, and they moved on, smoking.

"I can see you knitting socks," he said. "That would be just your speed. You know perfectly well you can't knit."

"I do worse," she said, soberly; "I write pieces advising other young women to knit and roll bandages and do without sugar and help win the war."

"Oh, well," said Adam, with the easy masculine morals in such questions, "that's merely your job, that doesn't count."

"I wonder," said Miranda. "How did you manage to get an extension of leave?"

"They just gave it," said Adam, "for no reason. The men are dying like flies out there, anyway. This funny new disease. Simply knocks you into a cocked hat."

"It seems to be a plague," said Miranda, "something out of the Middle Ages. Did you ever see so many funerals, ever?"

"Never did. Well, let's be strong minded and not have any of it. I've got four days more straight from the blue and not a blade of grass must grow under our feet. What about tonight?"

"Same thing," she told him, "but make it about half past one. I've got a special job beside my usual run of the mill."

"What a job you've got," said Adam, "nothing to do but run from one dizzy amusement to another and then write a piece about it."

"Yes, it's too dizzy for words," said Miranda. They stood while a funeral passed, and this time they watched it in silence. Miranda pulled her cap to an angle and winked in the sunlight, her head swimming slowly "like goldfish," she told Adam, "my head swims. I'm only half awake, I must have some coffee."

They lounged on their elbows over the counter of a drug store. "No more cream for the stay-at-homes," she said, "and only one lump of sugar. I'll have two or none; that's the kind of martyr I'm being. I mean to live on boiled cabbage and wear shoddy from now on and get in good shape for the next round. No war is going to sneak up on me again."

"Oh, there won't be any more wars, don't you read the newspapers?" asked Adam. "We're going to mop 'em up this time, and they're going to stay mopped, and this is going to be all."

"So they told me," said Miranda, tasting her bitter lukewarm brew and making a rueful face. Their smiles approved of each other, they felt they had got the right tone, they were taking the war properly. Above all, thought Miranda, no tooth-gnashing, no hair-tearing, it's noisy and unbecoming and it doesn't get you anywhere.

"Swill," said Adam rudely, pushing back his cup. "Is that all you're having for breakfast?"

"It's more than I want," said Miranda.

"I had buckwheat cakes, with sausage and maple syrup, and two bananas, and two cups of coffee, at eight o'clock, and right now, again, I feel like a famished orphan left in the ashcan. I'm all set," said Adam, "for broiled steak and fried potatoes and—"

"Don't go on with it," said Miranda, "it sounds delirious to me. Do all that after I'm gone." She slipped from the high seat, leaned against it slightly, glanced at her face in her round mirror, rubbed rouge on her lips and decided that she was past praying for.

"There's something terribly wrong," she told Adam. "I feel too rotten. It can't just be the weather, and the war."

"The weather is perfect," said Adam, "and the war is simply too good to be true. But since when? You were all right yesterday."

"I don't know," she said slowly, her voice sounding small and thin. They stopped as always at the open door before the flight of littered steps leading up to the newspaper loft. Miranda listened for a moment to the rattle of typewriters above, the steady rumble of presses below. "I wish we were going to spend the whole afternoon on a park bench," she said, "or drive to the mountains."

"I do too," he said; "let's do that tomorrow."

"Yes, tomorrow, unless something else happens. I'd like to run away," she told him; "let's both."

"Me?" said Adam. "Where I'm going there's no running to speak of. You mostly crawl about on your stomach here and there among the debris. You know, barbed wire and such stuff. It's going to be the kind of thing that happens once in a lifetime." He reflected a moment, and went on, "I don't know a darned thing about it, really, but they make it sound awfully messy. I've heard so much about it I feel as if I had been there and back. It's going to be an anticlimax," he said, "like seeing the pictures of a place so often you can't see it at all when you actually get there. Seems to me I've been in the army all my life."

Six months, he meant. Eternity. He looked so clear and fresh, and he had never had a pain in his life. She had seen them when they had been there and back and they never looked like this again. "Already the returned hero," she said, "and don't I wish you were."

"When I learned the use of the bayonet in my first training camp," said Adam, "I gouged the vitals out of more sandbags and sacks of hay than I could keep track of. They kept bawling at us, 'Get him, get that Boche, stick him before he sticks you'—and we'd go for those sandbags like wildfire, and honestly, sometimes I felt a perfect fool for getting so worked up when I saw the sand trickling out. I used to wake up in the night sometimes feeling silly about it."

"I can imagine," said Miranda. "It's perfect nonsense." They lingered, unwilling to say good-by. After a little pause, Adam, as if keeping up the conversation, asked, "Do you know what the average life expectation of a sapping party[4] is after it hits the job?"

"Something speedy, I suppose."

"Just nine minutes," said Adam; "I read that in your own newspaper not a week ago."

"Make it ten and I'll come along," said Miranda.

"Not another second," said Adam, "exactly nine minutes, take it or leave it."

"Stop bragging," said Miranda. "Who figured that out?"

"A noncombatant," said Adam, "a fellow with rickets."

This seemed very comic, they laughed and leaned towards each other and Miranda heard herself being a little shrill. She wiped the tears from her eyes. "My, it's a funny war," she said; "isn't it? I laugh every time I think about it."

Adam took her hand in both of his and pulled a little at the tips of her gloves and sniffed them. "What nice perfume you have," he said, "and such a lot of it, too. I like a lot of perfume on gloves and hair," he said, sniffing again.

"I've got probably too much," she said. "I can't smell or see or hear today. I must have a fearful cold."

"Don't catch cold," said Adam; "my leave is nearly up and it will be the last, the very last." She moved her fingers in her gloves as he pulled at the fingers and turned her hands as if they were something new and curious and of great value, and she turned shy and quiet. She liked him, she liked him, and there was more than this but it was no good even imagining, because he was not for her nor for any woman, being beyond experience already, committed without any knowledge or act of his own to death. She took back her hands. "Good-by," she said finally, "until tonight."

She ran upstairs and looked back from the top. He was still watching her, and raised his hand without smiling. Miranda hardly ever saw anyone look back after he had said good-by. She could not help turning sometimes for one glimpse more of the person she had been talking with, as if that would save too rude and too sudden a snapping of even the lightest bond. But people hurried away, their faces already changed, fixed, in their straining towards their next stopping place, already absorbed in planning their next act or encounter. Adam was waiting as if he expected her to turn, and under his brows fixed in a strained frown, his eyes were very black.

At her desk she sat without taking off jacket or cap, slitting envelopes and pretending to read the letters. Only Chuck Rouncivale, the sports reporter, and Ye Towne Gossyp were sitting on her desk today, and them she liked having there. She sat on theirs when she pleased. Towney and Chuck were talking and they went on with it.

"They say," said Towney, "that it is really caused by germs brought by a German ship to Boston, a camouflaged ship, naturally, it didn't come in under its own colors. Isn't that ridiculous?"

"Maybe it was a submarine," said Chuck, "sneaking in from the bottom of the sea in the dead of night. Now that sounds better."

"Yes, it does," said Towney; "they always slip up somewhere in these details . . . and they think the germs were sprayed over the city—it started in Boston, you know—and somebody reported seeing a strange, thick, greasy-looking cloud float up out of Boston Harbor and spread slowly all over that end of town. I think it was an old woman who saw it."

"Should have been," said Chuck.

"I read it in a New York newspaper," said Towney; "so it's bound to be true."

Chuck and Miranda laughed so loudly at this that Bill stood up and glared at them. "Towney still reads the newspapers," explained Chuck.

"Well, what's funny about that?" asked Bill, sitting down again and frowning into the clutter before him.

4. A small group of soldiers closely approaching the enemy's front lines.

"It was a noncombatant saw that cloud," said Miranda.

"Naturally," said Towney.

"Member of the Lusk Committee, maybe," said Miranda.

"The Angel of Mons," said Chuck, "or a dollar-a-year man."

Miranda wished to stop hearing, and talking, she wished to think for just five minutes of her own about Adam, really to think about him, but there was no time. She had seen him first ten days ago, and since then they had been crossing streets together, darting between trucks and limousines and pushcarts and farm wagons; he had waited for her in doorways and in little restaurants that smelled of stale frying fat; they had eaten and danced to the urgent whine and bray of jazz orchestras, they had sat in dull theaters because Miranda was there to write a piece about the play. Once they had gone to the mountains and, leaving the car, had climbed a stony trail, and had come out on a ledge upon a flat stone, where they sat and watched the lights change on a valley landscape that was, no doubt, Miranda said, quite apocryphal—"We need not believe it, but it is fine poetry," she told him; they had leaned their shoulders together there, and had sat quite still, watching. On two Sundays they had gone to the geological museum, and had pored in shared fascination over bits of meteors, rock formations, fossilized tusks and trees, Indian arrows, grottoes from the silver and gold lodes. "Think of those old miners washing out their fortunes in little pans beside the streams," said Adam, "and inside the earth there was this—" and he had told her he liked better those things that took long to make; he loved airplanes too, all sorts of machinery, things carved out of wood or stone. He knew nothing much about them, but he recognized them when he saw them. He had confessed that he simply could not get through a book, any kind of book except textbooks on engineering; reading bored him to crumbs; he regretted now he hadn't brought his roadster, but he hadn't thought he would need a car; he loved driving, he wouldn't expect her to believe how many hundreds of miles he could get over in a day . . . he had showed her snapshots of himself at the wheel of his roadster; of himself sailing a boat, looking very free and windblown, all angles, hauling on the ropes; he would have joined the air force, but his mother had hysterics every time he mentioned it. She didn't seem to realize that dog fighting in the air was a good deal safer than sapping parties on the ground at night. But he hadn't argued, because of course she did not realize about sapping parties. And here he was, stuck, on a plateau a mile high with no water for a boat and his car at home, otherwise they could really have had a good time. Miranda knew he was trying to tell her what kind of person he was when he had his machinery with him. She felt she knew pretty well what kind of person he was, and would have liked to tell him that if he thought he had left himself at home in a boat or an automobile, he was much mistaken. The telephones were ringing, Bill was shouting at somebody who kept saying, "Well, but listen, well, but listen—" but nobody was going to listen, of course, nobody. Old man Gibbons bellowed in despair, "Jarge, Jarge—"

"Just the same," Towney was saying in her most complacent patriotic voice. "Hut Service is a fine idea, and we should all volunteer even if they don't want us." Towney does well at this, thought Miranda, look at her; remembering the rose-colored sweater and the tight rebellious face in the cloakroom. Towney was now all open-faced glory and goodness, willing to sacrifice herself for her country. "After all," said Towney, "I *can* sing and dance well enough for the Little Theater, and I could write their letters for them, and at a pinch I might drive an ambulance. I have driven a Ford for years."

Miranda joined in: "Well, I can sing and dance too, but who's going to do the bed-making and the scrubbing up? Those huts are hard to keep, and it would be a dirty job and we'd be perfectly miserable; and as I've got a hard dirty job and am perfectly miserable, I'm going to stay at home."

"I think the women should keep out of it," said Chuck Rouncivale. "They just add skirts to the horrors of war." Chuck had bad lungs and fretted a good deal about missing the show. "I could have been there and back with a leg off by now; it would have served the old man right. Then he'd either have to buy his own hooch or sober up."

Miranda had seen Chuck on pay day giving the old man money for hooch. He was a good-humored ingratiating old scoundrel, too, that was the worst of him. He slapped his son on the back and beamed upon him with the bleared eye of paternal affection while he took his last nickel.

"It was Florence Nightingale[5] ruined wars," Chuck went on. What's the idea of petting soldiers and binding up their wounds and soothing their fevered brows? That's not war. Let 'em perish where they fall. That's what they're there for."

"You can talk," said Towney, with a slantwise glint at him.

"What's the idea?" asked Chuck, flushing and hunching his shoulders. "You know I've got this lung, or maybe half of it anyway by now."

"You're much too sensitive," said Towney. "I didn't mean a thing."

Bill had been raging about, chewing his half-smoked cigar, his hair standing up in a brush, his eyes soft and lambent but wild, like a stag's. He would never, thought Miranda, be more than fourteen years old if he lived for a century, which he would not, at the rate he was going. He behaved exactly like city editors in the moving pictures, even to the chewed cigar. Had he formed his style on the films, or had scenario writers seized once for all on the type Bill in its inarguable purity? Bill was shouting to Chuck: *"And* if he comes back here take him up the alley and saw his head off *by hand!"*

Chuck said, "He'll be back, don't worry." Bill said mildly, already off on another track, "Well, saw him off." Towney went to her own desk, but Chuck sat waiting amiably to be taken to the new vaudeville show. Miranda, with two tickets, always invited one of the reporters to go with her on Monday. Chuck was lavishly hardboiled and professional in his sports writing, but he had told Miranda that he didn't give a damn about sports, really; the job kept him out in the open, and paid him enough to buy the old man's hooch. He preferred shows and didn't see why women always had the job.

"Who does Bill want sawed today?" asked Miranda.

"That hoofer you panned in this morning's," said Chuck. "He was up here bright and early asking for the guy that writes up show business. He said he was going to take the goof who wrote that piece up the alley and bop him in the nose. He said . . ."

"I hope he's gone," said Miranda; "I do hope he had to catch a train."

Chuck stood up and arranged his maroon-colored turtle-necked sweater, glanced down at the peasoup tweed plus fours and the hobnailed tan boots which he hoped would help to disguise the fact that he had a bad lung and didn't care for sports, and said, "He's long gone by now, don't worry. Let's get going; you're late as usual."

Miranda, facing about, almost stepped on the toes of a little drab man in a derby hat. He might have been a pretty fellow once, but now his mouth drooped where he had lost his side teeth, and his sad red-rimmed eyes had given up coquetry. A thin brown wave of hair was combed out with brilliantine and curled against the rim of the derby. He didn't move his feet, but stood planted with a kind of inert resistance, and asked Miranda: "Are you the so-called dramatic critic on this hick newspaper?"

"I'm afraid I am," said Miranda.

"Well," said the little man, "I'm just asking for one minute of your valuable time." His underlip shot out, he began with shaking hands to fish about in his waistcoat pocket. "I just hate to let you get away with it, that's all." He riffled through a collection of shabby newspaper clippings. "Just give these the once-over, will you? And then let me ask you if you think I'm gonna stand for being knocked by a tanktown critic," he said, in a toneless voice; "look here, here's Buffalo, Chicago, Saint Looey, Philadelphia, Frisco, besides New York. Here's the best publications in the business, *Variety,* the *Billboard,* they all broke down and admitted that Danny Dickerson knows his stuff. So you don't think so, hey? That's all I wanta ask you."

"No, I don't," said Miranda, as bluntly as she could, "and I can't stop to talk about it."

5. English nurse (1820–1910), pioneer of modern   War (1853–1856).
   nursing, first earned fame during the Crimean

The little man leaned nearer, his voice shook as if he had been nervous for a long time. "Look here, what was there you didn't like about me? Tell me that."

Miranda said, "You shouldn't pay any attention at all. What does it matter what I think?"

"I don't care what you think, it ain't that," said the little man, "but these things get round and booking agencies back East don't know how it is out here. We get panned in the sticks and they think it's the same as getting panned in Chicago, see? They don't know the difference. They don't know that the more high class an act is the more the hick critics pan it. But I've been called the best in the business by the best in the business and I wanta know what you think is wrong with me."

Chuck said, "Come on, Miranda, curtain's going up." Miranda handed the little man his clippings, they were mostly ten years old, and tried to edge past him. He stepped before her again and said without much conviction, "If you was a man I'd knock your block off." Chuck got up at that and lounged over, taking his hands out of his pockets, and said, "Now you've done your song and dance you'd better get out. Get the hell out now before I throw you downstairs."

The little man pulled at the top of his tie, a small blue tie with red polka dots, slightly frayed at the knot. He pulled it straight and repeated as if he had rehearsed it, "Come out in the alley." The tears filled his thickened red lids. Chuck said, "Ah, shut up," and followed Miranda, who was running towards the stairs. He overtook her on the sidewalk. "I left him sniveling and shuffling his publicity trying to find the joker," said Chuck, "the poor old heel."

Miranda said, "There's too much of everything in this world just now. I'd like to sit down here on the curb, Chuck, and die, and never again see—I wish I could lose my memory and forget my own name . . . I wish—"

Chuck said, "Toughen up, Miranda. This is no time to cave in. Forget that fellow. For every hundred people in show business, there are ninety-nine like him. But you don't manage right, anyway. You bring it on yourself. All you have to do is play up the headliners, and you needn't even mention the also-rans. Try to keep in mind that Rypinsky has got show business cornered in this town; please Rypinsky and you'll please the advertising department, please them and you'll get a raise. Hand-in-glove, my poor dumb child, will you never learn?"

"I seem to keep learning all the wrong things," said Miranda, hopelessly.

"You do for a fact," Chuck told her cheerfully. "You are as good at it as I ever saw. Now do you feel better?"

"This is a rotten show you've invited me to," said Chuck. "Now what are you going to do about it? If I were writing it up, I'd—"

"Do write it up," said Miranda. "You write it up this time. I'm getting ready to leave, anyway, but don't tell anybody yet."

"You mean it? All my life," said Chuck, "I've yearned to be a so-called dramatic critic on a hick newspaper, and this is positively my first chance."

"Better take it," Miranda told him. "It may be your last." She thought, This is the beginning of the end of something. Something terrible is going to happen to me. I shan't need bread and butter where I'm going. I'll will it to Chuck, he has a venerable father to buy hooch for. I hope they let him have it. Oh, Adam, I hope I see you once more before I go under with whatever is the matter with me. "I wish the war were over," she said to Chuck, as if they had been talking about that. "I wish it were over and I wish it had never begun."

Chuck had got out his pad and pencil and was already writing his review. What she had said seemed safe enough but how would he take it? "I don't care how it started or when it ends," said Chuck, scribbling away, "I'm not going to be there."

All the rejected men talked like that, thought Miranda. War was the one thing they wanted, now they couldn't have it. Maybe they had wanted badly to go, some of them. All of them had a sidelong eye for the women they talked with about it, a guarded resentment which said, "Don't pin a white feather on me, you bloodthirsty female. I've offered my meat to the crows and they won't have it." The worst thing about war for the stay-at-homes is there isn't anyone to talk to any more. The Lusk Committee will get you if you don't watch out. Bread will win the war. Work will win, sugar will win, peach pits will win the war. Nonsense. *Not* nonsense, I tell you, there's some kind of valuable high explosive to be got out of peach pits. So all the happy housewives hurry during the canning season to lay their baskets of peach pits on the altar of their country. It keeps them busy and makes them feel useful, and all these women running wild with the men away are dangerous, if they aren't given something to keep their little minds out of mischief. So rows of young girls, the intact cradles of the future, with their pure serious faces framed becomingly in Red Cross wimples, roll cock-eyed bandages that will never reach a base hospital, and knit sweaters that will never warm a manly chest, their minds dwelling lovingly on all the blood and mud and the next dance at the Acanthus Club for the officers of the flying corps. Keeping still and quiet will win the war.

"I'm simply not going to be there," said Chuck, absorbed in his review. No, Adam will be there, thought Miranda. She slipped down in the chair and leaned her head against the dusty plush, closed her eyes and faced for one instant that was a lifetime the certain, the overwhelming and awful knowledge that there was nothing at all ahead for Adam and for her. Nothing. She opened her eyes and held her hands together palms up, gazing at them and trying to understand oblivion.

"Now look at this," said Chuck, for the lights had come on and the audience was rustling and talking again. "I've got it all done, even before the headliner comes on. It's old Stella Mayhew, and she's always good, she's been good for forty years, and she's going to sing 'O the blues ain't nothin' but the easy-going heart disease.' That's all you need to know about her. Now just glance over this. Would you be willing to sign it?"

Miranda took the pages and stared at them conscientiously, turning them over, she hoped, at the right moment, and gave them back. "Yes, Chuck, yes, I'd sign that. But I won't. We must tell Bill you wrote it, because it's your start, maybe."

"You don't half appreciate it," said Chuck. "You read it too fast. Here, listen to this—" and he began to mutter excitedly. While he was reading she watched his face. It was a pleasant face with some kind of spark of life in it, and a good severity in the modeling of the brow above the nose. For the first time since she had known him she wondered what Chuck was thinking about. He looked preoccupied and unhappy, he wasn't so frivolous as he sounded. The people were crowding into the aisle, bringing out their cigarette cases ready to strike a match the instant they reached the lobby; women with waved hair clutched at their wraps, men stretched their chins to ease them of their stiff collars, and Chuck said, "We might as well go now." Miranda, buttoning her jacket, stepped into the moving crowd, thinking, What did I ever know about them? There must be a great many of them here who think as I do, and we dare not say a word to each other of our desperation, we are speechless animals letting ourselves be destroyed, and why? Does anybody here believe the things we say to each other?

Stretched in unease on the ridge of the wicker couch in the cloakroom, Miranda waited for time to pass and leave Adam with her. Time seemed to proceed with more than usual eccentricity, leaving twilight gaps in her mind for thirty minutes which seemed like a second, and then hard flashes of light that shone clearly on her watch proving that three minutes is an intolerable stretch of waiting, as if she were hanging by her thumbs. At last it was reasonable to imagine Adam stepping out of the house in the early darkness into the blue mist that might soon be rain, he would be on the way, and there was nothing to think about him, after all. There was only the wish to see him and the fear, the present threat, of not seeing him again; for every step they took towards each other seemed perilous, drawing them apart instead of together, as a swimmer in spite of his most determined strokes is yet drawn slowly backward by the tide. "I don't want to love," she would think in spite of herself, "not Adam, there is no time and we are not ready for it and yet this is all we have—"

And there he was on the sidewalk, with his foot on the first step, and Miranda almost ran down to meet him. Adam, holding her hands, asked, "Do you feel well now? Are you hungry? Are you tired? Will you feel like dancing after the show?"

"Yes to everything," said Miranda, "yes, yes. . . ." Her head was like a feather, and she steadied herself on his arm. The mist was still mist that might be rain later, and though the air was sharp and clean in her mouth, it did not, she decided, make breathing any easier. "I hope the show is good, or at least funny," she told him, "but I promise nothing."

It was a long, dreary play, but Adam and Miranda sat very quietly together waiting patiently for it to be over. Adam carefully and seriously pulled off her glove and held her hand as if he were accustomed to holding her hand in theaters. Once they turned and their eyes met, but only once, and the two pairs of eyes were equally steady and noncommittal. A deep tremor set up in Miranda, and she set about resisting herself methodically as if she were closing windows and doors and fastening down curtains against a rising storm. Adam sat watching the monotonous play with a strange shining excitement, his face quite fixed and still.

When the curtain rose for the third act, the third act did not take place at once. There was instead disclosed a backdrop almost covered with an American flag improperly and disrespectfully exposed, nailed at each upper corner, gathered in the middle and nailed again, sagging dustily. Before it posed a local dollar-a-year man, now doing his bit as a Liberty Bond salesman. He was an ordinary man past middle life, with a neat little melon buttoned into his trousers and waistcoat, an opinionated tight mouth, a face and figure in which nothing could be read save the inept sensual record of fifty years. But for once in his life he was an important fellow in an impressive situation, and he reveled, rolling his words in an actorish tone.

"Looks like a penguin," said Adam. They moved, smiled at each other, Miranda reclaimed her hand, Adam folded his together and they prepared to wear their way again through the same old moldy speech with the same old dusty backdrop. Miranda tried not to listen, but she heard. These vile Huns—glorious Belleau Wood—our keyword is Sacrifice—Martyred Belgium—give till it hurts—our noble boys Over There—Big Berthas—the death of civilization—the Boche—

"My head aches," whispered Miranda. "Oh, why won't he hush?"

"He won't," whispered Adam. "I'll get you some aspirin."

"In Flanders Field the poppies grow, Between the crosses row on row"—"He's getting into the home stretch," whispered Adam—atrocities, innocent babes hoisted on Boche bayonets—your child and my child—if our children are spared these things, then let us say with all reverence that these dead have not died in vain—the war, the *war,* the WAR to end WAR, war for Democracy, for humanity, a safe world forever and ever—and to prove our faith in Democracy to each other, and to the world, let everybody get together and buy Liberty Bonds and do without sugar and wool socks—was that it? Miranda asked herself, Say that over, I didn't catch the last line. Did you mention Adam? If you didn't I'm not interested. What about Adam, you little pig? And what are we going to sing this time, "Tipperary" or "There's a Long, Long Trail"? Oh, please do let the show go on and get over with. I must write a piece about it before I can go dancing with Adam and we have no time. Coal, oil, iron, gold, international finance, why don't you tell us about them, you little liar?

The audience rose and sang, "There's a Long, Long Trail Awinding," their opened mouths black and faces pallid in the reflected footlights; some of the faces grimaced and wept and had shining streaks like snail's tracks on them. Adam and Miranda joined in at the tops of their voices, grinning shamefacedly at each other once or twice.

In the street, they lit their cigarettes and walked slowly as always. "Just another nasty old man who would like to see the young ones killed," said Miranda in a low voice; "the tom-cats try to eat the little tom-kittens, you know. They don't fool you really, do they, Adam?"

The young people were talking like that about the business by then. They felt they were seeing pretty clearly through that game. She went on, "I hate these potbellied baldheads, too fat, too old, too cowardly, to go to war themselves, they know they're safe; it's you they are sending instead—"

Adam turned eyes of genuine surprise upon her. "Oh, *that* one," he said. "Now what could the poor sap do if they did take him? It's not his fault," he explained, "he can't do anything but talk." His pride in his youth, his forbearance and tolerance and contempt for that unlucky being breathed out of his very pores as he strolled, straight and relaxed in his strength. "What *could* you expect of him, Miranda?"

She spoke his name often, and he spoke hers rarely. The little shock of pleasure the sound of her name in his mouth gave her stopped her answer. For a moment she hesitated, and began at another point of attack. "Adam," she said, "the worst of war is the fear and suspicion and the awful expression in all the eyes you meet . . . as if they had pulled down the shutters over their minds and their hearts and were peering out at you, ready to leap if you make one gesture or say one word they do not understand instantly. It frightens me; I live in fear too, and no one should have to live in fear. It's the skulking about, and the lying. It's what war does to the mind and the heart, Adam, and you can't separate these two—what it does to them is worse than what it can do to the body."

Adam said soberly, after a moment, "Oh, yes, but suppose one comes back whole? The mind and the heart sometimes get another chance, but if anything happens to the poor old human frame, why, it's just out of luck, that's all."

"Oh, yes," mimicked Miranda. "It's just out of luck, that's all."

"If I didn't go," said Adam, in a matter-of-fact voice, "I couldn't look myself in the face."

So that's all settled. With her fingers flattened on his arm, Miranda was silent, thinking about Adam. No, there was no resentment or revolt in him. Pure, she thought, all the way through, flawless, complete, as the sacrificial lamb must be. The sacrificial lamb strode along casually, accommodating his long pace to hers, keeping her on the inside of the walk in the good American style, helping her across street corners as if she were a cripple—"I hope we don't come to a mud puddle, he'll carry me over it"—giving off whiffs of tobacco smoke, a manly smell of scentless soap, freshly cleaned leather and freshly washed skin, breathing through his nose and carrying his chest easily. He threw back his head and smiled into the sky which still misted, promising rain. "Oh, boy," he said, "what a night. Can't you hurry that review of yours so we can get started?"

He waited for her before a cup of coffee in the restaurant next to the pressroom, nicknamed The Greasy Spoon. When she came down at last, freshly washed and combed and powdered, she saw Adam first, sitting near the dingy big window, face turned to the street, but looking down. It was an extraordinary face, smooth and fine and golden in the shabby light, but now set in a blind melancholy, a look of pained suspense and disillusion. For just one split second she got a glimpse of Adam when he would have been older, the face of the man he would not live to be. He saw her then, rose, and the bright glow was there.

Adam pulled their chairs together at their table; they drank hot tea and listened to the orchestra jazzing "Pack Up Your Troubles."

"In an old kit bag, and smoil, smoil, smoil," shouted half a dozen boys under the draft age, gathered around a table near the orchestra. They yelled incoherently, laughed in great hysterical bursts of something that appeared to be merriment, and passed around under the tablecloth flat bottles containing a clear liquid—for in this western city founded and built by roaring drunken miners, no one was allowed to take his alcohol openly—splashed it into their tumblers of ginger ale, and went on singing, "It's a Long Way to Tipperary." When the tune changed to "Madelon," Adam said, "Let's dance." It was a tawdry little place, crowded and hot and full of smoke, but there was nothing better. The music was gay; and life is completely crazy anyway, thought Miranda, so what does it matter? This is what we have, Adam and I, this is all we're going to get, this is the way it is with us. She wanted to say, "Adam, come out of your dream and listen to me. I have pains in my chest and my head and my heart and they're real. I am in pain all over, and you are in such danger as I can't bear to think about, and why can we not save each other?" When her hand tightened on his shoulder his arm tightened about her waist instantly, and stayed there, holding firmly. They said nothing but smiled continually at each other, odd changing smiles as though they had found a new language. Miranda, her face near Adam's shoulder, noticed a dark young pair sitting at a corner table, each with an arm around the waist of the other, their heads together, their eyes staring at the same thing, whatever it was, that hovered in space before them. Her right hand lay on the table, his hand over it, and her face was a blur with weeping. Now and then he raised her hand and kissed it, and set it down and held it, and her eyes would fill again. They were not shameless, they had merely forgotten where they were, or they had no other place to go, perhaps. They said not a word, and the small pantomime repeated itself, like a melancholy short film running monotonously over and over again. Miranda envied them. She envied that girl. At least she can weep if that helps, and he does not even have to ask, What is the matter? Tell me. They had cups of coffee before them, and after a long while—Miranda and Adam had danced and sat down again twice—when the coffee was quite cold, they drank it suddenly, then embraced as before, without a word and scarcely a glance at each other. Something was done and settled between them, at least; it was enviable, enviable, that they could sit quietly together and have the same expression on their faces while they looked into the hell they shared, no matter what kind of hell, it was theirs, they were together.

At the table nearest Adam and Miranda a young woman was leaning on her elbow, telling her young man a story. "And I don't like him because he's too fresh. He kept on asking me to take a drink and I kept telling him, I don't drink and he said, Now look here, I want a drink the worst way and I think it's mean of you not to drink with me, I can't sit up here and drink by myself, he said. I told him, You're not by yourself in the first place; I like that, I said, and if you want a drink go ahead and have it, I told him, why drag *me* in? So he called the waiter and ordered ginger ale and two glasses and I drank straight ginger ale like I always do but he poured a shot of hooch in his. He was awfully proud of that hooch, said he made it himself out of potatoes. Nice homemade likker, warm from the pipe, he told me, three drops of this and your ginger ale will taste like Mumm's Extry. But I said, No, and I mean no, can't you get that through your bean? He took another drink and said, Ah, come on, honey, don't be so stubborn, this'll make your shimmy shake. So I just got tired of the argument, and I said, I don't need to drink, to shake my shimmy, I can strut my stuff on tea, I said. Well, why don't you then, he wanted to know, and I just told him—"

She knew she had been asleep for a long time when all at once without even a warning footstep or creak of the door hinge, Adam was in the room turning on the light, and she knew it was he, though at first she was blinded and turned her head away. He came over at once and sat on the side of the bed and began to talk as if he were going on with something they had been talking about before. He crumpled a square of paper and tossed it in the fireplace.

"You didn't get my note," he said. "I left it under the door. I was called back suddenly to camp for a lot of inoculations. They kept me longer than I expected, I was late. I called the office and they told me you were not coming in today. I called Miss Hobbe here and she said you were in bed and couldn't come to the telephone. Did she give you my message?"

"No," said Miranda drowsily, "but I think I have been asleep all day. Oh, I do remember. There was a doctor here. Bill sent him. I was at the telephone once, for Bill told me he would send me an ambulance and have me taken to the hospital. The doctor tapped my chest and left a prescription and said he would be back, but he hasn't come."

"Where is it, the prescription?" asked Adam.

"I don't know. He left it, though, I saw him."

Adam moved about searching the tables and the mantelpiece. "Here it is," he said. "I'll be back in a few minutes. I must look for an all-night drug store. It's after one o'clock. Good-by."

Good-by, good-by. Miranda watched the door where he had disappeared for quite a while, then closed her eyes, and thought, When I am not here I cannot remember anything about this room where I have lived for nearly a year, except that the curtains are too thin and there was never any way of shutting out the morning light. Miss Hobbe had promised heavier curtains, but they had never appeared. When Miranda in her dressing gown had been at the telephone that morning, Miss Hobbe had passed through, carrying a tray. She was a little red-haired nervously friendly creature, and her manner said all too plainly that the place was not paying and she was on the ragged edge.

"My dear *child*," she said sharply, with a glance at Miranda's attire, "what is the matter?"

Miranda, with the receiver to her ear, said, "Influenza, I think."

"*Horrors*," said Miss Hobbe, in a whisper, and the tray wavered in her hands. "Go back to bed at once . . . go at *once!*"

"I must talk to Bill first," Miranda had told her, and Miss Hobbe had hurried on and had not returned. Bill had shouted directions at her, promising everything, doctor, nurse, ambulance, hospital, her check every week as usual, everything, but she was to get back to bed and stay there. She dropped into bed, thinking that Bill was the only person she had ever seen who actually tore his own hair when he was excited enough . . . I suppose I should ask to be sent home, she thought, it's a respectable old custom to inflict your death on the family if you can manage it. No, I'll stay here, this is my business, but not in this room, I hope . . . I wish I were in the cold mountains in the snow, that's what I should like best; and all about her rose the measured ranges of the Rockies wearing their perpetual snow, their majestic blue laurels of cloud, chilling her to the bone with their sharp breath. Oh, no, I must have warmth—and her memory turned and roved after another place she had known first and loved best, that now she could see only in drifting fragments of palm and cedar, dark shadows and a sky that warmed without dazzling, as this strange sky had dazzled without warming her; there was the long slow wavering of gray moss in the drowsy oak shade, the spacious hovering of buzzards overhead, the smell of crushed water herbs along a bank, and without warning a broad tranquil river into which flowed all the rivers she had known. The walls shelved away in one deliberate silent movement on either side, and a tall sailing ship was moored near by, with a gangplank weathered to blackness touching the foot of her bed. Back of the ship was jungle, and even as it appeared before her, she knew it was all she had ever read or had been told or felt or thought about jungles; a writhing terribly alive and secret place of death, creeping with tangles of spotted serpents, rainbow-colored birds with malign eyes, leopards with humanly wise faces and extravagantly crested lions; screaming long-armed monkeys tumbling among broad fleshy leaves that glowed with sulphur-colored light and exuded the ichor of death, and rotting trunks of unfamiliar trees sprawled in crawling slime. Without surprise, watching from her pillow, she saw herself run swiftly down this gangplank to the slanting deck, and standing there, she leaned on the rail and waved gaily to herself in bed, and the slender ship spread its wings and sailed away into the jungle. The air trembled with the shattering scream and the hoarse bellow of voices all crying together, rolling and colliding above her like ragged storm-clouds, and the words became two words only rising and falling and clamoring about her head. Danger, danger, danger, the voices said, and War, war, war. There was her door half open, Adam standing with his hand on the knob, and Miss Hobbe with her face all out of shape with terror was crying shrilly, "I tell you, they must come for her *now*, or I'll put her on the sidewalk . . . . I tell you, this is a plague, a plague, my God, and I've got a houseful of people to think about!"

Adam said, "I know that. They'll come for her tomorrow morning."

"Tomorrow morning, my God, they'd better come now!"

"They can't get an ambulance," said Adam, "and there aren't any beds. And we can't find a doctor or a nurse. They're all busy. That's all there is to it. You stay out of the room, and I'll look after her."

"Yes, you'll look after her, I can see that," said Miss Hobbe, in a particularly unpleasant tone.

"Yes, that's what I said," answered Adam, drily, "and you keep out."

He closed the door carefully. He was carrying an assortment of misshapen packages, and his face was astonishingly impassive.

"Did you hear that?" he asked, leaning over and speaking very quietly.

"Most of it," said Miranda, "it's a nice prospect, isn't it?"

"I've got your medicine," said Adam, "and you're to begin with it this minute. She can't put you out."

"So it's really as bad as that," said Miranda.

"It's as bad as anything can be," said Adam, "all the theaters and nearly all the shops and restaurants are closed, and the streets have been full of funerals all day and ambulances all night—"

"But not one for me," said Miranda, feeling hilarious and light-headed. She sat up and beat her pillow into shape and reached for her robe. "I'm glad you're here, I've been having a nightmare. Give me a cigarette, will you, and light one for yourself and open all the windows and sit near one of them. You're running a risk," she told him, "don't you know that? Why do you do it?"

"Never mind," said Adam, "take your medicine," and offered her two large cherry-colored pills. She swallowed them promptly and instantly vomited them up. *"Do* excuse me," she said, beginning to laugh. "I'm so sorry." Adam without a word and with a very concerned expression washed her face with a wet towel, gave her some cracked ice from one of the packages, and firmly offered her two more pills. "That's what they always did at home," she explained to him, "and it worked." Crushed with humiliation, she put her hands over her face and laughed again, painfully.

"There are two more kinds yet," said Adam, pulling her hands from her face and lifting her chin. "You've hardly begun. And I've got other things, like orange juice and ice cream—they told me to feed you ice cream—and coffee in a thermos bottle, and a thermometer. You have to work through the whole lot so you'd better take it easy."

"This time last night we were dancing," said Miranda, and drank something from a spoon. Her eyes followed him about the room, as he did things for her with an absent-minded face, like a man alone; now and again he would come back, and slipping his hand under her head, would hold a cup or a tumbler to her mouth, and she drank, and followed him with her eyes again, without a clear notion of what was happening.

"Adam," she said, "I've just thought of something. Maybe they forgot St. Luke's Hospital. Call the sisters there and ask them not to be so selfish with their silly old rooms. Tell them I only want a very small dark ugly one for three days, or less. Do try them, Adam."

He believed, apparently, that she was still more or less in her right mind, for she heard him at the telephone explaining in his deliberate voice. He was back again almost at once, saying, "This seems to be my day for getting mixed up with peevish old maids. The sister said that even if they had a room you couldn't have it without doctor's orders. But they didn't have one, anyway. She was pretty sour about it."

"Well," said Miranda in a thick voice, "I think that's abominably rude and mean, don't you?" She sat up with a wild gesture of both arms, and began to retch again, violently.

"Hold it, as you were," called Adam, fetching the basin. He held her head, washed her face and hands with ice water, put her head straight on the pillow, and went over and looked out of the window. "Well," he said at last, sitting beside her again, "they haven't got a room. They haven't got a bed. They haven't even got a baby crib, the way she talked. So I think that's straight enough, and we may as well dig in."

"Isn't the ambulance coming?"

"Tomorrow, maybe."

He took off his tunic and hung it on the back of a chair. Kneeling before the fireplace, he began carefully to set kindling sticks in the shape of an Indian tepee, with a little paper in the center for them to lean upon. He lighted this and placed other sticks upon them, and larger bits of wood. When they were going nicely he added still heavier wood, and coal a few lumps at a time, until there was a good blaze, and a fire that would not need rekindling. He rose and dusted his hands together, the fire illuminated him from the back and his hair shone.

"Adam," said Miranda, "I think you're very beautiful." He laughed out at this, and shook his head at her. "What a hell of a word," he said, "for me." "It was the first that occurred to me," she said, drawing up on her elbow to catch the warmth of the blaze. "That's a good job, that fire."

He sat on the bed again, dragging up a chair and putting his feet on the rungs. They smiled at each other for the first time since he had come in that night. "How do you feel now?" he asked.

"Better, much better," she told him. "Let's talk. Let's tell each other what we meant to do."

"You tell me first," said Adam. "I want to know about you."

"You'd get the notion I had a very sad life," she said, "and perhaps it was, but I'd be glad enough to have it now. If I could have it back, it would be easy to be happy about almost anything at all. That's not true, but that's the way I feel now." After a pause, she said, "There's nothing to tell, after all, if it ends now, for all this time I was getting ready for something that was going to happen later, when the time came. So now it's nothing much."

"But it must have been worth having until now, wasn't it?" he asked seriously as if it were something important to know.

"Not if this is all," she repeated obstinately.

"Weren't you ever—happy?" asked Adam, and he was plainly afraid of the word; he was shy of it as he was of the word *love*, he seemed never to have spoken it before, and was uncertain of its sound or meaning.

"I don't know," she said, "I just lived and never thought about it. I remember things I liked, though, and things I hoped for."

"I was going to be an electrical engineer," said Adam. He stopped short. "And I shall finish up when I get back," he added, after a moment.

"Don't you love being alive?" asked Miranda. "Don't you love weather and the colors at different times of the day, and all the sounds and noises like children screaming in the next lot, and automobile horns and little bands playing in the street and the smell of food cooking?"

"I love to swim, too," said Adam.

"So do I," said Miranda; "we never did swim together."

"Do you remember any prayers?" she asked him suddenly. "Did you ever learn anything at Sunday School?"

"Not much," confessed Adam without contrition. "Well, the Lord's Prayer."

"Yes, and there's Hail Mary," she said, "and the really useful one beginning, I confess to Almighty God and to blessed Mary ever virgin and to the holy Apostles Peter and Paul—"

"Catholic," he commented.

"Prayers just the same, you big Methodist. I'll bet you *are* a Methodist."

"No, Presbyterian."

"Well, what others do you remember?"

"Now I lay me down to sleep—" said Adam.

"Yes, that one, and Blessed Jesus meek and mild—you see that my religious education wasn't neglected either. I even know a prayer beginning O Apollo. Want to hear it?"

"No," said Adam, "you're making fun."

"I'm not," said Miranda, "I'm trying to keep from going to sleep. I'm afraid to go to sleep, I may not wake up. Don't let me go to sleep, Adam. Do you know Matthew, Mark, Luke and John? Bless the bed I lie upon?"

"If I should die before I wake, I pray the Lord my soul to take. Is that it?" asked Adam. "It doesn't sound right, somehow."

"Light me a cigarette, please, and move over and sit near the window. We keep forgetting about fresh air. You must have it." He lighted the cigarette and held it to her lips. She took it between her fingers and dropped it under the edge of her pillow. He found it and crushed it out in the saucer under the water tumbler. Her head swam in darkness for an instant, cleared, and she sat up in panic, throwing off the covers and breaking into a sweat. Adam leaped up with an alarmed face, and almost at once was holding a cup of hot coffee to her mouth.

"You must have some too," she told him, quiet again, and they sat huddled together on the edge of the bed, drinking coffee in silence.

Adam said, "You must lie down again. You're awake now."

"Let's sing," said Miranda. "I know an old spiritual, I can remember some of the words." She spoke in a natural voice. "I'm fine now." She began in a hoarse whisper, " 'Pale horse, pale rider, done taken my lover away . . .' Do you know that song?"

"Yes," said Adam, "I heard Negroes in Texas sing it, in an oil field."

"I heard them sing it in a cotton field," she said; "it's a good song."

They sang that line together. "But I can't remember what comes next," said Adam.

" 'Pale horse, pale rider,' " said Miranda, "(We really need a good banjo) 'done taken my lover away—' " Her voice cleared and she said, "But we ought to get on with it. What's the next line?"

"There's a lot more to it than that," said Adam, "about forty verses, the rider done taken away mammy, pappy, brother, sister, the whole family besides the lover—"

"But not the singer, not yet," said Miranda. "Death always leaves one singer to mourn. 'Death,' " she sang, " 'oh, leave one singer to mourn—' "

" 'Pale horse, pale rider,' " chanted Adam, coming in on the beat, " 'done taken my lover away!' (I think we're good, I think we ought to get up an act—)"

"Go in Hut Service," said Miranda, "entertain the poor defenseless heroes Over There."

"We'll play banjos," said Adam; "I always wanted to play the banjo."

Miranda sighed, and lay back on the pillow and thought, I must give up, I can't hold out any longer. There was only that pain, only that room, and only Adam. There were no longer any multiple planes of living, no tough filaments of memory and hope pulling taut backwards and forwards holding her upright between them. There was only this one moment and it was a dream of time, and Adam's face, very near hers, eyes still and intent, was a shadow, and there was to be nothing more. . . .

"Adam," she said out of the heavy soft darkness that drew her down, down, "I love you, and I was hoping you would say that to me, too."

He lay down beside her with his arm under her shoulder, and pressed his smooth face against hers, his mouth moved towards her mouth and stopped. "Can you hear what I am saying? . . . What do you think I have been trying to tell you all this time?"

She turned towards him, the cloud cleared and she saw his face for an instant. He pulled the covers about her and held her, and said, "Go to sleep, darling, darling, if you will go to sleep now for one hour I will wake you up and bring you hot coffee and tomorrow we will find somebody to help. I love you, go to sleep—"

Almost with no warning at all, she floated into the darkness, holding his hand, in sleep that was not sleep but clear evening light in a small green wood, an angry dangerous wood full of inhuman concealed voices singing sharply like the whine of arrows and she saw Adam transfixed by a flight of these singing arrows that struck him in the heart and passed shrilly cutting their path through the leaves. Adam fell straight back before her eyes, and rose again unwounded and alive; another flight of arrows loosed from the invisible bow struck him again and he fell, and yet he was there before her untouched in a perpetual death and resurrection. She threw herself before him, angrily and selfishly she interposed between him and the track of the arrow, crying, No, no, like a child cheated in a game, It's my turn now, why must you always be the one to die? and the arrows struck her cleanly through the heart and through his body and he lay dead, and she still lived, and the wood whistled and sang and shouted, every branch and leaf and blade of grass had its own terrible accusing voice. She ran then, and Adam caught her in the middle of the room, running, and said, "Darling, I must have been asleep too. What happened, you screamed terribly?"

After he had helped her to settle again, she sat with her knees drawn up under her chin, resting her head on her folded arms and began carefully searching for her words because it was important to explain clearly. "It was a very odd sort of dream, I don't know why it could have frightened me. There was something about an old-fashioned valentine. There were two hearts carved on a tree, pierced by the same arrow—you know, Adam—"

"Yes, I know, honey," he said in the gentlest sort of way, and sat kissing her on the cheek and forehead with a kind of accustomedness, as if he had been kissing her for years, "one of those lace paper things."

"Yes, and yet they were alive, and were us, you understand—this doesn't seem to be quite the way it was, but it was something like that. It was in a wood—"

"Yes," said Adam. He got up and put on his tunic and gathered up the thermos bottle. "I'm going back to that little stand and get us some ice cream and hot coffee," he told her, "and I'll be back in five minutes, and you keep quiet. Good-by for five minutes," he said, holding her chin in the palm of his hand and trying to catch her eye, "and you be very quiet."

"Good-by," she said. "I'm awake again." But she was not, and the two alert young internes from the County hospital who had arrived, after frantic urgings from the noisy city editor of the Blue Mountain *News*, to carry her away in a police ambulance, decided that they had better go down and get the stretcher. Their voices roused her, she sat up, got out of bed at once and stood glancing about brightly. "Why, you're all right," said the darker and stouter of the two young men, both extremely fit and competent-looking in their white clothes, each with a flower in his buttonhole. "I'll just carry you." He unfolded a white blanket and wrapped it around her. She gathered up the folds and asked, "But where is Adam?" taking hold of the doctor's arm. He laid a hand on her drenched forehead, shook his head, and gave her a shrewd look. "Adam?"

"Yes," Miranda told him, lowering her voice confidentially, "he was here and now he is gone."

"Oh, he'll be back," the interne told her easily, "he's just gone round the block to get cigarettes. Don't worry about Adam. He's the least of your troubles."

"Will he know where to find me?" she asked, still holding back.

"We'll leave him a note," said the interne. "Come now, it's time we got out of here."

He lifted and swung her up to his shoulder. "I feel very badly," she told him; "I don't know why."

"I'll bet you do," said he, stepping out carefully, the other doctor going before them, and feeling for the first step of the stairs. "Put your arms around my neck," he instructed her. "It won't do you any harm and it's a great help to me."

"What's your name?" Miranda asked as the other doctor opened the front door and they stepped out into the frosty sweet air.

"Hildesheim," he said, in the tone of one humoring a child.

"Well, Dr. Hildesheim, aren't we in a pretty mess?"

"We certainly are," said Dr. Hildesheim.

The second young interne, still quite fresh and dapper in his white coat, though his carnation was withering at the edges, was leaning over listening to her breathing through a stethoscope, whistling thinly, "There's a Long, Long Trail—" From time to time he tapped her ribs smartly with two fingers, whistling. Miranda observed him for a few moments until she fixed his bright busy hazel eye not four inches from hers. "I'm not unconscious," she explained, "I know what I want to say." Then to her horror she heard herself babbling nonsense, knowing it was nonsense though she could not hear what she was saying. The flicker of attention in the eye near her vanished, the second interne went on tapping and listening, hissing softly under his breath.

"I wish you'd stop whistling," she said clearly. The sound stopped. "It's a beastly tune," she added. Anything, anything at all to keep her small hold on the life of human beings, a clear line of communication, no matter what, between her and the receding world. "Please let me see Dr. Hildesheim," she said, "I have something important to say to him. I must say it now." The second interne vanished. He did not walk away, he fled into the air without a sound, and Dr. Hildesheim's face appeared in his stead.

"Dr. Hildesheim, I want to ask you about Adam."

"That young man? He's been here, and left you a note, and has gone again," said Dr. Hildesheim, "and he'll be back tomorrow and the day after." His tone was altogether too merry and flippant.

"I don't believe you," said Miranda, bitterly, closing her lips and eyes and hoping she might not weep.

"Miss Tanner," called the doctor, "have you got that note?"

Miss Tanner appeared beside her, handed her an unsealed envelope, took it back, unfolded the note and gave it to her.

"I can't see it," said Miranda, after a pained search of the page full of hasty scratches in black ink.

"Here, I'll read it," said Miss Tanner. "It says, 'They came and took you while I was away and now they will not let me see you. Maybe tomorrow they will, with my love, Adam,'" read Miss Tanner in a firm dry voice, pronouncing the words distinctly. "Now, do you see?" she asked soothingly.

Miranda, hearing the words one by one, forgot them one by one. "Oh, read it again, what does it say?" she called out over the silence that pressed upon her, reaching towards the dancing words that just escaped as she almost touched them. "That will do," said Dr. Hildesheim, calmly authoritarian. "Where is that bed?"

"There is no bed yet," said Miss Tanner, as if she said, We are short of oranges. Dr. Hildesheim said, "Well, we'll manage something," and Miss Tanner drew the narrow trestle with bright crossed metal supports and small rubbery wheels into a deep jut of the corridor, out of the way of the swift white figures darting about, whirling and skimming like water flies all in silence. The white walls rose sheer as cliffs, a dozen frosted moons followed each other in perfect self-possession down a white lane and dropped mutely one by one into a snowy abyss.

What is this whiteness and silence but the absence of pain? Miranda lay lifting the nap of her white blanket softly between eased fingers, watching a dance of tall deliberate shadows moving behind a wide screen of sheets spread upon a frame. It was there, near her, on her side of the wall where she could see it clearly and enjoy it, and it was so beautiful she had no curiosity as to its meaning. Two dark figures nodded, bent, curtsied to each other, retreated and bowed again, lifted long arms and spread great hands against the white shadow of the screen; then with a single round movement, the sheets were folded back, disclosing two speechless men in white, standing, and another speechless man in white, lying on the bare springs of a white iron bed. The man on the springs was swathed smoothly from head to foot in white, with folded bands across the face, and a large stiff bow like merry rabbit ears dangled at the crown of his head.

The two living men lifted a mattress standing hunched against the wall, spread it tenderly and exactly over the dead man. Wordless and white they vanished down the corridor, pushing the wheeled bed before them. It had been an entrancing and leisurely spectacle, but now it was over. A pallid white fog rose in their wake insinuatingly and floated before Miranda's eyes, a fog in which was concealed all terror and all weariness, all the wrung faces and twisted backs and broken feet of abused, outraged living things, all the shapes of their confused pain and their estranged hearts; the fog might part at any moment and loose the horde of human torments. She put up her hands and said, Not yet, not yet, but it was too late. The fog parted and two executioners, white clad, moved towards her pushing between them with marvelously deft and practiced hands the misshapen figure of an old man in filthy rags whose scanty beard waggled under his opened mouth as he bowed his back and braced his feet to resist and delay the fate they had prepared for him. In a high weeping voice he was trying to explain to them that the crime of which he was accused did not merit the punishment he was about to receive; and except for this whining cry there was silence as they advanced. The soiled cracked bowls of the old man's hands were held before him beseechingly as a beggar's as he said, "Before God I am not guilty," but they held his arms and drew him onward, passed, and were gone.

The road to death is a long march beset with all evils, and the heart fails little by little at each new terror, the bones rebel at each step, the mind sets up its own bitter resistance and to what end? The barriers sink one by one, and no covering of the eyes shuts out the landscape of disaster, nor the sight of crimes committed there. Across the field came Dr. Hildesheim, his face a skull beneath his German helmet, carrying a naked infant writhing on the point of his bayonet, and a huge stone pot marked Poison in Gothic letters. He stopped before the well that Miranda remembered in a pasture on her father's farm, a well once dry but now bubbling with living water, and into its pure depths he threw the child and the poison, and the violated water sank back soundlessly into the earth. Miranda, screaming, ran with her arms above her head; her voice echoed and came back to her like a wolf's howl, Hildesheim is a Boche, a spy, a Hun, kill him, kill him before he kills you. . . . She woke howling, she heard the foul words accusing Dr. Hildesheim tumbling from her mouth; opened her eyes and knew she was in a bed in a small white room, with Dr. Hildesheim sitting beside her, two firm fingers on her pulse. His hair was brushed sleekly and his buttonhole flower was fresh. Stars gleamed through the window, and Dr. Hildesheim seemed to be gazing at them with no particular expression, his stethoscope dangling around his neck. Miss Tanner stood at the foot of the bed writing something on a chart.

"Hello," said Dr. Hildesheim, "at least you take it out in shouting. You don't try to get out of bed and go running around." Miranda held her eyes open with a terrible effort, saw his rather heavy, patient face clearly even as her mind tottered and slithered again, broke from its foundation and spun like a cast wheel in a ditch. "I didn't mean it, I never believed it, Dr. Hildesheim, you mustn't remember it—" and was gone again, not being able to wait for an answer.

The wrong she had done followed her and haunted her dream: this wrong took vague shapes of horror she could not recognize or name, though her heart cringed at sight of them. Her mind, split in two, acknowledged and denied what she saw in the one instant, for across an abyss of complaining darkness her reasoning coherent self watched the strange frenzy of the other coldly, reluctant to admit the truth of its visions, its tenacious remorses and despairs.

"I know those are your hands," she told Miss Tanner, "I know it, but to me they are white tarantulas, don't touch me."

"Shut your eyes," said Miss Tanner.

"Oh, no," said Miranda, "for then I see worse things," but her eyes closed in spite of her will, and the midnight of her internal torment closed about her.

Oblivion, thought Miranda, her mind feeling among her memories of words she had been taught to describe the unseen, the unknowable, is a whirlpool of gray water turning upon itself for all eternity . . . eternity is perhaps more than the distance to the farthest star. She lay on a narrow ledge over a pit that she knew to be bottomless, though she could not comprehend it; the ledge was her childhood dream of danger, and she strained back against a reassuring wall of granite at her shoulders, staring into the pit, thinking. There it is, there it is at last, it is very simple; and soft carefully shaped words like oblivion and eternity are curtains hung before nothing at all. I shall not know when it happens, I shall not feel or remember, why can't I consent now, I am lost, there is no hope for me. Look, she told herself, there it is, that is death and there is nothing to fear. But she could not consent, still shrinking stiffly against the granite wall that was her childhood dream of safety, breathing slowly for fear of squandering breath, saying desperately, Look, don't be afraid, it is nothing, it is only eternity.

Granite walls, whirlpools, stars are things. None of them is death, nor the image of it. Death is death, said Miranda, and for the dead it has no attributes. Silenced she sank easily through deeps under deeps of darkness until she lay like a stone at the farthest bottom of life, knowing herself to be blind, deaf, speechless, no longer aware of the members of her own body, entirely withdrawn from all human concerns, yet alive with a peculiar lucidity and coherence; all notions of the mind, the reasonable inquiries of doubt, all ties of blood and the desires of the heart, dissolved and fell away from her, and there remained of her only a minute fiercely burning particle of being that knew itself alone, that relied upon nothing beyond itself for its strength; not susceptible to any appeal or inducement, being itself composed entirely of one single motive, the stubborn will to live. This fiery motionless particle set itself unaided to resist destruction, to survive and to be in its own madness of being, motiveless and planless beyond that one essential end. Trust me, the hard unwinking angry point of light said. Trust me. I stay.

At once it grew, flattened, thinned to a fine radiance, spread like a great fan and curved out into a rainbow through which Miranda, enchanted, altogether believing, looked upon a deep clear landscape of sea and sand, of soft meadow and sky, freshly washed and glistening with transparencies of blue. Why, of course, of course, said Miranda, without surprise but with serene rapture as if some promise made to her had been kept long after she had ceased to hope for it. She rose from her narrow ledge and ran lightly through the tall portals of the great bow that arched in its splendor over the burning blue of the sea and the cool green of the meadow on either hand.

The small waves rolled in and over unhurriedly, lapped upon the sand in silence and retreated; the grasses flurried before a breeze that made no sound. Moving towards her leisurely as clouds through the shimmering air came a great company of human beings, and Miranda saw in an amazement of joy that they were all the living she had known. Their faces were transfigured, each in its own beauty, beyond what she remembered of them, their eyes were clear and untroubled as good weather, and they cast no shadows. They were pure identities and she knew them every one without calling their names or remembering what relation she bore to them. They surrounded her smoothly on silent feet, then turned their entranced faces again towards the sea, and she moved among them easily as a wave among waves. The drifting circle widened, separated, and each figure was alone but not solitary; Miranda, alone too, questioning nothing, desiring nothing, in the quietude of her ecstasy, stayed where she was, eyes fixed on the overwhelming deep sky where it was always morning.

Lying at ease, arms under her head, in the prodigal warmth which flowed evenly from sea and sky and meadow, within touch but not touching the serenely smiling familiar beings about her, Miranda felt without warning a vague tremor of apprehension, some small flick of distrust in her joy; a thin frost touched the edges of this confident tranquillity; something, somebody, was missing, she had lost something, she had left something valuable in another country, oh, what could it be? There are no trees, no trees here, she said in fright, I have left something unfinished. A thought struggled at the back of her mind, came clearly as a voice in her ear. Where are the dead? We have forgotten the dead, oh, the dead, where are they? At once as if a curtain had fallen, the bright landscape faded, she was alone in a strange stony place of bitter cold, picking her way along a steep path of slippery snow, calling out, Oh, I must go back! But in what direction? Pain returned, a terrible compelling pain running through her veins like heavy fire, the stench of corruption filled her nostrils, the sweetish sickening smell of rotting flesh and pus; she opened her eyes and saw pale light through a coarse white cloth over her face, knew that the smell of death was in her own body, and struggled to lift her hand. The cloth was drawn away; she saw Miss Tanner filling a hypodermic needle in her methodical expert way, and heard Dr. Hildesheim saying, "I think that will do the trick. Try another." Miss Tanner plucked firmly at Miranda's arm near the shoulder, and the unbelievable current of agony ran burning through her veins again. She struggled to cry out, saying, Let me go, let me go; but heard only incoherent sounds of animal suffering. She saw doctor and nurse glance at each other with the glance of initiates at a mystery, nodding in silence, their eyes alive with knowledgeable pride. They looked briefly at their handiwork and hurried away.

Bells screamed all off key, wrangling together as they collided in mid air, horns and whistles mingled shrilly with cries of human distress; sulphur colored light exploded through the black window pane and flashed away in darkness. Miranda waking from a dreamless sleep asked without expecting an answer, "What is happening?" for there was a bustle of voices and footsteps in the corridor, and a sharpness in the air; the far clamor went on, a furious exasperated shrieking like a mob in revolt.

The light came on, and Miss Tanner said in a furry voice, "Hear that? They're celebrating. It's the Armistice. The war is over, my dear." Her hands trembled. She rattled a spoon in a cup, stopped to listen, held the cup out to Miranda. From the ward for old bedridden women down the hall floated a ragged chorus of cracked voices singing, "My country, 'tis of thee . . ."

Sweet land . . . oh, terrible land of this bitter world where the sound of rejoicing was a clamor of pain, where ragged tuneless old women, sitting up waiting for their evening bowl of cocoa, were singing, "Sweet land of Liberty—"

"Oh, say, can you see?" their hopeless voices were asking next, the hammer strokes of metal tongues drowning them out. "The war is over," said Miss Tanner, her underlip held firmly, her eyes blurred. Miranda said, "Please open the window, please, I smell death in here."

Now if real daylight such as I remember having seen in this world would only come again, but it is always twilight or just before morning, a promise of day that is never kept. What has become of the sun? That was the longest and loneliest night and yet it will not end and let the day come. Shall I ever see light again?

Sitting in a long chair, near a window, it was in itself a melancholy wonder to see the colorless sunlight slanting on the snow, under a sky drained of its blue. "Can this be my face?" Miranda asked her mirror. "Are these my own hands?" she asked Miss Tanner, holding them up to show the yellow tint like melted wax glimmering between the closed fingers. The body is a curious monster, no place to live in, how could anyone feel at home there? Is it possible I can ever accustom myself to this place? she asked herself. The human faces around her seemed dulled and tired, with no radiance of skin and eyes as Miranda remembered radiance; the once white walls of her room were now a soiled gray. Breathing slowly, falling asleep and waking again, feeling the splash of water on her flesh, taking food, talking in bare phrases with Dr. Hildesheim and Miss Tanner, Miranda looked about her with the covertly hostile eyes of an alien who does not like the country in which he finds himself, does not understand the language nor wish to learn it, does not mean to live there and yet is helpless, unable to leave it at his will.

"It is morning," Miss Tanner would say, with a sigh, for she had grown old and weary once for all in the past month, "morning again, my dear," showing Miranda the same monotonous landscape of dulled evergreens and leaden snow. She would rustle about in her starched skirts, her face bravely powdered, her spirit unbreakable as good steel, saying, "Look, my dear, what a heavenly morning, like a crystal," for she had an affection for the salvaged creature before her, the silent ungrateful human being whom she, Cornelia Tanner, a nurse who knew her business, had snatched back from death with her own hands. "Nursing is nine-tenths, just the same," Miss Tanner would tell the other nurses; "keep that in mind." Even the sunshine was Miss Tanner's own prescription for the further recovery of Miranda, this patient the doctors had given up for lost, and who yet sat here, visible proof of Miss Tanner's theory. She said, "Look at the sunshine, now," as she might be saying, "I ordered this for you, my dear, do sit up and take it."

"It's beautiful," Miranda would answer, even turning her head to look, thanking Miss Tanner for her goodness, most of all her goodness about the weather, "beautiful, I always loved it." And I might love it again if I saw it, she thought, but truth was, she could not see it. There was no light, there might never be light again, compared as it must always be with the light she had seen beside the blue sea that lay so tranquilly along the shore of her paradise. That was a child's dream of the heavenly meadow, the vision of repose that comes to a tired body in sleep, she thought, but I have seen it when I did not know it was a dream. Closing her eyes she would rest for a moment remembering that bliss which had repaid all the pain of the journey to reach it; opening them again she saw with a new anguish the dull world to which she was condemned, where the light seemed filmed over with cobwebs, all the bright surfaces corroded, the sharp planes melted and formless, all objects and beings meaningless, ah, dead and withered things that believed themselves alive!

At night, after the long effort of lying in her chair, in her extremity of grief for what she had so briefly won, she folded her painful body together and wept silently, shamelessly, in pity for herself and her lost rapture. There was no escape. Dr. Hildesheim, Miss Tanner, the nurses in the diet kitchen, the chemist, the surgeon, the precise machine of the hospital, the whole humane conviction and custom of society, conspired to pull her inseparable rack of bones and wasted flesh to its feet, to put in order her disordered mind, and to set her once more safely in the road that would lead her again to death.

Chuck Rouncivale and Mary Townsend came to see her, bringing her a bundle of letters they had guarded for her. They brought a basket of delicate small hothouse flowers, lilies of the valley with sweet peas and feathery fern, and above these blooms their faces were merry and haggard.

Mary said, "You *have* had a tussle, haven't you?" and Chuck said, "Well, you made it back, didn't you?" Then after an uneasy pause, they told her that everybody was waiting to see her again at her desk. "They've put me back on sports already, Miranda," said Chuck. For ten minutes Miranda smiled and told them how gay and what a pleasant surprise it was to find herself alive. For it will not do to betray the conspiracy and tamper with the courage of the living; there is nothing better than to be alive, everyone has agreed on that; it is past argument, and who attempts to deny it is justly outlawed. "I'll be back in no time at all," she said; "this is almost over."

Her letters lay in a heap in her lap and beside her chair. Now and then she turned one over to read the inscription, recognized this handwriting or that, examined the blotted stamps and the postmarks, and let them drop again. For two or three days they lay upon the table beside her, and she continued to shrink from them. "They will all be telling me again how good it is to be alive, they will say again they love me, they are glad I am living too, and what can I answer to that?" and her hardened, indifferent heart shuddered in despair at itself, because before it had been tender and capable of love.

Dr. Hildesheim said, "What, all these letters not opened yet?" and Miss Tanner said, "Read your letters, my dear, I'll open them for you." Standing beside the bed, she slit them cleanly with a paper knife. Miranda, cornered, picked and chose until she found a thin one in an unfamiliar handwriting. "Oh, no, now," said Miss Tanner, "take them as they come. Here, I'll hand them to you." She sat down, prepared to be helpful to the end.

What a victory, what triumph, what happiness to be alive, sang the letters in a chorus. The names were signed with flourishes like the circles in air of bugle notes, and they were the names of those she had loved best; some of those she had known well and pleasantly; and a few who meant nothing to her, then or now. The thin letter in the unfamiliar handwriting was from a strange man at the camp where Adam had been, telling her that Adam had died of influenza in the camp hospital. Adam had asked him, in case anything happened, to be sure to let her know.

If anything happened. To be sure to let her know. If anything happened. "Your friend, Adam Barclay," wrote the strange man. It had happened—she looked at the date—more than a month ago.

"I've been here a long time, haven't I?" she asked Miss Tanner, who was folding letters and putting them back in their proper envelopes.

"Oh, quite a while," said Miss Tanner, "but you'll be ready to go soon now. But you must be careful of yourself and not overdo, and you should come back now and then and let us look at you, because sometimes the aftereffects are very—"

Miranda, sitting up before the mirror, wrote carefully: "One lipstick, medium, one ounce flask Bois d'Hiver perfume, one pair of gray suède gauntlets without straps, two pairs gray sheer stockings without clocks—"

Towney, reading after her, said, "Everything without something so that it will be almost impossible to get?"

"Try it, though," said Miranda, "they're nicer without. One walking stick of silvery wood with a silver knob."

"That's going to be expensive," warned Towney. "Walking is hardly worth it."

"You're right," said Miranda, and wrote in the margin, "a nice one to match my other things. Ask Chuck to look for this, Mary. Good looking and not too heavy." Lazarus, come forth. Not unless you bring me my top hat and stick. Stay where you are then, you snob. Not at all. I'm coming forth. "A jar of cold cream," wrote Miranda, "a box of apricot powder—and, Mary, I don't need eye shadow, do I?" She glanced at her face in the mirror and away again. "Still, no one need pity this corpse if we look properly to the art of the thing."

Mary Townsend said, "You won't recognize yourself in a week."

"Do you suppose, Mary," asked Miranda, "I could have my old room back again?"

"That should be easy," said Mary. "We stored away all your things there with Miss Hobbe." Miranda wondered again at the time and trouble the living took to be helpful to the dead. But not quite dead now, she reassured herself, one foot in either world now; soon I shall cross back and be at home again. The light will seem real and I shall be glad when I hear that someone I know has escaped from death. I shall visit the escaped ones and help them dress and tell them how lucky they are, and how lucky I am still to have them. Mary will be back soon with my gloves and my walking stick, I must go now, I must begin saying good-by to Miss Tanner and Dr. Hildesheim. Adam, she said, now you need not die again, but still I wish you were here; I wish you had come back, what do you think I came back for, Adam, to be deceived like this?

At once he was there beside her, invisible but urgently present, a ghost but more alive than she was, the last intolerable cheat of her heart; for knowing it was false she still clung to the lie, the unpardonable lie of her bitter desire. She said, "I love you," and stood up trembling, trying by the mere act of her will to bring him to sight before her. If I could call you up from the grave I would, she said, if I could see your ghost I would say, I believe . . . "I believe," she said aloud. "Oh, let me see you once more." The room was silent, empty, the shade was gone from it, struck away by the sudden violence of her rising and speaking aloud. She came to herself as if out of sleep. Oh, no, that is not the way, I must never do that, she warned herself. Miss Tanner said, "Your taxicab is waiting, my dear," and there was Mary. Ready to go.

No more war, no more plague, only the dazed silence that follows the ceasing of the heavy guns; noiseless houses with the shades drawn, empty streets, the dead cold light of tomorrow. Now there would be time for everything.

1939

Zora Neale Hurston
(1891–1960)

Both as a person and as a writer, Hurston was marked by her birthplace—Eatonville, Florida, the first all-black town incorporated in the United States. Her father, the minister John Hurston, was three times mayor of Eatonville, and as a child she was never subject to the constraints of dealing with white authority. Though her mother, Lucy, died when Zora was young, maternal influence and the admonition to "jump at de sun" stayed with a child who was shunted from one relative to another before becoming a teenaged wardrobe girl with a traveling theater company. Later, supporting herself as a maid, Hurston attended Morgan Academy in Baltimore and Howard University in Washington, D.C.

With the encouragement of Alain Locke, whose anthology *The New Negro* (1925) heralded an artistic rebirth for black artists, Hurston moved to New York City. She worked as secretary and companion to Fanny Hurst, the popular white novelist, and helped edit *Fire*, a new quarterly cofounded by Langston Hughes. As the only black student of Barnard College's anthropologist Frank Boas, she determined to preserve the rich folklore of her birthplace and began collecting materials there in 1927.

The 1930s were Hurston's most productive decade, bracketed by two brief marriages. She began her graduate work in anthropology at Columbia and collected materials in Florida, Louisiana, and the Caribbean. Her first collection of folklore, *Mules and Men* (1935), and best-known novel, *Their Eyes Were Watching God* (1937), established Hurston's reputation as a writer. Other works published in the 1930s are *Jonah's Gourd Wine* (1934), a novel loosely based on her parents' lives; *Singing Steel* (1934), a play; *Tell My Horse* (1938), a gathering of Jamaican and Haitian folklore; and the novel *Moses, Man of the Mountain* (1939).

By the end of the decade, she was already under attack for her lack of interest in themes of racial conflict. Richard Wright dismissed *Their Eyes Were Watching God* as a "minstrel" novel intended for the amusement of white readers; Langston Hughes, with whom she had quarreled during their collaboration on the play *Mule Bone* (1931), denounced her relations with white patrons, and she was criticized for the conservatism of articles she wrote for popular magazines, including an attack on the Supreme Court school desegregation ruling (1954). The year she published her last novel, *Seraph on the Suwanee* (1948), she was charged with abuse of a minor, and though the charges were dropped, Hurston's life was on a downward spiral of ill health and poverty that ended with her death in a county welfare home and burial in an unmarked grave.

Increasing interest in issues of race and gender recently fostered a revitalization of Hurston's reputation. When *Their Eyes Were Watching God* was reissued in 1978, with an introduction by the Pulitzer Prize–winning novelist Alice Walker, it became a best-seller. Its detailed portrayal of small-town and rural black life and its preservation of dialect, folk sayings, and customs contributed to the recovery of African-American traditions. Hurston's heroines, especially Janie Woods of *Their Eyes*, by conquering the restrictions that make women—in Janie's grandmother's words—"de mule uh de world," provide inspirational alternatives to old stereotypes. At present there is more of Hurston's writing available in print than there ever was during her own lifetime, and her work has become the focus of serious critical attention.

Among scholarly treatments are Robert Hemenway, *Zora Neal Hurston: A Literary Biography* (1977), and Karla F. C. Holloway, *The Character of the Word, The Texts of Zora Neale Hurston* (1987).

The following text is from Chapter 6 of *Their Eyes Were Watching God.* Janie is married to her second husband, Joe Starks, a store owner and town mayor.

FROM THEIR EYES WERE WATCHING GOD

[The Yellow Mule]

6

Every morning the world flung itself over and exposed the town to the sun. So Janie had another day. And every day had a store in it, except Sundays. The store itself was a pleasant place if only she didn't have to sell things. When the people sat around on the porch and passed around the pictures of their thoughts for the others to look at and see, it was nice. The fact that the thought pictures were always crayon enlargements of life made it even nicer to listen to.

Take for instance the case of Matt Bonner's yellow mule. They had him up for conversation every day the Lord sent. Most especial if Matt was there himself to listen. Sam and Lige and Walter were the ringleaders of the mule-talkers. The others threw in whatever they could chance upon, but it seemed as if Sam and Lige and Walter could hear and see more about that mule than the whole county put together. All they needed was to see Matt's long spare shape coming down the street and by the time he got to the porch they were ready for him.

"Hello, Matt."

"Evenin', Sam."

"Mighty glad you come 'long right now, Matt. Me and some others wuz jus' about tuh come hunt yuh."

"Whut for, Sam?"

"Mighty serious matter, man. Serious!!"

"Yeah man," Lige would cut in, dolefully. "It needs yo' strict attention. You ought not tuh lose no time."

"Whut is it then? You oughta hurry up and tell me."

"Reckon we better not tell yuh heah at de store. It's too fur off tuh do any good. We better all walk on down by Lake Sabelia."

"Whut's wrong, man? Ah ain't after none uh y'alls foolishness now."

"Dat mule uh yourn, Matt. You better go see 'bout him. He's bad off."

"Where 'bouts? Did he wade in de lake and uh alligator ketch him?"

"Worser'n dat. De womenfolks got yo' mule. When Ah come round de lake 'bout noontime mah wife and some others had 'im flat on de ground usin' his sides fuh uh wash board."

The great clap of laughter that they have been holding in, bursts out. Sam never cracks a smile. "Yeah, Matt, dat mule so skinny till de women is usin' his rib bones fuh uh rub-board, and hangin' things out on his hock-bones tuh dry."

Matt realizes that they have tricked him again and the laughter makes him mad and when he gets mad he stammers.

"You'se uh stinkin' lie, Sam, and yo' feet ain't mates. Y-y-y-you!"

"Aw, man, 'tain't no use in you gittin' mad. Yuh know yuh don't feed de mule. How he gointuh git fat?"

"Ah-ah-ah d-d-does feed 'im! Ah g-g-gived 'im uh full cup uh cawn every feedin'."

"Lige knows all about dat cup uh cawn. He hid round yo' barn and watched yuh. 'Tain't no feed cup you measures dat cawn outa. It's uh tea cup."

"Ah does feed 'im. He's jus' too mean tuh git fat. He stay poor and rawbony jus' fuh spite. Skeered he'll hafta work some."

"Yeah, you feeds 'im. Feeds 'im offa 'come up' and seasons it wid raw-hide."

"Does feed de ornery varmint! Don't keer whut Ah do Ah can't git long wid 'im. He fights every inch in front uh de plow, and even lay back his ears tuh kick and bite when Ah go in de stall tuh feed 'im."

"Git reconciled, Matt," Lige soothed. "Us all knows he's mean. Ah seen 'im when he took after one uh dem Roberts chillun in de street and woulda caught 'im and maybe trompled 'im tuh death if de wind hadn't of changed all of a sudden. Yuh see de youngun wuz tryin' tuh make it tuh de fence uh Starks' onion patch and de mule wuz dead in behind 'im and gainin' on 'im every jump, when all of a sudden de wind changed and blowed de mule way off his course, him bein' so poor and everything, and before de ornery varmint could tack, de youngun had done got over de fence." The porch laughed and Matt got mad again.

"Maybe de mule takes out after everybody," Sam said, " 'cause he thinks everybody he hear comin' is Matt Bonner comin' tuh work 'im on uh empty stomach."

"Aw, naw, aw, naw. You stop dat right now," Walter objected. "Dat mule don't think Ah look lak no Matt Bonner. He ain't dat dumb. If Ah thought he didn't know no better Ah'd have mah picture took and give it tuh dat mule so's he could learn better. Ah ain't gointuh 'low 'im tuh hold nothin' lak dat against me."

Matt struggled to say something but his tongue failed him so he jumped down off the porch and walked away as mad as he could be. But that never halted the mule talk. There would be more stories about how poor the brute was; his age; his evil disposition and his latest caper. Everybody indulged in mule talk. He was next to the Mayor in prominence, and made better talking.

Janie loved the conversation and sometimes she thought up good stories on the mule, but Joe had forbidden her to indulge. He didn't want her talking after such trashy people. "You'se Mrs. Mayor Starks, Janie. I god, Ah can't see what uh woman uh yo' sability would want tuh be treasurin' all dat gum-grease from folks dat don't even own de house dey sleep in. 'Tain't no earthly use. They's jus' some puny humans playin' round de toes uh Time."

Janie noted that while he didn't talk the mule himself, he sat and laughed at it. Laughed his big heh, heh laugh too. But then when Lige or Sam or Walter or some of the other big picture talkers were using a side of the world for a canvas, Joe would hustle her off inside the store to sell something. Look like he took pleasure in doing it. Why couldn't he go himself sometimes? She had come to hate the inside of that store anyway. That Post Office too. People always coming and asking for mail at the wrong time. Just when she was trying to count up something or write in an account book. Get her so hackled she'd make the wrong change for stamps. Then too, she couldn't read everybody's writing. Some folks wrote so funny and spelt things different from what she knew about. As a rule, Joe put up the mail himself, but sometimes when he was off she had to do it herself and it always ended up in a fuss.

The store itself kept her with a sick headache. The labor of getting things down off of a shelf or out of a barrel was nothing. And so long as people wanted only a can of tomatoes or a pound of rice it was all right. But supposing they went on and said a pound and a half of bacon and a half pound of lard? The whole thing changed from a little walking and stretching to a mathematical dilemma. Or maybe cheese was thirty-seven cents a pound and somebody came and asked for a dime's worth. She went through many silent rebellions over things like that. Such a waste of life and time. But Joe kept saying that she could do it if she wanted to and he wanted her to use her privileges. That was the rock she was battered against.

This business of the head-rag irked her endlessly. But Jody was set on it. Her hair was NOT going to show in the store. It didn't seem sensible at all. That was because Joe never told Janie how jealous he was. He never told her how often he had seen the other men figuratively wallowing in it as she went about things in the store. And one night he had caught Walter standing behind Janie and brushing the back of his hand back and forth across the loose end of her braid ever so lightly so as to enjoy the feel of it without Janie knowing what he was doing. Joe was at the back of the store and Walter didn't see him. He felt like rushing forth with the meat knife and chopping off the offending hand. That night he ordered Janie to tie up her hair around the store. That was all. She was there in the store for *him* to look at, not those others. But he never said things like that. It just wasn't in him. Take the matter of the yellow mule, for instance.

Late one afternoon Matt came from the west with a halter in his hand. "Been huntin' fuh mah mule. Anybody seen 'im?" he asked.

"Seen 'im soon dis mornin' over behind de schoolhouse," Lum said. " 'Bout ten o'clock or so. He musta been out all night tuh be way over dere dat early."

"He wuz," Matt answered. "Seen 'im last night but Ah couldn't ketch 'im. Ah'm 'bliged tuh git 'im in tuhnight 'cause Ah got some plowin' fuh tuhmorrow. Done promised tuh plow Thompson's grove."

"Reckon you'll ever git through de job wid dat mule-frame?" Lige asked.

"Aw dat mule is plenty strong. Jus' evil and don't want tuh be led."

"Dat's right. Dey tell me he brought you heah tuh dis town. Say you started tuh Miccanopy but de mule had better sense and brung yuh on heah."

"It's uh l-l-lie! Ah set out fuh dis town when Ah left West Floridy."

"You mean tuh tell me you rode dat mule all de way from West Floridy down heah?"

"Sho he did, Lige. But he didn't mean tuh. He wuz satisfied up dere, but de mule wuzn't. So one mornin' he got straddle uh de mule and he took and brought 'im on off. Mule had sense. Folks up dat way don't eat biscuit bread but once uh week."

There was always a little seriousness behind the teasing of Matt, so when he got huffed and walked on off nobody minded. He was known to buy side-meat by the slice. Carried home little bags of meal and flour in his hand. He didn't seem to mind too much so long as it didn't cost him anything.

About half an hour after he left they heard the braying of the mule at the edge of the woods. He was coming past the store very soon.

"Less ketch Matt's mule fuh 'im and have some fun."

"Now, Lum, you know dat mule ain't aimin' tuh let hisself be caught. Less watch *you* do it."

When the mule was in front of the store, Lum went out and tackled him. The brute jerked up his head, laid back his ears and rushed to the attack. Lum had to run for safety. Five or six more men left the porch and surrounded the fractious beast, goosing him in the sides and making him show his temper. But he had more spirit left than body. He was soon panting and heaving from the effort of spinning his old carcass about. Everybody was having fun at the mule-baiting. All but Janie.

She snatched her head away from the spectacle and began muttering to herself. "They oughta be shamed uh theyselves! Teasin' dat poor brute beast lak they is! Done been worked tuh death; done had his disposition ruint wid mistreatment, and now they got tuh finish devilin' 'im tuh death. Wisht Ah had mah way wid 'em all."

She walked away from the porch and found something to busy herself with in the back of the store so she did not hear Jody when he stopped laughing. She didn't know that he had heard her, but she did hear him yell out, "Lum, I god, dat's enough! Y'all done had yo' fun now. Stop yo' foolishness and go tell Matt Bonner Ah wants tuh have uh talk wid him right away."

Janie came back out front and sat down. She didn't say anything and neither did Joe. But after a while he looked down at his feet and said, "Janie, Ah reckon you better go fetch me dem old black gaiters. Dese tan shoes sets mah feet on fire. Plenty room in 'em, but they hurts regardless."

She got up without a word and went off for the shoes. A little war of defense for helpless things was going on inside her. People ought to have some regard for helpless things. She wanted to fight about it. "But Ah hates disagreement and confusion, so Ah better not talk. It makes it hard tuh git along." She didn't hurry back. She fumbled around long enough to get her face straight. When she got back, Joe was talking with Matt.

"Fifteen dollars? I god you'se as crazy as uh betsy bug! Five dollars."

"L-l-less we strack uh compermise, Brother Mayor. Less m-make it ten."

"Five dollars." Joe rolled his cigar in his mouth and rolled his eyes away indifferently.

"If dat mule is wuth somethin' tuh *you* Brother Mayor, he's wuth mo' tuh me. More special when Ah got uh job uh work tuhmorrow."

"Five dollars."

"All right, Brother Mayor. If you wants tuh rob uh poor man lak me uh everything he got tuh make uh livin' wid, Ah'll take de five dollars. Dat mule been wid me twenty-three years. It's mighty hard."

Mayor Starks deliberately changed his shoes before he reached into his pocket for the money. By that time Matt was wringing and twisting like a hen on a hot brick. But as soon as his hand closed on the money his face broke into a grin.

"Beatyuh tradin' dat time, Starks! Dat mule is liable tuh be dead befo' de week is out. You won't git no work outa him."

"Didn't buy 'im fuh no work. I god, Ah bought dat varmint tuh let 'im rest. You didn't have gumption enough tuh do it."

A respectful silence fell on the place. Sam looked at Joe and said, "Dat's uh new idea 'bout varmints, Mayor Starks. But Ah laks it mah ownself. It's uh noble thing you done." Everybody agreed with that.

Janie stood still while they all made comments. When it was all done she stood in front of Joe and said, "Jody, dat wuz uh mighty fine thing fuh you tuh do. 'Tain't everybody would have thought of it, 'cause it ain't no everyday thought. Freein' dat mule makes uh mighty big man outa you. Something like George Washington and Lincoln. Abraham Lincoln, he had de whole United States tuh rule so he freed de Negroes. You got uh town so you freed uh mule. You have tuh have power tuh free things and dat makes you lak uh king uh something."

Hambo said, "Yo' wife is uh born orator, Starks. Us never knowed dat befo'. She put jus' de right words tuh our thoughts."

Joe bit down hard on his cigar and beamed all around, but he never said a word. The town talked it for three days and said that's just what they would have done if they had been rich men like Joe Starks. Anyhow a free mule in town was something new to talk about. Starks piled fodder under the big tree near the porch and the mule was usually around the store like the other citizens. Nearly everybody took the habit of fetching along a handful of fodder to throw on the pile. He almost got fat and they took a great pride in him. New lies sprung up about his free-mule doings. How he pushed open Lindsay's kitchen door and slept in the place one night and fought until they made coffee for his breakfast; how he stuck his head in the Pearsons' window while the family was at the table and Mrs. Pearson mistook him for Rev. Pearson and handed him a plate; he ran Mrs. Tully off of the croquet ground for having such an ugly shape; he ran and caught up with Becky Anderson on the way to Maitland so as to keep his head out of the sun under her umbrella; he got tired of listening to Redmond's long-winded prayer, and went inside the Baptist church and broke up the meeting. He did everything but let himself be bridled and visit Matt Bonner.

But way after awhile he died. Lum found him under the big tree on his rawbony back with all four feet up in the air. That wasn't natural and it didn't look right, but Sam said it would have been more unnatural for him to have laid down on his side and died like any other beast. He had seen Death coming and had stood his ground and fought it like a natural man. He had fought it to the last breath. Naturally he didn't have time to straighten himself out. Death had to take him like it found him.

When the news got around, it was like the end of a war or something like that. Everybody that could knocked off from work to stand around and talk. But finally there was nothing to do but drag him out like all other dead brutes. Drag him out to the edge of the hammock which was far enough off to satisfy sanitary conditions in the town. The rest was up to the buzzards. Everybody was going to the dragging-out. The news had got Mayor Starks out of bed before time. His pair of gray horses was out under the tree and the men were fooling with the gear when Janie arrived at the store with Joe's breakfast.

"I god, Lum, you fasten up dis store good befo' you leave, you hear me?" He was eating fast and talking with one eye out of the door on the operations.

"Whut you tellin' 'im tuh fasten up for, Jody?" Janie asked surprised.

" 'Cause it won't be nobody heah tuh look after de store. Ah'm goin' tuh de draggin'-out mahself."

" 'Tain't nothin' so important Ah got tuh do tuhday, Jody. How come Ah can't go long wid you tuh de draggin'-out?"

Joe was struck speechless for a minute. "Why, Janie! You wouldn't be seen at uh draggin'-out, wouldja? Wid any and everybody in uh passle pushin' and shovin' wid they no-manners selves? Naw, naw!"

"You would be dere wid me, wouldn't yuh?"

"Dat's right, but Ah'm uh man even if Ah is de Mayor. But de mayor's wife is somethin' different again. Anyhow they's liable tuh need me tuh say uh few words over de carcass, dis bein' uh special case. But *you* ain't goin' off in all dat mess uh commonness. Ah'm surprised at yuh fuh askin'."

He wiped his lips of ham gravy and put on his hat. "Shet de door behind yuh, Janie. Lum is too busy wid de hawses."

After more shouting of advice and orders and useless comments, the town escorted the carcass off. No, the carcass moved off with the town, and left Janie standing in the doorway.

Out in the swamp they made great ceremony over the mule. They mocked everything human in death. Starks led off with a great eulogy on our departed citizen, our most distinguished citizen and the grief he left behind him, and the people loved the speech. It made him more solid than building the schoolhouse had done. He stood on the distended belly of the mule for a platform and made gestures. When he stepped down, they hoisted Sam up and he talked about the mule as a school teacher first. Then he set his hat like John Pearson and imitated his preaching. He spoke of the joys of mule-heaven to which the dear brother had departed this valley of sorrow; the mule-angels flying around; the miles of green corn and cool water, a pasture of pure bran with a river of molasses running through it; and most glorious of all, *No* Matt Bonner with plow lines and halters to come in and corrupt. Up there, mule-angels would have people to ride on and from his place beside the glittering throne, the dear departed brother would look down into hell and see the devil plowing Matt Bonner all day long in a hell-hot sun and laying the raw-hide to his back.

With that the sisters got mock-happy and shouted and had to be held up by the menfolks. Everybody enjoyed themselves to the highest and then finally the mule was left to the already impatient buzzards. They were holding a great flying-meet way up over the heads of the mourners and some of the nearby trees were already peopled with the stoop-shouldered forms.

As soon as the crowd was out of sight they closed in in circles. The near ones got nearer and the far ones got near. A circle, a swoop and a hop with spread-out wings. Close in, close in till some of the more hungry or daring perched on the carcass. They wanted to begin, but the Parson wasn't there, so a messenger was sent to the ruler in a tree where he sat.

The flock had to wait the white-headed leader, but it was hard. They jostled each other and pecked at heads in hungry irritation. Some walked up and down the beast from head to tail, tail to head. The Parson sat motionless in a dead pine tree about two miles off. He had scented the matter as quickly as any of the rest, but decorum demanded that he sit oblivious until he was notified. Then he took off with ponderous flight and circled and lowered, circled and lowered until the others danced in joy and hunger at his approach.

He finally lit on the ground and walked around the body to see if it were really dead. Peered into its nose and mouth. Examined it well from end to end and leaped upon it and bowed, and the others danced a response. That being over, he balanced and asked:

"What killed this man?"
The chorus answered, "Bare, bare fat."
"What killed this man?"
"Bare, bare fat."
"What killed this man?"
"Bare, bare fat."
"Who'll stand his funeral?"
"We!!!!!"
"Well, all right now."

So he picked out the eyes in the ceremonial way and the feast went on. The yaller mule was gone from the town except for the porch talk, and for the children visiting his bleaching bones now and then in the spirit of adventure.

1937

Edna St. Vincent Millay

(1892–1950)

Born in Rockland, Maine, Edna St. Vincent Millay grew up there and in nearby Camden. After the breakup of her parents' marriage, she and her two sisters were raised by their mother, a practical nurse who encouraged the children in self-sufficiency and in their artistic talents. Later, she wrote to her mother, "I was telling somebody yesterday that the reason I am a poet is entirely because you wanted me to be and intended I should be, even from the very first. You brought me up in the tradition of poetry, and everything I did you encouraged." At 12, she saw her first poem in print in *St. Nicholas* magazine. At 20, she gained national attention with the poem "Renascence," published in *The Lyric Year;* as a result of a reading of that poem she found a sponsor to send her to college, first Barnard and then Vassar, from which she graduated in 1917.

In her late twenties, for several years after leaving Vassar, Millay entered freely into the bohemian life of Greenwich Village. Talented and independent, redhaired and green-eyed, her looks and personality fit the style of the era, and she seemed to many to embody the spirit of the jazz age, defined in 1920 in verse by her *A Few Figs from Thistles* and in prose by Fitzgerald's *This Side of Paradise*. She was active with the Provincetown Players, who produced her play *Aria da Capo* (1921). In

1923, she won the Pulitzer Prize for *The Harp-Weaver and Other Poems*. Notorious for her love affairs, she captivated Edmund Wilson, among others, but rejected his proposal of marriage. Writing as Nancy Boyd, she helped pay her bills with the magazine sketches and satires later gathered as *Distressing Dialogues* (1924).

In 1923, she married Eugen Boissevan, a Dutch-American importer widowed from his earlier marriage to the feminist Inez Mulholland. With Boissevan, she moved to the country home she called Steepletop, in Austerlitz, New York, where they lived for the rest of their lives. Supported by the warmth and nurturing personality of the older Boissevan, she continued to produce major collections of poems, although for many readers her reputation continued to rest upon her early work. From the late 1920s onward, she turned at times to political poetry, as in the poems on the Sacco-Vanzetti affair, including "Justice Denied in Massachusetts" in *The Buck in the Snow and Other Poems* (1928), and the poems on World War II in *Make Bright the Arrows* (1940).

Writing most often in carefully constricted forms, she was greatly influenced by Shelley and Keats in a time when the tide of American poetry was turning away from the Romantics and from what some considered the prison of form. Like Frost, she had a remarkable ability to put the sound of a human voice into an iambic pentameter line (and like Frost, she could construct compelling narratives, as, for example, in the sequence "Sonnets from an Ungrafted Tree," collected in *The Harp-Weaver*). As she matured, her voice matured also. Remembered by many primarily for the flippant lyrics of her youth, she became America's most accomplished writer of sonnets, one of the best ever to practice that form in English, and as her content deepened, her achievement became ever more remarkable as other poets of the twentieth century left that form largely ignored. *Fatal Interview* (1931) is a sequence recounting a foredoomed love affair. Important sonnets continued to appear even as late as the posthumous *Mine the Harvest* (1954).

Collected Poems (1956), the source of the texts below, was edited by the poet's sister, Norma Millay. *Selected Poems* (1991) was edited by Colin Falck. Earlier collections include *Collected Sonnets* (1941) and *Collected Lyrics* (1943). Individual books of verse, besides those named above, include *Renascence and Other Poems* (1917); *Wine from These Grapes* (1934); and *Huntsman, What Quarry?* (1939). *The Letters of Edna St. Vincent Millay* (1952) was edited by Allan Ross Macdougall.

Biographical and critical studies include Elizabeth Atkins, *Edna St. Vincent Millay and Her Times* (1936); Miriam Gurko, *Restless Spirit: The Life of Edna St. Vincent Millay* (1962); Norman A. Britten, *Edna St. Vincent Millay* (1967); and Jean Gould, *The Poet and Her Book: A Biography of Edna St. Vincent Millay* (1969).

First Fig

My candle burns at both ends;
   It will not last the night;
But ah, my foes, and oh, my friends—
   It gives a lovely light!

1920

Second Fig

Safe upon the solid rock the ugly houses stand:
Come and see my shining palace built upon the sand!

1920

Recuerdo[1]

We were very tired, we were very merry—
We had gone back and forth all night on the ferry.
It was bare and bright, and smelled like a stable—
But we looked into a fire, we leaned across a table,

---

1. "Memory" (Spanish).

We lay on a hill-top underneath the moon;   5
And the whistles kept blowing, and the dawn came soon.

We were very tired, we were very merry—
We had gone back and forth all night on the ferry;
And you ate an apple, and I ate a pear,
From a dozen of each we had bought somewhere;   10
And the sky went wan, and the wind came cold,
And the sun rose dripping, a bucketful of gold.

We were very tired, we were very merry,
We had gone back and forth all night on the ferry.
We hailed, "Good morrow, mother!" to a shawl-covered head,   15
And bought a morning paper, which neither of us read;
And she wept, "God bless you!" for the apples and pears,
And we gave her all our money but our subway fares.

                                                              1920

The Spring and the Fall

In the spring of the year, in the spring of the year,
I walked the road beside my dear.
The trees were black where the bark was wet.
I see them yet, in the spring of the year.
He broke me a bough of the blossoming peach   5
That was out of the way and hard to reach.

In the fall of the year, in the fall of the year,
I walked the road beside my dear.
The rooks went up with a raucous trill.
I hear them still, in the fall of the year.   10
He laughed at all I dared to praise,
And broke my heart, in little ways.

Year be springing or year be falling,
The bark will drip and the birds be calling.
There's much that's fine to see and hear   15
In the spring of a year, in the fall of a year.
'Tis not love's going hurts my days,
But that it went in little ways.

                                                              1923

[Oh, Oh, you will be sorry for that word!]

Oh, oh, you will be sorry for that word!
Give back my book and take my kiss instead.
Was it my enemy or my friend I heard,

"What a big book for such a little head!"
Come, I will show you now my newest hat,   5
And you may watch me purse my mouth and prink!
Oh, I shall love you still, and all of that.
I never again shall tell you what I think.
I shall be sweet and crafty, soft and sly;
You will not catch me reading any more: 10
I shall be called a wife to pattern by;
And some day when you knock and push the door,
Some sane day, not too bright and not too stormy,
I shall be gone, and you may whistle for me.

                                             1923

[What lips my lips have kissed, and where, and why,]

What lips my lips have kissed, and where, and why,
I have forgotten, and what arms have lain
Under my head till morning; but the rain
Is full of ghosts tonight, that tap and sigh
Upon the glass and listen for reply,   5
And in my heart there stirs a quiet pain
For unremembered lads that not again
Will turn to me at midnight with a cry.
Thus in the winter stands the lonely tree,
Nor knows what birds have vanished one by one,   10
Yet knows its boughs more silent than before:
I cannot say what loves have come and gone,
I only know that summer sang in me
A little while, that in me sings no more.

                                             1923

From Sonnets from an Ungrafted Tree[2]

VII

One way there was of muting in the mind
A little while the ever-clamorous care;
And there was rapture, of a decent kind,
In making mean and ugly objects fair:
Soft-sooted kettle-bottoms, that had been   5
Time after time set in above the fire,
Faucets, and candlesticks, corroded green,

---

2. A sequence of seventeen sonnets narrating a woman's loneliness as she cares for her dying husband, collected in *The Harp-Weaver and Other Poems.*

To mine again from quarry; to attire
The shelves in paper petticoats, and tack
New oilcloth in the ringed-and-rotten's place,   10
Polish the stove till you could see your face,
And after nightfall rear an aching back
In a changed kitchen, bright as a new pin,
An advertisement, far too fine to cook a supper in.

XIV

She had a horror he would die at night.
And sometimes when the light began to fade
She could not keep from noticing how white
The birches looked—and then she would be afraid,
Even with a lamp, to go about the house
And lock the windows; and as night wore on   5
Toward morning, if a dog howled, or a mouse
Squeaked in the floor, long after it was gone
Her flesh would sit awry on her. By day
She would forget somewhat, and it would seem
A silly thing to go with just this dream   10
And get a neighbor to come at night and stay.
But it would strike her sometimes, making the tea:
She had kept that kettle boiling all night long, for company.

                                                        1923

Justice Denied in Massachusetts[3]

Let us abandon then our gardens and go home
And sit in the sitting-room.
Shall the larkspur blossom or the corn grow under this cloud?
Sour to the fruitful seed
Is the cold earth under this cloud,   5
Fostering quack and weed, we have marched upon but cannot conquer;
We have bent the blades of our hoes against the stalks of them.

Let us go home, and sit in the sitting-room.
Not in our day
Shall the cloud go over and the sun rise as before,   10
Beneficent upon us
Out of the glittering bay,
And the warm winds be blown inward from the sea
Moving the blades of corn

3. A commentary on the execution of Nicola Sacco and Bartolomeo Vanzetti, on August 23, 1927. The case had been in the judicial system for nearly seven years. Many thought the two unjustly convicted of robbery and murder.

With a peaceful sound.   15
Forlorn, forlorn,
Stands the blue hay-rack by the empty mow.
And the petals drop to the ground,
Leaving the tree unfruited.
The sun that warmed our stooping backs and withered the weed uprooted—   20
We shall not feel it again.
We shall die in darkness, and be buried in the rain.

What from the splendid dead
We have inherited—
Furrows sweet to the grain, and the weed subdued—   25
See now the slug and the mildew plunder.
Evil does overwhelm
The larkspur and the corn;
We have seen them go under.

Let us sit here, sit still,   30
Here in the sitting-room until we die;
At the step of Death on the walk, rise and go;
Leaving to our children's children this beautiful doorway,
And this elm,
And a blighted earth to till   35
With a broken hoe.

                                                                    1928

From Fatal Interview[3]

II

This beast that rends me in the sight of all,
This love, this longing, this oblivious thing,
That has me under as the last leaves fall,
Will glut, will sicken, will be gone by spring.
The wound will heal, the fever will abate,   5
The knotted hurt will slacken in the breast;
I shall forget before the flickers mate
Your look that is today my east and west.
Unscathed, however, from a claw so deep
Though I should love again I shall not go: 10
Along my body, waking while I sleep,
Sharp to the kiss, cold to the hand as snow,
The scar of this encounter like a sword
Will lie between me and my troubled lord.

3.   A sequence of fifty-two sonnets, published under that title in 1931.

XIV

Since of no creature living the last breath
Is twice required, or twice the ultimate pain,
Seeing how to quit your arms is very death,
'Tis likely that I shall not die again;
And likely 'tis that Time whose gross decree   5
Sends now the dawn to clamour at our door,
Thus having done his evil worst to me,
Will thrust me by, will harry me no more.
When you are corn and roses and at rest
I shall endure, a dense and sanguine ghost,
To haunt the scene where I was happiest,   10
To bend above the thing I loved the most;
And rise, and wring my hands, and steal away
As I do now, before the advancing day.

XXX

Love is not all: it is not meat nor drink
Nor slumber nor a roof against the rain;
Nor yet a floating spar to men that sink
And rise and sink and rise and sink again;
Love can not fill the thickened lung with breath,   5
Nor clean the blood, nor set the fractured bone;
Yet many a man is making friends with death
Even as I speak, for lack of love alone.
It well may be that in a difficult hour,
Pinned down by pain and moaning for release,
Or nagged by want past resolution's power,
I might be driven to sell your love for peace,   10
Or trade the memory of this night for food.
It well may be. I do not think I would.

XLVI

Even in the moment of our earliest kiss,
When sighed the straitened bud into the flower,
Sat the dry seed of most unwelcome this;
And that I knew, though not the day and hour.
Too season-wise am I, being country-bred,
To tilt at autumn or defy the frost:
Snuffing the chill even as my fathers did,
I say with them, "What's out tonight is lost."   5
I only hoped, with the mild hope of all
Who watch the leaf take shape upon the tree,
A fairer summer and a later fall
Than in these parts a man is apt to see,
And sunny clusters ripened for the wine: 10
I tell you this across the blackened vine.

1931

[Those hours when happy hours were my estate,—]

Those hours when happy hours were my estate,—
Entailed, as proper, for the next in line,
Yet mine the harvest, and the title mine—
Those acres, fertile, and the furrow straight,
From which the lark would rise—all of my late   5
Enchantments, still, in brilliant colours, shine,
But striped with black, the tulip, lawn and vine,
Like gardens looked at through an iron gate.
Yet not as one who never sojourned there
I view the lovely segments of a past   10
I lived with all my senses, well aware
That this was perfect, and it would not last:
I smell the flower, though vacuum-still the air;
I feel its texture, though the gate is fast.

1954

[I will put Chaos into fourteen lines]

I will put Chaos into fourteen lines
And keep him there; and let him thence escape
If he be lucky; let him twist, and ape
Flood, fire, and demon—his adroit designs
Will strain to nothing in the strict confines   5
Of this sweet Order, where, in pious rape,
I hold his essence and amorphous shape,
Till he with Order mingles and combines.
Past are the hours, the years, of our duress,
His arrogance, our awful servitude: 10
I have him. He is nothing more nor less
Than something simple not yet understood;
I shall not even force him to confess;
Or answer. I will only make him good.

1954

Caroline Gordon

(1895–1981)

Caroline Gordon did not attend school formally until high school; prior to that she was educated at home and as the only female student of her father's classical school for boys in Clarksville, Kentucky. She began reading Latin at 10 and credited her intensive reading of the Greek classics for her interest in writing. After high school in Wilmington, Ohio, where her Southern accent set her apart, Gordon graduated from Bethany College in West Virginia.

She began writing for the *Chattanooga News* in 1920; as a reporter she wrote about the ideas of a group of intellectuals at Vanderbilt University, known as the Fugitives, who were expressing support for Southern agrarian values. One of the Fugitives was Allen Tate, the poet and literary critic, who became her husband in 1924. The young couple met the English novelist Ford Madox Ford in New York, and later in Paris, Gordon worked as Ford's secretary. He encouraged her writing and his enthusiastic praise of *Penhally*, her first novel (1931), helped bring her work to critical attention.

A literary critic and teacher of creative writing, Gordon studied the fictional technique of such writers as Gustave Flaubert, Henry James, and James Joyce and applied it in her own work. She tried to "show" rather than "tell" (as did her literary mentors), minimizing narratorial presence, and the significances conveyed by her spare dramatic presentation are, like theirs, left open to the reader's interpretation. Characteristically, Gordon's work is not "feminine"; the characters are often male and the presentation is markedly unsentimental. Her native Kentucky and Tennessee often provide the natural settings, and the ethos is grounded in the rural Southern experience.

Penhally deals with three generations of Kentucky planters. *Aleck Maury, Sportsman* (1934) introduces a professorial character, addicted to hunting and fishing, who also appears in several of her stories. *None Shall Look Back* (1937) deals with the Confederate general Nathan Bedford Forrest. Depression years on a Southern plantation are the subject of *The Garden of Adonis* (1937), and *Green Centuries* (1941) deals with pioneer life in Kentucky.

Other novels by Gordon include *The Woman on the Porch* (1944); *The Strange Children* (1951); *The Malefactors* (1956); and *The Glory of Hera* (1972). Stories are collected in *The Forest of the South* (1945); *Old Red and Other Stories* (1963); and *Collected Stories* (1981). *How to Read a Novel* (1957) is a work of literary criticism. A biography is Veronica A. Makowsky, *Caroline Gordon* (1989). Studies include William J. Stuckey, *Caroline Gordon* (1972); and Ann Waldron, *Close Connections: Caroline Gordon and the Southern Renaissance* (1989).

The Ice House[1]

Doug was waiting where the paths forked as Raeburn came through the woods. He had his Barlow out and was whittling a stick, but he threw it away and started striding along the path as soon as he saw Raeburn.

"I thought you wasn't coming," he said. "I thought you'd just about give it out and decided you wasn't coming."

"I had to get my breakfast," Raeburn told him. "I ain't going to work for nobody on a empty stomach." He cast an eye at the sun. " 'Tain't more'n six o'clock anyhow."

Doug slackened his pace a little. "Well," he said, "the way I look at it if you going to work for a man you ought to work for him. We don't know nothin' about this man. If we get there late he may not pay us what he said he would."

Raeburn watched his own skinny shadow racing with him, over the new green shoots of pokeberry and sassafras. It occurred to him that it was the middle of April. The dogwoods were in full flower. Channel cat ought to be biting.

"Wilmer was over to our house last night," he said. "He wanted to know if that man had

1. First collected in *The Forest of the South*, "The Ice House" was reprinted in *Collected Stories*,   the source of the present text.

asked us to work for him. He said *he* wouldn't tech it. He said he wouldn't tech it for *no* amount of money."

Doug laughed. "I don't reckon he would," he said. "I don't reckon anybody that once took a look at Wilmer would hire him for *this* job. He couldn't hold out to handle a pick . . ."

"You reckon we'll have to use a pick, Doug?"

Doug stopped short in the path. "You know who's in that ice house?" he asked.

"I don't know none of their names."

"I reckon you don't. They's Yankees. Every last one of 'em's Yankees. Course now if you don't want to you don't have to do it. I can git somebody else. Handlin' a dead Yankee ain't no more to *me* than handlin' a dead hawg, but of course now you don't have to go if you don't want to."

"Oh, I'll go," Raeburn said. "It ain't nothin' to me."

They emerged from the woods into the clearing. A hundred yards away the ice house stood, with around it the black, straight trunks of half a dozen oak trees. There were no leaves as yet on any of their branches, but a sugar tree at one corner of the house cast its yellowish green tassels low on the sloping roof.

The man was standing before the ice house door looking down into the pit. A short man, so plump that the waistband of his trousers seemed on the verge of bursting. He heard them coming and turned around. His eyes were gray. They looked pale in the creases of his red, round face.

"Well, boys," he said affably, "I see you're like me. Early risers."

He waved his hand at the unpainted pine coffins that curved in a long glistening line around one whole side of the ice house and back behind the sugar tree. "Now what we got to do is fill them boxes up. The sooner we get them boxes filled up the sooner we get done and the sooner we get done the sooner you get your money. . . . Ain't that right, Bud?"

"That's right," Doug said. He took a pick and stepped over the threshold of the ice house onto the little ledge of earth that ran all around the circular pit. Raeburn followed him.

The skeletons were level with the earth. There was a man's skull on top of the pile. The eye sockets turned toward the door, the ribs and long leg bones slanting away diagonally across the heap, as if the man had flung himself down face forward to look out over the field. Where the light from the open door fell the bones were pale, almost white, but the bones that showed here and there underneath were darker. There was moss on some of them.

Doug picked up one of the fingers. The joints still stuck together. But as he held them in his hand the little joint dropped from its socket and a wisp of dried tendon fell out on the heap.

Doug stooped and with both hands lifted the curved grayish ribs where they were joined to the backbone. "Here," he said, "I'll give 'em to you and you put 'em outside. That's the best way to do it."

Raeburn laid the ribs in the wheelbarrow that the contractor had drawn up to the door. When he turned around Doug had more bones ready to hand him. They worked there that way for a long while. When the barrow was full the contractor wheeled it around the corner and deposited the load in the pine boxes. Raeburn could hear the light clatter as the more fragile bones fell from the barrow into the coffin and could hear the contractor whistling as he went the rounds of the boxes arranging the skeletons.

Once when he knew the contractor was at the creek getting a drink Raeburn called down into the pit cautiously:

"Doug, how you reckon he knows when he's got a whole skeleton in one of them coffins?"

Doug raised a face curiously striped by the greenish light that filtered down through cracks in the planking. "I'd know," he said. "He can put a skull in each box, I reckon, even if he don't know where all them little bones belong. . . . Naw, he can't, either. Some of them fellers was put in here without any head!"

"Some of 'em was blowed clean to pieces," Raeburn said.

He looked out over the field where the new green was creeping up through the clumps of brown sedge grass. They had fought all over that field, and in the woods. In December. In the snow. When they went to bury the dead the next day the ground was frozen. A foot deep. They had to dig them out with pickaxes. They had buried a lot of them on the battlefield. In two big trenches. And then they had put all the rest in this ice house. . . . In 1862 that had been. Four years ago. . . .

The contractor's round, red face showed in the doorway. "Well, boys," he said, "time for a little snack, ain't it?"

Doug had heard him and was clambering up the side of the pit. Raeburn gave him a hand and pulled him up beside him. They walked around the side of the ice house and down the path to the creek. Both boys stretched themselves on the ground and lowered their faces into the water. It was clear and very cold. Raeburn gulped some down, then thrust his hands in wrist deep and let the cold water run over them. Doug was wiping his on some water grasses. "Wish I'd brought some soap," he said. He looked at Raeburn. "It ain't so hard when you just have to stand there and let me hand 'em up to you. It's getting 'em dug out and getting 'em loose from each other that's so hard."

"I'll get down in the pit after dinner," Raeburn told him.

The contractor was on his knees in the shade of the sugar tree when they came up the path. He had a trash fire going and was boiling coffee in a little bucket. Doug and Raeburn took their cold meat and biscuits and sat down on the grass. The contractor poured coffee into tin cups.

Raeburn drank the hot coffee down at a gulp. It warmed his insides and invigorated him. He decided that he would be able to eat something, after all, and bit into a biscuit, but the sick feeling swept over him again and he had to put it down quickly. He stretched out in the grass, supporting his head on one hand. Through a rift in the bushes he could see the creek shining in the noonday sun. It ran swiftly along here just above the falls, but there were good pools, all along here and higher up, too.

Doug was asking the man questions about his business. Had he ever worked for the government before? And how was he paid? By the day or so much for the job?

The contractor had finished eating his lunch and was lighting his pipe. "I ain't had much experience working for the government. Fact is, this is the first job I ever did fer 'em. Now on this job they pay me every time I take in a load of them boxes. Every time I take in a load of them boxes they count 'em and pay me so much a head." He took his pipe out of his mouth. "So much a head," he repeated meditatively.

"Channel cat ought to be biting now," Raeburn said. His voice that was not through changing yet, though he was nearly sixteen, broke unexpectedly into a deep bass. "I know a way to catch channel cat till the world looks level."

The contractor had got up and was standing beside one of the boxes. He had his stubby fingers spread out as if he were counting. "How's that?" he asked.

"Well," Raeburn said, "you have to do it at night." He fixed his large brown eyes intently on the man's face. "The channel cat, he's a night feeder, so you have to fix for him at night. . . ."

The contractor was looking at the boxes again, but he nodded politely. "What do you have to do, son?"

"Well, you fix you some limb lines. Get you a tree that has a branch over the creek, and just tie half a dozen lines on the limbs and leave 'em. Don't use too much sinker, because the channel cat he feeds on top of the water. Just fix 'em and leave 'em there and in the morning you'll have all the fish you can eat for breakfast."

The contractor came back and sat down. "Now that's right noticing, for a boy your age," he said.

"I'm fifteen," Raeburn told him. "I'm fifteen and Doug'll be sixteen next month."

"Well now . . ." the contractor said, "and what do you boys aim to do when you get through with this job?"

"Work for Mr. Foster out on the aidge of town here," Doug said, "if he needs any hands. Folks ain't hirin' many hands now, though."

The contractor shook his head. "Farm work's all right," he said. "Farm work's all right if you can't get nothing else to do, but a smart young feller like you wants to be looking out fer oppertunity.... Ain't everybody knows oppertunity when they see it. The folks at home all thought I was mighty foolish when I come down in this country, but I knew they was oppertunity in the South ... bound to be." He put out his pipe and rose briskly. "Well," he said, "I reckon we better be gettin' back to work."

Doug stood up. "One thing," he said, "we got to have a ladder. They're way down in there now. I don't know as I can get 'em up to Raeburn without a ladder."

The contractor looked at the Porter house, just visible through the trees. "Maybe them folks would lend us a ladder.... Supposing I walk over and see if they'd lend us a ladder."

"You reckon they'll lend him a ladder?" Raeburn asked when he was gone.

"Shore they will," Doug said. " 'Tain't nothin' to lend anybody a ladder."

Raeburn watched the rotund figure disappear in the bushes that fringed the slope. "Mrs. Porter hates Yankees," he said. "They was three of her boys killed by the Yankees."

Doug laughed. "This feller never killed no Confederates."

He stepped back into the ice house and slid quickly down into the pit.

Raeburn protested as he took his stand on the ledge. "I told you I was going to get down there after dinner."

Doug shook his head. "I'm used to it now. You have to kind of get the hang of it. It'd just be wasting time now if we changed places."

He stirred the bones vigorously with his pick and a rank odor rose and floated in the chill air. Raeburn drew it into his nostrils, wondering. It was several minutes before he knew where he had smelled it before—in the wooden walls and flooring of an abandoned slaughterhouse that had stood for a long time in one of Foster's fields.

The bones that Doug was piling up on the ledge now were different from the ones on top, grayish-green, matted, some of them, with strange fungus growths. Water had stood in the ice house a good deal of the time, it seemed. Doug had to keep shifting about to find a dry place to stand on.

He did not like it if Raeburn kept his face turned away from the pit to look over the field. He talked incessantly:

"You know what that Yankee done? ... He went down there in Blue Gum Hollow and asked Uncle Hooser's boys to work for him." He laughed. "Uncle Hooser told him them boys sho would be glad to make that money, but every one of them was away from home." He laughed again, so hard that he shook all over. "Every last one of them niggers was away from home!"

"Niggers is funny," Raeburn agreed. "When my Uncle Rod was killed ... over in Caroline County ... killed right there on his front porch ... there was a old nigger man standing there in the front yard. Old Uncle Lias Sims. And he wouldn't even help my mother carry Uncle Rod in the house. Naw, sir, he just turned around and ran. Niggers don't like to have nothin' to do with dead people."

"How come your Uncle Rod to get killed settin' on his front porch?" Doug inquired.

"He was so deaf he couldn't hear 'em shelling. The rest of the folks they all got down in the cellar, then somebody got to asking where Uncle Rod was. After it was over they went out on the front porch and there he was, settin' bolt up in his chair ..."

"Dead?"

"Dead as a herring." Raeburn looked off across the field. "There's that man coming," he said, "but he ain't got no ladder. How long you reckon he expects us to work? It'll be gettin' dark pretty soon."

"Must be past seven o'clock," Doug said. "I ain't going to work no longer."

The man came up just as Doug was climbing out of the ice house. He was panting and his round face wore a harassed look. "Them folks didn't have no ladder," he said; "more'n that they sent me off on a fool errant . . . said the Widow Hickman might have a ladder. And when I get to where they say the Widow Hickman lives there ain't nothing but an old house looks like nobody ain't lived in it these thirty years. . . . Either you boys ever hear of the Widow Hickman?"

"I don't know many folks over this way," Doug said. He laid his pick up against a tree. "Well," he said, "I reckon it's about quittin' time."

The man took a leather wallet from his pocket and counted silver out into their hands. "I don't believe I'll be needin' you boys tomorrow, after all," he said.

Doug stood looking at him a minute as if he wasn't sure he'd heard right, then he said, "Suit yourself," and started off across the field. Raeburn ran and caught up with him at the edge of the woods.

"I thought you said he wanted us to work three, four days, Doug. I thought you said he wanted us to get *all* of them skeletons out of that ice house."

"Hunh," Doug said.

He stopped and looked about him a minute, then turned off into the woods. Raeburn stood there waiting. When Doug did not come back he whistled, the soft, slow whistle that they used for calling each other. Doug's head appeared suddenly over a clump of buckberry bushes. "Shh!" he said, and beckoned Raeburn to come.

Raeburn made his way through the bushes. Doug was lying flat on his stomach behind the buckberries. Raeburn lay down beside him.

"What you doing this for?" he whispered.

Doug pushed a spray of buckberry a little to one side. "Look at that," he said.

The man was standing with his back to them. In front of the coffins. He had his hat off. They could see his bald head and the fringe of gray hair that came down on his blue shirt collar. He put his hand up and scratched his bald head, then he leaned over and lifted some bones out of one of the coffins. He held them in his hands a minute as if he didn't know what to do with them, then he laid them in one of the boxes farther down the line. He kept on doing this until he had put some bones in each of the empty boxes. Then he began fastening the lids and hammering them down.

"What you reckon he's doing, Doug?" Raeburn said.

Doug put his lips up close to Raeburn's ear. "He's dividing up them skeletons," he whispered. "He's dividing up them skeletons so he can git paid double."

He got to his feet and slipped off silently through the underbrush. Raeburn followed him. When they came to where the paths forked Doug stopped. "There ain't a whole man in ary one of them boxes," he said. He slapped his leg and rocked with laughter.

"If that ain't a Yankee fer ye!"

1945

Mari Sandoz
(1896–1966)

Although Mari Sandoz wrote both novels and short fiction, she regarded the multi-volume trans-Missouri historical series as her most important work; *Old Jules* (1935) and *Crazy Horse* (1942), two of her best-known titles, are part of the series. In it, she charted the transition of the western Nebraska prairie from prehistoric times to the atomic age. Individual volumes treat the history of the seven camps of the Teton Sioux, the encroachments of white settlers, the homesteading rush, wars between ranchers and homesteaders, and her own family's experience in coping with a harsh natural environment.

Mari was the oldest child of Jules and

Mary Elizabeth, his fourth wife. The parents emigrated from Switzerland in 1881 and took up land in Sheridan County on the Niobrara River three years later. Jules Sandoz had a Utopian vision and encouraged others to come to the region, helping them find suitable parcels of land and selling seed and supplies on credit to new arrivals. Marlizzie raised six children in a house 30 miles from the nearest settlement, doing most of the field work because her husband was crippled and often absent on his location trips.

Mari, starting school at age 9, was thrilled to find that the "little black marks were the key to wonderful stories." Her father did not approve of reading or writing fiction, so she kept her work a secret for years. She passed the rural teacher's examination at the age of 16 and taught for several years before enrolling in the University of Nebraska in 1922. She worked her way through college with various jobs, including researching for the State Historical Society and proofreading for the *State Journal*. All through this period, she was writing stories. Her first publication, a short story called "The Vine," appeared in the first issue of *Prairie Schooner* (January 1927).

When the first draft of *Old Jules*, a fictionalized biography of her father, was rejected by several publishers, Sandoz burned the manuscripts of eighty-five completed stories and left Lincoln to return to the sandhill country of her birth. There she built a shack-study, began on a novel, and revised *Old Jules*. On its second round of publishers, the work was accepted for publication and won the Atlantic Prize for Nonfiction in 1935.

In the 1940s and 1950s Sandoz taught writing at several universities and continued her work on the history of her region and fiction of frontier life. Other titles in the trans-Missouri series are *Cheyenne Autumn* (1952), *The Buffalo Hunters: The Story of the Hide Men* (1954), and *The Cattlemen: From the Rio Grande across the Far Marias* (1958). *Hostiles and Friendlies* (1959) and *Sandhill Sundays and Other Recollections* (1970) are collections of short pieces. Novels include *Slogum House* (1937), *Capital City* (1939), *The Tom-Walker* (1947), *Miss Morissa: Doctor of the Gold Trail* (1955), and *The Horsecatcher* (1956).

Though the events in *Crazy Horse* took place a generation before Mari Sandoz was born, she and her collaborator, Eleanor Hinman, were able to interview several Sioux who had known him, including his friend and contemporary He-Dog, his brother-in-law Red Feather, and White Calf, an eyewitness to his death (September 5, 1877). Combining these reminiscences with the interviews collected by Judge E. S. Ricker in the Nebraska State Historical Society Library, War Department and Bureau of Indian Affairs documents, correspondence of the period, Sioux pictographs, and memoirs and newspaper accounts, Sandoz was able to flesh out the saga of the fabled Lakota leader. As in *Old Jules*, her method is to dramatize events and invent conversations based on the central core of documentary information.

The following text is from Book I, Chapter 6, of *Crazy Horse*. It describes the coming of age of the young, light-skinned Oglala Sioux. His father, Crazy Horse the holy man, had given the teenager the name His Horse Looking, but because of his soft hair, the boy was still called by his childhood name, Curly. According to the Sioux custom, Curly had been adopted by the warrior High Back Bone, or Hump, who was to help train him in the skills of a warrior.

FROM CRAZY HORSE

The Song of a Good Name

With the first noisy gathering of the mountain jays for their flight south, the people began to scatter from the great council at Bear Butte. The Oglalas and Brules of the upper Platte country started first, moving off westward around the Black Hills, to separate later at some fork in the travois trail or to make their winter camps together. Then the Two Kettles and the No Bows left, and the Blackfoot and the Hunkpapas,[1] until only the poles of the great council lodge stood on the sacred place, to fall under some far-off winter storm, back to the earth from which they grew.

Crazy Horse and his son went out from the butte in a direction that had no trail. They rode alone, each leading a pack horse, and several times the father stopped to smoke and consider, the son quiet beside him. Finally he picked a high point and when they climbed to the top it was as he had wished: a place that looked far over a country stretching away in the sun like the shadow-marked flank of a buckskin horse, while just below them lay a sheltered little valley, with trees and a stream. Here the Lakota father sat and made a long smoke. And as he smoked he remembered many things of this place, and many things of his young Brule wife who bore him two sons before she died, sons that seemed like no others among the Oglalas, particularly this first-born beside him, whose eyes and whose way had long seemed chosen for sacred things, not only to him as the father but also to him as a holy man. He had waited several years for this son to speak of what was within him and now, because it seemed that he must make the words soon or lose his power, the father had brought him up here, for as the tree that does not leaf in its time, so it is with the man who does not use the power that rises in his youth.

When the father's pipe was out, he scraped it carefully and put it away in the beaded bag with the four fringings of pale hair from the horse like the one in his vision[2] that gave him the powers of a holy man. He got the hair from the mane of a wild sorrel mare who had long led her bunch with great cunning and wisdom into the Bad Lands whenever the horse-catchers came. But Crazy Horse had finally walked her down in a deep-snow winter and cut off this much of the mane hanging between the eyes, where lies the power to see beyond the things that are. She had never become gentle for the packs or the travois but she brought him colts in years too hard for any other, and always strong ones. When his young wife died he had led the sorrel mare out and shot her at the scaffold. It seemed good that the mother of his sons should have the proud red mare beside her.

Quietly, thoughtfully, the father stroked the hair of his pipe case for the wisdom he must have to speak to this son. Finally he began.

There, in the little valley below them, was the place where Curly had first come into the sunlight of a fall day like this. It was during the very bad times for the Lakotas of the Shell river, for all their relatives. The Brule camps were crazy from the white man's whisky, the lodges old and torn because the new skins were made into robes to trade for the burning cup, and many children went hungry because none would go far enough to make a good hunt. Many young Brules died; others, like Spotted Tail, vowed never to touch the whisky. Among his own people, the Oglalas, there was even greater trouble, with much quarreling and fighting, the blood of their brothers spilled on the ground. Since then there had been no man strong enough to bring them together. Now it was not only the Oglalas that must be brought together if their lands and people were to be saved, but all the Tetons, all brought together and held against the guns and the presents of the whites.

"Somewhere a good man must rise from the young ones among us," Crazy Horse told his son. "One who has had no part in the old troubles. It will not be enough for him to speak words of wisdom if he cannot give the people ears to hear and hearts to make them strong against the power of the white man's favor. He must be one who does great deeds for the young to see, great deeds for the people. It will take a very big, a very strong man, one the people can see standing above the others."

So the father spoke to young Curly, and because the boy could not bear to look into his face he got up and walked to the edge of the little hill, hot and ashamed under his blanket

---

1. The Teton circle of the Sioux included these camps and the Minneconjou.

2. Often a name or a course in life were derived from a coming-of-age vision.

that he was not a big man, big as his uncle, Spotted Tail, or his cousin, Touch the Clouds, the man who stood tall as a tree among the warriors.

But his father was not yet done. "Strength of arm and heart, even with every wisdom, will not be enough," he said. "The man must have the help of a great vision, one that drives him straight as the bowstring sends the arrow, one that brings together in him all the powers that are in the people."

The son looked out over the yellow plain below him and now it lay wide and far and empty as the whole earth and before it he was indeed small and weak, his heart as snow water. His father saw this happen and came to stand by the side of his son. "It is true that it will take a great man to save the people now," he said softly, as though speaking to himself, "a very great man, and many will hate him, and many try to get him killed—"

Still young Curly made no words of reply, but slowly his lean, sharp face lifted, his eyes looking beyond the fall-shadowed plain to the place where the earth and the sky meet, the earth and the sky and everything between, and suddenly now he was a part of them, a part of all things that are, and as he saw this, power surged through his breast.

Turning, the boy dropped his blanket and stood straight before his father, waiting.

So they built a sweat lodge near the creek and took a fast and a sweat and then they talked, young Curly telling all he could of the vision.[3] At first it was pale as an old dream, fogged in forgetting. But it became much clearer in the stinging breath of the sweat lodge, plainer even than when he sat under the cottonwood after the long waiting on the bluff the day before Conquering Bear[4] died. So he made the words for it, keeping back only what he thought the man of the vision would not have told, only the little about things that would make for sorrow before it must be. He told his father of seeing the dead-alive chief[5] between the legs of Hump and then running away to the high gravel hill, of the fast and the long wait, the hard work to keep from sleeping, the feeling that he was not fit for a vision because nothing came to him, no vision and no living thing, and then the giving up and going down to where his hobbled horse was feeding. But by then it seemed that all the earth was shaking around him, with a great sickness sitting in his belly, and because he was afraid of falling from his horse he waited a little in the shade of the cottonwood.

It seemed he must have slept because he had a feeling of giving up and letting himself go, and almost at once his horse that was hobbled out there eating started towards him, his neck high, his feet moving free. A man was on his back, sitting well forward, only the heel fringe of his moccasin stirring as he rode. It was not like the world the boy knew but the real world behind this one, the sky and the trees in it, the grass waving, but all in a strange and sacred way. Then he saw that the horse the man was riding changed to a bay and then yellow-spotted and many other colors too. And always it seemed to float, so light, and the man sitting on the horse seemed light too. He wore plain blue leggings and a white buckskin shirt, with no paint and only one feather in his long brown hair that hung loose below his waist. There were a few beads in his scalp lock and a small brown stone was tied behind his ear. He spoke no sounds but the boy heard him clearly, saying things that have no words.

And all the time the enemy shadows kept coming up before the man, but he rode straight into them, with streakings all about him, like arrows and lead balls, but always disappearing before they struck him. Several times he was held back, it seemed by some of his own people who came up from behind and caught his arms, but he shook them off and rode on, while behind him a storm cloud rolled and thunder was in the air and on the man's cheek a little

---

3. Curly has gone out without his father or his adopted warrior-father's approval to seek his vision.

4. A "paper chief" selected by the white man, Conquering Bear was shot during a conference

over a white man's cow, which was killed by the Sioux when it strayed into their camp.

5. Conquering Bear lingered for several days. Curley saw him being lifted by Hump and other warriors.

zigzag that seemed of lightning, and a few hail spots on his body that was stripped to the breechcloth now. Then the storm faded, the spots too, and he rode on, the people closer around him, making a great noise, some grabbing, grabbing, while over him flew the small hawk with red on his back, making his killy-killy crying.

Curly stopped and was silent, and when his father urged him on, he said that was all. Suddenly the man had faded, and everything of that other world with him. Out on the bottom near the cottonwood his horse moved slowly about, awkward as before in his eating hobbles, and on a purple thistle, swaying with its weight, a small red-backed hawk was saying "killy-killy" and beside him, looking at him with impatience, were Hump and his father.[6]

A long time Crazy Horse, the holy man of the Oglalas, sat silent over this. Finally he spoke to his son.

"Hou! It is as I saw it that day. You have been given a great vision, and you cannot move the load of it from you," he said. "The man on the horse is what you must become—did you not see his hair, how bright and long—or how he thought—?"

Yes, how he thought— It must have been himself, Curly saw now, for he knew what the man was thinking without any hearing of words at all.

So it was, the father agreed. And when young Curly went into battle he need only think of this vision to be like the man, unhit by enemy bullets. At all times he must do as the man did, dress like him, have a hawk over him, and the small stone behind his ear. He must be the first in the fighting, as the man was, and in the leading of the people, and he must do these things although often the road would seem dark and dangerous, the right way not clear. It would take much thought, and much trusting in the power of his vision, for it is only from the very high hill of death that all the rivers can be seen to run to the salt sea.

After the great Lakota council at Bear Butte broke up, some Minneconjous and Hunkpapas hunting buffalo west of the Black Hills found a soldier chief with many wagons along who said he was Lieutenant Warren, going through their country for the Great Father. The Lakotas were very angry, the warriors hot to kill them all. Bear Ribs and the other chiefs held them back and told the officer he must leave at once and tell everybody to keep away from the Indian country. If their annuities[7] were to pay for the whites coming into their lands they did not want the goods, and if they were given to stop the fighting against the Crows, they didn't want them either, for the war was to go on.

So it seemed that the northern Lakotas might be strong, but there was no heart in the Oglalas, with many still thinking about the little troubles of their own villages. Old Smoke lived down near the soldier town with the Loaf About the Forts, but his band, called Bad Faces now, was up north around the headquarters of the Cheyenne River, near Red Dog's Oyukhpes, Sitting Bear's True Oglalas, and the Hunkpatilas. White Beard,[8] angry at the independent way of Man Afraid, had made Bad Wound of the Bear people the paper chief of all the Oglalas. The old Indian let it be done, but he did not try to come near the councils of the northern Oglalas; instead he went south to Little Wound, the son of Bull Bear, hunting with the Brules in the Republican River country, still claimed by the Pawnees.

There were more soldiers coming up the Holy Road,[9] not only to fight the Cheyennes but going against the whites of the Salt Lake country. So the Mormons who had built houses and fields up where Deer Creek joins the Platte hurried away west to their people at the lake. As soon as this place was empty, Major Twiss moved the agency and his young Oglala woman up there. Janis, the trader, visiting with Man Afraid, said that the officers at Laramie were very angry with the agent for this. But he had been a soldier chief himself and knew how to talk to them.

6. Who had come looking for the missing teenager.
7. Yearly allotments of food and clothing promised by the government for access to Indian lands.
8. General William S. Harney (1800–1889).
9. The westward Oregon trail, running in this region along the North Platte river.

"You cannot come corporaling it over me!" the major had told them. And they let him go.

Crazy Horse and some of the others wondered about the story Janis told. They had seen soldiers do very hard and foolish things because a man they called their officer told them to.

Oh, but this was different, Janis said. The major belonged to another branch of the government, as though to another *akicita*[1] among the Indians or to another band. Perhaps someone from the Brules or the Minneconjous would come to tell Man Afraid to do something?

That made the Indians laugh, the women too, sitting back from the fire, softening deerskin between their hands, their small children beside them. It was funny. Not even the greatest chief among them told anybody what to do.

But it was good to have an agent like that, the older men said, between the whistlings of their pipes. Good to have their annuities given out near the buffalo ranges, and the traders once more coming to their villages with the coffee and the sweet lumps, the guns and the powder, as they did in the old days, before the Holy Road of the whites cut through their buffalo herds like a knife gash down the middle of a robe.

Hou! And it was good to be far enough from the soldiers so that they could not be counting everything that came in, every barrel hoop for the arrow points or palmful of powder for the guns. Even Richard[2] was back at his bridge over the Platte, and that meant the good Spanish blankets and other things from the people to the south.

Yes, and a little whisky for the belly cramps. As the stocky Richard with the many sons always said, no man was strong enough to keep him from selling anything he liked. Certainly it would not be the white-haired father at Deer Creek or the soldier chief down on the Laramie.

So that winter and spring the Oglalas scouted out new camping grounds along the headwaters of the Powder and the Belle Fourche and began to hunt in closer alliance with the Minneconjous and No Bows of the Black Hills, and with the northern Cheyennes of the upper Platte. The meat was fat up here, and the camps full of the roasting smells. They had sent word to the Crows to make all the arrows they could, for the Oglalas were coming, openly this time, and strong with men. The peace paper signed at the Big Council was forgotten by the Indians as it had been forgotten by the soldiers when they brought wagon guns into the Brule camp to kill their chief, more than four winters ago.

Some of Curly's friends had gone against the Crows last year, He Dog among them. Because the chiefs must pretend not to see, they could not make the war party parading through the village but had to slip out and back in the night-time, bringing in some good Crow horses and a couple of the white blanket capotes[3] with hoods for the winter storms. Best of all were the two new guns that the Crows dropped as they ran away. Even young He Dog got a horse and a Crow spear with an old Lakota scalp tied to the end. But nobody had been hurt and no coups[4] were counted, so it was nothing compared to the fight with the Omahas where Fontenelle was killed and Curly shot the woman,[5] or to seeing the strong medicine of the Cheyennes against the white man's guns broken by the charge with swords. But it was better than anything the boys of the Loafers had to tell, and it made the waiting for the next expedition seem very long.

Finally the sundance[6] and the summer hunt were done and a party got ready, openly, as agreed in the council at Bear Butte, with He Dog, Young Man Afraid, Lone Bear, and Curly along. Crazy Horse and Long Face had made a medicine bundle for the boy, and got him a brown stone to tie behind his ear and a red-backed hawk to put on his head for the fighting.

---

1. Warrior society. Each Sioux camp had several different societies.
2. A friendly trader.
3. Hooded cloaks.
4. Counting coups is the practice of touching the

enemy with a stick to show bravery.
5. He was unable to see in the dark that she was a woman and shot her by mistake.
6. Midsummer celebration.

The other warriors seemed as anxious as Hump to have him along now, for it was said he had been given a very strong medicine, and they wanted to see it tried.

But just before the party started, something bad happened. Curly was shot in the knee, not by an enemy, but by an Oglala in his own village. It was an accident and so to be forgotten as the water that falls on a stone is forgotten, but some saw it as part of the sacred vision come true. It was only by his own people that the son of Crazy Horse could be hurt.

The war party went out anyway, although it was considered a bad sign if anything happened to one of the warriors before they started. But Curly was only a boy, and so he had to listen to a night of drumming and dancing and the noise of the party leaving the next morning, the women calling out this name and that as the warriors rode by, making the trilling as the party started away. Curly buried his ears in the wolfskin pillow. He could bear the staying behind with a good face, but he disliked the noisy joys and griefs of his people more and more. Sometimes it seemed they must be as bad as the Crows, whose men, it was said, cried loud as the women for the dead. It made the Lakotas seem not brave, this noise over everything, and that Curly knew was not true.

Before the next moon the party was back, sneaking into the village in the night. They had found no coups and no horses, only big travois trails going north, beyond the Yellowstone.

While his knee was healing, young Curly limped around with the forked end of a long stick under his arm, what the traders' sons called a crutch. He spent much time listening to the father of Bad Heart Bull, the band historian. From him he learned the history of his people, the keeping of the winter counts and the picture histories that helped this man sing the great deeds of the Lakota heroes at the ceremonials and councils.

"A people without history is like the wind on the buffalo grass," the old man said over his paint stones and his quill and bone brushes.

"Hou! That is true!" Crazy Horse agreed.

As the geese and sandhill cranes went south and then came back, the Oglalas followed the path laid out through their new country the year before, every camp with wood and water close, the moves often enough for good grass and cleanness, everything done in the good way, without confusion or trouble. Now that there was no hanging around the whites of the Holy Road, no begging or grabbing at anything they could get, like dogs around the meat racks, Curly saw that many of his people were still the same as in the stories of his father and the band historian. Perhaps old-time white men like Le Beau and Bridger[7] who knew the Lakotas before the days of the whisky wagons and the Holy Road spoke true when they said the Indian got lazy, dirty, and lousy from the whites. It was strange that the lazier, lousier ones were given presents and that those who would hunt for their living were chased by the wagon guns.

So the buffalo dropped their red calves, the fork-tail bird, the swallow, came back from the south, and the eagle-catchers cleared out their pits. With the summer's passing there were stories of the buffalo gone from up around Heart River, where many Hunkpapas and Minneconjous lived, the people eating ponies. So a party of Oglalas went up with old Lone Horn of the North, taking pack horses of meat and robes, and invitations to their relatives to come visiting. Some men who had been far down the Missouri for a little visiting said they found not one buffalo all the way, or any chips. They found wheel tracks all the way up the Running Water too, right over the old camp ground where Conquering Bear died, and through all that country where so many of their dead ones lay. Here, too, the buffalo were leaving before the lengthening shadow of the whites.

Ahh-h, it seemed indeed so, the old ones agreed, and down along the Holy Road there was a cow-dying sickness this summer, one the Frenchmen called bloody murrain. Many wagons

7. Fur traders and guides. In 1843, Jim Bridger   Oregon Trail.
   (1804–1881) opened Fort Bridger on the

were left standing where the cattle fell down. The trail from Laramie far into the west was lined and stinking with the carcasses, particularly around the agency at Deer Creek, where the slopes above the road were yellow with fall flowers as if nothing at all had died. Some said the sickness might do like the others brought by the whites, spread through the Indian country. It might kill the horses or even the buffalo. There was a story of so many antelope already dead on the northern ranges that the sunburnt prairies were dark with them, and the wolves so fat they lay down to eat.

But in the new Oglala hunting lands the summer had been a good one, hot and a little dusty, with many of the sky pictures that the traders called mirages—pictures of shaking little lakes and green trees. In the nights there was the star with a long white tail to speak of good things, and it was true that the buffalo were plentiful clear down to the forks of the Platte, where the Bear people lived. When the wolves cleared away the stink of the dead cattle it was pleasant around the agency at Deer Creek, with always a few Indian lodges pitched near, the people trading, visiting, and then going away with their annuities. When the snows made the robes thick and the fur of the beaver and otter, too, the traders came to the villages as in the old days. There were several in each camp, for the white-haired agent had licensed enough to make the trade good again. Big Bat and a helper came with eight pack horses to Red Cloud's winter camp far west on the Wind River and took a full load, twenty robes to the horse, back to Richard. It was so in every village, clear up towards the Yellowstone, where Guerrier let a spark from his pipe fall into an open keg of powder he was measuring out for robes. When the Oglalas heard how he was blown to pieces they felt bad, but he was one of the soldier traders and so not like their own.

Towards spring Curly and Lone Bear found a white man dead in the Sweetwater country. He had no gun and nothing along to eat, but in a dirty little sack that smelled of tobacco hung around his neck were two stones of the yellow stuff, the gold that drove the whites crazy. Curly had seen great trains of these people go west when he was a small boy, all headed over the mountains to the salt sea, Bridger told them. Damn fools, he called them. Many came back and some, they heard, got caught in the snows and ate one another.[8] Truly these whites were a strange people.

Lately they had started to run down into the mountains in the country of the Black Men, the Utes. Even some of those married into the Oglalas went, like the Janises. The Cheyennes had found many of the gold-chasing white men lost and starving along the Smoky Hill River. They fed them and showed them how to get back to their people, but they would go on, although some of the wisest chiefs said that the yellow earth was not worth as much as the turnips the women dig, for those a hungry man could eat.

Now some of the gold-crazy ones must be coming to the Sweetwater, for where there is one, even a dead one, there will be others, bringing the bad things of the whites, scaring the game, scattering sickness. Already people were dying of the stinking spots over in the Beaverhead Valley, where a camp of trappers and traders' sons were living.

Yes, there would be many gold-hunting whites around, but the Crows and the Snakes were better fighting, the warriors said.

Up in the north country there was a stranger thing—several white buffaloes had been shot this fall, more than were sometimes seen in all the days of a man's life. Nobody understood this and so the robes were painted and given back to the earth, as was good with such sacred things. Then, the evening of a thawing winter day, Curly saw one. He was coming in alone from the mountains, his horse loaded with fresh elk. The buffalo stood on a south slope, almost as white as the snow patches about him. Curly was near enough for a good shot but before he raised his gun the animal threw up his fine, curly head, sniffed the wind, and was

---

8. The Donner party, trapped in the Sierra Nevada Mountains by snow in the winter of 1846–1847, were believed to have engaged in cannibalism.

gone over the ridge, his hoofs throwing snow and pounding on the dark, freezing earth. The boy whipped his loaded horse after the buffalo but he found nothing except tracks leading through a dusk-filled little valley. In a bare place they ended, as when the long-eared rabbit doubles back on his trail and then jumps to the side to sleep with his eyes open and watching. But the buffalo is not small and helpless and has no need for such tricks. It must have been a holy animal, so instead of searching for more tracks, the young Oglala hobbled his horse, made a wickiup of cedar branches where the trail ended, and spent the night there, hoping to dream. He slept well, awakened only once or twice by the howling of wolves drawn to his fire by the smell of the fresh meat. In the morning it was snowing, soft, warm, with the promise of a spring sun to break through and free the bowing cedars of their load. All the tracks were gone, everything covered, and he had dreamed nothing he could remember. So he started home.

The day he got back to the big Oglala village a crier went around calling everyone to the woman feast[9] for the niece of Red Cloud, Black Buffalo Woman as she was now called. Young Curly looked out to make certain he had heard right, and then hurried to dress himself for the feast. It was lucky he had not tried to hunt for the white buffalo or he would have missed this great time in the life of the pretty Oglala girl. He had not seen her very often the last few years, with all his visiting among the Brules and the Cheyennes. But she was always in his heart, as surely in a certain place as a warrior's weapons are, so even while sleeping he can grasp them at any strange thing in the night.

Curly had been a small boy when Black Buffalo Woman was born. He remembered it because the one he called mother had stayed back with a woman one day when her people were moving with them. Later the two came into camp with one who hadn't been with them before, a new little daughter for the brother of Red Cloud. Young Curly looked upon this small thing as somehow belonging to his own lodge, and when she got bigger he often stopped his playing to chase flies from her face as she swung in her cradleboard from a branch or leaned against the lodge while her mother scraped the hides. With the long spear of grass he used for playing he tickled the corners of her sober little mouth until she awoke and laughed, learning to look around for him with her round black eyes before she could make words. She had been one of the little girls in the ceremony when he was given the name of His Horse Looking, which no one used, although it was done with the parading through the village, the feasting, and the horses given away. Then there was the time he threw plums at the girl, his sister and brother teasing him about this, making him so warm and happy in his blanket. Since then he had been much away from the Oglalas, and often when he was home the Bad Face village of her people was not camped near. But the last year the girl had grown tall and was much alone. When the people were close together Curly sometimes loafed along the water path to walk a little with her, but the old woman of her lodge always chased him with such loud shouting and abuse that he ran, laughing much and pretending to be afraid. But sometimes it seemed the soft eyes of the girl sought him out, even in the daylight circle, where many were ready to see.

Now the old camp crier was running through the village announcing that the niece of Red Cloud had become a woman and that all the people were invited to visit her father's lodge. There was much excitement, much dressing up by the young men, much noisy moving down towards the lodge, for there would be feasting and ponies given away and a fine first woman-dress to see.

When Curly worked up through the crowd of men, women, and children, he found that the whole front of the lodge had been thrown open and behind the coals of ash wood, on a pile of robes, was Black Buffalo Woman. She was sitting in the woman's way, her feet to one side, and her hair smooth and shining, the part vermilioned, her slender young face too. Her dress was of white buckskin with a deep beaded yoke of blue, the wing sleeves and the bottom

9. Coming-of-age ceremony for a female.

fringed, the leggings beaded too, and the moccasins. On her breast hung many strings of beads, blue, red, and yellow, and on her arms were bracelets of copper and silver. Beside the girl stood an old man of the village, shouting advice in a voice loud enough for all to hear, earning the good pony he would receive for his work. He spoke first of her duty to her father and her brothers, to honor them by bringing a strong man into their family and giving them good sons, to hear them in all things.

"A Bad Face is speaking," some of the women of the other bands whispered, laughing a little among themselves, remembering the troubles of the son of Smoke. But the old man had words for the other things, too, the old, old things that make a good Lakota woman— diligence, modesty, virtue, and the mother heart for the people.

"Follow Mother Earth in all things," he counseled. "See how she feeds her children, clothes and shelters them, comforts them with her good silence when their hearts have fallen down. Be like Mother Earth in all things and so be a good woman of the Lakota!"

Hou! the people agreed, while the girl sat with lowered eyes. Once she looked up and, seeing young Curly so near, her cheeks turned ruddy under the vermilion as she dropped her head.

When the talk was done and the people crowded around her to see the fine new clothes, the young men passing before her in their best regalia, Curly pushed his way out, not waiting for the feasting. At the lodge he threw himself upon his bed, buried his face in the wolfskin that was his pillow, and thought of things that filled his breast hard with strength and greatness.

The next day Curly and Crazy Horse rode off into the hills for a smoke. There he told his father of the white buffalo and the way that it was lost. A long time the holy man of the Oglalas sat silent.

"It seems there are many sacred things happening to you, my son," the father said. "It is hard to tell what they will bring, but it seems they will be good things if you work alone like the buffalo you saw and do not try to carry anything back for yourself."

The next day Hump led a party out to raid a small tribe of Indians said to be relatives of the Snakes, but speaking a changed tongue. The Oglalas knew little of them, for they had seldom camped as far west as the Wind River country but the scouts said they lived in grass houses, so they would not be a fighting people like lodge Indians, and they had some very good horses. The warriors were hot to try their hearts against these strangers.

But the people of the unknown tongue evidently had scouts out and long before the Lakota party reached their houses their warriors started shooting from the top of a hill. It was a good fighting place they had selected, high up, covered with big rocks, and there seemed to be many guns among them. Hump and his warriors circled the place several times, whooping, shooting under the necks of their horses, but it seemed these people had seen such fighting before and did not waste much powder on running horses so far away. Then Hump led his warriors in a crawling up the hillside, but there was little to hide behind and some good men might be lost before they got into bow range, so they gave that up too, and tried charging a few times and more circling, still hoping to waste all the enemy powder.

It was a hard two-hour fight, the Lakotas losing some of their horses and getting a man hurt. They killed one or two men but couldn't drive the others from the rocks. Finally Curly's horse went down, and as he jumped from it, he remembered his vision and, catching a loose one of the enemy, he got on and was waiting for another circling when somebody behind him fired a shot. The horse was young and wild and it charged straight ahead, up the hill into the enemy. As in his vision he rode light and safe through the arrows and bullets that flew all around him making a wind past his bare breast, hitting stones and spurting up gravel. Flat against his horse he managed to draw his bow and drive an arrow into a warrior rising with a gun from a gully before him. The man fell back, the horse jumped him, and shying sideways from another one, swung off down the hill. There was a great whooping over this strong medicine from the Oglalas. Hump rode out to meet the boy, but before the warrior reached him, Curly had turned the horse and charged up the hill into the wall of shooting again. Once more he got a man, this time with the revolver from his belt, dropping him lower down in the gully, and as the whoop of approval went up from the Lakotas, Curly's heart swelled. Forgetting all his vision, he slipped off to take the scalp, and the other man's too, in full sight of the enemy. Just as he ripped up the second lock he was hit in the leg, the wild horse jerked loose, and so he had to flee down the hill afoot, jumping this way and that, the ground and the bushes on both sides cut by the flying lead. The Oglala warriors were in a half circle watching this thing—those with guns firing at the enemies who looked from behind their rocks at the boy getting away through all their shooting.

Only when the boy was back among the others did he remember about the hair he held in his hand. He should not have taken it, and because he did he was wounded. So he threw it away and sat down behind a rock to stop the bleeding. Hump looped the scalps under his belt, cut the iron arrow from the boy's leg, and tied it tightly with a fresh piece of skin from a dead horse. It was enough for today, the warriors said, and leaving the enemies in the rocks they started home.

Outside of the village the party stopped and sent a man ahead to announce their return. Then they came in, the two shield men leading, their spears bright in the sun. Behind them came the warriors in rows four abreast, their weapons in their hands, the war-bonnet men in their feathers. And in the back was the boy the village knew as Curly, without paint or feathers, only a red-backed hawk in his hair and the small brown stone half hidden behind his ear.

That night there was a big victory dance, for they had killed four, counted eight first coups, got some good horses, and lost no man at all. One after another the deeds were told, the people cheering each man for what he had done. Only Curly would not tell of his exploits. Twice he was pushed forward into the circle and each time he backed out. So they went on to dance the scalps, the mother of Curly, the only woman with two on her staff, leading them. Many eyes were on the boy, seventeen now but still small among the warriors, many eyes that were friendly—Hump's and his father's proud, his brother's excited and adoring, and those of Black Buffalo Woman soft and no longer so shy. But there were some eyes that were envious of this light-haired one and these, too, young Curly could not forget.

That night the boy did not sleep. His leg pained very little in its wet bandage of herbs that his father had cooked in a stone bowl in the old way, touching no iron or other metal, but there were so many things to think about, particularly his forgetting about the scalps. What good was a strong vision to a man if he forgot it in the first fight?

The next morning he still felt bad and so he lay still on his side of the lodge, so still that even his brother thought him sleeping. As his people got up they went out quietly, and finally young Curly slept. When the sun stood almost straight up, he awoke and was given a horn spoon of soup. Then Crazy Horse came in and took his ceremonial blanket from its case, the one with the beaded band across the middle showing all the sacred things of his holy vision. With this blanket about him, his braids long and fur-wrapped on his breast, the father walked slowly through the village, making a song as he went, singing it so all might hear:

> *My son has been against the people of unknown tongue.*
> *He has done a brave thing;*
> *For this I give him a new name, the name of his father,*
> *and of many fathers before him—*
> *I give him a great name*
> *I call him Crazy Horse.*

And behind the father came all those of the village who wished to honor the young man among them who had done a brave deed. By the time they came to the lodge where the boy sat, there was a mighty double line of the people until it seemed that everybody was walking in it: young men, old men, great men, wise ones, and all the women and the children too, all singing and laughing.

Then there was feasting and dancing all that day and late into the night, for among the Oglalas there was a new warrior, a warrior to be known by the great name of Crazy Horse.

1942

Louise Bogan

(1897–1970)

In a time dominated in verse by the high modernist mode and large ambitions of Ezra Pound and T. S. Eliot, women turned often to formal lyrics, more "feminine," less ambitious in scope than such works as *The Cantos* or *The Waste Land.* "Feminine," too, was the personal note frequently observed in the lyrics of the most popular women poets of the 1920s and 1930s. Poetry loose and irregular, intellectual, focused on large cultural matters, the times seemed to say, was the proper work of men. Shapely verse in small forms, personal and emotional, was for women. Against this paradigm, Louise Bogan was only half feminine, writing small lyric poems that were intense but impersonal, their emotional content bounded by a cool rationality. Her restricted output and her reserve in matters of content combined to limit her readership and her reputation during most of her life.

Born in Livermore Falls, Maine, she grew up embittered by family tensions, and by her mother's frequent infidelity to her father and abandonment of her family. "For half my life," she wrote, she was no more than "the semblance of a girl, in which some desires and illusions had early been assassinated: shot dead." She attended parochial school in Manchester, New Hampshire, graduated from Girls Latin School in Boston, and spent a year at Boston University before marrying a soldier and giving birth to a daughter in the Panama Canal Zone in 1917. Two years

later she left her husband, who soon died; she left her child with her parents when she moved to Greenwich Village to begin her life as a writer. Cautious in her personal relations, she married once more, but that marriage ended in divorce. Fighting off mental illness, hospitalized at times, she wrote relatively little verse that fully satisfied her. Her first book of verse, *Body of This Death* (1923) was followed by three more—*Dark Summer* (1929), *The Sleeping Fury* (1937), and *Poems and New Poems* (1941)—before the comprehensive *The Blue Estuaries, Poems: 1923–1968* (1968) gathered all her work in one slim volume containing 105 poems.

Much of her reputation while she lived was as a critic. From 1931 to 1968 she wrote poetry reviews for *The New Yorker,* earning a reputation for fair and incisive judgments. Yet it is probably in the lyric perfection of her best verse that she will be longest remembered.

The Blue Estuaries (1968) is the final complete collection and the source of the texts below. *Collected Poems, 1923–1953* appeared in 1953. Criticism is collected in *Achievement in American Poetry, 1900–1950* (1951) and *Selected Criticism: Poetry and Prose* (1955). Robert Phelps and Ruth Limmer edited *A Poet's Alphabet: Reflections on the Literary Art and Vocation* (1970). Ruth Limmer edited *Journey around My Room: The Autobiography of Louise Bogan, A Mosaic* (1980) and *What the Woman Lived: Selected Letters of Louise Bogan, 1920–1970* (1973).

A biography is Elizabeth Frank, *Louise Bogan: A Portrait* (1986). Studies include William Jay Smith, *Louise Bogan: A Woman's Words* (1971); and Gloria Bowles, *Louise Bogan's Aesthetic of Limitation* (1987).

The Alchemist

I burned my life, that I might find
A passion wholly of the mind,
Thought divorced from eye and bone,
Ecstasy come to breath alone.
I broke my life, to seek relief   5
From the flawed light of love and grief.

With mounting beat the utter fire
Charred existence and desire.
It died low, ceased its sudden thresh.
I had found unmysterious flesh—   10
Not the mind's avid substance—still
Passionate beyond the will.

                                        1923

Men Loved Wholly Beyond Wisdom

Men loved wholly beyond wisdom
Have the staff without the banner.
Like a fire in a dry thicket
Rising within women's eyes
Is the love men must return.   5
Heart, so subtle now, and trembling,
What a marvel to be wise,
To love never in this manner!
To be quiet in the fern
Like a thing gone dead and still,   10
Listening to the prisoned cricket
Shake its terrible, dissembling
Music in the granite hill.

                                        1923

The Crows

The woman who has grown old
And knows desire must die,
Yet turns to love again,
Hears the crows' cry.

She is a stem long hardened,   5
A weed that no scythe mows.
The heart's laughter will be to her
The crying of the crows,

Who slide in the air with the same voice
Over what yields not, and what yields,   10
Alike in spring, and when there is only bitter
Winter-burning in the fields.

1923

Women

Women have no wilderness in them,
They are provident instead,
Content in the tight hot cell of their hearts
To eat dusty bread.

They do not see cattle cropping red winter grass,   5
They do not hear
Snow water going down under culverts
Shallow and clear.

They wait, when they should turn to journeys,
They stiffen, when they should bend.   10
They use against themselves that benevolence
To which no man is friend.

They cannot think of so many crops to a field
Or of clean wood cleft by an axe.
Their love is an eager meaninglessness   15
Too tense, or too lax.

They hear in every whisper that speaks to them
A shout and a cry.
As like as not, when they take life over their door-sills
They should let it go by.   20

1923

Dark Summer

Under the thunder-dark, the cicadas resound.
The storm in the sky mounts, but is not yet heard.
The shaft and the flash wait, but are not yet found.

The apples that hang and swell for the late comer,
The simple spell, the rite not for our word,   5
The kisses not for our mouths,—light the dark summer.

1929

Roman Fountain

Up from the bronze, I saw
Water without a flaw
Rush to its rest in air,
Reach to its rest, and fall.

Bronze of the blackest shade,   5
An element man-made,
Shaping upright the bare
Clear gouts of water in air.

O, as with arm and hammer,
Still it is good to strive   10
To beat out the image whole,
To echo the shout and stammer
When full-gushed waters, alive,
Strike on the fountain's bowl
After the air of summer.   15

                                        1937

Evening in the Sanitarium[1]

The free evening fades, outside the windows fastened with decorative iron grilles.
The lamps are lighted; the shades drawn; the nurses are watching a little.
It is the hour of the complicated knitting on the safe bone needles; of the games of anagrams and bridge;
The deadly game of chess; the book held up like a mask.

The period of the wildest weeping, the fiercest delusion, is over.   5
The women rest their tired half-healed hearts; they are almost well.
Some of them will stay almost well always: the blunt-faced woman whose thinking dissolved
Under academic discipline; the manic-depressive girl
Now leveling off; one paranoiac afflicted with jealousy.
Another with persecution. Some alleviation has been possible.   10

O fortunate bride, who never again will become elated after childbirth!
O lucky older wife, who has been cured of feeling unwanted!
To the suburban railway station you will return, return,
To meet forever Jim home on the 5:35.
You will be again as normal and selfish and heartless as anybody else.   15

There is life left: the piano says it with its octave smile.
The soft carpets pad the thump and splinter of the suicide to be.
Everything will be splendid: the grandmother will not drink habitually.
The fruit salad will bloom on the plate like a bouquet
And the garden produce the blue-ribbon aquilegia.[2]   20

                                        1941

---

1. This poem was originally published with the subtitle "Imitated from Auden" [Bogan's note].

2. Columbine, a plant of the buttercup family.

The Dragonfly

You are made of almost nothing
But of enough
To be great eyes
And diaphanous double vans;
To be ceaseless movement,   5
Unending hunger
Grappling love.

Link between water and air,
Earth repels you.
Light touches you only to shift into iridescence 10
Upon your body and wings.

Twice-born, predator,
You split into the heat,
Swift beyond calculation or capture
You dart into the shadow   15
Which consumes you.

You rocket into the day.
But at last, when the wind flattens the grasses,
For you, the design and purpose stop.

And you fall   20
With the other husks of summer.

       1968

Night

The cold remote islands
And the blue estuaries
Where what breathes, breathes
The restless wind of the inlets,
And what drinks, drinks   5
The incoming tide;

Where shell and weed
Wait upon the salt wash of the sea,
And the clear nights of stars
Swing their lights westward   10
To set behind the land;

Where the pulse clinging to the rocks
Renews itself forever;
Where, again on cloudless nights,
The water reflects   15
The firmament's partial setting;

—O remember
In your narrowing dark hours
That more things move
Than blood in the heart.   20

1968

Meridel Le Sueur

(1900–)

A product of the Midwest, Le Sueur was born in Iowa, lived for a time in Kansas, and called St. Paul, Minnesota, home for most of her life. Early in life she was cared for by her grandmother and mother; later her mother, Marian Wharton, married the leftist lawyer Arthur Le Sueur. In her parents' home she met leaders of the radical and labor movement, including Eugene Debs, Emma Goldman, and Ella (Mother) Bloor, and absorbed the leftist ideal of the artist-worker. After dropping out of high school (1916), she studied dance in Chicago and acting at New York's American Academy of Dramatic Art. She appeared in New York stage productions before going to Hollywood where she worked as an actress and stunt woman in silent films. In San Francisco and Sacramento, she acted in little theater, supporting herself as a waitress.

All this time she was writing and having articles published in magazines such as *The Worker* and *Masses*; the story "Persephone" was published in the *Dial* in May 1927. The same year, imprisoned for protesting the trial of Sacco and Vanzetti, she made a decision to have a child, convinced that the bond between mother and child was the last vestige of common humanity in a ruined world. Rachel's birth in 1928 was followed by that of Deborah two years later. By the end of the decade she was back in Minnesota and had turned to the emphasis on women in myth and in society that was to characterize her most significant work.

She experienced considerable success as a journalist and fiction writer in the 1930s

and early 1940s. Sixteen of her short stories were chosen for reprint or listing in the best short story collections edited by Edward O'Brien; "I Was Marching," a chronicle of her involvement with a truckers' strike, appeared in *New Masses* in 1934; *Annunciation*, a meditation on pregnancy, was published in 1935, and *Salute to Spring*, a gathering of twelve stories and sketches, was published in 1940 with dust jacket tributes by Sinclair Lewis and Carl Sandburg. A grant from the Rockefeller Historical Research Fellowship enabled her to write an impressionistic history of her home region, *North Star Country* (1945).

The end of World War II and the onset of the Cold War, with its phobia against leftists and blacklisting of artists, forced her and others into retreat. For Le Sueur it meant a switch to writing biographies for young readers; she was able to get her books on figures such as Lincoln and his mother, Nancy Hanks, Johnny Appleseed, and Davy Crockett printed and the proceeds enabled her to survive financially while more political writing was, for the most part, stored away. In the mid-1950s, after her mother died, she began to spend time with Native Americans, both in Minnesota and in New Mexico. Many of the poems in her 1975 volume *Rites of Ancient Ripening* are spoken through the voices of Indian women and rooted in Native American myth.

With the rise of the women's movement and the freer climate of the 1960s, her feminist work was resurrected. In 1977, John Crawford, founder of West End Press, visited her and searched through her large collection of manuscripts, choosing material for several books: two volumes of short fiction, *Harvest* and *Song for My Time* (published by his press in 1977); two pamphlets, *Women on the Breadlines* (1977) and *Worker Writers* (1982); two longer stories, "The Bird" and "The Horse," included in a 1983 volume *I Hear Men Talking;* and a novel, *The Girl* (1978), completed in 1939. Some of the work had earlier been published in periodicals; other pieces had never seen print before.

In her "Afterword," dedicated to "the great and heroic women of the depression," Le Sueur makes clear that *The Girl* is a compilation of the experience of real women she interviewed in unemployment and relief offices, bars, drab rooming houses, and meetings of the Workers Alliance writers group. Some wrote out versions of their own lives, confident that the professional Le Sueur would correct their mistakes and, as she defined the writer's role, "mirror back the beauty of the people." The bank robbery sequence, for example, is attributed to a report by "the girl who drove the car," while Butch's death scene was written down by a different anonymous "girl," from the words of her lover killed in a bootleg shootout. The combined account appeared in *New Caravan* (1945) under the title "O Prairie Girl, Be Lonely." The following version is from the text as revised for the novel.

Ripening: Selected Work, 1927–1980 (1982), a chronologically arranged anthology, contains an informative biographical and critical essay on Le Sueur by the editor, Elaine Hedges.

FROM THE GIRL
[The Bank Robbery]

24

Belle said, Tomorrow night this time they might all be dead.

Stop it Belle, I said.[1]

Hoinck was playing poker with three other men.

Cut it out, Hoinck said, and have a drink. Hit me.

I wanted him to quit for years, I'm going to kill myself if he doesn't, Belle cried.

Have a drink, I said.

A fine way to talk the night before a big job, Hoinck said. We got to go to work tomorrow for sure.

Go to work, Belle said, in scorn. She began to cry. It isn't worth it, all the money in the world, it isn't worth it.

It'll be all right, Hoinck said. Play, he said to Ack, go on play.

It'll be all right, Belle said. A thief's phrase.

What do you want? Hoinck said. I take it.

What do I want? Belle shouted. Godlordchrist and the Virgin Mary, what do I want!

Cut that out, Hoinck said, what do you think this is? Because you have a fit I'm supposed to call everything off.

I'd be better off dead.

Stop saying that. What in the name of God, I'm giving you all I can.

What did you ever give me, living in ratholes from one minute to the next. Stop stealing.

Everybody steals, Hoinck said. My play.

1. The narrator, The Girl of the title, has come to the city to escape rural poverty and is working in a speakeasy run by Belle and her husband Hoinck.

Nuts! There must be some other way.

Well you know it as well as I do. Hit me. Go on hit me. We tried that.

We're better off dead and all our kind.

The men slapped down the cards.

Hoinck yelled, Here's a rod, blow your brains out, or else shut up and have a drink.

I'll never shut up, Belle screamed. Look, she said to me, I got him extradition papers, got a quick straw bond for him didn't I? I got him out of jail. I got bail for him. I hitchhiked from Baltimore, Maryland to Dallas, Texas to get him out of the can once. I took the rap for him. What else could I do? I might as well blow my brains out.

All right, Hoinck said, do it. If the women would only shut up.

Sure, say nothing. See everything blown to hell and sit quiet knitting, Belle cried. Sure, don't say a thing.

Have a drink.

I'll have a drink. Sure.

Butch came in and walked by me without speaking. He sat down and watched the game and Belle noticed it too and she said, What's the matter? Tomorrow we may all be dead and he can't speak to you.

He said, Shut up Belle, mind your own business.

Butch said to me, So you want a father and a husband? Well you won't be getting them. Nobody's going to get them.

I stood by the stove.

You want me to bring you something, give you something? Everybody could hear him. You goddamned chiseler, you lying whore. I wouldn't bring you anything.

The men playing cards looked at me.

Did you have a good lay, he said. Did you have to sell me down the river?

Shut up, Hoinck said. We want to be good for tomorrow.

Yeah, you all know it, Butch said, you all know it. I phoned here and you all knew she was lying up there with that skunk.

He was drunk. He would have a hangover.

Butch, I said, Come with me, come on out. I took hold of him and he came with me easy, I was surprised. He just followed me and we went outside in the hall. We stood against the wall and he put his body close to me. We stood there and I thought he had forgotten. It was good to smell him.

Why in hell did you do it? he said.

I felt cold. Do what? I said.

Instead of answering he struck me full in the face with the flat of his hand. I leaned against the wall. I couldn't see. Then I saw his face awful in front of me, as he came toward me and I put out my hand and pushed against his chest and when I touched him I loved him then.

Somebody was coming up the stairs. Don't Butch, I whispered, someone will see. I could see his hand lifted, this time in a fist and it struck me in the mouth. The man who had been coming up the stairs passed us and I tried to look like nothing had happened. But I couldn't help the blood coming out of the side of my mouth.

It's funny to be hit. Nobody ever hit me before but papa. He didn't hit like that. I took hold of Butch's arm and we went downstairs leaning on each other. It wasn't snowing.

Butch said, It isn't snowing, a good thing too. I hope it don't snow tomorrow.

I hope so too, I said. I could see my mouth. It was swelling. The inside of my lower lip was bleeding where my teeth had cut.

Butch said, What's the matter, your mouth is bleeding. He said, I'll hit you again, don't ever let me catch you again. Jesuschrist why did you have to do it?

You told me to do it, I said. You told me to be nice to him.

Sure, go on, blame it on me. That's my fault too. Everything's my fault. That's what my mother used to think. Sure I can take it, go ahead. I'll lead with my chin.

No! No! I cried and we walked along the dark, rotten streets. I didn't know where my legs were and fountains seemed to be rising and breaking behind my eyes. No, no, I cried, it's not your fault. I only thought I'd help with the money.

How much, he said, go on tell me how much?

I hadn't had a single drink but I felt drunk. I could hardly see.

Look Butch, I said, let's go to a hotel.

Listen, he said, I suppose you think I can't pay for a hotel. I suppose you think only that bloodsucker Ganz[2] can pay for a hotel. Well I want you to know that I got the dough, see? I can pay. I can pay my way. I always done that. I don't depend on no one on God's green earth, get me? Since I was eight years old I paid my way in this lousy world. You're not going to take *this* baby to any hotel, you're not going to pay for me. I can pay for my own room, and for my own girl, see?

Sure, I said, Butch, I know you can. I know that. I've never paid for you. I've never never paid for you.

All right, he said, don't act like it's any different.

Before we went in the hotel on St. Peter, Butch stopped by the pawn shop and took a drink.

Don't drink, Butch, I said pulling him. Remember in the morning. You got to have your wits.

I suppose you don't think I can drink either? I suppose you think I can't hold it. All right, belittle me, see? Go ahead, I'm used to it. I'll show this cockeyed world.

Sure you will Butch, sure you will. O I know you will. You're wonderful. You're a good mechanic, you're the best. I know that.

Do you, sweet? Do you?

Sure, sure, I cried, O I love you. I know it is going to be all right.

Do you love me? Honest?

Honest, Butch. O hurry, come on. Sure I love you. Better than anything.

All right, Butch said, that's enough for me. I know when I'm lucky. That's all I need to change my luck. That's absolutely all. I don't need a rabbit's foot. I don't need an eleven. I don't need nothing. Tomorrow is going to be silk. Look, he said, you help me get a picture of this. I stand by the pillars see, until Ganz gets in the side door, then I go in, step over the swinging gate and cover the clerks from the right.

I'll help you Butch, I cried pulling him, we'll get it all down.

And then I felt good. On my own I had done it.[3] I wouldn't tell him until after it was over. I had to smile. I had already robbed the bank. I had stolen the seed. I had it on deposit. It was cached. It was safe.

I had to laugh. It was in a safe. I had the key.

25

We went into the lobby and I stood back a little and he signed the register and then he looked in his pants pockets, and then his vest and then all his coat pockets, and he took out a bunch of letters and keys from his back pocket and then he started over and went through them again.

I said, gee honey, I forgot you gave me your purse to hold while you were changing the tire. I said, We had a blowout just outside the city, can you imagine, we came clean from Washington, D.C. without a blowout and then just before we get to the city we have one. I put a dollar on the counter and the clerk gave me the key and Butch leaned against me going upstairs and he said what number we got this time? The number on the door was 23.

Twenty-three skidoo, Butch said. Three and two is five. Five is a lucky number for me. Is it for you?

2. Leader of the planned bank robbery.
3. She is pregnant with Butch's baby and has decided not to get an abortion.

Yes, I said.

We went in and I didn't turn on the light. I laid Butch on the bed and he went to sleep like a baby. I sat on the edge of the bed. It was an inside room with a shaft. There was no outside window. The window led on the shaft and I could hear men talking in the room above. At first it sounded like wasps and then I heard one of them say, we got to be careful. And another said, But doughnuts is sure.

I didn't want to go to sleep because I dreamed about it every night. I could see it all plain. I've read about robberies but I didn't think anything of it. I have seen it in the papers, banks robbed and pictures of a young man or maybe a girl. I never thought anything of it. I can see myself sitting on the bed dim in the mirror. Tomorrow everyone will know it if we are caught. I am afraid to get up and look close to see if tomorrow already shows in the way I am made. This must show, make the bones go different, and the flesh different.

I am to drive the car. We are to meet Ack at the corner of Third and then we are to part. He is to go across the bridge for the transfer. I am to drive down Fourth and stop in front of the bank just six feet from the hydrant and from there I can see the cop directing traffic on the next corner. I am to watch him and watch behind me in the mirror and keep my foot on the clutch.

I wake up at night and dream that I've forgotten the shift. But that would be impossible. Then I dream I am paralyzed and have become rooted in the walk, like when we were kids and put our footprints in the fresh cement. Sometimes it is raining in the dream and sometimes the sun is shining. And I see people broken on the streets by an explosion.

It is awful to bear these things at night, and the horror in your dreams of things unknown to you, not thought of by you at all. I didn't think of these things. It isn't my own evil. I never dreamed of them nor looked to doing any of them. Was I evil? Was I a monster in my youth? Did my mother think of this? Who thought of these crimes and hatched them out to scatter our flesh?

I can see dead on the walk by the corner of that building. I never saw the corner of a building like that before. How far is six feet? How far is it from the door to the car, six feet from the hydrant? I must ask Butch to step that many feet for me. I never was good on distance. Distance is very important in this, time and distance. They blow up to big sizes in my dreams. One foot more, one foot back is the difference of a bullet. One minute more, one second less. I can see all this mixed up in time like a movie when you run it fast and then slow, or run it backward.

The voices above said, We got to have racks, we got to have a lot of racks to make it pay. Then the voices lowered.

I lay down beside Butch and he put his arm over me. In his sleep he did it. Some voices outside the door must have wakened me. I was dreaming that it came that moment when Butch was at the front door and Ganz came out the side door with three satchels of money and there were four coppers came around the corner at the same time. I shot at them and one officer pumped an automatic into Butch. In the light I saw Butch whirl, fire at the officer and then fall in a heap. I lifted a rifle and fired at the fourth officer again and he raised a shotgun and blasted away half my head.

I woke up crying and woke Butch. I said, That's funny I never fired a gun in my life.

He said, I hope it's clean tomorrow. I feel better. How about something to eat.

I said, You get it. I didn't want to see those streets again.

There was a commotion in the hall. A woman kept saying, Go on get going, go on, what's the matter. I won't take a thing! she cried, I don't want a thing. Then the man would mumble something like he was moved and ashamed, and then you could hear them kiss and then she shouted, Go on get going get out get going get along, and he didn't want to go. Voices in old hotels at night sound funny and finally he went back in with her, and we could hear them laughing. . . .

Butch turned on the light and killed a bedbug walking up the wall. He wanted to go out and get some beer. It was after twelve. I said, No you better not drink any more beer. We have to be out there at seven-thirty sharp.

Jesus, maybe we won't wake up, maybe we ought to stay up.

No, we got to get some rest.

He said, Have you got a dime I'll get you a hamburger. *I wait at the front, light a cigarette, lean against the pillars like I was just waiting. I can see through when Ganz gets the clerks covered and then I go in and cover them from the other side.*

I said, you put the money out of the drawer on the counter and sweep it into the satchel. Then you take the satchel to Ganz and watch the front door.

Yes, he said, that's right. It can't miss. We ought to make a cleanup.

Yes, I said. We ought to.

Why don't you be easy? he said.

I don't feel easy, I said. I feel awful.

You take everything too personal, he said. Look at me, I can stand anything.

Yes, I said, I'm looking at you. He was still pretty drunk and I knew nothing could keep him from getting drunker, nothing in heaven or hell.

26

He went out for the hamburger and didn't come back for a long time. They started a party next door. They must make these walls out of paper. I lay in bed listening. I thought if I didn't move I wouldn't remember. It was two o'clock. I thought I better get some sleep. I tried to figure things out. I couldn't figure it.

I could hear them through the wall moving like huge rats, like talking rats, very funny. I thought they would look like great rats with long snouts and blood hanging from their teeth. The shooting craps and the loud bad talk went on and the low roar and murmur of men's voices with the cries of the women riding them like birds on a wave.

The clock struck two-thirty and I could feel all this come into me like a misery.

I certainly wouldn't forget, if the copper moved, to look across the street, up at the empty windows, and one long and two short. Yes, I would remember that. One long and two short, you might say that on your deathbed. Last words—one long and two short.

Didn't anyone ever go to bed here? Were they all waiting for seven-thirty, for the holdup? The men upstairs kept figuring out how much it took to start a doughnut racket.

I went downstairs and it was snowing but the black street showed through. I had a cup of coffee and two hot dogs. I only had fifty cents left of the five bucks. I left twenty on the table.

I had only been upstairs ten minutes when Butch knocked and came in with a hot dog still warm in a paper. He was very drunk. He said he had been talking to a fellow who made two thousand a month before the depression. Think of that, he said, two grand a month selling shoes. Jesus!

You better get some sleep, I said, it's near three.

Do you think I can step over that swinging gate O.K.? he said. I'll have to step over it because it will be locked ten to one.

Sure, I said. How far is six feet from the hydrant?

Don't you know six feet? he said. Look, and he stepped it off from the window to the dresser. Not much smaller than the room. I looked at the space. Space could blow up, it could stretch like rubber.

I tried to eat the hot dog because he brought it.

Butch took off his pants and sat on the bed in his shirt, his strong legs hanging down. He was very drunk. His eyes were glazed.

I put on my coat and ran downstairs and brought up a milk bottle full of coffee. Now I only had fifteen cents left. The coffee cost ten with five deposit for the milk bottle. But that was enough until morning.

Here, I said, drink. I began pounding his arms. You got to eat, I said. You got to sober up.

So, Butch says to the air, I am your father.

Father, I almost screamed. Who was he talking to? A step came down the hall, somebody tiptoeing. He was talking in a low steady voice, the glare of the single light bulb fell on his black head.

I held the coffee to his mouth.

I am your father, he says. Go back to the grave, father, lie still. So, he says, my son, it was better for you not to be alive, it was better for you dead. You wouldn't be a white feather,[4] you would have made the big team. Pitcher for big time, you hear me, that's for certain. My lousy old man wouldn't have known you and you could pitch on Sunday.[5]

Drink, I cried, drink.

He pushed it away. I was scared. He kept on talking. He wasn't talking to me.

I will talk to you when you are dead, he said, when they lower you in the ground, when everything is dead.

We will have it, I cried, if it goes good tomorrow. Drink. We will have it. You got to sober up.

Too late, he said, it's against us.

No, no, I said. We're lucky.

Luck, he said, that bitch.

He swore to himself, like a wasp, ready to plunge it into you.

Drink, I shouted, drink. Somebody knocked on the wall. I was shaking like a gourd.

What's the matter? he said. This place smells like a perspiring corpse. Who's been in here? Has that nest robber been in here? I'll kill him!

Drink, I said, You got to be sober tomorrow. You got to be.

He looked at me. If the cop from the corner comes back we are going to be scattered, he said.

Don't think about it. Stop thinking about it.

All right, you stop too.

What time is it?

Almost four.

This time tomorrow we'll be through with it.

It will be all right. Everything will be all right.

Yes.

It won't though. It will be stinking. Lousy.

Don't say that.

Might as well look yourself in the eye.

It will be all right. We'll make it.

We'll be dead.

No, no.

We'll be dead and forgotten.

O, we will live forever, I cried.

Sure, nuts, forever. You sweet nut. Come here.

Don't Butch, you shouldn't. You got to sleep.

Come on, now honey, turn over, turn to me.

Not now.

The man and woman in the other room were laughing in bed. You can hear them strong, through the buggy walls, like grapes hanging in summer, like heavy wheat blowing in Wisconsin.

Now! Now! Butch cried. Before it is too late!

---

4. A coward.
5. Butch's father disapproved of his playing baseball on Sunday.

27

It's funny how when anything begins to happen how clear it gets. When it begins to happen you don't worry about it. When you are doing it you don't think about it.

At six-thirty I got Butch out and filled him with black coffee and walked him along the river. The street looked quiet and clear. It was a clear cold morning and it wasn't snowing. I walked him along the river and then he looked better and we went to the tavern and Belle was cooking coffee holding a wrapper over her breast and looking around from the stove, her ruined face frightened in a way I never saw it. What a life, she says, get up all hours of the night. Can't sleep a wink. Here's some coffee.

We can't stop, I said.

O yes you can, she says. It's only quarter after seven.

I gave Butch some more coffee and put a little brandy in it.

Ganz came in the kitchen and said, We can't stop here, it will look bad.

You look bad anyhow, Belle said, you look terrible.

All right, no remarks, give me some coffee. What's the matter with him? he said, pointing at Butch.

He's all right, I said.

Hoinck came in, his hair sticking up. He had a bag in his hand.

You can't use that, Ganz said.

What's the matter with it?

Jesus Christ man, you can't walk in a bank with a satchel like that. What a man.

Shut up will you, Belle said.

Belle, Hoinck said, get that bag upstairs will you?

Drink a cup of coffee, baby.

Ganz went into the bar which was still dark.

Don't do it honey, Belle said.

We'll quit after this, Belle. Don't rag me now, this is a hard one.

At seven-thirty we went out on the street. The car was in front, the one I had driven to have the license changed. I could see in the back, all the guns, rifles and shotguns on the floor.

The men all wore revolvers besides, I could see them under their coats. It made them all look funny.

I got in. Ganz sat beside me and I could feel Butch leaning forward from the back.

Drive easy Girl, Ganz said, like I told you in the middle of the street so nobody can see in and we don't have to put the curtains down. If we get nabbed now with all this arsenal we'd have to shoot it out.

I hope it's a nice job, Hoinck said, I hope it's clean.

Drive easy Girl. Don't break any rules today. We're dynamite.

Leave her alone, Butch said.

Who's talking?

I am, Butch said.

I screwed down the window. There was sweat on my head.

Speed between crossings, go slow at the crossing, Ganz said. Stop at all stop signs.

I could see both sides of the street at once like I had extra ways of seeing. A man moving down the street toward us walking to work struck me like a blow and I watched him. Everything looked so single, so clear.

A nice morning, Hoinck said. It looked like in a show, everything so clear and the buildings looked like they were painted on.

I saw three men talking on the corner. They raised their heads and looked at us. I can see one has a mustache like my father and a thin face. They go on talking. I look back and I can see the back of one's pants come down to a little peak behind, like my father's pants always were.

We came across the bridge to meet Ack where we were supposed to meet him with the car that they were to change to, and Ack wasn't there.

There was a tire store on the corner. Somebody was inside sweeping the floor.

Where is he? Ganz said. What the hell is this, a kindergarten? We drove around the block and back. He wasn't there.

Don't look, Ganz said. Don't gawk.

I drove around again slow and back, and the man was still sweeping the floor and he looked up this time.

Don't let him see you, Ganz said, cough in your handkerchief.

I felt like laughing, I didn't have a handkerchief.

We drove around again and this time the man came to the window and looked out at us, his broom in his hand.

I never saw everything before so clear and flat, as if it was the end of it, as if you could never get behind or around or even remember it. Like there was no place to go into, to hide. It was crazy. I kept saying to myself there's still time. We can stop now. Ganz leaned forward looking up and down the street. I could feel Butch at my back. I could see him there. I could see him plain.

I could see the street, tiny and sharp in the mirror behind me.

The police squad car was coming behind us. I saw it. I said, The squad car is coming behind us.

Ganz said, For Christ's sake!

I said, Sit still, look natural. It's nothing, they are going back to headquarters, around the block.

Ganz was white as a sheet. You're not so brave, I said to him, you're a rat.

The squad car drove alongside and past us and the two tired cops didn't even look at us.

It's a quarter of eight, Ganz said. What does he think this is?

He'll be here, Hoinck said.

Get off this street, Ganz said. Get the hell out of here, we'll drive a few blocks and come back. Get out of here, get off this street, get away, Ganz said.

All right, Butch said, you can speak decent to her.

To who? Ganz said. Don't be too sure about that.

What do you mean? Butch said.

Be still, I said. There's Ack. I could see him a block ahead.

Tail in half a block behind, Ganz said.

He saw us, I said. All we need to do is just pass him so he knows we're set.

O.K. We drove back to the tire store and Ack leaned out a little and raised his hand. I raised my hand. Stop, Ganz said. I pulled alongside. It wasn't necessary. Where you been? Ganz said, in a whisper. Where you been?

Never mind, Hoinck said, let's go.

Tell you later, Ack said.

All right, Hoinck said, let's take a gander at it, get it over with. It's not too late. We'll get something. . . .

Make it snappy, Ganz said.

The streets were beginning to have more cars. I drove fast. I drove very well. I turned down Fourth and drove slowly around the corner. I saw the cop a block ahead directing traffic like we knew he would be. When I saw the hydrant I jumped as if it was looking at me. I remember the wall of the bedroom. I stopped six feet away. I turned and looked at Butch and he smiled at me. I felt better.

The lights were on in the bank and we could see in clear. The doors weren't open yet. The sun struck across the pillars just like the morning we cased it. I left the engine running. Butch got out easy and just then I could see the steel vault opening.

There it goes! both Hoinck and Ganz said. Ganz opened the door, took out his briefcase and walked around the car, and back around the corner.

Hoinck got out and slowly followed him. Butch was leaning up against the pillar taking a cigarette out of the pack. He looked natural. Everything looked terribly natural. I saw a woman secretary clean off the desk of the president. She had a white lace collar on, very neat. The clerks came out with locked trays which they took to the cages and opened, sorting the bills into the open drawers.

I felt almost happy as if I knew all this would happen and now it was happening just like it should. I could feel my heart beating high up in me. A woman walked by Butch and he looked at her. I watched him look at her.

He put his hand up to his face so she couldn't see him clear. I remembered his saying, Cover your face honey, or I'll see you in the papers.

I saw Ganz inside.

Butch, I said softly to myself, just moving my lips. As if he heard me he threw his cigarette into the gutter, and turned his face, and went through the pillars into the bank. I could see the long hard nervous cat life in him. It was lonely now on all sides.

Now I couldn't tell what time it was, whether an hour passed or a minute. I felt light-headed. A man walked by and looked at me and I thought his eyes got larger.

It was very queer. Not many people seemed to be on the street. The cop kept turning full face to me and then sideways as the traffic went by him. I kept my foot on the clutch. I could see my foot far down as if it had gone to sleep. I couldn't feel it, as if it had been cut off, and was lying down there.

GET SET TO GO, Ganz's words kept going in my mind, GET THE HOT HEAP READY. TAKE OFF IN A MINUTE. SPEED, SPEED, THAT'S IT, LIKE HITLER.

I looked at the street behind, tiny in the mirror. I could see the buildings slanting a little, and darkening.

I said to myself for Butch, Step over the counter, counter ends at avenue window, small gate there, step over it, you're tall darling, step over it. Clerks and money drawers will be in line with you, cover them. Motion them back, give them their orders, keep them away from the alarms. Don't forget anything Butch, and if they hit it and start the big buzzer, remember, that's a lot of battle for us for sure, that's for sure. Be careful. Clean the drawer now as you come to each cage, throw the dough onto the counter and push it into the bag. That's right.

Hoinck has vaulted the other end at the second pay window. I didn't look in . . . the big windows flashed now like glasses in the sun.

A dog started across the street and stopped. He's afraid too, I thought, and he went back to the curb and stood by the hydrant and then lifted a leg.

I turned my head and looked at the door. I could see Butch standing by the door. Now Butch had emptied the drawers, given the satchel to Ganz, now he was watching the door. Don't let anybody in, Butch. Watch it!

A stout man with a briefcase was let out on the corner. A pretty girl was driving the car. She said, Goodbye, father. He pulled down his vest and pushed up his mustache with his fat finger, walked towards me without looking, and turned in between the pillars. Butch saw him too, and when he got in the door, I saw his head disappear like he had been dropped.

Everything was quiet. I could see the bank so clear like it was made of ice with the sun moving a little over the pillars, such lovely pillars.

Another man got out of a car, it stopped alongside. A chauffeur was driving. He got out, slammed the door, threw away a cigar and went towards the streak of light between the pillars.

I watched now like it was something in a story, something I was reading. He went inside and then almost instantly he ran out fast and squealing in a high voice like a stuck pig. Everything on the street changed. Someone was running. I raced the engine. I felt light-headed. I could see the air.

Then it broke like glass all round me and I heard the guns go off, and the repeater Ganz carried, and two single sharp cracks and the cop on the corner whirled like a doll, and then it was still again, with people running.

28

Butch came backward out the bank door. I kept my eyes on him. He came out with his back to me, and he was holding his side. He was bent over and then he straightened, turned toward me and ran four steps, then he turned again facing the door of the bank, through which people were running. I kept my eyes on the back of his head as he moved toward me. I raced the engine and when he was near I took hold of the door handle and opened the door. I held it open until I saw his head and the back of his ears, close to me.

People seemed to be running past him into the bank. No one seemed to be paying any attention to him. I held the door until he backed into it, then he opened it and got in. I could see the streets in front of me and in back of me in the mirror and everyone was running toward the bank.

I raced the engine and when he closed the door I threw in the shift, grating it a little because my foot had gone to sleep.

Butch said, They're both dead.

I didn't know who. I didn't ask him. I hoped it was Ganz anyway. No one seemed to notice us. I drove down to the end of the street, turned down the river hill. I drove fast and over the bridge without thinking because that was the way I was supposed to go. I drove *very* fast and I could see *very* well. Everything looked *very* clear like on a morning after a storm. I was over the bridge on the way to meet Ack before I thought of it, and then when I realized it, I turned off the road and kept going until we came to the country. Then I looked at Butch, he was very white and he was holding his side. I slowed up. Let me look. I pulled back his coat and his side looked like a tree that had been struck by lightning. He was almost split in two, the skin stripped down like bark.

I knew now nobody was following us. I couldn't figure it. I didn't even try to figure it, I just drove on as fast as I could but not too fast. I took off my coat. Put that on your side, I said, and try to stop the blood.

Where are we going now? he said. It don't much matter now, does it, go on blame me. I got you into this, go on blame me, I can take it.

Don't say anything, I said, it makes it worse.

We were driving through flat lands. I hoped we were going south. I tried to keep to the little roads so we wouldn't be seen, but I knew nobody was following us.

Well, you were right, go on tell me you were right. This is a fine end to come to.

We aren't coming to any end, I said.

He didn't say anything and it scared me.

We kept on driving and after awhile he said, We haven't got a bit of the haul. Nobody following us and we haven't a thing. After all that and not a thing. That bastard Ganz made it all up so he would carry the money. I could of just as well had a satchel but he would carry the money. It could of been every man with a satchel and his chances.

He seemed excited. I couldn't keep him from talking. I felt better now than I felt before the holdup. I felt light as if I dropped about a hundred pounds. He kept on talking and I was scared. I thought he was getting delirious.

There was a short fellow at the bar, he said, in a black mackinaw. He had a pointed nose and he was always having a fine time. He died of rotgut but he had a good time while it lasted. And he said, What kind of a cup is this? The chalice of McCarthy—he was a card—that was McCarthy's saloon, and he said, this is the chalice of McCarthy. I am going to wear a green tie, he said, if I have to bust a gut. I won't buy beer for any sons of guns that are drunk. If you are sober you need a beer—O he was a card all right—but if you are drunk you don't need a beer. He was the greatest gambler in town, used to gamble with Joe Hill[6] and he knew what it was all about and he knew the cards were stacked. He told me then—Butch, the cards are marked—when I was just a punk, he told me that, but I was smart—I was pretty smart all right.

There was no use to tell him to be quiet now. I had to find someplace to take him. I thought, should I take him to a doctor? I was afraid to take him. It seemed like we were against everybody now.

Now we haven't got a thing, Butch said, after all that, and all that money in my hands, I can still feel it, what we could have done with even a little bit of that sweet money.

You're alive, I said.

He looked at me.

I was thinking, he said, standing by them pillars before we went in, when that girl went by, there was a few seconds there, I could of walked out then, we could of lived our lives like you wanted. I could of walked out of there then.

Don't talk, I said. I kept on driving through the country going around the towns and villages. I just kept on going and then a river came up and I stopped and got out and took the extra gasoline can out and filled the tank and took off my petticoat and dipped it in the river and washed his side, and put the skirt in along the wound.

I kept driving and nobody was coming after us now for sure, and we must have been about a hundred fifty miles by afternoon and the land was very flat and I thought maybe we were in Iowa and it seemed so flat I looked at the sun and turned east because I had a crazy idea we would drive into the dark quicker and maybe get into Missouri or some wooded country. It was frightening to see it so flat with no place to go but into the ground.

I kept driving and nobody was coming after us. Farmers' wives came out and stood at the door. We drove past like lovers. Butch looked all right from the chest up and he leaned a little against me. The women stood in the doors of their houses, and children looked out the windows. All wives are beautiful.

I did everything just like we planned, Butch said, I couldn't catch hold of that fat bastard, he slipped out of my hands like a greased pig. He let out an awful squeal.

I heard him, I said. Don't talk. I'm going to stop now and get some gas before it is dark. Sit up, I said, pull that coat around.

You don't think it was my fault do you? Butch said, I mean the whole mess.

No, I said, it wasn't your fault. You couldn't help it, any of it. Be still now.

I drove into a service station. five gallons, I said. Could we fill our can too, we are going camping.

Sure, he said, going south?

Yes, I said, maybe it's warm in Arkansas. I hoped we were going towards Arkansas.

It didn't surprise him. Yes, he said, good hunting down there too.

He took our can from the back seat. It was a service station built like a cottage, there were paper geraniums at the window.

This is a swell place you got here, Butch said.

The young man looked at us, and went inside.

How much money you got Butch?

I got a fiver Ganz gave me for gas, he said.

Good, I said, that's one thing Ganz did that was O.K.

The young man came out and Butch said again that it was a fine place he had. He looked at us. O yes, he said wiping the windshield. Butch and I leaned together so he wouldn't see.

I put everything me and my wife had into this place, he said, and now the Standard Oil is going to take it away from me.

6. Joe Hill (1879–1915), born Joseph Hilstrom in Sweden, was a famous labor organizer and member of the Industrial Workers of the World (IWW). Executed by firing squad for a murder he claimed to be innocent of, he became legendary.

How can they do that, Butch said, didn't you get a lease on it?

O sure, he said, that's a racket, they make you feel like you got your place, like you're going to be the boss, a big shot. They take all your dough and they got it fixed so you can't make good. You could work twenty-eight hours out of twenty-four, you could starve your wife and kids and throw them in with it. They got you milked from both ends. It's a racket. They hold the cards, you can't win. And when you give up, when they've sucked you dry, they get another sucker.

Holy mackerel! Butch said.

It was getting night. He gave us the change and when we drove on down the road Butch began to swear. I never heard him swear like that.

Butch, I said, don't.

Oh, the Goddamned dirty bastards. They got you coming and going. They got you.

Be quiet, I said. Be quiet.

I had to stop somewhere. It was getting dark.

29

Once it began to snow a little and I was disappointed. I thought we were going south. I hoped we were going south.

I knew if we drove long enough we would come to a river, and rivers always have dark places near them, caves and trees.

Butch got very delirious. In the dark I couldn't see him but all the time I was looking for someplace to drive into I could hear him talking.

Yes, Butch said, honey it's got to show pretty soon. Where are we going? It's got to show soon. What are we looking forward to? You got to believe in the future. I knew a man, he wasn't my father, but he said, Son, I can't tell you anything but you will find out something. You'll learn something. He wasn't my father but he told me that. I wouldn't pay him no mind. I was a cocky buck.

We were coming to some trees and rolling hills. It was nice to drive into them and not see any road behind. I drove as good as I could and not jar him.

No, he wasn't my father, Butch said. *Do I owe my father any grief? Answer me that,* he said. *You don't owe your father anything. Here we are kicked around all our lives, what do you owe your father, spawning you in it.*

He began to sing. It sounded terrible. I cried a little so he wouldn't know it. He began to sing like he was drunk, to the tune of, My father's gone to sea, of thee I sing. . . . This is a dirty day, he said, a hell of a day. . . .

My mother, he said. *She was the darnedest bawler out and had all those lord there were kids everywhere like a brood of chicks. And where are mine? Where's my son? He'd make the big team wouldn't he? He wouldn't be a white feather. Got to take the old carcass somewhere. I sleep anywhere, don't worry about that, I can sleep anywhere. I'm pretty sleepy. Hell nobody'll bother you. One summer I slept in the morgue every night. Now that's a good place. Joe at the morgue don't like to stay alone with all the stiffs and it's cold in the summer, it's about the coolest place in summer, crawl up on a nice cool slab.*

Joe was good shakes once, going for a fare-you-well. It burnt him up. That's the trouble, you burn up. You don't bail out soon enough. I never saw anybody get out soon enough to save his hide. Joe was runner-up. He used to truck around Como and Rice in winter. I'd be coming down driving the truck, all bent out of shape with my kidneys killing me, and there'd be Joe warming up running like a dog. You can't hurt him now. Why should I be quiet? Can't I even speak? He's been knocked over so often his brains are addled. Jock Malone started a gym, that was a long time ago. Once Joe came back to town with a Packard. Boy-o-boy that was something! And then he didn't have a Packard, just like that, and I met him staggering down Fourth with a breath—got a nickel? he hollers. Damned if I know, I says, shake me and if you hear anything we'll split. Found a quarter and we split. My girl wants to go to a show, he says, and I went with him and I slept until a guy came along with a broom. That was another blank that's all. I've got a lot of blanks. I draw a lot of blanks. You gotta have. My mind doesn't register now. Have I been knocked over?

No, I says, you're all right, Butch.

I saw a bridge ahead and I thought there will be a road on the other side going down, to the river.

I know the porter at the union station, Butch said, he would help us. I know where you can get cheap gin. He would get us some. Five cents a pint, lay you in lavender for a week. And Mabel Martino the check girl is half baked, short and plump, keeps herself fried. It would help wouldn't it.

No, I said, we're all right.

O, we're fit as a fiddle, he shouted . . . and began to sing. The bellboy was drunk, he said, and started to lean where the old courthouse was and it was gone, the bells are gone now. I better hit the hay, honey. Come down close. This old carcass better get someplace, take this old carcass home wherever that is. . . .

We'll be home, I said and I drove across the bridge and turned to the left where the road went straight down in the brush by the river. It was a dirt road and I drove very slow and eased the car down the frozen ruts. I stopped and turned off the lights.

Butch said, Don't do that, don't make it dark, and I turned them on again.

Once, he said, we were coming into Oshkosh between games and there I saw two ballplayers at the bar. One was a guy named Pinkey. It was mahogany beams, pretty swanky. Pinkey said, Hello boy I'm in the big money I'm staying at the Fondulac over here. There was O'Leary and he was in the big money too and we had some drinks. We had ginrickys. Pinkey had pockets full of money, his old man just kicked off.

Say, he said, this must be the road to my mother's. My mother's goofy now. I used to go see the old girl it seemed to cheer her up so to see her best effort, this son of Erin. Does it cheer you up?

Yes, it does. I began to go on slow. Sometimes there are old shacks along a river.

Gee, he said, I remember it when I was young. I thought this old world couldn't love without me. Honest. I thought men couldn't live without me. I worked up until I was head of the route, I had to be in the alley back of the News at four o'clock in the morning. I thought I was doing a swell job. I didn't think they could get the paper out without me. Honest. I thought I was a public servant. I was a goof. Now a woman's got to give me food, hand-feed me. . . .

Charlie had three fingers from N.Y. came from Miami by freight. We flipped, Charlie and I had to sleep together, Red started telling about his kids. He was a steel worker too saved money and lived in a house and paid so much a month a steel rivet man worked with a boy friend didn't have to push the bell button often to warn the men below they always worked together Sam fell off the fifty-fourth floor of the empire state. Shouted I'm going down. I tried to grab his leg. All I could do then was ring bells. I had a pretty big funeral. All the gang. I felt terrible. I worked with a different fellow . . . worked in factories. . . . In October I met Charlie again, he was a sight, didn't care about anything but Baby Ruth candy bars. . . .

Remember my brother?

Yes, I said.

Bill was used to it. When he was a punk he climbed the company poles to fix wires in every kind of a gale so the hairs on his belly would freeze from the sweat of his armpits. I remember I met Bill. When I heard he was born I pulled up my didy and went out to give him howdy, and welcome to this mortal coil, and he was growing about one foot out of the linoleum in the kitchen and I was a little bigger than him. We had another boon companion named Sad Eye Morton and he was a bad boy. We were not good boys but he was a bad boy.

Where are you going?

I'll be back, I said. I got out easy and tried to prop him up. I thought I would walk down the road and look in the thicket. I walked down in the light. I could hear the river on my left. I saw a path and I turned off. It led to a shack close by the banks. I ran back and I could hear Butch still talking. I got in.

Butch said, *He was the greatest tipper over of outhouses and feeler under woman's skirts and now he is a bank teller, very respectable, it goes to show. Maybe he was that fat little squealing pig that got out of my hands.*

I said, We are almost there.

Where? he said.

I drove into a clearing where a car had been before.

I feel like my old man's feet that time, Butch said.

How? I said.

Well I was wandering around and the old man was sick and I happened to see his dogs sticking out of the bottom of the bed so I felt them and they were stone cold. The old man's feet were like stones. I told my old lady that and she let out a yell. It turned out he was dead.

I said, you'll have to help me. We are going to get out now.

I'll help you, he said, I'll do anything you say.

All right, I said. I opened the other door. You'll have to put your good arm around me.

Why that's easy, he said, that's a pleasure. Why that's cooperation.

I left the lights on and they pierced the bare winter trees that looked like the beard of a man.

30

When I got him on the cot in the shack his whole side was a big mouth opening and shutting, with his shirt and coat caked in it. I ran down and took off my undershirt and broke the thin ice and dipped it in the water and ran back putting it under my arm pits to warm it. I hated to put it on so cold. I put the cloth in and I didn't know how that mouth could ever be closed.

I went in to get some wood because it was cold. I ran in the brush like mad. Some of it wouldn't go in without the stove door staying open, but that was nice so I could watch Butch by the light of it.

He didn't say anything now. He slept and I watched to see that he was breathing. It was his being so quiet made me know.

Once he said, You better drive on honey, and leave me here.

I found an old stew pot and boiled some water. It seemed like it had been night for a long time. I thought I should have taken him to a doctor before. I must have been insane. Why didn't I do it, I thought as soon as it is light I will do it.

We did everything O.K., Butch said, except for that bastard slipped out of my hands like a greased pig. If it hadn't been for him.

Something else would have happened, I said.

It was funny, Butch said, there was a fat lady clerk and I told her to get down on the floor and when I was getting out of there to the door I almost stepped on her face and she looked at me. I didn't plan it, Butch said.

What? I said. Now he was going to tell it.

Take it on the natural out, Ganz told us, that's what I did. I came out of there natural and nobody followed us, I did that O.K. didn't I?

Yes, I said.

Well just before that little pig came in, Ganz said, O.K., boys, take it on the natural, get out now, natural, walk east, get that dough in the car. Hoinck had one satchel from the vault and Ganz had the one I gave him. The way I doped it, sometime in my sleep, was that Ganz was figuring with Hone to get all the dough one way or another.

Yes, I figured that too, I guess.

Ganz saw the pig slip out of my hands all right and he turned, and I saw Hoinck fall as he was making for the door, and it was Ganz shot Hoinck straight through the heart, from the back. It was Ganz. Hoinck fell by the door. I saw him. He was so big and he just fell like he was cracked from behind. Ganz took the money on the run from his hand so he had both satchels and I took aim and shot him in the back.

I didn't say anything. I took his hand.

I saw him and I shot him. I never liked to look at him from behind.

All right, I said, neither did I.

And he kind of twisted around spinning to the floor and he saw me, and raised his automatic, and shot the whole wad. Ganz could shoot straight, but I guess I got him bad.

All right, I said, try and sleep.

Sleep, he said, I been sleeping all my life. My God, do we belong to the human race or don't we?

Some people don't think so, I said.

To hell with them, I feel so tired.

Sleep, I said.

I had found a bottle of whiskey in the car. I put some in the hot water and made him drink it and I drank some. I began to rub his body. The bleeding had stopped but he was spitting blood like he was bleeding inside. I rubbed him all over slow, his feet, his thighs, his neck and shoulders. I thought of everything he ever told me.

His body had been good to me. It seemed like there was everything else bad, and our bodies good and sweet to us. He said, get in beside me, I'm so cold. I got in with him and put our coats over us and he held on to me and if I would move he would draw me back. It was a narrow cot and I felt the fever mount in him. Sometimes he talked serious and I talked to him.

I haven't been good to you.

You've been good to me. I said, The best.

I hate it the way my brother looked when he was dead. I went back and I saw him face down on the slab, and when I turned him over he looked at me.

There was Rafferty traveled and got his expenses paid, two thousand a month, think of that, met big men too. It brings the best out in you, Rafferty used to say, ten years in hotels, the best hotels, give a tip of one dollar as easy as sneezing. I saw his report it was two thousand for one month. What we couldn't do with that in one year even, if we had it. . . . The boy's doing well. I hope he makes a million.

Butch, I said, you know it wasn't anything with Ganz.

I know, Butch said, don't think about it. We're trapped honey.

Don't say anything.

This would happen anyway, he says, the sooner the better, eventually why not now? We couldn't do anything we didn't do. We put everything into it like they say. We shot the works. It was all in the cards.

Don't think of anything now, I said and began rubbing his back.

I haven't done you much, he said. . . .

O you're good, I said, haven't I done what you said, gone with you, followed you?

Yes, he said, you're sweet.

What was I doing all my life? Butch said. *What was I doing, what in high heaven and low hell was I up to? St. Peter Street, Wabasha, St. Paul, Third and Fourth and Fifth. Remember Hogan's used to be up two flights and in the back and Rifle Joe's, and Dodo? What in God's name? Three-story stone building, that's Belle's, I recognize that, an old stone building can be sweet, saloon tailor shop restaurant fruit stand hotel upstairs, rubber worn off, a red globe in the entrance, the alley was a blind, remember that. Smell of sour whiskey rotten fruits, horses, catgut and beer. I worked in a hat factory on that second floor when I was a punk, you didn't know me then, I hadn't slept with you then, I was looking for you. The girls used to hang out their towels in the hotel and we bet on how many towels, that was the first thing I bet on, and the machines made a steady-one-two-stop-one-two you got so you liked it, you would jig it, we used to do it.*

We both fell asleep. He woke me shouting: *What have they done to us, what have they done to this now? Where are the oats, the wheat, I was sure they were planted. Look, Mrs. Hinckley the wealth of the country, the iron-ore-wheat-with-my-body-I-thee-wed, with my worldly goods I thee endow. . . . What are they doing to you now honey? They own the town. They own the earth and the sweet marrow of your body. Watch out! They'll shoot at you from all the windows and blow up the town!*

All my life there—what in hell was I doing? Who said anything? What happened? Going around those streets year in and year out, boy and man, those narrow dark Godriddendevilhaunted whorish drunken grand streets upstairs and downstairs—oh Christ my God my heavens good morning good evening—with nothing Christ what was it who made it what got us we come to this bad end?

Be quiet, I said.

We didn't mean any of this we didn't think of any of this, he screamed.

I couldn't make him be quiet now.

He talked about other things, some he had told me, and some of it he hadn't. He thought of all the people he knew ending up with me and then he died.

1939   1978

Lillian Hellman

(1905–1984)

Equal doses of New Orleans, her birthplace, and Manhattan, where her family moved in 1911, seasoned the upbringing of Lillian Hellman. Her Jewish paternal grandfather had emigrated to New Orleans in 1848; her mother's family were the wealthy Newhouses of Demopolis, Alabama. When her father's shoe store failed, the Hellmans moved north, where Lillian graduated from high school and attended New York University and Columbia. She continued to spend a part of each year visiting relatives in the South.

As a publisher's reader and publicist for theater groups, she met several literary figures, including the playwright Arthur Kober, whom she married in 1925. For a time they lived in Paris, where Kober edited an English-language magazine and Hellman wrote apprentice stories. After their return to the United States, Hellman accepted a job with Metro-Goldwyn-Mayer and went to Hollywood in 1930. Her experiences in the movie capital are described in the first of her autobiographical volumes, *An Unfinished Woman* (1969), winner of the National Book Award.

The literary and theatrical relationships forged during this period were to have lasting effects on Hellman's career and her views. Writers such as Nathaniel West and Dorothy Parker were her friends. Herman Shumlin, the producer, for whom she read play manuscripts, encouraged her writing and helped get her work on the stage. Most important was Dashiell Hammett, the mystery writer, who became her companion after her divorce from Kober in 1932. Hammett dedicated his best-known novel *The Thin Man* (1934) to Hellman; the same year she dedicated her first play *The Children's Hour* to him. They were together until his death in 1961.

The Children's Hour centers on two college friends, struggling to run a girls' school, who are accused of homosexuality. Because of the subject matter, established actors were reluctant to take parts in the production. Staged by a cast of unknowns, it was an immediate sensation; it had a long run on Broadway and made a small fortune for the author. The fact that it was banned in Boston and London, and that the film version *These Three* (1936) had difficulty with the Hays office, Hollywood's censorship board, further added to its fame. When the Pulitzer Prize committee ignored it—members refusing to attend a performance—the New York drama critics formed the Drama Critics Circle to award their own set of prizes. It was a striking beginning for a new career.

Returning to Europe in 1934 and 1937, Hellman was shocked at the rising tide of fascism. Many of her friends, including Hammett, were already active in antifascist organizations; she soon enlisted in the cause, working with John Dos Passos, Archibald MacLeish, and Ernest Hemingway to support director Joris Ivens's film *The Spanish Earth*, a documentary of the Spanish Civil War that was shown to raise money for aid to refugees from the forces of Franco and Hitler.

In Europe, Hellman made contact with a girlhood friend who was a student of Freud's in Vienna and an antifascist activist. Called "Julia" in Hellman's autobiographical *Pentimento* (1973) and the movie (1977) made from the account, she was the daughter of a wealthy New York family. In 1934, Hellman visited her friend in the Viennese hospital where she was recuperating from the serious injuries she had received in the Austrian civil war. In 1937, Hellman agreed to smuggle $50,000 from Paris to Julia in Berlin; the funds were to be used for the relief of antifascists. Hellman's luggage was searched and, leaving Germany to travel to Moscow, she narrowly escaped arrest; a year later she learned that Julia had been murdered by the Nazis. Some aspects of this experience and of Julia's character turn up in Hellman's most outspoken antitotalitarian play *Watch on the Rhine* (1941), winner of the Drama Critics Circle Award.

Her best-known play, *The Little Foxes*, was staged in 1939 and filmed, with Bette Davis as the scheming Regina Hubbard

Giddens, in 1941. A story of intrigue and greed, it is set in the turn-of-the-century South. Its prequel *Another Part of the Forest*, dealing with Marcus Hubbard, founder of the fortune being contended for in *Foxes*, was staged in 1946 and filmed in 1948.

In 1943 she had written the screenplay for *The North Star*, describing the Nazi invasion of a Russian village. In 1944 she made a second trip to Moscow; and the same year the antifascist *The Searching Wind* (film, 1946) appeared on Broadway. By the end of the war, Hellman—like Dashiell Hammett and many other politically active artists—was the target of anticommunist zeal. She was one of those blacklisted by the movie industry (1948), and in 1952 she was called to testify before the House Un-American Activities Committee; she agreed to testify about her own activities but refused to discuss others. She described this experience in her third autobiographical volume, *Scoundrel Time* (1976).

In the 1950s she adapted works by Jean Anouilh (*The Lark*, 1955) and Voltaire (*Candide* libretto, 1956, with music by Leonard Bernstein and lyrics by Richard Wilbur), but her only original play was *The Autumn Garden* (1951), set in a Gulf Coast resort. *Toys in the Attic*, her last play, won the Drama Critics Circle Award in 1960.

Collected Plays appeared in 1972. Studies include R. Moody, *Lillian Hellman, Playwright* (1972) and K. Lederer, *Lillian Hellman* (1979).

Watch on the Rhine

Scene

The scene of the play is the living room of the Farrelly country house, about twenty miles from Washington. The time is late spring, 1940.

Act One

Early on a Wednesday morning.

Act Two

Ten days later.

Act Three

A half hour later.

Act One

SCENE: *The living room of the Farrelly house, about twenty miles from Washington, D. C., on a warm spring morning.*

    Center stage are large French doors leading to an elevated open terrace. On the terrace are chairs, tables, a large table for dining. Some of this furniture we can see; most of it is on the left side of the terrace, beyond our sight. Left stage is an arched entrance, leading to the oval reception hall. We can see the main staircase as it goes off to the back of the hall. Right stage is a door leading to a library. The Farrelly house was built in the early nineteenth century. It has space, simplicity, style. The living room is large. Up stage right is a piano; down stage left, a couch; down stage right, a couch and chairs; up stage a few smaller chairs. Four or five generations have furnished this room and they have all been people of taste. There are no styles, no periods; the room has never been refurnished. Each careless aristocrat has thrown into the room what he or she liked as a child, what he or she brought home when grown up. Therefore the furniture is of many periods: the desk is English, the couch is Victorian, some of the pictures are modern, some of the ornaments French. The room has too many things in it: vases, clocks, miniatures, boxes, china animals. On the right wall is a large portrait of a big kind-faced man in an evening suit of 1900. On another wall is a large, very ugly landscape. The room is crowded. But it is cool and clean and its fabrics and woods are in soft colors.

AT RISE: *Anise, a thin Frenchwoman of about sixty, in a dark housekeeper's dress, is standing at a table sorting mail. She takes the mail from a small basket, holds each letter to the light, reads each postal card, then places them in piles. On the terrace, Joseph, a tall, middle-aged Negro butler, wheels a breakfast wagon. As he appears, Fanny Farrelly comes in from the hall. She is a handsome woman of about sixty-three. She has on a fancy, good-looking dressing-gown.*

    Left and right are the audience's left and right.

FANNY: *(stops to watch Anise. Sees Joseph moving about on terrace. Calls)* Joseph! *(To Anise)* Morning.

ANISE: *(continues examining mail)* Good morning, Madame.

JOSEPH: *(comes to terrace door)* Yes'm?

FANNY: Everybody down?

JOSEPH: No'm. Nobody. I'll get your tea. *(He returns to breakfast wagon on terrace.)*

FANNY: Mr. David isn't down yet? But he knows he is to meet the train.

JOSEPH: *(comes in from the terrace with the cup of tea)* He's got plenty of time, Miss Fanny. The train ain't in till noon.

FANNY: Breakfast is at nine o'clock in this house and will be until the day after I die. Ring the bell.

JOSEPH: It ain't nine yet, Miss Fanny. It's eight-thirty.

FANNY: Well, put the clocks up to nine and ring the bell.

JOSEPH: Mr. David told me not to ring it any more. He says it's got too mean a ring, that bell. It disturbs folks.

FANNY: That's what it was put there for. I like to disturb folks.

JOSEPH: Yes'm.

FANNY: You slept well, Anise. You were asleep before I could dismantle myself.

ANISE: I woke several times during the night.

FANNY: Did you? Then you were careful not to stop snoring. We must finally get around to rearranging your room. *(Anise hands her three or four letters)* Even when you don't snore, it irritates me. *(Fanny opens a letter, begins to read it. After a minute)* What time is it?

ANISE: It is about eight-thirty. Joseph just told you.

FANNY: I didn't hear him. I'm nervous. Naturally. My mail looks dull. *(Reading the letter)* Jenny always tells you a piece of gossip three times, as if it grew fresher with the telling. Did you put flowers in their rooms?

ANISE: Certainly.

FANNY: David ought to get to the station by eleven-thirty.

ANISE: *(patiently)* The train does not draw in until ten minutes past noon.

FANNY: But it might come in early. It's been known.

ANISE: Never. Not in the Union Station in Washington, the District of Columbia.

FANNY: *(irritably)* But it might. It might. Don't argue with me about everything. What time is it?

ANISE: It's now twenty-seven minutes before nine. It will be impossible to continue telling you the time every three minutes from now until Miss Sara arrives. I think you are having a nervous breakdown. Compose yourself.

FANNY: It's been twenty years. Any mother would be nervous. If your daughter were coming home and you hadn't seen her, and a husband, *and* grandchildren—

ANISE: I do not say that it is wrong to be nervous. I, too, am nervous. I say only that you are.

FANNY: Very well. I heard you. *I* say that I am. *(She goes back to reading her letter. Looks up)* Jenny's still in California. She's lost her lavallière[1] again. Birdie Chase's daughter is still faire l'amouring[2] with that actor. Tawdry, Jenny says it is. An actor. Fashions in sin change. In my day, it was Englishmen. I don't understand infidelity. If you love a man, then why? If you don't love him, then why stay with him? *(Without turning, she points over her head to Joshua Farrelly's portrait)* Thank God, I was in love. I thought about Joshua last night. Three grandchildren. He would have liked that. I hope I will. *(Points to other letters)* Anything in anybody else's mail?

ANISE: Advertisements for Mr. David and legal things. For our Count and Countess, there is nothing but what seems an invitation to a lower-class embassy tea and letters asking for bills to get paid.

FANNY: That's every morning. *(Thoughtfully)* In the six weeks the Balkan nobility have been with us, they seem to have run up a great many bills.

ANISE: Yes. *I* told you that. Then there was a night-letter for Mr. David.

(A very loud, very unpleasant bell begins to ring.)

FANNY: *(through the noise)* Really? From whom?

ANISE: From her. I took it on the telephone, and—

(Bell drowns out her voice.)

FANNY: Who is "her"? *(Bell becomes very loud)* Go tell him to stop that noise—

ANISE: *(goes toward terrace, calling)* Joseph! Stop that bell. Miss Fanny says to stop it.

JOSEPH: *(calls)* Miss Fanny said to start it.

FANNY: *(shouts out to him)* I didn't tell you to hang yourself with it.

JOSEPH: *(appears on terrace)* I ain't hung. Your breakfast is ready. *(Disappears.)*

FANNY: *(to Anise)* Who is "her"?

ANISE: That Carter woman from Lansing, Michigan.

FANNY: Oh, my. Is she back in Washington again? What did the telegram say?

ANISE: It said the long sickness of her dear Papa had terminated in full recovery.

---

1. Ornamented pendant.   2. Having an affair.

FANNY: That's too bad.

ANISE: She was returning, and would Mr. David come for dinner a week from Thursday? "Love," it said, "to you and your charming mother." *(To Fanny))* That's you. I think Miss Carter from Lansing, Michigan, was unwise in attending the illness of her Papa.

FANNY: I hope so. Why?

ANISE: *(shrugs)* There is much winking of the eyes going on between our Countess and Mr. David.

FANNY: *(eagerly)* I know that. Anything new happen?

ANISE: *(too innocently)* Happen? I don't know what you mean?

FANNY: You know damn well what I mean.

ANISE: *That?* Oh, no, I don't think that.

JOSEPH: *(appears in the door)* The sausage cakes is shrinking.

FANNY: *(rises. To Anise)* I want everybody down here immediately. Is the car ready? *(Anise nods)* Did you order a good dinner? *(Shrieks)* David! Oh.
    (David Farrelly, a pleasant-looking man of thirty-nine, comes in from the entrance hall, almost bumps into Fanny.)

DAVID: Good morning, everybody.

ANISE: *(to Fanny)* Everything is excellent. You have been asking the same questions for a week. You have made the kitchen very nervous.

DAVID: *(to Joseph)* Why did you ring that air-raid alarm again?

JOSEPH: Ain't me, Mr. David. I don't like no noise. Miss Fanny told me.

FANNY: Good morning, David.

DAVID: *(to Joseph)* Tell Fred to leave the car. I'll drive to the station.

JOSEPH: *(nods)* Yes, sir. *(Exits.)*

DAVID: *(to Fanny, half amused, half annoyed, as he begins to read his mail)* Mama, I think we'll fix up the chicken-house for you as a playroom. We'll hang the room with bells and you can go into your second childhood in the proper privacy.

FANNY: I find it very interesting. You sleep soundly, you rise at your usual hour—although your sister, whom you haven't seen in years, is waiting at the station—

DAVID: She is not waiting at the station. *(Laughs)* The train does not come in until ten minutes past twelve.

FANNY: *(airily)* It's almost that now.

ANISE: *(turns to look at her)* Really, Miss Fanny, contain yourself. It is twenty minutes before nine.

DAVID: And I have *not* slept soundly. And I've been up since six o'clock.

FANNY: The Balkans aren't down yet. Where are they?

DAVID: I don't know.

ANISE: There's nothing in your mail, Mr. David. Only the usual advertisements.

DAVID: And for me, that is all that is ever likely to come—here.

ANISE: *(haughtily, as she starts toward hall)* I cannot, of course, speak for Miss Fanny. *I* have never opened a letter in my life.

DAVID: I know. You don't have to. For you they fly open.

FANNY: *(giggles)* It's true. You're a snooper, Anise. *(Anise exits. Fanny talks as Anise moves out)* I rather admire it. It shows an interest in life. *(She looks up at Joshua's portrait)* You know, I've been lying awake most of the night wondering what Papa would have thought about Sara. He'd have been very pleased, wouldn't he? I always find myself wondering what Joshua would have felt.

DAVID: Yes. But maybe it would be just as well if you didn't expect me to be wondering about it, too. I wasn't married to him, Mama. He was just my father.

FANNY: My. You got up on the wrong side of the bed. *(She moves past him. Points to the mail which he is still opening)* The bills are for our noble guests. Interesting, how many there are every morning. How much longer are they going to be with us?

DAVID: *(without looking at her)* I don't know.

FANNY: It's been six weeks. Now that Sara and her family are coming, even this house might be a little crowded— *(He looks up at her. Quickly)* Yes. I know I invited them. I felt sorry for Marthe, and Teck rather amused me. He plays good cribbage, and he tells good jokes. But that's not enough for a lifetime guest. If you've been urging her to stay, I wish you'd stop it. They haven't any money; all right, lend them some—

DAVID: I have been urging them to stay?

FANNY: I'm not so old I don't recognize flirting when I see it.

DAVID: But you're old enough not to be silly.

FANNY: I'm not silly. I'm charming.

(Marthe de Brancovis, an attractive woman of thirty-one or thirty-two, enters.)

MARTHE: Good morning, Fanny. Morning, David.

FANNY: Good morning, Marthe.

DAVID: *(warmly)* Good morning.

MARTHE: Fanny, darling, couldn't you persuade yourself to let me have a tray in bed and some cotton for my ears?

DAVID: Certainly not. My father ate breakfast at nine; and whatever my father did . . .

FANNY: *(carefully, to David)* There was a night-letter for you from that Carter woman in Lansing, Michigan. She is returning and you are to come to dinner next Thursday. *(As she exits on terrace)* C-A-R-T-E-R. *(Pronounces it carefully)* Lansing, Michigan.

DAVID: *(laughs)* I know how to spell Carter, but thank you. *(Fanny exits. David looks up at Marthe)* Do you understand my mother?

MARTHE: Sometimes.

DAVID: Miss Carter was done for your benefit.

MARTHE: *(smiles)* That means she has guessed that I would be jealous. And she has guessed right.

DAVID: *(looks at her)* Jealous?

MARTHE: I know I've no right to be, but I am. And Fanny knows it.

DAVID: *(carelessly)* Don't pay any attention to Mama. She has a sure instinct for the women I like, and she begins to hammer away early. Marthe—*(Goes to decanter on side-table)* I'm going to have a drink. I haven't had a drink before breakfast since the day I took my bar examination. *(Pours himself a drink, gulps it down)* What's it going to be like to stand on a station platform and see your sister after all these years? I'm afraid, I guess.

MARTHE: Why?

DAVID: I don't know. Afraid she won't like me—*(Shrugs)* We were very fond of each other, but it's been a long time.

MARTHE: I remember Sara. Mama brought me one day when your father was stationed in Paris. I was about six and Sara about fifteen and you were—

DAVID: You were a pretty little girl.

MARTHE: Do you really remember me? You never told me before.

FANNY: *(yelling from the terrace)* David! Come to breakfast.

DAVID: *(as if he had not been listening)* You know, I've never met Sara's husband. Mama did. I think the first day Sara met him, in Munich. Mama didn't like the marriage much in those days—and Sara didn't care, and Mama didn't like Sara not caring. Mama cut up about it, bad.

MARTHE: Why?

DAVID: Probably because they didn't let her arrange it. Why does Mama ever act badly? She doesn't remember ten minutes later.

MARTHE: Wasn't Mr. Müller poor?

DAVID: Oh, Mama wouldn't have minded that. If they'd only come home and let her fix their lives for them—(*Smiles*) But Sara didn't want it that way.

MARTHE: You'll have a house full of refugees—us and—

DAVID: Are you and Teck refugees? I'm not sure I know what you're refugees from.

MARTHE: From Europe.

DAVID: From what Europe?

MARTHE: (*smiles, shrugs*) I don't know. I don't know myself, really. Just Europe.
(*Quickly, comes to him*) Sara will like you. I like you. (*Laughs*) That doesn't make sense, does it?
    (*On her speech, Teck de Brancovis appears in the hall. He is a good-looking man of about forty-five. She stops quickly.*)

TECK: (*to Marthe and David*) Good morning.
    (*The bell gives an enormous ring.*)

DAVID: (*goes to terrace*) Good morning, Teck. For years I've been thinking they were coming for Mama with a net. I'm giving up hope. I may try catching her myself. (*Disappears, calling*) Mama? Stop that noise.

TECK: I wonder if science has a name for women who enjoy noise? (*Goes to table, picks up his mail*) Many mistaken people, Marthe, seem to have given you many charge accounts.

MARTHE: The Countess de Brancovis. That still does it. It would be nice to be able to pay bills again—

TECK: Do not act as if I refused to pay them. I did not sleep well last night. I was worried. We have eighty-seven dollars in American Express checks. (*Pleasantly, looking at her*) That's all we have, Marthe.

MARTHE: (*shrugs*) Maybe something will turn up. It's due.

TECK: (*carefully*) David? (*Then, as she turns to look at him*) The other relatives will arrive this morning?

MARTHE: Yes.

TECK: (*points to porch*) I think Madame Fanny and Mr. David may grow weary of accents and charity guests. Or is the husband of the sister a rich one?

MARTHE: No. He's poor. He had to leave Germany in '33.

TECK: A Jew?

MARTHE: No. I don't think so.

TECK: Why did he have to leave Germany?

MARTHE: (*still reading*) Oh, I don't know, Teck. He's an anti-Nazi.

TECK: A political?

MARTHE: No, I don't think so. He was an engineer. I don't know. I don't know much about him.

TECK: Did you sleep well?

MARTHE: Yes. Why not?

TECK: Money does not worry you?

MARTHE: It worries me very much. But I just lie still now and hope. I'm glad to be here.
(*Shrugs*) Maybe something good will happen. We've come to the end of a road.
That's been true for a long time. Things will have to go one way or the other. Maybe they'll go well, for a change.

TECK: I have not come to the end of any road.

MARTHE: (*looks at him*) No? I admire you.

TECK: I'm going into Washington tonight. Phili has a poker game every Wednesday evening. He has arranged for me to join it.

MARTHE: (*after a pause*) Have you been seeing Phili?

TECK: Once or twice. Why not? Phili and I are old friends. He may be useful. I do not want to stay in this country forever.

MARTHE: You can't leave them alone. Your favorite dream, isn't it, Teck? That they will let you play with them again? I don't think they will, and I don't think you should be seeing Phili, or that you should be seen at the Embassy.

TECK: *(smiles)* You have political convictions now?

MARTHE: I don't know what I have. I've never liked Nazis, as you know, and you should have had enough of them. They seem to have had enough of you, God knows. It would be just as well to admit they are smarter than you are and let them alone.

TECK: *(looking at her carefully, after a minute)* That is interesting.

MARTHE: What is interesting?

TECK: I think you are trying to say something to me. What is it?

MARTHE: That you ought not to be at the Embassy, and that it's insane to play cards in a game with Von Seitz with eighty-seven dollars in your pocket. I don't think he'd like your not being able to pay up. Suppose you lose?

TECK: I shall try not to lose.

MARTHE: But if you do lose and can't pay, it will be all over Washington in an hour. *(Points to terrace)* They'll find out about it, and we'll be out of here when they do.

TECK: I think I want to be out of here. I find that I do not like the picture of you and our host.

MARTHE: *(carefully)* There is no picture, as you put it, to like or dislike.

TECK: Not yet? I am glad to hear that. *(Comes toward her slowly)* Marthe, you understand that I am not really a fool? You understand that it is unwise to calculate me that way?

MARTHE: *(slowly, as if it were an effort)* Yes, I understand that. And I understand that I am getting tired. Just plain tired. The whole thing's too much for me. I've always meant to ask you, since you played on so many sides, why we didn't come out any better. I've always wanted to ask you what happened. *(Sharply)* I'm tired, see? And I just want to sit down. Just to sit down in a chair and stay.

TECK: *(carefully)* Here?

MARTHE: I don't know. Any place—

TECK: You have thus arranged it with David?

MARTHE: I've arranged nothing.

TECK: But you are trying, eh? *(He comes close to her)* I think not. I would not like that. Do not make any arrangements, Marthe. I may not allow you to carry them through. *(Smiles)* Come to breakfast now. *(He passes her, disappears on the terrace. She stands still and thoughtful. Then she, too, moves to the terrace, disappears. Joseph appears on the terrace, carrying a tray toward the unseen breakfast table. The stage is empty. After a minute, there are sounds of footsteps in the hall. Sara Müller appears in the doorway, comes toward the middle of the room as if expecting to find somebody, stops, looks around, begins to smile. Behind her in the doorway, are three children; behind them, Kurt Müller. They stand waiting, watching Sara. Sara is forty-one or forty-two, a good-looking woman, with a well-bred, serious face. She is very badly dressed. Her dress is too long, her shoes were bought a long time ago and have no relation to the dress, and the belt of her dress has become untied and is hanging down. She looks clean and dowdy. As she looks around the room, her face is gay and surprised. Smiling, without turning, absently, she motions to the children and Kurt. Slowly, the children come in. Bodo Müller, a boy of nine, comes first. He is carrying coats. Behind him, carrying two cheap valises, is Joshua Müller, a boy of fourteen. Behind him is Babette Müller, a pretty little girl of twelve. They are dressed for a much colder climate. They come forward, look at their mother, then move to a couch.*

*Behind them is Kurt Müller, a large, powerful, German-looking man of about
forty-seven. He is carrying a shabby valise and a brief-case. He stands watching Sara.
Joshua puts down the valises, goes to his father, takes the valise from Kurt, puts it
neatly near his, and puts the brief-case near Kurt. Babette goes to Sara, takes a
package from her, places it near the valise. Then she turns to Bodo, takes the coats he
is carrying, puts them neatly on top of the valises. After a second, Kurt sits down. As
he does so, we see that his movements are slow and careful, as if they are made with
effort.)*

BABETTE: *(points to a couch near which they are standing. She has a slight accent)* Is it
allowed?

KURT: *(smiles. He has an accent)* Yes. It is allowed. *(Babette and Bodo sit stiffly on the
couch.)*

JOSHUA: *(nervously. He has a slight accent)* But we did not sound the bell—

SARA: *(idly, as she wanders around the room, her face excited)* The door isn't locked. It
never was. Never since I can remember.

BODO: *(softly, puzzled)* The entrance of the home is never locked. So.

KURT: *(looks at him)* You find it curious to believe there are people who live and do not
need to watch, eh, Bodo?

BODO: Yes, Papa.

KURT: *(smiles)* You and I.

JOSHUA: *(smiles)* It is strange. But it must be good, I think.

KURT: Yes.

SARA: Sit back. Be comfortable. I—I wonder where Mama and David— *(Delighted, sees
portrait of Joshua Farrelly, points to it)* And that was my Papa. That was the famous
Joshua Farrelly. *(They all look up at it. She wanders around the room)* My goodness,
isn't it a fine room? I'd almost forgotten— *(Picks up a picture from the table)* And
this was my grandmother. *(Very nervously)* Shall I go and say we're here? They'd be
having breakfast, I think. Always on the side terrace in nice weather. I don't know.
Maybe— *(Picks up another picture)* "To Joshua and Fanny Farrelly. With admiration.
Alfonso,[3] May 7, 1910." I had an ermine boa and a pink coat. I was angry because it
was too warm in Madrid to wear it.

BODO: Alfons von Spanien? Der hat immer Bilder von sich verschenkt. Ein schlectes
Zeichen für einen Mann.

JOSHUA: Mama told you it is good manners to speak the language of the country you
visit. Therefore, speak in English.

BODO: I said he seemed always to give his photograph. I said that is a bad flag[4] on a
man. Grow fat on the poor people and give pictures of the face. *(Joshua sits down.)*

SARA: I remember a big party and cakes and a glass of champagne for me. I was ten, I
guess— *(Suddenly laughs)* That was when Mama said the first time a king got shot
at, he was a romantic, but the fifth time he was a comedian.[5] And when my father
gave his lecture in Madrid, he repeated it—right in Madrid. It was a great scandal.
You know, Alfonso was always getting shot at or bombed.

BODO: *(shrugs)* Certainement.

JOSHUA: Certainement? As-tu perdu la tête?[6]

BABETTE: Speak in English, please.

---

3. Alfonso XIII (1886–1941), King of Spain, went
into exile in 1931 to escape the political unrest
leading up to the Spanish Civil War
(1936–1939), a prelude to World War II.

4. *Zeichen* means sign, portent.

5. Many assassination attempts were made against
Alfonso, including one on his wedding day in
1906.

6. "Have you lost your head?"

KURT: *(without turning)* You are a terrorist, Bodo?

BODO: *(slowly)* No.

JOSHUA: Then since when has it become *natural* to shoot upon people?

BODO: Do not give me lessons. It is neither right nor natural to shoot upon people. I know that.

SARA: *(looks at Babette, thoughtfully)* An ermine boa. A boa is a scarf. I should like to have one for you, Babbie. Once, in Prague, I saw a pretty one. I wanted to buy it for you. But we had to pay our rent. *(Laughs)* But I almost bought it.

BABETTE: Yes, Mama. Thank you. Tie your sash, Mama.

SARA: *(thoughtfully)* Almost twenty years.

BODO: You were born here, Mama?

SARA: Upstairs. And I lived here until I went to live with your father. *(Looks out beyond terrace)* Your Uncle David and I used to have a garden, behind the terrace. I wonder if it's still there. I like a garden. I've always hoped we'd have a house some day and settle down— *(Stops, nervously, turns to stare at Kurt, who is looking at her)* I am talking so foolish. Sentimental. At my age. Gardens and ermine boas. I haven't wanted anything—

KURT: *(comes toward her, takes her hand)* Sara. Stop it. This is a fine room. A fine place to be. Everything is so pleasant and full of comfort. This will be a good piano on which to play again. And it is all so clean. I like that. Now, you shall not be a baby. You must enjoy your house, and not be afraid that you hurt me with it. Yes?

BABETTE: Papa, tie Mama's sash, please.

SARA: *(shyly smiles at him as he leans down to tie the belt)* Yes, of course. It's strange, that's all. We've never been in a place like this together—

KURT: That does not mean, and should not mean, that we do not remember how to enjoy what comes our way. We are on a holiday.

JOSHUA: A holiday? But for how long? And what plans afterward?

KURT: *(quietly)* We will have plans when the hour arrives to make them. *(Anise appears from the hall. She starts into the room, stops, bewildered. The Müllers have not seen her. Then, as Sara turns, Anise speaks. As she speaks, the children rise.)*

ANISE: What? What?

SARA: *(softly)* Anise. It's me. It's Sara.

ANISE: *(coming forward slowly)* What? *(Then as she approaches Sara, she begins to run toward her)* Miss Sara! Miss Sara! *(They reach each other, both laugh happily. Sara kisses Anise)* I would have known you. Yes, I would. I would have known— *(Excited, bewildered, nervous, she looks toward Kurt)* How do you do, sir? How do you do? *(Turns toward the children)* How do you do?

JOSHUA: Thank you, Miss Anise. We are in good health.

SARA: *(very happily)* You look the same. I think you look the same. Just the way I've always remembered. *(To the others)* This is the Anise I have told you about. She was here before I was born.

ANISE: But how— Did you just come in? What a way to come home! And after all the plans we've made! But you were to come on the twelve o'clock train, and Mr. David was to meet you—

BABETTE: The twelve o'clock train was most expensive. We could not have come with that train. We liked the train we came on. It was most luxurious.

ANISE: *(very nervously, very rattled)* But Madame Fanny will have a fit. I will call her— She will not be able to contain herself. She—

SARA: *(softly)* I wanted a few minutes. I'm nervous about coming home, I guess.

BODO: *(conversationally)* You are French, Madame Anise?

ANISE: Yes, I am from the Bas Rhin.[6] *(She looks past Sara, and bobs her head idiotically at Kurt)* Sara's husband. That is nice. That is nice.

BODO: Yes. Your accent is from the North. That is fine country. We were in hiding there once. *(Babette quickly pokes him.)*

ANISE: Hiding? You— *(Turns nervously to Kurt)* But here we stand and talk. You have not had your breakfast, sir!

BABETTE: *(simply, eagerly)* It would be nice to have breakfast.

ANISE: Yes, of course—I will go and order it.

SARA: *(to the children)* What would you like for breakfast?

BABETTE: *(surprised)* What would we like? Why, Mama, we will have anything that can be spared. If eggs are not too rare or too expensive—

ANISE: *(amazed)* Rare? Why— Oh, I—I must call Miss Fanny now. It is of a necessity. *(Excited, rushing toward terrace, calling)* Miss Fanny. Miss Fanny. *(Back to Sara)* Have you forgotten your Mama's nature? She cannot bear not knowing things. Miss Fanny! What a way to come home! After twenty years and nobody at the station—

FANNY'S VOICE: Don't yell at me. What is the matter with you?

ANISE: *(excitedly, as Fanny draws near)* She's here. They're here. Miss Sara. She's here, I tell you. *(Fanny comes up to her, stares at her, then looks slowly around until she sees Sara.)*

SARA: *(softly)* Hello, Mama.

FANNY: *(after a long pause, softly, coming toward her)* Sara. Sara, darling. You're here. You're really here. *(She reaches her, takes her arms, stares at her, smiles)* Welcome. Welcome. Welcome to your house. *(Slowly)* You're not young, Sara.

SARA: *(smiles)* No, Mama. I'm forty-one.

FANNY: *(softly)* Forty-one. Of course. *(Presses her arms again)* Oh, Sara, I'm— *(Then quickly)* You look more like Papa now. That's good. The years have helped you. *(Turns to look at Kurt)* Welcome to this house, sir.

KURT: *(warmly)* Thank you, Madame.

FANNY: *(turns to look at Sara again, nervously pats her arm. Nods, turns again to stare at Kurt. She is nervous and chatty)* You are a good-looking man, for a German. I didn't remember you that way. I like a good-looking man. I always have.

KURT: *(smiles)* I like a good-looking woman. I always have.

FANNY: Good. That's the way it should be.

BODO: *(to Sara)* Ist das Grossmama?

FANNY: *(looks down)* Yes. I am your grandmother. Also, I speak German, so do not talk about me. I speak languages very well. But there is no longer anybody to speak with. Anise has half forgotten her French, which was always bad; and I have nobody with whom to speak my Italian or German or—Sara, it's very good to have you home. I'm chattering away, I—

JOSHUA: Now you have us, Madame. We speak ignorantly, but fluently, in German, French, Italian, Spanish—

KURT: And boastfully in English.

BODO: There is never a need for boasting. If we are to fight for the good of all men, it is to be accepted that we must be among the most advanced.

ANISE: My God.

FANNY: *(to Sara)* Are these your *children*? Or are they dressed up midgets?

SARA: *(laughs)* These are my children, Mama. This, Babette. *(Babette bows)* This, Joshua. *(Joshua bows)* This is Bodo. *(Bodo bows.)*

---

6. Lower Rhineland, a part of the Alsace-Lorraine region disputed by France and Germany for hundreds of years. It was ceded to France after World War I, but the Germans reoccupied it in 1940.

FANNY: Joshua was named for Papa. You wrote me. *(Indicates picture of Joshua Farrelly)* You bear a great name, young man.

JOSHUA: *(smiles, indicates his father)* My name is Müller.

FANNY: *(looks at him, laughs)* Yes. You look a little like your grandfather. *(To Babette)* And so do you. You are a nice-looking girl. *(To Bodo)* You look like nobody.

BODO: *(proudly)* I am not beautiful.

FANNY: *(laughs)* Well, Sara, well. Three children. You have done well. *(To Kurt)* You, too, sir, of course. Are you quite recovered? Sara wrote that you were in Spain and—

BODO: Did Mama write that Papa was a great hero? He was brave, he was calm, he was expert, he was resourceful, he was—

KURT: *(laughs)* My biographer. And as unprejudiced as most of them.

SARA: Where is David? I am so anxious— Has he changed much? Does he . . .

FANNY: *(to Anise)* Don't stand there. Go and get him right away. Go get David. *(As Anise exits)* He's out having breakfast with the titled folk. Do you remember Marthe Randolph? I mean, do you remember Hortie Randolph, her mother, who was my friend? Can you follow what I'm saying? I'm not speaking well today.

SARA: *(laughs)* Of course I remember Marthe and Hortie. You and she used to scream at each other.

FANNY: Well, Marthe, her daughter, married Teck de Brancovis. *Count* de Brancovis. He was fancy when she married him. Not so fancy now, I suspect. Although still chic and tired. You know what I mean, the way they are in Europe. Well, they're here.

SARA: What's David like now? I—

FANNY: Like? Like? I don't know. He's a lawyer. You know that. Papa's firm. He's never married. You know that, too—

SARA: Why hasn't he married?

FANNY: Really, I don't know. I don't think he likes his own taste. Which is very discriminating of him. He's had a lot of girls, of course, one more ignorant and silly than the other— *(Goes toward terrace, begins to scream)* And where is he? David! David!

ANISE'S VOICE: He's coming, Miss Fanny. He's coming. Contain yourself. He was down at the garage getting ready to leave—

FANNY: I don't care where he is. Tell him to come.—David! *(Suddenly points to picture of Joshua)* That's my Joshua. Handsome, eh? We were very much in love. Hard to believe of people nowadays, isn't it?

SARA: Kurt and I love each other.

FANNY: Oh. You do? I daresay. But there are ways and ways of loving.

SARA: How dare you, Mama—

KURT: *(laughs)* Ladies, ladies.

SARA: *(giggles)* Why, I almost got mad then. You know, I don't think I've been mad since I last saw you.

BODO: My! You and Mama must not get angry. Anger is protest. And so you must direction it to the proper channels and then harness it for the good of other men. That is correct, Papa?

FANNY: *(peers down at him)* If you grow up to talk like that, and stay as ugly as you are, you are going to have one of those successful careers on the lecture platform. *(Joshua and Babette laugh.)*

JOSHUA: *(to Bodo)* Ah. It is a great pleasure to hear Grandma talk with you.

BODO: *(to Fanny, tenderly)* We will not like each other. *(Kurt has wandered to the piano. Standing, he touches the keys in the first bars of a Mozart Rondo.)*

FANNY: You are wrong. I think we are rather alike; if that is so, let us at least remember to admire each other. *(David comes running in from the entrance hall. At the door he stops, stares at Sara.)*

DAVID: *(to Sara)* Sara. Darling—

SARA: *(wheels, goes running toward him. She moves into his arms. He leans down, kisses her with great affection)* David. David.

DAVID: *(softly)* It's been a long, long time. I got to thinking it would never happen. *(He leans down, kisses her hair. After a minute, he smiles, presses her arm.)*

SARA: *(excited)* David, I'm excited. Isn't it strange? To be here, to see each other— But I am forgetting. This is my husband. These are my children. Babette, Joshua, Bodo. *(They all three advance, stand in line to shake hands.)*

BODO: *(shaking hand)* How do you do, Uncle David?

DAVID: How do you do, Bodo? *(David shakes hands with Joshua)* Boys can shake hands. But so pretty a girl must be kissed. *(He kisses Babette. She smiles, very pleased, and crosses to the side of Sara.)*

BABETTE: Thank you. Fix your hairpin, Mama. *(Sara shoves back a falling hairpin.)*

DAVID: *(crossing to Kurt)* I'm happy to meet you, sir, and to have you here.

KURT: Thank you. Sara has told me so much from you. You have a devoted sister.

DAVID: *(very pleased)* Have I? Still? That's mighty good to hear. *(Anise comes in from the library.)*

ANISE: Your breakfast is coming. Shall I wash the children, Miss Sara?

JOSHUA: *(amazed)* Wash us? Do people wash each other?

SARA: No, but the washing is a good idea. Go along now, and hurry. *(All three start for the hall)* And then we'll all have a fine, big breakfast again. *(The children exit.)*

FANNY: Again? Don't you usually have a good breakfast?

KURT: *(smiles)* No, Madame. Only sometimes.

SARA: *(laughs)* Oh, we do all right, usually. *(Very happily, very gaily)* Ah, it's good to be here. *(Puts her arm in David's)* We were kids. Now we're all grown up! I've got children, you're a lawyer, and a fine one, I bet—

FANNY: The name of Farrelly on the door didn't, of course, hurt David's career.

DAVID: *(smiles)* Sara, you might as well know Mama thinks of me only as a monument to Papa and a not very well-made monument at that. I am not the man Papa was.

SARA: *(to Fanny, smiles)* How do you know he's not?

FANNY: *(carefully)* I beg your pardon. That is the second time you have spoken disrespectfully of your father. *(Sara and David laugh. Fanny turns to Kurt)* I hope you will like me.

KURT: I hope so.

SARA: *(pulls him to the couch, sits down with him)* Now I want to hear about you— *(Looks at him, laughs)* I'm awfully nervous about seeing you. Are you, about me?

DAVID: Yes. I certainly am.

SARA: *(looks around)* I'm like an idiot. I want to see everything right away. The lake, and my old room—and I want to talk and ask questions . . .

KURT: *(laughs)* More slow, Sara. It is most difficult to have twenty years in a few minutes.

SARA: Yes, I know, but— Oh, well. Kurt's right. We'll say it all slowly. It's just nice being back. Haven't I fine children?

DAVID: Very fine. You're lucky. I wish I had them.

FANNY: How could you have them? All the women you like are too draughty, if you know what I mean. I'm sure that girl from Lansing, Michigan, would be sterile. Which is as God in his wisdom would have it.

SARA: Oh. So you have a girl?

DAVID: I have no girl. This amuses Mama.

FANNY: He's very attractive to some women. *(To Kurt)* Both my children are attractive, whatever else they're not. Don't you think so? *(Points to David)* He's flirting with our Countess now, Sara. You will see for yourself.

DAVID: *(sharply)* You are making nervous jokes this morning, Mama. And they're not very good ones.

FANNY: *(gaily)* I tell the truth. If it turns out to be a joke, all the better.

SARA: *(affectionately)* Ah, Mama hasn't changed. And that's good, too.

FANNY: Don't mind me, Sara. I, too, am nervous about seeing you. *(To Kurt)* You'll like it here. You are an engineer?

KURT: Yes.

FANNY: Do you remember the day we met in München?[7] The day Sara brought you to lunch? I thought you were rather a clod and that Sara would have a miserable life. I think I was wrong. *(To David)* You see? I always admit when I'm wrong.

DAVID: You are a woman who is noble in all things, at all times.

FANNY: Oh, you're mad at me. *(To Kurt)* As I say, you'll like it here. I've already made some plans. The new wing will be for you and Sara. The old turkey-house we'll fix up for the children. A nice, new bathroom, and we'll put in their own kitchen, and Anise will move in with them—

SARA: That's kind of you, Mama. But—but—we won't make any plans for a while— *(Very quietly)* A good, long vacation; God knows Kurt needs it—

FANNY: A vacation? You'll be staying here, of course. You don't have to worry about work—engineers can always get jobs, David says, and he's already begun to inquire—

KURT: I have not worked as an engineer since many years, Madame.

DAVID: Haven't you? I thought— Didn't you work for Dornier?

KURT: Yes. Before '33.

FANNY: But you have worked in other places. A great many other places, I should say. Every letter of Sara's seemed to have a new postmark.

KURT: *(smiles)* We move most often.

DAVID: You gave up engineering?

KURT: I gave it up? *(shrugs)* One could say it that way.

FANNY: What do you do?

SARA: Mama, we—

KURT: It is difficult to explain.

DAVID: *(after a slight pause)* If you'd rather not.

FANNY: No, I—I'm trying to find out something. *(To Kurt)* May I ask it, sir?

KURT: Let me help you, Madame. You wish to know whether not being an engineer buys adequate breakfasts for my family. It does not. I have no wish to make a mystery of what I have been doing; it is only that it is awkward to place neatly. *(Smiles, motions with his hand)* It sounds so big: it is so small. I am an Anti-Fascist. And that does not pay well.

FANNY: Do you mind questions?

SARA: Yes.

KURT: *(sharply)* Sara. *(To Fanny)* Perhaps I shall not answer them. But I shall try.

FANNY: Are you a radical?

KURT: You would have to tell me what that word means to you, Madame.

FANNY: *(after a slight pause)* That is just. Perhaps we all have private definitions. We all are Anti-Fascists, for example—

SARA: Yes. But Kurt works at it.

FANNY: What kind of work?

KURT: Any kind. Anywhere.

FANNY: *(sharply)* I will stop asking questions.

SARA: *(very sharply)* That would be sensible, Mama.

---

7. Munich.

DAVID: Darling, don't be angry. We've been worried about you, naturally. We knew so little, except that you were having a bad time.

SARA: I didn't have a bad time. We never—

KURT: Do not lie for me, Sara.

SARA: I'm not lying. I didn't have a bad time, the way they mean. I—

FANNY: *(slowly)* You had a bad time just trying to live, didn't you? That's obvious, Sara, and foolish to petend it isn't. Why wouldn't you take money from us? What kind of nonsense—

SARA: *(slowly)* We've lived the way we wanted to live. I don't know the language of rooms like this any more. And I don't want to learn it again.

KURT: Do not bristle about it.

SARA: I'm not bristling. *(To Fanny)* I married because I fell in love. You can understand that.

FANNY: *(slowly)* Yes.

SARA: For almost twelve years, Kurt went to work every morning and came home every night, and we lived modestly, and happily— *(Sharply)* As happily as people could in a starved Germany that was going to pieces—

KURT: Sara, please. You are angry. I do not like it that way. I will try to find a way to tell you with quickness. Yes. *(Sara turns, looks at him, starts to speak, stops)* I was born in a town called Fürth. *(Pauses. Looks up, smiles)* There is a holiday in my town. We call it Kirchweih. It was a gay holiday with games and music and a hot white sausage to eat with the wine. I grow up, I move away—to school, to work—but always I come back for Kirchweih. It is for me, the great day of the year. *(Slowly)* But after the war, that day begins to change. The sausage is made from bad stuff, the peasants come in without shoes, the children are too sick— *(Carefully)* It is bad for my people, those years, but always I have hope. In the festival of August, 1931, more than a year before the storm, I give up that hope. On that day, I see twenty-seven men murdered in a Nazi street fight. I cannot stay by now and watch. My time has come to move. I say with Luther, "Here I stand. I can do nothing else. God help me. Amen."[8]

SARA: It doesn't pay well to fight for what we believe in. But I wanted it the way Kurt wanted it. *(Shrugs)* They don't like us in Europe; I guess they never did. So Kurt brought us home. You've always said you wanted us. If you don't, I will understand.

DAVID: Darling, of course we want you—

FANNY: *(rises)* I am old. And made of dry cork. And bad-mannered. Please forgive me.

SARA: *(goes quickly to Fanny)* Shut up, Mama. We're all acting like fools. I'm glad to be home. That's all I know. So damned glad.

DAVID: And we're damned glad to have you. Come on. Let's walk to the lake. We've made it bigger and planted the island with blackberries— *(She smiles and goes to him. Together they move out the hall entrance.)*

FANNY: *(after a silence)* They've always liked each other. We're going to have Zwetschgen-Knoedel[9] for dinner. You like them?

KURT: Indeed.

FANNY: I hope you like decent food.

KURT: I do.

FANNY: That's a good sign in a man.

MARTHE: *(coming in from the terrace. Stops in the doorway)* Oh, I'm sorry, Fanny. We were waiting. I didn't want to interrupt the family reunion. I—

---

8. Quote from Martin Luther (1483–1546), Protestant reformer.

9. Plum dumplings.

FANNY: This is my son-in-law, Herr Müller. The Countess de Brancovis.

KURT AND MARTHE: *(together)* How do you do?

MARTHE: And how is Sara, Herr Müller? I haven't seen her since I was a little girl. She probably doesn't remember me at all. *(Teck comes in from the hall. She turns)* This is my husband, Herr Müller.

KURT: How do you do?

TECK: How do you do, sir? *(Kurt bows. They shake hands)* Would it be impertinent for one European to make welcome another?

KURT: *(smiles)* I do not think so. It would be friendly.

BODO: *(appears at the hall door)* Papa— *(Sees Teck and Marthe, bows)* Oh, good morning. Miss Anise says you are the Count and Countess. Once before we met a Count and Countess. They had a small room bordering on ours in Copenhagen. They were more older than you, and more poor. We shared with them our newspaper.

MARTHE: *(laughs)* It wasn't us, but it might have been. What's your name?

TECK: *(laughs)* We hope you will be as kind to us.

BODO: My name is Bodo. It's a strange name. No? *(To Kurt)* Papa, this is the house of great wonders. Each has his bed, each has his bathroom. The arrangement of it, that is splendorous.

FANNY: *(laughs)* You are a fancy talker, Bodo.

KURT: Oh, yes. In many languages.

BODO: *(to Fanny)* Please to correct me when I am wrong. Papa, the plumbing is such as you have never seen. Each implement is placed on the floor, and all are simultaneous in the same room. You will therefore see that being placed most solidly on the floor allows of no rats, rodents or crawlers, and is most sanitary. *(To the others)* Papa will be most interested. He likes to know how each thing of everything is put together. And he is so fond of being clean—

KURT: *(laughs. To Fanny)* I am a hero to my children. It bores everybody but me.

TECK: It is most interesting, Herr Müller. I thought I had a good ear for the accents of your country. But yours is most difficult to place. It is Bayrisch[1]? Or is it—

BODO: That's because Papa has worked in so many—

KURT: *(quickly)* German accents are the most difficult to identify. I, myself, when I try, am usually incorrect. It would be particularly difficult with me because I speak other languages. Yours would be Roumanian?

MARTHE: *(laughs)* My God, is it that bad?

KURT: *(smiles)* I am showing off. I know the Count de Brancovis is Roumanian.[2]

TECK: *(heartily)* So? We have met before? I thought so, but I cannot remember—

KURT: No, sir. We have not met before. I read your name in the newspapers.

TECK: *(to Kurt)* Strange. I was sure I had met you. I was in the Paris Legation for many years, and I thought perhaps—

KURT: Oh, no. If it is possible to believe, I am the exile who is not famous. *(To Fanny)* I have been thinking with pleasure, Madame Fanny, of breakfast on your porch. *(He points to the picture of Joshua Farrelly)* Your husband once wrote: "I am getting older now and Europe seems far away. Fanny and I will have an early breakfast on the porch and then I shall drive the bays into Washington." *(Remembering)* And then he goes on: "Henry Adams tells me he has been reading Karl Marx.[3] I shall have to tell him my father made me read Marx many years ago and that, since he proposes to exhibit himself to impress me, will spoil Henry's Sunday."

---

1. Bavarian.
2. Rumania was allied with Germany, Italy, and Japan in World War II.

3. Henry Adams (1838–1918), American historian; Karl Marx (1818–1883), German political theorist.

FANNY: *(laughs, delighted. Takes Kurt's arm)* And so it did. I had forgotten that. I am pleased with you. I shall come and serve you food myself. I had forgotten Joshua ever wrote it. *(They start out of the terrace doors together, followed by Bodo.)*

KURT: *(as they disappear)* I try to impress you. I learned it last night. *(Fanny laughs. They disappear.)*

TECK: *(smiles)* He is a clever man. A quotation from Joshua Farrelly is a sure road to Fanny's heart. Where did you say Herr Müller was from?

MARTHE: Germany.

TECK: I know that. *(Goes to a valise. He leans over, stares at it, looks at the labels, pushes the lock. The lock opens; he closes it. Then he turns and, as he speaks, picks up the brief-case)* What part of Germany?

MARTHE: I don't know. And I never knew you were an expert on accents.

TECK: I never knew it either. Are you driving into Washington with David this morning?

MARTHE: I was going to. But he may not be going to the office, now that Sara's here. I was to have lunch with Sally Tyne. *(Teck puts down the brief-case)* What are you doing?

TECK: Wondering why luggage is unlocked and a shabby brief-case is so carefully locked.

MARTHE: You're very curious about Mr. Müller.

TECK: Yes. And I do not know why. Something far away . . . I am curious about a daughter of the Farrellys' who marries a German who has bullet scars on his face and broken bones in his hands.

MARTHE: *(sharply)* Has he? There are many of them now, I guess.

TECK: So there are. But this one is in this house. *(He goes to the bell cord, pulls it. She watches him nervously.)*

MARTHE: Is it—is he any business of yours?

TECK: What is my business? Anything might be my business now.

MARTHE: Yes—unfortunately. You might inquire from your friend Von Seitz. They always know their nationals.

TECK: *(pleasantly, ignoring the sharpness with which she has spoken)* Oh, yes, I will do that, of course. But I do not like to ask questions without knowing the value of the answers.

MARTHE: Teck. This man is a little German Sara married years ago. I remember Mama talking about it. He was nothing then and he isn't now. They've had a tough enough time already without—

TECK: Have you— Have you been sleeping with David?

MARTHE: *(stops, stares at him, then simply)* No. I have not been. And that hasn't been your business for a good many years now.

TECK: You like him?

MARTHE: *(nervously)* What's this for, Teck?

TECK: Answer me, please.

MARTHE: I— *(She stops.)*

TECK: Yes? Answer me.

MARTHE: I do like him.

TECK: What does he feel about you?

MARTHE: I don't know.

TECK: But you are trying to find out. You have made plans with him?

MARTHE: Of course not. I—

TECK: But you will try to make him have plans. I have recognized it. Well, we have been together a long— *(Joseph enters, Teck stops)* Joseph, Miss Fanny wishes you to take the baggage upstairs.

JOSEPH: Yes, sir. I was going to. (*He begins to pick up the baggage. Marthe has turned sharply and is staring at Teck. Then she rises, watches Joseph pick up the baggage, turns again to look at Teck.*)

TECK: As I was saying. It is perhaps best that we had this talk.

MARTHE: (*she stops, waits for Joseph to move off. He exits, carrying the valises*) Why did you do that? Why did you tell Joseph that Fanny wanted him to take the baggage upstairs?

TECK: Obviously it is more comfortable to look at baggage behind closed doors.

MARTHE: (*very sharply*) What kind of silliness is this now? Leave these people alone— (*As he starts to exit*) I won't let you—

TECK: What? (*As he moves again, she comes after him.*)

MARTHE: I said I won't let you. You are not—

TECK: How many times have you seen me angry? (*Marthe looks up, startled*) You will not wish to see another. Run along now and have lunch with something you call Sally Tyne. But do not make plans with David. You will not be able to carry them out. You will go with me, when I am ready to go. You understand. (*He exits during his speech. The last words come as he goes through the door, and as the curtain falls.*)

Act Two

SCENE: *The same as Act One, about ten days later. During the act it will begin to grow dark; but the evening is warm and the terrace doors are open.*

AT RISE: *Sara is sitting on the couch, crocheting. Fanny and Teck are sitting at a small table playing cribbage. Bodo is sitting near them, at a large table, working on a heating pad. The cord is torn from the bag, the bag is ripped open. Anise sits next to him, anxiously watching him. Outside on the terrace, Joshua is going through baseball motions, coached by Joseph. From time to time they move out of sight, reappear, move off again.*

FANNY: (*playing a card*) One.

BODO: (*after a minute, to Teck*) The arrangement of this heating pad grows more complex.

TECK: (*smiles, moves on the cribbage board*) And the more wires you remove, the more complex it will grow.

BODO: (*points to bag*) Man has learned to make man comfortable. Yet all cannot have the comforts. (*To Anise*) How much did this cost you?

ANISE: It cost me ten dollars. And you have made a ruin of it.

BODO: That is not yet completely true. (*To Fanny*) Did I not install for you a twenty-five-cent button-push for your radio?

TECK: (*playing a card*) Two and two. (*Moves pegs on the cribbage board.*)

FANNY: Yes, you're quite an installer.

BODO: (*to Teck*) As I was wishing to tell you, Count de Brancovis, comfort and plenty exist. Yet all cannot have them it. Why?

TECK: I do not know. It has worried many men. Why?

ANISE: (*to Bodo*) Yes, why?

BODO: (*takes a deep breath, raises his finger as if about to lecture*) Why? (*Considers a moment, then deflates himself*) I am not as yet sure.

ANISE: I thought not.

FANNY: (*turns to look at Joshua and Joseph on the terrace*) Would you mind doing that dancing some place else?

JOSEPH: *(looking in)* Yes'm. That ain't dancing. I'm teaching Josh baseball.

FANNY: Then maybe he'd teach you how to clean the silver.

JOSEPH: I'm a good silver-cleaner, Miss Fanny.

FANNY: But you're getting out of practice.

JOSEPH: *(after a moment's thought)* Yes'm. I see what you mean. *(He exits.)*

FANNY: *(playing a card)* Three.

JOSHUA: It is my fault. I'm crazy about baseball.

BODO: Baseball players are among the most exploited people in this country. I read about it.

FANNY: You never should have learned to read.

BODO: Their exploited condition is foundationed on the fact that—

JOSHUA: *(bored)* All right, all right. I still like baseball.

SARA: Founded, Bodo, not foundationed.

JOSHUA: He does it always. He likes long words. In all languages.

TECK: How many languages do you children speak?

BODO: Oh, we do not really know any very well, except German and English. We speak bad French and—

SARA: And bad Danish and bad Czech.

TECK: You seem to have stayed close to the borders of Germany. Did Herr Müller have hopes, as so many did, that National Socialism[4] would be overthrown on every tomorrow?

SARA: We have not given up that hope. Have you, Count de Brancovis?

TECK: I never had it.

JOSHUA: *(pleasantly)* Then it must be most difficult for you to sleep.

TECK: I beg your pardon?

SARA: Schweig doch,[5] Joshua!

FANNY: *(to Teck)* Sara told Joshua to shut up. *(Playing a card)* Twelve.

TECK: I have offended you, Mrs. Müller. I am most sorry.

SARA: *(pleasantly)* No, sir, you haven't offended me. I just don't like polite political conversations any more.

TECK: *(nods)* All of us, in Europe, had too many of them.

SARA: Yes. Too much talk. By this time all of us must know where we are and what we have to do. It's an indulgence to sit in a room and discuss your beliefs as if they were a juicy piece of gossip.

FANNY: You know, Sara, I find it very pleasant that Kurt, considering his history, doesn't make platform speeches. He hasn't tried to convince anybody of anything.

SARA: *(smiles)* Why should he, Mama? You are quite old enough to have your own convictions—or Papa's.

FANNY: *(turns to look at her)* I am proud to have Papa's convictions.

SARA: Of course. But it might be well to have a few new ones, now and then.

FANNY: *(peers over at her)* Are you criticizing me?

SARA: *(smiles)* Certainly not.

BABETTE: *(comes running in from the right entrance door. She has on an apron and she is carrying a plate. She goes to Fanny)* Eat it while it's hot, Grandma.

(Fanny peers down, takes the fork, begins to eat. Anise and Bodo both rise, move to Fanny, inspect the plate.)

FANNY: *(to them)* Go away.

ANISE: It is a potato pancake.

---

4. Hitler's party; the name was shortened to Nazi.   5. Hush up!

FANNY: And the first good one I've eaten in many, many years. I love a good potato pancake.

BODO: I likewise.

BABETTE: I am making a great number for dinner. Move away, Bodo.

TECK: (playing a card) Fifteen and two.

ANISE: (who has followed Bodo back to the table, leans over to look at the heating pad) You've ruined it! I shall sue you.

JOSHUA: I told you not to let him touch it.

SARA: (laughs) I remember you were always saying that, Anise—that you were going to sue. That's very French. I was sick once in Paris, and Babbie stayed up for a whole night and day and finished a dress I was making for a woman in the Rue Jacob. I told her to tell the woman she'd done it—I thought perhaps the woman would give her a candy or something—and anyway, I was very proud of her work. But no. The woman admitted the dress was well done, but said she was going to sue because I hadn't done it myself. Fancy that.

FANNY: (slowly) You sewed for a living?

SARA: Not a very good one. But Babbie and I made a little something now and then. Didn't we, darling?

FANNY: (sharply) Really, Sara, were these—these things necessary? Why couldn't you have written?

SARA: (laughs) You've asked me that a hundred times in the last week.

JOSHUA: (gently) I think it is only that Grandma feels sorry for us. Grandma has not seen much of the world.

FANNY: Don't you start giving me lectures, Joshua. I'm fond of you. And of you, Babbie. (To Anise) Are there two desserts for dinner? And are they sweet?

ANISE: Yes.

FANNY: (turns to Bodo) I wish I were fond of you.

BODO: You are. (Happily) You are very fond of me.

FANNY: (playing a card) Twenty-five.

BABETTE: This is for you, Grandma. I'm making a bed-jacket. It is nice lace. Papa brought it to me from Spain and I mean for you to have it.

FANNY: (kisses Babette) Thank you, darling. A sequence and three. A pair and five. (To Teck, as they finish the cribbage game) There. That's two dollars off. I owe you eight-fifty.

TECK: Let us carry it until tomorrow. You shall give it to me as a going-away token.

FANNY: (too pleased) You're going away?

TECK: (laughs) Ah, Madame Fanny. Do not sound that happy.

FANNY: Did I? That's rude of me. When are you going?

TECK: In a few days, I think. (Turns to look at Sara) We're too many refugees, eh, Mrs. Müller?

SARA: (pleasantly) Perhaps.

TECK: Will you be leaving, also?

SARA: I beg your pardon?

TECK: I thought perhaps you, too, would be moving on. Herr Müller does not give me the feeling of a man who settles down. Men who have done his work, seldom leave it. Not for a quiet country house.

(All three children look up.)

SARA: (very quietly) What work do you think my husband has done, Count de Brancovis?

TECK: Engineering?

SARA: (slowly) Yes. Engineering.

FANNY: *(very deliberately to Teck)* I don't know what you're saying. They shall certainly not be leaving—ever. Is that understood, Sara?

SARA: Well, Mama—

FANNY: There are no wells about it. You've come home to see me die and you will wait until I'm ready.

SARA: *(laughs)* Really, Mama, that isn't the reason I came home.

FANNY: It's a good enough reason. I shall do a fine death. I intend to be a great deal of trouble to everybody.

ANISE: I daresay.

FANNY: I shall take to my bed early and stay for years. In great pain.

ANISE: I am sure of it. You will duplicate the disgrace of the birth of Miss Sara.

SARA: *(laughs)* Was I born in disgrace?

ANISE: It was not your fault. But it was disgusting. Three weeks before you were to come—all was excellent, of course, in so healthy a woman as Madame Fanny—a great dinner was given here and, most unexpectedly, attended by a beautiful lady from England.

FANNY: Do be still. You are dull and fanciful—

ANISE: Mr. Joshua made the great error of waltzing the beauty for two dances, Madame Fanny being unfitted for the waltz and under no circumstances being the most graceful of dancers.

FANNY: *(her voice rising)* Are you crazy? I danced magnificently.

ANISE: It is well you thought so. A minute did not elapse between the second of the waltzes and a scream from Madame Fanny. She was in labor. Two hundred people, and if we had left her alone, she would have remained in the ballroom—

FANNY: How you invent! How you invent!

ANISE: Do not call to me that I am a liar. For three weeks you are in the utmost agony—

FANNY: And so I was. I remember it to this day—

ANISE: *(to Sara, angrily)* Not a pain. Not a single pain. She would lie up there in state, stealing candy from herself. Then, when your Papa would rest himself for a minute at the dinner or with a book, a scream would dismantle the house—it was revolting. *(Spitefully to Fanny)* And now the years have passed I may disclose to you that Mr. Joshua knew you were going through the play-acting—

FANNY: *(rises)* He did not. You are a malicious—

ANISE: Once he said to me, "Anise, it is well that I am in love. This is of a great strain and her great-uncle Freddie was not right in the head, neither."

FANNY: *(screaming)* You will leave this house— You are a liar, a woman of—

SARA: Mama, sit down.

ANISE: I will certainly leave this house. I will—

SARA: *(sharply)* Both of you. Sit down. And be still.

ANISE: She has intimated that I lie—

FANNY: *(screaming)* Intimated! Is that what I was doing— *(Anise begins to leave the room)* All right. I beg your pardon. I apologize.

(Anise turns.)

SARA: Both of you. You are acting like children.

BODO: Really, Mama. You insult us.

ANISE: I accept your apology. Seat yourself.

(They both sit down.)

FANNY: *(after a silence)* I am unloved.

BABETTE: I love you, Grandma.

FANNY: Do you, Babbie?

JOSHUA: And I.

FANNY: *(nods, very pleased. To Bodo)* And you?

BODO: I loved you the primary second I saw you.

FANNY: You are a charlatan.

ANISE: As for me, I am fond of all the living creatures. It is true that the children cause me greater work, which in turn more greatly inconveniences the feet. However, I do not complain. I believe in children.

FANNY: Rather like believing in the weather, isn't it? *(David and Kurt come in from the terrace. Both are in work clothes, their sleeves rolled up)* Where have you been?

DAVID: Oh, we've been helping Mr. Chabeuf spray the fruit trees.

ANISE: Mr. Chabeuf says that Herr Müller has the makings of a good farmer. From a Frenchman that is a large thing to say.

KURT: *(who has looked around the room, looked at Teck, strolled over to Bodo)* Mr. Chabeuf and I have an excellent time exchanging misinformation. My father was a farmer. I have a wide knowledge of farmer's misinformation.

FANNY: This is good farm land. Perhaps, in time—

DAVID: *(laughs)* Mama would give you the place, Kurt, if you guaranteed that your great-grandchildren would die here.

KURT: *(smiles)* I would like to so guarantee.

TECK: A farmer. That is very interesting. Abandon your ideals, Herr Müller?

KURT: Ideals? *(Carefully)* Sara, heisst das auf deutsch "Ideale"?[6]

SARA: Yes.

KURT: Is that what I have now? I do not like the word. It gives to me the picture of a small, pale man at a seaside resort. *(To Bodo)* What are you doing?

BODO: Preparing an elderly electric pad for Miss Anise. I am confused.

KURT: *(wanders toward the piano)* So it seems.

BODO: Something has gone wrong with the principle on which I have been working. It is probably that I will ask your assistance.

KURT: *(bows to him)* Thank you. Whenever you are ready. *(Begins to pick out notes with one hand.)*

FANNY: We shall have a little concert tomorrow evening. In honor of Babbie's birthday. *(To Kurt)* Kurt, you and I will play "The Clock Symphony." Then Joshua and I will play the duet we've learned, and Babbie will sing. And I shall finish with a Chopin Nocturne.

DAVID: *(laughs)* I thought you'd be the last on the program.

TECK: Where is Marthe?

FANNY: She'll be back soon. She went into town to do an errand for me. *(To David)* Did you buy presents for everybody?

DAVID: I did.

SARA: *(smiles, to Babette)* We always did that here. If somebody had a birthday, we all got presents. Nice, isn't it?

DAVID: *(to Anise)* I shall buy you an electric pad. You will need it.

ANISE: Indeed.

FANNY: Did you buy me a good present?

DAVID: Pretty good. *(pats Babette's head)* The best present goes to Babbie; it's *her* birthday.

FANNY: Jewelry?

6. "Does it mean the same as the German Ideale?"

DAVID: No, not jewelry.

FANNY: Oh. Not jewelry.

DAVID: Why?

FANNY: *(too casually)* I just asked you.

TECK: *(gets up)* It was a natural mistake, David. You see, Mrs. Mellie Sewell told your mother that she had seen you and Marthe in Barstow's. And your mother said you were probably buying her a present, or one for Babbie.

DAVID: *(too sharply)* Yes.

TECK: *(laughs)* Yes what?

DAVID: *(slowly)* Just yes.

FANNY: *(too hurriedly)* Mellie gets everything wrong. She's very anxious to meet Marthe because she used to know Francie Cabot, her aunt. Marthe's aunt, I mean, not Mellie's.

SARA: *(too hurriedly)* She really came to inspect Kurt and me. But I saw her first. *(She looks anxiously at David, who has turned his back on the room and is facing the terrace)* You were lucky to be out, David.

DAVID: Oh, she calls every Saturday afternoon, to bring Mama all the Washington gossip of the preceding week. She gets it all wrong, you understand, but that doesn't make any difference to either Mama or her. Mama then augments it, wits it up, Papa used to say—

FANNY: Certainly. I sharpen it a little. Mellie has no sense of humor.

DAVID: So Mama sharpens it a little, and delivers it tomorrow afternoon to old lady Marcy down the road. Old lady Marcy hasn't heard a word in ten years, so she unsharpens it again, and changes the names. By Wednesday afternoon—

TECK: *(smiles)* By Wednesday afternoon it will not be you who were in Barstow's, and it will be a large diamond pin with four sapphires delivered to Gaby Deslys.

DAVID: *(turns, looks at him)* Exactly.

FANNY: *(very nervously)* Francie Cabot, Marthe's aunt, you understand— *(To Kurt)* Did you ever know Paul von Seitz, a German?

KURT: I have heard of him.

FANNY: *(speaking very rapidly)* Certainly. He was your Ambassador to somewhere, I've forgotten. Well, Francie Cabot married him. I could have. Any American, not crippled, whose father had money— He was crazy about me. I was better-looking than Francie. Well, years later when he was your Ambassador—my father was, too, as you probably know—not your Ambassador, of course, ours—but I am talking about Von Seitz.

DAVID: *(laughs to Kurt)* You can understand how it goes. Old lady Marcy is not entirely to blame.

FANNY: Somebody asked me if I didn't regret not marrying him. I said, "Madame, je le regrette tous les jours et j'en suis heureuse chaque soir." *(Fanny turns to David)* That means I regret it every day and am happy about it every night. You understand what I meant, by *night*? Styles in wit change so.

DAVID: I understood it, Mama.

JOSHUA: We, too, Grandma.

BABETTE: *(approvingly)* It was most witty.

BODO: I do not know that I understood. You will explain to me, Grandma?

SARA: Later.

FANNY: *(turns to look at Teck)* You remember the old Paul von Seitz?

TECK: *(nods)* He was stationed in Paris when I first was there.

FANNY: Of course. I always forget you were a diplomat.

TECK: It is just as well.

FANNY: There's something insane about a Roumanian diplomat. Pure insane. I knew another one, once. He wanted to marry me, too.

SARA: *(laughs)* All of Europe.

FANNY: Not all. Some. Naturally. I was rich, I was witty, my family was of the best. I was handsome, unaffected—

DAVID: And noble and virtuous and kind and elegant and fashionable and simple—it's hard to remember everything you were. I've often thought it must have been boring for Papa to have owned such perfection.

FANNY: *(shrieks)* What! Your father bored with me! Not for a second of our life—

DAVID: *(laughs)* Oh God, when will I learn?

BODO: Do not shriek, Grandma. It is an unpleasant sound for the ear.

FANNY: Where was I? Oh, yes. What I started out to say was— *(She turns, speaks carefully to Teck)* Mellie Sewell told me, when you left the room, that she had heard from Louis Chandler's child's governess that you had won quite a bit of money in a poker game with Sam Chandler and some Germans at the Embassy. *(Kurt, who has been playing the piano, stops playing very abruptly. Teck turns to look at him)* That's how I thought of Von Seitz. His nephew Philip was in on the game.

DAVID: *(looks at Teck)* It must have been a big game. Sam Chandler plays in big games.

TECK: Not big enough.

DAVID: Have you known Sam long?

TECK: For years. Every Embassy in Europe knew him.

DAVID: *(sharply)* Sam and Nazis must make an unpleasant poker game.

(Kurt begins to play a new melody.)

TECK: *(who has not looked away from Kurt)* I do not play poker to be amused.

DAVID: *(irritably)* What's Sam selling now?

TECK: Bootleg munitions. He always has.

DAVID: You don't mind?

TECK: Mind? I have not thought about it.

FANNY: Well, you ought to think about it. Sam Chandler has always been a scoundrel. All the Chandlers are. They're cousins of mine. Mama used to say they never should have learned to walk on two feet. They would have been more comfortable on four.

TECK: Do you know the young Von Seitz, Herr Müller? He was your military attaché in Spain.

KURT: He was the German government attaché in Spain. I know his name, of course. He is a famous artillery expert. But the side[7] on which I fought was not where he was stationed, Count de Brancovis.

ANISE: *(Babette and Joshua begin to hum the song Kurt is playing. Sara begins to hum)* It is time for the bath and the change of clothes. I will give you five more minutes—

FANNY: What is the song?

TECK: It was a German soldier's song. They sang it as they straggled back in '18. I remember hearing it in Berlin. Were you there then, Herr Müller?

KURT: *(the playing and the humming continue)* I was not in Berlin.

TECK: But you were in the war,[8] of course?

KURT: Yes. I was in the war.

FANNY: You didn't think then you'd live to see another war.

7. The Germans were allied with the Fascists led by Francisco Franco; Kurt fought with the anti-Fascist International Brigades, which rallied to support the democratically elected government besieged by the right-wing forces.

8. World War I.

KURT: Many of us were afraid we would.

FANNY: What are the words?

SARA: The Germans in Spain, in Kurt's Brigade, wrote new words for the song.

KURT: This was what you heard in Berlin, in 1918. *(Begins to sing.)*

"Wir zieh'n Heim, wir zieh'n Heim,
Mancher kommt nicht mit,
Mancher ging verschütt,
Aber Freunde sind wir stets."

(in English.)

"We come home. We come home.
Some of us are gone, and some of us are lost, but
    we are friends:
Our blood is on the earth together.
Some day. Some day we shall meet again.
Farewell."

(Stops singing) At a quarter before six on the morning of November 7th, 1936, eighteen years later, five hundred Germans walked through the Madrid streets on their way to defend the Manzanares River. We felt good that morning. You know how it is to be good when it is needed to be good? So we had need of new words to say that. I translate with awkwardness, you understand.

(Begins to sing.)

"And so we have met again.
The blood did not have time to dry.
We lived to stand and fight again.
This time we fight for people.
This time the bastards will keep their hands away.
Those who sell the blood of other men, this time,
They keep their hands away.
For us to stand.
For us to fight.
This time no farewell, no farewell."

(Music dies out. There is silence for a minute) We did not win. *(Looks up, gently)* It would have been a different world if we had.

SARA: Papa said so years ago. Do you remember, Mama? "For every man who lives without freedom, the rest of us must face the guilt."

FANNY: Yes. "We are liable in the conscience-balance for the tailor in Lodz,[9] the black man in our South, the peasant in—" *(Turns to Teck. Unpleasantly)* Your country, I think.

ANISE: *(rises)* Come. Baths for everybody. *(To Bodo)* Gather the wires. You have wrecked my cure.

BODO: If you would allow me a few minutes more—

ANISE: Come along. I have been duped for long enough. Come Joshua. Babette. Baths.

JOSHUA: *(starts out after Anise. Babette begins to gather up her sewing)* My tub is a thing of glory. But I do not like it so prepared for me and so announced by Miss Anise. *(He exits.)*

BODO: *(to Anise)* You are angry about this. I do not blame you with my heart or my head. I admit I have failed. But Papa will repair it, Anise. Will you not, Papa? In a few minutes—

TECK: *(to Bodo)* Your father is an expert electrician?

9. A city in Poland.

BODO: Oh yes, sir.

TECK: And as good with radio—

(Bodo begins to nod.)

KURT: *(sharply)* Count de Brancovis. Make your questions to me, please. Not to my children.

(The others look up, surprised.)

TECK: *(pleasantly)* Very well, Herr Müller.

ANISE: *(as she exits with Bodo)* Nobody can fix it. You have made a pudding of it.

BODO: *(as he follows her)* Do not worry. In five minutes tonight, you will have a pad far better— *(As Bodo reaches the door he bumps into Marthe who is carrying large dress boxes)* Oh. Your pardon. Oh, hello. *(He disappears.)*

MARTHE: *(gaily)* Hello. *(To Fanny)* I waited for them. I was afraid they wouldn't deliver this late in the day. *(To Sara)* Come on, Sara. I can't wait to see them.

SARA: What?

MARTHE: Dresses. From Fanny. A tan linen, and a dark green with wonderful buttons, a white net for Babbie, and a suit for you, and play dresses for Babbie, and a dinner dress in gray to wear for Babbie's birthday—gray should be good for you, Sara—all from Savitt's. We sneaked the measurements, Anise and I—

SARA: *(she goes toward Fanny)* How nice of you, Mama. How very kind of you. And of you, Marthe, to take so much trouble— *(She leans down, kisses Fanny)* You're a sweet woman, Mama.

DAVID: That's the first time Mama's ever heard that word. *(He takes the boxes from Marthe, puts them near the staircase. Marthe smiles at him, touches his hand, as Teck watches them.)*

FANNY: *(giggles)* I have a bottom sweetness, if you understand what I mean.

DAVID: I have been too close to the bottom to see it.

FANNY: That should be witty. I don't know why it isn't.

(Babette goes over to stare at the boxes.)

SARA: From Savitt's. Extravagant of you. They had such lovely clothes. I remember my coming-out dress— *(Goes to Kurt)* Do you remember the black suit with the braid, and the Milan hat? Not the *first* day we met, but the picnic day? *(He smiles up at her)* Well, they were from Savitt's. That was over twenty years ago—I've known you a long time. Me, in an evening dress. Now you'll have to take me into Washington. I want to show off. Next week, and we'll dance, maybe— *(Sees that he is not looking at her)* What's the matter, darling? *(No answer. Slowly he turns to look at her)* What's the matter, Kurt? *(Takes his arms, very unhappily)* What have I done? It isn't that dresses have ever mattered to me, it's just that—

KURT: Of course, they have mattered to you. As they should. I do not think of the dresses. *(Draws her to him)* How many years have I loved that face?

SARA: *(her face very happy)* So?

KURT: So. *(He leans down, kisses her, as if it were important.)*

SARA: *(pleased, unembarrassed)* There are other people here.

MARTHE: *(slowly)* And good for us to see.

TECK: Nostalgia?

MARTHE: No. Nostalgia is for something you have known.

(Fanny coughs.)

BABETTE: *(comes to Fanny)* Grandma, is it allowed to look at my dresses?

FANNY: Of course, child. Run along.

BABETTE: *(picks up the boxes, goes toward the hall entrance, stops near Fanny)* I love dresses, I have a great fondness for materials and colors. Thank you, Grandma. *(She runs out of the room.)*

(Joseph appears in the doorway.)

JOSEPH: There is a long-distance operator with a long-distance call for Mr. Müller. She wants to talk with him on the long-distance phone.

KURT: Oh— Excuse me, please—

(Kurt rises quickly. Sara turns sharply to look at him. Teck looks up. Kurt goes quickly out. Teck watches him go. Sara stands staring after him.)

MARTHE: *(laughs)* I feel the same way as Babbie. Come on, Sara. Let's try them on.

(Sara does not turn.)

TECK: You also have a new dress?

MARTHE: *(looks at him)* Yes. Fanny was kind to me, too.

TECK: You are a very generous woman, Madame Fanny. Did you also give her a sapphire bracelet from Barstow's?

FANNY: I beg your—

DAVID: *(slowly)* No. I gave Marthe the bracelet. And I understand that it is not any business of yours.

(Fanny rises. Sara turns.)

FANNY: Really, David—

DAVID: Be still, Mama.

TECK: *(after a second)* Did you tell him that, Marthe?

MARTHE: Yes.

TECK: *(looks up at her)* I shall not forgive you for that. *(Looks at David)* It is a statement which no man likes to hear from another man. You understand that? *(Playfully)* That is the type of thing about which we used to play at duels in Europe.

DAVID: *(comes toward him)* We are not so musical comedy here. And you are not in Europe.

TECK: Even if I were, I would not suggest any such action. I would have reasons for not wishing it.

DAVID: It would be well for you not to suggest *any* action. And the reason for *that* is you might get hurt.

TECK: *(slowly)* That would not be my reason. *(To Marthe)* Your affair has gone far enough—

MARTHE: *(sharply)* It is not an affair—

TECK: I do not care what it is. The time has come to leave here. Go upstairs and pack your things. *(She does not move. David turns toward her)* Go on, Marthe.

MARTHE: *(to David)* I am not going with him. I told you that.

DAVID: I don't want you to go with him.

FANNY: *(carefully)* Really, David, aren't you interfering in all this a good deal—

DAVID: *(carefully)* Yes, Mama. I am.

TECK: *(to Marthe)* When you are speaking to me, please say what you have to say
    to me.

MARTHE: *(comes to him)* You are trying to frighten me. But you are not going to frighten
    me any more. I will say it to you: I am not going with you. I am never going with
    you again.

TECK: *(softly)* If you do not fully mean what you say, or if you might change your mind,
    you are talking unwisely, Marthe.

MARTHE: I know that.

TECK: Shall we talk about it alone?

MARTHE: You can't make me go, can you, Teck?

TECK: No, I can't make you.

MARTHE: Then there's no sense talking about it.

TECK: Are you in love with him?

MARTHE: Yes.

FANNY: *(sharply)* Marthe! What is all this?

MARTHE: *(sharply)* I'll tell *you* about it in a minute.

DAVID: You don't have to explain anything to anybody.

TECK: *(ignores him)* Is he in love with you?

MARTHE: I don't think so. You won't believe it, because you can't believe anything that
    hasn't got tricks to it, but David hasn't much to do with this. I told you I would leave
    some day, and I remember where I said it—*(Slowly)*—and why I said it.

TECK: I also remember. But I did not believe you. I have not had much to offer you
    these last years. But if now we had some money and could go back—

MARTHE: No. I don't like you, Teck. I never have.

TECK: And I have always known it.

FANNY: *(stiffly)* I think your lack of affections should be discussed with more privacy.
    Perhaps—

DAVID: Mama—

MARTHE: There is nothing to discuss. Strange. I've talked to myself about this scene for
    almost fifteen years. I knew a lot of things to say to you and I used to lie awake at
    night or walk along the street and say them. Now I don't want to. I guess you only
    want to talk that way, when you're not sure what you can do. When you're sure, then
    what's the sense of saying it? "This is why and this is why and this—" *(Very happily)*
    But when you know you can do it, you don't have to say anything; you can just go.
    And I'm going. There is nothing you can do. I would like you to believe that now.

TECK: Very well, Marthe. I think I made a mistake. I should not have brought you here.
    I believe you now.

MARTHE: *(after a pause, she looks at David)* I'll move into Washington, and—

DAVID: Yes. Later. But I'd like you to stay here for a while, with us, if you wouldn't
    mind.

SARA: It would be better for you, Marthe—

FANNY: It's very interesting that I am not being consulted about this. *(To Marthe)* I have
    nothing against you, Marthe. I am sorry for you, but I don't think—

MARTHE: Thank you, Sara, David. But I'd rather move in now. *(Turns, comes toward
    Fanny)* But perhaps I have something against you. Do you remember my wedding?

FANNY: Yes.

MARTHE: Do you remember how pleased Mama was with herself? Brilliant Mama,
    handsome Mama—everybody thought so, didn't they? A seventeen-year-old
    daughter, marrying a pretty good title, about to secure herself in a world that Mama
    liked—she didn't ask me what I liked. And the one time I tried to tell her, she
    frightened me—*(Looks up)* Maybe I've always been frightened. All my life.

TECK: Of course.

MARTHE: *(to Fanny, as if she had not heard Teck)* I remember Mama's face at the wedding—it was *her* wedding, really, not mine.

FANNY: *(sharply)* You are very hard on your mother.

MARTHE: Nineteen hundred and twenty-five. No, I'm not hard on her. I only tell the truth. She wanted a life for me, I suppose. It just wasn't the life I wanted for myself. *(Sharply)* And that's what you have tried to do. With your children. In another way. Only Sara got away. And that made you angry—until so many years went by that you forgot.

FANNY: I don't usually mind people saying anything they think, but I find that—

MARTHE: I don't care what you mind or don't mind. I'm in love with your son—

FANNY: *(very sharply)* That's unfortunate—

MARTHE: And I'm sick of watching you try to make him into his father. I don't think you even know you do it any more and I don't think he knows it any more, either. And that's what's most dangerous about it.

FANNY: *(very angrily)* I don't know what you are talking about.

DAVID: I think you do. *(Smiles)* You shouldn't mind hearing the truth—and neither should I.

FANNY: *(worried, sharply)* David! What does all this nonsense mean? I—

MARTHE: *(to Fanny)* Look. That pretty world Mama got me into was a tough world, see? I'm used to trouble. So don't try to interfere with me, because I won't let you. *(She goes to David)* Let's just have a good time. *(He leans down, takes both her hands, kisses them. Then slowly, she turns away, starts to exit. To Teck)* You will also be going today?

TECK: Yes.

MARTHE: Then let us make sure we go in different directions, and do not meet again. Good-bye, Teck.

TECK: Good-bye, Marthe. You will not believe me, but I tried my best, and I am now most sorry to lose you.

MARTHE: Yes. I believe you. *(She moves out. There is silence for a minute.)*

FANNY: Well, a great many things have been said in the last few minutes.

DAVID: *(crosses to bell cord. To Teck)* I will get Joseph to pack for you.

TECK: Thank you. Do not bother. I will ring for him when I am ready. *(Kurt comes in from the study door. Sara turns, stares at him, waits. He does not look at her)* It will not take me very long. *(He starts for the door, looking at Kurt.)*

SARA: What is it, Kurt?

KURT: It is nothing of importance, darling— *(He looks quickly at Teck, who is moving very slowly.)*

SARA: Don't tell me it's nothing. I know the way you look when—

KURT: *(sharply)* I said it was of no importance. I must get to California for a few weeks. That is all.

SARA: I—

TECK: *(turns)* It is in the afternoon newspaper, Herr Müller. *(Points to paper on table)* I was waiting to find the proper moment to call it to your attention. *(He moves toward the table, as they all turn to watch him. He picks up the paper, turns it over, begins to read)* "Zurich, Switzerland: The Zurich papers today reprinted a despatch from the *Berliner Tageblatt* on the capture of Colonel Max Freidank. Freidank is said—*(Sara begins to move toward him)*—to be the chief of the Anti-Nazi Underground Movement. Colonel Friedank has long been an almost legendary figure. The son of the famous General Freidank, he was a World War officer and a distinguished physicist before the advent of Hitler." That is all.

SARA: Max—

KURT: Be still, Sara.

TECK: They told me of it at the Embassy last night. They also told me that with him they had taken a man who called himself Ebber, and a man who called himself Triste. They could not find a man called Gotter. *(He starts again toward the door)* I shall be a lonely man without Marthe. I am also a very poor one. I should like to have ten thousand dollars before I go.

DAVID: *(carefully)* You will make no loans in this house.

TECK: I was not speaking of a loan.

FANNY: *(carefully)* God made you not only a scoundrel but a fool. That is a dangerous combination.

DAVID: *(suddenly leaps toward Teck)* Damn you, you—

KURT: *(suddenly pounds on the top of the piano, as David almost reaches Teck)* Leave him alone. *(Moves quickly to stop David)* Leave him alone! David! Leave him alone!

DAVID: *(angrily to Kurt)* Keep out of it. *(Starts toward Teck again)* I'm beginning to see what Marthe meant. Blackmailing with your wife— You—

KURT: *(very sharply)* He is not speaking of his wife. Or you. He means me. *(Looks at Teck)* Is that correct?

(Sara moves toward Kurt. David draws back, bewildered.)

TECK: Good. It was necessary for me to hear you say it. You understand that?

KURT: I understand it.

SARA: *(frightened, softly)* Kurt—

DAVID: What is all this about? What the hell are you talking about?

TECK: *(sharply for the first time)* Be still. *(To Kurt)* At your convenience. Your hands are shaking, Herr Müller.

KURT: *(quietly)* My hands were broken; they are bad when I have fear.

TECK: I am sorry. I can understand that. It is not pleasant. *(Motions toward Fanny and David)* Perhaps you would like a little time to— I will go and pack, and be ready to leave. We will all find that more comfortable, I think. You should get yourself a smaller gun, Herr Müller. That pistol you have been carrying is big and awkward.

KURT: You saw the pistol when you examined our bags?

TECK: You knew that?

KURT: Oh, yes. I have the careful eye, through many years of needing it. And then you have not the careful eye. The pistol was lying to the left of a paper package and when you leave, it is to the right of the package.

SARA: Kurt! Do you mean that—

KURT: *(sharply)* Please, darling, do not do that.

TECK: It is a German Army Luger?

KURT: Yes.

TECK: Keep it in your pocket, Herr Müller. You will have no need to use it. And, in any case, I am not afraid of it. You understand that?

KURT: *(slowly)* I understand that you are not a man of fears. That is strange to me, because I am a man who has so many fears.

TECK: *(laughs, as he exits)* Are you? That is most interesting. *(He exits.)*

DAVID: *(softly)* What is this about, Kurt?

KURT: He knows who I am and what I do and what I carry with me.

SARA: *(carefully)* What about Max?

KURT: The telephone was from Mexico. Isle received a cable. Early on the morning of Monday, they caught Ebber and Triste. An hour after they took Max in Berlin. *(She looks up at him, begins to shake her head. He presses her arm)* Yes. It is hard.

FANNY: *(softly)* You said he knew who you were and what you carried with you. I don't understand.

KURT: I am going to tell you: I am an outlaw. I work with many others in an illegal organization. I have so worked for seven years. I am on what is called a desired list. But I did not know I was worth ten thousand dollars. My price has risen.

DAVID: *(slowly)* And what do you carry with you?

KURT: Twenty-three thousand dollars. It has been gathered from the pennies and the nickels of the poor who do not like Fascism, and who believe in the work we do. I came here to bring Sara home and to get the money. I had hopes to rest here for a while, and then—

SARA: *(slowly)* And I had hopes someone else would take it back and you would stay with us— *(Shakes her head, then)* Max is not dead?

KURT: No. The left side of his face is dead. *(Softly)* It was a good face.

SARA: *(to Fanny and David, as if she were going to cry)* It was a very good face. He and Kurt—in the old days— *(To Kurt)* After so many years. If Max got caught, then nobody's got a chance. Nobody. *(She suddenly sits down.)*

DAVID: *(points upstairs)* He wants to sell what he knows to you? Is that right?

KURT: Yes.

FANNY: Wasn't it careless of you to leave twenty-three thousand dollars lying around to be seen?

KURT: No, it was not careless of me. It is in a locked brief-case. I have thus carried money for many years. There seemed no safer place than Sara's home. It was careless of you to have in your house a man who opens baggage and blackmails.

DAVID: *(sharply)* Yes. It was very careless.

FANNY: But you said you knew he'd seen it—

KURT: Yes. I knew it the first day we were here. What was I to do about it? He is not a man who steals. This is a safer method. I knew that it would come some other way. I have been waiting to see what the way would be. That is all I could do.

DAVID: *(to Fanny)* What's the difference? It's been done. *(To Kurt)* If he wants to sell to you, he must have another buyer. Who?

KURT: The Embassy. Von Seitz, I think.

DAVID: You mean he has told Von Seitz about you and—

KURT: No. I do not think he has told him anything. As yet. It would be foolish of him. He has probably only asked most guarded questions.

DAVID: But you're here. You're in this country. They can't do anything to you. They wouldn't be crazy enough to try it. Is your passport all right?

KURT: Not quite.

FANNY: Why not? Why isn't it?

KURT: *(wearily, as if he were bored)* Because people like me are not given visas with such ease. And I was in a hurry to bring my wife and my children to safety. *(Sharply)* Madame Fanny, you must come to understand it is no longer the world you once knew.

DAVID: It doesn't matter. You're a political refugee. We don't turn back people like you. People who are in danger. You will give me your passport and tomorrow morning I'll see Barens. We'll tell him the truth— *(Points to the door)* Tell de Brancovis to go to hell. There's not a damn thing he or anybody else can do.

SARA: *(looks up at Kurt, who is staring at her)* You don't understand, David.

DAVID: There's a great deal I don't understand. But there's nothing to worry about.

SARA: Not much to worry about as long as Kurt is in this house. But he's not going to—

KURT: The Count has made the guess that—

SARA: That you will go back to get Ebber and Triste and Max. Is that right, Kurt? Is that right?

KURT: Yes, darling, I will try. They were taken to Sonnenburg. Guards can be bribed—
It has been done once before at Sonnenburg. We will try for it again. I must go back,
Sara. I must start.

SARA: Of course, you must go back. I guess I was trying to think it wouldn't come.
But— *(To Fanny and David)* Kurt's got to go back. He's got to go home. He's got to
buy them out. He'll do it, too. You'll see. *(She stops, breathes)* It's hard enough to get
back. Very hard. But if they knew he was coming— They want Kurt bad. Almost as
much as they wanted Max— And then there are hundreds of others, too— *(She gets
up, comes to him. He holds her, puts his face in her hair. She stands holding him,
trying to speak without crying. She puts her face down on his head)* Don't be scared,
darling. You'll get back. You'll see. You've done it before— You'll do it again. Don't
be scared. You'll get Max out all right. *(Gasps)* And then you'll do his work, won't
you? That's good. That's fine. You'll do a good job, the way you've always done. *(She
is crying very hard. To Fanny)* Kurt doesn't feel well. He was wounded and he gets
tired— *(To Kurt)* You don't feel well, do you? *(Slowly. She is crying too hard now to
be heard clearly)* Don't be scared, darling. You'll get home. Don't worry, you'll get
home. Yes, you will.

(The curtain falls.)

Act Three

SCENE: *The same. A half hour later.*

AT RISE: *Fanny is sitting in a chair. Kurt is at the piano, his head resting on one hand.
He is playing softly with the other hand. Sara is sitting very quietly on the couch.
David is pacing on the terrace.*

FANNY: *(to David)* David, would you stop that pacing, please? *(David comes in)* And
would you stop that one-hand piano playing? Either play, or get up.

*(Kurt gets up, crosses to the couch, sits. Sara looks at him, gets up, crosses to the
decanters, begins to make a drink.)*

SARA: *(to David)* A drink?

DAVID: What? Yes, please. *(To Kurt)* Do you intend to buy your friends out of jail?

KURT: I intend to try.

FANNY: It's all very strange to me. I thought things were so well run that bribery and—

KURT: *(smiles)* What a magnificent work Fascists have done in convincing the world that
they are men from legends.

DAVID: They have done very well for themselves—unfortunately.

KURT: Yes. But not by themselves. Does it make us all uncomfortable to remember that
they came in on the shoulders of the most powerful men in the world? Of course.
And so we would prefer to believe they are men from the planets. They are not. Let
me reassure you. They are smart, they are sick, and they are cruel. But given men
who know what they fight for— *(Shrugs)* I will console you. A year ago last month,
at three o'clock in the morning, Friedank and I, with two elderly pistols, raided the
home of the Gestapo chief in Konstanz, got what we wanted, and the following
morning Friedank was eating his breakfast three blocks away, and I was over the
Swiss border.

FANNY: *(slowly)* You are brave men.

KURT: *I* do not tell you the story to prove we are remarkable, but to prove they are *not.*

(Sara brings him a drink. Gives one to David.)

SARA: *(softly, touching Kurt's shoulder)* Kurt loves Max.

KURT: Always since I came here I have a dream: that he will come into this room some day. How he would like it here, eh, Sara? He loves good food and wine, and you have books— *(Laughs happily)* He is fifty-nine years of age. And when he was fifty-seven, he carried me on his back, seven miles across the border. I had been hurt— That takes a man, does it not?

FANNY: *(to Kurt)* You look like a sick man to me.

KURT: No. I'm only tired. I do not like to wait. It will go. It is the waiting that is always most bad for me.

DAVID: *(points upstairs)* Damn him! He's doing it deliberately.

KURT: It is then the corruption begins. Once in Spain I waited for two days until the planes would exhaust themselves. I think then why must our side fight always with naked hands. The spirit and the hands. All is against us but ourselves.

SARA: You will not think that when the time comes. It will go.

KURT: Of a certainty.

FANNY: But does it have to go on being your hands?

KURT: For each man, his own hands. He has to sleep with them.

DAVID: *(uncomfortably, as if he did not like to say it)* That's right. I guess it's the way all of us should feel. But—but you have a family. Isn't there somebody else who hasn't a wife and children—

KURT: Each could have his own excuse. Some love for the first time, some have bullet holes, some have fear of the camps, some are sick, many are getting older. *(Shrugs)* Each could find a reason. And many find it. My children are not the only children in the world, even to me.

FANNY: That's noble of you, of course. But they are your children, nevertheless. And Sara, she—

SARA: Mama—

KURT: *(after a slight pause)* One means always in English to insult with that word noble?

FANNY: Of course not, I—

KURT: It is not noble. It is the way I must live. Good or bad, it is what I am. *(Turns deliberately to look at Fanny)* And what I am is not what you wanted for your daughter, twenty years ago or now.

FANNY: You are misunderstanding me.

KURT: *(smiles)* For our girl, too, we want a safe and happy life. And it is thus I try to make it for her. We each have our way. I do not convert you to mine.

DAVID: You are very certain of your way.

KURT: *(smiles)* I seem so to you? Good.

(Joseph appears in the hall doorway. He is carrying valises and overcoats.)

JOSEPH: What'll I do with these, Miss Fanny?

FANNY: They're too large for eating, aren't they? What were you thinking of doing with them?

JOSEPH: I mean, it's Fred's day off.

DAVID: All right. You drive him into town.

JOSEPH: Then who's going to serve at dinner?

FANNY: *(impatiently)* Belle can do it alone tonight.

JOSEPH: No she can't. Belle's upstairs packing with Miss Marthe. My, there's quite a lot of departing, ain't there?

FANNY: *(very impatiently)* All right, then cook can bring in dinner.

JOSEPH: I wouldn't ask her to do that, if I were you. She's mighty mad: the sink pipe is leaking again. You just better wait for your dinner till I get back from Washington.

FANNY: *(shouting)* We are not cripples and we were eating dinner in this house before you arrived to show us how to use the knife and fork. *(Joseph laughs)* Go on. Put his things in the car. I'll ring for you when he's ready.

JOSEPH: You told me the next time you screamed to remind you to ask my pardon.

FANNY: You call that screaming?

JOSEPH: Yes'm.

FANNY: Very well. I ask your pardon. *(Waves him away)* Go on!

JOSEPH: Yes'm. *(Exits.)*

(Teck appears in the door. He is carrying his hat and the brief-case we have seen in Act One. Sara, seeing the brief-case, looks startled, looks quickly at Kurt. Kurt watches Teck as he comes toward him. Teck throws his hat on a chair, comes to the table at which Kurt is sitting, puts the brief-case on the table. Kurt puts out his hand, puts it on the brief-case, leaves it there.)

TECK: *(smiles at the gesture)* Nothing has been touched, Herr Müller. I brought it from your room, for your convenience.

FANNY: *(angrily)* Why didn't you steal it? Since you do not seem to—

TECK: That would have been very foolish of me, Madame Fanny.

KURT: Very.

TECK: I hope I have not kept you waiting too long. I wanted to give you an opportunity to make any explanations—

DAVID: *(angrily)* Does your price include listening to this tony conversation?

TECK: *(turns to look at him)* My price will rise if I have to spend the next few minutes being interrupted by your temper. I will do my business with Herr Müller. And you will understand, I will take from you no interruptions, no exclamations, no lectures, no opinions of what I am or what I am doing.

KURT: *(quietly)* You will not be interrupted.

TECK: *(sits down at table with Kurt)* I have been curious about you, Herr Müller. Even before you came here. Because Fanny and David either knew very little about you, which was strange, or wouldn't talk about you, which was just as strange. Have you ever had come to you one of those insistent half-memories of some person or some place?

KURT: *(quietly, without looking up)* You had such a half-memory of me?

TECK: Not even a memory, but something. The curiosity of one European for another, perhaps.

KURT: A most sharp curiosity. You lost no time examining—*(Pats the case)*—this. You are an expert with locks?

TECK: No, indeed. Only when I wish to be.

FANNY: *(angrily, to Teck)* I would like you out of this house as quickly as—

TECK: *(turns to her)* Madame Fanny, I have just asked Mr. David not to do that. I must now ask you. *(Leans forward to Kurt)* Herr Müller, I got one of the desired lists from Von Seitz, without, of course, revealing anything to him. As you probably know, they are quite easy to get. I simply told him that we refugees move in small circles and I might come across somebody on it. If, however, I have to listen to any more of this from any of you, I shall go immediately to him.

KURT: *(to David and Fanny)* Please allow the Count to do this in his own way. It will be best.

TECK: *(takes a sheet of paper from his pocket)* There are sixty-three names on this list. I read them carefully, I narrow the possibilities and under "G" I find Gotter. *(Begins to read)* "Age, forty to forty-five. About six feet. One hundred seventy pounds. Birthplace unknown to us. Original occupation unknown to us, although he seems to know Munich and Dresden. Schooling unknown to us. Family unknown to us. No known political connections. No known trade-union connections. Many descriptions, few of them in agreement and none of them of great reliability. Equally unreliable, though often asked for, were Paris, Copenhagen, Brussels police descriptions. Only points on which there is agreement: married to a foreign woman, either American or English; three children; has used name of Gotter, Thomas Bodmer, Karl Francis. Thought to have left Germany in 1933, and to have joined Max Freidank shortly after. Worked closely with Freidank, perhaps directly under his orders. Known to have crossed border in 1934—February, May, June, October. Known to have again crossed border with Max Friedank in 1935—August, twice in October, November, January—"

KURT: *(smiles)* The report is unreliable. It would have been impossible for God to have crossed the border that often.

TECK: *(looks up, laughs. Then looks back at list)* "In 1934, outlaw radio station announcing itself as Radio European, begins to be heard. Station was located in Düsseldorf: the house of a restaurant waiter was searched, and nothing was found. Radio heard during most of 1934 and 1935. In an attempt to locate it, two probable Communists killed in the tool-house of a farm near Bonn. In three of the broadcasts, Gotter known to have crossed border immediately before and after. Radio again became active in early part of 1936. Active attempt made to locate Freidank. Gotter believed to have then appeared in Spain with Madrid Government army, in one of the German brigades, and to have been a brigade commander under previously used name of Bodmer. Known to have stayed in France the first months of 1938. Again crossed German border some time during week when Hitler's Hamburg radio speech interrupted and went off the air." *(Looks up)* That was a daring deed, Herr Müller. It caused a great scandal. I remember. It amused me.

KURT: It was not done for that reason.

TECK: "Early in 1939, informer in Konstanz reported Gotter's entry, carrying money which had been exchanged in Paris and Brussels. Following day, home of Konstanz Gestapo chief raided for spy list by two men—" *(Kurt turns to look at Fanny and David, smiles)* My God, Herr Müller, that job took two good men.

SARA: *(angrily)* Even you admire them.

TECK: Even I. Now I conclude a week ago that you are Gotter, Karl Francis—

KURT: Please. Do not describe me to myself again.

TECK: And that you will be traveling home—*(Points to brief-case)*—with this. But you seem in no hurry, and so I must wait. Last night when I heard that Freidank has been taken, I guess that you will now be leaving. Not for California. I will tell you free of charge, Herr Müller, that they have got no information from Freidank or the others.

KURT: Thank you. But I was sure they would not. I know all three most well. They will take what will be given them.

TECK: *(looks down. Softly)* There is a deep sickness in the German character, Herr Müller. A pain-love, a death-love—

DAVID: *(very angrily)* Oh, for God's sake, spare us *your* moral judgments.

FANNY: *(very sharply)* Yes. They are sickening. Get on!

KURT: Fanny and David are Americans and they do not understand our world—as yet. *(Turns to David and Fanny)* All Fascists are not of one mind, one stripe. There are those who give the orders, those who carry out the orders, those who watch the orders being carried out. Then there are those who are half in, half hoping to come in. They are made to do the dishes and clean the boots. Frequently they come in high places and wish now only to survive. They come late: some because they did not jump in time, some because they were stupid, some because they were shocked at the crudity of the *German* evil, and preferred their own evils, and some because they were fastidious men. For those last, we may well some day have pity. They are lost men, their spoils are small, their day is gone. *(To Teck)* Yes?

TECK: *(slowly)* Yes. You have the understanding heart. It will get in your way some day.

KURT: *(smiles)* I will watch it.

TECK: We are both men in trouble, Herr Müller. The world, ungratefully, seems to like your kind even less than it does mine. *(Leans forward)* Now. Let us do business. You will not get back if Von Seitz knows you are going.

KURT: You are wrong. Instead of crawling a hundred feet an hour in deep night, I will walk across the border with as little trouble as if I were a boy again on a summer walking trip. There are many men they would like to have. I would be allowed to walk directly to them—until they had all the names and all the addresses. *(Laughs, points his finger at Teck)* Roumanians would pick me up ahead of time. *Germans* would not.

TECK: *(smiles)* Still the national pride?

KURT: Why not? For that which is good.

FANNY: *(comes over, very angrily, to Teck)* I have not often in my life felt what I feel now. Whatever you are, and however you became it, the picture of a man selling the lives of other men—

TECK: Is very ugly, Madame Fanny. I do not do it without some shame, and therefore I must sink my shame in large money. *(Puts his hand on the brief-case)* The money is here. For ten thousand, you go back to save your friends, nobody will know that you go, and I will give you my good wishes. *(Slowly, deliberately, Kurt begins to shake his head. Teck waits, then carefully)* No?

KURT: This money is going home with me. It was not given to me to save my life, and I shall not so use it. It is to save the lives and further the work of more than I. It is important to me to carry on that work and to save the lives of three valuable men, and to do that with all speed. But— *(Sharply)* Count de Brancovis, the first morning we arrived in this house, my children wanted their breakfast with great haste. That is because the evening before we had been able only to buy milk and buns for them. If I would not touch this money for them, I would not touch it for you. *(Very sharply)* It goes back with me. The way it is. And if it does not get back, it is because I will not get back.

(There is a long pause. Sara gets up, turns away.)

TECK: Then I do not think you will get back. You are a brave one, Herr Müller, but you will not get back.

KURT: *(as if he were very tired)* I will send to you a postal card and tell you about my bravery.

DAVID: *(coming toward Kurt)* Is it true that if this swine talks, you and the others will be—

SARA: *(very softly)* Caught and killed. Of course. If they're lucky enough to get killed quickly. *(Quietly, points to the table)* You should have seen his hands in 1935.

FANNY: *(violently, to David)* We'll give him the money. For God's sake, let's give it to him and get him out of here.

DAVID: *(to Sara)* Do you want Kurt to go back?

SARA: Yes. I do.

DAVID: All right. *(Goes to her, lifts her face)* You're a good girl.

KURT: That is true. Brave and good, my Sara. She is everything. She is handsome and gay and— *(Puts his hand over his eyes. Sara turns away.)*

DAVID: *(after a second, comes to stand near Teck)* If we give you the money, what is to keep you from selling to Von Seitz?

TECK: I do not like your thinking I would do that. But—

DAVID: *(tensely)* Look here. I'm sick of what you'd like or wouldn't like. And I'm sick of your talk. We'll get this over with now, without any more fancy talk from you, or as far as I am concerned, you can get out of here without my money and sell to any buyer you can find. I can't take much more of you at any cost.

TECK: *(smiles)* It is your anger which delays us. I was about to say that I understood your fear that I would go to Von Seitz, and I would suggest that you give me a small amount of cash now and a check dated a month from now. In a month, Herr Müller should be nearing home, and he can let you know. And if you should not honor the check because Herr Müller is already in Germany, Von Seitz will pay a little something for a reliable description. I will take my chance on that. You will now say that I could do that in any case—and that is the chance you will take.

DAVID: *(looks at Kurt, who does not look up)* Is a month enough? For you to get back?

KURT: *(shrugs)* I do not know.

DAVID: *(to Teck)* Two months from today. How do you want the cash and how do you want the check?

TECK: *One month from today.* That I will not discuss. One month. Please decide now.

DAVID: *(sharply)* All right. *(To Teck)* How do you want it?

TECK: Seventy-five hundred dollars in a check. Twenty-five hundred in cash.

DAVID: I haven't anywhere near that much cash in the house. Leave your address and I'll send it to you in the morning.

TECK: *(laughs)* Address? I have no address, and I wish it now. Madame Fanny has cash in her sitting-room safe.

FANNY: Have you investigated that, too?

TECK: *(laughs)* No. You once told me you always kept money in the house.

DAVID: *(to Fanny)* How much have you got upstairs?

FANNY: I don't know. About fifteen or sixteen hundred.

TECK: Very well. That will do. Make the rest in the check.

DAVID: Get it, Mama, please. *(He starts toward the library door. Fanny starts for the hall exit.)*

FANNY: *(turns, looks carefully at Teck)* Years ago, I heard somebody say that being Roumanian was not a nationality, but a profession. The years have brought no change.

KURT: *(softly)* Being a Roumanian aristocrat is a profession.

(Fanny exits. After her exit, there is silence. Kurt does not look up, Sara does not move.)

TECK: *(awkwardly)* The new world has left the room. *(Looks up at them)* I feel less discomfort with you. We are Europeans, born to trouble and understanding it.

KURT: My wife is not a European.

TECK: Almost. *(Points upstairs)* They are young. The world has gone well for most of them. For us— *(Smiles)* The three of us—we are like peasants watching the big frost. Work, trouble, ruin— *(Shrugs)* But no need to call curses at the frost. There it is, it will be again, always—for us.

SARA: *(gets up, moves to the window, looks out)* You mean my husband and I do not have angry words for you. What for? We know how many there are of you. They don't, yet. My mother and brother feel shocked that you are in their house. For us—we have seen you in so many houses.

TECK: I do not say you *want* to understand me, Mrs. Müller. I say only that you do.

SARA: Yes. You are not difficult to understand.

KURT: *(slowly gets up, stands stiffly. They he moves toward the decanter table)* A whiskey?

TECK: No, thank you. *(He turns his head to watch Kurt move. He turns back.)*

KURT: Sherry?

TECK: *(nods)* Thank you, I will.

KURT: *(as he pours)* You, too, wish to go back to Europe.

TECK: Yes.

KURT: But they do not much want you. Not since the Budapest oil deal of '31.

TECK: You seem as well informed about me as I am about you.

KURT: That must have been a conference of high comedy, that one. Everybody trying to guess whether Kessler was working for Fritz Thyssen, and what Thyssen *really* wanted—and whether this "National Socialism" was a smart blind of Thyssen's, and where was Wolff—I should like to have seen you and your friends. It is too bad: you guessed an inch off, eh?

TECK: More than an inch.

KURT: And Kessler has a memory? *(Almost playfully)* I do not think Von Seitz would pay you money for a description of a man who has a month to travel. But I think he would pay you in a visa and a cable to Kessler. I think you want a visa almost as much as you want money. Therefore, I conclude you will try for the money here, and the visa from Von Seitz. *(He comes toward the table carrying the sherry glass)* I cannot get anywhere near Germany in a month and you know it. *(He is about to place the glass on the table)* I have been bored with this talk of paying you money. If they are willing to try you on this fantasy, I am not. Whatever made you think I would take such a chance? Or *any* chance? You are a gambler. But you should not gamble with your life. *(Teck has turned to stare at him, made a half motion as if to rise. As he does so, and on the words, "gamble with your life," Kurt drops the glass, hits Teck in the face. Struggling, Teck makes a violent effort to rise. Kurt throws himself on Teck, knocking him to the floor. As Teck falls to the floor, Kurt hits him on the side of the head. At the fourth blow, Teck does not move. Kurt rises, takes the gun from his pocket, begins to lift Teck from the floor. As he does so, Joshua appears in the hall entrance. He is washed and ready for dinner. As he reaches the door, he stops, sees the scene, stands quietly as if he were waiting for orders. Kurt begins to balance Teck, to balance himself. (To Joshua) Hilf mir. (Joshua comes quickly to Kurt) Mach die Tür auf! (Joshua runs toward the doors, opens them, stands waiting) Bleib da! Mach die Tür zu!*[1] *(Kurt begins to move out through the terrace. When he is outside the doors, Joshua closes them quickly, stands looking at his mother.)*

SARA: There's trouble.

JOSHUA: Do not worry. I will go up now. I will pack. In ten minutes all will be ready. I will say nothing. I will get the children ready— *(He starts quickly for the hall, turns for a second to look toward the terrace doors. Then almost with a sob)* This was a nice house.

SARA: *(softly)* We're not going this time, darling. There's no need to pack.

JOSHUA: *(stares at her, puzzled)* But Papa—

SARA: Go upstairs, Joshua. Take Babbie and Bodo in your room, and close the door. Stay there until I call you. *(He looks at her, Sara sits down)* There's nothing to be frightened of, darling. Papa is all right. *(Then very softly)* Papa is going home.

JOSHUA: To Germany?

SARA: Yes.

JOSHUA: Oh. Alone?

SARA: Alone. *(Very softly)* Don't say anything to the children. He will tell them himself.

---

1. "Help me. Open the door. Stay there! Close the door!"

JOSHUA: I won't.

SARA: *(as he hesitates)* I'm all right. Go upstairs now. *(He moves slowly out, she watches him, he disappears. For a minute she sits quietly. Then she gets up, moves to the terrace doors, stands with her hands pressed against them. Then she crosses, picks up the overturned chair, places it by the table, picks up the glass, puts it on the table. As if without knowing what she is doing, she wipes the table with her handkerchief.)*

(Fanny comes in from hall. After a second, David comes in from library. Stops, looks around room.)

DAVID: Where is he? Upstairs?

SARA: No. They went outside.

FANNY: Outside? They went outside. What are they doing, picking a bouquet together?

SARA: *(without turning)* They just went outside.

DAVID: *(looks at her)* What's the matter, Sara?

(Sara shakes her head. Goes to the desk, opens the telephone book, looks at a number, begins to dial the telephone.)

FANNY: Eleven hundred, eleven hundred and fifty, twelve, twelve-fifty—

DAVID: For God's sake, stop counting that money.

FANNY: All right. I'm nervous. And I don't like to think of giving him too much.

SARA: It's very nice of you and Mama. All that money— *(Into the telephone)* Hello. What time is your next plane? Oh. To— South. To El Paso, or— Brownsville. Yes.

DAVID: *(to Fanny)* Is Joseph ready?

FANNY: I don't know. I told him I'd call him.

SARA: To Brownsville? Yes. Yes. That's all right. At what time? Yes. No. The ticket will be picked up at the airport. *(David begins to cross to the bell cord. She looks up)* No. David. Don't call Joseph. David! Please! *(He draws back, stares at her. Looking at him, she goes on with the conversation)* Ritter. R-I-T-T-E-R. From Chicago. Yes. Yes. *(She hangs up, walks away.)*

DAVID: Sara! What's happening? What is all this? *(She does not answer)* Where is Kurt? What— *(He starts for the terrace door.)*

SARA: David. *Don't* go out.

FANNY: *(rises)* Sara! What's happening—

SARA: For seven years now, day in, day out, men have crossed the German border. They are always in danger. They always may be going in to die. Did you ever see the face of a man who never knows if this day will be the last day? *(Softly)* Don't go out on the terrace, David. Leave Kurt alone.

FANNY: *(softly)* Sara! What is—

SARA: *(quietly)* For them, it may be torture, and it may be death. Some day, when it's all over, maybe there'll be a few of them left to celebrate. There aren't many of Kurt's age left. He couldn't take a chance on them. They wouldn't have liked it. *(Suddenly, violently)* He'd have had a bad time trying to explain to them that because of this house and this nice town and my mother and my brother, he took chances with their work and with their lives. *(Quietly)* Sit down, Mama. I think it's all over now. *(To David)* There's nothing you can do about it. It's the way it had to be.

DAVID: Sara—

FANNY: Do you mean what I think you— *(She sits down.)*

SARA: *(she turns, looks out toward the doors. After a pause)* He's going away tonight and he's never coming back any more. *(In a sing-song)* Never, never, never. *(She looks down at her hands, as if she were very interested in them)* I don't like to be alone at night. I guess everybody in the world's got a time they don't like. Me, it's right before I go to sleep. And now it's going to be for always. All the rest of my life. *(She looks up as Kurt comes in from the terrace)* I've told them. There is an eight-thirty plane going as far south as Brownsville. I've made you a reservation. In the name of Ritter.

KURT: *(stands looking at her)* Liebe Sara! *(Then he goes to the table at which Fanny is sitting. To Fanny)* It is hard for you, eh? *(He pats her hand)* I am sorry.

FANNY: *(without knowing why, she takes her hand away)* Hard? I don't know. I— I don't— I don't know what I want to say.

KURT: *(looks at the hand she has touched, then turns to look at David)* Before I come in, I stand and think. I say, I will make Fanny and David understand. I say, how can I? Does one understand a killing? No. To hell with it, I say. I do what must be done. I have long sickened of words when I see the men who live by them. What do you wish to make them understand, I ask myself. Wait. Stand here. Just stand here. What are you thinking? Say it to them just as it comes to you. And this is what came to me. When you kill in a war, it is not so lonely; and I remember a cousin I have not seen for many years; and a melody comes back and I begin to make it with my fingers; a staircase in a house in Bonn years ago; an old dog who used to live in our town; Sara in a hundred places— Shame on us. Thousands of years and we cannot yet make a world. Like a child I am. I have stopped a man's life. *(Points to the place on the couch where he had been sitting opposite Teck)* I sit here. I listen to him. You will not believe—but I pray that I will not have to touch him. Then I know I will have to, I know that if I do not, it is only that I pamper myself, and risk the lives of others. I want you from the room. I know what I must do. *(Loudly)* All right. Do I now pretend sorrow? Do I now pretend it is not I who act thus? No. I do it. I have done it. I will do it again. And I will keep my hope that we may make a world in which all men can die in bed. I have a great hate for the violent. They are the sick of the world. *(Softly)* Maybe I am sick now, too.

SARA: You aren't sick. Stop that. It's late. You must go soon.

KURT: *(he puts out his hands, she touches them)* I am going to say good-bye now to my children. Then I am going to take your car— *(Motions with his head)* I will take him with me. After that, it is up to you. Two ways: You can let me go and keep silent. I believe I can hide him and the car. At the end of two days, if they have not been found, you will tell as much of the truth as is safe for you to say. Tell them the last time you saw us we were on our way to Washington. You did not worry at the absence, we might have rested there. Two crazy foreigners fight, one gets killed, you know nothing of the reason. I will have left the gun, there will be no doubt who did the killing. If you will give me those two days, I think I will be far enough away from here. If the car is found before then—*(Shrugs)* I will still try to move with speed. And all that will make you, for yourselves, part of a murder. For the world, I do not think you will be in bad trouble. *(He pauses)* There is another way. You can call your police. You can tell them the truth. I will not get home. *(To Sara)* I wish to see the children now. *(She goes out into the hall and up the stairs. There is silence.)*

FANNY: What are you thinking, David?

DAVID: I don't know. What are you thinking?

FANNY: Me? Oh, I was thinking about my Joshua. I was thinking that a few months before he died, we were sitting out there. *(Points to terrace)* He said, "Fanny, the Renaissance American is dying, the Renaissance man is dying." I said what do you mean, although I knew what he meant, I always knew. "A Renaissance man," he said, "is a man who wants to know. He wants to know how fast a bird will fly, how thick is the crust of the earth, what made Iago evil, how to plow a field. He knows there is no dignity to a mountain, if there is no dignity to man. You can't put that in a man, but when it's *really* there, and he will fight for it, put your trust in him."

DAVID: *(gets up, smiles, looks at Fanny)* You're a smart woman sometimes. *(Sara enters with Joshua. To Kurt)* Don't worry about things here. My soul doesn't have to be so nice and clean. I'll take care of it. You'll have your two days. And good luck to you.

FANNY: You go with my blessing, too. I like you. *(Bodo enters.)*

SARA: See? I come from good stock. *(Kurt looks at David. Then he begins to smile. Nods to David. Turns, smiles at Fanny.)*

FANNY: Do you like me?

KURT: I like you, Madame, very much.

FANNY: Would you be able to cash that check?

KURT: *(laughs)* Oh, no.

FANNY: Then take the cash. I, too, would like to contribute to your work.

KURT: *(slowly)* All right. Thank you. *(He takes the money from the table, puts it in his pocket.)*

BODO: *(to Kurt)* You like Grandma? I thought you would, with time. I like her, too. Sometimes she dilates with screaming, but— Dilates is correct? *(Babette enters. Joshua stands away from the others, looking at his father. Kurt turns to look at him.)*

JOSHUA: Alles in Ordnung?[2]

KURT: Alles in Ordnung.

BODO: What? What does that mean, all is well? *(There is an awkward silence.)*

BABETTE: *(as if she sensed it)* We are all clean for dinner. But nobody else is clean. And I have on Grandma's dress to me—

FANNY: *(very nervously)* Of course. And you look very pretty. You're a pretty little girl, Babbie.

BODO: *(looks around the room)* What is the matter? Everybody is acting like such a ninny. I got that word from Grandma.

KURT: Come here. *(They look at him. Then slowly Babette comes toward him, followed by Bodo. Joshua comes more slowly, to stand at the side of Kurt's chair)* We have said many good-byes to each other, eh? We must now say another. *(As they stare at him, he smiles, slowly, as if it were difficult)* This time, I leave you with good people to whom I believe you also will be good. *(Half playfully)* Would you allow me to give away my share in you, until I come back?

BABETTE: *(slowly)* If you would like it.

KURT: Good. To your mother, her share. My share, to Fanny and David. It is all I have to give. *(Laughs)* There. I have made a will, eh? Now. We will not joke. I have something to say to you. It is important for me to say it.

JOSHUA: *(softly)* You are talking to us as if we were children.

KURT: *(turns to look at him)* Am I, Joshua? I wish you were children. I wish I could say love your mother, do not eat too many sweets, clean your teeth— *(Draws Bodo to him)* I cannot say these things. You are not children. I took it all away from you.

BABETTE: We have had a most enjoyable life, Papa.

KURT: *(smiles)* You are a gallant little liar. And I thank you for it. I have done something bad today—

FANNY: *(shocked, sharply)* Kurt—

SARA: Don't, Mama. *(Bodo and Babette have looked at Fanny and Sara, puzzled. Then they have turned again to look at Kurt.)*

KURT: It is not to frighten you. In a few days, your mother and David will tell you.

BODO: You could not do a bad thing.

BABETTE: *(proudly)* You could not.

KURT: *(shakes his head)* Now let us get straight together. The four of us. Do you

2. "Everything is in order?"

remember when we read "Les Misérables"? Do you remember that we talked about it afterward and Bodo got candy on Mama's bed?

BODO: I remember.

KURT: Well. He stole bread. The world is out of shape we said, when there are hungry men. And until it gets in shape, men will steal and lie and— *(A little more slowly)* —kill. But for whatever reason it is done, and whoever does it—you understand me—it is all bad. I want you to remember that. Whoever does it, it is bad. *(Then very gaily)* But you will live to see the day when it will not have to be. All over the world, in every place and every town, there are men who are going to make sure it will not have to be. They want what I want: a childhood for every child. For my children, and I for theirs. *(He picks Bodo up, rises)* Think of that. It will make you happy. In every town and every village and every mud hut in the world, there is always a man who loves children and who will fight to make a good world for them. And now good-bye. Wait for me. I shall try to come back for you. *(He moves toward the hall, followed by Babette, and more slowly, by Joshua)* Or you shall come to me. At Hamburg, the boat will come in. It will be a fine, safe land— I will be waiting on the dock. And there will be the three of you and Mama and Fanny and David. And I will have ordered an extra big dinner and we will show them what our Germany can be like— *(He has put Bodo down. He leans down, presses his face in Babette's hair. Tenderly, as her mother has done earlier, she touches his hair.)*

JOSHUA: Of course. That is the way it will be. Of course. But—but if you should find yourself delayed— *(Very slowly)* Then I will come to you. Mama.

SARA: *(she has turned away)* I heard you, Joshua.

KURT: *(he kisses Babette)* Gute Nacht, Liebling!

BABETTE: Gute Nacht, Papa. Mach's gut!

KURT: *(leans to kiss Bodo)* Good night, baby.

BODO: Good night, Papa. Mach's gut! *(Babette runs up the steps. Slowly Bodo follows her.)*

KURT: *(kisses Joshua)* Good night, son.

JOSHUA: Good night, Papa. Mach's gut! *(He begins to climb the steps. Kurt stands watching them, smiling. When they disappear, he turns to David.)*

KURT: Good-bye, and thank you.

DAVID: Good-bye, and good luck.

KURT: *(he moves to Fanny)* Good-bye. I have good children, eh?

FANNY: Yes, you have. *(Kurt kisses her hand.)*

KURT: *(slowly, he turns toward Sara)* Men who wish to live have the best chance to live. I wish to live. I wish to live with you. *(She comes toward him.)*

SARA: For twenty years. It is as much for me today— *(Takes his arms)* Just once, and for all my life. *(He pulls her toward him)* Come back for me, darling. If you can. *(Takes brief-case from table and gives it to him.)*

KURT: *(simply)* I will try. *(He turns)* Good-bye, to you all. *(He exits. After a second, there is the sound of a car starting. They sit listening to it. Gradually the noise begins to go off into the distance. A second later, Joshua appears.)*

JOSHUA: Mama— *(She looks up. He is very tense)* Bodo cries. Babette looks very queer. I think you should come.

SARA: *(gets up, slowly)* I'm coming.

JOSHUA: *(to Fanny and David. Still very tense)* Bodo talks so fancy, we forget sometimes he is a baby. *(He waits for Sara to come up to him. When she reaches him, she takes his hand, goes up the steps, disappears. Fanny and David watch them.)*

FANNY: *(after a minute)* Well, here we are. We're shaken out of the magnolias, eh?

DAVID: Yes. So we are.

FANNY: Tomorrow will be a hard day. But we'll have Babbie's birthday dinner. And we'll have music afterward. You can be the audience. I think you'd better go up to Marthe now. Be as careful as you can. She'd better stay here for a while. I daresay I can stand it.

DAVID: *(turns, smiles)* Even your graciousness is ungracious, Mama.

FANNY: I do my best. Well, I think I shall go and talk to Anise. I like Anise best when I don't feel well. *(She begins to move off.)*

DAVID: Mama. *(She turns)* We are going to be in for trouble. You understand that?

FANNY: I understand it very well. We will manage. You and I. I'm not put together with flour paste. And neither are you—I am happy to learn.

DAVID: Good night, Mama. *(As she moves out, the curtain falls.)*

1941

Eudora Welty
(1909–   )

Born in Jackson, Mississippi, Eudora Welty has lived most of her life in the same city, on the same street, in the same house to which her family moved when she was 6 years old. Her father was from Ohio and her mother was from West Virginia; the fact that her parents came from outside the Old South has suggested to some critics the reason why she seems unconcerned with Southern heritage except as it has played itself out within her personal view and hearing during a long, alert, and subtly perceptive life. Hers is not a world of guilt and magnolias, nor is it burdened overmuch with the remembered pain of Southern Reconstruction following the Civil War. Yet she is unmistakably a Southern writer, her people kin to those who inhabit the books of overlapping generations of Mississippi writers, from the slightly older William Faulkner to the much younger Barry Hannah.

Raised in Jackson, she attended Mississippi State College for Women in Columbus before transferring to the University of Wisconsin, where she received her B.A. in 1929. After a short stay in New York City, studying advertising at the Columbia University School of Business in 1930–1931, she returned to Jackson, to her parents' home, to face the prospect of earning a living in the Great Depression. For the next decade she worked in advertising and journalism, and for a while for the Works Progress Administration, a make-work program of the Roosevelt administration. From her WPA experience came the photographs of rural Mississippi shown briefly in New York in 1936 and later printed in *One Time, One Place* (1971). The same period inaugurated her life as a published writer, with her first story, "Death of a Traveling Salesman," published in *Manuscript* in 1936. Others soon followed in the *Southern Review* and *Atlantic Monthly*. Assisted by Cleanth Brooks, Robert Penn Warren, and Katherine Anne Porter (established Southern writers), she found a publisher for her first collection, *A Curtain of Green* (1941), containing several of her best-known stories. A Guggenheim Fellowship followed, and then the succession of books that have placed her among the most celebrated short story writers of her time. These include *The Wide Net* (1943); *The Golden Apples* (1949), linked stories exploring the lives of three generations of families in a Mississippi town; and *The Bride of Innisfallen* (1955), with the title story one of the few that Welty set outside of the South.

Her career as a novelist began with

The Robber Bridegroom (1942), a short work drawn in part from the history of pioneers on the Old Natchez Trace, but mixing in folklore and fairy tale motifs. This, together with *The Ponder Heart* (1954), *Losing Battles* (1970), and *The Optimist's Daughter* (1972), displays with special effectiveness her considerable comic gifts. Taking her all in all, short stories and longer fictions, many readers are particularly struck by the depth of her human sympathies, a quality in her work she discussed in the preface to *The Collected Stories* (1980):

I have been told, both in approval and in accusation, that I seem to love all my characters. What I do in writing of any character is to try to enter into the mind, heart, and skin of a human being who is not myself. Whether this happens to be a man or a woman, old or young, with skin black or white, the primary challenge lies in making the jump itself. It is the act of a writer's imagination that I set most high.

The Collected Stories (1980) contains the contents of the earlier collections and adds two stories previously unpublished. Other works, in addition to those named above, include *Delta Wedding* (1946), a novel; *Place in Fiction* (1957) and *The Eye of the Story* (1978), criticism; and *One Writer's Beginnings* (1984), autobiography. Peggy Whitman Prenshaw edited *Conversations with Eudora Welty* (1985).

A critical biography is Ruth Vande Kieft, *Eudora Welty* (1987). Other studies include Alfred Appel, Jr., *A Season of Dreams: The Fiction of Eudora Welty* (1965); Michael Kreyling, *Eudora Welty's Achievement of Order* (1980); Albert J. Devlin, *Eudora Welty's Chronicle: A Story of Mississippi Life* (1983); and Carol S. Manning, *With Ears Opening Like Morning Glories: Eudora Welty and the Love of Storytelling* (1987).

Livvie[1]

Solomon carried Livvie twenty-one miles away from her home when he married her. He carried her away up on the Old Natchez Trace[2] into the deep country to live in his house. She was sixteen—only a girl, then. Once people said he thought nobody would ever come along there. He told her himself that it had been a long time, and a day she did not know about, since that road was a traveled road with *people* coming and going. He was good to her, but he kept her in the house. She had not thought that she could not get back. Where she came from, people said an old man did not want anybody in the world to ever find his wife, for fear they would steal her back from him. Solomon asked her before he took her, would she be happy?—very dignified, for he was a colored man that owned his land and had it written down in the courthouse; and she said, "Yes, sir," since he was an old man and she was young and just listened and answered. He asked her, if she was choosing winter, would she pine for spring, and she said, "No indeed." Whatever she said, always, was because he was an old man . . . while nine years went by. All the time, he got older, and he got so old he gave out. At last he slept the whole day in bed, and she was young still.

It was a nice house, inside and outside both. In the first place, it had three rooms. The front room was papered in holly paper, with green palmettos from the swamp spaced at careful intervals over the walls. There was fresh newspaper cut with fancy borders on the mantelshelf, on which were propped photographs of old or very young men printed in faint yellow—Solomon's people. Solomon had a houseful of furniture. There was a double settee, a tall scrolled rocker and an organ in the front room, all around a three-legged table with a

1. An O. Henry Award story for 1943, "Livvie" was collected in *The Wide Net and Other Stories* (1943). The source of the present text is *The Collected Stories* (1980).
2. The road from Natchez, Mississippi, to Nashville, Tennessee—important to trade, settlement, and warfare from the late eighteenth to the early nineteenth century. It followed earlier Indian trails.

pink marble top, on which was set a lamp with three gold feet, besides a jelly glass with pretty hen feathers in it. Behind the front room, the other room had the bright iron bed with the polished knobs like a throne, in which Solomon slept all day. There were snow-white curtains of wiry lace at the window, and a lace bedspread belonged on the bed. But what old Solomon slept so sound under was a big feather-stitched piece-quilt in the pattern "Trip Around the World," which had twenty-one different colors, four hundred and forty pieces, and a thousand yards of thread, and that was what Solomon's mother made in her life and old age. There was a table holding the Bible, and a trunk with a key. On the wall were two calendars, and a diploma from somewhere in Solomon's family, and under that, Livvie's one possession was nailed, a picture of the little white baby of the family she worked for, back in Natchez before she was married. Going through that room and on to the kitchen, there was a big wood stove and a big round table always with a wet top and with the knives and forks in one jelly glass and the spoons in another, and a cut-glass vinegar bottle between, and going out from those, many shallow dishes of pickled peaches, fig preserves, watermelon pickles and blackberry jam always sitting there. The churn sat in the sun, the doors of the safe were always both shut, and there were four baited mousetraps in the kitchen, one in every corner.

The outside of Solomon's house looked nice. It was not painted, but across the porch was an even balance. On each side there was one easy chair with high springs, looking out, and a fern basket hanging over it from the ceiling, and a dishpan of zinnia seedlings growing at its foot on the floor. By the door was a plow-wheel, just a pretty iron circle, nailed up on one wall, and a square mirror on the other, a turquoise-blue comb stuck up in the frame, with the wash stand beneath it. On the door was a wooden knob with a pearl in the end, and Solomon's black hat hung on that, if he was in the house.

Out front was a clean dirt yard with every vestige of grass patiently uprooted and the ground scarred in deep whorls from the strike of Livvie's broom. Rose bushes with tiny blood-red roses blooming every month grew in threes on either side of the steps. On one side was a peach tree, on the other a pomegranate. Then coming around up the path from the deep cut of the Natchez Trace below was a line of bare crape-myrtle trees with every branch of them ending in a colored bottle, green or blue. There was no word that fell from Solomon's lips to say what they were for, but Livvie knew that there could be a spell put in trees, and she was familiar from the time she was born with the way bottle trees kept evil spirits from coming into the house—by luring them inside the colored bottles, where they cannot get out again. Solomon had made the bottle trees with his own hands over the nine years, in labor amounting to about a tree a year, and without a sign that he had any uneasiness in his heart, for he took as much pride in his precautions against spirits coming in the house as he took in the house, and sometimes in the sun the bottle trees looked prettier than the house did.

It was a nice house. It was in a place where the days would go by and surprise anyone that they were over. The lamplight and the firelight would shine out the door after dark, over the still and breathing country, lighting the roses and the bottle trees, and all was quiet there.

But there was nobody, nobody at all, not even a white person. And if there had been anybody, Solomon would not have let Livvie look at them, just as he would not let her look at a field hand, or a field hand look at her. There was no house near, except for the cabins of the tenants that were forbidden to her, and there was no house as far as she had been, stealing away down the still, deep Trace. She felt as if she waded a river when she went, for the dead leaves on the ground reached as high as her knees, and when she was all scratched and bleeding she said it was not like a road that went anywhere. One day, climbing up the high bank, she had found a graveyard without a church, with ribbon-grass growing about the foot of an angel (she had climbed up because she thought she saw angel wings), and in the sun, trees shining like burning flames through the great caterpillar nets which enclosed them.

Scarey thistles stood looking like the prophets in the Bible in Solomon's house. Indian paint brushes grew over her head, and the mourning dove made the only sound in the world. Oh, for a stirring of the leaves, and a breaking of the nets! But not by a ghost, prayed Livvie, jumping down the bank. After Solomon took to his bed, she never went out, except one more time.

Livvie knew she made a nice girl to wait on anybody. She fixed things to eat on a tray like a surprise. She could keep from singing when she ironed, and to sit by a bed and fan away the flies, she could be so still she could not hear herself breathe. She could clean up the house and never drop a thing, and wash the dishes without a sound, and she would step outside to churn, for churning sounded too sad to her, like sobbing, and if it made her homesick and not Solomon, she did not think of that.

But Solomon scarcely opened his eyes to see her, and scarcely tasted his food. He was not sick or paralyzed or in any pain that he mentioned, but he was surely wearing out in the body, and no matter what nice hot thing Livvie would bring him to taste, he would only look at it now, as if he were past seeing how he could add anything more to himself. Before she could beg him, he would go fast asleep. She could not surprise him any more, if he would not taste, and she was afraid that he was never in the world going to taste another thing she brought him—and so how could he last?

But one morning it was breakfast time and she cooked his eggs and grits, carried them in on a tray, and called his name. He was sound asleep. He lay in a dignified way with his watch beside him, on his back in the middle of the bed. One hand drew the quilt up high, though it was the first day of spring. Through the white lace curtains a little puffy wind was blowing as if it came from round cheeks. All night the frogs had sung out in the swamp, like a commotion in the room, and he had not stirred, though she lay wide awake and saying "Shh, frogs!" for fear he would mind them.

He looked as if he would like to sleep a little longer, and so she put back the tray and waited. When she tiptoed and stayed so quiet, she surrounded herself with a little reverie, and sometimes it seemed to her when she was so stealthy that the quiet she kept was for a sleeping baby, and that she had a baby and was its mother. When she stood at Solomon's bed and looked down at him, she would be thinking, "He sleeps so well," and she would hate to wake him up. And in some other way, too, she was afraid to wake him up because even in his sleep he seemed to be such a strict man.

Of course, nailed to the wall over the bed—only she would forget who it was—there was a picture of him when he was young. Then he had a fan of hair over his forehead like a king's crown. Now his hair lay down on his head, the spring had gone out of it. Solomon had a lightish face, with eyebrows scattered but rugged, the way privet grows, strong eyes, with second sight, a strict mouth, and a little gold smile. This was the way he looked in his clothes, but in bed in the daytime he looked a different and smaller man, even when he was wide awake, and holding the Bible. He looked like somebody kin to himself. And then sometimes when he lay in sleep and she stood fanning the flies away, and the light came in, his face was like new, so smooth and clear that it was like a glass of jelly held to the window, and she could almost look through his forehead and see what he thought.

She fanned him and at length he opened his eyes and spoke her name, but he would not taste the nice eggs she had kept warm under a pan.

Back in the kitchen she ate heartily, his breakfast and hers, and looked out the open door at what went on. The whole day, and the whole night before, she had felt the stir of spring close to her. It was as present in the house as a young man would be. The moon was in the last quarter and outside they were turning the sod and planting peas and beans. Up and down the red fields, over which smoke from the brush-burning hung showing like a little skirt of sky, a white horse and a white mule pulled the plow. At intervals hoarse shouts came through the air and roused her as if she dozed neglectfully in the shade, and they were telling her, "Jump up!" She could see how over each ribbon of field were moving men and girls, on foot and mounted on mules, with hats set on their heads and bright with tall hoes and forks as if they carried streamers on them and were going to some place on a journey—and how as if at a signal now and then they would all start at once shouting, hollering, cajoling, calling and answering back, running, being leaped on and breaking away, flinging to earth with a shout and lying motionless in the trance of twelve o'clock. The old women came out of the cabins and brought them the food they had ready for them, and then all worked together, spread evenly out. The little children came too, like a bouncing stream overflowing the fields, and set upon the men, the women, the dogs, the rushing birds, and the wave-like rows of earth, their little voices almost too high to be heard. In the middle distance like some white and gold towers were the haystacks, with black cows coming around to eat their edges. High above everything, the wheel of fields, house, and cabins, and the deep road surrounding like a moat to keep them in, was the turning sky, blue with long, far-flung white mare's-tail clouds, serene and still as high flames. And sound asleep while all this went around him that was his, Solomon was like a little still spot in the middle.

Even in the house the earth was sweet to breathe. Solomon had never let Livvie go any farther than the chicken house and the well. But what if she would walk now into the heart of the fields and take a hoe and work until she fell stretched out and drenched with her efforts, like other girls, and laid her cheek against the laid-open earth, and shamed the old man with her humbleness and delight? To shame him! A cruel wish could come in uninvited and so fast while she looked out the back door. She washed the dishes and scrubbed the table. She could hear the cries of the little lambs. Her mother, that she had not seen since her wedding day, had said one time, "I rather a man be anything, than a woman be mean."

So all morning she kept tasting the chicken broth on the stove, and when it was right she poured off a nice cupful. She carried it in to Solomon, and there he lay having a dream. Now what did he dream about? For she saw him sigh gently as if not to disturb some whole thing he held round in his mind, like a fresh egg. So even an old man dreamed about something pretty. Did he dream of her, while his eyes were shut and sunken, and his small hand with the wedding ring curled close in sleep around the quilt? He might be dreaming of what time it was, for even through his sleep he kept track of it like a clock, and knew how much of it went by, and waked up knowing where the hands were even before he consulted the silver watch that he never let go. He would sleep with the watch in his palm, and even holding it to his cheek like a child that loves a plaything. Or he might dream of journeys and travels on a steamboat to Natchez. Yet she thought he dreamed of her; but even while she scrutinized him, the rods of the foot of the bed seemed to rise up like a rail fence between them, and she could see that people never could be sure of anything as long as one of them was asleep and the other awake. To look at him dreaming of her when he might be going to die frightened her a little, as if he might carry her with him that way, and she wanted to run out of the room. She took hold of the bed and held on, and Solomon opened his eyes and called her name, but he did not want anything. He would not taste the good broth.

Just a little after that, as she was taking up the ashes in the front room for the last time in the year, she heard a sound. It was somebody coming. She pulled the curtains together and looked through the slit.

Coming up the path under the bottle trees was a white lady. At first she looked young, but then she looked old. Marvelous to see, a little car stood steaming like a kettle out in the field-track—it had come without a road.

Livvie stood listening to the long, repeated knockings at the door, and after a while she opened it just a little. The lady came in through the crack, though she was more than middle-sized and wore a big hat.

"My name is Miss Baby Marie," she said.

Livvie gazed respectfully at the lady and at the little suitcase she was holding close to her by the handle until the proper moment. The lady's eyes were running over the room, from palmetto to palmetto, but she was saying, "I live at home . . . out from Natchez . . . and get out and show these pretty cosmetic things to the white people and the colored people both . . . all around . . . years and years. . . . Both shades of powder and rouge . . . It's the kind of work a girl can do and not go clear 'way from home. . . ." And the harder she looked, the more she talked. Suddenly she turned up her nose and said, "It is not Christian or sanitary to put feathers in a vase," and then she took a gold key out of the front of her dress and began unlocking the locks on her suitcase. Her face drew the light, the way it was covered with intense white and red, with a little patty-cake of white between the wrinkles by her upper lip. Little red tassels of hair bobbed under the rusty wires of her picture-hat, as with an air of triumph and secrecy she now drew open her little suitcase and brought out bottle after bottle and jar after jar, which she put down on the table, the mantel-piece, the settee, and the organ.

"Did you ever see so many cosmetics in your life?" cried Miss Baby Marie.

"No'm," Livvie tried to say, but the cat had her tongue.

"Have you ever applied cosmetics?" asked Miss Baby Marie next.

"No'm," Livvie tried to say.

"Then look!" she said, and pulling out the last thing of all, "Try this!" she said. And in her hand was unclenched a golden lipstick which popped open like magic. A fragrance came out of it like incense, and Livvie cried out suddenly, "Chinaberry flowers!"

Her hand took the lipstick, and in an instant she was carried away in the air through the spring, and looking down with a half-drowsy smile from a purple cloud she saw from above a chinaberry tree, dark and smooth and neatly leaved, neat as a guinea hen in the dooryard, and there was her home that she had left. On one side of the tree was her mama holding up her heavy apron, and she could see it was loaded with ripe figs, and on the other side was her papa holding a fish-pole over the pond, and she could see it transparently, the little clear fishes swimming up to the brim.

"Oh, no, not chinaberry flowers—secret ingredients," said Miss Baby Marie. "My cosmetics have secret ingredients—not chinaberry flowers."

"It's purple," Livvie breathed, and Miss Baby Marie said, "Use it freely. Rub it on."

Livvie tiptoed out to the wash stand on the front porch and before the mirror put the paint on her mouth. In the wavery surface her face danced before her like a flame. Miss Baby Marie followed her out, took a look at what she had done, and said, "That's it."

Livvie tried to say "Thank you" without moving her parted lips where the paint lay so new.

By now Miss Baby Marie stood behind Livvie and looked in the mirror over her shoulder, twisting up the tassels of her hair. "The lipstick I can let you have for only two dollars," she said, close to her neck.

"Lady, but I don't have no money, never did have," said Livvie.

"Oh, but you don't pay the first time. I make another trip, that's the way I do. I come back again—later."

"Oh," said Livvie, pretending she understood everything so as to please the lady.

"But if you don't take it now, this may be the last time I'll call at your house," said Miss Baby Marie sharply. "It's far away from anywhere, I'll tell you that. You don't live close to anywhere."

"Yes'm. My husband, he keep the *money*," said Livvie, trembling. "He is strict as he can be. He don't know *you* walk in here—Miss Baby Marie!"

"Where is he?"

"Right now, he in yonder sound asleep, an old man. I wouldn't ever ask him for anything."

Miss Baby Marie took back the lipstick and packed it up. She gathered up the jars for both black and white and got them all inside the suitcase, with the same little fuss of triumph with which she had brought them out. She started away.

"Good-bye," she said, making herself look grand from the back, but at the last minute she turned around in the door. Her old hat wobbled as she whispered, "Let me see your husband."

Livvie obediently went on tiptoe and opened the door to the other room. Miss Baby Marie came behind her and rose on her toes and looked in.

"My, what a little tiny old, old man!" she whispered, clasping her hands and shaking her head over them. "What a beautiful quilt! What a tiny old, old man!"

"He can sleep like that all day," whispered Livvie proudly.

They looked at him awhile so fast asleep, and then all at once they looked at each other. Somehow that was as if they had a secret, for he had never stirred. Livvie then politely, but all at once, closed the door.

"Well! I'd certainly like to leave you with a lipstick!" said Miss Baby Marie vivaciously. She smiled in the door.

"Lady, but I told you I don't have no money, and never did have."

"And never will?" In the air and all around, like a bright halo around the white lady's nodding head, it was a true spring day.

"Would you take eggs, lady?" asked Livvie softly.

"No, I have plenty of eggs—plenty," said Miss Baby Marie.

"I still don't have no money," said Livvie, and Miss Baby Marie took her suitcase and went on somewhere else.

Livvie stood watching her go, and all the time she felt her heart beating in her left side. She touched the place with her hand. It seemed as if her heart beat and her whole face flamed from the pulsing color of her lips. She went to sit by Solomon and when he opened his eyes he could not see a change in her. "He's fixin' to die," she said inside. That was the secret. That was when she went out of the house for a little breath of air.

She went down the path and down the Natchez Trace a way, and she did not know how far she had gone, but it was not far, when she saw a sight. It was a man, looking like a vision—she standing on one side of the Old Natchez Trace and he standing on the other.

As soon as this man caught sight of her, he began to look himself over. Starting at the bottom with his pointed shoes, he began to look up, lifting his peg-top pants the higher to see fully his bright socks. His coat long and wide and leaf-green he opened like doors to see his high-up tawny pants and his pants he smoothed downward from the points of his collar, and he wore a luminous baby-pink satin shirt. At the end, he reached gently above his wide platter-shaped round hat, the color of a plum, and one finger touched at the feather, emerald green, blowing in the spring winds.

No matter how she looked, she could never look so fine as he did, and she was not sorry for that, she was pleased.

He took three jumps, one down and two up, and was by her side.

"My name is Cash," he said.

He had a guinea pig in his pocket. They began to walk along. She stared on and on at him, as if he were doing some daring spectacular thing, instead of just walking beside her. It was not simply the city way he was dressed that made her look at him and see hope in its insolence looking back. It was not only the way he moved along kicking the flowers as if he could break through everything in the way and destroy anything in the world, that made her eyes grow bright. It might be, if he had not appeared *that day* she would never have looked so closely at him, but the time people come makes a difference.

They walked through the still leaves of the Natchez Trace, the light and the shade falling through trees about them, the white irises shining like candles on the banks and the new ferns shining like green stars up in the oak branches. They came out at Solomon's house, bottle trees and all. Livvie stopped and hung her head.

Cash began whistling a little tune. She did not know what it was, but she had heard it before from a distance, and she had a revelation. Cash was a field hand. He was a transformed field hand. Cash belonged to Solomon. But he had stepped out of his overalls into this. There in front of Solomon's house he laughed. He had a round head, a round face, all of him was young, and he flung his head up, rolled it against the mare's-tail sky in his round hat, and he could laugh just to see Solomon's house sitting there. Livvie looked at it, and there was Solomon's black hat hanging on the peg on the front door, the blackest thing in the world.

"I been to Natchez," Cash said, wagging his head around against the sky. "I taken a trip, I ready for Easter!"

How was it possible to look so fine before the harvest? Cash must have stolen the money, stolen it from Solomon. He stood in the path and lifted his spread hand high and brought it down again and again in his laughter. He kicked up his heels. A little chill went through her. It was as if Cash was bringing that strong hand down to beat a drum or to rain blows upon a man, such an abandon and menace were in his laugh. Frowning, she went closer to him and his swinging arm drew her in at once and the fright was crushed from her body, as a little match-flame might be smothered out by what it lighted. She gathered the folds of his coat behind him and fastened her red lips to his mouth, and she was dazzled at herself then, the way he had been dazzled at himself to begin with.

In that instant she felt something that could not be told—that Solomon's death was at hand, that he was the same to her as if he were dead now. She cried out, and uttering little cries turned and ran for the house.

At once Cash was coming, following after, he was running behind her. He came close, and half-way up the path he laughed and passed her. He even picked up a stone and sailed it into the bottle trees. She put her hands over her head, and sounds clattered through the bottle trees like cries of outrage. Cash stamped and plunged zigzag up the front steps and in at the door.

When she got there, he had stuck his hands in his pockets and was turning slowly about in the front room. The little guinea pig peeped out. Around Cash, the pinned-up palmettos looked as if a lazy green monkey had walked up and down and around the walls leaving green prints of his hands and feet.

She got through the room and his hands were still in his pockets, and she fell upon the closed door to the other room and pushed it open. She ran to Solomon's bed, calling "Solomon! Solomon!" The little shape of the old man never moved at all, wrapped under the quilt as if it were winter still.

"Solomon!" She pulled the quilt away, but there was another one under that, and she fell on her knees beside him. He made no sound except a sigh, and then she could hear in the silence the light springy steps of Cash walking and walking in the front room, and the ticking of Solomon's silver watch, which came from the bed. Old Solomon was far away in his sleep, his face looked small, relentless, and devout, as if he were walking somewhere where she could imagine the snow falling.

Then there was a noise like a hoof pawing the floor, and the door gave a creak, and Cash appeared beside her. When she looked up, Cash's face was so black it was bright, and so bright and bare of pity that it looked sweet to her. She stood up and held up her head. Cash was so powerful that his presence gave her strength even when she did not need any.

Under their eyes Solomon slept. People's faces tell of things and places not known to the one who looks at them while they sleep, and while Solomon slept under the eyes of Livvie and Cash his face told them like a mythical story that all his life he had built, little scrap by little scrap, respect. A beetle could not have been more laborious or more ingenious in the task of its destiny. When Solomon was young, as he was in his picture overhead, it was the infinite thing with him, and he could see no end to the respect he would contrive and keep in a house. He had built a lonely house, the way he would make a cage, but it grew to be the same with him as a great monumental pyramid and sometimes in his absorption of getting it erected he was like the builder-slaves of Egypt who forgot or never knew the origin and meaning of the thing to which they gave all the strength of their bodies and used up all their days. Livvie and Cash could see that as a man might rest from a life-labor he lay in his bed, and they could hear how, wrapped in his quilt, he sighed to himself comfortably in sleep, while in his dreams he might have been an ant, a beetle, a bird, an Egyptian, assembling and carrying on his back and building with his hands, or he might have been an old man of India or a swaddled baby, about to smile and brush all away.

Then without warning old Solomon's eyes flew wide open under the hedge-like brows. He was wide awake.

And instantly Cash raised his quick arm. A radiant sweat stood on his temples. But he did not bring his arm down—it stayed in the air, as if something might have taken hold.

It was not Livvie—she did not move. As if something said "Wait," she stood waiting. Even while her eyes burned under motionless lids, her lips parted in a stiff grimace, and with her arms stiff at her sides she stood above the prone old man and the panting young one, erect and apart.

Movement when it came came in Solomon's face. It was an old and strict face, a frail face, but behind it, like a covered light, came an animation that could play hide and seek, that would dart and escape, had always escaped. The mystery flickered in him, and invited from his eyes. It was that very mystery that Cash with his quick arm would have to strike, and that Livvie could not weep for. But Cash only stood holding his arm in the air, when the gentlest flick of his great strength, almost a puff of his breath, would have been enough, if he had known how to give it, to send the old man over the obstruction that kept him away from death.

"Young ones can't wait," said Solomon.

Livvie shuddered violently, and then in a gush of tears she stooped for a glass of water and handed it to him, but he did not see her.

"So here come the young man Livvie wait for. Was no prevention. No prevention. Now I lay eyes on young man and it come to be somebody I know all the time, and been knowing since he were born in a cotton patch, and watched grow up year to year, Cash McCord, growed to size, growed up to come in my house in the end—ragged and barefoot."

Solomon gave a cough of distaste. Then he shut his eyes vigorously, and his lips began to move like a chanter's.

"When Livvie married, her husband were already somebody. He had paid great cost for his land. He spread sycamore leaves over the ground from wagon to door, day he brought her home, so her foot would not have to touch ground. He carried her through his door. Then he growed old and could not lift her, and she were still young."

Livvie's sobs followed his words like a soft melody repeating each thing as he stated it. His lips moved for a little without sound, or she cried too fervently, and unheard he might have been telling his whole life, and then he said, "God forgive Solomon for sins great and small. God forgive Solomon for carrying away too young girl for wife and keeping her away from her people and from all the young people would clamor for her back."

Then he lifted up his right hand toward Livvie where she stood by the bed and offered her his silver watch. He dangled it before her eyes, and she hushed crying; her tears stopped. For a moment the watch could be heard ticking as it always did, precisely in his proud hand. She lifted it away. Then he took hold of the quilt; then he was dead.

Livvie left Solomon dead and went out of the room. Stealthily, nearly without noise, Cash went beside her. He was like a shadow, but his shiny shoes moved over the floor in spangles, and the green downy feather shone like a light in his hat. As they reached the front room, he seized her deftly as a long black cat and dragged her hanging by the waist round and round him, while he turned in a circle, his face bent down to hers. The first moment, she kept one arm and its hand stiff and still, the one that held Solomon's watch. Then the fingers softly let go, all of her was limp, and the watch fell somewhere on the floor. It ticked away in the still room, and all at once there began outside the full song of a bird.

They moved around and around the room and into the brightness of the open door, then he stopped and shook her once. She rested in silence in his trembling arms, unprotesting as a bird on a nest. Outside the redbirds were flying and criss-crossing, the sun was in all the bottles on the prisoned trees, and the young peach was shining in the middle of them with the bursting light of spring.

1943

Mary McCarthy
(1912–1989)

Born in Seattle, Washington, Mary McCarthy was orphaned at 6, losing her mother on one day and her father on the next in the 1918 influenza epidemic remembered in literature especially in Katherine Anne Porter's "Pale Horse, Pale Rider." Raised by relatives in Minneapolis for the next few years, and then by grandparents in Seattle, she attended Catholic boarding schools in Seattle and Tacoma. At Vassar College, she was an undergraduate with Elizabeth Bishop and Muriel Rukeyser, editing a literary magazine with them.

Married for the first time almost immediately after college, she wrote reviews during the 1930s for *The New Republic, The Nation,* and *The Partisan Review,* but not until her marriage to Edmund Wilson in 1938 did she turn seriously to fiction. A first story, "Cruel and Barbarous Treatment," published in the *Southern Review* in 1939, led to her first book, *The Company She Keeps* (1942), partially autobiographical stories centered in New York in the 1930s. In later fictions she developed a similar practice, mixing self-analysis with clinical observation of character types and social trends in works that sometimes seem part essay, part story, and are usually witty and satiric. Most famous is the best-seller, *The Group* (1963), in which she follows the lives of Vassar graduates (and their mothers) as imagined from her own class of 1933. Other works of fiction include the stories of *Cast a Cold Eye* (1950) and the novels *The Oasis* (1949), *The Groves of Academe* (1952), *A Charmed Life* (1955), *Birds of America* (1971), and *Cannibals and Missionaries* (1979).

Some of McCarthy's most admired work is in her nonfiction, particularly her autobiographical *Memories of a Catholic Girlhood* (1957). An insightful journalist, she turned her sharp critical intelligence to discussions of a variety of subjects in books like *Venice Observed* (1956), *The Stones of Florence* (1959), *Vietnam* (1967), *Hanoi* (1968), and *The Mask of State: Watergate Portraits* (1974).

Books not named above include two collections of literary and cultural essays, *On the Contrary* (1961) and *The Writing on the Wall* (1978); essays on Vietnam and Watergate, *The Seventeenth Degree* (1974); *Mary McCarthy's Theatre Chronicles 1937–1962* (1963); *Ideas and the Novel* (1980); *Occasional Prose* (1985); the autobiographical *How I Grew* (1987); and *Intellectual Memoirs: New York 1936–1938* (1992).

Studies include Barbara McKenzie, *Mary McCarthy* (1966); Doris Grumbach, *The Company She Kept* (1967); Irwin Stock, *Mary McCarthy* (1967); Willena S. Hardy, *Mary McCarthy* (1981); and Carol Brightman, *Writing Dangerously: Mary McCarthy and Her World* (1992).

Artists in Uniform[1]

March, 1953

The Colonel went out sailing,
He spoke with Turk and Jew . . .

"Pour it on, Colonel," cried the young man in the Dacron suit excitedly, making his first sortie into the club-car conversation. His face was white as Roquefort and of a glistening, cheeselike texture; he had a shock of tow-colored hair, badly cut and greasy, and a snub nose with large gray pores. Under his darting eyes were two black craters. He appeared to be under some intense nervous strain and had sat the night before in the club car drinking bourbon with beer chasers and leafing through magazines which he frowningly tossed aside, like cards into a discard heap. This morning he had come in late, with a hangdog, hangover look, and had been sitting tensely forward on a settee, smoking cigarettes and following the conversation with little twitches of the nose and quivers of the body, as a dog follows a human conversation, veering its mistrustful eyeballs from one speaker to another and raising its head eagerly at its master's voice. The colonel's voice, rich and light and plausible, had in fact abruptly risen and swollen, as he pronounced his last sentence. "I can tell you one thing," he had said harshly. "They weren't named Ryan or Murphy!"

A sort of sigh, as of consummation, ran through the club car. "Pour it on, Colonel, give it to them, Colonel, that's right, Colonel," urged the young man in a transport of admiration. The colonel fingered his collar and modestly smiled. He was a thin, hawklike, black-haired handsome man with a bright blue bloodshot eye and a well-pressed, well-tailored uniform that did not show the effects of the heat—the train, westbound for St. Louis, was passing through Indiana, and, as usual in a heat wave, the air-conditioning had not met the test. He wore the Air Force insignia, and there was something in his light-boned, spruce figure and keen, knifelike profile that suggested a classic image of the aviator, ready to cut, piercing, into space. In base fact, however, the colonel was in procurement, as we heard him tell the mining engineer who had just bought him a drink. From several silken hints that parachuted into the talk, it was patent to us that the colonel was a man who knew how to enjoy this earth and its pleasures: he led, he gave us to think, a bachelor's life of abstemious dissipation and well-rounded sensuality. He had accepted the engineer's drink with a mere nod of the glass in acknowledgment, like a genial Mars quaffing a libation; there was clearly no prospect of his buying a second in return, not if the train were to travel from here to the Mojave Desert. In the same way, an understanding had arisen that I, the only woman in the club car, had become the colonel's perquisite; it was taken for granted, without an invitation's being issued, that I was to lunch with him in St. Louis, where we each had a wait between trains—my plans for seeing the city in a taxicab were dished.

From the beginning, as we eyed each other over my volume of Dickens (*"The Christmas Carol?"* suggested the colonel, opening relations), I had guessed that the colonel was of Irish stock, and this, I felt, gave me an advantage, for he did not suspect the same of me; strangely so, for I am supposed to have the map of Ireland written on my features. In fact, he had just wagered, with a jaunty, sidelong grin at the mining engineer, that my people "came from Boston from way back," and that I—narrowed glance, running, like steel measuring-tape, up and down my form—was a professional sculptress. I might have laughed this off, as a crudely

1.   Originally published in *Harper's* (February 1954), where it was called a "story," "Artists in Uniform" was collected in *On the Contrary* (1961), the source of the present text. McCarthy discussed the piece in an essay, "Settling the Colonel's Hash," also collected in *On the Contrary*. "I myself," she wrote, "would not know quite what to call it; it was a piece of reporting or a fragment of autobiography."

bad guess like his *Christmas Carol*, if I had not seen the engineer nodding gravely, like an idol, and the peculiar young man bobbing his head up and down in mute applause and agreement. I was wearing a bright apple-green raw silk blouse and a dark-green rather full raw silk skirt, plus a pair of pink glass earrings; my hair was done up in a bun. It came to me, for the first time, with a sort of dawning horror, that I had begun, in the course of years, without ever guessing it, to look irrevocably Bohemian. Refracted from the three men's eyes was a strange vision of myself as an artist, through and through, stained with my occupation like the dyer's hand. All I lacked, apparently, was a pair of sandals. My sick heart sank to my Ferragamo shoes; I had always particularly preened myself on being an artist in disguise. And it was not only a question of personal vanity—it seemed to me that the writer or intellectual had a certain missionary usefulness in just such accidental gatherings as this, if he spoke not as an intellectual but as a normal member of the public. Now, thanks to the colonel, I slowly became aware that my contributions to the club-car conversation were being watched and assessed as coming from *a certain quarter*. My costume, it seemed, carefully assembled as it had been at an expensive shop, was to these observers simply a uniform that blazoned a caste and allegiance just as plainly as the colonel's khaki and eagles. *"Gardez,"* I said to myself. But, as the conversation grew tenser and I endeavored to keep cool, I began to writhe within myself, and every time I looked down, my contrasting greens seemed to be growing more and more lurid and taking on an almost menacing light, like leaves just before a storm that lift their bright undersides as the air becomes darker. We had been speaking, of course, of Russia, and I had mentioned a study that had been made at Harvard of political attitudes among Iron Curtain refugees. Suddenly, the colonel had smiled. "They're pretty Red at Harvard, I'm given to understand," he observed in a comfortable tone, while the young man twitched and quivered urgently. The eyes of all the men settled on me and waited. I flushed as I saw myself reflected. The woodland greens of my dress were turning to their complementary red, like a color-experiment in psychology or a traffic light changing. Down at the other end of the club car, a man looked up from his paper. I pulled myself together. "Set your mind at rest, Colonel," I remarked dryly. "I know Harvard very well and they're conservative to the point of dullness. The only thing crimson is the football team." This disparagement had its effect. "So . . .?" queried the colonel. "I thought there was some professor. . . ." I shook my head. "Absolutely not. There used to be a few fellow-travelers, but they're very quiet these days, when they haven't absolutely recanted. The general atmosphere is more anti-Communist than the Vatican." The colonel and the mining engineer exchanged a thoughtful stare and seemed to agree that the Delphic oracle that had just pronounced knew whereof it spoke. "Glad to hear it," said the colonel. The engineer frowned and shook his fat wattles; he was a stately, gray-haired, plump man with small hands and feet and the pampered, finical tidiness of a small-town widow. "There's so much hearsay these days," he exclaimed vexedly. "You don't know *what* to believe."

I reopened my book with an air of having closed the subject and read a paragraph three times over. I exulted to think that I had made a modest contribution to sanity in our times, and I imagined my words pyramiding like a chain letter—the colonel telling a fellow-officer on the veranda of a club in Texas, the engineer halting a works-superintendent in a Colorado mine shaft: "I met a woman on the train who claims . . . Yes, absolutely. . . ." Of course, I did not know Harvard as thoroughly as I pretended, but I forgave myself by thinking it was the convention of such club-car symposia in our positivistic country to speak from the horse's mouth.

Meanwhile, across the aisle, the engineer and the colonel continued their talk in slightly lowered voices. From time to time, the colonel's polished index-fingernail scratched his burnished black head and his knowing blue eye forayed occasionally toward me. I saw that still I was a doubtful quantity to them, a movement in the bushes, a noise, a flicker, that was figuring in their crenelated thought as "she." The subject of Reds in our colleges had not, alas, been finished; they were speaking now of another university and a woman faculty-member who had been issuing Communist statements. This story somehow, I thought angrily, had managed to appear in the newspapers without my knowledge, while these men were conversant with it; I recognized a big chink in the armor of my authority. Looking up from my book, I began to question them sharply, as though they were reporting some unheard-of natural phenomenon. "When?" I demanded. "Where did you see it? What was her name?" This request for the professor's name was a headlong attempt on my part to buttress my position, the implication being that the identities of all university professors were known to me and that if I were but given the name I could promptly clarify the matter. To admit that there was a single Communist in our academic system whose activities were hidden from me imperiled, I instinctively felt, all the small good I had done here. Moreover, in the back of my mind, I had a supreme confidence that these men were wrong: the story, I supposed, was some tattered piece of misinformation they had picked up from a gossip column. Pride, as usual, preceded my fall. To the colonel, the demand for the name was not specific but generic: what *kind* of name was the question he presumed me to be asking. "Oh," he said slowly with a luxurious yawn, "Finkelstein or Fishbein or Feinstein." He lolled back in his seat with a side glance at the engineer, who deeply nodded. There was a voluptuary pause, as the implication sank in. I bit my lip, regarding this as a mere diversionary tactic. "Please!" I said impatiently. "Can't you remember exactly?" The colonel shook his head and then his spare cheekbones suddenly reddened and he looked directly at me. "I can tell you one thing," he exclaimed irefully. "They weren't named Ryan or Murphy."

The colonel went no further; it was quite unnecessary. In an instant, the young man was at his side, yapping excitedly and actually picking at the military sleeve. The poor thing was transformed, like some creature in a fairy tale whom a magic word releases from silence. "That's right, Colonel," he happily repeated. "I know them. *I* was at Harvard in the business school, studying accountancy. I left. I couldn't take it." He threw a poisonous glance at me, and the colonel, who had been regarding him somewhat doubtfully, now put on an alert expression and inclined an ear for his confidences. The man at the other end of the car folded his newspaper solemnly and took a seat by the young man's side. "They're all Reds, Colonel," said the young man. "They teach it in the classroom. I came back here to Missouri. It made me sick to listen to the stuff they handed out. If you didn't hand it back, they flunked you. Don't let anybody tell you different." "You are wrong," I said coldly and closed my book and rose. The young man was still talking eagerly, and the three men were leaning forward to catch his every gasping word, like three astute detectives over a dying informer, when I reached the door and cast a last look over my shoulder at them. For an instant, the colonel's eye met mine and I felt his scrutiny processing my green back as I tugged open the door and met a blast of hot air, blowing my full skirt wide. Behind me, in my fancy, I saw four sets of shrugging brows.

In my own car, I sat down, opposite two fat nuns, and tried to assemble my thoughts. I ought to have spoken, I felt, and yet what could I have said? It occurred to me that the four men had perhaps not realized why I had left the club car with such abruptness: was it possible that they thought I was a Communist, who feared to be unmasked? I spurned this possibility, and yet it made me uneasy. For some reason, it troubled my *amour-propre*[2] to think of my anti-Communist self living on, so to speak, green in their collective memory as a Communist or fellow-traveler. In fact, though I did not give a fig for the men, I hated the idea, while a few years ago I should have counted it a great joke. This, it seemed to me, was a measure of the change in the social climate. I had always scoffed at the notion of liberals "living in fear" of political demagoguery in America, but now I had to admit that if I was not fearful, I was at least uncomfortable in the supposition that anybody, anybody whatever, could think

2. "Self-respect" (French).

of me, precious me, as a Communist. A remoter possibility was, of course, that back there my departure was being ascribed to Jewishness, and this too annoyed me. I am in fact a quarter Jewish, and though I did not "hate" the idea of being taken for a Jew, I did not precisely like it, particularly under these circumstances. I wished it to be clear that I had left the club car for intellectual and principled reasons; I wanted those men to know that it was not I, but my principles, that had been offended. To let them conjecture that I had left because I was Jewish would imply that only a Jew could be affronted by an anti-Semitic outburst; a terrible idea. Aside from anything else, it voided the whole concept of transcendence, which was very close to my heart, the concept that man is more than his circumstances, more even than himself.

However you looked at the episode, I said to myself nervously, I had not acquitted myself well. I ought to have done or said something concrete and unmistakable. From this, I slid glassily to the thought that those men ought to be punished, the colonel, in particular, who occupied a responsible position. In a minute, I was framing a businesslike letter to the Chief of Staff, deploring the colonel's conduct as unbecoming to an officer and identifying him by rank and post, since unfortunately I did not know his name. Earlier in the conversation, he had passed some comments on "Harry"[3] that bordered positively on treason, I said to myself triumphantly. A vivid image of the proceedings against him presented itself to my imagination: the long military tribunal with a row of stern soldierly faces glaring down at the colonel. I myself occupied only an inconspicuous corner of this tableau, for, to tell the truth, I did not relish the role of the witness. Perhaps it would be wiser to let the matter drop . . . ? We were nearing St. Louis now; the colonel had come back into my car, and the young accountant had followed him, still talking feverishly. I pretended not to see them and turned to the two nuns, as if for sanctuary from this world and its hatred and revenges. Out of the corner of my eye, I watched the colonel, who now looked wry and restless; he shrank against the window as the young man made a place for himself amid the colonel's smart luggage and continued to express his views in a pale breathless voice. I smiled to think that the colonel was paying the piper. For the colonel, anti-Semitism was simply an aspect of urbanity, like a knowledge of hotels or women. This frantic psychopath of an accountant was serving him as a nemesis, just as the German people had been served by their psychopath, Hitler. Colonel, I adjured him, you have chosen, between him and me; measure the depth of your error and make the best of it! No intervention on my part was now necessary; justice had been meted out. Nevertheless, my heart was still throbbing violently, as if I were on the verge of some dangerous action. What was I to do, I kept asking myself, as I chatted with the nuns, if the colonel were to hold me to that lunch? And I slowly and apprehensively revolved this question, just as though it were a matter of the most serious import. It seemed to me that if I did not lunch with him—and I had no intention of doing so—I had the dreadful obligation of telling him why.

He was waiting for me as I descended the car steps. "Aren't you coming to lunch with me?" he called out and moved up to take my elbow. I began to tremble with audacity. "No," I said firmly, picking up my suitcase and draping an olive-green linen duster over my arm. "I can't lunch with you." He quirked a wiry black eyebrow. "Why not?" he said. "I understood it was all arranged." He reached for my suitcase. "No," I said, holding on to the suitcase. "I can't." I took a deep breath. "I have to tell you. I think you should be *ashamed* of yourself, Colonel, for what you said in the club car." The colonel stared: I mechanically waved for a redcap, who took my bag and coat and went off. The colonel and I stood facing each other on the emptying platform. "What do you mean?" he inquired in a low, almost clandestine tone. "Those anti-Semitic remarks," I muttered, resolutely. "You ought to be *ashamed.*" The colonel gave a quick, relieved laugh. "Oh, come now," he protested. "I'm sorry," I said. "I can't have lunch with anybody who feels that way about the Jews." The colonel put down his attaché case and scratched the back of his lean neck. "Oh, come now," he repeated, with a look of amusement. "You're not Jewish, are you?" "No," I said quickly. "Well, then . . ." said the colonel, spreading his hands in a gesture of bafflement. I saw that he was truly surprised and slightly hurt by my criticism, and this made me feel wretchedly embarrassed and even apologetic, on my side, as though I had called attention to some physical defect in him, of which he himself was unconscious. "But I might have been," I stammered. "You had no way of knowing. You oughtn't to talk like that." I recognized, too late, that I was strangely reducing the whole matter to a question of etiquette: "Don't start anti-Semitic talk before making sure there are no Jews present." "Oh, hell," said the colonel, easily. "I can tell a Jew." "No, you can't," I retorted, thinking of my Jewish grandmother, for by Nazi criteria I was Jewish. "Of course I can," he insisted. "So can you." We had begun to walk down the platform side by side, disputing with a restrained passion that isolated us like a pair of lovers. All at once, the colonel halted, as though struck with a thought. "What *are* you, anyway?" he said meditatively, regarding my dark hair, green blouse, and pink earrings. Inside myself, I began to laugh. "Oh," I said gaily, playing out the trump I had been saving. "I'm Irish, like you, Colonel." "How did you know?" he said amazedly. I laughed aloud. "I can tell an Irishman," I taunted. The colonel frowned. "What's your family name?" he said brusquely. "McCarthy." He lifted an eyebrow, in defeat, and then quickly took note of my wedding ring. "That your maiden name?" I nodded. Under this peremptory questioning, I had the peculiar sensation that I get when I am lying; I began to feel that "McCarthy" was a nom de plume, a coinage of my artistic personality. But the colonel appeared to be satisfied. "Hell," he said, "come on to lunch, then. With a fine name like that, you and I should be friends." I still shook my head, though by this time we were pacing outside the station restaurant; my baggage had been checked in a locker; sweat was running down my face and I felt exhausted and hungry. I knew that I was weakening and I wanted only an excuse to yield and go inside with him. The colonel seemed to sense this. "Hell," he conceded. "You've got me wrong. I've nothing against the Jews. Back there in the club car, I was just stating a simple fact: you won't find an Irishman sounding off for the Commies. You can't deny that, can you?"

His voice rose persuasively; he took my arm. In the heat, I wilted and we went into the air-conditioned cocktail lounge. The colonel ordered two old-fashioneds. The room was dark as a cave and produced, in the midst of the hot midday, a hallucinated feeling, as though time had ceased, with the weather, and we were in eternity together. As the colonel prepared to relax, I made a tremendous effort to guide the conversation along rational, purposive lines; my only justification for being here would be to convert the colonel. "There *have* been Irishmen associated with the Communist party." I said suddenly, when the drinks came. "I can think of two." "Oh, hell," said the colonel, "every race and nation has its traitors. What I mean is, you won't find them in numbers. You've got to admit the Communists in this country are ninety per cent Jewish." "But the Jews in this country aren't ninety per cent Communist," I retorted.

As he stirred his drink, restively, I began to try to show him the reasons why the Communist movement in America had attracted such a large number, relatively, of Jews: how the Communists had been anti-Nazi when nobody else seemed to care what happened to the Jews in Germany; how the Communists still capitalized on a Jewish fear of fascism; how many Jews had become, after Buchenwald, traumatized by this fear. . . .

But the colonel was scarcely listening. An impatient frown rested on his jaunty features. "I don't get it," he said slowly. "Why should you be for them, with a name like yours?" "I'm *not* for the Communists," I cried. "I'm just trying to explain to you—" "For the Jews," the colonel interrupted, irritable now himself. "I've heard of such people but I never met one before." "I'm not 'for' them," I protested. "You don't understand. I'm not for *any* race or nation. I'm against those who are against them." This word, *them*, with a sort of slurring circle drawn round it, was beginning to sound ugly to me. Automatically, in arguing with him, I seemed to have slipped into the colonel's style of thought. It occurred to me that defense of the Jews could be a subtle and safe form of anti-Semitism, an exercise of patronage: as a rational Gentile, one could feel superior both to the Jews and the anti-Semites. There could be no doubt that the Jewish question evoked a curious stealthy lust or concupiscence. I could feel it now vibrating between us over the dark table. If I had been a good person, I should unquestionably have got up and left.

"I don't get it," repeated the colonel. "How were you brought up? Were your people this way too?" It was manifest that an odd reversal had taken place; each of us regarded the other as "abnormal" and was attempting to understand the etiology of a disease. "Many of my people think just as you do," I said, smiling coldly. "It seems to be a sickness to which the Irish are prone. Perhaps it's due to the potato diet," I said sweetly, having divined that the colonel came from a social stratum somewhat lower than my own.

But the colonel's hide was tough. "You've got me wrong," he reiterated, with an almost plaintive laugh. "I don't dislike the Jews. I've got a lot of Jewish friends. Among themselves, they think just as I do, mark my words. I tell you what it is," he added ruminatively, with a thoughtful prod of his muddler, "I draw a distinction between a kike and a Jew." I groaned. "Colonel, I've never heard an anti-Semite who didn't draw that distinction. You know what Otto Kahn[4] said? 'A kike is a Jewish gentleman who has just left the room.' " The colonel did not laugh. "I don't hold it against some of them," he persisted, in a tone of pensive justice. "It's not their fault if they were born that way. That's what I tell them, and they respect me for my honesty. I've had a lot of discussions; in procurement, you have to do business with them, and the Jews are the first to admit that you'll find more chiselers among their race than among the rest of mankind." "It's not a race," I interjected wearily, but the colonel pressed on. "If I deal with a Jewish manufacturer, I can't bank on his word. I've seen it again and again, every damned time. When I deal with a Gentile, I can trust him to make delivery as promised. That's the difference between the two races. They're just a different breed. They don't have standards of honesty, even among each other." I sighed, feeling unequal to arguing the colonel's personal experience.

"Look," I said, "you may be dealing with an industry where the Jewish manufacturers are the most recent comers and feel they have to cut corners to compete with the established firms. I've heard that said about Jewish cattle-dealers, who are supposed to be extra sharp. But what I think, really, is that you notice it when a Jewish firm fails to meet an agreement and don't notice it when it's a Yankee." "Hah," said the colonel. "They'll tell you what I'm telling you themselves, if you get to know them and go into their homes. You won't believe it, but some of my best friends are Jews," he said, simply and thoughtfully, with an air of originality. "They may be *your* best friends, Colonel," I retorted, "but you are not theirs. I defy you to tell me that you talk to them as you're talking now." "Sure," said the Colonel, easily. "More or less." "They must be very queer Jews you know." I observed tartly, and I began to wonder whether there indeed existed a peculiar class of Jews whose function in life was to be "friends" with such people as the colonel. It was difficult to think that all the anti-Semites who made the colonel's assertion were the victims of a cruel self-deception.

A dispirited silence followed. I was not one of those liberals who believed that the Jews, alone among peoples, possessed no characteristics whatever of a distinguishing nature—this would mean they had no history and no culture, a charge which should be leveled against them only by an anti-Semite. Certainly, types of Jews could be noted and patterns of Jewish thought and feeling: Jewish humor, Jewish rationality, and so on, not that every Jew reflected every attribute of Jewish life or history. But somehow, with the colonel, I dared not concede that there was such a thing as a Jew: I saw the sad meaning of the assertion that a Jew was a person whom other people thought was Jewish.

Hopeless, however, to convey this to the colonel. The desolate truth was that the colonel was extremely stupid, and it came to me, as we sat there, glumly ordering lunch, that for extremely stupid people anti-Semitism was a form of intellectuality, the sole form of intellectuality of which they were capable. It represented, in a rudimentary way, the ability to make

4. Otto Hermann Kahn (1867–1934), German-born American banker and patron of the arts.

categories, to generalize. Hence a thing I had noted before but never understood: the fact that anti-Semitic statements were generally delivered in an atmosphere of profundity. Furrowed brows attended these speculative distinctions between a kike and a Jew, these little empirical laws that you can't know one without knowing them all. To arrive, indeed, at the idea of a Jew was, for these grouping minds, an exercise in Platonic thought, a discovery of essence, and to be able to add the great corollary, "Some of my best friends are Jews," was to find the philosopher's cleft between essence and existence. From this, it would seem, followed the querulous obstinacy with which the anti-Semite clung to his concept; to be deprived of this intellectual tool by missionaries of tolerance would be, for persons like the colonel, the equivalent of Western man's losing the syllogism: a lapse into animal darkness. In the club car, we had just witnessed an example: the colonel with his anti-Semitic observation had come to the mute young man like the paraclete, bearing the gift of tongues.

Here in the bar, it grew plainer and plainer that the colonel did not regard himself as an anti-Semite but merely as a heavy thinker. The idea that I considered him anti-Semitic sincerely outraged his feelings. "Prejudice" was the last trait he could have imputed to himself. He looked on me, almost respectfully, as a "Jew-lover," a kind of being he had heard of but never actually encountered, like a centaur or a Siamese twin, and the interest of relating this prodigy to the natural state of mankind overrode any personal distaste. There I sat, the exception which was "proving" or testing the rule, and he kept pressing me for details of my history that might explain my deviation in terms of the norm. On my side, of course, I had become fiercely resolved that he would learn nothing from me that would make it possible for him to dismiss my anti-anti-Semitism as the product of special circumstances: I was stubbornly sitting on the fact of my Jewish grandmother like a hen on a golden egg. I was bent on making *him* see himself as a monster, a deviation, a heretic from Church and State. Unfortunately, the colonel, owing perhaps to his military training, had not the glimmering of an idea of what democracy meant; to him, it was simply a slogan that was sometimes useful in war. The notion of an ordained inequality was to him "scientific."

"Honestly," he was saying in lowered tones, as our drinks were taken away and the waitress set down my sandwich and his corned-beef hash, "don't you, brought up the way you were, feel about them the way I do? Just between ourselves, isn't there a sort of inborn feeling of horror that the very word, Jew, suggests?" I shook my head, roundly. The idea of an *innate* anti-Semitism was in keeping with the rest of the colonel's thought, yet it shocked me more than anything he had yet said. "No," I sharply replied. "It doesn't evoke any feeling one way or the other." "Honest Injun?" said the colonel. "Think back; when you were a kid, didn't the word, Jew, make you feel sick?" There was a dreadful sincerity about this that made me answer in an almost kindly tone. "No, truthfully, I assure you. When we were children, we learned to call the old-clothes man a sheeny, but that was just a dirty word to us, like 'Hun' that we used to call after workmen we thought were Germans."

"I don't get it," pondered the colonel, eating a pickle. "There must be something wrong with you. Everybody is born with that feeling. It's natural; it's part of nature." "On the contrary," I said. "It's something very unnatural that you must have been taught as a child." "It's not something you're *taught*," he protested. "You must have been," I said. "You simply don't remember it. In any case, you're a man now; you must rid yourself of that feeling. It's psychopathic, like that horrible young man on the train." "You thought he was crazy?" mused the colonel, in an idle, dreamy tone. I shrugged my shoulders. "Of course. Think of his color. He was probably just out of a mental institution. People don't get that tattletale gray except in prison or mental hospitals." The colonel suddenly grinned. "You might be right," he said. "He was quite a case." He chuckled.

I leaned forward. "You know, Colonel," I said quickly, "anti-Semitism is contrary to the Church's teaching. God will make you do penance for hating the Jews. Ask your priest; he'll tell you I'm right. You'll have a long spell in Purgatory, if you don't rid yourself of this sin.

It's a deliberate violation of Christ's commandment, 'Love thy neighbor.' The Church holds that the Jews have a sacred place in God's design. Mary was a Jew and Christ was a Jew. The Jews are under God's special protection. The Church teaches that the millennium can't come until the conversion of the Jews; therefore, the Jews must be preserved that the Divine Will may be accomplished. Woe to them that harm them, for they controvert God's Will!" In the course of speaking, I had swept myself away with the solemnity of the doctrine. The Great Reconciliation between God and His chosen people, as envisioned by the Evangelist, had for me at that moment a piercing, majestic beauty, like some awesome Tintoretto.[5] I saw a noble spectacle of blue sky, thronged with gray clouds, and a vast white desert, across which God and Israel advanced to meet each other, while below in hell the demons of disunion shrieked and gnashed their teeth.

"Hell," said the colonel, jovially, "I don't believe in all that. I lost my faith when I was a kid. I saw that all this God stuff was a lot of bushwa." I gazed at him in stupefaction. His confidence had completely returned. The blue eyes glittered debonairly, the eagles glittered; the narrow polished head cocked and listened to itself like a trilling bird. I was up against an airman with a bird's-eye view, a man who believed in nothing but the law of kind: the epitome of godless materialism. "You still don't hold with that bunk?" the colonel inquired in an undertone, with an expression of stealthy curiosity. "No," I confessed, sad to admit to a meeting of minds. "You know what got me?" exclaimed the colonel. "That birth-control stuff. Didn't it kill you?" I made a neutral sound. "I was beginning to play around," said the colonel, with a significant beam of the eye, "and I just couldn't take that guff. When I saw through the birth-control talk, I saw through the whole thing. They claimed it was against nature, but I claim, if that's so, an operation's against nature. I told my old man that when he was having his kidney stones out. You ought to have heard him yell!" A rich, reminiscent satisfaction dwelt in the colonel's face.

This period of his life, in which he had thrown off the claims of the spiritual and adopted a practical approach, was evidently one of those "turning points" to which a man looks back with pride. He lingered over the story of his break with church and parents with a curious sort of heat, as though the flames of old sexual conquests stirred within his body at the memory of those old quarrels. The looks he rested on me, as a sharer of that experience, grew more and more lickerish and assaying. "What got *you* down?" he finally inquired, settling back in his chair and pushing his coffee cup aside. "Oh," I said wearily, "it's a long story. You can read it when it's published." "You're an author?" cried the colonel, who was really very slow-witted. I nodded, and the colonel regarded me afresh. "What do you write? Love stories?" He gave a half-wink. "No," I said. "Various things. Articles. Books. Highbrowish stories." A suspicion darkened in the colonel's sharp face. "That McCarthy," he said. "Is that your pen name?" "Yes," I said, "but it's my real name too. It's the name I write under *and* my maiden name." The colonel digested this thought. "Oh," he concluded.

A new idea seemed to visit him. Quite cruelly, I watched it take possession. He was thinking of the power of the press and the indiscretions of other military figures, who had been rewarded with demotion. The consciousness of the uniform he wore appeared to seep uneasily into his body. He straightened his shoulders and called thoughtfully for the check. We paid in silence, the colonel making no effort to forestall my dive into my pocketbook. I should not have let him pay in any case, but it startled me that he did not try to do so, if only for reasons of vanity. The whole business of paying, apparently, was painful to him; I watched his facial muscles contract as he pocketed the change and slipped two dimes for the waitress onto the table, not daring quite to hide them under the coffee cup—he had short-changed me on the bill and the tip, and we both knew it. We walked out into the steaming station and I took my baggage out of the checking locker. The colonel carried my

5. Venetian painter (1518–1596).

suitcase and we strolled along without speaking. Again, I felt horribly embarrassed for him. He was meditative, and I supposed that he too was mortified by his meanness about the tip.

"Don't get me wrong," he said suddenly, setting the suitcase down and turning squarely to face me, as though he had taken a big decision. "I may have said a few things back there about the Jews getting what they deserved in Germany." I looked at him in surprise; actually, he had not said that to me. Perhaps he had let it drop in the club car after I had left. "But that doesn't mean I approve of Hitler." "I should hope not," I said. "What I mean is," said the colonel, "that they probably gave the Germans a lot of provocation, but that doesn't excuse what Hitler did." "No," I said, somewhat ironically, but the colonel was unaware of anything satiric in the air. His face was grave and determined; he was sorting out his philosophy for the record. "I mean, I don't approve of his methods," he finally stated. "No," I agreed. "You mean, you don't approve of the gas chamber." The colonel shook his head very severely. "Absolutely not! That was terrible." He shuddered and drew out a handkerchief and slowly wiped his brow. "For God's sake," he said, "don't get me wrong. I think they're human beings." "Yes," I assented, and we walked along to my track. The colonel's spirits lifted, as though, having stated his credo, he had both got himself in line with public policy and achieved an autonomous thought. "I mean," he resumed, "you may not care for them, but that's not the same as killing them, in cold blood, like that." "No, Colonel," I said.

He swung my bag onto the car's platform and I climbed up behind it. He stood below, smiling, with upturned face. "I'll look for your article," he cried, as the train whistle blew. I nodded, and the colonel waved, and I could not stop myself from waving back at him and even giving him the corner of a smile. After all, I said to myself, looking down at him, the colonel was "a human being." There followed one of those inane intervals in which one prays for the train to leave. We both glanced at our watches. "See you some time," he called. "What's your married name?" "Broadwater," I called back. The whistle blew again. "Brodwater?" shouted the colonel, with a dazed look of unbelief and growing enlightenment; he was not the first person to hear it as a Jewish name, on the model of Goldwater. "B-r-o-a-d," I began, automatically, but then I stopped. I disdained to spell it out for him; the victory was his. "One of the chosen, eh?" his brief grimace seemed to commiserate. For the last time, and in the final fullness of understanding, the hawk eye patrolled the green dress, the duster, and the earrings; the narrow flue of his nostril contracted as he curtly turned away. The train commenced to move.

1954, 1961

Tillie Olsen
(1913?–   )

One of seven children born to immigrant parents who fled Russia after the 1905 rebellion, Tillie Lerner could not afford to continue attending high school in Omaha, Nebraska, after the eleventh grade. Working in factories, food processing plants, and slaughterhouses, she got her education from reading; in a 1972 interview she stated her debt to "books that contributed a comprehension of so many other human lives and human situations."

One particular narrative had a germinal influence on her writing. When she was 15 years old she bought a stack of used magazines, including a coverless *Atlantic Monthly* that contained a long narrative called *Life in the Iron Mills*. In keeping with the magazine's editorial policy, the piece was printed with no authorial attribution, and Olsen did not find out for thirty years that the work she so much admired had been written by another woman, Rebecca Harding Davis. The young reader's experience of seeing in print depictions of working people and the harsh industrial conditions they were exposed to demonstrated that the life she knew could become the subject for serious writing and that the effect on readers could be striking. Years later, in 1972, Olsen edited the nearly forgotten out-of-print work, with a long essay detailing Davis's experiences of conflict between family life and career and the personal, historical, and political significance of her book. The publication revived an early realist's female views for a new generation of readers.

Imprisoned in the early 1930s for her involvement in attempts to unionize packinghouse workers, Lerner became seriously ill. The forced rest gave her the opportunity to write for the first time, and she began a novel about a young girl's experiences in a Wyoming coal-mining town. Portions of the narrative were published in magazines, but the respite from her harsh struggle for existence was brief, and the germ of a novel was packed away for nearly forty years before its revision and publication as *Yonnondio: From the Thirties* in 1974.

In 1933 she moved to California, where she met and married Jack Olsen, a union organizer and printer. As she noted in *Silences* (1978), her life in the following years was absorbed with rearing five children, working as a secretary or waitress, and participating in union or political activities, so "the simplest circumstances for creation did not exist."

In the 1950s, with her youngest child in school, she was able to turn her attention to writing once again. The title novella of her collection *Tell Me a Riddle* (1961) won the O. Henry Award as the best American story of the year. Recognition for that book brought invitations to teach at universities as well as Guggenheim Foundation and National Endowment for the Humanities fellowships to encourage her writing. In a series of important essays, Olsen dealt with the crucial role of family and social circumstances in the careers of creative women.

Olsen also edited *Mother to Daughter, Daughter to Mother: A Daybook and Reader* (1984). Elaine Neil Orr's *Tillie Olsen and the Feminist Spiritual Vision* (1987) charts the significance of Olsen's thoughts for feminist readers.

A large portion of the following narrative was first printed as "The Iron Throat" by Tillie Lerner in the *Partisan Review* (April–May 1934). Revised and lengthened, it became the first chapter of *Yonnondio*. The text of the selection is from the novel.

FROM YONNONDIO
The Iron Throat

The whistles always woke Mazie. They pierced into her sleep like some guttural-voiced metal beast, tearing at her; breathing a terror. During the day if the whistle blew, she knew it meant death—somebody's poppa or brother, perhaps her own—in that fearsome place below the ground, the mine.

"God damn that blowhorn," she heard her father mutter. Creak of him getting out of bed. The door closed, with yellow light from the kerosene lamp making a long crack on the floor. Clatter of dishes. Her mother's tired, grimy voice.

"What'll ya have? Coffee and eggs? There aint no bacon."

"Dont bother with anything. Havent time. I gotta stop by Kvaternicks and get the kid. He's starting work today."

"What're they going to give him?"

"Little of everything at first, I guess, trap, throw switches. Maybe timberin."

"Well, he'll be starting one punch ahead of the old man. Chris began as a breaker boy." (Behind both stolid faces the claw of a buried thought—and maybe finish like him, buried under slaty roof that the company hadn't bothered to timber.)

"He's thirteen, ain't he?" asked Anna.

"I guess. Nearer to fourteen."

"Marie was tellin me, it would break Chris's heart if he only knew. He wanted the kid to be different, get an edjication."

"Yeah? Them foreigners do have funny ideas."

"Oh, I dunno. Then she says that she wants the girls to become nuns so they won't have to worry where the next meal's comin from, or have to have kids."

"Well, what other earthly use can a woman have, I'd like to know?"

"She says she doesnt want 'em raisin a lot of brats to get their heads blowed off in the mine. I guess she takes Chris's . . . passing away pretty hard. It's kinda affected her mind. She keeps talkin about the old country, the fields, and what they thought it would be like here—all buried in da bowels of earth, she finishes."

"Say, what does she think she is, a poet?"

"And she talks about the coal. Says it oughta be red, and let people see how they get it with blood."

"Quit your woman's blabbin," said Jim Holbrook, irritated suddenly. "I'm goin now."

Morning sounds. Scrunch of boots. The tinkle of his pail, swinging. Shouted greetings to fellow workers across the street. Her mother turning down the yellow light and creaking into bed. All the sounds of the morning weaving over the memory of the whistle like flowers growing lovely over a hideous corpse. Mazie slept again.

Anna Holbrook lay in the posture of sleep. Thoughts, like worms, crept within her. Of Marie Kvaternick, of Chris's dreams for the boys, of the paralyzing moment when the iron throat of the whistle shrieked forth its announcement of death, and women poured from every house to run for the tipple. Of her kids—Mazie, Will, Ben, the baby. Mazie for all her six and a half years was like a woman sometimes. It's living like this does it, she thought; makes 'em old before their time. Thoughts of the last accident writhed in her blood—there were whispered rumors that the new fire boss, the super's nephew, never made the trips to see if there was gas. Didn't the men care? They never let on. The whistle. In her a deep man's voice suddenly arose, moaning over and over, "God, God, God."

The sun sent its grimy light through the window of the three-room wooden shack, twitching over Mazie's face, filtering across to where Anna Holbrook bent over the washtub. Mazie awoke suddenly; the baby was crying. She stumbled over to the wooden box that held him, warming the infant to her body. Then she dressed, changed the baby's diaper with one of the old flour sacks her mother used for the purpose and went into the kitchen.

"Ma, what's there to eat?"

"Coffee. It's on the stove. Wake Will and Ben and dont bother me. I got washin to do." Later. "Ma?"

"Yes."

"What's an edication?"

"An edjication?" Mrs. Holbrook arose from amidst the shifting vapors of the washtub and, with the suds dripping from her red hands, walked over and stood impressively over Mazie. "An edjication is what you kids are going to get. It means your hands stay white and you read books and work in an office. Now, get the kids and scat. But dont go too far, or I'll knock your block off."

Mazie lay under the hot Wyoming sun, between the outhouse and the garbage dump. There was no other place for Mazie to lie, for the one patch of green in the yard was between these two spots. From the ground arose a nauseating smell. Food had been rotting in the garbage piles for years. Mazie pushed her mind hard against things half known, not known. "I am Mazie Holbrook," she said softly. "I am a-knowen things. I can diaper a baby. I can tell ghost stories. I know words and words. Tipple.[1] Edjication. Bug dust. Supertendent. My poppa can lick any man in this here town. Sometimes the whistle blows and everyone starts a-runnen. Things come a-blowen my hair and it is soft, like the baby laughin." A phrase trembled into her mind, "Bowels of earth." She shuddered. It was mysterious and terrible to her. "Bowels of earth. It means the mine. Bowels is the stummy. Earth is a stummy and mebbe she ets the men that come down. Men and daddy goin' in like the day and comin out black. Earth black and pop's face and hands black, and he spits from his mouth black. Night comes and it is black. Coal is black—it makes a fire. The sun is makin a fire on me, but it is not black. Some color I am not knowen it is," she said wistfully, "but I'll have that learnin' someday. Poppa says the ghosts down there start a fire. That's what blowed Sheen McEvoy's face off so it's red. It made him crazy. Night be comen and everything becomes like under the ground. I think I could find coal then. And a lamp like poppa's comes out, but in the sky. Momma looks all day as if she thinks she's goin to be hearin something. The whistle blows. Poppa says it is the ghosts laughin 'cause they have hit a man in the stummy, or on the head. Chris, that happenened too. Chris, who sang those funny songs. He was a furriner. Bowels of earth they put him in. Callin it dead. Mebbe it's for coal, more coal. That's one thing I'm not a-knowen. Day comes and night comes and the whistle blows and payday comes. Like the flats runnin on the tipple they come—one right a-followen the other. Mebbe I am black inside too. . . . The bowels of earth. . . . The things I know but am not knowen. . . . Sun on me and bowels of earth under . . ."

Andy Kvaternick stumbles through the night. The late September wind fills the night with lost and crying voices and drowns all but the largest stars. Chop, chop goes the black sea of his mind. How wild and stormy inside, how the shipwrecked thoughts plunge and whirl. Andy lifts his face to the stars and breathes frantic, like an almost drowned man.

But it is useless, Andy. The coal dust lies too far inside; it will lie there forever, like a hand squeezing your heart, choking at your throat. The bowels of earth have claimed you.

Breathe and breathe. How fresh the night. But the air you will know will only be sour with sweat, and this strong wind on your body turn to the clammy hands of sweat tickling under your underwear.

Breathe and breathe, Andy, turn your eyes to the stars. Their beauty, never known before, pricks like tears. You belong to a starless night now, unimaginably black, without light, like death. Perhaps the sweat glistening on the roof rock seen for an instant will seem like stars.

And no more can you stand erect. You lose that heritage of man, too. You are brought now to fit earth's intestines, stoop like a hunchback underneath, crawl like a child, do your man's work lying on your side, stretched and tense as a corpse. The rats shall be your birds, and the rocks plopping in the water your music. And death shall be your wife, who woos you in the brief moments when coal leaps from a bursting side, when a cross-piece falls and barely misses your head, when you barely catch the ladder to bring you up out of the hole you are dynamiting.

Breathe and lift your face to the night, Andy Kvaternick. Trying so vainly in some inarticulate way to purge your bosom of the coal dust. Your father had dreams. You too, like all boys, had dreams—vague dreams, of freedom and light and cheering throngs and happiness. The earth will take those too. You will leave them in, to replace the coal, to bear up the roof instead of the pillar the super

1. The structure above a mine shaft where the loaded cars are emptied by tipping.

ordered you to rob. Earth sucks you in, to spew out the coal, to make a few fat bellies fatter. Earth takes your dreams that a few may languidly lie on couches and trill "How exquisite" to paid dreamers.

Someday the bowels will grow monstrous and swollen with these old tired dreams, swell and break, and strong fists batter the fat bellies, and skeletons of starved children batter them, and perhaps you will be slugged by a thug hired by the fat bellies, Andy Kvaternick. Or death will take you to bed at last, or you will strangle with that old crony of miners, the asthma.

But walk in the night now, Andy Kvaternick, lift your face to the night, and desperately, like an almost drowned man, breathe and breathe. "Andy," they are calling to you, in their lusty voices, your fellow workers—it is an old story to them now. "Have one on us." The stuff burns down your throat. The thoughts lie shipwrecked and very still far underneath the black sea of your mind; you are gay and grave, knowing that you can never breathe the dust out. You have taken your man's burden, and you have the miner's only friend the earth gives, strong drink, Andy Kvaternick.

For several weeks Jim Holbrook had been in an evil mood. The whole household walked in terror. He had nothing but heavy blows for the children, and he struck Anna too often to remember. Every payday he clumped home, washed, went to town, and returned hours later, dead drunk. Once Anna had questioned him timidly concerning his work; he struck her on the mouth with a bellow of "Shut your damn trap."

Anna too became bitter and brutal. If one of the children was in her way, if they did not obey her instantly, she would hit at them in a blind rage, as if it were some devil she was exorcising. Afterward, in the midst of her work, regret would cramp her heart at the memory of the tear-stained little faces. " 'Twasn't them I was beatin up on. Somethin just seems to get into me when I have somethin to hit."

Friday came again. Jim returned with his pay, part money, most company script. Little Will, in high spirits, ran to meet him, not noticing his father's sullen face. Tugging on his pant's leg, Willie begged for a ghost story of the mine. He got a clout on the head that sent him sprawling. "Keep your damn brats from under my feet," Jim threatened in a violent rage, while Anna only stared at him, almost paralyzed, "and stop looking at me like a stuck pig."

The light from the dusk came in, cold, malignant. Anna sat in the half dark of the window, her head bent over her sewing in the attitude of a woman weeping. Willie huddled against her skirt, whimpering. Outside the wind gibbered and moaned. The room was suddenly chill. Some horror, some sense of evil seemed on everything.

It came to Mazie like dark juices of undefined pain, pouring into her, filling the heart in her breast till it felt big, like the world. Fear came that her heart would push itself out, roll out like a ball. She clutched the baby closer to her, tight, tight, to hold the swollen thing inside. Her dad stood in the washtub, nude, splashing water on his big chunky body. The menacing light was on him, too. Fear for him came to Mazie, yet some alien sweetness mixed with it, watching him there.

"I would be a-cryen," she whispered to herself, "but all the tears is stuck inside me. All the world is a-cryen, and I don't know for why. And the ghosts may get daddy. Now he's goin' away, but he'll come back with somethin sweet but sicklike hangin on his breath, and hit momma and start the baby a-bawlen. If it was all a dream, if I could only just wake up and daddy'd be smilin, and momma laughin, and us playin. All the world a-cryen and I don't know for why. . . . Maybe daddy'll know—daddy knowen everything." The huge question rose in her, impossible to express, too huge to understand. She ached with it. "I'll ask Daddy." To ask him—to force him into some recognition of her existence, her desire, her emotions.

As Jim Holbrook strode down the dirt street, he heard a fine patter-patter and a thin "Pop." He wheeled. It was Mazie. "You little brat," he said, the anger he had felt still smoldering in him. "What're you runnin away from home for? Get back or I'll skin you alive."

She came toward him, half cringing. "Pop, lemme go with you. Pop, I wanna know what ... what makes people a-cryen. Why don't you tell us ghost stories no more, Pop?" The first words had tumbled out, but now a silence came. "Don't send me home, Pop."

The rough retort Jim Holbrook had meant to make vanished before the undersized figure of Mazie, outlined so clearly against the cold sunset. In some vague way, the questions hurt him. What call's a kid got, he thought, asking questions like that? Though the cramp in his back from working, lying on his side all day, shot through him like hot needles, he stopped and took her hand.

"Don't be worryin your head with such things, Big-eyes—it'll bust. Wait'll you grow up."

"Pop, you said there was ghosts in the mine, black, not white, so's you couldn't see 'em. And they chased a feller, and then when they got him they laughed, but people think it's just the whistle. Pop, they wouldn't chase you, would they?" The fear was out at last.

"Why," chuckled Jim, "I'd like to see 'em try it. I'd just throw them over my shoulder, like this." He lifted her, swung her over his shoulder, set her down. "My right shoulder, or it wouldn't work. And then I'd pin 'em down with the crossbar so they'd have as much chance as a turkey at Thanksgiving. Now, how'd you like to ride to town on poppa's shouldiehorse and buggy, and get served with a sucker?"

Mazie smiled, but her heart was still sad. "Pop, does the boss man honest have a white shiny tub bigger than you and he turns somethin and the water comes out? Or is it a story? And does he honest have a toilet right inside the house? And silks on the floor?" She held her breath.

"Sure, Big-eyes. And they eat on white tablecloths, a new one, every night."

"How come he aint livin like we do? How come we aint livin like him, Pop?"

Why indeed? For a moment Jim was puzzled. " 'Cause he's a coal operator, that's why."

"Oh"—another wall of things not understood gone up. Something made the difference. A big word. Like what happened to Miss Tikas when she was cut up. But how could he cut up a mine? His knife would have to be awful big.

"But you could lick him, Pop, couldn't you? Couldn't you lick anybody?"

"Sure." And to prove it he told her an elaborate story of three dogs he fought, each big as a horse, finishing triumphantly, "Now, do you think anybody could lick your daddy?"

"Pop, I can make the bacon when I stand up on the box, and I can wash the baby, honest. Pop, momma says I'm gonna get an edjication, and my hands white. Is that a story, Pop?"

Fillin the kid's head with fool ideas, he thought wrathfully. But she could become a teacher. Aloud—"Sure you are. You'll go to college and read books and marry a—" his stomach revolted at the thought of a mine boss—"a doctor. And," he finished, "eat on white table-cloths."

She trotted along. Somehow the question she had meant to have answered could not be clamped into words. They reached the one street. Her dad went into the company store to buy her a sucker. Afterward when he went into the saloon, she slipped out to the culm[2] bank that rose like an enormous black mountain at the edge of the street. One side was on fire and weird; gorgeous colors flamed from it. The colors swirled against the night, reds and blues, oranges and yellows. "Like babies' tongues reachin out to you. Like what happens to the back of your eyes when you close 'em after seein the sun, only that hurts. Like all the world come a-colored," she whispered softly to herself. "Mazie Holbrook is a-watchin you," she whispered, "purty tongues." And gently, gently, the hard swollen lump of tears melted into a swell of wonder and awe.

It was cold and damp. Mazie shivered a little, but the shiver was pleasant. The wind came from the north, flinging fine bits of the coal dust from the culm against her face. They stung.

---

2. Piles of dust and waste from the mine.

Somehow it reminded her of the rough hand of her father when he caressed her, hurting her, but not knowing it, hurting with a pleasant hurt. "I am a-watching you, purty tongues."

Sheen McEvoy, lurching out of the saloon, saw a fluttering patch of white against the black culm. "Ghosts," he whispered to himself. His throat became dry. A lost ghost, sent out of the mine, and *white.* "God." The wind shivered against him. Against the culm he saw letters of fire dancing a devil's dance. For a paralyzing instant they danced together, writing a mine blowup. They seared Sheen McEvoy's eyes almost with the terrifying pain of the gas explosion that had blown his face off and taken his mind. The culm made a long finger of shadow toward him—the stars pointed, pointed. "No, no," he moaned, "don't make me have to save 'em."

In Sheen McEvoy's mind insanity dwelled, like a caged wind. Sometimes it was a hurricane, whistling crazily, tearing, making whirlpools of thought, driving his body to distorted movements. Sometimes an old forlorn wind, with the tired voice of dead people, barely touching him, creeping along the sensitive surface. Sometimes the wind spoke or laughed in him. Then awful prophecies came to his tongue. To him, the mine was alive—a thousand-armed creature, with ghosts hanging from the crossbeams, ghosts living in the coal swearing revenge when their homes were broken into. Once fire had risen from earth to sky, clutched at his face, borne it away. Looking in the mirror at himself, he thought now some ghost in the coal was wearing it, laughing.

The wind began its whining. He ran unsteadily for the white flutterflutter. Dazed, he saw it was a small child, with unholy eyes, green. A voice spoke in him, "A little child, pure of heart." *That* was it. The mine was hungry for a child; she was reaching her thousand arms for it. "She only takes men 'cause she aint got kids. All women want kids." Thoughts whirled in colors—licking to flame; exultation leaped up in him.

Sheen McEvoy will fill you, ol' lady. His laugh, horrible as the cracked thin laughter of old breastless women watching youth, sent the night unsteady. Mazie looked up. Sheen McEvoy was standing above her, laughing. Her heart congealed. The red mass of jelly that was his face was writhing, like a heart torn suddenly out of the breast, and he laughed and laughed. Mazie wanted to run; her mind fainted on the thought of her father, strong and tall, so far away. She turned to go.

He held her. His body was hot and putrid. Stinking. "You're the mine's baby now," he said, holding her tight. "The mine'll hold ya like that, pretty baby." Screams tore at Mazie's throat, caged there. Sweat poured over her. She closed her eyes. He strode toward the shaft. He kissed her with his shapeless face. In Mazie her heart fainted, and fainted, but her head stayed clear. "Make it a dream, Momma, Poppa, come here, make it a dream." But no words would come.

Instead another voice, thundering. "What are you doing with that kid, McEvoy?" No words would come. But he—his breath stinking, the jelly opening in the middle. "Stand out of my way. The mine is calling for her baby. Men'll die—but they'll live if she gets the baby. Stand back."

The night watchman's mouth came open. "Put her down."

Sheen McEvoy strode on, oblivious. Angels were singing in his head, men were singing—glad praise, saved men. Her body was soft and warm. "Lift my arms and throw her down the shaft and the mine'll forget about men."

"Put her down."

"Give her a sweet baby, and she'll want no more." Angels singing, men, strong-bodied men, marching and singing, saved. Her body, soft, trembled against him. Ecstasy sang. Now the shaft, hungry mouth.

"I am giving you your baby." He lifted his arms. Mazie saw down, but there was no bottom. Her scream sounded now, answered by his laughter: shrill, cracked, horrible.

Darkness came like lightning. His arms loosened. Mazie rolled, barely missing the shaft. Rising, she crawled, toward what she did not know. The tipple rose like a tree, without leaves, above her. Words came, drunken. Fear. "Poppa." Behind a figure rose, menacing; swung. A miner's pickax. Blindness on two men, fighting. The ax swings, misses. A gun spurts, one, two, three; lovely fire colored like on the culm, colored like the thoughts in McEvoy's head. One instant angels singing, men marching and singing, saved men; the mine yawning, hungry; soft body trembling to him. Blackness now. Black as the day in the mine. Over and over a body lurches, dips into a shaft, thuds thuds against the sides. The clouds, throwing their shadow, give for an instant a smile, inscrutable, to the mouth of the mine.

Into the saloon, like some apparition, came the nightman, bloody of face and clothes, carrying a child. The men looking up from their drink, laughter and oaths cut off, stared astounded. Breathing heavily, he walked to the center of the room and asked fiercely, "Whose kid is this?"

The whiskey making giddiness of his veins, Holbrook turned. The oath, so like a laugh, died on his lips. The kid was Mazie. "It's my kid," he answered gruffly. "What the hell are *you* doin with her?"

"You oughta thank your damn guts I am doin something with her. Why didn't you watch her, if she's your kid?"

The whiskey made a lovely golden fog in his head. Not understanding, he lurched to the nightman, taking the kid away. "What you been doin?" he asked sharply. "What did you run away for?" Her eyes opened for an instant. Questioning and impersonal like a wounded animal's, they stared at him. Uncomprehending, meaning to roar some oath, he looked toward the nightman. The tense, accusing face came like a wind, blowing the fog with cold sharp wings. "What happened?" he asked tersely, still shaking Mazie.

"Stop shaking the kid, she can't answer you, she's sick. And who wouldn't be? That bastard McEvoy went on another loony spree. Picked her up somewhere and gets the idea the mine wants a baby, as if it don't get enough grownups. Comes to the shaft laughing and singing about the men he's going to 'deliver.' When I looked for the kid she was crawlin like some blind animal. Scared to death."

"The sonofabitch," roared Holbrook, "I'll kill him. Where is he?"

"Keel him, leench him," one man muttered angrily.

"The mine done the job for you. He fell down the shaft he was aimin to throw her down."

Holbrook felt as if he were drowning. He felt weak, like a child. My baby, this happened too, he thought. He shook her again, but gently. The stirring of her body against him was insufferably sweet anguish.

"Geev her a sweeg dees," one of the Greeks offered roughly. "That waken her up."

"No, Nick, I'm taking her home. Anna'll fix her up. Got a coat, anybody?"

Tenderly he wrapped her in one, letting no one else touch her. Walking home, he still felt as if he were drowning. Once when she opened her eyes and in a dream-voice murmured, "Poppa, you came," tears stung his eyes.

"My baby, this had to happen too." A monstrous thought gripped him. Frightened, he shook her roughly. "What did he do to you, Mazie, Big-eyes, what did he do to you?" He ran for the yellow light that made a neat block on the road.

Anna was still by the window sewing, in the attitude of a woman weeping. But her eyes were tearless—they shone at him like hard bright steel. "You're home early. Get homesick?"

Remorse added to terror and shame. "Anna," he said, so broken, so tender, her heart leaped. "Jim?"

"The kid. She. Maybe . . ." He could not speak.

"Mazie?" cried Anna, shrill. "What happened? What've you done to her?" She snatched the child, spoke to her, took her to the light. There was a small bruise on her forehead, scratches on her face.

"You beat up on her, you dirty bastard."

"No, listen, Anna." He told her the story, tremblingly told his fear. He was like a child. Terrified, he heard Anna's hysterical laughter—then her calm.

"She hasn't been touched. She'd have been all bloody if he had. But God only knows how hurt she is. Put on hot water, you, and bring some whiskey into the bedroom." She carried Mazie onto their cot and tumbled hot whiskey and tea down her throat.

Jim sat and held the lamp. His wavering shadow looked at him from the wall. Feeling Mazie's burning head, her body moist with sweat, he asked, "Shouldn't I get a doctor?"

"Forget where you are? You know there's only the company doc—and a vets better'n him. She'll be all right. Looks like she might've hurt her head fallin, or maybe she's just scared. Poor baby, poor baby, I'll give her more hot whiskey."

The wind, starting up outside, shook against the house, and Mazie in the quiet of the bedroom began crying, tossing, calling out fragments of sentences, incoherent words. Will, waking, saw how his father sat so still and terrible. Still in his sleep, he began to whimper— "Dont hit me. Poppa, dont. I didn't mean nothing." Unsteadily Jim stood up. The waters seemed closing over his head again: a grimy face turned up to him, pleading, "A story, Pop," and a hand that had crashed down over it. Almost timidly he rubbed that hand against the soft head. "You're dreaming, Will boy," he whispered. "Sleep agin. Try to sleep."

He turned down the light. The new-made, concealing darkness came welcome to them both. "Listen." He gripped her shoulders. "We're clearin out in spring, you hear? We'll save every cent. We'll go to Dakota. Spring's the time to begin a new life, aint it? I'll farm. That's a good job—I could do it, tried my hand at everything else. Or maybe we'll go to Denver— get on at the slaughterhouse. No—it'll be farmin, workin with ground, not rock. Ground smells sweet. And it's good for the kids, right, Anna? We'll make it a new life in the spring?"

In her delirium Mazie laughed—terrible laughter, mocking, derisive, not her own. Anna and Jim, hearing it mix with their words, shuddered.

1934, 1974

Gwendolyn Brooks
(1917–   )

The first African American to win a Pulitzer Prize in poetry, and the first black woman to be elected to the National Institute of Arts and Letters and to be appointed as Poetry Consultant to the Library of Congress, Gwendolyn Brooks has also been honored by numerous other awards, including over fifty honorary degrees. Born in Topeka, Kansas, and brought to Chicago as an infant, she has lived mostly in Chicago ever since, writing poetry as early as age 7, when her mother proclaimed her the future "lady Paul Laurence Dunbar." Published in a children's magazine at 13, by 16 she was contributing poetry to the weekly *Chicago Defender*, which also published the work of James Weldon Johnson and Langston Hughes,

older poets who encouraged her and provided models of poetic accomplishment.

Graduated from Englewood High School in 1934 and from Wilson Junior College two years later, she worked a few years, then married in 1939. A poetry workshop run by Inez Cunningham Stark at the South Side Community Art Center helped her continue her development, and her first collection, *A Street in Bronzeville* (1945), was warmly received. With her second, *Annie Allen* (1949), she won the Pulitzer Prize. In her next book, the novel *Maud Martha* (1953), she showed her ability to capture in prose a ghetto woman's struggle with self-doubts concerning her personal worth. With *The Bean Eaters* (1960) she returned to verse, confirming her skill. All her work to the 1960s was focused on black life in Chicago, written, as she said of *A Street in Bronzeville,* in the hope that "people would recognize instantly that Negroes are just like other people; they have the same hates and loves and fears, the same tragedies and triumphs and deaths, as people of any race or religion or nationality."

Her career took a new turn, however, in 1967, in a personal reaction to changes in the 1960s that were wide-ranging in American poetry and American life. Poetry was opening up, dropping its deference both to the traditional metrics of Dickinson and Frost and to the elaborately multilayered intellectual constructions of the Pound and Eliot school of modernism. Desire for change was everywhere, with the special concerns of African Americans expressed variously as civil rights or Black Power. At a Fisk University Writers' Conference in the spring of 1967, not long before the devastating riots of that summer, Brooks found herself impressed by the energy of younger poets like Amiri Baraka, and by their message: "black poets should write as blacks, about blacks, and address themselves to blacks." Although she had never thought it necessary to be told that black is beautiful, beginning with her next book, *In the Mecca* (1968), she began to write more directly of black concerns. Somewhat later, she began to publish only with African-American publishers—with Dudley Randall's Broadside Press, Haki R. Madhubuti's Third World Press, and her own David Company. Books from this later phase include *Riot* (1969), *Family Pictures* (1970), *To Disembark* (1981), and *The Near Johannesburg Boy* (1987). Although the poems of this later period have not generally found the favor of her first books of verse, or of her novel, *Maud Martha,* they stand as continuing evidence of a lifelong commitment to art and to people.

Collections of Brooks's verse—none complete—include *Selected Poems* (1963); *The World of Gwendolyn Brooks* (1971); and *Blacks* (1987), the source of the texts below. *Report from Part One* (1972) is an autobiography.
Studies include Harry B. Shaw, *Gwendolyn Brooks* (1980); D. H. Melhem, *Gwendolyn Brooks: Poetry and the Heroic Voice* (1987); and George E. Kent, *A Life of Gwendolyn Brooks* (1990).

A Song in the Front Yard

I've stayed in the front yard all my life.
I want a peek at the back
Where it's rough and untended and hungry weed grows.
A girl gets sick of a rose.

I want to go in the back yard now   5
And maybe down the alley,
To where the charity children play.
I want a good time today.

They do some wonderful things.
They have some wonderful fun.   10
My mother sneers, but I say it's fine
How they don't have to go in at quarter to nine.
My mother, she tells me that Johnnie Mae
Will grow up to be a bad woman.
That George'll be taken to Jail soon or late   15
(On account of last winter he sold our back gate.)

But I say it's fine. Honest, I do.
And I'd like to be a bad woman, too,
And wear the brave stockings of night-black lace
And strut down the streets with paint on my face.   20

1945

The Vacant Lot

Mrs. Coley's three-flat brick
Isn't here any more.
All done with seeing her fat little form
Burst out of the basement door;
And with seeing her African son-in-law   5
(Rightful heir to the throne)
With his great white strong cold squares of teeth
And his little eyes of stone;
And with seeing the squat fat daughter
Letting in the men   10
When majesty has gone for the day—
And letting them out again.

1945

Queen of the Blues

Mame was singing
At the Midnight Club.
And the place was red
With blues.
She could shake her body   5
Across the floor.
For what did she have
To lose?

She put her mama
Under the ground   10
Two years ago.
(Was it three?)
She covered that grave
With roses and tears.
(A handsome thing   15
To see.)

She didn't have any
Legal pa
To glare at her,
To shame   20

Her off the floor
Of the Midnight Club.
Poor Mame.

She didn't have any
Big brother   25
To shout
"No sister of mine ! . ."
She didn't have any
Small brother
To think she was everything   30
Fine.

She didn't have any
Baby girl
With velvet
Pop-open eyes.   35
She didn't have any
Sonny boy
To tell sweet
Sonny boy lies.

"Show me a man   40
What will love me
Till I die.
Now show me a man
What will love me
Till I die.   45
Can't find no such a man
No matter how hard
You try.
Go 'long, baby.
Ain't a true man left   50
In Chi.

"I loved my daddy.
But what did my daddy
Do?
I loved my daddy.   55
But what did my daddy
Do?
Found him a brown-skin chicken
What's gonna be
Black and blue.   60

"I was good to my daddy.
Gave him all my dough.
I say, I was good to my daddy.
I gave him all of my dough.
Scrubbed hard in them white folks'   65
Kitchens
Till my knees was rusty
And so'."

The M.C. hollered,
"Queen of the blues!   70
Folks, this is strictly
The queen of the blues!"
She snapped her fingers.
She rolled her hips.
What did she have   75
To lose?

But a thought ran through her
Like a fire.
"Men don't tip their
Hats to me.   80
They pinch my arms
And they slap my thighs.
But when has a man
Tipped his hat to me?"

Queen of the blues!   85
Queen of the blues!
Strictly, strictly,
The queen of the blues!

Men are low down
Dirty and mean.   90
Why don't they tip
Their hats to a queen?

1945

The Bean Eaters

They eat beans mostly, this old yellow pair.
Dinner is a casual affair.
Plain chipware on a plain and creaking wood,
Tin flatware.

Two who are Mostly Good.   5
Two who have lived their day,
But keep on putting on their clothes
And putting things away.

And remembering . . .
Remembering, with twinklings and twinges,   10
As they lean over the beans in their rented back room that
     is full of beads and receipts and dolls and cloths,
     tobacco crumbs, vases and fringes.

1960

We Real Cool

The Pool Players.
Seven at the Golden Shovel.

We real cool. We
Left school. We

Lurk late. We
Strike straight. We

Sing sin. We   5
Thin gin. We

Jazz June. We
Die soon.

1960

Jessie Mitchell's Mother

Into her mother's bedroom to wash the ballooning body.
"My mother is jelly-hearted and she has a brain of jelly:
Sweet, quiver-soft, irrelevant. Not essential.
Only a habit would cry if she should die.
A pleasant sort of fool without the least iron....   5
Are you better, mother, do you think it will come today?"
The stretched yellow rag that was Jessie Mitchell's mother
Reviewed her. Young, and so thin, and so straight.
So straight! as if nothing could ever bend her.
But poor men would bend her, and doing things with poor men,   10
Being much in bed, and babies would bend her over,
And the rest of things in life that were for poor women,
Coming to them grinning and pretty with intent to bend and to kill.
Comparisons shattered her heart, ate at her bulwarks:
The shabby and the bright: she, almost hating her daughter,   15
Crept into an old sly refuge: "Jessie's black
And her way will be black, and jerkier even than mine.
Mine, in fact, because I was lovely, had flowers
Tucked in the jerks, flowers were here and there...."
She revived for the moment settled and dried-up triumphs,   20
Forced perfume into old petals, pulled up the droop,
Refueled
Triumphant long-exhaled breaths.
Her exquisite yellow youth. . . .

1960

The Lovers of the Poor

        arrive. The Ladies from the Ladies' Betterment
  League
Arrive in the afternoon, the late light slanting
In diluted gold bars across the boulevard brag
Of proud, seamed faces with mercy and murder hinting
Here, there, interrupting, all deep and debonair,   5
The pink paint on the innocence of fear;
Walk in a gingerly manner up the hall.
Cutting with knives served by their softest care,
Served by their love, so barbarously fair.
Whose mothers taught: You'd better not be cruel!   10
You had better not throw stones upon the wrens!
Herein they kiss and coddle and assault
Anew and dearly in the innocence
With which they baffle nature. Who are full,
Sleek, tender-clad, fit, fiftyish, a-glow, all   15
Sweetly abortive, hinting at fat fruit,
Judge it high time that fiftyish fingers felt
Beneath the lovelier planes of enterprise.
To resurrect. To moisten with milky chill.
To be a random hitching post or plush.   20
To be, for wet eyes, random and handy hem.
        Their guild is giving money to the poor.
The worthy poor. The very very worthy
And beautiful poor. Perhaps just not too swarthy?
Perhaps just not too dirty nor too dim   25
Nor—passionate. In truth, what they could wish
Is—something less than derelict or dull.
Not staunch enough to stab, though, gaze for gaze!
God shield them sharply from the beggar-bold!
The noxious needy ones whose battle's bald   30
Nonetheless for being voiceless, hits one down.
        But it's all so bad! and entirely too much for them.
The stench; the urine, cabbage, and dead beans,
Dead porridges of assorted dusty grains,
The old smoke, *heavy* diapers, and, they're told,   35
Something called chitterlings. The darkness. Drawn
Darkness, or dirty light. The soil that stirs.
The soil that looks the soil of centuries.
And for that matter the *general* oldness. Old
Wood. Old marble. Old tile. Old old old.   40
Not homekind Oldness! Not Lake Forest, Glencoe.
Nothing is sturdy, nothing is majestic,
There is no quiet drama, no rubbed glaze, no
Unkillable infirmity of such
A tasteful turn as lately they have left,   45
Glencoe, Lake Forest, and to which their cars

Must presently restore them. When they're done
With dullards and distortions of this fistic
Patience of the poor and put-upon.
                They've never seen such a make-do-ness as   50
Newspaper rugs before! In this, this "flat,"
Their hostess is gathering up the oozed, the rich
Rugs of the morning (tattered! the bespattered . . .),
Readies to spread clean rugs for afternoon,
Here is a scene for you. The Ladies look,   55
In horror, behind a substantial citizeness
Whose trains clank out across her swollen heart.
Who, arms akimbo, almost fills a door.
All tumbling children, quilts dragged to the floor
And tortured thereover, potato peelings, soft-   60
Eyed kitten, hunched-up, haggard, to-be-hurt.
                Their League is allotting largesse to the Lost.
But to put their clean, their pretty money, to put
Their money collected from delicate rose-fingers
Tipped with their hundred flawless rose-nails seems . . .   65
                They own Spode, Lowestoft, candelabra,
Mantels, and hostess gowns, and sunburst clocks,
Turtle soup, Chippendale, red satin "hangings,"
Aubussons and Hattie Carnegie. They Winter
In Palm Beach; cross the Water in June; attend,   70
When suitable, the nice Art Institute;
Buy the right books in the best bindings; saunter
On Michigan, Easter mornings, in sun or wind.
Oh Squalor! This sick four-story hulk, this fibre
With fissures everywhere! Why, what are bringings   75
Of loathe-love largesse? What shall peril hungers
So old old, what shall flatter the desolate?
Tin can, blocked fire escape and chitterling
And swaggering seeking youth and the puzzled wreckage
Of the middle passage, and urine and stale shames   80
And, again, the porridges of the underslung
And children children children. Heavens! That
Was a rat, surely, off there, in the shadows? Long
And long-tailed? Gray? The Ladies from the Ladies'
Betterment League agree it will be better   85
To achieve the outer air that rights and steadies,
To hie to a house that does not holler, to ring
Bells elsetime, better presently to cater
To no more Possibilities, to get
Away. Perhaps the money can be posted.   90
Perhaps they two may choose another Slum!
Some serious sooty half-unhappy home!—
Where loathe-love likelier may be invested.
                Keeping their scented bodies in the center
Of the hall as they walk down the hysterical hall,   95
They allow their lovely skirts to graze no wall,

Are off at what they manage of a canter,
And, resuming all the clues of what they were,
Try to avoid inhaling the laden air.

1960

The Crazy Woman

I shall not sing a May song.
A May song should be gay.
I'll wait until November
And sing a song of gray.

I'll wait until November.   5
That is the time for me.
I'll go out in the frosty dark
And sing most terribly.

And all the little people
Will stare at me and say,   10
"That is the Crazy Woman
Who would not sing in May."

1960

Amy Clampitt
(1920–   )

With her first major collection of verse published in her sixty-third year, Amy Clampitt became a poet of the 1980s, widely celebrated in a time when women's work generally was coming into closer scrutiny and greater appreciation than in some earlier decades. By 1990 she had published three more significant collections.

Born to a farm family in New Providence, Iowa, Clampitt attended public schools there before continuing her education at Grinnell College and Columbia University. In New York City, she worked at Oxford University Press, then, successively, as a librarian for the National Audubon Society, a free-lance researcher, and an editor for E. P. Dutton. Her poetry began to appear in *The New Yorker* in 1978.

Five years later, in her book *The Kingfisher* (1983) she established herself as a mature, accomplished poet. Later collections—*What the Light Was Like* (1985), *Archaic Figure* (1987), and *Westward* (1990)—confirmed her skill and her importance.

Her poetry is carefully crafted, intricate in its references to the landscapes of her life in Iowa, New York, Europe, New Jersey, and Maine, as well as in its allusions to her interest in nature and in cultural history. Especially prominent within her recent verses are her "Crossings," to use the name she gives to the first section of *Westward*, observations drawn from widely dispersed times and places that intersect within the fabric of a poem: Venice and New Providence, Iowa; *Potemkin* and Kent State; or, in the title of one poem, "John Donne in California." Among poets who have influenced her are Milton, Keats, Hopkins, Marianne Moore, and Elizabeth Bishop. Among prose writers, Thoreau, George Eliot, Henry James, and Virginia Woolf. Echoes in her work from these and other writers provide continual reminders of one of her recurring themes, the inescapable passage of time.

Major collections of verse are named above. *Predecessors, Et Cetera* (1991) is a collection of essays. A brief appraisal appears in *Dictionary of Literary Biography*, vol. 105, *American Poets Since World War II*, second series (1991).

The Kingfisher

In a year the nightingales were said to be so loud
they drowned out slumber, and peafowl strolled screaming
beside the ruined nunnery, through the long evening
of a dazzled pub crawl, the halcyon color, portholed
by those eye-spots' stunning tapestry, unsettled   5
the pastoral nightfall with amazements opening.

Months later, intermission in a pub on Fifty-fifth Street
found one of them still breathless, the other quizzical,
acting the philistine, puncturing Stravinsky[1]—"Tell
me, what *was* that racket in the orchestra about?"—   10
hauling down the Firebird, harum-scarum, like a kite,
a burnished, breathing wreck that didn't hurt at all.

Among the Bronx Zoo's exiled jungle fowl, they heard
through headphones of a separating panic, the bellbird
reiterate its single *chong*, a scream nobody answered.   15
When he mourned, "The poetry is gone," she quailed,
seeing how his hands shook, sobered into feeling old.
By midnight, yet another fifth would have been killed.

A Sunday morning, the November of their cataclysm.
(Dylan Thomas[2] brought in *in extremis*[3] to St. Vincent's,   20
that same week, a symptomatic datum) found them
wandering a downtown churchyard. Among its headstones,
while from unruined choirs the noise of Christendom
poured over Wall Street, a benison in vestments,

a late thrush paused, in transit from some grizzled   25
spruce bog to the humid equatorial fireside: berry-
eyed, bark-brown above, with dark hints of trauma
in the stigmata of its underparts—or so, too bruised
just then to have invented anything so fancy,
later, re-embroidering a retrospect, she had supposed.   30

In gray England, years of muted recrimination (then
dead silence) later, she could not have said how many
spoiled takeoffs, how many entanglements gone sodden,

1. Igor Stravinsky (1882–1971), Russian composer, whose works include the music for the ballet *The Firebird* (1910).

2. Welsh poet (1914–1953) who died in New York.

3. "Near death" (Latin).

how many gaudy evenings made frantic by just one
  insomniac nightingale, how many liaisons gone down   35
  screaming in a stroll beside the ruined nunnery;

a kingfisher's burnished plunge, the color
  of felicity afire, came glancing like an arrow
  through landscapes of untended memory: ardor
  illuminating with its terrifying currency   40
  now no mere glimpse, no porthole vista
  but, down on down, the uninhabitable sorrow.

1983

What the Light Was Like

For Louise Dickinson Rich
and the family of Ernest Woodward

Every year in June—up here, that's the month for lilacs—
  almost his whole front yard,
with lobster traps stacked out in back, atop the rise
  that overlooks the inlet
would be a Himalayan range of peaks of bloom,   5
  white or mauve-violet,

gusting a turbulence of perfume, and every year the same
  iridescent hummingbird,
or its descendant, would be at work among the mourning cloaks
  and swallowtails, its motor loud,   10
its burning gorget darkening at moments as though charred.
  He kept an eye out

for it, we learned one evening, as for everything that flapped
  or hopped or hovered
crepuscular under the firs: he'd heard the legendary   15
  trilling of the woodcock,
and watched the eiders, once rare along these coasts,
  making their comeback

so that now they're everywhere, in tribes, in families
  of aunts and cousins,   20
a knit-and-purl of irresistibly downy young behind them, riding
  every cove and inlet;
and yes, in answer to the question summer people always ask,
  he'd seen the puffins

that breed out on Tit Manan, in summer improbably clown-faced 25
  behind the striped scarlet
of Commedia dell' Arte[4] masks we'll never see except in
  Roger Tory Peterson's

4. Italian popular comedy.

field guide,[5] or childish wishful thinking. There was much
    else I meant to ask about 30

another summer. But in June, when we came limping up here
    again, looking forward
to easing up from a mean, hard, unaccommodating winter,
    we heard how he'd gone out
at dawn, one morning in October, unmoored the dinghy 35
    and rowed to his boat

as usual, the harbor already chugging with half a dozen
    neighbors' revved-up craft,
wet decks stacked abaft with traps, the bait and kegs stowed
    forward, a lifting weft 40
of fog spooled off in pearl-pink fleeces overhead with the first
    daylight, and steered,

as usual, past first the inner and then the outer bar, where in
    whatever kind of weather,
the red reef-bell yells, in that interminable treble, *Trouble,* 45
    out past where the Groaner[6]
lolls, its tempo and forte changing with the chop, played on
    by every wind shift,

straight into the sunrise, a surge of burning turning the
    whole ocean iridescent 50
fool's-gold over molten emerald, into the core of that
    day-after-day amazement—
a clue, one must suppose, to why lobstermen are often
    naturally gracious:

maybe, out there beside the wheel, the Baptist spire 55
    shrunk to a compass-
point, the town an interrupted circlet, feeble as an apron-
    string, for all the labor
it took to put it there, it's finding, out in that ungirdled
    wallowing and glitter, 60

finally, that what you love most is the same as what you're
    most afraid of—God,
in a word; whereas it seems they think they've got it licked
    (or used to), back there
in the Restricted Area for instance, where that huge hush- 65
    hush thing they say is radar

sits sprawling on the heath like Stonehenge, belittling every
    other man-made thing
in view, even the gargantuan pods of the new boat hulls you
    now and then see lying, 70
stark naked, crimson on the inside as a just-skinned carcass,
    in Young's boatyard,

even the gray Grange Hall, wood-heated by a yardarm of stovepipe
    across the ceiling.

5. Peterson wrote and illustrated a number of   6. A buoy that emits a warning sound.
field guides to the birds of North America.

Out there, from that wallowing perspective, all comparisons   75
    amount to nothing,
though once you've hauled your last trap, things tend to wander
    into shorter focus

as, around noon, you head back in: first 'Tit Manan lighthouse,
    a ghostly gimlet   80
on its ledge by day, but on clear nights expanding to a
    shout, to starboard,
the sunstruck rock pile of Cranberry Point to port; then
    you see the hamlet

rainbowed, above the blurring of the spray shield, by the   85
    hurrying herring gulls'
insatiable fandango of excitement—the spire first, then
    the crimson boat hulls,
the struts of the ill-natured gadget on the heath behind them
    as the face of things expands,   90

the hide-and-seek behind the velvet-shouldered, sparse
    tree-spined profiles,
as first the outer, then the inner bar appears, then the scree-
    beach under Crowley Island's
crowding firs and spruces, and you detect among the chimneys   95
    and the TV aerials,

yours. But by midafternoon of that October day,
    when all his neighbors'
boats had chugged back through the inlet, his
    was still out; at evening,   100
with half the town out looking, and a hard frost
    settling in among the alders,

there'd been no sign of him. The next day, and the next,
    the search went on,
and widened, joined by planes and helicopters from as   105
    far away as Boston.
When, on the third day, his craft was sighted
    finally, it had drifted,

with its engine running, till the last gulp of fuel
    spluttered and ran out,   110
beyond the town's own speckled noose of buoys, past
    the furred crest of Schoodic,
vivid in a skirt of aspens, the boglands cranberry-
    crimson at its foot,

past the bald brow the sunrise always strikes first, of   115
    the hulk of Cadillac,[7]
riding the current effortlessly as eiders tied to water
    by the summer molt,
for fifty miles southwestward to where, off Matinicus,
    out past the rock   120

---

7. Cadillac Mountain, Acadia National Park, where the sunrise first strikes the United States.

that, like 'Tit Manan, is a restricted area, off limits for
 all purposes but puffins',
they spotted him, slumped against the kegs. I find it
 tempting to imagine what,
when the blood roared, overflowing its cerebral sluiceway, 125
 and the iridescence

of his last perception, charring, gave way to unreversed,
 irrevocable dark,
the light out there was like, that's always shifting—from
 a nimbus gone berserk 130
to a single gorget, a cathedral train of blinking, or
 the fogbound shroud

that can turn anywhere into a nowhere. But it's useless.
 Among the mourning-cloak-
hovered-over lilac peaks, their whites and purples, 135
 when we pass his yard,
poignant to excess with fragrance, this year we haven't
 seen the hummingbird.

1985

Urn-Burial and the Butterfly Migration

Rest for the body's residue:
boxed ashes, earth pocket
under its lifted flap of turf
roofed by a black circumference
of Norway spruce, an old settler 5
now among old settlers, in their
numb stones' cooled silicates
the scar of memory benighted
alone articulate.

O friable repose of the organic! 10
Bark-creviced at the trunk's
foot, ladybirds' enameled herds
gather for the winter, red pearls
of an unsaid rosary to waking.
From the fenced beanfield, 15
crickets' brisk scrannel
plucks the worn reed of
individual survival.

Mulleins hunker to a hirsute
rosette about the taproot; from 20
frayed thistleheads, a liftoff
of aerial barbs begins; milkweed
spills on the wind its prodigal,
packed silks—slattern gondolas

whose wrecked stalks once   25
gave mooring to the sleep of
things terrestrial:

an urn of breathing jade, its
gilt-embossed exterior the
intact foreboding of a future   30
intricately contained, jet-
veined, spangle-margined,
birth-wet russet of the air-
traveling monarch emerging
from a torpid chrysalis. Oh,   35
we know nothing

of the universe we move through!
My dead brother, when we were
kids, fed milkweed caterpillars
in Mason jars, kept bees, ogled   40
the cosmos through a backyard
telescope. But then the rigor
of becoming throttled our pure
ignorance to mere haste
toward something else.   45

We scattered. Like the dandelion,
that quintessential successful
immigrant, its offspring gone
to fluff, dug-in hard-scrabble
nurtured a generation of   50
the mobile, nomads enamored
of cloverleafs, of hangars, of
that unrest whose home—*our*
home—is motion.

Here in the winds' terrain, the   55
glacier-abraded whetstone of their
keening knives, anvil of thunder,
its sabbaths one treacherous
long sob of apprehension, who
will rein in, harpoon or anchor   60
rest for the mind? Were the dead
to speak, were one day
these friable

residues to rise, would we hear
even that airborne murmur? Listen   65
as the monarchs' late-emerging
tribes ascend; you will hear
nothing. In wafted twos and threes
you may see them through the window
of a southbound Greyhound   70
bus, adrift across the
Minnesota border;

or in flickering clots, in dozens
above the parked cars of the
shopping malls of Kansas—this　75
miracle that will not live to
taste the scarce nectar, the
ample horror of another summer:
airborne marathon, elegiac
signature of nations who　80
have no language,

their landless caravans augment
among the blistered citadels
of Oklahoma; windborne along
the Dallas-Fort Worth airport's　85
utopian thoroughfares, their
hovering millenniums become
a mimic force of occupation,
a shadeless Vallombrosa,
forceless, autonomous.　90

O drifting apotheosis of dust
exhumed, who will unseal
the crypt locked up within
the shimmer of the chromosomes,
or harvest, from the alluvial　95
death-dance of these wrecked
galaxies, this risen residue
of milkweed leaf and honey,
rest for the body?

1985

Margaret Fuller, 1847

In this her thirty-seventh year, the Italy
she'd discerned already smoldering,
through some queer geological contortion,
beneath a New World crust, abruptly ceased
to be a metaphor. She was in Rome,　5
and from her lodgings on the Corso
she watched as things began to happen:
the torchlit procession to the Quirinal,[8]
the flung-out embrace of Pio Nono[9]
from his balcony seeming (at least)　10
to give the upheaval in the streets his blessing.

By September, in Florence, in Milan,
more demonstrations: that second spring
she'd once despaired of, the kernel

---

8. Seat of the Italian civil government.　　9. Pius IX (1792–1878), pope from 1846 to 1878.

lying dormant in the husk no longer,   15
the shattered chrysalis, the tidal
concourse in the streets and through the bloodstream
one and the same. Angelo Ossoli, whom
she'd met by chance—the faintly scandalous
perennial adventure that awaits a woman,   20
of whatever age or status, in such a place—
was now her lover. Without the cause he'd drawn

her into—a mutilated Italy made whole,
at peace within, left to itself at last,
the hated foreign uniforms gone home—   25
she'd once again have kept her head,
perhaps: remained unconscionably chaste,
seen the admirer she'd somehow led on
pull back bewildered as, her self-esteem
gone numb, she worked at being noble.   30
Not now. Not in this place. The furnace
that had scathed her solitude burned with the torches,
glowed in the votive banks lit by the faithful.

The two of them went frequently to Mass;
on long excursions into the countryside   35
inhaled the reek of grapes still on the vine,
observed the harvest. The violets and roses
that still bloomed made her bedroom sweet
all through November. "I have not been so well,"
she wrote her mother, "since I was a child, nor   40
so happy ever." *Nor so happy ever.* Short of money,
she lived now in one room, on fruit, bread,
a little wine; saw few acquaintances,
dissembled, as she'd so often done, even with those.

The mild days shrank. A season ended.   45
Nor so happy ever. In mid-December
a cold, steady rain began. Increasingly
the high-walled towers along the Corso
shut out the daylight. *Since I was a child:*
then there had been terror   50
in the night, as now: she'd wake
alone to find herself back in Nantasket,
where she'd dreamed her mother dead,
re-dreamed her best friend's body lying
on hard sand, until the waves reclaimed it,   55

drowned. Brave metaphor of tides became,
lodged in that sullen dark, a heaving
succubus of mud. The street-corner
flower vendors disappeared.
Lamplit all day, the stale cul-de-sac   60
she could not leave now stank of charcoal
and the chamber pot. Migraine, a vengeful
ever-since-childhood doppelgänger,
returned, with a new kind of nausea:

the body so little of her life had ever   65
found sweetness in, life for its own inexorable

purposes took over. "A strange lilting lean
old maid," Carlyle had called her—though
not nearly such a bore as he'd expected.
What would Carlyle, what would straitlaced   70
Horace Greeley, what would fastidious
Nathaniel Hawthorne, what would all Concord,
all New England and her own mother
say now? An actuality more fraught
than any nightmare: terrors of the sea,   75
of childbirth, the massive, slow,
unending heave of human trouble.

Injustice. Ridicule. What did she *do?*
it would be asked (as though that mattered).
Gave birth. Lived through a revolution.   80
Nursed its wounded. Saw it run aground.
Published a book or two.
And drowned.

1987

The Field Pansy

Yesterday, just before the first frost of the season,
I discovered a violet in bloom on the lawn—a white one,
with a mesh of faint purple pencil marks above the hollow
at the throat, where the petals join: an irregular, a waif,
out of sync with the ubiquity of the asters of New England,   5

or indeed with the johnny-jump-ups I stopped to look at,
last week, in a plot by the sidewalk: weedily prolific
common garden perennial whose lineage goes back to
the bi- or tri-colored native field pansy of Europe:
ancestor of the cloned ocher and aubergine, the cream-white,   10

the masked motley, the immaculate lilac-blue of the pansies
that thrive in the tended winter plots of tidewater Virginia,
where in spring the cutover fields at the timber's edge,
away from the boxwood and magnolia alleys, are populous
with an indigenous, white, just faintly suffused-with-violet   15

first cousin: a link with what, among the hollows of the
great dunes of Holland, out of reach of the slide and hurl
of the North Sea breakers, I found growing a summer ago—a
field pansy tinged not violet but pink, sometimes approaching
the hue of the bell of a foxglove: a gathering, a proliferation   20

on a scale that, for all its unobtrusiveness, seems to be
worldwide, of what I don't know how to read except as an

urge to give pleasure: a scale that may, for all our fazed
dubiety, indeed be universal. I know I'm leaving something out
when I write of this omnipresence of something like eagerness,   25

this gushing insouciance that appears at the same time capable
of an all but infinite particularity: sedulous, patient, though
in the end (so far as anyone can see) without consequence.
What is consequence? What difference do the minutiae
of that seeming inconsequence that's called beauty   30

add up to? Life was hard in the hinterland, where spring arrived
with a gush of violets, sky-blue out of the ground of the woodlot,
but where a woman was praised by others of her sex for being
Practical, and by men not at all, other than in a slow reddening
about the neck, a callowly surreptitious wolf-whistle: where the mode   35

was stoic, and embarrassment stood in the way of affect:
a mother having been alarmingly seen in tears, once only
we brought her a fistful of johnny-jump-ups from the garden,
"because you were crying"—and saw we'd done the wrong thing.

1990

A Winter Burial

From tall rooms, largesse of peonies,
the porches summercool, the bed upstairs
immaculate in its white counterpane,

to kerosene-lit evenings, the wind
an orphan roaming the silver maples,   5
sudden widowhood: to meaner comforts,

a trumpetvine above the kitchen door,
then one night her new husband didn't
come in from the milking: to the lot

she bought with what that place went   10
for, dwindlings in a doll's house: to
the high-rise efficiency condominium,

television on all day, to the cubicle
in the denominational home, to total
unprivacy of bed and bedpan, nurse shoes,   15

TV with no picture or else coming in waves,
a vertigo: to, one nightfall when the last
weak string gave way that had held whatever

she was, that mystery, together, the bier
that waited—there were no planes coming in,   20
not many made it to the funeral, the blizzard

had been so bad, the graveyard drifted
so deep, so many severed limbs of trees
thrown down, they couldn't get in to plow

an opening for the hearse, or shovel   25
the cold white counterpane from that cell
in the hibernal cupboard, till the day after.

                                    1990

Amherst[1]

May 15, 1987

The oriole, a charred and singing coal,
still burns aloud among the monuments,
its bugle call to singularity the same
unheard (she wrote) as to the crowd,
this graveyard gathering, the audience   5
            she never had.

Fame has its own dynamic, its smolderings
and ignitions, its necessary distance:
Colonel Higginson,[2] who'd braved the cannon,
admitted his relief not to live near such   10
breathless, hushed excess (you cannot
            fold a flood,

she wrote, and put it in a drawer), such
stoppered prodigies, compressions and
devastations within the atom—*all this*   15
world contains: his face—the civil
wars of just one stanza. A universe
            might still applaud,

the red at bases of the trees (she wrote)
like mighty footlights burn, God still   20
look on, his badge a raised hyperbole—
inspector general of all that carnage,
those gulfs, those fleets and crews
            of solid blood:

1. The profile of Norwottuck, a low hill south of
the town of Amherst that would have been
familiar to Emily Dickinson, may be viewed
from a site, new since her day, honoring
graduates of Amherst College who served in
the two world wars. The poet's death on May
15, 1886, has been commemorated in recent
years by a gathering in the cemetery where
she is buried.

Phrases lifted from the poems of Emily
Dickinson will be evident. The ones
represented include (using the numbers in *The*

Complete Poems of Emily Dickinson, edited by
Thomas H. Johnson) 526, 530, 663, 595, 658,
594, 601, 564, 593, 486. The most unlikely of
these is the poet's reference (in poem 564) to
"Vast Prairies of Air/Unbroken by a Settler."
Her work is, however, studded with allusions
to places she had never seen [Clampitt's note].
2. Thomas Wentworth Higginson (1823–1911),
friend, adviser, and editor of Emily Dickinson's
poems, had served as a colonel in the Civil
War.

the battle fought between the soul and No   25
One There, no one at all, where cities
ooze away: unbroken prairies of air
without a settlement. On Main Street
the hemlock hedge grows up untrimmed,
        the light that poured   30

in once like judgment (whether it was noon
at night, or only heaven at noon, she wrote,
she could not tell) cut off, the wistful,
the merely curious, in her hanging dress discern
an ikon; her ambiguities are made a shrine,   35
        then violated;

we've drunk champagne above her grave, declaimed
the lines of one who dared not live aloud.
I thought of writing her (Dear Emily, though,
seems too intrusive, Dear Miss Dickinson too prim)   40
to ask, not without irony, what, wherever she
        is now, is made

of all the racket, whether she's of two minds
still; and tell her how on one cleared hillside,
an ample peace that looks toward Norwottuck's   45
unaltered purple has been shaken since
by bloodshed on Iwo Jima, in Leyte Gulf
        and Belleau Wood.

        1990

Hisaye Yamamoto
(1921–   )

A Nisei, or child of Japanese immigrants, Yamamoto was born in Redondo Beach, California. When she entered school, she spoke no English, but she soon became an avid English reader. As a teenager she was a regular contributor to the English-language columns of the Japanese-American newspaper *Kashu Mainichi.*

After the bombing of Pearl Harbor (December 7, 1941), the federal government required all persons of Japanese heritage—regardless of citizenship—to abandon their homes and businesses and be confined in internment camps. The Yamamoto family was assigned to the camp in Poston, Arizona. Yamamoto describes the experience as "an episode of our collective life which wounded us more painfully than we realize," but she continued to write, serving as a reporter and columnist for the camp newspaper, the *Poston Chronicle.* She also contributed a serialized mystery, "Death Rides the Rails to Poston," to that publication. Her short story "The Legend of Miss Sasagawara" unfolds against an internment camp background. Yamamoto and two of her brothers left the camp to work for a short period in Springfield, Massachusetts, but they rejoined their parents when they learned that another brother had been killed in action in Italy.

After the war she was a reporter for the *Los Angeles Tribune,* an African-American weekly, and continued to write short stories, placing them both in Japanese publications and in such magazines as the *Partisan Review, Kenyon Review, Harper's Bazaar,* and the *Carleton Miscellany.* A Whitney Foundation Opportunity Fellowship (1950–1951) allowed her the brief luxury of writing full time. Four of her stories have been included in the lists of the year's best printed in the *Best American Short Story* annual volumes, and "Yoneko's Earthquake" was selected for publication in the 1952 collection. From 1953 to 1955 Yamamoto served as a volunteer at a Long Island rehabilitation farm operated by the *Catholic Worker* and wrote for that publication. For several years she has lived with her husband, Anthony De Soto, and their five children in southern California. In

1986, she was awarded the American Book Award for Lifetime Achievement by the Before Columbus Foundation.

"Seventeen Syllables" treats several of the dominant themes of Yamamoto's fiction: the restricted lives of first-generation (Issei) women, lack of communication between generations, and connections between various minority cultures. This story of a woman, isolated by geography and lack of sympathy, is recounted from the point of view of her adolescent daughter, Rosie, whose attention is distracted by romance. First published in the *Partisan Review* in November 1949, it is the title story of a collection of five pieces published in Tokyo in 1985 as well as the author's first American story collection (1988), containing fifteen selections, an introduction by King-Kok Cheung, and a bibliography.

Seventeen Syllables

The first Rosie knew that her mother had taken to writing poems was one evening when she finished one and read it aloud for her daughter's approval. It was about cats, and Rosie pretended to understand it thoroughly and appreciate it no end, partly because she hesitated to disillusion her mother about the quantity and quality of Japanese she had learned in all the years now that she had been going to Japanese school every Saturday (and Wednesday, too, in the summer). Even so, her mother must have been skeptical about the depth of Rosie's understanding, because she explained afterwards about the kind of poem she was trying to write.

See, Rosie, she said, it was a *haiku,* a poem in which she must pack all her meaning into seventeen syllables only, which were divided into three lines of five, seven, and five syllables. In the one she had just read, she had tried to capture the charm of a kitten, as well as comment on the superstition that owning a cat of three colors meant good luck.

"Yes, yes, I understand. How utterly lovely," Rosie said, and her mother, either satisfied or seeing through the deception and resigned, went back to composing.

The truth was that Rosie was lazy; English lay ready on the tongue but Japanese had to be searched for and examined, and even then put forth tentatively (probably to meet with laughter). It was so much easier to say yes, yes, even when one meant no, no. Besides, this was what was in her mind to say: I was looking through one of your magazines from Japan last night, Mother, and towards the back I found some *haiku* in English that delighted me. There was one that made me giggle off and on until I fell asleep—

It is morning, and lo!
I lie awake, comme il faut,
sighing for some dough.

Now, how to reach her mother, how to communicate the melancholy song? Rosie knew formal Japanese by fits and starts, her mother had even less English, no French. It was much more possible to say yes, yes.

It developed that her mother was writing the *haiku* for a daily newspaper, the *Mainichi Shimbun*, that was published in San Francisco. Los Angeles, to be sure, was closer to the farming community in which the Hayashi family lived and several Japanese vernaculars were printed there, but Rosie's parents said they preferred the tone of the northern paper. Once a week, the *Mainichi* would have a section devoted to *haiku*, and her mother became an extravagant contributor, taking for herself the blossoming pen name, Ume Hanazono.

So Rosie and her father lived for awhile with two women, her mother and Ume Hanazono. Her mother (Tome Hayashi by name) kept house, cooked, washed, and, along with her husband and the Carrascos, the Mexican family hired for the harvest, did her ample share of picking tomatoes out in the sweltering fields and boxing them in tidy strata in the cool packing shed. Ume Hanazono, who came to life after the dinner dishes were done, was an earnest, muttering stranger who often neglected speaking when spoken to and stayed busy at the parlor table as late as midnight scribbling with pencil on scratch paper or carefully copying characters on good paper with her fat, pale green Parker.

The new interest had some repercussions on the household routine. Before, Rosie had been accustomed to her parents and herself taking their hot baths early and going to bed almost immediately afterwards, unless her parents challenged each other to a game of flower cards or unless company dropped in. Now if her father wanted to play cards, he had to resort to solitaire (at which he always cheated fearlessly), and if a group of friends came over, it was bound to contain someone who was also writing *haiku*, and the small assemblage would be split in two, her father entertaining the non-literary members and her mother comparing ecstatic notes with the visiting poet.

If they went out, it was more of the same thing. But Ume Hanazono's life span, even for a poet's, was very brief—perhaps three months at most.

One night they went over to see the Hayano family in the neighboring town to the west, an adventure both painful and attractive to Rosie. It was attractive because there were four Hayano girls, all lovely and each one named after a season of the year (Haru, Natsu, Aki, Fuyu), painful because something had been wrong with Mrs. Hayano ever since the birth of her first child. Rosie would sometimes watch Mrs. Hayano, reputed to have been the belle of her native village, making her way about a room, stooped, slowly shuffling, violently trembling (*always* trembling), and she would be reminded that this woman, in this same condition, had carried and given issue to three babies. She would look wonderingly at Mr. Hayano, handsome, tall, and strong, and she would look at her four pretty friends. But it was not a matter she could come to any decision about.

On this visit, however, Mrs. Hayano sat all evening in the rocker, as motionless and unobtrusive as it was possible for her to be, and Rosie found the greater part of the evening practically anaesthetic. Too, Rosie spent most of it in the girls' room, because Haru, the garrulous one, said almost as soon as the bows and other greetings were over, "Oh, you must see my new coat!"

It was a pale plaid of grey, sand, and blue, with an enormous collar, and Rosie, seeing nothing special in it, said, "Gee, how nice."

"Nice?" said Haru, indignantly. "Is that all you can say about it? It's gorgeous! And so cheap, too. Only seventeen-ninety-eight, because it was a sale. The saleslady said it was twenty-five dollars regular."

"Gee," said Rosie. Natsu, who never said much and when she said anything said it shyly, fingered the coat covetously and Haru pulled it away.

"Mine," she said, putting it on. She minced in the aisle between the two large beds and smiled happily. "Let's see how your mother likes it."

She broke into the front room and the adult conversation and went to stand in front of Rosie's mother, while the rest watched from the door. Rosie's mother was properly envious. "May I inherit it when you're through with it?"

Haru, pleased, giggled and said yes, she could, but Natsu reminded gravely from the door. "You promised me, Haru."

Everyone laughed but Natsu, who shamefacedly retreated into the bedroom. Haru came in laughing, taking off the coat. "We were only kidding, Natsu," she said. "Here, you try it on now."

After Natsu buttoned herself into the coat, inspected herself solemnly in the bureau mirror, and reluctantly shed it, Rosie, Aki, and Fuyu got their turns, and Fuyu, who was eight, drowned in it while her sisters and Rosie doubled up in amusement. They all went into the front room later, because Haru's mother quaveringly called to her to fix the tea and rice cakes and open a can of sliced peaches for everybody. Rosie noticed that her mother and Mr. Hayano were talking together at the little table—they were discussing a *haiku* that Mr. Hayano was planning to send to the *Mainichi*, while her father was sitting at one end of the sofa looking through a copy of *Life*, the new picture magazine. Occasionally, her father would comment on a photograph, holding it toward Mrs. Hayano and speaking to her as he always did—loudly, as though he thought someone such as she must surely be at least a trifle deaf also.

The five girls had their refreshments at the kitchen table, and it was while Rosie was showing the sisters her trick of swallowing peach slices without chewing (she chased each slippery crescent down with a swig of tea) that her father brought his empty teacup and untouched saucer to the sink and said, "Come on, Rosie, we're going home now."

"Already?" asked Rosie.

"Work tomorrow," he said.

He sounded irritated, and Rosie, puzzled, gulped one last yellow slice and stood up to go, while the sisters began protesting, as was their wont.

"We have to get up at five-thirty," he told them, going into the front room quickly, so that they did not have their usual chance to hang onto his hands and plead for an extension of time.

Rosie, following, saw that her mother and Mr. Hayano were sipping tea and still talking together, while Mrs. Hayano concentrated, quivering, on raising the handleless Japanese cup to her lips with both her hands and lowering it back to her lap. Her father, saying nothing, went out the door, onto the bright porch, and down the steps. Her mother looked up and asked, "Where is he going?"

"Where is he going?" Rosie said. "He said we were going home now."

"Going home?" Her mother looked with embarrassment at Mr. Hayano and his absorbed wife and then forced a smile. "He must be tired," she said.

Haru was not giving up yet. "May Rosie stay overnight?" she asked, and Natsu, Aki, and Fuyu came to reinforce their sister's plea by helping her make a circle around Rosie's mother. Rosie, for once having no desire to stay, was relieved when her mother, apologizing to the perturbed Mr. and Mrs. Hayano for her father's abruptness at the same time, managed to shake her head no at the quartet, kindly but adamant, so that they broke their circle and let her go.

Rosie's father looked ahead into the windshield as the two joined him. "I'm sorry," her mother said. "You must be tired." Her father, stepping on the starter, said nothing. "You know how I get when it's *haiku*," she continued. "I forget what time it is." He only grunted.

As they rode homeward silently, Rosie, sitting between, felt a rush of hate for both—for her mother for begging, for her father for denying her mother. I wish this old Ford would crash, right now, she thought, then immediately, no, no, I wish my father would laugh, but it was too late: already the vision had passed through her mind of the green pick-up crumpled in the dark against one of the mighty eucalyptus trees they were just riding past, of the three contorted, bleeding bodies, one of them hers.

Rosie ran between two patches of tomatoes, her heart working more rambunctiously than she had ever known it to. How lucky it was that Aunt Taka and Uncle Gimpachi had come tonight, though, how very lucky. Otherwise she might not have really kept her half-promise to meet Jesus Carrasco. Jesus was going to be a senior in September at the same school she went to, and his parents were the ones helping with the tomatoes this year. She and Jesus, who hardly remembered seeing each other at Cleveland High where there were so many other people and two whole grades between them, had become great friends this summer— he always had a joke for her when he periodically drove the loaded pick-up up from the fields to the shed where she was usually sorting while her mother and father did the packing, and they laughed a great deal together over infinitesimal repartee during the afternoon break for chilled watermelon or ice cream in the shade of the shed.

What she enjoyed most was racing him to see which could finish picking a double row first. He, who could work faster, would tease her by slowing down until she thought she would surely pass him this time, then speeding up furiously to leave her several sprawling vines behind. Once he had made her screech hideously by crossing over, while her back was turned, to place atop the tomatoes in her green-stained bucket a truly monstrous, pale green worm (it had looked more like an infant snake). And it was when they had finished a contest this morning, after she had pantingly pointed a green finger at the immature tomatoes evident in the lugs at the end of his row and he had returned the accusation (with justice), that he had startlingly brought up the matter of their possibly meeting outside the range of both their parents' dubious eyes.

"What for?" she had asked.

"I've got a secret I want to tell you," he said.

"Tell me now," she demanded.

"It won't be ready till tonight," he said.

She laughed. "Tell me tomorrow then."

"It'll be gone tomorrow," he threatened.

"Well, for seven hakes, what is it?" she had asked, more than twice, and when he had suggested that the packing shed would be an appropriate place to find out, she had cautiously answered maybe. She had not been certain she was going to keep the appointment until the arrival of mother's sister and her husband. Their coming seemed a sort of signal of permission, of grace, and she had definitely made up her mind to lie and leave as she was bowing them welcome.

So as soon as everyone appeared settled back for the evening, she announced loudly that she was going to the privy outside, "I'm going to the *benjo!*" and slipped out the door. And now that she was actually on her way, her heart pumped in such an undisciplined way that she could hear it with her ears. It's because I'm running, she told herself, slowing to a walk. The shed was up ahead, one more patch away, in the middle of the fields. Its bulk, looming in the dimness, took on a sinisterness that was funny when Rosie reminded herself that it was only a wooden frame with a canvas roof and three canvas walls that made a slapping noise on breezy days.

Jesus was sitting on the narrow plank that was the sorting platform and she went around to the other side and jumped backwards to seat herself on the rim of a packing stand. "Well, tell me," she said without greeting, thinking her voice sounded reassuringly familiar.

"I saw you coming out the door," Jesus said. "I heard you running part of the way, too."

"Uh-huh," Rosie said. "Now tell me the secret."

"I was afraid you wouldn't come," he said.

Rosie delved around on the chicken-wire bottom of the stall for number two tomatoes, ripe, which she was sitting beside, and came up with a left-over that felt edible. She bit into it and began sucking out the pulp and seeds. "I'm here," she pointed out.

"Rosie, are you sorry you came?"

"Sorry? What for?" she said. "You said you were going to tell me something."

"I will, I will," Jesus said, but his voice contained disappointment, and Rosie fleetingly felt the older of the two, realizing a brand-new power which vanished without category under her recognition.

"I have to go back in a minute," she said. "My aunt and uncle are here from Wintersburg. I told them I was going to the privy."

Jesus laughed. "You funny thing," he said. "You slay me!"

"Just because you have a bathroom *inside*," Rosie said. "Come on, tell me."

Chuckling, Jesus came around to lean on the stand facing her. They still could not see each other very clearly, but Rosie noticed that Jesus became very sober again as he took the hollow tomato from her hand and dropped it back into the stall. When he took hold of her empty hand, she could find no words to protest; her vocabulary had become distressingly constricted and she thought desperately that all that remained intact now was yes and no and oh, and even these few sounds would not easily out. Thus, kissed by Jesus, Rosie fell for the first time entirely victim to a helplessness delectable beyond speech. But the terrible, beautiful sensation lasted no more than a second, and the reality of Jesus' lips and tongue and teeth and hands made her pull away with such strength that she nearly tumbled.

Rosie stopped running as she approached the lights from the windows of home. How long since she had left? She could not guess, but gasping yet, she went to the privy in back and locked herself in. Her own breathing deafened her in the dark, close space, and she sat and waited until she could hear at last the nightly calling of the frogs and crickets. Even then, all she could think to say was oh, my, and the pressure of Jesus' face against her face would not leave.

No one had missed her in the parlor, however, and Rosie walked in and through quickly, announcing that she was next going to take a bath. "Your father's in the bathhouse," her mother said, and Rosie, in her room, recalled that she had not seen him when she entered. There had been only Aunt Taka and Uncle Gimpachi with her mother at the table, drinking tea. She got her robe and straw sandals and crossed the parlor again to go outside. Her mother was telling them about the *haiku* competition in the *Mainichi* and the poem she had entered.

Rosie met her father coming out of the bathhouse. "Are you through, Father?" she asked. "I was going to ask you to scrub my back."

"Scrub your own back," he said shortly, going toward the main house.

"What have I done now?" she yelled after him. She suddenly felt like doing a lot of yelling. But he did not answer, and she went into the bathhouse. Turning on the dangling light, she removed her denims and T-shirt and threw them in the big carton for dirty clothes standing next to the washing machine. Her other things she took with her into the bath compartment to wash after her bath. After she had scooped a basin of hot water from the square wooden tub, she sat on the grey cement of the floor and soaped herself at exaggerated leisure, singing "Red Sails in the Sunset" at the top of her voice and using da-da-da where she suspected her words. Then, standing up, still singing, for she was possessed by the notion that any attempt now to analyze would result in spoilage and she believed that the larger her volume the less she would be able to hear herself think, she obtained more hot water and poured it on until she was free of lather. Only then did she allow herself to step into the steaming vat, one leg first, then the remainder of her body inch by inch until the water no longer stung and she could move around at will.

She took a long time soaking, afterwards remembering to go around outside to stoke the embers of the tin-lined fireplace beneath the tub and to throw on a few more sticks so that the water might keep its heat for her mother, and when she finally returned to the parlor, she found her mother still talking *haiku* with her aunt and uncle, the three of them on another round of tea. Her father was nowhere in sight.

At Japanese school the next day (Wednesday, it was), Rosie was grave and giddy by turns. Preoccupied at her desk in the row for students on Book Eight, she made up for it at recess by performing wild mimicry for the benefit of her friend Chizuko. She held her nose and whined a witticism or two in what she considered was the manner of Fred Allen; she assumed intoxication and a British accent to go over the climax of the Rudy Vallee recording of the pub conversation about William Ewart Gladstone; she was the child Shirley Temple piping, "On the Good Ship Lollipop"; she was the gentleman soprano of the Four Inkspots trilling, "If I Didn't Care."[1] And she felt reasonably satisfied when Chizuko wept and gasped, "Oh, Rosie, you ought to be in the movies!"

Her father came after her at noon, bringing her sandwiches of minced ham and two nectarines to eat while she rode, so that she could pitch right into the sorting when they got home. The lugs were piling up, he said, and the ripe tomatoes in them would probably have to be taken to the cannery tomorrow if they were not ready for the produce haulers tonight. "This heat's not doing them any good. And we've got no time for a break today."

It *was* hot, probably the hottest day of the year, and Rosie's blouse stuck damply to her back even under the protection of the canvas. But she worked as efficiently as a flawless machine and kept the stalls heaped, with one part of her mind listening in to the parental murmuring about the heat and the tomatoes and with another part planning the exact words she would say to Jesus when he drove up with the first load of the afternoon. But when at last she saw that the pick-up was coming, her hands went berserk and the tomatoes started falling in the wrong stalls, and her father said, "Hey, hey! Rosie, watch what you're doing!"

"Well, I have to go to the *benjo*," she said, hiding panic.

"Go in the weeds over there," he said, only half-joking.

"Oh, Father!" she protested.

"Oh, go on home," her mother said. "We'll make out for awhile."

In the privy Rosie peered through a knothole toward the fields, watching as much as she could of Jesus. Happily she thought she saw him look in the direction of the house from time to time before he finished unloading and went back toward the patch where his mother and father worked. As she was heading for the shed, a very presentable black car purred up the dirt driveway to the house and its driver motioned to her. Was this the Hayashi home, he wanted to know. She nodded. Was she a Hayashi? Yes, she said, thinking that he was a good-looking man. He got out of the car with a huge, flat package and she saw that he warmly wore a business suit. "I have something here for your mother then," he said, in a more elegant Japanese than she was used to.

She told him where her mother was and he came along with her, patting his face with an immaculate white handkerchief and saying something about the coolness of San Francisco. To her surprised mother and father, he bowed and introduced himself as, among other things, the *haiku* editor of the *Mainichi Shimbun*, saying that since he had been coming as far as Los Angeles anyway, he had decided to bring her the first prize she had won in the recent contest.

"First prize?" her mother echoed, believing and not believing, pleased and overwhelmed. Handed the package with a bow, she bobbed her head up and down numerous times to express her utter gratitude.

"It is nothing much," he added, "but I hope it will serve as a token of our great appreciation for your contributions and our great admiration of your considerable talent."

"I am not worthy," she said, falling easily into his style. "It is I who should make some sign of my humble thanks for being permitted to contribute."

1. Allen, Vallee, Temple, and the Inkspots were all popular entertainers of the 1930s. Gladstone was four times British prime minister between 1868 and 1894.

"No, no, to the contrary," he said, bowing again.

But Rosie's mother insisted, and then saying that she knew she was being unorthodox, she asked if she might open the package because her curiosity was so great. Certainly she might. In fact, he would like her reaction to it, for personally, it was one of his favorite *Hiroshiges*.[2]

Rosie thought it was a pleasant picture, which looked to have been sketched with delicate quickness. There were pink clouds, containing some graceful calligraphy, and a sea that was a pale blue except at the edges, containing four sampans with indications of people in them. Pines edged the water and on the far-off beach there was a cluster of thatched huts towered over by pine-dotted mountains of grey and blue. The frame was scalloped and gilt.

After Rosie's mother pronounced it without peer and somewhat prodded her father into nodding agreement, she said Mr. Kuroda must at least have a cup of tea after coming all this way, and although Mr. Kuroda did not want to impose, he soon agreed that a cup of tea would be refreshing and went along with her to the house, carrying the picture for her.

"Ha, your mother's crazy!" Rosie's father said, and Rosie laughed uneasily as she resumed judgment on the tomatoes. She had emptied six lugs when he broke into an imaginary conversation with Jesus to tell her to go and remind her mother of the tomatoes, and she went slowly.

Mr. Kuroda was in his shirtsleeves expounding some *haiku* theory as he munched a rice cake, and her mother was rapt. Abashed in the great man's presence, Rosie stood next to her mother's chair until her mother looked up inquiringly, and then she started to whisper the message, but her mother pushed her gently away and reproached, "You are not being very polite to our guest."

"Father says the tomatoes . . ." Rosie said aloud, smiling foolishly.

"Tell him I shall only be a minute," her mother said, speaking the language of Mr. Kuroda.

When Rosie carried the reply to her father, he did not seem to hear and she said again, "Mother says she'll be back in a minute."

"All right, all right," he nodded, and they worked again in silence. But suddenly, her father uttered an incredible noise, exactly like the cork of a bottle popping, and the next Rosie knew, he was stalking angrily toward the house, almost running in fact, and she chased after him crying, "Father! Father! What are you going to do?"

He stopped long enough to order her back to the shed. "Never mind!" he shouted. "Get on with the sorting!"

And from the place in the fields where she stood, frightened and vacillating, Rosie saw her father enter the house. Soon Mr. Kuroda came out alone, putting on his coat. Mr. Kuroda got into his car and backed out down the driveway onto the highway. Next her father emerged, also alone, something in his arms (it was the picture, she realized), and, going over to the bathhouse woodpile, he threw the picture on the ground and picked up the axe. Smashing the picture, glass and all (she heard the explosion faintly), he reached over for the kerosene that was used to encourage the bath fire and poured it over the wreckage. I am dreaming, Rosie said to herself, I am dreaming, but her father, having made sure that his act of cremation was irrevocable, was even then returning to the fields.

Rosie ran past him and toward the house. What had become of her mother? She burst into the parlor and found her mother at the back window watching the dying fire. They watched together until there remained only a feeble smoke under the blazing sun. Her mother was very calm.

"Do you know why I married your father?" she said without turning.

"No," said Rosie. It was the most frightening question she had ever been called upon to answer. Don't tell me now, she wanted to say, tell me tomorrow, tell me next week, don't tell me today. But she knew she would be told now, that the telling would combine with the other violence of the hot afternoon to level her life, her world to the very ground.

2. Work by Ando Hiroshige (1797–1858), famous Japanese landscape painter and printmaker.

It was like a story out of the magazines illustrated in sepia, which she had consumed so greedily for a period until the information had somehow reached her that those wretchedly unhappy autobiographies, offered to her as the testimonials of living men and women, were largely inventions: Her mother, at nineteen, had come to America and married her father as an alternative to suicide.

At eighteen she had been in love with the first son of one of the well-to-do families in her village. The two had met whenever and wherever they could, secretly, because it would not have done for his family to see him favor her—her father had no money; he was a drunkard and a gambler besides. She had learned she was with child; an excellent match had already been arranged for her lover. Despised by her family, she had given premature birth to a stillborn son, who would be seventeen now. Her family did not turn her out, but she could no longer project herself in any direction without refreshing in them the memory of her indiscretion. She wrote to Aunt Taka, her favorite sister in America, threatening to kill herself if Aunt Taka would not send for her. Aunt Taka hastily arranged a marriage with a young man of whom she knew, but lately arrived from Japan, a young man of simple mind, it was said, but of kindly heart. The young man was never told why his unseen betrothed was so eager to hasten the day of meeting.

The story was told perfectly, with neither groping for words nor untoward passion. It was as though her mother had memorized it by heart, reciting it to herself so many times over that its nagging vileness had long since gone.

"I had a brother then?" Rosie asked, for this was what seemed to matter now; she would think about the other later, she assured herself, pushing back the illumination which threatened all that darkness that had hitherto been merely mysterious or even glamorous. "A half-brother?"

"Yes."

"I would have liked a brother," she said.

Suddenly, her mother knelt on the floor and took her by the wrists. "Rosie," she said urgently, "Promise me you will never marry!" Shocked more by the request than the revelation, Rosie stared at her mother's face. Jesus, Jesus, she called silently, not certain whether she was invoking the help of the son of the Carrascos or of God, until there returned sweetly the memory of Jesus' hand, how it had touched her and where. Still her mother waited for an answer, holding her wrists so tightly that her hands were going numb. She tried to pull free. Promise, her mother whispered fiercely, promise. Yes, yes, I promise, Rosie said. But for an instant she turned away, and her mother, hearing the familiar glib agreement, released her. Oh, you, you, you, her eyes and twisted mouth said, you fool. Rosie, covering her face, began at last to cry, and the embrace and consoling hand came much later than she expected.

1949, 1988

Denise Levertov
(1923–   )

Included in an anthology of *The New British Poets* in 1949, by 1960 Denise Levertov had earned a place in Donald Allen's landmark *The New American Poetry: 1945–1960*. A lot had happened in the meantime in the world of poetry generally; emblematic of some of the changes was Levertov's transformation from a traditional British poet to a wholly American one, caught up in the postwar surge of innovation.

Born in Ilford, Essex, Levertov was raised in a multicultural family; her mother was Welsh, and her father was an immigrant Russian Jew who had converted to Christianity and become an Anglican priest. In a bookish family—her father, her mother, and her older sister Olga all wrote—she read widely but had no formal education, apart from ballet school. A civilian nurse in London during World War II, she published her first poems in *The Double Image* (1946). The next year she married the American writer Mitchell Goodman, and in 1948 the couple moved to the United States, where she soon began publishing poems in Cid Corman's *Origin* and Robert Creeley's *Black Mountain Review*. Grouped in Allen's anthology with the Black Mountain poets, she at that time considered two of them, Robert Duncan and Robert Creeley, "as the chief poets among my contemporaries."

Foremost among the influences that helped her become an American poet, however, was the example of William Carlos Williams, with his emphasis upon the rhythms of American speech. "His historical importance is, above all," she wrote, "that more than anyone else he made available to us the whole range of the language *** He cleared the ground, he gave us tools." Following from Williams was Creeley's dictum that "Form is never more than the extension of content," which Levertov, drawing on her own theories of inspiration, proposed revising as "Form is never more than a *revelation* of content." A resulting formal openness has characterized most of her work, beginning with her first American book, *Here and Now* (1957). With *The Sorrow Dance* (1967) and later books, however, though the principle of open form remains dominant, Levertov has become less often an introspective poet and more insistently a political one. Active in her opposition to the Vietnam War, she later turned her attention to other political and social causes, including Third World concerns and the women's movement.

Collections include *Collected Earlier Poems, 1940–1960* (1979); *Poems 1960–1967* (1983); and *Poems 1968–1972* (1987). Individual titles, in addition to those named above, include *With Eyes at the Back of Our Heads* (1959); *The Jacob's Ladder* (1961); *O Taste and See* (1964); *Relearning the Alphabet* (1970); *To Stay Alive* (1971); *Footprints* (1972); *The Freeing of the Dust* (1975); *Life in the Forest* (1978); *Oblique Prayers* (1984); *Breathing the Water* (1987); and *A Door in the Hive* (1989). Prose is collected in *The Poet in the World* (1973) and *Light Up the Cave* (1981).

Studies include Linda W. Wagner, *Denise Levertov* (1967); and Harry Marten, *Understanding Denise Levertov* (1988).

The Third Dimension

Who'd believe me if
I said, 'They took and

split me open from
scalp to crotch, and

still I'm alive, and   5
walk around pleased with

the sun and all
the world's bounty.' Honesty

isn't so simple:
a simple honesty is   10

nothing but a lie.
Don't the trees

hide the wind between
their leaves and

speak in whispers?   15
The third dimension

hides itself.
If the roadmen

crack stones, the
stones are stones: 20

but love
cracked me open

and I'm
alive to

tell the tale—but not   25
honestly:

the words
change it. Let it be—

here in the sweet sun
—a fiction, while I   30

breathe and
change pace.

1957

To the Snake

Green Snake, when I hung you round my neck
and stroked your cold, pulsing throat
        as you hissed to me, glinting
arrowy gold scales, and I felt
        the weight of you on my shoulders,   5
and the whispering silver of your dryness
        sounded close at my ears—

Green Snake—I swore to my companions that certainly
        you were harmless! But truly
I had no certainty, and no hope, only desiring   10
        to hold you, for that joy,
                        which left
a long wake of pleasure, as the leaves moved
and you faded into the pattern
of grass and shadows, and I returned   15
smiling and haunted, to a dark morning.

1959

Illustrious Ancestors

The Rav
of Northern White Russia[1] declined,
in his youth, to learn the
language of birds, because
the extraneous did not interest him; nevertheless   5
when he grew old it was found
he understood them anyway, having
listened well, and as it is said, 'prayed
          with the bench and the floor.' He used
what was at hand—as did   10
Angel Jones of Mold,[2] whose meditations
were sewn into coats and britches.
         Well, I would like to make
thinking some line still taut between me and them,
poems direct as what the birds said,   15
hard as a floor, sound as a bench,
mysterious as the silence when the tailor
would pause with his needle in the air.

                       1961

About Marriage

Don't lock me in wedlock, I want
marriage, an
encounter—

I told you about the
green light of   5
May

         (a veil of quiet befallen
         the downtown park,
         late

         Saturday after   10
         noon, long
         shadows and cool

         air, scent of
         new grass,
         fresh leaves,   15

         blossom on the threshold of
         abundance—

---

1. Schneour Zaiman (d. 1831), a Rabbi, or "Rav,"   2. Welsh tailor and mystic, an ancestor of
an ancestor of Levertov on her father's side.   Levertov on her mother's side.

and the birds I met there,
birds of passage breaking their journey,
three birds each of a different species: 20

the azalea-breasted with round poll, dark,
the brindled, merry, mousegliding one,
and the smallest, golden as gorse and wearing
a black Venetian mask

and with them the three douce hen-birds   25
feathered in tender, lively brown—

I stood
a half-hour under the enchantment,
no-one passed near,
the birds saw me and   30

let me be
near them.)

It's not
irrelevant:
I would be   35
met

and meet you
so,
in a green

airy space, not   40
locked in.

                                                  1964

In Mind

There's in my mind a woman
of innocence, unadorned but

fair-featured, and smelling of
apples or grass. She wears

a utopian smock or shift, her hair   5
is light brown and smooth, and she

is kind and very clean without
ostentation—
                    but she has
no imagination.   10
                    And there's a
turbulent moon-ridden girl

or old woman, or both,
dressed in opals and rags, feathers

and torn taffeta,   15
who knows strange songs—

but she is not kind.

1964

A Note to Olga[3] (1966)

i

Of lead and emerald
the reliquary
that knocks my breastbone,

slung round my neck
on a rough invisible rope   5
that rubs the knob of my spine.

Though I forget you
a red coal from your fire
burns in that box.

ii

On the Times Square sidewalk   10
we shuffle along, cardboard signs
—Stop the War—
slung round our necks.

The cops
hurry about,   15
shoulder to shoulder,
comic.

Your high soprano
sings out from just
in back of me—   20

We shall—I turn,
you're, I very well know,
not there,

and your voice, they say,
grew hoarse   25
from shouting at crowds . . .

yet *overcome*
sounds then hoarsely
from somewhere in front,

3. The poet's sister, Olga Levertoff (1914–1964).

the paddywagon   30
gapes.—It seems
you that is lifted

limp and ardent
off the dark snow
and shoved in, and driven away.   35

1967

Intrusion

After I had cut off my hands
and grown new ones

something my former hands had longed for
came and asked to be rocked.

After my plucked out eyes   5
had withered, and new ones grown

something my former eyes had wept for
came asking to be pitied.

1972

The 90th Year

for Lore Segal

High in the jacaranda shines the gilded thread
of a small bird's curlicue of song—too high
for her to see or hear.
                I've learned
not to say, these last years,   5
'O, look!—O, listen, Mother!'
as I used to.

        (It was she
who taught me to look;
to name the flowers when I was still close to the ground,   10
my face level with theirs;
or to watch the sublime metamorphoses
unfold and unfold
over the walled back gardens of our street . . .

It had not been given her   15
to know the flesh as good in itself,
as the flesh of a fruit is good. To her
the human body has been a husk,
a shell in which souls were prisoned.
Yet, from within it, with how much gazing   20
her life has paid tribute to the world's body!

How tears of pleasure
would choke her, when a perfect voice,
deep or high, clove to its note unfaltering!)

She has swept the crackling seedpods,   25
the litter of mauve blossoms, off the cement path,
tipped them into the rubbish bucket.
She's made her bed, washed up the breakfast dishes,
wiped the hotplate. I've taken the butter and milkjug
back to the fridge next door—but it's not my place,   30
visiting here, to usurp the tasks
that weave the day's pattern.
Now she is leaning forward in her chair,
      by the lamp lit in the daylight,
rereading *War and Peace.*   35
         When I look up
from her wellworn copy of *The Divine Milieu,*[4]
which she wants me to read, I see her hand
loose on the black stem of the magnifying glass,
she is dozing.   40
'I am so tired,' she has written to me, 'of appreciating
the gift of life.'

         1978

The Well

At sixteen I believed the moonlight
could change me if it would.
      I moved my head
on the pillow, even moved my bed
as the moon slowly   5
crossed the open lattice.

I wanted beauty, a dangerous
gleam of steel, my body thinner,
my pale face paler.
         I moonbathed   10
diligently, as others sunbathe.
But the moon's unsmiling stare
kept me awake. Mornings,
I was flushed and cross.

It was on dark nights of deep sleep   15
that I dreamed the most, sunk in the well,
and woke rested, and if not beautiful,
filled with some other power.

         1987

4. *War and Peace* is by Leo Tolstoy (1829–1910);   Chardin (1881–1955).
  The Divine Milieu is by Pierre Teilhard de

Flannery O'Connor

(1925–1964)

Mary Flannery O'Connor was born and lived the first thirteen years of her life in coastal Savannah, Georgia, but when her family moved to the smaller inland town of Milledgeville, that region became her emotional and fictional home. Her father died the year before her graduation from high school (1942), and she entered Georgia State College for Women (now Georgia College)—the local college—immediately, graduating in three years.

For the next five years she lived away from Georgia, earning a master of fine arts degree at the Iowa Writers' Workshop, publishing stories in mass circulation magazines, and staying briefly at the Yaddo artists' colony and in Manhattan, before moving into the Connecticut home of Sally and Robert Fitzgerald. There she suffered her first attack of disseminated lupus in December 1950; her illness sent her back home to her mother's farm, where she lived the rest of her short life.

In a predominantly Protestant region, O'Connor's family on both sides had been Roman Catholic for several generations; an ancestor had donated the land on which the Milledgeville church was built. She was a devoted practitioner, attending Mass daily when her health allowed and keeping religious books on her bedside table. Themes and symbols of Christianity dominate her work for, as she phrased it, "I see from the standpoint of Christian orthodoxy. This means that for me the meaning of life is centered in our Redemption by Christ, and what I see in the world I see in its relation to that."

This Christian perspective—which she saw in conflict with the surrounding secularism—influenced her use of grotesque characters and situations. As she explained in "The Fiction Writer and His Country" (1957), an artist whose orientation differs from that of the audience must distort in order to "make your vision apparent by shock—to the hard of hearing you shout, and for the almost-blind you draw large and startling figures." The resulting mixture of the comic and the serious has been compared to cartooning, an art O'Connor practiced as a high school and college student.

Wise Blood (1952), her first novel, depicted poor white Southern fundamentalists. The protagonist, Hazel Motes, finally accepts God and seeks to atone for his past transgressions by self-mutilation. The stories in the succeeding collection, *A Good Man Is Hard to Find* (1955), portray characters faced by malevolence or irrational violence who undergo spiritual awakening. In her second novel, *The Violent Bear It Away* (1960), a skeptic is brought to salvation when he is drugged and raped by a stranger. The posthumous *Everything That Rises Must Converge* (1965) deals with similar themes.

"On Her Own Work," an essay in the collection *Mystery and Manners* (1969), casts further light on O'Connor's methods with the assertion, "I have discovered that what is needed is an action that is totally unexpected, yet totally believable, and I have found that, for me, this is always an action which indicates that grace has been offered. And frequently it is an action in which the devil has been the unwilling instrument of grace. This is not a piece of knowledge that I consciously put into my stories; it is a discovery that I get out of them."

The Complete Stories appeared in 1971. *The Habit of Being* (1979), a collection of letters, was edited by Sally Fitzgerald. She also edited *Collected Works*, published in 1988. *Conversations with Flannery O'Connor* (1987) was edited by Rosemary M. Magee. Studies include Robert Coles, *Flannery O'Connor's South* (1980); Suzanne Morrow Paulson, *Flannery O'Connor: A Study of the Short Fiction* (1988); and Robert H. Brinkmeyer, Jr., *The Art and Vision of Flannery O'Connor* (1989).

The Life You Save May Be Your Own

The old woman and her daughter were sitting on their porch when Mr. Shiftlet came up their road for the first time. The old woman slid to the edge of her chair and leaned forward, shading her eyes from the piercing sunset with her hand. The daughter could not see far in front of her and continued to play with her fingers. Although the old woman lived in this desolate spot with only her daughter and she had never seen Mr. Shiftlet before, she could tell, even from a distance, that he was a tramp and no one to be afraid of. His left coat sleeve was folded up to show there was only half an arm in it and his gaunt figure listed slightly to the side as if the breeze were pushing him. He had on a black town suit and a brown felt hat that was turned up in the front and down in the back and he carried a tin tool box by a handle. He came on, at an amble, up her road, his face turned toward the sun which appeared to be balancing itself on the peak of a small mountain.

The old woman didn't change her position until he was almost into her yard; then she rose with one hand fisted on her hip. The daughter, a large girl in a short blue organdy dress, saw him all at once and jumped up and began to stamp and point and make excited speechless sounds.

Mr. Shiftlet stopped just inside the yard and set his box on the ground and tipped his hat at her as if she were not in the least afflicted; then he turned toward the old woman and swung the hat all the way off. He had long black slick hair that hung flat from a part in the middle to beyond the tips of his ears on either side. His face descended in forehead for more than half its length and ended suddenly with his features just balanced over a jutting steel-trap jaw. He seemed to be a young man but he had a look of composed dissatisfaction as if he understood life thoroughly.

"Good evening," the old woman said. She was about the size of a cedar fence post and she had a man's gray hat pulled down low over her head.

The tramp stood looking at her and didn't answer. He turned his back and faced the sunset. He swung both his whole and his short arm up slowly so that they indicated an expanse of sky and his figure formed a crooked cross. The old woman watched him with her arms folded across her chest as if she were the owner of the sun, and the daughter watched, her head thrust forward and her fat helpless hands hanging at the wrists. She had long pink-gold hair and eyes as blue as a peacock's neck.

He held the pose for almost fifty seconds and then he picked up his box and came on to the porch and dropped down on the bottom step. "Lady," he said in a firm nasal voice, "I'd give a fortune to live where I could see me a sun do that every evening."

"Does it every evening," the old woman said and sat back down. The daughter sat down too and watched him with a cautious sly look as if he were a bird that had come up very close. He leaned to one side, rooting in his pants pocket, and in a second he brought out a package of chewing gum and offered her a piece. She took it and unpeeled it and began to chew without taking her eyes off him. He offered the old woman a piece but she only raised her upper lip to indicate she had no teeth.

Mr. Shiftlet's pale sharp glance had already passed over everything in the yard—the pump near the corner of the house and the big fig tree that three or four chickens were preparing to roost in—and had moved to a shed where he saw the square rusted back of an automobile. "You ladies drive?" he asked.

"That car ain't run in fifteen year," the old woman said. "The day my husband died, it quit running."

"Nothing is like it used to be, lady," he said. "The world is almost rotten."

"That's right," the old woman said. "You from around here?"

"Name Tom T. Shiftlet," he murmured, looking at the tires.

"I'm pleased to meet you," the old woman said. "Name Lucynell Crater and daughter Lucynell Crater. What you doing around here, Mr. Shiftlet?"

He judged the car to be about a 1928 or '29 Ford. "Lady," he said, and turned and gave her his full attention, "lemme tell you something. There's one of these doctors in Atlanta that's taken a knife and cut the human heart—the human heart," he repeated, leaning forward, "out of a man's chest and held it in his hand," and he held his hand out, palm up, as if it were slightly weighted with the human heart, "and studied it like it was a day-old chicken, and lady," he said, allowing a long significant pause in which his head slid forward and his clay-colored eyes brightened, "he don't know no more about it than you or me."

"That's right," the old woman said.

"Why, if he was to take the knife and cut into every corner of it, he still wouldn't know no more than you or me. What you want to bet?"

"Nothing," the old woman said wisely. "Where you come from, Mr. Shiftlet?"

He didn't answer. He reached into his pocket and brought out a sack of tobacco and a package of cigarette papers and rolled himself a cigarette, expertly with one hand, and attached it in a hanging position to his upper lip. Then he took a box of wooden matches from his pocket and struck one on his shoe. He held the burning match as if he were studying the mystery of flame while it traveled dangerously toward his skin. The daughter began to make loud noises and to point to his hand and shake her finger at him, but when the flame was just before touching him, he leaned down with his hand cupped over it as if he were going to set fire to his nose and lit the cigarette.

He flipped away the dead match and blew a stream of gray into the evening. A sly look came over his face. "Lady," he said, "nowadays, people'll do anything anyways. I can tell you my name is Tom T. Shiftlet and I come from Tarwater, Tennessee, but you never have seen me before: how you know I ain't lying? How you know my name ain't Aaron Sparks, lady, and I come from Singleberry, Georgia, or how you know it's not George Speeds and I come from Lucy, Alabama, or how you know I ain't Thompson Bright from Toolafalls, Mississippi?"

"I don't know nothing about you," the old woman muttered, irked.

"Lady," he said, "people don't care how they lie. Maybe the best I can tell you is, I'm a man; but listen lady," he said and paused and made his tone more ominous still, "what is a man?"

The old woman began to gum a seed. "What you carry in that tin box, Mr. Shiftlet?" she asked.

"Tools," he said, put back. "I'm a carpenter."

"Well, if you come out here to work, I'll be able to feed you and give you a place to sleep but I can't pay. I'll tell you that before you begin," she said.

There was no answer at once and no particular expression on his face. He leaned back against the two-by-four that helped support the porch roof. "Lady," he said slowly, "there's some men that some things mean more to them than money." The old woman rocked without comment and the daughter watched the trigger that moved up and down in his neck. He told the old woman then that all most people were interested in was money, but he asked what a man was made for. He asked her if a man was made for money, or what. He asked her what she thought she was made for but she didn't answer, she only sat rocking and wondered if a one-armed man could put a new roof on her garden house. He asked a lot of questions that she didn't answer. He told her that he was twenty-eight years old and had lived a varied life. He had been a gospel singer, a foreman on the railroad, an assistant in an undertaking parlor, and he come over the radio for three months with Uncle Roy and his Red Creek Wranglers. He said he had fought and bled in the Arm Service of his country and visited every foreign land and that everywhere he had seen people that didn't care if they did a thing one way or another. He said he hadn't been raised thataway.

A fat yellow moon appeared in the branches of the fig tree as if it were going to roost there with the chickens. He said that a man had to escape to the country to see the world whole and that he wished he lived in a desolate place like this where he could see the sun go down every evening like God made it to do.

"Are you married or are you single?" the old woman asked.

There was a long silence. "Lady," he asked finally, "where would you find you an innocent woman today? I wouldn't have any of this trash I could just pick up."

The daughter was leaning very far down, hanging her head almost between her knees, watching him through a triangular door she had made in her overturned hair; and she suddenly fell in a heap on the floor and began to whimper. Mr. Shiftlet straightened her out and helped her get back in the chair.

"Is she your baby girl?" he asked.

"My only," the old woman said, "and she's the sweetest girl in the world. I wouldn't give her up for nothing on earth. She's smart too. She can sweep the floor, cook, wash, feed the chickens, and hoe. I wouldn't give her up for a casket of jewels."

"No," he said kindly, "don't ever let any man take her away from you."

"Any man come after her," the old woman said, " 'll have to stay around the place."

Mr. Shiftlet's eye in the darkness was focused on a part of the automobile bumper that glittered in the distance. "Lady," he said, jerking his short arm up as if he could point with it to her house and yard and pump, "there ain't a broken thing on this plantation that I couldn't fix for you, one-arm jackleg or not. I'm a man," he said with a sullen dignity, "even if I ain't a whole one. I got," he said, tapping his knuckles on the floor to emphasize the immensity of what he was going to say, "a moral intelligence!" and his face pierced out of the darkness into a shaft of doorlight and he stared at her as if he were astonished himself at this impossible truth.

The old woman was not impressed with the phrase. "I told you you could hang around and work for food," she said, "if you don't mind sleeping in that car yonder."

"Why listen, lady," he said with a grin of delight, "the monks of old slept in their coffins!"

"They wasn't as advanced as we are," the old woman said.

The next morning he began on the roof of the garden house while Lucynell, the daughter, sat on a rock and watched him work. He had not been around a week before the change he had made in the place was apparent. He had patched the front and back steps, built a new hog pen, restored a fence, and taught Lucynell, who was completely deaf and had never said a word in her life, to say the word "bird." The big rosy-faced girl followed him everywhere, saying "Burrttddt ddbirrrttdt." and clapping her hands. The old woman watched from a distance, secretly pleased. She was ravenous for a son-in-law.

Mr. Shiftlet slept on the hard narrow back seat of the car with his feet out the side window. He had his razor and a can of water on a crate that served him as a bedside table and he put up a piece of mirror against the back glass and kept his coat neatly on a hanger that he hung over one of the windows.

In the evenings he sat on the steps and talked while the old woman and Lucynell rocked violently in their chairs on either side of him. The old woman's three mountains were black against the dark blue sky and were visited off and on by various planets and by the moon after it had left the chickens. Mr. Shiftlet pointed out that the reason he had improved this plantation was because he had taken a personal interest in it. He said he was even going to make the automobile run.

He had raised the hood and studied the mechanism and he said he could tell that the car had been built in the days when cars were really built. You take now, he said, one man puts in one bolt and another man puts in another bolt and another man puts in another bolt so that it's a man for a bolt. That's why you have to pay so much for a car: you're paying all those men. Now if you didn't have to pay but one man, you could get you a cheaper car and one that had had a personal interest taken in it, and it would be a better car. The old woman agreed with him that this was so.

Mr. Shiftlet said that the trouble with the world was that nobody cared, or stopped and took any trouble. He said he never would have been able to teach Lucynell to say a word if he hadn't cared and stopped long enough.

"Teach her to say something else," the old woman said.

"What you want her to say next?" Mr. Shiftlet asked.

The old woman's smile was broad and toothless and suggestive. "Teach her to say 'sugarpie,'" she said.

Mr. Shiftlet already knew what was on her mind.

The next day he began to tinker with the automobile and that evening he told her that if she would buy a fan belt, he would be able to make the car run.

The old woman said she would give him the money. "You see that girl yonder?" she asked, pointing to Lucynell who was sitting on the floor a foot away, watching him, her eyes blue even in the dark. "If it was ever a man wanted to take her away, I would say, 'No man on earth is going to take that sweet girl of mine away from me!' but if he was to say, 'Lady, I don't want to take her away, I want her right here,' I would say, 'Mister, I don't blame you none. I wouldn't pass up a chance to live in a permanent place and get the sweetest girl in the world myself. You ain't no fool,' I would say."

"How old is she?" Mr. Shiftlet asked casually.

"Fifteen, sixteen," the old woman said. The girl was nearly thirty but because of her innocence it was impossible to guess.

"It would be a good idea to paint it too," Mr. Shiftlet remarked. "You don't want it to rust out."

"We'll see about that later," the old woman said.

The next day he walked into town and returned with the parts he needed and a can of gasoline. Late in the afternoon, terrible noises issued from the shed and the old woman rushed out of the house, thinking Lucynell was somewhere having a fit. Lucynell was sitting on a chicken crate, stamping her feet and screaming, "Burrddttt! bddurrddttt!" but her fuss was drowned out by the car. With a volley of blasts it emerged from the shed, moving in a fierce and stately way. Mr. Shiftlet was in the driver's seat, sitting very erect. He had an expression of serious modesty on his face as if he had just raised the dead.

That night, rocking on the porch, the old woman began her business at once. "You want you an innocent woman, don't you?" she asked sympathetically. "You don't want none of this trash."

"No'm, I don't," Mr. Shiftlet said.

"One that can't talk," she continued, "can't sass you back or use foul language. That's the kind for you to have. Right there," and she pointed to Lucynell sitting cross-legged in her chair, holding both feet in her hands.

"That's right," he admitted. "She wouldn't give me any trouble."

"Saturday," the old woman said, "you and her and me can drive into town and get married."

Mr. Shiftlet eased his position on the steps.

"I can't get married right now," he said. "Everything you want to do takes money and I ain't got any."

"What you need with money?" she asked.

"It takes money," he said. "Some people'll do anything anyhow these days, but the way I think, I wouldn't marry no woman that I couldn't take on a trip like she was somebody. I mean take her to a hotel and treat her. I wouldn't marry the Duchesser Windsor," he said firmly, "unless I could take her to a hotel and give her something good to eat.

"I was raised thataway and there ain't a thing I can do about it. My old mother taught me how to do."

"Lucynell don't even know what a hotel is," the old woman muttered. "Listen here, Mr. Shiftlet," she said, sliding forward in her chair, "you'd be getting a permanent house and a deep well and the most innocent girl in the world. You don't need no money. Lemme tell you something; there ain't any place in the world for a poor disabled friendless drifting man."

The ugly words settled in Mr. Shiftlet's head like a group of buzzards in the top of a tree. He didn't answer at once. He rolled himself a cigarette and lit it and then he said in an even voice, "Lady, a man is divided into parts, body and spirit."

The old woman clamped her gums together.

"A body and a spirit," he repeated. "The body, lady, is like a house: it don't go anywhere; but the spirit, lady, is like a automobile: always on the move, always . . ."

"Listen, Mr. Shiftlet," she said, "my well never goes dry and my house is always warm in the winter and there's no mortgage on a thing about this place. You can go to the courthouse and see for yourself. And yonder under that shed is a fine automobile." She laid the bait carefully. "You can have it painted by Saturday. I'll pay for the paint."

In the darkness, Mr. Shiftlet's smile stretched like a weary snake waking up by a fire. After a second he recalled himself and said, "I'm only saying a man's spirit means more to him than anything else. I would have to take my wife off for the week end without no regard at all for cost. I got to follow where my spirit says to go."

"I'll give you fifteen dollars for a week-end trip," the old woman said in a crabbed voice. "That's the best I can do."

"That wouldn't hardly pay for more than the gas and the hotel," he said. "It wouldn't feed her."

"Seventeen-fifty," the old woman said. "That's all I got so it isn't any use you trying to milk me. You can take a lunch."

Mr. Shiftlet was deeply hurt by the word "milk." He didn't doubt that she had more money sewed up in her mattress but he had already told her he was not interested in her money. "I'll make that do," he said and rose and walked off without treating with her further.

On Saturday the three of them drove into town in the car that the paint had barely dried on and Mr. Shiftlet and Lucynell were married in the Ordinary's office while the old woman witnessed. As they came out of the courthouse, Mr. Shiftlet began twisting his neck in his collar. He looked morose and bitter as if he had been insulted while someone held him. "That didn't satisfy me none," he said. "That was just something a woman in an office did, nothing but paper work and blood tests. What do they know about my blood? If they was to take my heart and cut it out," he said, "they wouldn't know a thing about me. It didn't satisfy me at all."

"It satisfied the law," the old woman said sharply.

"The law," Mr. Shiftlet said and spit. "It's the law that don't satisfy me."

He had painted the car dark green with a yellow band around it just under the windows. The three of them climbed in the front seat and the old woman said, "Don't Lucynell look pretty? Looks like a baby doll." Lucynell was dressed up in a white dress that her mother had uprooted from a trunk and there was a Panama hat on her head with a bunch of red wooden cherries on the brim. Every now and then her placid expression was changed by a sly isolated little thought like a shoot of green in the desert. "You got a prize!" the old woman said.

Mr. Shiftlet didn't even look at her.

They drove back to the house to let the old woman off and pick up the lunch. When they were ready to leave, she stood staring in the window of the car, with her fingers clenched around the glass. Tears began to seep sideways out of her eyes and run along the dirty creases in her face. "I ain't ever been parted with her for two days before," she said.

Mr. Shiftlet started the motor.

"And I wouldn't let no man have her but you because I seen you would do right. Good-by, Sugarbaby," she said, clutching at the sleeve of the white dress. Lucynell looked straight at her and didn't seem to see her there at all. Mr. Shiftlet eased the car forward so that she had to move her hands.

The early afternoon was clear and open and surrounded by pale blue sky. Although the car would go only thirty miles an hour, Mr. Shiftlet imagined a terrific climb and dip and swerve that went entirely to his head so that he forgot his morning bitterness. He had always wanted an automobile but he had never been able to afford one before. He drove very fast because he wanted to make Mobile by nightfall.

Occasionally he stopped his thoughts long enough to look at Lucynell in the seat beside him. She had eaten the lunch as soon as they were out of the yard and now she was pulling the cherries off the hat one by one and throwing them out the window. He became depressed in spite of the car. He had driven about a hundred miles when he decided that she must be hungry again and at the next small town they came to, he stopped in front of an aluminum-painted eating place called The Hot Spot and took her in and ordered her a plate of ham and grits. The ride had made her sleepy and as soon as she got up on the stool, she rested her head on the counter and shut her eyes. There was no one in The Hot Spot but Mr. Shiftlet and the boy behind the counter, a pale youth with a greasy rag hung over his shoulder. Before he could dish up the food, she was snoring gently.

"Give it to her when she wakes up," Mr. Shiftlet said. "I'll pay for it now."

The boy bent over her and stared at the long pink-gold hair and the half-shut sleeping eyes. Then he looked up and stared at Mr. Shiftlet. "She looks like an angel of Gawd," he murmured.

"Hitch-hiker," Mr. Shiftlet explained. "I can't wait. I got to make Tuscaloosa."

The boy bent over again and very carefully touched his finger to a strand of the golden hair and Mr. Shiftlet left.

He was more depressed than ever as he drove on by himself. The late afternoon had grown hot and sultry and the country had flattened out. Deep in the sky a storm was preparing very slowly and without thunder as if meant to drain every drop of air from the earth before it broke. There were times when Mr. Shiftlet preferred not to be alone. He felt too that a man with a car had a responsibility to others and he kept his eyes out for a hitchhiker. Occasionally he saw a sign that warned: "Drive carefully. The life you save may be your own."

The narrow road dropped off on either side into dry fields and here and there a shack or a filling station stood in a clearing. The sun began to set directly in front of the automobile. It was a reddening ball that through his windshield was slightly flat on the bottom and top. He saw a boy in overalls and a gray hat standing on the edge of the road and he slowed the car and stopped in front of him. The boy didn't have his hand raised to thumb the ride, he was only standing there, but he had a small cardboard suitcase and his hat was set on his head in a way to indicate that he had left somewhere for good. "Son," Mr. Shiftlet said, "I see you want a ride."

The boy didn't say he did or he didn't but he opened the door of the car and got in, and Mr. Shiftlet started driving again. The child held the suitcase on his lap and folded his arms on top of it. He turned his head and looked out the window away from Mr. Shiftlet. Mr. Shiftlet felt oppressed. "Son," he said after a minute, "I got the best old mother in the world so I reckon you only got the second best."

The boy gave him a quick dark glance and then turned his face back out the window.

"It's nothing so sweet," Mr. Shiftlet continued, "as a boy's mother. She taught him his first prayers at her knee, she give him love when no other would, she told him what was right and what wasn't, and she seen that he done the right thing. Son," he said, "I never rued a day in my life like the one I rued when I left that old mother of mine."

The boy shifted in his seat but he didn't look at Mr. Shiftlet. He unfolded his arms and put one hand on the door handle.

"My mother was a angel of Gawd," Mr. Shiftlet said in a very strained voice. "He took her from heaven and giver to me and I left her." His eyes were instantly clouded over with a mist of tears. The car was barely moving.

The boy turned angrily in the seat. "You go to the devil!" he cried. "My old woman is a flea bag and yours is a stinking pole cat!" and with that he flung the door open and jumped out with his suitcase into the ditch.

Mr. Shiftlet was so shocked that for about a hundred feet he drove along slowly with the door still open. A cloud, the exact color of the boy's hat and shaped like a turnip, had descended over the sun, and another, worse looking, crouched behind the car. Mr. Shiftlet felt that the rottenness of the world was about to engulf him. He raised his arm and let it fall again to his breast. "Oh Lord!" he prayed. "Break forth and wash the slime from this earth!"

The turnip continued slowly to descend. After a few minutes there was a guffawing peal of thunder from behind and fantastic raindrops, like tin-can tops, crashed over the rear of Mr. Shiftlet's car. Very quickly he stepped on the gas and with his stump sticking out the window he raced the galloping shower into Mobile.

1955

Maya Angelou
(1928–   )

Born in St. Louis, Marguerite Johnson became Maya Angelou when she combined her nickname with a name adopted for the stage when she was in her twenties. When she was 3, the marriage of her parents failed and she and her brother Bailey were shunted from one relative to another, living by turns with a grandmother in Stamps, Arkansas; with her mother in St. Louis, again for a period in Arkansas; and then in her high school years in San Francisco. Raped by her mother's boyfriend when she was 8, she became withdrawn and mute. Always she turned to literature for solace. She was educated in public schools of Arkansas and California, as well as by her wide reading. At 16 she became a single mother and, for the next few years, supported herself and her son with whatever jobs she could find. Then in 1954–1955, she won a part in the twenty-two-nation tour of *Porgy and Bess,* sponsored by the U.S. Department of State. Other stage and film roles took her from off Broadway in Jean Genet's *The Blacks* in 1960 to television in Alex Haley's *Roots* in 1977. She has written plays, film scripts, and television documentaries; been active in the civil rights movement; held a position at the University of Ghana for four years; and taught at various universities in the United States. She has achieved a wide following as a poet and lecturer.

Her multivolume autobiography ranks among the most extended in American literature. In *I Know Why the Caged Bird Sings* (1970) she tells her story up to age 16 and the birth of her son. Enormously popular, this and the two following were Book-of-the-Month Club selections. *Gather Together in My Name* (1974) and *Singin' and Swingin' and Gettin' Merry Like Christmas* (1976) cover late adolescence and young adulthood, prostitution, drug addiction, and her early stage career. In *The Heart of a Woman* (1981) she chronicles the years of her civil rights activity at home and abroad, and in *All God's Children Need Traveling Shoes* (1987) her experience in Ghana. In 1993 she was the featured poet at the inauguration of President Clinton.

Poems (1986) gathers the verse of earlier titles: *Just Give Me a Cool Drink of Water 'fore I Diiie* (1971); *Oh Pray My Wings Are Gonna Fit Me Well* (1975); *And Still I Rise* (1978); and *Shaker, Why Don't You Sing?* (1983). A brief appraisal appears in *Dictionary of Literary Biography,* vol. 38, *Afro-American Writers After 1955* (1985).

From I Know Why the Caged Bird Sings

11

I had decided that St. Louis was a foreign country. I would never get used to the scurrying sounds of flushing toilets, or the packaged foods, or doorbells or the noise of cars and trains and buses that crashed through the walls or slipped under the doors. In my mind I only stayed in St. Louis for a few weeks. As quickly as I understood that I had not reached my home, I sneaked away to Robin Hood's forest and the caves of Alley Oop where all reality was unreal and even that changed every day. I carried the same shield that I had used in Stamps: "I didn't come to stay."

Mother was competent in providing for us. Even if that meant getting someone else to furnish the provisions. Although she was a nurse, she never worked at her profession while we were with her. Mr. Freeman brought in the necessities and she earned extra money cutting poker games in gambling parlors. The straight eight-to-five world simply didn't have enough glamor for her, and it was twenty years later that I first saw her in a nurse's uniform.

Mr. Freeman was a foreman in the Southern Pacific yards and came home late sometimes, after Mother had gone out. He took his dinner off the stove where she had carefully covered it and which she had admonished us not to bother. He ate quietly in the kitchen while Bailey and I read separately and greedily our own Street and Smith pulp magazine. Now that we had spending money, we bought the illustrated paperbacks with their gaudy pictures. When Mother was away, we were put on an honor system. We had to finish our homework, eat dinner and wash the dishes before we could read or listen to *The Lone Ranger, Crime Busters* or *The Shadow.*

Mr. Freeman moved gracefully, like a big brown bear, and seldom spoke to us. He simply waited for Mother and put his whole self into the waiting. He never read the paper or patted his foot to radio. He waited. That was all.

If she came home before we went to bed, we saw the man come alive. He would start out of the big chair, like a man coming out of sleep, smiling. I would remember then that a few seconds before, I had heard a car door slam; then Mother's footsteps would signal from the concrete walk. When her key rattled the door, Mr. Freeman would have already asked his habitual question, "Hey, Bibbi, have a good time?"

His query would hang in the air while she sprang over to peck him on the lips. Then she turned to Bailey and me with the lipstick kisses. "Haven't you finished your homework?" If we had and were just reading—"O.K., say your prayers and go to bed." If we hadn't—"Then go to your room and finish . . . then say your prayers and go to bed."

Mr. Freeman's smile never grew, it stayed at the same intensity. Sometimes Mother would go over and sit on his lap and the grin on his face looked as if it would stay there forever.

From our rooms we could hear the glasses clink and the radio turned up. I think she must have danced for him on the good nights, because he couldn't dance, but before I fell asleep I often heard feet shuffling to dance rhythms.

I felt very sorry for Mr. Freeman. I felt as sorry for him as I had felt for a litter of helpless pigs born in our backyard sty in Arkansas. We fattened the pigs all year long for the slaughter on the first good frost, and even as I suffered for the cute little wiggly things, I knew how much I was going to enjoy the fresh sausage and hog's headcheese they could give me only with their deaths.

Because of the lurid tales we read and our vivid imaginations and, probably, memories of our brief but hectic lives, Bailey and I were afflicted—he physically and I mentally. He stuttered, and I sweated through horrifying nightmares. He was constantly told to slow down and start again, and on my particularly bad nights my mother would take me in to sleep with her, in the large bed with Mr. Freeman.

Because of a need for stability, children easily become creatures of habit. After the third time in Mother's bed, I thought there was nothing strange about sleeping there.

One morning she got out of bed for an early errand, and I fell asleep again. But I awoke to a pressure, a strange feeling on my left leg. It was too soft to be a hand, and it wasn't the touch of clothes. Whatever it was, I hadn't encountered the sensation in all the years of sleeping with Momma. It didn't move, and I was too startled to. I turned my head a little to the left to see if Mr. Freeman was awake and gone, but his eyes were open and both hands were above the cover. I knew, as if I had always known, it was his "thing" on my leg.

He said, "Just stay right here, Ritie, I ain't gonna hurt you." I wasn't afraid, a little apprehensive, maybe, but not afraid. Of course I knew that lots of people did "it" and they used their "things" to accomplish the deed, but no one I knew had ever done it to anybody. Mr. Freeman pulled me to him, and put his hand between my legs. He didn't hurt, but Momma had drilled into my head: "Keep your legs closed, and don't let nobody see your pocketbook."

"Now, I didn't hurt you. Don't get scared." He threw back the blankets and his "thing" stood up like a brown ear of corn. He took my hand and said, "Feel it." It was mushy and squirmy like the inside of a freshly killed chicken. Then he dragged me on top of his chest with his left arm, and his right hand was moving so fast and his heart was beating so hard that I was afraid that he would die. Ghost stories revealed how people who died wouldn't let go of whatever they were holding. I wondered if Mr. Freeman died holding me how I would ever get free. Would they have to break his arms to get me loose?

Finally he was quiet, and then came the nice part. He held me so softly that I wished he wouldn't ever let me go. I felt at home. From the way he was holding me I knew he'd never let me go or let anything bad ever happen to me. This was probably my real father and we had found each other at last. But then he rolled over, leaving me in a wet place and stood up.

"I gotta talk to you, Ritie." He pulled off his shorts that had fallen to his ankles, and went into the bathroom.

It was true the bed was wet, but I knew I hadn't had an accident. Maybe Mr. Freeman had one while he was holding me. He came back with a glass of water and told me in a sour voice, "Get up. You peed in the bed." He poured water on the wet spot, and it did look like my mattress on many mornings.

Having lived in Southern strictness, I knew when to keep quiet around adults, but I did want to ask him why he said I peed when I was sure he didn't believe that. If he thought I was naughty, would that mean that he would never hold me again? Or admit that he was my father? I had made him ashamed of me.

"Ritie, you love Bailey?" He sat down on the bed and I came close, hoping. "Yes." He was bending down, pulling on his socks, and his back was so large and friendly I wanted to rest my head on it.

"If you ever tell anybody what we did, I'll have to kill Bailey."

What had we done? We? Obviously he didn't mean my peeing in the bed. I didn't understand and didn't dare ask him. It had something to do with his holding me. But there was no chance to ask Bailey either, because that would be telling what we had done. The thought that he might kill Bailey stunned me. After he left the room I thought about telling Mother that I hadn't peed in the bed, but then if she asked me what happened I'd have to tell her about Mr. Freeman holding me, and that wouldn't do.

It was the same old quandary. I had always lived it. There was an army of adults, whose motives and movements I just couldn't understand and who made no effort to understand mine. There was never any question of my disliking Mr. Freeman, I simply didn't understand him either.

For weeks after, he said nothing to me, except the gruff hellos which were given without ever looking in my direction.

This was the first secret I had ever kept from Bailey and sometimes I thought he should be able to read it on my face, but he noticed nothing.

I began to feel lonely for Mr. Freeman and the encasement of his big arms. Before, my world had been Bailey, food, Momma, the Store, reading books and Uncle Willie. Now, for the first time, it included physical contact.

I began to wait for Mr. Freeman to come in from the yards, but when he did, he never noticed me, although I put a lot of feeling into "Good evening, Mr. Freeman."

One evening, when I couldn't concentrate on anything, I went over to him and sat quickly on his lap. He had been waiting for Mother again. Bailey was listening to *The Shadow* and didn't miss me. At first Mr. Freeman sat still, not holding me or anything, then I felt a soft lump under my thigh begin to move. It twitched against me and started to harden. Then he pulled me to his chest. He smelled of coal dust and grease and he was so close I buried my face in his shirt and listened to his heart, it was beating just for me. Only I could hear the thud, only I could feel the jumping on my face. He said, "Sit still, stop squirming." But all the time, he pushed me around on his lap, then suddenly he stood up and I slipped down to the floor. He ran to the bathroom.

For months he stopped speaking to me again. I was hurt and for a time felt lonelier than ever. But then I forgot about him, and even the memory of his holding me precious melted into the general darkness just beyond the great blinkers of childhood.

I read more than ever, and wished my soul that I had been born a boy. Horatio Alger was the greatest writer in the world. His heroes were always good, always won, and were always boys. I could have developed the first two virtues, but becoming a boy was sure to be difficult, if not impossible.

The Sunday funnies influenced me, and although I admired the strong heroes who always conquered in the end, I identified with Tiny Tim. In the toilet, where I used to take the papers, it was tortuous to look for and exclude the unnecessary pages so that I could learn how he would finally outwit his latest adversary. I wept with relief every Sunday as he eluded the evil men and bounded back from each seeming defeat as sweet and gentle as ever. The Katzenjammer kids were fun because they made the adults look stupid. But they were a little too smartalecky for my taste.

When spring came to St. Louis, I took out my first library card, and since Bailey and I seemed to be growing apart, I spent most of my Saturdays at the library (no interruptions) breathing in the world of penniless shoeshine boys who, with goodness and perseverance, became rich, rich men and gave baskets of goodies to the poor on holidays. The little princesses who were mistaken for maids, and the long-lost children mistaken for waifs, became more real to me than our house, our mother, our school or Mr. Freeman.

During those months we saw our grandparents and the uncles (our only aunt had gone to California to build her fortune), but they usually asked the same question, "Have you been good children?" for which there was only one answer. Even Bailey wouldn't have dared to answer No.

12

On a late spring Saturday, after our chores (nothing like those in Stamps) were done, Bailey and I were going out, he to play baseball and I to the library. Mr. Freeman said to me, after Bailey had gone downstairs, "Ritie, go get some milk for the house."

Mother usually brought milk when she came in, but that morning as Bailey and I straightened the living room her bedroom door had been open, and we knew that she hadn't come home the night before.

He gave me the money and I rushed to the store and back to the house. After putting the milk in the icebox, I turned and had just reached the front door when I heard, "Ritie." He was sitting in the big chair by the radio. "Ritie, come here." I didn't think about the holding time until I got close to him. His pants were open and his "thing" was standing out of his britches by itself.

"No, sir, Mr. Freeman." I started to back away. I didn't want to touch that mushy-hard thing again, and I didn't need him to hold me any more. He grabbed my arm and pulled me between his legs. His face was still and looked kind, but he didn't smile or blink his eyes. Nothing. He did nothing, except reach his left hand around to turn on the radio without even looking at it. Over the noise of music and static, he said, "Now, this ain't gonna hurt you much. You liked it before, didn't you?"

I didn't want to admit that I had in fact liked his holding me or that I had liked his smell or the hard heart-beating, so I said nothing. And his face became like the face of one of those mean natives the Phantom was always having to beat up.

His legs were squeezing my waist. "Pull down your drawers." I hesitated for two reasons: he was holding me too tight to move, and I was sure that any minute my mother or Bailey or the Green Hornet would bust in the door and save me.

"We was just playing before." He released me enough to snatch down my bloomers, and then he dragged me closer to him. Turning the radio up loud, too loud, he said, "If you scream, I'm gonna kill you. And if you tell, I'm gonna kill Bailey." I could tell he meant what he said. I couldn't understand why he wanted to kill my brother. Neither of us had done anything to him. And then.

Then there was the pain. A breaking and entering when even the senses are torn apart. The act of rape on an eight-year-old body is a matter of the needle giving because the camel[1] can't. The child gives, because the body can, and the mind of the violator cannot.

I thought I had died—I woke up in a white-walled world, and it had to be heaven. But Mr. Freeman was there and he was washing me. His hands shook, but he held me upright in the tub and washed my legs. "I didn't mean to hurt you, Ritie. I didn't mean it. But don't you tell . . . Remember, don't you tell a soul."

I felt cool and very clean and just a little tired. "No, sir, Mr. Freeman, I won't tell." I was somewhere above everything. "It's just that I'm so tired I'll just go and lay down a while, please," I whispered to him. I thought if I spoke out loud, he might become frightened and hurt me again. He dried me and handed me my bloomers. "Put these on and go to the library. Your momma ought to be coming home soon. You just act natural."

Walking down the street, I felt the wet on my pants, and my hips seemed to be coming out of their sockets. I couldn't sit long on the hard seats in the library (they had been constructed for children), so I walked by the empty lot where Bailey was playing ball, but he wasn't there. I stood for a while and watched the big boys tear around the dusty diamond and then headed home.

After two blocks, I knew I'd never make it. Not unless I counted every step and stepped on every crack. I had started to burn between my legs more than the time I'd wasted Sloan's Liniment on myself. My legs throbbed, or rather the insides of my thighs throbbed, with the same force that Mr. Freeman's heart had beaten. Thrum . . . step . . . thrum . . . step . . . STEP ON THE CRACK . . . thrum . . . step. I went up the stairs one at a, one at a, one at a time. No one was in the living room, so I went straight to bed, after hiding my red-and-yellow-stained drawers under the mattress.

When Mother came in she said, "Well, young lady, I believe this is the first time I've seen you go to bed without being told. You must be sick."

I wasn't sick, but the pit of my stomach was on fire—how could I tell her that? Bailey came

---

1. An allusion to Matthew 19:24: "And again I say to you, It is easier for a camel to go through the eye of a needle, than for a rich man to enter into the kingdom of God."

in later and asked me what the matter was. There was nothing to tell him. When Mother called us to eat and I said I wasn't hungry, she laid her cool hand on my forehead and cheeks. "Maybe it's the measles. They say they're going around the neighborhood." After she took my temperature she said, "You have a little fever. You've probably just caught them."

Mr. Freeman took up the whole doorway, "Then Bailey ought not to be in there with her. Unless you want a house full of sick children." She answered over her shoulder, "He may as well have them now as later. Get them over with." She brushed by Mr. Freeman as if he were made of cotton. "Come on, Junior. Get some cool towels and wipe your sister's face."

As Bailey left the room, Mr. Freeman advanced to the bed. He leaned over, his whole face a threat that could have smothered me. "If you tell . . ." And again so softly, I almost didn't hear it—"If you tell." I couldn't summon up the energy to answer him. He had to know that I wasn't going to tell anything. Bailey came in with the towels and Mr. Freeman walked out.

Later Mother made a broth and sat on the edge of the bed to feed me. The liquid went down my throat like bones. My belly and behind were as heavy as cold iron, but it seemed my head had gone away and pure air had replaced it on my shoulders. Bailey read to me from *The Rover Boys* until he got sleepy and went to bed.

That night I kept waking to hear Mother and Mr. Freeman arguing. I couldn't hear what they were saying, but I did hope that she wouldn't make him so mad that he'd hurt her too. I knew he could do it, with his cold face and empty eyes. Their voices came in faster and faster, the high sounds on the heels of the lows. I would have liked to have gone in. Just passed through as if I were going to the toilet. Just show my face and they might stop, but my legs refused to move. I could move the toes and ankles, but the knees had turned to wood.

Maybe I slept, but soon morning was there and Mother was pretty over my bed. "How're you feeling, baby?"

"Fine, Mother." An instinctive answer. "Where's Bailey?"

She said he was still asleep but that she hadn't slept all night. She had been in my room off and on to see about me. I asked her where Mr. Freeman was, and her face chilled with remembered anger. "He's gone. Moved this morning. I'm going to take your temperature after I put on your Cream of Wheat."

Could I tell her now? The terrible pain assured me that I couldn't. What he did to me, and what I allowed, must have been very bad if already God let me hurt so much. If Mr. Freeman was gone, did that mean Bailey was out of danger? And if so, if I told him, would he still love me?

After Mother took my temperature, she said she was going to bed for a while but to wake her if I felt sicker. She told Bailey to watch my face and arms for spots and when they came up he could paint them with calamine lotion.

That Sunday goes and comes in my memory like a bad connection on an overseas telephone call. Once, Bailey was reading *The Katzenjammer Kids* to me, and then without a pause for sleeping, Mother was looking closely at my face, and soup trickled down my chin and some got into my mouth and I choked. Then there was a doctor who took my temperature and held my wrist.

"Bailey!" I supposed I had screamed, for he materialized suddenly, and I asked him to help me and we'd run away to California or France or Chicago. I knew that I was dying and, in fact, I longed for death, but I didn't want to die anywhere near Mr. Freeman. I knew that even now he wouldn't have allowed death to have me unless he wished it to.

Mother said I should be bathed and the linens had to be changed since I had sweat so much. But when they tried to move me I fought, and even Bailey couldn't hold me. Then she picked me up in her arms and the terror abated for a while. Bailey began to change the bed. As he pulled off the soiled sheets he dislodged the panties I had put under the mattress. They fell at Mother's feet.

13

In the hospital, Bailey told me that I had to tell who did that to me, or the man would hurt another little girl. When I explained that I couldn't tell because the man would kill him, Bailey said knowingly, "He can't kill me. I won't let him." And of course I believed him. Bailey didn't lie to me. So I told him.

Bailey cried at the side of my bed until I started to cry too. Almost fifteen years passed before I saw my brother cry again.

Using the old brain he was born with (those were his words later on that day) he gave his information to Grandmother Baxter, and Mr. Freeman was arrested and was spared the awful wrath of my pistolwhipping uncles.

I would have liked to stay in the hospital the rest of my life. Mother brought flowers and candy. Grandmother came with fruit and my uncles clumped around and around my bed, snorting like wild horses. When they were able to sneak Bailey in, he read to me for hours.

The saying that people who have nothing to do become busybodies is not the only truth. Excitement is a drug, and people whose lives are filled with violence are always wondering where the next "fix" is coming from.

The court was filled. Some people even stood behind the churchlike benches in the rear. Overhead fans moved with the detachment of old men. Grandmother Baxter's clients were there in gay and flippant array. The gamblers in pin-striped suits and their makeup-deep women whispered to me out of blood-red mouths that now I knew as much as they did. I was eight, and grown. Even the nurses in the hospital had told me that now I had nothing to fear. "The worst is over for you," they had said. So I put the words in all the smirking mouths.

I sat with my family (Bailey couldn't come) and they rested still on the seats like solid, cold gray tombstones. Thick and forevermore unmoving.

Poor Mr. Freeman twisted in his chair to look empty threats over to me. He didn't know that he couldn't kill Bailey . . . and Bailey didn't lie . . . to me.

"What was the defendant wearing?" That was Mr. Freeman's lawyer.

"I don't know."

"You mean to say this man raped you and you don't know what he was wearing?" He snickered as if I had raped Mr. Freeman. "Do you know if you were raped?"

A sound pushed in the air of the court (I was sure it was laughter). I was glad that Mother had let me wear the navy-blue winter coat with brass buttons. Although it was too short and the weather was typical St. Louis hot, the coat was a friend that I hugged to me in the strange and unfriendly place.

"Was that the first time the accused touched you?" The question stopped me. Mr. Freeman had surely done something very wrong, but I was convinced that I had helped him to do it. I didn't want to lie, but the lawyer wouldn't let me think, so I used silence as a retreat.

"Did the accused try to touch you before the time he or rather you say he raped you?"

I couldn't say yes and tell them how he had loved me once for a few minutes and how he had held me close before he thought I had peed in my bed. My uncles would kill me and Grandmother Baxter would stop speaking, as she often did when she was angry. And all those people in the court would stone me as they had stoned the harlot in the Bible. And Mother, who thought I was such a good girl, would be so disappointed. But most important, there was Bailey. I had kept a big secret from him.

"Marguerite, answer the question. Did the accused touch you before the occasion on which you claim he raped you?"

Everyone in the court knew that the answer had to be No. Everyone except Mr. Freeman and me. I looked at his heavy face trying to look as if he would have liked me to say No. I said No.

The lie lumped in my throat and I couldn't get air. How I despised the man for making me lie. Old, mean, nasty thing. Old, black, nasty thing. The tears didn't soothe my heart as they usually did. I screamed, "Ole, mean, dirty thing, you. Dirty old thing." Our lawyer brought me off the stand and to my mother's arms. The fact that I had arrived at my desired destination by lies made it less appealing to me.

Mr. Freeman was given one year and one day, but he never got a chance to do his time. His lawyer (or someone) got him released that very afternoon.

In the living room, where the shades were drawn for coolness, Bailey and I played Monopoly on the floor. I played a bad game because I was thinking how I would be able to tell Bailey how I had lied and, even worse for our relationship, kept a secret from him. Bailey answered the doorbell, because Grandmother was in the kitchen. A tall white policeman asked for Mrs. Baxter. Had they found out about the lie? Maybe the policeman was coming to put me in jail because I had sworn on the Bible that everything I said would be the truth, the whole truth, so help me, God. The man in our living room was taller than the sky and whiter than my image of God. He just didn't have the beard.

"Mrs. Baxter, I thought you ought to know. Freeman's been found dead on the lot behind the slaughterhouse."

Softly, as if she were discussing a church program, she said, "Poor man." She wiped her hands on the dishtowel and just as softly asked, "Do they know who did it?"

The policeman said, "Seems like he was dropped there. Some say he was kicked to death."

Grandmother's color only rose a little. "Tom, thanks for telling me. Poor man. Well, maybe it's better this way. He *was* a mad dog. Would you like a glass of lemonade? Or some beer?"

Although he looked harmless, I knew he was a dreadful angel counting out my many sins.

"No, thanks, Mrs. Baxter. I'm on duty. Gotta be getting back."

"Well, tell your ma that I'll be over when I take up my beer and remind her to save some kraut for me."

And the recording angel was gone. He was gone, and a man was dead because I lied. Where was the balance in that? One lie surely wouldn't be worth a man's life. Bailey could have explained it all to me, but I didn't dare ask him. Obviously I had forfeited my place in heaven forever, and I was as gutless as the doll I had ripped to pieces ages ago. Even Christ Himself turned His back on Satan. Wouldn't He turn His back on me? I could feel the evilness flowing through my body and waiting, pent up, to rush off my tongue if I tried to open my mouth. I clamped my teeth shut, I'd hold it in. If it escaped, wouldn't it flood the world and all the innocent people?

Grandmother Baxter said, "Ritie and Junior, you didn't hear a thing. I never want to hear this situation nor that evil man's name mentioned in my house again. I mean that." She went back into the kitchen to make apple strudel for my celebration.

Even Bailey was frightened. He sat all to himself, looking at a man's death—a kitten looking at a wolf. Not quite understanding it but frightened all the same.

In those moments I decided that although Bailey loved me he couldn't help. I had sold myself to the Devil and there could be no escape. The only thing I could do was to stop talking to people other than Bailey. Instinctively, or somehow, I knew that because I loved him so much I'd never hurt him, but if I talked to anyone else that person might die too. Just my breath, carrying my words out, might poison people and they'd curl up and die like the black fat slugs that only pretended.

I had to stop talking.

I discovered that to achieve perfect personal silence all I had to do was to attach myself leechlike to sound. I began to listen to everything. I probably hoped that after I had heard all the sounds, really heard them and packed them down, deep in my ears, the world would be quiet around me. I walked into rooms where people were laughing, their voices hitting the walls like stones, and I simply stood still—in the midst of the riot of sound. After a minute or two, silence would rush into the room from its hiding place because I had eaten up all the sounds.

In the first weeks my family accepted my behavior as a post-rape, post-hospital affliction. (Neither the term nor the experience was mentioned in Grandmother's house, where Bailey and I were again staying.) They understood that I could talk to Bailey, but to no one else.

Then came the last visit from the visiting nurse, and the doctor said I was healed. That meant that I should be back on the sidewalks playing handball or enjoying the games I had been given when I was sick. When I refused to be the child they knew and accepted me to be, I was called impudent and my muteness sullenness.

For a while I was punished for being so uppity that I wouldn't speak; and then came the thrashings, given by any relative who felt himself offended.

We were on the train going back to Stamps, and this time it was I who had to console Bailey. He cried his heart out down the aisles of the coach, and pressed his little-boy body against the window pane looking for a last glimpse of his Mother Dear.[2]

I have never known if Momma[3] sent for us, or if the St. Louis family just got fed up with my grim presence. There is nothing more appalling than a constantly morose child.

I cared less about the trip than about the fact that Bailey was unhappy, and had no more thought of our destination than if I had simply been heading for the toilet.

1970

Anne Sexton
(1928–1974)

Anne Sexton's extraordinary rise from disturbed housewife to accomplished poet may be briefly encapsulated in several ways. Minimally educated, with little prior interest in poetry, in 1956 she watched Harvard professor I. A. Richards lecture on the sonnet on public television and decided she could write one; by 1959 her growing reputation earned her an invitation to read her poetry at Harvard. In John Holmes's poetry class in 1957–1958 she read the portions of W. D. Snodgrass's "Heart's Needle," published in the anthology New Poets of England and America, and derived from that poem the impetus to treat her deepest personal wounds as directly as Snodgrass had his; by 1960 her book To Bedlam and Part Way Back had to be counted with Snodgrass's Heart's Needle (1959) and Robert Lowell's Life Studies (1959) as foremost among works in the new "confessional" mode. In 1962 she earned inclusion in New Poets of England and America: Second Selection. Half a dozen

years after she began to write seriously, she had become one of her generation's most celebrated poets.

Born Anne Gray Harvey in Newton, Massachusetts, she was raised in a family blessed with moderate wealth but at least part of the time shadowed with emotional instability. Insecure and troubled in her childhood and youth (as she later recalled those years in numerous psychiatric sessions), she was educated at Rogers Hall, a boarding school in Lowell, Massachusetts, where she did not take the college preparatory curriculum. After a year at the Garland School, a finishing school in Boston, she eloped with Alfred Sexton. Not quite 20, she was married, and over the next eight years she was a housewife, a mother of two daughters, increasingly purposeless and depressed, from time to time hospitalized for emotional problems and an attempted suicide. In high school she had written a few poems. I. A. Richards got her started again. Her psychiatrist encouraged her to continue. For the rest of her life her

2. The children's mother, left behind in St. Louis. 3. Their paternal grandmother, in Stamps.

poetry came first, but her inner torments continued.

When she turned to poetry, she was fortunate to have immediate access to other poets. At John Holmes's poetry workshop at the Boston Center for Adult Education, she met Maxine Kumin, who became her closest friend. A summer workshop at Antioch College brought her under the tutelage of W. D. Snodgrass. Snodgrass was instrumental in getting her admitted to Robert Lowell's Boston University seminar, where she met Sylvia Plath, a fellow student, and James Wright, a visiting poet. She learned from all of these people, and some of them helped immensely.

When she showed the manuscript of *To Bedlam and Part Way Back* to Holmes, he advised her not to publish the hospital portions of it: "It bothers me that you use poetry this way. It's all a release for you, but what is it for anyone else except a spectacle of someone else experiencing release? *** Don't publish it in a book. You'll certainly outgrow it, and become another person, then this record will haunt you and hurt you. It will even haunt and hurt your children years from now." Rejecting his advice, in this and later books she drew many of her most powerful poems from the intimate details of her life, and from reference to subjects not then considered material for poetry. She wrote of her family, her lovers, her deepest unconscious images. "Letter Written on a Ferry While Crossing Long Island Sound" sprang from an adulterous affair with another poet. "With Mercy for the Greedy" is directed to a friend shocked to learn that she has had an illegal abortion; in it she writes "I

was born / doing reference work in sin, and born / confessing it."

Yet it would be a mistake to think that Sexton's fame rests solely on her sensational subject matter. Constructed by a poet who combined great intuitive gifts with hard-earned and sometimes matchless craftsmanship, many of her poems speak eloquently for her generation and for her position as a woman, rather than for her condition personally. As Maxine Kumin observed in her foreword to the *The Complete Poems*, "Women poets in particular owe a debt to Anne Sexton, who broke new ground, shattered taboos***. Anne delineated the problematic position of women—the neurotic reality of the time—though she was not able to cope in her own life with the personal trouble it created." Widely honored for her verse, she continued under psychiatric care, plagued with mental breakdowns. In 1973 she was divorced; a year later she died by inhaling carbon monoxide in her garage.

The Complete Poems (1981) is the source of the texts below. *Selected Poems of Anne Sexton* (1988) was edited by Diane Wood Middlebrook and Diana Hume George. Individual titles are *To Bedlam and Part Way Back* (1960); *All My Pretty Ones* (1962); *Live or Die* (1966); *Love Poems* (1969); *Transformations* (1971); *The Book of Folly* (1972); *The Death Notebooks* (1974); *The Awful Rowing Toward God* (1975); *45 Mercy Street* (1976); and *Words for Dr. Y.: Uncollected Poems* (1978). Linda Gray Sexton and Lois Ames edited *Anne Sexton: A Self-Portrait in Letters* (1977). Steven E. Colburn edited *No Evil Star: Selected Essays, Interviews, and Prose* (1985).

A full biography is Diane Wood Middlebrook, *Anne Sexton: A Biography* (1991). Studies include Diana Hume George, *Oedipus Anne: The Poetry of Anne Sexton* (1978); and Caroline King Barnard Hall, *Anne Sexton* (1989).

Her Kind

I have gone out, a possessed witch,
haunting the black air, braver at night;
dreaming evil, I have done my hitch

over the plain houses, light by light:
lonely thing, twelve-fingered, out of mind.   5
A woman like that is not a woman, quite.
I have been her kind.

I have found the warm caves in the woods,
filled them with skillets, carvings, shelves,
closets, silks, innumerable goods;   10
fixed the suppers for the worms and the elves:
whining, rearranging the disaligned.
A woman like that is misunderstood.
I have been her kind.

I have ridden in your cart, driver,   15
waved my nude arms at villages going by,
learning the last bright routes, survivor
where your flames still bite my thigh
and my ribs crack where your wheels wind.
A woman like that is not ashamed to die.   20
I have been her kind.

                                        1960

For John,[1] Who Begs Me Not to Enquire Further

Not that it was beautiful,
but that, in the end, there was
a certain sense of order there;
something worth learning
in that narrow diary of my mind,   5
in the commonplaces of the asylum
where the cracked mirror
or my own selfish death
outstared me.
And if I tried   10
to give you something else,
something outside of myself,
you would not know
that the worst of anyone
can be, finally,   15
an accident of hope.
I tapped my own head;
it was glass, an inverted bowl.
It is a small thing
to rage in your own bowl.   20
At first it was private.
Then it was more than myself;

1. John Holmes (1904–1962), Sexton's teacher   some of her more "confessional" poems.
and friend, had advised against publication of

it was you, or your house
or your kitchen.
And if you turn away   25
because there is no lesson here
I will hold my awkward bowl,
with all its cracked stars shining
like a complicated lie,
and fasten a new skin around it   30
as if I were dressing an orange
or a strange sun.
Not that it was beautiful,
but that I found some order there.
There ought to be something special   35
for someone
in this kind of hope.
This is something I would never find
in a lovelier place, my dear,
although your fear is anyone's fear,   40
like an invisible veil between us all . . .
and sometimes in private,
my kitchen, your kitchen,
my face, your face.

1960

The Double Image

1.

I am thirty this November.
You[2] are still small, in your fourth year.
We stand watching the yellow leaves go queer,
flapping in the winter rain,
falling flat and washed. And I remember   5
mostly the three autumns you did not live here.
They said I'd never get you back again.
I tell you what you'll never really know:
all the medical hypothesis
that explained my brain will never be as true as these   10
struck leaves letting go.

I, who chose two times
to kill myself, had said your nickname
the mewling months when you first came;
until a fever rattled   15
in your throat and I moved like a pantomime
above your head. Ugly angels spoke to me. The blame,
I heard them say, was mine. They tattled

―――――――――
2. Joyce Ladd Sexton, the poet's daughter.

like green witches in my head, letting doom
leak like a broken faucet;   20
as if doom had flooded my belly and filled your bassinet,
an old debt I must assume.

Death was simpler than I'd thought.
The day life made you well and whole
I let the witches take away my guilty soul.   25
I pretended I was dead
until the white men pumped the poison out,
putting me armless and washed through the rigamarole
of talking boxes and the electric bed.
I laughed to see the private iron in that hotel.   30
Today the yellow leaves
go queer. You ask me where they go. I say today believed
in itself, or else it fell.

Today, my small child, Joyce,
love your self's self where it lives.   40
There is no special God to refer to; or if there is,
why did I let you grow
in another place. You did not know my voice
when I came back to call. All the superlatives
of tomorrow's white tree and mistletoe   45
will not help you know the holidays you had to miss.
The time I did not love
myself, I visited your shoveled walks; you held my glove.
There was new snow after this.

2.

They sent me letters with news   50
of you and I made moccasins that I would never use.
When I grew well enough to tolerate
myself, I lived with my mother. Too late,
too late, to live with your mother, the witches said.
But I didn't leave. I had my portrait   55
done instead.

Part way back from Bedlam
I came to my mother's house in Gloucester,
Massachusetts. And this is how I came
to catch at her; and this is how I lost her.   60
I cannot forgive your suicide, my mother said.
And she never could. She had my portrait
done instead.

I lived like an angry guest,
like a partly mended thing, an outgrown child.   65
I remember my mother did her best.
She took me to Boston and had my hair restyled.
Your smile is like your mother's, the artist said.
I didn't seem to care. I had my portrait
done instead.   70

There was a church where I grew up
with its white cupboards where they locked us up,
row by row, like puritans or shipmates
singing together. My father passed the plate.
Too late to be forgiven now, the witches said.   75
I wasn't exactly forgiven. They had my portrait
done instead.

3.

All that summer sprinklers arched
over the seaside grass.
We talked of drought   80
while the salt-parched
field grew sweet again. To help time pass
I tried to mow the lawn
and in the morning I had my portrait done,
holding my smile in place, till it grew formal.   85
Once I mailed you a picture of a rabbit
and a postcard of Motif number one,[3]
as if it were normal
to be a mother and be gone.

They hung my portrait in the chill   90
north light, matching
me to keep me well.
Only my mother grew ill.
She turned from me, as if death were catching,
as if death transferred,   95
as if my dying had eaten inside of her.
That August you were two, but I timed my days with doubt.
On the first of September she looked at me
and said I gave her cancer.
They carved her sweet hills out   100
and still I couldn't answer.

4.

That winter she came
part way back
from her sterile suite
of doctors, the seasick   105
cruise of the X-ray,
the cells' arithmetic
gone wild. Surgery incomplete,
the fat arm, the prognosis poor, I heard
them say.   110

During the sea blizzards
she had her
own portrait painted.

3. A scene in Rockport, Massachusetts, a favorite of painters.

A cave of a mirror
placed on the south wall;   115
matching smile, matching contour.
And you resembled me; unacquainted
with my face, you wore it. But you were mine
after all.

I wintered in Boston,   120
childless bride,
nothing sweet to spare
with witches at my side.
I missed your babyhood,
tried a second suicide,   125
tried the sealed hotel a second year.
On April Fool you fooled me. We laughed and this
was good.

5.

I checked out for the last time
on the first of May;   130
graduate of the mental cases,
with my analyst's okay,
my complete book of rhymes,
my typewriter and my suitcases.

All that summer I learned life   135
back into my own
seven rooms, visited the swan boats,
the market, answered the phone,
served cocktails as a wife
should, made love among my petticoats   140

and August tan. And you came each
weekend. But I lie.
You seldom came. I just pretended
you, small piglet, butterfly
girl with jelly bean cheeks,   145
disobedient three, my splendid

stranger. And I had to learn
why I would rather
die than love, how your innocence
would hurt and how I gather   150
guilt like a young intern
his symptoms, his certain evidence.

That October day we went
to Gloucester the red hills
reminded me of the dry red fur fox   155
coat I played in as a child; stock-still
like a bear or a tent,
like a great cave laughing or a red fur fox.

We drove past the hatchery,
the hut that sells bait,   160
past Pigeon Cove, past the Yacht Club, past Squall's
Hill, to the house that waits
still, on the top of the sea,
and two portraits hang on opposite walls.

6.

In north light, my smile is held in place,   165
the shadow marks my bone.
What could I have been dreaming as I sat there,
all of me waiting in the eyes, the zone
of the smile, the young face,
the foxes' snare.   170

In south light, her smile is held in place,
her cheeks wilting like a dry
orchid; my mocking mirror, my overthrown
love, my first image. She eyes me from that face,
that stony head of death   175
I had outgrown.

The artist caught us at the turning;
we smiled in our canvas home
before we chose our foreknown separate ways.
The dry red fur fox coat was made for burning.   180
I rot on the wall, my own
Dorian Gray.[4]

And this was the cave of the mirror,
that double woman who stares
at herself, as if she were petrified   185
in time—two ladies sitting in umber chairs.
You kissed your grandmother
and she cried.

7.

I could not get you back
except for weekends. You came   190
each time, clutching the picture of a rabbit
that I had sent you. For the last time I unpack
your things. We touch from habit.
The first visit you asked my name.
Now you stay for good. I will forget   195
how we bumped away from each other like marionettes
on strings. It wasn't the same

4. In Oscar Wilde's *The Picture of Dorian Gray*   decline of his portrait.
   (1891), Gray's decline is mirrored in the

as love, letting weekends contain
us. You scrape your knee. You learn my name,
wobbling up the sidewalk, calling and crying.   200
You call me mother and I remember my mother again,
somewhere in greater Boston, dying.

I remember we named you Joyce
so we could call you Joy.
You came like an awkward guest   205
that first time, all wrapped and moist
and strange at my heavy breast.
I needed you. I didn't want a boy,
only a girl, a small milky mouse
of a girl, already loved, already loud in the house   210
of herself. We named you Joy.
I, who was never quite sure
about being a girl, needed another
life, another image to remind me.
And this was my worst guilt; you could not cure   215
nor soothe it. I made you to find me.

1960

The Truth the Dead Know

*For my mother, born March 1902, died March 1959
and my father, born February 1900, died June 1959*

Gone, I say and walk from church,
refusing the stiff procession to the grave,
letting the dead ride alone in the hearse.
It is June. I am tired of being brave.

We drive to the Cape. I cultivate   5
myself where the sun gutters from the sky,
where the sea swings in like an iron gate
and we touch. In another country people die.

My darling, the wind falls in like stones
from the whitehearted water and when we touch   10
we enter touch entirely. No one's alone.
Men kill for this, or for as much.

And what of the dead? They lie without shoes
in their stone boats. They are more like stone
than the sea would be if it stopped. They refuse   15
to be blessed, throat, eye and knucklebone.

1962

All My Pretty Ones[5]

Father, this year's jinx rides us apart
where you followed our mother to her cold slumber;
a second shock boiling its stone to your heart,
leaving me here to shuffle and disencumber
you from the residence you could not afford: 5
a gold key, your half of a woolen mill,
twenty suits from Dunne's, an English Ford,
the love and legal verbiage of another will,
boxes of pictures of people I do not know.
I touch their cardboard faces. They must go.   10

But the eyes, as thick as wood in this album,
hold me. I stop here, where a small boy
waits in a ruffled dress for someone to come . . .
for this soldier who holds his bugle like a toy
or for this velvet lady who cannot smile.   15
Is this your father's father, this commodore
in a mailman suit? My father, time meanwhile
has made it unimportant who you are looking for.
I'll never know what these faces are all about.
I lock them into their book and throw them out.   20

This is the yellow scrapbook that you began
the year I was born; as crackling now and wrinkly
as tobacco leaves: clippings where Hoover[6] outran
the Democrats, wiggling his dry finger at me
and Prohibition; news where the *Hindenburg*[7] went   25
down and recent years where you went flush
on war. This year, solvent but sick, you meant
to marry that pretty widow in a one-month rush.
But before you had that second chance, I cried
on your fat shoulder. Three days later you died.   30

These are the snapshots of marriage, stopped in places.
Side by side at the rail toward Nassau now;
here, with the winner's cup at the speedboat races,
here, in tails at the Cotillion, you take a bow,
here, by our kennel of dogs with their pink eyes,   35
running like show-bred pigs in their chain-link pen;
here, at the horseshow where my sister wins a prize;
and here, standing like a duke among groups of men.
Now I fold you down, my drunkard, my navigator,
my first lost keeper, to love or look at later.   40

I hold a five-year diary that my mother kept
for three years, telling all she does not say
of your alcoholic tendency. You overslept,

---

5. A quotation from Macduff's reaction when he
   learns his wife and children have been killed,
   Macbeth, 4.3:216.
6. Herbert Hoover (1874–1964), elected president
   in 1928, during prohibition.
7. German zeppelin that exploded and burned at
   Lakehurst, New Jersey, in 1937.

she writes. My God, father, each Christmas Day
with your blood, will I drink down your glass   45
of wine? The diary of your hurly-burly years
goes to my shelf to wait for my age to pass.
Only in this hoarded span will love persevere.
Whether you are pretty or not, I outlive you,
bend down my strange face to yours and forgive you.   50

1962

With Mercy for the Greedy

For my friend, Ruth, who urges me to make an
appointment for the Sacrament of Confession

Concerning your letter in which you ask
me to call a priest and in which you ask
me to wear The Cross that you enclose;
your own cross,
your dog-bitten cross,   5
no larger than a thumb,
small and wooden, no thorns, this rose—

I pray to its shadow,
that gray place
where it lies on your letter . . . deep, deep.   10
I detest my sins and I try to believe
in The Cross. I touch its tender hips, its dark jawed face,
its solid neck, its brown sleep.

True. There is
a beautiful Jesus.   15
He is frozen to his bones like a chunk of beef.
How desperately he wanted to pull his arms in!
How desperately I touch his vertical and horizontal axes!
But I can't. Need is not quite belief.

All morning long   20
I have worn
your cross, hung with package string around my throat.
It tapped me lightly as a child's heart might,
tapping secondhand, softly waiting to be born.
Ruth, I cherish the letter you wrote.   25

My friend, my friend, I was born
doing reference work in sin, and born
confessing it. This is what poems are:
with mercy
for the greedy,   30
they are the tongue's wrangle,
the world's pottage, the rat's star.

1962

Self in 1958

What is reality?
I am a plaster doll; I pose
with eyes that cut open without landfall or nightfall
upon some shellacked and grinning person,
eyes that open, blue, steel, and close.   5
Am I approximately an I. Magnin[8] transplant?
I have hair, black angel,
black-angel-stuffing to comb,
nylon legs, luminous arms
and some advertised clothes.   10

I live in a doll's house
with four chairs,
a counterfeit table, a flat roof
and a big front door.
Many have come to such a small crossroad.   15
There is an iron bed,
(Life enlarges, life takes aim)
a cardboard floor,
windows that flash open on someone's city,
and little more.   20

Someone plays with me,
plants me in the all-electric kitchen,
Is this what Mrs. Rombauer[9] said?
Someone pretends with me—
I am walled in solid by their noise—   25
or puts me upon their straight bed.
They think I am me!
Their warmth? Their warmth is not a friend!
They pry my mouth for their cups of gin
and their stale bread.   30

What is reality
to this synthetic doll
who should smile, who should shift gears,
should spring the doors open in a wholesome disorder,
and have no evidence of ruin or fears?   35
But I would cry,
rooted into the wall that
was once my mother,
if I could remember how
and if I had the tears.   40

1966

8. A department store.   9. Author of *The Joy of Cooking.*

Adrienne Rich

(1929–   )

"To write directly and overtly as a woman, out of a woman's body and experience, to take women's existence seriously as theme and source for art," Adrienne Rich wrote in 1983, "was something I had been hungering to do, needing to do, all my writing life." By that time she had been publishing for over thirty years; for many she had become the poet who stood as our chief contemporary exemplar of success won by extending the bounds of womanhood.

Born in Baltimore, the child of a Jewish father and non-Jewish mother, she grew up "vaguely episcopal" in a household directed toward cultural assimilation. At Radcliffe she was taught by male teachers and read male poets, her early models: "Frost, Dylan Thomas, Donne, Auden, MacNeice, Stevens, Yeats." By her senior year she had a book of verse, *A Change of World* (1951), selected by the Yale Series of Younger Poets; in his preface, W. H. Auden described her work as "neatly and modestly dressed." Two years later she married, and before she was 30 she was the mother of three children. A second book, *The Diamond Cutters,* appeared in 1955. By the time of her third, *Snapshots of a Daughter-in-Law* (1963), her poems were showing more clearly the stresses of women's roles. At this time also she began to date each poem, emphasizing its place in a continuum of change.

In 1966 she moved with her family from Cambridge to New York. There her life and her poems became increasingly political, involved with war resistance, the needs of the disadvantaged, the problems of the Third World, civil rights, and the women's movement. In 1970 she left her husband, who committed suicide not long after. Increasingly,

ideas of personal and cultural change began to dominate her work, as suggested in the title *The Will to Change* (1971), alluding to Charles Olson's lines "What does not change / is the will to change." At about the same time, in her influential essay "When We Dead Awaken: Writing as Re-Vision," she wrote that, for women,

Re-vision—the act of looking back, of seeing with fresh eyes, of entering an old text from a new critical direction—is for us more than a chapter in cultural history: it is an act of survival. Until we can understand the assumptions in which we are drenched we cannot know ourselves. And this drive to self-knowledge, for woman, is more than a search for identity: it is part of her refusal of the self-destructiveness of male-dominated society.

For several years in the 1970s, with Michelle Cliff she edited the feminist-lesbian journal *Sinister Wisdom* in western Massachusetts. More recently, she has lived, written, and taught in California.

The Fact of a Doorframe: Poems Selected and New 1950–1984 (1984), the source of the texts below, presents the author's selections from nine earlier books and includes some new poems. Other collections of verse, besides those named above, include *Necessities of Life* (1966); *Leaflets* (1969); *Diving into the Wreck* (1973); *The Dream of a Common Language* (1978); *A Wild Patience Has Taken Me This Far* (1981); *Your Native Land, Your Life* (1986); *Time's Power* (1989); and *An Atlas of the Difficult World* (1991). Prose works include *Of Woman Born: Motherhood as Experience and Institution* (1976); *On Lies, Secrets, and Silence* (1979); and *Blood, Bread, and Poetry* (1987).

Studies include Wendy Martin, *An American Triptych: Anne Bradstreet, Emily Dickinson, Adrienne Rich* (1984); and Claire Keyes, *The Aesthetics of Power: The Poetry of Adrienne Rich* (1986).

Aunt Jennifer's Tigers

Aunt Jennifer's tigers prance across a screen,
Bright topaz denizens of a world of green.
They do not fear the men beneath the tree;
They pace in sleek chivalric certainty.

Aunt Jennifer's fingers fluttering through her wool   5
Find even the ivory needle hard to pull.
The massive weight of Uncle's wedding band
Sits heavily upon Aunt Jennifer's hand.

When Aunt is dead, her terrified hands will lie
Still ringed with ordeals she was mastered by.   10
The tigers in the panel that she made
Will go on prancing, proud and unafraid.

                                                  1951

Living in Sin

She had thought the studio would keep itself;
no dust upon the furniture of love.
Half heresy, to wish the taps less vocal,
the panes relieved of grime. A plate of pears,
a piano with a Persian shawl, a cat   5
stalking the picturesque amusing mouse
had risen at his urging.
Not that at five each separate stair would writhe
under the milkman's tramp; that morning light
so coldly would delineate the scraps   10
of last night's cheese and three sepulchral bottles;
that on the kitchen shelf among the saucers
a pair of beetle-eyes would fix her own—
envoy from some village in the moldings . . .
Meanwhile, he, with a yawn,   15
sounded a dozen notes upon the keyboard,
declared it out of tune, shrugged at the mirror,
rubbed at his beard, went out for cigarettes;
while she, jeered by the minor demons,
pulled back the sheets and made the bed and found   20
a towel to dust the table-top,
and let the coffee-pot boil over on the stove.
By evening she was back in love again,
though not so wholly but throughout the night
she woke sometimes to feel the daylight coming   25
like a relentless milkman up the stairs.

                                                  1955

Snapshots of a Daughter-in-Law

1.

You, once a belle in Shreveport,
with henna-colored hair, skin like a peachbud,
still have your dresses copied from that time,
and play a Chopin prelude
called by Cortot: *"Delicious recollections*   5
float like perfume through the memory."[1]

Your mind now, moldering like wedding-cake,
heavy with useless experience, rich
with suspicion, rumor, fantasy,
crumbling to pieces under the knife-edge   10
of mere fact. In the prime of your life.

Nervy, glowering, your daughter
wipes the teaspoons, grows another way.

2.

Banging the coffee-pot into the sink
she hears the angels chiding, and looks out   15
past the raked gardens to the sloppy sky.
Only a week since They said: *Have no patience.*

The next time it was: *Be insatiable.*
Then: *Save yourself; others you cannot save.*
Sometimes she's let the tapstream scald her arm,   20
a match burn to her thumbnail,

or held her hand above the kettle's snout
right in the woolly steam. They are probably angels,
since nothing hurts her anymore, except
each morning's grit blowing into her eyes.   25

3.

A thinking woman sleeps with monsters.
The beak that grips her, she becomes. And Nature,
that sprung-lidded, still commodious
steamer-trunk of *tempora* and *mores*[2]
gets stuffed with it all: the mildewed orange-flowers,   30
the female pills, the terrible breasts
of Boadicea[3] beneath flat foxes' heads and orchids.

Two handsome women, gripped in argument,
each proud, acute, subtle, I hear scream

---

1. Alfred Cortot (1877–1962) in *Chopin: 24 Preludes* (1930). Frédéric Chopin (1810–1849) was a Polish composer and pianist who lived in France after 1831.

2. "Times" and "customs" (Latin).
3. British queen who led a revolt against the Romans. She died A.D. 61.

across the cut glass and majolica   35
like Furies[4] cornered from their prey:
The argument *ad feminam*,[5] all the old knives
that have rusted in my back, I drive in yours,
ma semblable, ma soeur![6]

4.

Knowing themselves too well in one another: 40
their gifts no pure fruition, but a thorn,
the prick filed sharp against a hint of scorn . . .
Reading while waiting
for the iron to heat,
writing, *My Life had stood—a Loaded Gun*—[7]   45
in that Amherst pantry while the jellies boil and scum,
or, more often,
iron-eyed and beaked and purposed as a bird,
dusting everything on the whatnot every day of life.

5.

Dulce ridens, dulce loquens,[8]   50
she shaves her legs until they gleam
like petrified mammoth-tusk.

6.

When to her lute Corinna sings[9]
neither words nor music are her own;
only the long hair dipping   55
over her cheek, only the song
of silk against her knees
and these
adjusted in reflections of an eye.

Poised, trembling and unsatisfied, before   60
an unlocked door, that cage of cages,
tell us, you bird, you tragical machine—
is this *fertilisante douleur*?[1] Pinned down
by love, for you the only natural action,
are you edged more keen   65
to prise the secrets of the vault? has Nature shown
her household books to you, daughter-in-law,
that her sons never saw?

---

4. Greek goddesses of vengeance.
5. An argument attacking the woman, not her
   ideas, on the model of *ad hominem*, attacking
   the man.
6. "My likeness, my sister" (French), alluding to
   a line in Baudelaire's *Flowers of Evil*, repeated
   in T. S. Eliot's *The Waste Land*, where the word

is "brother."
7. Poem by Emily Dickinson.
8. "Sweetly laughing, sweetly speaking" (Latin),
   from Horace's Ode 22.
9. A line quoted from Thomas Campion
   (1567–1620), British poet.
1. "Fertilizing sadness" (French).

7.

"To have in this uncertain world some stay
which cannot be undermined, is   70
of the utmost consequence."[2]
                                        Thus wrote
a woman, partly brave and partly good,
who fought with what she partly understood.
Few men about her would or could do more,   75
hence she was labeled harpy, shrew and whore.

8.

"You all die at fifteen," said Diderot,[3]
and turn part legend, part convention.
Still, eyes inaccurately dream
behind closed windows blankening with steam.   80
Deliciously, all that we might have been,
all that we were—fire, tears,
wit, taste, martyred ambition—
stirs like the memory of refused adultery
the drained and flagging bosom of our middle years. 85

9.

Not that it is done well, but
that it is done at all?[4] Yes, think
of the odds! or shrug them off forever.
This luxury of the precocious child,
Time's precious chronic invalid,—   90
would we, darlings, resign it if we could?
Our blight has been our sinecure:
mere talent was enough for us—
glitter in fragments and rough drafts.

Sigh no more, ladies.
                        Time is male   95
and in his cups drinks to the fair.
Bemused by gallantry, we hear
our mediocrities over-praised,
indolence read as abnegation,
slattern thought styled intuition,   100
every lapse forgiven, our crime
only to cast too bold a shadow
or smash the mold straight off.

2. Mary Wollstonecroft in *Thoughts on the*
Education of Daughters (London, 1787) [Sexton's
note].

3. Denis Diderot (1713–1784), French writer and
philosopher. The quotation is from his *Letters to*
Sophie Volland.

4. An allusion to Doctor Johnson's "Sir, a
woman's preaching is like a dog's walking on
his hind legs. It is not done well, but you are
surprised to find it done at all," reported in
James Boswell's *Life of Samuel Johnson.*

For that, solitary confinement,   105
tear gas, attrition shelling.
Few applicants for that honor.

10.

                              Well,
she's long about her coming, who must be
more merciless to herself than history.   110
Her mind full to the wind, I see her plunge
breasted and glancing through the currents,
taking the light upon her
at least as beautiful as any boy
or helicopter,   115
                    poised, still coming,
her fine blades making the air wince

but her cargo
no promise then:
delivered   120
palpable
ours.

1958–1960   1963

"I Am in Danger—Sir—"[5]

"Half-cracked" to Higginson, living,
afterward famous in garbled versions,
your hoard of dazzling scraps a battlefield,
now your old snood

mothballed at Harvard   5
and you in your variorum monument[6]
equivocal to the end—
who are you?

Gardening the day-lily,
wiping the wine-glass stems,   10
your thought pulsed on behind
a forehead battered paper-thin,

you, woman, masculine
in single-mindedness,
for whom the word was more   15
than a symptom—

<hr/>

5. From a letter from Emily Dickinson to her
friend and adviser Thomas Wentworth
Higginson (1823–1911), after he had criticized
the irregularities in her verse.

6. The variorum edition of her *Poems* (1955),
edited by Thomas H. Johnson, preserving all
her variations.

a condition of being.
Till the air buzzing with spoiled language
sang in your ears
of Perjury   20

and in your half-cracked way you chose
silence for entertainment,
chose to have it out at last
on your own premises.

1964   1966

Face to Face

Never to be lonely like that—
the Early American figure on the beach
in black coat and knee-breeches
scanning the didactic storm in privacy,

never to hear the prairie wolves   5
in their lunar hilarity
circling one's little all, one's claim
to be Law and Prophets

for all that lawlessness,
never to whet the appetite   10
weeks early, for a face, a hand
longed-for and dreaded—

How people used to meet!
starved, intense, the old
Christmas gifts saved up till spring,   15
and the old plain words,

and each with his God-given secret,
spelled out through months of snow and silence,
burning under the bleached scalp; behind dry lips
a loaded gun.   20

1965   1966

Diving into the Wreck

First having read the book of myths,
and loaded the camera,
and checked the edge of the knife-blade,
I put on
the body-armor of black rubber   5
the absurd flippers
the grave and awkward mask.

I am having to do this
not like Cousteau[7] with his
assiduous team   10
aboard the sun-flooded schooner
but here alone.

There is a ladder.
The ladder is always there
hanging innocently   15
close to the side of the schooner.
We know what it is for,
we who have used it.
Otherwise
it's a piece of maritime floss   20
some sundry equipment.

I go down.
Rung after rung and still
the oxygen immerses me
the blue light   25
the clear atoms
of our human air.
I go down.
My flippers cripple me,
I crawl like an insect down the ladder   30
and there is no one
to tell me when the ocean
will begin.

First the air is blue and then
it is bluer and then green and then   35
black I am blacking out and yet
my mask is powerful
it pumps my blood with power
the sea is another story
the sea is not a question of power   40
I have to learn alone
to turn my body without force
in the deep element.

And now: it is easy to forget
what I came for   45
among so many who have always
lived here
swaying their crenellated fans
between the reefs
and besides   50
you breathe differently down here.

I came to explore the wreck.
The words are purposes.
The words are maps.
I came to see the damage that was done   55

7. Jacques-Yves Cousteau, French underwater explorer.

and the treasures that prevail.
I stroke the beam of my lamp
slowly along the flank
of something more permanent
than fish or weed   60

the thing I came for:
the wreck and not the story of the wreck
the thing itself and not the myth
the drowned face always staring
toward the sun   65
the evidence of damage
worn by salt and sway into this threadbare beauty
the ribs of the disaster
curving their assertion
among the tentative haunters.   70

This is the place.
And I am here, the mermaid whose dark hair
streams black, the merman in his armored body
We circle silently
about the wreck   75
we dive into the hold.
I am she: I am he

whose drowned face sleeps with open eyes
whose breasts still bear the stress
whose silver, copper, vermeil cargo lies   80
obscurely inside barrels
half-wedged and left to rot
we are the half-destroyed instruments
that once held to a course
the water-eaten log   85
the fouled compass

We are, I am, you are
by cowardice or courage
the one who find our way
back to this scene   90
carrying a knife, a camera
a book of myths
in which
our names do not appear.

1972   1973

From a Survivor

The pact that we made was the ordinary pact
of men & women in those days

I don't know who we thought we were
that our personalities
could resist the failures of the race   5

Lucky or unlucky, we didn't know
the race had failures of that order
and that we were going to share them

Like everybody else, we thought of ourselves as special

Your body is as vivid to me   10
as it ever was: even more

since my feeling for it is clearer:
I know what it could and could not do

it is no longer
the body of a god   15
or anything with power over my life

Next year it would have been 20 years[8]
and you are wastefully dead
who might have made the leap
we talked, too late, of making   20

which I live now
not as a leap
but a succession of brief, amazing movements

each one making possible the next

1972   1973

For the Dead

I dreamed I called you on the telephone
to say: *Be kinder to yourself*
but you were sick and would not answer

The waste of my love goes on this way
trying to save you from yourself   5

I have always wondered about the leftover
energy, water rushing down a hill
long after the rains have stopped

or the fire you want to go to bed from
but cannot leave, burning-down but not burnt-down   10
the red coals more extreme, more curious
in their flashing and dying
than you wish they were
sitting there long after midnight

1972   1973

8. Since her marriage. Her husband, to whom the poem is addressed, had died a suicide in 1970.

From Twenty-One Love Poems

XVIII

Rain on the West Side Highway,
red light at Riverside:
the more I live the more I think
two people together is a miracle.
You're telling the story of your life   5
for once, a tremor breaks the surface of your words.
The story of our lives becomes our lives.
Now you're in fugue across what some I'm sure
Victorian poet[9] called the *salt estranging sea.*
Those are the words that come to mind.   10
I feel estrangement, yes. As I've felt dawn
pushing toward daybreak. Something: a cleft of light—?
Close between grief and anger, a space opens
where I am Adrienne alone. And growing colder.

1974–1976   1978

Upper Broadway

The leafbud straggles forth
toward the frigid light of the airshaft   this is faith
this pale extension of a day
when looking up   you know   something is changing
winter has turned   though the wind is colder   5
Three streets away   a roof collapses   onto people
who thought they still had time   Time out of mind

I have written so many words
wanting to live inside you
to be of use to you   10

Now I must write for myself   for this blind
woman scratching the pavement   with her wand of thought
this slippered crone   inching on icy streets
reaching into wire trashbaskets   pulling out
what was thrown away   and infinitely precious   15

I look at hands and see   they are still unfinished
I look at the vine and see the leafbud
inching towards life

I look at my face in the glass   and see
a halfborn woman   20

1975   1978

9. Matthew Arnold (1822–1888), English poet. The italicized words that follow end his "To
Marguerite."

Lorraine Hansberry

(1930–1965)

Lorraine Hansberry's play *A Raisin in the Sun* (1959) stands as a landmark in dramatic history: it was the first work by a black woman to be presented on Broadway; competing against plays by Tennessee Williams, Eugene O'Neill, and Archibald MacLeish, it won the 1959 New York Drama Critics Circle Award (the first drama by a black writer to be so honored); and the author was named in a *Variety* poll of critics as the season's "most promising" playwright. In the glow of her first play's success, Hansberry began work on several new works as well as the screenplay for *Raisin.* The movie, with a cast including Sidney Poitier, Ruby Dee, and Claudia McNeil, won a special award at the Cannes Film Festival (1961).

Everything pointed to a great career in the theater, but death was already stalking Lorraine Hansberry. Early in 1963 she was diagnosed with cancer of the duodenum; for the remaining two years of her life she was in pain from the disease and radiation treatment, and finally lapsed into blindness, then coma. She died on the same day that her second play, *The Sign in Sidney Brustein's Window,* closed on Broadway.

Hansberry was the youngest child of an upper middle-class Chicago family. Her father was a successful real estate owner-manager, and her mother was active in Republican politics. Her uncle William Leo Hansberry, an expert in African history, often visited and brought along exchange students; such well-known figures as Langston Hughes, W. E. B. Du Bois, Duke Ellington, and Paul Robeson were guests in the Hansberry home when Lorraine was young.

Though her family's financial success provided a partial shield against racial bigotry, an event that took place during her childhood made a strong impression on Hansberry. In 1938, trying to escape their cramped inner-city apartment, the family bought a house in a white residential area, where hostile neighbors harassed them; a brick thrown through the living room window narrowly missed Lorraine. When the Illinois courts found against them and the family was evicted, Carl Hansberry, Sr., and the NAACP appealed, finally winning a judgment against racial covenants in the Supreme Court (1940). Mr. Hansberry, embittered by his experience, bought a house in Mexico, but his plan to relocate his family there was thwarted when he died suddenly of a cerebral hemorrhage (1946).

Graduating from Englewood High School (1948), Hansberry enrolled at the University of Wisconsin, where she saw *Juno and the Paycock,* her first introduction to the work of Sean O'Casey, a writer who was influential in her evolving attitudes about drama. She was active in the college theater group, dated African exchange students, supported the independent candidacy of Henry Wallace for president, and was chair of the Young Progressives of America chapter.

After two years she left school and went to New York, where she wrote for Paul Robeson's *Freedom* magazine (1951–1953), studied African history with Du Bois (1953), and taught black literature. In 1952 she attended an international peace conference in Uruguay as a surrogate for Robeson, whose passport had been revoked in the McCarthyite atmosphere of the time. Her own passport was revoked when she returned to the United States.

The following year she met and married Robert Nemiroff, a song writer, and they moved to an apartment on Bleeker Street in Greenwich Village. When Nemiroff's song "Cindy, Oh Cindy" became a hit, Hansberry was able to quit her job and devote herself full time to writing. The stage and film success of *Raisin* allowed the couple to buy first a Greenwich Village brownstone and then a home in Croton-on-Hudson (1962).

The Sign in Sidney Brustein's Window opened on Broadway in 1964. While *Raisin* centered on the African-American Younger family's struggle against external racism and internal tensions, *Brustein* had a biracial cast and dealt with abstract ideas of human responsibility and interdependence. It evoked a mixed critical reaction, and only the support of actors and political activists enabled it to run for 101 performances.

At her death, Hansberry left behind three partial or finished plays: *The Drinking Gourd*, a treatment of slavery commissioned but never filmed by a television network;

What Use Are Flowers, a brief allegorical work; and *Les Blancs* ("The Whites"), set in Africa. Nemiroff, divorced from Hansberry at her death but designated her literary executor and still devoted to her work, edited the manuscripts and saw them published as *The Collected Last Plays of Lorraine Hansberry* (1972). He also put together selections from the plays, unpublished work, magazine essays, and letters under the title *To Be Young, Gifted, and Black: Lorraine Hansberry in Her Own Words* (1969).

Anne Cheney's *Lorraine Hansberry* (1984) is a biographical and critical study.

A Raisin in the Sun

To Mama: in gratitude for the dream

Characters

Ruth Younger
Travis Younger
Walter Lee Younger (Brother)
Beneatha Younger
Lena Younger (Mama)

Joseph Asagai
George Murchison
Karl Lindner
Bobo
Moving Men

(The action of the play is set in Chicago's Southside, sometime between World War II and the present)

Act One

Scene 1.   *Friday morning*

Scene 2.   *The following morning*

Act Two

Scene 1.   *Later, the same day.*

Scene 2.   *Friday night, a few weeks later.*

Scene 3.   *Moving day, one week later.*

Act Three

An hour later

What happens to a dream deferred?
Does it dry up
Like a raisin in the sun?
Or fester like a sore—
And then run?

Does it stink like rotten meat?
Or crust and sugar over—
Like a syrupy sweet?

Maybe it just sags
Like a heavy load.

Or does it explode?

Langston Hughes

Act One

Scene I

The Younger living room would be a comfortable and well ordered room if it were not for a number of indestructible contradictions to this state of being. Its furnishings are typical and undistinguished and their primary feature now is that they have clearly had to accommodate the living of too many people for too many years—and they are tired. Still, we can see that at some time, a time probably no longer remembered by the family (except perhaps for Mama), the furnishings of this room were actually selected with care and love and even hope—and brought to this apartment and arranged with taste and pride.

That was a long time ago. Now the once loved pattern of the couch upholstery has to fight to show itself from under acres of crocheted doilies and couch covers which have themselves finally come to be more important than the upholstery. And here a table or a chair has been moved to disguise the worn places in the carpet; but the carpet has fought back by showing its weariness, with depressing uniformity, elsewhere on its surface.

Weariness has, in fact, won in this room. Everything has been polished, washed, sat on, used, scrubbed too often. All pretenses but living itself have long since vanished from the very atmosphere of this room.

Moreover, a section of this room, for it is not really a room unto itself, though the landlord's lease would make it seem so, slopes backward to provide a small kitchen area, where the family prepares the meals that are eaten in the living room proper, which must also serve as dining room. The single window that has been provided for these "two" rooms is located in this kitchen area. The sole natural light the family may enjoy in the course of a day is only that which fights its way through this little window.

At left, a door leads to a bedroom which is shared by Mama and her daughter, Beneatha. At right, opposite, is a second room (which in the beginning of the life of this apartment was probably a breakfast room) which serves as a bedroom for Walter and his wife, Ruth.

Time: Sometime between World War II and the present.

Place: Chicago's Southside.

At Rise: It is morning dark in the living room. Travis is asleep on the make-down bed at center. An alarm clock sounds from within the bedroom at right, and presently Ruth enters from that room and closes the door behind her. She crosses sleepily toward the window. As she passes her sleeping son she reaches down and shakes him a little. At the window she raises the shade and a dusky Southside morning light comes in feebly. She fills a pot with water and puts it on to boil. She calls to the boy, between yawns, in a slightly muffed voice.

Ruth is about thirty. We can see that she was a pretty girl, even exceptionally so, but now it is apparent that life has been little that she expected, and disappointment has already begun to hang in her face. In a few years, before thirty-five even, she will be known among her people as a "settled woman."

She crosses to her son and gives him a good, final, rousing shake.

RUTH: Come on now, boy, it's seven thirty! *(Her son sits up at last, in a stupor of sleepiness)* I say hurry up, Travis! You ain't the only person in the world got to use a bathroom! *(The child, a sturdy, handsome little boy of ten or eleven, drags himself out of the bed and almost blindly takes his towels and "today's clothes" from drawers and a closet and goes out to the bathroom, which is in an outside hall and which is shared by another family or families on the same floor. Ruth crosses to the bedroom door at right and opens it and calls in to her husband.)* Walter Lee! . . . It's after seven thirty! Lemme see you do some waking up in there now! *(She waits)* You better get up from there, man! It's after seven thirty I tell you. *(She waits again)* All right, you just go ahead and lay there and next thing you know Travis be finished and Mr. Johnson'll be in there and you'll be fussing and cussing round here like a mad man! And be late too! *(She waits, at the end of patience)* Walter Lee—it's time for you to get up!

(She waits another second and then starts to go into the bedroom, but is apparently satisfied that her husband has begun to get up. She stops, pulls the door to, and returns to the kitchen area. She wipes her face with a moist cloth and runs her fingers through her sleep-disheveled hair in a vain effort and ties an apron around her housecoat. The bedroom door at right opens and her husband stands in the doorway in his pajamas, which are rumpled and mismated. He is a lean, intense young man in his middle thirties, inclined to quick nervous movements and erratic speech habits—and always in his voice there is a quality of indictment.)

WALTER: Is he out yet?

RUTH: What you mean *out?* He ain't hardly got in there good yet.

WALTER *(Wandering in, still more oriented to sleep than to a new day)*: Well, what was you doing all that yelling for if I can't even get in there yet? *(Stopping and thinking)* Check coming today?

RUTH: They *said* Saturday and this is just Friday and I hopes to God you ain't going to get up here first thing this morning and start talking to me 'bout no money—'cause I 'bout don't want to hear it.

WALTER: Something the matter with you this morning?

RUTH: No—I'm just sleepy as the devil. What kind of eggs you want?

WALTER: Not scrambled. *(Ruth starts to scramble eggs)* Paper come? *(Ruth points impatiently to the rolled up Tribune on the table, and he gets it and spreads it out and vaguely reads the front page)* Set off another bomb yesterday.

RUTH *(Maximum indifference)*: Did they?

WALTER *(Looking up)*: What's the matter with you?

RUTH: Ain't nothing the matter with me. And don't keep asking me that this morning.

WALTER: Ain't nobody bothering you. *(Reading the news of the day absently again)* Say Colonel McCormick[1] is sick.

RUTH *(Affecting tea-party interest)*: Is he now? Poor thing.

WALTER *(Sighing and looking at his watch)*: Oh, me. *(He waits)* Now what is that boy doing in that bathroom all this time? He just going to have to start getting up earlier. I can't be being late to work on account of him fooling around in there.

RUTH *(Turning on him)*: Oh, no he ain't going to be getting up no earlier no such thing! It ain't his fault that he can't get to bed no earlier nights 'cause he got a bunch of crazy good-for-nothing clowns sitting up running their mouths in what is supposed to be his bedroom after ten o'clock at night. . . .

---

1. Robert Rutherford McCormick (1880–1955), owner of *The Chicago Tribune*. His paper took positions against labor unions and for isolationism.

WALTER: That's what you mad about, ain't it? The things I want to talk about with my
friends just couldn't be important in your mind, could they?

(He rises and finds a cigarette in her handbag on the table and crosses to the little window
and looks out, smoking and deeply enjoying this first one)

RUTH (Almost matter of factly, a complaint too automatic to deserve emphasis): Why you
always got to smoke before you eat in the morning?
WALTER (At the window): Just look at 'em down there . . . Running and racing to work
. . . (He turns and faces his wife and watches her a moment at the stove, and then,
suddenly) You look young this morning, baby.
RUTH (Indifferently): Yeah?
WALTER: Just for a second—stirring them eggs. It's gone now—just for a second it
was—you looked real young again. (Then, drily) It's gone now—you look like
yourself again.
RUTH: Man, if you don't shut up and leave me alone.
WALTER (Looking out to the street again): First thing a man ought to learn in life is not
to make love to no colored woman first thing in the morning. You all some evil
people at eight o'clock in the morning.

(Travis appears in the hall doorway, almost fully dressed and quite wide awake now, his
towels and pajamas across his shoulders. He opens the door and signals for his father to
make the bathroom in a hurry.)

TRAVIS (Watching the bathroom): Daddy, come on!

(Walter gets his bathroom utensils and flies out to the bathroom)

RUTH: Sit down and have your breakfast, Travis.
TRAVIS: Mama, this is Friday. (Gleefully) Check coming tomorrow, huh?
RUTH: You get your mind off money and eat your breakfast.
TRAVIS (Eating): This is the morning we supposed to bring the fifty cents to school.
RUTH: Well, I ain't got no fifty cents this morning.
TRAVIS: Teacher say we have to.
RUTH: I don't care what teacher say. I ain't got it. Eat your breakfast, Travis.
TRAVIS: I am eating.
RUTH: Hush up now and just eat!

(The boy gives her an exasperated look for her lack of understanding, and eats grudgingly)

TRAVIS: You think Grandmama would have it?
RUTH: No! And I want you to stop asking your grandmother for money, you hear me?
TRAVIS (Outraged): Gaaaleee! I don't ask her, she just gimme it sometimes!
RUTH: Travis Willard Younger—I got too much on me this morning to be—
TRAVIS: Maybe Daddy—
RUTH: Travis!

(The boy hushes abruptly. They are both quiet and tense for several seconds.)

TRAVIS (Presently): Could I maybe go carry some groceries in front of the supermarket
for a little while after school then?
RUTH: Just hush, I said. (Travis jabs his spoon into his cereal bowl viciously, and rests his

head in anger upon his fists) If you through eating, you can get over there and make up your bed.

(The boy obeys stiffly and crosses the room, almost mechanically, to the bed and more or less carefully folds the covering. He carries the bedding into his mother's room and returns with his books and cap.)

TRAVIS *(Sulking and standing apart from her unnaturally)*: I'm gone.

RUTH *(Looking up from the stove to inspect him automatically)*: Come here. *(He crosses to her and she studies his head)* If you don't take this comb and fix this here head, you better! *(Travis puts down his books with a great sigh of oppression, and crosses to the mirror. His mother mutters under her breath about his "slubbornness")* 'Bout to march out of here with that head looking just like chickens slept in it! I just don't know where you get your slubborn ways . . . And get your jacket, too. Looks chilly out this morning.

TRAVIS *(With conspicuously brushed hair and jacket)*: I'm gone.

RUTH: Get carfare and milk money—*(Waving one finger)*—and not a single penny for no caps, you hear me?

TRAVIS *(With sullen politeness)*: Yes'm.

(He turns in outrage to leave. His mother watches after him as in his frustration he approaches the door almost comically. When she speaks to him, her voice has become a very gentle tease.)

RUTH *(Mocking; as she thinks he would say it)*: Oh, Mama makes me so mad sometimes, I don't know what to do! *(She waits and continues to his back as he stands stock-still in front of the door)* I wouldn't kiss that woman good-bye for nothing in this world this morning! *(The boy finally turns around and rolls his eyes at her, knowing the mood has changed and he is vindicated; he does not, however, move toward her yet)* Not for nothing in this world! *(She finally laughs aloud at him and holds out her arms to him and we see that it is a way between them, very old and practiced. He crosses to her and allows her to embrace him warmly but keeps his face fixed with masculine rigidity. She holds him back from her presently and looks at him and runs her fingers over the features of his face. With utter gentleness—)* Now—whose little old angry man are you?

TRAVIS *(The masculinity and gruffness start to fade at last)*: Aw gaalee—Mama . . .

RUTH *(Mimicking)*: Aw-gaaaaalleeeee, Mama! *(She pushes him, with rough playfulness and finality, toward the door)* Get on out of here or you going to be late.

TRAVIS *(In the face of love, new aggressiveness)*: Mama, could I *please* go carry groceries?

RUTH: Honey, it's starting to get so cold evenings.

WALTER *(Coming in from the bathroom and drawing a make-believe gun from a make-believe holster and shooting at his son)*: What is it he wants to do?

RUTH: Go carry groceries after school at the supermarket.

WALTER: Well, let him go . . .

TRAVIS *(Quickly, to the ally)*: I have to—she won't gimme the fifty cents . . .

WALTER *(To his wife only)*: Why not?

RUTH *(Simply, and with flavor)*: 'Cause we don't have it.

WALTER *(To Ruth only)*: What you tell the boy things like that for? *(Reaching down into his pants with a rather important gesture)* Here, son—

(He hands the boy the coin, but his eyes are directed to his wife's. Travis takes the money happily.)

TRAVIS: Thanks, Daddy.

(He starts out. Ruth watches both of them with murder in her eyes. Walter stands and stares back at her with defiance, and suddenly reaches into his pocket again on an afterthought.)

WALTER *(Without even looking at his son, still staring hard at his wife)*: In fact, here's another fifty cents . . . Buy yourself some fruit today—or take a taxi cab to school or something!

TRAVIS: Whoopee—

(He leaps up and clasps his father around the middle with his legs, and they face each other in mutual appreciation; slowly Walter Lee peeks around the boy to catch the violent rays from his wife's eyes and draws his head back as if shot)

WALTER: You better get down now—and get to school, man.

TRAVIS *(At the door)*: O.K. Good-bye.

(He exits)

WALTER *(After him, pointing with pride)*: That's *my* boy. *(She looks at him in disgust and turns back to her work)* You know what I was thinking 'bout in the bathroom this morning?

RUTH: No.

WALTER: How come you always try to be so pleasant!

RUTH: What is there to be pleasant 'bout!

WALTER: You want to know what I was thinking 'bout in the bathroom or not!

RUTH: I know what you was thinking 'bout.

WALTER *(Ignoring her)*: 'Bout what me and Willy Harris was talking about last night.

RUTH *(Immediately—a refrain)*: Willy Harris is a good-for-nothing loud mouth.

WALTER: Anybody who talks to me has got to be a good-for-nothing loud mouth, ain't he? And what you know about who is just a good-for-nothing loud mouth? Charlie Atkins was just a "good-for-nothing loud mouth" too, wasn't he! When he wanted me to go in the dry-cleaning business with him. And now—he's grossing a hundred thousand a year. A hundred thousand dollars a year! You still call *him* a loud mouth!

RUTH *(Bitterly)*: Oh, Walter Lee . . .

(She folds her head on her arms over on the table)

WALTER *(Rising and coming to her and standing over her)*: You tired, ain't you? Tired of everything. Me, the boy, the way we live—this beat-up hole—everything. Ain't you? *(She doesn't look up, doesn't answer)* So tired—moaning and groaning all the time, but you wouldn't do nothing to help, would you? You couldn't be on my side that long for nothing, could you?

RUTH: Walter, please leave me alone.

WALTER: A man needs for a woman to back him up . . .

RUTH: Walter—

WALTER: Mama would listen to you. You know she listen to you more than she do me and Bennie. She think more of you. All you have to do is just sit down with her when you drinking your coffee one morning and talking 'bout things like you do and—*(He sits down beside her and demonstrates graphically what he thinks her methods and tone should be)*—you just sip your coffee, see, and say easy like that you been thinking 'bout that deal Walter Lee is so interested in, 'bout the store and all, and sip some more coffee, like what you saying ain't really that important to you—And the next thing you know, she be listening good and asking you questions and when I come home—I can tell her the details. This ain't no fly-by-night proposition, baby. I mean we figured it out, me and Willy and Bobo.

RUTH (*With a frown*): Bobo?

WALTER: Yeah. You see, this little liquor store we got in mind cost seventy-five thousand and we figured the initial investment on the place be 'bout thirty thousand, see. That be ten thousand each. Course, there's a couple of hundred you got to pay so's you don't spend your life just waiting for them clowns to let your license get approved—

RUTH: You mean graft?

WALTER (*Frowning impatiently*): Don't call it that. See there, that just goes to show you what women understand about the world. Baby, don't *nothing* happen for you in this world 'less you pay *somebody* off!

RUTH: Walter, leave me alone! (*She raises her head and stares at him vigorously—then says, more quietly*) Eat your eggs, they gonna be cold.

WALTER (*Straightening up from her and looking off*): That's it. There you are. Man say to his woman: I got me a dream. His woman say: Eat your eggs. (*Sadly, but gaining in power*) Man say: I got to take hold of this here world, baby! And a woman will say: Eat your eggs and go to work. (*Passionately now*) Man say: I got to change my life, I'm choking to death, baby! And his woman say—(*In utter anguish as he brings his fists down on his thighs*)—Your eggs is getting cold!

RUTH (*Softly*): Walter, that ain't none of our money.

WALTER (*Not listening at all or even looking at her*): This morning, I was lookin' in the mirror and thinking about it . . . I'm thirty-five years old; I been married eleven years and I got a boy who sleeps in the living room—(*Very, very quietly*)—and all I got to give him is stories about how rich white people live. . . .

RUTH: Eat your eggs, Walter.

WALTER: *Damn my eggs . . . damn all the eggs that ever was!*

RUTH: Then go to work.

WALTER (*Looking up at her*): See—I'm trying to talk to you 'bout myself—(*Shaking his head with the repetition*)—and all you can say is eat them eggs and go to work.

RUTH (*Wearily*): Honey, you never say nothing new. I listen to you every day, every night and every morning, and you never say nothing new. (*Shrugging*) So you would rather *be* Mr. Arnold than be his chauffeur. So—I would *rather* be living in Buckingham Palace.

WALTER: That is just what is wrong with the colored woman in this world . . . Don't understand about building their men up and making 'em feel like they somebody. Like they can do something.

RUTH (*Drily, but to hurt*): There *are* colored men who do things.

WALTER: No thanks to the colored woman.

RUTH: Well, being a colored woman, I guess I can't help myself none.

(*She rises and gets the ironing board and sets it up and attacks a huge pile of rough-dried clothes, sprinkling them in preparation for the ironing and then rolling them into tight fat balls*)

WALTER (*Mumbling*): We one group of men tied to a race of women with small minds.

(*His sister Beneatha enters. She is about twenty, as slim and intense as her brother. She is not as pretty as her sister-in-law, but her lean, almost intellectual face has a handsomeness of its own. She wears a bright-red flannel nightie, and her thick hair stands wildly about her head. Her speech is a mixture of many things; it is different from the rest of the family's insofar as education has permeated her sense of English—and perhaps the Midwest rather than the South has finally—at last—won out in her inflection; but not altogether, because over all of it is a soft slurring and transformed use of vowels [which] is the decided influence of the Southside. She passes through the room without looking at either Ruth or Walter and goes to the outside door and looks, a little blindly, out to the bathroom. She sees that it has been lost to the Johnsons. She closes the door with a sleepy vengeance and crosses to the table and sits down a little defeated.)*

BENEATHA: I am going to start timing those people.

WALTER: You should get up earlier.

BENEATHA *(Her face in her hands. She is still fighting the urge to go back to bed)*: Really—would you suggest dawn? Where's the paper?

WALTER *(Pushing the paper across the table to her as he studies her almost clinically, as though he has never seen her before)*: You a horrible-looking chick at this hour.

BENEATHA *(Drily)*: Good morning, everybody.

WALTER *(Senselessly)*: How is school coming?

BENEATHA *(In the same spirit)*: Lovely. And you know, biology is the greatest. *(Looking up at him)* I dissected something that looked just like you yesterday.

WALTER: I just wondered if you've made up your mind and everything.

BENEATHA *(Gaining in sharpness and impatience)*: And what did I answer yesterday morning—and the day before that?

RUTH *(From the ironing board, like someone disinterested and old)*: Don't be so nasty, Bennie.

BENEATHA *(Still to her brother)*: And the day before that and the day before that!

WALTER *(Defensively)*: I'm interested in you. Something wrong with that? Ain't many girls who decide—

WALTER AND BENEATHA *(In unison)*: —"to be a doctor."

(Silence)

WALTER: Have we figured out yet just exactly how much medical school is going to cost?

RUTH: Walter Lee, why don't you leave that girl alone and get out of here to work?

BENEATHA *(Exits to the bathroom and bangs on the door)*: Come on out of there, please!

(She comes back into the room)

WALTER *(Looking at his sister intently)*: You know the check is coming tomorrow.

BENEATHA *(Turning on him with a sharpness all her own)*: That money belongs to Mama, Walter, and it's for her to decide how she wants to use it. I don't care if she wants to buy a house or a rocket ship or just nail it up somewhere and look at it. It's hers. Not ours—hers.

WALTER *(Bitterly)*: Now ain't that fine! You just got your mother's interest at heart, ain't you, girl? You such a nice girl—but if Mama got that money she can always take a few thousand and help you through school too—can't she?

BENEATHA: I have never asked anyone around here to do anything for me!

WALTER: No! And the line between asking and just accepting when the time comes is big and wide—ain't it!

BENEATHA *(With fury)*: What do you want from me, Brother—that I quit school or just drop dead, which!

WALTER: I don't want nothing but for you to stop acting holy 'round here. Me and Ruth done made some sacrifices for you—why can't you do something for the family!

RUTH: Walter, don't be dragging me in it.

WALTER: You are in it—Don't you get up and go work in somebody's kitchen for the last three years to help put clothes on her back?

RUTH: Oh, Walter—that's not fair . . .

WALTER: It ain't that nobody expects you to get on your knees and say thank you, Brother; thank you, Ruth; thank you, Mama—and thank you, Travis, for wearing the same pair of shoes for two semesters—

BENEATHA (Dropping to her knees): Well—I do—all right?—thank everybody . . . and forgive me for ever wanting to be anything at all . . . forgive me, forgive me!

RUTH: Please stop it! Your mama'll hear you.

WALTER: Who the hell told you you had to be a doctor? If you so crazy 'bout messing 'round with sick people—then go be a nurse like other women—or just get married and be quiet . . .

BENEATHA: Well—you finally got it said . . . It took you three years but you finally got it said. Walter, give up; leave me alone—it's Mama's money.

WALTER: He was my father, too!

BENEATHA: So what? He was mine, too—and Travis' grandfather—but the insurance money belongs to Mama. Picking on me is not going to make her give it to you to invest in any liquor stores—(Underbreath, dropping into a chair)—and I for one say, God bless Mama for that!

WALTER (To Ruth): See—did you hear? Did you hear!

RUTH: Honey, please go to work.

WALTER: Nobody in this house is ever going to understand me.

BENEATHA: Because you're a nut.

WALTER: Who's a nut?

BENEATHA: You—you are a nut. Thee is mad, boy.

WALTER (Looking at his wife and his sister from the door, very sadly): The world's most backward race of people, and that's a fact.

BENEATHA (Turning slowly in her chair): And then there are all those prophets who would lead us out of the wilderness—(Walter slams out of the house)—into the swamps!

RUTH: Bennie, why you always gotta be pickin' on your brother? Can't you be a little sweeter sometimes? (Door opens. Walter walks in)

WALTER (To Ruth): I need some money for carfare.

RUTH (Looks at him, then warms; teasing but tenderly): Fifty cents? (She goes to her bag and gets money) Here, take a taxi.

(Walter exits. Mama enters. She is a woman in her early sixties, full-bodied and strong. She is one of those women of a certain grace and beauty who wear it so unobtrusively that it takes a while to notice. Her dark-brown face is surrounded by the total whiteness of her hair, and, being a woman who has adjusted to many things in life and overcome many more, her face is full of strength. She has, we can see, wit and faith of a kind that keep her eyes lit and full of interest and expectancy. She is, in a word, a beautiful woman. Her bearing is perhaps most like the noble bearing of the women of the Hereros of Southwest Africa—rather as if she imagines that as she walks she still bears a basket or a vessel upon her head. Her speech, on the other hand, is as careless as her carriage is precise—she is inclined to slur everything—but her voice is perhaps not so much quiet as simply soft.)

MAMA: Who that 'round here slamming doors at this hour?

(She crosses through the room, goes to the window, opens it, and brings in a feeble little plant growing doggedly in a small pot on the window sill. She feels the dirt and puts it back out.)

RUTH: That was Walter Lee. He and Bennie was at it again.

MAMA: My children and they tempers. Lord, if this little old plant don't get more sun than it's been getting it ain't never going to see spring again. *(She turns from the window)* What's the matter with you this morning, Ruth? You looks right peaked. You aiming to iron all them things? Leave some for me. I'll get to 'em this afternoon. Bennie honey, it's too drafty for you to be sitting 'round half dressed. Where's your robe?

BENEATHA: In the cleaners.

MAMA: Well, go get mine and put it on.

BENEATHA: I'm not cold, Mama, honest.

MAMA: I know—but you so thin . . .

BENEATHA *(Irritably)*: Mama, I'm not cold.

MAMA *(Seeing the make-down bed as Travis has left it)*: Lord have mercy, look at that poor bed. Bless his heart—he tries, don't he?

(She moves to the bed Travis has sloppily made up)

RUTH: No—he don't half try at all 'cause he knows you going to come along behind him and fix everything. That's just how come he don't know how to do nothing right now—you done spoiled that boy so.

MAMA: Well—he's a little boy. Ain't supposed to know 'bout housekeeping. My baby, that's what he is. What you fix for his breakfast this morning?

RUTH *(Angrily)*: I feed my son, Lena!

MAMA: I ain't meddling—*(Underbreath; busy-bodyish)* I just noticed all last week he had cold cereal, and when it starts getting this chilly in the fall a child ought to have some hot grits or something when he goes out in the cold—

RUTH *(Furious)*: I gave him hot oats—is that all right!

MAMA: I ain't meddling. *(Pause)* Put a lot of nice butter on it? *(Ruth shoots her an angry look and does not reply)* He likes lots of butter.

RUTH *(Exasperated)*: Lena—

MAMA *(To Beneatha. Mama is inclined to wander conversationally sometimes)*: What was you and your brother fussing 'bout this morning?

BENEATHA: It's not important, Mama.

(She gets up and goes to look out at the bathroom, which is apparently free, and she picks up her towels and rushes out)

MAMA: What was they fighting about?

RUTH: Now you know as well as I do.

MAMA *(Shaking her head)*: Brother still worrying hisself sick about that money?

RUTH: You know he is.

MAMA: You had breakfast?

RUTH: Some coffee.

MAMA: Girl, you better start eating and looking after yourself better. You almost thin as Travis.

RUTH: Lena—

MAMA: Un-hunh?

RUTH: What are you going to do with it?

MAMA: Now don't you start, child. It's too early in the morning to be talking about money. It ain't Christian.

RUTH: It's just that he got his heart set on that store—

MAMA: You mean that liquor store that Willy Harris want him to invest in?

RUTH: Yes—

MAMA: We ain't no business people, Ruth. We just plain working folks.

RUTH: Ain't nobody business people till they go into business. Walter Lee say colored people ain't never going to start getting ahead till they start gambling on some different kinds of things in the world—investments and things.

MAMA: What done got into you, girl? Walter Lee done finally sold you on investing.

RUTH: No. Mama, something is happening between Walter and me. I don't know what it is—but he needs something—something I can't give him any more. He needs this chance, Lena.

MAMA (Frowning deeply): But liquor, honey—

RUTH: Well—like Walter say—I spec people going to always be drinking themselves some liquor.

MAMA: Well—whether they drinks it or not ain't none of my business. But whether I go into business selling it to 'em is, and I don't want that on my ledger this late in life. (Stopping suddenly and studying her daughter-in-law) Ruth Younger, what's the matter with you today? You look like you could fall over right there.

RUTH: I'm tired.

MAMA: Then you better stay home from work today.

RUTH: I can't stay home. She'd be calling up the agency and screaming at them, "My girl didn't come in today—send me somebody! My girl didn't come in!" Oh, she just have a fit. . . .

MAMA: Well, let her have it. I'll just call her up and say you got the flu—

RUTH (Laughing): Why the flu?

MAMA: 'Cause it sounds respectable to 'em. Something white people get, too. They know 'bout the flu. Otherwise they think you been cut up or something when you tell 'em you sick.

RUTH: I got to go in. We need the money.

MAMA: Somebody would of thought my children done all but starved to death the way they talk about money here late. Child, we got a great big old check coming tomorrow.

RUTH (Sincerely, but also self-righteously): Now that's your money. It ain't got nothing to do with me. We all feel like that—Walter and Bennie and me—even Travis.

MAMA (Thoughtfully, and suddenly very far away): Ten thousand dollars—

RUTH: Sure is wonderful.

MAMA: Ten thousand dollars.

RUTH: You know what you should do, Miss Lena? You should take yourself a trip somewhere. To Europe or South America or someplace—

MAMA (Throwing up her hands at the thought): Oh, child!

RUTH: I'm serious. Just pack up and leave! Go on away and enjoy yourself some. Forget about the family and have yourself a ball for once in your life—

MAMA (Drily): You sound like I'm just about ready to die. Who'd go with me? What I look like wandering 'round Europe by myself?

RUTH: Shoot—these here rich white women do it all the time. They don't think nothing of packing up they suitcases and piling on one of them big steamships and—swoosh!— they gone, child.

MAMA: Something always told me I wasn't no rich white woman.

RUTH: Well—what are you going to do with it then?

MAMA: I ain't rightly decided. (Thinking. She speaks now with emphasis) Some of it got to be put away for Beneatha and her schoolin'—and ain't nothing going to touch that part of it. Nothing. *(She waits several seconds, trying to make up her mind about something, and looks at Ruth a little tentatively before going on)* Been thinking that we maybe could meet the notes on a little old two-story somewhere, with a yard where Travis could play in the summertime, if we use part of the insurance for a down payment and everybody kind of pitch in. I could maybe take on a little day work again, few days a week—

RUTH *(Studying her mother-in-law furtively and concentrating on her ironing, anxious to encourage without seeming to)*: Well, Lord knows, we've put enough rent into this here rat trap to pay for four houses by now . . .

MAMA *(Looking up at the words "rat trap" and then looking around and leaning back and sighing—in a suddenly reflective mood—)*: "Rat trap"—yes, that's all it is. *(Smiling)* I remember just as well the day me and Big Walter moved in here. Hadn't been married but two weeks and wasn't planning on living here no more than a year. *(She shakes her head at the dissolved dream)* We was going to set away, little by little, don't you know, and buy a little place out in Morgan Park. We had even picked out the house. *(Chuckling a little)* Looks right dumpy today. But Lord, child, you should know all the dreams I had 'bout buying that house and fixing it up and making me a little garden in the back— *(She waits and stops smiling)* And didn't none of it happen.

(Dropping her hands in a futile gesture)

RUTH *(Keeps her head down, ironing)*: Yes, life can be a barrel of disappointments, sometimes.

MAMA: Honey, Big Walter would come in here some nights back then and slump down on that couch there and just look at the rug, and look at me and look at the rug and then back at me—and I'd know he was down then . . . really down. *(After a second very long and thoughtful pause; she is seeing back to times that only she can see)* And then, Lord, when I lost that baby—little Claude—I almost thought I was going to lose Big Walter too. Oh, that man grieved hisself! He was one man to love his children.

RUTH: Ain't nothin' can tear at you like losin' your baby.

MAMA: I guess that's how come that man finally worked hisself to death like he done. Like he was fighting his own war with this here world that took his baby from him.

RUTH: He sure was a fine man, all right. I always liked Mr. Younger.

MAMA: Crazy 'bout his children! God knows there was plenty wrong with Walter Younger—hard-headed, mean, kind of wild with women—plenty wrong with him. But he sure loved his children. Always wanted them to have something—be something. That's where Brother gets all these notions, I reckon. Big Walter used to say, he'd get right wet in the eyes sometimes, lean his head back with the water standing in his eyes and say, "Seem like God didn't see fit to give the black man nothing but dreams—but He did give us children to make them dreams seem worth while." *(She smiles)* He could talk like that, don't you know.

RUTH: Yes, he sure could. He was a good man, Mr. Younger.

MAMA: Yes, a fine man—just couldn't never catch up with his dreams, that's all.

(Beneatha comes in, brushing her hair and looking up to the ceiling, where the sound of a vacuum cleaner has started up)

BENEATHA: What could be so dirty on that woman's rugs that she has to vacuum them every single day?

RUTH: I wish certain young women 'round here who I could name would take inspiration about certain rugs in a certain apartment I could also mention.

BENEATHA (Shrugging): How much cleaning can a house need, for Christ's sakes.

MAMA (Not liking the Lord's name used thus): Bennie!

RUTH: Just listen to her—just listen!

BENEATHA: Oh, God!

MAMA: If you use the Lord's name just one more time—

BENEATHA (A bit of a whine): Oh, Mama—

RUTH: Fresh—just fresh as salt, this girl!

BENEATHA (Drily): Well—if the salt loses its savor—[2]

MAMA: Now that will do. I just ain't going to have you 'round here reciting the scriptures in vain—you hear me?

BENEATHA: How did I manage to get on everybody's wrong side by just walking into a room?

RUTH: If you weren't so fresh—

BENEATHA: Ruth, I'm twenty years old.

MAMA: What time you be home from school today?

BENEATHA: Kind of late. (With enthusiasm) Madeline is going to start my guitar lessons today.

(Mama and Ruth look up with the same expression)

MAMA: Your what kind of lessons?

BENEATHA: Guitar.

RUTH: Oh, Father!

MAMA: How come you done taken it in your mind to learn to play the guitar?

BENEATHA: I just want to, that's all.

MAMA (Smiling): Lord, child, don't you know what to do with yourself? How long it going to be before you get tired of this now—like you got tired of that little play-acting group you joined last year? (Looking at Ruth) And what was it the year before that?

RUTH: The horseback-riding club for which she bought that fifty-five-dollar riding habit that's been hanging in the closet ever since!

MAMA (To Beneatha): Why you got to flit so from one thing to another, baby?

BENEATHA (Sharply): I just want to learn to play the guitar. Is there anything wrong with that?

MAMA: Ain't nobody trying to stop you. I just wonders sometimes why you has to flit so from one thing to another all the time. You ain't never done nothing with all that camera equipment you brought home—

BENEATHA: I don't flit! I—I experiment with different forms of expression—

RUTH: Like riding a horse?

BENEATHA: People have to express themselves one way or another.

MAMA: What is it you want to express?

BENEATHA (Angrily): Me! (Mama and Ruth look at each other and burst into raucous laughter) Don't worry—I don't expect you to understand.

MAMA (To change the subject): Who you going out with tomorrow night?

BENEATHA (With displeasure): George Murchison again.

MAMA (Pleased): Oh—you getting a little sweet on him?

2. Matthew 5:13: "Ye are the salt of the earth: but   it be salted?"
   if the salt have lost his savour, wherewith shall

RUTH: You ask me, this child ain't sweet on nobody but herself—(*Underbreath*) Express herself!

(*They laugh*)

BENEATHA: Oh—I like George all right, Mama, I mean I like him enough to go out with him and stuff, but—

RUTH (*For devilment*): What does *and stuff* mean?

BENEATHA: Mind your own business.

MAMA: Stop picking at her now, Ruth. (*A thoughtful pause, and then a suspicious sudden look at her daughter as she turns in her chair for emphasis*) What *does* it mean?

BENEATHA (*Wearily*): Oh, I just mean I couldn't ever really be serious about George. He's—he's so shallow.

RUTH: Shallow—what do you mean he's shallow? He's *Rich!*

MAMA: Hush, Ruth.

BENEATHA: I know he's rich. He knows he's rich, too.

RUTH: Well—what other qualities a man got to have to satisfy you, little girl?

BENEATHA: You wouldn't even begin to understand. Anybody who married Walter could not possible understand.

MAMA (*Outraged*): What kind of way is that to talk about your brother?

BENEATHA: Brother is a flip—let's face it.

MAMA (*To Ruth, helplessly*): What's a flip?

RUTH (*Glad to add kindling*): She's saying he's crazy.

BENEATHA: Not crazy. Brother isn't really crazy yet—he—he's an elaborate neurotic.

MAMA: Hush your mouth!

BENEATHA: As for George. Well. George looks good—he's got a beautiful car and he takes me to nice places and, as my sister-in-law says, he is probably the richest boy I will ever get to know and I even like him sometimes—but if the Youngers are sitting around waiting to see if their little Bennie is going to tie up the family with the Murchisons, they are wasting their time.

RUTH: You mean you wouldn't marry George Murchison if he asked you someday? That pretty, rich thing? Honey, I knew you was odd—

BENEATHA: No I would not marry him if all I felt for him was what I feel now. Besides, George's family wouldn't really like it.

MAMA: Why not?

BENEATHA: Oh, Mama—the Murchisons are honest-to-God-real-*live*-rich colored people, and the only people in the world who are more snobbish than rich white people are rich colored people. I thought everybody knew that. I've met Mrs. Murchison. She's a scene!

MAMA: You must not dislike people 'cause they well off, honey.

BENEATHA: Why not? It makes just as much sense as disliking people 'cause they are poor, and lots of people do that.

RUTH (*A wisdom-of-the-ages manner. To Mama.*): Well, she'll get over some of this—

BENEATHA: Get over it? What are you talking about, Ruth? Listen, I'm going to be a doctor. I'm not worried about who I'm going to marry yet—if I ever get married.

MAMA *and* RUTH: *If!*

MAMA: Now, Bennie—

BENEATHA: Oh, I probably will . . . but first I'm going to be a doctor, and George, for one, still thinks that's pretty funny. I couldn't be bothered with that. I am going to be a doctor and everybody around here better understand that!

MAMA (*Kindly*): 'Course you going to be a doctor, honey, God willing.

BENEATHA (*Drily*): God hasn't got a thing to do with it.

MAMA: Beneatha—that just wasn't necessary.

BENEATHA: Well—neither is God. I get sick of hearing about God.

MAMA: Beneatha!

BENEATHA: I mean it! I'm just tired of hearing about God all the time. What has He got to do with anything? Does he pay tuition?

MAMA: You 'bout to get your fresh little jaw slapped!

RUTH: That's just what she needs, all right!

BENEATHA: Why? Why can't I say what I want to around here, like everybody else?

MAMA: It don't sound nice for a young girl to say things like that—you wasn't brought up that way. Me and your father went to trouble to get you and Brother to church every Sunday.

BENEATHA: Mama, you don't understand. It's all a matter of ideas, and God is just one idea I don't accept. It's not important. I am not going out and be immoral or commit crimes because I don't believe in God. I don't even think about it. It's just that I get tired of Him getting credit for all the things the human race achieves through its own stubborn effort. There simply is no blasted God—there is only man and it is he who makes miracles!

(Mama absorbs this speech, studies her daughter and rises slowly and crosses to Beneatha and slaps her powerfully across the face. After, there is only silence and the daughter drops her eyes from her mother's face, and Mama is very tall before her.)

MAMA: Now—you say after me, in my mother's house there is still God. *(There is a long pause and Beneatha stares at the floor wordlessly. Mama repeats the phrase with precision and cool emotion.)* In my mother's house there is still God.

BENEATHA: In my mother's house there is still God.

(A long pause)

MAMA *(Walking away from Beneatha, too disturbed for triumphant posture. Stopping and turning back to her daughter)*: There are some ideas we ain't going to have in this house. Not long as I am at the head of this family.

BENEATHA: Yes, ma'am.

(Mama walks out of the room)

RUTH *(Almost gently, with profound understanding)*: You think you a woman, Bennie—but you still a little girl. What you did was childish—so you got treated like a child.

BENEATHA: I see. *(Quietly)* I also see that everybody thinks it's all right for Mama to be a tyrant. But all the tyranny in the world will never put a God in the heavens!

(She picks up her books and goes out)

RUTH *(Goes to Mama's door)*: She said she was sorry.

MAMA *(Coming out, going to her plant)*: They frightens me, Ruth. My children.

RUTH: You got good children, Lena. They just a little off sometimes—but they're good.

MAMA: No—there's something come down between me and them that don't let us understand each other and I don't know what it is. One done almost lost his mind thinking 'bout money all the time and the other done commence to talk about things I can't seem to understand in no form or fashion. What is it that's changing, Ruth?

RUTH (Soothingly, older than her years): Now . . . you taking it all too seriously. You just got strong-willed children and it takes a strong woman like you to keep 'em in hand.

MAMA (Looking at her plant and sprinkling a little water on it): They spirited all right, my children. Got to admit they got spirit—Bennie and Walter. Like this little old plant that ain't never had enough sunshine or nothing—and look at it . . .

(She has her back to Ruth, who has had to stop ironing and lean against something and put the back of her hand to her forehead)

RUTH (Trying to keep Mama from noticing): You . . . sure . . . love that little old thing, don't you? . . .

MAMA: Well, I always wanted me a garden like I used to see sometimes at the back of the houses down home. This plant is close as I ever got to having one. (She looks out of the window as she replaces the plant) Lord, ain't nothing as dreary as the view from this window on a dreary day, is there? Why ain't you singing this morning, Ruth? Sing that "No Ways Tired." That song always lifts me up so—(She turns at last to see that Ruth has slipped quietly into a chair, in a state of semiconsciousness) Ruth! Ruth honey—what's the matter with you . . . Ruth!

Curtain

Scene 2

It is the following morning; a Saturday morning, and house cleaning is in progress at the Youngers. Furniture has been shoved hither and yon and Mama is giving the kitchen-area walls a washing down. Beneatha, in dungarees, with a handkerchief tied around her face, is spraying insecticide into the cracks in the walls. As they work, the radio is on and a Southside disk-jockey program is inappropriately filling the house with a rather exotic saxophone blues. Travis, the sole idle one, is leaning on his arms, looking out of the window.

TRAVIS: Grandmama, that stuff Bennie is using smells awful. Can I go downstairs, please?

MAMA: Did you get all them chores done already? I ain't seen you doing much.

TRAVIS: Yes'm—finished early. Where did Mama go this morning?

MAMA (Looking at Beneatha): She had to go on a little errand.

TRAVIS: Where?

MAMA: To tend to her business.

TRAVIS: Can I go outside then?

MAMA: Oh, I guess so. You better stay right in front of the house, though . . . and keep a good lookout for the postman.

TRAVIS: Yes'm. (He starts out and decides to give his Aunt Beneatha a good swat on the legs as he passes her) Leave them poor little old cockroaches alone, they ain't bothering you none.

(He runs as she swings the spray gun at him both viciously and playfully. Walter enters from the bedroom and goes to the phone.)

MAMA: Look out there, girl, before you be spilling some of that stuff on that child!

TRAVIS (Teasing): That's right—look out now!

(He exits)

BENEATHA (Drily): I can't imagine that it would hurt him—it has never hurt the roaches.

MAMA: Well little boys' hides ain't as tough as Southside roaches.

WALTER (Into phone): Hello—Let me talk to Willy Harris.

MAMA: You better get over there behind the bureau. I seen one marching out of there like Napoleon yesterday.

WALTER: Hello, Willy? It ain't come yet. It'll be here in a few minutes. Did the lawyer give you the papers?

BENEATHA: There's really only one way to get rid of them, Mama—

MAMA: How?

BENEATHA: Set fire to this building.

WALTER: Good. Good. I'll be right over.

BENEATHA: Where did Ruth go, Walter?

WALTER: I don't know.

(He exits abruptly)

BENEATHA: Mama, where did Ruth go?

MAMA (Looking at her with meaning): To the doctor, I think.

BENEATHA: The doctor? What's the matter? (They exchange glances) You don't think—

MAMA (With her sense of drama): Now I ain't saying what I think. But, I ain't never been wrong 'bout a woman neither.

(The phone rings)

BENEATHA (At the phone): Hay-lo . . . (Pause, and a moment of recognition) Well—when did you get back! . . . And how was it? . . . Of course I've missed you—in my way . . . This morning? No . . . house cleaning and all that and Mama hates it if I let people come over when the house is like this . . . You have? Well, that's different . . . What is it—Oh, what the hell, come on over . . . Right, see you then.

(She hangs up)

MAMA (Who has listened vigorously, as is her habit): Who is that you inviting over here with this house looking like this? You ain't got the pride you was born with!

BENEATHA: Asagai doesn't care how houses look, Mama—he's an intellectual.

MAMA: Who?

BENEATHA: Asagai—Joseph Asagai. He's an African boy I met on campus. He's been studying in Canada all summer.

MAMA: What's his name?

BENEATHA: Asagai, Joseph. As-sah-guy . . . He's from Nigeria.

MAMA: Oh, that's the little country that was founded by slaves way back . . .

BENEATHA: No, Mama—that's Liberia.

MAMA: I don't think I never met no African before.

BENEATHA: Well, do me a favor and don't ask him a whole lot of ignorant questions about Africans. I mean, do they wear clothes and all that—

MAMA: Well, now, I guess if you think we so ignorant 'round here maybe you shouldn't bring your friends here—

BENEATHA: It's just that people ask such crazy things. All anyone seems to know about when it comes to Africa is Tarzan—

MAMA (Indignantly): Why should I know anything about Africa?

BENEATHA: Why do you give money at church for the missionary work?

MAMA: Well, that's to help save people.

BENEATHA: You mean save them from *heathenism*—
MAMA *(Innocently)*: Yes.
BENEATHA: I'm afraid they need more salvation from the British and the French.

(Ruth comes in forlornly and pulls off her coat with dejection. They both turn to look at her.)

RUTH *(Dispiritedly)*: Well, I guess from all the happy faces—everybody knows.
BENEATHA: You pregnant?
MAMA: Lord have mercy, I sure hope it's a little old girl. Travis ought to have a sister.

(Beneatha and Ruth give her a hopeless look for this grandmotherly enthusiasm)

BENEATHA: How far along are you?
RUTH: Two months.
BENEATHA: Did you mean to? I mean did you plan it or was it an accident?
MAMA: What do you know about planning or not planning?
BENEATHA: Oh, Mama.
RUTH *(Wearily)*: She's twenty years old, Lena.
BENEATHA: Did you plan it, Ruth?
RUTH: Mind your own business.
BENEATHA: It is my business—where is he going to live, on the roof? *(There is silence following the remark as the three women react to the sense of it)* Gee—I didn't mean that, Ruth, honest. Gee, I don't feel like that at all. I—I think it is wonderful.
RUTH *(Dully)*: Wonderful.
BENEATHA: Yes—really.
MAMA *(Looking at Ruth, worried)*: Doctor say everything going to be all right?
RUTH *(Far away)*: Yes—she says everything is going to be fine . . .
MAMA *(Immediately suspicious)*: "She"—What doctor you went to?

(Ruth folds over, near hysteria)

MAMA *(Worriedly hovering over Ruth)*: Ruth honey—what's the matter with you—you sick?

(Ruth has her fists clenched on her thighs and is fighting hard to suppress a scream that seems to be rising in her)

BENEATHA: What's the matter with her, Mama?
MAMA *(Working her fingers in Ruth's shoulder to relax her)*: She be all right. Women gets right depressed sometimes when they get her way. *(Speaking softly, expertly, rapidly)* Now you just relax. That's right . . . just lean back, don't think 'bout nothing at all . . . nothing at all—
RUTH: I'm all right . . .

(The glassy-eyed look melts and then she collapses into a fit of heavy sobbing. The bell rings.)

BENEATHA: Oh, my God—that must be Asagai.
MAMA *(To Ruth)*: Come on now, honey. You need to lie down and rest awhile . . . then have some nice hot food.

(They exit, Ruth's weight on her mother-in-law. Beneatha, herself profoundly disturbed, opens the door to admit a rather dramatic-looking young man with a large package.)

ASAGAI: Hello, Alaiyo—

BENEATHA *(Holding the door open and regarding him with pleasure)*: Hello . . . *(Long pause)* Well—come in. And please excuse everything. My mother was very upset about my letting anyone come here with the place like this.

ASAGAI *(Coming into the room)*: You look disturbed too . . . Is something wrong?

BENEATHA *(Still at the door, absently)*: Yes . . . we've all got acute ghetto-itus. *(She smiles and comes toward him, finding a cigarette and sitting)* So—sit down! How was Canada?

ASAGAI *(A sophisticate)*: Canadian.

BENEATHA *(Looking at him)*: I'm very glad you are back.

ASAGAI *(Looking back at her in turn)*: Are you really?

BENEATHA: Yes—very.

ASAGAI: Why—you were quite glad when I went away. What happened?

BENEATHA: You went away.

ASAGAI: Ahhhhhhhh.

BENEATHA: Before—you wanted to be so serious before there was time.

ASAGAI: How much time must there be before one knows what one feels?

BENEATHA *(Stalling this particular conversation. Her hands pressed together, in a deliberately childish gesture.)*: What did you bring me?

ASAGAI *(Handing her the package)*: Open it and see.

BENEATHA *(Eagerly opening the package and drawing out some records and the colorful robes of a Nigerian woman)*: Oh, Asagai! . . . You got them for me! . . . How beautiful . . . and the records too! *(She lifts out the robes and runs to the mirror with them and holds the drapery up in front of herself)*

ASAGAI *(Coming to her at the mirror)*: I shall have to teach you how to drape it properly. *(He flings the material about her for the moment and stands back to look at her)* Ah—Oh-pay-gay-day, oh-gbah-mu-shay. *(A Yoruba exclamation for admiration)* You wear it well . . . very well . . . mutilated hair and all.

BENEATHA *(Turning suddenly)*: My hair—what's wrong with my hair?

ASAGAI *(Shrugging)*: Were you born with it like that?

BENEATHA *(Reaching up to touch it)*: No . . . of course not.

(She looks back to the mirror, disturbed)

ASAGAI *(Smiling)*: How then?

BENEATHA: You know perfectly well how . . . As crinkly as yours . . . that's how.

ASAGAI: And it is ugly to you that way?

BENEATHA *(Quickly)*: Oh, no—not ugly . . . *(More slowly, apologetically)* But it's so hard to manage when it's, well—raw.

ASAGAI: And so to accommodate that—you mutilate it every week?

BENEATHA: It's not mutilation!

ASAGAI *(Laughing aloud at her seriousness)*: Oh . . . please! I am only teasing you because you are so very serious about these things. *(He stands back from her and folds his arms across his chest as he watches her pulling at her hair and frowning in the mirror)* Do you remember the first time you met me at school? . . . *(He laughs)* You came up to me and you said—and I thought you were the most serious little thing I had ever seen—you said: *(He imitates her)* "Mr. Asagai—I want very much to talk with you. About Africa. You see, Mr. Asagai, I am looking for my *identity!*"

(He laughs)

BENEATHA *(Turning to him, not laughing)*: Yes—

(Her face is quizzical, profoundly disturbed)

ASAGAI *(Still teasing and reaching out and taking her face in his hands and turning her profile to him)*: Well . . . it is true that this is not so much a profile of a Hollywood queen as perhaps a queen of the Nile—*(A mock dismissal of the importance of the question)* But what does it matter? Assimilationism is so popular in your country.

BENEATHA *(Wheeling, passionately, sharply)*: I am not an assimilationist!

ASAGAI *(The protest hangs in the room for a moment and Asagai studies her, his laughter fading)*: Such a serious one. *(There is a pause)* So—you like the robes? You must take excellent care of them—they are from my sister's personal wardrobe.

BENEATHA *(With incredulity)*: You—you sent all the way home—for me?

ASAGAI *(With charm)*: For you—I would do much more . . . Well, that is what I came for. I must go.

BENEATHA: Will you call me Monday?

ASAGAI: Yes . . . We have a great deal to talk about. I mean about identity and time and all that.

BENEATHA: Time?

ASAGAI: Yes. About how much time one needs to know what one feels.

BENEATHA: You never understood that there is more than one kind of feeling which can exist between a man and a woman—or, at least, there should be.

ASAGAI *(Shaking his head negatively but gently)*: No. Between a man and a woman there need be only one kind of feeling. I have that for you . . . Now even . . . right this moment . . .

BENEATHA: I know—and by itself—it won't do. I can find that anywhere.

ASAGAI: For a woman it should be enough.

BENEATHA: I know—because that's what it says in all the novels that men write. But it isn't. Go ahead and laugh—but I'm not interested in being someone's little episode in America or—*(With feminine vengeance)*—one of them! *(Asagai has burst into laughter again)* That's funny as hell, huh!

ASAGAI: It's just that every American girl I have known has said that to me. White—black—in this you are all the same. And the same speech, too!

BENEATHA *(Angrily)*: Yuk, yuk, yuk!

ASAGAI: It's how you can be sure that the world's most liberated women are not liberated at all. You all talk about it too much!

(Mama enters and is immediately all social charm because of the presence of a guest)

BENEATHA: Oh—Mama—this is Mr. Asagai.

MAMA: How do you do?

ASAGAI *(Total politeness to an elder)*: How do you do, Mrs. Younger. Please forgive me for coming at such an outrageous hour on a Saturday.

MAMA: Well, you are quite welcome. I just hope you understand that our house don't always look like this. *(Chatterish)* You must come again. I would love to hear all about— *(Not sure of the name)* —your country. I think it's so sad the way our American Negroes don't know nothing about Africa 'cept Tarzan and all that. And all that money they pour into these churches when they ought to be helping you people over there drive out them French and Englishmen done taken away your land.

(The mother flashes a slightly superior look at her daughter upon completion of the recitation)

ASAGAI *(Taken aback by this sudden and acutely unrelated expression of sympathy)*: Yes . . . yes . . .

MAMA *(Smiling at him suddenly and relaxing and looking him over)*: How many miles is it from here to where you come from?

ASAGAI: Many thousands.

MAMA *(Looking at him as she would Walter)*: I bet you don't half look after yourself, being away from your mama either. I spec you better come 'round here from time to time and get yourself some decent home-cooked meals . . .

ASAGAI *(Moved)*: Thank you. Thank you very much. *(They are all quiet, then—)* Well . . . I must go. I will call you Monday, Alaiyo.

MAMA: What's that he call you?

ASAGAI: Oh—"Alaiyo." I hope you don't mind. It is what you would call a nickname, I think. It is a Yoruba word. I am a Yoruba.

MAMA *(Looking at Beneatha)*: I—I thought he was from—

ASAGAI *(Understanding)*: Nigeria is my country. Yoruba is my tribal origin—

BENEATHA: You didn't tell us what Alaiyo means . . . for all I know, you might be calling me Little Idiot or something . . .

ASAGAI: Well . . . let me see . . . I do not know how just to explain it . . . The sense of a thing can be so different when it changes languages.

BENEATHA: You're evading.

ASAGAI: No—really it is difficult . . . *(Thinking)* It means . . . it means One for Whom Bread—Food—Is Not Enough. *(He looks at her)* Is that all right?

BENEATHA *(Understanding, softly)*: Thank you.

MAMA *(Looking from one to the other and not understanding any of it)*: Well . . . that's nice . . . You must come see us again—Mr.—

ASAGAI: Ah-sah-guy . . .

MAMA: Yes . . . Do come again.

ASAGAI: Good-bye.

(He exits)

MAMA *(After him)*: Lord, that's a pretty thing just went out here! *(Insinuatingly, to her daughter)* Yes, I guess I see why we done commence to get so interested in Africa 'round here. Missionaries my aunt Jenny!

(She exits)

BENEATHA: Oh, Mama! . . .

(She picks up the Nigerian dress and holds it up to her in front of the mirror again. She sets the headdress on haphazardly and then notices her hair again and clutches at it and then replaces the headdress and frowns at herself. Then she starts to wriggle in front of the mirror as she thinks a Nigerian woman might. Travis enters and regards her.)

TRAVIS: You cracking up?

BENEATHA: Shut up.

(She pulls the headdress off and looks at herself in the mirror and clutches at her hair again and squinches her eyes as if trying to imagine something. Then, suddenly, she gets her raincoat and kerchief and hurriedly prepares for going out.)

MAMA *(Coming back into the room)*: She's resting now. Travis, baby, run next door and ask Miss Johnson to please let me have a little kitchen cleanser. This here can is empty as Jacob's kettle.

TRAVIS: I just came in.

MAMA: Do as you told. *(He exits and she looks at her daughter)* Where you going?

BENEATHA *(Halting at the door)*: To become a queen of the Nile!

(She exits in a breathless blaze of glory. Ruth appears in the bedroom doorway.)

MAMA: Who told you to get up?

RUTH: Ain't nothing wrong with me to be lying in no bed for. Where did Bennie go?

MAMA *(drumming her fingers)*: Far as I could make out—to Egypt. *(Ruth just looks at her)* What time is it getting to?

RUTH: Ten twenty. And the mailman going to ring that bell this morning just like he done every morning for the last umpteen years.

(Travis comes in with the cleanser can)

TRAVIS: She say to tell you that she don't have much.

MAMA *(Angrily)*: Lord, some people I could name sure is tight-fisted! *(Directing her grandson)* Mark two cans of cleanser down on the list there. If she that hard up for kitchen cleanser, I sure don't want to forget to get her none!

RUTH: Lena—maybe the woman is just short on cleanser—

MAMA *(Not listening)*: —Much baking powder as she done borrowed from me all these years, she could of done gone into the baking business!

(The bell sounds suddenly and sharply and all three are stunned—serious and silent— mid-speech. In spite of all the other conversations and distractions of the morning, this is what they have been waiting for, even Travis, who looks helplessly from his mother to his grandmother. Ruth is the first to come to life again.)

RUTH *(To Travis)*: Get down them steps, boy!

(Travis snaps to life and flies out to get the mail)

MAMA *(Her eyes wide, her hand to her breast)*: You mean it done really come?

RUTH *(Excited)*: Oh, Miss Lena!

MAMA *(Collecting herself)*: Well . . . I don't know what we all so excited about 'round here for. We known it was coming for months.

RUTH: That's a whole lot different from having it come and being able to hold it in your hands . . . a piece of paper worth ten thousand dollars . . . *(Travis bursts back into the room. He holds the envelope high above his head, like a little dancer, his face is radiant and he is breathless. He moves to his grandmother with sudden slow ceremony and puts the envelope into her hands. She accepts it, and then merely holds it and looks at it.)* Come on! Open it . . . Lord have mercy, I wish Walter Lee was here!

TRAVIS: Open it, Grandmama!

MAMA *(staring at it)*: Now you all be quiet. It's just a check.

RUTH: Open it . . .

MAMA (*still staring at it*): Now don't act silly . . . We ain't never been no people to act silly 'bout no money—
RUTH (*Swiftly*): We ain't never had none before—*open it!*

(*Mama finally makes a good strong tear and pulls out the thin blue slice of paper and inspects it closely. The boy and his mother study it raptly over Mama's shoulders.*)

MAMA: Travis! (*She is counting off with doubt*) Is that the right number of zeros.
TRAVIS: Yes'm . . . ten thousand dollars. Gaalee, Grandmama, you rich.
MAMA (*She holds the check away from her, still looking at it. Slowly her face sobers into a mask of unhappiness*): Ten thousand dollars. (*She hands it to Ruth*) Put it away somewhere, Ruth. (*She does not look at Ruth; her eyes seem to be seeing something somewhere very far off*) Ten thousand dollars they give you. Ten thousand dollars.
TRAVIS (*to his mother, sincerely*): What's the matter with Grandmama—don't she want to be rich?
RUTH (*Distractedly*): You go on out and play now, baby. (*Travis exits. Mama starts wiping dishes absently, humming intently to herself. Ruth turns to her, with kind exasperation.*) You've gone and got yourself upset.
MAMA (*not looking at her*): I spec if it wasn't for you all . . . I would just put that money away or give it to the church or something.
RUTH: Now what kind of talk is that. Mr. Younger would just be plain mad if he could hear you talking foolish like that.
MAMA (*Stopping and staring off*): Yes . . . he sure would. (*Sighing*) We got enough to do with that money, all right. (*She halts then, and turns and looks at her daughter-in-law hard; Ruth avoids her eyes and Mama wipes her hands with finality and starts to speak firmly to Ruth*) Where did you go today, girl?
RUTH: To the doctor.
MAMA (*Impatiently*): Now, Ruth . . . you know better than that. Old Doctor Jones is strange enough in his way but there ain't nothing 'bout him make somebody slip and call him "she"—like you done this morning.
RUTH: Well, that's what happened—my tongue slipped.
MAMA: You went to see that woman, didn't you?
RUTH (*Defensively, giving herself away*): What woman you talking about?
MAMA (*Angrily*): That woman who—

(*Walter enters in great excitement*)

WALTER: Did it come?
MAMA (*Quietly*): Can't you give people a Christian greeting before you start asking about money?
WALTER (*to Ruth*): Did it come? (*Ruth unfolds the check and lays it quietly before him, watching him intently with thoughts of her own. Walter sits down and grasps it close and counts off the zeros.*) Ten thousand dollars—(*He turns suddenly, frantically to his mother and draws some papers out of his breast pocket*) Mama—look. Old Willy Harris put everything on paper—
MAMA: Son—I think you ought to talk to your wife . . . I'll go on out and leave you alone if you want—
WALTER: I can talk to her later—Mama, look—
MAMA: Son—
WALTER: WILL SOMEBODY PLEASE LISTEN TO ME TODAY!
MAMA (*Quietly*): I don't 'low no yellin' in this house, Walter Lee, and you know it—(*Walter stares at them in frustration and starts to speak several times*) And there

ain't going to be no investing in no liquor stores. I don't aim to have to speak on that again.

(A long pause)

WALTER: Oh—so you don't aim to have to speak on that again? So *you* have decided . . . *(Crumpling his papers)* Well, *you* tell that to my boy tonight when you put him to sleep on the living-room couch . . . *(Turning to Mama and speaking directly to her)* Yeah—and tell it to my wife, Mama, tomorrow when she has to go out of here to look after somebody else's kids. And tell it to *me,* Mama, every time we need a new pair of curtains and I have to watch *you* go out and work in somebody's kitchen. Yeah, you tell me then!

(Walter starts out)

RUTH: Where you going?

WALTER: I'm going out!

RUTH: Where?

WALTER: Just out of this house somewhere—

RUTH *(Getting her coat)*: I'll come too.

WALTER: I don't want you to come!

RUTH: I got something to talk to you about, Walter.

WALTER: That's too bad.

MAMA *(Still quietly)*: Walter Lee— *(She waits and he finally turns and looks at her)* Sit down.

WALTER: I'm a grown man, Mama.

MAMA: Ain't nobody said you wasn't grown. But you still in my house and my presence. And as long as you are—you'll talk to your wife civil. Now sit down.

RUTH *(Suddenly)*: Oh, let him go on out and drink himself to death! He makes me sick to my stomach! *(She flings her coat against him)*

WALTER *(Violently)*: And you turn mine too, baby! *(Ruth goes into their bedroom and slams the door behind her)* That was my greatest mistake—

MAMA *(Still quietly)*: Walter, what is the matter with you?

WALTER: Matter with me? Ain't nothing the matter with *me!*

MAMA: Yes there is. Something eating you up like a crazy man. Something more than me not giving you this money. The past few years I been watching it happen to you. You get all nervous acting and kind of wild in the eyes—*(Walter jumps up impatiently at her words)* I said sit there now, I'm talking to you!

WALTER: Mama—I don't need no nagging at me today.

MAMA: Seem like you getting to a place where you always tied up in some kind of knot about something. But if anybody ask you 'bout it you just yell at 'em and bust out the house and go out and drink somewheres. Walter Lee, people can't live with that. Ruth's a good, patient girl in her way—but you getting to be too much. Boy, don't make the mistake of driving that girl away from you.

WALTER: Why—what she do for me?

MAMA: She loves you.

WALTER: Mama—I'm going out. I want to go off somewhere and be by myself for a while.

MAMA: I'm sorry 'bout your liquor store, son. It just wasn't the thing for us to do. That's what I want to tell you about—

WALTER: I got to go out, Mama—

(He rises)

MAMA: It's dangerous, son.

WALTER: What's dangerous?

MAMA: When a man goes outside his home to look for peace.

WALTER *(Beseechingly)*: Then why can't there never be no peace in this house then?

MAMA: You done found it in some other house?

WALTER: No—there ain't no woman! Why do women always think there's a woman somewhere when a man gets restless. *(Coming to her)* Mama—Mama—I want so many things. . . .

MAMA: Yes, son—

WALTER: I want so many things that they are driving me kind of crazy . . . Mama—look at me.

MAMA: I'm looking at you. You a good-looking boy. You got a job, a nice wife, a fine boy and—

WALTER: A job. *(Looks at her)* Mama, a job? I open and close car doors all day long. I drive a man around in his limousine and I say, "Yes, sir; no, sir; very good, sir; shall I take the Drive, sir?" Mama, that ain't no kind of job . . . that ain't nothing at all. *(Very quietly)* Mama, I don't know if I can make you understand.

MAMA: Understand what, baby?

WALTER *(Quietly)*: Sometimes it's like I can see the future stretched out in front of me—just plain as day. The future, Mama. Hanging over there at the edge of my days. Just waiting for me—a big, looming black space—full of *nothing.* Just waiting for *me.* *(Pause)* Mama—sometimes when I'm downtown and I pass them cool, quiet-looking restaurants where them white boys are sitting back and talking 'bout things . . . sitting there turning deals worth millions of dollars . . . sometimes I see guys don't look much older than me—

MAMA: Son—how come you talk so much 'bout money?

WALTER *(With immense passion)*: Because it is life, Mama!

MAMA *(Quietly)*: Oh—*(Very quietly)* So now it's life. Money is life. Once upon a time freedom used to be life—now it's money. I guess the world really do change . . .

WALTER: No—it was always money, Mama. We just didn't know about it.

MAMA: No . . . something has changed. *(She looks at him)* You something new, boy. In my time we was worried about not being lynched and getting to the North if we could and how to stay alive and still have a pinch of dignity too. . . . Now here come you and Beneatha—talking 'bout things we ain't never even thought about hardly, me and your daddy. You ain't satisfied or proud of nothing we done. I mean that you had a home; that we kept you out of trouble till you was grown; that you don't have to ride to work on the back of nobody's streetcar—You my children—but how different we done become.

WALTER: You just don't understand, Mama, you just don't understand.

MAMA: Son—do you know your wife is expecting another baby? *(Walter stands, stunned, and absorbs what his mother has said)* That's what she wanted to talk to you about. *(Walter sinks down into a chair)* This ain't for me to be telling—but you ought to know. *(She waits)* I think Ruth is thinking 'bout getting rid of that child.

WALTER *(Slowly understanding)*: No—no—Ruth wouldn't do that.

MAMA: When the world gets ugly enough—a woman will do anything for her family. *The part that's already living.*

WALTER: You don't know Ruth, Mama, if you think she would do that.

(Ruth opens the bedroom door and stands there a little limp)

RUTH (Beaten): Yes I would too, Walter. (Pause) I gave her a five-dollar down payment.

(There is total silence as the man stares at his wife and the mother stares at her son)

MAMA (Presently): Well— (Tightly) Well—son, I'm waiting to hear you say something.
. . . I'm waiting to hear how you be your father's son. Be the man he was. . . . (Pause)
Your wife say she going to destroy your child. And I'm waiting to hear you talk like
him and say we a people who give children life, not who destroys them— (She rises)
I'm waiting to see you stand up and look like your daddy and say we done give up
one baby to poverty and that we ain't going to give up nary another one. . . . I'm
waiting.

WALTER: Ruth—

MAMA: If you a son of mine, tell her! (Walter turns, looks at her and can say nothing.
She continues, bitterly) You . . . you are a disgrace to your father's memory.
Somebody get me my hat.

Act Two

Scene 1

Time: Later the same day.
At rise: Ruth is ironing again. She has the radio going. Presently Beneatha's bedroom door
opens and Ruth's mouth falls and she puts down the iron in fascination.

RUTH: What have we got on tonight!

BENEATHA (Emerging grandly from the doorway so that we can see her thoroughly robed in
the costume Asagai brought): You are looking at what a well-dressed Nigerian woman
wears—(She parades for Ruth, her hair completely hidden by the headdress; she is
coquettishly fanning herself with an ornate oriental fan, mistakenly more like Butterfly
than any Nigerian that ever was) Isn't it beautiful? (She promenades to the radio and,
with an arrogant flourish, turns off the good loud blues that is playing) Enough of this
assimilationist junk! (Ruth follows her with her eyes as she goes to the phonograph and
puts on a record and turns and waits ceremoniously for the music to come up. Then,
with a shout—) OCOMOGOSIAY!

(Ruth jumps. The music comes up, a lovely Nigerian melody. Beneatha listens, enraptured,
her eyes far away—"back to the past." She begins to dance. Ruth is dumfounded.)

RUTH: What kind of dance is that?

BENEATHA: A folk dance.

RUTH (Pearl Bailey): What kind of folks do that, honey?

BENEATHA: It's from Nigeria. It's a dance of welcome.

RUTH: Who you welcoming?

BENEATHA: The men back to the village.

RUTH: Where they been?

BENEATHA: How should I know—out hunting or something. Anyway, they are coming
back now. . . .

RUTH: Well, that's good.

BENEATHA (With the record):
Alundi, alundi
Alundi alunya
Jop pu a jeepua

Ang gu sooooooooooo
Ai yai yae . . .
Ayehaye—alundi. . . .

(Walter comes in during this performance; he has obviously been drinking. He leans against the door heavily and watches his sister, at first with distaste. Then his eyes look off—"back to the past"—as he lifts both his fists to the roof, screaming.)

WALTER: YEAH . . . AND ETHIOPIA STRETCH FORTH HER HANDS AGAIN! . . .
RUTH *(Drily, looking at him)*: Yes—and Africa sure is claiming her own tonight. *(She gives them both up and starts ironing again)*
WALTER *(All in a drunken, dramatic shout)*: Shut up! . . . I'm digging them drums . . . them drums move me . . . *(He makes his weaving way to his wife's face and leans in close to her)* In my heart of hearts— *(He thumps his chest)* —I am much warrior!
RUTH *(Without even looking up)*: In your heart of hearts you are much drunkard.
WALTER *(Coming away from her and starting to wander around the room, shouting)*: Me and Jomo . . . *(Intently, in his sister's face. She has stopped dancing to watch him in this unknown mood.)* That's my man, Kenyatta.[3] *(Shouting and thumping his chest)* FLAMING SPEAR! HOT DAMN! *(He is suddenly in possession of an imaginary spear and actively spearing enemies all over the room)* OCOMOGOSIAY . . . THE LION IS WAKING . . . OWIMOWEH! *(He pulls his shirt open and leaps up on a table and gestures with his spear. The bell rings. Ruth goes to answer.)*
BENEATHA *(To encourage Walter, thoroughly caught up with this side of him)*: OCOMOGOSIAY, FLAMING SPEAR!
WALTER *(On the table, very far gone, his eyes pure glass sheets. He sees what we cannot, that he is a leader of his people, a great chief, a descendant of Chaka,[4] and that the hour to march has come.)*: Listen, my black brothers—
BENEATHA: OCOMOGOSIAY!
WALTER: —Do you hear the waters rushing against the shores of the coastlands—
BENEATHA: OCOMOGOSIAY!
WALTER: —Do you hear the screeching of the cocks in yonder hills beyond where the chiefs meet in council for the coming of the mighty war—
BENEATHA: OCOMOGOSIAY!
WALTER: —Do you hear the beating of the wings of the birds flying low over the mountains and the low places of our land—

(Ruth opens the door. George Murchison enters.)

BENEATHA: OCOMOGOSIAY!
WALTER: —Do you hear the singing of the women, singing the war songs of our fathers to the babies in the great houses . . . singing the sweet war songs? OH, DO YOU HEAR, MY BLACK BROTHERS!
BENEATHA *(Completely gone)*: We hear you, Flaming Spear—
WALTER: Telling us to prepare for the greatness of the time—*(To George)* Black Brother!

(He extends his hand for the fraternal clasp)

3. Jomo Kenyatta (1893?–1978), first president of Kenya (1964). Following the Mau Mau uprising, he was imprisoned by the British (1953) and then exiled (1959). With Kwame Nkrumah he cofounded the Pan-African Federation after World War II.
4. Chaka (d. 1828), paramount chief of the Zulus.

GEORGE: Black Brother, hell!

RUTH (*Having had enough, and embarrassed for the family*): Beneatha, you got company—what's the matter with you? Walter Lee Younger, get down off that table and stop acting like a fool . . .

(*Walter comes down off the table suddenly and makes a quick exit to the bathroom*)

RUTH: He's had a little to drink . . . I don't know what her excuse is.

GEORGE (*To Beneatha*): Look honey, we're going *to* the theatre—we're not going to be *in* it . . . so go change, huh?

RUTH: You expect this boy to go out with you looking like that?

BENEATHA (*Looking at George*): That's up to George. If he's ashamed of his heritage—

GEORGE: Oh, don't be so proud of yourself, Bennie—just because you look eccentric.

BENEATHA: How can something that's natural be eccentric?

GEORGE: That's what being eccentric means—being natural. Get dressed.

BENEATHA: I don't like that, George.

RUTH: Why must you and your brother make an argument out of everything people say?

BENEATHA: Because I hate assimilationist Negroes!

RUTH: Will somebody please tell me what assimila-whoever means!

GEORGE: Oh, it's just a college girl's way of calling people Uncle Toms—but that isn't what it means at all.

RUTH: Well, what does it mean?

BENEATHA (*Cutting George off and staring at him as she replies to Ruth*): It means someone who is willing to give up his own culture and submerge himself completely in the dominant, and in this case, *oppressive* culture!

GEORGE: Oh, dear, dear, dear! Here we go! A lecture on the African past! On our Great West African Heritage! In one second we will hear all about the great Ashanti empires; the great Songhay civilizations; and the great sculpture of Bénin—and then some poetry in the Bantu⁵—and the whole monologue will end with the word *heritage*! (*Nastily*) Let's face it, baby, your heritage is nothing but a bunch of raggedy-assed spirituals and some grass huts!

BENEATHA: *Grass huts*! (*Ruth crosses to her and forcibly pushes her toward the bedroom*) See there . . . you are standing there in your splendid ignorance talking about people who were the first to smelt iron on the face of the earth! (*Ruth is pushing her through the door*) The Ashanti were performing surgical operations when the English—(*Ruth pulls the door to, with Beneatha on the other side, and smiles graciously at George. Beneatha opens the door and shouts the end of the sentence defiantly at George*)—were still tatooing themselves with blue dragons . . . (*She goes back inside*)

RUTH: Have a seat, George. (*They both sit. Ruth folds her hands rather primly on her lap, determined to demonstrate the civilization of the family.*) Warm, ain't it? I mean for September. (*Pause*) Just like they always say about Chicago weather: If it's too hot or cold for you, just wait a minute and it'll change. (*She smiles happily at this cliché of clichés*) Everybody say it's got to do with them bombs and things they keep setting off. (*Pause*) Would you like a nice cold beer?

GEORGE: No, thank you. I don't care for beer. (*He looks at his watch*) I hope she hurries up.

RUTH: What time is the show?

5. Ashanti, a West African state founded before the thirteenth century; Songhay, a state on the Middle Niger dating from about 700 A.D.; Benin, a West African kingdom founded in the thirteenth century that produced some of the greatest African art; Bantu, the language family of most of the continent south of the Congo. Zulu and Swahili are Bantu languages.

GEORGE: It's an eight-thirty curtain. That's just Chicago though. In New York standard curtain time is eight forty.

(He is rather proud of this knowledge)

RUTH *(Properly appreciating it)*: You get to New York a lot?
GEORGE *(Offhand)*: Few times a year.
RUTH: Oh—that's nice. I've never been to New York.

(Walter enters. We feel he has relieved himself, but the edge of unreality is still with him.)

WALTER: New York ain't got nothing Chicago ain't. Just a bunch of hustling people all squeezed up together—being "Eastern."

(He turns his face into a screw of displeasure)

GEORGE: Oh—you've been?
WALTER: *Plenty* of times.
RUTH *(Shocked at the lie)*: Walter Lee Younger!
WALTER *(Staring her down)*: Plenty! *(Pause)* What we got to drink in this house? Why don't you offer this man some refreshment. *(To George)* They don't know how to entertain people in this house, man.
GEORGE: Thank you—I don't really care for anything.
WALTER *(Feeling his head; sobriety coming)*: Where's Mama?
RUTH: She ain't come back yet.
WALTER *(Looking Murchison over from head to toe, scrutinizing his carefully casual tweed sports jacket over cashmere V-neck sweater over soft eyelet shirt and tie, and soft slacks, finished off with white buckskin shoes)*: Why all you college boys wear them fairyish-looking white shoes?
RUTH: Walter Lee!

(George Murchison ignores the remark)

WALTER *(To Ruth)*: Well, they look crazy as hell—white shoes, cold as it is.
RUTH *(Crushed)*: You have to excuse him—
WALTER: No he don't! Excuse me for what? What you always excusing me for! I'll excuse myself when I needs to be excused! *(A pause)* They look as funny as them black knee socks Beneatha wears out of here all the time.
RUTH: It's the college *style*, Walter.
WALTER: Style, hell. She looks like she got burnt legs or something!
RUTH: Oh, Walter—
WALTER *(An irritable mimic)*: Oh, Walter! Oh, Walter! *(To Murchison)* How's your old man making out? I understand you all going to buy that big hotel on the Drive? *(He finds a beer in the refrigerator, wanders over to Murchison, sipping and wiping his lips with the back of his hand, and straddling a chair backwards to talk to the other man)* Shrewd move. Your old man is all right, man. *(Tapping his head and half winking for emphasis)* I mean he knows how to operate. I mean he thinks *big*, you know what I mean, I mean for a *home*,[6] you know? But I think he's kind of running out of ideas now. I'd like to talk to him. Listen, man, I got some plans that could turn this city upside down. I mean I think like he does. *Big*. Invest big, gamble big, hell, lose *big* if

---

6. Someone from our local area.

you have to, you know what I mean. It's hard to find a man on this whole Southside
who understands my kind of thinking—you dig? *(He scrutinizes Murchison again,
drinks his beer, squints his eyes and leans in close, confidential, man to man)* Me and
you ought to sit down and talk sometimes, man. Man, I got me some ideas . . .

MURCHISON *(With boredom)*: Yeah—sometimes we'll have to do that, Walter.

WALTER *(Understanding the indifference, and offended)*: Yeah—well, when you get the
time, man, I know you a busy little boy.

RUTH: Walter, please—

WALTER *(Bitterly, hurt)*: I know ain't nothing in this world as busy as you colored
college boys with your fraternity pins and white shoes . . .

RUTH *(Covering her face with humiliation)*: Oh, Walter Lee—

WALTER: I see you all all the time—with the books tucked under your arms—going to
your *(British A—a mimic)* "clahsses." And for what! What the hell you learning over
there? Filling up your heads—*(Counting off on his fingers)*—with the sociology and
the psychology—but they teaching you how to be a man? How to take over and run
the world? They teaching you how to run a rubber plantation or a steel mill?
Naw—just to talk proper and read books and wear white shoes . . .

GEORGE *(Looking at him with distaste, a little above it all)*: You're all wacked up with
bitterness, man.

WALTER *(Intently, almost quietly, between the teeth, glaring at the boy)*: And you—ain't
you bitter, man? Ain't you just about had it yet? Don't you see no stars gleaming that
you can't reach out and grab? You happy?—you contented son-of-a-bitch—you
happy? You got it made? Bitter? Man, I'm a volcano. Bitter? Here I am a
giant—surrounded by ants! Ants who can't even understand what it is the giant is
talking about.

RUTH *(Passionately and suddenly)*: Oh, Walter—ain't you with nobody!

WALTER *(Violently)*: No! 'Cause ain't nobody with me! Not even my own mother!

RUTH: Walter, that's a terrible thing to say!

(Beneatha enters, dressed for the evening in a cocktail dress and earrings)

GEORGE: Well—hey, you look great.

BENEATHA: Let's go, George. See you all later.

RUTH: Have a nice time.

GEORGE: Thanks. Good night. *(To Walter, sarcastically)* Good night, *Prometheus.*[7]

(Beneatha and George exit)

WALTER *(To Ruth)*: Who is Prometheus?

RUTH: I don't know. Don't worry about it.

WALTER *(In fury, pointing after George)*: See there—they get to a point where they
can't insult you man to man—they got to go talk about something ain't nobody never
heard of!

RUTH: How you know it was an insult? *(To humor him)* Maybe Prometheus is a nice
fellow.

WALTER: Prometheus! I bet there ain't even no such thing! I bet that simpleminded
clown—

RUTH: Walter—

(She stops what she is doing and looks at him)

---

7. Greek mythological figure who stole fire from the gods to benefit humanity.

WALTER *(Yelling)*: Don't start!

RUTH: Start what?

WALTER: Your nagging! Where was I! Who was I with? How much money did I spend?

RUTH *(Plaintively)*: Walter Lee—why don't we just try to talk about it . . .

WALTER *(Not listening)*: I been out talking with people who understand me. People who care about the things I got on my mind.

RUTH *(Wearily)*: I guess that means people like Willy Harris.

WALTER: Yes, people like Willy Harris.

RUTH *(With a sudden flash of impatience)*: Why don't you all just hurry up and go into the banking business and stop talking about it!

WALTER: Why? You want to know why? 'Cause we all tied up in a race of people that don't know how to do nothing but moan, pray and have babies!

(The line is too bitter even for him and he looks at her and sits down)

RUTH: Oh, Walter . . . *(Softly)* Honey, why can't you stop fighting me?

WALTER *(Without thinking)*: Who's fighting you? Who even cares about you?

(This line begins the retardation of his mood)

RUTH: Well—*(She waits a long time, and then with resignation starts to put away her things)* I guess I might as well go on to bed . . . *(More or less to herself)* I don't know where we lost it . . . but we have . . . *(Then, to him)* I—I'm sorry about this new baby, Walter. I guess maybe I better go on and do what I started . . . I guess I just didn't realize how bad things was with us . . . I guess I just didn't really realize—*(She starts out to the bedroom and stops)* You want some hot milk?

WALTER: Hot milk?

RUTH: Yes—hot milk.

WALTER: Why hot milk?

RUTH: 'Cause after all that liquor you come home with you ought to have something hot in your stomach.

WALTER: I don't want no milk.

RUTH: You want some coffee then?

WALTER: No, I don't want no coffee. I don't want nothing hot to drink. *(Almost plaintively)* Why you always trying to give me something to eat?

RUTH *(Standing and looking at him helplessly)*: What else can I give you, Walter Lee Younger?

(She stands and looks at him and presently turns to go out again. He lifts his head and watches her going away from him in a new mood which began to emerge when he asked her "Who cares about you?")

WALTER: It's been rough, ain't it, baby? *(She hears and stops but does not turn around and he continues to her back)* I guess between two people there ain't never as much understood as folks generally thinks there is. I mean like between me and you—*(She turns to face him)* How we gets to the place where we scared to talk softness to each other. *(He waits, thinking hard himself)* Why you think it got to be like that? *(He is thoughtful, almost as a child would be)* Ruth, what is it gets into people ought to be close?

RUTH: I don't know, honey. I think about it a lot.

WALTER: On account of you and me, you mean? The way things are with us. The way something done come down between us.

RUTH: There ain't so much between us, Walter . . . Not when you come to me and try
to talk to me. Try to be with me . . . a little even.

WALTER *(Total honesty)*: Sometimes . . . Sometimes . . . I don't even know how to try.

RUTH: Walter—

WALTER: Yes?

RUTH *(Coming to him, gently and with misgiving, but coming to him)*: Honey . . . life
don't have to be like this. I mean sometimes people can do things so that things are
better . . . You remember how we used to talk when Travis was born . . . about the
way we were going to live . . . the kind of house . . . *(She is stroking his head)* Well,
it's all starting to slip away from us . . .

(Mama enters, and Walter jumps up and shouts at her)

WALTER: Mama, where have you been?

MAMA: My—them steps is longer than they used to be. Whew! *(She sits down and
ignores him)* How you feeling this evening, Ruth?

*(Ruth shrugs, disturbed some at having been prematurely interrupted and watching her
husband knowingly)*

WALTER: Mama, where have you been all day?

MAMA *(Still ignoring him and leaning on the table and changing to more comfortable
shoes)*: Where's Travis?

RUTH: I let him go out earlier and he ain't come back yet. Boy, is he going to get it!

WALTER: Mama!

MAMA *(As if she has heard him for the first time)*: Yes, son?

WALTER: Where did you go this afternoon?

MAMA: I went down town to tend to some business that I had to tend to.

WALTER: What kind of business?

MAMA: You know better than to question me like a child, Brother.

WALTER *(Rising and bending over the table)*: Where were you, Mama? *(Bringing his fists
down and shouting)* Mama, you didn't go do something with that insurance money,
something crazy?

*(The front door opens slowly, interrupting him, and Travis peeks his head in, less than
hopefully)*

TRAVIS *(To his mother)*: Mama, I—

RUTH: "Mama I" nothing! You're going to get it, boy! Get on in that bedroom and get
yourself ready!

TRAVIS: But I—

MAMA: Why don't you all never let the child explain hisself.

RUTH: Keep out of it now, Lena.

(Mama clamps her lips together, and Ruth advances toward her son menacingly)

RUTH: A thousand times I have told you not to go off like that—

MAMA *(Holding out her arms to her grandson)*: Well—at least let me tell him something.
I want him to be the first one to hear . . . Come here, Travis. *(The boy obeys, gladly)*
Travis—*(She takes him by the shoulders and looks into his face)*—you know that
money we got in the mail this morning?

TRAVIS: Yes'm—

MAMA: Well—what you think your grandmama gone and done with that money?

TRAVIS: I don't know, Grandmama.

MAMA (*Putting her finger on his nose for emphasis*): She went out and she bought you a house! (*The explosion comes from Walter at the end of the revelation and he jumps up and turns away from all of them in a fury. Mama continues, to Travis*) You glad about the house? It's going to be yours when you get to be a man.

TRAVIS: Yeah—I always wanted to live in a house.

MAMA: All right, gimme some sugar then—(*Travis puts his arms around her neck as she watches her son over the boy's shoulder. Then, to Travis, after the embrace*) Now when you say your prayers tonight, you thank God and your grandfather—'cause it was him who give you the house—in his way.

RUTH (*Taking the boy from Mama and pushing him toward the bedroom*): Now you get out of here and get ready for your beating.

TRAVIS: Aw, Mama—

RUTH: Get on in there— (*Closing the door behind him and turning radiantly to her mother-in-law*) So you went and did it!

MAMA (*Quietly, looking at her son with pain*): Yes, I did.

RUTH (*Raising both arms classically*): Praise God! (*Looks at Walter a moment, who says nothing. She crosses rapidly to her husband.*) Please, honey—let me be glad . . . you be glad too. (*She has laid her hands on his shoulders, but he shakes himself free of her roughly, without turning to face her*) Oh, Walter . . . a home . . . a home. (*She comes back to Mama*) Well—where is it? How big is it? How much it going to cost?

MAMA (*Well*—

RUTH: When we moving?

MAMA (*Smiling at her*): First of the month.

RUTH (*Throwing back her head with jubilance*): Praise God!

MAMA (*Tentatively, still looking at her son's back turned against her and Ruth*): It's—it's a nice house too . . . (*She cannot help speaking directly to him. An imploring quality in her voice, her manner, makes her almost like a girl now.*) Three bedrooms—nice big one for you and Ruth . . . Me and Beneatha still have to share our room, but Travis have one of his own—and—(*With difficulty*) I figures if the—new baby—is a boy, we could get one of them double-decker outfits . . . And there's a yard with a little patch of dirt where I could maybe get to grow me a few flowers . . . And a nice big basement . . .

RUTH: Walter honey, be glad—

MAMA (*Still to his back, fingering things on the table*): 'Course I don't want to make it sound fancier than it is . . . It's just a plain little old house—but it's made good and solid—and it will be ours. Walter Lee—it makes a difference in a man when he can walk on floors that belong to him . . .

RUTH: Where is it?

MAMA (*Frightened at this telling*): Well—well—it's out there in Clybourne Park—

(*Ruth's radiance fades abruptly, and Walter finally turns slowly to face his mother with incredulity and hostility*)

RUTH: Where?

MAMA (*Matter-of-factly*): Four o six Clybourne Street, Clybourne Park.

RUTH: Clybourne Park? Mama, there ain't no colored people living in Clybourne Park.

MAMA (*Almost idiotically*): Well, I guess there's going to be some now.

WALTER (*Bitterly*): So that's the peace and comfort you went out and bought for us today!

MAMA (*Raising her eyes to meet his finally*): Son—I just tried to find the nicest place for the least amount of money for my family.

RUTH (*Trying to recover from the shock*): Well—well—'course I ain't one never been 'fraid of no crackers, mind you—but—well, wasn't there no other houses nowhere?

MAMA: Them houses they put up for colored in them areas way out all seem to cost twice as much as other houses. I did the best I could.

RUTH (*Struck senseless with the news, in its various degrees of goodness and trouble, she sits a moment, her fists propping her chin in thought, and then she starts to rise, bringing her fists down with vigor, the radiance spreading from cheek to cheek again*): Well—well!—All I can say is—if this is my time in life—*my time*—to say good-bye—(*And she builds with momentum as she starts to circle the room with an exuberant, almost tearfully happy release*)—to these Goddamned cracking walls!—(*She pounds the walls*)—and these marching roaches!—(*She wipes at an imaginary army of marching roaches*)—and this cramped little closet which ain't now or never was no kitchen! . . . then I say it loud and good, *Hallelujah! and good-bye misery* . . . I don't never want to see your ugly face again! (*She laughs joyously, having practically destroyed the apartment, and flings her arms up and lets them come down happily, slowly, reflectively, over her abdomen, aware for the first time perhaps that the life therein pulses with happiness and not despair*) Lena?

MAMA (*Moved, watching her happiness*): Yes, honey?

RUTH (*Looking off*): Is there—is there a whole lot of sunlight?

MAMA (*Understanding*): Yes, child, there's a whole lot of sunlight.

(*Long pause*)

RUTH (*Collecting herself and going to the door of the room Travis is in*): Well—I guess I better see 'bout Travis. (*To Mama*) Lord, I sure don't feel like whipping nobody today!

(*She exits*)

MAMA (*The mother and son are left alone now and the mother waits a long time, considering deeply, before she speaks*): Son—you—you understand what I done, don't you? (*Walter is silent and sullen*) I—I just seen my family falling apart today . . . just falling to pieces in front of my eyes . . . We couldn't of gone on like we was today. We was going backwards 'stead of forwards—talking 'bout killing babies and wishing each other was dead . . . When it gets like that in life—you just got to do something different, push on out and do something bigger . . . (*She waits*) I wish you say something, son . . . I wish you'd say how deep inside you you think I done the right thing—

WALTER (*Crossing slowly to his bedroom door and finally turning there and speaking measuredly*): What you need me to say you done right for? *You* the head of this family. You run our lives like you want to. It was your money and you did what you wanted with it. So what you need for me to say it was all right for? (*Bitterly, to hurt her as deeply as he knows is possible*) So you butchered up a dream of mine—you— who always talking 'bout your children's dreams . . .

MAMA: Walter Lee—

(*He just closes the door behind him. Mama sits alone, thinking heavily.*)

Curtain

Scene 2

Time: Friday night. A few weeks later.
At rise: Packing crates mark the intention of the family to move. Beneatha and George
come in, presumably from an evening out again.

GEORGE: O.K. . . . O.K., whatever you say . . . *(They both sit on the couch. He tries to*
    kiss her. She moves away) Look, we've had a nice evening; let's not spoil it, huh? . . .

(He again turns her head and tries to nuzzle in and she turns away from him, not with
distaste but with momentary lack of interest; in a mood to pursue what they were talking
about)

BENEATHA: I'm *trying* to talk to you.
GEORGE: We always talk.
BENEATHA: Yes—and I love to talk.
GEORGE *(Exasperated; rising)*: I know it and I don't mind it sometimes . . . I want you to
    cut it out, see—The moody stuff, I mean. I don't like it. You're a nice-looking girl
    . . . all over. That's all you need, honey, forget the atmosphere. Guys aren't going to
    go for the atmosphere—they're going to go for what they see. Be glad for that. Drop
    the Garbo[8] routine. It doesn't go with you. As for myself, I want a nice—*(Groping)*—
    simple—*(Thoughtfully)*—sophisticated girl . . . not a poet—O.K.?

(She rebuffs him again and he starts to leave)

BENEATHA: Why are you angry?
GEORGE: Because this is stupid! I don't go out with you to discuss the nature of "quiet
    desperation" or to hear all about your thoughts—because the world will go on
    thinking what it thinks regardless—
BENEATHA: Then why read books? Why go to school?
GEORGE *(With artificial patience, counting on his fingers)*: It's simple. You read books—
    to learn facts—to get grades—to pass the course—to get a degree. That's all—it has
    nothing to do with thoughts.

(A long pause)

BENEATHA: I see. *(A longer pause as she looks at him)* Good night, George.

(George looks at her a little oddly, and starts to exit. He meets Mama coming in)

GEORGE: Oh—hello, Mrs. Younger.
MAMA: Hello, George, how you feeling?
GEORGE: Fine—fine, how are you?
MAMA: Oh, a little tired. You know them steps can get you after a day's work. You all
    have a nice time tonight?
GEORGE: Yes—a fine time. Well, good night.
MAMA: Good night. *(He exits. Mama closes the door behind her)* Hello, honey. What you
    sitting like that for?
BENEATHA: I'm just sitting.

8. Greta Garbo (1905–1990), film star born in Sweden, starred in both silent and sound movies. In later
life she was reclusive.

MAMA: Didn't you have a nice time?

BENEATHA: No.

MAMA: No? What's the matter?

BENEATHA: Mama, George is a fool—honest. (*She rises*)

MAMA (*Hustling around unloading the packages she has entered with. She stops.*): Is he, baby?

BENEATHA: Yes.

(*Beneatha makes up Travis' bed as she talks*)

MAMA: You sure?

BENEATHA: Yes.

MAMA: Well—I guess you better not waste your time with no fools.

(*Beneatha looks up at her mother, watching her put groceries in the refrigerator. Finally she gathers up her things and starts into the bedroom. At the door she stops and looks back at her mother.*)

BENEATHA: Mama—

MAMA: Yes, baby—

BENEATHA: Thank you.

MAMA: For what?

BENEATHA: For understanding me this time.

(*She exits quickly and the mother stands, smiling a little, looking at the place where Beneatha just stood. Ruth enters.*)

RUTH: Now don't you fool with any of this stuff, Lena—

MAMA: Oh, I just thought I'd sort a few things out.

(*The phone rings. Ruth answers.*)

RUTH (*At the phone*): Hello—Just a minute. (*Goes to door*) Walter, it's Mrs. Arnold. (*Waits. Goes back to the phone. Tense*) Hello. Yes, this is his wife speaking . . . He's lying down now. Yes . . . well, he'll be in tomorrow. He's been very sick. Yes—I know we should have called, but we were so sure he'd be able to come in today. Yes—yes, I'm very sorry. Yes . . . Thank you very much. (*She hangs up. Walter is standing in the doorway of the bedroom behind her.*) That was Mrs. Arnold.

WALTER (*Indifferently*): Was it?

RUTH: She said if you don't come in tomorrow that they are getting a new man . . .

WALTER: Ain't that sad—ain't that crying sad.

RUTH: She said Mr. Arnold has had to take a cab for three days . . . Walter, you ain't been to work for three days! (*This is a revelation to her*) Where you been, Walter Lee Younger? (*Walter looks at her and starts to laugh*) You're going to lose your job.

WALTER: That's right . . .

RUTH: Oh, Walter, and with your mother working like a dog every day—

WALTER: That's sad too—Everything is sad.

MAMA: What you been doing for these three days, son?

WALTER: Mama—you don't know all the things a man what got leisure can find to do in this city . . . What's this—Friday night? Well—Wednesday I borrowed Willy Harris' car and I went for a drive . . . just me and myself and I drove and drove . . . Way out . . . way past South Chicago, and I parked the car and I sat and looked at the steel mills all day long. I just sat in the car and looked at them big black chimneys for hours. Then I drove back and I went to the Green Hat. *(Pause)* And Thursday— Thursday I borrowed the car again and I got in it and I pointed it the other way and I drove the other way—for hours—way, way up to Wisconsin, and I looked at the farms. I just drove and looked at the farms. Then I drove back and I went to the Green Hat. *(Pause)* And today—today I didn't get the car. Today I just walked. All over the Southside. And I looked at the Negroes and they looked at me and finally I just sat down on the curb at Thirty-ninth and South Parkway and I just sat there and watched the Negroes go by. And then I went to the Green Hat. You all sad? You all depressed? And you know where I am going right now—

(Ruth goes out quietly)

MAMA: Oh, Big Walter, is this the harvest of our days?

WALTER: You know what I like about the Green Hat? *(He turns the radio on and a steamy, deep blues pours into the room)* I like this little cat they got there who blows a sax . . . He blows. He talks to me. He ain't but 'bout five feet tall and he's got a conked head and his eyes is always closed and he's all music—

MAMA *(Rising and getting some papers out of her handbag):* Walter—

WALTER: And there's this other guy who plays the piano . . . and they got a sound. I mean they can work on some music. . . . They got the best little combo in the world in the Green Hat . . . You can just sit there and drink and listen to them three men play and you realize that don't nothing matter worth a damn, but just being there—

MAMA: I've helped do it to you, haven't I, son? Walter, I been wrong.

WALTER: Naw—you ain't never been wrong about nothing, Mama.

MAMA: Listen to me, now. I say I been wrong, son. That I been doing to you what the rest of the world been doing to you. *(She stops and he looks up slowly at her and she meets his eyes pleadingly)* Walter—what you ain't never understood is that I ain't got nothing, don't own nothing, ain't never really wanted nothing that wasn't for you. There ain't nothing as precious to me . . . There ain't nothing worth holding on to, money, dreams, nothing else—if it means—if it means it's going to destroy my boy. *(She puts her papers in front of him and he watches her without speaking or moving)* I paid the man thirty-five hundred dollars down on the house. That leaves sixty-five hundred dollars. Monday morning I want you to take this money and take three thousand dollars and put it in a savings account for Beneatha's medical schooling. The rest you put in a checking account—with your name on it. And from now on any penny that come out of it or that go in it is for you to look after. For you to decide. *(She drops her hands a little helplessly)* It ain't much, but it's all I got in the world and I'm putting it in your hands. I'm telling you to be the head of this family from now on like you supposed to be.

WALTER *(Stares at the money):* You trust me like that, Mama?

MAMA: I ain't never stop trusting you. Like I ain't never stop loving you.

(She goes out, and Walter sits looking at the money on the table as the music continues in its idiom, pulsing in the room. Finally, in a decisive gesture, he gets up, and, in mingled joy and desperation, picks up the money. At the same moment, Travis enters for bed.)

TRAVIS: What's the matter, Daddy? You drunk?

WALTER *(Sweetly, more sweetly than we have ever known him):* No, Daddy ain't drunk. Daddy ain't going to never be drunk again. . . .

TRAVIS: Well, good night, Daddy.

(The Father has come from behind the couch and leans over, embracing his son)

WALTER: Son, I feel like talking to you tonight.

TRAVIS: About what?

WALTER: Oh, about a lot of things. About you and what kind of man you going to be when you grow up.... Son—son, what do you want to be when you grow up?

TRAVIS: A bus driver.

WALTER *(Laughing a little)*: A what? Man, that ain't nothing to want to be!

TRAVIS: Why not?

WALTER: 'Cause, man—it ain't big enough—you know what I mean.

TRAVIS: I don't know then. I can't make up my mind. Sometimes Mama asks me that too. And sometimes when I tell her I just want to be like you—she says she don't want me to be like that and sometimes she says she does....

WALTER *(Gathering him up in his arms)*: You know what, Travis? In seven years you going to be seventeen years old. And things is going to be very different with us in seven years, Travis.... One day when you are seventeen I'll come home—home from my office downtown somewhere—

TRAVIS: You don't work in no office, Daddy.

WALTER: No—but after tonight. After what your daddy gonna do tonight, there's going to be offices—a whole lot of offices....

TRAVIS: What you gonna do tonight, Daddy?

WALTER: You wouldn't understand yet, son, but your daddy's gonna make a transaction ... a business transaction that's going to change our lives.... That's how come one day when you 'bout seventeen years old I'll come home and I'll be pretty tired, you know what I mean, after a day of conferences and secretaries getting things wrong the way they do ... 'cause an executive's life is hell, man— *(The more he talks the farther away he gets)* And I'll pull the car up on the driveway ... just a plain black Chrysler, I think, with white walls—no—black tires. More elegant. Rich people don't have to be flashy ... though I'll have to get something a little sportier for Ruth— maybe a Cadillac convertible to do her shopping in.... And I'll come up the steps to the house and the gardener will be clipping away at the hedges and he'll say, "Good evening, Mr. Younger." And I'll say, "Hello Jefferson, how are you this evening?" And I'll go inside and Ruth will come downstairs and meet me at the door and we'll kiss each other and she'll take my arm and we'll go up to your room to see you sitting on the floor with the catalogues of all the great schools in America around you.... All the great schools in the world! And—and I'll say, all right son—it's your seventeenth birthday, what is it you've decided? ... Just tell me where you want to go to school and you'll go. Just tell me, what it is you want to be—and you'll *be* it.... Whatever you want to be—Yessir! *(He holds his arms open for Travis)* You just name it, son ... *(Travis leaps into them)* and I hand you the world!

(Walter's voice has risen in pitch and hysterical promise and on the last line he lifts Travis high)

(Blackout)

Scene 3

Time: Saturday, moving day, one week later.
Before the curtain rises, Ruth's voice, a strident, dramatic church alto, cuts through the silence.

It is, in the darkness, a triumphant surge, a penetrating statement of expectation: "Oh, Lord, I don't feel no ways tired! Children, Oh, glory hallelujah!"

As the curtain rises we see that Ruth is alone in the living room, finishing up the family's packing. It is moving day. She is nailing crates and tying cartons. Beneatha enters, carrying a guitar case, and watches her exuberant sister-in-law.

RUTH: Hey!

BENEATHA *(Putting away the case)*: Hi.

RUTH *(Pointing at a package)*: Honey—look in that package there and see what I found on sale this morning at the South Center. *(Ruth gets up and moves to the package and draws out some curtains)* Lookahere—hand-turned hems!

BENEATHA: How do you know the window size out there?

RUTH *(Who hadn't thought of that)*: Oh—Well, they bound to fit something in the whole house. Anyhow, they was too good a bargain to pass up. *(Ruth slaps her head, suddenly remembering something)* Oh, Bennie—I meant to put a special note on that carton over there. That's your mama's good china and she wants 'em to be very careful with it.

BENEATHA: I'll do it.

(Beneatha finds a piece of paper and starts to draw large letters on it)

RUTH: You know what I'm going to do soon as I get in that new house?

BENEATHA: What?

RUTH: Honey—I'm going to run me a tub of water up to here . . . *(With her fingers practically up to her nostrils)* And I'm going to get in it—and I am going to sit . . . and sit . . . and sit in that hot water and the first person who knocks to tell *me* to hurry up and come out—

BENEATHA: Gets shot at sunrise.

RUTH *(Laughing happily)*: You said it, sister! *(Noticing how large Beneatha is absentmindedly making the note)* Honey, they ain't going to read that from no airplane.

BENEATHA *(Laughing herself)*: I guess I always think things have more emphasis if they are big, somehow.

RUTH *(Looking up at her and smiling)*: You and your brother seem to have that as a philosophy of life. Lord, that man—done changed so 'round here. You know—you know what we did last night? Me and Walter Lee?

BENEATHA: What?

RUTH *(Smiling to herself)*: We went to the movies. *(Looking at Beneatha to see if she understands)* We went to the movies. You know the last time me and Walter went to the movies together?

BENEATHA: No.

RUTH: Me neither. That's how long it been. *(Smiling again)* But we went last night. The picture wasn't much good, but that didn't seem to matter. We went—and we held hands.

BENEATHA: Oh, Lord!

RUTH: We held hands—and you know what?

BENEATHA: What?

RUTH: When we come out of the show it was late and dark and all the stores and things was closed up . . . and it was kind of chilly and there wasn't many people on the streets . . . and we was still holding hands, me and Walter.

BENEATHA: You're killing me.

(*Walter enters with a large package. His happiness is deep in him; he cannot keep still with his new-found exuberance. He is singing and wiggling and snapping his fingers. He puts his package in a corner and puts a phonograph record, which he has brought in with him, on the record player. As the music comes up he dances over to Ruth and tries to get her to dance with him. She gives in at last to his raunchiness and in a fit of giggling allows herself to be drawn into his mood and together they deliberately burlesque an old social dance of their youth.*)

BENEATHA (*Regarding them a long time as they dance, then drawing in her breath for a deeply exaggerated comment which she does not particularly mean*): Talk about—olddddddddddd-fashionedddddddd—Negroes!

WALTER (*Stopping momentarily*): What kind of Negroes?

(*He says this in fun. He is not angry with her today, nor with anyone. He starts to dance with his wife again*)

BENEATHA: Old-fashioned.

WALTER (*As he dances with Ruth*): You know, when these *New Negroes* have their convention—(*Pointing at his sister*)—that is going to be the chairman of the Committee on Unending Agitation. (*He goes on dancing, then stops*) Race, race, race! . . . Girl, I do believe you are the first person in the history of the entire human race to successfully brainwash yourself. (*Beneatha breaks up and he goes on dancing. He stops again, enjoying his tease*) Damn, even the N double A C P takes a holiday sometimes! (*Beneatha and Ruth laugh. He dances with Ruth some more and starts to laugh and stops and pantomimes someone over an operating table.*) I can just see that chick someday looking down at some poor cat on an operating table before she starts to slice him, saying . . . (*Pulling his sleeves back maliciously*) "By the way, what are your views on civil rights down there? . . ."

(*He laughs at her again and starts to dance happily. The bell sounds.*)

BENEATHA: Sticks and stones may break my bones but . . . words will never hurt me!

(*Beneatha goes to the door and opens it as Walter and Ruth go on with the clowning. Beneatha is somewhat surprised to see a quiet-looking middle-aged white man in a business suit holding his hat and a briefcase in his hand and consulting a small piece of paper.*)

MAN: Uh—How do you do, miss. I am looking for a Mrs.— (*He looks at the slip of paper*) Mrs. Lena Younger?

BENEATHA (*Smoothing her hair with slight embarrassment*): Oh—yes, that's my mother. Excuse me. (*She closes the door and turns to quiet the other two*) Ruth! Brother! Somebody's here. (*Then she opens the door. The man casts a curious quick glance at all of them*) Uh—come in please.

MAN (*Coming in*): Thank you.

BENEATHA: My mother isn't here just now. Is it business?

MAN: Yes . . . well, of a sort.

WALTER (*Freely, the Man of the House*): Have a seat. I'm Mrs. Younger's son. I look after most of her business matters.

(*Ruth and Beneatha exchange amused glances*)

MAN (*Regarding Walter, and sitting*): Well—My name is Karl Lindner . . .

WALTER (*Stretching out his hand*): Walter Younger. This is my wife—(*Ruth nods politely*)—and my sister.

LINDNER: How do you do.

WALTER (*Amiably, as he sits himself easily on a chair, leaning with interest forward on his knees and looking expectantly into the newcomer's face*): What can we do for you, Mr. Lindner!

LINDNER (*Some minor shuffling of the hat and briefcase on his knees*): Well—I am a representative of the Clybourne Park Improvement Association—

WALTER (*Pointing*): Why don't you sit your things on the floor?

LINDNER: Oh—yes. Thank you. (*He slides the briefcase and hat under the chair*) And as I was saying—I am from the Clybourne Park Improvement Association and we have had it brought to our attention at the last meeting that you people—or at least your mother—has bought a piece of residential property at—(*He digs for the slip of paper again*)—four o six Clybourne Street . . .

WALTER: That's right. Care for something to drink? Ruth, get Mr. Lindner a beer.

LINDNER (*Upset for some reason*): Oh—no, really. I mean thank you very much, but no thank you.

RUTH (*Innocently*): Some coffee?

LINDNER: Thank you, nothing at all.

(*Beneatha is watching the man carefully*)

LINDNER: Well, I don't know how much you folks know about our organization. (*He is a gentle man; thoughtful and somewhat labored in his manner*) It is one of these community organizations set up to look after—oh, you know, things like block upkeep and special projects and we also have what we call our New Neighbors Orientation Committee . . .

BENEATHA (*Drily*): Yes—and what do they do?

LINDNER (*Turning a little to her and then returning the main force to Walter*): Well—it's what you might call a sort of welcoming committee, I guess. I mean they, we, I'm the chairman of the committee—go around and see the new people who move into the neighborhood and sort of give them the lowdown on the way we do things out in Clybourne Park.

BENEATHA (*With appreciation of the two meanings, which escape Ruth and Walter*): Un-huh.

LINDNER: And we also have the category of what the association calls—(*He looks elsewhere*)—uh—special community problems . . .

BENEATHA: Yes—and what are some of those?

WALTER: Girl, let the man talk.

LINDNER (*With understated relief*): Thank you. I would sort of like to explain this thing in my own way. I mean I want to explain to you in a certain way.

WALTER: Go ahead.

LINDNER: Yes. Well. I'm going to try to get right to the point. I'm sure we'll all appreciate that in the long run.

BENEATHA: Yes.

WALTER: Be still now!

LINDNER: Well—

RUTH (*Still innocently*): Would you like another chair—you don't look comfortable.

LINDNER (*more frustrated than annoyed*): No, thank you very much. Please. Well—to get right to the point. I—(*A great breath, and he is off at last*) I am sure you people must be aware of some of the incidents which have happened in various parts of the city when colored people have moved into certain areas—*(Beneatha exhales heavily and starts tossing a piece of fruit up and down in the air)* Well—because we have what I think is going to be a unique type of organization in American community life—not only do we deplore that kind of thing—but we are trying to do something about it. *(Beneatha stops tossing and turns with a new and quizzical interest to the man)* We feel—*(gaining confidence in his mission because of the interest in the faces of the people he is talking to)*—we feel that most of the trouble in this world, when you come right down to it—*(He hits his knee for emphasis)*—most of the trouble exists because people just don't sit down and talk to each other.

RUTH *(Nodding as she might in church, pleased with the remark)*: You can say that again, mister.

LINDNER *(More encouraged by such affirmation)*: That we don't try hard enough in this world to understand the other fellow's problem. The other guy's point of view.

RUTH: Now that's right.

(Beneatha and Walter merely watch and listen with genuine interest)

LINDNER: Yes—that's the way we feel out in Clybourne Park. And that's why I was elected to come here this afternoon and talk to you people. Friendly like, you know, the way people should talk to each other and see if we couldn't find some way to work this thing out. As I say, the whole business is a matter of *caring* about the other fellow. Anybody can see that you are a nice family of folks, hard working and honest I'm sure. *(Beneatha frowns slightly, quizzically, her head tilted regarding him)* Today everybody knows what it means to be on the outside of *something.* And of course, there is always somebody who is out to take the advantage of people who don't always understand.

WALTER: What do you mean?

LINDNER: Well—you see our community is made up of people who've worked hard as the dickens for years to build up that little community. They're not rich and fancy people; just hard-working, honest people who don't really have much but those little homes and a dream of the kind of community they want to raise their children in. Now, I don't say we are perfect and there is a lot wrong in some of the things they want. But you've got to admit that a man, right or wrong, has the right to want to have the neighborhood he lives in a certain kind of way. And at the moment the overwhelming majority of our people out there feel that people get along better, take more of a common interest in the life of the community, when they share a common background. I want you to believe me when I tell you that race prejudice simply doesn't enter into it. It is a matter of the people of Clybourne Park believing, rightly or wrongly, as I say, that for the happiness of all concerned that our Negro families are happier when they live in their *own* communities.

BENEATHA *(With a grand and bitter gesture)*: This, friends, is the Welcoming Committee!

WALTER *(Dumbfounded, looking at Lindner)*: Is this what you came marching all the way over here to tell us?

LINDNER: Well, now we've been having a fine conversation. I hope you'll hear me all the way through.

WALTER *(Tightly)*: Go ahead, man.

LINDNER: You see—in the face of all the things I have said, we are prepared to make your family a very generous offer . . .

BENEATHA: Thirty pieces and not a coin less!

WALTER: Yeah?

LINDNER *(Putting on his glasses and drawing a form out of the briefcase)*: Our association is prepared, through the collective effort of our people, to buy the house from you at a financial gain to your family.

RUTH: Lord have mercy, ain't this the living gall!

WALTER: All right, you through?

LINDNER: Well, I want to give you the exact terms of the financial arrangement—

WALTER: We don't want to hear no exact terms of no arrangements. I want to know if you got any more to tell us 'bout getting together?

LINDNER (*Taking off his glasses*): Well—I don't suppose that you feel . . .

WALTER: Never mind how I feel—you got any more to say 'bout how people ought to sit down and talk to each other? . . . Get out of my house, man.

(*He turns his back and walks to the door*)

LINDNER (*Looking around at the hostile faces and reaching and assembling his hat and briefcase*): Well—I don't understand why you people are reacting this way. What do you think you are going to gain by moving into a neighborhood where you just aren't wanted and where some elements—well—people can get awful worked up when they feel that their whole way of life and everything they've ever worked for is threatened.

WALTER: Get out.

LINDNER (*At the door, holding a small card*): Well—I'm sorry it went like this.

WALTER: Get out.

LINDNER (*Almost sadly regarding Walter*): You just can't force people to change their hearts, son.

(*He turns and puts his card on a table and exits. Walter pushes the door to with stinging hatred, and stands looking at it. Ruth just sits and Beneatha just stands. They say nothing. Mama and Travis enter.*)

MAMA: Well—this all the packing got done since I left out of here this morning. I testify before God that my children got all the energy of the dead. What time the moving men due?

BENEATHA: Four o'clock. You had a caller, Mama.

(*She is smiling, teasingly*)

MAMA: Sure enough—who?

BENEATHA (*Her arms folded saucily*): The Welcoming Committee.

(*Walter and Ruth giggle*)

MAMA (*Innocently*): Who?

BENEATHA: The Welcoming Committee. They said they're sure going to be glad to see you when you get there.

WALTER (*Devilishly*): Yeah, they said they can't hardly wait to see your face.

(*Laughter*)

MAMA (*Sensing their facetiousness*): What's the matter with you all?

WALTER: Ain't nothing the matter with us. We just telling you 'bout the gentleman who came to see you this afternoon. From the Clybourne Park Improvement Association.

MAMA: What he want?

RUTH (*In the same mood as Beneatha and Walter*): To welcome you, honey.

WALTER: He said they can't hardly wait. He said the one thing they don't have, that they just *dying* to have out there is a fine family of colored people! *(To Ruth and Beneatha)* Ain't that right!

RUTH and BENEATHA *(Mockingly)*: Yeah! He left his card in case—

(They indicate the card, and Mama picks it up and throws it on the floor—understanding and looking off as she draws her chair up to the table on which she has put her plant and some sticks and some cord)

MAMA: Father, give us strength. *(Knowingly—and without fun)* Did he threaten us?

BENEATHA: Oh—Mama—they don't do it like that any more. He talked Brotherhood. He said everybody ought learn how to sit down and hate each other with good Christian fellowship.

(She and Walter shake hands to ridicule the remark)

MAMA *(Sadly)*: Lord, protect us . . .

RUTH: You should hear the money those folks raised to buy the house from us. All we paid and then some.

BENEATHA: What they think we going to do—eat 'em?

RUTH: No, honey, marry 'em.

MAMA *(Shaking her head)*: Lord, Lord, Lord . . .

RUTH: Well—that's the way the crackers crumble. Joke.

BENEATHA *(Laughingly noticing what her mother is doing)*: Mama, what are you doing?

MAMA: Fixing my plant so it won't get hurt none on the way . . .

BENEATHA: Mama, you going to take *that* to the new house?

MAMA: Un-huh—

BENEATHA: That raggedy-looking old thing?

MAMA *(Stopping and looking at her)*: It expresses *me*.

RUTH *(With delight, to Beneatha)*: So there, Miss Thing!

(Walter comes to Mama suddenly and bends down behind her and squeezes her in his arms with all his strength. She is overwhelmed by the suddenness of it and, though delighted, her manner is like that of Ruth with Travis.)

MAMA: Look out now, boy! You make me mess up my thing here!

WALTER *(His face lit, he slips down on his knees beside her, his arms still about her)*: Mama . . . you know what it means to climb up in the chariot?

MAMA *(Gruffly, very happy)*: Get on away from me now . . .

RUTH *(Near the gift-wrapped package, trying to catch Walter's eye)*: Psst—

WALTER: What the old song say, Mama . . .

RUTH: Walter—Now?

(She is pointing at the package)

WALTER *(Speaking the lines, sweetly, playfully, in his mother's face)*:
I got wings . . . you got wings . . .
All God's children got wings . . .

MAMA: Boy—get out of my face and do some work . . .

WALTER: When I get to heaven gonna put on my wings,
Gonna fly all over God's heaven . . .

BENEATHA *(Teasingly, from across the room)*: Everybody talking 'bout heaven ain't going there!

WALTER (*To Ruth, who is carrying the box across to them*): I don't know, you think we ought to give her that . . . Seems to me she ain't been very appreciative around here.

MAMA (*Eying the box, which is obviously a gift*): What is that?

WALTER (*Taking it from Ruth and putting it on the table in front of Mama*): Well—what you all think. Should we give it to her?

RUTH: Oh—she was pretty good today.

MAMA: I'll good you—

(*She turns her eyes to the box again*)

BENEATHA: Open it, Mama.

(*She stands up, looks at it, turns and looks at all of them, and then presses her hands together and does not open the package*)

WALTER (*Sweetly*): Open it, Mama. It's for you. (*Mama looks in his eyes. It is the first present in her life without its being Christmas. Slowly she opens her package and lifts out, one by one, a brand-new sparkling set of gardening tools. Walter continues, prodding.*) Ruth made up the note—read it . . .

MAMA (*Picking up the card and adjusting her glasses*): "To our own Mrs. Miniver[9] —Love from Brother, Ruth and Beneatha." Ain't that lovely . . .

TRAVIS (*Tugging at his father's sleeve*): Daddy, can I give her mine now?

WALTER: All right, son. (*Travis flies to get his gift*) Travis didn't want to go in with the rest of us, Mama. He got his own. (*Somewhat amused*) We don't know what it is . . .

TRAVIS (*Racing back in the room with a large hatbox and putting it in front of his grandmother*): Here!

MAMA: Lord have mercy, baby. You done gone and bought your grandmother a hat?

TRAVIS (*Very proud*): Open it!

(*She does and lifts out an elaborate, but very elaborate, wide gardening hat, and all the adults break up at the sight of it*)

RUTH: Travis, honey, what is that?

TRAVIS (*Who thinks it is beautiful and appropriate*): It's a gardening hat! Like the ladies always have on in the magazines when they work in their gardens.

BENEATHA (*Giggling fiercely*): Travis—we were trying to make Mama Mrs. Miniver—not Scarlett O'Hara![1]

MAMA (*Indignantly*): What's matter with you all! This here is a beautiful hat! (*Absurdly*) I always wanted me one just like it!

(*She pops it on her head to prove it to her grandson, and the hat is ludicrous and considerably oversized*)

RUTH: Hot Dog! Go, Mama!

WALTER (*Doubled over with laughter*): I'm sorry, Mama—but you look like you ready to go out and chop you some cotton sure enough!

(*They all laugh except Mama, out of deference to Travis' feelings*)

9. The title character in a World War II movie (1942) about a British woman who endures hardship.

1. The southern belle of *Gone with the Wind* (1936, novel; 1939, film).

MAMA (*Gathering the boy up to her*): Bless your heart—this is the prettiest hat I ever owned— (*Walter, Ruth and Beneatha chime in—noisily, festively and insincerely congratulating Travis on his gift*) What are we standing around here for? We ain't finished packin' yet. Bennie, you ain't packed one book.

(*The bell rings*)

BENEATHA: That couldn't be the movers . . . it's not hardly two good yet—

(*Beneatha goes into her room. Mama starts for door*)

WALTER (*Turning, stiffening*): Wait—wait—I'll get it.

(*He stands and looks at the door*)

MAMA: You expecting company, son?
WALTER (*Just looking at the door*): Yeah—Yeah . . .

(*Mama looks at Ruth, and they exchange innocent and unfrightened glances*)

MAMA (*Not understanding*): Well, let them in, son.
BENEATHA (*From her room*): We need some more string.
MAMA: Travis—you run to the hardware and get me some string cord.

(*Mama goes out and Walter turns and looks at Ruth. Travis goes to a dish for money.*)

RUTH: Why don't you answer the door, man?
WALTER (*Suddenly bounding across the floor to her*): 'Cause sometimes it hard to let the future begin! (*Stooping down in her face*)
I got wings! You got wings!
All God's children got wings!

(*He crosses to the door and throws it open. Standing there is a very slight little man in a not too prosperous business suit and with haunted frightened eyes and a hat pulled down tightly, brim up, around his forehead. Travis passes between the men and exits. Walter leans deep in the man's face, still in his jubilance.*)

When I get to heaven gonna put on my wings,
Gonna fly all over God's heaven . . .

(*The little man just stares at him*)

Heaven—

(*Suddenly he stops and looks past the little man into the empty hallway*)

Where's Willy, man?
BOBO: He ain't with me.
WALTER (*Not disturbed*): Oh—come on in. You know my wife.
BOBO (*Dumbly, taking off his hat*): Yes—h'you, Miss Ruth.
RUTH (*Quietly, a mood apart from her husband already, seeing Bobo*): Hello, Bobo.
WALTER: You right on time today . . . Right on time. That's the way! (*He slaps Bobo on his back*) Sit down . . . lemme hear.

(Ruth stands stiffly and quietly in back of them, as though somehow she senses death, her eyes fixed on her husband)

BOBO *(His frightened eyes on the floor, his hat in his hands)*: Could I please get a drink a water, before I tell you about it, Walter Lee?

(Walter does not take his eyes off the man, Ruth goes blindly to the tap and gets a glass of water and brings it to Bobo)

WALTER: There ain't nothing wrong, is there?
BOBO: Lemme tell you—
WALTER: Man—didn't nothing go wrong?
BOBO: Lemme tell you—Walter Lee. *(Looking at Ruth and talking to her more than to Walter)* You know how it was. I got to tell you how it was. I mean first I got to tell you how it was all the way . . . I mean about the money I put in, Walter Lee . . .
WALTER *(With taut agitation now)*: What about the money you put in?
BOBO: Well—it wasn't much as we told you—me and Willy—*(He stops)* I'm sorry, Walter. I got a bad feeling about it. I got a real bad feeling about it . . .
WALTER: Man, what you telling me about all this for? . . . Tell me what happened in Springfield . . .
BOBO: Springfield.
RUTH *(Like a dead woman)*: What was supposed to happen in Springfield?
BOBO *(To her)*: This deal that me and Walter went into with Willy—Me and Willy was going to go down to Springfield and spread some money 'round so's we wouldn't have to wait so long for the liquor license . . . That's what we were going to do. Everybody said that was the way you had to do, you understand, Miss Ruth?
WALTER: Man—what happened down there?
BOBO *(A pitiful man, near tears)*: I'm trying to tell you, Walter.
WALTER *(Screaming at him suddenly)*: THEN TELL ME, GODDAMMIT . . . WHAT'S THE MATTER WITH YOU?
BOBO: Man . . . I didn't go to no Springfield, yesterday.
WALTER *(Halted, life hanging in the moment)*: Why not?
BOBO *(The long way, the hard way to tell)*: 'Cause I didn't have no reasons to . . .
WALTER: Man, what are you talking about!
BOBO: I'm talking about the fact that when I got to the train station yesterday morning—eight o'clock like we planned . . . Man—*Willy didn't never show up.*
WALTER: Why . . . where was he . . . where is he?
BOBO: That's what I'm trying to tell you . . . I don't know . . . I waited six hours . . . I called his house . . . and I waited . . . six hours . . . I waited in that train station six hours . . . *(Breaking into tears)* That was all the extra money I had in the world . . . *(Looking up at Walter with the tears running down his face)* Man, *Willy is gone.*
WALTER: Gone, what you mean Willy is gone? Gone where? You mean he went by himself. You mean he went off to Springfield by himself—to take care of getting the license—*(Turns and looks anxiously at Ruth)* You mean maybe he didn't want too many people in on the business down there? *(Looks to Ruth again, as before)* You know Willy got his own ways. *(Looks back to Bobo)* Maybe you was late yesterday and he just went on down there without you. Maybe—maybe—he's been callin' you at home tryin' to tell you what happened or something. Maybe—maybe—he just got sick. He's somewhere—he's got to be somewhere. We just got to find him—me and you got to find him. *(Grabs Bobo senselessly by the collar and starts to shake him)* We got to!

BOBO (*In sudden angry, frightened agony*): What's the matter with you, Walter! *When a cat take off with your money he don't leave you no maps!*

WALTER (*Turning madly, as though he is looking for Willy in the very room*): Willy! . . . Willy . . . don't do it . . . Please don't do it . . . Man, not with that money . . . Man, please, not with that money . . . Oh, God . . . Don't let it be true . . . (*He is wandering around, crying out for Willy and looking for him or perhaps for help from God*) Man . . . I trusted you . . . Man, I put my life in your hands . . . (*He starts to crumple down on the floor as Ruth just covers her face in horror. Mama opens the door and comes into the room, with Beneatha behind her*) Man . . . (*He starts to pound the floor with his fists, sobbing wildly*) That money is made out of my father's flesh . . .

BOBO (*Standing over him helplessly*): I'm sorry, Walter . . . (*Only Walter's sobs reply. Bobo puts on his hat*) I had my life staked on this deal, too . . .

(*He exits*)

MAMA (*To Walter*): Son—(*She goes to him, bends down to him, talks to his bent head*) Son . . . Is it gone? Son, I gave you sixty-five hundred dollars. Is it gone? All of it? Beneatha's money too?

WALTER (*Lifting his head slowly*): Mama . . . I never . . . went to the bank at all . . .

MAMA (*Not wanting to believe him*): You mean . . . your sister's school money . . . you used that too . . . Walter? . . .

WALTER: Yessss! . . . All of it . . . It's all gone . . .

(*There is total silence. Ruth stands with her face covered with her hands; Beneatha leans forlornly against a wall, fingering a piece of red ribbon from the mother's gift. Mama stops and looks at her son without recognition and then, quite without thinking about it, starts to beat him senselessly in the face. Beneatha goes to them and stops it.*)

BENEATHA: Mama!

(*Mama stops and looks at both of her children and rises slowly and wanders vaguely, aimlessly away from them*)

MAMA: I seen . . . him . . . night after night . . . come in . . . and look at that rug . . . and then look at me . . . the red showing in his eyes . . . the veins moving in his head . . . I seen him grow thin and old before he was forty . . . working and working and working like somebody's old horse . . . killing himself . . . and you—you give it all away in a day . . .

BENEATHA: Mama—

MAMA: Oh, God . . . (*She looks up to Him*) Look down here—and show me the strength.

BENEATHA: Mama—

MAMA (*Folding over*): Strength . . .

BENEATHA (*Plaintively*): Mama . . .

MAMA: Strength!

(*Curtain*)

Act Three

An hour later. At curtain, there is a sullen light of gloom in the living room, gray light not unlike that which began the first scene of Act One. At left we can see Walter within his room, alone with himself. He is stretched out on the bed, his shirt out and open, his arms under his head. He does not smoke, he does not cry out, he merely lies there, looking up at the ceiling, much as if he were alone in the world. In the living room Beneatha sits at the table, still surrounded by the now almost ominous packing crates. She sits looking off. We feel that this is a mood struck perhaps an hour before, and it lingers now, full of the empty sound of profound disappointment. We see on a line from her brother's bedroom the sameness of their attitudes. Presently the bell rings and Beneatha rises without ambition or interest in answering. It is Asagai, smiling broadly, striding into the room with energy and happy expectation and conversation.

ASAGAI: I came over . . . I had some free time. I thought I might help with the packing. Ah, I like the look of packing crates! A household in preparation for a journey! It depresses some people . . . but for me . . . it is another feeling. Something full of the flow of life, do you understand? Movement, progress . . . It makes me think of Africa.

BENEATHA: Africa!

ASAGAI: What kind of a mood is this? Have I told you how deeply you move me.

BENEATHA: He gave away the money, Asagai . . .

ASAGAI: Who gave away what money?

BENEATHA: The insurance money. My brother gave it away.

ASAGAI: Gave it away?

BENEATHA: He made an investment! With a man even Travis wouldn't have trusted.

ASAGAI: And it's gone?

BENEATHA: Gone!

ASAGAI: I'm very sorry . . . And you, now?

BENEATHA: Me? . . . Me? . . . Me I'm nothing . . . Me. When I was very small . . . we used to take our sleds out in the wintertime and the only hills we had were the ice-covered stone steps of some houses down the street. And we used to fill them in with snow and make them smooth and slide down them all day . . . and it was very dangerous you know . . . far too steep . . . and sure enough one day a kid named Rufus came down too fast and hit the sidewalk . . . and we saw his face just split open right there in front of us . . . And I remember standing there looking at his bloody open face thinking that was the end of Rufus. But the ambulance came and they took him to the hospital and they fixed the broken bones and they sewed it all up . . . and the next time I saw Rufus he just had a little line down the middle of his face . . . I never got over that . . .

(Walter sits up, listening on the bed. Throughout this scene it is important that we feel his reaction at all times, that he visibly respond to the words of his sister and Asagai.)

ASAGAI: What?

BENEATHA: That that was what one person could do for another, fix him up—sew up the problem, make him all right again. That was the most marvelous thing in the world . . . I wanted to do that. I always thought it was the one concrete thing in the world that a human being could do. Fix up the sick, you know—and make them whole again. This was truly being God. . . .

ASAGAI: You wanted to be God?

BENEATHA: No—I wanted to cure. It used to be so important to me. I wanted to cure. It used to matter. I used to care. I mean about people and how their bodies hurt . . .

ASAGAI: And you've stopped caring?

BENEATHA: Yes—I think so.

ASAGAI: Why?

(Walter rises, goes to the door of his room and is about to open it, then stops and stands listening, leaning on the door jamb)

BENEATHA: Because it doesn't seem deep enough, close enough to what ails mankind—I mean this thing of sewing up bodies or administering drugs. Don't you understand? It was a child's reaction to the world. I thought that doctors had the secret to all the hurts . . . That's the way a child sees things—or an idealist.

ASAGAI: Children see things very well sometimes—and idealists even better.

BENEATHA: I know that's what you think. Because you are still where I left off—you still care. This is what you see for the world, for Africa. You with the dreams of the future will patch up all Africa—you are going to cure the Great Sore of colonialism with Independence—

ASAGAI: Yes!

BENEATHA: Yes—and you think that one word is the penicillin of the human spirit: "Independence!" But then what?

ASAGAI: That will be the problem for another time. First we must get there.

BENEATHA: And where does it end?

ASAGAI: End? Who even spoke of an end? To life? To living?

BENEATHA: An end to misery!

ASAGAI *(Smiling)*: You sound like a French intellectual.

BENEATHA: No! I sound like a human being who just had her future taken right out of her hands! While I was sleeping in my bed in there, things were happening in this world that directly concerned me—and nobody asked me, consulted me—they just went out and did things—and changed my life. Don't you see there isn't any real progress, Asagai, there is only one large circle that we march in, around and around, each of us with our own little picture—in front of us—our own little mirage that we think is the future.

ASAGAI: That is the mistake.

BENEATHA: What?

ASAGAI: What you just said—about the circle. It isn't a circle—it is simply a long line—as in geometry, you know, one that reaches into infinity. And because we cannot see the end—we also cannot see how it changes. And it is very odd but those who see the changes are called "idealists"—and those who cannot, or refuse to think, they are the "realists." It is very strange, and amusing too, I think.

BENEATHA: You—you are almost religious.

ASAGAI: Yes . . . I think I have the religion of doing what is necessary in the world—and of worshipping man—because he is so marvelous, you see.

BENEATHA: Man is foul! And the human race deserves its misery!

ASAGAI: You see: *you* have become the religious one in the old sense. Already, and after such a small defeat, you are worshipping despair.

BENEATHA: From now on, I worship the truth—and the truth—is that people are puny, small and selfish. . . .

ASAGAI: Truth? Why is it that you despairing ones always think that only you have the truth? I never thought to see *you* like that. Your brother made a stupid, childish mistake—and you are grateful to him. So that now you can give up the ailing human race on account of it. You talk about what good is struggle; what good is anything? Where are we all going? And why are we bothering?

BENEATHA: *And you cannot answer it!* All your talk and dreams about Africa and Independence. Independence and then what? What about all the crooks and petty thieves and just plain idiots who will come into power to steal and plunder the same as before—only now they will be black, and do it in the name of the new Independence—You cannot answer that.

ASAGAI (*Shouting over her*): I live the answer! (*Pause*) In my village at home it is the exceptional man who can even read a newspaper . . . or who ever *sees* a book at all. I will go home and much of what I will have to say will seem strange to the people of my village . . . But I will teach and work and things will happen, slowly and swiftly. At times it will seem that nothing changes at all . . . and then again . . . the sudden dramatic events which make history leap into the future. And then quiet again. Retrogression even. Guns, murder, revolution. And I even will have moments when I wonder if the quiet was not better than all that death and hatred. But I will look about my village at the illiteracy and disease and ignorance and I will not wonder long. And perhaps . . . perhaps I will be a great man . . . I mean perhaps I will hold on to the substance of truth and find my way always with the right course . . . and perhaps for it I will be butchered in my bed some night by the servants of empire . . .

BENEATHA: *The martyr!*

ASAGAI: . . . or perhaps I shall live to be a very old man respected and esteemed in my new nation . . . And perhaps I shall hold office and this is what I'm trying to tell you, Alaiyo; perhaps the things I believe now for my country will be wrong and outmoded, and I will not understand and do terrible things to have things my way or merely to keep my power. Don't you see that there will be young men and women, not British soldiers then, but my own black countrymen . . . to step out of the shadows some evening and slit my then useless throat? Don't you see they have always been there . . . that they always will be. And that such a thing as my own death will be an advance? They who might kill me even . . . actually replenish me!

BENEATHA: Oh, Asagai, I know all that.

ASAGAI: Good! Then stop moaning and groaning and tell me what you plan to do.

BENEATHA: Do?

ASAGAI: I have a bit of a suggestion.

BENEATHA: What?

ASAGAI (*Rather quietly for him*): That when it is all over—that you come home with me—

BENEATHA (*Slapping herself on the forehead with exasperation born of misunderstanding*): Oh—Asagai—at this moment you decide to be romantic!

ASAGAI (*Quickly understanding the misunderstanding*): My dear, young creature of the New World—I do not mean across the city—I mean across the ocean; come—to Africa.

BENEATHA (*Slowly understanding and turning to him with murmured amazement*): To—to Nigeria?

ASAGAI: Yes! . . . (*Smiling and lifting his arms playfully*) Three hundred years later the African Prince rose up out of the seas and swept the maiden back across the middle passage over which her ancestors had come—

BENEATHA (*Unable to play*): Nigeria?

ASAGAI: Nigeria. Home. (*Coming to her with genuine romantic flippancy*) I will show you our mountains and our stars; and give you cool drinks from gourds and teach you the old songs and the ways of our people—and, in time, we will pretend that—(*Very softly*)—you have only been away for a day—

(*She turns her back to him, thinking. He swings her around and takes her full in his arms in a long embrace which proceeds to passion.*)

BENEATHA (*Pulling away*): You're getting me all mixed up—

ASAGAI: Why?

BENEATHA: Too many things—too many things have happened today. I must sit down and think. I don't know what I feel about anything right this minute.

(She promptly sits down and props her chin on her fist)

ASAGAI *(Charmed)*: All right, I shall leave you. No—don't get up. *(Touching her, gently, sweetly)* Just sit awhile and think . . . Never be afraid to sit awhile and think. *(He goes to door and looks at her)* How often I have looked at you and said, "Ah—so this is what the New World hath finally wrought . . ."

(He exits. Beneatha sits on alone. Presently Walter enters from his room and starts to rummage through things, feverishly looking for something. She looks up and turns in her seat.)

BENEATHA *(Hissingly)*: Yes—just look at what the New World hath wrought! . . . Just look! *(She gestures with bitter disgust)* There he is! *Monsieur le petit bourgeois noir*—himself! There he is—Symbol of a Rising Class! Entrepreneur! Titan of the system! *(Walter ignores her completely and continues frantically and destructively looking for something and hurling things to floor and tearing things out of their place in his search. Beneatha ignores the eccentricity of his actions and goes on with the monologue of insult.)* Did you dream of yachts on Lake Michigan, Brother? Did you see yourself on that Great Day sitting down at the Conference Table, surrounded by all the mighty bald-headed men in America? All halted, waiting, breathless, waiting for your pronouncements on industry? Waiting for you—Chairman of the Board? *(Walter finds what he is looking for—a small piece of white paper—and pushes it in his pocket and puts on his coat and rushes out without ever having looked at her. She shouts after him.)* I look at you and I see the final triumph of stupidity in the world!

(The door slams and she returns to just sitting again. Ruth comes quickly out of Mama's room.)

RUTH: Who was that?
BENEATHA: Your husband.
RUTH: Where did he go?
BENEATHA: Who knows—maybe he has an appointment at U.S. Steel.
RUTH *(Anxiously, with frightened eyes)*: You didn't say nothing bad to him, did you?
BENEATHA: Bad? Say anything bad to him? No—I told him he was a sweet boy and full of dreams and everything is strictly peachy keen, as the ofay[2] kids say!

(Mama enters from her bedroom. She is lost, vague, trying to catch hold, to make some sense of her former command of the world, but it still eludes her. A sense of waste overwhelms her gait; a measure of apology rides on her shoulders. She goes to her plant, which has remained on the table, looks at it, picks it up and takes it to the window sill and sits it outside, and she stands and looks at it a long moment. Then she closes the window, straightens her body with effort and turns around to her children.)

MAMA: Well—ain't it a mess in here, though? *(A false cheerfulness, a beginning of something)* I guess we all better stop moping around and get some work done. All this unpacking and everything we got to do. *(Ruth raises her head slowly in response to the*

2. White.

sense of the line; and Beneatha in similar manner turns very slowly to look at her mother) One of you all better call the moving people and tell 'em not to come.

RUTH: Tell 'em not to come?

MAMA: Of course, baby. Ain't no need in 'em coming all the way here and having to go back. They charges for that too. *(She sits down, fingers to her brow, thinking)* Lord, ever since I was a little girl, I always remembers people saying, "Lena—Lena Eggleston, you aims too high all the time. You needs to slow down and see life a little more like it is. Just slow down some." That's what they always used to say down home—"Lord, that Lena Eggleston is a highminded thing. She'll get her due one day!"

RUTH: No, Lena . . .

MAMA: Me and Big Walter just didn't never learn right.

RUTH: Lena, no! We gotta go. Bennie—tell her . . . *(She rises and crosses to Beneatha with her arms outstretched. Beneatha doesn't respond.)* Tell her we can still move . . . the notes ain't but a hundred and twenty five a month. We got four grown people in this house—we can work . . .

MAMA *(To herself)*: Just aimed too high all the time—

RUTH *(Turning and going to Mama fast—the words pouring out with urgency and desperation)*: Lena—I'll work . . . I'll work twenty hours a day in all the kitchens in Chicago . . . I'll strap my baby on my back if I have to and scrub all the floors in America and wash all the sheets in America if I have to—but we got to move . . . We got to get out of here . . .

(Mama reaches out absently and pats Ruth's hand)

MAMA: No—I sees things differently now. Been thinking 'bout some of the things we could do to fix this place up some. I seen a second-hand bureau over on Maxwell Street just the other day that could fit right there. *(She points to where the new furniture might go. Ruth wanders away from her)* Would need some new handles on it and then a little varnish and then it look like something brand-new. And—we can put them new curtains in the kitchen . . . Why this place be looking fine. Cheer us all up so that we forget trouble ever came . . . *(To Ruth)* And you could get some nice screens to put up in your room round the baby's bassinet . . . *(She looks at both of them, pleadingly)* Sometimes you just got to know when to give up some things . . . and hold on to what you got.

(Walter enters from the outside, looking spent and leaning against the door, his coat hanging from him)

MAMA: Where you been, son?

WALTER *(Breathing hard)*: Made a call.

MAMA: To who, son?

WALTER: To The Man.

MAMA: What man, baby?

WALTER: The Man, Mama. Don't you know who The Man is?

RUTH: Walter Lee?

WALTER: *The Man.* Like the guys in the streets say—The Man. Captain Boss—Mistuh Charley . . . Old Captain Please Mr. Bossman . . .

BENEATHA *(Suddenly)*: Lindner!

WALTER: That's right! That's good. I told him to come right over.

BENEATHA *(Fiercely, understanding)*: For what? What do you want to see him for!

WALTER *(Looking at his sister)*: We going to do business with him.

MAMA: What you talking 'bout, son?

WALTER: Talking 'bout life, Mama. You all always telling me to see life like it is. Well—I laid in there on my back today . . . and I figured it out. Life just like it is. Who gets and who don't get. *(He sits down with his coat on and laughs)* Mama, you know it's all divided up. Life is. Sure enough. Between the takers and the "tooken." *(He laughs)* I've figured it out finally. *(He looks around at them)* Yeah. Some of us always getting "tooken." *(He laughs)* People like Willy Harris, they don't never get "tooken." And you know why the rest of us do? 'Cause we all mixed up. Mixed up bad. We get to looking 'round for the right and the wrong; and we worry about it and cry about it and stay up nights trying to figure out 'bout the wrong and the right of things all the time . . . And all the time, man, them takers is out there operating, just taking and taking. Willy Harris? Shoot—Willy Harris don't even count. He don't even count in the big scheme of things. But I'll say one thing for old Willy Harris . . . he's taught me something. He's taught me to keep my eye on what counts in this world. Yeah—*(Shouting out a little)* Thanks, Willy!

RUTH: What did you call that man for, Walter Lee?

WALTER: Called him to tell him to come on over to the show. Gonna put on a show for the man. Just what he wants to see. You see, Mama, the man came here today and he told us that them people out there where you want us to move—well they so upset they willing to pay us not to move out there. *(He laughs again)* And—and oh, Mama—you would of been proud of the way me and Ruth and Bennie acted. We told him to get out . . . Lord have mercy! We told the man to get out. Oh, we was some proud folks this afternoon, yeah. *(He lights a cigarette)* We were still full of that old-time stuff . . .

RUTH *(Coming toward him slowly)*: You talking 'bout taking them people's money to keep us from moving in that house?

WALTER: I ain't just talking 'bout it, baby—I'm telling you that's what's going to happen.

BENEATHA: Oh, God! Where is the bottom! Where is the real honest-to-God bottom so he can't go any farther!

WALTER: See—that's the old stuff. You and that boy that was here today. You all want everybody to carry a flag and a spear and sing some marching songs, huh? You wanna spend your life looking into things and trying to find the right and the wrong part, huh? Yeah. You know what's going to happen to that boy someday—he'll find himself sitting in a dungeon, locked in forever—and the takers will have the key! Forget it, baby! There ain't no causes—there ain't nothing but taking in this world, and he who takes most is smartest—and it don't make a damn bit of difference *how*.

MAMA: You making something inside me cry, son. Some awful pain inside me.

WALTER: Don't cry, Mama. Understand. That white man is going to walk in that door able to write checks for more money than we ever had. It's important to him and I'm going to help him . . . I'm going to put on the show, Mama.

MAMA: Son—I come from five generations of people who was slaves and sharecroppers—but ain't nobody in my family never let nobody pay 'em no money that was a way of telling us we wasn't fit to walk the earth. We ain't never been that poor. *(Raising her eyes and looking at him)* We ain't never been that dead inside.

BENEATHA: Well—we are dead now. All the talk about dreams and sunlight that goes on in this house. All dead.

WALTER: What's the matter with you all! I didn't make this world! It was give to me this way! Hell, yes, I want me some yachts someday! Yes, I want to hang some real pearls 'round my wife's neck. Ain't she supposed to wear no pearls? Somebody tell me—tell me, who decides which women is suppose to wear pearls in this world. I tell you I am a *man*—and I think my wife should wear some pearls in this world!

(This last line hangs a good while and Walter begins to move about the room. The word "Man" has penetrated his consciousness; he mumbles it to himself repeatedly between strange agitated pauses as he moves about)

MAMA: Baby, how you going to feel on the inside?

WALTER: Fine! . . . Going to feel fine . . . a man . . .

MAMA: You won't have nothing left then, Walter Lee.

WALTER *(Coming to her)*: I'm going to feel fine, Mama. I'm going to look that son-of-a-bitch in the eyes and say—*(He falters)*—and say, "All right, Mr. Lindner—*(He falters even more)*—that's your neighborhood out there. You got the right to keep it like you want. You got the right to have it like you want. Just write the check and—the house is yours." And, and I am going to say—*(His voice almost breaks)* And you—you people just put the money in my hand and you won't have to live next to this bunch of stinking niggers! . . . *(He straightens up and moves away from his mother, walking around the room)* Maybe—maybe I'll just get down on my black knees . . . *(He does so; Ruth and Bennie and Mama watch him in frozen horror)* Captain, Mistuh, Bossman. *(He starts crying)* A-hee-hee-hee! *(Wringing his hands in profoundly anguished imitation)* Yasssssuh! Great White Father, just gi' ussen de money, fo' God's sake, and we's ain't gwine come out deh and dirty up yo' white folks neighborhood . . .

(He breaks down completely, then gets up and goes into the bedroom)

BENEATHA: That is not a man. That is nothing but a toothless rat.

MAMA: Yes—death done come in this here house. *(She is nodding, slowly, reflectively)* Done come walking in my house. On the lips of my children. You what supposed to be my beginning again. You—what supposed to be my harvest. *(To Beneatha)* You—you mourning your brother?

BENEATHA: He's no brother of mine.

MAMA: What you say?

BENEATHA: I said that the individual in that room is no brother of mine.

MAMA: That's what I thought you said. You feeling like you better than he is today? *(Beneatha does not answer)* Yes? What you tell him a minute ago? That he wasn't a man? Yes? You give him up for me? Yes? You done wrote his epitaph too—like the rest of the world? Well, who give you the privilege?

BENEATHA: Be on my side for once! You saw what he just did. Mama! You saw him—down on his knees. Wasn't it you who taught me—to despise any man who would do that. Do what he's going to do.

MAMA: Yes—I taught you that. Me and your daddy. But I thought I taught you something else too . . . I thought I taught you to love him.

BENEATHA: Love him? There is nothing left to love.

MAMA: There is always something left to love. And if you ain't learned that, you ain't learned nothing. *(Looking at her)* Have you cried for that boy today? I don't mean for yourself and for the family 'cause we lost the money. I mean for him; what he been through and what it done to him. Child, when do you think is the time to love somebody the most; when they done good and made things easy for everybody? Well then, you ain't through learning—because that ain't the time at all. It's when he's at his lowest and can't believe in hisself 'cause the world done whipped him so. When you starts measuring somebody, measure him right, child, measure him right. Make sure you done taken into account what hills and valleys he come through before he got to wherever he is.

(Travis bursts into the room at the end of the speech, leaving the door open)

TRAVIS: Grandmama—the moving men are downstairs! The truck just pulled up.
MAMA *(Turning and looking at him)*: Are they, baby? They downstairs?

(She sighs and sits. Lindner appears in the doorway. He peers in and knocks lightly, to gain attention, and comes in. All turn to look at him.)

LINDNER *(Hat and briefcase in hand)*: Uh—hello . . .

(Ruth crosses mechanically to the bedroom door and opens it and lets it swing open freely and slowly as the lights come up on Walter within, still in his coat, sitting at the far corner of the room. He looks up and out through the room to Lindner.)

RUTH: He's here.

(A long minute passes and Walter slowly gets up)

LINDNER *(Coming to the table with efficiency, putting his briefcase on the table and starting to unfold papers, and unscrew fountain pens)*: Well, I certainly was glad to hear from you people. *(Walter has begun the trek out of the room, slowly and awkwardly, rather like a small boy, passing the back of his sleeve across his mouth from time to time)* Life can really be so much simpler than people let it be most of the time. Well—with whom do I negotiate? You, Mrs. Younger, or your son here? *(Mama sits with her hands folded on her lap and her eyes closed as Walter advances. Travis goes close to Lindner and looks at the papers curiously.)* Just some official papers, sonny.
RUTH: Travis, you go downstairs.
MAMA *(Opening her eyes and looking into Walter's)*: No, Travis, you stay right here. And you make him understand what you doing, Walter Lee. You teach him good. Like Willy Harris taught you. You show where our five generations done come to. Go ahead, son—
WALTER *(Looks down into his boy's eyes. Travis grins at him merrily and Walter draws him beside him with his arm lightly around his shoulder.)*: Well, Mr. Lindner.
(Beneatha turns away) We called you—*(There is a profound, simple groping quality in his speech)*—because, well, me and my family *(He looks around and shifts from one foot to the other)* Well—we are very plain people . . .
LINDNER: Yes—
WALTER: I mean—I have worked as a chauffeur most of my life—and my wife here, she does domestic work in people's kitchens. So does my mother. I mean—we are plain people . . .
LINDNER: Yes, Mr. Younger—
WALTER *(Really like a small boy, looking down at his shoes and then up at the man)*: And—uh—well, my father, well, he was a laborer most of his life.
LINDNER *(Absolutely confused)*: Uh, yes—
WALTER *(Looking down at his toes once again)*: My father almost beat a man to death once because this man called him a bad name or something, you know what I mean?
LINDNER: No, I'm afraid I don't.
WALTER *(Finally straightening up)*: Well, what I mean is that we come from people who had a lot of pride. I mean—we are very proud people. And that's my sister over there and she's going to be a doctor—and we are very proud—
LINDNER: Well—I am sure that is very nice, but—

WALTER (*Starting to cry and facing the man eye to eye*): What I am telling you is that we called you over here to tell you that we are very proud and that this is—this is my son, who makes the sixth generation of our family in this country, and that we have all thought about your offer and we have decided to move into our house because my father—my father—he earned it. (*Mama has her eyes closed and is rocking back and forth as though she were in church, with her head nodding the amen yes*) We don't want to make no trouble for nobody or fight no causes—but we will try to be good neighbors. That's all we got to say. (*He looks the man absolutely in the eyes*) We don't want your money.

(*He turns and walks away from the man*)

LINDNER (*Looking around at all of them*): I take it then that you have decided to occupy.
BENEATHA: That's what the man said.
LINDNER (*To Mama in her reverie*): Then I would like to appeal to you, Mrs. Younger. You are older and wiser and understand things better I am sure . . .
MAMA (*Rising*): I am afraid you don't understand. My son said we was going to move and there ain't nothing left for me to say. (*Shaking her head with double meaning*) You know how these young folks is nowadays, mister. Can't do a thing with 'em. Good-bye.
LINDNER (*Folding up his materials*): Well—if you are that final about it . . . There is nothing left for me to say. (*He finishes. He is almost ignored by the family, who are concentrating on Walter Lee. At the door Lindner halts and looks around.*) I sure hope you people know what you're doing.

(*He shakes his head and exits*)

RUTH (*Looking around and coming to life*): Well, for God's sake—if the moving men are here—LET'S GET THE HELL OUT OF HERE!
MAMA (*Into action*): Ain't it the truth! Look at all this here mess. Ruth put Travis' good jacket on him . . . Walter Lee, fix your tie and tuck your shirt in, you look just like somebody's hoodlum. Lord have mercy, where is my plant? (*She flies to get it amid the general bustling of the family, who are deliberately trying to ignore the nobility of the past moment*) You all start on down . . . Travis child, don't go empty-handed . . . Ruth, where did I put that box with my skillets in it? I want to be in charge of it myself . . . I'm going to make us the biggest dinner we ever ate tonight . . . Beneatha, what's the matter with them stockings? Pull them things up, girl . . .

(*The family starts to file out as two moving men appear and begin to carry out the heavier pieces of furniture, bumping into the family as they move about*)

BENEATHA: Mama, Asagai—asked me to marry him today and go to Africa—
MAMA (*In the middle of her getting-ready activity*): He did? You ain't old enough to marry nobody—(*Seeing the moving men lifting one of her chairs precariously*) Darling, that ain't no bale of cotton, please handle it so we can sit in it again. I had that chair twenty-five years . . .

(*The movers sigh with exasperation and go on with their work*)

BENEATHA (*Girlishly and unreasonably trying to pursue the conversation*): To go to Africa, Mama—be a doctor in Africa . . .
MAMA (*Distracted*): Yes, baby—

WALTER: Africa! What he want you to go to Africa for?

BENEATHA: To practice there . . .

WALTER: Girl, if you don't get all them silly ideas out your head! You better marry
yourself a man with some loot . . .

BENEATHA (*Angrily, precisely as in the first scene of the play*): What have you got to do
with who I marry!

WALTER: Plenty. Now I think George Murchison—

(*He and Beneatha go out yelling at each other vigorously; Beneatha is heard saying that
she would not marry George Murchison if he were Adam and she were Eve, etc. The anger
is loud and real till their voices diminish. Ruth stands at the door and turns to Mama and
smiles knowingly.*)

MAMA (*Fixing her hat at last*): Yeah—they something all right, my children . . .

RUTH: Yeah—they're something. Let's go, Lena.

MAMA (*Stalling, starting to look around at the house*): Yes—I'm coming. Ruth—

RUTH: Yes?

MAMA (*Quietly, woman to woman*): He finally come into his manhood today, didn't he?
Kind of like a rainbow after the rain . . .

RUTH (*Biting her lip lest her own pride explode in front of Mama*): Yes, Lena.

(*Walter's voice calls for them raucously*)

MAMA (*Waving Ruth out vaguely*): All right, honey—go on down. I be down directly.

(*Ruth hesitates, then exits. Mama stands, at last alone in the living room, her plant on
the table before her as the lights start to come down. She looks around at all the walls and
ceilings and suddenly, despite herself, while the children call below, a great heaving thing
rises in her and she puts her fist to her mouth, takes a final desperate look, pulls her coat
about her, pats her hat and goes out. The lights dim down. The door opens and she comes
back in, grabs her plant, and goes out for the last time.*)

(*Curtain*)

1959

Toni Morrison
(1931–   )

With a richly lyrical style, Toni Morrison
details the lives of African Americans—
especially young women—in the segregated neighborhoods of small towns,
mostly in the Midwest, a location she describes as "an escape from stereotyped
black settings. It is neither plantation nor
ghetto."

Born Chloe Anthony Wofford in Lo-
rain, Ohio, Morrison learned early about
the struggle for survival. Her father often
worked three jobs during the Great Depression, to which the writer alludes when
she says of herself, "I never had to be
taught how to hold a job, how to make it
work, how to handle my time." She graduated from the local high school with honors, received her bachelor's degree from
Howard University (1953), and went right
on to graduate school at Cornell. She completed her master's degree in 1955, having
written a thesis on William Faulkner and

Virginia Woolf. She has taught at several universities, including Howard University where she met and married Harold Morrison, a Jamaican-born architect. They have since divorced and Ms. Morrison has raised her two sons. In 1989 she was named the Robert F. Goheen Professor of Humanities at Princeton. In 1993 she was awarded the Nobel Prize in Literature, the first African-American woman to be accorded that honor.

The Bluest Eye (1969), her first novel, chronicles the disparity between the adolescent Pecola Breedlove's emerging self-image and the images dominant in the surrounding white culture. *Sula* (1973) is the story of a friendship between two women, Sula Peace and Nel Wright, growing up in the 1920s and 1930s in a small Midwestern community. *Song of Solomon* (1977) won the National Book Critics Circle Award. Mixing the realistic and the fantastic, the novel begins with the birth of Macon "Milkman" Dead III in 1931 and reveals the history of generations of his family from the Civil War to the 1960s, as he comes to realize the importance of heritage and community. *Tar Baby* (1981) investigates the subtleties of race and class relations on a Caribbean island, in New York, and in the rural South by focusing on the love affair between Jadine, a light-skinned model with a degree from the Sorbonne in Paris, and Son, a fugitive from Southern poverty.

One of Morrison's most important projects for Random House was editing *The Black Book* (1974), an anthology of pieces illustrating the history of Black America. While she was researching materials for that work, Morrison found the true story of a runaway slave faced with recapture who killed her infant to save it from a lifetime of slavery. The incident haunted her with its revelation of the awful spiritual and physical suffering of enslavement and became the focus of *Beloved* (1987), her Pulitzer Prize–winning novel.

Sethe, the protagonist, has escaped a Kentucky plantation called Sweet Home where she was brought at 13 to be the sole female slave with five men. Later, when the master, Mr. Garner, dies, his widow calls in her brother-in-law, "Schoolteacher," a cruel and sadistic man who mistreats all the slaves and forces Sethe to escape. She is able to send her children north to join their freed grandmother but must abandon her husband Halle. Even in a free settlement on the outskirts of Cincinnati where she has been reunited with her children and her mother-in-law, Baby Suggs, the tortures of slavery are always present in Sethe's mind. When Schoolteacher appears on the road in front of her home, Sethe—fearful of recapture—cuts the throat of the baby she holds in her arms. The dead baby is the "Beloved" of the title, haunting the house and family and underlying the theme that humans cannot escape the past.

Studies include Bessie W. Jones and Audrey L. Vinson, *The World of Toni Morrison* (1985); Nellie McKay, ed., *Critical Essays on Toni Morrison* (1988); and David L. Middleton, *Toni Morrison, An Annotated Bibliography* (1988).

The following text is taken from Book One of *Beloved*.

FROM BELOVED

[Denver's Secrets]

Denver's secrets were sweet. Accompanied every time by wild veronica until she discovered cologne. The first bottle was a gift, the next she stole from her mother and hid among boxwood until it froze and cracked. That was the year winter came in a hurry at suppertime and stayed eight months. One of the War[1] years when Miss Bodwin, the whitewoman,

---

1. Civil War (1860–1865).

brought Christmas cologne for her mother and herself, oranges for the boys and another good wool shawl for Baby Suggs. Talking of a war full of dead people, she looked happy—flush-faced, and although her voice was heavy as a man's, she smelled like a roomful of flowers—excitement that Denver could have all for herself in the boxwood. Back beyond 124[2] was a narrow field that stopped itself at a wood. On the yonder side of these woods, a stream. In these woods, between the field and the stream, hidden by post oaks, five boxwood bushes, planted in a ring, had started stretching toward each other four feet off the ground to form a round, empty room seven feet high, its walls fifty inches of murmuring leaves.

Bent low, Denver could crawl into this room, and once there she could stand all the way up in emerald light.

It began as a little girl's houseplay, but as her desires changed, so did the play. Quiet, primate and completely secret except for the noisome cologne signal that thrilled the rabbits before it confused them. First a playroom (where the silence was softer), then a refuge (from her brothers' fright), soon the place became the point. In that bower, closed off from the hurt of the hurt world, Denver's imagination produced its own hunger and its own food, which she badly needed because loneliness wore her out. *Wore her out.* Veiled and protected by the live green walls, she felt ripe and clear, and salvation was as easy as a wish.

Once when she was in the boxwood, an autumn long before Paul D[3] moved into the house with her mother, she was made suddenly cold by a combination of wind and the perfume on her skin. She dressed herself, bent down to leave and stood up in snowfall: a thin and whipping snow very like the picture her mother had painted as she described the circumstances of Denver's birth in a canoe straddled by a whitegirl for whom she was named.

Shivering, Denver approached the house, regarding it, as she always did, as a person rather than a structure. A person that wept, sighed, trembled and fell into fits. Her steps and her gaze were the cautious ones of a child approaching a nervous, idle relative (someone dependent but proud). A breastplate of darkness hid all the windows except one. Its dim glow came from Baby Suggs' room. When Denver looked in, she saw her mother on her knees in prayer, which was not unusual. What was unusual (even for a girl who had lived all her life in a house peopled by the living activity of the dead) was that a white dress knelt down next to her mother and had its sleeve around her mother's waist. And it was the tender embrace of the dress sleeve that made Denver remember the details of her birth—that and the thin, whipping snow she was standing in, like the fruit of common flowers. The dress and her mother together looked like two friendly grown-up women—one (the dress) helping out the other. And the magic of her birth, its miracle in fact, testified to that friendliness as did her own name.

Easily she stepped into the told story that lay before her eyes on the path she followed away from the window. There was only one door to the house and to get to it from the back you had to walk all the way around to the front of 124, past the storeroom, past the cold house, the privy, the shed, on around to the porch. And to get to the part of the story she liked best, she had to start way back: hear the birds in the thick woods, the crunch of leaves underfoot; see her mother making her way up into the hills where no houses were likely to be. How Sethe was walking on two feet meant for standing still. How they were so swollen she could not see her arch or feel her ankles. Her leg shaft ended in a loaf of flesh scalloped by five toenails. But she could not, would not, stop, for when she did the little antelope rammed her with horns and pawed the ground of her womb with impatient hooves. While she was walking, it seemed to graze, quietly—so she walked, on two feet meant, in this sixth month of pregnancy, for standing still. Still, near a kettle; still, at the churn; still, at the tub and ironing board. Milk, sticky and sour on her dress, attracted every small flying thing from gnats to grasshoppers. By the time she

---

2. The number of the house where Sethe, her mother-in-law Baby Suggs, and the children lived.

3. One of the five male slaves from Sweet Home, he has sought Sethe out.

reached the hill skirt she had long ago stopped waving them off. The clanging in her head, begun as a churchbell heard from a distance, was by then a tight cap of pealing bells around her ears. She sank and had to look down to see whether she was in a hole or kneeling. Nothing was alive but her nipples and the little antelope. Finally, she was horizontal—or must have been because blades of wild onion were scratching her temple and her cheek. Concerned as she was for the life of her children's mother, Sethe told Denver, she remembered thinking: "Well, at least I don't have to take another step." A dying thought if ever there was one, and she waited for the little antelope to protest, and why she thought of an antelope Sethe could not imagine since she had never seen one. She guessed it must have been an invention held on to from before Sweet Home, when she was very young. Of that place where she was born (Carolina maybe? or was it Louisiana?) she remembered only song and dance. Not even her own mother, who was pointed out to her by the eight-year-old child who watched over the young ones—pointed out as the one among many backs turned away from her, stooping in a watery field. Patiently Sethe waited for this particular back to gain the row's end and stand. What she saw was a cloth hat as opposed to a straw one, singularity enough in that world of cooing women each of whom was called Ma'am.

"Seth—thuh."

"Ma'am."

"Hold on to the baby."

"Yes, Ma'am."

"Seth—thuh."

"Ma'am."

"Get some kindlin in here."

"Yes, Ma'am."

Oh but when they sang. And oh but when they danced and sometimes they danced the antelope. The men as well as the ma'ams, one of whom was certainly her own. They shifted shapes and became something other. Some unchained, demanding other whose feet knew her pulse better than she did. Just like this one in her stomach.

"I believe this baby's ma'am is gonna die in wild onions on the bloody[4] side of the Ohio River." That's what was on her mind and what she told Denver. Her exact words. And it didn't seem such a bad idea, all in all, in view of the step she would not have to take, but the thought of herself stretched out dead while the little antelope lived on—an hour? a day? a day and a night?—in her lifeless body grieved her so she made the groan that made the person walking on a path not ten yards away halt and stand right still. Sethe had not heard the walking, but suddenly she heard the standing still and then she smelled the hair. The voice, saying, "Who's in there?" was all she needed to know that she was about to be discovered by a whiteboy. That he too had mossy teeth, an appetite. That on a ridge of pine near the Ohio River, trying to get to her three children, one of whom was starving for the food she carried; that after her husband had disappeared; that after her milk had been stolen, her back pulped, her children orphaned, she was not to have an easeful death. No.

She told Denver that a *something* came up out of the earth into her—like a freezing, but moving too, like jaws inside. "Look like I was just cold jaws grinding," she said. Suddenly she was eager for his eyes, to bite into them; to gnaw his cheek.

"I was hungry," she told Denver, "just as hungry as I could be for his eyes. I couldn't wait."

So she raised up on her elbow and dragged herself, one pull, two, three, four, toward the young white voice talking about "Who that back in there?"

"'Come see,' I was thinking. 'Be the last thing you behold,' and sure enough here come the feet so I thought well that's where I'll have to start God do what He would, I'm gonna eat his feet off. I'm laughing now, but it's true. I wasn't just set to do it. I was hungry to do it. Like a snake. All jaws and hungry.

4. South side.

"It wasn't no whiteboy at all. Was a girl. The raggediest-looking trash you ever saw saying, 'Look there. A nigger. If that don't beat all.' "

And now the part Denver loved the best:

Her name was Amy and she needed beef and pot liquor like nobody in this world. Arms like cane stalks and enough hair for four or five heads. Slow-moving eyes. She didn't look at anything quick. Talked so much it wasn't clear how she could breathe at the same time. And those cane-stalk arms, as it turned out, were as strong as iron.

"You 'bout the scariest-looking something I ever seen. What you doing back up in here?"

Down in the grass, like the snake she believed she was, Sethe opened her mouth, and instead of fangs and a split tongue, out shot the truth.

"Running," Sethe told her. It was the first word she had spoken all day and it came out thick because of her tender tongue.[5]

"Them the feet you running on? My Jesus my." She squatted down and stared at Sethe's feet. "You got anything on you, gal, pass for food?"

"No." Sethe tried to shift to a sitting position but couldn't.

"I like to die I'm so hungry." The girl moved her eyes slowly, examining the greenery around her. "Thought there'd be huckleberries. Look like it. That's why I come up in here. Didn't expect to find no nigger woman. If they was any, birds ate em. You like huckleberries?"

"I'm having a baby, miss."

Amy looked at her. "That mean you don't have no appetite? Well I got to eat me something."

Combing her hair with her fingers, she carefully surveyed the landscape once more. Satisfied nothing edible was around, she stood up to go and Sethe's heart stood up too at the thought of being left alone in the grass without a fang in her head.

"Where you on your way to, miss?"

She turned and looked at Sethe with freshly lit eyes. "Boston. Get me some velvet. It's a store there called Wilson. I seen the pictures of it and they have the prettiest velvet. They don't believe I'm a get it, but I am."

Sethe nodded and shifted her elbow. "Your ma'am know you on the lookout for velvet?"

The girl shook her hair out of her face. "My mama worked for these here people to pay for her passage.[6] But then she had me and since she died right after, well, they said I had to work for em to pay it off. I did, but now I want me some velvet."

They did not look directly at each other, not straight into the eyes anyway. Yet they slipped effortlessly into yard chat about nothing in particular—except one lay on the ground.

"Boston," said Sethe. "Is that far?"

"Ooooh, yeah. A hundred miles. Maybe more."

"Must be velvet closer by."

"Not like in Boston. Boston got the best. Be so pretty on me. You ever touch it?"

"No, miss. I never touched no velvet." Sethe didn't know if it was the voice, or Boston or velvet, but while the whitegirl talked, the baby slept. Not one butt or kick, so she guessed her luck had turned.

"Ever see any?" she asked Sethe. "I bet you never even seen any."

"If I did I didn't know it. What's it like, velvet?"

Amy dragged her eyes over Sethe's face as though she would never give out so confidential a piece of information as that to a perfect stranger.

"What they call you?" she asked.

However far she was from Sweet Home, there was no point in giving out her real name to the first person she saw. "Lu," said Sethe. "They call me Lu."

"Well, Lu, velvet is like the world was just born. Clean and new and so smooth. The velvet I seen was brown, but in Boston they got all colors. Carmine. That means red but when you

---

5. Sethe had been punished by having an iron bit forced into her mouth.

6. She was an indentured servant.

talk about velvet you got to say 'carmine.' " She raised her eyes to the sky and then, as though she had wasted enough time away from Boston, she moved off saying, "I gotta go."

Picking her way through the brush she hollered back to Sethe, "What you gonna do, just lay there and foal?"

"I can't get up from here," said Sethe.

"What?" She stopped and turned to hear.

"I said I can't get up."

Amy drew her arm across her nose and came slowly back to where Sethe lay. "It's a house back yonder," she said.

"A house?"

"Mmmmm. I passed it. Ain't no regular house with people in it though. A lean-to, kinda."

"How far?"

"Make a difference, does it? You stay the night here snake get you."

"Well he may as well come on. I can't stand up let alone walk and God help me, miss, I can't crawl."

"Sure you can, Lu. Come on," said Amy and, with a toss of hair enough for five heads, she moved toward the path.

So she crawled and Amy walked alongside her, and when Sethe needed to rest, Amy stopped too and talked some more about Boston and velvet and good things to eat. The sound of that voice, like a sixteen-year-old boy's, going on and on and on, kept the little antelope quiet and grazing. During the whole hateful crawl to the lean-to, it never bucked once.

Nothing of Sethe's was intact by the time they reached it except the cloth that covered her hair. Below her bloody knees, there was no feeling at all; her chest was two cushions of pins. It was the voice full of velvet and Boston and good things to eat that urged her along and made her think that maybe she wasn't, after all, just a crawling graveyard for a six-month baby's last hours.

The lean-to was full of leaves, which Amy pushed into a pile for Sethe to lie on. Then she gathered rocks, covered them with more leaves and made Sethe put her feet on them, saying: "I know a woman had her feet cut off they was so swole." And she made sawing gestures with the blade of her hand across Sethe's ankles. "Zzz Zzz Zzz Zzz."

"I used to be a good size. Nice arms and everything. Wouldn't think it, would you? That was before they put me in the root cellar. I was fishing off the Beaver once. Catfish in Beaver River sweet as chicken. Well I was just fishing there and a nigger floated right by me. I don't like drowned people, you? Your feet remind me of him. All swole like."

Then she did the magic: lifted Sethe's feet and legs and massaged them until she cried salt tears.

"It's gonna hurt, now," said Amy. "Anything dead coming back to life hurts."

A truth for all times, thought Denver. Maybe the white dress holding its arm around her mother's waist was in pain. If so, it could mean the baby ghost had plans. When she opened the door, Sethe was just leaving the keeping room.

"I saw a white dress holding on to you," Denver said.

"White? Maybe it was my bedding dress. Describe it to me."

"Had a high neck. Whole mess of buttons coming down the back."

"Buttons. Well, that lets out my bedding dress. I never had a button on nothing."

"Did Grandma Baby?"

Sethe shook her head. "She couldn't handle them. Even on her shoes. What else?"

"A bunch at the back. On the sit-down part."

"A bustle? It had a bustle?"

"I don't know what it's called."

"Sort of gathered-like? Below the waist in the back?"

"Um hm."

"A rich lady's dress. Silk?"

"Cotton, look like."

"Lisle probably. White cotton lisle. You say it was holding on to me. How?"

"Like you. It looked just like you. Kneeling next to you while you were praying. Had its arm around your waist."

"Well, I'll be."

"What were you praying for, Ma'am?"

"Not *for* anything. I don't pray anymore. I just talk."

"What were you talking about?"

"You won't understand, baby."

"Yes, I will."

"I was talking about time. It's so hard for me to believe in it. Some things go. Pass on. Some things just stay. I used to think it was my rememory. You know. Some things you forget. Other things you never do. But it's not. Places, places are still there. If a house burns down, it's gone, but the place—the picture of it—stays, and not just in my rememory, but out there, in the world. What I remember is a picture floating around out there outside my head. I mean, even if I don't think it, even if I die, the picture of what I did, or knew, or saw is still out there. Right in the place where it happened."

"Can other people see it?" asked Denver.

"Oh, yes. Oh, yes, yes, yes. Someday you be walking down the road and you hear something or see something going on. So clear. And you think it's you thinking it up. A thought picture. But no. It's when you bump into a rememory that belongs to somebody else. Where I was before I came here, that place is real. It's never going away. Even if the whole farm—every tree and grass blade of it dies. The picture is still there and what's more, if you go there—you who never was there—if you go there and stand in the place where it was, it will happen again; it will be there for you, waiting for you. So, Denver, you can't never go there. Never. Because even though it's all over—over and done with—it's going to always be there waiting for you. That's how come I had to get all my children out. No matter what."

Denver picked at her fingernails. "If it's still there, waiting, that must mean that nothing ever dies."

Sethe looked right in Denver's face. "Nothing ever does," she said.

"You never told me all what happened. Just that they whipped you and you run off, pregnant. With me."

"Nothing to tell except schoolteacher. He was a little man. Short. Always wore a collar, even in the fields. A schoolteacher, she said. That made her feel good that her husband's sister's husband had book learning and was willing to come farm Sweet Home after Mr. Garner passed. The men could have done it, even with Paul F sold. But it was like Halle said. She didn't want to be the only white person on the farm and a woman too. So she was satisfied when the schoolteacher agreed to come. He brought two boys with him. Sons or nephews. I don't know. They called him Onka and had pretty manners, all of em. Talked soft and spit in handkerchiefs. Gentle in a lot of ways. You know, the kind who know Jesus by His first name, but out of politeness never use it even to His face. A pretty good farmer, Halle said. Not strong as Mr. Garner but smart enough. He liked the ink I made. It was her recipe, but he preferred how I mixed it and it was important to him because at night he sat down to write in his book. It was a book about us but we didn't know that right away. We just thought it was his manner to ask us questions. He commenced to carry round a notebook and write down what we said. I still think it was them questions that tore Sixo up. Tore him up for all time."

She stopped.

Denver knew that her mother was through with it—for now anyway. The single slow blink of her eyes; the bottom lip sliding up slowly to cover the top; and then a nostril sigh, like the snuff of a candle flame—signs that Sethe had reached the point beyond which she would not go.

"Well, I think the baby got plans," said Denver.

"What plans?"

"I don't know, but the dress holding on to you got to mean something."

"Maybe," said Sethe. "Maybe it does have plans."****

"You ain't got no business walking round these hills, miss."

"Looka here who's talking. I got more business here 'n you got. They catch you they cut your head off. Ain't nobody after me but I know somebody after you." Amy pressed her fingers into the soles of the slavewoman's feet. "Whose baby that?"

Sethe did not answer.

"You don't even know. Come here, Jesus," Amy sighed and shook her head. "Hurt?"

"A touch."

"Good for you. More it hurt more better it is. Can't nothing heal without pain, you know. What you wiggling for?"

Sethe raised up on her elbows. Lying on her back so long had raised a ruckus between her shoulder blades. The fire in her feet and the fire on her back made her sweat.

"My back hurt me," she said.

"Your back? Gal, you a mess. Turn over here and let me see."

In an effort so great it made her sick to her stomach, Sethe turned onto her right side. Amy unfastened the back of her dress and said, "Come here, Jesus," when she saw. Sethe guessed it must be bad because after that call to Jesus Amy didn't speak for a while. In the silence of an Amy struck dumb for a change, Sethe felt the fingers of those good hands lightly touch her back. She could hear her breathing but still the whitegirl said nothing. Sethe could not move. She couldn't lie on her stomach or her back, and to keep on her side meant pressure on her screaming feet. Amy spoke at last in her dreamwalker's voice.

"It's a tree, Lu. A chokecherry tree. See, here's the trunk—it's red and split wide open, full of sap, and this here's the parting for the branches. You got a mighty lot of branches. Leaves, too, look like, and dern if these ain't blossoms. Tiny little cherry blossoms, just as white. Your back got a whole tree on it. In bloom. What God have in mind, I wonder. I had me some whippings, but I don't remember nothing like this. Mr. Buddy had a right evil hand too. Whip you for looking at him straight. Sure would. I looked right at him one time and he hauled off and threw the poker at me. Guess he knew what I was a-thinking."

Sethe groaned and Amy cut her reverie short—long enough to shift Sethe's feet so the weight, resting on leaf-covered stones, was above the ankles.

"That better? Lord what a way to die. You gonna die in here, you know. Ain't no way out of it. Thank your Maker I come along so's you wouldn't have to die outside in them weeds. Snake come along he bite you. Bear eat you up. Maybe you should of stayed where you was, Lu. I can see by your back why you didn't ha ha. Whoever planted that tree beat Mr. Buddy by a mile. Glad I ain't you. Well, spiderwebs is 'bout all I can do for you. What's in here ain't enough. I'll look outside. Could use moss, but sometimes bugs and things is in it. Maybe I ought to break them blossoms open. Get that pus to running, you think? Wonder what God had in mind. You must of did something. Don't run off nowhere now."

Sethe could hear her humming away in the bushes as she hunted spiderwebs. A humming she concentrated on because as soon as Amy ducked out the baby began to stretch. Good question, she was thinking. What did He have in mind? Amy had left the back of Sethe's dress open and now a tail of wind hit it, taking the pain down a step. A relief that let her feel the lesser pain of her sore tongue. Amy returned with two palmfuls of web, which she cleaned of prey and then draped on Sethe's back, saying it was like stringing a tree for Christmas.

"We got a old nigger girl come by our place. She don't know nothing. Sews stuff for Mrs. Buddy—real fine lace but can't barely stick two words together. She don't know nothing, just like you. You don't know a thing. End up dead, that's what. Not me. I'm a get to Boston and get myself some velvet. Carmine. You don't even know about that, do you? Now you never will. Bet you never even sleep with the sun in your face. I did it a couple of times. Most times

I'm feeding stock before light and don't get to sleep till way after dark comes. But I was in the back of the wagon once and fell asleep. Sleeping with the sun in your face is the best old feeling. Two times I did it. Once when I was little. Didn't nobody bother me then. Next time, in back of the wagon, it happened again and doggone if the chickens didn't get loose. Mr. Buddy whipped my tail. Kentucky ain't no good place to be in. Boston's the place to be in. That's where my mother was before she was give to Mr. Buddy. Joe Nathan said Mr. Buddy is my daddy but I don't believe that, you?"

Sethe told her she didn't believe Mr. Buddy was her daddy.

"You know your daddy, do you?"

"No," said Sethe.

"Neither me. All I know is it ain't him." She stood up then, having finished her repair work, and weaving about the lean-to, her slow-moving eyes pale in the sun that lit her hair, she sang:

> "When the busy day is done
> And my weary little one
> Rocketh gently to and fro;
> When the night winds softly blow,
> And the crickets in the glen
> Chirp and chirp and chirp again;
> Where 'pon the haunted green
> Fairies dance around their queen,
> Then from yonder misty skies
> Cometh Lady Button Eyes."

Suddenly she stopped weaving and rocking and sat down, her skinny arms wrapped around her knees, her good good hands cupping her elbows. Her slow-moving eyes stopped and peered into the dirt at her feet. "That's my mama's song. She taught me it."

> "Through the muck and mist and gloam
> To our quiet cozy home,
> Where to singing sweet and low
> Rocks a cradle to and fro.
> Where the clock's dull monotone
> Telleth of the day that's done,
> Where the moonbeams hover o'er
> Playthings sleeping on the floor,
> Where my weary wee one lies
> Cometh Lady Button Eyes.
>
> "Layeth she her hands upon
> My dear weary little one,
> And those white hands overspread
> Like a veil the curly head,
> Seem to fondle and caress
> Every little silken tress.
> Then she smooths the eyelids down
> Over those two eyes of brown
> In such soothing tender wise
> Cometh Lady Button Eyes."

Amy sat quietly after her song, then repeated the last line before she stood, left the lean-to and walked off a little ways to lean against a young ash. When she came back the sun was in the valley below and they were way above it in blue Kentucky light.

"You ain't dead yet, Lu? Lu?"

"Not yet."

"Make you a bet. You make it through the night, you make it all the way." Amy rearranged the leaves for comfort and knelt down to massage the swollen feet again. "Give these one more real good rub," she said, and when Sethe sucked air through her teeth, she said, "Shut up. You got to keep your mouth shut."

Careful of her tongue, Sethe bit down on her lips and let the good hands go to work to the tune of "So bees, sing soft and bees, sing low." Afterward, Amy moved to the other side of the lean-to where, seated, she lowered her head toward her shoulder and braided her hair, saying, "Don't up and die on me in the night, you hear? I don't want to see your ugly black face hankering over me. If you do die, just go on off somewhere where I can't see you, hear?"

"I hear," said Sethe. "I'll do what I can, miss."

Sethe never expected to see another thing in this world, so when she felt toes prodding her hip it took a while to come out of a sleep she thought was death. She sat up, stiff and shivery, while Amy looked in on her juicy back.

"Looks like the devil," said Amy. "But you made it through. Come down here, Jesus, Lu made it through. That's because of me. I'm good at sick things. Can you walk, you think?"

"I have to let my water some kind of way."

"Let's see you walk on em."

It was not good, but it was possible, so Sethe limped, holding on first to Amy, then to a sapling.

"Was me did it. I'm good at sick things ain't I?"

"Yeah," said Sethe, "you good."

"We got to get off this here hill. Come on. I'll take you down to the river. That ought to suit you. Me, I'm going to the Pike. Take me straight to Boston. What's that all over your dress?"

"Milk."

"You one mess."

Sethe looked down at her stomach and touched it. The baby was dead. She had not died in the night, but the baby had. If that was the case, then there was no stopping now. She would get that milk to her baby girl if she had to swim.

"Ain't you hungry?" Amy asked her.

"I ain't nothing but in a hurry, miss."

"Whoa. Slow down. Want some shoes?"

"Say what?"

"I figured how," said Amy and so she had. She tore two pieces from Sethe's shawl, filled them with leaves and tied them over her feet, chattering all the while.

"How old are you, Lu? I been bleeding for four years but I ain't having nobody's baby. Won't catch me sweating milk cause . . ."

"I know," said Sethe. "You going to Boston."

At noon they saw it; then they were near enough to hear it. By late afternoon they could drink from it if they wanted to. Four stars were visible by the time they found, not a riverboat to stow Sethe away on, or a ferryman willing to take on a fugitive passenger—nothing like that—but a whole boat to steal. It had one oar, lots of holes and two bird nests.

"There you go, Lu. Jesus looking at you."

Sethe was looking at one mile of dark water, which would have to be split with one oar in a useless boat against a current dedicated to the Mississippi hundreds of miles away. It looked like home to her, and the baby (not dead in the least) must have thought so too. As soon as Sethe got close to the river her own water broke loose to join it. The break, followed by the redundant announcement of labor, arched her back.

"What you doing that for?" asked Amy. "Ain't you got a brain in your head? Stop that right now. I said stop it, Lu. You the dumbest thing on this here earth. Lu! Lu!"

Sethe couldn't think of anywhere to go but in. She waited for the sweet beat that followed the blast of pain. On her knees again, she crawled into the boat. It waddled under her and she had just enough time to brace her leaf-bag feet on the bench when another rip took her breath away. Panting under four summer stars, she threw her legs over the sides, because here come the head, as Amy informed her as though she did not know it—as though the rip was a breakup of walnut logs in the brace, or of lightning's jagged tear through a leather sky.

It was stuck. Face up and drowning in its mother's blood. Amy stopped begging Jesus and began to curse His daddy.

"Push!" screamed Amy.

"Pull," whispered Sethe.

And the strong hands went to work a fourth time, none too soon, for river water, seeping through any hole it chose, was spreading over Sethe's hips. She reached one arm back and grabbed the rope while Amy fairly clawed at the head. When a foot rose from the river bed and kicked the bottom of the boat and Sethe's behind, she knew it was done and permitted herself a short faint. Coming to, she heard no cries, just Amy's encouraging coos. Nothing happened for so long they both believed they had lost it. Sethe arched suddenly and the afterbirth shot out. Then the baby whimpered and Sethe looked. Twenty inches of cord hung from its belly and it trembled in the cooling evening air. Amy wrapped her skirt around it and the wet sticky women clambered ashore to see what, indeed, God had in mind.

Spores of bluefern growing in the hollows along the riverbank float toward the water in silver-blue lines hard to see unless you are in or near them, lying right at the river's edge when the sunshots are low and drained. Often they are mistook for insects—but they are seeds in which the whole generation sleeps confident of a future. And for a moment it is easy to believe each one has one—will become all of what is contained in the spore: will live out its days as planned. This moment of certainty lasts no longer than that; longer, perhaps, than the spore itself.

On a riverbank in the cool of a summer evening two women struggled under a shower of silvery blue. They never expected to see each other again in this world and at the moment couldn't care less. But there on a summer night surrounded by bluefern they did something together appropriately and well. A pateroller[7] passing would have sniggered to see two throw-away people, two lawless outlaws— a slave and a barefoot whitewoman with un-pinned hair—wrapping a ten-minute-old baby in the rags they wore. But no pateroller came and no preacher. The water sucked and swallowed itself beneath them. There was nothing to disturb them at their work. So they did it appropriately and well.

Twilight came on and Amy said she had to go; that she wouldn't be caught dead in daylight on a busy river with a runaway. After rinsing her hands and face in the river, she stood and looked down at the baby wrapped and tied to Sethe's chest.

"She's never gonna know who I am. You gonna tell her? Who brought her into this here world?" She lifted her chin, looked off into the place where the sun used to be. "You better tell her. You hear? Say Miss Amy Denver. Of Boston."

Sethe felt herself falling into a sleep she knew would be deep. On the lip of it, just before going under, she thought, "That's pretty. Denver. Real pretty."

1987

Sylvia Plath
(1932–1963)

Sylvia Plath was the daughter of Otto Plath, a German-speaking immigrant from Poland who taught German and zoology at Boston University. His death from dia-

---

7. A patroller or slave catcher.

betes when she was 8 proved a traumatic event that later informed some of her most powerful poems. Her mother, who had been a student of the father, moved the family from Winthrop, Massachusetts, to Wellesley, supporting them by teaching. Writing early, Sylvia published her first poem in the *Boston Sunday Herald* in 1940, the year of her father's death. In high school she was already submitting pieces to national magazines and had one accepted by *Seventeen* in her senior year. As a scholarship student at Smith College, she performed brilliantly, graduating *summa cum laude* in 1955 and winning a Fulbright fellowship to study at Cambridge University.

Her graduation had been delayed, however, by serious emotional problems. As a junior at Smith in 1953, she had won a prestigious appointment to the *Mademoiselle* college board, an award that brought her to Manhattan to work for a month in the magazine's editorial offices. At home in Wellesley in the same summer, she suffered a severe breakdown. Her three-day disappearance made national headlines; she had nearly died from an overdose of sleeping pills when her brother found her in the crawl space under the family breezeway. Hospitalization and electroconvulsive and insulin shock treatments followed as her return to Smith was postponed for several months. Later, the experience formed the basis for her novel *The Bell Jar* (1963).

In England she met and married a young poet, Ted Hughes, now Poet Laureate of England. The two came to the United States, where they taught a year at Smith, before they moved to Boston to pursue careers as writers. There Sylvia audited Robert Lowell's Boston University poetry seminar and met fellow student Anne Sexton, with whom she shared after-class drinks and discussions of poetry, psychotherapy, and suicide. Sylvia and Ted returned to England in 1959, the year that Robert Lowell's *Life Studies* provided great

impetus to the "confessional" mode of American poetry. Sexton's *To Bedlam and Part Way Back* appeared the next year, as did Plath's first collection, *The Colossus and Other Poems*.

In England, Plath became a mother (of a daughter in 1960, a son in 1962), worked on her novel, and wrote poems and a radio play. Life deteriorated, however, and she and her husband separated. She committed suicide with sleeping pills and gas from a kitchen stove in a cold London flat on February 11, 1963. Toward the end she had produced many of her best poems, writing to her mother, "I am writing the best poems of my life; they will make my name." And they did. In his foreword to the posthumously published *Ariel* (1965), Robert Lowell wrote of her "appalling and triumphant fulfillment." *Crossing the Water* (1971) and *Winter Trees* (1971) extended her reputation, as did *The Collected Poems* (1981), edited by Ted Hughes, which won a Pulitzer Prize two decades after her death.

Plath's poetry titles and her novel are listed above. Additional prose is collected in *Johnny Panic and the Bible of Dreams: Short Stories, Prose and Diary Excerpts* (1979). *Letters Home: Correspondence 1950–1963* (1975) was edited by her mother, Aurelia Schober Plath. *The Journals of Sylvia Plath* (1982) was edited by Ted Hughes and Frances McCullough.

Recent biographies include Linda Wagner-Martin, *Sylvia Plath: A Biography* (1987); Anne Stevenson, *Bitter Fame: A Life of Sylvia Plath* (1989); Ronald Hayman, *The Death and Life of Sylvia Plath* (1991); and Paul Alexander, *Rough Magic: A Biography of Sylvia Plath* (1991). Other critical and biographical studies include Eileen Aird, *Sylvia Plath: Her Life and Work* (1975); Edward Butscher, *Sylvia Plath: Method and Madness* (1976); David Holbrook, *Sylvia Plath: Poetry and Existence* (1976); Judith Kroll, *Chapters in a Mythology: The Poetry of Sylvia Plath* (1976); Margaret Dickie Uroff, *Sylvia Plath and Ted Hughes* (1979); Jon Rosenblatt, *Sylvia Plath: The Poetry of Initiation* (1979); Mary Lynn Broe, *Protean Poetic: The Poetry of Sylvia Plath* (1980); Lynda K. Bruntzen, *Plath's Incarnations: Woman and the Creative Process* (1985); Steven G. Axelrod, *Sylvia Plath: The Wound and the Cure of Words* (1990); and Jacqueline Rose, *The Haunting of Sylvia Plath* (1991).

Black Rook in Rainy Weather

On the stiff twig up there
Hunches a wet black rook
Arranging and rearranging its feathers in the rain.
I do not expect a miracle
Or an accident   5

To set the sight on fire
In my eye, nor seek
Any more in the desultory weather some design,
But let spotted leaves fall as they fall,
Without ceremony, or portent.   10

Although, I admit, I desire,
Occasionally, some backtalk
From the mute sky, I can't honestly complain:
A certain minor light may still
Lean incandescent   15

Out of kitchen table or chair
As if a celestial burning took
Possession of the most obtuse objects now and then—
Thus hallowing an interval
Otherwise inconsequent   20

By bestowing largesse, honor,
One might say love. At any rate, I now walk
Wary (for it could happen
Even in this dull, ruinous landscape); skeptical,
Yet politic; ignorant   25

Of whatever angel may choose to flare
Suddenly at my elbow. I only know that a rook
Ordering its black feathers can so shine
As to seize my senses, haul
My eyelids up, and grant   30

A brief respite from fear
Of total neutrality. With luck,
Trekking stubborn through this season
Of fatigue, I shall
Patch together a content   35

Of sorts. Miracles occur,
If you care to call those spasmodic
Tricks of radiance miracles. The wait's begun again,
The long wait for the angel,
For that rare, random descent.   40

1960

Morning Song

Love set you going like a fat gold watch.
The midwife slapped your footsoles, and your bald cry
Took its place among the elements.

Our voices echo, magnifying your arrival. New statue.
In a drafty museum, your nakedness   5
Shadows our safety. We stand round blankly as walls.

I'm no more your mother
Than the cloud that distills a mirror to reflect its own slow
Effacement at the wind's hand.

All night your moth-breath   10
Flickers among the flat pink roses. I wake to listen:
A far sea moves in my ear.

One cry, and I stumble from bed, cow-heavy and floral
In my Victorian nightgown.
Your mouth opens clean as a cat's. The window square   15

Whitens and swallows its dull stars. And now you try
Your handful of notes;
The clear vowels rise like balloons.

19 February 1961   1965

Blackberrying

Nobody in the lane, and nothing, nothing but blackberries,
Blackberries on either side, though on the right mainly,
A blackberry alley, going down in hooks, and a sea
Somewhere at the end of it, heaving. Blackberries
Big as the ball of my thumb, and dumb as eyes   5
Ebon in the hedges, fat
With blue-red juices. These they squander on my fingers.
I had not asked for such a blood sisterhood; they must love me.
They accommodate themselves to my milkbottle, flattening their sides.

Overhead go the choughs in black, cacophonous flocks—   10
Bits of burnt paper wheeling in a blown sky.
Theirs is the only voice, protesting, protesting.
I do not think the sea will appear at all.
The high, green meadows are glowing, as if lit from within.
I come to one bush of berries so ripe it is a bush of flies,   15
Hanging their bluegreen bellies and their wing panes in a Chinese screen.
The honey-feast of the berries has stunned them; they believe in heaven.
One more hook, and the berries and bushes end.

The only thing to come now is the sea.
From between two hills a sudden wind funnels at me,   20

Slapping its phantom laundry in my face.
These hills are too green and sweet to have tasted salt.
I follow the sheep path between them. A last hook brings me
To the hills' northern face, and the face is orange rock
That looks out on nothing, nothing but a great space   25
Of white and pewter lights, and a din like silversmiths
Beating and beating at an intractable metal.

23 September 1961   1971

The Arrival of the Bee Box

I ordered this, this clean wood box
Square as a chair and almost too heavy to lift.
I would say it was the coffin of a midget
Or a square baby
Were there not such a din in it.   5

The box is locked, it is dangerous.
I have to live with it overnight
And I can't keep away from it.
There are no windows, so I can't see what is in there.
There is only a little grid, no exit.   10

I put my eye to the grid.
It is dark, dark,
With the swarmy feeling of African hands
Minute and shrunk for export,
Black on black, angrily clambering.   15

How can I let them out?
It is the noise that appalls me most of all,
The unintelligible syllables.
It is like a Roman mob,
Small, taken one by one, but my god, together!   20

I lay my ear to furious Latin.
I am not a Caesar.
I have simply ordered a box of maniacs.
They can be sent back.
They can die, I need feed them nothing, I am the owner.   25

I wonder how hungry they are.
I wonder if they would forget me
If I just undid the locks and stood back and turned into a tree.
There is the laburnum, its blond colonnades,
And the petticoats of the cherry.   30

They might ignore me immediately
In my moon suit and funeral veil.

I am no source of honey
So why should they turn on me?
Tomorrow I will be sweet God, I will set them free.   35

The box is only temporary.

4 October 1962   1965

Wintering

This is the easy time, there is nothing doing.
I have whirled the midwife's extractor,[1]
I have my honey,
Six jars of it,
Six cat's eyes in the wine cellar,   5

Wintering in a dark without window
At the heart of the house
Next to the last tenant's rancid jam
And the bottles of empty glitters——
Sir So-and-so's gin.   10

This is the room I have never been in.
This is the room I could never breathe in.
The black bunched in there like a bat,
No light
But the torch and its faint   15

Chinese yellow on appalling objects——
Black asininity. Decay.
Possession.
It is they who own me.
Neither cruel nor indifferent,   20

Only ignorant.
This is the time of hanging on for the bees—the bees
So slow I hardly know them,
Filing like soldiers
To the syrup tin   25

To make up for the honey I've taken.
Tate and Lyle[2] keeps them going,
The refined snow.
It is Tate and Lyle they live on, instead of flowers.
They take it. The cold sets in.   30

Now they ball in a mass,
Black
Mind against all that white.
The smile of the snow is white.
It spreads itself out, a mile-long body of Meissen,[3]   35

---

1. Device for extracting honey from the comb.   3. A German porcelain.
2. A food for bees.

Into which, on warm days,
They can only carry their dead.
The bees are all women,
Maids and the long royal lady.
They have got rid of the men,   40

The blunt, clumsy stumblers, the boors.
Winter is for women——
The woman, still at her knitting,
At the cradle of Spanish walnut,
Her body a bulb in the cold and too dumb to think.   45

Will the hive survive, will the gladiolas
Succeed in banking their fires
To enter another year?
What will they taste of, the Christmas roses?
The bees are flying. They taste the spring.   50

9 October 1962   1965

Daddy

You do not do, you do not do
Any more, black shoe
In which I have lived like a foot
For thirty years, poor and white,
Barely daring to breathe or Achoo.   5

Daddy, I have had to kill you.
You died before I had time——
Marble-heavy, a bag full of God,
Ghastly statue with one gray toe[4]
Big as a Frisco seal   10

And a head in the freakish Atlantic
Where it pours bean green over blue
In the waters off beautiful Nauset.[5]
I used to pray to recover you.
Ach, du.[6]   15

In the German tongue, in the Polish town[7]
Scraped flat by the roller
Of wars, wars, wars.
But the name of the town is common.
My Polack friend   20

Says there are a dozen or two.
So I never could tell where you
Put your foot, your root,

4. The result of diabetes.   6. "Ah, you" (German).
5. A beach on Cape Cod.   7. Grabow, where her father was born.

I never could talk to you.
The tongue stuck in my jaw.   25

It stuck in a barb wire snare.
Ich, ich, ich, ich,[8]
I could hardly speak.
I thought every German was you.
And the language obscene   30

An engine, an engine
Chuffing me off like a Jew.
A Jew to Dachau, Auschwitz, Belsen.[9]
I began to talk like a Jew.
I think I may well be a Jew.   35

The snows of the Tyrol, the clear beer of Vienna
Are not very pure or true.
With my gipsy ancestress and my weird luck
And my Taroc[1] pack and my Taroc pack
I may be a bit of a Jew.   40

I have always been scared of *you*,
With your Luftwaffe,[2] your gobbledygoo.
And your neat mustache
And your Aryan eye, bright blue.
Panzer-man,[3] panzer-man, O You——   45

Not God but a swastika
So black no sky could squeak through.
Every woman adores a Fascist,
The boot in the face, the brute
Brute heart of a brute like you.   50

You stand at the blackboard, daddy,
In the picture I have of you,
A cleft in your chin instead of your foot
But no less a devil for that, no not
Any less the black man who   55

Bit my pretty red heart in two.
I was ten when they buried you.
At twenty I tried to die
And get back, back, back to you.
I thought even the bones would do.   60

But they pulled me out of the sack,
And they stuck me together with glue.
And then I knew what to do.
I made a model of you,
A man in black with a Meinkampf[4] look   65

8. "I."
9. Nazi death camps during World War II.
1. Usually "tarot," fortune-telling cards.
2. German air force.

3. A soldier in the German armored division.
4. Hitler's autobiography was titled *Mein Kampf*
("My struggle").

And a love of the rack and the screw.
And I said I do, I do.
So daddy, I'm finally through.
The black telephone's off at the root,
The voices just can't worm through.   70

If I've killed one man, I've killed two——
The vampire who said he was you
And drank my blood for a year,
Seven years, if you want to know.
Daddy, you can lie back now.   75

There's a stake in your fat black heart
And the villagers never liked you.
They are dancing and stamping on you.
They always *knew* it was you.
Daddy, daddy, you bastard, I'm through.   80

12 October 1962   1965

Lady Lazarus[5]

I have done it again.
One year in every ten
I manage it——

A sort of walking miracle, my skin
Bright as a Nazi lampshade,[6]   5
My right foot

A paperweight,
My face a featureless, fine
Jew linen.

Peel off the napkin   10
O my enemy.
Do I terrify?——

The nose, the eye pits, the full set of teeth?
The sour breath
Will vanish in a day.   15

Soon, soon the flesh
The grave cave ate will be
At home on me

And I a smiling woman.
I am only thirty.   20
And like the cat I have nine times to die.

5. The name of a man raised from the dead by
Jesus (John 11:39–44).

6. Sometimes made of human skin.

This is Number Three.
What a trash
To annihilate each decade.

What a million filaments.   25
The peanut-crunching crowd
Shoves in to see

Then unwrap me hand and foot——
The big strip tease.
Gentlemen, ladies   30

These are my hands
My knees.
I may be skin and bone,

Nevertheless, I am the same, identical woman.
The first time it happened I was ten.   35
It was an accident.

The second time I meant
To last it out and not come back at all.
I rocked shut

As a seashell.   40
They had to call and call
And pick the worms off me like sticky pearls.

Dying
Is an art, like everything else.
I do it exceptionally well.   45

I do it so it feels like hell.
I do it so it feels real.
I guess you could say I've a call.

It's easy enough to do it in a cell.
It's easy enough to do it and stay put.   50
It's the theatrical

Comeback in broad day
To the same place, the same face, the same brute
Amused shout:

'A miracle!'   55
That knocks me out.
There is a charge

For the eyeing of my scars, there is a charge
For the hearing of my heart——
It really goes.   60

And there is a charge, a very large charge
For a word or a touch
Or a bit of blood

Or a piece of my hair or my clothes.
So, so, Herr Doktor.   65
So, Herr Enemy.

I am your opus,
I am your valuable,
The pure gold baby

That melts to a shriek.   70
I turn and burn.
Do not think I underestimate your great concern.

Ash, ash—
You poke and stir.
Flesh, bone, there is nothing there——   75

A cake of soap,
A wedding ring,
A gold filling.

Herr God, Herr Lucifer
Beware   80
Beware.

Out of the ash[7]
I rise with my red hair
And I eat men like air.

23–29 October 1962   1965

Child

Your clear eye is the one absolutely beautiful thing.
I want to fill it with color and ducks,
The zoo of the new

Whose names you mediate—
April snowdrop, Indian pipe,   5
Little

Stalk without wrinkle,
Pool in which images
Should be grand and classical

Not this troublous   10
Wringing of hands, this dark
Ceiling without a star.

28 January 1963   1971

Mystic

The air is a mill of hooks—
Questions without answer,
Glittering and drunk as flies

---

7. Like the Phoenix, rising from the ashes of the fire that has consumed it.

Whose kiss stings unbearably
In the fetid wombs of black air under pines in summer.   5

I remember
The dead smell of sun on wood cabins,
The stiffness of sails, the long salt winding sheets.
Once one has seen God, what is the remedy?
Once one has been seized up   10

Without a part left over,
Not a toe, not a finger, and used,
Used utterly, in the sun's conflagrations, the stains
That lengthen from ancient cathedrals
What is the remedy?   15

The pill of the Communion tablet,
The walking beside still water? Memory?
Or picking up the bright pieces
Of Christ in the faces of rodents,
The tame flower-nibblers, the ones   20

Whose hopes are so low they are comfortable—
The humpback in his small, washed cottage
Under the spokes of the clematis.
Is there no great love, only tenderness?
Does the sea   25

Remember the walker upon it?
Meaning leaks from the molecules.
The chimneys of the city breathe, the window sweats,
The children leap in their cots.
The sun blooms, it is a geranium.   30

The heart has not stopped.

1 February 1963   1971

Words

Axes
After whose stroke the wood rings,
And the echoes!
Echoes traveling
Off from the center like horses.   5

The sap
Wells like tears, like the
Water striving
To re-establish its mirror
Over the rock   10

That drops and turns,
A white skull,
Eaten by weedy greens.

Years later I
Encounter them on the road——   15

Words dry and riderless,
The indefatigable hoof-taps.
While
From the bottom of the pool, fixed stars
Govern a life.   20

1 February 1963   1971

Joyce Carol Oates
(1938–   )

Joyce Carol Oates is easily described in superlatives. She has written more books, and more kinds of books, than any other serious contemporary American writer. In the words of John Updike, perhaps her chief rival in combining quality and quantity: "Joyce Carol Oates *** was perhaps born a hundred years too late; she needs a lustier audience, a race of Victorian word-eaters, to be worthy of her astounding productivity, her tireless gift of self-enthrallment." More prolific, in fact, than some of the great Victorians—than the Brontës or George Eliot, for example—she has published on the scale of a Dickens, a Trollope, a Howells, or a James, and, like them, has seldom fallen far from her level best. In the words of another of her contemporaries, John Gardner, she is "one of the great writers of her time."

Born outside of Lockport, New York, on the route of the old Erie Canal, she was raised in the rural and small-town environment that serves as setting for some of her most memorable fiction. It was, she has said, "a part of the world and an economic background where people don't even graduate from high school." As a scholarship student at Syracuse University, she astonished her writing teacher with her productivity: "About once a term she'd drop a 400-page novel on my desk." As a junior, she won *Mademoiselle*'s college fiction contest, and she graduated Phi Kappa Phi. Attending the University of Wiscon-

sin on a fellowship, she earned an M.A. in 1961 and in the same year married Raymond J. Smith, the literary scholar with whom she has shared her life since. Briefly a Ph.D. student at Rice University, she dropped out to devote herself to writing when she discovered that one of her stories had been placed on the honor roll of Martha Foley's *The Best American Short Stories*. In the 1960s and 1970s she taught at the University of Detroit and the University of Windsor, then from 1978 on at Princeton. In addition to her writing and teaching, she and her husband have established and run *The Ontario Review*, a literary journal, and The Ontario Review Press, publishing books of literary quality.

Like most of the nineteenth-century novelists, she has generally focused on the subject suggested by Trollope's title *The Way We Live Now*. For her, of course, the "we" and the "now" are Americans in the second half of the twentieth century, with only an occasional excursion into the past. Endowed with a large and varied imagination, she peoples her fiction with characters from all walks of life, all ages, all temperaments. Of her plots, which are almost relentlessly violent, she has said, "These things do not have to be contrived. This is America."

In *By the North Gate* (1963) she made her debut as a writer of short stories. In *With Shuddering Fall* (1964), about stock car racing, she began her career as a novelist. In every year since then, except for 1965, she has published at least one book, and sometimes more than one. The range of her subjects can be seen in some of her most successful novels: *A Garden of Earthly Delights* (1967), about migrant workers; *Them* (1969), telling of a family's life in Detroit from 1930s depression through 1967 riots; *Wonderland* (1971), about a boy who escapes his father's massacre of the rest of the family; *Do With Me What You Will* (1973), which opens with a small girl being abducted from a schoolyard; *Son of the Morning* (1978), focusing on an evangelical minister; *Unholy Loves* (1979), centered in university life; *Solstice* (1985), of women's friendship and victimization; *Marya: A Life* (1986), the story of a woman, dirt poor and abused as a child, who achieves intellectual success; *You Must Remember This* (1987), a family novel set in the 1950s; and *Because It Is Bitter, and Because It Is My Heart* (1990), of guilt shared by a white woman and a black man. Most of the above are more or less realistic in method; in works such as *Bellefleur* (1980), *A Bloodsmoor Romance* (1982), and *Mysteries of Winterthurn* (1984) she verges on gothic romance. Collections of stories appear with astonishing regularity, with similar breadth of subject matter and method, and she is also prolific as a poet and literary critic.

Novels, in addition to those named above, include *Expensive People* (1968); *The Assassins* (1975); *Childwold* (1976); *Cybele* (1979); *American Appetites* (1989); and *Foxfire* (1993). Short novels include *I Lock My Door upon Myself* (1990); and *The Rise of Life on Earth* (1991). Collections of short fiction include *Upon the Sweeping Flood* (1966); *The Wheel of Love* (1970); *Marriages and Infidelities* (1972); *The Goddess and Other Women* (1974); *Crossing the Border* (1976); *A Sentimental Education* (1981); *Raven's Wing* (1986); and *Heat* (1991). Collections of verse include *Invisible Women: New and Selected Poems, 1970–1982* (1982); and *The Time Traveler: Poems 1980–1989* (1990). Criticism and other nonfiction prose is collected in *The Edge of Impossibility: Tragic Forms in Literature* (1972); *New Heaven, New Earth: The Visionary Experience in Literature* (1974); *Contraries: Essays* (1981); *The Profane Art: Essays and Reviews* (1983); *On Boxing* (1987); and *(Woman) Writer: Occasions and Opportunities* (1988). Mysteries published under the pseudonym Rosamond Smith include *Lives of the Twins* (1987) and *Nemesis* (1990).

Studies include G. F. Waller, *Dreaming America: Obsession and Transcendence in the Fiction of Joyce Carol Oates* (1979); Joanne V. Creighton, *Joyce Carol Oates* (1979); Ellen G. Friedman, *Joyce Carol Oates* (1980); and Eileen T. Bender, *Joyce Carol Oates: Artist in Residence* (1987).

Nairobi[1]

Early Saturday afternoon the man who had introduced himself as Oliver took Ginny to several shops on Madison Avenue above Seventieth Street to buy her what he called an appropriate outfit. For an hour and forty-five minutes she modeled clothes, watching with critical interest her image in the three-way mirrors, and unable to decide if this was one of her really good days or only a mediocre day. Judging by Oliver's expression she looked all right but it was difficult to tell. The salesclerks saw too many beautiful young women to be impressed, though one told Ginny she envied her her hair—not just that shade of chestnut red but the thickness too. In the changing room she told Ginny that her own hair was "coming out in handfuls" but Ginny told her it didn't show. It will begin to show one of these days, the salesgirl said.

Ginny modeled a green velvet jumpsuit with a brass zipper and oversized buckles, and an Italian knit dress with bunchy sleeves in a zigzag pattern of beige, brown, and cream, and a

---

1. First published in *The Paris Review*. The source of the present text is *Raven's Wing* (1986).

ruffled organdy "tea dress" in pale orange, and a navy blue blazer made of Irish linen, with a pleated white linen skirt and a pale blue silk blouse. Assuming she could only have one costume, which seemed to be the case, she would have preferred the jumpsuit, not just because it was the most expensive outfit (the price tag read $475) but because the green velvet reflected in her eyes. Oliver decided on the Irish linen blazer and the skirt and blouse, however, and told the salesclerk to remove the tags and to pack up Ginny's own clothes, since she intended to wear the new outfit.

Strolling uptown he told her that with her hair down like that, and her bangs combed low on her forehead, she looked like a "convent schoolgirl." In theory, that was. Tangentially.

It was a balmy windy day in early April. Everyone was out. Ginny kept seeing people she almost knew, Oliver waved hello to several acquaintances. There were baby buggies, dogs being walked, sports cars with their tops down. In shop windows—particularly in the broad windows of galleries—Ginny's reflection in the navy blue blazer struck her as unfamiliar and quirky but not bad: the blazer with its built-up shoulders and wide lapels was more stylish than she'd thought at first. Oliver too was pleased. He had slipped on steel-frame tinted glasses. He said they had plenty of time. A pair of good shoes—really good shoes—might be an idea.

But first they went into a jewelry boutique at Seventy-sixth Street, where Oliver bought her four narrow silver bracelets, engraved in bird and animal heads, and a pair of conch-shaped silver earrings from Mexico. Ginny slipped her gold studs out and put on the new earrings as Oliver watched. "Doesn't it hurt to force those wires through your flesh?" he said. He was standing rather close.

"No," Ginny said. "My earlobes are numb, I don't feel a thing. It's easy."

"When did you get your ears pierced?" Oliver asked.

Ginny felt her cheeks color slightly—as if he were asking a favor of her and her instinct wasn't clear enough, whether to acquiesce or draw away just perceptibly. She drew away, still adjusting the earrings, but said, "I don't have any idea, maybe I was thirteen, maybe twelve, it was a long time ago. We all went out and had our ears pierced."

In a salon called Michel's she exchanged her chunky-heeled red shoes for a pair of kidskin sandals that might have been the most beautiful shoes she'd ever seen. Oliver laughed quizzically over them: they were hardly anything but a few straps and a price tag, he told the salesman, but they looked like the real thing, they were what he wanted. The salesman told Oliver that his taste was "unerring."

"Do you want to keep your old shoes?" Oliver asked Ginny.

"Of course," Ginny said, slightly hurt, but as the salesman was packing them she changed her mind. "No, the hell with them," she said. "They're too much trouble to take along." Which she might regret afterward: but it was the right thing to say at that particular moment.

In the cab headed west and then north along the park, Oliver gave her instructions in a low casual voice. The main thing was that she should say very little. She shouldn't smile unless it was absolutely necessary. While he and his friends spoke—if they spoke at any length; he couldn't predict Marguerite's attitude—Ginny might even drift away, pick up a magazine and leaf through it if something appropriate was available, not nervously, just idly, for something to do, as if she were bored: better yet, she might look out the window or even step out on the terrace since the afternoon was so warm. "Don't even look at me," Oliver said. "Don't give the impression that anything I say—anything the three of us say—matters very much to you."

"Yes," said Ginny.

"The important thing," Oliver said, squeezing her hand and releasing it, "is that you're basically not concerned. I mean with the three of us. With Marguerite. With anyone. Do you understand?"

"Yes," said Ginny. She was studying her new shoes. Kidskin in a shade called "vanilla," eight straps on each shoe, certainly the most beautiful shoes she'd ever owned. The price had taken her breath away too. She hadn't any questions to ask Oliver.

When Ginny had been much younger—which is to say a few years ago when she'd been new to the city—she might have had some questions to ask. In fact she'd had a number of questions to ask, then. But the answers had not been forthcoming. Or they'd been disappointing. The answers had contained so much less substance than her own questions she had learned by degrees it was wiser to ask nothing.

So she told Oliver a second time, to assure *him*, "Of course I understand."

The apartment building they entered at Fifth and Eighty-eighth Street was older than Ginny might have guessed from the exterior—the mosaic murals in the lobby were in a quaint ethereal style unknown to her. Perhaps they were meant to be amusing but she didn't think so. It was impressive that the uniformed doorman knew Oliver, whom he called "Mr. Leahy," and that he was so gracious about keeping their package for them, while they visited upstairs; it was impressive that the black elevator operator nodded and murmured hello in a certain tone. Smiles were measured and respectful all around but Ginny didn't trouble to smile, she knew it wasn't expected of her.

In the elevator—which was almost uncomfortably small—Oliver looked at Ginny critically, standing back to examine her from her toes upward and finding nothing wrong except a strand or two of hair out of place. "The Irish linen blazer was an excellent choice," he said. "The earrings too. The bracelets. The shoes." He spoke with assurance, though Ginny had the idea he was nervous, or excited. He turned to study his own reflection in the bronze-frosted mirror on the elevator wall, facing it with a queer childlike squint. This was his "mirror face," Ginny supposed, the way he had of confronting himself in the mirror so that it wasn't *really* himself but a certain habitual expression that protected him. Ginny hadn't any mirror face herself. She had gone beyond that, she knew better, those childish frowns and half smiles and narrowed eyes and heads turned coyly or hopefully to one side—ways of protecting her from seeing "Ginny" when the truth of "Ginny" was that she required being seen head-on. But it would have been difficult to explain to another person.

Oliver adjusted his handsome blue-striped cotton tie and ran his fingers deftly through his hair. It was pale, fine, airily colorless hair, blond perhaps, shading into premature silver, rather thin, Ginny thought, for a man his age. (She estimated his age at thirty-four, which seemed old to her in certain respects, but she knew it was reasonably young in others.) Oliver's skin was slightly coarse; his nose wide at the bridge, and the nostrils disfigured by a few dark hairs that should have been snipped off; his lower jaw was somewhat heavy. But he was a handsome man. In his steel-rimmed blue-tinted glasses he was a handsome man and Ginny saw for the first time that they made an attractive couple.

"Don't trouble to answer any questions they might ask," Oliver said. "In any case the questions won't be serious—just conversation."

"I understand," Ginny said.

A Hispanic maid answered the door. The elevator and the corridor had been so dimly lit, Ginny wasn't prepared for the flood of sunlight in the apartment. They were on the eighteenth floor overlooking the park and the day was still cloudless.

Oliver introduced Ginny to his friends Marguerite and Herbert—the last name sounded like Crews—and Ginny shook hands with them unhesitatingly, as if it were a customary gesture with her. The first exchanges were about the weather. Marguerite was vehement in her gratitude since the past winter, January in particular, had been uncommonly long and dark and depressing. Ginny assented without actually agreeing. For the first minute or two she felt thrown off balance, she couldn't have said why, by the fact that Marguerite Crews was so tall a woman—taller even than Ginny. And she was, or had been, a very beautiful woman as well, with a pale olive complexion and severely black hair parted in the center of her head and fixed in a careless knot at the nape of her neck.

Oliver was explaining apologetically that they couldn't stay. Not even for a drink, really: they were in fact already late for another engagement in the Village. Both the Crewses expressed disappointment. And Oliver's plans for the weekend had been altered as well, unavoidably. At this announcement the disappointment was keener, and Ginny looked away before Marguerite's eyes could lock with hers.

But Oliver was working too hard, Marguerite protested.

But he *must* come out to the Point as they'd planned, Herbert said, and bring his friend along.

Ginny eased discreetly away. She was aloof, indifferent, just slightly bored, but unfailingly courteous: a mark of good breeding. And the Irish linen blazer and skirt were just right.

After a brief while Herbert Crews came over to comment on the view and Ginny thought it wouldn't be an error to agree: the view of Central Park was, after all, something quite real. He told her they'd lived here for eleven years "off and on." They traveled a good deal, he was required to travel almost more than he liked, being associated with an organization Ginny might have heard of?—the Zieboldt Foundation. He had just returned from Nairobi, he said. Two days ago. And still feeling the strain, the fatigue. Ginny thought that his affable talkative "social" manner showed not the least hint of fatigue but did not make this observation to Herbert Crews.

She felt a small pinprick of pity for the way Marguerite Crews's collarbones showed through her filmy muslin "Indian" blouse, and for the extreme thinness of her waist (cinched tight with a belt of silver coins or medallions), and for the faint scolding voice— so conspicuously a "voice"—with which she was speaking to Oliver. She saw that Oliver, though smiling nervously and standing in a self-conscious pose with the thumb of his right hand hooked in his sports coat pocket, was enjoying the episode very much; she noted for the first time something vehement and cruel though at the same time unmistakably boyish in his face. Herbert Crews was telling her about Nairobi but she couldn't concentrate on his words. She was wondering if it might be proper to ask where Nairobi was—she assumed it was a country somewhere in Africa—but Herbert Crews continued, speaking now with zest of the wild animals, including great herds of "the most exquisitely beautiful antelopes," in the Kenya preserves. Had she ever been there? he asked. No, Ginny said. "Well," said Herbert, nodding vigorously, "it really *is* worth it. Next time Marguerite has promised to come along."

Ginny heard Oliver explain again that they were already late for an appointment in the Village, unfortunately they couldn't stay for a drink, yet it was a pity but he hoped they might do it another time: with which Marguerite warmly agreed. Though it was clearly all right for Oliver and Ginny to leave now, Herbert Crews was telling her about the various animals he'd seen—elands, giraffes, gnus, hippopotami, crocodiles, zebras, "feathered monkeys," impala— he had actually eaten impala and found it fairly good. But the trip was fatiguing and his business in Nairobi disagreeable. He'd discovered—as in fact the Foundation had known from certain clumsily fudged reports—not only that the microbiological research being subsidized there had come to virtually nothing but that vast sums of money had disappeared into nowhere. Ginny professed to feel some sympathy though at the same time, as she said, she wasn't surprised. "Well," she said, easing away from Herbert Crews's side, "that seems to be human nature, doesn't it. All around the world."

"Americans and Swedes this time," Herbert Crews said, "equally taken in."

It couldn't be avoided that Herbert tell Oliver what he'd been saying—Oliver in fact seemed to be interested, he might have had some indirect connection with the Foundation himself—but unfortunately they were late for their engagement downtown, and within five minutes they were out of the apartment and back in the elevator going down.

Oliver withdrew a handkerchief from his breast pocket, unfolded it, and carefully wiped his forehead. Ginny was studying her reflection in the mirror and felt a pinprick of disappointment—her eyes looked shadowed and tired, and her hair wasn't really all that wonderful, falling straight to her shoulders. Though she'd shampooed it only that morning it was already getting dirty—the wind had been so strong on their walk up Madison.

On Fifth Avenue, in the gusty sunlight, they walked together for several blocks. Ginny slid her arm through Oliver's as if they were being watched but at an intersection they were forced to walk at different paces and her arm slipped free. It was time in any case to say goodbye: she sensed that he wasn't going to ask her, even out of courtesy, to have a drink with him: and she had made up her mind not to feel even tangentially insulted. After all, she hadn't been insulted.

He signaled a cab for her. He handed over the pink cardboard box with her denim jumper and sweater in it and shook her hand vigorously. "You were lovely up there," Oliver said, "just perfect. Look, I'll call you, all right?"

She felt the weight, the subtle dizzying blow, of the "were." But she thanked him just the same. And got into the cab. And wasn't so stricken by a sudden fleeting sense of loss—of loss tinged with a queer cold sickish knowledge—that, as the cab pulled away into the traffic stream, she couldn't give him a final languid wave of her hand, and even shape her mouth into a puckish kiss. All she had really lost, in a sense, was her own pair of shoes.

1986

Maxine Hong Kingston
(1940–   )

Maxine Hong Kingston's first two books, *The Woman Warrior: Memoirs of a Girlhood among Ghosts* (1976) and *China Men* (1980), with their unique blending of legend, family history, and personal experience, do not fit easily into preset categories of fiction, nonfiction, or memoir. *Woman Warrior* won the National Book Critics Circle Award for nonfiction and *China Men* the American Book Award in the same category, but both contain plotted narratives, invented dialogue, and imagined events.

Kingston was the first of six American-born children of Chinese immigrants Ying Lan Chew and Tom Hong. Because of restrictive immigration policies, Kingston's mother—like most Chinese women—stayed behind in a village near Guangzhou (Canton) when her husband came to the United States to work. Ying Lan Chew was trained as an obstetrician in China, but in California she joined her husband in the family laundry business. Born in Stockton, Maxine Ting Ting Hong grew up in a segregated Chinese neighborhood where the family lived in the same building with

their laundry, was educated in English in the local public schools, and graduated from the University of California at Berkeley (1962). The year of her graduation she married Earll Kingston, an actor. They have one son. She has taught in several universities and is currently a professor at her alma mater.

Woman Warrior explores the dichotomy between traditional misogynist attitudes and myths about legendary heroines from the perspective of a woman trying to assess her place both in an immigrant family and in contemporary American society. The warrior of the title, Fa Mu Lan, led a peasant army in the overthrow of a corrupt emperor; as a child Kingston followed her mother around the house, both singing loudly about the soldier's glorious deeds. At the same time, she was told cautionary tales about nonconforming women and heard folk sayings about the uselessness of girls. Faced with these contradictions and the racism she experiences, the narrator resolves to become a writer, for "the swordswoman and I are not so dissimilar.

*** The reporting is the vengeance—not the beheading, not the gutting, but the words."

China Men recounts the stories of Chinese male immigrants, who came in search of the "Gold Mountain" but were met with bigotry, isolated in all-male communities, and often forced to work long hours in hazardous conditions in the building of the railroads and in mining.

Kingston's first wholly fictional work was *Tripmaster Monkey: His Fake Book* (1989). The monkey of the title is a mythical trickster character; in the sixteenth-century classical text *Journey to the West*, he serves as the protector of a monk on a quest for Buddhist scriptures. The novel's protagonist, Wittman Ah Sing, is a Berke-ley undergraduate during the Vietnam War era. Immersed in a psychedelic multicultural student society, Wittman is determined to write an important play and is trying to understand the implications of being an American of Chinese heritage. Kingston has said that though the major character is male, the narrative voice is female, that of the goddess of mercy, Kuan Yin.

Studies of Kingston's themes and techniques appear in Estelle Jelinek, ed., *Women's Autobiography: Essays in Criticism* (1980); Catherine Rainwater and William Scheik, eds., *Contemporary American Women Writers* (1985); Paul John Eakin, *Fictions in Autobiography: Studies in the Art of Self-Invention* (1985); and Sidonie Smith, *A Poetics of Women's Autobiography* (1987).

FROM THE WOMAN WARRIOR

No Name Woman

"You must not tell anyone," my mother said, "what I am about to tell you. In China your father had a sister who killed herself. She jumped into the family well. We say that your father has all brothers because it is as if she had never been born.

"In 1924 just a few days after our village celebrated seventeen hurry-up weddings—to make sure that every young man who went 'out on the road' would responsibly come home—your father and his brothers and your grandfather and his brothers and your aunt's new husband sailed for America, the Gold Mountain. It was your grandfather's last trip. Those lucky enough to get contracts waved good-bye from the decks. They fed and guarded the stowaways and helped them off in Cuba, New York, Bali, Hawaii. 'We'll meet in California next year,' they said. All of them sent money home.

"I remember looking at your aunt one day when she and I were dressing; I had not noticed before that she had such a protruding melon of a stomach. But I did not think, 'She's pregnant,' until she began to look like other pregnant women, her shirt pulling and the white tops of her black pants showing. She could not have been pregnant, you see, because her husband had been gone for years. No one said anything. We did not discuss it. In early summer she was ready to have the child, long after the time when it could have been possible.

"The village had also been counting. On the night the baby was to be born the villagers raided our house. Some were crying. Like a great saw, teeth strung with lights, files of people walked zigzag across our land, tearing the rice. Their lanterns doubled in the disturbed black water, which drained away through the broken bunds. As the villagers closed in, we could see that some of them, probably men and women we knew well, wore white masks. The people with long hair hung it over their faces. Women with short hair made it stand up on end. Some had tied white bands around their foreheads, arms, and legs.

"At first they threw mud and rocks at the house. Then they threw eggs and began slaughtering our stock. We could hear the animals scream their deaths—the roosters, the pigs, a last great roar from the ox. Familiar wild heads flared in our night windows; the villagers encircled us. Some of the faces stopped to peer at us, their eyes rushing like searchlights. The hands flattened against the panes, framed heads, and left red prints.

"The villagers broke in the front and the back doors at the same time, even though we had not locked the doors against them. Their knives dripped with the blood of our animals. They smeared blood on the doors and walls. One woman swung a chicken, whose throat she had slit, splattering blood in red arcs about her. We stood together in the middle of our house, in the family hall with the pictures and tables of the ancestors around us, and looked straight ahead.

"At that time the house had only two wings. When the men came back, we would build two more to enclose our courtyard and a third one to begin a second courtyard. The villagers pushed through both wings, even your grandparents' rooms, to find your aunt's, which was also mine until the men returned. From this room a new wing for one of the younger families would grow. They ripped up her clothes and shoes and broke her combs, grinding them underfoot. They tore her work from the loom. They scattered the cooking fire and rolled the new weaving in it. We could hear them in the kitchen breaking our bowls and banging the pots. They overturned the great waist-high earthenware jugs; duck eggs, pickled fruits, vegetables burst out and mixed in acrid torrents. The old woman from the next field swept a broom through the air and loosed the spirits-of-the-broom over our heads. 'Pig.' 'Ghost.' 'Pig,' they sobbed and scolded while they ruined our house.

"When they left, they took sugar and oranges to bless themselves. They cut pieces from the dead animals. Some of them took bowls that were not broken and clothes that were not torn. Afterward we swept up the rice and sewed it back up into sacks. But the smells from the spilled preserves lasted. Your aunt gave birth in the pigsty that night. The next morning when I went for the water, I found her and the baby plugging up the family well.

"Don't let your father know that I told you. He denies her. Now that you have started to menstruate, what happened to her could happen to you. Don't humiliate us. You wouldn't like to be forgotten as if you had never been born. The villagers are watchful."

Whenever she had to warn us about life, my mother told stories that ran like this one, a story to grow up on. She tested our strength to establish realities. Those in the emigrant generations who could not reassert brute survival died young and far from home. Those of us in the first American generations have had to figure out how the invisible world the emigrants built around our childhoods fit in solid America.

The emigrants confused the gods by diverting their curses, misleading them with crooked streets and false names. They must try to confuse their offspring as well, who, I suppose, threaten them in similar ways—always trying to get things straight, always trying to name the unspeakable. The Chinese I know hide their names; sojourners take new names when their lives change and guard their real names with silence.

Chinese-Americans, when you try to understand what things in you are Chinese, how do you separate what is peculiar to childhood, to poverty, insanities, one family, your mother who marked your growing with stories, from what is Chinese? What is Chinese tradition and what is the movies?

If I want to learn what clothes my aunt wore, whether flashy or ordinary, I would have to begin, "Remember Father's drowned-in-the-well sister?" I cannot ask that. My mother has told me once and for all the useful parts. She will add nothing unless powered by Necessity, a riverbank that guides her life. She plants vegetable gardens rather than lawns; she carries the odd-shaped tomatoes home from the fields and eats food left for the gods.

Whenever we did frivolous things, we used up energy; we flew high kites. We children came up off the ground over the melting cones our parents brought home from work and the American movie on New Year's Day—*Oh, You Beautiful Doll* with Betty Grable one year, and *She Wore a Yellow Ribbon* with John Wayne another year. After the one carnival ride each, we paid in guilt; our tired father counted his change on the dark walk home.

Adultery is extravagance. Could people who hatch their own chicks and eat the embryos and the heads for delicacies and boil the feet in vinegar for party food, leaving only the gravel, eating even the gizzard lining—could such people engender a prodigal aunt? To be a woman, to have a daughter in starvation time was a waste enough. My aunt could not have been the lone romantic who gave up everything for sex. Women in the old China did not choose. Some man had commanded her to lie with him and be his secret evil. I wonder whether he masked himself when he joined the raid on her family.

Perhaps she encountered him in the fields or on the mountain where the daughters-in-law collected fuel. Or perhaps he first noticed her in the marketplace. He was not a stranger because the village housed no strangers. She had to have dealings with him other than sex. Perhaps he worked an adjoining field, or he sold her the cloth for the dress she sewed and wore. His demand must have surprised, then terrified her. She obeyed him; she always did as she was told.

When the family found a young man in the next village to be her husband, she stood tractably beside the best rooster, his proxy, and promised before they met that she would be his forever. She was lucky that he was her age and she would be the first wife, an advantage secure now. The night she first saw him, he had sex with her. Then he left for America. She had almost forgotten what he looked like. When she tried to envision him, she only saw the black and white face in the group photograph the men had had taken before leaving.

The other man was not, after all, much different from her husband. They both gave orders: she followed. "If you tell your family, I'll beat you. I'll kill you. Be here again next week." No one talked sex, ever. And she might have separated the rapes from the rest of living if only she did not have to buy her oil from him or gather wood in the same forest. I want her fear to have lasted just as long as rape lasted so that the fear could have been contained. No drawn-out fear. But women at sex hazarded birth and hence lifetimes. The fear did not stop but permeated everywhere. She told the man, "I think I'm pregnant." He organized the raid against her.

On nights when my mother and father talked about their life back home, sometimes they mentioned an "outcast table" whose business they still seemed to be settling, their voices tight. In a commensal tradition, where food is precious, the powerful older people made wrongdoers eat alone. Instead of letting them start separate new lives like the Japanese, who could become samurais and geishas, the Chinese family, faces averted but eyes glowering sideways, hung on to the offenders and fed them leftovers. My aunt must have lived in the same house as my parents and eaten at an outcast table. My mother spoke about the raid as if she had seen it, when she and my aunt, a daughter-in-law to a different household, should not have been living together at all. Daughters-in-law lived with their husbands' parents, not their own; a synonym for marriage in Chinese is "taking a daughter-in-law." Her husband's parents could have sold her, mortgaged her, stoned her. But they had sent her back to her own mother and father, a mysterious act hinting at disgraces not told me. Perhaps they had thrown her out to deflect the avengers.

She was the only daughter; her four brothers went with her father, husband, and uncles "out on the road" and for some years became western men. When the goods were divided among the family, three of the brothers took land, and the youngest, my father, chose an education. After my grandparents gave their daughter away to her husband's family, they had dispensed all the adventure and all the property. They expected her alone to keep the traditional ways, which her brothers, now among the barbarians, could fumble without detection. The heavy, deep-rooted women were to maintain the past against the flood, safe for returning. But the rare urge west had fixed upon our family, and so my aunt crossed boundaries not delineated in space.

The work of preservation demands that the feelings playing about in one's guts not be turned into action. Just watch their passing like cherry blossoms. But perhaps my aunt, my forerunner, caught in a slow life, let dreams grow and fade and after some months or years went toward what persisted. Fear at the enormities of the forbidden kept her desires delicate, wire and bone. She looked at a man because she liked the way the hair was tucked behind his ears, or she liked the question-mark line of a long torso curving at the shoulder and straight at the hip. For warm eyes or a soft voice or a slow walk—that's all—a few hairs, a line, a brightness, a sound, a pace, she gave up family. She offered us up for a charm that vanished with tiredness, a pigtail that didn't toss when the wind died. Why, the wrong lighting could erase the dearest thing about him.

It could very well have been, however, that my aunt did not take subtle enjoyment of her friend, but, a wild woman, kept rollicking company. Imagining her free with sex doesn't fit, though. I don't know any women like that, or men either. Unless I see her life branching into mine, she gives me no ancestral help.

To sustain her being in love, she often worked at herself in the mirror, guessing at the colors and shapes that would interest him, changing them frequently in order to hit on the right combination. She wanted him to look back.

On a farm near the sea, a woman who tended her appearance reaped a reputation for eccentricity. All the married women blunt-cut their hair in flaps about their ears or pulled it back in tight buns. No nonsense. Neither style blew easily into heart-catching tangles. And at their weddings they displayed themselves in their long hair for the last time. "It brushed the backs of my knees," my mother tells me. "It was braided, and even so, it brushed the backs of my knees."

At the mirror my aunt combed individuality into her bob. A bun could have been contrived to escape into black streamers blowing in the wind or in quiet wisps about her face, but only the older women in our picture album wear buns. She brushed her hair back from her forehead, tucking the flaps behind her ears. She looped a piece of thread, knotted into a circle between her index fingers and thumbs, and ran the double strand across her forehead. When she closed her fingers as if she were making a pair of shadow geese bite, the string twisted together catching the little hairs. Then she pulled the thread away from her skin, ripping the hairs out neatly, her eyes watering from the needles of pain. Opening her fingers, she cleaned the thread, then rolled it along her hairline and the tops of her eyebrows. My mother did the same to me and my sisters and herself. I used to believe that the expression "caught by the short hairs" meant a captive held with a depilatory string. It especially hurt at the temples, but my mother said we were lucky we didn't have to have our feet bound when we were seven. Sisters used to sit on their beds and cry together, she said, as their mothers or their slaves removed the bandages for a few minutes each night and let the blood gush back into their veins. I hope that the man my aunt loved appreciated a smooth brow, that he wasn't just a tits-and-ass man.

Once my aunt found a freckle on her chin, at a spot that the almanac said predestined her for unhappiness. She dug it out with a hot needle and washed the wound with peroxide.

More attention to her looks than these pullings of hairs and pickings at spots would have caused gossip among the villagers. They owned work clothes and good clothes, and they wore good clothes for feasting the new seasons. But since a woman combing her hair hexes beginnings, my aunt rarely found an occasion to look her best. Women looked like great sea snails—the corded wood, babies, and laundry they carried were the whorls on their backs. The Chinese did not admire a bent back; goddesses and warriors stood straight. Still there must have been a marvelous freeing of beauty when a worker laid down her burden and stretched and arched.

Such commonplace loveliness, however, was not enough for my aunt. She dreamed of a lover for the fifteen days of New Year's, the time for families to exchange visits, money, and food. She plied her secret comb. And sure enough she cursed the year, the family, the village, and herself.

Even as her hair lured her imminent lover, many other men looked at her. Uncles, cousins, nephews, brothers would have looked, too, had they been home between journeys. Perhaps they had already been restraining their curiosity, and they left, fearful that their glances, like a field of nesting birds, might be startled and caught. Poverty hurt, and that was their first reason for leaving. But another, final reason for leaving the crowded house was the never-said.

She may have been unusually beloved, the precious only daughter, spoiled and mirror gazing because of the affection the family lavished on her. When her husband left, they welcomed the chance to take her back from the in-laws; she could live like the little daughter for just a while longer. There are stories that my grandfather was different from other people, "crazy ever since the little Jap bayoneted him in the head." He used to put his naked penis on the dinner table, laughing. And one day he brought home a baby girl, wrapped up inside his brown western-style greatcoat. He had traded one of his sons, probably my father, the youngest, for her. My grandmother made him trade back. When he finally got a daughter of his own, he doted on her. They must have all loved her, except perhaps my father, the only brother who never went back to China, having once been traded for a girl.

Brothers and sisters, newly men and women, had to efface their sexual color and present plain miens. Disturbing hair and eyes, a smile like no other threatened the ideal of five generations living under one roof. To focus blurs, people shouted face to face and yelled from room to room. The immigrants I know have loud voices, unmodulated to American tones even after years away from the village where they called their friendships out across the fields. I have not been able to stop my mother's screams in public libraries or over telephones. Walking erect (knees straight, toes pointed forward, not pigeon-toed, which is Chinese-feminine) and speaking in an inaudible voice, I have tried to turn myself American-feminine. Chinese communication was loud, public. Only sick people had to whisper. But at the dinner table, where the family members came nearest one another, no one could talk, not the outcasts nor any eaters. Every word that falls from the mouth is a coin lost. Silently they gave and accepted food with both hands. A preoccupied child who took his bowl with one hand got a sideways glare. A complete moment of total attention is due everyone alike. Children and lovers have no singularity here, but my aunt used a secret voice, a separate attentiveness.

She kept the man's name to herself throughout her labor and dying; she did not accuse him that he be punished with her. To save her inseminator's name she gave silent birth.

He may have been somebody in her own household, but intercourse with a man outside the family would have been no less abhorrent. All the village were kinsmen, and the titles shouted in loud country voices never let kinship be forgotten. Any man within visiting distance would have been neutralized as a lover—"brother," "younger brother," "older brother"—one hundred and fifteen relationship titles. Parents researched birth charts probably not so much to assure good fortune as to circumvent incest in a population that has but one hundred surnames. Everybody has eight million relatives. How useless then sexual mannerisms, how dangerous.

As if it came from an atavism deeper than fear, I used to add "brother" silently to boys' names. It hexed the boys, who would or would not ask me to dance, and made them less scary and as familiar and deserving of benevolence as girls.

But, of course, I hexed myself also—no dates. I should have stood up, both arms waving, and shouted out across libraries, "Hey, you! Love me back." I had no idea, though, how to make attraction selective, how to control its direction and magnitude. If I made myself American-pretty so that the five or six Chinese boys in the class fell in love with me, everyone else—the Caucasian, Negro, and Japanese boys—would too. Sisterliness, dignified and honorable, made much more sense.

Attraction eludes control so stubbornly that whole societies designed to organize relationships among people cannot keep order, not even when they bind people to one another from childhood and raise them together. Among the very poor and the wealthy, brothers married their adopted sisters, like doves. Our family allowed some romance, paying adult brides' prices and providing dowries so that their sons and daughters could marry strangers. Marriage promises to turn strangers into friendly relatives—a nation of siblings.

In the village structure, spirits shimmered among the live creatures, balanced and held in equilibrium by time and land. But one human being flaring up into violence could open up a black hole, a maelstrom that pulled in the sky. The frightened villagers, who depended on one another to maintain the real, went to my aunt to show her a personal, physical representation of the break she had made in the "roundness." Misallying couples snapped off the future, which was to be embodied in true offspring. The villagers punished her for acting as if she could have a private life, secret and apart from them.

If my aunt had betrayed the family at a time of large grain yields and peace, when many boys were born, and wings were being built on many houses, perhaps she might have escaped such severe punishment. But the men—hungry, greedy, tired of planting in dry soil, cuckolded—had had to leave the village in order to send food-money home. There were ghost plagues, bandit plagues, wars with the Japanese, floods. My Chinese brother and sister had died of an unknown sickness. Adultery, perhaps only a mistake during good times, became a crime when the village needed food.

The round moon cakes and round doorways, the round tables of graduated size that fit one roundness inside another, round windows and rice bowls—these talismen had lost their power to warn this family of the law: a family must be whole, faithfully keeping the descent line by having sons to feed the old and the dead, who in turn look after the family. The villagers came to show my aunt and her lover-in-hiding a broken house. The villagers were speeding up the circling of events because she was too shortsighted to see that her infidelity had already harmed the village, that waves of consequences would return unpredictably, sometimes in disguise, as now, to hurt her. This roundness had to be made coin-sized so that she would see its circumference: punish her at the birth of her baby. Awaken her to the inexorable. People who refused fatalism because they could invent small resources insisted on culpability. Deny accidents and wrest fault from the stars.

After the villagers left, their lanterns now scattering in various directions toward home, the family broke their silence and cursed her. "Aiaa, we're going to die. Death is coming. Death is coming. Look what you've done. You've killed us. Ghost! Dead ghost! Ghost! You've never been born." She ran out into the fields, far enough from the house so that she could no longer hear their voices, and pressed herself against the earth, her own land no more. When she felt the birth coming, she thought that she had been hurt. Her body seized together. "They've hurt me too much," she thought. "This is gall, and it will kill me." Her forehead and knees against the earth, her body convulsed and then released her onto her back. The black well of sky and stars went out and out and out forever; her body and her complexity seemed to disappear. She was one of the stars, a bright dot in blackness, without home, without a companion, in eternal cold and silence. An agoraphobia rose in her, speeding higher and higher, bigger and bigger; she would not be able to contain it; there would be no end to fear.

Flayed, unprotected against space, she felt pain return, focusing her body. This pain chilled her—a cold, steady kind of surface pain. Inside, spasmodically, the other pain, the pain of the child, heated her. For hours she lay on the ground, alternately body and space. Sometimes a vision of normal comfort obliterated reality: she saw the family in the evening gambling at the dinner table, the young people massaging their elders' backs. She saw them congratulating one another, high joy on the mornings the rice shoots came up. When these pictures burst, the stars drew yet further apart. Black space opened.

She got to her feet to fight better and remembered that old-fashioned women gave birth in their pigsties to fool the jealous, pain-dealing gods, who do not snatch piglets. Before the next spasms could stop her, she ran to the pigsty, each step a rushing out into emptiness. She climbed over the fence and knelt in the dirt. It was good to have a fence enclosing her, a tribal person alone.

Laboring, this woman who had carried her child as a foreign growth that sickened her every day, expelled it at last. She reached down to touch the hot, wet, moving mass, surely smaller than anything human, and could feel that it was human after all—fingers, toes, nails, nose. She pulled it up on to her belly, and it lay curled there, butt in the air, feet precisely tucked one under the other. She opened her loose shirt and buttoned the child inside. After resting, it squirmed and thrashed and she pushed it up to her breast. It turned its head this way and that until it found her nipple. There, it made little snuffling noises. She clenched her teeth at its preciousness, lovely as a young calf, a piglet, a little dog.

She may have gone to the pigsty as a last act of responsibility: she would protect this child as she had protected its father. It would look after her soul, leaving supplies on her grave. But how would this tiny child without family find her grave when there would be no marker for her anywhere, neither in the earth nor the family hall? No one would give her a family hall name. She had taken the child with her into the wastes. At its birth the two of them had felt the same raw pain of separation, a wound that only the family pressing tight could close. A child with no descent line would not soften her life but only trail after her, ghostlike, begging her to give it purpose. At dawn the villagers on their way to the fields would stand around the fence and look.

Full of milk, the little ghost slept. When it awoke, she hardened her breasts against the milk that crying loosens. Toward morning she picked up the baby and walked to the well.

Carrying the baby to the well shows loving. Otherwise abandon it. Turn its face into the mud. Mothers who love their children take them along. It was probably a girl; there is some hope of forgiveness for boys.

"Don't tell anyone you had an aunt. Your father does not want to hear her name. She has never been born." I have believed that sex was unspeakable and words so strong and fathers so frail that "aunt" would do my father mysterious harm. I have thought that my family, having settled among immigrants who had also been their neighbors in the ancestral land, needed to clean their name, and a wrong word would incite the kinspeople even here. But there is more to this silence: they want me to participate in her punishment. And I have.

In the twenty years since I heard this story I have not asked for details nor said my aunt's name; I do not know it. People who can comfort the dead can also chase after them to hurt them further—a reverse ancestor worship. The real punishment was not the raid swiftly inflicted by the villagers, but the family's deliberately forgetting her. Her betrayal so maddened them, they saw to it that she would suffer forever, even after death. Always hungry, always needing, she would have to beg food from other ghosts, snatch and steal it from those whose living descendants give them gifts. She would have to fight the ghosts massed at crossroads for the buns a few thoughtful citizens leave to decoy her away from village and home so that the ancestral spirits could feast unharassed. At peace, they could act like gods, not ghosts, their descent lines providing them with paper suits and dresses, spirit money, paper houses, paper automobiles, chicken, meat, and rice into eternity—essences delivered up in smoke and flames, steam and incense rising from each rice bowl. In an attempt to make the Chinese care for people outside the family, Chairman Mao encourages us now to give our paper replicas to the spirits of outstanding soldiers and workers, no matter whose ancestors they may be. My aunt remains forever hungry. Goods are not distributed evenly among the dead.

My aunt haunts me—her ghost drawn to me because now, after fifty years of neglect, I alone devote pages of paper to her, though not origamied into houses and clothes. I do not think she always means me well. I am telling on her, and she was a spite suicide, drowning herself in the drinking water. The Chinese are always very frightened of the drowned one, whose weeping ghost, wet hair hanging and skin bloated, waits silently by the water to pull down a substitute.

1976

Bobbie Ann Mason

(1940–)

Born and raised on a dairy farm near Mayfield, in western Kentucky, "a hundred and fifty miles from the nearest city, Nashville," Bobbie Ann Mason has made that region her special territory, not as it was in her girlhood, but as it has become. Lingering in the background of her stories is an earlier America, rural, isolated, tradition-bound, encased in values long sustained. In the foreground is an America of shopping malls and television, of soap operas, MTV, and Burger Kings, of people who have lost their past, live lonely in the present, work as cocktail waitresses or strip miners, or collect unemployment compensation while they try to connect with other humans. For them there is no better guidance than the flickering enlightenment of the TV talk shows or the lyrics of popular songs, and they expect little from the future. The literary result is a kind of social minimalism, portraits of lives severely diminished, but as in the social minimalism of Raymond Carver, with whom Mason has often been compared, it is clear that for the author these are lives that matter.

After graduating from the University of Kentucky in 1962, Mason wrote for movie and television fan magazines in New York before returning to school for an M.A. at the State University of New York at Binghamton. Married, she earned a Ph.D. from the University of Connecticut in 1972 with a dissertation on Vladimir Nabokov, and for the next several years she taught at Mansfield State College in Pennsylvania. Two books—*Nabokov's Garden: A Guide to Ada* (1974) and *The Girl Sleuth: A Feminist Guide to the Bobbsey Twins, Nancy Drew, and Their Sisters* (1975)—preceded her short stories. Her real vocation, however, was fiction, and after twenty rejections her story "Offerings" was published by *The New Yorker* in 1980. Two years later, with the appearance of her first collection, *Shiloh and Other Stories,* her mastery was established. Two novels followed. *In Country* (1985) tells of a family coming to grips with the wounds of Vietnam as they visit the Veterans Memorial in Washington. *Spence + Lila* (1988) portrays the tensions surrounding a woman's bout with breast cancer. A second collection of short stories, *Love Life* (1989), the source of the story below, confirms her place as one of the contemporary masters of the form.

A brief appraisal appears in *Dictionary of Literary Biography Yearbook; 1987* (1988).

Hunktown

Joann noticed that her daughter Patty had started parting her hair on the left, so that it fell over the right side of her forehead, hiding the scar from her recent car accident.

"That scar doesn't show, Mom," said Patty, when she caught Joann looking. Patty had the baby on her hip, and her little girl, Kristi, was on the floor, fooling with the cat.

"Where's Cody?" Patty asked.

"Gone to Nashville. He got tired of waiting for that big shot he met in Paducah to follow up on his word, so he's gone down with Will Ed and them to make a record album on his own." Joann's husband, Cody Swann, was going to make a record album. She could hardly believe it. Cody had always wanted to make a record album.

"Is it one of those deals where you pay the studio?" Patty asked suspiciously.

"He pays five hundred dollars for the studio, and then he gets ten percent after they sell the first thousand."

"That's a rip-off," said Patty. "Don't he know that? I saw that on 'Sixty Minutes.' "

"Well, he got tired of waiting to be discovered. You know how he is."

The baby, Rodney, started to cry, and Patty stuck a pacifier in his mouth. She said, "The thing is, will they distribute the record? Them companies get rich making records for every little two-bit band that can hitchhike to Nashville. And then they don't distribute the records."

"Cody says he can sell them to all his fans around here."

"He could sell them at the store," Patty said. She worked at a discount chain store.

"He took off this morning in that van with the muffler dragging. He had it wired up underneath and tied with a rope to the door handle on the passenger side."

"That sounds just like Cody. For God's sake, Kristi, what are you doing to that cat?"

Kristi had the cat upside down between her knees. "I'm counting her milkers. She's got four milkers."

"That's a tomcat, hon," said Joann gently.

Joann was taking her daughter shopping. Patty, who had gotten a ride to Joann's, was depending on her mother for transportation until the insurance money came through on her car. She had totaled it when she ran into a blue Buick, driven by an old woman on her way to a white sale in town. Patty's head had smashed against the steering wheel, and her face had been so bruised that for a while it resembled a ripe persimmon blackened by frost.

With the children in the back seat, Joann drove Patty around town on her errands. Patty didn't fasten her seat belt. She had had two wrecks before she was eighteen, but this latest accident was not her fault. Cody said Patty's middle name was Trouble. In high school, she became pregnant and had to get married, but a hay bale fell on her and caused a miscarriage. After that, she had two babies, but then she got divorced. Patty had a habit of flirting with Cody and teasing her mother for marrying such a good-looking man. Cody had grown up in a section of town known as Hunktown because so many handsome guys used to live there. That part of town—a couple of streets between Kroger's and the high school—was still known as Hunktown. The public housing project and the new health clinic were there now. Recently, a revival of pride in Hunktown had developed, as though it had been designated a historic area, and Cody had a Hunktown T-shirt. He wore cowboy outfits, and he hung his hats in a row on the scalloped trim of the china cabinet that Joann had antiqued.

Joann had known Cody since high school, but they had married only three years ago. After eighteen years of marriage to Joe Murphy, Joann found herself without a man—one of those women whose husbands suddenly leave them for someone younger. Last year, Phil Donahue had a show on that theme, and Joann remembered Phil saying something ironic like "It looks like you've got to keep tap-dancing in your negligee or the son of a gun is going to leave you." Joann was too indignant to sit around and feel sorry for herself. After filing for divorce, she got a new hairdo and new clothes and went out on weekends with some women. One night, she went to a place across the county line that sold liquor. Cody Swann was there, playing a fancy red electric guitar and singing about fickle women and trucks and heartache. At intermission, they reminisced about high school. Cody was divorced, and he had two grown children. Joann had two teenagers still living at home, and Patty had already left. In retrospect, Joann realized how impulsive their marriage had been, but she had been happy with Cody until he got laid off from his job, four months ago. He'd worked at the Crosbee plant, which manufactured electrical parts. Now he was drinking too much, but he assured Joann he couldn't possibly become an alcoholic on beer. Their situation was awkward, because she had a good job at the post office, and she knew he didn't like to depend on her. He had thrown himself into rehearsing for his album with his friends Will Ed and L.J. and Jimmy. "What we really need is a studio," Cody kept saying impatiently. They had been playing at county fairs and civic events around western Kentucky off and on for years. Every year, Cody played at the International Banana Festival, in Fulton, and recently he had played for the Wal-Mart grand opening and got a free toaster.

"Being out of work makes you lose your self-respect," Cody had told Joann matter-of-factly. "But I ain't going to let that happen to me. I've been fooling around too much. It's time to get serious about my singing."

"I don't want you to get your hopes up too much and then get disappointed," Joann said.

"Can't you imagine me with a television series? You could be on it with me. We'd play like we were Porter Wagoner and Dolly Parton. You could wear a big wig and balloons in your blouse."

"I can just see me—Miss Astor, in my plow shoes!" Joann said, squealing with laughter at the idea, playing along with Cody's dream.

"Do you care if we drive out to that truck patch and pick a few turnip greens before I take you home?" Joann asked Patty. "It's on the way."

"You're the driver. Beggars can't be choosers." Patty rummaged around on the floor under the bucket seat and found Rodney's pacifier, peppered with tobacco and dirt. She wiped it on her jeans and jammed it into the baby's mouth.

On the CB, a woman suddenly said, "Hey, Tomcat, you lost something back here. Come in, Tomcat. Over." A spurt of static followed. The woman said, "Tomcat, it looks like a big old sack of feed. You better get in reverse."

"She's trying to get something started with those cute guys in that green pickup we passed," Patty said.

"Everybody's on the make," Joann said uneasily. She knew what that was like.

At the truck patch, Patty stood there awkwardly in her high heels, like a scarecrow planted in the dirt.

"Let me show you how to pick turnip greens," Joann said. "Gather them like this. Just break them off partway down the stem, and clutch them in your hand till you get a big wad. Then pack them down in the sack."

"They're fuzzy, and they sting my hands. Is this a turnip green or a weed?" Patty held up a leaf.

"That's mustard. Go ahead and pick it. Mustard's good." Joann flicked the greens off expertly. "Don't get down into the stalk," she said. "And they wilt down when they're cooked, so pack them real good."

Kristi was looking for bugs, and Rodney was asleep in the car. Joann bent over, grabbing the greens. Some of the turnips were large enough to pull, their bulbs showing above ground like lavender pomanders. The okra plants in a row next to the turnip patch were as tall as corn, with yellow blossoms like roses. Where the blossoms had shriveled, the new okras thrust their points skyward. Joann felt the bright dizziness of the Indian-summer day, and she remembered many times when nothing had seemed important except picking turnip greens. She and Cody had lived on her parents' farm since her father died, two years before, but they had let it go. Cody wasn't a farmer. The field where her father used to grow turnips was wild now, spotted with burdock and thistles, and Cody was away in Nashville, seeking fame.

At a shed on the edge of the patch, Joann paid for the turnip greens and bought half a bushel of sweet potatoes from a black man in overalls, who was selling them from the back end of a pickup truck. The man measured the sweet potatoes in a half-bushel basket, then transferred them to grocery sacks. When he packed the sweet potatoes in the basket, he placed them so that their curves fit into one another, filling up the spaces. The man's carefulness was like Cody's when he was taping, recording a song over and over again. But Cody had tilled the garden last week in such a hurry that it looked as though cows had trampled the ground.

The man was saying, "When you get home with these, lay them in a basket and don't stir them. The sweet will settle in them, but if you disturb them, it will go away. Use them off the top. Don't root around in them."

"I'll put them in the basement," Joann said, as he set the sacks into her trunk. She said to

Patty, who was concentrating on a hangnail, "Sweet potatoes are hard to keep. They mold on you."

That evening, Joann discovered one of Cody's tapes that she had not heard before. On the tape, he sang "There Stands the Glass," a Webb Pierce song that made her cry, the way Cody sang it so convincingly. When Cody sang "The Wild Side of Life" on the tape, Joann recalled Kitty Wells's answer to that song. "It wasn't God who made honky-tonk angels," Kitty Wells had insisted, blaming unfaithful men for every woman's heartbreak. Joann admired the way Kitty Wells sang the song so matter-of-factly, transcending her pain. A man wrote that song, Cody had told her. Joann wondered if he was being unfaithful in Nashville. She regarded the idea in a detached way, the way she would look at a cabbage at Kroger's.

Now Cody was singing an unfamiliar song. Joann rewound the tape and listened.

> I was born in a place they call Hunktown,
> Good-lookin's my middle name—

The song startled her. He had been talking about writing his own material, and he had started throwing around terms like "backup vocals" and "sound mixing." In this song, he sang along with himself to get a multiple-voice effect. The song was a lonesome tune about being a misfit. It sounded strangely insincere.

When Cody returned from Nashville, his voice bubbled along enthusiastically, like a toilet tank that ran until the handle was jiggled. He had been drinking. Joann had missed him, but she realized she hadn't missed his hat. It was the one with the pheasant feathers. He hung it on the china cabinet again. Cody was happy. In Nashville, he had eaten surf-and-turf, toured the Ryman Auditorium, and met a guy who had once been a sideman for Ernest Tubb.

"And here's the best part," said Cody, smacking Joann on the lips again. She got a taste of his mint-flavored snuff. "We got a job playing at a little bar in Nashville on weekends. It just came out of the blue. Jimmy can't do it, because his daddy's real bad off, but Will Ed and L.J. and me could go. Their wives already said they could."

"What makes you think I'll let you?" she said, teasing.

"You're going with me."

"But I've got too much to do." She set his boots on a carpet sample near the door to the porch. Cold air was coming through the crack around the facing. Cody had pieced part of the facing with a broken yardstick when he installed the door, but he had neglected to finish the job.

Cody said, "It's just a little bar with a little stage and this great guy that runs it. He's got a motel next to it and we can stay free. Hey, we can live it up in Nashville! We can watch Home Box Office and everything."

"How can I go? Late beans are coming in, and all them tomatoes."

"This is my big chance! Don't you think I sing good?"

"You're as good as anybody on the 'Grand Ole Opry.'"

"Well, there you go," he said confidently.

"Patty says those studio deals are rip-offs. She saw it on 'Sixty Minutes.'"

"I don't care. The most I can lose is five hundred dollars. And at least I'll have a record album. I'm going to frame the cover and put it in the den."

In bed, they lay curled together, like sweet potatoes. Joann listened to Cody describe how they had made the album, laying down separate tracks and mixing the sound. Each little operation was done separately. They didn't just go into a studio and sing a song, Joann realized. They patched together layers of sound. She didn't mention the new song she had heard. She had put the tape back where she had found it. Now another of Cody's tapes was playing—"I'd Rather Die Young," a love song that seemed to have pointless suffering in it. Softly, Cody sang along with his taped voice. This was called a backup vocal, Joann reminded herself, trying to be very careful, taking one step at a time. Still, the idea of his singing with himself made her think of something self-indulgent and private, like masturbation. But country music was always like that, so personal.

"I'm glad you're home," she said, reaching for him.

"The muffler fell off about halfway home," Cody said, with a sudden hoot of laughter that made the covers quiver. "But we didn't get caught. I don't know why, though. It's as loud as a hundred amplifiers."

"Hold still," Joann said. "You're just like a wiggle-worm in hot ashes."

Cody was trying on his new outfit for the show, and Joann had the sewing machine out, to alter the pants. The pants resembled suede and had fringe.

"They feel tight in the crotch," Cody said. "But they didn't have the next size."

"Are you going to tell me what you paid for them?"

"I didn't pay for them. I charged them at Penney's."

Joann turned the hem up and jerked it forward so that it fell against his boot. "Is that too short?" she asked.

"Just a little longer."

Joann pulled the hem down about a quarter inch and pinned it. "Turn around," she said.

The pants were tan with dark-brown stitching. The vest was embroidered with butterflies. Cody turned around and around, examining himself in the long mirror.

"You look wonderful," she said.

He said, "We may get deeper in debt before it's over with, but one thing I've learned: You can't live with regret. You have to get on with your life. I know it's a big risk I'm taking, but I don't want to go around feeling sorry for myself because I've wasted so much time. And if I fail, at least I will have tried."

He sat on the bed and pulled his boots and then his pants off. The pants were too tight, but the seams were narrow, and there was no way Joann could let them out.

"You'll have to do something about that beer gut," she said.

The Bluebird Lounge looked as innocent as someone's kitchen: all new inside, with a country decor—old lanterns, gingham curtains, and a wagon wheel on the ceiling. It seemed odd to Joann that Cody had said he didn't want to live with regret, because his theme was country memories. He opened with "Walking the Floor Over You," then eased into "Your Cheatin' Heart," "The Wild Side of Life," and "I'd Rather Die Young." He didn't sing the new song she had heard on the tape, and she decided that he must be embarrassed by it. She liked his new Marty Robbins medley, a tribute to the late singer, though she had always detested the song "El Paso." In the pleasant atmosphere of the bar, Cody's voice sounded professional, more real there, somehow, than at home. Joann felt proud. She laughed when Will Ed and L.J. goofed around onstage, tripping over their electric cords and repeating things they had heard on "Hee Haw." L.J. had been kidding Joann, saying, "You better come to Nashville with us to keep the girls from falling all over Cody." Now Joann noticed the women, in twos and threes, sitting close to the stage, and she remembered the time she went across the county line and heard Cody sing. He still looked boyish, and he didn't have a single gray hair. She had cut his bangs too short, she realized now.

"They're really good," the cocktail waitress, Debbie, a slim, pretty woman in an embroidered cowboy shirt, said to Joann. "Most of the bands they get in here are so bad they really bum me out, but these guys are good."

"Cody just cut an album," Joann said proudly.

Debbie was friendly, and Joann felt comfortable with her, even though Debbie was only a little older than Patty. By the second night, Joann and Debbie were confiding in each other and trading notes on their hair. Joann's permanent was growing out strangely, and she was afraid getting a new permanent so soon would damage her hair, but Debbie got a permanent every three months and her hair stayed soft and manageable. In the rest room, Debbie fluffed her hair with her fingers and said, looking into the mirror, "I reckon I better put on some lipstick to keep the mortician away."

During the intermission, Debbie brought Joann a free Tequila Sunrise at her corner table. Cody was drinking beer at the bar with some musicians he had met.

"You've got a good-looking guy," Debbie said.

"He knows it, too," said Joann.

"He'd be blind if he didn't. It must be hard to be married to a guy like that."

"It wasn't so hard till he lost his job and got this notion that he has to get on the 'Grand Ole Opry.'"

"Well, he just might do it. He's good." Debbie told her about a man who had been in the bar once. He turned out to be a talent scout from a record company. "I wish I could remember his name," she said.

"I wish Cody would sing his Elvis songs," Joann said. "He can curl his lip exactly like Elvis, but he says he respects the memory of Elvis too much to do an Elvis act like everybody's doing. It would be exploitation."

"Cody sure is full of sad, lonesome songs," Debbie said. "You can tell he's a guy who's been through a lot. I always study people's faces. I'm fascinated by human nature."

"He went through a bad divorce," Joann said. "But right now he's acting like a kid."

"Men are such little boys," Debbie said knowingly.

Joann saw Cody talking with the men. Their behavior was easygoing, full of laughter. Women were so intense together. Joann could feel Cody's jubilation all the way across the room. It showed in the energetic way he sang the mournful music of all the old hillbilly singers.

Debbie said, "Making music must make you feel free. If I could make music, I'd feel that life was one big jam session."

Coming home on Sunday was disorienting. The cat looked impatient with them. The weather was changing, and the flowers were dying. Joann had meant to take the potted plants into the basement for the winter. There had been a cold snap, but not a killing frost. The garden was still producing, languidly, after a spurt of growth during the last spell of warm weather. After work, during the week, Joann gathered in lima beans and squash and dozens of new green tomatoes. She picked handfuls of dried Kentucky Wonder pole beans to save for seed. Burrs clung to the cuffs of her jeans. Her father used to fight the burdock, knowing that one plant could soon take over a field.

Cody stayed indoors, listening to tapes and playing his guitar. He collected his unemployment check, but when someone called about a job opening, he didn't go. As she worked in the garden, Joann tried to take out her anger on the dying plants that she pulled from the soil. She felt she had to hurry. Fall weather always filled her with a sense of urgency.

Patty stopped by in her new Lynx. She had come out ahead on the insurance deal. Cody paraded around the car, admiring it, stroking the fenders.

"When's your album coming out, Cody?" Patty asked.

"Any day now."

"I asked at the store if they could get it, but they said it would have to be nationally distributed for them to carry it."

"Do you want a mess of lima beans, Patty?" Joann asked. "There's not enough for a canning, so I'll let you have them."

"No, this bunch won't eat any beans but jelly beans." Patty turned to Cody, who was peering under the hood of her car. "I told all the girls at work about your album, Cody. We can't wait to hear it. What's on it?"

"It's a surprise," he said, looking up. "They swore I'd have it by Christmas. The assistant manager of the studio said he thought it was going to be big. He told that to the Oak Ridge Boys and he was right."

"Wow," said Patty.

When Cody patted the pinch of snuff under his lip, she said, "I think snuff's kind of sexy."

Joann hauled the baby out of the car seat and bounced him playfully on her shoulder. "Who's precious?" she asked the baby.

In the van on the way to Nashville that Friday, they sang gospel songs, changing the words crazily. "Swing Low, Sweet Chariot" became "Sweet 'n Low, Mr. Coffee pot, perking for to hurry my heart." Cody drove, and Joann sat in the back, where she could manage the food. She passed out beer and the sandwiches she had made before work that morning. She had been looking forward to the weekend, hoping to talk things over with Debbie.

Will Ed sat in the back with Joann, complaining about his wife, who was taking an interior-decorating course by correspondence. "She could come with us, but instead she wants to stay home and rearrange the furniture. I'm afraid to go home in the dark. I don't know where to walk." He added with a laugh, "And I don't know *who* I might stumble over."

"Joyce wouldn't cheat on you," said Joann.

"What do you think all these songs we sing are about?" he asked.

At that moment, Cody was humming "Pop a Top," a song about a wandering wife. He reached back for another beer, and Joann pulled the tab off for him. Cody set the can between his legs and said, "Poor Joann here's afraid we're going to get corrupted. She thinks I ought to be home spreading manure and milking cows."

"Don't 'poor Joann' me. I can take care of myself."

Cody laughed. "If men weren't tied down by women, what do you reckon they'd do with themselves? If they didn't have kids, a house, installments to pay?"

"Men want to marry and have a home just as much as women do, or they wouldn't do it," Joann said.

"Tell him, Joann," said L.J.

"Listen to this," said Will Ed. "I asked Joyce what was for supper? And she says, *I'm* having a hamburger. What are *you* going to have?' I mean you can't say a word now without 'em jumping on you."

"Y'all shut up," said Joann. "Let's sing another song. Let's sing 'The Old Rugged Cross.' "

"The old rugged cross" turned into "an old Chevrolet," a forlorn image, it seemed to Joann, like something of quality lost in the past. She imagined a handsome 1957 Chevrolet, its fins slashed by silver arrows, standing splendidly on top of a mountain.

"This is better than showing up at the plant with a lunch box!" Cody cried. "Ain't it, boys?" He blasted the horn twice at the empty highway and broke into joyous song.

At the Bluebird, Joann drank the Tequila Sunrise Debbie brought her. The drink was pretty, with an orange slice—a rising sun—on the rim of the glass. Between customers, Debbie sat with Joann and they talked about life. Debbie knew a lot about human nature, though Joann wasn't sure Debbie was right about Cody being a man who suffered. "If he's suffering, it's because I'm bringing in the paycheck," she said. "But instead of looking for work, he's singing songs."

"He's going through the change," Debbie said. "Men go through it, too. He's afraid he's missed out on life. I've seen a lot of guys like that."

"I don't understand what's happening to people, the way they can't hold together anymore," Joann said. "My daughter's divorced, and I think it's just now hitting me that I got divorced too. In my first marriage, I got shafted—eighteen years with a man, working my fingers to the bone, raising three kids—but I didn't make a federal case out of it. I was lucky Cody came along. Cody says don't live with regret, but it's awful hard to look forward when there's so little you can depend on."

Debbie jumped up to get a draft beer for a man who signaled her. When she returned, she suddenly confessed to Joann, "I had my tubes tied—but I was such an idiot! And now I've met this new guy, and he doesn't know. I think I'm serious about him, but I haven't got the heart to tell him what I did."

"When did you have it done?" Joann cried, horrified.

"Last spring." She lit a cigarette and exhaled smoke furiously. "You know why I got my tubes tied? Because I hate to be categorized. My ex-husband thought I had to have supper on the table at six on the dot, when he came home. I was working too, and I got home about five-thirty. I had to do all the shopping and cleaning and cooking. I hate it when people *assume* things like that—that I'm the one to make supper because I've got reproductive organs."

"I never thought of it that way exactly."

"I was going to add kids to those responsibilities? Like hell." Debbie punched holes in a cocktail napkin with her ballpoint pen. The napkin had jokes printed on it, and she punched out the jokes. "It's the little things," she said. "I don't care about equal pay as much as I care about people judging me by the way I keep house. It's nobody's damn business how I keep house."

Joann had never heard of anything like what Debbie had done. She hadn't known a woman would go that far to make a point to a man. Later, Debbie said, "You don't know what problems are till you go through tubal litigation." Joann had a feeling that that was the wrong term, but she didn't want to mention it.

"I hate to see you so upset," Joann said. "What can I do?"

"Tell them to stop playing those lovesick songs. All these country songs are so stupid. They tell you to stand by your man, but then they say he's just going to use you somehow."

Joann thought she understood how Debbie felt about telling her new boyfriend what she had done. It seemed like a dreadful secret. Debbie had had her tubes tied rather than tell her husband in plain English to treat her better. The country songs were open and confessional, but in reality people kept things to themselves. The songs were an invasion of privacy. Debbie must have felt something like that about her housekeeping and her husband's demands. Debbie should have sung a song about it, instead of getting herself butchered, Joann thought. But maybe Debbie couldn't sing. Joann was getting drunk.

The next afternoon, at the motel, Cody said to Joann, "They want us to play five nights a week at the bar. They've guaranteed me six months." He was smiling and slamming things around happily. He had just brought in some Cokes and Big Macs. "Will Ed and L.J. have to stay home and work, but I can get some backup men from here, easy. We could get a little apartment down here and put the house up for sale."

"I don't want to sell Daddy's place." Joann's stomach was churning.

"Well, we ain't doing nothing with it."

"They say they're going to hire again at the plant in the spring," Joann said.

"To hell with the plant. I gave 'em nineteen years and six months of my life and they cut me off without a pension. Screw *them.*"

Joann placed the Big Macs and Cokes on a tray. She and Cody sat on one of the two beds to eat. She nibbled at her hamburger. "You're telling me to quit my job," she said.

"You could find something in Nashville."

"And be a cocktail waitress like Debbie? No, thanks. That's a rough life. I like my job and I'm lucky to have it."

On TV, a preacher was blabbing about reservations for heaven. Cody got up and flipped the dial, testing all the channels. "Just look how many TV channels we could get if we lived down here," he said.

"Don't do it, Joann," Debbie said flatly that evening.

"Cody and I haven't been together that long," Joann said. "Sometimes I feel I don't even know him. We're still in that stage where I ought to be giving him encouragement, the way you should do when you're starting out with somebody." She added, sarcastically, "Stand by your man."

"We're always caught in one cliché or another," Debbie said. "But you've got to think about yourself, Joann."

"I should give him more of a chance. He's got his heart set on this, and I'm being so contrary."

"But look what he's asking you to do, girl! Look what-all you've worked for. You've got your daddy's homeplace and that good job. You don't want to lose all that."

"We wouldn't come out ahead, after we pay off the mortgage. Maybe he wants to move to Nashville because there's ninety-nine TV stations to choose from. Well, the cable's coming down our road next year, and we'll have ten channels. That's enough television for anybody. They're bidding on the franchise now."

"I never watch television," Debbie said. "I can't stand watching stuff that's straight out of my own life."

At home, Cody was restless, full of nervous energy. He repaired some fences, as if getting the place ready to sell, but Joann hadn't agreed to anything. In the den one evening, after "Dynasty" had ended, Cody turned the sound down and said, "Let's talk, Jo." She waited while he opened a beer. He had been drinking beer after beer, methodically. "I've been thinking a lot about the way things are going, and I feel bad about how I used to treat my first wife, Charlene. I'm afraid I'm doing you the same way."

"You don't treat me bad," Joann said.

"I've taken advantage of you, letting you pay all the bills. I know I should get a job, but damn it, there's got to be more to life than punching a time clock. I think I always expected a lot more out of life than most people. I used to be a real hell-raiser. I thought I could get away with anything because people always gave me things. All my life, people gave me things."

"What things?" Joann was sitting on the couch, and Cody was in the easy chair. The only light came from the television.

"In grade school, I'd get more valentines than anybody, and the valentines would have candy in them, little hearts with messages like 'Be Mine' and 'Cutie' and things like that. When I graduated from high school, all the storekeepers in town gave me stuff and took me in their back rooms and gave me whiskey. I had my first drink in the pharmacy in the back of the Rexall. I just breezed through life, letting people give me things, and it didn't dawn on me for a long time that people wanted something back. They expected something from me and I never gave it to them. I didn't live up to their expectations. Somehow, I want to give something back."

"People always admired you, Cody. You're so good-natured. Isn't that giving something?"

Cody belched loudly and laughed. "When I was about twelve, a man gave me five dollars to jack him off in the alley behind the old A and P."

"Did you do it?"

"Yep. And I didn't think a thing about it. I just did it. Five bucks was five bucks."

"Well, what do you owe *him*?" Joann said sharply.

"Nothing, I reckon, but the point is, I did a lot of stuff that wasn't right. Charlene was always thumping the Bible and hauling me off to church. I couldn't live with that. I treated her like dirt, the way I cheated on her. I always wanted what was free and available. It was what I was used to. I had a chance once, about fifteen years ago, to play in a little bar in Nashville, but the kids were little, and Charlene didn't want me to go. I've regretted that to this day. Don't you see why this chance means so much to me? I'm trying to *give* something of myself, instead of always taking. Just go along with me, Joann. Take this one risk with me."

"What can I say when you put it that way?"

"A person has to follow his dream."

"That sounds like some Elvis song," she said, sounding unexpectedly sarcastic. She was thinking of Elvis's last few years, when he got fat and corrupted. She rearranged some pillows on the couch. The weather news was on TV. The radar was showing rain in their area. Slowly, her eyes on the flashing lines of the radar map, she said, "What you want to do is be in the spotlight so people can adore you. That's the same thing as taking what's free."

"That's not true. Maybe you think it's easy to be in the spotlight. But it's not. Look what happened to Elvis."

"You're not Elvis. And selling the place is too extreme. Things can't be all one way or the other. There has to be some of both. That's what life is, when it's any good." Joann felt drained, as though she had just had to figure out all of life, like doing a complicated math problem in her head.

Cody turned the TV off, and the light vanished. In the dark, he said, "I cheated on Charlene, but I never cheated on you."

"I never said you did."

"But you expect it," he said.

Patty came over to ask Joann to keep the kids that weekend. She had a new boyfriend, who was taking her to St. Louis.

"If I can take 'em to Nashville," Joann told Patty. "I have to go along to keep the girls away from Cody." She looked meaningfully at Cody.

It was meant to be a casual, teasing remark, she thought, but it didn't come out that way. Cody glared at her, looking hurt.

"The kids will be in the way," he said. "You can't take them to the Bluebird Lounge."

"We'll stay in the motel room," Joann said. "I wanted to watch *On Golden Pond* on HBO anyway. Nashville has so much more to offer. Remember?"

She realized that taking the children to Nashville was a bad idea, but she felt she had to go with Cody. She didn't know what might happen. She hoped that having the kids along would make her and Cody feel they had a family to be responsible for. Besides, Patty was neglecting the kids. Joann had kept them three nights in a row last week while Patty went out with her new boyfriend.

In the van on the way down, Rodney cried because he was teething, and L.J. gave him a piece of rawhide to chew on. Kristi played with a bucket of plastic toys. Will Ed practiced the middle eight of a new song they had learned. It seemed pointless to Joann, since Cody planned to dump Will Ed and L.J. from his act. Will Ed played the passage over and over on his guitar, until Kristi screamed, "Shut up!" Cody said little. L.J. was driving, because Joann didn't want Cody to drive and drink beer, with the children along.

Daylight saving time had ended, and the dark came early. The bright lights at the edge of Nashville reminded Joann of how soon Christmas was.

She liked being alone in the motel room with the kids. It made her think of when she'd had small children and her first husband had worked a night shift. She had always tried to be quiet around sleeping children, but nowadays children had more tolerance for noise. The TV didn't bother them. She sat in bed, propped against pillows. The children were asleep. In the large mirror facing the bed, she could see herself, watching TV, with the sleeping bundles beside her. Joann felt expectant, as if some easy answers were waiting for her—from the movie, from the innocence of the children.

Suddenly Kristi sat straight up and shouted, "Where's Mommy?"

"Hush, Kristi! Mommy's gone to St. Louis. We'll see her Sunday."

Kristi hurled herself out of bed and ran around the room. She looked in the closet and in the bathroom. Then she began to shriek. Joann grabbed her and whispered, "Shush, you'll wake up your little brother!"

Kristi wiggled away from her and looked under the bed, but the bed was boxed in—a brilliant construction, Joann thought, so far as cleaning was concerned. Kristi bumped into a chair and fell down. She began bawling. Rodney stirred, and then he started to cry. Joann huddled both children in the center of the bed and began singing to them. She couldn't think of anything to sing except the Kitty Wells song about honky-tonk angels. The song was an absurd one to sing to kids, but she sang it anyway. It was her life. She sang it like an innocent bystander, angry that that was the way women were, that they looked on approvingly while some men went out and either did something big or made a fool of himself trying.

When Cody came in later, she had fallen asleep with the children. She woke up and glanced at the travel alarm. It was three. The TV was still on. Cody was missing the Burt Reynolds movie he had wanted to watch. He stumbled into the bathroom and then fell into the other bed with all his clothes on.

"I was rehearsing with those new guys," he said. "And then we went out to eat something." Joann heard his boots fall to the floor, and he said, "I called home around ten-thirty, between shows, to wish Mama a happy birthday, and she told me Daddy's in the Memphis hospital."

"Oh, what's wrong?" Joann sat up and pulled her pillow behind her. Cody's father, who was almost seventy-five, had always bragged about never being sick.

"It's cancer. He had some tests done. They never told me anything." Cody flung his shirt to the foot of the bed. "Lung cancer comes on sudden. They're going to operate next week."

"I was *so* afraid of that," Joann said. "The way he smoked."

Cody turned to face her across the aisle between the two beds. He reached over and searched for her hand. "I'll have to go to Memphis tomorrow night after the show. Mama's going down tomorrow."

Rodney squirmed beside Joann, and she pulled the covers around his shoulders. Then she crept into bed with Cody and lay close to him while he went on talking in a tone of disbelief about his father. "It makes me mad that I forgot it was Mama's birthday. I thought of it during the first show, when I was singing 'Blue Eyes Crying in the Rain.' I don't know how come me to think of it then."

"Do you want me to go to Memphis with you?"

"No. That's all right. You have to get the kids home. I'll take the bus and then come back here for the show Tuesday." Cody drew her near him. "Were you going to come back here with me?"

"I've been thinking about that. I don't want to quit my job or sell Daddy's place. That would be crazy."

"Sometimes it's good to act a little crazy."

"No. We have to reason things out, so we don't ruin anything between us." She was half-whispering, trying not to wake the children, and her voice trembled as though she were having a chill. "I think you should come down here by yourself first and see how it works out."

"What if my album's a big hit and we make a million dollars?" His eyes were on the TV. Burt Reynolds was speeding down an interstate.

"That would be different."

"Would you move to Nashville if I got on the 'Grand Ole Opry'?"

"Yes."

"Is that a promise?"

"Yes."

On Monday, Cody was still in Memphis. The operation was the next day, and Joann took off from work early in order to go down to be with Cody and his parents. She was ready to leave the house when the delivery truck brought the shipment of record albums. The driver brought two boxes, marked "1 of 3" and "2 of 3."

"I'll bring the third box tomorrow," the driver said. "We're not allowed to bring three at once."

"Why's that?" Joann asked, shivering in the open doorway to the porch.

"They want to keep us moving."

"Well, I don't understand that one bit."

Joann shoved the boxes across the threshold and closed the door. With a butcher knife, she ripped open one of the boxes and slipped out a record album. On the cover was a photograph of Cody and Will Ed and L.J. and Jimmy, sitting on a bench. Above them, the title of the album was a red-and-blue neon sign: "HUNKTOWN." Cody and his friends were all wearing Hunktown T-shirts, cowboy boots, and cowboy hats. They had a casual, slouchy look, like the group called Alabama. It was a terrible picture. Looking at her husband, Joann thought no one would say he was really handsome. She held the cover up to the glass door to get a better light on his face. He looked old. His expression seemed serious and unforgiving, as though he expected the world to be ready for him, as though this were his revenge, not his gift. That face was now on a thousand albums.

But the picture was not really Cody at all, she thought. It was only his wild side, not the part she loved. Seeing it was something like identifying a dead body: it was so unfamiliar that death was somehow acceptable. She had to laugh. Cody had meant the album to be a surprise, but he would be surprised to see how he looked.

Joann heard a noise outside. She touched her nose to the door glass and left a smudge. On the porch, the impatiens in a hanging basket had died in the recent freeze. She had forgotten to bring the plant inside. Now she watched it sway and twist in a little whirl of wind.

1989

Bharati Mukherjee
(1940–   )

Born in Calcutta, Mukherjee spent time as a child with her family in London and in Basel, Switzerland, before returning to India to receive her B.A. and M.A. from Indian universities. Coming to the United States, she received an M.F.A. from the Writers' Workshop at the University of Iowa, and met and married Clark Blaise, a novelist. In the 1960s the couple settled in Montreal and Toronto, where she completed her Iowa Ph.D. work. In 1980 they returned to the United States, where she has taught at Iowa, Skidmore, Queens College in New York City, and the University of California at Berkeley.

Questions of identity and examinations of cultures in transition inform the work of both Mukherjee and her husband (born in North Dakota, of French-Canadian descent), including their collaborative *Days and Nights in Calcutta* (1977), an account of a visit to the city of her birth. Mukherjee's writing, especially, is focused on the problems of Indian women suspended between two rapidly changing ways of life. Novels include *The Tiger's Daughter* (1972), in which an Indian woman educated in the United States goes home; *Wife* (1975), about a woman who comes from India to an arranged marriage in New York; and *Jasmine* (1989), with the woman experiencing both an Indian marriage and an American one. Stories are collected in *Darkness* (1985) and *The Middleman and Other Stories* (1989), the source of the selection below. She is also the author of *The Sorrow and the Terror: The Haunting Legacy of the Air India Tragedy* (1987).

The Management of Grief

A woman I don't know is boiling tea the Indian way in my kitchen. There are a lot of women I don't know in my kitchen, whispering, and moving tactfully. They open doors, rummage through the pantry, and try not to ask me where things are kept. They remind me of when my sons were small, on Mother's Day or when Vikram and I were tired, and they would make big, sloppy omelets. I would lie in bed pretending I didn't hear them.

Dr. Sharma, the treasurer of the Indo-Canada Society, pulls me into the hallway. He wants to know if I am worried about money. His wife, who has just come up from the basement with a tray of empty cups and glasses, scolds him. "Don't bother Mrs. Bhave with mundane details." She looks so monstrously pregnant her baby must be days overdue. I tell her she shouldn't be carrying heavy things. "Shaila," she says, smiling, "this is the fifth." Then she grabs a teenager by his shirttails. He slips his Walkman off his head. He has to be one of her four children, they have the same doomed and dented foreheads. "What's the official word now?" she demands. The boy slips the headphones back on. "They're acting evasive, Ma. They're saying it could be an accident or a terrorist bomb."

All morning, the boys have been muttering, Sikh Bomb, Sikh Bomb. The men, not using the word, bow their heads in agreement. Mrs. Sharma touches her forehead at such a word. At least they've stopped talking about space debris and Russian lasers.

Two radios are going in the dining room. They are tuned to different stations. Someone must have brought the radios down from my boys' bedrooms. I haven't gone into their rooms since Kusum came running across the front lawn in her bathrobe. She looked so funny, I was laughing when I opened the door.

The big TV in the den is being whizzed through American networks and cable channels. "Damn!" some man swears bitterly. "How can these preachers carry on like nothing's happened?" I want to tell him we're not that important. You look at the audience, and at the preacher in his blue robe with his beautiful white hair, the potted palm trees under a blue sky, and you know they care about nothing.

The phone rings and rings. Dr. Sharma's taken charge. "We're with her," he keeps saying. "Yes, yes, the doctor has given calming pills. Yes, yes, pills are having necessary effect." I wonder if pills alone explain this calm. Not peace, just a deadening quiet. I was always controlled, but never repressed. Sound can reach me, but my body is tensed, ready to scream. I hear their voices all around me. I hear my boys and Vikram cry, "Mommy, Shaila!" and their screams insulate me, like headphones.

The woman boiling water tells her story again and again. "I got the news first. My cousin called from Halifax before six A.M., can you imagine? He'd gotten up for prayers and his son was studying for medical exams and he heard on a rock channel that something had happened to a plane. They said first it had disappeared from the radar, like a giant eraser just reached out. His father called me, so I said to him, what do you mean, 'something bad'? You mean a hijacking? And he said, *behn*, there is no confirmation of anything yet, but check with your neighbors because a lot of them must be on that plane. So I called poor Kusum straightaway. I knew Kusum's husband and daughter were booked to go yesterday."

Kusum lives across the street from me. She and Satish had moved in less than a month ago. They said they needed a bigger place. All these people, the Sharmas and friends from the Indo-Canada Society had been there for the housewarming. Satish and Kusum made home-made tandoori on their big gas grill and even the white neighbors piled their plates high with that luridly red, charred, juicy chicken. Their younger daughter had danced, and even our boys had broken away from the Stanley Cup telecast to put in a reluctant appearance. Everyone took pictures for their albums and for the community newspapers—another of our families had made it big in Toronto—and now I wonder how many of those happy faces are gone. "Why does God give us so much if all along He intends to take it away?" Kusum asks me.

I nod. We sit on carpeted stairs, holding hands like children. "I never once told him that I loved him," I say. I was too much the well brought up woman. I was so well brought up I never felt comfortable calling my husband by his first name.

"It's all right," Kusum says. "He knew. My husband knew. They felt it. Modern young girls have to say it because what they feel is fake."

Kusum's daughter, Pam, runs in with an overnight case. Pam's in her McDonald's uniform. "Mummy! You have to get dressed!" Panic makes her cranky. "A reporter's on his way here."

"Why?"

"You want to talk to him in your bathrobe?" She starts to brush her mother's long hair. She's the daughter who's always in trouble. She dates Canadian boys and hangs out in the mall, shopping for tight sweaters. The younger one, the goody-goody one according to Pam, the one with a voice so sweet that when she sang *bhajans¹* for Ethiopian relief even a frugal man like my husband wrote out a hundred dollar check, *she* was on that plane. *She* was going to spend July and August with grandparents because Pam wouldn't go. Pam said she'd rather waitress at McDonald's. "If it's a choice between Bombay and Wonderland, I'm picking Wonderland," she'd said.

"Leave me alone," Kusum yells. "You know what I want to do? If I didn't have to look after you now, I'd hang myself."

Pam's young face goes blotchy with pain. "Thanks," she says, "don't let me stop you."

"Hush," pregnant Mrs. Sharma scolds Pam. "Leave your mother alone. Mr. Sharma will tackle the reporters and fill out the forms. He'll say what has to be said."

Pam stands her ground. "You think I don't know what Mummy's thinking? *Why ever?* that's what. That's sick! Mummy wishes my little sister were alive and I were dead."

Kusum's hand in mine is trembly hot. We continue to sit on the stairs.

She calls before she arrives, wondering if there's anything I need. Her name is Judith Templeton and she's an appointee of the provincial government. "Multiculturalism?" I ask, and she says, "partially," but that her mandate is bigger. "I've been told you knew many of the people on the flight," she says. "Perhaps if you'd agree to help us reach the others . . . ?"

She gives me time at least to put on tea water and pick up the mess in the front room. I have a few *samosas* from Kusum's housewarming that I could fry up, but then I think, why prolong this visit?

Judith Templeton is much younger than she sounded. She wears a blue suit with a white blouse and a polka dot tie. Her blond hair is cut short, her only jewelry is pearl drop earrings. Her briefcase is new and expensive looking, a gleaming cordovan leather. She sits with it across her lap. When she looks out the front windows onto the street, her contact lenses seem to float in front of her light blue eyes.

"What sort of help do you want from me?" I ask. She has refused the tea, out of politeness, but I insist, along with some slightly stale biscuits.

"I have no experience," she admits. "That is, I have an MSW and I've worked in liaison with accident victims, but I mean I have no experience with a tragedy of this scale—"

"Who could?" I ask.

"—and with the complications of culture, language, and customs. Someone mentioned that Mrs. Bhave is a pillar—because you've taken it more calmly."

At this, perhaps, I frown, for she reaches forward, almost to take my hand. "I hope you understand my meaning, Mrs. Bhave. There are hundreds of people in Metro directly affected, like you, and some of them speak no English. There are some widows who've never handled money or gone on a bus, and there are old parents who still haven't eaten or gone outside their bedrooms. Some houses and apartments have been looted. Some wives are still hysterical. Some husbands are in shock and profound depression. We want to help, but our

---

1. Religious songs.

hands are tied in so many ways. We have to distribute money to some people, and there are legal documents—these things can be done. We have interpreters, but we don't always have the human touch, or maybe the right human touch. We don't want to make mistakes, Mrs. Bhave, and that's why we'd like to ask you to help us."

"More mistakes, you mean," I say.

"Police matters are not in my hands," she answers.

"Nothing I can do will make any difference," I say. "We must all grieve in our own way."

"But you are coping very well. All the people said, Mrs. Bhave is the strongest person of all. Perhaps if the others could see you, talk with you, it would help them."

"By the standards of the people you call hysterical, I am behaving very oddly and very badly, Miss Templeton." I want to say to her, *I wish I could scream, starve, walk into Lake Ontario, jump from a bridge.* "They would not see me as a model. I do not see myself as a model."

I am a freak. No one who has ever known me would think of me reacting this way. This terrible calm will not go away.

She asks me if she may call again, after I get back from a long trip that we all must make. "Of course," I say. "Feel free to call, anytime."

Four days later, I find Kusum squatting on a rock overlooking a bay in Ireland. It isn't a big rock, but it juts sharply out over water. This is as close as we'll ever get to them. June breezes balloon out her sari and unpin her knee-length hair. She has the bewildered look of a sea creature whom the tides have stranded.

It's been one hundred hours since Kusum came stumbling and screaming across my lawn. Waiting around the hospital, we've heard many stories. The police, the diplomats, they tell us things thinking that we're strong, that knowledge is helpful to the grieving, and maybe it is. Some, I know, prefer ignorance, or their own versions. The plane broke into two, they say. Unconsciousness was instantaneous. No one suffered. My boys must have just finished their breakfasts. They loved eating on planes, they loved the smallness of plates, knives, and forks. Last year they saved the airline salt and pepper shakers. Half an hour more and they would have made it to Heathrow.

Kusum says that we can't escape our fate. She says that all those people—our husbands, my boys, her girl with the nightingale voice, all those Hindus, Christians, Sikhs, Muslims, Parsis, and atheists on that plane—were fated to die together off this beautiful bay. She learned this from a swami in Toronto.

I have my Valium.

Six of us "relatives"—two widows and four widowers—choose to spend the day today by the waters instead of sitting in a hospital room and scanning photographs of the dead. That's what they call us now: relatives. I've looked through twenty-seven photos in two days. They're very kind to us, the Irish are very understanding. Sometimes understanding means freeing a tourist bus for this trip to the bay, so we can pretend to spy our loved ones through the glassiness of waves or in sunspeckled cloud shapes.

I could die here, too, and be content.

"What is that, out there?" She's standing and flapping her hands and for a moment I see a head shape bobbing in the waves. She's standing in the water, I, on the boulder. The tide is low, and a round, black, head-sized rock has just risen from the waves. She returns, her sari end dripping and ruined and her face is a twisted remnant of hope, the way mine was a hundred hours ago, still laughing but inwardly knowing that nothing but the ultimate tragedy could bring two women together at six o'clock on a Sunday morning. I watch her face sag into blankness.

"That water felt warm, Shaila," she says at length.

"You can't," I say. "We have to wait for our turn to come."

I haven't eaten in four days, haven't brushed my teeth.

"I know," she says. "I tell myself I have no right to grieve. They are in a better place than we are. My swami says I should be thrilled for them. My swami says depression is a sign of our selfishness."

Maybe I'm selfish. Selfishly I break away from Kusum and run, sandals slapping against stones, to the water's edge. What if my boys aren't lying pinned under the debris? What if they aren't stuck a mile below that innocent blue chop? What if, given the strong currents. . . .

Now I've ruined my sari, one of my best. Kusum has joined me, knee-deep in water that feels to me like a swimming pool. I could settle in the water, and my husband would take my hand and the boys would slap water in my face just to see me scream.

"Do you remember what good swimmers my boys were, Kusum?"

"I saw the medals," she says.

One of the widowers, Dr. Ranganathan from Montreal, walks out to us, carrying his shoes in one hand. He's an electrical engineer. Someone at the hotel mentioned his work is famous around the world, something about the place where physics and electricity come together. He has lost a huge family, something indescribable. "With some luck," Dr. Ranganathan suggests to me, "a good swimmer could make it safely to some island. It is quite possible that there may be many, many microscopic islets scattered around."

"You're not just saying that?" I tell Dr. Ranganathan about Vinod, my elder son. Last year he took diving as well.

"It's a parent's duty to hope," he says. "It is foolish to rule out possibilities that have not been tested. I myself have not surrendered hope."

Kusum is sobbing once again. "Dear lady," he says, laying his free hand on her arm, and she calms down.

"Vinod is how old?" he asks me. He's very careful, as we all are. *Is*, not was.

"Fourteen. Yesterday he was fourteen. His father and uncle were going to take him down to the Taj and give him a big birthday party. I couldn't go with them because I couldn't get two weeks off from my stupid job in June." I process bills for a travel agent. June is a big travel month.

Dr. Ranganathan whips the pockets of his suit jacket inside out. Squashed roses, in darkening shades of pink, float on the water. He tore the roses off creepers in somebody's garden. He didn't ask anyone if he could pluck the roses, but now there's been an article about it in the local papers. When you see an Indian person, it says, please give him or her flowers.

"A strong youth of fourteen," he says, "can very likely pull to safety a younger one."

My sons, though four years apart, were very close. Vinod wouldn't let Mithun drown. *Electrical engineering,* I think, foolishly perhaps: this man knows important secrets of the universe, things closed to me. Relief spins me lightheaded. No wonder my boys' photographs haven't turned up in the gallery of photos of the recovered dead. "Such pretty roses," I say.

"My wife loved pink roses. Every Friday I had to bring a bunch home. I used to say, why? After twenty odd years of marriage you're still needing proof positive of my love?" He has identified his wife and three of his children. Then others from Montreal, the lucky ones, intact families with no survivors. He chuckles as he wades back to shore. Then he swings around to ask me a question. "Mrs. Bhave, you are wanting to throw in some roses for your loved ones? I have two big ones left."

But I have other things to float: Vinod's pocket calculator; a half-painted model B-52 for my Mithun. They'd want them on their island. And for my husband? For him I let fall into the calm, glassy waters a poem I wrote in the hospital yesterday. Finally he'll know my feelings for him.

"Don't tumble, the rocks are slippery," Dr. Ranganathan cautions. He holds out a hand for me to grab.

Then it's time to get back on the bus, time to rush back to our waiting posts on hospital benches.

Kusum is one of the lucky ones. The lucky ones flew here, identified in multiplicate their loved ones, then will fly to India with the bodies for proper ceremonies. Satish is one of the few males who surfaced. The photos of faces we saw on the walls in an office at Heathrow and here in the hospital are mostly of women. Women have more body fat, a nun said to me matter-of-factly. They float better.

Today I was stopped by a young sailor on the street. He had loaded bodies, he'd gone into the water when—he checks my face for signs of strength—when the sharks were first spotted. I don't blush, and he breaks down. "It's all right," I say. "Thank you." I had heard about the sharks from Dr. Ranganathan. In his orderly mind, science brings understanding, it holds no terror. It is the shark's duty. For every deer there is a hunter, for every fish a fisherman.

The Irish are not shy; they rush to me and give me hugs and some are crying. I cannot imagine reactions like that on the streets of Toronto. Just strangers, and I am touched. Some carry flowers with them and give them to any Indian they see.

After lunch, a policeman I have gotten to know quite well catches hold of me. He says he thinks he has a match for Vinod. I explain what a good swimmer Vinod is.

"You want me with you when you look at photos?" Dr. Ranganathan walks ahead of me into the picture gallery. In these matters, he is a scientist, and I am grateful. It is a new perspective. "They have performed miracles," he says. "We are indebted to them."

The first day or two the policemen showed us relatives only one picture at a time; now they're in a hurry, they're eager to lay out the possibles, and even the probables.

The face on the photo is of a boy much like Vinod; the same intelligent eyes, the same thick brows dipping into a V. But this boy's features, even his cheeks, are puffier, wider, mushier.

"No." My gaze is pulled by other pictures. There are five other boys who look like Vinod.

The nun assigned to console me rubs the first picture with a fingertip. "When they've been in the water for a while, love, they look a little heavier." The bones under the skin are broken, they said on the first day—try to adjust your memories. It's important.

"It's not him. I'm his mother. I'd know."

"I know this one!" Dr. Ranganathan cries out suddenly from the back of the gallery. "And this one!" I think he senses that I don't want to find my boys. "They are the Kutty brothers. They were also from Montreal." I don't mean to be crying. On the contrary, I am ecstatic. My suitcase in the hotel is packed heavy with dry clothes for my boys.

The policeman starts to cry. "I am so sorry, I am so sorry, ma'am. I really thought we had a match."

With the nun ahead of us and the policeman behind, we, the unlucky ones without our children's bodies, file out of the makeshift gallery.

From Ireland most of us go on to India. Kusum and I take the same direct flight to Bombay, so I can help her clear customs quickly. But we have to argue with a man in uniform. He has large boils on his face. The boils swell and glow with sweat as we argue with him. He wants Kusum to wait in line and he refuses to take authority because his boss is on a tea break. But Kusum won't let her coffins out of sight, and I shan't desert her though I know that my parents, elderly and diabetic, must be waiting in a stuffy car in a scorching lot.

"You bastard!" I scream at the man with the popping boils. Other passengers press closer. "You think we're smuggling contraband in those coffins!"

Once upon a time we were well brought up women; we were dutiful wives who kept our heads veiled, our voices shy and sweet.

In India, I become, once again, an only child of rich, ailing parents. Old friends of the family come to pay their respects. Some are Sikh, and inwardly, involuntarily, I cringe. My parents are progressive people; they do not blame communities for a few individuals.

In Canada it is a different story now.

"Stay longer," my mother pleads. "Canada is a cold place. Why would you want to be all by yourself?" I stay.

Three months pass. Then another.

"Vikram wouldn't have wanted you to give up things!" they protest. They call my husband by the name he was born with. In Toronto he'd changed to Vik so the men he worked with at his office would find his name as easy as Rod or Chris. "You know, the dead aren't cut off from us!"

My grandmother, the spoiled daughter of a rich *zamindar*,[2] shaved her head with rusty razor blades when she was widowed at sixteen. My grandfather died of childhood diabetes when he was nineteen, and she saw herself as the harbinger of bad luck. My mother grew up without parents, raised indifferently by an uncle, while her true mother slept in a hut behind the main estate house and took her food with the servants. She grew up a rationalist. My parents abhor mindless mortification.

The zamindar's daughter kept stubborn faith in Vedic rituals; my parents rebelled. I am trapped between two modes of knowledge. At thirty-six, I am too old to start over and too young to give up. Like my husband's spirit, I flutter between worlds.

Courting aphasia, we travel. We travel with our phalanx of servants and poor relatives. To hill stations and to beach resorts. We play contract bridge in dusty gymkhana clubs. We ride stubby ponies up crumbly mountain trails. At tea dances, we let ourselves be twirled twice round the ballroom. We hit the holy spots we hadn't made time for before. In Varanasi, Kalighat, Rishikesh, Hardwar, astrologers and palmists seek me out and for a fee offer me cosmic consolations.

Already the widowers among us are being shown new bride candidates. They cannot resist the call of custom, the authority of their parents and older brothers. They must marry; it is the duty of a man to look after a wife. The new wives will be young widows with children, destitute but of good family. They will make loving wives, but the men will shun them. I've had calls from the men over crackling Indian telephone lines. "Save me," they say, these substantial, educated, successful men of forty. "My parents are arranging a marriage for me." In a month they will have buried one family and returned to Canada with a new bride and partial family.

I am comparatively lucky. No one here thinks of arranging a husband for an unlucky widow.

Then, on the third day of the sixth month into this odyssey, in an abandoned temple in a tiny Himalayan village, as I make my offering of flowers and sweetmeats to the god of a tribe of animists, my husband descends to me. He is squatting next to a scrawny *sadhu*[3] in moth-eaten robes. Vikram wears the vanilla suit he wore the last time I hugged him. The *sadhu* tosses petals on a butter-fed flame, reciting Sanskrit mantras and sweeps his face of flies. My husband takes my hands in his.

You're beautiful, he starts. Then, *What are you doing here?*

Shall I stay? I ask. He only smiles, but already the image is fading. *You must finish alone what we started together.* No seaweed wreathes his mouth. He speaks too fast just as he used to when we were an envied family in our pink split-level. He is gone.

In the windowless altar room, smoky with joss sticks and clarified butter lamps, a sweaty hand gropes for my blouse. I do not shriek. The *sadhu* arranges his robe. The lamps hiss and sputter out.

When we come out of the temple, my mother says, "Did you feel something weird in there?"

My mother has no patience with ghosts, prophetic dreams, holy men, and cults.

---

2. A landholder.   3. Holy man.

"No," I lie. "Nothing."

But she knows that she's lost me. She knows that in days I shall be leaving.

Kusum's put her house up for sale. She wants to live in an ashram in Hardwar. Moving to Hardwar was her swami's idea. Her swami runs two ashrams, the one in Hardwar and another here in Toronto.

"Don't run away," I tell her.

"I'm not running away," she says. "I'm pursuing inner peace. You think you or that Ranganathan fellow are better off?"

Pam's left for California. She wants to do some modelling, she says. She says when she comes into her share of the insurance money she'll open a yoga-cum-aerobics studio in Hollywood. She sends me postcards so naughty I daren't leave them on the coffee table. Her mother has withdrawn from her and the world.

The rest of us don't lose touch, that's the point. Talk is all we have, says Dr. Ranganathan, who has also resisted his relatives and returned to Montreal and to his job, alone. He says, whom better to talk with than other relatives? We've been melted down and recast as a new tribe.

He calls me twice a week from Montreal. Every Wednesday night and every Saturday afternoon. He is changing jobs, going to Ottawa. But Ottawa is over a hundred miles away, and he is forced to drive two hundred and twenty miles a day. He can't bring himself to sell his house. The house is a temple, he says; the king-sized bed in the master bedroom is a shrine. He sleeps on a folding cot. A devotee.

There are still some hysterical relatives. Judith Templeton's list of those needing help and those who've "accepted" is in nearly perfect balance. Acceptance means you speak of your family in the past tense and you make active plans for moving ahead with your life. There are courses at Seneca and Ryerson we could be taking. Her gleaming leather briefcase is full of college catalogues and lists of cultural societies that need our help. She has done impressive work, I tell her.

"In the textbooks on grief management," she replies—I am her confidante, I realize, one of the few whose grief has not sprung bizarre obsessions—"there are stages to pass through: rejection, depression, acceptance, reconstruction." She has compiled a chart and finds that six months after the tragedy, none of us still reject reality, but only a handful are reconstructing. "Depressed Acceptance" is the plateau we've reached. Remarriage is a major step in reconstruction (though she's a little surprised, even shocked, over *how* quickly some of the men have taken on new families). Selling one's house and changing jobs and cities is healthy.

How do I tell Judith Templeton that my family surrounds me, and that like creatures in epics, they've changed shapes? She sees me as calm and accepting but worries that I have no job, no career. My closest friends are worse off than I. I cannot tell her my days, even my nights, are thrilling.

She asks me to help with families she can't reach at all. An elderly couple in Agincourt whose sons were killed just weeks after they had brought their parents over from a village in Punjab. From their names, I know they are Sikh. Judith Templeton and a translator have visited them twice with offers of money for air fare to Ireland, with bank forms, power-of-attorney forms, but they have refused to sign, or to leave their tiny apartment. Their sons' money is frozen in the bank. Their sons' investment apartments have been trashed by tenants, the furnishings sold off. The parents fear that anything they sign or any money they receive will end the company's or the country's obligations to them. They fear they are selling their sons for two airline tickets to a place they've never seen.

The high-rise apartment is a tower of Indians and West Indians, with a sprinkling of Orientals. The nearest bus stop kiosk is lined with women in saris. Boys practice cricket in the parking lot. Inside the building, even I wince a bit from the ferocity of onion fumes, the

1122 ᛭ Bharati Mukherjee

distinctive and immediate Indianness of frying *ghee*,[4] but Judith Templeton maintains a steady flow of information. These poor old people are in imminent danger of losing their place and all their services.

I say to her, "They are Sikh. They will not open up to a Hindu woman." And what I want to add is, as much as I try not to, I stiffen now at the sight of beards and turbans. I remember a time when we all trusted each other in this new country, it was only the new country we worried about.

The two rooms are dark and stuffy. The lights are off, and an oil lamp sputters on the coffee table. The bent old lady has let us in, and her husband is wrapping a white turban over his oiled, hip-length hair. She immediately goes to the kitchen, and I hear the most familiar sound of an Indian home, tap water hitting and filling a teapot.

They have not paid their utility bills, out of fear and the inability to write a check. The telephone is gone; electricity and gas and water are soon to follow. They have told Judith their sons will provide. They are good boys, and they have always earned and looked after their parents.

We converse a bit in Hindi. They do not ask about the crash and I wonder if I should bring it up. If they think I am here merely as a translator, then they may feel insulted. There are thousands of Punjabi-speakers, Sikhs, in Toronto to do a better job. And so I say to the old lady, "I too have lost my sons, and my husband, in the crash."

Her eyes immediately fill with tears. The man mutters a few words which sound like a blessing. "God provides and God takes away," he says.

I want to say, but only men destroy and give back nothing. "My boys and my husband are not coming back," I say. "We have to understand that."

Now the old woman responds. "But who is to say? Man alone does not decide these things." To this her husband adds his agreement.

Judith asks about the bank papers, the release forms. With a stroke of the pen, they will have a provincial trustee to pay their bills, invest their money, send them a monthly pension.

"Do you know this woman?" I ask them.

The man raises his hand from the table, turns it over and seems to regard each finger separately before he answers. "This young lady is always coming here, we make tea for her and she leaves papers for us to sign." His eyes scan a pile of papers in the corner of the room. "Soon we will be out of tea, then will she go away?"

The old lady adds, "I have asked my neighbors and no one else gets *angrezi* visitors. What have we done?"

"It's her job," I try to explain. "The government is worried. Soon you will have no place to stay, no lights, no gas, no water."

"Government will get its money. Tell her not to worry, we are honorable people."

I try to explain the government wishes to give money, not take. He raises his hand. "Let them take," he says. "We are accustomed to that. That is no problem."

"We are strong people," says the wife. "Tell her that."

"Who needs all this machinery?" demands the husband. "It is unhealthy, the bright lights, the cold air on a hot day, the cold food, the four gas rings. God will provide, not government."

"When our boys return," the mother says. Her husband sucks his teeth. "Enough talk," he says.

Judith breaks in. "Have you convinced them?" The snaps on her cordovan briefcase go off like firecrackers in that quiet apartment. She lays the sheaf of legal papers on the coffee table. "If they can't write their names, an X will do—I've told them that."

Now the old lady has shuffled to the kitchen and soon emerges with a pot of tea and two cups. "I think my bladder will go first on a job like this," Judith says to me, smiling. "If only there was some way of reaching them. Please thank her for the tea. Tell her she's very kind."

4. A liquid butter.

I nod in Judith's direction and tell them in Hindi, "She thanks you for the tea. She thinks you are being very hospitable but she doesn't have the slightest idea what it means."

I want to say, humor her. I want to say, my boys and my husband are with me too, more than ever. I look in the old man's eyes and I can read his stubborn, peasant's message: *I have protected this woman as best I can. She is the only person I have left. Give to me or take from me what you will, but I will not sign for it. I will not pretend that I accept.*

In the car, Judith says, "You see what I'm up against? I'm sure they're lovely people, but their stubbornness and ignorance are driving me crazy. They think signing a paper is signing their sons' death warrants, don't they?"

I am looking out the window. I want to say, *In our culture, it is a parent's duty to hope.*

"Now Shaila, this next woman is a real mess. She cries day and night, and she refuses all medical help. We may have to—"

"—Let me out at the subway," I say.

"I beg your pardon?" I can feel those blue eyes staring at me.

It would not be like her to disobey. She merely disapproves, and slows at a corner to let me out. Her voice is plaintive. "Is there anything I said? Anything I did?"

I could answer her suddenly in a dozen ways, but I choose not to. "Shaila? Let's talk about it," I hear, then slam the door.

A wife and mother begins her new life in a new country, and that life is cut short. Yet her husband tells her: Complete what we have started. We, who stayed out of politics and came halfway around the world to avoid religious and political feuding have been the first in the New World to die from it. I no longer know what we started, nor how to complete it. I write letters to the editors of local papers and to members of Parliament. Now at least they admit it was a bomb. One MP answers back, with sympathy, but with a challenge. You want to make a difference? Work on a campaign. Work on mine. Politicize the Indian voter.

My husband's old lawyer helps me set up a trust. Vikram was a saver and a careful investor. He had saved the boys' boarding school and college fees. I sell the pink house at four times what we paid for it and take a small apartment downtown. I am looking for a charity to support.

We are deep in the Toronto winter, gray skies, icy pavements. I stay indoors, watching television. I have tried to assess my situation, how best to live my life, to complete what we began so many years ago. Kusum has written me from Hardwar that her life is now serene. She has seen Satish and has heard her daughter sing again. Kusum was on a pilgrimage, passing through a village when she heard a young girl's voice, singing one of her daughter's favorite *bhajans*. She followed the music through the squalor of a Himalayan village, to a hut where a young girl, an exact replica of her daughter, was fanning coals under the kitchen fire. When she appeared, the girl cried out, "Ma!" and ran away. What did I think of that?

I think I can only envy her.

Pam didn't make it to California, but writes me from Vancouver. She works in a department store, giving make-up hints to Indian and Oriental girls. Dr. Ranganathan has given up his commute, given up his house and job, and accepted an academic position in Texas where no one knows his story and he has vowed not to tell it. He calls me now once a week.

I wait, I listen, and I pray, but Vikram has not returned to me. The voices and the shapes and the nights filled with visions ended abruptly several weeks ago.

I take it as a sign.

One rare, beautiful, sunny day last week, returning from a small errand on Yonge Street, I was walking through the park from the subway to my apartment. I live equidistant from the Ontario Houses of Parliament and the University of Toronto. The day was not cold, but something in the bare trees caught my attention. I looked up from the gravel, into the branches and the clear blue sky beyond. I thought I heard the rustling of larger forms, and I waited a moment for voices. Nothing.

"What?" I asked.

Then as I stood in the path looking north to Queen's Park and west to the university, I heard the voices of my family one last time. *Your time has come,* they said. *Go, be brave.*

I do not know where this voyage I have begun will end. I do not know which direction I will take. I dropped the package on a park bench and started walking.

1989

Louise Glück

(1943–   )

Born in New York City, raised on Long Island, Louise Glück (pronounced *Glick*) studied at Sarah Lawrence College and Columbia University. By her early twenties she was publishing poetry in literary journals, and her first collection, *Firstborn* (1968), showed her already as a skillful poet, with much of her attention focused on painful memories of childhood and adolescence. Her work was brooding, anxious, the poetry of a persona not entirely at home in the world. In her words, "From the first, I wanted to talk about death; also from the first I had an instinctive identification with the abandoned, the widowed, with all figures left behind." A sister who died before she was born left her, she has said, with "the guilty responsibility of the survivor." Anorexic as a teenager, she wrote the experience into poems like "Dedication to Hunger," collected in her third book, *Descending Figure* (1980).

If her poetry seems centered in self,

however, it is abstracted from the particularities of her personal existence in those poems where she seeks the "paradigm" rather than the "circumstantial," work sometimes tinged with myth and archetype. "It was clear to me long ago," she wrote in an essay published in 1985, "that any hope I had of writing real poetry depended on my living through common experiences." Thus, although the titles of her first three books (the second was *The House on Marshland,* 1975) could all be understood as having essentially personal reference, the next two titles allude insistently to elements of our common cultural heritage: *The Triumph of Achilles* (1985) and *Ararat* (1990). In the last named, through an intense focus on one family—mother, father, sisters—she again strives toward the emblematic.

Glück's books to date are named above. A brief appraisal appears in *Dictionary of Literary Biography*, volume 5, *American Poets Since World War II*, 1980.

The School Children

The children go forward with their little satchels.
And all morning the mothers have labored
to gather the late apples, red and gold,
like words of another language.

And on the other shore   5
are those who wait behind great desks
to receive these offerings.

How orderly they are—the nails
on which the children hang
their overcoats of blue or yellow wool.   10

And the teachers shall instruct them in silence
and the mothers shall scour the orchards for a way out,
drawing to themselves the gray limbs of the fruit trees
bearing so little ammunition.

           1975

Dedication to Hunger

I From the Suburbs

They cross the yard
and at the back door
the mother sees with pleasure
how alike they are, father and daughter—
I know something of that time.   5
The little girl purposefully
swinging her arms, laughing
her stark laugh:

It should be kept secret, that sound.
It means she's realized   10
that he never touches her.
She is a child; he could touch her
if he wanted to.

2 Grandmother

"Often I would stand at the window—
your grandfather   15
was a young man then—
waiting, in the early evening."

That is what marriage is,
I watch the tiny figure
changing to a man   20
as he moves toward her,
the last light rings in his hair.
I do not question
their happiness. And he rushes in
with his young man's hunger,   25
so proud to have taught her that:
his kiss would have been
clearly tender—

Of course, of course. Except
it might as well have been   30
his hand over her mouth.

3 Eros

To be male, always
to go to women
and be taken back
into the pierced flesh: 35

      I suppose
memory is stirred.
And the girl child
who wills herself
into her father's arms   40
likewise loved him
second. Nor is she told
what need to express.
There is a look one sees,
the mouth somehow desperate—   45

Because the bond
cannot be proven.

4 The Deviation

It begins quietly
in certain female children:
the fear of death, taking as its form   50
dedication to hunger,
because a woman's body
is a grave; it will accept
anything. I remember
lying in bed at night   55
touching the soft, digressive breasts,
touching, at fifteen,
the interfering flesh
that I would sacrifice
until the limbs were free   60
of blossom and subterfuge: I felt
what I feel now, aligning these words—
it is the same need to perfect,
of which death is the mere byproduct.

5 Sacred Objects

Today in the field I saw   65
the hard, active buds of the dogwood
and wanted, as we say, to capture them,
to make them eternal. That is the premise
of renunciation: the child,
having no self to speak of,   70
comes to life in denial—

I stood apart in that achievement,
in that power to expose

the underlying body, like a god
for whose deed   75
there is no parallel in the natural world.

1980

The Drowned Children

You see, they have no judgment.
So it is natural that they should drown,
first the ice taking them in
and then, all winter, their wool scarves
floating behind them as they sink   5
until at last they are quiet.
And the pond lifts them in its manifold dark arms.

But death must come to them differently,
so close to the beginning.
As though they had always been   10
blind and weightless. Therefore
the rest is dreamed, the lamp,
the good white cloth that covered the table,
their bodies.

And yet they hear the names they used   15
like lures slipping over the pond:
What are you waiting for
come home, come home, lost
in the waters, blue and permanent.

1980

Lamentations

1. The Logos[1]

They were both still,
the woman mournful, the man
branching into her body.

But god was watching.
They felt his gold eye   5
projecting flowers on the landscape.

Who knew what he wanted?
He was god, and a monster.
So they waited. And the world

---

1. "The Word" (Greek), here a reference to John   Word was with God, and the Word was God."
1:1: "In the beginning was the Word, and the

filled with his radiance,   10
as though he wanted to be understood.

Far away, in the void that he had shaped,
he turned to his angels.

2. Nocturne

A forest rose from the earth.
O pitiful, so needing   15
God's furious love—

Together they were beasts.
They lay in the fixed
dusk of his negligence;
from the hills, wolves came, mechanically   20
drawn to their human warmth,
their panic.

Then the angels saw
how He divided them:
the man, the woman, and the woman's body.   25

Above the churned reeds, the leaves let go
a slow moan of silver.

3. The Covenant

Out of fear, they built a dwelling place.
But a child grew between them
as they slept, as they tried   30
to feed themselves.

They set it on a pile of leaves,
the small discarded body
wrapped in the clean skin
of an animal. Against the black sky   35
they saw the massive argument of light.

Sometimes it woke. As it reached its hands
they understood they were the mother and father,
there was no authority above them.

4. The Clearing

Gradually, over many years,   40
the fur disappeared from their bodies
until they stood in the bright light
strange to one another.
Nothing was as before.
Their hands trembled, seeking   45
the familiar.

Nor could they keep their eyes
from the white flesh

on which wounds would show clearly
like words on a page.   50

And from the meaningless browns and greens
at last God arose, His great shadow
darkening the sleeping bodies of His children,
and leapt into heaven.

How beautiful it must have been,   55
the earth, that first time
seen from the air.

1980

Brooding Likeness

I was born in the month of the bull,
the month of heaviness,
or of the lowered, the destructive head,
or of purposeful blindness. So I know, beyond the shadowed
patch of grass, the stubborn one, the one who doesn't look up,   5
still senses the rejected world. It is
a stadium, a well of dust. And you who watch him
looking down in the face of death, what do you know
of commitment? If the bull lives
one controlled act of revenge, be satisfied   10
that in the sky, like you, he is always moving,
not of his own accord but through the black field
like grit caught on a wheel, like shining freight.

1985

Terminal Resemblance

When I saw my father for the last time, we both did the same thing.
He was standing in the doorway to the living room,
waiting for me to get off the telephone.
That he wasn't also pointing to his watch
was a signal he wanted to talk.   5

Talk for us always meant the same thing.
He'd say a few words. I'd say a few back.
That was about it.

It was the end of August, very hot, very humid.
Next door, workmen dumped new gravel on the driveway.   10

My father and I avoided being alone;
we didn't know how to connect, to make small talk—
there didn't seem to be

any other possibilities.
So this was special: when a man's dying,   15
he has a subject.

It must have been early morning. Up and down the street
sprinklers started coming on. The gardener's truck
appeared at the end of the block,
then stopped, parking.   20

My father wanted to tell me what it was like to be dying.
He told me he wasn't suffering.
He said he kept expecting pain, waiting for it, but it never came.
All he felt was a kind of weakness.
I said I was glad for him, that I thought he was lucky.   25

Some of the husbands were getting in their cars, going to work.
Not people we knew anymore. New families,
families with young children.
The wives stood on the steps, gesturing or calling.

We said goodbye in the usual way,   30
no embrace, nothing dramatic.
When the taxi came, my parents watched from the front door,
arm in arm, my mother blowing kisses as she always does,
because it frightens her when a hand isn't being used.
But for a change, my father didn't just stand there.   35
This time, he waved.

That's what I did, at the door to the taxi.
Like him, waved to disguise my hand's trembling.

                                                                    1990

Alice Walker
(1944–   )

The youngest child of sharecroppers Willie Lee and Minnie Grant Walker, Alice Walker was born in Eatonton, Georgia. An accidental shooting with a BB gun at age 8 left her scarred and blinded in one eye. Living "at the end of a long road in a house that was faced by the edge of the world on one side and nobody for miles on the other," experiencing the effects of racial segregation, and feeling set apart by her injury, Walker discovered what she has termed "the gift of loneliness," enabling her to observe keenly the life around her.

She attended Spelman College, a historically black institution, in Atlanta (1961–1963) before enrolling at Sarah Lawrence College, where the poet Muriel Rukeyser recognized her talent and called an editor's attention to her work. By the time she finished her degree in 1965, Walker was determined to become a writer.

First introduced to the civil rights movement as a Spelman student, she moved to Mississippi in 1967 where, along with her husband, attorney Mel Leventhal, she became actively involved in voter registration efforts.

Once (1968), her first book, contains many of the poems written under Rukeyser's tutelage. Other poetry collections include *Revolutionary Petunias and Other Poems* (1973), *Goodnight, Willie Lee, I'll See You in the Morning* (1979), and *Horses Make a Landscape Look More Beautiful* (1984). *The Third Life of Grange Copeland* (1970), her first novel, portrayed three generations of a sharecropper family. *In Love and Trouble,* a collection of short stories, appeared in 1973. The female protagonist of the novel *Meridian* (1976) dedicates her life to serving her rural black neighbors. Walker was awarded a Guggenheim Fellowship for fiction in 1977.

Divorced and bringing up her daughter alone, Walker taught African-American literature and creative writing at several universities and became an editor of *Ms.* magazine. Her enthusiastic introduction to *I Love Myself When I Am Laughing*** :A Zora Neale Hurston Reader* (1979) was crucial to the revival of Hurston's reputation.

The Color Purple (1982), her third novel, established Walker's place as an important writer. It won both the American Book Award and the Pulitzer Prize, enjoyed a long stay on the best-seller lists and was made into a popular movie. Told through letters written by the long-suffering Celie to God and her absent sister, the novel depicts brutality, racism, and poverty in the rural South but concludes on an optimistic feminist note.

Walker's other publications include *Langston Hughes: American Poet* (children's book, 1973), *You Can't Keep a Good Woman Down* (stories, 1981), *In Search of Our Mothers' Gardens: Womanist Prose* (1984), and *The Temple of My Familiar* (novel, 1989). *Alice Walker: An Annotated Bibliography 1968–1986* (1989) was edited by Erma Davis Banks and Keith Byerman.

Everyday Use

for your grandmama

I will wait for her in the yard that Maggie and I made so clean and wavy yesterday afternoon. A yard like this is more comfortable than most people know. It is not just a yard. It is like an extended living room. When the hard clay is swept clean as a floor and the fine sand around the edges lined with tiny, irregular grooves, anyone can come and sit and look up into the elm tree and wait for the breezes that never come inside the house.

Maggie will be nervous until after her sister goes: she will stand hopelessly in corners, homely and ashamed of the burn scars down her arms and legs, eyeing her sister with a mixture of envy and awe. She thinks her sister has held life always in the palm of one hand, that "no" is a word the world never learned to say to her.

You've no doubt seen those TV shows where the child who has "made it" is confronted, as a surprise, by her own mother and father, tottering in weakly from backstage. (A pleasant surprise, of course: What would they do if parent and child came on the show only to curse out and insult each other?) On TV mother and child embrace and smile into each other's faces. Sometimes the mother and father weep, the child wraps them in her arms and leans across the table to tell how she would not have made it without their help. I have seen these programs.

Sometimes I dream a dream in which Dee and I are suddenly brought together on a TV program of this sort. Out of a dark and soft-seated limousine I am ushered into a bright room filled with many people. There I meet a smiling, gray, sporty man like Johnny Carson who shakes my hand and tells me what a fine girl I have. Then we are on the stage and Dee is embracing me with tears in her eyes. She pins on my dress a large orchid, even though she has told me once that she thinks orchids are tacky flowers.

In real life I am a large, big-boned woman with rough, man-working hands. In the winter I wear flannel nightgowns to bed and overalls during the day. I can kill and clean a hog as mercilessly as a man. My fat keeps me hot in zero weather. I can work outside all day, breaking ice to get water for washing; I can eat pork liver cooked over the open fire minutes after it comes steaming from the hog. One winter I knocked a bull calf straight in the brain between the eyes with a sledge hammer and had the meat hung up to chill before nightfall. But of course all this does not show on television. I am the way my daughter would want me to be: a hundred pounds lighter, my skin like an uncooked barley pancake. My hair glistens in the hot bright lights. Johnny Carson has much to do to keep up with my quick and witty tongue.

But that is a mistake. I know even before I wake up. Who ever knew a Johnson with a quick tongue? Who can even imagine me looking a strange white man in the eye? It seems to me I have talked to them always with one foot raised in flight, with my head turned in whichever way is farthest from them. Dee, though. She would always look anyone in the eye. Hesitation was no part of her nature.

"How do I look, Mama?" Maggie says, showing just enough of her thin body enveloped in pink skirt and red blouse for me to know she's there, almost hidden by the door.

"Come out into the yard," I say.

Have you ever seen a lame animal, perhaps a dog run over by some careless person rich enough to own a car, sidle up to someone who is ignorant enough to be kind to him? That is the way my Maggie walks. She has been like this, chin on chest, eyes on ground, feet in shuffle, ever since the fire that burned the other house to the ground.

Dee is lighter than Maggie, with nicer hair and a fuller figure. She's a woman now, though sometimes I forget. How long ago was it that the other house burned? Ten, twelve years? Sometimes I can still hear the flames and feel Maggie's arms sticking to me, her hair smoking and her dress falling off her in little black papery flakes. Her eyes seemed stretched open, blazed open by the flames reflected in them. And Dee. I see her standing off under the sweet gum tree she used to dig gum out of; a look of concentration on her face as she watched the last dingy gray board of the house fall in toward the red-hot brick chimney. Why don't you do a dance around the ashes? I'd wanted to ask her. She had hated the house that much.

I used to think she hated Maggie, too. But that was before we raised the money, the church and me, to send her to Augusta to school. She used to read to us without pity; forcing words, lies, other folks' habits, whole lives upon us two, sitting trapped and ignorant underneath her voice. She washed us in a river of make-believe, burned us with a lot of knowledge we didn't necessarily need to know. Pressed us to her with the serious way she read, to shove us away at just the moment, like dimwits, we seemed about to understand.

Dee wanted nice things. A yellow organdy dress to wear to her graduation from high school; black pumps to match a green suit she'd made from an old suit somebody gave me. She was determined to stare down any disaster in her efforts. Her eyelids would not flicker for minutes at a time. Often I fought off the temptation to shake her. At sixteen she had a style of her own: and knew what style was.

I never had an education myself. After second grade the school was closed down. Don't ask my why: in 1927 colored asked fewer questions than they do now. Sometimes Maggie reads to me. She stumbles along good-naturedly but can't see well. She knows she is not bright. Like good looks and money, quickness passed her by. She will marry John Thomas (who has mossy teeth in an earnest face) and then I'll be free to sit here and I guess just sing church songs to myself. Although I never was a good singer. Never could carry a tune. I was always better at a man's job. I used to love to milk till I was hooked in the side in '49. Cows are soothing and slow and don't bother you, unless you try to milk them the wrong way.

I have deliberately turned my back on the house. It is three rooms, just like the one that burned, except the roof is tin; they don't make shingle roofs any more. There are no real windows, just some holes cut in the sides, like the portholes in a ship, but not round and not square, with rawhide holding the shutters up on the outside. This house is in a pasture, too, like the other one. No doubt when Dee sees it she will want to tear it down. She wrote me once that no matter where we "choose" to live, she will manage to come see us. But she will never bring her friends. Maggie and I thought about this and Maggie asked me, "Mama, when did Dee ever *have* any friends?"

She had a few. Furtive boys in pink shirts hanging about on washday after school. Nervous girls who never laughed. Impressed with her they worshiped the well-turned phrase, the cute shape, the scalding humor that erupted like bubbles in lye. She read to them.

When she was courting Jimmy T she didn't have much time to pay to us, but turned all her faultfinding power on him. He *flew* to marry a cheap city girl from a family of ignorant flashy people. She hardly had time to recompose herself.

When she comes I will meet—but there they are!

Maggie attempts to make a dash for the house, in her shuffling way, but I stay her with my hand. "Come back here," I say. And she stops and tries to dig a well in the sand with her toe.

It is hard to see them clearly through the strong sun. But even the first glimpse of leg out of the car tells me it is Dee. Her feet were always neat-looking, as if God himself had shaped them with a certain style. From the other side of the car comes a short, stocky man. Hair is all over his head a foot long and hanging from his chin like a kinky mule tail. I hear Maggie suck in her breath. "Uhnnnh," is what it sounds like. Like when you see the wriggling end of a snake just in front of your foot on the road. "Uhnnnh."

Dee next. A dress down to the ground, in this hot weather. A dress so loud it hurts my eyes. There are yellows and oranges enough to throw back the light of the sun. I feel my whole face warming from the heat waves it throws out. Earrings gold, too, and hanging down to her shoulders. Bracelets dangling and making noises when she moves her arm up to shake the folds of the dress out of her armpits. The dress is loose and flows, and as she walks closer, I like it. I hear Maggie go "Uhnnnh" again. It is her sister's hair. It stands straight up like the wool on a sheep. It is black as night and around the edges are two long pigtails that rope about like small lizards disappearing behind her ears.

"Wa-su-zo-Tean-o!" she says, coming on in that gliding way the dress makes her move. The short stocky fellow with the hair to his navel is all grinning and he follows up with "Asalamalakim, my mother and sister!" He moves to hug Maggie but she falls back, right up against the back of my chair. I feel her trembling there and when I look up I see the perspiration falling off her chin.

"Don't get up," says Dee. Since I am stout it takes something of a push. You can see me trying to move a second or two before I make it. She turns, showing white heels through her sandals, and goes back to the car. Out she peeks next with a Polaroid. She stoops down quickly and lines up picture after picture of me sitting there in front of the house with Maggie cowering behind me. She never takes a shot without making sure the house is included. When a cow comes nibbling around the edge of the yard she snaps it and me and Maggie *and* the house. Then she puts the Polaroid in the back seat of the car, and comes up and kisses me on the forehead.

Meanwhile Asalamalakim is going through motions with Maggie's hand. Maggie's hand is as limp as a fish, and probably as cold, despite the sweat, and she keeps trying to pull it back. It looks like Asalamalakim wants to shake hands but wants to do it fancy. Or maybe he don't know how people shake hands. Anyhow, he soon gives up on Maggie.

"Well," I say. "Dee."

"No, Mama," she says. "Not 'Dee,' Wangero Leewanika Kemanjo!"

"What happened to 'Dee'?" I wanted to know.

"She's dead," Wangero said. "I couldn't bear it any longer, being named after the people who oppress me."

"You know as well as me you was named after your aunt Dicie," I said. Dicie is my sister. She named Dee. We called her "Big Dee" after Dee was born.

"But who was *she* named after?" asked Wangero.

"I guess after Grandma Dee," I said.

"And who was she named after?" asked Wangero.

"Her mother," I said, and saw Wangero was getting tired. "That's about as far back as I can trace it," I said. Though, in fact, I probably could have carried it back beyond the Civil War through the branches.

"Well," said Asalamalakim, "there you are."

"Uhnnnh," I heard Maggie say.

"There I was not," I said, "before 'Dicie' cropped up in our family, so why should I try to trace it that far back?"

He just stood there grinning, looking down on me like somebody inspecting a Model A car. Every once in a while he and Wangero sent eye signals over my head.

"How do you pronounce this name?" I asked.

"You don't have to call me by it if you don't want to," said Wangero.

"Why shouldn't I?" I asked. "If that's what you want us to call you, we'll call you."

"I know it might sound awkward at first," said Wangero.

"I'll get used to it," I said. "Ream it out again."

Well, soon we got the name out of the way. Asalamalakim had a name twice as long and three times as hard. After I tripped over it two or three times he told me to just call him Hakim-a-barber. I wanted to ask him was he a barber, but I didn't really think he was, so I didn't ask.

"You must belong to those beef-cattle peoples down the road," I said. They said "Asalamalakim" when they met you, too, but they didn't shake hands. Always too busy: feeding the cattle, fixing the fences, putting up salt-lick shelters, throwing down hay. When the white folks poisoned some of the herd the men stayed up all night with rifles in their hands. I walked a mile and a half just to see the sight.

Hakim-a-barber said, "I accept some of their doctrines, but farming and raising cattle is not my style." (They didn't tell me, and I didn't ask, whether Wangero (Dee) had really gone and married him.)

We sat down to eat and right away he said he didn't eat collards and pork was unclean. Wangero, though, went on through the chitlins and corn bread, the greens and everything else. She talked a blue streak over the sweet potatoes. Everything delighted her. Even the fact that we still used the benches her daddy made for the table when we couldn't afford to buy chairs.

"Oh, Mama!" she cried. Then turned to Hakim-a-barber. "I never knew how lovely these benches are. You can feel the rump prints," she said, running her hands underneath her and along the bench. Then she gave a sigh and her hand closed over Grandma Dee's butter dish. "That's it!" she said. "I knew there was something I wanted to ask you if I could have." She jumped up from the table and went over in the corner where the churn stood, the milk in it clabber by now. She looked at the churn and looked at it.

"This churn top is what I need," she said. "Didn't Uncle Buddy whittle it out of a tree you all used to have?"

"Yes," I said.

"Uh huh," she said happily. "And I want the dasher, too."

"Uncle Buddy whittle that, too?" asked the barber.

Dee (Wangero) looked up at me.

"Aunt Dee's first husband whittled the dash," said Maggie so low you almost couldn't hear her. "His name was Henry, but they called him Stash."

"Maggie's brain is like an elephant's," Wangero said, laughing. "I can use the churn top as a centerpiece for the alcove table," she said, sliding a plate over the churn, "and I'll think of something artistic to do with the dasher."

When she finished wrapping the dasher the handle stuck out. I took it for a moment in my hands. You didn't even have to look close to see where hands pushing the dasher up and down to make butter had left a kind of sink in the wood. In fact, there were a lot of small sinks; you could see where thumbs and fingers had sunk into the wood. It was beautiful light yellow wood, from a tree that grew in the yard where Big Dee and Stash had lived.

After dinner Dee (Wangero) went to the trunk at the foot of my bed and started rifling through it. Maggie hung back in the kitchen over the dishpan. Out came Wangero with two quilts. They had been pieced by Grandma Dee and then Big Dee and me had hung them on the quilt frames on the front porch and quilted them. One was in the Lone Star pattern. The other was Walk Around the Mountain. In both of them were scraps of dresses Grandma Dee had worn fifty and more years ago. Bits and pieces of Grandpa Jarrell's Paisley shirts. And one teeny faded blue piece, about the size of a penny matchbox, that was from Great Grandpa Ezra's uniform that he wore in the Civil War.

"Mama," Wangero said sweet as a bird. "Can I have these old quilts?"

I heard something fall in the kitchen, and a minute later the kitchen door slammed.

"Why don't you take one or two of the others?" I asked. "These old things was just done by me and Big Dee from some tops your grandma pieced before she died."

"No," said Wangero. "I don't want those. They are stitched around the borders by machine."

"That'll make them last better," I said.

"That's not the point," said Wangero. "These are all pieces of dresses Grandma used to wear. She did all this stitching by hand. Imagine!" She held the quilts securely in her arms, stroking them.

"Some of the pieces, like those lavender ones, come from old clothes her mother handed down to her," I said, moving up to touch the quilts. Dee (Wangero) moved back just enough so that I couldn't reach the quilts. They already belonged to her.

"Imagine!" she breathed again, clutching them closely to her bosom.

"The truth is," I said, "I promised to give them quilts to Maggie, for when she marries John Thomas."

She gasped like a bee had stung her.

"Maggie can't appreciate these quilts!" she said. "She'd probably be backward enough to put them to everyday use."

"I reckon she would," I said. "God knows I been saving 'em for long enough with nobody using 'em. I hope she will!" I didn't want to bring up how I had offered Dee (Wangero) a quilt when she went away to college. Then she had told me they were old-fashioned, out of style.

"But they're *priceless!*" she was saying now, furiously; for she has a temper. "Maggie would put them on the bed and in five years they'd be in rags. Less than that!"

"She can always make some more," I said. "Maggie knows how to quilt."

Dee (Wangero) looked at me with hatred. "You just will not understand. The point is these quilts, *these* quilts!"

"Well," I said, stumped. "What would *you* do with them?"

"Hang them," she said. As if that was the only thing you *could* do with quilts.

Maggie by now was standing in the door. I could almost hear the sound her feet made as they scraped over each other.

"She can have them, Mama," she said, like somebody used to never winning anything, or having anything reserved for her. "I can 'member Grandma Dee without the quilts."

I looked at her hard. She had filled her bottom lip with checkerberry snuff and it gave her face a kind of dopey, hangdog look. It was Grandma Dee and Big Dee who taught her how to quilt herself. She stood there with her scarred hands hidden in the folds of her skirt. She looked at her sister with something like fear but she wasn't mad at her. This was Maggie's portion. This was the way she knew God to work.

When I looked at her like that something hit me in the top of my head and ran down to the soles of my feet. Just like when I'm in church and the spirit of God touches me and I get happy and shout. I did something I never had done before: hugged Maggie to me, then dragged her on into the room, snatched the quilts out of Miss Wangero's hands and dumped them into Maggie's lap. Maggie just sat there on my bed with her mouth open.

"Take one or two of the others," I said to Dee.

But she turned without a word and went out to Hakim-a-barber.

"You just don't understand," she said, as Maggie and I came out to the car.

"What don't I understand?" I wanted to know.

"Your heritage," she said. And then she turned to Maggie, kissed her, and said, "You ought to try to make something of yourself, too, Maggie. It's really a new day for us. But from the way you and Mama still live you'd never know it."

She put on some sunglasses that hid everything above the tip of her nose and her chin.

Maggie smiled; maybe at the sunglasses. But a real smile, not scared. After we watched the car dust settle I asked Maggie to bring me a dip of snuff. And then the two of us sat there just enjoying, until it was time to go in the house and go to bed.

1973

Ann Beattie
(1947–   )

Born in Washington, D.C., where her father worked for the Department of Health, Education and Welfare, Ann Beattie graduated from Washington's American University in 1969. The next year she earned an M.A. at the University of Connecticut, but although she began a Ph.D. there, she did not continue. Married, she turned to chronicling the lives of sophisticated young people on the East Coast. Coming of age as the 1960s were drawing to a close, her characters found themselves in a new decade that seemed empty and aimless in contrast to the social and intellectual turmoil of the one they had just lived through. Beattie has said, "I was watching the 1960s on my parents' television. I wasn't out getting gassed every day." Still, in her early works her characters are haunted by that decade. Bored in the milder 1970s, uncertain of goals or values, they spend their lives only superficially connected to family, careers, or loved ones. Often her plots, especially in her short stories, turn on nuances of feeling rather than events.

Her first novel, *Chilly Scenes of Winter*, and first collection of short stories, *Distor-*tions, both published in 1976, demonstrated the skill confirmed by later volumes. References to current events or popular songs fix the times of her fictions, much as they do in the work of Bobbie Ann Mason. Like Mason and Raymond Carver she has been called a minimalist, portraying in spare prose the lives of people who barely manage to hang on to existences marked by alienation and loss, whose victories, if they come, are minor. In *Chilly Scenes of Winter*, a man tries to hold his life together after his wife has left him. In *Falling in Place* (1980), characters whose lives are falling are measured metaphorically against the falling of Skylab. In *Love Always* (1985), a soap opera serves as metaphor for the actors and writers whose lives the novel explores. In *Picturing Will* (1990), a boy abandoned by his father comes to life, in part, as a subject for his mother's photographs. Later collections of stories include *Secrets and Surprises* (1978), *The Burning House* (1982), and *Where You'll Find Me* (1986).

A study is Christina Murphy, *Ann Beattie* (1986).

Skeletons[1]

Usually she was the artist. Today she was the model. She had on sweatpants—both she and Garrett wore medium, although his sweatpants fit her better than they did him, because she did not have his long legs—and a Chinese jacket, plum-colored, patterned with blue octagons, edged in silver thread, that seemed to float among the lavender flowers that were as big as the palm of a hand raised for the high-five. A *frog*, Nancy thought; that was what the piece was called—the near-knot she fingered, the little fastener she never closed.

It was late Saturday afternoon, and, as usual, Nancy Niles was spending the day with Garrett. She had met him in a drawing class she took at night. During the week, he worked in an artists' supply store, but he had the weekends off. Until recently, when the weather turned cold, they had often taken long walks on Saturday or Sunday, and sometimes Kyle Brown—an undergraduate at the University of Pennsylvania, who was the other tenant in the rooming house Garrett lived in, in a run-down neighborhood twenty minutes from the campus—had walked with them. It was Kyle who had told Garrett about the empty room in the house. His first week in Philadelphia, Garrett had been in line to pay his check at a coffee shop when the cashier asked Kyle for a penny, which he didn't have. Then she looked behind Kyle to Garrett and said, "Well, would *you* have a penny?" Leaving, Kyle and Garrett struck up the conversation that had led to Garrett's moving into the house. And now the cashier's question had become a running joke. Just that morning, Garrett was outside the bathroom, and when Kyle came out, wrapped in his towel, he asked, "Well, got a penny *now?*"

It was easy to amuse Kyle, and he had a lovely smile, Nancy thought. He once told her that he was the first member of his family to leave Utah to go to college. It had strained relations with his parents, but they couldn't argue with Kyle's insistence that the English department at Penn was excellent. The landlady's married daughter had gone to Penn, and Kyle felt sure that had been the deciding factor in his getting the room. That and the fact that when the landlady told him where the nearest Episcopal church was, he told her that he was a Mormon. "At least you have *some* religion," she said. When she interviewed Garrett and described the neighborhood and told him where the Episcopal church was, Kyle had already tipped him; Garrett flipped open a notebook and wrote down the address.

Now, as Garrett and Nancy sat talking as he sketched (Garrett cared so much about drawing that Nancy was sure that he was happy that the weather had turned, so he had an excuse to stay indoors), Kyle was frying chicken downstairs. A few minutes earlier, he had looked in on them and stayed to talk. He complained that he was tired of being known as "the Mormon" to the landlady. Not condescendingly, that he could see—she just said it the way a person might use the Latin name for a plant instead of its common one. He showed them a telephone message from his father she had written down, with "MORMON" printed at the top.

Kyle Brown lived on hydroponic tomatoes, Shake 'n Bake chicken, and Pepperidge Farm rolls. On Saturdays, Garrett and Nancy ate with him. They contributed apple cider—smoky, with a smell you could taste; the last pressing of the season—and sometimes turnovers from the corner bakery. Above the sputtering chicken Nancy could hear Kyle singing now, in his strong baritone: "The truth is, I *nev*-er left you . . ."

"Sit still," Garrett said, looking up from his sketchbook. "Don't you know your role in life?"

Nancy cupped her hands below her breasts, turned her head to the side, and pursed her lips.

"Don't do that," he said, throwing the crayon stub. "Don't put yourself down, even as a joke."

"Oh, don't analyze everything so seriously," she said, hopping off the window seat and

---

1. First published in *The New Yorker*, collected in *Where You'll Find Me* (1986), the source of the present text.

picking up the conté crayon. She threw it back to him. He caught it one-handed. He was the second person she had ever slept with. The other one, much to her embarrassment now, had been a deliberate experiment.

"Tell your shrink that your actions don't mean anything," he said.

"You hate it that I go to a shrink," she said, watching him bend over the sketchbook again. "Half the world sees a shrink. What are you worried about—that somebody might know something about me you don't know?"

He raised his eyebrows, as he often did when he was concentrating on something in a drawing. "I know a few things he doesn't know," he said.

"It's not a competition," she said.

"*Everything* is a competition. At some very serious, very deep level, every single thing—"

"You already made that joke," she said, sighing.

He stopped drawing and looked over at her in a different way. "I know," he said. "I shouldn't have taken it back. I really do believe that's what exists. One person jockeying for position, another person dodging."

"I can't tell when you're kidding. Now you're kidding, right?"

"No. I'm serious. I just took it back this morning because I could tell I was scaring you."

"Oh. Now are you going to tell me that you're in competition with me?"

"Why do you think I'm kidding?" he said. "It would *kill* me if you got a better grade in any course than I got. And you're so good. When you draw, you make strokes that look as if they were put on the paper with a feather. I'd take your technique away from you if I could. It's just that I know I can't, so I bite my tongue. Really. I envy you so much my heart races. I could never share a studio with you. I wouldn't be able to be in the same room with somebody who can be so patient and so exact at the same time. Compared to you, I might as well be wearing a catcher's mitt when I draw."

Nancy pulled her knees up to her chest and rested her cheek against one of them. She started to laugh.

"Really," he said.

"O.K.—*really*," she said, going poker-faced. "I know, darling Garrett. You really do mean it."

"I do," he said.

She stood up. "Then we don't have to share a studio," she said. "But you can't take it back that you said you wanted to marry me." She rubbed her hands through her hair and let one hand linger to massage her neck. Her body was cold from sitting on the window seat. Clasping her legs, she had realized that the thigh muscles ached.

"Maybe all that envy and anxiety has to be burnt away with constant passion," she said. "I mean—I really, *really* mean that." She smiled. "Really," she said. "Maybe you just want to give in to it—like scratching a mosquito bite until it's so sore you cry."

They were within seconds of touching each other, but just at the moment when she was about to step toward him they heard the old oak stairs creaking beneath Kyle's feet.

"This will come as no surprise to you," Kyle said, standing in the doorway, "but I'm checking to make sure that you know you're invited to dinner. I provide the chicken, sliced tomatoes, and bread—right? You bring dessert and something to drink."

Even in her disappointment, Nancy could smile at him. Of course he knew that he had stumbled into something. Probably he wanted to turn and run back down the stairs. It wasn't easy to be the younger extra person in a threesome. When she raised her head, Garrett caught her eye, and in that moment they both knew how embarrassed Kyle must be. His need for them was never masked as well as he thought. The two of them, clearly lovers, were forgoing candlelight and deliberately bumped knees and the intimacy of holding glasses to each other's lips in order to have dinner with him. Kyle had once told Nancy, on one of their late-fall walks, that one of his worst fears had always been that someone might be able to read his mind. It was clear to her that he had fantasies about them. At the time, Nancy had tried to pass it off lightly; she told him that when she was drawing she always sensed the model's bones and muscles, and what she did was stroke a soft surface over them until a body took form.

Kyle wanted to stay close to them—meant to stay close—but time passed, and after they all had moved several times he lost track of them. He knew nothing of Nancy Niles's life, had no idea that in October, 1985, she was out trick-or-treating with Garrett and their two-year-old child, Fraser, who was dressed up as a goblin for his first real Halloween. A plastic orange pumpkin, lit by batteries, bobbed in front of her as she walked a few steps ahead of them. She was dressed in a skeleton costume, but she might have been an angel, beaming salvation into the depths of the mines. Where she lived—their part of Providence, Rhode Island—was as grim and dark as an underground labyrinth.

It was ironic that men thought she could lead the way for them, because Nancy had realized all along that she had little sense of direction. She felt isolated, angry at herself for not pursuing her career as an artist, for no longer being in love. It would have surprised her to know that in a moment of crisis, late that night, in Warrenton, Virginia, when leaves, like shadows on an X ray, suddenly flew up and obscured his vision and his car went into a skid, Kyle Brown would see her again, in a vision. *Nancy Niles!* he thought, in that instant of fear and shock. There she was, for a split second—her face, ghostly pale under the gas-station lights, metamorphosed into brightness. In a flash, she was again the embodiment of beauty to him. As his car spun in a widening circle and then came to rest with its back wheels on an embankment, Nancy Niles the skeleton was walking slowly down the sidewalk. Leaves flew past her like footsteps, quickly descending the stairs.

1986

Leslie Marmon Silko
(1948–   )

Born in Albuquerque, New Mexico, Leslie Marmon was brought up on the nearby Laguna Pueblo, site of more than 500 years of human habitation. Her mixed ancestry includes Pueblo, European, Mexican, and Plains Indian forebears. She has speculated that "at the core of my writing is the attempt to identify what it is to be a half-breed or mixed-blooded person, what it is to grow up neither white nor fully traditional Indian."

As a child she attended Bureau of Indian Affairs schools and spent a lot of time with a great aunt and A'mooh, the great-grandmother who cared for her while her mother worked. Traditional and family stories were crucial to her development as an artist. She describes storytelling as "the heart of Pueblo people" and notes that knowing "all the stories within the com-

munity gives a certain distance, a useful perspective which brings incidents down to a level we can deal with. If others have done it before, it cannot be so terrible. If others have endured, so can we."

After high school in Albuquerque, she graduated with honors from the University of New Mexico (1969) and began law school, leaving after a year to pursue advanced study in English. She married John Silko, an attorney, when she was very young and had her first son at 18; a second son was born in 1972. Now divorced, Silko has taught at the Navajo Community College in Many Farms, Arizona, as well as the University of New Mexico and the University of Arizona.

Laguna Woman (1974), her first book, is a collection of poetry affirming the interdependence of humans and the surrounding environment. *Ceremony* (1977), her first novel, garnered for her critical recognition as a major Native American writer. The work centers on Tayo, a mixed-blood veteran of World War II whose combat experiences have caused a spiritual and emotional breakdown. Through the agency of an old man, Betonie, and other tribal healers who help him recapture his traditional heritage, Tayo is able to come to terms with his trauma.

The title story of her next book, *Storyteller* (1981), grew out of an extended stay among the Inuit of Bethel, Alaska, but her own Laguna Pueblo tradition is the major force in the book, a mélange of stories, photographs, and poems working together. Silko explained her method of communication in "Language and Literature from a Pueblo Indian Perspective," (1981):

For those of you accustomed to a structure that moves from point A to point B to point C, this presentation may be somewhat difficult to follow because the structure of Pueblo expression resembles something like a spider's web—with many little threads radiating from a center, criss-crossing each other. As with the web, the structure will emerge as it is made and you must simply listen and trust, as the Pueblo people do, that meaning will be made.

The year of *Storyteller*, Silko was awarded a fellowship by the MacArthur Foundation; the grant provided her support, enabling a leave from her teaching position and full-time devotion to her work. *Almanac of the Dead*, a massive work with more than seventy characters whose interlocking stories detail the ecological and social brutality of contemporary life, appeared in 1991.

Anne Wright edited the correspondence between her husband, the poet James Wright, and Silko in *The Delicacy and Strength of Lace* (1986). Per Seyerstad wrote a short study, *Leslie Marmon Silko* (1980). "Lullaby" is taken from *Storyteller*.

Lullaby

The sun had gone down but the snow in the wind gave off its own light. It came in thick tufts like new wool—washed before the weaver spins it. Ayah reached out for it like her own babies had, and she smiled when she remembered how she had laughed at them. She was an old woman now, and her life had become memories. She sat down with her back against the wide cottonwood tree, feeling the rough bark on her back bones; she faced east and listened to the wind and snow sing a high-pitched Yeibechei song. Out of the wind she felt warmer, and she could watch the wide fluffy snow fill in her tracks, steadily, until the direction she had come from was gone. By the light of the snow she could see the dark outline of the big arroyo a few feet away. She was sitting on the edge of Cebolleta Creek, where in the springtime the thin cows would graze on grass already chewed flat to the ground. In the wide deep creek bed where only a trickle of water flowed in the summer, the skinny cows would wander, looking for new grass along winding paths splashed with manure.

Ayah pulled the old Army blanket over her head like a shawl. Jimmie's blanket—the one he had sent to her. That was a long time ago and the green wool was faded, and it was unraveling on the edges. She did not want to think about Jimmie. So she thought about the weaving and the way her mother had done it. On the tall wooden loom set into the sand under a tamarack tree for shade. She could see it clearly. She had been only a little girl when her grandma gave her the wooden combs to pull the twigs and burrs from the raw, freshly washed wool. And while she combed the wool, her grandma sat beside her, spinning a silvery strand of yarn around the smooth cedar spindle. Her mother worked at the loom with yarns dyed bright yellow and red and gold. She watched them dye the yarn in boiling black pots full of beeweed petals, juniper berries, and sage. The blankets her mother made were soft and woven so tight that rain rolled off them like birds' feathers. Ayah remembered sleeping warm on cold windy nights, wrapped in her mother's blankets on the hogan's sandy floor.

The snow drifted now, with the northwest wind hurling it in gusts. It drifted up around her black overshoes—old ones with little metal buckles. She smiled at the snow which was trying to cover her little by little. She could remember when they had no black rubber overshoes; only the high buckskin leggings that they wrapped over their elkhide moccasins. If the snow was dry or frozen, a person could walk all day and not get wet; and in the evenings the beams of the ceiling would hang with lengths of pale buckskin leggings, drying out slowly.

She felt peaceful remembering. She didn't feel cold any more. Jimmie's blanket seemed warmer than it had ever been. And she could remember the morning he was born. She could remember whispering to her mother, who was sleeping on the other side of the hogan, to tell her it was time now. She did not want to wake the others. The second time she called to her, her mother stood up and pulled on her shoes; she knew. They walked to the old stone hogan together, Ayah walking a step behind her mother. She waited alone, learning the rhythms of the pains while her mother went to call the old woman to help them. The morning was already warm even before dawn and Ayah smelled the bee flowers blooming and the young willow growing at the springs. She could remember that so clearly, but his birth merged into the births of the other children and to her it became all the same birth. They named him for the summer morning and in English they called him Jimmie.

It wasn't like Jimmie died. He just never came back, and one day a dark blue sedan with white writing on its doors pulled up in front of the boxcar shack where the rancher let the Indians live. A man in a khaki uniform trimmed in gold gave them a yellow piece of paper and told them that Jimmie was dead. He said the Army would try to get the body back and then it would be shipped to them; but it wasn't likely because the helicopter had burned after it crashed. All of this was told to Chato because he could understand English. She stood inside the doorway holding the baby while Chato listened. Chato spoke English like a white man and he spoke Spanish too. He was taller than the white man and he stood straighter too. Chato didn't explain why; he just told the military man they could keep the body if they found it. The white man looked bewildered; he nodded his head and he left. Then Chato looked at her and shook his head, and then he told her, "Jimmie isn't coming home anymore," and when he spoke, he used the words to speak of the dead. She didn't cry then, but she hurt inside with anger. And she mourned him as the years passed, when a horse fell with Chato and broke his leg, and the white rancher told them he wouldn't pay Chato until he could work again. She mourned Jimmie because he would have worked for his father then; he would have saddled the big bay horse and ridden the fence lines each day, with wire cutters and heavy gloves, fixing the breaks in the barbed wire and putting the stray cattle back inside again.

She mourned him after the white doctors came to take Danny and Ella away. She was at the shack alone that day they came. It was back in the days before they hired Navajo women to go with them as interpreters. She recognized one of the doctors. She had seen him at the children's clinic at Cañoncito about a month ago. They were wearing khaki uniforms and they waved papers at her and a black ball-point pen, trying to make her understand their English words. She was frightened by the way they looked at the children, like the lizard watches the fly. Danny was swinging on the tire swing on the elm tree behind the rancher's house, and Ella was toddling around the front door, dragging the broomstick horse Chato made for her. Ayah could see they wanted her to sign the papers, and Chato had taught her to sign her name. It was something she was proud of. She only wanted them to go, and to take their eyes away from her children.

She took the pen from the man without looking at his face and she signed the papers in three different places he pointed to. She stared at the ground by their feet and waited for them to leave. But they stood there and began to point and gesture at the children. Danny stopped swinging. Ayah could see his fear. She moved suddenly and grabbed Ella into her arms; the child squirmed, trying to get back to her toys. Ayah ran with the baby toward Danny; she screamed for him to run and then she grabbed him around his chest and carried him too. She ran south into the foothills of juniper trees and black lava rock. Behind her she heard the doctors running, but they had been taken by surprise, and as the hills became steeper and the cholla cactus were thicker, they stopped. When she reached the top of the hill, she stopped to listen in case they were circling around her. But in a few minutes she heard a car engine start and they drove away. The children had been too surprised to cry while she ran with them. Danny was shaking and Ella's little fingers were gripping Ayah's blouse.

She stayed up in the hills for the rest of the day, sitting on a black lava boulder in the sunshine where she could see for miles all around her. The sky was light blue and cloudless, and it was warm for late April. The sun warmth relaxed her and took the fear and anger away. She lay back on the rock and watched the sky. It seemed to her that she could walk into the sky, stepping through clouds endlessly. Danny played with little pebbles and stones, pretending they were birds eggs and then little rabbits. Ella sat at her feet and dropped fistfuls of dirt into the breeze, watching the dust and particles of sand intently. Ayah watched a hawk soar high above them, dark wings gliding; hunting or only watching, she did not know. The hawk was patient and he circled all afternoon before he disappeared around the high volcanic peak the Mexicans called Guadalupe.

Late in the afternoon, Ayah looked down at the gray boxcar shack with the paint all peeled from the wood; the stove pipe on the roof was rusted and crooked. The fire she had built that morning in the oil drum stove had burned out. Ella was asleep in her lap now and Danny sat close to her, complaining that he was hungry; he asked when they would go to the house. "We will stay up here until your father comes," she told him, "because those white men were chasing us." The boy remembered then and he nodded at her silently.

If Jimmie had been there he could have read those papers and explained to her what they said. Ayah would have known then, never to sign them. The doctors came back the next day and they brought a BIA[1] policeman with them. They told Chato they had her signature and that was all they needed. Except for the kids. She listened to Chato sullenly; she hated him when he told her it was the old woman who died in the winter, spitting blood; it was her old grandma who had given the children this disease. "They don't spit blood," she said coldly. "The whites lie." She held Ella and Danny close to her, ready to run to the hills again. "I want a medicine man first," she said to Chato, not looking at him. He shook his head. "It's too late now. The policeman is with them. You signed the paper." His voice was gentle.

It was worse than if they had died: to lose the children and to know that somewhere, in a place called Colorado, in a place full of sick and dying strangers, her children were without her. There had been babies that died soon after they were born, and one that died before he could walk. She had carried them herself, up to the boulders and great pieces of the cliff that long ago crashed down from Long Mesa; she laid them in the crevices of sandstone and buried them in fine brown sand with round quartz pebbles that washed down the hills in the rain. She had endured it because they had been with her. But she could not bear this pain. She did not sleep for a long time after they took her children. She stayed on the hill where they had fled the first time, and she slept rolled up in the blanket Jimmie had sent her. She carried the pain in her belly and it was fed by everything she saw: the blue sky of their last day together and the dust and pebbles they played with; the swing in the elm tree and broomstick horse choked life from her. The pain filled her stomach and there was no room for food or for her lungs to fill with air. The air and the food would have been theirs.

She hated Chato, not because he let the policeman and doctors put the screaming children in the government car, but because he had taught her to sign her name. Because it was like the old ones always told her about learning their language or any of their ways: it endangered you. She slept alone on the hill until the middle of November when the first snows came.

---

1. Bureau of Indian Affairs

Then she made a bed for herself where the children had slept. She did not lie down beside Chato again until many years later, when he was sick and shivering and only her body could keep him warm. The illness came after the white rancher told Chato he was too old to work for him anymore, and Chato and his old woman should be out of the shack by the next afternoon because the rancher had hired new people to work there. That had satisfied her. To see how the white man repaid Chato's years of loyalty and work. All of Chato's fine-sounding English talk didn't change things.

It snowed steadily and the luminous light from the snow gradually diminished into the darkness. Somewhere in Cebolleta a dog barked and other village dogs joined with it. Ayah looked in the direction she had come, from the bar where Chato was buying the wine. Sometimes he told her to go on ahead and wait; and then he never came. And when she finally went back looking for him, she would find him passed out at the bottom of the wooden steps to Azzie's Bar. All the wine would be gone and most of the money too, from the pale blue check that came to them once a month in a government envelope. It was then that she would look at his face and his hands, scarred by ropes and the barbed wire of all those years, and she would think, this man is a stranger; for forty years she had smiled at him and cooked his food, but he remained a stranger. She stood up again, with the snow almost to her knees, and she walked back to find Chato.

It was hard to walk in the deep snow and she felt the air burn in her lungs. She stopped a short distance from the bar to rest and readjust the blanket. But this time he wasn't waiting for her on the bottom step with his old Stetson hat pulled down and his shoulders hunched up in his long wool overcoat.

She was careful not to slip on the wooden steps. When she pushed the door open, warm air and cigarette smoke hit her face. She looked around slowly and deliberately, in every corner, in every dark place that the old man might find to sleep. The bar owner didn't like Indians in there, especially Navajos, but he let Chato come in because he could talk Spanish like he was one of them. The men at the bar stared at her, and the bartender saw that she left the door open wide. Snowflakes were flying inside like moths and melting into a puddle on the oiled wood floor. He motioned to her to close the door, but she did not see him. She held herself straight and walked across the room slowly, searching the room with every step. The snow in her hair melted and she could feel it on her forehead. At the far corner of the room, she saw red flames at the mica window of the old stove door; she looked behind the stove just to make sure. The bar got quiet except for the Spanish polka music playing on the jukebox. She stood by the stove and shook the snow from her blanket and held it near the stove to dry. The wet wool smell reminded her of new-born goats in early March, brought inside to warm near the fire. She felt calm.

In past years they would have told her to get out. But her hair was white now and her face was wrinkled. They looked at her like she was a spider crawling slowly across the room. They were afraid; she could feel the fear. She looked at their faces steadily. They reminded her of the first time the white people brought her children back to her that winter. Danny had been shy and hid behind the thin white woman who brought them. And the baby had not known her until Ayah took her into her arms, and then Ella had nuzzled close to her as she had when she was nursing. The blonde woman was nervous and kept looking at a dainty gold watch on her wrist. She sat on the bench near the small window and watched the dark snow clouds gather around the mountains; she was worrying about the unpaved road. She was frightened by what she saw inside too: the strips of venison drying on a rope across the ceiling and the children jabbering excitedly in a language she did not know. So they stayed for only a few hours. Ayah watched the government car disappear down the road and she knew they were already being weaned from these lava hills and from this sky. The last time they came was in early June, and Ella stared at her the way the men in the bar were now staring. Ayah did not try to pick her up; she smiled at her instead and spoke cheerfully to Danny. When he tried to answer her, he could not seem to remember and he spoke English words with the Navajo. But he gave her a scrap of paper that he had found somewhere and carried in his pocket; it was folded in half, and he shyly looked up at her and said it was a bird. She asked Chato if they were home for good this time. He spoke to the white woman and she shook her head. "How much longer?" he asked, and she said she didn't know; but Chato saw how she stared at the boxcar shack. Ayah turned away then. She did not say good-bye.

She felt satisfied that the men in the bar feared her. Maybe it was her face and the way she held her mouth with teeth clenched tight, like there was nothing anyone could do to her now. She walked north down the road, searching for the old man. She did this because she had the blanket, and there would be no place for him except with her and the blanket in the old adobe barn near the arroyo. They always slept there when they came to Cebolleta. If the money and the wine were gone, she would be relieved because then they could go home again; back to the old hogan with a dirt roof and rock walls where she herself had been born. And the next day the old man could go back to the few sheep they still had, to follow along behind them, guiding them, into dry sandy arroyos where sparse grass grew. She knew he did not like walking behind old ewes when for so many years he rode big quarter horses and worked with cattle. But she wasn't sorry for him; he should have known all along what would happen.

There had not been enough rain for their garden in five years; and that was when Chato finally hitched a ride into the town and brought back brown boxes of rice and sugar and big tin cans of welfare peaches. After that, at the first of the month they went to Cebolleta to ask the postmaster for the check; and then Chato would go to the bar and cash it. They did this as they planted the garden every May, not because anything would survive the summer dust, but because it was time to do this. The journey passed the days that smelled silent and dry like the caves above the canyon with yellow painted buffaloes on their walls.

He was walking along the pavement when she found him. He did not stop or turn around when he heard her behind him. She walked beside him and she noticed how slowly he moved now. He smelled strong of woodsmoke and urine. Lately he had been forgetting. Sometimes he called her by his sister's name and she had been gone for a long time. Once she had found him wandering on the road to the white man's ranch, and she asked him why he was going that way; he laughed at her and said, "You know they can't run that ranch without me," and he walked on determined, limping on the leg that had been crushed many years before. Now he looked at her curiously, as if for the first time, but he kept shuffling along, moving slowly along the side of the highway. His gray hair had grown long and spread out on the shoulders of the long overcoat. He wore the old felt hat pulled down over his ears. His boots were worn out at the toes and he had stuffed pieces of an old red shirt in the holes. The rags made his feet look like little animals up to their ears in snow. She laughed at his feet; the snow muffled the sound of her laugh. He stopped and looked at her again. The wind had quit blowing and the snow was falling straight down; the southeast sky was beginning to clear and Ayah could see a star.

"Let's rest awhile," she said to him. They walked away from the road and up the slope to the giant boulders that had tumbled down from the red sandrock mesa throughout the centuries of rainstorms and earth tremors. In a place where the boulders shut out the wind, they sat down with their backs against the rock. She offered half of the blanket to him and they sat wrapped together.

The storm passed swiftly. The clouds moved east. They were massive and full, crowding together across the sky. She watched them with the feeling of horses—steely blue-gray horses startled across the sky. The powerful haunches pushed into the distances and the tail hairs streamed white mist behind them. The sky cleared. Ayah saw that there was nothing between her and the stars. The light was crystalline. There was no shimmer, no distortion through earth haze. She breathed the clarity of the night sky; she smelled the purity of the half moon and the stars. He was lying on his side with his knees pulled up near his belly for warmth. His eyes were closed now, and in the light from the stars and the moon, he looked young again.

She could see it descend out of the night sky: an icy stillness from the edge of the thin moon. She recognized the freezing. It came gradually, sinking snowflake by snowflake until the crust was heavy and deep. It had the strength of the stars in Orion, and its journey was endless. Ayah knew that with the wine he would sleep. He would not feel it. She tucked the blanket around him, remembering how it was when Ella had been with her; and she felt the rush so big inside her heart for the babies. And she sang the only song she knew to sing for babies. She could not remember if she had ever sung it to her children, but she knew that her grandmother had sung it and her mother had sung it:

> The earth is your mother,
>   she holds you.
> The sky is your father,
>   he protects you.
> Sleep,
> sleep.
> Rainbow is your sister,
>   she loves you.
> The winds are your brothers,
>   they sing to you.
> Sleep,
> sleep.
> We are together always
> We are together always
> There never was a time
> when this
> was not so.

1981

Rita Dove
(1952–   )

Born in Akron, Ohio, the daughter of a chemist, Rita Dove won a scholarship to Miami University in Ohio. Graduating from Miami summa cum laude, she went to Germany as a Fulbright scholar, studying modern European literature at the University of Tübingen in 1974–1975. Back in the United States, she earned an M.F.A. at the University of Iowa in 1977. In the next few years she was supported in her work by grants from the National Endowment for the Arts and the Ohio Arts Council and visited Germany again on a fellowship in 1980, the same year she published her first

book of verse, *The Yellow House on the Corner*. In the 1980s, she taught poetry, first at Arizona State University and then at the University of Virginia. In 1993 she was appointed poet laureate of the United States.

Her poetry is plain-spoken; it reflects in a relatively direct way her experiences as an African American in Akron, her interest in the lives of her forebears, and her observations of the world outside of the United States as derived from her travels and reading. After her first book, poems based largely on her youth, she turned in her second, *Museum* (1983), to a wider canvas. When she began it, she has said, "I was in Europe, and I had a way of looking back on America and distancing myself from my experience." In her third, *Thomas and Beulah* (1986), she began with stories of her grandparents and wove from them a collection of lyrics and brief narratives recounting the lives of Southern blacks, from Tennessee and Georgia, who move north to industrial Akron.

Additional titles by Dove include a fourth volume of verse, *Grace Notes* (1989), and a collection of short stories, *Fifth Sunday* (1985).

Ö

Shape the lips to an *o*, say *a*.
That's *island*.

One word of Swedish has changed the whole neighborhood.
When I look up, the yellow house on the corner
is a galleon stranded in flowers. Around it   5

the wind. Even the high roar of a leaf-mulcher
could be the horn-blast from a ship
as it skirts the misted shoals.

We don't need much more to keep things going.
Families complete themselves   10
and refuse to budge from the present,
the present extends its glass forehead to sea
(backyard breezes, scattered cardinals)

and if, one evening, the house on the corner
took off over the marshland,   15
neither I nor my neighbor
would be amazed. Sometimes

a word is found so right it trembles
at the slightest explanation.
You start out with one thing, end   20
up with another, and nothing's
like it used to be, not even the future.

1980

Dusting

Every day a wilderness—no
shade in sight. Beulah
patient among knickknacks,
the solarium a rage
of light, a grainstorm   5
as her gray cloth brings
dark wood to life.

Under her hand scrolls
and crests gleam
darker still. What　　　　10
was his name, that
silly boy at the fair with
the rifle booth? And his kiss and
the clear bowl with one bright
fish, rippling　　　　15
wound!

Not Michael—
something finer. Each dust
stroke a deep breath and
the canary in bloom.　　　　20
Wavery memory: home
from a dance, the front door
blown open and the parlor
in snow, she rushed
the bowl to the stove, watched　　25
as the locket of ice
dissolved and he
swam free.

That was years before
Father gave her up　　　　30
with her name, years before
her name grew to mean
Promise, then
Desert-in-Peace.
Long before the shadow and　　35
sun's accomplice, the tree.

Maurice.

　　　　　　　1983

Roast Possum

The possum's a greasy critter
that lives on persimmons and what
the Bible calls carrion.
So much from the 1909 Werner
Encyclopedia, three rows of deep green　　5
along the wall. A granddaughter
propped on each knee,
Thomas went on with his tale—

but it was for Malcolm, little
Red Delicious, that he invented　　10
embellishments: *We shined that possum*
with a torch and I shinnied up,

being the smallest,
to shake him down. He glared at me,
teeth bared like a shark's   15
in that torpedo snout.
Man he was tough but no match
for old-time know-how.

Malcolm hung back, studying them
with his gold hawk eyes. When the girls   20
got restless, Thomas talked horses:
Strolling Jim, who could balance
a glass of water on his back
and trot the village square
without spilling a drop. Who put   25
Wartrace[1] on the map and was buried
under a stone, like a man.

They liked that part.
He could have gone on to tell them
that the Werner admitted Negro children   30
to be intelligent, though briskness
clouded over at puberty, bringing
indirection and laziness. Instead,
he added: *You got to be careful*
with a possum when he's on the ground;   35
he'll turn on his back and play dead
till you give up looking. That's
what you'd call sullin'.

Malcolm interrupted to ask
who owned Strolling Jim,   40
and who paid for the tombstone.
They stared each other down
man to man, before Thomas,
as a grandfather, replied:
                                        Yessir,   45
we enjoyed that possum. We ate him
real slow, with sweet potatoes.

                                                        1986

Daystar

She wanted a little room for thinking:
but she saw diapers steaming on the line,
a doll slumped behind the door.

So she lugged a chair behind the garage
to sit out the children's naps.   5

Sometimes there were things to watch—
the pinched armor of a vanished cricket,

---

1. Tennessee town where the character Thomas was born in 1900.

a floating maple leaf. Other days
she stared until she was assured
when she closed her eyes   10
she'd see only her own vivid blood.

She had an hour, at best, before Liza appeared
pouting from the top of the stairs.
And just *what* was mother doing
out back with the field mice? Why,   15

building a palace. Later
that night when Thomas rolled over and
lurched into her, she would open her eyes
and think of the place that was hers
for an hour—where   20
she was nothing,
pure nothing, in the middle of the day.

                                              1986

Crab-Boil

(Ft. Myers, 1962)

Why do I remember the sky
above the forbidden beach,
why only blue and the scratch,
shell on tin, of their distress?
The rest   5

imagination supplies:
bucket and angry pink beseeching
claws. Why does Aunt Helen
laugh before saying "Look at that—

a bunch of niggers, not   10
a-one get out 'fore the others pull him
back." I don't believe her—

just as I don't believe *they* won't come
and chase us back to the colored-only shore
crisp with litter and broken glass.   15

"When do we kill them?"
"Kill 'em? Hell, the water does *that*.
They don't feel a thing . . . no nervous system."

I decide to believe this: I'm hungry.
Dismantled, they're merely exotic,   20
a blushing meat. After all, she *has*
grown old in the South. If
we're kicked out now, I'm ready.

                                              1989

Amy Tan
(1952–   )

A child of immigrant parents, Amy Tan grew up in Oakland, California. John Tan, an electrical engineer and Baptist minister, and Daisy Tan, a nurse, expected their three children to achieve great things. They hoped Amy would become a neurosurgeon who gave piano concerts on the side; her B.A. and M.A. degrees in English from San José State University and work toward a Ph.D. at the University of California, Berkeley, led her in a different direction.

Dissatisfied with the long hours she was working as a free-lance business writer, Tan turned to writing short fiction. Influenced by the parables her father used in his sermons and the Chinese fairy stories and family anecdotes she heard from her mother, Tan wove together traditional materials and contemporary observations. Encouraged by her husband, attorney Louis deMattei, and the members of her writing group, she engaged a literary agent and submitted several pieces for magazine publication. *The Atlantic, The Ladies Home Journal, Seventeen,* and others accepted pieces; she signed a contract with Putnam which enabled her to turn her attention exclusively to fiction and finish a first novel in about four months.

The Joy Luck Club was an immediate success; it hit the best-seller list in April 1989,

soon after publication, and stayed there through the summer. Softcover rights were sold for a record amount and the high volume sales continued; an audiotape of Tan reading her work was also successful.

The novel is composed of sixteen stories concerning four pairs of immigrant mothers and first generation daughters. Suyuan Woo, An-mei Hsu, Lindo Jong, and Ying-Ying St. Clair fled China in the 1940s and settled in San Francisco, where their daughters were born. Meeting weekly to play *mah-jong,* share food and gossip, and invest in the stock market, the four families have supported one another in a bicultural world. When the club's founder, Suyuan Woo, dies, the survivors ask Jing-mei, or June, to replace her mother at the gaming table. Their real need is for her to help them understand the transgenerational stresses they have all experienced. "The Rules of the Game" is the daughter portion of the Jong family story and is narrated by Waverly Jong.

Tan's second novel, *The Kitchen God's Wife,* appeared in 1991. It tells the intertwined stories of two women from contrasting classes and different regions of China who are thrown together by the events of war and remain friends after their arrival in the United States.

FROM THE JOY LUCK CLUB
Rules of the Game

I was six when my mother taught me the art of invisible strength. It was a strategy for winning arguments, respect from others, and eventually, though neither of us knew it at the time, chess games.

"Bite back your tongue," scolded my mother when I cried loudly, yanking her hand toward the store that sold bags of salted plums. At home, she said, "Wise guy, he not go against wind. In Chinese we say, Come from South, blow with wind—poom!—North will follow. Strongest wind cannot be seen."

The next week I bit back my tongue as we entered the store with the forbidden candies.

When my mother finished her shopping, she quietly plucked a small bag of plums from the rack and put it on the counter with the rest of the items.

My mother imparted her daily truths so she could help my older brothers and me rise above our circumstances. We lived in San Francisco's Chinatown. Like most of the other Chinese children who played in the back alleys of restaurants and curio shops, I didn't think we were poor. My bowl was always full, three five-course meals every day, beginning with a soup full of mysterious things I didn't want to know the names of.

We lived on Waverly Place, in a warm, clean, two-bedroom flat that sat above a small Chinese bakery specializing in steamed pastries and dim sum. In the early morning, when the alley was still quiet, I could smell fragrant red beans as they were cooked down to a pasty sweetness. By daybreak, our flat was heavy with the odor of fried sesame balls and sweet curried chicken crescents. From my bed, I would listen as my father got ready for work, then locked the door behind him, one-two-three clicks.

At the end of our two-block alley was a small sandlot playground with swings and slides well-shined down the middle with use. The play area was bordered by wood-slat benches where old-country people sat cracking roasted watermelon seeds with their golden teeth and scattering the husks to an impatient gathering of gurgling pigeons. The best playground, however, was the dark alley itself. It was crammed with daily mysteries and adventures. My brothers and I would peer into the medicinal herb shop, watching old Li dole out onto a stiff sheet of white paper the right amount of insect shells, saffron-colored seeds, and pungent leaves for his ailing customers. It was said that he once cured a woman dying of an ancestral curse that had eluded the best of American doctors. Next to the pharmacy was a printer who specialized in gold-embossed wedding invitations and festive red banners.

Farther down the street was Ping Yuen Fish Market. The front window displayed a tank crowded with doomed fish and turtles struggling to gain footing on the slimy green-tiled sides. A hand-written sign informed tourists, "Within this store, is all for food, not for pet." Inside, the butchers with their blood-stained white smocks deftly gutted the fish while customers cried out their orders and shouted, "Give me your freshest," to which the butchers always protested, "All are freshest." On less crowded market days, we would inspect the crates of live frogs and crabs which we were warned not to poke, boxes of dried cuttlefish, and row upon row of iced prawns, squid, and slippery fish. The sanddabs made me shiver each time; their eyes lay on one flattened side and reminded me of my mother's story of a careless girl who ran into a crowded street and was crushed by a cab. "Was smash flat," reported my mother.

At the corner of the alley was Hong Sing's, a four-table café with a recessed stairwell in front that led to a door marked "Tradesmen." My brothers and I believed the bad people emerged from this door at night. Tourists never went to Hong Sing's, since the menu was printed only in Chinese. A Caucasian man with a big camera once posed me and my playmates in front of the restaurant. He had us move to the side of the picture window so the photo would capture the roasted duck with its head dangling from a juice-covered rope. After he took the picture, I told him he should go into Hong Sing's and eat dinner. When he smiled and asked me what they served, I shouted, "Guts and duck's feet and octopus gizzards!" Then I ran off with my friends, shrieking with laughter as we scampered across the alley and hid in the entryway grotto of the China Gem Company, my heart pounding with hope that he would chase us.

My mother named me after the street that we lived on: Waverly Place Jong, my official name for important American documents. But my family called me Meimei, "Little Sister." I was the youngest, the only daughter. Each morning before school, my mother would twist and yank on my thick black hair until she had formed two tightly wound pigtails. One day, as she struggled to weave a hard-toothed comb through my disobedient hair, I had a sly thought.

I asked her, "Ma, what is Chinese torture?" My mother shook her head. A bobby pin was wedged between her lips. She wetted her palm and smoothed the hair above my ear, then pushed the pin in so that it nicked sharply against my scalp.

"Who say this word?" she asked without a trace of knowing how wicked I was being. I shrugged my shoulders and said, "Some boy in my class said Chinese people do Chinese torture."

"Chinese people do many things," she said simply. "Chinese people do business, do medicine, do painting. Not lazy like American people. We do torture. Best torture."

My older brother Vincent was the one who actually got the chess set. We had gone to the annual Christmas party held at the First Chinese Baptist Church at the end of the alley. The missionary ladies had put together a Santa bag of gifts donated by members of another church. None of the gifts had names on them. There were separate sacks for boys and girls of different ages.

One of the Chinese parishioners had donned a Santa Claus costume and a stiff paper beard with cotton balls glued to it. I think the only children who thought he was the real thing were too young to know that Santa Claus was not Chinese. When my turn came up, the Santa man asked me how old I was. I thought it was a trick question; I was seven according to the American formula and eight by the Chinese calendar. I said I was born on March 17, 1951. That seemed to satisfy him. He then solemnly asked if I had been a very, very good girl this year and did I believe in Jesus Christ and obey my parents. I knew the only answer to that. I nodded back with equal solemnity.

Having watched the other children opening their gifts, I already knew that the big gifts were not necessarily the nicest ones. One girl my age got a large coloring book of biblical characters, while a less greedy girl who selected a smaller box received a glass vial of lavender toilet water. The sound of the box was also important. A ten-year-old boy had chosen a box that jangled when he shook it. It was a tin globe of the world with a slit for inserting money. He must have thought it was full of dimes and nickels, because when he saw that it had just ten pennies, his face fell with such undisguised disappointment that his mother slapped the side of his head and led him out of the church hall, apologizing to the crowd for her son who had such bad manners he couldn't appreciate such a fine gift.

As I peered into the sack, I quickly fingered the remaining presents, testing their weight, imagining what they contained. I chose a heavy, compact one that was wrapped in shiny silver foil and a red satin ribbon. It was a twelve-pack of Life Savers and I spent the rest of the party arranging and rearranging the candy tubes in the order of my favorites. My brother Winston chose wisely as well. His present turned out to be a box of intricate plastic parts; the instructions on the box proclaimed that when they were properly assembled he would have an authentic miniature replica of a World War II submarine.

Vincent got the chess set, which would have been a very decent present to get at a church Christmas party, except it was obviously used and, as we discovered later, it was missing a black pawn and a white knight. My mother graciously thanked the unknown benefactor, saying, "Too good. Cost too much." At which point, an old lady with fine white, wispy hair nodded toward our family and said with a whistling whisper, "Merry, merry Christmas."

When we got home, my mother told Vincent to throw the chess set away. "She not want it. We not want it," she said, tossing her head stiffly to the side with a tight, proud smile. My brothers had deaf ears. They were already lining up the chess pieces and reading from the dog-eared instruction book.

I watched Vincent and Winston play during Christmas week. The chess board seemed to hold elaborate secrets waiting to be untangled. The chessmen were more powerful than Old Li's magic herbs that cured ancestral curses. And my brothers wore such serious faces that I was sure something was at stake that was greater than avoiding the tradesmen's door to Hong Sing's.

"Let me! Let me!" I begged between games when one brother or the other would sit back with a deep sigh of relief and victory, the other annoyed, unable to let go of the outcome. Vincent at first refused to let me play, but when I offered my Life Savers as replacements for the buttons that filled in for the missing pieces, he relented. He chose the flavors: wild cherry for the black pawn and peppermint for the white knight. Winner could eat both.

As our mother sprinkled flour and rolled out small doughy circles for the steamed dumplings that would be our dinner that night, Vincent explained the rules, pointing to each piece. "You have sixteen pieces and so do I. One king and queen, two bishops, two knights, two castles, and eight pawns. The pawns can only move forward one step, except on the first move. Then they can move two. But they can only take men by moving crossways like this, except in the beginning, when you can move ahead and take another pawn."

"Why?" I asked as I moved my pawn. "Why can't they move more steps?"

"Because they're pawns," he said.

"But why do they go crossways to take other men. Why aren't there any women and children?"

"Why is the sky blue? Why must you always ask stupid questions?" asked Vincent. "This is a game. These are the rules. I didn't make them up. See. Here. In the book." He jabbed a page with a pawn in his hand. "Pawn. P-A-W-N. Pawn. Read it yourself."

My mother patted the flour off her hands. "Let me see book," she said quietly. She scanned the pages quickly, not reading the foreign English symbols, seeming to search deliberately for nothing in particular.

"This American rules," she concluded at last. "Every time people come out from foreign country, must know rules. You not know, judge say, Too bad, go back. They not telling you why so you can use their way go forward. They say, Don't know why, you find out yourself. But they knowing all the time. Better you take it, find out why yourself." She tossed her head back with a satisfied smile.

I found out about all the whys later. I read the rules and looked up all the big words in a dictionary. I borrowed books from the Chinatown library. I studied each chess piece, trying to absorb the power each contained.

I learned about opening moves and why it's important to control the center early on; the shortest distance between two points is straight down the middle. I learned about the middle game and why tactics between two adversaries are like clashing ideas; the one who plays better has the clearest plans for both attacking and getting out of traps. I learned why it is essential in the endgame to have foresight, a mathematical understanding of all possible moves, and patience; all weaknesses and advantages become evident to a strong adversary and are obscured to a tiring opponent. I discovered that for the whole game one must gather invisible strengths and see the endgame before the game begins.

I also found out why I should never reveal "why" to others. A little knowledge withheld is a great advantage one should store for future use. That is the power of chess. It is a game of secrets in which one must show and never tell.

I loved the secrets I found within the sixty-four black and white squares. I carefully drew a handmade chessboard and pinned it to the wall next to my bed, where at night I would stare for hours at imaginary battles. Soon I no longer lost any games or Life Savers, but I lost my adversaries. Winston and Vincent decided they were more interested in roaming the streets after school in their Hopalong Cassidy cowboy hats.

On a cold spring afternoon, while walking home from school, I detoured through the playground at the end of our alley. I saw a group of old men, two seated across a folding table playing a game of chess, others smoking pipes, eating peanuts, and watching. I ran home and grabbed Vincent's chess set, which was bound in a cardboard box with rubber bands. I also carefully selected two prized rolls of Life Savers. I came back to the park and approached a man who was observing the game.

"Want to play?" I asked him. His face widened with surprise and he grinned as he looked at the box under my arm.

"Little sister, been a long time since I play with dolls," he said, smiling benevolently. I quickly put the box down next to him on the bench and displayed my retort.

Lau Po, as he allowed me to call him, turned out to be a much better player than my brothers. I lost many games and many Life Savers. But over the weeks, with each diminishing roll of candies, I added new secrets. Lau Po gave me the names. The Double Attack from the East and West Shores. Throwing Stones on the Drowning Man. The Sudden Meeting of the Clan. The Surprise from the Sleeping Guard. The Humble Servant Who Kills the King. Sand in the Eyes of Advancing Forces. A Double Killing Without Blood.

There were also the fine points of chess etiquette. Keep captured men in neat rows, as well-tended prisoners. Never announce "Check" with vanity, lest someone with an unseen sword slit your throat. Never hurl pieces into the sandbox after you have lost a game, because then you must find them again, by yourself, after apologizing to all around you. By the end of the summer, Lau Po had taught me all he knew, and I had become a better chess player.

A small weekend crowd of Chinese people and tourists would gather as I played and defeated my opponents one by one. My mother would join the crowds during these outdoor exhibition games. She sat proudly on the bench, telling my admirers with proper Chinese humility, "Is luck."

A man who watched me play in the park suggested that my mother allow me to play in local chess tournaments. My mother smiled graciously, an answer that meant nothing. I desperately wanted to go, but I bit back my tongue. I knew she would not let me play among strangers. So as we walked home I said in a small voice that I didn't want to play in the local tournament. They would have American rules. If I lost, I would bring shame on my family.

"Is shame you fall down nobody push you," said my mother.

During my first tournament, my mother sat with me in the front row as I waited for my turn. I frequently bounced my legs to unstick them from the cold metal seat of the folding chair. When my name was called, I leapt up. My mother unwrapped something in her lap. It was her *chang*, a small tablet of red jade which held the sun's fire. "Is luck," she whispered, and tucked it into my dress pocket. I turned to my opponent, a fifteen-year-old boy from Oakland. He looked at me, wrinkling his nose.

As I began to play, the boy disappeared, the color ran out of the room, and I saw only my white pieces and his black ones waiting on the other side. A light wind began blowing past my ears. It whispered secrets only I could hear.

"Blow from the South," it murmured. "The wind leaves no trail." I saw a clear path, the traps to avoid. The crowd rustled. "Shhh! Shhh!" said the corners of the room. The wind blew stronger. "Throw sand from the East to distract him." The knight came forward ready for the sacrifice. The wind hissed, louder and louder. "Blow, blow, blow. He cannot see. He is blind now. Make him lean away from the wind so he is easier to knock down."

"Check," I said, as the wind roared with laughter. The wind died down to little puffs, my own breath.

My mother placed my first trophy next to a new plastic chess set that the neighborhood Tao society had given to me. As she wiped each piece with a soft cloth, she said, "Next time win more, lose less."

"Ma, it's not how many pieces you lose," I said. "Sometimes you need to lose pieces to get ahead."

"Better to lose less, see if you really need."

At the next tournament, I won again, but it was my mother who wore the triumphant grin.

"Lost eight piece this time. Last time was eleven. What I tell you? Better off lose less!" I was annoyed, but I couldn't say anything.

I attended more tournaments, each one farther away from home. I won all games, in all divisions. The Chinese bakery downstairs from our flat displayed my growing collection of trophies in its window, amidst the dust-covered cakes that were never picked up. The day after I won an important regional tournament, the window encased a fresh sheet cake with whipped-cream frosting and red script saying, "Congratulations, Waverly Jong, Chinatown Chess Champion." Soon after that, a flower shop, headstone engraver, and funeral parlor offered to sponsor me in national tournaments. That's when my mother decided I no longer had to do the dishes. Winston and Vincent had to do my chores.

"Why does she get to play and we do all the work," complained Vincent.

"Is new American rules," said my mother. "Meimei play, squeeze all her brains out for win chess. You play, worth squeeze towel."

By my ninth birthday, I was a national chess champion. I was still some 429 points away from grand-master status, but I was touted as the Great American Hope, a child prodigy and a girl to boot. They ran a photo of me in *Life* magazine next to a quote in which Bobby Fischer said, "There will never be a woman grand master." "Your move, Bobby," said the caption.

The day they took the magazine picture I wore neatly plaited braids clipped with plastic barrettes trimmed with rhinestones. I was playing in a large high school auditorium that echoed with phlegmy coughs and the squeaky rubber knobs of chair legs sliding across freshly waxed wooden floors. Seated across from me was an American man, about the same age as Lau Po, maybe fifty. I remember that his sweaty brow seemed to weep at my every move. He wore a dark, malodorous suit. One of his pockets was stuffed with a great white kerchief on which he wiped his palm before sweeping his hand over the chosen chess piece with great flourish.

In my crisp pink-and-white dress with scratchy lace at the neck, one of two my mother had sewn for these special occasions, I would clasp my hands under my chin, the delicate points of my elbows poised lightly on the table in the manner my mother had shown me for posing for the press. I would swing my patent leather shoes back and forth like an impatient child riding on a school bus. Then I would pause, suck in my lips, twirl my chosen piece in midair as if undecided, and then firmly plant it in its new threatening place, with a triumphant smile thrown back at my opponent for good measure.

I no longer played in the alley of Waverly Place. I never visited the playground where the pigeons and old men gathered. I went to school, then directly home to learn new chess secrets, cleverly concealed advantages, more escape routes.

But I found it difficult to concentrate at home. My mother had a habit of standing over me while I plotted out my games. I think she thought of herself as my protective ally. Her lips would be sealed tight, and after each move I made, a soft "Hmmmmph" would escape from her nose.

"Ma, I can't practice when you stand there like that," I said one day. She retreated to the kitchen and made loud noises with the pots and pans. When the crashing stopped, I could see out of the corner of my eye that she was standing in the doorway. "Hmmmph!" Only this one came out of her tight throat.

My parents made many concessions to allow me to practice. One time I complained that the bedroom I shared was so noisy that I couldn't think. Thereafter, my brothers slept in a bed in the living room facing the street. I said I couldn't finish my rice; my head didn't work right when my stomach was too full. I left the table with half-finished bowls and nobody complained. But there was one duty I couldn't avoid. I had to accompany my mother on Saturday market days when I had no tournament to play. My mother would proudly walk with me, visiting many shops, buying very little. "This my daughter Wave-ly Jong," she said to whoever looked her way.

One day, after we left a shop I said under my breath, "I wish you wouldn't do that, telling everybody I'm your daughter." My mother stopped walking. Crowds of people with heavy bags pushed past us on the sidewalk, bumping into first one shoulder, then another.

"Aiii-ya. So shame be with mother?" She grasped my hand even tighter as she glared at me.

I looked down. "It's not that, it's just so obvious. It's just so embarrassing."

"Embarrass you be my daughter?" Her voice was cracking with anger.

"That's not what I meant. That's not what I said."

"What you say?"

I knew it was a mistake to say anything more, but I heard my voice speaking. "Why do you have to use me to show off? If you want to show off, then why don't you learn to play chess."

My mother's eyes turned into dangerous black slits. She had no words for me, just sharp silence.

I felt the wind rushing around my hot ears. I jerked my hand out of my mother's tight grasp and spun around, knocking into an old woman. Her bag of groceries spilled to the ground.

"Aii-ya! Stupid girl!" my mother and the woman cried. Oranges and tin cans careened down the sidewalk. As my mother stooped to help the old woman pick up the escaping food, I took off.

I raced down the street, dashing between people, not looking back as my mother screamed shrilly, "Meimei! Meimei!" I fled down an alley, past dark curtained shops and merchants washing the grime off their windows. I sped into the sunlight, into a large street crowded with tourists examining trinkets and souvenirs. I ducked into another dark alley, down another street, up another alley. I ran until it hurt and I realized I had nowhere to go, that I was not running from anything. The alleys contained no escape routes.

My breath came out like angry smoke. It was cold. I sat down on an upturned plastic pail next to a stack of empty boxes, cupping my chin with my hands, thinking hard. I imagined my mother, first walking briskly down one street or another looking for me, then giving up and returning home to await my arrival. After two hours, I stood up on creaking legs and slowly walked home.

The alley was quiet and I could see the yellow lights shining from our flat like two tiger's eyes in the night. I climbed the sixteen steps to the door, advancing quietly up each so as not to make any warning sounds. I turned the knob; the door was locked. I heard a chair moving, quick steps, the locks turning—click! click! click!—and then the door opened.

"About time you got home," said Vincent. "Boy, are you in trouble."

He slid back to the dinner table. On a platter were the remains of a large fish, its fleshy head still connected to bones swimming upstream in vain escape. Standing there waiting for my punishment, I heard my mother speak in a dry voice.

"We not concerning this girl. This girl not have concerning for us."

Nobody looked at me. Bone chopsticks clinked against the insides of bowls being emptied into hungry mouths.

I walked into my room, closed the door, and lay down on my bed. The room was dark, the ceiling filled with shadows from the dinnertime lights of neighboring flats.

In my head, I saw a chessboard with sixty-four black and white squares. Opposite me was my opponent, two angry black slits. She wore a triumphant smile. "Strongest wind cannot be seen," she said.

Her black men advanced across the plane, slowly marching to each successive level as a single unit. My white pieces screamed as they scurried and fell off the board one by one. As her men drew closer to my edge, I felt myself growing light. I rose up into the air and flew out the window. Higher and higher, above the alley, over the tops of tiled roofs, where I was gathered up by the wind and pushed up toward the night sky until everything below me disappeared and I was alone.

I closed my eyes and pondered my next move.

1989

Louise Erdrich

(1954–)

Chippewa, French, and German by ancestry, Louise Erdrich was born in Little Falls, Minnesota, and raised in Wahpeton, North Dakota, where her parents taught at the Bureau of Indian Affairs boarding school. Nearby on the Turtle Mountain Reservation her maternal grandmother served as tribal chairman. As a student at Dartmouth, she met Michael Dorris, himself of mixed American Indian descent, who headed the school's Native American studies program. In 1981 they married. Meanwhile, Erdrich graduated from Dartmouth (1976), earned an M.A. at Johns Hopkins University (1977), and began a career as a writer, supporting herself with a variety of jobs until she began to achieve success.

In 1984, she published both a collection of poems, *Jacklight*, and a novel, *Love Medicine*, the latter an immediate success. Widely praised in the United States, *Love Medicine* was also internationally acclaimed, translated into many languages. Weaving together discrete stories, Erdrich constructed a narrative covering the lives of three Chippewa families on a North Dakota reservation from the Depression years to the 1980s. In two novels since, she has demonstrated a continuing power, extending her broader story outside the reservation in *The Beet Queen* and moving backward in time to tell of an earlier generation of mixed-blood Americans in *Tracks*. Reminiscent of Faulkner in their generational reach, their exploration of place, and their narrative complexity, these novels have also reminded readers of the magical realism of recent Latin American writers.

Erdrich's husband, Michael Dorris, has also earned praise for books that include *A Yellow Raft in Blue Water* (1987), a novel, and *The Broken Cord* (1989), a nonfiction book about the couple's adopted son, a victim of fetal alcohol syndrome. Together, they have written *The Crown of Columbus* (1991), a novel about Dartmouth scholars seeking truths about Columbus, themselves, and America.

Erdrich's works, besides those named above, include *Baptism of Desire: Poems* (1989).

Fleur[1]

The first time she drowned in the cold and glassy waters of Lake Turcot, Fleur Pillager was only a girl. Two men saw the boat tip, saw her struggle in the waves. They rowed over to the place she went down, and jumped in. When they dragged her over the gunwales, she was cold to the touch and stiff, so they slapped her face, shook her by the heels, worked her arms back and forth, and pounded her back until she coughed up lake water. She shivered all over like a dog, then took a breath. But it wasn't long afterward that those two men disappeared. The first wandered off, and the other, Jean Hat, got himself run over by a cart.

It went to show, my grandma said. It figured to her, all right. By saving Fleur Pillager, those two men had lost themselves.

The next time she fell in the lake, Fleur Pillager was twenty years old and no one touched her. She washed onshore, her skin a dull dead gray, but when George Many Women bent to look closer, he saw her chest move. Then her eyes spun open, sharp black riprock, and she

---

1. First published in *Esquire*, August 1986, "Fleur" was slightly altered to become Chapter Two of *Tracks* (1989). Our text is the magazine version.

looked at him. "You'll take my place," she hissed. Everybody scattered and left her there, so no one knows how she dragged herself home. Soon after that we noticed Many Women changed, grew afraid, wouldn't leave his house, and would not be forced to go near water. For his caution, he lived until the day that his sons brought him a new tin bathtub. Then the first time he used the tub he slipped, got knocked out, and breathed water while his wife stood in the other room frying breakfast.

Men stayed clear of Fleur Pillager after the second drowning. Even though she was good-looking, nobody dared to court her because it was clear that Misshepeshu, the water-man, the monster, wanted her for himself. He's a devil, that one, love-hungry with desire and maddened for the touch of young girls, the strong and daring especially, the ones like Fleur.

Our mothers warn us that we'll think he's handsome, for he appears with green eyes, copper skin, a mouth tender as a child's. But if you fall into his arms, he sprouts horns, fangs, claws, fins. His feet are joined as one and his skin, brass scales, rings to the touch. You're fascinated, cannot move. He casts a shell necklace at your feet, weeps gleaming chips that harden into mica on your breasts. He holds you under. Then he takes the body of a lion or a fat brown worm. He's made of gold. He's made of beach moss. He's a thing of dry foam, a thing of death by drowning, the death a Chippewa cannot survive.

Unless you are Fleur Pillager. We all knew she couldn't swim. After the first time, we thought she'd never go back to Lake Turcot. We thought she'd keep to herself, live quiet, stop killing men off by drowning in the lake. After the first time, we thought she'd keep the good ways. But then, after the second drowning, we knew that we were dealing with something much more serious. She was haywire, out of control. She messed with evil, laughed at the old women's advice, and dressed like a man. She got herself into some half-forgotten medicine, studied ways we shouldn't talk about. Some say she kept the finger of a child in her pocket and a powder of unborn rabbits in a leather thong around her neck. She laid the heart of an owl on her tongue so she could see at night, and went out, hunting, not even in her own body. We know for sure because the next morning, in the snow or dust, we followed the tracks of her bare feet and saw where they changed, where the claws sprang out, the pad broadened and pressed into the dirt. By night we heard her chuffing cough, the bear cough. By day her silence and the wide grin she threw to bring down our guard made us frightened. Some thought that Fleur Pillager should be driven off the reservation, but not a single person who spoke like this had the nerve. And finally, when people were just about to get together and throw her out, she left on her own and didn't come back all summer. That's what this story is about.

During that summer, when she lived a few miles south in Argus, things happened. She almost destroyed that town.

When she got down to Argus in the year of 1920, it was just a small grid of six streets on either side of the railroad depot. There were two elevators, one central, the other a few miles west. Two stores competed for the trade of the three hundred citizens, and three churches quarreled with one another for their souls. There was a frame building for Lutherans, a heavy brick one for Episcopalians, and a long narrow shingled Catholic church. This last had a tall slender steeple, twice as high as any building or tree.

No doubt, across the low, flat wheat, watching from the road as she came near Argus on foot, Fleur saw that steeple rise, a shadow thin as a needle. Maybe in that raw space it drew her the way a lone tree draws lightning. Maybe, in the end, the Catholics are to blame. For if she hadn't seen that sign of pride, that slim prayer, that marker, maybe she would have kept walking.

But Fleur Pillager turned, and the first place she went once she came into town was to the back door of the priest's residence attached to the landmark church. She didn't go there for a handout, although she got that, but to ask for work. She got that too, or the town got her. It's hard to tell which came out worse, her or the men or the town, although the upshot of it all was that Fleur lived.

The four men who worked at the butcher's had carved up about a thousand carcasses between them, maybe half of that steers and the other half pigs, sheep, and game animals like deer, elk, and bear. That's not even mentioning the chickens, which were beyond counting. Pete Kozka owned the place, and employed Lily Veddar, Tor Grunewald, and my stepfather, Dutch James, who had brought my mother down from the reservation the year before she disappointed him by dying. Dutch took me out of school to take her place. I kept house half the time and worked the other in the butcher shop, sweeping floors, putting sawdust down, running a hambone across the street to a customer's bean pot or a package of sausage to the corner. I was a good one to have around because until they needed me, I was invisible. I blended into the stained brown walls, a skinny, big-nosed girl with staring eyes. Because I could fade into a corner or squeeze beneath a shelf, I knew everything, what the men said when no one was around, and what they did to Fleur.

Kozka's Meats served farmers for a fifty-mile area, both to slaughter, for it had a stock pen and chute, and to cure the meat by smoking it or spicing it in sausage. The storage locker was a marvel, made of many thicknesses of brick, earth insulation, and Minnesota timber, lined inside with sawdust and vast blocks of ice cut from Lake Turcot, hauled down from home each winter by horse and sledge.

A ramshackle board building, part slaughterhouse, part store, was fixed to the low, thick square of the lockers. That's where Fleur worked. Kozka hired her for her strength. She could lift a haunch or carry a pole of sausages without stumbling, and she soon learned cutting from Pete's wife, a string-thin blonde who chain-smoked and handled the razor-sharp knives with nerveless precision, slicing close to her stained fingers. Fleur and Fritzie Kozka worked afternoons, wrapping their cuts in paper, and Fleur hauled the packages to the lockers. The meat was left outside the heavy oak doors that were only opened at 5:00 each afternoon, before the men ate supper.

Sometimes Dutch, Tor, and Lily ate at the lockers, and when they did I stayed too, cleaned floors, restoked the fires in the front smokehouses, while the men sat around the squat cast-iron stove spearing slats of herring into hardtack bread. They played long games of poker or cribbage on a board made from the planed end of a salt crate. They talked and I listened, although there wasn't much to hear since almost nothing ever happened in Argus. Tor was married, Dutch had lost my mother, and Lily read circulars. They mainly discussed about the auctions to come, equipment, or women.

Every so often, Pete Kozka came out front to make a whist, leaving Fritzie to smoke cigarettes and fry raised doughnuts in the back room. He sat and played a few rounds but kept his thoughts to himself. Fritzie did not tolerate him talking behind her back, and the one book he read was the New Testament. If he said something, it concerned weather or a surplus of sheep stomachs, a ham that smoked green or the markets for corn and wheat. He had a good-luck talisman, the opal-white lens of a cow's eye. Playing cards, he rubbed it between his fingers. That soft sound and the slap of cards was about the only conversation.

Fleur finally gave them a subject.

Her cheeks were wide and flat, her hands large, chapped, muscular. Fleur's shoulders were broad as beams, her hips fishlike, slippery, narrow. An old green dress clung to her waist, worn thin where she sat. Her braids were thick like the tails of animals, and swung against her when she moved, deliberately, slowly in her work, held in and half-tamed, but only half. I could tell, but the others never saw. They never looked into her sly brown eyes or noticed her teeth, strong and curved and very white. Her legs were bare, and since she padded around in beadwork moccasins they never saw that her fifth toes were missing. They never knew she'd drowned. They were blinded, they were stupid, they only saw her in the flesh.

And yet it wasn't just that she was a Chippewa, or even that she was a woman, it wasn't that she was good-looking or even that she was alone that made their brains hum. It was how she played cards.

Women didn't usually play with men, so the evening that Fleur drew a chair up to the men's table without being so much as asked, there was a shock of surprise.

"What's this," said Lily. He was fat, with a snake's cold pale eyes and precious skin, smooth and lily-white, which is how he got his name. Lily had a dog, a stumpy mean little bull of a thing with a belly drum-tight from eating pork rinds. The dog liked to play cards just like Lily, and straddled his barrel thighs through games of stud, rum poker, vingt-un.[2] The dog snapped at Fleur's arm that first night, but cringed back, its snarl frozen, when she took her place.

"I thought," she said, her voice soft and stroking, "you might deal me in."

There was a space between the heavy bin of spiced flour and the wall where I just fit. I hunkered down there, kept my eyes open, saw her black hair swing over the chair, her feet solid on the wood floor. I couldn't see up on the table where the cards slapped down, so after they were deep in their game I raised myself up in the shadows, and crouched on a sill of wood.

I watched Fleur's hands stack and ruffle, divide the cards, spill them to each player in a blur, rake them up and shuffle again. Tor, short and scrappy, shut one eye and squinted the other at Fleur. Dutch screwed his lips around a wet cigar.

"Gotta see a man," he mumbled, getting up to go out back to the privy. The others broke, put their cards down, and Fleur sat alone in the lamplight that glowed in a sheen across the push of her breasts. I watched her closely, then she paid me a beam of notice for the first time. She turned, looked straight at me, and grinned the white wolf grin a Pillager turns on its victims, except that she wasn't after me.

"Pauline there," she said, "how much money you got?"

We'd all been paid for the week that day. Eight cents was in my pocket.

"Stake me," she said, holding out her long fingers. I put the coins in her palm and then I melted back to nothing, part of the walls and tables. It was a long time before I understood that the men would not have seen me no matter what I did, how I moved. I wasn't anything like Fleur. My dress hung loose and my back was already curved, an old woman's. Work had roughened me, reading made my eyes sore, caring for my mother before she died had hardened my face. I was not much to look at, so they never saw me.

When the men came back and sat around the table, they had drawn together. They shot each other small glances, stuck their tongues in their cheeks, burst out laughing at odd moments, to rattle Fleur. But she never minded. They played their vingt-un, staying even as Fleur slowly gained. Those pennies I had given her drew nickels and attracted dimes until there was a small pile in front of her.

Then she hooked them with five-card draw, nothing wild. She dealt, discarded, drew, and then she sighed and her cards gave a little shiver. Tor's eye gleamed, and Dutch straightened in his seat.

"I'll pay to see that hand," said Lily Veddar.

Fleur showed, and she had nothing there, nothing at all.

Tor's thin smile cracked open, and he threw his hand in too.

"Well, we know one thing," he said, leaning back in his chair, "the squaw can't bluff."

With that I lowered myself into a mound of swept sawdust and slept. I woke up during the night, but none of them had moved yet, so I couldn't either. Still later, the men must have gone out again, or Fritzie come out to break the game, because I was lifted, soothed, cradled in a woman's arms and rocked so quiet that I kept my eyes shut while Fleur rolled me into a closet of grimy ledgers, oiled paper, balls of string, and thick files that fit beneath me like a mattress.

2. Twenty-one, or blackjack.

The game went on after work the next evening. I got my eight cents back five times over, and Fleur kept the rest of the dollar she'd won for a stake. This time they didn't play so late, but they played regular, and then kept going at it night after night. They played poker now, or variations, for one week straight, and each time Fleur won exactly one dollar, no more and no less, too consistent for luck.

By this time, Lily and the other men were so lit with suspense that they got Pete to join the game with them. They concentrated, the fat dog sitting tense in Lily Veddar's lap, Tor suspicious, Dutch stroking his huge square brow, Pete steady. It wasn't that Fleur won that hooked them in so, because she lost hands too. It was rather that she never had a freak hand or even anything above a straight. She only took on her low cards, which didn't sit right. By chance, Fleur should have gotten a full or flush by now. The irritating thing was she beat with pairs and never bluffed, because she couldn't, and still she ended up each night with exactly one dollar, no more and no less. Lily couldn't believe, first of all, that a woman could be smart enough to play cards, but even if she was, that she would then be stupid enough to cheat for a dollar a night. By day I watched him turn the problem over, his hard white face dull, small fingers probing at his knuckles, until he finally thought he had Fleur figured out as a big-time player, caution her game. Raising the stakes would throw her.

More than anything now, he wanted Fleur to come away with something but a dollar. Two bits less or ten more, the sum didn't matter, just so he broke her streak.

Night after night she played, won her dollar, and left to stay in a place that just Fritzie and I knew about. Fleur bathed in the slaughtering tub, then slept in the unused brick smokehouse behind the lockers, a windowless place tarred on the inside with scorched fats. When I brushed against her skin I noticed that she smelled of the walls, rich and woody, slightly burnt. Since that night she put me in the closet I was no longer afraid of her, but followed her close, stayed with her, became her moving shadow that the men never noticed, the shadow that could have saved her.

August, the month that bears fruit, closed around the shop, and Pete and Fritzie left for Minnesota to escape the heat. Night by night, running, Fleur had won thirty dollars, and only Pete's presence had kept Lily at bay. But Pete was gone now, and one payday, with the heat so bad no one could move but Fleur, the men sat and played and waited while she finished work. The cards sweat, limp in their fingers, the table was slick with grease, and even the walls were warm to the touch. The air was motionless. Fleur was in the next room boiling heads.

Her green dress, drenched, wrapped her like a transparent sheet. A skin of lakeweed. Black snarls of veining clung to her arms. Her braids were loose, half-unraveled, tied behind her neck in a thick loop. She stood in steam, turning skulls through a vat with a wooden paddle. When scraps boiled to the surface, she bent with a round tin sieve and scooped them out. She'd filled two dishpans.

"Ain't that enough now?" called Lily. "We're waiting." The stump of a dog trembled in his lap, alive with rage. It never smelled me or noticed me above Fleur's smoky skin. The air was heavy in my corner, and pressed me down. Fleur sat with them.

"Now what do you say?" Lily asked the dog. It barked. That was the signal for the real game to start.

"Let's up the ante," said Lily, who had been stalking this night all month. He had a roll of money in his pocket. Fleur had five bills in her dress. The men had each saved their full pay.

"Ante a dollar then," said Fleur, and pitched hers in. She lost, but they let her scrape along, cent by cent. And then she won some. She played unevenly, as if chance was all she had. She reeled them in. The game went on. The dog was stiff now, poised on Lily's knees, a ball of vicious muscle with its yellow eyes slit in concentration. It gave advice, seemed to sniff the lay of Fleur's cards, twitched and nudged. Fleur was up, then down, saved by a scratch. Tor dealt seven cards, three down. The pot grew, round by round, until it held all the money. Nobody folded. Then it all rode on one last card and they went silent. Fleur picked hers up and blew a long breath. The heat lowered like a bell. Her card shook, but she stayed in.

Lily smiled and took the dog's head tenderly between his palms.

"Say, Fatso," he said, crooning the words, "you reckon that girl's bluffing?"

The dog whined and Lily laughed. "Me too," he said, "let's show." He swept his bills and coins into the pot and then they turned their cards over.

Lily looked once, looked again, then he squeezed the dog up like a fist of dough and slammed it on the table.

Fleur threw her arms out and drew the money over, grinning that same wolf grin that she'd used on me, the grin that had them. She jammed the bills in her dress, scooped the coins up in waxed white paper that she tied with string.

"Let's go another round," said Lily, his voice choked with burrs. But Fleur opened her mouth and yawned, then walked out back to gather slops for the one big hog that was waiting in the stock pen to be killed.

The men sat still as rocks, their hands spread on the oiled wood table. Dutch had chewed his cigar to damp shreds, Tor's eye was dull. Lily's gaze was the only one to follow Fleur. I didn't move. I felt them gathering, saw my stepfather's veins, the ones in his forehead that stood out in anger. The dog had rolled off the table and curled in a knot below the counter, where none of the men could touch it.

Lily rose and stepped out back to the closet of ledgers where Pete kept his private stock. He brought back a bottle, uncorked and tipped it between his fingers. The lump in his throat moved, then he passed it on. They drank, quickly felt the whiskey's fire, and planned with their eyes things they couldn't say out loud.

When they left, I followed. I hid out back in the clutter of broken boards and chicken crates beside the stock pen, where they waited. Fleur could not be seen at first, and then the moon broke and showed her, slipping cautiously along the rough board chute with a bucket in her hand. Her hair fell, wild and coarse, to her waist, and her dress was a floating patch in the dark. She made a pig-calling sound, rang the tin pail lightly against the wood, froze suspiciously. But too late. In the sound of the ring Lily moved, fat and nimble, stepped right behind Fleur and put out his creamy hands. At his first touch, she whirled and doused him with the bucket of sour slops. He pushed her against the big fence and the package of coins split, went clinking and jumping, winked against the wood. Fleur rolled over once and vanished in the yard.

The moon fell behind a curtain of ragged clouds, and Lily followed into the dark muck. But he tripped, pitched over the huge flank of the pig, who lay mired to the snout, heavily snoring. I sprang out of the weeds and climbed the side of the pen, stuck like glue. I saw the sow rise to her neat, knobby knees, gain her balance, and sway, curious, as Lily stumbled forward. Fleur had backed into the angle of rough wood just beyond, and when Lily tried to jostle past, the sow tipped up on her hind legs and struck, quick and hard as a snake. She plunged her head into Lily's thick side and snatched a mouthful of his shirt. She lunged again, caught him lower, so that he grunted in pained surprise. He seemed to ponder, breathing deep. Then he launched his huge body in a swimmer's dive.

The sow screamed as his body smacked over hers. She rolled, striking out with her knife-sharp hooves, and Lily gathered himself upon her, took her foot-long face by the ears and scraped her snout and cheeks against the trestles of the pen. He hurled the sow's tight skull against an iron post, but instead of knocking her dead, he merely woke her from her dream.

She reared, shrieked, drew him with her so that they posed standing upright. They bowed jerkily to each other, as if to begin. Then his arms swung and flailed. She sank her black fangs into his shoulder, clasping him, dancing him forward and backward through the pen. Their steps picked up pace, went wild. The two dipped as one, box-stepped, tripped each other. She ran her split foot through his hair. He grabbed her kinked tail. They went down and came up, the same shape and then the same color, until the men couldn't tell one from the other in that light and Fleur was able to launch herself over the gates, swing down, hit gravel.

The men saw, yelled, and chased her at a dead run to the smokehouse. And Lily too, once the sow gave up in disgust and freed him. That is where I should have gone to Fleur, saved her, thrown myself on Dutch. But I went stiff with fear and couldn't unlatch myself from the trestles or move at all. I closed my eyes and put my head in my arms, tried to hide, so there is nothing to describe but what I couldn't block out, Fleur's hoarse breath, so loud it filled me, her cry in the old language, and my name repeated over and over among the words.

The heat was still dense the next morning when I came back to work. Fleur was gone but the men were there, slack-faced, hung over. Lily was paler and softer than ever, as if his flesh had steamed on his bones. They smoked, took pulls off a bottle. It wasn't noon yet. I worked awhile, waiting shop and sharpening steel. But I was sick, I was smothered, I was sweating so hard that my hands slipped on the knives, and I wiped my fingers clean of the greasy touch of the customers' coins. Lily opened his mouth and roared once, not in anger. There was no meaning to the sound. His boxer dog, sprawled limp beside his foot, never lifted its head. Nor did the other men.

They didn't notice when I stepped outside, hoping for a clear breath. And then I forgot them because I knew that we were all balanced, ready to tip, to fly, to be crushed as soon as the weather broke. The sky was so low that I felt the weight of it like a yoke. Clouds hung down, witch teats, a tornado's green-brown cones, and as I watched one flicked out and became a delicate probing thumb. Even as I picked up my heels and ran back inside, the wind blew suddenly, cold, and then came rain.

Inside, the men had disappeared already and the whole place was trembling as if a huge hand was pinched at the rafters, shaking it. I ran straight through, screaming for Dutch or for any of them, and then I stopped at the heavy doors of the lockers, where they had surely taken shelter. I stood there a moment. Everything went still. Then I heard a cry building in the wind, faint at first, a whistle and then a shrill scream that tore through the walls and gathered around me, spoke plain so I understood that I should move, put my arms out, and slam down the great iron bar that fit across the hasp and lock.

Outside, the wind was stronger, like a hand held against me. I struggled forward. The bushes tossed, the awnings flapped off storefronts, the rails of porches rattled. The odd cloud became a fat snout that nosed along the earth and sniffled, jabbed, picked at things, sucked them up, blew them apart, rooted around as if it was following a certain scent, then stopped behind me at the butcher shop and bored down like a drill.

I went flying, landed somewhere in a ball. When I opened my eyes and looked, stranger things were happening.

A herd of cattle flew through the air like giant birds, dropping dung, their mouths opened in stunned bellows. A candle, still lighted, blew past, and tables, napkins, garden tools, a whole school of drifting eyeglasses, jackets on hangers, hams, a checkerboard, a lampshade, and at last the sow from behind the lockers, on the run, her hooves a blur, set free, swooping, diving, screaming as everything in Argus fell apart and got turned upside down, smashed, and thoroughly wrecked.

Days passed before the town went looking for the men. They were bachelors, after all, except for Tor, whose wife had suffered a blow to the head that made her forgetful. Everyone was occupied with digging out, in high relief because even though the Catholic steeple had been torn off like a peaked cap and sent across five fields, those huddled in the cellar were unhurt. Walls had fallen, windows were demolished, but the stores were intact and so were the bankers and shop owners who had taken refuge in their safes or beneath their cash registers. It was a fair-minded disaster, no one could be said to have suffered much more than the next, at least not until Fritzie and Pete came home.

Of all the businesses in Argus, Kozka's Meats had suffered worst. The boards of the front building had been split to kindling, piled in a huge pyramid, and the shop equipment was blasted far and wide. Pete paced off the distance the iron bathtub had been flung—a hundred feet. The glass candy case went fifty, and landed without so much as a cracked pane. There were other surprises as well, for the back rooms where Fritzie and Pete lived were undisturbed. Fritzie said the dust still coated her china figures, and upon her kitchen table, in the ashtray, perched the last cigarette she'd put out in haste. She lit it up and finished it, looking through the window. From there, she could see that the old smokehouse Fleur had slept in was crushed to a reddish sand and the stockpens were completely torn apart, the rails stacked helter-skelter. Fritzie asked for Fleur. People shrugged. Then she asked about the others and, suddenly, the town understood that three men were missing.

There was a rally of help, a gathering of shovels and volunteers. We passed boards from hand to hand, stacked them, uncovered what lay beneath the pile of jagged splinters. The lockers, full of the meat that was Pete and Fritzie's investment, slowly came into sight, still intact. When enough room was made for a man to stand on the roof, there were calls, a general urge to hack through and see what lay below. But Fritzie shouted that she wouldn't allow it because the meat would spoil. And so the work continued, board by board, until at last the heavy oak doors of the freezer were revealed and people pressed to the entry. Everyone wanted to be the first, but since it was my stepfather lost, I was let go in when Pete and Fritzie wedged through into the sudden icy air.

Pete scraped a match on his boot, lit the lamp Fritzie held, and then the three of us stood still in its circle. Light glared off the skinned and hanging carcasses, the crates of wrapped sausages, the bright and cloudy blocks of lake ice, pure as winter. The cold bit into us, pleasant at first, then numbing. We must have stood there a couple of minutes before we saw the men, or more rightly, the humps of fur, the iced and shaggy hides they wore, the bearskins they had taken down and wrapped around themselves. We stepped closer and tilted the lantern beneath the flaps of fur into their faces. The dog was there, perched among them, heavy as a doorstop. The three had hunched around a barrel where the game was still laid out, and a dead lantern and an empty bottle, too. But they had thrown down their last hands and hunkered tight, clutching one another, knuckles raw from beating at the door they had also attacked with hooks. Frost stars gleamed off their eyelashes and the stubble of their beards. Their faces were set in concentration, mouths open as if to speak some careful thought, some agreement they'd come to in each other's arms.

Power travels in the bloodlines, handed out before birth. It comes down through the hands, which in the Pillagers were strong and knotted, big, spidery, and rough, with sensitive fingertips good at dealing cards. It comes through the eyes, too, belligerent, darkest brown, the eyes of those in the bear clan, impolite as they gaze directly at a person.

In my dreams, I look straight back at Fleur, at the men. I am no longer the watcher on the dark sill, the skinny girl.

The blood draws us back, as if it runs through a vein of earth. I've come home and, except for talking to my cousins, live a quiet life. Fleur lives quiet too, down on Lake Turcot with her boat. Some say she's married to the waterman, Misshepeshu, or that she's living in shame with white men or windigos, or that she's killed them all. I'm about the only one here who ever goes to visit her. Last winter, I went to help out in her cabin when she bore the child, whose green eyes and skin the color of an old penny made more talk, as no one could decide if the child was mixed blood or what, fathered in a smokehouse, or by a man with brass scales, or by the lake. The girl is bold, smiling in her sleep, as if she knows what people wonder, as if she hears the old men talk, turning the story over. It comes up different every time and has no ending, no beginning. They get the middle wrong too. They only know that they don't know anything.

1986, 1989

Bibliography

For general reference purposes in American literature, the most comprehensive single-volume work is George Perkins, Barbara Perkins, and Phillip Leininger, eds., *Benet's Reader's Encyclopedia of American Literature*, 1991. Other general works in one volume include Arthur Hobson Quinn et al., *The Literature of the American People*, 1951; James D. Hart, ed., *The Oxford Companion to American Literature*, 5th edition, 1983; and Emory Elliott et al., eds., *The Columbia Liter-* *ary History of the United States*, 1988. Still useful is R. E. Spiller et al., eds., *Literary History of the United States*, 3 vols., 1948, with supplements. For women's literature as represented by the authors sampled in this volume, the introductory essays provide fundamental bibliographies. For women's literature generally, the bibliography that follows lists helpful reference works, volumes of literary history and criticism, and studies of political and social history.

Reference Works

Biblowitz, Iris, ed. *Women and Literature: An Annotated Bibliography of Women Writers*. 3rd ed. 1976.

Blain, Virginia, et al., eds. *The Feminist Companion to Literature in English*. 1990.

Chevalier, Tracy, ed. *Contemporary Poets*. 5th ed. 1991.

Contemporary Authors (a series, with various editors).

Contemporary Authors: Biographical Series. 1986–.

Dictionary of American Biography. Allen Johnson and Dumas Malone, eds. 20 vols. plus supplements. 1928–1973.

Dictionary of Literary Biography (a series, arranged by topics, beginning with *The American Renaissance in New England*, ed. Joel Myerson, 1978).

Ehrlich, Eugene, and Carruth, Gorton. *The Oxford Illustrated Literary Guide to the United States*. 1983.

Foner, Eric, and Garraty, John A., eds. *The Reader's Companion to American History*. 1991.

Gohdes, Clarence, and Marovitz, Sanford E. *Bibliographical Guide to the Study of the Literature of the U.S.A.* 5th ed. 1984.

Henderson, Lesley, ed. *Contemporary Novelists*. 5th ed. 1991.

Kirkpatrick, D. L., ed. *Reference Guide to American Literature*. 2d ed. 1987.

Koster, Donald N. *American Literature and Language: A Guide to Information Sources*. 1982.

Kunitz, S. J., and Haycraft, Howard, eds. *American Authors, 1600–1900* (a biographical dictionary).

———. *Twentieth Century Authors*. 1942 (a biographical dictionary). Supplement, 1955.

Leary, Lewis, ed. *Articles on American Literature, 1900–1950.* Supplements, 1970, 1979.

Ludwig, Richard M., and Nault, Clifford A., Jr. *Annals of American Literature 1602–1983.* 1986.

Mainero, Lina, ed. *American Women Writers: A Critical Reference Guide from Colonial Times to the Present.* 4 vols. 1979–1982.

Mitterling, Philip I. *United States Cultural History: A Guide to Information Sources.* 1980.

Poole's Index to Periodical Literature. Annual. 1802–1881. Supplements, 1882–1907.

Readers' Guide to Periodical Literature. Annual. 1900–.

Vinson, James, ed. *Contemporary Dramatists.* 3rd ed. 1982.

White, Barbara Anne, ed. *American Women Writers: An Annotated Bibliography of Criticism.* 1977.

Literary History and Criticism

Ammons, Elizabeth. *American Women Writers at the Turn into the Twentieth Century.* 1991.

Anzaldua, Gloria. *Borderlands: The New Mestiza—La Frontera.* 1987.

Auchincloss, Louis. *Pioneers and Caretakers: A Study of Nine American Women Novelists.* 1965.

Bardes, Barbara. *Declarations of Independence: Women and Political Power in Nineteenth-Century American Fiction.* 1990.

Baym, Nina. *Novels, Readers, and Reviewers.* 1984.

———. *Woman's Fiction.* 1978.

Bennett, Paula. *My Life, A Loaded Gun: Female Creativity and Feminist Poetics.* 1986.

Brown-Guillory, Elizabeth. *Their Place on the Stage: Black Women Playwrights in America.* 1990.

Carby, Hazel V. *Reconstructing Womanhood: The Emergence of the Afro-American Woman Novelist.* 1988.

Christian, Barbara. *Black Women Novelists: The Development of a Tradition, 1892–1976.* 1980.

Diehl, Joanne Feit. *Women Poets and the American Sublime.* 1990.

Drake, William. *The First Wave: Women Poets in America 1915–1945.* 1987.

DuPlessis, Rachel Blau. *Writing Beyond the Ending: Narrative Strategies of Twentieth-Century Women Writers.* 1985.

Fetterly, Judith. *The Resisting Reader: A Feminist Approach to American Fiction.* 1978.

Frye, Joanne S. *Living Stories, Telling Lives: Women and the Novel in Contemporary Experience.* 1986.

Gilbert, Sandra M., and Gubar, Susan. *The Madwoman in the Attic: The Woman Writer and the Nineteenth-Century Literary Imagination.* 1979.

———. *No Man's Land: The Place of the Woman Writer in the Twentieth Century.* 1988, 1989 (two volumes of three projected).

Gunn Allen, Paula. *The Sacred Hoop.* 1986.

Kolodny, Annette. *The Lay of the Land: Metaphor as Experience and History.* 1975.

Ling, Amy. *Between Worlds: Women Writers of Chinese Ancestry.* 1990.

Moraga, Cherrie. *The Bridge Called Me Back: Writings by Radical Women of Color.* 1983.

Ostriker, Alicia. *Stealing the Language: The Emergence of Women's Poetry in America.* 1986.

Pryse, Marjorie, and Spillers, Hortense J. *Conjuring: Black Women, Fiction, and Literary Tradition.* 1985.

Showalter, Elaine. *Sister's Choice: Traditions and Change in American Women's Writing.* 1991.

Tompkins, Jane. *Sensational Designs: The Cultural Work of American Fiction 1790–1860.* 1985.

Walker, Melissa. *Down from the Mountaintop: Black Women's Novels in the Wake of the Civil Rights Movement, 1966–1989.* 1991.

Washington, Mary Helen. *Invented Lives: Narratives of Black Women, 1860–1960.* 1987.

Willis, Susan. *Specifying: Black Women Writing the American Experience.* 1987.

Zimmerman, Bonnie. *The Safe Sea of Women: Lesbian Fiction, 1969–1989.* 1990.

Political and Social History

Cott, Nancy F. *The Grounding of Modern Feminism.* 1987.

Demos, John Putnam. *Entertaining Satan: Witchcraft and the Culture of Early New England.* 1983.

Donovan, Josephine. *Feminist Theory: The Intellectual Traditions of American Feminism.* 1985.

Ehrenreich, Barbara. *For Her Own Good: 150 Years of the Experts' Advice to Women.* 1979.

Flexner, Eleanor. *Century of Struggle: The Woman's Rights Movement in the United States.* 1979.

Fox Genovese, Elizabeth. *Within the Plantation Household: Black and White Women of the Old South.* 1988.

Goldin, Claudia. *Understanding the Gender Gap: An Economic History of American Women.* 1990.

Karlsen, Carol F. *The Devil in the Shape of a Woman: Witchcraft in Colonial New England.* 1987.

Lerner, Gerda. *The Majority Finds Its Past: Placing Women in History.* 1979.

Merchant, Carolyn. *Ecological Revolutions: Nature, Gender, and Science in New England.* 1989.

Mintz, Stephen, and Kellogg, Susan. *Domestic Revolutions: A Social History of American Family Life.* 1988.

Smith-Rosenberg, Carroll. *Disorderly Conduct.* 1985.

Solomon, Barbara Miller. *In the Company of Educated Women: A History of Women and Higher Education in America.* 1985.

Williamson, Chilton. *American Suffrage from Property to Democracy.* 1960.

Yellin, Jean Fagin. *Women and Sisters: Antislavery Feminists in American Culture.* 1989.

Acknowledgments

Abigail Adams   Selections reprinted by permission of the publishers from *The Book of Abigail and John: Selected Letters of The Adams Family, 1762–1784,* edited by L. H. Butterfield, Cambridge, Mass.: Harvard University Press, Copyright © 1975 by the Massachusetts Historical Society.

Maya Angelou   Excerpt from *I Know Why the Caged Bird Sings* by Maya Angelou. Copyright © 1969, 1970 by Maya Angelou. Reprinted by permission of Random House, Inc.

Ann Beattie   "Skeletons" from *Where You'll Find Me* by Ann Beattie. Copyright © 1986 by Ann Beattie. Reprinted by permission of Simon & Schuster, Inc.

Louise Bogan   "Dark Summer," "Evening in the Sanitarium," "Men Loved Wholly Beyond Wisdom," "Night," "Roman Fountain," "The Alchemist," "The Crows," "The Dragonfly," and "Women" from *The Blue Estuaries* by Louise Bogan. Copyright © 1968 by Louise Bogan. Reprinted by permission of Farrar, Straus & Giroux, Inc.

Anne Bradstreet   Selections reprinted by permission of the publishers from *The Works of Anne Bradstreet* edited by Jeannine Hensley, Cambridge, Mass.: The Belknap Press of Harvard University Press. Copyright © 1967 by the President and Fellows of Harvard College.

Gwendolyn Brooks   "a song in the front yard," "Jessie Mitchell's Mother," "Queen of the Blues," "The Bean Eaters," "The Crazy Woman," "The Lovers of the Poor," "the vacant lot," and "We Real Cool." All from *Blacks,* Gwendolyn Brooks, copyright © 1991. Published by Third World Press, Chicago, 1991.

Kate Chopin   "The Storm" reprinted by permission of Louisiana State University Press from *The Complete Works of Kate Chopin,* edited by Per Seyersted. Copyright © 1969 by Louisiana State University Press.

Amy Clampitt   "The Kingfisher" from *The Kingfisher* by Amy Clampitt. Copyright © 1983 by Amy Clampitt. Reprinted by permission of Alfred A. Knopf, Inc.

Amy Clampitt   "Urn-Burial and the Butterfly Migration" and "What the Light Was Like" from *What the Light Was Like* by Amy Clampitt. Copyright © 1985 by Amy Clampitt. Reprinted by permission of Alfred A. Knopf, Inc.

Amy Clampitt   "Margaret Fuller, 1847" from *Archaic Figure* by Amy Clampitt. Copyright © 1987 by Amy Clampitt. Reprinted by permission of Alfred A. Knopf, Inc.

Amy Clampitt   "A Winter Burial," "Amherst," and "The Field Pansy" from *Westward* by Amy Clampitt. Copyright © 1990 by Amy Clampitt. Reprinted by permission of Alfred A. Knopf, Inc.

H. D. (Hilda Doolittle)   "Garden," "Helen," "Mid-day," "Orchard," "Oread," "Pear Tree," and "Sea Rose" from *H. D.: Collected Poems, 1912–1944.* Copyright © 1982 by The Estate of Hilda Doolittle. Reprinted by permission of New Directions Publishing Corp.

H. D. (Hilda Doolittle)   Sections 1, 2, 3, 4, and 43 from "The Walls Do Not Fall" from *H. D.: Collected Poems, 1912–1944.* Copyright © 1982 by The Estate of Hilda Doolittle. Reprinted by permission of New Directions Publishing Corp.

warned that *Watch on the Rhine,* being fully protected under the copyright laws of the United States of America, the British Empire, including the Dominion of Canada, and all other countries of the copyright union, is subject to royalty. All rights, including professional, amateur, motion picture, recitation, public reading, radio broadcasting and the rights of translation into foreign languages, are strictly reserved. In its present form this play is dedicated to the reading public only. All inquiries regarding this play should be addressed to the author, care of Random House, Inc., 201 E. 50th Street, New York, NY 10022. The non-professional acting rights of *Watch on the Rhine* are controlled exclusively by the Dramatist's Play Service, 440 Park Avenue South, New York, NY 10016, without whose permission in writing no performance may be made.

Zora Neale Hurston Excerpt from *Their Eyes Were Watching God* by Zora Neale Hurston. Copyright 1937 by Harper & Row, Publishers, Inc. Copyright © renewed 1965 by John C. Hurston and Joel Hurston. Reprinted by permission of HarperCollins Publishers, Inc.

Maxine Hong Kingston "No Name Woman" from *The Woman Warrior* by Maxine Hong Kingston. Copyright © 1975, 1976 by Maxine Hong Kingston. Reprinted by permission of Alfred A. Knopf, Inc.

Meridel Le Sueur Excerpt from *The Girl.* Copyright © 1978, 1990 by Meridel Le Sueur. Reprinted by permission of West End Press.

Denise Levertov "The Well" from Denise Levertov: *Breathing the Water.* Copyright © 1987 by Denise Levertov. Reprinted by permission of New Directions Publishing Corp.

Denise Levertov "The 90th Year" from Denise Levertov: *Life in the Forest.* Copyright © 1976 by Denise Levertov. Reprinted by permission of New Directions Publishing Corp.

Denise Levertov "Intrusion" from Denise Levertov: *Footprints.* Copyright © 1970 by Denise Levertov Goodman. Reprinted by permission of New Directions Publishing Corp.

Denise Levertov "Illustrious Ancestors" and "To the Snake" from Denise Levertov: *Collected Earlier Poems 1940–1960.* Copyright © 1959 by Denise Levertov. First printed in *Poetry.* Reprinted by permission of New Directions Publishing Corp.

Denise Levertov "The Third Dimension" from Denise Levertov: *Collected Earlier Poems 1940– 1960.* Copyright © 1957 by Denise Levertov. Reprinted by permission of New Directions Publishing Corp.

Denise Levertov "A Note to Olga," "About Marriage," and "In Mind" from Denise Levertov: *Poems 1960–1970.* Copyright © 1964, 1966 by Denise Levertov Goodman. "About Marriage" and "In Mind" were first published in *Poetry.* Reprinted by permission of New Directions Publishing Corp.

Amy Lowell "Lilacs" and "Meeting-House Hill" from *The Complete Poetical Works of Amy Lowell.* Copyright © 1955 by Houghton Mifflin Company, © renewed 1983 by Houghton Mifflin Company, Brinton P. Roberts, and G. D'Andelot Belin, Esquire. Reprinted by permission of Houghton Mifflin Co. All rights reserved.

Bobbie Ann Mason "Hunktown" from *Love Life* by Bobbie Ann Mason. Copyright © 1988 by Bobbie Ann Mason. Reprinted by permission of HarperCollins Publishers, Inc.

Mary McCarthy "Artists in Uniform" from *On the Contrary.* Farrar, Straus & Giroux, 1961. Reprinted by permission of Mary McCarthy Literary Trust.

Edna St. Vincent Millay "First Fig," "Recuerdo," and "Second Fig." Copyright 1922, 1950 by Edna St. Vincent Millay. From *Collected Poems,* HarperCollins. Reprinted by permission of Elizabeth Barnett, literary executor.

Edna St. Vincent Millay "Oh, oh, you will be sorry for that word!," "The Spring and the Fall," "What lips my lips have kissed," and Sonnets VII and XIV of *Sonnets from an Ungrafted Tree.* Copyright 1923, 1951 by Edna St. Vincent Millay and Norma Millay Ellis. From *Collected Poems,* HarperCollins. Reprinted by permission of Elizabeth Barnett, literary executor.

Sylvia Plath "Daddy," "Lady Lazarus," "Morning Song," "The Arrival of the Bee Box," "Wintering," and "Words" from *Ariel* by Sylvia Plath. Copyright © 1961, 1963, 1965 by Ted Hughes. Reprinted by permission of HarperCollins Publishers, Inc.

Sylvia Plath "Child" and "Mystic" from *Winter Trees* by Sylvia Plath. Copyright © 1963, 1972 by Ted Hughes. Reprinted by permission of HarperCollins Publishers, Inc.

Katherine Anne Porter "Pale Horse, Pale Rider" from *Pale Horse, Pale Rider, Three Short Novels*, copyright 1937 and renewed 1965 by Katherine Anne Porter, reprinted by permission of Harcourt Brace & Company.

Adrienne Rich "Aunt Jennifer's Tigers," "Diving into the Wreck," "Face to Face," "For the Dead," "From a Survivor," "I Am in Danger—Sir—," "Living in Sin," "Snapshots of a Daughter-in-Law," "Upper Broadway," and XVIII from "Twenty-One Love Poems." Reprinted from *The Fact of a Doorframe, Poems Selected and New, 1950–1984*, by Adrienne Rich, by permission of W. W. Norton & Company, Inc. Copyright © 1984 by Adrienne Rich. Copyright © 1975, 1978 by W. W. Norton & Company, Inc. Copyright © 1981 by Adrienne Rich.

Mary Rowlandson *The Narrative of the Captivity and Restoration of Mrs. Mary Rowlandson*, edited by Robert Diebold. National Bicentennial Edition. Copyright © 1975, by Robert Diebold and The Town of Lancaster, Massachusetts. Reprinted by permission.

Mari Sandoz "The Song of a Good Name" from *Crazy Horse: The Strange Man of the Oglalas* by Mari Sandoz. Copyright © 1942 by Mari Sandoz. Copyright © renewed 1970 by Caroline Pifer. Reprinted by permission of McIntosh and Otis, Inc.

Anne Sexton "For John, Who Begs Me Not to Enquire Further," "Her Kind," and "The Double Image" from *To Bedlam and Part Way Back* by Anne Sexton. Copyright © 1960 by Anne Sexton, renewed 1988 by Linda G. Sexton. Reprinted by permission of Houghton Mifflin Co. All rights reserved.

Anne Sexton "All My Pretty Ones," "The Truth the Dead Know," and "With Mercy for the Greedy" from *All My Pretty Ones* by Anne Sexton. Copyright © 1962 by Anne Sexton, renewed 1990 by Linda G. Sexton. Reprinted by permission of Houghton Mifflin Co. All rights reserved.

Anne Sexton "Self in 1958" from *Live or Die* by Anne Sexton. Copyright © 1966 by Anne Sexton. Reprinted by permission of Houghton Mifflin Co. All rights reserved.

Leslie Marmon Silko "Lullaby." Copyright © 1981 by Leslie Marmon Silko. Reprinted from *Storyteller* by Leslie Marmon Silko, published by Seaver Books, New York, New York.

Amy Tan "Rules of the Game." Reprinted by permission of The Putnam Publishing Group from *The Joy Luck Club* by Amy Tan. Copyright © 1989 by Amy Tan.

Alice Walker "Everyday Use" from *In Love & Trouble: Stories of Black Women*, copyright © 1973 by Alice Walker, reprinted by permission of Harcourt Brace & Company.

Eudora Welty "Livvie" from *The Wide Net and Other Stories*, copyright 1942 and renewed 1970 by Eudora Welty, reprinted by permission of Harcourt Brace & Company.

Phillis Wheatley "On the Death of General Wooster" from *The Collected Works of Phillis Wheatley*, edited by John C. Shields. Copyright © 1988 by Oxford University Press, Inc. Reprinted by permission.

Sarah Payson Willis ("Fanny Fern") "Male Criticism on Ladies' Books," "The 'Coming' Woman," and "The Working-Girls of New York" from *Ruth Hall and Other Writings by Fanny Fern* edited by Joyce Warren. Copyright © 1986 by Rutgers, The State University.

Constance Fenimore Woolson "Miss Grief" from *Women Artists, Women Exiles: "Miss Grief" and Other Stories* edited by Joan M. Weimer. Copyright © 1988 by Rutgers, The State University.

Elinor Wylie "Sanctuary," "The Eagle and the Mole," and "Wild Peaches" from *Collected Poems* by Elinor Wylie. Copyright 1921 by Alfred A. Knopf, Inc., and renewed 1949 by William Rose Benét. Reprinted by permission of Alfred A. Knopf, Inc.

Elinor Wylie "Prophecy" from *Collected Poems* by Elinor Wylie. Copyright 1923 by Alfred A. Knopf, Inc., and renewed 1951 by Edwina C. Rubenstein. Reprinted by permission of Alfred A. Knopf, Inc.

Elinor Wylie "Let No Charitable Hope" from *Collected Poems* by Elinor Wylie. Copyright 1932 by Alfred A. Knopf, Inc. and renewed 1960 by Edwina C. Rubenstein. Reprinted by permission of Alfred A. Knopf, Inc.

Elinor Wylie "O Virtuous Light" and "Pastiche" from *Collected Poems* by Elinor Wylie. Copyright 1932 by Alfred A. Knopf, Inc. Reprinted by permission of the publisher.

Hisaye Yamamoto "Seventeen Syllables" from *Seventeen Syllables and Other Stories.* Copyright © 1988 by Hisaye Yamamoto. Used with permission of the author and Kitchen Table: Women of Color Press, P.O. Box 908, Latham, NY 12110.

Anzia Yezierska "The Free Vacation House" from *Hungry Hearts & Other Stories* by Anzia Yezierska. Copyright © 1985 by Louise Levitas Henriksen. Reprinted by permission of Persea Books.

Index

A

A Bird came down the Walk, 400
About Marriage, 967
Adams, Abigail, 97
After great pain, a formal feeling comes—, 401
After I had cut off my hands, 970
Alchemist, The, 848
Alcott, Louisa May, 440
All Greece hates, 767
All My Pretty Ones, 996
All things within this fading world hath end, 23
Although, great Queen, thou now in silence lie, 10
Amherst, 955
A narrow Fellow in the Grass, 408
Angelou, Maya, 979
An incident here and there, 768
Another, 25
Another armored animal—scale, 783
Antin, Mary, 745
Apparently with no surprise, 410
A private madness has prevailed, 761
A Route of Evanescence, 409
Arrival of the Bee Box, The, 1092
arrive. The Ladies from the Ladies' Betterment, 942
Artists in Uniform, 920
As imperceptibly as Grief, 409
As loving hind that (hartless) wants her deer, 25
As Weary Pilgrim, 32
As weary pilgrim, now at rest, 32
At sixteen I believed the moonlight, 971
ATTEND my lays, ye ever honour'd nine, 112
Aunt Jennifer's Tigers, 1000
Aunt Jennifer's tigers prance across a screen, 1000
Austin, Mary, 676
Author to Her Book, The, 23

Avoid the reeking herd, 758
A Word made Flesh is seldom, 410
Axes, 1089

B

Bean Eaters, The, 940
Beattie, Ann, 1136
Because I could not stop for Death—, 407
Before the Birth of One of Her Children, 23
Beloved, 1069
Blackberrying, 1081
Black Rook in Rainy Weather, 1080
Bogan, Louise, 847
Bradstreet, Anne, 8
Brooding Likeness, 1129
Brooks, Gwendolyn, 936

C

Cape Cod Folks, 633
Cary, Alice, 378
Cather, Willa, 683
Celestial choir! enthron'd in realms of light, 116
Charlotte Temple: A Tale of Truth, 120
Child, 1088
Chopin, Kate, 590
Civil War Diary of Sarah Morgan, The, 558
Clampitt, Amy, 944
Come slowly—Eden!, 397
"Coming" Woman, The, 244
Concerning your letter in which you ask, 997
Contemplations, 14
Cooke, Rose Terry, 383
Crab-Boil, 1149
Crazy Horse, 837
Crazy Woman, The, 944
Crippled Hope, A, 610
Crows, The, 848

D

Daddy, 1084
Dark Summer, 849
Davis, Rebecca Harding, 418

Daystar, 1148
Decade, A, 710
Dedication to Hunger, 1125
Denver's Secrets, 1069
Dickinson, Emily, 394
Diving into the Wreck, 1005
Don't lock me in wedlock, I want, 967
Doolittle, Hilda (H. D.), 762
Double Image, The, 990
Dove, Rita, 1145
Dover Street, 746
Dragonfly, The, 851
Drowned Children, The, 1127
Dusting, 1146

E

Eagle and the Mole, The, 758
Egyptian Pulled Glass Bottle in the Shape of
    a Fish, An, 780
Elysium is as far as to, 411
Erdrich, Louise, 1157
Evening in the Sanitarium, 850
Even in the moment of our earliest kiss, 830
Every day a wilderness—no, 1146
Everyday Use, 1131
Every year in June—up here, that's the
    month for lilacs—, 946

F

Face to Face, 1005
"Faith" is a fine invention, 397
Fakir, The, 677
Farewell dear babe, my heart's too much
    content, 28
Fatal Interview, 829
Father, this year's jinx rides us apart,
    996
Fern, Fanny [Sara Payson Willis], 224
Field Pansy, The, 953
First having read the book of myths, 1005
First Fig, 825
Flesh and the Spirit, The, 20
Fleur, 1157
For John, Who Begs Me Not to Enquire
    Further, 989
For the Dead, 1008
Freeman, Mary E. Wilkins, 615
Free Vacation House, The, 752
Frigate Pelican, The, 782
From a Survivor, 1007
From tall rooms, largesse of peonies, 954
From this the Muse rich consolation draws,
    117
Fuller, Margaret, 205

G

Gage, Frances D., 192
Garden, 765
Gentle Lena, The, 715
Gilman, Charlotte Perkins, 639
Girl, The, 853
Glasgow, Ellen, 696
Glaspell, Susan, 731
Glück, Louise, 1124
Gone, I say and walk from church, 995
Gordon, Caroline, 831
Grave, A, 779
Green, Sarah Pratt McLean, 632
Green Snake, when I hung you round my
    neck, 966
Group, The, 77

H

H. D. (Hilda Doolittle), 762
Hail, happy day, when, smiling like the
    morn, 113
Hail, happy saint, on thine immortal throne,
    111
"Half-cracked" to Higginson, living, 1004
Hansberry, Lorraine, 1010
He fumbles at your Soul, 399
Helen, 767
Hellman, Lillian, 868
He preached upon "Breadth" till it argued
    him narrow—, 409
Here Follows Some Verses upon the Burning
    of Our House July 10th, 1666. Copied
    out of a Loose Paper, 30
Here we have thirst, 780
Her Kind, 988
High in the jacaranda shines the gilded
    thread, 970
"Hope" is the thing with feathers—, 398
Hope Leslie, 178
Hopkins, Sarah Winnemucca, 576
How Celia Changed Her Mind, 383
Hunktown, 1103
Hurston, Zora Neale, 818
Hymn to the Evening, An, 113
Hymn to the Morning, An, 112

I

I Am in Danger—Sir—, 1004
I am thirty this November, 990
I burned my life, that I might find, 848
I cannot live with You—, 405
Ice House, The, 832
I died for Beauty—but was scarce, 402

I dreamed I called you on the telephone, 1008

I dwell in Possibility—, 406

I felt a Funeral, in my Brain, 398

If ever two were one, then surely we, 24

If external action is effete, 781

If you were coming in the Fall, 403

I had been hungry, all the Years—, 404

I had eight birds hatched in one nest, 26

I have done it again., 1086

I have gone out, a possessed witch, 988

I heard a Fly buzz—when I died—, 402

I know that He exists., 400

I Know Why the Caged Bird Sings, 980

I like a look of Agony, 398

I like to see it lap the Miles—, 405

Illustrious Ancestors, 967

I'm ceded—I've stopped being Theirs, 402

I'm Nobody! Who are you?, 399

I must be mad, or very tired, 710

In a year the nightingales were said to be so loud, 945

Incidents in the Life of a Slave Girl, 115

In Distrust of Merits, 787

I never lost as much but twice, 396

I never saw a Moor—, 408

In Honour of That High and Mighty Princess Queen Elizabeth of Happy Memory, 10

In Memory of My Dear Grandchild Anne Bradstreet, Who Deceased June 20, 1669, Being Three years and Seven Months Old, 29

In Memory of My Dear Grandchild Elizabeth Bradstreet, Who Deceased August, 1665, Being a Year and Half Old, 28

In Mind, 968

In Reference to Her Children, 23 June, 1659, 26

In secret place where once I stood, 20

In silent night when rest I took, 30

In the spring of the year, in the spring of the year, 826

In this her thirty-seventh year, the Italy, 951

Into her mother's bedroom to wash the ballooning body, 941

Intrusion, 970

In Winter in my Room, 410

I ordered this, this clean wood box, 1082

I reckon—when I count at all, 404

Iron Throat, The, 929

I shall not sing a May song, 944

is an enchanted thing, 786

I saw the first pear, 765

I shall lie hidden in a hut, 760

Is not the woman moulded by your wish, 762

I started Early—Took my Dog—, 403

I taste a liquor never brewed—, 397

I, too, dislike it; there are things that are important beyond all, 776

It was not Death, for I stood up, 403

I've seen a Dying Eye, 404

I've stayed in the front yard all my life, 937

I walk down the garden paths, 708

I was born in the month of the bull, 1129

I will put Chaos into fourteen lines, 831

J

Jacobs, Harriet, 313

Jelly-Fish, A, 789

Jessie Mitchell's Mother, 941

Jewett, Sarah Orne, 582

Jordan's End, 697

Journal of Madam Knight, The, 60

Joy Luck Club, The, 1150

Jury of Her Peers, A, 733

Justice Denied in Massachusetts, 828

K

Kingfisher, The, 945

King, Grace Elizabeth, 609

Kingston, Maxine Hong, 1095

Kirkland, Caroline Stansbury, 195

Knight, Sarah Kemble, 60

L

Lady, A, 707

Lady Lazarus, 1086

Lamentations, 1127

Le Sueur, Meridel, 852

Let No Charitable Hope, 761

Letter to Her Husband, Absent upon Public Employment, A, 24

Letters: to John Adams [Abigail Adams], 98, 100, 104, 108

Letters: to Mercy Otis Warren [Abigail Adams], 105

Letters: to recipient unknown [Emily Dickinson], 412, 413

Letters: to T. W. Higginson [Emily Dickinson], 414, 415, 416, 417

Let us abandon then our gardens and go home, 828

Levertov, Denise, 964

Life among the Piutes, 577

Life in the Iron Mills, 419

Life You Save May Be Your Own, The, 973

Lilacs, 711
Little Women, 442
Living in Sin, 1000
Livvie, 911
Love is not all; it is not meat nor drink, 830
Love set you going like a fat gold watch, 1081
Lovers of the Poor, The, 942
Lowell, Amy, 706
Lullaby, 1140

M

Male Criticism on Ladies' Books, 243
Mame was singing, 938
Management of Grief, The, 1115
Man looking into the sea, 779
Margaret Fuller, 1847, 951
Mason, Bobbie Ann, 1103
McCarthy, Mary, 919
Memoirs of Margaret Fuller Ossoli, 217
Men loved wholly beyond wisdom, 848
Meeting-House Hill, 710
Mid-day, 764
Millay, Edna St. Vincent, 824
Mind Is an Enchanting Thing, The, 786
Mine—by the Right of the White Election!, 404
"Miss Grief", 545
Moore, Marianne, 775
Morgan, Sarah, 557
Morning Song, 1081
Morrison, Toni, 1068
Mrs. Coley's three-flat brick, 938
Much Madness is divinest Sense—, 401
Mukherjee, Bharati, 1114
Murfree, Mary Noailles, 597
Muse's Tragedy, The, 657
My candle burns at both ends, 825
My father used to say, 781
My head, my heart, mine eyes, my life, nay, more, 24
My life closed twice before its close—, 411
My Life had stood—a Loaded Gun—, 408
Mystic, 1088

N

Nairobi, 1091
Narrative of the Captivity and Restoration of Mrs. Mary Rowlandson, The, 34
Never in Rome, 772
Nevertheless, 786
Never to be lonely like that—, 1005
New England Nun, A, 611
New Home, A, 196

Night, 851
90th year, The, 970
Nobody in the lane, and nothing, nothing but blackberries, 1081
No Name Woman, 1096
No sooner came, but gone, and fall'n asleep, 29
No Swan So Fine, 781
Note to Olga (1966), A, 969
Not that it was beautiful, 989
No water so still as the, 781
Now let no charitable hope, 761

O

Ö, 1146
Oates, Joyce Carol, 1090
O'Connor, Flannery, 972
Of all the Souls that stand create—, 406
Of Course—I prayed—, 401
Of lead and emerald, 969
Oh, Oh, you will be sorry for that word!, 826
Olsen, Tillie, 928
On the stiff twig up there, 1080
On Being Brought from Africa to America, 111
One need not be a Chamber—to be Haunted—, 406
One way there was of muting in the mind, 827
On My Dear Grandchild Simon Bradstreet, Who Died on 16 November, 1669, Being but a Month, and One Day Old, 29
On the Death of General Wooster, 117
On the Death of Dr. Samuel Marshall, 114
On the Death of the Reverend Mr. George Whitefield, 111
Opal, 710
Orchard, 765
Oread, 767
Other Two, The, 665
Over on the T'other Mounting, 598
O Virtuous Light, 761

P

Pain—has an Element of Blank—, 406
Pair of Silk Stockings, A, 591
Pale Horse, Pale Rider, 791
Pangolin, The, 783
Pastiche, 762
Past Is the Present, The, 781
Patterns, 708
Paul's Case, 685
Pear Tree, 766

Peter, 778
Plath, Sylvia, 1078
Poetry, 776
Porter, Katherine Anne, 790
Prologue, The, 9
Promised Land, The, 746
Prophecy, 760
Publication—is the Auction, 407

Q

Queen of the Blues, 938

R

Raisin in the Sun, A, 1011
Rain on the West Side Highway, 1009
Rapidly cruising or lying on the air there is a
  bird, 782
Rearrange a "Wife's" affection!, 411
Recuerdo, 825
Reminiscences by Frances D. Gage:
  Sojourner Truth, 192
Rest for the body's residue:, 949
Revolt of "Mother", The, 616
Rich, Adrienne, 999
Roast Possum, 1147
Roman Fountain, 850
Rose, harsh rose, 763
Rowlandson, Mary, 33
Rowson, Susanna Haswell, 118
Rules of the Game, 1150
Ruth Hall, 226

S

Safe in their Alabaster Chambers—, 397
Safe upon the solid rock the ugly houses
  stand, 825
Sanctuary, 760
Sandoz, Mari, 836
School Children, The, 1124
Sea Rose, 763
Second Fig, 825
Sedgwick, Catherine Maria, 177
Self in 1958, 998
Seventeen Syllables, 957
Sexton, Anne, 987
Shape the lips to an *o,* say *a,* 1146
She had thought the studio would keep itself,
  1000
She rose to His Requirement—dropt, 407
She wanted a little room for thinking, 1148
Silence, 781
Silko, Leslie Marmon, 1139
Silver dust, 766

Since of no creature living the last breath,
  830
Skeletons, 1137
Snapshots of a Daughter-in-Law, 1001
Some keep the Sabbath going to Church—,
  400
Some time now past in the autumnal tide, 14
Song in the Front Yard, A, 937
Song of a Good Name, The, 837
Sonnets from an Ungrafted Tree, 827
Soon as the sun forsook the eastern main,
  113
Spring and the Fall, The, 826
Stein, Gertrude, 713
Storm: A Sequel to "The 'Cadian Ball", The,
  594
Stowe, Harriet Beecher, 246
Strengthened to live, strengthened to die for,
  787
Strong and slippery, 778
Success is counted sweetest, 396

T

Tan, Amy, 1130
Tell all the Truth but tell it slant—, 409
Terminal Resemblance, 1129
The air is a mill of hooks—, 1088
The Bible is an antique Volume—, 410
The Brain—is wider than the Sky, 405
The Bustle in a House, 408
The children go forward with their little
  satchels, 1124
The cold remote islands, 851
The free evening fades, outside the windows
  fastened with decorative iron grilles,
  850
The Heart asks Pleasure—first—, 404
Their Eyes Were Watching God, 819
The Last Night that She lived, 409
The leafbud straggles forth, 1009
The light beats upon me, 764
The oriole, a charred and singing coat, 955
The pact that we made was the ordinary
  pact, 1007
The Pool Players, 941
The possum's a greasy critter, 1147
The Rav, 967
There came a Day at Summer's full, 399
There's a certain Slant of light, 398
There's in my mind a woman, 968
The Robin's my Criterion for Tune—, 399
These are the days when Birds come back—,
  396
The Soul selects her own Society, 399

The woman who has grown old, 848
They cross the yard, 1125
They eat beans mostly, this old yellow pair, 940
They were both still, 1127
Third Dimension, The, 965
This beast that rends me in the sight of all, 829
This is my letter to the World, 401
This is the bricklayer; hear the thud, 760
This is the easy time, there is nothing doing, 1083
This was a Poet—It is That, 401
This World is not Conclusion, 402
Those hours when happy hours were my estate, 831
Thou ill-formed offspring of my feeble brain, 23
Thou mighty God of sea and land, 30
Through thickest glooms look back, immortal shade, 114
To His Excellency General Washington, 116
To make a prairie it takes clover and one bee, 411
To My Dear and Loving Husband, 24
Town Poor, The, 583
To show the lab'ring bosom's deep intent, 115
To sing of wars, of captains, and of kings, 9
To S. M. a Young African Painter, on Seeing His Works, 115
To the Right Honourable WILLIAM, Earl of DARTMOUTH, His Majesty's Principal Secretary of State for North America, &c., 113
To the Snake, 966
To the University of Cambridge, in New-England, 110
Tribute to the Angels, 772
Truth the Dead Know, The, 995
Truth, Sojourner, 191
'Twas mercy brought me from my *Pagan* land, 111
Twenty-One Love Poems, 1009

U

Uncle Tom's Cabin, or Life among the Lowly, 248
Under the thunder-dark, the cicadas resound, 849
Up from the bronze, I saw, 850
Upon My Son Samuel His Going for England, Nov. 6, 1657, 30

Upper Broadway, 1009
Urn-Burial and the Butterfly Migration, 949

V

Vacant Lot, The, 938
Visible, invisible, 789

W

Walker, Alice
Walls Do Not Fall, The, 767
Warner, Susan, 350
Warren, Mercy Otis, 76
Watch on the Rhine, 869
Well, The, 971
Welty, Eudora, 910
We Real Cool, 941
We were very tired, we were very merry, 825
Wharton, Edith, 655
What is reality?, 998
What lips my lips have kissed, and where and why, 827
What Soft—Cherubic Creatures—, 401
What the Light Was Like, 946
What Time of Night It Is, 194
Wheatley, Phillis, 109
When I saw my father for the last time, we both did the same thing, 1129
When the world turns completely upside down, 758
When you came, you were like red wine and honey, 710
While an intrinsic ardor prompts to write, 110
Whirl up, sea—, 767
Who'd believe me if, 965
Why do I remember the sky, 1149
Wide, Wide World, The, 352
Wildermings, The, 378
Wild Nights—Wild Nights!, 398
Wild Peaches, 758
Willis, Sara Payson [Fanny Fern], 224
Winter Burial, The, 954
Wintering, 1083
With Mercy for the Greedy, 997
With troubled heart and trembling hand I write, 29
Woman in the Nineteenth Century, 206
Woman Warrior, The, 1096
Women, 849
Women have no wilderness in them, 849
Woolson, Constance Fenimore, 543
Words, 1089
Working-Girls of New York, The, 245
Wylie, Elinor, 757

Y

Yamamoto, Hisaye, 956
Yellow Wallpaper, The, 640
Yesterday, just before the first frost of the
    season, 953
Yezierska, Anzia, 751
Yonnondio, 929
You are beautiful and faded, 707
You are clear, 765

You are ice and fire, 710
You are made of almost nothing, 851
You do not do, you do not do, 1084
You, once a belle in Shreveport, 1001
Your clear eye is the one absolutely beautiful
    thing, 1088
You see, they have no judgment,
    1127
You've seen a strawberry, 786